William Shakespeare's First Folio

William Shakespeare's First Folio

A Photographic Facsimile

WAKING LION PRESS

ISBN 978-1-4341-0455-7

The images in this book are used by permission of the Folger Shakespeare Library under a Creative Commons Attribution-ShareAlike 4.0 International License. You can learn more here:

https://www.folger.edu/copyright-policy
https://www.folger.edu/permissions
https://creativecommons.org/licenses/by-sa/4.0/
https://www.folger.edu/the-shakespeare-first-folio-folger-copy-no-68#page/To+the+Reader/mode/2up

The publisher of this book, Waking Lion Press, has no affiliation with or endorsement by the Folger Shakespeare Library.

For the purposes of print publication, the images used in this book were converted from color to grayscale, cropped and reduced to fit on 8.5-by-11-inch paper, and digitally processed to enhance the legibility of the text.

Like the images themselves, this book is published under the Creative Commons Attribution-ShareAlike 4.0 International License (CC BY-SA 4.0).

The views expressed in this book are the responsibility of the author and do not necessarily represent the position of the publisher. The reader alone is responsible for the use of any ideas or information provided by this book.

This book is a work of fiction. The characters, places, and incidents in it are the products of the author's imagination or are represented fictitiously. Any resemblance of characters or events to actual persons or events is coincidental.

Published by Waking Lion Press, an imprint of The Editorium

Waking Lion Press™, the Waking Lion Press logo, and The Editorium™ are trademarks of The Editorium, LLC

The Editorium, LLC
West Jordan, UT 84081-6132
www.editorium.com

Publisher's Preface

The First Folio is a collection of plays published in 1623 as *Mr. William Shakespeare's Comedies, Histories, & Tragedies.* The contents of the book were compiled after Shakespeare's death by his friends and colleagues John Heminges and Henry Condell, both actors in the King's Men, the playing company for which Shakespeare wrote. The pair emphasized that the book was meant to replace earlier publications, which they characterised as "stol'n and surreptitious copies, maimed and deformed by frauds and stealths of injurious impostors," asserting that Shakespeare's true words "are now offer'd to your view cured, and perfect of their limbes; and all the rest, absolute in their numbers as he conceived them."

As you will see, "perfect of their limbes" is a bit of an overstatement; the book's printing has numerous imperfections, including inconsistent page positions, uneven ink distribution, and misnumbered pages. In addition, every copy of the First Folio has typographical errors—no copy is perfect—and every time an error was discovered while the book was being printed, the workers fixed it, which means that no two copies are identical. In spite of its faults, without the publication of the First Folio, eighteen of Shakespeare's plays, including *Macbeth, Twelfth Night, Julius Caesar, The Tempest*, and *Measure for Measure*, would probably not have survived. The hugely successful first edition was followed by others, referred to as the Second Folio, the Third Folio, and so on.

A folio is a book made up of sheets of paper on which four pages of text are printed, two pages on each side. Each sheet is then folded once to produce two leaves, each with two pages, one on the front and one on the back. The folded sheets are inserted inside one another to form a "gathering" or "quire" of leaves. The gatherings are then placed in order and bound as a book.

The images used in this book come from First Folio number 68 in the collection of the Folger Shakespeare Library in Washington, D.C. That copy is one of the cleanest and most complete available, and the Folger Shakespeare Library has done an outstanding job of photographing its pages. Many thanks to the library for creating the images and so generously making them available online. The library's doing so, of course, does not mean that it endorses or has any connection with the publication of this book.

The First Folio does present challenges for modern readers. In Shakespeare's time, the letters *i* and *j* were essentially the same, and the letters *u* and *v* were used interchangeably: "If Musicke be the food of Loue, play on." The "long *s*," with its similarity to the letter *f*, makes reading particularly difficult:

> He that fo generally is at all times good, muſt of neceſſitie hold his vertue to you, whoſe worthineſſe would ſtirre it vp where it wanted rather then lack it where there is ſuch abundance.

Nevertheless, using the First Folio gives players and directors a more accurate understanding of how the plays were originally meant to be acted and produced. As Megan Burnett of Bellarmine University writes, "The First Folio has visual clues for the actor, including capitalized words other than proper names; repeated use of specific consonants, words, and phrases; vowels added to words; changes in the spelling of some words and names; punctuation meant more for acting than reading; and split and shared lines and meter. These clues, along with others . . . , put the creative power of acting back in the hands of the actor. . . . Using a First Folio text can be a most thrilling and rewarding experience for the director, the actors, and the audience. Actors taught to look for and use the clues in a First Folio text are empowered to make fresh and exciting choices for their characters, mentally, vocally and physically, making the performance more entertaining and interesting for the production team, the acting company, and, most importantly, for the audience."[1]

---

1. "A Case for Using the First Folio as Directing and Acting Text," *Selected Papers of the Ohio Valley Shakespeare Conference:* Vol. 8, Article 2.

Collated : correct
See Lowndes Bibliographers Manual

Stephens 12 ¾ inches
by 8 ¼

[a copy 13¼ inches by 8 11/16" in "original calf binding"
in Quaritch catalogue Aug. 1855]

a² 12 11/16 × 8 inches
Ellis' catalogue 1891

Size = 12 ¾ × 8 ¼ in.

No.68

To the Reader.

This Figure, that thou here seest put,
    It was for gentle Shakespeare cut;
Wherein the Grauer had a strife
    with Nature, to out-doo the life:
O, could he but haue drawne his wit
    As well in brasse, as he hath hit
His face; the Print would then surpasse
    All, that was euer writ in brasse.
But, since he cannot, Reader, looke
    Not on his Picture, but his Booke.

                                  B. I.

Mr. WILLIAM SHAKESPEARES

COMEDIES, HISTORIES, & TRAGEDIES.

Published according to the True Originall Copies.

Martin Droeshout sculpsit London.

LONDON
Printed by Isaac Iaggard, and Ed. Blount. 1623.

TO THE MOST NOBLE
And
INCOMPARABLE PAIRE
OF BRETHREN.

WILLIAM
Earle of Pembroke, &c. Lord Chamberlaine to the
Kings most Excellent Maiesty.

AND

PHILIP
Earle of Montgomery, &c. Gentleman of his Maiesties
Bed-Chamber. Both Knights of the most Noble Order
of the Garter, and our singular good
LORDS.

Right Honourable,

Hilst we studie to be thankful in our particular, for the many fauors we haue receiued from your L.L. we are falne vpon the ill fortune, to mingle two the most diuerse things that can bee, feare, and rashnesse; rashnesse in the enterprize, and feare of the successe. For, when we valew the places your H.H. sustaine, we cannot but know their dignity greater, then to descend to the reading of these trifles: and, vvhile we name them trifles, we haue depriu'd our selues of the defence of our Dedication. But since your L.L. haue beene pleas'd to thinke these trifles some-thing, heeretofore; and haue prosequuted both them, and their Authour liuing, vvith so much fauour: we hope, that (they out-liuing him, and he not hauing the fate, common with some, to be exequutor to his owne writings) you will vse the like indulgence toward them, you haue done

The Epistle Dedicatorie.

vnto their parent. There is a great difference, whether any Booke choose his Patrones, or finde them: This hath done both. For, so much were your L.L. likings of the seuerall parts, when they were acted, as before they were published, the Volume ask'd to be yours. We haue but collected them, and done an office to the dead, to procure his Orphanes, Guardians; without ambition either of selfe-profit, or fame: onely to keepe the memory of so worthy a Friend, & Fellow aliue, as was our SHAKESPEARE, *by humble offer of his playes, to your most noble patronage. Wherein, as we haue iustly obserued, no man to come neere your L.L. but with a kind of religious addresse; it hath bin the height of our care, who are the Presenters, to make the present worthy of your H.H. by the perfection. But, there we must also craue our abilities to be considerd, my Lords. We cannot go beyond our owne powers. Country hands reach foorth milke, creame, fruites, or what they haue: and many Nations (we haue heard) that had not gummes & incense, obtained their requests with a leauened Cake. It was no fault to approch their Gods, by what meanes they could: And the most, though meanest, of things are made more precious, when they are dedicated to Temples. In that name therefore, we most humbly consecrate to your H.H. these remaines of your seruant* Shakespeare; *that what delight is in them, may be euer your L.L. the reputation his, & the faults ours, if any be committed, by a payre so carefull to shew their gratitude both to the liuing, and the dead, as is*

Your Lordshippes most bounden,

IOHN HEMINGE.
HENRY CONDELL.

To the great Variety of Readers.

From the most able, to him that can but spell: There you are number'd. We had rather you were weighd. Especially, when the fate of all Bookes depends vpon your capacities: and not of your heads alone, but of your purses. Well! It is now publique, & you wil stand for your priuiledges wee know: to read, and censure. Do so, but buy it first. That doth best commend a Booke, the Stationer saies. Then, how odde soeuer your braines be, or your wisedomes, make your licence the same, and spare not. Iudge your sixe-pen'orth, your shillings worth, your fiue shillings worth at a time, or higher, so you rise to the iust rates, and welcome. But, what euer you do, Buy. Censure will not driue a Trade, or make the Iacke go. And though you be a Magistrate of wit, and sit on the Stage at *Black-Friers*, or the *Cock-pit*, to arraigne Playes dailie, know, these Playes haue had their triall alreadie, and stood out all Appeales; and do now come forth quitted rather by a Decree of Court, then any purchas'd Letters of commendation.

It had bene a thing, we confesse, worthie to haue bene wished, that the Author himselfe had liu'd to haue set forth, and ouerseen his owne writings; But since it hath bin ordain'd otherwise, and he by death departed from that right, we pray you do not envie his Friends, the office of their care, and paine, to haue collected & publish'd them; and so to haue publish'd them, as where (before) you were abus'd with diuerse stolne, and surreptitious copies, maimed, and deformed by the frauds and stealthes of iniurious impostors, that expos'd them: euen those, are now offer'd to your view cur'd, and perfect of their limbes; and all the rest, absolute in their numbers, as he conceiued the. Who, as he was a happie imitator of Nature, was a most gentle expresser of it. His mind and hand went together: And what he thought, he vttered with that easinesse, that wee haue scarse receiued from him a blot in his papers. But it is not our prouince, who onely gather his works, and giue them you, to praise him. It is yours that reade him. And there we hope, to your diuers capacities, you will finde enough, both to draw, and hold you: for his wit can no more lie hid, then it could be lost. Reade him, therefore; and againe, and againe: And if then you doe not like him, surely you are in some manifest danger, not to vnderstand him. And so we leaue you to other of his Friends, whom if you need, can bee your guides: if you neede them not, you can leade your selues, and others. And such Readers we wish him.

Iohn Heminge.
Henrie Condell.

To the memory of my beloued,
The AVTHOR
Mr. WILLIAM SHAKESPEARE:
AND
what he hath left vs.

TO draw no enuy (Shakespeare) on thy name,
   Am I thus ample to thy Booke, and Fame:
While I confesse thy writings to be such,
   As neither Man, nor Muse, can praise too much.
'Tis true, and all mens suffrage. But these wayes
   Were not the paths I meant vnto thy praise:
For seeliest Ignorance on these may light,
   Which, when it sounds at best, but eccho's right;
Or blinde Affection, which doth ne're aduance
   The truth, but gropes, and vrgeth all by chance;
Or crafty Malice, might pretend this praise,
   And thinke to ruine, where it seem'd to raise.
These are, as some infamous Baud, or Whore,
   Should praise a Matron. What could hurt her more?
But thou art proofe against them, and indeed
   Aboue th'ill fortune of them, or the need.
I, therefore will begin. Soule of the Age!
   The applause! delight! the wonder of our Stage!
My Shakespeare, rise; I will not lodge thee by
   Chaucer, or Spenser, or bid Beaumont lye
A little further, to make thee a roome:
   Thou art a Moniment, without a tombe,
And art aliue still, while thy Booke doth liue,
   And we haue wits to read, and praise to giue.
That I not mixe thee so, my braine excuses;
   I meane with great, but disproportion'd Muses:
For, if I thought my iudgement were of yeeres,
   I should commit thee surely with thy peeres,
And tell, how farre thou didst our Lily out-shine,
   Or sporting Kid, or Marlowes mighty line.
And though thou hadst small Latine, and lesse Greeke,
   From thence to honour thee, I would not seeke
For names; but call forth thund'ring Æschilus,
   Euripides, and Sophocles to vs,
Paccuuius, Accius, him of Cordoua dead,
   To life againe, to heare thy Buskin tread,
And shake a Stage: Or, when thy Sockes were on,
   Leaue thee alone, for the comparison

Of all, that insolent Greece, or haughtie Rome
  sent forth, or since did from their ashes come.
Triumph, my Britaine, thou hast one to showe,
  To whom all Scenes of Europe homage owe.
He was not of an age, but for all time!
  And all the Muses still were in their prime,
When like Apollo he came forth to warme
  Our eares, or like a Mercury to charme!
Nature her selfe was proud of his designes,
  And ioy'd to weare the dressing of his lines!
Which were so richly spun, and wouen so fit,
  As, since, she will vouchsafe no other Wit.
The merry Greeke, tart Aristophanes,
  Neat Terence, witty Plautus, now not please;
But antiquated, and deserted lye
  As they were not of Natures family.
Yet must I not giue Nature all: Thy Art,
  My gentle Shakespeare, must enioy a part.
For though the Poets matter, Nature be,
  His Art doth giue the fashion. And, that he,
Who casts to write a liuing line, must sweat,
  (such as thine are) and strike the second heat
Vpon the Muses anuile: turne the same,
  (And himselfe with it) that he thinkes to frame;
Or for the lawrell, he may gaine a scorne,
  For a good Poet's made, as well as borne.
And such wert thou. Looke how the fathers face
  Liues in his issue, euen so, the race
Of Shakespeares minde, and manners brightly shines
  In his well torned, and true-filed lines:
In each of which, he seemes to shake a Lance,
  As brandish't at the eyes of Ignorance.
Sweet Swan of Auon! what a sight it were
  To see thee in our waters yet appeare,
And make those flights vpon the bankes of Thames,
  That so did take Eliza, and our Iames!
But stay, I see thee in the Hemisphere
  Aduanc'd, and made a Constellation there!
Shine forth, thou Starre of Poets, and with rage,
  Or influence, chide, or cheere the drooping Stage;
Which, since thy flight frō hence, hath mourn'd like night,
  And despaires day, but for thy Volumes light.

                                    BEN: IONSON.

Vpon the Lines and Life of the Famous Scenicke Poet, Master WILLIAM SHAKESPEARE.

THose hands, which you so clapt, go now, and wring
You *Britaines* braue; for done are *Shakespeares* dayes:
His dayes are done, that made the dainty Playes,
Which made the Globe of heau'n and earth to ring.
Dry'de is that veine, dry'd is the *Thespian* Spring,
Turn'd all to teares, and *Phœbus* clouds his rayes:
That corp's, that coffin now besticke those bayes,
Which crown'd him *Poet* first, then *Poets* King.
If *Tragedies* might any *Prologue* haue,
All those he made, would scarse make one to this:
Where *Fame*, now that he gone is to the graue
(Deaths publique tyring-house) the *Nuncius* is.
    For though his line of life went soone about,
    The life yet of his lines shall neuer out.

HVGH HOLLAND.

A CATALOGVE

of the seuerall Comedies, Histories, and Tragedies contained in this Volume.

COMEDIES.

The Tempest.	Folio 1.
The two Gentlemen of Verona.	20
The Merry Wiues of Windsor.	38
Measure for Measure.	61
The Comedy of Errours.	85
Much adoo about Nothing.	101
Loues Labour lost.	122
Midsommer Nights Dreame.	145
The Merchant of Venice.	163
As you Like it.	185
The Taming of the Shrew.	208
All is well, that Ends well.	230
Twelfe-Night, or what you will.	255
The Winters Tale.	304

HISTORIES.

The Life and Death of King John.	Fol. 1.
The Life & death of Richard the second.	23
The First part of King Henry the fourth.	46
The Second part of K. Henry the fourth.	74
The Life of King Henry the Fift.	69
The First part of King Henry the Sixt.	96
The Second part of King Hen. the Sixt.	120
The Third part of King Henry the Sixt.	147
The Life & Death of Richard the Third.	173
The Life of King Henry the Eight.	205

TRAGEDIES.

The Tragedy of Coriolanus.	Fol. 1.
Titus Andronicus.	31
Romeo and Juliet.	53
Timon of Athens.	80
The Life and death of Julius Cæsar.	109
The Tragedy of Macbeth.	131
The Tragedy of Hamlet.	152
King Lear.	283
Othello, the Moore of Venice.	310
Anthony and Cleopater.	346
Cymbeline King of Britaine.	369

TO THE MEMORIE
of the deceased Authour Maister
W. SHAKESPEARE.

Shake-speare, at length thy pious fellowes giue
The world thy Workes: thy Workes, by which, out-liue
Thy Tombe, thy name must: when that stone is rent,
And Time dissolues thy Stratford Moniment,
Here we aliue shall view thee still. This Booke,
When Brasse and Marble fade, shall make thee looke
Fresh to all Ages: when Posteritie
Shall loath what's new, thinke all is prodegie
That is not Shake-speares; eu'ry Line, each Verse
Here shall reuiue, redeeme thee from thy Herse.
Nor Fire, nor cankring Age, as Naso said,
Of his, thy wit-fraught Booke shall once inuade.
Nor shall I e're beleeue, or thinke thee dead
(Though mist) vntill our bankrout Stage be sped
(Impossible) with some new straine t'out-do
Passions of Iuliet, and her Romeo;
Or till I heare a Scene more nobly take,
Then when thy half-Sword parlying Romans spake.
Till these, till any of thy Volumes rest
Shall with more fire, more feeling be exprest,
Be sure, our Shake-speare, thou canst neuer dye,
But crown'd with Lawrell, liue eternally.

L. Digges.

To the memorie of M. W. Shake-speare.

WEE wondred (Shake-speare) that thou went'st so soone
From the Worlds-Stage, to the Graues-Tyring-roome.
Wee thought thee dead, but this thy printed worth,
Tels thy Spectators, that thou went'st but forth
To enter with applause. An Actors Art,
Can dye, and liue, to acte a second part.
That's but an Exit of Mortalitie;
This, a Re-entrance to a Plaudite.

I. M.

The Workes of William Shakespeare,

containing all his Comedies, Histories, and Tragedies: Truely set forth, according to their first ORIGINALL.

The Names of the Principall Actors
in all these Playes.

William Shakespeare.	Samuel Gilburne.
Richard Burbadge.	Robert Armin.
John Hemmings.	William Ostler.
Augustine Phillips.	Nathan Field.
William Kempt.	John Underwood.
Thomas Poope.	Nicholas Tooley.
George Bryan.	William Ecclestone.
Henry Condell.	Joseph Taylor.
William Slye.	Robert Benfield.
Richard Cowly.	Robert Goughe.
John Lowine.	Richard Robinson.
Samuell Crosse.	Iohn Shancke.
Alexander Cooke.	Iohn Rice.

THE TEMPEST.

Actus primus, Scena prima.

A tempestuous noise of Thunder and Lightning heard: Enter a Ship-master, and a Boteswaine.

Master.

Bote-swaine.

Botes. Heere Master: What cheere?

Mast. Good: Speake to th'Mariners: fall too't, yarely, or we run our selues a ground, bestirre, bestirre. *Exit.*

Enter Mariners.

Botes. Heigh my hearts, cheerely, cheerely my harts: yare, yare: Take in the toppe-sale: Tend to th'Masters whistle: Blow till thou burst thy winde, if roome enough.

Enter Alonso, Sebastian, Anthonio, Ferdinando, Gonzalo, and others.

Alon. Good Boteswaine haue care: where's the Master? Play the men.

Botes. I pray now keepe below.

Anth. Where is the Master, Boson?

Botes. Do you not heare him? you marre our labour, Keepe your Cabines: you do assist the storme.

Gonz. Nay, good be patient.

Botes. When the Sea is: hence, what cares these roarers for the name of King? to Cabine; silence: trouble vs not.

Gon. Good, yet remember whom thou hast aboord.

Botes. None that I more loue then my selfe. You are a Counsellor, if you can command these Elements to silence, and worke the peace of the present, wee will not hand a rope more, vse your authoritie: If you cannot, giue thankes you haue liu'd so long, and make your selfe readie in your Cabine for the mischance of the houre, if it so hap. Cheerely good hearts: out of our way I say. *Exit.*

Gon. I haue great comfort from this fellow: methinks he hath no drowning marke vpon him, his complexion is perfect Gallowes: stand fast good Fate to his hanging, make the rope of his destiny our cable, for our owne doth little aduantage: If he be not borne to bee hang'd, our case is miserable. *Exit.*

Enter Boteswaine.

Botes. Downe with the top-Mast: yare, lower, lower, bring her to Try with Maine-course. A plague——

A cry within. Enter Sebastian, Anthonio & Gonzalo.

vpon this howling: they are lowder then the weather, or our office: yet againe? What do you heere? Shal we giue ore and drowne, haue you a minde to sinke?

Sebas. A poxe o' your throat, you bawling, blasphemous incharitable Dog.

Botes. Worke you then.

Anth. Hang cur, hang, you whoreson insolent Noysemaker, we are lesse afraid to be drownde, then thou art.

Gonz. I'le warrant him for drowning, though the Ship were no stronger then a Nutt-shell, and as leaky as an vnstanched wench.

Botes. Lay her a hold, a hold, set her two courses off to Sea againe, lay her off.

Enter Mariners wet.

Mari. All lost, to prayers, to prayers, all lost.

Botes. What must our mouths be cold?

Gonz. The King, and Prince, at prayers, let's assist them, for our case is as theirs.

Sebas. I'am out of patience.

An. We are meerly cheated of our liues by drunkards, This wide-chopt-rascall, would thou mightst lye drowning the washing of ten Tides.

Gonz. Hee'l be hang'd yet,
Though euery drop of water sweare against it,
And gape at widst to glut him. *A confused noyse within.* Mercy on vs.
We split, we split, Farewell my wife, and children,
Farewell brother: we split, we split, we split.

Anth. Let's all sinke with' King

Seb. Let's take leaue of him. *Exit.*

Gonz. Now would I giue a thousand furlongs of Sea, for an Acre of barren ground: Long heath, Browne firrs, any thing: the wills aboue be done, but I would faine dye a dry death. *Exit.*

Scena Secunda.

Enter Prospero and Miranda.

Mira. If by your Art (my deerest father) you haue
Put the wild waters in this Rore; alay them:
The skye it seemes would powre down stinking pitch,
But that the Sea, mounting to th' welkins cheeke,
Dashes the fire out. Oh! I haue suffered
With those that I saw suffer: A braue vessell

(Who had no doubt some noble creature in her)
Dash'd all to peeces : O the cry did knocke
Against my very heart : poore soules, they perish'd.
Had I byn any God of power, I would
Haue suncke the Sea within the Earth, or ere
It should the good Ship so haue swallow'd, and
The fraughting Soules within her.

  Pros. Be collected,
No more amazement : Tell your pitteous heart
there's no harme done.

  Mira. O woe, the day.

  Pros. No harme :
I haue done nothing, but in care of thee
(Of thee my deere one ; thee my daughter) who
Art ignorant of what thou art . naught knowing
Of whence I am : nor that I am more better
Then *Prospero*, Master of a full poore cell,
And thy no greater Father.

  Mira. More to know
Did neuer medle with my thoughts.

  Pros. 'Tis time
I should informe thee farther : Lend thy hand
And plucke my Magick garment from me : So,
Lye there my Art : wipe thou thine eyes, haue comfort,
The direfull spectacle of the wracke which touch'd
The very vertue of compassion in thee :
I haue with such prouision in mine Art
So safely ordered, that there is no soule
No not so much perdition as an hayre
Betid to any creature in the vessell
Which thou heardst cry, which thou saw'st sinke : Sit
For thou must now know farther. [*downe,*

  Mira. You haue often
Begun to tell me what I am, but stopt
And left me to a booteleffe Inquisition,
Concluding, stay : not yet.

  Pros. The howr's now come
The very minute byds thee ope thine eare,
Obey, and be attentiue. Canst thou remember
A time before we came vnto this Cell ?
I doe not thinke thou canst, for then thou was't not
Out three yeeres old.

  Mira. Certainely Sir, I can.

  Pros. By what ? by any other house, or person ?
Of any thing the Image, tell me, that
Hath kept with thy remembrance.

  Mira. 'Tis farre off :
And rather like a dreame, then an assurance
That my remembrance warrants : Had I not
Fowre, or fiue women once, that tended me ?

  Pros. Thou hadst ; and more *Miranda* : But how is it
That this liues in thy minde ? What seest thou els
In the dark-backward and Abisme of Time ?
Yf thou remembrest ought ere thou cam'st here,
How thou cam'st here thou maist.

  Mira. But that I doe not.

  Pros. Twelue yere since(*Miranda*)twelue yere since,
Thy father was the Duke of *Millaine* and
A Prince of power :

  Mira. Sir, are not you my Father ?

  Pros. Thy Mother was a peece of vertue, and
She said thou wast my daughter ; and thy father
Was Duke of *Millaine*, and his onely heire,
And Princesse ; no worse Issued.

  Mira. O the heauens,
What fowle play had we, that we came from thence ?
Or blessed was't we did ?

  Pros. Both, both my Girle.
By fowle-play (as thou saist) were we heau'd thence,
But blessedly holpe hither.

  Mira. O my heart bleedes
To thinke oth' teene that I haue turn'd you to,
Which is from my remembrance, please you, farther ;

  Pros. My brother and thy vncle, call'd *Anthonio* :
I pray thee marke me, that a brother should
Be so perfidious : he, whom next thy selfe
Of all the world I lou'd, and to him put
The mannage of my state, as at that time
Through all the signories it was the first,
And *Prospero*, the prime Duke, being so reputed
In dignity ; and for the liberall Artes,
Without a paralell ; those being all my studie,
The Gouernment I cast vpon my brother,
And to my State grew stranger, being transported
And rapt in secret studies, thy false vncle
(Do'st thou attend me ?)

  Mira. Sir, most heedefully.

  Pros. Being once perfected how to graunt suites,
how to deny them : who t'aduance, and who
To trash for ouer-topping ; new created
The creatures that were mine, I say, or chang'd 'em,
Or els new form'd 'em ; hauing both the key,
Of Officer, and office, set all hearts i'th state
To what tune pleas'd his eare, that now he was
The Iuy which had hid my princely Trunck,
And suckt my verdure out on't : Thou attend'st not ?

  Mira. O good Sir, I doe.

  Pros. I pray thee marke me :
I thus neglecting worldly ends, all dedicated
To closenes, and the bettering of my mind
with that, which but by being so retir'd
Ore-priz'd all popular rate : in my false brother
Awak'd an euill nature, and my trust
Like a good parent, did beget of him
A falsehood in it's contrarie, as great
As my trust was, which had indeede no limit,
A confidence sans bound. He being thus Lorded,
Not onely with what my reuenew yeelded,
But what my power might els exact. Like one
Who hauing into truth, by telling of it,
Made such a synner of his memorie
To credite his owne lie, he did beleeue
He was indeed the Duke, out o'th' Substitution
And executing th'outward face of Roialtie
With all prerogatiue : hence his Ambition growing :
Do'st thou heare ?

  Mira. Your tale, Sir, would cure deafenesse.

  Pros. To haue no Schreene between this part he plaid,
And him he plaid it for, he needes will be
Absolute *Millaine*, Me (poore man) my Librarie
Was Dukedome large enough : of temporall roalties
He thinks me now incapable. Confederates
(so drie he was for Sway) with King of *Naples*
To giue him Annuall tribute, doe him homage
Subiect his Coronet, to his Crowne and bend
The Dukedom yet vnbow'd (alas poore *Millaine*)
To most ignoble stooping.

  Mira. Oh the heauens :

  Pros. Marke his condition, and th'euent, then tell me
If this might be a brother.

  Mira. I should sinne
To thinke but Noblie of my Grand-mother,

Good

The Tempest.

Good wombes haue borne bad sonnes.

 Pro. Now the Condition.
This King of *Naples* being an Enemy
To me inueterate, hearkens my Brothers suit,
Which was, That he in lieu o'th' premises,
Of homage, and I know not how much Tribute,
Should presently extirpate me and mine
Out of the Dukedome, and confer faire *Millaine*
With all the Honors, on my brother: Whereon
A treacherous Armie leuied, one mid-night
Fated to th' purpose, did *Anthonio* open
The gates of *Millaine*, and ith' dead of darkenesse
The ministers for th' purpose hurried thence
Me, and thy crying selfe.

 Mir. Alack, for pitty:
I not remembring how I cride out then
Will cry it ore againe: it is a hint
That wrings mine eyes too't.

 Pro. Heare a little further,
And then I'le bring thee to the present businesse
Which now's vpon's: without the which, this Story
Were most impertinent.

 Mir. Wherefore did they not
That howre destroy vs?

 Pro. Well demanded, wench:
My Tale prouokes that question: Deare, they durst not,
So deare the loue my people bore me: nor set
A marke so bloudy on the businesse; but
With colours fairer, painted their foule ends.
In few, they hurried vs a-boord a Barke,
Bore vs some Leagues to Sea, where they prepared
A rotten carkasse of a Butt, not rigg'd,
Nor tackle, sayle, nor mast, the very rats
Instinctiuely haue quit it: There they hoyst vs
To cry to th' Sea, that roard to vs; to sigh
To th' windes, whose pitty sighing backe againe
Did vs but louing wrong.

 Mir. Alack, what trouble
Was I then to you?

 Pro. O, a Cherubin
Thou was't that did preserue me; Thou didst smile,
Infused with a fortitude from heauen,
When I haue deck'd the sea with drops full salt,
Vnder my burthen groan'd, which rais'd in me
An vndergoing stomacke, to beare vp
Against what should ensue.

 Mir. How came we a shore?

 Pro. By prouidence diuine,
Some food, we had, and some fresh water, that
A noble *Neopolitan Gonzalo*
Out of his Charity, (who being then appointed
Master of this designe) did giue vs, with
Rich garments, linnens, stuffs, and necessaries
Which since haue steeded much, so of his gentlenesse
Knowing I lou'd my bookes, he furnish'd me
From mine owne Library, with volumes, that
I prize aboue my Dukedome.

 Mir. Would I might
But euer see that man.

 Pro. Now I arise,
Sit still, and heare the last of our sea-sorrow:
Heere in this Iland we arriu'd, and heere
Haue I, thy Schoolemaster, made thee more profit
Then other Princesse can, that haue more time
For vainer howres; and Tutors, not so carefull.

 Mir. Heuens thank you for't. And now I pray you Sir,
For still 'tis beating in my minde; your reason
For raysing this Sea-storme?

 Pro. Know thus far forth,
By accident most strange, bountifull *Fortune*
(Now my deere Lady) hath mine enemies
Brought to this shore: And by my prescience
I finde my *Zenith* doth depend vpon
A most auspitious starre, whose influence
If now I court not, but omit; my fortunes
Will euer after droope: Heare cease more questions,
Thou art inclinde to sleepe: 'tis a good dulnesse,
And giue it way: I know thou canst not chuse:
Come away, Seruant, come; I am ready now,
Approach my *Ariel*. Come.   *Enter Ariel.*

 Ari. All haile, great Master, graue Sir, haile: I come
To answer thy best pleasure; be't to fly,
To swim, to diue into the fire: to ride
On the curld clowds: to thy strong bidding, taske
Ariel, and all his Qualitie.

 Pro. Hast thou, Spirit,
Perform'd to point, the Tempest that I bad thee.

 Ar. To euery Article.
I boorded the Kings ship: now on the Beake,
Now in the Waste, the Decke, in euery Cabyn,
I flam'd amazement, sometime I'ld diuide
And burne in many places; on the Top-mast,
The Yards and Bore-spritt, would I flame distinctly,
Then meete, and ioyne. *Ioues* Lightning, the precursers
O'th dreadfull Thunder-claps more momentarie
And sight out-running were not; the fire, and cracks
Of sulphurous roaring, the most mighty *Neptune*
Seeme to besiege, and make his bold waues tremble,
Yea, his dread Trident shake.

 Pro. My braue Spirit,
Who was so firme, so constant, that this coyle
Would not infect his reason?

 Ar. Not a soule
But felt a Feauer of the madde, and plaid
Some tricks of desperation; all but Mariners
Plung'd in the foaming bryne, and quit the vessell;
Then all a fire with me the Kings sonne *Ferdinand*
With haire vp-staring (then like reeds, not haire)
Was the first man that leapt; cride hell is empty,
And all the Diuels are heere.

 Pro. Why that's my spirit:
But was not this nye shore?

 Ar. Close by, my Master.

 Pro. But are they (*Ariell*) safe?

 Ar. Not a haire perish'd:
On their sustaining garments not a blemish,
But fresher then before: and as thou badst me,
In troops I haue dispers'd them 'bout the Isle:
The Kings sonne haue I landed by himselfe,
Whom I left cooling of the Ayre with sighes,
In an odde Angle of the Isle, and sitting
His armes in this sad knot.

 Pro. Of the Kings ship,
The Marriners, say how thou hast dispos'd,
And all the rest o'th' Fleete?

 Ar. Safely in harbour
Is the Kings shippe, in the deepe Nooke, where once
Thou calldst me vp at midnight to fetch dewe
From the still-vext *Bermoothes*, there she's hid;
The Marriners all vnder hatches stowed,
Who, with a Charme ioynd to their suffred labour
I haue left asleep: and for the rest o'th' Fleet

(Which I dispers'd) they all haue met againe,
And are vpon the *Mediterranian* Flote
Bound sadly home for *Naples*,
Supposing that they saw the Kings ship wrackt,
And his great person perish.

Pro. *Ariel*, thy charge
Exactly is perform'd; but there's more worke:
What is the time o'th'day?

Ar. Past the mid season.

Pro. At least two Glasses: the time 'twixt six & now
Must by vs both be spent most preciously.

Ar. Is there more toyle? Since ỹ dost giue me pains,
Let me remember thee what thou hast promis'd,
Which is not yet perform'd me.

Pro. How now? moodie?
What is't thou canst demand?

Ar. My Libertie.

Pro. Before the time be out? no more:

Ar. I prethee,
Remember I haue done thee worthy seruice,
Told thee no lyes, made thee no mistakings, serv'd
Without or grudge, or grumblings; thou did promise
To bate me a full yeere.

Pro. Do'st thou forget
From what a torment I did free thee? *Ar.* No.

Pro. Thou do'st: & thinkst it much to tread ỹ Ooze
Of the salt deepe;
To run vpon the sharpe winde of the North,
To doe me businesse in the veines o'th' earth
When it is bak'd with frost.

Ar. I doe not Sir.

Pro. Thou liest, malignant Thing: hast thou forgot
The fowle Witch *Sycorax*, who with Age and Enuy
Was growne into a hoope? hast thou forgot her?

Ar. No Sir.

Pro. Thou hast: where was she born? speak: tell me:

Ar. Sir, in *Argier*.

Pro. Oh, was she so: I must
Once in a moneth recount what thou hast bin,
Which thou forgetst. This damn'd Witch *Sycorax*
For mischiefes manifold, and sorceries terrible
To enter humane hearing, from *Argier*
Thou know'st was banish'd: for one thing she did
They wold not take her life: Is not this true? *Ar.* I, Sir.

Pro. This blew ey'd hag, was hither brought with child,
And here was left by th' Saylors; thou my slaue,
As thou reportst thy selfe, was then her seruant,
And for thou wast a Spirit too delicate
To act her earthy, and abhord commands,
Refusing her grand hests, she did confine thee
By helpe of her more potent Ministers,
And in her most vnmittigable rage,
Into a clouen Pyne, within which rift
Imprison'd, thou didst painefully remaine
A dozen yeeres: within which space she di'd,
And left thee there: where thou didst vent thy groanes
As fast as Mill-wheeles strike: Then was this Island
(Saue for the Son, that he did littour heere,
A frekelld whelpe, hag-borne) not honour'd with
A humane shape.

Ar. Yes: *Caliban* her sonne.

Pro. Dull thing, I say so: he, that *Caliban*
Whom now I keepe in seruice, thou best know'st
What torment I did finde thee in; thy grones
Did make wolues howle, and penetrate the breasts
Of euer-angry Beares; it was a torment
To lay vpon the damn'd, which *Sycorax*
Could not againe vndoe: it was mine Art,
When I arriu'd, and heard thee, that made gape
The Pyne, and let thee out.

Ar. I thanke thee Master.

Pro. If thou more murmur'st, I will rend an Oake
And peg-thee in his knotty entrailes, till
Thou hast howl'd away twelue winters.

Ar. Pardon, Master,
I will be correspondent to command
And doe my spryting, gently.

Pro. Doe so: and after two daies
I will discharge thee.

Ar. That's my noble Master:
What shall I doe? say what? what shall I doe?

Pro. Goe make thy selfe like a Nymph o'th' Sea,
Be subiect to no sight but thine, and mine: inuisible
To euery eye-ball else: goe take this shape
And hither come in't: goe: hence
With diligence.   *Exit.*

Pro. Awake, deere hart awake, thou hast slept well,
Awake.

Mir. The strangenes of your story, put
Heauinesse in me.

Pro. Shake it off: Come on,
Wee'll visit *Caliban*, my slaue, who neuer
Yeelds vs kinde answere.

Mir. 'Tis a villaine Sir, I doe not loue to looke on.

Pro. But as 'tis
We cannot misse him: he do's make our fire,
Fetch in our wood, and serues in Offices
That profit vs: What hoa: slaue: *Caliban*:
Thou Earth, thou: speake.

Cal. within. There's wood enough within.

Pro. Come forth I say, there's other busines for thee:
Come thou Tortoys, when? *Enter Ariel like a water-*
Fine apparision: my queint *Ariel*,   *Nymph.*
Hearke in thine eare.

Ar. My Lord, it shall be done.   *Exit.*

Pro. Thou poysonous slaue, got by ỹ diuell himselfe
Vpon thy wicked Dam; come forth.   *Enter Caliban.*

Cal. As wicked dewe, as ere my mother brush'd
With Rauens feather from vnwholesome Fen
Drop on you both: A Southwest blow on yee,
And blister you all ore.

Pro. For this be sure, to night thou shalt haue cramps,
Side-stitches, that shall pen thy breath vp, Vrchins
Shall for that vast of night, that they may worke
All exercise on thee: thou shalt be pinch'd
As thicke as hony-combe, each pinch more stinging
Then Bees that made 'em.

Cal. I must eat my dinner:
This Island's mine by *Sycorax* my mother,
Which thou tak'st from me: when thou cam'st first
Thou stroakst me, & made much of me: wouldst giue me
Water with berries in't: and teach me how
To name the bigger Light, and how the lesse
That burne by day, and night: and then I lou'd thee
And shew'd thee all the qualities o'th' Isle,
The fresh Springs, Brine-pits; barren place and fertill,
Curs'd be I that did so: All the Charmes
Of *Sycorax*: Toades, Beetles, Batts light on you:
For I am all the Subiects that you haue,
Which first was min owne King: and here you sty-me
In this hard Rocke, whiles you doe keepe from me
The rest o'th' Island.

           Pro. Thou

The Tempest.

Pro. Thou most lying slaue,
Whom stripes may moue, not kindnes: I haue vs'd thee
(Filth as thou art) with humane care, and lodg'd thee
In mine owne Cell, till thou didst seeke to violate
The honor of my childe.

Cal. Oh ho, oh ho, would't had bene done:
Thou didst preuent me, I had peopel'd else
This Isle with *Calibans*.

Mira. Abhorred Slaue,
Which any print of goodnesse wilt not take,
Being capable of all ill: I pittied thee,
Took pains to make thee speak, taught thee each houre
One thing or other: when thou didst not (Sauage)
Know thine owne meaning; but wouldst gabble, like
A thing most brutish, I endow'd thy purposes
With words that made them knowne: But thy vild race
(Tho thou didst learn) had that in't, which good natures
Could not abide to be with; therefore wast thou
Deseruedly confin'd into this Rocke, who hadst
Deseru'd more then a prison.

Cal. You taught me Language, and my profit on't
Is, I know how to curse: the red-plague rid you
For learning me your language.

Pros. Hag-seed, hence:
Fetch vs in Fewell, and be quicke thou'rt best
To answer other businesse: shrug'st thou (Malice)
If thou neglectst, or dost vnwillingly
What I command, Ile racke thee with old Crampes,
Fill all thy bones with Aches, make thee rore,
That beasts shall tremble at thy dyn.

Cal. No, 'pray thee.
I must obey, his Art is of such pow'r,
It would controll my Dams god *Setebos*,
And make a vassaile of him.

Pro. So slaue, hence. *Exit Cal.*

Enter Ferdinand & Ariel, inuisible playing & singing.

Ariel Song. Come vnto these yellow sands,
    and then take hands:
Curtsied when you haue, and kist
    the wilde waues whist:
Foote it featly heere, and there, and sweete Sprights beare
    the burthen. *Burthen dispersedly.*
Harke, harke, bowgh wawgh: the watch-Dogges barke,
    bowgh-wawgh.

Ar. Hark, hark, I heare, the straine of strutting *Chanticlere*
    cry cockadidle-dowe.

Fer. Where shold this Musick be? I'th aire, or th'earth?
It sounds no more: and sure it waytes vpon
Some God 'oth'Iland, sitting on a banke,
Weeping againe the King my Fathers wracke.
This Musicke crept by me vpon the waters,
Allaying both their fury, and my passion
With it's sweet ayre: thence I haue follow'd it
(Or it hath drawne me rather) but 'tis gone.
No, it begins againe.

Ariell Song. Full fadom fiue thy Father lies,
    Of his bones are Corrall made:
    Those are pearles that were his eies,
    Nothing of him that doth fade,
    But doth suffer a Sea-change
    Into something rich, & strange:
    Sea-Nimphs hourly ring his knell.
        Burthen: ding dong.
Harke now I heare them, ding-dong bell.

Fer. The Ditty do's remember my drown'd father,
This is no mortall busines, nor no sound
That the earth owes: I heare it now aboue me.

Pro. The fringed Curtaines of thine eye aduance,
And say what thou see'st yond.

Mira. What is't a Spirit?
Lord, how it lookes about: Beleeue me sir,
It carries a braue forme. But 'tis a spirit.

Pro. No wench, it eats, and sleeps, & hath such senses
As we haue: such. This Gallant which thou seest
Was in the wracke: and but hee's something stain'd
With greefe (that's beauties canker) y' might'st call him
A goodly person: he hath lost his fellowes,
And strayes about to finde 'em.

Mir. I might call him
A thing diuine, for nothing naturall
I euer saw so Noble.

Pro. It goes on I see
As my soule prompts it: Spirit, fine spirit, Ile free thee
Within two dayes for this.

Fer. Most sure the Goddesse
On whom these ayres attend: Vouchsafe my pray'r
May know if you remaine vpon this Island,
And that you will some good instruction giue
How I may beare me heere: my prime request
(Which I do last pronounce) is (O you wonder)
If you be Mayd, or no?

Mir. No wonder Sir,
But certainly a Mayd.

Fer. My Language? Heauens:
I am the best of them that speake this speech,
Were I but where 'tis spoken.

Pro. How? the best?
What wer't thou if the King of *Naples* heard thee?

Fer. A single thing, as I am now, that wonders
To heare thee speake of *Naples*: he do's heare me,
And that he do's, I weepe: my selfe am *Naples*,
Who, with mine eyes (neuer since at ebbe) beheld
The King my Father wrack't.

Mir. Alacke, for mercy.

Fer. Yes faith, & all his Lords, the Duke of *Millaine*
And his braue sonne, being twaine.

Pro. The Duke of *Millaine*
And his more brauer daughter, could controll thee
If now 'twere fit to do't: At the first sight
They haue chang'd eyes: Delicate *Ariel*,
Ile set thee free for this. A word good Sir,
I feare you haue done your selfe some wrong: A word.

Mir. Why speakes my father so vngently? This
Is the third man that ere I saw: the first
That ere I sigh'd for: pitty moue my father
To be enclin'd my way.

Fer. O, if a Virgin,
And your affection not gone forth, Ile make you
The Queene of *Naples*.

Pro. Soft sir, one word more.
They are both in eythers pow'rs: But this swift busines
I must vneasie make, least too light winning
Make the prize light. One word more: I charge thee
That thou attend me: Thou do'st heere vsurpe
The name thou ow'st not, and hast put thy selfe
Vpon this Island, as a spy, to win it
From me, the Lord on't.

Fer. No, as I am a man.

Mir. Thet's nothing ill, can dwell in such a Temple,
If the ill-spirit haue so fayre a house,
Good things will striue to dwell with't.

Pro. Follow me.

Prof. Speake not you for him: hee's a Traitor: come,
Ile manacle thy necke and feete together:
Sea water shalt thou drinke: thy food shall be
The fresh-brooke Mussels, wither'd roots, and huskes
Wherein the Acorne cradled. Follow.

Fer. No,
I will resist such entertainment, till
Mine enemy ha's more pow'r.

He drawes, and is charmed from mouing.

Mira. O deere Father,
Make not too rash a triall of him, for
Hee's gentle, and not fearfull.

Prof. What I say,
My foote my Tutor? Put thy sword vp Traitor,
Who mak'st a shew, but dar'st not strike: thy conscience
Is so possest with guilt: Come, from thy ward,
For I can heere disarme thee with this sticke,
And make thy weapon drop.

Mira. Beseech you Father.

Prof. Hence: hang not on my garments.

Mira. Sir haue pity,
Ile be his surety.

Prof. Silence: One word more
Shall make me chide thee, if not hate thee: What,
An aduocate for an Impostor? Hush:
Thou think'st there is no more such shapes as he,
(Hauing seene but him and *Caliban:*) Foolish wench,
To th'most of men, this is a *Caliban*,
And they to him are Angels.

Mira. My affections
Are then most humble: I haue no ambition
To see a goodlier man.

Prof. Come on, obey:
Thy Nerues are in their infancy againe,
And haue no vigour in them.

Fer. So they are:
My spirits, as in a dreame, are all bound vp:
My Fathers losse, the weaknesse which I feele,
The wracke of all my friends, nor this mans threats,
To whom I am subdude, are but light to me,
Might I but through my prison once a day
Behold this Mayd: all corners else o'th'Earth
Let liberty make vse of: space enough
Haue I in such a prison.

Prof. It workes: Come on.
Thou hast done well, fine *Ariell*: follow me,
Harke what thou else shalt do mee.

Mira. Be of comfort,
My Fathers of a better nature (Sir)
Then he appeares by speech: this is vnwonted
Which now came from him.

Prof. Thou shalt be as free
As mountaine windes; but then exactly do
All points of my command.

Ariell. To th'syllable.

Prof. Come follow: speake not for him. *Exeunt.*

Actus Secundus. Scœna Prima.

Enter Alonso, Sebastian, Anthonio, Gonzalo, Adrian,
Francisco, and others.

Gonz. Beseech you Sir, be merry; you haue cause,
(So haue we all) of ioy; for our escape
Is much beyond our losse; our hint of woe
Is common, euery day, some Saylors wife,
The Masters of some Merchant, and the Merchant
Haue iust our Theame of woe: But for the miracle,
(I meane our preseruation) few in millions
Can speake like vs: then wisely (good Sir) weigh
Our sorrow, with our comfort.

Alons. Prethee peace.

Seb. He receiues comfort like cold porredge.

Ant. The Visitor will not giue him ore so.

Seb. Looke, hee's winding vp the watch of his wit,
By and by it will strike.

Gon. Sir.

Seb. One: Tell.

Gon. When euery greefe is entertaind,
That's offer'd comes to th'entertainer.

Seb. A dollor.

Gon. Dolour comes to him indeed, you haue spoken
truer then you purpos'd.

Seb. You haue taken it wiselier then I meant you
should.

Gon. Therefore my Lord.

Ant. Fie, what a spend-thrift is he of his tongue.

Alon. I pre-thee spare.

Gon. Well, I haue done: But yet

Seb. He will be talking.

Ant. Which, of he, or Adrian, for a good wager,
First begins to crow?

Seb. The old Cocke.

Ant. The Cockrell.

Seb. Done: The wager?

Ant. A Laughter.

Seb. A match.

Adr. Though this Island seeme to be desert,

Seb. Ha, ha, ha.

Ant. So: you'r paid.

Adr. Vninhabitable, and almost inaccessible.

Seb. Yet

Adr. Yet

Ant. He could not misse't.

Adr. It must needs be of subtle, tender, and delicate
temperance.

Ant. Temperance was a delicate wench.

Seb. I, and a subtle, as he most learnedly deliuer'd.

Adr. The ayre breathes vpon vs here most sweetly.

Seb. As if it had Lungs, and rotten ones.

Ant. Or, as 'twere perfum'd by a Fen.

Gon. Heere is euery thing aduantageous to life.

Ant. True, saue meanes to liue.

Seb. Of that there's none, or little.

Gon. How lush and lusty the grasse lookes?
How greene?

Ant. The ground indeed is tawny.

Seb. With an eye of greene in't.

Ant. He misses not much.

Seb. No: he doth but mistake the truth totally.

Gon. But the rariety of it is, which is indeed almost
beyond credit.

Seb. As many voucht rarieties are.

Gon. That our Garments being (as they were) drencht
in the Sea, hold notwithstanding their freshnesse and
glosses, being rather new dy'de then stain'd with salte
water.

Ant. If but one of his pockets could speake, would
it not say he lyes?

Seb. I, or very falsely pocket vp his report.

Gon.

Gon. Me thinkes our garments are now as fresh as when we put them on first in Affricke, at the marriage of the kings faire daughter *Claribel* to the king of *Tunis*.

Seb. 'Twas a sweet marriage, and we prosper well in our returne.

Adri. *Tunis* was neuer grac'd before with such a Paragon to their Queene.

Gon. Not since widdow *Dido's* time.

Ant. Widow? A pox o'that: how came that Widdow in? Widdow *Dido*!

Seb. What if he had said Widdower *Æneas* too? Good Lord, how you take it?

Adri. Widdow *Dido* said you? You make me study of that: She was of *Carthage*, not of *Tunis*.

Gon. This *Tunis* Sir was *Carthage*.

Adri. *Carthage*?   *Gon.* I assure you *Carthage*.

Ant. His word is more then the miraculous Harpe.

Seb. He hath rais'd the wall, and houses too.

Ant. What impossible matter wil he make easy next?

Seb. I thinke hee will carry this Island home in his pocket, and giue it his sonne for an Apple.

Ant. And sowing the kernels of it in the Sea, bring forth more Islands.

Gon. I.   *Ant.* Why in good time.

Gon. Sir, we were talking, that our garments seeme now as fresh as when we were at *Tunis* at the marriage of your daughter, who is now Queene.

Ant. And the rarest that ere came there.

Seb. Bate (I beseech you) widdow *Dido*.

Ant. O Widdow *Dido*? I, Widdow *Dido*.

Gon. Is not Sir my doublet as fresh as the first day I wore it? I meane in a sort.

Ant. That sort was well fish'd for.

Gon. When I wore it at your daughters marriage.

Alon. You cram these words into mine eares, against the stomacke of my sense: would I had neuer Married my daughter there: For comming thence My sonne is lost, and (in my rate) she too, Who is so farre from *Italy* remoued, I ne're againe shall see her: O thou mine heire Of *Naples* and of *Millaine*, what strange fish Hath made his meale on thee?

Fran. Sir he may liue, I saw him beate the surges vnder him, And ride vpon their backes; he trod the water Whose enmity he flung aside: and bresten The surge most swolne that met him: his bold head 'Boue the contentious waues he kept, and oared Himselfe with his good armes in lusty stroke To th'shore; that ore his waue-worne basis bowed As stooping to releeue him: I not doubt He came aliue to Land.

Alon. No, no, hee's gone.

Seb. Sir you may thank your selfe for this great losse, That would not blesse our Europe with your daughter, But rather loose her to an Affrican, Where she at least, is banish'd from your eye, Who hath cause to wet the greefe on't.

Alon. Pre-thee peace.

Seb. You were kneel'd too, & importun'd otherwise By all of vs: and the faire soule her selfe Waigh'd betweene loathnesse, and obedience, at Which end o'th'beame should bow: we haue lost your (son, I feare for euer: *Millaine* and *Naples* haue Mo widdowes in them of this businesse making, Then we bring men to comfort them:

The faults your owne.

Alon. So is the deer'st oth'losse.

Gon. My Lord *Sebastian*, The truth you speake doth lacke some gentlenesse, And time to speake it in: you rub the sore, When you should bring the plaister.

Seb. Very well.   *Ant.* And most Chirurgeonly.

Gon. It is foule weather in vs all, good Sir, When you are cloudy.

Seb. Fowle weather?   *Ant.* Very foule.

Gon. Had I plantation of this Isle my Lord.

Ant. Hee'd sow't with Nettle-seed.

Seb. Or dockes, or Mallowes.

Gon. And were the King on't, what would I do?

Seb. Scape being drunke, for want of Wine.

Gon. I'th'Commonwealth I would (by contraries) Execute all things: For no kinde of Trafficke Would I admit: No name of Magistrate: Letters should not be knowne: Riches, pouerty, And vse of seruice, none: Contract, Succession, Borne, bound of Land, Tilth, Vineyard none: No vse of Mettall, Corne, or Wine, or Oyle: No occupation, all men idle, all: And Women too, but innocent and pure: No Soueraignty.

Seb. Yet he would be King on't.

Ant. The latter end of his Common-wealth forgets the beginning.

Gon. All things in common Nature should produce Without sweat or endeuour: Treason, fellony, Sword, Pike, Knife, Gun, or neede of any Engine Would I not haue: but Nature should bring forth Of it owne kinde, all foyzon, all abundance To feed my innocent people.

Seb. No marrying 'mong his subiects?

Ant. None (man) all idle; Whores and knaues,

Gon. I would with such perfection gouerne Sir: T'Excell the Golden Age.

Seb. 'Saue his Maiesty.   *Ant.* Long liue *Gonzalo*.

Gon. And do you marke me, Sir?   (me.

Alon. Pre-thee no more: thou dost talke nothing to

Gon. I do well beleeue your Highnesse, and did it to minister occasion to these Gentlemen, who are of such sensible and nimble Lungs, that they alwayes vse to laugh at nothing.

Ant. 'Twas you we laugh'd at.

Gon. Who, in this kind of merry fooling am nothing to you: so you may continue, and laugh at nothing still.

Ant. What a blow was there giuen?

Seb. And it had not falne flat-long.

Gon. You are Gentlemen of braue mettal: you would lift the Moone out of her spheare, if she would continue in it fiue weekes without changing.

Enter Ariell playing solemne Musicke.

Seb. We would so, and then go a Bat-fowling.

Ant. Nay good my Lord, be not angry.

Gon. No I warrant you, I will not aduenture my discretion so weakly: Will you laugh me asleepe, for I am very heauy.

Ant. Go sleepe, and heare vs.

Alon. What, all so soone asleepe? I wish mine eyes Would (with themselues) shut vp my thoughts, I finde they are inclin'd to do so.

Seb. Please you Sir, Do not omit the heauy offer of it: It sildome visits sorrow, when it doth, it is a Comforter.

Ant.

The Tempest.

Ant. We two my Lord, will guard your person,
While you take your rest, and watch your safety.
Alon. Thanke you : Wondrous heauy.
Seb. What a strange drowsines possesses them?
Ant. It is the quality o'th'Clymate.
Seb. Why
Doth it not then our eye-lids sinke ? I finde
Not my selfe dispos'd to sleep.
Ant. Nor I, my spirits are nimble :
They fell together all, as by consent
They dropt, as by a Thunder-stroke : what might
Worthy *Sebastian?* O, what might? no more :
And yet, me thinkes I see it in thy face,
What thou should'st be : th'occasion speakes thee, and
My strong imagination see's a Crowne
Dropping vpon thy head.
Seb. What? art thou waking ?
Ant. Do you not heare me speake ?
Seb. I do, and surely
It is a sleepy Language ; and thou speak'st
Out of thy sleepe : What is it thou didst say?
This is a strange repose, to be asleepe
With eyes wide open : standing, speaking, mouing :
And yet so fast asleepe.
Ant. Noble *Sebastian*,
Thou let'st thy fortune sleepe : die rather : wink'st
Whiles thou art waking.
Seb. Thou do'st snore distinctly,
There's meaning in thy snores.
Ant. I am more serious then my custome : you
Must be so too, if heed me : which to do,
Trebbles thee o're.
Seb. Well : I am standing water.
Ant. Ile teach you how to flow.
Seb. Do so : to ebbe
Hereditary Sloth instructs me.
Ant. O !
If you but knew how you the purpose cherish
Whiles thus you mocke it : how in stripping it
You more inuest it : ebbing men, indeed
(Most often) do so neere the bottome run
By their owne feare, or sloth.
Seb. 'Pre-thee say on,
The setting of thine eye, and cheeke proclaime
A matter from thee ; and a birth, indeed,
Which throwes thee much to yeeld.
Ant. Thus Sir :
Although this Lord of weake remembrance; this
Who shall be of as little memory
When he is earth'd, hath here almost perswaded
(For hee's a Spirit of perswasion, onely
Professes to perswade) the King his sonne's aliue,
'Tis as impossible that hee's vndrown'd,
As he that sleepes heere, swims.
Seb. I haue no hope
That hee's vndrown'd.
Ant. O, out of that no hope,
What great hope haue you? No hope that way, Is
Another way so high a hope, that euen
Ambition cannot pierce a winke beyond
But doubt discouery there. Will you grant with me
That *Ferdinand* is drown'd.
Seb. He's gone.
Ant. Then tell me, who's the next heire of *Naples?*
Seb. *Claribell.*
Ant. She that is Queene of *Tunis* : she that dwels
Ten leagues beyond mans life : she that from *Naples*
Can haue no note, vnlesse the Sun were post :
The Man i'th'Moone's too slow, till new-borne chinnes
Be rough, and Razor-able : She that from whom
We all were sea-swallow'd, though some cast againe,
(And by that destiny) to performe an act
Whereof, what's past is Prologue ; what to come
In yours, and my discharge.
Seb. What stuffe is this ? How say you ?
'Tis true my brothers daughter's Queene of *Tunis*,
So is she heyre of *Naples*, 'twixt which Regions
There is some space.
Ant. A space, whose eu'ry cubit
Seemes to cry out, how shall that *Claribell*
Measure vs backe to *Naples* ? keepe in *Tunis*,
And let *Sebastian* wake. Say, this were death
That now hath seiz'd them, why they were no worse
Then now they are : There be that can rule *Naples*
As well as he that sleepes : Lords, that can prate
As amply, and vnnecessarily
As this *Gonzallo* : I my selfe could make
A Chough of as deepe chat : O, that you bore
The minde that I do ; what a sleepe were this
For your aduancement ? Do you vnderstand me ?
Seb. Me thinkes I do.
Ant. And how do's your content
Tender your owne good fortune?
Seb. I remember
You did supplant your Brother *Prospero.*
Ant. True :
And looke how well my Garments sit vpon me,
Much feater then before : My Brothers seruants
Were then my fellowes, now they are my men.
Seb. But for your conscience.
Ant. I Sir : where lies that ? If 'twere a kybe
'Twould put me to my slipper : But I feele not
This Deity in my bosome : 'Twentie consciences
That stand 'twixt me, and *Millaine*, candied be they,
And melt ere they mollest : Heere lies your Brother,
No better then the earth he lies vpon,
If he were that which now hee's like (that's dead)
Whom I with this obedient steele (three inches of it)
Can lay to bed for euer : whiles you doing thus,
To the perpetuall winke for aye might put
This ancient morsell : this Sir Prudence, who
Should not vpbraid our course : for all the rest
They'l take suggestion, as a Cat laps milke,
They'l tell the clocke, to any businesse that
We say befits the houre.
Seb. Thy case, deere Friend
Shall be my president : As thou got'st *Millaine*,
I'le come by *Naples* : Draw thy sword, one stroke
Shall free thee from the tribute which thou paiest,
And I the King shall loue thee.
Ant. Draw together :
And when I reare my hand, do you the like
To fall it on *Gonzalo.*
Seb. O, but one word.
Enter Ariell with Musicke and Song.
Ariel. My Master through his Art foresees the danger
That you (his friend) are in, and sends me forth
(For else his proiect dies) to keepe them liuing.
Sings in Gonzaloes eare.

While you here do snoaring lie,
Open-ey'd Conspiracie
His time doth take :

The Tempest.

If of Life you keepe a care,
Shake off slumber and beware.
Awake, awake.

Ant. Then let vs both be sodaine.

Gon. Now, good Angels preserue the King.

Alo. Why how now hoa; awake? why are you drawn?
Wherefore this ghastly looking?

Gon. What's the matter?

Seb. Whiles we stood here securing your repose,
(Euen now) we heard a hollow burst of bellowing
Like Buls, or rather Lyons, did't not wake you?
It strooke mine eare most terribly.

Alo. I heard nothing.

Ant. O, 'twas a din to fright a Monsters eare;
To make an earthquake: sure it was the roare
Of a whole heard of Lyons.

Alo. Heard you this *Gonzalo*?

Gon. Vpon mine honour, Sir, I heard a humming,
(And that a strange one too) which did awake me:
I shak'd you Sir, and cride: as mine eyes opend,
I saw their weapons drawne: there was a noyse,
That's verily: 'tis best we stand vpon our guard;
Or that we quit this place: let's draw our weapons.

Alo. Lead off this ground & let's make further search
For my poore sonne.

Gon. Heauens keepe him from these Beasts:
For he is sure i'th Island.

Alo. Lead away. (done.

Ariell. Prospero my Lord, shall know what I haue
So (King) goe safely on to seeke thy Son. *Exeunt.*

Scœna Secunda.

Enter Caliban, with a burthen of Wood (a noyse of Thunder heard.)

Cal. All the infections that the Sunne suckes vp
From Bogs, Fens, Flats, on *Prosper* fall, and make him
By ynch-meale a disease: his Spirits heare me,
And yet I needes must curse. But they'll nor pinch,
Fright me with Vrchyn-shewes, pitch me i'th mire,
Nor lead me like a fire-brand, in the darke
Out of my way, vnlesse he bid'em; but
For euery trifle, are they set vpon me,
Sometime like Apes, that moe and chatter at me,
And after bite me: then like Hedg-hogs, which
Lye tumbling in my bare-foote way, and mount
Their pricks at my foot-fall: sometime am I
All wound with Adders, who with clouen tongues
Doe hisse me into madnesse: Lo, now Lo, *Enter*
Here comes a Spirit of his, and to torment me *Trinculo.*
For bringing wood in slowly: I'le fall flat,
Perchance he will not minde me.

Tri. Here's neither bush, nor shrub to beare off any
weather at all: and another Storme brewing, I heare it
sing ith' winde: yond same blacke cloud, yond huge
one, lookes like a foule bumbard that would shed his
licquor: if it should thunder, as it did before, I know
not where to hide my head: yond same cloud cannot
choose but fall by paile-fuls. What haue we here, a man,
or a fish? dead or aliue? a fish, hee smels like a fish: a
very ancient and fish-like smell: a kinde of, not of the
newest poore-Iohn: a strange fish: were I in *England*
now (as once I was) and had but this fish painted; not
a holiday-foole there but would giue a peece of siluer:
there, would this Monster, make a man: any strange
beast there, makes a man: when they will not giue a
doit to relieue a lame Begger, they will lay out ten to see
a dead *Indian*: Leg'd like a man; and his Finnes like
Armes: warme o' my troth: I doe now let loose my o-
pinion; hold it no longer; this is no fish, but an Islan-
der, that hath lately suffered by a Thunderbolt: Alas,
the storme is come againe: my best way is to creepe vnder his Gaberdine: there is no other shelter here-a-
bout: Misery acquaints a man with strange bedfel-
lowes: I will here shrowd till the dregges of the storme
be past.

Enter Stephano singing.

Ste. I shall no more to sea, to sea, here shall I dye ashore.
This is a very scuruy tune to sing at a mans
Funerall: well, here's my comfort. *Drinkes.*

Sings. *The Master, the Swabber, the Boate-swaine & I;*
The Gunner, and his Mate
Lou'd Mall, Meg, and Marrian, and Margeris,
But none of vs car'd for Kate.
For she had a tongue with a tang,
Would cry to a Sailor goe hang:
She lou'd not the sauour of Tar nor of Pitch,
Yet a Tailor might scratch her where ere she did itch.
Then to Sea Boyes, and let her goe hang.
This is a scuruy tune too:
But here's my comfort. *drinks.*

Cal. Doe not torment me: oh.

Ste. What's the matter?
Haue we diuels here?
Doe you put trickes vpon's with Saluages, and Men of
Inde? ha? I haue not scap'd drowning, to be afeard
now of your foure legges: for it hath bin said; as proper a man as euer went on foure legs, cannot make him
giue ground: and it shall be said so againe, while *Ste-*
phano breathes at' nostrils.

Cal. The Spirit torments me: oh.

Ste. This is some Monster of the Isle, with foure legs;
who hath got (as I take it) an Ague: where the diuell
should he learne our language? I will giue him some reliefe if it be but for that: if I can recouer him, and keepe
him tame, and get to *Naples* with him, he's a Present for any Emperour that euer trod on Neates-lea-
ther.

Cal. Doe not torment me 'prethee: I'le bring my
wood home faster.

Ste. He's in his fit now; and doe's not talke after the
wisest; hee shall taste of my Bottle: if hee haue neuer
drunke wine afore, it will goe neere to remoue his Fit:
if I can recouer him, and keepe him tame, I will not take
too much for him; hee shall pay for him that hath him,
and that soundly.

Cal. Thou do'st me yet but little hurt; thou wilt a-
non, I know it by thy trembling: Now *Prosper* workes
vpon thee.

Ste. Come on your wayes: open your mouth: here
is that which will giue language to you Cat; open your
mouth; this will shake your shaking, I can tell you, and
that soundly: you cannot tell who's your friend; open
your chaps againe.

Tri. I should know that voyce:
It should be,

But

But hee is drownd; and these are diuels; O defend me.

Ste. Foure legges and two voyces; a most delicate Monster: his forward voyce now is to speake well of his friend; his backward voice, is to vtter foule speeches, and to detract: if all the wine in my bottle will recouer him, I will helpe his Ague: Come: Amen, I will poure some in thy other mouth.

Tri. Stephano.

Ste. Doth thy other mouth call me? Mercy, mercy: This is a diuell, and no Monster: I will leaue him, I haue no long Spoone.

Tri. Stephano: if thou beest *Stephano*, touch me, and speake to me: for I am *Trinculo*; be not afeard, thy good friend *Trinculo*.

Ste. If thou bee'st *Trinculo*: come foorth: I'le pull thee by the lesser legges: if any be *Trinculo's* legges, these are they: Thou art very *Trinculo* indeede: how cam'st thou to be the siege of this Moone-calfe? Can he vent *Trinculo's*?

Tri. I tooke him to be kil'd with a thunder-strok; but art thou not drownd *Stephano*: I hope now thou art not drownd: Is the Storme ouer-blowne? I hid mee vnder the dead Moone-Calfes Gaberdine, for feare of the Storme: And art thou liuing *Stephano*? O *Stephano*, two *Neapolitanes* scap'd?

Ste. 'Prethee doe not turne me about, my stomacke is not constant.

Cal. These be fine things, and if they be not sprights: that's a braue God, and beares Celestiall liquor: I will kneele to him.

Ste. How did'st thou scape?
How cam'st thou hither?
Sweare by this Bottle how thou cam'st hither: I escap'd vpon a But of Sacke, which the Saylors heaued o'reboord, by this Bottle which I made of the barke of a Tree, with mine owne hands, since I was cast a'-shore.

Cal. I'le sweare vpon that Bottle, to be thy true subiect, for the liquor is not earthly.

St. Heere: sweare then how thou escap'dst.

Tri. Swom ashore (man) like a Ducke: I can swim like a Ducke i'le be sworne.

Ste. Here, kisse the Booke.
Though thou canst swim like a Ducke, thou art made like a Goose.

Tri. O Stephano, ha'st any more of this?

Ste. The whole But (man) my Cellar is in a rocke by th'sea-side, where my Wine is hid:
How now Moone-Calfe, how do's thine Ague?

Cal. Ha'st thou not dropt from heauen?

Ste. Out o'th Moone I doe assure thee. I was the Man ith' Moone, when time was.

Cal. I haue seene thee in her: and I doe adore thee: My Mistris shew'd me thee, and thy Dog, and thy Bush.

Ste. Come, sweare to that: kisse the Booke: I will furnish it anon with new Contents: Sweare.

Tri. By this good light, this is a very shallow Monster: I afeard of him? a very weake Monster:
The Man ith' Moone?
A most poore creadulous Monster:
Well drawne Monster, in good sooth.

Cal. Ile shew thee euery fertill ynch 'oth Island: and I will kisse thy foote: I prethee be my god.

Tri. By this light, a most perfidious, and drunken Monster, when's god's asleepe he'll rob his Bottle.

Cal. Ile kisse thy foot. Ile sweare my selfe thy Subiect.

Ste. Come on then: downe and sweare.

Tri. I shall laugh my selfe to death at this puppi-headed Monster: a most scuruie Monster: I could finde in my heart to beate him.

Ste. Come, kisse.

Tri. But that the poore Monster's in drinke:
An abhominable Monster.

Cal. I'le shew thee the best Springs: I'le plucke thee Berries: I'le fish for thee; and get thee wood enough.
A plague vpon the Tyrant that I serue;
I'le beare him no more Stickes, but follow thee, thou wondrous man.

Tri. A most rediculous Monster, to make a wonder of a poore drunkard.

Cal. I' prethee let me bring thee where Crabs grow; and I with my long nayles will digge thee pig-nuts; show thee a Iayes nest, and instruct thee how to snare the nimble Marmazet: I'le bring thee to clustring Philbirts, and sometimes I'le get thee young Scamels from the Rocke: Wilt thou goe with me?

Ste. I pre'thee now lead the way without any more talking. *Trinculo*, the King, and all our company else being drownd, wee will inherit here: Here; beare my Bottle: Fellow *Trinculo*; we'll fill him by and by againe.

Caliban Sings drunkenly.
Farewell Master; farewell, farewell.

Tri. A howling Monster: a drunken Monster.

Cal. *No more dams I'le make for fish,*
 Nor fetch in firing, at requiring,
 Nor scrape trenchering, nor wash dish,
 Ban' ban' Ca-caliban
 Has a new Master, get a new Man.
Freedome, high-day, high-day freedome, freedome high-day, freedome.

Ste. O braue Monster; lead the way. *Exeunt.*

Actus Tertius. Scœna Prima.

Enter Ferdinand (bearing a Log.)

Fer. There be some Sports are painfull; & their labor
Delight in them set off: Some kindes of basenesse
Are nobly vndergon; and most poore matters
Point to rich ends: this my meane Taske
Would be as heauy to me, as odious, but
The Mistris which I serue, quickens what's dead,
And makes my labours, pleasures: O She is
Ten times more gentle, then her Father's crabbed;
And he's compos'd of harshnesse. I must remoue
Some thousands of these Logs, and pile them vp,
Vpon a sore iniunction; my sweet Mistris
Weepes when she sees me worke, & saies, such basenes
Had neuer like Executor: I forget:
But these sweet thoughts, doe euen refresh my labours,
Most busie lest, when I doe it. *Enter Miranda*

Mir. Alas, now pray you *and Prospero.*
Worke not so hard: I would the lightning had
Burnt vp those Logs that you are enioynd to pile:
Pray set it downe, and rest you: when this burnes
'Twill weepe for hauing wearied you: my Father
Is hard at study; pray now rest your selfe,

He's

The Tempest.

Hee's safe for these three houres.

 Fer. O most deere Mistris,
The Sun will set before I shall discharge
What I must striue to do.

 Mir. If you'l sit downe
Ile beare your Logges the while: pray giue me that,
Ile carry it to the pile.

 Fer. No precious Creature,
I had rather cracke my sinewes, breake my backe,
Then you should such dishonor vndergoe,
While I sit lazy by.

 Mir. It would become me
As well as it do's you; and I should do it
With much more ease: for my good will is to it,
And yours it is against.

 Pro. Poore worme thou art infected,
This visitation shewes it.

 Mir. You looke wearily.

 Fer. No, noble Mistris, 'tis fresh morning with me
When you are by at night: I do beseech you
Cheefely, that I might set it in my prayers,
What is your name?

 Mir. Miranda, O my Father,
I haue broke your hest to say so.

 Fer. Admir'd *Miranda,*
Indeede the top of Admiration, worth
What's deerest to the world: full many a Lady
I haue ey'd with best regard, and many a time
Th'harmony of their tongues, hath into bondage
Brought my too diligent eare: for seuerall vertues
Haue I lik'd seuerall women, neuer any
VVith so full soule, but some defect in her
Did quarrell with the noblest grace she ow'd,
And put it to the foile. But you, O you,
So perfect, and so peerlesse, are created
Of euerie Creatures best.

 Mir. I do not know
One of my sexe; no womans face remember,
Saue from my glasse, mine owne: Nor haue I seene
More that I may call men, then you good friend,
And my deere Father: how features are abroad
I am skillesse of; but by my modestie
(The iewell in my dower) I would not wish
Any Companion in the world but you:
Nor can imagination forme a shape
Besides your selfe, to like of: but I prattle
Something too wildely, and my Fathers precepts
I therein do forget.

 Fer. I am, in my condition
A Prince (*Miranda*) I do thinke a King
(I would not so) and would no more endure
This wodden slauerie, then to suffer
The flesh-flie blow my mouth: heare my soule speake.
The verie instant that I saw you, did
My heart flie to your seruice, there resides
To make me slaue to it, and for your sake
Am I this patient Logge-man.

 Mir. Do you loue me?

 Fer. O heauen; O earth, beare witnes to this sound,
And crowne what I professe with kinde euent
If I speake true: if hollowly, inuert
VVhat best is boaded me, to mischiefe: I,
Beyond all limit of what else i'th world
Do loue, prize, honor you.

 Mir. I am a foole
To weepe at what I am glad of.

 Pro. Faire encounter
Of two most rare affections: heauens raine grace
On that which breeds betweene 'em.

 Fer. VVherefore weepe you?

 Mir. At mine vnworthinesse, that dare not offer
VVhat I desire to giue; and much lesse take
VVhat I shall die to want: But this is trifling,
And all the more it seekes to hide it selfe,
The bigger bulke it shewes. Hence bashfull cunning,
And prompt me plaine and holy innocence.
I am your wife, if you will marrie me;
If not, Ile die your maid: to be your fellow
You may denie me, but Ile be your seruant
VVhether you will or no.

 Fer. My Mistris (deerest)
And I thus humble euer.

 Mir. My husband then?

 Fer. I, with a heart as willing
As bondage ere of freedome: heere's my hand.

 Mir. And mine, with my heart in't; and now farewel
Till halfe an houre hence.

 Fer. A thousand, thousand. *Exeunt.*

 Pro. So glad of this as they I cannot be,
VVho are surpriz'd with all; but my reioycing
At nothing can be more: Ile to my booke,
For yet ere supper time, must I performe
Much businesse appertaining. *Exit.*

Scœna Secunda.

Enter Caliban, Stephano, and Trinculo.

 Ste. Tell not me, when the But is out we will drinke water, not a drop before; therefore beare vp, & boord em' Seruant Monster, drinke to me.

 Trin. Seruant Monster? the folly of this Iland, they say there's but fiue vpon this Isle; we are three of them, if th' other two be brain'd like vs, the State totters.

 Ste. Drinke seruant Monster when I bid thee, thy eies are almost set in thy head.

 Trin. VVhere should they bee set else? hee were a braue Monster indeede if they were set in his taile.

 Ste. My man-Monster hath drown'd his tongue in sacke: for my part the Sea cannot drowne mee, I swam ere I could recouer the shore, fiue and thirtie Leagues off and on, by this light thou shalt bee my Lieutenant Monster, or my Standard.

 Trin. Your Lieutenant if you list, hee's no standard.

 Ste. VVeel not run Monsieur Monster.

 Trin. Nor go neither: but you'l lie like dogs, and yet say nothing neither.

 Ste. Moone-calfe, speak once in thy life, if thou beest a good Moone-calfe.

 Cal. How does thy honour? Let me licke thy shooe: Ile not serue him, he is not valiant.

 Trin. Thou liest most ignorant Monster, I am in case to iustle a Constable: why, thou debosh'd Fish thou, was there euer man a Coward, that hath drunk so much Sacke as I to day? wilt thou tell a monstrous lie, being but halfe a Fish, and halfe a Monster?

 Cal. Loe, how he mockes me, wilt thou let him my Lord?

Cal.

Trin. Lord, quoth he? that a Monster should be such a Naturall?

Cal. Loe, loe againe: bite him to death I prethee.

Ste. Trinculo, keepe a good tongue in your head: If you proue a mutineere, the next Tree: the poore Monster's my subiect, and he shall not suffer indignity.

Cal. I thanke my noble Lord. Wilt thou be pleas'd to hearken once againe to the suite I made to thee?

Ste. Marry will I: kneele, and repeate it, I will stand, and so shall *Trinculo*.

Enter Ariell inuisible.

Cal. As I told thee before, I am subiect to a Tirant, A Sorcerer, that by his cunning hath cheated me Of the Island.

Ariell. Thou lyest.

Cal. Thou lyest, thou iesting Monkey thou: I would my valiant Master would destroy thee. I do not lye.

Ste. Trinculo, if you trouble him any more in's tale, By this hand, I will supplant some of your teeth.

Trin. Why, I said nothing.

Ste. Mum then, and no more: proceed.

Cal. I say by Sorcery he got this Isle From me, he got it. If thy Greatnesse will Reuenge it on him, (for I know thou dar'st) But this Thing dare not.

Ste. That's most certaine.

Cal. Thou shalt be Lord of it, and Ile serue thee.

Ste. How now shall this be compast? Canst thou bring me to the party?

Cal. Yea, yea my Lord, Ile yeeld him thee asleepe, Where thou maist knocke a naile into his head.

Ariell. Thou liest, thou canst not.

Cal. What a py'de Ninnie's this? Thou scuruy patch: I do beseech thy Greatnesse giue him blowes, And take his bottle from him: When that's gone, He shall drinke nought but brine, for Ile not shew him Where the quicke Freshes are.

Ste. Trinculo, run into no further danger: Interrupt the Monster one word further, and by this hand, Ile turne my mercie out o'doores, and make a Stockfish of thee.

Trin. Why, what did I? I did nothing: Ile go farther off.

Ste. Didst thou not say he lyed?

Ariell. Thou liest.

Ste. Do I so? Take thou that, As you like this, giue me the lye another time.

Trin. I did not giue the lie: Out o'your wittes, and hearing too? A pox o'your bottle, this can Sacke and drinking doo: A murren on your Monster, and the diuell take your fingers.

Cal. Ha, ha, ha.

Ste. Now forward with your Tale: prethee stand further off.

Cal. Beate him enough: after a little time Ile beate him too.

Ste. Stand farther: Come proceede.

Cal. Why, as I told thee, 'tis a custome with him I'th afternoone to sleepe: there thou maist braine him, Hauing first seiz'd his bookes: Or with a logge Batter his skull, or paunch him with a stake, Or cut his wezand with thy knife. Remember First to possesse his Bookes; for without them

Hee's but a Sot, as I am; nor hath not One Spirit to command: they all do hate him As rootedly as I. Burne but his Bookes, He ha's braue Vtensils (for so he calles them) Which when he ha's a house, hee'l decke withall. And that most deeply to consider, is The beautie of his daughter: he himselfe Cals her a non-pareill: I neuer saw a woman But onely *Sycorax* my Dam, and she; But she as farre surpasseth *Sycorax*, As great'st do's least.

Ste. Is it so braue a Lasse?

Cal. I Lord, she will become thy bed, I warrant, And bring thee forth braue brood.

Ste. Monster, I will kill this man: his daughter and I will be King and Queene, saue our Graces: and *Trinculo* and thy selfe shall be Vice-royes: Dost thou like the plot *Trinculo*?

Trin. Excellent.

Ste. Giue me thy hand, I am sorry I beate thee: But while thou liu'st keepe a good tongue in thy head.

Cal. Within this halfe houre will he be asleepe, Wilt thou destroy him then?

Ste. I on mine honour.

Ariell. This will I tell my Master.

Cal. Thou mak'st me merry: I am full of pleasure, Let vs be iocond. Will you troule the Catch You taught me but whileare?

Ste. At thy request Monster, I will do reason, Any reason: Come on *Trinculo*, let vs sing.

Sings.

Flout 'em, and cout 'em: and skowt 'em, and flout 'em,
Thought is free.

Cal. That's not the tune.

Ariell plaies the tune on a Tabor and Pipe.

Ste. What is this same?

Trin. This is the tune of our Catch, plaid by the picture of No-body.

Ste. If thou beest a man, shew thy selfe in thy likenes: If thou beest a diuell, take't as thou list.

Trin. O forgiue me my sinnes.

Ste. He that dies payes all debts: I defie thee; Mercy vpon vs.

Cal. Art thou affeard?

Ste. No Monster, not I.

Cal. Be not affeard, the Isle is full of noyses, Sounds, and sweet aires, that giue delight and hurt not: Sometimes a thousand twangling Instruments Will hum about mine eares; and sometime voices, That if I then had wak'd after long sleepe, Will make me sleepe againe, and then in dreaming, The clouds methought would open, and shew riches Ready to drop vpon me, that when I wak'd I cri'de to dreame againe.

Ste. This will proue a braue kingdome to me, Where I shall haue my Musicke for nothing.

Cal. When *Prospero* is destroy'd.

Ste. That shall be by and by: I remember the storie.

Trin. The sound is going away, Lets follow it, and after do our worke.

Ste. Leade Monster, Wee'l follow: I would I could see this Taborer, He layes it on.

Trin. Wilt come?

Ile follow *Stephano*.
Exeunt.
Scena

The Tempest.

Scena Tertia.

Enter Alonso, Sebastian, Anthonio, Gonzallo, Adrian, Francisco, &c.

Gon. By'r lakin, I can goe no further, Sir,
My old bones akes: here's a maze trod indeede
Through fourth-rights, & Meanders: by your patience,
I needes must rest me.

Al. Old Lord, I cannot blame thee,
Who, am my selfe attach'd with wearinesse
To th'dulling of my spirits: Sit downe, and rest:
Euen here I will put off my hope, and keepe it
No longer for my Flatterer: he is droun'd
Whom thus we stray to finde, and the Sea mocks
Our frustrate search on land: well, let him goe.

Ant. I am right glad, that he's so out of hope:
Doe not for one repulse forgoe the purpose
That you resolu'd t'effect.

Seb. The next aduantage will we take throughly.

Ant. Let it be to night,
For now they are oppress'd with trauaile, they
Will not, nor cannot vse such vigilance
As when they are fresh.

Solemne and strange Musicke: and Prosper on the top (inuisible:) Enter seuerall strange shapes, bringing in a Banket; and dance about it with gentle actions of salutations, and inuiting the King, &c. to eate, they depart.

Seb. I say to night: no more.

Al. What harmony is this? my good friends, harke.

Gon. Maruellous sweet Musicke.

Alo. Giue vs kind keepers, heauẽs: what were these?

Seb. A liuing *Drolerie*: now I will beleeue
That there are Vnicornes: that in *Arabia*
There is one Tree, the Phœnix throne, one Phœnix
At this houre reigning there.

Ant. Ile beleeue both:
And what do's else want credit, come to me
And Ile besworne 'tis true: Trauellers nere did lye,
Though fooles at home condemne 'em.

Gon. If in *Naples*
I should report this now, would they beleeue me?
If I should say I saw such Islands;
(For certes, these are people of the Island)
Who though they are of monstrous shape, yet note
Their manners are more gentle, kinde, then of
Our humaine generation you shall finde
Many, nay almost any.

Pro. Honest Lord,
Thou hast said well: for some of you there present,
Are worse then diuels.

Al. I cannot too much muse
Such shapes, such gesture, and such sound expressing
(Although they want the vse of tongue) a kinde
Of excellent dumbe discourse.

Pro. Praise in departing.

Fr. They vanish'd strangely.

Seb. No matter, since (macks.
They haue left their Viands behinde; for wee haue sto-
Wilt please you taste of what is here?

Alo. Not I. (Boyes

Gon. Faith Sir, you neede not feare: when wee were
Who would beleeue that there were Mountayneeres,
Dew-lapt, like Buls, whose throats had hanging at'em
Wallets of flesh? or that there were such men
Whose heads stood in their brests? which now we finde
Each putter out of fiue for one, will bring vs
Good warrant of.

Al. I will stand to, and feede,
Although my last, no matter, since I feele
The best is past: brother: my Lord, the Duke,
Stand too, and doe as we.

Thunder and Lightning. Enter Ariell (like a Harpey) claps his wings vpon the Table, and with a quient deuice the Banquet vanishes.

Ar. You are three men of sinne, whom destiny
That hath to instrument this lower world,
And what is in't: the neuer surfeited Sea,
Hath caus'd to belch vp you; and on this Island,
Where man doth not inhabit, you 'mongst men,
Being most vnfit to liue: I haue made you mad;
And euen with such like valour, men hang, and drowne
Their proper selues: you fooles, I and my fellowes
Are ministers of Fate, the Elements
Of whom your swords are temper'd, may as well
Wound the loud windes, or with bemockt-at-Stabs
Kill the still closing waters, as diminish
One dowle that's in my plumbe: My fellow ministers
Are like-invulnerable: if you could hurt,
Your swords are now too massie for your strengths,
And will not be vplifted: But remember
(For that's my businesse to you) that you three
From *Millaine* did supplant good *Prospero*,
Expos'd vnto the Sea (which hath requit it)
Him, and his innocent childe: for which foule deed,
The Powres, delaying (not forgetting) haue
Incens'd the Seas, and Shores; yea, all the Creatures
Against your peace: Thee of thy Sonne, *Alonso*
They haue bereft; and doe pronounce by me
Lingring perdition (worse then any death
Can be at once) shall step, by step attend
You, and your wayes, whose wraths to guard you from,
Which here, in this most desolate Isle, else fals
Vpon your heads, is nothing but hearts-sorrow,
And a cleere life ensuing.

He vanishes in Thunder: then (to soft Musicke.) Enter the shapes againe, and daunce (with mockes and mowes) and carrying out the Table.

Pro. Brauely the figure of this *Harpie*, hast thou
Perform'd (my *Ariell*) a grace it had deuouring:
Of my Instruction, hast thou nothing bated
In what thou had'st to say: so with good life,
And obseruation strange, my meaner ministers
Their seuerall kindes haue done: my high charmes work,
And these (mine enemies) are all knit vp
In their distractions: they now are in my powre;
And in these fits, I leaue them, while I visit
Yong *Ferdinand* (whom they suppose is droun'd)
And his, and mine lou'd darling.

Gon. I'th name of something holy, Sir, why stand you
In this strange stare?

Al. O, it is monstrous: monstrous:
Me thought the billowes spoke, and told me of it,
The windes did sing it to me: and the Thunder
(That deepe and dreadfull Organ-Pipe) pronounc'd
The name of *Prosper*: it did base my Trespasse,
Therefore my Sonne i'th Ooze is bedded; and
I'le seeke him deeper then ere plummet sounded,
And with him there lye mudded. *Exit.*

Seb. But one feend at a time,
Ile fight their Legions ore.

B   *Ant.*

Ant. Ile be thy Second. *Exeunt.*

Gon. All three of them are desperate: their great guilt
(Like poyson giuen to worke a great time after)
Now gins to bite the spirits: I doe beseech you
(That are of suppler ioynts) follow them swiftly,
And hinder them from what this extasie
May now prouoke them to.

Ad. Follow, I pray you. *Exeunt omnes.*

Actus Quartus. Scena Prima.

Enter Prospero, Ferdinand, and Miranda.

Pro. If I haue too austerely punish'd you,
Your compensation makes amends, for I
Haue giuen you here, a third of mine owne life,
Or that for which I liue: who, once againe
I tender to thy hand: All thy vexations
Were but my trials of thy loue, and thou
Hast strangely stood the test: here, afore heauen
I ratifie this my rich guift: O *Ferdinand*,
Doe not smile at me, that I boast her of,
For thou shalt finde she will out-strip all praise
And make it halt, behinde her.

Fer. I doe beleeue it
Against an Oracle.

Pro. Then, as my guest, and thine owne acquisition
Worthily purchas'd, take my daughter: But
If thou do'st breake her Virgin-knot, before
All sanctimonious ceremonies may
With full and holy right, be ministred,
No sweet aspersion shall the heauens let fall
To make this contract grow; but barraine hate,
Sower-ey'd disdaine, and discord shall bestrew
The vnion of your bed, with weedes so loathly
That you shall hate it both: Therefore take heede,
As Hymens Lamps shall light you.

Fer. As I hope
For quiet dayes, faire Issue, and long life,
With such loue, as 'tis now the murkiest den,
The most opportune place, the strongst suggestion,
Our worser *Genius* can, shall neuer melt
Mine honor into lust, to take away
The edge of that dayes celebration,
When I shall thinke, or *Phœbus* Steeds are founderd,
Or Night kept chain'd below.

Pro. Fairely spoke;
Sit then, and talke with her, she is thine owne;
What *Ariell*; my industrious seruāt *Ariell.* *Enter Ariell.*

Ar. What would my potent master? here I am.

Pro. Thou, and thy meaner fellowes, your last seruice
Did worthily performe: and I must vse you
In such another tricke: goe bring the rabble
(Ore whom I giue thee powre) here, to this place:
Incite them to quicke motion, for I must
Bestow vpon the eyes of this yong couple
Some vanity of mine Art: it is my promise,
And they expect it from me.

Ar. Presently?

Pro. I: with a twincke.

Ar. Before you can say come, and goe,
And breathe twice; and cry, so, so:
Each one tripping on his Toe,
Will be here with mop, and mowe.
Doe you loue me Master? no?

Pro. Dearely, my delicate *Ariell*: doe not approach
Till thou do'st heare me call.

Ar. Well: I conceiue. *Exit.*

Pro. Looke thou be true: doe not giue dalliance
Too much the raigne: the strongest oathes, are straw
To th'fire ith' blood: be more abstenious,
Or else good night your vow.

Fer. I warrant you, Sir,
The white cold virgin Snow, vpon my heart
Abates the ardour of my Liuer.

Pro. Well.
Now come my *Ariell*, bring a Corolary,
Rather then want a Spirit; appear, & pertly. *Soft musick.*
No tongue: all eyes: be silent. *Enter Iris.*

Ir. *Ceres*, most bounteous Lady, thy rich Leas
Of Wheate, Rye, Barley, Fetches, Oates and Pease;
Thy Turphie-Mountaines, where liue nibling Sheepe,
And flat Medes thetchd with Stouer, them to keepe:
Thy bankes with pioned, and twilled brims
Which spungie *Aprill*, at thy hest betrims;
To make cold Nymphes chast crownes; & thy broome-
Whose shadow the dismissed Batchelor loues, (groues;
Being lasse-lorne: thy pole-clipt vineyard,
And thy Sea-marge stirrile, and rockey-hard,
Where thou thy selfe do'st ayre, the Queene o'th Skie,
Whose watry Arch, and messenger, am I.
Bids thee leaue these, & with her souersigne grace, *Iuno*
Here on this grasse-plot, in this very place *descends.*
To come, and sport: here Peacocks flye amaine:
Approach, rich *Ceres*, her to entertaine. *Enter Ceres.*

Cer. Haile, many-coloured Messenger, that nere
Do'st disobey the wife of *Iupiter*:
Who, with thy saffron wings, vpon my flowres
Diffusest hony drops, refreshing showres,
And with each end of thy blew bowe do'st crowne
My boskie acres, and my vnshrubd downe,
Rich scarph to my proud earth: why hath thy Queene
Summond me hither, to this short gras'd Greene?

Ir. A contract of true Loue, to celebrate,
And some donation freely to estate
On the bles'd Louers.

Cer. Tell me heauenly Bowe,
If *Venus* or her Sonne, as thou do'st know,
Doe now attend the Queene? since they did plot
The meanes, that duskie *Dis*, my daughter got,
Her, and her blind-Boyes scandald company,
I haue forsworne.

Ir. Of her societie
Be not afraid: I met her deitie
Cutting the clouds towards *Paphos*: and her Son
Doues drawn with her: here thought they to haue done
Some wanton charme, vpon this Man and Maide,
Whose vowes are, that no bed-right shall be paid
Till *Hymens* Torch be lighted: but in vaine,
Marses hot Minion is returnd againe,
Her waspish headed sonne, has broke his arrowes,
Swears he will shoote no more, but play with Sparrows,
And be a Boy right out.

Cer. Highest Queene of State,
Great *Iuno* comes, I know her by her gate.

Iu. How do's my bounteous sister? goe with me
To blesse this twaine, that they may prosperous be,
And honour'd in their Issue. *They Sing.*

Iu. Honor, riches, marriage, blessing,
Long continuance, and encreasing,
Hourely ioyes, be still vpon you,

Iuno

Iuno sings her blessings on you.
Earths increase, foyzon plentie,
Barnes, and Garners, neuer empty.
Vines, with clustring bunches growing,
Plants, with goodly burthen bowing:
Spring come to you at the farthest,
In the very end of Haruest.
Scarcity and want shall shun you,
Ceres blessing so is on you.

Fer. This is a most maiesticke vision, and
Harmonious charmingly: may I be bold
To thinke these spirits?

Pro. Spirits, which by mine Art
I haue from their confines call'd to enact
My present fancies.

Fer. Let me liue here euer,
So rare a wondred Father, and a wise
Makes this place Paradise.

Pro. Sweet now, silence:
Iuno and *Ceres* whisper seriously,
There's something else to doe: hush, and be mute
Or else our spell is mar'd.

Iuno and Ceres whisper, and send Iris on employment.

Iris. You Nimphs cald *Nayades* of ŷ windring brooks,
With your sedg'd crownes, and euer-harmelesse lookes,
Leaue your crispe channels, and on this greene-Land
Answere your summons, *Iuno* do's command.
Come temperate Nimphes, and helpe to celebrate
A Contract of true Loue: be not too late.

Enter Certaine Nimphes.

You Sun-burn'd Sicklemen of August weary,
Come hether from the furrow, and be merry,
Make holly day: your Rye-straw hats put on,
And these fresh Nimphes encounter euery one
In Country footing.

Enter certaine Reapers (properly habited:) they ioyne with the Nimphes, in a gracefull dance, towards the end whereof, Prospero starts sodainly and speakes, after which to a strange hollow and confused noyse, they heauily vanish.

Pro. I had forgot that foule conspiracy
Of the beast *Calliban*, and his confederates
Against my life: the minute of their plot
Is almost come: Well done, auoid: no more.

Fer. This is strange: your fathers in some passion
That workes him strongly.

Mir. Neuer till this day
Saw I him touch'd with anger, so distemper'd.

Pro. You doe looke (my son) in a mou'd sort,
As if you were dismaid: be cheerefull Sir,
Our Reuels now are ended: These our actors,
(As I foretold you) were all Spirits, and
Are melted into Ayre, into thin Ayre,
And like the baselesse fabricke of this vision
The Clowd-capt Towres, the gorgeous Pallaces,
The solemne Temples, the great Globe it selfe,
Yea, all which it inherit, shall dissolue,
And like this insubstantiall Pageant faded
Leaue not a racke behinde: we are such stuffe
As dreames are made on; and our little life
Is rounded with a sleepe: Sir, I am vext,
Beare with my weakenesse, my old braine is troubled:
Be not disturb'd with my infirmitie,
If you be pleas'd, retire into my Cell,
And there repose, a turne or two, Ile walke
To still my beating minde.

Fer. Mir. We wish your peace. *Exit.*

Pro. Come with a thought; I thank thee *Ariell*: come.

Enter Ariell.

Ar. Thy thoughts I cleaue to, what's thy pleasure?

Pro. Spirit: We must prepare to meet with *Caliban*.

Ar. I my Commander, when I presented *Ceres*
I thought to haue told thee of it, but I fear'd
Least I might anger thee.

Pro. Say again, where didst thou leaue these varlots?

Ar. I told you Sir, they were red-hot with drinking,
So full of valour, that they smote the ayre
For breathing in their faces: beate the ground
For kissing of their feete; yet alwaies bending
Towards their proiect: then I beate my Tabor,
At which like vnback't colts they prickt their eares,
Aduanc'd their eye-lids, lifted vp their noses
As they smelt musicke, so I charm'd their eares
That Calfe-like, they my lowing follow'd, through
Tooth'd briars, sharpe firzes, pricking gosse, & thorns,
Which entred their fraile shins: at last I left them
I'th' filthy mantled poole beyond your Cell,
There dancing vp to th' chins, that the sowle Lake
Ore-stunck their feet.

Pro. This was well done (my bird)
Thy shape inuisible retaine thou still:
The trumpery in my house, goe bring it hither
For stale to catch these theeues. *Ar.* I go, I goe. *Exit.*

Pro. A Deuill, a borne-Deuill, on whose nature
Nurture can neuer sticke: on whom my paines
Humanely taken, all, all lost, quite lost,
And, as with age, his body ouglier growes,
So his minde cankers: I will plague them all,
Euen to roaring: Come, hang on them this line.

Enter Ariell, loaden with glistering apparell, &c. Enter Caliban, Stephano, and Trinculo, all wet.

Cal. Pray you tread softly, that the blinde Mole may
not heare a foot fall: we now are neere his Cell.

St. Monster, your Fairy, ŵ you say is a harmles Fairy,
Has done little better then plaid the Iacke with vs.

Trin. Monster, I do smell all horse-pisse, at which
My nose is in great indignation.

Ste. So is mine. Do you heare Monster: If I should
Take a displeasure against you: Looke you.

Trin. Thou wert but a lost Monster.

Cal. Good my Lord, giue me thy fauour stil,
Be patient, for the prize Ile bring thee too
Shall hudwinke this mischance: therefore speake softly,
All's husht as midnight yet.

Trin. I, but to loose our bottles in the Poole.

Ste. There is not onely disgrace and dishonor in that
Monster, but an infinite losse.

Tr. That's more to me then my wetting:
Yet this is your harmlesse Fairy, Monster.

Ste. I will fetch off my bottle,
Though I be o're eares for my labour.

Cal. Pre-thee (my King) be quiet. Seest thou heere
This is the mouth o'th Cell: no noise, and enter:
Do that good mischeefe, which may make this Island
Thine owne for euer, and I thy *Caliban*
For aye thy foot-licker.

Ste. Giue me thy hand,
I do begin to haue bloody thoughts.

Trin. O King *Stephano*, O Peere: O worthy *Stephano*,
Looke what a wardrobe heere is for thee.

Cal. Let it alone thou foole, it is but trash.

Tri. Oh, ho, Monster: wee know what belongs to a
frippery, O King *Stephano*.

Ste. Put off that gowne (*Trinculo*) by this hand Ile haue that gowne.

Tri. Thy grace shall haue it. (meane

Cal. The dropsie drowne this foole, what doe you To doate thus on such luggage? let's alone And doe the murther first: if he awake, From toe to crowne hee'l fill our skins with pinches, Make vs strange stuffe.

Ste. Be you quiet (Monster) Mistris line, is not this my Ierkin? now is the Ierkin vnder the line: now Ierkin you are like to lose your haire, & proue a bald Ierkin.

Trin. Doe, doe; we steale by lyne and leuell, and't like your grace.

Ste. I thank thee for that iest; heer's a garment for't: Wit shall not goe vn-rewarded while I am King of this Country: Steale by line and leuell, is an excellent passe of pate: there's another garment for't.

Tri. Monster, come put some Lime vpon your fingers, and away with the rest.

Cal. I will haue none on't: we shall loose our time, And all be turn'd to Barnacles, or to Apes With foreheads villanous low.

Ste. Monster, lay to your fingers: helpe to beare this away, where my hogshead of wine is, or Ile turne you out of my kingdome: goe to, carry this.

Tri. And this.

Ste. I, and this.

A noyse of Hunters heard. Enter diuers Spirits in shape of Dogs and Hounds, hunting them about: Prospero and Ariel setting them on.

Pro. Hey Mountaine, hey.

Ari. Siluer: there it goes, Siluer.

Pro. Fury, Fury: there Tyrant, there: barke, harke. Goe, charge my Goblins that they grinde their ioynts With dry Convultions, shorten vp their sinewes With aged Cramps, & more pinch-spotted make them, Then Pard, or Cat o' Mountaine.

Ari. Harke, they rore.

Pro. Let them be hunted soundly: At this houre Lies at my mercy all mine enemies: Shortly shall all my labours end, and thou Shalt haue the ayre at freedome: for a little Follow, and doe me seruice. *Exeunt.*

Actus quintus: Scœna Prima.

Enter Prospero (in his Magicke robes) and Ariel.

Pro. Now do's my Proiect gather to a head: My charmes cracke not: my Spirits obey, and Time Goes vpright with his carriage: how's the day?

Ar. On the sixt hower, at which time, my Lord You said our worke should cease.

Pro. I did say so, When first I rais'd the Tempest: say my Spirit, How fares the King, and's followers?

Ar. Confin'd together In the same fashion, as you gaue in charge, Iust as you left them; all prisoners Sir In the *Line-groue* which weather-fends your Cell, They cannot boudge till your release: The King, His Brother, and yours, abide all three distracted, And the remainder mourning ouer them, Brim full of sorrow, and dismay: but chiefly Him that you term'd Sir, the good old Lord *Gonzallo*, His teares runs downe his beard like winters drops From eaues of reeds: your charm so strongly works 'em That if you now beheld them, your affections Would become tender.

Pro. Dost thou thinke so, Spirit?

Ar. Mine would, Sir, were I humane.

Pro. And mine shall. Hast thou (which art but aire) a touch, a feeling Of their afflictions, and shall not my selfe, One of their kinde, that rellish all as sharpely, Passion as they, be kindlier mou'd then thou art? Thogh with their high wrongs I am strook to th' quick, Yet, with my nobler reason, gainst my furie Doe I take part: the rarer Action is In vertue, then in vengeance: they, being penitent, The sole drift of my purpose doth extend Not a frowne further: Goe, release them *Ariell*, My Charmes Ile breake, their sences Ile restore, And they shall be themselues.

Ar. Ile fetch them, Sir. *Exit.*

Pro. Ye Elues of hils, brooks, stading lakes & groues, And ye, that on the sands with printlesse foote Doe chase the ebbing-*Neptune*, and doe flie him When he comes backe: you demy-Puppets, that By Moone-shine doe the greene sowre Ringlets make, Whereof the Ewe not bites: and you, whose pastime Is to make midnight-Mushrumps, that reioyce To heare the solemne Cursewe, by whose ayde (Weake Masters though ye be) I haue bedymn'd The Noone-tide Sun, call'd forth the mutenous windes, And twixt the greene Sea, and the azur'd vault Set roaring warre: To the dread ratling Thunder Haue I giuen fire, and rifted *Ioues* stowt Oke With his owne Bolt: The strong bass'd promontorie Haue I made shake, and by the spurs pluckt vp The Pyne, and Cedar. Graues at my command Haue wak'd their sleepers, op'd, and let 'em forth By my so potent Art. But this rough Magicke I heere abiure: and when I haue requir'd Some heauenly Musicke (which euen now I do) To worke mine end vpon their Sences, that This Ayrie-charme is for, I'le breake my staffe, Bury it certaine fadomes in the earth, And deeper then did euer Plummet sound Ile drowne my booke. *Solemne musicke.*

Heere enters Ariel *before: Then* Alonso *with a franticke gesture, attended by* Gonzalo. Sebastian *and* Anthonio *in like manner attended by* Adrian *and* Francisco: *They all enter the circle which* Prospero *had made, and there stand charm'd: which* Prospero *obseruing, speakes.*

A solemne Ayre, and the best comforter, To an vnsetled fancie, Cure thy braines (Now vselesse) boile within thy skull: there stand For you are Spell-stopt. Holy *Gonzallo*, Honourable man, Mine eyes ev'n sociable to the shew of thine Fall fellowly drops: The charme dissolues apace, And as the morning steales vpon the night (Melting the darkenesse) so their rising sences Begin to chace the ignorant fumes that mantle Their cleerer reason. O good *Gonzallo* My true preseruer, and a loyall Sir, To him thou follow'st; I will pay thy graces Home both in word, and deede: Most cruelly

Didst

The Tempest.

Did thou *Alonso*, vse me, and my daughter:
Thy brother was a furtherer in the Act,
Thou art pinch'd for't now *Sebastian*. Flesh, and bloud,
You, brother mine, that entertaine ambition,
Expelld remorse, and nature; whom, with *Sebastian*
(Whose inward pinches therefore are most strong)
Would heere haue kill'd your King: I do forgiue thee,
Vnnaturall though thou art: Their vnderstanding
Begins to swell, and the approching tide
Will shortly fill the reasonable shore
That now ly foule, and muddy: not one of them
That yet lookes on me, or would know me: *Ariell*,
Fetch me the Hat, and Rapier in my Cell,
I will discase me, and my selfe present
As I was sometime *Millaine*: quickly Spirit,
Thou shalt ere long be free.

Ariell sings; and helps to attire him.
   Where the Bee sucks, there suck I,
   In a Cowslips bell, I lie,
   There I cowch when Owles doe crie,
   On the Batts backe I doe flie
   after Sommer merrily.
   Merrily, merrily, shall I liue now,
   Vnder the blossom that hangs on the Bow.

Pro. Why that's my dainty *Ariell*: I shall misse
Thee, but yet thou shalt haue freedome: so, so, so.
To the Kings ship, inuisible as thou art,
There shalt thou finde the Marriners asleepe
Vnder the Hatches: the Master and the Boat-swaine
Being awake, enforce them to this place;
And presently, I pre'thee.

Ar. I drinke the aire before me, and returne
Or ere your pulse twice beate. *Exit.*

Gon. All torment, trouble, wonder, and amazement
Inhabits heere: some heauenly power guide vs
Out of this fearefull Country.

Pro. Behold Sir King
The wronged Duke of *Millaine*, *Prospero*:
For more assurance that a liuing Prince
Do's now speake to thee, I embrace thy body,
And to thee, and thy Company, I bid
A hearty welcome.

Alo. Where thou bee'st he or no,
Or some inchanted trifle to abuse me,
(As late I haue beene) I not know: thy Pulse
Beats as of flesh, and blood: and since I saw thee,
Th'affliction of my minde amends, with which
I feare a madnesse held me: this must craue
(And if this be at all) a most strange story.
Thy Dukedome I resigne, and doe entreat
Thou pardon me my wrongs: But how shold *Prospero*
Be liuing, and be heere?

Pro. First, noble Frend,
Let me embrace thine age, whose honor cannot
Be measur'd, or confin'd.

Gonz. Whether this be,
Or be not, I'le not sweare.

Pro. You doe yet taste
Some subtleties o'th'Isle, that will not let you
Beleeue things certaine: Wellcome, my friends all,
But you, my brace of Lords, were I so minded
I heere could plucke his Highnesse frowne vpon you
And iustifie you Traitors: at this time
I will tell no tales.

Seb. The Diuell speakes in him:

Pro. No:

For you (most wicked Sir) whom to call brother
Would euen infect my mouth, I do forgiue
Thy rankest fault; all of them: and require
My Dukedome of thee, which, perforce I know
Thou must restore.

Alo. If thou beest *Prospero*
Giue vs particulars of thy preseruation,
How thou hast met vs heere, whom three howres since
Were wrackt vpon this shore? where I haue lost
(How sharp the point of this remembrance is)
My deere sonne *Ferdinand*.

Pro. I am woe for't, Sir.

Alo. Irreparable is the losse, and patience
Saies, it is past her cure.

Pro. I rather thinke
You haue not sought her helpe, of whose soft grace
For the like losse, I haue her soueraigne aid,
And rest my selfe content.

Alo. You the like losse?

Pro. As great to me, as late, and supportable
To make the deere losse, haue I meanes much weaker
Then you may call to comfort you; for I
Haue lost my daughter.

Alo. A daughter?
Oh heauens, that they were liuing both in *Naples*
The King and Queene there, that they were, I wish
My selfe were mudded in that oo-zie bed
Where my sonne lies: when did you lose your daughter?

Pro. In this last Tempest. I perceiue these Lords
At this encounter doe so much admire,
That they deuoure their reason, and scarce thinke
Their eies doe offices of Truth: Their words
Are naturall breath: but howsoeu'r you haue
Beene iustled from your sences, know for certain
That I am *Prospero*, and that very Duke
Which was thrust forth of *Millaine*, who most strangely
Vpon this shore (where you were wrackt) was landed
To be the Lord on't: No more yet of this;
For 'tis a Chronicle of day by day,
Not a relation for a break-fast, nor
Besitting this first meeting: Welcome, Sir;
This Cell's my Court: heere haue I few attendants,
And Subiects none abroad: pray you looke in:
My Dukedome since you haue giuen me againe,
I will requite you with as good a thing,
At least bring forth a wonder, to content ye
As much, as me my Dukedome.

Here Prospero discouers Ferdinand and Miranda, playing at Chesse.

Mir. Sweet Lord, you play me false.

Fer. No my dearest loue,
I would not for the world. (wrangle,

Mir. Yes, for a score of Kingdomes, you should
And I would call it faire play.

Alo. If this proue
A vision of the Island, one deere Sonne
Shall I twice loose.

Seb. A most high miracle.

Fer. Though the Seas threaten they are mercifull,
I haue curs'd them without cause.

Alo. Now all the blessings
Of a glad father, compasse thee about:
Arise, and say how thou cam'st heere.

Mir. O wonder!
How many goodly creatures are there heere?
How beauteous mankinde is? O braue new world

B3   That

That has such people in't.
  Pro. 'Tis new to thee.
  Alo. What is this Maid, with whom thou was't at (play?
Your eld'st acquaintance cannot be three houres:
Is she the goddesse that hath seuer'd vs,
And brought vs thus together?
  Fer. Sir, she is mortall;
But by immortall prouidence, she's mine:
I chose her when I could not aske my Father
For his aduise: nor thought I had one: She
Is daughter to this famous Duke of *Millaine*,
Of whom, so often I haue heard renowne,
But neuer saw before: of whom I haue
Receiu'd a second life; and second Father
This Lady makes him to me.
  Alo. I am hers.
But O, how odly will it sound, that I
Must aske my childe forgiuenesse?
  Pro. There Sir stop,
Let vs not burthen our remembrances, with
A heauinesse that's gon.
  Gon. I haue inly wept,
Or should haue spoke ere this: looke downe you gods
And on this couple drop a blessed crowne;
For it is you, that haue chalk'd forth the way
Which brought vs hither.
  Alo. I say Amen, *Gonzallo*.
  Gon. Was *Millaine* thrust from *Millaine*, that his Issue
Should become Kings of *Naples*? O reioyce
Beyond a common ioy, and set it downe
With gold on lasting Pillers: In one voyage
Did *Claribell* her husband finde at *Tunis*,
And *Ferdinand* her brother, found a wife,
Where he himselfe was lost: *Prospero*, his Dukedome
In a poore Isle: and all of vs, our selues,
When no man was his owne.
  Alo. Giue me your hands:
Let griefe and sorrow still embrace his heart,
That doth not wish you ioy.
  Gon. Be it so, Amen.
  *Enter Ariell, with the Master and Boatswaine
    amazedly following.*
O looke Sir, looke Sir, here is more of vs:
I prophesi'd, if a Gallowes were on Land
This fellow could not drowne: Now blasphemy,
That swear'st Grace ore-boord, not an oath on shore,
Hast thou no mouth by land?
What is the newes?
  Bot. The best newes is, that we haue safely found
Our King, and company: The next: our Ship,
Which but three glasses since, we gaue out split,
Is tyte, and yare, and brauely rig'd, as when
We first put out to Sea.
  Ar. Sir, all this seruice
Haue I done since I went.
  Pro. My tricksey Spirit.
  Alo. These are not naturall euents, they strengthen
From strange, to stranger: say, how came you hither?
  Bot. If I did thinke, Sir, I were well awake,
I'ld striue to tell you: we were dead of sleepe,
And (how we know not) all clapt vnder hatches,
Where, but euen now, with strange, and seuerall noyses
Of roring, shreeking, howling, gingling chaines,
And mo diuersitie of sounds, all horrible.
We were awak'd: straight way, at liberty;
Where we, in all our trim, freshly beheld
Our royall, good, and gallant Ship: our Master
Capring to eye her: on a trice, so please you,
Euen in a dreame, were we diuided from them;
And were brought moaping hither.
  Ar. Was't well done?
  Pro. Brauely (my diligence) thou shalt be free.
  Alo. This is as strange a Maze, as ere men trod,
And there is in this businesse, more then nature
Was euer conduct of: some Oracle
Must rectifie our knowledge.
  Pro. Sir, my Leige,
Doe not infest your minde, with beating on
The strangenesse of this businesse, at pickt leisure
(Which shall be shortly single) I'le resolue you,
(Which to you shall seeme probable) of euery
These happend accidents: till when, be cheerefull
And thinke of each thing well: Come hither Spirit,
Set *Caliban*, and his companions free:
Vntye the Spell: How fares my gracious Sir?
There are yet missing of your Companie
Some few odde *Lads*, that you remember not.
  *Enter Ariell, driuing in Caliban, Stephano, and
    Trinculo in their stolne Apparell.*
  Ste. Euery man shift for all the rest, and let
No man take care for himselfe; for all is
But fortune: *Coragio* Bully-Monster *Corasio*.
  Tri. If these be true spies which I weare in my head,
here's a goodly sight.
  Cal. O *Setebos*, these be braue Spirits indeede:
How fine my Master is? I am afraid
He will chastise me.
  Seb. Ha, ha:
What things are these, my Lord *Anthonio*?
Will money buy em?
  Ant. Very like: one of them
Is a plaine Fish, and no doubt marketable.
  Pro. Marke but the badges of these men, my Lords,
Then say if they be true: This mishapen knaue;
His Mother was a Witch, and one so strong
That could controle the Moone; make flowes, and ebs,
And deale in her command, without her power:
These three haue robd me, and this demy-diuell;
(For he's a bastard one) had plotted with them
To take my life: two of these Fellowes, you
Must know, and owne, this Thing of darkenesse, I
Acknowledge mine.
  Cal. I shall be pincht to death.
  Alo. Is not this *Stephano*, my drunken Butler?
  Seb. He is drunke now;
Where had he wine?
  Alo. And *Trinculo* is reeling ripe: where should they
Finde this grand Liquor that hath gilded 'em?
How cam'st thou in this pickle?
  Tri. I haue bin in such a pickle since I saw you last,
That I feare me will neuer out of my bones:
I shall not feare fly-blowing.
  Seb. Why how now *Stephano*?
  Ste. O touch me not, I am not *Stephano*, but a Cramp.
  Pro. You'ld be King o'the Isle, Sirha?
  Ste. I should haue bin a sore one then.
  Alo. This is a strange thing as ere I look'd on.
  Pro. He is as disproportion'd in his Manners
As in his shape: Goe Sirha, to my Cell,
Take with you your Companions: as you looke
To haue my pardon, trim it handsomely.
  Cal. I that I will: and Ile be wise hereafter,

And

The Tempest.

And seeke for grace: what a thrice double Asse
Was I to take this drunkard for a god?
And worship this dull foole?

  Pro. Goe to, away.   (found it.
  Alo. Hence, and bestow your luggage where you
Seb. Or stole it rather.
  Pro. Sir, I inuite your Highnesse, and your traine
To my poore Cell: where you shall take your rest
For this one night, which part of it, Ile waste
With such discourse, as I not doubt, shall make it
Goe quicke away: The story of my life,
And the particular accidents, gon by
Since I came to this Isle: And in the morne
I'le bring you to your ship, and so to *Naples*,
Where I haue hope to see the nuptiall
Of these our deere-belou'd, solemnized,
And thence retire me to my *Millaine*, where
Euery third thought shall be my graue.

  Alo. I long
To heare the story of your life; which must
Take the eare strangely.

  Pro. I'le deliuer all,
And promise you calme Seas, auspicious gales,
And saile, so expeditious, that shall catch
Your Royall fleete farre off: My *Ariel*; chicke
That is thy charge: Then to the Elements
Be free, and fare thou well: please you draw neere.
                                 Exeunt omnes.

EPILOGVE,
spoken by *Prospero.*

Now my Charmes are all ore-throwne,
And what strength I haue's mine owne.
Which is most faint: now 'tis true
I must be heere confinde by you,
Or sent to Naples, Let me not
Since I haue my Dukedome got,
And pardon'd the deceiuer, dwell
In this bare Island, by your Spell,
But release me from my bands
With the helpe of your good hands:
Gentle breath of yours, my Sailes
Must fill, or else my proiect failes,
Which was to please: Now I want
Spirits to enforce: Art to inchant,
And my ending is despaire,
Vnlesse I be relieu'd by praier
Which pierces so, that it assaults
Mercy it selfe, and frees all faults.
  As you from crimes would pardon'd be,
  Let your Indulgence set me free.   *Exit.*

The Scene, an vn-inhabited Island

Names of the Actors.

Alonso, K. of Naples:
Sebastian his Brother.
Prospero, the right Duke of *Millaine.*
Anthonio his brother, the vsurping Duke of *Millaine.*
Ferdinand, Son to the King of *Naples.*
Gonzalo, an honest old Councellor.
Adrian, & *Francisco,* Lords.
Caliban, a saluage and deformed slaue.
Trinculo, a Iester.
Stephano, a drunken Butler.
Master of a Ship.
Boate-Swaine.
Marriners.
Miranda, daughter to *Prospero.*
Ariell, an ayrie spirit.
Iris
Ceres
Iuno   } Spirits.
Nymphes
Reapers

FINIS.

THE
Two Gentlemen of Verona.

Actus primus, Scena prima.

Valentine : Protheus, and Speed.

Valentine.

CEase to perswade, my louing *Protheus*;
Home-keeping youth, haue euer homely wits,
Wer't not affection chaines thy tender dayes
To the sweet glaunces of thy honour'd Loue,
I rather would entreat thy company,
To see the wonders of the world abroad,
Then (liuing dully sluggardiz'd at home)
Weare out thy youth with shapelesse idlenesse.
But since thou lou'st; loue still, and thriue therein,
Euen as I would, when I to loue begin.

Pro. Wilt thou be gone? Sweet *Valentine* adew,
Thinke on thy *Protheus*, when thou (hap'ly) seest
Some rare note-worthy obiect in thy trauaile.
Wish me partaker in thy happinesse,
When thou do'st meet good hap; and in thy danger,
(If euer danger doe enuiron thee)
Commend thy grieuance to my holy prayers,
For I will be thy beades-man, *Valentine*.

Val. And on a loue-booke pray for my successe?
Pro. Vpon some booke I loue, I'le pray for thee.
Val. That's on some shallow Storie of deepe loue,
How yong *Leander* crost the *Hellespont*.
Pro. That's a deepe Storie, of a deeper loue,
For he was more then ouer-shooes in loue.
Val. 'Tis true; for you are ouer-bootes in loue,
And yet you neuer swom the *Hellespont*.
Pro. Ouer the Bootes? nay giue me not the Boots.
Val. No, I will not; for it boots thee not.
Pro. What? (grones:
Val. To be in loue; where scorne is bought with
Coy looks, with hart-sore sighes: one fading moments
With twenty watchfull, weary, tedious nights; (mirth,
If hap'ly won, perhaps a haplesse gaine;
If lost, why then a grieuous labour won;
How euer: but a folly bought with wit,
Or else a wit, by folly vanquished.

Pro. So, by your circumstance, you call me foole.
Val. So, by your circumstance, I feare you'll proue.
Pro. 'Tis Loue you cauill at, I am not Loue.
Val. Loue is your master, for he masters you;
And he that is so yoked by a foole,
Me thinkes should not be chronicled for wise.
Pro. Yet Writers say; as in the sweetest Bud,
The eating Canker dwels; so eating Loue
Inhabits in the finest wits of all.
Val. And Writers say; as the most forward Bud

Is eaten by the Canker ere it blow,
Euen so by Loue, the yong, and tender wit
Is turn'd to folly, blasting in the Bud,
Loosing his verdure, euen in the prime,
And all the faire effects of future hopes.
But wherefore waste I time to counsaile thee
That art a votary to fond desire?
Once more adieu: my Father at the Road
Expects my comming, there to see me ship'd.

Pro. And thither will I bring thee *Valentine*.
Val. Sweet *Protheus*, no: Now let vs take our leaue:
To *Millaine* let me heare from thee by Letters
Of thy successe in loue; and what newes else
Betideth here in absence of thy Friend;
And I likewise will visite thee with mine.
Pro. All happinesse bechance to thee in *Millaine*.
Val. As much to you at home: and so farewell. *Exit*.
Pro. He after Honour hunts, I after Loue;
He leaues his friends, to dignifie them more;
I loue my selfe, my friends, and all for loue:
Thou *Iulia* thou hast metamorphis'd me:
Made me neglect my Studies, loose my time;
Warre with good counsaile; set the world at nought;
Made Wit with musing, weake; hart sick with thought.

Sp. Sir *Protheus*: 'saue you: saw you my Master?
Pro. But now he parted hence to embarque for *Millain*.
Sp. Twenty to one then, he is ship'd already,
And I haue plaid the Sheepe in loosing him.
Pro. Indeede a Sheepe doth very often stray,
And if the Shepheard be awhile away.
Sp. You conclude that my Master is a Shepheard then,
and I Sheepe?
Pro. I doe.
Sp. Why then my hornes are his hornes, whether I
wake or sleepe.
Pro. A silly answere, and fitting well a Sheepe.
Sp. This proues me still a Sheepe.
Pro. True: and thy Master a Shepheard.
Sp. Nay, that I can deny by a circumstance.
Pro. It shall goe hard but ile proue it by another.
Sp. The Shepheard seekes the Sheepe, and not the
Sheepe the Shepheard; but I seeke my Master, and my
Master seekes not me: therefore I am no Sheepe.
Pro. The Sheepe for fodder follow the Shepheard,
the Shepheard for foode followes not the Sheepe: thou
for wages followest thy Master, thy Master for wages
followes not thee: therefore thou art a Sheepe.
Sp. Such another proofe will make me cry baâ.
Pro. But do'st thou heare: gau'st thou my Letter
to *Iulia*?

Sp. I

The two Gentlemen of Verona.

Sp. I Sir: I (a lost-Mutton) gaue your Letter to her (a lac'd-Mutton) and she (a lac'd-Mutton) gaue mee (a lost-Mutton) nothing for my labour.

Pro. Here's too small a Pasture for such store of Muttons.

Sp. If the ground be ouer-charg'd, you were best sticke her.

Pro. Nay, in that you are astray: 'twere best pound you.

Sp. Nay Sir, lesse then a pound shall serue me for carrying your Letter.

Pro. You mistake; I meane the pound, a Pinfold.

Sp. From a pound to a pin? fold it ouer and ouer, 'Tis threefold too little for carrying a letter to your louer.

Pro. But what said she?

Sp. I.

Pro. Nod-I, why that's noddy.

Sp. You mistooke Sir: I say she did nod;
And you aske me if she did nod, and I say I.

Pro. And that set together is noddy.

Sp. Now you haue taken the paines to set it together, take it for your paines.

Pro. No, no, you shall haue it for bearing the letter.

Sp. Well, I perceiue I must be faine to beare with you.

Pro. Why Sir, how doe you beare with me?

Sp. Marry Sir, the letter very orderly,
Hauing nothing but the word noddy for my paines.

Pro. Beshrew me, but you haue a quicke wit.

Sp. And yet it cannot ouer-take your slow purse.

Pro. Come, come, open the matter in briefe; what said she.

Sp. Open your purse, that the money, and the matter may be both at once deliuered.

Pro. Well Sir: here is for your paines: what said she?

Sp. Truely Sir, I thinke you'll hardly win her.

Pro. Why? could'st thou perceiue so much from her?

Sp. Sir, I could perceiue nothing at all from her;
No, not so much as a ducket for deliuering your letter:
And being so hard to me, that brought your minde;
I feare she'll proue as hard to you in telling your minde.
Giue her no token but stones, for she's as hard as steele.

Pro. What said she, nothing?

Sp. No, not so much as take this for thy pains: (me;
To testifie your bounty, I thank you, you haue cestern'd
In requital whereof, henceforth, carry your letters your selfe; And so Sir, I'le commend you to my Master.

Pro. Go, go, be gone, to saue your Ship from wrack,
Which cannot perish hauing thee aboarde,
Being destin'd to a drier death on shore:
I must goe send some better Messenger,
I feare my *Iulia* would not daigne my lines,
Receiuing them from such a worthlesse post. *Exit.*

Scœna Secunda.

Enter Iulia and Lucetta.

Iul. But say *Lucetta* (now we are alone)
Would'st thou then counsaile me to fall in loue?

Luc. I Madam, so you stumble not vnheedfully.

Iul. Of all the faire resort of Gentlemen,
That euery day with par'le encounter me,
In thy opinion which is worthiest loue?

Lu. Please you repeat their names, ile shew my minde,
According to my shallow simple skill.

Iu. What thinkst thou of the faire sir *Eglamoure*?

Lu. As of a Knight, well-spoken, neat, and fine;
But were I you, he neuer should be mine.

Iu. What think'st thou of the rich *Mercatio*?

Lu. Well of his wealth; but of himselfe, so, so.

Iu. What think'st thou of the gentle *Protheus*?

Lu. Lord, Lord: to see what folly raignes in vs.

Iu. How now? what meanes this passion at his name?

Lu. Pardon deare Madam, 'tis a passing shame,
That I (vnworthy body as I am)
Should censure thus on louely Gentlemen.

Iu. Why not on *Protheus*, as of all the rest?

Lu. Then thus: of many good, I thinke him best.

Iul. Your reason?

Lu. I haue no other but a womans reason:
I thinke him so, because I thinke him so.

Iul. And would'st thou haue me cast my loue on him?

Lu. I: if you thought your loue not cast away.

Iul. Why he, of all the rest, hath neuer mou'd me.

Lu. Yet he, of all the rest, I thinke best loues ye.

Iul. His little speaking, shewes his loue but small.

Lu. Fire that's closest kept, burnes most of all.

Iul. They doe not loue, that doe not shew their loue.

Lu. Oh, they loue least, that let men know their loue.

Iul. I would I knew his minde.

Lu. Peruse this paper Madam.

Iul. To *Iulia*: say, from whom?

Lu. That the Contents will shew.

Iul. Say, say: who gaue it thee?

Lu. Sir *Valentines* page: & sent I think from *Protheus*;
He would haue giuen it you, but I being in the way,
Did in your name receiue it: pardon the fault I pray.

Iul. Now (by my modesty) a goodly Broker:
Dare you presume to harbour wanton lines?
To whisper, and conspire against my youth?
Now trust me, 'tis an office of great worth,
And you an officer fit for the place:
There: take the paper: see it be return'd,
Or else returne no more into my sight.

Lu. To plead for loue, deserues more fee, then hate.

Iul. Will ye be gon?

Lu. That you may ruminate. *Exit.*

Iul. And yet I would I had ore-look'd the Letter;
It were a shame to call her backe againe,
And pray her to a fault, for which I chid her.
What 'foole is she, that knowes I am a Maid,
And would not force the letter to my view?
Since Maides, in modesty, say no, to that,
Which they would haue the profferer construe, I.
Fie, fie: how way-ward is this foolish loue;
That (like a testie Babe) will scratch the Nurse,
And presently, all humbled kisse the Rod?
How churlishly, I chid *Lucetta* hence,
When willingly, I would haue had her here?
How angerly I taught my brow to frowne,
When inward ioy enforc'd my heart to smile?
My pennance is, to call *Lucetta* backe
And aske remission, for my folly past.
What hoe: *Lucetta*.

Lu. What would your Ladiship?

Iul. Is't neere dinner time?

Lu. I would it were,
That you might kill your stomacke on your meat,

And

And not vpon your Maid.
Iu. What is't that you
Tooke vp so gingerly?
Lu. Nothing.
Iu. Why didst thou stoope then?
Lu. To take a paper vp, that I let fall.
Iul. And is that paper nothing?
Lu. Nothing concerning me.
Iul. Then let it lye, for those that it concernes.
Lu. Madam, it will not lye where it concernes,
Vnlesse it haue a false Interpreter.
Iul. Some loue of yours, hath writ to you in Rime.
Lu. That I might sing it (Madam) to a tune:
Giue me a Note, your Ladiship can set.
Iul. As little by such toyes, as may be possible:
Best sing it to the tune of *Light O, Loue.*
Lu. It is too heauy for so light a tune.
Iu. Heauy? belike it hath some burden then?
Lu. I: and melodious were it, would you sing it,
Iu. And why not you?
Lu. I cannot reach so high.
Iu. Let's see your Song:
How now Minion?
Lu. Keepe tune there still; so you will sing it out:
And yet me thinkes I do not like this tune.
Iu. You doe not?
Lu. No (Madam) tis too sharpe.
Iu. You (Minion) are too saucie.
Lu. Nay, now you are too flat;
And marre the concord, with too harsh a descant:
There wanteth but a Meane to fill your Song.
Iu. The meane is dround with you vnruly base.
Lu. Indeede I bid the base for *Protheus.*
Iu. This babble shall not henceforth trouble me;
Here is a coile with protestation:
Goe, get you gone: and let the papers lye:
You would be fingring them, to anger me.
Lu. She makes it strage, but she would be best pleas'd
To be so angred with another Letter.
Iu. Nay, would I were so angred with the same:
Oh hatefull hands, to teare such louing words;
Iniurious Waspes, to feede on such sweet hony,
And kill the Bees that yeelde it, with your stings:
Ile kisse each seuerall paper, for amends:
Looke, here is writ, kinde *Iulia*: vnkinde *Iulia*,
As in reuenge of thy ingratitude,
I throw thy name against the bruzing-stones,
Trampling contemptuously on thy disdaine.
And here is writ, *Loue wounded Protheus.*
Poore wounded name: my bosome, as a bed,
Shall lodge thee till thy wound be throughly heal'd;
And thus I search it with a soueraigne kisse.
But twice, or thrice, was *Protheus* written downe:
Be calme (good winde) blow not a word away,
Till I haue found each letter, in the Letter,
Except mine own name: That, some whirle-winde beare
Vnto a ragged, fearefull, hanging Rocke,
And throw it thence into the raging Sea.
Loe, here in one line is his name twice writ:
Poore forlorne Protheus, passionate Protheus:
To the sweet Iulia: that ile teare away:
And yet I will not, sith so prettily
He couples it, to his complaining Names;
Thus will I fold them, one vpon another;
Now kisse, embrace, contend, doe what you will.
Lu. Madam: dinner is ready: and your father staies.

Iu. Well, let vs goe.
Lu. What, shall these papers lye, like Tel-tales here?
Iu. If you respect them; best to take them vp.
Lu. Nay, I was taken vp, for laying them downe.
Yet here they shall not lye, for catching cold.
Iu. I see you haue a months minde to them.
Lu. I (Madam) you may say what sights you see;
I see things too, although you iudge I winke.
Iu. Come, come, wilt please you goe. *Exeunt.*

Scœna Tertia.

Enter Antonio and Panthino. Protheus.

Ant. Tell me *Panthino*, what sad talke was that,
Wherewith my brother held you in the Cloyster?
Pan. 'Twas of his Nephew *Protheus*, your Sonne.
Ant. Why? what of him?
Pan. He wondred that your Lordship
Would suffer him, to spend his youth at home,
While other men, of slender reputation
Put forth their Sonnes, to seeke preferment out.
Some to the warres, to try their fortune there;
Some, to discouer Islands farre away:
Some, to the studious Vniuersities;
For any, or for all these exercises,
He said, that *Protheus*, your sonne, was meet;
And did request me, to importune you
To let him spend his time no more at home;
Which would be great impeachment to his age,
In hauing knowne no trauaile in his youth.
Ant. Nor need'st thou much importune me to that
Whereon, this month I haue bin hamering.
I haue consider'd well, his losse of time,
And how he cannot be a perfect man,
Not being tryed, and tutord in the world:
Experience is by industry atchieu'd,
And perfected by the swift course of time:
Then tell me, whether were I best to send him?
Pan. I thinke your Lordship is not ignorant
How his companion, youthfull *Valentino*,
Attends the Emperour in his royall Court.
Ant. I know it well. (thither,
Pan. 'Twere good, I thinke, your Lordship sent him
There shall he practise Tilts, and Turnaments;
Heare sweet discourse, conuerse with Noble-men,
And be in eye of euery Exercise
Worthy his youth, and noblenesse of birth.
Ant. I like thy counsaile: well hast thou aduis'd:
And that thou maist perceiue how well I like it,
The execution of it shall make knowne;
Euen with the speediest expedition,
I will dispatch him to the Emperors Court.
Pan. To morrow, may it please you, *Don Alphonso*,
With other Gentlemen of good esteeme
Are iournying, to salute the *Emperor*,
And to commend their seruice to his will.
Ant. Good company: with them shall *Protheus* go:
And in good time: now will we breake with him.
Pro. Sweet Loue, sweet lines, sweet life,
Here is her hand, the agent of her heart;
Here is her oath for loue, her honors pawne

O

The two Gentlemen of Verona. 23

O that our Fathers would applaud our loues
To seale our happinesse with their consents.

Pro. Oh heauenly *Iulia*.

Ant. How now? What Letter are you reading there?

Pro. May't please your Lordship, 'tis a word or two
Of commendations sent from *Valentine*;
Deliuer'd by a friend, that came from him.

Ant. Lend me the Letter: Let me see what newes.

Pro. There is no newes (my Lord) but that he writes
How happily he liues, how well-belou'd,
And daily graced by the Emperor;
Wishing me with him, partner of his fortune.

Ant. And how stand you affected to his wish?

Pro. As one relying on your Lordships will,
And not depending on his friendly wish.

Ant. My will is something sorted with his wish:
Muse not that I thus sodainly proceed;
For what I will, I will, and there an end:
I am resolu'd, that thou shalt spend some time
With *Valentinus*, in the Emperors Court:
What maintenance he from his friends receiues,
Like exhibition thou shalt haue from me,
To morrow be in readinesse, to goe,
Excuse it not: for I am peremptory.

Pro. My Lord I cannot be so soone prouided,
Please you deliberate a day or two.

Ant. Look what thou want'st shalbe sent after thee:
No more of stay: to morrow thou must goe;
Come on *Panthino*; you shall be imployd,
To hasten on his Expedition.

Pro. Thus haue I shund the fire, for feare of burning,
And drench'd me in the sea, where I am drown'd.
I fear'd to shew my Father *Iulias* Letter,
Least he should take exceptions to my loue,
And with the vantage of mine owne excuse
Hath he excepted most against my loue.
Oh, how this spring of loue resembleth
The vncertaine glory of an Aprill day,
Which now shewes all the beauty of the Sun,
And by and by a clowd takes all away.

Pan. Sir *Protheus*, your Fathers call's for you,
He is in haft, therefore I pray you go.

Pro. Why this it is: my heart accords thereto,
And yet a thousand times it answer's no.

Exeunt.   Finis.

Actus secundus: Scœna Prima.

Enter Valentine, Speed, Siluia.

Speed. Sir, your Gloue.

Valen. Not mine: my Gloues are on.

Sp. Why then this may be yours: for this is but one.

Val. Ha? Let me see: I, giue it me, it's mine:
Sweet Ornament, that deckes a thing diuine,
Ah *Siluia, Siluia*.

Speed. Madam *Siluia*: Madam *Siluia*.

Val. How now Sirha?

Speed. Shee is not within hearing Sir.

Val. Why sir, who bad you call her?

Speed. Your worship sir, or else I mistooke.

Val. Well: you'll still be too forward.

Speed. And yet I was last chidden for being too slow.

Val. Goe to, sir, tell me: do you know Madam *Silnia*?

Speed. Shee that your worship loues?

Val. Why, how know you that I am in loue?

Speed. Marry by these speciall markes: first, you haue learn'd (like Sir *Protheus*) to wreath your Armes like a Male-content: to rellish a Loue-song, like a *Robin*-red-breast: to walke alone like one that had the pestilence: to sigh, like a Schoole-boy that had lost his *A. B. C.* to weep like a yong wench that had buried her Grandam: to fast, like one that takes diet: to watch, like one that feares robbing: to speake puling, like a beggar at Hallow-Masse: You were wont, when you laughed, to crow like a cocke; when you walk'd, to walke like one of the Lions: when you fasted, it was presently after dinner: when you look'd sadly, it was for want of money: And now you are Metamorph's'd with a Mistris, that when I looke on you, I can hardly thinke you my Master.

Val. Are all these things perceiu'd in me?

Speed. They are all perceiu'd without ye.

Val. Without me? they cannot.

Speed. Without you? nay, that's certaine: for without you were so simple, none else would: but you are so without these follies, that these follies are within you, and shine through you like the water in an Vrinall: that not an eye that sees you, but is a Physician to comment on your Malady.

Val. But tell me: do'st thou know my Lady *Siluia*?

Speed. Shee that you gaze on so, as she sits at supper?

Val. Hast thou obseru'd that? euen she I meane.

Speed. Why sir, I know her not.

Val. Do'st thou know her by my gazing on her, and yet know'st her not?

Speed. Is she not hard-fauour'd, sir?

Val. Not so faire (boy) as well fauour'd.

Speed. Sir, I know that well enough.

Val. What dost thou know?

Speed. That shee is not so faire, as (of you) well-fauourd?

Val. I meane that her beauty is exquisite,
But her fauour infinite.

Speed. That's because the one is painted, and the other out of all count.

Val. How painted? and how out of count?

Speed. Marry sir, so painted to make her faire, that no man counts of her beauty.

Val. How esteem'st thou me? I account of her beauty.

Speed. You neuer saw her since she was deform'd.

Val. How long hath she beene deform'd?

Speed. Euer since you lou'd her.

Val. I haue lou'd her euer since I saw her,
And still I see her beautifull.

Speed. If you loue her, you cannot see her.

Val. Why?

Speed. Because Loue is blinde: O that you had mine eyes, or your owne eyes had the lights they were wont to haue, when you chidde at Sir *Protheus*, for going vngarter'd.

Val. What should I see then?

Speed. Your owne present folly, and her passing deformitie: for hee beeing in loue, could not see to garter his hose; and you, beeing in loue, cannot see to put on your hose.

Val. Belike (boy) then you are in loue, for last morning You could not see to wipe my shooes.

Speed. True sir: I was in loue with my bed, I thanke you, you swing'd me for my loue, which makes mee the bolder

bolder to chide you, for yours.

Val. In conclusion, I stand affected to her.

Speed. I would you were set, so your affection would cease.

Val. Last night she enioyn'd me,
To write some lines to one she loues.

Speed. And haue you?

Val. I haue.

Speed. Are they not lamely writt?

Val. No (Boy) but as well as I can do them:
Peace, here she comes.

Speed. Oh excellent motion; oh exceeding Puppet:
Now will he interpret to her.

Val. Madam & Mistres, a thousand good-morrows.

Speed. Oh, 'giue ye-good-ev'n : heer's a million of manners.

Sil. Sir *Valentine*, and seruant, to you two thousand.

Speed. He should giue her interest: & she giues it him.

Val. As you inioynd me; I haue writ your Letter
Vnto the secret, namelesse friend of yours:
Which I was much vnwilling to proceed in,
But for my duty to your Ladiship. (done.

Sil. I thanke you (gentle Seruant) 'tis very Clerkly.

Val. Now trust me (Madam) it came hardly-off:
For being ignorant to whom it goes,
I writ at randome, very doubtfully.

Sil. Perchance you think too much of so much pains?

Val. No (Madam) so it steed you, I will write
(Please you command) a thousand times as much:
And yet ⸻

Sil. A pretty period: well; I ghesse the sequell;
And yet I will not name it : and yet I care not.
And yet, take this againe : and yet I thanke you :
Meaning henceforth to trouble you no more.

Speed. And yet you will : and yet, another yet.

Val. What meanes your Ladiship?
Doe you not like it?

Sil. Yes, yes: the lines are very queintly writ,
But (since vnwillingly) take them againe.
Nay, take them.

Val. Madam, they are for you.

Sil. I, I: you writ them Sir, at my request,
But I will none of them : they are for you :
I would haue had them writ more mouingly :

Val. Please you, Ile write your Ladiship another.

Sil. And when it's writ : for my sake read it ouer,
And if it please you, so : if not : why so :

Val. If it please me, (Madam?) what then?

Sil. Why if it please you, take it for your labour;
And so good-morrow Seruant. *Exit. Sil.*

Speed. Oh Iest vnseene : inscrutible : inuisible,
As a nose on a mans face, or a Wethercocke on a steeple :
My Master sues to her: and she hath taught her Sutor,
He being her Pupill, to become her Tutor.
Oh excellent deuise, was there euer heard a better?
That my master being scribe,
To himselfe should write the Letter?

Val. How now Sir?
What are you reasoning with your selfe?

Speed. Nay; I was riming : 'tis you y haue the reason.

Val. To doe what?

Speed. To be a Spokes-man from Madam *Siluia*.

Val. To whom?

Speed. To your selfe : why, she woes you by a figure.

Val. What figure?

Speed. By a Letter, I should say.

Val. Why she hath not writ to me?

Speed. What need she,
When shee hath made you write to your selfe?
Why, doe you not perceiue the iest?

Val. No, beleeue me.

Speed. No beleeuing you indeed sir :
But did you perceiue her earnest?

Val. She gaue me none, except an angry word.

Speed. Why she hath giuen you a Letter.

Val. That's the Letter I writ to her friend.

Speed. And y letter hath she deliuer'd, & there an end.

Val. I would it were no worse.

Speed. Ile warrant you, 'tis as well :
For often haue you writ to her : and she in modesty,
Or else for want of idle time, could not againe reply,
Or fearing els some messenger, y might her mind discouer
Her self hath taught her Loue himself, to write vnto her
All this I speak in print, for in print I found it. (louer.
Why muse you sir, 'tis dinner time.

Val. I haue dyn'd.

Speed. I, but hearken sir : though the Cameleon Loue
can feed on the ayre, I am one that am nourish'd by my
victuals ; and would faine haue meate : oh bee not like
your Mistresse, be moued, be moued. *Exeunt.*

Scœna secunda.

Enter Protheus, Iulia, Panthion.

Pro. Haue patience, gentle *Iulia* :

Iul. I must where is no remedy.

Pro. When possibly I can, I will returne.

Iul. If you turne not : you will return the sooner :
Keepe this remembrance for thy *Iulia's* sake.

Pro. Why then wee'll make exchange;
Here, take you this.

Iul. And seale the bargaine with a holy kisse.

Pro. Here is my hand, for my true constancie:
And when that howre ore-slips me in the day,
Wherein I sigh not (*Iulia*) for thy sake,
The next ensuing howre, some foule mischance
Torment me for my Loues forgetfulnesse :
My father staies my comming : answere not :
The tide is now ; nay, not thy tide of teares,
That tide will stay me longer then I should,
Iulia, farewell : what, gon without a word?
I, so true loue should doe : it cannot speake,
For truth hath better deeds, then words to grace it.

Panth. Sir *Protheus* : you are staid for.

Pro. Goe : I come, I come :
Alas, this parting strikes poore Louers dumbe.
Exeunt.

Scœna Tertia.

Enter Launce, Panthion.

Launce. Nay, 'twill bee this howre ere I haue done
weeping : all the kinde of the *Launces*, haue this very
fault : I haue receiu'd my proportion, like the prodigious
sonne,

The two Gentlemen of Verona.   25

Sonne, and am going with Sir *Protheus* to the Imperialls Court: I thinke *Crab* my dog, be the sowrest natured dogge that liues: My Mother weeping: my Father wayling: my Sister crying: our Maid howling: our Catte wringing her hands, and all our house in a great perplexitie, yet did not this cruell-hearted Curre shedde one teare: he is a stone, a very pibble stone, and has no more pitty in him then a dogge: a Iew would haue wept to haue seene our parting: why my Grandam hauing no eyes, looke you, wept her selfe blinde at my parting: nay, Ile shew you the manner of it. This shooe is my father: no, this left shooe is my father; no, no, this left shooe is my mother: nay, that cannot bee so neyther: yes; it is so, it is so: it hath the worser sole: this shooe with the hole in it, is my mother: and this my father: a veng'ance on't, there 'tis: Now sir, this staffe is my sister: for, looke you, she is as white as a lilly, and as small as a wand: this hat is *Nan* our maid: I am the dogge: no, the dogge is himselfe, and I am the dogge: oh, the dogge is me, and I am my selfe: I; so, so: now come I to my Father; Father, your blessing: now should not the shooe speake a word for weeping: now should I kisse my Father; well, hee weepes on: Now come I to my Mother: Oh that she could speake now, like a would-woman: well, I kisse her: why there 'tis; heere's my mothers breath vp and downe: Now come I to my sister; marke the moane she makes: now the dogge all this while sheds not a teare: nor speakes a word: but see how I lay the dust with my teares.

Panth. *Launce*, away, away: a Boord: thy Master is ship'd, and thou art to post after with oares; what's the matter? why weep'st thou man? away asse, you'l loose the Tide, if you tarry any longer.

Laun. It is no matter if the tide were lost, for it is the vnkindest Tide, that euer any man tide.

Panth. What's the vnkindest tide?

Lau. Why, he that's tide here, *Crab* my dog.

Pant. Tut, man: I meane thou'lt loose the flood, and in loosing the flood, loose thy voyage, and in loosing thy voyage, loose thy Master, and in loosing thy Master, loose thy seruice, and in loosing thy seruice: —— why dost thou stop my mouth?

Laun. For feare thou shouldst loose thy tongue.

Panth. Where should I loose my tongue?

Laun. In thy Tale.

Panth. In thy Taile.

Laun. Loose the Tide, and the voyage, and the Master, and the Seruice, and the tide: why man, if the Riuer were drie, I am able to fill it with my teares: if the winde were downe, I could driue the boate with my sighes.

Panth. Come: come away man, I was sent to call thee.

Lau. Sir: call me what thou dar'st.

Pant. Wilt thou goe?

Laun. Well, I will goe.

Exeunt.

Scena Quarta.

Enter Valentine, Siluia, Thurio, Speed, Duke, Protheus.

Sil. Seruant.

Val. Mistris.

Spee. Master, Sir *Thurio* frownes on you.

Val. I Boy, it's for loue.

Spee. Not of you.

Val. Of my Mistresse then.

Spee. 'Twere good you knockt him.

Sil. Seruant, you are sad.

Val. Indeed, Madam, I seeme so.

Thu. Seeme you that you are not?

Val. Hap'ly I doe.

Thu. So doe Counterfeyts.

Val. So doe you.

Thu. What seeme I that I am not?

Val. Wise.

Thu. What instance of the contrary?

Val. Your folly.

Thu. And how quoat you my folly?

Val. I quoat it in your Ierkin.

Thu. My Ierkin is a doublet.

Val. Well then, Ile double your folly.

Thu. How?

Sil. What, angry, Sir *Thurio*, do you change colour?

Val. Giue him leaue, Madam, he is a kind of *Camelion*.

Thu. That hath more minde to feed on your bloud, then liue in your ayre.

Val. You haue said Sir.

Thu. I Sir, and done too for this time.

Val. I know it wel sir, you alwaies end ere you begin.

Sil. A fine volly of words, gentlemē, & quickly shot off

Val. 'Tis indeed, Madam, we thank the giuer.

Sil. Who is that Seruant?

Val. Your selfe (sweet Lady) for you gaue the fire,
Sir *Thurio* borrows his wit from your Ladiships lookes,
And spends what he borrowes kindly in your company.

Thu. Sir, if you spend word for word with me, I shall make your wit bankrupt.   (words,

Val. I know it well sir: you haue an Exchequer of
And I thinke, no other treasure to giue your followers:
For it appeares by their bare Liueries
That they liue by your bare words.

Sil. No more, gentlemen, no more:
Here comes my father.

Duk. Now, daughter *Siluia*, you are hard beset.
Sir *Valentine*, your father is in good health,
What say you to a Letter from your friends
Of much good newes?

Val. My Lord, I will be thankfull,
To any happy messenger from thence.

Duk. Know ye *Don Antonio*, your Countriman?

Val. I, my good Lord, I know the Gentleman
To be of worth, and worthy estimation,
And not without desert so well reputed.

Duk. Hath he not a Sonne?

Val. I, my good Lord, a Son, that well deserues
The honor, and regard of such a father.

Duk. You know him well?

Val. I knew him as my selfe: for from our Infancie
We haue conuerst, and spent our howres together,
And though my selfe haue beene an idle Trewant,
Omitting the sweet benefit of time
To cloath mine age with Angel-like perfection:
Yet hath Sir *Protheus* (for that's his name)
Made vse, and faire aduantage of his daies:
His yeares but yong, but his experience old:
His head vn-mellowed, but his Iudgement ripe;
And in a word (for far behinde his worth
Comes all the praises that I now bestow.)

C   He

He is compleat in feature, and in minde,
With all good grace, to grace a Gentleman.
  Duk. Beshrew me sir, but if he make this good
He is as worthy for an Empresse loue,
As meet to be an Emperors Councellor:
Well, Sir: this Gentleman is come to me
With Commendation from great Potentates,
And heere he meanes to spend his time a while,
I thinke 'tis no vn-welcome newes to you.
  Val. Should I haue wish'd a thing, it had beene he.
  Duk. Welcome him then according to his worth:
Siluia, I speake to you, and you Sir *Thurio*,
For *Valentine*, I need not cite him to it,
I will send him hither to you presently.
  Val. This is the Gentleman I told your Ladiship
Had come along with me, but that his Mistresse
Did hold his eyes, lockt in her Christall lookes.
  Sil. Be-like that now she hath enfranchis'd them
Vpon some other pawne for fealty.
  Val. Nay sure, I thinke she holds them prisoners stil.
  Sil. Nay then he should be blind, and being blind
How could he see his way to seeke out you?
  Val. Why Lady, Loue hath twenty paire of eyes.
  Thur. They say that Loue hath not an eye at all.
  Val. To see such Louers, *Thurio*, as your selfe,
Vpon a homely obiect, Loue can winke.
  Sil. Haue done, haue done: here comes ye gentleman.
  Val. Welcome, deer *Protheus*: Mistris, I beseech you
Confirme his welcome, with some speciall fauor.
  Sil. His worth is warrant for his welcome hether,
If this be he you oft haue wish'd to heare from.
  Val. Mistris, it is: sweet Lady, entertaine him
To be my fellow-seruant to your Ladiship.
  Sil. Too low a Mistres for so high a seruant.
  Pro. Not so, sweet Lady, but too meane a seruant
To haue a looke of such a worthy a Mistresse.
  Val. Leaue off discourse of disabilitie:
Sweet Lady, entertaine him for your Seruant.
  Pro. My dutie will I boast of, nothing else.
  Sil. And dutie neuer yet did want his meed.
Seruant, you are welcome to a worthlesse Mistresse.
  Pro. Ile die on him that saies so but your selfe.
  Sil. That you are welcome?
  Pro. That you are worthlesse.   (you.
  Thur. Madam, my Lord your father wold speak with
  Sil. I wait vpon his pleasure: Come Sir *Thurio*,
Goe with me: once more, new Seruant welcome;
Ile leaue you to confer of home affaires,
When you haue done, we looke too heare from you.
  Pro. Wee'll both attend vpon your Ladiship.
  Val. Now tell me: how do al from whence you came?
  Pro. Your frends are wel, & haue the much comended.
  Val. And how doe yours?
  Pro. I left them all in health.
  Val. How does your Lady? & how thriues your loue?
  Pro. My tales of Loue were wont to weary you,
I know you ioy not in a Loue-discourse.
  Val. I *Protheus*, but that life is alter'd now,
I haue done pennance for contemning Loue,
Whose high emperious thoughts haue punish'd me
With bitter fasts, with penitentiall grones,
With nightly teares, and daily hart-sore sighes,
For in reuenge of my contempt of loue,
Loue hath chas'd sleepe from my enthralled eyes,
And made them watchers of mine owne hearts sorrow.
O gentle *Protheus*, Loue's a mighty Lord,

And hath so humbled me, as I confesse
There is no woe to his correction,
Nor to his Seruice, no such ioy on earth:
Now, no discourse, except it be of loue:
Now can I breake my fast, dine, sup, and sleepe,
Vpon the very naked name of Loue.
  Pro. Enough; I read your fortune in your eye:
Was this the Idoll, that you worship so?
  Val. Euen She; and is she not a heauenly Saint?
  Pro. No; But she is an earthly Paragon.
  Val. Call her diuine.
  Pro. I will not flatter her.
  Val. O flatter me: for Loue delights in praises.
  Pro. When I was sick, you gaue me bitter pils,
And I must minister the like to you.
  Val. Then speake the truth by her; if not diuine,
Yet let her be a principalitie,
Soueraigne to all the Creatures on the earth.
  Pro. Except my Mistresse.
  Val. Sweet: except not any,
Except thou wilt except against my Loue.
  Pro. Haue I not reason to prefer mine owne?
  Val. And I will help thee to prefer her to:
Shee shall be dignified with this high honour,
To beare my Ladies traine, lest the base earth
Should from her vesture chance to steale a kisse,
And of so great a fauor growing proud,
Disdaine to roote the Sommer-swelling flowre,
And make rough winter euerlastingly.
  Pro. Why *Valentine*, what Bragadisme is this?
  Val. Pardon me (*Protheus*) all I can is nothing,
To her, whose worth, make other worthies nothing;
Shee is alone.
  Pro. Then let her alone.
  Val. Not for the world: why man, shee is mine owne,
And I as rich in hauing such a Iewell
As twenty Seas, if all their sand were pearle,
The water, Nectar, and the Rocks pure gold.
Forgiue me, that I doe not dreame on thee,
Because thou seest me doate vpon my loue:
My foolish Riuall that her Father likes
(Onely for his possessions are so huge)
Is gone with her along, and I must after,
For Loue (thou know'st is full of iealousie.)
  Pro. But she loues you?   (howre,
  Val. I, and we are betroathd: nay more, our mariage
With all the cunning manner of our flight
Determin'd of: how I must climbe her window,
The Ladder made of Cords, and all the means
Plotted, and 'greed on for my happinesse.
Good *Protheus* goe with me to my chamber,
In these affaires to aid me with thy counsaile.
  Pro. Goe on before: I shall enquire you forth:
I must vnto the Road, to dis-embarque
Some necessaries, that I needs must vse,
And then Ile presently attend you.
  Val. Will you make haste?   *Exit.*
  Pro. I will.
Euen as one heate, another heate expels,
Or as one naile, by strength driues out another.
So the remembrance of my former Loue
Is by a newer obiect quite forgotten,
It is mine, or *Valentines* praise?
Her true perfection, or my false transgression?
That makes me reasonlesse, to reason thus?
Shee is faire: and so is *Iulia* that I loue,

(That

(That I did loue, for now my loue is thaw'd,
Which like a waxen Image 'gainst a fire
Beares no impression of the thing it was.)
Me thinkes my zeale to *Valentine* is cold,
And that I loue him not as I was wont:
O, but I loue his Lady too-too much,
And that's the reason I loue him so little.
How shall I doate on her with more aduice,
That thus without aduice begin to loue her?
'Tis but her picture I haue yet beheld,
And that hath dazel'd my reasons light:
But when I looke on her perfections,
There is no reason, but I shall be blinde.
If I can checke my erring loue, I will,
If not, to compasse her Ile vse my skill.

Exeunt.

Scena Quinta.

Enter Speed *and* Launce.

Speed. Launce, by mine honesty welcome to *Padua*.

Laun. Forsweare not thy selfe, sweet youth, for I am not welcome. I reckon this alwaies, that a man is neuer vndon till hee be hang'd, nor neuer welcome to a place, till some certaine shot be paid, and the Hostesse say welcome.

Speed. Come-on you mad-cap: Ile to the Ale-house with you presently; where, for one shot of fiue pence, thou shalt haue fiue thousand welcomes: But sirha, how did thy Master part with Madam *Iulia*?

Lau. Marry after they cloas'd in earnest, they parted very fairely in iest.

Spee. But shall she marry him?

Lau. No.

Spee. How then? shall he marry her?

Lau. No, neither.

Spee. What, are they broken?

Lau. No; they are both as whole as a fish.

Spee. Why then, how stands the matter with them?

Lau. Marry thus, when it stands well with him, it stands well with her.

Spee. What an asse art thou, I vnderstand thee not.

Lau. What a blocke art thou, that thou canst not? My staffe vnderstands me?

Spee. What thou saist?

Lau. I, and what I do too: looke thee, Ile but leane, and my staffe vnderstands me.

Spee. It stands vnder thee indeed.

Lau. Why, stand-vnder: and vnder-stand is all one.

Spee. But tell me true, wil't be a match?

Lau. Aske my dogge, if he say I, it will: if hee say no, it will: if hee shake his taile, and say nothing, it will.

Spee. The conclusion is then, that it will.

Lau. Thou shalt neuer get such a secret from me, but by a parable.

Spee. 'Tis well that I get it so: but *Launce*, how saist thou that that my master is become a notable Louer?

Lau. I neuer knew him otherwise.

Spee. Then how?

Lau. A notable Lubber: as thou reportest him to bee.

Spee. Why, thou whorson Asse, thou mistak'st me,

Lau. Why Foole, I meant not thee, I meant thy Master.

Spee. I tell thee, my Master is become a hot Louer.

Lau. Why, I tell thee, I care not, though hee burne himselfe in Loue. If thou wilt goe with me to the Ale-house: if not, thou art an Hebrew, a Iew, and not worth the name of a Christian.

Spee. Why?

Lau. Because thou hast not so much charity in thee as to goe to the Ale with a Christian: Wilt thou goe?

Spee. At thy seruice.

Exeunt.

Scena Sexta.

Enter Protheus *solus.*

Pro. To leaue my *Iulia*, shall I be forsworne?
To loue faire *Siluia*, shall I be forsworne?
To wrong my friend, I shall be much forsworne.
And ev'n that Powre which gaue me first my oath
Prouokes me to this three-fold periurie.
Loue bad mee sweare, and Loue bids me for-sweare;
O sweet-suggesting Loue, if thou hast sin'd,
Teach me (thy tempted subiect) to excuse it.
At first I did adore a twinkling Starre,
But now I worship a celestiall Sunne:
Vn-heedfull vowes may heedfully be broken,
And he wants wit, that wants resolued will,
To learne his wit, t'exchange the bad for better;
Fie, fie, vnreuerend tongue, to call her bad,
Whose soueraignty so oft thou hast preferd,
With twenty thousand soule-confirming oathes.
I cannot leaue to loue; and yet I doe:
But there I leaue to loue, where I should loue.
Iulia I loose, and *Valentine* I loose,
If I keepe them, I needs must loose my selfe:
If I loose them, thus finde I by their losse,
For *Valentine*, my selfe: for *Iulia*, *Siluia*.
I to my selfe am deerer then a friend,
For Loue is still most precious in it selfe,
And *Siluia* (witnesse heauen that made her faire)
Shewes *Iulia* but a swarthy Ethiope.
I will forget that *Iulia* is aliue,
Remembring that my Loue to her is dead.
And *Valentine* Ile hold an Enemie,
Ayming at *Siluia* as a sweeter friend.
I cannot now proue constant to my selfe,
Without some treachery vs'd to *Valentine*.
This night he meaneth with a Corded-ladder
To climbe celestiall *Siluia's* chamber window,
My selfe in counsaile his competitor.
Now presently Ile giue her father notice
Of their disguising and pretended flight:
Who (all inrag'd) will banish *Valentine*:
For *Thurio* he intends shall wed his daughter,
But *Valentine* being gon, Ile quickely crosse
By some slie tricke, blunt *Thurio's* dull proceeding.
Loue lend me wings, to make my purpose swift
As thou hast lent me wit, to plot this drift.

Exit.

Scœna septima.

Enter *Iulia* and *Lucetta.*

Iul. Counsaile, *Lucetta*, gentle girle assist me,
And eu'n in kinde loue, I doe coniure thee,
Who art the Table wherein all my thoughts
Are visibly Character'd, and engrau'd,
To lesson me, and tell me some good meane
How with my honour I may vndertake
A iourney to my louing *Protheus*.

Luc. Alas, the way is wearisome and long.

Iul. A true-deuoted Pilgrime is not weary
To measure Kingdomes with his feeble steps,
Much lesse shall she that hath Loues wings to flie,
And when the flight is made to one so deere,
Of such diuine perfection as Sir *Protheus*.

Luc. Better forbeare, till *Protheus* make returne.

Iul. Oh, know'st y̆ not, his looks are my soules food?
Pitty the dearth that I haue pined in,
By longing for that food so long a time.
Didst thou but know the inly touch of Loue,
Thou wouldst as soone goe kindle fire with snow
As seeke to quench the fire of Loue with words.

Luc. I doe not seeke to quench your Loues hot fire,
But qualifie the fires extreame rage,
Lest it should burne aboue the bounds of reason.

Iul. The more thou dam'st it vp, the more it burnes:
The Current that with gentle murmure glides
(Thou know'st) being stop'd, impatiently doth rage:
But when his faire course is not hindered,
He makes sweet musicke with th'enameld stones,
Giuing a gentle kisse to euery sedge
He ouer-taketh in his pilgrimage.
And so by many winding nookes he straies
With willing sport to the wilde Ocean.
Then let me goe, and hinder not my course:
Ile be as patient as a gentle streame,
And make a pastime of each weary step,
Till the last step haue brought me to my Loue,
And there Ile rest, as after much turmoile
A blessed soule doth in *Elizium*.

Luc. But in what habit will you goe along?

Iul. Not like a woman, for I would preuent
The loose encounters of lasciuious men:
Gentle *Lucetta*, fit me with such weedes
As may beseeme some well reputed Page.

Luc. Why then your Ladiship must cut your haire.

Iul. No girle, Ile knit it vp in silken strings,
With twentie od-conceited true-loue knots:
To be fantastique, may become a youth
Of greater time then I shall shew to be. (ches?

Luc. What fashion (Madam) shall I make your bree-

Iul. That fits as well, as tell me (good my Lord)
What compasse will you weare your Farthingale?
Why eu'n what fashion thou best likes (*Lucetta*.)

Luc. You must needs haue the᷉ with a cod-peece (Ma-

Iul. Out, out, (*Lucetta*) that wilbe illfauourd. (dam)

Luc. A round hose (Madam) now's not worth a pin
Vnlesse you haue a cod-peece to stick pins on.

Iul. Lucetta, as thou lou'st me let me haue
What thou think'st meet, and is most mannerly.
But tell me (wench) how will the world repute me
For vndertaking so vnstaid a iourney?
I feare me it will make me scandaliz'd.

Luc. If you thinke so, then stay at home, and go not.

Iul. Nay, that I will not.

Luc. Then neuer dreame on Infamy, but go:
If *Protheus* like your iourney, when you come,
No matter who's displeas'd, when you are gone:
I feare me he will scarce be pleas'd with all.

Iul. That is the least (*Lucetta*) of my feare:
A thousand oathes, an Ocean of his teares,
And instances of infinite of Loue,
Warrant me welcome to my *Protheus*.

Luc. All these are seruants to deceitfull men.

Iul. Base men, that vse them to so base effect;
But truer starres did gouerne *Protheus* birth,
His words are bonds, his oathes are oracles,
His loue sincere, his thoughts immaculate,
His teares, pure messengers, sent from his heart,
His heart, as far from fraud, as heauen from earth.

Luc. Pray heau'n he proue so when you come to him.

Iul. Now, as thou lou'st me, do him not that wrong,
To beare a hard opinion of his truth:
Onely deserue my loue, by louing him,
And presently goe with me to my chamber
To take a note of what I stand in need of,
To furnish me vpon my longing iourney:
All that is mine I leaue at thy dispose,
My goods, my Lands, my reputation,
Onely, in lieu thereof, dispatch me hence:
Come; answere not: but to it presently,
I am impatient of my tarriance. *Exeunt.*

Actus Tertius, Scena Prima.

Enter *Duke, Thurio, Protheus, Valentine,
Launce, Speed.*

Duke. Sir *Thurio*, giue vs leaue (I pray) a while,
We haue some secrets to confer about.
Now tell me *Protheus*, what's your will with me?

Pro. My gracious Lord, that which I wold discouer,
The Law of friendship bids me to conceale,
But when I call to minde your gracious fauours
Done to me (vndeseruing as I am)
My dutie pricks me on to vtter that
Which else, no worldly good should draw from me:
Know (worthy Prince) Sir *Valentine* my friend
This night intends to steale away your daughter:
My selfe am one made priuy to the plot.
I know you haue determin'd to bestow her
On *Thurio*, whom your gentle daughter hates,
And should she thus be stolne away from you,
It would be much vexation to your age.
Thus (for my duties sake) I rather chose
To crosse my friend in his intended drift,
Then (by concealing it) heap on your head
A pack of sorrowes, which would presse you downe
(Being vnpreuented) to your timelesse graue.

Duke. Protheus, I thank thee for thine honest care,
Which to requite, command me while I liue.
This loue of theirs, my selfe haue often seene,
Haply when they haue iudg'd me fast asleepe,
And oftentimes haue purpos'd to forbid

The two Gentlemen of Verona. 29

Sir *Valentine* her companie, and my Court.
But fearing lest my iealous ayme might erre,
And so (vnworthily) disgrace the man
(A rashnesse that I euer yet haue shun'd)
I gaue him gentle lookes, thereby to finde
That which thy selfe hast now disclos'd to me.
And that thou maist perceiue my feare of this,
Knowing that tender youth is soone suggested,
I nightly lodge her in an vpper Towre,
The key whereof, my selfe haue euer kept:
And thence she cannot be conuay'd away.

Pro. Know (noble Lord) they haue deuis'd a meane
How he her chamber-window will ascend,
And with a Corded-ladder fetch her downe:
For which, the youthfull Louer now is gone,
And this way comes he with it presently.
Where (if it please you) you may intercept him.
But (good my Lord) doe it so cunningly
That my discouery be not aimed at:
For, loue of you, not hate vnto my friend,
Hath made me publisher of this pretence.

Duke. Vpon mine Honor, he shall neuer know
That I had any light from thee of this.

Pro. Adiew, my Lord, Sir *Valentine* is comming.

Duk. Sir *Valentine*, whether away so fast?

Val. Please it your Grace, there is a Messenger
That stayes to beare my Letters to my friends,
And I am going to deliuer them.

Duk. Be they of much import?

Val. The tenure of them doth but signifie
My health, and happy being at your Court.

Duk. Nay then no matter: stay with me a while,
I am to breake with thee of some affaires,
That touch me neere: wherein thou must be secret.
'Tis not vnknown to thee, that I haue sought
To match my friend Sir *Thurio*, to my daughter.

Val. I know it well (my Lord) and sure the Match
Were rich and honourable: besides, the gentleman
Is full of Vertue, Bounty, Worth, and Qualities
Beseeming such a Wife, as your faire daughter:
Cannot your Grace win her to fancie him?

Duk. No, trust me, She is peeuish, sullen, froward,
Prowd, disobedient, stubborne, lacking duty,
Neither regarding that she is my childe,
Nor fearing me, as if I were her father:
And may I say to thee, this pride of hers
(Vpon aduice) hath drawne my loue from her,
And where I thought the remnant of mine age
Should haue beene cherish'd by her child-like dutie,
I now am full resolu'd to take a wife,
And turne her out, to who will take her in:
Then let her beauty be her wedding dowre:
For me, and my possessions she esteemes not.

Val. What would your Grace haue me to do in this?

Duk. There is a Lady in *Verona* heere
Whom I affect: but she is nice, and coy,
And naught esteemes my aged eloquence.
Now therefore would I haue thee to my Tutor
(For long agone I haue forgot to court,
Besides the fashion of the time is chang'd)
How, and which way I may bestow my selfe
To be regarded in her sun-bright eye.

Val. Win her with gifts, if she respect not words,
Dumbe Iewels often in their silent kinde
More then quicke words, doe moue a womans minde.

Duk. But she did scorne a present that I sent her,

Val. A woman somtime scorns what best cōtents her,
Send her another: neuer giue her ore,
For scorne at first, makes after-loue the more.
If she doe frowne, 'tis not in hate of you,
But rather to beget more loue in you.
If she doe chide, 'tis not to haue you gone,
For why, the fooles are mad, if left alone.
Take no repulse, what euer she doth say,
For, get you gon, she doth not meane away.
Flatter, and praise, commend, extoll their graces:
Though nere so blacke, say they haue Angells faces,
That man that hath a tongue, I say is no man,
If with his tongue he cannot win a woman.

Duk. But she I meane, is promis'd by her friends
Vnto a youthfull Gentleman of worth,
And kept seuerely from resort of men,
That no man hath accesse by day to her.

Val. Why then I would resort to her by night.

Duk. I, but the doores be lockt, and keyes kept safe,
That no man hath recourse to her by night.

Val. What letts but one may enter at her window?

Duk. Her chamber is aloft, far from the ground,
And built so sheluing, that one cannot climbe it
Without apparant hazard of his life.

Val. Why then a Ladder quaintly made of Cords
To cast vp, with a paire of anchoring hookes,
Would serue to scale another *Hero's* towre,
So bold *Leander* would aduenture it.

Duk. Now as thou art a Gentleman of blood
Aduise me, where I may haue such a Ladder.

Val. When would you vse it? pray sir, tell me that.

Duk. This very night; for Loue is like a childe
That longs for euery thing that he can come by.

Val. By seauen a clock, ile get you such a Ladder.

Duk. But harke thee: I will goe to her alone,
How shall I best conuey the Ladder thither?

Val. It will be light (my Lord) that you may beare it
Vnder a cloake, that is of any length.

Duk. A cloake as long as thine will serue the turne?

Val. I my good Lord.

Duk. Then let me see thy cloake,
Ile get me one of such another length.

Val. Why any cloake will serue the turn (my Lord)

Duk. How shall I fashion me to weare a cloake?
I pray thee let me feele thy cloake vpon me.
What Letter is this same? what's here? to *Siluia*?
And heere an Engine fit for my proceeding,
Ile be so bold to breake the seale for once.

My thoughts do harbour with my Siluia *nightly,*
And slaues they are to me, that send them flying.
Oh, could their Master come, and goe as lightly,
Himselfe would lodge where (senceles) they are lying.
My Herald Thoughts, in thy pure bosome rest-them,
While I (their King) that thither them importune
Doe curse the grace, that with such grace hath blest them,
Because my selfe doe want my seruants fortune.
I curse my selfe, for they are sent by me,
That they should harbour where their Lord should be.

What's here? *Siluia*, this night I will enfranchise thee.
'Tis so: and heere's the Ladder for the purpose.
Why *Phaeton* (for thou art *Merops* sonne)
Wilt thou aspire to guide the heauenly Car?
And with thy daring folly burne the world?
Wilt thou reach stars, because they shine on thee?

C 3   Goe

The two Gentlemen of Verona.

Goe base Intruder, ouer-weening Slaue,
Bestow thy fawning smiles on equall mates,
And thinke my patience, (more then thy desert)
Is priuiledge for thy departure hence.
Thanke me for this, more then for all the fauors
Which (all too-much) I haue bestowed on thee.
But if thou linger in my Territories
Longer then swiftest expedition
Will giue thee time to leaue our royall Court,
By heauen, my wrath shall farre exceed the loue
I euer bore my daughter, or thy selfe.
Be gone, I will not heare thy vaine excuse,
But as thou lou'st thy life, make speed from hence.

Val. And why not death, rather then liuing torment?
To die, is to be banisht from my selfe,
And *Siluia* is my selfe: banish'd from her
Is selfe from selfe. A deadly banishment:
What light, is light, if *Siluia* be not seene?
What ioy is ioy, if *Siluia* be not by?
Vnlesse it be to thinke that she is by
And feed vpon the shadow of perfection.
Except I be by *Siluia* in the night,
There is no musicke in the Nightingale.
Vnlesse I looke on *Siluia* in the day,
There is no day for me to looke vpon.
Shee is my essence, and I leaue to be;
If I be not by her faire influence
Foster'd, illumin'd, cherish'd, kept aliue.
I flie not death, to flie his deadly doome;
Tarry I heere, I but attend on death,
But flie I hence, I flie away from life.

Pro. Run (boy) run, run, and seeke him out.
Lau. So-hough, Soa hough ———
Pro. What seest thou?
Lau. Him we goe to finde,
There's not a haire on's head, but t'is a *Valentine*.
Pro. *Valentine*?
Val. No.
Pro. Who then? his Spirit?
Val. Neither,
Pro. What then?
Val. Nothing.
Lau. Can nothing speake? Master, shall I strike?
Pro. Who wouldst thou strike?
Lau. Nothing.
Pro. Villaine, forbeare.
Lau. Why Sir, Ile strike nothing: I pray you.
Pro. Sirha, I say forbeare: friend *Valentine*, a word.
Val. My eares are stopt, & cannot hear good newes,
So much of bad already hath possest them.
Pro. Then in dumbe silence will I bury mine,
For they are harsh, vn-tuneable, and bad.
Val. Is *Siluia* dead?
Pro. No, *Valentine*.
Val. No *Valentine* indeed, for sacred *Siluia*,
Hath she forsworne me?
Pro. No, *Valentine*.
Val. No *Valentine*, if *Siluia* haue forsworne me.
What is your newes?
Lau. Sir, there is a proclamation, ỹ you are vanished.
Pro. That thou art banish'd: oh that's the newes,
From hence, from *Siluia*, and from me thy friend.
Val. Oh, I haue fed vpon this woe already,
And now excesse of it will make me surfet.
Doth *Siluia* know that I am banish'd?
Pro. I, I: and she hath offered to the doome
(Which vn-reuerst stands in effectuall force)
A Sea of melting pearle, which some call teares;
Those at her fathers churlish feete she tenderd,
With them vpon her knees, her humble selfe,
Wringing her hands, whose whitenes so became them,
As if but now they waxed pale for woe:
But neither bended knees, pure hands held vp,
Sad sighes, deepe grones, nor siluer-shedding teares
Could penetrate her vncompassionate Sire;
But *Valentine*, if he be tane, must die.
Besides, her intercession chaf'd him so,
When she for thy repeale was suppliant,
That to close prison he commanded her,
With many bitter threats of biding there.

Val. No more: vnles the next word that thou speak'st
Haue some malignant power vpon my life:
If so: I pray thee breath it in mine eare,
As ending Antheme of my endlesse dolor.

Pro. Cease to lament for that thou canst not helpe,
And study helpe for that which thou lament'st,
Time is the Nurse, and breeder of all good;
Here, if thou stay, thou canst not see thy loue:
Besides, thy staying will abridge thy life:
Hope is a louers staffe, walke hence with that
And manage it, against despairing thoughts:
Thy letters may be here, though thou art hence,
Which, being writ to me, shall be deliuer'd
Euen in the milke-white bosome of thy Loue.
The time now serues not to expostulate,
Come, Ile conuey thee through the City-gate.
And ere I part with thee, confer at large
Of all that may concerne thy Loue-affaires:
As thou lou'st *Siluia* (though not for thy selfe)
Regard thy danger, and along with me.

Val. I pray thee *Launce*, and if thou seest my Boy
Bid him make haste, and meet me at the North-gate.

Pro. Goe sirha, finde him out: Come *Valentine*.
Val. Oh my deere *Siluia*; haplesse *Valentine*.

Launce. I am but a foole, looke you, and yet I haue the wit to thinke my Master is a kinde of a knaue: but that's all one, if he be but one knaue: He liues not now that knowes me to be in loue, yet I am in loue, but a Teeme of horse shall not plucke that from me: nor who 'tis I loue: and yet 'tis a woman; but what woman, I will not tell my selfe: and yet 'tis a Milke-maid: yet 'tis not a maid: for shee hath had Gossips; yet 'tis a maid, for she is her Masters maid, and serues for wages. Shee hath more qualities then a Water-Spaniell, which is much in a bare Christian: Heere is the Cate-log of her Condition. *Inprimis*. Shee can fetch and carry: why a horse can doe no more; nay, a horse cannot fetch, but onely carry, therefore is shee better then a Iade. *Item*. She can milke, looke you, a sweet vertue in a maid with cleane hands.

Speed. How now Signior *Launce*? what newes with your Mastership?
La. With my Mastership? why, it is at Sea:
Sp. Well, your old vice still: mistake the word: what newes then in your paper?
La. The black'st newes that euer thou heard'st.
Sp. Why man? how blacke?
La. Why, as blacke as Inke.
Sp. Let me read them?
La. Fie on thee Iolt-head, thou canst not read.
Sp. Thou lyest: I can.
La. I will try thee: tell me this: who begot thee?
Sp. Marry,

Sp. Marry, the son of my Grand-father.

La. Oh illiterate loyterer; it was the sonne of thy Grand-mother: this proues that thou canst not read.

Sp. Come foole, come: try me in thy paper.

La. There: and S. *Nicholas* be thy speed.

Sp. Inprim:s she can milke.

La. I that she can.

Sp. Item, she brewes good Ale.

La. And thereof comes the prouerbe: (*Blessing of your heart, you brew good Ale.*)

Sp. Item, she can sowe.

La. That's as much as to say (*Can she so?*)

Sp. Item she can knit.

La. What neede a man care for a stock with a wench, When she can knit him a stocke?

Sp. Item, she can wash and scoure.

La. A speciall vertue: for then shee neede not be wash'd, and scowr'd.

Sp. Item, she can spin.

La. Then may I set the world on wheeles, when she can spin for her liuing.

Sp. Item, she hath many namelesse vertues.

La. That's as much as to say *Bastard-vertues*: that indeede know not their fathers; and therefore haue no names.

Sp. Here follow her vices.

La. Close at the heeles of her vertues.

Sp. Item, shee is not to be fasting in respect of her breath.

La. Well: that fault may be mended with a breakfast: read on.

Sp. Item, she hath a sweet mouth.

La. That makes amends for her soure breath.

Sp. Item, she doth talke in her sleepe.

La. It's no matter for that; so shee sleepe not in her talke.

Sp. Item, she is slow in words.

La. Oh villaine, that set this downe among her vices; To be slow in words, is a womans onely vertue: I pray thee out with't, and place it for her chiefe vertue.

Sp. Item, she is proud.

La. Out with that too: It was *Eues* legacie, and cannot be t'ane from her.

Sp. Item, she hath no teeth.

La. I care not for that neither: because I loue crusts.

Sp. Item, she is curst.

La. Well: the best is, she hath no teeth to bite.

Sp. Item, she will often praise her liquor.

La. If her liquor be good, she shall: if she will not, I will; for good things should be praised.

Sp. Item, she is too liberall.

La. Of her tongue she cannot; for that's writ downe she is slow of: of her purse, shee shall not, for that ile keepe shut: Now, of another thing shee may, and that cannot I helpe. Well, proceede.

Sp. Item, shee hath more haire then wit, and more faults then haires, and more wealth then faults.

La. Stop there: Ile haue her: she was mine, and not mine, twice or thrice in that last Article: rehearse that once more.

Sp. Item, she hath more haire then wit.

La. More haire then wit: it may be ile proue it: The couer of the salt, hides the salt, and therefore it is more then the salt; the haire that couers the wit, is more then the wit; for the greater hides the lesse: What's next?

Sp. And more faults then haires.

La. That's monstrous: oh that that were out.

Sp. And more wealth then faults.

La. Why that word makes the faults gracious: Well, ile haue her: and if it be a match, as nothing is impossible.

Sp. What then?

La. Why then, will I tell thee, that thy Master staies for thee at the *North gate*.

Sp. For me?

La. For thee? I, who art thou? he hath staid for a better man then thee.

Sp. And must I goe to him?

La. Thou must run to him; for thou hast staid so long, that going will scarce serue the turne.

Sp. Why didst not tell me sooner? 'pox of your loue Letters.

La. Now will he be swing'd for reading my Letter; An vnmannerly slaue, that will thrust himselfe into secrets: Ile after, to reioyce in the boyes correctiō. *Exeunt.*

Scena Secunda.

Enter Duke, Thurio, Protheus.

Du. Sir *Thurio*, feare not, but that she will loue you
Now *Valentine* is banish'd from her sight.

Th. Since his exile she hath despis'd me most,
Forsworne my company, and rail'd at me,
That I am desperate of obtaining her.

Du. This weake impresse of Loue, is as a figure
Trenched in ice, which with an houres heate
Dissolues to water, and doth loose his forme.
A little time will melt her frozen thoughts,
And worthlesse *Valentine* shall be forgot.
How now sir *Protheus*, is your countriman
(According to our Proclamation) gon?

Pro. Gon, my good Lord.

Du. My daughter takes his going grieuously?

Pro. A little time (my Lord) will kill that griefe.

Du. So I beleeue: but *Thurio* thinkes not so:
Protheus, the good conceit I hold of thee,
(For thou hast showne some signe of good desert)
Makes me the better to confer with thee.

Pro. Longer then I proue loyall to your Grace,
Let me not liue, to looke vpon your Grace.

Du. Thou know'st how willingly, I would effect
The match betweene sir *Thurio*, and my daughter?

Pro. I doe my Lord.

Du. And also, I thinke, thou art not ignorant
How she opposes her against my will?

Pro. She did my Lord, when *Valentine* was here.

Du. I, and peruersly, she perseuers so:
What might we doe to make the girle forget
The loue of *Valentine*, and loue sir *Thurio*?

Pro. The best way is, to slander *Valentine*,
With falsehood, cowardize, and poore discent:
Three things, that women highly hold in hate.

Du. I, but she'll thinke, that it is spoke in hate.

Pro. I, if his enemy deliuer it.
Therefore it must with circumstance be spoken
By one, whom she esteemeth as his friend.

Du. Then you must vndertake to slander him.

Pro.

Pro. And that (my Lord) I shall be loath to doe:
'Tis an ill office for a Gentleman,
Especially against his very friend.

Du. Where your good word cannot aduantage him,
Your slander neuer can endamage him;
Therefore the office is indifferent,
Being intreated to it by your friend.

Pro. You haue preuail'd (my Lord) if I can doe it
By ought that I can speake in his dispraise,
She shall not long continue loue to him:
But say this weede her loue from *Valentine*,
It followes not that she will loue sir *Thurio*.

Th. Therefore, as you vnwinde her loue from him;
Least it should rauell, and be good to none,
You must prouide to bottome it on me:
Which must be done, by praising me as much
As you, in worth dispraise, sir *Valentine*.

Du. And *Protheus*, we dare trust you in this kinde,
Because we know (on *Valentines* report:)
You are already loues firme votary,
And cannot soone reuolt, and change your minde.
Vpon this warrant, shall you haue accesse,
Where you, with *Siluia*, may conferre at large.
For she is lumpish, heauy, mellancholly,
And (for your friends sake) will be glad of you;
Where you may temper her, by your perswasion,
To hate yong *Valentine*, and loue my friend.

Pro. As much as I can doe, I will effect:
But you sir *Thurio*, are not sharpe enough:
You must lay Lime, to tangle her desires
By walefull Sonnets, whose composed Rimes
Should be full fraught with seruiceable vowes.

Du. I, much is the force of heauen-bred Poesie.

Pro. Say that vpon the altar of her beauty
You sacrifice your teares, your sighes, your heart:
Write till your inke be dry: and with your teares
Moist it againe: and frame some feeling line,
That may discouer such integrity:
For *Orpheus* Lute, was strung with Poets sinewes,
Whose golden touch could soften steele and stones;
Make Tygers tame, and huge *Leuiathans*
Forsake vnsounded deepes, to dance on Sands.
After your dire-lamenting Elegies,
Visit by night your Ladies chamber-window
With some sweet Consort; To their Instruments
Tune a deploring dumpe: the nights dead silence
Will well become such sweet complaining grieuance:
This, or else nothing, will inherit her.

Du. This discipline, showes thou hast bin in loue.

Th. And thy aduice, this night, ile put in practise:
Therefore, sweet *Protheus*, my direction-giuer,
Let vs into the City presently
To sort some Gentlemen, well skil'd in Musicke.
I haue a Sonnet, that will serue the turne
To giue the on-set to thy good aduise.

Du. About it Gentlemen.

Pro. We'll wait vpon your Grace, till after Supper,
And afterward determine our proceedings.

Du. Euen now about it, I will pardon you. *Exeunt.*

Actus Quartus. Scœna Prima.

Enter Valentine, Speed, and certaine Out-lawes.

1.*Out.* Fellowes, stand fast: I see a passenger.

2.*Out.* If there be ten, shrinke not, but down with'em.
3.*Out.* Stand sir, and throw vs that you haue about'ye.
If not: we'll make you sit, and rifle you.

Sp. Sir we are vndone; these are the Villaines
That all the Trauailers doe feare so much.

Val. My friends.
1.*Out.* That's not so, sir: we are your enemies.
2.*Out.* Peace: we'll heare him.
3.*Out.* I by my beard will we: for he is a proper man.

Val. Then know that I haue little wealth to loose;
A man I am, cros'd with aduersitie:
My riches, are these poore habiliments,
Of which, if you should here disfurnish me,
You take the sum and substance that I haue.

2.*Out.* Whether trauell you?
Val. To *Verona*.
1.*Out.* Whence came you?
Val. From *Millaine*.
3.*Out.* Haue you long soiourn'd there? (staid,
Val. Some sixteene moneths, and longer might haue
If crooked fortune had not thwarted me.
1.*Out.* What, were you banish'd thence?
Val. I was.
2.*Out.* For what offence?
Val. For that which now torments me to rehearse;
I kil'd a man, whose death I much repent,
But yet I slew him manfully, in fight,
Without false vantage, or base treachery.
1.*Out.* Why nere repent it, if it were done so;
But were you banisht for so small a fault?
Val. I was, and held me glad of such a doome.
2.*Out.* Haue you the Tongues?
Val. My youthfull trauaile, therein made me happy,
Or else I often had beene often miserable.
3.*Out.* By the bare scalpe of *Robin Hoods* fat Fryer,
This fellow were a King, for our wilde faction.
1.*Out.* We'll haue him: Sirs, a word.
Sp. Master, be one of them:
It's an honourable kinde of theeuery.
Val. Peace villaine.
2.*Out.* Tell vs this: haue you any thing to take to?
Val. Nothing but my fortune.
3.*Out.* Know then, that some of vs are Gentlemen,
Such as the fury of vngouern'd youth
Thrust from the company of awfull men.
My selfe was from *Verona* banished,
For practising to steale away a Lady,
And heire and Neece, alide vnto the Duke.
2.*Out.* And I from *Mantua*, for a Gentleman,
Who, in my moode, I stab'd vnto the heart.
1.*Out.* And I, for such like petty crimes as these.
But to the purpose: for we cite our faults,
That they may hold excus'd our lawlesse liues;
And partly seeing you are beautifide
With goodly shape; and by your owne report,
A Linguist, and a man of such perfection,
As we doe in our quality much want.
2.*Out.* Indeede because you are a banish'd man,
Therefore, aboue the rest, we parley to you:
Are you content to be our Generall?
To make a vertue of necessitie,
And liue as we doe in this wildernesse?
3.*Out.* What saist thou? wilt thou be of our consort?
Say I, and be the captaine of vs all:
We'll doe thee homage, and be rul'd by thee,
Loue thee, as our Commander, and our King.

1.*Out.*

1. *Out.* But if thou scorne our curtesie, thou dyest.
2. *Out.* Thou shalt not liue, to brag what we haue of-
Val. I take your offer, and will liue with you, (fer'd.
Prouided that you do no outrages
On silly women, or poore passengers.
3. *Out.* No, we detest such vile base practises.
Come, goe with vs, we'll bring thee to our Crewes,
And show thee all the Treasure we haue got;
Which, with our selues, all rest at thy dispose. *Exeunt.*

Scœna Secunda.

Enter Protheus, Thurio, Iulia, Host, Musitian, Siluia.

Pro. Already haue I bin false to *Valentine*,
And now I must be as vniust to *Thurio*,
Vnder the colour of commending him,
I haue accesse my owne loue to prefer.
But *Siluia* is too faire, too true, too holy,
To be corrupted with my worthlesse guifts;
When I protest true loyalty to her,
She twits me with my falsehood to my friend;
When to her beauty I commend my vowes,
She bids me thinke how I haue bin forsworne
In breaking faith with *Iulia*, whom I lou'd;
And notwithstanding all her sodaine quips,
The least whereof would quell a louers hope:
Yet (Spaniel-like) the more she spurnes my loue,
The more it growes, and fawneth on her still;
But here comes *Thurio*; now must we to her window,
And giue some euening Musique to her eare.

Th. How now, sir *Protheus*, are you crept before vs?
Pro. I gentle *Thurio*, for you know that loue
Will creepe in seruice, where it cannot goe.
Th. I, but I hope, Sir, that you loue not here.
Pro. Sir, but I doe: or else I would be hence.
Th. Who, *Siluia*?
Pro. I, *Siluia*, for your sake.
Th. I thanke you for your owne: Now Gentlemen
Let's tune: and to o it lustily a while.
Ho. Now, my yong guest; me thinks your' allycholly;
I pray you why is it?
Iu. Marry (mine *Host*) because I cannot be merry.
Ho. Come, we'll haue you merry: ile bring you where
you shall heare Musique, and see the Gentleman that
you ask'd for.
Iu. But shall I heare him speake.
Ho. I that you shall.
Iu. That will be Musique.
Ho. Harke, harke.
Iu. Is he among these?
Ho. I: but peace, let's heare'm.

Song. Who is *Siluia*? what is she?
That all our Swaines commend her?
Holy, faire, and wise is she,
The heauen such grace did lend her,
that she might admired be.
Is she kinde as she is faire?
For beauty liues with kindnesse:
Loue doth to her eyes repaire,
To helpe him of his blindnesse:
And being help'd, inhabits there.
Then to *Siluia*, let vs sing,
That *Siluia* is excelling;
She excels each mortall thing
Vpon the dull earth dwelling.
To her let vs Garlands bring.

Ho. How now? are you sadder then you were before;
How doe you, man? the Musicke likes you not.
Iu. You mistake: the Musitian likes me not.
Ho. Why, my pretty youth?
Iu. He plaies false (father.)
Ho. How, out of tune on the strings.
Iu. Not so: but yet
So false that he grieues my very heart-strings.
Ho. You haue a quicke eare. (heart.
Iu. I, I would I were deafe: it makes me haue a slow
Ho. I perceiue you delight not in Musique.
Iu. Not a whit, when it iars so.
Ho. Harke, what fine change is in the Musique.
Iu. I: that change is the spight.
Ho. You would haue them alwaies play but one thing.
Iu. I would alwaies haue one play but one thing.
But Host, doth this Sir *Protheus*, that we talke on,
Often resort vnto this Gentlewoman?
Ho. I tell you what *Launce* his man told me,
He lou'd her out of all nicke.
Iu. Where is *Launce*?
Ho. Gone to seeke his dog, which to morrow, by his
Masters command, hee must carry for a present to his
Lady.
Iu. Peace, stand aside, the company parts.
Pro. Sir *Thurio*, feare not you, I will so pleade,
That you shall say, my cunning drift excels.
Th. Where meete we?
Pro. At Saint *Gregories* well.
Th. Farewell.
Pro. Madam: good eu'n to your Ladiship.
Sil. I thanke you for your Musique (Gentlemen)
Who is that that spake?
Pro. One (Lady) if you knew his pure hearts truth,
You would quickly learne to know him by his voice.
Sil. Sir *Protheus*, as I take it.
Pro. Sir *Protheus* (gentle Lady) and your Seruant.
Sil. What's your will?
Pro. That I may compasse yours.
Sil. You haue your wish: my will is euen this,
That presently you hie you home to bed:
Thou subtile, periur'd, false, disloyall man:
Think'st thou I am so shallow, so conceitlesse,
To be seduced by thy flattery,
That has't deceiu'd so many with thy vowes?
Returne, returne, and make thy loue amends:
For me (by this pale queene of night I sweare)
I am so farre from granting thy request,
That I despise thee, for thy wrongfull suite;
And by and by intend to chide my selfe,
Euen for this time I spend in talking to thee.
Pro. I grant (sweet loue) that I did loue a Lady,
But she is dead.
Iu. 'Twere false, if I should speake it;
For I am sure she is not buried.
Sil. Say that she be: yet *Valentine* thy friend
Suruiues; to whom (thy selfe art witnesse)
I am betroth'd; and art thou not asham'd
To wrong him, with thy importunacy?

Pro.

Pro. I likewise heare that *Valentine* is dead.
Sil. And so suppose am I; for in her graue
Assure thy selfe, my loue is buried.
Pro. Sweet Lady, let me rake it from the earth.
Sil. Goe to thy Ladies graue and call hers thence,
Or at the least, in hers, sepulcher thine.
Iul. He heard not that.
Pro. Madam: if your heart be so obdurate:
Vouchsafe me yet your Picture for my loue,
The Picture that is hanging in your chamber:
To that ile speake, to that ile sigh and weepe:
For since the substance of your perfect selfe
Is else deuoted, I am but a shadow;
And to your shadow, will I make true loue.
Iul. If 'twere a substance you would sure deceiue it,
And make it but a shadow, as I am.
Sil. I am very loath to be your Idoll Sir;
But, since your falsehood shall become you well
To worship shadowes, and adore false shapes,
Send to me in the morning, and ile send it:
And so, good rest.
Pro. As wretches haue ore-night
That wait for execution in the morne.
Iul. Host, will you goe?
Ho. By my hallidome, I was fast asleepe.
Iul. Pray you, where lies Sir *Protheus*?
Ho. Marry, at my house:
Trust me, I thinke 'tis almost day.
Iul. Not so: but it hath bin the longest night
That ere I watch'd, and the most heauiest.

Scœna Tertia.

Enter Eglamore, Siluia.

Eg. This is the houre that Madam *Siluia*
Entreated me to call, and know her minde:
Ther's some great matter she'ld employ me in.
Madam, Madam.
Sil. Who cals?
Eg. Your seruant, and your friend;
One that attends your Ladiships command.
Sil. Sir *Eglamore*, a thousand times good morrow.
Eg. As many (worthy Lady) to your selfe:
According to your Ladiships impose,
I am thus early come, to know what seruice
It is your pleasure to command me in.
Sil. Oh *Eglamoure*, thou art a Gentleman:
Thinke not I flatter (for I sweare I doe not)
Valiant, wise, remorse-full, well accomplish'd.
Thou art not ignorant what deere good will
I beare vnto the banish'd *Valentine*:
Nor how my father would enforce me marry
Vaine *Thurio* (whom my very soule abhor'd.)
Thy selfe hast lou'd, and I haue heard thee say
No griefe did euer come so neere thy heart,
As when thy Lady, and thy true-loue dide,
Vpon whose Graue thou vow'dst pure chastitie:
Sir *Eglamoure*: I would to *Valentine*
To *Mantua*, where I heare, he makes aboad;
And for the waies are dangerous to passe,
I doe desire thy worthy company,
Vpon whose faith and honor, I repose.
Vrge not my fathers anger (*Eglamoure*)
But thinke vpon my griefe (a Ladies griefe)
And on the iustice of my flying hence,
To keepe me from a most vnholy match,
Which heauen and fortune still rewards with plagues,
I doe desire thee, euen from a heart
As full of sorrowes, as the Sea of sands,
To beare me company, and goe with me:
If not, to hide what I haue said to thee,
That I may venture to depart alone.
Egl. Madam, I pitty much your grieuances,
Which, since I know they vertuously are plac'd,
I giue consent to goe along with you,
Wreaking as little what betideth me,
As much, I wish all good befortune you.
When will you goe?
Sil. This euening comming.
Eg. Where shall I meete you?
Sil. At *Frier Patrickes* Cell,
Where I intend holy Confession.
Eg. I will not faile your Ladiship:
Good morrow (gentle Lady.)
Sil. Good morrow, kinde Sir *Eglamoure*. *Exeunt.*

Scena Quarta.

Enter Launce, Protheus, Iulia, Siluia.

Lau. When a mans seruant shall play the Curre with him (looke you) it goes hard: one that I brought vp of a puppy: one that I sau'd from drowning, when three or foure of his blinde brothers and sisters went to it: I haue taught him (euen as one would say precisely, thus I would teach a dog) I was sent to deliuer him, as a present to Mistris *Siluia*, from my Master; and I came no sooner into the dyning-chamber, but he steps me to her Trencher, and steales her Capons-leg: O, 'tis a foule thing, when a Cur cannot keepe himselfe in all companies: I would haue (as one should say) one that takes vpon him to be a dog indeede, to be, as it were, a dog at all things. If I had not had more wit then he, to take a fault vpon me that he did, I thinke verily hee had bin hang'd for't: sure as I liue he had suffer'd for't: you shall iudge: Hee thrusts me himselfe into the company of three or foure gentleman-like-dogs, vnder the Dukes table: hee had not bin there (blesse the marke) a pissing while, but all the chamber smelt him: out with the dog (saies one) what cur is that (saies another) whip him out (saies the third) hang him vp (saies the Duke.) I hauing bin acquainted with the smell before, knew it was Crab; and goes me to the fellow that whips the dogges: friend (quoth I) you meane to whip the dog: I marry doe I (quoth he) you doe him the more wrong (quoth I) 'twas I did the thing you wot of: he makes me no more adoe, but whips me out of the chamber: how many Masters would doe this for his Seruant? nay, ile be sworne I haue sat in the stockes, for puddings he hath stolne, otherwise he had bin executed: I haue stood on the Pillorie for Geese he hath kil'd, otherwise he had suffered for't: thou think'st not of this now: nay, I remember the tricke you seru'd me, when I tooke my leaue of Madam *Siluia*: did
not

The two Gentlemen of Verona.

not I bid thee still marke me, and doe as I do; when did'st thou see me heaue vp my leg, and make water against a Gentlewomans farthingale? did'st thou euer see me doe such a tricke?

Pro. *Sebastian* is thy name: I like thee well,
And will imploy thee in some seruice presently.

Iu. In what you please, ile doe what I can.

Pro. I hope thou wilt.
How now you whor-son pezant,
Where haue you bin these two dayes loytering?

La. Marry Sir, I carried Mistris *Siluia* the dogge you bad me.

Pro. And what saies she to my little Iewell?

La. Marry she saies your dog was a cur, and tels you currish thanks is good enough for such a present.

Pro. But she receiu'd my dog?

La. No indeede did she not:
Here haue I brought him backe againe.

Pro. What, didst thou offer her this from me?

La. I Sir, the other Squirrill was stolne from me
By the Hangmans boyes in the market place,
And then I offer'd her mine owne, who is a dog
As big as ten of yours, & therefore the guift the greater.

Pro. Goe, get thee hence, and finde my dog againe,
Or nere returne againe into my sight.
Away, I say: stayest thou to vexe me here;
A Slaue, that still an end, turnes me to shame:
Sebastian, I haue entertained thee,
Partly that I haue neede of such a youth,
That can with some discretion doe my businesse:
For 'tis no trusting to yond foolish Lowt;
But chiefely, for thy face, and thy behauiour,
Which (if my Augury deceiue me not)
Witnesse good bringing vp, fortune, and truth:
Therefore know thee, for this I entertaine thee.
Go presently, and take this Ring with thee,
Deliuer it to Madam *Siluia*;
She lou'd me well, deliuer'd it to me.

Iul. It seemes you lou'd not her, not leaue her token:
She is dead belike?

Pro. Not so: I thinke she liues.

Iul. Alas.

Pro. Why do'st thou cry alas?

Iul. I cannot choose but pitty her.

Pro. Wherefore should'st thou pitty her?

Iul. Because, me thinkes that she lou'd you as well
As you doe loue your Lady *Siluia*:
She dreames on him, that has forgot her loue,
You doate on her, that cares not for your loue.
'Tis pitty Loue, should be so contrary:
And thinking on it, makes me cry alas.

Pro. Well: giue her that Ring, and therewithall
This Letter: that's her chamber: Tell my Lady,
I claime the promise for her heauenly Picture:
Your message done, hye home vnto my chamber,
Where thou shalt finde me sad, and solitarie.

Iul. How many women would doe such a message?
Alas poore *Protheus*, thou hast entertain'd
A Foxe, to be the Shepheard of thy Lambs;
Alas, poore foole, why doe I pitty him
That with his very heart despiseth me?
Because he loues her, he despiseth me,
Because I loue him, I must pitty him.
This Ring I gaue him, when he parted from me,
To binde him to remember my good will:
And now am I (vnhappy Messenger)
To plead for that, which I would not obtaine;
To carry that, which I would haue refus'd;
To praise his faith, which I would haue disprais'd.
I am my Masters true confirmed Loue,
But cannot be true seruant to my Master,
Vnlesse I proue false traitor to my selfe.
Yet will I woe for him, but yet so coldly,
As (heauen it knowes) I would not haue him speed.
Gentlewoman, good day: I pray you be my meane
To bring me where to speake with Madam *Siluia*.

Sil. What would you with her, if that I be she?

Iul. If you be she, I doe intreat your patience
To heare me speake the message I am sent on.

Sil. From whom?

Iul. From my Master, Sir *Protheus*, Madam.

Sil. Oh: he sends you for a Picture?

Iul. I, Madam.

Sil. *Vrsula*, bring my Picture there,
Goe, giue your Master this: tell him from me,
One *Iulia*, that his changing thoughts forget
Would better fit his Chamber, then this Shadow.

Iul. Madam, please you peruse this Letter;
Pardon me (Madam) I haue vnaduis'd
Deliuer'd you a paper that I should not;
This is the Letter to your Ladiship.

Sil. I pray thee let me looke on that againe.

Iul. It may not be: good Madam pardon me.

Sil. There, hold:
I will not looke vpon your Masters lines:
I know they are stuft with protestations,
And full of new-found oathes, which he will breake
As easily as I doe teare his paper.

Iul. Madam, he sends your Ladiship this Ring.

Sil. The more shame for him, that he sends it me;
For I haue heard him say a thousand times,
His *Iulia* gaue it him, at his departure:
Though his false finger haue prophan'd the Ring,
Mine shall not doe his *Iulia* so much wrong.

Iul. She thankes you.

Sil. What sai'st thou?

Iul. I thanke you Madam, that you tender her:
Poore Gentlewoman, my Master wrongs her much.

Sil. Do'st thou know her?

Iul. Almost as well as I doe know my selfe.
To thinke vpon her woes, I doe protest
That I haue wept a hundred seuerall times.

Sil. Belike she thinks that *Protheus* hath forsook her?

Iul. I thinke she doth: and that's her cause of sorrow.

Sil. Is she not passing faire?

Iul. She hath bin fairer (Madam) then she is;
When she did thinke my Master lou'd her well;
She, in my iudgement, was as faire as you.
But since she did neglect her looking-glasse,
And threw her Sun-expelling Masque away,
The ayre hath staru'd the roses in her cheekes,
And pinch'd the lilly-tincture of her face,
That now she is become as blacke as I.

Sil. How tall was she?

Iul. About my stature: for at *Pentecost*,
When all our Pageants of delight were plaid,
Our youth got me to play the womans part,
And I was trim'd in Madam *Iulias* gowne,
Which serued me as fit, by all mens iudgements,
As if the garment had bin made for me:
Therefore I know she is about my height,
And at that time I made her weepe a good,

For I did play a lamentable part.
(Madam) 'twas *Ariadne*, passioning
For *Theseus* periury, and vniust flight;
Which I so liuely acted with my teares:
That my poore Mistris moued therewithall,
Wept bitterly: and would I might be dead,
If I in thought felt not her very sorrow.

Sil. She is beholding to thee (gentle youth)
Alas (poore Lady) desolate, and left;
I weepe my selfe to thinke vpon thy words:
Here youth: there is my purse; I giue thee this (well.
For thy sweet Mistris sake, because thou lou'st her. Fare-

Iul. And she shall thanke you for't, if ere you know
A vertuous gentlewoman, milde, and beautifull. (her.
I hope my Masters suit will be but cold,
Since she respects my Mistris loue so much.
Alas, how loue can trifle with it selfe:
Here is her Picture: let me see, I thinke
If I had such a Tyre, this face of mine
Were full as louely, as is this of hers;
And yet the Painter flatter'd her a little,
Vnlesse I flatter with my selfe too much.
Her haire is *Aburne*, mine is perfect *Yellow*;
If that be all the difference in his loue,
Ile get me such a coulour'd Perrywig:
Her eyes are grey as glasse, and so are mine:
I, but her fore-head's low, and mine's as high:
What should it be that he respects in her,
But I can make respectiue in my selfe?
If this fond Loue, were not a blinded god.
Come shadow, come, and take this shadow vp,
For 'tis thy riuall: O thou senceless forme,
Thou shalt be worship'd, kiss'd, lou'd, and ador'd;
And were there sence in his Idolatry,
My substance should be statue in thy stead.
Ile vse thee kindly, for thy Mistris sake
That vs'd me so: or else by *Ioue*, I vow,
I should haue scratch'd out your vnseeing eyes,
To make my Master out of loue with thee. *Exeunt.*

Actus Quintus. Scœna Prima.

Enter Eglamoure, Siluia.

Egl. The Sun begins to guild the westerne skie,
And now it is about the very houre
That *Siluia*, at Fryer *Patricks* Cell should meet me,
She will not faile; for Louers breake not houres,
Vnlesse it be to come before their time,
So much they spur their expedition.
See where she comes: Lady a happy euening.

Sil. Amen, Amen: goe on (good *Eglamoure*)
Out at the Posterne by the Abbey wall;
I feare I am attended by some Spies.

Egl. Feare not: the Forrest is not three leagues off,
If we recouer that, we are sure enough. *Exeunt.*

Scœna Secunda.

Enter Thurio, Protheus, Iulia, Duke.
Th. Sir *Protheus*, what saies *Siluia* to my suit?

Pro. Oh Sir, I finde her milder then she was,
And yet she takes exceptions at your person.
Thu. What? that my leg is too long?
Pro. No, that it is too little. (der.
Thu. Ile weare a Boote, to make it somewhat roun-
Pro. But loue will not be spur'd to what it loathes.
Thu. What saies she to my face?
Pro. She saies it is a faire one.
Thu. Nay then the wanton lyes: my face is blacke.
Pro. But Pearles are faire; and the old saying is,
Blacke men are Pearles, in beauteous Ladies eyes.
Thu. 'Tis true, such Pearles as put out Ladies eyes,
For I had rather winke, then looke on them.
Thu. How likes she my discourse?
Pro. Ill, when you talke of war.
Thu. But well, when I discourse of loue and peace.
Iul. But better indeede, when you hold you peace.
Thu. What sayes she to my valour?
Pro. Oh Sir, she makes no doubt of that.
Iul. She needes not, when she knowes it cowardize.
Thu. What saies she to my birth?
Pro. That you are well deriu'd.
Iul. True: from a Gentleman, to a foole.
Thu. Considers she my Possessions?
Pro. Oh, I: and pitties them.
Thu. Wherefore?
Iul. That such an Asse should owe them.
Pro. That they are out by Lease.
Iul. Here comes the Duke.
Du. How now sir *Protheus*; how now *Thurio*?
Which of you saw *Eglamoure* of late?
Thu. Not I.
Pro. Nor I.
Du. Saw you my daughter?
Pro. Neither.
Du. Why then
She's fled vnto that pezant, *Valentine*;
And *Eglamoure* is in her Company:
'Tis true: for Frier *Laurence* met them both
As he, in pennance wander'd through the Forrest:
Him he knew well: and guess'd that it was she,
But being mask'd, he was not sure of it.
Besides she did intend Confession
At *Patricks* Cell this euen, and there she was not.
These likelihoods confirme her flight from hence;
Therefore I pray you stand, not to discourse,
But mount you presently, and meete with me
Vpon the rising of the Mountaine foote
That leads toward *Mantua*, whether they are fled:
Dispatch (sweet Gentlemen) and follow me.

Thu. Why this it is, to be a peeuish Girle,
That flies her fortune when it followes her:
Ile after; more to be reueng'd on *Eglamoure*,
Then for the loue of reck-lesse *Siluia*.
Pro. And I will follow, more for *Siluas* loue
Then hate of *Eglamoure* that goes with her.
Iul. And I will follow, more to crosse that loue
Then hate for *Siluia*, that is gone for loue. *Exeunt.*

Scena Tertia.

Siluia, Out-lawes.
1.*Out.* Come, come be patient:

We

We must bring you to our Captaine.

Sil. A thousand more mischances then this one
Haue learn'd me how to brooke this patiently.

2 Out. Come, bring her away.

1 Out. Where is the Gentleman that was with her?

3 Out. Being nimble footed, he hath out-run vs.
But *Moyses* and *Valerius* follow him:
Goe thou with her to the West end of the wood,
There is our Captaine: Wee'll follow him that's fled,
The Thicket is beset, he cannot scape.

1 Out. Come, I must bring you to our Captains caue.
Feare not: he beares an honourable minde,
And will not vse a woman lawlesly.

Sil. O *Valentine*: this I endure for thee.

Exeunt.

Scœna Quarta.

Enter Valentine, Protheus, Siluia, Iulia, Duke, Thurio, Out-lawes.

Val. How vse doth breed a habit in a man?
This shadowy desart, vnfrequented woods
I better brooke then flourishing peopled Townes:
Here can I sit alone, vn-seene of any,
And to the Nightingales complaining Notes
Tune my distresses, and record my woes.
O thou that dost inhabit in my brest,
Leaue not the Mansion so long Tenant-lesse,
Lest growing ruinous, the building fall,
And leaue no memory of what it was,
Repaire me, with thy presence, *Siluia*;
Thou gentle Nimph, cherish thy for-lorne swaine.
What hallowing, and what stir is this to day?
These are my mates, that make their wills their Law,
Haue some vnhappy passenger in chace;
They loue me well: yet I haue much to doe
To keepe them from vnciuill outrages.
Withdraw thee *Valentine*: who's this comes heere?

Pro. Madam, this seruice I haue done for you
(Though you respect not aught your seruant doth)
To hazard life, and reskew you from him,
That would haue forc'd your honour, and your loue,
Vouchsafe me for my meed, but one faire looke:
(A smaller boone then this I cannot beg,
And lesse then this, I am sure you cannot giue.)

Val. How like a dreame is this? I see, and heare:
Loue, lend me patience to forbeare a while.

Sil. O miserable, vnhappy that I am.

Pro. Vnhappy were you (Madam) ere I came:
But by my comming, I haue made you happy.

Sil. By thy approach thou mak'st me most vnhappy.

Iul. And me, when he approcheth to your presence.

Sil. Had I beene ceazed by a hungry Lion,
I would haue beene a break-fast to the Beast,
Rather then haue false *Protheus* reskue me:
Oh heauen be iudge how I loue *Valentine*,
Whose life's as tender to me as my soule,
And full as much (for more there cannot be)
I doe detest false periur'd *Protheus*:
Therefore be gone, sollicit me no more.

Pro. What dangerous action, stood it next to death
Would I not vndergoe, for one calme looke:
Oh 'tis the curse in Loue, and still approu'd
When women cannot loue, where they're belou'd.

Sil. When *Protheus* cannot loue, where he's belou'd:
Read ouer *Iulia's* heart, (thy first best Loue)
For whose deare sake, thou didst then rend thy faith
Into a thousand oathes; and all those oathes,
Descended into periury, to loue me,
Thou hast no faith left now, vnlesse thou'dst two,
And that's farre worse then none: better haue none
Then plurall faith, which is too much by one:
Thou Counterfeyt, to thy true friend.

Pro. In Loue,
Who respects friend?

Sil. All men but *Protheus*.

Pro. Nay, if the gentle spirit of mouing words
Can no way change you to a milder forme;
Ile wooe you like a Souldier, at armes end,
And loue you 'gainst the nature of Loue: force ye.

Sil. Oh heauen.

Pro. Ile force thee yeeld to my desire.

Val. Ruffian: let goe that rude vnciuill touch,
Thou friend of an ill fashion.

Pro. *Valentine.*

Val. Thou comon friend, that's without faith or loue,
For such is a friend now: treacherous man,
Thou hast beguil'd my hopes; nought but mine eye
Could haue perswaded me: now I dare not say
I haue one friend aliue; thou wouldst disproue me:
Who should be trusted, when ones right hand
Is periured to the bosome? *Protheus*
I am sorry I must neuer trust thee more,
But count the world a stranger for thy sake:
The priuate wound is deepest: oh time, most accurst:
'Mongst all foes that a friend should be the worst?

Pro. My shame and guilt confounds me:
Forgiue me *Valentine*: if hearty sorrow
Be a sufficient Ransome for offence,
I tender't heere: I doe as truely suffer,
As ere I did commit.

Val. Then I am paid:
And once againe, I doe receiue thee honest;
Who by Repentance is not satisfied,
Is nor of heauen, nor earth; for these are pleas'd:
By Penitence th'Eternalls wrath's appeas'd:
And that my loue may appeare plaine and free,
All that was mine, in *Siluia*, I giue thee.

Iul. Oh me vnhappy.

Pro. Looke to the Boy.

Val. Why, Boy?
Why wag: how now? what's the matter? look vp: speak.

Iul. O good sir, my master charg'd me to deliuer a ring
to Madam *Siluia*: w̄ (out of my neglect) was neuer done.

Pro. Where is that ring? boy?

Iul. Heere 'tis: this is it.

Pro. How? let me see.
Why this is the ring I gaue to *Iulia*.

Iul. Oh, cry you mercy sir, I haue mistooke:
This is the ring you sent to *Siluia*.

Pro. But how cam'st thou by this ring? at my depart
I gaue this vnto *Iulia*.

Iul. And *Iulia* her selfe did giue it me,
And *Iulia* her selfe hath brought it hither.

Pro. How? *Iulia*?

Iul. Behold her, that gaue ayme to all thy oathes,
And entertain'd 'em deepely in her heart.
How oft hast thou with periury cleft the roote?
Oh *Protheus*, let this habit make thee blush.

Be thou asham'd that I haue tooke vpon me,
Such an immodest rayment; if shame liue
In a disguise of loue?
It is the lesser blot modesty findes,
Women to change their shapes, then men their minds.

  Pro. Then men their minds? tis true: oh heuen, were man
But Constant, he were perfect; that one error
Fils him with faults: makes him run through all th'sins;
Inconstancy falls-off, ere it begins:
What is in *Siluia's* face, but I may spie
More fresh in *Iulia's*, with a constant eye?

  Val. Come, come: a hand from either:
Let me be blest to make this happy close:
'Twere pitty two such friends should be long foes.

  Pro. Beare witnes (heauen) I haue my wish for euer.
  Iul. And I mine.
  Out-l. A prize: a prize: a prize.
  Val. Forbeare, forbeare I say: It is my Lord the *Duke*.
Your Grace is welcome to a man disgrac'd,
Banished *Valentine*.
  Duke. Sir *Valentine*?
  Thu. Yonder is *Siluia*: and *Siluia's* mine.
  Val. *Thurio* giue backe; or else embrace thy death:
Come not within the measure of my wrath:
Doe not name *Siluia* thine: if once againe,
Verona shall not hold thee: heere she stands,
Take but possession of her, with a Touch:
I dare thee, but to breath vpon my Loue.
  Thur. Sir *Valentine*, I care not for her, I:
I hold him but a foole that will endanger
His Body, for a Girle that loues him not:
I claime her not, and therefore she is thine.
  Duke. The more degenerate and base art thou
To make such meanes for her, as thou hast done,
And leaue her on such slight conditions.

Now, by the honor of my Ancestry,
I doe applaud thy spirit, *Valentine*,
And thinke thee worthy of an Empresse loue:
Know then, I heere forget all former greefes,
Cancell all grudge, repeale thee home againe,
Plead a new state in thy vn-riual'd merit,
To which I thus subscribe: Sir *Valentine*,
Thou art a Gentleman, and well deriu'd,
Take thou thy *Siluia*, for thou hast deseru'd her.
  Val. I thank your Grace, y gift hath made me happy:
I now beseech you (for your daughters sake)
To grant one Boone that I shall aske of you.
  Duke. I grant it (for thine owne) what ere it be.
  Val. These banish'd men, that I haue kept withall,
Are men endu'd with worthy qualities:
Forgiue them what they haue committed here,
And let them be recall'd from their Exile:
They are reformed, ciuill, full of good,
And fit for great employment (worthy Lord.)
  Duke. Thou hast preuaild, I pardon them and thee:
Dispose of them, as thou knowst their deserts.
Come, let vs goe, we will include all iarres,
With Triumphes, Mirth, and rare solemnity.
  Val. And as we walke along, I dare be bold
With our discourse, to make your Grace to smile.
What thinke you of this Page (my Lord?)
  Duke. I think the Boy hath grace in him, he blushes.
  Val. I warrant you (my Lord) more grace, then Boy.
  Duke. What meane you by that saying?
  Val. Please you, Ile tell you, as we passe along,
That you will wonder what hath fortuned:
Come *Protheus*, 'tis your pennance, but to heare
The story of your Loues discouered.
That done, our day of marriage shall be yours,
One Feast, one house, one mutuall happinesse.   *Exeunt*.

The names of all the Actors.

Duke: Father to Siluia.
Valentine. }
Protheus. } *the two Gentlemen.*
Anthonio: father to Protheus.
Thurio: a foolish riuall to Valentine.

Eglamoure: Agent for Siluia in her escape.
Host: where Iulia lodges.
Out-lawes with Valentine.
Speed: a clownish seruant to Valentine.
Launce: the like to Protheus.
Panthion: seruant to Antonio.
Iulia: beloued of Protheus.
Siluia: beloued of Valentine.
Lucetta: waighting-woman to Iulia.

FINIS.

THE
Merry Wiues of Windsor.

Actus primus, Scena prima.

Enter Iustice Shallow, Slender, *Sir* Hugh Euans, *Master* Page, Falstoffe, Bardolph, Nym, Pistoll, Anne Page, *Mistresse* Ford, *Mistresse* Page, Simple.

Shallow.

SIr *Hugh*, perswade me not: I will make a Star-Chamber matter of it, if hee were twenty Sir *Iohn Falstoffs*, he shall not abuse *Robert Shallow* Esquire. (*Coram.*

Slen. In the County of *Glocester*, Iustice of Peace and

Shal. I (Cosen *Slender*) and *Cust-alorum.*

Slen. I, and *Rato lorum* too; and a Gentleman borne (Master Parson) who writes himselfe *Armigero*, in any Bill, Warrant, Quittance, or Obligation, *Armigero.*

Shal. I that I doe, and haue done any time these three hundred yeeres.

Slen. All his successors (gone before him) hath don't: and all his Ancestors (that come after him) may: they may giue the dozen white Luces in their Coate.

Shal. It is an olde Coate.

Euans. The dozen white Lowses doe become an old Coat well: it agrees well passant: It is a familiar beast to man, and signifies Loue.

Shal. The Luse is the fresh-fish, the salt-fish, is an old Coate.

Slen. I may quarter (Coz).

Shal. You may, by marrying.

Euans. It is marring indeed, if he quarter it.

Shal. Not a whit.

Euan. Yes per-lady: if he ha's a quarter of your coat, there is but three Skirts for your selfe, in my simple coniectures; but that is all one: if Sir *Iohn Falstaffe* haue committed disparagements vnto you, I am of the Church and will be glad to do my beneuolence, to make attonements and compremises betweene you.

Shal. The Councell shall heare it, it is a Riot.

Euan. It is not meet the Councell heare a Riot: there is no feare of Got in a Riot: The Councell (looke you) shall desire to heare the feare of Got, and not to heare a Riot: take your viza-ments in that.

Shal. Ha; o'my life, if I were yong againe, the sword should end it.

Euans. It is petter that friends is the sword, and end it: and there is also another deuice in my praine, which peraduenture prings goot discretions with it. There is *Anne Page*, which is daughter to Master *Thomas Page*, which is pretty virginity.

Slen. Mistris Anne Page? she has browne haire, and speakes small like a woman.

Euans. It is that ferry person for all the orld, as iust as you will desire, and seuen hundred pounds of Moneyes, and Gold, and Siluer, is her Grand-sire vpon his deaths-bed, (Got deliuer to a ioyfull resurrections) giue, when she is able to ouertake seuenteene yeeres old. It were a goot motion, if we leaue our pribbles and prabbles, and desire a marriage betweene Master *Abraham*, and Mistris *Anne Page.*

Slen. Did her Grand-sire leaue her seauen hundred pound?

Euan. I, and her father is make her a petter penny.

Slen. I know the young Gentlewoman, she has good gifts.

Euan. Seuen hundred pounds, and possibilities, is goot gifts.

Shal. Wel, let vs see honest M.* Page*: is *Falstaffe* there?

Euan. Shall I tell you a lye? I doe despise a lyer, as I doe despise one that is false, or as I despise one that is not true: the Knight Sir *Iohn* is there, and I beseech you be ruled by your well-willers: I will peat the doore for M.* Page.* What hoa? Got-plesse your house heere.

M. Page.* Who's there?

Euan. Here is go't's plessing and your friend, and Iustice *Shallow*, and heere yong Master *Slender*: that peraduentures shall tell you another tale, if matters grow to your likings.

M. Page.* I am glad to see your Worships well: I thanke you for my Venison Master *Shallow.*

Shal. Master *Page*, I am glad to see you: much good doe it your good heart: I wish'd your Venison better, it was ill killd: how doth good Mistresse *Page*? and I thank you alwaies with my heart, la: with my heart.

M. Page. Sir, I thanke you.

Shal. Sir, I thanke you: by yea, and no I doe.

M. Pa. I am glad to see you, good Master *Slender.*

Slen. How do's your fallow Greyhound, Sir, I heard say he was out-run on *Cotsall.*

M. Pa. It could not be iudg'd, Sir.

Slen. You'll not confesse: you'll not confesse.

Shal. That he will not, 'tis your fault, 'tis your fault: 'tis a good dogge.

M. Pa. A Cur, Sir.

Shal. Sir: hee's a good dog, and a faire dog, can there be more said? he is good, and faire. Is Sir *Iohn Falstaffe* heere?

M. Pa. Sir, hee is within: and I would I could doe a good office be tweene you.

Euan. It is spoke as a Christians ought to speake.

Shal. He hath wrong'd me (Master *Page.*)

M. Pa. Sir, he doth in some sort confesse it.

D 2 *Sha.*

Shal. If it be confessed, it is not redressed; is not that so (*M. Page*?) he hath wrong'd me, indeed he hath, at a word he hath: beleeue me, *Robert Shallow* Esquire, saith he is wronged.

Ma. Pa. Here comes Sir *Iohn*.

Fal. Now, Master *Shallow*, you'll complaine of me to the King?

Shal. Knight, you haue beaten my men, kill'd my deere, and broke open my Lodge.

Fal. But not kiss'd your Keepers daughter?

Shal. Tut, a pin: this shall be answer'd.

Fal. I will answere it strait, I haue done all this: That is now answer'd.

Shal. The Councell shall know this.

Fal. 'Twere better for you if it were known in councell: you'll be laugh'd at.

Eu. Pauca verba; (Sir *Iohn*) good worts.

Fal. Good worts? good Cabidge; *Slender*, I broke your head: what matter haue you against me?

Slen. Marry sir, I haue matter in my head against you, and against your cony-catching Rascalls, *Bardolf, Nym*, and *Pistoll*.

Bar. You Banbery Cheese.

Slen. I, it is no matter.

Pist. How now, *Mephostophilus*?

Slen. I, it is no matter.

Nym. Slice, I say; *pauca, pauca*: Slice, that's my humor.

Slen. Where's *Simple* my man? can you tell, Cosen?

Eua. Peace, I pray you: now let vs vnderstand: there is three Vmpires in this matter, as I vnderstand; that is, Master *Page* (fidelicet Master *Page*,) & there is my selfe, (fidelicet my selfe) and the three party is (lastly, and finally) mine Host of the Gater.

Ma. Pa. We three to hear it, & end it between them.

Euan. Ferry goo't, I will make a priefe of it in my note-booke, and we wil afterwards orke vpon the cause, with as great discreetly as we can.

Fal. Pistoll.

Pist. He heares with eares.

Euan. The Teuill and his Tam: what phrase is this? he heares with eare? why, it is affectations.

Fal. Pistoll, did you picke M. *Slenders* purse?

Slen. I, by these gloues did hee, or I would I might neuer come in mine owne great chamber againe else, of seauen groates in mill-sixpences, and two *Edward* Shouelboords, that cost me two shilling and two pence a peece of *Yead Miller*: by these gloues.

Fal. Is this true, *Pistoll*?

Euan. No, it is false, if it is a picke-purse.

Pist. Ha, thou mountaine Forreyner: Sir *Iohn*, and Master mine, I combat challenge of this Latine Bilboe: word of deniall in thy *labras* here; word of denial; froth, and scum thou liest.

Slen. By these gloues, then 'twas he.

Nym. Be auis'd sir, and passe good humours: I will say marry trap with you, if you runne the nut-hooks humor on me, that is the very note of it.

Slen. By this hat, then he in the red face had it: for though I cannot remember what I did when you made me drunke, yet I am not altogether an asse.

Fal. What say you Scarlet, and Iohn?

Bar. Why sir, (for my part) I say the Gentleman had drunke himselfe out of his fiue sentences.

Eu. It is his fiue sences: fie, what the ignorance is.

Bar. And being sap, sir, was (as they say) casheerd: and so conclusions past the Car-eires.

Slen. I, you spake in Latten then to: but 'tis no matter; Ile nere be drunk whilst I liue againe, but in honest, ciuill, godly company for this tricke: if I be drunke, Ile be drunke with those that haue the feare of God, and not with drunken knaues.

Euan. So got-udge me, that is a vertuons minde.

Fal. You heare all these matters deni'd, Gentlemen; you heare it.

M^r. Page. Nay daughter, carry the wine in, wee'l drinke within.

Slen. Oh heauen: This is Mistresse *Anne Page*.

M^r. Page. How now Mistris *Ford*?

Fal. *Mistris Ford*, by my troth you are very wel met: by your leaue good Mistris.

M^r. Page. Wife, bid these gentlemen welcome: come, we haue a hot Venison pasty to dinner; Come gentlemen, I hope we shall drinke downe all vnkindnesse.

Slen. I had rather then forty shillings I had my booke of Songs and Sonnets heere: How now *Simple*, where haue you beene? I must wait on my selfe, must I? you haue not the booke of Riddles about you, haue you?

Sim. Booke of Riddles? why did you not lend it to *Alice Short-cake* vpon Alhallowmas last, a fortnight afore Michaelmas.

Shal. Come Coz, come Coz, we stay for you: a word with you Coz: marry this, Coz: there is as 'twere a tender, a kinde of tender, made a farre-off by Sir *Hugh* here; doe you vnderstand me?

Slen. I Sir, you shall finde me reasonable; if it be so, I shall doe that that is reason.

Shal. Nay, but vnderstand me.

Slen. So I doe Sir.

Euan. Giue eare to his motions; (M^r. *Slender*) I will description the matter to you, if you be capacity of it.

Slen. Nay, I will doe as my Cozen *Shallow* saies: I pray you pardon me, he's a Iustice of Peace in his Countrie, simple though I stand here.

Euan. But that is not the question: the question is concerning your marriage.

Shal. I, there's the point Sir.

Eu. Marry is it: the very point of it, to Mi. *An Page*.

Slen. Why if it be so; I will marry her vpon any reasonable demands.

Eu. But can you affection the 'o-man, let vs command to know that of your mouth, or of your lips: for diuers Philosophers hold, that the lips is parcell of the mouth: therfore precisely, cã you carry your good wil to ȳ maid?

Sh. Cosen *Abraham Slender*, can you loue her?

Slen. I hope sir, I will do as it shall become one that would doe reason.

Eu. Nay, got's Lords, and his Ladies, you must speake possitable, if you can carry-her your desires towards her.

Shal. That you must:
Will you, (vpon good dowry) marry her?

Slen. I will doe a greater thing then that, vpon your request (Cosen) in any reason.

Shal. Nay conceiue me, conceiue mee, (sweet Coz): what I doe is to pleasure you (Coz:) can you loue the maid?

Slen. I will marry her (Sir) at your request; but if there bee no great loue in the beginning, yet Heauen may decrease it vpon better acquaintance, when wee are married, and haue more occasion to know one another: I hope vpon familiarity will grow more content: but if you say mary-her, I will mary-her, that I am freely dissolued, and dissolutely.

Eu. It

Eu. It is a fery discretion-answere; saue the fall is in the'ord, dissolutely: the ort is (according to our meaning) resolutely: his meaning is good.

Sh. I: I thinke my Cosen meant well.

Sl. I, or else I would I might be hang'd (la.)

Sh. Here comes faire Mistris *Anne*; would I were yong for your sake, Mistris *Anne.*

An. The dinner is on the Table, my Father desires your worships company.

Sh. I will wait on him, (faire Mistris *Anne.*)

Eu. Od's plessed-wil: I wil not be absēce at the grace.

An. Wil't please your worship to come in, Sir?

Sl. No, I thank you forsooth, hartely; I am very well.

An. The dinner attends you, Sir.

Sl. I am not a-hungry, I thanke you, forsooth: goe, Sirha, for all you are my man, goe wait vpon my Cosen *Shallow*: a Iustice of peace sometime may be beholding to his friend, for a Man; I keepe but three Men, and a Boy yet, till my Mother be dead: but what though, yet I liue like a poore Gentleman borne.

An. I may not goe in without your worship: they will not sit till you come.

Sl. I'faith, ile eate nothing: I thanke you as much as though I did.

An. I pray you Sir walke in.

Sl. I had rather walke here (I thanke you) I bruiz'd my shin th'other day, with playing at Sword and Dagger with a Master of Fence (three veneys for a dish of stew'd Prunes) and by my troth, I cannot abide the smell of hot meate since. Why doe your dogs barke so? be there Beares ith' Towne?

An. I thinke there are, Sir, I heard them talk'd of.

Sl. I loue the sport well, but I shall as soone quarrell at it, as any man in *England*: you are afraid if you see the Beare loose, are you not?

An. I indeede Sir.

Sl. That's meate and drinke to me now: I haue seene *Sackerson* loose, twenty times, and haue taken him by the Chaine: but (I warrant you) the women haue so cride and shrekt at it, that it past: But women indeede, cannot abide 'em, they are very ill-fauour'd rough things.

Ma.Pa. Come, gentle M. *Slender*, come; we stay for you.

Sl. Ile eate nothing, I thanke you Sir.

Ma.Pa. By cocke and pie, you shall not choose, Sir: come, come.

Sl. Nay, pray you lead the way.

Ma.Pa. Come on, Sir.

Sl. Mistris *Anne*: your selfe shall goe first.

An. Not I Sir, pray you keepe on.

Sl. Truely I will not goe first: truely-la: I will not doe you that wrong.

An. I pray you Sir.

Sl. Ile rather be vnmannerly, then troublesome: you doe your selfe wrong indeede-la. *Exeunt.*

Scena Secunda.

Enter Euans, and Simple.

Eu. Go your waies, and aske of Doctor *Caius* house, which is the way; and there dwels one Mistris *Quickly*; which is in the manner of his Nurse; or his dry-Nurse; or his Cooke; or his Laundry; his Washer, and his Ringer.

Si. Well Sir.

Eu. Nay, it is petter yet: giue her this letter; for it is a'oman that altogeathers acquaintāce with Mistris *Anne Page*; and the Letter is to desire, and require her to solicite your Masters desires, to Mistris *Anne Page*: I pray you be gon: I will make an end of my dinner; ther's Pippins and Cheese to come. *Exeunt.*

Scena Tertia.

Enter Falstaffe, Host, Bardolfe, Nym, Pistoll, Page.

Fal. Mine *Host* of the *Garter*?

Ho. What saies my Bully Rooke? speake schollerly, and wisely.

Fal. Truely mine *Host*; I must turne away some of my followers.

Ho. Discard, (bully *Hercules*) casheere; let them wag; trot, trot.

Fal. I sit at ten pounds a weeke.

Ho. Thou'rt an Emperor (*Cesar, Keiser* and *Pheazar*) I will entertaine *Bardolfe*: he shall draw; he shall tap; said I well (bully *Hector*?)

Fa. Doe so (good mine *Host*.

Ho. I haue spoke: let him follow: let me see thee froth, and liue: I am at a word: follow.

Fal. Bardolfe, follow him: a *Tapster* is a good trade: an old Cloake, makes a new Ierkin: a wither'd Seruingman, a fresh Tapster: goe, adew.

Ba. It is a life that I haue desir'd: I will thriue.

Pist. O base hungarian wight: wilt ẏ the spigot wield.

Ni. He was gotten in drink: is not the humor cōceited?

Fal. I am glad I am so acquit of this Tinderbox: his Thefts were too open: his filching was like an vnskilfull Singer, he kept not time.

Ni. The good humor is to steale at a minutes rest.

Pist. Conuay: the wise it call: Steale? foh: a fico for the phrase.

Fal. Well sirs, I am almost out at heeles.

Pist. Why then let Kibes ensue.

Fal. There is no remedy: I must conicatch, I must shift.

Pist. Yong Rauens must haue foode.

Fal. Which of you know *Ford* of this Towne?

Pist. I ken the wight: he is of substance good.

Fal. My honest Lads, I will tell you what I am about.

Pist. Two yards, and more.

Fal. No quips now *Pistoll*: (Indeede I am in the waste two yards about: but I am now about no waste: I am about thrift) briefely: I doe meane to make loue to *Fords* wife: I spie entertainment in her: shee discourses: shee carues: she giues the leere of inuitation: I can construe the action of her familier stile, & the hardest voice of her behauior (to be english'd rightly) is, *I am Sir Iohn Falstafs.*

Pist. He hath studied her will; and translated her will: out of honesty, into English.

Ni. The Anchor is deepe: will that humor passe?

Fal. Now, the report goes, she has all the rule of her husbands Purse: he hath a legend of Angels.

Pist. As many diuels entertaine: and to her Boy say I.

Ni. The humor rises: it is good: humor me the angels.

Fal. I haue writ me here a letter to her: & here another to *Pages* wife, who euen now gaue mee good eyes too; examind my parts with most iudicious illiads: sometimes the beame of her view, guilded my foote: sometimes my portly belly.

Pist. Then did the Sun on dung-hill shine.

Ni. I thanke thee for that humour.

Fal. O she did so course o're my exteriors with such a greedy intention, that the appetite of her eye, did seeme to scorch me vp like a burning-glasse: here's another letter to her: She beares the Purse too: She is a Region in *Guiana*: all gold, and bountie: I will be Cheaters to them both, and they shall be Exchequers to mee: they shall be my East and West Indies, and I will trade to them both: Goe, beare thou this Letter to Mistris *Page*; and thou this to Mistris *Ford*: we will thriue (Lads) we will thriue.

Pist. Shall I Sir *Pandarus* of *Troy* become,
And by my side weare Steele? then Lucifer take all.

Ni. I will run no base humor: here take the humor-Letter; I will keepe the hauior of reputation.

Fal. Hold Sirha, beare you these Letters tightly,
Saile like my Pinnasse to these golden shores.
Rogues, hence, auaunt, vanish like haile-stones; goe,
Trudge; plod away ith' hoofe: seeke shelter, packe:
Falstaffe will learne the honor of the age,
French-thrift, you Rogues, my selfe, and skirted *Page*.

Pist. Let Vultures gripe thy guts: for gourd, and Fullam holds: & high and low beguiles the rich & poore,
Tester ile haue in pouch when thou shalt lacke,
Base *Phrygian* Turke.

Ni. I haue opperations,
Which be humors of reuenge.

Pist. Wilt thou reuenge?

Ni. By Welkin, and her Star.

Pist. With wit, or Steele?

Ni. With both the humors, I:
I will discusse the humour of this Loue to *Ford*.

Pist. And I to *Page* shall eke vnfold
How *Falstaffe* (varlet vile)
His Doue will proue; his gold will hold,
And his soft couch defile.

Ni. My humour shall not coole: I will incense *Ford* to deale with poyson: I will possesse him with yallow-nesse, for the reuolt of mine is dangerous: that is my true humour.

Pist. Thou art the *Mars* of *Malecontents*: I second thee: troope on. *Exeunt.*

Scœna Quarta.

Enter Mistris Quickly, Simple, Iohn Rugby, Doctor Caius, Fenton.

Qu. What, *Iohn Rugby*, I pray thee goe to the Casement, and see if you can see my Master, Master Docter *Caius* comming: if he doe (I'faith) and finde any body in the house; here will be an old abusing of Gods patience, and the Kings English.

Ru. Ile goe watch.

Qu. Goe, and we'll haue a posset for't soone at night, (in faith) at the latter end of a Sea-cole-fire: An honest, willing, kinde fellow, as euer seruant shall come in house withall: and I warrant you, no tel-tale, nor no breede-bate: his worst fault is, that he is giuen to prayer; hee is something peeuish that way: but no body but has his fault: but let that passe. *Peter Simple*, you say your name is?

Si. I: for fault of a better.

Qu. And Master *Slender's* your Master?

Si. I forsooth.

Qu. Do's he not weare a great round Beard, like a Glouers pairing-knife?

Si. No forsooth: he hath but a little wee-face; with a little yellow Beard: a Caine colourd Beard.

Qu. A softly-sprighted man, is he not?

Si. I forsooth: but he is as tall a man of his hands, as any is betweene this and his head: he hath fought with a Warrener.

Qu. How say you: oh, I should remember him: do's he not hold vp his head (as it were?) and strut in his gate?

Si. Yes indeede do's he.

Qu. Well, heauen send *Anne Page*, no worse fortune: Tell Master Parson *Euans*, I will doe what I can for your Master: *Anne* is a good girle, and I wish—

Ru. Out alas: here comes my Master.

Qu. We shall all be shent: Run in here, good young man: goe into this Closset: he will not stay long: what *Iohn Rugby*? *Iohn*: what *Iohn* I say? goe *Iohn*, goe enquire for my Master, I doubt he be not well, that hee comes not home: *(and downe, downe, adowne'a. &c.*

Ca. Vat is you sng? I doe not like des-toyes: pray you goe and vetch me in my Closset, vnboyteene verd; a Box, a greene-a-Box: do intend vat I speake? a greene-a-Box.

Qu. I forsooth ile fetch it you:
I am glad hee went not in himselfe: if he had found the yong man he would haue bin horne-mad.

Ca. Fe, se fe, fe, mai foy, il fait for chando, Ie man voi a le Court la grand affaires.

Qu. Is it this Sir?

Ca. Ouy mette le au mon pocket, de-peech quickly: Vere is dat knaue *Rugby*?

Qu. What *Iohn Rugby*, *Iohn*?

Ru. Here Sir.

Ca. You are *Iohn Rugby*, aad you are *Iacke Rugby*: Come, take-a-your Rapier, and come after my heele to the Court.

Ru. 'Tis ready Sir, here in the Porch.

Ca. By my trot: I tarry too long: od's-me: *que ay ie oublie:* dere is some Simples in my Closset, dat I vill not for the varld I shall leaue behinde.

Qu. Ay-me, he'll finde the yong man there, & be mad.

Ca. O *Diable, Diable:* vat is in my Closset? Villanie, La-roone: *Rugby*, my Rapier.

Qu. Good Master be content.

Ca. Wherefore shall I be content-a?

Qu. The yong man is an honest man.

Ca. What shall de honest man do in my Closset: dere is no honest man dat shall come in my Closset.

Qu. I beseech you be not so flegmaticke: heare the truth of it. He came of an errand to mee, from Parson *Hugh*.

Ca. Vell.

Si. I forsooth: to desire her to—

Qu. Peace, I pray you.

Ca. Peace-a-your tongue: speake-a-your Tale.

Si. To desire this honest Gentlewoman (your Maid) to speake a good word to Mistris *Anne Page*, for my Master in the way of Marriage.

Qu. This is all indeede-la: but ile nere put my finger in the fire, and neede not.

Ca. Sir *Hugh* send-a you? *Rugby*, ballow mee some paper: tarry you a littell-a-while.

Qui. I am glad he is so quiet: if he had bin throughly moued, you should haue heard him so loud, and so melancholly: but notwithstanding man, Ile doe yoe your Master what good I can: and the very yea, & the no is, ye French Doctor my Master, (I may call him my Master, looke you, for I keepe his house; and I wash, ring, brew, bake, scowre, dresse meat and drinke, make the beds, and doe all my selfe.)

Simp. 'Tis a great charge to come vnder one bodies hand.

Qui. Are you a-uis'd o' that? you shall finde it a great charge: and to be vp early, and down late: but notwithstanding, (to tell you in your eare, I wold haue no words of it) my Master himselfe is in loue with Mistris *Anne Page*: but notwithstanding that I know *Ans* mind, that's neither heere nor there.

Caius. You, Iack 'Nape: giue-'a this Letter to Sir *Hugh*, by gar it is a shallenge: I will cut his troat in de Parke, and I will teach a scuruy Iack-a-nape Priest to meddle, or make: ——— you may be gon: it is not good you tarry here: by gar I will cut all his two stones: by gar, he shall not haue a stone to throw at his dogge.

Qui. Alas: he speakes but for his friend.

Caius. It is no matter'a ver dat: do not you tell-a-me dat I shall haue *Anne Page* for my selfe? by gar, I vill kill de Iack-Priest: and I haue appointed mine Host of de Iarteer to measure our weapon: by gar, I wil my selfe haue *Anne Page*.

Qui. Sir, the maid loues you, and all shall bee well: We must giue folkes leaue to prate: what the good-ier.

Caius. Rugby, come to the Court with me: by gar, if I haue not *Anne Page*, I shall turne your head out of my dore: follow my heeles, *Rugby*.

Qui. You shall haue An-fooles head of your owne: No, I know *Ans* mind for that: neuer a woman in *Windsor* knowes more of *Ans* minde then I doe, nor can doe more then I doe with her, I thanke heauen.

Fenton. Who's with in there, hoa?

Qui. Who's there, I troa? Come neere the house I pray you.

Fen. How now (good woman) how dost thou?

Qui. The better that it pleases your good Worship to aske?

Fen. What newes? how do's pretty Mistris *Anne*?

Qui. In truth Sir, and shee is pretty, and honest, and gentle, and one that is your friend, I can tell you that by the way, I praise heauen for it.

Fen. Shall I doe any good thinkst thou? shall I not loose my suit?

Qui. Troth Sir, all is in his hands aboue: but notwithstanding (Master *Fenton*) Ile be sworne on a booke shee loues you: haue not your Worship a wart aboue your eye?

Fen. Yes marry haue I, what of that?

Qui. Wel, thereby hangs a tale: good faith, it is such another *Nan*; (but (I detest) an honest maid as euer broke bread: wee had an howres talke of that wart; I shall neuer laugh but in that maids company: but (indeed) shee is giuen too much to Allicholy and musing: but for you ——— well ——— goe too ———

Fen. Well: I shall see her to day: hold, there's money for thee: Let mee haue thy voice in my behalfe: if thou seest her before me, commend me.———

Qui. Will I? I faith that wee will: And I will tell your Worship more of the Wart, the next time we haue confidence, and of other wooers.

Fen. Well, fare-well, I am in great haste now.

Qui. Fare-well to your Worship: truely an honest Gentleman: but *Anne* loues hiim not: for I know *Ans* minde as well as another do's: out vpon't: what haue I forgot.

Exit.

Actus Secundus. Scœna Prima.

Enter Mistris Page, *Mistris* Ford, *Master* Page, *Master* Ford, Pistoll, Nim, Quickly, Host, Shallow.

Mist. Page. What, haue scap'd Loue-letters in the holly-day-time of my beauty, and am I now a subiect for them? let me see?

Aske me no reason why I loue you, for though Loue vse Reason for his precisian, hee admits him not for his Counsailour: you are not yong, no more am I: goe to then, there's simpathie: you are merry, so am I: ha, ha, then there's more simpathie: you loue sacke, and so do I: would you desire better simpathie? Let it suffice thee (Mistris Page) at the least if the Loue of Souldier can suffice, that I loue thee: I will not say pitty mee, 'tis not a Souldier-like phrase; but I say, loue me:

By me, thine owne true Knight, by day or night:
Or any kinde of light, with all his might,
For thee to fight.   *Iohn Falstaffe.*

What a *Herod* of *Iurie* is this? O wicked, wicked world: One that is well-nye worne to peeces with age To show himselfe a yong Gallant? What an vnwaied Behauiour hath this Flemish drunkard pickt (with The Deuills name) out of my conuersation, that he dares In this manner assay me? why, hee hath not beene thrice In my Company: what should I say to him? I was then Frugall of my mirth: (heauen forgiue mee:) why Ile Exhibit a Bill in the Parliament for the puting downe of men: how shall I be reueng'd on him? for reueng'd I will be? as sure as his guts are made of puddings.

Mis Ford. Mistris *Page*, trust me, I was going to your house.

Mis. Page. And trust me, I was comming to you: you looke very ill.

Mis. Ford. Nay, Ile nere beleeee that; I haue to shew to the contrary.

Mis. Page. 'Faith but you doe in my minde.

Mis. Ford. Well: I doe then: yet I say, I could shew you to the contrary: O Mistris *Page*, giue mee some counsaile.

Mis. Page. What's the matter, woman?

Mi. Ford. O woman: if it were not for one trifling respect, I could come to such honour.

Mi. Page. Hang the trifle (woman) take the honour: what is it? dispence with trifles: what is it?

Mi. Ford. If I would but goe to hell, for an eternall moment, or so: I could be knighted.

Mi. Page. What thou liest? Sir *Alice Ford*? these Knights will hacke, and so thou shouldst not alter the article of thy Gentry.

Mi. Ford. Wee burne day-light: heere, read, read: perceiue how I might bee knighted, I shall thinke the worse of fat men, as long as I haue an eye to make difference of mens liking: and yet hee would not sweare:

praise

praise womens modesty: and gaue such orderly and wel-behaued reproofe to al vncomelinesse, that I would haue sworne his disposition would haue gone to the truth of his words: but they doe no more adhere and keep place together, then the hundred Psalms to the tune of Greene-sleeues: What tempest (I troa) threw this Whale, (with so many Tuns of oyle in his belly) a'shoare at Windsor? How shall I bee reuenged on him? I thinke the best way were, to entertaine him with hope, till the wicked fire of lust haue melted him in his owne greace: Did you e-uer heare the like?

Mis. Page. Letter for letter; but that the name of *Page* and *Ford* differs: to thy great comfort in this my-stery of ill opinions, heere's the twyn-brother of thy Let-ter: but let thine inherit first, for I protest mine neuer shall: I warrant he hath a thousand of these Letters, writ with blancke-space for different names (sure more): and these are of the second edition: hee will print them out of doubt: for he cares not what hee puts into the presse, when he would put vs two: I had rather be a Giantesse, and lye vnder Mount *Pelion*: Well; I will find you twen-tie lasciuious Turtles ere one chaste man.

Mis. Ford. Why this is the very same: the very hand: the very words: what doth he thinke of vs?

Mis. Page. Nay I know not: it makes me almost rea-die to wrangle with mine owne honesty: Ile entertaine my selfe like one that I am not acquainted withall: for sure vnlesse hee know some straine in mee, that I know not my selfe, hee would neuer haue boorded me in this furie.

Mi. Ford. Boording, call you it? Ile bee sure to keepe him aboue decke.

Mi. Page. So will I: if hee come vnder my hatches, Ile neuer to Sea againe: Let's bee reueng'd on him: let's appoint him a meeting: giue him a show of comfort in his Suit, and lead him on with a fine baited delay, till hee hath pawn'd his horses to mine Host of the Garter.

Mi. Ford. Nay, I wil consent to act any villany against him, that may not sully the charinesse of our honesty: oh that my husband saw this Letter: it would giue eternall food to his iealousie.

Mis. Page. Why look where he comes; and my good man too: hee's as farre from iealousie, as I am from gi-uing him cause, and that (I hope) is an vnmeasurable di-stance.

Mis. Ford. You are the happier woman.

Mis. Page. Let's consult together against this greasie Knight: Come hither.

Ford. Well: I hope, it be not so.

Pist. Hope is a curtall-dog in some affaires:
Sir *Iohn* affects thy wife.

Ford. Why sir, my wife is not young.

Pist. He wooes both high and low, both rich & poor, both yong and old, one with another (*Ford*) he loues the Gally-mawfry (*Ford*) perpend.

Ford. Loue my wife?

Pist. With liuer, burning hot: preuent:
Or goe thou like Sir *Acteon* he, with
Ring-wood at thy heeles: O, odious is the name.

Ford. What name Sir?

Pist. The horne I say: Farewell:
Take heed, haue open eye, for theeues doe foot by night.
Take heed, ere sommer comes, or Cuckoo-birds do sing.
Away sir Corporall *Nim*:
Beleeue it (*Page*) he speakes sence.

Ford. I will be patient: I will find out this.

Nim. And this is true: I like not the humor of lying: hee hath wronged mee in some humors: I should haue borne the humour'd Letter to her: but I haue a sword: and it shall bite vpon my necessitie: he loues your wife; There's the short and the long: My name is Corporall *Nim*: I speak, and I auouch; 'tis true: my name is *Nim*: and *Falstaffe* loues your wife: adieu, I loue not the hu-mour of bread and cheese: adieu.

Page. The humour of it (quoth'a?) heere's a fellow frights English out of his wits.

Ford. I will seeke out *Falstaffe*.

Page. I neuer heard such a drawling-affecting rogue.

Ford. If I doe finde it: well.

Page. I will not beleeue such a *Cataian*, though the Priest o' th' Towne commended him for a true man.

Ford. 'Twas a good sensible fellow: well.

Page. How now *Meg*?

Mist. Page. Whether goe you (*George?*) harke you.

Mis. Ford. How now (sweet *Frank*) why art thou me-lancholy?

Ford. I melancholy? I am not melancholy:
Get you home: goe.

Mis. Ford. Faith, thou hast some crochets in thy head, Now: will you goe, *Mistris Page*?

Mis. Page. Haue with you: you'll come to dinner *George*? Looke who comes yonder: shee shall bee our Messenger to this paltrie Knight.

Mis. Ford. Trust me, I thought on her: shee'll fit it.

Mis. Page. You are come to see my daughter *Anne*?

Qui. I forsooth: and I pray how do's good Mistresse *Anne*?

Mis. Page. Go in with vs and see: we haue an houres talke with you.

Page. How now Master Ford?

For. You heard what this knaue told me, did you not?

Page. Yes, and you heard what the other told me?

Ford. Doe you thinke there is truth in them?

Pag. Hang 'em slaues: I doe not thinke the Knight would offer it: But these that accuse him in his intent towards our wiues, are a yoake of his discarded men: ve-ry rogues, now they be out of seruice.

Ford. Were they his men?

Page. Marry were they.

Ford. I like it neuer the beter for that,
Do's he lye at the Garter?

Page. I marry do's he: if hee should intend this voy-age toward my wife, I would turne her loose to him; and what hee gets more of her, then sharpe words, let it lye on my head.

Ford. I doe not misdoubt my wife: but I would bee loath to turne them together: a man may be too confi-dent: I would haue nothing lye on my head: I cannot be thus satisfied.

Page. Looke where my ranting-Host of the Garter comes: there is eyther liquor in his pate, or mony in his purse, when hee lookes so merrily: How now mine Host?

Host. How now Bully-Rooke: thou'rt a Gentleman Caueleiro Iustice, I say.

Shal. I follow, (mine Host) I follow: Good-euen, and twenty (good Master *Page*,) Master *Page*, wil you go with vs? we haue sport in hand.

Host. Tell him Caueleiro-Iustice: tell him Bully-Rooke.

Shal. Sir, there is a fray to be fought, betweene Sir *Hugh* the Welch Priest, and *Caius* the French Doctor.

Ford. Good

Ford. Good mine Host o'th' Garter: a word with you.

Host. What saist thou, my Bully-Rooke?

Shal. Will you goe with vs to behold it? My merry Host hath had the measuring of their weapons; and (I thinke) hath appointed them contrary places: for (beleeue mee) I heare the Parson is no Iester: harke, I will tell you what our sport shall be.

Host. Hast thou no suit against my Knight? my guest-Caualeire?

Shal. None, I protest: but Ile giue you a pottle of burn'd sacke, to giue me recourse to him, and tell him my name is *Broome*: onely for a iest.

Host. My hand, (Bully:) thou shalt haue egresse and regresse, (said I well?) and thy name shall be *Broome*. It is a merry Knight: will you goe An-heires?

Shal. Haue with you mine Host.

Page. I haue heard the French-man hath good skill in his Rapier.

Shal. Tut sir: I could haue told you more: In these times you stand on distance: your Passes, Stoccado's, and I know not what: 'tis the heart (Master *Page*) 'tis heere, 'tis heere: I haue seene the time, with my long-sword, I would haue made you fowre tall fellowes skippe like Rattes.

Host. Heere boyes, heere, heere: shall we wag?

Page. Haue with you: I had rather heare them scold, then fight.

Ford. Though *Page* be a secure foole, and stands so firmely on his wiues frailty; yet, I cannot put-off my opinion so easily: she was in his company at *Pages* house: and what they made there, I know not. Well, I wil looke further into't, and I haue a disguise, to sound *Falstaffe*; if I finde her honest, I loose not my labor: if she be otherwise, 'tis labour well bestowed. *Exeunt.*

Scœna Secunda.

Enter Falstaffe, Pistoll, Robin, Quickly, Bardolffe, Ford.

Fal. I will not lend thee a penny.

Pist. Why then the world's mine Oyster, which I, with sword will open.

Fal. Not a penny: I haue beene content (Sir,) you should lay my countenance to pawne: I haue grated vpon my good friends for three Repreeues for you, and your Coach-fellow *Nim*; or else you had look'd through the grate, like a Geminy of Baboones: I am damn'd in hell, for swearing to Gentlemen my friends, you were good Souldiers, and tall-fellowes. And when Mistresse *Briget* lost the handle of her Fan, I took't vpon mine honour thou hadst it not.

Pist. Didst not thou share? hadst thou not fifteene pence?

Fal. Reason, you roague, reason: thinkst thou Ile endanger my soule, *gratis*? at a word, hang no more about mee, I am no gibbet for you: goe, a short knife, and a throng, to your Mannor of *Pickt-hatch*: goe, you'll not beare a Letter for mee you roague? you stand vpon your honor: why, (thou vnconfinable basenesse) it is as much as I can doe to keepe the termes of my honnor precise: I, I, I my selfe sometimes, leauing the feare of heauen on the left hand, and hiding mine honor in my necessity, am faine to shuffle: to hedge, and to lurch, and yet, you Rogue, will en-sconce your raggs; your Cat-a-Mountaine-lookes, your red-lattice phrases, and your bold-beating-oathes, vnder the shelter of your honor? you will not doe it? you?

Pist. I doe relent: what would thou more of man?

Robin. Sir, here's a woman would speake with you.

Fal. Let her approach.

Qui. Giue your worship good morrow.

Fal. Good-morrow, good-wife.

Qui. Not so, and't please your worship.

Fal. Good maid then.

Qui. Ile be sworne,
As my mother was the first houre I was borne.

Fal. I doe beleeue the swearer; what with me?

Qui. Shall I vouch-safe your worship a word, or two?

Fal. Two thousand (faire woman) and ile vouchsafe thee the hearing.

Qui. There is one Mistresse *Ford*, (Sir) I pray come a little neerer this waies: I my selfe dwell with M. Doctor *Caius*:

Fal. Well, on; Mistresse *Ford*, you say.

Qui. Your worship saies very true: I pray your worship come a little neerer this waies.

Fal. I warrant thee, no-bodie heares: mine owne people, mine owne people.

Qui. Are they so? heauen-blesse them, and make them his Seruants.

Fal. Well; Mistresse *Ford*, what of her?

Qui. Why, Sir; shee's a good-creature; Lord, Lord, your Worship's a wanton: well: heauen forgiue you, and all of vs, I pray———.

Fal. Mistresse *Ford*: come, Mistresse *Ford*.

Qui. Marry this is the short, and the long of it: you haue brought her into such a Canaries, as 'tis wonderfull: the best Courtier of them all (when the Court lay at *Windsor*) could neuer haue brought her to such a Canarie: yet there has beene Knights, and Lords, and Gentlemen, with their Coaches; I warrant you Coach after Coach, letter after letter, gift after gift, smelling so sweetly; all Muske, and so rushling, I warrant you, in silke and golde, and in such alligant termes, and in such wine and suger of the best, and the fairest, that would haue wonne any womans heart: and I warrant you, they could neuer get an eye-winke of her: I had my selfe twentie Angels giuen me this morning, but I defie all Angels (in any such sort, as they say) but in the way of honesty: and I warrant you, they could neuer get her so much as sippe on a cup with the prowdest of them all, and yet there has beene Earles: nay, (which is more) Pentioners, but I warrant you all is one with her.

Fal. But what saies shee to mee? be briefe my good shee-*Mercurie*.

Qui. Marry, she hath receiu'd your Letter: for the which she thankes you a thousand times; and she giues you to notifie, that her husband will be absence from his house, betweene ten and eleuen.

Fal. Ten, and eleuen.

Qui. I, forsooth: and then you may come and see the picture (she sayes) that you wot of: Master *Ford* her husband will be from home: alas, the sweet woman leades an ill life with him: hee's a very iealousie-man; she leads a very frampold life with him, (good hart.)

Fal. Ten, and eleuen.

Woman, commend me to her, I will not faile her.

Qui. Why, you say well: But I haue another messenger to your worship: Mistresse *Page* hath her heartie commendations to you to: and let mee tell you in your eare, shee's as fartuous a ciuill modest wife, and one (I tell you) that will not misse you morning nor euening prayer, as any is in *Windsor*, who ere bee the other: and shee bade me tell your worship, that her husband is seldome from home, but she hopes there will come a time. I neuer knew a woman so doate vpon a man; surely I thinke you haue charmes, la: yes in truth.

Fal. Not I, I assure thee; setting the attraction of my good parts aside, I haue no other charmes.

Qui. Blessing on your heart for't.

Fal. But I pray thee tell me this: has *Fords* wife, and *Pages* wife acquainted each other, how they loue me?

Qui. That were a iest indeed: they haue not so little grace I hope, that were a tricke indeed: But Mistris *Page* would desire you to send her your little Page of al loues: her husband has a maruellous infectiō to the little Page: and truely Master *Page* is an honest man: neuer a wife in *Windsor* leades a better life then she do's: doe what shee will, say what she will, take all, pay all, goe to bed when she list, rise when she list, all is as she will: and truly she deserues it; for if there be a kinde woman in *Windsor*, she is one: you must send her your Page, no remedie.

Fal. Why, I will.

Qu. Nay, but doe so then, and looke you, hee may come and goe betweene you both: and in any case haue a nay-word, that you may know one anothers minde, and the Boy neuer neede to vnderstand any thing; for 'tis not good that children should know any wickednes: olde folkes you know, haue discretion, as they say, and know the world.

Fal. Fare-thee-well, commend mee to them both: there's my purse, I am yet thy debter: Boy, goe along with this woman, this newes distracts me.

Pist. This Puncke is one of *Cupids* Carriers,
Clap on more sailes, pursue: vp with your sights:
Giue fire: she is my prize, or Ocean whelme them all.

Fal. Saist thou so (old *Iacke*) go thy waies: Ile make more of thy olde body then I haue done: will they yet looke after thee? wilt thou after the expence of so much money, be now a gainer? good Body, I thanke thee: let them say 'tis grossely done, so it bee fairely done, no matter.

Bar. Sir *Iohn*, there's one Master *Broome* below would faine speake with you, and be acquainted with you; and hath sent your worship a mornings draught of Sacke.

Fal. *Broome* is his name?

Bar. I Sir.

Fal. Call him in: such *Broomes* are welcome to mee, that ore'flowes such liquor: ah ha, Mistresse *Ford* and Mistresse *Page*, haue I encompass'd you? goe to, *via*.

Ford. 'Blesse you sir.

Fal. And you sir: would you speake with me?

Ford. I make bold, to presse, with so little preparation vpon you.

Fal. You'r welcome, what's your will? giue vs leaue Drawer.

Ford. Sir, I am a Gentleman that haue spent much, my name is *Broome*.

Fal. Good Master *Broome*, I desire more acquaintance of you.

Ford. Good Sir *Iohn*, I sue for yours: not to charge you, for I must let you vnderstand, I thinke my selfe in better plight for a Lender, then you are: the which hath something embolded me to this vnseason'd intrusion: for they say, if money goe before, all waies doe lye open.

Fal. Money is a good Souldier (Sir) and will on.

Ford. Troth, and I haue a bag of money heere troubles me: if you will helpe to beare it (Sir *Iohn*) take all, or halfe, for easing me of the carriage.

Fal. Sir, I know not how I may deserue to bee your Porter.

Ford. I will tell you sir, if you will giue mee the hearing.

Fal. Speake (good Master *Broome*) I shall be glad to be your Seruant.

Ford. Sir, I heare you are a Scholler: (I will be briefe with you) and you haue been a man long knowne to me, though I had neuer so good means as desire, to make my selfe acquainted with you. I shall discouer a thing to you, wherein I must very much lay open mine owne imperfection: but (good Sir *Iohn*) as you haue one eye vpon my follies, as you heare them vnfolded, turne another into the Register of your owne, that I may passe with a reproofe the easier, sith you your selfe know how easie it is to be such an offender.

Fal. Very well Sir, proceed.

Ford. There is a Gentlewoman in this Towne, her husbands name is *Ford*.

Fal. Well Sir.

Ford. I haue long lou'd her, and I protest to you, bestowed much on her: followed her with a doating obseruance: Ingross'd opportunities to meete her: fee'd euery slight occasion that could but nigardly giue mee sight of her: not only bought many presents to giue her, but haue giuen largely to many, to know what shee would haue giuen: briefly, I haue pursu'd her, as Loue hath pursued mee, which hath beene on the wing of all occasions: but whatsoeuer I haue merited, either in my minde, or in my meanes, meede I am sure I haue receiued none, vnlesse Experience be a Iewell, that I haue purchased at an infinite rate, and that hath taught mee to say this,

" *Loue like a shadow flies, when substance Loue pursues,*
" *Pursuing that that flies, and flying what pursues.*

Fal. Haue you receiu'd no promise of satisfaction at her hands?

Ford. Neuer.

Fal. Haue you importun'd her to such a purpose?

Ford. Neuer.

Fal. Of what qualitie was your loue then?

Ford. Like a fair house, built on another mans ground, so that I haue lost my edifice, by mistaking the place, where I erected it.

Fal. To what purpose haue you vnfolded this to me?

For. When I haue told you that, I haue told you all: Some say, that though she appeare honest to mee, yet in other places shee enlargeth her mirth so farre, that there is shrewd construction made of her. Now (Sir *Iohn*) here is the heart of my purpose: you are a gentleman of excellent breeding, admirable discourse, of great admittance, authenticke in your place and person, generally allow'd for your many war-like, court-like, and learned preparations.

Fal. O Sir.

Ford. Beleeue it, for you know it: there is money, spend it, spend it, spend more; spend all I haue, onely giue

giue me so much of your time in enchange of it, as to lay an amiable siege to the honesty of this *Fords* wife : vse your Art of wooing ; win her to consent to you : if any man may, you may as soone as any.

Fal. Would it apply well to the vehemency of your affection that I should win what you would enioy ? Methinkes you prescribe to your selfe very preposterously.

Ford. O, vnderstand my drift : she dwells so securely on the excellency of her honor, that the folly of my soule dares not present it selfe : shee is too bright to be look'd against. Now, could I come to her with any detection in my hand ; my desires had instance and argument to commend themselues, I could driue her then from the ward of her purity, her reputation, her marriage-vow, and a thousand other her defences, which now are too-too strongly embattaild against me : what say you too't, Sir *Iohn* ?

Fal. Master *Broome*, I will first make bold with your money : next, giue mee your hand : and last, as I am a gentleman, you shall, if you will, enioy *Fords* wife.

Ford. O good Sir.

Fal. I say you shall.

Ford. Want no money (Sir *Iohn*) you shall want none.

Fal. Want no *Mistresse Ford* (Master *Broome*) you shall want none : I shall be with her (I may tell you) by her owne appointment, euen as you came in to me, her assistant, or goe-betweene, parted from me : I say I shall be with her betweene ten and eleuen : for at that time the iealious-rascally-knaue her husband will be forth : come you to me at night, you shall know how I speed.

Ford. I am blest in your acquaintance : do you know *Ford* Sir ?

Fal. Hang him (poore Cuckoldly knaue) I know him not : yet I wrong him to call him poore : They say the iealous wittolly-knaue hath masses of money, for the which his wife seemes to me well-fauourd : I will vse her as the key of the Cuckoldly-rogues Coffer, & thet's my haruest-home.

Ford. I would you knew *Ford*, sir, that you might auoid him, if you saw him.

Fal. Hang him, mechanicall-salt-butter rogue; I wil stare him out of his wits : I will awe him with my cudgell : it shall hang like a Meteor ore the Cuckolds horns: Master *Broome*, thou shalt know, I will predominate ouer the pezant, and thou shalt lye with his wife. Come to me soone at night : *Ford's* a knaue, and I will aggrauate his stile : thou (Master *Broome*) shalt know him for knaue, and Cuckold. Come to me soone at night.

Ford. What a damn'd Epicurian-Rascall is this ? my heart is ready to cracke with impatience : who saies this is improuident iealousie ? my wife hath sent to him, the howre is fixt, the match is made : would any man haue thought this ? see the hell of hauing a false woman : my bed shall be abus'd, my Coffers ransack'd, my reputation gnawne at, and I shall not onely receiue this villanous wrong, but stand vnder the adoption of abhominable termes, and by him that does mee this wrong : Termes, names : *Amaimon* sounds well : *Lucifer*, well : *Barbason*, well : yet they are Diuels additions, the names of fiends: But Cuckold, Wittoll, Cuckold ? the Diuell himselfe hath not such a name. *Page* is an Asse, a secure Asse ; hee will trust his wife, hee will not be iealous : I will rather trust a *Fleming* with my butter, Parson *Hugh* the *Welshman* with my Cheese, an *Irish-man* with my Aqua-vitæ-bottle, or a Theefe to walke my ambling gelding, then my wife with her selfe. Then she plots, then shee rumi-nates, then shee deuises : and what they thinke in their hearts they may effect ; they will breake their hearts but they will effect. Heauen bee prais'd for my iealousie: eleuen o' clocke the howre, I will preuent this, detect my wife, bee reueng'd on *Falstaffe*, and laugh at *Page*. I will about it, better three houres too soone, then a mynute too late : fie, fie, fie : Cuckold, Cuckold, Cuckold.

Exit.

Scena Tertia.

Enter Caius, Rugby, Page, Shallow, Slender, Host.

Caius. Iacke Rugby.

Rug. Sir.

Caius. Vat is the clocke, *Iack.*

Rug. 'Tis past the howre (Sir) that Sir *Hugh* promis'd to meet.

Cai. By gar, he has saue hi: soule, dat he is no-come: hee has pray his Pible well, dat he is no-come : by gar (*Iack Rugby*) he is dead already, if he be come.

Rug. Hee is wise Sir ; hee knew your worship would kill him if he came.

Cai. By gar, de herring is no dead, so as I vill kill him : take your Rapier, (*Iacke*) I vill tell you how I vill kill him.

Rug. Alas sir, I cannot fence.

Cai. Villanie, take your Rapier.

Rug. Forbeare : heer's company.

Host. 'Blesse thee, bully-Doctor.

Shal. 'Saue you M^r. Doctor *Caius*.

Page. Now good M^r. Doctor.

Slen. 'Giue you good-morrow, sir.

Caius. Vat be all you one, two, tree, fowre, come for?

Host. To see thee fight, to see thee foigne, to see thee trauerse, to see thee heere, to see thee there, to see thee passe thy puncto, thy stock, thy reuerse, thy distance, thy montant: Is he dead, my Ethiopian ? Is he dead, my Francisco ? ha Bully ? what saies my *Esculapius* ? my *Galien*? my heart of Elder ? ha ? is he dead bully-Stale? is he dead ?

Cai. By gar, he is de Coward-Iack-Priest of de vorld: he is not show his face.

Host. Thou art a Castalion-king-Vrinall : *Hector* of *Greece* (my Boy)

Cai. I pray you beare witnesse, that me haue stay, sixe or seuen, two tree howres for him, and hee is no-come.

Shal. He is the wiser man (M. Docto) he is a curer of soules, and you a curer of bodies : if you should fight, you goe against the haire of your professions : is it not true, Master *Page* ?

Page. Master *Shallow* ; you haue your selfe beene a great fighter, though now a man of peace.

Shal. Body-kins M. *Page*, though I now be old, and of the peace ; if I see a sword out, my finger itches to make one : though wee are Iustices, and Doctors, and Church-men (M. *Page*) wee haue some salt of our youth in vs, we are the sons of women (M. *Page*.)

Page. 'Tis true, M^r. *Shallow*.

Shal. It wil be found so, (M. *Page*:) M. Doctor *Caius*, I am come to fetch you home : I am sworn of the peace: you haue show'd your selfe a wise Physician, and Sir *Hugh* hath showne himselfe a wise and patient Churchman : you must goe with me, M. Doctor.

Host. Par-

Host. Pardon, Guest-Iustice; a Mounseur Mocke-water.

Cai. Mock-vater? vat is dat?

Host. Mock-water, in our English tongue, is Valour (Bully.)

Cai. By gar, then I haue as much Mock-vater as de Englishman: scuruy-Iack-dog-Priest: by gar, mee vill cut his eares.

Host. He will Clapper-claw thee tightly (Bully.)

Cai. Clapper-de-claw? vat is dat?

Host. That is, he will make thee amends.

Cai. By-gar, me doe looke hee shall clapper-de-claw me, for by-gar, me vill haue it.

Host. And I will prouoke him to't, or let him wag.

Cai. Me tanck you for dat.

Host. And moreouer, (Bully) but first, Mr. Ghuest, and M. Page, & eeke Caualeiro *Slender*, goe you through the Towne to *Frogmore*.

Page. Sir *Hugh* is there, is he?

Host. He is there, see what humor he is in: and I will bring the Doctor about by the Fields: will it doe well?

Shal. We will doe it.

All. Adieu, good M. Doctor.

Cai. By-gar, me vill kill de Priest, for he speake for a Iack-an-Ape to *Anne Page*.

Host. Let him die: sheath thy impatience: throw cold water on thy Choller: goe about the fields with mee through *Frogmore*, I will bring thee where Mistris *Anne Page* is, at a Farm-house a Feasting: and thou shalt wooe her: Cride-game, said I well?

Cai. By-gar, mee dancke you vor dat: by gar I loue you: and I shall procure'a you de good Guest: de Earle, de Knight, de Lords, de Gentlemen, my patients.

Host. For the which, I will be thy aduersary toward *Anne Page*: said I well?

Cai. By-gar, 'tis good: vell said.

Host. Let vs wag then.

Cai. Come at my heeles, *Iack Rugby*.

Exeunt.

Actus Tertius. Scœna Prima.

Enter Euans, Simple, Page, Shallow, Slender, Host, Caius, Rugby.

Euans. I pray you now, good Master *Slenders* seruing-man, and friend *Simple* by your name; which way haue you look'd for Master *Caius*, that calls himselfe Doctor of Phisicke.

Sim. Marry Sir, the pittie-ward, the Parke-ward: euery way: olde *Windsor* way, and euery way but the Towne-way.

Euan. I most fehemently desire you, you will also looke that way.

Sim. I will sir.

Euan. 'Plesse my soule: how full of Chollors I am, and trempling of minde: I shall be glad if he haue deceiued me: how melancholies I am? I will knog his Vrinalls about his knaues costard, when I haue good oportunities for the orke: 'Plesse my soule: *To shallow Riuers to whose falls: melodious Birds sings Madrigalls: There will we make our Peds of Roses: and a thousand fragrant posies. To Shallow:* 'Mercie on mee, I haue a great dispositions to cry.

Melodious birds sing Madrigalls: —— *When as I sat in Pabilon: and a thousand vagram Posies. To shallow, &c.*

Sim. Yonder he is comming, this way, Sir *Hugh*.

Euan. Hee's welcome: *To shallow Riuers, to whose fals*: Heauen prosper the right: what weapons is he?

Sim. No weapons, Sir: there comes my Master, Mr. *Shallow*, and another Gentleman; from *Frogmore*, ouer the stile, this way.

Euan. Pray you giue mee my gowne, or else keepe it in your armes.

Shal. How now Master Parson? good morrow good Sir *Hugh*: keepe a Gamester from the dice, and a good Studient from his booke, and it is wonderfull.

Slen. Ah sweet *Anne Page*.

Page. 'Saue you, good Sir *Hugh*.

Euan. 'Plesse you from his mercy-sake, all of you.

Shal. What? the Sword, and the Word? Doe you study them both, Mr. Parson?

Page. And youthfull still, in your doublet and hose, this raw-rumaticke day?

Euan. There is reasons, and causes for it.

Page. We are come to you, to doe a good office, Mr. Parson.

Euan. Fery-well: what is it?

Page. Yonder is a most reuerend Gentleman: who (be-like) hauing receiued wrong by some person, is at most odds with his owne grauity and patience, that euer you saw.

Shal. I haue liued foure-score yeeres, and vpward: I neuer heard a man of his place, grauity, and learning, so wide of his owne respect.

Euan. What is he?

Page. I thinke you know him: Mr. Doctor *Caius* the renowned French Physician.

Euan. Got's-will, and his passion of my heart: I had as lief you would tell me of a messe of porredge.

Page. Why?

Euan. He has no more knowledge in *Hibocrates* and *Galen*, and hee is a knaue besides: a cowardly knaue, as you would desires to be acquainted withall.

Page. I warrant you, hee's the man should fight with him.

Slen. O sweet *Anne Page*.

Shal. It appeares so by his weapons: keepe them a-sunder: here comes Doctor *Caius*.

Page. Nay good Mr. Parson, keepe in your weapon.

Shal. So doe you, good Mr. Doctor.

Host. Disarme them, and let them question: let them keepe their limbs whole, and hack our English.

Cai. I pray you let-a-mee speake a word with your eare; vherefore vill you not meet-a me?

Euan. Pray you vse your patience in good time.

Cai. By-gar, you are de Coward: de Iack dog: Iohn Ape.

Euan. Pray you let vs not be laughing-stocks to other mens humors: I desire you in friendship, and I will one way or other make you amends: I will knog your Vrinal about your knaues Cogs-combe.

Cai. Diable: Iack Rugby: mine *Host de Iarteer*: haue I not stay for him, to kill him? haue I not at de place I did appoint?

Euan. As I am a Christians-soule, now looke you: this is the place appointed, Ile bee iudgement by mine Host of the Garter.

Host. Peace, I say, *Gallia* and *Gaule*, French & Welch, Soule-Curer, and Body-Curer.

Cai. I,

Cai. I, dat is very good, excellant.

Host. Peace, I say: heare mine Host of the Garter, Am I politicke? Am I subtle? Am I a Machiuell? Shall I loose my Doctor? No, hee giues me the Potions and the Motions. Shall I loose my Parson? my Priest? my Sir *Hugh*? No, he giues me the Prouerbes, and the No-verbes. Giue me thy hand (Celestiall) so: Boyes of Art, I haue deceiu'd you both: I haue directed you to wrong places: your hearts are mighty, your skinnes are whole, and let burn'd Sacke be the issue: Come, lay their swords to pawne: Follow me, Lad of peace, follow, follow, follow.

Shal. Trust me, a mad Host: follow Gentlemen, follow.

Slen. O sweet *Anne Page*.

Cai. Ha'do I perceiue dat? Haue you make-a-de-sot of vs, ha, ha?

Eua. This is well, he has made vs his vlowting-stog: I desire you that we may be friends: and let vs knog our praines together to be reuenge on this same scall scuruy-cogging-companion the Host of the Garter.

Cai. By gar, with all my heart: he promise to bring me where is *Anne Page*: by gar he deceiue me too.

Euan. Well, I will smite his noddles: pray you follow.

Scena Secunda.

Mist. Page, Robin, Ford, Page, Shallow, Slender, Host, Euans, Caius.

Mist. Page. Nay keepe your way (little Gallant) you were wont to be a follower, but now you are a Leader: whether had you rather lead mine eyes, or eye your masters heeles?

Rob. I had rather (forsooth) go before you like a man, then follow him like a dwarfe.   (Courtier.

M. Pa. O you are a flattering boy, now I see you'l be a

Ford. Well met mistris *Page*, whether go you.

M. Pa. Truly Sir, to see your wife, is she at home?

Ford. I, and as idle as she may hang together for want of company: I thinke if your husbands were dead, you two would marry.

M. Pa. Be sure of that, two other husbands.

Ford. Where had you this pretty weather-cocke?

M. Pa. I cannot tell what (the dickens) his name is my husband had him of, what do you cal your Knights name

Rob. Sir *Iohn Falstaffe*.   (sirrah?

Ford. Sir *Iohn Falstaffe*.

M. Pa. He, he, I can neuer hit on's name; there is such a league betweene my goodman, and he: is your Wife at

Ford. Indeed she is.   (home indeed?

M. Pa. By your leaue sir, I am sicke till I see her.

Ford. Has *Page* any braines? Hath he any eies? Hath he any thinking? Sure they sleepe, he hath no vse of them: why this boy will carrie a letter twentie mile as easie, as a Canon will shoot point-blanke twelue score: hee peeces out his wiues inclination: he giues her folly motion and aduantage: and now she's going to my wife, & *Falstaffes* boy with her: A man may heare this showre sing in the winde; and *Falstaffes* boy with her: good plots, they are laide, and our reuolted wiues share damnation together: Well, I will take him, then torture my wife, plucke the borrowed vaile of modestie from the so-seeming Mist. *Page*, divulge *Page* himselfe for a secure and wilfull *Acteon*, and to these violent proceedings all my neighbors shall cry aime. The clocke giues me my Qu, and my assurance bids me search, there I shall finde *Falstaffe*: I shall be rather prais'd for this, then mock'd, for it is as possitiue, as the earth is firme, that *Falstaffe* is there: I will go.

Shal. Page, &c. Well met M. *Ford*.

Ford. Trust me, a good knotte; I haue good cheere at home, and I pray you all go with me.

Shal. I must excuse my selfe M. *Ford*.

Slen. And so must I Sir, We haue appointed to dine with Mistris *Anne*, And I would not breake with her for more mony Then Ile speake of.

Shal. We haue linger'd about a match betweene *An Page*, and my cozen *Slender*, and this day wee shall haue our answer.

Slen. I hope I haue your good will Father *Page*.

Pag. You haue M. *Slender*, I stand wholly for you, But my wife (M. Doctor) is for you altogether.

Cai. I be-gar, and de Maid is loue-a-me: my nursh-a-Quickly tell me so mush.

Host. What say you to yong M. *Fenton*? He capers, he dances, he has eies of youth: he writes verses, hee speakes holliday, he smels April and May, he wil carry't, he will carry't, 'tis in his buttons, he will carry't.

Page. Not by my consent I promise you. The Gentleman is of no hauing, hee kept companie with the wilde Prince, and *Pointz*: he is of too high a Region, he knows too much: no, hee shall not knit a knot in his fortunes, with the finger of my substance: if he take her, let him take her simply: the wealth I haue waits on my consent, and my consent goes not that way.

Ford. I beseech you heartily, some of you goe home with me to dinner: besides your cheere you shall haue sport, I will shew you a monster: M. Doctor, you shal go, so shall you M. *Page*, and you Sir *Hugh*.

Shal. Well, fare you well: We shall haue the freer woing at M. *Pages*.

Cai. Go home *Iohn Rugby*, I come anon.

Host. Farewell my hearts, I will to my honest Knight *Falstaffe*, and drinke Canarie with him.

Ford. I thinke I shall drinke in Pipe-wine first with him, Ile make him dance. Will you go, Gentles?

All. Haue with you, to see this Monster.   *Exeunt*

Scena Tertia.

Enter M. Ford, M. Page, Seruants, Robin, Falstaffe, Ford, Page, Caius, Euans.

Mist. Ford. What *Iohn*, what *Robert*.

M. Page. Quickly, quickly: Is the Buck-basket——

Mis. Ford. I warrant. What *Robin* I say.

Mis. Page. Come, come, come.

Mist. Ford. Heere, set it downe.

M. Pag. Giue your men the charge, we must be briefe.

M. Ford. Marrie, as I told you before (*Iohn* & *Robert*) be ready here hard-by in the Brew-house, & when I sodainly call you, come forth, and (without any pause, or staggering) take this basket on your shoulders: y done, trudge with it in all hast, and carry it among the Whitsters in *Dotchet* Mead, and there empty it in the muddie ditch, close by the Thames side.

M. Page. You will do it?   (direction.

M. Ford. I ha told them ouer and ouer, they lacke no

Be gone, and come when you are call'd.

M. Page. Here comes little *Robin*.

Mist. Ford. How now my Eyas-Musket, what newes (with you?

Rob. My M. Sir *Iohn* is come in at your backe doore (Mist. *Ford,* and requests your company.

M. Page. You litle Iack-a-lent, haue you bin true to vs

Rob. I, Ile be sworne: my Master knowes not of your being heere: and hath threatned to put me into euerlasting liberty, if I tell you of it: for he sweares he'll turne me away.

Mist. Pag. Thou'rt a good boy: this secrecy of thine shall be a Tailor to thee, and shal make thee a new doublet and hose. Ile go hide me.

Mi. Ford. Do so: go tell thy Master, I am alone: Mistris *Page,* remember you your *Qu.*

Mist. Pag. I warrant thee, if I do not act it, hisse me.

Mist. Ford. Go-too then: we'l vse this vnwholsome humidity, this grosse-watry Pumpion; we'll teach him to know Turtles from Iayes.

Fal. Haue I caught thee, my heauenly Iewell? Why now let me die, for I haue liu'd long enough: This is the period of my ambition: O this blessed houre.

Mist. Ford. O sweet Sir *Iohn.*

Fal. Mistris *Ford,* I cannot cog, I cannot prate (Mist. *Ford*) now shall I sin in my wish; I would thy Husband were dead, Ile speake it before the best Lord, I would make thee my Lady.

Mist. Ford. I your Lady Sir *Iohn*? Alas, I should bee a pittifull Lady.

Fal. Let the Court of France shew me such another: I see how thine eye would emulate the Diamond: Thou hast the right arched-beauty of the brow, that becomes the Ship-tyre, the Tyre-valiant, or any Tire of Venetian admittance.

Mist. Ford. A plaine Kerchiefe, Sir *Iohn*: My browes become nothing else, nor that well neither.

Fal. Thou art a tyrant to say so: thou wouldst make an absolute Courtier, and the firme fixture of thy foote, would giue an excellent motion to thy gate, in a semicircled Farthingale. I see what thou wert if Fortune thy foe, were not Nature thy friend: Come, thou canst not hide it.

Mist. Ford. Beleeue me, ther's no such thing in me.

Fal. What made me loue thee? Let that perswade thee. Ther's something extraordinary in thee: Come, I cannot cog, and say thou art this and that, like a-manie of these lisping-hauthorne buds, that come like women in mens apparrell, and smell like, Bucklers-berry in simple time: I cannot, but I loue thee, none but thee; and thou deseru'st it.

M. Ford. Do not betray me sir, I feare you loue M. *Page.*

Fal. Thou mightst as well say, I loue to walke by the Counter-gate, which is as hatefull to me, as the reeke of a Lime-kill.

Mis. Ford. Well, heauen knowes how I loue you, And you shall one day finde it.

Fal. Keepe in that minde, Ile deserue it.

Mist. Ford. Nay, I must tell you, so you doe; Or else I could not be in that minde.

Rob. Mistris *Ford,* Mistris *Ford*: heere's Mistris *Page* at the doore, sweating, and blowing, and looking wildely, and would needs speake with you presently.

Fal. She shall not see me, I will ensconce mee behinde the Arras.

M. Ford. Pray you do so, she's a very tatling woman. Whats the matter? How now?

Mist. Page. O mistris *Ford* what haue you done? You'r sham'd, y'are ouerthrowne, y'are vndone for euer.

M. Ford. What's the matter, good mistris *Page*?

M. Page. O weladay, mist. *Ford,* hauing an honest man to your husband, to giue him such cause of suspition.

M. Ford. What cause of suspition?

M. Page. What cause of suspition? Out vpon you: How am I mistooke in you?

M. Ford. Why (alas) what's the matter?

M. Page. Your husband's comming hether (Woman) with all the Officers in Windsor, to search for a Gentleman, that he sayes is heere now in the house; by your consent to take an ill aduantage of his absence: you are vndone.

M. Ford. 'Tis not so, I hope.

M. Page. Pray heauen it be not so, that you haue such a man heere: but 'tis most certaine your husband's comming, with halfe Windsor at his heeles, to serch for such a one, I come before to tell you: If you know your selfe cleere, why I am glad of it: but if you haue a friend here, conuey, conuey him out. Be not amaz'd, call all your senses to you, defend your reputation, or bid farwell to your good life for euer.

M. Ford. What shall I do? There is a Gentleman my deere friend: and I feare not mine owne shame so much, as his perill. I had rather then a thousand pound he were out of the house.

M. Page. For shame, neuer stand (you had rather, and you had rather:) your husband's heere at hand, bethinke you of some conueyance: in the house you cannot hide him. Oh, how haue you deceiu'd me? Looke, heere is a basket, if he be of any reasonable stature, he may creepe in heere, and throw fowle linnen vpon him, as if it were going to bucking: Or it is whiting time, send him by your two men to *Datchet*-Meade.

M. Ford. He's too big to go in there: what shall I do?

Fal. Let me see't, let me see't, O let me see't: Ile in, Ile in: Follow your friends counsell, Ile in.

M. Page. What Sir *Iohn Faistaffe*? Are these your Letters, Knight?

Fal. I loue thee, helpe mee away: let me creepe in heere: ile neuer——

M. Page. Helpe to couer your master (Boy:) Call your men (Mist. *Ford.*) You dissembling Knight.

M. Ford. What *Iohn, Robert, Iohn*; Go, take vp these cloathes heere, quickly: Wher's the Cowle-staffe? Look how you drumble? Carry them to the Landresse in Datchet mead: quickly, come.

Ford. 'Pray you come nere: if I suspect without cause, Why then make sport at me, then let me be your iest, I deserue it: How now? Whether beare you this?

Ser. To the Landresse forsooth?

M. Ford. Why, what haue you to doe whether they beare it? You were best meddle with buck-washing.

Ford. Buck? I would I could wash my selfe of ye Buck: Bucke, bucke, bucke, I bucke: I warrant you Bucke, And of the season too; it shall appeare. Gentlemen, I haue dream'd to night, Ile tell you my dreame: heere, heere, heere bee my keyes, ascend my Chambers, search, seeke, finde out: Ile warrant wee'le vnkennell the Fox. Let me stop this way first: so, now vncape.

Page. Good master *Ford,* be contented: You wrong your selfe too much.

Ford. True (master *Page*) vp Gentlemen, You shall see sport anon:

Follow

Follow me Gentlemen.

Euans. This is fery fantasticall humors and iealousies.

Caius. By gar, 'tis no-the fashion of France: It is not iealous in France.

Page. Nay follow him (Gentlemen) see the yssue of his search.

Mist. Page. Is there not a double excellency in this?

Mist. Ford. I know not which pleases me better, That my husband is decciued, or Sir *Iohn.*

Mist. Page. What a taking was hee in, when your husband askt who was in the basket?

Mist. Ford. I am halfe affraid he will haue neede of washing: so throwing him into the water, will doe him a benefit.

Mist. Page. Hang him dishonest rascall: I would all of the same straine, were in the same distresse.

Mist. Ford. I thinke my husband hath some speciall suspition of *Falstaffs* being heere: for I neuer saw him so grosse in his iealousie till now.

Mist. Page. I will lay a plot to try that, and wee will yet haue more trickes with *Falstaffe*: his dissolute disease will scarse obey this medicine.

Mis. Ford. Shall we send that foolishion Carion, Mist. *Quickly* to him, and excuse his throwing into the water, and giue him another hope, to betray him to another punishment?

Mist. Page. We will do it: let him be sent for to morrow eight a clocke to haue amends.

Ford. I cannot finde him: may be the knaue bragg'd of that he could not compasse.

Mis. Page. Heard you that?

Mis. Ford. You vse me well, M. *Ferd?* Do you?

Ford. I, I do so.

M. Ford. Heauen make you better then your thoghts

Ford. Amen.

Mi. Page. You do your selfe mighty wrong (M. *Ford*)

Ford. I, I: I must beare it.

Eu. If there be any pody in the house, & in the chambers, and in the coffers, and in the presses: heauen forgiue my sins at the day of iudgement.

Caius. Be gar, nor I too: there is no-bodies.

Page. Fy, fy, M. *Ford*, are you not ashem'd? What spirit, what diuell suggests this imagination? I wold not ha your distemper in this kind, for ẏ welth of *Windsor castle.*

Ford. 'Tis my fault (M. *Page*) I suffer for it.

Euans. You suffer for a pad conscience: your wife is as honest a o'mans, as I will desires among fiue thousand, and fiue hundred too.

Cai. By gar, I see 'tis an honest woman.

Ford. Well, I promis'd you a dinner: come, come, walk in the Parke, I pray you pardon me: I wil hereafter make knowne to you why I haue done this. Come wife, come Mi. *Page*, I pray you pardon me. Pray hartly pardon me.

Page. Let's go in Gentlemen, but (trust me) we'l mock him: I doe inuite you to morrow morning to my house to breakfast: after we'll a Birding together, I haue a fine Hawke for the bush. Shall it be so?

Ford. Any thing.

Eu. If there is one, I shall make two in the Companie

Ca. If there be one, or two, I shall make-a-the turd.

Ford. Pray you go, M. *Page.*

Eua. I pray you now remembrance to morrow on the lowsie knaue, mine Host.

Cai. Dat is good by gar, withall my heart.

Eua. A lowsie knaue, to haue his gibes, and his mockeries.

Exeunt.

Scœna Quarta.

Enter Fenton, Anne, Page, Shallow, Slender, Quickly, Page, Mist. Page.

Fen: I see I cannot get thy Fathers loue, Therefore no more turne me to him (sweet Nan.)

Anne. Alas, how then?

Fen. Why thou must be thy selfe. He doth obiect, I am too great of birth, And that my state being gall'd with my expence, I seeke to heale it onely by his wealth. Besides these, other barres he layes before me, My Riots past, my wilde Societies, And tels me 'tis a thing impossible I should loue thee, but as a property.

An. May be he tels you true.

No, heauen so speed me in my time to come, Albeit I will confesse, thy Fathers wealth Was the first motiue that I woo'd thee (*Anne:*) Yet wooing thee, I found thee of more valew Then stampes in Gold, or summes in sealed bagges: And 'tis the very riches of thy selfe, That now I ayme at.

An. Gentle M. *Fenton*, Yet seeke my Fathers loue, still seeke it sir, If opportunity and humblest suite Cannot attaine it, why then harke you hither.

Shal. Breake their talke Mistris *Quickly*, My Kinsman shall speake for himselfe.

Slen. Ile make a shaft or a bolt on't, slid, tis but iventu- (*ring.*

Shal. Be not dismaid.

Slen. No, she shall not dismay me: I care not for that, but that I am affeard.

Qui. Hark ye, M. *Slender* would speak a word with you

An. I come to him. This is my Fathers choice: O what a world of vilde ill-fauour'd faults Lookes handsome in three hundred pounds a yeere?

Qui. And how do's good Master *Fenton?* Pray you a word with you.

Shal. Shee's comming; to her Coz: O boy, thou hadst a father.

Slen. I had a father (M. *An*) my vncle can tel you good iests of him: pray you Vncle, tel Mist. *Anne* the iest how my Father stole two Geese out of a Pen, good Vnckle.

Shal. Mistris *Anne*, my Cozen loues you.

Slen. I that I do, as well as I loue any woman in Glocestershire.

Shal. He will maintaine you like a Gentlewoman.

Slen. I that I will, come cut and long-taile, vnder the degree of a Squire.

Shal. He will make you a hundred and fiftie pounds ioynture.

Anne. Good Maister *Shallow* let him woo for himselfe.

Shal. Marrie I thanke you for it: I thanke you for that good comfort: she cals you (Coz) Ile leaue you.

Anne. Now Master *Slender.*

Slen. Now good Mistris *Anne,*

Anne. What is your will?

Slen. My will? Odd's-hart-lings, that's a prettie iest indeede: I ne're made my Will yet (I thanke Heauen) I am not such a sickely creature, I giue Heauen praise.

Anne. I meane (M. *Slender*) what wold you with me?

Slen. Truely, for mine owne part, I would little or nothing with you: your father and my vncle hath made motions: if it be my lucke, so; if not, happy man bee his dole, they can tell you how things go, better then I can: you may aske your father, heere he comes.

Page. Now Mr *Slender*; Loue him daughter *Anne*, Why how now? What does Mr *Fenter* here? You wrong me Sir, thus still to haunt my house. I told you Sir, my daughter is dispos'd of.

Fen. Nay Mr *Page*, be not impatient.

Mist. Page. Good M. *Fenton*, come not to my child.

Page. She is no match for you.

Fen. Sir, will you heare me?

Page. No, good M. *Fenton*.
Come M. *Shallow*: Come sonne *Slender*, in;
Knowing my minde, you wrong me (M. *Fenton*.)

Qui. Speake to Mistris *Page*.

Fen. Good Mist. *Page*, for that I loue your daughter In such a righteous fashion as I do, Perforce, against all checkes, rebukes, and manners, I must aduance the colours of my loue, And not retire. Let me haue your good will.

An. Good mother, do not marry me to yond foole.

Mist. Page. I meane it not, I seeke you a better husband.

Qui. That's my master, M. Doctor.

An. Alas I had rather be set quick i'th earth, And bowl'd to death with Turnips.

Mist. Page. Come, trouble not your selfe good M. *Fenton*, I will not be your friend, nor enemy: My daughter will I question how she loues you, And as I finde her, so am I affected: Till then, farewell Sir, she must needs go in, Her father will be angry.

Fen. Farewell gentle Mistris: farewell *Nan*.

Qui. This is my doing now: Nay, saide I, will you cast away your childe on a Foole, and a Physitian: Looke on M. *Fenton*, this is my doing.

Fen. I thanke thee: and I pray thee once to night, Giue my sweet *Nan* this Ring: there's for thy paines.

Qui. Now heauen send thee good fortune, a kinde heart he hath: a woman would run through fire & water for such a kinde heart. But yet, I would my Maister had Mistris *Anne*, or I would M. *Slender* had her: or (in sooth) I would M. *Fenton* had her; I will do what I can for them all three, for so I haue promis'd, and Ile bee as good as my word, but speciously for M. *Fenton*. Well, I must of another errand to Sir *Iohn Falstaffe* from my two Mistresses: what a beast am I to slacke it. *Exeunt*

Scena Quinta.

Enter Falstaffe, Bardolfe, Quickly, Ford.

Fal. Bardolfe I say.

Bar. Heere Sir.

Fal. Go, fetch me a quart of Sacke, put a tost in't. Haue I liu'd to be carried in a Basket like a barrow of butchers Offall? and to be throwne in the Thames? Wel, if I be seru'd such another tricke, Ile haue my braines 'tane out and butter'd, and giue them to a dogge for a New-yeares gift. The rogues slighted me into the riuer with as little remorse, as they would haue drown'd a blinde bitches Puppies, fifteene i'th litter: and you may know by my size, that I haue a kinde of alacrity in sinking: if the bottome were as deepe as hell, I shold down. I had beene drown'd, but that the shore was sheluy and shallow: a death that I abhorre: for the water swelles a man; and what a thing should I haue beene, when I had beene swel'd? I should haue beene a Mountaine of Mummie.

Bar. Here's M. *Quickly* Sir to speake with you.

Fal. Come, let me poure in some Sack to the Thames water: for my bellies as cold as if I had swallow'd snowbals, for pilles to coole the reines. Call her in.

Bar. Come in woman.

Qui. By your leaue: I cry you mercy? Giue your worship good morrow.

Fal. Take away these Challices: Go, brew me a pottle of Sacke finely.

Bard. With Egges, Sir?

Fal. Simple of it selfe: Ile no Pullet-Spersme in my brewage. How now?

Qui. Marry Sir, I come to your worship from M. *Ford*.

Fal. Mist. Ford? I haue had Ford enough: I was thrown into the Ford; I haue my belly full of Ford.

Qui. Alas the day, (good-heart) that was not her fault: she do's so take on with her men; they mistooke their erection. (promise.

Fal. So did I mine, to build vpon a foolish Womans

Qui. Well, she laments Sir for it, that it would yern your heart to see it: her husband goes this morning a birding; she desires you once more to come to her, betweene eight and nine: I must carry her word quickely, she'll make you amends I warrant you.

Fal. Well, I will visit her, tell her so: and bidde her thinke what a man is: Let her consider his frailety, and then iudge of my merit.

Qui. I will tell her.

Fal. Do so. Betweene nine and ten saist thou?

Qui. Eight and nine Sir.

Fal. Well, be gone: I will not misse her.

Qui. Peace be with you Sir.

Fal. I meruaile I heare not of Mr *Broome*: he sent me word to stay within: I like his money well. Oh, heere he comes.

Ford. Blesse you Sir.

Fal. Now M. *Broome*, you come to know What hath past betweene me, and *Fords* wife.

Ford. That indeed (Sir *Iohn*) is my businesse.

Fal. M. Broome I will not lye to you, I was at her house the houre she appointed me.

Ford. And sped you Sir?

Fal. very ill-fauouredly M. *Broome*.

Ford. How so sir, did she change her determination?

Fal. No (M. *Broome*) but the peaking Curnuto her husband (M. *Broome*) dwelling in a continual larum of ielousie, coms me in the instant of our encounter, after we had embrast, kist, protested, & (as it were) spoke the prologue of our Comedy: and at his heeles, a rabble of his companions, thither prouoked and instigated by his distemper, and (forsooth) to serch his house for his wiues Loue.

Ford. What? While you were there?

Fal. While I was there.

For. And did he search for you, & could not find you?

Fal. You shall heare. As good lucke would haue it, comes in one *Mist. Page*, giues intelligence of *Fords* approch: and in her inuention, and *Fords* wiues distraction, they conuey'd me into a bucke-basket.

Ford

Ford. A Buck-basket?

Fal. Yes: a Buck-basket: ram'd mee in with foule Shirts and Smockes, Socks, foule Stockings, greasie Napkins, that (Master *Broome*) there was the rankest compound of villanous smell, that euer offended nostrill.

Ford. And how long lay you there?

Fal. Nay, you shall heare (Master *Broome*) what I haue sufferd, to bring this woman to euill, for your good: Being thus cram'd in the Basket, a couple of *Fords* knaues, his Hindes, were cald forth by their Mistris, to carry mee in the name of foule Cloathes to *Datchet-lane*: they tooke me on their shoulders: met the iealous knaue their Master in the doore; who ask'd them once or twice what they had in their Basket? I quak'd for feare least the Lunatique Knaue would haue search'd it: but Fate (ordaining he should be a Cuckold) held his hand: well, on went hee, for a search, and away went I for foule Cloathes: But marke the sequell (Master *Broome*) I suffered the pangs of three seuerall deaths: First, an intollerable fright, to be detected with a iealious rotten Bell-weather: Next to be compass'd like a good Bilbo in the circumference of a Pecke, hilt to point, heele to head. And then to be stopt in like a strong distillation with stinking Cloathes, that fretted in their owne grease: thinke of that, a man of my Kidney; thinke of that, that am as subiect to heate as butter; a man of continuall dissolution, and thaw: it was a miracle to scape suffocation. And in the height of this Bath (when I was more then halfe stew'd in grease (like a Dutch-dish) to be throwne into the Thames, and coold, glowing-hot, in that serge like a Horse-shoo; thinke of that; hissing hot: thinke of that(Master *Broome.*)

Ford. In good sadnesse Sir, I am sorry, that for my sake you haue sufferd all this.
My suite then is desperate: You'll vndertake her no more?

Fal. Master *Broome*: I will be throwne into *Etna*, as I haue beene into Thames, ere I will leaue her thus; her Husband is this morning gone a Birding: I haue receiued from her another ambassie of meeting: 'twixt eight and nine is the houre (Master *Broome.*)

Ford. 'Tis past eight already Sir.

Fal. Is it? I will then addresse mee to my appointment: Come to mee at your conuenient leisure, and you shall know how I speede: and the conclusion shall be crowned with your enioying her: adiew: you shall haue her (Master *Broome*) Master *Broome*, you shall cuckold *Ford*.

Ford. Hum: ha? Is this a vision? Is this a dreame? doe I sleepe? Master *Ford* awake, awake Master *Ford*: ther's a hole made in your best coate (Master *Ford*:) this 'tis to be married; this 'tis to haue Lynnen, and Buck-baskets: Well, I will proclaime my selfe what I am: I will now take the Leacher: hee is at my house: hee cannot scape me: 'tis impossible hee should: hee cannot creepe into a halfe-penny purse, nor into a Pepper-Boxe: But least the Diuell that guides him, should aide him, I will search impossible places: though what I am, I cannot auoide; yet to be what I would not, shall not make me tame: If I haue hornes, to make one mad, let the prouerbe goe with me, Ile be horne-mad. *Exeunt.*

Actus Quartus. Scœna Prima.

Enter Mistris Page, Quickly, William, Euans.

Mist.Pag. Is he at M. *Fords* already think'st thou?

Qui. Sure he is by this; or will be presently; but truely he is very couragious mad, about his throwing into the water. Mistris *Ford* desires you to come sodainely.

Mist.Pag. Ile be with her by and by: Ile but bring my yong-man here to Schoole: looke where his Master comes; 'tis a playing day I see: how now Sir *Hugh*, no Schoole to day?

Eua. No: Master *Slender* is let the Boyes leaue to play.

Qui. 'Blessing of his heart.

Mist.Pag. Sir *Hugh*, my husband saies my sonne profits nothing in the world at his Booke: I pray you aske him some questions in his Accidence.

Eu. Come hither *William*; hold vp your head; come.

Mist.Pag. Come-on Sirha; hold vp your head; answere your Master, be not afraid.

Eua. William, how many Numbers is in Nownes?

Will. Two.

Qui. Truely, I thought there had bin one Number more, because they say od's-Nownes.

Eua. Peace, your tatlings. What is (*Faire*)*William*?

Will. Pulcher.

Qu. Powlcats? there are fairer things then Powlcats, sure.

Eua. You are a very simplicity o'man: I pray you peace. What is (*Lapis*) *William*?

Will. A Stone.

Eua. And what is a Stone (*William*?)

Will. A Peeble.

Eua. No; it is *Lapis*: I pray you remember in your praine.

Will. Lapis.

Eua. That is a good *William*: what is he (*William*) that do's lend Articles.

Will. Articles are borrowed of the Pronoune; and be thus declined. *Singulariter nominatiuo hic, hæc, hoc.*

Eua. Nominatiuo hig, hag, hog: pray you marke: *genitiuo huius*: Well: what is your *Accusatiuo-case*?

Will. Accusatiuo hinc.

Eua. I pray you haue your remembrance (childe) *Accusatiuo hing, hang, hog.*

Qu. Hang-hog, is latten for Bacon, I warrant you.

Eua. Leaue your prables (o'man) What is the *Focatiue case* (*William?*)

Will. O, Vocatiuo, O.

Eua. Remember *William, Focatiue*, is *caret*.

Qu. And that's a good roote.

Eua. O'man, forbeare.

Mist.Pag. Peace.

Eua. What is your *Genitiue case plurall* (*William*?)

Will. Genitiue case?

Eua. I.

Will. Genitiue horum, harum, horum.

Qu. 'Vengeance of *Ginyes* case; fie on her; neuer name her (childe) if she be a whore.

Eua. For shame o'man.

Qu. You doe ill to teach the childe such words: hee teaches him to hic, and to hac; which they'll doe fast enough of themselues, and to call *horum*; fie vpon you.

Eua. 'Oman

Euans. O'man, art thou Lunaties? Hast thou no vnderstandings for thy Cases, & the numbers of the Genders? Thou art as foolish Christian creatures, as I would desires.

Mi. Page. Pre'thee hold thy peace.

Eu. Shew me now (*William*) some declensions of your Pronounes.

Will. Forsooth, I haue forgot.

Eu. It is *Qui*, *que*, *quod*; if you forget your *Quies*, your *Ques*, and your *Quods*, you must be preeches: Goe your waies and play, go.

M. Pag. He is a better scholler then I thought he was.

Eu. He is a good sprag-memory: Farewel *Mis. Page*.

Mis. Page. Adieu good Sir *Hugh*:
Get you home boy, Come we stay too long. *Exeunt.*

Scena Secunda.

Enter Falstoffe, Mist. Ford, Mist. Page, Seruants, Ford, Page, Caius, Euans, Shallow.

Fal. Mi. Ford, Your sorrow hath eaten vp my sufferance; I see you are obsequious in your loue, and I professe requitall to a haires bredth, not onely Mist. *Ford,* in the simple office of loue, but in all the accustrement, complement, and ceremony of it: But are you sure of your husband now?

Mis. Ford. Hee's a birding (sweet Sir *Iohn*.)

Mis. Page. What hoa, gossip *Ford* : what hoa.

Mis. Ford. Step into th'chamber, Sir *Iohn*.

Mis. Page. How now (sweete heart) whose at home besides your selfe?

Mis Ford. Why none but mine owne people.

Mis Page. Indeed?

Mis. Ford. No certainly: Speake louder.

Mist. Pag. Truly, I am so glad you haue no body here.

Mist. Ford. Why?

Mis Page. Why woman, your husband is in his olde lines againe : he so takes on yonder with my husband, so railes against all married mankinde ; so curses all *Eues* daughters, of what complexion soeuer ; and so buffettes himselfe on the for-head : crying peere-out, peere-out, that any madnesse I euer yet beheld, seem'd but tamenesse, ciuility, and patience to this his distemper he is in now : I am glad the fat Knight is not heere.

Mist. Ford. Why, do's he talke of him?

Mist. Page. Of none but him, and sweares he was caried out the last time hee search'd for him, in a Basket: Protests to my husband he is now heere, & hath drawne him and the rest of their company from their sport, to make another experiment of his suspition: But I am glad the Knight is not heere; now he shall see his owne foolerie.

Mist. Ford. How neere is he Mistris *Page?*

Mist. Pag. Hard by, at street end ; he wil be here anon.

Mist. Ford. I am vndone, the Knight is heere.

Mist. Page. Why then you are vtterly sham'd, & hee's but a dead man. What a woman are you ? Away with him, away with him : Better shame, then murther.

Mist. Ford. Which way should he go? How should I bestow him ? Shall I put him into the basket againe?

Fal. No, Ile come no more i'th Basket:
May I not go out ere he come?

Mist. Page. Alas : three of M*r. Fords* brothers watch the doore with Pistols, that none shall issue out : otherwise you might slip away ere hee came : But what make you heere ?

Fal. What shall I do ? Ile creepe vp into the chimney.

Mist. Ford. There they alwaies vse to discharge their Birding-peeces : creepe into the Kill-hole.

Fal. Where is it?

Mist. Ford. He will seeke there on my word : Neyther Presse, Coffer, Chest, Trunke, Well, Vault, but he hath an abstract for the remembrance of such places, and goes to them by his Note : There is no hiding you in the house.

Fal. Ile go out then.

Mist. Ford. If you goe out in your owne semblance, you die Sir *Iohn,* vnlesse you go out disguis'd.

Mist. Ford. How might we disguise him?

Mist. Page. Alas the day I know not, there is no womans gowne bigge enough for him : otherwise he might put on a hat, a muffler, and a kerchiefe, and so escape.

Fal. Good hearts, deuise something : any extremitie, rather then a mischiefe.

Mist. Ford. My Maids Aunt the fat woman of *Brainford,* has a gowne aboue.

Mist. Page. On my word it will serue him : shee's as big as he is : and there's her thrum'd hat, and her muffler too : run vp Sir *Iohn*.

Mist. Ford. Go, go, sweet Sir *Iohn* : *Mistris Page* and I will looke some linnen for your head.

Mist. Page. Quicke, quicke, wee'le come dresse you straight : put on the gowne the while.

Mist. Ford. I would my husband would meete him in this shape : he cannot abide the old woman of Brainford ; he sweares shee's a witch, forbad her my house, and hath threatned to beate her.

Mist. Page. Heauen guide him to thy husbands cudgell : and the diuell guide his cudgell afterwards.

Mist. Ford. But is my husband comming ?

Mist. Page. I in good sadnesse is he, and talkes of the basket too, howsoeuer he hath had intelligence.

Mist. Ford. Wee'l try that : for Ile appoint my men to carry the basket againe, to meete him at the doore with it, as they did last time.

Mist. Page. Nay, but hee'l be heere presently : let's go dresse him like the witch of *Brainford*.

Mist. Ford. Ile first direct direct my men, what they shall doe with the basket : Goe vp, Ile bring linnen for him straight.

Mist. Page. Hang him dishonest Varlet,
We cannot misuse enough :
We'll leaue a proofe by that which we will doo,
Wiues may be merry, and yet honest too :
We do not acte that often, iest, and laugh,
'Tis old, but true, Still Swine eats all the draugh.

Mist. Ford. Go Sirs, take the basket againe on your shoulders : your Master is hard at doore : if hee bid you set it downe, obey him ; quickly, dispatch.

1 Ser. Come, come, take it vp.

2 Ser. Pray heauen it be not full of Knight againe.

1 Ser. I hope not, I had liefe as beare so much lead.

Ford. I, but if it proue true (M*r. Page*) haue you any way then to vnfoole me againe. Set downe the basket villaine : some body call my wife : Youth in a basket : Oh you Panderly Rascals, there's a knot : a gin, a packe, a conspiracie against me : Now shall the diuel be sham'd. What wife I say : Come, come forth : behold what honest next cloathes you send forth to bleaching.

Page. Why, this passes M. *Ford*: you are not to goe loose any longer, you must be pinnion'd.

Euans. Why, this is Lunaticks: this is madde, as a mad dogge.

Shall. Indeed M. *Ford*, this is not well indeed.

Ford. So say I too Sir, come hither Mistris *Ford*, Mistris *Ford*, the honest woman, the modest wife, the vertuous creature, that hath the iealous foole to her husband: I suspect without cause (Mistris) do I?

Mist. Ford. Heauen be my witnesse you doe, if you suspect me in any dishouesty.

Ford. Well said Brazon-face, hold it out: Come forth sirrah.

Page. This passes.

Mist. Ford. Are you not asham'd, let the cloths alone.

Ford. I shall finde you anon.

Eua. 'Tis vnreasonable; will you take vp your wiues cloathes? Come, away.

Ford. Empty the basket I say.

M. Ford. Why man, why?

Ford. Master *Page*, as I am a man, there was one conuay'd out of my house yesterday in this basket: why may not he be there againe, in my house I am sure he is: my Intelligence is true, my iealousie is reasonable, pluck me out all the linnen.

Mist. Ford. If you find a man there, he shall dye a Fleas death.

Page. Heer's no man.

Shal. By my fidelity this is not well Mr. *Ford*: This wrongs you.

Euans. Mr *Ford*, you must pray, and not follow the imaginations of your owne heart: this is iealousies.

Ford. Well, hee's not heere I seeke for.

Page. No, nor no where else but in your braine.

Ford. Helpe to search my house this one time: if I find not what I seeke, shew no colour for my extremity: Let me for euer be your Table-sport: Let them say of me, as iealous as *Ford*, that search'd a hollow Wall-nut for his wiues Lemman. Satisfie me once more, once more serch with me.

M. Ford. What hoa (Mistris *Page*,) come you and the old woman downe: my husband will come into the Chamber.

Ford. Old woman? what old womans that?

M. Ford. Why it is my maids Aunt of *Brainford*.

Ford. A witch, a Queane, an olde couzening queane: Haue I not forbid her my house. She comes of errands do's she? We are simple men, wee doe not know what's brought to passe vnder the profession of Fortune-telling. She workes by Charmes, by Spels, by th'Figure, & such dawbry as this is, beyond our Element: wee know nothing. Come downe you Witch, you Hagge you, come downe I say.

Mist. Ford. Nay, good sweet husband, good Gentlemen, let him strike the old woman.

Mist. Page. Come mother *Prat*, Come giue me your hand.

Ford. Ile *Prat*-her: Out of my doore, you Witch, you Ragge, you Baggage, you Poulcat, you Runnion, out, out: Ile coniure you, Ile fortune-tell you.

Mist. Page. Are you not asham'd?
I thinke you haue kill'd the poore woman.

Mist. Ford. Nay he will do it, 'tis a goodly credite for you.

Ford. Hang her witch.

Eua. By yea, and no, I thinke the o'man is a witch indeede: I like not when a o'man has a great peard; I spie a great peard vnder his muffler.

Ford. Will you follow Gentlemen, I beseech you follow: see but the issue of my iealousie: If I cry out thus vpon no traile, neuer trust me when I open againe.

Page. Let's obey his humour a little further:
Come Gentlemen.

Mist. Page. Trust me he beate him most pittifully.

Mist. Ford. Nay by th'Masse that he did not: he beate him most vnpittifully, me thought.

Mist. Page. Ile haue the cudgell hallow'd, and hung ore the Altar, it hath done meritorious seruice.

Mist. Ford. What thinke you? May we with the warrant of woman-hood, and the witnesse of a good conscience, pursue him with any further reuenge?

M. Page. The spirit of wantonnesse is sure scar'd out of him, if the diuell haue him not in fee-simple, with fine and recouery, he will neuer (I thinke) in the way of waste, attempt vs againe.

Mist. Ford. Shall we tell our husbands how wee haue seru'd him?

Mist. Page. Yes, by all meanes: if it be but to scrape the figures out of your husbands braines: if they can find in their hearts, the poore vnuertuous fat Knight shall be any further afflicted, wee two will still bee the ministers.

Mist. Ford. Ile warrant, they'l haue him publiquely sham'd, and me thinkes there would be no period to the iest, should he not be publikely sham'd.

Mist. Page. Come, to the Forge with it, then shape it: I would not haue things coole.   *Exeunt*

Scena Tertia.

Enter Host and Bardolfe.

Bar. Sir, the Germane desires to haue three of your horses: the Duke himselfe will be to morrow at Court, and they are going to meet him.

Host. What Duke should that be comes so secretly? I heare not of him in the Court: let mee speake with the Gentlemen, they speake English?

Bar. I Sir? Ile call him to you.

Host. They shall haue my horses, but Ile make them pay: Ile sauce them, they haue had my houses a week at commaund: I haue turn'd away my other guests, they must come off, Ile sawce them, come.   *Exeunt*

Scena Quarta.

Enter Page, Ford, Mistris Page, Mistris Ford, and Euans.

Eua. 'Tis one of the best discretions of a o'man as euer I did looke vpon.

Page. And did he send you both these Letters at an instant?

Mist. Page. VVithin a quarter of an houre.

Ford. Pardon me (wife) henceforth do what ÿ wilt: I rather will suspect the Sunne with gold,
Then thee with wantonnes: Now doth thy honor stand

(In

(In him that was of late an Heretike)
As firme as faith.

Page. 'Tis well, 'tis well, no more:
Be not as extreme in submission, as in offence,
But let our plot go forward: Let our wiues
Yet once againe (to make vs publike sport)
Appoint a meeting with this old fat-fellow,
Where we may take him, and disgrace him for it.

Ford. There is no better way then that they spoke of.

Page. How? to send him word they'll meete him in the Parke at midnight? Fie, fie, he'll neuer come.

Eua. You say he has bin throwne in the Riuers: and has bin greeuously peaten, as an old o'man: me-thinkes there should be terrors in him, that he should not come: Me-thinkes his flesh is punish'd, hee shall haue no desires.

Page. So thinke I too.

M. Ford. Deuise but how you'l vse him whē he comes, And let vs two deuise to bring him thether.

Mis. Page. There is an old tale goes, that *Herne* the Hunter (sometime a keeper heere in Windsor Forrest) Doth all the winter time, at still midnight
Walke round about an Oake, with great rag'd-hornes,
And there he blasts the tree, and takes the cattle,
And make milch-kine yeeld blood, and shakes a chaine
In a most hideous and dreadfull manner.
You haue heard of such a Spirit, and well you know
The superstitious idle-headed-Eld
Receiu'd, and did deliuer to our age
This tale of *Herne* the Hunter, for a truth.

Page. Why yet there want not many that do feare
In deepe of night to walke by this Hernes Oake:
But what of this?

Mist. Ford. Marry this is our deuise,
That *Falstaffe* at that Oake shall meete with vs.

Page. Well, let it not be doubted but he'll come,
And in this shape, when you haue brought him thether,
What shall be done with him? What is your plot?

Mist. Pa. That likewise haue we thoght vpon: & thus:
Nan Page (my daughter) and my little sonne,
And three or foure more of their growth, wee'l dresse
Like Vrchins, Ouphes, and Fairies, greene and white,
With rounds of waxen Tapers on their heads,
And rattles in their hands; vpon a sodaine,
As *Falstaffe*, shee, and I, are newly met,
Let them from forth a saw-pit rush at once
With some diffused song: Vpon their sight
We two, in great amazednesse will flye:
Then let them all encircle him about,
And Fairy-like to pinch the vncleane Knight;
And aske him why that houre of Fairy Reuell,
In their so sacred pathes, he dares to tread
In shape prophane.

Ford. And till he tell the truth,
Let the supposed Fairies pinch him, sound,
And burne him with their Tapers.

Mist. Page. The truth being knowne,
We'll all present our selues; dis-horne the spirit,
And mocke him home to Windsor.

Ford. The children must
Be practis'd well to this, or they'd neu'r doo't.

Eua. I will teach the children their behauiours: and I will be like a Iacke-an-Apes also, to burne the Knight with my Taber.

Ford. That will be excellent,
Ile go buy them vizards.

Mist. Page. My *Nan* shall be the Queene of all the Fairies, finely attired in a robe of white.

Page. That silke will I go buy, and in that time Shall M. *Slender* steale my *Nan* away,
And marry her at *Eaton:* go, send to *Falstaffe* straight.

Ford. Nay, Ile to him againe in name of *Broome*,
Hee'l tell me all his purpose: sure hee'l come.

Mist. Page. Feare not you that: Go get vs properties And tricking for our Fayries.

Euans. Let vs about it,
It is admirable pleasures, and ferry honest knaueries.

Mist. Page. Go *Mist. Ford*,
Send quickly to Sir *Iohn*, to know his minde:
Ile to the Doctor, he hath my good will,
And none but he to marry with *Nan Page:*
That *Slender* (though well landed) is an Ideot:
And he, my husband best of all affects:
The Doctor is well monied, and his friends
Potent at Court: he, none but he shall haue her,
Though twenty thousand worthier come to craue her.

Scena Quinta.

Enter Host, Simple, Falstaffe, Bardolfe, Euans, Caius, Quickly.

Host. What wouldst thou haue? (Boore) what? (thick skin) speake, breathe, discusse: breefe, short, quicke, snap.

Simp. Marry Sir, I come to speake with Sir *Iohn Falstaffe* from M. *Slender*.

Host. There's his Chamber, his House, his Castle, his standing-bed and truckle-bed: 'tis painted about with the story of the Prodigall, fresh and new: go, knock and call: hee'l speake like an Anthropophaginian vnto thee: Knocke I say.

Simp. There's an olde woman, a fat woman gone vp into his chamber: Ile be so bold as stay Sir till she come downe: I come to speake with her indeed.

Host. Ha? A fat woman? The Knight may be robb'd: Ile call. Bully-Knight, Bully Sir *Iohn:* speake from thy Lungs Military: Art thou there? It is thine Host, thine Ephesian cals.

Fal. How now, mine Host?

Host. Here's a Bohemian-Tartar taries the comming downe of thy fat-woman: Let her descend (Bully) let her descend: my Chambers are honourable: Fie, priuacy? Fie.

Fal. There was (mine Host) an old-fat-woman euen now with me, but she's gone.

Simp. Pray you Sir, was't not the Wise-woman of *Brainford?*

Fal. I marry was it (Mussel-shell) what would you with her?

Simp. My Master (Sir) my master *Slender*, sent to her seeing her go thorough the streets, to know (Sir) whether one *Nim* (Sir) that beguil'd him of a chaine, had the chaine, or no.

Fal. I spake with the old woman about it.

Sim. And what sayes she, I pray Sir?

Fal. Marry shee sayes, that the very same man that beguil'd Master *Slender* of his Chaine, cozon'd him of it.

Simp. I would I could haue spoken with the Woman her

The Merry Wiues of Windsor.

her selfe, I had other things to haue spoken with her too, from him.

Fal. What are they? let vs know.

Host. I: come: quicke.

Fal. I may not conceale them (Sir.)

Host. Conceale them, or thou di'st.

Sim. Why sir, they were nothing but about Mistris *Anne Page*, to know if it were my Masters fortune to haue her, or no.

Fal. 'Tis, 'tis his fortune.

Sim. What Sir?

Fal. To haue her, or no: goe; say the woman told me so.

Sim. May I be bold to say so Sir?

Fal. I Sir: like who more bold.

Sim. I thanke your worship: I shall make my Master glad with these tydings.

Host. Thou are clearkly: thou art clearkly (Sir *Iohn*) was there a wise woman with thee?

Fal. I that there was (mine *Host*) one that hath taught me more wit, then euer I learn'd before in my life: and I paid nothing for it neither, but was paid for my learning.

Bar. Out alas (Sir) cozonage: meere cozonage.

Host. Where be my horses? speake well of them varletto.

Bar. Run away with the cozoners: for so soone as I came beyond *Eaton*, they threw me off, from behinde one of them, in a slough of myre; and set spurres, and away; like three *Germane*-diuels; three *Doctor Faustasses*.

Host. They are gone but to meete the Duke (villaine) doe not say they be fled: *Germanes* are honest men.

Euan. Where is mine *Host*?

Host. What is the matter Sir?

Euan. Haue a care of your entertainments: there is a friend of mine come to Towne, tels mee there is three Cozen-Iermans, that has cozend all the *Hosts* of *Readins*, of *Maidenhead*, of *Cole-brooke*, of horses and money: I tell you for good will (looke you) you are wise, and full of gibes, and vlouting-stocks: and 'tis not conuenient you should be cozoned. Fare you well.

Cai. Ver' is mine *Host de Iarteere*?

Host. Here (Master *Doctor*) in perplexitie, and doubtfull delemma.

Cai. I cannot tell vat is dat: but it is tell-a-me, dat you make grand preparation for a Duke *de Iamanie*: by my trot: der is no Duke that the Court is know, to come: I tell you for good will: adieu.

Host. Huy and cry, (villaine) goe: assist me Knight, I am vndone: fly, run: huy, and cry (villaine) I am vndone.

Fal. I would all the world might be cozond, for I haue beene cozond and beaten too: if it should come to the eare of the Court, how I haue beene transformed; and how my transformation hath beene washd, and cudgeld, they would melt mee out of my fat drop by drop, and liquor Fishermens-boots with me: I warrant they would whip me with their fine wits, till I were as crest-falne as a dride-peare: I neuer prosper'd, since I forswore my selfe at *Primero*: well, if my winde were but long enough; I would repent: Now? Whence come you?

Qui. From the two parties forsooth.

Fal. The Diuell take one partie, and his Dam the other: and so they shall be both bestowed; I haue suf-

fer'd more for their sakes; more then the villanous inconstancy of mans disposition is able to beare.

Qui. And haue not they suffer'd? Yes, I warrant; speciously one of them; Mistris *Ford* (good heart) is beaten blacke and blew, that you cannot see a white spot about her.

Fal. What tell'st thou mee of blacke, and blew? I was beaten my selfe into all the colours of the Raine-bow: and I was like to be apprehended for the Witch of *Braineford*, but that my admirable dexteritie of wit, my counterfeiting the action of an old woman deliuer'd me, the knaue Constable had set me ith' Stocks, ith' common Stocks, for a Witch.

Qu. Sir: let me speake with you in your Chamber, you shall heare how things goe, and (I warrant) to your content: here is a Letter will say somewhat: (goodhearts) what a-doe here is to bring you together? Sure, one of you do's not serue heauen well, that you are so crost'd.

Fal. Come vp into my Chamber. *Exeunt.*

Scena Sexta.

Enter Fenton, Host.

Host. Master *Fenton*, talke not to mee, my minde is heauy: I will giue ouer all.

Fen. Yet heare me speake: assist me in my purpose,
And (as I am a gentleman) ile giue thee
A hundred pound in gold, more then your losse.

Host. I will heare you (Master *Fenton*) and I will (at the least) keepe your counsell.

Fen. From time to time, I haue acquainted you
With the deare loue I beare to faire *Anne Page*,
Who, mutually, hath answer'd my affection,
(So farre forth, as her selfe might be her chooser)
Euen to my wish; I haue a letter from her
Of such contents, as you will wonder at;
The mirth whereof, so larded with my matter,
That neither (singly) can be manifested
Without the shew of both: fat *Falstaffe*
Hath a great Scene; the image of the iest
Ile show you here at large (harke good mine *Host*:)
To night at *Hernes-Oke*, iust 'twixt twelue and one,
Must my sweet *Nan* present the *Faerie-Queene*:
The purpose why, is here: in which disguise
While other Iests are something ranke on foote,
Her father hath commanded her to slip
Away with *Slender*, and with him, at *Eaton*
Immediately to Marry: She hath consented: Now Sir,
Her Mother, (euen strong against that match
And firme for Doctor *Caius*) hath appointed
That he shall likewise shuffle her away,
While other sports are tasking of their mindes,
And at the *Deanry*, where a *Priest* attends
Strait marry her: to this her Mothers plot
She seemingly obedient) likewise hath
Made promise to the *Doctor*: Now, thus it rests,
Her Father meanes she shall be all in white;
And in that habit, when *Slender* sees his time
To take her by the hand, and bid her goe,
She shall goe with him: her Mother hath intended
(The better to deuote her to the *Doctor*;
For they must all be mask'd, and vizarded)

That

That quaint in greene, she shall be loose en-roab'd,
With Ribonds-pendant, flaring 'bout her head;
And when the Doctor spies his vantage ripe,
To pinch her by the hand, and on that token,
The maid hath giuen consent to go with him.

Host. Which meanes she to deceiue? Father, or Mother.

Fen. Both (my good Host) to go along with me:
And heere it rests, that you'l procure the Vicar
To stay for me at Church, 'twixt twelue, and one,
And in the lawfull name of marrying,
To giue our hearts vnited ceremony.

Host. Well, husband your deuice; Ile to the Vicar,
Bring you the Maid, you shall not lacke a Priest.

Fen. So shall I euermore be bound to thee;
Besides, Ile make a present recompence.   *Exeunt*

Actus Quintus. Scœna Prima.

Enter Falstoffe, Quickly, and Ford.

Fal. Pre'thee no more pratling: go, Ile hold, this is the third time: I hope good lucke lies in odde numbers: Away, go, they say there is Diuinity in odde Numbers, either in natiuity, chance, or death: away.

Qui. Ile prouide you a chaine, and Ile do what I can to get you a paire of hornes.

Fal. Away I say, time weares, hold vp your head & mince. How now M. Broome? Master Broome, the matter will be knowne to night, or neuer. Bee you in the Parke about midnight, at Hernes-Oake, and you shall see wonders.

Ford. Went you not to her yesterday (Sir) as you told me you had appointed?

Fal. I went to her (Master *Broome*) as you see, like a poore-old-man, but I came from her (Master *Broome*) like a poore-old-woman; that same knaue (*Ford* hir husband) hath the finest mad diuell of iealousie in him (Master *Broome*) that euer gouern'd Frensie. I will tell you, he beate me greeuously, in the shape of a woman: (for in the shape of Man (Master *Broome*) I feare not Goliah with a Weauers beame, because I know also, life is a Shuttle) I am in hast, go along with mee, Ile tell you all (Master *Broome*:) since I pluckt Geese, plaide Trewant, and whipt Top, I knew not what 'twas to be beaten, till lately. Follow mee, Ile tell you strange things of this knaue *Ford*, on whom to night I will be reuenged, and I will deliuer his wife into your hand. Follow, straunge things in hand (M. *Broome*) follow.   *Exeunt.*

Scena Secunda.

Enter Page, Shallow, Slender.

Page. Come, come: wee'll couch i'th Castle-ditch, till we see the light of our Fairies. Remember son *Slender*, my

Slen. I forsooth, I haue spoke with her, & we haue a nay-word, how to know one another. I come to her in white, and cry Mum; she cries Budget, and by that we know one another.

Shal. That's good too: But what needes either your Mum, or her Budget? The white will decipher her well enough. It hath strooke ten a'clocke.

Page. The night is darke, Light and Spirits will become it wel: Heauen prosper our sport. No man means euill but the deuill, and we shal know him by his hornes. Lets away: follow me.   *Exeunt.*

Scena Tertia.

Enter Mist. Page, Mist. Ford, Caius.

Mist. Page. Mr Doctor, my daughter is in green, when you see your time, take her by the hand, away with her to the Deanerie, and dispatch it quickly: go before into the Parke: we two must go together.

Cai. I know vat I haue to do, adieu.

Mist. Page. Fare you well (Sir:) my husband will not reioyce so much at the abuse of *Falstaffe*, as he will chafe at the Doctors marrying my daughter: But 'tis no matter; better a little chiding, then a great deale of heart-breake.

Mist. Ford. Where is *Nan* now? and her troop of Fairies? and the Welch-deuill Herne?

Mist. Page. They are all couch'd in a pit hard by Hernes Oake, with obscur'd Lights; which at the very instant of *Falstaffes* and our meeting, they will at once display to the night.

Mist. Ford. That cannot choose but amaze him.

Mist. Page. If he be not amaz'd he will be mock'd: If he be amaz'd, he will euery way be mock'd.

Mist. Ford. Wee'll betray him finely.

Mist. Page. Against such Lewdsters, and their lechery, Those that betray them, do no treachery.

Mist. Ford. The houre drawes-on: to the Oake, to the Oake.   *Exeunt,*

Scena Quarta.

Enter Euans and Fairies.

Euans. Trib, trib Fairies: Come, and remember your parts: be pold (I pray you) follow me into the pit, and when I giue the watch-'ords, do as I pid you : Come, come, trib, trib.   *Exeunt*

Scena Quinta.

Enter Falstaffe, Mistris Page, Mistris Ford, Euans, Anne Page, Fairies, Page, Ford, Quickly, Slender, Fenton, Caius, Pistoll.

Fal. The Windsor-bell hath stroke twelue: the Minute drawes-on: Now the hot-bloodied-Gods assist me: Remember *Ioue*, thou was't a Bull for thy *Europa*, Loue set on thy hornes. O powerfull Loue, that in some respects makes a Beast a Man: in som other, a Man a beast. You were also (Iupiter) a Swan, for the loue of *Leda*: O

omnipotent

omnipotent Loue, how nere the God drew to the complexion of a Goose: a fault done first in the forme of a beast,(O Ioue, a beastly fault:) and then another fault, in the semblance of a Fowle, thinke on't (Ioue) a fowle-fault. When Gods haue hot backes, what shall poore men do? For me, I am heere a Windsor Stagge, and the fattest (I thinke) i'th Forrest. Send me a coole rut-time (Ioue) or who can blame me to pisse my Tallow? Who comes heere? my Doe?

  M.Ford. Sir *Iohn?* Art thou there (my Deere?) My male-Deere?

  Fal. My Doe, with the blacke Scut? Let the skie raine Potatoes: let it thunder, to the tune of Greene-sleeues, haile-kissing Comfits, and snow Eringoes: Let there come a tempest of prouocation, I will shelter mee heere.

  M.Ford. Mistris *Page* is come with me(sweet hart.)

  Fal. Diuide me like a brib'd-Bucke,each a Haunch: I will keepe my sides to my selfe, my shoulders for the fellow of this walke; and my hornes I bequeath your husbands. Am I a Woodman, ha? Speake I like *Herne* the Hunter? Why, now is Cupid a child of conscience, he makes restitution. As I am a true spirit, welcome.

  M.Page. Alas, what noise?

  M.Ford. Heauen forgiue our sinnes.

  Fal. What should this be?

  M.Ford. M.Page. Away, away.

  Fal. I thinke the diuell wil not haue me damn'd, Least the oyle that's in me should set hell on fire; He would neuer else crosse me thus.

Enter Fairies.

  Qui. Fairies blacke, gray, greene, and white,
You Moone-shine reuellers,and shades of night.
You Orphan heires of fixed destiny,
Attend your office, and your quality.
Crier Hob-goblyn, make the Fairy Oyes.

  Pist. Elues, list your names: Silence you aiery toyes.
Cricket, to Windsor-chimnies shalt thou leape;
Where fires thou find'st vnrak'd, and hearths vnswept,
There pinch the Maids as blew as Bill-berry,
Our radiant Queene, hates Sluts, and Sluttery.

  Fal. They are Fairies, he that speaks to them shall die, Ile winke, and couch: No man their workes must eie.

  Eu. Wher's *Bede?* Go you, and where you find a maid That ere she sleepe has thrice her prayers said,
Raise vp the Organs of her fantasie,
Sleepe she as sound as carelesse infancie,
But those as sleepe, and thinke not on their sins,
Pinch them armes, legs, backes, shoulders, sides, & shins.

  Qu. About, about:
Search Windsor Castle (Elues) within, and out.
Strew good lucke (Ouphes) on euery sacred roome,
That it may stand till the perpetuall doome,
In state as wholsome, as in state 'tis fit,
Worthy the Owner, and the Owner it.
The seuerall Chaires of Order, looke you scowre
With iuyce of Balme; and euery precious flowre,
Each faire Instalment, Coate, and seu'rall Crest,
With loyall Blazon, euermore be blest.
And Nightly-meadow-Fairies, looke you sing
Like to the *Garters*-Compasse, in a ring,
Th'expressure that it beares: Greene let it be,
Mote fertile-fresh then all the Field to see:
And, *Hony Soit Qui Mal-y-Pence*, write
In Emrold-tuffes, Flowres purple, blew, and white,
Like Saphire-pearle, and rich embroiderie,
Buckled below faire Knight-hoods bending knee;
Fairies vse Flowres for their characterie.
Away, disperse: But till 'tis one a clocke,
Our Dance of Custome, round about the Oke
Of *Herne* the Hunter, let vs not forget. (set:

  Euan. Pray you lock hand in hand: your selues in order And twenty glow-wormes shall our Lanthornes bee To guide our Measure round about the Tree.
But stay, I smell a man of middle earth.

  Fal. Heauens defend me from that Welsh Fairy, Least he transforme me to a peece of Cheese.

  Pist. Vilde worme, thou wast ore-look'd euen in thy birth.

  Qu. With Triall-fire touch me his finger end:
If he be chaste, the flame will backe descend
And turne him to no paine: but if he start,
It is the flesh of a corrupted hart.

  Pist. A triall, come.

  Eua. Come: will this wood take fire?

  Fal. Oh, oh, oh.

  Qui. Corrupt, corrupt, and tainted in desire.
About him (Fairies) sing a scornfull rime,
And as you trip, still pinch him to your time.

The Song.

Fie on sinnefull phantasie: Fie on Lust, and Luxurie:
Lust is but a bloudy fire, kindled with vnchaste desire,
    Fed in heart whose flames aspire,
    As thoughts do blow them higher and higher.
Pinch him (Fairies) mutually: Pinch him for his villanie.
    Pinch him, and burne him, and turne him about,
    Till Candles, & Star-light, & Moone-shine be out.

  Page. Nay do not flye, I thinke we haue watcht you now: Will none but *Herne* the Hunter serue your turne?

  M.Page. I pray you come, hold vp the iest no higher. Now (good Sir *Iohn*) how like you *Windsor* wiues? See you these husband? Do not these faire yoakes Become the Forrest better then the Towne?

  Ford. Now Sir, whose a Cuckold now?
M: *Broome, Falstaffes* a Knaue, a Cuckoldly knaue, Heere are his hornes Master *Broome*:
And Master *Broome*, he hath enioyed nothing of *Fords*, but his Buck-basket, his cudgell, and twenty pounds of money, which must be paid to M: *Broome*, his horses are arrested for it, M: *Broome*.

  M.Ford. Sir *Iohn*, we haue had ill lucke: wee could neuer meete: I will neuer take you for my Loue againe, but I will alwayes count you my Deere.

  Fal. I do begin to perceiue that I am made an Asse.

  Ford. I, and an Oxe too: both the proofes are extant.

  Fal. And these are not Fairies:
I was three or foure times in the thought they were not Fairies, and yet the guiltinesse of my minde, the sodaine surprize of my powers, droue the grossenesse of the foppery into a receiu'd beleefe, in despight of the teeth of all rime and reason, that they were Fairies. See now how wit may be made a Iacke-a-Lent, when 'tis vpon ill imployment.

  Euant. Sir *Iohn Falstaffe*, serue Got, and leaue your desires, and Fairies will not pinse you.

  Ford. Well said Fairy *Hugh*.

  Euans. And leaue you your iealouzies too, I pray you.

Ford.

Ford. I will neuer mistrust my wife againe, till thou art able to woo her in good English.

Fal. Haue I laid my braine in the Sun, and dri'de it, that it wants matter to preuent so grosse ore-reaching as this? Am I ridden with a Welch Goate too? Shal I haue a Coxcombe of Frize? Tis time I were choak'd with a peece of toasted Cheese.

Eu. Seese is not good to giue putter; your belly is al putter.

Fal. Seese, and Putter? Haue I liu'd to stand at the taunt of one that makes Fritters of English? This is enough to be the decay of lust and late-walking through the Realme.

Mist.Page. Why Sir *Iohn*, do you thinke though wee would haue thrust vertue out of our hearts by the head and shoulders, and haue giuen our selues without scruple to hell, that euer the deuill could haue made you our delight?

Ford. What, a hodge-pudding? A bag of flax?

Mist.Page. A puft man?

Page. Old, cold, wither'd, and of intollerable entrailes?

Ford. And one that is as slanderous as Sathan?

Page. And as poore as Iob?

Ford. And as wicked as his wife?

Euan. And giuen to Fornications, and to Tauernes, and Sacke, and Wine, and Metheglins, and to drinkings and swearings, and starings? Pribles and prables?

Fal. Well, I am your Theame: you haue the start of me, I am deiected: I am not able to answer the Welch Flannell, Ignorance it selfe is a plummet ore me, vse me as you will.

Ford. Marry Sir, wee'l bring you to Windsor to one Mr *Broome*, that you haue cozon'd of money, to whom you should haue bin a Pander: ouer and aboue that you haue suffer'd, I thinke, to repay that money will be a biting affliction.

Page. Yet be cheerefull Knight: thou shalt eat a posset to night at my house, wher I will desire thee to laugh at my wife, that now laughes at thee: Tell her Mr *Slender* hath married her daughter.

Mist.Page. Doctors doubt that;
If *Anne Page* be my daughter, she is (by this) Doctour *Caius* wife.

Slen. Whoa hoe, hoe, Father *Page*.

Page. Sonne? How now? How now Sonne,
Haue you dispatch'd?

Slen. Dispatch'd? Ile make the best in' Glostershire know on't: would I were hang'd la, else.

Page. Of what sonne?

Slen. I came yonder at *Eaton* to marry Mistris *Anne Page*, and she's a great lubberly boy. If it had not bene i'th Church, I would haue swing'd him, or hee should haue swing'd me. If I did not thinke it had beene *Anne Page*, would I might neuer stirre, and 'tis a Post-masters Boy.

Page. Vpon my life then, you tooke the wrong.

Slen. What neede you tell me that? I think so, when I tooke a Boy for a Girle: If I had bene married to him, (for all he was in womans apparrell) I would not haue had him.

Page. Why this is your owne folly,
Did not I tell you how you should know my daughter,
By her garments?

Slen. I went to her in greene, and cried Mum, and she cride budget, as *Anne* and I had appointed, and yet it was not *Anne*, but a Post-masters boy.

Mist.Page. Good *George* be not angry, I knew of your purpose: turn'd my daughter into white, and indeede she is now with the Doctor at the Deanrie, and there married.

Cai. Ver is Mistris *Page*: by gar I am cozened, I ha married oon Garsoon, a boy; oon pesant, by gar. A boy, it is not *An Page*, by gar, I am cozened.

M.Page. VVhy? did you take her in white?

Cai. I bee gar, and 'tis a boy: be gar, Ile raise all Windsor.

Ford. This is strange: Who hath got the right *Anne*?

Page. My heart misgiues me, here comes Mr *Fenton*.
How now Mr *Fenton*?

Anne. Pardon good father, good my mother pardon

Page. Now Mistris:
How chance you went not with Mr *Slender*?

M.Page. Why went you not with Mr Doctor, maid?

Fen. You do amaze her: heare the truth of it,
You would haue married her most shamefully,
Where there was no proportion held in loue:
The truth is, she and I (long since contracted)
Are now so sure that nothing can dissolue vs:
Th'offence is holy, that she hath committed,
And this deceit looses the name of craft,
Of disobedience, or vnduteous title,
Since therein she doth euitate and shun
A thousand irreligious cursed houres
Which forced marriage would haue brought vpon her.

Ford. Stand not amaz'd, here is no remedie:
In Loue, the heauens themselues do guide the state,
Money buyes Lands, and wiues are sold by fate.

Fal. I am glad, though you haue tane a special stand to strike at me, that your Arrow hath glanc'd.

Page. Well, what remedy? *Fenton*, heauen giue thee ioy, what cannot be eschew'd, must be embrac'd.

Fal. When night-dogges run, all sorts of Deere are chac'd.

Mist.Page. Well, I will muse no further: Mr *Fenton*,
Heauen giue you many, many merry dayes:
Good husband, let vs euery one go home,
And laugh this sport ore by a Countrie fire,
Sir *Iohn* and all.

Ford. Let it be so (Sir *Iohn*:)
To Master *Broome*, you yet shall hold your word,
For he, to night, shall lye with Mistris *Ford*: *Exeunt.*

FINIS.

MEASVRE, For Measure.

Actus primus, Scena prima.

Enter Duke, Escalus, Lords.

Duke. Escalus.

Esc. My Lord.

Duk. Of Gouernment, the properties to vn-fold,
Would seeme in me t'affect speech & discourse,
Since I am put to know, that your owne Science
Exceedes (in that) the lists of all aduice
My strength can giue you: Then no more remaines
But that, to your sufficiency, as your worth is able,
And let them worke: The nature of our People,
Our *Cities Institutions*, and the Termes
For Common Iustice, y'are as pregnant in
As Art, and practise, hath inriched any
That we remember: There is our Commission,
From which, we would not haue you warpe; call hither,
I say, bid come before vs *Angelo*:
What figure of vs thinke you, he will beare.
For you must know, we haue with speciall soule
Elected him our absence to supply;
Lent him our terror, drest him with our loue,
And giuen his Deputation all the Organs
Of our owne powre: What thinke you of it?

Esc. If any in *Vienna* be of worth
To vndergoe such ample grace, and honour,
It is Lord *Angelo*.

Enter Angelo.

Duk. Looke where he comes.

Ang. Alwayes obedient to your Graces will,
I come to know your pleasure.

Duke. Angelo:
There is a kinde of Character in thy life,
That to th'obseruer, doth thy history
Fully vnfold: Thy selfe, and thy belongings
Are not thine owne so proper, as to waste
Thy selfe vpon thy vertues; they on thee:
Heauen doth with vs, as we, with Torches doe,
Not light them for themselues: For if our vertues
Did not goe forth of vs, 'twere all alike
As if we had them not: Spirits are not finely toucht'd,
But to fine issues: nor nature neuer lends
The smallest scruple of her excellence,
But like a thrifty goddesse, she determines
Her selfe the glory of a creditour,
Both thanks, and vse; but I do bend my speech
To one that can my part in him aduertise;
Hold therefore *Angelo*:
In our remoue, be thou at full, our selfe:
Mortallitie and Mercie in *Vienna*
Liue in thy tongue, and heart: Old *Escalus*
Though first in question, is thy secondary.
Take thy Commission.

Ang. Now good my Lord
Let there be some more test, made of my mettle,
Before so noble, and so great a figure
Be stamp't vpon it.

Duk. No more euasion:
We haue with a leauen'd, and prepared choice
Proceeded to you; therefore take your honors:
Our haste from hence is of so quicke condition,
That it prefers it selfe, and leaues vnquestion'd
Matters of needfull value: We shall write to you
As time, and our concernings shall importune,
How it goes with vs, and doe looke to know
What doth befall you here. So fare you well:
To th' hopefull execution doe I leaue you,
Of your Commissions.

Ang. Yet giue leaue (my Lord,)
That we may bring you something on the way.

Duk. My haste may not admit it,
Nor neede you (on mine honor) haue to doe
With any scruple: your scope is as mine owne,
So to inforce, or qualifie the Lawes
As to your soule seemes good: Giue me your hand,
Ile priuily away: I loue the people,
But doe not like to stage me to their eyes:
Though it doe well, I doe not rellish well
Their lowd applause, and Aues vehement:
Nor doe I thinke the man of safe discretion
That do's affect it. Once more fare you well.

Ang. The heauens giue safety to your purposes.

Esc. Lead forth, and bring you backe in happinesse. *Exit.*

Duk. I thanke you, fare you well.

Esc. I shall desire you, Sir, to giue me leaue
To haue free speech with you; and it concernes me
To looke into the bottome of my place:
A powre I haue, but of what strength and nature,
I am not yet instructed.

Ang. 'Tis so with me: Let vs with-draw together,
And we may soone our satisfaction haue
Touching that point.

Esc. Ile wait vpon your honor. *Exeunt.*

F *Scœna*

Scena Secunda.

Enter Lucio, and two other Gentlemen.

Luc. If the *Duke*, with the other Dukes, come not to composition with the King of *Hungary*, why then all the Dukes fall vpon the King.

1. Gent. Heauen grant vs its peace, but not the King of *Hungaries*.

2. Gent. Amen.

Luc. Thou conclud'st like the Sanctimonious Pirat, that went to sea with the ten Commandements, but scrap'd one out of the Table.

2. Gent. Thou shalt not Steale?

Luc. I, that he raz'd.

1. Gent. Why? 'twas a commandement, to command the Captaine and all the rest from their functions: they put forth to steale: There's not a Souldier of vs all, that in the thankf-giuing before meate, do rallish the petition well, that praies for peace.

2. Gent. I neuer heard any Souldier dislike it.

Luc. I beleeue thee: for I thinke thou neuer was't where Grace was said.

2. Gent. No? a dozen times at least.

1. Gent. What? In meeter?

Luc. In any proportion, or in any language.

1. Gent. I thinke, or in any Religion.

Luc. I, why not? Grace, is Grace, despight of all controuersie: as for example; Thou thy selfe art a wicked villaine, despight of all Grace.

1. Gent. Well: there went but a paire of sheeres betweene vs.

Luc. I grant: as there may betweene the Lifts, and the Veluet. Thou art the List.

1. Gent. And thou the Veluet; thou art good veluet; thou'rt a three pil'd-peece I warrant thee: I had as liefe be a Lyst of an English Kersey, as be pil'd, as thou art pil'd, for a French Veluet. Do I speake feelingly now?

Luc. I thinke thou do'st: and indeed with most painfull feeling of thy speech: I will, out of thine owne confession, learne to begin thy health; but, whilst I liue forget to drinke after thee.

1. Gen. I think I haue done my selfe wrong, haue I not?

2. Gent. Yes, that thou hast; whether thou art tainted, or free. *Enter Bawde.*

Luc. Behold, behold, where Madam *Mitigation* comes. I haue purchas'd as many diseases vnder her Roofe, As come to

2. Gent. To what, I pray?

Luc. Iudge.

2. Gent. To three thousand Dollours a yeare.

1. Gent. I, and more.

Luc. A French crowne more.

1. Gent. Thou art alwayes figuring diseases in me; but thou art full of error, I am sound.

Luc. Nay, not (as one would say) healthy: but so sound, as things that are hollow; thy bones are hollow; Impiety has made a feast of thee.

1. Gent. How now, which of your hips has the most profound Ciatica?

Bawd. Well, well: there's one yonder arrested, and carried to prison, was worth fiue thousand of you all.

2. Gent. Who's that I pray 'thee?

Bawd. Marry Sir, that's *Claudio*, Signior *Claudio*.

1. Gent. Claudio to prison? 'tis not so.

Bawd. Nay, but I know 'tis so: I saw him arrested: saw him carried away: and which is more, within these three daies his head to be chop'd off.

Luc. But, after all this fooling, I would not haue it so: Art thou sure of this?

Bawd. I am too sure of it: and it is for getting Madam *Iulietta* with childe.

Luc. Beleeue me this may be: he promis'd to meete me two howres since, and he was euer precise in promise keeping.

2. Gent. Besides you know, it drawes somthing neere to the speech we had to such a purpose.

1. Gent. But most of all agreeing with the proclamatiō.

Luc. Away: let's goe learne the truth of it. *Exit.*

Bawd. Thus, what with the war; what with the sweat, what with the gallowes, and what with pouerty, I am Custom-shrunke. How now? what's the newes with you. *Enter Clowne.*

Clo. Yonder man is carried to prison.

Baw. Well: what has he done?

Clo. A Woman.

Baw. But what's his offence?

Clo. Groping for Trowts, in a peculiar Riuer.

Baw. What? is there a maid with child by him?

Clo. No: but there's a woman with maid by him: you haue not heard of the proclamation, haue you?

Baw. What proclamation, man?

Clow. All howses in the Suburbs of *Vienna* must bee pluck'd downe.

Bawd. And what shall become of those in the Citie?

Clow. They shall stand for seed: they had gon down to, but that a wise Burger put in for them.

Bawd. But shall all our houses of resort in the Suburbs be puld downe?

Clow. To the ground, Mistris.

Bawd. Why heere's a change indeed in the Commonwealth: what shall become of me?

Clow. Come: feare not you: good Counsellors lacke no Clients: though you change your place, you neede not change your Trade: Ile bee your Tapster still; courage, there will bee pitty taken on you; you that haue worne your eyes almost out in the seruice, you will bee considered.

Bawd. What's to doe heere, *Thomas* Tapster? let's withdraw?

Clo. Here comes Signior *Claudio*, led by the Prouost to prison: and there's Madam *Iuliet*. *Exeunt.*

Scena Tertia.

Enter Prouost, Claudio, Iuliet, Officers, Lucio, & 2. Gent.

Cla. Fellow, why do'st thou show me thus to th'world? Beare me to prison, where I am committed.

Pro. I do it not in euill disposition,
But from Lord *Angelo* by speciall charge.

Clau. Thus can the demy-god (Authority)
Make vs pay downe, for our offence, by waight
The words of heauen; on whom it will, it will,
On whom it will not (soe) yet still 'tis iust. (straint.

Luc. Why how now *Claudio*? whence comes this re-

Cla. From too much liberty, (my *Lucio*) Liberty
As surfet is the father of much fast,
So euery Scope by the immoderate vse
Turnes to restraint: Our Natures doe pursue

Like

Like Rats that rauyn downe their proper Bane,
A thirsty euill, and when we drinke, we die.

  Luc. If I could speake so wisely vnder an arrest, I would send for certaine of my Creditors: and yet, to say the truth, I had as lief haue the foppery of freedome, as the mortality of imprisonment: what's thy offence, *Claudio*?

  Cla. What (but to speake of) would offend againe.

  Luc. What, is't murder?

  Cla. No.

  Luc. Lecherie?

  Cla. Call it so.

  Pro. Away, Sir, you must goe.

  Cla. One word, good friend:
Lucio, a word with you.

  Luc. A hundred:
If they'll doe you any good: Is *Lechery* so look'd after?

  Cla. Thus stands it with me: vpon a true contract
I got possession of *Iulietas* bed,
You know the Lady, she is fast my wife,
Saue that we doe the denunciation lacke
Of outward Order. This we came not to,
Onely for propogation of a Dowre
Remaining in the Coffer of her friends,
From whom we thought it meet to hide our Loue
Till Time had made them for vs. But it chances
The stealth of our most mutuall entertainment
With Character too grosse, is writ on *Iuliet*.

  Luc. With childe, perhaps?

  Cla. Vnhappely, euen so.
And the new Deputie, now for the Duke,
Whether it be the fault and glimpse of newnes,
Or whether that the body publique, be
A horse whereon the Gouernor doth ride,
Who newly in the Seate, that it may know
He can command; lets it strait feele the spur:
Whether the Tirranny be in his place,
Or in his Eminence that fills it vp
I stagger in: But this new Gouernor
Awakes me all the inrolled penalties
Which haue (like vn-scowr'd Armor) hung by th' wall
So long, that ninteene Zodiacks haue gone round,
And none of them beene worne; and for a name
Now puts the drowsie and neglected Act
Freshly on me: 'tis surely for a name.

  Luc. I warrant it is: And thy head stands so tickle on thy shoulders, that a milke-maid, if she be in loue, may sigh it off: Send after the Duke, and appeale to him.

  Cla. I haue done so, but hee's not to be found.
I pre'thee (*Lucio*) doe me this kinde seruice:
This day, my sister should the Cloyster enter,
And there receiue her approbation.
Acquaint her with the danger of my state,
Implore her, in my voice, that she make friends
To the strict deputie: bid her selfe assay him,
I haue great hope in that: for in her youth
There is a prone and speechlesse dialect,
Such as moue men: beside, she hath prosperous Art
When she will play with reason, and discourse,
And well she can perswade.

  Luc. I pray shee may; aswell for the encouragement of the like, which else would stand vnder greeuous imposition: as for the enioying of thy life, who I would be sorry should bee thus foolishly lost, at a game of ticke-tacke: Ile to her.

  Cla. I thanke you good friend *Lucio*.

  Luc. Within two houres.

  Cla. Come Officer, away.   *Exeunt.*

Scena Quarta.

Enter Duke and Frier Thomas.

  Duk. No: holy Father, throw away that thought,
Beleeue not that the dribling dart of Loue
Can pierce a compleat bosome: why, I desire thee
To giue me secret harbour, hath a purpose
More graue, and wrinkled, then the aimes, and ends
Of burning youth.

  Fri. May your Grace speake of it?

  Duk. My holy Sir, none better knowes then you
How I haue euer lou'd the life remoued
And held in idle price, to haunt assemblies
Where youth, and cost, witlesse brauery keepes.
I haue deliuerd to Lord *Angelo*
(A man of stricture and firme abstinence)
My absolute power, and place here in *Vienna*,
And he supposes me trauaild to *Poland*,
(For so I haue strewd it in the common eare)
And so it is receiu'd: Now (pious Sir)
You will demand of me, why I do this.

  Fri. Gladly, my Lord.

  Duk. We haue strict Statutes, and most biting Laws,
(The needfull bits and curbes to headstrong weedes,)
Which for this foureteene yeares, we haue let slip,
Euen like an ore-growne Lyon in a Caue
That goes not out to prey: Now, as fond Fathers,
Hauing bound vp the threatning twigs of birch,
Onely to sticke it in their childrens sight,
For terror, not to vse: in time the rod
More mock'd, then fear'd: so our Decrees,
Dead to infliction, to themselues are dead,
And libertie, plucks Iustice by the nose;
The Baby beates the Nurse, and quite athwart
Goes all decorum.

  Fri. It rested in your Grace
To vnloose this tyde-vp Iustice, when you pleas'd:
And it in you more dreadfull would haue seem'd
Then in Lord *Angelo*.

  Duk. I doe feare: too dreadfull:
Sith 'twas my fault, to giue the people scope,
'T would be my tirranny to strike and gall them,
For what I bid them doe: For, we bid this be done
When euill deedes haue their permissiue passe,
And not the punishment: therefore indeede (my father)
I haue on *Angelo* impos'd the office,
Who may in th' ambush of my name, strike home,
And yet, my nature neuer in the fight
To do in slander: And to behold his sway
I will, as 'twere a brother of your Order,
Visit both Prince, and People: Therefore I pre'thee
Supply me with the habit, and instruct me
How I may formally in person beare
Like a true *Frier*: Moe reasons for this action
At our more leysure, shall I render you;
Onely, this one: Lord *Angelo* is precise,
Stands at a guard with Enuie: scarce confesses
That his blood flowes: or that his appetite
Is more to bread then stone: hence shall we see
If power change purpose: what our Seemers be.   *Exit.*

F 2   *Scœna*

Scena Quinta.

Enter Isabell and Francisca a Nun.

Isa. And haue you Nuns no farther priuiledges?
Nun. Are not these large enough?
Isa. Yes truely; I speake not as desiring more,
But rather wishing a more strict restraint
Vpon the Sisterstood, the Votarists of Saint *Clare*.
    Lucio within.
Luc. Hoa? peace be in this place.
Isa. Who's that which cals?
Nun. It is a mans voice: gentle *Isabella*
Turne you the key, and know his businesse of him;
You may; I may not: you are yet vnsworne:
When you haue vowd, you must not speake with men,
But in the presence of the *Prioresse*;
Then if you speake, you must not show your face;
Or if you show your face, you must not speake:
He cals againe: I pray you answere him.
Isa. Peace and prosperitie: who is't that cals?
Luc. Haile Virgin, (if you be) as those cheeke-Roses
Proclaime you are no lesse: can you so steed me,
As bring me to the sight of *Isabella*,
A Nouice of this place, and the faire Sister
To her vnhappie brother *Claudio*?
Isa. Why her vnhappy Brother? Let me aske,
The rather for I now must make you know
I am that *Isabella*, and his Sister.
Luc. Gentle & faire: your Brother kindly greets you;
Not to be weary with you; he's in prison.
Isa. Woe me; for what?
Luc. For that, which if my selfe might be his Iudge,
He should receiue his punishment, in thankes:
He hath got his friend with childe.
Isa. Sir, make me not your storie.
Luc. 'Tis true; I would not, though 'tis my familiar sin,
With Maids to seeme the Lapwing, and to iest
Tongue, far from heart: play with all Virgins so:
I hold you as a thing en-skied, and sainted,
By your renouncement, an immortall spirit
And to be talk'd with in sincerity,
As with a Saint.
Isa. You doe blaspheme the good, in mocking me.
Luc. Doe not beleeue it: fewnes, and truth; tis thus,
Your brother, and his louer haue embrac'd;
As those that feed, grow full: as blossoming Time
That from the seednes, the bare fallow brings
To teemiug foyson: euen so her plenteous wombe
Expresseth his full Tilth, and husbandry.
Isa. Some one with childe by him? my cosen *Iuliet*?
Luc. Is she your cosen?
Isa. Adoptedly, as schoole-maids change their names
By vaine, though apt affection.
Luc. She it is.
Isa. Oh, let him marry her.
Luc. This is the point.
The Duke is very strangely gone from hence;
Bore many gentlemen (my selfe being one)
In hand, and hope of action: but we doe learne,
By those that know the very Nerues of State,
His giuing-out, were of an infinite distance
From his true meant designe: vpon his place,
(And with full line of his authority)
Gouernes Lord *Angelo*; A man, whose blood
Is very snow-broth: one, who neuer feeles
The wanton stings, and motions of the sence;
But doth rebate, and blunt his naturall edge
With profits of the minde: Studie, and fast
He (to giue feare to vse, and libertie,
Which haue, for long, run-by the hideous law,
As Myce, by Lyons) hath pickt out an act,
Vnder whose heauy sence, your brothers life
Fals into forfeit: he arrests him on it,
And followes close the rigor of the Statute
To make him an example: all hope is gone,
Vnlesse you haue the grace, by your faire praier
To soften *Angelo*: And that's my pith of businesse
'Twixt you, and your poore brother.
Isa. Doth he so,
Seeke his life?
Luc. Has censur'd him already,
And as I heare, the Prouost hath a warrant
For's execution.
Isa. Alas: what poore
Abilitie's in me, to doe him good.
Luc. Assay the powre you haue.
Isa. My power? alas, I doubt.
Luc. Our doubts are traitors
And makes vs loose the good we oft might win,
By fearing to attempt: Goe to Lord *Angelo*
And let him learne to know, when Maidens sue
Men giue like gods: but when they weepe and kneele,
All their petitions, are as freely theirs
As they themselues would owe them.
Isa. Ile see what I can doe.
Luc. But speedily.
Isa. I will about it strait;
No longer staying, but to giue the Mother
Notice of my affaire: I humbly thanke you:
Commend me to my brother: soone at night
Ile send him certaine word of my successe.
Luc. I take my leaue of you.
Isa. Good sir, adieu. *Exeunt.*

Actus Secundus. Scœna Prima.

Enter Angelo, Escalus, and seruants, Iustice.

Ang. We must not make a scar-crow of the Law,
Setting it vp to feare the Birds of prey,
And let it keepe one shape, till custome make it
Their pearch, and not their terror.
Esc. I, but yet
Let vs be keene, and rather cut a little
Then fall, and bruise to death: alas, this gentleman
Whom I would saue, had a most noble father,
Let but your honour know
(Whom I beleeue to be most strait in vertue)
That in the working of your owne affections,
Had time coheard with Place, or place with wishing,
Or that the resolute acting of our blood
Could haue attain'd th'effect of your owne purpose,
Whether you had not sometime in your life
Er'd in this point, which now you censure him,
And puld the Law vpon you.
Ang. 'Tis one thing to be tempted (*Escalus*)
Another

Another thing to fall: I not deny
The Iury passing on the Prisoners life
May in the sworne-twelue haue a thiefe, or two
Guiltier then him they try; what's open made to Iustice,
That Iustice ceizes; What knowes the Lawes
That theeues do passe on theeues? 'Tis very pregnant,
The Iewell that we finde, we stoope, and take't,
Because we see it; but what we doe not see,
We tread vpon, and neuer thinke of it.
You may not so extenuate his offence,
For I haue had such faults; but rather tell me
When I, that censure him, do so offend,
Let mine owne Iudgement patterne out my death,
And nothing come in partiall. Sir, he must dye.

Enter Prouost.

Esc. Be it as your wisedome will.

Ang. Where is the *Prouost*?

Pro. Here if it like your honour.

Ang. See that *Claudio*
Be executed by nine to morrow morning,
Bring him his Confessor, let him be prepar'd,
For that's the vtmost of his pilgrimage.

Esc. Well: heauen forgiue him; and forgiue vs all:
Some rise by sinne, and some by vertue fall:
Some run from brakes of Ice, and answere none,
And some condemned for a fault alone.

Enter Elbow, Froth, Clowne, Officers.

Elb. Come, bring them away: if these be good people in a Common-weale, that doe nothing but vse their abuses in common houses, I know no law: bring them away.

Ang. How now Sir, what's your name? And what's the matter?

Elb. If it please your honour, I am the poore Dukes Constable, and my name is *Elbow*; I doe leane vpon Iustice Sir, and doe bring in here before your good honor, two notorious Benefactors.

Ang. Benefactors? Well: What Benefactors are they? Are they not Malefactors?

Elb. If it please your honour, I know not well what they are: But precise villaines they are, that I am sure of, and void of all prophanation in the world, that good Christians ought to haue.

Esc. This comes off well: here's a wise Officer.

Ang. Goe to: What quality are they of? *Elbow* is your name? Why do'st thou not speake *Elbow*?

Clo. He cannot Sir: he's out at Elbow.

Ang. What are you Sir?

Elb. He Sir: a Tapster Sir: parcell Baud: one that serues a bad woman: whose house Sir was (as they say) pluckt downe in the Suburbs: and now shee professes a hot-house; which, I thinke is a very ill house too.

Esc. How know you that?

Elb. My wife Sir? whom I detest before heauen, and your honour.

Esc. How? thy wife?

Elb. I Sir: whom I thanke heauen is an honest woman.

Esc. Do'st thou detest her therefore?

Elb. I say sir, I will detest my selfe also, as well as she, that this house, if it be not a Bauds house, it is pitty of her life, for it is a naughty house.

Esc. How do'st thou know that, Constable?

Elb. Marry sir, by my wife, who, if she had bin a woman Cardinally giuen, might haue bin accus'd in fornication, adultery, and all vncleanlinesse there.

Esc. By the womans meanes?

Elb. I sir, by Mistris *Ouer-dons* meanes: but as she spit in his face, so she defide him.

Clo. Sir, if it please your honor, this is not so.

Elb. Proue it before these varlets here, thou honorable man, proue it.

Esc. Doe you heare how he misplaces?

Clo. Sir, she came in great with childe: and longing (sauing your honors reuerence) for stew'd prewyns; sir, we had but two in the house, which at that very distant time stood, as it were in a fruit dish (a dish of some three pence; your honours haue seene such dishes) they are not China-dishes, but very good dishes.

Esc. Go too: go too: no matter for the dish sir.

Clo. No indeede sir not of a pin; you are therein in the right: but, to the point: As I say, this Mistris *Elbow*, being (as I say) with childe, and being great bellied, and longing (as I said) for prewyns: and hauing but two in the dish (as I said) Master *Froth* here, this very man, hauing eaten the rest (as I said) & (as I say) paying for them very honestly: for, as you know Master *Froth*, I could not giue you three pence againe.

Fro. No indeede.

Clo. Very well: you being then (if you be remembred) cracking the stones of the foresaid prewyns.

Fro. I, so I did indeede.

Clo. Why, very well: I telling you then (if you be remembred) that such a one, and such a one, were past cure of the thing you wot of, vnlesse they kept very good diet, as I told you.

Fro. All this is true.

Clo. Why very well then.

Esc. Come: you are a tedious foole: to the purpose: what was done to *Elbowes* wife, that hee hath cause to complaine of? Come me to what was done to her.

Clo. Sir, your honor cannot come to that yet.

Esc. No sir, nor I meane it not.

Clo. Sir, but you shall come to it, by your honours leaue: And I beseech you, looke into Master *Froth* here sir, a man of foure-score pound a yeare; whose father died at *Hallowmas*: Was't not at *Hallowmas* Master *Froth*?

Fro. Allhallond-Eue.

Clo. Why very well: I hope here be truthes: he Sir, sitting (as I say) in a lower chaire, Sir, 'twas in the bunch of Grapes, where indeede you haue a delight to sit, haue you not?

Fro. I haue so, because it is an open roome, and good for winter.

Clo. Why very well then: I hope here be truthes.

Ang. This will last out a night in *Russia*
When nights are longest there: Ile take my leaue,
And leaue you to the hearing of the cause;
Hoping youle finde good cause to whip them all. *Exit.*

Esc. I thinke no lesse: good morrow to your Lordship. Now Sir, come on: What was done to *Elbowes* wife, once more?

Clo. Once Sir? there was nothing done to her once.

Elb. I beseech you Sir, aske him what this man did to my wife.

Clo. I beseech your honor, aske me.

Esc. Well sir, what did this Gentleman to her?

Clo. I beseech you sir, looke in this Gentlemans face: good Master *Froth* looke vpon his honor; 'tis for a good purpose: doth your honor marke his face?

Esc. I sir, very well.

Clo. Nay, I beseech you marke it well.

Esc. Well, I doe so.

Clo. Doth your honor see any harme in his face?

Esc. Why no.

Clo. Ile be suppos'd vpon a booke, his face is the worst thing about him: good then: if his face be the worst thing about him, how could Master *Froth* doe the Constables wife any harme? I would know that of your honour.

Esc. He's in the right (Constable) what say you to it?

Elb. First, and it like you, the house is a respected house; next, this is a respected fellow; and his Mistris is a respected woman.

Clo. By this hand Sir, his wife is a more respected person then any of vs all.

Elb. Varlet, thou lyest; thou lyest wicked varlet: the time is yet to come that shee was euer respected with man, woman, or childe.

Clo. Sir, she was respected with him, before he married with her.

Esc. Which is the wiser here; *Iustice* or *Iniquitie*? Is this true?

Elb. O thou caytiffe: O thou varlet: O thou wicked *Hanniball*; I respected with her, before I was married to her? If euer I was respected with her, or she with me, let not your worship thinke mee the poore *Dukes* Officer: proue this, thou wicked *Hanniball*, or ile haue mine action of battry on thee.

Esc. If he tooke you a box 'oth'eare, you might haue your action of slander too.

Elb. Marry I thanke your good worship for it: what is't your Worships pleasure I shall doe with this wicked Caitiffe?

Esc. Truly Officer, because he hath some offences in him, that thou wouldst discouer, if thou couldst, let him continue in his courses, till thou knowst what they are.

Elb. Marry I thanke your worship for it: Thou seest thou wicked varlet now, what's come vpon thee. Thou art to continue now thou Varlet, thou art to continue.

Esc. Where were you borne, friend?

Froth. Here in *Vienna*, Sir.

Esc. Are you of fourescore pounds a yeere?

Froth. Yes, and't please you sir.

Esc. So: what trade are you of, sir?

Clo. A Tapster, a poore widdowes Tapster.

Esc. Your Mistris name?

Clo. Mistris *Ouer-don*.

Esc. Hath she had any more then one husband?

Clo. Nine, sir: *Ouer-don* by the last.

Esc. Nine? come hether to me, Master *Froth*; Master *Froth*, I would not haue you acquainted with Tapsters; they will draw you Master *Froth*, and you wil hang them: get you gon, and let me heare no more of you.

Fro. I thanke your worship: for mine owne part, I neuer come into any roome in a Tap-house, but I am drawne in.

Esc. Well: no more of it Master *Froth*: farewell: Come you hether to me, Mr. Tapster: what's your name Mr. Tapster?

Clo. Pompey.

Esc. What else?

Clo. Bum, Sir.

Esc. Troth, and your bum is the greatest thing about you, so that in the beastliest sence, you are *Pompey* the great; *Pompey*, you are partly a bawd, *Pompey*; howsoeuer you colour it in being a Tapster, are you not? come, tell me true, it shall be the better for you.

Clo. Truly sir, I am a poore fellow that would liue.

Esc. How would you liue *Pompey*? by being a bawd? what doe you thinke of the trade *Pompey*? is it a lawfull trade?

Clo. If the Law would allow it, sir.

Esc. But the Law will not allow it *Pompey*; nor it shall not be allowed in *Vienna*.

Clo. Do's your Worship meane to geld and splay all the youth of the City?

Esc. No, *Pompey*.

Clo. Truely Sir, in my poore opinion they will too't then: if your worship will take order for the drabs and the knaues, you need not to feare the bawds.

Esc. There is pretty orders beginning I can tell you: It is but heading, and hanging.

Clo. If you head, and hang all that offend that way but for ten yeare together; you'll be glad to giue out a Commission for more heads: if this law hold in *Vienna* ten yeare, ile rent the fairest house in it after three pence a Bay: if you liue to see this come to passe, say *Pompey* told you so.

Esc. Thanke you good *Pompey*; and in requitall of your prophesie, harke you: I aduise you let me not finde you before me againe vpon any complaint whatsoeuer; no, not for dwelling where you doe: if I doe *Pompey*, I shall beat you to your Tent, and proue a shrewd *Cæsar* to you: in plaine dealing *Pompey*, I shall haue you whipt; so for this time, *Pompey*, fare you well.

Clo. I thanke your Worship for your good counsell; but I shall follow it as the flesh and fortune shall better determine. Whip me? no, no, let Carman whip his Iade, The valiant heart's not whipt out of his trade. *Exit.*

Esc. Come hether to me, Master *Elbow*: come hither Master Constable: how long haue you bin in this place of Constable?

Elb. Seuen yeere, and a halfe sir.

Esc. I thought by the readinesse in the office, you had continued in it some time: you say seauen yeares together.

Elb. And a halfe sir.

Esc. Alas, it hath beene great paines to you: they do you wrong to put you so oft vpon't. Are there not men in your Ward sufficient to serue it?

Elb. 'Faith sir, few of any wit in such matters: as they are chosen, they are glad to choose me for them; I do it for some peece of money, and goe through with all.

Esc. Looke you bring mee in the names of some sixe or seuen, the most sufficient of your parish.

Elb. To your Worships house sir?

Esc. To my house: fare you well: what's a clocke, thinke you?

Iust. Eleuen, Sir.

Esc. I pray you home to dinner with me.

Iust. I humbly thanke you.

Esc. It grieues me for the death of *Claudio*
But there's no remedie:

Iust. Lord *Angelo* is seuere.

Esc. It is but needfull.
Mercy is not it selfe, that oft lookes so,
Pardon is still the nurse of second woe:
But yet, poore *Claudio*; there is no remedie.
Come Sir. *Exeunt.*

Scena

Scena Secunda.

Enter Prouost, Seruant.

Ser. Hee's hearing of a Cause; he will come straight,
I'le tell him of you.

Pro. 'Pray you doe; Ile know
His pleasure, may be he will relent; alas
He hath but as offended in a dreame,
All Sects, all Ages smack of this vice, and he
To die for't?

Enter Angelo.

Ang. Now, what's the matter *Prouost?*

Pro. Is it your will *Claudio* shall die to morrow?

Ang. Did not I tell thee yea? hadst thou not order?
Why do'st thou aske againe?

Pro. Lest I might be too rash:
Vnder your good correction, I haue seene
When after execution, Iudgement hath
Repented ore his doome.

Ang. Goe to; let that be mine,
Doe you your office, or giue vp your Place,
And you shall well be spar'd.

Pro. I craue your Honours pardon:
What shall be done Sir, with the groaning *Iuliet?*
Shee's very neere her howre.

Ang. Dispose of her
To some more fitter place; and that with speed.

Ser. Here is the sister of the man condemn'd,
Desires accesse to you.

Ang. Hath he a Sister?

Pro. I my good Lord, a very vertuous maid,
And to be shortlie of a Sister-hood,
If not alreadie.

Ang. Well: let her be admitted,
See you the Fornicatresse be remou'd,
Let her haue needfull, but not lauish meanes,
There shall be order for't.

Enter Lucio and Isabella.

Pro. 'Saue your Honour. (will?

Ang. Stay a little while: y'are welcome: what's your

Isab. I am a wofull Sutor to your Honour,
'Please but your Honor heare me.

Ang. Well: what's your suite.

Isab. There is a vice that most I doe abhorre,
And most desire should meet the blow of Iustice;
For which I would not plead, but that I must,
For which I must not plead, but that I am
At warre, twixt will, and will not.

Ang. Well: the matter?

Isab. I haue a brother is condemn'd to die,
I doe beseech you let it be his fault,
And not my brother.

Pro. Heauen giue thee mouing graces.

Ang. Condemne the fault, and not the actor of it,
Why euery fault's condemnd ere it be done:
Mine were the verie Cipher of a Function
To fine the faults, whose fine stands in record,
And let goe by the Actor.

Isab. Oh iust, but seuere Law:
I had a brother then; heauen keepe your honour.

Luc. Giue't not ore so: to him againe, entreat him,
Kneele downe before him, hang vpon his gowne,
You are too cold: if you should need a pin,
You could not with more tame a tongue desire it:
To him, I say.

Isab. Must he needs die?

Ang. Maiden, no remedie.

Isab. Yes: I doe thinke that you might pardon him,
And neither heauen, nor man grieue at the mercy.

Ang. I will not doe't.

Isab. But can you if you would?

Ang. Looke what I will not, that I cannot doe.

Isab. But might you doe't & do the world no wrong
If so your heart were touch'd with that remorse,
As mine is to him?

Ang. Hee's sentenc'd, tis too late.

Luc. You are too cold.

Isab. Too late? why no: I that doe speak a word
May call it againe: well, beleeue this
No ceremony that to great ones longs,
Not the Kings Crowne; nor the deputed sword,
The Marshalls Truncheon, nor the Iudges Robe
Become them with one halfe so good a grace
As mercie does: If he had bin as you, and you as he,
You would haue slipt like him, but he like you
Would not haue beene so sterne.

Ang. Pray you be gone.

Isab. I would to heauen I had your potencie,
And you were *Isabell*: should it then be thus?
No: I would tell what 'twere to be a Iudge,
And what a prisoner.

Luc. I, touch him: there's the vaine.

Ang. Your Brother is a forfeit of the Law,
And you but waste your words.

Isab. Alas, alas:
Why all the soules that were, were forfeit once,
And he that might the vantage best haue tooke,
Found out the remedie: how would you be,
If he, which is the top of Iudgement, should
But iudge you, as you are? Oh, thinke on that,
And mercie then will breathe within your lips
Like man new made.

Ang. Be you content, (faire Maid)
It is the Law, not I, condemne your brother,
Were he my kinsman, brother, or my sonne,
It should be thus with him: he must die to morrow.

Isab. To morrow? oh, that's sodaine,
Spare him, spare him:
Hee's not prepar'd for death; euen for our kitchins
We kill the fowle of season: shall we serue heauen
With lesse respect then we doe minister
To our grosse-selues? good, good my Lord, bethink you;
Who is it that hath di'd for this offence?
There's many haue committed it.

Luc. I, well said.

Ang. The Law hath not bin dead, thogh it hath slept
Those many had not dar'd to doe that euill
If the first, that did th' Edict infringe
Had answer'd for his deed: Now 'tis awake,
Takes note of what is done, and like a Prophet
Lookes in a glasse that shewes what future euils
Either now, or by remissenesse, new conceiu'd,
And so in progresse to be hatch'd, and borne,
Are now to haue no successiue degrees,
But here they liue to end.

Isab. Yet shew some pittie.

Ang. I shew it most of all, when I show Iustice;
For then I pittie those I doe not know,
Which a dismis'd offence, would after gaule

And

And doe him right, that answering one foule wrong
Liues not to act another. Be satisfied;
Your Brother dies to morrow; be content.
　Isab. So you must be ye first that giues this sentence,
And hee, that suffers: Oh, it is excellent
To haue a Giants strength: but it is tyrannous
To vse it like a Giant.
　Luc. That's well said.
　Isab. Could great men thunder
As *Ioue* himselfe do's, *Ioue* would neuer be quiet,
For euery pelting petty Officer
Would vse his heauen for thunder;
Nothing but thunder: Mercifull heauen,
Thou rather with thy sharpe and sulpherous bolt
Splits the vn-wedgable and gnarled Oke,
Then the soft Mertill: But man, proud man,
Drest in a little briefe authoritie,
Most ignorant of what he's most assur'd,
(His glassie Essence) like an angry Ape
Plaies such phantastique tricks before high heauen,
As makes the Angels weepe: who with our spleenes,
Would all themselues laugh mortall.
　Luc. Oh, to him, to him wench: he will relent,
Hee's comming: I perceiue't.
　Pro. Pray heauen she win him.
　Isab. We cannot weigh our brother with our selfe,
Great men may iest with Saints: tis wit in them,
But in the lesse fowle prophanation.
　Luc. Thou'rt i'th right (Girle) more o'that.
　Isab. That in the Captaine's but a chollericke word,
Which in the Souldier is flat blasphemie.
　Luc. Art auis'd o'that? more on't.
　Ang. Why doe you put these sayings vpon me?
　Isab. Because Authoritie, though it erre like others,
Hath yet a kinde of medicine in it selfe
That skins the vice o'th top; goe to your bosome,
Knock there, and aske your heart what it doth know
That's like my brothers fault: if it confesse
A naturall guiltinesse, such as is his,
Let it not sound a thought vpon your tongue
Against my brothers life.
　Ang. Shee speakes, and 'tis such sence
That my Sence breeds with it; fare you well.
　Isab. Gentle my Lord, turne backe.
　Ang. I will bethinke me: come againe to morrow.
　Isa. Hark, how Ile bribe you: good my Lord turn back.
　Ang. How? bribe me?
　Is. I, with such gifts that heauen shall share with you.
　Luc. You had mar'd all else.
　Isab. Not with fond Sickles of the tested-gold,
Or Stones, whose rate are either rich, or poore
As fancie values them: but with true prayers,
That shall be vp at heauen, and enter there
Ere Sunne rise: prayers from preserued soules,
From fasting Maides, whose mindes are dedicate
To nothing temporall.
　Ang. Well: come to me to morrow.
　Luc. Goe to: 'tis well; away.
　Isab. Heauen keepe your honour safe.
　Ang. Amen.
For I am that way going to temptation,
Where prayers crosse.
　Isab. At what hower to morrow,
Shall I attend your Lordship?
　Ang. At any time 'fore-noone.
　Isab. 'Saue your Honour.

　Ang. From thee: euen from thy vertue.
What's this? what's this? is this her fault, or mine?
The Tempter, or the Tempted, who sins most? ha?
Not she: nor doth she tempt: but it is I,
That, lying by the Violet in the Sunne,
Doe as the Carrion do's, not as the flowre,
Corrupt with vertuous season: Can it be,
That Modesty may more betray our Sence
Then womans lightnesse? hauing waste ground enough,
Shall we desire to raze the Sanctuary
And pitch our euils there? oh fie, fie, fie:
What dost thou? or what art thou *Angelo*?
Dost thou desire her fowly, for those things
That make her good? oh, let her brother liue:
Theeues for their robbery haue authority,
When Iudges steale themselues: what, doe I loue her,
That I desire to heare her speake againe?
And feast vpon her eyes? what is't I dreame on?
Oh cunning enemy, that to catch a Saint,
With Saints dost bait thy hooke: most dangerous
Is that temptation, that doth goad vs on
To sinne, in louing vertue: neuer could the Strumpet
With all her double vigor, Art, and Nature
Once stir my temper: but this vertuous Maid
Subdues me quite: Euer till now
When men were fond, I smild, and wondred how. *Exit.*

Scena Tertia.

Enter Duke and Prouost.

　Duke. Haile to you, *Prouost*, so I thinke you are.
　Pro. I am the Prouost: whats your will, good Frier?
　Duke. Bound by my charity, and my blest order,
I come to visite the afflicted spirits
Here in the prison: doe me the common right
To let me see them: and to make me know
The nature of their crimes, that I may minister
To them accordingly.
　Pro. I would doe more then that, if more were needfull
　Enter Iuliet.
Looke here comes one: a Gentlewoman of mine,
Who falling in the flawes of her owne youth,
Hath blisterd her report: She is with childe,
And he that got it, sentenc'd: a yong man,
More fit to doe another such offence,
Then dye for this.
　Duk. When must he dye?
　Pro. As I do thinke to morrow.
I haue prouided for you, stay a while
And you shall be conducted.
　Duk. Repent you (faire one) of the sin you carry?
　Iul. I doe; and beare the shame most patiently.
　Du. Ile teach you how you shal araign your consciēce
And try your penitence, if it be sound,
Or hollowly put on.
　Iul. Ile gladly learne.
　Duk. Loue you the man that wrong'd you?
　Iul. Yes, as I loue the woman that wrong'd him.
　Duk. So then it seemes your most offence full act
Was mutually committed.
　Iul. Mutually.
　Duk. Then was your sin of heauier kinde then his.
　Iul. I doe confesse it, and repent it (Father.)
　　　　　　　　　　　　　　　　　　Du. 'Tis

Duke. 'Tis meet so (daughter) but least you do repent
As that the sin hath brought you to this shame,
Which sorrow is alwaies toward our selues, not heauen,
Showing we would not spare heauen, as we loue it,
But as we stand in feare.

Iul. I doe repent me, as it is an euill,
And take the shame with ioy.

Duke. There rest:
Your partner (as I heare) must die to morrow,
And I am going with instruction to him:
Grace goe with you, *Benedicite.* *Exit.*

Iul. Must die to morrow? oh iniurious Loue
That respits me a life, whose very comfort
Is still a dying horror.

Pro. 'Tis pitty of him. *Exeunt.*

Scena Quarta.

Enter Angelo.

An. When I would pray, & think, I thinke, and pray
To seuerall subiects: heauen hath my empty words,
Whilst my Inuention, hearing not my Tongue,
Anchors on *Isabell:* heauen in my mouth,
As if I did but onely chew his name,
And in my heart the strong and swelling euill
Of my conception: the state whereon I studied
Is like a good thing, being often read
Growne feard, and tedious: yea, my Grauitie
Wherein (let no man heare me) I take pride,
Could I, with boote, change for an idle plume
Which the ayre beats for vaine: oh place, oh forme,
How often dost thou with thy case, thy habit
Wrench awe from fooles, and tye the wiser soules
To thy false seeming? Blood, thou art blood,
Let's write good Angell on the Deuills horne
'Tis not the Deuills Crest: how now? who's there?

Enter Seruant.

Ser. One *Isabell,* a Sister, desires accesse to you.

Ang. Teach her the way: oh, heauens
Why doe's my bloud thus muster to my heart,
Making both it vnable for it selfe,
And dispossessing all my other parts
Of necessary fitnesse?
So play the foolish throngs with one that swounds,
Come all to help him, and so stop the ayre
By which hee should reuiue: and euen so
The generall subiect to a wel-wisht King
Quit their owne part, and in obsequious fondnesse
Crowd to his presence, where their vn-taught loue
Must needs appear offence: how now faire Maid.

Enter Isabella.

Isab. I am come to know your pleasure.

An. That you might know it, wold much better please (me,
Then to demand what 'tis: your Brother cannot liue.

Isab. Euen so: heauen keepe your Honor.

Ang. Yet may he liue a while: and it may be
As long as you, or I: yet he must die.

Isab. Vnder your Sentence?

Ang. Yea.

Isab. When, I beseech you: that in his Reprieue
(Longer, or shorter) he may be so fitted
That his soule sicken not.

Ang. Ha? fie, these filthy vices: It were as good
To pardon him, that hath from nature stolne
A man already made, as to remit
Their sawcie sweetnes, that do coyne heauens Image
In stamps that are forbid: 'tis all as easie,
Falsely to take away a life true made,
As to put mettle in restrained meanes
To make a false one.

Isab. 'Tis set downe so in heauen, but not in earth.

Ang. Say you so: then I shall poze you quickly.
Which had you rather, that the most iust Law
Now tooke your brothers life, and to redeeme him
Giue vp your body to such sweet vncleannesse
As she that he hath staind?

Isab. Sir, beleeue this,
I had rather giue my body, then my soule.

Ang. I talke not of your soule: our compel'd sins
Stand more for number, then for accompt.

Isab. How say you?

Ang. Nay Ile not warrant that: for I can speake
Against the thing I say: Answere to this,
I (now the voyce of the recorded Law)
Pronounce a sentence on your Brothers life,
Might there not be a charitie in sinne,
To saue this Brothers life?

Isab. Please you to doo't,
Ile take it as a perill to my soule,
It is no sinne at all, but charitie.

Ang. Pleas'd you to doo't, at perill of your soule
Were equall poize of sinne, and charitie.

Isab. That I do beg his life, if it be sinne
Heauen let me beare it: you granting of my suit,
If that be sin, Ile make it my Morne-praier,
To haue it added to the faults of mine,
And nothing of your answere.

Ang. Nay, but heare me,
Your sence pursues not mine: either you are ignorant,
Or seeme so crafty; and that's not good.

Isab. Let be ignorant, and in nothing good,
But graciously to know I am no better.

Ang. Thus wisdome wishes to appeare most bright,
When it doth taxe it selfe: As these blacke Masques
Proclaime an en-shield beauty ten times louder
Then beauty could displaied: But marke me,
To be receiued plaine, Ile speake more grosse:
Your Brother is to dye.

Isab. So.

Ang. And his offence is so, as it appeares,
Accountant to the Law, vpon that paine.

Isab. True.

Ang. Admit no other way to saue his life
(As I subscribe not that, nor any other,
But in the losse of question) that you, his Sister,
Finding your selfe desir'd of such a person,
Whose creadit with the Iudge, or owne great place,
Could fetch your Brother from the Manacles
Of the all-building-Law: and that there were
No earthly meane to saue him, but that either
You must lay downe the treasures of your body,
To this supposed, or else to let him suffer:
What would you doe?

Isab. As much for my poore Brother, as my selfe;
That is: were I vnder the tearmes of death,
Th'impression of keene whips, I'ld weare as Rubies,
And strip my selfe to death, as to a bed,
That longing haue bin sicke for, ere I'ld yeeld
My body vp to shame.

Ang. That

Ang. Then must your brother die.
Isa. And 'twer the cheaper way:
Better it were a brother dide at once,
Then that a sister, by redeeming him
Should die for euer.

Ang. Were not you then as cruell as the Sentence,
That you haue slander'd so?

Isa. Ignomie in ransome, and free pardon
Are of two houses: lawfull mercie,
Is nothing kin to fowle redemption.

Ang. You seem'd of late to make the Law a tirant,
And rather prou'd the sliding of your brother
A merriment, then a vice.

Isa. Oh pardon me my Lord, it oft fals out
To haue, what we would haue,
We speake not what vve meane;
I something do excuse the thing I hate,
For his aduantage that I dearely loue.

Ang. We are all fraile.

Isa. Else let my brother die,
If not a fedarie but onely he
Owe, and succeed thy weakenesse.

Ang. Nay, women are fraile too.

Isa. I, as the glasses where they view themselues,
Which are as easie broke as they make formes:
Women? Helpe heauen; men their creation marre
In profiting by them: Nay, call vs ten times fraile,
For we are soft, as our complexions are,
And credulous to false prints.

Ang. I thinke it well:
And from this testimonie of your owne sex
(Since I suppose we are made to be no stronger
Then faults may shake our frames) let me be bold;
I do arrest your words. Be that you are,
That is a woman; if you be more, you'r none.
If you be one (as you are well exprest
By all externall warrants) shew it now,
By putting on the destin'd Liuerie.

Isa. I haue no tongue but one; gentle my Lord,
Let me entreate you speake the former language.

Ang. Plainlie conceiue I loue you.

Isa. My brother did loue *Iuliet*,
And you tell me that he shall die for't.

Ang. He shall not *Isabell* if you giue me loue.

Isa. I know your vertue hath a licence in't,
Which seemes a little fouler then it is,
To plucke on others.

Ang. Beleeue me on mine Honor,
My words expresse my purpose.

Isa. Ha? Little honor, to be much beleeu'd,
And most pernitious purpose: Seeming, seeming.
I will proclaime thee *Angelo*, looke for't:
Signe me a present pardon for my brother,
Or with an out-stretcht throate Ile tell the world aloud
What man thou art.

Ang. Who will beleeue thee *Isabell*?
My vnsoild name, th'austeerenesse of my life,
My vouch against you, and my place i'th State,
Will so your accusation ouer-weigh,
That you shall stifle in your owne report,
And smell of calumnie. I haue begun,
And now I giue my sensuall race, the reine,
Fit thy consent to my sharpe appetite,
Lay by all nicetie, and prolixious blushes
That banish what they sue for: Redeeme thy brother,
By yeelding vp thy bodie to my will,
Or else he must not onelie die the death,
But thy vnkindnesse shall his death draw out
To lingring sufferance: Answer me to morrow,
Or by the affection that now guides me most,
Ile proue a Tirant to him. As for you,
Say what you can; my false, ore-weighs your true. *Exit*

Isa. To whom should I complaine? Did I tell this,
Who would beleeue me? O perilous mouthes
That beare in them, one and the selfesame tongue,
Either of condemnation, or approofe,
Bidding the Law make curtsie to their will,
Hooking both right and wrong to th'appetite,
To follow as it drawes. Ile to my brother,
Though he hath falne by prompture of the blood,
Yet hath he in him such a minde of Honor,
That had he twentie heads to tender downe
On twentie bloodie blockes, hee'ld yeeld them vp,
Before his sister should her bodie stoope
To such abhord pollution.
Then *Isabell* liue chaste, and brother die;
"More then our Brother, is our Chastitie.
Ile tell him yet of *Angelo's* request,
And fit his minde to death, for his soules rest. *Exit.*

Actus Tertius. Scena Prima.

Enter Duke, Claudio, and Prouost.

Du. So then you hope of pardon from Lord *Angelo*?

Cla. The miserable haue no other medicine
But onely hope: I'haue hope to liue, and am prepar'd to die.

Duke. Be absolute for death: either death or life
Shall thereby be the sweeter. Reason thus with life:
If I do loose thee, I do loose a thing
That none but fooles would keepe: a breath thou art,
Seruile to all the skyie-influences,
That dost this habitation where thou keepst
Hourely afflict: Meerely, thou art deaths foole,
For him thou labourst by thy flight to shun,
And yet runst toward him still. Thou art not noble,
For all th'accommodations that thou bearst,
Are nurst by basenesse: Thou'rt by no meanes valiant,
For thou dost feare the soft and tender forke
Of a poore worme: thy best of rest is sleepe,
And that thou oft prouoakst, yet grosselie fearst
Thy death, which is no more. Thou art not thy selfe,
For thou exists on manie a thousand graines
That issue out of dust. Happie thou art not,
For what thou hast not, still thou striu'st to get,
And what thou hast forgetst. Thou art not certaine,
For thy complexion shifts to strange effects,
After the Moone: If thou art rich, thou'rt poore,
For like an Asse, whose backe with Ingots bowes;
Thou bearst thy heauie riches but a iournie,
And death vnloads thee; Friend hast thou none.
For thine owne bowels which do call thee, sire
The meere effusion of thy proper loines
Do curse the Gowt, Sapego, and the Rheume
For ending thee no sooner. Thou hast nor youth, nor age
But as it were an after-dinners sleepe
Dreaming on both, for all thy blessed youth
Becomes as aged, and doth begge the almes
Of palsied-Eld: and when thou art old, and rich

Thou

Measure for Measure. 71

Thou hast neither heate, affection, limbe, nor beautie
To make thy riches pleasant: what's yet in this
That beares the name of life? Yet in this life
Lie hid moe thousand deaths; yet death we feare
That makes these oddes, all euen.

Cla. I humblie thanke you.
To sue to liue, I finde I seeke to die,
And seeking death, finde life: Let it come on.

Enter Isabella.

Isab. What hoa? Peace heere; Grace, and good companie.

Pro. Who's there? Come in, the wish deserues a welcome.

Duke. Deere sir, ere long Ile visit you againe.

Cla. Most holie Sir, I thanke you.

Isa. My businesse is a word or two with *Claudio*.

Pro. And verie welcom: looke Signior, here's your sister.

Duke. Prouost, a word with you.

Pro. As manie as you please.

Duke. Bring them to heare me speak, where I may be conceal'd.

Cla. Now sister, what's the comfort?

Isa. Why,
As all comforts are: most good, most good indeede,
Lord *Angelo* hauing affaires to heauen
Intends you for his swift Ambassador,
Where you shall be an euerlasting Leiger;
Therefore your best appointment make with speed,
To Morrow you set on.

Clau. Is there no remedie?

Isa. None, but such remedie, as to saue a head
To cleaue a heart in twaine:

Clau. But is there anie?

Isa. Yes brother, you may liue;
There is a diuellish mercie in the Iudge,
If you'l implore it, that will free your life,
But fetter you till death.

Cla. Perpetuall durance?

Isa. I iust, perpetuall durance, a restraint
Through all the worlds vastiditie you had
To a determin'd scope.

Clau. But in what nature?

Isa. In such a one, as you consenting too't,
Would barke your honor from that trunke you beare,
And leaue you naked.

Clau. Let me know the point.

Isa. Oh, I do feare thee *Claudio*, and I quake,
Least thou a feauorous life shouldst entertaine,
And six or seuen winters more respect
Then a perpetuall Honor. Dar'st thou die?
The sence of death is most in apprehension,
And the poore Beetle that we treade vpon
In corporall sufferance, finds a pang as great,
As when a Giant dies.

Cla. Why giue you me this shame?
Thinke you I can a resolution fetch
From flowrie tendernesse? If I must die,
I will encounter darknesse as a bride,
And hugge it in mine armes.

Isa. There spake my brother: there my fathers graue
Did vtter forth a voice. Yes, thou must die:
Thou art too noble, to conserue a life
In base appliances. This outward sainted Deputie,
Whose setled visage, and deliberate word
Nips youth i'th head, and follies doth emmew

As Falcon doth the Fowle, is yet a diuell:
His filth within being cast, he would appeare
A pond, as deepe as hell.

Cla. The prenzie, *Angelo*?

Isa. Oh 'tis the cunning Liuerie of hell,
The damnest bodie to inuest, and couer
In prenzie gardes; dost thou thinke *Claudio*,
If I would yeeld him my virginitie
Thou might'st be freed?

Cla. Oh heauens, it cannot be.

Isa. Yes, he would giu't thee; from this rank offence
So to offend him still. This night's the time
That I should do what I abhorre to name,
Or else thou diest to morrow.

Clau. Thou shalt not do't.

Isa. O, were it but my life,
I'de throw it downe for your deliuerance
As frankely as a pin.

Clau. Thankes deere *Isabell*.

Isa. Be readie *Claudio*, for your death to morrow.

Clau. Yes. Has he affections in him,
That thus can make him bite the Law by th'nose,
When he would force it? Sure it is no sinne,
Or of the deadly seuen it is the least.

Isa. Which is the least?

Cla. If it were damnable, he being so wise,
Why would he for the momentarie tricke
Be perdurablie fin'de? Oh *Isabell*.

Isa. What saies my brother?

Cla. Death is a fearefull thing.

Isa. And shamed life, a hatefull.

Cla. I, but to die, and go we know not where,
To lie in cold obstruction, and to rot,
This sensible warme motion, to become
A kneaded clod; And the delighted spirit
To bath in fierie floods, or to reside
In thrilling Region of thicke-ribbed Ice,
To be imprison'd in the viewlesse windes
And blowne with restlesse violence round about
The pendant world: or to be worse then worst
Of those, that lawlesse and incertaine thought,
Imagine howling, 'tis too horrible.
The weariest, and most loathed worldly life
That Age, Ache, periury, and imprisonment
Can lay on nature, is a Paradise
To what we feare of death.

Isa. Alas, alas.

Cla. Sweet Sister, let me liue.
What sinne you do, to saue a brothers life,
Nature dispenses with the deede so farre,
That it becomes a vertue.

Isa. Oh you beast,
Oh faithlesse Coward, oh dishonest wretch,
Wilt thou be made a man, out of my vice?
Is't not a kinde of Incest, to take life
From thine owne sisters shame? What should I thinke,
Heauen shield my Mother plaid my Father faire:
For such a warped slip of wildernesse
Nere issu'd from his blood. Take my defiance,
Die, perish: Might but my bending downe
Repreeue thee from thy fate, it should proceede.
Ile pray a thousand praiers for thy death,
No word to saue thee.

Cla. Nay heare me *Isabell*.

Isa. Oh fie, fie, fie:
Thy sinn's not accidentall, but a Trade;

Mercie

Mercy to thee would proue it selfe a Bawd,
'Tis best that thou diest quickly.

Cla. Oh heare me *Isabella*.

Duk. Vouchsafe a word, yong sister, but one word.

Isa. What is your Will.

Duk. Might you dispense with your leysure, I would by and by haue some speech with you: the satisfaction I would require, is likewise your owne benefit.

Isa. I haue no superfluous leysure, my stay must be stolen out of other affaires: but I will attend you a while.

Duke. Son, I haue ouer-heard what hath past betweene you & your sister. *Angelo* had neuer the purpose to corrupt her; onely he hath made an assay of her vertue, to practise his iudgement with the disposition of natures. She (hauing the truth of honour in her) hath made him that gracious deniall, which he is most glad to receiue: I am Confessor to *Angelo*, and I know this to be true, therefore prepare your selfe to death: do not satisfie your resolution with hopes that are fallible, to morrow you must die, goe to your knees, and make ready.

Cla. Let me ask my sister pardon, I am so out of loue with life, that I will sue to be rid of it.

Duke. Hold you there: farewell: *Prouost*, a word with you.

Pro. What's your will (father?)

Duk. That now you are come, you wil be gone: leaue me a while with the Maid, my minde promises with my habit, no losse shall touch her by my company.

Pro. In good time.   *Exit.*

Duk. The hand that hath made you faire, hath made you good: the goodnes that is cheape in beauty, makes beauty briefe in goodnes; but grace being the soule of your complexion, shall keepe the body of it euer faire: the assault that *Angelo* hath made to you, Fortune hath conuaid to my vnderstanding; and but that frailty hath examples for his falling, I should wonder at *Angelo*: how will you doe to content this Substitute, and to saue your Brother?

Isab. I am now going to resolue him: I had rather my brother die by the Law, then my sonne should be vnlawfullie borne. But (oh) how much is the good Duke deceiu'd in *Angelo*: if euer he returne, and I can speake to him, I will open my lips in vaine, or discouer his gouernment.

Duke. That shall not be much amisse: yet, as the matter now stands, he will auoid your accusation: he made triall of you onelie. Therefore fasten your eare on my aduisings, to the loue I haue in doing good; a remedie presents it selfe. I doe make my selfe beleeue that you may most vprighteously do a poor wronged Lady a merited benefit; redeem your brother from the angry Law; doe no staine to your owne gracious person, and much please the absent Duke, if peraduenture he shall euer returne to haue hearing of this businesse.

Isab. Let me heare you speake farther; I haue spirit to do any thing that appeares not fowle in the truth of my spirit.

Duke. Vertue is bold, and goodnes neuer fearefull: Haue you not heard speake of *Mariana* the sister of *Fredericke* the great Souldier, who miscarried at Sea?

Isa. I haue heard of the Lady, and good words went with her name.

Duke. Shee should this *Angelo* haue married: was affianced to her oath, and the nuptiall appointed: betweene which time of the contract, and limit of the solemnitie, her brother *Fredericke* was wrackt at Sea, hauing in that perished vessell, the dowry of his sister: but marke how heauily this befell to the poore Gentlewoman, there she lost a noble and renowned brother, in his loue toward her, euer most kinde, and naturall: with him the portion and sinew of her fortune, her marriage dowry: with both, her combynate-husband, this well-seeming *Angelo*.

Isab. Can this be so? did *Angelo* so leaue her?

Duke. Left her in her teares, & dried not one of them with his comfort: swallowed his vowes whole, pretending in her, discoueries of dishonor: in few, bestow'd her on her owne lamentation, which she yet weares for his sake: and he, a marble to her teares, is washed with them, but relents not.

Isab. What a merit were it in death to take this poore maid from the world? what corruption in this life, that it will let this man liue? But how out of this can shee auaile?

Duke. It is a rupture that you may easily heale: and the cure of it not onely saues your brother, but keepes you from dishonor in doing it.

Isab. Shew me how (good Father.)

Duk. This fore-named Maid hath yet in her the continuance of her first affection: his vniust vnkindenesse (that in all reason should haue quenched her loue) hath (like an impediment in the Current) made it more violent and vnruly: Goe you to *Angelo*, answere his requiring with a plausible obedience, agree with his demands to the point: onely referre your selfe to this aduantage; first, that your stay with him may not be long: that the time may haue all shadow, and silence in it: and the place answere to conuenience: this being granted in course, and now followes all: wee shall aduise this wronged maid to steed vp your appointment, goe in your place: if the encounter acknowledge it selfe heereafter, it may compell him to her recompence; and heere, by this is your brother saued, your honor vntainted, the poore *Mariana* aduantaged, and the corrupt Deputy scaled. The Maid will I frame, and make fit for his attempt: if you thinke well to carry this as you may, the doublenes of the benefit defends the deceit from reproofe. What thinke you of it?

Isab. The image of it giues me content already, and I trust it will grow to a most prosperous perfection.

Duk. It lies much in your holding vp: haste you speedily to *Angelo*, if for this night he intreat you to his bed, giue him promise of satisfaction: I will presently to S. *Lukes*, there at the moated-Grange recides this deiected *Mariana*; at that place call vpon me, and dispatch with *Angelo*, that it may be quickly.

Isab. I thank you for this comfort: fare you well good father.   *Exit.*

Enter Elbow, Clowne, Officers.

Elb. Nay, if there be no remedy for it, but that you will needes buy and sell men and women like beasts, we shall haue all the world drinke browne & white bastard.

Duk. Oh heauens, what stuffe is heere.

Clow. Twas neuer merry world since of two vsuries the merriest was put downe, and the worser allow'd by order of Law; a fur'd gowne to keepe him warme; and furd with Foxe and Lamb-skins too, to signifie, that craft being richer then Innocency, stands for the facing.

Elb. Come your way sir: 'blesse you good Father Frier.

Duk. And you good Brother Father; what offence hath this man made you, Sir?

                                    Elb. Marry

Elb. Marry Sir, he hath offended the Law; and Sir, we take him to be a Theefe too Sir: for wee haue found vpon him Sir, a strange Pick-lock, which we haue sent to the Deputie.

Duke. Fie, sirrah, a Bawd, a wicked bawd,
The euill that thou causest to be done,
That is thy meanes to liue. Do thou but thinke
What 'tis to cram a maw, or cloath a backe
From such a filthie vice: say to thy selfe,
From their abhominable and beastly touches
I drinke, I eate away my selfe, and liue:
Canst thou beleeue thy liuing is a life,
So stinkingly depending? Go mend, go mend.

Clo. Indeed, it do's stinke in some sort, Sir:
But yet Sir I would proue.

Duke. Nay, if the diuell haue giuen thee proofs for sin Thou wilt proue his. Take him to prison Officer: Correction, and Instruction must both worke Ere this rude beast will profit.

Elb. He must before the Deputy Sir, he ha's giuen him warning: the Deputy cannot abide a Whore-master: if he be a Whore-monger, and comes before him, he were as good go a mile on his errand.

Duke. That we were all, as some would seeme to bee From our faults, as faults from seeming free.

Enter Lucio.

Elb. His necke will come to your wast, a Cord sir.

Clo. I spy comfort, I cry baile: Here's a Gentleman, and a friend of mine.

Luc. How now noble *Pompey*? What, at the wheels of *Cæsar*? Art thou led in triumph? What is there none of *Pigmalions* Images newly made woman to bee had now, for putting the hand in the pocket, and extracting clutch'd? What reply? Ha? What saist thou to this Tune, Matter, and Method? Is't not drown'd i'th last raine? Ha? What saist thou Trot? Is the world as it was Man? Which is the vvay? Is it sad, and few words? Or how? The tricke of it?

Duke. Still thus, and thus: still vvorse?

Luc. How doth my deere Morseil, thy Mistris? Procures she still? Ha?

Clo. Troth sir, shee hath eaten vp all her beefe, and she is her selfe in the tub.

Luc. Why 'tis good: It is the right of it: it must be so. Euer your fresh Whore, and your pouder'd Baud, an vnshun'd consequence, it must be so. Art going to prison *Pompey*?

Clo. Yes faith sir.

Luc. Why 'tis not amisse *Pompey*: farewell: goe say I sent thee thether: for debt *Pompey*? Or how?

Elb. For being a baud, for being a baud.

Luc. Well, then imprison him: If imprisonment be the due of a baud, why 'tis his right. Baud is he doubtlesse, and of antiquity too: Baud borne. Farwell good *Pompey*: Commend me to the prison *Pompey*, you will turne good husband now *Pompey*, you vvill keepe the house.

Clo. I hope Sir, your good Worship wil be my baile?

Luc. No indeed vvil I not *Pompey*, it is not the wear: I will pray (*Pompey*) to encrease your bondage if you take it not patiently: Why, your mettle is the more: Adieu trustie *Pompey*.
Blesse you Friar.

Duke. And you.

Luc. Do's *Bridget* paint still, *Pompey*? Ha?

Elb. Come your waies sir, come.

Clo. You will not baile me then Sir?

Luc. Then *Pompey*, nor now: what newes abroad Frier? What newes?

Elb. Come your waies sir, come.

Luc. Goe to kennell (*Pompey*) goe:
What newes Frier of the Duke?

Duke. I know none: can you tell me of any?

Luc. Some say he is with the Emperor of *Russia*: other some, he is in *Rome*: but where is he thinke you?

Duke. I know not where: but wheresoeuer, I wish him well.

Luc. It was a mad fantasticall tricke of him to steale from the State, and vsurpe the beggerie hee was neuer borne to: Lord *Angelo* Dukes it well in his absence: he puts transgression too't.

Duke. He do's well in't.

Luc. A little more lenitie to Lecherie would doe no harme in him: Something too crabbed that way, Frier.

Duk. It is too general a vice, and seueritie must cure it.

Luc. Yes in good sooth, the vice is of a great kindred; it is vvell allied, but it is impossible to extirpe it quite, Frier, till eating and drinking be put downe. They say this *Angelo* vvas not made by Man and Woman, after this downe-right vvay of Creation: is it true, thinke you?

Duke. How should he be made then?

Luc. Some report, a Sea-maid spawn'd him. Some, that he vvas begot betweene two Stock-fishes. But it is certaine, that when he makes water, his Vrine is congeal'd ice, that I know to bee true: and he is a motion generatiue, that's infallible.

Duke. You are pleasant sir, and speake apace.

Luc. Why, what a ruthlesse thing is this in him, for the rebellion of a Cod-peece, to take away the life of a man? Would the Duke that is absent haue done this? Ere he vvould haue hang'd a man for the getting a hundred Bastards, he vvould haue paide for the Nursing a thousand. He had some feeling of the sport, hee knew the seruice, and that instructed him to mercie.

Duke. I neuer heard the absent Duke much detected for Women, he was not enclin'd that vvay.

Luc. Oh Sir, you are deceiu'd.

Duke. 'Tis not possible.

Luc. Who, not the Duke? Yes, your beggar of fifty: and his vse was, to put a ducket in her Clack-dish; the Duke had Crochets in him. Hee would be drunke too, that let me informe you.

Duke. You do him wrong, surely.

Luc. Sir, I vvas an inward of his: a shie fellow vvas the Duke, and I beleeue I know the cause of his vvithdrawing.

Duke. What (I prethee) might be the cause?

Luc. No, pardon: 'Tis a secret must bee lockt within the teeth and the lippes: but this I can let you vnderstand, the greater file of the subiect held the Duke to be vvise.

Duke. Wise? Why no question but he was.

Luc. A very superficiall, ignorant, vnweighing fellow

Duke. Either this is Enuie in you, Folly, or mistaking: The very streame of his life, and the businesse he hath helmed, must vppon a warranted neede, giue him a better proclamation. Let him be but testimonied in his owne bringings forth, and hee shall appeare to the enuious, a Scholler, a Statesman, and a Soldier: therefore you speake vnskilfully: or, if your knowledge bee more, it is much darkned in your malice.

Luc. Sir, I know him, and I loue him.

Duke. Loue talkes with better knowledge, & knowledge with deare loue.

Luc. Come Sir, I know what I know.

Duke. I can hardly beleeue that, since you know not what you speake. But if euer the Duke returne (as our praiers are he may) let mee desire you to make your answer before him: if it bee honest you haue spoke, you haue courage to maintaine it; I am bound to call vppon you, and I pray you your name?

Luc. Sir my name is *Lucio*, wel known to the Duke.

Duke. He shall know you better Sir, if I may liue to report you.

Luc. I feare you not.

Duke. O, you hope the Duke will returne no more: or you imagine me to vnhurtfull an opposite: but indeed I can doe you little harme: You'll for-sweare this againe?

Luc. Ile be hang'd first: Thou art deceiu'd in mee Friar. But no more of this: Canst thou tell if *Claudio* die to morrow, or no?

Duke. Why should he die Sir?

Luc. Why? For filling a bottle with a Tunne-dish: I would the Duke we talke of were return'd againe: this vngenitur'd Agent will vn-people the Prouince with Continencie. Sparrowes must not build in his house-eeues, because they are lecherous: The Duke yet would haue darke deeds darkelie answered, hee would neuer bring them to light: would hee were return'd. Marrie this *Claudio* is condemned for vntrussing. Farwell good Friar, I prethee pray for me: The Duke (I say to thee againe) would eate Mutton on Fridaies. He's now past it, yet (and I say to thee) hee would mouth with a beggar, though she smelt browne-bread and Garlicke: say that I said so: Farewell. *Exit.*

Duke. No might, nor greatnesse in mortality
Can censure scape: Back-wounding calumnie
The whitest vertue strikes. What King so strong,
Can tie the gall vp in the slanderous tong?
But who comes heere?

Enter Escalus, Prouost, and Bawd.

Esc. Go, away with her to prison.

Bawd. Good my Lord be good to mee, your Honor is accounted a mercifull man: good my Lord.

Esc. Double, and trebble admonition, and still forfeite in the same kinde? This would make mercy sweare and play the Tirant.

Pro. A Bawd of eleuen yeares continuance, may it please your Honor.

Bawd. My Lord, this is one *Lucio*'s information against me, Mistris *Kate Keepe-downe* was with childe by him in the Dukes time, he promis'd her marriage: his Childe is a yeere and a quarter olde come *Philip* and *Iacob*: I haue kept it my selfe; and see how hee goes about to abuse me.

Esc. That fellow is a fellow of much License: Let him be call'd before vs, Away with her to prison: Goe too, no more words. Prouost, my Brother *Angelo* will not be alter'd, *Claudio* must die to morrow: Let him be furnish'd with Diuines, and haue all charitable preparation. If my brother wrought by my pitie, it should not be so with him.

Pro. So please you, this Friar hath beene with him, and aduis'd him for th'entertainment of death.

Esc. Good'euen, good Father.

Duke. Blisse, and goodnesse on you.

Esc. Of whence are you?

Duke. Not of this Countrie, though my chance is now To vse it for my time: I am a brother
Of gracious Order, late come from the Sea,
In speciall businesse from his Holinesse.

Esc. What newes abroad i'th World?

Duke. None, but that there is so great a Feauor on goodnesse, that the dissolution of it must cure it. Noueltie is onely in request, and as it is as dangerous to be aged in any kinde of course, as it is vertuous to be constant in any vndertaking. There is scarse truth enough aliue to make Societies secure, but Securitie enough to make Fellowships accurst: Much vpon this riddle runs the wisedome of the world: This newes is old enough, yet it is euerie daies newes. I pray you Sir, of what disposition was the Duke?

Esc. One, that aboue all other strifes,
Contended especially to know himselfe.

Duke. What pleasure was he giuen to?

Esc. Rather reioycing to see another merry, then merrie at anie thing which profest to make him reioice. A Gentleman of all temperance. But leaue wee him to his euents, with a praier they may proue prosperous, & let me desire to know, how you finde *Claudio* prepar'd? I am made to vnderstand, that you haue lent him visitation.

Duke. He professes to haue receiued no sinister measure from his Iudge, but most willingly humbles himselfe to the determination of Iustice: yet had he framed to himselfe (by the instruction of his frailty) manie deceyuing promises of life, which I (by my good leisure) haue discredited to him, and now is he resolu'd to die.

Esc. You haue paid the heauens your Function, and the prisoner the verie debt of your Calling. I haue labour'd for the poore Gentleman, to the extremest shore of my modestie, but my brother-Iustice haue I found so seuere, that he hath forc'd me to tell him, hee is indeede Iustice.

Duke. If his owne life,
Answere the straitnesse of his proceeding,
It shall become him well: wherein if he chance to faile he hath sentenc'd himselfe.

Esc. I am going to visit the prisoner, Fare you well.

Duke. Peace be with you.
He who the sword of Heauen will beare,
Should be as holy, as seuere:
Patterne in himselfe to know,
Grace to stand, and Vertue go:
More, nor lesse to others paying,
Then by selfe-offences weighing.
Shame to him, whose cruell striking,
Kils for faults of his owne liking:
Twice trebble shame on *Angelo*,
To vveede my vice, and let his grow.
Oh, what may Man within him hide,
Though Angel on the outward side?
How may likenesse made in crimes,
Making practise on the Times,
To draw with ydle Spiders strings
Most ponderous and substantiall things?
Craft against vice, I must applie.
With *Angelo* to night shall lye
His old betroathed (but despised:)
So disguise shall by th'disguised
Pay with falshood, false exacting,
And performe an olde contracting. *Exit*

Actus

Actus Quartus. Scœna Prima.

Enter Mariana, and Boy singing.

Song. *Take, oh take those lips away,*
    that so sweetly were forsworne,
  And those eyes: the breake of day
    lights that doe mislead the Morne;
  But my kisses bring againe, bring againe,
  Seales of loue, but seal'd in vaine, seal'd in vaine.

Enter Duke.

Mar. Breake off thy song, and haste thee quick away,
Here comes a man of comfort, whose aduice
Hath often still'd my brawling discontent.
I cry you mercie, Sir, and well could wish
You had not found me here so musicall.
Let me excuse me, and beleeue me so,
My mirth it much displeas'd, but pleas'd my woe.

Duk. 'Tis good; though Musick oft hath such a charme
To make bad, good; and good prouoake to harme.
I pray you tell me, hath any body enquir'd for mee here
to day; much vpon this time haue I promis'd here to
meete.

Mar. You haue not bin enquir'd after: I haue sat
here all day.

Enter Isabell.

Duk. I doe constantly beleeue you: the time is come
euen now. I shall craue your forbearance alittle, may be
I will call vpon you anone for some aduantage to your
selfe.

Mar. I am alwayes bound to you.   *Exit.*

Duk. Very well met, and well come:
What is the newes from this good Deputie?

Isab. He hath a Garden circummur'd with Bricke,
Whose westerne side is with a Vineyard back't;
And to that Vineyard is a planched gate,
That makes his opening with this bigger Key:
This other doth command a little doore,
Which from the Vineyard to the Garden leades,
There haue I made my promise, vpon the
Heauy midle of the night, to call vpon him.

Duk. But shall you on your knowledge find this way?

Isab. I haue t'ane a due, and wary note vpon't,
With whispering, and most guiltie diligence,
In action all of precept, he did show me
The way twice ore.

Duk. Are there no other tokens
Betweene you 'greed, concerning her obseruance?

Isab. No: none but onely a repaire ith' darke,
And that I haue possest him, my most stay
Can be but briefe: for I haue made him know,
I haue a Seruant comes with me along
That staies vpon me; whose perswasion is,
I come about my Brother.

Duk. 'Tis well borne vp.
I haue not yet made knowne to *Mariana*

Enter Mariana.

A word of this: what hoa, within; come forth,
I pray you be acquainted with this Maid,
She comes to doe you good.

Isab. I doe desire the like.

Duk. Do you perswade your selfe that I respect you?

Mar. Good Frier, I know you do, and haue found it.

Duke. Take then this your companion by the hand
Who hath a storie readie for your eare:
I shall attend your leisure, but make haste
The vaporous night approaches.

Mar. Wilt please you walke aside.   *Exit.*

Duke. Oh Place, and greatnes: millions of false eies
Are stucke vpon thee: volumes of report
Run with these false, and most contrarious Quest
Vpon thy doings: thousand escapes of wit
Make thee the father of their idle dreame,
And racke thee in their fancies. Welcome, how agreed?

Enter Mariana and Isabella.

Isab. Shee'll take the enterprize vpon her father,
If you aduise it.

Duke. It is not my consent,
But my entreaty too.

Isa. Little haue you to say
When you depart from him, but soft and low,
Remember now my brother.

Mar. Feare me not.

Duk. Nor gentle daughter, feare you not at all:
He is your husband on a pre-contract:
To bring you thus together 'tis no sinne,
Sith that the Iustice of your title to him
Doth flourish the deceit. Come, let vs goe,
Our Corne's to reape, for yet our Tithes to sow. *Exeunt.*

Scena Secunda.

Enter Prouost and Clowne.

Pro. Come hither sirha; can you cut off a mans head?

Clo. If the man be a Bachelor Sir, I can:
But if he be a married man, he's his wiues head,
And I can neuer cut off a womans head.

Pro. Come sir, leaue me your snatches, and yeeld mee
a direct answere. To morrow morning are to die *Claudio* and *Barnardine*: heere is in our prison a common executioner, who in his office lacks a helper, if you will take
it on you to assist him, it shall redeeme you from your
Gyues: if not, you shall haue your full time of imprisonment, and your deliuerance with an vnpittied whipping;
for you haue beene a notorious bawd.

Clo. Sir, I haue beene an vnlawfull bawd, time out of
minde, but yet I will bee content to be a lawfull hangman: I would bee glad to receiue some instruction from
my fellow partner.

Pro. What hoa, *Abhorson*: where's *Abhorson* there?

Enter Abhorson.

Abh. Doe you call sir?

Pro. Sirha, here's a fellow will helpe you to morrow
in your execution: if you thinke it meet, compound with
him by the yeere, and let him abide here with you, if not,
vse him for the present, and dismisse him, hee cannot
plead his estimation with you: he hath beene a Bawd.

Abh. A Bawd Sir? fie vpon him, he will discredit our
mysterie.

Pro. Goe too Sir, you waigh equallie: a feather will
turne the Scale.   *Exit.*

Clo. Pray sir, by your good fauor: for surely sir, a
good fauor you haue, but that you haue a hanging look:
Doe you call sir, your occupation a Mysterie?

Abh. I Sir, a Misterie.

Clo. Painting Sir, I haue heard say, is a Misterie; and your Whores sir, being members of my occupation, vsing painting, do proue my Occupation, a Misterie: but what Misterie there should be in hanging, if I should be hang'd, I cannot imagine.

Abh. Sir, it is a Misterie.

Clo. Proofe.

Abh. Euerie true mans apparrell fits your Theefe.

Clo. If it be too little for your theefe, your true man thinkes it bigge enough. If it bee too bigge for your Theefe, your Theefe thinkes it little enough: So euerie true mans apparrell fits your Theefe.

Enter Prouost.

Pro. Are you agreed?

Clo. Sir, I will serue him: For I do finde your Hangman is a more penitent Trade then your Bawd: he doth oftner aske forgiuenesse.

Pro. You sirrah, prouide your blocke and your Axe to morrow, foure a clocke.

Abh. Come on (Bawd) I will instruct thee in my Trade: follow.

Clo. I do desire to learne sir: and I hope, if you haue occasion to vse me for your owne turne, you shall finde me y'are. For truly sir, for your kindnesse, I owe you a good turne. *Exit*

Pro. Call hether *Barnardine* and *Claudio*:
Th'one has my pitie; not a iot the other,
Being a Murtherer, though he were my brother.

Enter Claudio.

Looke, here's the Warrant *Claudio*, for thy death,
'Tis now dead midnight, and by eight to morrow
Thou must be made immortall. Where's *Barnardine*?

Cla. As fast lock'd vp in sleepe, as guiltlesse labour,
When it lies starkely in the Traueilers bones,
He will not wake.

Pro. Who can do good on him?
Well, go, prepare your selfe. But harke, what noise?
Heauen giue your spirits comfort: by, and by,
I hope it is some pardon, or repreeue
For the most gentle *Claudio*. Welcome Father.

Enter Duke.

Duke. The best, and wholsomst spirits of the night,
Inuellop you, good Prouost: who call'd heere of late?

Pro. None since the Curphew rung.

Duke. Not *Isabell*?

Pro. No.

Duke. They will then er't be long.

Pro. What comfort is for *Claudio*?

Duke. There's some in hope.

Pro. It is a bitter Deputie.

Duke. Not so, not so: his life is paralel'd
Euen with the stroke and line of his great Iustice:
He doth with holie abstinence subdue
That in himselfe, which he spurres on his powre
To qualifie in others: were he meal'd with that
Which he corrects, then were he tirrannous,
But this being so, he's iust. Now are they come.
This is a gentle Prouost, sildome when
The steeled Gaoler is the friend of men:
How now? what noise? That spirit's possest with haste,
That wounds th'vnsisting Posterne with these strokes.

Pro. There he must stay vntil the Officer
Arise to let him in: he is call'd vp.

Duke. Haue you no countermand for *Claudio* yet?
But he must die to morrow?

Pro. None Sir, none.

Duke. As neere the dawning Prouost, as it is,
You shall heare more ere Morning.

Pro. Happely
You something know: yet I beleeue there comes
No countermand: no such example haue we:
Besides, vpon the verie siege of Iustice,
Lord *Angelo* hath to the publike eare
Profest the contrarie.

Enter a Messenger.

Duke. This is his Lords man.

Pro. And heere comes *Claudio's* pardon.

Mess. My Lord hath sent you this note,
And by mee this further charge;
That you swerue not from the smallest Article of it,
Neither in time, matter, or other circumstance.
Good morrow: for as I take it, it is almost day.

Pro. I shall obey him.

Duke. This is his Pardon purchas'd by such sin,
For which the Pardoner himselfe is in:
Hence hath offence his quicke celeritie,
When it is borne in high Authority.
When Vice makes Mercie; Mercie's so extended,
That for the faults loue, is th'offender friended.
Now Sir, what newes?

Pro. I told you:
Lord *Angelo* (be-like) thinking me remisse
In mine Office, awakens mee
With this vnwonted putting on, methinks strangely:
For he hath not vs'd it before.

Duk. Pray you let's heare.

The Letter.

Whatsoeuer you may heare to the contrary, let Claudio be executed by foure of the clocke, and in the afternoone Bernardine: For my better satisfaction, let mee haue Claudios head sent me by fiue. Let this be duely performed with a thought that more depends on it, then we must yet deliuer. Thus faile not to doe your Office, as you will answere it at your perill.

What say you to this Sir?

Duke. What is that *Barnardine*, who is to be executed in th'afternoone?

Pro. A Bohemian borne: But here nurst vp & bred,
One that is a prisoner nine yeeres old.

Duke. How came it, that the absent Duke had not either deliuer'd him to his libertie, or executed him? I haue heard it was euer his manner to do so.

Pro. His friends still wrought Repreeues for him:
And indeed his fact till now in the gouernment of Lord *Angelo*, came not to an vndoubtfull proofe.

Duke. It is now apparant?

Pro. Most manifest, and not denied by himselfe.

Duke. Hath he borne himselfe penitently in prison?
How seemes he to be touch'd?

Pro. A man that apprehends death no more dreadfully, but as a drunken sleepe, carelesse, wreaklesse, and feareless of what's past, present, or to come: insensible of mortality, and desperately mortall.

Duke. He wants aduice.

Pro. He wil heare none: he hath euermore had the liberty of the prison: giue him leaue to escape hence, hee would not. Drunke many times a day, if not many daies entirely drunke. We haue verie oft awak'd him, as if to carrie him to execution, and show'd him a seeming warrant for it, it hath not moued him at all.

Duke.

Duke. More of him anon: There is written in your brow Prouost, honesty and constancie; if I reade it not truly, my ancient skill beguiles me: but in the boldnes of my cunning, I will lay my selfe in hazard: *Claudio*, whom heere you haue warrant to execute, is no greater forfeit to the Law, then *Angelo* who hath sentenc'd him. To make you vnderstand this in a manifested effect, I craue but foure daies respit: for the which, you are to do me both a present, and a dangerous courtesie.

Pro. Pray Sir, in what?

Duke. In the delaying death.

Pro. Alacke, how may I do it? Hauing the houre limited, and an expresse command, vnder penaltie, to deliuer his head in the view of *Angelo*? I may make my case as *Claudio's*, to crosse this in the smallest.

Duke. By the vow of mine Order, I warrant you, If my instructions may be your guide, Let this *Barnardine* be this morning executed, And his head borne to *Angelo*.

Pro. *Angelo* hath seene them both, And will discouer the fauour.

Duke. Oh, death's a great disguiser, and you may adde to it; Shaue the head, and tie the beard, and say it was the desire of the penitent to be so bar'de before his death: you know the course is common. If any thing fall to you vpon this, more then thankes and good fortune, by the Saint whom I professe, I will plead against it with my life.

Pro. Pardon me, good Father, it is against my oath.

Duke. Were you sworne to the Duke, or to the Deputie?

Pro. To him, and to his Substitutes.

Duke. You will thinke you haue made no offence, if the Duke auouch the iustice of your dealing?

Pro. But what likelihood is in that?

Duke. Not a resemblance, but a certainty; yet since I see you fearfull, that neither my coate, integrity, nor perswasion, can with ease attempt you, I wil go further then I meant, to plucke all feares out of you. Looke you Sir, heere is the hand and Seale of the Duke: you know the Charracter I doubt not, and the Signet is not strange to you?

Pro. I know them both.

Duke. The Contents of this, is the returne of the Duke; you shall anon ouer-reade it at your pleasure: where you shall finde within these two daies, he wil be heere. This is a thing that *Angelo* knowes not, for hee this very day receiues letters of strange tenor, perchance of the Dukes death, perchance entering into some Monasterie, but by chance nothing of what is writ. Looke, th'vnfolding Starre calles vp the Shepheard: put not your selfe into amazement, how these things should be; all difficulties are but easie when they are knowne. Call your executioner, and off with *Barnardines* head: I will giue him a present shrift, and aduise him for a better place. Yet you are amaz'd, but this shall absolutely resolue you: Come away, it is almost cleere dawne. *Exit*.

Scena Tertia.

Enter Clowne.

Clo. I am as well acquainted heere, as I was in our house of profession: one would thinke it were Mistris Ouer-dons owne house, for heere be manie of her olde Customers. First, here's yong Mr *Rash*, hee's in for a commoditie of browne paper, and olde Ginger, nine score and seuenteene pounds, of which hee made fiue Markes readie money: marrie then, Ginger was not much in request, for the olde Women were all dead. Then is there heere one Mr *Caper*, at the suite of Master *Three-Pile* the Mercer, for some foure suites of Peach-colour'd Satten, which now peaches him a beggar. Then haue vve heere, yong *Dizie*, and yong Mr *Deepe-vow*, and Mr *Copperspurre*, and Mr *Starue-Lackey* the Rapier and dagger man, and yong *Drop-heire* that kild lustie *Pudding*, and Mr *Forthlight* the Tilter, and braue Mr *Shootie* the great Traueller, and wilde *Halfe-Canne* that stabb'd Pots, and I thinke fortie more, all great doers in our Trade, and are now for the Lords sake.

Enter Abhorson.

Abh. Sirrah, bring *Barnardine* hether.

Clo. Mr *Barnardine*, you must rise and be hang'd, Mr *Barnardine*.

Abh. What hoa *Barnardine*.

Barnardine within.

Bar. A pox o'your throats: who makes that noyse there? What are you?

Clo. Your friends Sir, the Hangman: You must be so good Sir to rise, and be put to death.

Bar. Away you Rogue, away, I am sleepie.

Abh. Tell him he must awake, And that quickly too.

Clo: Pray Master *Barnardine*, awake till you are executed, and sleepe afterwards.

Ab. Go in to him, and fetch him out.

Clo. He is comming Sir, he is comming: I heare his Straw russle.

Enter Barnardine.

Abh. Is the Axe vpon the blocke, sirrah?

Clo. Verie readie Sir.

Bar. How now *Abhorson*? What's the newes vvith you?

Abh. Truly Sir, I would desire you to clap into your prayers: for looke you, the Warrants come.

Bar. You Rogue, I haue bin drinking all night, I am not fitted for't.

Clo. Oh, the better Sir: for he that drinkes all night, and is hanged betimes in the morning, may sleepe the sounder all the next day.

Enter Duke.

Abh. Looke you Sir, heere comes your ghostly Father: do we iest now thinke you?

Duke. Sir, induced by my charitie, and hearing how hastily you are to depart, I am come to aduise you, Comfort you, and pray with you.

Bar. Friar, not I: I haue bin drinking hard all night, and I will haue more time to prepare mee, or they shall beat out my braines with billets: I will not consent to die this day, that's certaine.

Duke. Oh sir, you must: and therefore I beseech you Looke forward on the iournie you shall go.

Bar. I sweare I will not die to day for anie mans perswasion.

Duke. But heare you:

Bar. Not a word: if you haue anie thing to say to me, come to my Ward: for thence will not I to day. *Exit*

Enter Prouost.

Duke. Vnfit to liue, or die: oh grauell heart.

After him (Fellowes) bring him to the blocke.

Pro. Now Sir, how do you finde the prisoner?

Duke. A creature vnpre-par'd, vnmeet for death,
And to transport him in the minde he is,
Were damnable.

Pro. Heere in the prison, Father,
There died this morning of a cruell Feauor,
One *Ragozine*, a most notorious Pirate,
A man of *Claudio's* yeares : his beard, and head
Iust of his colour. What if we do omit
This Reprobate, til he were wel enclin'd,
And satisfie the Deputie with the visage
Of *Ragozine*, more like to *Claudio*?

Duke. Oh, 'tis an accident that heauen prouides :
Dispatch it presently, the houre drawes on
Prefixt by *Angelo* : See this be done,
And sent according to command, whiles I
Perswade this rude wretch willingly to die.

Pro. This shall be done (good Father) presently :
But *Barnardine* must die this afternoone,
And how shall we continue *Claudio*,
To saue me from the danger that might come,
If he were knowne aliue?

Duke. Let this be done,
Put them in secret holds, both *Barnardine* and *Claudio*,
Ere twice the Sun hath made his iournall greeting
To yond generation, you shal finde
Your safetie manifested.

Pro. I am your free dependant.   *Exit.*

Duke. Quicke, dispatch, and send the head to *Angelo*
Now wil I write Letters to *Angelo*,
(The Prouost he shal beare them) whose contents
Shal witnesse to him I am neere at home :
And that by great Iniunctions I am bound
To enter publikely : him Ile desire
To meet me at the consecrated Fount,
A League below the Citie : and from thence,
By cold gradation, and weale-ballanc'd forme,
We shal proceed with *Angelo*.

Enter Prouost.

Pro. Heere is the head, Ile carrie it my selfe.

Duke. Conuenient is it : Make a swift returne,
For I would commune with you of such things,
That want no eare but yours.

Pro. Ile make all speede.   *Exit*

Isabell within.

Isa. Peace hoa, be heere.

Duke. The tongue of *Isabell.* She's come to know,
If yet her brothers pardon be come hither :
But I will keepe her ignorant of her good,
To make her heauenly comforts of dispaire,
When it is least expected.

Enter Isabella.

Isa. Hoa, by your leaue.

Duke. Good morning to you, faire, and gracious daughter.

Isa. The better giuen me by so holy a man,
Hath yet the Deputie sent my brothers pardon?

Duke. He hath releas'd him, *Isabell*, from the world,
His head is off, and sent to *Angelo*.

Isa. Nay, but it is not so.

Duke. It is no other,
Shew your wisedome daughter in your close patience.

Isa. Oh, I wil to him, and plucke out his eies.

Duke. You shal not be admitted to his sight.

Isa. Vnhappie *Claudio*, wretched *Isabell*,

Iniurious world, most damned *Angelo*.

Duke. This nor hurts him, nor profits you a iot,
Forbeare it therefore, giue your cause to heauen,
Marke what I say, which you shal finde
By euery sillable a faithful veritie.
The Duke comes home to morrow : nay drie your eyes,
One of our Couent, and his Confessor
Giues me this instance : Already he hath carried
Notice to *Escalus* and *Angelo*,
Who do prepare to meete him at the gates,   (dome,
There to giue vp their powre : If you can pace your wis-
In that good path that I would wish it go,
And you shal haue your bosome on this wretch,
Grace of the Duke, reuenges to your heart,
And general Honor.

Isa. I am directed by you.

Duk. This Letter then to Friar *Peter* giue,
'Tis that he sent me of the Dukes returne :
Say, by this token, I desire his companie
At *Mariana's* house to night. Her cause, and yours
Ile perfect him withall, and he shal bring you
Before the Duke ; and to the head of *Angelo*
Accuse him home and home. For my poore selfe,
I am combined by a sacred Vow,
And shall be absent. Wend you with this Letter :
Command these fretting waters from your eies
With a light heart ; trust not my holie Order
If I peruert your course : whose heere?

Enter Lucio.

Luc. Good'euen ;
Frier, where's the Prouost?

Duke. Not within Sir.

Luc. Oh prettie *Isabella*, I am pale at mine heart, to
see thine eyes so red : thou must be patient ; I am faine
to dine and sup with water and bran : I dare not for my
head fill my belly. One fruitful Meale would set mee
too't : but they say the Duke will be heere to Morrow.
By my troth *Isabell* I lou'd thy brother, if the olde fantastical Duke of darke corners had bene at home, he had
liued.

Duke. Sir, the Duke is maruellous little beholding
to your reports, but the best is, he liues not in them.

Luc. Friar, thou knowest not the Duke so wel as I
do : he's a better woodman then thou tak'st him for.

Duke. Well : you'l answer this one day. Fare ye well.

Luc. Nay tarrie, Ile go along with thee,
I can tel thee pretty tales of the Duke.

Duke. You haue told me too many of him already sir
if they be true : if not true, none were enough.

Lucio. I was once before him for getting a Wench
with childe.

Duke. Did you such a thing?

Luc. Yes marrie did I ; but I was faine to forswear it,
They would else haue married me to the rotten Medler.

Duke. Sir your company is fairer then honest, rest you well.

Lucio. By my troth Ile go with thee to the lanes end:
if baudy talke offend you, we'el haue very litle of it: nay
Friar, I am a kind of Burre, I shal sticke.   *Exeunt*

Scena Quarta.

Enter Angelo & Escalus.

Esc. Euery Letter he hath writ, hath disuouch'd other.

Ang.

An. In most vneuen and distracted manner, his actions show much like to madnesse, pray heauen his wisedome bee not tainted: and why meet him at the gates and reliuer ou rauthorities there?

Esc. I ghesse not.

Ang. And why should wee proclaime it in an howre before his entring, that if any craue redresse of iniustice, they should exhibit their petitions in the street?

Esc. He showes his reason for that: to haue a dispatch of Complaints, and to deliuer vs from deuices heereafter, which shall then haue no power to stand against vs.

Ang. Well: I beseech you let it bee proclaim'd betimes i'th' morne, Ile call you at your house: giue notice to such men of sort and suite as are to meete him.

Esc. I shall sir: fareyouwell.   *Exit.*

Ang. Good night.
This deede vnshapes me quite, makes me vnpregnant
And dull to all proceedings. A deflowred maid,
And by an eminent body, that enforc'd
The Law against it? But that her tender shame
Will not proclaime against her maiden losse,
How might she tongue me? yet reason dares her no,
For my Authority beares of a credent bulke,
That no particular scandall once can touch
But it confounds the breather. He should haue liu'd,
Saue that his riotous youth with dangerous sense
Might in the times to come haue ta'ne reuenge
By so receiuing a dishonor'd life
With ransome of such shame: would yet he had liued.
Alack, when once our grace we haue forgot,
Nothing goes right, we would, and we would not. *Exit.*

Scena Quinta.

Enter Duke and Frier Peter.

Duke. These Letters at fit time deliuer me,
The Prouost knowes our purpose and our plot,
The matter being afoote, keepe your instruction
And hold you euer to our speciall drift,
Though sometimes you doe blench from this to that
As cause doth minister: Goe call at *Flauia's* house,
And tell him where I stay: giue the like notice
To *Valencius, Rowland*, and to *Crassus*,
And bid them bring the Trumpets to the gate:
But send me *Flauius* first.

Peter. It shall be speeded well.

Enter Varrius.

Duke. I thank thee *Varrius*, thou hast made good hast,
Come, we will walke: There's other of our friends
Will greet vs heere anon: my gentle *Varrius*.   *Exeunt.*

Scena Sexta.

Enter Isabella and Mariana.

Isab. To speak so indirectly I am loath,
I would say the truth, but to accuse him so
That is your part, yet I am aduis'd to doe it,
He saies, to vaile full purpose.

Mar. Be rul'd by him.

Isab. Besides he tells me, that if peraduenture
He speake against me on the aduerse side,
I should not thinke it strange, for 'tis a physicke
That's bitter, to sweet end.

Enter Peter.

Mar. I would *Frier Peter—*

Isab. Oh peace, the *Frier* is come.

Peter. Come I haue found you out a stand most fit,
Where you may haue such vantage on the *Duke*
He shall not passe you:
Twice haue the Trumpets sounded.
The generous, and graueft Citizens
Haue hent the gates, and very neere vpon
The *Duke* is entring:
Therefore hence away.   *Exeunt.*

Actus Quintus. Scœna Prima.

Enter Duke, Varrius, Lords, Angelo, Esculus, Lucio, Citizens at seuerall doores.

Duk. My very worthy Cosen, fairely met,
Our old, and faithfull friend, we are glad to see you.

Ang. Esc. Happy returne be to your royall grace.

Duk. Many and harty thankings to you both:
We haue made enquiry of you, and we heare
Such goodnesse of your Iustice, that our soule
Cannot but yeeld you forth to publique thankes
Forerunning more requitall.

Ang. You make my bonds still greater.

Duk. Oh your desert speaks loud, & I should wrong it
To locke it in the wards of couert bosome
When it deserues with characters of brasse
A forted residence 'gainst the tooth of time,
And razure of obliuion: Giue we your hand
And let the Subiect see, to make them know
That outward curtesies would faine proclaime
Fauours that keepe within: Come *Escalus*,
You must walke by vs, on our other hand:
And good supporters are you.

Enter Peter and Isabella.

Peter. Now is your time
Speake loud, and kneele before him.

Isab. Iustice, O royall *Duke*, vaile your regard
Vpon a wrong'd (I would faine haue said a Maid)
Oh worthy Prince, dishonor not your eye
By throwing it on any other obiect,
Till you haue heard me, in my true complaint,
And giuen me Iustice, Iustice, Iustice, Iustice.

Duk. Relate your wrongs;
In what, by whom? be briefe:
Here is Lord *Angelo* shall giue you Iustice,
Reueale your selfe to him.

Isab. Oh worthy *Duke*,
You bid me seeke redemption of the diuell,
Heare me your selfe: for that which I must speake
Must either punish me, not being beleeu'd,
Or wring redresse from you:
Heare me: oh heare me, heere.

Ang. My Lord, her wits I feare me are not firme:
She hath bin a suitor to me, for her Brother
Cut off by course of Iustice.

Isab. By course of Iustice.

Ang. And she will speake most bitterly, and strange.

Isab. Most

Isab. Most strange: but yet most truely wil I speake,
That *Angelo's* forsworne, is it not strange?
That *Angelo's* a murtherer, is't not strange?
That *Angelo* is an adulterous thiefe,
An hypocrite, a virgin violator,
Is it not strange? and strange?

Duke. Nay it is ten times strange?

Isa. It is not truer he is *Angelo*,
Then this is all as true, as it is strange;
Nay, it is ten times true, for truth is truth
To th'end of reckning.

Duke. Away with her: poore soule
She speakes this, in th'infirmity of sence.

Isa. Oh Prince, I coniure thee, as thou beleeu'st
There is another comfort, then this world,
That thou neglect me not, with that opinion
That I am touch'd with madnesse: make not impossible
That which but seemes vnlike, 'tis not impossible
But one, the wickedst caitiffe on the ground
May seeme as shie, as graue, as iust, as absolute:
As *Angelo*, euen so may *Angelo*
In all his dressings, caracts, titles, formes,
Be an arch-villaine: Beleeue it, royall Prince
If he be lesse, he's nothing, but he's more,
Had I more name for badnesse.

Duke. By mine honesty
If she be mad, as I beleeue no other,
Her madnesse hath the oddest frame of sense,
Such a dependancy of thing, on thing,
As ere I heard in madnesse.

Isab. Oh gracious Duke
Harpe not on that; nor do not banish reason
For inequality, but let your reason serue
To make the truth appeare, where it seemes hid,
And hide the false seemes true.

Duk. Many that are not mad
Haue sure more lacke of reason:
What would you say?

Isab. I am the Sister of one *Claudio*,
Condemnd vpon the Act of Fornication
To loose his head, condemn'd by *Angelo*,
I, (in probation of a Sisterhood)
Was sent to by my Brother; one *Lucio*
As then the Messenger.

Luc. That's I, and't like your Grace:
I came to her from *Claudio*, and desir'd her,
To try her gracious fortune with Lord *Angelo*,
For her poore Brothers pardon.

Isab. That's he indeede.

Duk. You were not bid to speake.

Luc. No, my good Lord,
Nor wish'd to hold my peace.

Duk. I wish you now then,
Pray you take note of it: and when you haue
A businesse for your selfe: pray heauen you then
Be perfect.

Luc. I warrant your honor.

Duk. The warrant's for your selfe: take heede to't.

Isab. This Gentleman told somewhat of my Tale.

Luc. Right.

Duk. It may be right, but you are i'the wrong
To speake before your time: proceed,

Isab. I went
To this pernicious Caitiffe Deputie.

Duk. That's somewhat madly spoken.

Isab. Pardon it,
The phrase is to the matter.

Duke. Mended againe: the matter: proceed.

Isab. In briefe, to set the needlesse processe by:
How I perswaded, how I praid, and kneel'd,
How he refeld me, and how I replide
(For this was of much length) the vild conclusion
I now begin with griefe, and shame to vtter.
He would not, but by gift of my chaste body
To his concupiscible intemperate lust
Release my brother; and after much debatement,
My sisterly remorse, confutes mine honour,
And I did yeeld to him: But the next morne betimes,
His purpose surfetting, he sends a warrant
For my poore brothers head.

Duke. This is most likely.

Isab. Oh that it were as like as it is true. (speak'st,

Duk. By heauen (fond wretch) ỹ knowst not what thou
Or else thou art suborn'd against his honor
In hatefull practise: first his Integritie
Stands without blemish: next it imports no reason,
That with such vehemency he should pursue
Faults proper to himselfe: if he had so offended
He would haue waigh'd thy brother by himselfe,
And not haue cut him off: some one hath set you on:
Confesse the truth, and say by whose aduice
Thou com'st heere to complaine.

Isab. And is this all?
Then oh you blessed Ministers aboue
Keepe me in patience, and with ripened time
Vnfold the euill, which is heere wrapt vp
In countenance: heauen shield your Grace from woe,
As I thus wrong'd, hence vnbeleeued goe.

Duke. I know you'ld faine be gone: An Officer:
To prison with her: Shall we thus permit
A blasting and a scandalous breath to fall,
On him so neere vs? This needs must be a practise;
Who knew of your intent and comming hither?

Isa. One that I would were heere, *Frier Lodowick*.

Duk. A ghostly Father, belike:
Who knowes that *Lodowicke*?

Luc. My Lord, I know him, 'tis a medling Fryer,
I doe not like the man: had he been Lay my Lord,
For certaine words he spake against your Grace
In your retirment, I had swing'd him soundly.

Duke. Words against mee? this 'a good Fryer belike
And to set on this wretched woman here
Against our Substitute: Let this Fryer be found.

Luc. But yesternight my Lord, she and that Fryer
I saw them at the prison; a sawcy Fryar,
A very scuruy fellow.

Peter. Blessed be your Royall Grace:
I haue stood by my Lord, and I haue heard
Your royall eare abus'd: first hath this woman
Most wrongfully accus'd your Substitute,
Who is as free from touch, or soyle with her
As she from one vngot.

Duke. We did beleeue no lesse.
Know you that Frier *Lodowick* that she speakes of?

Peter. I know him for a man diuine and holy,
Not scuruy, nor a temporary medler
As he's reported by this Gentleman:
And on my trust, a man that neuer yet
Did (as he vouches) mis-report your Grace.

Luc. My Lord, most villanously, beleeue it.

Peter. Well: he in time may come to cleere himselfe;
But at this instant he is sicke, my Lord:

Of

Of a strange Feauor: vpon his meere request
Being come to knowledge, that there was complaint
Intended 'gainst Lord *Angelo*, came I hether
To speake as from his mouth, what he doth know
Is true, and false: And what he with his oath
And all probation will make vp full cleare
Whensoeuer he's conuented: First for this woman,
To iustifie this worthy Noble man,
So vulgarly and personally accus'd,
Her shall you heare disproued to her eyes,
Till she her selfe confesse it.

  Duk. Good Frier, let's heare it:
Doe you not smile at this, Lord *Angelo*?
Oh heauen, the vanity of wretched fooles.
Giue vs some seates, Come cosen *Angelo*,
In this I'll be impartiall: be you Iudge
Of your owne Cause: Is this the Witnes Frier?

Enter Mariana.

First, let her shew your face, and after, speake.
  Mar. Pardon my Lord, I will not shew my face
Vntill my husband bid me.
  Duke. What, are you married?
  Mar. No my Lord.
  Duke. Are you a Maid?
  Mar. No my Lord.
  Duk. A Widow then?
  Mar. Neither, my Lord.
  Duk. Why you are nothing then: neither Maid, Widow, nor Wife?
  Luc. My Lord, she may be a Puncke: for many of them, are neither Maid, Widow, nor Wife.
  Duk. Silence that fellow: I would he had some cause to prattle for himselfe.
  Luc. Well my Lord.
  Mar. My Lord, I doe confesse I nere was married,
And I confesse besides, I am no Maid,
I haue known my husband, yet my husband
Knowes not, that euer he knew me.
  Luc. He was drunk then, my Lord, it can be no better.
  Duk. For the benefit of silence, would thou wert so to.
  Luc. Well, my Lord.
  Duk. This is no witnesse for Lord *Angelo*.
  Mar. Now I come to't, my Lord.
Shee that accuses him of Fornication,
In selfe-same manner, doth accuse my husband,
And charges him, my Lord, with such a time,
When I'le depose I had him in mine Armes
With all th'effect of Loue.
  Ang. Charges she moe then me?
  Mar. Not that I know.
  Duk. No? you say your husband.
  Mar. Why iust, my Lord, and that is *Angelo*,
Who thinkes he knowes, that he nere knew my body,
But knows, he thinkes, that he knowes *Isabels*.
  Ang. This is a strange abuse: Let's see thy face.
  Mar. My husband bids me, now I will vnmaske.
This is that face, thou cruell *Angelo*
Which once thou sworst, was worth the looking on:
This is the hand, which with a vowd contract
Was fast belockt in thine: This is the body
That tooke away the match from *Isabell*,
And did supply thee at thy garden-house
In her Imagin'd person.
  Duke. Know you this woman?
  Luc. Carnallie she saies.

  Duk. Sirha, no more.
  Luc. Enoug my Lord.
  Ang. My Lord, I must confesse, I know this woman,
And fiue yeres since there was some speech of marriage
Betwixt my selfe, and her: which was broke off,
Partly for that her promis'd proportions
Came short of Composition: But in chiefe
For that her reputation was dis-valued
In leuitie: Since which time of fiue yeres
I neuer spake with her, saw her, nor heard from her
Vpon my faith, and honor.
  Mar. Noble Prince,
As there comes light from heauen, and words frō breath,
As there is sence in truth, and truth in vertue,
I am affianced this mans wife, as strongly
As words could make vp vowes: And my good Lord,
But Tuesday night last gon, in's garden house,
He knew me as a wife. As this is true,
Let me in safety raise me from my knees,
Or else for euer be confixed here
A Marble Monument.
  Ang. I did but smile till now,
Now, good my Lord, giue me the scope of Iustice,
My patience here is touch'd: I doe perceiue
These poore informall women, are no more
But instruments of some more mightier member
That sets them on. Let me haue way, my Lord
To finde this practise out.
  Duke. I, with my heart,
And punish them to your height of pleasure.
Thou foolish Frier, and thou pernicious woman
Compact with her that's gone: thinkst thou, thy oathes,
Though they would sweare downe each particular Saint,
Were testimonies against his worth, and credit
That's seal'd in approbation? you, Lord *Escalus*
Sit with my Cozen, lend him your kinde paines
To finde out this abuse, whence 'tis deriu'd.
There is another Frier that set them on,
Let him be sent for.
  Peter. Would he were here, my Lord, for he indeed
Hath set the women on to this Complaint;
Your Prouost knowes the place where he abides,
And he may fetch him.
  Duke. Goe, doe it instantly:
And you, my noble and well-warranted Cosen
Whom it concernes to heare this matter forth,
Doe with your iniuries as seemes you best
In any chastisement; I for a while
Will leaue you; but stir not you till you haue
Well determin'd vpon these Slanderers.   *Exit.*
  Esc. My Lord, wee'll doe it throughly: Signior *Lucio*, did not you say you knew that Frier *Lodowick* to be a dishonest person?
  Luc. Cucullus non facit Monachum, honest in nothing but in his Clothes, and one that hath spoke most villanous speeches of the Duke.
  Esc. We shall intreat you to abide heere till he come, and inforce them against him: we shall finde this Frier a notable fellow.
  Luc. As any in *Vienna*, on my word.
  Esc. Call that same *Isabell* here once againe, I would speake with her: pray you, my Lord, giue mee leaue to question, you shall see how Ile handle her.
  Luc. Not better then he, by her owne report.
  Esc. Say you?
  Luc. Marry sir, I thinke, if you handled her priuately
                              shee

She would sooner confesse, perchance publikely she'll be asham'd.

Enter Duke, Prouost, Isabella.

Esc. I will goe darkely to worke with her.

Luc. That's the way: for women are light at midnight.

Esc. Come on Mistris, here's a Gentlewoman, Denies all that you haue said.

Luc. My Lord, here comes the rascall I spoke of, Here, with the *Prouost*.

Esc. In very good time: speake not you to him, till we call vpon you.

Luc. Mum.

Esc. Come Sir, did you set these women on to slander Lord *Angelo*? they haue confes'd you did.

Duk. 'Tis false.

Esc. How? Know you where you are?

Duk. Respect to your great place; and let the diuell Be sometime honour'd, for his burning throne. Where is the *Duke*? 'tis he should heare me speake.

Esc. The *Duke's* in vs: and we will heare you speake, Looke you speake iustly.

Duk. Boldly, at least. But oh poore soules, Come you to seeke the Lamb here of the Fox; Good night to your redresse: Is the *Duke* gone? Then is your cause gone too: The *Duke's* vniust, Thus to retort your manifest Appeale, And put your triall in the villaines mouth, Which here you come to accuse.

Luc. This is the rascall: this is he I spoke of.

Esc. Why thou vnreuerend, and vnhallowed Fryer: Is't not enough thou hast suborn'd these women, To accuse this worthy man? but in foule mouth, And in the witnesse of his proper eare, To call him villaine; and then to glance from him, To th'*Duke* himselfe, to taxe him with Iniustice? Take him hence; to th' racke with him: we'll towze you Ioynt by ioynt, but we will know his purpose: What? vniust?

Duk. Be not so hot: the *Duke* dare No more stretch this finger of mine, then he Dare racke his owne: his Subiect am I not, Nor here Prouinciall: My businesse in this State Made me a looker on here in *Vienna*, Where I haue seene corruption boyle and bubble, Till it ore-run the Stew: Lawes, for all faults, But faults so countenanc'd, that the strong Statutes Stand like the forfeites in a Barbers shop, As much in mocke, as marke.

Esc. Slander to th' State: Away with him to prison.

Ang. What can you vouch against him Signior *Lucio*? Is this the man that you did tell vs of?

Luc. 'Tis he, my Lord: come hither goodman baldpate, doe you know me?

Duk. I remember you Sir, by the sound of your voice, I met you at the Prison, in the absence of the *Duke*.

Luc. Oh, did you so? and do you remember what you said of the *Duke*.

Duk. Most notedly Sir.

Luc. Do you so Sir: And was the *Duke* a flesh-monger, a foole, and a coward, as you then reported him to be?

Duk. You must (Sir) change persons with me, ere you make that my report: you indeede spoke so of him, and much more, much worse.

Luc. Oh thou damnable fellow: did not I plucke thee by the nose, for thy speeches?

Duk. I protest, I loue the *Duke*, as I loue my selfe.

Ang. Harke how the villaine would close now, after his treasonable abuses.

Esc. Such a fellow is not to be talk'd withall: Away with him to prison: Where is the *Prouost*? away with him to prison: lay bolts enough vpon him: let him speak no more: away with those Giglets too, and with the other confederate companion.

Duk. Stay Sir, stay a while.

Ang. What, resists he? helpe him *Lucio*.

Luc. Come sir, come sir, come sir: foh sir, why you bald-pated lying rascall, you must be hooded must you? shew your knaues visage with a poxe to you: show your sheepe-biting face, and be hang'd an houre: will't not off?

Duk. Thou art the first knaue, that ere mad'st a Duke. First *Prouost*, let me bayle these gentle three: Sneake not away Sir, for the Fryer, and you, Must haue a word anon: lay hold on him.

Luc. This may proue worse then hanging.

Duk. What you haue spoke, I pardon: sit you downe, We'll borrow place of him; Sir, by your leaue: Ha'st thou or word, or wit, or impudence, That yet can doe thee office? If thou ha'st Rely vpon it, till my tale be heard, And hold no longer out.

Ang. Oh, my dread Lord, I should be guiltier then my guiltinesse, To thinke I can be vndiscerneable, When I perceiue your grace, like powre diuine, Hath look'd vpon my passes. Then good Prince, No longer Session hold vpon my shame, But let my Triall, be mine owne Confession: Immediate sentence then, and sequent death, Is all the grace I beg.

Duk. Come hither *Mariana*, Say: was't thou ere contracted to this woman?

Ang. I was my Lord.

Duk. Goe take her hence, and marry her instantly. Doe you the office (*Fryer*) which consummate, Returne him here againe: goe with him *Prouost*. *Exit.*

Esc. My Lord, I am more amaz'd at his dishonor, Then at the strangenesse of it.

Duk. Come hither *Isabell*, Your *Frier* is now your Prince: As I was then Aduertysing, and holy to your businesse, (Not changing heart with habit) I am still, Atturnied at your seruice.

Isab. Oh giue me pardon That I, your vassaile, haue imploid, and pain'd Your vnknowne Soueraigntie.

Duk. You are pardon'd *Isabell*: And now, deere Maide, be you as free to vs. Your Brothers death I know sits at your heart: And you may maruaile, why I obscur'd my selfe, Labouring to saue his life: and would not rather Make rash remonstrance of my hidden powre, Then let him so be lost: oh most kinde Maid, It was the swift celeritie of his death, Which I did thinke, with slower foot came on, That brain'd my purpose: but peace be with him, That life is better life past fearing death, Then that which liues to feare: make it your comfort, So

So happy is your Brother.

Enter Angelo, Maria, Peter, Prouost.

Isab. I doe my Lord.

Duk. For this new-maried man, approaching here,
Whose salt imagination yet hath wrong'd
Your well defended honor: you must pardon
For *Mariana's* sake: But as he adiudg'd your Brother,
Being criminall, in double violation
Of sacred Chastitie, and of promise-breach,
Thereon dependant for your Brothers life,
The very mercy of the Law cries out
Most audible, euen from his proper tongue.
An *Angelo* for *Claudio*, death for death:
Haste still paies haste, and leasure, answers leasure;
Like doth quit like, and *Measure* still for *Measure*:
Then *Angelo*, thy fault's thus manifested;
Which though thou would'st deny, denies thee vantage.
We doe condemne thee to the very Blocke
Where *Claudio* stoop'd to death, and with like haste.
Away with him.

Mar. Oh my most gracious Lord,
I hope you will not mocke me with a husband?

Duk. It is your husband mock't you with a husband,
Consenting to the safe-guard of your honor,
I thought your marriage fit: else Imputation,
For that he knew you, might reproach your life,
And choake your good to come: For his Possessions,
Although by confutation they are ours;
We doe en-state, and widow you with all,
To buy you a better husband.

Mar. Oh my deere Lord,
I craue no other, nor no better man.

Duke. Neuer craue him, we are definitiue.

Mar. Gentle my Liege.

Duke. You doe but loose your labour.
Away with him to death: Now Sir, to you.

Mar. Oh my good Lord, sweet *Isabell*, take my part,
Lend me your knees, and all my life to come,
I'll lend you all my life to doe you seruice.

Duke. Against all sence you doe importune her,
Should she kneele downe, in mercie of this fact,
Her Brothers ghost, his paued bed would breake,
And take her hence in horror.

Mar. Isabell:
Sweet *Isabel*, doe yet but kneele by me,
Hold vp your hands, say nothing: I'll speake all.
They say best men are moulded out of faults,
And for the most, become much more the better
For being a little bad: So may my husband.
Oh *Isabel*: will you not lend a knee?

Duke. He dies for *Claudio's* death.

Isab. Most bounteous Sir.
Looke if it please you, on this man condemn'd,
As if my Brother liu'd: I partly thinke,
A due sinceritie gouerned his deedes,
Till he did looke on me: Since it is so,
Let him not die: my Brother had but Iustice,
In that he did the thing for which he dide.
For *Angelo*, his Act did not ore-take his bad intent,
And must be buried but as an intent
That perish'd by the way: thoughts are no subiects
Intents, but meerely thoughts.

Mar. Meerely my Lord.

Duk. Your suite's vnprofitable: stand vp I say:
I haue bethought me of another faule.
Prouost, how came it *Claudio* was beheaded
At an vnusuall howre?

Pro. It was commanded so.

Duke. Had you a speciall warrant for the deed?

Pro. No my good Lord: it was by priuate message.

Duk. For which I doe discharge you of your office,
Giue vp your keyes.

Pro. Pardon me, noble Lord,
I thought it was a fault, but knew it not,
Yet did repent me after more aduice,
For testimony whereof, one in the prison
That should by priuate order else haue dide,
I haue reseru'd aliue.

Duk. What's he?

Pro. His name is *Barnardine*.

Duke. I would thou hadst done so by *Claudio*:
Goe fetch him hither, let me looke vpon him.

Esc. I am sorry, one so learned, and so wise
As you, Lord *Angelo*, haue stil appear'd,
Should slip so grosselie, both in the heat of bloud
And lacke of temper'd iudgement afterward.

Ang. I am sorrie, that such sorrow I procure,
And so deepe sticks it in my penitent heart,
That I craue death more willingly then mercy,
'Tis my deseruing, and I doe entreat it.

Enter Barnardine and Prouost, Claudio, Iulietta.

Duke. Which is that *Barnardine*?

Pro. This my Lord.

Duke. There was a Friar told me of this man.
Sirha, thou art said to haue a stubborne soule
That apprehends no further then this world,
And squar'st thy life according: Thou'rt condemn'd,
But for those earthly faults, I quit them all,
And pray thee take this mercie to prouide
For better times to come: Frier aduise him,
I leaue him to your hand. What muffeld fellow's that?

Pro. This is another prisoner that I sau'd,
Who should haue di'd when *Claudio* lost his head,
As like almost to *Claudio*, as himselfe.

Duke. If he be like your brother, for his sake
Is he pardon'd, and for your louelie sake
Giue me your hand, and say you will be mine,
He is my brother too: But fitter time for that:
By this Lord *Angelo* perceiues he's safe,
Methinkes I see a quickning in his eye:
Well *Angelo*, your euill quits you well.
Looke that you loue your wife: her worth, worth yours
I finde an apt remission in my selfe:
And yet heere's one in place I cannot pardon,
You sirha, that knew me for a foole, a Coward,
One all of Luxurie, an asse, a mad man:
Wherein haue I so deseru'd of you
That you extoll me thus?

Luc. 'Faith my Lord, I spoke it but according to the
trick: if you will hang me for it you may: but I had rather it would please you, I might be whipt.

Duke. Whipt first, sir, and hang'd after.
Proclaime it Prouost round about the Citie,
If any woman wrong'd by this lewd fellow
(As I haue heard him sweare himselfe there's one
whom he begot with childe) let her appeare,
And he shall marry her: the nuptiall finish'd,
Let him be whipt and hang'd.

Luc. I beseech your Highnesse doe not marry me to
a Whore: your Highnesse said euen now I made you a
Duke, good my Lord do not recompence me, in making
me a Cuckold.

Duk. Vpon

Duke. Vpon mine honor thou shalt marrie her.
Thy slanders I forgiue, and therewithall
Remit thy other forfeits: take him to prison,
And see our pleasure herein executed.

Luc. Marrying a punke my Lord, is pressing to death,
Whipping and hanging.

Duke. Slandering a Prince deserues it.
She *Claudio* that you wrong'd, looke you restore.
Ioy to you *Mariana*, loue her *Angelo*:
I haue confes'd her, and I know her vertue.
Thanks good friend, *Escalus*, for thy much goodnesse,
There's more behinde that is more gratulate.
Thanks *Prouost* for thy care, and secrecie,
We shall imploy thee in a worthier place.
Forgiue him *Angelo*, that brought you home
The head of *Ragozine* for *Claudio's*,
Th'offence pardons it selfe. Deere *Isabell*,
I haue a motion much imports your good,
Whereto if you'll a willing eare incline;
What's mine is yours, and what is yours is mine.
So bring vs to our Pallace, where wee'll show
What's yet behinde, that meete you all should know.

The Scene Vienna.

The names of all the Actors.

Vincentio: the Duke.
Angelo, the Deputie.
Escalus, an ancient Lord.
Claudio, a yong Gentleman.
Lucio, a fantastique.
2. Other like Gentlemen.
Prouost.

Thomas. ⎫
Peter. ⎬ *2. Friers.*
Elbow, a simple Constable.
Froth, a foolish Gentleman.
Clowne.
Abhorson, an Executioner.
Barnardine, a dissolute prisoner.
Isabella, sister to Claudio.
Mariana, betrothed to Angelo.
Iuliet, beloued of Claudio.
Francisca, a Nun.
Mistris Ouer-don, a Bawd.

FINIS.

The Comedie of Errors.

Actus primus, Scena prima.

Enter the Duke of Ephesus, with the Merchant of Siracusa, Iaylor, and other attendants.

Marchant.

PRoceed *Solinus* to procure my fall,
And by the doome of death end woes and all.
  Duke. Merchant of *Siracusa*, plead no more.
I am not partiall to infringe our Lawes;
The enmity and discord which of late
Sprung from the rancorous outrage of your Duke,
To Merchants our well-dealing Countrimen,
Who wanting gilders to redeeme their liues,
Haue seal'd his rigorous statutes with their blouds,
Excludes all pitty from our threatning lookes:
For since the mortall and intestine iarres
Twixt thy seditious Countrimen and vs,
It hath in solemne Synodes beene decreed,
Both by the *Siracusians* and our selues,
To admit no trafficke to our aduerse townes:
Nay more, if any borne at *Ephesus*
Be seene at any *Siracusian* Marts and Fayres:
Againe, if any *Siracusian* borne
Come to the Bay of *Ephesus*, he dies:
His goods confiscate to the Dukes dispose,
Vnlesse a thousand markes be leuied
To quit the penalty, and to ransome him:
Thy substance, valued at the highest rate,
Cannot amount vnto a hundred Markes,
Therefore by Law thou art condemn'd to die.
  Mer. Yet this my comfort, when your words are done,
My woes end likewise with the euening Sonne.
  Duk. Well *Siracusian*; say in briefe the cause
Why thou departedst from thy natiue home?
And for what cause thou cam'st to *Ephesus*.
  Mer. A heauier taske could not haue beene impos'd,
Then I to speake my griefes vnspeakeable:
Yet that the world may witnesse that my end
Was wrought by nature, not by vile offence,
Ile vtter what my sorrow giues me leaue.
In *Syracusa* was I borne, and wedde
Vnto a woman, happy but for me,
And by me; had not our hap beene bad:
With her I liu'd in ioy, our wealth increast
By prosperous voyages I often made
To *Epidamium*, till my factors death,
And he great care of goods at randone left,
Drew me from kinde embracements of my spouse;
From whom my absence was not sixe moneths olde,
Before her selfe (almost at fainting vnder
The pleasing punishment that women beare)
Had made prouision for her following me,
And soone, and safe, arriued where I was:
There had she not beene long, but she became
A ioyfull mother of two goodly sonnes:
And, which was strange, the one so like the other,
As could not be distinguish'd but by names.
That very howre, and in the selfe-same Inne,
A meane woman was deliuered
Of such a burthen Male, twins both alike:
Those, for their parents were exceeding poore,
I bought, and brought vp to attend my sonnes.
My wife, not meanely prowd of two such boyes,
Made daily motions for our home returne:
Vnwilling I agreed, alas, too soone wee came aboord.
A league from *Epidamium* had we saild
Before the alwaies winde-obeying deepe
Gaue any Tragicke Instance of our harme:
But longer did we not retaine much hope;
For what obscured light the heauens did grant,
Did but conuay vnto our fearefull mindes
A doubtfull warrant of immediate death,
Which though my selfe would gladly haue imbrac'd,
Yet the incessant weepings of my wife,
Weeping before for what she saw must come,
And pitteous playnings of the prettie babes
That mourn'd for fashion, ignorant what to feare,
Forst me to seeke delayes for them and me,
And this it was: (for other meanes was none)
The Sailors sought for safety by our boate,
And left the ship then sinking ripe to vs.
My wife, more carefull for the latter borne,
Had fastned him vnto a small spare Mast,
Such as sea-faring men prouide for stormes:
To him one of the other twins was bound,
Whil'st I had beene like heedfull of the other.
The children thus dispos'd, my wife and I,
Fixing our eyes on whom our care was fixt,
Fastned our selues at eyther end the mast,
And floating straight, obedient to the streame,
Was carried towards *Corinth*, as we thought.
At length the sonne gazing vpon the earth,
Disperst those vapours that offended vs,
And by the benefit of his wished light
The seas waxt calme, and we discouered
Two shippes from farre, making amaine to vs:
Of *Corinth* that, of *Epidarus* this,
But ere they came, oh let me say no more,
Gather the sequell by that went before.
  Duk. Nay forward old man, doe not breake off so,

H   For

For we may pitty, though not pardon thee.

Merch. Oh had the gods done so, I had not now
Worthily tearm'd them mercilesse to vs:
For ere the ships could meet by twice fiue leagues,
We were encountred by a mighty rocke,
Which being violently borne vp,
Our helpefull ship was splitted in the midst;
So that in this vniust diuorce of vs,
Fortune had left to both of vs alike,
What to delight in, what to sorrow for,
Her part, poore soule, seeming as burdened
With lesser waight, but not with lesser woe,
Was carried with more speed before the winde,
And in our sight they three were taken vp
By Fishermen of *Corinth*, as we thought.
At length another ship had seiz'd on vs,
And knowing whom it was their hap to saue,
Gaue healthfull welcome to their ship-wrackt guests,
And would haue reft the Fishers of their prey,
Had not their backe beene very slow of saile;
And therefore homeward did they bend their course.
Thus haue you heard me seuer'd from my blisse,
That by misfortunes was my life prolong'd,
To tell sad stories of my owne mishaps.

Duke. And for the sake of them thou sorrowest for,
Doe me the fauour to dilate at full,
What haue befalne of them and they till now.

Merch. My yongest boy, and yet my eldest care,
At eighteene yeeres became inquisitiue
After his brother; and importun'd me
That his attendant, so his case was like,
Reft of his brother, but retain'd his name,
Might beare him company in the quest of him:
Whom whil'st I laboured of a loue to see,
I hazarded the losse of whom I lou'd.
Fiue Sommers haue I spent in farthest *Greece*,
Roming cleane through the bounds of *Asia*,
And coasting homeward, came to *Ephesus*:
Hopelesse to finde, yet loth to leaue vnsought
Or that, or any place that harbours men:
But heere must end the story of my life,
And happy were I in my timelie death,
Could all my trauells warrant me they liue.

Duke. Haplesse *Egeon* whom the fates haue markt
To beare the extremitie of dire mishap:
Now trust me, were it not against our Lawes,
Against my Crowne, my oath, my dignity,
Which Princes would they may not disanull,
My soule should sue as aduocate for thee:
But though thou art adiudged to the death,
And passed sentence may not be recal'd
But to our honours great disparagement:
Yet will I fauour thee in what I can;
Therefore Marchant, Ile limit thee this day
To seeke thy helpe by beneficiall helpe,
Try all the friends thou hast in *Ephesus*,
Beg thou, or borrow, to make vp the summe,
And liue: if no, then thou art doom'd to die:
Iaylor, take him to thy custodie.

Iaylor. I will my Lord.

Merch. Hopelesse and helpelesse doth *Egean* wend,
But to procrastinate his liuelesse end. *Exeunt.*

Enter Antipholis Erotes, a Marchant, and Dromio.

Mer. Therefore giue out you are of *Epidamium*,
Lest that your goods too soone be confiscate:
This very day a *Syracusian* Marchant
Is apprehended for a riuall here,
And not being able to buy out his life,
According to the statute of the towne,
Dies ere the wearie sunne set in the West:
There is your monie that I had to keepe.

Ant. Goe beare it to the Centaure, where we host,
And stay there *Dromio*, till I come to thee;
Within this houre it will be dinner time,
Till that Ile view the manners of the towne,
Peruse the traders, gaze vpon the buildings,
And then returne and sleepe within mine Inne,
For with long trauaile I am stiffe and wearie.
Get thee away.

Dro. Many a man would take you at your word,
And goe indeede, hauing so good a meane. *Exit Dromio.*

Ant. A trustie villaine sir, that very oft,
When I am dull with care and melancholly,
Lightens my humour with his merry iests:
What will you walke with me about the towne,
And then goe to my Inne and dine with me?

E.Mar. I am inuited sir to certaine Marchants,
Of whom I hope to make much benefit:
I craue your pardon, soone at fiue a clocke,
Please you, Ile meete with you vpon the Mart,
And afterward consort you till bed time:
My present businesse cals me from you now.

Ant. Farewell till then: I will goe loose my selfe,
And wander vp and downe to view the Citie.

E.Mar. Sir, I commend you to your owne content. *Exeunt.*

Ant. He that commends me to mine owne content,
Commends me to the thing I cannot get:
I to the world am like a drop of water,
That in the Ocean seekes another drop,
Who falling there to finde his fellow forth,
(Vnseene, inquisitiue) confounds himselfe.
So I, to finde a Mother and a Brother,
In quest of them (vnhappie a) loose my selfe.

Enter Dromio of Ephesus.

Here comes the almanacke of my true date:
What now? How chance thou art return'd so soone.

E.Dro. Return'd so soone, rather approacht too late:
The Capon burnes, the Pig fals from the spit;
The clocke hath strucken twelue vpon the bell:
My Mistris made it one vpon my cheeke:
She is so hot because the meate is colde:
The meate is colde, because you come not home:
You come not home, because you haue no stomacke:
You haue no stomacke, hauing broke your fast:
But we that know what 'tis to fast and pray,
Are penitent for your default to day.

Ant. Stop in your winde sir, tell me this I pray?
Where haue you left the mony that I gaue you.

E.Dro. Oh sixe pence that I had a wensday last,
To pay the Sadler for my Mistris crupper:
The Sadler had it Sir, I kept it not.

Ant. I am not in a sportiue humor now:
Tell me, and dally not, where is the monie?
We being strangers here, how dar'st thou trust
So great a charge from thine owne custodie.

E.Dro. I pray you iest sir as you sit at dinner:
I from my Mistris come to you in post:
If I returne I shall be post indeede.

For she will scoure your fault vpon my pate:
Me thinkes your maw, like mine, should be your cooke,
And strike you home without a messenger.

Ant. Come Dromio, come, these iests are out of season,
Reserue them till a merrier houre then this:
Where is the gold I gaue in charge to thee?

E.Dro. To me sir? why you gaue no gold to me?

Ant. Come on sir knaue, haue done your foolishnes,
And tell me how thou hast dispos'd thy charge.

E.Dro. My charge was but to fetch you frō the Mart
Home to your house, the *Phœnix* sir, to dinner;
My Mistris and her sister staies for you.

Ant. Now as I am a Christian answer me,
In what safe place you haue bestow'd my monie;
Or I shall breake that merrie sconce of yours
That stands on tricks, when I am vndispos'd:
Where is the thousand Markes thou hadst of me?

E.Dro. I haue some markes of yours vpon my pate:
Some of my Mistris markes vpon my shoulders:
But not a thousand markes betweene you both.
If I should pay your worship those againe,
Perchance you will not beare them patiently.

Ant. Thy Mistris markes? what Mistris slaue hast thou?

E.Dro. Your worships wife, my Mistris at the *Phœnix*;
She that doth fast till you come home to dinner:
And praies that you will hie you home to dinner.

Ant. What wilt thou flout me thus vnto my face
Being forbid? There take you that sir knaue.

E.Dro. What meane you sir, for God sake hold your
Nay, and you will not sir, Ile take my heeles. (hands:
Exeunt Dromio Ep.

Ant. Vpon my life by some deuise or other,
The villaine is ore-wrought of all my monie.
They say this towne is full of cosenage:
As nimble Iuglers that deceiue the eie:
Darke working Sorcerers that change the minde:
Soule-killing Witches, that deforme the bodie:
Disguised Cheaters, prating Mountebankes;
And manie such like liberties of sinne:
If it proue so, I will be gone the sooner:
Ile to the Centaur to goe seeke this slaue,
I greatly feare my monie is not safe. *Exit.*

Actus Secundus.

Enter Adriana, wife to Antipholis Sereptus, with Luciana her Sister.

Adr. Neither my husband nor the slaue return'd,
That in such haste I sent to seeke his Master?
Sure *Luciana* it is two a clocke.

Luc. Perhaps some Merchant hath inuited him,
And from the Mart he's somewhere gone to dinner:
Good Sister let vs dine, and neuer fret;
A man is Master of his libertie:
Time is their Master, and when they see time,
They'll goe or come; if so, be patient Sister.

Adr. Why should their libertie then ours be more?

Luc. Because their businesse still lies out adore.

Adr. Looke when I serue him so, he takes it thus.

Luc. Oh, know he is the bridle of your will.

Adr. There's none but asses will be bridled so.

Luc. Why, headstrong liberty is lasht with woe:
There's nothing situate vnder heauens eye,
But hath his bound in earth, in sea, in skie.
The beasts, the fishes, and the winged fowles
Are their males subiects, and at their controules:
Man more diuine, the Master of all these,
Lord of the wide world, and wilde watry seas,
Indued with intellectuall sence and soules,
Of more preheminence then fish and fowles,
Are masters to their females, and their Lords:
Then let your will attend on their accords.

Adri. This seruitude makes you to keepe vnwed.

Luci. Not this, but troubles of the marriage bed.

Adr. But were you wedded, you wold bear some sway

Luc. Ere I learne loue, Ile practise to obey.

Adr. How if your husband start some other where?

Luc. Till he come home againe, I would forbeare.

Adr. Patience vnmou'd, no maruel though she pause,
They can be meeke, that haue no other cause:
A wretched soule bruis'd with aduersitie,
We bid be quiet when we heare it crie.
But were we burdned with like waight of paine,
As much, or more, we should our selues complaine:
So thou that hast no vnkinde mate to greeue thee,
With vrging helpelesse patience would releeue me;
But if thou liue to see like right bereft,
This foole-beg'd patience in thee will be left.

Luci. Well, I will marry one day but to trie:
Heere comes your man, now is your husband nie.

Enter Dromio Eph.

Adr. Say, is your tardie master now at hand?

E.Dro. Nay, hee's at too hands with mee, and that my two eares can witnesse.

Adr. Say, didst thou speake with him? knowst thou his minde?

E. Dro. I, I, he told his minde vpon mine eare,
Beshrew his hand, I scarce could vnderstand it.

Luc. Spake hee so doubtfully, thou couldst not feele his meaning.

E. Dro. Nay, hee strooke so plainly, I could too well feele his blowes; and withall so doubtfully, that I could scarce vnderstand them.

Adri. But say, I prethee, is he comming home?
It seemes he hath great care to please his wife.

E. Dro. Why Mistresse, sure my Master is horne mad.

Adri. Horne mad, thou villaine?

E. Dro. I meane not Cuckold mad,
But sure he is starke mad:
When I desir'd him to come home to dinner,
He ask'd me for a hundred markes in gold:
'Tis dinner time, quoth I: my gold, quoth he:
Your meat doth burne, quoth I: my gold quoth he:
Will you come, quoth I: my gold, quoth he;
Where is the thousand markes I gaue thee villaine?
The Pigge quoth I, is burn'd: my gold, quoth he:
My mistresse, sir, quoth I: hang vp thy Mistresse:
I know not thy mistresse, out on thy mistresse.

Luci. Quoth who?

E. Dr. Quoth my Master, I know quoth he, no house,
no wife, no mistresse: so that my arrant due vnto my
tongue, I thanke him, I bare home vpon my shoulders:
for in conclusion, he did beat me there.

Adri. Go back againe, thou slaue, & fetch him home.

Dro. Goe backe againe, and be new beaten home?
For Gods sake send some other messenger.

Adri. Backe

Adri. Backe slaue, or I will breake thy pate a-crosse.
Dro. And he will blesse ẙ crosse with other beating:
Betweene you, I shall haue a holy head.
Adri. Hence prating pesant, fetch thy Master home.
Dro. Am I so round with you, as you with me,
That like a foot-ball you doe spurne me thus:
You spurne me hence, and he will spurne me hither,
If I last in this seruice, you must case me in leather.
Luci. Fie how impatience lowreth in your face.
Adri. His company must do his minions grace,
Whil'st I at home starue for a merrie looke:
Hath homelie age th'alluring beauty tooke
From my poore cheeke? then he hath wasted it.
Are my discourses dull? Barren my wit,
If voluble and sharpe discourse be mar'd,
Vnkindnesse blunts it more then marble hard.
Doe their gay vestments his affections baite?
That's not my fault, hee's master of my state.
What ruines are in me that can be found,
By him not ruin'd? Then is he the ground
Of my defeatures. My decayed faire,
A sunnie looke of his, would soone repaire.
But, too vnruly Deere, he breakes the pale,
And feedes from home; poore I am but his stale.
Luci. Selfe-harming Iealousie; fie beat it hence.
Ad. Vnfeeling fools can with such wrongs dispence:
I know his eye doth homage other-where,
Or else, what lets it but he would be here?
Sister, you know he promis'd me a chaine,
Would that alone, a loue he would detaine,
So he would keepe faire quarter with his bed:
I see the Iewell best enamaled
Will loose his beautie: yet the gold bides still
That others touch, and often touching will,
Where gold and no man that hath a name,
By falshood and corruption doth it shame:
Since that my beautie cannot please his eie,
Ile weepe (what's left away) and weeping die.
Luci. How manie fond fooles serue mad Ielousie?

Exit.

Enter Antipholis Errotis.

Ant. The gold I gaue to *Dromio* is laid vp
Safe at the *Centaur*, and the heedfull slaue
Is wandred forth in care to seeke me out
By computation and mine hosts report.
I could not speake with *Dromio*, since at first
I sent him from the Mart? see here he comes.

Enter Dromio Siracusia.

How now sir, is your merrie humor alter'd?
As you loue stroakes, so iest with me againe:
You know no *Centaur*? you receiu'd no gold?
Your Mistresse sent to haue me home to dinner?
My house was at the *Phœnix*? Wast thou mad,
That thus so madlie thou did didst answere me?
S.Dro. What answer sir? when spake I such a word?
E.Ant. Euen now, euen here, not halfe an howre since.
S.Dro. I did not see you since you sent me hence
Home to the *Centaur* with the gold you gaue me.
Ant. Villaine, thou didst denie the golds receit,
And toldst me of a Mistresse, and a dinner,
For which I hope thou feltst I was displeas'd.
S.Dro. I am glad to see you in this merrie vaine,
What meanes this iest, I pray you Master tell me?
Ant. Yea, dost thou ieere & flowt me in the teeth?
Think'st ẙ I iest? hold, take thou that, & that. *Beats Dro.*
S.Dr. Hold sir, for Gods sake, now your iest is earnest,
Vpon what bargaine do you giue it me?
Antiph. Because that I familiarlie sometimes
Doe vse you for my foole, and chat with you,
Your sawcinesse will iest vpon my loue,
And make a Common of my serious howres,
When the sunne shines, let foolish gnats make sport,
But creepe in crannies, when he hides his beames:
If you will iest with me, know my aspect,
And fashion your demeanor to my lookes,
Or I will beat this method in your sconce.
S.Dro. Sconce call you it? so you would leaue battering, I had rather haue it a head, and you vse these blows long, I must get a sconce for my head, and Insconce it to, or else I shall seek my wit in my shoulders, but I pray sir, why am I beaten?
Ant. Dost thou not know?
S.Dro. Nothing sir, but that I am beaten.
Ant. Shall I tell you why?
S.Dro. I sir, and wherefore; for they say, euery why hath a wherefore.
Ant. Why first for flowting me, and then wherefore, for vrging it the second time to me.
S.Dro. Was there euer anie man thus beaten out of season, when in the why and the wherefore, is neither rime nor reason. Well sir, I thanke you.
Ant. Thanke me sir, for what?
S.Dro. Marry sir, for this something that you gaue me for nothing.
Ant. Ile make you amends next, to giue you nothing for something. But say sir, is it dinner time?
S.Dro. No sir, I thinke the meat wants that I haue.
Ant. In good time sir: what's that?
S.Dro. Basting.
Ant. Well sir, then 'twill be drie.
S.Dro. If it be sir, I pray you eat none of it.
Ant. Your reason?
S.Dro. Lest it make you chollericke, and purchase me another drie basting.
Ant. Well sir, learne to iest in good time, there's a time for all things.
S.Dro. I durst haue denied that before you vvere so chollericke.
Anti. By what rule sir?
S.Dro. Marry sir, by a rule as plaine as the plaine bald pate of Father time himselfe.
Ant. Let's heare it.
S.Dro. There's no time for a man to recouer his haire that growes bald by nature.
Ant. May he not doe it by fine and recouerie?
S.Dro. Yes, to pay a fine for a perewig, and recouer the lost haire of another man.
Ant. Why, is Time such a niggard of haire, being (as it is) so plentifull an excrement?
S.Dro. Because it is a blessing that hee bestowes on beasts, and what he hath scanted them in haire, hee hath giuen them in wit.
Ant. Why, but theres manie a man hath more haire then wit.
S.Dro. Not a man of those but he hath the wit to lose his haire.
Ant. Why thou didst conclude hairy men plain dealers without wit.
S.Dro. The plainer dealer, the sooner lost; yet he looseth it in a kinde of iollitie.
An. For what reason.
S.Dro. For two, and sound ones to.

An. Nay

An. Nay not found I pray you.
S.Dro. Sure ones then.
An. Nay, not sure in a thing falsing.
S.Dro. Certaine ones then.
An. Name them.
S.Dro. The one to saue the money that he spends in trying: the other, that at dinner they should not drop in his porrage.
An. You would all this time haue prou'd, here is no time for all things.
S.Dro. Marry and did sir: namely, in no time to recouer haire lost by Nature.
An. But your reason was not substantiall, why there is no time to recouer.
S.Dro. Thus I mend it: Time himselfe is bald, and therefore to the worlds end, will haue bald followers.
An. I knew'twould be a bald conclusion: but soft, who wafts vs yonder.

Enter Adriana and Luciana.

Adri. I, I, *Antipholus*, looke strange and frowne,
Some other Mistresse hath thy sweet aspects:
I am not *Adriana*, nor thy wife.
The time was once, when thou vn-vrg'd wouldst vow,
That neuer words were musicke to thine eare,
That neuer obiect pleasing in thine eye,
That neuer touch well welcome to thy hand,
That neuer meat sweet-sauour'd in thy taste,
Vnlesse I spake, or look'd, or touch'd, or caru'd to thee.
How comes it now, my Husband, oh how comes it,
That thou art then estranged from thy selfe?
Thy selfe I call it, being strange to me:
That vndiuidable Incorporate
Am better then thy deere selfes better part.
Ah doe not teare away thy selfe from me;
For know my loue: as easie maist thou fall
A drop of water in the breaking gulfe,
And take vnmingled thence that drop againe
Without addition or diminishing,
As take from me thy selfe, and not me too.
How deerely would it touch thee to the quicke,
Shouldst thou but heare I were licencious?
And that this body consecrate to thee,
By Ruffian Lust should be contaminate?
Wouldst thou not spit at me, and spurne at me,
And hurle the name of husband in my face,
And teare the stain'd skin of my Harlot brow,
And from my false hand cut the wedding ring,
And breake it with a deepe-diuorcing vow?
I know thou canst, and therefore see thou doe it.
I am possest with an adulterate blot,
My bloud is mingled with the crime of lust:
For if we two be one, and thou play false,
I doe digest the poison of thy flesh,
Being strumpeted by thy contagion:
Keepe then faire league and truce with thy true bed,
I liue distain'd, thou vndishonoured.

Antip. Plead you to me faire dame? I know you not:
In *Ephesus* I am but two houres old,
As strange vnto your towne, as to your talke,
Who euery word by all my wit being scan'd,
Wants wit in all, one word to vnderstand.

Luci. Fie brother, how the world is chang'd with you:
When were you wont to vse my sister thus?
She sent for you by *Dromio* home to dinner.

Ant. By *Dromio*? *Drom.* By me.
Adr. By thee, and this thou didst returne from him,
That he did buffet thee, and in his blowes,
Denied my house for his, me for his wife.

Ant. Did you conuerse sir with this gentlewoman:
What is the course and drift of your compact?
S.Dro. I sir? I neuer saw her till this time.
Ant. Villaine thou liest, for euen her verie words,
Didst thou deliuer to me on the Mart.
S.Dro. I neuer spake with her in all my life.
Ant. How can she thus then call vs by our names?
Vnlesse it be by inspiration.

Adri. How ill agrees it with your grauitie,
To counterfeit thus grosely with your slaue,
Abetting him to thwart me in my moode;
Be it my wrong, you are from me exempt,
But wrong not that wrong with a more contempt.
Come I will fasten on this sleeue of thine:
Thou art an Elme my husband, I a Vine:
Whose weaknesse married to thy stranger state,
Makes me with thy strength to communicate:
If ought possesse thee from me, it is drosse,
Vsurping Iuie, Brier, or idle Mosse,
Who all for want of pruning, with intrusion,
Infect thy sap, and liue on thy confusion.

Ant. To mee shee speakes, shee moues mee for her theame;
What, was I married to her in my dreame?
Or sleepe I now, and thinke I heare all this?
What error driues our eies and eares amisse?
Vntill I know this sure vncertaintie,
Ile entertaine the free'd fallacie.

Luc. *Dromio*, goe bid the seruants spred for dinner.
S.Dro. Oh for my beads, I crosse me for a sinner.
This is the Fairie land, oh spight of spights,
We talke with Goblins, Owles and Sprights;
If we obay them not, this will insue:
They'll sucke our breath, or pinch vs blacke and blew.

Luc. Why prat'st thou to thy selfe, and answer'st not?
Dromio, thou *Dromio*, thou snaile, thou slug, thou sot.

S.Dro. I am transformed Master, am I not?
Ant. I thinke thou art in minde, and so am I.
S.Dro. Nay Master, both in minde, and in my shape.
Ant. Thou hast thine owne forme.
S.Dro. No, I am an Ape.
Luc. If thou art chang'd to ought, 'tis to an Asse.
S.Dro. 'Tis true she rides me, and I long for grasse.
'Tis so, I am an Asse, else it could neuer be,
But I should know her as well as she knowes me.

Adr. Come, come, no longer will I be a foole,
To put the finger in the eie and weepe;
Whil'st man and Master laughes my woes to scorne:
Come sir to dinner, *Dromio* keepe the gate:
Husband Ile dine aboue with you to day,
And shriue you of a thousand idle prankes:
Sirra, if any aske you for your Master,
Say he dines forth, and let no creature enter:
Come sister, *Dromio* play the Porter well.

Ant. Am I in earth, in heauen, or in hell?
Sleeping or waking, mad or well aduisde:
Knowne vnto these, and to my selfe disguisde:
Ile say as they say, and perseuer so:
And in this mist at all aduentures go.

S.Dro. Master, shall I be Porter at the gate?
Adr. I, and let none enter, least I breake your pate.
Luc. Come, come, *Antipholus*, we dine to late.

Actus Tertius. Scena Prima.

Enter Antipholus of Ephesus, his man Dromio, Angelo the Goldsmith, and Balthaser the Merchant.

E. Anti. Good signior *Angelo* you must excuse vs all,
My wife is shrewish when I keepe not howres;
Say that I lingerd with you at your shop
To see the making of her Carkanet,
And that to morrow you will bring it home.
But here's a villaine that would face me downe
He met me on the Mart, and that I beat him,
And charg'd him with a thousand markes in gold,
And that I did denie my wife and house;
Thou drunkard thou, what didst thou meane by this?

E. Dro. Say what you wil sir, but I know what I know,
That you beat me at the Mart I haue your hand to show;
If ỹ skin were parchment, & ỹ blows you gaue were ink,
Your owne hand-writing would tell you what I thinke.

E. Ant. I thinke thou art an asse.

E. Dro. Marry so it doth appeare
By the wrongs I suffer, and the blowes I beare,
I should kicke being kickt, and being at that passe,
You would keepe from my heeles, and beware of an asse.

E. An. Y'are sad signior *Balthazar*, pray God our cheer
May answer my good will, and your good welcom here.

Bal. I hold your dainties cheap sir, & your welcom deer.

E. An. Oh signior *Balthazar*, either at flesh or fish,
A table full of welcome, makes scarce one dainty dish.

Bal. Good meat sir is cōmon that euery churle affords.

Anti. And welcome more common, for thats nothing but words.

Bal. Small cheere and great welcome, makes a merrie feast.

Anti. I, to a niggardly Host, and more sparing guest:
But though my cates be meane, take them in good part,
Better cheere may you haue, but not with better hart.
But soft, my doore is lockt; goe bid them let vs in.

E. Dro. Maud, Briget, Marian, Cisley, Gillian, Ginn.

S. Dro. Mome, Malthorse, Capon, Coxcombe, Idiot, Patch,
Either get thee from the dore, or sit downe at the hatch:
Dost thou coniure for wenches, that ỹ calst for such store,
When one is one too many, goe get thee from the dore.

E. Dro. What patch is made our Porter? my Master stayes in the street.

S. Dro. Let him walke from whence he came, lest hee catch cold on's feet.

E. Ant. Who talks within there? hoa, open the dore.

S. Dro. Right sir, Ile tell you when, and you'll tell me wherefore.

Ant. Wherefore? for my dinner: I haue not din'd to day.

S. Dro. Nor to day here you must not come againe when you may.

Anti. What art thou that keep'st mee out from the howse I owe?

S. Dro. The Porter for this time Sir, and my name is *Dromio.*

E. Dro. O villaine, thou hast stolne both mine office and my name,
The one nere got me credit, the other mickle blame:
If thou hadst beene *Dromio* to day in my place,
Thou wouldst haue chang'd thy face for a name, or thy name for an asse.

Enter Luce.

Luce. What a coile is there *Dromio*? who are those at the gate?

E. Dro. Let my Master in *Luce*.

Luce. Faith no, hee comes too late, and so tell your Master.

E. Dro. O Lord I must laugh, haue at you with a Prouerbe,
Shall I set in my staffe.

Luce. Haue at you with another, that's when? can you tell?

S. Dro. If thy name be called *Luce*, *Luce* thou hast answer'd him well.

Anti. Doe you heare you minion, you'll let vs in I hope?

Luce. I thought to haue askt you.

S. Dro. And you said no.

E. Dro. So come helpe, well strooke, there was blow for blow.

Anti. Thou baggage let me in.

Luce. Can you tell for whose sake?

E. Drom. Master, knocke the doore hard.

Luce. Let him knocke till it ake.

Anti. You'll crie for this minion, if I beat the doore downe.

Luce. What needs all that, and a paire of stocks in the towne?

Enter Adriana.

Adr. Who is that at the doore ỹ keeps all this noise?

S. Dro. By my troth your towne is troubled with vnruly boies.

Anti. Are you there Wife? you might haue come before.

Adri. Your wife sir knaue? go get you from the dore.

E. Dro. If you went in paine Master, this knaue wold goe sore.

Angelo. Heere is neither cheere sir, nor welcome, we would faine haue either.

Baltz. In debating which was best, wee shall part with neither.

E. Dro. They stand at the doore, Master, bid them welcome hither.

Anti. There is something in the winde, that we cannot get in.

E. Dro. You would say so Master, if your garments were thin.
Your cake here is warme within: you stand here in the cold.
It would make a man mad as a Bucke to be so bought and sold.

Ant. Go fetch me something, Ile break ope the gate.

S. Dro. Breake any breaking here, and Ile breake your knaues pate.

E. Dro. A man may breake a word with your sir, and words are but winde:
I and breake it in your face, so he break it not behinde.

S. Dro. It seemes thou want'st breaking, out vpon thee hinde.

E. Dro. Here's too much out vpon thee, I pray thee let me in.

S. Dro. I, when fowles haue no feathers, and fish haue no fin.

Ant. Well, Ile breake in: go borrow me a crow.

E. Dro. A crow without feather, Master meane you so;
For

For a fish without a finne, ther's a fowle without a fether,
If a crow help vs in sirra, wee'll plucke a crow together.

Ant. Go, get thee gon, fetch me an iron Crow.

Balth. Haue patience sir, oh let it not be so,
Heerein you warre against your reputation,
And draw within the compasse of suspect
Th'vnuiolated honor of your wife.
Once this your long experience of your wisedome,
Her sober vertue, yeares, and modestie,
Plead on your part some cause to you vnknowne;
And doubt not sir, but she will well excuse
Why at this time the dores are made against you.
Be rul'd by me, depart in patience,
And let vs to the Tyger all to dinner,
And about euening come your selfe alone,
To know the reason of this strange restraint:
If by strong hand you offer to breake in
Now in the stirring passage of the day,
A vulgar comment will be made of it;
And that supposed by the common rowt
Against your yet vngalled estimation,
That may with foule intrusion enter in,
And dwell vpon your graue when you are dead;
For slander liues vpon succession;
For euer hows'd, where it gets possession.

Anti. You haue preuail'd, I will depart in quiet,
And in despight of mirth meane to be merrie:
I know a wench of excellent discourse,
Prettie and wittie; wilde, and yet too gentle;
There will we dine: this woman that I meane
My wife (but I protest without desert)
Hath oftentimes vpbraided me withall:
To her will we to dinner, get you home
And fetch the chaine, by this I know 'tis made,
Bring it I pray you to the *Porpentine*,
For there's the house: That chaine will I bestow
(Be it for nothing but to spight my wife)
Vpon mine hostesse there, good sir make haste:
Since mine owne doores refuse to entertaine me,
Ile knocke else-where, to see if they'll disdaine me.

Ang. Ile meet you at that place some houre hence.

Anti. Do so, this iest shall cost me some expence.

Exeunt.

Enter Iuliana, with Antipholus of Siracusia.

Iulia. And may it be that you haue quite forgot
A husbands office? shall *Antipholus*
Euen in the spring of Loue, thy Loue-springs rot?
Shall loue in buildings grow so ruinate?
If you did wed my sister for her wealth,
Then for her wealths-sake vse her with more kindnesse:
Or if you like else-where doe it by stealth,
Muffle your false loue with some shew of blindnesse:
Let not my sister read it in your eye:
Be not thy tongue thy owne shames Orator:
Looke sweet, speake faire, become disloyaltie:
Apparell vice like vertues harbenger:
Beare a faire presence, though your heart be tainted,
Teach sinne the carriage of a holy Saint,
Be secret false: what need she be acquainted?
What simple thiefe brags of his owne attaine?
'Tis double wrong to truant with your bed,
And let her read it in thy lookes at boord:
Shame hath a bastard fame, well managed,
Ill deeds is doubled with an euill word:
Alas poore women, make vs not beleeue
(Being compact of credit) that you loue vs,
Though others haue the arme, shew vs the sleeue:
We in your motion turne, and you may moue vs.
Then gentle brother get you in againe;
Comfort my sister, cheere her, call her wife;
'Tis holy sport to be a little vaine,
When the sweet breath of flatterie conquers strife.

S. Anti. Sweete Mistris, what your name is else I know not;
Nor by what wonder you do hit of mine:
Lesse in your knowledge, and your grace you show not,
Then our earths wonder, more then earth diuine.
Teach me deere creature how to thinke and speake:
Lay open to my earthie grosse conceit:
Smothred in errors, feeble, shallow, weake,
The foulded meaning of your words deceit:
Against my soules pure truth, why labour you,
To make it wander in an vnknowne field?
Are you a god? would you create me new?
Transforme me then, and to your powre Ile yeeld.
But if that I am I, then well I know,
Your weeping sister is no wife of mine,
Nor to her bed no homage doe I owe:
Farre more, farre more, to you doe I decline:
Oh traine me not sweet Mermaide with thy note,
To drowne me in thy sister floud of teares:
Sing Siren for thy selfe, and I will dote:
Spread ore the siluer waues thy golden haires;
And as a bud Ile take thee, and there lie:
And in that glorious supposition thinke,
He gaines by death, that hath such meanes to die:
Let Loue, being light, be drowned if she sinke.

Luc. What are you mad, that you doe reason so?

Ant. Not mad, but mated, how I doe not know.

Luc. It is a fault that springeth from your eie.

Ant. For gazing on your beames faire sun being by.

Luc. Gaze when you should, and that will cleere your sight.

Ant. As good to winke sweet loue, as looke on night.

Luc. Why call you me loue? Call my sister so.

Ant. Thy sisters sister.

Luc. That's my sister.

Ant. No: it is thy selfe, mine owne selfes better part:
Mine eies cleere eie, my deere hearts deerer heart;
My foode, my fortune, and my sweet hopes aime;
My sole earths heauen, and my heauens claime.

Luc. All this my sister is, or else should be.

Ant. Call thy selfe sister sweet, for I am thee.
Thee will I loue, and with thee lead my life;
Thou hast no husband yet, nor I no wife:
Giue me thy hand.

Luc. Oh soft sir, hold you still:
Ile fetch my sister to get her good will. *Exit.*

Enter Dromio, Siracusia.

Ant. Why how now *Dromio*, where run'st thou so fast?

S. Dro. Doe you know me sir? Am I *Dromio*? Am I your man? Am I my selfe?

Ant. Thou art *Dromio*, thou art my man, thou art thy selfe.

Dro. I am an asse, I am a womans man, and besides my selfe.

Ant. What womans man? and how besides thy selfe?

Dro. Marrie sir, besides my selfe, I am due to a woman: One that claimes me, one that haunts me, one that will haue me.

Ant. What

Anti. What claime laies she to thee?

Dro. Marry sir, such claime as you would lay to your horse, and she would haue me as a beast, not that I beeing a beast she would haue me, but that she being a verie beastly creature layes claime to me.

Anti. What is she?

Dro. A very reuerent body: I such a one, as a man may not speake of, without he say sir reuerence, I haue but leane lucke in the match, and yet is she a wondrous fat marriage.

Anti. How dost thou meane a fat marriage?

Dro. Marry sir, she's the Kitchin wench, & al grease, and I know not what vse to put her too, but to make a Lampe of her, and run from her by her owne light. I warrant, her ragges and the Tallow in them, will burne a *Poland* Winter: If she liues till doomesday, she'l burne a weeke longer then the whole World.

Anti. What complexion is she of?

Dro. Swart like my shoo, but her face nothing like so cleane kept: for why? she sweats a man may goe ouer-shooes in the grime of it.

Anti. That's a fault that water will mend.

Dro. No sir, 'tis in graine, *Noahs* flood could not do it.

Anti. What's her name?

Dro. *Nell* Sir: but her name is three quarters, that's an Ell and three quarters, will not measure her from hip to hip.

Anti. Then she beares some bredth?

Dro. No longer from head to foot, then from hippe to hippe: she is sphericall, like a globe: I could find out Countries in her.

Anti. In what part of her body stands *Ireland*?

Dro. Marry sir in her buttockes, I found it out by the bogges.

Ant. Where *Scotland*?

Dro. I found it by the barrennesse, hard in the palme of the hand.

Ant. Where *France*?

Dro. In her forhead, arm'd and reuerted, making warre against her heire.

Ant. Where *England*?

Dro. I look'd for the chalkie Cliffes, but I could find no whitenesse in them. But I guesse, it stood in her chin by the salt rheume that ranne betweene *France*, and it.

Ant. Where *Spaine*?

Dro. Faith I saw it not: but I felt it hot in her breth.

Ant. Where *America*, the *Indies*?

Dro. Oh sir, vpon her nose, all ore embellished with Rubies, Carbuncles, Saphires, declining their rich Aspect to the hot breath of Spaine, who sent whole Armadoes of Carrects to be ballast at her nose.

Anti. Where stood *Belgia*, the *Netherlands*?

Dro. Oh sir, I did not looke so low. To conclude, this drudge or Diuiner layd claime to mee, call'd mee *Dromio*, swore I was assur'd to her, told me what priuie markes I had about mee, as the marke of my shoulder, the Mole in my necke, the great Wart on my left arme, that I amaz'd ranne from her as a witch. And I thinke, if my brest had not beene made of faith, and my heart of steele, she had transform'd me to a Curtull dog, & made me turne i'th wheele.

Anti. Go hie thee presently, post to the rode, And if the winde blow any way from shore, I will not harbour in this Towne to night. If any Barke put forth, come to the Mart, Where I will walke till thou returne to me: If euerie one knowes vs, and we know none, 'Tis time I thinke to trudge, packe, and be gone.

Dro. As from a Beare a man would run for life, So flie I from her that would be my wife.   *Exit.*

Anti. There's none but Witches do inhabite heere, And therefore 'tis hie time that I were hence: She that doth call me husband, euen my soule Doth for a wife abhorre. But her faire sister Possest with such a gentle soueraigne grace, Of such inchanting presence and discourse, Hath almost made me Traitor to my selfe: But least my selfe be guilty to selfe wrong, Ile stop mine eares against the Mermaids song.

Enter Angelo with the Chaine.

Ang. Mr *Antipholus*.

Anti. I that's my name.

Ang. I know it well sir, loe here's the chaine, I thought to haue tane you at the *Porpentine*, The chaine vnfinish'd made me stay thus long.

Anti. What is your will that I shal do with this?

Ang. What please your selfe sir: I haue made it for you.

Anti. Made it for me sir, I bespoke it not.

Ang. Not once, nor twice, but twentie times you haue: Go home with it, and please your Wife withall, And soone at supper time Ile visit you, And then receiue my money for the chaine.

Anti. I pray you sir receiue the money now, For feare you ne're see chaine, nor mony more.

Ang. You are a merry man sir, fare you well.   *Exit.*

Ant. What I should thinke of this, I cannot tell: But this I thinke, there's no man is so vaine, That would refuse so faire an offer'd Chaine. I see a man heere needs not liue by shifts, When in the streets he meetes such Golden gifts: Ile to the Mart, and there for *Dromio* stay, If any ship put out, then straight away.   *Exit.*

Actus Quartus. Scœna Prima.

Enter a Merchant, Goldsmith, and an Officer.

Mar. You know since Pentecost the sum is due, And since I haue not much importun'd you, Nor now I had not, but that I am bound To *Persia*, and want Gilders for my voyage: Therefore make present satisfaction, Or Ile attach you by this Officer.

Gold. Euen iust the sum that I do owe to you, Is growing to me by *Antipholus*, And in the instant that I met with you, He had of me a Chaine, at fiue a clocke I shall receiue the money for the same: Pleaseth you walke with me downe to his house, I will discharge my bond, and thanke you too.

Enter Antipholus Ephes. Dromio from the Courtizans.

Offi. That labour may you saue: See where he comes.

Ant. While I go to the Goldsmiths house, go thou
And

The Comedie of Errors.

And buy a ropes end, that will I bestow
Among my wife, and their confederates,
For locking me out of my doores by day:
But soft I see the Goldsmith; get thee gone,
Buy thou a rope, and bring it home to me.

Dro. I buy a thousand pound a yeare, I buy a rope.
Exit Dromio

Eph. Ant. A man is well holpe vp that trusts to you,
I promised your presence, and the Chaine,
But neither Chaine nor Goldsmith came to me:
Belike you thought our loue would last too long
If it were chain'd together: and therefore came not.

Gold. Sauing your merrie humor: here's the note
How much your Chaine weighs to the vtmost charect,
The finenesse of the Gold, and chargefull fashion,
Which doth amount to three odde Duckets more
Then I stand debted to this Gentleman,
I pray you see him presently discharg'd,
For he is bound to Sea, and stayes but for it.

Anti. I am not furnish'd with the present monie:
Besides I haue some businesse in the towne,
Good Signior take the stranger to my house,
And with you take the Chaine, and bid my wife
Disburse the summe, on the receit thereof,
Perchance I will be there as soone as you.

Gold. Then you will bring the Chaine to her your selfe.

Anti. No beare it with you, least I come not time enough.

Gold. Well sir, I will? Haue you the Chaine about you?

Ant. And if I haue not sir, I hope you haue:
Or else you may returne without your money.

Gold. Nay come I pray you sir, giue me the Chaine:
Both winde and tide stayes for this Gentleman,
And I too blame haue held him heere too long.

Anti. Good Lord, you vse this dalliance to excuse
Your breach of promise to the *Porpentine*,
I should haue chid you for not bringing it,
But like a shrew you first begin to brawle.

Mar. The houre steales on, I pray you sir dispatch.

Gold. You heare how he importunes me, the Chaine.

Ant. Why giue it to my wife, and fetch your mony.

Gold. Come, come, you know I gaue it you euen now.
Either send the Chaine, or send me by some token.

Ant. Fie, now you run this humor out of breath,
Come where's the Chaine, I pray you let me see it.

Mar. My businesse cannot brooke this dalliance,
Good sir say, whe'r you'l answer me, or no:
If not, Ile leaue him to the Officer.

Ant. I answer you? What should I answer you.

Gold. The monie that you owe me for the Chaine.

Ant. I owe you none, till I receiue the Chaine.

Gold. You know I gaue it you halfe an houre since.

Ant. You gaue me none, you wrong mee much to say so.

Gold. You wrong me more sir in denying it.
Consider how it stands vpon my credit.

Mar. Well Officer, arrest him at my suite.

Offi. I do, and charge you in the Dukes name to obey me.

Gold. This touches me in reputation.
Either consent to pay this sum for me,
Or I attach you by this Officer.

Ant. Consent to pay thee that I neuer had:
Arrest me foolish fellow if thou dar'st.

Gold. Heere is thy fee, arrest him Officer.
I would not spare my brother in this case,
If he should scorne me so apparantly.

Offi. I do arrest you sir, you heare the suite.

Ant. I do obey thee, till I giue thee baile.
But sirrah, you shall buy this sport as deere,
As all the mettall in your shop will answer.

Gold. Sir, sir, I shall haue Law in *Ephesus*,
To your notorious shame, I doubt it not.

Enter Dromio Sira. from the Bay.

Dro. Master, there's a Barke of *Epidamium*,
That staies but till her Owner comes aboord,
And then sir she beares away. Our fraughtage sir,
I haue conuei'd aboord, and I haue bought
The Oyle, the *Balsamum*, and Aqua-vitæ.
The ship is in her trim, the merrie winde
Blowes faire from land: they stay for nought at all,
But for their Owner, Master, and your selfe.

An. How now? a Madman? Why thou peeuish sheep
What ship of *Epidamium* staies for me.

S. Dro. A ship you sent me too, to hier waftage.

Ant. Thou drunken slaue, I sent thee for a rope,
And told thee to what purpose, and what end.

S. Dro. You sent me for a ropes end as soone,
You sent me to the Bay sir, for a Barke.

Ant. I will debate this matter at more leisure
And teach your eares to list me with more heede:
To *Adriana* Villaine hie thee straight:
Giue her this key, and tell her in the Deske
That's couer'd o're with Turkish Tapistrie,
There is a purse of Duckets, let her send it:
Tell her, I am arrested in the streete,
And that shall baile me: hie thee slaue, be gone,
On Officer to prison, till it come. *Exeunt*

S. Dromio. To *Adriana*, that is where we din'd,
Where *Dowsabell* did claime me for her husband,
She is too bigge I hope for me to compasse,
Thither I must, although against my will:
For seruants must their Masters mindes fulfill. *Exit*

Enter Adriana and Luciana.

Adr. Ah *Luciana*, did he tempt thee so?
Might'st thou perceiue austeerely in his eie,
That he did plead in earnest, yea or no:
Look'd he or red or pale, or sad or merrily?
What obseruation mad'st thou in this case?
Oh, his hearts Meteors tilting in his face.

Luc. First he deni'de you had in him no right.

Adr. He meant he did me none: the more my spight

Luc. Then swore he that he was a stranger heere.

Adr. And true he swore, though yet forsworne hee were.

Luc. Then pleaded I for you.

Adr. And what said he?

Luc. That loue I begg'd for you, he begg'd of me.

Adr. With what perswasion did he tempt thy loue?

Luc. With words, that in an honest suit might moue.
First, he did praise my beautie, then my speech.

Adr. Did'st speake him faire?

Luc. Haue patience I beseech.

Adr. I cannot, nor I will not hold me still,
My tongue, though not my heart, shall haue his will.
He is deformed, crooked, old, and sere,
Ill-fac'd, worse bodied, shapelesse euery where:
Vicious, vngentle, foolish, blunt, vnkinde,

Stigma-

Stigmaticall in making worse in minde.

  Luc. Who would be iealous then of such a one?
No euill lost is wail'd, when it is gone.

  Adr. Ah but I thinke him better then I say:
And yet would herein others eies were worse:
Farre from her nest the Lapwing cries away;
My heart praies for him, though my tongue doe curse.

Enter S. Dromio.

  Dro. Here goe: the deske, the purse, sweet now make haste.

  Luc. How hast thou lost thy breath?

  S. Dro. By running fast.

  Adr. Where is thy Master *Dromio*? Is he well?

  S. Dro. No, he's in Tartar limbo, worse then hell:
A diuell in an euerlasting garment hath him;
On whose hard heart is button'd vp with steele:
A Feind, a Fairie, pittilesse and ruffe:
A Wolfe, nay worse, a fellow all in buffe:
A back friend, a shoulder-clapper, one that countermads
The passages of allies, creekes, and narrow lans:
A hound that runs Counter, and yet draws drifoot well,
One that before the Iudgmét carries poore soules to hel.

  Adr. Why man, what is the matter?

  S. Dro. I doe not know the matter, hee is rested on the case.

  Adr. What is he arrested? tell me at whose suite?

  S. Dro. I know not at whose suite he is arested well;
but is in a suite of buffe which rested him, that can I tell,
will you send him Mistris redemption, the monie in his deske.

  Adr. Go fetch it Sister: this I wonder at.
                                Exit Luciana.
Thus he vnknowne to me should be in debt:
Tell me, was he arested on a band?

  S. Dro. Not on a band, but on a stronger thing:
A chaine, a chaine, doe you not here it ring.

  Adria. What, the chaine?

  S. Dro. No, no, the bell, 'tis time that I were gone:
It was two ere I left him, and now the clocke strikes one.

  Adr. The houres come backe, that did I neuer here.

  S. Dro. Oh yes, if any houre meete a Serieant, a turnes backe for verie feare.

  Adri. As if time were in debt: how fondly do'st thou reason?

  S. Dro. Time is a verie bankerout, and owes more then he's worth to season.
Nay, he's a theefe too: haue you not heard men say,
That time comes stealing on by night and day?
If I be in debt and theft, and a Serieant in the way,
Hath he not reason to turne backe an houre in a day?

Enter Luciana.

  Adr. Go *Dromio*, there's the monie, beare it straight,
And bring thy Master home imediately.
Come sister, I am prest downe with conceit:
Conceit, my comfort and my iniurie.   *Exit.*

Enter Antipholus Siracusian.

There's not a man I meete but doth salute me
As if I were their well acquainted friend,
And euerie one doth call me by my name:
Some tender monie to me, some inuite me;
Some other giue me thankes for kindnesses;
Some offer me Commodities to buy.
Euen now a tailor cal'd me in his shop,
And show'd me Silkes that he had bought for me,
And therewithall tooke measure of my body.
Sure these are but imaginarie wiles,
And lapland Sorcerers inhabite here.

Enter Dromio. Sir.

  S. Dro. Master, here's the gold you sent me for: what haue you got the picture of old *Adam* new apparel'd?

  Ant. What gold is this? What *Adam* do'st thou meane?

  S. Dro. Not that *Adam* that kept the Paradise: but that *Adam* that keepes the prison; hee that goes in the calues-skin, that was kil'd for the Prodigall: hee that came behinde you sir, like an euill angel, and bid you forsake your libertie.

  Ant. I vnderstand thee not.

  S. Dro. No? why 'tis a plaine case: he that went like a Base-Viole in a case of leather; the man sir, that when gentlemen are tired giues them a sob, and rests them: he sir, that takes pittie on decaied men, and giues them suites of durance: he that sets vp his rest to doe more exploits with his Mace, then a Moris Pike.

  Ant. What thou mean'st an officer?

  S. Dro. I sir, the Serieant of the Band: he that brings any man to answer it that breakes his Band: one that thinkes a man alwaies going to bed, and saies, God giue you good rest.

  Ant. Well sir, there rest in your foolerie:
Is there any ships puts forth to night? may we be gone?

  S. Dro. Why sir, I brought you word an houre since, that the Barke *Expedition* put forth to night, and then were you hindred by the Serieant to tarry for the *Hoy* delay: Here are the angels that you sent for to deliuer you.

  Ant. The fellow is distract, and so am I,
And here we wander in illusions:
Some blessed power deliuer vs from hence.

Enter a Curtizan.

  Cur. Well met, well met, Master *Antipholus*:
I see sir you haue found the Gold-smith now:
Is that the chaine you promis'd me to day.

  Ant. Sathan auoide, I charge thee tempt me not.

  S. Dro. Master, is this Mistris *Sathan*?

  Ant. It is the diuell.

  S. Dro. Nay, she is worse, she is the diuels dam:
And here she comes in the habit of a light wench, and thereof comes, that the wenches say God dam me, That's as much to say, God make me a light wench: It is written, they appeare to men like angels of light, light is an effect of fire, and fire will burne: *ergo*, light wenches will burne, come not neere her.

  Cur. Your man and you are maruailous merrie sir.
Will you goe with me, wee'll mend our dinner here?

  S. Dro. Master, if do expect spoon-meate, or bespeake a long spoone.

  Ant. Why *Dromio*?

  S. Dro. Marrie he must haue a long spoone that must eate with the diuell.

  Ant. Auoid then fiend, what tel'st thou me of supping?
Thou art, as you are all a sorceresse:
I coniure thee to leaue me, and be gon.

  Cur. Giue me the ring of mine you had at dinner,
Or for my Diamond the Chaine you promis'd,
And Ile be gone sir, and not trouble you.

  S. Dro. Some diuels aske but the parings of ones naile,

The Comedie of Errors.

a rush, a haire, a drop of blood, a pin, a nut, a cherrie-stone: but she more couetous, wold haue a chaine: Master be wise, and if you giue it her, the diuell will shake her Chaine, and fright vs with it.

Cur. I pray you sir my Ring, or else the Chaine, I hope you do not meane to cheate me so?

Ant. Auant thou witch: Come *Dromio* let vs go.

S.Dro. Flie pride saies the Pea-cocke, Mistris that you know. *Exit.*

Cur. Now out of doubt *Antipholus* is mad,
Else would he neuer so demeane himselfe,
A Ring he hath of mine worth fortie Duckets,
And for the same he promis'd me a Chaine,
Both one and other he denies me now:
The reason that I gather he is mad,
Besides this present instance of his rage,
Is a mad tale he told to day at dinner,
Of his owne doores being shut against his entrance.
Belike his wife acquainted with his fits,
On purpose shut the doores against his way:
My way is now to hie home to his house,
And tell his wife, that being Lunaticke,
He rush'd into my house, and tooke perforce
My Ring away. This course I fittest choose,
For fortie Duckets is too much to loose.

Enter Antipholus Ephes. with a Iailor.

An. Feare me not man, I will not breake away,
Ile giue thee ere I leaue thee so much money
To warrant thee as I am rested for.
My wife is in a wayward moode to day,
And will not lightly trust the Messenger,
That I should be attach'd in *Ephesus*,
I tell you 'twill sound harshly in her eares.

Enter Dromio Eph. with a ropes end.

Heere comes my Man, I thinke he brings the monie.
How now sir? Haue you that I sent you for?

E.Dro. Here's that I warrant you will pay them all.

Anti. But where's the Money?

E.Dro. Why sir, I gaue the Monie for the Rope.

Ant. Fiue hundred Duckets villaine for a rope?

E.Dro. Ile serue you sir fiue hundred at the rate.

Ant. To what end did I bid thee hie thee home?

E.Dro. To a ropes end sir, and to that end am I return'd.

Ant. And to that end sir, I will welcome you.

Off. Good sir be patient.

E.Dro. Nay 'tis for me to be patient, I am in aduersitie.

Off. Good now hold thy tongue.

E.Dro. Nay, rather perswade him to hold his hands.

Anti. Thou whoreson senselesse Villaine.

E.Dro. I would I were senselesse sir, that I might not feele your blowes.

Anti. Thou art sensible in nothing but blowes, and so is an Asse.

E.Dro. I am an Asse indeede, you may prooue it by my long eares. I haue serued him from the houre of my Natiuitie to this instant, and haue nothing at his hands for my seruice but blowes: When I am cold, he heates me with beating: when I am warme, he cooles me with beating: I am wak'd with it when I sleepe, rais'd with it when I sit, driuen out of doores with it when I goe from home, welcom'd home with it when I returne, nay I beare it on my shoulders, as a begger woont her brat: and I thinke when he hath lam'd me, I shall begge with it from doore to doore.

Enter Adriana, Luciana, Courtizan, and a Schoole-master, call'd Pinch.

Ant. Come goe along, my wife is comming yonder.

E.Dro. Mistris *respice finem*, respect your end, or rather the prophesie like the Parrat, beware the ropes end.

Anti. Wilt thou still talke? *Beats Dro.*

Curt. How say you now? Is not your husband mad?

Adri. His inciuility confirmes no lesse:
Good Doctor *Pinch*, you are a Coniurer,
Establish him in his true sence againe,
And I will please you what you will demand.

Luc. Alas how fiery, and how sharpe he lookes.

Cur. Marke, how he trembles in his extasie.

Pinch. Giue me your hand, and let mee feele your pulse.

Ant. There is my hand, and let it feele your eare.

Pinch. I charge thee Sathan, hous'd within this man,
To yeeld possession to my holie praiers,
And to thy state of darknesse hie thee straight,
I coniure thee by all the Saints in heauen.

Anti. Peace doting wizard, peace; I am not mad.

Adr. Oh that thou wer't not, poore distressed soule.

Anti. You Minion you, are these your Customers?
Did this Companion with the saffron face
Reuell and feast it at my house to day,
Whil'st vpon me the guiltie doores were shut,
And I denied to enter in my house.

Adr. O husband, God doth know you din'd at home
Where would you had remain'd vntill this time,
Free from these slanders, and this open shame.

Anti. Din'd at home? Thou Villaine, what sayest thou?

Dro. Sir sooth to say, you did not dine at home.

Ant. Were not my doores lockt vp, and I shut out?

Dro. Perdie, your doores were lockt, and you shut out.

Anti. And did not she her selfe reuile me there?

Dro. Sans Fable, she her selfe reuil'd you there.

Anti. Did not her Kitchen maide raile, taunt, and scorne me?

Dro. Certis she did, the kitchin vestall scorn'd you.

Ant. And did not I in rage depart from thence?

Dro. In veritie you did, my bones beares witnesse,
That since haue felt the vigor of his rage.

Adr. Is't good to sooth him in these crontraries?

Pinch. It is no shame, the fellow finds his vaine,
And yeelding to him, humors well his frensie.

Ant. Thou hast subborn'd the Goldsmith to arrest mee.

Adr. Alas, I sent you Monie to redeeme you,
By *Dromio* heere, who came in hast for it.

Dro. Monie by me? Heart and good will you might,
But surely Master not a ragge of Monie.

Ant. Wentst not thou to her for a purse of Duckets.

Adri. He came to me, and I deliuer'd it.

Luci. And I am witnesse with her that she did.

Dro. God and the Rope-maker beare me witnesse,
That I was sent for nothing but a rope.

Pinch. Mistris, both Man and Master is possest,
I know it by their pale and deadly lookes,

They

They muſt be bound and laide in ſome darke roome.
  Ant. Say wherefore didſt thou locke me forth to day,
And why doſt thou denie the bagge of gold?
  Adr. I did not gentle husband locke thee forth.
  Dro. And gentle Mr I receiu'd no gold:
But I confeſſe ſir, that we were lock'd out.
  Adr. Diſſembling Villain, thou ſpeak'ſt falſe in both
  Ant. Diſſembling harlot, thou art falſe in all,
And art confederate with a damned packe,
To make a loathſome abiect ſcorne of me:
But with theſe nailes, Ile plucke out theſe falſe eyes,
That would behold in me this ſhamefull ſport.

Enter three or foure, and offer to binde him:
Hee ſtriues.

  Adr. Oh binde him, binde him, let him not come neere me.
  Pinch. More company, the fiend is ſtrong within him
  Luc. Aye me poore man, how pale and wan he looks.
  Ant. What will you murther me, thou Iailor thou?
I am thy priſoner, wilt thou ſuffer them to make a reſcue?
  Offi. Maſters let him go: he is my priſoner, and you ſhall not haue him.
  Pinch. Go binde this man, for he is franticke too.
  Adr. What wilt thou do, thou peeuiſh Officer?
Haſt thou delight to ſee a wretched man
Do outrage and diſpleaſure to himſelfe?
  Offi. He is my priſoner, if I let him go,
The debt he owes will be requir'd of me.
  Adr. I will diſcharge thee ere I go from thee,
Beare me forthwith vnto his Creditor,
And knowing how the debt growes I will pay it.
Good Maſter Doctor ſee him ſafe conuey'd
Home to my houſe, oh moſt vnhappy day.
  Ant. Oh moſt vnhappie ſtrumpet.
  Dro. Maſter, I am heere entred in bond for you.
  Ant. Out on thee Villaine, wherefore doſt thou mad mee?
  Dro. Will you be bound for nothing, be mad good Maſter, cry the diuell.
  Luc. God helpe poore ſoules, how idlely doe they talke.
  Adr. Go beare him hence, ſiſter go you with me:
Say now, whoſe ſuite is he arreſted at?

Exeunt. Manet Offic. Adri. Luci. Courtizan

  Off. One *Angelo* a Goldſmith, do you know him?
  Adr. I know the man: what is the ſumme he owes?
  Off. Two hundred Duckets.
  Adr. Say, how growes it due.
  Off. Due for a Chaine your husband had of him.
  Adr. He did beſpeake a Chain for me, but had it not.
  Cur. When as your husband all in rage to day,
Came to my houſe, and tooke away my Ring,
The Ring I ſaw vpon his finger now,
Straight after did I meete him with a Chaine.
  Adr. It may be ſo, but I did neuer ſee it.
Come Iailor, bring me where the Goldſmith is,
I long to know the truth heereof at large.

Enter Antipholus Siracuſia with his Rapier drawne,
and Dromio Sirac.

  Luc. God for thy mercy, they are looſe againe.
  Adr. And come with naked ſwords,
Let's call more helpe to haue them bound againe.
Runne all out.

  Off. Away, they'l kill vs.
Exeunt omnes, as faſt as may be, frighted.
  S. Ant. I ſee theſe Witches are affraid of ſwords.
  S. Dro. She that would be your wife, now ran from you.
  Ant. Come to the Centaur, fetch our ſtuffe from thence:
I long that we were ſafe and ſound aboord.
  Dro. Faith ſtay heere this night, they will ſurely do vs no harme: you ſaw they ſpeake vs faire, giue vs gold:
me thinkes they are ſuch a gentle Nation, that but for the Mountaine of mad fleſh that claimes mariage of me,
I could finde in my heart to ſtay heere ſtill, and turne Witch.
  Ant. I will not ſtay to night for all the Towne,
Therefore away, to get our ſtuffe aboord. *Exeunt*

Actus Quintus. Scœna Prima.

Enter the Merchant and the Goldſmith.

  Gold. I am ſorry Sir that I haue hindred you,
But I proteſt he had the Chaine of me,
Though moſt diſhoneſtly he doth denie it.
  Mar. How is the man eſteem'd heere in the Citie?
  Gold. Of very reuerent reputation ſir,
Of credit infinite, highly belou'd,
Second to none that liues heere in the Citie:
His word might beare my wealth at any time.
  Mar. Speake ſoftly, yonder as I thinke he walkes.

Enter Antipholus and Dromio againe.

  Gold. 'Tis ſo: and that ſelfe chaine about his necke,
Which he forſwore moſt monſtrouſly to haue.
Good ſir draw neere to me, Ile ſpeake to him:
Signior *Antipholus*, I wonder much
That you would put me to this ſhame and trouble,
And not without ſome ſcandall to your ſelfe,
With circumſtance and oaths, ſo to denie
This Chaine, which now you weare ſo openly.
Beſide the charge, the ſhame, impriſonment,
You haue done wrong to this my honeſt friend,
Who but for ſtaying on our Controuerſie,
Had hoiſted ſaile, and put to ſea to day:
This Chaine you had of me, can you deny it?
  Ant. I thinke I had, I neuer did deny it.
  Mar. Yes that you did ſir, and forſwore it too.
  Ant. Who heard me to denie it or forſweare it?
  Mar. Theſe eares of mine thou knowſt did hear thee:
Fie on thee wretch, 'tis pitty that thou liu'ſt
To walke where any honeſt men reſort.
  Ant. Thou art a Villaine to impeach me thus,
Ile proue mine honor, and mine honeſtie
Againſt thee preſently, if thou dar'ſt ſtand:
  Mar. I dare and do defie thee for a villaine.

They draw. Enter Adriana, Luciana, Courtezan, & others.
  Adr. Hold, hurt him not for God ſake, he is mad,
Some get within him, take his ſword away:
Binde *Dromio* too, and beare them to my houſe.
  S. Dro. Runne maſter run, for Gods ſake take a houſe,
This is ſome Priorie, in, or we are ſpoyl'd.
Exeunt to the Priorie.
Enter

The Comedie of Errors. 97

Enter Ladie Abbesse.

Ab. Be quiet people, wherefore throng you hither?
Adr. To fetch my poore distracted husband hence,
Let vs come in, that we may binde him fast,
And beare him home for his recouerie.

Gold. I knew he was not in his perfect wits.

Mar. I am sorry now that I did draw on him.

Ab. How long hath this possession held the man.

Adr. This weeke he hath beene heauie, sower sad,
And much different from the man he was:
But till this afternoone his passion
Ne're brake into extremity of rage.

Ab. Hath he not lost much wealth by wrack of sea,
Buried some deere friend, hath not else his eye
Stray'd his affection in vnlawfull loue,
A sinne preuailing much in youthfull men,
Who giue their eies the liberty of gazing.
Which of these sorrowes is he subiect too?

Adr. To none of these, except it be the last,
Namely, some loue that drew him oft from home.

Ab. You should for that haue reprehended him.

Adr. Why so I did.

Ab. I but not rough enough.

Adr. As roughly as my modestie would let me.

Ab. Haply in priuate.

Adr. And in assemblies too.

Ab. I, but not enough.

Adr. It was the copie of our Conference,
In bed he slept not for my vrging it,
At boord he fed not for my vrging it:
Alone, it was the subiect of my Theame:
In company I often glanced it:
Still did I tell him, it was vilde and bad.

Ab. And thereof came it, that the man was mad.
The venome clamors of a iealous woman,
Poisons more deadly then a mad dogges tooth.
It seemes his sleepes were hindred by thy railing,
And thereof comes it that his head is light.
Thou saist his meate was sawc'd with thy vpbraidings,
Vnquiet meales make ill digestions,
Thereof the raging fire of feauer bred,
And what's a Feauer, but a fit of madnesse?
Thou sayest his sports were hindred by thy bralles.
Sweet recreation barr'd, what doth ensue
But moodie and dull melancholly,
Kinsman to grim and comfortlesse dispaire,
And at her heeles a huge infectious troope
Of pale distemperatures, and foes to life?
In food, in sport, and life-preseruing rest
To be disturb'd, would mad or man, or beast:
The consequence is then, thy iealous fits
Hath scar'd thy husband from the vse of wits.

Luc. She neuer reprehended him but mildely,
When he demean'd himselfe, rough, rude, and wildly,
Why beare you these rebukes, and answer not?

Adri. She did betray me to my owne reproofe,
Good people enter, and lay hold on him.

Ab. No, not a creature enters in my house.

Ad. Then let your seruants bring my husband forth.

Ab. Neither: he tooke this place for sanctuary,
And it shall priuiledge him from your hands,
Till I haue brought him to his wits againe,
Or loose my labour in assaying it.

Adr. I will attend my husband, be his nurse,
Diet his sicknesse, for it is my Office,
And will haue no atturney but my selfe,
And therefore let me haue him home with me.

Ab. Be patient, for I will not let him stirre,
Till I haue vs'd the approoued meanes I haue,
With wholsome sirrups, drugges, and holy prayers
To make of him a formall man againe:
It is a branch and parcell of mine oath,
A charitable dutie of my order,
Therefore depart, and leaue him heere with me.

Adr. I will not hence, and leaue my husband heere:
And ill it doth beseeme your holinesse
To separate the husband and the wife.

Ab. Be quiet and depart, thou shalt not haue him.

Luc. Complaine vnto the Duke of this indignity.

Adr. Come go, I will fall prostrate at his feete,
And neuer rise vntill my teares and prayers
Haue won his grace to come in person hither,
And take perforce my husband from the Abbesse.

Mar. By this I thinke the Diall points at fiue:
Anon I'me sure the Duke himselfe in person
Comes this way to the melancholly vale;
The place of depth, and sorrie execution,
Behinde the ditches of the Abbey heere.

Gold. Vpon what cause?

Mar. To see a reuerent *Siracusian* Merchant,
Who put vnluckily into this Bay
Against the Lawes and Statutes of this Towne,
Beheaded publikely for his offence.

Gold. See where they come, we wil behold his death

Luc. Kneele to the Duke before he passe the Abbey.

Enter the Duke of Ephesus, and the Merchant of Siracuse bare head, with the Headsman, & other Officers.

Duke. Yet once againe proclaime it publikely,
If any friend will pay the summe for him,
He shall not die, so much we tender him.

Adr. Iustice most sacred Duke against the Abbesse.

Duke. She is a vertuous and a reuerend Lady,
It cannot be that she hath done thee wrong.

Adr. May it please your Grace, *Antipholus* my husbād,
Who I made Lord of me, and all I had,
At your important Letters this ill day,
A most outragious fit of madnesse tooke him:
That desp'rately he hurried through the streete,
With him his bondman, all as mad as he,
Doing displeasure to the Citizens,
By rushing in their houses: bearing thence
Rings, Iewels, any thing his rage did like.
Once did I get him bound, and sent him home,
Whil'st to take order for the wrongs I went,
That heere and there his furie had committed,
Anon I wot not, by what strong escape
He broke from those that had the guard of him,
And with his mad attendant and himselfe,
Each one with irefull passion, with drawne swords
Met vs againe, and madly bent on vs
Chac'd vs away: till raising of more aide
We came againe to binde them: then they fled
Into this Abbey, whether we pursu'd them,
And heere the Abbesse shuts the gates on vs,
And will not suffer vs to fetch him out,
Nor send him forth, that we may beare him hence.

I Therefore

Therefore most gracious Duke with thy command,
Let him be brought forth, and borne hence for helpe.

  Duke. Long since thy husband feru'd me in my wars
And I to thee ingag'd a Princes word,
When thou didst make him Master of thy bed,
To do him all the grace and good I could.
Go some of you, knocke at the Abbey gate,
And bid the Lady Abbesse come to me:
I will determine this before I stirre.

  Enter a Messenger.

Oh Mistris, Mistris, shift and saue your selfe,
My Master and his man are both broke loose,
Beaten the Maids a-row, and bound the Doctor,
Whose beard they haue singd'd off with brands of fire,
And euer as it blaz'd, they threw on him
Great pailes of puddled myre to quench the haire;
My M.r preaches patience to him, and the while
His man with Cizers nickes him like a foole:
And sure (vnlesse you send some present helpe)
Betweene them they will kill the Coniurer.

  Adr. Peace foole, thy Master and his man are here,
And that is false thou dost report to vs.

  Mess. Mistris, vpon my life I tel you true,
I haue not breath'd almost since I did see it.
He cries for you, and vowes if he can take you,
To scorch your face, and to disfigure you:

  Cry within.

Harke, harke, I heare him Mistris: flie, be gone.

  Duke. Come stand by me, feare nothing: guard with Halberds.

  Adr. Ay me, it is my husband: witnesse you,
That he is borne about inuisible,
Euen now we hous'd him in the Abbey heere.
And now he's there, past thought of humane reason.

  Enter Antipholus, and E. Dromio of Ephesus.

  E. Ant. Iustice most gracious Duke, oh grant me iu- (stice,
Euen for the seruice that long since I did thee,
When I bestrid thee in the warres, and tooke
Deepe scarres to saue thy life; euen for the blood
That then I lost for thee, now grant me iustice.

  Mar. Fat. Vnlesse the feare of death doth make me dote, I see my sonne *Antipholus* and *Dromio.*

  E. Ant. Iustice (sweet Prince) against ỹ Woman there:
She whom thou gau'st to me to be my wife;
That hath abused and dishonored me,
Euen in the strength and height of iniurie:
Beyond imagination is the wrong
That she this day hath shamelesse throwne on me.

  Duke. Discouer how, and thou shalt finde me iust.

  E. Ant. This day (great Duke) she shut the doores vpon me,
While she with Harlots feasted in my house.

  Duke. A greeuous fault: say woman, didst thou so?

  Adr. No my good Lord. My selfe, he, and my sister,
To day did dine together: so befall my soule,
As this is false he burthens me withall.

  Luc. Nere may I looke on day, nor sleepe on night,
But she tels to your Highnesse simple truth.

  Gold. O periur'd woman! They are both forsworne,
In this the Madman iustly chargeth them.

  E. Ant. My Liege, I am aduised what I say,
Neither disturbed with the effect of Wine,
Nor headie-rash prouoak'd with raging ire,
Albeit my wrongs might make one wiser mad.

This woman lock'd me out this day from dinner;
That Goldsmith there, were he not pack'd with her,
Could witnesse it: for he was with me then,
Who parted with me to go fetch a Chaine,
Promising to bring it to the Porpentine,
Where *Balthasar* and I did dine together.
Our dinner done, and he not comming thither,
I went to seeke him. In the street I met him,
And in his companie that Gentleman.
There did this periur'd Goldsmith sweare me downe,
That I this day of him receiu'd the Chaine,
Which God he knowes, I saw not. For the which,
He did arrest me with an Officer.
I did obey, and sent my Pesant home
For certaine Duckets: he with none return'd.
Then fairely I bespoke the Officer
To go in person with me to my house.
By th' way, we met my wife, her sister, and a rabble more
Of vilde Confederates: Along with them
They brought one *Pinch*, a hungry leane-fac'd Villaine;
A meere Anatomie, a Mountebanke,
A thred-bare Iugler, and a Fortune-teller,
A needy-hollow-ey'd-sharpe-looking-wretch;
A liuing dead man. This pernicious slaue,
Forsooth tooke on him as a Coniurer:
And gazing in mine eyes, feeling my pulse,
And with no-face (as 'twere) out-facing me,
Cries out, I was possest. Then altogether
They fell vpon me, bound me, bore me thence,
And in a darke and dankish vault at home
There left me and my man, both bound together,
Till gnawing with my teeth my bonds in sunder,
I gain'd my freedome; and immediately
Ran hether to your Grace, whom I beseech
To giue me ample satisfaction
For these deepe shames, and great indignities.

  Gold. My Lord, in truth, thus far I witnes with him:
That he din'd not at home, but was lock'd out.

  Duke. But had he such a Chaine of thee, or no?

  Gold. He had my Lord, and when he ran in heere,
These people saw the Chaine about his necke.

  Mar. Besides, I will be sworne these eares of mine,
Heard you confesse you had the Chaine of him,
After you first forswore it on the Mart,
And thereupon I drew my sword on you:
And then you fled into this Abbey heere,
From whence I thinke you are come by Miracle.

  E. Ant. I neuer came within these Abbey wals,
Nor euer didst thou draw thy sword on me:
I neuer saw the Chaine, so helpe me heauen:
And this is false you burthen me withall.

  Duke. Why what an intricate impeach is this?
I thinke you all haue drunke of *Circes* cup:
If heere you hous'd him, heere he would haue bin.
If he were mad, he would not pleade so coldly:
You say he din'd at home, the Goldsmith heere
Denies that saying. Sirra, what say you?

  E. Dro. Sir he din'de with her there, at the Porpen- (tine.

  Cur. He did, and from my finger snacht that Ring.

  E. Anti. Tis true (my Liege) this Ring I had of her.

  Duke. Saw'st thou him enter at the Abbey heere?

  Curt. As sure (my Liege) as I do see your Grace.

  Duke. Why this is straunge: Go call the Abbesse hi- (ther.
I thinke you are all mated, or starke mad.

Exit

The Comedie of Errors.

Exit one to the Abbesse.

Fa. Most mighty Duke, vouchsafe me speak a word:
Haply I see a friend will saue my life,
And pay the sum that may deliuer me.

Duke. Speake freely *Siracusian* what thou wilt.

Fath. Is not your name sir call'd *Antipholus*?
And is not that your bondman *Dromio*?

E. Dro. Within this houre I was his bondman sir,
But he I thanke him gnaw'd in two my cords,
Now am I *Dromio*, and his man, vnbound.

Fath. I am sure you both of you remember me.

Dro. Our selues we do remember sir by you:
For lately we were bound as you are now.
You are not *Pinches* patient, are you sir?

Father. Why looke you strange on me? you know me well.

E. Ant. I neuer saw you in my life till now.

Fa. Oh! griefe hath chang'd me since you saw me last,
And carefull houres with times deformed hand,
Haue written strange defeatures in my face:
But tell me yet, dost thou not know my voice?

Ant. Neither.

Fat. *Dromio*, nor thou?

Dro. No trust me sir, nor I.

Fa. I am sure thou dost?

E. Dromio. I sir, but I am sure I do not, and whatsoeuer a man denies, you are now bound to beleeue him.

Fath. Not know my voice, oh times extremity
Hast thou so crack'd and splitted my poore tongue
In seuen short yeares, that heere my onely sonne
Knowes not my feeble key of vntun'd cares?
Though now this grained face of mine be hid
In sap-consuming Winters drizled snow,
And all the Conduits of my blood froze vp:
Yet hath my night of life some memorie:
My wasting lampes some fading glimmer left;
My dull deafe eares a little vse to heare:
All these old witnesses, I cannot erre.
Tell me, thou art my sonne *Antipholus*.

Ant. I neuer saw my Father in my life.

Fa. But seuen yeares since, in *Siracusa* boy
Thou know'st we parted, but perhaps my sonne,
Thou sham'st to acknowledge me in miserie.

Ant. The Duke, and all that know me in the City,
Can witnesse with me that it is not so.
I ne're saw *Siracusa* in my life.

Duke. I tell thee *Siracusian*, twentie yeares
Haue I bin Patron to *Antipholus*,
During which time, he ne're saw *Siracusa*:
I see thy age and dangers make thee dote.

Enter the Abbesse with Antipholus Siracusa, and Dromio Sir.

Abbesse. Most mightie Duke, behold a man much wrong'd.

All gather to see them.

Adr. I see two husbands, or mine eyes deceiue me.

Duke. One of these men is *genius* to the other:
And so of these, which is the naturall man,
And which the spirit? Who deciphers them?

S. Dromio. I Sir am *Dromio*, command him away.

E. Dro. I Sir am *Dromio*, pray let me stay.

S. Ant. *Egeon* art thou not? or else his ghost.

S. Drom. Oh my olde Master, who hath bound him heere?

Abb. Who euer bound him, I will lose his bonds,
And gaine a husband by his libertie:
Speake olde *Egeon*, if thou bee'st the man
That hadst a wife once call'd *Æmilia*,
That bore thee at a burthen two faire sonnes?
Oh if thou bee'st the same *Egeon*, speake:
And speake vnto the same *Æmilia*.

Duke. Why heere begins his Morning storie right:
These two *Antipholus*, these two so like,
And these two *Dromio's*, one in semblance:
Besides her vrging of her wracke at sea,
These are the parents to these children,
Which accidentally are met together.

Fa. If I dreame not, thou art *Æmilia*,
If thou art she, tell me, where is that sonne
That floated with thee on the fatall rafte.

Abb. By men of *Epidamium*, he, and I,
And the twin *Dromio*, all were taken vp;
But by and by, rude Fishermen of *Corinth*
By force tooke *Dromio*, and my sonne from them,
And me they left with those of *Epidamium*.
What then became of them, I cannot tell:
I, to this fortune that you see mee in.

Duke. *Antipholus* thou cam'st from *Corinth* first.

S. Ant. No sir, not I, I came from *Siracuse*.

Duke. Stay, stand apart, I know not which is which.

E. Ant. I came from *Corinth* my most gracious Lord

E. Dro. And I with him.

E. Ant. Brought to this Town by that most famous Warriour,
Duke *Menaphon*, your most renowned Vnckle.

Adr. Which of you two did dine with me to day?

S. Ant. I, gentle Mistris.

Adr. And are not you my husband?

E. Ant. No, I say nay to that.

S. Ant. And so do I, yet did she call me so:
And this faire Gentlewoman her sister heere
Did call me brother. What I told you then,
I hope I shall haue leisure to make good,
If this be not a dreame I see and heare.

Goldsmith. That is the Chaine sir, which you had of mee.

S. Ant. I thinke it be sir, I denie it not.

E. Ant. And you sir for this Chaine arrested me.

Gold. I thinke I did sir, I deny it not.

Adr. I sent you monie sir to be your baile
By *Dromio*, but I thinke he brought it not.

E. Dro. No, none by me.

S. Ant. This purse of Duckets I receiu'd from you,
And *Dromio* my man did bring them me:
I see we still did meete each others man,
And I was tane for him, and he for me,
And thereupon these errors are arose.

E. Ant. These Duckets pawne I for my father heere.

Duke. It shall not neede, thy father hath his life.

Cur. Sir I must haue that Diamond from you.

E. Ant. There take it, and much thanks for my good cheere.

Abb. Renowned Duke, vouchsafe to take the paines
To go with vs into the Abbey heere,
And heare at large discoursed all our fortunes,
And all that are assembled in this place:
That by this simpathized one daies error
Haue suffer'd wrong. Goe, keepe vs companie,

And

And we shall make full satisfaction.
Thirtie three yeares haue I but gone in trauaile
Of you my sonnes, and till this present houre
My heauie burthen are deliuered:
The Duke my husband, and my children both,
And you the Kalenders of their Natiuity,
Go to a Gossips feast, and go with mee,
After so long greefe such Natiuitie.

Duke. With all my heart, Ile Gossip at this feast.

Exeunt omnes. Manet the two Dromio's and two Brothers.

S.Dro. Mast, shall I fetch your stuffe from shipbord?
E.An.Dromio, what stuffe of mine hast thou imbarkt
S.Dro. Your goods that lay at host sir in the Centaur.
S.Ant. He speakes to me, I am your master *Dromio.*

Come go with vs, wee'l looke to that anon,
Embrace thy brother there, reioyce with him. *Exit*

S.Dro. There is a fat friend at your masters house,
That kitchin'd me for you to day at dinner:
She now shall be my sister, not my wife.

E.D. Me thinks you are my glasse, & not my brother:
I see by you, I am a sweet-fac'd youth,
Will you walke in to see their gossipping?

S.Dro. Not I sir, you are my elder.
E.Dro. That's a question, how shall we trie it.
S.Dro. Wee'l draw Cuts for the Signior, till then, lead thou first.
E.Dro. Nay then thus:
We came into the world like brother and brother:
And now let's go hand in hand, not one before another.
Exeunt.

FINIS.

Much adoe about Nothing.

Actus primus, Scena prima.

Enter Leonato Gouernour of Messina, Innogen his wife, Hero his daughter, and Beatrice his Neece, with a messenger.

Leonato.
I Learne in this Letter, that *Don Peter* of *Arragon*, comes this night to *Messina*.

Mess. He is very neere by this : he was not three Leagues off when I left him.

Leon. How many Gentlemen haue you lost in this action?

Mess. But few of any sort, and none of name.

Leon. A victorie is twice it selfe, when the atchieuer brings home full numbers: I finde heere, that Don *Peter* hath bestowed much honor on a yong *Florentine*, called *Claudio*.

Mess. Much deseru'd on his part, and equally remembred by Don *Pedro*, he hath borne himselfe beyond the promise of his age, doing in the figure of a Lambe, the feats of a Lion, he hath indeede better bettred expectation, then you must expect of me to tell you how.

Leo. He hath an Vnckle heere in *Messina*, wil be very much glad of it.

Mess. I haue alreadie deliuered him letters, and there appeares much ioy in him, euen so much, that ioy could not shew it selfe modest enough, without a badg of bitternesse.

Leo. Did he breake out into teares?

Mess. In great measure.

Leo. A kinde ouerflow of kindnesse, there are no faces truer, then those that are so wash'd, how much better is it to weepe at ioy, then to ioy at weeping?

Bea. I pray you, is Signior *Mountanto* return'd from the warres, or no?

Mess. I know none of that name, Lady, there was none such in the armie of any sort.

Leon. What is he that you aske for Neece?

Hero. My cousin meanes Signior Benedick of *Padua*.

Mess. O he's return'd, and as pleasant as euer he was.

Beat. He set vp his bils here in *Messina*, & challeng'd Cupid at the Flight: and my Vnckles foole reading the Challenge, subscrib'd for Cupid, and challeng'd him at the Burbolt. I pray you, how many hath hee kil'd and eaten in these warres? But how many hath he kil'd? for indeed, I promis'd to eate all of his killing.

Leon. 'Faith Neece, you taxe Signior Benedicke too much, but hee'l be meet with you, I doubt it not.

Mess. He hath done good seruice Lady in these wars.

Beat. You had musty victuall, and he hath holpe to ease it: he's a very valiant Trencher-man, hee hath an excellent stomacke.

Mess. And a good souldier too Lady.

Beat. And a good souldier to a Lady. But what is he to a Lord?

Mess. A Lord to a Lord, a man to a man, stuft with all honourable vertues.

Beat. It is so indeed, he is no lesse then a stuft man: but for the stuffing well, we are all mortall.

Leon. You must not (sir) mistake my Neece, there is a kind of merry war betwixt Signior Benedick, & her: they neuer meet, but there's a skirmish of wit between them.

Bea. Alas, he gets nothing by that. In our last conflict, foure of his fiue wits went halting off, and now is the whole man gouern'd with one: so that if hee haue wit enough to keepe himselfe warme, let him beare it for a difference betweene himselfe and his horse: For it is all the wealth that he hath left, to be knowne a reasonable creature. Who is his companion now? He hath euery month a new sworne brother.

Mess. I'st possible?

Beat. Very easily possible: he weares his faith but as the fashion of his hat, it euer changes with ý next block.

Mess. I see (Lady) the Gentleman is not in your bookes.

Bea. No, and he were, I would burne my study. But I pray you, who is his companion? Is there no young squarer now, that will make a voyage with him to the diuell?

Mess. He is most in the company of the right noble *Claudio*.

Beat. O Lord, he will hang vpon him like a disease: he is sooner caught then the pestilence, and the taker runs presently mad. God helpe the noble *Claudio*, if hee haue caught the Benedict, it will cost him a thousand pound ere he be cur'd.

Mess. I will hold friends with you Lady.

Bea. Do good friend.

Leo. You'l ne're run mad Neece.

Bea. No, not till a hot Ianuary.

Mess. Don *Pedro* is approach'd.

Enter don Pedro, Claudio, Benedicke, Balthasar, and Iohn the bastard.

Pedro. Good Signior *Leonato*, you are come to meet your trouble: the fashion of the world is to auoid cost, and you encounter it.

Leon. Neuer came trouble to my house in the likenes of your Grace: for trouble being gone, comfort should remaine: but when you depart from me, sorrow abides, and happinesse takes his leaue.

Pedro.

Pedro. You embrace your charge too willingly: I thinke this is your daughter.

Leonato. Her mother hath many times told me so.

Bened. Were you in doubt that you askt her?

Leonato. Signior *Benedicke*, no, for then were you a childe.

Pedro. You haue it full *Benedicke*, we may ghesse by this, what you are, being a man, truely the Lady fathers her selfe: be happie Lady, for you are like an honorable father.

Ben. If Signior *Leonato* be her father, she would not haue his head on her shoulders for al *Messina*, as like him as she is.

Beat. I wonder that you will still be talking, signior *Benedicke*, no body markes you.

Ben. What my deere Ladie Disdaine! are you yet liuing?

Beat. Is it possible Disdaine should die, while shee hath such meete foode to feede it, as Signior *Benedicke*? Curtesie it selfe must conuert to Disdaine, if you come in her presence.

Bene. Then is curtesie a turne-coate, but it is certaine I am loued of all Ladies, onely you excepted: and I would I could finde in my heart that I had not a hard heart, for truely I loue none.

Beat. A deere happinesse to women, they would else haue beene troubled with a pernitious Suter, I thanke God and my cold blood, I am of your humour for that, I had rather heare my Dog barke at a Crow, than a man sweare he loues me.

Bene. God keepe your Ladiship still in that minde, so some Gentleman or other shall scape a predestinate scratcht face.

Beat. Scratching could not make it worse, and 'twere such a face as yours were.

Bene. Well, you are a rare Parrat teacher.

Beat. A bird of my tongue, is better than a beast of your.

Ben. I would my horse had the speed of your tongue, and so good a continuer, but keepe your way a Gods name, I haue done.

Beat. You alwaies end with a Iades tricke, I know you of old.

Pedro. This is the summe of all: *Leonato*, signior *Claudio*, and signior *Benedicke*; my deere friend *Leonato*, hath inuited you all, I tell him we shall stay here, at the least a moneth, and he heartily praies some occasion may detaine vs longer: I dare sweare hee is no hypocrite, but praies from his heart.

Leon. If you sweare, my Lord, you shall not be forsworne, let mee bid you welcome, my Lord, being reconciled to the Prince your brother: I owe you all duetie.

Iohn. I thanke you, I am not of many words, but I thanke you.

Leon. Please it your grace leade on?

Pedro. Your hand *Leonato*, we will goe together.

    Exeunt. Manet Benedicke and Claudio.

Clau. *Benedicke*, didst thou note the daughter of signior *Leonato*?

Bene. I noted her not, but I lookt on her.

Clau. Is she not a modest yong Ladie?

Bene. Doe you question me as an honest man should doe, for my simple true iudgement? or would you haue me speake after my custome, as being a professed tyrant to their sexe?

Clau. No, I pray thee speake in sober iudgement.

Bene. Why yfaith me thinks shee's too low for a hie praise, too browne for a faire praise, and too little for a great praise, onely this commendation I can affoord her, that were shee other then she is, she were vnhandsome, and being no other, but as she is, I doe not like her.

Clau. Thou think'st I am in sport, I pray thee tell me truely how thou lik'st her.

Bene. Would you buie her, that you enquier after her?

Clau. Can the world buie such a iewell?

Ben. Yea, and a case to put it into, but speake you this with a sad brow? Or doe you play the flowting iacke, to tell vs Cupid is a good Hare-finder, and Vulcan a rare Carpenter: Come, in what key shall aman take you to goe in the song?

Clau. In mine eie, she is the sweetest Ladie that euer I lookt on.

Bene. I can see yet without spectacles, and I see no such matter: there's her cosin, and she were not possest with a furie, exceedes her as much in beautie, as the first of Maie doth the last of December: but I hope you haue no intent to turne husband, haue you?

Clau. I would scarce trust my selfe, though I had sworne the contrarie, if *Hero* would be my wife.

Bene. Ist come to this? in faith hath not the world one man but he will weare his cap with suspition? shall I neuer see a batcheller of three score againe? goe to yfaith, and thou wilt needes thrust thy necke into a yoke, weare the print of it, and sigh away sundaies: looke, *don Pedro* is returned to seeke you.

    Enter don Pedro, Iohn the bastard.

Pedr. What secret hath held you here, that you followed not to *Leonatoes*?

Bened. I would your Grace would constraine mee to tell.

Pedro. I charge thee on thy allegeance.

Ben. You heare, Count *Claudio*, I can be secret as a dumbe man, I would haue you thinke so (but on my allegiance, marke you this, on my allegiance) hee is in loue, With who? now that is your Graces part: marke how short his answere is, with *Hero*, *Leonatoes* short daughter.

Clau. If this were so, so were it vttred.

Bened. Like the old tale, my Lord, it is not so, nor 'twas not so: but indeede, God forbid it should be so.

Clau. If my passion change not shortly, God forbid it should be otherwise.

Pedro. Amen, if you loue her, for the Ladie is verie well worthie.

Clau. You speake this to fetch me in, my Lord.

Pedr. By my troth I speake my thought.

Clau. And in faith, my Lord, I spoke mine.

Bened. And by my two faiths and troths, my Lord, I speake mine.

Clau. That I loue her, I feele.

Pedr. That she is worthie, I know.

Bened. That I neither feele how shee should be loued, nor know how shee should be worthie, is the opinion that fire cannot melt out of me, I will die in it at the stake.

Pedr. Thou wast euer an obstinate heretique in the despight of Beautie.

Clau. And neuer could maintaine his part, but in the force of his will.

                             Bene. That

Ben. That a woman conceiued me, I thanke her: that she brought mee vp, I likewise giue her most humble thankes: but that I will haue a rechate winded in my forehead, or hang my bugle in an inuisible baldricke, all women shall pardon me: because I will not do them the wrong to mistrust any, I will doe my selfe the right to trust none: and the fine is, (for the which I may goe the finer) I will liue a Batchellor.

Pedro. I shall see thee ere I die, looke pale with loue.

Bene. With anger, with sicknesse, or with hunger, my Lord, not with loue: proue that euer I loose more blood with loue, then I will get againe with drinking, picke out mine eyes with a Ballet-makers penne, and hang me vp at the doore of a brothel-house for the signe of blinde Cupid.

Pedro. Well, if euer thou doost fall from this faith, thou wilt proue a notable argument.

Bene. If I do, hang me in a bottle like a Cat, & shoot at me, and he that hit's me, let him be clapt on the shoulder, and cal'd *Adam*.

Pedro. Well, as time shall trie: In time the sauage Bull doth beare the yoake.

Bene. The sauage bull may, but if euer the sensible *Benedicke* beare it, plucke off the bulles hornes, and set them in my forehead, and let me be vildely painted, and in such great Letters as they write, heere is good horse to hire: let them signifie vnder my signe, here you may see *Benedicke* the married man.

Clau. If this should euer happen, thou wouldst bee horne mad.

Pedro. Nay, if Cupid haue not spent all his Quiuer in Venice, thou wilt quake for this shortly.

Bene. I looke for an earthquake too then.

Pedro. Well, you will temporize with the houres, in the meane time, good Signior *Benedicke*, repaire to *Leonatoes*, commend me to him, and tell him I will not faile him at supper, for indeede he hath made great preparation.

Bene. I haue almost matter enough in me for such an Embassage, and so I commit you.

Clau. To the tuition of God. From my house, if I had it.

Pedro. The sixt of Iuly. Your louing friend, *Benedick*.

Bene. Nay mocke not, mocke not; the body of your discourse is sometime guarded with fragments, and the guardes are but slightly basted on neither, ere you flout old ends any further, examine your conscience, and so I leaue you. *Exit.*

Clau. My Liege, your Highnesse now may doe mee good.

Pedro. My loue is thine to teach, teach it but how,
And thou shalt see how apt it is to learne
Any hard Lesson that may do thee good.

Clau. Hath *Leonato* any sonne my Lord?

Pedro. No childe but *Hero*, she's his onely heire.
Dost thou affect her *Claudio*?

Clau. O my Lord,
When you went onward on this ended action,
I look'd vpon her with a souldiers eie,
That lik'd, but had a rougher taske in hand,
Than to driue liking to the name of loue:
But now I am return'd, and that warre-thoughts
Haue left their places vacant: in their roomes,
Come thronging soft and delicate desires,
All prompting mee how faire yong *Hero* is,
Saying I lik'd her ere I went to warres.

Pedro. Thou wilt be like a louer presently,
And tire the hearer with a booke of words:
If thou dost loue faire *Hero*, cherish it,
And I will breake with her: wast not to this end,
That thou beganst to twist so fine a story?

Clau. How sweetly doe you minister to loue,
That know loues griefe by his complexion!
But lest my liking might too sodaine seeme,
I would haue salu'd it with a longer treatise.

Ped. What need ÿ bridge much broder then the flood?
The fairest graunt is the necessitie:
Looke what will serue, is fit: 'tis once, thou louest,
And I will fit thee with the remedie,
I know we shall haue reuelling to night,
I will assume thy part in some disguise,
And tell faire *Hero* I am *Claudio*,
And in her bosome Ile vnclaspe my heart,
And take her hearing prisoner with the force
And strong incounter of my amorous tale:
Then after, to her father will I breake,
And the conclusion is, shee shall be thine,
In practise let vs put it presently. *Exeunt.*

Enter Leonato and an old man, brother to Leonato.

Leo. How now brother, where is my cosen your son: hath he prouided this musicke?

Old. He is very busie about it, but brother, I can tell you newes that you yet dreamt not of.

Lo. Are they good?

Old. As the euents stamps them, but they haue a good couer: they shew well outward, the Prince and Count *Claudio* walking in a thick pleached alley in my orchard, were thus ouer-heard by a man of mine: the Prince discouered to *Claudio* that hee loued my niece your daughter, and meant to acknowledge it this night in a dance, and if hee found her accordant, hee meant to take the present time by the top, and instantly breake with you of it.

Leo. Hath the fellow any wit that told you this?

Old. A good sharpe fellow, I will send for him, and question him your selfe.

Leo. No, no; wee will hold it as a dreame, till it appeare it selfe: but I will acquaint my daughter withall, that she may be the better prepared for an answer, if peraduenture this bee true: goe you and tell her of it: coosins, you know what you haue to doe, O I crie you mercie friend, goe you with mee and I will vse your skill, good cosin haue a care this busie time. *Exeunt.*

Enter Sir Iohn the Bastard, and Conrade his companion.

Con. What the good yeere my Lord, why are you thus out of measure sad?

Ioh. There is no measure in the occasion that breeds, therefore the sadnesse is without limit.

Con. You should heare reason.

Iohn. And when I haue heard it, what blessing bringeth it?

Con. If not a present remedy, yet a patient sufferance.

Ioh. I wonder that thou (being as thou saist thou art, borne vnder *Saturne*) goest about to apply a morall medicine, to a mortifying mischiefe: I cannot hide what I am: I must bee sad when I haue cause, and smile at no mans iests, eat when I haue stomacke, and wait for no mans leisure: sleepe when I am drowsie, and tend on no mans businesse, laugh when I am merry, and claw no man in his humor.

Con. Yea, but you must not make the ful show of this, till you may doe it without controllment, you haue of
late

late stood out against your brother, and hee hath tane you newly into his grace, where it is impossible you should take root, but by the faire weather that you make your selfe, it is needful that you frame the season for your owne haruest.

Iohn. I had rather be a canker in a hedge, then a rose in his grace, and it better fits my bloud to be disdain'd of all, then to fashion a carriage to rob loue from any: in this (though I cannot be said to be a flattering honest man) it must not be denied but I am a plaine dealing villaine, I am trusted with a mussell, and enfranchisde with a clog, therefore I haue decreed, not to sing in my cage: if I had my mouth, I would bite: if I had my liberty, I would do my liking: in the meane time, let me be that I am, and seeke not to alter me.

Con. Can you make no vse of your discontent?

Iohn. I will make all vse of it, for I vse it onely. Who comes here? what newes *Borachio*?

Enter Borachio.

Bor. I came yonder from a great supper, the Prince your brother is royally entertained by *Leonato*, and I can giue you intelligence of an intended marriage.

Iohn. Will it serue for any Modell to build mischiefe on? What is hee for a foole that betrothes himselfe to vnquietnesse?

Bor. Mary it is your brothers right hand.

Iohn. Who, the most exquisite *Claudio*?

Bor. Euen he.

Iohn. A proper squier, and who, and whe, which way lookes he?

Bor. Mary on *Hero*, the daughter and Heire of *Leonato*.

Iohn. A very forward March-chicke, how came you to this?

Bor. Being entertain'd for a perfumer, as I was smoaking a musty roome, comes me the Prince and *Claudio*, hand in hand in sad conference: I whipt behind the Arras, and there heard it agreed vpon, that the Prince should wooe *Hero* for himselfe, and hauing obtain'd her, giue her to Count *Claudio*.

Iohn. Come, come, let vs thither, this may proue food to my displeasure, that young start-vp hath all the glorie of my ouerthrow: if I can crosse him any way, I blesse my selfe euery way, you are both sure, and will assist mee?

Conr. To the death my Lord.

Iohn. Let vs to the great supper, their cheere is the greater that I am subdued, would the Cooke were of my minde: shall we goe proue whats to be done?

Bor. Wee'll wait vpon your Lordship.

Exeunt.

Actus Secundus.

Enter Leonato, his brother, his wife, Hero his daughter, and Beatrice his neece, and a kinswoman.

Leonato. Was not Count *Iohn* here at supper?

Brother. I saw him not.

Beatrice. How tartly that Gentleman lookes, I neuer can see him, but I am heart-burn'd an howre after.

Hero. He is of a very melancholy disposition.

Beatrice. Hee were an excellent man that were made iust in the mid-way betweene him and *Benedicke*, the one is too like an image and saies nothing, and the other too like my Ladies eldest sonne, euermore tatling.

Leon. Then halfe signior *Benedicks* tongue in Count *Iohns* mouth, and halfe Count *Iohns* melancholy in Signior *Benedicks* face.

Beat. With a good legge, and a good foot vnckle, and money enough in his purse, such a man would winne any woman in the world, if he could get her good will.

Leon. By my troth Neece, thou wilt neuer get thee a husband, if thou be so shrewd of thy tongue.

Brother. Infaith shee's too curst.

Beat. Too curst is more then curst, I shall lessen Gods sending that way: for it is said, God sends a curst Cow short hornes, but to a Cow too curst he sends none.

Leon. So, by being too curst, God will send you no hornes.

Beat. Iust, if he send me no husband, for the which blessing, I am at him vpon my knees euery morning and euening: Lord, I could not endure a husband with a beard on his face, I had rather lie in the woollen.

Leonato. You may light vpon a husband that hath no beard.

Batrice. What should I doe with him? dresse him in my apparell, and make him my waiting gentlewoman? he that hath a beard, is more then a youth: and he that hath no beard, is lesse then a man: and hee that is more then a youth, is not for mee: and he that is lesse then a man, I am not for him: therefore I will euen take sixepence in earnest of the Berrord, and leade his Apes into hell.

Leon. Well then, goe you into hell.

Beat. No, but to the gate, and there will the Deuill meete mee like an old Cuckold with hornes on his head, and say, get you to heauen *Beatrice*, get you to heauen, heere's no place for you maids, so deliuer I vp my Apes, and away to S. *Peter*: for the heauens, hee shewes mee where the Batchellers sit, and there liue wee as merry as the day is long.

Brother. Well neece, I trust you will be rul'd by your father.

Beatrice. Yes faith, it is my cosens dutie to make cursie, and say, as it please you: but yet for all that cosin, let him be a handsome fellow, or else make an other cursie, and say, father, as it please me.

Leonato. Well neece, I hope to see you one day fitted with a husband.

Beatrice. Not till God make men of some other mettall then earth, would it not grieue a woman to be ouermastred with a peece of valiant dust? to make account of her life to a clod of waiward marle? no vnckle, ile none: *Adams* sonnes are my brethren, and truly I hold it a sinne to match in my kinred.

Leon. Daughter, remember what I told you, if the Prince doe solicit you in that kinde, you know your answere.

Beatrice. The fault will be in the musicke cosin, if you be not woed in good time: if the Prince bee too important, tell him there is measure in euery thing, & so dance out the answere, for heare me *Hero*, wooing, wedding, & repenting, is as a Scotch ijgge, a measure, and a cinquepace: the first suite is hot and hasty like a Scotch ijgge (and full as fantasticall) the wedding manerly modest, (as a measure) full of state & aunchentry, and then comes repentance, and with his bad legs falls into the cinquepace faster and faster, till he sinkes into his graue.

Leonato.

Much adoe about Nothing.

Leonato. Cosin you apprehend passing shrewdly.

Beatrice. I haue a good eye vnckle, I can see a Church by daylight.

Leon. The reuellers are entring brother, make good roome.

Enter Prince, Pedro, Claudio, and Benedicke, and Balthasar, or dumbe Iohn, Maskers with a drum.

Pedro. Lady, will you walke about with your friend?

Hero. So you walke softly, and looke sweetly, and say nothing, I am yours for the walke, and especially when I walke away.

Pedro. With me in your company.

Hero. I may say so when I please.

Pedro. And when please you to say so?

Hero. When I like your fauour, for God defend the Lute should be like the case.

Pedro. My visor is Philemons roofe, within the house is Loue.

Hero. Why then your visor should be thatcht.

Pedro. Speake low if you speake Loue.

Bene. Well, I would you did like me.

Mar. So would not I for your owne sake, for I haue manie ill qualities.

Bene. Which is one?

Mar. I say my prayers alowd.

Ben. I loue you the better, the hearers may cry Amen.

Mar. God match me with a good dauncer.

Balt. Amen.

Mar. And God keepe him out of my sight when the daunce is done: answer Clarke.

Balt. No more words, the Clarke is answered.

Vrsula. I know you well enough, you are Signior Anthonio.

Anth. At a word, I am not.

Vrsula. I know you by the wagling of your head.

Anth. To tell you true, I counterfet him.

Vrsu. You could neuer doe him so ill well, vnlesse you were the very man: here's his dry hand vp & down, you are he, you are he.

Anth. At a word I am not.

Vrsula. Come, come, doe you thinke I doe not know you by your excellent wit? can vertue hide it selfe? goe to, mumme, you are he, graces will appeare, and there's an end.

Beat. Will you not tell me who told you so?

Bene. No, you shall pardon me.

Beat. Nor will you not tell me who you are?

Bened. Not now.

Beat. That I was disdainfull, and that I had my good wit out of the hundred merry tales: well, this was Signior Benedicke that said so.

Bene. What's he?

Beat. I am sure you know him well enough.

Bene. Not I, beleeue me.

Beat. Did he neuer make you laugh?

Bene. I pray you what is he?

Beat. Why he is the Princes iester, a very dull foole, onely his gift is, in deuising impossible slanders, none but Libertines delight in him, and the commendation is not in his witte, but in his villanie, for hee both pleaseth men and angers them, and then they laugh at him, and beat him: I am sure he is in the Fleet, I would he had boorded me.

Bene. When I know the Gentleman, Ile tell him what you say.

Beat. Do, do, hee'l but breake a comparison or two on me, which peraduenture (not markt, or not laugh'd at) strikes him into melancholly, and then there's a Partridge wing saued, for the foole will eate no supper that night. We must follow the Leaders.

Ben. In euery good thing.

Bea. Nay, if they leade to any ill, I will leaue them at the next turning. *Exeunt.*

Musicke for the dance.

Iohn. Sure my brother is amorous on *Hero*, and hath withdrawne her father to breake with him about it: the Ladies follow her, and but one visor remaines.

Borachio. And that is *Claudio*, I know him by his bearing.

Iohn. Are not you signior *Benedicke*?

Clau. You know me well, I am hee.

Iohn. Signior, you are verie neere my Brother in his loue, he is enamor'd on *Hero*, I pray you disswade him from her, she is no equall for his birth: you may do the part of an honest man in it.

Claudio. How know you he loues her?

Iohn. I heard him sweare his affection.

Bor. So did I too, and he swore he would marrie her to night.

Iohn. Come, let vs to the banquet. *Ex. manet Clau.*

Clau. Thus answere I in name of Benedicke,
But heare these ill newes with the eares of *Claudio*:
'Tis certaine so, the Prince woes for himselfe:
Friendship is constant in all other things,
Saue in the Office and affaires of loue:
Therefore all hearts in loue vse their owne tongues.
Let euerie eye negotiate for it selfe,
And trust no Agent: for beautie is a witch,
Against whose charmes, faith melteth into blood:
This is an accident of hourely proofe,
Which I mistrusted not. Farewell therefore *Hero*.

Enter Benedicke.

Ben. Count *Claudio*.

Clau. Yea, the same.

Ben. Come, will you go with me?

Clau. Whither?

Ben. Euen to the next Willow, about your own businesse, Count. What fashion will you weare the Garland off? About your necke, like an Vsurers chaine? Or vnder your arme, like a Lieutenants scarfe? You must weare it one way, for the Prince hath got your *Hero*.

Clau. I wish him ioy of her.

Ben. Why that's spoken like an honest Drouier, so they sel Bullockes: but did you thinke the Prince wold haue serued you thus?

Clau. I pray you leaue me.

Ben. Ho now you strike like the blindman, 'twas the boy that stole your meate, and you'l beat the post.

Clau. If it will not be, Ile leaue you. *Exit.*

Ben. Alas poore hurt fowle, now will he creepe into sedges: But that my Ladie *Beatrice* should know me, & not know me: the Princes foole! Hah? It may be I goe vnder that title, because I am merrie: yea but so I am apt to do my selfe wrong: I am not so reputed, it is the base (though bitter) disposition of *Beatrice*, that putt's the world into her person, and so giues me out: well, Ile be reuenged as I may.

Enter the Prince.

Pedro. Now Signior, where's the Count, did you see him?

Ben

Bene. Troth my Lord, I haue played the part of Lady Fame, I found him heere as melancholy as a Lodge in a Warren, I told him, and I thinke, told him true, that your grace had got the will of this young Lady, and I offered him my company to a willow tree, either to make him a garland, as being forsaken, or to binde him a rod, as being worthy to be whipt.

Pedro. To be whipt, what's his fault?

Bene. The flat transgression of a Schoole-boy, who being ouer-ioyed with finding a birds nest, shewes it his companion, and he steales it.

Pedro. Wilt thou make a trust, a transgression? the transgression is in the stealer.

Ben. Yet it had not beene amisse the rod had beene made, and the garland too, for the garland he might haue worne himselfe, and the rod hee might haue bestowed on you, who (as I take it) haue stolne his birds nest.

Pedro. I will but teach them to sing, and restore them to the owner.

Bene. If their singing answer your saying, by my faith you say honestly.

Pedro. The Lady *Beatrice* hath a quarrell to you, the Gentleman that daunst with her, told her shee is much wrong'd by you.

Bene. O she misusde me past the indurance of a block: an oake but with one greene leafe on it, would haue answered her: my very visor began to assume life, and scold with her: shee told mee, not thinking I had beene my selfe, that I was the Princes Iester, and that I was duller then a great thaw, hudling iest vpon iest, with such impossible conueiance vpon me, that I stood like a man at a marke, with a whole army shooting at me: shee speakes poynyards, and euery word stabbes: if her breath were as terrible as terminations, there were no liuing neere her, she would infect to the north starre: I would not marry her, though she were indowed with all that *Adam* had left him before he transgrest, she would haue made *Hercules* haue turnd spit, yea, and haue cleft his club to make the fire too: come, talke not of her, you shall finde her the infernall Ate in good apparell. I would to God some scholler would coniure her, for certainely while she is heere, a man may liue as quiet in hell, as in a sanctuary, and people sinne vpon purpose, because they would goe thither, so indeed all disquiet, horror, and perturbation followes her.

Enter Claudio and Beatrice, Leonato, Hero.

Pedro. Looke heere she comes.

Bene. Will your Grace command mee any seruice to the worlds end? I will goe on the slightest arrand now to the Antypodes that you can deuise to send me on: I will fetch you a tooth-picker now from the furthest inch of Asia: bring you the length of *Prester Iohns* foot: fetch you a hayre off the great *Chams* beard: doe you any embassage to the Pigmies, rather then hould three words conference, with this Harpy: you haue no employment for me?

Pedro. None, but to desire your good company.

Bene. O God sir, heeres a dish I loue not, I cannot indure this Lady tongue. *Exit.*

Pedr. Come Lady, come, you haue lost the heart of Signior *Benedicke*.

Beatr. Indeed my Lord, hee lent it me a while, and I gaue him vse for it, a double heart for a single one, marry once before he wonne it of mee, with false dice, therefore your Grace may well say I haue lost it.

Pedro. You haue put him downe Lady, you haue put him downe.

Beat. So I would not he should do me, my Lord, lest I should prooue the mother of fooles: I haue brought Count *Claudio*, whom you sent me to seeke.

Pedro. Why how now Count, wherfore are you sad?

Claud. Not sad my Lord.

Pedro. How then? sicke?

Claud. Neither, my Lord.

Beat. The Count is neither sad, nor sicke, nor merry, nor well: but ciuill Count, ciuill as an Orange, and something of a iealous complexion.

Pedro. Ifaith Lady, I thinke your blazon to be true, though Ile be sworne, if hee be so, his conceit is false: heere *Claudio*, I haue wooed in thy name, and faire *Hero* is won, I haue broke with her father, and his good will obtained, name the day of marriage, and God giue thee ioy.

Leona. Count, take of me my daughter, and with her my fortunes: his grace hath made the match, & all grace say, Amen to it.

Beatr. Speake Count, tis your Qu.

Claud. Silence is the perfectest Herault of ioy, I were but little happy if I could say, how much? Lady, as you are mine, I am yours, I giue away my selfe for you, and doat vpon the exchange.

Beat. Speake cosin, or (if you cannot) stop his mouth with a kisse, and let not him speake neither.

Pedro. Infaith Lady you haue a merry heart.

Beatr. Yea my Lord I thanke it, poore foole it keepes on the windy side of Care, my coosin tells him in his eare that he is in my heart.

Clau. And so she doth coosin.

Beat. Good Lord for alliance: thus goes euery one to the world but I, and I am sun-burn'd, I may sit in a corner and cry, heigh ho for a husband.

Pedro. Lady *Beatrice*, I will get you one.

Beat. I would rather haue one of your fathers getting: hath your Grace ne're a brother like you? your father got excellent husbands, if a maid could come by them.

Prince. Will you haue me? Lady.

Beat. No, my Lord, vnlesse I might haue another for working-daies, your Grace is too costly to weare euerie day: but I beseech your Grace pardon mee, I was borne to speake all mirth, and no matter.

Prince. Your silence most offends me, and to be merry, best becomes you, for out of question, you were born in a merry howre.

Beatr. No sure my Lord, my Mother cried, but then there was a starre daunst, and vnder that was I borne: cosins God giue you ioy.

Leonato. Neece, will you looke to those things I told you of?

Beat. I cry you mercy Vncle, by your Graces pardon.
Exit Beatrice.

Prince. By my troth a pleasant spirited Lady.

Leon. There's little of the melancholy element in her my Lord, she is neuer sad, but when she sleepes, and not euer sad then: for I haue heard my daughter say, she hath often dreamt of vnhappinesse, and wakt her selfe with laughing.

Pedro. Shee cannot indure to heare tell of a husband.

Leonato. O, by no meanes, she mocks all her wooers out of suite.

Prince. She were an excellent wife for *Benedick*.

Leonato. O Lord, my Lord, if they were but a weeke married,

married, they would talke themselues madde.

Prince. Counte *Claudio*, when meane you to goe to Church?

Clau. To morrow my Lord, Time goes on crutches, till Loue haue all his rites.

Leonato. Not till monday, my deare sonne, which is hence a iust seuen night, and a time too briefe too, to haue all things answer minde.

Prince. Come, you shake the head at so long a breathing, but I warrant thee *Claudio*, the time shall not goe dully by vs, I will in the *interim*, vndertake one of *Hercules* labors, which is, to bring Signior *Benedicke* and the Lady *Beatrice* into a mountaine of affection, th'one with th'other, I would faine haue it a match, and I doubt not but to fashion it, if you three will but minister such assistance as I shall giue you direction.

Leonato. My Lord, I am for you, though it cost mee ten nights watchings.

Claud. And I my Lord.

Prin. And you to gentle *Hero*?

Hero. I will doe any modest office, my Lord, to helpe my cosin to a good husband.

Prin. And *Benedick* is not the vnhopefullest husband that I know: thus farre can I praise him, hee is of a noble straine, of approued valour, and confirm'd honesty, I will teach you how to humour your cosin, that shee shall fall in loue with *Benedicke*, and I, with your two helpes, will so practise on *Benedicke*, that in despight of his quicke wit, and his queasie stomacke, hee shall fall in loue with *Beatrice*: if wee can doe this, *Cupid* is no longer an Archer, his glory shall be ours, for wee are the onely louegods, goe in with me, and I will tell you my drift. *Exit.*

Enter Iohn and Borachio.

Ioh. It is so, the Count *Claudio* shal marry the daughter of *Leonato*.

Bora. Yea my Lord, but I can crosse it.

Iohn. Any barre, any crosse, any impediment, will be medicinable to me, I am sicke in displeasure to him, and whatsoeuer comes athwart his affection, ranges euenly with mine, how canst thou crosse this marriage?

Bor. Not honestly my Lord, but so couertly, that no dishonesty shall appeare in me.

Iohn. Shew me breefely how.

Bor. I thinke I told your Lordship a yeere since, how much I am in the fauour of *Margaret*, the waiting gentlewoman to *Hero*.

Iohn. I remember.

Bor. I can at any vnseasonable instant of the night, appoint her to look out at her Ladies chamber window.

Iohn. What life is in that, to be the death of this marriage?

Bor. The poyson of that lies in you to temper, goe you to the Prince your brother, spare not to tell him, that hee hath wronged his Honor in marrying the renowned *Claudio*, whose estimation do you mightily hold vp, to a contaminated stale, such a one as *Hero*.

Iohn. What proofe shall I make of that?

Bor. Proofe enough, to misuse the Prince, to vexe *Claudio*, to vndoe *Hero*, and kill *Leonato*, looke you for any other issue?

Iohn. Onely to despight them, I will endeauour any thing.

Bor. Goe then, finde me a meete howre, to draw on *Pedro* and the Count *Claudio* alone, tell them that you know that *Hero* loues me, intend a kinde of zeale both to the Prince and *Claudio* (as in a loue of your brothers honor who hath made this match) and his friends reputation, who is thus like to be cosen'd with the semblance of a maid, that you haue discouer'd thus: they will scarcely beleeue this without triall: offer them instances which shall beare no lesse likelihood, than to see mee at her chamber window, heare me call *Margaret*, *Hero*; heare *Margaret* terme me *Claudio*, and bring them to see this the very night before the intended wedding, for in the meane time, I will so fashion the matter, that *Hero* shall be absent, and there shall appeare such seeming truths of *Heroes* disloyaltie, that iealousie shall be cal'd assurance, and all the preparation ouerthrowne.

Iohn. Grow this to what aduerse issue it can, I will put it in practise: be cunning in the working this, and thy fee is a thousand ducates.

Bor. Be thou constant in the accusation, and my cunning shall not shame me.

Iohn. I will presentlie goe learne their day of marriage. *Exit.*

Enter Benedicke alone.

Bene. Boy.

Boy. Signior.

Bene. In my chamber window lies a booke, bring it hither to me in the orchard.

Boy. I am heere already sir. *Exit.*

Bene. I know that, but I would haue thee hence, and heere againe. I doe much wonder, that one man seeing how much another man is a foole, when he dedicates his behauiours to loue, will after hee hath laught at such shallow follies in others, become the argument of his owne scorne, by falling in loue, & such a man is *Claudio*, I haue known when there was no musicke with him but the drum and the fife, and now had hee rather heare the taber and the pipe: I haue knowne when he would haue walkt ten mile afoot, to see a good armor, and now will he lie ten nights awake caruing the fashion of a new doublet: he was wont to speake plaine, & to the purpose (like an honest man & a souldier) and now is he turn'd orthography, his words are a very fantasticall banquet, iust so many strange dishes: may I be so conuerted, & see with these eyes? I cannot tell, I thinke not: I will not bee sworne, but loue may transforme me to an oyster, but Ile take my oath on it, till he haue made an oyster of me, he shall neuer make me such a foole: one woman is faire, yet I am well: another is wise, yet I am well: another vertuous, yet I am well: but till all graces be in one woman, one woman shall not come in my grace: rich shee shall be, that's certaine: wise, or Ile none: vertuous, or Ile neuer cheapen her: faire, or Ile neuer looke on her: milde, or come not neere me: Noble, or not for an Angell: of good discourse: an excellent Musitian, and her haire shal be of what colour it please God, hah! the Prince and Monsieur Loue, I will hide me in the Arbor.

Enter Prince, Leonato, Claudio, and Iacke Wilson.

Prin. Come, shall we heare this musicke?

Claud. Yea my good Lord: how still the euening is, As husht on purpose to grace harmonie.

Prin. See you where *Benedicke* hath hid himselfe?

Clau. O very well my Lord: the musicke ended, Wee'll fit the kid-foxe with a penny worth.

Prince. Come *Balthasar*, wee'll heare that song againe.

Balth. O good my Lord, taxe not so bad a voyce, To slander musicke any more then once.

Prin. It is the witnesse still of excellency,

To slander Musicke any more then once.

Prince. It is the witnesse still of excellencie,
To put a strange face on his owne perfection,
I pray thee sing, and let me woe no more.

Balth. Because you talke of wooing, I will sing,
Since many a wooer doth commence his suit,
To her he thinkes not worthy, yet he wooes,
Yet will he sweare he loues.

Prince. Nay pray thee come,
Or if thou wilt hold longer argument,
Doe it in notes.

Balth. Note this before my notes,
Theres not a note of mine that's worth the noting.

Prince. Why these are very crotchets that he speaks,
Note notes forsooth, and nothing.

Bene. Now diuine aire, now is his soule rauisht, is it not strange that sheepes guts should hale soules out of mens bodies? well, a horne for my money when all's done.

The Song.

Sigh no more Ladies, sigh no more,
Men were deceiuers euer,
One foote in Sea, and one on shore,
To one thing constant neuer,
Then sigh not so, but let them goe,
And be you blithe and bonnie,
Conuerting all your sounds of woe,
Into hey nony nony.

Sing no more ditties, sing no moe,
Of dumps so dull and heauy,
The fraud of men were euer so,
Since summer first was leauy,
Then sigh not so, &c.

Prince. By my troth a good song.
Balth. And an ill singer, my Lord.
Prince. Ha, no, no faith, thou singst well enough for a shift.

Ben. And he had been a dog that should haue howld thus, they would haue hang'd him, and I pray God his bad voyce bode no mischiefe, I had as liefe haue heard the night-rauen, come what plague could haue come after it.

Prince. Yea marry, dost thou heare *Balthasar*? I pray thee get vs some excellent musick: for to morrow night we would haue it at the Lady *Heroes* chamber window.

Balth. The best I can, my Lord.   *Exit Balthasar.*

Prince. Do so, farewell. Come hither *Leonato*, what was it you told me of to day, that your Niece *Beatrice* was in loue with signior *Benedicke*?

Cla. O I, stalke on, stalke on, the foule sits. I did neuer thinke that Lady would haue loued any man.

Leon. No, nor I neither, but most wonderful, that she should so dote on Signior *Benedicke*, whom shee hath in all outward behauiours seemed euer to abhorre.

Bene. Is't possible? sits the winde in that corner?

Leo. By my troth my Lord, I cannot tell what to thinke of it, but that she loues him with an inraged affection, it is past the infinite of thought.

Prince. May be she doth but counterfeit.
Claud. Faith like enough.

Leon. O God! counterfeit? there was neuer counterfeit of passion, came so neere the life of passion as she discouers it.

Prince. Why what effects of passion shewes she?
Claud. Baite the hooke well, this fish will bite.
Leon. What effects my Lord? shee will sit you, you heard my daughter tell you how.
Clau. She did indeed.

Prin. How, how I pray you? you amaze me, I would haue thought her spirit had beene inuincible against all assaults of affection.

Leo. I would haue sworne it had, my Lord, especially against *Benedicke*.

Bene. I should thinke this a gull, but that the whitebearded fellow speakes it: knauery cannot sure hide himselfe in such reuerence.

Claud. He hath tane th'infection, hold it vp.
Prince. Hath shee made her affection known to *Benedicke*?

Leonato. No, and sweares she neuer will, that's her torment.

Claud. 'Tis true indeed, so your daughter saies: shall I, saies she, that haue so oft encountred him with scorne, write to him that I loue him?

Leo. This saies shee now when shee is beginning to write to him, for shee'll be vp twenty times a night, and there will she sit in her smocke, till she haue writ a sheet of paper: my daughter tells vs all.

Clau. Now you talke of a sheet of paper, I remember a pretty iest your daughter told vs of.

Leon. O when she had writ it, & was reading it ouer, she found *Benedicke* and *Beatrice* betweene the sheete.

Clau. That.

Leon. O she tore the letter into a thousand halfpence, raild at her self, that she should be so immodest to write, to one that shee knew would flout her: I measure him, saies she, by my owne spirit, for I should flout him if hee writ to mee, yea though I loue him, I should.

Clau. Then downe vpon her knees she falls, weepes, sobs, beates her heart, teares her hayre, praies, curses, O sweet *Benedicke*, God giue me patience.

Leon. She doth indeed, my daughter saies so, and the extasie hath so much ouerborne her, that my daughter is somtime afeard she will doe a desperate out-rage to her selfe, it is very true.

Prin. It were good that *Benedicke* knew of it by some other, if she will not discouer it.

Clau. To what end? he would but make a sport of it, and torment the poore Lady worse.

Prin. And he should, it were an almes to hang him, shee's an excellent sweet Lady, and (out of all suspition,) she is vertuous.

Claudio. And she is exceeding wise.
Prince. In euery thing, but in louing *Benedicke*.

Leon. O my Lord, wisedome and bloud combating in so tender a body, we haue ten proofes to one, that bloud hath the victory, I am sorry for her, as I haue iust cause, being her Vncle, and her Guardian.

Prince. I would shee had bestowed this dotage on mee, I would haue daft all other respects, and made her halfe my selfe: I pray you tell *Benedicke* of it, and heare what he will say.

Leon. Were it good thinke you?

Clau. Hero thinkes surely she wil die, for she saies she will die, if hee loue her not, and shee will die ere shee make her loue knowne, and she will die if hee wooe her, rather than shee will bate one breath of her accustomed crossenesse.

Prin. She doth well, if she should make tender of her loue,

loue, 'tis very possible hee'l scorne it, for the man (as you know all) hath a contemptible spirit.

Clau. He is a very proper man.
Prin. He hath indeed a good outward happines.
Clau. 'Fore God, and in my minde very wise.
Prin. He doth indeed shew some sparkes that are like wit.
Leon. And I take him to be valiant.
Prin. As *Hector*, I assure you, and in the managing of quarrels you may see hee is wise, for either hee auoydes them with great discretion, or vndertakes them with a Christian-like feare.
Leon. If hee doe feare God, a must necessarilie keepe peace, if hee breake the peace, hee ought to enter into a quarrell with feare and trembling.
Prin. And so will he doe, for the man doth fear God, howsoeuer it seemes not in him, by some large ieasts hee will make: well, I am sorry for your niece, shall we goe see *Benedicke*, and tell him of her loue.
Claud. Neuer tell him, my Lord, let her weare it out with good counsell.
Leon. Nay that's impossible, she may weare her heart out first.
Prin. Well, we will heare further of it by your daughter, let it coole the while, I loue *Benedicke* well, and I could wish he would modestly examine himselfe, to see how much he is vnworthy to haue so good a Lady.
Leon. My Lord, will you walke? dinner is ready.
Clau. If he do not doat on her vpon this, I wil neuer trust my expectation.
Prin. Let there be the same Net spread for her, and that must your daughter and her gentlewoman carry: the sport will be, when they hold one an opinion of anothers dotage, and no such matter, that's the Scene that I would see, which will be meerely a dumbe shew : let vs send her to call him into dinner. *Exeunt.*

Bene. This can be no tricke, the conference was sadly borne, they haue the truth of this from *Hero*, they seeme to pittie the Lady : it seemes her affections haue the full bent : loue me? why it must be requited : I heare how I am censur'd, they say I will beare my selfe proudly, if I perceiue the loue come from her : they say too, that she will rather die than giue any signe of affection: I did neuer thinke to marry, I must not seeme proud, happy are they that heare their detractions, and can put them to mending : they say the Lady is faire, 'tis a truth, I can beare them witnesse : and vertuous, tis so, I cannot reprooue it, and wise, but for louing me, by my troth it is no addition to her witte, nor no great argument of her folly; for I wil be horribly in loue with her, I may chance haue some odde quirkes and remnants of witte broken on mee, because I haue rail'd so long against marriage: but doth not the appetite alter? a man loues the meat in his youth, that he cannot indure in his age. Shall quips and sentences, and these paper bullets of the braine awe a man from the careere of his humour ? No, the world must be peopled. When I said I would die a batcheler, I did not think I should liue till I were maried, here comes *Beatrice* : by this day, shee's a faire Lady, I doe spie some markes of loue in her.

Enter Beatrice.

Beat. Against my wil I am sent to bid you come in to dinner.
Bene. Faire *Beatrice*, I thanke you for your paines.

Beat. I tooke no more paines for those thankes, then you take paines to thanke me, if it had been painefull, I would not haue come.
Bene. You take pleasure then in the message.
Beat. Yea iust so much as you may take vpon a kniues point, and choake a daw withall : you haue no stomacke signior, fare you well. *Exit.*
Bene. Ha, against my will I am sent to bid you come into dinner: there's a double meaning in that : I tooke no more paines for those thankes then you tooke paines to thanke me, that's as much as to say, any paines that I take for you is as easie as thankes : if I do not take pitty of her I am a villaine, if I doe not loue her I am a Iew, I will goe get her picture. *Exit.*

Actus Tertius.

Enter Hero and two Gentlemen, Margaret, and Vrsula.

Hero. Good *Margaret* runne thee to the parlour,
There shalt thou finde my Cosin *Beatrice*,
Proposing with the Prince and *Claudio*,
Whisper her eare, and tell her I and *Vrsula*,
Walke in the Orchard, and our whole discourse
Is all of her, say that thou ouer-heardst vs,
And bid her steale into the pleached bower,
Where hony-suckles ripened by the sunne,
Forbid the sunne to enter : like fauourites,
Made proud by Princes, that aduance their pride,
Against that power that bred it, there will she hide her,
To listen our purpose, this is thy office,
Beare thee well in it, and leaue vs alone.
Marg. Ile make her come I warrant you presently.
Hero. Now *Vrsula*, when *Beatrice* doth come,
As we do trace this alley vp and downe,
Our talke must onely be of *Benedicke*,
When I doe name him, let it be thy part,
To praise him more then euer man did merit,
My talke to thee must be how *Benedicke*
Is sicke in loue with *Beatrice* : of this matter,
Is little *Cupids* crafty arrow made,
That onely wounds by heare-say: now begin,

Enter Beatrice.

For looke where *Beatrice* like a Lapwing runs
Close by the ground, to heare our conference.
Vrs. The pleasant'st angling is to see the fish
Cut with her golden ores the siluer streame,
And greedily deuoure the treacherous baite:
So angle we for *Beatrice*, who euen now,
Is couched in the wood-bine couerture,
Feare you not my part of the Dialogue.
Her. Then go we neare her that her eare loose nothing,
Of the false sweete baite that we lay for it :
No truely *Vrsula*, she is too disdainfull,
I know her spirits are as coy and wilde,
As Haggerds of the rocke.
Vrsula. But are you sure,
That *Benedicke* loues *Beatrice* so intirely ?
Her. So saies the Prince, and my new trothed Lord.
Vrs. And did they bid you tell her of it, Madam?
Her. They did intreate me to acquaint her of it,
But I perswaded them, if they lou'd *Benedicke*,

To wish him wrastle with affection,
And neuer to let *Beatrice* know of it.

　Vrsula. Why did you so, doth not the Gentleman
Deserue as full as fortunate a bed,
As euer *Beatrice* shall couch vpon?

　Hero. O God of loue! I know he doth deserue,
As much as may be yeelded to a man:
But Nature neuer fram'd a womans heart,
Of prowder stuffe then that of *Beatrice*:
Disdaine and Scorne ride sparkling in her eyes,
Mis-prizing what they looke on, and her wit
Values it selfe so highly, that to her
All matter else seemes weake: she cannot loue,
Nor take no shape nor proiect of affection,
Shee is so selfe indeared.

　Vrsula. Sure I thinke so,
And therefore certainely it were not good
She knew his loue, lest she make sport at it.

　Hero. Why you speake truth, I neuer yet saw man,
How wise, how noble, yong, how rarely featur'd,
But she would spell him backward: if faire fac'd,
She would sweare the gentleman should be her sister:
If blacke, why Nature drawing of an anticke,
Made a foule blot: if tall, a launce ill headed:
If low, an agot very vildlie cut:
If speaking, why a vane blowne with all windes:
If silent, why a blocke moued with none.
So turnes she euery man the wrong side out,
And neuer giues to Truth and Vertue, that
Which simplenesse and merit purchaseth.

　Vrsu. Sure, sure, such carping is not commendable.

　Hero. No, not to be so odde, and from all fashions,
As *Beatrice* is, cannot be commendable,
But who dare tell her so? if I should speake,
She would mocke me into ayre, O she would laugh me
Out of my selfe, presse me to death with wit,
Therefore let *Benedicke* like couered fire,
Consume away in sighes, waste inwardly:
It were a better death, to die with mockes,
Which is as bad as die with tickling.

　Vrsu. Yet tell her of it, heare what shee will say.

　Hero. No, rather I will goe to *Benedicke*,
And counsaile him to fight against his passion,
And truly Ile deuise some honest slanders,
To staine my cosin with, one doth not know,
How much an ill word may impoison liking.

　Vrsu. O doe not doe your cosin such a wrong,
She cannot be so much without true iudgement,
Hauing so swift and excellent a wit
As she is prisde to haue, as to refuse
So rare a Gentleman as signior *Benedicke*.

　Hero. He is the onely man of Italy,
Alwaies excepted, my deare *Claudio*.

　Vrsu. I pray you be not angry with me, Madame,
Speaking my fancy: Signior *Benedicke*,
For shape, for bearing argument and valour,
Goes formost in report through Italy.

　Hero. Indeed he hath an excellent good name.

　Vrsu. His excellence did earne it ere he had it:
When are you married Madame?

　Hero. Why euerie day to morrow, come goe in,
Ile shew thee some attires, and haue thy counsell,
Which is the best to furnish me to morrow.

　Vrsu. Shee's tane I warrant you,
We haue caught her Madame?

　Hero. If it proue so, then louing goes by haps,
Some *Cupid* kills with arrowes, some with traps. *Exit.*

　Beat. What fire is in mine eares? can this be true?
Stand I condemn'd for pride and scorne so much?
Contempt, farewell, and maiden pride, adew,
No glory liues behinde the backe of such.
And *Benedicke*, loue on, I will requite thee,
Taming my wilde heart to thy louing hand:
If thou dost loue, my kindenesse shall incite thee
To binde our loues vp in a holy band.
For others say thou dost deserue, and I
Beleeue it better then reportingly. *Exit.*

Enter Prince, Claudio, Benedicke, and Leonato.

　Prince. I doe but stay till your marriage be consummate, and then go I toward Arragon.

　Clau. Ile bring you thither my Lord, if you'l vouch-safe me.

　Prin. Nay, that would be as great a soyle in the new glosse of your marriage, as to shew a childe his new coat and forbid him to weare it, I will onely bee bold with *Benedicke* for his companie, for from the crowne of his head, to the sole of his foot, he is all mirth, he hath twice or thrice cut *Cupids* bow-string, and the little hang-man dare not shoot at him, he hath a heart as sound as a bell, and his tongue is the clapper, for what his heart thinkes, his tongue speakes.

　Bene. Gallants, I am not as I haue bin.

　Leo. So say I, methinkes you are sadder.

　Claud. I hope he be in loue.

　Prin. Hang him truant, there's no true drop of bloud in him to be truly toucht with loue, if he be sad, he wants money.

　Bene. I haue the tooth-ach.

　Prin. Draw it.

　Bene. Hang it.

　Claud. You must hang it first, and draw it afterwards.

　Prin. What? sigh for the tooth-ach.

　Leon. Where is but a humour or a worme.

　Bene. Well, euery one cannot master a griefe, but hee that has it.

　Clau. Yet say I, he is in loue.

　Prin. There is no appearance of fancie in him, vnlesse it be a fancy that he hath to strange disguises, as to bee a Dutchman to day, a Frenchman to morrow: vnlesse hee haue a fancy to this foolery, as it appeares hee hath, hee is no foole for fancy, as you would haue it to appeare he is.

　Clau. If he be not in loue vvith some vvoman, there is no beleeuing old signes, a brushes his hat a mornings, What should that bode?

　Prin. Hath any man seene him at the Barbers?

　Clau. No, but the Barbers man hath beene seen with him, and the olde ornament of his cheeke hath alreadie stuft tennis balls.

　Leon. Indeed he lookes yonger than hee did, by the losse of a beard.

　Prin. Nay a rubs himselfe vvith Ciuit, can you smell him out by that?

　Clau. That's as much as to say, the sweet youth's in loue.

　Prin. The greatest note of it is his melancholy.

　Clau. And vvhen vvas he vvont to vvash his face?

　Prin. Yea, or to paint himselfe? for the which I heare vvhat they say of him.

　Clau. Nay, but his iesting spirit, vvhich is now crept into a lute-string, and now gouern'd by stops.

Princ.

Prin. Indeed that tels a heauy tale for him: conclude, he is in loue.

Clau. Nay, but I know who loues him.

Prince. That would I know too, I warrant one that knowes him not.

Cla. Yes, and his ill conditions, and in despight of all, dies for him.

Prin. Shee shall be buried with her face vpwards.

Bene. Yet is this no charme for the tooth-ake, old signior, walke aside with mee, I haue studied eight or nine wise words to speake to you, which these hobby-horses must not heare.

Prin. For my life to breake with him about *Beatrice*.

Clau. 'Tis euen so, *Hero* and *Margaret* haue by this played their parts with *Beatrice*, and then the two Beares will not bite one another when they meete.

Enter Iohn the Bastard.

Bast. My Lord and brother, God saue you.

Prin. Good den brother.

Bast. If your leisure seru'd, I would speake with you.

Prince. In priuate?

Bast. If it please you, yet Count *Claudio* may heare, for what I would speake of, concernes him.

Prin. What's the matter?

Basta. Meanes your Lordship to be married to morrow?

Prin. You know he does.

Bast. I know not that when he knowes what I know.

Clau. If there be any impediment, I pray you discouer it.

Bast. You may thinke I loue you not, let that appeare hereafter, and ayme better at me by that I now will manifest, for my brother (I thinke, he holds you well, and in dearenesse of heart) hath holpe to effect your ensuing marriage: surely sute ill spent, and labour ill bestowed.

Prin. Why, what's the matter?

Bastard. I came hither to tell you, and circumstances shortned, (for she hath beene too long a talking of) the Lady is disloyall.

Clau. Who *Hero*?

Bast. Euen shee, *Leonatoes Hero*, your *Hero*, euery mans *Hero*.

Clau. Disloyall?

Bast. The word is too good to paint out her wickednesse, I could say she were worse, thinke you of a worse title, and I will fit her to it: wonder not till further warrant: goe but with mee to night, you shal see her chamber window entred, euen the night before her wedding day, if you loue her, then to morrow wed her: But it would better fit your honour to change your minde.

Claud. May this be so?

Prince. I will not thinke it.

Bast. If you dare not trust that you see, confesse not that you know: if you will follow mee, I will shew you enough, and when you haue seene more, & heard more, proceed accordingly.

Clau. If I see any thing to night, why I should not marry her to morrow in the congregation, where I shold wedde, there will I shame her.

Prin. And as I wooed for thee to obtaine her, I will ioyne with thee to disgrace her.

Bast. I will disparage her no farther, till you are my witnesses, beare it coldly but till night, and let the issue shew it selfe.

Prin. O day vntowardly turned!

Claud. O mischiefe strangelie thwarting!

Bastard. O plague right well preuented! so will you say, when you haue seene the sequele. *Exit.*

Enter Dogbery and his compartner with the watch.

Dog. Are you good men and true?

Verg. Yea, or else it were pitty but they should suffer saluation body and soule.

Dogb. Nay, that were a punishment too good for them, if they should haue any allegiance in them, being chosen for the Princes watch.

Verges. Well, giue them their charge, neighbour *Dogbery*.

Dog. First, who thinke you the most desartlesse man to be Constable?

Watch.1. *Hugh Ote-cake* sir, or *George Sea-coale*, for they can write and reade.

Dogb. Come hither neighbour Sea-coale, God hath blest you with a good name: to be a wel-fauoured man, is the gift of Fortune, but to write and reade, comes by Nature.

Watch 2. Both which Master Constable

Dogb. You haue: I knew it would be your answere: well, for your fauour sir, why giue God thankes, & make no boast of it, and for your writing and reading, let that appeare when there is no need of such vanity, you are thought heere to be the most senslesse and fit man for the Constable of the watch: therefore beare you the lanthorne: this is your charge: You shall comprehend all vagrom men, you are to bid any man stand in the Princes name.

Watch 2. How if a will not stand?

Dogb. Why then take no note of him, but let him go, and presently call the rest of the Watch together, and thanke God you are ridde of a knaue.

Verges. If he will not stand when he is bidden, hee is none of the Princes subiects.

Dogb. True, and they are to meddle with none but the Princes subiects: you shall also make no noise in the streetes: for, for the Watch to babble and talke, is most tollerable, and not to be indured.

Watch. We will rather sleepe than talke, wee know what belongs to a Watch.

Dog. Why you speake like an ancient and most quiet watchman, for I cannot see how sleeping should offence: only haue a care that your bills be not stolne: well, you are to call at all the Alehouses, and bid them that are drunke get them to bed.

Watch. How if they will not?

Dogb. Why then let them alone till they are sober, if they make you not then the better answere, you may say, they are not the men you tooke them for.

Watch. Well sir.

Dogb. If you meet a theefe, you may suspect him, by vertue of your office, to be no true man: and for such kinde of men, the lesse you meddle or make with them, why the more is for your honesty.

Watch. If wee know him to be a thiefe, shall wee not lay hands on him.

Dogb. Truly by your office you may, but I think they that touch pitch will be defil'd: the most peaceable way for you, if you doe take a theefe, is, to let him shew himselfe what he is, and steale out of your company.

Ver. You haue bin alwaies cal'd a merciful mã partner.

Dog. Truely I would not hang a dog by my will, much more a man who hath anie honestie in him.

K 2 *Verges.*

Verges. If you heare a child crie in the night you must call to the nurse, and bid her still it.

Watch. How if the nurse be asleepe and will not heare vs?

Dog. Why then depart in peace, and let the childe wake her with crying, for the ewe that will not heare her Lambe when it baes, will neuer answere a calfe when he bleates.

Verges. 'Tis verie true.

Dog. This is the end of the charge: you constable are to present the Princes owne person, if you meete the Prince in the night, you may staie him.

Verges. Nay birladie that I thinke a cannot.

Dog. Fiue shillings to one on't with anie man that knowes the Statues, he may staie him, marrie not without the prince be willing, for indeed the watch ought to offend no man, and it is an offence to stay a man against his will.

Verges. Birladie I thinke it be so.

Dog. Ha, ah ha, well masters good night, and there be anie matter of weight chances, call vp me, keepe your fellowes counsailes, and your owne, and good night, come neighbour.

Watch. Well masters, we heare our charge, let vs go sit here vpon the Church bench till two, and then all to bed.

Dog. One word more, honest neighbors. I pray you watch about signior *Leonatoes* doore, for the wedding being there to morrow, there is a great coyle to night, adiew, be vigitant I beseech you. *Exeunt.*

Enter Borachio and Conrade.

Bor. What, *Conrade?*

Watch. Peace, stir not.

Bor. Conrade I say.

Con. Here man, I am at thy elbow.

Bor. Mas and my elbow itcht, I thought there would a scabbe follow.

Con. I will owe thee an answere for that, and now forward with thy tale.

Bor. Stand thee close then vnder this penthouse, for it drissels raine, and I will, like a true drunkard, vtter all to thee.

Watch. Some treason masters, yet stand close.

Bor. Therefore know, I haue earned of *Don Iohn* a thousand Ducates.

Con. Is it possible that anie villanie should be so deare?

Bor. Thou should'st rather aske if it were possible anie villanie should be so rich? for when rich villains haue neede of poore ones, poore ones may make what price they will.

Con. I wonder at it.

Bor. That shewes thou art vnconfirm'd, thou knowest that the fashion of a doublet, or a hat, or a cloake, is nothing to a man.

Con. Yes, it is apparell.

Bor. I meane the fashion.

Con. Yes the fashion is the fashion.

Bor. Tush, I may as well say the foole's the foole, but seest thou not what a deformed theefe this fashion is?

Watch. I know that deformed, a has bin a vile theefe, this vii. yeares, a goes vp and downe like a gentle man: I remember his name.

Bor. Did'st thou not heare some bodie?

Con. No, 'twas the vaine on the house.

Bor. Seest thou not (I say) what a deformed theefe this fashion is, how giddily a turnes about all the Hotblouds, betweene fourteene & fiue & thirtie, sometimes fashioning them like *Pharaoes* souldiours in the rechie painting, sometime like god *Bels* priests in the old Church window, sometime like the shauen *Hercules* in the smircht worm-eaten tapestrie, where his cod-peece seemes as massie as his club.

Con. All this I see, and see that the fashion weares out more apparrell then the man; but art not thou thy selfe giddie with the fashion too that thou hast shifted out of thy tale into telling me of the fashion?

Bor. Not so neither, but know that I haue to night wooed *Margaret* the Lady *Heroes* gentle-woman, by the name of *Hero*, she leanes me out at her mistris chamber-vvindow, bids me a thousand times good night: I tell this tale vildly. I should first tell thee how the Prince *Claudio* and my Master planted, and placed, and possessed by my Master *Don Iohn*, saw a far off in the Orchard this amiable incounter.

Con. And thought thy *Margaret* was *Hero*?

Bor. Two of them did, the Prince and *Claudio*, but the diuell my Master knew she was *Margaret* and partly by his oathes, which first possest them, partly by the darke night which did deceiue them, but chiefely, by my villanie, which did confirme any slander that *Don Iohn* had made, away vvent *Claudio* enraged, sware hee vvould meete her as he was apointed next morning at the Temple, and there, before the whole congregation shame her with vvhat he saw o're night, and send her home againe vvithout a husband.

Watch.1. We charge you in the Princes name stand.

Watch.2. Call vp the right master Constable, vve haue here recouered the most dangerous peece of lechery, that euer vvas knowne in the Common-wealth.

Watch.1. And one Deformed is one of them, I know him, a vveares a locke.

Conr. Masters, masters.

Watch.2. Youle be made bring deformed forth I warrant you,

Conr. Masters, neuer speake, vve charge you, let vs obey you to goe vvith vs.

Bor. We are like to proue a goodly commoditie, being taken vp of these mens bils.

Conr. A commoditie in question I warrant you, come vveele obey you. *Exeunt.*

Enter Hero, and Margaret, and Vrsula.

Hero. Good *Vrsula* wake my cosin *Beatrice*, and desire her to rise.

Vrsu. I will Lady.

Her. And bid her come hither.

Vrs. Well.

Mar. Troth I thinke your other rebato were better.

Hero. No pray thee good *Meg*, Ile vveare this.

Marg. By my troth's not so good, and I vvarrant your cosin vvill say so.

Hero. My cosin's a foole, and thou art another, ile vveare none but this.

Mar. I like the new tire vvithin excellently, if the haire vvere a thought browner: and your gown's a most rare fashion yfaith, I saw the Dutchesse of *Millaines* gowne that they praise so.

Hero. O that exceedes they say.

Mar. By my troth's but a night-gowne in respect of yours, cloth a gold and curs, and lac'd with siluer, set with pearles, downe sleeues, side sleeues, and skirts, round vnderborn with a blewish tinsel, but for a fine queint gracefull and excellent fashion, yours is worth ten on't.

Hero. God

Much adoe about Nothing.

Hero. God giue mee ioy to weare it, for my heart is exceeding heauy.

Marga. 'Twill be heauier soone, by the waight of a man.

Hero. Fie vpon thee, art not asham'd?

Marg. Of what Lady? of speaking honourably? is not marriage honourable in a beggar? is not your Lord honourable without marriage? I thinke you would haue me say, sauing your reuerence a husband: and bad thinking doe not wrest true speaking, Ile offend no body, is there any harme in the heauier for a husband? none I thinke, and it be the right husband, and the right wife, otherwise 'tis light and not heauy, aske my Lady *Beatrice* else, here she comes.

Enter Beatrice.

Hero. Good morrow Coze.

Beat. Good morrow sweet *Hero.*

Hero. Why how now? do you speake in the sick tune?

Beat. I am out of all other tune, me thinkes.

Mar. Claps into Light a loue, (that goes without a burden,) do you sing it and Ile dance it.

Beat. Ye Light aloue with your heeles, then if your husband haue stables enough, you'll looke he shall lacke no barnes.

Mar. O illegitimate construction! I scorne that with my heeles.

Beat. 'Tis almost fiue a clocke cosin, 'tis time you were ready, by my troth I am exceeding ill, hey ho.

Mar. For a hauke, a horse, or a husband?

Beat. For the letter that begins them all, H.

Mar. Well, and you be not turn'd Turke, there's no more sayling by the starre.

Beat. What meanes the foole trow?

Mar. Nothing I, but God send euery one their harts desire.

Hero. These gloues the Count sent mee, they are an excellent perfume.

Beat. I am stuft cosin, I cannot smell.

Mar. A maid and stuft! there's goodly catching of colde.

Beat. O God helpe me, God help me, how long haue you profest apprehension?

Mar. Euer since you left it, doth not my wit become me rarely?

Beat. It is not seene enough, you should weare it in your cap, by my troth I am sicke.

Mar. Get you some of this distill'd *carduus benedictus* and lay it to your heart, it is the onely thing for a qualm.

Hero. There thou prickst her with a thissell.

Beat. Benedictus, why *benedictus*? you haue some morall in this *benedictus*.

Mar. Morall? no by my troth, I haue no morall meaning, I meant plaine holy thissell, you may thinke perchance that I thinke you are in loue, nay birlady I am not such a foole to thinke what I list, nor I list not to thinke what I can, nor indeed I cannot thinke, if I would thinke my hart out of thinking, that you are in loue, or that you will be in loue, or that you can be in loue: yet *Benedicke* was such another, and now is he become a man, he swore hee would neuer marry, and yet now in despight of his heart he eates his meat without grudging, and how you may be conuerted I know not, but me thinkes you looke with your eies as other women doe.

Beat. What pace is this that thy tongue keepes.

Mar. Not a false gallop.

Enter Vrsula.

Vrsula. Madam, withdraw, the Prince, the Count, signior *Benedicke,* Don *Iohn,* and all the gallants of the towne are come to fetch you to Church.

Hero. Helpe to dresse mee good coze, good *Meg,* good *Vrsula.*

Enter Leonato, and the Constable, and the Headborough.

Leonato. What would you with mee, honest neighbour?

Const. Dog. Mary sir I would haue some confidence with you, that decernes you nearely.

Leon. Briefe I pray you, for you see it is a busie time with me.

Const. Dog. Mary this it is sir.

Headb. Yes in truth it is sir.

Leon. What is it my good friends?

Con. Do. Goodman Verges sir speakes a little of the matter, an old man sir, and his wits are not so blunt, as God helpe I would desire they were, but infaith honest as the skin betweene his browes.

Head. Yes I thank God, I am as honest as any man liuing, that is an old man, and no honester then I.

Con. Dog. Comparisons are odorous, palabras, neighbour Verges.

Leon. Neighbours, you are tedious.

Con. Dog. It pleases your worship to say so, but we are the poore Dukes officers, but truely for mine owne part, if I were as tedious as a King I could finde in my heart to bestow it all of your worship.

Leon. All thy tediousnesse on me, ah?

Const. Dog. Yea, and 'twere a thousand times more than 'tis, for I heare as good exclamation on your Worship as of any man in the Citie, and though I bee but a poore man, I am glad to heare it.

Head. And so am I.

Leon. I would faine know what you haue to say.

Head. Marry sir our watch to night, excepting your worships presence, haue tane a couple of as arrant knaues as any in Messina.

Con. Dog. A good old man sir, hee will be talking as they say, when the age is in the wit is out, God helpe vs, it is a world to see: well said yfaith neighbour *Verges,* well, God's a good man, and two men ride of a horse, one must ride behinde, an honest soule yfaith sir, by my troth he is, as euer broke bread, but God is to bee worshipt, all men are not alike, alas good neighbour.

Leon. Indeed neighbour he comes too short of you.

Con. Do. Gifts that God giues.

Leon. I must leaue you.

Con. Dog. One word sir, our watch sir haue indeede comprehended two aspitious persons, & we would haue them this morning examined before your worship.

Leon. Take their examination your selfe, and bring it me, I am now in great haste, as may appeare vnto you.

Const. It shall be suffigance.   (*Exit.*

Leon. Drinke some wine ere you goe: fare you well.

Messenger. My Lord, they stay for you to giue your daughter to her husband.

Leon. Ile wait vpon them, I am ready.

Dogb. Goe good partner, goe get you to *Francis Seacoale,* bid him bring his pen and inkehorne to the Gaole: we are now to examine those men.

Verges. And we must doe it wisely.

Dogb. Wee will spare for no witte I warrant you:

K 3   heere

heere's that shall driue some of them to a non-come, onely get the learned writer to set downe our excommunication, and meet me at the Iaile. *Exeunt.*

Actus Quartus.

Enter Prince, Bastard, Leonato, Frier, Claudio, Benedicke, Hero, and Beatrice.

Leonato. Come Frier *Francis*, be briefe, onely to the plaine forme of marriage, and you shal recount their particular duties afterwards.

Fran. You come hither, my Lord, to marry this Lady.

Clau. No.

Leo. To be married to her: Frier, you come to marrie her.

Frier. Lady, you come hither to be married to this Count.

Hero. I doe.

Frier. If either of you know any inward impediment why you should not be conioyned, I charge you on your soules to vtter it.

Claud. Know you anie, *Hero*?

Hero. None my Lord.

Frier. Know you anie, Count?

Leon. I dare make his answer, None.

Clau. O what men dare do! what men may do! what men daily do!

Bene. How now! interiections? why then, some be of laughing, as ha, ha, he.

Clau. Stand thee by Frier, father, by your leaue,
Will you with free and vnconstrained soule
Giue me this maid your daughter?

Leon. As freely sonne as God did giue her me.

Cla. And what haue I to giue you back, whose worth
May counterpoise this rich and precious gift?

Prin. Nothing, vnlesse you render her againe.

Clau. Sweet Prince, you learn me noble thankfulnes:
There *Leonato*, take her backe againe,
Giue not this rotten Orenge to your friend,
Shee's but the signe and semblance of her honour:
Behold how like a maid she blushes heere!
O what authoritie and shew of truth
Can cunning sinne couer it selfe withall!
Comes not that bloud, as modest euidence,
To witnesse simple Vertue? would you not sweare
All you that see her, that she were a maide,
By these exterior shewes? But she is none:
She knowes the heat of a luxurious bed:
Her blush is guiltinesse, not modestie.

Leonato. What doe you meane, my Lord?

Clau. Not to be married,
Not to knit my soule to an approued wanton.

Leon. Deere my Lord, if you in your owne proofe,
Haue vanquisht the resistance of her youth,
And made defeat of her virginitie.

Clau. I know what you would say: if I haue knowne her,
You will say, she did imbrace me as a husband,
And so extenuate the forehand sinne: No *Leonato*,
I neuer tempted her with word too large,
But as a brother to his sister, shewed
Bashfull sinceritie and comely loue.

Hero. And seem'd I euer otherwise to you?

Clau. Out on thee seeming, I will write against it,
You seeme to me as *Diane* in her Orbe,
As chaste as is the budde ere it be blowne:
But you are more intemperate in your blood,
Than *Venus*, or those pampred animalls,
That rage in sauage sensualitie.

Hero. Is my Lord well, that he doth speake so wide?

Leon. Sweete Prince, why speake not you?

Prin. What should I speake?
I stand dishonour'd that haue gone about,
To linke my deare friend to a common stale.

Leon. Are these things spoken, or doe I but dreame?

Bast. Sir, they are spoken, and these things are true.

Bene. This lookes not like a nuptiall.

Hero. True, O God!

Clau. Leonato, stand I here?
Is this the Prince? is this the Princes brother?
Is this face *Heroes*? are our eies our owne?

Leon. All this is so, but what of this my Lord?

Clau. Let me but moue one question to your daughter,
And by that fatherly and kindly power,
That you haue in her, bid her answer truly.

Leo. I charge thee doe, as thou art my childe.

Hero. O God defend me how am I beset,
What kinde of catechizing call you this?

Clau. To make you answer truly to your name.

Hero. Is it not *Hero*? who can blot that name
With any iust reproach?

Claud. Marry that can *Hero*,
Hero it selfe can blot out *Heroes* vertue.
What man was he, talkt with you yesternight,
Out at your window betwixt twelue and one?
Now if you are a maid, answer to this.

Hero. I talkt with no man at that howre my Lord.

Prince. Why then you are no maiden. *Leonato*,
I am sorry you must heare: vpon mine honor,
My selfe, my brother, and this grieued Count
Did see her, heare her, at that howre last night,
Talke with a ruffian at her chamber window,
Who hath indeed most like a liberall villaine,
Confest the vile encounters they haue had
A thousand times in secret.

Iohn. Fie, fie, they are not to be named my Lord,
Not to be spoken of,
There is not chastitie enough in language,
Without offence to vtter them: thus pretty Lady
I am sorry for thy much misgouernment.

Claud. O *Hero*! what a *Hero* hadst thou beene
If halfe thy outward graces had beene placed
About thy thoughts and counsailes of thy heart?
But fare thee well, most foule, most faire, farewell
Thou pure impiety, and impious puritie,
For thee Ile locke vp all the gates of Loue,
And on my eie-lids shall Coniecture hang,
To turne all beauty into thoughts of harme,
And neuer shall it more be gracious.

Leon. Hath no mans dagger here a point for me?

Beat. Why how now cosin, wherfore sink you down?

Bast. Come, let vs go: these things come thus to light,
Smother her spirits vp.

Bene. How doth the Lady?

Beat. Dead I thinke, helpe vncle,
Hero, why *Hero*, Vncle, Signor *Benedicke*, Frier.

Leonato. O Fate! take not away thy heauy hand,
Death is the fairest couer for her shame
That may be wisht for.

Beat. How

Much adoe about Nothing.

Beatr. How now cosin *Hero*?
Fri. Haue comfort Ladie.
Leon. Dost thou looke vp?
Frier. Yea, wherefore should she not?
Leon. Wherfore? Why doth not euery earthly thing
Cry shame vpon her? Could she heere denie
The storie that is printed in her blood?
Do not liue *Hero*, do not ope thine eyes:
For did I thinke thou wouldst not quickly die,
Thought I thy spirits were stronger then thy shames,
My selfe would on the reward of reproaches
Strike at thy life. Grieu'd I, I had but one?
Chid I, for that at frugal Natures frame?
O one too much by thee: why had I one?
Why euer was't thou louelie in my eies?
Why had I not with charitable hand
Tooke vp a beggars issue at my gates,
Who smeered thus, and mir'd with infamie,
I might haue said, no part of it is mine:
This shame deriues it selfe from vnknowne loines,
But mine, and mine I lou'd, and mine I prais'd,
And mine that I was proud on mine so much,
That I my selfe, was to my selfe not mine:
Valewing of her, why she, O she is falne
Into a pit of Inke, that the wide sea
Hath drops too few to wash her cleane againe,
And salt too little, which may season giue
To her foule tainted flesh.

Ben. Sir, sir, be patient: for my part, I am so attired
in wonder, I know not what to say.

Bea. O on my soule my cosin is belied.

Ben. Ladie, were you her bedfellow last night?

Bea. No truly: not although vntill last night,
I haue this tweluemonth bin her bedfellow.

Leon. Confirm'd, confirm'd, O that is stronger made
Which was before barr'd vp with ribs of iron.
Would the Princes lie, and *Claudio* lie,
Who lou'd her so, that speaking of her foulnesse,
Wash'd it with teares? Hence from her, let her die.

Fri. Heare me a little, for I haue onely bene silent so
long, and giuen way vnto this course of fortune, by no-
ting of the Ladie, I haue markt.
A thousand blushing apparitions,
To start into her face, a thousand innocent shames,
In Angel whitenesse beare away those blushes,
And in her eie there hath appear'd a fire
To burne the errors that these Princes hold
Against her maiden truth. Call me a foole,
Trust not my reading, nor my obseruations,
Which with experimental seale doth warrant
The tenure of my booke: trust not my age,
My reuerence, calling, nor diuinitie,
If this sweet Ladie lye not guiltlesse heere,
Vnder some biting error.

Leo. Friar, it cannot be:
Thou seest that all the Grace that she hath left,
Is, that she wil not adde to her damnation,
A sinne of periury, she not denies it:
Why seek'st thou then to couer with excuse,
That which appeares in proper nakednesse?

Fri. Ladie, what man is he you are accus'd of?

Hero. They know that do accuse me, I know none:
If I know more of any man aliue
Then that which maiden modestie doth warrant,
Let all my sinnes lacke mercy. O my Father,
Proue you that any man with me conuerst,

At houres vnmeete, or that I yesternight
Maintain'd the change of words with any creature,
Refuse me, hate me, torture me to death.

Fri. There is some strange misprision in the Princes.

Ben. Two of them haue the verie bent of honor,
And if their wisedomes be misled in this:
The practise of it liues in *Iohn* the bastard,
Whose spirits toile in frame of villanies.

Leo. I know not: if they speake but truth of her,
These hands shall teare her: If they wrong her honour,
The proudest of them shall wel heare of it.
Time hath not yet so dried this bloud of mine,
Nor age so eate vp my inuention,
Nor Fortune made such hauocke of my meanes,
Nor my bad life reft me so much of friends,
But they shall finde, awak'd in such a kinde,
Both strength of limbe, and policie of minde,
Ability in meanes, and choise of friends,
To quit me of them throughly.

Fri. Pause awhile:
And let my counsell sway you in this case,
Your daughter heere the Princesse (left for dead)
Let her awhile be secretly kept in,
And publish it, that she is dead indeed:
Maintaine a mourning ostentation,
And on your Families old monument,
Hang mournfull Epitaphes, and do all rites,
That appertaine vnto a buriall.

Leon. What shall become of this? What wil this do?

Fri. Marry this wel carried, shall on her behalfe,
Change slander to remorse, that is some good,
But not for that dreame I on this strange course,
But on this trauaile looke for greater birth:
She dying, as it must be so maintain'd,
Vpon the instant that she was accus'd,
Shal be lamented, pittied, and excus'd
Of euery hearer: for it so fals out,
That what we haue, we prize not to the worth,
Whiles we enioy it; but being lack'd and lost,
Why then we racke the value, then we finde
The vertue that possession would not shew vs
Whiles it was ours, so will it fare with *Claudio*:
When he shal heare she dyed vpon his words,
Th'Idea of her life shal sweetly creepe
Into his study of imagination.
And euery louely Organ of her life,
Shall come apparel'd in more precious habite:
More mouing delicate, and ful of life,
Into the eye and prospect of his soule
Then when she liu'd indeed: then shal he mourne,
If euer Loue had interest in his Liuer,
And wish he had not so accused her:
No, though he thought his accusation true:
Let this be so, and doubt not but successe
Wil fashion the euent in better shape,
Then I can lay it downe in likelihood.
But if all ayme but this be leuelld false,
The supposition of the Ladies death,
Will quench the wonder of her infamie.
And if it sort not well, you may conceale her,
As best befits her wounded reputation,
In some reclusiue and religious life,
Out of all eyes, tongnes, mindes and iniuries.

Bene. Signior *Leonato*, let the Frier aduise you,
And though you know my inwardnesse and loue
Is very much vnto the Prince and *Claudio*.

Yet

Yet, by mine honor, I will deale in this,
As secretly and iustlie, as your soule
Should with your bodie.

Leon. Being that I flow in greefe,
The smallest twine may lead me.

Frier. 'Tis well consented, presently away,
For to strange sores, strangely they straine the cure,
Come Lady, die to liue, this wedding day
Perhaps is but prolong'd, haue patience & endure. *Exit.*

Bene. Lady *Beatrice*, haue you wept all this while?

Beat. Yea, and I will weepe a while longer.

Bene. I will not desire that.

Beat. You haue no reason, I doe it freely.

Bene. Surelie I do beleeue your fair cosin is wrong'd.

Beat. Ah, how much might the man deserue of mee that would right her!

Bene. Is there any way to shew such friendship?

Beat. A verie euen way, but no such friend.

Bene. May a man doe it?

Beat. It is a mans office, but not yours.

Bene. I doe loue nothing in the world so well as you, is not that strange?

Beat. As strange as the thing I know not, it were as possible for me to say, I loued nothing so well as you, but beleeue me not, and yet I lie not, I confesse nothing, nor I deny nothing, I am sorry for my cousin.

Bene. By my sword *Beatrice* thou lou'st me.

Beat. Doe not sweare by it and eat it.

Bene. I will sweare by it that you loue mee, and I will make him eat it that sayes I loue not you.

Beat. Will you not eat your word?

Bene. With no sawce that can be deuised to it, I protest I loue thee.

Beat. Why then God forgiue me.

Bene. What offence sweet Beatrice?

Beat. You haue stayed me in a happy howre, I was about to protest I loued you.

Bene. And doe it with all thy heart.

Beat. I loue you with so much of my heart, that none is left to protest.

Bened. Come, bid me doe any thing for thee.

Beat. Kill *Claudio*.

Bene. Ha, not for the wide world.

Beat. You kill me to denie, farewell.

Bene. Tarrie sweet *Beatrice*.

Beat. I am gone, though I am heere, there is no loue in you, nay I pray you let me goe.

Bene. Beatrice.

Beat. Infaith I will goe.

Bene. Wee'll be friends first.

Beat. You dare easier be friends with mee, than fight with mine enemy.

Bene. Is *Claudio* thine enemie?

Beat. Is a not approued in the height a villaine, that hath slandered, scorned, dishonoured my kinswoman? O that I were a man! what, beare her in hand vntill they come to take hands, and then with publike accusation vncouered slander, vnmittigated rancour? O God that I were a man! I would eat his heart in the market-place.

Bene. Heare me *Beatrice*.

Beat. Talke with a man out at a window, a proper saying.

Bene. Nay but *Beatrice*.

Beat. Sweet *Hero*, she is wrong'd, shee is slandered, she is vndone.

Bene. Beat?

Beat. Princes and Counties! surelie a Princely testimonie, a goodly Count, Comfect, a sweet Gallant surelie, O that I were a man for his sake! or that I had any friend would be a man for my sake! But manhood is melted into cursies, valour into complement, and men are onelie turned into tongue, and trim ones too: he is now as valiant as *Hercules*, that only tells a lie, and sweares it: I cannot be a man with wishing, therfore I will die a woman with grieuing.

Bene. Tarry good *Beatrice*, by this hand I loue thee.

Beat. Vse it for my loue some other way then swearing by it.

Bened. Thinke you in your soule the Count *Claudio* hath wrong'd *Hero*?

Beat. Yea, as sure as I haue a thought, or a soule.

Bene. Enough, I am engagde, I will challenge him, I will kisse your hand, and so leaue you: by this hand *Claudio* shall render me a deere account: as you heare of me, so thinke of me: goe comfort your coosin, I must say she is dead, and so farewell.

Enter the Constables, Borachio, and the Towne Clerke in gownes.

Keeper. Is our whole dissembly appeard?

Cowley. O a stoole and a cushion for the Sexton.

Sexton. Which be the malefactors?

Andrew. Marry that am I, and my partner.

Cowley. Nay that's certaine, wee haue the exhibition to examine.

Sexton. But which are the offenders that are to be examined, let them come before master Constable.

Kemp. Yea marry, let them come before mee, what is your name, friend?

Bor. Borachio.

Kem. Pray write downe *Borachio*. Yours sirra.

Con. I am a Gentleman sir, and my name is *Conrade*.

Kee. Write downe Master gentleman *Conradei*: maisters, doe you serue God: maisters, it is proued alreadie that you are little better than false knaues, and it will goe neere to be thought so shortly, how answer you for your selues?

Con. Marry sir, we say we are none.

Kemp. A maruellous witty fellow I assure you, but I will goe about with him: come you hither sirra, a word in your eare sir, I say to you, it is thought you are false knaues.

Bor. Sir, I say to you, we are none.

Kemp. Well, stand aside, 'fore God they are both in a tale: haue you writ downe that they are none?

Sext. Master Constable, you goe not the way to examine, you must call forth the watch that are their accusers.

Kemp. Yea marry, that's the eftest way, let the watch come forth: masters, I charge you in the Princes name, accuse these men.

Watch 1. This man said sir, that *Don Iohn* the Princes brother was a villaine.

Kemp. Write down, Prince *Iohn* a villaine: why this is flat periurie, to call a Princes brother villaine.

Bors. Master Constable.

Kemp. Pray thee fellow peace, I do not like thy looke I promise thee.

Sexton. What heard you him say else?

Watch 2. Mary that he had receiued a thousand Dukates of *Don Iohn*, for accusing the Lady *Hero* wrongfully.

Kem.

Much adoe about Nothing.

Kemp. Flat Burglarie as euer was committed.
Const. Yea by th'masse that it is.
Sexton. What else fellow?
Watch 1. And that Count *Claudio* did meane vpon his words, to disgrace *Hero* before the whole assembly, and not marry her.
Kemp. O villaine! thou wilt be condemn'd into euerlasting redemption for this.
Sexton. What else?
Watch. This is all.
Sexton. And this is more masters then you can deny, Prince *Iohn* is this morning secretly stolne away: *Hero* was in this manner accus'd, in this very manner refus'd, and vpon the griefe of this sodainely died: Master Constable, let these men be bound, and brought to *Leonato*, I will goe before, and shew him their examination.
Const. Come, let them be opinion'd.
Sex. Let them be in the hands of *Coxcombe*.
Kem. Gods my life, where's the Sexton? let him write downe the Princes Officer *Coxcombe*: come, binde them thou naughty varlet.
Couley. Away, you are an asse, you are an asse.
Kemp. Dost thou not suspect my place? dost thou not suspect my yeeres? O that hee were heere to write mee downe an asse! but masters, remember that I am an asse: though it be not written down, yet forget not ỹ I am an asse: No thou villaine, ỹ art full of piety as shall be prou'd vpon thee by good witnesse, I am a wise fellow, and which is more, an officer, and which is more, a houshoulder, and which is more, as pretty a peece of flesh as any in Messina, and one that knowes the Law, goe to, & a rich fellow enough, goe to, and a fellow that hath had losses, and one that hath two gownes, and euery thing handsome about him: bring him away: O that I had been writ downe an asse! *Exit.*

Actus Quintus.

Enter Leonato and his brother.

Brother. If you goe on thus, you will kill your selfe,
And 'tis not wisedome thus to second griefe,
Against your selfe.
Leon. I pray thee cease thy counsaile,
Which falls into mine eares as profitlesse,
As water in a siue: giue not me counsaile,
Nor let no comfort delight mine eare,
But such a one whose wrongs doth sute with mine.
Bring me a father that so lou'd his childe,
Whose ioy of her is ouer-whelmed like mine,
And bid him speake of patience,
Measure his woe the length and bredth of mine,
And let it answere euery straine for straine,
As thus for thus, and such a griefe for such,
In euery lineament, branch, shape, and forme:
If such a one will smile and stroke his beard,
And sorrow, wagge, crie hem, when he should grone,
Patch griefe with prouerbs, make misfortune drunke,
With candle-wasters: bring him yet to me,
And I of him will gather patience:
But there is no such man, for brother, men
Can counsaile, and speake comfort to that griefe,
Which they themselues not feele, but tasting it,
Their counsaile turnes to passion, which before,
Would giue preceptiall medicine to rage,
Fetter strong madnesse in a silken thred,
Charme ache with ayre, and agony with words,
No, no, 'tis all mens office, to speake patience
To those that wring vnder the load of sorrow:
But no mans vertue nor sufficiencie
To be so morall, when he shall endure
The like himselfe: therefore giue me no counsaile,
My griefs cry lowder then aduertisement.
Broth. Therein do men from children nothing differ.
Leonato. I pray thee peace, I will be flesh and bloud,
For there was neuer yet Philosopher,
That could endure the tooth-ake patiently,
How euer they haue writ the stile of gods,
And made a push at chance and sufferance.
Brother. Yet bend not all the harme vpon your selfe,
Make those that doe offend you, suffer too.
Leon. There thou speak'st reason, nay I will doe so,
My soule doth tell me, *Hero* is belied,
And that shall *Claudio* know, so shall the Prince,
And all of them that thus dishonour her.

Enter Prince and Claudio.

Bro. Here comes the *Prince* and *Claudio* hastily.
Prin. Good den, good den.
Clau. Good day to both of you.
Leon. Heare you my Lords?
Prin. We haue some haste *Leonato*.
Leo. Some haste my Lord! wel, fareyouwel my Lord,
Are you so hasty now? well, all is one.
Prin. Nay, do not quarrell with vs, good old man.
Brot. If he could rite himselfe with quarrelling,
Some of vs would lie low.
Claud. Who wrongs him?
Leon. Marry ỹ dost wrong me, thou dissembler, thou:
Nay, neuer lay thy hand vpon thy sword,
I feare thee not.
Claud. Marry beshrew my hand,
If it should giue your age such cause of feare,
Infaith my hand meant nothing to my sword.
Leonato. Tush, tush, man, neuer fleere and iest at me,
I speake not like a dotard, nor a foole,
As vnder priuiledge of age to bragge,
What I haue done being yong, or what would doe,
Were I not old, know *Claudio* to thy head,
Thou hast so wrong'd my innocent childe and me,
That I am forc'd to lay my reuerence by,
And with grey haires and bruise of many daies,
Doe challenge thee to triall of a man,
I say thou hast belied mine innocent childe.
Thy slander hath gone through and through her heart,
And she lies buried with her ancestors:
O in a tombe where neuer scandall slept,
Saue this of hers, fram'd by thy villanie.
Claud. My villany?
Leonato. Thine *Claudio*, thine I say.
Prin. You say not right old man.
Leon. My Lord, my Lord,
Ile proue it on his body if he dare,
Despight his nice fence, and his actiue practise,
His Maie of youth, and bloome of lustihood.
Claud. Away, I will not haue to do with you.
Leo. Canst thou so daffe me? thou hast kild my child,
If thou kilst me, boy, thou shalt kill a man.
Bro. He shall kill two of vs, and men indeed,
But that's no matter, let him kill one first:

Win me and weare me, let him answere me,
Come follow me boy, come sir boy, come follow me
Sir boy, ile whip you from your foyning fence,
Nay, as I am a gentleman, I will.

Leon. Brother.

Brot. Content your self, God knows I lou'd my neece,
And she is dead, slander'd to death by villaines,
That dare as well answer a man indeede,
As I d are take a serpent by the tongue.
Boyes, apes, braggarts, Iackes, milke-sops.

Leon. Brother *Anthony*.

Brot. Hold you content, what man? I know them, yea
And what they weigh, euen to the vtmost scruple,
Scambling, out-facing, fashion-monging boyes,
That lye, and cog, and flout, depraue, and slander,
Goe antiquely, and show outward hidiousnesse,
And speake of halfe a dozen dang'rous words,
How they might hurt their enemies, if they durst.
And this is all.

Leon. But brother *Anthonie*.

Ant. Come, 'tis no matter,
Do not you meddle, let me deale in this.

Pri. Gentlemen both, we will not wake your patience
My heart is sorry for your daughters death:
But on my honour she was charg'd with nothing
But what was true, and very full of proofe.

Leon. My Lord, my Lord.

Prin. I will not heare you.

Enter Benedicke.

Leo. No come brother, away, I will be heard.

Exeunt ambo.

Bro. And shall, or some of vs will smart for it.

Prin. See, see, here comes the man we went to seeke.

Clau. Now signior, what newes?

Ben. Good day my Lord.

Prin. Welcome signior, you are almost come to part almost a fray.

Clau. Wee had like to haue had our two noses snapt off with two old men without teeth.

Prin. Leonato and his brother, what think'st thou? had wee fought, I doubt we should haue beene too yong for them.

Ben. In a false quarrell there is no true valour, I came to seeke you both.

Clau. We haue beene vp and downe to seeke thee, for we are high proofe melancholly, and would faine haue it beaten away, wilt thou vse thy wit?

Ben. It is in my scabberd, shall I draw it?

Prin. Doest thou weare thy wit by thy side?

Clau. Neuer any did so, though verie many haue been beside their wit, I will bid thee drawe, as we do the minstrels, draw to pleasure vs.

Prin. As I am an honest man he lookes pale, art thou sicke, or angrie?

Clau. What, courage man: what though care kil'd a cat, thou hast mettle enough in thee to kill care.

Ben. Sir, I shall meete your wit in the careere, and you charge it against me, I pray you chuse another subiect.

Clau. Nay then giue him another staffe, this last was broke crosse.

Prin. By this light, he changes more and more, I thinke he be angrie indeede.

Clau. If he be, he knowes how to turne his girdle.

Ben. Shall I speake a word in your eare?

Clau. God blesse me from a challenge.

Ben. You are a villaine, I iest not, I will make it good how you dare, with what you dare, and when you dare: do me right, or I will protest your cowardise: you haue kill'd a sweete Ladie, and her death shall fall heauie on you, let me heare from you.

Clau. Well, I will meete you, so I may haue good cheare.

Prin. What, a feast, a feast?

Clau. I faith I thanke him, he hath bid me to a calues head and a Capon, the which if I doe not carue most curiously, say my knife's naught, shall I not finde a woodcocke too?

Ben. Sir, your wit ambles well, it goes easily.

Prin. Ile tell thee how *Beatrice* prais'd thy wit the other day: I said thou hadst a fine wit: true saies she, a fine little one: no said I, a great wit: right saies shee, a great grosse one: nay said I, a good wit: iust said she, it hurts no body: nay said I, the gentleman is wise: certain said she, a wise gentleman: nay said I, he hath the tongues: that I beleeue said shee, for hee swore a thing to me on munday night, which he forswore on tuesday morning: there's a double tongue, there's two tongues: thus did shee an howre together trans-shape thy particular vertues, yet at last she concluded with a sigh, thou wast the proprest man in Italie.

Claud. For the which she wept heartily, and said shee car'd not.

Prin. Yea that she did, but yet for all that, and if shee did not hate him deadlie, shee would loue him dearely, the old mans daughter told vs all.

Clau. All, all, and moreouer, God saw him when he was hid in the garden.

Prin. But when shall we set the sauage Bulls hornes on the sensible *Benedicks* head?

Clau. Yea and text vnder-neath, heere dwells *Benedicke* the married man.

Ben. Fare you well, Boy, you know my minde, I will leaue you now to your gossep-like humor, you breake iests as braggards do their blades, which God be thanked hurt not: my Lord, for your manie courtesies I thank you, I must discontinue your companie, your brother the Bastard is fled from *Messina*: you haue among you, kill'd a sweet and innocent Ladie: for my Lord Lackebeard there, he and I shall meete, and till then peace be with him.

Prin. He is in earnest.

Clau. In most profound earnest, and Ile warrant you, for the loue of Beatrice.

Prin. And hath challeng'd thee.

Clau. Most sincerely.

Prin. What a prettie thing man is, when he goes in his doublet and hose, and leaues off his wit.

Enter Constable, Conrade, and Borachio.

Clau. He is then a Giant to an Ape, but then is an Ape a Doctor to such a man.

Prin. But soft you, let me be, plucke vp my heart, and be sad, did he not say my brother was fled?

Const. Come you sir, if iustice cannot tame you, shee shall nere weigh more reasons in her ballance, nay, and you be a cursing hypocrite once, you must be lookt to.

Prin. How now, two of my brothers men bound? *Borachio* one.

Clau. Harken after their offence my Lord.

Prin. Officers, what offence haue these men done?

Con. Marrie

Const. Marrie sir, they haue committed false report, moreouer they haue spoken vntruths, secondarily they are slanders, sixt and lastly, they haue belyed a Ladie, thirdly, they haue verified vniust things, and to conclude they are lying knaues.

Prin. First I aske thee what they haue done, thirdlie I aske thee what's their offence, sixt and lastlie why they are committed, and to conclude, what you lay to their charge.

Clau. Rightlie reasoned, and in his owne diuision, and by my troth there's one meaning vvell suted.

Prin. Who haue you offended masters, that you are thus bound to your answer? this learned Constable is too cunning to be vnderstood, vvhat's your offence?

Bor. Sweete Prince, let me go no farther to mine answere: do you heare me, and let this Count kill mee: I haue deceiued euen your verie eies: vvhat your wisedomes could not discouer, these shallow fooles haue brought to light, vvho in the night ouerheard me confessing to this man, how *Don Iohn* your brother incensed me to slander the Ladie *Hero*, how you were brought into the Orchard, and saw mee court *Margaret* in *Heroes* garments, how you disgrac'd her vvhen you should marrie her: my villanie they haue vpon record, vvhich I had rather seale vvith my death, then repeate ouer to my shame: the Ladie is dead vpon mine and my masters false accusation: and briefelie, I desire nothing but the reward of a villaine.

Prin. Runs not this speech like yron through your bloud?

Clau. I haue drunke poison whiles he vtter'd it.

Prin. But did my Brother set thee on to this?

Bor. Yea, and paid me richly for the practise of it.

Prin. He is compos'd and fram'd of treacherie, And fled he is vpon this villanie.

Clau. Sweet *Hero*, now thy image doth appeare In the rare semblance that I lou'd it first.

Const. Come, bring away the plaintiffes, by this time our *Sexton* hath reformed *Signior Leonato* of the matter: and masters, do not forget to specifie when time & place shall serue, that I am an Asse.

Con. 2. Here, here comes master *Signior Leonato*, and the *Sexton* too.

Enter Leonato.

Leon. Which is the villaine? let me see his eies, That when I note another man like him, I may auoide him: vvhich of these is he?

Bor. If you vvould know your wronger, looke on me.

Leon. Art thou thou the slaue that with thy breath hast kild mine innocent childe?

Bor. Yea, euen I alone.

Leo. No, not so villaine, thou beliest thy selfe, Here stand a paire of honourable men, A third is fled that had a hand in it: I thanke you Princes for my daughters death, Record it with your high and worthie deedes, 'Twas brauely done, if you bethinke you of it.

Clau. I know not how to pray your patience, Yet I must speake, choose your reuenge your selfe, Impose me to what penance your inuention Can lay vpon my sinne, yet sinn'd I not, But in mistaking.

Prin. By my soule nor I, And yet to satisfie this good old man, I vvould bend vnder anie heauie vvaight, That heele enioyne me to.

Leon. I cannot bid you bid my daughter liue, That vvere impossible, but I praie you both, Possesse the people in *Messina* here, How innocent she died, and if your loue Can labour aught in sad inuention, Hang her an epitaph vpon her toomb, And sing it to her bones, sing it to night: To morrow morning come you to my house, And since you could not be my sonne in law, Be yet my Nephew: my brother hath a daughter, Almost the copie of my childe that's dead, And she alone is heire to both of vs, Giue her the right you should haue giu'n her cosin, And so dies my reuenge.

Clau. O noble sir! Your ouerkindnesse doth wring teares from me, I do embrace your offer, and dispose For henceforth of poore *Claudio*.

Leon. To morrow then I will expect your comming, To night I take my leaue, this naughtie man Shall face to face be brought to *Margaret*, Who I beleeue was packt in all this wrong, Hired to it by your brother.

Bor. No by my soule she was not, Nor knew not what she did when she spoke to me, But alwaies hath bin iust and vertuous, In anie thing that I do know by her.

Const. Moreouer sir, which indeede is not vnder white and black, this plaintiffe here, the offendour did call mee asse, I beseech you let it be remembred in his punishment, and also the vvatch heard them talke of one *Deformed*, they say he weares a key in his eare and a lock hanging by it, and borrowes monie in Gods name, the which he hath vs'd so long, and neuer paied, that now men grow hard-harted and will lend nothing for Gods sake: praie you examine him vpon that point.

Leon. I thanke thee for thy care and honest paines.

Const. Your vvorship speakes like a most thankefull and reuerend youth, and I praise God for you.

Leon. There's for thy paines.

Const. God saue the foundation.

Leon. Goe, I discharge thee of thy prisoner, and I thanke thee.

Const. I leaue an arrant knaue vvith your vvorship, which I beseech your worship to correct your selfe, for the example of others: God keepe your vvorship, I wish your worship vvell, God restore you to health, I humblie giue you leaue to depart, and if a merrie meeting may be wisht, God prohibite it: come neighbour.

Leon. Vntill to morrow morning, Lords, farewell. *Exeunt.*

Brot. Farewell my Lords, vve looke for you to morrow.

Prin. We will not faile.

Clau. To night ile mourne with *Hero*.

Leon. Bring you these fellowes on, weel talke vvith *Margaret*, how her acquaintance grew vvith this lewd fellow. *Exeunt.*

Enter Benedicke and Margaret.

Ben. Praie thee sweete Mistris *Margaret*, deserue vvell at my hands, by helping mee to the speech of *Beatrice*.

Mar. Will

Mar. Will you then write me a Sonnet in praise of my beautie?

Bene. In so high a stile *Margaret*, that no man liuing shall come ouer it, for in most comely truth thou deseruest it.

Mar. To haue no man come ouer me, why, shall I alwaies keepe below staires?

Bene. Thy wit is as quicke as the grey-hounds mouth, it catches.

Mar. And yours, as blunt as the Fencers foiles, which hit, but hurt not.

Bene. A most manly wit *Margaret*, it will not hurt a woman: and so I pray thee call *Beatrice*, I giue thee the bucklers.

Mar. Giue vs the swords, wee haue bucklers of our owne.

Bene. If you vse them *Margaret*, you must put in the pikes with a vice, and they are dangerous weapons for Maides.

Mar. Well, I will call *Beatrice* to you, who I thinke hath legges. *Exit Margarite.*

Ben. And therefore will come. The God of loue that sits aboue, and knowes me, and knowes me, how pittifull I deserue. I meane in singing, but in louing, Leander the good swimmer, Troilous the first imploier of pandars, and a whole booke full of these quondam carpet-mongers, whose name yet runne smoothly in the euen rode of a blanke verse, why they were neuer so truely turned ouer and ouer as my poore selfe in loue: marrie I cannot shew it rime, I haue tried, I can finde out no rime to Ladie but babie, an innocent rime: for scorne, horne, a hard time: for schoole foole, a babling time: verie ominous endings, no, I was not borne vnder a riming Plannet, for I cannot wooe in festiuall tearmes: *Enter Beatrice.*

sweete *Beatrice* would'st thou come when I cal'd thee?

Beat. Yea Signior, and depart when you bid me.

Bene. O stay but till then.

Beat. Then, is spoken: fare you well now, and yet ere I goe, let me goe with that I came, which is, with knowing what hath past betweene you and *Claudio*.

Bene. Onely foule words, and thereupon I will kisse thee.

Beat. Foule words is but foule wind, and foule wind is but foule breath, and foule breath is noisome, therefore I will depart vnkist.

Bene. Thou hast frighted the word out of his right sence, so forcible is thy wit, but I must tell thee plainely, *Claudio* vndergoes my challenge, and either I must shortly heare from him, or I will subscribe him a coward, and I pray thee now tell me, for which of my bad parts didst thou first fall in loue with me?

Beat. For them all together, which maintain'd so politique a state of euill, that they will not admit any good part to intermingle with them: but for which of my good parts did you first suffer loue for me?

Bene. Suffer loue! a good epithite, I do suffer loue indeede, for I loue thee against my will.

Beat. In spight of your heart I think, alas poore heart, if you spight it for my sake, I will spight it for yours, for I will neuer loue that which my friend hates.

Bened. Thou and I are too wise to wooe peaceablie.

Bea. It appeares not in this confession, there's not one wise man among twentie that will praise himselfe.

Bene. An old, an old instance *Beatrice*, that liu'd in the time of good neighbours, if a man doe not erect in this age his owne tombe ere he dies, hee shall liue no longer in monuments, then the Bels ring, & the Widdow weepes.

Beat. And how long is that thinke you?

Ben. Question, why an hower in clamour and a quarter in rhewme, therfore is it most expedient for the wise, if Don worme (his conscience) finde no impediment to the contrarie, to be the trumpet of his owne vertues, as I am to my selfe so much for praising my selfe, who I my selfe will beare witnesse is praise worthie, and now tell me, how doth your cosin?

Beat. Verie ill.

Bene. And how doe you?

Beat. Verie ill too.

Enter Vrsula.

Bene. Serue God, loue me, and mend, there will I leaue you too, for here comes one in haste.

Vrs. Madam, you must come to your Vncle, yonders old coile at home, it is prooued my Ladie *Hero* hath bin falselie accusde, the *Prince* and *Claudio* mightilie abusde, and *Don Iohn* is the author of all, who is fled and gone: will you come presentlie?

Beat. Will you go heare this newes Signior?

Bene. I will liue in thy heart, die in thy lap, and be buried in thy eies: and moreouer, I will goe with thee to thy Vncles. *Exeunt.*

Enter Claudio, Prince, and three or foure with Tapers.

Clau. Is this the monument of *Leonato*?

Lord. It is my Lord. *Epitaph.*

> Done to death by slanderous tongues,
> Was the Hero that here lies:
> Death in guerdon of her wrongs,
> Giues her fame which neuer dies:
> So the life that dyed with shame,
> Liues in death with glorious fame.
>   Hang thou there vpon the tombe,
>   Praising her when I am dombe.

Clau. Now musick sound & sing your solemn hymne

Song.
> Pardon goddesse of the night,
> Those that slew thy virgin knight,
> For the which with songs of woe,
> Round about her tombes they goe:
> Midnight assist our mone, helpe vs to sigh and grone.
> Heauily, heauily.
> Graues yawne and yeelde your dead,
> Till death be vttered,
> Heauenly, heauenly.

(this right.

Lo. Now vnto thy bones good night, yeerely will I do

Prin. Good morrow masters, put your Torches out, The wolues haue preied, and looke, the gentle day Before the wheeles of Phœbus, round about Dapples the drowsie East with spots of grey: Thanks to you all, and leaue vs, fare you well.

Clau. Good morrow masters, each his seuerall way.

Prin. Come let vs hence, and put on other weedes, And then to *Leonatoes* we will goe.

Clau. And Hymen now with luckier issue speeds,

Then

Then this for whom we rendred vp this woe. *Exeunt.*

Enter Leonato, Bene. Marg. Vrsula, old man, Frier, Hero.

Frier. Did I not tell you she was innocent?

Leo. So are the *Prince* and *Claudio* who accuz'd her,
Vpon the errour that you heard debated:
But *Margaret* was in some fault for this,
Although against her will as it appeares,
In the true course of all the question.

Old. Well, I am glad that all things sort so well.

Bene. And so am I, being else by faith enforc'd
To call young *Claudio* to a reckoning for it.

Leo. Well daughter, and you gentlewomen all,
Withdraw into a chamber by your selues,
And when I send for you, come hither mask'd:
The *Prince* and *Claudio* promis'd by this howre
To visit me, you know your office Brother,
You must be father to your brothers daughter,
And giue her to young *Claudio*. *Exeunt Ladies.*

Old. Which I will doe with confirm'd countenance.

Bene. Frier, I must intreat your paines, I thinke.

Frier. To doe what Signior?

Bene. To binde me, or vndoe me, one of them:
Signior *Leonato*, truth it is good Signior,
Your neece regards me with an eye of fauour.

Leo. That eye my daughter lent her, 'tis most true.

Bene. And I doe with an eye of loue requite her.

Leo. The sight whereof I thinke you had from me,
From *Claudio*, and the *Prince*, but what's your will?

Bened. Your answer sir is Enigmaticall,
But for my will, my will is, your good will
May stand with ours, this day to be conioyn'd,
In the state of honourable marriage,
In which (good Frier) I shall desire your helpe.

Leon. My heart is with your liking.

Frier. And my helpe.

Enter Prince and Claudio, with attendants.

Prin. Good morrow to this faire assembly.

Leo. Good morrow Prince, good morrow *Claudio*:
We heere attend you, are you yet determin'd,
To day to marry with my brothers daughter?

Claud. Ile hold my minde were she an Ethiope.

Leo. Call her forth brother, heres the Frier ready.

Prin. Good morrow *Benedike*, why what's the matter?
That you haue such a Februarie face,
So full of frost, of storme, and clowdinesse.

Claud. I thinke he thinkes vpon the sauage bull:
Tush, feare not man, wee'll tip thy hornes with gold,
And all Europa shall reioyce at thee,
As once *Europa* did at lusty *Ioue*,
When he would play the noble beast in loue.

Ben. Bull *Ioue* sir, had an amiable low,
And some such strange bull leapt your fathers Cow,
A got a Calfe in that same noble feat,
Much like to you, for you haue iust his bleat.

Enter brother, Hero, Beatrice, Margaret, Vrsula.

Cla. For this I owe you: here comes other reckning.
Which is the Lady I must seize vpon?

Leo. This same is she, and I doe giue you her.

Cla. Why then she's mine, sweet let me see your face.

Leon. No that you shal not, till you take her hand,
Before this Frier, and sweare to marry her.

Clau. Giue me your hand before this holy Frier,
I am your husband if you like of me.

Hero. And when I liu'd I was your other wife,
And when you lou'd, you were my other husband.

Clau. Another *Hero*?

Hero. Nothing certainer.
One *Hero* died, but I doe liue,
And surely as I liue, I am a maid.

Prin. The former *Hero*, *Hero* that is dead.

Leon. Shee died my Lord, but whiles her slander liu'd.

Frier. All this amazement can I qualifie,
When after that the holy rites are ended,
Ile tell you largely of faire *Heroes* death:
Meane time let wonder seeme familiar,
And to the chappell let vs presently.

Ben. Soft and faire Frier, which is *Beatrice*?

Beat. I answer to that name, what is your will?

Bene. Doe not you loue me?

Beat. Why no, no more then reason.

Bene. Why then your Vncle, and the Prince, & *Claudio*, haue beene deceiued, they swore you did.

Beat. Doe not you loue mee?

Bene. Troth no, no more then reason.

Beat. Why then my Cosin *Margaret* and *Vrsula*
Are much deceiu'd, for they did sweare you did.

Bene. They swore you were almost sicke for me.

Beat. They swore you were wel-nye dead for me.

Bene. 'Tis no matter, then you doe not loue me?

Beat. No truly, but in friendly recompence.

Leon. Come Cosin, I am sure you loue the gentlemā.

Clau. And Ile be sworne vpon't, that he loues her,
For heres a paper written in his hand,
A halting sonnet of his owne pure braine,
Fashioned to *Beatrice*.

Hero. And heeres another,
Writ in my cosins hand, stolne from her pocket,
Containing her affection vnto *Benedicke*.

Bene. A miracle, here's our owne hands against our hearts: come I will haue thee, but by this light I take thee for pittie.

Beat. I would not denie you, but by this good day, I yeeld vpon great perswasion, & partly to saue your life, for I was told, you were in a consumption.

Leon. Peace I will stop your mouth.

Prin. How dost thou *Benedicke* the married man?

Bene. Ile tell thee what Prince: a Colledge of witte-crackers cannot flout mee out of my humour, dost thou think I care for a Satyre or an Epigram? no, if a man will be beaten with braines, a shall weare nothing handsome about him: in briefe, since I do purpose to marry, I will thinke nothing to any purpose that the world can say a-gainst it, and therefore neuer flout at me, for I haue said against it: for man is a giddy thing, and this is my con-clusion: for thy part *Claudio*, I did thinke to haue beaten thee, but in that thou art like to be my kinsman, liue vn-bruis'd, and loue my cousin.

Cla. I had well hop'd ÿ wouldst haue denied *Beatrice*, ÿ I might haue cudgel'd thee out of thy single life, to make thee a double dealer, which out of questiō thou wilt be, if my Cousin do not looke exceeding narrowly to thee.

Bene. Come, come, we are friends, let's haue a dance ere we are married, that we may lighten our own hearts, and our wiues heeles.

Leon. Wee'll haue dancing afterward.

Bene. First, of my vvord, therfore play musick. *Prince*, thou art sad, get thee a vvife, get thee a vvife, there is no staff more reuerend then one tipt with horn. *Enter Mes.*

Messen. My Lord, your brother *Iohn* is tane in flight,
And brought with armed men backe to *Messina*.

Bene. Thinke not on him till to morrow, ile deuise thee braue punishments for him: strike vp Pipers. *Dance.*

FINIS.

Loues Labour's lost.

Actus primus.

Enter Ferdinand King of Nauarre, Berowne, Longauill, and Dumane.

Ferdinand.

Et *Fame*, that all hunt after in their liues,
Liue regiſtred vpon our brazen Tombes,
And then grace vs in the diſgrace of death:
when ſpight of cormorant deuouring Time,
Th'endeuour of this preſent breath may buy:
That honour which ſhall bate his ſythes keene edge,
And make vs heyres of all eternitie.
Therefore braue Conquerours, for ſo you are,
That warre againſt your owne affections,
And the huge Armie of the worlds deſires.
Our late edict ſhall ſtrongly ſtand in force,
Nauar ſhall be the wonder of the world.
Our Court ſhall be a little Achademe,
Still and contemplatiue in liuing Art.
You three, *Berowne, Dumaine,* and *Longauill,*
Haue ſworne for three yeeres terme, to liue with me:
My fellow Schollers, and to keepe thoſe ſtatutes
That are recorded in this ſcedule heere.
Your oathes are paſt, and now ſubſcribe your names:
That his owne hand may ſtrike his honour downe,
That violates the ſmalleſt branch heerein:
If you are arm'd to doe, as ſworne to do,
Subſcribe to your deepe oathes, and keepe it to.

Longauill. I am reſolu'd, 'tis but a three yeeres faſt:
The minde ſhall banquet, though the body pine,
Fat paunches haue leane pates: and dainty bits,
Make rich the ribs, but bankerout the wits.

Dumane. My louing Lord, *Dumane* is mortified,
The groſſer manner of theſe worlds delights,
He throwes vpon the groſſe worlds baſer ſlaues:
To loue, to wealth, to pompe, I pine and die,
With all theſe liuing in Philoſophie.

Berowne. I can but ſay their proteſtation ouer,
So much deare Liege, I haue already ſworne,
That is, to liue and ſtudy heere three yeeres.
But there are other ſtrict obſeruances:
As not to ſee a woman in that terme,
Which I hope well is not enrolled there.
And one day in a weeke to touch no foode:
And but one meale on euery day beſide:
The which I hope is not enrolled there.
And then to ſleepe but three houres in the night,
And not be ſeene to winke of all the day.
When I was wont to thinke no harme all night,
And make a darke night too of halfe the day:
Which I hope well is not enrolled there.
O, theſe are barren taskes, too hard to keepe,
Not to ſee Ladies, ſtudy, faſt, not ſleepe.

Ferd. Your oath is paſt, to paſſe away from theſe.

Berow. Let me ſay no my Liedge, and if you pleaſe,
I onely ſwore to ſtudy with your grace,
And ſtay heere in your Court for three yeeres ſpace.

Longa. You ſwore to that *Berowne*, and to the reſt.

Berow. By yea and nay ſir, than I ſwore in ieſt,
What is the end of ſtudy, let me know?

Fer. Why that to know which elſe wee ſhould not know.

Ber. Things hid & bard (you meane) frō cōmon ſenſe.

Ferd. I, that is ſtudies god-like recompence.

Bero. Come on then, I will ſweare to ſtudie ſo,
To know the thing I am forbid to know:
As thus, to ſtudy where I well may dine,
When I to faſt expreſſely am forbid.
Or ſtudie where to meet ſome Miſtreſſe fine,
When Miſtreſſes from common ſenſe are hid.
Or hauing ſworne too hard a keeping oath,
Studie to breake it, and not breake my troth.
If ſtudies gaine be thus, and this be ſo,
Studie knowes that which yet it doth not know,
Sweare me to this, and I will nere ſay no.

Ferd. Theſe be the ſtops that hinder ſtudie quite,
And traine our intellects to vaine delight.

Ber. Why? all delights are vaine, and that moſt vaine
Which with paine purchas'd, doth inherit paine,
As painefully to poare vpon a Booke,
To ſeeke the light of truth, while truth the while
Doth falſely blinde the eye-ſight of his looke:
Light ſeeeking light, doth light of light beguile:
So ere you finde where light in darkeneſſe lies,
Your light growes darke by loſing of your eyes.
Studie me how to pleaſe the eye indeede,
By fixing it vpon a fairer eye,
Who dazling ſo, that eye ſhall be his heed,
And giue him light that it was blinded by.
Studie is like the heauens glorious Sunne,
That will not be deepe ſearch'd with ſawcy lookes:
Small haue continuall plodders euer wonne,
Saue baſe authoritie from others Bookes.
Theſe earthly Godfathers of heauens lights,
That giue a name to euery fixed Starre,
Haue no more profit of their ſhining nights,
Then thoſe that walke and wot not what they are.
Too much to know, is to know nought but fame:
And euery Godfather can giue a name.

Fer. How well hee's read, to reaſon againſt reading.

Dum.

Dum. Proceeded well, to stop all good proceeding.
Lon. Hee weedes the corne, and still lets grow the weeding.
Ber. The Spring is neare when greene geesse are a breeding.
Dum. How followes that?
Ber. Fit in his place and time.
Dum. In reason nothing.
Ber. Something then in rime.
Ferd. *Berowne* is like an enuious sneaping Frost,
That bites the first borne infants of the Spring.
Ber. Wel, say I am, why should proud Summer boast,
Before the Birds haue any cause to sing?
Why should I ioy in any abortiue birth?
At Christmas I no more desire a Rose,
Then wish a Snow in Mayes new fangled showes:
But like of each thing that in season growes.
So you to studie now it is too late,
That were to clymbe ore the house to vnlocke the gate.
Fer. Well, fit you out: go home *Berowne*: adue.
Ber. No my good Lord, I haue sworn to stay with you.
And though I haue for barbarisme spoke more,
Then for that Angell knowledge you can say,
Yet confident Ile keepe what I haue sworne,
And bide the pennance of each three yeares day.
Giue me the paper, let me reade the same,
And to the strictest decrees Ile write my name.
Fer. How well this yeelding rescues thee from shame.
Ber. Item. That no woman shall come within a mile of my Court.
Hath this bin proclaimed?
Lon. Foure dayes agoe.
Ber. Let's see the penaltie.
On paine of loosing her tongue.
Who deuis'd this penaltie?
Lon. Marry that did I.
Ber. Sweete Lord, and why?
Lon. To fright them hence with that dread penaltie,
A dangerous law against gentilitie.
Item, If any man be seene to talke with a woman within the tearme of three yeares, hee shall indure such publique shame as the rest of the Court shall possibly deuise.
Ber. This Article my Liedge your selfe must breake,
For well you know here comes in Embassie
The *French* Kings daughter, with your selfe to speake:
A Maide of grace and compleate maiestie,
About surrender vp of *Aquitaine*:
To her decrepit, sicke, and bed-rid Father:
Therefore this Article is made in vaine,
Or vainly comes th'admired Princesse hither.
Fer. What say you Lords?
Why, this was quite forgot.
Ber. So Studie euermore is ouershot,
While it doth study to haue what it would,
It doth forget to doe the thing it should:
And when it hath the thing it hunteth most,
'Tis won as townes with fire, so won, so lost.
Fer. We must of force dispence with this Decree,
She must lye here on meere necessitie.
Ber. Necessity will make vs all forsworne,
Three thousand times within this three yeeres space:
For euery man with his affects is borne,
Not by might mastred, but by speciall grace.
If I breake faith, this word shall breake for me,
I am forsworne on meere necessitie.

So to the Lawes at large I write my name,
And he that breakes them in the least degree,
Stands in attainder of eternall shame.
Suggestions are to others as to me:
But I beleeue although I seeme so loth,
I am the last that will last keepe his oth.
But is there no quicke recreation granted?
Fer. I that there is, our Court you know is hanted
With a refined trauailer of *Spaine*,
A man in all the worlds new fashion planted,
That hath a mint of phrases in his braine:
One, who the musicke of his owne vaine tongue,
Doth rauish like inchanting harmonie:
A man of complements whom right and wrong
Haue chose as vmpire of their mutinie.
This childe of fancie that *Armado* hight,
For interim to our studies shall relate,
In high-borne words the worth of many a Knight:
From tawnie *Spaine* lost in the worlds debate.
How you delight my Lords, I know not I,
But I protest I loue to heare him lie,
And I will vse him for my Minstrelsie.
Bero. *Armado* is a most illustrious wight,
A man of fire, new words, fashions owne Knight.
Lon. *Costard* the swaine and he, shall be our sport,
And so to studie, three yeeres is but short.

Enter a Constable with Costard with a Letter.

Const. Which is the Dukes owne person.
Ber. This fellow, What would'st?
Con. I my selfe reprehend his owne person, for I am his graces Tharborough: But I would see his own person in flesh and blood.
Ber. This is he.
Con. Signeor *Arme*, *Arme* commends you:
Ther's villanie abroad, this letter will tell you more.
Clow. Sir the Contempts thereof are as touching mee.
Fer. A letter from the magnificent *Armado*.
Ber. How low soeuer the matter, I hope in God for high words.
Lon. A high hope for a low heauen, God grant vs patience.
Ber. To heare, or forbeare hearing.
Lon. To heare meekely sir, and to laugh moderately, or to forbeare both.
Ber. Well sir, be it as the stile shall giue vs cause to clime in the merrinesse.
Clo. The matter is to me sir, as concerning *Iaquenetta*.
The manner of it is, I was taken with the manner.
Ber. In what manner?
Clo. In manner and forme following sir all those three.
I was seene with her in the Mannor house, sitting with her vpon the Forme, and taken following her into the Parke: which put to gether, is in manner and forme following. Now sir for the manner; It is the manner of a man to speake to a woman, for the forme in some forme.
Ber. For the following sir.
Clo. As it shall follow in my correction, and God defend the right.
Fer. Will you heare this Letter with attention?
Ber. As we would heare an Oracle.
Clo. Such is the simplicitie of man to harken after the flesh.

Fer. Great

Ferdinand.

GReat Deputie, the Welkins Vicegerent, and sole dominater of Nauar, my soules earths God, and bodies fostring patrone:

Cost. Not a vvord of *Costard* yet.

Ferd. So it is.

Cost. It may be so: but if he say it is so, he is in telling true: but so.

Ferd. Peace,

Clow. Be to me, and euery man that dares not fight.

Ferd. No words,

Clow. Of other mens secrets I beseech you.

Ferd. So it is besieged with sable coloured melancholie, I did commend the blacke oppressing humour to the most wholesome Physicke of thy health-giuing ayre: And as I am a Gentleman, betooke my selfe to walke: the time When? about the sixt houre, When beasts most grase, birds best pecke, and men sit downe to that nourishment which is called supper: So much for the time When. Now for the ground Which? which I meane I walkt vpon, it is yclipe'd, Thy Parke. Then for the place Where? where I meane I did encounter that obscene and most preposterous euent that draweth from my snow-white pen the ebon coloured Inke, which heere thou viewest, beholdest, suruayest, or seest. But to the place Where? It standeth North North-east and by East from the West corner of thy curious knotted garden; There did I see that low spirited Swaine, that base Minow of thy myrth, (*Clown.* Mee?) that vnletered small knowing soule, (*Clow* Me?) that shallow vassall (*Clow.* Still mee?) which as I remember, hight Costard, (*Clow.* O me) sorted and consorted contrary to thy established proclaymed Edict and Continet, Cannon: Which with, ô with, but with this I passion to say wherewith:

Clo. With a Wench.

Ferd. With a childe of our Grandmother Eue, a female; or for thy more sweet vnderstanding a woman: him, I (as my euer esteemed dutie prickes me on) haue sent to thee, to receiue the meed of punishment by thy sweet Graces Officer Anthony Dull, a man of good repute, carriage, bearing, & estimation.

Anth. Me, an't shall please you? I am *Anthony Dull.*

Ferd. For Iaquenetta (so is the weaker vessell called) which I apprehended with the aforesaid Swaine, I keeper her as a vessell of thy Lawes furie, and shall at the least of thy sweet notice, bring her to triall. Thine in all complements of deuoted and heart-burning heat of dutie.

Don Adriana de Armado.

Ber. This is not so well as I looked for, but the best that euer I heard.

Fer. I the best, for the worst. But sirra, What say you to this?

Clo. Sir I confesse the Wench.

Fer. Did you heare the Proclamation?

Clo. I doe confesse much of the hearing it, but little of the marking of it.

Fer. It was proclaimed a yeeres imprisoment to bee taken with a Wench.

Clow. I was taken with none sir, I was taken vvith a Damosell.

Fer. Well, it was proclaimed Damosell.

Clo. This was no Damosell neyther sir, shee was a Virgin.

Fer. It is so varried to, for it was proclaimed Virgin.

Clo. If it were, I denie her Virginitie: I was taken with a Maide.

Fer. This Maid will not serue your turne sir.

Clo. This Maide will serue my turne sir.

Kin. Sir I will pronounce your sentence: You shall fast a Weeke with Branne and water.

Clo. I had rather pray a Moneth with Mutten and Porridge.

Kin. And Don *Armado* shall be your keeper. My Lord *Berowne*, see him deliuer'd ore, And goe we Lords to put in practice that, Which each to other hath so strongly sworne.

Bero. Ile lay my head to any good mans hat, These oathes and lawes will proue an idle scorne. Sirra, come on.

Clo. I suffer for the truth sir: for true it is, I was taken with *Iaquenetta*, and *Iaquenetta* is a true girle, and therefore welcome the sowre cup of prosperitie, affliction may one day smile againe, and vntill then sit downe sorrow. *Exit.*

Enter Armado and Moth his Page.

Arma. Boy, What signe is it when a man of great spirit growes melancholy?

Boy. A great signe sir, that he will looke sad.

Brag. Why? sadnesse is one and the selfe-same thing deare impe.

Boy. No no, O Lord sir no.

Brag. How canst thou part sadnesse and melancholy my tender *Iuuenall*?

Boy. By a familiar demonstration of the working, my tough signeur.

Brag. Why tough signeur? Why tough signeur?

Boy. Why tender *Iuuenall*? Why tender *Iuuenall*?

Brag. I spoke it tender *Iuuenall*, as a congruent apathaton, appertaining to thy young daies, which we may nominate tender.

Boy. And I tough signeur, as an appertinent title to your olde time, which we may name tough.

Brag. Pretty and apt.

Boy. How meane you sir, I pretty, and my saying apt? or I apt, and my saying prettie?

Brag. Thou pretty because little.

Boy. Little pretty, because little: wherefore apt?

Brag. And therefore apt, because quicke.

Boy. Speake you this in my praise Master?

Brag. In thy condigne praise.

Boy. I will praise an Eele with the same praise.

Brag. What? that an Eele is ingenuous.

Boy. That an Eeele is quicke.

Brag. I doe say thou art quicke in answeres. Thou heat'st my bloud.

Boy. I am answer'd sir.

Brag. I loue not to be crost. (him.

Boy. He speakes the meere contrary, crosses loue not

Br. I haue promis'd to study iij. yeres with the Duke.

Boy. You may doe it in an houre sir.

Brag. Impossible.

Boy. How many is one thrice told?

Bra. I am ill at reckning, it fits the spirit of a Tapster.

Boy. You are a gentleman and a gamester sir.

Brag. I confesse both, they are both the varnish of a compleat man.

Boy. Then I am sure you know how much the grosse summe of deus-ace amounts to.

Brag. It doth amount to one more then two.

Boy. Which the base vulgar call three.

Br. True. *Boy.* Why sir is this such a peece of study? Now here's three studied, ere you'l thrice wink, & how easie it is to put yeres to the word three, and study three yeeres in two words, the dancing horse will tell you.

Brag. A

Brag. A most fine Figure.
Boy. To proue you a Cypher.
Brag. I will heereupon confesse I am in loue: and as it is base for a Souldier to loue; so am I in loue with a base wench. If drawing my sword against the humour of affection, would deliuer mee from the reprobate thought of it, I would take Desire prisoner, and ransome him to any French Courtier for a new deuis'd curtsie. I thinke scorne to sigh, me thinkes I should out-sweare *Cupid*. Comfort me Boy, What great men haue beene in loue?

Boy. Hercules Master.

Brag. Most sweete *Hercules*: more authority deare Boy, name more; and sweet my childe let them be men of good repute and carriage.

Boy. *Sampson* Master, he was a man of good carriage, great carriage: for hee carried the Towne-gates on his backe like a Porter: and he was in loue.

Brag. O well-knit *Sampson*, strong ioynted *Sampson*; I doe excell thee in my rapier, as much as thou didst mee in carrying gates. I am in loue too. Who was *Sampsons* loue my deare *Moth*?

Boy. A Woman, Master.

Brag. Of what complexion?

Boy. Of all the foure, or the three, or the two, or one of the foure.

Brag. Tell me precisely of what complexion?

Boy. Of the sea-water Greene sir.

Brag. Is that one of the foure complexions?

Boy. As I haue read sir, and the best of them too.

Brag. Greene indeed is the colour of Louers: but to haue a Loue of that colour, methinkes *Sampson* had small reason for it. He surely affected her for her wit.

Boy. It was so sir, for she had a greene wit.

Brag. My Loue is most immaculate white and red.

Boy. Most immaculate thoughts Master, are mask'd vnder such colours.

Brag. Define, define, well educated infant.

Boy. My fathers witte, and my mothers tongue assist mee.

Brag. Sweet inuocation of a childe, most pretty and patheticall.

Boy. If shee be made of white and red,
Her faults will nere be knowne:
For blush-in cheekes by faults are bred,
And feares by pale white showne:
Then if she feare, or be to blame,
By this you shall not know,
For still her cheekes possesse the same,
Which natiue she doth owe:
A dangerous rime master against the reason of white and redde.

Brag. Is there not a ballet Boy, of the King and the Begger?

Boy. The world was very guilty of such a Ballet some three ages since, but I thinke now 'tis not to be found: or if it were, it would neither serue for the writing, nor the tune.

Brag. I will haue that subiect newly writ ore, that I may example my digression by some mighty president. Boy, I doe loue that Countrey girle that I tooke in the Parke with the rationall hinde *Costard*: she deserues well.

Boy. To bee whip'd: and yet a better loue then my Master.

Brag. Sing Boy, my spirit grows heauy in loue.

Boy. And that's great maruell, louing a light wench.

Brag. I say sing.

Boy. Forbeare till this company be past.

Enter Clowne, Constable, and Wench.

Const. Sir, the Dukes pleasure, is that you keepe *Costard* safe, and you must let him take no delight, nor no penance, but hee must fast three daies a weeke: for this Damsell, I must keepe her at the Parke, shee is alowd for the Day-woman. Fare you well. *Exit.*

Brag. I do betray my selfe with blushing: Maide.

Maid. Man.

Brag. I wil visit thee at the Lodge.

Maid. That's here by.

Brag. I know where it is situate.

Mai. Lord how wise you are!

Brag. I will tell thee wonders.

Ma. With what face?

Brag. I loue thee.

Mai. So I heard you say.

Brag. And so farewell.

Mai. Faire weather after you.

Clo. Come *Iaquenetta*, away. *Exeunt.*

Brag. Villaine, thou shalt fast for thy offences ere thou be pardoned.

Clo. Well sir, I hope when I doe it, I shall doe it on a full stomacke.

Brag. Thou shalt be heauily punished.

Clo. I am more bound to you then your fellowes, for they are but lightly rewarded.

Clo. Take away this villaine, shut him vp.

Boy. Come you transgressing slaue, away.

Clow. Let mee not bee pent vp sir, I will fast being loose.

Boy. No sir, that were fast and loose: thou shalt to prison.

Clow. Well, if euer I do see the merry dayes of desolation that I haue seene, some shall see.

Boy. What shall some see?

Clow. Nay nothing, Master *Moth*, but what they looke vpon. It is not for prisoners to be silent in their words, and therefore I will say nothing: I thanke God, I haue as little patience as another man, and therefore I can be quiet. *Exit.*

Brag. I doe affect the very ground (which is base) where her shooe (which is baser) guided by her foote (which is basest) doth tread. I shall be forsworn (which is a great argument of falshood) if I loue. And how can that be true loue, which is falsly attempted? Loue is a familiar, Loue is a Diuell. There is no euill Angell but Loue, yet *Sampson* was so tempted, and he had an excellent strength: Yet was *Salomon* so seduced, and hee had a very good witte. *Cupids* Butshaft is too hard for *Hercules* Clubbe, and therefore too much ods for a Spaniards Rapier: The first and second cause will not serue my turne: the *Passado* hee respects not, the *Duello* he regards not; his disgrace is to be called Boy, but his glorie is to subdue men. Adue Valour, rust Rapier, bee still Drum, for your manager is in loue; yea hee loueth. Assist me some extemporall god of Rime, for I am sure I shall turne Sonnet. Deuise Wit, write Pen, for I am for whole volumes in folio. *Exit.*

Finis Actus Primus.

Actus Secunda.

Enter the Princesse of France, with three attending Ladies, and three Lords.

Boyet. Now Madam summon vp your dearest spirits,
Consider who the King your father sends:
To whom he sends, and what's his Embassie.
Your selfe, held precious in the worlds esteeme,
To parlee with the sole inheritour
Of all perfections that a man may owe,
Matchlesse *Nauarre*, the plea of no lesse weight
Then *Aquitaine*, a Dowrie for a Queene.
Be now as prodigall of all deare grace,
As Nature was in making Graces deare,
When she did starue the generall world beside,
And prodigally gaue them all to you.

Queen. Good L. *Boyet*, my beauty though but mean,
Needs not the painted flourish of your praise:
Beauty is bought by iudgement of the eye,
Not vttred by base sale of chapmens tongues:
I am lesse proud to heare you tell my worth,
Then you much wiling to be counted wise,
In spending your wit in the praise of mine.
But now to taske the tasker, good *Boyet*,

Prin. You are not ignorant all-telling fame
Doth noyse abroad *Nauar* hath made a vow,
Till painefull studie shall out-weare three yeares,
No woman may approach his silent Court:
Therefore to's seemeth it a needfull course,
Before we enter his forbidden gates,
To know his pleasure, and in that behalfe
Bold of your worthinesse, we single you,
As our best mouing faire soliciter:
Tell him, the daughter of the King of France,
On serious businesse crauing quicke dispatch,
Importunes personall conference with his grace.
Haste, signifie so much while we attend,
Like humble visag'd suters his high will.

Boy. Proud of imployment, willingly I goe. *Exit.*

Prin. All pride is willing pride, and yours is so:
Who are the Votaries my louing Lords, that are vow-fellowes with this vertuous Duke?

Lor. *Longauill* is one.

Prin. Know you the man?

1 Lady. I know him Madame at a marriage feast,
Betweene L. *Perigort* and the beautious heire
Of *Iaques Fauconbridge* solemnized.
In *Normandie* saw I this *Longauill*,
A man of soueraigne parts he is esteem'd:
Well fitted in Arts, glorious in Armes:
Nothing becomes him ill that he would well.
The onely soyle of his faire vertues glosse,
If vertues glosse will staine with any soile,
Is a sharp wit match'd with too blunt a Will:
Whose edge hath power to cut whose will still willes,
It should none spare that come within his power.

Prin. Some merry mocking Lord belike, ist so?

Lad. 1. They say so most, that most his humors know.

Prin. Such short liu'd wits do wither as they grow.
Who are the rest?

2. Lad. The yong *Dumaine*, a well accomplisht youth,
Of all that Vertue loue, for Vertue loued.
Most power to doe most harme, least knowing ill:
For he hath wit to make an ill shape good,
And shape to win grace though she had no wit.
I saw him at the Duke *Alansoes* once,
And much too little of that good I saw,
Is my report to his great worthinesse.

Rossa. Another of these Students at that time,
Was there with him, as I haue heard a truth.
Berowne they call him, but a merrier man,
Within the limit of becomming mirth,
I neuer spent an houres talke withall.
His eye begets occasion for his wit,
For euery obiect that the one doth catch,
The other turnes to a mirth-mouing iest.
Which his faire tongue (conceits expositor)
Deliuers in such apt and gracious words,
That aged eares play treuant at his tales,
And yonger hearings are quite rauished.
So sweet and voluble is his discourse.

Prin. God blesse my Ladies, are they all in loue?
That euery one her owne hath garnished,
With such bedecking ornaments of praise.

Ma. Heere comes *Boyet*.

Enter Boyet.

Prin. Now, what admittance Lord?

Boyet. *Nauar* had notice of your faire approach,
And he and his competitors in oath,
Were all addrest to meete you gentle Lady
Before I came: Marrie thus much I haue learnt,
He rather meanes to lodge you in the field,
Like one that comes heere to besiege his Court,
Then seeke a dispensation for his oath:
To let you enter his vnpeopled house.

Enter Nauar, Longauill, Dumaine, and Berowne.

Heere comes *Nauar*.

Nau. Faire Princesse, welcom to the Court of *Nauar*.

Prin. Faire I giue you backe againe, and welcome I haue not yet: the roofe of this Court is too high to bee yours, and welcome to the wide fields, too base to be mine.

Nau. You shall be welcome Madam to my Court.

Prin. I wil be welcome then, Conduct me thither.

Nau. Heare me deare Lady, I haue sworne an oath.

Prin. Our Lady helpe my Lord, he'll be forsworne.

Nau. Not for the world faire Madam, by my will.

Prin. Why, will shall breake it will, and nothing els.

Nau. Your Ladiship is ignorant what it is.

Prin. Were my Lord so, his ignorance were wise,
Where now his knowledge must proue ignorance.
I heare your grace hath sworne out Houseekeeping:
'Tis deadly sinne to keepe that oath my Lord,
And sinne to breake it:
But pardon me, I am too sodaine bold,
To teach a Teacher ill beseemeth me.
Vouchsafe to read the purpose of my comming,
And sodainly resolue me in my suite.

Nau. Madam, I will, if sodainly I may.

Prin. You will the sooner that I were away,
For you'll proue periur'd if you make me stay.

Berow. Did not I dance with you in *Brabant* once?

Rosa. Did not I dance with you in *Brabant* once?

Ber. I know you did.
Rosa. How needlesse was it then to aske the question?
Ber. You must not be so quicke.
Rosa. 'Tis long of you y ̄ spur me with such questions.
Ber. Your wit's too hot, it speeds too fast, 'twill tire.
Rosa. Not till it leaue the Rider in the mire.
Ber. What time a day?
Rosa. The howre that fooles should aske.
Ber. Now faire befall your maske.
Rosa. Faire fall the face it couers.
Ber. And send you many louers.
Rosa. Amen, so you be none.
Ber. Nay then will I be gone.

Kin. Madame, your father heere doth intimate,
The paiment of a hundred thousand Crownes,
Being but th'one halfe, of an intire summe,
Disbursed by my father in his warres,
But say that he, or we, as neither haue
Receiu'd that summe; yet there remaines vnpaid
A hundred thousand more: in surety of the which,
One part of *Aquitaine* is bound to vs,
Although not valued to the moneys worth.
If then the King your father will restore
But that one halfe which is vnsatisfied,
We will giue vp our right in *Aquitaine*,
And hold faire friendship with his Maiestie:
But that it seemes he little purposeth,
For here he doth demand to haue repaie,
An hundred thousand Crownes, and not demands
One paiment of a hundred thousand Crownes,
To haue his title liue in *Aquitaine*.
Which we much rather had depart withall,
And haue the money by our father lent,
Then *Aquitane*, so guelded as it is.
Deare Princesse, were not his requests so farre
From reasons yeelding, your faire selfe should make
A yeelding 'gainst some reason in my brest,
And goe well satisfied to *France* againe.

Prin. You doe the King my Father too much wrong,
And wrong the reputation of your name,
In so vnseeming to confesse receyt
Of that which hath so faithfully beene paid.

Kin. I doe protest I neuer heard of it,
And if you proue it, Ile repay it backe,
Or yeeld vp *Aquitaine*.

Prin. We arrest your word:
Boyet, you can produce acquittances
For such a summe, from speciall Officers,
Of *Charles* his Father.

Kin. Satisfie me so.

Boyet. So please your Grace, the packet is not come
Where that and other specialties are bound,
To morrow you shall haue a sight of them.

Kin. It shall suffice me; at which enteruiew,
All liberall reason would I yeeld vnto:
Meane time, receiue such welcome at my hand,
As Honour, without breach of Honour may
Make tender of, to thy true worthinesse.
You may not come faire Princesse in my gates,
But heere without you shall be so receiu'd,
As you shall deeme your selfe lodg'd in my heart,
Though so deni'd farther harbour in my house:
Your owne good thoughts excuse me, and farewell,
To morrow we shall visit you againe.

Prin. Sweet health & faire desires consort your grace.

Kin. Thy own wish wish I thee, in euery place. *Exit.*

Boy. Lady, I will commend you to my owne heart.
La.Ro. Pray you doe my commendations,
I would be glad to see it.
Boy. I would you heard it grone.
La.Ro. Is the soule sicke?
Boy. Sicke at the heart.
La.Ro. Alacke, let it bloud.
Boy. Would that doe it good?
La.Ro. My Phisicke saies I.
Boy. Will you prick't with your eye.
La.Ro. No poynt, with my knife.
Boy. Now God saue thy life.
La.Ro. And yours from long liuing.
Ber. I cannot stay thanks-giuing. *Exit.*

Enter Dumane.

Dum. Sir, I pray you a word: What Lady is that same?
Boy. The heire of *Alanson*, *Rosalin* her name.
Dum. A gallant Lady, Mounsier fare you well.
Long. I beseech you a word: what is she in the white?
Boy. A woman somtimes, if you saw her in the light.
Long. Perchance light in the light: I desire her name.
Boy. Shee hath but one for her selfe,
To desire that were a shame.
Long. Pray you sir, whose daughter?
Boy. Her Mothers, I haue heard.
Long. Gods blessing a your beard.
Boy. Good sir be not offended,
Shee is an heyre of *Faulconbridge*.
Long. Nay, my choller is ended:
Shee is a most sweet Lady. *Exit.Long.*
Boy. Not vnlike sir, that may be.

Enter Beroune.

Ber. What's her name in the cap.
Boy. *Katherine* by good hap.
Ber. Is she wedded, or no.
Boy. To her will sir, or so.
Ber. You are welcome sir, adiew.
Boy. Fare well to me sir, and welcome to you. *Exit.*
La.Ma. That last is *Beroune*, the mery mad-cap Lord.
Not a word with him, but a iest.
Boy. And euery iest but a word.
Pri. It was well done of you to take him at his word.
Boy. I was as willing to grapple, as he was to boord.
La.Ma. Two hot Sheepes marie:
And wherefore not Ships? (lips.
Boy. No Sheepe (sweet Lamb) vnlesse we feed on your
La. You Sheep & I pasture: shall that finish the iest?
Boy. So you grant pasture for me.
La. Not so gentle beast.
My lips are no Common, though seuerall they be.
Bo. Belonging to whom?
La. To my fortunes and me.
Prin. Good wits wil be iangling, but gentles agree.
This ciuill warre of wits were much better vsed
On *Nauar* and his bookemen, for heere 'tis abus'd.
Bo. If my obseruation (which very seldome lies
By the hearts still rhetoricke, disclosed with eyes)
Deceiue me not now, *Nauar* is infected.
Prin. With what?
Bo. With that which we Louers intitle affected.
Prin. Your reason.
Bo. Why all his behauiours doe make their retire,
To the court of his eye, peeping thorough desire.
His hart like an Agot with your print impressed,

Proud

Proud with his forme, in his eie pride expressed.
His tongue all impatient to speake and not see,
Did stumble with haste in his eie-sight to be,
All sences to that sence did make their repaire,
To feele onely looking on fairest of faire:
Me thought all his sences were lockt in his eye,
As Iewels in Christall for some Prince to buy. (glass,
Who tendring their own worth from whence they were
Did point out to buy them along as you past.
His faces owne margent did coate such amazes,
That all eyes saw his eies inchanted with gazes.
Ile giue you *Aquitaine*, and all that is his,
And you giue him for my sake, but one louing Kisse.

  Prin. Come to our Pauillion, *Boyet* is disposde.

  Bro. But to speak that in words, which his eie hath dis-
I onelie haue made a mouth of his eie, (clos'd.
By adding a tongue, which I know will not lie.

  Lad. Ro. Thou art an old Loue-monger, and speakest skilfully.

  Lad. Ma. He is *Cupids* Grandfather, and learnes news of him.

  Lad. 2. Then was *Venus* like her mother, for her father is but grim.

  Boy. Do you heare my mad wenches?

  La. 1. No.

  Boy. What then, do you see?

  Lad. 2. I, our way to be gone.

  Boy. You are too hard for me. *Exeunt omnes.*

Actus Tertius.

Enter Broggart and Boy.
  Song.

  Bra. Warble childe, make passionate my sense of hearing.

  Boy. Concolinel.

  Brag. Sweete Ayer, go tendernesse of yeares: take this Key, giue enlargement to the swaine, bring him festinatly hither: I must imploy him in a letter to my Loue.

  Boy. Will you win your loue with a French braule?

  Bra. How meanest thou, brauling in French?

  Boy. No my compleat master, but to Iigge off a tune at the tongues end, canarie to it with the feete, humour it with turning vp your eie: sigh a note and sing a note, sometime through the throate: if you swallowed loue with singing, loue sometime through: nose as if you snuft vp loue by smelling loue with your hat penthouse-like ore the shop of your eies, with your armes crost on your thinbellie doublet, like a Rabbet on a spit, or your hands in your pocket, like a man after the old painting, and keepe not too long in one tune, but a snip and away: these are complements, these are humours, these betraie nice wenches that would be betraied without these, and make them men of note: do you note men that most are affected to these?

  Brag. How hast thou purchased this experience?

  Boy. By my penne of obseruation.

  Brag. But O, but O.

  Boy. The Hobbie-horse is forgot.

  Bra. Cal'st thou my loue Hobbi-horse.

  Boy. No Master, the Hobbie-horse is but a Colt, and and your Loue perhaps, a Hacknie:

But haue you forgot your Loue?

  Brag. Almost I had.

  Boy. Negligent student, learne her by heart.

  Brag. By heart, and in heart Boy.

  Boy. And out of heart Master: all those three I will proue.

  Brag. What wilt thou proue?

  Boy. A man, if I liue (and this) by, in, and without, vpon the instant: by heart you loue her, because your heart cannot come by her: in heart you loue her, because your heart is in loue with her: and out of heart you loue her, being out of heart that you cannot enioy her.

  Brag. I am all these three.

  Boy. And three times as much more, and yet nothing at all.

  Brag. Fetch hither the Swaine, he must carrie mee a letter.

  Boy. A message well simpathis'd, a Horse to be embassadour for an Asse.

  Brag. Ha, ha, What saiest thou?

  Boy. Marrie sir, you must send the Asse vpon the Horse for he is verie slow gated: but I goe.

  Brag. The way is but short, away.

  Boy. As swift as Lead sir.

  Brag. Thy meaning prettie ingenious, is not Lead a mettall heauie, dull, and slow?

  Boy. Minnime honest Master, or rather Master no.

  Brad. I say Lead is slow.

  Boy. You are too swift sir to say so.
Is that Lead slow which is fir'd from a Gunne?

  Brag. Sweete smoke of Rhetorike,
He reputes me a Cannon, and the Bullet that's he:
I shoote thee at the Swaine.

  Boy. Thump then, and I flee.

  Bra. A most acute iuuenall, voluble and free of grace,
By thy fauour sweet Welkin, I must sigh in thy face.
Most rude melancholie, Valour giues thee place.
My Herald is return'd.

Enter Page and Clowne.

  Pag. A wonder Master, here's a *Costard* broken in a shin.

  Ar. Some enigma, some riddle, come, thy *Lenuoy* begin.

  Clo. No egma, no riddle, no *lenuoy*, no salue, in thee male sir. Or sir, Plantan, a plaine Plantan: no *lenuoy*, no *lenuoy*, no Salue sir, but a Plantan.

  Ar. By vertue thou inforcest laughter, thy sillie thought, my spleene, the heauing of my lunges prouokes me to rediculous smyling: O pardon me my stars, doth the inconsiderate take *salue* for *lenuoy*, and the word *lenuoy* for a *salue*?

  Pag. Doe the wise thinke them other, is not *lenuoy* a *salue*? (plaine,

  Ar. No *Page*, it is an epilogue or discourse to make some obscure precedence that hath tofore bin saine.
Now will I begin your morrall, and do you follow with my *lenuoy*.

  The Foxe, the Ape, and the Humble-Bee,
    Were still at oddes, being but three.

  Arm. Vntill the Goose came out of doore,
    Staying the oddes by adding foure.

  Pag. A good *Lenuoy*, ending in the Goose: would you desire more?

  Clo. The Boy hath sold him a bargaine, a Goose, that's flat

Sir, your penny-worth is good, and your Goose be fat.
To sell a bargaine well is as cunning as fast and loose:
Let me see a fat L'enuoy, I that's a fat Goose.

  Ar. Come hither, come hither:
How did this argument begin?
  Boy. By saying that a Costard was broken in a shin.
Then cal'd you for the L'enuoy.
  Clow. True, and I for a Plantan:
Thus came your argument in:
Then the Boyes fat L'enuoy, the Goose that you bought,
And he ended the market.
  Ar. But tell me: How was there a Costard broken in a shin?
  Pag. I will tell you sencibly.
  Clow. Thou hast no feeling of it Moth,
I will speake that L'enuoy.
I Costard running out, that was safely within,
Fell ouer the threshold, and broke my shin.
  Arm. We will talke no more of this matter.
  Clow. Till there be more matter in the shin.
  Arm. Sirra Costard, I will infranchise thee.
  Clow. O, marrie me to one Francis, I smell some L'enuoy, some Goose in this.
  Arm. By my sweete soule, I meane, setting thee at libertie. Enfreedoming thy person: thou wert emured, restrained, captiuated, bound.
  Clow. True, true, and now you will be my purgation, and let me loose.
  Arm. I giue thee thy libertie, set thee from durance, and in lieu thereof, impose on thee nothing but this: Beare this significant to the countrey Maide Iaquenetta: there is remuneration, for the best ward of mine honours is rewarding my dependants. Moth, follow.
  Pag. Like the sequell I,
Signeur Costard adew.   Exit.
  Clow. My sweete ounce of mans flesh, my in-conie Iew: Now will I looke to his remuneration. Remuneration, O, that's the Latine word for three-farthings: Three-farthings remuration, What's the price of this yncle? i.d.no, Ile giue you a remuneration: Why? It carries it remuneration: Why? It is a fairer name then a French-Crowne. I will neuer buy and sell out of this word.

Enter Berowne.

  Ber. O my good knaue Costard, exceedingly well met.
  Clow. Pray you sir, How much Carnation Ribbon may a man buy for a remuneration?
  Ber. What is a remuneration?
  Cost. Marrie sir, halfe pennie farthing.
  Ber. O, Why then threefarthings worth of Silke.
  Cost. I thanke your worship, God be wy you.
  Ber. O stay slaue, I must employ thee:
As thou wilt win my fauour, good my knaue,
Doe one thing for me that I shall intreate.
  Clow. When would you haue it done sir?
  Ber. O this after-noone.
  Clo. Well, I will doe it sir: Fare you well.
  Ber. O thou knowest not what it is.
  Clo. I shall know sir, when I haue done it.
  Ber. Why villaine thou must know first.
  Clo. I wil come to your worship to morrow merning.
  Ber. It must be done this after-noone,
Harke slaue, it is but this:
The Princesse comes to hunt here in the Parke,
And in her traine there is a gentle Ladie:
When tongues speak sweetly, then they name her name,
And Rosaline they call her, aske for her:
And to her white hand see thou do commend
This seal'd-vp counsaile. Ther's thy guerdon: goe.
  Clo. Gardon, O sweete gardon, better then remuneration, a leuenpence-farthing better: most sweete gardon. I will doe it sir in print: gardon, remuneration.
                                                              Exit.

  Ber. O, and I forsooth in loue,
I that haue beene loues whip?
A verie Beadle to a humerous sigh: A Criticke,
Nay, a night-watch Constable.
A domineering pedant ore the Boy,
Then whom no mortall so magnificent.
This wimpled, whyning, purblinde waiward Boy,
This signior Iunios gyant dwarfe, don Cupid,
Regent of Loue-rimes, Lord of folded armes,
Th'annointed soueraigne of sighes and groanes:
Liedge of all loyterers and malecontents:
Dread Prince of Placcats, King of Codpeeces.
Sole Emperator and great generall
Of trotting Parrators (O my little heart.)
And I to be a Corporall of his field,
And weare his colours like a Tumblers hoope.
What? I loue, I sue, I seeke a wife,
A woman that is like a Germane Cloake,
Still a repairing: euer out of frame,
And neuer going a right, being a Watch:
But being watcht, that it may still goe right.
Nay, to be periurde, which is worst of all:
And among three, to loue the worst of all,
A whitly wanton, with a veluet brow.
With two pitch bals stucke in her face for eyes.
I, and by heauen, one that will doe the deede,
Though Argus were her Eunuch and her garde.
And I to sigh for her, to watch for her,
To pray for her, go to: it is a plague
That Cupid will impose for my neglect,
Of his almighty dreadfull little might.
Well, I will loue, write, sigh, pray, shue, grone,
Some men must loue my Lady, and some Ione.

Actus Quartus.

Enter the Princesse, a Forrester, her Ladies, and her Lords.

  Qu. Was that the King that spurd his horse so hard,
Against the steepe vprising of the hill?
  Boy. I know not, but I thinke it was not he.
  Qu. Who ere a was, a shew'd a mounting minde:
Well Lords, to day we shall haue our dispatch,
On Saterday we will returne to France.
Then Forrester my friend, Where is the Bush
That we must stand and play the murtherer in?
  For. Hereby vpon the edge of yonder Coppice,
A Stand where you may make the fairest shoote.
  Qu. I thanke my beautie, I am faire that shoote,
And thereupon thou speak'st the fairest shoote.
  For. Pardon me Madam, for I meant not so.
  Qu. What, what? First praise me, & then againe say no.
O short liu'd pride. Not faire? alacke for woe.
                                                              For. Yes

For. Yes Madam faire.
Qu. Nay, neuer paint me now,
Where faire is not, praise cannot mend the brow.
Here (good my glasse) take this for telling true:
Faire paiment for foule words, is more then due.

For. Nothing but faire is that which you inherit.
Qu. See, see, my beautie will be sau'd by merit.
O heresie in faire, fit for these dayes,
A giuing hand, though foule, shall haue faire praise.
But come, the Bow: Now Mercie goes to kill,
And shooting well, is then accounted ill:
Thus will I saue my credit in the shoote,
Not wounding, pittie would not let me do't:
If wounding, then it was to shew my skill,
That more for praise, then purpose meant to kill.
And out of question, so it is sometimes:
Glory growes guiltie of detested crimes,
When for Fames sake, for praise an outward part,
We bend to that, the working of the hart.
As I for praise alone now seeke to spill
The poore Deeres blood, that my heart meanes no ill.

Boy. Do not curst wiues hold that selfe-soueraigntie
Onely for praise sake, when they striue to be
Lords ore their Lords?
Qu. Onely for praise, and praise we may afford,
To any Lady that subdewes a Lord.

Enter Clowne.

Boy. Here comes a member of the common-wealth.
Clo. God dig-you-den all, pray you which is the head Lady?
Qu. Thou shalt know her fellow, by the rest that haue no heads.
Clo. Which is the greatest Lady, the highest?
Qu. The thickest, and the tallest.
Clo. The thickest, & the tallest: it is so, truth is truth.
And your waste Mistris, were as slender as my wit,
One a these Maides girdles for your waste should be fit.
Are not you the chiefe womã? You are the thickest here?
Qu. What's your will sir? What's your will?
Clo. I haue a Letter from Monsier *Berowne*,
To one Lady *Rosaline*.
Qu. O thy letter, thy letter: He's a good friend of mine.
Stand a side good bearer.
Boyet, you can carue,
Breake vp this Capon.
Boyet. I am bound to serue.
This Letter is mistooke: it importeth none here:
It is writ to *Iaquenetta*.
Qu. We will reade it, I sweare.
Breake the necke of the Waxe, and euery one giue eare.

Boyet reades.

BY heauen, that thou art faire, is most infallible: true that thou art beauteous, truth it selfe that thou art louely: more fairer then faire, beautifull then beautious, truer then truth it selfe: haue comiseration on thy heroicall Vassall. The magnanimous and most illustrate King *Cophetua* set eie vpon the pernicious and indubitate Begger *Zenelophon*: and he it was that might rightly say, *Veni, vidi, vici*: Which to annothanize in the vulgar, O base and obscure vulgar; *videlicet*, He came, See, and ouercame: hee came one; see, two; ouercame three: Who came? the King. Why did he come? to see. Why did he see? to ouercome. To whom came he? to the Begger. What saw he? the Begger. Who ouercame he? the Begger. The conclusion is victorie: On whose side? the King: the captiue is inricht: On whose side? the Beggers. The catastrophe is a Nuptiall: on whose side? the Kings: no, on both in one, or one in both. I am the King (for so stands the comparison) thou the Begger, for so witnesseth thy lowlinesse. Shall I command thy loue? I may. Shall I enforce thy loue? I could. Shall I entreate thy loue? I will. What, shalt thou exchange for ragges, roabes: for tittles titles, for thy selfe mee. Thus expecting thy reply, I prophane my lips on thy foote, my eyes on thy picture, and my heart on thy euerie part.

Thine in the dearest designe of industrie,

Don *Adriana de Armatho*.

Thus dost thou heare the Nemean Lion roare,
Gainst thee thou Lambe, that standest as his pray:
Submissiue fall his princely feete before,
And he from forrage will incline to play.
But if thou striue (poore soule) what art thou then?
Foode for his rage, repasture for his den.

Qu. What plume of feathers is hee that indited this Letter? What veine? What Wethercocke? Did you euer heare better?
Boy. I am much deceiued, but I remember the stile.
Qu. Else your memorie is bad, going ore it erewhile.
Boy. This *Armado* is a *Spaniard* that keeps here in court
A Phantasime, a Monarcho, and one that makes sport
To the Prince and his Booke-mates.
Qu. Thou fellow, a word.
Who gaue thee this Letter?
Clow. I told you, my Lord.
Qu. To whom should'st thou giue it?
Clo. From my Lord to my Lady.
Qu. From which Lord, to which Lady?
Clo. From my Lord *Berowne*, a good master of mine,
To a Lady of *France*, that he call'd *Rosaline*.
Qu. Thou hast mistaken his letter. Come Lords away.
Here sweete, put vp this, 'twill be thine another day. *Exeunt.*

Boy. Who is the shooter? Who is the shooter?
Rosa. Shall I teach you to know.
Boy. I my continent of beautie.
Rosa. Why she that beares the Bow. Finely put off.
Boy. My Lady goes to kill hornes, but if thou marrie,
Hang me by the necke, if hornes that yeare miscarrie.
Finely put on.
Rosa. Well then, I am the shooter.
Boy. And who is your Deare?
Rosa. If we choose by the hornes, your selfe come not neare. Finely put on indeede.
Maria. You still wrangle with her *Boyet*, and shee strikes at the brow.
Boyet. But she her selfe is hit lower:
Haue I hit her now.
Rosa. Shall I come vpon thee with an old saying, that was a man when King *Pippin* of *France* was a little boy, as touching the hit it.
Boyet. So I may answere thee with one as old that was a woman when Queene *Guinouer* of *Brittaine* was a little wench, as touching the hit it.
Rosa. Thou

Rosa. Thou canst not hit it, hit it, hit it,
Thou canst not hit it my good man.

Boy. I cannot, cannot, cannot:
And I cannot, another can. *Exit.*

Clo. By my troth most pleasant, how both did fit it.

Mar. A marke marueilous well shot, for they both did hit.

Boy. A mark, O marke but that marke: a marke saies my Lady.
Let the mark haue a pricke in't, to meat at, if it may be.

Mar. Wide a'th bow hand, yfaith your hand is out.

Clo. Indeede a'must shoote nearer, or heele ne're hit the clout.

Boy. And if my hand be out, then belike your hand is in.

Clo. Then will shee get the vpshoot by cleauing the is in.

Ma. Come, come, you talke greasely, your lips grow foule.

Clo. She's too hard for you at pricks, sir challenge her to boule.

Boy. I feare too much rubbing: good night my good Oule.

Clo. By my soule a Swaine, a most simple Clowne.
Lord, Lord, how the Ladies and I haue put him downe.
O my troth most sweete iests, most inconie vulgar wit,
When it comes so smoothly off, so obscenely, as it were, so fit.
Armathor ath to the side, O a most dainty man.
To see him walke before a Lady, and to beare her Fan.
To see him kisse his hand, and how most sweetly a will sweare:
And his Page atother side, that handfull of wit,
Ah heauens, it is most patheticall nit.
Sowla, sowla. *Exeunt.*

Shoote within.

Enter Dull, Holofernes, the Pedant and Nathaniel.

Nat. Very reuerent sport truely, and done in the testimony of a good conscience.

Ped. The Deare was (as you know) sanguis in blood, ripe as a Pomwater, who now hangeth like a Iewell in the eare of *Celo* the skie; the welken the heauen, and anon falleth like a Crab on the face of *Terra*, the soyle, the land, the earth.

Curat. Nath. Truely M. *Holofernes*, the epythithes are sweetly varied like a scholler at the least: but sir I assure ye, it was a Bucke of the first head.

Hol. Sir *Nathaniel*, haud credo.

Dul. 'Twas not a haud credo, 'twas a Pricket.

Hol. Most barbarous intimation: yet a kinde of insinuation, as it were *in via*, in way of explication *facere*: as it were replication, or rather *ostentare*, to show as it were his inclination after his vndressed, vnpolished, vneducated, vnpruned, vntrained, or rather vnlettered, or rather est vnconfirmed fashion, to insert againe my *haud credo* for a Deare.

Dul. I said the Deare was not a *haud credo*, 'twas a Pricket.

Hol. Twice sod simplicitie, *bis coctus*, O thou monster Ignorance, how deformed doost thou looke.

Nath. Sir hee hath neuer fed of the dainties that are bred in a booke.
He hath not eate paper as it were;
He hath not drunke inke.

His intellect is not replenished, hee is onely an animall, onely sensible in the duller parts: and such barren plants are set before vs, that we thankfull should be: which we taste and feeling, are for those parts that doe fructifie in vs more then he.
For as it would ill become me to be vaine, indiscreet, or a foole;
So were there a patch set on Learning, to see him in a Schoole.
But *omne bene* say I, being of an old Fathers minde,
Many can brooke the weather, that loue not the winde.

Dul. You two are book-men: Can you tell by your wit, What was a month old at *Cains* birth, that's not fiue weekes old as yet?

Hol. Dictisima goodman *Dull, dictisima* goodman *Dull.*

Dul. What is *dictima*?

Nath. A title to *Phebe*, to *Luna*, to the *Moone*.

Hol. The Moone was a month old when *Adam* was no more. (score.
And wrought not to fiue-weekes when he came to fiue-
Th'allusion holds in the Exchange.

Dul. 'Tis true indeede, the Collusion holds in the Exchange.

Hol. God comfort thy capacity, I say th'allusion holds in the Exchange.

Dul. And I say the polusion holds in the Exchange: for the Moone is neuer but a month old: and I say beside that, 'twas a Pricket that the Princesse kill'd.

Hol. Sir *Nathaniel*, will you heare an extemporall Epytaph on the death of the Deare, and to humour the ignorant call'd the Deare, the Princesse kill'd a Pricket.

Nath. Perge, good M. *Holofernes, perge*, so it shall please you to abrogate scurilitie.

Hol I will something affect the letter, for it argues facilitie.

> The prayfull Princesse pearst and pricks
>   a prettie pleasing Pricket,
> Some say a Sore, but not a sore,
>   till now made sore with shooting.
> The Dogges did yell, put ell to Sore,
>   then Sorell iumps from thicket:
> Or Pricket-sore, or else Sorell,
>   the people fall a hooting.
> If Sore be sore, then ell to Sore,
>   makes fiftie sores O forell:
> Of one sore I an hundred make
>   by adding but one more L.

Nath. A rare talent.

Dul. If a talent be a claw, looke how he clawes him with a talent.

Nath. This is a gift that I haue simple: simple, a foolish extrauagant spirit, full of formes, figures, shapes, obiects, Ideas, apprehensions, motions, reuolutions. These are begot in the ventricle of memorie, nourisht in the wombe of primater, and deliuered vpon the mellowing of occasion: but the gift is good in those in whom it is acute, and I am thankfull for it.

Hol. Sir, I praise the Lord for you, and so may my parishioners, for their Sonnes are well tutor'd by you, and their Daughters profit very greatly vnder you: you are a good member of the common-wealth.

Nath. Me herele, If their Sonnes be ingennous, they shall

shall want no instruction: If their Daughters be capable, I will put it to them. But *Vir sapis qui pauca loquitur*, a soule Feminine saluteth vs.

Enter Iaquenetta and the Clowne.

Iaqu. God giue you good morrow M. *Person.*
Nath. Master Person, *quasi* Person? And if one should be perst, Which is the one?
Clo. Marry M. Schoolemaster, hee that is likest to a hogshead.
Nath. Of persing a Hogshead, a good luster of conceit in a turph of Earth, Fire enough for a Flint, Pearle enough for a Swine: 'tis prettie, it is well.
Iaqu. Good Master Parson be so good as reade mee this Letter, it was giuen mee by *Costard*, and sent mee from *Don Armatho*: I beseech you reade it.
Nath. Facile precor gellida, quando pecas omnia sub vmbra ruminat, and so forth. Ah good old *Mantuan*, I may speake of thee as the traueiler doth of *Venice, vemchie, vencha, que non te vnde, que non te perresche.* Old *Mantuam*, old *Mantuan*. Who vnderstandeth thee not, *vt re sol la mi fa*: Vnder pardon sir, What are the contents? or rather as *Horrace* sayes in his, What my soule verses.
Hol. I sir, and very learned.
Nath. Let me heare a staffe, a stanze, a verse, *Lege domine.*

If Loue make me forsworne, how shall I sweare to loue?
Ah neuer faith could hold, if not to beautie vowed.
Though to my selfe forsworn, to thee Ile faithfull proue.
Those thoughts to mee were Okes, to thee like Osiers bowed.
Studie his byas leaues, and makes his booke thine eyes,
Where all those pleasures liue, that Art would comprehend.
If knowledge be the marke, to know thee shall suffice.
Well learned is that tongue, that well can thee comend.
All ignorant that soule, that sees thee without wonder.
Which is to me some praise, that I thy parts admire;
Thy eye *Ioues* lightning beares, thy voyce his dreadfull thunder.
Which not to anger bent, is musique, and sweet fire.
Celestiall as thou art, Oh pardon loue this wrong,
That sings heauens praise, with such an earthly tongue.

Ped. You finde not the apostraphas, and so misse the accent. Let me superuise the cangenet.
Nath. Here are onely numbers ratified, but for the elegancy, facility, & golden cadence of poesie *caret*: *Oviddius Naso* was the man. And why in deed *Naso*, but for smelling out the odoriferous flowers of fancy? the ierkes of inuention imitarie is nothing: So doth the Hound his master, the Ape his keeper, the tyred Horse his rider: But *Damosella virgin*, Was this directed to you?
Iaq. I sir from one mounsier *Berowne*, one of the strange Queenes Lords.
Nath. I will ouerglance the superscript.
To the snow-white hand of the most beautious Lady Rosaline.
I will looke againe on the intellect of the Letter, for the nomination of the partie written to the person written vnto.
Your Ladiships in all desired imployment, Berowne.
Per. Sir *Holofernes*, this *Berowne* is one of the Votaries with the King, and here he hath framed a Letter to a sequent of the stranger Queenes: which accidentally, or by the way of progression, hath miscarried. Trip and goe my sweete, deliuer this Paper into the hand of the King, it may concerne much: stay not thy complement, I forgiue thy duetie, adue.
Maid. Good *Costard* go with me:
Sir God saue your life.
Cost. Haue with thee my girle. *Exit.*
Hol. Sir you haue done this in the feare of God very religiously: and as a certaine Father saith
Ped. Sir tell not me of the Father, I do feare colourable colours. But to returne to the Verses, Did they please you sir *Nathaniel*?
Nath. Marueilous well for the pen.
Peda. I do dine to day at the fathers of a certaine Pupill of mine, where if (being repast) it shall please you to gratifie the table with a Grace, I will on my priuiledge I haue with the parents of the foresaid Childe or Pupill, vndertake your *bien vonuto*, where I will proue those Verses to be very vnlearned, neither sauouring of Poetrie, Wit, nor Inuention. I beseech your Societie.
Nat. And thanke you to: for societie (saith the text) is the happinesse of life.
Peda. And certes the text most infallibly concludes it. Sir I do inuite you too, you shall not say me nay: *pauca verba*.
Away, the gentles are at their game, and we will to our recreation. *Exeunt.*

Enter Berowne with a Paper in his hand, alone.

Bero. The King he is hunting the Deare,
I am coursing my selfe.
They haue pitcht a Toyle, I am toyling in a pytch, pitch that defiles; defile, a foule word: Well, set thee downe sorrow; for so they say the foole said, and so say I, and I the foole: Well proued wit. By the Lord this Loue is as mad as *Aiax*, it kils sheepe, it kils mee, I a sheepe: Well proued againe a my side. I will not loue; if I do hang me: yfaith I will not. O but her eye: by this light, but for her eye, I would not loue her; yes, for her two eyes. Well, I doe nothing in the world but lye, and lye in my throate. By heauen I doe loue, and it hath taught mee to Rime, and to be mallicholie: and here is part of my Rime, and heere my mallicholie. Well, she hath one a'my Sonnets already, the Clowne bore it, the Foole sent it, and the Lady hath it: sweet Clowne, sweeter Foole, sweetest Lady. By the world, I would not care a pin, if the other three were in. Here comes one with a paper, God giue him grace to grone.

He stands aside. *The King entreth.*
Kin. Ay mee!
Ber. Shot by heauen: proceede sweet *Cupid*, thou hast thumpt him with thy Birdbolt vnder the left pap: in faith secrets.
King. So sweete a kisse the golden Sunne giues not,
To those fresh morning drops vpon the Rose,
As thy eye beames, when their fresh rayse haue smot.
The night of dew that on my cheekes downe flowes.
Nor shines the siluer Moone one halfe so bright,
Through the transparent bosome of the deepe,
As doth thy face through teares of mine giue light:
Thou shin'st in euery teare that I doe weepe,
No drop, but as a Coach doth carry thee:
So ridest thou triumphing in my woe.
Do but behold the teares that swell in me,
And they thy glory through my griefe will show:

But

But doe not loue thy selfe, then thou wilt keepe
My teares for glasses, and still make me weepe.
O Queene of Queenes, how farre dost thou excell,
No thought can thinke, nor tongue of mortall tell.
How shall she know my griefes? Ile drop the paper.
Sweet leaues shade folly. Who is he comes heere?

Enter Longauile. The King steps aside.

What *Longauill*, and reading: listen eare.

Ber. Now in thy likenesse, one more foole appeare.

Long. Ay me, I am forsworne.

Ber. Why he comes in like a periure, wearing papers.

Long. In loue I hope, sweet fellowship in shame.

Ber. One drunkard loues another of the name.

Lon. Am I the first y haue been periur'd so? (know,

Ber. I could put thee in comfort, not by two that I
Thou makest the triumphery, the corner cap of societie,
The shape of Loues Tiburne, that hangs vp simplicitie.

Lon. I feare these stubborn lines lack power to moue.
O sweet *Maria*, Empresse of my Loue,
These numbers will I teare, and write in prose.

Ber. O, Rimes are gards on wanton *Cupids* hose,
Disfigure not his Shop.

Lon. This same shall goe. *He reades the Sonnet.*
Did not the heauenly Rhetoricke of thine eye,
'Gainst whom the world cannot hold argument,
Perswade my heart to this false periurie?
Vowes for thee broke deserue not punishment.
A Woman I forswore, but I will proue,
Thou being a Goddesse, I forswore not thee.
My Vow was earthly, thou a heauenly Loue.
Thy grace being gain'd, cures all disgrace in me.
Vowes are but breath, and breath a vapour is.
Then thou faire Sun, which on my earth doest shine,
Exhalest this vapor-vow, in thee it is:
If broken then, it is no fault of mine:
If by me broke, What foole is not so wise,
To loose an oath, to win a Paradise?

Ber. This is the liuer veine, which makes flesh a deity.
A greene Goose, a Goddesse, pure pure Idolatry.
God amend vs, God amend, we are much out o'th' way.

Enter Dumaine.

Lon. By whom shall I send this (company?) Stay.

Bero. All hid, all hid, an old infant play,
Like a demie God, here sit I in the skie,
And wretched fooles secrets heedfully ore-eye.
More Sacks to the myll. O heauens I haue my wish,
Dumaine transform'd, foure Woodcocks in a dish.

Dum. O most diuine *Kate*.

Bero. O most prophane coxcombe.

Dum. By heauen the wonder of a mortall eye.

Bero. By earth she is not, corporall, there you lye.

Dum. Her Amber haires for foule hath amber coted.

Ber. An Amber coloured Rauen was well noted.

Dum. As vpright as the Cedar.

Ber. Stoope I say, her shoulder is with-child.

Dum. As faire as day.

Ber. I as some daies, but then no sunne must shine.

Dum. O that I had my wish?

Lon. And I had mine.

Kin. And mine too good Lord.

Ber. Amen, so I had mine: Is not that a good word?

Dum. I would forget her, but a Feuer she
Raignes in my bloud, and will remembred be.

Ber. A Feuer in your bloud, why then incision
Would let her out in Sawcers, sweet misprision.

Dum. Once more Ile read the Ode that I haue writ.

Ber. Once more Ile marke how Loue can varry Wit.

Dumane reades his Sonnet.

On a day, alack the day:
Loue, whose Month is euery May,
Spied a blossome passing faire,
Playing in the wanton ayre:
Through the Veluet, leaues the winde,
All vnseene, can passage finde,
That the Louer sicke to death,
Wish himselfe the heauens breath.
Ayre (quoth he) thy cheekes may blowe,
Ayre, would I might triumph so.
But alacke my hand is sworne,
Nere to plucke thee from thy throne:
Vow alacke for youth vnmeete,
Youth so apt to plucke a sweet.
Doe not call it sinne in me,
That I am forsworne for thee.
Thou for whom Ioue would sweare,
Iuno but an Æthiop were,
And denie himselfe for Ioue.
Turning mortall for thy Loue.

This will I send, and something else more plaine.
That shall expresse my true-loues fasting paine.
O would the *King*, *Berowne* and *Longauill*,
Were Louers too, ill to example ill,
Would from my forehead wipe a periur'd note:
For none offend, where all alike doe dote.

Lon. *Dumaine*, thy Loue is farre from charitie,
That in Loues griefe desir'st societie:
You may looke pale, but I should blush I know,
To be ore-heard, and taken napping so.

Kin. Come sir, you blush: as his, your case is such,
You chide at him, offending twice as much.
You doe not loue *Maria*? *Longauile*,
Did neuer Sonnet for her sake compile;
Nor neuer lay his wreathed armes athwart
His louing bosome, to keepe downe his heart.
I haue beene closely shrowded in this bush,
And markt you both, and for you both did blush.
I heard your guilty Rimes, obseru'd your fashion:
Saw sighes reeke from you, noted well your passion.
Aye me, sayes one! O *Ioue*, the other cries!
On her haires were Gold, Christall the others eyes.
You would for Paradise breake Faith and troth,
And *Ioue* for your Loue would infringe an oath.
What will *Berowne* say when that he shall heare
Faith infringed, which such zeale did sweare.
How will he scorne? how will he spend his wit?
How will he triumph, leape, and laugh at it?
For all the wealth that euer I did see,
I would not haue him know so much by me.

Bero. Now step I forth to whip hypocrisie.
Ah good my Liedge, I pray thee pardon me.
Good heart, What grace hast thou thus to reproue
These wormes for louing, that art most in loue?
Your eyes doe make no couches in your teares.
There is no certaine Princesse that appeares.
You'll not be periur'd, 'tis a hatefull thing:
Tush, none but Minstrels like of Sonnetting.
But are you not asham'd? nay, are you not

All three of you, to be thus much ore'shot?
You found his Moth, the King your Moth did see:
But I a Beame doe finde in each of three.
O what a Scene of fool'ry haue I seene.
Of sighes, of grones, of sorrow, and of teene:
O me, with what strict patience haue I sat,
To see a King transformed to a Gnat?
To see great *Hercules* whipping a Gigge,
And profound *Salomon* tuning a Iygge?
And *Nestor* play at push-pin with the boyes,
And *Critticke Tymon* laugh at idle toyes.
Where lies thy griefe? O tell me good *Dumaine*;
And gentle *Longauill*, where lies thy paine?
And where my Liedges? all about the brest:
 A Candle hoa!
 Kin. Too bitter is thy iest.
Are wee betrayed thus to thy ouer-view?
 Ber. Not you by me, but I betrayed to you.
I that am honest, I that hold it sinne
To breake the vow I am ingaged in.
I am betrayed by keeping company
With men, like men of inconstancie.
When shall you see me write a thing in rime?
Or grone for *Ioane*? or spend a minutes time,
In pruning mee, when shall you heare that I will praise a hand, a foot, a face, an eye: a gate, a state, a brow, a brest, a waste, a legge, a limme.
 Kin. Soft, Whither a-way so fast?
A true man, or a theefe, that gallops so.
 Ber. I post from Loue, good Louer let me go.

 Enter Iaquenetta and Clowne.
 Iaqu. God blesse the King.
 Kin. What Present hast thou there?
 Clo. Some certaine treason.
 Kin. What makes treason heere?
 Clo. Nay it makes nothing sir.
 Kin. If it marre nothing neither,
The treason and you goe in peace away together.
 Iaqu. I beseech your Grace let this Letter be read,
Our person mis-doubts it: it was treason he said.
 Kin. Berowne, read it ouer.   *He reades the Letter.*
 Kin. Where hadst thou it?
 Iaqu. Of *Costard*.
 King. Where hadst thou it?
 Cost. Of *Dun Adramadio, Dun Adramadio*.
 Kin. How now, what is in you? why dost thou tear it?
 Ber. A toy my Liedge, a toy: your grace needes not feare it.
 Long. It did moue him to passion, and therefore let's heare it.
 Dum. It is *Berowns* writing, and heere is his name.
 Ber. Ah you whoreson loggerhead, you were borne to doe me shame.
Guilty my Lord, guilty: I confesse, I confesse.
 Kin. What?
 Ber. That you three fooles, lackt mee foole, to make vp the messe.
He, he, and you: and you my Liedge, and I,
Are picke-purses in Loue, and we deserue to die.
O dismisse this audience, and I shall tell you more.
 Dum. Now the number is euen.
 Berow. True true, we are sowre: will these Turtles be gone?
 Kin. Hence sirs, away.
 Clo. Walk aside the true folke, & let the traytors stay.

 Ber. Sweet Lords, sweet Louers, O let vs imbrace,
As true we are as flesh and bloud can be,
The Sea will ebbe and flow, heauen will shew his face:
Young bloud doth not obey an old decree,
We cannot crosse the cause why we are borne:
Therefore of all hands must we be forsworne.
 King. What, did these rent lines shew some loue of thine?   (*Rosaline.*
 Ber. Did they, quoth you? Who sees the heauenly
That (like a rude and sauage man of *Inde*,)
At the first opening of the gorgeous East,
Bowes not his vassall head, and strooken blinde,
Kisses the base ground with obedient brest?
What peremptory Eagle-sighted eye
Dares looke vpon the heauen of her brow,
That is not blinded by her maiestie?
 Kin. What zeale, what furie, hath inspir'd thee now?
My Loue (her Mistres) is a gracious Moone,
Shee (an attending Starre) scarce seene a light.
 Ber. My eyes are then no eyes, nor I *Berowne*.
O, but for my Loue, day would turne to night,
Of all complexions the cul'd soueraignty,
Doe meet as at a faire in her faire cheeke,
Where seuerall Worthies make one dignity,
Where nothing wants, that want it selfe doth seeke.
Lend me the flourish of all gentle tongues,
Fie painted Rethoricke, O she needs it not,
To things of sale, a sellers praise belongs:
She passes prayse, then prayse too short doth blot.
A withered Hermite, fiuescore winters worne,
Might shake off fiftie, looking in her eye:
Beauty doth varnish Age, as if new borne,
And giues the Crutch the Cradles infancie.
O 'tis the Sunne that maketh all things shine.
 King. By heauen, thy Loue is blacke as Ebonie.
 Berow. Is Ebonie like her? O word diuine?
A wife of such wood were felicitie.
O who can giue an oth? Where is a booke?
That I may sweare Beauty doth beauty lacke,
If that she learne not of her eye to looke:
No face is faire that is not full so blacke.
 Kin. O paradoxe, Blacke is the badge of hell,
The hue of dungeons, and the Schoole of night:
And beauties crest becomes the heauens well.
 Ber. Diuels soonest tempt resembling spirits of light.
O if in blacke my Ladies browes be deckt,
It mournes, that painting vsurping haire
Should rauish doters with a false aspect:
And therfore is she borne to make blacke, faire.
Her fauour turnes the fashion of the dayes,
For natiue bloud is counted painting now:
And therefore red that would auoyd dispraise,
Paints it selfe blacke, to imitate her brow.
 Dum. To look like her are Chimny-sweepers blacke.
 Lon. And since her time, are Colliers counted bright.
 King. And Æthiops of their sweet complexion crake.
 Dum. Dark needs no Candles now, for dark is light.
 Ber. Your mistresses dare neuer come in raine,
For feare their colours should be washt away.
 Kin. 'Twere good yours did: for sir to tell you plaine,
Ile finde a fairer face not washt to day.
 Ber. Ile proue her faire, or talke till dooms-day here.
 Kin. No Diuell will fright thee then so much as shee.
 Duma. I neuer knew man hold vile stuffe so deere.
 Lon. Looke, heer's thy loue, my foot and her face see.
 Ber. O if the streets were paued with thine eyes,

Her feet were much too dainty for such tread.

Duma. O vile, then as she goes what vpward lyes?
The street should see as she walk'd ouer head.

Kin. But what of this, are we not all in loue?

Ber. O nothing so sure, and thereby all forsworne.

Kin. Then leaue this chat, & good *Berown* now proue
Our louing lawfull, and our fayth not torne.

Dum. I marie there, some flattery for this euill.

Long. O some authority how to proceed,
Some tricks, some quillets, how to cheat the diuell.

Dum. Some salue for periurie.

Ber. O 'tis more then neede.
Haue at you then affections men at armes,
Consider what you first did sweare vnto:
To fast, to study, and to see no woman:
Flat treason against the Kingly state of youth.
Say, Can you fast? your stomacks are too young:
And abstinence ingenders maladies.
And where that you haue vow'd to studie (Lords)
In that each of you haue forsworne his Booke.
Can you still dreame and pore, and thereon looke.
For when would you my Lord, or you, or you,
Haue found the ground of studies excellence,
Without the beauty of a womans face;
From womens eyes this doctrine I deriue,
They are the Ground, the Bookes, the Achademes,
From whence doth spring the true *Promethean* fire.
Why, vniuersall plodding poysons vp
The nimble spirits in the arteries,
As motion and long during action tyres
The sinnowy vigour of the trauailer.
Now for not looking on a womans face,
You haue in that forsworne the vse of eyes:
And studie too, the causer of your vow.
For where is any Author in the world,
Teaches such beauty as a womans eye:
Learning is but an adiunct to our seife,
And where we are, our Learning likewise is.
Then when our selues we see in Ladies eyes,
With our selues.
Doe we not likewise see our learning there?
O we haue made a Vow to studie, Lords,
And in that vow we haue forsworne our Bookes:
For when would you (my Leege) or you, or you?
In leaden contemplation haue found out
Such fiery Numbers as the prompting eyes,
Of beauties tutors haue inrich'd you with:
Other slow Arts intirely keepe the braine:
And therefore finding barraine practizers,
Scarce shew a haruest of their heauy toyle.
But Loue first learned in a Ladies eyes,
Liues not alone emured in the braine:
But with the motion of all elements,
Courses as swift as thought in euery power,
And giues to euery power a double power,
Aboue their functions and their offices.
It addes a precious seeing to the eye:
A Louers eyes will gaze an Eagle blinde.
A Louers eare will heare the lowest sound.
When the suspicious head of theft is stopt.
Loues feeling is more soft and sensible,
Then are the tender hornes of Cockled Snayles.
Loues tongue proues dainty, *Bachus* grosse in taste,
For Valour, is not Loue a *Hercules*?
Still climing trees in the *Hesporides*.
Subtill as *Sphinx*, as sweet and musicall,

As bright *Apollo's* Lute, strung with his haire.
And when Loue speakes, the voyce of all the Gods,
Make heauen drowsie with the harmonie.
Neuer durst Poet touch a pen to write,
Vntill his Inke were tempred with Loues sighes:
O then his lines would rauish sauage eares,
And plant in Tyrants milde humilitie.
From womens eyes this doctrine I deriue.
They sparcle still the right promethean fire,
They are the Bookes, the Arts, the Achademes,
That shew, containe, and nourish all the world.
Else none at all in ought proues excellent.
Then fooles you were these women to forsweare:
Or keeping what is sworne, you will proue fooles,
For Wisedomes sake, a word that all men loue:
Or for Loues sake, a word that loues all men.
Or for Mens sake, the author of these Women:
Or Womens sake, by whom we men are Men.
Let's once loose our oathes to finde our selues,
Or else we loose our selues, to keepe our oathes:
It is religion to be thus forsworne.
For Charity it selfe fulfills the Law:
And who can seuer loue from Charity.

Kin. Saint *Cupid* then, and Souldiers to the field.

Ber. Aduance your standards, & vpon them Lords.
Pell, mell, downe with them: but be first aduis'd,
In conflict that you get the Sunne of them.

Long. Now to plaine dealing, Lay these glozes by,
Shall we resolue to woe these girles of France?

Kin. And winne them too, therefore let vs deuise,
Some entertainment for them in their Tents.

Ber. First from the Park let vs conduct them thither,
Then homeward euery man attach the hand
Of his faire Mistresse, in the afternoone
We will with some strange pastime solace them:
Such as the shortnesse of the time can shape,
For Reuels, Dances, Maskes, and merry houres,
Fore-runne faire Loue, strewing her way with flowres.

Kin. Away, away, no time shall be omitted,
That will be time, and may by vs be fitted.

Ber. Alone, alone sowed Cockell, reap'd no Corne,
And Iustice alwaies whirles in equall measure:
Light Wenches may proue plagues to men forsworne,
If so, our Copper buyes no better treasure. *Exeunt.*

Actus Quartus.

Enter the Pedant, Curate and Dull.

Pedant. Satis quid sufficit.

Curat. I praise God for you sir, your reasons at dinner haue beene sharpe & sententious: pleasant without scurrillity, witty without affection, audacious without impudency, learned without opinion, and strange without heresie: I did conuerse this *quondam* day with a companion of the Kings, who is intituled, nominated, or called, *Don Adriano de Armatho.*

Ped. Noui hominum tanquam te, His humour is lofty, his discourse peremptorie: his tongue filed, his eye ambitious, his gate maiesticall, and his generall behauiour vaine, ridiculous, and thrasonicall. He is too picked, too spruce, too affected, too odde, as it were, too peregrinat, as I may call it.

Curat. A most singular and choise Epithat,
Draw out his Table-booke.

Peda. He draweth out the thred of his verbositie, finer then the staple of his argument. I abhor such phanaticall phantasims, such insociable and poynt deuise companions, such rackers of ortagriphie, as to speake dout fine, when he should say doubt; det, when he shold pronounce debt; d e b t, not der: he clepeth a Calf, Caufe: halfe, haufe: neighbour *vocatur* nebour; neigh abreuiated ne: this is abhominable, which he would call abhominable: it insinuateth me of infamie: *ne inteligis domine*, to make franticke, lunaticke?

Cura. Laus deo, bene intelligo.

Peda. Bome boon for boon prescian, a little scratcht, 'twil serue.

Enter Bragart, Boy.

Curat. Vides ne quis venit?

Peda. Video, & gaudio.

Brag. Chirra.

Peda. Quari Chirra, not Sirra?

Brag. Men of peace well incountred.

Ped. Most millitarie sir salutation.

Boy. They haue beene at a great feast of Languages, and stolne the scraps.

Clow. O they haue liu'd long on the almes-basket of words. I maruell thy M.hath not eaten thee for a word, for thou art not so long by the head as honorificabilitudinitatibus: Thou art easier swallowed then a flapdragon.

Page. Peace, the peale begins.

Brag. Mounsier, are you not lettred?

Page. Yes, yes, he teaches boyes the Horne-booke: What is Ab speld backward with the horn on his head?

Peda. Ba, *pueritia* with a horne added.

Pag. Ba most seely Sheepe, with a horne: you heare his learning.

Peda. Quis quis, thou Consonant?

Pag. The last of the fiue Vowels if You repeat them, or the fift if I.

Peda. I will repeot them: a e I.

Pag. The Sheepe, the other two concludes it o u.

Brag. Now by the salt waue of the mediteranium, a sweet tutch, a quicke vene we of wit, snip snap, quick & home, it reioyceth my intellect, true wit.

Page. Offered by a childe to an olde man: which is wit-old.

Peda. What is the figure? What is the figure?

Page. Hornes.

Peda. Thou disputes like an Infant: goe whip thy Gigge.

Pag. Lend me your Horne to make one, and I will whip about your Infamie *unum cita* a gigge of a Cuckolds horne.

Clow. And I had but one penny in the world, thou shouldst haue it to buy Ginger bread: Hold, there is the very Remuneration I had of thy Maister, thou halfpenny purse of wit, thou Pidgeon-egge of discretion. O & the heauens were so pleased, that thou wert but my Bastard; What a ioyfull father wouldst thou make mee? Goe to, thou hast it *ad dungil*, at the fingers ends, as they say.

Peda. Oh I smell false Latine, *dunghel* for *unguem*.

Brag. Arts-man preambulat, we will bee singled from the barbarous. Do you not educate youth at the Charg-house on the top of the Mountaine?

Peda. Or *Mons* the hill.

Brag. At your sweet pleasure, for the Mountaine.

Peda. I doe *sans question*.

Bra. Sir, it is the Kings most sweet pleasure and affection, to congratulate the Princesse at her Pauilion, in the *posteriors* of this day, which the rude multitude call the after-noone.

Ped. The *posterior* of the day, most generous sir, is liable, congruent, and measurable for the after-noone: the word is well culd, chose, sweet, and apt I doe assure you sir, I doe assure.

Brag. Sir, the King is a noble Gentleman, and my familiar, I doe assure ye very good friend: for what is inward betweene vs, let it passe. I doe beseech thee remember thy curtesie. I beseech thee apparell thy head: and among other importunate & most serious designes, and of great import indeed too: but let that passe, for I must tell thee it will please his Grace (by the world) sometime to leane vpon my poore shoulder, and with his royall finger thus dallie with my excrement, with my mustachio: but sweet heart let that passe. By the world I recount no fable, some certaine speciall honours it pleaseth his greatnesse to impart to *Armado* a Souldier, a man of trauell, that hath seene the world: but let that passe; the very all of all is: but sweet heart, I do implore secrecie, that the King would haue mee present the Princesse (sweet chucke) with some delightfull ostentation, or show, or pageant, or anticke, or fire-worke: Now, vnderstanding that the Curate and your sweet self are good at such eruptions, and sodaine breaking out of myrth (as it were) I haue acquainted you withall, to the end to craue your assistance.

Peda. Sir, you shall present before her the Nine Worthies. Sir *Holofernes*, as concerning some entertainment of time, some show in the posterior of this day, to bee rendred by our assistants the Kings command: and this most gallant, illustrate and learned Gentleman, before the Princesse: I say none so fit as to present the Nine Worthies.

Curat. Where will you finde men worthy enough to present them?

Peda. Iosua, your selfe: my selfe, and this gallant gentleman *Iudas Machabeus*; this Swaine (because of his great limme or ioynt) shall passe *Pompey* the great, the Page *Hercules*.

Brag. Pardon sir, error: He is not quantitie enough for that Worthies thumb, hee is not so big as the end of his Club.

Peda. Shall I haue audience? he shall present *Hercules* in minoritie: his *enter* and *exit* shall bee strangling a Snake; and I will haue an Apologie for that purpose.

Pag. An excellent deuice: so if any of the audience hisse, you may cry, Well done *Hercules*, now thou crushest the Snake; that is the way to make an offence gracious, though few haue the grace to doe it.

Brag. For the rest of the Worthies?

Peda. I will play three my selfe.

Pag. Thrice worthy Gentleman.

Brag. Shall I tell you a thing?

Peda. We attend.

Brag. We will haue, if this fadge not, an Antique. I beseech you follow.

Ped. Via good-man *Dull*, thou hast spoken no word all this while.

Dull. Nor vnderstood none neither sir.

Ped. Alone, we will employ thee.

Dull. Ile make one in a dance, or so: or I will play on

on the taber to the Worthies, & let them dance the hey.
 Ped. Most *Dull*, honest *Dull*, to our sport away. *Exit.*

Enter Ladies.

 Qu. Sweet hearts we shall be rich ere we depart,
If fairings come thus plentifully in.
A Lady wal'd about with Diamonds: Look you, what I
haue from the louing King.
 Rosa. Madam, came nothing else along with that?
 Qu. Nothing but this: yes as much loue in Rime,
As would be cram'd vp in a sheet of paper
Writ on both sides the leafe, margent and all,
That he was faine to seale on *Cupids* name.
 Rosa. That was the way to make his god-head wax:
For he hath beene fiue thousand yeeres a Boy.
 Kath. I, and a shrewd vnhappy gallowes too.
 Ros. You'll nere be friends with him, a kild your sister.
 Kath. He made her melancholy, sad, and heauy, and
so she died: had she beene Light like you, of such a mer-
rie nimble stirring spirit, she might a bin a Grandam ere
she died. And so may you: For a light heart liues long.
 Ros. What's your darke meaning mouse, of this light
word?
 Kat. A light condition in a beauty darke.
 Ros. We need more light to finde your meaning out.
 Kat. You'll marre the light by taking it in snuffe:
Therefore Ile darkely end the argument.
 Ros. Look what you doe, you doe it stil i'th darke.
 Kat. So do not you, for you are a light Wench.
 Ros. Indeed I waigh not you, and therefore light.
 Ka. You waigh me not, O that's you care not for me.
 Ros. Great reason: for past care, is still past cure.
 Qu. Well bandied both, a set of Wit well played.
But *Rosaline*, you haue a Fauour too?
Who sent it? and what is it?
 Ros. I would you knew.
And if my face were but as faire as yours,
My Fauour were as great, be witnesse this.
Nay, I haue Verses too, I thanke *Berowne*,
The numbers true, and were the numbring too,
I were the fairest goddesse on the ground.
I am compar'd to twenty thousand fairs.
O he hath drawne my picture in his letter.
 Qu. Any thing like?
 Ros. Much in the letters, nothing in the praise.
 Qu. Beauteous as Incke: a good conclusion.
 Kat. Faire as a text B. in a Coppie booke.
 Ros. Ware pensals. How? Let me not die your debtor,
My red Dominicall, my golden letter.
O that your face were full of Oes.
 Qu. A Pox of that iest, and I beshrew all Shrowes:
But *Katherine*, what was sent to you
From faire *Dumaine*?
 Kat. Madame, this Gloue.
 Qu. Did he not send you twaine?
 Kat. Yes Madame: and moreouer,
Some thousand Verses of a faithfull Louer.
A huge translation of hypocrisie,
Vildly compiled, profound simplicitie.
 Mar. This, and these Pearls, to me sent *Longauile*.
The Letter is too long by halfe a mile.
 Qu. I thinke no lesse: Dost thou wish in heart
The Chaine were longer, and the Letter short.
 Mar. I, or I would these hands might neuer part.
 Quee. We are wise girles to mocke our Louers so.
 Ros. They are worse fooles to purchase mocking so.

That same *Berowne* ile torture ere I goe.
O that I knew he were but in by th'weeke,
How I would make him fawne, and begge, and seeke,
And wait the season, and obserue the times,
And spend his prodigall wits in booteles rimes.
And shape his seruice wholly to my deuice,
And make him proud to make me proud that iests.
So pertaunt like would I o'resway his state,
That he shold be my foole, and I his fate.
 Qu. None are so surely caught, when they are catcht,
As Wit turn'd foole, follie in Wisedome hatch'd:
Hath wisedoms warrant, and the helpe of Schoole,
And Wits owne grace to grace a learned Foole?
 Ros. The bloud of youth burns not with such excesse,
As grauities reuolt to wantons be.
 Mar. Follie in Fooles beares not so strong a note,
As fool'ry in the Wise, when Wit doth dote:
Since all the power thereof it doth apply,
To proue by Wit, worth in simplicitie.

Enter Boyet.

 Qu. Heere comes *Boyet*, and mirth in his face.
 Boy. O I am stab'd with laughter, Wher's her Grace?
 Qu. Thy newes *Boyet*?
 Boy. Prepare Madame, prepare.
Arme Wenches arme, incounters mounted are,
Against your Peace, Loue doth approach, disguis'd:
Armed in arguments, you'll be surpriz'd.
Muster your Wits, stand in your owne defence,
Or hide your heads like Cowards, and flie hence.
 Qu. Saint *Dennis* to S. *Cupid*: What are they,
That charge their breath against vs? Say scout say.
 Boy. Vnder the coole shade of a Siccamore,
I thought to close mine eyes some halfe an houre:
When lo to interrupt my purpos'd rest,
Toward that shade I might behold addrest,
The King and his companions: warely
I stole into a neighbour thicket by,
And ouer-heard, what you shall ouer-heare:
That by and by disguis'd they will be heere.
Their Herald is a pretty knauish Page:
That well by heart hath con'd his embassage,
Action and accent did they teach him there,
Thus must thou speake, and thus thy body beare.
And euer and anon they made a doubt,
Presence maiesticall would put him out:
For quoth the King, an Angell shalt thou see:
Yet feare not thou, but speake audaciously.
The Boy reply'd, An Angell is not euill:
I should haue fear'd her, had she beene a deuill.
With that all laugh'd, and clap'd him on the shoulder,
Making the bold wagg by their praises bolder.
One rub'd his elboe thus, and fleer'd, and swore,
A better speech was neuer spoke before.
Another with his finger and his thumb,
Cry'd *via*, we will doo't, come what will come.
The third he caper'd and cried, All goes well.
The fourth turn'd on the toe, and downe he fell:
With that they all did tumble on the ground,
With such a zelous laughter so profound,
That in this spleene ridiculous appeares,
To checke their folly passions solemne teares.
 Quee. But what, but what, come they to visit vs?
 Boy. They do, they do; and are apparel'd thus,
Like *Muscouites*, or *Russians*, as I gesse.
Their purpose is to parlee, to court, and dance,

M 3 And

And euery one his Loue-feat will aduance,
Vnto his seuerall Mistresse: which they'll know
By fauours seuerall, which they did bestow.
  Queen. And will they so? the Gallants shall be taskt:
For Ladies; we will euery one be maskt,
And not a man of them shall haue the grace
Despight of sute, to see a Ladies face.
Hold *Rosaline*, this Fauour thou shalt weare,
And then the King will court thee for his Deare:
Hold, take thou this my sweet, and giue me thine,
So shall *Berowne* take me for *Rosaline*.
And change your Fauours too, so shall your Loues
Woo contrary, deceiu'd by these remoues.
  Rosa. Come on then, weare the fauours most in sight.
  Kath. But in this changing, What is your intent?
  Queen. The effect of my intent is to crosse theirs:
They doe it but in mocking merriment,
And mocke for mocke is onely my intent.
Their seuerall counsels they vnbosome shall,
To Loues mistooke, and so be mockt withall.
Vpon the next occasion that we meete,
With Visages display'd to talke and greete.
  Ros. But shall we dance, if they desire vs too't?
  Quee. No, to the death we will not moue a foot,
Nor to their pen'd speech render we no grace:
But while 'tis spoke, each turne away his face.
  Boy. Why that contempt will kill the keepers heart,
And quite diuorce his memory from his part.
  Quee. Therefore I doe it, and I make no doubt,
The rest will ere come in, if he be out.
Theres no such sport, as sport by sport orethrowne:
To make theirs ours, and ours none but our owne.
So shall we stay mocking entended game,
And they well mockt, depart away with shame. *Sound.*
  Boy. The Trompet sounds, be maskt, the maskers
come.

*Enter Black-moores with musicke, the Boy with a speech,
and the rest of the Lords disguised.*

  Page. All haile, the richest Beauties on the earth.
  Ber. Beauties no richer then rich Taffata.
  Pag. A holy parcell of the fairest dames that euer turn'd
their backes to mortall viewes.
    The Ladies turne their backes to him.
  Ber. Their eyes villaine, their eyes.
  Pag. That euer turn'd their eyes to mortall viewes.
Out
  Boy. True, out indeed.
  Pag. Out of your fauours heauenly spirits vouchsafe
Not to beholde.
  Ber. Once to behold, rogue.
  Pag. Once to behold with your Sunne beamed eyes,
With your Sunne beamed eyes.
  Boy. They will not answer to that Epythite,
You were best call it Daughter beamed eyes.
  Pag. They do not marke me, and that brings me out.
  Bero. Is this your perfectnesse? be gon you rogue.
  Rosa. What would these strangers?
Know their mindes *Boyet.*
If they doe speake our language, 'tis our will
That some plaine man recount their purposes.
Know what they would?
  Boyet. What would you with the Princes?
  Ber. Nothing but peace, and gentle visitation.
  Ros. What would they, say they?

  Boy. Nothing but peace, and gentle visitation.
  Rosa. Why that they haue, and bid them so be gon.
  Boy. She saies you haue it, and you may be gon.
  Kin. Say to her we haue measur'd many miles,
To tread a Measure with you on the grasse.
  Boy. They say that they haue measur'd many a mile,
To tread a Measure with you on this grasse.
  Rosa. It is not so. Aske them how many inches
Is in one mile? If they haue measur'd manie,
The measure then of one is easlie told.
  Boy. If to come hither, you haue measur'd miles,
And many miles: the Princesse bids you tell,
How many inches doth fill vp one mile?
  Ber. Tell her we measure them by weary steps.
  Boy. She heares her selfe.
  Rosa. How manie wearie steps,
Of many wearie miles you haue ore-gone,
Are numbred in the trauell of one mile?
  Bero. We number nothing that we spend for you,
Our dutie is so rich, so infinite,
That we may doe it still without accompt.
Vouchsafe to shew the sunshine of your face,
That we (like sauages) may worship it.
  Rosa. My face is but a Moone and clouded too.
  Kin. Blessed are clouds, to doe as such clouds do.
Vouchsafe bright Moone, and these thy stars to shine,
(Those clouds remooued) vpon our waterie eyne.
  Rosa. O vaine peticioner, beg a greater matter,
Thou now requests but Mooneshine in the water.
  Kin. Then in our measure, vouchsafe but one change.
Thou bidst me begge, this begging is not strange.
  Rosa. Play musicke then: nay you must doe it soone.
Not yet no dance: thus change I like the Moone.
  Kin. Will you not dance? How come you thus e-
stranged?
  Rosa. You tooke the Moone at full, but now shee's
changed?
  Kin. Yet still she is the Moone, and I the Man.
  Rosa. The musick playes, vouchsafe some motion to
it: Our eares vouchsafe it.
  Kin. But your legges should doe it.
  Ros. Since you are strangers, & come here by chance,
Wee'll not be nice, take hands, we will not dance.
  Kin. Why take you hands then?
  Rosa. Onelie to part friends.
Curtsie sweet hearts, and so the Measure ends.
  Kin. More measure of this measure, be not nice.
  Rosa. We can afford no more at such a price.
  Kin. Prise your selues: What buyes your companie?
  Rosa. Your absence onelie.
  Kin. That can neuer be.
  Rosa. Then cannot we be bought: and so adue,
Twice to your Visore, and halfe once to you.
  Kin. If you denie to dance, let's hold more chat.
  Ros. In priuate then.
  Kin. I am best pleas'd with that.
  Be. White handed Mistris, one sweet word with thee.
  Qu. Hony, and Milke, and Suger: there is three.
  Ber. Nay then two treyes, an if you grow so nice
Metheglinne, Wort, and Malmsey; well runne dice:
There's halfe a dozen sweets.
  Qu. Seuenth sweet adue, since you can cogg,
Ile play no more with you.
  Ber. One word in secret.
  Qu. Let it not be sweet.
  Ber. Thou greeu'st my gall.

Qu. Gall, bitter.
Ber. Therefore meete.
Du. Will you vouchsafe with me to change a word?
Mar. Name it.
Dum. Faire Ladie:
Mar. Say you so? Faire Lord:
Take you that for your faire Lady.
Du. Please it you,
As much in priuate, and Ile bid adieu.
Mar. What, was your vizard made without a tong?
Long. I know the reason Ladie why you aske.
Mar. O for your reason, quickly sir, I long.
Long. You haue a double tongue within your mask.
And would affoord my speechlesse vizard halfe.
Mar. Veale quoth the Dutch-man: is not Veale a Calfe?
Long. A Calfe faire Ladie?
Mar. No, a faire Lord Calfe.
Long. Let's part the word.
Mar. No, Ile not be your halfe:
Take all and weane it, it may proue an Oxe.
Long. Looke how you but your selfe in these sharpe mockes.
Will you giue hornes chast Ladie? Do not so.
Mar. Then die a Calfe before your horns do grow.
Lon. One word in priuate with you ere I die.
Mar. Bleat softly then, the Butcher heares you cry.
Boyet. The tongues of mocking wenches are as keen
As is the Razors edge, inuisible:
Cutting a smaller haire then may be seene,
Aboue the sense of sence so sensible:
Seemeth their conference, their conceits haue wings,
Fleeter then arrows, bullets wind, thoght, swifter things
Rosa. Not one word more my maides, breake off, breake off.
Ber. By heauen, all drie beaten with pure scoffe.
King. Farewell madde Wenches, you haue simple wits. *Exeunt.*
Qu. Twentie adieus my frozen Muscouits.
Are these the breed of wits so wondred at?
Boyet. Tapers they are, with your sweete breathes puft out.
Rosa. Wel-liking wits they haue, grosse, grosse, fat, fat.
Qu. O pouertie in wit, Kingly poore flout.
Will they not (thinke you) hang themselues to night?
Or euer but in vizards shew their faces:
This pert *Berowne* was out of count'nance quite.
Rosa. They were all in lamentable cases.
The King was vveeping ripe for a good word.
Qu. *Berowne* did sweare himselfe out of all suite.
Mar. *Dumaine* was at my seruice, and his sword:
No point (quoth I:) my seruant straight vvas mute.
Ka. Lord *Longauill* said I came ore his hart:
And trow you vvhat he call'd me?
Qu. Qualme perhaps.
Kat. Yes in good faith.
Qu. Go sicknesse as thou art.
Ros. Well, better wits haue worne plain statute caps,
But vvil you heare; the King is my loue sworne.
Qu. And quicke *Berowne* hath plighted faith to me.
Kat. And *Longauill* was for my seruice borne.
Mar. *Dumaine* is mine as sure as barke on tree.
Boyet. Madam, and prettie mistresses giue eare,
Immediately they will againe be heere
In their owne shapes: for it can neuer be,
They will digest this harsh indignitie.

Qu. Will they returne?
Boy. They will they will, God knowes,
And leape for ioy, though they are lame with blowes:
Therefore change Fauours, and when they repaire,
Blow like sweet Roses, in this summer aire.
Qu. How blovv? how blovv? Speake to bee vnderstood.
Boy. Faire Ladies maskt, are Roses in their bud:
Dismaskt, their damaske sweet commixture showne,
Are Angels vailing clouds, or Roses blowne.
Qu. Auant perplexitie: What shall vve do,
If they returne in their owne shapes to wo?
Rosa. Good Madam, if by me you'l be aduis'd,
Let's mocke them still as well knowne as disguis'd:
Let vs complaine to them vvhat fooles were heare,
Disguis'd like Muscouites in shapelesse geare:
And wonder what they were, and to what end
Their shallow showes, and Prologue vildely pen'd:
And their rough carriage so ridiculous,
Should be presented at our Tent to vs.
Boyet. Ladies, withdraw: the gallants are at hand.
Quee. Whip to our Tents, as Roes runnes ore Land.
Exeunt.

Enter the King and the rest.

King. Faire sir, God saue you. Wher's the Princesse?
Boy. Gone to her Tent.
Please it your Maiestie command me any seruice to her?
King. That she vouchsafe me audience for one word.
Boy. I will, and so will she, I know my Lord. *Exit.*
Ber. This fellow pickes vp wit as Pigeons pease,
And vtters it againe, when *Ioue* doth please.
He is Wits Pedler, and retailes his Wares,
At Wakes, and Wassels, Meetings, Markets, Faires.
And we that sell by grosse, the Lord doth know,
Haue not the grace to grace it with such show.
This Gallant pins the Wenches on his sleeue.
Had he bin *Adam*, he had tempted *Eue*.
He can carue too, and lispe: Why this is he,
That kist away his hand in courtesie.
This is the Ape of Forme, Monsieur the nice,
That when he plaies at Tables, chides the Dice
In honorable tearmes: Nay he can sing
A meane most meanly, and in Vshering
Mend him who can: the Ladies call him sweete.
The staires as he treads on them kisse his feete.
This is the flower that smiles on euerie one,
To shew his teeth as white as Whales bone.
And consciences that wil not die in debt,
Pay him the dutie of honie-tongued *Boyet*.
King. A blister on his sweet tongue with my hart,
That put *Armathoes* Page out of his part.

Enter the Ladies.

Ber. See where it comes. Behauiour what wer't thou,
Till this madman shew'd thee? And what art thou now?
King. All haile sweet Madame, and faire time of day.
Qu. Faire in all Haile is foule, as I conceiue.
King. Construe my speeches better, if you may.
Qu. Then wish me better, I wil giue you leaue.
King. We came to visit you, and purpose now
To leade you to our Court, vouchsafe it then.
Qu. This field shal hold me, and so hold your vow:
Nor God, nor I, delights in periur'd men.
King. Rebuke me not for that which you prouoke:
The

The vertue of your eie must breake my oth.

Qu. You nickname vertue: vice you should haue spoke:
For vertues office neuer breakes men troth.
Now by my maiden honor, yet as pure
As the vnsallied Lilly, I protest,
A world of torments though I should endure,
I would not yeeld to be your houses guest:
So much I hate a breaking cause to be
Of heauenly oaths, vow'd with integritie.

Kin. O you haue liu'd in desolation heere,
Vnseene, vnuisited, much to our shame.

Qu. Not so my Lord, it is not so I sweare,
We haue had pastimes heere, and pleasant game,
A messe of Russians left vs but of late.

Kin. How Madam? Russians?

Qu. I in truth, my Lord.
Trim gallants, full of Courtship and of state.

Rosa. Madam speake true. it is not so my Lord:
My Ladie (to the manner of the daies)
In curtesie giues vndeseruing praise.
We foure indeed confronted were with foure
In Russia habit: Heere they stayed an houre,
And talk'd apace: and in that houre (my Lord)
They did not blesse vs with one happy word.
I dare not call them fooles; but this I thinke,
When they are thirstie, fooles would faine haue drinke.

Ber. This iest is drie to me. Gentle sweete,
Your wits makes wise things foolish when we greete
With eies best seeing, heauens fierie eie:
By light we loose light; your capacitie
Is of that nature, that to your huge stoore,
Wise things seeme foolish, and rich things but poore.

Ros. This proues you wise and rich: for in my eie

Ber. I am a foole, and full of pouertie.

Ros. But that you take what doth to you belong,
It were a fault to snatch words from my tongue.

Ber. O, I am yours, and all that I possesse.

Ros. All the foole mine.

Ber. I cannot giue you lesse.

Ros. Which of the Vizards what it that you wore?

Ber. Where? when? What Vizard?
Why demand you this?

Ros. There, then, that vizard, that superfluous case,
That hid the worse, and shew'd the better face.

Kin. We are discried,
They'l mocke vs now downeright.

Du. Let vs confesse, and turne it to a iest.

Que. Amaz'd my Lord? Why lookes your Highnes
sadde?

Rosa. Helpe hold his browes, hee'l sound: why looke
you pale?
Sea-sicke I thinke comming from Muscouie.

Ber. Thus poure the stars down plagues for periury.
Can any face of brasse hold longer out?
Heere stand I, Ladie dart thy skill at me,
Bruise me with scorne, confound me with a flout.
Thrust thy sharpe wit quite through my ignorance.
Cut me to peeces with thy keene conceit:
And I will wish thee neuer more to dance,
Nor neuer more in Russian habit waite.
O! neuer will I trust to speeches pen'd,
Nor to the motion of a Schoole-boies tongue.
Nor neuer come in vizard to my friend,
Nor woo in rime like a blind-harpers songue,
Taffata phrases, silken tearmes precise,
Three-pil'd Hyperboles, spruce affection;
Figures pedanticall, these summer flies,
Haue blowne me full of maggot ostentation.
I do forsweare them, and I heere protest,
By this white Gloue (how white the hand God knows)
Henceforth my woing minde shall be exprest
In russet yeas, and honest kersie noes.
And to begin Wench, so God helpe me law,
My loue to thee is sound, *sans* cracke or flaw.

Rosa. Sans, sans, I pray you.

Ber. Yet I haue a tricke
Of the old rage: beare with me, I am sicke.
Ile leaue it by degrees: soft, let vs see,
Write *Lord haue mercie on vs*, on those three,
They are infected, in their hearts it lies:
They haue the plague, and caught it of your eyes:
These Lords are visited, you are not free:
For the Lords tokens on you do I see.

Qu. No, they are free that gaue these tokens to vs.

Ber. Our states are forfeit, seeke not to vndo vs.

Ros. It is not so; for how can this be true,
That you stand forfeit, being those that sue.

Ber. Peace, for I will not haue to do with you.

Ros. Nor shall not, if I do as I intend.

Ber. Speake for your selues, my wit is at an end.

King. Teach vs sweete Madame, for our rude transgression, some faire excuse.

Qu. The fairest is confession.
Were you not heere but euen now, disguis'd?

Kin. Madam, I was.

Qu. And were you well aduis'd?

Kin. I was faire Madam.

Qu. When you then were heere,
What did you whisper in your Ladies eare?

King. That more then all the world I did respect her

Qu. When shee shall challenge this, you will reiect her.

King. Vpon mine Honor no.

Qu. Peace, peace, forbeare:
your oath once broke, you force not to forsweare.

King. Despise me when I breake this oath of mine.

Qu. I will, and therefore keepe it. *Rosaline*,
What did the Russian whisper in your eare?

Ros. Madam, he swore that he did hold me deare
As precious eye-sight, and did value me
Aboue this World: adding thereto moreouer,
That he vvould Wed me, or else die my Louer.

Qu. God giue thee ioy of him: the Noble Lord
Most honorably doth vphold his word.

King. What meane you Madame?
By my life, my troth,
I neuer swore this Ladie such an oth.

Ros. By heauen you did; and to confirme it plaine,
you gaue me this: But take it sir againe.

King. My faith and this, the Princesse I did giue,
I knew her by this Iewell on her sleeue.

Qu. Pardon me sir, this Iewell did she weare,
And Lord *Berowne* (I thanke him) is my deare.
What? Will you haue me, or your Pearle againe?

Ber. Neither of either, I remit both twaine.
I see the tricke on't: Heere was a consent,
Knowing aforehand of our merriment,
To dash it like a Christmas Comedie.
Some carry-tale, some please-man, some slight Zanie,
Some mumble-newes, some trencher-knight, som Dick
That smiles his cheeke in yeares, and knowes the trick
To make my Lady laugh, when she's dispos'd;

Told

Told our intents before: which once disclos'd,
The Ladies did change Fauours; and then we
Following the signes, woo'd but the signe of she.
Now to our periurie, to adde more terror,
We are againe forsworne in will and error.
Much vpon this tis: and might not you
Forestall our sport, to make vs thus vntrue?
Do not you know my Ladies foot by'th squier?
And laugh vpon the apple of her eie?
And stand betweene her backe sir, and the fire,
Holding a trencher, iesting merrilie?
You put our Page out : go, you are alowd.
Die when you will, a smocke shall be your shrowd.
You leere vpon me, do you? There's an eie
Wounds like a Leaden sword.

Boy. Full merrily hath this braue manager, this carreere bene run.

Ber. Loe, he is tilting straight. Peace, I haue don.

Enter Clowne.

Welcome pure wit, thou part'st a faire fray.

Clo. O Lord sir, they would kno,
Whether the three worthies shall come in, or no.

Ber. What, are there but three?

Clo. No sir, but it is vara fine,
For euerie one pursents three.

Ber. And three times thrice is nine.

Clo. Not so sir, vnder correction sir, I hope it is not so.
You cannot beg vs sir, I can assure you sir, we know what
we know : I hope sir three times thrice sir.

Ber. Is not nine.

Clo. Vnder correction sir, wee know where-vntill it
doth amount.

Ber. By Ioue, I alwaies tooke three threes for nine.

Clow. O Lord sir, it were pittie you should get your
liuing by reckning sir.

Ber. How much is it?

Clo. O Lord sir, the parties themselues, the actors sir
will shew where-vntill it doth amount : for mine owne
part, I am (as they say, but to perfect one man in one
poore man) *Pompion* the great sir.

Ber. Art thou one of the Worthies?

Clo. It pleased them to thinke me worthie of *Pompey*
the great : for mine owne part, I know not the degree of
the Worthie, but I am to stand for him.

Ber. Go, bid them prepare. *Exit.*

Clo. We will turne it finely off sir, we wil take some
care.

King. Berowne, they will shame vs :
Let them not approach.

Ber. We are shame-proofe my Lord : and 'tis some
policie, to haue one shew worse then the Kings and his
companie.

Kin. I say they shall not come.

Qu. Nay my good Lord, let me ore-rule you now;
That sport best pleases, that doth least know how.
Where Zeale striues to content, and the contents
Dies in the Zeale of that which it presents :
Their forme confounded, makes most forme in mirth,
When great things labouring perish in their birth.

Ber. A right description of our sport my Lord.

Enter Braggart.

Brag. Annointed, I implore so much expence of thy
royall sweet breath, as will vtter a brace of words.

Qu. Doth this man serue God?

Ber. Why aske you?

Qu. He speak's not like a man of God's making.

Brag. That's all one my faire sweet honie Monarch:
For I protest, the Schoolmaster is exceeding fantasticall:
Too too vaine, too too vaine. But we wil put it (as they
say) to *Fortuna delaguar*, I wish you the peace of minde
most royall cupplement.

King. Here is like to be a good presence of Worthies;
He presents *Hector* of Troy, the Swaine *Pompey* y great,
the Parish Curate *Alexander*, Armadoes Page *Hercules*,
the Pedant *Iudas Machabeus* : And if these foure Worthies in their first shew thriue, these foure will change
habites, and present the other fiue.

Ber. There is fiue in the first shew.

Kin. You are deceiued, tis not so.

Ber. The Pedant, the Braggart, the Hedge-Priest, the
Foole, and the Boy,
Abate throw at *Novum*, and the whole world againe,
Cannot pricke out fiue such, take each one in's vaine.

Kin. The ship is vnder saile, and here she coms amain.

Enter Pompey.

Clo. I *Pompey* am.

Ber. You lie, you are not he.

Clo. I *Pompey* am.

Boy. With Libbards head on knee.

Ber. Well said old mocker,
I must needs be friends with thee.

Clo. I *Pompey* am, *Pompey* surnam'd the big.

Du. The great.

Clo. It is great sir : *Pompey* surnam'd the great :
That oft in field, with Targe and Shield,
  did make my foe to sweat :
And trauailing along this coast, I heere am come by chance,
And lay my Armes before the legs of this sweet Lasse of
France.
If your Ladiship would say thankes *Pompey*, I had done.

La. Great thankes great *Pompey*.

Clo. Tis not so much worth : but I hope I was perfect. I made a little fault in great.

Ber. My hat to a halfe-penie, *Pompey* prooues the
best Worthie.

Enter Curate for Alexander.

Curat. When in the world I liu'd, I was the worldes Com-
mander :
By East, West, North, & South, I spred my conquering might
My Scutcheon plaine declares that I am *Alisander*.

Boiet. Your nose saies no, you are not :
For it stands too right.

Ber. Your nose smels no, in this most tender smelling Knight.

Qu. The Conqueror is dismaid :
Proceede good *Alexander*.

Cur. When in the world I liued, I was the worldes Commander.

Boiet. Most true, 'tis right : you were so *Alisander*.

Ber. Pompey the great.

Clo. your seruant and *Costard*.

Ber. Take away the Conqueror, take away *Alisander*

Clo. O sir, you haue ouerthrowne *Alisander* the conqueror : you will be scrap'd out of the painted cloth for
this.

this: your Lion that holds his Pollax sitting on a close stoole, will be giuen to Aiax. He will be the ninth worthie. A Conqueror, and affraid to speake? Runne away for shame Alisander. There an't shall please you: a foolish milde man, an honest man, looke you, & soon dasht. He is a maruellous good neighbour insooth, and a verie good Bowler: but for Alisander, alas you see, how 'tis a little ore-parted. But there are Worthies a comming, will speake their minde in some other sort. *Exit Cu.*

  Qu. Stand aside good Pompey.

  Enter Pedant for Iudas, and the Boy for Hercules.

  Ped. Great Hercules is presented by this Impe,
Whose Club kil'd Cerberus that three-headed Canus,
And when he was a babe, a childe, a shrimpe,
Thus did he strangle Serpents in his Manus:
Quoniam, he seemeth in minoritie,
Ergo, I come with this Apologie.
Keepe some state in thy exit, and vanish. *Exit Boy*

  Ped. Iudas I am.
  Dum. A Iudas?
  Ped. Not Iscariot sir.
Iudas I am, ycliped Machabeus.
  Dum. Iudas Machabeus clipt, is plaine Iudas.
  Ber. A kissing traitor. How art thou prou'd Iudas?
  Ped. Iudas I am.
  Dum. The more shame for you Iudas.
  Ped. What meane you sir?
  Boi. To make Iudas hang himselfe.
  Ped. Begin sir, you are my elder.
  Ber. Well follow'd, Iudas was hang'd on an Elder.
  Ped. I will not be put out of countenance.
  Ber. Because thou hast no face.
  Ped. What is this?
  Boi. A Citterne head.
  Dum. The head of a bodkin.
  Ber. A deaths face in a ring.
  Lon. The face of an old Roman coine, scarce seene.
  Boi. The pummell of Cæsars Faulchion.
  Dum. The caru'd-bone face on a Flaske.
  Ber. S. Georges halfe cheeke in a brooch.
  Dum. I, and in a brooch of Lead.
  Ber. I, and worne in the cap of a Tooth-drawer.
And now forward, for we haue put thee in countenance
  Ped. You haue put me out of countenance.
  Ber. False, we haue giuen thee faces.
  Ped. But you haue out-fac'd them all.
  Ber. And thou wer't a Lion, we would do so.
  Boy. Therefore as he is, an Asse, let him go:
And so adieu sweet Iude. Nay, why dost thou stay?
  Dum. For the latter end of his name.
  Ber. For the Asse to the Iude: giue it him. Iud-as away.
  Ped. This is not generous, not gentle, not humble.
  Boy. A light for monsieur Iudas, it growes darke, he may stumble.
  Que. Alas poore Machabeus, how hath hee beene baited.

  Enter Braggart.

  Ber. Hide thy head Achilles, heere comes Hector in Armes.
  Dum. Though my mockes come home by me, I will now be merrie.
  King. Hector was but a Troyan in respect of this.
  Boi. But is this Hector?
  Kin. I thinke Hector was not so cleane timber'd.
  Lon. His legge is too big for Hector.
  Dum. More Calfe certaine.
  Boi. No, he is best indued in the small.
  Ber. This cannot be Hector.
  Dum. He's a God or a Painter, for he makes faces.
  Brag. The Armipotent Mars, of Launces the almighty, gaue Hector a gift.
  Dum. A gilt Nutmegge.
  Ber. A Lemmon.
  Lon. Stucke with Cloues.
  Dum. No clouen.
  Brag. The Armipotent Mars of Launces the almighty,
Gaue Hector a gift, the heire of Illion;
A man so breathed, that certaine he would fight: yea
From morne till night, out of his Pauillion.
I am that Flower.
  Dum. That Mint.
  Long. That Cullambine.
  Brag. Sweet Lord Longauill reine thy tongue.
  Lon. I must rather giue it the reine: for it runnes against Hector.
  Dum. I, and Hector's a Grey-hound.
  Brag. The sweet War-man is dead and rotten,
Sweet chuckes, beat not the bones of the buried:
But I will forward with my deuice;
Sweet Royaltie bestow on me the sence of hearing.

  Berowne steppes forth.

  Qu. Speake braue Hector, we are much delighted.
  Brag. I do adore thy sweet Graces slipper.
  Boy. Loues her by the foot.
  Dum. He may not by the yard.
  Brag. This Hector farre surmounted Hanniball.
  The partie is gone.
  Clo. Fellow Hector, she is gone; she is two moneths on her way.
  Brag. What meanest thou?
  Clo. Faith vnlesse you play the honest Troyan, the poore Wench is cast away: she's quick, the child brags in her belly alreadie: tis yours.
  Brag. Dost thou infamonize me among Potentates? Thou shalt die.
  Clo. Then shall Hector be whipt for Iaquenetta that is quicke by him, and hang'd for Pompey, that is dead by him.
  Dum. Most rare Pompey.
  Boi. Renowned Pompey.
  Ber. Greater then great, great, great, great Pompey: Pompey the huge.
  Dum. Hector trembles.
  Ber. Pompey is moued, more Atees more Atees stirre them, or stirre them on.
  Dum. Hector will challenge him.
  Ber. I, if a'haue no more mans blood in's belly, then will sup a Flea.
  Brag. By the North-pole I do challenge thee.
  Clo. I wil not fight with a pole like a Northern man; Ile slash, Ile do it by the sword: I pray you let mee borrow my Armes againe.
  Dum. Roome for the incensed Worthies.
  Clo. Ile do it in my shirt.
  Dum. Most resolute Pompey.
  Page. Master, let me take you a button hole lower:
Do you not see Pompey is vncasing for the combat: what
meane

meane you? you will lose your reputation.

Brag. Gentlemen and Souldiers pardon me, I will not combat in my shirt.

Du. You may not denie it, *Pompey* hath made the challenge.

Brag. Sweet bloods, I both may, and will.

Ber. What reason haue you for't?

Brag. The naked truth of it is, I haue no shirt, I go woolward for penance.

Boy. True, and it was inioyned him in *Rome* for want of Linnen: since when, Ile be sworne he wore none, but a dishclout of *Iaquenettas*, and that hee weares next his heart for a fauour.

Enter a Messenger, Monsieur Marcade.

Mar. God saue you Madame.

Qu. Welcome *Marcade*, but that thou interruptest our merriment.

Marc. I am sorrie Madam, for the newes I bring is heauie in my tongue. The King your father

Qu. Dead for my life.

Mar. Euen so: My tale is told.

Ber. Worthies away, the Scene begins to cloud.

Brag. For mine owne part, I breath free breath: I haue seene the day of wrong, through the little hole of discretion, and I will right my selfe like a Souldier.

Exeunt Worthies

Kin. How fare's your Maiestie?

Qu. Boyet prepare, I will away to night.

Kin. Madame not so, I do beseech you stay.

Qu. Prepare I say. I thanke you gracious Lords
For all your faire endeuours and entreats:
Out of a new sad-soule, that you vouchsafe,
In your rich wisedome to excuse, or hide,
The liberall opposition of our spirits,
If ouer-boldly we haue borne our selues,
In the conuerse of breath (your gentlenesse
Was guiltie of it,) Farewell worthie Lord:
A heauie heart beares not a humble tongue.
Excuse me so, comming so short of thankes,
For my great suite, so easily obtain'd.

Kin. The extreme parts of time, extremelie formes
All causes to the purpose of his speed:
And often at his verie loose decides
That, which long processe could not arbitrate.
And though the mourning brow of progenie
Forbid the smiling curtesie of Loue:
The holy suite which faine it would conuince,
Yet since loues argument was first on foote,
Let not the cloud of sorrow iustle it
From what it purpos'd: since to waile friends lost,
Is not by much so wholsome profitable,
As to reioyce at friends but newly found.

Qu. I vnderstand you not, my greefes are double.

Ber. Honest plain words, best pierce the ears of griefe
And by these badges vnderstand the King,
For your faire sakes haue we neglected time,
Plaid foule play with our oaths: your beautie Ladies
Hath much deformed vs, fashioning our humors
Euen to the opposed end of our intents.
And what in vs hath seem'd ridiculous:
As Loue is full of vnbefitting straines,
All wanton as a childe, skipping and vaine.
Form'd by the eie, and therefore like the eie.
Full of straying shapes, of habits, and of formes
Varying in subiects as the eie doth roule,
To euerie varied obiect in his glance:
Which partie-coated presence of loose loue
Put on by vs, if in your heauenly eies,
Haue misbecom'd our oathes and grauities.
Those heauenlie eies that looke into these faults,
Suggested vs to make: therefore Ladies
Our loue being yours, the error that Loue makes
Is likewise yours. We to our selues proue false,
By being once false, for euer to be true
To those that make vs both, faire Ladies you.
And euen that falshood in it selfe a sinne,
Thus purifies it selfe, and turnes to grace.

Qu. We haue receiu'd your Letters, full of Loue:
Your Fauours, the Ambassadors of Loue.
And in our maiden counsaile rated them,
At courtship, pleasant iest, and curtesie,
As bumbast and as lining to the time:
But more deuout then these are our respects
Haue we not bene, and therefore met your loues
In their owne fashion, like a merriment.

Du. Our letters Madam, shew'd much more then iest.

Lon. So did our lookes.

Rosa. We did not coat them so.

Kin. Now at the latest minute of the houre,
Grant vs your loues.

Qu. A time me thinkes too short,
To make a world-without-end bargaine in:
No, no my Lord, your Grace is periur'd much,
Full of deare guiltinesse, and therefore this:
If for my Loue (as there is no such cause)
You will do ought, this shall you do for me.
Your oth I will not trust: but go with speed
To some forlorne and naked Hermitage,
Remote from all the pleasures of the world:
There stay, vntill the twelue Celestiall Signes
Haue brought about their annuall reckoning,
If this austere insociable life,
Change not your offer made in heate of blood:
If frosts, and fasts, hard lodging, and thin weeds
Nip not the gaudie blossomes of your Loue,
But that it beare this triall, and last loue:
Then at the expiration of the yeare,
Come challenge me, challenge me by these deserts,
And by this Virgin palme, now kissing thine,
I will be thine: and till that instant shut
My wofull selfe vp in a mourning house,
Raining the teares of lamentation,
For the remembrance of my Fathers death.
If this thou do denie, let our hands part,
Neither intitled in the others hart.

Kin. If this, or more then this, I would denie,
To flatter vp these powers of mine with rest,
The sodaine hand of death close vp mine eie.
Hence euer then, my heart is in thy brest.

Ber. And what to me my Loue? and what to me?

Ros. You must be purged too, your sins are rack'd.
You are attaint with faults and periurie:
Therefore if you my fauor meane to get,
A twelue month shall you spend, and neuer rest,
But seeke the wearie beds of people sicke.

Du. But what to me my loue? but what to me?

Kat. A wife? a beard, faire health, and honestie,
With three-fold loue, I wish you all these three.

Du. O shall I say, I thanke you gentle wife?

Kat. Not so my Lord, a twelue month and a day,

Ile marke no words that smoothfac'd wooers say.
Come when the King doth to my Ladie come:
Then if I haue much loue, Ile giue you some.

 Dum. Ile serue thee true and faithfully till then.
 Kath. Yet sweare not, least ye be forsworne agen.
 Lon. What saies *Maria*?
 Mari. At the tweluemonths end,
Ile change my blacke Gowne, for a faithfull friend.
 Lon. Ile stay with patience: but the time is long.
 Mari. The liker you, few taller are so yong.
 Ber. Studies my Ladie? Mistresse, looke on me,
Behold the window of my heart, mine eie:
What humble suite attends thy answer there,
Impose some seruice on me for my loue.
 Rof. Oft haue I heard of you my Lord *Berowne*,
Before I saw you: and the worlds large tongue
Proclaimes you for a man repleate with mockes,
Full of comparisons, and wounding floutes:
Which you on all estates will execute,
That lie within the mercie of your wit.
To weed this Wormewood from your fruitfull braine,
And therewithall to win me, if you please,
Without the which I am not to be won:
You shall this tweluemonth terme from day to day,
Visite the speechlesse sicke, and still conuerse
With groaning wretches: and your taske shall be,
With all the fierce endeuour of your wit,
To enforce the pained impotent to smile.
 Ber. To moue wilde laughter in the throate of death?
It cannot be, it is impossible.
Mirth cannot moue a soule in agonie.
 Rof. Why that's the way to choke a gibing spirit,
Whose influence is begot of that loose grace,
Which shallow laughing hearers giue to fooles:
A iests prosperitie, lies in the eare
Of him that heares it, neuer in the tongue
Of him that makes it: then, if sickly eares,
Deaft with the clamors of their owne deare grones,
Will heare your idle scornes; continue then,
And I will haue you, and that fault withall.
But if they will not, throw away that spirit,
And I shal finde you emptie of that fault,
Right ioysull of your reformation.
 Ber. A tweluemonth? Well: befall what will befall,
Ile iest a tweluemonth in an Hospitall.
 Qu. I sweet my Lord, and so I take my leaue.
 King. No Madam, we will bring you on your way.
 Ber. Our woing doth not end like an old Play:
Iacke hath not Gill: these Ladies courtesie
Might wel haue made our sport a Comedie.
 Kin. Come sir, it wants a tweluemonth and a day,
And then 'twil end.
 Ber. That's too long for a play.

Enter Braggart.
 Brag. Sweet Maiesty vouchsafe me.
 Qu. Was not that Hector?
 Dum. The worthie Knight of Troy.
 Brag. I wil kisse thy royal finger, and take leaue.
I am a Votarie, I haue vow'd to *Iaquenetta* to holde the
Plough for her sweet loue three yeares. But most estee-
med greatnesse, wil you heare the Dialogue that the two
Learned men haue compiled, in praise of the Owle and
the Cuckow? It should haue followed in the end of our
shew.
 Kin. Call them forth quickely, we will do so.
 Brag. Holla, Approach.

Enter all.
This side is *Hiems*, Winter.
This *Ver*, the Spring: the one maintained by the Owle,
Th'other by the Cuckow.
Ver, begin.

The Song.

When Dasies pied, and Violets blew,
And Cuckow-buds of yellow hew:
And Ladie-smockes all siluer white,
Do paint the Medowes with delight.
The Cuckow then on euerie tree,
Mockes married men, for thus sings he,
Cuckow.
Cuckow, Cuckow: O word of feare,
Vnpleasing to a married eare.

When Shepheards pipe on Oaten strawes,
And merrie Larkes are Ploughmens clockes:
When Turtles tread, and Rookes and Dawes,
And Maidens bleach their summer smockes:
The Cuckow then on euerie tree
Mockes married men; for thus sings he,
Cuckow.
Cuckow, Cuckow: O word of feare,
Vnpleasing to a married eare.

Winter.
When Isicles hang by the wall,
And Dicke the Sphepheard blowes his naile;
And Tom beares Logges into the hall,
And Milke comes frozen home in paile:
When blood is nipt, and waies be fowle,
Then nightly sings the staring Owle
Tu-whit to-who.
 A merrie note,
 While greasie Ione doth keele the pot.

When all aloud the winde doth blow,
And coffing drownes the Parsons saw:
And birds sit brooding in the snow,
And Marrians nose lookes red and raw:
When roasted Crabs hisse in the bowle,
Then nightly sings the staring Owle,
Tu-whit to who:
 A merrie note,
 While greasie Ione doth keele the pot.

 Brag. The Words of Mercurie,
Are harsh after the songs of Apollo:
You that way; we this way.

Exeunt omnes.

FINIS.

A MIDSOMMER Nights Dreame.

Actus primus.

Enter Theseus, Hippolita, with others.

Theseus.

Ow faire Hippolita, our nuptiall houre
Drawes on apace: foure happy daies bring in
Another Moon: but oh, me thinkes, how slow
This old Moon wanes; She lingers my desires
Like to a Step-dame, or a Dowager,
Long withering out a yong mans revennew.

Hip. Foure daies wil quickly steep thēselues in nights
Foure nights wil quickly dreame away the time:
And then the Moone, like to a siluer bow,
Now bent in heauen, shal behold the night
Of our solemnities.

The. Go *Philostrate*,
Stirre vp the Athenian youth to merriments,
Awake the pert and nimble spirit of mirth,
Turne melancholy forth to Funerals:
The pale companion is not for our pompe.
Hippolita, I woo'd thee with my sword,
And wonne thy loue, doing thee iniuries:
But I will wed thee in another key,
With pompe, with triumph, and with reuelling.

*Enter Egeus and his daughter Hermia, Lysander,
and Demetrius.*

Ege. Happy be *Theseus*, our renowned Duke.
The. Thanks good *Egeus*: what's the news with thee?
Ege. Full of vexation, come I, with complaint
Against my childe, my daughter Hermia.
Stand forth Demetrius.
My Noble Lord,
This man hath my consent to marrie her.
Stand forth Lysander.
And my gracious Duke,
This man hath bewitch'd the bosome of my childe:
Thou, thou *Lysander*, thou hast giuen her rimes,
And interchang'd loue-tokens with my childe:
Thou hast by Moone-light at her window sung,
With fainting voice, verses of faining loue,
And stolne the impression of her fantasie,
With bracelets of thy haire, rings, gawdes, conceits,
Knackes, trifles, Nose-gaies, sweet meats (messengers
Of strong preuailment in vnhardned youth)
With cunning hast thou filch'd my daughters heart,
Turn'd her obedience (which is due to me)
To stubborne harshnesse. And my gracious Duke,
Be it so she will not heere before your Grace,
Consent to marrie with *Demetrius*,
I beg the ancient priuiledge of Athens;
As she is mine, I may dispose of her;
Which shall be either to this Gentleman,
Or to her death, according to our Law,
Immediately prouided in that case.

The. What say you Hermia? be aduis'd faire Maide,
To you your Father should be as a God;
One that compos'd your beauties; yea and one
To whom you are but as a forme in waxe
By him imprinted: and within his power,
To leaue the figure, or disfigure it:
Demetrius is a worthy Gentleman.

Her. So is *Lysander*.
The. In himselfe he is.
But in this kinde, wanting your fathers voyce,
The other must be held the worthier.
Her. I would my father look'd but with my eyes.
The. Rather your eies must with his iudgment looke.
Her. I do entreat your Grace to pardon me.
I know not by what power I am made bold,
Nor how it may concerne my modestie
In such a presence heere to pleade my thoughts:
But I beseech your Grace, that I may know
The worst that may befall me in this case,
If I refuse to wed *Demetrius*.

The. Either to dye the death, or to abiure
For euer the society of men.
Therefore faire Hermia question your desires,
Know of your youth, examine well your blood,
Whether (if you yeeld not to your fathers choice)
You can endure the liuerie of a Nunne,
For aye to be in shady Cloister mew'd,
To liue a barren sister all your life,
Chanting faint hymnes to the cold fruitlesse Moone,
Thrice blessed they that master so their blood,
To vndergo such maiden pilgrimage,
But earthlier happie is the Rose distil'd,
Then that which withering on the virgin thorne,
Growes, liues, and dies, in single blessednesse.

Her. So will I grow, so liue, so die my Lord,
Ere I will yeeld my virgin Patent vp
Vnto his Lordship, whose vnwished yoake,
My soule consents not to giue soueraignty.

The. Take time to pause, and by the next new Moon
The sealing day betwixt my loue and me,
For euerlasting bond of fellowship:
Vpon that day either prepare to dye,
For disobedience to your fathers will,
Or else to wed *Demetrius* as hee would,
Or on *Dianaes* Altar to protest
For aie, austerity, and single life.

Dem. Relent sweet *Hermia*, and *Lysander*, yeelde
Thy crazed title to my certaine right.

Lys. You haue her fathers loue, *Demetrius*:
Let me haue *Hermiaes*: do you marry him.

Egeus. Scornfull *Lysander*, true, he hath my Loue;
Aud what is mine, my loue shall render him.
And she is mine, and all my right of her,
I do estate vnto *Demetrius*.

Lys. I am my Lord, as well deriu'd as he,
As well possest: my loue is more then his:
My fortunes euery way as fairely rank'd
(If not with vantage) as *Demetrius*:
And (which is more then all these boasts can be)
I am belou'd of beauteous *Hermia*.
Why should not I then prosecute my right?
Demetrius, Ile auouch it to his head,
Made loue to *Nedars* daughter, *Helena*,
And won her soule: and she (sweet Ladie) dotes,
Deuoutly dotes, dotes in Idolatry,
Vpon this spotted and inconstant man.

The. I must confesse, that I haue heard so much,
And with *Demetrius* thought to haue spoke thereof:
But being ouer-full of selfe-affaires,
My minde did lose it. But *Demetrius* come,
And come *Egeus*, you shall go with me,
I haue some priuate schooling for you both.
For you faire *Hermia*, looke you arme your selfe,
To fit your fancies to your Fathers will;
Or else the Law of Athens yeelds you vp
(Which by no meanes we may extenuate)
To death, or to a vow of single life.
Come my *Hippolita*, what cheare my loue?
Demetrius and *Egeus* go along:
I must imploy you in some businesse
Against our nuptiall, and conferre with you
Of something, neerely that concernes your selues.

Ege. With dutie and desire we follow you. *Exeunt*

Manet Lysander and Hermia.

Lys. How now my loue? Why is your cheek so pale?
How chance the Roses there do fade so fast?

Her. Belike for want of raine, which I could well
Beteeme them, from the tempest of mine eyes.

Lys. For ought that euer I could reade,
Could euer heare by tale or historie,
The course of true loue neuer did run smooth,
But either it was different in blood.

Her. O crosse! too high to be enthral'd to loue.

Lys. Or else misgraffed, in respect of yeares.

Her. O spight! too old to be ingag'd to yong.

Lys. Or else it stood vpon the choise of merit.

Her. O hell! to choose loue by anothers eie.

Lys. Or if there were a simpathie in choise,
Warre, death, or sicknesse, did lay siege to it;
Making it momentarie, as a sound:
Swift as a shadow, short as any dreame,
Briefe as the lightning in the collied night,
That (in a spleene) vnfolds both heauen and earth;
And ere a man hath power to say, behold,
The iawes of darknesse do deuoure it vp:
So quicke bright things come to confusion.

Her. If then true Louers haue beene euer crost,
It stands as an edict in destinie:
Then let vs teach our triall patience,
Because it is a customarie crosse,
As due to loue, as thoughts, and dreames, and sighes,
Wishes and teares; poore Fancies followers.

Lys. A good perswasion; therefore heare me *Hermia*,
I haue a Widdow Aunt, a dowager,
Of great reuennew, and she hath no childe,
From Athens is her house remou'd seuen leagues,
And she respects me, as her onely sonne:
There gentle *Hermia*, may I marrie thee,
And to that place, the sharpe Athenian Law
Cannot pursue vs. If thou lou'st me, then
Steale forth thy fathers house to morrow night:
And in the wood, a league without the towne,
(Where I did meete thee once with *Helena*,
To do obseruance for a morne of May)
There will I stay for thee.

Her. My good *Lysander*,
I sweare to thee, by Cupids strongest bow,
By his best arrow with the golden head,
By the simplicitie of Venus Doues,
By that which knitteth soules, and prospers loue,
And by that fire which burn'd the Carthage Queene,
When the false Troyan vnder saile was seene,
By all the vowes that euer men haue broke,
(In number more then euer women spoke)
In that same place thou hast appointed me,
To morrow truly will I meete with thee.

Lys. Keepe promise loue: looke here comes *Helena*.

Enter Helena.

Her. God speede faire *Helena*, whither away?

Hel. Cal you me faire? that faire againe vnsay,
Demetrius loues you faire: O happie faire!
Your eyes are loadstarres, and your tongues sweet ayre
More tuneable then Larke to shepheards eare,
When wheate is greene, when hauthorne buds appeare,
Sicknesse is catching: O were fauor so,
Your words I catch, faire *Hermia* ere I go,
My eare should catch your voice, my eye, your eye,
My tongue should catch your tongues sweet melodie,
Were the world mine, *Demetrius* being bated,
The rest Ile giue to be to you translated.
O teach me how you looke, and with what art
You sway the motion of *Demetrius* hart.

Her. I frowne vpon him, yet he loues me still.

Hel. O that your frownes would teach my smiles such skil.

Her. I giue him curses, yet he giues me loue.

Hel. O that my prayers could such affection mooue.

Her. The more I hate, the more he followes me.

Hel. The more I loue, the more he hateth me.

Her. His folly *Helena* is none of mine.

Hel. None but your beauty, wold that fault wer mine

Her. Take comfort: he no more shall see my face,
Lysander and my selfe will flie this place.
Before the time I did *Lysander* see,
Seem'd Athens like a Paradise to mee.

O then, what graces in my Loue do dwell,
That he hath turn'd a heauen into hell.

Lys. Helen, to you our mindes we will vnfold,
To morrow night, when Phœbe doth behold
Her siluer visage, in the watry glasse,
Decking with liquid pearle, the bladed grasse
(A time that Louers flights doth still conceale)
Through Athens gates, haue we deuis'd to steale.

Her. And in the wood, where often you and I,
Vpon faint Primrose beds, were wont to lye,
Emptying our bosomes, of their counsell sweld:
There my *Lysander*, and my selfe shall meete,
And thence from Athens turne away our eyes
To seeke new friends and strange companions,
Farwell sweet play-fellow, pray thou for vs,
And good lucke grant thee thy *Demetrius*.
Keepe word *Lysander* we must starue our sight,
From louers foode, till morrow deepe midnight.
Exit Hermia.

Lys. I will my *Hermia*, *Helena* adieu,
As you on him, *Demetrius* dotes on you. *Exit Lysander.*

Hele. How happy some, ore othersome can be?
Through Athens I am thought as faire as she.
But what of that? *Demetrius* thinkes not so:
He will not know, what all, but he doth know,
And as hee erres, doting on *Hermias* eyes;
So I, admiring of his qualities:
Things base and vilde, holding no quantity,
Loue can transpose to forme and dignity,
Loue lookes not with the eyes, but with the minde,
And therefore is wing'd *Cupid* painted blinde.
Nor hath loues minde of any iudgement taste:
Wings and no eyes, figure, vnheedy haste.
And therefore is Loue said to be a childe,
Because in choise he is often beguil'd,
As waggish boyes in game themselues forsweare;
So the boy Loue is periur'd euery where.
For ere *Demetrius* lookt on *Hermias* eyne,
He hail'd downe oathes that he was onely mine.
And when this Haile some heat from *Hermia* felt,
So he dissolu'd, and showres of oathes did melt,
I will goe tell him of faire *Hermias* flight:
Then to the wood will he, to morrow night
Pursue her; and for his intelligence,
If I haue thankes, it is a deere expence:
But heerein meane I to enrich my paine,
To haue his sight thither, and backe againe. *Exit.*

Enter Quince the Carpenter, Snug the Ioyner, Bottome the Weauer, Flute the bellowes-mender, Snout the Tinker, and Starueling the Taylor.

Quin. Is all our company heere?

Bot. You were best to call them generally, man by man, according to the scrip.

Qui. Here is the scrowle of euery mans name, which is thought fit through all Athens, to play in our Enterlude before the Duke and the Dutches, on his wedding day at night.

Bot. First, good *Peter Quince*, say what the play treats on: then read the names of the Actors: and so grow on to a point.

Quin. Marry our play is the most lamentable Comedy, and most cruell death of *Pyramus* and *Thisbie*.

Bot. A very good peece of worke I assure you, and a merry. Now good *Peter Quince*, call forth your Actors by the scrowle. Masters spread your selues.

Quince. Answere as I call you. *Nick Bottome* the Weauer.

Bottome. Ready; name what part I am for, and proceed.

Quince. You *Nicke Bottome* are set downe for *Pyramus*.

Bot. What is *Pyramus*, a louer, or a tyrant?

Quin. A Louer that kills himselfe most gallantly for loue.

Bot. That will aske some teares in the true performing of it: if I do it, let the audience looke to their eies: I will mooue stormes; I will condole in some measure. To the rest yet, my chiefe humour is for a tyrant. I could play *Ercles* rarely, or a part to teare a Cat in, to make all split the raging Rocks; and shiuering shocks shall break the locks of prison gates, and *Phibbus* carre shall shine from farre, and make and marre the foolish Fates. This was lofty. Now name the rest of the Players. This is *Ercles* vaine, a tyrants vaine: a louer is more condoling.

Quin. Francis Flute the Bellowes-mender.

Flu. Heere *Peter Quince*.

Quin. You must take *Thisbie* on you.

Flut. What is *Thisbie*, a wandring Knight?

Quin. It is the Lady that *Pyramus* must loue.

Flut. Nay faith, let not mee play a woman, I haue a beard comming.

Qui. That's all one, you shall play it in a Maske, and you may speake as small as you will.

Bot. And I may hide my face, let me play *Thisbie* too: Ile speake in a monstrous little voyce; *Thisne, Thisne*, ah *Pyramus* my louer deare, thy *Thisbie* deare, and Lady deare.

Quin. No no, you must play *Pyramus*, and *Flute*, you *Thisby*.

Bot. Well, proceed.

Qu. Robin Starueling the Taylor.

Star. Heere *Peter Quince*.

Quince. Robin Starueling, you must play *Thisbies* mother?

Tom Snowt, the Tinker.

Snowt. Heere *Peter Quince*.

Quin. You, *Pyramus* father; my self, *Thisbies* father; *Snugge* the Ioyner, you the Lyons part: and I hope there is a play fitted.

Snug. Haue you the Lions part written? pray you if be, giue it me, for I am slow of studie.

Quin. You may doe it *extempore*, for it is nothing but roaring.

Bot. Let mee play the Lyon too, I will roare that I will doe any mans heart good to heare me. I will roare, that I will make the Duke say, Let him roare againe, let him roare againe.

Quin. If you should doe it too terribly, you would fright the Dutchesse and the Ladies, that they would shrike, and that were enough to hang vs all.

All. That would hang vs euery mothers sonne.

Bottome. I graunt you friends, if that you should fright the Ladies out of their Wittes, they would haue no more discretion but to hang vs: but I will aggrauate my voyce so, that I will roare you as gently as any sucking Doue; I will roare and 'twere any Nightingale.

Quin. You can play no part but *Piramus*, for *Piramus*

mus is a sweet-fac'd man, a proper man as one shall see in a summers day; a most louely Gentleman-like man, therfore you must needs play *Piramus*.

Bot. Well, I will vndertake it. What beard were I best to play it in?

Quin. Why, what you will.

Bot. I will discharge it, in either your straw-colour beard, your orange tawnie beard, your purple in graine beard, or your French-crowne colour'd beard, your perfect yellow.

Quin. Some of your French Crownes haue no haire at all, and then you will play bare-fac'd. But masters here are your parts, and I am to intreat you, request you, and desire you, to con them by too morrow night: and meet me in the palace wood, a mile without the Towne, by Moone-light, there we will rehearse: for if we meete in the Citie, we shalbe dog'd with company, and our deuises knowne. In the meane time, I wil draw a bil of properties, such as our play wants. I pray you faile me not.

Bottom. We will meete, and there we may rehearse more obscenely and couragiously. Take paines, be perfect, adieu.

Quin. At the Dukes oake we meete.

Bot. Enough, hold or cut bow-strings. *Exeunt*

Actus Secundus.

Enter a Fairie at one doore, and Robin good-fellow at another.

Rob. How now spirit, whether wander you?

Fai. Ouer hil, ouer dale, through bush, through briar,
Ouer parke, ouer pale, through flood, through fire,
I do wander euerie where, swifter then ỹ Moons sphere;
And I serue the Fairy Queene, to dew her orbs vpon the
The Cowslips tall, her pensioners bee, (greene.
In their gold coats, spots you see,
Those be Rubies, Fairie fauors,
In those freckles, liue their sauors,
I must go seeke some dew drops heere,
And hang a pearle in euery cowslips eare.
Farewell thou Lob of spirits, Ile be gon,
Our Queene and all her Elues come heere anon.

Rob. The King doth keepe his Reuels here to night,
Take heed the Queene come not within his sight,
For *Oberon* is passing fell and wrath,
Because that she, as her attendant, hath
A louely boy stolne from an Indian King,
She neuer had so sweet a changeling,
And iealous *Oberon* would haue the childe
Knight of his traine, to trace the Forrests wilde.
But she (perforce) with-holds the loued boy,
Crownes him with flowers, and makes him all her ioy.
And now they neuer meete in groue, or greene,
By fountaine cleere, or spangled star-light sheene,
But they do square, that all their Elues for feare
Creepe into Acorne cups and hide them there.

Fai. Either I mistake your shape and making quite,
Or else you are that shrew'd and knauish spirit
Cal'd Robin Good-fellow. Are you not hee,
That frights the maidens of the Villagree,
Skim milke, and sometimes labour in the querne,
And bootlesse make the breathlesse huswife cherne,
And sometime make the drinke to beare no barme,
Misleade night-wanderers, laughing at their harme,
Those that Hobgoblin call you, and sweet Pucke,
You do their worke, and they shall haue good lucke.
Are not you he?

Rob. Thou speak'st aright;
I am that merrie wanderer of the night:
I iest to *Oberon*, and make him smile,
When I a fat and beane-fed horse beguile,
Neighing in likenesse of a silly foale,
And sometime lurke I in a Gossips bole,
In very likenesse of a roasted crab:
And when she drinkes, against her lips I bob,
And on her withered dewlop poure the Ale.
The wisest Aunt telling the saddest tale,
Sometime for three-foot stoole, mistaketh me,
Then slip I from her bum, downe topples she,
And tailour cries, and fals into a coffe.
And then the whole quire hold their hips, and losse,
And waxen in their mirth, and neeze, and sweare,
A merrier houre vvas neuer wasted there.
But roome Fairy, heere comes *Oberon*.

Fair. And heere my Mistris:
Would that he vvere gone.

Enter the King of Fairies at one doore with his traine, and the Queene at another with hers.

Ob. Ill met by Moone-light,
Proud *Tytania*.

Qu. What, iealous *Oberon*? Fairy skip hence.
I haue forsworne his bed and companie.

Ob. Tarrie rash Wanton; am not I thy Lord?

Qu. Then I must be thy Lady: but I know
When thou vvast stolne away from Fairy Land,
And in the shape of *Corin*, sate all day,
Playing on pipes of Corne, and versing loue
To amorous *Phillida*. Why art thou heere
Come from the farthest steepe of *India*?
But that forsooth the bouncing *Amazon*
Your buskin'd Mistresse, and your Warrior loue,
To *Theseus* must be Wedded; and you come,
To giue their bed ioy and prosperitie.

Ob. How canst thou thus for shame *Tytania*,
Glance at my credite, vvith *Hippolita*?
Knowing I knovv thy loue to *Theseus*?
Didst thou not leade him through the glimmering night
From *Peregenia*, whom he rauished?
And make him vvith faire Eagles breake his faith
With *Ariadne*, and *Atiopa*?

Que. These are the forgeries of iealousie,
And neuer since the middle Summers spring
Met vve on hil, in dale, forrest, or mead,
By paued fountaine, or by rushie brooke,
Or in the beached margent of the sea,
To dance our ringlets to the whistling Winde,
But vvith thy braules thou hast disturb'd our sport.
Therefore the Windes, piping to vs in vaine,
As in reuenge, haue suck'd vp from the sea
Contagious fogges: Which falling in the Land,
Hath euerie petty Riuer made so proud,
That they haue ouer-borne their Continents.
The Oxe hath therefore stretch'd his yoake in vaine,
The Ploughman lost his sweat, and the greene Corne
Hath rotted, ere his youth attain'd a beard:
The fold stands empty in the drowned field,
And Crowes are fatted vvith the murrion flocke,

The nine mens Morris is fild vp with mud,
And the queint Mazes in the wanton greene,
For lacke of tread are vndistinguishable.
The humane mortals want their winter heere,
No night is now with hymne or caroll blest;
Therefore the Moone (the gouernesse of floods)
Pale in her anger, washes all the aire;
That Rheumaticke diseases doe abound.
And through this distemperature, we see
The seasons alter; hoared headed frosts
Fall in the fresh lap of the crimson Rose,
And on old *Hyems* chinne and Icie crowne,
An odorous Chaplet of sweet Sommer buds
Is as in mockry set. The Spring, the Sommer,
The childing Autumne, angry Winter change
Their wonted Liueries, and the mazed world,
By their increase, now knowes not which is which;
And this same progeny of euills,
Comes from our debate, from our dissention,
We are their parents and originall.

 Ober. Do you amend it then, it lies in you,
Why should *Titania* crosse her *Oberon*?
I do but beg a little changeling boy,
To be my Henchman.

 Qu. Set your heart at rest,
The Fairy land buyes not the childe of me,
His mother was a Votresse of my Order,
And in the spiced *Indian* aire, by night
Full often hath she gossipt by my side,
And sat with me on *Neptunes* yellow sands,
Marking th'embarked traders on the flood,
When we haue laught to see the sailes conceiue,
And grow big bellied with the wanton winde:
Which she with pretty and with swimming gate,
Following (her wombe then rich with my yong squire)
Would imitate, and saile vpon the Land,
To fetch me trifles, and returne againe,
As from a voyage, rich with merchandize.
But she being mortall, of that boy did die,
And for her sake I doe reare vp her boy,
And for her sake I will not part with him.

 Ob. How long within this wood intend you stay?

 Qu. Perchance till after *Theseus* wedding day.
If you will patiently dance in our Round,
And see our Moone-light reuels, goe with vs;
If not, shun me and I will spare your haunts.

 Ob. Giue me that boy, and I will goe with thee.

 Qu. Not for thy Fairy Kingdome. Fairies away:
We shall chide downe right, if I longer stay. *Exeunt.*

 Ob. Wel, go thy way: thou shalt not from this groue,
Till I torment thee for this iniury.
My gentle *Pucke* come hither; thou remembrest
Since once I sat vpon a promontory,
And heard a Meare-maide on a Dolphins backe,
Vttering such dulcet and harmonious breath,
That the rude sea grew ciuill at her song,
And certaine starres shot madly from their Spheares,
To heare the Sea-maids musicke.

 Puc. I remember.

 Ob. That very time I say (but thou couldst not)
Flying betweene the cold Moone and the earth,
Cupid all arm'd; a certaine aime he tooke
At a faire Vestall, throned by the West,
And loos'd his loue-shaft smartly from his bow,
As it should pierce a hundred thousand hearts,
But I might see young *Cupids* fiery shaft

Quencht in the chaste beames of the watry Moone;
And the imperiall Votresse passed on,
In maiden meditation, fancy free.
Yet markt I where the bolt of *Cupid* fell.
It fell vpon a little westerne flower;
Before, milke-white; now purple with loues wound,
And maidens call it, Loue in idlenesse.
Fetch me that flower; the hearb I shew'd thee once,
The iuyce of it, on sleeping eye-lids laid,
Will make or man or woman madly dote
Vpon the next liue creature that it sees.
Fetch me this hearbe, and be thou heere againe,
Ere the *Leuiathan* can swim a league.

 Pucke. Ile put a girdle about the earth, in forty minutes.

 Ober. Hauing once this iuyce,
Ile watch *Titania*, when she is asleepe,
And drop the liquor of it in her eyes:
The next thing when she waking lookes vpon,
(Be it on Lyon, Beare, or Wolfe, or Bull,
On medling Monkey, or on busie Ape)
Shee shall pursue it, with the soule of loue.
And ere I take this charme off from her sight,
(As I can take it with another hearbe)
Ile make her render vp her Page to me.
But who comes heere? I am inuisible,
And I will ouer-heare their conference.

Enter Demetrius, Helena following him.

 Deme. I loue thee not, therefore pursue me not,
Where is *Lysander*, and faire *Hermia*?
The one Ile stay, the other stayeth me.
Thou toldst me they were stolne into this wood;
And heere am I, and wood within this wood,
Because I cannot meet my *Hermia*.
Hence, get thee gone, and follow me no more.

 Hel. You draw me, you hard-hearted Adamant,
But yet you draw not Iron, for my heart
Is true as steele. Leaue you your power to draw,
And I shall haue no power to follow you.

 Deme. Do I entice you? do I speake you faire?
Or rather doe I not in plainest truth,
Tell you I doe not, nor I cannot loue you?

 Hel. And euen for that doe I loue thee the more;
I am your spaniell, and *Demetrius*,
The more you beat me, I will fawne on you.
Vse me but as your spaniell; spurne me, strike me,
Neglect me, lose me; onely giue me leaue
(Vnworthy as I am) to follow you.
What worser place can I beg in your loue,
(And yet a place of high respect with me)
Then to be vsed as you doe your dogge.

 Dem. Tempt not too much the hatred of my spirit,
For I am sicke when I do looke on thee.

 Hel. And I am sicke when I looke not on you.

 Dem. You doe impeach your modesty too much,
To leaue the Citty, and commit your selfe
Into the hands of one that loues you not,
To trust the opportunity of night,
And the ill counsell of a desert place,
With the rich worth of your virginity.

 Hel. Your vertue is my priuiledge: for that
It is not night when I doe see your face.
Therefore I thinke I am not in the night,
Nor doth this wood lacke worlds of company,

For you in my respect are all the world.
Then how can it be said I am alone,
When all the world is heere to looke on me?

Dem. Ile run from thee, and hide me in the brakes,
And leaue thee to the mercy of wilde beasts.

Hel. The wildest hath not such a heart as you;
Runne when you will, the story shall be chang'd:
Apollo flies, and *Daphne* holds the chase;
The Doue pursues the Griffin, the milde Hinde
Makes speed to catch the Tyger. Bootlesse speede,
When cowardise pursues, and valour flies.

Demet. I will not stay thy questions, let me go;
Or if thou follow me, doe not beleeue,
But I shall doe thee mischiefe in the wood.

Hel. I, in the Temple, in the Towne, and Field
You doe me mischiefe. Fye *Demetrius*,
Your wrongs doe set a scandall on my sexe:
We cannot fight for loue, as men may doe;
We should be woo'd, and were not made to wooe.
I follow thee, and make a heauen of hell,
To die vpon the hand I loue so well. *Exit.*

Ob. Fare thee well Nymph, ere he do leaue this groue,
Thou shalt flie him, and he shall seeke thy loue.
Hast thou the flower there? Welcome wanderer.

Enter Pucke.

Puck. I, there it is.

Ob. I pray thee giue it me.
I know a banke where the wilde time blowes,
Where Oxslips and the nodding Violet growes,
Quite ouer-cannoped with luscious woodbine,
With sweet muske roses, and with Eglantine;
There sleepes *Tytania*, sometime of the night,
Lul'd in these flowers, with dances and delight:
And there the snake throwes her enammel'd skinne,
Weed wide enough to rap a Fairy in.
And with the iuyce of this Ile streake her eyes,
And make her full of hatefull fantasies.
Take thou some of it, and seek through this groue;
A sweet *Athenian* Lady is in loue
With a disdainefull youth: annoint his eyes,
But doe it when the next thing he espies,
May be the Lady. Thou shalt know the man,
By the *Athenian* garments he hath on.
Effect it with some care, that he may proue
More fond on her, then she vpon her loue;
And looke thou meet me ere the first Cocke crow.

Pu. Feare not my Lord, your seruant shall do so. *Exit.*

Enter Queene of Fairies, with her traine.

Queen. Come, now a Roundell, and a Fairy song;
Then for the third part of a minute hence,
Some to kill Cankers in the muske rose buds,
Some warre with Reremise, for their leathern wings,
To make my small Elues coates, and some keepe backe
The clamorous Owle that nightly hoots and wonders
At our queint spirits: Sing me now asleepe,
Then to your offices, and let me rest.

Fairies Sing.

You spotted Snakes with double tongue,
Thorny Hedgehogges be not seene,
Newts and blinde wormes do no wrong,
Come not neere our Fairy Queene.
Philomele with melodie,
Sing in your sweet Lullaby,
Lulla, lulla, lullaby, lulla, lulla, lullaby,
Neuer harme, nor spell, nor charme,
Come our louely Lady nye,
So good night with Lullaby.

2. Fairy. Weauing Spiders come not heere,
Hence you long leg'd Spinners, hence:
Beetles blacke approach not neere,
Worme nor Snayle doe no offence.
Philomele with melody, &c.

1. Fairy. Hence away, now all is well;
One aloofe, stand Centinell. *Shee sleepes.*

Enter Oberon.

Ober. What thou seest when thou dost wake,
Doe it for thy true Loue take:
Loue and languish for his sake.
Be it Ounce, or Catte, or Beare,
Pard, or Boare with bristled haire,
In thy eye that shall appeare,
When thou wak'st, it is thy deare,
Wake when some vile thing is neere.

Enter Lisander and Hermia.

Lis. Faire loue, you faint with wandring in y woods,
And to speake troth I haue forgot our way:
Wee'll rest vs *Hermia*, if you thinke it good,
And tarry for the comfort of the day.

Her. Be it so *Lysander*; finde you out a bed,
For I vpon this banke will rest my head.

Lys. One turfe shall serue as pillow for vs both,
One heart, one bed, two bosomes, and one troth.

Her. Nay good *Lysander*, for my sake my deere
Lie further off yet, doe not lie so neere.

Lys. O take the sence sweet, of my innocence,
Loue takes the meaning, in loues conference,
I meane that my heart vnto yours is knit,
So that but one heart can you make of it.
Two bosomes interchanged with an oath,
So then two bosomes, and a single troth.
Then by your side, no bed-roome me deny,
For lying so. *Hermia*, I doe not lye.

Her. Lysander riddles very prettily;
Now much beshrew my manners and my pride,
If *Hermia* meant to say, *Lysander* lied.
But gentle friend, for loue and courtesie
Lie further off, in humane modesty,
Such separation, as may well be said,
Becomes a vertuous batchelour, and a maide,
So farre be distant, and good night sweet friend;
Thy loue nere alter, till thy sweet life end.

Lys. Amen, amen, to that faire prayer, say I,
And then end life, when I end loyalty:
Heere is my bed, sleepe giue thee all his rest.

Her. With halfe that wish, the wishers eyes be prest.

Enter Pucke. *They sleepe.*

Puck. Through the Forrest haue I gone,
But *Athenian* finde I none,
One whose eyes I might approue
This flowers force in stirring loue.
Night and silence: who is heere?
Weedes of *Athens* he doth weare:
This is he (my master said)
Despised the *Athenian* maide:
And heere the maiden sleeping found,

On

A Midsomer nights Dreame.

On the danke and durty ground.
Pretty soule, she durst not lye
Neere this lacke-loue, this kill-curtesie.
Churle, vpon thy eyes I throw
All the power this charme doth owe:
When thou wak'st, let loue forbid
Sleepe his seate on thy eye-lid.
So awake when I am gone:
For I must now to *Oberon*. *Exit.*

Enter Demetrius and Helena running.

Hel. Stay, though thou kill me, sweete *Demetrius*.
De. I charge thee hence, and do not haunt me thus.
Hel. O wilt thou darkling leaue me? do not so.
De. Stay on thy perill, I alone will goe.
Exit Demetrius.

Hel. O I am out of breath, in this fond chace,
The more my prayer, the lesser is my grace,
Happy is *Hermia*, wheresoere she lies;
For she hath blessed and attractiue eyes.
How came her eyes so bright? Not with salt teares.
If so, my eyes are oftner washt then hers.
No, no, I am as vgly as a Beare;
For beasts that meete me, runne away for feare,
Therefore no maruaile, though *Demetrius*
Doe as a monster, flie my presence thus.
What wicked and dissembling glasse of mine,
Made me compare with *Hermias* sphery eyne?
But who is here? *Lysander* on the ground;
Deade or asleepe? I see no bloud, no wound,
Lysander, if you liue, good sir awake.

Lys. And run through fire I will for thy sweet sake.
Transparent *Helena*, nature her shewes art,
That through thy bosome makes me see thy heart.
Where is *Demetrius*? oh how fit a word
Is that vile name, to perish on my sword!

Hel. Do not say so *Lysander*, say not so:
What though he loue your *Hermia*? Lord, what though?
Yet *Hermia* still loues you; then be content.

Lys. Content with *Hermia*? No, I do repent
The tedious minutes I with her haue spent.
Not *Hermia*, but *Helena* now I loue;
Who will not change a Rauen for a Doue?
The will of man is by his reason sway'd:
And reason saies you are the worthier Maide.
Things growing are not ripe vntill their season;
So I being yong, till now ripe not to reason,
And touching now the point of humane skill,
Reason becomes the Marshall to my will,
And leades me to your eyes, where I orelooke
Loues stories, written in Loues richest booke.

Hel. Wherefore was I to this keene mockery borne?
When at your hands did I deserue this scorne?
Ist not enough, ist not enough, yong man,
That I did neuer, no nor neuer can,
Deserue a sweete looke from *Demetrius* eye,
But you must flout my insufficiency?
Good troth you do me wrong (good-sooth you do)
In such disdainfull manner, me to wooe.
But fare you well; perforce I must confesse,
I thought you Lord of more true gentlenesse.
Oh, that a Lady of one man refus'd,
Should of another therefore be abus'd. *Exit.*

Lys. She sees not *Hermia*: *Hermia* sleepe thou there,
And neuer maist thou come *Lysander* neere;

For as a surfeit of the sweetest things
The deepest loathing to the stomacke brings:
Or as the heresies that men do leaue,
Are hated most of those that did deceiue:
So thou, my surfeit, and my heresie,
Of all be hated; but the most of me;
And all my powers addresse your loue and might,
To honour *Helen*, and to be her Knight. *Exit.*

Her. Helpe me *Lysander*, helpe me; do thy best
To plucke this crawling serpent from my brest.
Aye me, for pitty; what a dreame was here?
Lysander looke, how I do quake with feare:
Me-thought a serpent eate my heart away,
And yet sat smiling at his cruell prey.
Lysander, what remoou'd? *Lysander*, Lord,
What, out of hearing, gone? No sound, no word?
Alacke where are you? speake and if you heare;
Speake of all loues; I sound almost with feare.
No, then I well perceiue you are not nye,
Either death or you Ile finde immediately. *Exit.*

Actus Tertius.

Enter the Clownes.

Bot. Are we all met?

Quin. Pat, pat, and here's a maruailous conuenient place for our rehearsall. This greene plot shall be our stage, this hauthorne brake our tyring house, and we will do it in action, as we will do it before the Duke.

Bot. Peter quince?

Peter. What saist thou, bully *Bottome*?

Bot. There are things in this Comedy of *Piramus* and *Thisby*, that will neuer please. First, *Piramus* must draw a sword to kill himselfe; which the Ladies cannot abide. How answere you that?

Snout. Berlaken, a parlous feare.

Star. I beleeue we must leaue the killing out, when all is done.

Bot. Not a whit, I haue a deuice to make all well. Write me a Prologue, and let the Prologue seeme to say, we will do no harme with our swords, and that *Pyramus* is not kill'd indeede: and for the more better assurance, tell them, that I *Piramus* am not *Piramus*, but *Bottome* the Weauer; this will put them out of feare.

Quin. Well, we will haue such a Prologue, and it shall be written in eight and sixe.

Bot. No, make it two more, let it be written in eight and eight.

Snout. Will not the Ladies be afear'd of the Lyon?

Star. I feare it, I promise you.

Bot. Masters, you ought to consider with your selues, to bring in (God shield vs) a Lyon among Ladies, is a most dreadfull thing. For there is not a more fearefull wilde foule then your Lyon liuing: and wee ought to looke to it.

Snout. Therefore another Prologue must tell he is not a Lyon.

Bot. Nay, you must name his name, and halfe his face must be seene through the Lyons necke, and he himselfe must speake through, saying thus, or to the same defect; Ladies, or faire Ladies, I would wish you, or I would
request

request you, or I would entreat you, not to feare, not to tremble: my life for yours. If you thinke I come hither as a Lyon, it were pitty of my life. No, I am no such thing, I am a man as other men are; and there indeed let him name his name, and tell him plainly hee is *Snug* the ioyner.

Quin. Well, it shall be so: but there is two hard things, that is, to bring the Moone-light into a chamber: for you know, *Piramus* and *Thisby* meete by Moone-light.

Sn. Doth the Moone shine that night wee play our play?

Bot. A Calender, a Calender, looke in the Almanack, finde out Moone-shine, finde out Moone-shine.

Enter Pucke.

Quin. Yes, it doth shine that night.

Bot. Why then may you leaue a casement of the great chamber window (where we play) open, and the Moone may shine in at the casement.

Quin. I, or else one must come in with a bush of thornes and a lanthorne, and say he comes to disfigure, or to present the person of Moone-shine. Then there is another thing, we must haue a wall in the great Chamber; for *Piramus* and *Thisby* (saies the story) did talke through the chinke of a wall.

Sn. You can neuer bring in a wall. What say you *Bottome*?

Bot. Some man or other must present wall, and let him haue some Plaster, or some Lome, or some rough cast about him, to signifie wall; or let him hold his fingers thus; and through that cranny, shall *Piramus* and *Thisby* whisper.

Quin. If that may be, then all is well. Come, sit downe euery mothers sonne, and rehearse your parts. *Piramus*, you begin; when you haue spoken your speech, enter into that Brake, and so euery one according to his cue.

Enter Robin.

Rob. What hempen home-spuns haue we swaggering here,
So neere the Cradle of the Faierie Queene?
What, a Play toward? Ile be an auditor,
An Actor too perhaps, if I see cause.

Quin. Speake *Piramus*: *Thisby* stand forth.

Pir. Thisby, the flowers of odious sauors sweete.

Quin. Odours, odours.

Pir. Odours sauors sweete,
So hath thy breath, my dearest *Thisby* deare.
But harke, a voyce: stay thou but here a while,
And by and by I will to thee appeare. *Exit. Pir.*

Puck. A stranger *Piramus*, then ere plaid here.

Thiſ. Must I speake now?

Pet. I marry must you. For you must vnderstand he goes but to see a noyse that he heard, and is to come againe.

Thiſ. Most radiant *Piramus*, most Lilly white of hue,
Of colour like the red rose on triumphant bryer,
Most brisky Iuuenall, and eke most louely Iew,
As true as truest horse, that yet would neuer tyre,
Ile meete thee *Piramus*, at *Ninnies* toombe.

Pet. Ninus toombe man: why, you must not speake that yet; that you answere to *Piramus*: you speake all your part at once, cues and all. *Piramus* enter, your cue is past; it is neuer tyre.

Thiſ. O, as true as truest horse, that yet would neuer tyre:

Pir. If I were faire, *Thisby* I were onely thine.

Pet. O monstrous. O strange. We are hanted; pray masters, flye masters, helpe.

The Clownes all Exit.

Puk. Ile follow you, Ile leade you about a Round,
Through bogge, through bush, through brake, through bryer,
Sometime a horse Ile be, sometime a hound:
A hogge, a headlesse beare, sometime a fire,
And neigh, and barke, and grunt, and rore, and burne,
Like horse, hound, hog, beare, fire, at euery turne. *Exit.*

Enter Piramus with the Asse head.

Bot. Why do they run away? This is a knauery of them to make me afeard. *Enter Snowt.*

Sn. O *Bottom*, thou art chang'd; What doe I see on thee?

Bot. What do you see? You see an Asse-head of your owne, do you?

Enter Peter Quince.

Pet. Blesse thee *Bottome*, blesse thee; thou art translated. *Exit.*

Bot. I see their knauery; this is to make an asse of me, to fright me if they could; but I will not stirre from this place, do what they can. I will walke vp and downe here, and I will sing that they shall heare I am not afraid.

The Woosell cocke, so blacke of hew,
With Orenge-tawny bill.
The Throstle, with his note so true,
The Wren and little quill.

Tyta. What Angell wakes me from my flowry bed?

Bot. The Finch, the Sparrow, and the Larke,
The plainsong Cuckow gray;
Whose note full many a man doth marke,
And dares not answere, nay.
For indeede, who would set his wit to so foolish a bird?
Who would giue a bird the lye, though he cry Cuckow, neuer so?

Tyta. I pray thee gentle mortall, sing againe,
Mine eare is much enamored of thy note;
On the first view to say, to sweare I loue thee.
So is mine eye enthralled to thy shape,
And thy faire vertues force (perforce) doth moue me.

Bot. Me-thinkes mistresse, you should haue little reason for that: and yet to say the truth, reason and loue keepe little company together, now-adayes. The more the pittie, that some honest neighbours will not make them friends. Nay, I can gleeke vpon occasion.

Tyta. Thou art as wise, as thou art beautifull.

Bot. Not so neither: but if I had wit enough to get out of this wood, I haue enough to serue mine owne turne.

Tyta. Out of this wood, do not desire to goe,
Thou shalt remaine here, whether thou wilt or no.
I am a spirit of no common rate:
The Summer still doth tend vpon my state,
And I doe loue thee; therefore goe with me,
Ile giue thee Fairies to attend on thee;
And they shall fetch thee Iewels from the deepe,
And sing, while thou on pressed flowers dost sleepe:
And I will purge thy mortall grossenesse so,
That thou shalt like an airie spirit go.

Enter Pease-blossome, Cobweb, Moth, Mustard-seede, and foure Fairies.

Fai. Ready; and I, and I, and I, Where shall we go?
Tita. Be

Tita. Be kinde and curteous to this Gentleman,
Hop in his walkes, and gambole in his eies,
Feede him with Apricocks, and Dewberries,
With purple Grapes, greene Figs, and Mulberries,
The honie-bags steale from the humble Bees,
And for night-tapers crop their waxen thighes,
And light them at the fierie-Glow-wormes eyes,
To haue my loue to bed, and to arise:
And plucke the wings from painted Butterflies,
To fan the Moone-beames from his sleeping eies.
Nod to him Elues, and doe him curtesies.

  1. *Fai.* Haile mortall, haile.
  2. *Fai.* Haile.
  3. *Fai.* Haile.

  Bot. I cry your worships mercy hartily; I beseech your worships name.

  Cob. Cobweb.

  Bot. I shall desire you of more acquaintance, good Master *Cobweb*: if I cut my finger, I shall make bold with you.
Your name honest Gentleman?

  Peas. Pease blossome.

  Bot. I pray you commend mee to mistresse *Squash*, your mother, and to master *Peascod* your father. Good master *Pease-blossome*, I shal desire of you more acquaintance to. Your name I beseech you sir?

  Mus. Mustard-seede.

  Peas. Pease-blossome.

  Bot. Good master *Mustard seede*, I know your patience well: that same cowardly gyant-like Oxe-beefe hath deuoured many a gentleman of your house. I promise you, your kindred hath made my eyes water ere now. I desire you more acquaintance, good Master *Mustard-seede*.

  Tita. Come waite vpon him, lead him to my bower.
The Moone me-thinks, lookes with a watrie eie,
And when she weepes, weepe euerie little flower,
Lamenting some enforced chastitie.
Tye vp my louers tongue, bring him silently. *Exit.*

Enter King of Pharies, solus.

  Ob. I wonder if *Titania* be awak't;
Then what it was that next came in her eye,
Which she must dote on, in extremitie.

Enter Pucke.

Here comes my messenger: how now mad spirit,
What night-rule now about this haunted groue?

  Puck. My Mistris with a monster is in loue,
Neere to her close and consecrated bower,
While she was in her dull and sleeping hower,
A crew of patches, rude Mechanicals,
That worke for bread vpon Athenian stals,
Were met together to rehearse a Play,
Intended for great *Theseus* nuptiall day:
The shallowest thick-skin of that barren sort,
Who *Piramus* presented, in their sport,
Forsooke his Scene, and entred in a brake,
When I did him at this aduantage take,
An Asses nole I fixed on his head.
Anon his *Thisbie* must be answered,
And forth my Mimmick comes: when they him spie,
As Wilde-geese, that the creeping Fowler eye,
Or russed-pated choughes, many in sort
(Rising and cawing at the guns report)
Seuer themselues, and madly sweepe the skye:
So at his sight, away his fellowes flye,
And at our stampe, here ore and ore one fals;
He murther cries, and helpe from *Athens* cals.
Their sense thus weake, lost with their fears thus strong,
Made senselesse things begin to do them wrong.
For briars and thornes at their apparell snatch,
Some sleeues, some hats, from yeelders all things catch,
I led them on in this distracted feare,
And left sweete *Piramus* translated there:
When in that moment (so it came to passe)
Tytania waked, and straightway lou'd an Asse.

  Ob. This fals out better then I could deuise:
But hast thou yet lacht the *Athenians* eyes,
With the loue iuyce, as I did bid thee doe?

  Rob. I tooke him sleeping (that is finisht to)
And the *Athenian* woman by his side,
That when he wak't, of force she must be eyde.

Enter Demetrius and Hermia.

  Ob. Stand close, this is the same *Athenian*.
  Rob. This is the woman, but not this the man.
  Dem. O why rebuke you him that loues you so?
Lay breath so bitter on your bitter foe.
  Her. Now I but chide, but I should vse thee worse.
For thou (I feare) hast giuen me cause to curse,
If thou hast slaine *Lysander* in his sleepe,
Being ore shooes in bloud, plunge in the deepe, and kill me too:
The Sunne was not so true vnto the day,
As he to me. Would he haue stollen away,
From sleeping *Hermia*? Ile beleeue as soone
This whole earth may be bord, and that the Moone
May through the Center creepe, and so displease
Her brothers noonetide, with th' *Antipodes*.
It cannot be but thou hast murdred him,
So should a mutrherer looke, so dead, so grim.
  Dem. So should the murderer looke, and so should I,
Pierst through the heart with your sterne cruelty:
Yet you the murderer looks as bright as cleare,
As yonder *Venus* in her glimmering sphere.
  Her. What's this to my *Lysander*? where is he?
Ah good *Demetrius*, wilt thou giue him me?
  Dem. I'de rather giue his carkasse to my hounds.
  Her. Out dog, out cur, thou driu'st me past the bounds
Of maidens patience. Hast thou slaine him then?
Henceforth be neuer numbred among men.
Oh, once tell true, euen for my sake,
Durst thou a lookt vpon him, being awake?
And hast thou kill'd him sleeping? O braue tutch:
Could not a worme, an Adder do so much?
An Adder did it: for with doubler tongue
Then thine (thou serpent) neuer Adder stung.
  Dem. You spend your passion on a mispri'sd mood,
I am not guiltie of *Lysanders* blood:
Nor is he dead for ought that I can tell.
  Her. I pray thee tell me then that he is well.
  Dem. And if I could, what should I get therefore?
  Her. A priuiledge, neuer to see me more;
And from thy hated presence part I; see me no more
Whether he be dead or no. *Exit.*
  Dem. There is no following her in this fierce vaine,
Here therefore for a while I will remaine.
So sorrowes heauinesse doth heauier grow:
For debt that bankrout slip doth sorrow owe,
Which now in some slight measure it will pay,

If for his tender here I make some stay.   *Lie downe.*

  Ob. What hast thou done? Thou hast mistaken quite
And laid the loue iuyce on some true loues sight:
Of thy misprision, must perforce ensue
Some true loue turn'd, and not a false turn'd true.
  Rob. Then fate ore-rules, that one man holding troth,
A million faile, confounding oath on oath.
  Ob. About the wood, goe swifter then the winde,
And *Helena* of *Athens* looke thou finde.
All fancy sicke she is, and pale of cheere,
With sighes of loue, that costs the fresh bloud deare.
By some illusion see thou bring her heere,
Ile charme his eyes against she doth appeare.
  Robin. I go, I go, looke how I goe,
Swifter then arrow from the *Tartars* bowe.   *Exit.*
  Ob. Flower of this purple die,
Hit with *Cupids* archery,
Sinke in apple of his eye,
When his loue he doth espie,
Let her shine as gloriously
As the *Venus* of the sky.
When thou wak'st if she be by,
Beg of her for remedy.

Enter Pucke.

  Puck. Captaine of our Fairy band,
Helena is heere at hand,
And the youth, mistooke by me,
Pleading for a Louers fee.
Shall we their fond Pageant see?
Lord, what fooles these mortals be!
  Ob. Stand aside: the noyse they make,
Will cause *Demetrius* to awake.
  Puck. Then will two at once wooe one,
That must needs be sport alone:
And those things doe best please me,
That befall preposterously.

Enter Lysander and Helena.

  Lys. Why should you think y̑ I should wooe in scorn?
Scorne and derision neuer comes in teares:
Looke when I vow I weepe; and vowes so borne,
In their natiuity all truth appeares.
How can these things in me, seeme scorne to you?
Bearing the badge of faith to proue them true.
  Hel. You doe aduance your cunning more & more,
When truth kils truth, O diuelish holy fray!
These vowes are *Hermias.* Will you giue her ore?
Weigh oath with oath, and you will nothing weigh.
Your vowes to her, and me, (put in two scales)
Will euen weigh, and both as light as tales.
  Lys. I had no iudgement, when to her I swore.
  Hel. Nor none in my minde, now you giue her ore.
  Lys. Demetrius loues her, and he loues not you. *Awa.*
  Dem. O *Helen,* goddesse, nimph, perfect, diuine,
To what my, loue, shall I compare thine eyne!
Christall is muddy, O how ripe in show,
Thy lips, those kissing cherries, tempting grow!
That pure congealed white, high *Taurus* snow,
Fan'd with the Easterne winde, turnes to a crow,
When thou holdst vp thy hand. O let me kisse
This Princesse of pure white, this seale of blisse.
  Hell. O spight! O hell! I see you are all bent
To set against me, for your merriment:
If you were ciuill, and knew curtesie,
You would not doe me thus much iniury.

Can you not hate me, as I know you doe,
But you must ioyne in soules to mocke me to?
If you are men, as men you are in show,
You would not vse a gentle Lady so;
To vow, and sweare, and superpraise my parts,
When I am sure you hate me with your hearts.
You both are Riuals, and loue *Hermia*;
And now both Riuals to mocke *Helena.*
A trim exploit, a manly enterprize,
To coniure teares vp in a poore maids eyes,
With your derision; none of noble sort,
Would so offend a Virgin, and extort
A poore soules patience, all to make you sport.
  Lysa. You are vnkind *Demetrius*; be not so,
For you loue *Hermia*; this you know I know;
And here with all good will, with all my heart,
In *Hermias* loue I yeeld you vp my part;
And yours of *Helena,* to me bequeath,
Whom I do loue, and will do to my death.
  Hel. Neuer did mockers wast more idle breth.
  Dem. Lysander, keep thy *Hermia,* I will none:
If ere I lou'd her, all that loue is gone.
My heart to her, but as guest-wise soiourn'd,
And now to *Helen* it is home return'd,
There to remaine.
  Lys. It is not so.
  De. Disparage not the faith thou dost not know,
Lest to thy perill thou abide it deare.
Looke where thy Loue comes, yonder is thy deare.

Enter Hermia.

  Her. Dark night, that from the eye his function takes,
The eare more quicke of apprehension makes,
Wherein it doth impaire the seeing sense,
It paies the hearing double recompence.
Thou art not by mine eye, *Lysander* found,
Mine eare (I thanke it) brought me to that sound.
But why vnkindly didst thou leaue me so?   (to go?
  Lysan. Why should hee stay whom Loue doth presse
  Her. What loue could presse *Lysander* from my side?
  Lys. Lysanders loue (that would not let him bide)
Faire *Helena*; who more engilds the night,
Then all yon fierie oes, and eies of light.
Why seek'st thou me? Could not this make thee know,
The hate I bare thee made me leaue thee so?
  Her. You speake not as you thinke; it cannot be.
  Hel. Loe, she is one of this confederacy,
Now I perceiue they haue conioyn'd all three,
To fashion this false sport in spight of me.
Iniurious Hermia, most vngratefull maid,
Haue you conspir'd, haue you with these contriu'd
To baite me, with this foule derision?
Is all the counsell that we two haue shar'd,
The sisters vowes, the houres that we haue spent,
When wee haue chid the hasty footed time,
For parting vs; O, is all forgot?
All schooledaies friendship, child-hood innocence?
We Hermia, like two Artificiall gods,
Haue with our needles, created both one flower,
Both on one sampler, sitting on one cushion,
Both warbling of one song, both in one key;
As if our hands, our sides, voices, and mindes
Had beene incorporate. So we grew together,
Like to a double cherry, seeming parted,
But yet a vnion in partition,

Two

Two louely berries molded on one stem,
So with two seeming bodies, but one heart,
Two of the first life coats in Heraldry,
Due but to one and crowned with one crest.
And will you rent our ancient loue asunder,
To ioyne with men in scorning your poore friend?
It is not friendly,'tis not maidenly.
Our sexe as well as I, may chide you for it,
Though I alone doe feele the iniurie.

Her. I am amazed at your passionate words,
I scorne you not; It seemes that you scorne me.

Hel. Haue you not set *Lysander*, as in scorne
To follow me, and praise my eies and face?
And made your other loue, *Demetrius*
(Who euen but now did spurne me with his foote)
To call me goddesse, nimph, diuine, and rare,
Precious, celestiall? Wherefore speakes he this
To her he hates? And wherefore doth *Lysander*
Denie your loue (so rich within his soule)
And tender me (forsooth) affection,
But by your setting on, by your consent?
What though I be not so in grace as you,
So hung vpon with loue, so fortunate?
(But miserable most, to loue vnlou'd)
This you should pittie, rather then despise.

Her. I vnderstand not what you meane by this.

Hel. I, doe, perseuer, counterfeit sad lookes,
Make mouthes vpon me when I turne my backe,
Winke each at other, hold the sweete iest vp:
This sport well carried, shall be chronicled.
If you haue any pittie, grace, or manners,
You would not make me such an argument:
But fare ye well, 'tis partly mine owne fault,
Which death or absence soone shall remedie.

Lys. Stay gentle *Helena*, heare my excuse,
My loue, my life, my soule, faire *Helena*.

Hel. O excellent!

Her. Sweete, do not scorne her so.

Dem. If she cannot entreate, I can compell.

Lys. Thou canst compell, no more then she entreate.
Thy threats haue no more strength then her weak praise.
Helen, I loue thee; by my life I doe;
I sweare by that which I will lose for thee,
To proue him false, that saies I loue thee not.

Dem. I say, I loue thee more then he can do.

Lys. If thou say so, with-draw and proue it too.

Dem. Quick, come.

Her. *Lysander*, whereto tends all this?

Lys. Away, you Ethiope.

Dem. No, no, Sir, seeme to breake loose;
Take on as you would follow,
But yet come not: you are a tame man, go.

Lys. Hang off thou cat, thou bur; vile thing let loose,
Or I will shake thee from me like a serpent.

Her. Why are you growne so rude?
What change is this sweete Loue?

Lys. Thy loue? out tawny *Tartar*, out;
Out loathed medicine; O hated poison hence.

Her. Do you not iest?

Hel. Yes sooth, and so do you.

Lys. Demetrius, I will keepe my word with thee.

Dem. I would I had your bond: for I perceiue
A weake bond holds you; Ile not trust your word.

Lys. What, should I hurt her, strike her, kill her dead?
Although I hate her, Ile not harme her so.

Her. What, can you do me greater harme then hate?
Hate me, wherefore? O me, what newes my Loue?
Am not I *Hermia*? Are not you *Lysander*?
I am as faire now, as I was ere while.
Since night you lou'd me; yet since night you left me.
Why then you left me (O the gods forbid)
In earnest, shall I say?

Lys. I, by my life;
And neuer did desire to see thee more.
Therefore be out of hope, of question, of doubt;
Be certaine, nothing truer: 'tis no iest,
That I doe hate thee, and loue *Helena*.

Her. O me, you iugler, you canker blossome,
You theefe of loue; What, haue you come by night,
And stolne my loues heart from him?

Hel. Fine yfaith:
Haue you no modesty, no maiden shame,
No touch of bashfulnesse? What, will you teare
Impatient answers from my gentle tongue?
Fie, fie, you counterfeit, you puppet, you.

Her. Puppet? why so? I, that way goes the game.
Now I perceiue that she hath made compare
Betweene our statures, she hath vrg'd her height,
And with her personage, her tall personage,
Her height (forsooth) she hath preuail'd with him.
And are you growne so high in his esteeme,
Because I am so dwarfish, and so low?
How low am I, thou painted May-pole? Speake,
How low am I? I am not yet so low,
But that my nailes can reach vnto thine eyes.

Hel. I pray you though you mocke me, gentlemen,
Let her not hurt me; I was neuer curst:
I haue no gift at all in shrewishnesse;
I am a right maide for my cowardize;
Let her not strike me: you perhaps may thinke,
Because she is something lower then my selfe,
That I can match her.

Her. Lower? harke againe.

Hel. Good *Hermia*, do not be so bitter with me,
I euermore did loue you *Hermia*,
Did euer keepe your counsels, neuer wronged you,
Saue that in loue vnto *Demetrius*,
I told him of your stealth vnto this wood.
He followed you, for loue I followed him,
But he hath chid me hence, and threatned me
To strike me, spurne me, nay to kill me too;
And now, so you will let me quiet go,
To *Athens* will I beare my folly backe,
And follow you no further. Let me go.
You see how simple, and how fond I am.

Her. Why get you gone: who ist that hinders you?

Hel. A foolish heart, that I leaue here behinde.

Her. What, with *Lysander*?

Her. With *Demetrius*.

Lys. Be not afraid, she shall not harme thee *Helena*.

Dem. No sir, she shall not, though you take her part.

Hel. O when she's angry, she is keene and shrewd,
She was a vixen when she went to schoole,
And though she be but little, she is fierce.

Her. Little againe? Nothing but low and little?
Why will you suffer her to flout me thus?
Let me come to her.

Lys. Get you gone you dwarfe,
You *minimus*, of hindring knot-grasse made,
You bead, you acorne.

Dem. You are too officious,
In her behalfe that scornes your seruices.

Let

Let her alone, speake not of *Helena*,
Take not her part. For if thou dost intend
Neuer so little shew of loue to her,
Thou shalt abide it.

Lyf. Now she holds me not,
Now follow if thou dar'st, to try whose right,
Of thine or mine is most in *Helena*.

Dem. Follow? Nay, Ile goe with thee cheeke by iowle. *Exit Lysander and Demetrius.*

Her. You Mistris, all this coyle is long of you.
Nay, goe not backe.

Hel. I will not trust you I,
Nor longer stay in your curst companie.
Your hands then mine, are quicker for a fray,
My legs are longer though to runne away.

Enter Oberon and Pucke.

Ob. This is thy negligence, still thou mistak'st,
Or else committ'st thy knaueries willingly.

Puck. Beleeue me, King of shadowes, I mistooke,
Did not you tell me, I should know the man,
By the *Athenian* garments he hath on?
And so farre blamelesse proues my enterpize,
That I haue nointed an Athenians eies,
And so farre am I glad, it so did sort,
As this their iangling I esteeme a sport.

Ob. Thou seest these Louers seeke a place to fight,
Hie therefore *Robin*, ouercast the night,
The starrie Welkin couer thou anon,
With drooping fogge as blacke as *Acheron*,
And lead these testie Riuals so astray,
As one come not within anothers way.
Like to *Lysander*, sometime frame thy tongue,
Then stirre *Demetrius* vp with bitter wrong;
And sometime raile thou like *Demetrius*;
And from each other looke thou leade them thus,
Till ore their browes, death-counterfeiting sleepe
With leaden legs, and Battie-wings doth creepe;
Then crush this hearbe into *Lysanders* eie,
Whose liquor hath this vertuous propertie,
To take from thence all error, with his might,
And make his eie-bals role with wonted sight.
When they next wake, all this derision
Shall seeme a dreame, and fruitlesse vision,
And backe to *Athens* shall the Louers wend
With league, whose date till death shall neuer end.
Whiles I in this affaire do thee imply,
Ile to my Queene, and beg her *Indian* Boy;
And then I will her charmed eie release
From monsters view, and all things shall be peace.

Puck. My Fairie Lord, this must be done with haste,
For night-swift Dragons cut the Clouds full fast,
And yonder shines *Auroras* harbinger;
At whose approach Ghosts wandring here and there,
Troope home to Church-yards; damned spirits all,
That in crosse-waies and flouds haue buriall,
Alreadie to their wormie beds are gone;
For feare least day should looke their shames vpon,
They wilfully themselues exile from light,
And must for aye consort with blacke browd night.

Ob. But we are spirits of another sort:
I, with the mornings loue haue oft made sport;
And like a Forrester, the groues may tread,
Euen till the Easterne gate all fierie red,
Opening on *Neptune*, with faire blessed beames,
Turnes into yellow gold, his salt greene streames.
But notwithstanding haste, make no delay:
We may effect this businesse, yet ere day.

Puck. Vp and downe, vp and downe, I will leade them vp and downe: I am fear'd in field and towne.
Goblin, lead them vp and downe: here comes one.

Enter Lysander.

Lys. Where art thou, proud *Demetrius*?
Speake thou now.

Rob. Here villaine, drawne & readie. Where art thou?

Lys. I will be with thee straight.

Rob. Follow me then to plainer ground.

Enter Demetrius.

Dem. *Lysander*, speake againe;
Thou runaway, thou coward, art thou fled?
Speake in some bush: Where dost thou hide thy head?

Rob. Thou coward, art thou bragging to the stars,
Telling the bushes that thou look'st for wars,
And wilt not come? Come recreant, come thou childe,
Ile whip thee with a rod. He is defil'd
That drawes a sword on thee.

Dem. Yea, art thou there?

Ro. Follow my voice, we'l try no manhood here. *Exit.*

Lys. He goes before me, and still dares me on,
When I come where he cals, then he's gone.
The villaine is much lighter heel'd then I:
I followed fast, but faster he did flye; *shifting places.*
That fallen am I in darke vneuen way,
And here wil rest me. Come thou gentle day: *lye down.*
For if but once thou shew me thy gray light,
Ile finde *Demetrius*, and reuenge this spight.

Enter Robin and Demetrius.

Rob. Ho, ho, ho; coward, why com'st thou not?

Dem. Abide me, if thou dar'st. For well I wot,
Thou runst before me, shifting euery place,
And dar'st not stand, nor looke me in the face.
Where art thou?

Rob. Come hither, I am here.

Dem. Nay then thou mock'st me; thou shalt buy this deere,
If euer I thy face by day-light see.
Now goe thy way; faintnesse constraineth me,
To measure out my length on this cold bed,
By daies approach looke to be visited.

Enter Helena.

Hel. O weary night, O long and tedious night,
Abate thy houres, shine comforts from the East,
That I may backe to *Athens* by day-light,
From these that my poore companie detest;
And sleepe that sometime shuts vp sorrowes eie,
Steale me a while from mine owne companie. *Sleepe.*

Rob. Yet but three? Come one more,
Two of both kindes makes vp foure.
Here she comes, curst and sad,
Cupid is a knauish lad,

Enter Hermia.

Thus to make poore females mad.

Her. Neuer so wearie, neuer so in woe,
Bedabbled with the dew, and torne with briars,
I can no further crawle, no further goe;
My legs can keepe no pace with my desires.
Here will I rest me till the breake of day,
Heauens shield *Lysander*, if they meane a fray.

Rob. On the ground sleepe sound,
Ile apply your eie gentle louer, remedy.
When thou wak'st, thou tak'st
True delight in the sight of thy former Ladies eye,

And

And the Country Prouerb knowne,
That euery man should take his owne,
In your waking shall be showne.
Iacke shall haue Iill, nought shall goe ill,
The man shall haue his Mare againe, and all shall bee
well.

They sleepe all the Act.

Actus Quartus.

Enter Queene of Fairies, and Clowne, and Fairies, and the King behinde them.

Tita. Come, sit thee downe vpon this flowry bed,
While I thy amiable cheekes doe coy,
And sticke muske roses in thy sleeke smoothe head,
And kisse thy faire large eares, my gentle ioy.

Clow. Where's *Pease blossome*?

Peas. Ready.

Clow. Scratch my head, *Pease-blossome*. Wher's Mounsieur *Cobweb.*

Cob. Ready.

Clowne. Mounsieur *Cobweb*, good Mounsier get your weapons in your hand, & kill me a red hipt humble-Bee, on the top of a thistle; and good Mounsieur bring mee the hony bag. Doe not fret your selfe too much in the action, Mounsieur; and good Mounsieur haue a care the hony bag breake not, I would be loth to haue yon ouerflowne with a hony-bag signiour. Where's Mounsieur *Mustardseed*?

Mus. Ready.

Clo. Giue me your neafe, Mounsieur *Mustardseed*. Pray you leaue your courtesie good Mounsieur.

Mus. What's your will?

Clo. Nothing good Mounsieur, but to help Caualery *Cobweb* to scratch. I must to the Barbers Mounsieur, for me-thinkes I am maruellous hairy about the face. And I am such a tender asse, if my haire do but tickle me, I must scratch.

Tita. What, wilt thou heare some musicke, my sweet loue.

Clow. I haue a reasonable good eare in musicke. Let vs haue the tongs and the bones.

Musicke Tongs, Rurall Musicke.

Tita. Or say sweete Loue, what thou desirest to eat.

Clowne. Truly a pecke of Prouender; I could munch your good dry Oates. Me-thinkes I haue a great desire to a bottle of hay: good hay, sweete hay hath no fellow.

Tita. I haue a venturous Fairy,
That shall seeke the Squirrels hoard,
And fetch thee new Nuts.

Clown. I had rather haue a handfull or two of dried pease. But I pray you let none of your people stirre me, I haue an exposition of sleepe come vpon me.

Tyta. Sleepe thou, and I will winde thee in my arms,
Fairies be gone, and be alwaies away.
So doth the woodbine, the sweet Honisuckle,
Gently entwist; the female Iuy so
Enrings the barky fingers of the Elme.
O how I loue thee! how I dote on thee!

Enter Robin goodfellow and Oberon.

Ob. Welcome good *Robin:*
Seest thou this sweet sight?
Her dotage now I doe begin to pitty.
For meeting her of late behinde the wood,
Seeking sweet sauors for this hatefull foole,
I did vpbraid her, and fall out with her.
For she his hairy temples then had rounded,
With coronet of fresh and fragrant flowers.
And that same dew which somtime on the buds,
Was wont to swell like round and orient pearles;
Stood now within the pretty flouriets eyes,
Like teares that did their owne disgrace bewaile.
When I had at my pleasure taunted her,
And she in milde termes beg'd my patience,
I then did aske of her, her changeling childe,
Which straight she gaue me, and her Fairy sent
To beare him to my Bower in Fairy Land.
And now I haue the Boy, I will vndoe
This hatefull imperfection of her eyes.
And gentle *Pucke* take this transformed scalpe,
From off the head of this *Athenian* swaine;
That he awaking when the other doe,
May all to *Athens* backe againe repaire,
And thinke no more of this nights accidents,
But as the fierce vexation of a dreame.
But first I will release the Fairy Queene.

Be thou as thou wast wont to be;
See as thou wast wont to see.
Dians bud, or Cupids flower,
Hath such force and blessed power.

Now my *Titania* wake you my sweet Queene.

Tita. My *Oberon*, what visions haue I seene!
Me-thought I was enamoured of an Asse.

Ob. There lies your loue.

Tita. How came these things to passe?
Oh, how mine eyes doth loath this visage now!

Ob. Silence a while. *Robin* take off his head:
Titania musick call, and strike more dead
Then common sleepe; of all these, fine the sense.

Tita. Musicke, ho musicke, such as charmeth sleepe.

Musick still.

Rob. When thou wak'st, with thine owne fooles eies peepe.

Ob. Sound musick; come my Queen, take hands with me
And rocke the ground whereon these sleepers be.
Now thou and I are new in amity,
And will to morrow midnight, solemnly
Dance in Duke *Theseus* house triumphantly,
And blesse it to all faire posterity.
There shall the paires of faithfull Louers be
Wedded, with *Theseus*, all in iollity.

Rob. Faire King attend, and marke,
I doe heare the morning Larke.

Ob. Then my Queene in silence sad,
Trip we after the nights shade;
We the Globe can compasse soone,
Swifter then the wandring Moone.

Tita. Come my Lord, and in our flight,
Tell me how it came this night,
That I sleeping heere was found,

Sleepers Lye still.

With these mortals on the ground. *Exeunt.*
Winde Hornes.

Enter Theseus, Egeus, Hippolita and all his traine.

Thef. Goe one of you, finde out the Forrester,
For now our obseruation is perform'd;
And since we haue the vaward of the day,
My Loue shall heare the musicke of my hounds.
Vncouple in the Westerne valley, let them goe;
Dispatch I say, and finde the Forrester.
We will faire Queene, vp to the Mountaines top,
And marke the musicall confusion
Of hounds and eccho in coniunction.

Hip. I was with *Hercules* and *Cadmus* once,
When in a wood of *Creete* they bayed the Beare
With hounds of *Sparta*; neuer did I heare
Such gallant chiding. For besides the groues,
The skies, the fountaines, euery region neere,
Seeme all one mutuall cry. I neuer heard
So musicall a discord, such sweet thunder.

Thef. My hounds are bred out of the *Spartan* kinde,
So flew'd, so sanded, and their heads are hung
With eares that sweepe away the morning dew,
Crooke kneed, and dew-lapt, like *Thessalian* Buls,
Slow in pursuit, but match'd in mouth like bels,
Each vnder each. A cry more tuneable
Was neuer hallowed to, nor cheer'd with horne,
In *Creete*, in *Sparta*, nor in *Thessaly*;
Iudge when you heare. But soft, what nimphs are these?

Egeus. My Lord, this is my daughter heere asleepe,
And this *Lysander*, this *Demetrius* is,
This *Helena*, olde *Nedars Helena*,
I wonder of this being heere together.

The. No doubt they rose vp early, to obserue
The right of May; and hearing our intent,
Came heere in grace of our solemnity.
But speake *Egeus*, is not this the day
That *Hermia* should giue answer of her choice?

Egeus. It is, my Lord.

Thef. Goe bid the huntf-men wake them with their hornes.

Hornes and they wake.
Shout within, they all start vp.

Thef. Good morrow friends: Saint *Valentine* is past,
Begin these wood birds but to couple now?

Lys. Pardon my Lord.

Thef. I pray you all stand vp.
I know you two are Riuall enemies.
How comes this gentle concord in the world,
That hatred is so farre from iealousie,
To sleepe by hate, and feare no enmity.

Lys. My Lord, I shall reply amazedly,
Halfe sleepe, halfe waking. But as yet, I sweare,
I cannot truly say how I came heere.
But as I thinke (for truly would I speake)
And now I doe bethinke me, so it is;
I came with *Hermia* hither. Our intent
Was to be gone from *Athens*, where we might be
Without the perill of the *Athenian* Law.

Ege. Enough, enough, my Lord: you haue enough;
I beg the Law, the Law, vpon his head:
They would haue stolne away, they would *Demetrius*,
Thereby to haue defeated you and me:
You of your wife, and me of my consent;
Of my consent, that she should be your wife.

Dem. My Lord, faire *Helen* told me of their stealth,
Of this their purpose hither, to this wood,
And I in furie hither followed them;
Faire *Helena*, in fancy followed me.
But my good Lord, I wot not by what power,
(But by some power it is) my loue
To *Hermia* (melted as the snow)
Seems to me now as the remembrance of an idle gaude,
Which in my childehood I did doat vpon:
And all the faith, the vertue of my heart,
The obiect and the pleasure of mine eye,
Is onely *Helena*. To her, my Lord,
Was I betroth'd, ere I see *Hermia*,
But like a sickenesse did I loath this food,
But as in health, come to my naturall taste,
Now doe I wish it, loue it, long for it,
And will for euermore be true to it.

Thef. Faire Louers, you are fortunately met;
Of this discourse we shall heare more anon.
Egeus, I will ouer-beare your will;
For in the Temple, by and by with vs,
These couples shall eternally be knit.
And for the morning now is something worne,
Our purpos'd hunting shall be set aside.
Away, with vs to *Athens*; three and three,
Wee'll hold a feast in great solemnitie.
Come *Hippolita*. *Exit Duke and Lords.*

Dem. These things seeme small & vndistinguishable,
Like farre off mountaines turned into Clouds.

Her. Me-thinks I see these things with parted eye,
When euery things seemes double.

Hel. So me-thinkes:
And I haue found *Demetrius*, like a iewell,
Mine owne, and not mine owne.

Dem. It seemes to mee,
That yet we sleepe, we dreame. Do not you thinke,
The Duke was heere, and bid vs follow him?

Her. Yea, and my Father.

Hel. And *Hippolita*.

Lys. And he bid vs follow to the Temple.

Dem. Why then we are awake; lets follow him, and by the way let vs recount our dreames.

Bottome wakes. *Exit Louers.*

Clo. When my cue comes, call me, and I will answer. My next is, most faire *Piramus*. Hey ho. *Peter Quince*? *Flute* the bellowes-mender? *Snout* the tinker? *Starueling*? Gods my life! Stolne hence, and left me asleepe: I haue had a most rare vision. I had a dreame, past the wit of man, to say, what dreame it was. Man is but an Asse, if he goe about to expound this dreame. Me-thought I was, there is no man can tell what. Me-thought I was, and me-thought I had. But man is but a patch'd foole, if he will offer to say, what me-thought I had. The eye of man hath not heard, the eare of man hath not seen, mans hand is not able to taste, his tongue to conceiue, nor his heart to report, what my dreame was. I will get *Peter Quince* to write a ballet of this dreame, it shall be called *Bottomes Dreame*, because it hath no bottome; and I will sing it in the latter end of a play, before the Duke. Peraduenture, to make it the more gracious, I shall sing it at her death. *Exit.*

Enter Quince, Flute, Thisbie, Snout, and Starueling.

Quin. Haue you sent to *Bottomes* house? Is he come home yet?

Staru. He cannot be heard of. Out of doubt hee is transported.

Thif. If

Thiſ. If he come not, then the play is mar'd. It goes not forward, doth it?

Quin. It is not poſſible: you haue not a man in all *Athens*, able to diſcharge *Piramus* but he.

Thiſ. No, hee hath ſimply the beſt wit of any handy-craft man in *Athens*.

Quin. Yea, and the beſt perſon too, and hee is a very *Paramour*, for a ſweet voyce.

Thiſ. You muſt ſay, Paragon. A Paramour is (God bleſſe vs) a thing of nought.

Enter Snug the Ioyner.

Snug. Maſters, the Duke is comming from the Temple, and there is two or three Lords & Ladies more married. If our ſport had gone forward, we had all bin made men.

Thiſ. O ſweet bully *Bottome*: thus hath he loſt ſixepence a day, during his life; he could not haue ſcaped ſixpence a day. And the Duke had not giuen him ſixpence a day for playing *Piramus*, Ile be hang'd. He would haue deſerued it. Sixpence a day in *Piramus*, or nothing.

Enter Bottome.

Bot. Where are theſe Lads? Where are theſe hearts?

Quin. *Bottome*, ô moſt couragious day! O moſt happie houre!

Bot. Maſters, I am to diſcourſe wonders; but ask me not what. For if I tell you, I am no true *Athenian*. I will tell you euery thing as it fell out.

Qu. Let vs heare, ſweet *Bottome*.

Bot. Not a word of me: all that I will tell you, is, that the Duke hath dined. Get your apparell together, good ſtrings to your beards, new ribbands to your pumps, meete preſently at the Palace, euery man looke ore his part: for the ſhort and the long is, our play is preferred: In any caſe let *Thisby* haue cleane linnen: and let not him that playes the Lion, paire his nailes, for they ſhall hang out for the Lions clawes. And moſt deare Actors, eate no Onions, nor Garlicke; for wee are to vtter ſweete breath, and I doe not doubt but to heare them ſay, it is a ſweet Comedy. No more words: away, go away.

Exeunt.

Actus Quintus.

Enter Theſeus, Hippolita, Egeus and his Lords.

Hip. 'Tis ſtrange my *Theſeus*, ỹ theſe louers ſpeake of.

The. More ſtrange then true. I neuer may beleeue
Theſe anticke fables, nor theſe Fairy toyes,
Louers and mad men haue ſuch ſeething braines,
Such ſhaping phantaſies, that apprehend more
Then coole reaſon euer comprehends.
The Lunaticke, the Louer, and the Poet,
Are of imagination all compact:
One ſees more diuels then vaſte hell can hold;
That is the mad man. The Louer, all as franticke,
Sees *Helens* beauty in a brow of *Egipt*.
The Poets eye in a fine frenzy rolling, doth glance
From heauen to earth, from earth to heauen.
And as imagination bodies forth the forms of things
Vnknowne; the Poets pen turnes them to ſhapes,
And giues to aire nothing, a locall habitation,
And a name. Such tricks hath ſtrong imagination,
That if it would but apprehend ſome ioy,
It comprehends ſome bringer of that ioy.
Or in the night, imagining ſome feare,
How eaſie is a buſh ſuppos'd a Beare?

Hip. But all the ſtorie of the night told ouer,
And all their minds transfigur'd ſo together,
More witneſſeth than fancies images,
And growes to ſomething of great conſtancie;
But howſoeuer, ſtrange, and admirable.

Enter louers, Lyſander, Demetrius, Hermia, and Helena.

The. Heere come the louers, full of ioy and mirth:
Ioy, gentle friends, ioy and freſh dayes
Of loue accompany your hearts.

Lyſ. More then to vs, waite in your royall walkes, your boord, your bed.

The. Come now, what maſkes, what dances ſhall we haue,
To weare away this long age of three houres,
Between our after ſupper, and bed-time?
Where is our vſuall manager of mirth?
What Reuels are in hand? Is there no play,
To eaſe the anguiſh of a torturing houre?
Call *Egeus*.

Ege. Heere mighty *Theſeus*.

The. Say, what abridgement haue you for this euening?
What maſke? What muſicke? How ſhall we beguile
The lazie time, if not with ſome delight?

Ege. There is a breefe how many ſports are rife:
Make choiſe of which your Highneſſe will ſee firſt.

Liſ. The battell with the Centaurs to be ſung
By an Athenian Eunuch, to the Harpe.

The. Wee'l none of that. That haue I told my Loue
In glory of my kinſman Hercules.

Liſ. The riot of the tipſie Bachanals,
Tearing the Thracian ſinger, in their rage?

The. That is an old deuice, and it was plaid
When I from *Thebes* came laſt a Conqueror.

Liſ. The thrice three Muſes, mourning for the death of learning, late deceaſt in beggerie.

The. That is ſome Satire keene and criticall,
Not ſorting with a nuptiall ceremonie.

Liſ. A tedious breefe Scene of yong *Piramus*,
And his loue *Thisby*; very tragicall mirth.

The. Merry and tragicall? Tedious, and briefe? That is, hot ice, and wondrous ſtrange ſnow. How ſhall wee finde the concord of this diſcord?

Ege. A play there is, my Lord, ſome ten words long,
Which is as breefe, as I haue knowne a play;
But by ten words, my Lord, it is too long;
Which makes it tedious. For in all the play,
There is not one word apt, one Player fitted.
And tragicall my noble Lord it is: for *Piramus*
Therein doth kill himſelfe. Which when I ſaw
Rehearſt, I muſt confeſſe, made mine eyes water:
But more merrie teares, the paſſion of loud laughter
Neuer ſhed.

Theſ. What are they that do play it?

Ege. Hard handed men, that worke in Athens heere,
Which neuer labour'd in their mindes till now;
And now haue toyled their vnbreathed memories
With this ſame play, againſt your nuptiall.

The. And we will heare it.

Phi. No, my noble Lord, it is not for you. I haue heard
It ouer, and it is nothing, nothing in the world;
Vnlesse you can finde sport in their intents,
Extreamely stretcht, and cond with cruell paine,
To doe you seruice.

Thes. I will heare that play. For neuer any thing
Can be amisse, when simplenesse and duty tender it.
Goe bring them in, and take your places, Ladies.

Hip. I loue not to see wretchednesse orecharged;
And duty in his seruice perishing.

Thes. Why gentle sweet, you shall see no such thing.

Hip. He saies, they can doe nothing in this kinde.

Thes. The kinder we, to giue them thanks for nothing
Our sport shall be, to take what they mistake;
And what poore duty cannot doe, noble respect
Takes it in might, not merit.
Where I haue come, great Clearkes haue purposed
To greete me with premeditated welcomes;
Where I haue seene them shiuer and looke pale,
Make periods in the midst of sentences,
Throttle their practiz'd accent in their feares,
And in conclusion, dumbly haue broke off,
Not paying me a welcome. Trust me sweete,
Out of this silence yet, I pickt a welcome:
And in the modesty of fearefull duty,
I read as much, as from the ratling tongue
Of saucy and audacious eloquence.
Loue therefore, and tongue-tide simplicity,
In least, speake most, to my capacity.

Egeus. So please your Grace, the Prologue is addrest.

Duke. Let him approach. *Flor. Trum.*

Enter the Prologue. Quince.

Pro. If we offend, it is with our good will.
That you should thinke, we come not to offend,
But with good will. To shew our simple skill,
That is the true beginning of our end.
Consider then, we come but in despight.
We do not come, as minding to content you,
Our true intent is. All for your delight,
We are not heere. That you should here repent you,
The Actors are at hand; and by their show,
You shall know all, that you are like to know.

Thes. This fellow doth not stand vpon points.

Lys. He hath rid his Prologue, like a rough Colt: he
knowes not the stop. A good morall my Lord. It is not
enough to speake, but to speake true.

Hip. Indeed hee hath plaid on his Prologue, like a
childe on a Recorder, a sound, but not in gouernment.

Thes. His speech was like a tangled chaine: nothing
impaired, but all disordered. Who is next?

Tawyer with a Trumpet before them.

Enter Pyramus and Thisby, Wall, Moone-shine, and Lyon.

Prol. Gentles, perchance you wonder at this show,
But wonder on, till truth make all things plaine.
This man is *Piramus*, if you would know;
This beauteous Lady, *Thisby* is certaine.
This man, with lyme and rough-cast, doth present
Wall, that vile wall, which did these louers sunder:
And through walls chink (poor soules) they are content
To whisper. At the which, let no man wonder.
This man, with Lanthorne, dog, and bush of thorne,
Presenteth moone-shine. For if you will know,
By moone-shine did these Louers thinke no scorne
To meet at *Ninus* toombe, there, there to wooe:
This grizy beast (which Lyon hight by name)
The trusty *Thisby*, comming first by night,
Did scarre away, or rather did affright:
And as she fled, her mantle she did fall;
Which Lyon vile with bloody mouth did staine.
Anon comes *Piramus*, sweet youth and tall,
And findes his *Thisbies* Mantle slaine;
Whereat, with blade, with bloody blamefull blade,
He brauely broacht his boiling bloudy breast,
And *Thisby*, tarrying in Mulberry shade,
His dagger drew, and died. For all the rest,
Let *Lyon, Moone-shine, Wall*, and Louers twaine,
At large discourse, while here they doe remaine.

Exit all but Wall.

Thes. I wonder if the Lion be to speake.

Deme. No wonder, my Lord: one Lion may, when
many Asses doe.

Exit Lyon, Thisbie, and Mooneshine.

Wall. In this same Interlude, it doth befall,
That I, one *Snowt* (by name) present a wall:
And such a wall, as I would haue you thinke,
That had in it a crannied hole or chinke:
Through which the Louers, *Piramus* and *Thisbie*
Did whisper often, very secretly.
This loame, this rough-cast, and this stone doth shew,
That I am that same Wall; the truth is so.
And this the cranny is, right and sinister,
Through which the fearefull Louers are to whisper.

Thes. Would you desire Lime and Haire to speake
better?

Deme. It is the wittiest partition, that euer I heard
discourse, my Lord.

Thes. Pyramus drawes neere the Wall, silence.

Enter Pyramus.

Pir. O grim lookt night, ô night with hue so blacke,
O night, which euer art, when day is not:
O night, ô night, alacke, alacke, alacke,
I feare my *Thisbies* promise is forgot.
And thou ô wall, thou sweet and louely wall,
That stands betweene her fathers ground and mine,
Thou wall, ô wall, ô sweet and louely wall,
Shew me thy chinke, to blinke through with mine eine.
Thankes courteous wall. *Ioue* shield thee well for this.
But what see I? No *Thisbie* doe I see.
O wicked wall, through whom I see no blisse,
Curst be thy stones for thus decceiuing mee.

Thes. The wall me-thinkes being sensible, should
curse againe.

Pir. No in truth sir, he should not. *Deceiuing me*,
Is *Thisbies* cue; she is to enter, and I am to spy
Her through the wall. You shall see it will fall.

Enter Thisbie.

Pat as I told you; yonder she comes.

Thisb. O wall, full often hast thou heard my mones,
For parting my faire *Piramus*, and me.
My cherry lips haue often kist thy stones;
Thy stones with Lime and Haire knit vp in thee.

Pyra. I see a voyce; now will I to the chinke,
To spy and I can heare my *Thisbies* face. *Thisbie?*

Thisb. My Loue thou art, my Loue I thinke.

Pir. Thinke what thou wilt, I am thy Louers grace,
And like *Limander* am I trusty still.

Thisb. And like *Helen* till the Fates me kill.

Pir. Not *Shafalus* to *Procrus*, was so true.

Thisb. As *Shafalus* to *Procrus*, I to you.

Pir. O

Pir. O kisse me through the hole of this vile wall.
Thisb. I kisse the wals hole, not your lips at all.
Pir. Wilt thou at *Ninnies* tombe meete me straight way?
Thisb. Tide life, tide death, I come without delay.
Wall. Thus haue I *Wall*, my part discharged so;
And being done, thus *Wall* away doth go. *Exit Claw.*

Du. Now is the morall downe betweene the two Neighbors.

Dem. No remedie my Lord, when Wals are so wilfull, to heare without vvarning.

Dut. This is the silliest stuffe that ere I heard.

Du. The best in this kind are but shadowes, and the worst are no worse, if imagination amend them.

Dut. It must be your imagination then, & not theirs.

Duk. If wee imagine no worse of them then they of themselues, they may passe for excellent men. Here com two noble beasts, in a man and a Lion.

Enter Lyon and Moone-shine.

Lyon. You Ladies, you (whose gentle harts do feare
The smallest monstrous mouse that creepes on floore)
May now perchance, both quake and tremble heere,
When Lion rough in wildest rage doth roare.
Then know that I, one *Snug* the Ioyner am
A Lion fell, nor else no Lions dam:
For if I should as Lion come in strife
Into this place, 'twere pittie of my life.

Du. A verie gentle beast, and of a good conscience.

Dem. The verie best at a beast, my Lord, ỹ ere I saw.

Lis. This Lion is a verie Fox for his valor.

Du. True, and a Goose for his discretion.

Dem. Not so my Lord: for his valor cannot carrie his discretion, and the Fox carries the Goose.

Du. His discretion, I am sure cannot carrie his valor: for the Goose carries not the Fox. It is well; leaue it to his discretion, and let vs hearken to the Moone.

Moon. This Lanthorne doth the horned Moone present.

De. He should haue worne the hornes on his head.

Du. Hee is no crescent, and his hornes are inuisible, within the circumference.

Moon. This lanthorne doth the horned Moone present: My selfe, the man i'th Moone doth seeme to be.

Du. This is the greatest error of all the rest; the man should be put into the Lanthorne. How is it els the man i'th Moone?

Dem. He dares not come there for the candle. For you see, it is already in snuffe.

Dut. I am vvearie of this Moone; vvould he would change.

Du. It appeares by his smal light of discretion, that he is in the wane: but yet in courtesie, in all reason, vve must stay the time.

Lys. Proceed Moone.

Moon. All that I haue to say, is to tell you, that the Lanthorne is the Moone; I, the man in the Moone; this thorne bush, my thorne bush; and this dog, my dog.

Dem. Why all these should be in the Lanthorne: for they are in the Moone. But silence, heere comes *Thisby*.

Enter Thisby.

Thisb. This is old *Ninnies* tombe: where is my loue?

Lyon. Oh.

The Lion roares, Thisby runs off.

Dem. Well roar'd Lion.

Du. Well run *Thisby*.

Dut. Well shone Moone.

Truly the Moone shines with a good grace.

Du. Wel mouz'd Lion.

Dem. And then came *Piramus*.

Lys. And so the Lion vanisht.

Enter Piramus.

Pyr. Sweet Moone, I thank thee for thy sunny beames,
I thanke thee Moone, for shining now so bright:
For by thy gracious, golden, glittering beames,
I trust to taste of truest *Thisbies* sight.
But stay: O spight! but marke, poore Knight,
What dreadful dole is heere?
Eyes do you see! How can it be!
O dainty Ducke: O Deere!
Thy mantle good; what staind with blood!
Approch you Furies fell:
O Fates! come, come: Cut thred and thrum,
Quaile, crush, conclude, and quell.

Du. This passion, and the death of a deare friend, Would go neere to make a man looke sad.

Dut. Beshrew my heart, but I pittie the man.

Pir. O wherefore Nature, did'st thou Lions frame?
Since Lion vilde hath heere deflour'd my deere:
Which is: no, no, which was the fairest Dame
That liu'd, that lou'd, that lik'd, that look'd with cheere.
Come teares, confound: Out sword, and wound
The pap of *Piramus*:
I, that left pap, where heart doth hop;
Thus dye I, thus, thus, thus.
Now am I dead, now am I fled, my soule is in the sky,
Tongue lose thy light, Moone take thy flight,
Now dye, dye, dye, dye, dye.

Dem. No Die, but an ace for him; for he is but one.

Lys. Lesse then an ace man. For he is dead, he is nothing.

Du. With the helpe of a Surgeon, he might yet recouer, and proue an Asse.

Dut. How chance Moone-shine is gone before? *Thisby* comes backe, and findes her Louer.

Enter Thisby.

Duke. She wil finde him by starre-light.
Heere she comes, and her passion ends the play.

Dut. Me thinkes shee should not vse a long one for such a *Piramus*: I hope she will be breefe.

Dem. A Moth wil turne the ballance, which *Piramus* which *Thisby* is the better. (eyes.

Lys. She hath spyed him already, with those sweete

Dem. And thus she meanes, *videlicit.*

This. Asleepe my Loue? What, dead my Doue?
O *Piramus* arise:
Speake, Speake. Quite dumbe? Dead, dead? A tombe
Must couer thy sweet eyes.
These Lilly Lips, this cherry nose,
These yellow Cowslip cheekes
Are gone, are gone: Louers make mone:
His eyes were greene as Leekes.
O sisters three, come, come to mee,
With hands as pale as Milke,
Lay them in gore, since you haue shore
With sheeres, his thred of silke.
Tongue not a word: Come trusty sword:
Come blade, my brest imbrue:

And farwell friends, thus *Thisbie* ends;
Adieu, adieu, adieu.

Duk. Moon-shine & Lion are left to burie the dead.
Deme. I, and Wall too.
Bot. No, I assure you, the wall is downe, that parted their Fathers. Will it please you to see the Epilogue, or to heare a Bergomask dance, betweene two of our company?

Duk. No Epilogue, I pray you; for your play needs no excuse. Neuer excuse; for when the plaiers are all dead, there need none to be blamed. Marry, if hee that writ it had plaid *Piramus*, and hung himselfe in *Thisbies* garter, it would haue beene a fine Tragedy: and so it is truely, and very notably discharg'd. But come, your Burgomaske; let your Epilogue alone.
The iron tongue of midnight hath told twelue.
Louers to bed, 'tis almost Fairy time.
I feare we shall out-sleepe the comming morne,
As much as we this night haue ouer-watcht.
This palpable grosse play hath well beguil'd
The heauy gate of night. Sweet friends to bed.
A fortnight hold we this solemnity.
In nightly Reuels; and new iollitie. *Exeunt.*

Enter Pucke.

Puck. Now the hungry Lyons rores,
And the Wolfe beholds the Moone:
Whilest the heauy ploughman snores,
All with weary taske fore-done.
Now the wasted brands doe glow,
Whil'st the scritch-owle, scritching loud,
Puts the wretch that lies in woe,
In remembrance of a shrowd.
Now it is the time of night,
That the graues, all gaping wide,
Euery one lets forth his spright,
In the Church-way paths to glide.
And we Fairies, that do runne,
By the triple *Hecates* teame,
From the presence of the Sunne,
Following darkenesse like a dreame,
Now are frollicke; not a Mouse
Shall disturbe this hallowed house.
I am sent with broome before,
To sweep the dust behinde the doore.

Enter King and Queene of Fairies, with their traine.

Ob. Through the house giue glimmering light,
By the dead and drowsie fier,
Euerie Elfe and Fairie spright,
Hop as light as bird from brier,
And this Ditty after me, sing and dance it trippinglie.

Tita. First rehearse this song by roate,
To each word a warbling note.
Hand in hand, with Fairie grace,
Will we sing and blesse this place.

The Song.

Now vntill the breake of day,
Through this house each Fairy stray.
To the best Bride-bed will we,
Which by vs shall blessed be:
And the issue there create,
Euer shall be fortunate:
So shall all the couples three,
Euer true in louing be:
And the blots of Natures hand,
Shall not in their issue staud.
Neuer mole, harelip, nor scarre,
Nor marke prodigious, such as are
Despised in Natiuitie,
Shall vpon their children be.
With this field dew consecrate,
Euery Fairy take his gate,
And each seuerall chamber blesse,
Through this Pallace with sweet peace,
Euer shall in safety rest,
And the owner of it blest.
Trip away, make no stay;
Meet me all by breake of day.

Robin. If we shadowes haue offended,
Thinke but this (and all is mended)
That you haue but slumbred heere,
While these visions did appeare.
And this weake and idle theame,
No more yeelding but a dreame,
Centles, doe not reprehend.
If you pardon, we will mend.
And as I am an honest *Pucke*,
If we haue vnearned lucke,
Now to scape the Serpents tongue,
We will make amends ere long:
Else the *Pucke* a lyar call.
So good night vnto you all.
Giue me your hands, if we be friends,
And *Robin* shall restore amends.

FINIS.

The Merchant of Venice.

Actus primus.

Enter Anthonio, Salarino, and Salanio.

Anthonio.

IN sooth I know not why I am so sad,
It wearies me: you say it wearies you;
But how I caught it, found it, or came by it,
What stuffe 'tis made of, whereof it is borne,
I am to learne: and such a Want-wit sadnesse makes of
     mee,
That I haue much ado to know my selfe.

Sal. Your minde is tossing on the Ocean,
There where your Argosies with portly saile
Like Signiors and rich Burgers on the flood,
Or as it were the Pageants of the sea,
Do ouer-peere the pettie Traffiquers
That curtsie to them, do them reuerence
As they flye by them with their wouen wings.

Salar. Beleeue me sir, had I such venture forth,
The better part of my affections, would
Be with my hopes abroad. I should be still
Plucking the grasse to know where sits the winde,
Peering in Maps for ports, and peers, and rodes:
And euery obiect that might make me feare
Misfortune to my ventures, out of doubt
Would make me sad.

Sal. My winde cooling my broth,
Would blow me to an Ague, when I thought
What harme a winde too great might doe at sea.
I should not see the sandie houre-glasse runne,
But I should thinke of shallows, and of flats,
And see my wealthy *Andrew* docks in sand,
Vailing her high top lower then her ribs
To kisse her buriall; should I goe to Church
And see the holy edifice of stone,
And not bethinke me straight of dangerous rocks,
Which touching but my gentle Vessels side
Would scatter all her spices on the streame,
Enrobe the roring waters with my silkes,
And in a word, but euen now worth this,
And now worth nothing. Shall I haue the thought
To thinke on this, and shall I lacke the thought
That such a thing bechaunc'd would make me sad?
But tell not me, I know *Anthonio*
Is sad to thinke vpon his merchandize.

Anth. Beleeue me no, I thanke my fortune for it,
My ventures are not in one bottome trusted,
Nor to one place; nor is my whole estate
Vpon the fortune of this present yeere:
Therefore my merchandize makes me not sad.

Sola. Why then you are in loue.
Anth. Fie, fie.
Sola. Not in loue neither: then let vs say you are sad
Because you are not merry; and 'twere as easie
For you to laugh and leape, and say you are merry
Because you are not sad. Now by two-headed *Ianus*,
Nature hath fram'd strange fellowes in her time:
Some that will euermore peepe through their eyes,
And laugh like Parrats at a bag-piper.
And other of such vineger aspect,
That they'il not shew their teeth in way of smile,
Though *Nestor* sweare the iest be laughable.

Enter Bassanio, Lorenso, and Gratiano.

Sola. Heere comes *Bassanio*,
Your most noble Kinsman,
Gratiano, and *Lorenso.* Faryewell,
We leaue you now with better company.

Sala. I would haue staid till I had made you merry,
If worthier friends had not preuented me.

Ant. Your worth is very deere in my regard.
I take it your owne busines calls on you,
And you embrace th'occasion to depart.

Sal. Good morrow my good Lords.   (when?
Bass. Good signiors both, when shall we laugh? say,
You grow exceeding strange: must it be so?

Sal. Wee'll make our leysures to attend on yours.
        Exeunt Salarino, and Solanio.

Lor. My Lord *Bassanio*, since you haue found *Anthonio*
We two will leaue you, but at dinner time
I pray you haue in minde where we must meete.

Bass. I will not faile you.

Grat. You looke not well signior *Anthonio*,
You haue too much respect vpon the world:
They loose it that doe buy it with much care,
Beleeue me you are maruellously chang'd.

Ant. I hold the world but as the world *Gratiano*,
A stage, where euery man must play a part,
And mine a sad one.

Grati. Let me play the foole,
With mirth and laughter let old wrinckles come,
And let my Liuer rather heate with wine,
Then my heart coole with mortifying grones.
Why should a man whose bloud is warme within,
Sit like his Grandsire, cut in Alablaster?
Sleepe when he wakes? and creep into the Iaundies

By

By being peeuish? I tell thee what *Anthonio*,
I loue thee, and it is my loue that speakes:
There are a sort of men, whose visages
Do creame and mantle like a standing pond,
And do a wilfull stilnesse entertaine,
With purpose to be drest in an opinion
Of wisedome, grauity, profound conceit,
As who should say, I am sir an Oracle,
And when I ope my lips, let no dogge barke.
O my *Anthonio*, I do know of these
That therefore onely are reputed wise,
For saying nothing; when I am verie sure
If they should speake, would almost dam those eares
Which hearing them would call their brothers fooles:
Ile tell thee more of this another time.
But fish not with this melancholly baite
For this foole Gudgin, this opinion:
Come good *Lorenzo*, faryewell a while,
Ile end my exhortation after dinner.

  Lor. Well, we will leaue you then till dinner time,
I must be one of these same dumbe wise men,
For *Gratiano* neuer let's me speake.

  Gra. Well, keepe me company but two yeares mo,
Thou shalt not know the sound of thine owne tongue.

  Ant. Far you well, Ile grow a talker for this geare.

  Gra. Thankes ifaith, for silence is onely commendable
In a neats tongue dri'd, and a maid not vendible. *Exit*.

  Ant. It is that any thing now.

  Bas. *Gratiano* speakes an infinite deale of nothing,
more then any man in all Venice, his reasons are two
graines of wheate hid in two bushels of chaffe: you shall
seeke all day ere you finde them, & when you haue them
they are not worth the search.

  An. Well: tel me now, what Lady is the same
To whom you swore a secret Pilgrimage
That you to day promis'd to tel me of?

  Bas. Tis not vnknowne to you *Anthonio*
How much I haue disabled mine estate,
By something shewing a more swelling port
Then my faint meanes would grant continuance:
Nor do I now make mone to be abridg'd
From such a noble rate, but my cheefe care
Is to come fairely off from the great debts
Wherein my time something too prodigall
Hath left me gag'd: to you *Anthonio*
I owe the most in money, and in loue,
And from your loue I haue a warrantie
To vnburthen all my plots and purposes,
How to get cleere of all the debts I owe.

  An. I pray you good *Bassanio* let me know it,
And if it stand as you your selfe still do,
Within the eye of honour, be assur'd
My purse, my person, my extreamest meanes
Lye all vnlock'd to your occasions.

  Bas. In my schoole dayes, when I had lost one shaft
I shot his fellow of the selfesame flight
The selfesame way, with more aduised watch
To finde the other forth, and by aduenturing both,
I oft found both. I vrge this child-hoode proofe,
Because what followes is pure innocence.
I owe you much, and like a wilfull youth,
That which I owe is lost: but if you please
To shoote another arrow that selfe way
Which you did shoot the first, I do not doubt,
As I will watch the ayme: Or to finde both,
Or bring your latter hazard backe againe,

And thankfully rest debter for the first.

  An. You know me well, and herein spend but time
To winde about my loue with circumstance,
And out of doubt you doe more wrong
In making question of my vttermost
Then if you had made waste of all I haue:
Then doe but say to me what I should doe
That in your knowledge may by me be done,
And I am prest vnto it: therefore speake.

  Bass. In *Belmont* is a Lady richly left,
And she is faire, and fairer then that word,
Of wondrous vertues, sometimes from her eyes
I did receiue faire speechlesse messages:
Her name is *Portia*, nothing vndervallewd
To *Cato*'s daughter, *Brutus Portia*,
Nor is the wide world ignorant of her worth,
For the foure windes blow in from euery coast
Renowned sutors, and her sunny locks
Hang on her temples like a golden fleece,
Which makes her seat of *Belmont Cholchos* strond,
And many *Iasons* come in quest of her.
O my *Anthonio*, had I but the meanes
To hold a riuall place with one of them,
I haue a minde presages me such thrift,
That I should questionlesse be fortunate.

  Anth. Thou knowst that all my fortunes are at sea,
Neither haue I money, nor commodity
To raise a present summe, therefore goe forth
Try what my credit can in *Venice* doe,
That shall be rackt euen to the vttermost,
To furnish thee to *Belmont* to faire *Portia*.
Goe presently enquire, and so will I
Where money is, and I no question make
To haue it of my trust, or for my sake. *Exeunt*.

Enter Portia with her waiting woman Nerissa.

  Portia. By my troth *Nerrissa*, my little body is a wearie of this great world.

  Ner. You would be sweet Madam, if your miseries
were in the same abundance as your good fortunes are:
and yet for ought I see, they are as sicke that surfet with
too much, as they that starue with nothing; it is no smal
happinesse therefore to bee seated in the meane, superfluitie comes sooner by white haires, but competencie
liues longer.

  Portia. Good sentences, and well pronounc'd.

  Ner. They would be better if well followed.

  Portia. If to doe were as easie as to know what were
good to doe, Chappels had beene Churches, and poore
mens cottages Princes Pallaces: it is a good Diuine that
followes his owne instructions; I can easier teach twentie what were good to be done, then be one of the twentie to follow mine owne teaching: the braine may deuise lawes for the blood, but a hot temper leapes ore a
colde decree, such a hare is madnesse the youth, to skip
ore the meshes of good counsaile the cripple; but this
reason is not in fashion to choose me a husband: O mee,
the word choose, I may neither choose whom I would,
nor refuse whom I dislike, so is the wil of a liuing daughter curb'd by the will of a dead father: it is not hard *Nerrissa*, that I cannot choose one, nor refuse none.

  Ner. Your father was euer vertuous, and holy men
at their death haue good inspirations, therefore the lotterie that hee hath deuised in these three chests of gold,
siluer, and leade, whereof who chooses his meaning,
chooses

chooses you, wil no doubt neuer be chosen by any right-ly, but one who you shall rightly loue: but what warmth is there in your affection towards any of these Princely suters that are already come?

Por. I pray thee ouer-name them, and as thou namest them, I will describe them, and according to my description leuell at my affection.

Ner. First there is the Neopolitane Prince.

Por. I that's a colt indeede, for he doth nothing but talke of his horse, and hee makes it a great appropriation to his owne good parts that he can shoo him himselfe: I am much afraid my Ladie his mother plaid false with a Smyth.

Ner. Than is there the Countie Palentine.

Por. He doth nothing but frowne (as who should say, and you will not haue me, choose: he heares merrie tales and smiles not, I feare hee will proue the weeping Phylosopher when he growes old, being so full of vnmannerly sadnesse in his youth.) I had rather to be married to a deaths head with a bone in his mouth, then to either of these: God defend me from these two.

Ner. How say you by the French Lord, Mounsier Le Bonne?

Pro. God made him, and therefore let him passe for a man, in truth I know it is a sinne to be a mocker, but he, why he hath a horse better then the Neopolitans, a better bad habite of frowning then the Count Palentine, he is euery man in no man, if a Trassell sing, he fals straight a capring, he will fence with his own shadow. If I should marry him, I should marry twentie husbands: if hee would despise me, I would forgiue him, for if he loue me to madnesse, I should neuer requite him.

Ner. What say you then to *Fauconbridge*, the yong Baron of *England*?

Por. You know I say nothing to him, for hee vnderstands not me, nor I him: he hath neither *Batine*, *French*, nor *Italian*, and you will come into the Court & sweare that I haue a poore pennie-worth in the *English*: hee is a proper mans picture, but alas who can conuerse with a dumbe show? how odly he is suited, I thinke he bought his doublet in *Italie*, his round hose in *France*, his bonnet in *Germanie*, and his behauiour euery where.

Ner. What thinke you of the other Lord his neighbour?

Por. That he hath a neighbourly charitie in him, for he borrowed a boxe of the eare of the *Englishman*, and swore he would pay him againe when hee was able: I thinke the *Frenchman* became his suretie, and seald vnder for another.

Ner. How like you the yong *Germaine*, the Duke of *Saxonies* Nephew?

Por. Very vildely in the morning when hee is sober, and most vildely in the afternoone when hee is drunke: when he is best, he is a little worse then a man, and when he is worst, he is little better then a beast: and the worst fall that euer fell, I hope I shall make shift to goe without him.

Ner. If he should offer to choose, and choose the right Casket, you should refuse to performe your Fathers will, if you should refuse to accept him.

Por. Therefore for feare of the worst, I pray thee set a deepe glasse of Reinish-wine on the contrary Casket, for if the diuell be within, and that temptation without, I know he will choose it. I will doe any thing *Nerrissa* ere I will be married to a spunge.

Ner. You neede not feare Lady the hauing any of these Lords, they haue acquainted me with their determinations, which is indeede to returne to their home, and to trouble you with no more suite, vnlesse you may be won by some other sort then your Fathers imposition, depending on the Caskets.

Por. If I liue to be as olde as *Sibilla*, I will dye as chaste as *Diana*: vnlesse I be obtained by the manner of my Fathers will: I am glad this parcell of wooers are so reasonable, for there is not one among them but I doate on his verie absence: and I wish them a faire departure.

Ner. Doe you not remember Ladie in your Fathers time, a *Venecian*, a Scholler and a Souldior that came hither in companie of the Marquesse of *Mountferrat*?

Por. Yes, yes, it was *Bassanio*, as I thinke, so was hee call'd.

Ner. True Madam, hee of all the men that euer my foolish eyes look'd vpon, was the best deseruing a faire Lady.

Por. I remember him well, and I remember him worthy of thy praise.

Enter a Seruingman.

Ser. The foure Strangers seeke you Madam to take their leaue: and there is a fore-runner come from a fift, the Prince of *Moroco*, who brings word the Prince his Maister will be here to night.

Por. If I could bid the fift welcome with so good heart as I can bid the other foure farewell, I should be glad of his approach: if he haue the condition of a Saint, and the complexion of a diuell, I had rather hee should shriue me then wiue me. Come *Nerrissa*, sirra go before; whiles wee shut the gate vpon one wooer, another knocks at the doore. *Exeunt.*

Enter Bassanio with Shylocke the Iew.

Shy. Three thousand ducates, well.

Bass. I sir, for three months.

Shy. For three months, well.

Bass. For the which, as I told you, *Anthonio* shall be bound.

Shy. *Anthonio* shall become bound, well.

Bass. May you sted me? Will you pleasure me? Shall I know your answere.

Shy. Three thousand ducats for three months, and *Anthonio* bound.

Bass. Your answere to that.

Shy. *Anthonio* is a good man.

Bass. Haue you heard any imputation to the contrary.

Shy. Ho no, no, no, no: my meaning in saying he is a good man, is to haue you vnderstand me that he is sufficient, yet his meanes are in supposition: he hath an Argosie bound to Tripolis, another to the Indies, I vnderstand moreouer vpon the Ryalta, he hath a third at Mexico, a fourth for England, and other ventures hee hath squandred abroad, but ships are but boords, Saylers but men, there be land rats, and water rats, water theeues, and land theeues, I meane Pyrats, and then there is the perrill of waters, windes, and rocks: the man is notwithstanding sufficient, three thousand ducats, I thinke I may take his bond.

Bas. Be assured you may.

Iew. I

Iew. I will be assured I may: and that I may be assured, I will bethinke mee, may I speake with *Anthonio*?

Bass. If it please you to dine with vs.

Iew. Yes, to smell porke, to eate of the habitation which your Prophet the Nazarite coniured the diuell into: I will buy with you, sell with you, talke with you, walke with you, and so following: but I will not eate with you, drinke with you, nor pray with you. What newes on the Ryalta, who is he comes here?

Enter Anthonio.

Bass. This is signior *Anthonio*.

Iew. How like a fawning publican he lookes.
I hate him for he is a Christian:
But more, for that in low simplicitie
He lends out money gratis, and brings downe
The rate of vsance here with vs in *Venice*.
If I can catch him once vpon the hip,
I will feede fat the ancient grudge I beare him.
He hates our sacred Nation, and he railes
Euen there where Merchants most doe congregate
On me, my bargaines, and my well-worne thrift,
Which he cals interrest: Cursed be my Trybe
If I forgiue him.

Bass. Shylock, doe you heare.

Shy. I am debating of my present store,
And by the neere gesse of my memorie
I cannot instantly raise vp the grosse
Of full three thousand ducats: what of that?
Tuball a wealthy Hebrew of my Tribe
Will furnish me; but soft, how many months
Doe you desire? Rest you faire good signior,
Your worship was the last man in our mouthes.

Ant. Shylocke, albeit I neither lend nor borrow
By taking, nor by giuing of excesse,
Yet to supply the ripe wants of my friend,
Ile breake a custome: is he yet possest
How much he would?

Shy. I, I, three thousand ducats.

Ant. And for three months.

Shy. I had forgot, three months, you told me so.
Well then, your bond: and let me see, but heare you,
Me thoughts you said, you neither lend nor borrow
Vpon aduantage.

Ant. I doe neuer vse it.

Shy. When *Iacob* graz'd his Vncle *Labans* sheepe,
This *Iacob* from our holy *Abram* was
(As his wife mother wrought in his behalfe)
The third possesser; I, he was the third.

Ant. And what of him, did he take interrest?

Shy. No, not take interest, not as you would say
Directly interest, marke what *Iacob* did,
When *Laban* and himselfe were compremyz'd
That all the eanelings which were streakt and pied
Should fall as *Iacobs* hier, the Ewes being rancke,
In end of Autumne turned to the Rammes,
And when the worke of generation was
Betweene these woolly breeders in the act,
The skilfull shepheard pil'd me certaine wands,
And in the dooing of the deede of kinde,
He stucke them vp before the fulsome Ewes,
Who then conceauing, did in eaning time
Fall party-colour'd lambs, and those were *Iacobs*.
This was a way to thriue, and he was blest:
And thrift is blessing if men steale it not.

Ant. This was a venture sir that *Iacob* seru'd for,
A thing not in his power to bring to passe,
But sway'd and fashion'd by the hand of heauen.
Was this inserted to make interrest good?
Or is your gold and siluer Ewes and Rams?

Shy. I cannot tell, I make it breede as fast,
But note me signior.

Ant. Marke you this *Bassanio*,
The diuell can cite Scripture for his purpose,
An euill soule producing holy witnesse,
Is like a villaine with a smiling cheeke,
A goodly apple rotten at the heart.
O what a goodly outside falsehood hath.

Shy. Three thousand ducats, 'tis a good round sum.
Three months from twelue, then let me see the rate.

Ant. Well *Shylocke*, shall we be beholding to you?

Shy. Signior *Anthonio*, many a time and oft
In the Ryalto you haue rated me
About my monies and my vsances:
Still haue I borne it with a patient shrug,
(For sufrance is the badge of all our Tribe.)
You call me misbeleeuer, cut-throate dog,
And spet vpon my Iewish gaberdine,
And all for vse of that which is mine owne.
Well then, it now appeares you neede my helpe:
Goe to then, you come to me, and you say,
Shylocke, we would haue moneyes, you say so:
You that did voide your rume vpon my beard,
And foote me as you spurne a stranger curre
Ouer your threshold, moneyes is your suite.
What should I say to you? Should I not say,
Hath a dog money? Is it possible
A curre should lend three thousand ducats? or
Shall I bend low, and in a bond-mans key
With bated breath, and whispring humblenesse,
Say this: Faire sir, you spet on me on Wednesday last;
You spurn'd me such a day; another time
You cald me dog: and for these curtesies
Ile lend you thus much moneyes.

Ant. I am as like to call thee so againe,
To spet on thee againe, to spurne thee too.
If thou wilt lend this money, lend it not
As to thy friends, for when did friendship take
A breede of barraine mettall of his friend?
But lend it rather to thine enemie,
Who if he breake, thou maist with better face
Exact the penalties.

Shy. Why looke you how you storme,
I would be friends with you, and haue your loue,
Forget the shames that you haue staind me with,
Supplie your present wants, and take no doite
Of vsance for my moneyes, and youle not heare me,
This is kinde I offer.

Bass. This were kindnesse.

Shy. This kindnesse will I showe,
Goe with me to a Notarie, seale me there
Your single bond, and in a merrie sport,
If you repaie me not on such a day,
In such a place, such sum or sums as are
Exprest in the condition, let the forfeite
Be nominated for an equall pound
Of your faire flesh, to be cut off and taken
In what part of your bodie it pleaseth me.

Ant. Content infaith, Ile seale to such a bond,
And say there is much kindnesse in the Iew.

Bass. You

Bass. You shall not seale to such a bond for me,
Ile rather dwell in my necessitie.

Ant. Why feare not man, I will not forfaite it,
Within these two months, that's a month before
This bond expires, I doe expect returne
Of thrice three times the valew of this bond.

Shy. O father *Abram*, what these Christians are,
Whose owne hard dealings teaches them suspect
The thoughts of others: Praie you tell me this,
If he should breake his daie, what should I gaine
By the exaction of the forfeiture?
A pound of mans flesh taken from a man,
Is not so estimable, profitable neither
As flesh of Muttons, Beefes, or Goates, I say
To buy his fauour, I extend this friendship,
If he will take it, so: if not adiew,
And for my loue I praie you wrong me not.

Ant. Yes *Shylocke*, I will seale vnto this bond.

Shy. Then meete me forthwith at the Notaries,
Giue him direction for this merrie bond,
And I will goe and purse the ducats straite.
See to my house left in the fearefull gard
Of an vnthriftie knaue: and presentlie
Ile be with you. *Exit.*

Ant. Hie thee gentle *Iew.* This Hebrew will turne
Christian, he growes kinde.

Bass. I like not faire teames, and a villaines minde.

Ant. Come on, in this there can be no dismaie,
My Shippes come home a month before the daie.
Exeunt.

Actus Secundus.

Enter Morochus a tawnie Moore all in white, and three or foure followers accordingly, with Portia, Nerrissa, and their traine.
Flo. Cornets.

Mor. Mislike me not for my complexion,
The shadowed liuerie of the burnisht sunne,
To whom I am a neighbour, and neere bred.
Bring me the fairest creature North-ward borne,
Where *Phœbus* fire scarce thawes the ysicles,
And let vs make incision for your loue,
To proue whose blood is reddest, his or mine.
I tell thee Ladie this aspect of mine
Hath feard the valiant, (by my loue I sweare)
The best regarded Virgins of our Clyme
Haue lou'd it to: I would not change this hue,
Except to steale your thoughts my gentle Queene.

Por. In tearmes of choise I am not solie led
By nice direction of a maidens eies:
Besides, the lottrie of my destenie
Bars me the right of voluntarie choosing:
But if my Father had not scanted me,
And hedg'd me by his wit to yeelde my selfe
His wife, who wins me by that meanes I told you,
Your selfe (renowned Prince) than stood as faire
As any commer I haue look'd on yet
For my affection.

Mor. Euen for that I thanke you,
Therefore I pray you leade me to the Caskets
To trie my fortune: By this Symitare
That slew the Sophie, and a Persian Prince
That won three fields of Sultan Solyman,
I would ore-stare the sternest eies that looke:
Out-braue the heart most daring on the earth:
Plucke the yong sucking Cubs from the she Beare,
Yea, mocke the Lion when he rores for pray
To win the Ladie. But alas, the while
If *Hercules* and *Lychas* plaie at dice
Which is the better man, the greater throw
May turne by fortune from the weaker hand:
So is *Alcides* beaten by his rage,
And so may I, blinde fortune leading me
Misse that which one vnworthier may attaine,
And die with grieuing.

Port. You must take your chance,
And either not attempt to choose at all,
Or sweare before you choose, if you choose wrong
Neuer to speake to Ladie afterward
In way of marriage, therefore be aduis'd.

Mor. Nor will not, come bring me vnto my chance.

Por. First forward to the temple, after dinner
Your hazard shall be made.

Mor. Good fortune then, *Cornets.*
To make me blest or cursed'st among men. *Exeunt.*

Enter the Clowne alone.

Clo. Certainely, my conscience will serue me to run from this Iew my Maister: the fiend is at mine elbow, and tempts me, saying to me, *Iobbe, Launcelet Iobbe*, good *Launcelet*, or good *Iobbe*, or good *Launcelet Iobbe*, vse your legs, take the start, run awaie: my conscience saies no; take heede honest *Launcelet*, take heed honest *Iobbe*, or as afore-said honest *Launcelet Iobbe*, doe not runne, scorne running with thy heeles; well, the most coragious fiend bids me packe, *fia* saies the fiend, away saies the fiend, for the heauens rouse vp a braue minde saies the fiend, and run; well, my conscience hanging about the necke of my heart, saies verie wisely to me: my honest friend *Launcelet*, being an honest mans sonne, or rather an honest womans sonne, for indeede my Father did something smack, something grow too; he had a kinde of taste; wel, my conscience saies *Lancelet* bouge not, bouge saies the fiend, bouge not saies my conscience, conscience say I you counsaile well, fiend say I you counsaile well, to be rul'd by my conscience I should stay with the *Iew* my Maister, (who God blesse the marke) is a kinde of diuell; and to run away from the *Iew* I should be ruled by the fiend, who sauing your reuerence is the diuell himselfe: certainely the *Iew* is the verie diuell incarnation, and in my conscience, my conscience is a kinde of hard conscience, to offer to counsaile me to stay with the *Iew*; the fiend giues the more friendly counsaile: I will runne fiend, my heeles are at your commandement, I will runne.

Enter old Gobbo with a Basket.

Gob. Maister yong-man, you I praie you, which is the waie to Maister *Iewes*?

Lan. O heauens, this is my true begotten Father, who being more then sand-blinde, high grauel blinde, knows me not, I will trie confusions with him.

Gob. Maister yong Gentleman, I praie you which is the waie to Maister *Iewes*.

Laun. Turne vpon your right hand at the next turning

ning, but at the next turning of all on your left; marrie at the verie next turning, turne of no hand, but turn down indirectlie to the *Iewes* house.

Gob. Be Gods sonties 'twill be a hard waie to hit, can you tell me whether one *Launcelet* that dwels with him, dwell with him or no.

Laun. Talke you of yong Maister *Launcelet*, marke me now, now will I raise the waters; talke you of yong Maister *Launcelet*?

Gob. No Maister sir, but a poore mans sonne, his Father though I say't is an honest exceeding poore man, and God be thanked well to liue.

Lan. Well, let his Father be what a will, wee talke of yong Maister *Launcelet*.

Gob. Your worships friend and *Launcelet*.

Laun. But I praie you *ergo* old man, *ergo* I beseech you, talke you of yong Maister *Launcelet*.

Gob. Of *Launcelet*, an't please your maistership.

Lan. Ergo Maister *Lancelet*, talke not of maister *Lancelet* Father, for the yong gentleman according to fates and destinies, and such odde sayings, the sisters three, & such branches of learning, is indeede deceased, or as you would say in plaine tearmes, gone to heauen.

Gob. Marrie God forbid, the boy was the verie staffe of my age, my verie prop.

Lau. Do I look like a cudgell or a houell-post, a staffe or a prop: doe you know me Father.

Gob. Alacke the day, I know you not yong Gentleman, but I praie you tell me, is my boy God rest his soule aliue or dead.

Lan. Doe you not know me Father.

Gob. Alacke sir I am sand blinde, I know you not.

Lan. Nay, indeede if you had your eies you might faile of the knowing me: it is a wise Father that knowes his owne childe. Well, old man, I will tell you newes of your son, giue me your blessing, truth will come to light, murder cannot be hid long, a mans sonne may, but in the end truth will out.

Gob. Praie you sir stand vp, I am sure you are not *Lancelet* my boy.

Lan. Praie you let's haue no more fooling about it, but giue mee your blessing: I am *Lancelet* your boy that was, your sonne that is, your childe that shall be.

Gob. I cannot thinke you are my sonne.

Lan. I know not what I shall thinke of that: but I am *Lancelet* the *Iewes* man, and I am sure *Margerie* your wife is my mother.

Gob. Her name is *Margerie* indeede, Ile be sworne if thou be *Lancelet*, thou art mine owne flesh and blood: Lord worshipt might he be, what a beard hast thou got; thou hast got more haire on thy chin, then Dobbin my philhorse has on his taile.

Lan. It should seeme then that Dobbins taile growes backeward. I am sure he had more haire of his taile then I haue of my face when I lost saw him.

Gob. Lord how art thou chang'd: how doost thou and thy Maister agree, I haue brought him a present; how gree you now?

Lan. Well, well, but for mine owne part, as I haue set vp my rest to run awaie, so I will not rest till I haue run some ground; my Maister's a verie *Iew*, giue him a present, giue him a halter, I am famisht in his seruice. You may tell euerie finger I haue with my ribs: Father I am glad you are come, giue me your present to one Maister *Bassanio*, who indeede giues rare new Liueries, if I serue

not him, I will run as far as God has anie ground. O rare fortune, here comes the man, to him Father, for I am a *Iew* if I serue the *Iew* anie longer.

Enter Bassanio with a follower or two.

Bass. You may doe so, but let it be so hasted that supper be readie at the farthest by fiue of the clocke: see these Letters deliuered, put the Liueries to making, and desire *Gratiano* to come anone to my lodging.

Lan. To him Father.

Gob. God blesse your worship.

Bass. Gramercie, would'st thou ought with me.

Gob. Here's my sonne sir, a poore boy.

Lan. Not a poore boy sir, but the rich *Iewes* man that would sir as my Father shall specifie.

Gob. He hath a great infection sir, as one would say to serue.

Lan. Indeede the short and the long is, I serue the *Iew*, and haue a desire as my Father shall specifie.

Gob. His Maister and he (sauing your worships reuerence) are scarce catercosins.

Lan. To be briefe, the verie truth is, that the *Iew* hauing done me wrong, doth cause me as my Father being I hope an old man shall frutifie vnto you.

Gob. I haue here a dish of Doues that I would bestow vpon your worship, and my suite is.

Lan. In verie briefe, the suite is impertinent to my selfe, as your worship shall know by this honest old man, and though I say it, though old man, yet poore man my Father.

Bass. One speake for both, what would you?

Lan. Serue you sir.

Gob. That is the verie defect of the matter sir.

Bass. I know thee well, thou hast obtain'd thy suite, *Shylocke* thy Maister spoke with me this daie, And hath prefer'd thee, if it be preferment To leaue a rich *Iewes* seruice, to become The follower of so poore a Gentleman.

Clo. The old prouerbe is verie well parted betweene my Maister *Shylocke* and you sir, you haue the grace of God sir, and he hath enough.

Bass. Thou speak'st it well; go Father with thy Son, Take leaue of thy old Maister, and enquire My lodging out, giue him a Liuerie More garded then his fellowes: see it done.

Clo. Father in, I cannot get a seruice, no, I haue nere a tongue in my head, well: if anie man in *Italie* haue a fairer table which doth offer to sweare vpon a booke, I shall haue good fortune; goe too, here's a simple line of life, here's a small trifle of wiues, alas, fifteene wiues is nothing, a leuen widdowes and nine maides is a simple comming in for one man, and then to scape drowning thrice, and to be in perill of my life with the edge of a featherbed, here are simple scapes: well, if Fortune be a woman, she's a good wench for this gere: Father come, Ile take my leaue of the *Iew* in the twinkling. *Exit Clowne.*

Bass. I praie thee good *Leonardo* thinke on this, These things being bought and orderly bestowed Returne in haste, for I doe feast to night My best esteemd acquaintance, hie thee goe.

Leon. My best endeuors shall be done herein. *Exit Le.*

Enter Gratiano.

Gra. Where's your Maister.

Leon. Yonder

Leon. Yonder sir he walkes.
Gra. Signior *Bassanio*.
Bass. Gratiano.
Gra. I haue a sute to you.
Bass. You haue obtain'd it.
Gra. You must not denie me, I must goe with you to Belmont.
Bass. Why then you must: but heare thee *Gratiano*,
Thou art to wilde, to rude, and bold of voyce,
Parts that become thee happily enough,
And in such eyes as ours appeare not faults;
But where they are not knowne, why there they show
Something too liberall, pray thee take paine
To allay with some cold drops of modestie
Thy skipping spirit, least through thy wilde behauiour
I be misconsterd in the place I goe to,
And loose my hopes.
Gra. Signor *Bassanio*, heare me,
If I doe not put on a sober habite,
Talke with respect, and sweare but now and than,
Weare prayer bookes in my pocket, looke demurely,
Nay more, while grace is saying hood mine eyes
Thus with my hat, and sigh and say Amen:
Vse all the obseruance of ciuillitie
Like one well studied in a sad ostent
To please his Grandam, neuer trust me more.
Bass. Well, we shall see your bearing.
Gra. Nay but I barre to night, you shall not gage me
By what we doe to night.
Bass. No that were pittie,
I would intreate you rather to put on
Your boldest suite of mirth, for we haue friends
That purpose merriment: but far you well,
I haue some businesse.
Gra. And I must to *Lorenso* and the rest,
But we will visite you at supper time. *Exeunt*.

Enter Iessica and the Clowne.

Ies. I am sorry thou wilt leaue my Father so,
Our house is hell, and thou a merrie diuell
Did'st rob it of some taste of tediousnesse;
But far thee well, there is a ducat for thee,
And *Lancelet*, soone at supper shalt thou see
Lorenzo, who is thy new Maisters guest,
Giue him this Letter, doe it secretly,
And so farwell: I would not haue my Father
See me talke with thee.
Clo. Adue, teares exhibit my tongue, most beautifull
Pagan, most sweete Iew, if a Christian doe not play the
knaue and get thee, I am much deceiued; but adue, these
foolish drops doe somewhat drowne my manly spirit:
adue. *Exit*.
Ies. Farewell good *Lancelet*.
Alacke, what hainous sinne is it in mee
To be ashamed to be my Fathers childe,
But though I am a daughter to his blood,
I am not to his manners: O *Lorenzo*,
If thou keepe promise I shall end this strife,
Become a Christian, and thy louing wife. *Exit*.

Enter Gratiano, Lorenzo, Slarino, and Salanio.

Lor. Nay, we will slinke away in supper time,
Disguise vs at my lodging, and returne all in an houre.
Gra. We haue not made good preparation.
Sal. We haue not spoke vs yet of Torch-bearers.

Sol. 'Tis vile vnlesse it may be quaintly ordered,
And better in my minde not vndertooke.
Lor. 'Tis now but foure of clock, we haue two houres
To furnish vs; friend *Lancelet* what's the newes.

Enter Launcelet with a Letter.

Lan. And it shall please you to breake vp this, shall it seeme to signifie.
Lor. I know the hand, in faith 'tis a faire hand
And whiter then the paper it writ on,
I the faire hand that writ.
Gra. Loue newes in faith.
Lan. By your leaue sir.
Lor. Whither goest thou?
Lan. Marry sir to bid my old Master the *Iew* to sup
to night with my new Master the Christian.
Lor. Hold here, take this, tell gentle *Iessica*
I will not faile her, speake it priuately:
Go Gentlemen, will you prepare you for this Maske to
   night,
I am prouided of a Torch-bearer. *Exit. Clowne*.
Sal. I marry, ile be gone about it strait.
Sol. And so will I.
Lor. Meete me and *Gratiano* at *Gratianos* lodging
Some houre hence.
Sal. 'Tis good we do so. *Exit*.
Gra. Was not that Letter from faire *Iessica*?
Lor. I must needes tell thee all, she hath directed
How I shall take her from her Fathers house,
What gold and iewels she is furnisht with,
What Pages suite she hath in readinesse:
If ere the *Iew* her Father come to heauen,
It will be for his gentle daughters sake;
And neuer dare misfortune crosse her foote,
Vnlesse she doe it vnder this excuse,
That she is issue to a faithlesse *Iew*:
Come goe with me, peruse this as thou goest,
Faire *Iessica* shall be my Torch-bearer. *Exit*.

Enter Iew, and his man that was the Clowne.

Iew. Well, thou shall see, thy eyes shall be thy iudge,
The difference of old *Shylocke* and *Bassanio*;
What *Iessica*, thou shalt not gurmandize
As thou hast done with me: what *Iessica*?
And sleepe, and snore, and rend apparrell out.
Why *Iessica* I say.
Clo. Why *Iessica*.
Shy. Who bids thee call? I do not bid thee call.
Clo. Your worship was wont to tell me
I could doe nothing without bidding.

Enter Iessica.

Ies. Call you? what is your will?
Shy. I am bid forth to supper *Iessica*,
There are my Keyes: but wherefore should I go?
I am not bid for loue, they flatter me,
But yet Ile goe in hate, to feede vpon
The prodigall Christian. *Iessica* my girle,
Looke to my house, I am right loath to goe,
There is some ill a bruing towards my rest,
For I did dreame of money bags to night.
Clo. I beseech you sir goe, my yong Master
Doth expect your reproach.
Shy. So doe I his.
Clo. And they haue conspired together, I will not say
you shall see a Maske, but if you doe, then it was not for
nothing that my nose fell a bleeding on blacke monday

P   last,

last, at six a clocke ith morning, falling out that yeere on ashwensday was foure yeere in th'afternoone.

Shy. What are their maskes? heare you me *Iessica*,
Lock vp my doores, and when you heare the drum
And the vile squealing of the wry-neckt Fife,
Clamber not you vp to the casements then,
Nor thrust your head into the publique streete
To gaze on Christian fooles with varnisht faces:
But stop my houses eares, I meane my casements,
Let not the sound of shallow fopperie enter
My sober house. By *Iacobs* staffe I sweare,
I haue no minde of feasting forth to night:
But I will goe: goe you before me sirra,
Say I will come.

Clo. I will goe before sir.
Mistris looke out at window for all this;
There will come a Christian by,
Will be worth a Iewes eye.

Shy. What saies that foole of *Hagars* off-spring? ha.

Ies. His words were farewell mistris, nothing else.

Shy. The patch is kinde enough, but a huge feeder:
Snaile-slow in profit, but he sleepes by day
More then the wilde-cat: drones hiue not with me,
Therefore I part with him, and part with him
To one that I would haue him helpe to waste
His borrowed purse. Well *Iessica* goe in,
Perhaps I will returne immediately;
Doe as I bid you, shut dores after you, fast binde, fast finde,
A prouerbe neuer stale in thriftie minde. *Exit.*

Ies. Farewell, and if my fortune be not crost,
I haue a Father, you a daughter lost. *Exit.*

Enter the Maskers, Gratiano and Salino.

Gra. This is the penthouse vnder which *Lorenzo*
Desired vs to make a stand.

Sal. His houre is almost past.

Gra. And it is meruaile he out-dwels his houre,
For louers euer run before the clocke.

Sal. O ten times faster *Venus* Pidgions flye
To steale loues bonds new made, then they are wont
To keepe obliged faith vnforfaited.

Gra. That euer holds, who riseth from a feast
With that keene appetite that he sits downe?
Where is the horse that doth vntread againe
His tedious measures with the vnbated fire,
That he did pace them first: all things that are,
Are with more spirit chased then enioy'd.
How like a yonger or a prodigall
The skarfed barke puts from her natiue bay,
Hudg'd and embraced by the strumpet winde:
How like a prodigall doth she returne
With ouer-wither'd ribs and ragged sailes,
Leane, rent, and begger'd by the strumpet winde?

Enter Lorenzo.

Salino. Heere comes *Lorenzo*, more of this hereafter.

Lor. Sweete friends, your patience for my long abode,
Not I, but my affaires haue made you wait:
When you shall please to play the theeues for wiues
Ile watch as long for you then: approach
Here dwels my father Iew. Hoa, who's within?

Iessica aboue.

Iess. Who are you? tell me for more certainty,
Albeit Ile sweare that I do know your tongue.

Lor. Lorenzo, and thy Loue.

Ies. Lorenzo certaine, and my loue indeed,
For who loue I so much? and now who knowes
But you *Lorenzo*, whether I am yours?

Lor. Heauen and thy thoughts are witness that thou art.

Ies. Heere, catch this casket, it is worth the paines,
I am glad 'tis night, you do not looke on me,
For I am much asham'd of my exchange:
But loue is blinde, and louers cannot see
The pretty follies that themselues commit,
For if they could, *Cupid* himselfe would blush
To see me thus transformed to a boy.

Lor. Descend, for you must be my torch-bearer.

Ies. What, must I hold a Candle to my shames?
They in themselues goodsooth are too too light.
Why, 'tis an office of discouery Loue,
And I should be obscur'd.

Lor. So you are sweet,
Euen in the louely garnish of a boy: but come at once,
For the close night doth play the run-away,
And we are staid for at *Bassanio's* feast.

Ies. I will make fast the doores and guild my selfe
With some more ducats, and be with you straight.

Gra. Now by my hood, a gentle, and no Iew.

Lor. Beshrew me but I loue her heartily.
For she is wise, if I can iudge of her,
And faire she is, if that mine eyes be true,
And true she is, as she hath prou'd her selfe:
And therefore like her selfe, wise, faire, and true,
Shall she be placed in my constant soule.

Enter Iessica.

What, art thou come? on gentlemen, away,
Our masking mates by this time for vs stay. *Exit.*

Enter Anthonio.

Ant. Who's there?
Gra. Signior *Anthonio*?
Ant. Fie, fie, *Gratiano*, where are all the rest?
'Tis nine a clocke, our friends all stay for you,
No maske to night, the winde is come about,
Bassanio presently will goe aboord,
I haue sent twenty out to seeke for you.

Gra. I am glad on't, I desire no more delight
Then to be vnder saile, and gone to night. *Exeunt.*

Enter Portia with Morrocho, and both their traines.

Por. Goe, draw aside the curtaines, and discouer
The seuerall Caskets to this noble Prince:
Now make your choyse.

Mor. The first of gold, who this inscription beares,
Who chooseth me, shall gaine what men desire.
The second siluer, which this promise carries,
Who chooseth me, shall get as much as he deserues.
This third, dull lead, with warning all as blunt,
Who chooseth me, must giue and hazard all he hath.
How shall I know if I doe choose the right?

Por. The

How shall I know if I doe choose the right.
　Por. The one of them containes my picture Prince,
If you choose that, then I am yours withall.
　Mor. Some God direct my iudgement, let me see,
I will suruay the inscriptions, backe againe:
What saies this leaden casket?
Who chooseth me, must giue and hazard all he hath.
Must giue, for what? for lead, hazard for lead?
This casket threatens men that hazard all
Doe it in hope of faire aduantages:
A golden minde stoopes not to showes of drosse,
Ile then nor giue nor hazard ought for lead.
What saies the Siluer with her virgin hue?
Who chooseth me, shall get as much as he deserues.
As much as he deserues; pause there *Morocho*,
And weigh thy value with an euen hand,
If thou beest rated by thy estimation
Thou doost deserue enough, and yet enough
May not extend so farre as to the Ladie:
And yet to be afeard of my deseruing,
Were but a weake disabling of my selfe.
As much as I deserue, why that's the Lady.
I doe in birth deserue her, and in fortunes,
In graces, and in qualities of breeding:
But more then these, in loue I doe deserue.
What if I strai'd no farther, but chose here?
Let's see once more this saying grau'd in gold.
Who chooseth me shall gaine what many men desire:
Why that's the Lady, all the world desires her:
From the foure corners of the earth they come
To kisse this shrine, this mortall breathing Saint.
The Hircanion deserts, and the vaste wildes
Of wide Arabia are as throughfares now
For Princes to come view faire *Portia*.
The waterie Kingdome, whose ambitious head
Spets in the face of heauen, is no barre
To stop the forraine spirits, but they come
As ore a brooke to see faire *Portia*.
One of these three containes her heauenly picture.
Is't like that Lead containes her? 'twere damnation
To thinke so base a thought, it were too grose
To rib her searecloath in the obscure graue:
Or shall I thinke in Siluer she's immur'd
Being ten times vndervalued to tride gold;
O sinfull thought, neuer so rich a Iem
Was set in worse then gold! They haue in England
A coyne that beares the figure of an Angell
Stampt in gold, but that's insculpt vpon:
But here an Angell in a golden bed
Lies all within. Deliuer me the key:
Here doe I choose, and thriue I as I may.
　Por. There take it Prince, and if my forme lye there
Then I am yours.
　Mor. O hell! what haue we here, a carrion death,
Within whose emptie eye there is a written scroule;
Ile reade the writing.

　　All that glisters is not gold,
　　Often haue you heard that told;
　　Many a man his life hath sold
　　But my out side to behold;
　　Guilded timber doe wormes infolde,
　　Had you beene as wise as bold,
　　Yong in limbs, in iudgement old,
　　Your answere had not beene inscrold,
　　Fare you well, your suite is cold.

　Mor. Cold indeede, and labour lost,
Then farewell heate, and welcome frost:
Portia adew, I haue too grieu'd a heart
To take a tedious leaue: thus loosers part.　　*Exit.*
　Por. A gentle riddance: draw the curtaines, go:
Let all of his complexion choose me so.　　*Exeunt.*

Enter Salarino and Solanio.
Flo. Cornets.

　Sal. Why man I saw *Bassanio* vnder sayle,
With him is *Gratiano* gone along;
And in their ship I am sure *Lorenzo* is not.
　Sol. The villaine *Iew* with outcries rais'd the Duke,
Who went with him to search *Bassanios* ship.
　Sal. He comes too late, the ship was vndersaile;
But there the Duke was giuen to vnderstand
That in a Gondilo were seene together
Lorenzo and his amorous *Iessica*.
Besides, *Anthonio* certified the Duke
They were not with *Bassanio* in his ship.
　Sol. I neuer heard a passion so confus'd,
So strange, outragious, and so variable,
As the dogge *Iew* did vtter in the streets;
My daughter, O my ducats, O my daughter,
Fled with a Christian, O my Christian ducats!
Iustice, the law, my ducats, and my daughter;
A sealed bag, two sealed bags of ducats,
Of double ducats, stolne from me by my daughter,
And iewels, two stones, two rich and precious stones,
Stolne by my daughter: iustice, finde the girle,
She hath the stones vpon her, and the ducats.
　Sal. Why all the boyes in Venice follow him,
Crying his stones, his daughter, and his ducats.
　Sol. Let good *Anthonio* looke he keepe his day
Or he shall pay for this.
　Sal. Marry well remembred,
I reason'd with a Frenchman yesterday,
Who told me, in the narrow seas that part
The French and English, there miscaried
A vessell of our countrey richly fraught:
I thought vpon *Anthonio* when he told me,
And wisht in silence that it were not his.
　Sol. Yo were best to tell *Anthonio* what you heare,
Yet doe not suddainely, for it may grieue him.
　Sal. A kinder Gentleman treads not the earth,
I saw *Bassanio* and *Anthonio* part,
Bassanio told him he would make some speede
Of his returne: he answered, doe not so,
Slubber not businesse for my sake *Bassanio*,
But stay the very riping of the time,
And for the *Iewes* bond which he hath of me,
Let it not enter in your minde of loue:
Be merry, and imploy your chiefest thoughts
To courtship, and such faire ostents of loue
As shall conueniently become you there;
And euen there his eye being big with teares,
Turning his face, he put his hand behinde him,
And with affection wondrous sencible
He wrung *Bassanios* hand, and so they parted.
　Sol. I thinke he onely loues the world for him,
I pray thee let vs goe and finde him out
And quicken his embraced heauinesse
With some delight or other.
　Sal. Doe we so.　　*Exeunt.*

Enter Nerrissa and a Seruiture.
　Ner. Quick, quick I pray thee, draw the curtain strait,

The Prince of Arragon hath tane his oath,
And comes to his election presently.

Enter Arragon, his traine, and Portia.
Flor. Cornets.

Por. Behold, there stand the caskets noble Prince,
If you choose that wherein I am contain'd,
Straight shall our nuptiall rights be solemniz'd:
But if thou faile, without more speech my Lord,
You must be gone from hence immediately.

Ar. I am enioynd by oath to obserue three things;
First, neuer to vnfold to any one
Which casket 'twas I chose; next, if I faile
Of the right casket, neuer in my life
To wooe a maide in way of marriage:
Lastly, if I doe faile in fortune of my choyse,
Immediately to leaue you, and be gone.

Por. To these iniunctions euery one doth sweare
That comes to hazard for my worthlesse selfe.

Ar. And so haue I addrest me, fortune now
To my hearts hope: gold, siluer, and base lead.
Who chooseth me must giue and hazard all he hath.
You shall looke fairer ere I giue or hazard.
What saies the golden chest, ha, let me see:
Who chooseth me, shall gaine what many men desire:
What many men desire, that many may be meant
By the foole multitude that choose by show,
Not learning more then the fond eye doth teach,
Which pries not to th'interior, but like the Martlet
Builds in the weather on the outward wall,
Euen in the force and rode of casualtie.
I will not choose what many men desire,
Because I will not iumpe with common spirits,
And ranke me with the barbarous multitudes.
Why then to thee thou Siluer treasure house,
Tell me once more, what title thou doost beare;
Who chooseth me shall get as much as he deserues:
And well said too; for who shall goe about
To cosen Fortune, and be honourable
Without the stampe of merrit, let none presume
To weare an vndeserued dignitie:
O that estates, degrees, and offices,
Were not deriu'd corruptly, and that cleare honour
Were purchast by the merrit of the wearer;
How many then should couer that stand bare?
How many be commanded that command?
How much low pleasantry would then be gleaned
From the true seede of honor? And how much honor
Pickt from the chaffe and ruine of the times,
To be new varnisht: Well, but to my choise.
Who chooseth me shall get as much as he deserues.
I will assume desert; giue me a key for this,
And instantly vnlocke my fortunes here.

Por. Too long a pause for that which you finde there.

Ar. What's here, the portrait of a blinking idiot
Presenting me a scedule, I will reade it:
How much vnlike art thou to *Portia*?
How much vnlike my hopes and my deseruings?
Who chooseth me, shall haue as much as he deserues.
Did I deserue no more then a fooles head,
Is that my prize, are my deserts no better?

Por. To offend and iudge are distinct offices,
And of opposed natures.

Ar. What is here?

The fier seauen times tried this,
Seauen times tried that iudgement is,
That did neuer choose amis,
Some there be that shadowes kisse,
Such haue but a shadowes blisse:
There be fooles aliue Iwis
Siluer'd o're, and so was this:
Take what wife you will to bed,
I will euer be your head:
So be gone, you are sped.

Ar. Still more foole I shall appeare
By the time I linger here,
With one fooles head I came to woo,
But I goe away with two.
Sweet adue, Ile keepe my oath,
Patiently to beare my wroath.

Por. Thus hath the candle sing'd the moath:
O these deliberate fooles when they doe choose,
They haue the wisdome by their wit to loose.

Ner. The ancient saying is no heresie,
Hanging and wiuing goes by destinie.

Por. Come draw the curtaine *Nerrissa*.

Enter Messenger.

Mes. Where is my Lady?

Por. Here, what would my Lord?

Mes. Madam, there is a-lighted at your gate
A yong Venetian, one that comes before
To signifie th'approaching of his Lord,
From whom he bringeth sensible regreets;
To wit (besides commends and curteous breath)
Gifts of rich value; yet I haue not seene
So likely an Embassador of loue.
A day in Aprill neuer came so sweete
To show how costly Sommer was at hand,
As this fore-spurrer comes before his Lord.

Por. No more I pray thee, I am halfe a-feard
Thou wilt say anone he is some kin to thee,
Thou spend'st such high-day wit in praising him:
Come, come *Nerryssa*, for I long to see
Quicke *Cupids* Post, that comes so mannerly.

Ner. *Bassanio* Lord, loue if thy will it be. *Exeunt.*

Actus Tertius.

Enter Solanio and Salarino.

Sol. Now, what newes on the Ryalto?

Sal. Why yet it liues there vncheckt, that *Anthonio*
hath a ship of rich lading wrackt on the narrow seas; the
Goodwins I thinke they call the place, a very dangerous
flat, and fatall, where the carcasses of many a tall ship, lye
buried, as they say, if my gossips report be an honest woman of her word.

Sol. I would she were as lying a gossip in that, as euer
knapt Ginger, or made her neighbours beleeue she wept
for the death of a third husband: but it is true, without
any flips of prolixity, or crossing the plaine high-way of
talke, that the good *Anthonio*, the honest *Anthonio*; ô that
I had a title good enough to keepe his name company!

Sal. Come, the full stop.

Sol. Ha, what sayest thou, why the end is, he hath lost
a ship.

Sal. I

Sal. I would it might proue the end of his losses.

Sol. Let me say Amen betimes, least the diuell crosse my praier, for here he comes in the likenes of a *Iew.* How now *Shylocke*, what newes among the Merchants?

Enter Shylocke.

Shy. You knew none so well, none so well as you, of my daughters flight.

Sal. That's certaine, I for my part knew the Tailor that made the wings she flew withall.

Sol. And *Shylocke* for his own part knew the bird was fledg'd, and then it is the complexion of them al to leaue the dam.

Shy. She is damn'd for it.

Sal. That's certaine, if the diuell may be her Iudge.

Shy. My owne flesh and blood to rebell.

Sol. Out vpon it old carrion, rebels it at these yeeres.

Shy. I say my daughter is my flesh and bloud.

Sal. There is more difference betweene thy flesh and hers, then betweene Iet and Iuorie, more betweene your bloods, then there is betweene red wine and rennish: but tell vs, doe you heare whether *Anthonio* haue had anie losse at sea or no?

Shy. There I haue another bad match, a bankrout, a prodigall, who dare scarce shew his head on the Ryalto, a begger that was vsd to come so smug vpon the Mart: let him look to his bond, he was wont to call me Vsurer, let him looke to his bond, he was wont to lend money for a Christian curtsie, let him looke to his bond.

Sal. Why I am sure if he forfaite, thou wilt not take his flesh, what's that good for?

Shy. To baite fish withall, if it will feede nothing else, it will feede my reuenge; he hath disgrac'd me, and hindred me halfe a million, laught at my losses, mockt at my gaines, scorned my Nation, thwarted my bargaines, cooled my friends, heated mine enemies, and what's the reason? I am a *Iewe*: Hath not a *Iew* eyes? hath not a *Iew* hands, organs, dementions, sences, affections, passions, fed with the same foode, hurt with the same weapons, subiect to the same diseases, healed by the same meanes, warmed and cooled by the same Winter and Sommmer as a Christian is: if you pricke vs doe we not bleede? if you tickle vs, doe we not laugh? if you poison vs doe we not die? and if you wrong vs shall we not reuenge? if we are like you in the rest, we will resemble you in that. If a *Iew* wrong a *Christian*, what is his humility, reuenge? If a *Christian* wrong a *Iew*, what should his sufferance be by Christian example, why reuenge? The villanie you teach me I will execute, and it shall goe hard but I will better the instruction.

Enter a man from Anthonio.

Gentlemen, my maister *Anthonio* is at his house, and desires to speake with you both.

Sal. We haue beene vp and downe to seeke him.

Enter Tuball.

Sol. Here comes another of the Tribe, a third cannot be matcht, vnlesse the diuell himselfe turne *Iew*.

Exeunt Gentlemen.

Shy. How now *Tuball*, what newes from *Genowa*? hast thou found my daughter?

Tub. I often came where I did heare of her, but cannot finde her.

Shy. Why there, there, there, there, a diamond gone cost me two thousand ducats in Franckford, the curse neuer fell vpon our Nation till now, I neuer felt it till now, two thousand ducats in that, and other precious, precious iewels: I would my daughter were dead at my foot, and the iewels in her eare: would she were hearst at my foote, and the duckets in her coffin: no newes of them, why so? and I know not how much is spent in the search: why thou losse vpon losse, the theefe gone with so much, and so much to finde the theefe, and no satisfaction, no reuenge, nor no ill luck stirring but what lights a my shoulders, no sighes but a my breathing, no teares but a my shedding.

Tub. Yes, other men haue ill lucke too, *Anthonio* as I heard in Genowa?

Shy. What, what, what, ill lucke, ill lucke.

Tub. Hath an Argosie cast away comming from Tripolis.

Shy. I thanke God, I thanke God, is it true, is it true?

Tub. I spoke with some of the Saylers that escaped the wracke.

Shy. I thanke thee good *Tuball*, good newes, good newes: ha, ha, here in Genowa.

Tub. Your daughter spent in Genowa, as I heard, one night fourescore ducats.

Shy. Thou stick'st a dagger in me, I shall neuer see my gold againe, fourescore ducats at a sitting, fourescore ducats.

Tub. There came diuers of *Anthonios* creditors in my company to Venice, that sweare hee cannot choose but breake.

Shy. I am very glad of it, ile plague him, ile torture him, I am glad of it.

Tub. One of them shewed me a ring that hee had of your daughter for a Monkie.

Shy. Out vpon her, thou torturest me *Tuball*, it was my Turkies, I had it of *Leah* when I was a Batcheler: I would not haue giuen it for a wildernesse of Monkies.

Tub. But *Anthonio* is certainely vndone.

Shy. Nay, that's true, that's very true, goe *Tuball*, fee me an Officer, bespeake him a fortnight before, I will haue the heart of him if he forfeit, for were he out of Venice, I can make what merchandize I will: goe *Tuball*, and meete me at our Sinagogue, goe good *Tuball*, at our Sinagogue *Tuball*. *Exeunt.*

Enter Bassanio, Portia, Gratiano, and all their traine.

Por. I pray you tarrie, pause a day or two
Before you hazard, for in choosing wrong
I loose your companie; therefore forbeare a while,
There's something tels me (but it is not loue)
I would not loose you, and you know your selfe,
Hate counsailes not in such a quallitie;
But least you should not vnderstand me well,
And yet a maiden hath no tongue, but thought,
I would detaine you here some month or two
Before you venture for me. I could teach you
How to choose right, but then I am forsworne,
So will I neuer be, so may you misse me,
But if you doe, youle make me wish a sinne,
That I had beene forsworne: Beshrow your eyes,
They haue ore-lookt me and deuided me,
One halfe of me is yours, the other halfe yours,
Mine owne I would say: but of mine then yours,
And so all yours; O these naughtie times
Puts bars betweene the owners and their rights.
And so though yours, not yours (proue it so)
Let Fortune goe to hell for it, not I.
I speake too long, but 'tis to peize the time,
To ich it, and to draw it out in length,
To stay you from election.

Bass. Let me choose,
For as I am, I liue vpon the racke.

Por. Vpon the racke *Bassanio*, then confesse
What treason there is mingled with your loue.

Bass. None but that vglie treason of mistrust,
Which makes me feare the enioying of my loue:
There may as well be amitie and life,
'Tweene snow and fire, as treason and my loue:

Por. I, but I feare you speake vpon the racke,
Where men enforced doth speake any thing.

Bass. Promise me life, and ile confesse the truth.

Por. Well then, confesse and liue.

Bass. Confesse and loue
Had beene the verie sum of my confession:
O happie torment, when my torturer
Doth teach me answers for deliuerance:
But let me to my fortune and the caskets.

Por. Away then, I am lockt in one of them,
If you doe loue me, you will finde me out.
Nerryssa and the rest, stand all aloofe,
Let musicke sound while he doth make his choise,
Then if he loose he makes a Swan-like end,
Fading in musique. That the comparison
May stand more proper, my eye shall be the streame
And watrie death-bed for him: he may win,
And what is musique than? Than musique is
Euen as the flourish, when true subiects bowe
To a new crowned Monarch: Such it is,
As are those dulcet sounds in breake of day,
That creepe into the dreaming bride-groomes eare,
And summon him to marriage. Now he goes
With no lesse presence, but with much more loue
Then yong *Alcides*, when he did redeeme
The virgine tribute, paied by howling *Troy*
To the Sea-monster: I stand for sacrifice,
The rest aloofe are the Dardanian wiues:
With bleared visages come forth to view
The issue of th'exploit: Goe *Hercules*,
Liue thou, I liue with much more dismay
I view the fight, then thou that mak'st the fray.

Here Musicke.

A Song the whilst Bassanio *comments on the Caskets to himselfe.*

Tell me where is fancie bred,
Or in the heart, or in the head:
How begot, how nourished.   *Replie, replie.*
It is engendred in the eyes,
With gazing fed, and Fancie dies,
In the cradle where it lies:
Let vs all ring Fancies knell.
Ile begin it.
Ding, dong, bell.

All. Ding, dong, bell.

Bass. So may the outward showes be least themselues
The world is still deceiu'd with ornament.
In Law, what Plea so tanted and corrupt,
But being season'd with a gracious voice,
Obscures the show of euill? In Religion,
What damned error, but some sober brow
Will blesse it, and approue it with a text,
Hiding the grosenesse with faire ornament:
There is no voice so simple, but assumes
Some marke of vertue on his outward parts;
How manie cowards, whose hearts are all as false
As stayers of sand, weare yet vpon their chins
The beards of *Hercules* and frowning *Mars*,
Who inward searcht, haue lyuers white as milke,
And these assume but valors excrement,
To render them redoubted. Looke on beautie,
And you shall see 'tis purchast by the weight,
Which therein workes a miracle in nature,
Making them lightest that weare most of it:
So are those crisped snakie golden locks
Which makes such wanton gambols with the winde
Vpon supposed fairenesse, often knowne
To be the dowrie of a second head,
The scull that bred them in the Sepulcher.
Thus ornament is but the guiled shore
To a most dangerous sea: the beautious scarfe
Vailing an Indian beautie; In a word,
The seeming truth which cunning times put on
To intrap the wisest. Therefore then thou gaudie gold,
Hard food for *Midas*, I will none of thee,
Nor none of thee thou pale and common drudge
'Tweene man and man: but thou, thou meager lead
Which rather threatnest then dost promise ought,
Thy palenesse moues me more then eloquence,
And here choose I, ioy be the consequence.

Por. How all the other passions fleet to ayre,
As doubtfull thoughts, and rash imbrac'd despaire:
And shuddring feare, and greene-eyed iealousie.
O loue be moderate, allay thy extasie,
In measure raine thy ioy, scant this excesse,
I feele too much thy blessing, make it lesse,
For feare I surfeit.

Bass. What finde I here?
Faire *Portias* counterfeit. What demie God
Hath come so neere creation? moue these eies?
Or whether riding on the bals of mine
Seeme they in motion? Here are seuer'd lips
Parted with suger breath, so sweet a barre
Should sunder such sweet friends: here in her haires
The Painter plaies the Spider, and hath wouen
A golden mesh t'intrap the hearts of men
Faster then gnats in cobwebs: but her eies,
How could he see to doe them? hauing made one,
Me thinkes it should haue power to steale both his
And leaue it selfe vnfurnisht: Yet looke how farre
The substance of my praise doth wrong this shadow
In vnderprising it, so farre this shadow
Doth limpe behinde the substance. Here's the scroule,
The continent, and summarie of my fortune.

> You that choose not by the view
> Chance as faire, and choose as true:
> Since this fortune fals to you,
> Be content, and seeke no new.
> If you be well pleas'd with this,
> And hold your fortune for your blisse,
> Turne you where your Lady is,
> And claime her with a louing kisse.

Bass. A gentle scroule: Faire Lady, by your leaue,
I come by note to giue, and to receiue,
Like one of two contending in a prize
That thinks he hath done well in peoples eies:
Hearing applause and vniuersall shout,
Giddie in spirit, still gazing in a doubt
Whether those peales of praise be his or no.

The Merchant of Venice.

So thrice faire Lady stand I euen so,
As doubtfull whether what I see be true,
Vntill confirm'd, sign'd, ratified by you.

Por. You see my Lord *Bassiano* where I stand,
Such as I am; though for my selfe alone
I would not be ambitious in my wish,
To wish my selfe much better, yet for you,
I would be trebled twenty times my selfe,
A thousand times more faire, ten thousand times
More rich, that onely to stand high in your account,
I might in vertues, beauties, liuings, friends,
Exceed account: but the full summe of me
Is sum of nothing: which to terme in grosse,
Is an vnlessoned girle, vnschool'd, vnpractiz'd,
Happy in this, she is not yet so old,
But she may learne: happier then this,
Shee is not bred so dull but she can learne;
Happiest of all, is that her gentle spirit
Commits it selfe to yours to be directed,
As from her Lord, her Gouernour, her King.
My selfe, and what is mine, to you and yours
Is now conuerted. But now I was the Lord
Of this faire mansion, master of my seruants,
Queene ore my selfe: and euen now, but now,
This house, these seruants, and this same my selfe
Are yours, my Lord, I giue them with this ring,
Which when you part from, leose, or giue away,
Let it presage the ruine of your loue,
And be my vantage to exclaime on you.

Bass. Maddam, you haue bereft me of all words,
Onely my bloud speakes to you in my vaines,
And there is such confusion in my powers,
As after some oration fairely spoke
By a beloued Prince, there doth appeare
Among the buzzing pleased multitude,
Where euery something being blent together,
Turnes to a wilde of nothing, saue of ioy
Exprest, and not exprest: but when this ring
Parts from this finger, then parts life from hence,
O then be bold to say *Bassanio's* dead.

Ner. My Lord and Lady, it is now our time
That haue stood by and seene our wishes prosper,
To cry good ioy, good ioy my Lord and Lady.

Gra. My Lord *Bassanio*, and my gentle Lady,
I wish you all the ioy that you can wish:
For I am sure you can wish none from me:
And when your Honours meane to solemnize
The bargaine of your faith: I doe beseech you
Euen at that time I may be married too.

Bass. With all my heart, so thou canst get a wife.

Gra. I thanke your Lordship, you gaue got me one.
My eyes my Lord can looke as swift as yours:
You saw the mistres, I beheld the maid:
You lou'd, I lou'd for intermission,
No more pertaines to me my Lord then you;
Your fortune stood vpon the caskets there,
And so did mine too, as the matter falls:
For wooing heere vntill I swet againe,
And swearing till my very rough was dry
With oathes of loue, at last, if promise last,
I got a promise of this faire one heere
To haue her loue: prouided that your fortune
Atchieu'd her mistresse.

Por. Is this true *Nerrissa*?

Ner. Madam it is so, so you stand pleas'd withall.

Bass. And doe you *Gratiano* meane good faith?

Gra. Yes faith my Lord.

Bass. Our feast shall be much honored in your marriage.

Gra. Weele play with them the first boy for a thousand ducats.

Ner. What and stake downe?

Gra. No, we shal nere win at that sport, and stake downe.
But who comes heere? *Lorenzo* and his Infidell?
What and my old Venetian friend *Salerio*?

Enter Lorenzo, Iessica, and Salerio.

Bass. *Lorenzo* and *Salerio*, welcome hether,
If that the youth of my new interest heere
Haue power to bid you welcome: by your leaue
I bid my verie friends and Countrimen
Sweet *Portia* welcome.

Por. So do I my Lord, they are intirely welcome.

Lor. I thanke your honor; for my part my Lord,
My purpose was not to haue seene you heere,
But meeting with *Salerio* by the way,
He did intreate mee past all saying nay
To come with him along.

Sal. I did my Lord,
And I haue reason for it, Signior *Anthonio*
Commends him to you.

Bass. Ere I ope his Letter
I pray you tell me how my good friend doth.

Sal. Not sicke my Lord, vnlesse it be in minde,
Nor wel, vnlesse in minde: his Letter there
Wil shew you his estate.

Opens the Letter.

Gra. *Nerrissa*, cheere yond stranger, bid her welcom,
Your hand *Salerio*, what's the newes from Venice?
How doth that royal Merchant good *Anthonio*;
I know he vvil be glad of our successe,
We are the *Iasons*, we haue won the fleece.

Sal. I would you had vvon the fleece that hee hath lost.

Por. There are some shrewd contents in yond same Paper,
That steales the colour from *Bassianos* cheeke,
Some deere friend dead, else nothing in the world
Could turne so much the constitution
Of any constant man. What, worse and worse?
With leaue *Bassanio* I am halfe your selfe,
And I must freely haue the halfe of any thing
That this same paper brings you.

Bass. O sweet *Portia*,
Heere are a few of the vnpleasant'st words
That euer blotted paper. Gentle Ladie
When I did first impart my loue to you,
I freely told you all the wealth I had
Ran in my vaines: I was a Gentleman,
And then I told you true: and yet deere Ladie,
Rating my selfe at nothing, you shall see
How much I was a Braggart, when I told you
My state was nothing, I should then haue told you
That I vvas worse then nothing: for indeede
I haue ingag'd my selfe to a deere friend,
Ingag'd my friend to his meere enemie
To feede my meanes. Heere is a Letter Ladie,
The paper as the bodie of my friend,
And euerie word in it a gaping wound
Issuing life blood. But is it true *Salerio*,

Hath

Hath all his ventures faild, what not one hit,
From Tripolis, from Mexico and England,
From Lisbon, Barbary, and India,
And not one vessell scape the dreadfull touch
Of Merchant-marring rocks?

Sal. Not one my Lord.
Besides, it should appeare, that if he had
The present money to discharge the Iew,
He would not take it: neuer did I know
A creature that did beare the shape of man
So keene and greedy to confound a man.
He plyes the Duke at morning and at night,
And doth impeach the freedome of the state
If they deny him iustice. Twenty Merchants,
The Duke himselfe, and the Magnificoes
Of greatest port haue all perswaded with him,
But none can driue him from the enuious plea
Of forfeiture, of iustice, and his bond.

Iessi. When I was with him, I haue heard him sweare
To *Tuball* and to *Chus*, his Countri-men,
That he would rather haue *Anthonio's* flesh,
Then twenty times the value of the summe
That he did owe him: and I know my Lord,
If law, authoritie, and power denie not,
It will goe hard with poore *Anthonio*.

Por. Is it your deere friend that is thus in trouble?

Bass. The deerest friend to me, the kindest man,
The best condition'd, and vnwearied spirit
In doing curtesies: and one in whom
The ancient Romane honour more appeares
Then any that drawes breath in Italie.

Por. What summe owes he the Iew?

Bass. For me three thousand ducats.

Por. What, no more?
Pay him sixe thousand, and deface the bond:
Double sixe thousand, and then treble that,
Before a friend of this description
Shall lose a haire through *Bassano's* fault.
First goe with me to Church, and call me wife,
And then away to Venice to your friend:
For neuer shall you lie by *Portias* side
With an vnquiet soule. You shall haue gold
To pay the petty debt twenty times ouer.
When it is payd, bring your true friend along,
My maid *Nerrissa*, and my selfe meane time
Will liue as maids and widdowes; come away,
For you shall hence vpon your wedding day:
Bid your friends welcome, show a merry cheere,
Since you are deere bought, I will loue you deere.
But let me heare the letter of your friend.

Sweet Bassanio, my ships haue all miscarried, my Creditors grow cruell, my estate is very low, my bond to the Iew is forfeit, and since in paying it, it is impossible I should liue, all debts are cleerd betweene you and I, if I might see you at my death: notwithstanding, vse your pleasure, if your loue doe not perswade you to come, let not my letter.

Por. O loue! dispach all busines and be gone.

Bass. Since I haue your good leaue to goe away,
I will make hast; but till I come againe,
No bed shall ere be guilty of my stay,
Nor rest be interposer twixt vs twaine. *Exeunt.*

Enter the Iew, and Solanio, and Anthonio, and the Iaylor.

Iew. Iaylor, looke to him, tell not me of mercy,
This is the foole that lends out money *gratis*.
Iaylor, looke to him.

Ant. Heare me yet good *Shylok*.

Iew. Ile haue my bond, speake not against my bond,
I haue sworne an oath that I will haue my bond:
Thou call'dst me dog before thou hadst a cause,
But since I am a dog, beware my phangs,
The Duke shall grant me iustice, I do wonder
Thou naughty Iaylor, that thou art so fond
To come abroad with him at his request.

Ant. I pray thee heare me speake.

Iew. Ile haue my bond, I will not heare thee speake,
Ile haue my bond, and therefore speake no more,
Ile not be made a soft and dull ey'd foole,
To shake the head, relent, and sigh, and yeeld
To Christian intercessors: follow not,
Ile haue no speaking, I will haue my bond. *Exit Iew.*

Sol. It is the most impenetrable curre
That euer kept with men.

Ant. Let him alone,
Ile follow him no more with bootlesse prayers:
He seekes my life, his reason well I know;
I oft deliuer'd from his forfeitures
Many that haue at times made mone to me,
Therefore he hates me.

Sol. I am sure the Duke will neuer grant
this forfeiture to hold.

An. The Duke cannot deny the course of law:
For the commoditie that strangers haue
With vs in Venice, if it be denied,
Will much impeach the iustice of the State,
Since that the trade and profit of the citty
Consisteth of all Nations. Therefore goe,
These greefes and losses haue so bated mee,
That I shall hardly spare a pound of flesh
To morrow; to my bloudy Creditor.
Well Iaylor, on, pray God *Bassanio* come
To see me pay his debt, and then I care not. *Exeunt.*

Enter Portia, Nerrissa, Lorenzo, Iessica, and a man of Portias.

Lor. Madam, although I speake it in your presence,
You haue a noble and a true conceit
Of god-like amity, which appeares most strongly
In bearing thus the absence of your Lord.
But if you knew to whom you shew this honour,
How true a Gentleman you send releefe,
How deere a louer of my Lord your husband,
I know you would be prouder of the worke
Then customary bounty can enforce you.

Por. I neuer did repent for doing good,
Nor shall not now: for in companions
That do conuerse and waste the time together,
Whose soules doe beare an egal yoke of loue,
There must be needs a like proportion
Of lyniaments, of manners, and of spirit;
Which makes me thinke that this *Anthonio*
Being the bosome louer of my Lord,
Must needs be like my Lord. If it be so,
How little is the cost I haue bestowed
In purchasing the semblance of my soule;
From out the state of hellish cruelty,
This comes too neere the praising of my selfe,
Therefore no more of it: heere other things
Lorenso I commit into your hands,

The husbandry and mannage of my house,
Vntill my Lords returne; for mine owne part
I haue toward heauen breath'd a secret vow,
To liue in prayer and contemplation,
Onely attended by *Nerrissa* heere,
Vntill her husband and my Lords returne:
There is a monastery too miles off,
And there we will abide. I doe desire you
Not to denie this imposition,
The which my loue and some necessity
Now layes vpon you.

Lorenf. Madame, with all my heart,
I shall obey you in all faire commands.

Por. My people doe already know my minde,
And will acknowledge you and *Iessica*
In place of Lord *Bassanio* and my selfe.
So far you well till we shall meete againe.

Lor. Faire thoughts & happy houres attend on you.

Iessi. I wish your Ladiship all hearts content.

Por. I thanke you for your wish, and am well pleas'd
To wish it backe on you: far you well *Iessica*. *Exeunt.*
Now *Balthaser*, as I haue euer found thee honest true,
So let me finde thee still: take this same letter,
And vse thou all the indeauor of a man,
In speed to Mantua, see thou render this
Into my cosins hand, Doctor *Belario*,
And looke what notes and garments he doth giue thee,
Bring them I pray thee with imagin'd speed
Vnto the Tranect, to the common Ferrie
Which trades to Venice; waste no time in words,
But get thee gone, I shall be there before thee.

Balth. Madam, I goe with all conuenient speed.

Por. Come on *Nerissa*, I haue worke in hand
That you yet know not of; wee'll see our husbands
Before they thinke of vs?

Nerrissa. Shall they see vs?

Portia. They shall *Nerrissa*: but in such a habit,
That they shall thinke we are accomplished
With that we lacke; Ile hold thee any wager
When we are both accoutered like yong men,
Ile proue the prettier fellow of the two,
And weare my dagger with the brauer grace,
And speake betweene the change of man and boy,
With a reede voyce, and turne two minsing steps
Into a manly stride; and speake of frayes
Like a fine bragging youth: and tell quaint lyes
How honourable Ladies sought my loue,
Which I denying, they fell sicke and died.
I could not doe withall: then Ile repent,
And wish for all that, that I had not kil'd them;
And twentie of these punie lies Ile tell,
That men shall sweare I haue discontinued schoole
Aboue a twelue moneth: I haue within my minde
A thousand raw tricks of these bragging Iacks,
Which I will practise.

Nerris. Why, shall wee turne to men?

Portia. Fie, what a questions that?
If thou wert nere a lewd interpreter:
But come, Ile tell thee all my whole deuice
When I am in my coach, which stayes for vs
At the Parke gate; and therefore haste away,
For we must measure twentie miles to day. *Exeunt.*

Enter Clowne and Iessica.

Clowne. Yes truly; for looke you, the sinnes of the Father are to be laid vpon the children, therefore I promise
you, I feare you, I was alwaies plaine with you, and so
now I speake my agitation of the matter: therfore be of
good cheere, for truly I thinke you are damn'd, there is
but one hope in it that can doe you anie good, and that is
but a kinde of bastard hope neither.

Iessica. And what hope is that I pray thee?

Clow. Marrie you may partlie hope that your father
got you not, that you are not the Iewes daughter.

Ief. That were a kinde of bastard hope indeed, so the
sins of my mother should be visited vpon me.

Clow. Truly then I feare you are damned both by father and mother: thus when I shun *Scilla* your father, I
fall into *Charibdis* your mother; well, you are gone both
waies.

Ief. I shall be sau'd by my husband, he hath made me
a Christian.

Clow. Truly the more to blame he, we were Christians enow before, e'ne as many as could well liue one by a-
nother: this making of Christians will raise the price of
Hogs, if wee grow all to be porke-eaters, wee shall not
shortlie haue a rasher on the coales for money.

Enter Lorenzo.

Ief. Ile tell my husband *Lancelet* what you say, heere
he comes.

Loren. I shall grow iealous of you shortly *Lancelet*,
if you thus get my wife into corners?

Ief. Nay, you need not feare vs *Lorenzo*, *Launcelet*
and I are out, he tells me flatly there is no mercy for mee
in heauen, because I am a Iewes daughter: and hee saies
you are no good member of the common wealth, for
in conuerting Iewes to Christians, you raise the price
of Porke.

Loren. I shall answere that better to the Common-
wealth, than you can the getting vp of the Negroes bel-
lie: the Moore is with childe by you *Launcelet*?

Clow. It is much that the Moore should be more then
reason: but if she be lesse then an honest woman, shee is
indeed more then I tooke her for.

Loren. How euerie foole can play vpon the word, I
thinke the best grace of witte will shortly turne into silence, and discourse grow commendable in none onely
but Parrats: goe in sirra, bid them prepare for dinner?

Clow. That is done sir, they haue all stomacks?

Loren. Goodly Lord, what a witte-snapper are you,
then bid them prepare dinner.

Clow. That is done to sir, onely couer is the word.

Loren. Will you couer than sir?

Clow. Not so sir neither, I know my dutie.

Loren. Yet more quarreling with occasion, wilt thou
shew the whole wealth of thy wit in an instant; I pray
thee vnderstand a plaine man in his plaine meaning: goe
to thy fellowes, bid them couer the table, serue in the
meat, and we will come in to dinner.

Clow. For the table sir, it shall be seru'd in, for the
meat sir, it shall bee couered, for your comming in to
dinner sir, why let it be as humors and conceits shall gouerne. *Exit Clowne.*

Lor. O deare discretion, how his words are suted,
The foole hath planted in his memory
An Armie of good words, and I doe know
A many fooles that stand in better place,
Garnisht like him, that for a trickfie word
Defie the matter: how cheer'st thou *Iessica*,
And now good sweet say thy opinion,

How

How dost thou like the Lord *Bassanio's* wife?
　Iessi. Past all expressing, it is very meete
The Lord *Bassanio* liue an vpright life
For hauing such a blessing in his Lady,
He findes the ioyes of heauen heere on earth,
And if on earth he doe not meane it, it
Is reason he should neuer come to heauen?
Why, if two gods should play some heauenly match,
And on the wager lay two earthly women,
And *Portia* one: there must be something else
Paund with the other, for the poore rude world
Hath not her fellow.
　Loren. Euen such a husband
Hast thou of me, as she is for a wife.
　Ies. Nay, but aske my opinion to of that?
　Lor. I will anone, first let vs goe to dinner?
　Ies. Nay, let me praise you while I haue a stomacke?
　Lor. No pray thee, let it serue for table talke,
Then how som ere thou speakst 'mong other things,
I shall digest it?
　Iessi. Well, Ile set you forth.　　*Exeunt.*

Actus Quartus.

Enter the Duke, the Magnificoes, Anthonio, Bassanio, and Gratiano.

　Duke. What, is *Anthonio* heere?
　Ant. Ready, so please your grace?
　Duke. I am sorry for thee, thou art come to answere
A stonie aduersary, an inhumane wretch,
Vncapable of pitty, voyd, and empty
From any dram of mercie.
　Ant. I haue heard
Your Grace hath tane great paines to qualifie
His rigorous course: but since he stands obdurate,
And that no lawful meanes can carrie me
Out of his enuies reach, I do oppose
My patience to his fury, and am arm'd
To suffer with a quietnesse of spirit,
The very tiranny and rage of his.
　Du. Go one and cal the Iew into the Court.
　Sal. He is ready at the doore, he comes my Lord.

Enter Shylocke.

　Du. Make roome, and let him stand before our face.
Shylocke the world thinkes, and I thinke so to
That thou but leadest this fashion of thy mallice
To the last houre of act, and then 'tis thought
Thou'lt shew thy mercy and remorse more strange,
Than is thy strange apparant cruelty;
And where thou now exact'st the penalty,
Which is a pound of this poore Merchants flesh,
Thou wilt not onely loose the forfeiture,
But touch'd with humane gentlenesse and loue:
Forgiue a moytie of the principall,
Glancing an eye of pitty on his losses
That haue of late so hudled on his backe,
Enow to presse a royall Merchant downe;
And plucke commiseration of his state
From brassie bosomes, and rough hearts of flints,
From stubborne Turkes and Tarters neuer traind
To offices of tender curtesie,
We all expect a gentle answer Iew?
　Iew. I haue possest your grace of what I purpose,
And by our holy Sabbath haue I sworne
To haue the due and forfeit of my bond.
If you denie it, let the danger light
Vpon your Charter, and your Cities freedome.
You'l aske me why I rather choose to haue
A weight of carrion flesh, then to receiue
Three thousand Ducats? Ile not answer that:
But say it is my humor; Is it answered?
What if my house be troubled with a Rat,
And I be pleas'd to giue ten thousand Ducates
To haue it bain'd? What, are you answer'd yet?
Some men there are loue not a gaping Pigge:
Some that are mad, if they behold a Cat:
And others, when the bag-pipe sings i'th nose,
Cannot containe their Vrine for affection.
Masters of passion swayes it to the moode
Of what it likes or loaths, now for your answer:
As there is no firme reason to be rendred
Why he cannot abide a gaping Pigge?
Why he a harmlesse necessarie Cat?
Why he a woollen bag-pipe: but of force
Must yeeld to such ineuitable shame,
As to offend himselfe being offended:
So can I giue no reason, nor I will not,
More then a lodg'd hate, and a certaine loathing
I beare *Anthonio*, that I follow thus
A loosing suite against him? Are you answered?
　Bass. This is no answer thou vnfeeling man,
To excuse the currant of thy cruelty.
　Iew. I am not bound to please thee with my answer.
　Bass. Do all men kil the things they do not loue?
　Iew. Hates any man the thing he would not kill?
　Bass. Euerie offence is not a hate at first.
　Iew. What wouldst thou haue a Serpent sting thee twice?
　Ant. I pray you thinke you question with the Iew:
You may as well go stand vpon the beach,
And bid the maine flood baite his vsuall height,
Or euen as well vse question with the Wolfe,
The Ewe bleate for the Lambe:
You may as well forbid the Mountaine Pines
To wagge their high tops, and to make no noise
When they are fretted with the gusts of heauen:
You may as well do any thing most hard,
As seeke to soften that, then which what harder?
His Iewish heart. Therefore I do beseech you
Make no more offers, vse no farther meanes,
But with all briefe and plaine conueniencie
Let me haue iudgement, and the Iew his will.
　Bas. For thy three thousand Ducates heereis six.
　Iew. If euerie Ducat in sixe thousand Ducates
Were in sixe parts, and euery part a Ducate,
I would not draw them, I would haue my bond?
　Du. How shalt thou hope for mercie, rendring none?
　Iew. What iudgement shall I dread doing no wrong?
You haue among you many a purchast slaue,
Which like your Asses, and your Dogs and Mules,
You vse in abiect and in slauish parts,
Because you bought them. Shall I say to you,
Let them be free, marrie them to your heires?
Why sweate they vnder burthens? Let their beds
Be made as soft as yours: and let their pallats
Be season'd with such Viands; you will answer

The

The Merchant of Venice.

The slaues are ours. So do I answer you.
The pound of flesh which I demand of him
Is deerely bought, 'tis mine, and I will haue it.
If you deny me; fie vpon your Law,
There is no force in the decrees of Venice;
I stand for iudgement, answer, Shall I haue it?

Du. Vpon my power I may dismisse this Court,
Vnlesse *Bellario* a learned Doctor,
Whom I haue sent for to determine this,
Come heere to day.

Sal. My Lord, heere stayes without
A Messenger with Letters from the Doctor,
New come from Padua.

Du. Bring vs the Letters, Call the Messengers.

Bass. Good cheere *Anthonio*. What man, corage yet:
The Iew shall haue my flesh, blood, bones, and all,
Ere thou shalt loose for me one drop of blood.

Ant. I am a tainted Weather of the flocke,
Meetest for death, the weakest kinde of fruite
Drops earliest to the ground, and so let me;
You cannot better be employ'd *Bassanio*,
Then to liue still, and write mine Epitaph.

Enter Nerrissa.

Du. Came you from Padua from *Bellario*?

Ner. From both.
My Lord *Bellario* greets your Grace.

Bass. Why dost thou whet thy knife so earnestly?

Iew. To cut the forfeiture from that bankrout there.

Gra. Not on thy soale: but on thy soule harsh Iew
Thou mak'st thy knife keene: but no mettall can,
No, not the hangmans Axe beare halfe the keennesse
Of thy sharpe enuy. Can no prayers pierce thee?

Iew. No, none that thou hast wit enough to make.

Gra. O be thou damn'd, inexecrable dogge,
And for thy life let iustice be accus'd:
Thou almost mak'st me wauer in my faith;
To hold opinion with *Pythagoras*,
That soules of Animals infuse themselues
Into the trunkes of men. Thy currish spirit
Gouern'd a Wolfe, who hang'd for humane slaughter,
Euen from the gallowes did his fell soule fleet;
And whil'st thou layest in thy vnhallowed dam,
Infus'd it selfe in thee: For thy desires
Are Woluish, bloody, steru'd, and rauenous.

Iew. Till thou canst raile the seale from off my bond
Thou but offend'st thy Lungs to speake so loud:
Repaire thy wit good youth, or it will fall
To endlesse ruine. I stand heere for Law.

Du. This Letter from *Bellario* doth commend
A yong and Learned Doctor in our Court;
Where is he?

Ner. He attendeth heere hard by
To know your answer, whether you'l admit him.

Du. With all my heart. Some three or four of you
Go giue him curteous conduct to this place,
Meane time the Court shall heare *Bellarioes* Letter.

Your Grace shall vnderstand, that at the receite of your Letter I am very sicke: but in the instant that your messenger came, in louing visitation, was with me a young Doctor of Rome, his name is Balthasar: I acquained him with the cause in Controuersie, betweene the Iew and Anthonio the Merchant: We turn'd ore many Bookes together: hee is furnished with my opinion, which bettred with his owne learning, the greatnesse whereof I cannot enough commend, comes with him at my importunity, to fill vp your Graces request in my sted. I beseech you, let his lacke of yeares be no impediment to let him lacke a reuerend estimation: for I neuer knewe so yong a body, with so old a head. I leaue him to your gracious acceptance, whose triall shall better publish his commendation.

Enter Portia for Balthazar.

Duke. You heare the learn'd *Bellario* what he writes,
And heere (I take it) is the Doctor come.
Giue me your hand: Came you from old *Bellario*?

Por. I did my Lord.

Du. You are welcome: take your place;
Are you acquainted with the difference
That holds this present question in the Court.

Por. I am enformed throughly of the cause.
Which is the Merchant heere? and which the Iew?

Du. *Anthonio* and old *Shylocke*, both stand forth.

Por. Is your name *Shylocke*?

Iew. *Shylocke* is my name.

Por. Of a strange nature is the sute you follow,
Yet in such rule, that the Venetian Law
Cannot impugne you as you do proceed.
You stand within his danger, do you not?

Ant. I, so he sayes.

Por. Do you confesse the bond?

Ant. I do.

Por. Then must the Iew be mercifull.

Iew. On what compulsion must I? Tell me that.

Por. The quality of mercy is not strain'd,
It droppeth as the gentle raine from heauen
Vpon the place beneath. It is twice blest,
It blesseth him that giues, and him that takes,
'Tis mightiest in the mightiest, it becomes
The throned Monarch better then his Crowne.
His Scepter shewes the force of temporall power,
The attribute to awe and Maiestie,
Wherein doth sit the dread and feare of Kings:
But mercy is aboue this sceptred sway,
It is enthroned in the hearts of Kings,
It is an attribute to God himselfe;
And earthly power doth then shew likest Gods
When mercie seasons Iustice. Therefore Iew,
Though Iustice be thy plea, consider this,
That in the course of Iustice, none of vs
Should see saluation: we do pray for mercie,
And that same prayer, doth teach vs all to render
The deeds of mercie. I haue spoke thus much
To mittigate the iustice of thy plea:
Which if thou follow, this strict course of Venice
Must needes giue sentence 'gainst the Merchant there.

Shy. My deeds vpon my head, I craue the Law,
The penaltie and forfeite of my bond.

Por. Is he not able to discharge the money?

Bass. Yes, heere I tender it for him in the Court,
Yea, twice the summe, if that will not suffice,
I will be bound to pay it ten times ore,
On forfeit of my hands, my head, my heart:
If this will not suffice, it must appeare
That malice beares downe truth. And I beseech you
Wrest once the Law to your authority.
To do a great right, do a little wrong,
And curbe this cruell diuell of his will.

Por. It must not be, there is no power in Venice
Can alter a decree established:
'Twill be recorded for a President,

And

And many an error by the same example,
Will rush into the state: It cannot be.
  Iew. A *Daniel* come to iudgement, yea a *Daniel*.
O wise young Iudge, how do I honour thee.
  Por. I pray you let me looke vpon the bond.
  Iew. Heere 'tis most reuerend Doctor, heere it is.
  Por. Shylocke, there's thrice thy monie offered thee.
  Shy. An oath, an oath, I haue an oath in heauen:
Shall I lay periurie vpon my soule?
No not for Venice.
  Por. Why this bond is forfeit,
And lawfully by this the Iew may claime
A pound of flesh, to be by him cut off
Neerest the Merchants heart: be mercifull,
Take thrice thy money, bid me teare the bond.
  Iew. When it is paid according to the tenure.
It doth appeare you are a worthy Iudge:
you know the Law, your exposition
Hath beene most sound. I charge you by the Law,
Whereof you are a well-deseruing pillar,
Proceede to iudgement: By my soule I sweare,
There is no power in the tongue of man
To alter me: I stay heere on my bond.
  An. Most heartily I do beseech the Court
To giue the iudgement.
  Por. Why then thus it is:
you must prepare your bosome for his knife.
  Iew. O noble Iudge, O excellent yong man.
  Por. For the intent and purpose of the Law
Hath full relation to the penaltie,
Which heere appeareth due vpon the bond.
  Iew. 'Tis verie true: O wise and vpright Iudge,
How much more elder art thou then thy lookes?
  Por. Therefore lay bare your bosome.
  Iew. I, his brest,
So sayes the bond, doth it not noble Iudge?
Neerest his heart, those are the very words.
  Por. It is so: Are there ballance heere to weigh the
flesh?
  Iew. I haue them ready.
  Por. Haue by some Surgeon *Shylock* on your charge
To stop his wounds, least he should bleede to death.
  Iew. It is not nominated in the bond?
  Por. It is not so exprest: but what of that?
'Twere good you do so much for charitie.
  Iew. I cannot finde it, 'tis not in the bond.
  Por. Come Merchant, haue you any thing to say?
  Ant. But little: I am arm'd and well prepar'd.
Giue me your hand *Bassanio,* fare you well,
Greeue not that I am falne to this for you:
For heerein fortune shewes her selfe more kinde
Then is her custome. It is still her vse
To let the wretched man out-liue his wealth,
To view with hollow eye, and wrinkled brow
An age of pouerty. From which lingring penance
Of such miserie, doth she cut me off:
Commend me to your honourable Wife,
Tell her the processe of *Anthonio's* end:
Say how I lou'd you, speake me faire in death:
And when the tale is told, bid her be iudge,
Whether *Bassanio* had not once a Loue:
Repent not you that you shall loose your friend,
And he repents not that he payes your debt.
For if the Iew do cut but deepe enough,
Ile pay it instantly, with all my heart.
  Baß. Anthonio, I am married to a wife,

Which is as deere to me as life it selfe,
But life it selfe, my wife, and all the world,
Are not with me esteem'd aboue thy life.
I would loose all, I sacrifice them all
Heere to this deuill, to deliuer you.
  Por. Your wife would giue you little thanks for that
If she were by to heare you make the offer.
  Gra. I haue a wife whom I protest I loue,
I would she were in heauen, so she could
Intreat some power to change this currish Iew.
  Ner. 'Tis well you offer it behinde her backe,
The wish would make else an vnquiet house.
  Iew. These be the Christian husbands: I haue a daugh-
Would any of the stocke of *Barrabas*   (ter
Had beene her husband, rather then a Christian.
We trifle time, I pray thee pursue sentence.
  Por. A pound of that same marchants flesh is thine,
The Court awards it, and the law doth giue it.
  Iew. Most rightfull Iudge.
  Por. And you must cut this flesh from off his breast,
The Law allowes it, and the Court awards it.
  Iew. Most learned Iudge, a sentence, come prepare.
  Por. Tarry a little, there is something else,
This bond doth giue thee heere no iot of bloud,
The words expresly are a pound of flesh:
Then take thy bond, take thou thy pound of flesh,
But in the cutting it, if thou dost shed
One drop of Christian bloud, thy lands and goods
Are by the Lawes of Venice confiscate
Vnto the state of Venice.
  Gra. O vpright Iudge,
Marke Iew, ô learned Iudge.
  Shy. Is that the law?
  Por. Thy selfe shalt see the Act:
For as thou vrgest iustice, be assur'd
Thou shalt haue iustice more then thou desirest.
  Gra. O learned Iudge, mark Iew, a learned Iudge.
  Iew. I take this offer then, pay the bond thrice,
And let the Christian goe.
  Baß. Heere is the money.
  Por. Soft, the Iew shall haue all iustice, soft, no haste,
He shall haue nothing but the penalty.
  Gra. O Iew, an vpright Iudge, a learned Iudge.
  Por. Therefore prepare thee to cut off the flesh,
Shed thou no bloud, nor cut thou lesse nor more
But iust a pound of flesh: if thou tak'st more
Or lesse then a iust pound, be it so much
As makes it light or heauy in the substance,
Or the deuision of the twentieth part
Of one poore scruple, nay if the scale doe turne
But in the estimation of a hayre,
Thou diest, and all thy goods are confiscate.
  Gra. A second *Daniel,* a *Daniel* Iew,
Now infidell I haue thee on the hip.
  Por. Why doth the Iew pause, take thy forfeiture.
  Shy. Giue me my principall, and let me goe.
  Baß. I haue it ready for thee, heere it is.
  Por. He hath refus'd it in the open Court,
He shall haue meerly iustice and his bond.
  Gra. A *Daniel* still say I, a second *Daniel,*
I thanke thee Iew for teaching me that word.
  Shy. Shall I not haue barely my principall?
  Por. Thou shalt haue nothing but the forfeiture,
To be taken so at thy perill Iew.
  Shy. Why then the Deuill giue him good of it:
Ile stay no longer question.

Por. Tarry

Por. Tarry Iew,
The Law hath yet another hold on you.
It is enacted in the Lawes of Venice,
If it be proued against an Alien,
That by direct, or indirect attempts
He seeke the life of any Citizen,
The party gainst the which he doth contriue,
Shall seaze one halfe his goods, the other halfe
Comes to the priuie coffer of the State,
And the offenders life lies in the mercy
Of the Duke onely, gainst all other voice.
In which predicament I say thou standst:
For it appeares by manifest proceeding,
That indirectly, and directly to,
Thou hast contriu'd against the very life
Of the defendant: and thou hast incur'd
The danger formerly by me rehearst.
Downe therefore, and beg mercy of the Duke.

Gra. Beg that thou maist haue leaue to hang thy selfe,
And yet thy wealth being forfeit to the state,
Thou hast not left the value of a cord,
Therefore thou must be hang'd at the states charge.

Duk. That thou shalt see the difference of our spirit,
I pardon thee thy life before thou aske it:
For halfe thy wealth, it is *Anthonio's*,
The other halfe comes to the generall state,
Which humblenesse may driue vnto a fine.

Por. I for the state, not for *Anthonio*.

Shy. Nay, take my life and all, pardon not that,
You take my house, when you do take the prop
That doth sustaine my house: you take my life
When you doe take the meanes whereby I liue.

Por. What mercy can you render him *Anthonio*?

Gra. A halter *gratis*, nothing else for Gods sake.

Ant. So please my Lord the Duke, and all the Court
To quit the fine for one halfe of his goods,
I am content: so he will let me haue
The other halfe in vse, to render it
Vpon his death, vnto the Gentleman
That lately stole his daughter.
Two things prouided more, that for this fauour
He presently become a Christian:
The other, that he doe record a gift
Heere in the Court of all he dies possest
Vnto his sonne *Lorenzo*, and his daughter.

Duk. He shall doe this, or else I doe recant
The pardon that I late pronounced heere.

Por. Art thou contented Iew? what dost thou say?

Shy. I am content.

Por. Clarke, draw a deed of gift.

Shy. I pray you giue me leaue to goe from hence,
I am not well, send the deed after me,
And I will signe it.

Duke. Get thee gone, but doe it.

Gra. In christning thou shalt haue two godfathers,
Had I been iudge, thou shouldst haue had ten more,
To bring thee to the gallowes, not to the font. *Exit.*

Du. Sir I intreat you with me home to dinner.

Por. I humbly doe desire your Grace of pardon,
I must away this night toward Padua,
And it is meete I presently set forth.

Duk. I am sorry that your leysure serues you not:
Anthonio, gratifie this gentleman,
For in my minde, you are much bound to him.
Exit Duke and his traine.

Bass. Most worthy gentleman, I and my friend

Haue by your wisedome beene this day acquitted
Of greeuous penalties, in lieu whereof,
Three thousand Ducats due vnto the Iew
We freely cope your curteous paines withall.

An. And stand indebted ouer and aboue
In loue and seruice to you euermore.

Por. He is well paid that is well satisfied,
And I deliuering you, am satisfied,
And therein doe account my selfe well paid,
My minde was neuer yet more mercinarie.
I pray you know me when we meete againe,
I wish you well, and so I take my leaue.

Bass. Deare sir, of force I must attempt you further,
Take some remembrance of vs as a tribute,
Not as fee: grant me two things, I pray you
Not to denie me, and to pardon me.

Por. You presse mee farre, and therefore I will yeeld,
Giue me your gloues, Ile weare them for your sake,
And for your loue Ile take this ring from you,
Doe not draw backe your hand, ile take no more,
And you in loue shall not deny me this?

Bass. This ring good sir, alas it is a trifle,
I will not shame my selfe to giue you this.

Por. I wil haue nothing else but onely this,
And now methinkes I haue a minde to it.

Bas. There's more depends on this then on the valew,
The dearest ring in Venice will I giue you,
And finde it out by proclamation,
Onely for this I pray you pardon me.

Por. I see sir you are liberall in offers,
You taught me first to beg, and now me thinkes
You teach me how a beggar should be answer'd.

Bas. Good sir, this ring was giuen me by my wife,
And when she put it on, she made me vow
That I should neither sell, nor giue, nor lose it.

Por. That scuse serues many men to saue their gifts,
And if your wife be not a mad woman,
And know how well I haue deseru'd this ring,
Shee would not hold out enemy for euer
For giuing it to me: well, peace be with you. *Exeunt.*

Ant. My L. *Bassanio*, let him haue the ring,
Let his deseruings and my loue withall
Be valued against your wiues commandement.

Bass. Goe *Gratiano*, run and ouer-take him,
Giue him the ring, and bring him if thou canst
Vnto *Anthonies* house, away, make haste. *Exit Grati.*
Come, you and I will thither presently,
And in the morning early will we both
Flie toward *Belmont*, come *Anthonio*. *Exeunt.*

Enter Portia and Nerrissa.

Por. Enquire the Iewes house out, giue him this deed,
And let him signe it, wee'll away to night,
And be a day before our husbands home:
This deed will be well welcome to *Lorenzo*.

Enter Gratiano.

Gra. Faire sir, you are well ore-tane:
My L. *Bassanio* vpon more aduice,
Hath sent you heere this ring, and doth intreat
Your company at dinner.

Por. That cannot be;
His ring I doe accept most thankfully,
And so I pray you tell him: furthermore,
I pray you shew my youth old *Shylockes* house.

Gra. That will I doe.

Ner. Sir, I would speake with you:

Ile see if I can get my husbands ring
Which I did make him sweare to keepe for euer.
   Por. Thou maist I warrant, we shal haue old swearing
That they did giue the rings away to men;
But weele out-face them, and out-sweare them to:
Away, make haste, thou know'st where I will tarry.
   Ner. Come good sir, will you shew me to this house.
                                           Exeunt.

Actus Quintus.

Enter Lorenzo and Iessica.

   Lor. The moone shines bright. In such a night as this,
When the sweet winde did gently kisse the trees,
And they did make no nnyse, in such a night
Troylus me thinkes mounted the Troian walls,
And sigh'd his soule toward the Grecian tents
Where *Cressed* lay that night.
   Iess. In such a night
Did *Thisbie* fearefully ore-trip the dewe,
And saw the Lyons shadow ere himselfe,
And ranne dismayed away.
   Loren. In such a night
Stood *Dido* with a Willow in her hand
Vpon the wilde sea bankes, and waft her Loue
To come againe to Carthage.
   Iess. In such a night
Medea gathered the inchanted hearbs
That did renew old *Eson*.
   Loren. In such a night
Did *Iessica* steale from the wealthy Iewe,
And with an Vnthrift Loue did runne from Venice,
As farre as Belmont.
   Iess. In such a night
Did young *Lorenzo* sweare he lou'd her well,
Stealing her soule with many vowes of faith,
And nere a true one.
   Loren. In such a night
Did pretty *Iessica* (like a little shrow)
Slander her Loue, and he forgaue it her.
   Iessi. I would out-night you did no body come:
But harke, I heare the footing of a man.

Enter Messenger.

   Lor. Who comes so fast in silence of the night?
   Mes. A friend.   (friend?
   Loren. A friend, what friend? your name I pray you
   Mes. Stephano is my name, and I bring word
My Mistresse will before the breake of day
Be heere at Belmont, she doth stray about
By holy crosses where she kneeles and prayes
For happy wedlocke houres.
   Loren. Who comes with her?
   Mes. None but a holy Hermit and her maid:
I pray you it my Master yet return'd?
   Loren. He is not, nor we haue not heard from him,
But goe we in I pray thee *Iessica*,
And ceremoniously let vs vs prepare
Some welcome for the Mistresse of the house,

Enter Clowne.

   Clo. Sola, sola: wo ha ho, sola, sola.
   Loren. Who calls?
   Clo. Sola, did you see M. *Lorenzo*, & M. *Lorenzo*, sola,
   Lor. Leaue hollowing man, heere.   (sola,
   Clo. Sola, where, where?
   Lor. Heere?
   Clo. Tel him ther's a Post come from my Master, with
his horne full of good newes, my Master will be here ere
morning sweet soule.
   Loren. Let's in, and there expect their comming.
And yet no matter: why should we goe in?
My friend *Stephen*, signifie pray you
Within the house, your Mistresse is at hand,
And bring your musique foorth into the ayre.
How sweet the moone-light sleepes vpon this banke,
Heere will we sit, and let the sounds of musicke
Creepe in our eares soft stilnes, and the night
Become the tutches of sweet harmonie:
Sit *Iessica*, looke how the floore of heauen
Is thicke inlayed with pattens of bright gold,
There's not the smallest orbe which thou beholdst
But in his motion like an Angell sings,
Still quiring to the young eyed Cherubins;
Such harmonie is in immortall soules,
But whilst this muddy vesture of decay
Doth grosly close in it, we cannot heare it:
Come hoe, and wake *Diana* with a hymne,
With sweetest tutches pearce your Mistresse eare,
And draw her home with musicke.
   Iessi. I am neuer merry when I heare sweet musique.
                                     Play musicke.
   Lor. The reason is, your spirits are attentiue:
For doe but note a wilde and wanton heard
Or race of youthful and vnhandled colts,
Fetching mad bounds, bellowing and neighing loud,
Which is the hot condition of their bloud,
If they but heare perchance a trumpet sound,
Or any ayre of musicke touch their eares,
You shall perceiue them make a mutuall stand,
Their sauage eyes turn'd to a modest gaze,
By the sweet power of musicke: therefore the Poet
Did faine that *Orpheus* drew trees, stones, and floods,
Since naught so stockish, hard, and full of rage,
But musicke for time doth change his nature,
The man that hath no musicke in himselfe,
Nor is not moued with concord of sweet sounds,
Is fit for treasons, stratagems, and spoyles,
The motions of his spirit are dull as night,
And his affections darke as *Erobus*,
Let no such man be trusted: marke the musicke.

Enter Portia and Nerrissa.

   Por. That light we see is burning in my hall:
How farre that little candell throwes his beames,
So shines a good deed in a naughty world.   (dle
   Ner. When the moone shone we did not see the can
   Por. So doth the greater glory dim the lesse,
A substitute shines brightly as a King
Vntill a King be by, and then his state
Empties it selfe, as doth an inland brooke
Into the maine of waters: musique, harke,   *Musicke.*
   Ner. It is your musicke Madame of the house.
   Por. Nothing is good I see without respect,
Methinkes it sounds much sweeter then by day?
   Ner. Silence bestowes that vertue on it Madam.
   Por. The Crow doth sing as sweetly as the Larke
                                              When

When neither is attended: and I thinke
The Nightingale if she should sing by day
When euery Goose is cackling, would be thought
No better a Musitian then the Wren?
How many things by season, season'd are
To their right praise, and true perfection:
Peace, how the Moone sleepes with Endimion,
And would not be awak'd.

Musicke ceases.

Lor. That is the voice,
Or I am much deceiu'd of *Portia.*

Por. He knowes me as the blinde man knowes the
Cuckow by the bad voice?

Lor. Deere Lady welcome home?

Por. We haue bene praying for our husbands welfare
Which speed we hope the better for our words,
Are they return'd?

Lor. Madam, they are not yet:
But there is come a Messenger before
To signifie their comming.

Por. Go in *Nerrissa,*
Giue order to my seruants, that they take
No note at all of our being absent hence,
Nor you *Lorenzo*, *Iessica* nor you.

A Tucket sounds.

Lor. Your husband is at hand, I heare his Trumpet,
We are no tell-tales Madam, feare you not.

Por. This night methinkes is but the daylight sicke,
It lookes a little paler, 'tis a day,
Such as the day is, when the Sun is hid.

*Enter Bassanio, Anthonio, Gratiano, and their
Followers.*

Bas. We should hold day with the Antipodes,
If you would walke in absence of the sunne.

Por. Let me giue light, but let me not be light,
For a light wife doth make a heauie husband,
And neuer be *Bassanio* so for me,
But God sort all: you are welcome home my Lord.

Bass. I thanke you Madam, giue welcom to my friend
This is the man, this is *Anthonio,*
To whom I am so infinitely bound.

Por. You should in all sence be much bound to him,
For as I heare he was much bound for you.

Anth. No more then I am wel acquitted of.

Por. Sir, you are verie welcome to our house:
It must appeare in other waies then words,
Therefore I scant this breathing curtesie.

Gra. By yonder Moone I sweare you do me wrong,
Infaith I gaue it to the Iudges Clearke,
Would he were gelt that had it for my part,
Since you do take it Loue so much at hart.

Por. A quarrel hoe alreadie, what's the matter?

Gra. About a hoope of Gold, a paltry Ring
That she did giue me, whose Poesie was
For all the world like Cutlers Poetry
Vpon a knife; *Loue mee, and leaue mee not.*

Ner. What talke you of the Poesie or the valew:
You swore to me when I did giue it you,
That you would weare it til the houre of death,
And that it should lye with you in your graue,
Though not for me, yet for your vehement oaths,
You should haue beene respectiue and haue kept it.
Gaue it a Iudges Clearke: but wel I know
The Clearke wil nere weare haire on's face that had it.

Gra. He wil, and if he liue to be a man.

Nerrissa. I, if a Woman liue to be a man.

Gra. Now by this hand I gaue it to a youth,
A kinde of boy, a little scrubbed boy,
No higher then thy selfe, the Iudges Clearke,
A prating boy that begg'd it as a Fee,
I could not for my heart deny it him.

Por. You were too blame, I must be plaine with you,
To part so slightly with your wiues first gift,
A thing stucke on with oathes vpon your finger,
And so riueted with faith vnto your flesh.
I gaue my Loue a Ring, and made him sweare
Neuer to part with it, and heere he stands:
I dare be sworne for him, he would not leaue it,
Nor plucke it from his finger, for the wealth
That the world masters. Now in faith *Gratiano,*
You giue your wife too vnkinde a cause of greefe,
And 'twere to me I should be mad at it.

Bass. Why I were best to cut my left hand off,
And sweare I lost the Ring defending it.

Gre. My Lord *Bassanio* gaue his Ring away
Vnto the Iudge that beg'd it, and indeede
Deseru'd it too: and then the Boy his Clearke
That tooke some paines in writing, he begg'd mine,
And neyther man nor master would take ought
But the two Rings.

Por. What Ring gaue you my Lord?
Not that I hope which you receiu'd of me.

Bass. If I could adde a lie vnto a fault,
I would deny it: but you see my finger
Hath not the Ring vpon it, it is gone.

Por. Euen so voide is your false heart of truth.
By heauen I wil nere come in your bed
Vntil I see the Ring.

Ner. Nor I in yours, til I againe see mine.

Bass. Sweet *Portia,*
If you did know to whom I gaue the Ring,
If you did know for whom I gaue the Ring,
And would conceiue for what I gaue the Ring,
And how vnwillingly I left the Ring,
When nought would be accepted but the Ring,
You would abate the strength of your displeasure?

Por. If you had knowne the vertue of the Ring,
Or halfe her worthinesse that gaue the Ring,
Or your owne honour to containe the Ring,
You would not then haue parted with the Ring:
What man is there so much vnreasonable,
If you had pleas'd to haue defended it
With any termes of Zeale: wanted the modestie
To vrge the thing held as a ceremonie:
Nerrissa teaches me what to beleeue,
Ile die for't, but some Woman had the Ring?

Bass. No by mine honor Madam, by my soule
No Woman had it, but a ciuill Doctor,
Which did refuse three thousand Ducates of me,
And beg'd the Ring; the which I did denie him,
And suffer'd him to go displeas'd away:
Euen he that had held vp the verie life
Of my deere friend. What should I say sweete Lady?
I was inforc'd to send it after him,
I was beset with shame and curtesie,
My honor would not let ingratitude
So much besmeare it. Pardon me good Lady,
And by these blessed Candles of the night,
Had you bene there, I thinke you would haue beg'd
The Ring of me, to giue the worthie Doctor?

Por. Let not that Doctor ere come neere my house,
Since he hath got the iewell that I loued,
And that which you did sweare to keepe for me,
I will become as liberall as you,
Ile not deny him any thing I haue,
No, not my body, nor my husbands bed:
Know him I shall, I am well sure of it.
Lie not a night from home. Watch me like Argos,
If you doe not, if I be left alone,
Now by mine honour which is yet mine owne,
Ile haue the Doctor for my bedfellow.

Nerrissa. And I his Clarke: therefore be well aduis'd
How you doe leaue me to mine owne protection.

Gra. Well, doe you so: let not me take him then,
For if I doe, ile mar the yong Clarks pen.

Ant. I am th'vnhappy subiect of these quarrels.

Por. Sir, grieue not you,
You are welcome notwithstanding.

Bass. Portia, forgiue me this enforced wrong,
And in the hearing of these manie friends
I sweare to thee, euen by thine owne faire eyes
Wherein I see my selfe.

Por. Marke you but that?
In both my eyes he doubly sees himselfe:
In each eye one, sweare by your double selfe,
And there's an oath of credit.

Bass. Nay, but heare me.
Pardon this fault, and by my soule I sweare
I neuer more will breake an oath with thee.

Anth. I once did lend my bodie for thy wealth,
Which but for him that had your husbands ring
Had quite miscarried. I dare be bound againe,
My soule vpon the forfeit, that your Lord
Will neuer more breake faith aduisedlie.

Por. Then you shall be his suretie: giue him this,
And bid him keepe it better then the other.

Ant. Heere Lord *Bassanio*, swear to keep this ring.

Bass. By heauen it is the same I gaue the Doctor.

Por. I had it of him: pardon *Bassanio*,
For by this ring the Doctor lay with me.

Ner. And pardon me my gentle *Gratiano*,
For that same scrubbed boy the Doctors Clarke
In liew of this, last night did lye with me.

Gra. Why this is like the mending of high waies
In Sommer, where the waies are faire enough:
What, are we Cuckolds ere we haue deseru'd it.

Por. Speake not so grossely, you are all amaz'd;
Heere is a letter, reade it at your leysure,
It comes from Padua from *Bellario*,
There you shall finde that *Portia* was the Doctor,
Nerrissa there her Clarke. *Lorenzo* heere
Shall witnesse I set forth as soone as you,
And but eu'n now return'd: I haue not yet
Entred my house. *Anthonio* you are welcome,
And I haue better newes in store for you
Then you expect: vnseale this letter soone,
There you shall finde three of your Argosies
Are richly come to harbour sodainlie.
You shall not know by what strange accident
I chanced on this letter.

Antho. I am dumbe.

Bass. Were you the Doctor, and I knew you not?

Gra. Were you the Clark that is to make me cuckold.

Ner. I, but the Clark that neuer meanes to doe it,
Vnlesse he liue vntill he be a man.

Bass. (Sweet Doctor) you shall be my bedfellow,
When I am absent, then lie with my wife.

An. (Sweet Ladie) you haue giuen me life & liuing;
For heere I reade for certaine that my ships
Are safelie come to Rode.

Por. How now *Lorenzo*?
My Clarke hath some good comforts to for you.

Ner. I, and Ile giue them him without a fee.
There doe I giue to you and *Iessica*
From the rich Iewe, a speciall deed of gift
After his death, of all he dies possess'd of.

Loren. Faire Ladies you drop Manna in the way
Of starued people.

Por. It is almost morning,
And yet I am sure you are not satisfied
Of these euents at full. Let vs goe in,
And charge vs there vpon intergatories,
And we will answer all things faithfully.

Gra. Let it be so, the first intergatory
That my *Nerrissa* shall be sworne on, is,
Whether till the next night she had rather stay,
Or goe to bed, now being two houres to day,
But were the day come, I should wish it darke,
Till I were couching with the Doctors Clarke.
Well, while I liue, Ile feare no other thing
So sore, as keeping safe *Nerrissas* ring.

Exeunt.

FINIS.

As you Like it.

Actus primus. Scœna Prima.

Enter Orlando and Adam.

Orlando.

AS I remember *Adam*, it was vpon this fashion bequeathed me by will, but poore a thousand Crownes, and as thou saist, charged my brother on his blessing to breed mee well: and there begins my sadnesse: My brother *Iaques* he keepes at schoole, and report speakes goldenly of his profit: for my part, he keepes me rustically at home, or (to speak more properly) staies me heere at home vnkept: for call you that keeping for a gentleman of my birth, that differs not from the stalling of an Oxe? his horses are bred better, for besides that they are faire with their feeding, they are taught their mannage, and to that end Riders deerely hir'd: but I (his brother) gaine nothing vnder him but growth, for the which his Animals on his dunghils are as much bound to him as I: besides this nothing that he so plentifully giues me, the something that nature gaue mee, his countenance seemes to take from me: hee lets mee feede with his Hindes, barres mee the place of a brother, and as much as in him lies, mines my gentility with my education. This is it *Adam* that grieues me, and the spirit of my Father, which I thinke is within mee, begins to mutinie against this seruitude. I will no longer endure it, though yet I know no wise remedy how to auoid it.

Enter Oliuer.

Adam. Yonder comes my Master, your brother.

Orlan. Goe a-part *Adam*, and thou shalt heare how he will shake me vp.

Oli. Now Sir, what make you heere?

Orl. Nothing: I am not taught to make any thing.

Oli. What mar you then sir?

Orl. Marry sir, I am helping you to mar that which God made, a poore vnworthy brother of yours with idlenesse.

Oliuer. Marry sir be better employed, and be naught a while.

Orlan. Shall I keepe your hogs, and eat huskes with them? what prodigall portion haue I spent, that I should come to such penury?

Oli. Know you where you are sir?

Orl. O sir, very well: heere in your Orchard.

Oli. Know you before whom sir?

Orl. I, better then him I am before knowes mee: I know you are my eldest brother, and in the gentle condition of bloud you should so know me: the courtesie of nations allowes you my better, in that you are the first borne, but the same tradition takes not away my bloud, were there twenty brothers betwixt vs: I haue as much of my father in mee, as you, albeit I confesse your comming before me is neerer to his reuerence.

Oli. What Boy.

Orl. Come, come elder brother, you are too yong in this.

Oli. Wilt thou lay hands on me villaine?

Orl. I am no villaine: I am the yongest sonne of Sir *Rowland de Boys*, he was my father, and he is thrice a villaine that saies such a father begot villaines: wert thou not my brother, I would not take this hand from thy throat, till this other had puld out thy tongue for saying so, thou hast raild on thy selfe.

Adam. Sweet Masters bee patient, for your Fathers remembrance, be at accord.

Oli. Let me goe I say.

Orl. I will not till I please: you shall heare mee: my father charg'd you in his will to giue me good education: you haue train'd me like a pezant, obscuring and hiding from me all gentleman-like qualities: the spirit of my father growes strong in mee, and I will no longer endure it: therefore allow me such exercises as may become a gentleman, or giue mee the poore allottery my father left me by testament, with that I will goe buy my fortunes.

Oli. And what wilt thou do? beg when that is spent? Well sir, get you in. I will not long be troubled with you: you shall haue some part of your will, I pray you leaue me.

Orl. I will no further offend you, then becomes mee for my good.

Oli. Get you with him, you olde dogge.

Adam. Is old dogge my reward: most true, I haue lost my teeth in your seruice: God be with my olde master, he would not haue spoke such a word. *Ex. Orl. Ad.*

Oli. Is it euen so, begin you to grow vpon me? I will physicke your ranckenesse, and yet giue no thousand crownes neyther: holla *Dennis*.

Enter Dennis.

Den. Calls your worship?

Oli. Was not *Charles* the Dukes Wrastler heere to speake with me?

Den. So please you, he is heere at the doore, and importunes accesse to you.

Oli. Call him in: 'twill be a good way: and to morrow the wrastling is.

Enter Charles.

Cha. Good morrow to your worship.

Oli. Good Mounsier *Charles*: what's the new newes at the new Court?

Charles. There's no newes at the Court Sir, but the olde newes: that is, the old Duke is banished by his yonger brother the new Duke, and three or foure louing

Lords haue put themselues into voluntary exile with him, whose lands and reuenues enrich the new Duke, therefore he giues them good leaue to wander.

Oli. Can you tell if *Rosalind* the Dukes daughter bee banished with her Father?

Cha. O no; for the Dukes daughter her Cosen so loues her, being euer from their Cradles bred together, that hee would haue followed her exile, or haue died to stay behind her; she is at the Court, and no lesse beloued of her Vncle, then his owne daughter, and neuer two Ladies loued as they doe.

Oli. Where will the old Duke liue?

Cha. They say hee is already in the Forrest of *Arden*, and a many merry men with him; and there they liue like the old *Robin Hood* of *England*: they say many yong Gentlemen flocke to him euery day, and fleet the time carelesly as they did in the golden world.

Oli. What, you wrastle to morrow before the new Duke.

Cha. Marry doe I sir: and I came to acquaint you with a matter: I am giuen sir secretly to vnderstand, that your yonger brother *Orlando* hath a disposition to come in disguis'd against mee to try a fall: to morrow sir I wrastle for my credit, and hee that escapes me without some broken limbe, shall acquit him well: your brother is but young and tender, and for your loue I would bee loth to foyle him, as I must for my owne honour if hee come in: therefore out of my loue to you, I came hither to acquaint you withall, that either you might stay him from his intendment, or brooke such disgrace well as he shall runne into, in that it is a thing of his owne search, and altogether against my will.

Oli. *Charles*, I thanke thee for thy loue to me, which thou shalt finde I will most kindly requite: I had my selfe notice of my Brothers purpose heerein, and haue by vnder-hand meanes laboured to disswade him from it; but he is resolute. Ile tell thee *Charles*, it is the stubbornest yong fellow of France, full of ambition, an enuious emulator of euery mans good parts, a secret & villanous contriuer against mee his naturall brother: therefore vse thy discretion, I had as liefe thou didst breake his necke as his finger. And thou wert best looke to't; for if thou dost him any slight disgrace, or if hee doe not mightilie grace himselfe on thee, hee will practise against thee by poyson, entrap thee by some treacherous deuise, and neuer leaue thee till he hath tane thy life by some indirect meanes or other: for I assure thee, (and almost with teares I speake it) there is not one so young, and so villanous this day liuing. I speake but brotherly of him, but should I anathomize him to thee, as hee is, I must blush, and weepe, and thou must looke pale and wonder.

Cha. I am heartily glad I came hither to you: if hee come to morrow, Ile giue him his payment: if euer hee goe alone againe, Ile neuer wrastle for prize more: and so God keepe your worship. *Exit.*

Farewell good *Charles*. Now will I stirre this Gamester: I hope I shall see an end of him; for my soule (yet I know not why) hates nothing more then he: yet hee's gentle, neuer school'd, and yet learned, full of noble deuise, of all sorts enchantingly beloued, and indeed so much in the heart of the world, and especially of my owne people, who best know him, that I am altogether misprised: but it shall not be so long, this wrastler shall cleare all: nothing remaines, but that I kindle the boy thither, which now Ile goe about. *Exit.*

Scœna Secunda.

Enter Rosalind, and Cellia.

Cel. I pray thee *Rosalind*, sweet my Coz, be merry.

Ros. Deere *Cellia*; I show more mirth then I am mistresse of, and would you yet were merrier: vnlesse you could teach me to forget a banished father, you must not learne mee how to remember any extraordinary pleasure.

Cel. Heerein I see thou lou'st mee not with the full waight that I loue thee; if my Vncle thy banished father had banished thy Vncle the Duke my Father, so thou hadst beene still with mee, I could haue taught my loue to take thy father for mine; so wouldst thou, if the truth of thy loue to me were so righteously temper'd, as mine is to thee.

Ros. Well, I will forget the condition of my estate, to reioyce in yours.

Cel. You know my Father hath no childe, but I, nor none is like to haue; and truely when he dies, thou shalt be his heire; for what hee hath taken away from thy father perforce, I will render thee againe in affection: by mine honor I will, and when I breake that oath, let mee turne monster: therefore my sweet *Rose*, my deare *Rose*, be merry.

Ros. From henceforth I will Coz, and deuise sports: let me see, what thinke you of falling in Loue?

Cel. Marry I prethee doe, to make sport withall: but loue no man in good earnest, nor no further in sport reyther, then with safety of a pure blush, thou maist in honor come off againe.

Ros. What shall be our sport then?

Cel. Let vs sit and mocke the good housewife *Fortune* from her wheele, that her gifts may henceforth bee bestowed equally.

Ros. I would wee could doe so: for her benefits are mightily misplaced, and the bountifull blinde woman doth most mistake in her gifts to women.

Cel. 'Tis true, for those that she makes faire, she scarce makes honest, & those that she makes honest, she makes very illfauouredly.

Ros. Nay now thou goest from Fortunes office to Natures: Fortune reignes in gifts of the world, not in the lineaments of Nature.

Enter Clowne.

Cel. No; when Nature hath made a faire creature, may she not by Fortune fall into the fire? though nature hath giuen vs wit to flout at Fortune, hath not Fortune sent in this foole to cut off the argument?

Ros. Indeed there is fortune too hard for nature, when fortune makes natures naturall, the cutter off of natures witte.

Cel. Peraduenture this is not Fortunes work neither, but Natures, who perceiueth our naturall wits too dull to reason of such goddesses, hath sent this Naturall for our whetstone, for alwaies the dulnesse of the foole, is the whetstone of the wits. How now Witte, whether wander you?

Clow. Mistresse, you must come away to your father.

Cel. Were you made the messenger?

Clo. No by mine honor, but I was bid to come for you

Ros. Where learned you that oath foole?

Clo. Of a certaine Knight, that swore by his Honour they were good Pan-cakes, and swore by his Honor the Mustard was naught: Now Ile stand to it, the Pancakes were naught, and the Mustard was good, and yet was not the Knight forsworne.

Cel. How proue you that in the great heape of your knowledge?

Ros. I marry, now vnmuzzle your wisedome.

Clo. Stand you both forth now: stroke your chinnes, and sweare by your beards that I am a knaue.

Cel. By our beards (if we had them) thou art.

Clo. By my knauerie (if I had it) then I were: but if you sweare by that that is not, you are not forsworn : no more was this knight swearing by his Honor, for he neuer had anie; or if he had, he had sworne it away, before euer he saw those Pancakes, or that Mustard.

Cel. Prethee, who is't that thou means't?

Clo. One that old *Fredericke* your Father loues.

Ros. My Fathers loue is enough to honor him enough; speake no more of him, you'l be whipt for taxation one of these daies.

Clo. The more pittie that fooles may not speak wisely, what Wisemen do foolishly.

Cel. By my troth thou saiest true: For, since the little wit that fooles haue was silenced, the little foolerie that wise men haue makes a great shew; Heere comes Monsieur the *Beu.*

Enter le Beau.

Ros. With his mouth full of newes.

Cel. Which he vvill put on vs, as Pigeons feed their young.

Ros. Then shal we be newes-cram'd.

Cel. All the better: we shalbe the more Marketable. Boon-iour Monsieur le *Beu,* what's the newes?

Le Beu. Faire Princesse, you haue lost much good sport.

Cel. Sport : of what colour?

Le Beu. What colour Madame? How shall I aunswer you?

Ros. As wit and fortune will.

Clo. Or as the destinies decrees.

Cel. Well said, that was laid on with a trowell.

Clo. Nay, if I keepe not my ranke.

Ros. Thou loosest thy old smell.

Le Beu. You amaze me Ladies: I would haue told you of good wrastling, which you haue lost the sight of.

Ros. Yet tell vs the manner of the Wrastling.

Le Beu. I wil tell you the beginning: and if it please your Ladiships, you may see the end, for the best is yet to doe, and heere where you are, they are comming to performe it.

Cel. Well, the beginning that is dead and buried.

Le Beu. There comes an old man, and his three sons.

Cel. I could match this beginning with an old tale.

Le Beu. Three proper yong men, of excellent growth and presence.

Ros. With bils on their neckes : Be it knowne vnto all men by these presents.

Le Beu. The eldest of the three, wrastled with *Charles* the Dukes Wrastler, which *Charles* in a moment threw him, and broke three of his ribbes, that there is little hope of life in him : So he seru'd the second, and so the third: yonder they lie, the poore old man their Father, making such pittiful dole ouer them, that all the beholders take his part with weeping.

Ros. Alas.

Clo. But what is the sport Monsieur, that the Ladies haue lost?

Le Beu. Why this that I speake of.

Clo. Thus men may grow wiser euery day. It is the first time that euer I heard breaking of ribbes was sport for Ladies.

Cel. Or I, I promise thee.

Ros. But is there any else longs to see this broken Musicke in his sides? Is there yet another doates vpon rib-breaking? Shall we see this wrastling Cosin?

Le Beu. You must if you stay heere, for heere is the place appointed for the wrastling, and they are ready to performe it.

Cel. Yonder sure they are comming. Let vs now stay and see it.

Flourish. Enter Duke, Lords, Orlando, Charles, and Attendants.

Duke. Come on, since the youth will not be intreated His owne perill on his forwardnesse.

Ros. Is yonder the man?

Le Beu. Euen he, Madam.

Cel. Alas, he is too yong : yet he looks successfully

Du. How now daughter, and Cousin: Are you crept hither to see the wrastling?

Ros. I my Liege, so please you giue vs leaue.

Du. You wil take little delight in it, I can tell you there is such oddes in the man : In pitie of the challengers youth, I would faine disswade him, but he will not bee entreated. Speake to him Ladies, see if you can mooue him.

Cel. Call him hether good Monsieuer Le *Beu.*

Duke. Do so: Ile not be by.

Le Beu. Monsieur the Challenger, the Princesse cals for you.

Orl. I attend them with all respect and dutie.

Ros. Young man, haue you challeng'd *Charles* the Wrastler?

Orl. No faire Princesse : he is the generall challenger, I come but in as others do, to try with him the strength of my youth.

Cel. Yong Gentleman, your spirits are too bold for your yeares : you haue seene cruell proofe of this mans strength, if you saw your selfe with your eies, or knew your selfe with your iudgment, the feare of your aduenture would counsel you to a more equall enterprise. We pray you for your owne sake to embrace your own safetie, and giue ouer this attempt.

Ros. Do yong Sir, your reputation shall not therefore be misprised : we wil make it our suite to the Duke, that the wrastling might not go forward.

Orl. I beseech you, punish mee not with your harde thoughts, wherein I confesse me much guiltie to denie so faire and excellent Ladies anie thing. But let your faire eies, and gentle wishes go with mee to my triall; wherein if I bee foil'd, there is but one sham'd that vvas neuer gracious : if kil'd, but one dead that is willing to be so : I shall do my friends no wrong, for I haue none to lament me: the world no iniurie, for in it I haue nothing: onely in the world I fil vp a place, which may bee better supplied, when I haue made it emptie.

Ros. The little strength that I haue, I would it vvere with you.

Cel. And mine to eeke out hers.

Rof. Fare you well: praie heauen I be deceiu'd in you.

Cel. Your hearts desires be with you.

Char. Come, where is this yong gallant, that is so desirous to lie with his mother earth?

Orl. Readie Sir, but his will hath in it a more modest working.

Duk. You shall trie but one fall.

Cha. No, I warrant your Grace you shall not entreat him to a second, that haue so mightilie perswaded him from a first.

Orl. You meane to mocke me after: you should not haue mockt me before: but come your waies.

Rof. Now Hercules, be thy speede yong man.

Cel. I would I were inuisible, to catch the strong fellow by the legge. *Wrastle.*

Rof. Oh excellent yong man.

Cel. If I had a thunderbolt in mine eie, I can tell who should downe. *Shout.*

Duk. No more, no more.

Orl. Yes I beseech your Grace, I am not yet well breath'd.

Duk. How do'st thou *Charles*?

Le Beu. He cannot speake my Lord.

Duk. Beare him awaie:
What is thy name yong man?

Orl. Orlando my Liege, the yongest sonne of Sir *Roland de Boys*.

Duk. I would thou hadst beene son to some man else,
The world esteem'd thy father honourable,
But I did finde him still mine enemie:
Thou should'st haue better pleas'd me with this deede,
Hadst thou descended from another house:
But fare thee well, thou art a gallant youth,
I would thou had'st told me of another Father.
Exit Duke.

Cel. Were I my Father (Coze) would I do this?

Orl. I am more proud to be Sir *Rolands* sonne,
His yongest sonne, and would not change that calling
To be adopted heire to *Fredricke*.

Rof. My Father lou'd Sir *Roland* as his soule,
And all the world was of my Fathers minde,
Had I before knowne this yong man his sonne,
I should haue giuen him teares vnto entreaties,
Ere he should thus haue ventur'd.

Cel. Gentle Cosen,
Let vs goe thanke him, and encourage him:
My Fathers rough and enuious disposition
Sticks me at heart: Sir, you haue well deseru'd,
If you doe keepe your promises in loue;
But iustly as you haue exceeded all promise,
Your Mistris shall be happie.

Rof. Gentleman,
Weare this for me: one out of suites with fortune
That could giue more, but that her hand lacks meanes.
Shall we goe Coze?

Cel. I: fare you well faire Gentleman.

Orl. Can I not say, I thanke you? My better parts
Are all throwne downe, and that which here stands vp
Is but a quintine, a meere liuelesse blocke.

Rof. He cals vs back: my pride fell with my fortunes,
Ile aske him what he would: Did you call Sir?
Sir, you haue wrastled well, and ouerthrowne
More then your enemies.

Cel. Will you goe Coze?

Rof. Haue with you: fare you well. *Exit.*

Orl. What passion hangs these waights vpō my toong?
I cannot speake to her, yet she vrg'd conference.

Enter Le Beu.

O poore *Orlando*! thou art ouerthrowne
Or *Charles*, or something weaker masters thee.

Le Beu. Good Sir, I do in friendship counsaile you
To leaue this place; Albeit you haue deseru'd
High commendation, true applause, and loue;
Yet such is now the Dukes condition,
That he misconsters all that you haue done:
The Duke is humorous, what he is indeede
More suites you to conceiue, then I to speake of.

Orl. I thanke you Sir; and pray you tell me this,
Which of the two was daughter of the Duke,
That here was at the Wrastling?

Le Beu. Neither his daughter, if we iudge by manners,
But yet indeede the taller is his daughter,
The other is daughter to the banish'd Duke,
And here detain'd by her vsurping Vncle
To keepe his daughter companie, whose loues
Are deerer then the naturall bond of Sisters:
But I can tell you, that of late this Duke
Hath tane displeasure 'gainst his gentle Neece,
Grounded vpon no other argument,
But that the people praise her for her vertues,
And pittie her, for her good Fathers sake;
And on my life his malice 'gainst the Lady
Will sodainly breake forth: Sir, fare you well,
Hereafter in a better world then this,
I shall desire more loue and knowledge of you.

Orl. I rest much bounden to you: fare you well.
Thus must I from the smoake into the smother,
From tyrant Duke, vnto a tyrant Brother.
But heauenly *Rosaline*. *Exit*

Scena Tertius.

Enter Celia and Rosaline.

Cel. Why Cosen, why *Rosaline*: *Cupid* haue mercie, Not a word?

Rof. Not one to throw at a dog.

Cel. No, thy words are too precious to be cast away vpon curs, throw some of them at me; come lame mee with reasons.

Rof. Then there were two Cosens laid vp, when the one should be lam'd with reasons, and the other mad without any.

Cel. But is all this for your Father?

Rof. No, some of it is for my childes Father: Oh how full of briers is this working day world.

Cel. They are but burs, Cosen, throwne vpon thee in holiday foolerie, if we walke not in the trodden paths our very petty-coates will catch them.

Rof. I could shake them off my coate, these burs are in my heart.

Cel. Hem them away.

Rof. I would try if I could cry hem, and haue him.

Cel. Come, come, wrastle with thy affections.

Rof. O they take the part of a better wrastler then my selfe.

Cel. O, a good wish vpon you: you will trie in time
in

in dispight of a fall: but turning these iests out of seruice, let vs talke in good earnest: Is it possible on such a sodaine, you should fall into so strong a liking with old Sir *Rowlands* yongest sonne?

Ros. The Duke my Father lou'd his Father deerelie.

Cel. Doth it therefore ensue that you should loue his Sonne deerelie? By this kinde of chase, I should hate him, for my father hated his father deerely; yet I hate not *Orlando*.

Ros. No faith, hate him not for my sake.

Cel. Why should I not? doth he not deserue well?

Enter Duke with Lords.

Ros. Let me loue him for that, and do you loue him Because I doe. Looke, here comes the Duke.

Cel. With his eies full of anger.

Duk. Mistris, dispatch you with your safest haste, And get you from our Court.

Ros. Me Vncle.

Duk. You Cosen, Within these ten daies if that thou beest found So neere our publike Court as twentie miles, Thou diest for it.

Ros. I doe beseech your Grace Let me the knowledge of my fault beare with me: If with my selfe I hold intelligence, Or haue acquaintance with mine owne desires, If that I doe not dreame, or be not franticke, (As I doe trust I am not) then deere Vncle, Neuer so much as in a thought vnborne, Did I offend your highnesse.

Duk. Thus doe all Traitors, If their purgation did consist in words, They are as innocent as grace it selfe; Let it suffice thee that I trust thee not.

Ros. Yet your mistrust cannot make me a Traitor; Tell me whereon the likelihoods depends?

Duk. Thou art thy Fathers daughter, there's enough.

Ros. So was I when your highnes took his Dukdome, So was I when your highnesse banisht him; Treason is not inherited my Lord, Or if we did deriue it from our friends, What's that to me, my Father was no Traitor, Then good my Leige, mistake me not so much, To thinke my pouertie is treacherous.

Cel. Deere Soueraigne heare me speake.

Duk. I *Celia*, we staid her for your sake, Else had she with her Father rang'd along.

Cel. I did not then intreat to haue her stay, It was your pleasure, and your owne remorse, I was too yong that time to value her, But now I know her: if she be a Traitor, Why so am I: we still haue slept together, Rose at an instant, learn'd, plaid, eate together, And wheresoere we went, like *Iunos* Swans, Still we went coupled and inseperable.

Duk. She is too subtile for thee, and her smoothnes; Her verie silence, and per patience, Speake to the people, and they pittie her: Thou art a foole, she robs thee of thy name, And thou wilt show more bright, & seem more vertuous When she is gone: then open not thy lips Firme, and irreuocable is my doombe, Which I haue past vpon her, she is banish'd.

Cel. Pronounce that sentence then on me my Leige, I cannot liue out of her companie.

Duk. You are a foole: you Neice prouide your selfe, If you out-stay the time, vpon mine honor, And in the greatnesse of my word you die.

Exit Duke, &c.

Cel. O my poore *Rosaline*, whether wilt thou goe? Wilt thou change Fathers? I will giue thee mine: I charge thee be not thou more grieu'd then I am.

Ros. I haue more cause.

Cel. Thou hast not Cosen, Prethee be cheerefull; know'st thou not the Duke Hath banish'd me his daughter?

Ros. That he hath not.

Cel. No, hath not? *Rosaline* lacks then the loue Which teacheth thee that thou and I am one, Shall we be sundred? shall we part sweete girle? No, let my Father seeke another heire: Therefore deuise with me how we may flie Whether to goe, and what to beare with vs, And doe not seeke to take your change vpon you, To beare your griefes your selfe, and leaue me out: For by this heauen, now at our sorrowes pale; Say what thou canst, Ile goe along with thee.

Ros. Why, whether shall we goe?

Cel. To seeke my Vncle in the Forrest of *Arden*.

Ros. Alas, what danger will it be to vs, (Maides as we are) to trauell forth so farre? Beautie prouoketh theeues sooner then gold.

Cel. Ile put my selfe in poore and meane attire, And with a kinde of vmber smirch my face, The like doe you, so shall we passe along, And neuer stir assailants.

Ros. Were it not better, Because that I am more then common tall, That I did suite me all points like a man, A gallant curtelax vpon my thigh, A bore-speare in my hand, and in my heart Lye there what hidden womans feare there will, Weele haue a swashing and a martiall outside, As manie other mannish cowards haue, That doe outface it with their semblances.

Cel. What shall I call thee when thou art a man?

Ros. Ile haue no worse a name then *Ioues* owne Page, And therefore looke you call me *Ganimed*. But what will you by call'd?

Cel. Something that hath a reference to my state: No longer *Celia*, but *Aliena*.

Ros. But Cosen, what if we assaid to steale The clownish Foole out of your Fathers Court: Would he not be a comfort to our trauaile?

Cel. Heele goe along ore the wide world with me, Leaue me alone to woe him; Let's away And get our Iewels and our wealth together, Deuise the fittest time, and safest way To hide vs from pursuite that will be made After my flight: now goe in we content To libertie, and not to banishment. *Exeunt.*

Actus Secundus. Scœna Prima.

Enter Duke Senior: Amyens, and two or three Lords like Forresters.

Duk.Sen. Now my Coe-mates, and brothers in exile: Hath not old custome made this life more sweete

Then

Then that of painted pompe? Are not these woods
More free from perill then the enuious Court?
Heere feele we not the penaltie of *Adam*,
The seasons difference, as the Icie phange
And churlish chiding of the winters winde,
Which when it bites and blowes vpon my body
Euen till I shrinke with cold, I smile, and say
This is no flattery: these are counsellors
That feelingly perswade me what I am:
Sweet are the vses of aduersitie
Which like the toad, ougly and venemous,
Weares yet a precious Iewell in his head:
And this our life exempt from publike haunt,
Findes tongues in trees, bookes in the running brookes,
Sermons in stones, and good in euery thing.
  Amien. I would not change it, happy is your Grace
That can translate the stubbornnesse of fortune
Into so quiet and so sweet a stile.
  Du.Sen. Come, shall we goe and kill vs venison?
And yet it irkes me the poore dapled fooles
Being natiue Burgers of this desert City,
Should in their owne confines with forked heads
Haue their round hanches goard.
  1.*Lord.* Indeed my Lord
The melancholy *Iaques* grieues at that,
And in that kinde sweares you doe more vsurpe
Then doth your brother that hath banish'd you:
To day my Lord of *Amiens*, and my selfe,
Did steale behinde him as he lay along
Vnder an oake, whose anticke roote peepes out
Vpon the brooke that brawles along this wood,
To the which place a poore sequestred Stag
That from the Hunters aime had tane a hurt,
Did come to languish; and indeed my Lord
The wretched annimall heau'd forth such groanes
That their discharge did stretch his leatherne coat
Almost to bursting, and the big round teares
Cours'd one another downe his innocent nose
In pitteous chase: and thus the hairie foole,
Much marked of the melancholie *Iaques*,
Stood on th'extremest verge of the swift brooke,
Augmenting it with teares.
  Du.Sen. But what said *Iaques*?
Did he not moralize this spectacle?
  1.*Lord.* O yes, into a thousand similies.
First, for his weeping into the needlesse streame;
Poore Deere quoth he, thou mak'st a testament
As worldlings doe, giuing thy sum of more
To that which had too must: then being there alone,
Left and abandoned of his veluet friend;
'Tis right quoth he, thus miserie doth part
The Fluxe of companie: anon a carelesse Heard
Full of the pasture, iumps along by him
And neuer staies to greet him: I quoth *Iaques*,
Sweepe on you fat and greazie Citizens,
'Tis iust the fashion; wherefore doe you looke
Vpon that poore and broken bankrupt there?
Thus most inuectiuely he pierceth through
The body of Countrie, Citie, Court,
Yea, and of this our life, swearing that we
Are meere vsurpers, tyrants, and whats worse
To fright the Annimals, and to kill them vp
In their assign'd and natiue dwelling place.
  D.Sen. And did you leaue him in this contemplation?
  2.*Lord.* We did my Lord, weeping and commenting
Vpon the sobbing Deere.

  Du.Sen. Show me the place,
I loue to cope him in these sullen fits,
For then he's full of matter.
  1.*Lor.* Ile bring you to him strait. *Exeunt.*

Scena Secunda.

Enter Duke, with Lords.

  Duk. Can it be possible that no man saw them?
It cannot be, some villaines of my Court
Are of consent and sufferance in this.
  1.*Lo.* I cannot heare of any that did see her,
The Ladies her attendants of her chamber
Saw her a bed, and in the morning early,
They found the bed vntreasur'd of their Mistris.
  2.*Lor.* My Lord, the roynish Clown, at whom so oft,
Your Grace was wont to laugh is also missing,
Hisperia the Princesse Gentlewoman
Confesses that she secretly ore-heard
Your daughter and her Cosen much commend
The parts and graces of the Wrastler
That did but lately foile the synowie *Charles*,
And she beleeues where euer they are gone
That youth is surely in their companie.
  Duk. Send to his brother, fetch that gallant hither,
If he be absent, bring his Brother to me,
Ile make him finde him: do this sodainly;
And let not search and inquisition quaile,
To bring againe these foolish runawaies. *Exeunt.*

Scena Tertia.

Enter Orlando and Adam.

  Orl. Who's there?
  Ad. What my yong Master, oh my gentle master,
Oh my sweet master, O you memorie
Of old Sir *Rowland*; why, what make you here?
Why are you vertuous? Why do people loue you?
And wherefore are you gentle, strong, and valiant?
Why would you be so fond to ouercome
The bonnie priser of the humorous Duke?
Your praise is come too swiftly home before you.
Know you not Master, to seeme kinde of men,
Their graces serue them but as enemies,
No more doe yours: your vertues gentle Master
Are sanctified and holy traitors to you:
Oh what a world is this, when what is comely
Enuenoms him that beares it?
Why, what's the matter?
  Ad. O vnhappie youth,
Come not within these doores: within this roofe
The enemie of all your graces liues
Your brother, no, no brother, yet the sonne
(Yet not the son, I will not call him son)
Of him I was about to call his Father,
Hath heard your praises, and this night he meanes,
To burne the lodging where you vse to lye,
And you within it: if he faile of that

He

He will haue other meanes to cut you off;
I ouerheard him: and his practises:
This is no place, this house is but a butcherie;
Abhorre it, feare it, doe not enter it.

  Ad. Why whecher *Adam* would'st thou haue me go?
  Ad. No matter whether, so you come not here.
  Orl. What, would'st thou haue me go & beg my food,
Or with a base and boistrous Sword enforce
A theeuish liuing on the common rode?
This I must do, or know not what to do:
Yet this I will not do, do how I can,
I rather will subiect me to the malice
Of a diuerted blood, and bloudie brother.

  Ad. But do not so: I haue fiue hundred Crownes,
The thriftie hire I saued vnder your Father,
Which I did store to be my foster Nurse,
When seruice should in my old limbs lie lame,
And vnregarded age in corners throwne,
Take that, and he that doth the Rauens feede,
Yea prouidently caters for the Sparrow,
Be comfort to my age: here is the gold,
All this I giue you, let me be your seruant,
Though I looke old, yet I am strong and lustie;
For in my youth I neuer did apply
Hot, and rebellious liquors in my bloud,
Nor did not with vnbashfull forehead woe,
The meanes of weaknesse and debilitie,
Therefore my age is as a lustie winter,
Frostie, but kindely; let me goe with you,
Ile doe the seruice of a yonger man
In all your businesse and necessities.

  Orl. Oh good old man, how well in thee appeares
The constant seruice of the antique world,
When seruice sweate for dutie, not for meede:
Thou art not for the fashion of these times,
Where none will sweate, but for promotion,
And hauing that do choake their seruice vp,
Euen with the hauing, it is not so with thee:
But poore old man, thou prun'st a rotten tree,
That cannot so much as a blossome yeelde,
In lieu of all thy paines and husbandrie,
But come thy waies, weele goe along together,
And ere we haue thy youthfull wages spent,
Weele light vpon some setled low content.

  Ad. Master goe on, and I will follow thee
To the last gaspe with truth and loyaltie,
From seauentie yeeres, till now almost fourescore
Here liued I, but now liue here no more
At seauenteene yeeres, many their fortunes seeke
But at fourescore, it is too late a weeke,
Yet fortune cannot recompence me better
Then to die well, and not my Masters debter. *Exeunt.*

Scena Quarta.

Enter Rosaline for Ganimed, Celia for Aliena, and Clowne, alias Touchstone.

  Ros. O *Iupiter*, how merry are my spirits?
  Clo. I care not for my spirits, if my legges were not wearie.
  Ros. I could finde in my heart to disgrace my mans apparell, and to cry like a woman: but I must comfort the weaker vessell, as doublet and hose ought to show it selfe coragious to petty-coate; therefore courage, good *Aliena*.
  Cel. I pray you beare with me, I cannot goe no further.
  Clo. For my part, I had rather beare with you, then beare you: yet I should beare no crosse if I did beare you, for I thinke you haue no money in your purse.
  Ros. Well, this is the Forrest of *Arden*.
  Clo. I, now am I in *Arden*, the more foole I, when I was at home I was in a better place, but Trauellers must be content.

Enter Corin and Siluius.

  Ros. I, be so good *Touchstone*: Look you, who comes here, a yong man and an old in solemne talke.
  Cor. That is the way to make her scorne you still.
  Sil. Oh *Corin*, that thou knew'st how I do loue her.
  Cor. I partly guesse: for I haue lou'd ere now.
  Sil. No *Corin*, being old, thou canst not guesse,
Though in thy youth thou wast as true a louer
As euer sigh'd vpon a midnight pillow:
But if thy loue were euer like to mine,
As sure I thinke did neuer man loue so:
How many actions most ridiculous,
Hast thou beene drawne to by thy fantasie?
  Cor. Into a thousand that I haue forgotten.
  Sil. Oh thou didst then neuer loue so hartily,
If thou remembrest not the slightest folly,
That euer loue did make thee run into,
Thou hast not lou'd.
Or if thou hast not sat as I doe now,
Wearing thy hearer in thy Mistris praise,
Thou hast not lou'd.
Or if thou hast not broke from companie,
Abruptly as my passion now makes me,
Thou hast not lou'd.
O *Phebe, Phebe, Phebe*. *Exit.*
  Ros. Alas poore Shepheard searching of they would,
I haue by hard aduenture found mine owne.
  Clo. And I mine: I remember when I was in loue, I broke my sword vpon a stone, and bid him take that for comming a night to *Iane Smile*, and I remember the kissing of her batler, and the Cowes dugs that her prettie chopt hands had milk'd; and I remember the wooing of a peascod instead of her, from whom I tooke two cods, and giuing her them againe, said with weeping teares, weare these for my sake: wee that are true Louers, runne into strange capers; but as all is mortall in nature, so is all nature in loue, mortall in folly.
  Ros. Thou speak'st wiser then thou art ware of.
  Clo. Nay, I shall nere be ware of mine owne wit, till I breake my shins against it.
  Ros. *Ioue, Ioue*, this Shepherds passion,
Is much vpon my fashion.
  Clo. And mine, but it growes something stale with mee.
  Cel. I pray you, one of you question yon'd man,
If he for gold will giue vs any foode,
I faint almost to death.
  Clo. Holla; you Clowne.
  Ros. Peace foole, he's not thy kinsman.
  Cor. Who cals?
  Clo. Your betters Sir.
  Cor. Else are they very wretched.

Ros. Peace I say; good euen to your friend.
Cor. And to you gentle Sir, and to you all.
Ros. I prethee Shepheard, if that loue or gold
Can in this desert place buy entertainment,
Bring vs where we may rest our selues, and feed:
Here's a yong maid with trauaile much oppressed,
And faints for succour.

Cor. Faire Sir, I pittie her,
And wish for her sake more then for mine owne,
My fortunes were more able to releeue her:
But I am shepheard to another man,
And do not sheere the Fleeces that I graze:
My master is of churlish disposition,
And little wreakes to finde the way to heauen
By doing deeds of hospitalitie.
Besides his Coate, his Flockes, and bounds of feede
Are now on sale, and at our sheep-coat now
By reason of his absence there is nothing
That you will feed on: but what is, come see,
And in my voice most welcome shall you be.

Ros. What is he that shall buy his flocke and pasture?
Cor. That yong Swaine that you saw heere but erewhile,
That little cares for buying any thing.
Ros. I pray thee, if it stand with honestie,
Buy thou the Cottage, pasture, and the flocke,
And thou shalt haue to pay for it of vs.
Cel. And we will mend thy wages:
I like this place, and willingly could
Waste my time in it.
Cor. Assuredly the thing is to be sold:
Go with me, if you like vpon report,
The soile, the profit, and this kinde of life,
I will your very faithfull Feeder be,
And buy it with your Gold right sodainly. *Exeunt.*

Scena Quinta.

Enter, Amyens, Iaques, & others.
Song.
Vnder the greene wood tree,
who loues to lye with mee,
And turne his merrie Note,
vnto the sweet Birds throte:
Come hither, come hither, come hither:
Heere shall he see no enemie,
But Winter and rough Weather.

Iaq. More, more, I pre'thee more.
Amy. It will make you melancholly Monsieur *Iaques*.
Iaq. I thanke it: More, I prethee more,
I can sucke melancholly out of a song,
As a Weazel suckes egges: More, I pre'thee more.
Amy. My voice is ragged, I know I cannot please you.
Iaq. I do not desire you to please me,
I do desire you to sing:
Come, more, another stanzo: Cal you 'em stanzo's?
Amy. What you wil Monsieur *Iaques*.
Iaq. Nay, I care not for their names, they owe mee nothing. Wil you sing?
Amy. More at your request, then to please my selfe.
Iaq. Well then, if euer I thanke any man, Ile thanke you: but that they cal complement is like th'encounter of two dog-Apes. And when a man thankes me hartily, me thinkes I haue giuen him a penie, and he renders me the beggerly thankes. Come sing; and you that wil not hold your tongues.

Amy. Wel, Ile end the song. Sirs, couer the while, the Duke wil drinke vnder this tree; he hath bin all this day to looke you.
Iaq. And I haue bin all this day to auoid him: He is too disputeable for my companie:
I thinke of as many matters as he, but I giue Heauen thankes, and make no boast of them.
Come, warble, come.

Song. *Altogether heere.*
Who doth ambition shunne,
and loues to liue i'th Sunne:
Seeking the food he eates,
and pleas'd with what he gets:
Come hither, come hither, come hither,
Heere shall he see. &c.

Iaq. Ile giue you a verse to this note,
That I made yesterday in despight of my Inuention.
Amy. And Ile sing it.
Amy. Thus it goes.
If it do come to passe, that any man turne Asse:
Leauing his wealth and ease,
A stubborne will to please,
Ducdame, ducdame, ducdame:
Heere shall he see, grosse fooles as he,
And if he will come to me.
Amy. What's that Ducdame?
Iaq. 'Tis a Greeke inuocation, to call fools into a circle. Ile go sleepe if I can: if I cannot, Ile raile against all the first borne of Egypt.
Amy. And Ile go seeke the Duke,
His banket is prepar'd. *Exeunt.*

Scena Sexta.

Enter Orlando, & Adam.

Adam. Deere Master, I can go no further:
O I die for food. Heere lie I downe,
And measure out my graue. Farwel kinde master.
Orl. Why how now *Adam*? No greater heart in thee:
Liue a little, comfort a little, cheere thy selfe a little.
If this vncouth Forrest yeeld any thing sauage,
I wil either be food for it, or bring it for foode to thee:
Thy conceite is neerer death, then thy powers.
For my sake be comfortable, hold death a while
At the armes end: I wil heere be with thee presently,
And if I bring thee not something to eate,
I wil giue thee leaue to die: but if thou diest
Before I come, thou art a mocker of my labor.
Wel said, thou look'st cheerely,
And Ile be with thee quickly: yet thou liest
In the bleake aire. Come, I wil beare thee
To some shelter, and thou shalt not die
For lacke of a dinner,
If there liue any thing in this Desert.
Cheerely good *Adam*. *Exeunt*
Scena

Scena Septima.

Enter Duke Sen. & Lord, like Out-lawes.

Du.Sen. I thinke he be transform'd into a beast,
For I can no where finde him, like a man.

1.Lord. My Lord, he is but euen now gone hence,
Heere was he merry, hearing of a Song.

Du.Sen. If he compact of iarres, grow Musicall,
We shall haue shortly discord in the Spheares:
Go seeke him, tell him I would speake with him.

Enter Iaques.

1.Lord. He saues my labor by his owne approach.

Du.Sen. Why how now Monsieur, what a life is this
That your poore friends must woe your companie?
What, you looke merrily.

Iaq. A Foole, a foole: I met a foole i'th Forrest,
A motley Foole (a miserable world:)
As I do liue by foode, I met a foole,
Who laid him downe, and bask'd him in the Sun,
And rail'd on Lady Fortune in good termes,
In good set termes, and yet a motley foole.
Good morrow foole (quoth I:) no Sir, quoth he,
Call me not foole, till heauen hath sent me fortune,
And then he drew a diall from his poake,
And looking on it, with lacke-lustre eye,
Sayes, very wisely, it is ten a clocke:
Thus we may see (quoth he) how the world wagges:
'Tis but an houre agoe, since it was nine,
And after one houre more, 'twill be eleuen,
And so from houre to houre, we ripe, and ripe,
And then from houre to houre, we rot, and rot,
And thereby hangs a tale. When I did heare
The motley Foole, thus morall on the time,
My Lungs began to crow like Chanticleere,
That Fooles should be so deepe contemplatiue:
And I did laugh, sans intermission
An houre by his diall. Oh noble foole,
A worthy foole: Motley's the onely weare.

Du.Sen. What foole is this?

Iaq. O worthie Foole: One that hath bin a Courtier
And sayes, if Ladies be but yong, and faire,
They haue the gift to know it: and in his braine,
Which is as drie as the remainder bisket
After a voyage: He hath strange places cram'd
With obseruation, the which he vents
In mangled formes. O that I were a foole,
I am ambitious for a motley coat.

Du.Sen. Thou shalt haue one.

Iaq. It is my onely suite,
Prouided that you weed your better iudgements
Of all opinion that growes ranke in them,
That I am wise. I must haue liberty
Wiithall, as large a Charter as the winde,
To blow on whom I please, for so fooles haue:
And they that are most gauled with my folly,
They most must laugh: And why sir must they so?
The why is plaine, as way to Parish Church:
Hee, that a Foole doth very wisely hit,
Doth very foolishly, although he smart
Seeme senselesse of the bob. If not,
The Wise-mans folly is anathomiz'd
Euen by the squandring glances of the foole.
Inuest me in my motley: Giue me leaue
To speake my minde, and I will through and through
Cleanse the foule bodie of th'infected world,
If they will patiently receiue my medicine.

Du.Sen. Fie on thee. I can tell what thou wouldst do.

Iaq. What, for a Counter, would I do, but good?

Du.Sen. Most mischeeuous foule sin, in chiding sin:
For thou thy selfe hast bene a Libertine,
As sensuall as the brutish sting it selfe,
And all th'imbossed sores, and headed euils,
That thou with license of free foot hast caught,
Would'st thou disgorge into the generall world.

Iaq. Why who cries out on pride,
That can therein taxe any priuate party:
Doth it not flow as hugely as the Sea,
Till that the wearie verie meanes do ebbe.
What woman in the Citie do I name,
When that I say the City woman beares
The cost of Princes on vnworthy shoulders?
Who can come in, and say that I meane her,
When such a one as shee, such is her neighbor?
Or what is he of basest function,
That sayes his brauerie is not on my cost,
Thinking that I meane him, but therein suites
His folly to the mettle of my speech,
There then, how then, what then, let me see wherein
My tongue hath wrong'd him: if it do him right,
Then he hath wrong'd himselfe: if he be free,
Why then my taxing like a wild-goose flies
Vnclaim'd of any. man But who come here?

Enter Orlando.

Orl. Forbeare, and eate no more.

Iaq. Why I haue eate none yet.

Orl. Nor shalt not, till necessity be seru'd.

Iaq. Of what kinde should this Cocke come of?

Du.Sen. Art thou thus bolden'd man by thy distres?
Or else a rude despiser of good manners,
That in ciuility thou seem'st so emptie?

Orl. You touch'd my veine at first, the thorny point
Of bare distresse, hath tane from me the shew
Of smooth ciuility: yet am I in-land bred,
And know some nourture: But forbeare, I say,
He dies that touches any of this fruite,
Till I, and my affaires are answered.

Iaq. And you will not be answer'd with reason,
I must dye.

Du.Sen. What would you haue?
Your gentlenesse shall force, more then your force
Moue vs to gentlenesse.

Orl. I almost die for food, and let me haue it.

Du.Sen. Sit downe and feed, & welcom to our table

Orl. Speake you so gently? Pardon me I pray you,
I thought that all things had bin sauage heere,
And therefore put I on the countenance
Of sterne command'ment. But what ere you are
That in this desert inaccessible,
Vnder the shade of melancholly boughes,
Loose, and neglect the creeping houres of time:
If euer you haue look'd on better dayes:
If euer beene where bels haue knoll'd to Church:
If euer sate at any good mans feast:
If euer from your eye-lids wip'd a teare,
And know what 'tis to pittie, and be pitried:
Let gentlenesse my strong enforcement be,
In the which hope, I blush, and hide my Sword.

R   *Duke*

Du. Sen. True is it, that we haue seene better dayes,
And haue with holy bell bin knowld to Church,
And sat at good mens feasts, and wip'd our eies
Of drops, that sacred pity hath engendred:
And therefore sit you downe in gentlenesse,
And take vpon command, what helpe we haue
That to your wanting may be ministred.

Orl. Then but forbeare your food a little while:
Whiles (like a Doe) I go to finde my Fawne,
And giue it food. There is an old poore man,
Who after me, hath many a weary steppe
Limpt in pure loue: till he be first suffic'd,
Opprest with two weake euils, age, and hunger,
I will not touch a bit.

Duke Sen. Go finde him out,
And we will nothing waste till you returne.

Orl. I thanke ye, and be blest for your good comfort.

Du Sen. Thou seest, we are not all alone vnhappie:
This wide and vniuersall Theater
Presents more wofull Pageants then the Sceane
Wherein we play in.

Ia. All the world's a stage,
And all the men and women, meerely Players;
They haue their *Exits* and their *Entrances*,
And one man in his time playes many parts,
His Acts being seuen ages. At first the Infant,
Mewling, and puking in the Nurses armes:
Then, the whining Schoole-boy with his Satchell
And shining morning face, creeping like snaile
Vnwillingly to schoole. And then the Louer,
Sighing like Furnace, with a wofull ballad
Made to his Mistresse eye-brow. Then, a Soldier,
Full of strange oaths, and bearded like the Pard,
Ielous in honor, sodaine, and quicke in quarrell,
Seeking the bubble Reputation
Euen in the Canons mouth: And then, the Iustice,
In faire round belly, with good Capon lin'd,
With eyes seuere, and beard of formall cut,
Full of wise sawes, and moderne instances,
And so he playes his part. The sixt age shifts
Into the leane and slipper'd Pantaloone,
With spectacles on nose, and pouch on side,
His youthfull hose well sau'd, a world too wide,
For his shrunke shanke, and his bigge manly voice,
Turning againe toward childish trebble pipes,
And whistles in his sound. Last Scene of all,
That ends this strange euentfull historie,
Is second childishnesse, and meere obliuion,
Sans teeth, sans eyes, sans taste, sans euery thing.

Enter Orlando with Adam.

Du Sen. Welcome: set downe your venerable burthen, and let him feede.

Orl. I thanke you most for him.

Ad. So had you neede,
I scarce can speake to thanke you for my selfe.

Du. Sen. Welcome, fall too: I wil not trouble you,
As yet to question you about your fortunes:
Giue vs some Musicke, and good Cozen, sing.

Song.

*Blow, blow, thou winter winde,
Thou art not so vnkinde, as mans ingratitude
Thy tooth is not so keene, because thou art not seene,
although thy breath be rude.*

*Heigh ho, sing heigh ho, vnto the greene holly,
Most frendship, is fayning; most Louing, meere folly:
The heigh ho, the holly,
This Life is most iolly.*

*Freize, freize, thou bitter skie that dost not bight so nigh
as benefitts forgot:
Though thou the waters warpe, thy sting is not so sharpe,
as freind remembred not.
Heigh ho, sing, &c.*

Duke Sen. If that you were the good Sir *Rowlands* son,
As you haue whisper'd faithfully you were,
And as mine eye doth his effigies witnesse,
Most truly limn'd, and liuing in your face,
Be truly welcome hither: I am the Duke
That lou'd your Father, the residue of your fortune,
Go to my Caue, and tell mee. Good old man,
Thou art right welcome, as thy masters is:
Support him by the arme: giue me your hand,
And let me all your fortunes vnderstand. *Exeunt.*

Actus Tertius. Scena Prima.

Enter Duke, Lords, & Oliuer.

Du. Not see him since? Sir, sir, that cannot be:
But were I not the better part made mercie,
I should not seeke an absent argument
Of my reuenge, thou present: but looke to it,
Finde out thy brother wheresoere he is,
Seeke him with Candle: bring him dead, or liuing
Within this twelue month, or turne thou no more
To seeke a liuing in our Territorie.
Thy Lands and all things that thou dost call thine,
Worth seizure, do we seize into our hands,
Till thou canst quit thee by thy brothers mouth,
Of what we thinke against thee.

Ol. Oh that your Highnesse knew my heart in this:
I neuer lou'd my brother in my life.

Duke. More villaine thou. Well push him out of dores
And let my officers of such a nature
Make an extent vpon his house and Lands:
Do this expediently, and turne him going. *Exeunt*

Scena Secunda.

Enter Orlando.

Orl. Hang there my verse, in witnesse of my loue,
And thou thrice crowned Queene of night suruey
With thy chaste eye, from thy pale spheare aboue
Thy Huntresse name, that my full life doth sway.
O *Rosalind*, these Trees shall be my Bookes,
And in their barkes my thoughts Ile charracter,
That euerie eye, which in this Forrest lookes,
Shall see thy vertue witnest euery where.
Run, run *Orlando*, carue on euery Tree,
The faire, the chaste, and vnexpressiue shee. *Exit*

Enter Corin & Clowne.

Co. And how like you this shepherds life Mr *Touchstone*?
Clo.

Clow. Truely Shepheard, in respect of it selfe, it is a good life; but in respect that it is a shepheards life, it is naught. In respect that it is solitary, I like it verie well: but in respect that it is priuate, it is a very vild life. Now in respect it is in the fields, it pleaseth mee well: but in respect it is not in the Court, it is tedious. As it is a spare life (looke you) it fits my humor well: but as there is no more plentie in it, it goes much against my stomacke. Has't any Philosophie in thee shepheard?

Cor. No more, but that I know the more one sickens, the worse at ease he is: and that hee that wants money, meanes, and content, is without three good frends. That the propertie of raine is to wet, and fire to burne: That good pasture makes fat sheepe: and that a great cause of the night, is lacke of the Sunne: That hee that hath learned no wit by Nature, nor Art, may complaine of good breeding, or comes of a very dull kindred.

Clo. Such a one is a naturall Philosopher: Was't euer in Court, Shepheard?

Cor. No truly.

Clo. Then thou art damn'd.

Cor. Nay, I hope.

Clo. Truly thou art damn'd, like an ill roasted Egge, all on one side.

Cor. For not being at Court? your reason.

Clo. Why, if thou neuer was't at Court, thou neuer saw'st good manners: if thou neuer saw'st good maners, then thy manners must be wicked, and wickednes is sin, and sinne is damnation: Thou art in a parlous state shepheard.

Cor. Not a whit *Touchstone*, those that are good maners at the Court, are as ridiculous in the Countrey, as the behauiour of the Countrie is most mockeable at the Court. You told me, you salute not at the Court, but you kisse your hands; that courtesie would be vncleanlie if Courtiers were shepheards.

Clo. Instance, briefly: come, instance.

Cor. Why we are still handling our Ewes, and their Fels you know are greasie.

Clo. Why do not your Courtiers hands sweate? and is not the grease of a Mutton, as wholesome as the sweat of a man? Shallow, shallow: A better instance I say: Come.

Cor. Besides, our hands are hard.

Clo. Your lips wil feele them the sooner. Shallow agen: a more sounder instance, come.

Cor. And they are often tarr'd ouer, with the surgery of our sheepe: and would you haue vs kisse Tarre? The Courtiers hands are perfum'd with Ciuet.

Clo. Most shallow man: Thou wormes meate in respect of a good peece of flesh indeed: learne of the wise and perpend: Ciuet is of a baser birth then Tarre, the verie vncleanly fluxe of a Cat. Mend the instance Shepheard.

Cor. You haue too Courtly a wit for me, Ile rest.

Clo. Wilt thou rest damn'd? God helpe thee shallow man: God make incision in thee, thou art raw.

Cor. Sir, I am a true Labourer, I earne that I eate: get that I weare; owe no man hate, enuie no mans happinesse: glad of other mens good content with my harme: and the greatest of my pride, is to see my Ewes graze, & my Lambes sucke.

Clo. That is another simple sinne in you, to bring the Ewes and the Rammes together, and to offer to get your liuing, by the copulation of Cattle, to be bawd to a Belweather, and to betray a shee-Lambe of a twelue month to a crooked-pated olde Cuckoldly Ramme, out of all reasonable match. If thou bee'st not damn'd for this, the diuell himselfe will haue no shepherds, I cannot see else how thou shouldst scape.

Cor. Heere comes yong M[r] *Ganimed*, my new Mistrisses Brother.

Enter Rosalind.

Ros. *From the east to westerne Inde,*
no iewel is like Rosalinde,
Hir worth being mounted on the winde,
through all the world beares Rosalinde.
All the pictures fairest Linde,
are but blacke to Rosalinde:
Let no face bee kept in mind,
but the faire of Rosalinde.

Clo. Ile rime you so, eight yeares together; dinners, and suppers, and sleeping houres excepted: it is the right Butter-womens ranke to Market.

Ros. Out Foole.

Clo. For a taste.
If a Hart doe lacke a Hinde,
Let him seeke out Rosalinde:
If the Cat will after kinde,
so be sure will Rosalinde:
Wintred garments must be linde,
so must slender Rosalinde:
They that reap must sheafe and binde,
then to cart with Rosalinde.
Sweetest nut, hath sowrest rinde,
such a nut is Rosalinde.
He that sweetest rose will finde,
must finde Loues pricke, & Rosalinde.

This is the verie false gallop of Verses, why doe you infect your selfe with them?

Ros. Peace you dull foole, I found them on a tree.

Clo. Truely the tree yeelds bad fruite.

Ros. Ile graffe it with you, and then I shall graffe it with a Medler: then it will be the earliest fruit i'th country: for you'l be rotten ere you bee halfe ripe, and that's the right vertue of the Medler.

Clo. You haue said: but whether wisely or no, let the Forrest iudge.

Enter Celia with a writing.

Ros. Peace, here comes my sister reading, stand aside.

Cel. *Why should this Desert bee,*
for it is vnpeopled? Noe:
Tonges Ile hang on euerie tree,
that shall ciuill sayings shoe.
Some, how briefe the Life of man
runs his erring pilgrimage,
That the stretching of a span,
buckles in his summe of age.
Some of violated vowes,
twixt the soules of friend, and friend:
But vpon the fairest bowes,
or at euerie sentence end;
Will I Rosalinda write,
teaching all that reade, to know
The quintessence of euerie sprite,
heauen would in little show.
Therefore heauen Nature charg'd,
that one bodie should be fill'd
With all Graces wide enlarg'd,
nature presently distill'd

R 2 *Helens*

Helens cheeke, but not his heart,
    Cleopatra's *Maiestie*:
Attalanta's *better part*,
    sad Lucrecia's *Modestie*.
Thus Rosalinde *of manie parts*,
    by Heauenly Synode was deuis'd,
Of manie faces, eyes, and hearts,
    to haue the touches deerest pris'd.
Heauen would that shee these gifts should haue,
    and I to liue and die her slaue.

Ros. O most gentle Iupiter, what tedious homilie of Loue haue you wearied your parishioners withall, and neuer cri'de, haue patience good people.

Cel. How now backe friends: Shepheard, go off a little: go with him sirrah.

Clo. Come Shepheard, let vs make an honorable retreit, though not with bagge and baggage, yet with scrip and scrippage. *Exit.*

Cel. Didst thou heare these verses?

Ros. O yes, I heard them all, and more too, for some of them had in them more feete then the Verses would beare.

Cel. That's no matter: the feet might beare ẏ verses.

Ros. I, but the feet were lame, and could not beare themselues without the verse, and therefore stood lamely in the verse.

Cel. But didst thou heare without wondering, how thy name should be hang'd and carued vpon these trees?

Ros. I was seuen of the nine daies out of the wonder, before you came: for looke heere what I found on a Palme tree; I was neuer so berim'd since *Pythagoras* time that I was an Irish Rat, which I can hardly remember.

Cel. Tro you, who hath done this?

Ros. Is it a man?

Cel. And a chaine that you once wore about his neck: change you colour?

Ros. I pre'thee who?

Cel. O Lord, Lord, it is a hard matter for friends to meete; but Mountaines may bee remoou'd with Earthquakes, and so encounter.

Ros. Nay, but who is it?

Cel. Is it possible?

Ros. Nay, I pre'thee now, with most petitionary vehemence, tell me who it is.

Cel. O wonderfull, wonderfull, and most wonderfull wonderfull, and yet againe wonderful, and after that out of all hooping.

Ros. Good my complection, dost thou think though I am caparison'd like a man, I haue a doublet and hose in my disposition? One inch of delay more, is a South-sea of discouerie. I pre'thee tell me, who is it quickely, and speake apace: I would thou couldst stammer, that thou might'st powre this conceal'd man out of thy mouth, as Wine comes out of a narrow-mouth'd bottle: either too much at once, or none at all. I pre'thee take the Corke out of thy mouth, that I may drinke thy tydings.

Cel. So you may put a man in your belly.

Ros. Is he of Gods making? What manner of man? Is his head worth a hat? Or his chin worth a beard?

Cel. Nay, he hath but a little beard.

Ros. Why God will send more, if the man will bee thankful: let me stay the growth of his beard, if thou delay me not the knowledge of his chin.

Cel. It is yong *Orlando*, that tript vp the Wrastlers heeles, and your heart, both in an instant.

Ros. Nay, but the diuell take mocking: speake sadde brow, and true maid.

Cel. I'faith (Coz) tis he.

Ros. *Orlando*?

Cel. *Orlando*.

Ros. Alas the day, what shall I do with my doublet & hose? What did he when thou saw'st him? What sayde he? How look'd he? Wherein went he? What makes hee heere? Did he aske for me? Where remaines he? How parted he with thee? And when shalt thou see him againe? Answer me in one vvord.

Cel. You must borrow me Gargantuas mouth first: 'tis a Word too great for any mouth of this Ages size, to say I and no, to these particulars, is more then to answer in a Catechisme.

Ros. But doth he know that I am in this Forrest, and in mans apparrell? Looks he as freshly, as he did the day he Wrastled?

Cel. It is as easie to count Atomies as to resolue the propositions of a Louer: but take a taste of my finding him, and rellish it with good obseruance. I found him vnder a tree like a drop'd Acorne.

Ros. It may vvel be cal'd Ioues tree, when it droppes forth fruite.

Cel. Giue me audience, good Madam.

Ros. Proceed.

Cel. There lay hee stretch'd along like a Wounded knight.

Ros. Though it be pittie to see such a sight, it vvell becomes the ground.

Cel. Cry holla, to the tongue, I prethee: it curuettes vnseasonably. He was furnish'd like a Hunter.

Ros. O ominous, he comes to kill my Hart.

Cel. I would sing my song without a burthen, thou bring'st me out of tune.

Ros. Do you not know I am a woman, when I thinke, I must speake: sweet, say on.

Enter Orlando & Iaques.

Cel. You bring me out. Soft, comes he not heere?

Ros. 'Tis he, slinke by, and note him.

Iaq. I thanke you for your company, but good faith I had as liefe haue beene my selfe alone.

Orl. And so had I: but yet for fashion sake I thanke you too, for your societie.

Iaq. God buy you, let's meet as little as we can.

Orl. I do desire we may be better strangers.

Iaq. I pray you marre no more trees vvith Writing Loue-songs in their barkes.

Orl. I pray you marre no moe of my verses with reading them ill-fauouredly.

Iaq. *Rosalinde* is your loues name? *Orl.* Yes, Iust.

Iaq. I do not like her name.

Orl. There was no thought of pleasing you when she was christen'd.

Iaq. What stature is she of?

Orl. Iust as high as my heart.

Iaq. You are ful of prety answers: haue you not bin acquainted with goldsmiths wiues, & cond thē out of rings

Orl. Not so: but I answer you right painted cloath, from whence you haue studied your questions.

Iaq. You haue a nimble wit; I thinke 'twas made of *Attalanta's* heeles. Will you sitte downe with me, and wee two, will raile against our Mistris the world, and all our miserie.

Orl. I wil chide no breather in the world but my selfe
                                                    against

against whom I know most faults.

Iaq. The worst fault you haue, Is to be in loue.

Orl. 'Tis a fault I will not change, for your best vertue: I am wearie of you.

Iaq. By my troth, I was seeking for a Foole, when I found you.

Orl. He is drown'd in the brooke, looke but in, and you shall see him.

Iaq. There I shal see mine owne figure.

Orl. Which I take to be either a foole, or a Cipher.

Iaq. Ile tarrie no longer with you, farewell good signior Loue.

Orl. I am glad of your departure: Adieu good Monsieur Melancholly.

Ros. I wil speake to him like a sawcie Lacky, and vnder that habit play the knaue with him, do you hear Forester.

Orl. Verie wel, what would you?

Ros. I pray you, what i'st a clocke?

Orl. You should aske me what time o'day: there's no clocke in the Forrest.

Ros. Then there is no true Louer in the Forrest, else sighing euerie minute, and groaning euerie houre wold detect the lazie foot of time, as wel as a clocke.

Orl. And why not the swift foote of time? Had not that bin as proper?

Ros. By no meanes sir; Time trauels in diuers paces, with diuers persons: Ile tel you who Time ambles withall, who Time trots withal, who Time gallops withal, and who he stands stil withall.

Orl. I prethee, who doth he trot withal?

Ros. Marry he trots hard with a yong maid, betweene the contract of her marriage, and the day it is solemnizd: if the interim be but a sennight, Times pace is so hard, that it seemes the length of seuen yeare.

Orl. Who ambles Time withal?

Ros. With a Priest that lacks Latine, and a rich man that hath not the Gowt: for the one sleepes easily because he cannot study, and the other liues merrily, because he feeles no paine: the one lacking the burthen of leane and wasteful Learning; the other knowing no burthen of heauie tedious penurie. These Time ambles withal.

Orl. Who doth he gallop withal?

Ros. With a theefe to the gallowes: for though hee go as softly as foot can fall, he thinkes himselfe too soon there.

Orl. Who staies it stil withal?

Ros. With Lawiers in the vacation: for they sleepe betweene Terme and Terme, and then they perceiue not how time moues.

Orl. Where dwel you prettie youth?

Ros. With this Shepheardesse my sister: heere in the skirts of the Forrest, like fringe vpon a petticoat.

Orl. Are you natiue of this place?

Ros. As the Conie that you see dwell where shee is kindled.

Orl. Your accent is something finer, then you could purchase in so remoued a dwelling.

Ros. I haue bin told so of many: but indeed, an olde religious Vnckle of mine taught me to speake, who was in his youth an inland man, one that knew Courtship too well: for there he fel in loue. I haue heard him read many Lectors against it, and I thanke God, I am not a Woman to be touch'd with so many giddie offences as hee hath generally tax'd their whole sex withal.

Orl. Can you remember any of the principall euils, that he laid to the charge of women?

Ros. There were none principal, they were all like one another, as halfe pence are, euerie one fault seeming monstrous, til his fellow-fault came to match it.

Orl. I prethee recount some of them.

Ros. No: I wil not cast away my physick, but on those that are sicke. There is a man haunts the Forrest, that abuses our yong plants with caruing *Rosalinde* on their barkes; hangs Oades vpon Hauthornes, and Elegies on brambles; all (forsooth) defying the name of *Rosalinde*. If I could meet that Fancie-monger, I would giue him some good counsel, for he seemes to haue the Quotidian of Loue vpon him.

Orl. I am he that is so Loue-shak'd, I pray you tel me your remedie.

Ros. There is none of my Vnckles markes vpon you: he taught me how to know a man in loue: in which cage of rushes, I am sure you are not prisoner.

Orl. What were his markes?

Ros. A leane cheeke, which you haue not: a blew eie and sunken, which you haue not: an vnquestionable spirit, which you haue not: a beard neglected, which you haue not: (but I pardon you for that, for simply your hauing in beard, is a yonger brothers reuennew) then your hose should be vngarter'd, your bonnet vnbanded, your sleeue vnbutton'd, your shoo vnti'de, and euerie thing about you, demonstrating a carelesse desolation: but you are no such man; you are rather point deuice in your accoustrements, as louing your selfe, then seeming the Louer of any other.

Orl. Faire youth, I would I could make thee beleeue I Loue.

Ros. Me beleeue it? You may assoone make her that you Loue beleeue it, which I warrant she is apter to do, then to confesse she do's: that is one of the points, in the which women stil giue the lie to their consciences. But in good sooth, are you he that hangs the verses on the Trees, wherein *Rosalind* is so admired?

Orl. I sweare to thee youth, by the white hand of *Rosalind*, I am that he, that vnfortunate he.

Ros. But are you so much in loue, as your rimes speak?

Orl. Neither rime nor reason can expresse how much.

Ros. Loue is meerely a madnesse, and I tel you, deserues as wel a darke house, and a whip, as madmen do: and the reason why they are not so punish'd and cured, is that the Lunacie is so ordinarie, that the whippers are in loue too: yet I professe curing it by counsel.

Orl. Did you euer cure any so?

Ros. Yes one, and in this manner. Hee was to imagine me his Loue, his Mistris: and I set him euerie day to woe me At which time would I, being but a moonish youth, greeue, be effeminate, changeable, longing, and liking, proud, fantastical, apish, shallow, inconstant, ful of teares, full of smiles; for euerie passion something, and for no passion truly any thing, as boyes and women are for the most part, cattle of this colour: would now like him, now loath him: then entertaine him, then forswear him: now weepe for him, then spit at him; that I draue my Sutor from his mad humor of loue, to a liuing humor of madnes, w was to forsweare the ful stream of $\S$ world, and to liue in a nooke meerly Monastick: and thus I cur'd him, and this way wil I take vpon mee to wash your Liuer as cleane as a sound sheepes heart, that there shal not be one spot of Loue in't.

Orl. I would not be cured, youth.

Ros. I would cure you, if you would but call me *Rosalind*, and come euerie day to my Coat, and woe me.

Orlan. Now by the faith of my loue, I will; Tel me where it is.

Ros. Go with me to it, and Ile shew it you: and by the way, you shal tell me, where in the Forrest you liue: Wil you go?

Orl. With all my heart, good youth.

Ros. Nay, you must call mee *Rosalind*: Come sister, will you go? *Exeunt.*

Scœna Tertia.

Enter Clowne, Audrey, & Iaques.

Clo. Come apace good *Audrey*, I wil fetch vp your Goates, *Audrey*: and how *Audrey* am I the man yet? Doth my simple feature content you?

Aud. Your features, Lord warrant vs: what features?

Clo. I am heere with thee, and thy Goats, as the most capricious Poet honest *Ouid* was among the Gothes.

Iaq. O knowledge ill inhabited, worse then Ioue in a thatch'd house.

Clo. When a mans verses cannot be vnderstood, nor a mans good wit seconded with the forward childe, vnderstanding: it strikes a man more dead then a great reckoning in a little roome: truly, I would the Gods hadde made thee poeticall.

Aud. I do not know what Poetical is: is it honest in deed and word: is it a true thing?

Clo. No trulie: for the truest poetrie is the most faining, and Louers are giuen to Poetrie: and what they sweare in Poetrie, may be said as Louers, they do feigne.

Aud. Do you wish then that the Gods had made me Poeticall?

Clow. I do truly: for thou swear'st to me thou art honest: Now if thou wert a Poet, I might haue some hope thou didst feigne.

Aud. Would you not haue me honest?

Clo. No truly, vnlesse thou wert hard fauour'd: for honestie coupled to beautie, is to haue Honie a sawce to Sugar.

Iaq. A materiall foole.

Aud. Well, I am not faire, and therefore I pray the Gods make me honest.

Clo. Truly, and to cast away honestie vppon a foule slut, were to put good meate into an vncleane dish.

Aud. I am not a slut, though I thanke the Goddes I am foule.

Clo. Well, praised be the Gods, for thy foulnesse; sluttishnesse may come heereafter. But be it, as it may bee, I wil marrie thee: and to that end, I haue bin with Sir *Oliuer Mar-text*, the Vicar of the next village, who hath promis'd to meete me in this place of the Forrest, and to couple vs.

Iaq. I would faine see this meeting.

Aud. Wel, the Gods giue vs ioy.

Clo. Amen. A man may if he were of a fearful heart, stagger in this attempt: for heere wee haue no Temple but the wood, no assembly but horne-beasts. But what though? Courage. As hornes are odious, they are necessarie. It is said, many a man knowes no end of his goods; right: Many a man has good Hornes, and knows no end of them. Well, that is the dowrie of his wife, 'tis none of his owne getting; hornes, euen so poore men alone: No, no, the noblest Deere hath them as huge as the Rascall: Is the single man therefore blessed? No, as a wall'd Towne is more worthier then a village, so is the forehead of a married man, more honourable then the bare brow of a Batcheller: and by how much defence is better then no skill, by so much is a horne more precious then to want.

Enter Sir Oliuer Mar-text.

Heere comes Sir *Oliuer*: Sir *Oliuer Mar-text* you are wel met. Will you dispatch vs heere vnder this tree, or shal we go with you to your Chappell?

Ol. Is there none heere to giue the woman?

Clo. I wil not take her on guift of any man.

Ol. Truly she must be giuen, or the marriage is not lawfull.

Iaq. Proceed, proceede: Ile giue her.

Clo. Good euen good Mr what ye cal't: how do you Sir, you are verie well met: goddild you for your last companie, I am verie glad to see you, euen a toy in hand keere Sir: Nay, pray be couer'd.

Iaq. Wil you be married, Motley?

Clo. As the Oxe hath his bow sir, the horse his curb, and the Falcon her bels, so man hath his desires, and as Pigeons bill, so wedlocke would be nibling.

Iaq. And wil you (being a man of your breeding) be married vnder a bush like a begger? Get you to church, and haue a good Priest that can tel you what marriage is, this fellow wil but ioyne you together, as they ioyne Wainscot, then one of you wil proue a shrunke pannell, and like greene timber, warpe, warpe.

Clo. I am not in the minde, but I were better to bee married of him then of another, for he is not like to marrie me wel: and not being wel married, it wil be a good excuse for me heereafter, to leaue my wife.

Iaq. Goe thou with mee,
And let me counsel thee.

Ol. Come sweete *Audrey*,
We must be married, or we must liue in baudrey:
Farewel good Mr *Oliuer*: Not O sweet *Oliuer*, O braue *Oliuer* leaue me not behind thee: But winde away, bee gone I say, I wil not to wedding with thee.

Ol. 'Tis no matter; Ne're a fantasticall knaue of them all shal flout me out of my calling. *Exeunt*

Scœna Quarta.

Enter Rosalind & Celia.

Ros. Neuer talke to me, I wil weepe.

Cel. Do I prethee, but yet haue the grace to consider, that teares do not become a man.

Ros. But haue I not cause to weepe?

Cel. As good cause as one would desire,
Therefore weepe.

Ros. His very haire
Is of the dissembling colour.

Cel. Something browner then Iudasses:
Marrie his kisses are Iudasses owne children.

Ros. I'faith his haire is of a good colour.

Cel. An excellent colour:
Your Chessenut was euer the onely colour:

Ros. And his kissing is as ful of sanctitie,
As the touch of holy bread.

Cel.

Cel. Hee hath bought a paire of cast lips of *Diana*: a Nun of winters sisterhood kisses not more religiouslie, the very yce of chastity is in them.

Rosa. But why did hee sweare hee would come this morning, and comes not?

Cel. Nay certainly there is no truth in him.

Ros. Doe you thinke so?

Cel. Yes, I thinke he is not a picke purse, nor a horse-stealer, but for his verity in loue, I doe thinke him as concaue as a couered goblet, or a Worme-eaten nut.

Ros. Not true in loue?

Cel. Yes, when he is in, but I thinke he is not in.

Ros. You haue heard him sweare downright he was.

Cel. Was, is not is: besides, the oath of Louer is no stronger then the word of a Tapster, they are both the confirmer of false reckonings, he attends here in the forrest on the Duke your father.

Ros. I met the Duke yesterday, and had much question with him: he askt me of what parentage I was; I told him of as good as he, so he laugh'd and let mee goe. But what talke wee of Fathers, when there is such a man as *Orlando*?

Cel. O that's a braue man, hee writes braue verses, speakes braue words, sweares braue oathes, and breakes them brauely, quite trauers athwart the heart of his louer, as a puisny Tilter, ỹ spurs his horse but on one side, breakes his staffe like a noble goose; but all's braue that youth mounts, and folly guides: who comes heere?

Enter Corin.

Corin. Mistresse and Master, you haue oft enquired After the Shepheard that complain'd of loue,
Who you saw sitting by me on the Turph,
Praising the proud disdainfull Shepherdesse
That was his Mistresse.

Cel. Well: and what of him?

Cor. If you will see a pageant truely plaid
Betweene the pale complexion of true Loue,
And the red glowe of scorne and prowd disdaine,
Goe hence a little, and I shall conduct you
If you will marke it.

Ros. O come, let vs remoue,
The sight of Louers feedeth those in loue:
Bring vs to this sight, and you shall say
Ile proue a busie actor in their play. *Exeunt.*

Scena Quinta.

Enter Siluius and Phebe.

Sil. Sweet *Phebe* doe not scorne me, do not *Phebe*
Say that you loue me not, but say not so
In bitternesse; the common executioner
Whose heart th'accustom'd sight of death makes hard
Falls not the axe vpon the humbled neck,
But first begs pardon: will you sterner be
Then he that dies and liues by bloody drops?

Enter Rosalind, Celia, and Corin.

Phe. I would not be thy executioner,
I flye thee, for I would not iniure thee:
Thou tellst me there is murder in mine eye,
'Tis pretty sure, and very probable,
That eyes that are the frail'st, and softest things,
Who shut their coward gates on atomyes,
Should be called tyrants, butchers, murtherers.
Now I doe frowne on thee with all my heart,
And if mine eyes can wound, now let them kill thee:
Now counterfeit to swound, why now fall downe,
Or if thou canst not, oh for shame, for shame,
Lye not, to say mine eyes are murtherers:
Now shew the wound mine eye hath made in thee,
Scratch thee but with a pin, and there remaines
Some scarre of it: Leane vpon a rush
The Cicatrice and capable impressure
Thy palme some moment keepes: but now mine eyes
Which I haue darted at thee, hurt thee not,
Nor I am sure there is no force in eyes
That can doe hurt.

Sil. O deere *Phebe*,
If euer (as that euer may be neere)
You meet in some fresh cheeke the power of fancie,
Then shall you know the wounds inuisible
That Loues keene arrowes make.

Phe. But till that time
Come not thou neere me: and when that time comes,
Afflict me with thy mockes, pitty me not,
As till that time I shall not pitty thee.

Ros. And why I pray you? who might be your mother
That you insult, exult, and all at once
Ouer the wretched? what though you haue no beauty
As by my faith, I see no more in you
Then without Candle may goe darke to bed:
Must you be therefore prowd and pittilesse?
Why what meanes this? why do you looke on me?
I see no more in you then in the ordinary
Of Natures sale-worke? 'ods my little life,
I thinke she meanes to tangle my eies too:
No faith proud Mistresse, hope not after it,
'Tis not your inkie browes, your blacke silke haire,
Your bugle eye-balls, nor your cheeke of creame
That can entame my spirits to your worship:
You foolish Shepheard, wherefore do you follow her
Like foggy South, puffing with winde and raine,
You are a thousand times a properer man
Then she a woman. 'Tis such fooles as you
That makes the world full of ill-fauourd children:
'Tis not her glasse, but you that flatters her,
And out of you she sees her selfe more proper
Then any of her lineaments can show her:
But Mistris, know your selfe, downe on your knees
And thanke heauen, fasting, for a good mans loue;
For I must tell you friendly in your eare,
Sell when you can, you are not for all markets:
Cry the man mercy, loue him, take his offer,
Foule is most foule, being foule to be a scoffer.
So take her to thee Shepheard, fareyouwell.

Phe. Sweet youth, I pray you chide a yere together,
I had rather here you chide, then this man wooe.

Ros. Hees falne in loue with your foulnesse, & shee'l
Fall in loue with my anger. If it be so, as fast
As she answeres thee with frowning lookes, ile sauce
Her with bitter words: why looke you so vpon me?

Phe. For no ill will I beare you.

Ros. I pray you do not fall in loue with mee,
For I am falser then vowes made in wine:
Besides, I like you not: if you will know my house,
'Tis at the tuft of Oliues, here hard by:
Will you goe Sister? Shepheard ply her hard:

Come

Come Sister: Shepheardesse, looke on him better
And be not proud, though all the world could see,
None could be so abus'd in sight as hee.
Come, to our flocke, *Exit.*

Phe. Dead Shepheard, now I find thy saw of might,
Who euer lov'd, that lou'd not at first sight?

Sil. Sweet *Phebe*.

Phe. Hah: what saist thou *Siluius*?

Sil. Sweet *Phebe* pitty me.

Phe. Why I am sorry for thee gentle *Siluius*.

Sil. Where euer sorrow is, reliefe would be:
If you doe sorrow at my griefe in loue,
By giuing loue your sorrow, and my griefe
Were both extermin'd.

Phe. Thou hast my loue, is not that neighbourly?

Sil. I would haue you.

Phe. Why that were couetousnesse:
Siluius; the time was, that I hated thee;
And yet it is not, that I beare thee loue,
But since that thou canst talke of loue so well,
Thy company, which erst was irkesome to me
I will endure; and Ile employ thee too:
But doe not looke for further recompence
Then thine owne gladnesse, that thou art employd.

Sil. So holy, and so perfect is my loue,
And I in such a pouerty of grace,
That I shall thinke it a most plenteous crop
To gleane the broken eares after the man
That the maine haruest reapes: loose now and then
A scattred smile, and that Ile liue vpon. (while?

Phe. Know'st thou the youth that spoke to mee yere-

Sil. Not very well, but I haue met him oft,
And he hath bought the Cottage and the bounds
That the old *Carlot* once was Master of.

Phe. Thinke not I loue him, though I ask for him,
'Tis but a peeuish boy, yet he talkes well,
But what care I for words? yet words do well
When he that speakes them pleases those that heare:
It is a pretty youth, not very prettie,
But sure hee's proud, and yet his pride becomes him;
Hee'll make a proper man: the best thing in him
Is his complexion: and faster then his tongue
Did make offence, his eye did heale it vp:
He is not very tall, yet for his yeeres hee's tall:
His leg is but so so, and yet 'tis well:
There was a pretty rednesse in his lip,
A little riper, and more lustie red
Then that mixt in his cheeke: 'twas iust the difference
Betwixt the constant red, and mingled Damaske.
There be some women *Siluius*, had they markt him
In parcells as I did, would haue gone neere
To fall in loue with him: but for my part
I loue him not, nor hate him not: and yet
Haue more cause to hate him then to loue him,
For what had he to doe to chide at me?
He said mine eyes were black, and my haire blacke,
And now I am remembred, scorn'd at me:
I maruell why I answer'd not againe,
But that's all one: omittance is no quittance:
Ile write to him a very tanting Letter,
And thou shalt beare it, wilt thou *Siluius*?

Sil. *Phebe*, with all my heart.

Phe. Ile write it strait:
The matter's in my head, and in my heart,
I will be bitter with him, and passing short;
Goe with me *Siluius*. *Exeunt.*

Actus Quartus. Scena Prima.

Enter Rosalind, and Celia, and Iaques.

Iaq. I prethee, pretty youth, let me better acquainted with thee.

Ros. They say you are a melancholly fellow.

Iaq. I am so: I doe loue it better then laughing.

Ros. Those that are in extremity of either, are abhominable fellowes, and betray themselues to euery moderne censure, worse then drunkards.

Iaq. Why, 'tis good to be sad and say nothing.

Ros. Why then 'tis good to be a poste.

Iaq. I haue neither the Schollers melancholy, which is emulation: nor the Musitians, which is fantasticall; nor the Courtiers, which is proud: ner the Souldiers, which is ambitious: nor the Lawiers, which is politick: nor the Ladies, which is nice: nor the Louers, which is all these: but it is a melancholy of mine owne, compounded of many simples, extracted from many obiects, and indeed the sundrie contemplation of my trauells, in which by often rumination, wraps me in a most humorous sadnesse.

Ros. A Traueller: by my faith you haue great reason to be sad: I feare you haue sold your owne Lands, to see other mens; then to haue seene much, and to haue nothing, is to haue rich eyes and poore hands.

Iaq. Yes, I haue gain'd my experience.

Enter Orlando.

Ros. And your experience makes you sad: I had rather haue a foole to make me merrie, then experience to make me sad, and to trauaile for it too.

Orl. Good day, and happinesse, deere *Rosalind*.

Iaq. Nay then God buy you, and you talke in blanke verse.

Ros. Farewell Mounsieur Trauellor: looke you lispe, and weare strange suites; disable all the benefits of your owne Countrie: be out of loue with your natiuitie, and almost chide God for making you that countenance you are; or I will scarce thinke you haue swam in a Gundello. Why how now *Orlando*, where haue you bin all this while? you a louer? and you serue me such another tricke, neuer come in my sight more.

Orl. My faire *Rosalind*, I come within an houre of my promise.

Ros. Breake an houres promise in loue? hee that will diuide a minute into a thousand parts, and breake but a part of the thousand part of a minute in the affairs of loue, it may be said of him that *Cupid* hath clapt him oth' shoulder, but Ile warrant him heart hole.

Orl. Pardon me deere *Rosalind*.

Ros. Nay, and you be so tardie, come no more in my sight, I had as liefe be woo'd of a Snaile.

Orl. Of a Snaile?

Ros. I, of a Snaile: for though he comes slowly, hee carries his house on his head; a better ioyncture I thinke then you make a woman: besides, he brings his destinie with him.

Orl. What's that?

Ros. Why hornes: w such as you are faine to be beholding to your wiues for: but he comes armed in his fortune, and preuents the slander of his wife.

Orl. Vertue

Orl. Vertue is no horne-maker: and my *Rosalind* is vertuous.

Ros. And I am your *Rosalind*.

Cel. It pleases him to call you so: but he hath a *Rosalind* of a better leere then you.

Ros. Come, wooe me, wooe mee: for now I am in a holy-day humor, and like enough to consent: What would you say to me now, and I were your verie, verie *Rosalind*?

Orl. I would kisse before I spoke.

Ros. Nay, you were better speake first, and when you were grauel'd, for lacke of matter, you might take occasion to kisse: verie good Orators when they are out, they will spit, and for louers, lacking (God warne vs) matter, the cleanliest shift is to kisse.

Orl. How if the kisse be denide?

Ros. Then she puts you to entreatie, and there begins new matter.

Orl. Who could be out, being before his beloued Mistris?

Ros. Marrie that should you if I were your Mistris, or I should thinke my honestie ranker then my wit.

Orl. What, of my suite?

Ros. Not out of your apparrell, and yet out of your suite:
Am not I your *Rosalind*?

Orl. I take some ioy to say you are, because I would be talking of her.

Ros. Well, in her person, I say I will not haue you.

Orl. Then in mine owne person, I die.

Ros. No faith, die by Attorney: the poore world is almost six thousand yeeres old, and in all this time there was not anie man died in his owne person (*videlicet*) in a loue cause: *Troilous* had his braines dash'd out with a Grecian club, yet he did what hee could to die before, and he is one of the patternes of loue. *Leander*, he would haue liu'd manie a faire yeere though *Hero* had turn'd Nun; if it had not bin for a hot Midsomer-night, for (good youth) he went but forth to wash him in the Hellespont, and being taken with the crampe, was droun'd, and the foolish Chronoclers of that age, found it was *Hero* of Cestos. But these are all lies, men haue died from time to time, and wormes haue eaten them, but not for loue.

Orl. I would not haue my right *Rosalind* of this mind, for I protest her frowne might kill me.

Ros. By this hand, it will not kill a flie: but come, now I will be your *Rosalind* in a more comming-on disposition: and aske me what you will, I will grant it.

Orl. Then loue me *Rosalind*.

Ros. Yes faith will I, fridaies and saterdaies, and all.

Orl. And wilt thou haue me?

Ros. I, and twentie such.

Orl. What saiest thou?

Ros. Are you not good?

Orl. I hope so.

Rosalind. Why then, can one desire too much of a good thing: Come sister, you shall be the Priest, and marrie vs: giue me your hand *Orlando*: What doe you say sister?

Orl. Pray thee marrie vs.

Cel. I cannot say the words.

Ros. You must begin, will you *Orlando*.

Cel. Goe too: wil you *Orlando*, haue to wife this *Rosalind*?

Orl. I will.

Ros. I, but when?

Orl. Why now, as fast as she can marrie vs.

Ros. Then you must say, I take thee *Rosalind* for wife.

Orl. I take thee *Rosalind* for wife.

Ros. I might aske you for your Commission, But I doe take thee *Orlando* for my husband: there's a girle goes before the Priest, and certainely a Womans thought runs before her actions.

Orl. So do all thoughts, they are wing'd.

Ros. Now tell me how long you would haue her, after you haue possest her?

Orl. For euer, and a day.

Ros. Say a day, without the euer: no, no *Orlando*, men are Aprill when they woe, December when they wed: Maides are May when they are maides, but the sky changes when they are wiues: I will bee more iealous of thee, then a Barbary cocke-pidgeon ouer his hen, more clamorous then a Parrat against raine, more new-fangled then an ape, more giddy in my desires, then a monkey: I will weepe for nothing, like *Diana* in the Fountaine, & I wil do that when you are dispos'd to be merry: I will laugh like a Hyen, and that when thou art inclin'd to sleepe.

Orl. But will my *Rosalind* doe so?

Ros. By my life, she will doe as I doe.

Orl. O but she is wise.

Ros. Or else shee could not haue the wit to doe this: the wiser, the waywarder: make the doores vpon a womans wit, and it will out at the casement: shut that, and 'twill out at the key-hole: stop that, 'twill flie with the smoake out at the chimney.

Orl. A man that had a wife with such a wit, he might say, wit whether wil't?

Ros. Nay, you might keepe that checke for it, till you met your wiues wit going to your neighbours bed.

Orl. And what wit could wit haue, to excuse that?

Rosa. Marry to say, she came to seeke you there: you shall neuer take her without her answer, vnlesse you take her without her tongue: ô that woman that cannot make her fault her husbands occasion, let her neuer nurse her childe her selfe, for she will breed it like a foole.

Orl. For these two houres *Rosalinde*, I wil leaue thee.

Ros. Alas, deere loue, I cannot lacke thee two houres.

Orl. I must attend the Duke at dinner, by two a clock I will be with thee againe.

Ros. I, goe your waies, goe your waies: I knew what you would proue, my friends told mee as much, and I thought no lesse: that flattering tongue of yours wonne me: 'tis but one cast away, and so come death: two o' clocke is your howre.

Orl. I, sweet *Rosalind*.

Ros. By my troth, and in good earnest, and so God mend mee, and by all pretty oathes that are not dangerous, if you breake one iot of your promise, or come one minute behinde your houre, I will thinke you the most patheticall breake-promise, and the most hollow louer, and the most vnworthy of her you call *Rosalinde*, that may bee chosen out of the grosse band of the vnfaithfull: therefore beware my censure, and keep your promise.

Orl. With no lesse religion, then if thou wert indeed my *Rosalind*: so adieu.

Ros. Well, Time is the olde Iustice that examines all such offenders, and let time try: adieu. *Exit.*

Cel. You haue simply misus'd our sexe in your loue-
prate:

prate: we must haue your doublet and hose pluckt ouer your head, and shew the world what the bird hath done to her owne neast.

Ros. O coz, coz, coz: my pretty little coz, that thou didst know how many fathome deepe I am in loue: but it cannot bee sounded: my affection hath an vnknowne bottome, like the Bay of Portugall.

Cel. Or rather bottomlesse, that as fast as you poure affection in, in runs out.

Ros. No, that same wicked Bastard of *Venus*, that was begot of thought, conceiu'd of spleene, and borne of madnesse, that blinde rascally boy, that abuses euery ones eyes, because his owne are out, let him bee iudge, how deepe I am in loue: ile tell thee *Aliena*, I cannot be out of the sight of *Orlando*: Ile goe finde a shadow, and sigh till he come.

Cel. And Ile sleepe. *Exeunt.*

Scena Secunda.

Enter Iaques and Lords, Forresters.

Iaq. Which is he that killed the Deare?
Lord. Sir, it was I.
Iaq. Let's present him to the Duke like a Romane Conquerour, and it would doe well to set the Deares horns vpon his head, for a branch of victory; haue you no song Forrester for this purpose?
Lord. Yes Sir.
Iaq. Sing it: 'tis no matter how it bee in tune, so it make noyse enough.

Musicke, Song.

What shall he haue that kild the Deare?
His Leather skin, and hornes to weare:
Then sing him home, the rest shall beare this burthen;
Take thou no scorne to weare the horne,
It was a crest ere thou wast borne,
Thy fathers father wore it,
And thy father bore it,
The horne, the horne, the lusty horne,
Is not a thing to laugh to scorne. *Exeunt.*

Scœna Tertia.

Enter Rosalind and Celia.

Ros. How say you now, is it not past two a clock? And heere much *Orlando*.

Cel. I warrant you, with pure loue, & troubled brain,
Enter Siluius.
He hath t'ane his bow and arrowes, and is gone forth
To sleepe: looke who comes heere.

Sil. My errand is to you, faire youth,
My gentle *Phebe*, did bid me giue you this:
I know not the contents, but as I guesse
By the sterne brow, and waspish action
Which she did vse, as she was writing of it,
It beares an angry tenure; pardon me,
I am but as a guiltlesse messenger.

Ros. Patience her selfe would startle at this letter,
And play the swaggerer, beare this, beare all:
Shee saies I am not faire, that I lacke manners,
She calls me proud, and that she could not loue me
Were man as rare as Phenix: 'od's my will,
Her loue is not the Hare that I doe hunt,
Why writes she so to me? well Shepheard, well,
This is a Letter of your owne deuice.

Sil. No, I protest, I know not the contents,
Phebe did write it.

Ros. Come, come, you are a foole,
And turn'd into the extremity of loue.
I saw her hand, she has a leatherne hand,
A freestone coloured hand: I verily did thinke
That her old gloues were on, but twas her hands:
She has a huswiues hand, but that's no matter:
I say she neuer did inuent this letter,
This is a mans inuention, and his hand.

Sil. Sure it is hers.

Ros. Why, tis a boysterous and a cruell stile,
A stile for challengers: why, she defies me,
Like Turke to Christian: vvomens gentle braine
Could not drop forth such giant rude inuention,
Such Ethiop vvords, blacker in their effect
Then in their countenance: vvill you heare the letter?

Sil. So please you, for I neuer heard it yet:
Yet heard too much of *Phebes* crueltie.

Ros. She *Phebes* me: marke how the tyrant vvrites.
Read. *Art thou god, to Shepherd turn'd?*
That a maidens heart hath burn'd.
Can a vvoman raile thus?

Sil. Call you this railing?

Ros. Read. *Why, thy godhead laid a part,*
War'st thou with a womans heart?
Did you euer heare such railing?
Whiles the eye of man did wooe me,
That could do no vengeance to me.
Meaning me a beast.
If the scorne of your bright eine
Haue power to raise such loue in mine,
Alacke, in me, what strange effect
Would they worke in milde aspect?
Whiles you chid me, I did loue,
How then might your praiers moue?
He that brings this loue to thee,
Little knowes this Loue in me:
And by him seale vp thy minde,
Whether that thy youth and kinde
Will the faithfull offer take
Of me, and all that I can make,
Or else by him my loue denie,
And then Ile studie how to die.

Sil. Call you this chiding?

Cel. Alas poore Shepheard.

Ros. Doe you pitty him? No, he deserues no pitty: wilt thou loue such a woman? what to make thee an instrument, and play false straines vpon thee? not to be endur'd. Well, goe your way to her; (for I see Loue hath made thee a tame snake) and say this to her; That if she loue me, I charge her to loue thee: if she will not, I will neuer haue her, vnlesse thou intreat for her: if you bee a true louer hence, and not a word; for here comes more company. *Exit. Sil.*

Enter Oliuer.
Oliu. Good morrow, faire ones: pray you, (if you know)
Where in the Purlews of this Forrest, stands

A sheep-coat, fenc'd about with Oliue-trees.

Cel. West of this place, down in the neighbor bottom
The ranke of Oziers, by the murmuring streame
Left on your right hand, brings you to the place:
But at this howre, the house doth keepe it selfe,
There's none within.

Oli. If that an eye may profit by a tongue,
Then should I know you by description,
Such garments, and such yeeres: the boy is faire,
Of femall fauour, and bestowes himselfe
Like a ripe sister: the woman low
And browner then her brother: are not you
The owner of the house I did enquire for?

Cel. It is no boast, being ask'd, to say we are.

Oli. Orlando doth commend him to you both,
And to that youth hee calls his *Rosalind*,
He sends this bloudy napkin; are you he?

Ros. I am: what must we vnderstand by this?

Oli. Some of my shame, if you will know of me
What man I am, and how, and why, and where
This handkercher was stain'd.

Cel. I pray you tell it.

Oli. When last the yong *Orlando* parted from you,
He left a promise to returne againe
Within an houre, and pacing through the Forrest,
Chewing the food of sweet and bitter fancie,
Loe what befell: he threw his eye aside,
And marke what obiect did present it selfe
Vnder an old Oake, whose bows were moss'd with age
And high top, bald with drie antiquitie:
A wretched ragged man, ore-growne with haire
Lay sleeping on his back; about his necke
A greene and guilded snake had wreath'd it selfe,
Who with her head, nimble in threats approach'd
The opening of his mouth: but sodainly
Seeing *Orlando*, it vnlink'd it selfe,
And with indented glides, did slip away
Into a bush, vnder which bushes shade
A Lyonnesse, with vdders all drawne drie,
Lay cowching head on ground, with catlike watch
When that the sleeping man should stirre; for 'tis
The royall disposition of that beast
To prey on nothing, that doth seeme as dead:
This seene, *Orlando* did approach the man,
And found it was his brother, his elder brother.

Cel. O I haue heard him speake of that same brother,
And he did render him the most vnnaturall
That liu'd amongst men.

Oli. And well he might so doe,
For well I know he was vnnaturall.

Ros. But to *Orlando*: did he leaue him there
Foed to the suck'd and hungry Lyonnesse?

Oli. Twice did he turne his backe, and purpos'd so:
But kindnesse, nobler euer then reuenge,
And Nature stronger then his iust occasion,
Made him giue battell to the Lyonnesse:
Who quickly fell before him, in which hurtling
From miserable slumber I awaked.

Cel. Are you his brother?

Ros. Was't you he rescu'd?

Cel. Was't you that did so oft contriue to kill him?

Oli. 'Twas I: but 'tis not I: I doe not shame
To tell you what I was, since my conuersion
So sweetly tastes, being the thing I am.

Ros. But for the bloody napkin?

Oli. By and by:
When from the first to last betwixt vs two,
Teares our recountments had most kindely bath'd,
As how I came into that Desert place.
I briefe, he led me to the gentle Duke,
Who gaue me fresh aray, and entertainment,
Committing me vnto my brothers loue,
Who led me instantly vnto his Caue,
There stript himselfe, and heere vpon his arme
The Lyonnesse had torne some flesh away,
Which all this while had bled; and now he fainted,
And cride in fainting vpon *Rosalinde*.
Briefe, I recouer'd him, bound vp his wound,
And after some small space, being strong at heart,
He sent me hither, stranger as I am
To tell this story, that you might excuse
His broken promise, and to giue this napkin
Died in this bloud, vnto the Shepheard youth,
That he in sport doth call his *Rosalind*.

Cel. Why how now *Ganimed*, sweet *Ganimed*.

Oli. Many will swoon when they do look on bloud.

Cel. There is more in it; Cosen *Ganimed*.

Oli. Looke, he recouers.

Ros. I would I were at home.

Cel. Wee'll lead you thither:
I pray you will you take him by the arme.

Oli. Be of good cheere youth: you a man?
You lacke a mans heart.

Ros. I doe so, I confesse it:
Ah, sirra, a body would thinke this was well counterfeited, I pray you tell your brother how well I counterfeited: heigh-ho.

Oli. This was not counterfeit, there is too great testimony in your complexion, that it was a passion of earnest.

Ros. Counterfeit, I assure you.

Oli. Well then, take a good heart, and counterfeit to be a man.

Ros. So I doe: but yfaith, I should haue beene a woman by right.

Cel. Come, you looke paler and paler: pray you draw homewards: good sir, goe with vs.

Oli. That will I: for I must beare answere backe
How you excuse my brother, *Rosalind*.

Ros. I shall deuise something: but I pray you commend my counterfeiting to him: will you goe?

Exeunt.

Actus Quintus. Scena Prima.

Enter Clowne and Awdrie.

Clow. We shall finde a time *Awdrie*, patience gentle *Awdrie*.

Awd. Faith the Priest was good enough, for all the olde gentlemans saying.

Clow. A most wicked Sir *Oliuer*, *Awdrie*, a most vile *Mar-text*. But *Awdrie*, there is a youth heere in the Forrest layes claime to you.

Awd. I, I know who 'tis: he hath no interest in mee in the world: here comes the man you meane.

Enter William.

Clo. It is meat and drinke to me to see a Clowne, by
my

my troth, we that haue good wits, haue much to answer for : we shall be flouting : we cannot hold.

Will. Good eu'n *Audrey.*

Aud. God ye good eu'n *William.*

Will. And good eu'n to you Sir.

Clo. Good eu'n gentle friend. Couer thy head, couer thy head : Nay prethee bee couer'd. How olde are you Friend?

Will. Fiue and twentie Sir.

Clo. A ripe age : Is thy name *William*?

Will. William, sir.

Clo. A faire name. Was't borne i'th Forrest heere?

Will. I sir, I thanke God.

Clo. Thanke God : A good answer : Art rich?

Will. Faith sir, so, so.

Clo. So, so, is good, very good, very excellent good : and yet it is not, it is but so, so : Art thou wise?

Will. I sir, I haue a prettie wit.

Clo. Why, thou saist well. I do now remember a saying : The Foole doth thinke he is wise, but the wiseman knowes himselfe to be a Foole. The Heathen Philosopher, when he had a desire to eate a Grape, would open his lips when he put it into his mouth, meaning thereby, that Grapes were made to eate, and lippes to open. You do loue this maid?

Will. I do sir.

Clo. Giue me your hand : Art thou Learned?

Will. No sir.

Clo. Then learne this of me, To haue, is to haue. For it is a figure in Rhetoricke, that drink being powr'd out of a cup into a glasse, by filling the one, doth empty the other. For all your Writers do consent, that *ipse* is hee : now you are not *ipse*, for I am he.

Will. Which he sir?

Clo. He sir, that must marrie this woman : Therefore you Clowne, abandon : which is in the vulgar, leaue the societie : which in the boorish, is companie, of this female : which in the common, is woman : which together, is, abandon the society of this Female, or Clowne thou perishest : or to thy better vnderstanding, dyest ; or (to wit) I kill thee, make thee away, translate thy life into death, thy libertie into bondage : I will deale in poyson with thee, or in bastinado, or in steele : I will bandy with thee in faction, I will ore-run thee with policie : I will kill thee a hundred and fifty wayes, therefore tremble and depart.

Aud. Do good *William.*

Will. God rest you merry sir. *Exit*

Enter Corin.

Cor. Our Master and Mistresse seekes you : come away, away.

Clo. Trip *Audry,* trip *Audry,* I attend, I attend. *Exeunt*

Scœna Secunda.

Enter Orlando & Oliuer.

Orl. Is't possible, that on so little acquaintance you should like her? that, but seeing, you should loue her? And louing woo? and wooing, she should graunt? And will you perseuer to enioy her?

Ol. Neither call the giddinesse of it in question ; the pouertie of her, the small acquaintance, my sodaine wooing, nor sodaine consenting : but say with mee, I loue *Aliena* : say with her, that she loues mee ; consent with both, that we may enioy each other : it shall be to your good : for my fathers house, and all the reuennew, that was old Sir *Rowlands* will I estate vpon you, and heere liue and die a Shepherd.

Enter Rosalind.

Orl. You haue my consent. Let your Wedding be to morrow : thither will I Inuite the Duke, and all's contented followers : Go you, and prepare *Aliena*; for looke you, Heere comes my *Rosalinde.*

Ros. God saue you brother.

Ol. And you faire sister.

Ros. Oh my deere *Orlando,* how it greeues me to see thee weare thy heart in a scarfe.

Orl. It is my arme.

Ros. I thought thy heart had beene wounded with the clawes of a Lion.

Orl. Wounded it is, but with the eyes of a Lady.

Ros. Did your brother tell you how I counterfeyted to sound, when he shew'd me your handkercher?

Orl. I, and greater wonders then that.

Ros. O, I know where you are : nay, tis true : there was neuer any thing so sodaine, but the fight of two Rammes, and *Cesars* Thrasonicall bragge of I came, saw, and ouercome. For your brother, and my sister, no sooner met, but they look'd : no sooner look'd, but they lou'd ; no sooner lou'd, but they sigh'd : no sooner sigh'd but they ask'd one another the reason : no sooner knew the reason, but they sought the remedie : and in these degrees, haue they made a paire of staires to marriage, which they will climbe incontinent, or else bee incontinent before marriage ; they are in the verie wrath of loue, and they will together. Clubbes cannot part them.

Orl. They shall be married to morrow : and I will bid the Duke to the Nuptiall. But O, how bitter a thing it is, to looke into happines through another mans eies : by so much the more shall I to morrow be at the height of heart heauinesse, by how much I shal thinke my brother happie, in hauing what he wishes for.

Ros. Why then to morrow, I cannot serue your turne for *Rosalind?*

Orl. I can liue no longer by thinking.

Ros. I will wearie you then no longer with idle talking. Know of me then (for now I speake to some purpose) that I know you are a Gentleman of good conceit : I speake not this, that you should beare a good opinion of my knowledge : insomuch (I say) I know you are : neither do I labor for a greater esteeme then may in some little measure draw a beleefe from you, to do your selfe good, and not to grace me. Beleeue then, if you please, that I can do strange things : I haue since I was three yeare old conuerst with a Magitian, most profound in his Art, and yet not damnable. If you do loue *Rosalinde* so neere the hart, as your gesture cries it out : when your brother marries *Aliena,* shall you marrie her. I know into what straights of Fortune she is driuen, and it is not impossible to me, if it appeare not inconuenient to you,
to

As you like it.

to set her before your eyes to morrow, humane as she is, and without any danger.

Orl. Speak'st thou in sober meanings?

Ros. By my life I do, which I tender deerly, though I say I am a Magitian: Therefore put you in your best array, bid your friends: for if you will be married to morrow, you shall: and to *Rosalind* if you will.

Enter Silvius & Phebe.

Looke, here comes a Louer of mine, and a louer of hers.

Phe. Youth, you haue done me much vngentlenesse, To shew the letter that I writ to you.

Ros. I care not if I haue: it is my studie To seeme despightfull and vngentle to you: you are there followed by a faithfull shepheard, Looke vpon him, loue him: he worships you.

Phe. Good shepheard, tell this youth what 'tis to loue

Sil. It is to be all made of sighes and teares, And so am I for *Phebe*.

Phe. And I for *Ganimed*.

Orl. And I for *Rosalind*.

Ros. And I for no woman.

Sil. It is to be all made of faith and seruice, And so am I for *Phebe*.

Phe. And I for *Ganimed*.

Orl. And I for *Rosalind*.

Ros. And I for no woman.

Sil. It is to be all made of fantasie, All made of passion, and all made of wishes, All adoration, dutie, and obseruance, All humblenesse, all patience, and impatience, All puritie, all triall, all obseruance: And so am I for *Phebe*.

Phe. And so am I for *Ganimed*.

Orl. And so am I for *Rosalind*.

Ros. And so am I for no woman.

Phe. If this be so, why blame you me to loue you?

Sil. If this be so, why blame you me to loue you?

Orl. If this be so, why blame you me to loue you?

Ros. Why do you speake too, Why blame you mee to loue you.

Orl. To her, that is not heere, nor doth not heare.

Ros. Pray you no more of this, 'tis like the howling of Irish Wolues against the Moone: I will helpe you if I can: I would loue you if I could: To morrow meet me altogether: I wil marrie you, if euer I marrie Woman, and Ile be married to morrow: I will satisfie you, if euer I satisfi'd man, and you shall bee married to morrow. I wil content you, if what pleases you contents you, and you shal be married to morrow. As you loue *Rosalind* meet, as you loue *Phebe* meet, and as I loue no woman, Ile meet: so fare you wel: I haue left you commands.

Sil. Ile not faile, if I liue.

Phe. Nor I.

Orl. Nor I.   *Exeunt.*

Scœna Tertia.

Enter Clowne and Audrey.

Cl. To morrow is the ioyfull day *Audrey*, to morrow will we be married.

Aud. I do desire it with all my heart: and I hope it is no dishonest desire, to desire to be a woman of ȳ world?

Heere come two of the banish'd Dukes Pages.

Enter two Pages.

1.Pa. Wel met honest Gentleman.

Clo. By my troth well met: come, sit, sit, and a song.

2.Pa. We are for you, sit i'th middle.

1.Pa. Shal we clap into't roundly, without hauking, or spitting, or saying we are hoarse, which are the onely prologues to a bad voice.

2.Pa. I faith, y'faith, and both in a tune like two gipsies on a horse.

Song.

It was a Louer, and his lasse,
  With a hey, and a ho, and a hey nonino,
That o're the greene corne feild did passe,
  In the spring time, the onely pretty rang time,
When Birds do sing, hey ding a ding, ding.
Sweet Louers loue the spring,
  And therefore take the present time,
With a hey, & a ho, and a hey nonino,
For loue is crowned with the prime.
  In spring time, &c.

Betweene the acres of the Rie,
With a hey, and a ho, & a hey nonino:
These prettie Country folks would lie,
  In spring time, &c.

This Carroll they began that houre,
With a hey and a ho, & a hey nonino:
How that a life was but a Flower,
  In spring time, &c.

Clo. Truly yong Gentlemen, though there vvas no great matter in the dittie, yet ȳ note was very vntunable

1.Pa. you are deceiu'd Sir, we kept time, we lost not our time.

Clo. By my troth yes: I count it but time lost to heare such a foolish song. God buy you, and God mend your voices. Come *Audrie*.   *Exeunt.*

Scena Quarta.

Enter Duke Senior, Amyens, Iaques, Orlando, Oliuer, Celia.

Du.Sen. Dost thou beleeue *Orlando*, that the boy Can do all this that he hath promised?

Orl. I sometimes do beleeue, and somtimes do not, As those that feare they hope, and know they feare.

Enter Rosalinde, Silvius, & Phebe.

Ros. Patience once more, whiles our cōpact is vrg'd: You say, if I bring in your *Rosalinde*, You wil bestow her on *Orlando* heere?

Du.Se. That would I, had I kingdoms to giue with hir.

Ros. And you say you wil haue her, when I bring hir?

Orl. That would I, were I of all kingdomes King.

Ros. You say, you'l marrie me, if I be willing.

Phe. That will I, should I die the houre after.

Ros. But if you do refuse to marrie me, You'l giue your selfe to this most faithfull Shepheard.

Phe. So is the bargaine.

Ros. You say that you'l haue *Phebe* if she will.

Sil. Though to haue her and death, were both one thing.

S   *Ros.*

Ros. I haue promis'd to make all this matter euen:
Keepe you your word, O Duke, to giue your daughter,
You yours *Orlando*, to receiue his daughter:
Keepe you your word *Phebe*, that you'l marrie me,
Or else refusing me to wed this shepheard:
Keepe your word *Siluius*, that you'l marrie her
If she refuse me, and from hence I go
To make these doubts all euen. *Exit Ros. and Celia.*

Du.Sen. I do remember in this shepheard boy,
Some liuely touches of my daughters fauour.

Orl. My Lord, the first time that I euer saw him,
Me thought he was a brother to your daughter:
But my good Lord, this Boy is Forrest borne,
And hath bin tutor'd in the rudiments
Of many desperate studies, by his vnckle,
Whom he reports to be a great Magitian.

Enter Clowne and Audrey.

Obscured in the circle of this Forrest.

Iaq. There is sure another flood toward, and these couples are comming to the Arke. Here comes a payre of verie strange beasts, which in all tongues, are call'd Fooles.

Clo. Salutation and greeting to you all.

Iaq. Good my Lord, bid him welcome: This is the Motley-minded Gentleman, that I haue so often met in the Forrest: he hath bin a Courtier he sweares.

Clo. If any man doubt that, let him put mee to my purgation, I haue trod a measure, I haue flattred a Lady, I haue bin politicke with my friend, smooth with mine enemie, I haue vndone three Tailors, I haue had foure quarrels, and like to haue fought one.

Iaq. And how was that tane vp?

Clo. 'Faith we met, and found the quarrel was vpon the seuenth cause.

Iaq. How seuenth cause? Good my Lord, like this fellow.

Du.Se. I like him very well.

Clo. God'ild you sir, I desire you of the like: I presse in heere sir, amongst the rest of the Country copulatiues to sweare, and to forsweare, according as mariage binds and blood breakes: a poore virgin sir, an il-fauor'd thing sir, but mine owne, a poore humour of mine sir, to take that that no man else will: rich honestie dwels like a miser sir, in a poore house, as your Pearle in your foule oyster.

Du.Se. By my faith, he is very swift, and sententious

Clo. According to the fooles bolt sir, and such dulcet diseases.

Iaq. But for the seuenth cause. How did you finde the quarrell on the seuenth cause?

Clo. Vpon a lye, seuen times remoued: (beare your bodie more seeming *Audry*) as thus sir: I did dislike the cut of a certaine Courtiers beard: he sent me word, if I said his beard was not cut well, hee was in the minde it was: this is call'd the retort courteous. If I sent him word againe, it was not well cut, he wold send me word he cut it to please himselfe: this is call'd the quip modest. If againe, it was not well cut, he disabled my iudgment: this is called, the reply churlish. If againe it was not well cut, he would answer I spake not true: this is call'd the reproofe valiant. If againe, it was not well cut, he wold say, I lie: this is call'd the counter-checke quarrelsome: and so to lye circumstantiall, and the lye direct.

Iaq. And how oft did you say his beard was not well cut?

Clo. I durst go no further then the lye circumstantial: nor he durst not giue me the lye direct: and so wee measur'd swords, and parted.

Iaq. Can you nominate in order now, the degrees of the lye.

Clo. O sir, we quarrel in print, by the booke: as you haue bookes for good manners: I will name you the degrees. The first, the Retort courteous: the second, the Quip-modest: the third, the reply Churlish: the fourth, the Reproofe valiant: the fift, the Countercheck quarrelsome: the sixt, the Lye with circumstance: the seauenth, the Lye direct: all these you may auoyd, but the Lye direct: and you may auoide that too, with an If. I knew when seuen Iustices could not take vp a Quarrell, but when the parties were met themselues, one of them thought but of an If; as if you saide so, then I saide so: and they shooke hands, and swore brothers. Your If, is the onely peace-maker: much vertue in if.

Iaq. Is not this a rare fellow my Lord? He's as good at any thing, and yet a foole.

Du.Se. He vses his folly like a stalking-horse, and vnder the presentation of that he shoots his wit.

Enter Hymen, Rosalind, and Celia.
Still Musicke.

Hymen. *Then is there mirth in heauen,*
When earthly things made euen
attone together.
Good Duke receiue thy daughter,
Hymen from Heauen brought her,
Yea brought her hether.
That thou mightst ioyne his hand with his,
Whose heart within his bosome is.

Ros. To you I giue my selfe, for I am yours.
To you I giue my selfe, for I am yours.

Du.Se. If there be truth in sight, you are my daughter,
Orl. If there be truth in sight, you are my *Rosalind*.
Phe. If sight & shape be true, why then my loue adieu
Ros. Ile haue no Father, if you be not he:
Ile haue no Husband, if you be not he:
Nor ne're wed woman, if you be not shee.

Hy. Peace hoa: I barre confusion,
'Tis I must make conclusion
Of these most strange euents:
Here's eight that must take hands,
To ioyne in *Hymens* bands,
If truth holds true contents.
You and you, no crosse shall part;
You and you, are hart in hart:
You, to his loue must accord,
Or haue a Woman to your Lord.
You and you, are sure together,
As the Winter to fowle Weather:
Whiles a Wedlocke Hymne we sing,
Feede your selues with questioning:
That reason, wonder may diminish
How thus we met, and these things finish.

Song.
Wedding is great Iunos crowne,
O blessed bond of boord and bed:
'Tis Hymen peoples euerie towne,
High wedlock then be honored:
Honor, high honor and renowne
To Hymen, God of euerie Towne.

Du.Se. O my deere Neece, welcome thou art to me,
Euen daughter welcome, in no lesse degree.
Phe.

As you like it.

Phe. I wil not eate my word, now thou art mine,
Thy faith, my fancie to thee doth combine.

Enter Second Brother.

2.Bro. Let me haue audience for a word or two:
I am the second sonne of old *Sir Rowland*,
That bring these tidings to this faire assembly.
Duke Frederick hearing how that euerie day
Men of great worth resorted to this forrest,
Addrest a mightie power, which were on foote
In his owne conduct, purposely to take
His brother heere, and put him to the sword:
And to the skirts of this wilde Wood he came;
Where, meeting with an old Religious man,
After some question with him, was conuerted
Both from his enterprize, and from the world:
His crowne bequeathing to his banish'd Brother,
And all their Lands restor'd to him againe
That were with him exil'd. This to be true,
I do engage my life.

Du.Se. Welcome yong man:
Thou offer'st fairely to thy brothers wedding:
To one his lands with-held, and to the other
A land it selfe at large, a potent Dukedome.
First, in this Forrest, let vs do those ends
That heere were well begun, and wel begot:
And after, euery of this happie number
That haue endur'd shrew'd daies, and nights with vs,
Shal share the good of our returned fortune,
According to the measure of their states.
Meane time, forget this new-falne dignitie,
And fall into our Rusticke Reuelrie:
Play Musicke, and you Brides and Bride-groomes all,
With measure heap'd in ioy, to'th Measures fall.

Iaq. Sir, by your patience: if I heard you rightly,
The Duke hath put on a Religious life,
And throwne into neglect the pompous Court.

2.Bri. He hath.

Iaq. To him will I: out of these conuertites,
There is much matter to be heard, and learn'd:
you to your former Honor, I bequeath
your patience, and your vertue, well deserues it.
you to a loue, that your true faith doth merit:
you to your land, and loue, and great allies:
you to a long, and well-deserued bed:
And you to wrangling, for thy louing voyage
Is but for two moneths victuall'd: So to your pleasures,
I am for other, then for dancing meazures.

Du.Se. Stay, *Iaques*, stay.

Iaq. To see no pastime, I: what you would haue,
Ile stay to know, at your abandon'd caue. *Exit.*

Du.Se. Proceed, proceed: wee'l begin these rights,
As we do trust, they'l end in true delights. *Exit*

Ros. It is not the fashion to see the Ladie the Epilogue: but it is no more vnhandsome, then to see the Lord the Prologue. If it be true, that good wine needs no bush, 'tis true, that a good play needes no Epilogue. Yet to good wine they do vse good bushes: and good playes proue the better by the helpe of good Epilogues: What a case am I in then, that am neither a good Epilogue, nor cannot insinuate with you in the behalfe of a good play. I am not furnish'd like a Begger, therefore to begge will not become mee. My way is to coniure you, and Ile begin with the Women. I charge you (O women) for the loue you beare to men, to like as much of this Play, as please you: And I charge you (O men) for the loue you beare to women (as I perceiue by your simpring, none of you hates them) that betweene you, and the women, the play may please. If I were a Woman, I would kisse as many of you as had beards that pleas'd me, complexions that lik'd me, and breaths that I defi'de not: And I am sure, as many as haue good beards, or good faces, or sweet breaths, will for my kind offer, when I make curt'sie, bid me farewell. *Exit.*

FINIS.

THE
Taming of the Shrew.

Actus primus. Scœna Prima.

Enter Begger and Hostes, Christophero Sly.

Begger.

Ile pheeze you infaith.

Host. A paire of stockes you rogue.

Beg. Y'are a baggage, the *Slies* are no Rogues. Looke in the Chronicles, we came in with *Richard Conqueror*: therefore *Paucas pallabris*, let the world slide: Sessa.

Host. You will not pay for the glasses you haue burst?

Beg. No, not a deniere: go by S. *Ieronimie*, goe to thy cold bed, and warme thee.

Host. I know my remedie, I must go fetch the Headborough.

Beg. Third, or fourth, or fift Borough, Ile answere him by Law. Ile not budge an inch boy: Let him come, and kindly. *Falles asleepe.*

Winde hornes. Enter a Lord from hunting, with his traine.

Lo. Huntsman I charge thee, tender wel my hounds, Brach *Meriman*, the poore Curre is imbost, And couple *Clowder* with the deepe-mouth'd brach, Saw'st thou not boy how *Siluer* made it good At the hedge corner, in the couldest fault, I would not loose the dogge for twentie pound.

Hunts. Why *Belman* is as good as he my Lord, He cried vpon it at the meerest losse, And twice to day pick'd out the dullest sent, Trust me, I take him for the better dogge.

Lord. Thou art a Foole, if *Eccho* were as fleete, I would esteeme him worth a dozen such: But sup them well, and looke vnto them all, To morrow I intend to hunt againe.

Hunts. I will my Lord.

Lord. What's heere? One dead, or drunke? See doth he breath?

2. Hun. He breath's my Lord. Were he not warm'd with Ale, this were a bed but cold to sleep so soundly.

Lord. Oh monstrous beast, how like a swine he lyes. Grim death, how foule and loathsome is thine image: Sirs, I will practise on this drunken man. What thinke you, if he were conuey'd to bed, Wrap'd in sweet cloathes: Rings put vpon his fingers: A most delicious banquet by his bed, And braue attendants neere him when he wakes, Would not the begger then forget himselfe?

1. Hun. Beleeue me Lord, I thinke he cannot choose.

2. H. It would seem strange vnto him when he wak'd

Lord. Euen as a flatt'ring dreame, or worthles fancie.

Then take him vp, and manage well the iest: Carrie him gently to my fairest Chamber, And hang it round with all my wanton pictures: Balme his foule head in warme distilled waters, And burne sweet Wood to make the Lodging sweete: Procure me Musicke readie when he wakes, To make a dulcet and a heauenly sound: And if he chance to speake, be readie straight (And with a lowe submissiue reuerence) Say, what is it your Honor wil command: Let one attend him with a siluer Bason Full of Rose-water, and bestrew'd with Flowers, Another beare the Ewer: the third a Diaper, And say wilt please your Lordship coole your hands. Some one be readie with a costly suite, And aske him what apparrel he will weare: Another tell him of his Hounds and Horse, And that his Ladie mournes at his disease, Perswade him that he hath bin Lunaticke, And when he sayes he is, say that he dreames, For he is nothing but a mightie Lord: This do, and do it kindly, gentle sirs, It wilbe pastime passing excellent, If it be husbanded with modestie.

1. Hunts. My Lord I warrant you we wil play our part As he shall thinke by our true diligence He is no lesse then what we say he is.

Lord. Take him vp gently, and to bed with him, And each one to his office when he wakes.

Sound trumpets.

Sirrah, go see what Trumpet 'tis that sounds, Belike some Noble Gentleman that meanes (Trauelling some iourney) to repose him heere.

Enter Seruingman.

How now? who is it?

Ser. An't please your Honor, Players That offer seruice to your Lordship.

Enter Players.

Lord. Bid them come neere: Now fellowes, you are welcome.

Players. We thanke your Honor.

Lord. Do you intend to stay with me to night?

2. Player. So please your Lordshippe to accept our dutie.

Lord. With all my heart. This fellow I remember, Since once he plaide a Farmers eldest sonne, 'Twas where you woo'd the Gentlewoman so well: I haue forgot your name: but sure that part

The Taming of the Shrew.

Was aptly fitted, and naturally perform'd.
  Sincklo. I thinke 'twas *Soto* that your honor meanes.
  Lord. 'Tis verie true, thou didst it excellent:
Well you are come to me in happie time,
The rather for I haue some sport in hand,
Wherein your cunning can assist me much.
There is a Lord will heare you play to night;
But I am doubtfull of your modesties,
Least (ouer-eying of his odde behauiour,
For yet his honor neuer heard a play)
You breake into some merrie passion,
And so offend him: for I tell you sirs,
If you should smile, he growes impatient.
  Plai. Feare not my Lord, we can contain our selues,
Were he the veriest anticke in the world.
  Lord. Go sirra, take them to the Butterie,
And giue them friendly welcome euerie one,
Let them want nothing that my house affoords.

Exit one with the Players.

Sirra go you to Bartholmew my Page,
And see him drest in all suites like a Ladie:
That done, conduct him to the drunkards chamber,
And call him Madam, do him obeisance:
Tell him from me (as he will win my loue)
He beare himselfe with honourable action,
Such as he hath obseru'd in noble Ladies
Vnto their Lords, by them accomplished,
Such dutie to the drunkard let him do:
With soft lowe tongue, and lowly curtesie,
And say: What is't your Honor will command,
Wherein your Ladie, and your humble wife,
May shew her dutie, and make knowne her loue.
And then with kinde embracements, tempting kisses,
And with declining head into his bosome
Bid him shed teares, as being ouer-ioyed
To see her noble Lord restor'd to health,
Who for this seuen yeares hath esteemed him
No better then a poore and loathsome begger:
And if the boy haue not a womans guift
To raine a shower of commanded teares,
An Onion wil do well for such a shift,
Which in a Napkin (being close conuei'd)
Shall in despight enforce a waterie eie:
See this dispatch'd with all the hast thou canst,
Anon Ile giue thee more instructions.

Exit a seruingman.

I know the boy will wel vsurpe the grace,
Voice, gate, and action of a Gentlewoman:
I long to heare him call the drunkard husband,
And how my men will stay themselues from laughter,
When they do homage to this simple peasant,
Ile into counsell them: haply my presence
May well abate the ouer-merrie spleene,
Which otherwise would grow into extreames.

*Enter aloft the drunkard with attendants, some with apparel,
Bason and Ewer, & other appurtenances, & Lord.*

  Beg. For Gods sake a pot of small Ale.
  1. Ser. Wilt please your Lord drink a cup of sacke?
  2. Ser. Wilt please your Honor taste of these Conserues?
  3. Ser. What raiment wil your honor weare to day.
  Beg. I am *Christophero Sly*, call not mee Honour nor Lordship: I ne're drank sacke in my life: and if you giue me any Conserues, giue me conserues of Beefe: nere ask me what raiment Ile weare, for I haue no more doublets then backes: no more stockings then legges: nor no more shooes then feet, nay sometime more feete then shooes, or such shooes as my toes looke through the ouer-leather.
  Lord. Heauen cease this idle humor in your Honor.
Oh that a mightie man of such discent,
Of such possessions, and so high esteeme
Should be infused with so foule a spirit.
  Beg. What would you make me mad? Am not I *Christopher Slie*, old *Sies* sonne of Burton-heath, by byrth a Pedler, by education a Cardmaker, by transmutation a Beare-heard, and now by present profession a Tinker. Aske *Marrian Hacket* the fat Alewife of Wincot, if shee know me not: if she say I am not xiiii.d. on the score for sheere Ale, score me vp for the lyingst knaue in Christendome. What I am not bestraught: here's——
  3. Man. Oh this it is that makes your Ladie mourne.
  2. Man. Oh this is it that makes your seruants droop.
  Lord. Hence comes it, that your kindred shuns your house
As beaten hence by your strange Lunacie.
Oh Noble Lord, bethinke thee of thy birth,
Call home thy ancient thoughts from banishment,
And banish hence these abiect lowlie dreames:
Looke how thy seruants do attend on thee,
Each in his office readie at thy becke.
Wilt thou haue Musicke? Harke Apollo plaies, *Musick*
And twentie caged Nightingales do sing.
Or wilt thou sleepe? Wee'l haue thee to a Couch,
Softer and sweeter then the lustfull bed
On purpose trim'd vp for Semiramis.
Say thou wilt walke: we wil bestrow the ground.
Or wilt thou ride? Thy horses shal be trap'd,
Their harnesse studded all with Gold and Pearle.
Dost thou loue hawking? Thou hast hawkes will soare
Aboue the morning Larke. Or wilt thou hunt,
Thy hounds shall make the Welkin answer them
And fetch shrill ecchoes from the hollow earth.
  1 Man. Say thou wilt course, thy gray-hounds are as swift
As breathed Stags: I fleeter then the Roe.
  2 M. Dost thou loue pictures? we wil fetch thee strait
Adonis painted by a running brooke,
And *Citherea* all in sedges hid,
Which seeme to moue and wanton with her breath,
Euen as the wauing sedges play with winde.
  Lord. Wee'l shew thee *Io*, as she was a Maid,
And how she was beguiled and surpriz'd,
As liuelie painted, as the deede was done.
  3. Man. Or *Daphne* roming through a thornie wood,
Scratching her legs, that one shal sweare she bleeds,
And at that sight shal sad Apollo weepe,
So workmanlie the blood and teares are drawne.
  Lord. Thou art a Lord, and nothing but a Lord:
Thou hast a Ladie farre more Beautifull,
Then any woman in this waining age.
  1 Man. And til the teares that she hath shed for thee,
Like enuious flouds ore-run her louely face,
She was the fairest creature in the world,
And yet shee is inferiour to none.
  Beg. Am I a Lord, and haue I such a Ladie?
Or do I dreame? Or haue I dream'd till now?
I do not sleepe: I see, I heare, I speake:
I smel sweet sauours, and I feele soft things:
Vpon my life I am a Lord indeede,
And not a Tinker, nor Christopher Slie.
Well, bring our Ladie hither to our sight,
And once againe a pot o'th smallest Ale.

2. *Man.* Wilt please your mightinesse to wash your hands:
Oh how we ioy to see your wit restor'd,
Oh that once more you knew but what you are:
These fifteene yeeres you haue bin in a dreame,
Or when you wak'd, so wak'd as if you slept.

Beg. These fifteene yeeres, by my fay, a goodly nap,
But did I neuer speake of all that time.

1 *Man.* Oh yes my Lord, but verie idle words,
For though you lay heere in this goodlie chamber,
Yet would you say, ye were beaten out of doore,
And raile vpon the Hostesse of the house,
And say you would present her at the Leete,
Because she brought stone-Iugs, and no seal'd quarts:
Sometimes you would call out for Cicely Hacket.

Beg. I, the womans maide of the house.

3. *man.* Why sir you know no house, nor no such maid
Nor no such men as you haue reckon'd vp,
As *Stephen Slie*, and old *Iohn Naps* of Greece,
And *Peter Turph*, and *Henry Pimpernell*,
And twentie more such names and men as these,
Which neuer were, nor no man euer saw.

Beg. Now Lord be thanked for my good amends.
All. Amen.

Enter Lady with Attendants.

Beg. I thanke thee, thou shalt not loose by it.
Lady. How fares my noble Lord?
Beg. Marrie I fare well, for heere is cheere enough.
Where is my wife?
La. Heere noble Lord, what is thy will with her?
Beg. Are you my wife, and will not cal me husband?
My men should call me Lord, I am your good-man.
La. My husband and my Lord, my Lord and husband
I am your wife in all obedience.
Beg. I know it well, what must I call her?
Lord. Madam.
Beg. Alce Madam, or Ione Madam?
Lord. Madam, and nothing else, so Lords cal Ladies
Beg. Madame wife, they say that I haue dream'd,
And slept aboue some fifteene yeare or more.
Lady. I, and the time seeme's thirty vnto me,
Being all this time abandon'd from your bed.
Beg. 'Tis much, seruants leaue me and her alone:
Madam vndresse you, and come now to bed.
La. Thrice noble Lord, let me intreat of you
To pardon me yet for a night or two:
Or if not so, vntill the Sun be set.
For your Physitians haue expressely charg'd,
In perill to incurre your former malady,
That I should yet absent me from your bed:
I hope this reason stands for my excuse.
Beg. I, it stands so that I may hardly tarry so long:
But I would be loth to fall into my dreames againe: I
wil therefore tarrie in despight of the flesh & the blood

Enter a Messenger.

Mes. Your Honors Players hearing your amendment,
Are come to play a pleasant Comedie,
For so your doctors hold it very meete,
Seeing too much sadnesse hath congeal'd your blood,
And melancholly is the Nurse of frenzie,
Therefore they thought it good you heare a play,
And frame your minde to mirth and merriment,
Which barres a thousand harmes, and lengthens life.

Beg. Marrie I will let them play, it is not a Comon-tie, a Christmas gambold, or a tumbling tricke?
Lady. No my good Lord, it is more pleasing stuffe.
Beg. What, houshold stuffe.
Lady. It is a a kinde of history.
Beg. Well, we'l see't:
Come Madam wife sit by my side,
And let the world slip, we shall nere be yonger.

Flourish. Enter Lucentio, and his man Tranio.

Luc. *Tranio*, since for the great desire I had
To see faire *Padua*, nurserie of Arts,
I am arriu'd for fruitfull *Lumbardie*,
The pleasant garden of great *Italy*,
And by my fathers loue and leaue am arm'd
With his good will, and thy good companie.
My trustie seruant well approu'd in all,
Heere let vs breath, and haply institute
A course of Learning, and ingenious studies.
Pisa renowned for graue Citizens
Gaue me my being, and my father first
A Merchant of great Trafficke through the world:
Vincentio's come of the *Bentiuolij*,
Vincentio's sonne, brough vp in *Florence*,
It shall become to serue all hopes conceiu'd
To decke his fortune with his vertuous deedes:
And therefore *Tranio*, for the time I studie,
Vertue and that part of Philosophie
Will I applie, that treats of happinesse,
By vertue specially to be atchieu'd.
Tell me thy minde, for I haue *Pisa* left,
And am to *Padua* come, as he that leaues
A shallow plash, to plunge him in the deepe,
And with sacietie seekes to quench his thirst.

Tra. *Me Pardonato*, gentle master mine:
I am in all affected as your selfe,
Glad that you thus continue your resolue,
To sucke the sweets of sweete Philosophie.
Onely (good master) while we do admire
This vertue, and this morall discipline,
Let's be no Stoickes, nor no stockes I pray,
Or so deuote to *Aristotles* checkes
As *Ouid*; be an out-cast quite abiur'd:
Balke Lodgicke with acquaintaince that you haue,
And practise Rhetoricke in your common talke,
Musicke and Poesie vse, to quicken you,
The Mathematickes, and the Metaphysickes
Fall to them as you finde your stomacke serues you:
No profit growes, where is no pleasure tane:
In briefe sir, studie what you most affect.

Luc. Gramercies *Tranio*, well dost thou aduise,
If *Biondello* thou wert come ashore,
We could at once put vs in readinesse,
And take a Lodging fit to entertaine
Such friends (as time) in *Padua* shall beget.
But stay a while, what companie is this?

Tra. Master some shew to welcome vs to Towne.

Enter Baptista with his two daughters, Katerina & Bianca, Gremio a Pantelowne, Hortentio sister to Bianca. Lucen. Tranio, stand by.

Bap. Gentlemen, importune me no farther,
For how I firmly am resolu'd you know:
That is, not to bestow my yongest daughter,
Before I haue a husband for the elder:
If either of you both loue *Katherina*,

Because

Because I know you well, and loue you well,
Leaue shall you haue to court her at your pleasure.
 Gre. To cart her rather. She's to rough for mee,
There, there *Hortensio*, will you any Wife?
 Kate. I pray you sir, is it your will
To make a stale of me amongst these mates?
 Hor. Mates maid, how meane you that?
No mates for you,
Vnlesse you were of gentler milder mould.
 Kate. I'faith sir, you shall neuer neede to feare,
I-wis it is not halfe way to her heart:
But if it were, doubt not, her care should be,
To combe your noddle with a three-legg'd stoole,
And paint your face, and vse you like a foole.
 Hor. From all such diuels, good Lord deliuer vs.
 Gre. And me too, good Lord.
 Tra. Husht master, heres some good pastime toward;
That wench is starke mad, or wonderfull froward.
 Lucen. But in the others silence do I see,
Maids milde behauiour and sobrietie.
Peace *Tranio*.
 Tra. Well said Mr. mum, and gaze your fill.
 Bap. Gentlemen, that I may soone make good
What I haue said, *Bianca* get you in,
And let it not displease thee good *Bianca*,
For I will loue thee nere the lesse my girle.
 Kate. A pretty peate, it is best put finger in the eye,
and she knew why.
 Bian. Sister content you, in my discontent.
Sir, to your pleasure humbly I subscribe:
My bookes and instruments shall be my companie,
On them to looke, and practise by my selfe.
 Luc. Harke *Tranio*, thou maist heare *Minerua* speak.
 Hor. Signior *Baptista*, will you be so strange,
Sorrie am I that our good will effects
Bianca's greefe.
 Gre. Why will you mew her vp
(Signior *Baptista*) for this fiend of hell,
And make her beare the pennance of her tongue.
 Bap. Gentlemen content ye: I am resould:
Go in *Bianca*.
And for I know she taketh most delight
In Musicke, Instruments, and Poetry,
Schoolemasters will I keepe within my house,
Fit to instruct her youth. If you *Hortensio*,
Or signior *Gremio* you know any such,
Preferre them hither: for to cunning men,
I will be very kinde and liberall,
To mine owne children, in good bringing vp,
And so farewell: *Katherina* you may stay,
For I haue more to commune with *Bianca*. *Exit.*
 Kate. Why, and I trust I may go too, may I not?
What shall I be appointed houres, as though
(Belike) I knew not what to take,
And what to leaue? Ha. *Exit*
 Gre. You may go to the diuels dam: your guifts are
so good heere's none will holde you: Their loue is not
so great *Hortensio*, but we may blow our nails together,
and fast it fairely out. Our cakes dough on both sides.
Farewell: yet for the loue I beare my sweet *Bianca*, if
I can by any meanes light on a fit man to teach her that
wherein she delights, I will wish him to her father.
 Hor. So will I signiour *Gremio*: but a word I pray:
Though the nature of our quarrell yet neuer brook'd
parle, know now vpon aduice, it toucheth vs both: that
we may yet againe haue accesse to our faire Mistris, and
be happie riuals in *Bianca's* loue, to labour and effect
one thing specially.
 Gre. What's that I pray?
 Hor. Marrie sir to get a husband for her Sister.
 Gre. A husband: a diuell.
 Hor. I say a husband.
 Gre. I say, a diuell: Think'st thou *Hortensio*, though
her father be verie rich, any man is so verie a foole to be
married to hell?
 Hor. Tush *Gremio*: though it passe your patience &
mine to endure her lowd alarums, why man there bee
good fellowes in the world, and a man could light on
them, would take her with all faults, and mony enough.
 Gre. I cannot tell: but I had as lief take her dowrie
with this condition; To be whipt at the hie crosse euerie
morning.
 Hor. Faith (as you say) there's small choise in rotten
apples: but come, since this bar in law makes vs friends,
it shall be so farre forth friendly maintain'd, till by helping *Baptistas* eldest daughter to a husband, wee set his
yongest free for a husband, and then haue too t afresh:
Sweet *Bianca*, happy man be his dole: hee that runnes
fastest, gets the Ring: How say you signior *Gremio*?
 Grem. I am agreed, and would I had giuen him the
best horse in *Padua* to begin his woing that would thoroughly woe her, wed her, and bed her, and ridde the
house of her. Come on.

Exeunt ambo. Manet Tranio and Lucentio
 Tra. I pray sir tel me, is it possible
That loue should of a sodaine take such hold.
 Luc. Oh *Tranio*, till I found it to be true,
I neuer thought it possible or likely.
But see, while idely I stood looking on,
I found the effect of Loue in idlenesse,
And now in plainnesse do confesse to thee
That art to me as secret and as deere
As *Anna* to the Queene of Carthage was:
Tranio I burne, I pine, I perish *Tranio*,
If I atchieue not this yong modest gyrle:
Counsaile me *Tranio*, for I know thou canst:
Assist me *Tranio*, for I know thou wilt.
 Tra. Master, it is no time to chide you now,
Affection is not rated from the heart:
If loue haue touch'd you, naught remaines but so,
Redime te captam quam queas minimo.
 Luc. Gramercies Lad: Go forward, this contents,
The rest wil comfort, for thy counsels sound.
 Tra. Master, you look'd so longly on the maide,
Perhaps you mark'd not what's the pith of all.
 Luc. Oh yes, I saw sweet beautie in her face,
Such as the daughter of *Agenor* had,
That made great *Ioue* to humble him to her hand,
When with his knees he kist the Cretan strond.
 Tra. Saw you no more? Mark'd you not how hir sister
Began to scold, and raise vp such a storme,
That mortal eares might hardly indure the din.
 Luc. Tranio, I saw her corrall lips to moue,
And with her breath she did perfume the ayre,
Sacred and sweet was all I saw in her.
 Tra. Nay, then 'tis time to stirre him frō his trance:
I pray awake sir: if you loue the Maide,
Bend thoughts and wits to atcheeue her. Thus it stands:
Her elder sister is so curst and shrew'd,
That til the Father rid his hands of her,
Master, your Loue must liue a maide at home,
And therefore has he closely meu'd her vp,

Because

Because she will not be annoy'd with suters.

Luc. Ah *Tranio*, what a cruell Fathers he:
But art thou not aduis'd, he tooke some care
To get her cunning Schoolemasters to instruct her.

Tra. I marry am I sir, and now 'tis plotted.

Luc. I haue it *Tranio*.

Tra. Master, for my hand,
Both our inuentions meet and iumpe in one.

Luc. Tell me thine first.

Tra. You will be schoole-master,
And vndertake the teaching of the maid:
That's your deuice.

Luc. It is: May it be done?

Tra. Not possible: for who shall beare your part,
And be in *Padua* heere *Vincentio's* sonne,
Keepe house, and ply his booke, welcome his friends,
Visit his Countrimen, and banquet them?

Luc. Basta, content thee: for I haue it full.
We haue not yet bin seene in any house,
Nor can we be distinguish'd by our faces,
For man or master: then it followes thus;
Thou shalt be master, *Tranio* in my sted:
Keepe house, and port, and seruants, as I should,
I will some other be, some *Florentine*,
Some *Neapolitan*, or meaner man of *Pisa*.
'Tis hatch'd, and shall be so: *Tranio* at once
Vncase thee: take my Conlord hat and cloake,
When *Biondello* comes, he waites on thee,
But I will charme him first to keepe his tongue.

Tra. So had you neede:
In breefe Sir, sith it your pleasure is,
And I am tyed to be obedient,
For so your father charg'd me at our parting:
Be seruiceable to my sonne (quoth he)
Although I thinke 'twas in another sence,
I am content to bee *Lucentio*,
Because so well I loue *Lucentio*.

Luc. Tranio be so, because *Lucentio* loues,
And let me be a slaue, t'atchieue that maide,
Whose sodaine sight hath thral'd my wounded eye.

Enter Biondello.

Heere comes the rogue. Sirra, where haue you bin?

Bion. Where haue I beene? Nay how now, where
are you? Maister, ha's my fellow *Tranio* stolne your
cloathes, or you stolne his, or both? Pray what's the
newes?

Luc. Sirra come hither, 'tis no time to iest,
And therefore frame your manners to the time
Your fellow *Tranio* heere to saue my life,
Puts my apparrell, and my count'nance on,
And I for my escape haue put on his:
For in a quarrell since I came a-shore,
I kil'd a man, and feare I was descried:
Waite you on him, I charge you, as becomes:
While I make way from hence to saue my life:
You vnderstand me?

Bion. I sir, ne're a whit.

Luc. And not a iot of *Tranio* in your mouth,
Tranio is chang'd into *Lucentio*.

Bion. The better for him, would I were so too.

Tra. So could I 'faith boy, to haue the next wish after, that *Lucentio* indeede had *Baptistas* yongest daughter. But sirra, not for my sake, but your masters, I aduise you vse your manners discreetly in all kind of companies: When I am alone, why then I am *Tranio*: but in
all places else, you master *Lucentio*.

Luc. Tranio let's go:
One thing more rests, that thy selfe execute,
To make one among these wooers: if thou ask me why,
Sufficeth my reasons are both good and waighty.
Exeunt.   *The Presenters aboue speakes.*

1. *Man.* My Lord you nod, you do not minde the play.

Beg. Yes by Saint Anne do I, a good matter surely:
Comes there any more of it?

Lady. My Lord, 'tis but begun.

Beg. 'Tis a verie excellent peece of worke, Madame
Ladie: would 'twere done.   *They sit and marke.*

Enter Petruchio, and his man Grumio.

Petr. Verona, for a while I take my leaue,
To see my friends in *Padua*; but of all
My best beloued and approued friend
Hortensio: & I trow this is his house:
Heere sirra *Grumio*, knocke I say.

Gru. Knocke sir? whom should I knocke? Is there
any man ha's rebus'd your worship?

Petr. Villaine I say, knocke me heere soundly.

Gru. Knocke you heere sir? Why sir, what am I sir,
that I should knocke you heere sir.

Petr. Villaine I say, knocke me at this gate,
And rap me well, or Ile knocke your knaues pate.

Gru. My M'r is growne quarrelsome:
I should knocke you first,
And then I know after who comes by the worst.

Petr. Will it not be?
'Faith sirrah, and you'l not knocke, Ile ring it,
Ile trie how you can *Sol, Fa*, and sing it.
           He rings him by the eares

Gru. Helpe mistris helpe, my master is mad.

Petr. Now knocke when I bid you: sirrah villaine.

Enter Hortensio.

Hor. How now, what's the matter? My olde friend
Grumio, and my good friend *Petruchio*? How do you all
at *Verona*?

Petr. Signior *Hortensio*, come you to part the fray?
Contutti le core bene trobatto, may I say.

*Hor. Alla nostra casa bene venuto multo honorata signi-
or mio Petruchio*.
Rise *Grumio* rise, we will compound this quarrell.

Gru. Nay 'tis no matter sir, what he leges in Latine.
If this be not a lawfull cause for me to leaue his seruice,
looke you sir: He bid me knocke him, & rap him soundly sir. Well, was it fit for a seruant to vse his master so,
being perhaps (for ought I see) two and thirty, a peepe
out? Whom would to God I had well knockt at first,
then had not *Grumio* come by the worst.

Petr. A sencelesse villaine: good *Hortensio*,
I bad the rascall knocke vpon your gate,
And could not get him for my heart to do it.

Gru. Knocke at the gate? O heauens: spake you not
these words plaine? Sirra, Knocke me heere: rappe me
heere: knocke me well, and knocke me soundly? And
come you now with knocking at the gate?

Petr. Sirra be gone, or talke not I aduise you.

Hor. Petruchio patience, I am *Grumio's* pledge:
Why this a heauie chance twixt him and you,
Your ancient trustie pleasant seruant *Grumio*:
And tell me now (sweet friend) what happie gale
Blowes you to *Padua* heere, from old *Verona*?

Petr. Such wind as scatters yongmen throgh ȳ world,
                          To

To seeke their fortunes farther then at home,
Where small experience growes but in a few.
Signior *Hortensio*, thus it stands with me,
Antonio my father is deceast,
And I haue thrust my selfe into this maze,
Happily to wiue and thriue, as best I may:
Crownes in my purse I haue, and goods at home,
And so am come abroad to see the world.

Hor. *Petruchio*, shall I then come roundly to thee,
And wish thee to a shrew'd ill-fauour'd wife?
Thou'dst thanke me but a little for my counsell:
And yet Ile promise thee she shall be rich,
And verie rich: but th'art too much my friend,
And Ile not wish thee to her.

Petr. Signior *Hortensio*, 'twixt such friends as wee,
Few words suffice: and therefore, if thou know
One rich enough to be *Petruchio's* wife:
(As wealth is burthen of my woing dance)
Be she as foule as was *Florentius* Loue,
As old as *Sibell*, and as curst and shrow'd
As *Socrates Zentippe*, or a worse:
She moues me not, or not remoues at least
Affections edge in me. Were she is as rough
As are the swelling *Adriaticke* seas.
I come to wiue it wealthily in *Padua*:
If wealthily, then happily in *Padua*.

Gru. Nay looke you sir, hee tels you flatly what his
minde is: why giue him Gold enough, and marrie him
to a Puppet or an Aglet babie, or an old trot with ne're a
tooth in her head, though she haue as manie diseases as
two and fiftie horses. Why nothing comes amisse, so
monie comes withall.

Hor. *Petruchio*, since we are stept thus farre in,
I will continue that I broach'd in iest,
I can *Petruchio* helpe thee to a wife
With wealth enough, and yong and beautious,
Brought vp as best becomes a Gentlewoman.
Her onely fault, and that is faults enough,
Is, that she is intollerable curst,
And shrow'd, and froward, so beyond all measure,
That were my state farre worser then it is,
I would not wed her for a mine of Gold.

Petr. *Hortensio* peace: thou knowst not golds effect,
Tell me her fathers name, and 'tis enough:
For I will boord her, though she chide as loud
As thunder, when the clouds in Autumne cracke.

Hor. Her father is *Baptista Minola*,
An affable and courteous Gentleman,
Her name is *Katherina Minola*,
Renown'd in *Padua* for her scolding tongue.

Petr. I know her father, though I know not her,
And he knew my deceased father well:
I wil not sleepe *Hortensio* til I see her,
And therefore let me be thus bold with you,
To giue you ouer at this first encounter,
Vnlesse you wil accompanie me thither.

Gru. I pray you sir let him go while the humor lasts.
A my word, and she knew him as wel as I do, she would
thinke scolding would doe little good vpon him. Shee
may perhaps call him halfe a score Knaues, or so: Why
that's nothing; and he begin once, hee'l raile in his rope
trickes. Ile tell you what sir, and she stand him but a litle, he wil throw a figure in her face, and so disfigure hir
with it, that shee shal haue no more eies to see withall
then a Cat: you know him not sir.

Hor. Tarrie *Petruchio*, I must go with thee,
For in *Baptistas* keepe my treasure is:
He hath the Iewel of my life in hold,
His yongest daughter, beautiful *Bianca*,
And her with-holds from me. Other more
Suters to her, and riuals in my Loue:
Supposing it a thing impossible,
For those defects I haue before rehearst,
That euer *Katherina* wil be woo'd:
Therefore this order hath *Baptista* tane,
That none shal haue accesse vnto *Bianca*,
Til *Katherine* the Curst, haue got a husband.

Gru. *Katherine* the curst,
A title for a maide, of all titles the worst.

Hor. Now shal my friend *Petruchio* do me grace,
And offer me disguis'd in sober robes,
To old *Baptista* as a schoole-master
Well seene in Musicke, to instruct *Bianca*,
That so I may by this deuice at least
Haue leaue and leisure to make loue to her,
And vnsuspected court her by her selfe.

Enter Gremio and Lucentio disguised.

Gru. Heere's no knauerie. See, to beguile the olde-
folkes, how the young folkes lay their heads together.
Master, master, looke about you: Who goes there? ha.

Hor. Peace *Grumio*, it is the riuall of my Loue,
Petruchio stand by a while.

Grumio. A proper stripling, and an amorous.

Gremio. O very well, I haue perus'd the note:
Hearke you sir, Ile haue them verie fairely bound,
All bookes of Loue, see that at any hand,
And see you reade no other Lectures to her:
You vnderstand me. Ouer and beside
Signior *Baptistas* liberalitie,
Ile mend it with a Largesse. Take your paper too,
And let me haue them verie wel perfum'd;
For she is sweeter then perfume it selfe
To whom they go to: what wil you reade to her.

Luc. What ere I reade to her, Ile pleade for you,
As for my patron, stand you so assur'd,
As firmely as your selfe were still in place,
Yea and perhaps with more successefull words
Then you; vnlesse you were a scholler sir.

Gre. Oh this learning, what a thing it is.

Gru. Oh this Woodcocke, what an Asse it is.

Petru. Peace sirra.

Hor. *Grumio* mum: God saue you signior *Gremio*.

Gre. And you are wel met, Signior *Hortensio*.
Trow you whither I am going? To *Baptista Minola*,
I promist to enquire carefully
About a schoolemaster for the faire *Bianca*,
And by good fortune I haue lighted well
On this yong man: For learning and behauiour
Fit for her turne, well read in Poetrie
And other bookes, good ones, I warrant ye.

Hor. 'Tis well: and I haue met a Gentleman
Hath promist me to helpe one to another,
A fine Musitian to instruct our Mistris,
So shal I no whit be behinde in dutie
To faire *Bianca*, so beloued of me.

Gre. Beloued of me, and that my deeds shal proue.

Gru. And that his bags shal proue.

Hor. *Gremio*, 'tis now no time to vent our loue,
Listen to me, and if you speake me faire,
Ile tel you newes indifferent good for either.
Heere is a Gentleman whom by chance I met

Vpon agreement from vs to his liking,
Will vndertake to woo curst *Katherine*,
Yea, and to marrie her, if her dowrie please.

  Gre. So said, so done, is well:
Hortensio, haue you told him all her faults?

  Petr. I know she is an irkesome brawling scold:
If that be all Masters, I heare no harme.

  Gre. No, sayst me so, friend? What Countreyman?

  Petr. Borne in *Verona*, old *Butonios* sonne:
My father dead, my fortune liues for me,
And I do hope, good dayes and long, to see.

  Gre. Oh sir, such a life with such a wife, were strange:
But if you haue a stomacke, too't a Gods name,
You shal haue me assisting you in all.
But will you woo this Wilde-cat?

  Petr. Will I liue?

  Gru. Wil he woo her? I: or Ile hang her.

  Petr. Why came I hither, but to that intent?
Thinke you, a little dinne can daunt mine eares?
Haue I not in my time heard Lions rore?
Haue I not heard the sea, puft vp with windes,
Rage like an angry Boare, chafed with sweat?
Haue I not heard great Ordnance in the field?
And heauens Artillerie thunder in the skies?
Haue I not in a pitched battell heard
Loud larums, neighing steeds, & trumpets clangue?
And do you tell me of a womans tongue?
That giues not halfe so great a blow to heare,
As wil a Chesse-nut in a Farmers fire.
Tush, tush, feare boyes with bugs.

  Gru. For he feares none.

  Grem. Hortensio hearke:
This Gentleman is happily arriu'd,
My minde presumes for his owne good, and yours.

  Hor. I promist we would be Contributors,
And beare his charge of wooing whatsoere.

  Gremio. And so we wil, prouided that he win her.

  Gru. I would I were as sure of a good dinner.

  Enter Tranio braue, and Biondello.

  Tra. Gentlemen God saue you. If I may be bold
Tell me I beseech you, which is the readiest way
To the house of Signior *Baptista Minola*?

  Bion. He that ha's the two faire daughters: ist he you
meane?

  Tra. Euen he *Biondello*.

  Gre. Hearke you sir, you meane not her to———

  Tra. Perhaps him and her sir, what haue you to do?

  Petr. Not her that chides sir, at any hand I pray.

  Tranio. I loue no chiders sir: *Biondello*, let's away.

  Luc. Well begun *Tranio*.

  Hor. Sir, a word ere you go:
Are you a sutor to the Maid you talke of, yea or no?

  Tra. And if I be sir, is it any offence?

  Gremio. No: if without more words you will get you
hence.

  Tra. Why sir, I pray are not the streets as free
For me, as for you?

  Gre. But so is not she.

  Tra. For what reason I beseech you.

  Gre. For this reason if you'l kno,
That she's the choise loue of Signior *Gremio*.

  Hor. That she's the chosen of signior *Hortensio*.

  Tra. Softly my Masters: If you be Gentlemen
Do me this right: heare me with patience.
Baptista is a noble Gentleman,

To whom my Father is not all vnknowne,
And were his daughter fairer then she is,
She may more sutors haue, and me for one.
Faire *Ledaes* daughter had a thousand wooers,
Then well one more may faire *Bianca* haue;
And so she shall: *Lucentio* shal make one,
Though *Paris* came, in hope to speed alone.

  Gre. What, this Gentleman will out-talke vs all.

  Luc. Sir giue him head, I know hee'l proue a Iade.

  Petr. Hortensio, to what end are all these words?

  Hor. Sir, let me be so bold as aske you,
Did you yet euer see *Baptistas* daughter?

  Tra. No sir, but heare I do that he hath two:
The one, as famous for a scolding tongue,
As is the other, for beauteous modestie.

  Petr. Sir, sir, the first's for me, let her go by.

  Gre. Yea, leaue that labour to great *Hercules*,
And let it be more then *Alcides* twelue.

  Petr. Sir vnderstand you this of me (insooth)
The yongest daughter whom you hearken for,
Her father keepes from all accesse of sutors,
And will not promise her to any man,
Vntill the elder sister first be wed.
The yonger then is free, and not before.

  Tranio. If it be so sir, that you are the man
Must steed vs all, and me amongst the rest:
And if you breake the ice, and do this seeke,
Atchieue the elder: set the yonger free,
For our accesse, whose hap shall be to haue her,
Wil not so gracelesse be, to be ingrate.

  Hor. Sir you say wel, and wel you do conceiue,
And since you do professe to be a sutor,
You must as we do, gratifie this Gentleman,
To whom we all rest generally beholding.

  Tranio. Sir, I shal not be slacke, in signe whereof,
Please ye we may contriue this afternoone,
And quaffe carowses to our Mistresse health,
And do as aduersaries do in law,
Striue mightily, but eate and drinke as friends.

  Gru. Bion. Oh excellent motion: fellowes let's be gon.

  Hor. The motions good indeed, and be it so,
Petruchio, I shal be your *Been venuto*.   *Exeunt.*

  Enter Katherina and Bianca.

  Bian. Good sister wrong me not, nor wrong your self,
To make a bondmaide and a slaue of mee,
That I disdaine: but for these other goods,
Vnbinde my hands, Ile pull them off my selfe,
Yea all my raiment, to my petticoate,
Or what you will command me, wil I do,
So well I know my dutie to my elders.

  Kate. Of all thy sutors heere I charge tel
Whom thou lou'st best: see thou dissemble not.

  Bianca. Beleeue me sister, of all the men aliue,
I neuer yet beheld that speciall face,
Which I could fancie, more then any other.

  Kate. Minion thou lyest: Is't not *Hortensio*?

  Bian. If you affect him sister, heere I sweare
Ile pleade for you my selfe, but you shal haue him.

  Kate. Oh then belike you fancie riches more,
You wil haue *Gremio* to keepe you faire.

  Bian. Is it for him you do enuie me so?
Nay then you iest, and now I wel perceiue
You haue but iested with me all this while:
I prethee sister *Kate*, vntie my hands.

  Ka. If that be iest, then all the rest was so.   *Strikes her*
Enter

Enter Baptista.

Bap. Why how now Dame, whence growes this infolence?
Bianca stand aside, poore gyrle she weepes:
Go ply thy Needle, meddle not with her.
For shame thou Hilding of a diuellish spirit,
Why dost thou wrong her, that did nere wrong thee?
When did she crosse thee with a bitter word?

Kate. Her silence flouts me, and Ile be reueng'd.
Flies after Bianca

Bap. What in my sight? *Bianca* get thee in. *Exit.*

Kate. What will you not suffer me: Nay now I see
She is your treasure, she must haue a husband,
I must dance bare-foot on her wedding day,
And for your loue to her, leade Apes in hell.
Talke not to me, I will go sit and weepe,
Till I can finde occasion of reuenge.

Bap. Was euer Gentleman thus greeu'd as I?
But who comes heere.

*Enter Gremio, Lucentio, in the habit of a meane man,
Petruchio with Tranio, with his boy
bearing a Lute and Bookes.*

Gre. Good morrow neighbour *Baptista.*

Bap. Good morrow neighbour *Gremio*: God saue you Gentlemen.

Pet. And you good sir: pray haue you not a daughter, cal'd *Katerina*, faire and vertuous.

Bap. I haue a daughter sir, cal'd *Katerina*.

Gre. You are too blunt, go to it orderly.

Pet. You wrong me signior *Gremio*, giue me leaue.
I am a Gentleman of *Verona* sir,
That hearing of her beautie, and her wit,
Her affability and bashfull modestie:
Her wondrous qualities, and milde behauiour,
Am bold to shew my selfe a forward guest
Within your house, to make mine eye the witnesse
Of that report, which I so oft haue heard,
And for an entrance to my entertainment,
I do present you with a man of mine
Cunning in Musicke, and the Mathematickes,
To instruct her fully in those sciences,
Whereof I know she is not ignorant,
Accept of him, or else you do me wrong.
His name is *Litio*, borne in *Mantua*.

Bap. Y'are welcome sir, and he for your good sake.
But for my daughter *Katerine*, this I know,
She is not for your turne, the more my greefe.

Pet. I see you do not meane to part with her,
Or else you like not of my companie.

Bap. Mistake me not, I speake but as I finde,
Whence are you sir? What may I call your name.

Pet. Petruchio is my name, *Antonio's* sonne,
A man well knowne throughout all Italy.

Bap. I know him well: you are welcome for his sake.

Gre. Sauing your tale *Petruchio*, I pray let vs that are poore petitioners speake too? *Bacare*, you are meruaylous forward.

Pet. Oh, Pardon me signior *Gremio*, I would faine be doing.

Gre. I doubt it not sir. But you will curse
Your wooing neighbors: this is a guift
Very gratefull, I am sure of it, to expresse
The like kindnesse my selfe, that haue beene
More kindely beholding to you then any:
Freely giue vnto this yong Scholler, that hath
Beene long studying at *Rhemes*, as cunning
In Greeke, Latine, and other Languages,
As the other in Musicke and Mathematickes:
His name is *Cambio*: pray accept his seruice.

Bap. A thousand thankes signior *Gremio*:
Welcome good *Cambio*. But gentle sir,
Me thinkes you walke like a stranger,
May I be so bold, to know the cause of your comming?

Tra. Pardon me sir, the boldnesse is mine owne,
That being a stranger in this Cittie heere,
Do make my selfe a sutor to your daughter,
Vnto *Bianca*, faire and vertuous:
Nor is your firme resolue vnknowne to me,
In the preferment of the eldest sister.
This liberty is all that I request,
That vpon knowledge of my Parentage,
I may haue welcome 'mongst the rest that woo,
And free accesse and fauour as the rest.
And toward the education of your daughters:
I heere bestow a simple instrument,
And this small packet of Greeke and Latine bookes:
If you accept them, then their worth is great:

Bap. Lucentio is your name, of whence I pray.

Tra. Of *Pisa* sir, sonne to *Vincentio*.

Bap. A mightie man of *Pisa* by report,
I know him well: you are verie welcome sir:
Take you the Lute, and you the set of bookes,
You shall go see your Pupils presently.
Holla, within.

Enter a Seruant.
Sirrah, leade these Gentlemen
To my daughters, and tell them both
These are their Tutors, bid them vse them well,
We will go walke a little in the Orchard,
And then to dinner: you are passing welcome,
And so I pray you all to thinke your selues.

Pet. Signior *Baptista*, my businesse asketh haste,
And euerie day I cannot come to woo,
You knew my father well, and in him me,
Left solie heire to all his Lands and goods,
Which I haue bettered rather then decreast,
Then tell me, if I get your daughters loue,
What dowrie shall I haue with her to wife.

Bap. After my death, the one halfe of my Lands,
And in possession twentie thousand Crownes.

Pet. And for that dowrie, Ile assure her of
Her widdow-hood, be it that she suruiue me
In all my Lands and Leases whatsoeuer,
Let specialties be therefore drawne betweene vs,
That couenants may be kept on either hand.

Bap. I, when the speciall thing is well obtain'd,
That is her loue: for that is all in all.

Pet. Why that is nothing: for I tell you father,
I am as peremptorie as she proud minded:
And where two raging fires meete together,
They do consume the thing that feedes their furie.
Though little fire growes great with little winde,
Yet extreme gusts will blow out fire and all:
So I to her, and so she yeelds to me,
For I am rough, and woo not like a babe.

Bap. Well maist thou woo, and happy be thy speed:
But be thou arm'd for some vnhappie words.

Pet. I to the proofe, as Mountaines are for windes,
That shakes not, though they blow perpetually.

Enter Hortensio with his head broke.

Bap. How now my friend, why dost thou looke so pale?

Hor. For feare I promise you, if I looke pale.

Bap. What, will my daughter proue a good Musitian?

Hor. I thinke she'l sooner proue a souldier, Iron may hold with her, but neuer Lutes.

Bap. Why then thou canst not break her to the Lute?

Hor. Why no, for she hath broke the Lute to me:
I did but tell her she mistooke her frets,
And bow'd her hand to teach her fingering,
When (with a most impatient diuellish spirit)
Frets call you these? (quoth she) Ile fume with them:
And with that word she stroke me on the head,
And through the instrument my pate made way,
And there I stood amazed for a while,
As on a Pillorie, looking through the Lute,
While she did call me Rascall, Fidler,
And twangling Iacke, with twentie such vilde tearmes,
As had she studied to misvse me so.

Pet. Now by the world, it is a lustie Wench,
I loue her ten times more then ere I did,
Oh how I long to haue some chat with her.

Bap. Wel go with me, and be not so discomfited.
Proceed in practise with my yonger daughter,
She's apt to learne, and thankefull for good turnes:
Signior *Petruchio*, will you go with vs,
Or shall I send my daughter *Kate* to you.
Exit. Manet Petruchio.

Pet. I pray you do. Ile attend her heere,
And woo her with some spirit when she comes,
Say that she raile, why then Ile tell her plaine,
She sings as sweetly as a Nightinghale:
Say that she frowne, Ile say she lookes as cleere
As morning Roses newly washt with dew:
Say she be mute, and will not speake a word,
Then Ile commend her volubility,
And say she vttereth piercing eloquence:
If she do bid me packe, Ile giue her thankes,
As though she bid me stay by her a weeke:
If she denie to wed, Ile craue the day
When I shall aske the banes, and when be married.
But heere she comes, and now *Petruchio* speake.

Enter Katerina.

Good morrow *Kate*, for thats your name I heare.

Kate. Well haue you heard, but something hard of hearing:
They call me *Katerine*, that do talke of me.

Pet. You lye infaith, for you are call'd plaine *Kate*,
And bony *Kate*, and sometimes *Kate* the curst:
But *Kate*, the prettiest *Kate* in Christendome,
Kate of *Kate*-hall, my super-daintie *Kate*,
For dainties are all *Kates*, and therefore *Kate*
Take this of me, *Kate* of my consolation,
Hearing thy mildnesse prais'd in euery Towne,
Thy vertues spoke of, and thy beautie sounded,
Yet not so deepely as to thee belongs,
My selfe am moou'd to woo thee for my wife.

Kate. Mou'd, in good time, let him that mou'd you hether
Remoue you hence: I knew you at the first
You were a moueable.

Pet. Why, what's a moueable?

Kat. A ioyn'd stoole.

Pet. Thou hast hit it: come sit on me.

Kate. Asses are made to beare, and so are you.

Pet. Women are made to beare, and so are you.

Kate. No such Iade as you, if me you meane.

Pet. Alas good *Kate*, I will not burthen thee,
For knowing thee to be but yong and light.

Kate. Too light for such a swaine as you to catch,
And yet as heauie as my waight should be.

Pet. Shold be, should: buzze.

Kate. Well tane, and like a buzzard.

Pet. Oh slow-wing'd Turtle, shal a buzard take thee?

Kat. I for a Turtle, as he takes a buzard.

Pet. Come, come you Waspe, y'faith you are too angrie.

Kate. If I be waspish, best beware my sting.

Pet. My remedy is then to plucke it out.

Kate. I, if the foole could finde it where it lies.

Pet. Who knowes not where a Waspe does weare his sting? In his taile.

Kate. In his tongue?

Pet. Whose tongue.

Kate. Yours if you talke of tales, and so farewell.

Pet. What with my tongue in your taile.
Nay, come againe, good *Kate*, I am a Gentleman.

Kate. That Ile trie. *she strikes him*

Pet. I sweare Ile cuffe you, if you strike againe.

Kate. So may you loose your armes,
If you strike me, you are no Gentleman,
And if no Gentleman, why then no armes.

Pet. A Herald *Kate*? Oh put me in thy bookes.

Kate. What is your Crest, a Coxcombe?

Pet. A comblesse Cocke, so *Kate* will be my Hen.

Kate. No Cocke of mine, you crow too like a crauen

Pet. Nay come *Kate*, come: you must not looke so sowre.

Kate. It is my fashion when I see a Crab.

Pet. Why heere's no crab, and therefore looke not sowre.

Kate. There is, there is.

Pet. Then shew it me.

Kate. Had I a glasse, I would.

Pet. What, you meane my face.

Kate. Well aym'd of such a yong one.

Pet. Now by S. George I am too yong for you.

Kate. Yet you are wither'd.

Pet. 'Tis with cares.

Kate. I care not.

Pet. Nay heare you *Kate*. Insooth you scape not so.

Kate. I chafe you if I tarrie. Let me go.

Pet. No, not a whit, I finde you passing gentle:
'Twas told me you were rough, and coy, and sullen,
And now I finde report a very liar:
For thou art pleasant, gamesome, passing courteous,
But slow in speech: yet sweet as spring-time flowers.
Thou canst not frowne, thou canst not looke a sconce,
Nor bite the lip, as angry wenches will,
Nor hast thou pleasure to be crosse in talke:
But thou with mildnesse entertain'st thy wooers,
With gentle conference, soft, and affable.
Why does the world report that *Kate* doth limpe?
Oh sland'rous world: *Kate* like the hazle twig
Is straight, and slender, and as browne in hue
As hazle nuts, and sweeter then the kernels:
Oh let me see thee walke: thou dost not halt.

Kate. Go foole, and whom thou keep'st command.

Pet. Did euer *Dian* so become a Groue
As *Kate* this chamber with her princely gate:
O be thou *Dian*, and let her be *Kate*,

And

The Taming of the Shrew. 217

And then let *Kate* be chaste, and *Dian* sportfull.
Kate. Where did you study all this goodly speech?
Petr. It is *extempore*, from my mother wit.
Kate. A witty mother, witlesse else her sonne.
Pet. Am I not wise?
Kat. Yes, keepe you warme.
Pet. Marry so I meane sweet *Katherine* in thy bed:
And therefore setting all this chat aside,
Thus in plaine termes: your father hath consented
That you shall be my wife; your dowry greed on,
And will you, nill you, I will marry you.
Now *Kate*, I am a husband for your turne,
For by this light, whereby I see thy beauty,
Thy beauty that doth make me like thee well,
Thou must be married to no man but me,

Enter Baptista, Gremio, Trayno.

For I am he am borne to tame you *Kate*,
And bring you from a wilde *Kate* to a *Kate*
Conformable as other houshold *Kates*:
Heere comes your father, neuer make deniall,
I must, and will haue *Katherine* to my wife. (daughter?
Bap. Now Signior *Petruchio*, how speed you with my
Pet. How but well sir? how but well?
It were impossible I should speed amisse. (dumps?
Bap. Why how now daughter *Katherine*, in your
Kat. Call you me daughter? now I promise you
You haue shewd a tender fatherly regard,
To wish me wed to one halfe Lunaticke,
A mad-cap ruffian, and a swearing Iacke,
That thinkes with oathes to face the matter out.
Pet. Father, 'tis thus, your selfe and all the world
That talk'd of her, haue talk'd amisse of her:
If she be curst, it is for pollicie,
For shee's not froward, but modest as the Doue,
Shee is not hot, but temperate as the morne,
For patience shee will proue a second *Grissell*,
And Romane *Lucrece* for her chastitie:
And to conclude, we haue greed so well together,
That vpon sonday is the wedding day.
Kate. Ile see thee hang'd on sonday first. (first.
Gre. Hark *Petruchio*, she saies shee'll see thee hang'd
Tra. Is this your speeding? nay thē godnight our part.
Pet. Be patient gentlemen, I choose her for my selfe,
If she and I be pleas'd, what's that to you?
'Tis bargain'd twixt vs twaine being alone,
That she shall still be curst in company.
I tell you 'tis incredible to beleeue
How much she loues me: oh the kindest *Kate*,
Shee hung about my necke, and kisse on kisse
Shee vi'd so fast, protesting oath on oath,
That in a twinke she won me to her loue.
Oh you are nouices, 'tis a world to see
How tame when men and women are alone,
A meacocke wretch can make the curstest shrew:
Giue me thy hand *Kate*, I will vnto *Venice*
To buy apparell 'gainst the wedding day;
Prouide the feast father, and bid the guests,
I will be sure my *Katherine* shall be fine.
Bap. I know not what to say, but giue me your hāds,
God send you ioy, *Petruchio*, 'tis a match.
Gre. Tra. Amen say we, we will be witnesses.
Pet. Father, and wife, and gentlemen adieu,
I will to *Venice*, sonday comes apace,
We will haue rings, and things, and fine array,
And kisse me *Kate*, we will be married a sonday.
    Exit Petruchio and Katherine.
Gre. Was euer match clapt vp so sodainly?
Bap. Faith Gentlemen now I play a marchants part,
And venture madly on a desperate Mart.
Tra. Twas a commodity lay fretting by you,
'Twill bring you gaine, or perish on the seas.
Bap. The gaine I seeke, is quiet me the match.
Gre. No doubt but he hath got a quiet catch:
But now *Baptista*, to your yonger daughter,
Now is the day we long haue looked for,
I am your neighbour, and was suter first.
Tra. And I am one that loue *Bianca* more
Then words can witnesse, or your thoughts can guesse.
Gre. Yongling thou canst not loue so deare as I.
Tra. Gray-beard thy loue doth freeze.
Gre. But thine doth frie,
Skipper stand backe, 'tis age that nourisheth.
Tra. But youth in Ladies eyes that florisheth.
Bap. Content you gentlemen, I wil cōpound this strife
'Tis deeds must win the prize, and he of both
That can assure my daughter greatest dower,
Shall haue my *Biancas* loue.
Say signior *Gremio*, what can you assure her?
Gre. First, as you know, my house within the City
Is richly furnished with plate and gold,
Basons and ewers to laue her dainty hands:
My hangings all of *tirian* tapestry:
In Iuory cofers I haue stuft my crownes:
In Cypres chests my arras counterpoints,
Costly apparell, tents, and Canopies,
Fine Linnen, Turky cushions bost with pearle,
Vallens of Venice gold, in needle worke:
Pewter and brasse, and all things that belongs
To house or house-keeping: then at my farme
I haue a hundred milch-kine to the pale,
Sixe-score fat Oxen standing in my stalls,
And all things answerable to this portion.
My selfe am strooke in yeeres I must confesse,
And if I die to morrow this is hers,
If whil'st I liue she will be onely mine.
Tra. That only came well in: sir, list to me,
I am my fathers heyre and onely sonne,
If I may haue your daughter to my wife,
Ile leaue her houses three or foure as good
Within rich *Pisa* walls, as any one
Old Signior *Gremio* has in *Padua*,
Besides, two thousand Duckets by the yeere
Of fruitfull land, all which shall be her ioynter.
What, haue I pincht you Signior *Gremio*?
Gre. Two thousand Duckets by the yeere of land,
My Land amounts not to so much in all:
That she shall haue, besides an Argosie
That now is lying in Marcellus roade:
What, haue I choakt you with an Argosie?
Tra. Gremio, 'tis knowne my father hath no lesse
Then three great Argosies, besides two Galliasses
And twelue tire Gallies, these I will assure her,
And twice as much what ere thou offrest next.
Gre. Nay, I haue offred all, I haue no more,
And she can haue no more then all I haue,
If you like me, she shall haue me and mine.
Tra. Why then the maid is mine from all the world
By your firme promise, *Gremio* is out-vied.
Bap. I must confesse your offer is the best,
And let your father make her the assurance,

T   Shee

Shee is your owne, else you must pardon me:
If you should die before him, where's her dower?

Tra. That's but a cauill: he is olde, I young.

Gre. And may not yong men die as well as old?

Bap. Well gentlemen, I am thus resolu'd,
On sonday next, you know
My daughter *Katherine* is to be married:
Now on the sonday following, shall *Bianca*
Be Bride to you, if you make this assurance:
If not, to Signior *Gremio*:
And so I take my leaue, and thanke you both. *Exit.*

Gre. Adieu good neighbour: now I feare thee not:
Sirra, yong gamester, your father were a foole
To giue thee all, and in his wayning age
Set foot vnder thy table: tut, a toy,
An olde Italian foxe is not so kinde my boy. *Exit.*

Tra. A vengeance on your crafty withered hide,
Yet I haue fac'd it with a card of ten:
'Tis in my head to doe my master good:
I see no reason but suppos'd *Lucentio*
Must get a father, call'd suppos'd *Vincentio*,
And that's a wonder: fathers commonly
Doe get their children: but in this case of woing,
A childe shall get a sire, if I faile not of my cunning. *Exit.*

Actus Tertia.

Enter Lucentio, Hortentio, and Bianca.

Luc. Fidler forbeare, you grow too forward Sir,
Haue you so soone forgot the entertainment
Her sister *Katherine* welcom'd you withall.

Hort. But wrangling pedant, this is
The patronesse of heauenly harmony:
Then giue me leaue to haue prerogatiue,
And when in Musicke we haue spent an houre,
Your Lecture shall haue leisure for as much.

Luc. Preposterous Asse that neuer read so farre,
To know the cause why musicke was ordain'd:
Was it not to refresh the minde of man
After his studies, or his vsuall paine?
Then giue me leaue to read Philosophy,
And while I pause, serue in your harmony.

Hort. Sirra, I will not beare these braues of thine.

Bianc. Why gentlemen, you doe me double wrong,
To striue for that which resteth in my choice:
I am no breeching scholler in the schooles,
Ile not be tied to howres, nor pointed times,
But learne my Lessons as I please my selfe,
And to cut off all strife: heere sit we downe,
Take you your instrument, play you the whiles,
His Lecture will be done ere you haue tun'd.

Hort. You'll leaue his Lecture when I am in tune?

Luc. That will be neuer, tune your instrument.

Bian. Where left we last?

Luc. Heere Madam: *Hic Ibat Simois, hic est sigeria tellus, hic steterat Priami regia Celsa senis.*

Bian. Conster them.

Luc. Hic Ibat, as I told you before, *Simois,* I am Lucentio, *hic est,* sonne vnto Vincentio of Pisa, *Sigeria tellus,* disguised thus to get your loue, *hic steterat,* and that Lucentio that comes a wooing, *priami,* is my man Tranio, *regia,* bearing my port, *celsa senis* that we might beguile the old Pantalowne.

Hort. Madam, my Instrument's in tune.

Bian. Let's heare, oh fie, the treble iarres.

Luc. Spit in the hole man, and tune againe.

Bian. Now let mee see if I can conster it. *Hic ibat simois,* I know you not, *hic est sigeria tellus,* I trust you not, *hic staterat priami,* take heede he heare vs not, *regia* presume not, *Celsa senis,* despaire not.

Hort. Madam, tis now in tune.

Luc. All but the base.

Hort. The base is right, 'tis the base knaue that iars.

Luc. How fiery and forward our Pedant is,
Now for my life the knaue doth court my loue,
Pedascule, Ile watch you better yet:
In time I may beleeue, yet I mistrust.

Bian. Mistrust it not, for sure *Æacides*
Was *Aiax* cald so from his grandfather.

Hort. I must beleeue my master, else I promise you,
I should be arguing still vpon that doubt,
But let it rest, now *Litio* to you:
Good master take it not vnkindly pray
That I haue beene thus pleasant with you both.

Hort. You may go walk, and giue me leaue a while,
My Lessons make no musicke in three parts.

Luc. Are you so formall sir, well I must waite
And watch withall, for but I be deceiu'd,
Our fine Musitian groweth amorous.

Hor. Madam, before you touch the instrument,
To learne the order of my fingering,
I must begin with rudiments of Art,
To teach you gamoth in a briefer sort,
More pleasant, pithy, and effectuall,
Then hath beene taught by any of my trade,
And there it is in writing fairely drawne.

Bian. Why, I am past my gamouth long agoe.

Hor. Yet read the gamouth of *Hortentio.*

Bian. Gamouth I am, the ground of all accord:
Are, to plead *Hortensio*'s passion:
Beeme, Bianca take him for thy Lord
Cfavt, that loues with all affection:
D solre, one Cliffe, two notes haue I,
Ela mi, show pitty or I die.
Call you this gamouth? tut I like it not,
Old fashions please me best, I am not so nice
To charge true rules for old inuentions.

Enter a Messenger.

Nicke. Mistresse, your father prayes you leaue your books,
And helpe to dresse your sisters chamber vp,
You know to morrow is the wedding day.

Bian. Farewell sweet masters both, I must be gone.

Luc. Faith Mistresse then I haue no cause to stay.

Hor. But I haue cause to pry into this pedant,
Methinkes he lookes as though he were in loue:
Yet if thy thoughts *Bianca* be so humble
To cast thy wandring eyes on euery stale:
Seize thee that List, if once I finde thee ranging,
Hortensio will be quit with thee by changing. *Exit.*

Enter Baptista, Gremio, Tranio, Katherine, Bianca, and others, attendants.

Bap. Signior *Lucentio,* this is the pointed day
That *Katherine* and *Petruchio* should be married,
And yet we heare not of our sonne in Law:
What will be said, what mockery will it be?
To want the Bride-groome when the Priest attends
To speake the ceremoniall rites of marriage?
What saies *Lucentio* to this shame of ours?

Kate. No shame but mine, I must forsooth be forst
To giue my hand oppos'd against my heart
Vnto a mad-braine rudesby, full of spleene,
Who woo'd in haste, and meanes to wed at leysure:
I told you I, he was a franticke foole,
Hiding his bitter iests in blunt behauiour,
And to be noted for a merry man;
Hee'll wooe a thousand, point the day of marriage,
Make friends, inuite, and proclaime the banes,
Yet neuer meanes to wed where he hath woo'd:
Now must the world point at poore *Katherine*,
And say, loe, there is mad *Petruchio's* wife
If it would please him come and marry her.

Tra. Patience good *Katherine* and *Baptista* too,
Vpon my life *Petruchio* meanes but well,
Whateuer fortune stayes him from his word,
Though he be blunt, I know him passing wise,
Though he be merry, yet withall he 's honest.

Kate. Would *Katherine* had neuer seene him though.
Exit weeping.

Bap. Goe girle, I cannot blame thee now to weepe,
For such an iniurie would vexe a very saint,
Much more a shrew of impatient humour.

Enter Biondello.

Bion. Master, master, newes, and such newes as you neuer heard of,

Bap. Is it new and olde too? how may that be?

Bion. Why, is it not newes to heard of *Petruchio's*

Bap. Is he come? *(comming?*

Bion. Why no sir.

Bap. What then?

Bion. He is comming.

Bap. When will he be heere?

Bion. When he stands where I am, and sees you there.

Tra. But say, what to thine olde newes?

Bion. Why *Petruchio* is comming, in a new hat and an old ierkin, a paire of olde breeches thrice turn'd; a paire of bootes that haue beene candle-cases, one buckled, another lac'd: an olde rusty sword tane out of the Towne Armory, with a broken hilt, and chapelesse: with two broken points: his horse hip'd with an olde mothy saddle, and stirrops of no kindred: besides possest with the glanders, and like to mose in the chine, troubled with the Lampasse, infected with the fashions, full of Windegalls, sped with Spauins, raied with the Yellowes, past cure of the Fiues, starke spoyl'd with the Staggers, begnawne with the Bots, Waid in the backe, and shoulder-shotten, neere leg'd before, and with a halfe-chekt Bitte, & a headstall of sheepes leather, which being restrain'd to keepe him from stumbling, hath been often burst, and now repaired with knots: one girth sixe times peec'd, and a womans Crupper of velure, which hath two letters for her-name, fairely set down in studs, and heere and there peec'd with packthred.

Bap. Who comes with him?

Bion. Oh sir, his Lackey, for all the world Caparison'd like the horse: with a linnen stock on one leg, and a kersey boot-hose on the other, gartred with a red and blew list; an old hat, & the humor of forty fancies prickt in't for a feather: a monster, a very monster in apparell, & not like a Christian foot-boy, or a gentlemans Lacky.

Tra. 'Tis some od humor pricks him to this fashion,
Yet oftentimes he goes but meane apparel'd.

Bap. I am glad he's come, howsoere he comes.

Bion. Why sir, he comes not.

Bap. Didst thou not say hee comes?

Bion. Who, that *Petruchio* came?

Bap. I, that *Petruchio* came. *(backe.*

Bion. No sir, I say his horse comes with him on his

Bap. Why that's all one.

Bion. Nay by S. *Iamy*, I hold you a penny, a horse and a man is more then one, and yet not many.

Enter Petruchio and Grumio.

Pet. Come, where be these gallants? who's at home?

Bap. You are welcome sir.

Petr. And yet I come not well.

Bap. And yet you halt not.

Tra. Not so well apparell'd as I wish you were.

Petr. Were it better I should rush in thus:
But where is *Kate*? where is my louely Bride?
How does my father? gentles methinkes you frowne,
And wherefore gaze this goodly company,
As if they saw some wondrous monument,
Some Commet, or vnusuall prodigie?

Bap. Why sir, you know this is your wedding day:
First were we sad, fearing you would not come,
Now sadder that you come so vnprouided:
Fie, doff this habit, shame to your estate,
An eye-sore to our solemne festiuall.

Tra. And tell vs what occasion of import
Hath all so long detain'd you from your wife,
And sent you hither so vnlike your selfe?

Petr. Tedious it were to tell, and harsh to heare,
Sufficeth I am come to keepe my word,
Though in some part inforced to digresse,
Which at more leysure I will so excuse,
As you shall well be satisfied with all.
But where is *Kate*? I stay too long from her,
The morning weares, 'tis time we were at Church.

Tra. See not your Bride in these vnreuerent robes,
Goe to my chamber, put on clothes of mine.

Pet. Not I, beleeue me, thus Ile visit her.

Bap. But thus I trust you will not marry her. *(words,*

Pet. Good sooth euen thus: therefore ha done with
To me she's married, not vnto my cloathes:
Could I repaire what she will weare in me,
As I can change these poore accoutrements,
'Twere well for *Kate*, and better for my selfe.
But what a foole am I to chat with you,
When I should bid good morrow to my Bride?
And seale the title with a louely kisse. *Exit.*

Tra. He hath some meaning in his mad attire,
We will perswade him be it possible,
To put on better ere he goe to Church.

Bap. Ile after him, and see the euent of this. *Exit.*

Tra. But sir, Loue concerneth vs to adde
Her fathers liking, which to bring to passe
As before imparted to your worship,
I am to get a man what ere he be,
It skills not much, weele fit him to our turne,
And he shall be *Vincentio* of *Pisa*,
And make assurance heere in *Padua*
Of greater summes then I haue promised,
So shall you quietly enioy your hope,
And marry sweet *Bianca* with consent.

Luc. Were it not that my fellow schoolemaster
Doth watch *Bianca's* steps so narrowly:
'Twere good me-thinkes to steale our marriage,
Which once perform'd, let all the world say no,
Ile keepe mine owne despite of all the world.

Tra. That by degrees we meane to looke into,

T 2 And

And watch our vantage in this businesse,
Wee'll ouer-reach the grey-beard Gremio,
The narrow prying father Minola,
The quaint Musician, amorous Litio,
All for my Masters sake Lucentio.

Enter Gremio.

Signior *Gremio*, came you from the Church?
  Gre. As willingly as ere I came from schoole.
  Tra. And is the Bride & Bridegroom coming home?
  Gre. A bridegroome say you? 'tis a groome indeed,
A grumlling groome, and that the girle shall finde.
  Tra. Curster then she, why 'tis impossible.
  Gre. Why hee's a deuill, a deuill, a very fiend.
  Tra. Why she's a deuill, a deuill, the deuils damme.
  Gre. Tut, she's a Lambe, a Doue, a foole to him:
Ile tell you sir *Lucentio*; when the Priest
Should aske if *Katherine* should be his wife,
I, by goggs woones quoth he, and swore so loud,
That all amaz'd the Priest let fall the booke,
And as he stoop'd againe to take it vp,
This mad-brain'd bridegroome tooke him such a cuffe,
That downe fell Priest and booke, and booke and Priest,
Now take them vp quoth he, if any list.
  Tra. What said the wench when he rose againe?
  Gre. Trembled and shooke: for why, he stamp'd and
swore, as if the Vicar meant to cozen him: but after ma-
ny ceremonies done, hee calls for wine, a health quoth
he, as if he had beene aboord carowsing to his Mates after a storme, quaft off the Muscadell, and threw the sops
all in the Sextons face: hauing no other reason, but that
his beard grew thinne and hungerly, and seem'd to aske
him sops as hee was drinking: This done, hee tooke the
Bride about the necke, and kist her lips with such a clamorous smacke, that at the parting all the Church did
eccho: and I seeing this, came thence for very shame, and
after mee I know the rout is comming, such a mad marriage neuer was before: harke, harke, I heare the minstrels play.   *Musicke playes.*

Enter Petruchio, Kate, Bianca, Hortensio, Baptista.

  Petr. Gentlemen & friends, I thank you for your pains,
I know you thinke to dine with me to day,
And haue prepar'd great store of wedding cheere,
But so it is, my haste doth call me hence,
And therefore heere I meane to take my leaue.
  Bap. Is't possible you will away to night?
  Pet. I must away to day before night come,
Make it no wonder: if you knew my businesse,
You would intreat me rather goe then stay:
And honest company, I thanke you all,
That haue beheld me giue away my selfe
To this most patient, sweet, and vertuous wife,
Dine with my father, drinke a health to me,
For I must hence, and farewell to you all.
  Tra. Let vs intreat you stay till after dinner.
  Pet. It may not be.
  Gra. Let me intreat you.
  Pet. It cannot be.
  Kat. Let me intreat you.
  Pet. I am content.
  Kat. Are you content to stay?
  Pet. I am content you shall entreat me stay,
But yet not stay, entreat me how you can.
  Kat. Now if you loue me stay.
  Pet. *Grumio*, my horse.
  Gru. I sir, they be ready, the Oates haue eaten the
horses.
  Kate. Nay then,
Doe what thou canst, I will not goe to day,
No, nor to morrow, not till I please my selfe,
The dore is open sir, there lies your way,
You may be iogging whiles your bootes are greene:
For me, Ile not be gone till I please my selfe,
'Tis like you'll proue a iolly surly groome,
That take it on you at the first so roundly.
  Pet. O *Kate* content thee, prethee be not angry.
  Kat. I will be angry, what hast thou to doe?
Father, be quiet, he shall stay my leisure.
  Gre. I marry sir, now it begins to worke.
  Kat. Gentlemen, forward to the bridall dinner,
I see a woman may be made a foole
If she had not a spirit to resist.
  Pet. They shall goe forward *Kate* at thy command,
Obey the Bride you that attend on her.
Goe to the feast, reuell and domineere,
Carowse full measure to her maiden-head,
Be madde and merry, or goe hang your selues:
But for my bonny *Kate*, she must with me:
Nay, looke not big, nor stampe, nor stare, nor fret,
I will be master of what is mine owne,
Shee is my goods, my chattels, she is my house,
My houshold-stuffe, my field, my barne,
My horse, my oxe, my asse, my any thing,
And heere she stands, touch her who euer dare,
Ile bring mine action on the proudest he
That stops my way in *Padua*: *Grumio*
Draw forth thy weapon, we are beset with theeues,
Rescue thy Mistresse if thou be a man:
Feare not sweet wench, they shall not touch thee *Kate*,
Ile buckler thee against a Million.   *Exeunt. P.Ka.*
  Bap. Nay, let them goe, a couple of quiet ones. (ing.
  Gre. Went they not quickly, I should die with laugh-
  Tra. Of all mad matches neuer was the like.
  Luc. Mistresse, what's your opinion of your sister?
  Bian. That being mad her selfe, she's madly mated.
  Gre. I warrant him *Petruchio* is Kated.
  Bap. Neighbours and friends, though Bride & Bride-
For to supply the places at the table,   (groom wants
You know there wants no iunkets at the feast:
Lucentio, you shall supply the Bridegroomes place,
And let *Bianca* take her sisters roome.
  Tra. Shall sweet *Bianca* practise how to bride it?
  Bap. She shall *Lucentio*: come gentlemen lets goe.
                Enter Grumio.   *Exeunt.*
  Gru. Fie, fie on all tired Iades, on all mad Masters, &
all foule waies: was euer man so beaten? was euer man
so raide? was euer man so weary? I am sent before to
make a fire, and they are comming after to warme them:
now were not I a little pot, & soone hot; my very lippes
might freeze to my teeth, my tongue to the roofe of my
mouth, my heart in my belly, ere I should come by a fire
to thaw me: but I with blowing the fire shall warme my
selfe: for considering the weather, a taller man then I
will take cold: Holla, hoa *Curtis*.

Enter Curtis.

  Curt. Who is that calls so coldly?
  Gru. A piece of Ice: if thou doubt it, thou maist
slide from my shoulder to my heele, with no
                                            greater

greater a run but my head and my necke. A fire good *Curtis*.

Cur. Is my master and his wife comming *Grumio*?

Gru. Oh I *Curtis* I, and therefore fire, fire, cast on no water.

Cur. Is she so hot a shrew as she's reported.

Gru. She was good *Curtis* before this frost: but thou know'st winter tames man, woman, and beast: for it hath tam'd my old master, and my new mistris, and my selfe fellow *Curtis*.

Gru. Away you three inch foole, I am no beast.

Gru. Am I but three inches? Why thy horne is a foot and so long am I at the least. But wilt thou make a fire, or shall I complaine on thee to our mistris, whose hand (she being now at hand) thou shalt soone feele, to thy cold comfort, for being slow in thy hot office.

Cur. I prethee good *Grumis*, tell me, how goes the world?

Gru. A cold world *Curtis* in euery office but thine, & therefore fire: do thy duty, and haue thy dutie, for my Master and mistris are almost frozen to death.

Cur. There's fire readie, and therefore good *Grumio* the newes.

Gru. Why Iacke boy, ho boy, and as much newes as wilt thou.

Cur. Come, you are so full of conicatching.

Gru. Why therefore fire, for I haue caught extreme cold. Where's the Cooke, is supper ready, the house trim'd, rushes strew'd, cobwebs swept, the seruingmen in their new fustian, the white stockings, and euery officer his wedding garment on? Be the Iackes faire within, the Gils faire without, the Carpets laide, and euerie thing in order?

Cur. All readie: and therefore I pray thee newes.

Gru. First know my horse is tired, my master & mistris falne out. *Cur.* How?

Gru. Out of their saddles into the durt, and thereby hangs a tale.

Cur. Let's ha't good *Grumio*.

Gru. Lend thine eare.

Cur. Heere.

Gru. There.

Cur. This 'tis to feele a tale, not to heare a tale.

Gru. And therefore 'tis cal'd a sensible tale: and this Cuffe was but to knocke at your eare, and beseech listning: now I begin, Inprimis wee came downe a fowle hill, my Master riding behinde my Mistris.

Cur. Both of one horse?

Gru. What's that to thee?

Cur. Why a horse.

Gru. Tell thou the tale: but hadst thou not crost me, thou shouldst haue heard how her horse fel, and she vnder her horse: thou shouldst haue heard in how miery a place, how she was bemoil'd, how hee left her with the horse vpon her, how he beat me because her horse stumbled, how she waded through the durt to plucke him off me: how he swore, how she prai'd, that neuer prai'd before: how I cried, how the horses ranne away, how her bridle was burst: how I lost my crupper, with manie things of worthy memorie, which now shall die in obliuion, and thou returne vnexperienc'd to thy graue.

Cur. By this reckning he is more shrew than she.

Gru. I, and that thou and the proudest of you all shall finde when he comes home. But what talke I of this? Call forth *Nathaniel, Ioseph, Nicholas, Phillip, Walter, Sugersop* and the rest: let their heads bee slickely comb'd, their blew coats brush'd, and their garters of an indifferent knit, let them curtsie with their left legges, and not presume to touch a haire of my Masters horse-taile, till they kisse their hands. Are they all readie?

Cur. They are.

Gru. Call them forth.

Cur. Do you heare ho? you must meete my maister to countenance my mistris.

Gru. Why she hath a face of her owne.

Cur. Who knowes not that?

Gru. Thou it seemes, that cals for company to countenance her.

Cur. I call them forth to credit her.

Enter foure or fiue seruingmen.

Gru. Why she comes to borrow nothing of them.

Nat. Welcome home *Grumio*.

Phil. How now *Grumio*.

Ios. What *Grumio*.

Nick. Fellow *Grumio*.

Nat. How now old lad.

Gru. Welcome you: how now you: what you: fellow you: and thus much for greeting. Now my spruce companions, is all readie, and all things neate?

Nat. All things is readie, how neere is our master?

Gre. E'ne at hand, alighted by this: and therefore be not———Cockes passion, silence, I heare my master.

Enter Petruchio and Kate.

Pet. Where be these knaues? What no man at doore
To hold my stirrop, nor to take my horse?
Where is *Nathaniel, Gregory, Phillip*.

All ser. Heere, heere sir, heere sir.

Pet. Heere sir, heere sir, heere sir, heere sir.
You logger-headed and vnpollisht groomes:
What? no attendance? no regard? no dutie?
Where is the foolish knaue I sent before?

Gru. Heere sir, as foolish as I was before.

Pet. You pezant, swain, you horson malt-horse drudg
Did I not bid thee meete me in the Parke,
And bring along these rascal knaues with thee?

Grumio. Nathaniels coate sir was not fully made,
And *Gabrels* pumpes were all vnpinkt i'th heele:
There was no Linke to colour *Peters* hat,
And *Walters* dagger was not come from sheathing:
There were none fine, but *Adam, Rafe*, and *Gregory*,
The rest were ragged, old, and beggerly,
Yet as they are, heere are they come to meete you.

Pet. Go rascals, go, and fetch my supper in. *Ex. Ser.*
Where is the life that late I led?
Where are those? Sit downe *Kate*,
And welcome. Soud, soud, soud, soud.

Enter seruants with supper.

Why when I say? Nay good sweete *Kate* be merrie.
Off with my boots, you rogues: you villaines, when?
It was the Friar of Orders gray,
As he forth walked on his way.
Out you rogue, you plucke my foote awrie,
Take that, and mend the plucking of the other.
Be merrie *Kate*: Some water heere: what hoa.

Enter one with water.

Where's my Spaniel *Troilus*? Sirra, get you hence,
And bid my cozen *Ferdinand* come hither:
One *Kate* that you must kisse, and be acquainted with.
Where are my Slippers? Shall I haue some water?
Come *Kate* and wash, & welcome heartily:
you horson villaine, will you let it fall?

Kate. Patience I pray you, 'twas a fault vnwilling.

Pet. A horson beetle-headed flap-ear'd knaue:
Come *Kate* sit downe, I know you haue a stomacke,
Will you giue thankes, sweete *Kate*, or else shall I?
What's this, Mutton?

1. Ser. I.

Pet. Who brought it?

Peter. I.

Pet. 'Tis burnt, and so is all the meate:
What dogges are these? Where is the rascall Cooke?
How durst you villaines bring it from the dresser
And serue it thus to me that loue it not?
There, take it to you, trenchers, cups, and all:
You heedlesse iolt-heads, and vnmanner'd slaues.
What, do you grumble? Ile be with you straight.

Kate. I pray you husband be not so disquiet,
The meate was well, if you were so contented.

Pet. I tell thee *Kate*, 'twas burnt and dried away,
And I expressely am forbid to touch it:
For it engenders choller, planteth anger,
And better'twere that both of vs did fast,
Since of our selues, our selues are chollericke,
Then feede it with such ouer-rosted flesh:
Be patient, to morrow't shalbe mended,
And for this night we'l fast for companie.
Come I wil bring thee to thy Bridall chamber. *Exeunt.*

Enter Seruants seuerally.

Nath. Peter didst euer see the like.

Peter. He kils her in her owne humor.

Grumio. Where is he?

Enter Curtis a Seruant.

Cur. In her chamber, making a sermon of continencie to her, and railes, and sweares, and rates, that shee
(poore soule) knowes not which way to stand, to looke,
to speake, and sits as one new risen from a dreame. A-
way, away, for he is comming hither.

Enter Petruchio.

Pet. Thus haue I politickely begun my reigne,
And 'tis my hope to end successefully:
My Faulcon now is sharpe, and passing emptie,
And til she stoope, she must not be full gorg'd,
For then she neuer lookes vpon her lure.
Another way I haue to man my Haggard,
To make her come, and know her Keepers call:
That is, to watch her, as we watch these Kites,
That baite, and beate, and will not be obedient:
She eate no meate to day, nor none shall eate.
Last night she slept not, nor to night she shall not:
As with the meate, some vndeserued fault
Ile finde about the making of the bed,
And heere Ile fling the pillow, there the boulster,
This way the Couerlet, another way the sheets:
I, and amid this hurlie I intend,
That all is done in reuerend care of her,
And in conclusion, she shal watch all night,
And if she chance to nod, Ile raile and brawle,
And with the clamor keepe her stil awake:
This is a way to kil a Wife with kindnesse,
And thus Ile curbe her mad and headstrong humor:
He that knowes better how to tame a shrew,
Now let him speake, 'tis charity to shew. *Exit*

Enter Tranio and Hortensio.

Tra. Is't possible friend *Lisio*, that mistris *Bianca*
Doth fancie any other but *Lucentio*,
I tel you sir, she beares me faire in hand.

Luc. Sir, to satisfie you in what I haue said,
Stand by, and marke the manner of his teaching.

Enter Bianca.

Hor. Now Mistris, profit you in what you reade?

Bian. What Master reade you first, resolue me that?

Hor. I reade, that I professe the Art to loue.

Bian. And may you proue sir Master of your Art.

Luc. While you sweet deere proue Mistresse of my
heart.

Hor. Quicke proceeders marry, now tel me I pray,
you that durst sweare that your mistris *Bianca*
Lou'd me in the World so wel as *Lucentio*.

Tra. Oh despightful Loue, vnconstant womankind,
I tel thee *Lisio* this is wonderfull.

Hor. Mistake no more, I am not *Lisio*,
Nor a Musitian as I seeme to bee,
But one that scorne to liue in this disguise,
For such a one as leaues a Gentleman,
And makes a God of such a Cullion;
Know sir, that I am cal'd *Hortensio*.

Tra. Signior *Hortensio*, I haue often heard
Of your entire affection to *Bianca*,
And since mine eyes are witnesse of her lightnesse,
I wil with you, if you be so contented,
Forsweare *Bianca*, and her loue for euer.

Hor. See how they kisse and court: Signior *Lucentio*,
Heere is my hand, and heere I firmly vow
Neuer to woo her more, but do forsweare her
As one vnworthie all the former fauours
That I haue fondly flatter'd them withall.

Tra. And heere I take the like vnfained oath,
Neuer to marrie with her, though she would intreate,
Fie on her, see how beastly she doth court him.

Hor. Would all the world but he had quite forsworn
For me, that I may surely keepe mine oath.
I wil be married to a wealthy Widdow,
Ere three dayes passe, which hath as long lou'd me,
As I haue lou'd this proud disdainful Haggard,
And so farewel signior *Lucentio*,
Kindnesse in women, not their beauteous lookes
Shal win my loue, and so I take my leaue,
In resolution, as I swore before.

Tra. Mistris *Bianca*, blesse you with such grace,
As longeth to a Louers blessed case:
Nay, I haue tane you napping gentle Loue,
And haue forsworne you with *Hortensio*.

Bian. *Tranio* you iest, but haue you both forsworne
mee?

Tra. Mistris we haue.

Luc. Then we are rid of *Lisio*.

Tra. I'faith hee'l haue a lustie Widdow now,
That shalbe woo'd, and wedded in a day.

Bian. God giue him ioy.

Tra. I, and hee'l tame her.

Bianca. He sayes so *Tranio*.

Tra. Faith he is gone vnto the taming schoole.

Bian. The taming schoole: what is there such a place?

Tra. I mistris, and *Petruchio* is the master,
That teacheth trickes eleuen and twentie long,
To tame a shrew, and charme her chattering tongue.

Enter Biondello.

Bion. Oh Master, master I haue watcht so long,
That I am dogge-wearie, but at last I spied
An ancient Angel comming downe the hill,
Wil serue the turne.

Tra. What is he *Biondello*?

Bio. Master, a Marcantant, or a pedant,

I know not what, but formall in apparrell,
In gate and countenance surely like a Father.

 Luc. And what of him *Tranio*?

 Tra. If he be credulous, and trust my tale,
Ile make him glad to seeme *Vincentio*,
And giue assurance to *Baptista Minola*.
As if he were the right *Vincentio*.

 Par. Take me your loue, and then let me alone.

Enter a Pedant.

 Ped. God saue you sir.

 Tra. And you sir, you are welcome,
Trauaile you farre on, or are you at the farthest?

 Ped. Sir at the farthest for a weeke or two,
But then vp farther, and as farre as Rome,
And so to Tripolie, if God lend me life.

 Tra. What Countreyman I pray?

 Ped. Of *Mantua*.

 Tra. Of *Mantua* Sir, marrie God forbid,
And come to Padua carelesse of your life.

 Ped. My life sir? how I pray? for that goes hard.

 Tra. 'Tis death for any one in Mantua
To come to Padua, know you not the cause?
Your ships are staid at Venice, and the Duke
For priuate quarrel 'twixt your Duke and him,
Hath publish'd and proclaim'd it openly:
'Tis meruaile, but that you are but newly come,
you might haue heard it else proclaim'd about.

 Ped. Alas sir, it is worse for me then so,
For I haue bils for monie by exchange
From Florence, and must heere deliuer them.

 Tra. Wel sir, to do you courtesie,
This wil I do, and this I wil aduise you.
First tell me, haue you euer beene at Pisa?

 Ped. I sir, in Pisa haue I often bin,
Pisa renowned for graue Citizens.

 Tra. Among them know you one *Vincentio*?

 Ped. I know him not, but I haue heard of him:
A Merchant of incomparable wealth.

 Tra. He is my father sir, and sooth to say,
In count'nance somewhat doth resemble you.

 Bion. As much as an apple doth an oyster, & all one.

 Tra. To saue your life in this extremitie,
This fauor wil I do you for his sake,
And thinke it not the worst of all your fortunes,
That you are like to Sir *Vincentio*.
His name and credite shal you vndertake,
And in my house you shal be friendly lodg'd,
Looke that you take vpon you as you should,
you vnderstand me sir : so shal you stay
Til you haue done your businesse in the Citie :
If this be court'sie sir, accept of it.

 Ped. Oh sir I do, and wil repute you euer
The patron of my life and libertie.

 Tra. Then go with me, to make the matter good,
This by the way I let you vnderstand,
My father is heere look'd for euerie day,
To passe assurance of a dowre in marriage
'Twixt me, and one *Baptistas* daughter heere:
In all these circumstances Ile instruct you,
Go with me to cloath you as becomes you. *Exeunt.*

Actus Quartus. Scena Prima.

Enter Katherina and Grumio.

 Gru. No, no forsooth I dare not for my life.

 Ka. The more my wrong, the more his spite appears.
What, did he marrie me to famish me?
Beggers that come vnto my fathers doore,
Vpon intreatie haue a present almes,
If not, elsewhere they meete with charitie:
But I, who neuer knew how to intreat,
Nor neuer needed that I should intreate,
Am staru'd for meate, giddie for lacke of sleepe:
With oathes kept waking, and with brawling fed,
And that which spights me more then all these wants,
He does it vnder name of perfect loue:
As who should say, if I should sleepe or eate
'Twere deadly sicknesse, or else present death.
I prethee go, and get me some repast,
I care not what, so it be holsome foode.

 Gru. What say you to a Neats foote?

 Kate. 'Tis passing good, I prethee let me haue it.

 Gru. I feare it is too chollericke a meate.
How say you to a fat Tripe finely broyl'd?

 Kate. I like it well, good Grumio fetch it me.

 Gru. I cannot tell, I feare 'tis chollericke.
What say you to a peece of Beefe and Mustard?

 Kate. A dish that I do loue to feede vpon.

 Gru. I, but the Mustard is too hot a little.

 Kate. Why then the Beefe, and let the Mustard rest.

 Gru. Nay then I wil not, you shal haue the Mustard
Or else you get no beefe of Grumio.

 Kate. Then both or one, or any thing thou wilt.

 Gru. Why then the Mustard without the beefe.

 Kate. Go get thee gone, thou false deluding slaue,
Beats him.
That feed'st me with the verie name of meate.
Sorrow on thee, and all the packe of you
That triumph thus vpon my misery:
Go get thee gone, I say.

Enter Petruchio, and Hortensio with meate.

 Petr. How fares my Kate, what sweeting all a-mort?

 Hor. Mistris, what cheere?

 Kate. Faith as cold as can be.

 Pet. Plucke vp thy spirits, looke cheerfully vpon me.
Heere Loue, thou seest how diligent I am,
To dresse thy meate my selfe, and bring it thee.
I am sure sweet Kate, this kindnesse merites thankes.
What, not a word? Nay then, thou lou'st it not:
And all my paines is sorted to no proofe.
Heere take away this dish.

 Kate. I pray you let it stand.

 Pet. The poorest seruice is repaide with thankes,
And so shall mine before you touch the meate.

 Kate. I thanke you sir.

 Hor. Signior *Petruchio*, fie you are too blame:
Come Mistris Kate, Ile beare you companie.

 Petr. Eate it vp all *Hortensio*, if thou louest mee:
Much good do it vnto thy gentle heart:
Kate eate apace; and now my honie Loue,
Will we returne vnto thy Fathers house,
And reuell it as brauely as the best,
With silken coats and caps, and golden Rings,
With Ruffes and Cuffes, and Fardingales, and things:
With Scarfes, and Fannes, & double change of brau'ry,
With Amber Bracelets, Beades, and all this knau'ry.
What hast thou din'd? The Tailor staies thy leasure,
To decke thy bodie with his ruffling treasure.

Enter Tailor.

Come Tailor, let vs see these ornaments.
Enter Haberdasher.
Lay forth the gowne. What newes with you sir?

Fel. Heere is the cap your Worship did bespeake.

Pet. Why this was moulded on a porrenger,
A Veluet dish: Fie, fie, 'tis lewd and filthy,
Why 'tis a cockle or a walnut-shell,
A knacke, a toy, a tricke, a babies cap:
Away with it, come let me haue a bigger.

Kate. Ile haue no bigger, this doth fit the time,
And Gentlewomen weare such caps as these.

Pet. When you are gentle, you shall haue one too,
And not till then.

Hor. That will not be in haste.

Kate. Why sir I trust I may haue leaue to speake,
And speake I will. I am no childe, no babe,
Your betters haue indur'd me say my minde,
And If you cannot, best you stop your eares.
My tongue will tell the anger of my heart,
Or els my heart concealing it wil breake,
And rather then it shall, I will be free,
Euen to the vttermost as I please in words.

Pet. Why thou saist true, it is paltrie cap,
A custard coffen, a bauble, a silken pie,
I loue thee well in that thou lik'st it not.

Kate. Loue me, or loue me not, I like the cap,
And it I will haue, or I will haue none.

Pet. Thy gowne, why I: come Tailor let vs see't.
Oh mercie God, what masking stuffe is heere?
Whats this? a sleeue? 'tis like demi cannon,
What, vp and downe caru'd like an apple Tart?
Heers snip, and nip, and cut, and slish and slash,
Like to a Censor in a barbers shoppe:
Why what a deuils name Tailor cal'st thou this?

Hor. I see shees like to haue neither cap nor gowne.

Tai. You bid me make it orderlie and well,
According to the fashion, and the time.

Pet. Marrie and did: but if you be remembred,
I did not bid you marre it to the time.
Go hop me ouer euery kennell home,
For you shall hop without my custome sir:
Ile none of it; hence, make your best of it.

Kate. I neuer saw a better fashion'd gowne,
More queint, more pleasing, nor more commendable:
Belike you meane to make a puppet of me.

Pet. Why true, he meanes to make a puppet of thee.

Tail. She saies your Worship meanes to make a
puppet of her.

Pet. Oh monstrous arrogance:
Thou lyest, thou thred, thou thimble,
Thou yard three quarters, halfe yard, quarter, naile,
Thou Flea, thou Nit, thou winter cricket thou:
Brau'd in mine owne house with a skeine of thred:
Away thou Ragge, thou quantitie, thou remnant,
Or I shall so be-mete thee with thy yard,
As thou shalt thinke on prating whil'st thou liu'st:
I tell thee I, that thou hast marr'd her gowne.

Tail. Your worship is deceiu'd, the gowne is made
Iust as my master had direction:
Grumio gaue order how it should be done.

Gru. I gaue him no order, I gaue him the stuffe.

Tail. But how did you desire it should be made?

Gru. Marrie sir with needle and thred.

Tail. But did you not request to haue it cut?

Gru. Thou hast fac'd many things.

Tail. I haue.

Gru. Face not mee: thou hast brau'd manie men,
braue not me; I will neither bee fac'd nor brau'd. I say
vnto thee, I bid thy Master cut out the gowne, but I did
not bid him cut it to peeces. Ergo thou liest.

Tail. Why heere is the note of the fashion to testify.

Pet. Reade it.

Gru. The note lies in's throate if he say I said so.

Tail. Inprimis, a loose bodied gowne.

Gru. Master, if euer I said loose-bodied gowne, sow
me in the skirts of it, and beate me to death with a bottome of browne thred: I said a gowne.

Pet. Proceede.

Tai. With a small compast cape.

Gru. I confesse the cape.

Tai. With a trunke sleeue.

Gru. I confesse two sleeues.

Tai. The sleeues curiously cut.

Pet. I there's the villanie.

Gru. Error i'th bill sir, error i'th bill? I commanded
the sleeues should be cut out, and sow'd vp againe, and
that Ile proue vpon thee, though thy little finger be armed in a thimble.

Tail. This is true that I say, and I had thee in place
where thou shouldst know it.

Gru. I am for thee straight: take thou the bill, giue
me thy meat-yard, and spare not me.

Hor. God-a-mercie *Grumio*, then hee shall haue no
oddes.

Pet. Well sir in breefe the gowne is not for me.

Gru. You are i'th right sir, 'tis for my mistris.

Pet. Go take it vp vnto thy masters vse.

Gru. Villaine, not for thy life: Take vp my Mistresse
gowne for thy masters vse.

Pet. Why sir, what's your conceit in that?

Gru. Oh sir, the conceit is deeper then you think for:
Take vp my Mistris gowne to his masters vse.
Oh fie, fie, fie.

Pet. Hortensio, say thou wilt see the Tailor paide:
Go take it hence, be gone, and say no more.

Hor. Tailor, Ile pay thee for thy gowne to morrow,
Take no vnkindnesse of his hastie words:
Away I say, commend me to thy master. *Exit Tail.*

Pet. Well, come my *Kate*, we will vnto your fathers,
Euen in these honest meane habiliments:
Our purses shall be proud, our garments poore:
For 'tis the minde that makes the bodie rich.
And as the Sunne breakes through the darkest clouds,
So honor peereth in the meanest habit.
What is the Iay more precious then the Larke?
Because his feathers are more beautifull.
Or is the Adder better then the Eele,
Because his painted skin contents the eye.
Oh no good *Kate*: neither art thou the worse
For this poore furniture, and meane array.
If thou accountedst it shame, lay it on me,
And therefore frolicke, we will hence forthwith,
To feast and sport vs at thy fathers house,
Go call my men, and let vs straight to him,
And bring our horses vnto Long-lane end,
There wil we mount, and thither walke on foote,
Let's see, I thinke 'tis now some seuen a clocke,
And well we may come there by dinner time.

Kate. I dare assure you sir, 'tis almost two,
And 'twill be supper time ere you come there.

Pet. It shall be seuen ere I go to horse:
Looke what I speake, or do, or thinke to doe,

You

The Taming of the Shrew.

You are still crossing it, sirs let't alone,
I will not goe to day, and ere I doe,
It shall be what a clock I say it is.

Hor. Why so this gallant will command the sunne.

Enter Tranio, and the Pedant drest like Vincentio.

Tra. Sirs, this is the house, please it you that I call.
Ped. I what else, and but I be deceiued,
Signior *Baptista* may remember me
Neere twentie yeares a goe in *Genoa*.
Tra. Where we were lodgers, at the *Pegasus*,
Tis well, and hold your owne in any case
With such austeritie as longeth to a father.

Enter Biondello.

Ped. I warrant you : but sir here comes your boy,
Twere good he were school'd.
Tra. Feare you not him: sirra *Biondello*,
Now doe your dutie throughlie I aduise you :
Imagine 'twere the right *Vincentio*.
Bion. Tut, feare not me.
Tra. But hast thou done thy errand to *Baptista*.
Bion. I told him that your father was at *Venice*,
And that you look't for him this day in *Padua*.
Tra. Th'art a tall fellow, hold thee that to drinke,
Here comes *Baptista* : set your countenance sir.

*Enter Baptista and Lucentio : Pedant booted
and bare headed.*

Tra. Signior *Baptista* you are happilie met :
Sir, this is the gentleman I told you of,
I pray you stand good father to me now,
Giue me *Bianca* for my patrimony.
Ped. Soft son: sir by your leaue, hauing com to *Padua*
To gather in some debts, my son *Lucentio*
Made me acquainted with a waighty cause
Of loue betweene your daughter and himselfe :
And for the good report I heare of you,
And for the loue he beareth to your daughter,
And she to him : to stay him not too long,
I am content in a good fathers care
To haue him matcht, and if you please to like
No worse then I, vpon some agreement
Me shall you finde readie and willing
With one consent to haue her so bestowed :
For curious I cannot be with you
Signior *Baptista*, of whom I heare so well.
Bap. Sir, pardon me in what I haue to say,
Your plainnesse and your shortnesse please me well :
Right true it is your sonne *Lucentio* here
Doth loue my daughter, and she loueth him,
Or both dissemble deepely their affections :
And therefore if you say no more then this,
That like a Father you will deale with him,
And passe my daughter a sufficient dower,
The match is made, and all is done,
Your sonne shall haue my daughter with consent.
Tra. I thanke you sir, where then doe you know best
We be affied and such assurance tane,
As shall with either parts agreement stand.
Bap. Not in my house *Lucentio*, for you know
Pitchers haue eares, and I haue manie seruants,
Besides old *Gremio* is harkning still,
And happilie we might be interrupted.
Tra. Then at my lodging, and it like you,
There doth my father lie : and there this night

Weele passe the businesse priuately and well :
Send for your daughter by your seruant here,
My Boy shall fetch the Scriuener presentlie,
The worst is this that at so slender warning,
You are like to haue a thin and slender pittance.
Bap. It likes me well :
Cambio hie you home, and bid *Bianca* make her readie
    straight :
And if you will tell what hath hapned,
Lucentios Father is arriued in *Padua*,
And how she's like to be *Lucentios* wife.
Biond. I praie the gods she may withall my heart.
                                                    Exit.
Tran. Dallie not with the gods, but get thee gone.
Enter Peter.
Signior *Baptista*, shall I leade the way,
Welcome, one messe is like to be your cheere,
Come sir, we will better it in *Pisa*.
Bap. I follow you.   *Exeunt.*

Enter Lucentio and Biondello.

Bion. Cambio.
Luc. What saist thou *Biondello*.
Biond. You saw my Master winke and laugh vpon
you?
Luc. *Biondello*, what of that?
Biond. Faith nothing : but has left mee here behinde
to expound the meaning or morrall of his signes and to-
kens.
Luc. I pray thee moralize them.
Biond. Then thus : *Baptista* is safe talking with the
deceiuing Father of a deceitfull sonne.
Luc. And what of him?
Biond. His daughter is to be brought by you to the
supper.
Luc. And then.
Bio. The old Priest at Saint *Lukes* Church is at your
command at all houres.
Luc. And what of all this.
Bion. I cannot tell, expect they are busied about a
counterfeit assurance : take you assurance of her, *Cum
preuilegio ad Impremendum solem*, to th' Church take the
Priest, Clarke, and some sufficient honest witnesses :
If this be not that you looke for, I haue no more to say,
But bid *Bianca* farewell for euer and a day.
Luc. Hear'st thou *Biondello*.
Biond. I cannot tarry : I knew a wench maried in an
afternoone as shee went to the Garden for Parseley to
stuffe a Rabit, and so may you sir : and so adew sir, my
Master hath appointed me to goe to Saint *Lukes* to bid
the Priest be readie to come against you come with your
appendix.   *Exit.*
Luc. I may and will, if she be so contented :
She will be pleas'd, then wherefore should I doubt :
Hap what hap may, Ile roundly goe about her :
It shall goe hard if *Cambio* goe without her.   *Exit.*

Enter Petruchio, Kate, Hortentio.

Petr. Come on a Gods name, once more toward our
    fathers :
Good Lord how bright and goodly shines the Moone.
Kate. The Moone, the Sunne : it is not Moonelight
    now.
Pet. I say it is the Moone that shines so bright.
Kate. I know it is the Sunne that shines so bright.
Pet. Now by my mothers sonne, and that's my selfe,
                                                    It

It shall be moone, or starre, or what I list,
Or ere I iourney to your Fathers house:
Goe on, and fetch our horses backe againe,
Euermore crost and crost, nothing but crost.

Hort. Say as he saies, or we shall neuer goe.

Kate. Forward I pray, since we haue come so farre,
And be it moone, or sunne, or what you please:
And if you please to call it a rush Candle,
Henceforth I vowe it shall be so for me.

Petr. I say it is the Moone.

Kate. I know it is the Moone.

Petr. Nay then you lye: it is the blessed Sunne.

Kate. Then God be blest, it in the blessed sun,
But sunne it is not, when you say it is not,
And the Moone changes euen as your minde:
What you will haue it nam'd, euen that it is,
And so it shall be so for Katherine.

Hort. Petruchio, goe thy waies, the field is won.

Petr. Well, forward, forward, thus the bowle should run,
And not vnluckily against the Bias:
But soft, Company is comming here.

Enter Vincentio.

Good morrow gentle Mistris, where away?
Tell me sweete Kate, and tell me truely too,
Hast thou beheld a fresher Gentlewoman:
Such warre of white and red within her cheekes:
What stars do spangle heauen with such beautie,
As those two eyes become that heauenly face?
Faire louely Maide, once more good day to thee:
Sweete Kate embrace her for her beauties sake.

Hort. A will make the man mad to make the woman of him.

Kate. Yong budding Virgin, faire, and fresh, & sweet,
Whether away, or whether is thy aboade?
Happy the Parents of so faire a childe;
Happier the man whom fauourable stars
A lots thee for his louely bedfellow.

Petr. Why how now Kate, I hope thou art not mad,
This is a man old, wrinckled, faded, withered,
And not a Maiden, as thou saist he is.

Kate. Pardon old father my mistaking eies,
That haue bin so bedazled with the sunne,
That euery thing I looke on seemeth greene:
Now I perceiue thou art a reuerent Father:
Pardon I pray thee for my mad mistaking.

Petr. Do good old grandsire, & withall make known
Which way thou trauellest, if along with vs,
We shall be ioyfull of thy companie.

Vin. Faire Sir, and you my merry Mistris,
That with your strange encounter much amasde me:
My name is call'd Vincentio, my dwelling Pisa,
And bound I am to Padua, there to visite
A sonne of mine, which long I haue not seene.

Petr. What is his name?

Vinc. Lucentio gentle sir.

Petr. Happily met, the happier for thy sonne:
And now by Law, as well as reuerent age,
I may intitle thee my louing Father,
The sister to my wife, this Gentlewoman,
Thy Sonne by this hath married: wonder not,
Nor be not grieued, she is of good esteeme,
Her dowrie wealthie, and of worthie birth;
Beside, so qualified, as may beseeme
The Spouse of any noble Gentleman:
Let me imbrace with old Vincentio.

And wander we to see thy honest sonne,
Who will of thy arriuall be full ioyous.

Vinc. But is this true, or is it else your pleasure,
Like pleasant trauailors to breake a Iest
Vpon the companie you ouertake?

Hort. I doe assure thee father so it is.

Petr. Come goe along and see the truth hereof,
For our first merriment hath made thee iealous. *Exeunt.*

Hor. Well Petruchio, this has put me in heart;
Haue to my Widdow, and if she froward,
Then hast thou taught Hortentio to be vntoward. *Exit.*

Enter Biondello, Lucentio and Bianca, Gremio is out before.

Biond. Softly and swiftly sir, for the Priest is ready.

Luc. I flie Biondello; but they may chance to neede
thee at home, therefore leaue vs. *Exit.*

Biond. Nay faith, Ile see the Church a your backe,
and then come backe to my mistris as soone as I can.

Gre. I maruaile Cambio comes not all this while.

Enter Petruchio, Kate, Vincentio, Grumio with Attendants.

Petr. Sir heres the doore, this is Lucentios house,
My Fathers beares more toward the Market place,
Thither must I, and here I leaue you sir.

Vin. You shall not choose but drinke before you go,
I thinke I shall command your welcome here;
And by all likelihood some cheere is toward. *Knock.*

Grem. They're busie within, you were best knocke lowder.

Pedant lookes out of the window.

Ped. What's he that knockes as he would beat downe the gate?

Vin. Is Signior Lucentio within sir?

Ped. He's within sir, but not to be spoken withall.

Vinc. What if a man bring him a hundred pound or two to make merrie withall.

Ped. Keepe your hundred pounds to your selfe, hee shall neede none so long as I liue.

Petr. Nay, I told you your sonne was well beloued in Padua: doe you heare sir, to leaue friuolous circumstances, I pray you tell signior Lucentio that his Father is come from Pisa, and is here at the doore to speake with him.

Ped. Thou liest his Father is come from Padua, and here looking out at the window.

Vin. Art thou his father?

Ped. I sir, so his mother saies, if I may beleeue her.

Petr. Why how now gentleman: why this is flat knauerie to take vpon you another mans name.

Peda. Lay hands on the villaine, I beleeue a meanes to cosen some bodie in this Citie vnder my countenance.

Enter Biondello.

Bio. I haue seene them in the Church together, God send'em good shipping: but who is here? mine old Master Vincentio: now wee are vndone and brought to nothing.

Vin. Come hither crackhempe.

Bion. I hope I may choose Sir.

Vin. Come hither you rogue, what haue you forgot mee?

Biond. Forgot you, no sir: I could not forget you, for I neuer saw you before in all my life.

Vinc. What, you notorious villaine, didst thou neuer see thy Mistris father, Vincentio?

Bion. What

Bion. What my old worshipfull old master? yes marie sir see where he lookes out of the window.

Vin. Ist so indeede. *He beates Biondello.*

Bion. Helpe, helpe, helpe, here's a mad man will murder me.

Vdan. Helpe, sonne, helpe signior *Baptista*.

Ker. Pree the *Kate* let's stand aside and see the end of this controuersie.

Enter Pedant with seruants, Baptista, Tranio.

Tra. Sir, what are you that offer to beate my seruant?

Vinc. What am I sir: nay what are you sir: oh immortall Goddes: oh fine villaine, a silken doubtlet, a veluet hose, a scarlet cloake, and a copataine hat: oh I am vndone, I am vndone: while I plaie the good husband at home, my sonne and my seruant spend all at the vniuersitie.

Tra. How now, what's the matter?

Bapt. What is the man lunaticke?

Tra. Sir, you seeme a sober ancient Gentleman by your habit: but your words shew you a mad man: why sir, what cernes it you, if I weare Pearle and gold: I thank my good Father, I am able to maintaine it.

Vin. Thy father: oh villaine, he is a Saile-maker in *Bergamo*.

Bap. You mistake sir, you mistake sir, praie what do you thinke is his name?

Vin. His name, as if I knew not his name: I haue brought him vp euer since he was three yeeres old, and his name is *Tronio*.

Ped. Awaie, awaie mad asse, his name is *Lucentio*, and he is mine onelie sonne and heire to the Lands of me signior *Vincentio*.

Ven. *Lucentio*: oh he hath murdred his Master; laie hold on him I charge you in the Dukes name: oh my sonne, my sonne: tell me thou villaine, where is my son *Lucentio*?

Tra. Call forth an officer: Carrie this mad knaue to the Iaile: father *Baptista*, I charge you see that hee be forth comming.

Vinc. Carrie me to the Iaile?

Gre. Staie officer, he shall not go to prison.

Bap. Talke not signior *Gremio*: I saie he shall goe to prison.

Gre. Take heede signior *Baptista*, least you be conicatcht in this businesse: I dare sweare this is the right *Vincentio*.

Ped. Sweare if thou dar'st.

Gre. Naie, I dare not sweare it.

Tran. Then thou wert best saie that I am not *Lucentio*.

Gre. Yes, I know thee to be signior *Lucentio*.

Bap. Awaie with the dotard, to the Iaile with him.

Enter Biondello, Lucentio and Bianca.

Vin. Thus strangers may be haild and abus'd: oh monstrous villaine.

Bion. Oh we are spoil'd, and yonder he is, denie him, forsweare him, or else we are all vndone.

Exit Biondello, Tranio and Pedant as fast as may be.

Luc. Pardon sweete father. *Kneele.*

Vin. Liues my sweete sonne?

Bian. Pardon deere father.

Bap. How hast thou offended, where is *Lucentio*?

Luc. Here's *Lucentio*, right sonne to the right *Vincentio*,

That haue by marriage made thy daughter mine, While counterfeit supposes bleer'd thine eine.

Gre. Here's packing with a witnesse to deceiue vs all.

Vin. Where is that damned villaine *Tranio*, That fac'd and braued me in this matter so?

Bap. Why, tell me is not this my *Cambio*?

Bian. *Cambio* is chang'd into *Lucentio*.

Luc. Loue wrought these miracles. *Biancas* loue Made me exchange my state with *Tranio*, While he did beare my countenance in the towne; And happilie I haue arriued at the last Vnto the wished hauen of my blisse : What *Tranio* did, my selfe enforst him to ; Then pardon him sweete Father for my sake.

Vin. Ile slit the villaines nose that would haue sent me to the Iaile.

Bap. But doe you heare sir, haue you married my daughter without asking my good will?

Vin. Feare not *Baptista*, we will content you, goe to: but I will in to be reueng'd for this villanie. *Exit.*

Bap. And I to sound the depth of this knauerie. *Exit.*

Luc. Looke not pale *Bianca*, thy father will not frown. *Exeunt.*

Gre. My cake is dough, but Ile in among the rest, Out of hope of all, but my share of the feast.

Kate. Husband let's follow, to see the end of this adoe.

Petr. First kisse me *Kate*, and we will.

Kate. What in the midst of the streete?

Petr. What art thou asham'd of me?

Kate. No sir, God forbid, but asham'd to kisse.

Petr. Why then let's home againe: Come Sirra let's awaie.

Kate. Nay, I will giue thee a kisse, now praie thee Loue staie.

Petr. Is not this well? come my sweete *Kate*. Better once then neuer, for neuer to late. *Exeunt.*

Actus Quintus.

Enter Baptista, Vincentio, Gremio, the Pedant, Lucentio, and Bianca. Tranio, Biondello Grumio, and Widdow: The Seruingmen with Tranio bringing in a Banquet.

Luc. At last, though long, our iarring notes agree, And time it is when raging warre is come, To smile at scapes and perils ouerblowne: My faire *Bianca* bid my father welcome, While I with selfesame kindnesse welcome thine: Brother *Petruchio*, sister *Katerina*, And thou *Hortentio* with thy louing *Widdow*: Feast with the best, and welcome to my house, My Banket is to close our stomakes vp After our great good cheere: praie you sit downe, For now we sit to chat as well as eate.

Petr. Nothing but sit and sit, and eate and eate.

Bap. *Padua* affords this kindnesse, sonne *Petruchio*.

Petr. *Padua* affords nothing but what is kinde.

Hor. For both our sakes I would that word were true.

Pet. Now for my life *Hortentio* feares his Widow.

Wid. Then neuer trust me if I be affeard.

Petr. You are verie sencible, and yet you misse my sence:

I meane *Hortentio* is afeard of you.

Wid. He

Wid. He that is giddie thinks the world turns round.
Petr. Roundlie replied.
Kat. Mistris, how meane you that?
Wid. Thus I conceiue by him.
Petr. Conceiues by me, how likes *Hortentio* that?
Hor. My Widdow saies, thus she conceiues her tale.
Petr. Verie well mended: kisse him for that good
    Widdow.
Kat. He that is giddie thinkes the world turnes round,
I praie you tell me what you meant by that.
Wid. Your housband being troubled with a shrew,
Measures my husbands sorrow by his woe:
And now you know my meaning.
Kate. A verie meane meaning.
Wid. Right, I meane you.
Kat. And I am meane indeede, respecting you.
Petr. To her *Kate*.
Hor. To her *Widdow*.
Petr. A hundred markes, my *Kate* does put her down.
Hor. That's my office.
Petr. Spoke like an Officer: ha to the lad.
    Drinkes to Hortentio.
Bap. How likes *Gremio* these quicke witted folkes?
Gre. Beleeue me sir, they But together well.
Bian. Head, and but an hastie witted bodie,
Would say your Head and But were head and horne.
Vin. I Mistris Bride, hath that awakened you?
Bian. I, but not frighted me, therefore Ile sleepe a-
gaine.
Petr. Nay that you shall not since you haue begun:
Haue at you for a better iest or too.
Bian. Am I your Bird, I meane to shift my bush,
And then pursue me as you draw your Bow.
You are welcome all.   *Exit Bianca.*
Petr. She hath preuented me, here signior *Tranis*,
This bird you aim'd at, though you hit her not,
Therefore a health to all that shot and mist.
Tri. Oh sir, *Lucentio* slipt me like his Gray-hound,
Which runs himselfe, and catches for his Master.
Petr. A good swift simile, but something currish.
Tra. 'Tis well sir that you hunted for your selfe:
'Tis thought your Deere does hold you at a baie.
Bap. Oh, oh *Petruchio*, *Tranio* hits you now.
Luc. I thanke thee for that gird good *Tranio*.
Hor. Confesse, confesse, hath he not hit you here?
Petr. A has a little gald me I confesse:
And as the Iest did glaunce awaie from me,
'Tis ten to one it maim'd you too out right.
Bap. Now in good sadnesse sonne *Petruchio*,
I thinke thou hast the veriest shrew of all.
Petr. Well, I say no: and therefore sir assurance,
Let's each one send vnto his wife,
And he whose wife is most obedient,
To come at first when he doth send for her,
Shall win the wager which we will propose.
Hort. Content, what's the wager?
Luc. Twentie crownes.
Petr. Twentie crownes,
Ile venture so much of my Hawke or Hound,
But twentie times so much vpon my Wife.
Luc. A hundred then.
Hor. Content.
Petr. A match, 'tis done.
Hor. Who shall begin?
Luc. That will I.
Goe *Biondello*, bid your Mistris come to me.

Bio. I goe.   *Exit.*
Bap. Sonne, Ile be your halfe, *Bianca* comes.
Luc. Ile haue no halues: Ile beare it all my selfe,
    Enter Biondello.
How now, what newes?
Bio. Sir, my Mistris sends you word
That she is busie, and she cannot come.
Petr. How? she's busie, and she cannot come:
an answere?
Gre. I, and a kinde one too:
Praie God sir your wife send you not a worse.
Petr. I hope better.
Hor. Sirra *Biondello*, goe and intreate my wife to
come to me forthwith.   *Exit. Bion.*
Pet. Oh ho, intreate her, nay then shee must needes
come.
Hor. I am affraid sir, doe what you can
    Enter Biondello.
Yours will not be entreated: Now, where's my wife?
Bion. She saies you haue some goodly Iest in hand,
She will not come: she bids you come to her.
Petr. Worse and worse, she will not come:
Oh vilde, intollerable, not to be indur'd:
Sirra *Grumio*, goe to your Mistris,
Say I command her come to me.   *Exit.*
Hor. I know her answere.
Pet. What?
Hor. She will not.
Petr. The fouler fortune mine, and there an end.

    Enter Katerina.
Bap. Now by my hollidam here comes *Katerina*.
Kat. What is your will sir, that you send for me?
Petr. Where is your sister, and *Hortensios* wife?
Kate. They sit conferring by the Parler fire.
Petr. Goe fetch them hither, if they denie to come,
Swinge me them soundly forth vnto their husbands:
Away I say, and bring them hither straight.
Luc. Here is a wonder, if you talke of a wonder.
Hor. And so it is: I wonder what it boads.
Petr. Marrie peace it boads, and loue, and quiet life,
An awfull rule, and right supremicie:
And to be short, what not, that's sweete and happie.
Bap. Now faire befall thee good *Petruchio*;
The wager thou hast won, and I will adde
Vnto their losses twentie thousand crownes,
Another dowrie to another daughter,
For she is chang'd as she had neuer bin.
Petr. Nay, I will win my wager better yet,
And show more signe of her obedience,
Her new built vertue and obedience.
    Enter Kate, Bianca, and Widdow.
See where she comes, and brings your froward Wiues
As prisoners to her womanlie perswasion:
Katerine, that Cap of yours becomes you not,
Off with that bable, throw it vnderfoote.
Wid. Lord let me neuer haue a cause to sigh,
Till I be brought to such a sillie passe.
Bian. Fie what a foolish dutie call you this?
Luc. I would your dutie were as foolish too:
The wisdome of your dutie faire *Bianca*,
Hath cost me fiue hundred crownes since supper time.
Bian. The more foole you for laying on my dutie.
Pet. *Katherine* I charge thee tell these head-strong
women, what dutie they doe owe their Lords and hus-
bands.
    Wid. Come,

Wid. Come, come, your mocking: we will haue no telling.

Pet. Come on I say, and first begin with her.

Wid. She shall not.

Pet. I say she shall, and first begin with her.

Kate. Fie, fie, vnknit that threatning vnkinde brow,
And dart not scornefull glances from those eies,
To wound thy Lord, thy King, thy Gouernour.
It blots thy beautie, as frosts doe bite the Meads,
Confounds thy fame, as whirlewinds shake faire budds,
And in no sence is meete or amiable.
A woman mou'd, is like a fountaine troubled,
Muddie, ill seeming, thicke, bereft of beautie,
And while it is so, none so dry or thirstie
Will daigne to sip, or touch one drop of it.
Thy husband is thy Lord, thy life, thy keeper,
Thy head, thy soueraigne: One that cares for thee,
And for thy maintenance. Commits his body
To painfull labour, both by sea and land:
To watch the night in stormes, the day in cold,
Whil'st thou ly'st warme at home, secure and safe,
And craues no other tribute at thy hands,
But loue, faire lookes, and true obedience;
Too little payment for so great a debt.
Such dutie as the subiect owes the Prince,
Euen such a woman oweth to her husband:
And when she is froward, peeuish, sullen, sowre,
And not obedient to his honest will,
What is she but a foule contending Rebell,
And gracelesse Traitor to her louing Lord?
I am asham'd that women are so simple,
To offer warre, where they should kneele for peace:
Or seeke for rule, supremacie, and sway,
When they are bound to serue, loue, and obay.
Why are our bodies soft, and weake, and smooth,
Vnapt to toyle and trouble in the world,
But that our soft conditions, and our harts,
Should well agree with our externall parts?
Come, come, you froward and vnable wormes,
My minde hath bin as bigge as one of yours,
My heart as great, my reason haplie more,
To bandie word for word, and frowne for frowne;
But now I see our Launces are but strawes:
Our strength as weake, our weakenesse past compare,
That seeming to be most, which we indeed least are.
Then vale your stomackes, for it is no boote,
And place your hands below your husbands foote:
In token of which dutie, if he please,
My hand is readie, may it do him ease.

Pet. Why there's a wench: Come on, and kisse mee Kate.

Luc. Well go thy waies olde Lad for thou shalt ha't.

Vin. Tis a good hearing, when children are toward.

Luc. But a harsh hearing, when women are froward,

Pet. Come Kate, weee'le to bed,
We three are married, but you two are sped.
'Twas I wonne the wager, though you hit the white,
And being a winner, God giue you good night.

Exit Petruchio

Horten. Now goe thy wayes, thou hast tam'd a curst Shrew.

Luc. Tis a wonder, by your leaue, she wil be tam'd so.

FINIS.

Vv

ALL'S Well, that Ends Well.

Actus primus. Scœna Prima.

Enter yong Bertram Count of Rossillion, his Mother, and Helena, Lord Lafew, all in blacke.

Mother.

IN deliuering my sonne from me, I burie a second husband.

Ros. And I in going Madam, weep ore my fathers death anew; but I must attend his maiesties command, to whom I am now in Ward, euermore in subiection.

Laf. You shall find of the King a husband Madame, you sir a father. He that so generally is at all times good, must of necessitie hold his vertue to you, whose worthinesse would stirre it vp where it wanted rather then lack it where there is such abundance.

Mo. What hope is there of his Maiesties amendment?

Laf. He hath abandon'd his Phisitions Madam, vnder whose practises he hath persecuted time with hope, and finds no other aduantage in the processe, but onely the loosing of hope by time.

Mo. This yong Gentlewoman had a father, O that had, how sad a passage tis, whose skill was almost as great as his honestie, had it stretch'd so far, would haue made nature immortall, and death should haue play for lacke of worke. Would for the Kings sake hee were liuing, I thinke it would be the death of the Kings disease.

Laf. How call'd you the man you speake of Madam?

Mo. He was famous sir in his profession, and it was his great right to be so: *Gerard de Narbon.*

Laf. He was excellent indeed Madam, the King very latelie spoke of him admiringly, and mourningly: hee was skilfull enough to haue liu'd stil, if knowledge could be set vp against mortallitie.

Ros. What is it (my good Lord) the King languishes of?

Laf. A Fistula my Lord.

Ros. I heard not of it before.

Laf. I would it were not notorious. Was this Gentlewoman the Daughter of *Gerard de Narbon*?

Mo. His sole childe my Lord, and bequeathed to my ouer looking. I haue those hopes of her good, that her education promises her dispositions shee inherits, which makes faire gifts fairer: for where an vncleane mind carries vertuous qualities, there commendations go with pitty, they are vertues and traitors too: in her they are the better for their simplenesse; she deriues her honestie, and atcheeues her goodnesse.

Lafew. Your commendations Madam get from her teares.

Mo. 'Tis the best brine a Maiden can season her praise in. The remembrance of her father neuer approches her heart, but the tirrany of her sorrowes takes all liuelihood from her cheeke. No more of this *Helena*, go too, no more least it be rather thought you affect a sorrow, then to haue——

Hell. I doe affect a sorrow indeed, but I haue it too.

Laf. Moderate lamentation is the right of the dead, excessiue greefe the enemie to the liuing.

Mo. If the liuing be enemie to the greefe, the excesse makes it soone mortall.

Ros. Maddam I desire your holie wishes.

Laf. How vnderstand we that?

Mo. Be thou blest *Bertrame*, and succeed thy father In manners as in shape: thy blood and vertue Contend for Empire in thee, and thy goodnesse Share with thy birth-right. Loue all, trust a few, Doe wrong to none: be able for thine enemie Rather in power then vse: and keepe thy friend Vnder thy owne lifes key. Be checkt for silence, But neuer tax'd for speech. What heauen more wil, That thee may furnish, and my prayers plucke downe, Fall on thy head. Farwell my Lord, 'Tis an vnseason'd Courtier, good my Lord Aduise him.

Laf. He cannot want the best That shall attend his loue.

Mo. Heauen blesse him: Farwell *Bertram.*

Ro. The best wishes that can be forg'd in your thoghts be seruants to you: be comfortable to my mother, your Mistris, and make much of her.

Laf. Farewell prettie Lady, you must hold the credit of your father.

Hell. O were that all, I thinke not on my father, And these great teares grace his remembrance more Then those I shed for him. What was he like? I haue forgott him. My imagination Carries no fauour in't but *Bertrams.* I am vndone, there is no liuing, none, If *Bertram* be away. 'Twere all one, That I should loue a bright particuler starre, And think to wed it, he is so aboue me In his bright radience and colaterall light,

Must

Must I be comforted, not in his sphere;
Th'ambition in my loue thus plagues it selfe:
The hind that would be mated by the Lion
Must die for loue. 'Twas prettie, though a plague
To see him euerie houre to sit and draw
His arched browes, his hawking eie, his curles
In our hearts table: heart too capeable
Of euerie line and tricke of his sweet fauour.
But now he's gone, and my idolatrous fancie
Must sanctifie his Reliques. Who comes heere?

Enter Parrolles.

One that goes with him: I loue him for his sake,
And yet I know him a notorious Liar,
Thinke him a great way foole, solie a coward,
Yet these fixt euils sit so fit in him,
That they take place, when Vertues steely bones
Lookes bleake i'th cold wind: withall, full ofte we see
Cold wisedome waighting on superfluous follie.

  Par. Saue you faire Queene.
  Hel. And you Monarch.
  Par. No.
  Hel. And no.
  Par. Are you meditating on virginitie?
  Hel. I: you haue some staine of souldier in you: Let mee aske you a question. Man is enemie to virginitie, how may we barracado it against him?
  Par. Keepe him out.
  Hel. But he assailes, and our virginitie though valiant, in the defence yet is weak: vnfold to vs some warlike resistance.
  Par. There is none: Man setting downe before you, will vndermine you, and blow you vp.
  Hel. Blesse our poore Virginity from vnderminers and blowers vp. Is there no Military policy how Virgins might blow vp men?
  Par. Virginity beeing blowne downe, Man will quicklier be blowne vp: marry in blowing him downe againe, with the breach your selues made, you lose your Citty. It is not politicke, in the Common-wealth of Nature, to preserue virginity. Losse of Virginitie, is rationall encrease, and there was neuer Virgin goe, till virginitie was first lost. That you were made of, is mettall to make Virgins. Virginitie, by beeing once lost, may be ten times found: by being euer kept, it is euer lost: 'tis too cold a companion: Away with't.
  Hel. I will stand for't a little, though therefore I die a Virgin.
  Par. There's little can bee saide in't, 'tis against the rule of Nature. To speake on the part of virginitie, is to accuse your Mothers; which is most infallible disobedience. He that hangs himselfe is a Virgin: Virginitie murthers it selfe, and should be buried in highwayes out of all sanctified limit, as a desperate Offendresse against Nature. Virginitie breedes mites, much like a Cheese, consumes it selfe to the very payring, and so dies with feeding his owne stomacke. Besides, Virginitie is peeuish, proud, ydle, made of selfe-loue, which is the most inhibited sinne in the Cannon. Keepe it not, you cannot choose but loose by't. Out with't: within ten yeare it will make it selfe two, which is a goodly increase, and the principall it selfe not much the worse. Away with't.
  Hel. How might one do sir, to loose it to her owne liking?
  Par. Let mee see. Marry ill, to like him that ne're it likes. 'Tis a commodity wil lose the glosse with lying: The longer kept, the lesse worth: Off with't while 'tis vendible. Answer the time of request, Virginitie like an olde Courtier, weares her cap out of fashion, richly suted, but vnsuteable, iust like the brooch & the toothpick, which were not now: your Date is better in your Pye and your Porredge, then in your cheeke: and your virginity, your old virginity, is like one of our French wither'd peares, it lookes ill, it eates drily, marry 'tis a wither'd peare: it was formerly better, marry yet 'tis a wither'd peare: Will you any thing with it?
  Hel. Not my virginity yet:
There shall your Master haue a thousand loues,
A Mother, and a Mistresse, and a friend,
A Phenix, Captaine, and an enemy,
A guide, a Goddesse, and a Soueraigne,
A Counsellor, a Traitoresse, and a Deare:
His humble ambition, proud humility:
His iarring, concord: and his discord, dulcet:
His faith, his sweet disaster: with a world
Of pretty fond adoptious christendomes
That blinking Cupid gossips. Now shall he:
I know not what he shall, God send him well,
The Courts a learning place, and he is one.
  Par. What one ifaith?
  Hel. That I wish well, 'tis pitty.
  Par. What's pitty?
  Hel. That wishing well had not a body in't,
Which might be felt, that we the poorer borne,
Whose baser starres do shut vs vp in wishes,
Might with effects of them follow our friends,
And shew what we alone must thinke, which neuer
Returnes vs thankes.

Enter Page.

  Pag. Monsieur *Parrolles*,
My Lord cals for you.
  Par. Little *Hellen* farewell, if I can remember thee, I will thinke of thee at Court.
  Hel. Monsieur *Parolles*, you were borne vnder a charitable starre.
  Par. Vnder *Mars* I.
  Hel. I especially thinke, vnder *Mars*.
  Par. Why vnder *Mars*?
  Hel. The warres hath so kept you vnder, that you must needes be borne vnder *Mars*.
  Par. When he was predominant.
  Hel. When he was retrograde I thinke rather.
  Par. Why thinke you so?
  Hel. You go so much backward when you fight.
  Par. That's for aduantage.
  Hel. So is running away,
When feare proposes the safetie:
But the composition that your valour and feare makes in you, is a vertue of a good wing, and I like the weare well.
  Paroll. I am so full of businesses, I cannot answere thee acutely: I will returne perfect Courtier, in the which my instruction shall serue to naturalize thee, so thou wilt be capeable of a Courtiers councell, and vnderstand what aduice shall thrust vppon thee, else thou diest in thine vnthankfulnes, and thine ignorance makes thee away, farewell: When thou hast leysure, say thy praiers: when thou hast none, remember thy Friends:

Get thee a good husband, and vse him as he vses thee:
So farewell.

Hel. Our remedies oft in our selues do lye,
Which we ascribe to heauen: the fated skye
Giues vs free scope, onely doth backward pull
Our slow designes, when we our selues are dull.
What power is it, which mounts my loue so hye,
That makes me see, and cannot feede mine eye?
The mightiest space in fortune, Nature brings
To ioyne like, likes; and kisse like natiue things.
Impossible be strange attempts to those
That weigh their paines in sence, and do suppose
What hath beene, cannot be. Who euer stroue
To shew her merit, that did misse her loue?
(The Kings disease) my proiect may deceiue me,
But my intents are fixt, and will not leaue me. *Exit*

Flourish Cornets.
Enter the King of France with Letters, and diuers Attendants.

King. The *Florentines* and *Senoys* are by th'eares,
Haue fought with equall fortune, and continue
A brauing warre.

1.Lo.G. So tis reported sir.

King. Nay tis most credible, we heere receiue it,
A certaintie vouch'd from our Cosin *Austria*,
With caution, that the *Florentine* will moue vs
For speedie ayde: wherein our deerest friend
Preiudicates the businesse, and would seeme
To haue vs make deniall.

1.Lo.G. His loue and wisedome
Approu'd so to your Maiesty, may pleade
For amplest credence.

King. He hath arm'd our answer,
And *Florence* is deni'de before he comes:
Yet for our Gentlemen that meane to see
The *Tuscan* seruice, freely haue they leaue
To stand on either part.

2.Lo.E. It well may serue
A nursserie to our Gentrie, who are sicke
For breathing, and exploit.

King. What's he comes heere.

Enter Bertram, Lafew, and Parolles.

1.Lor.G. It is the Count *Rosignoll* my good Lord,
Yong *Bertram*.

King. Youth, thou bear'st thy Fathers face,
Franke Nature rather curious then in hast
Hath well compos'd thee: Thy Fathers morall parts
Maist thou inherit too: Welcome to *Paris*.

Ber. My thankes and dutie are your Maiesties.

Kin. I would I had that corporall soundnesse now,
As when thy father, and my selfe, in friendship
First tride our souldiership: he did looke farre
Into the seruice of the time, and was
Discipled of the brauest. He lasted long,
But on vs both did haggish Age steale on,
And wore vs out of act: It much repaires me
To talke of your good father; in his youth
He had the wit, which I can well obserue
To day in our yong Lords: but they may iest
Till their owne scorne returne to them vnnoted
Ere they can hide their leuitie in honour:
So like a Courtier, contempt nor bitternesse
Were in his pride, or sharpnesse; if they were,
His equall had awak'd them, and his honour
Clocke to it selfe, knew the true minute when
Exception bid him speake; and at this time
His tongue obey'd his hand. Who were below him
He vs'd as creatures of another place,
And bow'd his eminent top to their low rankes,
Making them proud of his humilitie,
In their poore praise he humbled: Such a man
Might be a copie to these yonger times;
Which followed well, would demonstrate them now
But goers backward.

Ber. His good remembrance sir
Lies richer in your thoughts, then on his tombe:
So in approofe liues not his Epitaph,
As in your royall speech.

King. Would I were with him he would alwaies say,
(Me thinkes I heare him now) his plausiue words
He scatter'd not in eares, but grafted them
To grow there and to beare: Let me not liue,
This his good melancholly oft began
On the Catastrophe and heele of pastime
When it was out: Let me not liue (quoth hee)
After my flame lackes oyle, to be the snuffe
Of yonger spirits, whose apprehensiue senses
All but new things disdaine; whose iudgements are
Meere fathers of their garments: whose constancies
Expire before their fashions: this he wish'd.
I after him, do after him wish too:
Since I nor wax nor honie can bring home,
I quickly were dissolued from my hiue
To giue some Labourers roome.

L.2.E. You'r loued Sir,
They that least lend it you, shall lacke you first.

Kin. I fill a place I know't: how long ist Count
Since the Physitian at your fathers died?
He was much fam'd.

Ber. Some six moneths since my Lord.

Kin. If he were liuing, I would try him yet.
Lend me an arme: the rest haue worne me out
With seuerall applications: Nature and sicknesse
Debate it at their leisure. Welcome Count,
My sonne's no deerer.

Ber. Thanke your Maiesty. *Exit*

Flourish.

Enter Countesse, Steward, and Clowne.

Coun. I will now heare, what say you of this gentle-woman.

Ste. Maddam the care I haue had to euen your content, I wish might be found in the Kalender of my past endeuours, for then we wound our Modestie, and make foule the clearnesse of our deseruings, when of our selues we publish them.

Coun. What doe's this knaue heere? Get you gone sirra: the complaints I haue heard of you I do not all beleeue, 'tis my slownesse that I doe not: For I know you lacke not folly to commit them, & haue abilitie enough to make such knaueries yours.

Clo. 'Tis not vnknown to you Madam, I am a poore fellow.

Coun. Well sir.

Clo. No maddam,
'Tis not so well that I am poore, though manie of

of the rich are damn'd, but if I may haue your Ladiships good will to goe to the world, *Isbell* the woman and w will doe as we may.

Coun. Wilt thou needes be a begger?

Clo. I doe beg your good will in this case.

Cou. In what case?

Clo. In *Isbels* case and mine owne: seruice is no heritage, and I thinke I shall neuer haue the blessing of God, till I haue issue a my bodie: for they say barnes are blessings.

Cou. Tell me thy reason why thou wilt marrie?

Clo. My poore bodie Madam requires it, I am driuen onby the flesh, and hee must needes goe that the diuell driues.

Cou. Is this all your worships reason?

Clo. Faith Madam I haue other holie reasons, such as they are.

Cou. May the world know them?

Clo. I haue beene Madam a wicked creature, as you and all flesh and blood are, and indeede I doe marrie that I may repent.

Cou. Thy marriage sooner then thy wickednesse.

Clo. I am out a friends Madam, and I hope to haue friends for my wiues sake.

Cou. Such friends are thine enemies knaue.

Clo. Y'are shallow Madam in great friends, for the knaues come to doe that for me which I am a wearie of: he that eres my Land, spares my teame, and giues mee leaue to Inne the crop: if I be his cuckold hee's my drudge; he that comforts my wife, is the cherisher of my flesh and blood; hee that cherishes my flesh and blood, loues my flesh and blood; he that loues my flesh and blood is my friend: *ergo*, he that kisses my wife is my friend: if men could be contented to be what they are, there were no feare in marriage, for yong *Charbon* the Puritan, and old *Poysam* the Papist, how somere their hearts are seuer'd in Religion, their heads are both one, they may ioule horns together like any Deare i'th Herd.

Cou. Wilt thou euer be a foule mouth'd and calumnious knaue?

Clo. A Prophet I Madam, and I speake the truth the next waie, for I the Ballad will repeate, which men full true shall finde, your marriage comes by destinie, your Cuckow sings by kinde.

Cou. Get you gone sir, Ile talke with you more anon.

Stew. May it please you Madam, that hee bid *Hellen* come to you, of her I am to speake.

Cou. Sirra tell my gentlewoman I would speake with her, *Hellen* I meane.

Clo. Was this faire face the cause, quoth she,
Why the Grecians sacked *Troy*,
Fond doue, done, fond was this King *Priams* ioy,
With that she sighed as she stood, *bis*
And gaue this sentence then, among nine bad if one be good, among nine bad if one be good, there's yet one good in ten.

Cou. What, one good in tenne? you corrupt the song sirra.

Clo. One good woman in ten Madam, which is a purifying ath' song: would God would serue the world so all the yeere, weed finde no fault with the tithe woman if I were the Parson, one in ten queth a? and wee might haue a good woman borne but ore euerie blazing starre, or at an earthquake, 'twould mend the Lotterie well, a man may draw his heart out ere a plucke one.

Cou. Youle begone sir knaue, and doe as I command you?

Clo. That man should be at womans command, and yet no hurt done, though honestie be no Puritan, yet it will doe no hurt, it will weare the Surplis of humilitie ouer the blacke-Gowne of a bigge heart: I am going forsooth, the businesse is for *Helen* to come hither.
Exit.

Cou. Well now.

Stew. I know Madam you loue your Gentlewoman intirely.

Cou. Faith I doe: her Father bequeath'd her to mee, and she her selfe without other aduantage, may lawfullie make title to as much loue as shee findes, there is more owing her then is paid, and more shall be paid her then sheele demand.

Stew. Madam, I was verie late more neere her then I thinke shee wisht mee, alone shee was, and did communicate to her selfe her owne words to her owne eares, shee thought, I dare vowe for her, they touch not anie stranger sence, her matter was, shee loued your Sonne; Fortune shee said was no goddesse, that had put such difference betwixt their two estates: Loue no god, that would not extend his might onelie, where qualities were leuell, Queene of Virgins, that would suffer her poore Knight surpris'd without rescue in the first assault or ransome afterward: This shee deliuer'd in the most bitter touch of sorrow that ere I heard Virgin exclaime in, which I held my dutie speedily to acquaint you withall, sithence in the losse that may happen, it concernes you something to know it.

Cou. You haue discharg'd this honestlie, keepe it to your selfe, manie likelihoods inform'd mee of this before, which hung so tottring in the ballance, that I could neither beleeue nor misdoubt: praie you leaue mee, stall this in your bosome, and I thanke you for your honest care: I will speake with you further anon.
Exit Steward.

Enter Hellen.

Old.Cou. Euen so it vvas vvith me when I was yong:
If euer vve are natures, these are ours, this thorne
Doth to our Rose of youth righlie belong
Our bloud to vs, this to our blood is borne,
It is the show, and seale of natures truth,
Where loues strong passion is imprest in youth,
By our remembrances of daies forgon,
Such were our faults, or then we thought them none,
Her eie is sicke on't, I obserue her now.

Hell. What is your pleasure Madam?

Ol.Cou. You know *Hellen* I am a mother to you.

Hell. Mine honorable Mistris.

Ol.Cou. Nay a mother, why not a mother? when I
  sed a mother
Me thought you saw a serpent, what's in mother,
That you start at it? I say I am your mother,
And put you in the Catalogue of those
That were enwombed mine, 'tis often seene
Adoption striues vvith nature, and choise breedes
A natiue slip to vs from forraine seedes:
You nere opprest me with a mothers groane,
Yet I expresse to you a mothers care,
(Gods mercie maiden) dos it curd thy blood
To say I am thy mother? vvhat's the matter,
That this distempered messenger of wet?

The manie colour'd Iris rounds thine eye?
——————Why, that you are my daughter?

Hell. That I am not.

Old. Cou. I say I am your Mother.

Hell. Pardon Madam.
The Count *Rosillion* cannot be my brother:
I am from humble, he from honored name:
No note vpon my Parents, his all noble,
My Master, my deere Lord he is, and I
His seruant liue, and will his vassall die:
He must not be my brother.

Ol. Cou. Nor I your Mother.

Hell. You are my mother Madam, would you were
So that my Lord your sonne were not my brother,
Indeede my mother, or were you both our mothers,
I care no more for, then I doe for heauen,
So I were not his sister, can't no other,
But I your daughter, he must be my brother.

Old. Cou. Yes *Hellen*, you might be my daughter in law,
God shield you meane it not, daughter and mother
So striue vpon your pulse; vvhat pale agen?
My feare hath catcht your fondnesse! now I see
The mistrie of your louelinesse, and finde
Your salt teares head, now to all sence 'tis grosse:
You loue my sonne, inuention is asham'd
Against the proclamation of thy passion
To say thou doost not: therefore tell me true,
But tell me then 'tis so, for looke, thy cheekes
Confesse it 'ton tooth to th'other, and thine eies
See it so grosely showne in thy behauiours,
That in their kinde they speake it, onely sinne
And hellish obstinacie tye thy tongue
That truth should be suspected, speake, ist so?
If it be so, you haue wound a goodly clewe:
If it be not, forsweare't how ere I charge thee,
As heauen shall worke in me for thine auaile
To tell me truelie.

Hell. Good Madam pardon me.

Cou. Do you loue my Sonne?

Hell. Your pardon noble Mistris.

Cou. Loue you my Sonne?

Hell. Doe not you loue him Madam?

Cou. Goe not about; my loue hath in't a bond
Whereof the world takes note: Come, come, disclose:
The state of your affection, for your passions
Haue to the full appeach'd.

Hell. Then I confesse
Here on my knee, before high heauen and you,
That before you, and next vnto high heauen, I loue your
  Sonne:
My friends were poore but honest, so's my loue:
Be not offended, for it hurts not him
That he is lou'd of me; I follow him not
By any token of presumptuous suite,
Nor would I haue him, till I doe deserue him,
Yet neuer know how that desert should be:
I know I loue in vaine, striue against hope:
Yet in this captious, and intemible Siue,
I still poure in the waters of my loue
And lacke not to loose still; thus *Indian* like
Religious in mine error, I adore
The Sunne that lookes vpon his worshipper,
But knowes of him no more. My deerest Madam,
Let not your hate incounter with my loue,
For louing where you doe; but if your selfe,
Whose aged honor cites a vertuous youth,

Did euer, in so true a flame of liking,
Wish chastly, and loue dearely, that your *Dian*
Was both her selfe and loue, O then giue pittie
To her whose state is such, that cannot choose
But lend and giue where she is sure to loose;
That seekes not to finde that, her search implies,
But riddle like, liues sweetely where she dies.

Cou. Had you not lately an intent, speake truely,
To goe to *Paris*?

Hell. Madam I had.

Cou. Wherefore? tell true.

Hell. I will tell truth, by grace it selfe I sweare:
You know my Father left me some prescriptions
Of rare and prou'd effects, such as his reading
And manifest experience, had collected
For generall soueraigntie: and that he wil'd me
In heedefull'st reseruation to bestow them,
As notes, whose faculties inclusiue were,
More then they were in note: Amongst the rest,
There is a remedie, approu'd, set downe,
To cure the desperate languishings whereof
The King is render'd lost.

Cou. This was your motiue for *Paris*, was it, speake?

Hell. My Lord, your sonne, made me to think of this;
Else *Paris*, and the medicine, and the King,
Had from the conuersation of my thoughts,
Happily beene absent then.

Cou. But thinke you *Hellen*,
If you should tender your supposed aide,
He would receiue it? He and his Phisitions
Are of a minde, he, that they cannot helpe him:
They, that they cannot helpe, how shall they credit
A poore vnlearned Virgin, when the Schooles
Embowel'd of their doctrine, haue left off
The danger to it selfe.

Hell. There's something in't
More then my Fathers skill, which was the great'st
Of his profession, that his good receipt,
Shall for my legacie be sanctified
By th' luckiest stars in heauen, and would your honor
But giue me leaue to trie successe, I'de venture
The well lost life of mine, on his Graces cure,
By such a day, an houre.

Cou. Doo'st thou beleeue't?

Hell. I Madam knowingly.

Cou. Why *Hellen* thou shalt haue my leaue and loue,
Meanes and attendants, and my louing greetings
To those of mine in Court, Ile staie at home
And praie Gods blessing into thy attempt:
Begon to morrow, and be sure of this,
What I can helpe thee to, thou shalt not misse. *Exeunt.*

Actus Secundus.

*Enter the King with diuers yong Lords, taking leaue for
the Florentine warre: Count, Rosse, and
Parrolles. Florish Cornets.*

King. Farewell yong Lords, these warlike principles
Doe not throw from you, and you my Lords farewell:
Share the aduice betwixt you, if both gaine, all
The guift doth stretch it selfe as tis receiu'd,
And is enough for both.

Lord. G. 'Tis our hope sir,

After

After well entred souldiers, to returne
And finde your grace in health.

King. No, no, it cannot be; and yet my heart
Will not confesse he owes the mallady
That doth my life besiege : farewell yong Lords,
Whether I liue or die, be you the sonnes
Of worthy French men : let higher Italy
(Those bated that inherit but the fall
Of the last Monarchy) see that you come
Not to wooe honour, but to wed it, when
The brauest questant shrinkes : finde what you seeke,
That fame may cry you loud: I say farewell.

L.G. Health at your bidding serue your Maiesty.

King. Those girles of Italy, take heed of them,
They say our French, lacke language to deny
If they demand : beware of being Capriues
Before you serue.

Bo. Our hearts receiue your warnings.

King. Farewell, come hether to me.

1.Lo.G. Oh my sweet Lord ỹ you wil stay behind vs.

Parr. 'Tis not his fault the spark.

2.Lo.E. Oh 'tis braue warres.

Parr. Most admirable, I haue seene those warres.

Rossill. I am commanded here, and kept a coyle with,
Too young, and the next yeere, and 'tis too early.

Parr. And thy minde stand too't boy,
Steale away brauely.

Rossill. I shal stay here the fot-horse to a smocke,
Creeking my shooes on the plaine Masonry,
Till honour be bought vp, and no sword worne
But one to dance with: by heauen, Ile steale away.

1.Lo.G. There's honour in the theft.

Parr. Commit it Count.

2.Lo.E. I am your accessary, and so farewell.

Ros. I grow to you, & our parting is a tortur'd body.

1.Lo.G. Farewll Captaine.

2.Lo.E. Sweet Mounsier *Parolles.*

Parr. Noble *Heroes*; my sword and yours are kinne,
good sparkes and lustrous, a word good mettals. You
shall finde in the Regiment of the Spinij, one Captaine
Spurio his sicatrice, with an Embleme of warre heere on
his sinister cheeke; it was this very sword entrench'd it:
say to him I liue, and obserue his reports for me.

Lo.G. We shall noble Captaine.

Parr. Mars doate on you for his nouices, what will
ye doe?

Ross. Stay the King.

Parr. Vse a more spacious ceremonie to the Noble
Lords, you haue restrain'd your selfe within the List of
too cold an adieu: be more expressiue to them; for they
weare themselues in the cap of the time, there do muster
true gate; eat, speake, and moue vnder the influence of
the most receiu'd starre, and though the deuill leade the
measure, such are to be followed: after them, and take a
more dilated farewell.

Ross. And I will doe so.

Parr. Worthy fellowes, and like to prooue most si-
newie sword-man. *Exeunt.*

Enter Lafew.

L.Laf. Pardon my Lord for mee and for my tidings.

King. Ile see thee to stand vp. (pardon,

L.Laf. Then heres a man stands that has brought his
I would you had kneel'd my Lord to aske me mercy,
And that at my bidding you could so stand vp.

King. I would I had, so I had broke thy pate
And askt thee mercy for't.

Laf. Goodfaith a-crosse, but my good Lord 'tis thus,
Will you be cur'd of your infirmitie?

King. No.

Laf. O will you eat no grapes my royall foxe?
Yes but you will, my noble grapes, and if
My royall foxe could reach them: I haue seene a medicine
That's able to breath life into a stone,
Quicken a rocke, and make you dance Canari
With sprightly fire and motion, whose simple touch
Is powerfull to arayse King *Pippen,* nay
To giue great *Charlemaine* a pen in's hand
And write to her a loue-line.

King. What her is this?

Laf. Why doctor she : my Lord, there's one arriu'd,
If you will see her: now by my faith and honour,
If seriously I may conuay my thoughts
In this my light deliuerance, I haue spoke
With one, that in her sexe, her yeeres, profession,
Wisedome and constancy, hath amaz'd mee more
Then I dare blame my weakenesse : will you see her?
For that is her demand, and know her businesse?
That done, laugh well at me.

King. Now good *Lafew,*
Bring in the admiration, that we with thee
May spend our wonder too, or take off thine
By wondring how thou tookst it.

Laf. Nay, Ile fit you,
And not be all day neither.

King. Thus he his speciall nothing euer prologues.

Laf. Nay, come your waies.

Enter Hellen.

King. This haste hath wings indeed.

Laf. Nay, come your waies,
This is his Maiestie, say your minde to him,
A Traitor you doe looke like, but such traitors
His Maiesty seldome seares, I am *Cresseds* Vncle,
That dare leaue two together, far you well. *Exit.*

King. Now faire one, do's your busines follow vs?

Hel. I my good Lord,
Gerard de Narbon was my father,
In what he did professe, well found.

King. I knew him.

Hel. The rather will I spare my praises towards him,
Knowing him is enough : on's bed of death,
Many receits he gaue me, chieflie one,
Which as the dearest issue of his practice
And of his olde experience, th'onlie darling,
He bad me store vp, as a triple eye,
Safer then mine owne two : more deare I haue so,
And hearing your high Maiestie is toucht
With that malignant cause, wherein the honour
Of my deare fathers gift, stands cheefe in power,
I come to tender it, and my appliance,
With all bound humblenesse.

King. We thanke you maiden,
But may not be so credulous of cure,
When our most learned Doctors leaue vs, and
The congregated Colledge haue concluded,
That labouring Art can neuer ransome nature
From her inaydible estate : I say we must not
So staine our iudgement, or corrupt our hope,
To prostitute our past-cure malladie
To empericks, or to disseuer so
Our great selfe and our credit, to esteeme
A sencelesse helpe, when helpe past sence we deeme.

Hel. My

Hell. My dutie then shall pay me for my paines:
I will no more enforce mine office on you,
Humbly intreating from your royall thoughts,
A modest one to beare me backe againe.

King. I cannot giue thee lesse to be cal'd gratefull:
Thou thoughtst to helpe me, and such thankes I giue,
As one neere death to those that wish him liue:
But what at full I know, thou knowst no part,
I knowing all my perill, thou no Art.

Hell. What I can doe, can doe no hurt to try,
Since you set vp your rest 'gainst remedie:
He that of greatest workes is finisher,
Oft does them by the weakest minister:
So holy Writ, in babes hath iudgement showne,
When Iudges haue bin babes; great flouds haue flowne
From simple sources: and great Seas haue dried
When Miracles haue by the great'st beene denied.
Oft expectation failes, and most oft there
Where most it promises: and oft it hits,
Where hope is coldest, and despaire most shifts.

King. I must not heare thee, fare thee wel kind maide,
Thy paines not vs'd, must by thy selfe be paid,
Proffers not tooke, reape thanks for their reward.

Hel. Inspired Merit so by breath is bard,
It is not so with him that all things knowes
As 'tis with vs, that square our guesse by showes:
But most it is presumption in vs, when
The help of heauen we count the act of men.
Deare sir, to my endeauors giue consent,
Of heauen, not me, make an experiment.
I am not an Impostrue, that proclaime
My selfe against the leuill of mine aime,
But know I thinke, and thinke I know most sure,
My Art is not past power, nor you past cure.

King. Art thou so confident? Within what space
Hop'st thou my cure?

Hel. The greatest grace lending grace,
Ere twice the horses of the sunne shall bring
Their fiery torcher his diurnall ring,
Ere twice in murke and occidentall dampe
Moist *Hesperus* hath quench'd her sleepy Lampe:
Or foure and twenty times the Pylots glasse
Hath told the theeuish minutes, how they passe:
What is infirme, from your sound parts shall flie,
Health shall liue free, and sickenesse freely dye.

King. Vpon thy certainty and confidence,
What dar'st thou venter?

Hell. Taxe of impudence,
A strumpets boldnesse, a divulged shame
Traduc'd by odious ballads: my maidens name
Seard otherwise, ne worse of worst extended
With vildest torture, let my life be ended.

Kin. Methinks in thee some blessed spirit doth speak
His powerfull sound, within an organ weake:
And what impossibility would slay
In common sence, sence saues another way:
Thy life is deere, for all that life can rate
Worth name of life, in thee hath estimate:
Youth, beauty, wisedome, courage, all
That happines and prime, can happy call:
Thou this to hazard, needs must intimate
Skill infinite, or monstrous desperate,
Sweet practiser, thy Physicke I will try,
That ministers thine owne death if I die.

Hel. If I breake time, or flinch in property
Of what I spoke, vnpittied let me die,
And well deseru'd: not helping, death's my fee,
But if I helpe, what doe you promise me.

Kin. Make thy demand.

Hel. But will you make it euen?

Kin. I by my Scepter, and my hopes of helpe.

Hel. Then shalt thou giue me with thy kingly hand
What husband in thy power I will command:
Exempted be from me the arrogance
To choose from forth the royall bloud of France,
My low and humble name to propagate
With any branch or image of thy state:
But such a one thy vassall, whom I know
Is free for me to aske, thee to bestow.

Kin. Heere is my hand, the premisses obseru'd,
Thy will by my performance shall be seru'd:
So make the choice of thy owne time, for I
Thy resolv'd Patient, on thee still relye:
More should I question thee, and more I must,
Though more to know, could not be more to trust:
From whence thou cam'st, how tended on, but rest
Vnquestion'd welcome, and vndoubted blest.
Giue me some helpe heere hoa, if thou proceed,
As high as word, my deed shall match thy deed.

Florish. Exit.

Enter Countesse and Clowne.

Lady. Come on sir, I shall now put you to the height of your breeding.

Clown. I will shew my selfe highly fed, and lowly taught, I know my businesse is but to the Court.

Lady. To the Court, why what place make you speciall, when you put off that with such contempt, but to the Court?

Clo. Truly Madam, if God haue lent a man any manners, hee may easilie put it off at Court: hee that cannot make a legge, put off's cap, kisse his hand, and say nothing, has neither legge, hands, lippe, nor cap; and indeed such a fellow, to say precisely, were not for the Court, but for me, I haue an answere will serue all men.

Lady. Marry that's a bountifull answere that fits all questions.

Clo. It is like a Barbers chaire that fits all buttockes, the pin buttocke, the quatch-buttocke, the brawn buttocke, or any buttocke.

Lady. Will your answere serue fit to all questions?

Clo. As fit as ten groats is for the hand of an Atturney, as your French Crowne for your taffety punke, as *Tibs* rush for *Toms* fore-finger, as a pancake for Shrouetuesday, a Morris for May-day, as the naile to his hole, the Cuckold to his horne, as a scolding queane to a wrangling knaue, as the Nuns lip to the Friers mouth, nay as the pudding to his skin.

Lady. Haue you, I say, an answere of such fitnesse for all questions?

Clo. From below your Duke, to beneath your Constable, it will fit any question.

Lady. It must be an answere of most monstrous size, that must fit all demands.

Clo. But a trifle neither in good faith, if the learned should speake truth of it: heere it is, and all that belongs to't. Aske mee if I am a Courtier, it shall doe you no harme to learne.

Lady. To be young againe if we could: I will bee a foole in question, hoping to bee the wiser by your answer.

Lady.

All's Well that ends Well.

La. I pray you sir, are you a Courtier?

Clo. O Lord sir there's a simple putting off: more, more, a hundred of them.

La. Sir I am a poore freind of yours, that loues you.

Clo. O Lord sir, thicke, thicke, spare not me.

La. I thinke sir, you can eate none of this homely meate.

Clo. O Lord sir; nay put me too't, I warrant you.

La. You were lately whipt sir as I thinke.

Clo. O Lord sir, spare not me.

La. Doe you crie O Lord sir at your whipping, and spare not me? Indeed your O Lord sir, is very sequent to your whipping: you would answere very well to a whipping if you were but bound too't.

Clo. I nere had worse lucke in my life in my O Lord sir; I see things may serue long, but not serue euer.

La. I play the noble huswife with the time, to entertaine it so merrily with a foole.

Clo. O Lord sir, why there't serues well agen.

La. And end sir to your businesse: giue *Hellen* this, And vrge her to a present answer backe, Commend me to my kinsmen, and my sonne, This is not much.

Clo. Not much commendation to them.

La. Not much imployement for you, you vnderstand me.

Clo. Most fruitfully, I am there, before my legges.

La. Hast you agen. *Exeunt*

Enter Counts, Lafew, and Parolles.

Ol.Laf. They say miracles are past, and we haue our Philosophicall persons, to make moderne and familiar things supernaturall and causelesse. Hence is it, that we make trifles of terrours, ensconcing our selues into seeming knowledge, when we should submit our selues to an vnknowne feare.

Par. Why 'tis the rarest argument of wonder, that hath shot out in our latter times.

Rof. And so 'tis.

Ol.Laf. To be relinquisht of the Artists.

Par. So I say both of *Galen* and *Paracelsus*.

Ol.Laf. Of all the learned and authenticke fellowes.

Par. Right so I say.

Ol.Laf. That gaue him out incureable.

Par. Why there 'tis, so say I too.

Ol.Laf. Not to be help'd.

Par. Right, as 'twere a man assur'd of a——

Ol.Laf. Vncertaine life, and sure death.

Par. Iust, you say well: so would I haue said.

Ol.Laf. I may truly say, it is a nouelcie to the world.

Par. It is indeede if you will haue it in shewing, you shall reade it in what do ye call there.

Ol.Laf. A shewing of a heauenly effect in an earthly Actor.

Par. That's it, I would haue said, the verie same.

Ol.Laf. Why your Dolphin is not lustier: fore mee I speake in respect——

Par. Nay 'tis strange, 'tis very straunge, that is the breefe and the tedious of it, and he's of a most facinerious spirit, that will not acknowledge it to be the——

Ol.Laf. Very hand of heauen.

Par. I, so I say.

Ol.Laf. In a most weake——

Par. And debile minister great power, great trancendence, which should indeede giue vs a further vse to be made, then alone the recou'ry of the king, as to bee

Old Laf. Generally thankfull.

Enter King, Hellen, and attendants.

Par. I would haue said it, you say well: heere comes the King.

Ol.Laf. Lustique, as the Dutchman saies: Ile like a maide the Better whil'st I haue a tooth in my head: why he's able to leade her a Carranto.

Par. Mor du vinager, is not this *Helen*?

Ol.Laf. Fore God I thinke so.

King. Goe call before mee all the Lords in Court,
Sit my preseruer by thy patients side,
And with this healthfull hand whose banisht sence
Thou hast repeal'd, a second time receyue
The confirmation of my promis'd guift,
Which but attends thy naming.

Enter 3 or 4 Lords.

Faire Maide send forth thine eye, this yourhfull parcell
Of Noble Batchellors, stand at my bestowing,
Ore whom both Soueraigne power, and fathers voice
I haue to vse; thy franke election make,
Thou hast power to choose, and they none to forsake.

Hel. To each of you, one faire and vertuous Mistris;
Fall when loue please, marry to each but one.

Old Laf. I'de giue bay curtall, and his furniture
My mouth no more were broken then these boyes,
And writ as little beard.

King. Peruse them well:
Not one of those, but had a Noble father.

She addresses her to a Lord.

Hel. Gentlemen, heauen hath through me, restor'd the king to health.

All. We vnderstand it, and thanke heauen for you.

Hel. I am a simple Maide, and therein wealthiest
That I protest, I simply am a Maide:
Please it your Maiestie, I haue done already:
The blushes in my cheekes thus whisper mee,
We blush that thou shouldst choose, but be refused;
Let the white death sit on thy cheeke for euer,
Wee'l nere come there againe.

King. Make choise and see,
Who shuns thy loue, shuns all his loue in mee.

Hel. Now *Dian* from thy Altar do I fly,
And to imperiall loue, that God most high
Do my sighes streame: Sir, wil you heare my suite?

1.Lo. And grant it.

Hel. Thankes sir, all the rest is mute.

Ol.Laf. I had rather be in this choise, then throw Ames-ace for my life.

Hel. The honor sir that flames in your faire eyes,
Before I speake too threatningly replies:
Loue make your fortunes twentie times aboue
Her that so wishes, and her humble loue.

2.Lo. No better if you please.

Hel. My wish receiue,
Which great loue grant, and so I take my leaue.

Ol.Laf. Do all they denie her? And they were sons of mine, I'de haue them whip'd, or I would send them to'th Turke to make Eunuches of.

Hel. Be not afraid that I your hand should take,
Ile neuer do you wrong for your owne sake:
Blessing vpon your vowes, and in your bed
Finde fairer fortune, if you euer wed.

Old Laf. These boyes are boyes of Ice, they'le none haue

haue beene: sure they are bastards to the English, the French nere got em.

La. You are too young, too happie, and too good To make your selfe a sonne out of my blood.

4.Lord. Faire one, I thinke not so.

Ol.Lord There's one grape yet, I am sure thy father drunke wine. But if thou be'st not an asse, I am a youth of fourteene: I haue knowne thee already.

Hel. I dare not say I take you, but I giue Me and my seruice, euer whilst I liue Into your guiding power: This is the man.

King. Why then young *Bertram* take her shee's thy wife.

Ber. My wife my Leige? I shal beseech your highnes In such a busines, giue me leaue to vse The helpe of mine owne eies.

King. Know'st thou not *Bertram* what shee ha's done for mee?

Ber. Yes my good Lord, but neuer hope to know why I should marrie her.

King. Thou know'st shee ha's rais'd me from my sickly bed.

Ber. But followes it my Lord, to bring me downe Must answer for your raising? I knowe her well: Shee had her breeding at my fathers charge: A poore Physitians daughter my wife? Disdaine Rather corrupt me euer.

King. Tis onely title thou disdainst in her, the which I can build vp: strange is it that our bloods Of colour, waight, and heat, pour'd all together, Would quite confound distinction: yet stands off In differences so mightie. If she bee All that is vertuous (saue what thou dislik'st) A poore Phisitians daughter, thou dislik'st Of vertue for the name: but doe not so: From lowest place, whence vertuous things proceed, The place is dignified by th' doers deede. Where great additions swell's, and vertue none, It is a dropsied honour. Good alone, Is good without a name? Vilenesse is so: The propertie by what it is, should go, Not by the title. Shee is young, wise, faire, In these, to Nature shee's immediate heire: And these breed honour: that is honours scorne, Which challenges it selfe as honours borne, And is not like the sire: Honours thriue, When rather from our acts we them deriue Then our fore-goers: the meere words, a slaue Debosh'd on euerie tombe, on euerie graue: A lying Trophee, and as oft is dumbe, Where dust, and damn'd obliuion is the Tombe. Of honour'd bones indeed, what should be saide? If thou canst like this creature, as a maide, I can create the rest: Vertue, and shee Is her owne dower: Honour and wealth, from mee.

Ber. I cannot loue her, nor will striue to doo't.

King. Thou wrong'st thy selfe, if thou shold'st striue to choose.

Hel. That you are well restor'd my Lord, I'me glad: Let the rest go.

King. My Honor's at the stake, which to defeate I must produce my power. Heere, take her hand, Proud scornfull boy, vnworthie this good gift, That dost in vile misprision shackle vp My loue, and her desert: that canst not dreame, We poizing vs in her defectiue scale,

Shall weigh thee to the beame: That wilt not know, It is in Vs to plant thine Honour, where We please to haue it grow. Checke thy contempt: Obey Our will, which trauailes in thy good: Beleeue not thy disdaine, but presentlie Do thine owne fortunes that obedient right Which both thy dutie owes, and Our power claimes, Or I will throw thee from my care for euer Into the staggers, and the carelesse lapse Of youth and ignorance: both my reuenge and hate Loosing vpon thee, in the name of iustice, Without all termes of pittie. Speake, thine answer.

Ber. Pardon my gracious Lord: for I submit My fancie to your eies, when I consider What great creation, and what dole of honour Flies where you bid it: I finde that she which late Was in my Nobler thoughts, most base: is now The praised of the King, who so ennobled, Is as 'twere borne so.

King. Take her by the hand, And tell her she is thine: to whom I promise A counterpoize: If not to thy estate, A ballance more repleat.

Ber. I take her hand.

Kin. Good fortune, and the fauour of the King Smile vpon this Contract: whose Ceremonie Shall seeme expedient on the now borne briefe, And be perform'd to night: the solemne Feast Shall more attend vpon the coming space, Expecting absent friends. As thou lou'st her, Thy loue's to me Religious: else, do's erre. *Exeunt*

Parolles and Lafew stay behind, commenting of this wedding.

Laf. Do you heare Monsieur? A word with you.

Par. Your pleasure sir.

Laf. Your Lord and Master did well to make his recantation.

Par. Recantation? My Lord? my Master?

Laf. I: Is it not a Language I speake?

Par. A most harsh one, and not to bee vnderstoode without bloudie succeeding My Master?

Laf. Are you Companion to the Count *Rosillion*?

Par. To any Count, to all Counts: to what is man.

Laf. To what is Counts man: Counts maister is of another stile.

Par. You are too old sir: Let it satisfie you, you are too old.

Laf. I must tell thee sirrah, I write Man: to which title age cannot bring thee.

Par. What I dare too well do, I dare not do.

Laf. I did thinke thee for two ordinaries: to bee a prettie wise fellow, thou didst make tollerable vent of thy trauell, it might passe: yet the scarffes and the bannerets about thee, did manifoldlie disswade me from beleeuing thee a vessell of too great a burthen. I haue now found thee, when I loose thee againe, I care not: yet art thou good for nothing but taking vp, and that th' oure scarce worth.

Par. Hadst thou not the priuiledge of Antiquity vpon thee.

Laf. Do not plundge thy selfe to farre in anger, least thou hasten thy triall: which if, Lord haue mercie on thee for a hen, so my good window of Lettice fare thee well, thy casement I neede not open, for I look through thee. Giue me thy hand.

Par. My Lord, you giue me most egregious indignity.

Laf.

All's Well, that Ends Well.

Laf. I with all my heart, and thou art worthy of it.

Par. I haue not my Lord deseru'd it.

Laf. Yes good faith, eu'ry dramme of it, and I will not bate thee a scruple.

Par. Well, I shall be wiser.

Laf. Eu'n as soone as thou can'st, for thou hast to pull at a smacke a'th contrarie. If euer thou bee'st bound in thy skarfe and beaten, thou shall finde what it is to be proud of thy bondage, I haue a desire to holde my acquaintance with thee, or rather my knowledge, that I may say in the default, he is a man I know.

Par. My Lord you do me most insupportable vexation.

Laf. I would it were hell paines for thy sake, and my poore doing eternall: for doing I am past, as I will by thee, in what motion age will giue me leaue. *Exit.*

Par. Well, thou hast a sonne shall take this disgrace off me; scuruy, old, filthy, scuruy Lord: Well, I must be patient, there is no fettering of authority. Ile beate him (by my life) if I can meete him with any conuenience, and he were double and double a Lord. Ile haue no more pittie of his age then I would haue of―――Ile beate him, and if I could but meet him agen.

Enter Lafew.

Laf. Sirra, your Lord and masters married, there's newes for you: you haue a new Mistris.

Par. I most vnfainedly beseech your Lordshippe to make some reseruation of your wrongs. He is my good Lord, whom I serue aboue is my master.

Laf. Who? God.

Par. I sir.

Laf. The deuill it is, that's thy master. Why dooest thou garter vp thy armes a this fashion? Dost make hose of thy sleeues? Do other seruants so? Thou wert best set thy lower part where thy nose stands. By mine Honor, if I were but two houres yonger, I'de beate thee: methink'st thou art a generall offence, and euery man shold beate thee: I thinke thou wast created for men to breath themselues vpon thee.

Par. This is hard and vndeserued measure my Lord.

Laf. Go too sir, you were beaten in *Italy* for picking a kernell out of a Pomgranat, you are a vagabond, and no true traueller: you are more sawcie with Lordes and honourable personages, then the Commission of your birth and vertue giues you Heraldry. You are not worth another word, else I'de call you knaue. I leaue you. *Exit*

Enter Count Rossillion.

Par. Good, very good, it is so then: good, very good, let it be conceal'd awhile.

Ros. Vndone, and forfeited to cares for euer.

Par. What's the matter sweet-heart?

Rossill. Although before the solemne Priest I haue sworne, I will not bed her.

Par. What? what sweet heart?

Ros. O my *Parrolles*, they haue married me: Ile to the *Tuscan* warres, and neuer bed her.

Par. *France* is a dog-hole, and it no more merits, The tread of a mans foot: too'th warres.

Ros. There's letters from my mother: What th'import is, I know not yet.

Par. I that would be knowne: too'th warrs my boy, too'th warres:

He weares his honor in a boxe vnseene, That hugges his kickie wickie heare at home, Spending his manlie marrow in her armes Which should sustaine the bound and high curuet Of *Marses* fierie steed: to other Regions, *France* is a stable, wee that dwell in't Iades, Therefore too'th warre.

Ros. It shall be so, Ile send her to my house, Acquaint my mother with my hate to her, And wherefore I am fled: Write to the King That which I durst not speake. His present gift Shall furnish me to those Italian fields Where noble fellowes strike: Warres is no strife To the darke house, and the detected wife.

Par. Will this Caprichio hold in thee, art sure?

Ros. Go with me to my chamber, and aduice me: Ile send her straight away: To morrow, Ile to the warres, she to her single sorrow.

Par. Why these bals bound, ther's noise in it. Tis hard A yong man maried, is a man that's mard: Therefore away, and leaue her brauely: go, The King ha's done you wrong: but hush 'tis so. *Exit*

Enter Helena and Clowne.

Hel. My mother greets me kindly, is she well?

Clo. She is not well, but yet she has her health, she's very merrie, but yet she is not well: but thankes be giuen she's very well, and wants nothing i'th world: but yet she is not well.

Hel. If she be verie wel, what do's she ayle, that she's not verie well?

Clo. Truly she's very well indeed, but for two things

Hel. What two things?

Clo. One, that she's not in heauen, whether God send her quickly: the other, that she's in earth, from whence God send her quickly.

Enter Parolles.

Par. Blesse you my fortunate Ladie.

Hel. I hope sir I haue your good will to haue mine owne good fortune.

Par. You had my prayers to leade them on, and to keepe them on, haue them still. O my knaue, how do's my old Ladie?

Clo. So that you had her wrinkles, and I her money, I would she did as you say.

Par. Why I say nothing.

Clo. Marry you are the wiser man: for many a mans tongue shakes out his masters vndoing: to say nothing, to do nothing, to know nothing, and to haue nothing, is to be a great part of your title, which is within a verie little of nothing.

Par. Away, th'art a knaue.

Clo. You should haue said sir before a knaue, th'art a knaue, that's before me th'art a knaue: this had beene truth sir.

Par. Go too, thou art a wittie foole, I haue found thee.

Clo. Did you finde me in your selfe sir, or were you taught to finde me?

Clo. The search sir was profitable, and much Foole may you find in you, euen to the worlds pleasure, and the encrease of laughter.

Par. A good knaue ifaith, and well fed. Madam, my Lord will go awaie to night,

A

A verie serrious businesse call's on him:
The great prerogatiue and rite of loue,
Which as your due time claimes, he do's acknowledge,
But puts it off to a compell'd restraint:
Whose want, and whose delay, is strew'd with sweets
Which they distill now in the curbed time,
To make the comming houre oreflow with ioy,
And pleasure drowne the brim.

   Hel. What's his will else?
   Par. That you will take your instant leaue a'th king,
And make this hast as your owne good proceeding,
Strengthned with what Apologie you thinke
May make it probable neede.
   Hel. What more commands hee?
   Par. That hauing this obtain'd, you presentlie
Attend his further pleasure.
   Hel. In euery thing I waite vpon his will.
   Par. I shall report it so.   *Exit Par.*
   Hell. I pray you come sirrah.   *Exit*

Enter Lafew and Bertram.

   Laf. But I hope your Lordshippe thinkes not him a souldier.
   Ber. Yes my Lord and of verie valiant approofe.
   Laf. You haue it from his owne deliuerance.
   Ber. And by other warranted testimonie.
   Laf. Then my Diall goes not true, I tooke this Larke for a bunting.
   Ber. I do assure you my Lord he is very great in knowledge, and accordinglie valiant.
   Laf. I haue then sinn'd against his experience, and transgrest against his valour, and my state that way is dangerous, since I cannot yet find in my heart to repent: Heere he comes, I pray you make vs freinds, I will pursue the amitie.

Enter Parolles.

   Par. These things shall be done sir.
   Laf. Pray you sir whose his Tailor?
   Par. Sir?
   Laf. O I know him well, I sir, hee sirs a good workeman, a verie good Tailor.
   Ber. Is shee gone to the king?
   Par. Shee is.
   Ber. Will shee away to night?
   Par. As you'le haue her.
   Ber. I haue writ my letters, casketted my treasure, Giuen order for our horses, and to night,
When I should take possession of the Bride,
And ere I doe begin.
   Laf. A good Trauailer is something at the latter end of a dinner, but on that lies three thirds, and vses a knowne truth to passe a thousand nothings with, should bee once hard, and thrice beaten. God saue you Captaine.
   Ber. Is there any vnkindnes betweene my Lord and you Monsieur?
   Par. I know not how I haue deserued to run into my Lords displeasure.
   Laf. You haue made shift to run into't, bootes and spurres and all; like him that leapt into the Custard, and out of it you'le runne againe, rather then suffer question for your residence.
   Ber. It may bee you haue mistaken him my Lord.
   Laf. And shall doe so euer, though I tooke him at's prayers. Fare you well my Lord, and beleeue this of me, there can be no kernell in this light Nut: the soule of this man is his cloathes: Trust him not in matter of heauie consequence: I haue kept of them tame, & know their natures. Farewell Monsieur, I haue spoken better of you, then you haue or will to deserue at my hand, but we must do good against euill.
   Par. An idle Lord, I sweare.
   Ber. I thinke so.
   Par. Why do you not know him?
   Ber. Yes, I do know him well, and common speech Giues him a worthy passe. Heere comes my clog.

Enter Helena.

   Hel. I haue sir as I was commanded from you Spoke with the King, and haue procur'd his leaue For present parting, onely he desires
Some priuate speech with you.
   Ber. I shall obey his will.
You must not meruaile *Helen* at my course,
Which holds not colour with the time, nor does
The ministration, and required office
On my particular. Prepar'd I was not
For such a businesse, therefore am I found
So much vnsetled: This driues me to intreate you,
That presently you take your way for home,
And rather muse then aske why I intreate you,
For my respects are better then they seeme,
And my appointments haue in them a neede
Greater then shewes it selfe at the first view,
To you that know them not. This to my mother,
'Twill be two daies ere I shall see you, so
I leaue you to your wisedome.
   Hel. Sir, I can nothing say,
But that I am your most obedient seruant.
   Ber. Come, come, no more of that.
   Hel. And euer shall
With true obseruance seeke to eeke out that
Wherein toward me my homely starres haue faild
To equall my great fortune.
   Ber. Let that goe: my hast is verie great. Farwell: Hie home.
   Hel. Pray sir your pardon.
   Ber. Well, what would you say?
   Hel. I am not worthie of the wealth I owe,
Nor dare I say 'tis mine: and yet it is,
But like a timorous theefe, most faine would steale
What law does vouch mine owne.
   Ber. What would you haue?
   Hel. Something, and scarse so much: nothing indeed, I would not tell you what I would my Lord: Faith yes, Strangers and foes do sunder, and not kisse.
   Ber. I pray you stay not, but in hast to horse.
   Hel. I shall not breake your bidding, good my Lord: Where are my other men? Monsieur, farwell.   *Exit*
   Ber. Go thou toward home, where I wil neuer come, Whilst I can shake my sword, or heare the drumme: Away, and for our flight.
   Par. Brauely, Coragio.

Actus Tertius.

Flourish. Enter the Duke of Florence, the two Frenchmen, with a troope of Souldiers.

   Duke. So that from point to point, now haue you heard
The

All's Well, that Ends Well.

The fundamentall reasons of this warre,
Whose great decision hath much blood let forth
And more thirsts after.

1. Lord. Holy seemes the quarrell
Vpon your Graces part: blacke and fearefull
On the opposer.

Duke. Therefore we meruaile much our Cosin France
Would in so iust a businesse, shut his bosome
Against our borrowing prayers.

French E. Good my Lord,
The reasons of our state I cannot yeelde,
But like a common and an outward man,
That the great figure of a Counsaile frames,
By selfe vnable motion, therefore dare not
Say what I thinke of it, since I haue found
My selfe in my incertaine grounds to faile
As often as I guest.

Duke. Be it his pleasure.

Fren. G. But I am sure the yonger of our nature,
That surfet on their ease, will day by day
Come heere for Physicke.

Duke. Welcome shall they bee:
And all the honors that can flye from vs,
Shall on them settle: you know your places well,
When better fall, for your auailes they fell,
To morrow to'th field. *Flourish.*

Enter Countesse and Clowne.

Count. It hath happen'd all, as I would haue had it, saue that he comes not along with her.

Clo. By my troth I take my young Lord to be a verie melancholly man.

Count. By what obseruance I pray you.

Clo. Why he will looke vppon his boote, and sing: mend the Ruffe and sing, aske questions and sing, picke his teeth, and sing: I know a man that had this tricke of melancholy hold a goodly Mannor for a song.

Lad. Let me see what he writes, and when he meanes to come.

Clow. I haue no minde to *Isbell* since I was at Court. Our old Lings, and our *Isbels* a'th Country, are nothing like your old Ling and your *Isbels* a'th Court: the brains of my Cupid's knock'd out, and I beginne to loue, as an old man loues money, with no stomacke.

Lad. What haue we heere?

Clo. In that you haue there. *exit*

A Letter.

I haue sent you a daughter-in-Law, shee hath recouered the King, and vndone me: I haue wedded her, not bedded her, and sworne to make the not eternall. You shall heare I am runne away, know it before the report come. If there bee bredth enough in the world, I will hold a long distance. My duty to you.
Your vnfortunate sonne,
Bertram.

This is not well rash and vnbridled boy,
To flye the fauours of so good a King,
To plucke his indignation on thy head,
By the misprising of a Maide too vertuous
For the contempt of Empire.

Enter Clowne.

Clow. O Madam, yonder is heauie newes within betweene two souldiers, and my yong Ladie.

La. What is the matter.

Clo. Nay there is some comfort in the newes, some comfort, your sonne will not be kild so soone as I thoght he would.

La. Why should he be kill'd?

Clo. So say I Madame, if he runne away, as I heare he does, the danger is in standing too't, that's the losse of men, though it be the getting of children. Heere they come will tell you more. For my part I onely heare your sonne was run away.

Enter Hellen and two Gentlemen.

French E. Saue you good Madam.
Hel. Madam, my Lord is gone, for euer gone.
French G. Do not say so.
La. Thinke vpon patience, pray you Gentlemen,
I haue felt so many quirkes of ioy and greefe,
That the first face of neither on the start
Can woman me vntoo't. Where is my sonne I pray you?
Fren. G. Madam he's gone to serue the Duke of Florence,
We met him thitherward, for thence we came:
And after some dispatch in hand at Court,
Thither we bend againe.
Hel. Looke on his Letter Madam, here's my Pasport.

When thou canst get the Ring vpon my finger, which neuer shall come off, and shew mee a childe begotten of thy bodie, that I am father too, then call me husband: but in such a (then) I write a Neuer.

This is a dreadfull sentence.
La. Brought you this Letter Gentlemen?
1. G. I Madam, and for the Contents sake are sorrie for our paines.
Old La. I prethee Ladie haue a better cheere,
If thou engrossest, all the greefes are thine,
Thou robst me of a moity: He was my sonne,
But I do wash his name out of my blood,
And thou art all my childe. Towards Florence is he?
Fren. G. I Madam.
La. And to be a souldier.
Fren. G. Such is his noble purpose, and beleeu't
The Duke will lay vpon him all the honor
That good conuenience claimes.
La. Returne you thither.
Fren. E. I Madam, with the swiftest wing of speed.
Hel. Till I haue no wife, I haue nothing in France,
'Tis bitter.
La. Finde you that there?
Hel. I Madame.
Fren. E. 'Tis but the boldnesse of his hand haply, which his heart was not consenting too.
Lad. Nothing in France, vntill he haue no wife:
There's nothing heere that is too good for him
But onely she, and she deserues a Lord
That twenty such rude boyes might tend vpon,
And call her hourely Mistris. Who was with him?
Fren. E. A seruant onely, and a Gentleman: which I haue sometime knowne.
La. Parolles was it not?
Fren. E. I my good Ladie, hee.
La. A verie tainted fellow, and full of wickednesse,
My sonne corrupts a well deriued nature
With his inducement.
Fren. E. Indeed good Ladie the fellow has a deale of that, too much, which holds him much to haue.
La. Y'are welcome Gentlemen, I will intreate you when you see my sonne, to tell him that his sword can neuer winne the honor that he looses: more Ile intreate

X   you

you written to beare along.

Fren. G. We serue you Madam in that and all your worthiest affaires.

La. Not so, but as we change our courtesies,
Will you draw neere? *Exit.*

Hel. Till I haue no wife I haue nothing in France,
Nothing in France vntill he has no wife:
Thou shalt haue none *Rossillion*, none in France,
Then hast thou all againe: poore Lord, is't I
That chase thee from thy Countrie, and expose
Those tender limbes of thine, to the euent
Of the none-sparing warre? And is it I,
That driue thee from the sportiue Court, where thou
Was't shot at with faire eyes, to be the marke
Of smoakie Muskets? O you leaden messengers,
That ride vpon the violent speede of fire,
Fly with false ayme, moue the still-peering aire
That sings with piercing, do not touch my Lord:
Who euer shoots at him, I set him there.
Who euer charges on his forward brest
I am the Caitiffe that do hold him too't,
And though I kill him not, I am the cause
His death was so effected: Better 'twere
I met the rauine Lyon when he roar'd
With sharpe constraint of hunger: better 'twere,
That all the miseries which nature owes
Were mine at once. No come thou home *Rossillion*,
Whence honor but of danger winnes a scarre,
As oft it looses all. I will be gone:
My being heere it is, that holds thee hence,
Shall I stay heere to doo't? No, no, although
The ayre of Paradise did fan the house,
And Angles offic'd all: I will be gone,
That pittifull rumour may report my flight
To consolate thine eare. Come night, end day,
For with the darke (poore theefe) Ile steale away. *Exit.*

*Flourish. Enter the Duke of Florence, Rossillion,
drum and trumpets, soldiers, Parrolles.*

Duke. The Generall of our horse thou art, and we
Great in our hope, lay our best loue and credence
Vpon thy promising fortune.

Ber. Sir it is
A charge too heauy for my strength, but yet
Wee'l striue to beare it for your worthy sake,
To th'extreme edge of hazard.

Duke. Then go thou forth,
And fortune play vpon thy prosperous helme
As thy auspicious mistris.

Ber. This very day
Great Mars I put my selfe into thy file,
Make me but like my thoughts, and I shall proue
A louer of thy drumme, hater of loue. *Exeunt omnes*

Enter Countesse & Steward.

La. Alas! and would you take the letter of her:
Might you not know she would do, as she has done,
By sending me a Letter. Reade it agen.

Letter.
I am S. *Iaques* Pilgrim, thither gone:
Ambitious loue hath so in me offended,
That bare-foot plod I the cold ground vpon
With sainted vow my faults to haue amended.
Write, write, that from the bloodie course of warre,
My deerest Master your deare sonne, may hie,
Blesse him at home in peace. Whilst I from farre,
His name with zealous feruour sanctifie:
His taken labours bid him me forgiue:
I his despightfull Iuno sent him forth,
From Courtly friends, with Camping foes to liue,
Where death and danger dogges the heeles of worth.
He is too good and faire for death, and mee,
Whom I my selfe embrace, to set him free.

Ah what sharpe stings are in her mildest words?
Rynaldo, you did neuer lacke aduice so much,
As letting her passe so: had I spoke with her,
I could haue well diuerted her intents,
Which thus she hath preuented.

Ste. Pardon me Madam,
If I had giuen you this at ouer-night,
She might haue beene ore-tane: and yet she writes
Pursuite would be but vaine.

La. What Angell shall
Blesse this vnworthy husband, he cannot thriue,
Vnlesse her prayers, whom heauen delights to heare
And loues to grant, repreeue him from the wrath
Of greatest Iustice. Write, write *Rynaldo*,
To this vnworthy husband of his wife,
Let euerie word waigh heauie of her worth,
That he does waigh too light: my greatest greefe,
Though little he do feele it, set downe sharpely.
Dispatch the most conuenient messenger,
When haply he shall heare that she is gone,
He will returne, and hope I may that shee
Hearing so much, will speede her foote againe,
Led hither by pure loue : which of them both
Is deerest to me, I haue no skill in sence
To make distinction : prouide this Messenger:
My heart is heauie, and mine age is weake,
Greefe would haue teares, and sorrow bids me speake. *Exeunt*

A Tucket afarre off.

*Enter old Widdow of Florence, her daughter, Violenta
and Mariana, with other
Citizens.*

Widdow. Nay come,
For if they do approach the Citty,
We shall loose all the sight.

Diana. They say, the French Count has done
Most honourable seruice.

Wid. It is reported,
That he has taken their great'st Commander,
And that with his owne hand he slew
The Dukes brother: we haue lost our labour,
They are gone a contrarie waye harke,
you may know by their Trumpets.

Maria. Come lets returne againe,
And suffice our selues with the report of it.
Well *Diana*, take heed of this French Earle,
The honor of a Maide is her name,
And no Legacie is so rich
As honestie.

Widdow. I haue told my neighbour
How you haue beene solicited by a Gentleman,
His Companion.

Mari.

Maria. I know that knaue, hang him, one *Parolles*, a filthy Officer he is in those suggestions for the young Earle, beware of them *Diana*; their promises, entisements, oathes, tokens, and all these engines of lust, are not the things they go vnder: many a maide hath beene seduced by them, and the miserie is example, that so terrible shewes in the wracke of maiden-hood, cannot for all that disswade succession, but that they are limed with the twigges that threatens them. I hope I neede not to aduise you further, but I hope your owne grace will keepe you where you are, though there were no further danger knowne, but the modestie which is so lost.

Dia. You shall not neede to feare me.

Enter Hellen.

Wid. I hope so: looke here comes a pilgrim, I know she will lye at my house, thither they send one another, Ile question her. God saue you pilgrim, whether are bound?

Hel. To S. *Iaques la grand.*
Where do the Palmers lodge, I do beseech you?

Wid. At the S. *Francis* heere beside the Port.

Hel. Is this the way? *A march afarre.*

Wid. I marrie ist. Harke you, they come this way: If you will tarrie holy Pilgrime
But till the troopes come by,
I will conduct you where you shall be lodg'd,
The rather for I thinke I know your hostesse
As ample as my selfe.

Hel. Is it your selfe?

Wid. If you shall please so Pilgrime.

Hel. I thanke you, and will stay vpon your leisure.

Wid. you came I thinke from *France*?

Hel. I did so.

Wid. Heere you shall see a Countriman of yours That has done worthy seruice.

Hel. His name I pray you?

Dia. The Count *Rossillion*: know you such a one?

Hel. But by the eare that heares most nobly of him: His face I know not.

Dia. What somere he is
He's brauely taken heere. He stole from *France* As 'tis reported: for the King had married him Against his liking. Thinke you it is so?

Hel. I surely meere the truth, I know his Lady.

Dia. There is a Gentleman that serues the Count, Reports but coursely of her.

Hel. What's his name?

Dia. Monsieur *Parolles.*

Hel. Oh I beleeue with him,
In argument of praise, or to the worth
Of the great Count himselfe, she is too meane
To haue her name repeated, all her deseruing
Is a reserued honestie, and that
I haue not heard examin'd.

Dian. Alas poore Ladie,
Tis a hard bondage to become the wife
Of a detesting Lord.

Wid. I write good creature, wheresoere she is,
Her hart waighes sadly: this yong maid might do her
A shrewd turne if she pleas'd.

Hel. How do you meane?
May be the amorous Count solicites her
In the vnlawfull purpose.

Wid. He does indeede,
And brokes with all that can in such a suite
Corrupt the tender honour of a Maide:
But she is arm'd for him, and keepes her guard
In honestest defence.

Drumme and Colours.
Enter Count Rossillion, Parrolles, and the whole Armie.

Mar. The goddes forbid else.

Wid. So, now they come:
That is *Anthonio* the Dukes eldest sonne,
That *Escalus.*

Hel. Which is the Frenchman?

Dia. Hee,
That with the plume, 'tis a most gallant fellow,
I would he lou'd his wife: if he were honester
He were much goodlier. Is't not a handsom Gentleman

Hel. I like him well.

Di. 'Tis pitty he is not honest: yonds that same knaue
That leades him to these places: were I his Ladie,
I would poison that vile Rascall.

Hel. Which is he?

Dia. That Iacke an-apes with scarfes. Why is hee melancholly?

Hel. Perchance he's hurt i'th battaile.

Par. Loose our drum? Well.

Mar. He's shrewdly vext at something. Looke he has spyed vs.

Wid. Marrie hang you.

Mar. And your curtesie, for a ring-carrier. *Exit.*

Wid. The troope is past: Come pilgrim, I wil bring you, Where you shall host: Of inioyn'd penitents There's foure or fiue, to great S. *Iaques* bound, Alreadie at my house.

Hel. I humbly thanke you:
Please it this Matron, and this gentle Maide
To eate with vs to night, the charge and thanking
Shall be for me. and to requite you further,
I will bestow some precepts of this Virgin,
Worthy the note.

Both. Wee'l take your offer kindly. *Exeunt.*

Enter Count Rossillion and the Frenchmen, as at first.

Cap. E. Nay good my Lord put him too't: let him haue his way.

Cap. G. If your Lordshippe finde him not a Hilding, hold me no more in your respect.

Cap. E. On my life my Lord a bubble.

Ber. Do you thinke I am so farre Deceiued in him.

Cap. E. Beleeue it my Lord, in mine owne direct knowledge, without any malice, but to speake of him as my kinsman, hee's a most notable Coward, an infinite and endlesse Lyar, an hourely promise-breaker, the owner of no one good qualitie, worthy your Lordships entertainment.

Cap. G. It were fit you knew him, least reposing too farre in his vertue which he hath not, he might at some great and trustie businesse, in a maine daunger, fayle you.

Ber. I would I knew in what particular action to try him.

Cap. G. None better then to let him fetch off his drumme, which you heare him so confidently vndertake to do.

C. E. I with a troope of Florentines wil sodainly surprize

prize him; such I will haue whom I am sure he knowes not from the enemie: wee will binde and hoodwinke him so, that he shall suppose no other but that he is carried into the Leager of the aduersaries, when we bring him to our owne tents: be but your Lordship present at his examination, if he do not for the promise of his life, and in the highest compulsion of base feare, offer to betray you, and deliuer all the intelligence in his power against you, and that with the diuine forfeite of his soule vpon oath, neuer trust my iudgement in anie thing.

Cap.G. O for the loue of laughter, let him fetch his drumme, he sayes he has a stratagem for't: when your Lordship sees the bottome of this successe in't, and to what mettle this counterfeyt lump of ours will be melted if you giue him not Iohn drummes entertainement, your inclining cannot be remoued. Heere he comes.

Enter Parrolles.

Cap.E. O for the loue of laughter hinder not the honor of his designe, let him fetch off his drumme in any hand.

Ber. How now Monsieur? This drumme sticks sorely in your disposition.

Cap.G. A pox on't, let it go, 'tis but a drumme.

Par. But a drumme: Ist but a drumme? A drum so lost. There was excellent command, to charge in with our horse vpon our owne wings, and to rend our owne souldiers.

Cap.G. That was not to be blam'd in the command of the seruice: it was a disaster of warre that *Cæsar* him selfe could not haue preuented, if he had beene there to command.

Ber. Well, wee cannot greatly condemne our successe: some dishonor wee had in the losse of that drum, but it is not to be recouered.

Par. It might haue beene recouered.

Ber. It might, but it is not now.

Par. It is to be recouered, but that the merit of seruice is sildome attributed to the true and exact performer, I would haue that drumme or another, or *hic iacet.*

Ber. Why if you haue a stomacke, too't Monsieur: if you thinke your mysterie in stratagem, can bring this instrument of honour againe into his natiue quarter, be magnanimious in the enterprize and go on, I wil grace the attempt for a worthy exploit: if you speede well in it, the Duke shall both speake of it, and extend to you what further becomes his greatnesse, euen to the vtmost syllable of your worthinesse.

Par. By the hand of a souldier I will vndertake it.

Ber. But you must not now slumber in it.

Par. Ile about it this euening, and I will presently pen downe my dilemma's, encourage my selfe in my certaintie, put my selfe into my mortall preparation: and by midnight looke to heare further from me.

Ber. May I bee bold to acquaint his grace you are gone about it.

Par. I know not what the successe wil be my Lord, but the attempt I vow.

Ber. I know th'art valiant,
And to the possibility of thy souldiership,
Will subscribe for thee: Farewell.

Par. I loue not many words. *Exit*

Cap.E. No more then a fish loues water. Is not this a strange fellow my Lord, that so confidently seemes to vndertake this businesse, which he knowes is not to be done, damnes himselfe to do, & dares better be damnd then to doo't.

Cap.G. You do not know him my Lord as we doe, certaine it is that he will steale himselfe into a mans fauour, and for a weeke escape a great deale of discoueries, but when you finde him out, you haue him euer after.

Ber. Why do you thinke he will make no deede at all of this that so seriouslie hee dooes addresse himselfe vnto?

Cap.E. None in the world, but returne with an inuention, and clap vpon you two or three probable lies: but we haue almost imbost him, you shall see his fall to night; for indeede he is not for your Lordshippes respect.

Cap.G. Weele make you some sport with the Foxe ere we case him. He was first smoak'd by the old Lord *Lafew*, when his disguise and he is parted, tell me what a sprat you shall finde him, which you shall see this verie night.

Cap.E. I must go looke my twigges,
He shall be caught.

Ber. Your brother he shall go along with me.

Cap.G. As't please your Lordship, Ile leaue you.

Ber. Now wil I lead you to the house, and shew you
The Lasse I spoke of.

Cap.E. But you say she's honest.

Ber. That's all the fault: I spoke with hir but once,
And found her wondrous cold, but I sent to her
By this same Coxcombe that we haue i'th winde
Tokens and Letters, which she did resend,
And this is all I haue done: She's a faire creature,
Will you go see her?

Cap.E. With all my heart my Lord. *Exeunt*

Enter Hellen, and Widdow.

Hel. If you misdoubt me that I am not shee,
I know not how I shall assure you further,
But I shall loose the grounds I worke vpon.

Wid. Though my estate be falne, I was well borne,
Nothing acquainted with these businesses,
And would not put my reputation now
In any staining act.

Hel. Nor would I wish you.
First giue me trust, the Count he is my husband,
And what to your sworne counsaile I haue spoken,
Is so from word to word: and then you cannot
By the good ayde that I of you shall borrow,
Erre in bestowing it.

Wid. I should beleeue you,
For you haue shew'd me that which well approues
Y'are great in fortune.

Hel. Take this purse of Gold,
And let me buy your friendly helpe thus farre,
Which I will ouer-pay, and pay againe
When I haue found it. The Count he woes your
daughter,
Layes downe his wanton siedge before her beautie,
Resolue to carrie her: let her in fine consent
As wee'l direct her how 'tis best to beare it:
Now his important blood will naught denie,
That shee'l demand: a ring the Countie weares,
That downward hath succeeded in his house

from sonne to sonne, some foure or fiue discents,
Since the first father wore it. This Ring he holds
In most rich choice: yet in his idle fire,
To buy his will, it would not seeme too deere,
How ere repented after.

  Wid. Now I see the bottome of your purpose.
  Hel. You see it lawfull then, it is no more,
But that your daughter ere she seemes as wonne,
Desires this Ring; appoints him an encounter;
In fine, deliuers me to fill the time,
Her selfe most chastly absent: after
To marry her, Ile adde three thousand Crownes
To what is past already.

  Wid. I haue yeelded:
Instruct my daughter how she shall perseuer,
That time and place with this deceite so lawfull
May proue coherent. Euery night he comes
With Musickes of all sorts, and songs compos'd
To her vnworthinesse: It nothing steeds vs
To chide him from our eeues, for he persists
As if his life lay on't.

  Hel. Why then to night
Let vs assay our plot, which if it speed,
Is wicked meaning in a lawfull deede;
And lawfull meaning in a lawfull act,
Where both not sinne, and yet a sinfull fact.
But let's about it.

Actus Quartus.

Enter one of the Frenchmen, with fiue or sixe other souldiers in ambush.

  1.*Lord E.* He can come no other way but by this hedge corner: when you sallie vpon him, speake what terrible Language you will: though you vnderstand it not your selues, no matter: for we must not seeme to vnderstand him, vnlesse some one among vs, whom wee must produce for an Interpreter.
  1.*Sol.* Good Captaiue, let me be th'Interpreter.
  Lor.E. Art not acquainted with him? knowes he not thy voice?
  1.*Sol.* No sir I warrant you.
  Lo.E. But what linsie wolsy hast thou to speake to vs againe.
  1.*Sol.* E'n such as you speake to me.
  Lo.E. He must thinke vs some band of strangers, i'th aduersaries entertainment. Now he hath a smacke of all neighbouring Languages: therefore we must euery one be a man of his owne fancie, not to know what we speak one to another: so we seeme to know, is to know straight our purpose: Choughs language, gabble enough, and good enough. As for you interpreter, you must seeme very politicke. But couch hoa, heere hee comes, to beguile two houres in a sleepe, and then to returne & sweare the lies he forges.

Enter Parrolles.

  Par. Ten a clocke: Within these three houres 'twill be time enough to goe home. What shall I say I haue done? It must bee a very plausiue inuention that carries it. They beginne to smoake mee, and disgraces haue of late, knock'd too often at my doore: I finde my tongue is too foole-hardie, but my heart hath the feare of Mars before it, and of his creatures, not daring the reports of my tongue.
  Lo.E. This is the first truth that ere thine own tongue was guiltie of.
  Par. What the diuell should moue mee to vndertake the recouerie of this drumme, being not ignorant of the impossibility, and knowing I had no such purpose? I must giue my selfe some hurts, and say I got them in exploit: yet slight ones will not carrie it. They will say, came you off with so little? And great ones I dare not giue, wherefore what's the instance. Tongue, I must put you into a Butter-womans mouth, and buy my selfe another of *Baiazeths* Mule, if you prattle mee into these perilles.
  Lo.E. Is it possible he should know what hee is, and be that he is.
  Par. I would the cutting of my garments wold serue the turne, or the breaking of my Spanish sword.
  Lo.E. We cannot affoord you so.
  Par. Or the baring of my beard, and to say it was in stratagem.
  Lo.E. 'Twould not do.
  Par. Or to drowne my cloathes, and say I was stript.
  Lo.E. Hardly serue.
  Par. Though I swore I leapt from the window of the Citadell.
  Lo.E. How deepe?
  Par. Thirty fadome.
  Lo.E. Three great oathes would scarse make that be beleeued.
  Par. I would I had any drumme of the enemies, I would sweare I recouer'd it.
  Lo.E. You shall heare one anon.
  Par. A drumme now of the enemies.

Alarum within.

  Lo.E. Throca movousus, cargo, cargo, cargo.
  All. Cargo, cargo, cargo, villianda par corbo, cargo.
  Par. O ransome, ransome,
Do not hide mine eyes.
  Inter. Boskos thromuldo boskos.
  Par. I know you are the *Muskos* Regiment,
And I shall loose my life for want of language.
If there be heere German or Dane, Low Dutch,
Italian, or French, let him speake to me,
Ile discouer that, which shal vndo the Florentine.
  Int. Boskos vauvado, I vnderstand thee, & can speake thy tongue: *Kerelybonto* sir, betake thee to thy faith, for seuenteene ponyards are at thy bosome.
  Par. Oh.
  Inter. Oh pray, pray, pray,
Manka reuania dulche.
  Lo.E. Oscorbidulchos voliuorco.
  Int. The Generall is content to spare thee yet,
And hoodwinkt as thou art, will leade thee on
To gather from thee. Haply thou mayst informe
Something to saue thy life.
  Par. O let me liue,
And all the secrets of our campe Ile shew,
Their force, their purposes: Nay, Ile speake that,
Which you will wonder at.
  Inter. But wilt thou faithfully?
  Par. If I do not, damne me.
  Inter. Acordo linta.
Come on, thou are granted space.   *Exit.*
A short Alarum within.

L.E. Go tell the Count *Rossillion* and my brother,
We haue caught the woodcocke, and will keepe him
Till we do heare from them. (mufled

Sol. Captaine I will.

L.E. A will betray vs all vnto our selues,
Informe on that.

Sol. So I will sir.

L.E. Till then Ile keepe him darke and safely lockt.
Exit

Enter Bertram, and the Maide called Diana.

Ber. They told me that your name was *Fontybell*.

Dia. No my good Lord, *Diana*.

Ber. Titled Goddesse,
And worth it with addition: but faire soule,
In your fine frame hath loue no qualitie?
If the quicke fire of youth light not your minde,
You are no Maiden but a monument
When you are dead you should be such a one
As you are now: for you are cold and sterne,
And now you should be as your mother was
When your sweet selfe was got.

Dia. She then was honest.

Ber. So should you be.

Dia. No:
My mother did but dutie, such (my Lord)
As you owe to your wife.

Ber. No more a'that:
I prethee do not striue against my vowes:
I was compell'd to her, but I loue thee
By loues owne sweet constraint, and will for euer
Do thee all rights of seruice.

Dia. I so you serue vs
Till we serue you: But when you haue our Roses,
You barely leaue our thornes to pricke our selues,
And mocke vs with our barenesse.

Ber. How haue I sworne.

Dia. Tis not the many oathes that makes the truth,
But the plaine single vow, that is vow'd true:
What is not holie, that we sweare not by,
But take the high'st to witnesse: then pray you tell me,
If I should sweare by Ioues great attributes,
I lou'd you deerely, would you beleeue my oathes,
When I did loue you ill? This ha's no holding
To sweare by him whom I protest to loue
That I will worke against him. Therefore your oathes
Are words and poore conditions, but vnseal'd
At lest in my opinion.

Ber. Change it, change it:
Be not so holy cruell: Loue is holie,
And my integritie ne're knew the crafts
That you do charge men with: Stand no more off,
But giue thy selfe vnto my sicke desires,
Who then recouers. Say thou art mine, and euer
My loue as it beginnes, shall so perseuer.

Dia. I see that men make rope's in such a scarre,
That wee'l forsake our selues. Giue me that Ring.

Ber. Ile lend it thee my deere; but haue no power
To giue it from me.

Dia. Will you not my Lord?

Ber. It is an honour longing to our house,
Bequeathed downe from manie Ancestors,
Which were the greatest obloquie i'th world,
In me to loose.

Dia. Mine Honors such a Ring,
My chastities the Iewell of our house,
Bequeathed downe from many Ancestors,
Which were the greatest obloquie i'th world,
In mee to loose. Thus your owne proper wisedome
Brings in the Champion honor on my part,
Against your vaine assault.

Ber. Heere, take my Ring,
My house, mine honor, yea my life be thine,
And Ile be bid by thee.

Dia. When midnight comes, knocke at my chamber window:
Ile order take, my mother shall not heare.
Now will I charge you in the band of truth,
When you haue conquer'd my yet maiden-bed,
Remaine there but an houre, nor speake to mee:
My reasons are most strong, and you shall know them,
When backe againe this Ring shall be deliuer'd:
And on your finger in the night, Ile put
Another Ring, that what in time proceeds,
May token to the future, our past deeds.
Adieu till then, then faile not: you haue wonne
A wife of me, though there my hope be done.

Ber. A heauen on earth I haue won by wooing thee.
Exit.

Di. For which, liue long to thank both heauen & me,
You may so in the end.
My mother told me iust how he would woo,
As if she sate in's heart. She sayes, all men
Haue the like oathes: He had sworne to marrie me
When his wife's dead: therfore Ile lye with him
When I am buried. Since Frenchmen are so braide,
Marry that will, I liue and die a Maid:
Onely in this disguise, I think't no sinne,
To cosen him that would vniustly winne. *Exit*

Enter the two French Captaines, and some two or three Souldiours.

Cap.G. You haue not giuen him his mothers letter.

Cap.E. I haue deliu'red it an houre since, there is something in't that stings his nature: for on the reading it, he chang'd almost into another man.

Cap.G. He has much worthy blame laid vpon him, for shaking off so good a wife, and so sweet a Lady.

Cap.E. Especially, hee hath incurred the euerlasting displeasure of the King, who had euen tun'd his bounty to sing happinesse to him. I will tell you a thing, but you shall let it dwell darkly with you.

Cap.G. When you haue spoken it 'tis dead, and I am the graue of it.

Cap.E. Hee hath peruerted a young Gentlewoman heere in *Florence*, of a most chaste renown, & this night he fleshes his will in the spoyle of her honour: hee hath giuen her his monumentall Ring, and thinkes himselfe made in the vnchaste composition.

Cap.G. Now God delay our rebellion as we are our selues, what things are we.

Cap.E. Meerely our owne traitours. And as in the common course of all treasons, we still see them reueale themselues, till they attaine to their abhorr'd ends: so he that in this action contriues against his owne Nobility in his proper streame, ore-flowes himselfe.

Cap.G. Is it not meant damnable in vs, to be Trumpeters of our vnlawfull intents? We shall not then haue his company to night?

Cap.E. Not till after midnight: for hee is dieted to his houre.

Cap.G. That approaches apace: I would gladly haue him see his company anathomiz'd, that hee might take a measure of his owne iudgements, wherein so curiously he had set this counterfeit.

Cap.E. We will not meddle with him till he come; for his presence must be the whip of the other.

Cap.G. In the meane time, what heare you of these Warres?

Cap.E. I heare there is an ouerture of peace.

Cap.G. Nay, I assure you a peace concluded.

Cap.E. What will Count *Rossillion* do then? Will he trauaile higher, or returne againe into France?

Cap.G. I perceiue by this demand, you are not altogether of his councell.

Cap.E. Let it be forbid sir, so should I bee a great deale of his act.

Cap.G. Sir, his wife some two months since fledde from his house, her pretence is a pilgrimage to Saint *Iaques le grand*; which holy vndertaking, with most austere sanctimonie she accomplisht: and there residing, the tendernesse of her Nature, became as a prey to her greefe: in fine, made a groane of her last breath, & now she sings in heauen.

Cap.E. How is this iustified?

Cap.G. The stronger part of it by her owne Letters, which makes her storie true, euen to the poynt of her death: her death it selfe, which could not be her office to say, is come: was faithfully confirm'd by the Rector of the place.

Cap.E. Hath the Count all this intelligence?

Cap.G. I, and the particular confirmations, point from point, to the full arming of the veritie.

Cap.E. I am heartily sorrie that hee'l bee gladde of this.

Cap.G. How mightily sometimes, we make vs comforts of our losses.

Cap.E. And how mightily some other times, wee drowne our gaine in teares, the great dignitie that his valour hath here acquir'd for him, shall at home be encountred with a shame as ample.

Cap.G. The webbe of our life, is of a mingled yarne, good and ill together: our vertues would bee proud, if our faults whipt them not, and our crimes would dispaire if they were not cherish'd by our vertues.

Enter a Messenger.

How now? Where's your master?

Ser. He met the Duke in the street sir, of whom hee hath taken a solemne leaue: his Lordshippe will next morning for France. The Duke hath offered him Letters of commendations to the King.

Cap.E. They shall bee no more then needfull there, if they were more than they can commend.

Enter Count Rossillion.

Ber. They cannot be too sweete for the Kings tartnesse, heere's his Lordship now. How now my Lord, i'st not after midnight?

Ber. I haue to night dispatch'd sixteene businesses, a moneths length a peece, by an abstract of successe: I haue congied with the Duke, done my adieu with his neerest: buried a wife, mourn'd for her, writ to my Ladie mother, I am returning, entertain'd my Conuoy, & betweene these maine parcels of dispatch, affected many nicer needs: the last was the greatest, but that I haue not ended yet.

Cap.E. If the businesse bee of any difficulty, and this morning your departure hence, it requires hast of your Lordship.

Ber. I meane the businesse is not ended, as fearing to heare of it hereafter: but shall we haue this dialogue betweene the Foole and the Soldiour. Come, bring forth this counterfet module, ha's deceiu'd mee, like a double-meaning Prophesier.

Cap.E. Bring him forth, ha's sate i'th stockes all night poore gallant knaue.

Ber. No matter, his heeles haue deseru'd it, in vsurping his spurres so long. How does he carry himselfe?

Cap.E. I haue told your Lordship alreadie: The stockes carrie him. But to answer you as you would be vnderstood, hee weepes like a wench that had shed her milke, he hath confest himselfe to *Morgan*, whom hee supposes to be a Friar, frō the time of his remembrance to this very instant disaster of his setting i'th stockes: and what thinke you he hath confest?

Ber. Nothing of me, ha's a?

Cap.E. His confession is taken, and it shall bee read to his face, if your Lordshippe be in't, as I beleeue you are, you must haue the patience to heare it.

Enter Parolles with his Interpreter.

Ber. A plague vpon him, muffeld; he can say nothing of me: hush, hush.

Cap.G. Hoodman comes: *Portotartarossa*.

Inter. He calles for the tortures, what will you say without em.

Par. I will confesse what I know without constraint, If ye pinch me like a Pasty, I can say no more.

Int. Bosko Chimurcho.

Cap. Boblibindo chicurmurco.

Int. You are a mercifull Generall: Our Generall bids you answer to what I shall aske you out of a Note.

Par. And truly, as I hope to liue.

Int. First demand of him, how many horse the Duke is strong. What say you to that?

Par. Fiue or sixe thousand, but very weake and vnseruiceable: the troopes are all scattered, and the Commanders verie poore rogues, vpon my reputation and credit, and as I hope to liue.

Int. Shall I set downe your answer so?

Par. Do, Ile take the Sacrament on't, how & which way you will: all's one to him.

Ber. What a past-sauing slaue is this?

Cap.G. Y'are deceiu'd my Lord, this is Mounsieur *Parrolles* the gallant militarist, that was his owne phrase that had the whole theoricke of warre in the knot of his scarfe, and the practise in the chape of his dagger.

Cap.E. I will neuer trust a man againe, for keeping his sword cleane, nor beleeue he can haue euerie thing in him, by wearing his apparrell neatly.

Int. Well, that's set downe.

Par. Fiue or six thousand horse I sed, I will say true, or thereabouts set downe, for Ile speake truth.

Cap.G. He's very neere the truth in this.

Ber. But I con him no thankes for't in the nature he deliuers it.

Par. Poore rogues, I pray you say.

Int. Well, that's set downe.

Par. I humbly thanke you sir, a truth's a truth, the Rogues are maruailous poore.

Interp. Demaund of him of what strength they are a foot. What say you to that?

Par. By my troth sir, if I were to liue this present houre, I will tell true. Let me see, *Spurio* a hundred & fiftie,

fiftie, *Sebastian* so many, *Corambus* so many, *Iaques* so many: *Guiltian, Cosmo, Lodowicke,* and *Gratij,* two hundred fiftie each: Mine owne Company, *Chistopher, Vaumond, Bentij,* two hundred fiftie each: so that the muster file, rotten and sound, vppon my life amounts not to fifteene thousand pole, halfe of the which, dare not shake the snow from off their Cassockes, least they shake themselues to peeces.

Ber. What shall be done to him?

Cap.G. Nothing, but let him haue thankes. Demand of him my condition: and what credite I haue with the Duke.

Int. Well that's set downe: you shall demaund of him, whether one Captaine *Dumaine* bee i'th Campe, a Frenchman: what his reputation is with the Duke, what his valour, honestie, and expertnesse in warres: or whether he thinkes it were not possible with well-waighing summes of gold to corrupt him to a reuolt. What say you to this? What do you know of it?

Par. I beseech you let me answer to the particular of the intergatories. Demand them singly.

Int. Do you know this Captaine *Dumaine?*

Par. I know him, a was a Botchers Prentize in *Paris,* from whence he was whipt for getting the Shrieues fool with childe, a dumbe innocent that could not say him nay.

Ber. Nay, by your leaue hold your hands, though I know his braines are forfeite to the next tile that fals.

Int. Well, is this Captaine in the Duke of Florences campe?

Par. Vpon my knowledge he is, and lowsie.

Cap.G. Nay looke not so vpon me: we shall heare of your Lord anon.

Int. What is his reputation with the Duke?

Par. The Duke knowes him for no other, but a poore Officer of mine, and writ to mee this other day, to turne him out a'th band. I thinke I haue his Letter in my pocket.

Int. Marry we'll search.

Par. In good sadnesse I do not know, either it is there, or it is vpon a file with the Dukes other Letters, in my Tent.

Int. Heere'tis, heere's a paper, shall I reade it to you?

Par. I do not know if it be it or no.

Ber. Our Interpreter do's it well.

Cap.G. Excellently.

Int. Dian, the Counts a foole, and full of gold.

Par. That is not the Dukes letter sir: that is an aduertisement to a proper maide in Florence, one *Diana,* to take heede of the allurement of one Count *Rossillion,* a foolish idle boy: but for all that very ruttish. I pray you sir put it vp againe.

Int. Nay, Ile reade it first by your fauour.

Par. My meaning in't I protest was very honest in the behalfe of the maid: for I knew the young Count to be a dangerous and lasciuious boy, who is a whale to Virginity, and deuours vp all the fry it finds.

Ber. Damnable both-sides rogue.

Int. Let. When he sweares oathes, bid him drop gold, and take it:
After he scores, he neuer payes the score:
Halfe won is match well made, match and well make it,
He nere payes after-debts, take it before,
And say a souldier (Dian) told thee this:
Men are to mell with, boyes are not to kis.
For count of this, the Counts a Foole I know it,
Who payes before, but not when he does owe it.
    Thine as he vow'd to thee in thine eare,
                                    Parolles.

Ber. He shall be whipt through the Armie with this rime in's forehead.

Cap.E. This is your deuoted friend sir, the manifold Linguist, and the army-potent souldier.

Ber. I could endure any thing before but a Cat, and now he's a Cat to me.

Int. I perceiue sir by your Generals lookes, wee shall be faine to hang you.

Par. My life sir in any case: Not that I am afraide to dye, but that my offences beeing many, I would repent out the remainder of Nature. Let me liue sir in a dungeon, i'th stockes, or any where, so I may liue.

Int. Wee'le see what may bee done, so you confesse freely: therefore once more to this Captaine *Dumaine:* you haue answer'd to his reputation with the Duke, and to his valour. What is his honestie?

Par. He will steale sir an Egge out of a Cloister: for rapes and rauishments he paralels *Nessus.* Hee professes not keeping of oaths, in breaking em he is stronger then *Hercules.* He will lye sir, with such volubilitie, that you would thinke truth were a foole: drunkennesse is his best vertue, for he will be swine-drunke, and in his sleepe he does little harme, saue to his bed-cloathes about him: but they know his conditions, and lay him in straw. I haue but little more to say sir of his honesty, he ha's euerie thing that an honest man should not haue; what an honest man should haue, he has nothing.

Cap.G. I begin to loue him for this.

Ber. For this description of thine honestie? A pox vpon him for me, he's more and more a Cat.

Int. What say you to his expertnesse in warre?

Par. Faith sir, ha's led the drumme before the English Tragedians: to belye him I will not, and more of his souldiership I know not, except in that Country, he had the honour to be the Officer at a place there called *Mileend,* to instruct for the doubling of files. I would doe the man what honour I can, but of this I am not certaine.

Cap.G. He hath out-villain'd villanie so farre, that the raritie redeemes him.

Ber. A pox on him, he's a Cat still.

Int. His qualities being at this poore price, I neede not to aske you, if Gold will corrupt him to reuolt.

Par. Sir, for a Cardceue he will sell the fee-simple of his saluation, the inheritance of it, and cut th'intaile from all remainders, and a perpetuall succession for it perpetually.

Int. What's his Brother, the other Captain *Dumain?*

Cap.E. Why do's he aske him of me?

Int. What's he?

Par. E'ne a Crow a'th same nest: not altogether so great as the first in goodnesse, but greater a great deale in euill. He excels his Brother for a coward, yet his Brother is reputed one of the best that is. In a retreate hee out-runnes any Lackey; marrie in comming on, hee ha's the Crampe.

Int. If your life be saued, will you vndertake to betray the Florentine.

Par. I, and the Captaine of his horse, Count *Rossillion.*

Int. Ile whisper with the Generall, and knowe his pleasure.

Par. Ile no more drumming, a plague of all drummes, onely to seeme to deserue well, and to beguile the supposition

All's Well, that Ends Well.

sition of that lasciuious yong boy the Count, haue I run into this danger: yet who would haue suspected an ambush where I was taken?

Int. There is no remedy sir, but you must dye: the Generall sayes, you that haue so traitorously discouer'd the secrets of your army, and made such pestifferous reports of men very nobly held, can serue the world for no honest vse: therefore you must dye. Come headesman, off with his head.

Par. O Lord sir let me liue, or let me see my death.

Int. That shall you, and take your leaue of all your friends:

So, looke about you, know you any heere?

Count. Good morrow noble Captaine.

Lo.E. God blesse you Captaine *Parolles*.

Cap.G. God saue you noble Captaine.

Lo.E. Captain, what greeting will you to my Lord *Lafew*? I am for *France*.

Cap.G. Good Captaine will you giue me a Copy of the sonnet you writ to *Diana* in behalfe of the Count *Rossillion*, and I were not a verie Coward, I'de compell it of you, but far you well. *Exeunt.*

Int. You are vndone Captaine all but your scarfe, that has a knot on't yet.

Par. Who cannot be crush'd with a plot?

Inter. If you could finde out a Countrie where but women were that had receiued so much shame, you might begin an impudent Nation. Fare yee well sir, I am for *France* too, we shall speake of you there. *Exit*

Par. Yet am I thankfull: if my heart were great 'Twould burst at this: Captaine Ile be no more,
But I will eate, and drinke, and sleepe as soft
As Captaine shall. Simply the thing I am
Shall make me liue: who knowes himselfe a braggart
Let him feare this; for it will come to passe,
That euery braggart shall be found an Asse.
Rust sword, coole blushes, and *Parrolles* liue
Safest in shame: being fool'd, by fool'rie thriue;
There's place and meanes for euery man aliue.
Ile after them. *Exit.*

Enter Hellen, Widdow, and Diana.

Hel. That you may well perceiue I haue not wrong'd you,
One of the greatest in the Christian world
Shall be my suretie: for whose throne 'tis needfull
Ere I can perfect mine intents, to kneele.
Time was, I did him a desired office
Deere almost as his life, which gratitude
Through flintie Tartars bosome would peepe forth,
And answer thankes. I duly am inform'd,
His grace is at *Marcella*, to which place
We haue conuenient conuoy: you must know
I am supposed dead, the Army breaking,
My husband hies him home, where heauen ayding,
And by the leaue of my good Lord the King,
Wee'l be before our welcome.

Wid. Gentle Madam,
You neuer had a seruant to whose trust
Your busines was more welcome.

Hel. Nor your Mistris
Euer a friend, whose thoughts more truly labour
To recompence your loue: Doubt not but heauen
Hath brought me vp to be your daughters dower,
As it hath fated her to be my motiue

And helper to a husband. But O strange men,
That can such sweet vse make of what they hate,
When sawcie trusting of the cosin'd thoughts
Defiles the pitchy night, so lust doth play
With what it loathes, for that which is away,
But more of this heereafter: you *Diana*,
Vnder my poore instructions yet must suffer
Something in my behalfe.

Dia. Let death and honestie
Go with your impositions, I am yours
Vpon your will to suffer.

Hel. Yet I pray you:
But with the word the time will bring on summer,
When Briars shall haue leaues as well as thornes,
And be as sweet as sharpe: we must away,
Our Wagon is prepar'd, and time reuiues vs,
All's well that ends well, still the fines the Crowne;
What ere the course, the end is the renowne. *Exeunt*

Enter Clowne, old Lady, and Lafew.

Laf. No, no, no, your sonne was misled with a snipt taffata fellow there, whose villanous saffron wold haue made all the vnbak'd and dowy youth of a nation in his colour: your daughter-in-law had beene aliue at this houre, and your sonne heere at home, more aduanc'd by the King, then by that red-tail'd humble Bee I speak of.

La. I would I had not knowne him, it was the death of the most vertuous gentlewoman, that euer Nature had praise for creating. If she had pertaken of my flesh and cost mee the deerest groanes of a mother, I could not haue owed her a more rooted loue.

Laf. 'Twas a good Lady, 'twas a good Lady. Wee may picke a thousand sallets ere wee light on such another hearbe.

Clo. Indeed sir she was the sweete Margerom of the sallet, or rather the hearbe of grace.

Laf. They are not hearbes you knaue, they are nose-hearbes.

Clowne. I am no great *Nabuchadnezar* sir, I haue not much skill in grace.

Laf. Whether doest thou professe thy selfe, a knaue or a foole?

Clo. A foole sir at a womans seruice, and a knaue at a mans.

Laf. Your distinction.

Clo. I would cousen the man of his wife, and do his seruice.

Laf. So you were a knaue at his seruice indeed.

Clo. And I would giue his wife my bauble sir to doe her seruice.

Laf. I will subscribe for thee, thou art both knaue and foole.

Clo. At your seruice.

Laf. No, no, no.

Clo. Why sir, if I cannot serue you, I can serue as great a prince as you are.

Laf. Whose that, a Frenchman?

Clo. Faith sir a has an English maine, but his fisnomie is more hotter in France then there.

Laf. What prince is that?

Clo. The blacke prince sir, alias the prince of darkenesse, alias the diuell.

Laf. Hold thee there's my purse, I giue thee not this to suggest thee from thy master thou talk'st off, serue him still.

Clow

Clo. I am a woodland fellow sir, that alwaies loued a great fire, and the master I speak of euer keeps a good fire, but sure he is the Prince of the world, let his Nobilitie remaine in's Court. I am for the house with the narrow gate, which I take to be too little for pompe to enter: some that humble themselues may, but the manie will be too chill and tender, and theyle bee for the flowrie way that leads to the broad gate, and the great fire.

Laf. Go thy waies, I begin to bee a wearie of thee, and I tell thee so before, because I would not fall out with thee. Go thy wayes, let my horses be wel look'd too, without any trickes.

Clo. If I put any trickes vpon em sir, they shall bee Iades trickes, which are their owne right by the law of Nature. *exit*

Laf. A shrewd knaue and an vnhappie.

Lady. So a is. My Lord that's gone made himselfe much sport out of him, by his authoritie hee remaines heere, which he thinkes is a pattent for his sawcinesse, and indeede he has no pace, but runnes where he will.

Laf. I like him well, 'tis not amisse: and I was about to tell you, since I heard of the good Ladies death, and that my Lord your sonne was vpon his returne home. I moued the King my master to speake in the behalfe of my daughter, which in the minoritie of them both, his Maiestie out of a selfe gracious remembrance did first propose, his Highnesse hath promis'd me to doe it, and to stoppe vp the displeasure he hath conceiued against your sonne, there is no fitter matter. How do's your Ladyship like it?

La. With verie much content my Lord, and I wish it happily effected.

Laf. His Highnesse comes post from *Marcellus*, of as able bodie as when he number'd thirty, a will be heere to morrow, or I am deceiu'd by him that in such intelligence hath seldome fail'd.

La. It reioyces me, that I hope I shall see him ere I die. I haue letters that my sonne will be heere to night: I shall beseech your Lordship to remaine with mee, till they meete together.

Laf. Madam, I was thinking with what manners I might safely be admitted.

Lad. You neede but pleade your honourable priuiledge.

Laf. Ladie, of that I haue made a bold charter, but I thanke my God, it holds yet.

Enter Clowne.

Clo. O Madam, yonders my Lord your sonne with a patch of veluet on's face, whether there bee a scar vnder't or no, the Veluet knowes, but 'tis a goodly patch of Veluet, his left cheeke is a cheeke of two pile and a halfe, but his right cheeke is worne bare.

Laf. A scarre nobly got,
Or a noble scarre, is a good liu'rie of honor,
So belike is that.

Clo. But it is your carbinado'd face.

Laf. Let vs go see
your sonne I pray you, I long to talke
With the yong noble souldier.

Clowne. 'Faith there's a dozen of em, with delicate fine hats, and most courteous feathers, which bow the head, and nod at euerie man. *Exeunt*

Actus Quintus.

Enter Hellen, Widdow, and Diana, with two Attendants.

Hel. But this exceeding posting day and night,
Must wear your spirits low, we cannot helpe it:
But since you haue made the daies and nights as one,
To weare your gentle limbes in my affayres,
Be bold you do so grow in my requitall,
As nothing can vnroote you. In happie time,

Enter a gentle Astringer.

This man may helpe me to his Maiesties eare,
If he would spend his power. God saue you sir.

Gent. And you.

Hel. Sir, I haue seene you in the Court of France.

Gent. I haue beene sometimes there.

Hel. I do presume sir, that you are not falne
From the report that goes vpon your goodnesse,
And therefore goaded with most sharpe occasions,
Which lay nice manners by, I put you to
The vse of your owne vertues, for the which
I shall continue thankefull.

Gent. What's your will?

Hel. That it will please you
To giue this poore petition to the King,
And ayde me with that store of power you haue
To come into his presence.

Gen. The Kings not heere.

Hel. Not heere sir?

Gen. Not indeed,
He hence remou'd last night, and with more hast
Then is his vse.

Wid. Lord how we loose our paines.

Hel. All's well that ends well yet,
Though time seeme so aduerse, and meanes vnfit:
I do beseech you, whither is he gone?

Gent. Marrie as I take it to *Rossillion*,
Whither I am going.

Hel. I do beseech you sir,
Since you are like to see the King before me,
Commend the paper to his gracious hand,
Which I presume shall render you no blame,
But rather make you thanke your paines for it,
I will come after you with what good speede
Our meanes will make vs meanes.

Gent. This Ile do for you.

Hel. And you shall finde your selfe to be well thankt what e're falles more. We must to horse againe, Go, go, prouide.

Enter Clowne and Parrolles.

Par. Good Mr *Lauatch* giue my Lord *Lafew* this letter, I haue ere now sir beene better knowne to you, when I haue held familiaritie with fresher cloathes: but I am now sir muddied in fortunes mood, and smell somewhat strong of her strong displeasure.

Clo. Truely, Fortunes displeasure is but sluttish if it smell so strongly as thou speak'st of: I will henceforth eate no Fish of Fortunes butt'ring. Pre thee alow the winde.

Par. Nay you neede not to stop your nose sir: I spake but by a Metaphor.

Clo. Indeed sir, if your Metaphor stinke, I will stop my nose, or against any mans Metaphor. Prethe get thee further. *Par.*

Par. Pray you sir deliuer me this paper.

Clo. Foh, prethee stand away : a paper from fortunes close-stoole, to giue to a Nobleman. Looke heere he comes himselfe.

Enter Lafew.

Clo. Heere is a purre of Fortunes sir, or of Fortunes Cat, but not a Muscat, that ha's falne into the vncleane fish-pond of her displeasure, and as he sayes is muddied withall. Pray you sir, vse the Carpe as you may, for he lookes like a poore decayed, ingenious, foolish, rascally knaue. I doe pittie his distresse in my smiles of comfort, and leaue him to your Lordship.

Par. My Lord I am a man whom fortune hath cruelly scratch'd.

Laf. And what would you haue me to doe? 'Tis too late to paire her nailes now. Wherein haue you played the knaue with fortune that she should scratch you, who of her selfe is a good Lady, and would not haue knaues thriue long vnder? There's a Cardecue for you: Let the Iustices make you and fortune friends ; I am for other businesse.

Par. I beseech your honour to heare mee one single word.

Laf. you begge a single peny more : Come you shall ha't, saue your word.

Par. My name my good Lord is *Parrolles*.

Laf. You begge more then word then. Cox my passion, giue me your hand : How does your drumme?

Par. O my good Lord, you were the first that found mee.

Laf. Was I insooth? And I was the first that lost thee.

Par. It lies in you my Lord to bring me in some grace for you did bring me out.

Laf. Out vpon thee knaue, doest thou put vpon mee at once both the office of God and the diuel: one brings thee in grace, and the other brings thee out. The Kings comming I know by his Trumpets. Sirrah, inquire further after me, I had talke of you last night, though you are a foole and a knaue, you shall eate, go too, follow.

Par. I praise God for you.

Flourish. Enter King, old Lady, Lafew; the two French Lords, with attendants.

Kin. We lost a Iewell of her, and our esteeme Was made much poorer by it : but your sonne, As mad in folly, lack'd the sence to know Her estimation home.

Old La. 'Tis past my Liege, And I beseech your Maiestie to make it Naturall rebellion, done i'th blade of youth, When oyle and fire, too strong for reasons force, Ore-beares it, and burnes on.

Kin. My honour'd Lady, I haue forgiuen and forgotten all, Though my reuenges were high bent vpon him, And watch'd the time to shoote.

Laf. This I must say, But first I begge my pardon : the yong Lord Did to his Maiesty, his Mother, and his Ladie, Offence of mighty note; but to himselfe The greatest wrong of all. He lost a wife, Whose beauty did astonish the suruey Of richest eies : whose words all eares tooke captiue, Whose deere perfection, hearts that scorn'd to serue,

Humbly call'd Mistris.

Kin. Praising what is lost, Makes the remembrance deere. Well, call him hither, We are reconcil'd, and the first view shall kill All repetition : Let him not aske our pardon, The nature of his great offence is dead, And deeper then obliuion, we do burie Th'incensing reliques of it. Let him approach A stranger, no offender ; and informe him So 'tis our will he should.

Gent. I shall my Liege.

Kin. What sayes he to your daughter, Haue you spoke?

Laf. All that he is, hath reference to your Highnes.

Kin. Then shall we haue a match, I haue letters sent me, that sets him high in fame.

Enter Count Bertram.

Laf. He lookes well on't.

Kin. I am not a day of season, For thou maist see a sun-shine, and a haile In me at once : But to the brightest beames Distracted clouds giue way, so stand thou forth, The time is faire againe.

Ber. My high repented blames Deere Soueraigne pardon to me.

Kin. All is whole, Not one word more of the consumed time, Let's take the instant by the forward top : For we are old, and on our quick'st decrees Th'inaudible, and noiselesse foot of time Steales, ere we can effect them. You remember The daughter of this Lord?

Ber. Admiringly my Liege, at first I stucke my choice vpon her, ere my heart Durst make too bold a herauld of my tongue : Where the impression of mine eye enfixing, Contempt his scornfull Perspectiue did lend me, Which warpt the line, of euerie other fauour, Scorn'd a faire colour, or exprest it stolne, Extended or contracted all proportions To a most hideous obiect. Thence it came, That she whom all men prais'd, and whom my selfe, Since I haue lost, haue lou'd; was in mine eye The dust that did offend it.

Kin. Well excus'd: That thou didst loue her, strikes some scores away From the great compt : but loue that comes too late, Like a remorsefull pardon slowly carried To the great sender, turnes a sowre offence, Crying, that's good that's gone : Our rash faults, Make triuiall price of serious things we haue, Not knowing them, vntill we know their graue. Oft our displeasures to our selues vniust, Destroy our friends, and after weepe their dust: Our owne loue waking, cries to see what's don,e While shamefull hate sleepes out the afternoone. Be this sweet *Helens* knell, and now forget her. Send forth your amorous token for faire *Mandlin*, The maine consents are had, and heere wee'l stay To see our widdowers second marriage day : Which better then the first, O deere heauen blesse, Or, ere they meete in me, O Nature cesse.

Laf. Come on my sonne, in whom my houses name Must be digested : giue a fauour from you To sparkle in the spirits of my daughter,

That

That she may quickly come. By my old beard,
And eu'rie haire that's on't, *Helen* that's dead
Was a sweet creature: such a ring as this,
The last that ere I tooke her leaue at Court,
I saw vpon her finger.

Ber. Hers it was not.

King. Now pray you let me see it. For mine eye,
While I was speaking, oft was fasten'd too't:
This Ring was mine, and when I gaue it *Hellen*,
I bad her if her fortunes euer stoode
Necessitied to helpe, that by this token
I would releeue her. Had you that craft to reaue her
Of what should stead her most?

Ber. My gracious Soueraigne,
How ere it pleases you to take it so,
The ring was neuer hers.

Old La. Sonne, on my life
I haue seene her weare it, and she reckon'd it
At her liues rate.

Laf. I am sure I saw her weare it.

Ber. You are deceiu'd my Lord, she neuer saw it:
In Florence was it from a casement throwne mee,
Wrap'd in a paper, which contain'd the name
Of her that threw it: Noble she was, and thought
I stood ingag'd. but when I had subscrib'd
To mine owne fortune, and inform'd her fully,
I could not answer in that course of Honour
As she had made the ouerture, she ceast
In heauie satisfaction, and would neuer
Receiue the Ring againe.

Kin. *Platus* himselfe,
That knowes the tinct and multiplying med'cine,
Hath not in natures mysterie more science,
Then I haue in this Ring. 'Twas mine, 'twas *Helens*,
Who euer gaue it you: then if you know
That you are well acquainted with your selfe,
Confesse 'twas hers, and by what rough enforcement
You got it from her. She call'd the Saints to suretie,
That she would neuer put it from her finger,
Vnlesse she gaue it to your selfe in bed,
Where you haue neuer come: or sent it vs
Vpon her great disaster.

Ber. She neuer saw it.

Kin. Thou speak'st it falsely: as I loue mine Honor,
And mak'st connecturall feares to come into me,
Which I would faine shut out, if it should proue
That thou art so inhumane, 'twill not proue so:
And yet I know not, thou didst hate her deadly,
And she is dead, which nothing but to close
Her eyes my selfe, could win me to beleeue,
More then to see this Ring. Take him away,
My fore-past proofes, how ere the matter fall
Shall taze my feares of little vanitie,
Hauing vainly fear'd too little. Away with him,
Wee'l sift this matter further.

Ber. If you shall proue
This Ring was euer hers, you shall as easie
Proue that I husbanded her bed in Florence,
Where yet she neuer was.

Enter a Gentleman.

King. I am wrap'd in dismall thinkings.

Gen. Gracious Soueraigne.
Whether I haue beene too blame or no, I know not,
Here's a petition from a Florentine,
Who hath for foure or fiue remoues come short,
To tender it her selfe. I vndertooke it,
Vanquish'd thereto by the faire grace and speech
Of the poore suppliant, who by this I know
Is heere attending: her businesse lookes in her
With an importing visage, and she told me
In a sweet verball breefe, it did concerne
Your Highnesse with her selfe.

A Letter.
Vpon his many protestations to marrie mee when his wife was dead, I blush to say it, he wonne me. Now is the Count Rossillion a Widdower, his vowes are forfeited to mee, and my honors payed to him. Hee stole from Florence, taking no leaue, and I follow him to his Countrey for Iustice: Grant it me, O King, in you it best lies, otherwise a seducer flourishes, and a poore Maid is vndone.

Diana Capilet.

Laf. I will buy me a sonne in Law in a faire, and toule for this. Ile none of him.

Kin. The heauens haue thought well on thee *Lafew*,
To bring forth this discou'rie, seeke these sutors:
Go speedily, and bring againe the Count.

Enter Bertram.
I am a-feard the life of *Hellen* (Ladie)
Was fowly snatcht.

Old La. Now iustice on the doers.

King. I wonder sir, sir, wiues are monsters to you,
And that you flye them as you sweare them Lordship,
Yet you desire to marry. What woman's that?

Enter Widdow, Diana, and Parrolles.

Dia. I am my Lord a wretched Florentine,
Deriued from the ancient Capilet,
My suite as I do vnderstand you know,
And therefore know how farre I may be pittied.

Wid. I am her Mother sir, whose age and honour
Both suffer vnder this complaint we bring,
And both shall cease, without your remedie.

King. Come hether Count, do you know these Women?

Ber. My Lord, I neither can nor will denie,
But that I know them, do they charge me further?

Dia. Why do you looke so strange vpon your wife?

Ber. She's none of mine my Lord.

Dia. If you shall marrie
You giue away this hand, and that is mine,
You giue away heauens vowes, and those are mine:
You giue away my selfe, which is knowne mine:
For I by vow am so embodied yours,
That she which marries you, must marrie me,
Either both or none.

Laf. your reputation comes too short for my daughter, you are no husband for her.

Ber. My Lord, this is a fond and desp'rate creature,
Whom sometime I haue laugh'd with: Let your highnes
Lay a more noble thought vpon mine honour,
Then for to thinke that I would sinke it heere.

Kin. Sir for my thoughts, you haue them il to friend,
Till your deeds gaine them fairer: proue your honor,
Then in my thought it lies.

Dian. Good my Lord,
Aske him vpon his oath, if hee do's thinke
He had not my virginity.

Kin. What saist thou to her?

Ber. She's impudent my Lord,
And was a common gamester to the Campe.

Dia. He do's me wrong my Lord: If I were so,
He might haue bought me at a common price.

Do not beleeue him. O behold this Ring,
Whose high respect and rich validitie
Did lacke a Paralell: yet for all that
He gaue it to a Commoner a'th Campe
If I be one.
  Coun. He blushes, and 'tis hit:
Of sixe preceding Ancestors, that Iemme
Conferr'd by testament to'th sequent issue
Hath it beene owed and worne. This is his wife,
That Ring's a thousand proofes.
  King. Me thought you saide
You saw one heere in Court could witnesse it.
  Dia. I did my Lord, but loath am to produce
So bad an instrument, his names *Parrolles*.
  Laf. I saw the man to day, if man he bee.
  Kin. Finde him, and bring him hether.
  Ros. What of him:
He's quoted for a most perfidious slaue
With all the spots a'th world, taxt and debosh'd,
Whose nature sickens: but to speake a truth,
Am I, or that or this for what he'l vtter,
That will speake any thing.
  Kin. She hath that Ring of yours.
  Ros. I thinke she has; certaine it is I lyk'd her,
And boorded her i'th wanton way of youth:
She knew her distance, and did angle for mee,
Madding my eagernesse with her restraint,
As all impediments in fancies course
Are motiues of more fancie, and in fine,
Her insuite comming with her moderne grace,
Subdu'd me to her rate, she got the Ring,
And I had that which any inferiour might
At Market price haue bought.
  Dia. I must be patient:
You that haue turn'd off a first so noble wife,
May iustly dyet me. I pray you yet,
(Since you lacke vertue, I will loose a husband)
Send for your Ring, I will returne it home,
And giue me mine againe.
  Ros. I haue it not.
  Kin. What Ring was yours I pray you?
  Dian. Sir much like the same vpon your finger.
  Kin. Know you this Ring, this Ring was his of late.
  Dia. And this was it I gaue him being a bed.
  Kin. The story then goes false, you threw it him
Out of a Casement.
  Dia. I haue spoke the truth.   *Enter Parolles.*
  Ros. My Lord, I do confesse the ring was hers.
  Kin. You boggle shrewdly, euery feather starts you:
Is this the man you speake of?
  Dia. I, my Lord.
  Kin. Tell me sirrah, but tell me true I charge you,
Not fearing the displeasure of your master:
Which on your iust proceeding, Ile keepe off,
By him and by this woman heere, what know you?
  Par. So please your Maiesty, my master hath bin an
honourable Gentleman. Trickes hee hath had in him,
which Gentlemen haue.
  Kin. Come, come, to'th'purpose: Did hee loue this
woman?
  Par. Faith sir he did loue her, but how.
  Kin. How I pray you?
  Par. He did loue her sir, as a Gent. loues a Woman.
  Kin. How is that?
  Par. He lou'd her sir, and lou'd her not.
  Kin. As thou art a knaue and no knaue, what an equi-

uocall Companion is this?
  Par. I am a poore man, and at your Maiesties command.
  Laf. Hee's a good drumme my Lord, but a naughtie Orator.
  Dian. Do you know he promist me marriage?
  Par. Faith I know more then Ile speake.
  Kin. But wilt thou not speake all thou know'st?
  Par. Yes so please your Maiesty: I did goe betweene them as I said, but more then that he loued her, for indeede he was madde for her, and talkt of Sathan, and of Limbo, and of Furies, and I know not what: yet I was in that credit with them at that time, that I knewe of their going to bed, and of other motions, as promising her marriage, and things which would deriue mee ill will to speake of, therefore I will not speake what I know.
  Kin. Thou hast spoken all alreadie, vnlesse thou canst say they are maried, but thou art too fine in thy euidence, therefore stand aside. This Ring you say was yours.
  Dia. I my good Lord.
  Kin. Where did you buy it? Or who gaue it you?
  Dia. It was not giuen me, nor I did not buy it.
  Kin. Who lent it you?
  Dia. It was not lent me neither.
  Kin. Where did you finde it then?
  Dia. I found it not.
  Kin. If it were yours by none of all these wayes,
How could you giue it him?
  Dia. I neuer gaue it him.
  Laf. This womans an easie gloue my Lord, she goes off and on at pleasure.
  Kin. This Ring was mine, I gaue it his first wife.
  Dia. It might be yours or hers for ought I know.
  Kin. Take her away, I do not like her now,
To prison with her: and away with him,
Vnlesse thou telst me where thou hadst this Ring,
Thou diest within this houre.
  Dia. Ile neuer tell you.
  Kin. Take her away.
  Dia. Ile put in baile my liedge.
  Kin. I thinke thee now some common Customer.
  Dia. By Ioue if euer I knew man 'twas you.
  King. Wherefore hast thou accusde him al this while.
  Dia. Because he's guiltie, and he is not guilty:
He knowes I am no Maid, and hee'l sweare too't:
Ile sweare I am a Maid, and he knowes not.
Great King I am no strumpet, by my life,
I am either Maid, or else this old mans wife.
  Kin. She does abuse our eares, to prison with her.
  Dia. Good mother fetch my bayle. Stay Royall sir,
The Ieweller that owes the Ring is sent for,
And he shall surety me. But for this Lord,
Who hath abus'd me as he knowes himselfe,
Though yet he neuer harm'd me, heere I quit him.
He knowes himselfe my bed he hath defil'd,
And at that time he got his wife with childe:
Dead though she be, she feeles her yong one kicke:
So there's my riddle, one that's dead is quicke,
And now behold the meaning.

Enter Hellen and Widdow.

  Kin. Is there no exorcist
Beguiles the truer Office of mine eyes?
Is't reall that I see?
  Hel. No my good Lord,

254 Alls Well, that Ends Well.

'Tis but the shadow of a wife you see,
The name, and not the thing.

Ros. Both, both, O pardon.

Hel. Oh my good Lord, when I was like this Maid,
I found you wondrous kinde, there is your Ring,
And looke you, heeres your letter: this it sayes,
When from my finger you can get this Ring,
And is by me with childe, &c. This is done,
Will you be mine now you are doubly wonne?

Ros. If she my Liege can make me know this clearly,
Ile loue her dearely, euer, euer dearly.

Hel. If it appeare not plaine, and proue vntrue,
Deadly diuorce step betweene me and you.
O my deere mother do I see you liuing?

Laf. Mine eyes smell Onions, I shall weepe anon:
Good Tom Drumme lend me a handkercher.
So I thanke thee, waite on me home, Ile make sport with
thee: Let thy curtsies alone, they are scuruy ones.

King. Let vs from point to point this storie know,
To make the euen truth in pleasure flow:
If thou beest yet a fresh vncropped flower,
Choose thou thy husband, and Ile pay thy dower.
For I can guesse, that by thy honest ayde,
Thou kept'st a wife her selfe, thy selfe a Maide.
Of that and all the progresse more and lesse,
Resolduedly more leasure shall expresse:
All yet seemes well, and if it end so meete,
The bitter past, more welcome is the sweet.
Flourish.

THe Kings a Begger, now the Play is done,
All is well ended, if this suite be wonne,
That you expresse Content: which we willpay,
With strift to please you, day exceeding day:
Ours be your patience then, and yours our parts,
Your gentle hands lend vs, and take our hearts. *Exeunt omn.*

FINIS.

Twelfe Night, Or vvhat you vvill.

Actus Primus, Scæna Prima.

Enter Orsino Duke of Illyria, Curio, and other Lords.

Duke.
IF Musicke be the food of Loue, play on,
Giue me excesse of it: that surfetting,
The appetite may sicken, and so dye.
That straine agen, it had a dying fall:
O, it came ore my eare, like the sweet sound
That breathes vpon a banke of Violets;
Stealing, and giuing Odour. Enough, no more,
Tis not so sweet now, as it was before.
O spirit of Loue, how quicke and fresh art thou,
That notwithstanding thy capacitie,
Receiueth as the Sea. Nought enters there,
Of what validity, and pitch so ere,
But falles into abatement, and low price
Euen in a minute; so full of shapes is fancie,
That it alone, is high fantasticall.

Cu. Will you go hunt my Lord?
Du. What *Curio*?
Cu. The Hart.
Du. Why so I do, the Noblest that I haue:
O when mine eyes did see *Oliuia* first,
Methought she purg'd the ayre of pestilence;
That instant was I turn'd into a Hart,
And my desires like fell and cruell hounds,
Ere since pursue me. How now what newes from her?

Enter Valentine.

Val. So please my Lord, I might not be admitted,
But from her handmaid do returne this answer:
The Element it selfe, till seuen yeares heate,
Shall not behold her face at ample view:
But like a Cloystresse she will vailed walke,
And water once a day her Chamber round
With eye-offending brine: all this to season
A brothers dead loue, which she would keepe fresh
And lasting, in her sad remembrance.

Du. O she that hath a heart of that fine frame
To pay this debt of loue but to a brother,
How will she loue, when the rich golden shaft
Hath kill'd the flocke of all affections else
That liue in her. When Liuer, Braine, and Heart,
These soueraigne thrones, are all supply'd and fill'd
Her sweete perfections with one selfe king:
Away before me, to sweet beds of Flowres,
Loue-thoughts lye rich, when canopy'd with bowres.

Exeunt

Scena Secunda.

Enter Viola, a Captaine, and Saylors.

Vio. What Country (Friends) is this?
Cap. This is Illyria Ladie.
Vio. And what should I do in Illyria?
My brother he is in Elizium,
Perchance he is not drown'd: What thinke you saylors?
Cap. It is perchance that you your selfe were saued.
Vio. O my poore brother, and so perchance may he be.
Cap. True Madam, and to comfort you with chance,
Assure your selfe, after our ship did split,
When you, and those poore number saued with you,
Hung on our driuing boate: I saw your brother
Most prouident in perill, binde himselfe,
(Courage and hope both teaching him the practise)
To a strong Maste, that liu'd vpon the sea:
Where like *Orion* on the Dolphines backe,
I saw him hold acquaintance with the waues,
So long as I could see.

Vio. For saying so, there's Gold:
Mine owne escape vnfoldeth to my hope,
Whereto thy speech serues for authoritie
The like of him. Know'st thou this Countrey?
Cap. I Madam well, for I was bred and borne
Not three houres trauaile from this very place:
Vio. Who gouernes heere?
Cap. A noble Duke in nature, as in name.
Vio. What is his name?
Cap. Orsino.
Vio. *Orsino*: I haue heard my father name him.
He was a Batchellor then.
Cap. And so is now, or was so very late:
For but a month ago I went from hence,
And then 'twas fresh in murmure (as you know
What great ones do, the lesse will prattle of,)
That he did seeke the loue of faire *Oliuia*.
Vio. What's shee?
Cap. A vertuous maid, the daughter of a Count
That dide some twelue month since, then leauing her
In the protection of his sonne, her brother,
Who shortly also dide: for whose deere loue
(They say) she hath abiur'd the sight
And company of men.
Vio. O that I seru'd that Lady,
And might not be deliuered to the world

Till

Till I had made mine owne occasion mellow
What my estate is.

Cap. That were hard to compasse,
Because she will admit no kinde of suite,
No, not the Dukes.

Vio. There is a faire behauiour in thee Captaine,
And though that nature, with a beauteous wall
Doth oft close in pollution : yet of thee
I will beleeue thou hast a minde that suites
With this thy faire and outward charracter.
I prethee (and Ile pay thee bounteously)
Conceale me what I am, and be my ayde,
For such disguise as haply shall become
The forme of my intent. Ile serue this Duke,
Thou shalt present me as an Eunuch to him,
It may be worth thy paines : for I can sing,
And speake to him in many sorts of Musicke,
That will allow me very worth his seruice.
What else may hap, to time I will commit,
Onely shape thou thy silence to my wit.

Cap. Be you his Eunuch, and your Mute Ile bee,
When my tongue blabs, then let mine eyes not see.

Vio. I thanke thee : Lead me on. *Exeunt*

Scæna Tertia.

Enter Sir Toby, and Maria.

Sir To. What a plague meanes my Neece to take the death of her brother thus ? I am sure care's an enemie to life.

Mar. By my troth sir *Toby*, you must come in earlyer a nights : your Cosin, my Lady, takes great exceptions to your ill houres.

To. Why let her except, before excepted.

Ma. I, but you must confine your selfe within the modest limits of order.

To. Confine? Ile confine my selfe no finer then I am : these cloathes are good enough to drinke in, and so bee these boots too : and they be not, let them hang themselues in their owne straps.

Ma. That quaffing and drinking will vndoe you : I heard my Lady talke of it yesterday : and of a foolish knight that you brought in one night here, to be hir woer

To. Who, Sir *Andrew Ague-cheeke* ?

Ma. I he.

To. He's as tall a man as any's in Illyria.

Ma. What's that to th'purpose ?

To. Why he ha's three thousand ducates a yeare.

Ma. I, but hee'l haue but a yeare in all these ducates : He's a very foole, and a prodigall.

To. Fie, that you'l say so : he playes o'th Viol-de-gam-boys, and speaks three or four languages word for word without booke, & hath all the good gifts of nature.

Ma. He hath indeed, almost naturall : for besides that he's a foole, he's a great quarreller : and but that hee hath the gift of a Coward, to allay the gust he hath in quarrelling, 'tis thought among the prudent, he would quickly haue the gift of a graue.

Tob. By this hand they are scoundrels and substractors that say so of him. Who are they?

Ma. They that adde moreour, hee's drunke nightly in your company.

To. With drinking healths to my Neece : Ile drinke to her as long as there is a passage in my throat, & drinke in Illyria : he's a Coward and a Coystrill that will not drinke to my Neece. till his braines turne o'th toe, like a parish top. What wench? *Castiliano vulgo*: for here coms Sir *Andrew Agueface.*

Enter Sir Andrew.

And. Sir *Toby Belch.* How now sir *Toby Belch*?

To. Sweet sir *Andrew.*

And. Blesse you faire Shrew.

Mar. And you too sir.

Tob. Accost Sir *Andrew*, accost.

And. What's that?

To. My Neeces Chamber-maid.

Ma. Good Mistris accost, I desire better acquaintance

Ma. My name is *Mary* sir.

And. Good mistris *Mary*, accost.

To. You mistake knight : Accost, is front her, boord her, woe her, assayle her.

And. By my troth I would not vndertake her in this company. Is that the meaning of Accost ?

Ma. Far you well Gentlemen.

To. And thou let part so Sir *Andrew*, would thou mightst neuer draw sword agen.

And. And you part so mistris, I would I might neuer draw sword agen : Faire Lady, doe you thinke you haue fooles in hand?

Ma. Sir, I haue not you by'th hand.

An. Marry but you shall haue, and heeres my hand.

Ma. Now sir, thought is free : I pray you bring your hand to'th Buttry barre, and let it drinke.

An. Wherefore (sweet-heart?) What's your Metaphor ?

Ma. It's dry sir.

And. Why I thinke so : I am not such an asse, but I can keepe my hand dry. But what's your iest ?

Ma. A dry iest Sir.

And. Are you full of them ?

Ma. I Sir, I haue them at my fingers ends: marry now I let go your hand, I am barren. *Exit Maria*

To. O knight, thou lack'st a cup of Canarie: when did I see thee so put downe?

An. Neuer in your life I thinke, vnlesse you see Canarie put me downe : mee thinkes sometimes I haue no more wit then a Christian, or an ordinary man ha's : but I am a great eater of beefe, and I beleeue that does harme to my wit.

To. No question.

An. And I thought that, I'de forsweare it. Ile ride home to morrow sir *Toby*.

To. Pur-quoy my deere knight?

An. What is *purquoy*? Do, or not do? I would I had bestowed that time in the tongues, that I haue in fencing dancing, and beare-bayting : O had I but followed the Arts.

To. Then hadst thou had an excellent head of haire.

An. Why, would that haue mended my haire?

To. Past question, for thou seest it will not coole my

An. But it becoms we wel enough, dost not? (nature

To. Excellent, it hangs like flax on a distaffe: & I hope to see a huswife take thee between her legs, & spin it off.

An. Faith Ile home to morrow sir *Toby*, your niece wil not be seene, or if she be it's four to one, she'l none of me: the Count himselfe here hard by, wooes her.

To. Shee'l none o'th Count, she'l not match aboue hir degree, neither in estate, yeares, nor wit : I haue heard her swear t. Tut there's life in't man.

And.

Twelfe Night, or, What you will.

And. Ile ſtay a moneth longer. I am a fellow o'th ſtrangeſt minde i'th world: I delight in Maskes and Reuels ſometimes altogether.

To. Art thou good at theſe kicke-chawſes Knight?

And. As any man in Illyria, whatſoeuer he be, vnder the degree of my betters, & yet I will not compare with an old man.

To. What is thy excellence in a galliard, knight?

And. Faith, I can cut a caper.

To. And I can cut the Mutton too't.

And. And I thinke I haue the backe-tricke, ſimply as ſtrong as any man in Illyria.

To. Wherefore are theſe things hid? Wherefore haue theſe gifts a Curtaine before 'em? Are they like to take duſt, like miſtris *Mals* picture? Why doſt thou not goe to Church in a Galliard, and come home in a Carranto? My verie walke ſhould be a Iigge: I would not ſo much as make water but in a Sinke-a-pace: What dooeſt thou meane? Is it a world to hide vertues in? I did thinke by the excellent conſtitution of thy legge, it was form'd vnder the ſtarre of a Galliard.

And. I, 'tis ſtrong, and it does indifferent well in a dam'd colour'd ſtocke. Shall we ſit about ſome Reuels?

To. What ſhall we do elſe: were we not borne vnder Taurus?

And. Taurus? That ſides and heart.

To. No ſir, it is leggs and thighes: let me ſee thee caper. Ha, higher: ha, ha, excellent. *Exeunt*

Scena Quarta.

Enter Valentine, and Viola in mans attire.

Val. If the Duke continue theſe fauours towards you *Ceſario*, you are like to be much aduanc'd, he hath known you but three dayes, and already you are no ſtranger.

Vio. You either feare his humour, or my negligence, that you call in queſtion the continuance of his loue. Is he inconſtant ſir, in his fauours. *Val.* No beleeue me.

Enter Duke, Curio, and Attendants.

Vio. I thanke you: heere comes the Count.

Duke. Who ſaw *Ceſario* hoa?

Vio. On your attendance my Lord heere.

Du. Stand you a-while aloofe. *Ceſario*,
Thou knowſt no leſſe, but all: I haue vnclaſp'd
To thee the booke euen of my ſecret ſoule.
Therefore good youth, addreſſe thy gate vnto her,
Be not deni'de acceſſe, ſtand at her doores,
And tell them, there thy fixed foot ſhall grow
Till thou haue audience.

Vio. Sure my Noble Lord,
If ſhe be ſo abandon'd to her ſorrow
As it is ſpoke, ſhe neuer will admit me.

Du. Be clamorous, and leape all ciuill bounds,
Rather then make vnprofited returne,

Vio. Say I do ſpeake with her (my Lord) what then?

Du. O then, vnfold the paſſion of my loue,
Surprize her with diſcourſe of my deere faith;
It ſhall become thee well to act my woes:
She will attend it better in thy youth,
Then in a Nuntio's of more graue aſpect.

Vio. I thinke not ſo, my Lord.

Du. Deere Lad, beleeue it;
For they ſhall yet belye thy happy yeeres,
That ſay thou art a man: *Dianas* lip
Is not more ſmooth, and rubious: thy ſmall pipe
Is as the maidens organ, ſhrill, and ſound,
And all is ſemblatiue a womans part.
I know thy conſtellation is right apt
For this affayre: ſome foure or fiue attend him;
All if you will: for I my ſelfe am beſt
When leaſt in companie: proſper well in this,
And thou ſhalt liue as freely as thy Lord,
To call his fortunes thine.

Vio. Ile do my beſt
To woe your Lady: yet a barrefull ſtrife,
Who ere I woe, my ſelfe would be his wife. *Exeunt.*

Scena Quinta.

Enter Maria, and Clowne.

Ma. Nay, either tell me where thou haſt bin, or I will not open my lippes ſo wide as a briſtle may enter, in way of thy excuſe: my Lady will hang thee for thy abſence.

Clo. Let her hang me: hee that is well hang'de in this world, needs to feare no colours.

Ma. Make that good.

Clo. He ſhall ſee none to feare.

Ma. A good lenton anſwer: I can tell thee where ẏ ſaying was borne, of I feare no colours.

Clo. Where good miſtris *Mary*?

Ma. In the warrs, & that may you be bolde to ſay in your foolerie.

Clo. Well, God giue them wiſedome that haue it: & thoſe that are fooles, let them vſe their talents.

Ma. Yet you will be hang'd for being ſo long abſent, or to be turn'd away: is not that as good as a hanging to you?

Clo. Many a good hanging, preuents a bad marriage: and for turning away, let ſummer beare it out.

Ma. You are reſolute then?

Clo. Not ſo neyther, but I am reſolu'd on two points

Ma. That if one breake, the other will hold: or if both breake, your gaskins fall.

Clo. Apt in good faith, very apt: well go thy way, if ſir *Toby* would leaue drinking, thou wert as witty a piece of *Eues* fleſh, as any in Illyria.

Ma. Peace you rogue, no more o'that: here comes my Lady: make your excuſe wiſely, you were beſt.

Enter Lady Oliuia, with Maluolio.

Clo. Wit, and't be thy will, put me into good fooling: thoſe wits that thinke they haue thee, doe very oft proue fooles: and I that am ſure I lacke thee, may paſſe for a wiſe man. For what ſaies *Quinapalus*, Better a witty foole, then a fooliſh wit. God bleſſe thee Lady.

Ol. Take the foole away.

Clo. Do you not heare fellowes, take away the Ladie.

Ol. Go too, y'are a dry foole: Ile no more of you: beſides you grow diſ-honeſt.

Clo. Two faults Madona, that drinke & good counſell wil amend: for giue the dry foole drink, then is the foole not dry: bid the diſhoneſt man mend himſelf, if he mend, he is no longer diſhoneſt; if hee cannot, let the Botcher mend him: any thing that's mended, is but patch'd: vertu that tranſgreſſes, is but patcht with ſinne, and ſin that amends, is but patcht with vertue. If that this ſimple Sillogiſme will ſerue, ſo: if it will not, vvhat remedy?

As there is no true Cuckold but calamity, so beauties a flower; The Lady bad take away the foole, therefore I say againe, take her away.

Ol. Sir, I bad them take away you.

Clo. Misprision in the highest degree. Lady, *Cucullus non facit monachum*: that's as much to say, as I weare no motley in my braine: good *Madona*, giue mee leaue to proue you a foole.

Ol. Can you do it?

Clo. Dexteriously, good Madona.

Ol. Make your proofe.

Clo. I must catechize you for it Madona, Good my Mouse of vertue answer mee.

Ol. Well sir, for want of other idlenesse, Ile bide your proofe.

Clo. Good Madona, why mournst thou?

Ol. Good foole, for my brothers death.

Clo. I thinke his soule is in hell, Madona.

Ol. I know his soule is in heauen, foole.

Clo. The more foole (Madona) to mourne for your Brothers soule, being in heauen. Take away the Foole, Gentlemen.

Ol. What thinke you of this foole *Maluolio*, doth he not mend?

Mal. Yes, and shall do, till the pangs of death shake him: Infirmity that decaies the wise, doth euer make the better foole.

Clow. God send you sir, a speedie Infirmity, for the better increasing your folly: Sir *Toby* will be sworn that I am no Fox, but he wil not passe his word for two pence that you are no Foole.

Ol. How say you to that *Maluolio*?

Mal. I maruell your Ladyship takes delight in such a barren rascall: I saw him put down the other day, with an ordinary foole, that has no more braine then a stone. Looke you now, he's out of his gard already: vnles you laugh and minister occasion to him, he is gag'd. I protest I take these Wisemen, that crow so at these set kinde of fooles, no better then the fooles Zanies.

Ol. O you are sicke of selfe-loue *Maluolio*, and taste with a distemper'd appetite. To be generous, guiltlesse, and of free disposition, is to take those things for Bird-bolts, that you deeme Cannon bullets: There is no slander in an allow'd foole, though he do nothing but rayle; nor no rayling, in a knowne discreet man, though hee do nothing but reproue.

Clo. Now Mercury indue thee with leasing, for thou speak'st well of fooles.

Enter Maria.

Mar. Madam, there is at the gate, a young Gentleman, much desires to speake with you.

Ol. From the Count *Orsino*, is it?

Ma. I know not (Madam) 'tis a faire young man, and well attended.

Ol. Who of my people hold him in delay?

Ma. Sir *Toby* Madam, your kinsman.

Ol. Fetch him off I pray you, he speakes nothing but madman: Fie on him. Go you *Maluolio*; If it be a suit from the Count, I am sicke, or not at home. What you will, to dismisse it. *Exit Malu.*

Now you see sir, how your fooling growes old, & people dislike it.

Clo. Thou hast spoke for vs (Madona) as if thy eldest sonne should be a foole: whose scull, Ioue cramme with braines, for heere he comes. *Enter Sir Toby.*

One of thy kin has a most weake *Pia-mater*.

Ol. By mine honor halfe drunke. What is he at the gate Cosin?

To. A Gentleman.

Ol. A Gentleman? What Gentleman?

To. 'Tis a Gentleman heere. A plague o' these pickle herring: How now Sot.

Clo. Good Sir *Toby*.

Ol. Cosin, Cosin, how haue you come so earely by this Lethargie?

To. Letcherie, I defie Letchery: there's one at the gate.

Ol. I marry, what is he?

To. Let him be the diuell and he will, I care not: giue me faith say I. Well, it's all one. *Exit*

Ol. What's a drunken man like, foole?

Clo. Like a drown'd man, a foole, and a madde man: One draught aboue heate, makes him a foole, the second maddes him, and a third drownes him.

Ol. Go thou and seeke the Crowner, and let him sitte o' my Coz: for he's in the third degree of drinke: hee's drown'd: go looke after him.

Clo. He is but mad yet Madona, and the foole shall looke to the madman.

Enter Maluolio.

Mal. Madam, yond young fellow sweares hee will speake with you. I told him you were sicke, he takes on him to vnderstand so much, and therefore comes to speak with you. I told him you were asleepe, he seems to haue a fore knowledge of that too, and therefore comes to speake with you. What is to be said to him Ladie, hee's fortified against any deniall.

Ol. Tell him, he shall not speake with me.

Mal. Ha's beene told so: and hee sayes hee'l stand at your doore like a Sheriffes post, and be the supporter to a bench, but hee'l speake with you.

Ol. What kinde o' man is he?

Mal. Why of mankinde.

Ol. What manner of man?

Mal. Of verie ill manner: hee'l speake with you, will you, or no.

Ol. Of what personage, and yeeres is he?

Mal. Not yet old enough for a man, nor yong enough for a boy: as a squash is before tis a pescod, or a Codling when tis almost an Apple: Tis with him in standing water, betweene boy and man. He is verie well-fauour'd, and he speakes verie shrewishly: One would thinke his mothers milke were scarse out of him.

Ol. Let him approach: Call in my Gentlewoman.

Mal. Gentlewoman, my Lady calles. *Exit.*

Enter Maria.

Ol. Giue me my vaile: come throw it ore my face, Wee'l once more heare *Orsinos* Embassie.

Enter Violenta.

Vio. The honorable Ladie of the house, which is she?

Ol. Speake to me, I shall answer for her: your will.

Vio. Most radiant, exquisite, and vnmatchable beautie. I pray you tell me if this bee the Lady of the house, for I neuer saw her. I would bee loath to cast away my speech: for besides that it is excellently well pend, I haue taken great paines to con it. Good Beauties, let mee sustaine no scorne; I am very comptible, euen to the least sinister vsage.

Ol. Whence came you sir?

Vio. I can say little more then I haue studied, & that question's out of my part. Good gentle one, giue mee modest assurance, if you be the Ladie of the house, that may proceede in my speech.

Ol. Are you a Comedian?

Vio. No my profound heart : and yet (by the verie phangs of malice, I sweare) I am not that I play. Are you the Ladie of the house?

Ol. If I do not vsurpe my selfe, I am.

Vio. Most certaine, if you are shee, you do vsurp your selfe: for what is yours to bestowe, is, not yours to reserue. But this is from my Commission: I will on with my speech in your praise, and then shew you the heart of my message.

Ol. Come to what is important in't: I forgiue you the praise.

Vio. Alas, I tooke great paines to studie it, and 'tis Poeticall.

Ol. It is the more like to be feigned, I pray you keep it in. I heard you were sawcy at my gates, & allowd your approach rather to wonder at you, then to heare you. If you be not mad, be gone: if you haue reason, be breefe: 'tis not that time of Moone with me, to make one in so skipping a dialogue.

Ma. Will you hoyst sayle sir, here lies your way.

Vio. No good swabber, I am to hull here a little longer. Some mollification for your Giant, sweete Ladie; tell me your minde, I am a messenger.

Ol. Sure you haue some hiddeous matter to deliuer, when the curtesie of it is so fearefull. Speake your office.

Vio. It alone concernes your eare: I bring no ouerture of warre, no taxation of homage; I hold the Olyffe in my hand: my words are as full of peace, as matter.

Ol. Yet you began rudely. What are you? What would you?

Vio. The rudenesse that hath appear'd in mee, haue I learn'd from my entertainment. What I am, and what I would, are as secret as maiden-head: to your eares, Diuinity; to any others, prophanation.

Ol. Giue vs the place alone, We will heare this diuinitie. Now sir, what is your text?

Vio. Most sweet Ladie.

Ol. A comfortable doctrine, and much may bee saide of it. Where lies your Text?

Vio. In *Orsinoes* bosome.

Ol. In his bosome? In what chapter of his bosome?

Vio. To answer by the method, in the first of his hart.

Ol. O, I haue read it: it is heresie. Haue you no more to say?

Vio. Good Madam, let me see your face.

Ol. Haue you any Commission from your Lord, to negotiate with my face: you are now out of your Text: but we will draw the Curtain, and shew you the picture. Looke you sir, such a one I was this present: Ist not well done?

Vio. Excellently done, if God did all.

Ol. 'Tis in graine sir, 'twill endure winde and weather.

Vio. Tis beauty truly blent, whose red and white, Natures owne sweet, and cunning hand laid on: Lady, you are the cruell'st shee aliue, If you will leade these graces to the graue, And leaue the world no copie.

Ol. O sir, I will not be so hard-hearted: I will giue out diuers scedules of my beautie. It shalbe Inuentoried and euery particle and vtensile labell'd to my will: As, Item two lippes indifferent redde, Item two grey eyes, with lids to them: Item, one necke, one chin, & so forth. Were you sent hither to praise me?

Vio. I see you what you are, you are too proud: But if you were the diuell, you are faire: My Lord, and master loues you: O such loue Could be but recompenc'd, though you were crown'd The non-pareil of beautie.

Ol. How does he loue me?

Vio. With adorations, fertill teares, With groanes that thunder loue, with sighes of fire.

Ol. Your Lord does know my mind, I cannot loue him Yet I suppose him vertuous, know him noble, Of great estate, of fresh and stainlesse youth; In voyces well divulg'd, free, learn'd, and valiant, And in dimension, and the shape of nature, A gracious person; But yet I cannot loue him: He might haue tooke his answer long ago.

Vio. If I did loue you in my masters flame, With such a suffring, such a deadly life: In your deniall, I would finde no sence, I would not vnderstand it.

Ol. Why, what would you?

Vio. Make me a willow Cabine at your gate, And call vpon my soule within the house, Write loyall Cantons of contemned loue, And sing them lowd euen in the dead of night: Hallow your name to the reuerberate hilles, And make the babling Gossip of the aire, Cry out *Oliuia*: O you should not rest Betweene the elements of ayre, and earth, But you should pittie me.

Ol. You might do much: What is your Parentage?

Vio. Aboue my fortunes, yet my state is well: I am a Gentleman.

Ol. Get you to your Lord: I cannot loue him: let him send no more, Vnlesse (perchance) you come to me againe, To tell me how he takes it: Fare you well: I thanke you for your paines: spend this for mee.

Vio. I am no feede post, Lady; keepe your purse, My Master, not my selfe, lackes recompence. Loue make his heart of flint, that you shal loue, And let your feruour like my masters be, Plac'd in contempt: Farwell fayre crueltie. *Exit*

Ol. What is your Parentage? Aboue my fortunes, yet my state is well; I am a Gentleman. Ile be sworne thou art, Thy tongue, thy face, thy limbes, actions, and spirit, Do giue thee fiue-fold blazon: not too fast: soft, soft, Vnlesse the Master were the man. How now? Euen so quickly may one catch the plague? Me thinkes I feele this youths perfections With an inuisible, and subtle stealth To creepe in at mine eyes. Well, let it be. What hoa, *Maluolio*.

Enter Maluolio.

Mal. Heere Madam, at your seruice.

Ol. Run after that same peeuish Messenger The Countes man: he left this Ring behinde him Would I, or not: tell him, Ile none of it. Desire him not to flatter with his Lord, Nor hold him vp with hopes, I am not for him: If that the youth will come this way to morrow, Ile giue him reasons for't: hie thee *Maluolio*.

Mal. Madam, I will. *Exit.*

Ol. I do I know not what, and feare to finde Mine eye too great a flatterer for my minde:

Fate

Fate, shew thy force, our selues we do not owe,
What is decreed, must be: and be this so.

Finis, Actus primus.

Actus Secundus, Scæna prima.

Enter Antonio & Sebastian.

Ant. Will you stay no longer: nor will you not that I go with you.

Seb. By your patience, no: my starres shine darkely ouer me; the malignancie of my fate, might perhaps distemper yours; therefore I shall craue of you your leaue, that I may beare my euils alone. It were a bad recompence for your loue, to lay any of them on you.

An. Let me yet know of you, whither you are bound.

Seb. No sooth sir: my determinate voyage is meere extrauagancie. But I perceiue in you so excellent a touch of modestie, that you will not extort from me, what I am willing to keepe in: therefore it charges me in manners, the rather to expresse my selfe: you must know of mee then *Antonio*, my name is *Sebastian* (which I call'd *Rodorigo*) my father was that *Sebastian* of *Messaline*, whom I know you haue heard of. He left behinde him, my selfe, and a sister, both borne in an houre: if the Heauens had beene pleas'd, would we had so ended. But you sir, alter'd that, for some houre before you tooke me from the breach of the sea, was my sister drown'd.

Ant. Alas the day.

Seb. A Lady sir, though it was said shee much resembled me, was yet of many accounted beautiful: but thogh I could not with such estimable wonder ouer-farre beleeue that, yet thus farre I will boldly publish her, shee bore a minde that enuy could not but call faire: Shee is drown'd already sir with salt water, though I seeme to drowne her remembrance againe with more.

Ant. Pardon me sir, your bad entertainment.

Seb. O good *Antonio*, forgiue me your trouble.

Ant. If you will not murther me for my loue, let mee be your seruant.

Seb. If you will not vndo what you haue done, that is kill him, whom you haue recouer'd, desire it not. Fare ye well at once, my bosome is full of kindnesse, and I am yet so neere the manners of my mother, that vpon the least occasion more, mine eyes will tell tales of me: I am bound to the Count Orsino's Court, farewell. *Exit*

Ant. The gentlenesse of all the gods go with thee:
I haue many enemies in Orsino's Court,
Else would I very shortly see thee there:
But come what may, I do adore thee so,
That danger shall seeme sport, and I will go. *Exit.*

Scæna Secunda.

Enter Viola and Maluolio, at seuerall doores.

Mal. Were not you eu'n now, with the Countesse Oliuia?

Vio. Euen now sir, on a moderate pace, I haue since arriu'd but hither.

Mal. She returnes this Ring to you (sir) you might haue saued mee my paines, to haue taken it away your selfe. She adds moreouer, that you should put your Lord into a desperate assurance, she will none of him. And one thing more, that you be neuer so hardie to come againe in his affaires, vnlesse it bee to report your Lords taking of this: receiue it so.

Vio. She tooke the Ring of me, Ile none of it.

Mal. Come sir, you peeuishly threw it to her: and her will is, it should be so return'd: If it bee worth stooping for, there it lies, in your eye: if not, bee it his that findes it. *Exit.*

Vio. I left no Ring with her: what meanes this Lady?
Fortune forbid my out-side haue not charm'd her:
She made good view of me, indeed so much,
That me thought her eyes had lost her tongue,
For she did speake in starts distractedly.
She loues me sure, the cunning of her passion
Inuites me in this churlish messenger:
None of my Lords Ring? Why he sent her none;
I am the man, if it be so, as tis,
Poore Lady, she were better loue a dreame:
Disguise, I see thou art a wickednesse,
Wherein the pregnant enemie does much.
How easie is it, for the proper false
In womens waxen hearts to set their formes:
Alas, O frailtie is the cause, not wee,
For such as we are made, if such we bee:
How will this fadge? My master loues her deerely,
And I (poore monster) fond asmuch on him:
And she (mistaken) seemes to dote on me:
What will become of this? As I am man,
My state is desperate for my maisters loue:
As I am woman (now alas the day)
What thriftlesse sighes shall poore *Oliuia* breath?
O time, thou must vntangle this, not I,
It is too hard a knot for me t'vnty.

Scæna Tertia.

Enter Sir Toby, and Sir Andrew.

To. Approach Sir *Andrew*: not to bee a bedde after midnight, is to be vp betimes, and *Deliculo surgere*, thou know'st.

And. Nay by my troth I know not: but I know, to be vp late, is to be vp late.

To. A false conclusion: I hate it as an vnfill'd Canne. To be vp after midnight, and to go to bed then is early: so that to go to bed after midnight, is to goe to bed betimes. Does not our liues consist of the foure Elements?

And. Faith so they say, but I thinke it rather consists of eating and drinking.

To. Th'art a scholler; let vs therefore eate and drinke, *Marian* I say, a stoope of wine.

Enter Clowne.

And. Heere comes the foole yfaith.

Clo. How now my harts: Did you neuer see the Picture of we three?

To. Welcome asse, now let's haue a catch.

And. By my troth the foole has an excellent breast. I had rather then forty shillings I had such a legge, and so sweet a breath to sing, as the foole has. In sooth thou wast in very gracious fooling last night, when thou spok'st of *Pigrogromitus*, of the *Vapians* passing the Equinoctial of *Queubus*: 'twas very good yfaith: I sent thee sixe pence for

Twelfe Night, or, What you will.

for thy Lemon, hadst it?

Clo. I did impeticos thy gratillity: for *Maluolios* nose is no Whip-stocke. My Lady has a white hand, and the Mermidons are no bottle-ale houses.

An. Excellent: Why this is the best fooling, when all is done. Now a song.

To. Come on, there is sixe pence for you. Let's haue a song.

An. There's a testrill of me too: if one knight giue a

Clo. Would you haue a loue-song, or a song of good life?

To. A loue song, a loue song.

An. I, I. I care not for good life.

Clowne sings.

O Mistris mine where are you roming?
O stay and heare, your true loues coming,
That can sing both high and low.
Trip no further prettie sweeting.
Iourneys end in louers meeting,
Euery wise mans sonne doth know.

An. Excellent good, ifaith.

To. Good, good.

Clo. What is loue, tis not heereafter,
Present mirth, hath present laughter:
What's to come, is still vnsure.
In delay there lies no plentie,
Then come kisse me sweet and twentie:
Youths a stuffe will not endure.

An. A mellifluous voyce, as I am true knight.

To. A contagious breath.

An. Very sweet, and contagious ifaith.

To. To heare by the nose, it is dulcet in contagion. But shall we make the Welkin dance indeed? Shall wee rowze the night-Owle in a Catch, that will drawe three soules out of one Weauer? Shall we do that?

And. And you loue me, let's doo't: I am dogge at a Catch.

Clo. Byrlady sir, and some dogs will catch well.

An. Most certaine: Let our Catch be, *Thou Knaue.*

Clo. *Hold thy peace, thou Knaue* knight. I shall be constrain'd in't, to call thee knaue, Knight.

An. Tis not the first time I haue constrained one to call me knaue. Begin foole: it begins, *Hold thy peace.*

Clo. I shall neuer begin if I hold my peace.

An. Good ifaith: Come begin. *Catch sung*

Enter Maria.

Mar. What a catterwalling doe you keepe heere? If my Ladie haue not call'd vp her Steward *Maluolio,* and bid him turne you out of doores, neuer trust me.

To. My Lady's a *Catayan,* we are politicians, *Maluolios* a Peg-a-ramsie, and *Three merry men be wee.* Am not I consanguinious? Am I not of her blood: tilly vally. Ladie, *There dwelt a man in Babylon, Lady, Lady.*

Clo. Beshrew me, the knights in admirable fooling.

An. I, he do's well enough if he be dispos'd, and so do I too: he does it with a better grace, but I do it more naturall.

To. O *the twelfe day of December.*

Mar. For the loue o'God peace.

Enter Maluolio.

Mal. My masters are you mad? Or what are you? Haue you no wit, manners, nor honestie, but to gabble like Tinkers at this time of night? Do yee make an Alehouse of my Ladies house, that ye squeak out your Coziers Catches without any mitigation or remorse of voice? Is there no respect of place, persons, nor time in you?

To. We did keepe time sir in our Catches. Snecke vp.

Mal. Sir *Toby,* I must be round with you. My Lady bad me tell you, that though she harbors you as her kinsman, she's nothing ally'd to your disorders. If you can separate your selfe and your misdemeanors, you are welcome to the house: if not, and it would please you to take leaue of her, she is very willing to bid you farewell.

To. Farewell deere heart, since I must needs be gone.

Mar. Nay good Sir *Toby.*

Clo. His eyes do shew his dayes are almost done.

Mal. Is't euen so?

To. But I will neuer dye.

Clo. Sir *Toby* there you lye.

Mal. This is much credit to you.

To. Shall I bid him go.

Clo. What and if you do?

To. Shall I bid him go, and spare not?

Clo. O no, no, no, no, you dare not.

To. Out o'tune sir, ye lye: Art any more then a Steward? Dost thou thinke because thou art vertuous, there shall be no more Cakes and Ale?

Clo. Yes by S. Anne, and Ginger shall bee hotte y'th mouth too.

To. Th'art i'th right. Goe sir, rub your Chaine with crums. A stope of Wine *Maria.*

Mal. Mistris Mary, if you priz'd my Ladies fauour at any thing more then contempt, you would not giue meanes for this vnciuill rule; she shall know of it by this hand. *Exit*

Mar. Go shake your eares.

An. 'Twere as good a deede as to drink when a mans a hungrie, to challenge him the field, and then to breake promise with him, and make a foole of him.

To. Doo't knight, Ile write thee a Challenge: or Ile deliuer thy indignation to him by word of mouth.

Mar. Sweet Sir *Toby* be patient for to night: Since the youth of the Counts was to day with my Lady, she is much out of quiet. For Monsieur Maluolio, let me alone with him: If I do not gull him into an ayword, and make him a common recreation, do not thinke I haue witte enough to lye straight in my bed: I know I can do it.

To. Possesse vs, possesse vs, tell vs something of him.

Mar. Marrie sir, sometimes he is a kinde of Puritane.

An. O, if I thought that, Ide beate him like a dogge.

To. What for being a Puritan, thy exquisite reason, deere knight.

An. I haue no exquisite reason for't, but I haue reason good enough.

Mar. The diu'll a Puritane that hee is, or any thing constantly but a time-pleaser, an affection'd Asse, that cons State without booke, and vtters it by great swarths. The best perswaded of himselfe: so cram'd (as he thinkes) with excellencies, that it is his grounds of faith, that all that looke on him, loue him: and on that vice in him, will my reuenge finde notable cause to worke.

To. What wilt thou do?

Mar. I will drop in his way some obscure Epistles of loue, wherein by the colour of his beard, the shape of his legge, the manner of his gate, the expressure of his eye, forehead, and complection, he shall finde himselfe most feelingly personated. I can write very like my Ladie your Neece, on a forgotten matter wee can hardly make distinction of our hands.

To. Excellent, I smell a deuice.

An. I hau't in my nose too.

To. He shall thinke by the Letters that thou wilt drop

that they come from my Neece, and that shee's in loue with him.

Mar. My purpose is indeed a horse of that colour.

An. And your horse now would make him an Asse.

Mar. Asse, I doubt not.

An. O twill be admirable.

Mar. Sport royall I warrant you: I know my Physicke will worke with him, I will plant you two, and let the Foole make a third, where he shall finde the Letter: obserue his construction of it: For this night to bed, and dreame on the euent: Farewell. *Exit*

To. Good night *Penthisilea*.

An. Before me shee's a good wench.

To. She's a beagle true bred, and one that adores me: what o'that?

An. I was ador'd once too.

To. Let's to bed knight: Thou hadst neede send for more money.

An. If I cannot recouer your Neece, I am a foule way out.

To. Send for money knight, if thou hast her not i'th end, call me Cut.

An. If I do not, neuer trust me, take it how you will.

To. Come, come, Ile go burne some Sacke, tis too late to go to bed now: Come knight, come knight. *Exeunt*

Scena Quarta.

Enter Duke, Viola, Curio, and others.

Du. Giue me some Musick; Now good morow frends.
Now good *Cesario*, but that peece of song,
That old and Anticke song we heard last night;
Me thought it did releeue my passion much,
More then light ayres, and recollected termes
Of these most briske and giddy-paced times.
Come, but one verse.

Cur. He is not heere (so please your Lordshippe) that should sing it?

Du. Who was it?

Cur. Feste the Iester my Lord, a foole that the Ladie *Oliuiaes* Father tooke much delight in. He is about the house.

Du. Seeke him out, and play the tune the while.
Musicke playes.

Come hither Boy, if euer thou shalt loue
In the sweet pangs of it, remember me:
For such as I am, all true Louers are,
Vnstaid and skittish in all motions else,
Saue in the constant image of the creature
That is belou'd. How dost thou like this tune?

Vio. It giues a verie eccho to the seate
Where loue is thron'd.

Du. Thou dost speake masterly,
My life vpon't, yong though thou art, thine eye
Hath staid vpon some fauour that it loues:
Hath it not boy?

Vio. A little, by your fauour.

Du. What kinde of woman ist?

Vio. Of your complection.

Du. She is not worth thee then. What yeares ifaith?

Vio. About your yeeres my Lord.

Du. Too old by heauen: Let still the woman take
An elder then her selfe, so weares she to him;
So swayes she leuell in her husbands heart:
For boy, howeuer we do praise our selues,
Our fancies are more giddie and vnfirme,
More longing, wauering, sooner lost and worne,
Then womens are.

Vio. I thinke it well my Lord.

Du. Then let thy Loue be yonger then thy selfe,
Or thy affection cannot hold the bent:
For women are as Roses, whose faire flowre
Being once displaid, doth fall that verie howre.

Vio. And so they are: alas, that they are so:
To die, euen when they to perfection grow.

Enter Curio & Clowne.

Du. O fellow come, the song we had last night:
Marke it Cesario, it is old and plaine;
The Spinsters and the Knitters in the Sun,
And the free maides that weaue their thred with bones,
Do vse to chaunt it: it is silly sooth,
And dallies with the innocence of loue,
Like the old age.

Clo. Are you ready Sir?

Duke. I prethee sing. *Musicke.*

The Song.

Come away, come away death,
And in sad cypresse let me be laide.
Fye away, fie away breath,
I am slaine by a faire cruell maide:
My shrowd of white, stuck all with Ew, O prepare it,
My part of death no one so true did share it.

Not a flower, not a flower sweete
On my blacke coffin, let there be strewne,
Not a friend, not a friend greet
My poore corpes, where my bones shall be throwne:
A thousand thousand sighes to saue, lay me ô where
Sad true louer neuer find my graue, to weepe there.

Du. There's for thy paines.

Clo. No paines sir, I take pleasure in singing sir.

Du. Ile pay thy pleasure then.

Clo. Truely sir, and pleasure will be paide one time, or another.

Du. Giue me now leaue, to leaue thee.

Clo. Now the melancholly God protect thee, and the Tailor make thy doublet of changeable Taffata, for thy minde is a very Opall. I would haue men of such constancie put to Sea, that their businesse might be euery thing, and their intent euerie where, for that's it, that alwayes makes a good voyage of nothing. Farewell. *Exit*

Du. Let all the rest giue place: Once more *Cesario*,
Get thee to yond same soueraigne crueltie:
Tell her my loue, more noble then the world
Prizes not quantitie of dirtie lands,
The parts that fortune hath bestow'd vpon her:
Tell her I hold as giddily as Fortune:
But 'tis that miracle, and Queene of Iems
That nature prankes her in, attracts my soule.

Vio. But if she cannot loue you sir.

Du. It cannot be so answer'd.

Vio. Sooth but you must.
Say that some Lady, as perhappes there is,
Hath for your loue as great a pang of heart
As you haue for *Oliuia*: you cannot loue her:
You tel her so: Must she not then be answer'd?

Du. There is no womans sides

Can bide the beating of so strong a passion,
As loue doth giue my heart: no womans heart
So bigge, to hold so much, they lacke retention.
Alas, their loue may be call'd appetite,
No motion of the Liuer, but the Pallat,
That suffer surfet, cloyment, and reuolt,
But mine is all as hungry as the Sea,
And can digest as much, make no compare
Betweene that loue a woman can beare me,
And that I owe *Oliuia.*

Vio. I but I know.

Du. What dost thou knowe?

Vio. Too well what loue women to men may owe:
In faith they are as true of heart, as we.
My Father had a daughter lou'd a man
As it might be perhaps, were I a woman
I should your Lordship.

Du. And what's her history?

Vio. A blanke my Lord: she neuer told her loue,
But let concealment like a worme i'th budde
Feede on her damaske cheeke: she pin'd in thought,
And with a greene and yellow melancholly,
She sate like Patience on a Monument,
Smiling at greefe. Was not this loue indeede?
We men may say more, sweare more, but indeed
Our shewes are more then will: for still we proue
Much in our vowes, but little in our loue.

Du. But di'de thy sister of her loue my Boy?

Vio. I am all the daughters of my Fathers house,
And all the brothers too: and yet I know not.
Sir, shall I to this Lady?

Du. I that's the Theame,
To her in haste: giue her this Iewell: say,
My loue can giue no place, bide no denay. *exeunt*

Scena Quinta.

Enter Sir Toby, Sir Andrew, and Fabian.

To. Come thy wayes Signior *Fabian.*

Fab. Nay Ile come: if I loose a scruple of this sport, let me be boyl'd to death with Melancholly.

To. Wouldst thou not be glad to haue the niggardly Rascally sheepe-biter, come by some notable shame?

Fa. I would exult man: you know he brought me out o'fauour with my Lady, about a Beare-baiting heere.

To. To anger him wee'l haue the Beare againe, and we will foole him blacke and blew, shall we not sir *Andrew*?

An. And we do not, it is pittie of our liues.

Enter Maria.

To. Heere comes the little villaine: How now my Mettle of India?

Mar. Get ye all three into the box tree: *Maluolio's* comming downe this walke, he has beene yonder i'the Sunne practising behauiour to his own shadow this halfe houre: obserue him for the loue of Mockerie: for I know this Letter wil make a contemplatiue Ideot of him. Close in the name of ieasting, lye thou there: for heere comes the Trowt, that must be caught with tickling. *Exit*

Enter Maluolio.

Mal. 'Tis but Fortune, all is fortune. *Maria* once told me she did affect me, and I haue heard her self come thus neere, that should shee fancie, it should bee one of my complection. Besides she vses me with a more exalted respect, then any one else that followes her. What should I thinke on't?

To. Heere's an ouer-weening rogue.

Fa. Oh peace: Contemplation makes a rare Turkey Cocke of him, how he iets vnder his aduanc'd plumes.

And. Slight I could so beate the Rogue.

To. Peace I say.

Mal. To be Count *Maluolio.*

To. Ah Rogue.

An. Pistoll him, pistoll him.

To. Peace, peace.

Mal. There is example for't: The Lady of the *Strachy*, matried the yeoman of the wardrobe.

An. Fie on him Iezabel.

Fa. O peace, now he's deepely in: looke how imagination blowes him.

Mal. Hauing beene three moneths married to her, sitting in my state.

To. O for a stone-bow to hit him in the eye.

Mal. Calling my Officers about me, in my branch'd Veluet gowne: hauing come from a day bedde, where I haue left *Oliuia* sleeping.

To. Fire and Brimstone.

Fa. O peace, peace.

Mal. And then to haue the humor of state: and after a demure trauaile of regard: telling them I knowe my place, as I would they should doe theirs; to aske for my kinsman *Toby.*

To. Boltes and shackles.

Fa. Oh peace, peace, peace, now, now.

Mal. Seauen of my people with an obedient start, make out for him: I frowne the while, and perchance winde vp my watch, or play with my some rich Iewell: *Toby* approaches; curtsies there to me.

To. Shall this fellow liue?

Fa. Though our silence be drawne from vs with cars, yet peace.

Mal. I extend my hand to him thus: quenching my familiar smile with an austere regard of controll.

To. And do's not *Toby* take you a blow o'the lippes, then?

Mal. Saying, Cosine *Toby*, my Fortunes hauing cast me on your Neece, giue me this prerogatiue of speech.

To. What, what?

Mal. You must amend your drunkennesse.

To. Out scab.

Fab. Nay patience, or we breake the sinewes of our plot?

Mal. Besides you waste the treasure of your time, with a foolish knight.

And. That's mee I warrant you.

Mal. One sir *Andrew.*

And. I knew 'twas I, for many do call mee foole.

Mal. What employment haue we heere?

Fa. Now is the Woodcocke neere the gin.

To. Oh peace, and the spirit of humors intimate reading aloud to him.

Mal. By my life this is my Ladies hand: these bee her very *C's*, her *V's*, and her *T's*, and thus makes shee her great *P's*. It is in contempt of question her hand.

An. Her *C's*, her *V's*, and her *T's*: why that?

Mal. To the vnknowne belou'd, this, and my good Wishes: Her very Phrases: By your leaue wax. Soft, and the impressure her *Lucrece*, with which she vses to seale: tis my Lady: To whom should this be?

Fab. This winnes him, Liuer and all.

Mal.

Mal. Ioue knowes I loue, but who, Lips do not mooue, no man must know. No man must know. What followes? The numbers alter'd: No man must know. If this should be thee *Maluolio?*

To. Marrie hang thee brocke.

Mal. I may command where I adore, but silence like a Lucresse knife:
With bloodlesse stroke my heart doth gore, *M.O.A.I.* doth sway my life.

Fa. A fustian riddle.

To. Excellent Wench, say I.

Mal. *M.O.A.I.* doth sway my life. Nay but first let me see, let me see, let me see.

Fab. What dish a poyson has she drest him?

To. And with what wing the stallion checkes at it?

Mal. *I may command, where I adore*: Why shee may command me: I serue her, she is my Ladie. Why this is euident to any formall capacitie. There is no obstruction in this, and the end: What should that Alphabeticall position portend, if I could make that resemble something in me? Softly, *M.O.A.I.*

To. O I, make vp that, he is now at a cold sent.

Fab. Sowter will cry vpon't for all this, though it bee as ranke as a Fox.

Mal. *M. Maluolio, M.* why that begins my name.

Fab. Did not I say he would worke it out, the Curre is excellent at faults.

Mal. *M.* But then there is no consonancy in the sequell that suffers vnder probation: *A.* should follow, but *O.* does.

Fa. And *O* shall end, I hope.

To. I, or Ile cudgell him, and make him cry O.

Mal. And then *I.* comes behind.

Fa. I, and you had any eye behinde you, you might see more detraction at your heeles, then Fortunes before you.

Mal. *M,O,A,I.* This simulation is not as the former: and yet to crush this a little, it would bow to mee, for euery one of these Letters are in my name. Soft, here followes prose: *If this fall into thy hand, reuolue.* In my stars I am aboue thee, but be not affraid of greatnesse: Some are become great, some atcheeues greatnesse, and some haue greatnesse thrust vppon em. Thy fates open theyr hands, let thy blood and spirit embrace them, and to inure thy selfe to what thou art like to be: cast thy humble slough, and appeare fresh. Be opposite with a kinsman, surly with seruants: Let thy tongue tang arguments of state; put thy selfe into the tricke of singularitie. Shee thus aduises thee, that sighes for thee. Remember who commended thy yellow stockings, and wish'd to see thee euer crosse garter'd: I say remember, goe too, thou art made if thou desir'st to be so: If not, let me see thee a steward still, the fellow of seruants, and not woorthie to touch Fortunes fingers Farewell, Shee that would alter seruices with thee, the fortunate vnhappy daylight and champian discouers not more: This is open, I will bee proud, I will reade politicke Authours, I will baffle Sir *Toby*, I will wash off grosse acquaintance, I will be point deuise, the very man. I do not now foole my selfe, to let imagination iade mee; for euery reason excites to this, that my Lady loues me. She did commend my yellow stockings of late, shee did praise my legge being crosse-garter'd, and in this she manifests her selfe to my loue, & with a kinde of iniunction driues mee to these habites of her liking. I thanke my starres, I am happy: I will bee strange, stout, in yellow stockings, and crosse Garter'd, euen with the swiftnesse of putting on. Ioue, and my starres be praised. Heere is yet a postscript. *Thou canst not choose but know who I am. If thou entertainst my loue, let it appeare in thy smiling, thy smiles become thee well.* Therefore in my presence still smile, deero my sweete, I prethee. Ioue I thanke thee, I will smile, I wil do euery thing that thou wilt haue me. *Exit*

Fab. I will not giue my part of this sport for a pension of thousands to be paid from the Sophy.

To. I could marry this wench for this deuice.

An. So could I too.

To. And aske no other dowry with her, but such another iest.

Enter Maria.

An. Nor I neither.

Fab. Heere comes my noble gull catcher.

To. Wilt thou set thy foote o'my necke.

An. Or o'mine either?

To. Shall I play my freedome at tray-trip, and becom thy bondslaue?

An. Ifaith, or I either?

Tob. Why, thou hast put him in such a dreame, that when the image of it leaues him, he must run mad.

Ma. Nay but say true, do's it worke vpon him?

To. Like Aqua vite with a Midwife.

Mar. If you will then see the fruites of the sport, mark his first approach before my Lady: hee will come to her in yellow stockings, and 'tis a colour shee abhorres, and crosse garter'd, a fashion shee detests: and hee will smile vpon her, which will now be so vnsuteable to her disposition, being addicted to a melancholly, as shee is, that it cannot but turn him into a notable contempt: if you wil see it follow me.

To. To the gates of Tartar, thou most excellent diuell of wit.

And. Ile make one too. *Exeunt.*

Finis Actus secundus.

Actus Tertius, Scæna prima.

Enter Viola and Clowne.

Vio. Saue thee Friend and thy Musick: dost thou liue by thy Tabor?

Clo. No sir, I liue by the Church.

Vio. Art thou a Churchman?

Clo. No such matter sir, I do liue by the Church: For, I do liue at my house, and my house dooth stand by the Church.

Vio. So thou maist say the Kings lyes by a begger, if a begger dwell neer him: or the Church stands by thy Tabor, if thy Tabor stand by the Church.

Clo. You haue said sir: To see this age: A sentence is but a cheu'rill gloue to a good witte, how quickely the wrong side may be turn'd outward.

Vio. Nay that's certaine: they that dally nicely with words, may quickely make them wanton.

Clo. I would therefore my sister had had no name Sir.

Vio. Why man?

Clo. Why sir, her names a word, and to dallie with that word, might make my sister wanton: But indeede, words are very Rascals, since bonds disgrac'd them.

Vio. Thy reason man?

Clo.

Twelfe Night, or, What you will.

Clo. Troth sir, I can yeeld you none without wordes, and wordes are growne so false, I am loath to proue reason with them.

Vio. I warrant thou art a merry fellow, and car'st for nothing.

Clo. Not so sir, I do care for something: but in my conscience sir, I do not care for you: if that be to care for nothing sir, I would it would make you inuisible.

Vio. Art not thou the Lady *Oliuia's* foole?

Clo. No indeed sir, the Lady *Oliuia* has no folly, shee will keepe no foole sir, till she be married, and fooles are as like husbands, as Pilchers are to Herrings, the Husbands the bigger, I am indeede not her foole, but hir corrupter of words.

Vio. I saw thee late at the Count *Orsino's*.

Clo. Foolery sir, does walke about the Orbe like the Sun, it shines euery where. I would be sorry sir, but the Foole should be as oft with your Master, as with my Mistris: I thinke I saw your wisedome there.

Vio. Nay, and thou passe vpon me, Ile no more with thee: Hold there's expences for thee.

Clo. Now Ioue in his next commodity of hayre, send thee a beard.

Vio. By my troth Ile tell thee, I am almost sicke for one, though I would not haue it grow on my chinne. Is thy Lady within?

Clo. Would not a paire of these haue bred sir?

Vio. Yes being kept together, and put to vse.

Clo. I would play Lord *Pandarus* of *Phrygia* sir, to bring a *Cressida* to this *Troylus*.

Vio. I vnderstand you sir, tis well begg'd.

Clo. The matter I hope is not great sir; begging, but a begger: *Cressida* was a begger. My Lady is within sir. I will conster to them whence you come, who you are, and what you would are out of my welkin, I might say Element, but the word is ouer-worne. *exit*

Vio. This fellow is wise enough to play the foole,
And to do that well, craues a kinde of wit:
He must obserue their mood on whom he iests,
The quality of persons, and the time:
And like the Haggard, checke at euery Feather
That comes before his eye. This is a practice,
As full of labour as a Wise-mans Art:
For folly that he wisely shewes, is fit;
But wisemens folly falne, quite taint their wit.

Enter Sir Toby and Andrew.

To. Saue you Gentleman.

Vio. And you sir.

And. *Dieu vou guard Monsieur.*

Vio. *Et vouz ousie vostre seruiture.*

An. I hope sir, you are, and I am yours.

To. Will you incounter the house, my Neece is desirous you should enter, if your trade be to her.

Vio. I am bound to your Neece sir, I meane she is the list of my voyage.

To. Taste your legges sir, put them to motion.

Vio. My legges do better vnderstand me sir, then I vnderstand what you meane by bidding me taste my legs.

To. I meane to go sir, to enter.

Vio. I will answer you with gate and entrance, but we are preuented.

Enter Oliuia, and Gentlewoman.

Most excellent accomplish'd Lady, the heauens raine Odours on you.

And. That youth's a rare Courtier, raine odours, wel.

Vio. My matter hath no voice Lady, but to your owne most pregnant and vouchsafed eare.

And. Odours, pregnant, and vouchsafed: Ile get 'em all three already.

Ol. Let the Garden doore be shut, and leaue mee to my hearing. Giue me your hand sir.

Vio. My dutie Madam, and most humble seruice.

Ol. What is your name?

Vio. *Cesario* is your seruants name, faire Princesse.

Ol. My seruant sir? 'Twas neuer merry world,
Since lowly feigning was call'd complement:
y'are seruant to the Count *Orsino* youth.

Vio. And he is yours, and his must needs be yours:
your seruants seruant, is your seruant Madam.

Ol. For him, I thinke not on him: for his thoughts,
Would they were blankes, rather then fill'd with me.

Vio. Madam, I come to whet your gentle thoughts
On his behalfe.

Ol. O by your leaue I pray you,
I bad you neuer speake againe of him;
But would you vndertake another suite
I had rather heare you, to solicit that,
Then Musicke from the spheares.

Vio. Deere Lady.

Ol. Giue me leaue, beseech you: I did send,
After the last enchantment you did heare,
A Ring in chace of you. So did I abuse
My selfe, my seruant, and I feare me you:
Vnder your hard construction must I sit,
To force that on you in a shamefull cunning
Which you knew none of yours. What might you think?
Haue you not set mine Honor at the stake,
And baited it with all th'vnmuzled thoughts
That tyrannous heart can thinke? To one of your receiuing
Enough is shewne, a Cipresse, not a bosome,
Hides my heart: so let me heare you speake.

Vio. I pittie you.

Ol. That's a degree to loue.

Vio. No not a grize: for tis a vulgar proofe
That verie oft we pitty enemies.

Ol. Why then me thinkes 'tis time to smile agen:
O world, how apt the poore are to be proud?
If one should be a prey, how much the better
To fall before the Lion, then the Wolfe?

Clocke strikes.

The clocke vpbraides me with the waste of time:
Be not affraid good youth, I will not haue you,
And yet when wit and youth is come to haruest,
your wife is like to reape a proper man:
There lies your way, due West.

Vio. Then Westward hoe:
Grace and good disposition attend your Ladyship:
you'l nothing Madam to my Lord, by me:

Ol. Stay: I prethee tell me what thou thinkst of me?

Vio. That you do thinke you are not what you are.

Ol. If I thinke so, I thinke the same of you.

Vio. Then thinke you right: I am not what I am.

Ol. I would you were, as I would haue you be.

Vio. Would it be better Madam, then I am?
I wish it might, for now I am your foole.

Ol. O what a deale of scorne, lookes beautifull?
In the contempt and anger of his lip,
A murdrous guilt shewes not it selfe more soone,
Then loue that would seeme hid: Loues night, is noone.
Cesario, by the Roses of the Spring,
By maid-hood, honor, truth, and euery thing,
I loue thee so, that maugre all thy pride,

Nor wit, nor reason, can my passion hide:
Do not extort thy reasons from this clause,
For that I woo, thou therefore hast no cause:
But rather reason thus, with reason fetter;
Loue sought, is good: but giuen vnsought, is better.

Vio. By innocence I sweare, and by my youth,
I haue one heart, one bosome, and one truth,
And that no woman has, nor neuer none
Shall mistris be of it, saue I alone.
And so adieu good Madam, neuer more,
Will I my Masters teares to you deplore.

Ol. Yet come againe: for thou perhaps mayst moue
That heart which now abhorres, to like his loue. *Exeunt*

Scœna Secunda.

Enter Sir Toby, Sir Andrew, and Fabian.

And. No faith, Ile not stay a iot longer:

To. Thy reason deere venom, giue thy reason.

Fab. You must needes yeelde your reason, Sir *Andrew*?

And. Marry I saw your Neece do more fauours to the Counts Seruing-man, then euer she bestow'd vpon mee: I saw't i'th Orchard.

To. Did she see the while, old boy, tell me that.

And. As plaine as I see you now.

Fab. This was a great argument of loue in her toward you.

And. S'light; will you make an Asse o'me.

Fab. I will proue it legitimate sir, vpon the Oathes of iudgement, and reason.

To. And they haue beene grand Iurie men, since before *Noah* was a Saylor.

Fab. Shee did shew fauour to the youth in your sight, onely to exasperate you, to awake your dormouse valour, to put fire in your Heart, and brimstone in your Liuer: you should then haue accosted her, and with some excellent iests, fire-new from the mint, you should haue bangd the youth into dumbenesse: this was look'd for at your hand, and this was baulkt: the double gilt of this opportunitie you let time wash off, and you are now sayld into the North of my Ladies opinion, where you will hang like an ysickle on a Dutchmans beard, vnlesse you do redeeme it, by some laudable attempt, either of valour or policie.

And. And't be any way, it must be with Valour, for policie I hate: I had as liefe be a Brownist, as a Politician.

To. Why then build me thy fortunes vpon the basis of valour. Challenge me the Counts youth to fight with him, hurt him in eleuen places, my Neece shall take note of it, and assure thy selfe, there is no loue-Broker in the world, can more preuaile in mans commendation with woman, then report of valour.

Fab. There is no way but this sir *Andrew*.

An. Will either of you beare me a challenge to him?

To. Go, write it in a martial hand, be curst and briefe: it is no matter how wittie, so it bee eloquent, and full of inuention: taunt him with the license of Inke: if thou thou'st him some thrice, it shall not be amisse, and as many Lyes, as will lye in thy sheete of paper, although the sheete were bigge enough for the bedde of *Ware* in England, set 'em downe, go about it. Let there bee gaulle enough in thy inke, though thou write with a Goose-pen, no matter: about it.

And. Where shall I finde you?

To. Wee'l call thee at the Cubiculo: Go.

Exit Sir Andrew.

Fa. This is a deere Manakin to you Sir *Toby*.

To. I haue beene deere to him lad, some two thousand strong, or so.

Fa. We shall haue a rare Letter from him; but you'le not deliuer't.

To. Neuer trust me then: and by all meanes stirre on the youth to an answer. I thinke Oxen and waine-ropes cannot hale them together. For *Andrew*, if he were open'd and you finde so much blood in his Liuer, as will clog the foote of a flea, Ile eate the rest of th'anatomy.

Fab. And his opposit the youth beares in his visage no great presage of cruelty.

Enter Maria.

To. Looke where the youngest Wren of mine comes.

Mar. If you desire the spleene, and will laughe your selues into stitches, follow me; yond gull *Maluolio* is turned Heathen, a verie Renegatho; for there is no christian that meanes to be saued by beleeuing rightly, can euer beleeue such impossible passages of grossenesse. Hee's in yellow stockings.

To. And crosse garter'd?

Mar. Most villanously: like a Pedant that keepes a Schoole i'th Church: I haue dogg'd him like his murtherer. He does obey euery point of the Letter that I dropt, to betray him: He does smile his face into more lynes, then is in the new Mappe, with the augmentation of the Indies: you haue not seene such a thing as tis: I can hardly forbeare hurling things at him, I know my Ladie will strike him: if shee doe, hee'l smile, and take't for a great fauour.

To. Come bring vs, bring vs where he is.

Exeunt Omnes.

Scœna Tertia.

Enter Sebastian and Anthonio.

Seb. I would not by my will have troubled you,
But since you make your pleasure of your paines,
I will no further chide you.

Ant. I could not stay behinde you: my desire
(More sharpe then filed steele) did spurre me forth,
And not all loue to see you (though so much
As might haue drawne one to a longer voyage)
But iealousie, what might befall your trauell,
Being skillesse in these parts: which to a stranger,
Vnguided, and vnfriended, often proue
Rough, and vnhospitable. My willing loue,
The rather by these arguments of feare
Set forth in your pursuite.

Seb. My kinde *Anthonio*,
I can no other answer make, but thankes,
And thankes: and euer oft good turnes,
Are shuffel'd off with such vncurrant pay:
But were my worth, as is my conscience firme,

You should finde better dealing: what's to do?
Shall we go see the reliques of this Towne?

Ant. To morrow sir, best first go see your Lodging?

Seb. I am not weary, and 'tis long to night
I pray you let vs satisfie our eyes
With the memorials, and the things of fame
That do renowne this City.

Ant. Would you'ld pardon me:
I do not without danger walke these streetes.
Once in a sea-fight 'gainst the Count his gallies,
I did some seruice, of such note indeede,
That were I tane heere, it would scarse be answer'd.

Seb. Belike you slew great number of his people.

Ant. Th offence is not of such a bloody nature,
Albeit the quality of the time, and quarrell
Might well haue giuen vs bloody argument:
It might haue since bene answer'd in repaying
What we tooke from them, which for Traffiques sake
Most of our City did. Onely my selfe stood out,
For which if I be lapsed in this place
I shall pay deere.

Seb. Do not then walke too open.

Ant. It doth not fit me: hold sir, here's my purse,
In the South Suburbes at the Elephant
Is best to lodge: I w ll bespeake our dyet,
Whiles you beguile the time, and feed your knowledge
With viewing of the Towne, there shall you haue me.

Seb. Why I your purse?

Ant. Haply your eye shall light vpon some toy
You haue desire to purchase: and your store
I thinke is not for idle Markets, sir.

Seb. Ile be your purse-bearer, and leaue you
For an houre.

Ant. To th'Elephant.

Seb. I do remember. *Exeunt.*

Scœna Quarta.

Enter Oliuia and Maria.

Ol. I haue sent after him, he sayes hee'l come:
How shall I feast him? What bestow of him?
For youth is bought more oft, then begg'd, or borrow'd.
I speake too loud: Where's *Maluolio*, he is sad, and ciuill,
And suites well for a seruant with my fortunes,
Where is *Maluolio*?

Mar. He's comming Madame:
But in very strange manner. He is sure possest Madam.

Ol. Why what's the matter, does he raue?

Mar. No Madam, he does nothing but smile: your Ladyship were best to haue some guard about you, if hee come, for sure the man is tainted in's wits.

Ol. Go call him hither.

Enter Maluolio.

I am as madde as hee,
If sad and merry madnesse equall bee.
How now *Maluolio*?

Mal. Sweet Lady, ho, ho.

Ol. Smil'st thou? I sent for thee vpon a sad occasion.

Mal. Sad Lady, I could be sad:
This does make some obstruction in the blood:
This crosse-gartering, but what of that?
If it please the eye of one, it is with me as the very true Sonnet is: Please one, and please all.

Mal. Why how doest thou man?
What is the matter with thee?

Mal. Not blacke in my mindei, though yellow in my legges: It did come to his hands, and Commaunds shall be executed. I thinke we doe know the sweet Romane hand.

Ol. Wilt thou go to bed *Maluolio*?

Mal. To bed? I sweet heart, and Ile come to thee.

Ol. God comfort thee: Why dost thou smile so, and kisse thy hand so oft?

Mar. How do you *Maluolio*?

Maluo. At your request:
Yes Nightingales answere Dawes.

Mar. Why appeare you with this ridiculous boldnesse before my Lady.

Mal. Be not afraid of greatnesse: 'twas well writ.

Ol. What meanst thou by that *Maluolio*?

Mal. Some are borne great.

Ol. Ha?

Mal. Some atcheeue greatnesse.

Ol. What sayst thou?

Mal. And some haue greatnesse thrust vpon them.

Ol. Heauen restore thee.

Mal. Remember who commended thy yellow stockings.

Ol. Thy yellow stockings?

Mal. And wish'd to see thee crosse garter'd.

Ol. Crosse garter'd?

Mal. Go too, thou art made, if thou desir'st to be so.

Ol. Am I made?

Mal. If not, let me see thee a seruant still.

Ol. Why this is verie Midsommer madnesse.

Enter Seruant.

Ser. Madame, the young Gentleman of the Count *Orsino's* is return'd, I could hardly entreate him backe: he attends your Ladyships pleasure.

Ol. Ile come to him.
Good *Maria*, let this fellow be look'd too. Where's my Cosine *Toby*, let some of my people haue a speciall care of him, I would not haue him miscarrie for the halfe of my Dowry. *exit*

Mal. Oh ho, do you come neere me now: no worse man then sir *Toby* to looke to me. This concurres directly with the Letter, she sends him on purpose, that I may appeare stubborne to him: for she incites me to that in the Letter. Cast thy humble slough sayes she: be opposite with a Kinsman, surly with seruants, let thy tongue langer with arguments of state, put thy selfe into the tricke of singularity: and consequently setts downe the manner how: as a sad face, a reuerend carriage, a slow tongue, in the habite of some Sir of note, and so foorth. I haue lymde her, but it is Ioues doing, and Ioue make me thankefull. And when she went away now, let this Fellow be look'd too: Fellow? not *Maluolio*, nor after my degree, but Fellow. Why euery thing adheres togither, that no dramme of a scruple, no scruple of a scruple, no obstacle, no incredulous or vnsafe circumstance: What can be saide? Nothing that can be, can come betweene me, and the full prospect of my hopes. Well Ioue, not I, is the doer of this, and he is to be thanked.

Enter Toby, Fabian, and Maria.

To. Which way is hee in the name of sanctity. If all the diuels of hell be drawne in little, and Legion himselfe possest him, yet Ile speake to him.

Fab. Heere he is, heere he is: how ist with you sir? How ist with you man?

Mal. Go off, I discard you: let me enioy my priuate: go off.

Mar. Lo, how hollow the fiend speakes within him; did not I tell you? Sir *Toby*, my Lady prayes you to haue a care of him.

Mal. Ah ha, does she so?

To. Go too, go too: peace, peace, wee must deale gently with him: Let me alone. How do you *Maluolio*? How ist with you? What man, defie the diuell: consider, he's an enemy to mankinde.

Mal. Do you know what you say?

Mar. La you, and you speake ill of the diuell, how he takes it at heart. Pray God he be not bewitch'd.

Fab. Carry his water to th'wise woman.

Mar. Marry and it shall be done to morrow morning if I liue. My Lady would not loose him for more then ile say.

Mal. How now mistris?

Mar. Oh Lord.

To. Prethee hold thy peace, this is not the way: Doe you not see you moue him? Let me alone with him.

Fa. No way but gentlenesse, gently, gently: the Fiend is rough, and will not be roughly vs'd.

To. Why how now my bawcock? how dost ÿ chuck?

Mal. Sir.

To. I biddy, come with me. What man, tis not for grauity to play at cherrie-pit with sathan. Hang him foul Colliar.

Mar. Get him to say his prayers, good sir *Toby* gette him to pray.

Mal. My prayers Minx.

Mar. No I warrant you, he will not heare of godlynesse.

Mal. Go hang your selues all: you are ydle shallowe things, I am not of your element, you shall knowe more heereafter. *Exit*

To. Ist possible?

Fa. If this were plaid vpon a stage now, I could condemne it as an improbable fiction.

To. His very genius hath taken the infection of the deuice man.

Mar. Nay pursue him now, least the deuice take ayre, and taint.

Fa. Why we shall make him mad indeede.

Mar. The house will be the quieter.

To. Come, wee'l haue him in a darke room & bound. My Neece is already in the beleefe that he's mad: we may carry it thus for our pleasure, and his pennance, til our very pastime tyred out of breath, prompt vs to haue mercy on him: at which time, we wil bring the deuice to the bar and crowne thee for a finder of madmen: but see, but see.

Enter Sir Andrew.

Fa. More matter for a May morning.

An. Heere's the Challenge, reade it: I warrant there's vinegar and pepper in't.

Fab. Ist so sawcy?

And. I, ist? I warrant him: do but read.

To. Giue me.

Youth, whatsoeuer thou art, thou art but a scuruy fellow.

Fa. Good, and valiant.

To. Wonder not, nor admire not in thy minde why I doe call thee so, for I will shew thee no reason for't.

Fa. A good note, that keepes you from the blow of § Law.

To. Thou comst to the Lady Oliuia, and in my sight shee vses thee kindly: but thou lyest in thy throat, that is not the matter I challenge thee for.

Fa. Very breefe, and to exceeding good sence-lesse.

To. I will way-lay thee going home, where if it be thy chance to kill me.

Fa. Good.

To. Thou kilst me like a rogue and a villaine.

Fa. Still you keepe o'th windie side of the Law: good.

Tob. Fartheewell, and God haue mercie vpon one of our soules. He may haue mercie vpon mine, but my hope is better, and so looke to thy selfe. Thy friend as thou vsest him, & thy sworne enemie, Andrew Ague-cheeke.

To. If this Letter moue him not, his legges cannot: Ile giu't him.

Mar. You may haue verie fit occasion for't: he is now in some commerce with my Ladie, and will by and by depart.

To. Go sir *Andrew*: scout mee for him at the corner of the Orchard like a bum-Baylie: so soone as euer thou seest him, draw, and as thou draw'st, sweare horrible: for t comes to passe oft, that a terrible oath, with a swaggering accent sharpely twang'd off, giues manhoode more approbation, then euer proofe it selfe would haue earn'd him. Away.

And. Nay let me alone for swearing. *Exit*

To. Now will not I deliuer his Letter: for the behauiour of the yong Gentleman, giues him out to be of good capacity, and breeding: his employment betweene his Lord and my Neece, confirmes no lesse. Therefore, this Letter being so excellently ignorant, will breed no terror in the youth: he will finde it comes from a Clodde-pole. But sir, I will deliuer his Challenge by word of mouth; set vpon *Ague-cheeke* a notable report of valor, and driue the Gentleman (as I know his youth will aptly receiue it) into a most hideous opinion of his rage, skill, furie, and impetuositie. This will so fright them both, that they wil kill one another by the looke, like Cockatrices.

Enter Oliuia and Viola.

Fab. Heere he comes with your Neece, giue them way till he take leaue, and presently after him.

To. I wil meditate the while vpon some horrid message for a Challenge.

Ol. I haue said too much vnto a hart of stone,
And laid mine honour too vnchary on't:
There's something in me that reproues my fault:
But such a head-strong potent fault it is,
That it but mockes reproofe.

Vio. With the same hauiour that your passion beares,
Goes on my Masters greefes.

Ol. Heere, weare this Iewell for me, tis my picture:
Refuse it not, it hath no tongue, to vex you:
And I beseech you come againe to morrow.
What shall you aske of me that Ile deny,
That honour (sau'd) may vpon asking giue.

Vio. Nothing but this, your true loue for my master.

Ol. How with mine honor may I giue him that,
Which I haue giuen to you.

Vio. I will acquit you.

Ol. Well, come againe to morrow: far-thee-well,
A Fiend like thee might beare my soule to hell.

Enter Toby and Fabian.

To. Gentleman, God saue thee.

Vio. And you sir.

To. That defence thou hast, betake the too't: of what nature the wrongs are thou hast done him, I knowe not: but thy intercepter full of despight, bloody as the Hunter, attends thee at the Orchard end: dismount thy tucke, be yare in thy preparation, for thy assaylant is quick, skilfull, and deadly.

Vio. You mistake sir I am sure, no man hath any quarrell to me: my remembrance is very free and cleere from any image of offence done to any man.

To. You'l finde it otherwise I assure you: therefore, if you hold your life at any price, betake you to your gard: for your opposite hath in him what youth, strength, skill, and wrath, can furnish man withall.

Vio. I pray you sir what is he?

To. He is knight dubb'd with vnhatch'd Rapier, and on carpet consideration, but he is a diuell in priuate brall, soules and bodies hath he diuorc'd three, and his incensement at this moment is so implacable, that satisfaction can be none, but by pangs of death and sepulcher: Hob, nob, is his word: giu't or take't.

Vio. I will returne againe into the house, and desire some conduct of the Lady. I am no fighter, I haue heard of some kinde of men, that put quarrells purposely on others, to taste their valour: belike this is a man of that quirke.

To. Sir, no: his indignation deriues it selfe out of a very competent iniurie, therefore get you on, and giue him his desire. Backe you shall not to the house, vnlesse you vndertake that with me, which with as much safetie you might answer him: therefore on, or strippe your sword starke naked: for meddle you must that's certain, or forsweare to weare iron about you.

Vio. This is as vnciuill as strange. I beseech you doe me this courteous office, as to know of the Knight what my offence to him is: it is something of my negligence, nothing of my purpose.

To. I will doe so. Signiour *Fabian*, stay you by this Gentleman, till my returne. *Exit Toby.*

Vio. Pray you sir, do you know of this matter?

Fab. I know the knight is incenst against you, euen to a mortall arbitrement, but nothing of the circumstance more.

Vio. I beseech you what manner of man is he?

Fab. Nothing of that wonderfull promise to read him by his forme, as you are like to finde him in the proofe of his valour. He is indeede sir, the most skilfull, bloudy, & fatall opposite that you could possibly haue found in anie part of Illyria: will you walke towards him, I will make your peace with him, if I can.

Vio. I shall bee much bound to you for't: I am one, that had rather go with sir Priest, then sir knight: I care not who knowes so much of my mettle. *Exeunt.*

Enter Toby and Andrew.

To. Why man hee s a verie diuell, I haue not seen such a firago: I had a passe with him, rapier, scabberd, and all: and he giues me the stucke in with such a mortall motion that it is ineuitable: and on the answer, he payes you as surely, as your feete hits the ground they step on. They say, he has bin Fencer to the Sophy.

And. Pox on't, Ile not meddle with him.

To. I but he will not now be pacified, *Fabian* can scarse hold him yonder.

An. Plague on't, and I thought he had beene valiant, and so cunning in Fence, I'de haue seene him damn'd ere I'de haue challeng'd him. Let him let the matter slip, and Ile giue him my horse, gray Capilet.

To. Ile make the motion: stand heere, make a good shew on't, this shall end without the perdition of soules, marry Ile ride your horse as well as I ride you.

Enter Fabian and Viola.

I haue his horse to take vp the quarrell, I haue perswaded him the youths a diuell.

Fa. He is as horribly conceited of him: and pants, & lookes pale, as if a Beare were at his heeles.

To. There's no remedie sir, he will fight with you for's oath sake: marrie hee hath better bethought him of his quarrell, and hee findes that now scarse to bee worth talking of: therefore draw for the supportance of his vowe, he protests he will not hurt you.

Vio. Pray God defend me: a little thing would make me tell them how much I lacke of a man.

Fab. Giue ground if you see him furious.

To. Come sir *Andrew*, there's no remedie, the Gentleman will for his honors sake haue one bowt with you: he cannot by the Duello auoide it: but hee has promised me, as he is a Gentleman and a Soldiour, he will not hurt you. Come on, too't.

And. Pray God he keepe his oath.

Enter Antonio.

Vio. I do assure you tis against my will.

Ant. Put vp your sword: if this yong Gentleman Haue done offence, I take the fault on me: If you offend him, I for him defie you.

To. You sir? Why, what are you?

Ant. One sir, that for his loue dares yet do more Then you haue heard him brag to you he will.

To. Nay, if you be an vndertaker, I am for you.

Enter Officers.

Fab. O good sir *Toby* hold: heere come the Officers.

To. Ile be with you anon.

Vio. Pray sir, put your sword vp if you please.

And. Marry will I sir: and for that I promis'd you Ile be as good as my word. Hee will beare you easily, and raines well.

1.Off. This is the man, do thy Office.

2 Off. *Anthonio*, I arrest thee at the suit of Count *Orsino*

An. You do mistake me sir.

1.Off. No sir, no iot: I know your fauour well: Though now you haue no sea-cap on your head: Take him away, he knowes I know him well.

Ant. I must obey. This comes with seeking you: But there's no remedie, I shall answer it: What will you do: now my necessitie Makes me to aske you for my purse. It greeues mee Much more, for what I cannot do for you, Then what befals my selfe: you stand amaz'd, But be of comfort.

2 Off. Come sir away.

Ant. I must entreat of you some of that money.

Vio. What money sir? For the fayre kindnesse you haue shew'd me heere, And part being prompted by your present trouble, Out of my leane and low ability Ile lend you something: my hauing is not much, Ile make diuision of my present with you: Hold, there's halfe my Coffer.

Ant. Will you deny me now, Ist possible that my deserts to you Can lacke perswasion. Do not tempt my misery, Least that it make me so vnsound a man As to vpbraid you with those kindnesses

That I haue done for you.

Vio. I know of none,
Nor know I you by voyce, or any feature:
I hate ingratitude more in a man,
Then lying, vainnesse, babling drunkennesse,
Or any taint of vice, whose strong corruption
Inhabites our fraile blood.

Ant. Oh heauens themselues.

2. Off. Come sir, I pray you go.

Ant. Let me speake a little. This youth that you see
I snatch'd one halfe out of the iawes of death,
Releeu'd him with such sanctitie of loue; (heere,
And to his image, which me thought did promise
Most venerable worth, did I deuotion.

1. Off. What's that to vs, the time goes by: Away.

Ant. But oh, how vilde an idoll proues this God:
Thou hast *Sebastian* done good feature, shame,
In Nature, there's no blemish but the minde:
None can be call'd deform'd, but the vnkinde.
Vertue is beauty, but the beauteous euill
Are empty trunkes, ore-flourish'd by the deuill.

1. Off. The man growes mad, away with him:
Come, come sir.

Ant. Leade me on. *Exit*

Vio. Me thinkes his words do from such pasion flye
That he beleeues himselfe, so do not I:
Proue true imagination, oh proue true,
That I deere brother, be now tane for you.

To. Come hither Knight, come hither *Fabian*: Weel
whisper ore a couplet or two of most sage sawes.

Vio. He nam'd *Sebastian*: I my brother know
Yet liuing in my glasse: euen such, and so
In fauour was my Brother, and he went
Still in this fashion, colour, ornament,
For him I imitate: Oh if it proue,
Tempests are kinde, and salt waues fresh in loue.

To. A very dishonest paltry boy, and more a coward
then a Hare, his dishonesty appeares, in leauing his frend
heere in necessity, and denying him: and for his coward-
ship aske *Fabian*.

Fab. A Coward, a most deuout Coward, religious in
it.

And. Slid Ile after him againe, and beate him.

To. Do, cuffe him soundly, but neuer draw thy sword

And. And I do not.

Fab. Come, let's see the euent.

To. I dare lay any money, twill be nothing yet. *Exit*

Actus Quartus, Scæna prima.

Enter Sebastian and Clowne.

Clo. Will you make me beleeue, that I am not sent for
you?

Seb. Go too, go too, thou art a foolish fellow,
Let me be cleere of thee.

Clo. Well held out yfaith: No, I do not know you,
nor I am not sent to you by my Lady, to bid you come
speake with her: nor your name is not Master *Cesario*,
nor this is not my nose neyther: Nothing that is so, is so.

Seb. I prethee vent thy folly some-where else, thou
know'st not me.

Clo. Vent my folly: He has heard that word of some
great man, and now applyes it to a foole. Vent my folly: I am affraid this great lubber the World will proue a
Cockney: I prethee now vngird thy strangenes, and tell
me what I shall vent to my Lady? Shall I vent to hir that
thou art comming?

Seb. I prethee foolish greeke depart from me, there's
money for thee, if you tarry longer, I shall giue worse
paiment.

Clo. By my troth thou hast an open hand: these Wisemen that giue fooles money, get themselues a good report, after foureteene yeares purchase.

Enter Andrew, Toby, and Fabian.

And. Now sir, haue I met you again: ther's for you.

Seb. Why there's for thee, and there, and there,
Are all the people mad?

To. Hold sir, or Ile throw your dagger ore the house.

Clo. This will I tell my Lady straight, I would not be
in some of your coats for two pence.

To. Come on sir, hold.

An. Nay let him alone, Ile go another way to worke
with him: Ile haue an action of Battery against him, if
there be any law in Illyria: though I stroke him first, yet
it's no matter for that.

Seb. Let go thy hand.

To. Come sir, I will not let you go. Come my yong
souldier put vp your yron: you are well flesh'd: Come
on.

Seb. I will be free from thee. What wouldst ỹ now?
If thou dar'st tempt me further, draw thy sword.

To. What, what? Nay then I must haue an Ounce or
two of this malapert blood from you.

Enter Oliuia.

Ol. Hold *Toby*, on thy life I charge thee hold.

To. Madam.

Ol. Will it be euer thus? Vngracious wretch,
Fit for the Mountaines, and the barbarous Caues,
Where manners nere were preach'd: out of my sight.
Be not offended, deere *Cesario*:
Rudesbey be gone. I prethee gentle friend,
Let thy fayre wisedome, not thy pasion sway
In this vnciuill, and vniust extent
Against thy peace. Go with me to my house,
And heare thou there how many fruitlesse prankes
This Ruffian hath botch'd vp, that thou thereby
Mayst smile at this: Thou shalt not choose but goe:
Do not denie, beshrew his soule for mee,
He started one poore heart of mine, in thee.

Seb. What rellish is in this? How runs the streame?
Or I am mad, or else this is a dreame:
Let fancie still my sense in Lethe steepe,
If it be thus to dreame, still let me sleepe.

Ol. Nay come I prethee, would thoud'st be rul'd by me

Seb. Madam, I will.

Ol. O say so, and so be. *Exeunt*

Scæna Secunda.

Enter Maria and Clowne.

Mar. Nay, I prethee put on this gown, & this beard,
make him beleeue thou art sir *Topas* the Curate, doe it
quickly. Ile call sir *Toby* the whilst.

Clo. Well, Ile put it on, and I will dissemble my selfe
in't, and I would I were the first that euer dissembled in
such

Twelfe Night, or, What you will.

in such a gowne. I am not tall enough to become the function well, nor leane enough to bee thought a good Student: but to be said an honest man and a good houskeeper goes as fairely, as to say, a carefull man, & a great scholler. The Competitors enter.

Enter Toby.

To. Ioue blesse thee M. Parson.

Clo. Bonos dies sir *Toby*: for as the old hermit of *Prage* that neuer saw pen and inke, very wittily sayd to a Neece of King *Gorbodacke*, that that is, is : so I being M. Parson, am M. Parson; for what is that, but that? and is, but is?

To. To him sir *Topas*.

Clow. What hoa, I say, Peace in this prison.

To. The knaue counterfets well: a good knaue.

Maluolio within.

Mal. Who cals there?

Clo. Sir *Topas* the Curate, who comes to visit *Maluolio* the Lunaticke.

Mal. Sir *Topas*, sir *Topas*, good sir *Topas* goe to my Ladie.

Clo. Out hyperbolicall fiend, how vexest thou this man? Talkest thou nothing but of Ladies?

Tob. Well said M. Parson.

Mal. Sir *Topas*, neuer was man thus wronged, good sir *Topas* do not thinke I am mad: they haue layde mee heere in hideous darknesse.

Clo. Fye, thou dishonest sathan: I call thee by the most modest termes, for I am one of those gentle ones, that will vse the diuell himselfe with curtesie: sayst thou that house is darke?

Mal. As hell sir *Topas*.

Clo. Why it hath bay Windowes transparant as baricadoes, and the cleere stores toward the South north, are as lustrous as Ebony: and yet complainest thou of obstruction?

Mal. I am not mad sir *Topas*, I say to you this house is darke.

Clo. Madman thou errest: I say there is no darknesse but ignorance, in which thou art more puzel'd then the Ægyptians in their fogge.

Mal. I say this house is as darke as Ignorance, thogh Ignorance were as darke as hell; and I say there was neuer man thus abus'd, I am no more madde then you are, make the triall of it in any constant question.

Clo. What is the opinion of *Pythagoras* concerning Wilde-fowle?

Mal. That the soule of our grandam, might happily inhabite a bird.

Clo. What thinkst thou of his opinion?

Mal. I thinke nobly of the soule, and no way aproue his opinion.

Clo. Fare thee well: remaine thou still in darknesse, thou shalt hold th'opinion of *Pythagoras*, ere I will allow of thy wits, and feare to kill a Woodcocke, lest thou dispossesse the soule of thy grandam. Fare thee well.

Mal. Sir *Topas*, sir *Topas*.

Tob. My most exquisite sir *Topas*.

Clo. Nay I am for all waters.

Mar. Thou mightst haue done this without thy berd and gowne, he sees thee not.

To. To him in thine owne voyce, and bring me word how thou findst him: I would we were well ridde of this knauery. If he may bee conueniently deliuer'd, I would he were, for I am now so farre in offence with my Niece, that I cannot pursue with any safety this sport the vppeshot. Come by and by to my Chamber. *Exit*

Clo. Hey Robin, iolly Robin, tell me how thy Lady does.

Mal. Foole.

Clo. My Lady is vnkind, *perdie*.

Mal. Foole.

Clo. Alas why is she so?

Mal. Foole, I say.

Clo. She loues another. Who calles, ha?

Mal. Good foole, as euer thou wilt deserue well at my hand, helpe me to a Candle, and pen, inke, and paper: as I am a Gentleman, I will liue to bee thankefull to thee for't.

Clo. M. *Maluolio*?

Mal. I good Foole.

Clo. Alas sir, how fell you besides your fiue witts?

Mall. Foole, there was neuer man so notoriouslie abus'd: I am as well in my wits (foole) as thou art.

Clo. But as well: then you are mad indeede, if you be no better in your wits then a foole.

Mal. They haue heere propertied me: keepe mee in darkenesse, send Ministers to me, Asses, and doe all they can to face me out of my wits.

Clo. Aduise you what you say: the Minister is heere. *Maluolio, Maluolio*, thy wittes the heauens restore: endeauour thy selfe to sleepe, and leaue thy vaine bibble babble.

Mal. Sir *Topas*.

Clo. Maintaine no words with him good fellow. Who I sir, not I sir, God buy you good sir Topas: Marry Amen. I will sir, I will.

Mal. Foole, foole, foole I say.

Clo. Alas sir be patient. What say you sir, I am shent for speaking to you.

Mal. Good foole, helpe me to some light, and some paper, I tell thee I am as well in my wittes, as any man in Illyria.

Clo. Well-a-day, that you were sir.

Mal. By this hand I am: good foole, some inke, paper, and light: and conuey what I will set downe to my Lady: it shall aduantage thee more, then euer the bearing of Letter did.

Clo. I will help you too't. But tel me true, are you not mad indeed, or do you but counterfeit.

Mal. Beleeue me I am not, I tell thee true.

Clo. Nay, Ile nere beleeue a madman till I see his brains I will fetch you light, and paper, and inke.

Mal. Foole, Ile requite it in the highest degree: I prethee be gone.

Clo. I am gone sir, and anon sir,
Ile be with you againe:
In a trice, like to the old vice,
   your neede to sustaine.
Who with dagger of lath, in his rage and his wrath,
   cries ah ha, to the diuell:
Like a mad lad, paire thy nayles dad,
   Adieu good man diuell. *Exit*

Scæna Tertia.

Enter Sebastian.

This is the ayre, that is the glorious Sunne,
This pearle she gaue me, I do feel't, and see't,
And though tis wonder that enwraps me thus,

Yet

Yet 'tis not madnesse. Where's *Anthonio* then,
I could not finde him at the Elephant,
Yet there he was, and there I found this credite,
That he did range the towne to seeke me out,
His councell now might do me golden seruice,
For though my soule disputes well with my sence,
That this may be some error, but no madnesse,
Yet doth this accident and flood of Fortune,
So farre exceed all instance, all discourse,
That I am readie to distrust mine eyes,
And wrangle with my reason that perswades me
To any other trust, but that I am mad,
Or else the Ladies mad; yet if 'twere so,
She could not sway her house, command her followers,
Take, and giue backe affayres, and their dispatch,
With such a smooth, discreet, and stable bearing
As I perceiue she do's: there's something in't
That is deceiueable. But heere the Lady comes.

Enter Oliuia, and Priest.

Ol. Blame not this haste of mine: if you meane well
Now go with me, and with this holy man
Into the Chantry by: there before him,
And vnderneath that consecrated roofe,
Plight me the full assurance of your faith,
That my most iealious, and too doubtfull soule
May liue at peace. He shall conceale it,
Whiles you are willing it shall come to note,
What time we will our celebration keepe
According to my birth, what do you say?

Seb. Ile follow this good man, and go with you,
And hauing sworne truth, euer will be true.

Ol. Then lead the way good father, & heauens so shine,
That they may fairely note this acte of mine. *Exeunt.*

Finis Actus Quartus.

Actus Quintus. Scena Prima.

Enter Clowne and Fabian.

Fab. Now as thou lou'st me, let me see his Letter.
Clo. Good M. *Fabian*, grant me another request.
Fab. Any thing.
Clo. Do not desire to see this Letter.
Fab. This is to giue a dogge, and in recompence desire my dogge againe.

Enter Duke, Viola, Curio, and Lords.

Duke. Belong you to the Lady *Oliuia*, friends?
Clo. I sir, we are some of her trappings.
Duke. I know thee well: how doest thou my good Fellow?
Clo. Truely sir, the better for my foes, and the worse for my friends.
Du. Iust the contrary: the better for thy friends.
Clo. No sir, the worse.
Du. How can that be?
Clo. Marry sir, they praise me, and make an asse of me, now my foes tell me plainly, I am an Asse: so that by my foes sir, I profit in the knowledge of my selfe, and by my friends I am abused: so that conclusions to be as kisses, if your foure negatiues make your two affirmatiues, why then the worse for my friends, and the better for my foes.

Du. Why this is excellent.
Clo. By my troth sir, no: though it please you to be one of my friends.
Du. Thou shalt not be the worse for me, there's gold.
Clo. But that it would be double dealing sir, I would you could make it another.
Du. O you giue me ill counsell.
Clo. Put your grace in your pocket sir, for this once, and let your flesh and blood obey it.
Du. Well, I will be so much a sinner to be a double dealer: there's another.
Clo. *Primo, secundo, tertio*, is a good play, and the olde saying is, the third payes for all: the triplex sir, is a good tripping measure, or the belles of S. *Bennet* sir, may put you in minde, one, two, three.
Du. You can foole no more money out of mee at this throw: if you will let your Lady know I am here to speak with her, and bring her along with you, it may awake my bounty further.
Clo. Marry sir, lullaby to your bountie till I come agen. I go sir, but I would not haue you to thinke, that my desire of hauing is the sinne of couetousnesse: but as you say sir, let your bounty take a nappe, I will awake it anon. *Exit*

Enter Anthonio and Officers.

Vio. Here comes the man sir, that did rescue mee.
Du. That face of his I do remember well,
yet when I saw it last, it was besmear'd
As blacke as Vulcan, in the smoake of warre:
A bawbling Vessell was he Captaine of,
For shallow draught and bulke vnprizable,
With which such scathfull grapple did he make,
With the most noble bottome of our Fleete,
That very enuy, and the tongue of losse
Cride fame and honor on him: What's the matter?
1 Offi. *Orsino*, this is that *Anthonio*
That tooke the *Phœnix*, and her fraught from *Candy*,
And this is he that did the *Tiger* boord,
When your yong Nephew *Titus* lost his legge;
Heere in the streets, desperate of shame and state,
In priuate brabble did we apprehend him.
Vio. He did me kindnesse sir, drew on my side,
But in conclusion put strange speech vpon me,
I know not what 'twas, but distraction.
Du. Notable Pyrate, thou salt-water Theefe,
What foolish boldnesse brought thee to their mercies,
Whom thou in termes so bloudie, and so deere
Hast made thine enemies?
Ant. *Orsino*: Noble sir,
Be pleas'd that I shake off these names you giue mee:
Anthonio neuer yet was Theefe, or Pyrate,
Though I confesse, on base and ground enough
Orsino's enemie. A witchcraft drew me hither:
That most ingratefull boy there by your side,
From the rude seas enrag'd and foamy mouth
Did I redeeme: a wracke past hope he was:
His life I gaue him, and did thereto adde
My loue without retention, or restraint,
All his in dedication. For his sake,
Did I expose my selfe (pure for his loue)
Into the danger of this aduerse Towne,
Drew to defend him, when he was beset:
Where being apprehended, his false cunning
(Not meaning to partake with me in danger)
Taught him to face me out of his acquaintance,

And

Twelfe Night, or, What you will.

And grew a twentie yeeres remoued thing
While one would winke: denide me mine owne purse,
Which I had recommended to his vse,
Not halfe an houre before.

Vio. How can this be?

Du. When came he to this Towne?

Ant. To day my Lord: and for three months before,
No *intrim*, not a minutes vacancie,
Both day and night did we keepe companie.

Enter Oliuia and attendants.

Du. Heere comes the Countesse, now heauen walkes on earth:
But for thee fellow, fellow thy words are madnesse,
Three monthes this youth hath tended vpon mee,
But more of that anon. Take him aside.

Ol. What would my Lord, but that he may not haue,
Wherein *Oliuia* may seeme seruiceable?
Cesario, you do not keepe promise with me.

Vio. Madam:

Du. Gracious *Oliuia*.

Ol. What do you say *Cesario*? Good my Lord.

Vio. My Lord would speake, my dutie hushes me.

Ol. If it be ought to the old tune my Lord,
It is as fat and fulsome to mine eare
As howling after Musicke.

Du. Still so cruell?

Ol. Still so constant Lord.

Du. What to peruersenesse? you vnciuill Ladie
To whose ingrate, and vnauspicious Altars
My soule the faithfull'st offrings haue breath'd out
That ere deuotion tender'd. What shall I do?

Ol. Euen what it please my Lord, that shal becom him

Du. Why should I not, (had I the heart to do it)
Like to th'Egyptian theefe, at point of death
Kill what I loue: (a sauage iealousie,
That sometime sauours nobly) but heare me this:
Since you to non-regardance cast my faith,
And that I partly know the instrument
That screwes me from my true place in your fauour:
Liue you the Marble-brested Tirant still.
But this your Minion, whom I know you loue,
And whom, by heauen I sweare, I tender deerely,
Him will I teare out of that cruell eye,
Where he sits crowned in his masters spight.
Come boy with me, my thoughts are ripe in mischiefe:
Ile sacrifice the Lambe that I do loue,
To spight a Rauens heart within a Doue.

Vio. And I most iocund, apt, and willinglie,
To do you rest, a thousand deaths would dye.

Ol. Where goes *Cesario*?

Vio. After him I loue,
More then I loue these eyes, more then my life,
More by all mores, then ere I shall loue wife.
If I do feigne, you witnesses aboue
Punish my life, for tainting of my loue.

Ol. Aye me detested, how am I beguil'd?

Vio. Who does beguile you? who does do you wrong?

Ol. Hast thou forgot thy selfe? Is it so long?
Call forth the holy Father.

Du. Come, away.

Ol. Whether my Lord? *Cesario*, Husband, stay.

Du. Husband?

Ol. I Husband. Can he that deny?

Du. Her husband, sirrah?

Vio. No my Lord, not I.

Ol. Alas, it is the basenesse of thy feare,
That makes thee strangle thy propriety:
Feare not *Cesario*, take thy fortunes vp,
Be that thou know'st thou art, and then thou art
As great as that thou fear'st.

Enter Priest.

O welcome Father:
Father, I charge thee by thy reuerence
Heere to vnfold, though lately we intended
To keepe in darkenesse, what occasion now
Reueales before 'tis ripe: what thou dost know
Hath newly past, betweene this youth, and me.

Priest. A Contract of eternall bond of loue,
Confirm'd by mutuall ioynder of your hands,
Attested by the holy close of lippes,
Strengthned by enterchangement of your rings,
And all the Ceremonie of this compact
Seal'd in my function, by my testimony:
Since when, my watch hath told me, toward my graue
I haue trauail'd but two houres.

Du. O thou dissembling Cub: what wilt thou be
When time hath sow'd a grizzle on thy case?
Or will not else thy craft so quickely grow,
That thine owne trip shall be thine ouerthrow:
Farewell, and take her, but direct thy feete,
Where thou, and I (henceforth) may neuer meet.

Vio. My Lord, I do protest.

Ol. O do not sweare,
Hold little faith, though thou hast too much feare.

Enter Sir Andrew.

And. For the loue of God a Surgeon, send one presently to sir *Toby*.

Ol. What's the matter?

And. H'as broke my head a-crosse, and has giuen Sir *Toby* a bloody Coxcombe too: for the loue of God your helpe, I had rather then forty pound I were at home.

Ol. Who has done this sir *Andrew*?

And. The Counts Gentleman, one *Cesario*: we tooke him for a Coward, but hee's the verie diuell incardinate.

Du. My Gentleman *Cesario*?

And. Odd's lifelings heere he is: you broke my head for nothing, and that that I did, I was set on to do't by sir *Toby*.

Vio. Why do you speake to me, I neuer hurt you:
you drew your sword vpon me without cause,
But I bespake you faire, and hurt you not.

Enter Toby and Clowne.

And. If a bloody coxcombe be a hurt, you haue hurt me: I thinke you set nothing by a bloody Coxcombe.
Heere comes sir *Toby* halting, you shall heare more: but if he had not beene in drinke, hee would haue tickel'd you other gates then he did.

Du. How now Gentleman? how ist with you?

To. That's all one, has hurt me, and there's th'end on't:
Sot, didst see Dicke Surgeon, sot?

Clo. O he's drunke sir *Toby* an houre agone: his eyes were set at eight i'th morning.

To. Then he's a Rogue, and a passy measures panyn: I hate a drunken rogue.

Ol. Away with him? Who hath made this hauocke with them?

And. Ile helpe you sir *Toby*, because we'll be drest together.

To. Will you helpe an Asse-head, and a coxcombe, & a knaue: a thin fac'd knaue, a gull?

Ol. Get him to bed, and let his hurt be look'd too.

Enter Sebastian.

Seb. I am sorry Madam I haue hurt your kinsman:
But had it beene the brother of my blood,
I must haue done no lesse with wit and safety.
You throw a strange regard vpon me, and by that
I do perceiue it hath offended you:
Pardon me (sweet one) euen for the vowes
We made each other, but so late ago.

Du. One face, one voice, one habit, and two persons,
A naturall Perspectiue, that is, and is not.

Seb. Anthonio: O my deere *Anthonio*,
How haue the houres rack'd, and tortur'd me,
Since I haue lost thee?

Ant. *Sebastian* are you?

Seb. Fear'st thou that *Anthonio*?

Ant. How haue you made diuision of your selfe,
An apple cleft in two, is not more twin
Then these two creatures. Which is *Sebastian*?

Ol. Most wonderfull.

Seb. Do I stand there? I neuer had a brother:
Nor can there be that Deity in my nature
Of heere, and euery where. I had a sister,
Whom the blinde waues and surges haue deuour'd:
Of charity, what kinne are you to me?
What Countreyman? What name? What Parentage?

Vio. Of *Messaline*: *Sebastian* was my Father,
Such a *Sebastian* was my brother too:
So went he suited to his watery tombe:
If spirits can assume both forme and suite,
You come to fright vs.

Seb. A spirit I am indeed,
But am in that dimension grossely clad,
Which from the wombe I did participate.
Were you a woman, as the rest goes euen,
I should my teares let fall vpon your cheeke,
And say, thrice welcome drowned *Viola*.

Vio. My father had a moale vpon his brow.

Seb. And so had mine.

Vio. And dide that day when *Viola* from her birth
Had numbred thirteene yeares.

Seb. O that record is liuely in my soule,
He finished indeed his mortall acte
That day that made my sister thirteene yeares.

Vio. If nothing lets to make vs happie both,
But this my masculine vsurp'd attyre:
Do not embrace me, till each circumstance,
Of place, time, fortune, do co-here and iumpe
That I am *Viola*, which to confirme,
Ile bring you to a Captaine in this Towne,
Where lye my maiden weeds: by whose gentle helpe,
I was preseru'd to serue this Noble Count:
All the occurrence of my fortune since
Hath beene betweene this Lady, and this Lord.

Seb. So comes it Lady, you haue beene mistooke:
But Nature to her bias drew in that.
You would haue bin contracted to a Maid,
Nor are you therein (by my life) deceiu'd,
You are betroth'd both to a maid and man.

Du. Be not amaz'd, right noble is his blood:
If this be so, as yet the glasse seemes true,
I shall haue share in this most happy wracke,
Boy, thou hast saide to me a thousand times,
Thou neuer should'st loue woman like to me.

Vio. And all those sayings, will I ouer sweare,
And all those swearings keepe as true in soule,

As doth that Orbed Continent, the fire,
That seuers day from night.

Du. Giue me thy hand,
And let me see thee in thy womans weedes.

Vio. The Captaine that did bring me first on shore
Hath my Maides garments: he vpon some Action
Is now in durance, at *Maluolio's* suite,
A Gentleman, and follower of my Ladies.

Ol. He shall inlarge him: fetch *Maluolio* hither,
And yet alas, now I remember me,
They say poore Gentleman, he's much distract.

Enter Clowne with a Letter, and Fabian.

A most extracting frensie of mine owne
From my remembrance, clearly banisht his.
How does he sirrah?

Cl. Truely Madam, he holds *Belzebub* at the staues end as
well as a man in his case may do: has heere writ a letter to
you, I should haue giuen't you to day morning. But as a
madmans Epistles are no Gospels, so it skilles not much
when they are deliuer'd.

Ol. Open't, and read it.

Clo. Looke then to be well edified, when the Foole
deliuers the Madman. *By the Lord Madam.*

Ol. How now, art thou mad?

Clo. No Madam, I do but reade madnesse: and your
Ladyship will haue it as it ought to bee, you must allow
Vox.

Ol. Prethee reade i'thy right wits.

Clo. So I do Madona: but to reade his right wits, is to
reade thus: therefore, perpend my Princesse, and giue
eare.

Ol. Read it you, sirrah.

Fab. Reads. By the Lord Madam, you wrong me, and
the world shall know it: Though you haue put mee into
darkenesse, and giuen your drunken Cosine rule ouer me,
yet haue I the benefit of my senses as well as your Ladie-
ship. I haue your owne letter, that induced mee to the
semblance I put on; with the which I doubt not, but to
do my selfe much right, or you much shame: thinke of
me as you please. I leaue my duty a little vnthought of,
and speake out of my iniury. *The madly vs'd Maluolio.*

Ol. Did he write this?

Clo. I Madame.

Du. This sauours not much of distraction.

Ol. See him deliuer'd *Fabian*, bring him hither:
My Lord, so please you, these things further thought on,
To thinke me as well a sister, as a wife,
One day shall crowne th'alliance on't, so please you,
Heere at my house, and at my proper cost.

Du. Madam, I am most apt t'embrace your offer:
Your Master quits you: and for your seruice done him,
So much against the mettle of your sex,
So farre beneath your soft and tender breeding,
And since you call'd me Master, for so long:
Heere is my hand, you shall from this time bee
your Masters Mistris.

Ol. A sister, you are she.

Enter Maluolio.

Du. Is this the Madman?

Ol. I my Lord, this same: How now *Maluolio*?

Mal. Madam, you haue done me wrong,
Notorious wrong.

Ol. Haue I *Maluolio*? No.

Mal. Lady you haue, pray you peruse that Letter.
You must not now denie it is your hand,
Write from it if you can, in hand, or phrase,

Twelfe Night, or, What you will.

Or say, tis not your seale, not your inuention:
You can say none of this. Well, grant it then,
And tell me in the modestie of honor,
Why you haue giuen me such cleare lights of fauour,
Bad me come smiling, and crosse-garter'd to you,
To put on yellow stockings, and to frowne
Vpon sir *Toby*, and the lighter people:
And acting this in an obedient hope,
Why haue you suffer'd me to be imprison'd,
Kept in a darke house, visited by the Priest,
And made the most notorious gecke and gull,
That ere inuention plaid on? Tell me why?

Ol. Alas *Maluolio*, this is not my writing,
Though I confesse much like the Charracter:
But out of question, tis *Marias* hand.
And now I do bethinke me, it was shee
First told me thou wast mad; then cam'st in smiling,
And in such formes, which heere were presuppos'd
Vpon thee in the Letter: prethee be content,
This practice hath most shrewdly past vpon thee:
But when we know the grounds, and authors of it,
Thou shalt be both the Plaintiffe and the Iudge
Of thine owne cause.

Fab. Good Madam heare me speake,
And let no quarrell, nor no braule to come,
Taint the condition of this present houre,
Which I haue wondred at. In hope it shall not,
Most freely I confesse my selfe, and *Toby*
Set this deuice against *Maluolio* heere,
Vpon some stubborne and vncourteous parts
We had conceiu'd against him. *Maria* writ
The Letter, at sir *Tobyes* great importance,
In recompence whereof, he hath married her:
How with a sportfull malice it was follow'd,
May rather plucke on laughter then reuenge,
If that the iniuries be iustly weigh'd,
That haue on both sides past.

Ol. Alas poore Foole, how haue they baffel'd thee?
Clo. Why some are borne great, some atchieue greatnesse, and some haue greatnesse throwne vpon them. I
was one sir, in this Enterlude, one sir *Topas* sir, but that's
all one: By the Lord Foole, I am not mad: but do you remember, Madam, why laugh you at such a barren rascall,
and you smile not he's gag'd: and thus the whirlegigge
of time, brings in his reuenges.

Mal. Ile be reueng'd on the whole packe of you?
Ol. He hath bene most notoriously abus'd.
Du. Pursue him, and entreate him to a peace:
He hath not told vs of the Captaine yet,
When that is knowne, and golden time conuents
A solemne Combination shall be made
Of our deere soules. Meane time sweet sister,
We will not part from hence. *Cesario* come
(For so you shall be while you are a man:)
But when in other habites you are seene,
Orsino's Mistris, and his fancies Queene. *Exeunt*

Clowne sings.
When that I was and a little tine boy,
  with hey, ho, the winde and the raine:
A foolish thing was but a toy,
  for the raine it raineth euery day.

But when I came to mans estate,
  with hey ho, &c.
Gainst Knaues and Theeues men shut their gate,
  for the raine, &c.

But when I came alas to wiue,
  with hey ho, &c.
By swaggering could I neuer thriue,
  for the raine, &c.

But when I came vnto my beds,
  with hey ho, &c.
With tospottes still had drunken heades,
  for the raine, &c.

A great while ago the world begon,
  hey ho, &c.
But that's all one, our Play is done,
  and wee'l striue to please you euery day.

FINIS.

The Winters Tale.

Actus Primus. Scœna Prima.

Enter Camillo and Archidamus.

Arch. IF you shall chance (*Camillo*) to visit *Bohemia*, on the like occasion whereon my seruices are now on-foot, you shall see (as I haue said) great difference betwixt our *Bohemia*, and your *Sicilia*.

Cam. I thinke, this comming Summer, the King of *Sicilia* meanes to pay *Bohemia* the Visitation, which hee iustly owes him.

Arch. Wherein our Entertainment shall shame vs: we will be iustified in our Loues: for indeed——

Cam. 'Beseech you———

Arch. Verely I speake it in the freedome of my knowledge: we cannot with such magnificence——in so rare——I know not what to say——Wee will giue you sleepie Drinkes, that your Sences (vn-intelligent of our insufficience) may, though they cannot prayse vs, as little accuse vs.

Cam. You pay a great deale to deare, for what's giuen freely.

Arch. 'Beleeue me, I speake as my vnderstanding instructs me, and as mine honestie puts it to vtterance.

Cam. Sicilia cannot shew himselfe ouer-kind to *Bohemia*: They were trayn'd together in their Child-hoods; and there rooted betwixt them then such an affection, which cannot chuse but braunch now. Since their more mature Dignities, and Royall Necessities, made seperation of their Societie, their Encounters (though not Personall) hath been Royally attornyed with enter-change of Gifts, Letters, louing Embassies, that they haue seem'd to be together, though absent: shooke hands, as ouer a Vast; and embrac'd as it were from the ends of opposed Winds. The Heauens continue their Loues.

Arch. I thinke there is not in the World, either Malice or Matter, to alter it. You haue an vnspeakable comfort of your young Prince *Mamillius*: it is a Gentleman of the greatest Promise, that euer came into my Note.

Cam. I very well agree with you, in the hopes of him: it is a gallant Child; one, that (indeed) Physicks the Subiect, makes old hearts fresh: they that went on Crutches ere he was borne, desire yet their life, to see him a Man.

Arch. Would they else be content to die?

Cam. Yes; if there were no other excuse, why they should desire to liue.

Arch. If the King had no Sonne, they would desire to liue on Crutches till he had one.   *Exeunt.*

Scœna Secunda.

Enter Leontes, Hermione, Mamillius, Polixenes, Camillo.

Pol. Nine Changes of the Watry-Starre hath been The Shepheards Note, since we haue left our Throne Without a Burthen: Time as long againe Would be fill'd vp (my Brother) with our Thanks, And yet we should, for perpetuitie, Goe hence in debt: And therefore, like a Cypher (Yet standing in rich place) I multiply With one we thanke you, many thousands moe, That goe before it.

Leo. Stay your Thanks a while, And pay them when you part.

Pol. Sir, that's to morrow: I am question'd by my feares, of what may chance, Or breed vpon our absence, that may blow No sneaping Winds at home, to make vs say, This is put forth too truly: besides, I haue stay'd To tyre your Royaltie.

Leo. We are tougher (Brother) Then you can put vs to't.

Pol. No longer stay.

Leo. One Seue'night longer.

Pol. Very sooth, to morrow.

Leo. Wee'le part the time betweene's then: and in that Ile no gaine-saying.

Pol. Presse me not ('beseech you) so: There is no Tongue that moues; none, none i'th' World So soone as yours, could win me: so it should now, Were there necessitie in your request, although 'Twere needfull I deny'd it. My Affaires Doe euen drag me home-ward: which to hinder, Were (in your Loue) a Whip to me; my stay, To you a Charge, and Trouble: to saue both, Farewell (our Brother.)

Leo. Tongue-ty'd our Queene? speake you.

Her. I had thought (Sir) to haue held my peace, vntill You had drawne Oathes from him, not to stay: you (Sir) Charge him too coldly. Tell him, you are sure All in *Bohemia*'s well: this satisfaction, The by-gone-day proclaym'd, say this to him, He's beat from his best ward.

Leo. Well said, *Hermione*.

Her. To tell, he longs to see his Sonne, were strong: But let him say so then, and let him goe; But let him sweare so, and he shall not stay, Wee'l thwack him hence with Distaffes. Yet of your Royall presence, Ile aduenture The borrow of a Weeke. When at *Bohemia* You take my Lord, Ile giue him my Commission, To let him there a Moneth, behind the Gest Prefix'd for's parting: yet (good-deed) *Leontes*, I loue thee not a Iarre o'th' Clock, behind

What Lady she her Lord. You'le stay?
　Pol. No, Madame.
　Her. Nay, but you will?
　Pol. I may not verely.
　Her. Verely?
You put me off with limber Vowes: but I,
Though you would seek t'vnsphere the Stars with Oaths,
Should yet say, Sir, no going: Verely
You shall not goe; a Ladyes Verely' is
As potent as a Lords. Will you goe yet?
Force me to keepe you as a Prisoner,
Not like a Guest: so you shall pay your Fees
When you depart, and saue your Thanks. How say you?
My Prisoner? or my Guest? by your dread Verely,
One of them you shall be.
　Pol. Your Guest then, Madame:
To be your Prisoner, should import offending;
Which is for me, lesse easie to commit,
Then you to punish.
　Her. Not your Gaoler then,
But your kind Hostesse. Come, Ile question you
Of my Lords Tricks, and yours, when you were Boyes:
You were pretty Lordings then?
　Pol. We were (faire Queene)
Two Lads, that thought there was no more behind,
But such a day to morrow, as to day,
And to be Boy eternall.
　Her. Was not my Lord
The veryer Wag o'th' two?
　Pol. We were as twyn'd Lambs, that did frisk i'th' Sun,
And bleat the one at th'other: what we chang'd,
Was Innocence, for Innocence: we knew not
The Doctrine of ill-doing, nor dream'd
That any did: Had we pursu'd that life,
And our weake Spirits ne're been higher rear'd
With stronger blood, we should haue answer'd Heauen
Boldly, not guilty; the Imposition clear'd,
Hereditarie ours.
　Her. By this we gather
You haue tript since.
　Pol. O my most sacred Lady,
Temptations haue since then been borne to's: for
In those vnfledg'd dayes, was my Wife a Girle;
Your precious selfe had then not cross'd the eyes
Of my young Play-fellow.
　Her. Grace to boot:
Of this make no conclusion, least you say
Your Queene and I are Deuils: yet goe on,
Th'offences we haue made you doe, wee'le answere,
If you first sinn'd with vs: and that with vs
You did continue fault; and that you slipt not
With any, but with vs.
　Leo. Is he woon yet?
　Her. Hee'le stay (my Lord.)
　Leo. At my request, he would not:
Hermione (my dearest) thou neuer spoak'st
To better purpose.
　Her. Neuer?
　Leo. Neuer, but once.
　Her. What? haue I twice said well? when was't before?
I prethee tell me: cram's with prayse, and make's
As fat as tame things: One good deed, dying tonguelesse,
Slaughters a thousand, wayting vpon that.
Our prayses are our Wages. You may ride's
With one soft Kisse a thousand Furlongs, ere
With Spur we heat an Acre. But to th' Goale:

My last good deed, was to entreat his stay.
What was my first? it ha's an elder Sister,
Or I mistake you: O, would her Name were *Grace*.
But once before I spoke to th' purpose? when?
Nay, let me haue't: I long.
　Leo. Why, that was when
Three crabbed Monaths had sowr'd themselues to death,
Ere I could make thee open thy white Hand:
A clap thy selfe my Loue; then didst thou vtter,
I am yours for euer.
　Her. 'Tis Grace indeed.
Why lo-you now; I haue spoke to th' purpose twice:
The one, for euer earn'd a Royall Husband;
Th'other, for some while a Friend.
　Leo. Too hot, too hot:
To mingle friendship farre, is mingling bloods.
I haue *Tremor Cordis* on me: my heart daunces,
But not for ioy; not ioy. This Entertainment
May a free face put on: deriue a Libertie
From Heartinesse, from Bountie, fertile Bosome,
And well become the Agent:'t may; I graunt:
But to be padling Palmes, and pinching Fingers,
As now they are, and making practis'd Smiles
As in a Looking-Glasse; and then to sigh, as 'twere
The Mort o'th' Deere: oh, that is entertainment
My Bosome likes not, nor my Browes. *Mamillius*,
Art thou my Boy?
　Mam. I, my good Lord.
　Leo. I'fecks:
Why that's my Bawcock: what? has't smutch'd thy Nose?
They say it is a Coppy out of mine. Come Captaine,
We must be neat; not neat, but cleanly, Captaine:
And yet the Steere, the Heycfer, and the Calfe,
Are all call'd Neat. Still Virginalling
Vpon his Palme? How now (you wanton Calfe)
Art thou my Calfe?
　Mam. Yes, if you will (my Lord.)
　Leo. Thou want'st a rough pash, & the shoots that I haue
To be full, like me: yet they say we are
Almost as like as Egges; Women say so,
(That will say any thing.) But were they false
As o're-dy'd Blacks, as Wind, as Waters; false
As Dice are to be wish'd, by one that fixes
No borne 'twixt his and mine; yet were it true,
To say this Boy were like me. Come (Sir Page)
Looke on me with your Welkin eye: sweet Villaine,
Most dear'st, my Collop: Can thy Dam, may't be
Affection? thy Intention stabs the Center.
Thou do'st make possible things not so held,
Communicat'st with Dreames (how can this be?)
With what's vnreall: thou coactiue art,
And fellow'st nothing. Then 'tis very credent,
Thou may'st co-ioyne with something, and thou do'st,
(And that beyond Commission) and I find it,
(And that to the infection of my Braines,
And hardning of my Browes.)
　Pol. What meanes *Sicilia*?
　Her. He something seemes vnsetled.
　Pol. How? my Lord?
　Leo. What cheere? how is't with you, best Brother?
　Her. You look as if you held a Brow of much distraction:
Are you mou'd (my Lord?)
　Leo. No, in good earnest.
How sometimes Nature will betray it's folly?
It's tendernesse? and make it selfe a Pastime
To harder bosomes? Looking on the Lynes

Of my Boyes face, me thoughts I did requoyle
Twentie three yeeres, and saw my selfe vn-breech'd,
In my greene Veluet Coat; my Dagger muzzel'd,
Least it should bite it's Master, and so proue
(As Ornaments oft do's) too dangerous:
How like (me thought) I then was to this Kernell,
This Squash, this Gentleman. Mine honest Friend,
Will you take Egges for Money?

Mam. No (my Lord) Ile fight.

Leo. You will: why happy man be's dole. My Brother
Are you so fond of your young Prince, as we
Doe seeme to be of ours?

Pol. If at home (Sir)
He's all my Exercise, my Mirth, my Matter;
Now my sworne Friend, and then mine Enemy;
My Parasite, my Souldier: States-man; all:
He makes a Iulyes day, short as December,
And with his varying child-nesse, cures in me
Thoughts, that would thick my blood.

Leo. So stands this Squire
Offic'd with me: We two will walke (my Lord)
And leaue you to your grauer steps. *Hermione,*
How thou lou'st vs, shew in our Brothers welcome;
Let what is deare in Sicily, be cheape:
Next to thy selfe, and my young Rouer, he's
Apparant to my heart.

Her. If you would seeke vs,
We are yours i'th' Garden: shall's attend you there?

Leo. To your owne bents dispose you: you'le be found,
Be you beneath the Sky: I am angling now,
(Though you perceiue me not how I giue Lyne)
Goe too, goe too.
How she holds vp the Neb? the Byll to him?
And armes her with the boldnesse of a Wife
To her allowing Husband. Gone already,
Ynch-thick, knee-deepe; ore head and eares a fork'd one.
Goe play (Boy) play: thy Mother playes, and I
Play too: but so disgrac'd a part, whose issue
Will hisse me to my Graue: Contempt and Clamor
Will be my Knell. Goe play (Boy) play, there haue been
(Or I am much deceiu'd) Cuckolds ere now,
And many a man there is (euen at this present,
Now, while I speake this) holds his Wife by th' Arme,
That little thinkes she ha's been sluyc'd in's absence,
And his Pond fish'd by his next Neighbor (by
Sir *Smile,* his Neighbor:) nay, there's comfort in't,
Whiles other men haue Gates, and those Gates open'd
(As mine) against their will. Should all despaire
That haue reuolted Wiues, the tenth of Mankind
Would hang themselues. Physick for't, there's none:
It is a bawdy Planet, that will strike
Where 'tis predominant; and 'tis powrefull: thinke it:
From East, West, North, and South, be it concluded,
No Barricado for a Belly. Know't,
It will let in and out the Enemy,
With bag and baggage: many thousand on's
Haue the Disease, and feele't not. How now Boy?

Mam. I am like you say.

Leo. Why, that's some comfort.
What? *Camillo* there?

Cam. I, my good Lord.

Leo. Goe play (*Mamillius*) thou'rt an honest man:
Camillo, this great Sir will yet stay longer.

Cam. You had much adoe to make his Anchor hold,
When you cast out, it still came home.

Leo. Didst note it?

Cam. He would not stay at your Petitions, made
His Businesse more materiall.

Leo. Didst perceiue it?
They're here with me already; whisp'ring, rounding:
Sicilia is a so-forth: 'tis farre gone,
When I shall gust it last. How cam't (*Camillo*)
That he did stay?

Cam. At the good Queenes entreatie.

Leo. At the Queenes be't: Good should be pertinent,
But so it is, it is not. Was this taken
By any vnderstanding Pate but thine?
For thy Conceit is soaking, will draw in
More then the common Blocks. Not noted, is't,
But of the finer Natures? by some Seuералls
Of Head-peece extraordinarie? Lower Messes
Perchance are to this Businesse purblind? say.

Cam. Businesse, my Lord? I thinke most vnderstand
Bohemia stayes here longer.

Leo. Ha?

Cam. Stayes here longer.

Leo. I, but why?

Cam. To satisfie your Highnesse, and the Entreaties
Of our most gracious Mistresse.

Leo. Satisfie?
Th' entreaties of your Mistresse? Satisfie?
Let that suffice. I haue trusted thee (*Camillo*)
With all the neerest things to my heart, as well
My Chamber-Councels, wherein (Priest-like) thou
Hast cleans'd my Bosome: I, from thee departed
Thy Penitent reform'd: but we haue been
Deceiu'd in thy Integritie, deceiu'd
In that which seemes so.

Cam. Be it forbid (my Lord.)

Leo. To bide vpon't: thou art not honest: or
If thou inclin'st that way, thou art a Coward,
Which hoxes honestie behind, restrayning
From Course requir'd: or else thou must be counted
A Seruant, grafted in my serious Trust,
And therein negligent: or else a Foole,
That seest a Game play'd home, the rich Stake drawne,
And tak'st it all for ieast.

Cam. My gracious Lord,
I may be negligent, foolish, and fearefull,
In euery one of these, no man is free,
But that his negligence, his folly, feare,
Among the infinite doings of the World,
Sometime puts forth in your affaires (my Lord.)
If euer I were wilfull-negligent,
It was my folly: if industriously
I play'd the Foole, it was my negligence,
Not weighing well the end: if euer fearefull
To doe a thing, where I the issue doubted,
Whereof the execution did cry out
Against the non-performance, 'twas a feare
Which oft infects the wisest: these (my Lord)
Are such allow'd Infirmities, that honestie
Is neuer free of. But beseech your Grace
Be plainer with me, let me know my Trespas
By it's owne visage; if I then deny it,
'Tis none of mine.

Leo. Ha' not you seene *Camillo*?
(But that's past doubt: you haue, or your eye-glasse
Is thicker then a Cuckolds Horne) or heard?
(For to a Vision so apparant, Rumor
Cannot be mute) or thought? (for Cogitation
Resides not in that man, that do's not thinke)

My Wife is slipperie? If thou wilt confesse,
Or else be impudently negatiue,
To haue nor Eyes, nor Eares, nor Thought, then say
My Wife's a Holy-Horse, deserues a Name
As ranke as any Flax-Wench, that puts to
Before her troth-plight: say't, and iustify't.

Cam. I would not be a stander-by, to heare
My Soueraigne Mistresse clouded so, without
My present vengeance taken: 'shrew my heart,
You neuer spoke what did become you lesse
Then this; which to reiterate, were sin
As deepe as that, though true.

Leo. Is whispering nothing?
Is leaning Cheeke to Cheeke? is meating Noses?
Kissing with in-side Lip? stopping the Cariere
Of Laughter, with a sigh? (a Note infallible
Of breaking Honestie) horsing foot on foot?
Skulking in corners? wishing Clocks more swift?
Houres, Minutes? Noone, Mid-night? and all Eyes
Blind with the Pin and Web, but theirs; theirs onely,
That would vnseene be wicked? Is this nothing?
Why then the World, and all that's in't, is nothing,
The couering Skie is nothing, Bohemia nothing,
My Wife is nothing, nor Nothing haue these Nothings,
If this be nothing.

Cam. Good my Lord, be cur'd
Of this diseas'd Opinion, and betimes,
For 'tis most dangerous.

Leo. Say it be, 'tis true.

Cam. No, no, my Lord.

Leo. It is: you lye, you lye:
I say thou lyest *Camillo*, and I hate thee,
Pronounce thee a grosse Lowt, a mindlesse Slaue,
Or else a houering Temporizer, that
Canst with thine eyes at once see good and euill,
Inclining to them both: were my Wiues Liuer
Infected (as her life) she would not liue
The running of one Glasse.

Cam. Who do's infect her?

Leo. Why he that weares her like her Medull, hanging
About his neck (Bohemia) who, if I
Had Seruants true about me, that bare eyes
To see alike mine Honor, as their Profits,
(Their owne particular Thrifts) they would doe that
Which should vndoe more doing: I, and thou
His Cup-bearer, whom I from meaner forme
Haue Bench'd, and rear'd to Worship, who may'st see
Plainely, as Heauen sees Earth, and Earth sees Heauen,
How I am gall'd, might'st be-spice a Cup,
To giue mine Enemy a lasting Winke:
Which Draught to me, were cordiall.

Cam. Sir (my Lord)
I could doe this, and that with no rash Potion,
But with a lingring Dram, that should not worke
Maliciously, like Poyson: But I cannot
Beleeue this Crack to be in my dread Mistresse
(So soueraignely being Honorable.)
I haue lou'd thee,

Leo Make that thy question, and goe rot:
Do'st thinke I am so muddy, so vnsetled,
To appoint my selfe in this vexation?
Sully the puritie and whitenesse of my Sheetes
(Which to preserue, is Sleepe; which being spotted,
Is Goades, Thornes, Nettles, Tayles of Waspes)
Giue scandall to the blood o'th' Prince, my Sonne,
(Who I doe thinke is mine, and loue as mine)
Without ripe mouing to't? Would I doe this?
Could man so blench?

Cam. I must beleeue you (Sir)
I doe, and will fetch off *Bohemia* for't:
Prouided, that when hee's remou'd, your Highnesse
Will take againe your Queene, as yours at first,
Euen for your Sonnes sake, and thereby for sealing
The Iniurie of Tongues, in Courts and Kingdomes
Knowne, and ally'd to yours.

Leo. Thou do'st aduise me,
Euen so as I mine owne course haue set downe:
Ile giue no blemish to her Honor, none.

Cam. My Lord,
Goe then; and with a countenance as cleare
As Friendship weares at Feasts, keepe with *Bohemia*,
And with your Queene: I am his Cup-bearer,
If from me he haue wholesome Beueridge,
Account me not your Seruant.

Leo. This is all:
Do't, and thou hast the one halfe of my heart;
Do't not, thou splitt'st thine owne.

Cam. Ile do't, my Lord.

Leo. I wil seeme friendly, as thou hast aduis'd me. *Exit*

Cam. O miserable Lady. But for me,
What case stand I in? I must be the poysoner
Of good *Polixenes*, and my ground to do't,
Is the obedience to a Master; one,
Who in Rebellion with himselfe, will haue
All that are his, so too. To doe this deed,
Promotion followes: If I could find example
Of thousand's that had struck anoynted Kings,
And flourish'd after, Il'd not do't: But since
Nor Brasse, nor Stone, nor Parchment beares not one,
Let Villanie it selfe forswear't. I must
Forsake the Court: to do't, or no, is certaine
To me a breake-neck. Happy Starre raigne now,
Here comes Bohemia. *Enter Polixenes.*

Pol. This is strange: Me thinkes
My fauor here begins to warpe. Not speake?
Good day *Camillo*.

Cam. Hayle most Royall Sir.

Pol. What is the Newes i'th' Court?

Cam. None rare (my Lord.)

Pol. The King hath on him such a countenance,
As he had lost some Prouince, and a Region
Lou'd, as he loues himselfe: euen now I met him
With customarie complement, when hee
Wafting his eyes to th' contrary, and falling
A Lippe of much contempt, speedes from me, and
So leaues me, to consider what is breeding,
That changes thus his Manners.

Cam. I dare not know (my Lord.)

Pol. How, dare not? doe not? doe you know, and dare not?
Be intelligent to me, 'tis thereabouts:
For to your selfe, what you doe know, you must,
And cannot say, you dare not. Good *Camillo*,
Your chang'd complexions are to me a Mirror,
Which shewes me mine chang'd too: for I must be
A partie in this alteration, finding
My selfe thus alter'd with't.

Cam. There is a sicknesse
Which puts some of vs in distemper, but
I cannot name the Disease, and it is caught
Of you, that yet are well.

Pol. How caught of me?
Make me not sighted like the Basilisque.

I haue

I haue look'd on thousands, who haue sped the better
By my regard, but kill'd none so: Camillo,
As you are certainely a Gentleman, thereto
Clerke-like experienc'd, which no lesse adornes
Our Gentry, then our Parents Noble Names,
In whose successe we are gentle: I beseech you,
If you know ought which do's behoue my knowledge,
Thereof to be inform'd, imprison't not
In ignorant concealement.

Cam. I may not answere.

Pol. A Sicknesse caught of me, and yet I well?
I must be answer'd. Do'st thou heare *Camillo*,
I coniure thee, by all the parts of man,
Which Honor do's acknowledge, whereof the least
Is not this Suit of mine, that thou declare
What incidencie thou do'st ghesse of harme
Is creeping toward me; how farre off, how neere,
Which way to be preuented, if to be:
If not, how best to beare it.

Cam. Sir, I will tell you,
Since I am charg'd in Honor, and by him
That I thinke Honorable: therefore marke my counsaile,
Which must be eu'n as swiftly followed, as
I meane to vtter it; or both your selfe, and me,
Cry lost, and so good night.

Pol. On, good *Camillo*.

Cam. I am appointed him to murther you.

Pol. By whom, *Camillo*?

Cam. By the King.

Pol. For what?

Cam. He thinkes, nay with all confidence he sweares,
As he had seen't, or beene an Instrument
To vice you to't, that you haue toucht his Queene
Forbiddenly.

Pol. Oh then, my best blood turne
To an infected Gelly, and my Name
Be yoak'd with his, that did betray the Best:
Turne then my freshest Reputation to
A sauour, that may strike the dullest Nosthrill
Where I arriue, and my approch be shun'd,
Nay hated too, worse then the great'st Infection
That ere was heard, or read.

Cam. Sweare his thought ouer
By each particular Starre in Heauen, and
By all their Influences; you may as well
Forbid the Sea for to obey the Moone,
As (or by Oath) remoue, or (Counsaile) shake
The Fabrick of his Folly, whose foundation
Is pyl'd vpon his Faith, and will continue
The standing of his Body.

Pol. How should this grow?

Cam. I know not: but I am sure 'tis safer to
Auoid what's growne, then question how 'tis borne.
If therefore you dare trust my honestie,
That lyes enclosed in this Trunke, which you
Shall beare along impawnd, away to Night,
Your Followers I will whisper to the Businesse,
And will by twoes, and threes, at seuerall Posternes,
Cleare them o'th' Citie: For my selfe, Ile put
My fortunes to your seruice (which are here
By this discouerie lost.) Be not vncertaine,
For by the honor of my Parents, I
Haue vttred Truth: which if you seeke to proue,
I dare not stand by; nor shall you be safer,
Then one condemn'd by the Kings owne mouth:
Thereon his Execution sworne.

Pol. I doe beleeue thee:
I saw his heart in's face. Giue me thy hand,
Be Pilot to me, and thy places shall
Still neighbour mine. My Ships are ready, and
My people did expect my hence departure
Two dayes agoe. This Iealousie
Is for a precious Creature: as shee's rare,
Must it be great; and, as his Person's mightie,
Must it be violent: and, as he do's conceiue,
He is dishonor'd by a man, which euer
Profess'd to him: why his Reuenges must
In that be made more bitter. Feare ore-shades me:
Good Expedition be my friend, and comfort
The gracious Queene, part of his Theame; but nothing
Of his ill-ta'ne suspition. Come *Camillo*,
I will respect thee as a Father, if
Thou bear'st my life off, hence: Let vs auoid.

Cam. It is in mine authoritie to command
The Keyes of all the Posternes: Please your Highnesse
To take the vrgent houre. Come Sir, away. *Exeunt.*

Actus Secundus. Scena Prima.

Enter Hermione, Mamillius, Ladies: Leontes,
Antigonus, Lords.

Her. Take the Boy to you: he so troubles me,
'Tis past enduring.

Lady. Come (my gracious Lord)
Shall I be your play-fellow?

Mam. No, Ile none of you.

Lady. Why (my sweet Lord?)

Mam. You'le kisse me hard, and speake to me, as if
I were a Baby still. I loue you better.

2. Lady. And why so (my Lord?)

Mam. Not for because
Your Browes are blacker (yet black-browes they say
Become some Women best, so that there be not
Too much haire there, but in a Cemicircle,
Or a halfe-Moone, made with a Pen.)

2. Lady. Who taught 'this?

Mam. I learn'd it out of Womens faces: pray now,
What colour are your eye-browes?

Lady. Blew (my Lord.)

Mam. Nay, that's a mock: I haue seene a Ladies Nose
That ha's beene blew, but not her eye-browes.

Lady. Harke ye,
The Queene (your Mother) rounds apace: we shall
Present our seruices to a fine new Prince
One of these dayes, and then youl'd wanton with vs,
If we would haue you.

2. Lady. She is spread of late
Into a goodly Bulke (good time encounter her.)

Her. What wisdome stirs amongst you? Come Sir, now
I am for you againe: 'Pray you sit by vs,
And tell's a Tale.

Mam. Merry, or sad, shal't be?

Her. As merry as you will.

Mam. A sad Tale's best for Winter:
I haue one of Sprights, and Goblins.

Her. Let's haue that (good Sir.)
Come-on, sit downe, come-on, and doe your best,
To fright me with your Sprights: you're powrefull at it.

Mam. There

Mam. There was a man.

Her. Nay, come sit downe: then on.

Mam. Dwelt by a Church-yard: I will tell it softly,
Yond Crickets shall not heare it.

Her. Come on then, and giu't me in mine eare.

Leon. Was hee met there? his Traine? *Camillo* with him?

Lord. Behind the tuft of Pines I met them, neuer
Saw I men scowre so on their way: I eyed them
Euen to their Ships.

Leo. How blest am I
In my iust Censure? in my true Opinion?
Alack, for lesser knowledge, how accurs'd,
In being so blest? There may be in the Cup
A Spider steep'd, and one may drinke; depart,
And yet partake no venome: (for his knowledge
Is not infected) but if one present
Th'abhor'd Ingredient to his eye, make knowne
How he hath drunke, he cracks his gorge, his sides
With violent Hefts: I haue drunke, and seene the Spider.
Camillo was his helpe in this, his Pandar:
There is a Plot against my Life, my Crowne;
All's true that is mistrusted: that false Villaine,
Whom I employ'd, was pre-employ'd by him:
He ha's discouer'd my Designe, and I
Remaine a pinch'd Thing; yea, a very Trick
For them to play at will: how came the Posternes
So easily open?

Lord. By his great authority,
Which often hath no lesse preuail'd, then so,
On your command.

Leo. I know't too well.
Giue me the Boy, I am glad you did not nurse him:
Though he do's beare some signes of me, yet you
Haue too much blood in him.

Her. What is this? Sport?

Leo. Beare the Boy hence, he shall not come about her,
Away with him, and let her sport her selfe
With that shee's big-with, for 'tis *Polixenes*
Ha's made thee swell thus.

Her. But Il'd say he had not;
And Ile be sworne you would beleeue my saying,
How e're you leane to th'Nay-ward.

Leo. You (my Lords)
Looke on her, marke her well: be but about
To say she is a goodly Lady, and
The iustice of your hearts will thereto adde
'Tis pitty shee's not honest: Honorable;
Prayse her but for this her without-dore-Forme,
(Which on my faith deserues high speech) and straight
The Shrug, the Hum, or Ha, (these Petty-brands
That Calumnie doth vse; Oh, I am out,
That Mercy do's, for Calumnie will seare
Vertue it selfe) these Shrugs, these Hum's, and Ha's,
When you haue said shee's goodly, come betweene,
Ere you can say shee's honest: But be't knowne
(From him that ha's most cause to grieue it should be)
Shee's an Adultresse.

Her. Should a Villaine say so,
(The most replenish'd Villaine in the World)
He were as much more Villaine: you (my Lord)
Doe but mistake.

Leo. You haue mistooke (my Lady)
Polixenes for *Leontes*: O thou Thing,
(Which Ile not call a Creature of thy place,
Least Barbarisme (making me the precedent)
Should a like Language vse to all degrees,
And mannerly distinguishment leaue out,
Betwixt the Prince and Begger:) I haue said
Shee's an Adultresse, I haue said with whom:
More; shee's a Traytor, and *Camillo* is
A Federarie with her, and one that knowes
What she should shame to know her selfe,
But with her most vild Principall: that shee's
A Bed-swaruer, euen as bad as those
That Vulgars giue bold'st Titles; I, and priuy
To this their late escape.

Her. No (by my life)
Priuy to none of this: how will this grieue you,
When you shall come to clearer knowledge, that
You thus haue publish'd me? Gentle my Lord,
You scarce can right me throughly, then, to say
You did mistake.

Leo. No: if I mistake
In those Foundations which I build vpon,
The Centre is not bigge enough to beare
A Schoole-Boyes Top. Away with her, to Prison:
He who shall speake for her, is a farre-off guiltie,
But that he speakes.

Her. There's some ill Planet raignes:
I must be patient, till the Heauens looke
With an aspect more sauorable. Good my Lords,
I am not prone to weeping (as our Sex
Commonly are) the want of which vaine dew
Perchance shall dry your pitties: but I haue
That honorable Griefe lodg'd here, which burnes
Worse then Teares drowne:'beseech you all (my Lords)
With thoughts so qualified, as your Charities
Shall best instruct you, measure me; and so
The Kings will be perform'd.

Leo. Shall I be heard?

Her. Who is't that goes with me? beseech your Highnes
My Women may be with me, for you see
My plight requires it. Doe not weepe (good Fooles)
There is no cause: When you shall know your Mistris
Ha's deseru'd Prison, then abound in Teares,
As I come out; this Action I now goe on,
Is for my better grace. Adieu (my Lord)
I neuer wish'd to see you sorry, now
I trust I shall: my Women come, you haue leaue.

Leo. Goe, doe our bidding: hence.

Lord. Beseech your Highnesse call the Queene againe.

Antig. Be certaine what you do (Sir) least your Iustice
Proue violence, in the which three great ones suffer,
Your Selfe, your Queene, your Sonne.

Lord. For her (my Lord)
I dare my life lay downe, and will do't (Sir)
Please you t'accept it, that the Queene is spotlesse
I'th' eyes of Heauen, and to you (I meane
In this, which you accuse her.)

Antig. If it proue
Shee's otherwise, Ile keepe my Stables where
I lodge my Wife, Ile goe in couples with her:
Then when I feele, and see her, no farther trust her:
For euery ynch of Woman in the World,
I, euery dram of Womans flesh is false,
If she be.

Leo. Hold your peaces.

Lord. Good my Lord,

Antig. It is for you we speake, not for our selues:
You are abus'd, and by some putter on,
That will be damn'd for't: would I knew the Villaine,
I would

I would Land-damne him: be she honor-flaw'd,
I haue three daughters: the eldest is eleuen;
The second, and the third, nine: and some fiue:
If this proue true, they'l pay for't. By mine Honor
Ile gell'd em all: fourteene they shall not see
To bring false generations: they are co-heyres,
And I had rather glib my selfe, then they
Should not produce faire issue.

 Leo. Cease, no more:
You smell this businesse with a sence as cold
As is a dead-mans nose: but I do see't, and feel't,
As you feele doing thus: and see withall
The Instruments that feele.

 Antig. If it be so,
We neede no graue to burie honesty,
There's not a graine of it, the face to sweeten
Of the whole dungy-earth.

 Leo. What? lacke I credit?

 Lord. I had rather you did lacke then I (my Lord)
Vpon this ground: and more it would content me
To haue her Honor true, then your suspition
Be blam'd for't how you might.

 Leo. Why what neede we
Commune with you of this? but rather follow
Our forcefull instigation? Our prerogatiue
Cals not your Counsailes, but our naturall goodnesse
Imparts this: which, if you, or stupified,
Or seeming so, in skill, cannot, or will not
Rellish a truth, like vs: informe your selues,
We neede no more of your aduice: the matter,
The losse, the gaine, the ord'ring on't,
Is all properly ours.

 Antig. And I wish (my Liege)
You had onely in your silent iudgement tride it,
Without more ouerture.

 Leo. How could that be?
Either thou art most ignorant by age,
Or thou wer't borne a foole: *Camillo's* flight
Added to their Familiarity
(Which was as grosse, as euer touch'd coniecture,
That lack'd sight onely, nought for approbation
But onely seeing, all other circumstances
Made vp to'th deed) doth push-on this proceeding.
Yet, for a greater confirmation
(For in an Acte of this importance, 'twere
Most pitteous to be wilde) I haue dispatch'd in post,
To sacred *Delphos*, to *Appollo's* Temple,
Cleomines and *Dion*, whom you know
Of stuff'd-sufficiency: Now, from the Oracle
They will bring all, whose spirituall counsaile had
Shall stop, or spurre me. Haue I done well?

 Lord. Well done (my Lord.)

 Leo. Though I am satisfide, and neede no more
Then what I know, yet shall the Oracle
Giue rest to th'mindes of others; such as he
Whose ignorant credulitie, will not
Come vp to th'truth. So haue we thought it good
From our free person, she should be confinde,
Least that the treachery of the two, fled hence,
Be left her to performe. Come follow vs,
We are to speake in publique: for this businesse
Will raise vs all.

 Antig. To laughter, as I take it,
If the good truth, were knowne.   *Exeunt*

Scena Secunda.

Enter Paulina, a Gentleman, Gaoler, Emilia.

 Paul. The Keeper of the prison, call to him:
Let him haue knowledge who I am. Good Lady,
No Court in Europe is too good for thee,
What dost thou then in prison? Now good Sir,
You know me, do you not?

 Gao. For a worthy Lady,
And one, who much I honour.

 Pau. Pray you then,
Conduct me to the Queene.

 Gao. I may not (Madam)
To the contrary I haue expresse commandment.

 Pau. Here's a-do, to locke vp honesty & honour from
Th'accesse of gentle visitors. Is't lawfull pray you
To see her Women? Any of them? *Emilia*?

 Gao. So please you (Madam)
To put a-part these your attendants, I
Shall bring *Emilia* forth.

 Pau. I pray now call her:
With-draw your selues.

 Gao. And Madam,
I must be present at your Conference.

 Pau. Well: be't so: prethee.
Heere's such a-doe, to make no staine, a staine,
As passes colouring. Deare Gentlewoman,
How fares our gracious Lady?

 Emil. As well as one so great, and so forlorne
May hold together: On her frights, and greefes
(Which neuer tender Lady hath borne greater)
She is, something before her time, deliuer'd.

 Pau. A boy?

 Emil. A daughter, and a goodly babe,
Lusty, and like to liue: the Queene receiues
Much comfort in't: Sayes, my poore prisoner,
I am innocent as you.

 Pau. I dare be sworne:
These dangerous, vnsafe Lunes i'th'King, beshrew them:
He must be told on't, and he shall: the office
Becomes a woman best. Ile take't vpon me,
If I proue hony-mouth'd, let my tongue blister.
And neuer to my red-look'd Anger bee
The Trumpet any more: pray you (*Emilia*)
Commend my best obedience to the Queene,
If she dares trust me with her little babe,
I'le shew't the King, and vndertake to bee
Her Aduocate to th'lowd'st. We do not know
How he may soften at the sight o'th'Childe:
The silence often of pure innocence
Perswades, when speaking failes.

 Emil. Most worthy Madam,
your honor, and your goodnesse is so euident,
That your free vndertaking cannot misse
A thriuing yssue: there is no Lady liuing
So meete for this great errand; please your Ladiship
To visit the next roome, Ile presenrly
Acquaint the Queene of your most noble offer;
Who, but to day hammered of this designe,
But durst not tempt a minister of honour
Least she should be deny'd.

Paul. Tell her (*Emilia*)
Ile vse that tongue I haue: If wit flow from't
As boldnesse from my bosome, le't not be doubted
I shall do good,

Emil. Now be you blest for it.
Ile to the Queene: please you come something neerer.

Gao. Madam, if't please the Queene to send the babe,
I know not what I shall incurre, to passe it,
Hauing no warrant.

Pau. You neede not feare it (sir)
This Childe was prisoner to the wombe, and is
By Law and processe of great Nature, thence
Free'd, and enfranchis'd, not a partie to
The anger of the King, nor guilty of
(If any be) the trespasse of the Queene.

Gao. I do beleeue it.

Paul. Do not you feare: vpon mine honor, I
Will stand betwixt you, and danger. *Exeunt*

Scæna Tertia.

Enter Leontes, Seruants, Paulina, Antigonus, and Lords.

Leo. Nor night, nor day, no rest: It is but weaknesse
To beare the matter thus: meere weaknesse, if
The cause were not in being: part o'th'cause,
She, th'Adultresse: for the harlot-King
Is quite beyond mine Arme, out of the blanke
And leuell of my braine: plot-proofe: but shee,
I can hooke to me: say that she were gone,
Giuen to the fire, a moity of my rest
Might come to me againe. Whose there?

Ser. My Lord.

Leo. How do's the boy?

Ser. He tooke good rest to night: 'tis hop'd
His sicknesse is discharg'd.

Leo. To see his Noblenesse,
Conceyuing the dishonour of his Mother.
He straight declin'd, droop'd, tooke it deeply,
Fasten'd, and fix'd the shame on't in himselfe:
Threw-off his Spirit, his Appetite, his Sleepe,
And down-right languish'd. Leaue me solely: goe,
See how he fares: Fie, fie, no thought of him,
The very thought of my Reuenges that way
Recoyle vpon me: in himselfe too mightie,
And in his parties, his Alliance; Let him be,
Vntill a time may serue. For present vengeance
Take it on her: *Camillo*, and *Polixenes*
Laugh at me: make their pastime at my sorrow:
They should not laugh, if I could reach them, nor
Shall she, within my powre.

Enter Paulina.

Lord. You must not enter.

Paul. Nay rather (good my Lords) be second to me:
Feare you his tyrannous passion more (alas)
Then the Queenes life? A gracious innocent soule,
More free, then he is iealous.

Antig. That's enough.

Ser. Madam; he hath not slept to night, commanded
None should come at him.

Pau. Not so hot (good Sir)
I come to bring him sleepe. 'Tis such as you
That creepe like shadowes by him, and do sighe
At each his needlesse heauings: such as you
Nourish the cause of his awaking. I
Do come with words, as medicinall, as true;
(Honest, as either;) to purge him of that humor,
That presses him from sleepe.

Leo. Who noyse there, hoe?

Pau. No noyse (my Lord) but needfull conference,
About some Gossips for your Highnesse.

Leo. How?
Away with that audacious Lady. *Antigonus*,
I charg'd thee that she should not come about me,
I knew she would.

Ant. I told her so (my Lord)
On your displeasures perill, and on mine,
She should not visit you.

Leo. What? canst not rule her?

Paul. From all dishonestie he can: in this
(Vnlesse he take the course that you haue done)
Commit me, for committing honor, trust it,
He shall not rule me:

Ant. La-you now, you heare,
When she will take the raine, I let her run,
But shee'l not stumble.

Paul. Good my Liege, I come:
And I beseech you heare me, who professes
My selfe your loyall Seruant, your Physitian,
Your most obedient Counsailor: yet that dares
Lesse appeare so, in comforting your Euilles,
Then such as most seeme yours. I say, I come
From your good Queene.

Leo. Good Queene?

Paul. Good Queene (my Lord) good Queene,
I say good Queene,
And would by combate, make her good so, were I
A man, the worst about you.

Leo. Force her hence.

Pau. Let him that makes but trifles of his eyes
First hand me: on mine owne accord, Ile off,
But first, Ile do my errand. The good Queene
(For she is good) hath brought you forth a daughter,
Heere 'tis: Commends it to your blessing.

Leo. Out:
A mankinde Witch? Hence with her, out o'dore:
A most intelligencing bawd.

Paul. Not so:
I am as ignorant in that, as you,
In so entit'ling me: and no lesse honest
Then you are mad: which is enough, Ile warrant
(As this world goes) to passe for honest:

Leo. Traitors;
Will you not push her out? Giue her the Bastard,
Thou dotard, thou art woman-tyr'd: vnroosted
By thy dame *Partlet* heere. Take vp the Bastard,
Take't vp, I say: giue't to thy Crone.

Paul. For euer
Vnvenerable be thy hands, if thou
Tak'st vp the Princesse, by that forced basenesse
Which he ha's put vpon't.

Leo. He dreads his Wife.

Paul. So I would you did: then 'twere past all doubt
You'ld call your children, yours.

Leo. A nest of Traitors.

Ant. I am none, by this good light.

Pau. Nor I: nor any
But one that's heere: and that's himselfe: for he,

The

The Winters Tale.

The sacred Honor of himselfe, his Queenes,
His hopefull Sonnes, his Babes, betrayes to Slander,
Whose sting is sharper then the Swords; and will not
(For as the case now stands, it is a Curse
He cannot be compell'd too't) once remoue
The Root of his Opinion, which is rotten,
As euer Oake, or Stone was sound.

Leo. A Callat
Of boundlesse tongue, who late hath beat her Husband,
And now bayts me: This Brat is none of mine,
It is the Issue of *Polixenes*.
Hence with it, and together with the Dam,
Commit them to the fire.

Paul. It is yours:
And might we lay th'old Prouerb to your charge,
So like you, 'tis the worse. Behold (my Lords)
Although the Print be little, the whole Matter
And Coppy of the Father: (Eye, Nose, Lippe,
The trick of's Frowne, his Fore-head, nay, the Valley,
The pretty dimples of his Chin, and Cheeke; his Smiles:
The very Mold, and frame of Hand, Nayle, Finger.)
And thou good Goddesse *Nature*, which hast made it
So like to him that got it, if thou hast
The ordering of the Mind too, 'mongst all Colours
No Yellow in't, least she suspect, as he do's,
Her Children, not her Husbands.

Leo. A grosse Hagge:
And Lozell, thou art worthy to be hang'd,
That wilt not stay her Tongue.

Antig. Hang all the Husbands
That cannot doe that Feat, you'le leaue your selfe
Hardly one Subiect.

Leo. Once more take her hence.

Paul. A most vnworthy, and vnnaturall Lord
Can doe no more.

Leo. Ile ha' thee burnt.

Paul. I care not:
It is an Heretique that makes the fire,
Not she which burnes in't. Ile not call you Tyrant:
But this most cruell vsage of your Queene
(Not able to produce more accusation
Then your owne weake-hindg'd Fancy) somthing sauors
Of Tyrannie, and will ignoble make you,
Yea, scandalous to the World.

Leo. On your Allegeance,
Out of the Chamber with her. Were I a Tyrant,
Where were her life? she durst not call me so,
If she did know me one. Away with her.

Paul. I pray you doe not push me, Ile be gone.
Looke to your Babe (my Lord) 'tis yours: *Ioue* send her
A better guiding Spirit. What needs these hands?
You that are thus so tender o're his Follyes,
Will neuer doe him good, not one of you.
So, so: Farewell, we are gone. *Exit.*

Leo. Thou (Traytor) hast set on thy Wife to this.
My Child? away with't? euen thou, that hast
A heart so tender o're it, take it hence,
And see it instantly consum'd with fire.
Euen thou, and none but thou. Take it vp straighte:
Within this houre bring me word 'tis done,
(And by good testimonie) or Ile seize thy life,
With what thou else call'st thine: if thou refuse,
And wilt encounter with my Wrath, say so;
The Bastard-braynes with these my proper hands
Shall I dash out. Goe, take it to the fire,
For thou sett'st on thy Wife.

Antig. I did not, Sir:
These Lords, my Noble Fellowes, if they please,
Can cleare me in't.

Lords. We can: my Royall Liege,
He is not guiltie of her comming hither.

Leo. You're lyers all.

Lord. Beseech your Highnesse, giue vs better credit:
We haue alwayes truly seru'd you, and beseech'
So to esteeme of vs: and on our knees we begge,
(As recompence of our deare seruices
Past, and to come) that you doe change this purpose,
Which being so horrible, so bloody, must
Lead on to some foule Issue. We all kneele.

Leo. I am a Feather for each Wind that blows:
Shall I liue on, to see this Bastard kneele,
And call me Father? better burne it now,
Then curse it then. But be it: let it liue.
It shall not neyther. You Sir, come you hither:
You that haue beene so tenderly officious
With Lady *Margerie*, your Mid-wife there,
To saue this Bastards life; for 'tis a Bastard,
So sure as this Beard's gray. What will you aduenture,
To saue this Brats life?

Antig. Any thing (my Lord)
That my abilitie may vndergoe,
And Noblenesse impose: at least thus much;
Ile pawne the little blood which I haue left,
To saue the Innocent: any thing possible.

Leo. It shall be possible: Sweare by this Sword
Thou wilt performe my bidding.

Antig. I will (my Lord.)

Leo. Marke, and performe it: seest thou? for the faile
Of any point in't, shall not onely be
Death to thy selfe, but to thy lewd-tongu'd Wife,
(Whom for this time we pardon) We enioyne thee,
As thou art Liege-man to vs, that thou carry
This female Bastard hence, and that thou beare it
To some remote and desart place, quite out
Of our Dominions; and that there thou leaue it
(Without more mercy) to it owne protection,
And fauour of the Climate: as by strange fortune
It came to vs, I doe in Iustice charge thee,
On thy Soules perill, and thy Bodyes torture,
That thou commend it strangely to some place,
Where Chance may nurse, or end it: take it vp.

Antig. I sweare to doe this: though a present death
Had beene more mercifull. Come on (poore Babe)
Some powerfull Spirit instruct the Kytes and Rauens
To be thy Nurses. Wolues and Beares, they say,
(Casting their sauagenesse aside) haue done
Like offices of Pitty. Sir, be prosperous
In more then this deed do's require; and Blessing
Against this Crueltie, fight on thy side
(Poore Thing, condemn'd to losse.) *Exit.*

Leo. No: Ile not reare
Anothers Issue. *Enter a Seruant.*

Seru. Please' your Highnesse, Posts
From those you sent to th'Oracle, are come
An houre since: *Cleomines* and *Dion*,
Being well arriu'd from Delphos, are both landed,
Hasting to th' Court.

Lord. So please you (Sir) their speed
Hath beene beyond accompt.

Leo. Twentie three dayes
They haue beene absent: 'tis good speed: fore-tells
The great *Apollo* suddenly will haue

The

The truth of this appeare: Prepare you Lords,
Summon a Session, that we may arraigne
Our most disloyall Lady: for as she hath
Been publikely accus'd, so shall she haue
A iust and open Triall. While she liues,
My heart will be a burthen to me. Leaue me,
And thinke vpon my bidding. *Exeunt.*

Actus Tertius. Scena Prima.

Enter Cleomines and Dion.

Cleo. The Clymat's delicate, the Ayre most sweet,
Fertile the Isle, the Temple much surpassing
The common prayse it beares.

Dion. I shall report,
For most it caught me, the Celestiall Habits,
(Me thinkes I so should terme them) and the reuerence
Of the graue Wearers. O, the Sacrifice,
How ceremonious, solemne, and vn-earthly
It was i'th'Offring?

Cleo. But of all, the burst
And the eare-deaff'ning Voyce o'th'Oracle,
Kin to *Ioues* Thunder, so surpriz'd my Sence,
That I was nothing.

Dio. If th'euent o'th'Iourney
Proue as successefull to the Queene (O be't so)
As it hath beene to vs, rare, pleasant, speedie,
The time is worth the vse on't.

Cleo. Great *Apollo*
Turne all to th'best: these Proclamations,
So forcing faults vpon *Hermione*,
I little like.

Dio. The violent carriage of it
Will cleare, or end the Businesse, when the Oracle
(Thus by *Apollo's* great Diuine seal'd vp)
Shall the Contents discouer: something rare
Euen then will rush to knowledge. Goe: fresh Horses,
And gracious be the issue. *Exeunt.*

Scoena Secunda.

Enter Leontes, Lords, Officers: Hermione (as to her Triall) Ladies: Cleomines, Dion.

Leo. This Sessions (to our great griefe we pronounce)
Euen pushes 'gainst our heart. The partie try'd,
The Daughter of a King, our Wife, and one
Of vs too much belou'd. Let vs be clear'd
Of being tyrannous, since we so openly
Proceed in Iustice, which shall haue due course,
Euen to the Guilt, or the Purgation:
Produce the Prisoner.

Officer. It is his Highnesse pleasure, that the Queene
Appeare in person, here in Court. *Silence.*

Leo. Reade the Indictment.

Officer. Hermione, Queene to the worthy Leontes, King of Sicilia, thou art here accused and arraigned of High Treason, in committing Adultery with Polixenes King of Bohemia, and conspiring with Camillo to take away the Life of our Soueraigne Lord the King, thy Royall Husband: the pretence whereof being by circumstances partly layd open, thou (Hermione) contrary to the Faith and Allegeance of a true Subiect, didst counsaile and ayde them, for their better safetie, to flye away by Night.

Her. Since what I am to say, must be but that
Which contradicts my Accusation, and
The testimonie on my part, no other
But what comes from my selfe, it shall scarce boot me
To say, Not guiltie: mine Integritie
Being counted Falsehood, shall (as I expresse it)
Be so receiu'd. But thus, if Powres Diuine
Behold our humane Actions (as they doe)
I doubt not then, but Innocence shall make
False Accusation blush, and Tyrannie
Tremble at Patience. You (my Lord) best know
(Whom least will seeme to doe so) my past life
Hath beene as continent, as chaste, as true,
As I am now vnhappy; which is more
Then Historie can patterne, though deuis'd,
And play'd, to take Spectators. For behold me,
A Fellow of the Royall Bed, which owe
A Moitie of the Throne: a great Kings Daughter,
The Mother to a hopefull Prince, here standing
To prate and talke for Life, and Honor, fore
Who please to come, and heare. For Life, I prize it
As I weigh Griefe (which I would spare:) For Honor,
'Tis a deriuatiue from me to mine,
And onely that I stand for. I appeale
To your owne Conscience (Sir) before *Polixenes*
Came to your Court, how I was in your grace,
How merited to be so: Since he came,
With what encounter so vncurrant, I
Haue strayn'd t'appeare thus; if one iot beyond
The bound of Honor, or in act, or will
That way enclining, hardned be the hearts
Of all that heare me, and my neer'st of Kin
Cry fie vpon my Graue.

Leo. I ne're heard yet,
That any of these bolder Vices wanted
Lesse Impudence to gaine-say what they did,
Then to performe it first.

Her. That's true enough,
Though 'tis a saying (Sir) not due to me.

Leo. You will not owne it.

Her. More then Mistresse of,
Which comes to me in name of Fault, I must not
At all acknowledge. For *Polixenes*
(With whom I am accus'd) I doe confesse
I lou'd him, as in Honor he requir'd:
With such a kind of Loue, as might become
A Lady like me; with a Loue, euen such,
So, and no other, as your selfe commanded:
Which, not to haue done, I thinke had been in me
Both Disobedience, and Ingratitude
To you, and toward your Friend, whose Loue had spoke,
Euen since it could speake, from an Infant, freely,
That it was yours. Now for Conspiracie,
I know not how it tastes, though it be dish'd
For me to try how: All I know of it,
Is, that *Camillo* was an honest man;
And why he left your Court, the Gods themselues
(Wotting no more then I) are ignorant.

Leo. You knew of his departure, as you know
What you haue vnderta'ne to doe in's absence.

Her. Sir,

Her. Sir,
You speake a Language that I vnderstand not:
My Life stands in the leuell of your Dreames,
Which Ile lay downe.

Leo. Your Actions are my Dreames.
You had a Bastard by *Polixenes,*
And I but dream'd it: As you were past all shame,
(Those of your Fact are so) so past all truth;
Which to deny, concernes more then auailes: for as
Thy Brat hath been cast out; like to it selfe,
No Father owning it (which is indeed
More criminall in thee, then it) so thou
Shalt feele our Iustice; in whose easiest passage,
Looke for no lesse then death.

Her. Sir, spare your Threats:
The Bugge which you would fright me with, I seeke:
To me can Life be no commoditie;
The crowne and comfort of my Life (your Fauor)
I doe giue lost, for I doe feele it gone,
But know not how it went. My second Ioy,
And first Fruits of my body, from his presence
I am bar'd, like one infectious. My third comfort
(Star'd most vnluckily) is from my breast
(The innocent milke in it most innocent mouth)
Hal'd out to murther. My selfe on euery Post
Proclaym'd a Strumpet: With immodest hatred
The Child-bed priuiledge deny'd, which longs
To Women of all fashion. Lastly, hurried
Here, to this place, i'th' open ayre, before
I haue got strength of limit. Now (my Liege)
Tell me what blessings I haue here aliue,
That I should feare to die? Therefore proceed:
But yet heare this: mistake me not: no Life,
(I prize it not a straw) but for mine Honor,
Which I would free: if I shall be condemn'd
Vpon surmizes (all proofes sleeping else,
But what your Iealousies awake) I tell you
'Tis Rigor, and not Law. Your Honors all,
I doe referre me to the Oracle:
Apollo be my Iudge.

Lord. This your request
Is altogether iust: therefore bring forth
(And in *Apollo's* Name) his Oracle.

Her. The Emperor of Russia was my Father.
Oh that he were aliue, and here beholding
His Daughters Tryall: that he did but see
The flatnesse of my miserie; yet with eyes
Of Pitty, not Reuenge.

Officer. You here shal sweare vpon this Sword of Iustice,
That you (*Cleomines* and *Dion*) haue
Been both at Delphos, and from thence haue brought
This seal'd-vp Oracle, by the Hand deliuer'd
Of great *Apollo's* Priest; and that since then,
You haue not dar'd to breake the holy Seale,
Nor read the Secrets in't.

Cleo. Dio. All this we sweare.

Leo. Breake vp the Seales, and read.

Officer. Hermione *is chast,* Polixenes *blamelesse,* Camillo
a true Subiect, Leontes *a iealous Tyrant, his innocent Babe
truly begotten, and the King shall liue without an Heire, if that
which is lost, be not found.*

Lords. Now blessed be the great *Apollo.*

Her. Praysed.

Leo. Hast thou read truth?

Offic. I (my Lord) euen so as it is here set downe.

Leo. There is no truth at all i'th' Oracle:
The Sessions shall proceed: this is meere falsehood.

Ser. My Lord the King: the King?

Leo. What is the businesse?

Ser. O Sir, I shall be hated to report it.
The Prince your Sonne, with meere conceit, and feare
Of the Queenes speed, is gone.

Leo. How? gone?

Ser. Is dead.

Leo. Apollo's angry, and the Heauens themselues
Doe strike at my Iniustice. How now there?

Paul. This newes is mortall to the Queene: Look downe
And see what Death is doing.

Leo. Take her hence:
Her heart is but o're-charg'd: she will recouer.
I haue too much beleeu'd mine owne suspition:
'Beseech you tenderly apply to her
Some remedies for life. *Apollo* pardon
My great prophanenesse 'gainst thine Oracle.
Ile reconcile me to *Polixenes,*
New woe my Queene, recall the good *Camillo*
(Whom I proclaime a man of Truth, of Mercy:)
For being transported by my Iealousies
To bloody thoughts, and to reuenge, I chose
Camillo for the minister, to poyson
My friend *Polixenes*: which had been done,
But that the good mind of *Camillo* tardied
My swift command: though I with Death, and with
Reward, did threaten and encourage him,
Not doing it, and being done: he (most humane,
And fill'd with Honor) to my Kingly Guest
Vnclasp'd my practise, quit his fortunes here
(Which you knew great) and to the hazard
Of all Incertainties, himselfe commended,
No richer then his Honor: How he glisters
Through my Rust? and how his Pietie
Do's my deeds make the blacker?

Paul. Woe the while:
O cut my Lace, least my heart (cracking it)
Breake too.

Lord. What fit is this? good Lady?

Paul. What studied torments (Tyrant) hast for me?
What Wheeles? Racks? Fires? What flaying? boyling?
In Leads, or Oyles? What old, or newer Torture
Must I receiue? whose euery word deserues
To taste of thy most worst. Thy Tyranny
(Together working with thy Iealousies,
Fancies too weake for Boyes, too greene and idle
For Girles of Nine) O thinke what they haue done,
And then run mad indeed: starke-mad: for all
Thy by-gone fooleries were but spices of it.
That thou betrayed'st *Polixenes,* 'twas nothing,
(That did but shew thee, of a Foole, inconstant,
And damnable ingratefull:) Nor was't much,
Thou would'st haue poyson'd good *Camillo's* Honor,
To haue him kill a King: poore Trespasses,
More monstrous standing by: whereof I reckon
The casting forth to Crowes, thy Baby-daughter,
To be or none, or little; though a Deuill
Would haue shed water out of fire, ere don't:
Nor is't directly layd to thee, the death
Of the young Prince, whose honorable thoughts
(Thoughts high for one so tender) cleft the heart
That could conceiue a grosse and foolish Sire
Blemish'd his gracious Dam: this is not, no,
Layd to thy answere: but the last: O Lords,
When I haue said, cry woe: the Queene, the Queene,

The sweet'st, deer'st creature's dead: & vengeance for't
Not drop'd downe yet.

Lord. The higher powres forbid.

Pau. I say she's dead: Ile swear't. If word, nor oath
Preuaile not, go and see: if you can bring
Tincture, or lustre in her lip, her eye
Heate outwardly, or breath within, Ile serue you
As I would do the Gods. But, O thou Tyrant,
Do not repent these things, for they are heauier
Then all thy woes can stirre: therefore betake thee
To nothing but dispaire. A thousand knees,
Ten thousand yeares together, naked, fasting,
Vpon a barren Mountaine, and still Winter
In storme perpetuall, could not moue the Gods
To looke that way thou wer't.

Leo. Go on, go on:
Thou canst not speake too much, I haue deseru'd
All tongues to talke their bittrest.

Lord. Say no more;
How ere the businesse goes, you haue made fault
I'th boldnesse of your speech.

Pau. I am sorry for't;
All faults I make, when I shall come to know them,
I do repent: Alas, I haue shew'd too much
The rashnesse of a woman: he is toucht
To th'Noble heart. What's gone, and what's past helpe
Should be past greefe: Do not receiue affliction
At my petition; I beseech you, rather
Let me be punish'd, that haue minded you
Of what you should forget. Now (good my Liege)
Sir, Royall Sir, forgiue a foolish woman:
The loue I bore your Queene (Lo, foole againe)
Ile speake of her no more, nor of your Children:
Ile not remember you of my owne Lord,
(Who is lost too:) take your patience to you,
And Ile say nothing.

Leo. Thou didst speake but well,
When most the truth: which I receyue much better,
Then to be pittied of thee. Prethee bring me
To the dead bodies of my Queene, and Sonne,
One graue shall be for both: Vpon them shall
The causes of their death appeare (vnto
Our shame perpetuall) once a day, Ile visit
The Chappell where they lye, and teares shed there
Shall be my recreation. So long as Nature
Will beare vp with this exercise, so long
I dayly vow to vse it. Come, and leade me
To these sorrowes. *Exeunt*

Scæna Tertia.

*Enter Antigonus, a Marriner, Babe, Sheepe-
heard, and Clowne.*

Ant. Thou art perfect then, our ship hath toucht vpon
The Deserts of *Bohemia.*

Mar. I (my Lord) and feare
We haue Landed in ill time: the skies looke grimly,
And threaten present blusters. In my conscience
The heauens with that we haue in hand, are angry,
And frowne vpon's.

Ant. Their sacred wil's be done: go get a-boord,
Looke to thy barke, Ile not be long before
I call vpon thee.

Mar. Make your best haste, and go not
Too-farre i'th Land: 'tis like to be lowd weather,
Besides this place is famous for the Creatures
Of prey, that keepe vpon't.

Antig. Go thou away,
Ile follow instantly.

Mar. I am glad at heart
To be so ridde o'th businesse. *Exit*

Ant. Come, poore babe;
I haue heard (but not beleeu'd) the Spirits o'th'dead
May walke againe: if such thing be, thy Mother
Appear'd to me last night: for ne're was dreame
So like a waking. To me comes a creature,
Sometimes her head on one side, some another,
I neuer saw a vessell of like sorrow
So fill'd, and so becomming: in pure white Robes
Like very sanctity she did approach
My Cabine where I lay: thrice bow'd before me,
And (gasping to begin some speech) her eyes
Became two spouts; the furie spent, anon
Did this breake from her. Good *Antigonus*,
Since Fate (against thy better disposition)
Hath made thy person for the Thower-out
Of my poore babe, according to thine oath,
Places remote enough are in *Bohemia*,
There weepe, and leaue it crying: and for the babe
Is counted lost for euer, *Perdita*
I prethee call't: For this vngentle businesse
Put on thee, by my Lord, thou ne're shalt see
Thy Wife *Paulina* more: and so, with shriekes
She melted into Ayre. Affrighted much,
I did in time collect my selfe, and thought
This was so, and no slumber: Dreames, are toyes,
Yet for this once, yea superstitiously,
I will be squar'd by this. I do beleeue
Hermione hath suffer'd death, and that
Apollo would (this being indeede the issue
Of King *Polixenes*) it should heere be laide
(Either for life, or death) vpon the earth
Of it's right Father. Blossome, speed thee well,
There lye, and there thy charracter: there these,
Which may if Fortune please, both breed thee (pretty)
And still rest thine. The storme beginnes, poore wretch,
That for thy mothers fault, art thus expos'd
To losse, and what may follow. Weepe I cannot,
But my heart bleedes: and most accurst am I
To be by oath enioyn'd to this. Farewell,
The day frownes more and more: thou'rt like to haue
A lullabie too rough: I neuer saw
The heauens so dim, by day. A sauage clamor?
Well may I get a-boord: This is the Chace,
I am gone for euer. *Exit pursued by a Beare.*

Shep. I would there were no age betweene ten and
three and twenty, or that youth would sleep out the rest:
for there is nothing (in the betweene) but getting wenches with childe, wronging the Auncientry, stealing,
fighting, hearke you now: would any but these boylde-
braines of nineteene, and two and twenty hunt this weather? They haue scarr'd away two of my best Sheepe,
which I feare the Wolfe will sooner finde then the Maister; if any where I haue them, 'tis by the sea-side, brou-
zing of Iuy. Good-lucke (and't be thy will) what haue
we heere? Mercy on's, a Barne? A very pretty barne; A
boy, or a Childe I wonder? (A pretty one, a verie prettie
one) sure some Scape; Though I am not bookish, yet I
can

can reade Waiting-Gentlewoman in the scape: this has beene some staire-worke, some Trunke-worke, some behinde-doore worke: they were warmer that got this, then the poore Thing is heere. Ile take it vp for pity, yet Ile tarry till my sonne come: he hallow'd but euen now. Whoa-ho-hoa.

Enter Clowne.

Clo. Hilloa, loa.

Shep. What? art so neere? If thou'lt see a thing to talke on, when thou art dead and rotten, come hither: what ayl'st thou, man?

Clo. I haue seene two such sights, by Sea & by Land: but I am not to say it is a Sea, for it is now the skie, betwixt the Firmament and it, you cannot thrust a bodkins point.

Shep. Why boy, how is it?

Clo. I would you did but see how it chafes, how it rages, how it takes vp the shore, but that's not to the point: Oh, the most pitteous cry of the poore soules, sometimes to see 'em, and not to see 'em: Now the Shippe boaring the Moone with her maine Mast, and anon swallowed with yest and froth, as you'ld thrust a Corke into a hogshead. And then for the Land-seruice, to see how the Beare tore out his shoulder-bone, how he cride to mee for helpe, and said his name was *Antigonus*, a Nobleman: But to make an end of the Ship, to see how the Sea flapdragon'd it: but first, how the poore soules roared, and the sea mock'd them: and how the poore Gentleman roared, and the Beare mock'd him, both roaring lowder then the sea, or weather.

Shep. Name of mercy, when was this boy?

Clo. Now, now: I haue not wink'd since I saw these sights: the men are not yet cold vnder water, nor the Beare halfe din'd on the Gentleman: he's at it now.

Shep. Would I had bin by, to haue help'd the olde man.

Clo. I would you had beene by the ship side, to haue help'd her; there your charity would haue lack'd footing.

Shep. Heauy matters, heauy matters: but looke thee heere boy. Now blesse thy selfe: thou met'st with things dying, I with things new borne. Here's a sight for thee: Looke thee, a bearing-cloath for a Squires childe: looke thee heere, take vp, take vp (Boy:) open't: so, let's see, it was told me I should be rich by the Fairies. This is some Changeling: open't: what's within, boy?

Clo. You're a mad olde man: If the sinnes of your youth are forgiuen you, you're well to liue. Golde, all Gold.

Shep. This is Faiery Gold boy, and 'twill proue so: vp with't, keepe it close: home, home, the next way. We are luckie (boy) and to bee so still requires nothing but secrecie. Let my sheepe go: Come (good boy) the next way home.

Clo. Go you the next way with your Findings, Ile go see if the Beare bee gone from the Gentleman, and how much he hath eaten: they are neuer curst but when they are hungry: if there be any of him left, Ile bury it.

Shep. That's a good deed: if thou mayest discerne by that which is left of him, what he is, fetch me to th'sight of him.

Clowne. 'Marry will I: and you shall helpe to put him i'th' ground.

Shep. 'Tis a lucky day, boy, and wee'l do good deeds on't. *Exeunt*

Actus Quartus. Scena Prima.

Enter Time, the Chorus.

Time. I that please some, try all: both ioy and terror Of good, and bad: that makes, and vnfolds error,
Now take vpon me (in the name of Time)
To vse my wings: Impute it not a crime
To me, or my swift passage, that I slide
Ore sixteene yeeres, and leaue the growth vntride
Of that wide gap, since it is in my powre
To orethrow Law, and in one selfe-borne howre
To plant, and ore-whelme Custome. Let me passe
The same I am, ere ancient'st Order was,
Or what is now receiu'd. I witnesse to
The times that brought them in, so shall I do
To th'freshest things now reigning, and make stale
The glistering of this present, as my Tale
Now seemes to it: your patience this allowing,
I turne my glasse, and giue my Scene such growing
As you had slept betweene: *Leontes* leauing
Th'effects of his fond iealousies, so greeuing
That he shuts vp himselfe. Imagine me
(Gentle Spectators) that I now may be
In faire Bohemia, and remember well,
I mentioned a sonne o'th'Kings, which *Florizell*
I now name to you: and with speed so pace
To speake of *Perdita*, now growne in grace
Equall with wond'ring. What of her insues
I list not prophesie: but let Times newes
Be knowne when 'tis brought forth. A shepherds daughter
And what to her adheres, which followes after,
Is th'argument of Time: of this allow,
If euer you haue spent time worse, ere now:
If neuer, yet that Time himselfe doth say,
He wishes earnestly, you neuer may. *Exit.*

Scena Secunda.

Enter Polixenes, and Camillo.

Pol. I pray thee (good *Camillo*) be no more importunate: 'tis a sicknesse denying thee any thing: a death to grant this.

Cam. It is fifteene yeeres since I saw my Countrey: though I haue (for the most part) bin ayred abroad, I desire to lay my bones there. Besides, the penitent King (my Master) hath sent for me, to whose feeling sorrowes I might be some allay, or I oreweene to thinke so) which is another spurre to my departure.

Pol. As thou lou'st me (*Camillo*) wipe not out the rest of thy seruices, by leauing me now: the neede I haue of thee, thine owne goodnesse hath made: better not to haue had thee, then thus to want thee, thou hauing made me Businesses, (which none (without thee) can sufficiently manage) must either stay to execute them thy selfe, or take away with thee the very seruices thou hast done: which if I haue not enough considered (as too much I cannot) to bee more thankefull to thee, shall bee my studie, and my profite therein, the heaping friendshippes. Of that fatall Countrey Sicillia, prethee speake no more, whose very naming, punnishes me with the remembrance of that penitent (as thou calst him) and reconciled King my brother, whose losse of his most precious Queene & Children, are euen now to be a-fresh lamented. Say to me, when saw'st thou the Prince *Florizell* my son? Kings are no lesse vnhappy, their issue, not being gracious, then they are in loosing them, when they haue approued their Vertues.

Cam. Sir, it is three dayes since I saw the Prince: what his happier affayres may be, are to me vnknowne : but I haue (missingly) noted, he is of late much retyred from Court, and is lesse frequent to his Princely exercises then formerly he hath appeared.

Pol. I haue considered so much (*Camillo*) and with some care, so farre, that I haue eyes vnder my seruice, which looke vpon his remouednesse: from whom I haue this Intelligence, that he is seldome from the house of a most homely shepheard: a man (they say) that from very nothing, and beyond the imagination of his neighbors, is growne into an vnspeakable estate.

Cam. I haue heard (sir) of such a man, who hath a daughter of most rare note: the report of her is extended more, then can be thought to begin from such a cottage

Pol. That's likewise part of my Intelligence : but (I feare) the Angle that pluckes our sonne thither. Thou shalt accompany vs to the place, where we will (not appearing what we are) haue some question with the shepheard; from whose simplicity, I thinke it not vneasie to get the cause of my sonnes resort thether. 'Prethe be my present partner in this busines, and lay aside the thoughts of Sicillia.

Cam. I willingly obey your command.

Pol. My best *Camillo*, we must disguise our selues. *Exit*

Scena Tertia.

Enter Autolicus singing.

When Daffadils begin to peere,
With heigh the Doxy ouer the dale,
Why then comes in the sweet o' the yeere,
For the red blood raigns in y winters pale.

The white sheete bleaching on the hedge,
With hey the sweet birds, O how they sing:
Doth set my pugging tooth an edge,
For a quart of Ale is a dish for a King.

The Larke, that tirra-Lyra chaunts,
With heigh, the Thrush and the Iay:
Are Summer songs for me and my Aunts
While we lye tumbling in the hay.

I haue seru'd Prince *Florizell*, and in my time wore three pile, but now I am out of seruice.

But shall I go mourne for that (my deere)
the pale Moone shines by night:
And when I wander here, and there
I then do most go right.

If Tinkers may haue leaue to liue,
and beare the Sow-skin Bowget,
Then my account I well may giue,
and in the Stockes auouch-it.

My Trafficke is sheetes: when the Kite builds, looke to lesser Linnen. My Father nam'd me *Autolicus*, who being (as I am) lytter'd vnder *Mercurie*, was likewise a snapper-vp of vnconsidered trifles: With Dye and drab, I purchas'd this Caparison, and my Reuennew is the silly Cheate. Gallowes, and Knocke, are too powerfull on the Highway: Beating and hanging are terrors to mee: For the life to come, I sleepe out the thought of it. A prize, a prize.

Enter Clowne.

Clo. Let me see, euery Leauen-weather toddes, euery tod yeeldes pound and odde shilling: fifteene hundred shorne, what comes the wooll too?

Aut. If the sprindge hold, the Cocke's mine.

Clo. I cannot do't without Compters. Let mee see, what am I to buy for our Sheepe-shearing-Feast? Three pound of Sugar, fiue pound of Currence, Rice: What will this sister of mine do with Rice? But my father hath made her Mistris of the Feast, and she layes it on. Shee hath made me four and twenty Nose-gayes for the shearers (three-man song-men, all, and very good ones) but they are most of them Meanes and Bases; but one Puritan amongst them, and he sings Psalmes to horne-pipes. I must haue Saffron to colour the Warden Pies, Mace: Dates, none: that's out of my note: Nutmegges, seuen; a Race or two of Ginger, but that I may begge: Foure pound of Prewyns, and as many of Reysons o'th Sun.

Aut. Oh, that euer I was borne.

Clo. I'th'name of me.

Aut. Oh helpe me, helpe mee: plucke but off these ragges: and then, death, death.

Clo. Alacke poore soule, thou hast need of more rags to lay on thee, rather then haue these off.

Aut. Oh sir, the loathsomnesse of them offend mee, more then the stripes I haue receiued, which are mightie ones and millions.

Clo. Alas poore man, a million of beating may come to a great matter.

Aut. I am rob'd sir, and beaten: my money, and apparrell tane from me, and these detestable things put vpon me.

Clo. What, by a horse-man, or a foot-man?

Aut. A footman (sweet sir) a footman.

Clo. Indeed, he should be a footman, by the garments he has left with thee: If this bee a horsemans Coate, it hath seene very hot seruice. Lend me thy hand, Ile helpe thee. Come, lend me thy hand.

Aut. Oh good sir, tenderly, oh.

Clo. Alas poore soule.

Aut. Oh good sir, softly, good sir: I feare (sir) my shoulder-blade is out.

Clo. How now? Canst stand?

Aut. Softly, deere sir: good sir, softly: you ha done me a charitable office.

Clo. Doest lacke any mony? I haue a little mony for thee.

Aut. No, good sweet sir: no, I beseech you sir: I haue a Kinsman not past three quarters of a mile hence, vnto whome I was going: I shall there haue money, or anie thing I want: Offer me no money I pray you, that killes my heart.

Clow. What manner of Fellow was hee that robb'd you?

Aut. A fellow (sir) that I haue knowne to goe about with Troll-my-dames: I knew him once a seruant of the Prince: I cannot tell good sir, for which of his Vertues it was, but hee was certainely Whipt out of the Court.

Clo.

Clo. His vices you would say: there's no vertue whipt out of the Court: they cherish it to make it stay there; and yet it will no more but abide.

Aut. Vices I would say (Sir.) I know this man well, he hath bene since an Ape-bearer, then a Processe-seruer (a Bayliffe) then hee compast a Motion of the Prodigall sonne, and married a Tinkers wife, within a Mile where my Land and Liuing lyes; and (hauing flowne ouer many knauish professions) he setled onely in Rogue: some call him *Autolicus.*

Clo. Out vpon him: Prig, for my life Prig: he haunts Wakes, Faires, and Beare-baitings.

Aut. Very true sir: he sir hee: that's the Rogue that put me into this apparrell.

Clo. Not a more cowardly Rogue in all *Bohemia*; If you had but look'd bigge, and spit at him, hee'ld haue runne.

Aut. I must confesse to you (sir) I am no fighter: I am false of heart that way, & that he knew I warrant him.

Clo. How do you now?

Aut. Sweet sir, much better then I was: I can stand, and walke: I will euen take my leaue of you, & pace softly towards my Kinsmans.

Clo. Shall I bring thee on the way?

Aut. No, good fac'd sir, no sweet sir.

Clo. Then fartheewell, I must go buy Spices for our sheepe-shearing. *Exit.*

Aut. Prosper you sweet sir. Your purse is not hot enough to purchase your Spice: Ile be with you at your sheepe-shearing too: If I make not this Cheat bring out another, and the sheerers proue sheepe, let me be vnrold, and my name put in the booke of Vertue.

Song. *Iog-on, Iog-on, the foot-path way,*
And merrily hent the Stile-a:
A merry heart goes all the day,
Your sad tyres in a Mile-a. *Exit.*

Scena Quarta.

Enter Florizell, Perdita, Shepherd, Clowne, Polixenes, Camillo, Mopsa, Dorcas, Seruants, Autolicus.

Flo. These your vnusuall weeds, to each part of you
Do's giue a life: no Shepherdesse, but *Flora*
Peering in Aprils front. This your sheepe-shearing,
Is as a meeting of the petty Gods,
And you the Queene on't.

Perd. Sir: my gracious Lord,
To chide at your extreames, it not becomes me:
(Oh pardon, that I name them:) your high selfe
The gracious marke o'th'Land, you haue obscur'd
With a Swaines wearing: and me (poore lowly Maide)
Most Goddesse-like prank'd vp: But that our Feasts
In euery Messe, haue folly; and the Feeders
Digest with a Custome, I should blush
To see you so attyr'd: sworne I thinke,
To shew my selfe a glasse.

Flo. I blesse the time,
When my good Falcon, made her flight a-crosse
Thy Fathers ground.

Perd. Now Ioue affoord you cause:
To me the difference forges dread (your Greatnesse
Hath not beene vs'd to feare:) euen now I tremble
To thinke your Father, by some accident
Should passe this way, as you did: Oh the Fates,
How would he looke, to see his worke, so noble,
Vildely bound vp? What would he say? Or how
Should I (in these my borrowed Flaunts) behold
The sternnesse of his presence?

Flo. Apprehend
Nothing but iollity: the Goddes themselues
(Humbling their Deities to loue) haue taken
The shapes of Beasts vpon them. Iupiter,
Became a Bull, and bellow'd: the greene Neptune
A Ram, and bleated: and the Fire-roab'd-God
Golden Apollo, a poore humble Swaine,
As I seeme now. Their transformations,
Were neuer for a peece of beauty, rarer,
Nor in a way so chaste: since my desires
Run not before mine honor: nor my Lusts
Burne hotter then my Faith.

Perd. O but Sir,
Your resolution cannot hold, when 'tis
Oppos'd (as it must be) by th'powre of the King:
One of these two must be necessities,
Which then will speake, that you must change this purpose,
Or I my life.

Flo. Thou deer'st *Perdita,*
With these forc'd thoughts, I prethee darken not
The Mirth o'th'Feast: Or Ile be thine (my Faire)
Or not my Fathers. For I cannot be
Mine owne, nor any thing to any, if
I be not thine. To this I am most constant,
Though destiny say no. Be merry (Gentle)
Strangle such thoughts as these, with any thing
That you behold the while. Your guests are comming:
Lift vp your countenance, as it were the day
Of celebration of that nuptiall, which
We two haue sworne shall come.

Perd. O Lady Fortune,
Stand you auspicious.

Flo. See, your Guests approach,
Addresse your selfe to entertaine them sprightly,
And let's be red with mirth.

Shep. Fy (daughter) when my old wife liu'd: vpon
This day, she was both Pantler, Butler, Cooke,
Both Dame and Seruant: Welcom'd all: seru'd all,
Would sing her song, and dance her turne: now heere
At vpper end o'th'Table; now, i'th'middle:
On his shoulder, and his: her face o'fire
With labour, and the thing she tooke to quench it
She would to each one sip. You are retyred,
As if you were a feasted one: and not
The Hostesse of the meeting: Pray you bid
These vnknowne friends to's welcome, for it is
A way to make vs better Friends, more knowne.
Come, quench your blushes, and present your selfe
That which you are, Mistris o'th'Feast. Come on,
And bid vs welcome to your sheepe-shearing,
As your good flocke shall prosper.

Perd. Sir, welcome:
It is my Fathers will, I should take on mee
The Hostesseship o'th'day: you're welcome sir.
Giue me those Flowres there (*Dorcas.*) Reuerend Sirs,
For you, there's Rosemary, and Rue, these keepe
Seeming, and sauour all the Winter long:
Grace, and Remembrance be to you both,
And welcome to our Shearing.

Pol.

Pol. Shepherdesse,
(A faire one are you:) well you fit our ages
With flowres of Winter.

Perd. Sir, the yeare growing ancient,
Not yet on summers death, nor on the birth
Of trembling winter, the fayrest flowres o'th season
Are our Carnations, and streak'd Gilly-vors,
(Which some call Natures bastards) of that kind
Our rusticke Gardens barren, and I care not
To get slips of them.

Pol. Wherefore (gentle Maiden)
Do you neglect them.

Perd. For I haue heard it said,
There is an Art, which in their pidenesse shares
With great creating-Nature.

Pol. Say there be:
Yet Nature is made better by no meane,
But Nature makes that Meane: so ouer that Art,
(Which you say addes to Nature) is an Art.
That Nature makes: you see (sweet Maid) we marry
A gentler Sien, to the wildest Stocke,
And make conceyue a barke of baser kinde
By bud of Nobler race. This is an Art
Which do's mend Nature: change it rather, but
The Art it selfe, is Nature.

Perd. So it is.

Pol. Then make you Garden rich in Gilly'vors,
And do not call them bastards.

Perd. Ile not put
The Dible in earth, to set one slip of them:
No more then were I painted, I would wish
This youth should say 'twer well: and onely therefore
Desire to breed by me. Here's flowres for you:
Hot Lauender, Mints, Sauory, Mariorum,
The Mary-gold, that goes to bed with Sun,
And with him rises, weeping: These are flowres
Of middle summer, and I thinke they are giuen
To men of middle age. Y'are very welcome.

Cam. I should leaue grasing, were I of your flocke,
And onely liue by gazing.

Perd. Out alas:
You'ld be so leane, that blasts of Ianuary
Would blow you through and through. Now (my fairst Friend,
I would I had some Flowres o'th Spring, that might
Become your time of day: and yours, and yours,
That weare vpon your Virgin-branches yet
Your Maiden-heads growing: O *Proserpina*,
For the Flowres now, that (frighted) thou let'st fall
From *Dysses* Waggon: Daffadils,
That come before the Swallow dares, and take
The windes of March with beauty: Violets (dim,
But sweeter then the lids of *Iuno's* eyes,
Or *Cytherea's* breath) pale Prime-roses,
That dye vnmarried, ere they can behold
Bright Phœbus in his strength (a Maladie
Most incident to Maids:) bold Oxlips, and
The Crowne Imperiall: Lillies of all kinds,
(The Flowre-de-Luce being one.) O, these I lacke,
To make you Garlands of) and my sweet friend,
To strew him o're, and ore.

Flo. What? like a Coarse?

Perd. No, like a banke, for Loue to lye, and play on:
Not like a Coarse: or if: not to be buried,
But quicke, and in mine armes. Come, take your flours,
Me thinkes I play as I haue seene them do
In Whitson-Pastorals: Sure this Robe of mine
Do's change my disposition:

Flo. What you do,
Still betters what is done. When you speake (Sweet)
I'ld haue you do it euer: When you sing,
I'ld haue you buy, and sell so: so giue Almes,
Pray so: and for the ord'ring your Affayres,
To sing them too. When you do dance, I wish you
A waue o'th Sea, that you might euer do
Nothing but that: moue still, still so:
And owne no other Function. Each your doing,
(So singular, in each particular)
Crownes what you are doing, in the present deeds,
That all your Actes, are Queenes.

Perd. O *Doricles*,
Your praises are too large: but that your youth
And the true blood which peepes fairely through't,
Do plainly giue you out an vnstain'd Sphepherd
With wisedome, I might feare (my *Doricles*)
You woo'd me the false way.

Flo. I thinke you haue
As little skill to feare, as I haue purpose
To put you to't. But come, our dance I pray,
Your hand (my *Perdita*:) so Turtles paire
That neuer meane to part.

Perd. Ile sweare for 'em.

Po'. This is the prettiest Low-borne Lasse, that euer
Ran on the greene-sord: Nothing she do's, or seemes
But smackes of something greater then her selfe,
Too Noble for this place.

Cam. He tels her something
That makes her blood looke on't: Good sooth she is
The Queene of Curds and Creame.

Clo. Come on: strike vp.

Dorcas *Mopsa* must be your Mistris: marry Garlick
to mend her kissing with.

Mop. Now in good time.

Clo. Not a word, a word, we stand vpon our manners,
Come, strike vp.

Heere a Daunce of Shepheards and Shephearddesses.

Pol. Pray good Shepheard, what faire Swaine is this,
Which dances with your daughter?

Shep. They call him *Doricles*, and boasts himselfe
To haue a worthy Feeding; but I haue it
Vpon his owne report, and I beleeue it:
He lookes like sooth: he sayes he loues my daughter,
I thinke so too; for neuer gaz'd the Moone
Vpon the water, as hee'l stand and reade
As 'twere my daughters eyes: and to be plaine,
I thinke there is not halfe a kisse to choose
Who loues another best.

Pol. She dances featly.

Shep. So she do's any thing, though I report it
That should be silent: If yong *Doricles*
Do light vpon her, she shall bring him that
Which he not dreames of. *Enter Seruant.*

Ser. O Master: if you did but heare the Pedler at the
doore, you would neuer dance againe after a Tabor and
Pipe: no, the Bag-pipe could not moue you: hee singes
seuerall Tunes, faster then you'l tell money: hee vtters
them as he had eaten ballads, and all mens eares grew to
his Tunes.

Clo. He could neuer come better: hee shall come in:
I loue a ballad but euen too well, if it be dolefull matter
merrily set downe: or a very pleasant thing indeede, and
sung lamentably.

Ser.

Ser. He hath songs for man, or woman, of all sizes: No Milliner can so fit his customers with Gloues: he has the prettiest Loue-songs for Maids, so without bawdrie (which is strange,) with such delicate burthens of Dildo's and Fadings: Iump-her, and thump-her; and where some stretch-mouth'd Rascall, would (as it were) meane mischeefe, and breake a sowle gap into the Matter, hee makes the maid to answere, *Whoop, doe me no harme good man:* put's him off, slights him, with *Whoop, doe mee no harme good man.*

Pol. This is a braue fellow.

Clo. Beleeee mee, thou talkest of an admirable conceited fellow, has he any vnbraided Wares?

Ser. Hee hath Ribbons of all the colours i'th Raine-bow; Points, more then all the Lawyers in *Bohemia*, can learnedly handle, though they come to him by th'grosse: Inckles, Caddysses, Cambrickes, Lawnes: (why he sings em ouer, as they were Gods, or Goddesses: you would thinke a Smocke were a shee-Angell, he so chauntes to the sleeue-hand, and the worke about the square on't.

Clo. Pre'thee bring him in, and let him approach singing.

Perd. Forewarne him, that he vse no scurrilous words in's tunes.

Clow. You haue of these Pedlers, that haue more in them, then you'l'd thinke (Sister.)

Perd. I, good brother, or go about to thinke.

Enter *Autolicus* singing.
Lawne as white as driuen Snow,
Cypresse blacke as ere was Crow,
Gloues as sweete as Damaske Roses,
Maskes for faces, and for noses:
Bugle-bracelet, Necke-lace Amber,
Perfume for a Ladies Chamber:
Golden Quoifes, and Stomachers
For my Lads, to giue their deers:
Pins, and poaking-stickes of steele.
What Maids lacke from head to heele:
   Come buy of me, come: come buy, come buy,
   Buy Lads, or else your Lasses cry: Come buy.

Clo. If I were not in loue with *Mopsa*, thou shouldst take no money of me, but being enthrall'd as I am, it will also be the bondage of certaine Ribbons and Gloues.

Mop. I was promis'd them against the Feast, but they come not too late now.

Dor. He hath promis'd you more then that, or there be lyars.

Mop. He hath paid you all he promis'd you: May be he has paid you more, which will shame you to giue him againe.

Clo. Is there no manners left among maids? Will they weare their plackets, where they should bear their faces? Is there not milking-time? When you are going to bed? Or kill-hole? To whistle of these secrets, but you must be tittle-tatling before all our guests? 'Tis well they are whispring: clamor your tongues, and not a word more.

Mop. I haue done; Come you promis'd me a tawdry-lace, and a paire of sweet Gloues.

Clo. Haue I not told thee how I was cozen'd by the way, and lost all my money.

Aut. And indeed Sir, there are Cozeners abroad, therefore it behooues men to be wary.

Clo. Feare not thou man, thou shalt lose nothing here.

Aut. I hope so sir, for I haue about me many parcels of charge.

Clo. What hast heere? Ballads?

Mop. Pray now buy some: I loue a ballet in print, a life, for then we are sure they are true.

Aut. Here's one, to a very dolefull tune, how a Vsurers wife was brought to bed of twenty money baggs at a burthen, and how she long'd to eate Adders heads, and Toads carbonado'd.

Mop. Is it true, thinke you?

Aut. Very true, and but a moneth old.

Dor. Blesse me from marrying a Vsurer.

Aut. Here's the Midwiues name to't: one Mist. *Tale-Porter,* and fiue or six honest Wiues, that were present. Why should I carry lyes abroad?

Mop. 'Pray you now buy it.

Clo. Come-on, lay it by: and let's first see moe Ballads: Wee'l buy the other things anon.

Aut. Here's another ballad of a Fish, that appeared vpon the coast, on wensday the fourescore of April, fortie thousand fadom aboue water, & sung this ballad against the hard hearts of maids: it was thought she was a Woman, and was turn'd into a cold fish, for she wold not exchange flesh with one that lou'd her: The Ballad is very pittifull, and as true.

Dor. Is it true too, thinke you.

Autol. Fiue Iustices hands at it, and witnesses more then my packe will hold.

Clo. Lay it by too; another.

Aut. This is a merry ballad, but a very pretty one.

Mop. Let's haue some merry ones.

Aut. Why this is a passing merry one, and goes to the tune of two maids wooing a man: there's scarse a Maide westward but she sings it: 'tis in request, I can tell you.

Mop. We can both sing it: if thou'lt beare a part, thou shalt heare, 'tis in three parts.

Dor. We had the tune on't, a month agoe.

Aut. I can beare my part, you must know 'tis my occupation: Haue at it with you.

Song   *Get you hence, for I must goe.*
Aut.   *Where it fits not you to know.*
Dor.   *Whether?*
Mop   *O whether?*
Dor.   *Whether?*
Mop.   *It becomes thy oath full well,*
       Thou to me thy secrets tell.
Dor.   *Me too: Let me go thether:*
Mop   *Or thou goest to th' Grange, or Mill,*
Dor: *If to either thou dost ill.*
Aut: *Neither.*
Dor: *What neither?*
Aut: *Neither:*
Dor: *Thou hast sworne my Loue to be,*
Mop   *Thou hast sworne it more to mee.*
       Then whether goest? Say whether?

Clo. Wee'l haue this song out anon by our selues: My Father, and the Gent. are in sad talke, & wee'll not trouble them: Come bring away thy pack after me, Wenches Ile buy for you both: Pedler let's haue the first choice; folow me girles.   *Aut:* And you shall pay well for 'em.
Song. *Will you buy any Tape, or Lace for your Cape?*
      My dainty Ducke, my deere-a?
      Any Silke, any Thred, any Toyes for your head
      Of the news't, and fins't, fins't weare-a.
      Come to the Pedler, Money's a medler,
      That doth vtter all mens ware-a.   Exit

Seruant. Mayster, there is three Carters, three Shepherds, three Neat-herds, three Swine-herds y haue made them themselues all men of haire, they cal themselues Saltiers, and they haue a Dance, which the Wenches say is a gally-maufrey of Gambols, because they are not in't : but they themselues are o'th'minde (if it bee not too rough for some, that know little but bowling) it will please plentifully.

Shep. Away : Wee'l none on't; heere has beene too much homely foolery already. I know (Sir) wee wearie you.

Pol. You wearie those that refresh vs : pray let's see these foure-threes of Heardsmen.

Ser. One three of them, by their owne report (Sir,) hath danc'd before the King : and not the worst of the three, but iumpes twelue foote and a halfe by th'squire.

Shep. Leaue your prating, since these good men are pleas'd, let them come in : but quickly now.

Ser. Why, they stay at doore Sir.

Heere a Dance of twelue Satyres.

Pol. O Father, you'l know more of that heereafter:
Is it not too farre gone? 'Tis time to part them,
He's simple, and tels much. How now (faire shepheard)
Your heart is full of something, that do's take
Your minde from feasting. Sooth, when I was yong,
And handed loue, as you do; I was wont
To load my Shee with knackes : I would haue ransackt
The Pedlers silken Treasury, and haue powr'd it
To her acceptance : you haue let him go,
And nothing marted with him. If your Lasse
Interpretation should abuse, and call this
Your lacke of loue, or bounty, you were straited
For a reply at least, if you make a care
Of happie holding her.

Flo. Old Sir, I know
She prizes not such trifles as these are :
The gifts she lookes from me, are packt and lockt
Vp in my heart, which I haue giuen already,
But not deliuer'd. O heare me breath my life
Before this ancient Sir, whom (it should seeme)
Hath sometime lou'd : I take thy hand, this hand,
As soft as Doues-downe, and as white as it,
Or Ethyopians tooth, or the fan'd snow, that's bolted
By th'Northerne blasts, twice ore.

Pol. What followes this?
How prettily th'yong Swaine seemes to wash
The hand, was faire before? I haue put you out,
But to your protestation : Let me heare
What you professe.

Flo. Do, and be witnesse too't.

Pol. And this my neighbour too?

Flo. And he, and more
Then he, and men : the earth, the heauens, and all;
That were I crown'd the most Imperiall Monarch
Thereof most worthy : were I the fayrest youth
That euer made eye swerue, had force and knowledge
More then was euer mans, I would not prize them
Without her Loue; for her, employ them all,
Commend them, and condemne them to her seruice,
Or to their owne perdition.

Pol. Fairely offer'd.

Cam. This shewes a sound affection.

Shep. But my daughter,
Say you the like to him.

Per. I cannot speake
So well, (nothing so well) no, nor meane better
By th'patterne of mine owne thoughts, I cut out
The puritie of his.

Shep. Take hands, a bargaine;
And friends vnknowne, you shall beare witnesse to't:
I giue my daughter to him, and will make
Her Portion, equall his.

Flo. O, that must bee
I'th Vertue of your daughter : One being dead,
I shall haue more then you can dreame of yet,
Enough then for your wonder : but come-on,
Contract vs fore these Witnesses.

Shep. Come, your hand :
And daughter, yours.

Pol. Soft Swaine a-while, beseech you,
Haue you a Father?

Flo. I haue : but what of him?

Pol. Knowes he of this?

Flo. He neither do's, nor shall.

Pol. Me-thinkes a Father,
Is at the Nuptiall of his sonne, a guest
That best becomes the Table : Pray you once more
Is not your Father growne incapeable
Of reasonable affayres? Is he not stupid
With Age, and altring Rheumes? Can he speake? heare?
Know man, from man? Dispute his owne estate?
Lies he not bed-rid? And againe, do's nothing
But what he did, being childish?

Flo. No good Sir :
He has his health, and ampler strength indeede
Then most haue of his age.

Pol. By my white beard,
You offer him (if this be so) a wrong
Something vnfilliall : Reason my sonne
Should choose himselfe a wife, but as good reason
The Father (all whose ioy is nothing else
But faire posterity) should hold some counsaile
In such a businesse.

Flo. I yeeld all this;
But for some other reasons (my graue Sir)
Which 'tis not fit you know, I not acquaint
My Father of this businesse.

Pol. Let him know't.

Flo He shall not.

Pol. Prethee let him.

Flo No, he must not.

Shep. Let him (my sonne) he shall not need to greeue
At knowing of thy choice.

Flo. Come, come, he must not :
Marke our Contract.

Pol. Marke your diuorce (yong sir)
Whom sonne I dare not call : Thou art too base
To be acknowledge. Thou a Scepters heire,
That thus affects a sheepe-hooke? Thou, old Traitor,
I am sorry, that by hanging thee, I can
but shorten thy life one weeke. And thou, fresh peece
Of excellent Witchcraft, whom of force must know
The royall Foole thou coap'st with.

Shep. Oh my heart.

Pol. Ile haue thy beauty scratcht with briers & made
More homely then thy state. For thee (fond boy)
If I may euer know thou dost but sigh,
That thou no more shalt neuer see this knacke (as neuer
I meane thou shalt) wee'l barre thee from succession,
Not hold thee of our blood, no not our Kin,
Farre then *Deucalion* off : (marke thou my words)
Follow vs to the Court. Thou Churle, for this time
(Though full of our displeasure) yet we free thee
From the dead blow of it. And you Enchantment,

Worthy enough a Heardsman: yea him too,
That makes himselfe (but for our Honor therein)
Vnworthy thee. If euer henceforth, thou
These rurall Latches, to his entrance open,
Or hope his body more, with thy embraces,
I will deuise a death, as cruell for thee
As thou art tender to't. *Exit.*

Ferd. Euen heere vndone:
I was not much a-fear'd: for once, or twice
I was about to speake, and tell him plainely,
The selfe-same Sun, that shines vpon his Court,
Hides not his visage from our Cottage, but
Lookes on alike. Wilt please you (Sir) be gone?
I told you what would come of this: Beseech you
Of your owne state take care: This dreame of mine
Being now awake, Ile Queene it no inch farther,
But milke my Ewes, and weepe.

Cam. Why how now Father,
Speake ere thou dyest.

Shep. I cannot speake, nor thinke,
Nor dare to know, that which I know: O Sir,
You haue vndone a man of fourescore three,
That thought to fill his graue in quiet: yea,
To dye vpon the bed my father dy'de,
To lye close by his honest bones; but now
Some Hangman must put on my shrowd, and lay me
Where no Priest shouels-in dust. Oh cursed wretch,
That knew'st this was the Prince, and wouldst aduenture
To mingle faith with him. Vndone, vndone:
If I might dye within this houre, I haue liu'd
To die when I desire. *Exit.*

Flo. Why looke you so vpon me?
I am but sorry, not affear'd: delaid,
But nothing altred: What I was, I am:
More straining on, for plucking backe; not following
My leash vnwillingly.

Cam. Gracious my Lord,
You know my Fathers temper: at this time
He will allow no speech: (which I do ghesse
You do not purpose to him:) and as hardly
Will he endure your sight, as yet I feare;
Then till the fury of his Highnesse settle
Come not before him.

Flo. I not purpose it:
I thinke *Camillo.*

Cam. Euen he, my Lord.

Per. How often haue I told you 'twould be thus?
How often said my dignity would last
But till 'twer knowne?

Flo. It cannot faile, but by
The violation of my faith, and then
Let Nature crush the sides o'th earth together,
And marre the seeds within. Lift vp thy lookes:
From my succession wipe me (Father) I
Am heyre to my affection.

Cam. Be aduis'd.

Flo. I am: and by my fancie, if my Reason
Will thereto be obedient: I haue reason:
If not, my sences better pleas'd with madnesse,
Do bid it welcome.

Cam. This is desperate (sir.)

Flo. So call it: but it do's fulfill my vow:
I needs must thinke it honesty. *Camillo,*
Not for *Bohemia,* nor the pompe that may
Be thereat gleaned: for all the Sun sees, or
The close earth wombes, or the profound seas, hides
In vnknowne fadomes, will I breake my oath
To this my faire belou'd: Therefore, I pray you,
As you haue euer bin my Fathers honour'd friend,
When he shall misse me, as (in faith I meane not
To see him any more) cast your good counsailes
Vpon his passion: Let my selfe, and Fortune
Tug for the time to come. This you may know,
And so deliuer, I am put to Sea
With her, who heere I cannot hold on shore:
And most opportune to her neede, I haue
A Vessell rides fast by, but not prepar'd
For this designe. What course I meane to hold
Shall nothing benefit your knowledge, nor
Concerne me the reporting.

Cam. O my Lord,
I would your spirit were easier for aduice,
Or stronger for your neede.

Flo. Hearke *Perdita,*
Ile heare you by and by.

Cam. Hee's irremoueable,
Resolu'd for flight: Now were I happy if
His going, I could frame to serue my turne,
Saue him from danger, do him loue and honor,
Purchase the sight againe of deere *Sicillia,*
And that vnhappy King, my Master, whom
I so much thirst to see.

Flo. Now good *Camillo,*
I am so fraught with curious businesse, that
I leaue out ceremony.

Cam. Sir, I thinke
You haue heard of my poore seruices, i'th loue
That I haue borne your Father?

Flo. Very nobly
Haue you deseru'd: It is my Fathers Musicke
To speake your deeds: not little of his care
To haue them recompenc'd, as thought on.

Cam. Well (my Lord)
If you may please to thinke I loue the King,
And through him, what's neerest to him, which is
Your gracious selfe; embrace but my direction,
If your more ponderous and setled proiect
May suffer alteration. On mine honor,
Ile point you where you shall haue such receiuing
As shall become your Highnesse, where you may
Enioy your Mistris; from the whom, I see
There's no disiunction to be made, but by
(As heauens forefend) your ruine: Marry her,
And with my best endeuours, in your absence,
Your discontenting Father, striue to qualifie
And bring him vp to liking.

Flo. How *Camillo*
May this (almost a miracle) be done?
That I may call thee something more then man,
And after that trust to thee.

Cam. Haue you thought on
A place whereto you'l go?

Flo. Not any yet:
But as th'vnthought-on accident is guiltie
To what we wildely do, so we professe
Our selues to be the slaues of chance, and flyes
Of euery winde that blowes.

Cam. Then list to me:
This followes, if you will not change your purpose
But vndergo this flight; make for *Sicillia,*
And there present your selfe, and your fayre Princesse,
(For so I see she must be) 'fore *Leontes*;

She shall be habited, as it becomes
The partner of your Bed. Me thinkes I see
Leontes opening his free Armes, and weeping
His Welcomes forth: asks thee there Sonne forgiuenesse,
As 'twere i'th' Fathers person: kisses the hands
Of your fresh Princesse; ore and ore diuides him,
'Twixt his vnkindnesse, and his Kindnesse: th'one
He chides to Hell, and bids the other grow
Faster then Thought, or Time.

Flo. Worthy *Camillo*,
What colour for my Visitation, shall I
Hold vp before him?

Cam. Sent by the King your Father
To greet him, and to giue him comforts. Sir,
The manner of your bearing towards him, with
What you (as from your Father) shall deliuer,
Things knowne betwixt vs three, Ile write you downe,
The which shall point you forth at euery sitting
What you must say: that he shall not perceiue,
But that you haue your Fathers Bosome there,
And speake his very Heart.

Flo. I am bound to you:
There is some sappe in this.

Cam. A Course more promising,
Then a wild dedication of your selues
To vnpath'd Waters, vndream'd Shores; most certaine,
To Miseries enough: no hope to helpe you,
But as you shake off one, to take another:
Nothing so certaine, as your Anchors, who
Doe their best office, if they can but stay you,
Where you'le be loth to be: besides you know,
Prosperitie's the very bond of Loue,
Whose fresh complexion, and whose heart together,
Affliction alters.

Perd. One of these is true:
I thinke Affliction may subdue the Cheeke,
But not take-in the Mind.

Cam. Yea? say you so?
There shall not, at your Fathers House, these seuen yeeres
Be borne another such.

Flo. My good *Camillo*,
She's as forward, of her Breeding, as
She is i'th' reare 'our Birth.

Cam. I cannot say, 'tis pitty
She lacks Instructions, for she seemes a Mistresse
To most that teach.

Perd. Your pardon Sir, for this,
Ile blush you Thanks.

Flo. My prettiest *Perdita*.
But O, the Thornes we stand vpon: (*Camillo*)
Preseruer of my Father, now of me,
The Medicine of our House: how shall we doe?
We are not furnish'd like *Bohemia's* Sonne,
Nor shall appeare in *Sicilia*.

Cam. My Lord,
Feare none of this: I thinke you know my fortunes
Doe all lye there: it shall be so my care,
To haue you royally appointed, as if
The Scene you play, were mine. For instance Sir,
That you may know you shall not want: one word.

Enter Autolicus.

Aut. Ha, ha, what a Foole Honestie is? and Trust (his
sworne brother) a very simple Gentleman. I haue sold
all my Tromperie: not a counterfeit Stone, not a Ribbon,
Glasse, Pomander, Browch, Table-booke, Ballad, Knife,
Tape, Gloue, Shooe-tye, Bracelet, Horne-Ring, to keepe
my Pack from fasting: they throng who should buy first,
as if my Trinkets had beene hallowed, and brought a benediction to the buyer: by which meanes, I saw whose
Purse was best in Picture; and what I saw, to my good
vse, I remembred. My Clowne (who wants but something to be a reasonable man) grew so in loue with the
Wenches Song, that hee would not stirre his Petty-toes,
till he had both Tune and Words, which so drew the rest
of the Heard to me, that all their other Sences stucke in
Eares: you might haue pinch'd a Placket, it was sencelesse; 'twas nothing to gueld a Cod-peece of a Purse: I
would haue fill'd Keyes of that hung in Chaynes: no
hearing, no feeling, but my Sirs Song, and admiring the
Nothing of it. So that in this time of Lethargie, I pickd
and cut most of their Festiuall Purses: And had not the
old-man come in with a Whoo-bub against his Daughter, and the Kings Sonne, and scar'd my Chowghes from
the Chaffe, I had not left a Purse aliue in the whole
Army.

Cam. Nay, but my Letters by this meanes being there
So soone as you arriue, shall cleare that doubt.

Flo. And those that you'le procure from King *Leontes*

Cam. Shall satisfie your Father.

Perd. Happy be you:
All that you speake, shewes faire.

Cam. Who haue we here?
Wee'le make an Instrument of this: omit
Nothing may giue vs aide.

Aut. If they haue ouer-heard me now: why hanging.

Cam. How now (good Fellow)
Why shak'st thou so? Feare not (man)
Here's no harme intended to thee.

Aut. I am a poore Fellow, Sir.

Cam. Why, be so still: here's no body will steale that
from thee: yet for the out-side of thy pouertie, we must
make an exchange; therefore dis-case thee instantly (thou
must thinke there's a necessitie in't) and change Garments
with this Gentleman: Though the penny-worth (on his
side) be the worst, yet hold thee, there's some boot.

Aut. I am a poore Fellow, Sir: (I know ye well
enough.)

Cam. Nay prethee dispatch: the Gentleman is halfe
fled already.

Aut. Are you in earnest, Sir? (I smell the trick on't.)

Flo. Dispatch, I prethee.

Aut. Indeed I haue had Earnest, but I cannot with
conscience take it.

Cam. Vnbuckle, vnbuckle.
Fortunate Mistresse (let my prophecie
Come home to ye:) you must retire your selfe
Into some Couert; take your sweet-hearts Hat
And pluck it ore your Browes, muffle your face,
Dis-mantle you, and (as you can) dissliken
The truth of your owne seeming, that you may
(For I doe feare eyes ouer) to Ship-boord
Get vndescry'd.

Perd. I see the Play so lyes,
That I must beare a part.

Cam. No remedie:
Haue you done there?

Flo. Should I now meet my Father,
He would not call me Sonne.

Cam. Nay, you shall haue no Hat:
Come Lady, come: Farewell (my friend.)

Aut. Adieu, Sir.

Flo. O *Perdita*: what haue we twaine forgot?

Pray

Pray you a word.
Cam. What I doe next, shall be to tell the King
Of this escape, and whither they are bound;
Wherein, my hope is, I shall so preuaile,
To force him after: in whose company
I shall re-view *Sicilia*; for whose sight,
I haue a Womans Longing.

Flo. Fortune speed vs:
Thus we set on (*Camillo*) to th' Sea-side.

Cam. The swifter speed, the better. *Exit.*

Aut. I vnderstand the businesse, I heare it: to haue an open eare, a quick eye, and a nimble hand, is necessary for a Cut-purse; a good Nose is requisite also, to smell out worke for th'other Sences. I see this is the time that the vniust man doth thriue. What an exchange had this been, without boot? What a boot is here, with this exchange? Sure the Gods doe this yeere conniue at vs, and we may doe any thing extempore. The Prince himselfe is about a peece of Iniquitie (stealing away from his Father, with his Clog at his heeles:) if I thought it were a peece of honestie to acquaint the King withall, I would not do't: I hold it the more knauerie to conceale it; and therein am I constant to my Profession.

Enter Clowne and Shepheard.

Aside, aside, here is more matter for a hot braine: Euery Lanes end, euery Shop, Church, Session, Hanging, yeelds a carefull man worke.

Clowne. See, see: what a man you are now? there is no other way, but to tell the King she's a Changeling, and none of your flesh and blood.

Shep. Nay, but heare me.

Clow. Nay; but heare me.

Shep. Goe too then.

Clow. She being none of your flesh and blood, your flesh and blood ha's not offended the King, and so your flesh and blood is not to be punish'd by him. Shew those things you found about her (those secret things, all but what she ha's with her:) This being done, let the Law goe whistle: I warrant you.

Shep. I will tell the King all, euery word, yea, and his Sonnes prancks too; who, I may say, is no honest man, neither to his Father, nor to me, to goe about to make me the Kings Brother in Law.

Clow. Indeed Brother in Law was the farthest off you could haue beene to him, and then your Blood had beene the dearer, by I know how much an ounce.

Aut. Very wisely (Puppies.)

Shep. Well: let vs to the King: there is that in this Farthell, will make him scratch his Beard.

Aut. I know not what impediment this Complaint may be to the flight of my Master.

Clo. 'Pray heartily he be at' Pallace.

Aut. Though I am not naturally honest, I am so sometimes by chance: Let me pocket vp my Pedlers excrement. How now (Rustiques) whither are you bound?

Shep. To th' Pallace (and it like your Worship.)

Aut. Your Affaires there? what? with whom? the Condition of that Farthell? the place of your dwelling? your names? your ages? of what hauing? breeding, and any thing that is fitting to be knowne, discouer?

Clo. We are but plaine fellowes, Sir.

Aut. A Lye; you are rough, and hayrie: Let me haue no lying; it becomes none but Tradef-men, and they often giue vs (Souldiers) the Lye, but wee pay them for it with stamped Coyne, not stabbing Steele, therefore they doe not giue vs the Lye.

Clo. Your Worship had like to haue giuen vs one, if you had not taken your selfe with the manner.

Shep. Are you a Courtier, and 't like you Sir?

Aut. Whether it lke me, or no, I am a Courtier. Seest thou not the ayre of the Court, in these enfoldings? Hath not my gate in it, the measure of the Court? Receiues not thy Nose Court-Odour from me? Reflect I not on thy Basenesse, Court-Contempt? Think'st thou, for that I insinuate, at toaze from thee thy Businesse, I am therefore no Courtier? I am Courtier *Cap-a-pe*; and one that will eyther push-on, or pluck-back, thy Businesse there: whereupon I command thee to open thy Affaire.

Shep. My Businesse, Sir, is to the King.

Aut. What Aduocate ha'st thou to him?

Shep. I know not (and't like you.)

Clo. Aduocate's the Court-word for a Pheazant: say you haue none.

Shep. None, Sir: I haue no Pheazant Cock, nor Hen.

Aut. How blessed are we, that are not simple men?
Yet Nature might haue made me as these are,
Therefore I will not disdaine.

Clo. This cannot be but a great Courtier.

Shep. His Garments are rich, but he weares them not handsomely.

Clo. He seemes to be the more Noble, in being fantasticall: A great man, Ile warrant; I know by the picking on's Teeth.

Aut. The Farthell there? What's i'th' Farthell? Wherefore that Box?

Shep. Sir, there lyes such Secrets in this Farthell and Box, which none must know but the King, and which hee shall know within this houre, if I may come to th' speech of him.

Aut. Age, thou hast lost thy labour.

Shep. Why Sir?

Aut. The King is not at the Pallace, he is gone aboord a new Ship, to purge Melancholy, and ayre himselfe: for if thou bee'st capable of things serious, thou must know the King is full of griefe.

Shep. So 'tis said (Sir:) about his Sonne, that should haue marryed a Shepheards Daughter.

Aut. If that Shepheard be not in hand-fast, let him flye; the Curses he shall haue, the Tortures he shall feele, will breake the back of Man, the heart of Monster.

Clo. Thinke you so, Sir?

Aut. Not hee alone shall suffer what Wit can make heauie, and Vengeance bitter; but those that are Iermaine to him (though remou'd fiftie times) shall all come vnder the Hang-man: which, though it be great pitty, yet it is necessarie. An old Sheepe-whistling Rogue, a Ram-tender, to offer to haue his Daughter come into grace? Some say hee shall be ston'd: but that death is too soft for him (say I:) Draw our Throne into a Sheep-Coat? all deaths are too few, the sharpest too easie.

Clo. Ha's the old-man ere a Sonne Sir (doe you heare) and 't like you, Sir?

Aut. Hee ha's a Sonne: who shall be flayd aliue, then 'noynted ouer with Honey, set on the head of a Waspes Nest, then stand till he be three quarters and a dram dead; then recouer'd againe with Aquavite, or some other hot Infusion: then, raw as he is (and in the hotest day Prognostication proclaymes) shall he be set against a Brick-wall, (the Sunne looking with a South-ward eye vpon him; where hee is to behold him, with Flyes blown to death.) But what talke we of these Traitorly-Rascals, whose miseries are to be smil'd at, their offences being so capitall?

Tell me (for you seeme to be honest plaine men) what you haue to the King: being something gently consider'd, Ile bring you where he is aboord, tender your persons to his presence, whisper him in your behalfes; and if it be in man, besides the King, to effect your Suites, here is man shall doe it.

Clow. He seemes to be of great authoritie: close with him, giue him Gold; and though Authoritie be a stubborne Beare, yet hee is oft led by the Nose with Gold: shew the in-side of your Purse to the out-side of his hand, and no more adoe. Remember ston'd, and flay'd aliue.

Shep. And't please you (Sir) to vndertake the Businesse for vs, here is that Gold I haue: Ile make it as much more, and leaue this young man in pawne, till I bring it you.

Aut. After I haue done what I promised?

Shep. I Sir.

Aut. Well, giue me the Moitie: Are you a partie in this Businesse?

Clow. In some sort, Sir: but though my case be a pittifull one, I hope I shall not be flayd out of it.

Aut. Oh, that's the case of the Shepheards Sonne: hang him, hee'le be made an example.

Clow. Comfort, good comfort: We must to the King, and shew our strange sights: he must know 'tis none of your Daughter, nor my Sister: wee are gone else. Sir, I will giue you as much as this old man do's, when the Businesse is performed, and remaine (as he sayes) your pawne till it be brought you.

Aut. I will trust you. Walke before toward the Sea-side, goe on the right hand, I will but looke vpon the Hedge, and follow you.

Clow. We are bless'd, in this man: as I may say, euen bless'd.

Shep. Let's before, as he bids vs: he was prouided to doe vs good.

Aut. If I had a mind to be honest, I see *Fortune* would not suffer mee: shee drops Booties in my mouth. I am courted now with a double occasion: (Gold, and a means to doe the Prince my Master good; which, who knowes how that may turne backe to my aduancement?) I will bring these two Moales, these blind-ones, aboord him. if he thinke it fit to shoare them againe, and that the Complaint they haue to the King, concernes him nothing, let him call me Rogue, for being so farre officious, for I am proofe against that Title, and what shame else belongs to't: To him will I present them, there may be matter in it. *Exeunt.*

Actus Quintus. Scena Prima.

Enter Leontes, Cleomines, Dion, Paulina, Seruants: Florizel, Perdita.

Cleo. Sir, you haue done enough, and haue perform'd A Saint-like Sorrow: No fault could you make, Which you haue not redeem'd; indeed pay'd downe More penitence, then done trespas: At the last Doe, as the Heauens haue done; forget your euill, With them, forgiue your selfe.

Leo. Whilest I remember Her, and her Vertues, I cannot forget My blemishes in them, and so still thinke of The wrong I did my selfe: which was so much, That Heire-lesse it hath made my Kingdome, and Destroy'd the sweet'st Companion, that ere man Bred his hopes out of, true.

Paul. Too true (my Lord:) If one by one, you wedded all the World, Or from the All that are, tooke something good, To make a perfect Woman; she you kill'd, Would be vnparallell'd.

Leo. I thinke so. Kill'd? She I kill'd? I did so: but thou strik'st me Sorely, to say I did: it is as bitter Vpon thy Tongue, as in my Thought. Now, good now, Say so but seldome.

Cleo. Not at all, good Lady: You might haue spoken a thousand things, that would Haue done the time more benefit, and grac'd Your kindnesse better.

Paul. You are one of those Would haue him wed againe.

Dio. If you would not so, You pitty not the State, nor the Remembrance Of his most Soueraigne Name: Consider little, What Dangers, by his Highnesse faile of Issue, May drop vpon his Kingdome, and deuoure Incertaine lookers on. What were more holy, Then to reioyce the former Queene is well? What holyer, then for Royalties repayre, For present comfort, and for future good, To blesse the Bed of Maiestie againe With a sweet Fellow to't?

Paul. There is none worthy, (Respecting her that's gone:) besides the Gods Will haue fulfill'd their secret purposes: For ha's not the Diuine *Apollo* said? Is't not the tenor of his Oracle, That King *Leontes* shall not haue an Heire, Till his lost Child be found? Which, that it shall, Is all as monstrous to our humane reason, As my *Antigonus* to breake his Graue, And come againe to me: who, on my life, Did perish with the Infant. 'Tis your councell, My Lord should to the Heauens be contrary, Oppose against their wills. Care not for Issue, The Crowne will find an Heire. Great *Alexander* Left his to th' Worthiest: so his Successor Was like to be the best.

Leo. Good *Paulina,* Who hast the memorie of *Hermione* I know in honor: O, that euer I Had squar'd me to thy councell: then, euen now, I might haue look'd vpon my Queenes full eyes, Haue taken Treasure from her Lippes.

Paul. And left them More rich, for what they yeelded.

Leo. Thou speak'st truth: No more such Wiues, therefore no Wife: one worse, And better vs'd, would make her Sainted Spirit Againe possesse her Corps, and on this Stage (Where we Offendors now appeare) Soule-vext, And begin, why to me?

Paul. Had she such power, She had iust such cause.

Leo. She had, and would incense me To murther her I marryed.

Paul. I should so:
Were I the Ghost that walk'd, Il'd bid you marke
Her eye, and tell me for what dull part in't
You chose her: then Il'd shrieke, that euen your eares
Should rift to heare me, and the words that follow'd,
Should be, Remember mine.

Leo. Starres, Starres,
And all eyes else, dead coales: feare thou no Wife;
Ile haue no Wife, *Paulina*.

Paul. Will you sweare
Neuer to marry, but by my free leaue?

Leo. Neuer (*Paulina*) so be bless'd my Spirit.

Paul. Then good my Lords, beare witnesse to his Oath.

Cleo. You tempt him ouer-much.

Paul. Vnlesse another,
As like *Hermione*, as is her Picture,
Affront his eye.

Cleo. Good Madame, I haue done.

Paul. Yet if my Lord will marry: if you will, Sir;
No remedie but you will: Giue me the Office
To chuse you a Queene: she shall not be so young
As was your former, but she shall be such
As (walk'd your first Queenes Ghost) it should take ioy
To see her in your armes.

Leo. My true *Paulina*,
We shall not marry, till thou bidst vs.

Paul. That
Shall be when your first Queene's againe in breath:
Neuer till then.

Enter a Seruant.

Ser. One that giues out himselfe Prince *Florizell*,
Sonne of *Polixenes*, with his Princesse (she
The fairest I haue yet beheld) desires accesse
To your high presence.

Leo. What with him? he comes not
Like to his Fathers Greatnesse: his approach
(So out of circumstance, and suddaine) tells vs,
Tis not a Visitation fram'd, but forc'd
By need, and accident. What Trayne?

Ser. But few,
And those but meane.

Leo. His Princesse (say you) with him?

Ser. I: the most peerelesse peece of Earth, I thinke,
That ere the Sunne shone bright on.

Paul. Oh *Hermione*,
As euery present Time doth boast it selfe
Aboue a better, gone; so must thy Graue
Giue way to what's seene now. Sir, you your selfe
Haue said, and writ so; but your writing now
Is colder then that Theame: she had not beene,
Nor was not to be equall'd, thus your Verse
Flow'd with her Beautie once; 'tis shrewdly ebb'd,
To say you haue seene a better.

Ser. Pardon, Madame:
The one, I haue almost forgot (your pardon:)
The other, when she ha's obtayn'd your Eye,
Will haue your Tongue too. This is a Creature,
Would she begin a Sect, might quench the zeale
Of all Professors else; make Proselytes
Of who she but bid follow.

Paul. How? not women?

Ser. Women will loue her, that she is a Woman
More worth then any Man: Men, that she is
The rarest of all Women.

Leo. Goe *Cleomines*,
Your selfe (assisted with your honor'd Friends)
Bring them to our embracement. Still 'tis strange,
He thus should steale vpon vs. *Exit.*

Paul. Had our Prince
(Iewell of Children) seene this houre, he had payr'd
Well with this Lord; there was not full a moneth
Betweene their births.

Leo. 'Prethee no more; cease: thou know'st
He dyes to me againe, when talk'd-of: sure
When I shall see this Gentleman, thy speeches
Will bring me to consider that, which may
Vnfurnish me of Reason. They are come.

Enter Florizell, Perdita, Cleomines, and others.

Your Mother was most true to Wedlock, Prince,
For she did print your Royall Father off,
Conceiuing you. Were I but twentie one,
Your Fathers Image is so hit in you,
(His very ayre) that I should call you Brother,
As I did him, and speake of something wildly
By vs perform'd before. Most dearely welcome,
And your faire Princesse (Goddesse) oh: alas,
I lost a couple, that 'twixt Heauen and Earth
Might thus haue stood, begetting wonder, as
You (gracious Couple) doe: and then I lost
(All mine owne Folly) the Societie,
Amitie too of your braue Father, whom
(Though bearing Miserie) I desire my life
Once more to looke on him.

Flo. By his command
Haue I here touch'd *Sicilia*, and from him
Giue you all greetings, that a King (at friend)
Can send his Brother: and but Infirmitie
(Which waits vpon worne times) hath something seiz'd
His wish'd Abilitie, he had himselfe
The Lands and Waters, 'twixt your Throne and his,
Measur'd, to looke vpon you; whom he loues
(He bad me say so) more then all the Scepters,
And those that beare them, liuing.

Leo. Oh my Brother,
(Good Gentleman) the wrongs I haue done thee, stirre
Afresh within me: and these thy offices
(So rarely kind) are as Interpreters
Of my behind-hand slacknesse. Welcome hither,
As is the Spring to th' Earth. And hath he too
Expos'd this Paragon to th' fearefull vsage
(At least vngentle) of the dreadfull *Neptune*,
To greet a man, not worth her paines; much lesse,
Th' aduenture of her person?

Flo. Good my Lord,
She came from *Libia*.

Leo. Where the Warlike *Smalus*,
That Noble honor'd Lord, is fear'd, and lou'd?

Flo. Most Royall Sir,
From thence: from him, whose Daughter
His Teares proclaym'd his parting with her: thence
(A prosperous South-wind friendly) we haue cros'd,
To execute the Charge my Father gaue me,
For visiting your Highnesse: My best Traine
I haue from your *Sicilian* Shores dismiss'd;
Who for *Bohemia* bend, to signifie
Not onely my successe in *Libia* (Sir)
But my arriuall, and my Wifes, in safetie
Here, where we are.

Leo. The blessed Gods
Purge all Infection from our Ayre, whilest you
Doe Clymate here: you haue a holy Father,
A gracefull Gentleman, against whose person

(So

(So sacred as it is) I haue done sinne,
For which, the Heauens (taking angry note)
Haue left me Issue-lesse: and your Father's bless'd
(As he from Heauen merits it) with you,
Worthy his goodnesse. What might I haue been,
Might I a Sonne and Daughter now haue look'd on,
Such goodly things as you?

Enter a Lord.

Lord. Most Noble Sir,
That which I shall report, will beare no credit,
Were not the proofe so nigh. Please you (great Sir)
Bohemia greets you from himselfe, by me:
Desires you to attach his Sonne, who ha's
(His Dignitie, and Dutie both cast off)
Fled from his Father, from his Hopes, and with
A Shepheards Daughter.

Leo. Where's *Bohemia*? speake.

Lord. Here, in your Citie: I now came from him.
I speake amazedly, and it becomes
My meruaile, and my Message. To your Court
Whiles he was hastning (in the Chase, it seemes,
Of this faire Couple) meetes he on the way
The Father of this seeming Lady, and
Her Brother, hauing both their Countrey quitted,
With this young Prince.

Flo. Camillo ha's betray'd me;
Whose honor, and whose honestie till now,
Endur'd all Weathers.

Lord. Lay't so to his charge:
He's with the King your Father.

Leo. Who? *Camillo*?

Lord. Camillo (Sir:) I spake with him: who now
Ha's these poore men in question. Neuer saw I
Wretches so quake: they kneele, they kisse the Earth;
Forsweare themselues as often as they speake:
Bohemia stops his eares, and threatens them
With diuers deaths, in death.

Perd. Oh my poore Father:
The Heauen sets Spyes vpon vs, will not haue
Our Contract celebrated.

Leo. You are marryed?

Flo. We are not (Sir) nor are we like to be:
The Starres (I see) will kisse the Valleyes first:
The oddes for high and low's alike.

Leo. My Lord,
Is this the Daughter of a King?

Flo. She is,
When once she is my Wife.

Leo. That once (I see) by your good Fathers speed,
Will come-on very slowly. I am sorry
(Most sorry) you haue broken from his liking,
Where you were ty'd in dutie: and as sorry,
Your Choise is not so rich in Worth, as Beautie,
That you might well enioy her.

Flo. Deare, looke vp:
Though *Fortune*, visible an Enemie,
Should chase vs, with my Father; powre no iot
Hath she to change our Loues. Beseech you (Sir)
Remember, since you ow'd no more to Time
Then I doe now: with thought of such Affections,
Step forth mine Aduocate: at your request,
My Father will graunt precious things, as Trifles.

Leo. Would he doe so, I'ld beg your precious Mistris,
Which he counts but a Trifle.

Paul. Sir (my Liege)
Your eye hath too much youth in't: not a moneth
'Fore your Queene dy'd, she was more worth such gazes,
Then what you looke on now.

Leo. I thought of her,
Euen in these Lookes I made. But your Petition
Is yet vn-answer'd: I will to your Father:
Your Honor not o're-throwne by your desires,
I am friend to them, and you: Vpon which Errand
I now goe toward him: therefore follow me,
And marke what way I make: Come good my Lord.

Exeunt.

Scœna Secunda.

Enter Autolicus, and a Gentleman.

Aut. Beseech you (Sir) were you present at this Relation?

Gent.1. I was by at the opening of the Farthell, heard the old Shepheard deliuer the manner how he found it: Whereupon (after a little amazednesse) we were all commanded out of the Chamber: onely this (me thought) I heard the Shepheard say, he found the Child.

Aut. I would most gladly know the issue of it.

Gent.1. I make a broken deliuerie of the Businesse; but the changes I perceiued in the King, and *Camillo*, were very Notes of admiration: they seem'd almost, with staring on one another, to teare the Cases of their Eyes. There was speech in their dumbnesse, Language in their very gesture: they look'd as they had heard of a World ransom'd, or one destroyed: a notable passion of Wonder appeared in them: but the wisest beholder, that knew no more but seeing, could not say, if th'importance were Ioy, or Sorrow; but in the extremitie of the one, it must needs be.

Enter another Gentleman.

Here comes a Gentleman, that happily knowes more: The Newes, *Rogero*.

Gent.2. Nothing but Bon-fires: the Oracle is fulfill'd: the Kings Daughter is found: such a deale of wonder is broken out within this houre, that Ballad-makers cannot be able to expresse it.

Enter another Gentleman.

Here comes the Lady *Paulina*'s Steward, hee can deliuer you more. How goes it now (Sir.) This Newes (which is call'd true) is so like an old Tale, that the veritie of it is in strong suspition: Ha's the King found his Heire?

Gent.3. Most true, if euer Truth were pregnant by Circumstance: That which you heare, you'le sweare you see, there is such vnitie in the proofes. The Mantle of Queene *Hermiones*: her Iewell about the Neck of it: the Letters of *Antigonus* found with it, which they know to be his Character: the Maiestie of the Creature, in resemblance of the Mother: the Affection of Noblenesse, which Nature shewes aboue her Breeding, and many other Euidences, proclayme her, with all certaintie, to be the Kings Daughter. Did you see the meeting of the two Kings?

Gent.2. No.

Gent.3. Then haue you lost a Sight which was to bee seene, cannot bee spoken of. There might you haue beheld one Ioy crowne another, so and in such manner, that it seem'd Sorrow wept to take leaue of them: for their Ioy waded in teares. There was casting vp of Eyes, holding vp of Hands, with Countenance of such distraction, that they were to be knowne by Garment, not by Fauor.
Our

Our King being ready to leape out of himselfe, for ioy of his found Daughter; as if that Ioy were now become a Losse, cryes, Oh, thy Mother, thy Mother: then askes *Bohemia* forgiuenesse, then embraces his Sonne-in-Law: then againe worryes he his Daughter, with clipping her. Now he thanks the old Shepheard (which stands by, like a Weather-bitten Conduit, of many Kings Reignes.) I neuer heard of such another Encounter, which lames Report to follow it, and vndo's description to doe it.

Gent.2. What, 'pray you, became of *Antigonus*, that carryed hence the Child?

Gent.3. Like an old Tale still, which will haue matter to rehearse, though Credit be asleepe, and not an eare open; he was torne to pieces with a Beare: This auouches the Shepheards Sonne; who ha's not onely his Innocence (which seemes much) to iustifie him, but a Hand-kerchief and Rings of his, that *Paulina* knowes.

Gent.1. What became of his Barke, and his Followers?

Gent.3. Wrackt the same instant of their Masters death, and in the view of the Shepheard: so that all the Instruments which ayded to expose the Child, were euen then lost, when it was found. But oh the Noble Combat, that twixt Ioy and Sorrow was fought in *Paulina*. Shee had one Eye declin'd for the losse of her Husband, another eleuated, that the Oracle was fulfill'd: Shee lifted the Princesse from the Earth, and so locks her in embracing, as if shee would pin her to her heart, that shee might no more be in danger of loosing.

Gent.1. The Dignitie of this Act was worth the audience of Kings and Princes, for by such was it acted.

Gent.3. One of the prettyest touches of all, and that which angl'd for mine Eyes (caught the Water, though not the Fish) was, when at the Relation of the Queenes death (with the manner how shee came to't, brauely confess'd, and lamented by the King) how attentiuenesse wounded his Daughter, till (from one signe of dolour to another) shee did (with an *Alas*) I would faine say, bleed Teares; for I am sure, my heart wept blood. Who was most Marble, there changed colour: some swownded, all sorrowed: if all the World could haue seen't, the Woe had beene vniuersall.

Gent.1. Are they returned to the Court?

Gent.3. No: The Princesse hearing of her Mothers Statue (which is in the keeping of *Paulina*) a Peece many yeeres in doing, and now newly perform'd, by that rare Italian Master, *Iulio Romano*, who (had he himselfe Eternitie, and could put Breath into his Worke) would beguile Nature of her Custome, so perfectly he is her Ape: He so neere to *Hermione*, hath done *Hermione*, that they say one would speake to her, and stand in hope of answer. Thither (with all greedinesse of affection) are they gone, and there they intend to Sup.

Gent.2. I thought shee had some great matter there in hand, for shee hath priuately, twice or thrice a day, euer since the death of *Hermione*, visited that remoued House. Shall wee thither, and with our companie peece the Reioycing?

Gent.1. Who would be thence, that ha's the benefit of Accesse? euery winke of an Eye, some new Grace will be borne: our Absence makes vs vnthriftie to our Knowledge. Let's along. *Exit.*

Aut. Now (had I not the dash of my former life in me) would Preferment drop on my head. I brought the old man and his Sonne aboord the Prince; told him, I heard them talke of a Farthell, and I know not what: but he at that time ouer-fond of the Shepheards Daughter (so he then tooke her to be) who began to be much Sea-sick, and himselfe little better, extremitie of Weather continuing, this Mysterie remained vndiscouer'd. But 'tis all one to me: for had I beene the finder-out of this Secret, it would not haue rellish'd among my other discredits.

Enter Shepheard and Clowne.

Here come those I haue done good to against my will, and alreadie appearing in the blossomes of their Fortune.

Shep. Come Boy, I am past moe Children: but thy Sonnes and Daughters will be all Gentlemen borne.

Clow. You are well met (Sir:) you deny'd to fight with mee this other day, because I was no Gentleman borne. See you these Clothes? say you see them not, and thinke me still no Gentleman borne: You were best say these Robes are not Gentlemen borne. Giue me the Lye: doe: and try whether I am not now a Gentleman borne.

Aut. I know you are now (Sir) a Gentleman borne.

Clow. I, and haue been so any time these foure houres.

Shep. And so haue I, Boy.

Clow. So you haue: but I was a Gentleman borne before my Father: for the Kings Sonne tooke me by the hand, and call'd mee Brother: and then the two Kings call'd my Father Brother: and then the Prince (my Brother) and the Princesse (my Sister) call'd my Father, Father; and so wee wept: and there was the first Gentleman-like teares that euer we shed.

Shep. We may liue (Sonne) to shed many more.

Clow. I: or else 'twere hard luck, being in so preposterous estate as we are.

Aut. I humbly beseech you (Sir) to pardon me all the faults I haue committed to your Worship, and to giue me your good report to the Prince my Master.

Shep. 'Prethee Sonne doe: for we must be gentle, now we are Gentlemen.

Clow. Thou wilt amend thy life?

Aut. I, and it like your good Worship.

Clow. Giue me thy hand: I will sweare to the Prince, thou art as honest a true Fellow as any is in *Bohemia*.

Shep. You may say it, but not sweare it.

Clow. Not sweare it, now I am a Gentleman? Let Bootes and Francklins say it, Ile sweare it.

Shep. How if it be false (Sonne?)

Clow. If it be ne're so false, a true Gentleman may sweare it, in the behalfe of his Friend: And Ile sweare to the Prince, thou art a tall Fellow of thy hands, and that thou wilt not be drunke: but I know thou art no tall Fellow of thy hands, and that thou wilt be drunke: but Ile sweare it, and I would thou would'st be a tall Fellow of thy hands.

Aut. I will proue so (Sir) to my power.

Clow. I, by any meanes proue a tall Fellow: if I do not wonder, how thou dar'st venture to be drunke, not being a tall Fellow, trust me not. Harke, the Kings and the Princes (our Kindred) are going to see the Queenes Picture. Come, follow vs: wee'le be thy good Masters. *Exeunt.*

Scæna Tertia.

Enter Leontes, Polixenes, Florizell, Perdita, Camillo, Paulina: Hermione (like a Statue:) Lords, &c.

Leo. O graue and good *Paulina*, the great comfort
That I haue had of thee?

Paul. What (Soueraigne Sir)
I did not well, I meant well: all my Seruices
You haue pay'd home. But that you haue vouchsaf'd
(With your Crown'd Brother, and these your contracted
Heires of your Kingdomes) my poore House to visit;
It is a surplus of your Grace, which neuer
My life may last to answere.

Leo. O *Paulina*,
We honor you with trouble: but we came
To see the Statue of our Queene. Your Gallerie
Haue we pass'd through, not without much content
In many singularities; but we saw not
That which my Daughter came to looke vpon,
The Statue of her Mother.

Paul. As she liu'd peerelesse,
So her dead likenesse I doe well beleeue
Excells what euer yet you look'd vpon,
Or hand of Man hath done: therefore I keepe it
Louely, apart. But here it is: prepare
To see the Life as liuely mock'd, as euer
Still Sleepe mock'd Death: behold, and say 'tis well.
I like your silence, it the more shewes-off
Your wonder: but yet speake, first you (my Liege)
Comes it not something neere?

Leo. Her naturall Posture.
Chide me (deare Stone) that I may say indeed
Thou art *Hermione*; or rather, thou art she,
In thy not chiding: for she was as tender
As Infancie, and Grace. But yet (*Paulina*)
Hermione was not so much wrinckled, nothing
So aged as this seemes.

Pol. Oh, not by much.

Paul. So much the more our Caruers excellence,
Which lets goe-by some sixteene yeeres, and makes her
As she liu'd now.

Leo. As now she might haue done,
So much to my good comfort, as it is
Now piercing to my Soule. Oh, thus she stood,
Euen with such Life of Maiestie (warme Life,
As now it coldly stands) when first I woo'd her.
I am asham'd: Do's not the Stone rebuke me,
For being more Stone then it? Oh Royall Peece:
There's Magick in thy Maiestie, which ha's
My Euils coniur'd to remembrance; and
From thy admiring Daughter tooke the Spirits,
Standing like Stone with thee.

Perd. And giue me leaue,
And doe not say 'tis Superstition, that
I kneele, and then implore her Blessing. Lady,
Deere Queene, that ended when I but began,
Giue me that hand of yours, to kisse.

Paul. O, patience:
The Statue is but newly fix'd; the Colour's
Not dry.

Cam. My Lord, your Sorrow was too sore lay'd-on,
Which sixteene Winters cannot blow away,
So many Summers dry: scarce any Ioy
Did euer so long liue; no Sorrow,
But kill'd it selfe much sooner.

Pol. Deere my Brother,
Let him, that was the cause of this, haue powre
To take-off so much griefe from you, as he
Will peece vp in himselfe.

Paul. Indeed my Lord,
If I had thought the sight of my poore Image
Would thus haue wrought you (for the Stone is mine)
I'd not haue shew'd it.

Leo. Doe not draw the Curtaine.

Paul. No longer shall you gaze on't, least your Fancie
May thinke anon, it moues.

Leo. Let be, let be:
Would I were dead, but that me thinkes alreadie.
(What was he that did make it?) See (my Lord)
Would you not deeme it breath'd? and that those veines
Did verily beare blood?

Pol. 'Masterly done:
The very Life seemes warme vpon her Lippe.

Leo. The fixure of her Eye ha's motion in't,
As we are mock'd with Art.

Paul. Ile draw the Curtaine:
My Lord's almost so farre transported, that
Hee'le thinke anon it liues.

Leo. Oh sweet *Paulina*,
Make me to thinke so twentie yeeres together:
No setled Sences of the World can match
The pleasure of that madnesse. Let't alone.

Paul. I am sorry (Sir) I haue thus farre stir'd you: but
I could afflict you farther.

Leo. Doe *Paulina*:
For this Affliction ha's a taste as sweet
As any Cordiall comfort. Still me thinkes
There is an ayre comes from her. What fine Chizzell
Could euer yet cut breath? Let no man mock me,
For I will kisse her.

Paul. Good my Lord, forbeare:
The ruddinesse vpon her Lippe, is wet:
You'le marre it, if you kisse it; stayne your owne
With Oyly Painting: shall I draw the Curtaine.

Leo. No: not these twentie yeeres.

Perd. So long could I
Stand-by, a looker-on.

Paul. Either forbeare,
Quit presently the Chappell, or resolue you
For more amazement: if you can behold it,
Ile make the Statue moue indeed; descend,
And take you by the hand: but then you'le thinke
(Which I protest against) I am assisted
By wicked Powers.

Leo. What you can make her doe,
I am content to looke on: what to speake,
I am content to heare: for 'tis as easie
To make her speake, as moue.

Paul. It is requir'd
You doe awake your Faith: then, all stand still:
On: those that thinke it is vnlawfull Businesse,
I am about, let them depart.

Leo. Proceed:
No foot shall stirre.

Paul. Musick; awake her: Strike:
'Tis time: descend: be Stone no more: approach:
Strike all that looke vpon with meruaile: Come:
Ile fill your Graue vp: stirre: nay, come away:
Bequeath to Death your numnesse: (for from him,
Deare Life redeemes you) you perceiue she stirres:
Start not: her Actions shall be holy, as
You heare my Spell is lawfull: doe not shun her,
Vntill you see her dye againe; for then
You kill her double: Nay, present your Hand:
When she was young, you woo'd her: now, in age,
Is she become the Suitor?

Leo. Oh, she's warme:
If this be Magick, let it be an Art

The Winters Tale.

Lawfull as Eating.
  Pol. She embraces him,
  Cam. She hangs about his necke,
If she pertaine to life, let her speake too.
  Pol. I, and make it manifest where she ha's liu'd,
Or how stolne from the dead?
  Paul. That she is liuing,
Were it but told you, should be hooted at
Like an old Tale : but it appeares she liues,
Though yet she speake not. Marke a little while:
Please you to interpose (faire Madam) kneele,
And pray your Mothers blessing : turne good Lady,
Our *Perdita* is found.
  Her. You Gods looke downe,
And from your sacred Viols poure your graces
Vpon my daughters head : Tell me (mine owne)
Where hast thou bin preseru'd? Where liu'd? How found
Thy Fathers Court? For thou shalt heare that I
Knowing by *Paulina*, that the Oracle
Gaue hope thou wast in being, haue preseru'd
My selfe, to see the yssue.
  Paul. There's time enough for that,
Least they desire (vpon this push) to trouble
Your ioyes, with like Relation. Go together
You precious winners all : your exultation

Partake to euery one : I (an old Turtle)
Will wing me to some wither'd bough, and there
My Mate (that's neuer to be found againe)
Lament, till I am lost.
  Leo. O peace *Paulina*:
Thou shouldst a husband take by my consent,
As I by thine a Wife. This is a Match,
And made betweene's by Vowes. Thou hast found mine,
But how, is to be question'd : for I saw her
(As I thought) dead : and haue (in vaine) said many
A prayer vpon her graue. Ile not seeke farre
(For him, I partly know his minde) to finde thee
An honourable husband. Come *Camillo*,
And take her by the hand : whose worth, and honesty
Is richly noted : and heere iustified
By Vs, a paire of Kings. Let's from this place.
What? looke vpon my Brother : both your pardons,
That ere I put betweene your holy lookes
My ill suspition : This your Son-in-law,
And Sonne vnto the King, whom heauens directing
Is troth-plight to your daughter. Good *Paulina*,
Leade vs from hence, where we may leysurely
Each one demand, and answere to his part
Perform'd in this wide gap of Time, since first
We were disseuer'd : Hastily lead away. *Exeunt.*

The Names of the Actors.

Leontes, *King of Sicillia.*
Mamillus, *yong Prince of Sicillia.*
Camillo.
Antigonus. }
Cleomines. } *Foure Lords of Sicillia.*
Dion.
Hermione, *Queene to Leontes.*
Perdita, *Daughter to Leontes and Hermione.*
Paulina, *wife to Antigonus.*

Emilia, *a Lady.*
Polixenes, *King of Bohemia.*
Florizell, *Prince of Bohemia.*
Old Shephsard, *reputed Father of Perdita.*
Clowne, *his Sonne.*
Autolicus, *a Rogue.*
Archidamus, *a Lord of Bohemia.*
Other Lords, *and Gentlemen, and Seruants.*
Shepheards, *and Shephearddesses.*

FINIS.

The life and death of King Iohn.

Actus Primus, Scæna Prima.

Enter King Iohn, Queene Elinor, Pembroke, Essex, and Salisbury, with the Chattylion of France.

King Iohn.

NOw say *Chatillion*, what would *France* with vs?
Chat. Thus (after greeting) speakes the King of France,
In my behauiour to the Maiesty,
The borrowed Maiesty of *England* heere.
Elea. A strange beginning: borrowed Maiesty?
K.Iohn. Silence (good mother) heare the Embassie.
Chat. Philip of France, in right and true behalfe
Of thy deceased brother, *Geffreyes* sonne,
Arthur Plantaginet, laies most lawfull claime
To this faire Iland, and the Territories:
To *Ireland, Poyctiers, Aniowe, Torayne, Maine*,
Desiring thee to lay aside the sword
Which swaies vsurpingly these seuerall titles,
And put the same into yong *Arthurs* hand,
Thy Nephew, and right royall Soueraigne.
K.Iohn. What followes if we disallow of this?
Chat. The proud controle of fierce and bloudy warre,
To inforce these rights, so forcibly with-held,
K.Io. Heere haue we war for war, & bloud for bloud,
Controlement for controlement: so answer *France*.
Chat. Then take my Kings defiance from my mouth,
The farthest limit of my Embassie.
K.Iohn. Beare mine to him, and so depart in peace,
Be thou as lightning in the eies of *France*;
For ere thou canst report, I will be there:
The thunder of my Cannon shall be heard.
So hence: be thou the trumpet of our wrath,
And sullen presage of your owne decay:
An honourable conduct let him haue,
Pembroke looke too't: farewell *Chattillion*.
Exit Chat. and Pem.
Ele. What now my sonne, haue I not euer said
How that ambitious *Constance* would not cease
Till she had kindled *France* and all the world,
Vpon the right and party of her sonne.
This might haue beene preuented, and made whole
With very easie arguments of loue,
Which now the mannage of two kingdomes must
With fearefull bloudy issue arbitrate.
K.Iohn. Our strong possession, and our right for vs.
Eli. Your strong possession much more then your right,
Or else it must go wrong with you and me,
So much my conscience whispers in your eare,

Which none but heauen, and you, and I, shall heare.
Enter a Sheriffe.
Essex. My Liege, here is the strangest controuersie
Come from the Country to be iudg'd by you
That ere I heard: shall I produce the men?
K.Iohn. Let them approach:
Our Abbies and our Priories shall pay
This expeditious charge: what men are you?
Enter Robert Faulconbridge, and Philip.
Philip. Your faithfull subiect, I a gentleman,
Borne in *Northamptonshire*, and eldest sonne
As I suppose, to *Robert Faulconbridge*,
A Souldier by the Honor-giuing-hand
Of *Cordelion*, Knighted in the field.
K.Iohn. What art thou?
Robert. The son and heire to that same *Faulconbridge*.
K.Iohn. Is that the elder, and art thou the heyre?
You came not of one mother then it seemes.
Philip. Most certain of one mother, mighty King,
That is well knowne, and as I thinke one father:
But for the certaine knowledge of that truth,
I put you o're to heauen, and to my mother;
Of that I doubt, as all mens children may.
Eli. Out on thee rude man, & dost shame thy mother,
And wound her honor with this diffidence.
Phil. I Madame? No, I haue no reason for it,
That is my brothers plea, and none of mine,
The which if he can proue, a pops me out,
At least from faire fiue hundred pound a yeere:
Heauen guard my mothers honor, and my Land.
K.Iohn. A good blunt fellow: why being yonger born
Doth he lay claime to thine inheritance?
Phil. I know not why, except to get the land:
But once he slanderd me with bastardy:
But where I be as true begot or no,
That still I lay vpon my mothers head,
But that I am as well begot my Liege
(Faire fall the bones that tooke the paines for me)
Compare our faces, and be Iudge your selfe
If old Sir *Robert* did beget vs both,
And were our father, and this sonne like him:
O old sir *Robert* Father, on my knee
I giue heauen thankes I was not like to thee.
K.Iohn. Why what a mad-cap hath heauen lent vs here?
Elea. He hath a tricke of *Cordelions* face,
The accent of his tongue affecteth him:
Doe you not read some tokens of my sonne
In the large composition of this man?

K. Iohn. Mine eye hath well examined his parts,
And findes them perfect *Richard*: sirra speake,
What doth moue you to claime your brothers land.

Philip. Because he hath a half-face like my father?
With halfe that face would he haue all my land,
A halfe-fac'd groat, fiue hundred pound a yeere?

Rob. My gracious Liege, when that my father liu'd,
Your brother did imploy my father much.

Phil. Well sir, by this you cannot get my land,
Your tale must be how he employ'd my mother.

Rob. And once dispatch'd him in an Embassie
To *Germany*, there with the Emperor
To treat of high affaires touching that time:
Th'aduantage of his absence tooke the King,
And in the meane time soiourn'd at my fathers;
Where how he did preuaile, I shame to speake:
But truth is truth, large lengths of seas and shores
Betweene my father, and my mother lay,
As I haue heard my father speake himselfe
When this same lusty gentleman was got:
Vpon his death-bed he by will bequeath'd
His lands to me, and tooke it on his death
That this my mothers sonne was none of his;
And if he were, he came into the world
Full fourteene weekes before the course of time:
Then good my Liedge let me haue what is mine,
My fathers land, as was my fathers will.

K. Iohn. Sirra, your brother is Legittimate,
Your fathers wife did after wedlocke beare him:
And if she did play false, the fault was hers,
Which fault lyes on the hazards of all husbands
That marry wiues: tell me, how if my brother
Who as you say, tooke paines to get this sonne,
Had of your father claim'd this sonne for his,
Insooth, good friend, your father might haue kept
This Calfe, bred from his Cow from all the world:
Insooth he might: then if he were my brothers,
My brother might not claime him, nor your father
Being none of his, refuse him: this concludes,
My mothers sonne did get your fathers heyre,
Your fathers heyre must haue your fathers land.

Rob. Shal then my fathers Will be of no force,
To dispossesse that childe which is not his.

Phil. Of no more force to dispossesse me sir,
Then was his will to get me, as I think.

Eli. Whether hadst thou rather be a *Faulconbridge*,
And like thy brother to enioy thy land:
Or the reputed sonne of *Cordelion*,
Lord of thy presence, and no land beside.

Bast. Madam, and if my brother had my shape
And I had his, sir *Roberts* his like him,
And if my legs were two such riding rods,
My armes, such eele-skins stuft, my face so thin,
That in mine eare I durst not sticke a rose,
Lest men should say, looke where three farthings goes,
And to his shape were heyre to all this land,
Would I might neuer stirre from off this place,
I would giue it euery foot to haue this face:
It would not be sir nobbe in any case.

Elinor. I like thee well: wilt thou forsake thy fortune,
Bequeath thy land to him, and follow me?
I am a Souldier, and now bound to *France*.

Bast. Brother, take you my land, Ile take my chance;
Your face hath got fiue hundred pound a yeere,
Yet sell your face for fiue pence and 'tis deere:
Madam, Ile follow you vnto the death.

Elinor. Nay, I would haue you go before me thither.

Bast. Our Country manners giue our betters way.

K. Iohn. What is thy name?

Bast. Philip my Liege, so is my name begun,
Philip, good old Sir *Roberts* wiues eldest sonne.

K. Iohn. From henceforth beare his name
Whose forme thou bearest:
Kneele thou downe *Philip*, but rise more great,
Arise Sir *Richard*, and *Plantagenet*.

Bast. Brother by th' mothers side, giue me your hand,
My father gaue me honor, yours gaue land:
Now blessed be the houre by night or day
When I was got, Sir *Robert* was away.

Ele. The very spirit of *Plantaginet*:
I am thy grandame *Richard*, call me so.

Bast. Madam by chance, but not by truth, what tho;
Something about a little from the right,
In at the window, or else ore the hatch:
Who dares not stirre by day, must walke by night,
And haue is haue, how euer men doe catch:
Neere or farre off, well wonne is still well shot,
And I am I, how ere I was begot.

K. Iohn. Goe, *Faulconbridge*, now hast thou thy desire,
A landlesse Knight, makes thee a landed Squire:
Come Madam, and come *Richard*, we must speed
For *France*, for *France*, for it is more then need.

Bast. Brother adieu, good fortune come to thee,
For thou wast got i'th way of honesty.
Exeunt all but bastard.

Bast. A foot of Honor better then I was,
But many a many foot of Land the worse.
Well, now can I make any *Ioane* a Lady,
Good den Sir *Richard*, Godamercy fellow,
And if his name be *George*, Ile call him *Peter*;
For new made honor doth forget mens names:
'Tis two respectiue, and too sociable
For your conuersion, now your traueller,
Hee and his tooth-picke at my worships messe,
And when my knightly stomacke is suffis'd,
Why then I sucke my teeth, and catechize
My picked man of Countries: my deare sir,
Thus leaning on mine elbow I begin,
I shall beseech you; that is question now,
And then comes answer like an Absey booke:
O sir, sayes answer, at your best command,
At your employment, at your seruice sir:
No sir, saies question, I sweet sir at yours,
And so ere answer knowes what question would,
Sauing in Dialogue of Complement,
And talking of the Alpes and Appenines,
The Perennean and the riuer *Poe*,
It drawes toward supper in conclusion so.
But this is worshipfull society,
And fits the mounting spirit like my selfe;
For he is but a bastard to the time
That doth not smoake of obseruation,
And so am I whether I smacke or no:
And not alone in habit and deuice,
Exterior forme, outward accoutrement;
But from the inward motion to deliuer
Sweet, sweet, sweet poyson for the ages tooth,
Which though I will not practice to deceiue,
Yet to auoid deceit I meane to learne;
For it shall strew the footsteps of my rising:
But who comes in such haste in riding robes?

What woman post is this? hath she no husband
That will take paines to blow a horne before her?
O me, 'tis my mother: how now good Lady,
What brings you heere to Court so hastily?

Enter Lady Faulconbridge and Iames Gurney.

Lady. Where is that slaue thy brother? where is he?
That holds in chase mine honour vp and downe.

Bast. My brother *Robert*, old Sir *Roberts* sonne:
Colbrand the Gyant, that same mighty man,
Is it Sir *Roberts* sonne that you seeke so?

Lady. Sir *Roberts* sonne, I thou vnreuerend boy,
Sir *Roberts* sonne? why scorn'st thou at sir *Robert*?
He is Sir *Roberts* sonne, and so art thou.

Bast. *Iames Gournie*, wilt thou giue vs leaue a while?

Gur. Good leaue good *Philip*.

Bast. *Philip*, sparrow, *Iames*,
There's toyes abroad, anon Ile tell thee more.
Exit Iames.
Madam, I was not old Sir *Roberts* sonne,
Sir *Robert* might haue eat his part in me
Vpon good Friday, and nere broke his fast:
Sir *Robert* could doe well, marrie to confesse
Could get me sir *Robert* could not doe it;
We know his handy-worke, therefore good mother
To whom am I beholding for these limmes?
Sir *Robert* neuer holpe to make this legge.

Lady. Hast thou conspired with thy brother too,
That for thine owne gaine shouldst defend mine honor?
What meanes this scorne, thou most vntoward knaue?

Bast. Knight, knight good mother, Basilisco-like:
What, I am dub'd, I haue it on my shoulder:
But mother, I am not Sir *Roberts* sonne,
I haue disclaim'd Sir *Robert* and my land,
Legitimation, name, and all is gone;
Then good my mother, let me know my father,
Some proper man I hope, who was it mother?

Lady. Hast thou denied thy selfe a *Faulconbridge*?

Bast. As faithfully as I denie the deuill.

Lady. King *Richard Cordelion* was thy father,
By long and vehement suit I was seduc'd
To make roome for him in my husbands bed:
Heauen lay not my transgression to my charge,
That art the issue of my deere offence
Which was so strongly vrg'd past my defence.

Bast. Now by this light were I to get againe,
Madam I would not wish a better father:
Some sinnes doe beare their priuiledge on earth,
And so doth yours: your fault, was not your follie,
Needs must you lay your heart at his dispose,
Subiected tribute to commanding loue,
Against whose furie and vnmatched force,
The awlesse Lion could not wage the fight,
Nor keepe his Princely heart from *Richards* hand:
He that perforce robs Lions of their hearts,
May easily winne a womans: aye my mother,
With all my heart I thanke thee for my father:
Who liues and dares but say, thou didst not well
When I was got, Ile send his soule to hell.
Come Lady I will shew thee to my kinne,
And they shall say, when *Richard* me begot,
If thou hadst sayd him nay, it had beene sinne;
Who sayes it was, he lyes, I say twas not.
Exeunt.

Scæna Secunda.

Enter before Angiers, Philip King of France, Lewis, Daulphin, Austria, Constance, Arthur.

Lewis. Before *Angiers* well met braue *Austria*,
Arthur that great fore-runner of thy bloud,
Richard that rob'd the Lion of his heart,
And fought the holy Warres in *Palestine*,
By this braue Duke came early to his graue:
And for amends to his posteritie,
At our importance hether is he come,
To spread his colours boy, in thy behalfe,
And to rebuke the vsurpation
Of thy vnnaturall Vncle, English *Iohn*,
Embrace him, loue him, giue him welcome hether.

Arth. God shall forgiue you *Cordelions* death
The rather, that you giue his off-spring life,
Shadowing their right vnder your wings of warre:
I giue you welcome with a powerlesse hand,
But with a heart full of vnstained loue,
Welcome before the gates of *Angiers* Duke.

Lewis. A noble boy, who would not doe thee right?

Aust. Vpon thy cheeke lay I this zelous kisse,
As seale to this indenture of my loue:
That to my home I will no more returne
Till *Angiers*, and the right thou hast in *France*,
Together with that pale, that white-fac'd shore,
Whose foot spurnes backe the Oceans roaring tides,
And coopes from other lands her Ilanders,
Euen till that *England* hedg'd in with the maine,
That Water-walled Bulwarke, still secure
And confident from forreine purposes,
Euen till that vtmost corner of the West
Salute thee for her King, till then faire boy
Will I not thinke of home, but follow Armes.

Const. O take his mothers thanks, a widdows thanks,
Till your strong hand shall helpe to giue him strength,
To make a more requitall to your loue.

Aust. The peace of heauen is theirs y lift their swords
In such a iust and charitable warre.

King. Well, then to worke our Cannon shall be bent
Against the browes of this resisting towne,
Call for our cheefest men of discipline,
To cull the plots of best aduantages:
Wee'll lay before this towne our Royal bones,
Wade to the market-place in *French*-mens bloud,
But we will make it subiect to this boy.

Con. Stay for an answer to your Embassie,
Lest vnaduis'd you staine your swords with bloud,
My Lord *Chattilion* may from *England* bring
That right in peace which heere we vrge in warre,
And then we shall repent each drop of bloud,
That hot rash haste so indirectly shedde.
Enter Chattilion.

King. A wonder Lady: lo vpon thy wish
Our Messenger *Chattilion* is arriu'd,
What *England* saies, say breefely gentle Lord,
We coldly pause for thee, *Chatilion* speake.

Chat. Then turne your forces from this paltry siege,
And stirre them vp against a mightier taske:
England impatient of your iust demands,
Hath put himselfe in Armes, the aduerse windes

Whose leisure I haue staid, haue giuen him time
To land his Legions all as soone as I:
His marches are expedient to this towne,
His forces strong, his Souldiers confident:
With him along is come the Mother Queene,
An Ace stirring him to bloud and strife,
With her her Neece, the Lady *Blanch of Spaine*,
With them a Bastard of the Kings deceast,
And all th'vnsetled humors of the Land,
Rash, inconsiderate, fiery voluntaries,
With Ladies faces, and fierce Dragons spleenes,
Haue sold their fortunes at their natiue homes,
Bearing their birth-rights proudly on their backs,
To make a hazard of new fortunes heere:
In briefe, a brauer choyse of dauntlesse spirits
Then now the *English* bottomes haue wast o're,
Did neuer flote vpon the swelling tide,
To doe offence and scathe in Christendome:
The interruption of their churlish drums
Cuts off more circumstance, they are at hand,

Drum beats.

To parlie or to fight, therefore prepare.

Kin. How much vnlook'd for, is this expedition.

Aust. By how much vnexpected, by so much
We must awake indeuor for defence,
For courage mounteth with occasion,
Let them be welcome then, we are prepar'd.

Enter K. of England, Bastard, Queene, Blanch, Pembroke, and others.

K.Iohn. Peace be to *France*: If *France* in peace permit
Our iust and lineall entrance to our owne;
If not, bleede *France*, and peace ascend to heauen,
Whiles we Gods wrathfull agent doe correct
Their proud contempt that beats his peace to heauen.

Fran. Peace be to *England*, if that warre returne
From *France* to *England*, there to liue in peace:
England we loue, and for that *Englands* sake,
With burden of our armor heere we sweat:
This toyle of ours should be a worke of thine;
But thou from louing *England* art so farre,
That thou hast vnder-wrought his lawfull King,
Cut off the sequence of posterity,
Out-faced Infant State, and done a rape
Vpon the maiden vertue of the Crowne:
Looke heere vpon thy brother *Geffreyes* face,
These eyes, these browes, were moulded out of his;
This little abstract doth containe that large,
Which died in *Geffrey*: and the hand of time,
Shall draw this breefe into as huge a volume:
That *Geffrey* was thy elder brother borne,
And this his sonne, *England* was *Geffreys* right,
And this is *Geffreyes* in the name of God:
How comes it then that thou art call'd a King,
When liuing blood doth in these temples beat
Which owe the crowne, that thou ore-masterest?

K.Iohn. From whom hast thou this great commission
To draw my answer from thy Articles? (*France*,

Fra. Frō that supernal Iudge that stirs good thoughts
In any beast of strong authoritie,
To looke into the blots and staines of right,
That Iudge hath made me guardian to this boy,
Vnder whose warrant I impeach thy wrong,
And by whose helpe I meane to chastise it.

K.Iohn. Alack thou dost vsurpe authoritie.

Fran. Excuse it is to beat vsurping downe.

Queen. Who is it thou dost call vsurper *France?*

Const. Let me make answer: thy vsurping sonne.

Queen. Out insolent, thy bastard shall be King,
That thou maist be a Queen, and checke the world.

Con. My bed was euer to thy sonne as true
As thine was to thy husband, and this boy
Liker in feature to his father *Geffrey*
Then thou and *Iohn*, in manners being as like,
As raine to water, or deuill to his damme;
My boy a bastard? by my soule I thinke
His father neuer was so true begot,
It cannot be, and if thou wert his mother. (ther

Queen. Theres a good mother boy, that blots thy fa-

Const. There's a good grandame boy
That would blot thee.

Aust. Peace.

Bast. Heare the Cryer.

Aust. What the deuill art thou?

Bast. One that wil play the deuill sir with you,
And a may catch your hide and you alone:
You are the Hare of whom the Prouerb goes
Whose valour plucks dead Lyons by the beard;
Ile smoake your skin-coat and I catch you right,
Sirra looke too't, yfaith I will, yfaith.

Blan. O well did he become that Lyons robe,
That did distrobe the Lion of that robe.

Bast. It lies as sightly on the backe of him
As great *Alcides* shooes vpon an Asse:
But Asse, Ile take that burthen from your backe,
Or lay on that shall make your shoulders cracke.

Aust. What cracker is this same that deafes our eares
With this abundance of superfluous breath?
King *Lewis*, determine what we shall doe strait.

Lew. Women & fooles, breake off your conference.
King *Iohn*, this is the very summe of all:
England and *Ireland*, *Angiers*, *Toraine*, *Maine*,
In right of *Arthur* doe I claime of thee:
Wilt thou resigne them, and lay downe thy Armes?

Iohn. My life as soone: I doe defie thee *France*,
Arthur of *Britaine*, yeeld thee to my hand,
And out of my deere loue Ile giue thee more,
Then ere the coward hand of *France* can win;
Submit thee boy.

Queen. Come to thy grandame child.

Const. Doe childe, goe to yt grandame childe,
Giue grandame kingdome, and it grandame will
Giue yt a plum, a cherry, and a figge,
There's a good grandame.

Arthur. Good my mother peace,
I would that I were low laid in my graue,
I am not worth this coyle that's made for me. (weepes.

Qu. Mo. His mother shames him so, poore boy hee

Con. Now shame vpon you where she does or no,
His grandames wrongs, and not his mothers shames
Drawes those heauen-mouing pearles frō his poor eies,
Which heauen shall take in nature of a fee:
I, with these Christall beads heauen shall be brib'd
To doe him Iustice, and reuenge on you.

Qu. Thou monstrous slanderer of heauen and earth.

Con. Thou monstrous Iniurer of heauen and earth,
Call not me slanderer, thou and thine vsurpe
The Dominations, Royalties, and rights
Of this oppressed boy; this is thy eldest sonnes sonne,
Infortunate in nothing but in thee:

Thy

The life and death of King Iohn.

Thy sinnes are visited in this poore childe,
The Canon of the Law is laide on him,
Being but the second generation
Remoued from thy sinne-conceiuing wombe.

Iohn. Bedlam haue done.

Con. I haue but this to say,
That he is not onely plagued for her sin,
But God hath made her sinne and her, the plague
On this remoued issue, plagued for her,
And with her plague her sinne: his iniury
Her iniurie the Beadle to her sinne,
All punish'd in the person of this childe,
And all for her, a plague vpon her.

Que. Thou vnaduised scold, I can produce
A Will, that barres the title of thy sonne.

Con. I who doubts that, a Will: a wicked will,
A womans will, a cankred Grandams will.

Fra. Peace Lady, pause, or be more temperate,
It ill beseemes this presence to cry ayme
To these ill-tuned repetitions:
Some Trumpet summon hither to the walles
These men of Angiers, let vs heare them speake,
Whose title they admit, *Arthurs* or *Iohns*.

Trumpet sounds.
Enter a Citizen vpon the walles.

Cit. Who is it that hath warn'd vs to the walles?

Fra. 'Tis France, for England.

Iohn. England for it selfe:
You men of Angiers, and my louing subiects.

Fra. You louing men of Angiers, *Arthurs* subiects,
Our Trumpet call'd you to this gentle parle.

Iohn. For our aduantage, therefore heare vs first:
These flagges of France that are aduanced heere
Before the eye and prospect of your Towne,
Haue hither march'd to your endamagement.
The Canons haue their bowels full of wrath,
And ready mounted are they to spit forth
Their Iron indignation 'gainst your walles:
All preparation for a bloody siedge
And merciles proceeding, by these French.
Comfort yours Citties eies, your winking gates:
And but for our approch, those sleeping stones,
That as a waste doth girdle you about
By the compulsion of their Ordinance,
By this time from their fixed beds of lime
Had bin dishabited, and wide hauocke made
For bloody power to rush vppon your peace.
But on the sight of vs your lawfull King,
Who painefully with much expedient march
Haue brought a counter-checke before your gates,
To saue vnscratch'd your Citties threatned cheekes:
Behold the French amaz'd vouchsafe a parle,
And now insteed of bullets wrapt in fire
To make a shaking feuer in your walles,
They shoote but calme words, folded vp in smoake,
To make a faithlesse errour in your eares,
Which trust accordingly kinde Cittizens,
And let vs in. Your King, whose labour'd spirits
Fore-wearied in this action of swift speede,
Craues harbourage within your Citie walles.

France. When I haue saide, make answer to vs both.
Loe in this right hand, whose protection
Is most diuinely vow'd vpon the right
Of him it holds, stands yong *Plantagenet*,
Sonne to the elder brother of this man,
And King ore him, and all that he enioyes:
For this downe-troden equity, we tread
In warlike march, these greenes before your Towne,
Being no further enemy to you
Then the constraint of hospitable zeale,
In the releefe of this oppressed childe,
Religiously prouokes. Be pleased then
To pay that dutie which you truly owe,
To him that owes it, namely, this yong Prince,
And then our Armes, like to a muzled Beare,
Saue in aspect, hath all offence seal'd vp:
Our Cannons malice vainly shall be spent
Against th'inuolurable clouds of heauen,
And with a blessed and vn-vext retyre,
With vnhack'd swords, and Helmets all vnbruis'd,
We will beare home that lustie blood againe,
Which heere we came to spout against your Towne,
And leaue your children, wiues, and you in peace.
But if you fondly passe our proffer'd offer,
'Tis not the rounder of your old-fac'd walles,
Can hide you from our messengers of Warre,
Though all these English, and their discipline
Were harbour'd in their rude circumference:
Then tell vs, Shall your Citie call vs Lord,
In that behalfe which we haue challeng'd it?
Or shall we giue the signall to our rage,
And stalke in blood to our possession?

Cit. In breefe, we are the King of Englands subiects
For him, and in his right, we hold this Towne.

Iohn. Acknowledge then the King, and let me in.

Cit. That can we not: but he that proues the King
To him will we proue loyall, till that time
Haue we ramm'd vp our gates against the world.

Iohn. Doth not the Crowne of England, prooue the King?
And if not that, I bring you Witnesses
Twice fifteene thousand hearts of Englands breed.

Bast. Bastards and else.

Iohn. To verifie our title with their liues.

Fran. As many and as well-borne bloods as those.

Bast. Some Bastards too.

Fran. Stand in his face to contradict his claime.

Cit. Till you compound whose right is worthiest,
We for the worthiest hold the right from both.

Iohn. Then God forgiue the sinne of all those soules,
That to their euerlasting residence,
Before the dew of euening fall, shall fleete
In dreadfull triall of our kingdomes King.

Fran. Amen, Amen, mount Cheualiers to Armes.

Bast. Saint *George* that swindg'd the Dragon,
And ere since sit's on's horsebacke at mine Hostesse dore
Teach vs some fence. Sirrah, were I at home
At your den sirrah, with your Lionnesse,
I would set an Oxe-head to your Lyons hide:
And make a monster of you.

Aust. Peace, no more.

Bast. O tremble: for you heare the Lyon rore.

Iohn. Vp higher to the plaine, where we'l set forth
In best appointment all our Regiments.

Bast. Speed then to take aduantage of the field.

Fra. It shall be so, and at the other hill
Command the rest to stand, God and our right. *Exeunt*

Heere after excursions, Enter the Herald of France
with Trumpets to the gates.

F. Her. You men of Angiers open wide your gates,
And let yong *Arthur* Duke of Britaine in,

Who by the hand of France, this day hath made
Much worke for teares in many an English mother,
Whose sonnes lye scattered on the bleeding ground:
Many a widdowes husband groueling lies,
Coldly embracing the discoloured earth,
And victorie with little losse doth play
Vpon the dancing banners of the French,
Who are at hand triumphantly displayed
To enter Conquerors, and to proclaime
Arthur of Britaine, Englands King, and yours.

Enter English Herald with Trumpet.

E.Har. Reioyce you men of Angiers, ring your bels,
King *Iohn*, your king and Englands, doth approach,
Commander of this hot malicious day,
Their Armours that march'd hence so siluer bright,
Hither returne all gilt with Frenchmens blood:
There stucke no plume in any English Crest,
That is remoued by a staffe of France.
Our colours do returne in those same hands
That did display them when we first marcht forth:
And like a iolly troope of Huntsmen come
Our lustie English, all with purpled hands,
Dide in the dying slaughter of their foes,
Open your gates, and giue the Victors way.

Hubert. Heralds, from off our towres we might behold
From first to last, the on-set and retyre,
Of both your Armies, whose equality
By our best eyes cannot be censured: (blowes:
Blood hath bought blood, and blowes haue answerd
Strength matcht with strength, and power confronted
    power,
Both are alike, and both alike we like:
One must proue greatest. While they weigh so euen,
We hold our Towne for neither: yet for both.

Enter the two Kings with their powers,
at seuerall doores.

Iohn. France, hast thou yet more blood to cast away?
Say, shall the currant of our right rome on,
Whose passage vext with thy impediment,
Shall leaue his natiue channell, and ore-swell
With course disturb'd euen thy confining shores,
Vnlesse thou let his siluer Water, keepe
A peacefull progresse to the Ocean.

Fra. England thou hast not sau'd one drop of blood
In this hot triall more then we of France,
Rather lost more. And by this hand I sweare
That swayes the earth this Climate ouer-lookes,
Before we will lay downe our iust-borne Armes,
Wee'l put thee downe, 'gainst whom these Armes wee
Or adde a royall number to the dead: (beare,
Gracing the scroule that tels of this warres losse,
With slaughter coupled to the name of kings.

Bast. Ha Maiesty: how high thy glory towres,
When the rich blood of kings is set on fire:
Oh now doth death line his dead chaps with steele,
The swords of souldiers are his teeth, his phangs,
And now he feasts, mousing the flesh of men
In vndetermin'd differences of kings.
Why stand these royall fronts amazed thus:
Cry hauocke kings, backe to the stained field
You equall Potents, fierie kindled spirits,
Then let confusion of one part confirm
The others peace: till then, blowes, blood, and death.

Iohn. Whose party do the Townesmen yet admit?

Fra. Speake Citizens for England, whose your king.
Hub. The king of England, when we know the king.
Fra. Know him in vs, that heere hold vp his right.
Iohn. In Vs, that are our owne great Deputie,
And beare possession of our Person heere,
Lord of our presence Angiers, and of you.

Fra. A greater powre then We denies all this,
And till it be vndoubted, we do locke
Our former scruple in our strong barr'd gates:
Kings of our feare, vntill our feares resolu'd
Be by some certaine king, purg'd and depos'd.

Bast. By heauen, these scroyles of Angiers flout you
And stand securely on their battlements, (kings,
As in a Theater, whence they gape and point
At your industrious Scenes and acts of death.
Your Royall presences be rul'd by mee,
Do like the Mutines of Ierusalem,
Be friends a-while, and both conioyntly bend
Your sharpest Deeds of malice on this Towne.
By East and West let France and England mount,
Their battering Canon charged to the mouthes,
Till their soule-fearing clamours haue braul'd downe
The flintie ribbes of this contemptuous Citie,
I'de play incessantly vpon these Iades,
Euen till vnfenced desolation
Leaue them as naked as the vulgar ayre:
That done, disseuer your vnited strengths,
And part your mingled colours once againe,
Turne face to face, and bloody point to point:
Then in a moment Fortune shall cull forth
Out of one side her happy Minion,
To whom in fauour she shall giue the day,
And kisse him with a glorious victory:
How like you this wilde counsell mighty States,
Smackes it not something of the policie.

Iohn. Now by the sky that hangs aboue our heads,
I like it well. France, shall we knit our powres,
And lay this Angiers euen with the ground,
Then after fight who shall be king of it?

Bast. And if thou hast the mettle of a king,
Being wrong'd as we are by this peeuish Towne:
Turne thou the mouth of thy Artillerie,
As we will ours, against these sawcie walles,
And when that we haue dash'd them to the ground,
Why then defie each other, and pell-mell,
Make worke vpon our selues, for heauen or hell.

Fra. Let it be so: say, where will you assault?
Iohn. We from the West will send destruction
Into this Cities bosome.
Aust. I from the North.
Fran. Our Thunder from the South,
Shall raine their drift of bullets on this Towne.
Bast. O prudent discipline! From North to South:
Austria and France shoot in each others mouth.
Ile stirre them to it: Come, away, away.

Hub. Heare vs great kings, vouchsafe awhile to stay
And I shall shew you peace, and faire-fac'd league:
Win you this Citie without stroke, or wound,
Rescue those breathing liues to dye in beds,
That heere come sacrifices for the field.
Perseuer not, but heare me mighty kings.

Iohn. Speake on with fauour, we are bent to heare.
Hub. That daughter there of Spaine, the Lady *Blanch*
Is neere to England, looke vpon the yeeres
Of *Lewes* the Dolphin, and that louely maid.
If lustie loue should go in quest of beautie,

Where

Where should he finde it fairer, then in *Blanch*:
If zealous loue should go in search of vertue,
Where should he finde it purer then in *Blanch*?
If loue ambitious, sought a match of birth,
Whose veines bound richer blood then Lady *Blanch*?
Such as she is, in beautie, vertue, birth,
Is the yong Dolphin euery way compleat,
If not compleat of, say he is not shee,
And she againe wants nothing, to name want,
If want it be not, that she is not hee:
He is the halfe part of a blessed man,
Left to be finished by such as shee,
And she a faire diuided excellence,
Whose fulnesse of perfection lyes in him.
O two such siluer currents when they ioyne
Do glorifie the bankes that bound them in:
And two such shores, to two such streames made one,
Two such controlling bounds shall you be, kings,
To these two Princes, if you marrie them:
This Vnion shall do more then batterie can
To our fast closed gates: for at this match,
With swifter spleene then powder can enforce
The mouth of passage shall we fling wide ope,
And giue you entrance: but without this match,
The sea enraged is not halfe so deafe,
Lyons more confident, Mountaines and rockes
More free from motion, no not death himselfe
In mortall furie halfe so peremptorie,
As we to keepe this Citie.

Bast. Heeres a stay,
That shakes the rotten carkasse of old death
Out of his ragges. Here's a large mouth indeede,
That spits forth death, and mountaines, rockes, and seas,
Talkes as familiarly of roaring Lyons,
As maids of thirteene do of puppi-dogges.
What Cannoneere begot this lustie blood,
He speakes plaine Cannon fire, and smoake, and bounce,
He giues the bastinado with his tongue:
Our eares are cudgel'd, not a word of his
But buffets better then a fist of France:
Zounds, I was neuer so bethumpt with words,
Since I first cal'd my brothers father Dad.

Old Qu. Son, list to this coniunction, make this match
Giue with our Neece a dowrie large enough,
For by this knot, thou shalt so surely tye
Thy now vnsur'd assurance to the Crowne,
That yon greene boy shall haue no Sunne to ripe
The bloome that promiseth a mightie fruite.
I see a yeelding in the lookes of France:
Marke how they whisper, vrge them while their soules
Are capeable of this ambition,
Least zeale now melted by the windie breath
Of soft petitions, pittie and remorse,
Coole and congeale againe to what it was.

Hub. Why answer not the double Maiesties,
This friendly treatie of our threatned Towne.

Fra. Speake England first, that hath bin forward first
To speake vnto this Cittie: what say you?

Iohn. If that the Dolphin there thy Princely sonne,
Can in this booke of beautie read, I loue:
Her Dowrie shall weigh equall with a Queene:
For *Angiers*, and faire *Toraine Maine*, *Poyctiers*,
And all that we vpon this side the Sea,
(Except this Cittie now by vs besiedg'd)
Finde liable to our Crowne and Dignitie,
Shall gild her bridall bed and make her rich
In titles, honors, and promotions,
As she in beautie, education, blood,
Holdes hand with any Princesse of the world.

Fra. What sai'st thou boy? looke in the Ladies face.

Dol. I do my Lord, and in her eie I find
A wonder, or a wondrous miracle,
The shadow of my selfe form'd in her eye,
Which being but the shadow of your sonne,
Becomes a sonne and makes your sonne a shadow:
I do protest I neuer lou'd my selfe
Till now, infixed I beheld my selfe,
Drawne in the flattering table of her eie.
Whispers with Blanch.

Bast. Drawne in the flattering table of her eie,
Hang'd in the frowning wrinkle of her brow,
And quarter'd in her heart, hee doth espie
Himselfe loues traytor, this is pittie now;
That hang'd, and drawne, and quarter'd there should be
In such a loue, so vile a Lout as he.

Blan. My vnckles will in this respect is mine,
If he see ought in you that makes him like,
That any thing he see's which moues his liking,
I can with ease translate it to my will:
Or if you will, to speake more properly,
I will enforce it easlie to my loue.
Further I will not flatter you, my Lord,
That all I see in you is worthie loue,
Then this, that nothing do I see in you,
Though churlish thoughts themselues should bee your
    Iudge,
That I can finde, should merit any hate.

Iohn. What saie these yong-ones? What say you my
Neece?

Blan. That she is bound in honor still to do
What you in wisedome still vouchsafe to say.

Iohn. Speake then Prince Dolphin, can you loue this
Ladie?

Dol. Nay aske me if I can refraine from loue,
For I doe loue her most vnfainedly.

Iohn. Then do I giue *Volquessen*, *Torsine*, *Maine*,
Poyctiers, and *Aniow*, these fiue Prouinces
With her to thee, and this addition more,
Full thirty thousand Markes of English coyne:
Phillip of France, if thou be pleas'd withall,
Command thy sonne and daughter to ioyne hands.

Fra. It likes vs well young Princes: close your hands

Aust. And your lippes too, for I am well assur'd,
That I did so when I was first assur'd.

Fra. Now Cittizens of Angiers ope your gates,
Let in that amitie which you haue made,
For at Saint Maries Chappell presently,
The rights of marriage shallbe solemniz'd.
Is not the Ladie *Constance* in this troope?
I know she is not for this match made vp,
Her presence would haue interrupted much.
Where is she and her sonne, tell me, who knowes?

Dol. She is sad and passionate at your highnes Tent.

Fra. And by my faith, this league that we haue made
Will giue her sadnesse very little cure:
Brother of England, how may we content
This widdow Lady? In her right we came,
Which we God knowes, haue turn'd another way,
To our owne vantage.

Iohn. We will heale vp all,
For wee'l create yong *Arthur* Duke of Britaine
And Earle of Richmond, and this rich faire Towne

We

We make him Lord of. Call the Lady *Constance*,
Some speedy Messenger bid her repaire
To our solemnity : I trust we shall,
(If not fill vp the measure of her will)
Yet in some measure satisfie her so,
That we shall stop her exclamation,
Go we as well as hast will suffer vs,
To this vnlook'd for vnprepared pompe.   *Exeunt.*

Bast. Mad world, mad kings, mad composition:
Iohn to stop *Arthurs* Title in the whole,
Hath willingly departed with a part,
And France, whose armour Conscience buckled on,
Whom zeale and charitie brought to the field,
As Gods owne souldier, rounded in the eare,
With that same purpose-changer, that slye diuel,
That Broker, that still breakes the pate of faith,
That dayly breake-vow, he that winnes of all,
Of kings, of beggers, old men, yong men, maids,
Who hauing no externall thing to loose,
But the word Maid, cheats the poore Maide of that.
That smooth-fac'd Gentleman, tickling commoditie,
Commoditie, the byas of the world,
The world, who of it selfe is peysed well,
Made to run euen, vpon euen ground;
Till this aduantage, this vile drawing byas,
This sway of motion, this commoditie,
Makes it take head from all indifferency,
From all direction, purpose, course, intent.
And this same byas, this Commoditie,
This Bawd, this Broker, this all-changing-word,
Clap'd on the outward eye of fickle France,
Hath drawne him from his owne determin'd ayd,
From a resolu'd and honourable warre,
To a most base and vile-concluded peace.
And why rayle I on this Commoditie?
But for because he hath not wooed me yet:
Not that I haue the power to clutch my hand,
When his faire Angels would salute my palme,
But for my hand, as vnattempted yet,
Like a poore begger, raileth on the rich.
Well, whiles I am a begger, I will raile,
And say there is no sin but to be rich:
And being rich, my vertue then shall be,
To say there is no vice, but beggerie:
Since Kings breake faith vpon commoditie,
Gaine be my Lord, for I will worship thee.   *Exit.*

Actus Secundus

Enter Constance, Arthur, and Salisbury.

Con. Gone to be married? Gone to sweare a peace?
False blood to false blood ioyn'd. Gone to be freinds?
Shall *Lewis* haue *Blaunch*, and *Blaunch* those Prouinces?
It is not so, thou hast mispoke, misheard,
Be well aduis'd, tell ore thy tale againe.
It cannot be, thou do'st but say 'tis so.
I trust I may not trust thee, for thy word
Is but the vaine breath of a common man:
Beleeue me, I doe not beleeue thee man,
I haue a Kings oath to the contrarie.
Thou shalt be punish'd for thus frighting me,
For I am sicke, and capeable of feares,

Opprest with wrongs, and therefore full of feares,
A widdow, husbandles, subiect to feares,
A woman naturally borne to feares;
And though thou now confesse thou didst but iest
With my vext spirits, I cannot take a Truce,
But they will quake and tremble all this day.
What dost thou meane by shaking of thy head?
Why dost thou looke so sadly on my sonne?
What meanes that hand vpon that breast of thine?
Why holdes thine eie that lamentable rhewme,
Like a proud riuer peering ore his bounds?
Be these sad signes confirmers of thy words?
Then speake againe, not all thy former tale,
But this one word, whether thy tale be true.

Sal. As true as I beleeue you thinke them false,
That giue you cause to proue my saying true.

Con. Oh if thou teach me to beleeue this sorrow,
Teach thou this sorrow, how to make me dye,
And let beleefe, and life encounter so,
As doth the furie of two desperate men,
Which in the very meeting fall, and dye.
Lewes marry *Blaunch*? O boy, then where art thou?
France friend with *England*, what becomes of me?
Fellow be gone: I cannot brooke thy sight,
This newes hath made thee a most vgly man.

Sal. What other harme haue I good Lady done,
But spoke the harme, that is by others done?

Con. Which harme within it selfe so heynous is,
As it makes harmefull all that speake of it.

Ar. I do beseech you Madam be content.

Con. If thou that bidst me be content, wert grim
Vgly, and slandrous to thy Mothers wombe,
Full of vnpleasing blots, and sightlesse staines,
Lame, foolish, crooked, swart, prodigious,
Patch'd with foule Moles, and eye-offending markes,
I would not care, I then would be content,
For then I should not loue thee: no, nor thou
Become thy great birth, nor deserue a Crowne.
But thou art faire, and at thy birth (deere boy)
Nature and Fortune ioyn'd to make thee great.
Of Natures guifts, thou mayst with Lillies boast,
And with the halfe-blowne Rose. But Fortune, oh,
She is corrupted, chang'd, and wonne from thee,
Sh'adulterates hourely with thine Vnckle *Iohn*,
And with her golden hand hath pluckt on France
To tread downe faire respect of Soueraigntie,
And made his Maiestie the bawd to theirs.
France is a Bawd to Fortune, and king *Iohn*,
That strumpet Fortune, that vsurping *Iohn*:
Tell me thou fellow, is not France forsworne?
Euenom him with words, or get thee gone,
And leaue those woes alone, which I alone
Am bound to vnder-beare.

Sal. Pardon me Madam,
I may not goe without you to the kings.

Con. Thou maist, thou shalt, I will not go with thee,
I will instruct my sorrowes to bee proud,
For greefe is proud, and makes his owner stoope,
To me and to the state of my great greefe,
Let kings assemble: for my greefe's so great,
That no supporter but the huge firme earth
Can hold it vp: here I and sorrowes sit,
Heere is my Throne, bid kings come bow to it.

Actus Tertius, Scæna prima.

Enter King Iohn, France, Dolphin, Blanch, Elianor, Philip, Austria, Constance.

Fran. 'Tis true (faire daughter) and this blessed day,
Euer in *France* shall be kept festiuall:
To solemnize this day the glorious sunne
Stayes in his course, and playes the Alchymist,
Turning with splendor of his precious eye
The meager cloddy earth to glittering gold:
The yearely course that brings this day about,
Shall neuer see it, but a holy day.

Const. A wicked day, and not a holy day.
What hath this day deseru'd? what hath it done,
That it in golden letters should be set
Among the high tides in the Kalender?
Nay, rather turne this day out of the weeke,
This day of shame, oppression, periury.
Or if it must stand still, let wiues with childe
Pray that their burthens may not fall this day,
Lest that their hopes prodigiously be crost:
But (on this day) let Sea-men feare no wracke,
No bargaines breake that are not this day made;
This day all things begun, come to ill end,
Yea, faith it selfe to hollow falshood change.

Fra. By heauen Lady, you shall haue no cause
To curse the faire proceedings of this day:
Haue I not pawn'd to you my Maiesty?

Const. You haue beguil'd me with a counterfeit
Resembling Maiesty, which being touch'd and tride,
Proues valuelesse: you are forsworne, forsworne,
You came in Armes to spill mine enemies bloud,
But now in Armes, you strengthen it with yours.
The grapling vigor, and rough frowne of Warre
Is cold in amitie, and painted peace,
And our oppression hath made vp this league:
Arme, arme, you heauens, against these periur'd Kings,
A widdow cries, be husband to me (heauens)
Let not the howres of this vngodly day
Weare out the daies in Peace; but ere Sun-set,
Set armed discord 'twixt these periur'd Kings,
Heare me, Oh, heare me.

Aust. Lady *Constance*, peace.

Const. War, war, no peace, peace is to me a warre:
O *Lymoges*, O *Austria*, thou dost shame
That bloudy spoyle: thou slaue, thou wretch, y coward,
Thou little valiant, great in villanie,
Thou euer strong vpon the stronger side;
Thou Fortunes Champion, that do'st neuer fight
But when her humourous Ladiship is by
To teach thee safety: thou art periur'd too,
And sooth'st vp greatnesse. What a foole art thou,
A ramping foole, to brag, and stamp, and sweare,
Vpon my partie: thou cold blooded slaue,
Hast thou not spoke like thunder on my side?
Beene sworne my Souldier, bidding me depend
Vpon thy starres, thy fortune, and thy strength,
And dost thou now fall ouer to my foes?
Thou weare a Lyons hide, doff it for shame,
And hang a Calues skin on those recreant limbes.

Aus. O that a man should speake those words to me.

Phil. And hang a Calues-skin on those recreant limbs

Aus. Thou dar'st not say so villaine for thy life.

Phil. And hang a Calues-skin on those recreant limbs.

Iohn. We like not this, thou dost forget thy selfe.

Enter Pandulph.

Fra. Heere comes the holy Legat of the Pope.

Pan. Haile you annointed deputies of heauen;
To thee King *Iohn* my holy errand is:
I *Pandulph*, of faire *Millane* Cardinall,
And from Pope *Innocent* the Legate heere,
Doe in his name religiously demand
Why thou against the Church, our holy Mother,
So wilfully dost spurne; and force perforce
Keepe *Stephen Langton* chosen Arshbishop
Of *Canterbury* from that holy Sea:
This in our foresaid holy Fathers name
Pope *Innocent*, I doe demand of thee.

Iohn. What earthie name to Interrogatories
Can tast the free breath of a sacred King?
Thou canst not (Cardinall) deuise a name
So slight, vnworthy, and ridiculous
To charge me to an answere, as the Pope:
Tell him this tale, and from the mouth of *England*,
Adde thus much more, that no *Italian* Priest
Shall tythe or toll in our dominions:
But as we, vnder heauen, are supreame head,
So vnder him that great supremacy
Where we doe reigne, we will alone vphold
Without th'assistance of a mortall hand:
So tell the Pope, all reuerence set apart
To him and his vsurp'd authoritie.

Fra. Brother of *England*, you blaspheme in this.

Iohn. Though you, and all the Kings of Christendom
Are led so grossely by this medling Priest,
Dreading the curse that money may buy out,
And by the merit of vilde gold, drosse, dust,
Purchase corrupted pardon of a man,
Who in that sale sels pardon from himselfe:
Though you, and al the rest so grossely led,
This iugling witchcraft with reuennue cherish,
Yet I alone, alone doe me oppose
Against the Pope, and count his friends my foes.

Pand. Then by the lawfull power that I haue,
Thou shalt stand curst, and excommunicate,
And blessed shall he be that doth reuolt
From his Allegeance to an heretique,
And meritorious shall that hand be call'd,
Canonized and worship'd as a Saint,
That takes away by any secret course
Thy hatefull life.

Con. O lawfull let it be
That I haue roome with *Rome* to curse a while,
Good Father Cardinall, cry thou Amen
To my keene curses; for without my wrong
There is no tongue hath power to curse him right.

Pan. There's Law and Warrant (Lady) for my curse.

Const. And for mine too, when Law can do no right.
Let it be lawfull, that Law barre no wrong:
Law cannot giue my childe his kingdome heere;
For he that holds his Kingdome, holds the Law:
Therefore since Law it selfe is perfect wrong,
How can the Law forbid my tongue to curse?

Pand. *Philp* of *France*, on perill of a curse,
Let goe the hand of that Arch-heretique,
And raise the power of *France* vpon his head,
Vnlesse he doe submit himselfe to *Rome*.

Elea. Look'st thou pale *France*? do not let go thy hand.

Con. Looke to that Deuill, lest that *France* repent,

And

And by disioyning hands hell lose a soule.

Aust. King *Philip*, listen to the Cardinall.

Bast. And hang a Calues-skin on his recreant limbs.

Aust. Well ruffian, I must pocket vp these wrongs,
Because.

Bast. Your breeches best may carry them.

Iohn. *Philip*, what saist thou to the Cardinall?

Con. What should he say, but as the Cardinall?

Dolph. Bethinke you father, for the difference
Is purchase of a heauy curse from *Rome*,
Or the light losse of *England*, for a friend:
Forgoe the easier.

Bla. That's the curse of *Rome*.

Con. O *Lewis*, stand fast, the deuill tempts thee heere
In likenesse of a new vntrimmed Bride.

Bla. The Lady *Constance* speakes not from her faith,
But from her need.

Con. Oh, if thou grant my need,
Which onely liues but by the death of faith,
That need, must needs inferre this principle,
That faith would liue againe by death of need:
O then tread downe my need, and faith mounts vp,
Keepe my need vp, and faith is trodden downe.

Iohn. The king is mou'd, and answers not to this.

Con. O be remou'd from him, and answere well.

Aust. Doe so king *Philip*, hang no more in doubt.

Bast. Hang nothing but a Calues skin most sweet lout.

Fra. I am perplext, and know not what to say.

Pan. What canst thou say, but wil perplex thee more?
If thou stand excommunicate, and curst?

Fra. Good reuerend father, make my person yours,
And tell me how you would bestow your selfe?
This royall hand and mine are newly knit,
And the coniunction of our inward soules
Married in league, coupled, and link'd together
With all religous strength of sacred vowes,
The latest breath that gaue the sound of words
Was deepe-sworne faith, peace, amity, true loue
Betweene our kingdomes and our royall selues,
And euen before this truce, but new before,
No longer then we well could wash our hands,
To clap this royall bargaine vp of peace,
Heauen knowes they were besmear'd and ouer-staind
With slaughters pencill; where reuenge did paint
The fearefull difference of incensed kings:
And shall these hands so lately purg'd of bloud?
So newly ioyn'd in loue? so strong in both,
Vnyoke this seysure, and this kinde regreete?
Play fast and loose with faith? so iest with heauen,
Make such vnconstant children of our selues
As now againe to snatch our palme from palme:
Vn-sweare faith sworne, and on the marriage bed
Of smiling peace to march a bloody hoast,
And make a ryot on the gentle brow
Of true sincerity? O holy Sir
My reuerend father, let it not be so;
Out of your grace, deuise, ordaine, impose
Some gentle order, and then we shall be blest
To doe your pleasure, and continue friends.

Pand. All forme is formelesse, Order orderlesse,
Saue what is opposite to *Englands* loue.
Therefore to Armes, be Champion of our Church,
Or let the Church our mother breathe her curse,
A mothers curse, on her reuolting sonne:
France, thou maist hold a serpent by the tongue,
A cased Lion by the mortall paw,
A fasting Tyger safer by the tooth,
Then keepe in peace that hand which thou dost hold.

Fra. I may dis-ioyne my hand, but not my faith.

Pand. So mak'st thou faith an enemy to faith,
And like a ciuill warre setst oath to oath,
Thy tongue against thy tongue. O let thy vow
First made to heauen, first be to heauen perform'd,
That is, to be the Champion of our Church,
What since thou sworst, is sworne against thy selfe,
And may not be performed by thy selfe,
For that which thou hast sworne to doe amisse,
Is not amisse when it is truely done:
And being not done, where doing tends to ill,
The truth is then most done not doing it:
The better Act of purposes mistooke,
Is to mistake again, though indirect,
Yet indirection thereby growes direct,
And falshood, falshood cures, as fire cooles fire
Within the scorched veines of one new burn'd:
It is religion that doth make vowes kept,
But thou hast sworne against religion:
By what thou swear'st against the thing thou swear'st,
And mak'st an oath the suretie for thy truth,
Against an oath the truth, thou art vnsure
To sweare, sweares onely not to be forsworne,
Else what a mockerie should it be to sweare?
But thou dost sweare, onely to be forsworne,
And most forsworne, to keepe what thou dost sweare,
Therefore thy later vowes, against thy first,
Is in thy selfe rebellion to thy selfe:
And better conquest neuer canst thou make,
Then arme thy constant and thy nobler parts
Against these giddy loose suggestions:
Vpon which better part, our prayrs come in,
If thou vouchsafe them. But if not, then know
The perill of our curses light on thee
So heauy, as thou shalt not shake them off
But in despaire, dye vnder their blacke weight.

Aust. Rebellion, flat rebellion.

Bast. Wil't not be?
Will not a Calues-skin stop that mouth of thine?

Daul. Father, to Armes.

Blanch. Vpon thy wedding day?
Against the blood that thou hast married?
What, shall our feast be kept with slaughtered men?
Shall braying trumpets, and loud churlish drums
Clamors of hell, be measures to our pomp?
O husband heare me: aye, alacke, how new
Is husband in my mouth? euen for that name
Which till this time my tongue did nere pronounce;
Vpon my knee I beg, goe not to Armes
Against mine Vncle.

Const. O, vpon my knee made hard with kneeling,
I doe pray to thee, thou vertuous *Daulphin*,
Alter not the doome fore-thought by heauen.

Blan. Now shall I see thy loue, what motiue may
Be stronger with thee, then the name of wife?

Con. That which vpholdeth him, that thee vpholds,
His Honor, Oh thine Honor, *Lewis* thine Honor.

Dolph. I muse your Maiesty doth seeme so cold,
When such profound respects doe pull you on?

Pand. I will denounce a curse vpon his head.

Fra. Thou shalt not need. *England*, I will fall frō thee.

Const. O faire returne of banish'd Maiestie.

Elea. O foule reuolt of French inconstancy.

Eng. France, ỹ shalt rue this houre within this houre.

Bast.

The life and death of King John.

Bast. Old Time the clocke setter, y^t bald sexton Time:
Is it as he will? well then, *France* shall rue.
  Bla. The Sun's orecast with bloud: faire day adieu,
Which is the side that I must goe withall?
I am with both, each Army hath a hand,
And in their rage, I hauing hold of both,
They whurle a-sunder, and dismember mee.
Husband, I cannot pray that thou maist winne:
Vncle, I needs must pray that thou maist lose:
Father, I may not wish the fortune thine:
Grandam, I will not wish thy wishes thriue:
Who-euer wins, on that side shall I lose:
Assured losse, before the match be plaid.
  Dolph. Lady, with me, with me thy fortune lies.
  Bla. There where my fortune liues, there my life dies.
  Iohn. Cosen, goe draw our puisance together,
France, I am burn'd vp with inflaming wrath,
A rage, whose heat hath this condition;
That nothing can allay, nothing but blood,
The blood and deerest valued bloud of *France.*
  Fra. Thy rage shall burne thee vp, & thou shalt turne
To ashes, ere our blood shall quench that fire:
Looke to thy selfe, thou art in ieopardie.
  Iohn. No more then he that threats. To Arms le'ts hie.
        Exeunt.

Scœna Secunda.

Allarums, Excursions: Enter Bastard with Austria's head.

  Bast. Now by my life, this day grows wondrous hot,
Some ayery Deuill houers in the skie,
And pour's downe mischiefe. *Austrias* head lye there,
    Enter Iohn, Arthur, Hubert.
While *Philip* breathes.
  Iohn. Hubert, keepe this boy: *Philip* make vp,
My Mother is assayled in our Tent,
And tane I feare.
  Bast. My Lord I rescued her,
Her Highnesse is in safety, feare you not:
But on my Liege, for very little paines
Will bring this labor to an happy end.   *Exit.*

Alarums, excursions, Retreat. Enter Iohn, Eleanor, Arthur Bastard, Hubert, Lords.

  Iohn. So shall it be: your Grace shall stay behinde
So strongly guarded: *Cosen,* looke not sad,
Thy Grandame loues thee, and thy Vnkle will
As deere be to thee, as thy father was.
  Arth. O this will make my mother die with griefe.
  Iohn. Cosen away for *England,* haste before,
And ere our comming see thou shake the bags
Of hoording Abbots, imprisoned angells
Set at libertie: the fat ribs of peace
Must by the hungry now be fed vpon:
Vse our Commission in his vtmost force.
  Bast. Bell, Booke, & Candle, shall not driue me back,
When gold and siluer becks me to come on.
I leaue your highnesse: Grandame, I will pray
(If euer I remember to be holy)
For your faire safety: so I kisse your hand.
  Ele. Farewell gentle Cosen.

  Iohn. Coz, farewell.
  Ele. Come hether little kinsman, harke, a worde.
  Iohn. Come hether *Hubert.* O my gentle *Hubert,*
We owe thee much: within this wall of flesh
There is a soule counts thee her Creditor,
And with aduantage meanes to pay thy loue:
And my good friend, thy voluntary oath
Liues in this bosome, deerely cherished.
Giue me thy hand, I had a thing to say,
But I will fit it with some better tune.
By heauen *Hubert,* I am almost asham'd
To say what good respect I haue of thee.
  Hub. I am much bounden to your Maiesty.
  Iohn. Good friend, thou hast no cause to say so yet,
But thou shalt haue: and creepe time nere so slow,
Yet it shall come, for me to doe thee good.
I had a thing to say, but let it goe:
The Sunne is in the heauen, and the proud day,
Attended with the pleasures of the world,
Is all too wanton, and too full of gawdes
To giue me audience: If the mid-night bell
Did with his yron tongue, and brazen mouth
Sound on into the drowzie race of night:
If this same were a Church-yard where we stand,
And thou possessed with a thousand wrongs:
Or if that surly spirit melancholy
Had bak'd thy bloud, and made it heauy, thicke,
Which else runnes tickling vp and downe the veines,
Making that idiot laughter keepe mens eyes,
And straine their cheekes to idle merriment,
A passion hatefull to my purposes:
Or if that thou couldst see me without eyes,
Heare me without thine eares, and make reply
Without a tongue, vsing conceit alone,
Without eyes, eares, and harmefull sound of words:
Then, in despight of brooded watchfull day,
I would into thy bosome poure my thoughts:
But (ah) I will not, yet I loue thee well,
And by my troth I thinke thou lou'st me well.
  Hub. So well, that what you bid me vndertake,
Though that my death were adiunct to my Act,
By heauen I would doe it.
  Iohn. Doe not I know thou wouldst?
Good *Hubert, Hubert, Hubert* throw thine eye
On yon young boy: Ile tell thee what my friend,
He is a very serpent in my way,
And wheresoere this foot of mine doth tread,
He lies before me: dost thou vnderstand me?
Thou art his keeper.
  Hub. And Ile keepe him so,
That he shall not offend your Maiesty.
  Iohn. Death.
  Hub. My Lord.
  Iohn. A Graue.
  Hub. He shall not liue.
  Iohn. Enough.
I could be merry now, *Hubert,* I loue thee.
Well, Ile not say what I intend for thee:
Remember: Madam, Fare you well,
Ile send those powers o're to your Maiesty.
  Ele. My blessing goe with thee.
  Iohn. For *England* Cosen, goe,
Hubert shall be your man, attend on you
With al true duetie: On toward *Callice,* hoa.
        Exeunt.

Scæna Tertia.

Enter France, Dolphin, Pandulpho, Attendants.

Fra. So by a roaring Tempest on the flood,
A whole Armado of conuicted saile
Is scattered and dis-ioyn'd from fellowship.

Pand. Courage and comfort, all shall yet goe well.

Fra. What can goe well, when we haue runne so ill?
Are we not beaten? Is not *Angiers* lost?
Arthur tane prisoner? diuers deere friends slaine?
And bloudy *England* into *England* gone,
Ore-bearing interruption spight of *France*?

Dol. What he hath won, that hath he fortified:
So hot a speed, with such aduice dispos'd,
Such temperate order in so fierce a cause,
Doth want example: who hath read, or heard
Of any kindred-action like to this?

Fra. Well could I beare that *England* had this praise,
So we could finde some patterne of our shame:

Enter Constance.

Looke who comes heere? a graue vnto a soule,
Holding th'eternall spirit against her will,
In the vilde prison of afflicted breath:
I prethee Lady goe away with me.

Con. Lo; now: now see the issue of your peace.

Fra. Patience good Lady, comfort gentle *Constance*.

Con. No, I defie all Counsell, all redresse,
But that which ends all counsell, true Redresse:
Death, death, O amiable, louely death,
Thou odoriferous stench: sound rottennesse,
Arise forth from the couch of lasting night,
Thou hate and terror to prosperitie,
And I will kisse thy detestable bones,
And put my eye-balls in thy vaultie browes,
And ring these fingers with thy houshold wormes,
And stop this gap of breath with fulsome dust,
And be a Carrion Monster like thy selfe;
Come, grin on me, and I will thinke thou smil'st,
And busse thee as thy wife: Miseries Loue,
O come to me.

Fra. O faire affliction, peace.

Con. No, no, I will not, hauing breath to cry:
O that my tongue were in the thunders mouth,
Then with a passion would I shake the world,
And rowze from sleepe that fell Anatomy
Which cannot heare a Ladies feeble voyce,
Which scornes a moderne Inuocation.

Pand. Lady, you vtter madnesse, and not sorrow.

Con. Thou art holy to belye me so,
I am not mad: this haire I teare is mine,
My name is *Constance*, I was *Geffreyes* wife,
Yong *Arthur* is my sonne, and he is lost:
I am not mad, I would to heauen I were,
For then 'tis like I should forget my selfe:
O, if I could, what griefe should I forget?
Preach some Philosophy to make me mad,
And thou shalt be Canoniz'd (Cardinall.)
For, being not mad, but sensible of greefe,
My reasonable part produces reason
How I may be deliuer'd of these woes,
And teaches mee to kill or hang my selfe:
If I were mad, I should forget my sonne,
Or madly thinke a babe of clowts were he;
I am not mad: too well, too well I feele
The different plague of each calamitie.

Fra. Binde vp those tresses: O what loue I note
In the faire multitude of those her haires;
Where but by chance a siluer drop hath falne,
Euen to that drop ten thousand wiery fiends
Doe glew themselues in sociable griefe,
Like true, inseparable, faithfull loues,
Sticking together in calamitie.

Con. To *England*, if you will.

Fra. Binde vp your haires.

Con. Yes that I will: and wherefore will I do it?
I tore them from their bonds, and cride aloud,
O, that these hands could so redeeme my sonne,
As they haue giuen these hayres their libertie:
But now I enuie at their libertie,
And will againe commit them to their bonds,
Because my poore childe is a prisoner.
And Father Cardinall, I haue heard you say
That we shall see and know our friends in heauen:
If that be true, I shall see my boy againe;
For since the birth of *Caine*, the first male-childe
To him that did but yesterday suspire,
There was not such a gracious creature borne:
But now will Canker-sorrow eat my bud,
And chase the natiue beauty from his cheeke,
And he will looke as hollow as a Ghost,
As dim and meager as an Agues fitte,
And so hee'll dye: and rising so againe,
When I shall meet him in the Court of heauen
I shall not know him: therefore neuer, neuer
Must I behold my pretty *Arthur* more.

Pand. You hold too heynous a respect of greefe.

Const. He talkes to me, that neuer had a sonne.

Fra. You are as fond of greefe, as of your childe.

Con. Greefe fils the roome vp of my absent childe:
Lies in his bed, walkes vp and downe with me,
Puts on his pretty lookes, repeats his words,
Remembers me of all his gracious parts,
Stuffes out his vacant garments with his forme;
Then, haue I reason to be fond of griefe?
Fareyouwell: had you such a losse as I,
I could giue better comfort then you doe.
I will not keepe this forme vpon my head,
When there is such disorder in my witte:
O Lord, my boy, my *Arthur*, my faire sonne,
My life, my ioy, my food, my all the world:
My widow-comfort, and my sorrowes cure. *Exit.*

Fra. I feare some out-rage, and Ile follow her. *Exit.*

Dol. There's nothing in this world can make me ioy,
Life is as tedious as a twice-told tale,
Vexing the dull eare of a drowsie man;
And bitter shame hath spoyl'd the sweet words taste,
That it yeelds nought but shame and bitternesse.

Pand. Before the curing of a strong disease,
Euen in the instant of repaire and health,
The fit is strongest: Euils that take leaue
On their departure, most of all shew euill:
What haue you lost by losing of this day?

Dol. All daies of glory, ioy, and happinesse.

Pan. If you had won it, certainely you had.
No, no: when Fortune meanes to men most good,
Shee lookes vpon them with a threatning eye;
'Tis strange to thinke how much King *Iohn* hath lost
In this which he accounts so clearely wonne:

Are not you grieu'd that *Arthur* is his prisoner?
　Dol. As heartily as he is glad he hath him.
　Pan. Your minde is all as youthfull as your blood.
Now heare me speake with a propheticke spirit:
For euen the breath of what I meane to speake,
Shall blow each dust, each straw, each little rub
Out of the path which shall directly lead
Thy foote to Englands Throne. And therefore marke:
Iohn hath seiz'd *Arthur*, and it cannot be,
That whiles warme life playes in that infants veines,
The mis-plac'd-*Iohn* should entertaine an houre,
One minute, nay one quiet breath of rest.
A Scepter snatch'd with an vnruly hand,
Must be as boysterously maintain'd as gain'd.
And he that stands vpon a slipp'ry place,
Makes nice of no vilde hold to stay him vp:
That *Iohn* may stand, then *Arthur* needs must fall,
So be it, for it cannot be but so.
　Dol. But what shall I gaine by yong *Arthurs* fall?
　Pan. You, in the right of Lady *Blanch* your wife,
May then make all the claime that *Arthur* did.
　Dol. And loose it, life and all, as *Arthur* did.
　Pan. How greene you are, and fresh in this old world?
Iohn layes you plots: the times conspire with you,
For he that steepes his safetie in true blood,
Shall finde but bloodie safety, and vntrue.
This Act so euilly borne shall coole the hearts
Of all his people, and freeze vp their zeale,
That none so small aduantage shall step forth
To checke his reigne, but they will cherish it.
No naturall exhalation in the skie,
No scope of Nature, no distemper'd day,
No common winde, no customed euent,
But they will plucke away his naturall cause,
And call them Meteors, prodigies, and signes,
Abbortiues, presages, and tongues of heauen,
Plainly, denouncing vengeance vpon *Iohn*.
　Dol. May be he will not touch yong *Arthurs* life,
But hold himselfe safe in his prisonment.
　Pan. O Sir, when he shall heare of your approach,
If that yong *Arthur* be not gone alreadie,
Euen at that newes he dies: and then the hearts
Of all his people shall reuolt from him,
And kisse the lippes of vnacquainted change,
And picke strong matter of reuolt, and wrath
Out of the bloody fingers ends of *Iohn*.
Me thinkes I see this hurley all on foot;
And O, what better matter breeds for you,
Then I haue nam'd. The Bastard *Falconbridge*
Is now in England ransacking the Church,
Offending Charity: If but a dozen French
Were there in Armes, they would be as a Call
To traine ten thousand English to their side;
Or, as a little snow, tumbled about,
Anon becomes a Mountaine. O noble Dolphine,
Go with me to the King, 'tis wonderfull,
What may be wrought out of their discontent,
Now that their soules are topfull of offence,
For England go; I will whet on the King.
　Dol. Strong reasons makes strange actions: let vs go,
If you say I, the King will not say no. *Exeunt.*

Actus Quartus, Scæna prima.

Enter Hubert and Executioners.

　Hub. Heate me these Irons hot, and looke thou stand
Within the Arras: when I strike my foot
Vpon the bosome of the ground, rush forth
And binde the boy, which you shall finde with me
Fast to the chaire: be heedfull: hence, and watch.
　Exec. I hope your warrant will beare out the deed.
　Hub. Vncleanly scruples feare not you: looke too't.
Yong Lad come forth; I haue to say with you.
Enter Arthur.
　Ar. Good morrow *Hubert*.
　Hub. Good morrow, little Prince.
　Ar. As little Prince, hauing so great a Title
To be more Prince, as may be: you are sad.
　Hub. Indeed I haue beene merrier.
　Art. 'Mercie on me:
Me thinkes no body should be sad but I:
Yet I remember, when I was in France,
Yong Gentlemen would be as sad as night
Onely for wantonnesse: by my Christendome,
So I were out of prison, and kept Sheepe
I should be as merry as the day is long:
And so I would be heere, but that I doubt
My Vnckle practises more harme to me:
He is affraid of me, and I of him:
Is it my fault, that I was *Geffreyes* sonne?
No in deede is't not: and I would to heauen
I were your sonne, so you would loue me, *Hubert*.
　Hub. If I talke to him, with his innocent prate
He will awake my mercie, which lies dead:
Therefore I will be sodaine, and dispatch.
　Ar. Are you sicke *Hubert*? you looke pale to day,
Insooth I would you were a little sicke,
That I might sit all night, and watch with you.
I warrant I loue you more then you do me.
　Hub. His words do take possession of my bosome.
Reade heere yong *Arthur*. How now foolish rheume?
Turning dispitious torture out of doore?
I must be breefe, least resolution drop
Out at mine eyes, in tender womanish teares.
Can you not reade it? Is it not faire writ?
　Ar. Too fairely *Hubert*, for so foule effect,
Must you with hot Irons, burne out both mine eyes?
　Hub. Yong Boy, I must.
　Art. And will you?
　Hub. And I will.
　Art. Haue you the heart? When your head did but ake,
I knit my hand-kercher about your browes
(The best I had, a Princesse wrought it me)
And I did neuer aske it you againe:
And with my hand, at midnight held your head;
And like the watchfull minutes, to the houre,
Still and anon cheer'd vp the heauy time;
Saying, what lacke you? and where lies your greefe?
Or what good loue may I performe for you?
Many a poore mans sonne would haue lyen still,
And nere haue spoke a louing word to you:
But you, at your sicke seruice had a Prince:
Nay, you may thinke my loue was craftie loue,
And call it cunning. Do, and if you will,

If heauen be pleas'd that you must vse me ill,
Why then you must. Will you put out mine eyes?
These eyes, that neuer did, nor neuer shall
So much as frowne on you.

  Hub. I haue sworne to do it:
And with hot Irons must I burne them out.

  Ar. Ah, none but in this Iron Age, would do it:
The Iron of it selfe, though heate red hot,
Approaching neere these eyes, would drinke my teares,
And quench this fierie indignation,
Euen in the matter of mine innocence:
Nay, after that, consume away in rust,
But for containing fire to harme mine eye:
Are you more stubborne hard, then hammer'd Iron?
And if an Angell should haue come to me,
And told me *Hubert* should put out mine eyes,
I would not haue beleeu'd him: no tongue but *Huberts*.

  Hub. Come forth: Do as I bid you do.

  Art. O saue me *Hubert*, saue me: my eyes are out
Euen with the fierce lookes of these bloody men.

  Hub. Giue me the Iron I say, and binde him heere.

  Art. Alas, what neede you be so boistrous rough?
I will not struggle, I will stand stone still:
For heauen sake *Hubert* let me not be bound:
Nay heare me *Hubert*, driue these men away,
And I will sit as quiet as a Lambe.
I will not stirre, nor winch, nor speake a word,
Nor looke vpon the Iron angerly:
Thrust but these men away, and Ile forgiue you,
What euer torment you do put me too.

  Hub. Go stand within: let me alone with him.

  Exec. I am best pleas'd to be from such a deede.

  Art. Alas, I then haue chid away my friend,
He hath a sterne looke, but a gentle heart:
Let him come backe, that his compassion may
Giue life to yours.

  Hub. Come (Boy) prepare your selfe.

  Art. Is there no remedie?

  Hub. None, but to lose your eyes.

  Art. O heauen: that there were but a moth in yours,
A graine, a dust, a gnat, a wandering haire,
Any annoyance in that precious sense:
Then feeling what small things are boysterous there,
Your vilde intent must needs seeme horrible.

  Hub. Is this your promise? Go too, hold your toong.

  Art. Hubert, the vtterance of a brace of tongues,
Must needes want pleading for a paire of eyes:
Let me not hold my tongue: let me not *Hubert*,
Or *Hubert*, if you will cut out my tongue,
So I may keepe mine eyes. O spare mine eyes,
Though to no vse, but still to looke on you.
Loe, by my troth, the Instrument is cold,
And would not harme me.

  Hub. I can heate it, Boy.

  Art. No, in good sooth: the fire is dead with griefe,
Being create for comfort, to be vs'd
In vndeserued extreames: See else your selfe,
There is no malice in this burning cole,
The breath of heauen, hath blowne his spirit out,
And strew'd repentant ashes on his head.

  Hub. But with my breath I can reuiue it Boy.

  Art. And if you do, you will but make it blush,
And glow with shame of your proceedings, *Hubert*:
Nay, it perchance will sparkle in your eyes:
And, like a dogge that is compell'd to fight,
Snatch at his Master that doth tarre him on.

All things that you should vse to do me wrong
Deny their office: onely you do lacke
That mercie, which fierce fire, and Iron extends,
Creatures of note for mercy, lacking vses.

  Hub. Well, see to liue: I will not touch thine eye,
For all the Treasure that thine Vnckle owes,
Yet am I sworne, and I did purpose, Boy,
With this same very Iron, to burne them out.

  Art. O now you looke like *Hubert*. All this while
You were disguis'd.

  Hub. Peace: no more. Adieu,
Your Vnckle must not know but you are dead.
Ile fill these dogged Spies with false reports:
And, pretty childe, sleepe doubtlesse, and secure,
That *Hubert* for the wealth of all the world,
Will not offend thee.

  Art. O heauen! I thanke you *Hubert*.

  Hub. Silence, no more; go closely in with mee,
Much danger do I vndergo for thee.   *Exeunt.*

Scena Secunda.

Enter Iohn, Pembroke, Salisbury, and other Lordes.

  Iohn. Heere once againe we sit: once against crown'd
And look'd vpon, I hope, with chearefull eyes.

  Pem. This once again (but that your Highnes pleas'd)
Was once superfluous: you were Crown'd before,
And that high Royalty was nere pluck'd off:
The faiths of men, nere stained with reuolt:
Fresh expectation troubled not the Land
With any long'd-for-change, or better State.

  Sal. Therefore, to be possess'd with double pompe,
To guard a Title, that was rich before;
To gilde refined Gold, to paint the Lilly;
To throw a perfume on the Violet,
To smooth the yce, or adde another hew
Vnto the Raine-bow; or with Taper-light
To seeke the beauteous eye of heauen to garnish,
Is wastefull, and ridiculous excesse.

  Pem. But that your Royall pleasure must be done,
This acte, is as an ancient tale new told,
And, in the last repeating, troublesome,
Being vrged at a time vnseasonable.

  Sal. In this the Anticke, and well noted face
Of plaine old forme, is much disfigured,
And like a shifted winde vnto a saile,
It makes the course of thoughts to fetch about,
Startles, and frights consideration:
Makes sound opinion sicke, and truth suspected,
For putting on so new a fashion'd robe.

  Pem. When Workemen striue to do better then wel,
They do confound their skill in couetousnesse,
And oftentimes excusing of a fault,
Doth make the fault the worse by th'excuse:
As patches set vpon a little breach,
Discredite more in hiding of the fault,
Then did the fault before it was so patch'd.

  Sal. To this effect, before you were new crown'd
We breath'd our Councell: but it pleas'd your Highnes
To ouer-beare it, and we are all well pleas'd,
Since all, and euery part of what we would
Doth make a stand, at what your Highnesse will.

Iohn.

Ioh. Some reasons of this double Coronation
I haue possest you with, and thinke them strong,
And more, more strong, then lesser is my feare
I shall indue you with: Meane time, but aske
What you would haue reform'd, that is not well,
And well shall you perceiue, how willingly
I will both heare, and grant you your requests.

Pem. Then I, as one that am the tongue of these
To sound the purposes of all their hearts,
Both for my selfe, and them: but chiefe of all
Your safety: for the which, my selfe and them
Bend their best studies, heartily request
Th'infranchisement of *Arthur*, whose restraint
Doth moue the murmuring lips of discontent
To breake into this dangerous argument.
If what in rest you haue, in right you hold,
Why then your feares, which (as they say) attend
The steppes of wrong, should moue you to mew vp
Your tender kinsman, and to choake his dayes
With barbarous ignorance, and deny his youth
The rich aduantage of good exercise,
That the times enemies may not haue this
To grace occasions: let it be our suite,
That you haue bid vs aske his libertie,
Which for our goods, we do no further aske,
Then, whereupon our weale on you depending,
Counts it your weale: he haue his liberty.

Enter Hubert.

Ioh. Let it be so: I do commit his youth
To your direction: *Hubert*, what newes with you?

Pem. This is the man should do the bloody deed:
He shew'd his warrant to a friend of mine,
The image of a wicked heynous fault
Liues in his eye: that close aspect of his,
Do shew the mood of a much troubled brest,
And I do fearefully beleeue 'tis done,
What we so fear'd he had a charge to do.

Sal. The colour of the King doth come, and go
Betweene his purpose and his conscience,
Like Heralds 'twixt two dreadfull battailes set:
His passion is so ripe, it needs must breake.

Pem. And when it breakes, I feare will issue thence
The foule corruption of a sweet childes death.

Iohn. We cannot hold mortalities strong hand.
Good Lords, although my will to giue, is liuing,
The suite which you demand is gone, and dead.
He tels vs *Arthur* is deceas'd to night.

Sal. Indeed we fear'd his sicknesse was past cure.

Pem. Indeed we heard how neere his death he was,
Before the childe himselfe felt he was sicke:
This must be answer'd either heere, or hence.

Ioh. Why do you bend such solemne browes on me?
Thinke you I beare the Sheeres of destiny?
Haue I commandement on the pulse of life?

Sal. It is apparant foule-play, and 'tis shame
That Greatnesse should so grossely offer it;
So thriue it in your game, and so farewell.

Pem. Stay yet (Lord Salisbury) Ile go with thee,
And finde th'inheritance of this poore childe,
His little kingdome of a forced graue.
That blood which ow'd the bredth of all this Ile,
Three foot of it doth hold; bad world the while:
This must not be thus borne, this will breake out
To all our sorrowes, and ere long I doubt. *Exeunt*

Io. They burn in indignation: I repent: *Enter Mes.*
There is no sure foundation set on blood:
No certaine life atchieu'd by others death:
A fearefull eye thou hast. Where is that blood,
That I haue seene inhabite in those cheekes?
So foule a skie, cleeres not without a storme,
Poure downe thy weather: how goes all in France?

Mes. From France to England, neuer such a powre
For any forraigne preparation,
Was leuied in the body of a land.
The Copie of your speede is learn'd by them:
For when you should be told they do prepare,
The tydings comes, that they are all arriu'd.

Ioh. Oh where hath our Intelligence bin drunke?
Where hath it slept? Where is my Mothers care?
That such an Army could be drawne in France,
And she not heare of it?

Mes. My Liege, her eare
Is stopt with dust: the first of Aprill di'de
Your noble mother; and as I heare, my Lord,
The Lady *Constance* in a frenzie di'de
Three dayes before: but this from Rumors tongue
I idely heard: if true, or false I know not.

Iohn. With-hold thy speed, dreadfull Occasion:
O make a league with me, 'till I haue pleas'd
My discontented Peeres. What? Mother dead?
How wildely then walkes my Estate in France?
Vnder whose conduct came those powres of France,
That thou for truth giu'st out are landed heere?

Mes. Vnder the Dolphin.

Enter Bastard and Peter of Pomfret.

Ioh. Thou hast made me giddy
With these ill tydings: Now? What sayes the world
To your proceedings? Do not seeke to stuffe
My head with more ill newes: for it is full.

Bast. But if you be a-feard to heare the worst,
Then let the worst vn-heard, fall on your head.

Iohn. Beare with me Cosen, for I was amaz'd
Vnder the tide; but now I breath againe
Aloft the flood, and can giue audience
To any tongue, speake it of what it will.

Bast. How I haue sped among the Clergy men,
The summes I haue collected shall expresse:
But as I trauail'd hither through the land,
I finde the people strangely fantasied,
Possest with rumors, full of idle dreames,
Not knowing what they feare, but full of feare.
And here's a Prophet that I brought with me
From forth the streets of Pomfret, whom I found
With many hundreds treading on his heeles:
To whom he sung in rude harsh sounding rimes,
That ere the next Ascension day at noone,
Your Highnes should deliuer vp your Crowne.

Iohn. Thou idle Dreamer, wherefore didst thou so?

Pet. Fore-knowing that the truth will fall out so.

Iohn. *Hubert*, away with him: imprison him,
And on that day at noone, whereon he sayes
I shall yeeld vp my Crowne, let him be hang'd.
Deliuer him to safety, and returne,
For I must vse thee. O my gentle Cosen,
Hear'st thou the newes abroad, who are arriu'd?

Bast. The French (my Lord) mens mouths are ful of it:
Besides I met Lord *Bigot*, and Lord *Salisburie*
With eyes as red as new enkindled fire,
And others more, going to seeke the graue
Of *Arthur*, whom they say is kill'd to night, on your

Iohn. Gentle kinsman, go (suggestion.
And thrust thy selfe into their Companies,

I haue a way to winne their loues againe:
Bring them before me.
  Bast. I will seeke them out.
  Iohn. Nay, but make haste: the better foote before.
O, let me haue no subiect enemies,
When aduerse Forreyners affright my Townes
With dreadfull pompe of stout inuasion.
Be Mercurie, set feathers to thy heeles,
And flye (like thought) from them, to me againe.
  Bast. The spirit of the time shall teach me speed. Exit
  Iohn. Spoke like a sprightfull Noble Gentleman.
Go after him: for he perhaps shall neede
Some Messenger betwixt me, and the Peeres,
And be thou hee.
  Mes. With all my heart, my Liege.
  Iohn. My mother dead?

            Enter Hubert.

  Hub. My Lord, they say fiue Moones were seene to
Foure fixed, and the fift did whirle about   (night:
The other foure, in wondrous motion.
  Ioh. Fiue Moones?
  Hub. Old men, and Beldames, in the streets
Do prophesie vpon it dangerously:
Yong Arthurs death is common in their mouths,
And when they talke of him, they shake their heads,
And whisper one another in the eare.
And he that speakes, doth gripe the hearers wrist,
Whilst he that heares, makes fearefull action
With wrinkled browes, with nods, with rolling eyes.
I saw a Smith stand with his hammer (thus)
The whilst his Iron did on the Anuile coole,
With open mouth swallowing a Taylors newes,
Who with his Sheeres, and Measure in his hand,
Standing on slippers, which his nimble haste
Had falsely thrust vpon contrary feete,
Told of a many thousand warlike French,
That were embattailed, and rank'd in Kent.
Another leane, vnwash'd Artificer,
Cuts off his tale, and talkes of Arthurs death.
  Io. Why seek'st thou to possesse me with these feares?
Why vrgest thou so oft yong Arthurs death?
Thy hand hath murdred him: I had a mighty cause
To wish him dead, but thou hadst none to kill him.
  H. No had (my Lord?) why, did you not prouoke me?
  Iohn. It is the curse of Kings, to be attended
By slaues, that take their humors for a warrant,
To breake within the bloody house of life,
And on the winking of Authoritie
To vnderstand a Law; to know the meaning
Of dangerous Maiesty, when perchance it frownes
More vpon humor, then aduis'd respect.
  Hub. Heere is your hand and Seale for what I did.
  Ioh. Oh, when the last accompt twixt heauen & earth
Is to be made, then shall this hand and Seale
Witnesse against vs to damnation.
How oft the sight of meanes to do ill deeds,
Make deeds ill done? Had'st not thou beene by,
A fellow by the hand of Nature mark'd,
Quoted, and sign'd to do a deede of shame,
This murther had not come into my minde.
But taking note of thy abhorr'd Aspect,
Finding thee fit for bloody villanie:
Apt, liable to be employ'd in danger,
I faintly broke with thee of Arthurs death:
And thou, to be endeered to a King,
Made it no conscience to destroy a Prince.
  Hub. My Lord.
  Ioh. Had'st thou but shooke thy head, or made a pause
When I spake darkely, what I purposed:
Or turn'd an eye of doubt vpon my face;
As bid me tell my tale in expresse words:
Deepe shame had struck me dumbe, made me break off,
And those thy feares, might haue wrought feares in me.
But, thou didst vnderstand me by my signes,
And didst in signes againe parley with sinne,
Yea, without stop, didst let thy heart consent,
And consequently, thy rude hand to acte
The deed, which both our tongues held vilde to name.
Out of my sight, and neuer see me more:
My Nobles leaue me, and my State is braued,
Euen at my gates, with rankes of forraigne powres;
Nay, in the body of this fleshly Land,
This kingdome, this Confine of blood, and breathe
Hostilitie, and ciuill tumult reignes
Betweene my conscience, and my Cosins death.
  Hub. Arme you against your other enemies:
Ile make a peace betweene your soule, and you.
Yong Arthur is aliue: This hand of mine
Is yet a maiden, and an innocent hand.
Not painted with the Crimson spots of blood.
Within this bosome, neuer entred yet
The dreadfull motion of a murderous thought,
And you haue slander'd Nature in my forme,
Which howsoeuer rude exteriorly,
Is yet the couer of a fayrer minde,
Then to be butcher of an innocent childe.
  Ioh. Doth Arthur liue? O haste thee to the Peeres,
Throw this report on their incensed rage,
And make them tame to their obedience.
Forgiue the Comment that my passion made
Vpon thy feature, for my rage was blinde,
And foule immaginarie eyes of blood
Presented thee more hideous then thou art.
Oh, answer not; but to my Closset bring
The angry Lords, with all expedient haste,
I coniure thee but slowly: run more fast. Exeunt.

Scœna Tertia.

          Enter Arthur on the walles.
  Ar. The Wall is high, and yet will I leape downe.
Good ground be pittifull, and hurt me not:
There's few or none do know me, if they did,
This Ship-boyes semblance hath disguis'd me quite.
I am afraide, and yet Ile venture it.
If I get downe, and do not breake my limbes,
Ile finde a thousand shifts to get away;
As good to dye, and go; as dye, and stay.
Oh me, my Vnckles spirit is in these stones,
Heauen take my soule, and England keep my bones. Dies

        Enter Pembroke, Salisbury, & Bigot.
  Sal. Lords, I will meet him at S. Edmondsbury,
It is our safetie, and we must embrace
This gentle offer of the perillous time.
  Pem. Who brought that Letter from the Cardinall?
  Sal. The Count Meloone, a Noble Lord of France,
Whose priuate with me of the Dolphines loue,
Is much more generall, then these lines import.
                                              Big.

The life and death of King John. 17

Big. To morrow morning let vs meete him then.
Sal. Or rather then set forward, for 'twill be
Two long dayes iourney (Lords) or ere we meete.

Enter Bastard.

Bast. Once more to day well met, distemper'd Lords,
The King by me requests your presence straight.
Sal. The king hath dispossest himselfe of vs,
We will not lyne his thin-bestained cloake
With our pure Honors: nor attend the foote
That leaues the print of blood where ere it walkes.
Returne, and tell him so: we know the worst.
Bast. What ere you thinke, good words I thinke
were best.
Sal. Our greefes, and not our manners reason now.
Bast. But there is little reason in your greefe.
Therefore 'twere reason you had manners now.
Pem. Sir, sir, impatience hath his priuiledge.
Bast. 'Tis true, to hurt his master, no mans else.
Sal. This is the prison: What is he lyes heere?
P. Oh death, made proud with pure & princely beuty,
The earth had not a hole to hide this deede.
Sal. Murther, as hating what himselfe hath done,
Doth lay it open to vrge on reuenge.
Big. Or when he doom'd this Beautie to a graue,
Found it too precious Princely, for a graue.
Sal. Sir *Richard*, what thinke you? you haue beheld,
Or haue you read, or heard, or could you thinke?
Or do you almost thinke, although you see,
That you do see? Could thought, without this obiect
Forme such another? This is the very top,
The heighth, the Crest: or Crest vnto the Crest
Of murthers Armes: This is the bloodiest shame,
The wildest Sauagery, the vildest stroke
That euer wall-ey'd wrath, or staring rage
Presented to the teares of soft remorse.
Pem. All murthers past, do stand excus'd in this:
And this so sole, and so vnmatcheable,
Shall giue a holinesse, a puritie,
To the yet vnbegotten sinne of times;
And proue a deadly blood-shed, but a iest,
Exampled by this heynous spectacle.
Bast. It is a damned, and a bloody worke,
The gracelesse action of a heauy hand,
If that it be the worke of any hand.
Sal. If that it be the worke of any hand?
We had a kinde of light, what would ensue:
It is the shamefull worke of *Huberts* hand,
The practice, and the purpose of the king:
From whose obedience I forbid my soule,
Kneeling before this ruine of sweete life,
And breathing to his breathlesse Excellence
The Incense of a Vow, a holy Vow:
Neuer to taste the pleasures of the world,
Neuer to be infected with delight,
Nor conuersant with Ease, and Idlenesse,
Till I haue set a glory to this hand,
By giuing it the worship of Reuenge.
Pem. Big. Our soules religiously confirme thy words.

Enter Hubert.

Hub. Lords, I am hot with haste, in seeking you,
Arthur doth liue, the king hath sent for you.
Sal. Oh he is bold, and blushes not at death,
Auant thou hatefull villain, get thee gone. (the Law?
Hu. I am no villaine. *Sal.* Must I rob
Bast. Your sword is bright sir, put it vp againe.
Sal. Not till I sheath it in a murtherers skin.

Hub. Stand backe Lord Salsbury, stand backe I say:
By heauen, I thinke my sword's as sharpe as yours.
I would not haue you (Lord) forget your selfe,
Nor tempt the danger of my true defence;
Least I, by marking of your rage, forget
your Worth, your Greatnesse, and Nobility.
Big. Out dunghill: dar'st thou braue a Nobleman?
Hub. Not for my life: But yet I dare defend
My innocent life against an Emperor.
Sal. Thou art a Murtherer.
Hub. Do not proue me so:
Yet I am none. Whose tongue so ere speakes false,
Not truely speakes: who speakes not truly, Lies.
Pem. Cut him to peeces.
Bast. Keepe the peace, I say.
Sal. Stand by, or I shall gaul you *Faulconbridge*.
Bast. Thou wer't better gaul the diuell Salsbury.
If thou but frowne on me, or stirre thy foote,
Or teach thy hastie spleene to do me shame,
Ile strike thee dead. Put vp thy sword betime,
Or Ile so maule you, and your tosting-Iron,
That you shall thinke the diuell is come from hell.
Big. What wilt thou do, renowned *Faulconbridge*?
Second a Villaine, and a Murtherer?
Hub. Lord *Bigot*, I am none.
Big. Who kill'd this Prince?
Hub. 'Tis not an houre since I left him well:
I honour'd him, I lou'd him, and will weepe
My date of life out, for his sweete liues losse.
Sal. Trust not those cunning waters of his eyes,
For villanie is not without such rheume,
And he, long traded in it, makes it seeme
Like Riuers of remorse and innocencie.
Away with me, all you whose soules abhorre
Th'vncleanly sauours of a Slaughter-house,
For I am stifled with this smell of sinne.
Big. Away, toward *Burie*, to the Dolphin there.
P. There tel the king, he may inquire vs out. *Ex Lords.*
Ba. Here's a good world: knew you of this faire work?
Beyond the infinite and boundlesse reach of mercie,
(If thou didst this deed of death) art ÿ damn'd *Hubert*.
Hub Do but heare me sir.
Bast. Ha? Ile tell thee what.
Thou'rt damn'd as blacke, nay nothing is so blacke,
Thou art more deepe damn'd then Prince Lucifer:
There is not yet so vgly a fiend of hell
As thou shalt be, if thou didst kill this childe.
Hub. Vpon my soule.
Bast. If thou didst but consent
To this most cruell Act: do but dispaire,
And if thou want'st a Cord, the smallest thred
That euer Spider twisted from her wombe
Will serue to strangle thee: A rush will be a beame
To hang thee on. Or wouldst thou drowne thy selfe,
Put but a little water in a spoone,
And it shall be as all the Ocean,
Enough to stifle such a villaine vp.
I do suspect thee very greeuously.
Hub. If I in act, consent, or sinne of thought,
Be guiltie of the stealing that sweete breath
Which was embounded in this beauteous clay,
Let hell want paines enough to torture me:
I left him well.
Bast. Go, beare him in thine armes:
I am amaz'd me thinkes, and loose my way
Among the thornes, and dangers of this world.

How easie dost thou take all *England* vp,
From forth this morcell of dead Royaltie?
The life, the right, and truth of all this Realme
Is fled to heauen : and *England* now is left
To tug and scamble, and to part by th'teeth
The vn-owed interest of proud swelling State :
Now for the bare-prickt bone of Maiesty,
Doth dogged warre bristle his angry crest,
And snarleth in the gentle eyes of peace :
Now Powers from home, and discontents at home
Meet in one line : and vast confusion waites
As doth a Rauen on a sicke-falne beast,
The iminent decay of wrested pompe.
Now happy he, whose cloake and center can
Hold out this tempest. Beare away that childe,
And follow me with speed : Ile to the King :
A thousand businesses are briefe in hand,
And heauen it selfe doth frowne vpon the Land. *Exit.*

Actus Quartus, Scæna prima.

Enter King Iohn and Pandolph, attendants.

K. Iohn. Thus haue I yeelded vp into your hand
The Circle of my glory.
  Pan. Take againe
From this my hand, as holding of the Pope
Your Soueraigne greatnesse and authoritie.
  Iohn. Now keep your holy word, go meet the *French*,
And from his holinesse vse all your power
To stop their marches 'fore we are enflam'd :
Our discontented Counties doe reuolt :
Our people quarrell with obedience,
Swearing Allegiance, and the loue of soule
To stranger-bloud, to forren Royalty :
This inundation of mistempred humor,
Rests by you onely to be qualified.
Then pause not : for the present time's so sicke,
That present medcine must be ministred,
Or ouerthrow incureable ensues.
  Pand. It was my breath that blew this Tempest vp,
Vpon your stubborne vsage of the Pope :
But since you are a gentle conuertite,
My tongue shall hush againe this storme of warre,
And make faire weather in your blustring land :
On this Ascension day, remember well,
Vpon your oath of seruice to the Pope,
Goe I to make the *French* lay downe their Armes. *Exit.*
  Iohn. Is this Ascension day ? did not the Prophet
Say, that before Ascension day at noone,
My Crowne I should giue off ? euen so I haue :
I did suppose it should be on constraint,
But (heau'n be thank'd) it is but voluntary.
  Enter Bastard.
  Bast. All Kent hath yeelded : nothing there holds out
But Douer Castle : London hath receiu'd
Like a kinde Host, the Dolphin and his powers.
Your Nobles will not heare you, but are gone
To offer seruice to your enemy :
And wilde amazement hurries vp and downe
The little number of your doubtfull friends.
  Iohn. Would not my Lords returne to me againe
After they heard yong *Arthur* was aliue ?

  Bast. They found him dead, and cast into the streets,
An empty Casket, where the Iewell of life
By some damn'd hand was rob'd, and tane away.
  Iohn. That villaine *Hubert* told me he did liue.
  Bast. So on my soule he did, for ought he knew :
But wherefore doe you droope ? why looke you sad ?
Be great in act, as you haue beene in thought :
Let not the world see feare and sad distrust
Gouerne the motion of a kinglye eye :
Be stirring as the time, be fire with fire,
Threaten the threatner, and out-face the brow
Of bragging horror : So shall inferior eyes
That borrow their behauiours from the great,
Grow great by your example, and put on
The dauntlesse spirit of resolution.
Away, and glister like the god of warre
When he intendeth to become the field :
Shew boldnesse and aspiring confidence :
What, shall they seeke the Lion in his denne,
And fright him there ? and make him tremble there ?
Oh let it not be said : forrage, and runne
To meet displeasure farther from the dores,
And grapple with him ere he come so nye.
  Iohn. The Legat of the Pope hath beene with mee,
And I haue made a happy peace with him,
And he hath promis'd to dismisse the Powers
Led by the Dolphin.
  Bast. Oh inglorious league :
Shall we vpon the footing of our land,
Send fayre-play-orders, and make comprimise,
Insinuation, parley, and base truce
To Armes Inuasiue ? Shall a beardlesse boy,
A cockred-silken wanton braue our fields,
And flesh his spirit in a warre-like soyle,
Mocking the ayre with colours idlely spred,
And finde no checke ? Let vs my Liege to Armes :
Perchance the Cardinall cannot make your peace ;
Or if he doe, let it at least be said
They saw we had a purpose of defence.
  Iohn. Haue thou the ordering of this present time.
  Bast. Away then with good courage : yet I know
Our Partie may well meet a prowder foe. *Exeunt.*

Scæna Secunda.

Enter (in Armes) Dolphin, Salisbury, Meloone, Pembroke, Bigot, Souldiers.

  Dol. My Lord *Melloone*, let this be coppied out,
And keepe it safe for our remembrance :
Returne the president to these Lords againe,
That hauing our faire order written downe,
Both they and we, perusing ore these notes
May know wherefore we tooke the Sacrament,
And keepe our faithes firme and inuiolable.
  Sal. Vpon our sides it neuer shall be broken.
And Noble Dolphin, albeit we sweare
A voluntary zeale, and an vn-urg'd Faith
To your proceedings : yet beleeue me Prince,
I am not glad that such a sore of Time
Should seeke a plaster by contemn'd reuolt,
And heale the inueterate Canker of one wound,

By making many: Oh it grieues my soule,
That I must draw this mettle from my side
To be a widdow-maker: oh, and there
Where honourable rescue, and defence
Cries out vpon the name of *Salisbury*.
But such is the infection of the time,
That for the health and Physicke of our right,
We cannot deale but with the very hand
Of sterne Iniustice, and confused wrong:
And is't not pitty, (oh my grieued friends)
That we, the sonnes and children of this Isle,
Was borne to see so sad an houre as this,
Wherein we step after a stranger, march
Vpon her gentle bosom, and fill vp
Her Enemies rankes? I must withdraw, and weepe
Vpon the spot of this inforced cause,
To grace the Gentry of a Land remote,
And follow vnacquainted colours heere:
What heere? O Nation that thou couldst remoue,
That *Neptunes* Armes who clippeth thee about,
Would beare thee from the knowledge of thy selfe,
And cripple thee vnto a Pagan shore,
Where these two Christian Armies might combine
The bloud of malice, in a vaine of league,
And not to spend it so vn-neighbourly.

  Dolph. A noble temper dost thou shew in this,
And great affections wrastling in thy bosome
Doth make an earth-quake of Nobility:
Oh, what a noble combat hast fought
Between compulsion, and a braue respect:
Let me wipe off this honourable dewe,
That siluerly doth progresse on thy cheekes:
My heart hath melted at a Ladies teares,
Being an ordinary Inundation:
But this effusion of such manly drops,
This showre, blowne vp by tempest of the soule,
Startles mine eyes, and makes me more amaz'd
Then had I seene the vaultie top of heauen
Figur'd quite ore with burning Meteors.
Lift vp thy brow (renowned *Salisburie*)
And with a great heart heaue away this storme:
Commend these waters to those baby-eyes
That neuer saw the giant-world enrag'd,
Nor met with Fortune, other then at feasts,
Full warm of blood, of mirth, of gossipping:
Come, come; for thou shalt thrust thy hand as deepe
Into the purse of rich prosperity
As *Lewis* himselfe: so (Nobles) shall you all,
That knit your sinewes to the strength of mine.

  Enter Pandulpho.

And euen there, methinkes an Angell spake,
Looke where the holy Legate comes apace,
To giue vs warrant from the hand of heauen,
And on our actions set the name of right
With holy breath.

  Pand. Haile noble Prince of *France*:
The next is this: King *Iohn* hath reconcil'd
Himselfe to *Rome*, his spirit is come in,
That so stood out against the holy Church,
The great Metropolis and Sea of *Rome*:
Therefore thy threatning Colours now winde vp,
And tame the sauage spirit of wilde warre,
That like a Lion fostered vp at hand,
It may lie gently at the foot of peace,
And be no further harmefull then in shewe.

  Dol. Your Grace shall pardon me, I will not backe:
I am too high-borne to be proportied
To be a secondary at controll,
Or vsefull seruing-man, and Instrument
To any Soueraigne State throughout the world.
Your breath first kindled the dead coale of warres,
Betweene this chastiz'd kingdome and my selfe,
And brought in matter that should feed this fire;
And now 'tis farre too huge to be blowne out
With that same weake winde, which enkindled it:
You taught me how to know the face of right,
Acquainted me with interest to this Land,
Yea, thrust this enterprize into my heart,
And come ye now to tell me *Iohn* hath made
His peace with *Rome*? what is that peace to me?
I (by the honour of my marriage bed)
After yong *Arthur*, claime this Land for mine,
And now it is halfe conquer'd, must I backe,
Because that *Iohn* hath made his peace with *Rome*?
Am I *Romes* slaue? What penny hath *Rome* borne?
What men prouided? What munition sent
To vnder-prop this Action? Is't not I
That vnder-goe this charge? Who else but I,
And such as to my claime are liable,
Sweat in this businesse, and maintaine this warre?
Haue I not heard these Islanders shout out
Viue le Roy, as I haue bank'd their Townes?
Haue I not heere the best Cards for the game
To winne this easie match, plaid for a Crowne?
And shall I now giue ore the yeelded Set?
No, no, on my soule it neuer shall be said.

  Pand. You looke but on the out-side of this worke.

  Dol. Out-side or in-side, I will not returne
Till my attempt so much be glorified,
As to my ample hope was promised,
Before I drew this gallant head of warre,
And cull'd these fiery spirits from the world
To out-looke Conquest, and to winne renowne
Euen in the iawes of danger, and of death:
What lusty Trumpet thus doth summon vs?

  Enter Bastard.

  Bast. According to the faire-play of the world,
Let me haue audience: I am sent to speake:
My holy Lord of Millane, from the King
I come to learne how you haue dealt for him:
And, as you answer, I doe know the scope
And warrant limited vnto my tongue.

  Pand. The *Dolphin* is too wilfull opposite
And will not temporize with my intreaties:
He flatly saies, hee'll not lay downe his Armes.

  Bast. By all the bloud that euer fury breath'd,
The youth saies well. Now heare our *English* King,
For thus his Royaltie doth speake in me:
He is prepar'd, and reason to he should,
This apish and vnmannerly approach,
This harness'd Maske, and vnaduised Reuell,
This vn-heard sawcinesse and boyish Troopes,
The King doth smile at, and is well prepar'd
To whip this dwarfish warre, this Pigmy Armes
From out the circle of his Territories.
That hand which had the strength, euen at your dore,
To cudgell you, and make you take the hatch,
To diue like Buckets in concealed Welles,
To crowch in litter of your stable plankes,
To lye like pawnes, lock'd vp in chests and truncks,
To hug with swine, to seeke sweet safety out
In vaults and prisons, and to thrill and shake,

Euen at the crying of your Nations crow,
Thinking this voyce an armed Englishman.
Shall that victorious hand be feebled heere,
That in your Chambers gaue you chasticement?
No: know the gallant Monarch is in Armes,
And like an Eagle, o're his ayerie towres,
To sowsse annoyance that comes neere his Nest;
And you degenerate, you ingrate Reuolts,
you bloudy Nero's, ripping vp the wombe
Of your deere Mother-England: blush for shame:
For your owne Ladies, and pale-visag'd Maides,
Like *Amazons*, come tripping after drummes:
Their thimbles into armed Gantlets change,
Their Needl's to Lances, and their gentle hearts
To fierce and bloody inclination.

 Dol. There end thy braue, and turn thy face in peace,
We grant thou canst out-scold vs: Far thee well,
We hold our time too precious to be spent
With such a brabler.

 Pan. Giue me leaue to speake.

 Bast. No, I will speake.

 Dol. We will attend to neyther:
Strike vp the drummes, and let the tongue of warre
Pleade for our interest, and our being heere.

 Bast. Indeede your drums being beaten, wil cry out;
And so shall you, being beaten: Do but start
An eccho with the clamor of thy drumme,
And euen at hand, a drumme is readie brac'd,
That shall reuerberate all, as lowd as thine.
Sound but another, and another shall
(As lowd as thine) rattle the Welkins eare,
And mocke the deepe mouth'd Thunder: for at hand
(Not trusting to this halting Legate heere,
Whom he hath vs'd rather for sport, then neede)
Is warlike *Iohn*: and in his fore-head sits
A bare-rib'd death, whose office is this day
To feast vpon whole thousands of the French.

 Dol. Strike vp our drummes, to finde this danger out.

 Bast. And thou shalt finde it (Dolphin) do not doubt
 Exeunt.

Scæna Tertia.

Alarums. Enter Iohn and Hubert.

 Iohn. How goes the day with vs? oh tell me *Hubert*.

 Hub. Badly I feare; how fares your Maiesty?

 Iohn. This Feauer that hath troubled me so long,
Lyes heauie on me: oh, my heart is sicke.

 Enter a Messenger.

 Mes. My Lord: your valiant kinsman *Falconbridge*,
Desires your Maiestie to leaue the field,
And send him word by me, which way you go.

 Iohn. Tell him toward *Swinsted*, to the Abbey there.

 Mes. Be of good comfort: for the great supply,
That was expected by the Dolphin heere,
Are wrack'd three nights ago on *Goodwin* sands.
This newes was brought to *Richard* but euen now,
The French fight coldly, and retyre themselues.

 Iohn. Aye me, this tyrant Feauer burnes mee vp,
And will not let me welcome this good newes.
Set on toward *Swinsted*: to my Litter straight,
Weaknesse possesseth me, and I am faint. *Exeunt*.

Scena Quarta.

Enter Salisbury, Pembroke, and Bigot.

 Sal. I did not thinke the King so stor'd with friends.

 Pem. Vp once againe: put spirit in the French,
If they miscarry: we miscarry too.

 Sal. That misbegotten diuell *Falconbridge*,
In spight of spight, alone vpholds the day.

 Pem. They say King *Iohn* sore sick, hath left the field.

 Enter Meloon wounded.

 Mel. Lead me to the Reuolts of England heere.

 Sal. When we were happie, we had other names.

 Pem. It is the Count *Meloone*.

 Sal. Wounded to death.

 Mel. Fly Noble English, you are bought and sold,
Vnthred the rude eye of Rebellion,
And welcome home againe discarded faith,
Seeke out King *Iohn*, and fall before his feete:
For if the French be Lords of this loud day,
He meanes to recompence the paines you take,
By cutting off your heads: Thus hath he sworne,
And I with him, and many moe with mee,
Vpon the Altar at S. *Edmondsbury*,
Euen on that Altar, where we swore to you
Deere Amity, and euerlasting loue.

 Sal. May this be possible? May this be true?

 Mel. Haue I not hideous death within my view,
Retaining but a quantity of life,
Which bleeds away, euen as a forme of waxe
Resolueth from his figure 'gainst the fire?
What in the world should make me now deceiue,
Since I must loose the vse of all deceite?
Why should I then be false, since it is true
That I must dye heere, and liue hence, by Truth?
I say againe, if *Lewis* do win the day,
He is forsworne, if ere those eyes of yours
Behold another day breake in the East:
But euen this night, whose blacke contagious breath
Already smoakes about the burning Crest
Of the old, feeble, and day-wearied Sunne,
Euen this ill night, your breathing shall expire,
Paying the fine of rated Treachery,
Euen with a treacherous fine of all your liues:
If *Lewis*, by your assistance win the day.
Commend me to one *Hubert*, with your King;
The loue of him, and this respect besides
(For that my Grandsire was an Englishman)
Awakes my Conscience to confesse all this.
In lieu whereof, I pray you beare me hence
From forth the noise and rumour of the Field;
Where I may thinke the remnant of my thoughts
In peace: and part this bodie and my soule
With contemplation, and deuout desires.

 Sal. We do beleeue thee, and beshrew my soule,
But I do loue the fauour, and the forme
Of this most faire occasion, by the which
We will vntread the steps of damned flight,
And like a bated and retired Flood,
Leauing our ranknesse and irregular course,
Stoope lowe within those bounds we haue ore-look'd,
And calmely run on in obedience
Euen to our Ocean, to our great King *Iohn*.
My arme shall giue thee helpe to beare thee hence,

For I do see the cruell pangs of death
Right in thine eye. Away, my friends, new flight,
And happie newnesse, that intends old right. *Exeunt*

Scena Quinta.

Enter Dolphin, and his Traine.

Dol. The Sun of heauen (me thought) was loth to set;
But staid, and made the Westerne Welkin blush,
When English measure backward their owne ground
In faint Retire: Oh brauely came we off,
When with a volley of our needlesse shot,
After such bloody toile, we bid good night,
And woon'd our tott'ring colours clearly vp,
Last in the field, and almost Lords of it.

Enter a Messenger.

Mes. Where is my Prince, the Dolphin?
Dol. Heere: what newes?
Mes. The Count Meloone is slaine: The English Lords
By his perswasion, are againe falne off,
And your supply, which you haue wish'd so long,
Are cast away, and sunke on Goodwin sands.
Dol. Ah fowle, shrew'd newes. Beshrew thy very hart:
I did not thinke to be so sad to night
As this hath made me. Who was he that said
King *Iohn* did flie an houre or two before
The stumbling night did part our wearie powres?
Mes. Who euer spoke it, it is true my Lord.
Dol. Well: keepe good quarter, & good care to night,
The day shall not be vp so soone as I,
To try the faire aduenture of to morrow. *Exeunt*

Scena Sexta.

Enter Bastard and Hubert, seuerally.

Hub. Whose there? Speake hoa, speake quickely, or
I shoote.
Bast. A Friend. What art thou?
Hub. Of the part of England.
Bast. Whether doest thou go?
Hub. What's that to thee?
Why may not I demand of thine affaires,
As well as thou of mine?
Bast. Hubert, I thinke.
Hub. Thou hast a perfect thought:
I will vpon all hazards well beleeue
Thou art my friend, that know'st my tongue so well:
Who art thou?
Bast. Who thou wilt: and if thou please
Thou maist be-friend me so much, as to thinke
I come one way of the *Plantagenets*.
Hub. Vnkinde remembrance: thou, & endles night,
Haue done me shame: Braue Soldier, pardon me,
That any accent breaking from thy tongue,
Should scape the true acquaintance of mine eare.
Bast. Come, come: sans complement, What newes
abroad?
Hub. Why heere walke I, in the black brow of night
To finde you out.

Bast. Breefe then: and what's the newes?
Hub. O my sweet sir, newes fitting to the night,
Blacke, fearefull, comfortlesse, and horrible.
Bast. Shew me the very wound of this ill newes,
I am no woman, Ile not swound at it.
Hub. The King I feare is poyson'd by a Monke,
I left him almost speechlesse, and broke out
To acquaint you with this euill, that you might
The better arme you to the sodaine time,
Then if you had at leisure knowne of this.
Bast. How did he take it? Who did taste to him?
Hub. A Monke I tell you, a resolued villaine
Whose Bowels sodainly burst out: The King
Yet speakes, and peraduenture may recouer.
Bast. Who didst thou leaue to tend his Maiesty?
Hub. Why know you not? The Lords are all come
backe,
And brought Prince *Henry* in their companie,
At whose request the king hath pardon'd them,
And they are all about his Maiestie.
Bast. With-hold thine indignation, mighty heauen,
And tempt vs not to beare aboue our power.
Ile tell thee *Hubert*, halfe my power this night
Passing these Flats, are taken by the Tide,
These Lincolne-Washes haue deuoured them,
My selfe, well mounted, hardly haue escap'd.
Away before: Conduct me to the king,
I doubt he will be dead, or ere I come. *Exeunt*

Scena Septima.

Enter Prince Henry, Salisburie, and Bigot.

Hen. It is too late, the life of all his blood
Is touch'd, corruptibly: and his pure braine
(Which some suppose the soules fraile dwelling house)
Doth by the idle Comments that it makes,
Fore-tell the ending of mortality.

Enter Pembroke.

Pem. His Highnesse yet doth speak, & holds beleefe,
That being brought into the open ayre,
It would allay the burning qualitie
Of that fell poison which assayleth him.
Hen. Let him be brought into the Orchard heere:
Doth he still rage?
Pem. He is more patient
Then when you left him; euen now he sung.
Hen. Oh vanity of sicknesse: fierce extreames
In their continuance, will not feele themselues.
Death hauing praide vpon the outward parts
Leaues them inuisible, and his seige is now
Against the winde, the which he prickes and wounds
With many legions of strange fantasies,
Which in their throng, and presse to that last hold,
Counfound themselues. 'Tis strange y death shold sing:
I am the Symet to this pale faint Swan,
Who chaunts a dolefull hymne to his owne death,
And from the organ-pipe of frailety sings
His soule and body to their lasting rest.
Sal. Be of good comfort (Prince) for you are borne
To set a forme vpon that indigest
Which he hath left so shapelesse, and so rude.

Iohn brought in.

Iohn. I marrie, now my soule hath elbow roome,

It would not out at windowes, nor at doores,
There is so hot a summer in my bosome,
That all my bowels crumble vp to dust:
I am a scribled forme drawne with a pen
Vpon a Parchment, and against this fire
Do I shrinke vp.

Hen. How fares your Maiesty?

Ioh. Poyson'd, ill fare: dead, forsooke, cast off,
And none of you will bid the winter come
To thrust his ycie fingers in my maw;
Nor let my kingdomes Riuers take their course
Through my burn'd bosome: nor intreat the North
To make his bleake windes kisse my parched lips,
And comfort me with cold. I do not aske you much,
I begge cold comfort: and you are so straight
And so ingratefull, you deny me that.

Hen. Oh that there were some vertue in my teares,
That might releeue you.

Iohn. The salt in them is hot.
Within me is a hell, and there the poyson
Is, as a fiend, confin'd to tyrannize,
On vnrepreeuable condemned blood.

Enter Bastard.

Bast. Oh, I am scalded with my violent motion
And spleene of speede, to see your Maiesty.

Iohn. Oh Cozen, thou art come to set mine eye:
The tackle of my heart, is crack'd and burnt,
And all the shrowds wherewith my life should saile,
Are turned to one thred, one little haire:
My heart hath one poore string to stay it by,
Which holds but till thy newes be vttered,
And then all this thou seest, is but a clod,
And module of confounded royalty.

Bast. The Dolphin is preparing hither-ward,
Where heauen he knowes how we shall answer him,
For in a night the best part of my powre,
As I vpon aduantage did remoue,
Were in the *Washes* all vnwarily,
Deuoured by the vnexpected flood.

Sal. You breath these dead newes in as dead an eare
My Liege, my Lord: but now a King, now thus.

Hen. Euen so must I run on, and euen so stop.
What surety of the world, what hope, what stay,
When this was now a King, and now is clay?

Bast. Art thou gone so? I do but stay behinde,
To do the office for thee, of reuenge,
And then my soule shall waite on thee to heauen,
As it on earth hath bene thy seruant still.
Now, now you Starres, that moue in your right spheres,
Where be your powres? Shew now your mended faiths,
And instantly returne with me againe.
To push destruction, and perpetuall shame
Out of the weake doore of our fainting Land:
Straight let vs seeke, or straight we shall be sought,
The Dolphine rages at our verie heeles.

Sal. It seemes you know not then so much as we,
The Cardinall *Pandulph* is within at rest,
Who halfe an houre since came from the Dolphin,
And brings from him such offers of our peace,
As we with honor and respect may take,
With purpose presently to leaue this warre.

Bast. He will the rather do it, when he sees
Our selues well sinew'd to our defence.

Sal. Nay, 'tis in a manner done already,
For many carriages hee hath dispatch'd
To the sea side, and put his cause and quarrell
To the disposing of the Cardinall,
With whom your selfe, my selfe, and other Lords,
If you thinke meete, this afternoone will post
To consummate this businesse happily.

Bast. Let it be so, and you my noble Prince,
With other Princes that may best be spar'd,
Shall waite vpon your Fathers Funerall.

Hen. At Worster must his bodie be interr'd,
For so he will'd it.

Bast. Thither shall it then,
And happily may your sweet selfe put on
The lineall state, and glorie of the Land,
To whom with all submission on my knee,
I do bequeath my faithfull seruices
And true subiection euerlastingly.

Sal. And the like tender of our loue wee make
To rest without a spot for euermore.

Hen. I haue a kinde soule, that would giue thankes,
And knowes not how to do it, but with teares.

Bast. Oh let vs pay the time: but needfull woe,
Since it hath beene before hand with our greefes.
This England neuer did, nor neuer shall
Lye at the proud foote of a Conqueror,
But when it first did helpe to wound it selfe.
Now, these her Princes are come home againe,
Come the three corners of the world in Armes,
And we shall shocke them: Naught shall make vs rue,
If England to it selfe, do rest but true. *Exeunt.*

The life and death of King Richard the Second.

Actus Primus, Scæna Prima.

Enter King Richard, Iohn of Gaunt, with other Nobles and Attendants.

King Richard.
Ld *Iohn of Gaunt*, time-honoured Lancaster,
Hast thou according to thy oath and band
Brought hither *Henry Herford* thy bold son:
Heere to make good § boistrous late-appeale,
Which then our leysure would not let vs heare,
Against the Duke of Norfolke, *Thomas Mowbray*?

Gaunt. I haue my Liege.

King. Tell me moreouer, hast thou sounded him,
If he appeale the Duke on ancient malice,
Or worthily as a good subiect should
On some knowne ground of treacherie in him.

Gaunt. As neere as I could sift him on that argument,
On some apparant danger seene in him,
Aym'd at your Highnesse, no inueterate malice.

Kin. Then call them to our presence face to face,
And frowning brow to brow, our selues will heare
Th'accuser, and the accused, freely speake;
High stomack'd are they both, and full of ire,
In rage, deafe as the sea; hastie as fire.

Enter Bullingbrooke and Mowbray.

Bul. Many yeares of happy dayes befall
My gracious Soueraigne, my most louing Liege.

Mow. Each day still better others happinesse,
Vntill the heauens enuying earths good hap,
Adde an immortall title to your Crowne.

King. We thanke you both, yet one but flatters vs,
As well appeareth by the cause you come,
Namely, to appeale each other of high treason.
Coosin of Hereford, what dost thou obiect
Against the Duke of Norfolke, *Thomas Mowbray*?

Bul. First, heauen be the record to my speech,
In the deuotion of a subiects loue,
Tendering the precious safetie of my Prince,
And free from other misbegotten hate,
Come I appealant to this Princely presence.
Now *Thomas Mowbray* do I turne to thee,
And marke my greeting well: for what I speake,
My body shall make good vpon this earth,
Or my diuine soule answer it in heauen.
Thou art a Traitor, and a Miscreant;
Too good to be so, and too bad to liue,
Since the more faire and christall is the skie,

The vglier seeme the cloudes that in it flye:
Once more, the more to aggrauate the note,
With a foule Traitors name stuffe I thy throte,
And wish (so please my Soueraigne) ere I moue,
What my tong speaks, my right drawn sword may proue.

Mow. Let not my cold words heere accuse my zeale:
'Tis not the triall of a Womans warre,
The bitter clamour of two eager tongues,
Can arbitrate this cause betwixt vs twaine:
The blood is hot that must be cool'd for this.
Yet can I not of such tame patience boast,
As to be husht, and nought at all to say.
First the faire reuerence of your Highnesse curbes mee,
From giuing reines and spurres to my free speech,
Which else would post, vntill it had return'd
These tearmes of treason, doubly downe his throat.
Setting aside his high bloods royalty,
And let him be no Kinsman to my Liege,
I do defie him, and I spit at him,
Call him a slanderous Coward, and a Villaine:
Which to maintaine, I would allow him oddes,
And meete him, were I tide to runne afoote,
Euen to the frozen ridges of the Alpes,
Or any other ground inhabitable,
Where euer Englishman durst set his foote.
Meane time, let this defend my loyaltie,
By all my hopes most falsely doth he lie.

Bul. Pale trembling Coward, there I throw my gage,
Disclaiming heere the kindred of a King,
And lay aside my high bloods Royalty,
Which feare, not reuerence makes thee to except,
If guilty dread hath left thee so much strength,
As to take vp mine Honors pawne, then stoope.
By that, and all the rites of Knight-hood else,
Will I make good against thee arme to arme,
What I haue spoken, or thou canst deuise.

Mow. I take it vp, and by that sword I sweare,
Which gently laid my Knight-hood on my shoulder,
Ile answer thee in any faire degree,
Or Chiualrous designe of knightly triall:
And when I mount, aliue may I not light,
If I be Traitor, or vniustly fight.

King. What doth our Cosin lay to *Mowbraies* charge?
It must be great that can inherite vs,
So much as of a thought of ill in him.

Bul. Looke what I said, my life shall proue it true,
That *Mowbray* hath receiu'd eight thousand Nobles,

In

In name of lendings for your Highnesse Soldiers,
The which he hath detain'd for lewd employments,
Like a false Traitor, and iniurious Villaine.
Besides I say, and will in battaile proue,
Or heere, or elsewhere to the furthest Verge
That euer was suruey'd by English eye,
That all the Treasons for these eighteene yeeres
Complotted, and contriued in this Land,
Fetch'd from false *Mowbray* their first head and spring.
Further I say, and further will maintaine
Vpon his bad life, to make all this good.
That he did plot the Duke of Gloufters death,
Suggest his soone beleeuing aduersaries,
And consequently, like a Traitor Coward,
Sluc'd out his innocent soule through streames of blood:
Which blood, like sacrificing *Abels* cries,
(Euen from the toonglesse cauerns of the earth)
To me for iustice, and rough chasticement:
And by the glorious worth of my discent,
This arme shall do it, or this life be spent.

 King. How high a pitch his resolution soares:
Thomas of Norfolke, what sayest thou to this?

 Mow. Oh let my Soueraigne turne away his face,
And bid his eares a little while be deafe,
Till I haue told this slander of his blood,
How God, and good men, hate so foule a lyar.

 King. Mowbray, impartiall are our eyes and eares,
Were he my brother, nay our kingdomes heyre,
As he is but my fathers brothers sonne;
Now by my Scepters awe, I make a vow,
Such neighbour-neerenesse to our sacred blood,
Should nothing priuiledge him, nor partialize
The vn-stooping firmenesse of my vpright soule.
He is our subiect (*Mowbray*) so art thou,
Free speech, and fearelesse, I to thee allow.

 Mow. Then *Bullingbrooke*, as low as to thy heart,
Through the false passage of thy throat; thou lyest:
Three parts of that receipt I had for Callice,
Disburst I to his Highnesse souldiers;
The other part reseru'd I by consent,
For that my Soueraigne Liege was in my debt,
Vpon remainder of a deere Accompt,
Since last I went to France to fetch his Queene:
Now swallow downe that Lye. For Gloufters death,
I slew him not; but (to mine owne disgrace)
Neglected my sworne duty in that case:
For you my noble Lord of *Lancaster*,
The honourable Father to my foe,
Once I did lay an ambush for your life,
A trespasse that doth vex my greeued soule:
But ere I last receiu'd the Sacrament,
I did confesse it, and exactly begg'd
Your Graces pardon, and I hope I had it.
This is my fault: as for the rest appeal'd,
It issues from the rancour of a Villaine,
A recreant, and most degenerate Traitor,
Which in my selfe I boldly will defend,
And interchangeably hurle downe my gage
Vpon this ouer-weening Traitors foote,
To proue my selfe a loyall Gentleman,
Euen in the best blood chamber'd in his bosome.
In hast whereof, most heartily I pray
Your Highnesse to assigne our Triall day.

 King. Wrath-kindled Gentlemen be rul'd by me:
Let's purge this choller without letting blood:
This we prescribe, though no Physition,
Deepe malice makes too deepe incision.
Forget, forgiue, conclude, and be agreed,
Our Doctors say, This is no time to bleed.
Good Vnckle, let this end where it begun,
Wee'l calme the Duke of Norfolke; you, your son.

 Gaunt. To be a make-peace shall become my age,
Throw downe (my sonne) the Duke of Norfolkes gage.

 King. And Norfolke, throw downe his.

 Gaunt. When *Harrie* when? Obedience bids,
Obedience bids I should not bid agen.

 King. Norfolke, throw downe, we bidde; there is
no boote.

 Mow. My selfe I throw (dread Soueraigne) at thy foot.
My life thou shalt command, but not my shame,
The one my dutie owes, but my faire name
Despight of death, that liues vpon my graue
To darke dishonours vse, thou shalt not haue.
I am disgrac'd, impeach'd, and baffel'd heere,
Pierc'd to the soule with slanders venom'd speare:
The which no balme can cure, but his heart blood
Which breath'd this poyson.

 King. Rage must be withstood:
Giue me his gage: Lyons make Leopards tame.

 Mo. Yea, but not change his spots: take but my shame,
And I resigne my gage. My deere, deere Lord,
The purest treasure mortall times afford
Is spotlesse reputation: that away,
Men are but gilded loame, or painted clay.
A Iewell in a ten times barr'd vp Chest,
Is a bold spirit, in a loyall brest.
Mine Honor is my life; both grow in one:
Take Honor from me, and my life is done.
Then (deere my Liege) mine Honor let me trie,
In that I liue; and for that will I die.

 King. Coosin, throw downe your gage,
Do you begin.

 Bul. Oh heauen defend my soule from such foule sin.
Shall I seeme Crest-falne in my fathers sight,
Or with pale beggar-feare impeach my hight
Before this out-dar'd dastard? Ere my toong,
Shall wound mine honor with such feeble wrong;
Or sound so base a parle: my teeth shall teare
The slauish motiue of recanting feare,
And spit it bleeding in his high disgrace,
Where shame doth harbour, euen in *Mowbrayes* face.
                                                   Exit Gaunt.

 King. We were not borne to sue, but to command,
Which since we cannot do to make you friends,
Be readie, (as your liues shall answer it)
At Couentree, vpon S. *Lamberts* day:
There shall your swords and Lances arbitrate
The swelling difference of your setled hate:
Since we cannot attone you, you shall see
Iustice designe the Victors Chiualrie.
Lord Marshall, command our Officers at Armes,
Be readie to direct these home Alarmes. *Exeunt.*

Scæna Secunda.

Enter Gaunt, and Dutchesse of Gloucester.

 Gaunt. Alas, the part I had in Gloufters blood,
Doth more solicite me then your exclaimes,
To stirre against the Butchers of his life.

But since correction lyeth in those hands
Which made the fault that we cannot correct,
Put we our quarrell to the will of heauen,
Who when they see the houres ripe on earth,
Will raigne hot vengeance on offenders heads.

  Dut. Findes brotherhood in thee no sharper spurre?
Hath loue in thy old blood no liuing fire?
Edwards seuen sonnes (whereof thy selfe art one)
Were as seuen violles of his Sacred blood,
Or seuen faire branches springing from one roote:
Some of those seuen are dride by natures course,
Some of those branches by the destinies cut:
But *Thomas*, my deere Lord, my life, my Glouster,
One Violl full of *Edwards* Sacred blood,
One flourishing branch of his most Royall roote
Is crack'd, and all the precious liquor spilt;
Is hackt downe, and his summer leafes all vaded
By Enuies hand, and Murders bloody Axe.
Ah *Gaunt*! His blood was thine, that bed, that wombe,
That mettle, that selfe-mould that fashion'd thee,
Made him a man: and though thou liu'st, and breath'st,
Yet art thou slaine in him: thou dost consent
In some large measure to thy Fathers death,
In that thou seest thy wretched brother dye,
Who was the modell of thy Fathers life.
Call it not patience (*Gaunt*) it is dispaire,
In suffring thus thy brother to be slaughter'd,
Thou shew'st the naked pathway to thy life,
Teaching sterne murther how to butcher thee:
That which in meane men we intitle patience
Is pale cold cowardice in noble brests:
What shall I say, to safegard thine owne life,
The best way is to venge my Glousters death.

  Gaunt. Heauens is the quarrell: for heauens substitute
His Deputy annointed in his sight,
Hath caus'd his death, the which if wrongfully
Let heauen reuenge: for I may neuer lift
An angry arme against his Minister.

  Dut. Where then (alas may I) complaint my selfe?
  Gau. To heauen, the widdowes Champion to defence
  Dut. Why then I will: farewell old *Gaunt*.
Thou go'st to Couentrie, there to behold
Our Cosine Herford, and fell Mowbray fight:
O sit my husbands wrongs on Herfords speare,
That it may enter butcher Mowbrayes brest:
Or if misfortune misse the first carreere,
Be Mowbrayes sinnes so heauy in his bosome,
That they may breake his foaming Coursers backe,
And throw the Rider headlong in the Lists,
A Caytiffe recreant to my Cosine Herford:
Farewell old *Gaunt*, thy sometimes brothers wife
With her companion Greefe, must end her life.

  Gau. Sister farewell: I must to Couentree,
As much good stay with thee, as go with mee.

  Dut. Yet one word more: Greefe boundeth where it
Not with the emptie hollownes, but weight: (falls,
I take my leaue, before I haue begun,
For sorrow ends not, when it seemeth done.
Commend me to my brother *Edmund Yorke*.
Loe, this is all: nay, yet depart not so,
Though this be all, do not so quickly go,
I shall remember more. Bid him, Oh, what?
With all good speed at Plashie visit mee.
Alacke, and what shall good old *Yorke* there see
But empty lodgings, and vnfurnish'd walles,
Vn-peopel'd Offices, vntroden stones?

And what heare there for welcome, but my grones?
Therefore commend me, let him not come there,
To seeke out sorrow, that dwels euery where:
Desolate, desolate will I hence, and dye,
The last leaue of thee, takes my weeping eye. *Exeunt*

Scena Tertia.

Enter Marshall, and Aumerle.

  Mar. My L. *Aumerle*, is *Harry Herford* arm'd.
  Aum. Yea, at all points, and longs to enter in.
  Mar. The Duke of Norfolke, sprightfully and bold,
Stayes but the summons of the Appealants Trumpet.
  Au. Why then the Champions, are prepar'd, and stay
For nothing but his Maiesties approach. *Flourish.*

*Enter King, Gaunt, Bushy, Bagot, Greene, &
others: Then Mowbray in Ar-
mor, and Harrold.*

  Rich. Marshall, demand of yonder Champion
The cause of his arriuall heere in Armes,
Aske him his name, and orderly proceed
To sweare him in the iustice of his cause.

  Mar. In Gods name, and the Kings, say who y art,
And why thou com'st thus knightly clad in Armes?
Against what man thou com'st, and what's thy quarrell,
Speake truly on thy knighthood, and thine oath,
As so defend thee heauen, and thy valour.

  Mow. My name is *Tho. Mowbray*, Duke of Norfolk,
Who hither comes engaged by my oath
(Which heauen defend a knight should violate)
Both to defend my loyalty and truth,
To God, my King, and his succeeding issue,
Against the Duke of Herford, that appeales me:
And by the grace of God, and this mine arme,
To proue him (in defending of my selfe)
A Traitor to my God, my King, and me,
And as I truly fight, defend me heauen.

Tucket. Enter Hereford, and Harold.

  Rich. Marshall: Aske yonder Knight in Armes,
Both who he is, and why he commeth hither,
Thus placed in habiliments of warre:
And formerly according to our Law
Depose him in the iustice of his cause.

  Mar. What is thy name? and wherfore comst y hither
Before King *Richard* in his Royall Lifts?
Against whom com'st thou? and what's thy quarrell?
Speake like a true Knight, so defend thee heauen.

  Bul. Harry of Herford, Lancaster, and Derbie,
Am I: who ready heere do stand in Armes,
To proue by heauens grace, and my bodies valour,
In Lifts, on *Thomas Mowbray* Duke of Norfolke,
That he's a Traitor foule, and dangerous,
To God of heauen, King *Richard*, and to me,
And as I truly fight, defend me heauen.

  Mar. On paine of death, no person be so bold,
Or daring hardie as to touch the Lifts,
Except the Marshall, and such Officers
Appointed to direct these faire designes.

  Bul. Lord Marshall, let me kisse my Soueraigns hand,
And bow my knee before his Maiestie:
For *Mowbray* and my selfe are like two men,
That vow a long and weary pilgrimage,

Then

Then let vs take a ceremonious leaue
And louing farwell of our seuerall friends.

  Mar. The Appealant in all duty greets your Highnes,
And craues to kisse your hand, and take his leaue.

  Rich. We will descend, and fold him in our armes.
Cosin of Herford, as thy cause is iust,
So be thy fortune in this Royall fight:
Farewell, my blood, which if to day thou shead,
Lament we may, but not reuenge thee dead.

  Bull. Oh let no noble eye prophane a teare
For me, if I be gor'd with *Mowbrayes* speare:
As confident, as is the Falcons flight
Against a bird, do I with *Mowbray* fight.
My louing Lord, I take my leaue of you,
Of you (my Noble Cosin) Lord *Aumerle*;
Not sicke, although I haue to do with death,
But lustie, yong, and cheerely drawing breath.
Loe, as at English Feasts, so I regreete
The daintiest last, to make the end most sweet.
Oh thou the earthy author of my blood,
Whose youthfull spirit in me regenerate,
Doth with a two-fold rigor lift mee vp
To reach at victory aboue my head,
Adde proofe vnto mine Armour with thy prayres,
And with thy blessings steele my Lances point,
That it may enter *Mowbrayes* waxen Coate,
And furnish new the name of *Iohn a Gaunt*,
Euen in the lusty hauiour of his sonne.

  Gaunt. Heauen in thy good cause make thee prosp'rous
Be swift like lightning in the execution,
And let thy blowes doubly redoubled,
Fall like amazing thunder on the Caske
Of thy amaz'd pernicious enemy.
Rouze vp thy youthfull blood, be valiant, and liue.

  Bul. Mine innocence, and S. *George* to thriue.

  Mow. How euer heauen or fortune cast my lot,
There liues, or dies, true to Kings *Richards* Throne,
A loyall, iust, and vpright Gentleman:
Neuer did Captiue with a freer heart,
Cast off his chaines of bondage, and embrace
His golden vncontroul'd enfranchisement,
More then my dancing soule doth celebrate
This Feast of Battell, with mine Aduersarie.
Most mighty Liege, and my companion Peeres,
Take from my mouth, the wish of happy yeares,
As gentle, and as iocond, as to iest,
Go I to fight: Truth, hath a quiet brest.

  Rich. Farewell, my Lord, securely I espy
Vertue with Valour, couched in thine eye:
Order the triall Marshall, and begin.

  Mar. *Harrie* of *Herford*, *Lancaster*, and *Derby*,
Receiue thy Launce, and heauen defend thy right.

  Bul. Strong as a towre in hope, I cry Amen.

  Mar. Go beare this Lance to *Thomas* D. of Norfolke.

  1. *Har.* *Harry* of *Herford*, *Lancaster*, and *Derbie*,
Stands heere for God, his Soueraigne, and himselfe,
On paine to be found false, and recreant,
To proue the Duke of Norfolke, *Thomas Mowbray*,
A Traitor to his God, his King, and him,
And dares him to set forwards to the fight.

  2. *Har.* Here standeth *Tho: Mowbray* Duke of Norfolk
On paine to be found false and recreant,
Both to defend himselfe, and to approue
Henry of *Herford*, *Lancaster*, and *Derby*,
To God, his Soueraigne, and to him disloyall:
Couragiously, and with a free desire
Attending but the signall to begin. *A charge sounded*

  Mar. Sound Trumpets, and set forward Combatants:
Stay, the King hath throwne his Warder downe.

  Rich. Let them lay by their Helmets & their Speares,
And both returne backe to their Chaires againe:
Withdraw with vs, and let the Trumpets sound,
While we returne these Dukes what we decree.

A long Flourish.

Draw neere and list
What with our Councell we haue done.
For that our kingdomes earth should not be soyld
With that deere blood which it hath fostered,
And for our eyes do hate the dire aspect
Of ciuill wounds plowgh'd vp with neighbors swords,
Which so rouz'd vp with boystrous vntun'd drummes,
With harsh resounding Trumpets dreadfull bray,
And grating shocke of wrathfull yron Armes,
Might from our quiet Confines fright faire peace,
And make vs wade euen in our kindreds blood:
Therefore, we banish you our Territories.
You Cosin Herford, vpon paine of death,
Till twice fiue Summers haue enrich'd our fields,
Shall not regreet our faire dominions,
But treade the stranger pathes of banishment.

  Bul. Your will be done: This must my comfort be,
That Sun that warmes you heere, shall shine on me:
And those his golden beames to you heere lent,
Shall point on me, and gild my banishment.

  Rich. Norfolke: for thee remaines a heauier dombe,
Which I with some vnwillingnesse pronounce,
The slye slow houres shall not determinate
The datelesse limit of thy deere exile:
The hopelesse word, of Neuer to returne,
Breath I against thee, vpon paine of life.

  Mow. A heauy sentence, my most Soueraigne Liege,
And all vnlook'd for from your Highnesse mouth:
A deerer merit, not so deepe a maime,
As to be cast forth in the common ayre
Haue I deserued at your Highnesse hands.
The Language I haue learn'd these forty yeares
(My natiue English) now I must forgo,
And now my tongues vse is to me no more,
Then an vnstringed Vyall, or a Harpe,
Or like a cunning Instrument cas'd vp,
Or being open, put into his hands
That knowes no touch to tune the harmony.
Within my mouth you haue engaol'd my tongue,
Doubly percullist with my teeth and lippes,
And dull, vnfeeling, barren ignorance,
Is made my Gaoler to attend on me:
I am too old to fawne vpon a Nurse,
Too farre in yeeres to be a pupill now:
What is thy sentence then, but speechlesse death,
Which robs my tongue from breathing natiue breath?

  Rich. It boots thee not to be compassionate,
After our sentence, plaining comes too late.

  Mow. Then thus I turne me from my countries light
To dwell in solemne shades of endlesse night.

  Ric. Returne againe, and take an oath with thee,
Lay on our Royall sword, your banisht hands;
Sweare by the duty that you owe to heauen
(Our part therein we banish with your selues)
To keepe the Oath that we administer:
You neuer shall (so helpe you Truth, and Heauen)
Embrace each others loue in banishment,
Nor euer looke vpon each others face,

Nor euer write, regreete, or reconcile
This lowring tempest of your home-bred hate,
Nor euer by aduised purpose meete,
To plot, contriue, or complot any ill,
'Gainst Vs, our State, our Subiects, or our Land.

Bull. I sweare.

Mow. And I, to keepe all this.

Bul. Norfolke, so farre, as to mine enemie,
By this time (had the King permitted vs)
One of our soules had wandred in the ayre,
Banish'd this fraile sepulchre of our flesh,
As now our flesh is banish'd from this Land.
Confesse thy Treasons, ere thou flye this Realme,
Since thou hast farre to go, beare not along
The clogging burthen of a guilty soule.

Mow. No *Bullingbroke*: If euer I were Traitor,
My name be blotted from the booke of Life,
And I from heauen banish'd, as from hence:
But what thou art, heauen, thou, and I do know,
And all too soone (I feare) the King shall rue.
Farewell (my Liege) now no way can I stray,
Saue backe to England, all the worlds my way. *Exit.*

Rich. Vncle, euen in the glasses of thine eyes
I see thy greeued heart: thy sad aspect,
Hath from the number of his banish'd yeares
Pluck'd foure away: Six frozen Winters spent,
Returne with welcome home, from banishment.

Bul. How long a time lyes in one little word:
Foure lagging Winters, and foure wanton springs
End in a word, such is the breath of Kings.

Gaunt. I thanke my Liege, that in regard of me
He shortens foure yeares of my sonnes exile:
But little vantage shall I reape thereby.
For ere the sixe yeares that he hath to spend
Can change their Moones, and bring their times about,
My oyle-dride Lampe, and time-bewasted light
Shall be extinct with age, and endlesse night:
My inch of Taper, will be burnt, and done,
And blindfold death, not let me see my sonne.

Rich. Why Vncle, thou hast many yeeres to liue.

Gaunt. But not a minute (King) that thou canst giue;
Shorten my dayes thou canst with sudden sorow,
And plucke nights from me, but not lend a morrow:
Thou canst helpe time to furrow me with age,
But stop no wrinkle in his pilgrimage:
Thy word is currant with him, for my death,
But dead, thy kingdome cannot buy my breath.

Ric. Thy sonne is banish'd vpon good aduice,
Whereto thy tongue a party-verdict gaue,
Why at our Iustice seem'st thou then to lowre?

Gau. Things sweet to tast, proue in digestion sowre:
You vrg'd me as a Iudge, but I had rather
you would haue bid me argue like a Father.
Alas, I look'd when some of you should say,
I was too strict to make mine owne away:
But you gaue leaue to my vnwilling tong,
Against my will, to do my selfe this wrong.

Rich. Cosine farewell: and Vncle bid him so:
Six yeares we banish him, and he shall go. *Exit.*

Flourish.

Au. Cosine farewell: what presence must not know
From where you do remaine, let paper show.

Mar. My Lord, no leaue take I, for I will ride
As farre as land will let me, by your side.

Gaunt. Oh to what purpose dost thou hord thy words,
That thou returnst no greeting to thy friends?

Bull. I haue too few to take my leaue of you,
When the tongues office should be prodigall,
To breath th'abundant dolour of the heart.

Gau. Thy greefe is but thy absence for a time.

Bull. Ioy absent, greefe is present for that time.

Gau. What is sixe Winters, they are quickely gone?

Bul. To men in ioy, but greefe makes one houre ten.

Gau. Call it a trauell that thou tak'st for pleasure.

Bul. My heart will sigh, when I miscall it so,
Which findes it an inforced Pilgrimage.

Gau. The sullen passage of thy weary steppes
Esteeme a foyle, wherein thou art to set
The precious Iewell of thy home returne.

Bul. Oh who can hold a fire in his hand
By thinking on the frostie *Caucasus*?
Or cloy the hungry edge of appetite,
by bare imagination of a Feast?
Or Wallow naked in December snow
by thinking on fantasticke summers heate?
Oh no, the apprehension of the good
Giues but the greater feeling to the worse:
Fell sorrowes tooth, doth euer ranckle more
Then when it bites, but lanceth not the sore.

Gau. Come, come (my son) Ile bring thee on thy way
Had I thy youth, and cause, I would not stay.

Bul. Then Englands ground farewell: sweet soil adieu,
My Mother, and my Nurse, which beares me yet:
Where ere I wander, boast of this I can,
Though banish'd, yet a true-borne Englishman.

Scœna Quarta.

Enter King, Aumerle, Greene, and Bagot.

Rich. We did obserue. Cosine *Aumerle*,
How far brought you high Herford on his way?

Aum. I brought high Herford (if you call him so)
but to the next high way, and there I left him.

Rich. And say, what store of parting teares were shed?

Aum. Faith none for me: except the Northeast wind
Which then grew bitterly against our face,
Awak'd the sleepie rhewme, and so by chance
Did grace our hollow parting with a teare.

Rich. What said our Cosin when you parted with him?

Au. Farewell: and for my hart disdained ÿ my tongue
Should so prophane the word, that taught me craft
To counterfeit oppression of such greefe,
That word seem'd buried in my sorrowes graue.
Marry, would the word Farwell, haue lengthen'd houres,
And added yeeres to his short banishment,
He should haue had a volume of Farwels,
but since it would not, he had none of me.

Rich. He is our Cosin (Cosin) but 'tis doubt,
When time shall call him home from banishment,
Whether our kinsman come to see his friends,
Our selfe, and *Bushy*: heere *Bagot* and *Greene*
Obseru'd his Courtship to the common people:
How he did seeme to diue into their hearts,
With humble, and familiar courtesie,
What reuerence he did throw away on slaues;
Wooing poore Craftes-men, with the craft of soules,
And patient vnder-bearing of his Fortune,
As 'twere to banish their affects with him.
Off goes his bonnet to an Oyster-wench,

A brace of Dray-men bid God speed him well,
And had the tribute of his supple knee,
With thankes my Countrimen, my louing friends,
As were our England in reuersion his,
And he our subiects next degree in hope.

Gr. Well, he is gone, & with him go these thoughts:
Now for the Rebels, which stand out in Ireland,
Expedient manage must be made my Liege
Ere further leysure, yeeld them further meanes
For their aduantage, and your Highnesse losse.

Ric. We will our selfe in person to this warre,
And for our Coffers, with too great a Court,
And liberall Largesse, are growne somewhat light,
We are inforc'd to farme our royall Realme,
The Reuennew whereof shall furnish vs
For our affayres in hand: if that come short
Our Substitutes at home shall haue Blanke-charters:
Whereto, when they shall know what men are rich,
They shall subscribe them for large summes of Gold,
And send them after to supply our wants:
For we will make for Ireland presently.

Enter Bushy.

Bushy, what newes?

Bu. Old *Iohn of Gaunt* is verie sicke my Lord,
Sodainly taken, and hath sent post haste
To entreat your Maiesty to visit him.

Ric. Where lyes he?

Bu. At Ely house.

Ric. Now put it (heauen) in his Physitians minde,
To helpe him to his graue immediately:
The lining of his coffers shall make Coates
To decke our souldiers for these Irish warres.
Come Gentlemen, let's all go visit him:
Pray heauen we may make hast, and come too late. *Exit.*

Actus Secundus. Scena Prima.

Enter Gaunt, sicke with Yorke.

Gau. Will the King come, that I may breath my last
In wholsome counsell to his vnstaid youth?

Yor. Vex not your selfe, nor striue not with your breth,
For all in vaine comes counsell to his eare.

Gau. Oh but (they say) the tongues of dying men
Inforce attention like deepe harmony;
Where words are scarse, they are seldome spent in vaine,
For they breath truth, that breath their words in paine.
He that no more must say, is listen'd more,
Then they whom youth and ease haue taught to glose,
More are mens ends markt, then their liues before,
The setting Sun, and Musicke is the close
As the last taste of sweetes, is sweetest last,
Writ in remembrance, more then things long past;
Though *Richard* my liues counsell would not heare,
My deaths sad tale, may yet vndeafe his eare.

Yor. No, it is stopt with other flatt'ring sounds
As praises of his state: then there are found
Lasciuious Meeters, to whose venom sound
The open eare of youth doth alwayes listen.
Report of fashions in proud Italy,
Whose manners still our tardie apish Nation
Limpes after in base imitation.
Where doth the world thrust forth a vanity,
So it be new, there's no respect how vile,
That is not quickly buz'd into his eares?
That all too late comes counsell to be heard,
Where will doth mutiny with wits regard:
Direct not him, whose way himselfe will choose,
Tis breath thou lackst, and that breath wilt thou loose.

Gaunt. Me thinkes I am a Prophet new inspir'd,
And thus expiring, do foretell of him,
His rash fierce blaze of Ryot cannot last,
For violent fires soone burne out themselues,
Small showres last long, but sodaine stormes are short,
He tyres betimes, that spurs too fast betimes;
With eager feeding, food doth choake the feeder:
Light vanity, insatiate cormorant,
Consuming meanes soone preyes vpon it selfe.
This royall Throne of Kings, this sceptred Isle,
This earth of Maiesty, this seate of Mars,
This other Eden, demy paradise,
This Fortresse built by Nature for her selfe,
Against infection, and the hand of warre:
This happy breed of men, this little world,
This precious stone, set in the siluer sea,
Which serues it in the office of a wall,
Or as a Moate defensiue to a house,
Against the envy of lesse happier Lands,
This blessed plot, this earth, this Realme, this England,
This Nurse, this teeming wombe of Royall Kings,
Fear'd by their breed, and famous for their birth,
Renowned for their deeds, as farre from home,
For Christian seruice, and true Chiualrie,
As is the sepulcher in stubborne *Iury*
Of the Worlds ransome, blessed *Maries* Sonne.
This Land of such deere soules, this deere-deere Land,
Deere for her reputation through the world,
Is now Leas'd out (I dye pronouncing it)
Like to a Tenement or pelting Farme.
England bound in with the triumphant sea,
Whose rocky shore beates backe the enuious siedge
Of watery Neptune, is now bound in with shame,
With Inky blottes, and rotten Parchment bonds.
That England, that was wont to conquer others,
Hath made a shamefull conquest of it selfe.
Ah! would the scandall vanish with my life,
How happy then were my ensuing death?

Enter King, Queene, Aumerle, Bushy, Greene,
Bagot, Ros, and Willoughby.

Yor. The King is come, deale mildly with his youth,
For young hot Colts, being rag'd, do rage the more.

Qu. How fares our noble Vncle Lancaster?

Ri. What comfort man? How ist with aged *Gaunt*?

Ga. Oh how that name befits my composition:
Old *Gaunt* indeed, and gaunt in being old:
Within me greefe hath kept a tedious fast,
And who abstaynes from meate, that is not gaunt?
For sleeping England long time haue I watcht,
Watching breeds leannesse, leannesse is all gaunt.
The pleasure that some Fathers feede vpon,
Is my strict fast, I meane my Childrens lookes,
And therein fasting, hast thou made me gaunt:
Gaunt am I for the graue, gaunt as a graue,
Whose hollow wombe inherits naught but bones.

Ric. Can sicke men play so nicely with their names?

Gau. No, misery makes sport to mocke it selfe:
Since thou dost seeke to kill my name in mee,

I mocke my name (great King) to flatter thee.
  Ric. Should dying men flatter those that liue?
  Gau. No, no, men liuing flatter those that dye.
  Rich. Thou now a dying, sayst thou flatter'st me.
  Gau. Oh no, thou dyest, though I the sicker be.
  Rich. I am in health, I breath, I see thee ill.
  Gau. Now he that made me, knowes I see thee ill:
Ill in my selfe to see, and in thee, seeing ill,
Thy death-bed is no lesser then the Land,
Wherein thou lyest in reputation sicke,
And thou too care-lesse patient as thou art,
Commit'st thy'anointed body to the cure
Of those Physitians, that first wounded thee.
A thousand flatterers sit within thy Crowne,
Whose compasse is no bigger then thy head,
And yet incaged in so small a Verge,
The waste is no whit lesser then thy Land:
Oh had thy Grandsire with a Prophets eye,
Seene how his sonnes sonne, should destroy his sonnes,
From forth thy reach he would haue laid thy shame,
Deposing thee before thou wert possest,
Which art possest now to depose thy selfe.
Why (Cosine) were thou Regent of the world,
It were a shame to let his Land by lease:
But for thy world enioying but this Land,
Is it not more then shame, to shame it so?
Landlord of England art thou, and not King:
Thy state of Law, is bondslaue to the law,
And——

  Rich. And thou, a lunaticke leane-witted foole,
Presuming on an Agues priuiledge,
Dar'st with thy frozen admonition
Make pale our cheeke, chasing the Royall blood
With fury, from his natiue residence?
Now by my Seates right Royall Maiestie,
Wer't thou not Brother to great *Edwards* sonne,
This tongue that runs so roundly in thy head,
Should run thy head from thy vnreuerent shoulders.

  Gau. Oh spare me not, my brothers *Edwards* sonne,
For that I was his Father *Edwards* sonne:
That blood already (like the Pellican)
Thou hast tapt out, and drunkenly carows'd.
My brother Gloucester, plaine well meaning soule
(Whom faire befall in heauen 'mongst happy soules)
May be a president, and witnesse good,
That thou respect'st not spilling *Edwards* blood:
Ioyne with the present sicknesse that I haue,
And thy vnkindnesse be like crooked age,
To crop at once a too-long wither'd flowre.
Liue in thy shame, but dye not shame with thee,
These words heereafter, thy tormentors bee.
Conuey me to my bed, then to my graue,
Loue they to liue, that loue and honor haue. *Exit*

  Rich. And let them dye, that age and sullens haue,
For both hast thou, and both become the graue.

  Yor. I do beseech your Maiestie impute his words
To wayward sicklinesse, and age in him:
He loues you on my life, and holds you deere
As *Harry* Duke of *Herford*, were he heere.

  Rich. Right, you say true: as *Herfords* loue, so his;
As theirs, so mine: and all be as it is.

Enter Northumberland.

  Nor. My Liege, olde *Gaunt* commends him to your
Maiestie.

  Rich. What sayes he?
  Nor. Nay nothing, all is said:
His tongue is now a stringlesse instrument,
Words, life, and all, old Lancaster hath spent.
  Yor. Be Yorke the next, that must be bankrupt so,
Though death be poore, it ends a mortall wo.
  Rich. The ripest fruit first fals, and so doth he,
His time is spent, our pilgrimage must be:
So much for that. Now for our Irish warres,
We must supplant those rough rug-headed Kernes,
Which liue like venom, where no venom else
But onely they, haue priuiledge to liue.
And for these great affayres do aske some charge
Towards our assistance, we do seize to vs
The plate, coine, reuennewes, and moueables,
Whereof our Vncle *Gaunt* did stand possest.

  Yor. How long shall I be patient? Oh how long
Shall tender dutie make me suffer wrong?
Not *Gloisters* death, nor *Herfords* banishment,
Nor *Gauntes* rebukes, nor Englands priuate wrongs,
Nor the preuention of poore *Bullingbrooke*,
About his marriage, nor my owne disgrace
Haue euer made me sowre my patient cheeke,
Or bend one wrinckle on my Soueraignes face:
I am the last of noble *Edwards* sonnes,
Of whom thy Father Prince of Wales was first,
In warre was neuer Lyon rag'd more fierce:
In peace, was neuer gentle Lambe more milde,
Then was that yong and Princely Gentleman,
His face thou hast, for euen so look'd he
Accomplish'd with the number of thy howers:
But when he frown'd, it was against the French,
And not against his friends: his noble hand
Did win what he did spend: and spent not that
Which his triumphant fathers hand had won:
His hands were guilty of no kindreds blood,
But bloody with the enemies of his kinne:
Oh *Richard*, *Yorke* is too farre gone with greefe,
Or else he neuer would compare betweene.

  Rich. Why Vncle,
What's the matter?

  Yor. Oh my Liege, pardon me if you please, if not
I pleas'd not to be pardon'd, am content with all:
Seeke you to seize, and gripe into your hands
The Royalties and Rights of banish'd Herford?
Is not *Gaunt* dead? and doth not Herford liue?
Was not *Gaunt* iust? and is not *Harry* true?
Did not the one deserue to haue an heyre?
Is not his heyre a well-deseruing sonne?
Take Herfords rights away, and take from time
His Charters, and his customarie rights:
Let not to morrow then insue to day,
Be not thy selfe. For how art thou a King
But by faire sequence and succession?
Now afore God, God forbid I say true,
If you do wrongfully seize Herfords right,
Call in his Letters Patents that he hath
By his Atturneyes generall, to sue
His Liuerie, and denie his offer'd homage,
You plucke a thousand dangers on your head,
You loose a thousand well-disposed hearts,
And pricke my tender patience to those thoughts
Which honor and allegeance cannot thinke.

  Ric. Thinke what you will: we seise into our hands,
His plate, his goods, his money, and his lands.

  Yor. Ile not be by the while: My Liege farewell,

What will ensue heereof, there's none can tell.
But by bad courses may be vnderstood,
That their euents can neuer fall out good. *Exit.*

Rich. Go *Bushie* to the Earle of *Wiltshire* streight,
Bid him repaire to vs to *Ely* house,
To see this businesse: to morrow next
We will for *Ireland*, and 'tis time, I trow:
And we create in absence of our selfe
Our Vncle *Yorke*, Lord Gouernor of England:
For he is iust, and alwayes lou'd vs well.
Come on our Queene, to morrow must we part,
Be merry, for our time of stay is short. *Flourish.*

Manet North. Willoughby, & Rosse.

Nor. Well Lords, the Duke of Lancaster is dead.
Ross. And liuing too, for now his sonne is Duke.
Wil. Barely in title, not in reuennew.
Nor. Richly in both, if iustice had her right.
Ross. My heart is great: but it must break with silence,
Er't be disburthen'd with a liberall tongue.
Nor. Nay speake thy mind: & let him ne'r speak more
That speakes thy words againe to do thee harme.
Wil. Tends that thou'dst speake to th'Du. of Hereford,
If it be so, out with it boldly man,
Quicke is mine eare to heare of good towards him.
Ross. No good at all that I can do for him,
Vnlesse you call it good to pitie him,
Bereft and gelded of his patrimonie.
Nor. Now afore heauen, 'tis shame such wrongs are borne,
In him a royall Prince, and many moe
Of noble blood in this declining Land;
The King is not himselfe, but basely led
By Flatterers, and what they will informe
Meerely in hate 'gainst any of vs all,
That will the King seuerely prosecute
'Gainst vs, our liues, our children, and our heires.
Ros. The Commons hath he pil'd with greeuous taxes
And quite lost their hearts: the Nobles hath he finde
For ancient quarrels, and quite lost their hearts.
Wil. And daily new exactions are deuis'd,
As blankes, beneuolences, and I wot not what:
But what o'Gods name doth become of this?
Nor. Wars hath not wasted it, for war'd he hath not,
But basely yeelded vpon comprimize,
That which his Ancestors atchieu'd with blowes:
More hath he spent in peace, then they in warres.
Ros. The Earle of Wiltshire hath the realme in Farme.
Wil. The Kings growne bankrupt like a broken man.
Nor. Reproach, and dissolution hangeth ouer him.
Ros. He hath not monie for these Irish warres:
(His burthenous taxations notwithstanding)
But by the robbing of the banish'd Duke.
Nor. His noble Kinsman, most degenerate King:
But Lords, we heare this fearefull tempest sing,
Yet seeke no shelter to auoid the storme:
We see the winde sit sore vpon our sailes,
And yet we strike not, but securely perish.
Ros. We see the very wracke that we must suffer,
And vnauoyded is the danger now
For suffering so the causes of our wracke.
Nor. Not so: euen through the hollow eyes of death,
I spie life peering: but I dare not say
How neere the tidings of our comfort is.
Wil. Nay let vs share thy thoughts, as thou dost ours
Ros. Be confident to speake Northumberland,
We three, are but thy selfe, and speaking so,
Thy words are but as thoughts, therefore be bold.
Nor. Then thus: I haue from Port *le Blan*,
A Bay in *Britaine*, receiu'd intelligence,
That *Harry* Duke of *Herford*, *Rainald* Lord *Cobham*,
That late broke from the Duke of *Exeter*,
His brother Archbishop, late of *Canterbury*,
Sir *Thomas Erpingham*, Sir *Iohn Rainston*,
Sir *Iohn Norberie*, Sir *Robert Waterton*, & *Francis Quoint*,
All these well furnish'd by the Duke of *Britaine*,
With eight tall ships, three thousand men of warre
Are making hither with all due expedience,
And shortly meane to touch our Northerne shore:
Perhaps they had ere this, but that they stay
The first departing of the King for Ireland.
If then we shall shake off our slauish yoake,
Impe out our drooping Countries broken wing,
Redeeme from broaking pawne the blemish'd Crowne,
Wipe off the dust that hides our Scepters gilt,
And make high Maiestie looke like it selfe,
Away with me in poste to *Rauenspurgh*,
But if you faint, as fearing to do so,
Stay, and be secret, and my selfe will go.
Ros. To horse, to horse, vrge doubts to them y feare.
Wil. Hold out my horse, and I will first be there.
Exeunt.

Scena Secunda.

Enter Queene, Bushy, and Bagot.

Bush. Madam, your Maiesty is too much sad,
You promis'd when you parted with the King,
To lay aside selfe-harming heauinesse,
And entertaine a cheerefull disposition.
Qu. To please the King, I did: to please my selfe
I cannot do it: yet I know no cause
Why I should welcome such a guest as greefe,
Saue bidding farewell to so sweet a guest
As my sweet *Richard*; yet againe me thinkes,
Some vnborne sorrow, ripe in fortunes wombe
Is comming towards me, and my inward soule
With nothing trembles, at something it greeues,
More then with parting from my Lord the King.
Bush. Each substance of a greefe hath twenty shadows
Which shewes like greefe it selfe, but is not so:
For sorrowes eye, glazed with blinding teares,
Diuides one thing intire, to many obiects,
Like perspectiues, which rightly gaz'd vpon
Shew nothing but confusion, ey'd awry,
Distinguish forme: so your sweet Maiestie
Looking awry vpon your Lords departure,
Finde shapes of greefe, more then himselfe to waile,
Which look'd on as it is, is naught but shadowes
Of what it is not: then thrice-gracious Queene,
More then your Lords departure weep not, more's not
Or if it be, 'tis with false sorrowes eie, (seene;
Which for things true, weepe things imaginary.
Qu. It may be so: but yet my inward soule
Perswades me it is otherwise: how ere it be,
I cannot but be sad: so heauy sad,
As though on thinking on no thought I thinke,
Makes me with heauy nothing faint and shrinke.
Bush. 'Tis nothing but conceit (my gracious Lady.)
Queene.

Qu. 'Tis nothing lesse: conceit is still deriu'd
From some fore-father greefe, mine is not so,
For nothing hath begot my something greefe,
Or something, hath the nothing that I greeue,
'Tis in reuersion that I do possesse,
But what it is, that is not yet knowne, what
I cannot name, 'tis namelesse woe I wot.

Enter Greene.

Gree. Heauen saue your Maiesty, and wel met Gentle-
I hope the King is not yet shipt for Ireland. (men:

Qu. Why hop'st thou so? Tis better hope he is:
For his designes craue hast, his hast good hope,
Then wherefore dost thou hope he is not shipt?

Gre. That he our hope, might haue retyr'd his power,
and driuen into dispaire an enemies hope,
Who strongly hath set footing in this Land.
The banish'd *Bullingbrooke* repeales himselfe,
And with vp-lifted Armes is safe arriu'd
At *Rauenspurg*.

Qu. Now God in heauen forbid.

Gr. O Madam 'tis too true: and that is worse,
The L.Northumberland,his yong sonne *Henrie Percie*,
The Lords of *Rosse, Beaumond*, and *Willoughby*,
With all their powrefull friends are fled to him.

Bush. Why haue you not proclaim'd Northumberland
And the rest of the reuolted faction, Traitors?

Gre. We haue: whereupon the Earle of Worcester
Hath broke his staffe, resign'd his Stewardship,
And al the houshold seruants fled with him to *Bullinbrook*

Qu. So *Greene*, thou art the midwife of my woe,
And *Bullinbrooke* my sorrowes dismall heyre:
Now hath my soule brought forth her prodegie,
And I a gasping new deliuered mother,
Haue woe to woe, sorrow to sorrow ioyn'd.

Bush. Dispaire not Madam.

Qu. Who shall hinder me?
I will dispaire, and be at enmitie
With couzening hope; he is a Flatterer,
A Parasite, a keeper backe of death,
Who gently would dissolue the bands of life,
Which false hopes linger in extremity.

Enter Yorke

Gre. Heere comes the Duke of Yorke.

Qu. With signes of warre about his aged necke,
Oh full of carefull businesse are his lookes:
Vncle, for heauens sake speake comfortable words:

Yor. Comfort's in heauen, and we are on the earth,
Where nothing liues but crosses, care and greefe:
Your husband he is gone to saue farre off,
Whilst others come to make him loose at home:
Heere am I left to vnder-prop his Land,
Who weake with age, cannot support my selfe:
Now comes the sicke houre that his surfet made,
Now shall he try his friends that flattered him.

Enter a seruant.

Ser. My Lord, your sonne was gone before I came.

Yor. He was: why so: go all which way it will:
The Nobles they are fled, the Commons they are cold,
And will I feare reuolt on Herfords side.
Sirra, get thee to Plashie to my sister Gloster,
Bid her send me presently a thousand pound,
Hold, take my Ring.

Ser. My Lord, I had forgot
To tell your Lordship, to day I came by, and call'd there,
But I shall greeue you to report the rest.

Yor. What is't knaue?

Ser. An houre before I came, the Dutchesse di'de.

Yor. Heau'n for his mercy, what a tide of woes
Come rushing on this wofull Land at once?
I know not what to do: I would to heauen
(So my vntruth had not prouok'd him to it)
The King had cut off my head with my brothers.
What, are there postes dispatcht for Ireland?
How shall we do for money for these warres?
Come sister (Cozen I would say) pray pardon me.
Go fellow, get thee home, prouide some Carts,
And bring away the Armour that is there.
Gentlemen, will you muster men?
If I know how, or which way to order these affaires
Thus disorderly thrust into my hands,
Neuer beleeue me. Both are my kinsmen,
Th'one is my Soueraigne, whom both my oath
And dutie bids defend: th'other againe
Is my kinsman, whom the King hath wrong'd,
Whom conscience, and my kindred bids to right:
Well, somewhat we must do: Come Cozen,
Ile dispose of you. Gentlemen, go muster vp your men,
And meet me presently at Barkley Castle:
I should to Plashy too: but time will not permit,
All is vneuen, and euery thing is left at six and seuen. *Exit*

Bush. The winde sits faire for newes to go to Ireland,
But none returnes: For vs to leuy power
Proportionable to th'enemy, is all impossible.

Gr. Besides our neerenesse to the King in loue,
Is neere the hate of those loue not the King.

Ba. And that's the wauering Commons, for their loue
Lies in their purses, and who so empties them,
By so much fils their hearts with deadly hate.

Bush. Wherein the king stands generally condemn'd

Bag. If iudgement lye in them, then so do we,
Because we haue beene euer neere the King.

Gr. Well: I will for refuge straight to Bristoll Castle,
The Earle of Wiltshire is alreadie there.

Bush. Thither will I with you, for little office
Will the hatefull Commons performe for vs,
Except like Curres, to teare vs all in peeces:
Will you go along with vs?

Bag. No, I will to Ireland to his Maiestie:
Farewell, if hearts presages be not vaine,
We three here part, that neu'r shall meete againe.

Bu. That's as Yorke thriues to beate back *Bullinbroke*

Gr. Alas poore Duke, the taske he vndertakes
Is numbring sands, and drinking Oceans drie,
Where one on his side fights, thousands will flye.

Bush. Farewell at once, for once, for all, and euer.
Well, we may meete againe.

Bag. I feare me neuer. *Exit.*

Scæna Tertia.

Enter the Duke of Hereford, and Northum-
berland.

Bul. How farre is it my Lord to Berkley now?

Nor. Beleeue me noble Lord,
I am a stranger heere in Gloustershire,
These high wilde hilles, and rough vneuen waies,
Drawes out our miles, and makes them wearisome:
And yet our faire discourse hath beene as sugar,

Mak in

Making the hard way sweet and delectable:
But I bethinke me, what a wearie way
From Rauenspurgh to Cottshold will be found,
In *Rosse* and *Willoughby*, wanting your companie,
Which I protest hath very much beguild
The tediousnesse, and processe of my trauell:
But theirs is sweetned with the hope to haue
The present benefit that I possesse;
And hope to ioy, is little lesse in ioy,
Then hope enioy'd: By this, the wearie Lords
Shall make their way seeme short, as mine hath done,
By sight of what I haue, your Noble Companie.

  Bull. Of much lesse value is my Companie,
Then your good words: but who comes here?

            Enter H. Percie.

  North. It is my Sonne, young *Harry Percie*,
Sent from my Brother *Worcester*: Whence soeuer.
Harry, how fares your Vnckle?

  Percie. I had thought, my Lord, to haue learn'd his
health of you.

  North. Why, is he not with the Queene?

  Percie. No, my good Lord, he hath forsook the Court,
Broken his Staffe of Office, and disperst
The Houshold of the King.

  North. What was his reason?
He was not so resolu'd, when we last spake together.

  Percie Because your Lordship was proclaimed Traitor.
But hee, my Lord, is gone to Rauenspurgh,
To offer seruice to the Duke of Hereford,
And sent me ouer by Barkely, to discouer
What power the Duke of Yorke had leuied there,
Then with direction to repaire to Rauenspurgh.

  North. Haue you forgot the Duke of Hereford (Boy.)

  Percie. No, my good Lord; for that is not forgot
Which ne're I did remember: to my knowledge,
I neuer in my life did looke on him.

  North. Then learne to know him now: this is the
Duke.

  Percie. My gracious Lord, I tender you my seruice,
Such as it is, being tender, raw, and young,
Which elder dayes shall ripen, and confirme
To more approued seruice, and desert.

  Bull. I thanke thee gentle *Percie*, and be sure
I count my selfe in nothing else so happy,
As in a Soule remembring my good Friends:
And as my Fortune ripens with thy Loue,
It shall be still thy true Loues recompence,
My Heart this Couenant makes, my Hand thus seales it.

  North. How farre is it to Barkely? and what stirre
Keepes good old *Yorke* there, with his Men of Warre?

  Percie. There stands the Castle, by yond tuft of Trees,
Mann'd with three hundred men, as I haue heard,
And in it are the Lords of *Yorke*, *Barkely*, and *Seymor*,
None else of Name, and noble estimate.

          Enter Rosse and Willoughby.

  North. Here come the Lords of *Rosse* and *Willoughby*,
Bloody with spurring, fierie red with haste.

  Bull. Welcome my Lords, I wot your loue pursues
A banisht Traytor; all my Treasurie
Is yet but vnfelt thankes, which more enrich'd,
Shall be your loue, and labours recompence.

  Ross. Your presence makes vs rich, most Noble Lord.

  Willo. And farre surmounts our labour to attaine it.

  Bull. Euermore thankes, th'Exchequer of the poore,
Which till my infant-fortune comes to yeeres,
Stands for my Bountie: but who comes here?

            Enter Barkely.

  North. It is my Lord of Barkely, as I ghesse.

  Bark. My Lord of Hereford, my Message is to you.

  Bull. My Lord, my Answere is to *Lancaster*,
And I am come to seeke that Name in England,
And I must finde that Title in your Tongue,
Before I make reply to aught you say.

  Bark. Mistake me not, my Lord, 'tis not my meaning
To raze one Title of your Honor out.
To you, my Lord, I come (what Lord you will)
From the most glorious of this Land,
The Duke of Yorke, to know what pricks you on
To take aduantage of the absent time,
And fright our Natiue Peace with selfe-borne Armes.

            Enter Yorke.

  Bull. I shall not need transport my words by you,
Here comes his Grace in Person. My Noble Vnckle,

  York. Shew me thy humble heart, and not thy knee,
Whose dutie is deceiuable, and false.

  Bull My gracious Vnckle.

  York. Tut, tut, Grace me no Grace, nor Vnckle me,
I am no Traytors Vnckle; and that word Grace,
In an vngracious mouth, is but prophane.
Why haue these banish'd, and forbidden Legges,
Dar'd once to touch a Dust of Englands Ground?
But more then why, why haue they dar'd to march
So many miles vpon her peacefull Bosome,
Frighting her pale-fac'd Villages with Warre,
And ostentation of despised Armes?
Com'st thou because th'anoynted King is hence?
Why foolish Boy, the King is left behind,
And in my loyall Bosome lyes his power.
Were I but now the Lord of such hot youth,
As when braue *Gaunt*, thy Father, and my selfe
Rescued the *Black Prince*, that yong *Mars* of men,
From forth the Rankes of many thousand French:
Oh then, how quickly should this Arme of mine,
Now Prisoner to the Palsie, chastise thee,
And minister correction to thy Fault.

  Bull. My gracious Vnckle, let me know my Fault,
On what Condition stands it, and wherein?

  York. Euen in Condition of the worst degree,
In grosse Rebellion, and detested Treason:
Thou art a banish'd man, and here art come
Before th'expiration of thy time,
In brauing Armes against thy Soueraigne.

  Bull. As I was banish'd, I was banish'd *Hereford*,
But as I come, I come for *Lancaster*.
And Noble Vnckle, I beseech your Grace
Looke on my Wrongs with an indifferent eye:
You are my Father, for me thinkes in you
I see old *Gaunt* aliue. Oh then my Father,
Will you permit, that I shall stand condemn'd
A wandring Vagabond; my Rights and Royalties
Pluckt from my armes perforce, and giuen away
To vpstart Vnthrifts? Wherefore was I borne?
If that my Cousin King, be King of England,
It must be graunted, I am Duke of Lancaster.
You haue a Sonne, *Aumerle*, my Noble Kinsman,
Had you first died, and he beene thus trod downe,
He should haue found his Vnckle *Gaunt* a Father,
To rowze his Wrongs, and chase them to the bay.
I am denyde to sue my Liuerie here,
And yet my Letters Patents giue me leaue:
My Fathers goods are all distraynd, and sold,
And these, and all, are all amisse imployd.

What

What would you haue me doe? I am a Subiect,
And challenge Law: Attorneyes are deny'd me;
And therefore personally I lay my claime
To my Inheritance of free Discent.

North. The Noble Duke hath been too much abus'd.

Ross. It stands your Grace vpon, to doe him right.

Willo. Base men by his endowments are made great.

York. My Lords of England, let me tell you this,
I haue had feeling of my Cosens Wrongs,
And labour'd all I could to doe him right:
But in this kind, to come in brauing Armes,
Be his owne Caruer, and cut out his way,
To find out Right with Wrongs, it may not be;
And you that doe abett him in this kind,
Cherish Rebellion, and are Rebels all.

North. The Noble Duke hath sworne his comming is
But for his owne; and for the right of that,
Wee all haue strongly sworne to giue him ayd,
And let him neu'r see Ioy, that breakes that Oath.

York. Well, well, I see the issue of these Armes,
I cannot mend it, I must needes confesse,
Because my power is weake, and all ill left:
But if I could, by him that gaue me life,
I would attach you all, and make you stoope
Vnto the Soueraigne Mercy of the King.
But since I cannot, be it knowne to you,
I doe remaine as Neuter. So fare you well,
Vnlesse you please to enter in the Castle,
And there repose you for this Night.

Bull. An offer Vnckle, that wee will accept:
But wee must winne your Grace to goe with vs
To Bristow Castle, which they say is held
By *Bushie, Bagot,* and their Complices,
The Caterpillers of the Commonwealth,
Which I haue sworne to weed, and plucke away.

York. It may be I will go with you: but yet Ile pawse,
For I am loth to breake our Countries Lawes:
Nor Friends, nor Foes, to me welcome you are,
Things past redresse, are now with me past care. *Exeunt.*

Scœna Quarta.

Enter Salisbury, and a Captaine.

Capt. My Lord of Salisbury, we haue stayd ten dayes,
And hardly kept our Countreymen together,
And yet we heare no tidings from the King;
Therefore we will disperse our selues: farewell.

Sal. Stay yet another day, thou trustie Welchman,
The King reposeth all his confidence in thee.

Capt. 'Tis thought the King is dead, we will not stay;
The Bay-trees in our Countrey all are wither'd,
And Meteors fright the fixed Starres of Heauen;
The pale-fac'd Moone lookes bloody on the Earth,
And leane-look'd Prophets whisper fearefull change;
Rich men looke sad, and Ruffians dance and leape,
The one in feare, to loose what they enioy,
The other to enioy by Rage, and Warre:
These signes fore-run the death of Kings.
Farewell, our Countreymen are gone and fled,
As well assur'd *Richard* their King is dead. *Exit.*

Sal. Ah *Richard,* with eyes of heauie mind,
I see thy Glory, like a shooting Starre,
Fall to the base Earth, from the Firmament:
Thy Sunne sets weeping in the lowly West,
Witnessing Stormes to come, Woe, and Vnrest:
Thy Friends are fled, to wait vpon thy Foes,
And crossely to thy good, all fortune goes. *Exit.*

Actus Tertius. Scena Prima.

*Enter Bullingbrooke, Yorke, Northumberland,
Rosse, Percie, Willoughby, with Bushie
and Greene Prisoners.*

Bull. Bring forth these men:
Bushie and *Greene,* I will not vex your soules,
(Since presently your soules must part your bodies)
With too much vrging your pernitious liues,
For 'twere no Charitie: yet to wash your blood
From off my hands, here in the view of men,
I will vnfold some causes of your deaths.
You haue mis-led a Prince, a Royall King,
A happie Gentleman in Blood, and Lineaments,
By you vnhappied, and disfigur'd cleane:
You haue in manner with your sinfull houres
Made a Diuorce betwixt his Queene and him,
Broke the possession of a Royall Bed,
And stayn'd the beautie of a faire Queenes Cheekes,
With teares drawn frō her eyes, with your foule wrongs.
My selfe a Prince, by fortune of my birth,
Neere to the King in blood, and neere in loue,
Till you did make him mis-interprete me,
Haue stoopt my neck vnder your iniuries,
And sigh'd my English breath in forraine Clouds,
Eating the bitter bread of banishment;
While you haue fed vpon my Seignories,
Dis-park'd my Parkes, and fell'd my Forrest Woods;
From mine owne Windowes torne my Household Coat,
Raz'd out my Impresse, leauing me no signe,
Saue mens opinions, and my liuing blood,
To shew the World I am a Gentleman.
This, and much more, much more then twice all this,
Condemnes you to the death: see them deliuered ouer
To execution, and the hand of death.

Bushie. More welcome is the stroake of death to me,
Then *Bullingbrooke* to England.

Greene. My comfort is, that Heauen will take our soules,
And plague Iniustice with the paines of Hell.

Bull. My Lord *Northumberland,* see them dispatch'd:
Vnckle, you say the Queene is at your House,
For Heauens sake fairely let her be entreated,
Tell her I send to her my kind commends;
Take speciall care my Greetings be deliuer'd.

York. A Gentleman of mine I haue dispatch'd
With Letters of your loue, to her at large.

Bull. Thankes gentle Vnckle: come Lords away,
To fight with *Glendoure,* and his Complices;
A while to worke, and after holliday. *Exeunt.*

Scena Secunda.

Drums: Flourish, and Colours.

Enter Richard, Aumerle, Carlile, and Souldiers.

Rich. Barkloughly Castle call you this at hand?
Au. Yea, my Lord: how brooks your Grace the ayre,
After your late tossing on the breaking Seas?
 Rich. Needs must I like it well: I weepe for ioy
To stand vpon my Kingdome once againe.
Deere Earth, I doe salute thee with my hand,
Though Rebels wound thee with their Horses hoofes:
As a long parted Mother with her Child,
Playes fondly with her teares, and smiles in meeting;
So weeping, smiling, greet I thee my Earth,
And doe thee fauor with my Royall hands.
Feed not thy Soueraignes Foe, my gentle Earth,
Nor with thy Sweetes, comfort his rauenous sence:
But let thy Spiders, that suck vp thy Venome,
And heauie-gated Toades lye in their way,
Doing annoyance to the trecherous feete,
Which with vsurping steps doe trample thee.
Yeeld stinging Nettles to mine Enemies;
And when they from thy Bosome pluck a Flower,
Guard it I prethee with a lurking Adder,
Whose double tongue may with a mortall touch
Throw death vpon thy Soueraignes Enemies.
Mock not my senceless Coniuration, Lords;
This Earth shall haue a feeling, and these Stones
Proue armed Souldiers, ere her Natiue King
Shall falter vnder foule Rebellious Armes.
 Car. Feare not my Lord, that Power that made you King
Hath power to keepe you King, in spight of all.
 Aum. He meanes, my Lord, that we are too remisse,
Whilest *Bullingbrooke* through our securitie,
Growes strong and great, in substance and in friends.
 Rich. Discomfortable Cousin, knowest thou not,
That when the searching Eye of Heauen is hid
Behind the Globe, that lights the lower World,
Then Theeues and Robbers raunge abroad vnseene,
In Murthers and in Out-rage bloody here:
But when from vnder this Terrestriall Ball
He fires the prowd tops of the Easterne Pines,
And darts his Lightning through eu'ry guiltie hole,
Then Murthers, Treasons, and detested sinnes
(The Cloake of Night being pluckt from off their backs)
Stand bare and naked, trembling at themselues.
So when this Theefe, this Traytor *Bullingbrooke*,
Who all this while hath reuell'd in the Night,
Shall see vs rising in our Throne, the East,
His Treasons will sit blushing in his face,
Not able to endure the sight of Day;
But selfe-affrighted, tremble at his sinne.
Not all the Water in the rough rude Sea
Can wash the Balme from an anoynted King;
The breath of worldly men cannot depose
The Deputie elected by the Lord:
For euery man that *Bullingbrooke* hath prest,
To lift shrewd Steele against our Golden Crowne,
Heauen for his *Richard* hath in heauenly pay
A glorious Angell: then if Angels fight,
Weake men must fall, for Heauen still guards the right.

Enter Salisbury.

Welcome my Lord, how farre off lyes your Power?
 Salisb. Nor neere, nor farther off, my gracious Lord,
Then this weake arme: discomfort guides my tongue,
And bids me speake of nothing but despaire:
One day too late, I feare (my Noble Lord)
Hath clouded all thy happie dayes on Earth:
Oh call backe Yesterday, bid Time returne,
And thou shalt haue twelue thousand fighting men:
To day, to day, vnhappie day too late
Orethrowes thy Ioyes, Friends, Fortune, and thy State;
For all the Welchmen hearing thou wert dead,
Are gone to *Bullingbrooke*, disperst, and fled.
 Aum. Comfort my Liege, why lookes your Grace so pale?
 Rich. But now the blood of twentie thousand men
Did triumph in my face, and they are fled,
And till so much blood thither come againe,
Haue I not reason to looke pale, and dead?
All Soules that will be safe, flye from my side,
For Time hath set a blot vpon my pride.
 Aum. Comfort my Liege, remember who you are.
 Rich. I had forgot my selfe. Am I not King?
Awake thou sluggard Maiestie, thou sleepest:
Is not the Kings Name fortie thousand Names?
Arme, arme my Name: a punie subiect strikes
At thy great glory. Looke not to the ground,
Ye Fauorites of a King: are wee not high?
High be our thoughts: I know my Vnckle *Yorke*
Hath Power enough to serue our turne.
But who comes here? *Enter Scroope.*
 Scroope. More health and happinesse betide my Liege,
Then can my care-tun'd tongue deliuer him.
 Rich. Mine eare is open, and my heart prepar'd:
The worst is worldly losse, thou canst vnfold:
Say, Is my Kingdome lost? why 'twas my Care:
And what losse is it to be rid of Care?
Striues *Bullingbrooke* to be as Great as wee?
Greater he shall not be: If hee serue God,
Wee'l serue him too, and be his Fellow so.
Reuolt our Subiects? That we cannot mend,
They breake their Faith to God, as well as vs:
Cry Woe, Destruction, Ruine, Losse, Decay,
The worst is Death, and Death will haue his day.
 Scroope. Glad am I, that your Highnesse is so arm'd
To beare the tidings of Calamitie.
Like an vnseasonable stormie day,
Which make the Siluer Riuers drowne their Shores,
As if the World were all dissolu'd to teares:
So high, aboue his Limits, swells the Rage
Of *Bullingbrooke*, couering your fearefull Land
With hard bright Steele, and hearts harder then Steele:
White Beares haue arm'd their thin and hairelesse Scalps
Against thy Maiestie, and Boyes with Womens Voyces,
Striue to speake bigge, and clap their female ioints
In stiffe vnwieldie Armes: against thy Crowne
Thy very Beads-men learne to bend their Bowes
Of double fatall Eugh: against thy State
Yea Distaffe-Women manage rustie Bills:
Against thy Seat both young and old rebell,
And all goes worse then I haue power to tell.
 Rich. Too well, too well thou tell'st a Tale so ill.
Where is the Earle of Wiltshire? where is *Bagot*?
What is become of *Bushie*? where is *Greene*?

That they haue let the dangerous Enemie
Measure our Confines with such peacefull steps?
If we preuaile, their heads shall pay for it.
I warrant they haue made peace with *Bullingbrooke*.

  Scroope. Peace haue they made with him indeede (my
Lord.)
  Rich. Oh Villains, Vipers, damn'd without redemption,
Dogges, easily woon to fawne on any man,
Snakes in my heart blood warm'd, that sting my heart,
Three Iudasses, each one thrice worse then *Iudas*,
Would they make peace? terrible Hell make warre
Vpon their spotted Soules for this Offence.
  Scroope. Sweet Loue (I see) changing his propertie,
Turnes to the sowrest, and most deadly hate:
Againe vncurse their Soules; their peace is made
With Heads, and not with Hands: those whom you curse
Haue felt the worst of Deaths destroying hand,
And lye full low, grau'd in the hollow ground.
  Aum. Is *Bushie*, *Greene*, and the Earle of Wiltshire
dead?
  Scroope. Yea, all of them at Bristow lost their heads.
  Aum. Where is the Duke my Father with his Power?
  Rich. No matter where; of comfort no man speake:
Let's talke of Graues, of Wormes, and Epitaphs,
Make Dust our Paper, and with Raynie eyes
Write Sorrow on the Bosome of the Earth.
Let's chuse Executors, and talke of Wills:
And yet not so; for what can we bequeath,
Saue our deposed bodies to the ground?
Our Lands, our Liues, and all are *Bullingbrookes*,
And nothing can we call our owne, but Death,
And that small Modell of the barren Earth,
Which serues as Paste, and Couer to our Bones:
For Heauens sake let vs sit vpon the ground,
And tell sad stories of the death of Kings:
How some haue been depos'd, some slaine in warre,
Some haunted by the Ghosts they haue depos'd,
Some poyson'd by their Wiues, some sleeping kill'd,
All murther'd. For within the hollow Crowne
That rounds the mortall Temples of a King,
Keepes Death his Court, and there the Antique sits
Scoffing his State, and grinning at his Pompe,
Allowing him a breath, a little Scene,
To Monarchize, be fear'd, and kill with lookes,
Infusing him with selfe and vaine conceit,
As if this Flesh, which walls about our Life,
Were Brasse impregnable: and humor'd thus,
Comes at the last, and with a little Pinne
Bores through his Castle Walls, and farwell King.
Couer your heads, and mock not flesh and blood
With solemne Reuerence: throw away Respect,
Tradition, Forme, and Ceremonious dutie,
For you haue but mistooke me all this while:
I liue with Bread like you, feele Want,
Taste Griefe, need Friends: subiected thus,
How can you say to me, I am a King?
  Carl. My Lord, wise men ne're waile their present woes,
But presently preuent the wayes to waile:
To feare the Foe, since feare oppresseth strength,
Giues in your weakenesse, strength vnto your Foe;
Feare, and be slaine, no worse can come to fight,
And fight and die, is death destroying death,
Where fearing, dying, payes death seruile breath.
  Aum. My Father hath a Power, enquire of him,
And learne to make a Body of a Limbe.
  Rich. Thou chid'st me well: proud *Bullingbrooke* I come
To change Blowes with thee, for our day of Doome:
This ague fit of feare is ouer-blowne,
An easie taske it is to winne our owne.
Say *Scroope*, where lyes our Vnckle with his Power?
Speake sweetly man, although thy lookes be sowre.
  Scroope. Men iudge by the complexion of the Skie
The state and inclination of the day;
So may you by my dull and heauie Eye:
My Tongue hath but a heauier Tale to say:
I play the Torturer, by small and small
To lengthen out the worst, that must be spoken.
Your Vnckle *Yorke* is ioyn'd with *Bullingbrooke*,
And all your Northerne Castles yeelded vp,
And all your Southerne Gentlemen in Armes
Vpon his Faction.
  Rich. Thou hast said enough.
Beshrew thee Cousin, which didst lead me forth
Of that sweet way I was in, to despaire:
What say you now? What comfort haue we now?
By Heauen Ile hate him euerlastingly,
That bids me be of comfort any more.
Goe to Flint Castle, there Ile pine away,
A King, Woes slaue, shall Kingly Woe obey:
That Power I haue, discharge, and let 'em goe
To eare the Land, that hath some hope to grow,
For I haue none. Let no man speake againe
To alter this, for counsaile is but vaine.
  Aum. My Liege, one word.
  Rich. He does me double wrong,
That wounds me with the flatteries of his tongue.
Discharge my followers: let them hence away,
From *Richards* Night, to *Bullingbrookes* faire Day.
                              Exeunt.

Scæna Tertia.

Enter with Drum and Colours, Bullingbrooke,
Yorke, Northumberland, Attendants.

  Bull. So that by this intelligence we learne
The Welchmen are dispers'd, and *Salisbury*
Is gone to meet the King, who lately landed
With some few priuate friends, vpon this Coast.
  North. The newes is very faire and good, my Lord,
Richard, not farre from hence, hath hid his head.
  York. It would beseeme the Lord Northumberland,
To say King *Richard*: alack the heauie day,
When such a sacred King should hide his head.
  North. Your Grace mistakes: onely to be briefe,
Left I his Title out.
  York. The time hath beene,
Would you haue beene so briefe with him, he would
Haue beene so briefe with you, to shorten you,
For taking so the Head, your whole heads length.
  Bull. Mistake not (Vnckle) farther then you should.
  York. Take not (good Cousin) farther then you should.
Least you mistake the Heauens are ore your head.
  Bull. I know it (Vnckle) and oppose not my selfe
Against their will. But who comes here?
            Enter Percie.
Welcome *Harry*: what, will not this Castle yeeld?
  Per. The Castle royally is mann'd, my Lord,
Against thy entrance.
                              Bull. Roy-

Bull. Royally? Why, it containes no King?

Per. Yes (my good Lord)
It doth containe a King: King *Richard* lyes
Within the limits of yond Lime and Stone,
And with him, the Lord *Aumerle*, Lord *Salisbury*,
Sir *Stephen Scroope*, besides a Clergie man
Of holy reuerence; who, I cannot learne.

North. Oh, belike it is the Bishop of Carlile.

Bull. Noble Lord,
Goe to the rude Ribs of that ancient Castle,
Through Brazen Trumpet send the breath of Parle
Into his ruin'd Eares, and thus deliuer:
Henry Bullingbrooke vpon his knees doth kisse
King *Richards* hand, and sends allegeance
And true faith of heart to his Royall Person: hither come
Euen at his feet, to lay my Armes and Power,
Prouided, that my Banishment repeal'd,
And Lands restor'd againe, be freely graunted:
If not, Ile vse th'aduantage of my Power,
And lay the Summers dust with showers of blood,
Rayn'd from the wounds of slaughter'd Englishmen;
The which, how farre off from the mind of *Bullingbrooke*
It is, such Crimson Tempest should bedrench
The fresh greene Lap of faire King *Richards* Land,
My stooping dutie tenderly shall shew.
Goe signifie as much, while here we march
Vpon the Grassie Carpet of this Plaine:
Let's march without the noyse of threatning Drum,
That from this Castles tatter'd Battlements
Our faire Appointments may be well perus'd.
Me thinkes King *Richard* and my selfe should meet
With no lesse terror then the Elements
Of Fire and Water, when their thundring smoake
At meeting teares the cloudie Cheekes of Heauen:
Be he the fire, Ile be the yeelding Water;
The Rage be his, while on the Earth I raine
My Waters on the Earth, and not on him.
March on, and marke King *Richard* how he lookes.

Parle without, and answere within: then a Flourish.
Enter on the Walls, Richard, Carlile, Aumerle, Scroop,
Salisbury.

See, see, King *Richard* doth himselfe appeare
As doth the blushing discontented Sunne,
From out the fierie Portall of the East,
When he perceiues the enuious Clouds are bent
To dimme his glory, and to staine the tract
Of his bright passage to the Occident.

York. Yet lookes he like a King: behold his Eye
(As bright as is the Eagles) lightens forth
Controlling Maiestie: alack, alack, for woe,
That any harme should staine so faire a shew.

Rich. Wee are amaz'd, and thus long haue we stood
To watch the fearefull bending of thy knee,
Because we thought our selfe thy lawfull King:
And if we be, how dare thy ioynts forget
To pay their awfull dutie to our presence?
If we be not, shew vs the Hand of God,
That hath dismiss'd vs from our Stewardship,
For well wee know, no Hand of Blood and Bone
Can gripe the sacred Handle of our Scepter,
Vnlesse he doe prophane, steale, or vsurpe.
And though you thinke, that all, as you haue done,
Haue torne their Soules, by turning them from vs,
And we are barren, and bereft of Friends:
Yet know, my Master, God Omnipotent,
Is mustring in his Clouds, on our behalfe,
Armies of Pestilence, and they shall strike
Your Children yet vnborne, and vnbegot,
That lift your Vassall Hands against my Head,
And threat the Glory of my precious Crowne.
Tell *Bullingbrooke*, for yond me thinkes he is,
That euery stride he makes vpon my Land,
Is dangerous Treason: He is come to ope
The purple Testament of bleeding Warre;
But ere the Crowne he lookes for, liue in peace,
Ten thousand bloody crownes of Mothers Sonnes
Shall ill become the flower of Englands face,
Change the complexion of her Maid-pale Peace
To Scarlet Indignation, and bedew
Her Pastors Grasse with faithfull English Blood.

North. The King of Heauen forbid our Lord the King
Should so with ciuill and vnciuill Armes
Be rush'd vpon: Thy thrice-noble Cousin,
Harry Bullingbrooke, doth humbly kisse thy hand,
And by the Honorable Tombe he sweares,
That stands vpon your Royall Grandsires Bones,
And by the Royalties of both your Bloods,
(Currents that spring from one most gracious Head)
And by the buried Hand of Warlike *Gaunt*,
And by the Worth and Honor of himselfe,
Comprising all that may be sworne, or said,
His comming hither hath no further scope,
Then for his Lineall Royalties, and to begge
Infranchisement immediate on his knees:
Which on thy Royall partie graunted once,
His glittering Armes he will commend to Rust,
His barbed Steedes to Stables, and his heart
To faithfull seruice of your Maiestie:
This sweares he, as he is a Prince, is iust,
And as I am a Gentleman, I credit him.

Rich. Northumberland, say thus: The King returnes,
His Noble Cousin is right welcome hither,
And all the number of his faire demands
Shall be accomplish'd without contradiction:
With all the gracious vtterance thou hast,
Speake to his gentle hearing kind commends.
We doe debase our selfe (Cousin) doe we not,
To looke so poorely, and to speake so faire?
Shall we call back *Northumberland*, and send
Defiance to the Traytor, and so die?

Aum. No, good my Lord, let's fight with gentle words,
Till time lend friends, and friends their helpeful Swords.

Rich. Oh God, oh God, that ere this tongue of mine,
That layd the Sentence of dread Banishment
On yond prowd man, should take it off againe
With words of sooth: Oh that I were as great
As is my Griefe, or lesser then my Name,
Or that I could forget what I haue beene,
Or not remember what I must be now:
Swell'st thou prowd heart? Ile giue thee scope to beat,
Since Foes haue scope to beat both thee and me.

Aum. Northumberland comes backe from *Bullingbrooke.*

Rich. What must the King doe now? must he submit?
The King shall doe it: Must he be depos'd?
The King shall be contented: Must he loose
The Name of King? o' Gods Name let it goe.
Ile giue my Iewels for a sett of Beades,
My gorgeous Pallace, for a Hermitage,
My gay Apparrell, for an Almes-mans Gowne,
My figur'd Goblets, for a Dish of Wood,
My Scepter, for a Palmers walking Staffe,

My

My Subiects, for a payre of carued Saints,
And my large Kingdome, for a little Graue,
A little little Graue, an obscure Graue.
Or Ile be buryed in the Kings high-way,
Some way of common Trade, where Subiects feet
May howrely trample on their Soueraignes Head:
For on my heart they tread now, whilest I liue;
And buryed once, why not vpon my Head?
Aumerle, thou weep'st (my tender-hearted Cousin)
Wee'le make foule Weather with despised Teares:
Our sighes, and they, shall lodge the Summer Corne,
And make a Dearth in this reuolting Land.
Or shall we play the Wantons with our Woes,
And make some prettie Match, with shedding Teares?
As thus: to drop them still vpon one place,
Till they haue fretted vs a payre of Graues,
Within the Earth: and therein lay'd, there lyes
Two Kinsmen, digg'd their Graues with weeping Eyes?
Would not this ill, doe well? Well, well, I see
I talke but idly, and you mock at mee.
Most mightie Prince, my Lord *Northumberland*,
What sayes King *Bullingbrooke*? Will his Maiestie
Giue *Richard* leaue to liue, till *Richard* die?
You make a Legge, and *Bullingbrooke* sayes I.

 North. My Lord, in the base Court he doth attend
To speake with you, may it please you to come downe.

 Rich. Downe, downe I come, like glist'ring *Phaeton*,
Wanting the manage of vnruly Iades.
In the base Court? base Court, where Kings grow base,
To come at Traytors Calls, and doe them Grace.
In the base Court come down: down Court, down King,
For night-Owls shrike, where mouting Larks should sing.

 Bull. What sayes his Maiestie?

 North. Sorrow, and griefe of heart
Makes him speake fondly, like a frantick man:
Yet he is come.

 Bull. Stand all apart,
And shew faire dutie to his Maiestie.
My gracious Lord.

 Rich. Faire Cousin,
You debase your Princely Knee,
To make the base Earth prowd with kissing it.
Me rather had, my Heart might feele your Loue,
Then my vnpleas'd Eye see your Courtesie.
Vp Cousin, vp, your Heart is vp, I know,
Thus high at least, although your Knee be low.

 Bull. My gracious Lord, I come but for mine
owne.

 Rich. Your owne is yours, and I am yours, and
all.

 Bull. So farre be mine, my most redoubted Lord,
As my true seruice shall deserue your loue.

 Rich. Well you deseru'd:
They well deserue to haue,
That know the strong'st, and surest way to get.
Vnckle giue me your Hand: nay, drie your Eyes,
Teares shew their Loue, but want their Remedies.
Cousin, I am too young to be your Father,
Though you are old enough to be my Heire.
What you will haue, Ile giue, and willing to,
For doe we must, what force will haue vs doe.
Set on towards London:
Cousin, is it so?

 Bull. Yea, my good Lord.

 Rich. Then I must not say, no.

Flourish. Exeunt.

Scena Quarta.

Enter the Queene, and two Ladies.

 Qu. What sport shall we deuise here in this Garden,
To driue away the heauie thought of Care?

 La. Madame, wee'le play at Bowles.

 Qu. 'Twill make me thinke the World is full of Rubs,
And that my fortune runnes against the Byas.

 La. Madame, wee'le Dance.

 Qu. My Legges can keepe no measure in Delight,
When my poore Heart no measure keepes in Griefe.
Therefore no Dancing (Girle) some other sport.

 La. Madame, wee'le tell Tales.

 Qu. Of Sorrow, or of Griefe?

 La. Of eyther, Madame.

 Qu. Of neyther, Girle.
For if of Ioy, being altogether wanting,
It doth remember me the more of Sorrow:
Or if of Griefe, being altogether had,
It addes more Sorrow to my want of Ioy:
For what I haue, I need not to repeat;
And what I want, it bootes not to complaine.

 La. Madame, Ile sing.

 Qu. 'Tis well that thou hast cause:
But thou should'st please me better, would'st thou weepe.

 La. I could weepe, Madame, would it doe you good.

 Qu. And I could sing, would weeping doe me good,
And neuer borrow any Teare of thee.

Enter a Gardiner, and two Seruants.

But stay, here comes the Gardiners,
Let's step into the shadow of these Trees.
My wretchednesse, vnto a Rowe of Pinnes,
They'le talke of State: for euery one doth so,
Against a Change; Woe is fore-runne with Woe.

 Gard. Goe binde thou vp yond dangling Apricocks,
Which like vnruly Children, make their Syre
Stoupe with oppression of their prodigall weight:
Giue some supportance to the bending twigges.
Goe thou, and like an Executioner
Cut off the heads of too fast growing sprayes,
That looke too loftie in our Common-wealth:
All must be euen, in our Gouernment.
You thus imploy'd, I will goe root away
The noysome Weedes, that without profit sucke
The Soyles fertilitie from wholesome flowers.

 Ser. Why should we, in the compasse of a Pale,
Keepe Law and Forme, and due Proportion,
Shewing as in a Modell our firme Estate?
When our Sea-walled Garden, the whole Land,
Is full of Weedes, her fairest Flowers choakt vp,
Her Fruit-trees all vnpruin'd, her Hedges ruin'd,
Her Knots disorder'd, and her wholesome Hearbes
Swarming with Caterpillers.

 Gard. Hold thy peace.
He that hath suffer'd this disorder'd Spring,
Hath now himselfe met with the Fall of Leafe.
The Weeds that his broad-spreading Leaues did shelter,
That seem'd, in eating him, to hold him vp,
Are pull'd vp, Root and all, by *Bullingbrooke*:
I meane, the Earle of Wiltshire, *Bushie, Greene*.

Ser. What

The Life and Death of Richard the Second.

Ser. What are they dead?
Gard. They are,
And *Bullingbrooke* hath seiz'd the wastefull King.
Oh, what pitty is it, that he had not so trim'd
And drest his Land, as we this Garden, at time of yeare,
And wound the Barke, the skin of our Fruit-trees,
Least being ouer-proud with Sap and Blood,
With too much riches it confound it selfe?
Had he done so, to great and growing men,
They might haue liu'd to beare, and he to taste
Their fruites of dutie. Superfluous branches
We lop away, that bearing boughes may liue:
Had he done so, himselfe had borne the Crowne,
Which waste and idle houres, hath quite throwne downe.

Ser. What thinke you the King shall be depos'd?
Gar. Deprest he is already, and depos'd
'Tis doubted he will be. Letters came last night
To a deere Friend of the Duke of Yorkes,
That tell blacke tydings.

Qu. Oh I am prest to death through want of speaking:
Thou old *Adams* likenesse, set to dresse this Garden:
How dares thy harsh rude tongue sound this vnpleasing
What Eue? what Serpent hath suggested thee, (newes
To make a second fall of cursed man?
Why do'st thou say, King *Richard* is depos'd,
Dar'st thou, thou little better thing then earth,
Diuine his downfall? Say, where, when, and how
Cam'st thou by this ill-tydings? Speake thou wretch.

Gard. Pardon me Madam. Little ioy haue I
To breath these newes; yet what I say, is true;
King *Richard*, he is in the mighty hold
Of *Bullingbrooke*, their Fortunes both are weigh'd:
In your Lords Scale, is nothing but himselfe,
And some few Vanities, that make him light:
But in the Ballance of great *Bullingbrooke*,
Besides himselfe, are all the English Peeres,
And with that oddes he weighes King *Richard* downe.
Poste you to London, and you'l finde it so,
I speake no more, then euery one doth know.

Qu. Nimble mischance, that art so light of foote,
Doth not thy Embassage belong to me?
And am I last that knowes it? Oh thou think'st
To serue me last, that I may longest keepe
Thy sorrow in my breast. Come Ladies goe,
To meet at London, Londons King in woe.
What was I borne to this: that my sad looke,
Should grace the Triumph of great *Bullingbrooke*.
Gard'ner, for telling me this newes of woe,
I would the Plants thou graft'st, may neuer grow. *Exit.*

G Poore Queen, so that thy State might be no worse,
I would my skill were subiect to thy curse:
Heere did she drop a teare, heere in this place
Ile set a Banke of Rew, sowre Herbe of Grace:
Rue, eu'n for ruth, heere shortly shall be seene,
In the remembrance of a Weeping Queene. *Exit.*

Actus Quartus. Scœna Prima.

Enter as to the Parliament, Bullingbrooke, Aumerle, Northumberland, Percie, Fitz-Water, Surrey, Carlile, Abbot of Westminster. Herauld, Officers, and Bagot.

Bullingbrooke. Call forth *Bagot.*
Now *Bagot*, freely speake thy minde,
What thou do'st know of Noble *Gloufters* death:
Who wrought it with the King, and who perform'd
The bloody Office of his Timelesse end.

Bag. Then set before my face, the Lord *Aumerle.*
Bul. Cosin, stand forth, and looke vpon that man.
Bag. My Lord *Aumerle*, I know your daring tongue
Scornes to vnsay, what it hath once deliuer'd,
In that dead time, when *Gloufters* death was plotted,
I heard you say, Is not my arme of length,
That reacheth from the restfull English Court
As farre as Callis, to my Vnkles head.
Amongst much other talke, that very time,
I heard you say, that you had rather refuse
The offer of an hundred thousand Crownes,
Then *Bullingbrookes* returne to England; adding withall,
How blest this Land would be, in this your Cosins death.

Aum. Princes, and Noble Lords:
What answer shall I make to this base man?
Shall I so much dishonor my faire Starres,
On equall termes to giue him chasticement?
Either I must, or haue mine honor soyl'd
With th' Attaindor of his sland'rous Lippes.
There is my Gage, the manuall Seale of death
That markes thee out for Hell. Thou lyest,
And will maintaine what thou hast said, is false,
In thy heart blood, though being all too base
To staine the temper of my Knightly sword.

Bul. Bagot forbeare, thou shalt not take it vp.
Aum. Excepting one, I would he were the best
In all this presence, that hath mou'd me so.

Fitz. If that thy valour stand on sympathize:
There is my Gage, *Aumerle*, in Gage to thine:
By that faire Sunne, that shewes me where thou stand'st,
I heard thee say (and vauntingly thou spak'st it)
That thou wer't cause of Noble *Gloufters* death.
If thou deniest it, twenty times thou lyest,
And I will turne thy falshood to thy hart,
Where it was forged with my Rapiers point.

Aum. Thou dar'st not (Coward) liue to see the day.
Fitz. Now by my Soule, I would it were this houre.
Aum. *Fitzwater* thou art damn'd to hell for this.
Per. Aumerle, thou lye'st: his Honor is as true
In this Appeale, as thou art all vniust:
And that thou art so, there I throw my Gage
To proue it on thee, to th' extreamest point
Of mortall breathing. Seize it, if thou dar'st.

Aum. And if I do not, may my hands rot off,
And neuer brandish more reuengefull Steele,
Ouer the glittering Helmet of my Foe.

Surrey. My Lord *Fitz water*:
I do remember well, the very time
Aumerle, and you did talke.

Fitz. My Lord,
'Tis very true: You were in presence then,
And you can witnesse with me, this is true.

Surrey. As false, by heauen,
As Heauen it selfe is true.

Fitz. Surrey, thou Lyest.

Surrey. Dishonourable Boy;
That Lye, shall lie so heauy on my Sword,
That it shall render Vengeance, and Reuenge,
Till thou the Lye-giuer, and that Lye, doe lye
In earth as quiet, as thy Fathers Scull.
In proofe whereof, there is mine Honors pawne,
Engage it to the Triall, if thou dar'st.

Fitz.

Fitzw. How fondly do'st thou spurre a forward Horse?
If I dare eate, or drinke, or breathe, or liue,
I dare meete *Surrey* in a Wildernesse,
And spit vpon him, whilest I say he Lyes,
And Lyes, and Lyes: there is my Bond of Faith,
To tye thee to my strong Correction.
As I intend to thriue in this new World,
Aumerle is guiltie of my true Appeale.
Besides, I heard the banish'd *Norfolke* say,
That thou *Aumerle* didst send two of thy men,
To execute the Noble Duke at Callis.

Aum. Some honest Christian trust me with a Gage,
That *Norfolke* lyes: here doe I throw downe this,
If he may be repeal'd, to trie his Honor.

Bull. These differences shall all rest vnder Gage,
Till *Norfolke* be repeal'd: repeal'd he shall be;
And (though mine Enemie) restor'd againe
To all his Lands and Seignories: when hee's return'd,
Against *Aumerle* we will enforce his Tryall.

Carl. That honorable day shall ne're be seene.
Many a time hath banish'd *Norfolke* fought
For Iesu Christ, in glorious Christian field
Streaming the Ensigne of the Christian Crosse,
Against black Pagans, Turkes, and Saracens:
And toyl'd with workes of Warre, retyr'd himselfe
To Italy, and there at Venice gaue
His Body to that pleasant Countries Earth,
And his pure Soule vnto his Captaine Christ,
Vnder whose Colours he had fought so long.

Bull. Why Bishop, is *Norfolke* dead?

Carl. As sure as I liue, my Lord.

Bull. Sweet peace conduct his sweet Soule
To the Bosome of good old *Abraham*.
Lords Appealants, your differēces shal all rest vnder gage,
Till we assigne you to your dayes of Tryall.

Enter Yorke.

Yorke. Great Duke of Lancaster, I come to thee
From plume-pluckt *Richard*, who with willing Soule
Adopts thee Heire, and his high Scepter yeelds
To the possession of thy Royall Hand.
Ascend his Throne, descending now from him,
And long liue *Henry*, of that Name the Fourth.

Bull. In Gods Name, Ile ascend the Regall Throne.

Carl. Mary, Heauen forbid.
Worst in this Royall Presence may I speake,
Yet best beseeming me to speake the truth.
Would God, that any in this Noble Presence
Were enough Noble, to be vpright Iudge
Of Noble *Richard*: then true Noblenesse would
Learne him forbearance from so foule a Wrong.
What Subiect can giue Sentence on his King?
And who sits here, that is not *Richards* Subiect?
Theeues are not iudg'd, but they are by to heare,
Although apparant guilt be seene in them:
And shall the figure of Gods Maiestie,
His Captaine, Steward, Deputie elect,
Anoynted, Crown'd, planted many yeeres,
Be iudg'd by subiect, and inferior breathe,
And he himselfe not present? Oh, forbid it, God,
That in a Christian Climate, Soules refin'de
Should shew so heynous, black, obscene a deed.
I speake to Subiects, and a Subiect speakes,
Stirr'd vp by Heauen, thus boldly for his King.
My Lord of Hereford here, whom you call King,
Is a foule Traytor to prowd *Herefords* King.
And if you Crowne him, let me prophecie,
The blood of English shall manure the ground,
And future Ages groane for his foule Act.
Peace shall goe sleepe with Turkes and Infidels,
And in this Seat of Peace, tumultuous Warres
Shall Kinne with Kinne, and Kinde with Kinde confound.
Disorder, Horror, Feare, and Mutinie
Shall here inhabite, and this Land be call'd
The field of Golgotha, and dead mens Sculls.
Oh, if you reare this House, against this House
It will the wofullest Diuision proue,
That euer fell vpon this cursed Earth.
Preuent it, resist it, and let it not be so,
Least Child, Childs Children cry against you, Woe.

North. Well haue you argu'd Sir: and for your paines,
Of Capitall Treason we arrest you here.
My Lord of Westminster, be it your charge,
To keepe him safely, till his day of Tryall.
May it please you, Lords, to grant the Commons Suit?

Bull. Fetch hither *Richard*, that in common view
He may surrender: so we shall proceede
Without suspition.

Yorke. I will be his Conduct. *Exit.*

Bull. Lords, you that here are vnder our Arrest,
Procure your Sureties for your Dayes of Answer:
Little are we beholding to your Loue,
And little look'd for at your helping Hands.

Enter Richard and Yorke.

Rich. Alack, why am I sent for to a King,
Before I haue shooke off the Regall thoughts
Wherewith I reign'd? I hardly yet haue learn'd
To insinuate, flatter, bowe, and bend my Knee.
Giue Sorrow leaue a while, to tuture me
To this submission. Yet I well remember
The fauors of these men: were they not mine?
Did they not sometime cry, All hayle to me?
So *Iudas* did to Christ: but he in twelue,
Found truth in all, but one; I, in twelue thousand, none.
God saue the King: will no man say, Amen?
Am I both Priest, and Clarke? well then, Amen.
God saue the King, although I be not hee:
And yet Amen, if Heauen doe thinke him meet.
To doe what seruice, am I sent for hither?

Yorke. To doe that office of thine owne good will,
Which tyred Maiestie did make thee offer:
The Resignation of thy State and Crowne
To *Henry Bullingbrooke*.

Rich. Giue me the Crown. Here Cousin, seize ȳ Crown:
Here Cousin, on this side my Hand, on that side thine.
Now is this Golden Crowne like a deepe Well,
That owes two Buckets, filling one another,
The emptier euer dancing in the ayre,
The other downe, vnseene, and full of Water:
That Bucket downe, and full of Teares am I,
Drinking my Griefes, whil'st you mount vp on high.

Bull. I thought you had been willing to resigne.

Rich. My Crowne I am, but still my Griefes are mine:
You may my Glories and my State depose,
But not my Griefes; still am I King of those.

Bull. Part of your Cares you giue me with your Crowne.

Rich. Your Cares set vp, do not pluck my Cares downe.
My Care, is losse of Care, by old Care done,
Your Care, is gaine of Care, by new Care wonne:
The Cares I giue, I haue, though giuen away,
They 'tend the Crowne, yet still with me they stay:

Bull. Are you contented to resigne the Crowne?

Rich. I,

Rich. I, no; no, I: for I must nothing bee:
Therefore no, no, for I resigne to thee.
Now, marke me how I will vndoe my selfe.
I giue this heauie Weight from off my Head,
And this vnwieldie Scepter from my Hand,
The pride of Kingly sway from out my Heart,
With mine owne Teares I wash away my Balme,
With mine owne Hands I giue away my Crowne,
With mine owne Tongue denie my Sacred State,
With mine owne Breath release all dutious Oathes;
All Pompe and Maiestie I doe forsweare:
My Manors, Rents, Reuenues, I forgoe;
My Acts, Decrees, and Statutes I denie:
God pardon all Oathes that are broke to mee,
God keepe all Vowes vnbroke are made to thee.
Make me, that nothing haue, with nothing grieu'd,
And thou with all pleas'd, that hast all atchieu'd.
Long may'st thou liue in *Richards* Seat to sit,
And soone lye *Richard* in an Earthie Pit.
God saue King *Henry*, vn-King'd *Richard* sayes,
And send him many yeeres of Sunne-shine dayes.
What more remaines?

North. No more: but that you reade
These Accusations, and these grieuous Crymes,
Committed by your Person, and your followers,
Against the State, and Profit of this Land:
That by confessing them, the Soules of men
May deeme, that you are worthily depos'd.

Rich. Must I doe so? and must I rauell out
My weau'd-vp follyes? Gentle *Northumberland*,
If thy Offences were vpon Record,
Would it not shame thee, in so faire a troupe,
To reade a Lecture of them? If thou would'st,
There should'st thou finde one heynous Article,
Contayning the deposing of a King,
And cracking the strong Warrant of an Oath,
Mark'd with a Blot, damn'd in the Booke of Heauen.
Nay, all of you, that stand and looke vpon me,
Whil'st that my wretchednesse doth bait my selfe,
Though some of you, with *Pilate*, wash your hands,
Shewing an outward pittie: yet you *Pilates*
Haue here deliuer'd me to my sowre Crosse,
And Water cannot wash away your sinne.

North. My Lord dispatch, reade o're these Articles.

Rich. Mine Eyes are full of Teares, I cannot see:
And yet salt-Water blindes them not so much,
But they can see a sort of Traytors here.
Nay, if I turne mine Eyes vpon my selfe,
I finde my selfe a Traytor with the rest:
For I haue giuen here my Soules consent,
T'vndeck the pompous Body of a King;
Made Glory base; a Soueraigntie, a Slaue;
Prowd Maiestie, a Subiect; State, a Pesant.

North. My Lord.

Rich. No Lord of thine, thou haught-insulting man;
No, nor no mans Lord: I haue no Name, no Title;
No, not that Name was giuen me at the Font,
But 'tis vsurpt: alack the heauie day,
That I haue worne so many Winters out,
And know not now, what Name to call my selfe.
Oh, that I were a Mockerie, King of Snow,
Standing before the Sunne of *Bullingbrooke*,
To melt my selfe away in Water-drops.
Good King, great King, and yet not greatly good,
And if my word be Sterling yet in England,
Let it command a Mirror hither straight,
That it may shew me what a Face I haue,
Since it is Bankrupt of his Maiestie.

Bull. Goe some of you, and fetch a Looking-Glasse.

North. Read o're this Paper, while § Glasse doth come.

Rich. Fiend, thou torments me, ere I come to Hell.

Bull. Vrge it no more, my Lord *Northumberland*.

North. The Commons will not then be satisfy'd.

Rich. They shall be satisfy'd: Ile reade enough,
When I doe see the very Booke indeede,
Where all my sinnes are writ, and that's my selfe.

Enter one with a Glasse.

Giue me that Glasse, and therein will I reade.
No deeper wrinkles yet? hath Sorrow strucke
So many Blowes vpon this Face of mine,
And made no deeper Wounds? Oh flatt'ring Glasse,
Like to my followers in prosperitie,
Thou do'st beguile me. Was this Face, the Face
That euery day, vnder his House-hold Roofe,
Did keepe ten thousand men? Was this the Face,
That like the Sunne, did make beholders winke?
Is this the Face, which fac'd so many follyes,
That was at last out-fac'd by *Bullingbrooke*?
A brittle Glory shineth in this Face,
As brittle as the Glory, is the Face,
For there it is, crackt in an hundred shiuers.
Marke silent King, the Morall of this sport,
How soone my Sorrow hath destroy'd my Face.

Bull. The shadow of your Sorrow hath destroy'd
The shadow of your Face.

Rich. Say that againe.
The shadow of my Sorrow: ha, let's see,
'Tis very true, my Griefe lyes all within,
And these externall manner of Laments,
Are meerely shadowes, to the vnseene Griefe,
That swells with silence in the tortur'd Soule.
There lyes the substance: and I thanke thee King
For thy great bountie, that not onely giu'st
Me cause to wayle, but teachest me the way
How to lament the cause. Ile begge one Boone,
And then be gone, and trouble you no more.
Shall I obtaine it?

Bull. Name it, faire Cousin.

Rich. Faire Cousin? I am greater then a King:
For when I was a King, my flatterers
Were then but subiects; being now a subiect,
I haue a King here to my flatterer:
Being so great, I haue no neede to begge.

Bull. Yet aske.

Rich. And shall I haue?

Bull. You shall.

Rich. Then giue me leaue to goe.

Bull. Whither?

Rich. Whither you will, so I were from your sights.

Bull. Goe some of you, conuey him to the Tower.

Rich. Oh good: conuey: Conueyers are you all,
That rise thus nimbly by a true Kings fall.

Bull. On Wednesday next, we solemnly set downe
Our Coronation: Lords, prepare your selues. *Exeunt.*

Abbot. A wofull Pageant haue we here beheld.

Carl. The Woes to come, the Children yet vnborne,
Shall feele this day as sharpe to them as Thorne.

Aum. You holy Clergie-men, is there no Plot
To rid the Realme of this pernicious Blot.

Abbot. Before I freely speake my minde herein,
You shall not onely take the Sacrament,
To bury mine intents, but also to effect

What euer I shall happen to deuise.
I see your Browes are full of Discontent,
Your Heart of Sorrow, and your Eyes of Teares.
Come home with me to Supper, Ile lay a Plot
Shall shew vs all a merry day. *Exeunt.*

Actus Quintus. Scena Prima.

Enter Queene, and Ladies.

Qu. This way the King will come: this is the way
To *Iulius Cæsars* ill-erected Tower:
To whose flint Bosome, my condemned Lord
Is doom'd a Prisoner, by prowd *Bullingbrooke*.
Here let vs rest, if this rebellious Earth
Haue any resting for her true Kings Queene.

Enter Richard, and Guard.

But soft, but see, or rather doe not see,
My faire Rose wither: yet looke vp; behold,
That you in pittie may dissolue to dew,
And wash him fresh againe with true-loue Teares.
Ah thou, the Modell where old Troy did stand,
Thou Mappe of Honor, thou King *Richards* Tombe,
And not King *Richard*: thou most beauteous Inne,
Why should hard-fauor'd Griefe be lodg'd in thee,
When Triumph is become an Ale-house Guest.

Rich. Ioyne not with griefe, faire Woman, do not so,
To make my end too sudden: learne good Soule,
To thinke our former State a happie Dreame,
From which awak'd, the truth of what we are,
Shewes vs but this. I am sworne Brother (Sweet)
To grim Necessitie; and hee and I
Will keepe a League till Death. High thee to France,
And Cloyster thee in some Religious House:
Our holy liues must winne a new Worlds Crowne,
Which our prophane houres here haue stricken downe.

Qu. What, is my *Richard* both in shape and minde
Transform'd, and weaken'd? Hath *Bullingbrooke*
Depos'd thine Intellect? hath he beene in thy Heart?
The Lyon dying, thrusteth forth his Paw,
And wounds the Earth, if nothing else, with rage
To be o're-powr'd: and wilt thou, Pupill-like,
Take thy Correction mildly, kisse the Rodde,
And fawne on Rage with base Humilitie,
Which art a Lyon, and a King of Beasts?

Rich. A King of Beasts indeed: if aught but Beasts,
I had beene still a happy King of Men.
Good (sometime Queene) prepare thee hence for France:
Thinke I am dead, and that euen here thou tak'st,
As from my Death-bed, my last liuing leaue.
In Winters tedious Nights sit by the fire
With good old folkes, and let them tell thee Tales
Of wofull Ages, long agoe betide:
And ere thou bid good-night, to quit their griefe,
Tell thou the lamentable fall of me,
And send the hearers weeping to their Beds:
For why? the senceless Brands will sympathize
The heauie accent of thy mouing Tongue,
And in compassion, weepe the fire out:
And some will mourne in ashes, some coale-black,
For the deposing of a rightfull King.

Enter Northumberland.

North. My Lord, the mind of *Bullingbrooke* is chang'd.
You must to Pomfret, not vnto the Tower.
And Madame, there is order ta'ne for you:
With all swift speed, you must away to France.

Rich. Northumberland, thou Ladder wherewithall
The mounting *Bullingbrooke* ascends my Throne,
The time shall not be many houres of age,
More then it is, ere foule sinne, gathering head,
Shall breake into corruption: thou shalt thinke,
Though he diuide the Realme, and giue thee halfe,
It is too little, helping him to all:
He shall thinke, that thou which know'st the way
To plant vnrightfull Kings, wilt know againe,
Being ne're so little vrg'd another way,
To pluck him headlong from the vsurped Throne.
The Loue of wicked friends conuerts to Feare;
That Feare, to Hate; and Hate turnes one, or both,
To worthie Danger, and deserued Death.

North. My guilt be on my Head, and there an end:
Take leaue, and part, for you must part forthwith.

Rich. Doubly diuorc'd? (bad men) ye violate
A two-fold Marriage; 'twixt my Crowne, and me,
And then betwixt me, and my marryed Wife.
Let me vn-kisse the Oath 'twixt thee, and me;
And yet not so, for with a Kisse 'twas made.
Part vs, *Northumberland*: I, towards the North,
Where shiuering Cold and Sicknesse pines the Clyme:
My Queene to France: from whence, set forth in pompe,
She came adorned hither like sweet May;
Sent back like Hollowmas, or short'st of day.

Qu. And must we be diuided? must we part?
Rich. I, hand from hand (my Loue) and heart frō heart.
Qu. Banish vs both, and send the King with me.
North. That were some Loue, but little Pollicy.
Qu. Then whither he goes, thither let me goe.
Rich. So two together weeping, make one Woe.
Weepe thou for me in France; I, for thee heere:
Better farre off, then neere, be ne're the neere.
Goe, count thy Way with Sighes; I, mine with Groanes.

Qu. So longest Way shall haue the longest Moanes.
Rich. Twice for one step Ile groane, ÿ Way being short,
And peece the Way out with a heauie heart.
Come, come, in wooing Sorrow let's be briefe,
Since wedding it, there is such length in Griefe:
One Kisse shall stop our mouthes, and dumbely part;
Thus giue I mine, and thus take I thy heart.

Qu. Giue me mine owne againe: 'twere no good part,
To take on me to keepe, and kill thy heart.
So, now I haue mine owne againe, be gone,
That I may striue to kill it with a groane.

Rich. We make Woe wanton with this fond delay:
Once more adieu; the rest, let Sorrow say. *Exeunt.*

Scœna Secunda.

Enter Yorke, and his Duchesse.

Duch. My Lord, you told me you would tell the rest,
When weeping made you breake the story off,
Of our two Cousins comming into London.

Yorke. Where did I leaue?
Duch. At that sad stoppe, my Lord,
Where rude mis-gouern'd hands, from Windowes tops,
Threw dust and rubbish on King *Richards* head.

Yorke. Then

Yorke. Then, as I said, the Duke, great *Bullingbrooke,*
Mounted vpon a hot and fierie Steed,
Which his aspiring Rider seem'd to know,
With slow, but stately pace, kept on his course:
While all tongues cride, God saue thee *Bullingbrooke.*
You would haue thought the very windowes spake,
So many greedy lookes of yong and old,
Through Casements darted their desiring eyes
Vpon his visage: and that all the walles,
With painted Imagery had said at once,
Iesu preserue thee, welcom *Bullingbrooke.*
Whil'st he, from one side to the other turning,
Bare-headed, lower then his proud Steeds necke,
Bespake them thus: I thanke you Countrimen:
And thus still doing, thus he past along.

Dutch. Alas poore *Richard,* where rides he the whilst?

Yorke. As in a Theater, the eyes of men
After a well grac'd Actor leaues the Stage,
Are idlely bent on him that enters next,
Thinking his prattle to be tedious:
Euen so, or with much more contempt, mens eyes
Did scowle on *Richard*: no man cride, God saue him:
No ioyfull tongue gaue him his welcome home,
But dust was throwne vpon his Sacred head,
Which with such gentle sorrow he shooke off,
His face still combating with teares and smiles
(The badges of his greefe and patience)
That had not God (for some strong purpose) steel'd
The hearts of men, they must perforce haue melted,
And Barbarisme it selfe haue pittied him.
But heauen hath a hand in these euents,
To whose high will we bound our calme contents.
To *Bullingbrooke,* are we sworne Subiects now,
Whose State, and Honor, I for aye allow.

Enter Aumerle.

Dut. Heere comes my sonne *Aumerle.*

Yor. Aumerle that was,
But that is lost, for being *Richards* Friend.
And Madam, you must call him *Rutland* now:
I am in Parliament pledge for his truth,
And lasting fealtie to the new-made King.

Dut. Welcome my sonne: who are the Violets now,
That strew the greene lap of the new-come Spring?

Aum. Madam, I know not, nor I greatly care not,
God knowes, I had as liefe be none, as one.

Yorke. Well, beare you well in this new-spring of time
Least you be cropt before you come to prime.
What newes from Oxford? Hold those Iusts & Triumphs?

Aum. For ought I know my Lord, they do.

Yorke. You will be there I know.

Aum. If God preuent not, I purpose so.

Yor. What Seale is that that hangs without thy bosom?
Yea, look'st thou pale? Let me see the Writing.

Aum. My Lord, 'tis nothing.

Yorke. No matter then who sees it,
I will be satisfied, let me see the Writing.

Aum. I do beseech your Grace to pardon me,
It is a matter of small consequence,
Which for some reasons I would not haue seene.

Yorke. Which for some reasons sir, I meane to see:
I feare, I feare.

Dut. What should you feare?
'Tis nothing but some bond, that he is enter'd into
For gay apparrell, against the Triumph.

Yorke. Bound to himselfe? What doth he with a Bond
That he is bound to? Wife, thou art a foole.
Boy, let me see the Writing.

Aum. I do beseech you pardon me, I may not shew it.

Yor. I will be satisfied: let me see it I say. *Snatches it*
Treason, foule Treason, Villaine, Traitor, Slaue.

Dut. What's the matter, my Lord?

Yorke. Hoa, who's within there? Saddle my horse.
Heauen for his mercy: what treachery is heere?

Dut. Why, what is't my Lord?

Yorke. Giue me my boots, I say: Saddle my horse:
Now by my Honor, my life, my troth,
I will appeach the Villaine.

Dut. What is the matter?

Yorke. Peace foolish Woman.

Dut. I will not peace. What is the matter Sonne?

Aum. Good Mother be content, it is no more
Then my poore life must answer.

Dut. Thy life answer?

Enter Seruant with Boots.

Yor. Bring me my Boots, I will vnto the King.

Dut. Strike him *Aumerle.* Poore boy, y art amaz'd,
Hence Villaine, neuer more come in my sight.

Yor. Giue me my Boots, I say.

Dut. Why Yorke, what wilt thou do?
Wilt thou not hide the Trespasse of thine owne?
Haue we more Sonnes? Or are we like to haue?
Is not my teeming date drunke vp with time?
And wilt thou plucke my faire Sonne from mine Age,
And rob me of a happy Mothers name?
Is he not like thee? Is he not thine owne?

Yor. Thou fond mad woman:
Wilt thou conceale this darke Conspiracy?
A dozen of them heere haue tane the Sacrament,
And interchangeably set downe their hands
To kill the King at Oxford.

Dut. He shall be none:
Wee'l keepe him heere: then what is that to him?

Yor. Away fond woman: were hee twenty times my
Son, I would appeach him.

Dut. Hadst thou groan'd for him as I haue done,
Thou wouldest be more pittifull:
But now I know thy minde; thou do'st suspect
That I haue bene disloyall to thy bed,
And that he is a Bastard, not thy Sonne:
Sweet Yorke, sweet husband, be not of that minde:
He is as like thee, as a man may bee,
Not like to me, nor any of my Kin,
And yet I loue him.

Yorke. Make way, vnruly Woman. *Exit*

Dut. After *Aumerle.* Mount thee vpon his horse,
Spurre post, and get before him to the King,
And begge thy pardon, ere he do accuse thee,
Ile not be long behind: though I be old,
I doubt not but to ride as fast as Yorke:
And neuer will I rise vp from the ground,
Till *Bullingbrooke* haue pardon'd thee: Away be gone. *Exit*

Scœna Tertia.

Enter Bullingbrooke, Percie, and other Lords.

Bul. Can no man tell of my vnthriftie Sonne?
'Tis full three monthes since I did see him last.
If any plague hang ouer vs, 'tis he,
I would to heauen (my Lords) he might be found:
Enquire at London, 'mongst the Tauernes there:

The Life and Death of Richard the Second.

For there (they say) he dayly doth frequent,
With vnrestrained loose Companions,
Euen such (they say) as stand in narrow Lanes,
And rob our Watch, and beate our passengers,
Which he, yong wanton, and effeminate Boy
Takes on the point of Honor, to support
So dissolute a crew.

Per. My Lord, some two dayes since I saw the Prince,
And told him of these Triumphes held at Oxford.

Bul. And what said the Gallant?

Per. His answer was: he would vnto the Stewes,
And from the common'st creature plucke a Gloue
And weare it as a fauour, and with that
He would vnhorse the lustiest Challenger.

Bul. As dissolute as desp'rate, yet through both,
I see some sparkes of better hope: which elder dayes
May happily bring forth. But who comes heere?

Enter Aumerle.

Aum. Where is the King?

Bul. What meanes our Cosin, that hee stares
And lookes so wildely?

Aum. God saue your Grace. I do beseech your Maiesty
To haue some conference with your Grace alone.

Bul. Withdraw your selues, and leaue vs here alone:
What is the matter with our Cosin now?

Aum. For euer may my knees grow to the earth,
My tongue cleaue to my roofe within my mouth,
Vnlesse a Pardon, ere I rise, or speake.

Bul. Intended, or committed was this fault?
If on the first, how heynous ere it bee,
To win thy after loue, I pardon thee.

Aum. Then giue me leaue, that I may turne the key,
That no man enter, till my tale me done.

Bul. Haue thy desire. *Yorke within.*

Yor. My Liege beware, looke to thy selfe,
Thou hast a Traitor in thy presence there.

Bul. Villaine, Ile make thee safe.

Aum. Stay thy reuengefull hand, thou hast no cause to feare.

Yorke. Open the doore, secure foole-hardy King:
Shall I for loue speake treason to thy face?
Open the doore, or I will breake it open.

Enter Yorke.

Bul. What is the matter (Vnkle) speak, recouer breath,
Tell vs how neere is danger,
That we may arme vs to encounter it.

Yor. Peruse this writing heere, and thou shalt know
The reason that my haste forbids me show.

Aum. Remember as thou read'st, thy promise past:
I do repent me, reade not my name there,
My heart is not confederate with my hand.

Yor. It was (villaine) ere thy hand did set it downe.
I tore it from the Traitors bosome, King.
Feare, and not Loue, begets his penitence;
Forget to pitty him, least thy pitty proue
A Serpent, that will sting thee to the heart.

Bul. Oh heinous, strong, and bold Conspiracie,
O loyall Father of a treacherous Sonne:
Thou sheere, immaculate, and siluer fountaine,
From whence this streame, through muddy passages
Hath had his current, and defil'd himselfe.
Thy ouerflow of good, conuerts to bad,
And thy abundant goodnesse shall excuse
This deadly blot, in thy digressing sonne.

Yorke. So shall my Vertue be his Vices bawd,
And he shall spend mine Honour, with his Shame;
As thriftlesse Sonnes, their scraping Fathers Gold.
Mine honor liues, when his dishonor dies,
Or my sham'd life, in his dishonor lies:
Thou kill'st me in his life, giuing him breath,
The Traitor liues, the true man's put to death.

Dutchesse within.

Dut. What hoa (my Liege) for heauens sake let me in.

Bul. What shrill-voic'd Suppliant, makes this eager cry?

Dut. A woman, and thine Aunt (great King) 'tis I.
Speake with me, pitty me, open the dore,
A Begger begs, that neuer begg'd before.

Bul. Our Scene is alter'd from a serious thing,
And now chang'd to the Begger, and the King.
My dangerous Cosin, let your Mother in,
I know she's come, to pray for your foule sin.

Yorke. If thou do pardon, whosoeuer pray,
More sinnes for this forgiuenesse, prosper may.
This fester'd ioynt cut off, the rest rests sound,
This let alone, will all the rest confound.

Enter Dutchesse.

Dut. O King, beleeue not this hard-hearted man,
Loue, louing not it selfe, none other can.

Yor. Thou franticke woman, what dost y make here,
Shall thy old dugges, once more a Traitor reare?

Dut. Sweet Yorke be patient, heare m: gentle Liege.

Bul. Rise vp good Aunt.

Dut. Not yet, I thee beseech.
For euer will I kneele vpon my knees,
And neuer see day, that the happy sees,
Till thou giue ioy: vntill thou bid me ioy,
By pardoning Rutland, my transgressing Boy.

Aum. Vnto my mothers prayres, I bend my knee.

Yorke. Against them both, my true ioynts bended be.

Dut. Pleades he in earnest? Looke vpon his Face,
His eyes do drop no teares: his prayres are in iest:
His words come from his mouth, ours from our brest.
He prayes but faintly, and would be denide,
We pray with heart, and soule, and all beside:
His weary ioynts would gladly rise, I know,
Our knees shall kneele, till to the ground they grow:
His prayers are full of false hypocrisie,
Ours of true zeale, and deepe integritie:
Our prayers do out-pray his, then let them haue
That mercy, which true prayers ought to haue.

Bul. Good Aunt stand vp.

Dut. Nay, do not say stand vp;
But Pardon first, and afterwards stand vp.
And if I were thy Nurse, thy tongue to teach,
Pardon should be the first word of thy speach.
I neuer long'd to heare a word till now:
Say Pardon (King,) let pitty teach thee how.
The word is short: but not so short as sweet,
No word like Pardon, for Kings mouth's so meet.

Yorke. Speake it in French (King) say *Pardon'ne moy.*

Dut. Dost thou teach pardon, Pardon to destroy?
Ah my sowre husband, my hard-hearted Lord,
That set's the word it selfe, against the word.
Speake Pardon, as 'tis currant in our Land,
The chopping French we do not vnderstand.
Thine eye begins to speake, set thy tongue there,
Or in thy pitteous heart, plant thou thine eare,
That hearing how our plaints and prayres do pearce,
Pitty may moue thee, Pardon to rehearse.

Bul. Good Aunt, stand vp.

Dut. I do not sue to stand,
Pardon is all the suite I haue in hand.

Bul.

Bul. I pardon him, as heauen shall pardon mee.
Dut. O happy vantage of a kneeling knee:
Yet am I sicke for feare: Speake it againe,
Twice saying Pardon, doth not pardon twaine,
But makes one pardon strong.
Bul. I pardon him with all my hart.
Dut. A God on earth thou art.
Bul. But for our trusty brother-in-Law, the Abbot,
With all the rest of that consorted crew,
Destruction straight shall dogge them at the heeles:
Good Vnckle helpe to order seuerall powres
To Oxford, or where ere these Traitors are:
They shall not liue within this world I sweare,
But I will haue them, if I once know where.
Vnckle farewell, and Cosin adieu:
Your mother well hath praid, and proue you true.
Dut. Come my old son, I pray heauen make thee new. *Exeunt.*

Enter Exton and Seruants.

Ext. Didst thou not marke the King what words hee spake?
Haue I no friend will rid me of this liuing feare:
Was it not so?
Ser. Those were his very words.
Ex. Haue I no Friend? (quoth he:) he spake it twice,
And vrg'd it twice together, did he not?
Ser. He did.
Ex. And speaking it, he wistly look'd on me,
As who should say, I would thou wer't the man
That would diuorce this terror from my heart,
Meaning the King at Pomfret: Come, let's goe;
I am the Kings Friend, and will rid his Foe. *Exit.*

Scæna Quarta.

Enter Richard.

Rich. I haue bin studying, how to compare
This Prison where I liue, vnto the World:
And for because the world is populous,
And heere is not a Creature, but my selfe,
I cannot do it: yet Ile hammer't out.
My Braine, Ile proue the Female to my Soule,
My Soule, the Father: and these two beget
A generation of still breeding Thoughts;
And these same Thoughts, people this Little World
In humors, like the people of this world,
For no thought is contented. The better sort,
As thoughts of things Diuine, are intermixt
With scruples, and do set the Faith it selfe
Against the Faith: as thus: Come litle ones:& then againe,
It is as hard to come, as for a Camell
To thred the posterne of a Needles eye.
Thoughts tending to Ambition, they do plot
Vnlikely wonders; how these vaine weake nailes
May teare a passage through the Flinty ribbes
Of this hard world, my ragged prison walles:
And for they cannot, dye in their owne pride.
Thoughts tending to Content, flatter themselues,
That they are not the first of Fortunes slaues,
Nor shall not be the last. Like silly Beggars,
Who sitting in the Stockes, refuge their shame
That many haue, and others must sit there;
And in this Thought, they finde a kind of ease,
Bearing their owne misfortune on the backe
Of such as haue before indur'd the like.
Thus play I in one Prison, many people,
And none contented. Sometimes am I King;
Then Treason makes me wish my selfe a Beggar,
And so I am. Then crushing penurie,
Perswades me, I was better when a King:
Then am I king'd againe: and by and by,
Thinke that I am vn-king'd by *Bullingbrooke*,
And straight am nothing. But what ere I am, *Musick*
Nor I, nor any man, that but man is,
With nothing shall be pleas'd, till he be eas'd
With being nothing. Musicke do I heare?
Ha, ha? keepe time: How sowre sweet Musicke is,
When Time is broke, and no Proportion kept?
So is it in the Musicke of mens liues:
And heere haue I the daintinesse of eare,
To heare time broke in a disorder'd string:
But for the Concord of my State and Time,
Had not an eare to heare my true Time broke.
I wasted Time, and now doth Time waste me:
For now hath Time made me his numbring clocke;
My Thoughts, are minutes; and with Sighes they iarre,
Their watches on vnto mine eyes, the outward Watch,
Whereto my finger, like a Dialls point,
Is pointing still, in cleansing them from teares.
Now sir, the sound that tels what houre it is,
Are clamorous groanes, that strike vpon my heart,
Which is the bell: so Sighes, and Teares, and Grones,
Shew Minutes, Houres, and Times; but my Time
Runs poasting on, in *Bullingbrookes* proud ioy,
While I stand fooling heere, his iacke o'th'Clocke.
This Musicke mads me, let it sound no more,
For though it haue holpe madmen to their wits,
In me it seemes, it will make wise-men mad:
Yet blessing on his heart that giues it me;
For 'tis a signe of loue, and loue to *Richard*,
Is a strange Brooch, in this all-hating world.

Enter Groome.

Groo. Haile Royall Prince.
Rich. Thankes Noble Peere,
The cheapest of vs, is ten groates too deere.
What art thou? And how com'st thou hither?
Where no man euer comes, but that sad dogge
That brings me food, to make misfortune liue?
Groo. I was a poore Groome of thy Stable (King)
When thou wer't King: who trauelling towards Yorke,
With much adoo, at length haue gotten leaue
To looke vpon my (sometimes Royall) masters face.
O how it yern'd my heart, when I beheld
In London streets, that Coronation day,
When *Bullingbrooke* rode on Roane *Barbary*,
That horse, that thou so often hast bestrid,
That horse, that I so carefully haue drest.
Rich. Rode he on *Barbary*? Tell me gentle Friend,
How went he vnder him?
Groo. So proudly, as if he had disdain'd the ground.
Rich. So proud, that *Bullingbrooke* was on his backe;
That Iade hath eate bread from my Royall hand.
This hand hath made him proud with clapping him.
Would he not stumble? Would he not fall downe
(Since Pride must haue a fall) and breake the necke
Of that proud man, that did vsurpe his backe?
Forgiuenesse horse: Why do I raile on thee,
Since thou created to be aw'd by man
Was't borne to beare? I was not made a horse,

And yet I beare a burthen like an Asse,
Spur-gall'd, and tyrd by iauncing *Bullingbrooke*.

Enter Keeper with a Dish.

Keep. Fellow, giue place, heere is no longer stay.
Rich. If thou loue me, 'tis time thou wer't away.
Groo. What my tongue dares not, that my heart shall say. *Exit.*
Keep. My Lord, wilt please you to fall too?
Rich. Taste of it first, as thou wer't wont to doo.
Keep. My Lord I dare not: Sir *Pierce* of Exton,
Who lately came from th'King, commands the contrary.
Rich. The diuell take *Henrie* of Lancaster, and thee;
Patience is stale, and I am weary of it.
Keep. Helpe, helpe, helpe.

Enter Exton and Seruants.

Ri. How now? what meanes Death in this rude assalt?
Villaine, thine owne hand yeelds thy deaths instrument,
Go thou and fill another roome in hell.

Exton strikes him downe.

That hand shall burne in neuer-quenching fire,
That staggers thus my person. *Exton*, thy fierce hand,
Hath with the Kings blood, stain'd the Kings own land.
Mount, mount my soule, thy seate is vp on high,
Whil'st my grosse flesh sinkes downward, heere to dye.

Exton. As full of Valor, as of Royall blood,
Both haue I spilt: Oh would the deed were good.
For now the diuell, that told me I did well,
Sayes, that this deede is chronicled in hell.
This dead King to the liuing King Ile beare,
Take hence the rest, and giue them buriall heere. *Exit.*

Scœna Quinta.

Flourish. Enter Bullingbrooke, Yorke, with other Lords & attendants.

Bul. Kinde Vnkle Yorke, the latest newes we heare,
Is that the Rebels haue consum'd with fire
Our Towne of Ciceter in Gloucestershire,
But whether they be tane or slaine, we heare not.

Enter Northumberland.

Welcome my Lord: What is the newes?
Nor. First to thy Sacred State, wish I all happinesse:
The next newes is, I haue to London sent
The heads of *Salsbury*, *Spencer*, *Blunt*, and *Kent*:
The manner of their taking may appeare
At large discoursed in this paper heere.
Bul. We thank thee gentle *Percy* for thy paines,
And to thy worth will adde right worthy gaines.

Enter Fitz-waters.

Fitz. My Lord, I haue from Oxford sent to London,
The heads of *Broccas*, and Sir *Bennet Seely*,
Two of the dangerous consorted Traitors,
That sought at Oxford, thy dire ouerthrow.
Bul. Thy paines *Fitzwaters* shall not be forgot,
Right Noble is thy merit, well I wot.

Enter Percy and Carlile.

Per. The grand Conspirator, Abbot of Westminster,
With clog of Conscience, and sowre Melancholly,
Hath yeelded vp his body to the graue:
But heere is *Carlile*, liuing to abide
Thy Kingly doome, and sentence of his pride.
Bul. Carlile, this is your doome:
Choose out some secret place, some reuerend roome
More then thou hast, and with it ioy thy life:
So as thou liu'st in peace, dye free from strife:
For though mine enemy, thou hast euer beene,
High sparkes of Honor in thee haue I seene.

Enter Exton with a Coffin.

Exton. Great King, within this Coffin I present
Thy buried feare. Heerein all breathlesse lies
The mightiest of thy greatest enemies
Richard of Burdeaux, by me hither brought.
Bul. Exton, I thanke thee not, for thou hast wrought
A deede of Slaughter, with thy fatall hand,
Vpon my head, and all this famous Land.
Ex. From your owne mouth my Lord, did I this deed.
Bul. They loue not poyson, that do poyson neede,
Nor do I thee: though I did wish him dead,
I hate the Murtherer, loue him murthered:
The guilt of conscience take thou for thy labour,
But neither my good word, nor Princely fauour.
With *Caine* go wander through the shade of night,
And neuer shew thy head by day, nor light.
Lords, I protest my soule is full of woe,
That blood should sprinkle me, to make me grow.
Come mourne with me, for that I do lament,
And put on sullen Blacke incontinent:
Ile make a voyage to the Holy-land,
To wash this blood off from my guilty hand.
March sadly after, grace my mourning heere,
In weeping after this vntimely Beere. *Exeunt*

FINIS.

The First Part of Henry the Fourth,
with the Life and Death of HENRY Sirnamed HOT-SPVRRE.

Actus Primus. Scœna Prima.

Enter the King, Lord Iohn of Lancaster, Earle of Westmerland, with others.

King.

SO shaken as we are, so wan with care,
Finde we a time for frighted Peace to pant,
And breath shortwinded accents of new broils
To be commenc'd in Stronds a-farre remote:
No more the thirsty entrance of this Soile,
Shall daube her lippes with her owne childrens blood:
No more shall trenching Warre channell her fields,
Nor bruise her Flowrets with the Armed hoofes
Of hostile paces. Those opposed eyes,
Which like the Meteors of a troubled Heauen,
All of one Nature, of one Substance bred,
Did lately meete in the intestine shocke,
And furious cloze of ciuill Butchery,
Shall now in mutuall well-beseeming rankes
March all one way, and be no more oppos'd
Against Acquaintance, Kindred, and Allies.
The edge of Warre, like an ill-sheathed knife,
No more shall cut his Master. Therefore Friends,
As farre as to the Sepulcher of Christ,
Whose Souldier now vnder whose blessed Crosse
We are impressed and ingag'd to fight,
Forthwith a power of English shall we leuie,
Whose armes were moulded in their Mothers wombe,
To chace these Pagans in those holy Fields,
Ouer whose Acres walk'd those blessed feete
Which fourteene hundred yeares ago were nail'd
For our aduantage on the bitter Crosse.
But this our purpose is a twelue month old,
And bootlesse 'tis to tell you we will go:
Therefore we meete not now. Then let me heare
Of you my gentle Cousin Westmerland,
What yesternight our Councell did decree,
In forwarding this deere expedience.

West. My Liege: This haste was hot in question,
And many limits of the Charge set downe
But yesternight: when all athwart there came
A Post from Wales, loaden with heauy Newes;
Whose worst was, That the Noble *Mortimer*,
Leading the men of Herefordshire to fight
Against the irregular and wilde *Glendower*,
Was by the rude hands of that Welshman taken,
And a thousand of his people butchered:
Vpon whose dead corpes there was such misuse,
Such beastly, shamelesse transformation,
By those Welshwomen done, as may not be
(Without much shame) re-told or spoken of.

King. It seemes then, that the tidings of this broile,
Brake off our businesse for the Holy land.

West. This matcht with other like, my gracious Lord,
Farre more vneuen and vnwelcome Newes
Came from the North, and thus it did report:
On Holy-roode day, the gallant *Hotspurre* there,
Young *Harry Percy*, and braue *Archibald*,
That euer-valiant and approoued Scot,
At *Holmeden* met, where they did spend
A sad and bloody houre:
As by discharge of their Artillerie,
And shape of likely-hood the newes was told:
For he that brought them, in the very heate
And pride of their contention, did take horse,
Vncertaine of the issue any way.

King. Heere is a deere and true industrious friend,
Sir *Walter Blunt*, new lighted from his Horse,
Strain'd with the variation of each soyle,
Betwixt that *Holmedon*, and this Seat of ours:
And he hath brought vs smooth and welcome newes.
The Earle of *Dowglas* is discomfited,
Ten thousand bold Scots, two and twenty Knights
Balk'd in their owne blood did Sir *Walter* see
On *Holmedons* Plaines. Of Prisoners, *Hotspurre* tooke
Mordake Earle of Fife, and eldest sonne
To beaten *Dowglas*, and the Earle of *Atholl*,
Of *Murry*, *Angus*, and *Menteith*.
And is not this an honourable spoyle?
A gallant prize? Ha Cosin, is it not? Infaith it is.

West. A Conquest for a Prince to boast of.

King. Yea, there thou mak'st me sad, & mak'st me sin,
In enuy, that my Lord Northumberland
Should be the Father of so blest a Sonne:
A Sonne, who is the Theame of Honors tongue;
Among'st a Groue, the very straightest Plant,
Who is sweet Fortunes Minion, and her Pride:
Whil'st I by looking on the praise of him,
See Ryot and Dishonor staine the brow
Of my yong *Harry*. O that it could be prou'd,
That some Night-tripping-Faiery, had exchang'd
In Cradle-clothes, our Children where they lay,
And call'd mine *Percy*, his *Plantagenet*:

The

Then would I haue his *Harry*, and he mine:
But let him from my thoughts. What thinke you Coze
Of this young *Percies* pride? The Prisoners
Which he in this aduenture hath surpriz'd,
To his owne vse he keepes, and sends me word
I shall haue none but *Mordake* Earle of *Fife*.

  West. This is his Vnckles teaching. This is Worcester
Maleuolent to you in all Aspects:
Which makes him prune himselfe, and bristle vp
The crest of Youth against your Dignity.

  King. But I haue sent for him to answer this:
And for this cause a-while we must neglect
Our holy purpose to *Ierusalem*.
Cosin, on Wednesday next, our Councell we will hold
At Windsor, and so informe the Lords:
But come your selfe with speed to vs againe,
For more is to be said, and to be done,
Then out of anger can be vttered.

  West. I will my Liege.   *Exeunt*

Scæna Secunda.

Enter Henry Prince of Wales, Sir Iohn Falstaffe, and Pointz.

  Fal. Now *Hal*, what time of day is it Lad?

  Prince. Thou art so fat-witted with drinking of olde Sacke, and vnbuttoning thee after Supper, and sleeping vpon Benches in the afternoone, that thou hast forgotten to demand that truely, which thou wouldest truly know. What a diuell hast thou to do with the time of the day? vnlesse houres were cups of Sacke, and minutes Capons, and clockes the tongues of Bawdes, and dialls the signes of Leaping-houses, and the blessed Sunne himselfe a faire hot Wench in Flame-coloured Taffata; I see no reason, why thou shouldest bee so superfluous, to demaund the time of the day.

  Fal. Indeed you come neere me now *Hal*, for we that take Purses, go by the Moone and seuen Starres, and not by *Phœbus* hee, that wand'ring Knight so faire. And I prythee sweet Wagge, when thou art King, as God saue thy Grace, Maiesty I should say, for Grace thou wilte haue none.

  Prin. What, none?

  Fal. No, not so much as will serue to be Prologue to an Egge and Butter.

  Prin. Well, how then? Come roundly, roundly.

  Fal. Marry then, sweet Wagge, when thou art King, let not vs that are Squires of the Nights bodie, bee call'd Theeues of the Dayes beautie. Let vs be *Dianaes* Forresters, Gentlemen of the Shade, Minions of the Moone; and let men say, we be men of good Gouernment, being gouerned as the Sea is, by our noble and chast mistris the Moone, vnder whose countenance we steale.

  Prin. Thou say'st well, and it holds well too: for the fortune of vs that are the Moones men, doeth ebbe and flow like the Sea, beeing gouerned as the Sea is, by the Moone: as for proofe. Now a Purse of Gold most resolutely snatch'd on Monday night, and most dissolutely spent on Tuesday Morning; got with swearing, Lay by: and spent with crying, Bring in; now, in as low an ebbe as the foot of the Ladder, and by and by in as high a flow as the ridge of the Gallowes.

  Fal. Thou say'st true Lad: and is not my Hostesse of the Tauerne a most sweet Wench?

  Prin. As is the hony, my old Lad of the Castle: and is not a Buffe Ierkin a most sweet robe of durance?

  Fal. How now? how now mad Wagge? What in thy quips and thy quiddities? What a plague haue I to doe with a Buffe-Ierkin?

  Prin. Why, what a poxe haue I to doe with my Hostesse of the Tauerne?

  Fal. Well, thou hast call'd her to a reck'ning many a time and oft.

  Prin. Did I euer call for thee to pay thy part?

  Fal. No, Ile giue thee thy due, thou hast paid al there.

  Prin. Yea and elsewhere, so farre as my Coine would stretch, and where it would not, I haue vs'd my credit.

  Fal. Yea, and so vs'd it, that were it heere apparant, that thou art Heire apparant. But I prythee sweet Wag, shall there be Gallowes standing in England when thou art King? and resolution thus fobb'd as it is, with the rustie curbe of old Father Anticke the Law? Doe not thou when thou art a King, hang a Theefe.

  Prin. No, thou shalt.

  Fal. Shall I? O rare! Ile be a braue Iudge.

  Prin. Thou iudgest false already. I meane, thou shalt haue the hanging of the Theeues, and so become a rare Hangman.

  Fal. Well *Hal*, well: and in some sort it iumpes with my humour, as well as waiting in the Court, I can tell you.

  Prin. For obtaining of suites?

  Fal. Yea, for obtaining of suites, whereof the Hangman hath no leane Wardrobe. I am as Melancholly as a Gyb-Cat, or a lugg'd Beare.

  Prin. Or an old Lyon, or a Louers Lute.

  Fal. Yea, or the Drone of a Lincolnshire Bagpipe.

  Prin. What say'st thou to a Hare, or the Melancholly of Moore Ditch?

  Fal. Thou hast the most vnsauoury smiles, and art indeed the most comparatiue rascalleft sweet yong Prince. But *Hal*, I prythee trouble me no more with vanity, I wold thou and I knew, where a Commodity of good names were to be bought: an olde Lord of the Councell rated me the other day in the street about you sir; but I mark'd him not, and yet hee talk'd very wisely, but I regarded him not, and yet he talkt wisely, and in the street too.

  Prin. Thou didst well: for no man regards it.

  Fal. O, thou hast damnable iteration, and art indeede able to corrupt a Saint. Thou hast done much harme vnto me *Hall*, God forgiue thee for it. Before I knew thee *Hal*, I knew nothing: and now I am (if a man shold speake truly) little better then one of the wicked. I must giue o-uer this life, and I will giue it ouer: and I do not, I am a Villaine. Ile be damn'd for neuer a Kings sonne in Christendome.

  Prin. Where shall we take a purse to morrow, Iacke?

  Fal. Where thou wilt Lad, Ile make one: and I doe not, call me Villaine, and baffle me.

  Prin. I see a good amendment of life in thee: From Praying, to Purse-taking.

  Fal. Why, *Hal*, 'tis my Vocation *Hal*: 'Tis no sin for a man to labour in his Vocation.

  Pointz. Now shall wee know if Gads hill haue set a Watch. O, if men were to be saued by merit, what hole in Hell were hot enough for him? This is the most omnipotent Villaine, that euer cryed, Stand, to a true man.

  Prin. Good morrow *Ned*.

                                                              Pointz.

Poines. Good morrow sweet *Hal.* What saies Monsieur Remorse? What sayes Sir Iohn Sacke and Sugar: Iacke? How agrees the Diuell and thee about thy Soule, that thou soldest him on Good-Friday last, for a Cup of Madera, and a cold Capons legge?

Prin. Sir Iohn stands to his word, the diuel shall haue his bargaine, for he was neuer yet a Breaker of Prouerbs: *He will giue the diuell his due.*

Poin. Then art thou damn'd for keeping thy word with the diuell.

Prin. Else he had damn'd for cozening the diuell.

Poy. But my Lads, my Lads, to morrow morning, by foure a clocke early at Gads hill, there are Pilgrimes going to Canterbury with rich Offerings, and Traders riding to London with fat Purses. I haue vizards for you all; you haue horses for your selues: Gads-hill lyes to night in Rochester, I haue bespoke Supper to morrow in Eastcheape; we may doe it as secure as sleepe: if you will go, I will stuffe your Purses full of Crownes: if you will not, tarry at home and be hang'd.

Fal. Heare ye Yedward, if I tarry at home and go not, Ile hang you for going.

Poy. You will chops.

Fal. Hal, wilt thou make one?

Prin. Who, I rob? I a Theefe? Not I.

Fal. There's neither honesty, manhood, nor good fellowship in thee, nor thou cam'st not of the blood-royall, if thou dar'st not stand for ten shillings.

Prin. Well then, once in my dayes Ile be a mad-cap.

Fal. Why, that's well said.

Prin. Well, come what will, Ile tarry at home.

Fal. Ile be a Traitor then, when thou art King.

Prin. I care not.

Poyn. Sir *Iohn*, I prythee leaue the Prince & me alone, I will lay him downe such reasons for this aduenture, that he shall go.

Fal. Well, maist thou haue the Spirit of perswasion; and he the eares of profiting, that what thou speakest, may moue; and what he heares may be beleeued, that the true Prince, may (for recreation sake) proue a false theefe; for the poore abuses of the time, want countenance. Farwell, you shall finde me in Eastcheape.

Prin. Farwell the latter Spring. Farewell Alhollown Summer.

Poy. Now, my good sweet Hony Lord, ride with vs to morrow. I haue a iest to execute, that I cannot manage alone. *Falstaffe, Haruey, Rossill,* and *Gads-hill,* shall robbe those men that wee haue already way-layde, your selfe and I, wil not be there: and when they haue the booty, if you and I do not rob them, cut this head from my shoulders.

Prin. But how shal we part with them in setting forth?

Poyn. Why, we wil set forth before or after them, and appoint them a place of meeting, wherin it is at our pleasure to faile; and then will they aduenture vppon the exploit themselues, which they shall haue no sooner atchieued, but wee'l set vpon them.

Prin. I, but tis like that they will know vs by our horses, by our habits, and by euery other appointment to be our selues.

Poy. Tut our horses they shall not see, Ile tye them in the wood, our vizards wee will change after wee leaue them: and sirrah, I haue Cases of Buckram for the nonce, to immaske our noted outward garments.

Prin. But I doubt they will be too hard for vs.

Poin. Well, for two of them, I know them to bee as true bred Cowards as euer turn'd backe: and for the third if he fight longer then he sees reason, Ile forswear Armes. The vertue of this Iest will be, the incomprehensible lyes that this fat Rogue will tell vs, when we meete at Supper: how thirty at least he fought with, what Wardes, what blowes, what extremities he endured; and in the reproofe of this, lyes the iest.

Prin. Well, Ile goe with thee, prouide vs all things necessary, and meete me to morrow night in Eastcheape, there Ile sup. Farewell.

Poyn. Farewell, my Lord. *Exit Pointz*

Prin. I know you all, and will a-while vphold
The vnyoak'd humor of your idlenesse:
Yet heerein will I imitate the Sunne,
Who doth permit the base contagious cloudes
To smother vp his Beauty from the world,
That when he please againe to be himselfe,
Being wanted, he may be more wondred at,
By breaking through the foule and vgly mists
Of vapours, that did seeme to strangle him.
If all the yeare were playing holidaies,
To sport, would be as tedious as to worke;
But when they seldome come, they wisht-for come,
And nothing pleaseth but rare accidents.
So when this loose behauiour I throw off,
And pay the debt I neuer promised;
By how much better then my word I am,
By so much shall I falsifie mens hopes,
And like bright Mettall on a sullen ground:
My reformation glittering o're my fault,
Shall shew more goodly, and attract more eyes,
Then that which hath no foyle to set it off.
Ile so offend, to make offence a skill,
Redeeming time, when men thinke least I will.

Scœna Tertia.

Enter the King, Northumberland, Worcester, Hotspurre, Sir Walter Blunt, and others.

King. My blood hath beene too cold and temperate,
Vnapt to stirre at these indignities,
And you haue found me; for accordingly,
You tread vpon my patience: But be sure,
I will from henceforth rather be my Selfe,
Mighty, and to be fear'd, then my condition
Which hath beene smooth as Oyle, soft as yong Downe,
And therefore lost that Title of respect,
Which the proud soule ne're payes, but to the proud.

Wor. Our house (my Soueraigne Liege) little deserues
The scourge of greatnesse to be vsed on it,
And that same greatnesse too, which our owne hands
Haue holpe to make so portly.

Nor. My Lord.

King. Worcester get thee gone: for I do see
Danger and disobedience in thine eye.
O sir, your presence is too bold and peremptory,
And Maiestie might neuer yet endure
The moody Frontier of a seruant brow,
You haue good leaue to leaue vs. When we need
Your vse and counsell, we shall send for you.
You were about to speake.

North. Yes, my good Lord.

Those

Those Prisoners in your Highnesse demanded,
Which *Harry Percy* heere at *Holmedon* tooke,
Were (as he sayes) not with such strength denied
As was deliuered to your Maiesty:
Who either through enuy, or misprision,
Was guilty of this fault; and not my Sonne.

  Hot. My Liege, I did deny no Prisoners.
But, I remember when the fight was done,
When I was dry with Rage, and extreame Toyle,
Breathlesse, and Faint, leaning vpon my Sword,
Came there a certaine Lord, neat and trimly drest;
Fresh as a Bride-groome, and his Chin new reapt,
Shew'd like a stubble Land at Haruest home.
He was perfumed like a Milliner,
And 'twixt his Finger and his Thumbe, he held
A Pouncet-box: which euer and anon
He gaue his Nose, and took't away againe:
Who therewith angry, when it next came there,
Tooke it in Snuffe. And still he smil'd and talk'd:
And as the Souldiers bare dead bodies by,
He call'd them vntaught Knaues, Vnmannerly,
To bring a slouenly vnhandsome Coarse
Betwixt the Winde, and his Nobility.
With many Holiday and Lady tearme
He question'd me: Among the rest, demanded
My Prisoners, in your Maiesties behalfe.
I then, all smarting, with my wounds being cold,
(To be so pestered with a Popingay)
Out of my Greefe, and my Impatience,
Answer'd (neglectingly) I know not what,
He should, or should not: For he made me mad,
To see him shine so briske, and smell so sweet,
And talke so like a Waiting-Gentlewoman,
Of Guns, & Drums, and Wounds: God saue the marke;
And telling me, the Soueraign'st thing on earth
Was Parmacity, for an inward bruise:
And that it was great pitty, so it was,
That villanous Salt-peter should be digg'd
Out of the Bowels of the harmlesse Earth,
Which many a good Tall Fellow had destroy'd
So Cowardly. And but for these vile Gunnes,
He would himselfe haue beene a Souldier.
This bald, vnioynted Chat of his (my Lord)
Made me to answer indirectly (as I said.)
And I beseech you, let not this report
Come currant for an Accusation,
Betwixt my Loue, and your high Maiesty.

  Blunt. The circumstance considered, good my Lord,
What euer *Harry Percie* then had said,
To such a person, and in such a place,
At such a time, with all the rest retold,
May reasonably dye, and neuer rise
To do him wrong, or any way impeach
What then he said, so he vnsay it now.

  King. Why yet doth deny his Prisoners,
But with Prouiso and Exception,
That we at our owne charge, shall ransome straight
His Brother-in-Law, the foolish *Mortimer*,
Who (in my soule) hath wilfully betraid
The liues of those, that he did leade to Fight,
Against the great Magitian, damn'd *Glendower*:
Whose daughter (as we heare) the Earle of March
Hath lately married. Shall our Coffers then,
Be emptied, to redeeme a Traitor home?
Shall we buy Treason? and indent with Feares,
When they haue lost and forfeyted themselues.
No: on the barren Mountaine let him sterue:
For I shall neuer hold that man my Friend,
Whose tongue shall aske me for one peny cost
To ransome home reuolted *Mortimer*.

  Hot. Reuolted *Mortimer*?
He neuer did fall off, my Soueraigne Liege,
But by the chance of Warre: to proue that true,
Needs no more but one tongue. For all those Wounds,
Those mouthed Wounds, which valiantly he tooke,
When on the gentle Seuernes siedgie banke,
In single Opposition hand to hand,
He did confound the best part of an houre
In changing hardiment with great *Glendower*:
Three times they breath'd, and three times did they drink
Vpon agreement, of swift Seuernes flood;
Who then affrighted with their bloody lookes,
Ran fearefully among the trembling Reeds,
And hid his crispe-head in the hollow banke,
Blood-stained with these Valiant Combatants.
Neuer did base and rotten Policy
Colour her working with such deadly wounds;
Nor neuer could the Noble *Mortimer*
Receiue so many, and all willingly:
Then let him not be sland'red with Reuolt.

  King. Thou do'st bely him *Percy*, thou dost bely him;
He neuer did encounter with *Glendower*:
I tell thee, he durst as well haue met the diuell alone,
As *Owen Glendower* for an enemy.
Art thou not asham'd? But Sirrah, henceforth
Let me not heare you speake of *Mortimer*.
Send me your Prisoners with the speediest meanes,
Or you shall heare in such a kinde from me
As will displease ye. My Lord *Northumberland*,
We License your departure with your sonne,
Send vs your Prisoners, or you'l heare of it. *Exit King.*

  Hot. And if the diuell come and roare for them
I will not send them. I will after straight
And tell him so: for I will ease my heart,
Although it be with hazard of my head.

  Nor. What? drunke with choller? Stay & pause awhile,
Heere comes your Vnckle. *Enter Worcester.*

  Hot. Speake of *Mortimer*?
Yes, I will speake of him, and let my soule
Want mercy, if I do not ioyne with him.
In his behalfe, Ile empty all these Veines,
And shed my deere blood drop by drop i'th dust,
But I will lift the downfall *Mortimer*
As high i'th Ayre, as this Vnthankfull King,
As this Ingrate and Cankred *Bullingbrooke*.

  Nor. Brother, the King hath made your Nephew mad
  Wor. Who strooke this heate vp after I was gone?

  Hot. He will (forsooth) haue all my Prisoners:
And when I vrg'd the ransom once againe
Of my Wiues Brother, then his cheeke look'd pale,
And on my face he turn'd an eye of death,
Trembling euen at the name of *Mortimer*.

  Wor. I cannot blame him: was he not proclaim'd
By *Richard* that dead is, the next of blood?

  Nor. He was: I heard the Proclamation,
And then it was, when the vnhappy King
(Whose wrongs in vs God pardon) did set forth
Vpon his Irish Expedition:
From whence he intercepted, did returne
To be depos'd, and shortly murthered.

  Wor. And for whose death, we in the worlds wide mouth
Liue scandaliz'd, and fouly spoken of.

Hot. But soft I pray you; did King *Richard* then
Proclaime my brother *Mortimer*,
Heyre to the Crowne?

Nor. He did, my selfe did heare it.

Hot. Nay then I cannot blame his Cousin King,
That wish'd him on the barren Mountaines staru'd.
But shall it be, that you that set the Crowne
Vpon the head of this forgetfull man,
And for his sake, wore the detested blot
Of murtherous subornation? Shall it be,
That you a world of curses vndergoe,
Being the Agents, or base second meanes,
The Cords, the Ladder, or the Hangman rather?
O pardon, if that I descend so low,
To shew the Line, and the Predicament
Wherein you range vnder this subtill King.
Shall it for shame, be spoken in these dayes,
Or fill vp Chronicles in time to come,
That men of your Nobility and Power,
Did gage them both in an vniust behalfe
(As Both of you, God pardon it, haue done)
To put downe *Richard*, that sweet louely Rose,
And plant this Thorne, this Canker *Bullingbrooke*?
And shall it in more shame be further spoken,
That you are fool'd, discarded, and shooke off
By him, for whom these shames ye vnderwent?
No: yet time serues, wherein you may redeeme
Your banish'd Honors, and restore your selues
Into the good Thoughts of the world againe.
Reuenge the geering and disdain'd contempt
Of this proud King, who studies day and night
To answer all the Debt he owes vnto you,
Euen with the bloody Payment of your deaths:
Therefore I say——

Wor. Peace Cousin, say no more.
And now I will vnclaspe a Secret booke,
And to your quicke conceyuing Discontents,
Ile reade you Matter, deepe and dangerous,
As full of perill and aduenturous Spirit,
As to o're-walke a Current, roaring loud
On the vnstedfast footing of a Speare.

Hot. If he fall in, good night, or sinke or swimme:
Send danger from the East vnto the West,
So Honor crosse it from the North to South,
And let them grapple: The blood more stirres
To rowze a Lyon, then to start a Hare.

Nor. Imagination of some great exploit,
Driues him beyond the bounds of Patience.

Hot. By heauen, me thinkes it were an easie leap,
To plucke bright Honor from the pale-fac'd Moone,
Or diue into the bottome of the deepe,
Where Fadome-line could neuer touch the ground,
And plucke vp drowned Honor by the Lockes:
So he that doth redeeme her thence, might weare
Without Co-riuall, all her Dignities:
But out vpon this halfe-fac'd Fellowship.

Wor. He apprehends a World of Figures here,
But not the forme of what he should attend:
Good Cousin giue me audience for a-while,
And list to me.

Hot. I cry you mercy.

Wor. Those same Noble Scottes
That are your Prisoners.

Hot. Ile keepe them all.
By heauen, he shall not haue a Scot of them:
No, if a Scot would saue his Soule, he shall not.
Ile keepe them, by this Hand.

Wor. You start away,
And lend no eare vnto my purposes.
Those Prisoners you shall keepe.

Hot. Nay, I will; that's flat:
He said, he would not ransome *Mortimer*:
Forbad my tongue to speake of *Mortimer*.
But I will finde him when he lyes asleepe,
And in his eare, Ile holla *Mortimer*.
Nay, Ile haue a Starling shall be taught to speake
Nothing but *Mortimer*, and giue it him,
To keepe his anger still in motion.

Wor. Heare you Cousin: a word.

Hot. All studies heere I solemnly defie,
Saue how to gall and pinch this *Bullingbrooke*,
And that same Sword and Buckler Prince of Wales.
But that I thinke his Father loues him not,
And would be glad he met with some mischance,
I would haue poyson'd him with a pot of Ale.

Wor. Farewell Kinsman: Ile talke to you
When you are better temper'd to attend.

Nor. Why what a Waspe-tongu'd & impatient foole
Art thou, to breake into this Womans mood,
Tying thine eare to no tongue but thine owne?

Hot. Why look you, I am whipt & scourg'd with rods,
Netled, and stung with Pismires, when I heare
Of this vile Politician *Bullingbrooke*.
In *Richards* time: What de'ye call the place?
A plague vpon't, it is in Gloustershire:
'Twas, where the madcap Duke his Vncle kept,
His Vncle Yorke, where I first bow'd my knee
Vnto this King of Smiles, this *Bullingbrooke*:
When you and he came backe from Rauenspurgh.

Nor. At Barkley Castle.

Hot. You say true:
Why what a caudie deale of curtesie,
This fawning Grey-hound then did proffer me.
Looke when his infant Fortune came to age,
And gentle *Harry Percy*, and kinde Cousin:
O, the Diuell take such Couzeners, God forgiue me,
Good Vncle tell your tale, for I haue done.

Wor. Nay, if you haue not, too't againe,
Wee'l stay your leysure.

Hot. I haue done insooth.

Wor. Then once more to your Scottish Prisoners.
Deliuer them vp without their ransome straight,
And make the *Dowglas* sonne your onely meane
For powres in Scotland: which for diuers reasons
Which I shall send you written, be assur'd
Will easily be granted you, my Lord.
Your Sonne in Scotland being thus impl y'd,
Shall secretly into the bosome creepe
Of that same noble Prelate, well belou'd,
The Archbishop.

Hot. Of Yorke, is't not?

Wor. True, who beares hard
His Brothers death at *Bristow*, the Lord *Stroope*.
I speake not this in estimation,
As what I thinke might be, but what I know
Is ruminated, plotted, and set downe,
And onely stayes but to behold the face
Of that occasion that shall bring it on.

Hot. I smell it:
Vpon my life, it will do wond'rous well.

Nor. Before the game's a-foot, thou still let'st slip.

Hot. Why, it cannot choose but be a Noble plot,

And then the power of Scotland, and of Yorke
To ioyne with *Mortimer*, Ha.

Wor. And so they shall.

Hot. Infaith it is exceedingly well aym'd.

Wor. And 'tis no little reason bids vs speed,
To saue our heads, by raising of a Head :
For, beare our selues as euen as we can,
The King will alwayes thinke him in our debt,
And thinke, we thinke our selues vnsatisfied,
Till he hath found a time to pay vs home.
And see already, how he doth beginne
To make vs strengers to his lookes of loue.

Hot. He does, he does; wee'l be reueng'd on him.

Wor. Cousin, farewell. No further go in this,
Then I by Letters shall direct your course
When time is ripe, which will be sodainly:
Ile steale to *Glendower*, and loe, *Mortimer*,
Where you, and *Dowglas*, and our powres at once,
As I will fashion it, shall happily meete,
To beare our fortunes in our owne strong armes,
Which now we hold at much vncertainty.

Nor. Farewell good Brother, we shall thriue, I trust.

Hot. Vncle, adieu : O let the houres be short,
Till fields, and blowes, and grones, applaud our sport. *exit*

Actus Secundus. Scena Prima.

Enter a Carrier with a Lanterne in his hand.

1.Car. Heigh-ho, an't be not foure by the day, Ile be hang'd. *Charles waine* is ouer the new Chimney, and yet our horse not packt. What Ostler ?

Ost. Anon, anon.

1.Car. I prethee Tom, beate Cuts Saddle, put a few Flockes in the point : the poore Iade is wrung in the withers, out of all cesse.

Enter another Carrier.

2.Car. Pease and Beanes are as danke here as a Dog, and this is the next way to giue poore Iades the Bottes: This house is turned vpside downe since *Robin* the Ostler dyed.

1.Car. Poore fellow neuer ioy'd since the price of oats rose, it was the death of him.

2.Car. I thinke this is the most villanous house in al London rode for Fleas: I am stung like a Tench.

1.Car. Like a Tench? There is ne're a King in Christendome, could be better bit, then I haue beene since the first Cocke.

2.Car. Why, you will allow vs ne're a' Iourden, and then we leake in your Chimney : and your Chamber-lye breeds Fleas like a Loach.

1.Car. What Ostler, come away, and be hang'd: come away.

2.Car. I haue a Gammon of Bacon, and two razes of Ginger, to be deliuered as farre as Charing-crosse.

1.Car. The Turkies in my Pannier are quite starued. What Ostler? A plague on thee, hast thou neuer an eye in thy head? Can'st not heare ? And t'were not as good a deed as drinke, to break the pate of thee, I am a very Villaine. Come and be hang'd, hast no faith in thee ?

Enter Gads-hill.

Gad. Good-morrow Carriers. What's a clocke?

Car. I thinke it be two a clocke.

Gad. I prethee lend me thy Lanthorne to see my Gelding in the stable.

1.Car. Nay soft I pray ye, I know a trick worth two of that.

Gad. I prethee lend me thine.

2.Car. I, when, canst tell ? Lend mee thy Lanthorne (quoth-a) marry Ile see thee hang'd first.

Gad. Sirra Carrier: What time do you meane to come to London ?

2.Car. Time enough to goe to bed with a Candle, I warrant thee. Come neighbour *Mugges*, wee'll call vp the Gentlemen, they will along with company, for they haue great charge. *Exeunt*

Enter Chamberlaine.

Gad. What ho, Chamberlaine ?

Cham. At hand quoth Pick-purse.

Gad. That's euen as faire, as at hand quoth the Chamberlaine : For thou variest no more from picking of Purses, then giuing direction, doth from labouring. Thou lay'st the plot, how.

Cham. Good morrow Master *Gads-Hill*, it holds currant that I told you yesternight. There's a Franklin in the wilde of Kent, hath brought three hundred Markes with him in Gold: I heard him tell it to one of his company last night at Supper ; a kinde of Auditor, one that hath abundance of charge too (God knowes what) they are vp already, and call for Egges and Butter. They will away presently.

Gad. Sirra, if they meete not with S. Nicholas Clarks, Ile giue thee this necke.

Cham. No, Ile none of it : I prythee keep that for the Hangman, for I know thou worshipst S. Nicholas as truly as a man of falshood may.

Gad. What talkest thou to me of the Hangman? If I hang, Ile make a fat payre of Gallowes. For, if I hang, old Sir *Iohn* hangs with mee, and thou know'st hee's no Starueling. Tut, there are other Troians that y dream'st not of, the which (for sport sake) are content to doe the Profession some grace ; that would (if matters should bee look'd into) for their owne Credit sake, make all Whole. I am ioyned with no Foot-land-Rakers, no Long-staffe six-penny strikers, none of these mad Mustachio-purple-hu'd-Maltwormes, but with Nobility, and Tranquilitie; Bourgomasters, and great Oneyers, such as can holde in, such as will strike sooner then speake ; and speake sooner then drinke, and drinke sooner then pray: and yet I lye, for they pray continually vnto their Saint the Commonwealth ; or rather, not to pray to her, but prey on her:for they ride vp & downe on her, and make hir their Boots.

Cham. What, the Commonwealth their Bootes? Will she hold out water in foule way?

Gad. She will, she will; Iustice hath liquor'd her. We steale as in a Castle, cocksure : we haue the receit of Fern-seede, we walke inuisible.

Cham. Nay, I thinke rather, you are more beholding to the Night, then to the Fernseed, for your walking inuisible.

Gad. Giue me thy hand.
Thou shalt haue a share in our purpose,
As I am a true man.

Cham. Nay, rather let mee haue it, as you are a false Theefe.

Gad. Goe too : *Homo* is a common name to all men. Bid the Ostler bring the Gelding out of the stable. Farewell, ye muddy Knaue. *Exeunt.*

Scæna Secunda.

Enter Prince, Poynes, and Peto.

Poines. Come shelter, shelter, I haue remoued *Falstaffs* Horse, and he frets like a gum'd Veluet.

Prin. Stand close.

Enter Falstaffe.

Fal. Poines, Poines, and be hang'd Poines.

Prin. Peace ye fat-kidney'd Rascall, what a brawling dost thou keepe.

Fal. What *Poines. Hal*?

Prin. He is walk'd vp to the top of the hill, Ile go seek him.

Fal. I am accurst to rob in that Theefe company: that Rascall hath remoued my Horse, and tied him I know not where. If I trauell but foure foot by the squire further a foote, I shall breake my winde. Well, I doubt not but to dye a faire death for all this, if I scape hanging for killing that Rogue, I haue forsworne his company hourely any time this two and twenty yeare, & yet I am bewitcht with the Rogues company. If the Rascall haue not giuen me medicines to make me loue him, Ile behang'd; it could not be else: I haue drunke Medicines. *Poines, Hal*, a Plague vpon you both. *Bardolph, Peto*: Ile starue ere I rob a foote further. And 'twere not as good a deede as to drinke, to turne True-man, and to leaue these Rogues, I am the veriest Varlet that euer chewed with a Tooth. Eight yards of vneuen ground, is threescore & ten miles afoot with me: and the stony-hearted Villaines knowe it well enough. A plague vpon't, when Theeues cannot be true one to another. *They whistle.* Whew: a plague light vpon you all. Giue my Horse you Rogues: giue me my Horse, and be hang'd.

Prin. Peace ye fat guttes, lye downe, lay thine eare close to the ground, and list if thou can heare the tread of Trauellers.

Fal. Haue you any Leauers to lift me vp again being downe? Ile not beare mine owne flesh so far afoot again, for all the coine in thy Fathers Exchequer. What a plague meane ye to colt me thus?

Prin. Thou ly'st, thou art not colted, thou art vncolted.

Fal. I prethee good Prince *Hal*, help me to my horse, good Kings sonne.

Prin. Out you Rogue, shall I be your Ostler?

Fal. Go hang thy selfe in thine owne heire-apparant-Garters: If I be tane, Ile peach for this: and I haue not Ballads made on all, and sung to filthy tunes, let a Cup of Sacke be my poyson: when a iest is so forward, & a foote too, I hate it.

Enter Gads-hill.

Gad. Stand.

Fal. So I do against my will.

Poin. O 'tis our Setter, I know his voyce: *Bardolfe*, what newes?

Bar. Case ye, case ye; on with your Vizards, there's mony of the Kings comming downe the hill, 'tis going to the Kings Exchequer.

Fal. You lie you rogue, 'tis going to the Kings Tauern.

Gad. There's enough to make vs all.

Fal. To be hang'd.

Prin. You foure shall front them in the narrow Lane: Ned and I, will walke lower; if they scape from your encounter, then they light on vs.

Peto. But how many be of them?

Gad. Some eight or ten.

Fal. Will they not rob vs?

Prin. What, a Coward Sir *Iohn* Paunch?

Fal. Indeed I am not *Iohn of Gaunt* your Grandfather; but yet no Coward, *Hal*.

Prin. Wee'l leaue that to the proofe.

Poin. Sirra Iacke, thy horse stands behinde the hedg, when thou need'st him, there thou shalt finde him. Farewell, and stand fast.

Fal. Now cannot I strike him, if I should be hang'd.

Prin. Ned, where are our disguises?

Poin. Heere hard by: Stand close.

Fal. Now my Masters, happy man be his dole, say I: euery man to his businesse.

Enter Trauellers.

Tra. Come Neighbor: the boy shall leade our Horses downe the hill: Wee'l walke a-foot a while, and ease our Legges.

Theeues. Stay.

Tra. Iesu blesse vs.

Fal. Strike down with them, cut the villains throats; a whorson Caterpillars: Bacon-fed Knaues, they hate vs youth; downe with them, fleece them.

Tra. O, we are vndone, both we and ours for euer.

Fal. Hang ye gorbellied knaues, are you vndone? No ye Fat Chuffes, I would your store were heere. On Bacons, on, what ye knaues? Yong men must liue, you are Grand Iurers, are ye? Wee'l iure ye ifaith.

Heere they rob them, and binde them. Enter the Prince and Poines.

Prin. The Theeues haue bound the True-men: Now could thou and I rob the Theeues, and go merily to London, it would be argument for a Weeke, Laughter for a Moneth, and a good iest for euer.

Poynes. Stand close, I heare them comming.

Enter Theeues againe.

Fal. Come my Masters, let vs share, and then to horsse before day: and the Prince and Poynes bee not two arrand Cowards, there's no equity stirring. There's no moe valour in that Poynes, than in a wilde Ducke.

Prin. Your money.

Poin. Villaines.

As they are sharing, the Prince and Poynes set vpon them. They all run away, leauing the booty behind them.

Prince. Got with much ease. Now merrily to Horse: The Theeues are scattred, and possest with fear so strongly, that they dare not meet each other: each takes his fellow for an Officer. Away good Ned, *Falstaffe* sweates to death, and Lards the leane earth as he walkes along: wer't not for laughing, I should pitty him.

Poin. How the Rogue roar'd. *Exeunt.*

Scæna Tertia.

Enter Hotspurre solus, reading a Letter.

But for mine owne part, my Lord, I could bee well contented to be there, in respect of the loue I beare your house.

He

He could be contented: Why is he not then? in respect of the loue he beares our house. He shewes in this, he loues his owne Barne better then he loues our house. Let me see some more. *The purpose you vndertake is dangerous.* Why that's certaine: 'Tis dangerous to take a Colde, to sleepe, to drinke: but I tell you (my Lord foole) out of this Nettle, Danger; we plucke this Flower, Safety. *The purpose you vndertake is dangerous, the Friends you haue named vncertaine, the Time it selfe vnsorted, and your whole Plot too light, for the counterpoize of so great an Opposition.* Say you so, say you so: I say vnto you againe, you are a shallow cowardly Hinde, and you Lye. What a lackebraine is this? I protest, our plot is as good a plot as euer was laid; our Friend true and constant: A good Plotte, good Friends, and full of expectation: An excellent plot, very good Friends. What a Frosty-spirited rogue is this? Why, my Lord of Yorke commends the plot, and the generall course of the action. By this hand, if I were now by this Rascall, I could braine him with his Ladies Fan. Is there not my Father, my Vnckle, and my Selfe, Lord *Edmund Mortimer*, my Lord of *Yorke*, and *Owen Glendour*? Is there not besides, the *Dowglas*? Haue I not all their letters, to meete me in Armes by the ninth of the next Moneth? and are they not some of them set forward already? What a Pagan Rascall is this? An Infidell. Ha, you shall see now in very sincerity of Feare and Cold heart, will he to the King, and lay open all our proceedings. O, I could diuide my selfe, and go to buffets, for mouing such a dish of skim'd Milk with so honourable an Action. Hang him, let him tell the King we are prepared. I will set forwards to night.

Enter his Lady.

How now Kate, I must leaue you within these two hours.
 La. O my good Lord, why are you thus alone?
For what offence haue I this fortnight bin
A banish'd woman from my *Harries* bed?
Tell me (sweet Lord) what is't that takes from thee
Thy stomacke, pleasure, and thy golden sleepe?
Why dost thou bend thine eyes vpon the earth?
And start so often when thou sitt'st alone?
Why hast thou lost the fresh blood in thy cheekes?
And giuen my Treasures and my rights of thee,
To thicke-ey'd musing, and curst melancholly?
In my faint-slumbers, I by thee haue watcht,
And heard thee murmore tales of Iron Warres:
Speake tearmes of manage to thy bounding Steed,
Cry courage to the field. And thou hast talk'd
Of Sallies, and Retires; Trenches, Tents,
Of Palizadoes, Frontiers, Parapets,
Of Basiliskes, of Canon, Culuerin,
Of Prisoners ransome, and of Souldiers slaine,
And all the current of a headdy fight.
Thy spirit within thee hath beene so at Warre,
And thus hath so bestirr'd thee in thy sleepe,
That beds of sweate hath stood vpon thy Brow,
Like bubbles in a late-disturbed Streame;
And in thy face strange motions haue appear'd,
Such as we see when men restraine their breath
On some great sodaine hast. O what portents are these?
Some heauie businesse hath my Lord in hand,
And I must know it: else he loues me not.
 Hot. What ho; Is *Gilliams* with the Packet gone?
 Ser. He is my Lord, an houre agone.
 Hot. Hath *Butler* brought those horses frō the Sheriffe?
 Ser. One horse, my Lord, he brought euen now.
 Hot. What Horse? A Roane, a crop eare, is it not.
 Ser. It is my Lord.
 Hot. That Roane shall be my Throne. Well, I will backe him straight. *Esperance*, bid *Butler* lead him forth into the Parke.
 La. But heare you, my Lord.
 Hot. What say'st thou my Lady?
 La. What is it carries you away?
 Hot. Why, my horse (my Loue) my horse.
 La. Out you mad-headed Ape, a Weazell hath not such a deale of Spleene, as you are tost with. In sooth Ile know your businesse *Harry*, that I will. I feare my Brother *Mortimer* doth stirre about his Title, and hath sent for you to line his enterprize. But if you go——
 Hot. So farre a foot, I shall be weary, Loue.
 La. Come, come, you Paraquito, answer me directly vnto this question, that I shall aske. Indeede Ile breake thy little finger *Harry*, if thou wilt not tel me true.
 Hot. Away, away you trifler: Loue, I loue thee not,
I care not for thee *Kate*: this is no world
To play with Mammets, and to tilt with lips.
We must haue bloodie Noses, and crack'd Crownes,
And passe them currant too. Gods me, my horse.
What say'st thou *Kate*? what wold'st thou haue with me?
 La. Do ye not loue me? Do ye not indeed?
Well, do not then. For since you loue me not,
I will not loue my selfe. Do you not loue me?
Nay, tell me if thou speak'st in iest, or no.
 Hot. Come, wilt thou see me ride?
And when I am a horsebacke, I will sweare
I loue thee infinitely. But hearke you *Kate*,
I must not haue you henceforth, question me,
Whether I go: nor reason whereabout.
Whether I must, I must: and to conclude,
This Euening must I leaue thee, gentle *Kate*.
I know you wise, but yet no further wise
Then *Harry Percies* wife. Constant you are,
But yet a woman: and for secrecie,
No Lady closer. For I will beleeue
Thou wilt not vtter what thou do'st not know,
And so farre wilt I trust thee, gentle Kate.
 La. How so farre?
 Hot. Not an inch further. But harke you *Kate*,
Whither I go, thither shall you go too:
To day will I set forth, to morrow you.
Will this content you *Kate*?
 La. It must of force. *Exeunt*

Scena Quarta.

Enter Prince and Poines.

 Prin. Ned, prethee come out of that fat roome, & lend me thy hand to laugh a little.
 Poines. Where hast bene Hall?
 Prin. With three or foure Logger-heads, amongst 3. or fourescore Hogsheads. I haue sounded the verie base string of humility. Sirra, I am sworn brother to a leash of Drawers, and can call them by their names, as *Tom, Dicke*, and *Francis*. They take it already vpon their confidence, that though I be but Prince of Wales, yet I am the King of Curtesie: telling me flatly I am no proud Iack like *Falstaffe*, but a Corinthian, a lad of mettle, a good boy, and when I am King of England, I shall command al the good Laddes in East-cheape. They call drinking deepe, dying Scarlet; and when you breath in your watering, then

they cry hem, and bid you play it off. To conclude, I am so good a proficient in one quarter of an houre, that I can drinke with any Tinker in his owne Language during my life. I tell thee *Ned*, thou hast lost much honor, that thou wer't not with me in this action: but sweet *Ned*, to sweeten which name of *Ned*, I giue thee this peniworth of Sugar, clapt euen now into my hand by an vnder Skinker, one that neuer spake other English in his life, then *Eight shillings and six pence*, and, *You are welcome*: with this shril addition, *Anon, Anon sir, Score a Pint of Bastard in the Halfe Moone*, or so. But *Ned*, to driue away time till *Falstaffe* come, I prythee doe thou stand in some by-roome, while I question my puny Drawer, to what end hee gaue me the Sugar, and do neuer leaue calling *Francis*, that his Tale to me may be nothing but, Anon: step aside, and Ile shew thee a President.

Poines. Francis.
Prin. Thou art perfect.
Poin. Francis.

Enter Drawer.

Fran. Anon, anon sir; looke downe into the Pomgarnet, *Ralfe*.
Prince. Come hither *Francis*.
Fran. My Lord.
Prin. How long hast thou to serue, *Francis*?
Fran. Forsooth fiue yeares, and as much as to——
Poin. Francis.
Fran. Anon, anon sir.
Prin. Fiue yeares: Berlady a long Lease for the clinking of Pewter. But Francis, darest thou be so valiant, as to play the coward with thy Indenture, & shew it a faire paire of heeles, and run from it?
Fran. O Lord sir, Ile be sworne vpon all the Books in England, I could finde in my heart.
Poin. Francis.
Fran. Anon, anon sir.
Prin. How old art thou, *Francis*?
Fran. Let me see, about Michaelmas next I shalbe——
Poin. Francis.
Fran. Anon sir, pray you stay a little, my Lord.
Prin. Nay but harke you Francis, for the Sugar thou gauest me, 'twas a penyworth, was't not?
Fran. O Lord sir, I would it had bene two.
Prin. I will giue thee for it a thousand pound: Aske me when thou wilt, and thou shalt haue it.
Poin. Francis.
Fran. Anon, anon.
Prin. Anon Francis? No Francis, but to morrow Francis: or Francis, on thursday: or indeed Francis when thou wilt. But Francis.
Fran. My Lord.
Prin. Wilt thou rob this Leatherne Ierkin, Christall button, Not-pated, Agat ring, Puke stocking, Caddice garter, Smooth tongue, Spanish pouch.
Fran. O Lord sir, who do you meane?
Prin. Why then your browne Bastard is your onely drinke: for looke you Francis, your white Canuas doublet will sulley. In Barbary sir, it cannot come to so much.
Fran. What sir?
Poin. Francis.
Prin. Away you Rogue, dost thou heare them call?
Heere they both call him, the Drawer stands amazed, not knowing which way to go.

Enter Vintner.

Vint. What, stand'st thou still, and hear'st such a calling? Looke to the Guests within: My Lord, olde Sir *Iohn* with halfe a dozen more, are at the doore: shall I let them in?
Prin. Let them alone awhile, and then open the doore. *Poines*.

Enter Poines.

Poin. Anon, anon sir.
Prin. Sirra, *Falstaffe* and the rest of the Theeues, are at the doore, shall we be merry?
Poin. As merrie as Crickets my Lad. But harke yee, What cunning match haue you made with this iest of the Drawer? Come, what's the issue?
Prin. I am now of all humors, that haue shewed themselues humors, since the old dayes of goodman *Adam*, to the pupill age of this present twelue a clock at midnight. What's a clocke Francis?
Fran. Anon, anon sir.
Prin. That euer this Fellow should haue fewer words then a Parret, and yet the sonne of a Woman. His industry is vp-staires and down-staires, his eloquence the parcell of a reckoning. I am not yet of *Percies* mind, the Hotspurre of the North, he that killes me some sixe or seauen dozen of Scots at a Breakfast, washes his hands, and saies to his wife; Fie vpon this quiet life, I want worke. O my sweet *Harry* sayes she, how many hast thou kill'd to day? Giue my Roane horse a drench (sayes hee) and answeres, some fourteene, an houre after: a trifle, a trifle. I prethee call in *Falstaffe*, Ile play *Percy*, and that damn'd Brawne shall play Dame *Mortimer* his wife. *Riuo*, sayes the drunkard. Call in Ribs, call in Tallow.

Enter Falstaffe.

Poin. Welcome Iacke, where hast thou beene?
Fal. A plague of all Cowards I say, and a Vengeance too, marry and Amen. Giue me a cup of Sacke Boy. Ere I leade this life long, Ile sowe nether stockes, and mend them too. A plague of all cowards. Giue me a Cup of Sacke, Rogue. Is there no Vertue extant?
Prin. Didst thou neuer see Titan kisse a dish of Butter, pittifull hearted Titan that melted at the sweete Tale of the Sunne? If thou didst, then behold that compound.
Fal. You Rogue, heere's Lime in this Sacke too: there is nothing but Roguery to be found in Villanous man; yet a Coward is worse then a Cup of Sack with lime. A villanous Coward, go thy wayes old Iacke, die when thou wilt, if manhood, good manhood be not forgot vpon the face of the earth, then am I a shotten Herring: there liues not three good men vnhang'd in England, & one of them is fat, and growes old, God helpe the while, a bad world I say. I would I were a Weauer, I could sing all manner of songs. A plague of all Cowards, I say still.
Prin. How now Woolsacke, what mutter you?
Fal. A Kings Sonne? If I do not beate thee out of thy Kingdome with a dagger of Lath, and driue all thy Subiects afore thee like a flocke of Wilde-geese, Ile neuer weare haire on my face more. You Prince of Wales?
Prin. Why you horson round man? what's the matter?
Fal. Are you not a Coward? Answer me to that, and *Poines* there?
Prin. Ye fatch paunch, and yee call mee Coward, Ile stab thee.
Fal. I call thee Coward? Ile see thee damn'd ere I call the Coward: but I would giue a thousand pound I could run as fast as thou canst. You are straight enough in the shoulders, you care not who sees your backe: Call you

that backing of your friends? a plague vpon such backing: giue me them that will face me. Giue me a Cup
of Sack, I am a Rogue if I drunke to day.

Prince. O Villaine, thy Lippes are scarce wip'd, since
thou drunk'st last.

Falst. All's one for that.   *He drinkes.*
A plague of all Cowards still, say I.

Prince. What's the matter?

Falst. What's the matter? here be foure of vs, haue
ta'ne a thousand pound this Morning.

Prince. Where is it, *Iack*? where is it?

Falst. Where is it? taken from vs, it is: a hundred
vpon poore foure of vs.

Prince. What, a hundred, man?

Falst. I am a Rogue, if I were not at halfe Sword with
a dozen of them two houres together. I haue scaped by
miracle. I am eight times thrust through the Doublet,
foure through the Hose, my Buckler cut through and
through, my Sword hackt like a Hand-saw, *ecce signum*.
I neuer dealt better since I was a man: all would not doe.
A plague of all Cowards: let them speake; if they speake
more or lesse then truth, they are villaines, and the sonnes
of darknesse.

Prince. Speake sirs, how was it?

Gad. We foure set vpon some dozen.

Falst. Sixteene, at least, my Lord.

Gad. And bound them.

Peto. No, no, they were not bound.

Falst. You Rogue, they were bound, euery man of
them, or I am a Iew else, an Ebrew Iew.

Gad. As we were sharing, some sixe or seuen fresh men
set vpon vs.

Falst. And vnbound the rest, and then come in the
other.

Prince. What, fought yee with them all?

Falst. All? I know not what yee call all: but if I
fought not with fiftie of them, I am a bunch of Radish:
if there were not two or three and fiftie vpon poore olde
Iack, then am I no two-legg'd Creature.

Poin. Pray Heauen, you haue not murthered some of
them.

Falst. Nay, that's past praying for, I haue pepper'd
two of them: Two I am sure I haue payed, two Rogues
in Buckrom Sutes. I tell thee what, *Hal*, if I tell thee a
Lye, spit in my face, call me Horse: thou knowest my olde
word: here I lay, and thus I bore my point; foure Rogues
in Buckrom let driue at me.

Prince. What, foure? thou sayd'st but two, euen now.

Falst. Foure *Hal*, I told thee foure.

Poin. I, I, he said foure.

Falst. These foure came all a-front, and mainely thrust
at me; I made no more adoe, but tooke all their seuen
points in my Targuet, thus.

Prince. Seuen? why there were but foure, euen now.

Falst. In Buckrom.

Poin. I, foure, in Buckrom Sutes.

Falst. Seuen, by these Hilts, or I am a Villaine else.

Prin. Prethee let him alone, we shall haue more anon.

Falst. Doest thou heare me, *Hal*?

Prin. I, and marke thee too, *Iack*.

Falst. Doe so, for it is worth the listning too: these
nine in Buckrom, that I told thee of.

Prin. So, two more alreadie.

Falst. Their Points being broken.

Poin. Downe fell his Hose.

Falst. Began to giue me ground: but I followed me
close, came in foot and hand; and with a thought, seuen of
the eleuen I pay'd.

Prin. O monstrous! eleuen Buckrom men growne
out of two?

Falst. But as the Deuill would haue it, three mis-begotten Knaues, in Kendall Greene, came at my Back, and
let driue at me; for it was so darke, *Hal*, that thou could'st
not see thy Hand.

Prin. These Lyes are like the Father that begets them,
grosse as a Mountaine, open, palpable. Why thou Clay-
brayn'd Guts, thou Knotty-pated Foole, thou Horson obscene greasie Tallow Catch.

Falst. What, art thou mad? art thou mad? is not the
truth, the truth?

Prin. Why, how could'st thou know these men in
Kendall Greene, when it was so darke, thou could'st not
see thy Hand? Come, tell vs your reason: what say'st thou
to this?

Poin. Come, your reason *Iack*, your reason.

Falst. What, vpon compulsion? No: were I at the
Strappado, or all the Racks in the World, I would not
tell you on compulsion. Giue you a reason on compulsion? If Reasons were as plentie as Black-berries, I would
giue no man a Reason vpon compulsion, I.

Prin. Ile be no longer guiltie of this sinne. This sanguine Coward, this Bed-presser, this Horse-back-breaker,
this huge Hill of Flesh.

Falst. Away you Starueling, you Elfe-skin, you dried
Neats tongue, Bulles-pissell, you stocke-fish: O for breth
to vtter. What is like thee? You Tailors yard, you sheath
you Bow-case, you vile standing tucke.

Prin. Well, breath a-while, and then to't againe: and
when thou hast tyr'd thy selfe in base comparisons, heare
me speake but thus.

Poin. Marke *Iacke*.

Prin. We two, saw you foure set on foure, and bound
them, and were Masters of their Wealth: mark now how
a plaine Tale shall put you downe. Then did we two, set
on you foure, and with a word, outfac'd you from your
prize, and haue it: yea, and can shew it you in the House.
And *Falstaffe*, you caried your Guts away as nimbly, with
as quicke dexteritie, and roared for mercy, and still ranne
and roar'd, as euer I heard Bull-Calfe. What a Slaue art
thou, to hacke thy sword as thou hast done, and then say
it was in fight. What trick? what deuice? what starting
hole canst thou now find out, to hide thee from this open
and apparant shame?

Poines. Come, let's heare Iacke: What tricke hast
thou now?

Fal. I knew ye as well as he that made ye. Why heare
ye my Masters, was it for me to kill the Heire apparant?
Should I turne vpon the true Prince? Why, thou knowest
I am as valiant as *Hercules*: but beware Instinct, the Lion
will not touch the true Prince: Instinct is a great matter.
I was a Coward on Instinct: I shall thinke the better of
my selfe, and thee, during my life: I, for a valiant Lion,
and thou for a true Prince. But Lads, I am glad you haue
the Mony. Hostesse, clap to the doores: watch to night,
pray to morrow. Gallants, Lads, Boyes, Harts of Gold,
all the good Titles of Fellowship come to you. What,
shall we be merry? shall we haue a Play extempory.

Prin. Content, and the argument shall be, thy runing
away.

Fal. A, no more of that *Hall*, and thou louest me.
Enter Hostesse.

Host. My Lord, the Prince?

Prin.

Prin. How now my Lady the Hostesse, what say'st thou to me?

Hostesse. Marry, my Lord, there is a Noble man of the Court at doore would speake with you: hee sayes, hee comes from your Father.

Prin. Giue him as much as will make him a Royall man, and send him backe againe to my Mother.

Falst. What manner of man is hee?

Hostesse. An old man.

Falst. What doth Grauitie out of his Bed at Midnight? Shall I giue him his answere?

Prin. Prethee doe *Iacke*.

Falst. 'Faith, and Ile send him packing. *Exit.*

Prince. Now Sirs: you fought faire; so did you *Peto*, so did you *Bardol*: you are Lyons too, you ranne away vpon instinct: you will not touch the true Prince; no, fie.

Bard. 'Faith, I ranne when I saw others runne.

Prin. Tell mee now in earnest, how came *Falstaffes* Sword so hackt?

Peto. Why, he hackt it with his Dagger, and said, hee would sweare truth out of England, but hee would make you beleeue it was done in fight, and perswaded vs to doe the like.

Bard. Yea, and to tickle our Noses with Spear-grasse, to make them bleed, and then to beslubber our garments with it, and sweare it was the blood of true men. I did that I did not this seuen yeeres before, I blusht to heare his monstrous deuices.

Prin. O Villaine, thou stolest a Cup of Sacke eighteene yeeres agoe, and wert taken with the manner, and euer since thou hast blusht extempore: thou hadst fire and sword on thy side, and yet thou ranst away; what instinct hadst thou for it?

Bard. My Lord, doe you see these Meteors? doe you behold these Exhalations?

Prin. I doe.

Bard. What thinke you they portend?

Prin. Hot Liuers, and cold Purses.

Bard. Choler, my Lord, if rightly taken.

Prin. No, if rightly taken, Halter.

Enter Falstaffe.

Heere comes leane *Iacke*, heere comes bare-bone. How now my sweet Creature of Bombast, how long is't agoe, *Iacke*, since thou saw'st thine owne Knee?

Falst. My owne Knee? When I was about thy yeeres (Hal) I was not an Eagles Talent in the Waste, I could haue crept into any Aldermans Thumbe-Ring: a plague of sighing and griefe, it blowes a man vp like a Bladder. There's villanous Newes abroad: heere was Sir *Iohn Braby* from your Father; you must goe to the Court in the Morning. The same mad fellow of the North, *Percy*; and hee of Wales, that gaue *Amamon* the Bastinado, and made *Lucifer* Cuckold, and swore the Deuill his true Liege-man vpon the Crosse of a Welch-hooke; what a plague call you him?

Poin. O, *Glendower*.

Falst. Owen, Owen; the same, and his Sonne in Law *Mortimer*, and old *Northumberland*, and the sprightly Scot of Scots, *Dowglas*, that runnes a Horse-backe vp a Hill perpendicular.

Prin. Hee that rides at high speede, and with a Pistoll kills a Sparrow flying.

Falst. You haue hit it.

Prin. So did he neuer the Sparrow.

Falst. Well, that Rascall hath good mettall in him, hee will not runne.

Prin. Why, what a Rascall art thou then, to prayse him so for running?

Falst. A Horse-backe (ye Cuckoe) but a foot hee will not budge a foot.

Prin. Yes *Iacke*, vpon instinct.

Falst. I grant ye, vpon instinct: Well, hee is there too, and one *Mordake*, and a thousand blew-Cappes more. *Worcester* is stolne away by Night: thy Fathers Beard is turn'd white with the Newes; you may buy Land now as cheape as stinking Mackrell.

Prin. Then 'tis like, if there come a hot Sunne, and this ciuill buffetting hold, wee shall buy Maiden-heads as they buy Hob-nayles, by the Hundreds.

Falst. By the Masse Lad, thou say'st true, it is like wee shall haue good trading that way. But tell me *Hal*, art not thou horrible afear'd? thou being Heire apparant, could the World picke thee out three such Enemyes againe, as that Fiend *Dowglas*, that Spirit *Percy*, and that Deuill *Glendower*? Art not thou horrible afraid? Doth not thy blood thrill at it?

Prin. Not a whit: I lacke some of thy instinct.

Falst. Well, thou wilt be horrible chidde to morrow, when thou commest to thy Father: if thou doe loue me, practise an answere.

Prin. Doe thou stand for my Father, and examine mee vpon the particulars of my Life.

Falst. Shall I? content: This Chayre shall bee my State, this Dagger my Scepter, and this Cushion my Crowne.

Prin. Thy State is taken for a Ioyn'd-Stoole, thy Golden Scepter for a Leaden Dagger, and thy precious rich Crowne, for a pittifull bald Crowne.

Falst. Well, and the fire of Grace be not quite out of thee, now shalt thou be moued. Giue me a Cup of Sacke to make mine eyes looke redde, that it may be thought I haue wept, for I must speake in passion, and I will doe it in King *Cambyses* vaine.

Prin. Well, heere is my Legge.

Falst. And heere is my speech: stand aside Nobilitie.

Hostesse. This is excellent sport, yfaith.

Falst. Weepe not, sweet Queene, for trickling teares are vaine.

Hostesse. O the Father, how hee holdes his countenance?

Falst. For Gods sake Lords, conuey my trustfull Queen, For teares doe stop the floud-gates of her eyes.

Hostesse. O rare, he doth it as like one of these harlotry Players, as euer I see.

Falst. Peace good Pint-pot, peace good Tickle-braine. Harry, I doe not onely maruell where thou spendest thy time; but also, how thou art accompanied: For though the Camomile, the more it is troden, the faster it growes; yet Youth, the more it is wasted, the sooner it weares. Thou art my Sonne: I haue partly thy Mothers Word, partly my Opinion; but chiefely, a villanous tricke of thine Eye, and a foolish hanging of thy nether Lippe, that doth warrant me. If then thou be Sonne to mee, heere lyeth the point: why, being Sonne to me, art thou so poynted at? Shall the blessed Sonne of Heauen proue a Micher, and eate Black-berryes? a question not to bee askt. Shall the Sonne of England proue a Theefe, and take Purses? a question to be askt. There is a thing, Harry, which thou hast often heard of, and it is knowne to many

many in our Land, by the Name of Pitch: this Pitch (as ancient Writers doe report) doth defile; so doth the companie thou keepest: for Harry, now I doe not speake to thee in Drinke, but in Teares; not in Pleasure, but in Passion; not in Words onely, but in Woes also: and yet there is a vertuous man, whom I haue often noted in thy companie, but I know not his Name.

Prin. What manner of man, and it like your Maiestie?

Falst. A goodly portly man yfaith, and a corpulent, of a chearefull Looke, a pleasing Eye, and a most noble Carriage, and as I thinke, his age some fiftie, or (byrlady) inclining to threescore; and now I remember mee, his Name is *Falstaffe*: if that man should be lewdly giuen, hee deceiues mee; for *Harry*, I see Vertue in his Lookes. If then the Tree may be knowne by the Fruit, as the Fruit by the Tree, then peremptorily I speake it, there is Vertue in that *Falstaffe*: him keepe with, the rest banish. And tell mee now, thou naughtie Varlet, tell mee, where hast thou beene this moneth?

Prin. Do'st thou speake like a King? doe thou stand for mee, and Ile play my Father.

Falst. Depose me: if thou do'st it halfe so grauely, so maiestically, both in word and matter, hang me vp by the heeles for a Rabbet-sucker, or a Poulters Hare.

Prin. Well, heere I am set.

Falst. And heere I stand: iudge my Masters.

Prin. Now *Harry*, whence come you?

Falst. My Noble Lord, from East-cheape.

Prin. The complaints I heare of thee, are grieuous.

Falst. Yfaith, my Lord, they are false: Nay, Ile tickle ye for a young Prince.

Prin. Swearest thou, vngracious Boy? henceforth ne're looke on me: thou art violently carryed away from Grace: there is a Deuill haunts thee, in the likenesse of a fat old Man; a Tunne of Man is thy Companion: Why do'st thou conuerse with that Trunke of Humors, that Boulting-Hutch of Beastlinesse, that swolne Parcell of Dropsies, that huge Bombard of Sacke, that stuft Cloake-bagge of Guts, that rosted Manning Tree Oxe with the Pudding in his Belly, that reuerend Vice, that grey Iniquitie, that Father Ruffian, that Vanitie in yeeres? wherein is he good, but to taste Sacke, and drinke it? wherein neat and cleanly, but to carue a Capon, and eat it? wherein Cunning, but in Craft? wherein Craftie, but in Villanie? wherein Villanous, but in all things? wherein worthy, but in nothing?

Falst. I would your Grace would take me with you: whom meanes your Grace?

Prince. That villanous abhominable mis-leader of Youth, *Falstaffe*, that old white-bearded Sathan.

Falst. My Lord, the man I know.

Prince. I know thou do'st.

Falst. But to say, I know more harme in him then in my selfe, were to say more then I know. That hee is olde (the more the pittie) his white hayres doe witnesse it: but that hee is (sauing your reuerence) a Whore-master, that I vtterly deny. If Sacke and Sugar bee a fault, Heauen helpe the Wicked: if to be olde and merry, be a sinne, then many an olde Hoste that I know, is damn'd: if to be fat, be to be hated, then *Pharaohs* leane Kine are to be loued. No, my good Lord, banish *Peto*, banish *Bardolph*, banish *Poines*: but for sweete *Iacke Falstaffe*, kinde *Iacke Falstaffe*, true *Iacke Falstaffe*, valiant *Iacke Falstaffe*, and therefore more valiant, being as hee is olde *Iack Falstaffe*, banish not him thy *Harryes* companie, banish not him thy *Harryes* companie; banish plumpe *Iacke*, and banish all the World.

Prince. I doe, I will.

Enter Bardolph running.

Bard. O, my Lord, my Lord, the Sherife, with a most most monstrous Watch, is at the doore.

Falst. Out you Rogue, play out the Play: I haue much to say in the behalfe of that *Falstaffe*.

Enter the Hostesse.

Hostesse. O, my Lord, my Lord.

Falst. Heigh, heigh, the Deuill rides vpon a Fiddle-sticke: what's the matter?

Hostesse. The Sherife and all the Watch are at the doore: they are come to search the House, shall I let them in?

Falst. Do'st thou heare *Hal*, neuer call a true peece of Gold a Counterfeit: thou art essentially made, without seeming so.

Prince. And thou a naturall Coward, without instinct.

Falst. I deny your *Maior*: if you will deny the Sherife, so: if not, let him enter. If I become not a Cart as well as another man, a plague on my bringing vp: I hope I shall as soone be strangled with a Halter, as another.

Prince. Goe hide thee behinde the Arras, the rest walke vp aboue. Now my Masters, for a true Face and good Conscience.

Falst. Both which I haue had: but their date is out, and therefore Ile hide me. *Exit.*

Prince. Call in the Sherife.

Enter Sherife and the Carrier.

Prince. Now Master Sherife, what is your will with mee?

She. First pardon me, my Lord. A Hue and Cry hath followed certaine men vnto this house.

Prince. What men?

She. One of them is well knowne, my gracious Lord, a grosse fat man.

Car. As fat as Butter.

Prince. The man, I doe assure you, is not heere, For I my selfe at this time haue imploy'd him: And Sherife, I will engage my word to thee, That I will by to morrow Dinner time, Send him to answere thee, or any man, For any thing he shall be charg'd withall: And so let me entreat you, leaue the house.

She. I will, my Lord: there are two Gentlemen Haue in this Robberie lost three hundred Markes.

Prince. It may be so: if he haue robb'd these men, He shall be answerable: and so farewell.

She. Good Night, my Noble Lord.

Prince. I thinke it is good Morrow, is it not?

She. Indeede, my Lord, I thinke it be two a Clocke. *Exit.*

Prince. This oyly Rascall is knowne as well as Poules: goe call him forth.

Peto. *Falstaffe*? fast asleepe behinde the Arras, and snorting like a Horse.

Prince. Harke, how hard he fetches breath: search his Pockets. He

He searcheth his Pockets, and findeth certaine Papers.

Prince. What hast thou found?

Peto. Nothing but Papers, my Lord.

Prince. Let's see, what be they? reade them.

Peto. Item, a Capon. ii.s.ii.d.
Item, Sawce. iiii.d.
Item, Sacke, two Gallons. v.s.viii.d.
Item, Anchoues and Sacke after Supper. ii.s.vi.d.
Item, Bread. ob.

Prince. O monstrous, but one halfe penny-worth of Bread to this intollerable deale of Sacke? What there is else, keepe close, wee'le reade it at more aduantage: there let him sleepe till day. Ile to the Court in the Morning: Wee must all to the Warres, and thy place shall be honorable. Ile procure this fat Rogue a Charge of Foot, and I know his death will be a Match of Twelue-score. The Money shall be pay'd backe againe with aduantage. Be with me betimes in the Morning: and so good morrow *Peto*.

Peto. Good morrow, good my Lord. *Exeunt.*

Actus Tertius. Scena Prima.

Enter Hotspurre, Worcester, Lord Mortimer, Owen Glendower.

Mort. These promises are faire, the parties sure,
And our induction full of prosperous hope.

Hotsp. Lord *Mortimer*, and Cousin *Glendower*,
Will you sit downe?
And Vnckle *Worcester*; a plague vpon it,
I haue forgot the Mappe.

Glend. No, here it is:
Sit Cousin *Percy*, sit good Cousin *Hotspurre*:
For by that Name, as oft as *Lancaster* doth speake of you,
His Cheekes looke pale, and with a rising sigh,
He wisheth you in Heauen.

Hotsp. And you in Hell, as oft as he heares *Owen Glendower* spoke of.

Glend. I cannot blame him: At my Natiuitie,
The front of Heauen was full of fierie shapes,
Of burning Cressets: and at my Birth,
The frame and foundation of the Earth
Shak'd like a Coward.

Hotsp. Why so it would haue done at the same season,
if your Mothers Cat had but kitten'd, though your selfe had neuer beene borne.

Glend. I say the Earth did shake when I was borne.

Hotsp. And I say the Earth was not of my minde,
If you suppose, as fearing you, it shooke.

Glend. The Heauens were all on fire, the Earth did tremble.

Hotsp. Oh, then the Earth shooke
To see the Heauens on fire,
And not in feare of your Natiuitie.
Diseased Nature oftentimes breakes forth
In strange eruptions; and the teeming Earth
Is with a kinde of Collick pincht and vext,
By the imprisoning of vnruly Winde
Within her Wombe: which for enlargement striuing,
Shakes the old Beldame Earth, and tombles downe
Steeples, and mosse-growne Towers. At your Birth,
Our Grandam Earth, hauing this distemperature,
In passion shooke.

Glend. Cousin: of many men
I doe not beare these Crossings: Giue me leaue
To tell you once againe, that at my Birth
The front of Heauen was full of fierie shapes,
The Goates ranne from the Mountaines, and the Heards
Were strangely clamorous to the frighted fields:
These signes haue markt me extraordinarie,
And all the courses of my Life doe shew,
I am not in the Roll of common men.
Where is the Liuing, clipt in with the Sea,
That chides the Bankes of England, Scotland, and Wales,
Which calls me Pupill, or hath read to me?
And bring him out, that is but Womans Sonne,
Can trace me in the tedious wayes of Art,
And hold me pace in deepe experiments.

Hotsp. I thinke there's no man speakes better Welsh:
Ile to Dinner.

Mort. Peace Cousin *Percy*, you will make him mad.

Glend. I can call Spirits from the vastie Deepe.

Hotsp. Why so can I, or so can any man:
But will they come, when you doe call for them?

Glend. Why, I can teach thee, Cousin, to command the Deuill.

Hotsp. And I can teach thee, Cousin, to shame the Deuil,
By telling truth. *Tell truth, and shame the Deuill.*
If thou haue power to rayse him, bring him hither,
And Ile be sworne, I haue power to shame him hence.
Oh, while you liue, tell truth, and shame the Deuill.

Mort. Come, come, no more of this vnprofitable Chat.

Glend. Three times hath *Henry Bullingbrooke* made head
Against my Power: thrice from the Banks of Wye,
And sandy-bottom'd Seuerne, haue I hent him
Bootlesse home, and Weather-beaten backe.

Hotsp. Home without Bootes,
And in foule Weather too,
How scapes he Agues in the Deuils name?

Glend. Come, heere's the Mappe:
Shall wee diuide our Right,
According to our three-fold order ta'ne?

Mort. The Arch-Deacon hath diuided it
Into three Limits, very equally:
England, from Trent, and Seuerne, bitherto,
By South and East, is to my part assign'd:
All Westward, Wales, beyond the Seuerne shore,
And all the fertile Land within that bound,
To *Owen Glendower*: And deare Couze, to you
The remnant Northward, lying off from Trent.
And our Indentures Tripartite are drawne:
Which being sealed enterchangeably,
(A Businesse that this Night may execute)
To morrow, Cousin *Percy*, you and I,
And my good Lord of Worcester, will set forth,
To meete your Father, and the Scottish Power,
As is appointed vs at Shrewsbury.
My Father *Glendower* is not readie yet,
Nor shall wee neede his helpe these foureteene dayes:
Within that space, you may haue drawne together
Your Tenants, Friends, and neighbouring Gentlemen.

Glend. A shorter time shall send me to you, Lords:
And in my Conduct shall your Ladies come,
From whom you now must steale, and take no leaue,
For there will be a World of Water shed,

Vpon

Vpon the parting of your Wiues and you.

Hotsp. Me thinks my Moity, North from Burton here,
In quantitie equals not one of yours:
See, how this Riuer comes me cranking in,
And cuts me from the best of all my Land,
A huge halfe Moone, a monstrous Cantle out.
Ile haue the Currant in this place damn'd vp,
And here the smug and Siluer Trent shall runne,
In a new Channell, faire and euenly:
It shall not winde with such a deepe indent,
To rob me of so rich a Bottome here.

Glend. Not winde? it shall, it must, you see it doth.

Mort. Yea, but marke how he beares his course,
And runnes me vp, with like aduantage on the other side,
Gelding the opposed Continent as much,
As on the other side it takes from you.

Worc. Yea, but a little Charge will trench him here,
And on this North side winne this Cape of Land,
And then he runnes straight and euen.

Hotsp. Ile haue it so, a little Charge will doe it.

Glend. Ile not haue it alter'd.

Hotsp. Will not you?

Glend. No, nor you shall not.

Hotsp. Who shall say me nay?

Glend. Why, that will I.

Hotsp. Let me not vnderstand you then, speake it in Welsh.

Glend. I can speake English, Lord, as well as you:
For I was trayn'd vp in the English Court;
Where, being but young, I framed to the Harpe
Many an English Dittie, louely well,
And gaue the Tongue a helpefull Ornament;
A Vertue that was neuer seene in you.

Hotsp. Marry, and I am glad of it with all my heart,
I had rather be a Kitten, and cry mew,
Then one of these same Meeter Ballad-mongers:
I had rather heare a Brazen Candlestick turn'd,
Or a dry Wheele grate on the Axle-tree,
And that would set my teeth nothing an edge,
Nothing so much, as mincing Poetrie;
Tis like the forc't gate of a shuffling Nagge.

Glend. Come, you shall haue Trent turn'd.

Hotsp. I doe not care: Ile giue thrice so much Land
To any well-deseruing friend;
But in the way of Bargaine, marke ye me,
Ile cauill on the ninth part of a hayre.
Are the Indentures drawne? shall we be gone?

Glend. The Moone shines faire,
You may away by Night:
Ile haste the Writer; and withall,
Breake with your Wiues, of your departure hence:
I am afraid my Daughter will runne madde,
So much she doteth on her *Mortimer*. *Exit.*

Mort. Fie, Cousin *Percy*, how you crosse my Father.

Hotsp. I cannot chuse: sometime he angers me,
With telling me of the Moldwarpe and the Ant,
Of the Dreamer *Merlin*, and his Prophecies;
And of a Dragon, and a finne-lesse Fish,
A clip-wing'd Griffin, and a moulten Rauen,
A couching Lyon, and a ramping Cat,
And such a deale of skimble-skamble Stuffe,
As puts me from my Faith. I tell you what,
He held me last Night, at least, nine howres,
In reckning vp the seuerall Deuils Names,
That were his Lacqueyes:
I cry'd hum, and well, goe too,
But mark'd him not a word. O, he is as tedious
As a tyred Horse, a rayling Wife,
Worse then a smoakie House. I had rather liue
With Cheese and Garlick in a Windmill farre,
Then feede on Cates, and haue him talke to me,
In any Summer-House in Christendome.

Mort. In faith he was a worthy Gentleman,
Exceeding well read, and profited,
In strange Concealements:
Valiant as a Lyon, and wondrous affable,
And as bountifull, as Mynes of India.
Shall I tell you, Cousin,
He holds your temper in a high respect,
And curbes himselfe, euen of his naturall scope,
When you doe crosse his humor: faith he does.
I warrant you, that man is not aliue,
Might so haue tempted him, as you haue done,
Without the taste of danger, and reproofe:
But doe not vse it oft, let me entreat you.

Worc. In faith, my Lord, you are too wilfull blame,
And since your comming hither, haue done enough,
To put him quite besides his patience.
You must needes learne, Lord, to amend this fault:
Though sometimes it shew Greatnesse, Courage, Blood,
And that's the dearest grace it renders you;
Yet oftentimes it doth present harsh Rage,
Defect of Manners, want of Gouernment,
Pride, Haughtinesse, Opinion, and Disdaine:
The least of which, haunting a Nobleman,
Loseth mens hearts, and leaues behinde a stayne
Vpon the beautie of all parts besides,
Beguiling them of commendation.

Hotsp. Well, I am school'd:
Good-manners be your speede;
Heere come your Wiues, and let vs take our leaues

Enter Glendower, with the Ladies.

Mort. This is the deadly spight, that angers me,
My Wife can speake no English, I no Welsh.

Glend. My Daughter weepes, shee'le not part with you,
Shee'le be a Souldier too, shee'le to the Warres.

Mort. Good Father tell her, that she and my Aunt *Percy*
Shall follow in your Conduct speedily.

Glendower speakes to her in Welsh, and she answeres him in the same.

Glend. Shee is desperate heere:
A peeuish selfe-will'd Harlotry,
One that no perswasion can doe good vpon.

The Lady speakes in Welsh.

Mort. I vnderstand thy Lookes: that pretty Welsh
Which thou powr'st down from these swelling Heauens,
I am too perfect in: and but for shame,
In such a parley should I answere thee.

The Lady againe in Welsh.

Mort. I vnderstand thy Kisses, and thou mine,
And that's a feeling disputation:
But I will neuer be a Truant, Loue,
Till I haue learn'd thy Language: for thy tongue

Makes

Makes Welsh as sweet as Ditties highly penn'd,
Sung by a faire Queene in a Summers Bowre,
With rauishing Diuision to her Lute.

  Glend. Nay, if thou melt, then will she runne madde.

The Lady speakes againe in Welsh.

  Mort. O, I am Ignorance it selfe in this.
  Glend. She bids you,
On the wanton Rushes lay you downe,
And rest your gentle Head vpon her Lappe,
And she will sing the Song that pleaseth you,
And on your Eye-lids Crowne the God of Sleepe,
Charming your blood with pleasing heauinesse;
Making such difference betwixt Wake and Sleepe,
As is the difference betwixt Day and Night,
The houre before the Heauenly Harneis'd Teeme
Begins his Golden Progresse in the East.

  Mort. With all my heart Ile sit, and heare her sing:
By that time will our Booke, I thinke, be drawne.

  Glend. Doe so:
And those Musitians that shall play to you,
Hang in the Ayre a thousand Leagues from thence;
And straight they shall be here: sit, and attend.

  Hotsp. Come *Kate*, thou art perfect in lying downe:
Come, quicke, quicke, that I may lay my Head in thy
Lappe.

  Lady. Goe, ye giddy-Goose.

The Musicke playes.

  Hotsp. Now I perceiue the Deuill vnderstands Welsh,
And 'tis no maruell he is so humorous:
Byrlady hee's a good Musitian.

  Lady. Then would you be nothing but Musicall,
For you are altogether gouerned by humors:
Lye still ye Theefe, and heare the Lady sing in Welsh.

  Hotsp. I had rather heare (Lady) my Brach howle in
Irish.

  Lady. Would'st haue thy Head broken?
  Hotsp. No.
  Lady. Then be still.
  Hotsp. Neyther 'tis a Womans fault.
  Lady. Now God helpe thee.
  Hotsp. To the Welsh Ladies Bed.
  Lady. What's that?
  Hotsp. Peace, shee sings.

Heere the Lady sings a Welsh Song.

  Hotsp. Come, Ile haue your Song too.
  Lady. Not mine, in good sooth.
  Hotsp. Not yours, in good sooth?
You sweare like a Comfit-makers Wife:
Not you, in good sooth; and, as true as I liue;
And, as God shall mend me; and, as sure as day:
And giuest such Sarcenet suretie for thy Oathes,
As if thou neuer walk'st further then Finsbury.
Sweare me, *Kate*, like a Lady, as thou art,
A good mouth-filling Oath: and leaue in sooth,
And such protest of Pepper Ginger-bread,
To Veluet-Guards, and Sunday-Citizens.
Come, sing.

  Lady. I will not sing.
  Hotsp. 'Tis the next way to turne Taylor, or be Red-brest teacher: and the Indentures be drawne, Ile away within these two howres: and so come in, when yee will.   *Exit.*

  Glend. Come, come, Lord *Mortimer*, you are as slow,
As hot Lord *Percy* is on fire to goe.
By this our Booke is drawne: wee'le but seale,
And then to Horse immediately.

  Mort. With all my heart.   *Exeunt.*

Scæna Secunda.

Enter the King, Prince of Wales, and others.

  King. Lords, giue vs leaue:
The Prince of Wales, and I,
Must haue some priuate conference:
But be neere at hand,
For wee shall presently haue neede of you.

  Exeunt Lords.

I know not whether Heauen will haue it so,
For some displeasing seruice I haue done;
That in his secret Doome, out of my Blood,
Hee'le breede Reuengement, and a Scourge for me:
But thou do'st in thy passages of Life,
Make me beleeue, that thou art onely mark'd
For the hot vengeance, and the Rod of heauen
To punish my Mistreadings. Tell me else,
Could such inordinate and low desires,
Such poore, such bare, such lewd, such meane attempts,
Such barren pleasures, rude societie,
As thou art matcht withall, and grafted too,
Accompanie the greatnesse of thy blood,
And hold their leuell with thy Princely heart?

  Prince. So please your Maiesty, I would I could
Quit all offences with as cleare excuse,
As well as I am doubtlesse I can purge
My selfe of many I am charg'd withall:
Yet such extenuation let me begge,
As in reproofe of many Tales deuis'd,
Which oft the Eare of Greatnesse needes must heare,
By smiling Pick-thankes, and base Newes-mongers;
I may for some things true, wherein my youth
Hath faultie wandred, and irregular,
Finde pardon on my true submission.

  King. Heauen pardon thee:
Yet let me wonder, *Harry*,
At thy affections, which doe hold a Wing
Quite from the flight of all thy ancestors.
Thy place in Councell thou hast rudely lost,
Which by thy younger Brother is supply'de;
And art almost an alien to the hearts
Of all the Court and Princes of my blood.
The hope and expectation of thy time
Is ruin'd, and the Soule of euery man
Prophetically doe fore-thinke thy fall.
Had I so lauish of my presence beene,
So common hackney'd in the eyes of men,
So stale and cheape to vulgar Company;
Opinion, that did helpe me to the Crowne,
Had still kept loyall to possession,
And left me in reputelesse banishment,
A fellow of no marke, nor likelyhood.
By being seldome seene, I could not stirre,
But like a Comet, I was wondred at,

That men would tell their Children, This is hee:
Others would say; Where, Which is *Bullingbrooke*.
And then I stole all Courtesie from Heauen,
And drest my selfe in such Humilitie,
That I did plucke Allegeance from mens hearts,
Lowd Showts and Salutations from their mouthes,
Euen in the presence of the Crowned King.
Thus I did keepe my Person fresh and new,
My Presence like a Robe Pontificall,
Ne're seene, but wondred at: and so my State,
Seldome but sumptuous, shewed like a Feast,
And wonne by rarenesse such Solemnitie.
The skipping King hee ambled vp and downe,
With shallow Iesters, and rash Bauin Wits,
Soone kindled, and soone burnt, carded his State,
Mingled his Royaltie with Carping Fooles,
Had his great Name prophaned with their Scornes,
And gaue his Countenance, against his Name,
To laugh at gybing Boyes, and stand the push
Of euery Beardlesse vaine Comparatiue;
Grew a Companion to the common Streetes,
Enfeoff'd himselfe to Popularitie:
That being dayly swallowed by mens Eyes,
They surfeted with Honey, and began to loathe
The taste of Sweetnesse, whereof a little
More then a little, is by much too much.
So when he had occasion to be seene,
He was but as the Cuckow is in Iune,
Heard, not regarded: seene but with such Eyes,
As sicke and blunted with Communitie,
Affoord no extraordinarie Gaze,
Such as is bent on Sunne-like Maiestie,
When it shines seldome in admiring Eyes:
But rather drowz'd, and hung their eye-lids downe,
Slept in his Face, and rendred such aspect
As Cloudie men vse to doe to their aduersaries,
Being with his presence glutted, gorg'd, and full.
And in that very Line, *Harry*, standest thou:
For thou hast lost thy Princely Priuiledge,
With vile participation. Not an Eye
But is awearie of thy common sight,
Saue mine, which hath desir'd to see thee more:
Which now doth that I would not haue it doe,
Make blinde it selfe with foolish tendernesse.

 Prince. I shall hereafter, my thrice gracious Lord,
Be more my selfe.

 King. For all the World,
As thou art to this houre, was *Richard* then,
When I from France set foot at Rauenspurgh;
And euen as I was then, is *Percy* now:
Now by my Scepter, and my Soule to boot,
He hath more worthy interest to the State
Then thou, the shadow of Succession;
For of no Right, nor colour like to Right.
He doth fill fields with Harneis in the Realme,
Turnes head against the Lyons armed Iawes;
And being no more in debt to yeeres, then thou,
Leades ancient Lords, and reuerent Bishops on
To bloody Battailes, and to brusing Armes.
What neuer-dying Honor hath he got,
Against renowned *Dowglas*? whose high Deedes,
Whose hot Incursions, and great Name in Armes,
Holds from all Souldiers chiefe Maioritie,
And Militarie Title Capitall.
Through all the Kingdomes that acknowledge Christ,
Thrice hath the Hotspur *Mars*, in swathing Clothes,
This Infant Warrior, in his Enterprises,
Discomfited great *Dowglas*, ta'ne him once,
Enlarged him, and made a friend of him,
To fill the mouth of deepe Defiance vp,
And shake the peace and safetie of our Throne.
And what say you to this? *Percy*, *Northumberland*,
The Arch-bishops Grace of *Yorke*, *Dowglas*, *Mortimer*,
Capitulate against vs, and are vp.
But wherefore doe I tell these Newes to thee?
Why, *Harry*, doe I tell thee of my Foes,
Which art my neer'st and dearest Enemie?
Thou, that art like enough, through vassall Feare,
Base Inclination, and the start of Spleene,
To fight against me vnder *Percies* pay,
To dogge his heeles, and curtsie at his frownes,
To shew how much thou art degenerate.

 Prince. Doe not thinke so, you shall not finde it so:
And Heauen forgiue them, that so much haue sway'd
Your Maiesties good thoughts away from me:
I will redeeme all this on *Percies* head,
And in the closing of some glorious day,
Be bold to tell you, that I am your Sonne,
When I will weare a Garment all of Blood,
And staine my fauours in a bloody Maske:
Which washt away, shall scowre my shame with it.
And that shall be the day, when ere it lights,
That this same Child of Honor and Renowne,
This gallant *Hotspur*, this all-praysed Knight,
And your vnthought-of *Harry* chance to meet:
For euery Honor sitting on his Helme,
Would they were multitudes, and on my head
My shames redoubled. For the time will come,
That I shall make this Northerne Youth exchange
His glorious Deedes for my Indignities:
Percy is but my Factor, good my Lord,
To engrosse vp glorious Deedes on my behalfe:
And I will call him to so strict account,
That he shall render euery Glory vp,
Yea, euen the sleightest worship of his time,
Or I will teare the Reckoning from his Heart.
This, in the Name of Heauen, I promise here:
The which, if I performe, and doe suruiue,
I doe beseech your Maiestie, may salue
The long-growne Wounds of my intemperature:
If not, the end of Life cancells all Bands,
And I will dye a hundred thousand Deaths,
Ere breake the smallest parcell of this Vow.

 King. A hundred thousand Rebels dye in this:
Thou shalt haue Charge, and soueraigne trust herein.

Enter Blunt.

How now good *Blunt*? thy Lookes are full of speed.

 Blunt. So hath the Businesse that I come to speake of.
Lord *Mortimer* of Scotland hath sent word,
That *Dowglas* and the English Rebels met
The eleuenth of this moneth, at Shrewsbury:
A mightie and a fearefull Head they are,
(If Promises be kept on euery hand)
As euer offered foule play in a State.

 King. The Earle of Westmerland set forth to day:
With him my sonne, Lord *Iohn* of Lancaster,
For this aduertisement is fiue dayes old.
On Wednesday next, *Harry* thou shalt set forward:
On Thursday, wee our selues will march.
Our meeting is Bridgenorth: and *Harry*, you shall march

Through

Through Glocestershire: by which account,
Our Businesse valued some twelue dayes hence,
Our generall Forces at Bridgenorth shall meete.
Our Hands are full of Businesse: let's away,
Aduantage feedes him fat, while men delay. *Exeunt.*

Scena Tertia.

Enter Falstaffe and Bardolph.

Falst. Bardolph, am I not falne away vilely, since this last action? doe I not bate? doe I not dwindle? Why my skinne hangs about me like an olde Ladies loose Gowne: I am withered like an olde Apple *Iohn*. Well, Ile repent, and that suddenly, while I am in some liking: I shall be out of heart shortly, and then I shall haue no strength to repent. And I haue not forgotten what the in-side of a Church is made of, I am a Pepper-Corne, a Brewers Horse, the in-side of a Church. Company, villanous Company hath beene the spoyle of me.

Bard. Sir *Iohn*, you are so fretfull, you cannot liue long.

Falst. Why there is it: Come, sing me a bawdy Song, make me merry: I was as vertuously giuen, as a Gentleman need to be; vertuous enough, swore little, dic'd not aboue seuen times a weeke, went to a Bawdy-house not aboue once in a quarter of an houre, payd Money that I borrowed, three or foure times; liued well, and in good compasse: and now I liue out of all order, out of compasse.

Bard. Why, you are so far, Sir *Iohn*, that you must needes bee out of all compasse; out of all reasonable compasse, Sir *Iohn*.

Falst. Doe thou amend thy Face, and Ile amend thy Life: Thou art our Admirall, thou bearest the Lanterne in the Poope, but 'tis in the Nose of thee; thou art the Knight of the burning Lampe.

Bard. Why, Sir *Iohn*, my Face does you no harme.

Falst. No, Ile be sworne: I make as good vse of it, as many a man doth of a Deaths-Head, or a *Memento Mori*. I neuer see thy Face, but I thinke vpon Hell fire, and *Diues* that liued in Purple; for there he is in his Robes burning, burning. If thou wert any way giuen to vertue, I would sweare by thy Face; my Oath should bee, *By this Fire*: But thou art altogether giuen ouer; and wert indeede, but for the Light in thy Face, the Sunne of vtter Darkenesse. When thou ran'st vp Gads-Hill in the Night, to catch my Horse, if I did not thinke that thou hadst beene an *Ignis fatuus*, or a Ball of Wild-fire, there's no Purchase in Money. O thou art a perpetuall Triumph, an euerlasting Bone-fire-Light: thou hast saued me a thousand Markes in Linkes and Torches, walking with thee in the Night betwixt Tauerne and Tauerne: But the Sack that thou hast drunke me, would haue bought me Lights as good cheape, as the dearest Chandlers in Europe. I haue maintain'd that Salamander of yours with fire, any time this two and thirtie yeeres, Heauen reward me for it.

Bard. I would my Face were in your Belly.

Falst. So should I be sure to be heart-burn'd.

Enter Hostesse.

How now, Dame *Partlet* the Hen, haue you enquir'd yet who pick'd my Pocket?

Hostesse. Why Sir *Iohn*, what doe you thinke, Sir *Iohn*? doe you thinke I keepe Theeues in my House? I haue search'd, I haue enquired, so haz my Husband, Man by Man, Boy by Boy, Seruant by Seruant: the tight of a hayre was neuer lost in my house before.

Falst. Ye lye Hostesse: *Bardolph* was shau'd, and lost many a hayre; and Ile be sworne my Pocket was pick'd: goe to, you are a Woman, goe.

Hostesse. Who I? I defie thee: I was neuer call'd so in mine owne house before.

Falst. Goe to, I know you well enough.

Hostesse. No, Sir *Iohn*, you doe not know me, Sir *Iohn*: I know you, Sir *Iohn*: you owe me Money, Sir *Iohn*, and now you picke a quarrell, to beguile me of it: I bought you a dozen of Shirts to your Backe.

Falst. Doulas, filthy Doulas: I haue giuen them away to Bakers Wiues, and they haue made Boulters of them.

Hostesse. Now as I am a true Woman, Holland of eight shillings an Ell: You owe Money here besides, Sir *Iohn*, for your Dyet, and by-Drinkings, and Money lent you, foure and twentie pounds.

Falst. Hee had his part of it, let him pay.

Hostesse. Hee? alas hee is poore, hee hath nothing.

Falst. How? Poore? Looke vpon his Face: What call you Rich? Let them coyne his Nose, let them coyne his Cheekes, Ile not pay a Denier. What, will you make a Younker of me? Shall I not take mine ease in mine Inne, but I shall haue my Pocket pick'd? I haue lost a Seale-Ring of my Grand-fathers, worth fortie Marke.

Hostesse. I haue heard the Prince tell him, I know not how oft, that that Ring was Copper.

Falst. How? the Prince is a Iacke, a Sneake-Cuppe: and if hee were heere, I would cudgell him like a Dogge, if hee would say so.

Enter the Prince marching, and Falstaffe meets him, playing on his Trunchion like a Fife.

Falst. How now Lad? is the Winde in that Doore? Must we all march?

Bard. Yea, two and two, Newgate fashion.

Hostesse. My Lord, I pray you heare me.

Prince. What say'st thou, Mistresse *Quickly*? How does thy Husband? I loue him well, hee is an honest man.

Hostesse. Good, my Lord, heare mee.

Falst. Prethee let her alone, and list to mee.

Prince. What say'st thou, *Iacke*?

Falst. The other Night I fell asleepe heere behind the Arras, and had my Pocket pickt: this House is turn'd Bawdy-house, they picke Pockets.

Prince. What didst thou lose, *Iacke*?

Falst. Wilt thou beleeue me, *Hal*? Three or foure Bonds of fortie pound apeece, and a Seale-Ring of my Grand-fathers.

Prince. A Trifle, some eight-penny matter.

Host. So I told him, my Lord; and I said, I heard your Grace say so: and (my Lord) hee speakes most vilely of you, like a foule-mouth'd man as hee is, and said, hee would cudgell you.

Prince. What hee did not?

Host. There's neyther Faith, Truth, nor Woman-hood in me else.

Falst. There's

The First Part of King Henry the Fourth.

Falſt. There's no more faith in thee then a ſtu'de Prune, nor no more truth in thee, then in a drawne Fox: and for Wooman-hood, Maid-marian may be the Deputies wife of the Ward to thee. Go you nothing: go.

Hoſt. Say, what thing? what thing?

Falſt. What thing? why a thing to thanke heauen on.

Hoſt. I am no thing to thanke heauen on, I wold thou ſhouldſt know it: I am an honeſt mans wife: and ſetting thy Knighthood aſide, thou art a knaue to call me ſo.

Falſt. Setting thy woman-hood aſide, thou art a beaſt to ſay otherwiſe.

Hoſt. Say, what beaſt, thou knaue thou?

Fal. What beaſt? Why an Otter.

Prin. An Otter, ſir *Iohn*? Why an Otter?

Fal. Why? She's neither fiſh nor fleſh; a man knowes not where to haue her.

Hoſt. Thou art vniuſt man in ſaying ſo; thou, or anie man knowes where to haue me, thou knaue thou.

Prince. Thou ſay'ſt true Hoſteſſe, and he ſlanders thee moſt groſſely.

Hoſt. So he doth you, my Lord, and ſayde this other day, You ought him a thouſand pound.

Prince. Sirrah, do I owe you a thouſand pound?

Falſt. A thouſand pound *Hal*? A Million. Thy loue is worth a Million: thou ow'ſt me thy loue.

Hoſt. Nay my Lord, he call'd you Iacke, and ſaid hee would cudgell you.

Fal. Did I, *Bardolph*?

Bar. Indeed Sir *Iohn*, you ſaid ſo.

Fal. Yea, if he ſaid my Ring was Copper.

Prince. I ſay 'tis Copper. Dar'ſt thou bee as good as thy word now?

Fal. Why *Hal*? thou know'ſt, as thou art but a man, I dare: but, as thou art a Prince, I feare thee, as I feare the roaring of the Lyons Whelpe.

Prince. And why not as the Lyon?

Fal. The King himſelfe is to bee feared as the Lyon: Do'ſt thou thinke Ile feare thee, as I feare thy Father? nay if I do, let my Girdle breake.

Prin. O, if it ſhould, how would thy guttes fall about thy knees. But ſirra: There's no roome for Faith, Truth, nor Honeſty, in this boſome of thine: it is all fill'd vppe with Guttes and Midriffe. Charge an honeſt Woman with picking thy pocket? Why thou horſon impudent imboſt Raſcall, if there were any thing in thy Pocket but Tauerne Recknings, *Memorandums* of Bawdie-houſes, and one poore peny-worth of Sugar-candie to make thee long-winded: if thy pocket were enrich'd with anie other iniuries but theſe, I am a Villaine: And yet you will ſtand to it, you will not Pocket vp wrong. Art thou not aſham'd?

Fal. Do'ſt thou heare *Hal*? Thou know'ſt in the ſtate of Innocency, *Adam* fell: and what ſhould poore *Iacke Falſtaffe* do, in the dayes of Villany? Thou ſeeſt, I haue more fleſh then another man, and therefore more frailty. You confeſſe then you pickt my Pocket?

Prin. It appeares ſo by the Story.

Fal. Hoſteſſe, I forgiue thee:
Go make ready Breakfaſt, loue thy Husband,
Looke to thy Seruants, and cheriſh thy Gueſts:
Thou ſhalt find me tractable to any honeſt reaſon:
Thou ſeeſt, I am pacified ſtill.
Nay, I prethee be gone.
Exit Hoſteſſe.

Now *Hal*, to the newes at Court for the Robbery, Lad? How is that anſwered?

Prin. O my ſweet Beefe:
I muſt ſtill be good Angell to thee.
The Monie is paid backe againe.

Fal. O, I do not like that paying backe, 'tis a double Labour.

Prin. I am good Friends with my Father, and may do any thing.

Fal. Rob me the Exchequer the firſt thing thou do'ſt, and do it with vnwaſh'd hands too.

Bard. Do my Lord.

Prin. I haue procured thee *Iacke*, a Charge of Foot.

Fal. I would it had beene of Horſe. Where ſhal I finde one that can ſteale well? O, for a fine theefe, of two and twentie, or thereabout: I am heynouſly vnprouided. Wel God be thanked for theſe Rebels, they offend none but the Vertuous. I laud them, I praiſe them.

Prin. Bardolph.

Bar. My Lord.

Prin. Go beare this Letter to Lord *Iohn* of Lancaſter
To my Brother *Iohn*. This to my Lord of Weſtmerland,
Go *Peto*, to horſe: for thou, and I,
Haue thirtie miles to ride yet ere dinner time.
Iacke, meet me to morrow in the Temple Hall
At two a clocke in the afternoone,
There ſhalt thou know thy Charge, and there receiue
Money and Order for their Furniture.
The Land is burning, *Percie* ſtands on hye,
And either they, or we muſt lower lye.

Fal. Rare words! braue world.
Hoſteſſe, my breakfaſt, come:
Oh, I could wiſh this Tauerne were my drumme.
Exeunt omnes.

Actus Quartus. Scœna Prima.

Enter Harrie Hotſpurre, Worceſter, and Dowglas.

Hot. Well ſaid, my Noble Scot, if ſpeaking truth
In this fine Age, were not thought flatterie,
Such attribution ſhould the *Dowglas* haue,
As not a Souldiour of this ſeaſons ſtampe,
Should go ſo generall currant through the world.
By heauen I cannot flatter: I defie
The Tongues of Soothers. But a Brauer place
In my hearts loue, hath no man then your Selfe.
Nay, taske me to my word: approue me Lord.

Dow. Thou art the King of Honor:
No man ſo potent breathes vpon the ground,
But I will Beard him.

Enter a Meſſenger.

Hot. Do ſo, and 'tis well. What Letters haſt there?
I can but thanke you.

Meſſ. Theſe Letters come from your Father.

Hot. Letters from him?
Why comes he not himſelfe?

Meſ. He cannot come, my Lord,
He is greeuous ſicke.

Hot. How? haz he the leyſure to be ſicke now,
In ſuch a iuſtling time? Who leades his power?
Vnder whoſe Gouernment come they along?

Mess. His Letters beares his minde, not I his minde.
Wor. I prethee tell me, doth he keepe his Bed?
Mess. He did, my Lord, foure dayes ere I set forth:
And at the time of my departure thence,
He was much fear'd by his Physician.
Wor. I would the state of time had first beene whole,
Ere he by sicknesse had beene visited:
His health was neuer better worth then now.
Hotsp. Sicke now? droope now? this sicknes doth infect
The very Life-blood of our Enterprise,
'Tis catching hither, euen to our Campe.
He writes me here, that inward sicknesse,
And that his friends by deputation
Could not so soone be drawne: nor did he thinke it meet,
To lay so dangerous and deare a trust
On any Soule remou'd, but on his owne.
Yet doth he giue vs bold aduertisement,
That with our small coniunction we should on,
To see how Fortune is dispos'd to vs:
For, as he writes, there is no quailing now,
Because the King is certainely possest
Of all our purposes. What say you to it?
Wor. Your Fathers sicknesse is a mayme to vs.
Hotsp. A perillous Gash, a very Limme lopt off:
And yet, in faith, it is not his present want
Seemes more then we shall finde it.
Were it good, to set the exact wealth of all our states
All at one Cast? To set so rich a mayne
On the nice hazard of one doubtfull houre,
It were not good: for therein should we reade
The very Bottome, and the Soule of Hope,
The very List, the very vtmost Bound
Of all our fortunes.
Dowg. Faith, and so wee should,
Where now remaines a sweet reuersion.
We may boldly spend, vpon the hope
Of what is to come in:
A comfort of retyrement liues in this.
Hotsp. A Randeuous, a Home to flye vnto,
If that the Deuill and Mischance looke bigge
Vpon the Maydenhead of our Affaires.
Wor. But yet I would your Father had beene here:
The Qualitie and Heire of our Attempt
Brookes no diuision: It will be thought
By some, that know not why he is away,
That wisedome, loyaltie, and meere dislike
Of our proceedings, kept the Earle from hence.
And thinke, how such an apprehension
May turne the tyde of fearefull Faction,
And breede a kinde of question in our cause:
For well you know, wee of the offring side,
Must keepe aloofe from strict arbitrement,
And stop all sight-holes, euery loope, from whence
The eye of reason may prie in vpon vs:
This absence of your Father drawes a Curtaine,
That shewes the ignorant a kinde of feare,
Before not dreamt of.
Hotsp. You strayne too farre.
I rather of his absence make this vse:
It lends a Lustre, and more great Opinion,
A larger Dare to your great Enterprize,
Then if the Earle were here: for men must thinke,
If we without his helpe, can make a Head
To push against the Kingdome; with his helpe,
We shall o're-turne it topsie-turuy downe:
Yet all goes well, yet all our ioynts are whole.

Dowg. As heart can thinke:
There is not such a word spoke of in Scotland,
At this Dreame of Feare.

Enter Sir Richard Vernon.

Hotsp. My Cousin *Vernon*, welcome by my Soule.
Vern. Pray God my newes be worth a welcome, Lord,
The Earle of Westmerland, seuen thousand strong,
Is marching hither-wards, with Prince *Iohn*.
Hotsp. No harme: what more?
Vern. And further, I haue learn'd,
The King himselfe in person hath set forth,
Or hither-wards intended speedily,
With strong and mightie preparation.
Hotsp. He shall be welcome too.
Where is his Sonne,
The nimble-footed Mad-Cap, Prince of Wales,
And his Cumrades, that daft the World aside,
And bid it passe?
Vern. All furnisht, all in Armes,
All plum'd like Estridges, that with the Winde
Bayted like Eagles, hauing lately bath'd,
Glittering in Golden Coates, like Images,
As full of spirit as the Moneth of May,
And gorgeous as the Sunne at Mid-summer,
Wanton as youthfull Goates, wilde as young Bulls.
I saw young *Harry* with his Beuer on,
His Cushes on his thighes, gallantly arm'd,
Rise from the ground like feathered *Mercury*,
And vaulted with such ease into his Seat,
As if an Angell dropt downe from the Clouds,
To turne and winde a fierie *Pegasus*,
And witch the World with Noble Horsemanship.
Hotsp. No more, no more,
Worse then the Sunne in March:
This prayse doth nourish Agues: let them come,
They come like Sacrifices in their trimme,
And to the fire-ey'd Maid of smoakie Warre,
All hot, and bleeding, will wee offer them:
The mayled *Mars* shall on his Altar sit
Vp to the eares in blood. I am on fire,
To heare this rich reprizall is so nigh,
And yet not ours. Come, let me take my Horse,
Who is to beare me like a Thunder-bolt,
Against the bosome of the Prince of Wales.
Harry to *Harry*, shall not Horse to Horse
Meete, and ne're part, till one drop downe a Coarse?
Oh, that *Glendower* were come.
Ver. There is more newes:
I learned in Worcester, as I rode along,
He cannot draw his Power this foureteene dayes.
Dowg. That's the worst Tidings that I heare of yet.
Wor. I by my faith, that beares a frosty sound.
Hotsp. What may the Kings whole Battaile reach vnto?
Ver. To thirty thousand.
Hot. Forty let it be,
My Father and *Glendower* being both away,
The powres of vs, may serue so great a day.
Come, let vs take a muster speedily:
Doomesday is neere; dye all, dye merrily.
Dow. Talke not of dying, I am out of feare
Of death, or deaths hand, for this one halfe yeare.

Exeunt Omnes.
Scena

Scæna Secunda.

Enter Falstaffe and Bardolph.

Falst. Bardolph, get thee before to Couentry, fill me a Bottle of Sack, our Souldiers shall march through: wee'le to Sutton-cop-hill to Night.

Bard. Will you giue me Money, Captaine?

Falst. Lay out, lay out.

Bard. This Bottle makes an Angell.

Falst. And if it doe, take it for thy labour: and if it make twentie, take them all, Ile answere the Coynage. Bid my Lieutenant *Peto* meete me at the Townes end.

Bard. I will Captaine: farewell.   *Exit.*

Falst. If I be not asham'd of my Souldiers, I am a sowc't-Gurnet: I haue mis-vs'd the Kings Presse damnably. I haue got, in exchange of a hundred and fiftie Souldiers, three hundred and odde Pounds. I presse me none but good House-holders, Yeomens Sonnes: enquire me out contracted Batchelers, such as had beene ask'd twice on the Banes: such a Commoditie of warme slaues, as had as lieue heare the Deuill, as a Drumme; such as feare the report of a Caliuer, worse then a struck-Foole, or a hurt wilde-Ducke. I prest me none but such Tostes and Butter, with Hearts in their Bellyes no bigger then Pinnes heads, and they haue bought out their seruices: And now, my whole Charge consists of Ancients, Corporals, Lieutenants, Gentlemen of Companies, Slaues as ragged as *Lazarus* in the painted Cloth, where the Gluttons Dogges licked his Sores; and such, as indeed were neuer Souldiers, but dis-carded vniust Seruingmen, younger Sonnes to younger Brothers, reuolted Tapsters and Ostlers, Trade-falne, the Cankers of a calme World, and long Peace, tenne times more dis-honorable ragged, then an old-fac'd Ancient; and such haue I to fill vp the roomes of them that haue bought out their seruices: that you would thinke, that I had a hundred and fiftie totter'd Prodigalls, lately come from Swine-keeping, from eating Draffe and Huskes. A mad fellow met me on the way, and told me, I had vnloaded all the Gibbets, and prest the dead bodyes. No eye hath seene such skar-Crowes: Ile not march through Couentry with them, that's flat. Nay, and the Villaines march wide betwixt the Legges, as if they had Gyues on; for indeede, I had the most of them out of Prison. There's not a Shirt and a halfe in all my Company: and the halfe Shirt is two Napkins tackt together, and throwne ouer the shoulders like a Heralds Coat, without sleeues: and the Shirt, to say the truth, stolne from my Host of S. Albones, or the Red-Nose Inne-keeper of Dauintry. But that's all one, they'le finde Linnen enough on euery Hedge.

Enter the Prince, and the Lord of Westmerland.

Prince. How now blowne *Iack*? how now Quilt?

Falst. What *Hal*? How now mad Wag, what a Deuill do'st thou in Warwickshire? My good Lord of Westmerland, I cry you mercy, I thought your Honour had already beene at Shrewsbury.

West. 'Faith, Sir *Iohn*, 'tis more then time that I were there, and you too: but my Powers are there alreadie. The King, I can tell you, lookes for vs all: we must away all to Night.

Falst. Tut, neuer feare me, I am as vigilant as a Cat, to steale Creame.

Prince. I thinke to steale Creame indeed, for thy theft hath alreadie made thee Butter: but tell me, *Iack*, whose fellowes are these that come after?

Falst. Mine, *Hal*, mine.

Prince. I did neuer see such pittifull Rascals.

Falst. Tut, tut, good enough to tosse: foode for Powder, foode for Powder: they'le fill a Pit, as well as better: tush man, mortall men, mortall men.

Westm. I, but Sir *Iohn*, me thinkes they are exceeding poore and bare, too beggarly.

Falst. Faith, for their pouertie, I know not where they had that; and for their barenesse, I am sure they neuer learn'd that of me.

Prince. No, Ile be sworne, vnlesse you call three fingers on the Ribbes bare. But sirra, make haste, *Percy* is already in the field.

Falst. What, is the King encamp'd?

Westm. Hee is, Sir *Iohn*, I feare wee shall stay too long.

Falst. Well, to the latter end of a Fray, and the beginning of a Feast, fits a dull fighter, and a keene Guest.

Exeunt.

Scæna Tertia.

Enter Hotspur, Worcester, Dowglas, and Vernon.

Hotsp. Wee'le fight with him to Night.

Worc. It may not be.

Dowg. You giue him then aduantage.

Vern. Not a whit.

Hotsp. Why say you so? lookes he not for supply?

Vern. So doe wee.

Hotsp. His is certaine, ours is doubtfull.

Worc. Good Cousin be aduis'd, stirre not to night.

Vern. Doe not, my Lord.

Dowg. You doe not counsaile well:
You speake it out of feare, and cold heart.

Vern. Doe me no slander, *Dowglas:* by my Life,
And I dare well maintaine it with my Life,
If well-respected Honor bid me on,
I hold as little counsaile with weake feare,
As you, my Lord, or any Scot that this day liues,
Let it be seene to morrow in the Battell,
Which of vs feares.

Dowg. Yea, or to night.

Vern. Content.

Hotsp. To night, say I.

Vern. Come, come, it may not be.
I wonder much, being mē of such great leading as you are
That you fore-see not what impediments
Drag backe our expedition: certaine Horse
Of my Cousin *Vernons* are not yet come vp,
Your Vnckle *Worcesters* Horse came but to day,
And now their pride and mettall is asleepe,
Their courage with hard labour tame and dull,
That not a Horse is halfe the halfe of himselfe.

Hotsp. So are the Horses of the Enemie
In generall iourney bated, and brought low:
The better part of ours are full of rest.

Worc. The number of the King exceedeth ours:
For Gods sake, Cousin, stay till all come in.

The Trumpet sounds a Parley. Enter Sir Walter Blunt.

Blunt. I come with gracious offers from the King,
If you vouchsafe me hearing, and respect.

Hotsp. Welcome, Sir *Walter Blunt*:
And would to God you were of our determination.
Some of vs loue you well: and euen those some
Enuie your great deseruings, and good name,
Because you are not of our qualitie,
But stand against vs like an Enemie.

Blunt. And Heauen defend, but still I should stand so,
So long as out of Limit, and true Rule,
You stand against anoynted Maiestie.
But to my Charge.
The King hath sent to know
The nature of your Griefes, and whereupon
You coniure from the Brest of Ciuill Peace,
Such bold Hostilitie, teaching his dutious Land
Audacious Crueltie. If that the King
Haue any way your good Deserts forgot,
Which he confesseth to be manifold,
He bids you name your Griefes, and with all speed
You shall haue your desires, with interest;
And Pardon absolute for your selfe, and these,
Herein mis-led, by your suggestion.

Hotsp. The King is kinde:
And well wee know, the King
Knowes at what time to promise, when to pay.
My Father, my Vnckle, and my selfe,
Did giue him that same Royaltie he weares:
And when he was not sixe and twentie strong,
Sicke in the Worlds regard, wretched, and low,
A poore vnminded Out-law, sneaking home,
My Father gaue him welcome to the shore:
And when he heard him sweare, and vow to God,
He came but to be Duke of Lancaster,
To sue his Liuerie, and begge his Peace,
With teares of Innocencie, and tearmes of Zeale;
My Father, in kinde heart and pitty mou'd,
Swore him assistance, and perform'd it too.
Now, when the Lords and Barons of the Realme
Perceiu'd *Northumberland* did leane to him,
The more and lesse came in with Cap and Knee,
Met him in Boroughs, Cities, Villages,
Attended him on Bridges, stood in Lanes,
Layd Gifts before him, proffer'd him their Oathes,
Gaue him their Heires, as Pages followed him,
Euen at the heeles, in golden multitudes.
He presently, as Greatnesse knowes it selfe,
Steps me a little higher then his Vow
Made to my Father, while his blood was poore,
Vpon the naked shore at Rauenspurgh:
And now (forsooth) takes on him to reforme
Some certaine Edicts, and some strait Decrees,
That lay too heauie on the Common-wealth;
Cryes out vpon abuses, seemes to weepe
Ouer his Countries Wrongs: and by this Face,
This seeming Brow of Iustice, did he winne
The hearts of all that hee did angle for.
Proceeded further, cut me off the Heads
Of all the Fauorites, that the absent King
In deputation left behinde him heere,

When hee was personall in the Irish Warre.

Blunt. Tut, I came not to heare this.

Hotsp. Then to the point.
In short time after, hee depos'd the King,
Soone after that, depriu'd him of his Life:
And in the neck of that, task't the whole State,
To make that worse, suffer'd his Kinsman *March*,
Who is, if euery Owner were plac'd,
Indeede his King, to be engag'd in Wales,
There, without Ransome, to lye forfeited:
Disgrac'd me in my happie Victories,
Sought to intrap me by intelligence,
Rated my Vnckle from the Councell-Boord,
In rage dismiss'd my Father from the Court,
Broke Oath on Oath, committed Wrong on Wrong,
And in conclusion, droue vs to seeke out
This Head of safetie; and withall, to prie
Into his Title: the which wee finde
Too indirect, for long continuance.

Blunt. Shall I returne this answer to the King?

Hotsp. Not so, Sir *Walter*.
Wee'le with-draw a while:
Goe to the King, and let there be impawn'd
Some suretie for a safe returne againe,
And in the Morning early shall my Vnckle
Bring him our purpose: and so farewell.

Blunt. I would you would accept of Grace and Loue.

Hotsp. And't may be, so wee shall.

Blunt. Pray Heauen you doe. *Exeunt.*

Scena Quarta.

Enter the Arch-Bishop of Yorke, and Sir Michell.

Arch. Hie, good Sir *Michell*, beare this sealed Briefe
With winged haste to the Lord Marshall,
Thus to my Cousin *Scroope*, and all the rest
To whom they are directed.
If you knew how much they doe import,
You would make haste.

Sir Mich. My good Lord, I guesse their tenor.

Arch. Like enough you doe.
To morrow, good Sir *Michell*, is a day,
Wherein the fortune of ten thousand men
Must bide the touch. For Sir, at Shrewsbury,
As I am truly giuen to vnderstand,
The King, with mightie and quick-raysed Power,
Meetes with Lord *Harry*: and I feare, Sir *Michell*,
What with the sicknesse of *Northumberland*,
Whose Power was in the first proportion;
And what with *Owen Glendowers* absence thence,
Who with them was rated firmely too,
And comes not in, ouer-rul'd by Prophecies,
I feare the Power of *Percy* is too weake,
To wage an instant tryall with the King.

Sir Mich. Why, my good Lord, you need not feare,
There is *Dowglas*, and Lord *Mortimer*.

Arch. No, *Mortimer* is not there.

Sir Mic. But there is *Mordake*, *Vernon*, Lord *Harry Percy*,
And there is my Lord of Worcester,
And a Head of gallant Warriors,
Noble Gentlemen.

Arch. And

Arch. And so there is, but yet the King hath drawne
The speciall head of all the Land together:
The Prince of Wales, Lord *Iohn* of Lancaster,
The Noble Westmerland, and warlike *Blunt*;
And many moe Corriuals, and deare men
Of estimation, and command in Armes.

  Sir M. Doubt not my Lord, he shall be well oppos'd
  Arch. I hope no lesse? Yet needfull 'tis to feare,
And to preuent the worst, Sir *Michell* speed;
For if Lord *Percy* thriue not, ere the King
Dismisse his power, he meanes to visit vs:
For he hath heard of our Confederacie,
And, 'tis but Wisedome to make strong against him:
Therefore make hast, I must go write againe
To other Friends: and so farewell, Sir *Michell*. *Exeunt.*

Actus Quintus. Scena Prima.

Enter the King, Prince of Wales, Lord Iohn of Lancaster, Earle of Westmerland, Sir Walter Blunt, and Falstaffe.

  King. How bloodily the Sunne begins to peere
Aboue yon busky hill: the day lookes pale
At his distemperature.
  Prin. The Southerne winde
Doth play the Trumpet to his purposes,
And by his hollow whistling in the Leaues,
Fortels a Tempest, and a blust'ring day.
  King. Then with the losers let it sympathize,
For nothing can seeme foule to those that win.
The Trumpet sounds.
Enter Worcester.

  King. How now my Lord of Worster? 'Tis not well
That you and I should meet vpon such tearmes,
As now we meet. You haue deceiu'd our trust,
And made vs doffe our easie Robes of Peace,
To crush our old limbes in vngentle Steele:
This is not well, my Lord, this is not well.
What say you to it? Will you againe vnknit
This churlish knot of all-abhorred Warre?
And moue in that obedient Orbe againe,
Where you did giue a faire and naturall light,
And be no more an exhall'd Meteor,
A prodigie of Feare, and a Portent
Of broached Mischeefe, to the vnborne Times?
  Wor. Heare me, my Liege:
For mine owne part, I could be well content
To entertaine the Lagge-end of my life
With quiet houres: For I do protest,
I haue not sought the day of this dislike.
  King. You haue not sought it: how comes it then?
  Fal. Rebellion lay in his way, and he found it.
  Prin. Peace, Chewet, peace.
  Wor. It pleas'd your Maiesty, to turne your lookes
Of Fauour, from my Selfe, and all our House;
And yet I must remember you my Lord,
We were the first, and dearest of your Friends:
For you, my staffe of Office did I breake
In *Richards* time, and poasted day and night
To meete you on the way, and kisse your hand,
When yet you were in place, and in account
Nothing so strong and fortunate, as I;
It was my Selfe, my Brother, and his Sonne,
That brought you home, and boldly did out-dare
The danger of the time. You swore to vs,
And you did sweare that Oath at Doncaster,
That you did nothing of purpose 'gainst the State,
Nor claime no further, then your new-falne right,
The seate of *Gaunt*, Dukedome of Lancaster,
To this, we sware our aide: But in short space,
It rain'd downe Fortune showring on your head,
And such a floud of Greatnesse fell on you,
What with our helpe, what with the absent King,
What with the iniuries of wanton time,
The seeming sufferances that you had borne,
And the contrarious Windes that held the King
So long in the vnlucky Irish Warres,
That all in England did repute him dead:
And from this swarme of faire aduantages,
You tooke occasion to be quickly woo'd,
To gripe the generall sway into your hand,
Forgot your Oath to vs at Doncaster,
And being fed by vs, you vs'd vs so,
As that vngentle gull the Cuckowes Bird,
Vseth the Sparrow, did oppresse our Nest,
Grew by our Feeding, to so great a bulke,
That euen our Loue durst not come neere your sight
For feare of swallowing: But with nimble wing
We were inforc'd for safety sake, to flye
Out of your sight, and raise this present Head,
Whereby we stand opposed by such meanes
As you your selfe, haue forg'd against your selfe,
By vnkinde vsage, dangerous countenance,
And violation of all faith and troth
Sworne to vs in yonger enterprize.
  Kin. These things indeede you haue articulated,
Proclaim'd at Market Crosses, read in Churches,
To face the Garment of Rebellion
With some fine colour, that may please the eye
Of fickle Changelings, and poore Discontents,
Which gape, and rub the Elbow at the newes
Of hurly burly Innouation:
And neuer yet did Insurrection want
Such water-colours, to impaint his cause:
Nor moody Beggars, staruing for a time
Of pell-mell hauocke, and confusion.
  Prin. In both our Armies, there is many a soule
Shall pay full dearely for this encounter,
If once they ioyne in triall. Tell your Nephew,
The Prince of Wales doth ioyne with all the world
In praise of *Henry Percie*: By my Hopes,
This present enterprize set off his head,
I do not thinke a brauer Gentleman,
More actiue, valiant, or more valiant yong,
More daring, or more bold, is now aliue,
To grace this latter Age with Noble deeds.
For my part, I may speake it to my shame,
I haue a Truant beene to Chiualry,
And so I heare, he doth account me too:
Yet this before my Fathers Maiesty,
I am content that he shall take the oddes
Of his great name and estimation,
And will, to saue the blood on either side,
Try fortune with him, in a Single Fight.
  King. And Prince of Wales, so dare we venter thee,
Albeit, considerations infinite

Do make against it: No good Worster, no,
We loue our people well; euen those we loue
That are misled vpon your Cousins part:
And will they take the offer of our Grace:
Both he, and they, and you; yea, euery man
Shall be my Friend againe, and Ile be his.
So tell your Cousin, and bring me word,
What he will do. But if he will not yeeld,
Rebuke and dread correction waite on vs,
And they shall do their Office. So bee gone,
We will not now be troubled with reply,
We offer faire, take it aduisedly. *Exit Worcester.*

Prin. It will not be accepted, on my life,
The *Dowglas* and the *Hotspurre* both together,
Are confident against the world in Armes.

King. Hence therefore, euery Leader to his charge,
For on their answer will we set on them;
And God befriend vs, as our cause is iust. *Exeunt.*

Manet Prince and Falstaffe.

Fal. Hal, if thou see me downe in the battell,
And bestride me, so; 'tis a point of friendship.

Prin. Nothing but a Colossus can do thee that frendship
Say thy prayers, and farewell.

Fal. I would it were bed time *Hal*, and all well.

Prin. Why, thou ow'st heauen a death.

Falst. 'Tis not due yet: I would bee loath to pay him
before his day. What neede I bee so forward with him,
that call's not on me? Well, 'tis no matter, Honor prickes
me on. But how if Honour pricke me off when I come
on? How then? Can Honour set too a legge? No: or an
arme? No: Or take away the greefe of a wound? No.
Honour hath no skill in Surgerie, then? No. What is Honour? A word. What is that word Honour? Ayre: A
trim reckoning. Who hath it? He that dy'de a Wednesday. Doth he feele it? No. Doth hee heare it? No. Is it
insensible then? yea, to the dead. But wil it not liue with
the liuing? No. Why? Detraction wil not suffer it, therfore Ile none of it. Honour is a meere Scutcheon, and so
ends my Catechisme. *Exit.*

Scena Secunda.

Enter Worcester, and Sir Richard Vernon.

Wor. O no, my Nephew must not know, Sir *Richard*,
The liberall kinde offer of the King.

Ver. 'Twere best he did.

Wor. Then we are all vndone.
It is not possible, it cannot be,
The King would keepe his word in louing vs,
He will suspect vs still, and finde a time
To punish this offence in others faults:
Supposition, all our liues, shall be stucke full of eyes;
For Treason is but trusted like the Foxe,
Who ne're so tame, so cherisht, and lock'd vp,
Will haue a wilde tricke of his Ancestors:
Looke how he can, or sad or merrily,
Interpretation will misquote our lookes,
And we shall feede like Oxen at a stall,
The better cherisht, still the nearer death.
My Nephewes trespasse may be well forgot,
It hath the excuse of youth, and heate of blood,
And an adopted name of Priuiledge,
A haire-brain'd *Hotspurre*, gouern'd by a Spleene:
All his offences liue vpon my head,
And on his Fathers. We did traine him on,
And his corruption being tane from vs,
We as the Spring of all, shall pay for all:
Therefore good Cousin, let not *Harry* know
In any case, the offer of the King.

Ver. Deliuer what you will, Ile say 'tis so.
Heere comes your Cosin.

Enter Hotspurre.

Hot. My Vnkle is return'd,
Deliuer vp my Lord of Westmerland.
Vnkle, what newe-?

Wor. The King will bid you battell presently.

Dow. Defie him by the Lord of Westmerland.

Hot. Lord *Dowglas*: Go you and tell him so.

Dow. Marry and shall, and verie willingly. *Exit Dowglas.*

Wor. There is no seeming mercy in the King.

Hot. Did you begge any? God forbid.

Wor. I told him gently of our greeuances,
Of his Oath-breaking: which he mended thus,
By now forswearing that he is forsworne,
He cals vs Rebels, Traitors, and will scourge
With haughty armes, this hatefull name in vs.

Enter Dowglas.

Dow. Arme Gentlemen, to Armes, for I haue thrown
A braue defiance in King *Henries* teeth:
And Westmerland that was ingag'd did beare it,
Which cannot choose but bring him quickly on.

Wor. The Prince of Wales stept forth before the king,
And Nephew, challeng'd you to single fight.

Hot. O, would the quarrell lay vpon our heads,
And that no man might draw short breath to day,
But I and *Harry Monmouth*. Tell me, tell mee,
How shew'd his Talking? Seem'd it in contempt?

Ver. No, by my Soule: I neuer in my life
Did heare a Challenge vrg'd more modestly,
Vnlesse a Brother should a Brother dare
To gentle exercise, and proofe of Armes.
He gaue you all the Duties of a Man,
Trimm'd vp your praises with a Princely tongue,
Spoke your deseruings like a Chronicle,
Making you euer better then his praise,
By still dispraising praise, valew'd with you:
And which became him like a Prince indeed,
He made a blushing citall of himselfe,
And chid his Trewant youth with such a *Grace*,
As if he mastred there a double spirit
Of teaching, and of learning instantly:
There did he pause. But let me tell the World,
If he out-liue the enuie of this day,
England did neuer owe so sweet a hope,
So much misconstrued in his Wantonnesse.

Hot. Cousin, I thinke thou art enamored
On his Follies: neuer did I heare
Of any Prince so wilde at Liberty.
But be he as he will, yet once ere night,
I will imbrace him with a Souldiers arme,
That he shall shrinke vnder my curtesie.
Arme, arme with speed. And Fellow's, Soldiers, Friends,
Better consider what you haue to do,
That I that haue not well the gift of Tongue,

Can lift your blood vp with perswasion.

Enter a Messenger.

Mes. My Lord, heere are Letters for you.
Hot. I cannot reade them now.
O Gentlemen, the time of life is short;
To spend that shortnesse basely, were too long.
If life did ride vpon a Dials point,
Still ending at the arriuall of an houre,
And if we liue, we liue to treade on Kings:
If dye; braue death, when Princes dye with vs.
Now for our Consciences, the Armes is faire,
When the intent for bearing them is iust.

Enter another Messenger.

Mes. My Lord prepare, the King comes on apace.
Hot. I thanke him, that he cuts me from my tale:
For I professe not talking: Onely this,
Let each man do his best. And heere I draw a Sword,
Whose worthy temper I intend to staine
With the best blood that I can meete withall,
In the aduenture of this perillous day.
Now Esperance *Percy*, and set on:
Sound all the lofty Instruments of Warre,
And by that Musicke, let vs all imbrace:
For heauen to earth, some of vs neuer shall,
A second time do such a curtesie.

They embrace, the Trumpets sound, the King entereth with his power, alarum vnto the battell. Then enter Dowglas, and Sir Walter Blunt.

Blu. What is thy name, that in battel thus ȳ crossest me?
What honor dost thou seeke vpon my head?
Dow. Know then my name is *Dowglas*,
And I do haunt thee in the battell thus,
Because some tell me, that thou art a King.
Blunt. They tell thee true.
Dow. The Lord of Stafford deere to day hath bought
Thy likenesse: for insted of thee King *Harry*,
This Sword hath ended him, so shall it thee,
Vnlesse thou yeeld thee as a Prisoner.
Blu. I was not borne to yeeld, thou haughty Scot,
And thou shalt finde a King that will reuenge
Lords Staffords death.

Fight, Blunt is slaine, then enters Hotspur.

Hot. O *Dowglas*, hadst thou fought at Holmedon thus
I neuer had triumphed o're a Scot.
Dow. All's done, all's won, here breathles lies the king
Hot. Where?
Dow. Heere.
Hot. This *Dowglas*? No, I know this face full well:
A gallant Knight he was, his name was *Blunt*,
Semblably furnish'd like the King himselfe.
Dow. Ah foole: go with thy soule whether it goes,
A borrowed Title hast thou bought too deere.
Why didst thou tell me, that thou wer't a King?
Hot. The King hath many marching in his Coates.
Dow. Now by my Sword, I will kill all his Coates,
Ile murder all his Wardrobe peece by peece,
Vntill I meet the King.
Hot. Vp, and away,
Our Souldiers stand full fairely for the day. *Exeunt*

Alarum, and enter Falstaffe solus.

Fal. Though I could scape shot-free at London, I fear
the shot heere: here's no scoring, but vpon the pate. Soft
who are you? Sir *Walter Blunt*, there's Honour for you:
here's no vanity, I am as hot as molten Lead, and as heauy too; heauen keepe Lead out of mee, I neede no more weight then mine owne Bowelles. I haue led my rag of Muffins where they are pepper'd: there's not three of my 150. left aliue, and they for the Townes end, to beg during life. But who comes heere?

Enter the Prince.

Pri. What, stand'st thou idle here? Lend me thy sword,
Many a Nobleman likes starke and stiffe
Vnder the hooues of vaunting enemies,
Whose deaths are vnreueng'd. Prethy lend me thy sword
Fal. O *Hal*, I prethee giue me leaue to breath awhile:
Turke *Gregory* neuer did such deeds in Armes, as I haue done this day. I haue paid *Percy*, I haue made him sure.
Prin. He is indeed, and liuing to kill thee:
I prethee lend me thy sword.
Falst. Nay *Hal*, if *Percy* bee aliue, thou getst not my Sword; but take my Pistoll if thou wilt.
Prin. Giue it me: What, is it in the Case?
Fal. I *Hal*, 'tis hot: There's that will Sacke a City.

The Prince drawes out a Bottle of Sacke.

Prin. What, is it a time to iest and dally now. *Exit.*

Throwes it at him.

Fal. If *Percy* be aliue, Ile pierce him: if he do come in my way, so: if he do not, if I come in his (willingly) let him make a Carbonado of me. I like not such grinning honour as Sir *Walter* hath: Giue mee life, which if I can saue, so: if not, honour comes vnlook'd for, and ther's an end. *Exit*

Scena Tertia.

Alarum, excursions, enter the King, the Prince, Lord Iohn of Lancaster, and Earle of Westmerland.

King. I prethee *Harry* withdraw thy selfe, thou bleedest too much: Lord *Iohn of Lancaster*, go you with him.
P. Ioh. Not I, my Lord, vnlesse I did bleed too.
Prin. I beseech your Maiesty make vp,
Least your retirement do amaze your friends.
King. I will do so:
My Lord of Westmerland leade him to his Tent.
West. Come my Lord, Ile leade you to your Tent.
Prin. Lead me my Lord? I do not need your helpe;
And heauen forbid a shallow scratch should driue
The Prince of Wales from such a field as this,
Where stain'd Nobility lyes troden on,
And Rebels Armes triumph in massacres.
Ioh. We breath too long: Come cosin Westmerland,
Our duty this way lies, for heauens sake come.
Prin. By heauen thou hast deceiu'd me Lancaster,
I did not thinke thee Lord of such a spirit:
Before, I lou'd thee as a Brother, *Iohn*;
But now, I do respect thee as my Soule.
King. I saw him hold Lord *Percy* at the point,
With lustier maintenance then I did looke for
Of such an vngrowne Warriour.
Prin. O this Boy, lends mettall to vs all. *Exit.*

Enter Dowglas.

Dow. Another King? They grow like Hydra's heads:
I am the *Dowglas*, fatall to all those
That weare those colours on them. What art thou
That counterfeit'st the person of a King?
King. The King himselfe: who *Dowglas* grieues at hart

So

So many of his shadowes thou hast met,
And not the very King. I haue two Boyes
Seeke Percy and thy selfe about the Field:
But seeing thou fall'st on me so luckily,
I will assay thee: so defend thy selfe.

Dow. I feare thou art another counterfeit:
And yet infaith thou bear'st thee like a King:
But mine I am sure thou art, whoere thou be,
And thus I win thee. *They fight, the K.being in danger,*
Enter Prince.

Prin. Hold vp they head vile Scot, or thou art like
Neuer to hold it vp againe: the Spirits
Of valiant *Sherly, Stafford, Blunt,* are in my Armes;
It is the Prince of Wales that threatens thee,
Who neuer promiseth, but he meanes to pay.
They Fight, Dowglas flyeth.
Cheerely My Lord: how fare's your Grace?
Sir *Nicholas Gawsey* hath for succour sent,
And so hath *Clifton*: Ile to *Clifton* straight.

King. Stay, and breath awhile.
Thou hast redeem'd thy lost opinion,
And shew'd thou mak'st some tender of my life
In this faire rescue thou hast brought to mee.

Prin. O heauen, they did me too much iniury,
That euer said I hearkned to your death.
If it were so, I might haue let alone
The insulting hand of *Dowglas* ouer you,
Which would haue bene as speedy in your end,
As all the poysonous Potions in the world,
And sau'd the Treacherous labour of your Sonne.

K. Make vp to *Clifton,* Ile to Sir *Nicholas Gausey. Exit*
Enter Hotspur.

Hot. If I mistake not, thou art *Harry Monmouth.*
Prin. Thou speak'st as if I would deny my name.
Hot. My name is *Harrie Percie.*
Prin. Why then I see a very valiant rebel of that name.
I am the Prince of Wales, and thinke not *Percy,*
To share with me in glory any more:
Two Starres keepe not their motion in one Sphere,
Nor can one England brooke a double reigne,
Of *Harry Percy,* and the Prince of Wales.

Hot. Nor shall it *Harry,* for the houre is come
To end the one of vs; and would to heauen,
Thy name in Armes, were now as great as mine.

Prin. Ile make it greater, ere I part from thee,
And all the budding Honors on thy Crest,
Ile crop, to make a Garland for my head.

Hot. I can no longer brooke thy Vanities. *Fight.*
Enter Falstaffe.

Fal. Well said *Hal,* to it *Hal.* Nay you shall finde no
Boyes play heere, I can tell you.
Enter Dowglas, he fights with Falstaffe, who fals downe
as if he were dead. The Prince killeth Percie.

Hot. Oh *Harry,* thou hast rob'd me of my youth:
I better brooke the losse of brittle life,
Then those proud Titles thou hast wonne of me,
They wound my thoghts worse, then the sword my flesh:
But thought's the slaue of Life, and Life, Times foole;
And Time, that takes suruey of all the world,
Must haue a stop. O, I could Prophesie,
But that the Earth, and the cold hand of death,
Lyes on my Tongue: No *Percy,* thou art dust
And food for ——

Prin. For Wormes, braue *Percy.* Farewell great heart:
Ill-weau'd Ambition, how much art thou shrunke?
When that this bodie did containe a spirit,
A Kingdome for it was too small a bound:
But now two paces of the vilest Earth
Is roome enough. This Earth that beares the dead,
Beares not aliue so stout a Gentleman.
If thou wer't sensible of curtesie,
I should not make so great a shew of Zeale:
But let my fauours hide thy mangled face,
And euen in thy behalfe, Ile thanke my selfe
For doing these fayre Rites of Tendernesse.
Adieu, and take thy praise with thee to heauen,
Thy ignomy sleepe with thee in the graue,
But not remembred in thy Epitaph.
What? Old Acquaintance? Could not all this flesh
Keepe in a little life? Poore *Iacke,* farewell:
I could haue better spar'd a better man.
O, I should haue a heauy misse of thee,
If I were much in loue with Vanity.
Death hath not strucke so fat a Deere to day,
Though many dearer in this bloody Fray:
Imbowell'd will I see thee by and by,
Till then, in blood, by Noble *Percie* lye. *Exit.*
Falstaffe riseth vp.

Falst. Imbowell'd? If thou imbowell mee to day, Ile
giue you leaue to powder me, and eat me too to morow.
'Twas time to counterfet, or that hotte Termagant Scot,
had paid me scot and lot too, Counterfeit? I am no counterfeit; to dye, is to be a counterfeit, for hee is but the
counterfeit of a man, who hath not the life of a man: But
to counterfeit dying, when a man thereby liueth, is to be
no counterfeit, but the true and perfect image of life indeede. The better part of Valour, is Discretion; in the
which better part, I haue saued my life. I am affraide of
this Gun-powder *Percy* though he be dead. How if hee
should counterfeit too, and rise? I am afraid hee would
proue the better counterfeit: therefore Ile make him sure:
yea, and Ile sweare I kill'd him. Why may not hee rise as
well as I: Nothing confutes me but eyes, and no-bodie
sees me. Therefore sirra, with a new wound in your thigh
come you along me. *Takes Hotspurre on his back.*
Enter Prince and Iohn of Lancaster.

Prin. Come Brother *Iohn,* full brauely hast thou flesht
thy Maiden sword.

Iohn. But soft, who haue we heere?
Did you not tell me this Fat man was dead?

Prin. I did, I saw him dead,
Breathlesse, and bleeding on the ground: Art thou aliue?
Or is it fantasie that playes vpon our eye-sight?
I prethee speake, we will not trust our eyes
Without our eares. Thou art not what thou seem'st.

Fal. No, that's certaine: I am not a double man: but
if I be not *Iacke Falstaffe,* then am I a Iacke: There is *Per-*
cy, if your Father will do me any Honor, so: if not, let him
kill the next *Percie* himselfe. I looke to be either Earle or
Duke, I can assure you.

Prin. Why, *Percy* I kill'd my selfe, and saw thee dead.

Fal. Did'st thou? Lord, Lord, how the world is giuen
to Lying? I graunt you I was downe, and out of Breath,
and so was he, but we rose both at an instant, and fought
a long houre by Shrewsburie clocke. If I may bee beleeued, so: if not, let them that should reward Valour, beare
the sinne vpon their owne heads. Ile take't on my death
I gaue him this wound in the Thigh: if the man were a-
liue, and would deny it, I would make him eate a peece
of my sword.

Iohn. This is the strangest Tale that e're I heard.

Prin. This is the strangest Fellow, Brother *Iohn.*
Come

Come bring your luggage Nobly on your backe:
For my part, if a lye may do thee grace,
Ile gil'd it with the happiest tearmes I haue.
A Retreat is sounded.
The Trumpets sound Retreat, the day is ours:
Come Brother, let's to the highest of the field,
To see what Friends are liuing, who are dead. *Exeunt*

Fal. Ile follow as they say, for Reward. Hee that rewards me, heauen reward him. If I do grow great againe, Ile grow lesse? For Ile purge, and leaue Sacke, and liue cleanly, as a Nobleman should do. *Exit*

Scæna Quarta.

The Trumpets sound.
Enter the King, Prince of Wales, Lord Iohn of Lancaster,
Earle of Westmerland, with Worcester &
Vernon Prisoners.

King. Thus euer did Rebellion finde Rebuke.
Ill-spirited Worcester, did we not send Grace,
Pardon, and tearmes of Loue to all of you?
And would'st thou turne our offers contrary?
Misuse the tenor of thy Kinsmans trust?
Three Knights vpon our party slaine to day,
A Noble Earle, and many a creature else,
Had beene aliue this houre,
If like a Christian thou had'st truly borne
Betwixt our Armies, true Intelligence.

Wor. What I haue done, my safety vrg'd me to,
And I embrace this fortune patiently,
Since not to be auoyded, it fals on mee.

King. Beare Worcester to death, and *Vernon* too:
Other Offenders we will pause vpon.
Exit Worcester and Vernon.
How goes the Field?

Prin. The Noble Scot Lord *Dowglas*, when hee saw
The fortune of the day quite turn'd from him,
The Noble *Percy* slaine, and all his men,
Vpon the foot of feare, fled with the rest;
And falling from a hill, he was so bruiz'd
That the pursuers tooke him. At my Tent
The *Dowglas* is, and I beseech your Grace,
I may dispose of him.

King. With all my heart.

Prin. Then Brother *Iohn* of Lancaster,
To you this honourable bounty shall belong:
Go to the *Dowglas*, and deliuer him
Vp to his pleasure, ransomlesse and free:
His Valour shewne vpon our Crests to day,
Hath taught vs how to cherish such high deeds,
Euen in the bosome of our Aduersaries.

King. Then this remaines: that we diuide our Power.
You Sonne *Iohn*, and my Cousin Westmerland
Towards Yorke shall bend you, with your deerest speed
To meet Northumberland, and the Prelate *Scroope*,
Who (as we heare) are busily in Armes.
My Selfe, and you Sonne *Harry* will towards Wales,
To fight with *Glendower*, and the Earle of March.
Rebellion in this Land shall lose his way,
Meeting the Checke of such another day:
And since this Businesse so faire is done,
Let vs not leaue till all our owne be wonne. *Exeunt.*

FINIS.

The Second Part of Henry the Fourth,
Containing his Death: and the Coronation of King Henry the Fift.

Actus Primus. Scœna Prima.

INDVCTION.

Enter Rumour.

Pen your Eares: For which of you will stop
The vent of Hearing, when loud *Rumor* speakes?
I, from the Orient, to the drooping West
(Making the winde my Post-horse) still vnfold
The Acts commenced on this Ball of Earth.
Vpon my Tongue, continuall Slanders ride,
The which, in euery Language, I pronounce,
Stuffing the Eares of them with false Reports:
I speake of Peace, while couert Enmitie
(Vnder the smile of Safety) wounds the World:
And who but *Rumour*, who but onely I
Make fearfull Musters, and prepar'd Defence,
Whil'st the bigge yeare, swolne with some other griefes,
Is thought with childe, by the sterne Tyrant, Warre,
And no such matter? *Rumour*, is a Pipe
Blowne by Surmises, Ielousies, Coniectures;
And of so easie, and so plaine a stop,
That the blunt Monster, with vncounted heads,
The still discordant, wauering Multitude,
Can play vpon it. But what neede I thus
My well-knowne Body to Anathomize
Among my houshold? Why is *Rumour* heere?
I run before King *Harries* victory,
Who in a bloodie field by Shrewsburie
Hath beaten downe yong *Hotspurre*, and his Troopes,
Quenching the flame of bold Rebellion,
Euen with the Rebels blood. But what meane I
To speake so true at first? My Office is
To noyse abroad, that *Harry Monmouth* fell
Vnder the Wrath of Noble *Hotspurres* Sword:
And that the King, before the *Dowglas* Rage
Stoop'd his Annointed head, as low as death.
This haue I rumour'd through the peasant-Townes,
Betweene the Royall Field of Shrewsburie,
And this Worme-eaten-Hole of ragged Stone,
Where *Hotspurres* Father, old Northumberland,
Lyes crafty sicke. The Postes come tyring on,
And not a man of them brings other newes
Then they haue learn'd of Me. From *Rumours* Tongues,
They bring smooth-Comforts-false, worse then True-wrongs. *Exit.*

Scena Secunda.

Enter Lord Bardolfe, and the Porter.

L.Bar. Who keepes the Gate heere hoa?
Where is the Earle?
Por. What shall I say you are?
Bar. Tell thou the Earle
That the Lord *Bardolfe* doth attend him heere.
Por. His Lordship is walk'd forth into the Orchard,
Please it your Honor, knocke but at the Gate,
And he himselfe will answer.
Enter Northumberland.
L.Bar. Heere comes the Earle.
Nor. What newes Lord *Bardolfe*? Eu'ry minute now
Should be the Father of some Stratagem;
The Times are wilde: Contention (like a Horse
Full of high Feeding) madly hath broke loose,
And beares downe all before him.
L.Bar. Noble Earle,
I bring you certaine newes from Shrewsbury.
Nor. Good, and heauen will.
L.Bar. As good as heart can wish:
The King is almost wounded to the death:
And in the Fortune of my Lord your Sonne,
Prince *Harrie* slaine out-right: and both the *Blunts*
Kill'd by the hand of *Dowglas*. Yong Prince *Iohn*,
And Westmerland, and Stafford, fled the Field.
And *Harrie Monmouth's* Brawne (the Hulke Sir *Iohn*)
Is prisoner to your Sonne. O, such a Day,
(So fought, so follow'd, and so fairely wonne)
Came not, till now, to dignifie the Times
Since *Cæsars* Fortunes.
Nor. How is this deriu'd?
Saw you the Field? Came you from Shrewsbury?
L.Bar. I spake with one (my L.) that came frō thence,
A Gentleman well bred, and of good name,
That freely render'd me these newes for true.
Nor. Heere comes my Seruant *Trauers*, whom I sent
On Tuesday last, to listen after Newes.
Enter Trauers.
L.Bar. My Lord, I ouer-rod him on the way,
And he is furnish'd with no certainties,
More then he (haply) may retaile from me.
Nor. Now *Trauers*, what good tidings comes frō you?

Tra. My Lord, Sir *Iohn Vmfreuill* turn'd me backe
With ioyfull tydings; and (being better hors'd)
Out-rod me. After him, came spurring head
A Gentleman (almost fore-spent with speed)
That stopp'd by me, to breath his bloodied horse.
He ask'd the way to *Chester* : And of him
I did demand what Newes from *Shrewsbury*:
He told me, that Rebellion had ill lucke,
And that yong *Harry Percies* Spurre was cold.
With that he gaue his able Horse the head,
And bending forwards strooke his able heeles
Agsinst the panting sides of his poore Iade
Vp to the Rowell head, and starting so,
He seem'd in running, to deuoure the way,
Staying no longer question.

North. Ha? Againe:
Said he yong *Harrie Percyes* Spurre was cold?
(Of *Hot-Spurre*, cold-Spurre?) that Rebellion,
Had met ill lucke?

L.Bar. My Lord : Ile tell you what,
If my yong Lord your Sonne, haue not the day,
Vpon mine Honor, for a silken point
Ile giue my Barony. Neuer talke of it.

Nor. Why should the Gentleman that rode by *Trauers*
Giue then such instances of Losse?

L.Bar. Who, he?
He was some hielding Fellow, that had stolne
The Horse he rode-on : and vpon my life
Speake at aduenture. Looke, here comes more Newes.

Enter Morton.

Nor. Yea, this mans brow, like to a Title-leafe,
Fore-tels the Nature of a Tragicke Volume:
So lookes the Strond, when the Imperious Flood
Hath left a witnest Vsurpation.
Say *Morton*, did'st thou come from *Shrewsbury*?

Mor. I ran from *Shrewsbury* (my Noble Lord)
Where hatefull death put on his vgliest Maske
To fright our party.

North. How doth my Sonne, and Brother?
Thou trembl'st; and the whitenesse in thy Cheeke
Is apter then thy Tongue, to tell thy Errand.
Euen such a man, so faint, so spiritlesse,
So dull, so dead in looke, so woe-be-gone,
Drew *Priams* Curtaine, in the dead of night,
And would haue told him, Halfe his Troy was burn'd.
But *Priam* found the Fire, ere he his Tongue:
And I, my *Percies* death, ere thou report'st it.
This, thou would'st say : Your Sonne did thus, and thus :
Your Brother, thus . So fought the Noble *Dowglas*,
Stopping my greedy eare, with their bold deeds.
But in the end (to stop mine Eare indeed)
Thou hast a Sigh, to blow away this Praise,
Ending with Brother, Sonne, and all are dead.

Mor. *Dowglas* is liuing, and your Brother, yet:
But for my Lord, your Sonne.

North. Why, he is dead.
See what a ready tongue Suspition hath :
He that but feares the thing, he would not know,
Hath by Instinct, knowledge from others Eyes,
That what he feard, is chanc'd. Yet speake (*Morton*)
Tell thou thy Earle, his Diuination Lies,
And I will take it, as a sweet Disgrace,
And make thee rich, for doing me such wrong.

Mor. You are too great, to be (by me) gainsaid :
Your Spirit is too true, your Feares too certaine.

North. Yet for all this, say not that *Percies* dead.
I see a strange Confession in thine Eye:
Thou shak'st thy head, and hold'st it Feare, or Sinne,
To speake a truth. If he be slaine, say so :
The Tongue offends not, that reports his death :
And he doth sinne that doth belye the dead :
Not he, which sayes the dead is not aliue :
Yet the first bringer of vnwelcome Newes
Hath but a loosing Office : and his Tongue,
Sounds euer after as a sullen Bell
Remembred, knolling a departing Friend.

L.Bar. I cannot thinke (my Lord) your son is dead.

Mor. I am sorry, I should force you to beleeue
That, which I would to heauen, I had not seene.
But these mine eyes, saw him in bloody state,
Rend'ring faint quittance (wearied, and out-breath'd)
To *Henrie Monmouth*, whose swift wrath beate downe
The neuer-daunted *Percie* to the earth,
From whence (with life) he neuer more sprung vp.
In few; his death (whose spirit lent a fire,
Euen to the dullest Peazant in his Campe)
Being bruited once, tooke fire and heate away
From the best temper'd Courage in his Troopes.
For from his Mettle, was his Party steel'd ;
Which once, in him abated, all the rest
Turn'd on themselues, like dull and heauy Lead :
And as the Thing, that's heauy in it selfe,
Vpon enforcement, flyes with greatest speede,
So did our Men, heauy in *Hotspurres* losse,
Lend to this weight, such lightnesse with their Feare,
That Arrowes fled not swifter toward their ayme,
Then did our Soldiers (ayming at their safety)
Fly from the field. Then was that Noble *Worcester*
Too soone ta'ne prisoner : and that furious Scot,
(The bloody *Dowglas*) whose well-labouring sword
Had three times slaine th'appearance of the King,
Gan vaile his stomacke, and did grace the shame
Of those that turn'd their backes : and in his flight,
Stumbling in Feare, was tooke. The summe of all,
Is, that the King hath wonne : and hath sent out
A speedy power, to encounter you my Lord,
Vnder the Conduct of yong *Lancaster*
And *Westmerland*. This is the Newes at full.

North. For this, I shall haue time enough to mourne.
In Poyson, there is Physicke : and this newes
(Hauing beene well) that would haue made me sicke,
Being sicke, haue in some measure, made me well.
And as the Wretch, whose Feauer-weakned ioynts,
Like strengthlesse Hindges, buckle vnder life,
Impatient of his Fit, breakes like a fire
Out of his keepers armes : Euen so, my Limbes
(Weak'ned with greefe) being now inrag'd with greefe,
Are thrice themselues. Hence therefore thou nice crutch,
A scalie Gauntlet now, with ioynts of Steele
Must gloue this hand. And hence thou sickly Quoife,
Thou art a guard too wanton for the head,
Which Princes, flesh'd with Conquest, ayme to hit.
Now binde my Browes with Iron, and approach
The ragged'st houre, that Time and Spight dare bring
To frowne vpon th'enrag'd *Northumberland*.
Let Heauen kisse Earth : now let not Natures hand
Keepe the wilde Flood confin'd : Let Order dye,
And let the world no longer be a stage
To feede Contention in a ling'ring Act :
But let one spirit of the First-borne *Caine*

Reigne

Reigne in all bosomes, that each heart being set
On bloody Courses, the rude Scene may end,
And darknesse be the burier of the dead. (Honor.

L. Bar. Sweet Earle, diuorce not wisedom from your

Mor. The liues of all your louing Complices
Leane-on your health, the which if you giue-o're
To stormy Passion, must perforce decay.
You cast th'euent of Warre (my Noble Lord)
And summ'd the accompt of Chance, before you said
Let vs make head: It was your presurmize,
That in the dole of blowes, your Son might drop.
You knew he walk'd o're perils, on an edge
More likely to fall in, then to get o're:
You were aduis'd his flesh was capeable
Of Wounds, and Scarres; and that his forward Spirit
Would lift him, where most trade of danger rang'd,
Yet did you say go forth: and none of this
(Though strongly apprehended) could restraine
The stiffe-borne Action: What hath then befalne?
Or what hath this bold enterprize bring forth,
More then that Being, which was like to be?

L. Bar. We all that are engaged to this losse,
Knew that we ventur'd on such dangerous Seas,
That if we wrought out life, was ten to one:
And yet we ventur'd for the gaine propos'd,
Choak'd the respect of likely perill fear'd,
And since we are o're-set, venture againe.
Come, we will all put forth; Body, and Goods,

Mor. 'Tis more then time: And (my most Noble Lord)
I heare for certaine, and do speake the truth:
The gentle Arch-bishop of Yorke is vp
With well appointed Powres: he is a man
Who with a double Surety bindes his Followers.
My Lord (your Sonne) had onely but the Corpes,
But shadowes, and the shewes of men to fight.
For that same word (Rebellion) did diuide
The action of their bodies, from their soules;
And they did fight with queasinesse, constrain'd
As men drinke Potions; that their Weapons only
Seem'd on our side: but for their Spirits and Soules,
This word (Rebellion) it had froze them vp,
As Fish are in a Pond. But now the Bishop
Turnes Insurrection to Religion,
Suppos'd sincere, and holy in his Thoughts:
He's follow'd both with Body, and with Minde:
And doth enlarge his Rising, with the blood
Of faire King *Richard*, scrap'd from Pomfret stones,
Deriues from heauen, his Quarrell, and his Cause:
Tels them, he doth bestride a bleeding Land,
Gasping for life, vnder great *Bullingbrooke*,
And more, and lesse, do flocke to follow him.

North. I knew of this before. But to speake truth,
This present greefe had wip'd it from my minde.
Go in with me, and councell euery man
The aptest way for safety, and reuenge:
Get Posts, and Letters, and make Friends with speed,
Neuer so few, nor neuer yet more need. *Exeunt.*

Scena Tertia.

Enter Falstaffe, and Page.

Fal. Sirra, you giant, what saies the Doct. to my water?

Pag. He said sir, the water it selfe was a good healthy water: but for the party that ow'd it, he might haue more diseases then he knew for.

Fal. Men of all sorts take a pride to gird at mee: the braine of this foolish compounded Clay-man, is not able to inuent any thing that tends to laughter, more then I inuent, or is inuented on me. I am not onely witty in my selfe, but the cause that wit is in other men. I doe heere walke before thee, like a Sow, that hath o'rewhelm'd all her Litter, but one. If the Prince put thee into my Seruice for any other reason, then to set mee off, why then I haue no iudgement. Thou horson Mandrake, thou art fitter to be worne in my cap, then to wait at my heeles. I was neuer mann'd with an Agot till now: but I will sette you neyther in Gold, nor Siluer, but in vilde apparell, and send you backe againe to your Master, for a Iewell. The *Iuuenall* (the Prince your Master) whose Chin is not yet fledg'd, I will sooner haue a beard grow in the Palme of my hand, then he shall get one on his cheeke: yet he will not sticke to say, his Face is a Face-Royall. Heauen may finish it when he will, it is not a haire amisse yet: he may keepe it still at a Face-Royall, for a Barber shall neuer earne six pence out of it; and yet he will be crowing, as if he had writ man euer since his Father was a Batchellour. He may keepe his owne Grace, but he is almost out of mine, I can assure him. What said M. *Dombledon*, about the Satten for my short Cloake, and Slops?

Pag. He said sir, you should procure him better Assurance, then *Bardolfe*: he wold not take his Bond & yours, he lik'd not the Security.

Fal. Let him bee damn'd like the Glutton, may his Tongue be hotter, a horson *Achitophel*; a Rascally-yea-forsooth-knaue, to beare a Gentleman in hand, and then stand vpon Security? The horson smooth-pates doe now weare nothing but high shoes, and bunches of Keyes at their girdles: and if a man is through with them in honest Taking-vp, then they must stand vpon Securitie: I had as liefe they would put Rats-bane in my mouth, as offer to stoppe it with Security. I look'd hee should haue sent me two and twenty yards of Satten (as I am true Knight) and he sends me Security. Well, he may sleep in Security, for he hath the horne of Abundance: and the lightnesse of his Wife shines through it, and yet cannot he see, though he haue his owne Lanthorne to light him. Where's *Bardolfe*?

Pag. He's gone into Smithfield to buy your worship a horse.

Fal. I bought him in Paules, and bee'l buy mee a horse in Smithfield. If I could get mee a wife in the Stewes, I were Mann'd, Hors'd, and Wiu'd.

Enter Chiefe Iustice, and Seruant.

Pag. Sir, heere comes the Nobleman that committed the Prince for striking him, about *Bardolfe*.

Fal. Wait close, I will not see him.

Ch. Iust. What's he that goes there?

Ser. Falstaffe, and't please your Lordship.

Iust. He that was in question for the Robbery?

Ser. He my Lord, but he hath since done good seruice at Shrewsbury: and (as I heare) tis now going with some Charge, to the Lord *Iohn of Lancaster*.

Iust. What to Yorke? Call him backe againe.

Ser. Sir *Iohn Falstaffe*.

Fal. Boy, tell him, I am deafe.

Pag. You must speake lowder, my Master is deafe.

Iust. I am sure he is, to the hearing of any thing good. Go plucke him by the Elbow, I must speake with him.

Ser. Sir *Iohn*.

Fal. What? a yong knaue and beg? Is there not wars? Is there not imployment? Doth not the K. lack subiects? Do not the Rebels want Soldiers? Though it be a shame to be on on any side but one, it is worse shame to begge, then to be on the worst side, were it worse then the name of Rebellion can tell how to make it.

Ser. You mistake me Sir.

Fal. Why sir? Did I say you were an honest man? Setting my Knight-hood, and my Souldiership aside, I had lyed in my throat, if I had said so.

Ser. I pray you (Sir) then set your Knighthood and your Souldier-ship aside, and giue mee leaue to tell you, you lye in your throat, if you say I am any other then an honest man.

Fal. I giue thee leaue to tell me so? I lay a-side that which growes to me? If thou get'st any leaue of me, hang me: if thou tak'st leaue, thou wer't better be hang'd: you Hunt-counter, hence: Auant.

Ser. Sir, my Lord would speake with you.

Iust. Sir *Iohn Falstaffe*, a word with you.

Fal. My good Lord: giue your Lordship good time of the day. I am glad to see your Lordship abroad: I heard say your Lordship was sicke. I hope your Lordship goes abroad by aduise. Your Lordship (though not clean past your youth) hath yet some smack of age in you: some relish of the saltnesse of Time, and I most humbly beseech your Lordship, to haue a reuerend care of your health.

Iust. Sir *Iohn*, I sent you before your Expedition, to Shrewsburie.

Fal. If it please your Lordship, I heare his Maiestie is return'd with some discomfort from Wales.

Iust. I talke not of his Maiesty: you would not come when I sent for you?

Fal. And I heare moreouer, his Highnesse is falne into this same whorson Apoplexie. (you.

Iust. Well, heauen mend him. I pray let me speak with

Fal. This Apoplexie is (as I take it) a kind of Lethargie, a sleeping of the blood, a horson Tingling.

Iust. What tell you me of it? be it as it is.

Fal. It hath it originall from much greefe; from study and perturbation of the braine. I haue read the cause of his effects in *Galen*. It is a kinde of deafenesse.

Iust. I thinke you are falne into the disease: For you heare not what I say to you.

Fal. Very well (my Lord) very well: rather an't please you) it is the disease of not Listning, the malady of not Marking, that I am troubled withall.

Iust. To punish you by the heeles, would amend the attention of your eares, & I care not if I be your Physitian

Fal. I am as poore as *Iob*, my Lord; but not so Patient: your Lordship may minister the Potion of imprisonment to me, in respect of Pouertie: but how I should bee your Patient, to follow your prescriptions, the wise may make some dram of a scruple, or indeede, a scruple it selfe.

Iust. I sent for you (when there were matters against you for your life) to come speake with me.

Fal. As I was then aduised by my learned Councel, in the lawes of this Land-seruice, I did not come.

Iust. Wel, the truth is (sir *Iohn*) you liue in great infamy

Fal. He that buckles him in my belt, cãnot liue in lesse.

Iust. Your Meanes is very slender, and your wast great.

Fal. I would it were otherwise: I would my Meanes were greater, and my waste slenderer.

Iust. You haue misled the youthfull Prince.

Fal. The yong Prince hath misled mee. I am the Fellow with the great belly, and he my Dogge.

Iust. Well, I am loth to gall a new-heal'd wound: your daies seruice at Shrewsbury, hath a little gilded ouer your Nights exploit on Gads-hill. You may thanke the vnquiet time, for your quiet o're-posting that Action.

Fal. My Lord? (Wolfe.

Iust. But since all is wel, keep it so: wake not a sleeping

Fal. To wake a Wolfe, is as bad as to smell a Fox.

Iu. What? you are as a candle, the better part burnt out

Fal. A Wassell-Candle, my Lord; all Tallow: if I did say of wax, my growth would approue the truth.

Iust. There is not a white haire on your face, but shold haue his effect of grauity.

Fal. His effect of grauy, grauy, grauy.

Iust. You follow the yong Prince vp and downe, like his euill Angell.

Fal. Not so (my Lord) your ill Angell is light: but I hope, he that lookes vpon mee, will take mee without, weighing: and yet, in some respects I grant, I cannot go: I cannot tell. Vertue is of so little regard in these Costor-mongers, that true valor is turn'd Beare-heard. Pregnancie is made a Tapster, and hath his quicke wit wasted in giuing Recknings: all the other gifts appertinent to man (as the malice of this Age shapes them) are not woorth a Gooseberry. You that are old, consider not the capacities of vs that are yong: you measure the heat of our Liuers, with the bitternes of your gals: & we that are in the vaward of our youth, I must confesse, are wagges too.

Iust. Do you set downe your name in the scrowle of youth, that are written downe old, with all the Charracters of age? Haue you not a moist eye? a dry hand? a yellow cheeke? a white beard? a decreasing leg? an incresing belly? Is not your voice broken? your winde short? your wit single? and euery part about you blasted with Antiquity? and wil you cal your selfe yong? Fy, fy, fy, sir *Iohn*.

Fal. My Lord, I was borne with a white head, & something a round belly. For my voice, I haue lost it with hallowing and singing of Anthemes. To approue my youth farther, I will not: the truth is, I am onely olde in iudgement and vnderstanding: and he that will caper with mee for a thousand Markes, let him lend me the mony, & haue at him. For the boxe of th'eare that the Prince gaue you, he gaue it like a rude Prince, and you tooke it like a sensible Lord. I haue checkt him for it, and the yong Lion repents: Marry not in ashes and sacke-cloath, but in new Silke, and old Sacke.

Iust. Wel, heauen send the Prince a better companion.

Fal. Heauen send the Companion a better Prince: I cannot rid my hands of him.

Iust. Well, the King hath seuer'd you and Prince *Harry*, I heare you are going with Lord *Iohn* of Lancaster, against the Archbishop, and the Earle of Northumberland

Fal. Yes, I thanke your pretty sweet wit for it: but looke you pray, (all you that kisse my Ladie Peace, at home) that our Armies ioyn not in a hot day: for if I take but two shirts out with me, and I meane not to sweat extraordinarily: if it bee a hot day, if I brandish any thing but my Bottle, would I might neuer spit white againe: There is not a daungerous Action can peepe out his head, but I am thrust vpon it. Well, I cannot last euer.

Iust. Well, be honest, be honest, and heauen blesse your Expedition.

Fal. Will your Lordship lend mee a thousand pound, to furnish me forth?

Iust. Not a peny, not a peny: you are too impatient to beare crosses. Fare you well. Commend mee to my Cosin Westmerland.

Fal. If I do, fillop me with a three-man-Beetle. A man can no more separate Age and Couetousnesse, then he can part yong limbes and letchery: but the Gowt galles the

g 2   on:

one, and the pox pinches the other; and so both the Degrees preuent my curses. Boy?

Page. Sir.

Fal. What money is in my purse?

Page. Seuen groats, and two pence.

Fal. I can get no remedy against this Consumption of the purse. Borrowing onely lingers, and lingers it out, but the disease is incureable. Go beare this letter to my Lord of Lancaster, this to the Prince, this to the Earle of Westmerland, and this to old Mistris *Vrsula*, whome I haue weekly sworne to marry, since I perceiu'd the first white haire on my chin. About it: you know where to finde me. A pox of this Gowt, or a Gowt of this Poxe: for the one or th'other playes the rogue with my great toe: It is no matter, if I do halt, I haue the warres for my colour, and my Pension shall seeme the more reasonable. A good wit will make vse of any thing: I will turne diseases to commodity. *Exeunt*

Scena Quarta.

Enter Archbishop, Hastings, Mowbray, and Lord Bardolfe.

Ar. Thus haue you heard our causes, & kno our Means:
And my most noble Friends, I pray you all
Speake plainly your opinions of our hopes,
And first (Lord Marshall) what say you to it?

Mow. I well allow the occasion of our Armes,
But gladly would be better satisfied,
How (in our Meanes) we should aduance our selues
To looke with forhead bold and big enough
Vpon the Power and puisance of the King.

Hast. Our present Musters grow vpon the File
To fiue and twenty thousand men of choice:
And our Supplies, liue largely in the hope
Of great Northumberland, whose bosome burnes
With an incensed Fire of Iniuries.

L. Bar. The question then (Lord *Hastings*) standeth thus,
Whether our present fiue and twenty thousand
May hold-vp-head, without Northumberland:

Hast. With him, we may.

L. Bar. I marry, there's the point:
But if without him we be thought to feeble,
My iudgement is, we should not step too farre
Till we had his Asistance by the hand.
For in a Theame so bloody fac'd, as this,
Coniecture, Expectation, and Surmise
Of Aydes incertaine, should not be admitted.

Arch. 'Tis very true Lord *Bardolfe*, for indeed
It was yong *Hotspurres* case, at Shrewsbury.

L. Bar. It was (my Lord) who lin'd himself with hope,
Eating the ayre, on promise of Supply,
Flatt'ring himselfe with Proiect of a power,
Much smaller, then the smallest of his Thoughts,
And so with great imagination
(Proper to mad men) led his Powers to death,
And (winking) leap'd into destruction.

Hast. But (by your leaue) it neuer yet did hurt,
To lay downe likely-hoods, and formes of hope.

L. Bar. Yes, if this present quality of warre,
Indeed the instant action: a cause on foot,
Liues so in hope: As in an early Spring,
We see th'appearing buds, which to proue fruite,
Hope giues not so much warrant, as Dispaire
That Frosts will bite them. When we meane to build,
We first suruey the Plot, then draw the Modell,
And when we see the figure of the house,
Then must we rate the cost of the Erection,
Which if we finde out-weighes Ability,
What do we then, but draw a-new the Modell
In fewer offices? Or at least, desist
To builde at all? Much more, in this great worke,
(Which is (almost) to plucke a Kingdome downe,
And set another vp) should we suruey
The plot of Situation, and the Modell;
Consent vpon a sure Foundation:
Question Surueyors, know our owne estate,
How able such a Worke to vndergo,
To weigh against his Opposite? Or else,
We fortifie in Paper, and in Figures,
Vsing the Names of men, instead of men:
Like one, that drawes the Modell of a house
Beyond his power to builde it; who (halfe through)
Giues o're, and leaues his part-created Cost
A naked subiect to the Weeping Clouds,
And waste, for churlish Winters tyranny.

Hast. Grant that our hopes (yet likely of faire byrth)
Should be still-borne: and that we now possest
The vtmost man of expectation:
I thinke we are a Body strong enough
(Euen as we are) to equall with the King.

L. Bar. What is the King but fiue & twenty thousand?

Hast. To vs no more: nay not so much Lord *Bardolf*.
For his diuisions (as the Times do brawl)
Are in three Heads: one Power against the French,
And one against *Glendower*: Perforce a third
Must take vp vs: So is the vnfirme King
In three diuided: and his Coffers sound
With hollow Pouerty, and Emptinesse.

Ar. That he should draw his seuerall strengths togither
And come against vs in full puissance
Need not be dreaded.

Hast. If he should do so,
He leaues his backe vnarm'd, the French, and Welch
Baying him at the heeles: neuer feare that.

L. Bar. Who is it like should lead his Forces hither?

Hast. The Duke of Lancaster, and Westmerland:
Against the Welsh himselfe, and *Harrie Monmouth*.
But who is substituted 'gainst the French,
I haue no certaine notice.

Arch. Let vs on:
And publish the occasion of our Armes.
The Common-wealth is sicke of their owne Choice,
Their ouer-greedy loue hath surfetted:
An habitation giddy, and vnsure
Hath he that buildeth on the vulgar heart.
O thou fond Many, with what loud applause
Did'st thou beate heauen with blessing *Bullingbrooke*,
Before he was, what thou would'st haue him be?
And being now trimm'd in thine owne desires,
Thou (beastly Feeder) art so full of him,
That thou prouok'st thy selfe to cast him vp.
So, so, (thou common Dogge) did'st thou disgorge
Thy glutton-bosome of the Royall *Richard*,
And now thou would'st eate thy dead vomit vp,
And howl'st to finde it. What trust is in these Times?
They, that when *Richard* liu'd, would haue him dye,
Are now become enamour'd on his graue.
Thou that threw'st dust vpon his goodly head
When through proud London he came sighing on,
After th'admired heeles of *Bullingbrooke*,
Cri'st now, O Earth, yeeld vs that King agine,

And

The second Part of King Henry the Fourth. 79

And take thou this (O thoughts of men accurs'd):
Past, and to Come, seemes best; things Present, worst.

Mow. Shall we go draw our numbers, and set on?

Hast. We are Times subiects, and Time bids, be gon.

Actus Secundus. Scœna Prima.

Enter Hostesse, with two Officers, Fang, and Snare.

Hostesse. Mr. *Fang*, haue you entred the Action?

Fang. It is enter'd.

Hostesse. Whers's your Yeoman? Is it a lusty yeoman? Will he stand to it?

Fang. Sirrah, where's *Snare*?

Hostesse. I,I, good M. *Snare*.

Snare. Heere, heere.

Fang. *Snare*, we must Arrest Sir *Iohn Falstaffe*.

Host. I good M. *Snare*, I haue enter'd him, and all.

Sn. It may chance cost some of vs our liues: he wil stab.

Hostesse. Alas the day: take heed of him: he stabd me in mine owne house, and that most beastly: he cares not what mischeefe he doth, if his weapon be out. Hee will foyne like any diuell, he will spare neither man, woman, nor childe.

Fang. If I can close with him, I care not for his thrust.

Hostesse. No, nor I neither: Ile be at your elbow.

Fang. If I but fist him once: if he come but within my Vice.

Host. I am vndone with his going: I warrant he is an infinitiue thing vpon my score. Good M.*Fang* hold him sure: good M. *Snare* let him not scape, he comes continually to Py-Corner (sauing your manhoods) to buy a saddle, and hee is indited to dinner to the Lubbars head in Lombardstreet, to M. *Smoothes* the Silkman. I pra'ye, since my Exion is enter'd, and my Case so openly knowne to the world, let him be brought in to his answer: A 100. Marke is a long one, for a poore lone woman to beare: & I haue borne, and borne, and borne, and haue bin fub'd off, and fub'd-off, from this day to that day, that it is a shame to be thought on. There is no honesty in such dealing, vnles a woman should be made an Asse and a Beast, to beare euery Knaues wrong. *Enter Falstaffe and Bardolfe.*
Yonder he comes, and that arrant Malmesey-Nose *Bardolfe* with him, Do your Offices, do your offices: M.*Fang*, & M.*Snare*, do me, do me, do me your Offices.

Fal. How now? whose Mare's dead? what's the matter?

Fang. Sir *Iohn*, I arrest you, at the suit of Mist. *Quickly*.

Falst. Away Varlets, draw *Bardolfe* : Cut me off the Villaines head: throw the Queane in the Channel.

Host. Throw me in the channell? Ile throw thee there. Wilt thou? wilt thou? thou bastardly rogue. Murder, murder, O thou Hony-suckle villaine, wilt thou kill Gods officers, and the Kings? O thou hony-seed Rogue, thou art a honyseed, a Man-queller, and a woman-queller.

Falst. Keep them off, *Bardolfe*. *Fang.* A rescu, a rescu.

Host. Good people bring a rescu. Thou wilt not? thou wilt not? Do, do thou Rogue: Do thou Hempseed.

Page. Away you Scullion, you Rampallian, you Fustillirian: Ile tucke your Catastrophe. *Enter. Ch. Iustice.*

Iust. What's the matter? Keepe the Peace here, hoa.

Host. Good my Lord be good to mee. I beseech you stand to me.

Ch.Iust. How now sir *Iohn*? What are you brauling here? Doth this become your place, your time, and businesse? You should haue bene well on your way to Yorke. Stand from him Fellow; wherefore hang'st vpon him?

Host. Oh my most worshipfull Lord, and't please your Grace, I am a poore widdow of Eastcheap, and he is arrested at my suit. *Ch. Iust.* For what summe?

Host. It is more then for some (my Lord) it is for all: all I haue, he hath eaten me out of house and home; hee hath put all my substance into that fat belly of his: but I will haue some of it out againe, or I will ride thee o'Nights, like the Mare.

Falst. I thinke I am as like to ride the Mare, if I haue any vantage of ground, to get vp.

Ch.Iust. How comes this, Sir *Iohn*? Fy, what a man of good temper would endure this tempest of exclamation? Are you not asham'd to inforce a poore Widdowe to so rough a course, to come by her owne?

Falst. What is the grosse summe that I owe thee?

Host. Marry (if thou wer't an honest man) thy selfe, & the mony too. Thou didst sweare to mee vpon a parcell gilt Goblet, sitting in my Dolphin-chamber at the round table, by a sea-cole fire, on Wednesday in Whitson week, when the Prince broke thy head for lik'ning him to a singing man of Windsor; Thou didst sweare to me then (as I was washing thy wound) to marry me, and make mee my Lady thy wife. Canst ỹ deny it? Did not goodwife *Keech* the Butchers wife come in then, and cal me gossip *Quickly*? comming in to borrow a messe of Vinegar: telling vs, she had a good dish of Prawnes: whereby ỹ didst desire to eat some: whereby I told thee they were ill for a greene wound? And didst not thou (when she was gone downe staires) desire me to be no more familiar with such poore people, saying, that ere long they should call me Madam? And did'st ỹ not kisse me, and bid mee fetch thee 30.s? I put thee now to thy Book-oath, deny it if thou canst?

Fal. My Lord, this is a poore mad soule: and she sayes vp & downe the town, that her eldest son is like you. She hath bin in good case, & the truth is, pouerty hath distracted her: but for these foolish Officers, I beseech you, I may haue redresse against them.

Iust. Sir *Iohn*, sir *Iohn*, I am well acquainted with your maner of wrenching the true cause, the false way. It is not a confident brow, nor the throng of wordes, that come with such (more then impudent) sawcines from you, can thrust me from a leuell consideration, I know you ha' practis'd vpon the easie-yeelding spirit of this woman.

Host. Yes in troth my Lord.

Iust. Prethee peace: pay her the debt you owe her, and vnpay the villany you haue done her: the one you may do with sterling mony, & the other with currant repentance.

Fal. My Lord, I will not vndergo this sneape without reply. You call honorable Boldnes, impudent Sawcinesse: If a man wil curt'sie, and say nothing, he is vertuous: No, my Lord (your humble duty remẽbred) I will not be your sutor. I say to you, I desire deliu'rance from these Officers being vpon hasty employment in the Kings Affaires.

Iust. You speake, as hauing power to do wrong: But answer in the effect of your Reputation, and satisfie the poore woman.

Falst. Come hither Hostesse. *Enter M. Gower*

Ch. Iust. Now Master *Gower*; What newes?

Gow. The King (my Lord) and *Henrie* Prince of Wales Are neere at hand: The rest the Paper telles.

Falst. As I am a Gentleman.

Host. Nay, you said so before.

Fal. As I am a Gentleman. Come, no more words of it

Host. By this Heauenly ground I tread on, I must be faine to pawne both my Plate, and the Tapistry of my dyning Chambers.

g3 *Falst.*

Fal. Glasses, glasses, is the onely drinking: and for thy walles a pretty slight Drollery, or the Storie of the Prodigall, or the Germane hunting in Waterworke, is worth a thousand of these Bed-hangings, and these Fly-bitten Tapistries. Let it be tenne pound (if thou canst.) Come, if it were not for thy humors, there is not a better Wench in England. Go, wash thy face, and draw thy Action: Come, thou must not bee in this humour with me, come, I know thou was't set on to this.

Host. Prethee (Sir *Iohn*) let it be but twenty Nobles, I loath to pawne my Plate, in good earnest la.

Fal. Let it alone, Ile make other shift: you'l be a fool still.

Host. Well, you shall haue it although I pawne my Gowne. I hope you'l come to Supper: You'l pay me altogether?

Fal. Will I liue? Go with her, with her: hooke-on, hooke-on.

Host. Will you haue *Doll Teare-sheet* meet you at supper?

Fal. No more words. Let's haue her.

Ch. Iust. I haue heard bitter newes.

Fal. What's the newes (my good Lord?)

Ch. Iu. Where lay the King last night?

Mes. At Basingstoke my Lord.

Fal. I hope (my Lord) all's well. What is the newes my Lord?

Ch. Iust. Come all his Forces backe?

Mes. No: Fifteene hundred Foot, fiue hundred Horse Are march'd vp to my Lord of Lancaster, Against Northumberland, and the Archbishop.

Fal. Comes the King backe from Wales, my noble L?

Ch. Iust. You shall haue Letters of me presently. Come, go along with me, good M. *Gowre.*

Fal. My Lord.

Ch. Iust. What's the matter?

Fal. Master *Gowre*, shall I entreate you with mee to dinner?

Gow. I must waite vpon my good Lord heere. I thanke you, good Sir *Iohn.*

Ch. Iust. Sir *Iohn*, you loyter heere too long, being you are to take Souldiers vp, in Countries as you go.

Fal. Will you sup with me, Master *Gowre*?

Ch. Iust. What foolish Master taught you these manners, Sir *Iohn*?

Fal. Master *Gower*, if they become mee not, hee was a Foole that taught them mee. This is the right Fencing grace (my Lord) tap for tap, and so part faire.

Ch. Iust. Now the Lord lighten thee, thou art a great Foole. *Exeunt*

Scena Secunda.

Enter Prince Henry, Pointz, Bardolfe, and Page.

Prin. Trust me, I am exceeding weary.

Poin. Is it come to that? I had thought wearines durst not haue attach'd one of so high blood.

Prin. It doth me: though it discolours the complexion of my Greatnesse to acknowledge it. Doth it not shew vildely in me, to desire small Beere?

Poin. Why, a Prince should not be so loosely studied, as to remember so weake a Composition.

Prince. Belike then, my Appetite was not Princely got: for (in troth) I do now remember the poore Creature, Small Beere. But indeede these humble considerations make me out of loue with my Greatnesse. What a disgrace is it to me, to remember thy name? Or to know thy face to morrow? Or to take note how many paire of Silk stockings ȳ hast? (Viz. these, and those that were thy peach-colour'd ones:) Or to beare the Inuentorie of thy shirts, as one for superfluity, and one other, for vse. But that the Tennis-Court-keeper knowes better then I, for it is a low ebbe of Linnen with thee, when thou kept'st not Racket there, as thou hast not done a great while, because the rest of thy Low Countries, haue made a shift to eate vp thy Holland.

Poin. How ill it followes, after you haue labour'd so hard, you should talke so idlely? Tell me how many good yong Princes would do so, their Fathers lying so sicke, as yours is?

Prin. Shall I tell thee one thing, *Pointz*?

Poin. Yes: and let it be an excellent good thing.

Prin. It shall serue among wittes of no higher breeding then thine.

Poin. Go to: I stand the push of your one thing, that you'l tell.

Prin. Why, I tell thee, it is not meet, that I should be sad now my Father is sicke: albeit I could tell to thee (as to one it pleases me, for fault of a better, to call my friend) I could be sad, and sad indeed too.

Poin. Very hardly vpon such a subiect.

Prin. Thou think'st me as farre in the Diuels Booke, as thou, and *Falstaffe*, for obduracie and persistencie. Let the end try the man. But I tell thee, my hart bleeds inwardly, that my Father is so sicke: and keeping such vild company as thou art, hath in reason taken from me, all ostentation of sorrow.

Poin. The reason?

Prin. What would'st thou think of me, if I shold weep?

Poin. I would thinke thee a most Princely hypocrite.

Prin. It would be euery mans thought: and thou art a blessed Fellow, to thinke as euery man thinkes: neuer a mans thought in the world, keepes the Rode-way better then thine: euery man would thinke me an Hypocrite indeede. And what accites your most worshipful thought to thinke so?

Poin. Why, because you haue beene so lewde, and so much ingraffed to *Falstaffe.*

Prin. And to thee.

Pointz. Nay, I am well spoken of, I can heare it with mine owne eares: the worst that they can say of me is, that I am a second Brother, and that I am a proper Fellowe of my hands: and those two things I confesse I canot helpe. Looke, looke, here comes *Bardolfe.*

Prince. And the Boy that I gaue *Falstaffe*, he had him from me Christian, and see if the fat villain haue not transform'd him Ape.

Enter Bardolfe.

Bar. Saue your Grace.

Prin. And yours, most Noble *Bardolfe.*

Poin. Come you pernitious Asse, you bashfull Foole, must you be blushing? Wherefore blush you now? what a Maidenly man at Armes are you become? Is it such a matter to get a Pottle-pots Maiden-head?

Page. He call'd me euen now (my Lord) through a red Lattice, and I could discerne no part of his face from the window:

window: at last I spy'd his eyes, and me thought he had made two holes in the Ale-wiues new Petticoat, & peeped through.

Prin. Hath not the boy profited?

Bar. Away, you horson vpright Rabbet, away.

Page. Away, you rascally *Althea*s dreame, away.

Prin. Instruct vs Boy: what dreame, Boy?

Page. Marry (my Lord) *Althea* dream'd, she was deliuer'd of a Firebrand, and therefore I call him hir dreame.

Prince. A Crownes-worth of good Interpretation: There it is, Boy.

Poin. O that this good Blossome could bee kept from Cankers: Well, there is six pence to preserue thee.

Bard. If you do not make him be hang'd among you, the gallowes shall be wrong'd.

Prince. And how doth thy Master, *Bardolph*?

Bar. Well, my good Lord: he heard of your Graces comming to Towne. There's a Letter for you.

Poin. Deliuer'd with good respect: And how doth the Martlemas, your Master?

Bard. In bodily health Sir.

Poin. Marry, the immortall part needes a Physitian: but that moues not him: though that bee sicke, it dyes not.

Prince. I do allow this Wen to bee as familiar with me, as my dogge: and he holds his place, for looke you he writes.

Poin.Letter. Iohn Falstaffe Knight: (Euery man must know that, as oft as hee hath occasion to name himselfe:) Euen like those that are kinne to the King, for they neuer pricke their finger, but they say, there is som of the kings blood spilt. How comes that (sayes he) that takes vpon him not to conceiue? the answer is as ready as a borrowed cap: I am the Kings poore Cosin, Sir.

Prince. Nay, they will be kin to vs, but they wil fetch it from *Iaphet*. But to the Letter: ——— Sir *Iohn Falstaffe*, Knight, to the Sonne of the King, neerest his Father, Harrie Prince of Wales, greeting.

Poin. Why this is a Certificate.

Prin. Peace.

I will imitate the honourable Romaines in breuitie.

Poin. Sure he meanes breuity in breath: short-winded.

I commend me to thee, I commend thee, and I leaue thee. Bee not too familiar with Pointz, *for hee misuses thy Fauours so much, that he sweares thou art to marrie his Sister* Nell. *Repent at idle times as thou mayst, and so farewell.*

Thine, by yea and no: which is as much as to say, as thou vsest him. Iacke Falstaffe *with my Familiars:* Iohn *with my Brothers and Sister: & Sir* Iohn, *with all Europe.*

My Lord, I will steepe this Letter in Sack, and make him eate it.

Prin. That's to make him eate twenty of his Words. But do you vse me thus *Ned*? Must I marry your Sister?

Poin. May the Wench haue no worse Fortune. But I neuer said so.

Prin. Well, thus we play the Fooles with the time, & the spirits of the wise, sit in the clouds, and mocke vs: Is your Master heere in London?

Bard. Yes my Lord.

Prin. Where suppes he? Doth the old Sore, feede in the old Franke?

Bard. At the old place my Lord, in East-cheape.

Prin. What Company?

Page. Ephesians my Lord, of the old Church.

Prin. Sup any women with him?

Page. None my Lord, but old Mistris *Quickly*, and M. Doll *Teare-sheet*.

Prin. What Pagan may that be?

Page. A proper Gentlewoman, Sir, and a Kinswoman of my Masters.

Prin. Euen such Kin, as the Parish Heyfors are to the Towne-Bull? Shall we steale vpon them (*Ned*) at Supper?

Poin. I am your shadow, my Lord, Ile follow you.

Prin. Sirrah, you boy, and *Bardolph*, no word to your Master that I am yet in Towne. There's for your silence.

Bar. I haue no tongue, sir.

Page. And for mine Sir, I will gouerne it.

Prin. Fare ye well: go.

This *Doll Teare-sheet* should be some Rode.

Poin. I warrant you, as common as the way betweene S. Albans, and London.

Prin. How might we see *Falstaffe* bestow himselfe to night, in his true colours, and not our selues be seene?

Poin. Put on two Leather Ierkins, and Aprons, and waite vpon him at his Table, like Drawers.

Prin. From a God, to a Bull? A heauie declension! It was *Ioues* case. From a Prince, to a Prentice, a low transformation, that shall be mine: for in euery thing, the purpose must weigh with the folly. Follow me *Ned*. *Exeunt*

Scena Tertia.

Enter Northumberland, his Ladie, and Harrie Percies Ladie.

North. I prethee louing Wife, and gentle Daughter,
Giue an euen way vnto my rough Affaires:
Put not you on the visage of the Times,
And be like them to *Percie*, troublesome.

Wife. I haue giuen ouer, I will speak no more,
Do what you will: your Wisedome, be your guide.

North. Alas (sweet Wife) my Honor is at pawne,
And but my going, nothing can redeeme it.

La. Oh yet, for heauens sake, go not to these Warrs;
The Time was (Father) when you broke your word,
When you were more endeer'd to it, then now,
When your owne Percy, when my heart-deere *Harry*,
Threw many a Northward looke, to see his Father
Bring vp his Powres: but he did long in vaine.
Who then perswaded you to stay at home?
There were two Honors lost; Yours, and your Sonnes.
For Yours, may heauenly glory brighten it:
For His, it stucke vpon him, as the Sunne
In the gray vault of Heauen: and by his Light
Did all the Cheualrie of England moue
To do braue Acts. He was (indeed) the Glasse
Wherein the Noble-Youth did dresse themselues.
He had no Legges, that practic'd not his Gate:
And speaking thicke (which Nature made his blemish)
Became the Accents of the Valiant.
For those that could speake low, and tardily,
Would turne their owne Perfection, to Abuse,
To seeme like him. So that in Speech, in Gate,
In Diet, in Affections of delight,
In Militarie Rules, Humors of Blood,

He was the Marke, and Glasse, Coppy, and Booke,
That fashion'd others. And him, O wondrous! him,
O Miracle of Men! Him did you leaue
(Second to none) vn-seconded by you,
To looke vpon the hideous God of Warre,
In dis-aduantage, to abide a field,
Where nothing but the sound of *Hotspurs* Name
Did seeme defensible: so you left him.
Neuer, O neuer doe his Ghost the wrong,
To hold your Honor more precise and nice
With others, then with him. Let them alone:
The Marshall and the Arch-bishop are strong.
Had my sweet *Harry* had but halfe their Numbers,
To day might I (hanging on *Hotspurs* Necke)
Haue talk'd of *Monmouth's* Graue.

North. Beshrew your heart,
(Faire Daughter) you doe draw my Spirits from me,
With new lamenting ancient Ouer-sights.
But I must goe, and meet with Danger there,
Or it will seeke me in another place,
And finde me worse prouided.

Wife. O flye to Scotland,
Till that the Nobles, and the armed Commons,
Haue of their Puissance made a little taste.

Lady. If they get ground, and vantage of the King,
Then ioyne you with them, like a Ribbe of Steele,
To make Strength stronger. But, for all our loues,
First let them trye themselues. So did your Sonne,
He was so suffer'd: so came I a Widow:
And neuer shall haue length of Life enough,
To raine vpon Remembrance with mine Eyes,
That it may grow, and sprowt, as high as Heauen,
For Recordation to my Noble Husband.

North. Come, come, go in with me: 'tis with my Minde
As with the Tyde, swell'd vp vnto his height,
That makes a still-stand, running neyther way.
Faine would I goe to meet the Arch-bishop,
But many thousand Reasons hold me backe.
I will resolue for Scotland: there am I,
Till Time and Vantage craue my company. *Exeunt.*

Scæna Quarta.

Enter two Drawers.

1. Drawer. What hast thou brought there? Apple-Iohns? Thou know'st Sir *Iohn* cannot endure an Apple-Iohn.

2. Draw. Thou say'st true: the Prince once set a Dish of Apple-Iohns before him, and told him there were fiue more Sir *Iohns*: and, putting off his Hat, said, I will now take my leaue of these sixe drie, round, old-wither'd Knights. It anger'd him to the heart: but hee hath forgot that.

1. Draw. Why then couer, and set them downe: and see if thou canst finde out *Sneakes* Noyse; Mistris *Tearesheet* would faine haue some Musique.

2. Draw. Sirrha, heere will be the Prince, and Master *Points*, anon: and they will put on two of our Ierkins, and Aprons, and Sir *Iohn* must not know of it: *Bardolph* hath brought word.

1. Draw. Then here will be old *Vtis*: it will be an excellent stratagem.

2. Draw. Ile see if I can finde out *Sneake*. *Exit.*

Enter Hostesse, and Dol.

Host. Sweet-heart, me thinkes now you are in an excellent good temperalitie: your Pulsidge beates as extraordinarily, as heart would desire; and your Colour (I warrant you) is as red as any Rose: But you haue drunke too much Canaries, and that's a maruellous searching Wine; and it perfumes the blood, ere wee can say what's this. How doe you now?

Dol. Better then I was: Hem.

Host. Why that was well said: A good heart's worth Gold. Looke, here comes Sir *Iohn*.

Enter Falstaffe.

Falst. When Arthur first in Court---(emptie the Iordan) *and was a worthy King*: How now Mistris *Dol*?

Host. Sick of a Calme: yea, good-sooth.

Falst. So is all her Sect: if they be once in a Calme, they are sick.

Dol. You muddie Rascall, is that all the comfort you giue me?

Falst. You make fat Rascalls, Mistris *Dol*.

Dol. I make them? Gluttonie and Diseases make them, I make them not.

Falst. If the Cooke make the Gluttonie, you helpe to make the Diseases (*Dol*) we catch of you (*Dol*) we catch of you: Grant that, my poore Vertue, grant that.

Dol. I marry, our Chaynes, and our Iewels.

Falst. Your Brooches, Pearles, and Owches: For to serue brauely, is to come halting off: you know, to come off the Breach, with his Pike bent brauely, and to Surgerie brauely; to venture vpon the charg'd-Chambers brauely.

Host. Why this is the olde fashion: you two neuer meete, but you fall to some discord: you are both (in good troth) as Rheumatike as two drie Tostes, you cannot one beare with anothers Confirmities. What the good-yere? One must beare, and that must bee you: you are the weaker Vessell; as they say, the emptier Vessell.

Dol. Can a weake emptie Vessell beare such a huge full Hogs-head? There's a whole Marchants Venture of Burdeux-Stuffe in him: you haue not seene a Hulke better stufft in the Hold. Come, Ile be friends with thee *Iacke*: Thou art going to the Warres, and whether I shall euer see thee againe, or no, there is no body cares.

Enter Drawer.

Drawer. Sir, Ancient *Pistoll* is below, and would speake with you.

Dol. Hang him, swaggering Rascall, let him not come hither: it is the foule-mouth'dst Rogue in England.

Host. If hee swagger, let him not come here: I must liue amongst my Neighbors, Ile no Swaggerers: I am in good name, and fame, with the very best: shut the doore, there comes no Swaggerers heere: I haue not liu'd all this while, to haue swaggering now: shut the doore, I pray you.

Falst. Do'st thou heare, Hostesse?

Host. Pray you pacifie your selfe (Sir *Iohn*) there comes no Swaggerers heere.

Falst. Do'st

Falst. Do'st thou heare? it is mine Ancient.

Host. Tilly-fally (Sir *Iohn*) neuer tell me, your ancient Swaggerer comes not in my doores. I was before Master *Tisick* the Deputie, the other day: and as hee said to me, it was no longer agoe then Wednesday last: Neighbour *Quickly* (sayes hee;) Master *Dombe*, our Minister, was by then: Neighbour *Quickly* (sayes hee) receiue those that are Ciuill; for (sayth hee) you are in an ill Name: now hee said so, I can tell whereupon: for (sayes hee) you are an honest Woman, and well thought on; therefore take heede what Guests you receiue: Receiue (sayes hee) no swaggering Companions. There comes none heere. You would blesse you to heare what hee said. No, Ile no Swaggerers.

Falst. Hee's no Swaggerer (Hostesse:) a tame Cheater, hee: you may stroake him as gently, as a Puppie Grey-hound: hee will not swagger with a Barbarie Henne, if her feathers turne backe in any shew of resistance. Call him vp (Drawer.)

Host. Cheater, call you him? I will barre no honest man my house, nor no Cheater: but I doe not loue swaggering; I am the worse when one sayes, swagger: Feele Masters, how I shake: looke you, I warrant you.

Dol. So you doe, Hostesse.

Host. Doe I? yea, in very truth doe I, if it were an Aspen Leafe: I cannot abide Swaggerers.

Enter Pistol, and Bardolph and his Boy.

Pist. 'Saue you, Sir *Iohn*.

Falst. Welcome Ancient *Pistol*. Here (*Pistol*) I charge you with a Cup of Sacke: doe you discharge vpon mine Hostesse.

Pist. I will discharge vpon her (Sir *Iohn*) with two Bullets.

Falst. She is Pistoll-proofe (Sir) you shall hardly offend her.

Host. Come, Ile drinke no Proofes, nor no Bullets: I will drinke no more then will doe me good, for no mans pleasure, I.

Pist. Then to you (Mistris *Dorothie*) I will charge you.

Dol. Charge me? I scorne you (scuruie Companion) what? you poore, base, rascally, cheating, lacke-Linnen-Mate: away you mouldie Rogue, away; I am meat for your Master.

Pist. I know you, Mistris *Dorothie*.

Dol. Away you Cut-purse Rascall, you filthy Bung, away: By this Wine, Ile thrust my Knife in your mouldie Chappes, if you play the sawcie Cuttle with me. Away you Bottle-Ale Rascall, you Basket-hilt stale Iugler, you. Since when, I pray you, Sir? what, with two Points on your shoulder? much.

Pist. I will murther your Ruffe, for this.

Host. No, good Captaine *Pistol*: not heere, sweete Captaine.

Dol. Captaine? thou abhominable damn'd Cheater, art thou not asham'd to be call'd Captaine? If Captaines were of my minde, they would trunchion you out, for taking their Names vpon you, before you haue earn'd them. You a Captaine? you slaue, for what? for tearing a poore Whores Ruffe in a Bawdy-house? Hee a Captaine? hang him Rogue, hee liues vpon mouldie stew'd-Pruines, and dry'de Cakes. A Captaine? These Villaines will make the word Captaine odious: Therefore Captaines had neede looke to it.

Bard. 'Pray thee goe downe, good Ancient.

Falst. Hearke thee hither, Mistris *Dol*.

Pist. Not I: I tell thee what, Corporall *Bardolph*, I could teare her: Ile be reueng'd on her.

Page. 'Pray thee goe downe.

Pist. Ile see her damn'd first: to *Pluto's* damn'd Lake, to the Infernall Deepe, where *Erebus* and Tortures vilde also. Hold Hooke and Line, say I: Downe: downe Dogges, downe Fates: haue wee not *Hiren* here?

Host. Good Captaine *Peesel* be quiet, it is very late: I beseeke you now, aggrauate your Choler.

Pist. These be good Humors indeede. Shall Pack-Horses, and hollow-pamper'd Iades of Asia, which cannot goe but thirtie miles a day, compare with *Cæsar*, and with Caniballs, and Troian Greekes? nay, rather damne them with King *Cerberus*, and let the Welkin roare: shall wee fall foule for Toyes?

Host. By my troth Captaine, these are very bitter words.

Bard. Be gone, good Ancient: this will grow to a Brawle anon.

Pist. Die men, like Dogges; giue Crownes like Pinnes: Haue we not *Hiren* here?

Host. On my word (Captaine) there's none such here. What the good-yere, doe you thinke I would denye her? I pray be quiet.

Pist. Then feed, and be fat (my faire *Calipolis*.) Come, giue me some Sack, *Si fortune me tormente, sperato me contente*. Feare wee broad-sides? No, let the Fiend giue fire: Giue me some Sack: and Sweet-heart lye thou there: Come wee to full Points here, and are *et cetera's* nothing?

Fal. *Pistol*, I would be quiet.

Pist. Sweet Knight, I kisse thy Neaffe: what? wee haue seene the seuen Starres.

Dol. Thrust him downe stayres, I cannot endure such a Fustian Rascall.

Pist. Thrust him downe stayres? know we not Galloway Nagges?

Fal. Quoit him downe (*Bardolph*) like a shoue-groat shilling: nay, if hee doe nothing but speake nothing, hee shall be nothing here.

Bard. Come, get you downe stayres.

Pist. What? shall wee haue Incision? shall wee embrew? then Death rocke me asleepe, abridge my dolefull dayes: why then let grieuous, gastly, gaping Wounds, vntwin'd the Sisters three: Come *Atropos*, I say.

Host. Here's good stuffe toward.

Fal. Giue me my Rapier, Boy.

Dol. I prethee *Iack*, I prethee doe not draw.

Fal. Get you downe stayres.

Host. Here's a goodly tumult: Ile forsweare keeping house, before Ile be in these tirrits, and frights. So: Murther I warrant now. Alas, alas, put vp your naked Weapons, put vp your naked Weapons.

Dol. I prethee *Iack* be quiet, the Rascall is gone: ah, you whorson little valiant Villaine, you.

Host. Are you not hurt i'th' Groyne? me thought hee made a threwd Thrust at your Belly.

Fal. Haue you turn'd him out of doores?

Bard. Yes Sir: the Rascall's drunke: you haue hurt him (Sir) in the shoulder.

Fal. A Rascall to braue me.

Dol. Ah, you sweet little Rogue, you: alas, poore Ape, how thou sweat'st? Come, let me wipe thy Face: Come on, you whorson Chops: Ah Rogue, I loue thee: Thou art as valorous as *Hector* of Troy, worth fiue of *Agamemnon*, and tenne times better then the nine Worthies: ah Villaine.

Fal. A rascally Slaue, I will tosse the Rogue in a Blanket.

Dol. Doe, if thou dar'st for thy heart: if thou doo'st, Ile canuas thee betweene a paire of Sheetes.

Enter Musique.

Page. The Musique is come, Sir.

Fal. Let them play: play Sirs. Sit on my Knee, *Dol.* A Rascall bragging Slaue: the Rogue fled from me like Quick-siluer.

Dol. And thou followd'st him like a Church: thou whorson little tydie Bartholmew Bore-pigge, when wilt thou leaue fighting on dayes, and foyning on nights, and begin to patch vp thine old Body for Heauen?

Enter the Prince and Poines disguis'd.

Fal. Peace (good *Dol*) doe not speake like a Deaths-head: doe not bid me remember mine end.

Dol. Sirrha, what humor is the Prince of?

Fal. A good shallow young fellow: hee would haue made a good Pantler, hee would haue chipp'd Bread well.

Dol. They say *Poines* hath a good Wit.

Fal. Hee a good Wit? hang him Baboone, his Wit is as thicke as Tewksburie Mustard: there is no more conceit in him, then is in a Mallet.

Dol. Why doth the Prince loue him so then?

Fal. Because their Legges are both of a bignesse: and hee playes at Quoits well, and eates Conger and Fennell, and drinkes off Candles ends for Flap-dragons, and rides the wilde-Mare with the Boyes, and iumpes vpon Ioyn'd-stooles, and sweares with a good grace, and weares his Boot very smooth, like vnto the Signe of the Legge; and breedes no bate with telling of discreete stories: and such other Gamboll Faculties hee hath, that shew a weake Minde, and an able Body, for the which the Prince admits him; for the Prince himselfe is such another: the weight of an hayre will turne the Scales betweene their *Haber-de-pois*.

Prince. Would not this Naue of a Wheele haue his Eares cut off?

Poin. Let vs beat him before his Whore.

Prince. Looke, if the wither'd Elder hath not his Poll claw'd like a Parrot.

Poin. Is it not strange, that Desire should so many yeeres out-liue performance?

Fal. Kisse me *Dol*.

Prince. Saturne and *Venus* this yeere in Coniunction? What sayes the Almanack to that?

Poin. And looke whether the fierie *Trigon*, his Man, be not lisping to his Masters old Tables, his Note-Booke, his Councell-keeper?

Fal. Thou do'st giue me flatt'ring Busses.

Dol. Nay truely, I kisse thee with a most constant heart.

Fal. I am olde, I am olde.

Dol. I loue thee better, then I loue ere a scuruie young Boy of them all.

Fal. What Stuffe wilt thou haue a Kirtle of? I shall receiue Money on Thursday: thou shalt haue a Cappe to morrow. A merrie Song, come: it growes late, wee will to Bed. Thou wilt forget me, when I am gone.

Dol. Thou wilt set me a weeping, if thou say'st so: proue that euer I dresse my selfe handsome, till thy returne: well, hearken the end.

Fal. Some Sack, *Francis*.

Prin. Poin. Anon, anon, Sir.

Fal. Ha? a Bastard Sonne of the Kings? And art not thou *Poines*, his Brother?

Prince. Why thou Globe of sinfull Continents, what a Life do'st thou lead?

Fal. A better then thou: I am a Gentleman, thou art a Drawer.

Prince. Very true, Sir: and I come to draw you out by the Eares.

Host. Oh, the Lord preserue thy good Grace: Welcome to London. Now Heauen blesse that sweete Face of thine: what, are you come from Wales?

Fal. Thou whorson mad Compound of Maiestie: by this light Flesh, and corrupt Blood, thou art welcome.

Dol. How? you fat Foole, I scorne you.

Poin. My Lord, hee will driue you out of your reuenge, and turne all to a merryment, if you take not the heat.

Prince. You whorson Candle-myne you, how vildly did you speake of me euen now, before this honest, vertuous, ciuill Gentlewoman?

Host. 'Blessing on your good heart, and so shee is by my troth.

Fal. Didst thou heare me?

Prince. Yes: and you knew me, as you did when you ranne away by Gads-hill: you knew I was at your back, and spoke it on purpose, to trie my patience.

Fal. No, no, no: not so: I did not thinke, thou wast within hearing.

Prince. I shall driue you then to confesse the wilfull abuse, and then I know how to handle you.

Fal. No abuse (*Hall*) on mine Honor, no abuse.

Prince. Not to disprayse me? and call me Pantler, and Bread-chopper, and I know not what?

Fal. No abuse (*Hal.*)

Poin. No abuse?

Fal. No abuse (*Ned*) in the World: honest *Ned* none. I disprays'd him before the Wicked, that the Wicked might not fall in loue with him: In which doing, I haue done the part of a carefull Friend, and a true Subiect, and thy Father is to giue me thankes for it. No abuse (*Hal*:) none (*Ned*) none; no Boyes, none.

Prince. See now whether pure Feare, and entire Cowardise, doth not make thee wrong this vertuous Gentlewoman, to close with vs? Is shee of the Wicked? Is thine Hostesse heere, of the Wicked? Or is the Boy of the Wicked? Or honest *Bardolph* (whose Zeale burnes in his Nose) of the Wicked?

Poin. Answere thou dead Elme, answere.

Fal. The Fiend hath prickt downe *Bardolph* irrecouerable, and his Face is *Lucifers* Priuy-Kitchin, where hee doth nothing but rost Mault-Wormes: for the Boy, there is a good Angell about him, but the Deuill out-bids him too.

Prince. For the Women?

Fal. For one of them, shee is in Hell alreadie, and burnes poore Soules: for the other, I owe her Money; and whether shee bee damn'd for that, I know not.

Host. No, I warrant you.

Fal. No,

Fal. No, I thinke thou art not: I thinke thou art quit for that. Marry, there is another Indictment vpon thee, for suffering flesh to bee eaten in thy house, contrary to the Law, for the which I thinke thou wilt howle.

Host. All Victuallers doe so: What is a Ioynt of Mutton, or two, in a whole Lent?

Prince. You, Gentlewoman.

Dol. What sayes your Grace?

Falst. His Grace sayes that, which his flesh rebells against.

Host. Who knocks so lowd at doore? Looke to the doore there, *Francis*?

Enter Peto.

Prince. Peto, how now? what newes?

Peto. The King, your Father, is at Westminster, And there are twentie weake and wearied Postes, Come from the North: and as I came along, I met, and ouer-tooke a dozen Captaines, Bare-headed, sweating, knocking at the Tauernes, And asking euery one for Sir *Iohn Falstaffe*.

Prince. By Heauen (*Poines*) I feele me much to blame, So idly to prophane the precious time, When Tempest of Commotion, like the South, Borne with black Vapour, doth begin to melt, And drop vpon our bare vnarmed heads. Giue me my Sword, and Cloake: *Falstaffe*, good night.   *Exit.*

Falst. Now comes in the sweetest Morsell of the night, and wee must hence, and leaue it vnpickt. More knocking at the doore? How now? what's the matter?

Bard. You must away to Court, Sir, presently, A dozen Captaines stay at doore for you.

Falst. Pay the Musitians, Sirrha: farewell Hostesse, farewell *Dol*. You see (my good Wenches) how men of Merit are sought after: the vndeseruer may sleepe, when the man of Action is call'd on. Farewell good Wenches: if I be not sent away poste, I will see you againe, ere I goe.

Dol. I cannot speake: if my heart bee not readie to burst--- Well (sweete *Iacke*) haue a care of thy selfe.

Falst. Farewell, farewell.   *Exit.*

Host. Well, fare thee well: I haue knowne thee these twentie nine yeeres, come Pescod-time: but an honester, and truer-hearted man---- Well, fare thee well.

Bard. Mistris *Teare-sheet*.

Host. What's the matter?

Bard. Bid Mistris *Teare-sheet* come to my Master.

Host. Oh runne *Dol*, runne: runne, good *Dol*.
                            Exeunt.

Actus Tertius. Scena Prima.

Enter the King, with a Page.

King. Goe, call the Earles of Surrey, and of Warwick: But ere they come, bid them ore-reade these Letters, And well consider of them: make good speed. *Exit.*

How many thousand of my poorest Subiects Are at this howre asleepe? O Sleepe, O gentle Sleepe, Natures soft Nurse, how haue I frighted thee, That thou no more wilt weigh my eye-lids downe, And steepe my Sences in Forgetfulnesse? Why rather (Sleepe) lyest thou in smoakie Cribs, Vpon vneasie Pallads stretching thee, And huisht with bussing Night, flyes to thy slumber, Then in the perfum'd Chambers of the Great? Vnder the Canopies of costly State, And lull'd with sounds of sweetest Melodie? O thou dull God, why lyest thou with the vilde, In loathsome Beds, and leau'st the Kingly Couch, A Watch-case, or a common Larum-Bell? Wilt thou, vpon the high and giddie Mast, Seale vp the Ship-boyes Eyes, and rock his Braines, In Cradle of the rude imperious Surge, And in the visitation of the Windes, Who take the Ruffian Billowes by the top, Curling their monstrous heads, and hanging them With deaff'ning Clamors in the slipp'ry Clouds, That with the hurley, Death it selfe awakes? Canst thou (O partiall Sleepe) giue thy Repose To the wet Sea-Boy, in an houre so rude: And in the calmest, and most stillest Night, With all appliances, and meanes to boote, Deny it to a King? Then happy Lowe, lye downe, Vneasie lyes the Head, that weares a Crowne.

Enter Warwicke and Surrey.

War. Many good-morrowes to your Maiestie.

King. Is it good-morrow, Lords?

War. 'Tis One a Clock, and past.

King. Why then good-morrow to you all (my Lords:) Haue you read o're the Letters that I sent you?

War. We haue (my Liege.)

King. Then you perceiue the Body of our Kingdome, How foule it is: what ranke Diseases grow, And with what danger, neere the Heart of it?

War. It is but as a Body, yet distemper'd, Which to his former strength may be restor'd, With good aduice, and little Medicine: My Lord *Northumberland* will soone be cool'd.

King. Oh Heauen, that one might read the Book of Fate, And see the reuolution of the Times Make Mountaines leuell, and the Continent (Wearie of solide firmenesse) melt it selfe Into the Sea: and other Times, to see The beachie Girdle of the Ocean Too wide for *Neptunes* hippes; how Chances mocks And Changes fill the Cuppe of Alteration With diuers Liquors. 'Tis not tenne yeeres gone, Since *Richard*, and *Northumberland*, great friends, Did feast together; and in two yeeres after, Were they at Warres. It is but eight yeeres since, This *Percie* was the man, neerest my Soule, Who, like a Brother, toyl'd in my Affaires, And layd his Loue and Life vnder my foot: Yea, for my sake, euen to the eyes of *Richard* Gaue him defiance. But which of you was by (You Cousin *Neuil*, as I may remember) When *Richard*, with his Eye, brim-full of Teares, (Then check'd, and rated by *Northumberland*) Did speake these words (now prou'd a Prophecie:) *Northumberland*, thou Ladder, by the which

My

My Cousin *Bullingbrooke* ascends my Throne:
(Though then, Heauen knowes, I had no such intent,
But that necessitie so bow'd the State,
That I and Greatnesse were compell'd to kisse:)
The Time shall come (thus did hee follow it)
The Time will come, that foule Sinne gathering head,
Shall breake into Corruption: so went on,
Fore-telling this same Times Condition,
And the diuision of our Amitie.

War. There is a Historie in all mens Liues,
Figuring the nature of the Times deceas'd:
The which obseru'd, a man may prophecie
With a neere ayme, of the maine chance of things,
As yet not come to Life, which in their Seedes
And weake beginnings lye entreasured:
Such things become the Hatch and Brood of Time;
And by the necessarie forme of this,
King *Richard* might create a perfect guesse,
That great *Northumberland*, then false to him,
Would of that Seed, grow to a greater falsenesse,
Which should not finde a ground to roote vpon,
Vnlesse on you.

King. Are these things then Necessities?
Then let vs meete them like Necessities;
And that same word, euen now cryes out on vs:
They say, the Bishop and *Northumberland*
Are fiftie thousand strong.

War. It cannot be (my Lord:)
Rumor doth double, like the Voice, and Eccho,
The numbers of the feared. Please it your Grace
To goe to bed, vpon my Life (my Lord)
The Pow'rs that you alreadie haue sent forth,
Shall bring this Prize in very easily.
To comfort you the more, I haue receiu'd
A certaine instance, that *Glendour* is dead.
Your Maiestie hath beene this fort-night ill,
And these vnseason'd howres perforce must adde
Vnto your Sicknesse.

King. I will take your counsaile:
And were these inward Warres once out of hand,
Wee would (deare Lords) vnto the Holy-Land.
Exeunt.

Scena Secunda.

Enter Shallow and Silence: with Mouldie, Shadow, Wart, Feeble, Bull-calfe.

Shal. Come-on, come-on, come-on: giue mee your Hand, Sir; giue mee your Hand, Sir: an early stirrer, by the Rood. And how doth my good Cousin *Silence*?

Sil. Good-morrow, good Cousin *Shallow*.

Shal. And how doth my Cousin, your Bed-fellow? and your fairest Daughter, and mine, my God-Daughter *Ellen*?

Sil. Alas, a blacke Ouzell (Cousin *Shallow*.)

Shal. By yea and nay, Sir, I dare say my Cousin *William* is become a good Scholler? hee is at Oxford still, is hee not?

Sil. Indeede Sir, to my cost.

Shal. Hee must then to the Innes of Court shortly: I was once of *Clements* Inne; where (I thinke) they will talke of mad *Shallow* yet.

Sil. You were call'd lustie *Shallow* then (Cousin.)

Shal. I was call'd any thing: and I would haue done any thing indeede too, and roundly too. There was I, and little *Iohn Doit* of Staffordshire, and blacke *George Bare*, and *Francis Pick-bone*, and *Will Squele* a Cot-sal-man, you had not foure such Swindge-bucklers in all the Innes of Court againe: And I may say to you, wee knew where the *Bona-Roba's* were, and had the best of them all at commandement. Then was *Iacke Falstaffe* (now Sir *Iohn*) a Boy, and Page to *Thomas Mowbray*, Duke of Norfolke.

Sil. This Sir *Iohn* (Cousin) that comes hither anon about Souldiers?

Shal. The same Sir *Iohn*, the very same: I saw him breake *Scoggan's* Head at the Court-Gate, when hee was a Crack, not thus high: and the very same day did I fight with one *Sampson Stock-fish*, a Fruiterer, behinde Greyes-Inne. Oh the mad dayes that I haue spent! and to see how many of mine olde Acquaintance are dead?

Sil. Wee shall all follow (Cousin.)

Shal. Certaine: 'tis certaine: very sure, very sure: Death is certaine to all, all shall dye. How a good Yoke of Bullocks at Stamford Fayre?

Sil. Truly Cousin, I was not there.

Shal. Death is certaine. Is old *Double* of your Towne liuing yet?

Sil. Dead, Sir.

Shal. Dead? See, see: hee drew a good Bow: and dead? hee shot a fine shoote. *Iohn* of Gaunt loued him well, and betted much Money on his head. Dead? hee would haue clapt in the Clowt at Twelue-score, and carryed you a fore-hand Shaft at foureteene, and foureteene and a halfe, that it would haue done a mans heart good to see. How a score of Ewes now?

Sil. Thereafter as they be: a score of good Ewes may be worth tenne pounds.

Shal. And is olde *Double* dead?

Enter Bardolph and his Boy.

Sil. Heere come two of Sir *Iohn Falstaffes* Men (as I thinke.)

Shal. Good-morrow, honest Gentlemen.

Bard. I beseech you, which is Iustice *Shallow*?

Shal. I am *Robert Shallow* (Sir) a poore Esquire of this Countie, and one of the Kings Iustices of the Peace: What is your good pleasure with me?

Bard. My Captaine (Sir) commends him to you: my Captaine, Sir *Iohn Falstaffe*: a tall Gentleman, and a most gallant Leader.

Shal. Hee greetes me well: (Sir) I knew him a good Back-Sword-man. How doth the good Knight? may I aske, how my Lady his Wife doth?

Bard. Sir, pardon: a Souldier is better accommodated, then with a Wife.

Shal. It is well said, Sir; and it is well said, indeede, too: Better accommodated? it is good, yea indeede is it: good phrases are surely, and euery where very commendable. Accommodated, it comes of *Accommodo*: very good, a good Phrase.

Bard. Pardon, Sir, I haue heard the word. Phrase call you it? by this Day, I know not the Phrase: but I will maintaine the Word with my Sword, to bee a Souldier-like Word, and a Word of exceeding good Command. Accommodated: that is, when a man is (as they say) accommodated: or, when a man is, being
whereby

whereby he thought to be accommodated, which is an excellent thing.

Enter Falstaffe.

Shal. It is very iust: Looke, heere comes good Sir *Iohn*. Giue me your hand, giue me your Worships good hand: Trust me, you looke well: and beare your yeares very well. Welcome, good Sir *Iohn*.

Fal. I am glad to see you well, good M. *Robert Shallow*: Master *Sure-card* as I thinke?

Shal. No sir *Iohn*, it is my Cosin *Silence*: in Commission with mee.

Fal. Good M. *Silence*, it well befits you should be of the peace.

Sil. Your good Worship is welcome.

Fal. Fye, this is hot weather (Gentlemen) haue you prouided me heere halfe a dozen of sufficient men?

Shal. Marry haue we sir: Will you sit?

Fal. Let me see them, I beseech you.

Shal. Where's the Roll? Where's the Roll? Where's the Roll? Let me see, let me see, let me see: so, so, so, so: yea marry Sir. *Raphe Mouldie*: let them appeare as I call: let them do so, let them do so: Let mee see, Where is *Mouldie*?

Moul. Heere, if it please you.

Shal. What thinke you (Sir *Iohn*) a good limb'd fellow: yong, strong, and of good friends.

Fal. Is thy name *Mouldie*?

Moul. Yea, if it please you.

Fal. 'Tis the more time thou wert vs'd.

Shal. Ha,ha,ha, most excellent. Things that are mouldie, lacke vse: very singular good. Well saide Sir *Iohn*, very well said.

Fal. Pricke him.

Moul. I was prickt well enough before, if you could haue let me alone: my old Dame will be vndone now, for one to doe her Husbandry, and her Drudgery; you need not to haue prickt me, there are other men fitter to goe out, then I.

Fal. Go too: peace *Mouldie*, you shall goe. *Mouldie*, it is time you were spent.

Moul. Spent?

Shallow. Peace, fellow, peace; stand aside: Know you where you are? For the other sir *Iohn*: Let me see: *Simon Shadow*.

Fal. I marry, let me haue him to sit vnder: he's like to be a cold souldier.

Shal. Where's *Shadow*?

Shad. Heere sir.

Fal. Shadow, whose sonne art thou?

Shad. My Mothers sonne, Sir.

Falst. Thy Mothers sonne: like enough, and thy Fathers shadow; so the sonne of the Female, is the shadow of the Male: it is often so indeede, but not of the Fathers substance.

Shal. Do you like him, sir *Iohn*?

Falst. Shadow will serue for Summer: pricke him: For wee haue a number of shadowes to fill vppe the Muster-Booke.

Shal. Thomas Wart?

Falst. Where's he?

Wart. Heere sir.

Falst. Is thy name *Wart*?

Wart. Yea sir.

Fal. Thou art a very ragged *Wart*.

Shal. Shall I pricke him downe, Sir *Iohn*?

Falst. It were superfluous: for his apparrel is built vpon his backe, and the whole frame stands vpon pins: prick him no more.

Shal. Ha,ha,ha, you can do it sir: you can doe it: I commend you well.

Francis Feeble.

Feeble. Heere sir.

Shal. What Trade art thou *Feeble*?

Feeble. A Womans Taylor sir.

Shal. Shall I pricke him, sir?

Fal. You may:
But if he had beene a mans Taylor, he would haue prick'd you. Wilt thou make as many holes in an enemies Battaile, as thou hast done in a Womans petticote?

Feeble. I will doe my good will sir, you can haue no more.

Falst. Well said, good Womans Tailour: Well sayde Couragious *Feeble*: thou wilt bee as valiant as the wrathfull Doue, or most magnanimous Mouse. Pricke the womans Taylour well Master *Shallow*, deepe Maister *Shallow*.

Feeble. I would *Wart* might haue gone sir.

Fal. I would thou wert a mans Tailor, that y might'st mend him, and make him fit to goe. I cannot put him to a priuate souldier, that is the Leader of so many thousands. Let that suffice, most Forcible *Feeble*.

Feeble. It shall suffice.

Falst. I am bound to thee, reuerend *Feeble*. Who is the next?

Shal. Peter Bulcalfe of the Greene.

Falst. Yea marry, let vs see *Bulcalfe*.

Bul. Heere sir.

Fal. Trust me, a likely Fellow. Come, pricke me *Bulcalfe* till he roare againe.

Bul. Oh, good my Lord Captaine.

Fal. What? do'st thou roare before th'art prickt.

Bul. Oh sir, I am a diseased man.

Fal. What disease hast thou?

Bul. A whorson cold sir, a cough sir, which I caught with Ringing in the Kings affayres, vpon his Coronation day, sir.

Fal. Come, thou shalt go to the Warres in a Gowne: we will haue away thy Cold, and I will take such order, that thy friends shall ring for thee. Is heere all?

Shal. There is two more called then your number: you must haue but foure heere sir, and so I pray you go in with me to dinner.

Fal. Come, I will goe drinke with you, but I cannot tarry dinner. I am glad to see you in good troth, Master *Shallow*.

Shal. O sir *Iohn*, doe you remember since wee lay all night in the Winde-mill, in S Georges Field.

Falstaffe. No more of that good Master *Shallow*: No more of that.

Shal. Ha? it was a merry night. And is *Iane Nightworke* aliue?

Fal. She liues, M. *Shallow*.

Shal. She neuer could away with me.

Fal. Neuer, neuer: she would alwayes say shee could not abide M. *Shallow*.

Shal. I could anger her to the heart: shee was then a *Bona-Roba*. Doth she hold her owne well.

Fal. Old, old, M. *Shallow*.

Shal. Nay, she must be old, she cannot choose but be old:

old: certaine shee's old: and had *Robin Night-worke*, by old *Night-worke*, before I came to *Clements* Inne.

Sil. That's fiftie fiue yeeres agoe.

Shal. Hah, Cousin *Silence*, that thou hadst seene that, that this Knight and I haue seene: hah, Sir *Iohn*, said I well?

Falst. Wee haue heard the Chymes at mid-night, Master *Shallow.*

Shal. That wee haue, that wee haue; in faith, Sir *Iohn*, wee haue: our watch-word was, Hem-Boyes. Come, let's to Dinner; come, let's to Dinner: Oh the dayes that wee haue seene. Come, come.

Bull. Good Master Corporate *Bardolph*, stand my friend, and heere is foure *Harry* tenne shillings in French Crownes for you: in very truth, sir, I had as lief be hang'd sir, as goe: and yet, for mine owne part, sir, I do not care; but rather, because I am vnwilling, and for mine owne part, haue a desire to stay with my friends: else, sir, I did not care, for mine owne part, so much.

Bard. Go-too: stand aside.

Mould. And good Master Corporall Captaine, for my old Dames sake, stand my friend: shee hath no body to doe any thing about her, when I am gone: and she is old, and cannot helpe her selfe: you shall haue fortie, sir.

Bard. Go-too: stand aside.

Feeble. I care not, a man can die but once: wee owe a death. I will neuer beare a base minde: if it be my destinie, so: if it be not, so: no man is too good to serue his Prince: and let it goe which way it will, he that dies this yeere, is quit for the next.

Bard. Well said, thou art a good fellow.

Feeble. Nay, I will beare no base minde.

Falst. Come sir, which men shall I haue?

Shal. Foure of which you please.

Bard. Sir, a word with you: I haue three pound, to free *Mouldie* and *Bull-calfe.*

Falst. Go-too: well.

Shal. Come, sir *Iohn*, which foure will you haue?

Falst. Doe you chuse for me.

Shal. Marry then, *Mouldie*, *Bull-calfe*, *Feeble*, and *Shadow.*

Falst. *Mouldie*, and *Bull-calfe*: for you *Mouldie*, stay at home, till you are past seruice: and for your part, *Bull-calfe*, grow till you come vnto it: I will none of you.

Shal. Sir *Iohn*, Sir *Iohn*, doe not your selfe wrong, they are your likelyest men, and I would haue you seru'd with the best.

Falst. Will you tell me (Master *Shallow*) how to chuse a man? Care I for the Limbe, the Thewes, the stature, bulke, and bigge assemblance of a man? giue mee the spirit (Master *Shallow*.) Where's *Wart*? you see what a ragged appearance it is: hee shall charge you, and discharge you, with the motion of a Pewterers Hammer: come off, and on, swifter then hee that gibbets on the Brewers Bucket. And this same halfe-fac'd fellow, *Shadow*, giue me this man: hee presents no marke to the Enemie, the foe-man may with as great ayme leuell at the edge of a Pen-knife: and for a Retrait, how swiftly will this *Feeble*, the Womans Taylor, runne off. O, giue me the spare men, and spare me the great ones. Put me a Calyuer into *Warts* hand, *Bardolph.*

Bard. Hold *Wart*, Trauerse: thus, thus, thus.

Falst. Come, manage me your Calyuer: so: very well, go-too, very good, exceeding good. O, giue me alwayes a little, leane, old, chopt, bald Shot. Well said *Wart*, thou art a good Scab: hold, there is a Tester for thee.

Shal. Hee is not his Crafts-master, hee doth not doe it right. I remember at Mile-end-Greene, when I lay at *Clements* Inne, I was then Sir *Dagonet* in *Arthurs* Show: there was a little quiuer fellow, and hee would manage you his Peece thus: and hee would about, and about, and come you in, and come you in: Rah, tah, tah, would hee say, Bownce would hee say, and away againe would hee goe, and againe would he come: I shall neuer see such a fellow.

Falst. These fellowes will doe well, Master *Shallow*. Farewell Master *Silence*, I will not vse many wordes with you: fare you well, Gentlemen both: I thanke you: I must a dozen mile to night. *Bardolph*, giue the Souldiers Coates.

Shal. Sir *Iohn*, Heauen blesse you, and prosper your Affaires, and send vs Peace. As you returne, visit my house. Let our old acquaintance be renewed: peraduenture I will with you to the Court.

Falst. I would you would, Master *Shallow.*

Shal. Go-too: I haue spoke at a word. Fare you well.   *Exit.*

Falst. Fare you well, gentle Gentlemen. On *Bardolph*, leade the men away. As I returne, I will fetch off these Iustices: I doe see the bottome of Iustice *Shallow*. How subiect wee old men are to this vice of Lying? This same staru'd Iustice hath done nothing but prate to me of the wildenesse of his Youth, and the Feates hee hath done about Turnball-street, and euery third word a Lye, duer pay'd to the hearer, then the Turkes Tribute. I doe remember him at *Clements* Inne, like a man made after Supper, of a Cheese-paring. When hee was naked, hee was, for all the world, like a forked Radish, with a Head fantastically caru'd vpon it with a Knife. Hee was so forlorne, that his Dimensions (to any thicke sight) were inuincible. Hee was the very *Genius* of Famine: hee came euer in the rere-ward of the Fashion: And now is this Vices Dagger become a Squire, and talkes as familiarly of *Iohn* of Gaunt, as if hee had beene sworne Brother to him: and Ile be sworne hee neuer saw him but once in the Tilt-yard, and then he burst his Head, for crowding among the Marshals men. I saw it, and told *Iohn* of Gaunt, hee beat his owne Name, for you might haue truss'd him and all his Apparrell into an Eele-skinne: the Case of a Treble Hoeboy was a Mansion for him: a Court: and now hath hee Land, and Beeues. Well, I will be acquainted with him, if I returne: and it shall goe hard, but I will make him a Philosophers two Stones to me. If the young Dace be a Bayt for the old Pike, I see no reason, in the Law of Nature, but I may snap at him. Let time shape, and there an end.   *Exeunt.*

Actus Quartus. Scena Prima.

Enter the Arch-bishop, Mowbray, Hastings, Westmerland, Coleuile.

Bish. What is this Forrest call'd?

Hast. 'Tis Gaultree Forrest, and't shall please your Grace.

Bish. Here stand (my Lords) and send discouerers forth, To know the numbers of our Enemies.

Hast. Wee

Hast. Wee haue sent forth alreadie.
Bish. 'Tis well done.
My Friends, and Brethren (in these great Affaires)
I must acquaint you, that I haue receiu'd
New-dated Letters from *Northumberland*:
Their cold intent, tenure, and substance thus.
Here doth hee wish his Person, with such Powers
As might hold sortance with his Qualitie,
The which hee could not leuie: whereupon
Hee is retyr'd, to ripe his growing Fortunes,
To Scotland; and concludes in heartie prayers,
That your Attempts may ouer-liue the hazard,
And fearefull meeting of their Opposite.

Mow. Thus do the hopes we haue in him, touch ground,
And dash themselues to pieces.

Enter a Messenger.

Hast. Now? what newes?
Mess. West of this Forrest, scarcely off a mile,
In goodly forme, comes on the Enemie:
And by the ground they hide, I iudge their number
Vpon, or neere, the rate of thirtie thousand.

Mow. The iust proportion that we gaue them out.
Let vs sway-on, and face them in the field.

Enter Westmerland.

Bish. What well-appointed Leader fronts vs here?
Mow. I thinke it is my Lord of Westmerland.
West. Health, and faire greeting from our Generall,
The Prince, Lord *Iohn*, and Duke of Lancaster.
Bish. Say on (my Lord of Westmerland) in peace:
What doth concerne your comming?
West. Then (my Lord)
Vnto your Grace doe I in chiefe addresse
The substance of my Speech. If that Rebellion
Came like it selfe, in base and abiect Routs,
Led on by bloodie Youth, guarded with Rage,
And countenanc'd by Boyes, and Beggerie:
I say, if damn'd Commotion so appeare,
In his true, natiue, and most proper shape,
You (Reuerend Father, and these Noble Lords)
Had not beene here, to dresse the ougly forme
Of base, and bloodie Insurrection,
With your faire Honors. You, Lord Arch-bishop,
Whose Sea is by a Ciuill Peace maintain'd,
Whose Beard, the Siluer Hand of Peace hath touch'd,
Whose Learning, and good Letters, Peace hath tutor'd,
Whose white Inuestments figure Innocence,
The Doue, and very blessed Spirit of Peace.
Wherefore doe you so ill translate your selfe,
Out of the Speech of Peace, that beares such grace,
Into the harsh and boystrous Tongue of Warre?
Turning your Bookes to Graues, your Inke to Blood,
Your Pennes to Launces, and your Tongue diuine
To a lowd Trumpet, and a Point of Warre.

Bish. Wherefore doe I this? so the Question stands.
Briefely to this end: Wee are all diseas'd,
And with our surfetting, and wanton howres,
Haue brought our selues into a burning Feuer,
And wee must bleede for it: of which Disease,
Our late King *Richard* (being infected) dy'd.
But (my most Noble Lord of Westmerland)
I take not on me here as a Physician,
Nor doe I, as an Enemie to Peace,
Troope in the Throngs of Militarie men:
But rather shew a while like fearefull Warre,
To dyet ranke Mindes, sicke of happinesse,
And purge th'obstructions, which begin to stop
Our very Veines of Life: heare me more plainely.
I haue in equall ballance iustly weigh'd,
What wrongs our Armes may do, what wrongs we suffer,
And finde our Griefes heauier then our Offences.
Wee see which way the streame of Time doth runne,
And are enforc'd from our most quiet there,
By the rough Torrent of Occasion,
And haue the summarie of all our Griefes
(When time shall serue) to shew in Articles;
Which long ere this, wee offer'd to the King,
And might, by no Suit, gayne our Audience:
When wee are wrong'd, and would vnfold our Griefes,
Wee are deny'd accesse vnto his Person,
Euen by those men, that most haue done vs wrong.
The dangers of the dayes but newly gone,
Whose memorie is written on the Earth
With yet appearing blood; and the examples
Of euery Minutes instance (present now)
Hath put vs in these ill-beseeming Armes:
Not to breake Peace, or any Branch of it,
But to establish here a Peace indeede,
Concurring both in Name and Qualitie.

West. When euer yet was your Appeale deny'd?
Wherein haue you beene galled by the King?
What Peere hath beene suborn'd, to grate on you,
That you should seale this lawlesse bloody Booke
Of forg'd Rebellion, with a Seale diuine?

Bish. My Brother generall, the Common-wealth,
I make my Quarrell, in particular.

West. There is no neede of any such redresse:
Or if there were, it not belongs to you.

Mow. Why not to him in part, and to vs all,
That feele the bruizes of the dayes before,
And suffer the Condition of these Times
To lay a heauie and vnequall Hand vpon our Honors?

West. O my good Lord *Mowbray*,
Construe the Times to their Necessities,
And you shall say (indeede) it is the Time,
And not the King, that doth you iniuries.
Yet for your part, it not appeares to me,
Either from the King, or in the present Time,
That you should haue an ynch of any ground
To build a Griefe on: were you not restor'd
To all the Duke of Norfolkes Seignories,
Your Noble, and right well-remembred Fathers?

Mow. What thing, in Honor, had my Father lost,
That need to be reuiu'd, and breath'd in me?
The King that lou'd him, as the State stood then,
Was forc'd, perforce compell'd to banish him:
And then, that *Henry Bullingbrooke* and hee
Being mounted, and both rowsed in their Seates,
Their neighing Coursers daring of the Spurre,
Their armed Staues in charge, their Beauers downe,
Their eyes of fire, sparkling through sights of Steele,
And the lowd Trumpet blowing them together:
Then, then, when there was nothing could haue stay'd
My Father from the Breast of *Bullingbrooke*;
O, when the King did throw his Warder downe,
(His owne Life hung vpon the Staffe hee threw)
Then threw hee downe himselfe, and all their Liues,
That by Indictment, and by dint of Sword,
Haue since mis-carryed vnder *Bullingbrooke.*

West. You

West. You speake (Lord *Mowbray*) now you know not what.
The Earle of Hereford was reputed then
In England the most valiant Gentleman.
Who knowes, on whom Fortune would then haue smil'd?
But if your Father had beene Victor there,
Hee ne're had borne it out of Couentry.
For all the Countrey, in a generall voyce,
Cry'd hate vpon him: and all their prayers, and loue,
Were set on *Herford*, whom they doted on,
And bless'd, and grac'd, and did more then the King.
But this is meere digression from my purpose.
Here come I from our Princely Generall,
To know your Griefes; to tell you, from his Grace,
That hee will giue you Audience: and wherein
It shall appeare, that your demands are iust,
You shall enioy them, euery thing set off,
That might so much as thinke you Enemies.

Mow. But hee hath forc'd vs to compell this Offer,
And it proceedes from Pollicy, not Loue.

West. *Mowbray*, you ouer-weene to take it so:
This Offer comes from Mercy, not from Feare.
For loe, within a Ken our Army lyes,
Vpon mine Honor, all too confident
To giue admittance to a thought of feare.
Our Battaile is more full of Names then yours,
Our Men more perfect in the vse of Armes,
Our Armor all as strong, our Cause the best;
Then Reason will, our hearts should be as good.
Say you not then, our Offer is compell'd.

Mow. Well, by my will, wee shall admit no Parley.

West. That argues but the shame of your offence:
A rotten Case abides no handling.

Hast. Hath the Prince *Iohn* a full Commission,
In very ample vertue of his Father,
To heare, and absolutely to determine
Of what Conditions wee shall stand vpon?

West. That is intended in the Generals Name:
I muse you make so slight a Question.

Bish. Then take (my Lord of Westmerland) this Schedule,
For this containes our generall Grieuances:
Each seuerall Article herein redress'd,
All members of our Cause, both here, and hence,
That are insinewed to this Action,
Acquitted by a true substantiall forme,
And present execution of our wills,
To vs, and to our purposes consin'd,
Wee come within our awfull Banks againe,
And knit our Powers to the Arme of Peace.

West. This will I shew the Generall. Please you Lords,
In sight of both our Battailes, wee may meete
At either end in peace: which Heauen so frame,
Or to the place of difference call the Swords,
Which must decide it.

Bish. My Lord, wee will doe so.

Mow. There is a thing within my Bosome tells me,
That no Conditions of our Peace can stand.

Hast. Feare you not, that if wee can make our Peace
Vpon such large termes, and so absolute,
As our Conditions shall consist vpon,
Our Peace shall stand as firme as Rockie Mountaines.

Mow. I, but our valuation shall be such,
That euery slight, and false-deriued Cause,
Yea, euery idle, nice, and wanton Reason,
Shall, to the King, taste of this Action:
That were our Royall faiths, Martyrs in Loue,
Wee shall be winnowed with so rough a winde,
That euen our Corne shall seeme as light as Chaffe,
And good from bad finde no partition.

Bish. No, no (my Lord) note this: the King is wearie
Of daintie, and such picking Grieuances:
For hee hath found, to end one doubt by Death,
Reuiues two greater in the Heires of Life.
And therefore will hee wipe his Tables cleane,
And keepe no Tell-tale to his Memorie,
That may repeat, and Historie his losse,
To new remembrance. For full well hee knowes,
Hee cannot so precisely weede this Land,
As his mis-doubts present occasion:
His foes are so en-rooted with his friends,
That plucking to vnfixe an Enemie,
Hee doth vnfasten so, and shake a friend.
So that this Land, like an offensiue wife,
That hath enrag'd him on, to offer strokes,
As he is striking, holds his Infant vp,
And hangs resolu'd Correction in the Arme,
That was vprear'd to execution.

Hast. Besides, the King hath wasted all his Rods,
On late Offenders, that he now doth lacke
The very Instruments of Chasticement:
So that his power, like to a Fanglesse Lion
May offer, but not hold.

Bish. 'Tis very true:
And therefore be assur'd (my good Lord Marshal)
If we do now make our attonement well,
Our Peace, will (like a broken Limbe vnited)
Grow stronger, for the breaking.

Mow. Be it so:
Heere is return'd my Lord of Westmerland.

Enter Westmerland.

West. The Prince is here at hand: pleaseth your Lordship
To meet his Grace, iust distance 'tweene our Armies?

Mow. Your Grace of Yorke, in heauen's name then
forward.

Bish. Before, and greet his Grace (my Lord) we come.

Enter Prince Iohn.

Iohn. You are wel encountred here (my cosin *Mowbray*)
Good day to you, gentle Lord Archbishop,
And so to you Lord *Hastings*, and to all.
My Lord of Yorke, it better shew'd with you,
When that your Flocke (assembled by the Bell)
Encircled you, to heare with reuerence
Your exposition on the holy Text,
Then now to see you heere an Iron man
Chearing a rowt of Rebels with your Drumme,
Turning the Word, to Sword; and Life to death?
That man that sits within a Monarches heart,
And ripens in the Sunne-shine of his fauor,
Would hee abuse the Countenance of the King,
Alack, what Mischiefes might hee set abroach,
In shadow of such Greatnesse? With you, Lord Bishop,
It is euen so. Who hath not heard it spoken,
How deepe you were within the Bookes of Heauen?
To vs, the Speaker in his Parliament;
To vs, th'imagine Voyce of Heauen it selfe:
The very Opener, and Intelligencer,
Betweene the Grace, the Sanctities of Heauen;
And our dull workings. O, who shall beleeue,
But you mis-vse the reuerence of your Place,
Employ the Countenance, and Grace of Heauen,
As a false Fauorite doth his Princes Name,
In deedes dis-honorable? You haue taken vp,

Vnder

Vnder the counterfeited Zeale of Heauen,
The Subiects of Heauens Substitute, my Father,
And both against the Peace of Heauen, and him,
Haue here vp-swarmed them.

Bish. Good my Lord of Lancaster,
I am not here against your Fathers Peace:
But (as I told my Lord of Westmerland)
The Time (mis-order'd) doth in common sence
Crowd vs, and crush vs, to this monstrous Forme,
To hold our safetie vp. I sent your Grace
The parcels, and particulars of our Griefe,
The which hath been with scorne shou'd from the Court:
Whereon this *Hydra*-Sonne of Warre is borne,
Whose dangerous eyes may well be charm'd asleepe,
With graunt of our most iust and right desires;
And true Obedience, of this Madnesse cur'd,
Stoope tamely to the foot of Maiestie.

Mow. If not, wee readie are to trye our fortunes,
To the last man.

Hast. And though wee here fall downe,
Wee haue Supplyes, to second our Attempt:
If they mis-carry, theirs shall second them.
And so, successe of Mischiefe shall be borne,
And Heire from Heire shall hold this Quarrell vp,
Whiles England shall haue generation.

Iohn. You are too shallow (*Hastings*)
Much too shallow,
To sound the bottome of the after-Times.

West. Pleaseth your Grace, to answere them directly,
How farre-forth you doe like their Articles.

Iohn. I like them all, and doe allow them well:
And sweare here, by the honor of my blood,
My Fathers purposes haue beene mistooke,
And some, about him, haue too lauishly
Wrested his meaning, and Authoritie.
My Lord, these Griefes shall be with speed redrest:
Vpon my Life, they shall. If this may please you,
Discharge your Powers vnto their seuerall Counties,
As wee will ours: and here, betweene the Armies,
Let's drinke together friendly, and embrace,
That all their eyes may beare those Tokens home,
Of our restored Loue, and Amitie.

Bish. I take your Princely word, for these redresses.

Iohn. I giue it you, and will maintaine my word:
And thereupon I drinke vnto your Grace.

Hast. Goe Captaine, and deliuer to the Armie
This newes of Peace: let them haue pay, and part:
I know, it will well please them.
High thee Captaine. *Exit.*

Bish. To you, my Noble Lord of Westmerland.

West. I pledge your Grace:
And if you knew what paines I haue bestow'd,
To breede this present Peace,
You would drinke freely: but my loue to ye,
Shall shew it selfe more openly hereafter.

Bish. I doe not doubt you.

West. I am glad of it.
Health to my Lord, and gentle Cousin *Mowbray*.

Mow. You wish me health in very happy season,
For I am, on the sodaine, something ill.

Bish. Against ill Chances, men are euer merry,
But heauinesse fore-runnes the good euent.

West. Therefore be merry (Cooze) since sodaine sorrow
Serues to say thus: some good thing comes to morrow.

Bish. Beleeue me, I am passing light in spirit.

Mow. So much the worse, if your owne Rule be true.

Iohn. The word of Peace is render'd: hearke how they showt.

Mow. This had been chearefull, after Victorie.

Bish. A Peace is of the nature of a Conquest:
For then both parties nobly are subdu'd,
And neither partie looser.

Iohn. Goe (my Lord)
And let our Army be discharged too:
And good my Lord (so please you) let our Traines
March by vs, that wee may peruse the men *Exit.*
Wee should haue coap'd withall.

Bish. Goe, good Lord *Hastings:*
And ere they be dismiss'd, let them march by. *Exit.*

Iohn. I trust (Lords) wee shall lye to night together.
Enter Westmerland.
Now Cousin, wherefore stands our Army still?

West. The Leaders hauing charge from you to stand,
Will not goe off, vntill they heare you speake.

Iohn. They know their duties. *Enter Hastings.*

Hast. Our Army is dispers'd:
Like youthfull Steeres, vnyoak'd, they tooke their course
East, West, North, South: or like a Schoole, broke vp,
Each hurryes towards his home, and sporting place.

West. Good tidings (my Lord *Hastings*) for the which,
I doe arrest thee (Traytor) of high Treason:
And you Lord Arch-bishop, and you Lord *Mowbray*,
Of Capitall Treason, I attach you both.

Mow. Is this proceeding iust, and honorable?

West. Is your Assembly so?

Bish. Will you thus breake your faith?

Iohn. I pawn'd thee none:
I promis'd you redresse of these same Grieuances
Whereof you did complaine; which, by mine Honor,
I will performe, with a most Christian care.
But for you (Rebels) looke to taste the due
Meet for Rebellion, and such Acts as yours.
Most shallowly did you these Armes commence,
Fondly brought here, and foolishly sent hence.
Strike vp our Drummes, pursue the scatter'd stray,
Heauen, and not wee, haue safely fought to day.
Some guard these Traitors to the Block of Death,
Treasons true Bed, and yeelder vp of breath. *Exeunt.*

Enter Falstaffe and Colleuile.

Falst. What's your Name, Sir? of what Condition are you? and of what place, I pray?

Col. I am a Knight, Sir:
And my Name is *Colleuile* of the Dale.

Falst. Well then, *Colleuile* is your Name, a Knight is your Degree, and your Place, the Dale. *Colleuile* shall still be your Name, a Traytor your Degree, and the Dungeon your Place, a place deepe enough: so shall you be still *Colleuile* of the Dale.

Col. Are not you Sir *Iohn Falstaffe?*

Falst. As good a man as he sir, who ere I am: doe yee yeelde sir, or shall I sweate for you? if I doe sweate, they are the drops of thy Louers, and they weep for thy death, therefore rowze vp Feare and Trembling, and do obseruance to my mercy.

Col. I thinke you are Sir *Iohn Falstaffe*, & in that thought yeeld me.

Fal. I haue a whole Schoole of tongues in this belly of mine, and not a Tongue of them all, speakes anie other word but my name: and I had but a belly of any indifferencie, I were simply the most actiue fellow in Europe: my wombe, my wombe, my wombe vndoes mee. Heere comes our Generall.

Enter Prince Iohn, and Westmerland.

Iohn. The heat is past, follow no farther now:
Call in the Powers, good Cousin *Westmerland*.
Now *Falstaffe*, where haue you beene all this while?
When euery thing is ended, then you come.
These tardie Tricks of yours will (on my life)
One time, or other, breake some Gallowes back.

Falst. I would bee sorry (my Lord) but it should bee thus: I neuer knew yet, but rebuke and checke was the reward of Valour. Doe you thinke me a Swallow, an Arrow, or a Bullet? Haue I, in my poore and olde Motion, the expedition of Thought? I haue speeded hither with the very extremest ynch of possibilitie. I haue sowndred nine score and odde Postes: and heere (trauell-tainted as I am) haue, in my pure and immaculate Valour, taken Sir *Iohn Colleuile* of the Dale, a most furious Knight, and valorous Enemie: But what of that? hee saw mee, and yeelded: that I may iustly say with the hooke-nos'd fellow of Rome, I came, saw, and ouer-came.

Iohn. It was more of his Courtesie, then your deseruing.

Falst. I know not: heere hee is, and heere I yeeld him: and I beseech your Grace, let it be book'd, with the rest of this dayes deedes; or I sweare, I will haue it in a particular Ballad, with mine owne Picture on the top of it (*Colleuile* kissing my foot:) To the which course, if I be enforc'd, if you do not all shew like gilt two-pences to me; and I, in the cleare Skie of Fame, o're-shine you as much as the Full Moone doth the Cynders of the Element (which shew like Pinnes-heads to her) beleeue not the Word of the Noble: therefore let mee haue right, and let desert mount.

Iohn. Thine's too heauie to mount.
Falst. Let it shine then.
Iohn. Thine's too thick to shine.
Falst. Let it doe something (my good Lord) that may doe me good, and call it what you will.
Iohn. Is thy Name *Colleuile*?
Col. It is (my Lord.)
Iohn. A famous Rebell art thou, *Colleuile*.
Falst. And a famous true Subiect tooke him.
Col. I am (my Lord) but as my Betters are,
That led me hither: had they beene rul'd by me,
You should haue wonne them dearer then you haue.
Falst. I know not how they sold themselues, but thou like a kinde fellow, gau'st thy selfe away; and I thanke thee, for thee.

Enter Westmerland.

Iohn. Haue you left pursuit?
West. Retreat is made, and Execution stay'd.
Iohn. Send *Colleuile*, with his Confederates,
To Yorke, to present Execution.
Blunt, leade him hence, and see you guard him sure.

Exit with Colleuile.

And now dispatch we toward the Court (my Lords)
I heare the King, my Father, is sore sicke.
Our Newes shall goe before vs, to his Maiestie,
Which (Cousin) you shall beare, to comfort him:
And wee with sober speede will follow you.

Falst. My Lord, I beseech you, giue me leaue to goe through Gloucestershire: and when you come to Court, stand my good Lord, 'pray, in your good report.

Iohn. Fare you well, *Falstaffe*: I, in my condition,
Shall better speake of you, then you deserue.   *Exit.*

Falst. I would you had but the wit: 'twere better then your Dukedome. Good faith, this same young sober-blooded Boy doth not loue me, nor a man cannot make him laugh: but that's no maruaile, hee drinkes no Wine. There's neuer any of these demure Boyes come to any proofe: for thinne Drinke doth so ouer-coole their blood, and making many Fish-Meales, that they fall into a kinde of Male Greene-sicknesse: and then, when they marry, they get Wenches. They are generally Fooles, and Cowards; which some of vs should be too, but for inflamation. A good Sherris-Sack hath a two-fold operation in it: it ascends me into the Braine, dryes me there all the foolish, and dull, and cruddie Vapours, which enuiron it: makes it apprehensiue, quicke, forgetiue, full of nimble, fierie, and delectable shapes; which deliuer'd o're to the Voyce, the Tongue, which is the Birth, becomes excellent Wit. The second propertie of your excellent Sherris, is, the warming of the Blood: which before (cold, and setled) left the Liuer white, and pale; which is the Badge of Pusillanimitie, and Cowardize: but the Sherris warmes it, and makes it course from the inwards, to the parts extremes: it illuminateth the Face, which (as a Beacon) giues warning to all the rest of this little Kingdome (Man) to Arme: and then the Vitall Commoners, and in-land pettie Spirits, muster me all to their Captaine, the Heart; who great, and puft vp with his Retinue, doth any Deed of Courage: and this Valour comes of Sherris. So, that skill in the Weapon is nothing, without Sack (for that sets it a-worke:) and Learning, a meere Hoord of Gold, kept by a Deuill, till Sack commences it, and sets it in act, and vse. Hereof comes it, that Prince *Harry* is valiant: for the cold blood hee did naturally inherite of his Father, hee hath, like leane, stirrill, and bare Land, manured, husbanded, and tyll'd, with excellent endeauour of drinking good, and good store of fertile Sherris, that hee is become very hot, and valiant. If I had a thousand Sonnes, the first Principle I would teach them, should be to forsweare thinne Potions, and to addict themselues to Sack.   *Enter Bardolph.*
How now *Bardolph*?

Bard. The Armie is discharged all, and gone.
Falst. Let them goe: Ile through Gloucestershire, and there will I visit Master *Robert Shallow*, Esquire: I haue him alreadie tempering betweene my finger and my thombe, and shortly will I seale with him. Come away.

Exeunt.

Scena Secunda.

Enter King, Warwicke, Clarence, Gloucester.

King. Now Lords, if Heauen doth giue successefull end
To this Debate, that bleedeth at our doores,
Wee will our Youth lead on to higher Fields,
And draw no Swords, but what are sanctify'd.
Our Nauie is addressed, our Power collected,
Our Substitutes, in absence, well inuested,
And euery thing lyes leuell to our wish;
Onely wee want a little personall Strength:
And pawse vs, till these Rebels, now a-foot,
Come vnderneath the yoake of Gouernment.

War. Both which we doubt not, but your Maiestie
Shall soone enioy.

King. Hum-

The second Part of King Henry the Fourth.   93

King. Humphrey (my Sonne of Gloucester) where is the Prince, your Brother?

Glo. I thinke hee's gone to hunt (my Lord) at Windsor.

King. And how accompanied?

Glo. I doe not know (my Lord.)

King. Is not his Brother, *Thomas* of Clarence, with him?

Glo. No (my good Lord) hee is in presence heere.

Clar. What would my Lord, and Father?

King. Nothing but well to thee, *Thomas* of Clarence.
How chance thou art not with the Prince, thy Brother?
Hee loues thee, and thou do'st neglect him (*Thomas*.)
Thou hast a better place in his Affection,
Then all thy Brothers: cherish it (my Boy)
And Noble Offices thou may'st effect
Of Mediation (after I am dead)
Betweene his Greatnesse, and thy other Brethren.
Therefore omit him not: blunt not his Loue,
Nor loose the good aduantage of his Grace,
By seeming cold, or carelesse of his will.
For hee is gracious, if hee be obseru'd:
Hee hath a Teare for Pitie, and a Hand
Open (as Day) for melting Charitie:
Yet notwithstanding, being incens'd, hee's Flint,
As humorous as Winter, and as sudden,
As Flawes congealed in the Spring of day.
His temper therefore must be well obseru'd:
Chide him for faults, and doe it reuerently,
When you perceiue his blood enclin'd to mirth:
But being moodie, giue him Line, and scope,
Till that his passions (like a Whale on ground)
Confound themselues with working. Learne this *Thomas*,
And thou shalt proue a shelter to thy friends,
A Hoope of Gold, to binde thy Brothers in:
That the vnited Vessell of their Blood
(Mingled with Venome of Suggestion,
As force, perforce, the Age will powre it in)
Shall neuer leake, though it doe worke as strong
As *Aconitum*, or rash Gun-powder.

Clar. I shall obserue him with all care, and loue.

King. Why art thou not at Windsor with him (*Thomas*?)

Clar. Hee is not there to day: hee dines in London.

King. And how accompanyed? Canst thou tell that?

Clar. With *Pointz*, and other his continuall followers.

King. Most subiect is the fattest Soyle to Weedes:
And hee (the Noble Image of my Youth)
Is ouer-spread with them: therefore my griefe
Stretches it selfe beyond the howre of death.
The blood weepes from my heart, when I doe shape
(In formes imaginarie) th' vnguided Dayes,
And rotten Times, that you shall looke vpon,
When I am sleeping with my Ancestors.
For when his head-strong Riot hath no Curbe,
When Rage and hot-Blood are his Counsailors,
When Meanes and lauish Manners meete together;
Oh, with what Wings shall his Affections flye
Towards fronting Perill, and oppos'd Decay?

War. My gracious Lord, you looke beyond him quite:
The Prince but studies his Companions,
Like a strange Tongue: wherein, to gaine the Language,
'Tis needfull, that the most immodest word
Be look'd vpon, and learn'd: which once attayn'd,
Your Highnesse knowes, comes to no farther vse,
But to be knowne, and hated. So, like grosse termes,
The Prince will, in the perfectnesse of time,
Cast off his followers: and their memorie
Shall as a Patterne, or a Measure, liue,
By which his Grace must mete the liues of others,
Turning past-euills to aduantages.

King. 'Tis seldome, when the Bee doth leaue her Combe
In the dead Carrion.

Enter Westmerland.

Who's heere? *Westmerland*?

West. Health to my Soueraigne, and new happinesse
Added to that, that I am to deliuer.
Prince *Iohn*, your Sonne, doth kisse your Graces Hand:
Mowbray, the Bishop, *Scroope*, *Hastings*, and all,
Are brought to the Correction of your Law.
There is not now a Rebels Sword vnsheath'd,
But Peace puts forth her Oliue euery where:
The manner how this Action hath beene borne,
Here (at more leysure) may your Highnesse reade,
With euery course, in his particular.

King. O *Westmerland*, thou art a Summer Bird,
Which euer in the haunch of Winter sings
The lifting vp of day.

Enter Harcourt.

Looke, heere's more newes.

Harc. From Enemies, Heauen keepe your Maiestie:
And when they stand against you, may they fall,
As those that I am come to tell you of.
The Earle *Northumberland*, and the Lord *Bardolfe*,
With a great Power of English, and of Scots,
Are by the Sherife of Yorkeshire ouerthrowne:
The manner, and true order of the fight,
This Packet (please it you) containes at large.

King. And wherefore should these good newes
Make me sicke?
Will Fortune neuer come with both hands full,
But write her faire words still in foulest Letters?
Shee eyther giues a Stomack, and no Foode,
(Such are the poore, in health) or else a Feast,
And takes away the Stomack (such are the Rich,
That haue aboundance, and enioy it not.)
I should reioyce now, at this happy newes,
And now my Sight fayles, and my Braine is giddie.
O me, come neere me, now I am much ill.

Glo. Comfort your Maiestie.

Cla. Oh, my Royall Father.

West. My Soueraigne Lord, cheare vp your selfe, looke vp.

War. Be patient (Princes) you doe know, these Fits
Are with his Highnesse very ordinarie.
Stand from him, giue him ayre:
Hee'le straight be well.

Clar. No, no, hee cannot long hold out: these pangs,
Th' incessant care, and labour of his Minde,
Hath wrought the Mure, that should confine it in,
So thinne, that Life lookes through, and will breake out.

Glo. The people feare me: for they doe obserue
Vnfather'd Heires, and loathly Births of Nature:
The Seasons change their manners, as the Yeere
Had found some Moneths asleepe, and leap'd them ouer.

Clar. The Riuer hath thrice flow'd, no ebbe betweene:
And the old folke (Times doting Chronicles)
Say it did so, a little time before
That our great Grand-sire *Edward* sick'd, and dy'de.

War. Speake

The second Part of King Henry the Fourth.

War. Speake lower (Princes) for the King recouers.

Glo. This Apoplexie will (certaine) be his end.

King. I pray you take me vp, and beare me hence
Into some other Chamber: softly 'pray.
Let there be no noyse made (my gentle friends)
Vnlesse some dull and fauourable hand
Will whisper Musicke to my wearie Spirit.

War. Call for the Musicke in the other Roome.

King. Set me the Crowne vpon my Pillow here.

Clar. His eye is hollow, and hee changes much.

War. Lesse noyse, lesse noyse.

Enter Prince Henry.

P.Hen. Who saw the Duke of Clarence?

Clar. I am here (Brother) full of heauinesse.

P.Hen. How now? Raine within doores, and none abroad? How doth the King?

Glo. Exceeding ill.

P.Hen. Heard hee the good newes yet?
Tell it him.

Glo. Hee alter'd much, vpon the hearing it.

P.Hen. If hee be sicke with Ioy,
Hee'le recouer without Physicke.

War. Not so much noyse (my Lords)
Sweet Prince speake lowe.
The King, your Father, is dispos'd to sleepe.

Clar. Let vs with-draw into the other Roome.

War. Wil't please your Grace to goe along with vs?

P.Hen. No: I will sit, and watch here, by the King.
Why doth the Crowne lye there, vpon his Pillow,
Being so troublesome a Bed-fellow?
O pollish'd Perturbation! Golden Care!
That keep'st the Ports of Slumber open wide,
To many a watchfull Night: sleepe with it now,
Yet not so sound, and halfe so deepely sweete,
As hee whose Brow (with homely Biggen bound)
Snores out the Watch of Night. O Maiestie!
When thou do'st pinch thy Bearer, thou do'st sit
Like a rich Armor, worne in heat of day,
That scald'st with safetie: by his Gates of breath,
There lyes a dowlney feather, which stirres not:
Did hee suspire, that light and weightlesse dowlne
Perforce must moue. My gracious Lord, my Father,
This sleepe is sound indeede: this is a sleepe,
That from this Golden Rigoll hath diuorc'd
So many English Kings. Thy due, from me,
Is Teares, and heauie Sorrowes of the Blood,
Which Nature, Loue, and filiall tendernesse,
Shall (O deare Father) pay thee plenteously.
My due, from thee, is this Imperiall Crowne,
Which (as immediate from thy Place, and Blood)
Deriues it selfe to me. Loe, heere it sits,
Which Heauen shall guard:
And put the worlds whole strength into one gyant Arme,
It shall not force this Lineall Honor from me.
This, from thee, will I to mine leaue,
As 'tis left to me. *Exit.*

Enter Warwicke, Gloucester, Clarence.

King. Warwicke, Gloucester, Clarence.

Clar. Doth the King call?

War. What would your Maiestie? how fares your Grace?

King. Why did you leaue me here alone (my Lords?)

Cla. We left the Prince (my Brother) here (my Liege)
Who vndertooke to sit and watch by you.

King. The Prince of Wales? where is hee? let mee see him.

War. This doore is open, hee is gone this way.

Glo. Hee came not through the Chamber where wee stayd.

King. Where is the Crowne? who tooke it from my Pillow?

War. When wee with-drew (my Liege) wee left it heere.

King. The Prince hath ta'ne it hence:
Goe seeke him out.
Is hee so hastie, that hee doth suppose
My sleepe, my death? Finde him (my Lord of Warwick)
Chide him hither: this part of his conioynes
With my disease, and helpes to end me.
See Sonnes, what things you are:
How quickly Nature falls into reuolt,
When Gold becomes her Obiect?
For this, the foolish ouer-carefull Fathers
Haue broke their sleepes with thoughts,
Their braines with care, their bones with industry.
For this, they haue ingrossed and pyl'd vp
The canker'd heepes of strange-atchieued Gold:
For this, they haue beene thoughtfull, to inuest
Their Sonnes with Arts, and Martiall Exercises:
When, like the Bee, culling from euery flower
The vertuous Sweetes, our Thighes packt with Waxe,
Our Mouthes with Honey, wee bring it to the Hiue:
And like the Bees, are murthered for our paines.
This bitter taste yeelds his engrossements,
To the ending Father.

Enter Warwicke.

Now, where is hee, that will not stay so long,
Till his Friend Sicknesse hath determin'd me?

War. My Lord, I found the Prince in the next Roome,
Washing with kindly Teares his gentle Cheekes,
With such a deepe demeanure, in great sorrow,
That Tyranny, which neuer quafft but blood,
Would (by beholding him) haue wash'd his Knife
With gentle eye-drops. Hee is comming hither.

King. But wherefore did hee take away the Crowne?

Enter Prince Henry.

Loe, where hee comes. Come hither to me (*Harry.*)
Depart the Chamber, leaue vs heere alone. *Exit.*

P.Hen. I neuer thought to heare you speake againe.

King. Thy wish was Father (*Harry*) to that thought:
I stay too long by thee, I wearie thee.
Do'st thou so hunger for my emptie Chayre,
That thou wilt needes inuest thee with mine Honors,
Before thy howre be ripe? O foolish Youth!
Thou seek'st the Greatnesse, that will ouer-whelme thee.
Stay but a little: for my Cloud of Dignitie
Is held from falling, with so weake a winde,
That it will quickly drop: my Day is dimme.
Thou hast stolne that, which after some few howres
Were thine, without offence: and at my death
Thou hast seal'd vp my expectation.
Thy Life did manifest, thou lou'dst me not,
And thou wilt haue me dye assur'd of it.
Thou hid'st a thousand Daggers in thy thoughts,
Which thou hast whetted on thy stonie heart,
To stab at halfe an howre of my Life.
What? canst thou not forbeare me halfe an howre?

Then

Then get thee gone, and digge my graue thy selfe,
And bid the merry Bels ring to thy eare
That thou art Crowned, not that I am dead.
Let all the Teares, that should bedew my Hearse
Be drops of Balme, to sanctifie thy head:
Onely compound me with forgotten dust.
Giue that, which gaue thee life, vnto the Wormes:
Plucke downe my Officers, breake my Decrees;
For now a time is come, to mocke at Forme.
Henry the fift is Crown'd: Vp Vanity,
Downe Royall State: All you sage Counsailors, hence:
And to the English Court, assemble now
From eu'ry Region, Apes of Idlenesse.
Now neighbor-Confines, purge you of your Scum:
Haue you a Ruffian that swill sweare? drinke? dance?
Reuell the night? Rob? Murder? and commit
The oldest sinnes, the newest kinde of wayes?
Be happy, he will trouble you no more:
England, shall double gill'd, his trebble guilt.
England, shall giue him Office, Honor, Might:
For the Fift *Harry*, from curb'd License pluckes
The muzzle of Restraint; and the wilde Dogge
Shall flesh his tooth in euery Innocent.
O my poore Kingdome (sicke, with ciuill blowes)
When that my Care could not with-hold thy Ryots,
What wilt thou do, when Ryot is thy Care?
O, thou wilt be a Wildernesse againe,
Peopled with Wolues (thy old Inhabitants.)

  Prince. O pardon me (my Liege)
But for my Teares,
The most Impediments vnto my Speech,
I had fore-stall'd this deere, and deepe Rebuke,
Ere you (with greefe) had spoke, and I had heard
The course of it so farre. There is your Crowne,
And he that weares the Crowne immortally,
Long guard it yours. If I affect it more,
Then as your Honour, and as your Renowne,
Let me no more from this Obedience rise,
Which my most true, and inward duteous Spirit
Teacheth this prostrate, and exteriour bending.
Heauen witnesse with me, when I heere came in,
And found no course of breath within your Maiestie,
How cold it strooke my heart. If I do faine,
O let me, in my present wildenesse, dye,
And neuer liue, to shew th'incredulous World,
The Noble change that I haue purposed.
Comming to looke on you, thinking you dead,
(And dead almost (my Liege) to thinke you were)
I spake vnto the Crowne (as hauing sense)
And thus vpbraided it. The Care on thee depending,
Hath fed vpon the body of my Father,
Therefore, thou best of Gold, art worst of Gold.
Other, lesse fine in Charract, is more precious,
Preseruing life, in Med'cine potable:
But thou, most Fine, most Honour'd, most Renown'd,
Hast eate the Bearer vp.
Thus (my Royall Liege)
Accusing it, I put it on my Head,
To try with it (as with an Enemie,
That had before my face murdred my Father)
The Quarrell of a true Inheritor.
But if it did infect my blood with Ioy,
Or swell my Thoughts, to any straine of Pride,
If any Rebell, or vaine spirit of mine,
Did, with the least Affection of a Welcome,
Giue entertainment to the might of it,

Let heauen, for euer, keepe it from my head,
And make me, as the poorest Vassaile is,
That doth with awe, and terror kneele to it.

  King. O my Sonne!
Heauen put it in thy minde to take it hence,
That thou might'st ioyne the more, thy Fathers loue,
Pleading so wisely, in excuse of it.
Come hither *Harrie*, sit thou by my bedde,
And heare (I thinke, the very latest Counsell
That euer I shall breath: Heauen knowes, my Sonne)
By what by-pathes, and indirect crook'd-wayes
I met this Crowne: and I my selfe know well
How troublesome it sate vpon my head.
To thee, it shall descend with better Quiet,
Better Opinion, better Confirmation:
For all the soyle of the Atchieuement goes
With me, into the Earth. It seem'd in mee,
But as an Honour snatch'd with boystrous hand,
And I had many liuing, to vpbraide
My gaine of it, by their Assistances,
Which dayly grew to Quarrell, and to Blood-shed,
Wounding supposed Peace.
All these bold Feares,
Thou seest (with perill) I haue answered:
For all my Reigne, hath beene but as a Scene
Acting that argument. And now my death
Changes the Moode: For what in me, was purchas'd,
Falles vpon thee, in a more Fayrer sort.
So thou, the Garland wear'st successiuely.
Yet, though thou stand'st more sure, then I could do,
Thou art not firme enough, since greefes are greene:
And all thy Friends, which thou must make thy Friends
Haue but their stings, and teeth, newly tak'n out,
By whose fell working, I was first aduanc'd,
And by whose power, I well might lodge a Feare
To be againe displac'd. Which to auoyd,
I cut them off: and had a purpose now
To leade out many to the Holy Land;
Least rest, and lying still, might make them looke
Too neere vnto my State.
Therefore (my *Harrie*)
Be it thy course to basie giddy Mindes
With Forraigne Quarrels: that Action hence borne out,
May waste the memory of the former dayes.
More would I, but my Lungs are wasted so,
That strength of Speech is vtterly deni'de mee.
How I came by the Crowne, O heauen forgiue:
And grant it may, with thee, in true peace liue.

  Prince. My gracious Liege:
You wonne it, wore it: kept it, gaue it me,
Then plaine and right must my possession be;
Which I, with more, then with a Common paine,
'Gainst all the World, will rightfully maintaine.

Enter Lord Iohn of Lancaster,
and Warwicke.

  King. Looke, looke,
Heere comes my *Iohn* of Lancaster:
  Iohn. Health, Peace, and Happinesse,
To my Royall Father.
  King. Thou bring'st me happinesse and Peace
(Sonne *Iohn*:
But health (alacke) with youthfull wings is flowne
From this bare, wither'd Trunke. Vpon thy sight
My worldly businesse makes a period.

Where

Where is my Lord of Warwicke?

Prin. My Lord of Warwicke.

King. Doth any name particular, belong
Vnto the Lodging, where I first did swoon'd?

War. 'Tis call'd *Ierusalem*, my Noble Lord.

King. Laud be to heauen:
Euen there my life must end.
It hath beene prophesi'de to me many yeares,
I should not dye, but in *Ierusalem*:
Which (vainly) I suppos'd the Holy-Land.
But beare me to that Chamber, there Ile lye:
In that *Ierusalem*, shall *Harry* dye. *Exeunt.*

Actus Quintus. Scœna Prima.

Enter Shallow, Silence, Falstaffe, Bardolfe, Page, and Dauie.

Shal. By Cocke and Pye, you shall not away to night. What *Dauy*, I say.

Fal. You must excuse me, M. *Robert Shallow*.

Shal. I will not excuse you: you shall not be excused. Excuses shall not be admitted: there is no excuse shall serue: you shall not be excus'd.
Why *Dauie*.

Dauie. Heere sir.

Shal. Dauy, Dauy, Dauy, let me see *(Dauy)* let me see: *William* Cooke, bid him come hither. Sir *Iohn*, you shal not be excus'd.

Dauy. Marry sir, thus: those Precepts cannot bee seru'd: and againe sir, shall we sowe the head-land with Wheate?

Shal. With red Wheate *Dauy*. But for *William* Cook: are there no yong Pigeons?

Dauy. Yes Sir.
Heere is now the Smithes note, for Shooing,
And Plough-Irons.

Shal. Let it be cast, and payde: Sir *Iohn*, you shall not be excus'd.

Dauy. Sir, a new linke to the Bucket must needes bee had: And Sir, doe you meane to stoppe any of *Williams* Wages, about the Sacke he lost the other day, at *Hinckley* Fayre?

Shal. He shall answer it:
Some Pigeons *Dauy*, a couple of short-legg'd Hennes: a ioynt of Mutton, and any pretty little tine Kickshawes, tell *William* Cooke.

Dauy. Doth the man of Warre, stay all night sir?

Shal. Yes *Dauy*:
I will vse him well. A Friend i'th Court, is better then a penny in purse. Vse his men well *Dauy*, for they are arrant Knaues, and will backe-bite.

Dauy. No worse then they are bitten. sir: For they haue maruellous fowle linnen.

Shallow. Well conceited *Dauy*: about thy Businesse, *Dauy*.

Dauy. I beseech you sir,
To countenance *William Visor* of Woncot, against *Clement Perkes* of the hill.

Shal. There are many Complaints *Dauy*, against that *Visor*, that *Visor* is an arrant Knaue, on my knowledge.

Dauy. I graunt your Worship, that he is a knaue Sir:) But yet heauen forbid Sir, but a Knaue should haue some Countenance, at his Friends request. An honest man sir, is able to speake for himselfe, when a Knaue is not. I haue seru'd your Worshippe truely sir, these eight yeares: and if I cannot once or twice in a Quarter beare out a knaue, against an honest man, I haue but a very litle credite with your Worshippe. The Knaue is mine honest Friend Sir, therefore I beseech your Worship, let him bee Countenanc'd.

Shal. Go too,
I say he shall haue no wrong: Looke about *Dauy*.
Where are you Sir *Iohn*? Come, off with your Boots.
Giue me your hand M. *Bardolfe.*

Bard. I am glad to see your Worship.

Shal. I thanke thee, with all my heart, kinde Master *Bardolfe*: and welcome my tall Fellow:
Come Sir *Iohn*.

Falstaffe. Ile follow you, good Master *Robert Shallow*. *Bardolfe*, looke to our Horsses. If I were saw'de into Quantities, I should make foure dozen of such bearded Hermites staues, as Master *Shallow*. It is a wonderfull thing to see the semblable Coherence of his mens spirits, and his: They, by obseruing of him, do beare themselues like foolish Iustices: Hee, by conuersing with them, is turn'd into a Iustice-like Seruingman. Their spirits are so married in Coniunction, with the participation of Society, that they flocke together in consent, like so many Wilde-Geese. If I had a suite to Mayster *Shallow*, I would humour his men, with the imputation of beeing neere their Mayster. If to his Men, I would currie with Maister *Shallow*, that no man could better command his Seruants. It is certaine, that either wise bearing, or ignorant Carriage is caught, as men take diseases, one of another: therefore, let men take heede of their Companie. I will deuise matter enough out of this *Shallow*, to keepe Prince *Harry* in continuall Laughter, the wearing out of sixe Fashions (which is foure Tearmes) or two Actions, and he shall laugh with *Interuallums*. O it is much that a Lye (with a slight Oath) and a iest (with a sadde brow) will doe, with a Fellow, that neuer had the Ache in his shoulders. O you shall see him laugh, till his Face be like a wet Cloake, ill laid vp.

Shal. Sir *Iohn*.

Falst. I come Master *Shallow*, I come Master *Shallow*. *Exeunt*

Scena Secunda.

Enter the Earle of Warwicke, and the Lord Chiefe Iustice.

Warwicke. How now, my Lord Chiefe Iustice, whether away?

Ch. Iust. How doth the King?

Warw. Exceeding well: his Cares
Are now, all ended.

Ch. Iust. I hope, not dead.

Warw. Hee's walk'd the way of Nature,
And to our purposes, he liues no more.

Ch. Iust. I would his Maiesty had call'd me with him,
The seruice, that I truly did his life,
Hath left me open to all iniuries.

War. Indeed I thinke the yong King loues you not.
Ch. Iust. I know he doth not, and do arme my selfe
To welcome the condition of the Time,
Which cannot looke more hideously vpon me,
Then I haue drawne it in my fantasie.

Enter Iohn of Lancaster, Gloucester, and Clarence.

War. Heere come the heauy Issue of dead *Harrie*:
O, that the liuing *Harrie* had the temper
Of him, the worst of these three Gentlemen:
How many Nobles then, should hold their places,
That must strike saile, to Spirits of vilde sort?
Ch. Iust. Alas, I feare, all will be ouer-turn'd.
Iohn. Good morrow Cosin *Warwick*, good morrow.
Glou. Cla. Good morrow, Cosin.
Iohn. We meet, like men, that had forgot to speake.
War. We do remember: but our Argument
Is all too heauy, to admit much talke.
Ioh. Well: Peace be with him, that hath made vs heauy
Ch. Iust. Peace be with vs, least we be heauier.
Glou. O, good my Lord, you haue lost a friend indeed:
And I dare sweare, you borrow not that face
Of seeming sorrow, it is sure your owne.
Iohn. Though no man be assur'd what grace to finde,
You stand in coldest expectation.
I am the sorrier, would 'twere otherwise.
Cla. Wel, you must now speake Sir *Iohn Falstaffe* faire,
Which swimmes against your streame of Quality.
Ch. Iust. Sweet Princes: what I did, I did in Honor,
Led by th' Imperiall Conduct of my Soule,
And neuer shall you see, that I will begge
A ragged, and fore-stall'd Remission.
If Troth, and vpright Innocency fayle me,
Ile to the King (my Master) that is dead,
And tell him, who hath sent me after him.
War. Heere comes the Prince.

Enter Prince Henrie.

Ch. Iust. Good morrow: and heauen saue your Maiesty
Prince. This new, and gorgeous Garment, Maiesty,
Sits not so easie on me, as you thinke.
Brothers, you mixe your Sadnesse with some Feare:
This is the English, not the Turkish Court:
Not *Amurath*, an *Amurah* succeeds,
But *Harry*, *Harry*: Yet be sad (good Brothers)
For (to speake truth) it very well becomes you:
Sorrow, so Royally in you appeares,
That I will deeply put the Fashion on,
And weare it in my heart. Why then be sad,
But entertaine no more of it (good Brothers)
Then a ioynt burthen, laid vpon vs all.
For me, by Heauen (I bid you be assur'd)
Ile be your Father, and your Brother too:
Let me but beare your Loue, Ile beare your Cares;
But weepe that *Harrie*'s dead, and so will I.
But *Harry* liues, that shall conuert those Teares
By number, into houres of Happinesse.
Iohn, &c. We hope no other from your Maiesty.
Prin. You all looke strangely on me: and you most,
You are (I thinke) assur'd, I loue you not.
Ch. Iust. I am assur'd (if I be measur'd rightly)
Your Maiesty hath no iust cause to hate mee.
Pr. No? How might a Prince of my great hopes forget
So great Indignities you laid vpon me?
What? Rate? Rebuke? and roughly send to Prison
Th' immediate Heire of England? Was this easie?
May this be wash'd in *Lethe*, and forgotten?
Ch. Iust. I then did vse the Person of your Father:
The Image of his power, lay then in me,
And in th' administration of his Law,
Whiles I was busie for the Commonwealth,
Your Highnesse pleased to forget my place,
The Maiesty, and power of Law, and Iustice,
The Image of the King, whom I presented,
And strooke me in my very Seate of Iudgement:
Whereon (as an Offender to your Father)
I gaue bold way to my Authority,
And did commit you. If the deed were ill,
Be you contented, wearing now the Garland,
To haue a Sonne, set your Decrees at naught?
To plucke downe Iustice from your awefull Bench?
To trip the course of Law, and blunt the Sword
That guards the peace, and safety of your Person?
Nay more, to spurne at your most Royall Image,
And mocke your workings, in a Second body?
Question your Royall Thoughts, make the case yours:
Be now the Father, and propose a Sonne:
Heare your owne dignity so much prophan'd,
See your most dreadfull Lawes, so loosely slighted;
Behold your selfe, so by a Sonne disdained:
And then imagine me, taking you part,
And in your power, soft silencing your Sonne:
After this cold consideance, sentence me;
And, as you are a King, speake in your State,
What I haue done, that misbecame my place,
My person, or my Lieges Soueraigntie.
Prin. You are right Iustice, and you weigh this well:
Therefore still beare the Ballance, and the Sword:
And I do wish your Honors may encrease,
Till you do liue, to see a Sonne of mine
Offend you, and obey you, as I did.
So shall I liue, to speake my Fathers words:
Happy am I, that haue a man so bold,
That dares do Iustice, on my proper Sonne;
And no lesse happy, hauing such a Sonne,
That would deliuer vp his Greatnesse so,
Into the hands of Iustice. You did commit me:
For which, I do commit into your hand,
Th' vnstained Sword that you haue vs'd to beare:
With this Remembrance; That you vse the same
With the like bold, iust, and impartiall spirit
As you haue done 'gainst me. There is my hand,
You shall be as a Father, to my Youth:
My voice shall sound, as you do prompt mine eare,
And I will stoope, and humble my Intents,
To your well-practis'd, wise Directions.
And Princes all, beleeue me, I beseech you:
My Father is gone wilde into his Graue,
(For in his Tombe, lye my Affections)
And with his Spirits, sadly I suruiue,
To mocke the expectation of the World;
To frustrate Prophesies, and to race out
Rotten Opinion, who hath writ me downe
After my seeming. The Tide of Blood in me,
Hath prowdly flow'd in Vanity, till now.
Now doth it turne, and ebbe backe to the Sea,
Where it shall mingle with the state of Floods,
And flow henceforth in formall Maiesty.
Now call we our High Court of Parliament,
And let vs choose such Limbes of Noble Counsaile,

That

That the great Body of our State may go
In equall ranke, with the best gouern'd Nation,
That Warre, or Peace, or both at once may be
As things acquainted and familiar to vs,
In which you (Father) shall haue formost hand.
Our Coronation done, we will accite
(As I before remembred) all our State,
And heauen (consigning to my good intents)
No Prince, nor Peere, shall haue iust cause to say,
Heauen shorten *Harries* happy life, one day.   *Exeunt.*

Scena Tertia.

Enter Falstaffe, Shallow, Silence, Bardolfe,
Page, and Pistoll.

Shal. Nay, you shall see mine Orchard: where, in an Arbor we will eate a last yeares Pippin of my owne graffing, with a dish of Carrawayes, and so forth. (Come Cosin *Silence*, and then to bed.

Fal. You haue heere a goodly dwelling, and a rich.

Shal. Barren, barren, barren : Beggers all, beggers all Sir *Iohn*: Marry, good ayre. Spread *Dauy*, spread *Dauie*: Well said *Dauie*.

Falst. This *Dauie* serues you for good vses: he is your Seruingman, and your Husband.

Shal. A good Varlet, a good Varlet, a very good Varlet, Sir *Iohn*: I haue drunke too much Sacke at Supper. A good Varlet. Now sit downe, now sit downe : Come Cosin.

Sil. Ah sirra (quoth-a) we shall doe nothing but eate, and make good cheere, and praise heauen for the merrie yeere: when flesh is cheape, and Females deere, and lustie Lads rome heere, and there : so merrily, and euer among so merrily.

Fal. There's a merry heart, good M. *Silence*, Ile giue you a health for that anon.

Shal. Good M. *Bardolfe*: some wine, *Dauie*.

Da. Sweet sir, sit: Ile be with you anon : most sweete sir, sit. Master Page, good M. Page, sit: Proface. What you want in meate, wee'l haue in drinke : but you beare, the heart's all.

Shal. Be merry M. *Bardolfe*, and my little Souldiour there, be merry.

Sil. Be merry, be merry, my wife ha's all.
For women are Shrewes, both short, and tall :
'Tis merry in Hall, when Beards wagge all ;
And welcome merry Shrouetide. Be merry, be merry.

Fal. I did not thinke M. *Silence* had bin a man of this Mettle.

Sil. Who I? I haue beene merry twice and once, ere now.

Dauy. There is a dish of Lether-coats for you.

Shal. Dauie.

Dau. Your Worship: Ile be with you straight, A cup of Wine, sir?

Sil. A Cup of Wine, that's briske and fine, & drinke vnto the Leman mine: and a merry heart liues long-a.

Fal. Well said, M. *Silence*.

Sil. If we shall be merry, now comes in the sweete of the night.

Fal. Health, and long life to you, M. *Silence*.

Sil. Fill the Cuppe, and let it come. Ile pledge you a mile to the bottome.

Shal. Honest *Bardolfe*, welcome : If thou want'st any thing, and wilt not call, beshrew thy heart. Welcome my little tyne theefe, and welcome indeed too : Ile drinke to M. *Bardolfe*, and to all the Cauileroes about London.

Dau. I hope to see London, once ere I die.

Bar. If I might see you there, *Dauie*.

Shal. You'l cracke a quart together? Ha, will you not M. *Bardolfe*?

Bar. Yes Sir, in a pottle pot.

Shal. I thanke thee : the knaue will sticke by thee, I can assure thee that. He will not out, he is true bred.

Bar. And Ile sticke by him, sir.

Shal. Why there spoke a King: lack nothing, be merry. Looke, who's at doore there, ho : who knockes?

Fal. Why now you haue done me right.

Sil. Do me right, and dub me Knight, *Samingo*. Is't not so?

Fal. 'Tis so.

Sil. Is't so? Why then say an old man can do somwhat.

Dau. If it please your Worshippe, there's one *Pistoll* come from the Court with newes.

Fal. From the Court? Let him come in.

Enter Pistoll.

How now Pistoll?

Pist. Sir *Iohn*, 'saue you sir.

Fal. What winde blew you hither, Pistoll?

Pist. Not the ill winde which blowes none to good, sweet Knight : Thou art now one of the greatest men in the Realme.

Sil. Indeed, I thinke he bee, but Goodman *Puffe* of Batson.

Pist. Puffe? puffe in thy teeth, most recreant Coward base. Sir *Iohn*, I am thy Pistoll, and thy Friend : helter skelter haue I rode to thee, and tydings do I bring, and luckie ioyes, and golden Times, and happie Newes of price.

Fal. I prethee now deliuer them, like a man of this World.

Pist. A footra for the World, and Worldlings base, I speake of Affrica, and Golden ioyes.

Fal. O base Assyrian Knight, what is thy newes ? Let King *Couitha* know the truth thereof.

Sil. And Robin-hood, Scarlet, and Iohn.

Pist. Shall dunghill Curres confront the *Hellicons*?
And shall good newes be baffel'd?
Then Pistoll lay thy head in Furies lappe.

Shal. Honest Gentleman,
I know not your breeding.

Pist. Why then Lament therefore.

Shal. Giue me pardon, Sir.
If sir, you come with news from the Court, I take it, there is but two wayes, either to vtter them, or to conceale them. I am Sir, vnder the King, in some Authority.

Pist. Vnder which King?
Bezonian, speake, or dye.

Shal. Vnder King *Harry*.

Pist. *Harry* the Fourth? or Fift ?

Shal. *Harry* the Fourth.

Pist. A footra for thine Office.
Sir *Iohn*, thy tender Lamb-kinne, now is King:
Harry the Fift's the man, I speake the truth.
When Pistoll lyes, do this, and figge-me, like
The bragging Spaniard.

                                                                                                Fal.

Fal. What, is the old King dead?
Pist. As naile in doore.
The things I speake, are iust.
Fal. Away *Bardolfe*, Sadle my Horse,
Master *Robert Shallow*, choose what Office thou wilt
In the Land, 'tis thine. *Pistol*, I will double charge thee
With Dignities.
Bard. O ioyfull day:
I would not take a Knighthood for my Fortune.
Pist. What? I do bring good newes.
Fal. Carrie Master *Silence* to bed: Master *Shallow*, my
Lord *Shallow*, be what thou wilt, I am Fortunes Steward.
Get on thy Boots, wee'l ride all night. Oh sweet *Pistoll*:
Away *Bardolfe*: Come *Pistoll*, vtter more to mee: and
withall deuise something to do thy selfe good. Boote,
boote Master *Shallow*, I know the young King is sick for
mee. Let vs take any mans Horsses: The Lawes of England are at my command'ment. Happie are they, which
haue beene my Friendes: and woe vnto my Lord Chiefe
Iustice.
Pist. Let Vultures vil'de seize on his Lungs also:
Where is the life that late I led, say they?
Why heere it is, welcome those pleasant dayes. *Exeunt*

Scena Quarta.

Enter Hostesse Quickly, Dol Teare-sheete, and Beadles.

Hostesse. No, thou arrant knaue: I would I might dy,
that I might haue thee hang'd: Thou hast drawne my
shoulder out of ioynt.
Off. The Constables haue deliuer'd her ouer to mee:
and shee shall haue Whipping cheere enough, I warrant
her. There hath beene a man or two (lately) kill'd about
her.
Dol. Nut-hooke, nut-hooke, you Lye: Come on, Ile
tell thee what, thou damn'd Tripe-visag'd Rascall, if the
Childe I now go with, do miscarrie, thou had'st better
thou had'st strooke thy Mother, thou Paper-fac'd Villaine.
Host. O that Sir *Iohn* were come, hee would make
this a bloody day to some body. But I would the Fruite
of her Wombe might miscarry.
Officer. If it do, you shall haue a dozen of Cushions
againe, you haue but eleuen now. Come, I charge you
both go with me: for the man is dead, that you and Pistoll beate among you.
Dol. Ile tell thee what, thou thin man in a Censor; I
will haue you as soundly swindg'd for this, you blew-Bottel'd Rogue: you filthy famish'd Correctioner, if you
be not swing'd, Ile forsweare halfe Kirtles.
Off. Come, come, you shee-Knight-arrant, come.
Host. O, that right should thus o'recome might. Wel
of sufferance, comes ease.
Dol. Come you Rogue, come:
Bring me to a Iustice.
Host. Yes, come you staru'd Blood-hound.
Dol. Goodman death, goodman Bones.
Host. Thou Anatomy, thou.
Dol. Come you thinne Thing:
Come you Rascall.
Off. Very well. *Exeunt.*

Scena Quinta.

Enter two Groomes.

1. *Groo.* More Rushes, more Rushes.
2. *Groo.* The Trumpets haue sounded twice.
1. *Groo.* It will be two of the Clocke, ere they come
from the Coronation. *Exit Groo.*

Enter Falstaffe, Shallow, Pistoll, Bardolfe, and Page.

Falstaffe. Stand heere by me, M. *Robert Shallow*, I will
make the King do you Grace. I will leere vpon him, as
he comes by: and do but marke the countenance that hee
will giue me.
Pistol. Blesse thy Lungs good Knight.
Falst. Come heere *Pistol*, stand behind me. O if I had
had time to haue made new Liueries, I would haue bestowed the thousand pound I borrowed of you. But it is
no matter, this poore shew doth better: this doth inferre
the zeale I had to see him.
Shal. It doth so.
Falst. It shewes my earnestnesse in affection.
Pist. It doth so.
Fal. My deuotion.
Pist. It doth, it doth, it doth.
Fal. As it were, to ride day and night,
And not to deliberate, not to remember,
Not to haue patience to shift me.
Shal. It is most certaine.
Fal. But to stand stained with Trauaile, and sweating
with desire to see him, thinking of nothing else, putting
all affayres in obliuion, as if there were nothing els to bee
done, but to see him.
Pist. 'Tis *semper idem*: for *obsque hoc nihil est.* 'Tis all
in euery part.
Shal. 'Tis so indeed.
Pist. My Knight, I will enflame thy Noble Liuer, and
make thee rage. Thy *Dol*, and *Helen* of thy noble thoghts
is in base Durance, and contagious prison: Hall'd thither by most Mechanicall and durty hand. Rowze vppe
Reuenge from Ebon den, with fell *Alecto's* Snake, for
Dol is in. Pistol, speakes nought but troth.
Fal. I will deliuer her.
Pistol. There roar'd the Sea: and Trumpet Clangour
sounds.

*The Trumpets sound. Enter King Henrie the
Fift, Brothers, Lord Chiefe
Iustice.*

Falst. Saue thy Grace, King *Hall*, my Royall *Hal*.
Pist. The heauens thee guard, and keepe, most royall
Impe of Fame.
Fal. 'Saue thee my sweet Boy.
King. My Lord Chiefe Iustice, speake to that vaine
man.
Ch.Iust. Haue you your wits?
Know you what 'tis you speake?
Falst. My King, my Ioue; I speake to thee, my heart.
King. I know thee not, old man: Fall to thy Prayers:
How ill white haires become a Foole, and Iester?

I haue

I haue long dream'd of such a kinde of man,
So surfeit-swell'd, so old, and so prophane:
But being awake, I do despise my dreame.
Make lesse thy body (hence) and more thy Grace,
Leaue gourmandizing; Know the Graue doth gape
For thee, thrice wider then for other men.
Reply not to me, with a Foole-borne Iest,
Presume not, that I am the thing I was,
For heauen doth know (so shall the world perceiue)
That I haue turn'd away my former Selfe,
So will I those that kept me Companie.
When thou dost heare I am, as I haue bin,
Approach me, and thou shalt be as thou was't
The Tutor and the Feeder of my Riots:
Till then, I banish thee, on paine of death,
As I haue done the rest of my Misleaders,
Not to come neere our Person, by ten mile.
For competence of life, I will allow you,
That lacke of meanes enforce you not to euill:
And as we heare you do reforme your selues,
We will according to your strength, and qualities,
Giue you aduancement. Be it your charge (my Lord)
To see perform'd the tenure of our word. Set on.
                                                                    Exit King.

  Fal. Master *Shallow*, I owe you a thousand pound.
  Shal. I marry Sir *Iohn*, which I beseech you to let me
haue home with me.
  Fal. That can hardly be, M. *Shallow*, do not you grieue
at this: I shall be sent for in priuate to him: Looke you,
he must seeme thus to the world: feare not your aduancement: I will be the man yet, that shall make you great.

  Shal. I cannot well perceiue how, vnlesse you should
giue me your Doublet, and stuffe me out with Straw. I
beseech you, good Sir *Iohn*, let mee haue fiue hundred of
my thousand.
  Fal. Sir, I will be as good as my word. This that you
heard, was but a colour.
  Shall. A colour I feare, that you will dye, in Sir *Iohn*.
  Fal. Feare no colours, go with me to dinner:
Come Lieutenant *Pistol*, come *Bardolfe*,
I shall be sent for soone at night.
  Ch. Iust. Go carry Sir *Iohn Falstaffe* to the Fleete,
Take all his Company along with him.
  Fal. My Lord, my Lord.
  Ch. Iust. I cannot now speake, I will heare you soone:
Take them away.
  Pist. *Si fortuna me tormento, spera me contento.*
                          Exit. Manet Lancaster and Chiefe Iustice.
  Iohn. I like this faire proceeding of the Kings:
He hath intent his wonted Followers
Shall all be very well prouided for:
But all are banisht, till their conuersations
Appeare more wise, and modest to the world.
  Ch. Iust. And so they are.
  Iohn. The King hath call'd his Parliament,
My Lord.
  Ch. Iust. He hath.
  Iohn. I will lay oddes, that ere this yeere expire,
We beare our Ciuill Swords, and Natiue fire
As farre as France. I heare a Bird so sing,
Whose Musicke (to my thinking) pleas'd the King.
Come, will you hence?
                                                                    Exeunt

FINIS.

EPILOGVE.

FIRST, *my Feare*: then, *my Curtsie*: last, *my Speech*. *My Feare, is your Displeasure*: *My Curtsie, my Dutie*: *And my Speech, to Begge your Pardons*. If you looke for a good Speech now, you vndoe me: For what I haue to say, is of mine owne making: and what (indeed) I should say, will (I doubt) prooue mine owne marring. But to the Purpose, and so to the Venture. Be it knowne to you (as it is very well) I was lately heere in the end of a displeasing Play, to pray your Patience for it, and to promise you a Better: I did meane (indeede) to pay you with this, which if (like an ill Venture) it come vnluckily home, I breake; and you, my gentle Creditors lose. Heere I promist you I would be, and heere I commit my Bodie to your Mercies: Bate me some, and I will pay you some, and (as most Debtors do) promise you infinitely.

If my Tongue cannot entreate you to acquit me: Will you command me to vse my Legges? And yet that were but light payment, to Dance out of your debt: But a good Conscience, will make any possible satisfaction, and so will I. All the Gentlewomen heere, haue forgiuen me, if the Gentlemen will not, then the Gentlemen do not agree with the Gentlewomen, which was neuer seene before, in such an Assembly.

One word more, I beseech you: if you be not too much cloid with Fat Meate, our humble Author will continue the Story (with Sir *Iohn* in it) and make you merry, with faire *Katherine* of *France*: where (for any thing I know) *Falstaffe* shall dye of a sweat, vnlesse already he be kill'd with your hard Opinions: For *Old-Castle* dyed a Martyr, and this is not the man. My Tongue is wearie, when my Legs are too, I will bid you good night; and so kneele downe before you: But (indeed) to pray for the *Queene*.

THE ACTORS NAMES.

RVMOVR the Presentor.
King *Henry* the Fourth.
Prince *Henry*, afterwards Crowned King *Henrie* the Fift.
Prince *Iohn* of Lancaster. ⎫
Humphrey of Gloucester. ⎬ Sonnes to *Henry* the Fourth, & brethren to *Henry* 5.
Thomas of Clarence. ⎭

Northumberland.
The Arch-Byshop of Yorke.
Mowbray.
Hastings.
Lord Bardolfe.
Trauers.
Morton.
Coleuile.
} Opposites against King *Henrie* the Fourth.

Warwicke.
Westmerland.
Surrey.
Gowre.
Harecourt.
Lord Chiefe Iustice.
} Of the Kings Partie.

Pointz.
Falstaffe.
Bardolphe.
Pistoll.
Peto.
Page.
} Irregular Humorists.

Shallow. ⎱ Both Country
Silence. ⎰ Iustices.
Dauie, Seruant to Shallow.
Phang, and Snare, 2. Serieants
Mouldie.
Shadow.
Wart. } Country Soldiers
Feeble.
Bullcalfe.

Drawers
Beadles.
Groomes

Northumberlands Wife.
Percies Widdow.
Hostesse Quickly.
Doll Teare-sheete.
Epilogue.

The Life of Henry the Fift.

Enter Prologue.

O For a Muse of Fire, that would ascend
The brightest Heauen of Inuention:
A Kingdome for a Stage, Princes to Act,
And Monarchs to behold the swelling Scene.
Then should the Warlike Harry, like himselfe,
Assume the Port of Mars, and at his heeles
(Leasht in, like Hounds) should Famine, Sword, and Fire
Crouch for employment. But pardon, Gentles all:
The flat vnraysed Spirits, that hath dar'd,
On this vnworthy Scaffold, to bring forth
So great an Obiect. Can this Cock-Pit hold
The vastie fields of France? Or may we cramme
Within this Wodden O, the very Caskes
That did affright the Ayre at Agincourt?
O pardon: since a crooked Figure may
Attest in little place a Million,
And let vs, Cyphers to this great Accompt,
On your imaginarie Forces worke.
Suppose within the Girdle of these Walls
Are now confin'd two mightie Monarchies,
Whose high, vp-reared, and abutting Fronts,
The perillous narrow Ocean parts asunder.
Peece out our imperfections with your thoughts:
Into a thousand parts diuide one Man,
And make imaginarie Puissance.
Thinke when we talke of Horses, that you see them
Printing their prowd Hoofes i'th' receiuing Earth:
For 'tis your thoughts that now must deck our Kings,
Carry them here and there: Iumping o're Times;
Turning th' accomplishment of many yeeres
Into an Howre-glasse: for the which supplie,
Admit me Chorus to this Historie;
Who Prologue-like, your humble patience pray,
Gently to heare, kindly to iudge our Play. *Exit.*

Actus Primus. Scœna Prima.

Enter the two Bishops of Canterbury and Ely.

Bish. Cant.
MY Lord, Ile tell you, that selfe Bill is vrg'd,
Which in th' eleueth yere of ye last Kings reign
Was like, and had indeed against vs past,
But that the scambling and vnquiet time
Did push it out of farther question.

Bish. Ely. But how my Lord shall we resist it now?

Bish. Cant. It must be thought on: if it passe against vs,
We loose the better halfe of our Possession:
For all the Temporall Lands, which men deuout
By Testament haue giuen to the Church,
Would they strip from vs; being valu'd thus,
As much as would maintaine, to the Kings honor,
Full fifteene Earles, and fifteene hundred Knights,
Six thousand and two hundred good Esquires:
And to reliefe of Lazars, and weake age
Of indigent faint Soules, past corporall toyle,
A hundred Almes-houses, right well supply'd:
And to the Coffers of the King beside,
A thousand pounds by th' yeere. Thus runs the Bill.

Bish. Ely. This would drinke deepe.

Bish. Cant. 'Twould drinke the Cup and all.

Bish. Ely. But what preuention?

Bish. Cant. The King is full of grace, and faire regard.

Bish. Ely. And a true louer of the holy Church.

Bish. Cant. The courses of his youth promis'd it not.
The breath no sooner left his Fathers body,
But that his wildnesse, mortify'd in him,
Seem'd to dye too: yea, at that very moment,
Consideration like an Angell came,
And whipt th' offending Adam out of him;
Leauing his body as a Paradise,
T' inuelop and containe Celestiall Spirits.
Neuer was such a sodaine Scholler made:
Neuer came Reformation in a Flood,
With such a heady currance scowring faults:
Nor neuer Hidra-headed Wilfulnesse
So soone did loose his Seat; and all at once;
As in this King.

Bish. Ely. We are blessed in the Change.

Bish. Cant. Heare him but reason in Diuinitie;
And all-admiring, with an inward wish
You would desire the King were made a Prelate:
Heare him debate of Common-wealth Affaires;
You would say, it hath been all in all his study:
List his discourse of Warre; and you shall heare
A fearefull Battaile rendred you in Musique.

Turne

Turne him to any Cause of Pollicy,
The Gordian Knot of it he will vnloose,
Familiar as his Garter: that when he speakes,
The Ayre, a Charter'd Libertine, is still,
And the mute Wonder lurketh in mens eares,
To steale his sweet and honyed Sentences:
So that the Art and Practique part of Life,
Must be the Mistresse to this Theorique.
Which is a wonder how his Grace should gleane it,
Since his addiction was to Courses vaine,
His Companies vnletter'd, rude, and shallow,
His Houres fill'd vp with Ryots, Banquets, Sports;
And neuer noted in him any studie,
Any retyrement, any sequestration,
From open Haunts and Popularitie.

 B. Ely. The Strawberry growes vnderneath the Nettle,
And holesome Berryes thriue and ripen best,
Neighbour'd by Fruit of baser qualitie:
And so the Prince obscur'd his Contemplation
Vnder the Veyle of Wildnesse, which (no doubt)
Grew like the Summer Grasse, fastest by Night,
Vnseene, yet cressiue in his facultie.

 B. Cant. It must be so; for Miracles are ceast:
And therefore we must needes admit the meanes,
How things are perfected.

 B. Ely. But my good Lord:
How now for mittigation of this Bill,
Vrg'd by the Commons? doth his Maiestie
Incline to it, or no?

 B. Cant. He seemes indifferent:
Or rather swaying more vpon our part,
Then cherishing th'exhibiters against vs:
For I haue made an offer to his Maiestie,
Vpon our Spirituall Conuocation,
And in regard of Causes now in hand,
Which I haue open'd to his Grace at large,
As touching France, to giue a greater Summe,
Then euer at one time the Clergie yet
Did to his Predecessors part withall.

 B. Ely. How did this offer seeme receiu'd, my Lord?

 B. Cant. With good acceptance of his Maiestie:
Saue that there was not time enough to heare,
As I perceiu'd his Grace would faine haue done,
The seuerals and vnhidden passages
Of his true Titles to some certaine Dukedomes,
And generally, to the Crowne and Seat of France,
Deriu'd from *Edward*, his great Grandfather.

 B. Ely. What was th'impediment that broke this off?

 B. Cant. The French Embassador vpon that instant
Crau'd audience; and the howre I thinke is come,
To giue him hearing: Is it foure a Clock?

 B. Ely. It is.

 B. Cant. Then goe we in, to know his Embassie:
Which I could with a ready guesse declare,
Before the Frenchman speake a word of it.

 B. Ely. Ile wait vpon you, and I long to heare it.

Exeunt.

*Enter the King, Humfrey, Bedford, Clarence,
Warwick, Westmerland, and Exeter.*

 King. Where is my gracious Lord of Canterbury?

 Exeter. Not here in presence.

 King. Send for him, good Vnckle.

 Westm. Shall we call in th'Ambassador, my Liege?

 King. Not yet, my Cousin: we would be resolu'd,
Before we heare him, of some things of weight,
That taske our thoughts, concerning vs and France.

Enter two Bishops.

 B. Cant. God and his Angels guard your sacred Throne,
And make you long become it.

 King. Sure we thanke you.
My learned Lord, we pray you to proceed,
And iustly and religiously vnfold,
Why the Law *Salike*, that they haue in France,
Or should or should not barre vs in our Clayme:
And God forbid, my deare and faithfull Lord,
That you should fashion, wrest, or bow your reading,
Or nicely charge your vnderstanding Soule,
With opening Titles miscreate, whose right
Sutes not in natiue colours with the truth:
For God doth know, how many now in health,
Shall drop their blood, in approbation
Of what your reuerence shall incite vs to.
Therefore take heed how you impawne our Person,
How you awake our sleeping Sword of Warre;
We charge you in the Name of God take heed:
For neuer two such Kingdomes did contend,
Without much fall of blood, whose guiltlesse drops
Are euery one, a Woe, a sore Complaint,
'Gainst him, whose wrongs giues edge vnto the Swords,
That makes such waste in briefe mortalitie.
Vnder this Coniuration, speake my Lord:
For we will heare, note, and beleeue in heart,
That what you speake, is in your Conscience washt,
As pure as sinne with Baptisme.

 B. Can. Then heare me gracious Soueraign, & you Peers,
That owe your selues, your liues, and seruices,
To this Imperiall Throne. There is no barre
To make against your Highnesse Clayme to France,
But this which they produce from *Pharamond*,
In terram Salicam Mulieres ne succedant,
No Woman shall succeed in *Salike* Land:
Which *Salike* Land, the French vniustly gloze
To be the Realme of France, and *Pharamond*
The founder of this Law, and Female Barre.
Yet their owne Authors faithfully affirme,
That the Land *Salike* is in Germanie,
Betweene the Flouds of Sala and of Elue:
Where *Charles* the Great hauing subdu'd the Saxons,
There left behind and settled certaine French:
Who holding in disdaine the German Women,
For some dishonest manners of their life,
Establisht then this Law; to wit, No Female
Should be Inheritrix in *Salike* Land:
Which *Salike* (as I said) twixt Elue and Sala,
Is at this day in Germanie, call'd *Meisen*.
Then doth it well appeare, the *Salike* Law
Was not deuised for the Realme of France:
Nor did the French possesse the *Salike* Land,
Vntill foure hundred one and twentie yeeres
After defunction of King *Pharamond*,
Idly suppos'd the founder of this Law,
Who died within the yeere of our Redemption,
Foure hundred twentie six: and *Charles* the Great
Subdu'd the Saxons, and did seat the French
Beyond the Riuer Sala, in the yeere
Eight hundred fiue. Besides, their Writers say,
King *Pepin*, which deposed *Childerike*,
Did as Heire Generall, being descended
Of *Blithild*, which was Daughter to King *Clothair*,
Make Clayme and Title to the Crowne of France.
Hugh Capet also, who vsurpt the Crowne

Of *Charles* the Duke of Loraine, sole Heire male
Of the true Line and Stock of *Charles* the Great:
To find his Title with some shewes of truth,
Though in pure truth it was corrupt and naught,
Conuey'd himselfe as th'Heire to th' Lady *Lingare*,
Daughter to *Charlemaine*, who was the Sonne
To *Lewes* the Emperour, and *Lewes* the Sonne
Of *Charles* the Great: also King *Lewes* the Tenth,
Who was sole Heire to the Vsurper *Capet*,
Could not keepe quiet in his conscience,
Wearing the Crowne of France, 'till satisfied,
That faire Queene *Isabel*, his Grandmother,
Was Lineall of the Lady *Ermengare*,
Daughter to *Charles* the foresaid Duke of Loraine:
By the which Marriage, the Lyne of *Charles* the Great
Was re-vnited to the Crowne of France.
So, that as cleare as is the Summers Sunne,
King *Pepins* Title, and *Hugh Capets* Clayme,
King *Lewes* his satisfaction, all appeare
To hold in Right and Title of the Female:
So doe the Kings of France vnto this day.
Howbeit, they would hold vp this Salique Law,
To barre your Highnesse clayming from the Female,
And rather chuse to hide them in a Net,
Then amply to imbarre their crooked Titles,
Vsurpt from you and your Progenitors.

  King. May I with right and conscience make this claim?
  Bish. Cant. The sinne vpon my head, dread Soueraigne:
For in the Booke of *Numbers* is it writ,
When the man dyes, let the Inheritance
Descend vnto the Daughter. Gracious Lord,
Stand for your owne, vnwind your bloody Flagge,
Looke back into your mightie Ancestors:
Goe my dread Lord, to your great Grandsires Tombe,
From whom you clayme; inuoke his Warlike Spirit,
And your Great Vnckles, *Edward* the Black Prince,
Who on the French ground play'd a Tragedie,
Making defeat on the full Power of France,
Whiles his most mightie Father on a Hill
Stood smiling, to behold his Lyons Whelpe
Forrage in blood of French Nobilitie.
O Noble English, that could entertaine
With halfe their Forces, the full pride of France,
And let another halfe stand laughing by,
All out of worke, and cold for action.

  Bish. Awake remembrance of these valiant dead,
And with your puissant Arme renew their Feats;
You are their Heire, you sit vpon their Throne:
The Blood and Courage that renowned them,
Runs in your Veines: and my thrice-puissant Liege
Is in the very May-Morne of his Youth,
Ripe for Exploits and mightie Enterprises.

  Exe. Your Brother Kings and Monarchs of the Earth
Doe all expect, that you should rowse your selfe,
As did the former Lyons of your Blood.

  West. They know your Grace hath cause, and means, and might;
So hath your Highnesse: neuer King of England
Had Nobles richer, and more loyall Subiects,
Whose hearts haue left their bodyes here in England,
And lye pauillion'd in the fields of France.

  Bish. Can. O let their bodyes follow my deare Liege
With Bloods, and Sword and Fire, to win your Right:
In ayde whereof, we of the Spiritualtie
Will rayse your Highnesse such a mightie Summe,
As neuer did the Clergie at one time
Bring in to any of your Ancestors.

  King. We must not onely arme t'inuade the French,
But lay downe our proportions, to defend
Against the Scot, who will make roade vpon vs,
With all aduantages.

  Bish. Can. They of those Marches, gracious Soueraign,
Shall be a Wall sufficient to defend
Our in-land from the pilfering Borderers.

  King. We do not meane the coursing snatchers onely,
But feare the maine intendment of the Scot,
Who hath been still a giddy neighbour to vs:
For you shall reade, that my great Grandfather
Neuer went with his forces into France,
But that the Scot, on his vnfurnisht Kingdome,
Came pouring like the Tyde into a breach,
With ample and brim fulnesse of his force,
Galling the gleaned Land with hot Assayes,
Girding with grieuous siege, Castles and Townes:
That England being emptie of defence,
Hath shooke and trembled at th'ill neighbourhood.

  B. Can. She hath bin the more fear'd the harm'd, my Liege:
For heare her but exampl'd by her selfe,
When all her Cheualrie hath been in France,
And shee a mourning Widdow of her Nobles,
Shee hath her selfe not onely well defended,
But taken and impounded as a Stray,
The King of Scots: whom shee did send to France,
To fill King *Edwards* fame with prisoner Kings,
And make their Chronicle as rich with prayse,
As is the Owse and bottome of the Sea
With sunken Wrack, and sum-lesse Treasuries.

  Bish. Ely. But there's a saying very old and true,
If that you will France win, then with Scotland first begin.
For once the Eagle (England) being in prey,
To her vnguarded Nest, the Weazell (Scot)
Comes sneaking, and so sucks her Princely Egges,
Playing the Mouse in absence of the Cat,
To tame and hauocke more then she can eate.

  Exet. It followes then, the Cat must stay at home,
Yet that is but a crush'd necessity,
Since we haue lockes to safegard necessaries,
And pretty traps to catch the petty theeues.
While that the Armed hand doth fight abroad,
Th'aduised head defends it selfe at home:
For Gouernment, though high, and low, and lower,
Put into parts, doth keepe in one consent,
Congreeing in a full and natural close,
Like Musicke.

  Cant. Therefore doth heauen diuide
The state of man in diuers functions,
Setting endeuour in continual motion:
To which is fixed as an ayme or butt,
Obedience: for so worke the Hony Bees,
Creatures that by a rule in Nature teach
The Act of Order to a peopled Kingdome.
They haue a King, and Officers of sorts,
Where some like Magistrates correct at home:
Others, like Merchants venter Trade abroad:
Others, like Souldiers armed in their stings,
Make boote vpon the Summers Veluet buddes:
Which pillage, they with merry march bring home
To the Tent-royal of their Emperor:
Who busied in his Maiesties surueyes
The singing Masons building roofes of Gold,
The ciuil Citizens kneading vp the hony;
The poore Mechanicke Porters, crowding in
Their heauy burthens at his narrow gate:

The sad-ey'd Iustice with his surly humme,
Deliuering ore to Executors pale
The lazie yawning Drone: I this inferre,
That many things hauing full reference
To one consent, may worke contrariously,
As many Arrowes loosed seuerall wayes
Come to one marke: as many wayes meet in one towne,
As many fresh streames meet in one salt sea;
As many Lynes close in the Dials center:
So may a thousand actions once a foote,
And in one purpose, and be all well borne
Without defeat. Therefore to France, my Liege,
Diuide your happy England into foure,
Whereof, take you one quarter into France,
And you withall shall make all Gallia shake.
If we with thrice such powers left at home,
Cannot defend our owne doores from the dogge,
Let vs be worried, and our Nation lose
The name of hardinesse and policie.

  King. Call in the Messengers sent from the Dolphin.
Now are we well resolu'd, and by Gods helpe
And yours, the noble sinewes of our power,
France being ours, wee'l bend it to our Awe,
Or breake it all to peeces. Or there wee'l sit,
(Ruling in large and ample Emperie,
Ore France, and all her (almost) Kingly Dukedomes)
Or lay these bones in an vnworthy Vrne,
Tomblesse, with no remembrance ouer them:
Either our History shall with full mouth
Speake freely of our Acts, or else our graue
Like Turkish mute, shall haue a tonguelesse mouth,
Not worshipt with a waxen Epitaph.

    Enter Ambassadors of France.

Now are we well prepar'd to know the pleasure
Of our faire Cosin Dolphin: for we heare,
Your greeting is from him, not from the King.

  Amb. May't please your Maiestie to giue vs leaue
Freely to render what we haue in charge:
Or shall we sparingly shew you farre off
The Dolphins meaning, and our Embassie.

  King. We are no Tyrant, but a Christian King,
Vnto whose grace our passion is as subiect
As is our wretches fettred in our prisons,
Therefore with franke and with vncurbed plainnesse,
Tell vs the *Dolphins* minde.

  Amb. Thus than in few:
Your Highnesse lately sending into France,
Did claime some certaine Dukedomes, in the right
Of your great Predecessor, King *Edward* the third.
In answer of which claime, the Prince our Master
Sayes, that you sauour too much of your youth,
And bids you be aduis'd: There's nought in France,
That can be with a nimble Galliard wonne:
You cannot reuell into Dukedomes there.
He therefore sends you meeter for your spirit
This Tun of Treasure; and in lieu of this,
Desires you let the dukedomes that you claime
Heare no more of you. This the *Dolphin* speakes.

  King. What Treasure Vncle?
  Exe. Tennis balles, my Liege.
  Kin. We are glad the *Dolphin* is so pleasant with vs,
His Present, and your paines we thanke you for:
When we haue matcht our Rackets to these Balles,
We will in France (by Gods grace) play a set,
Shall strike his fathers Crowne into the hazard.
Tell him, he hath made a match with such a Wrangler,
That all the Courts of France will be disturb'd
With Chaces. And we vnderstand him well,
How he comes o're vs with our wilder dayes,
Not measuring what vse we made of them.
We neuer valew'd this poore seate of England,
And therefore liuing hence, did giue our selfe
To barbarous licence: As 'tis euer common,
That men are merriest, when they are from home.
But tell the *Dolphin*, I will keepe my State,
Be like a King, and shew my sayle of Greatnesse,
When I do rowse me in my Throne of France.
For that I haue layd by my Maiestie,
And plodded like a man for working dayes:
But I will rise there with so full a glorie,
That I will dazle all the eyes of France,
Yea strike the *Dolphin* blinde to looke on vs,
And tell the pleasant Prince, this Mocke of his
Hath turn'd his balles to Gun-stones, and his soule
Shall stand sore charged, for the wastefull vengeance
That shall flye with them: for many a thousand widows
Shall this his Mocke, mocke out of their deer husbands;
Mocke mothers from their sonnes, mock Castles downe:
And some are yet vngotten and vnborne,
That shal haue cause to curse the *Dolphins* scorne.
But this lyes all within the wil of God,
To whom I do appeale, and in whose name
Tel you the *Dolphin*, I am comming on,
To venge me as I may, and to put forth
My rightfull hand in a wel-hallow'd cause.
So get you hence in peace: And tell the *Dolphin*,
His Iest will sauour but of shallow wit,
When thousands weepe more then did laugh at it.
Conuey them with safe conduct. Fare you well.
                    Exeunt Ambassadors.

  Exe. This was a merry Message.
  King. We hope to make the Sender blush at it:
Therefore, my Lords, omit no happy howre,
That may giue furth'rance to our Expedition:
For we haue now no thought in vs but France,
Saue those to God, that runne before our businesse.
Therefore let our proportions for these Warres
Be soone collected, and all things thought vpon,
That may with reasonable swiftnesse adde
More Feathers to our Wings: for God before,
Wee'le chide this *Dolphin* at his fathers doore.
Therefore let euery man now taske his thought,
That this faire Action may on foot be brought. *Exeunt.*

    Flourish.   Enter Chorus.
Now all the Youth of England are on fire,
And silken Dalliance in the Wardrobe lyes:
Now thriue the Armorers, and Honors thought
Reignes solely in the breast of euery man.
They sell the Pasture now, to buy the Horse;
Following the Mirror of all Christian Kings,
With winged heeles, as English *Mercuries.*
For now sits Expectation in the Ayre,
And hides a Sword, from Hilts vnto the Point,
With Crownes Imperiall, Crownes and Coronets,
Promis'd to *Harry*, and his followers.
The French aduis'd by good intelligence
Of this most dreadfull preparation,
Shake in their feare, and with pale Pollicy
Seeke to diuert the English purposes.
O England: Modell to thy inward Greatnesse,
Like little Body with a mightie Heart:
                                              What

The Life of Henry the Fift.

What mightst thou do, that honour would thee do,
Were all thy children kinde and naturall:
But see, thy fault France hath in thee found out,
A nest of hollow bosomes, which he filles
With treacherous Crownes, and three corrupted men:
One, *Richard* Earle of Cambridge, and the second
Henry Lord Scroope of *Masham*, and the third
Sir *Thomas Grey* Knight of Northumberland,
Haue for the Gilt of France (O guilt indeed)
Confirm'd Conspiracy with fearefull France,
And by their hands, this grace of Kings must dye.
If Hell and Treason hold their promises,
Ere he take ship for France; and in Southampton.
Linger your patience on, and wee'l digest
Th'abuse of distance; force a play:
The summe is payde, the Traitors are agreed,
The King is set from London, and the Scene
Is now transported (Gentles) to Southampton,
There is the Play-house now, there must you sit,
And thence to France shall we conuey you safe,
And bring you backe: Charming the narrow seas
To giue you gentle Passe: for if we may,
Wee'l not offend one stomacke with our Play.
But till the King come forth, and not till then,
Vnto Southampton do we shift our Scene. *Exit*

Enter Corporall Nym, and Lieutenant Bardolfe.

Bar. Well met Corporall *Nym*.

Nym. Good morrow Lieutenant *Bardolfe*.

Bar. What, are Ancient *Pistoll* and you friends yet?

Nym. For my part, I care not: I say little: but when time shall serue, there shall be smiles, but that shall be as it may. I dare not fight, but I will winke and holde out mine yron: it is a simple one, but what though? It will toste Cheese, and it will endure cold, as another mans sword will: and there's an end.

Bar. I will bestow a breakfast to make you friendes, and wee'l bee all three sworne brothers to France: Let't be so good Corporall *Nym*.

Nym. Faith, I will liue so long as I may, that's the certaine of it: and when I cannot liue any longer, I will doe as I may: That is my rest, that is the rendeuous of it.

Bar. It is certaine Corporall, that he is marryed to *Nell Quickly*, and certainly she did you wrong, for you were troth-plight to her.

Nym. I cannot tell, Things must be as they may: men may sleepe, and they may haue their throates about them at that time, and some say, kniues haue edges: It must be as it may, though patience be a tyred name, yet shee will plodde, there must be Conclusions, well, I cannot tell.

Enter Pistoll, & Quickly.

Bar. Heere comes Ancient *Pistoll* and his wife: good Corporall be patient heere. How now mine Hoaste *Pistoll*?

Pist. Base Tyke, cal'st thou mee Hoste, now by this hand I sweare I scorne the terme: nor shall my *Nel* keep Lodgers.

Host. No by my troth, not long: For we cannot lodge and board a dozen or fourteene Gentlewomen that liue honestly by the pricke of their Needles, but it will bee thought we keepe a Bawdy-house straight. O welliday Lady, if he be not hewne now, we shall see wilful adultery and murther committed.

Bar. Good Lieutenant, good Corporal offer nothing heere.

Nym. Pish.

Pist. Pish for thee, Island dogge: thou prickeard cur of Island.

Host. Good Corporall *Nym* shew thy valor, and put vp your sword.

Nym. Will you shogge off? I would haue you solus.

Pist. Solus, egregious dog? O Viper vile; The solus in thy most meruailous face, the solus in thy teeth, and in thy throate, and in thy hatefull Lungs, yea in thy Maw perdy; and which is worse, within thy nastie mouth. I do retort the solus in thy bowels, for I can take, and *Pistols* cocke is vp, and flashing fire will follow.

Nym. I am not *Barbason*, you cannot coniure mee: I haue an humor to knocke you indifferently well: If you grow fowle with me Pistoll, I will scoure you with my Rapier, as I may, in fayre tearmes. If you would walke off, I would pricke your guts a little in good tearmes, as I may, and that's the humor of it.

Pist. O Braggard vile, and damned furious wight,
The Graue doth gape, and doting death is neere,
Therefore exhale.

Bar. Heare me, heare me what I say: Hee that strikes the first stroake, Ile run him vp to the hilts, as I am a souldier.

Pist. An oath of mickle might, and fury shall abate.
Giue me thy fist, thy fore-foote to me giue: Thy spirites are most tall.

Nym. I will cut thy throate one time or other in faire termes, that is the humor of it.

Pistoll. Couple a gorge, that is the word. I defie thee againe. O hound of Creet, think'st thou my spouse to get? No, to the spittle goe, and from the Poudring tub of infamy, fetch forth the Lazar Kite of *Cressids* kinde, *Doll Teare-sheete*, she by name, and her espouse. I haue, and I will hold the *Quondam Quickely* for the onely shee: and *Pauca*, there's enough to go to.

Enter the Boy.

Boy. Mine Hoast *Pistoll*, you must come to my Mayster, and your Hostesse: He is very sicke, & would to bed. Good *Bardolfe*, put thy face betweene his sheets, and do the Office of a Warming-pan: Faith, he's very ill.

Bard. Away you Rogue.

Host. By my troth he'l yeeld the Crow a pudding one of these dayes: the King has kild his heart. Good Husband come home presently. *Exit*

Bar. Come, shall I make you two friends. Wee must to France together: why the diuel should we keep kniues to cut one anothers throats?

Pist. Let floods ore-swell, and fiends for food howle on.

Nym. You'l pay me the eight shillings I won of you at Betting?

Pist. Base is the Slaue that payes.

Nym. That now I wil haue: that's the humor of it.

Pist. As manhood shal compound: push home. *Draw*

Bard. By this sword, hee that makes the first thrust, Ile kill him: By this sword, I wil.

Pi. Sword is an Oath, & Oaths must haue their course

Bar. Coporall *Nym*, & thou wilt be friends be frends, and thou wilt not, why then be enemies with me to: prethee put vp.

Pist. A Noble shalt thou haue, and present pay, and Liquor likewise will I giue to thee, and friendshippe shall combyne, and brotherhood. Ile liue by *Nymme*, & *Nymme* shall liue by me, is not this iust? For I shal Sutler be vnto the Campe, and profits will accrue. Giue mee thy hand.

Nym. I shall haue my Noble?
Pist. In cash, most iustly payd.
Nym. Well, then that the humor of't.

Enter Hostesse.

Host. As euer you come of women, come in quickly to sir *Iohn*: A poore heart, hee is so shak'd of a burning quotidian Tertian, that it is most lamentable to behold. Sweet men, come to him.

Nym. The King hath run bad humors on the Knight, that's the euen of it.

Pist. Nym, thou hast spoke the right, his heart is fracted and corroborate.

Nym. The King is a good King, but it must bee as it may: he passes some humors, and carreeres.

Pist. Let vs condole the Knight, for (Lambekins) we will liue.

Enter Exeter, Bedford, & Westmerland.

Bed. Fore God his Grace is bold to trust these traitors
Exe. They shall be apprehended by and by.
West. How smooth and euen they do beare themselues,
As if allegeance in their bosomes sate
Crowned with faith, and constant loyalty.

Bed. The King hath note of all that they intend,
By interception, which they dreame not of.

Exe. Nay, but the man that was his bedfellow,
Whom he hath dull'd and cloy'd with gracious fauours;
That he should for a forraigne purse, so sell
His Soueraignes life to death and treachery.

Sound Trumpets.

Enter the King, Scroope, Cambridge, and Gray.

King. Now sits the winde faire, and we will aboord.
My Lord of *Cambridge*, and my kinde Lord of *Masham*,
And you my gentle Knight, giue me your thoughts:
Thinke you not that the powres we beare with vs
Will cut their passage through the force of France?
Doing the execution, and the acte,
For which we haue in head assembled them.

Scro. No doubt my Liege, if each man do his best.

King. I doubt not that, since we are well perswaded
We carry not a heart with vs from hence,
That growes not in a faire consent with ours:
Nor leaue not one behinde, that doth not wish
Successe and Conquest to attend on vs.

Cam. Neuer was Monarch better fear'd and lou'd,
Then is your Maiesty; there's not I thinke a subiect
That sits in heart-greefe and vneasinesse
Vnder the sweet shade of your gouernment.

Kni. True: those that were your Fathers enemies,
Haue steep'd their gauls in hony, and do serue you
With hearts create of duty, and of zeale.

King. We therefore haue great cause of thankfulnes,
And shall forget the office of our hand
Sooner then quittance of desert and merit,
According to the weight and worthinesse.

Scro. So seruice shall with steeled sinewes toyle,
And labour shall refresh it selfe with hope
To do your Grace incessant seruices.

King. We Iudge no lesse, Vnkle of *Exeter*,
Inlarge the man committed yesterday,
That rayl'd against our person: We consider
It was excesse of Wine that set him on,
And on his more aduice, We pardon him.

Scro. That's mercy, but too much security:
Let him be punish'd Soueraigne, least example
Breed (by his sufferance) more of such a kind.

King. O let vs yet be mercifull.

Cam. So may your Highnesse, and yet punish too.
Grey. Sir, you shew great mercy if you giue him life,
After the taste of much correction.

King. Alas, your too much loue and care of me,
Are heauy Orisons 'gainst this poore wretch:
If little faults proceeding on distemper,
Shall not be wink'd at, how shall we stretch our eye
When capitall crimes, chew'd, swallow'd, and digested,
Appeare before vs? Wee'l yet inlarge that man,
Though *Cambridge*, *Scroope*, and *Gray*, in their deere care
And tender preseruation of our person
Wold haue him punish'd. And now to our French causes,
Who are the late Commissioners?

Cam. I one my Lord,
Your Highnesse bad me aske for it to day.

Scro. So did you me my Liege.
Gray. And I my Royall Soueraigne.

King. Then *Richard* Earle of *Cambridge*, there is yours:
There yours Lord *Scroope* of *Masham*, and Sir Knight:
Gray of *Northumberland*, this same is yours:
Reade them, and know I know your worthinesse.
My Lord of *Westmerland*, and Vnkle *Exeter*,
We will aboord to night. Why how now Gentlemen?
What see you in those papers, that you loose
So much complexion? Looke ye how they change:
Their cheekes are paper. Why, what reade you there,
That haue so cowarded and chac'd your blood
Out of apparance.

Cam. I do confesse my fault,
And do submit me to your Highnesse mercy.

Gray. Scro. To which we all appeale.

King. The mercy that was quicke in vs but late,
By your owne counsaile is suprest and kill'd:
You must not dare (for shame) to talke of mercy,
For your owne reasons turne into your bosomes,
As dogs vpon their maisters, worrying you:
See you my Princes, and my Noble Peeres,
These English monsters: My Lord of *Cambridge* heere,
You know how apt our loue was, to accord
To furnish with all appertinents
Belonging to his Honour; and this man,
Hath for a few light Crownes, lightly conspir'd
And sworne vnto the practises of France
To kill vs heere in Hampton. To the which,
This Knight no lesse for bounty bound to Vs
Then Cambridge is, hath likewise sworne. But O,
What shall I say to thee Lord *Scroope*, thou cruell,
Ingratefull, sauage, and inhumane Creature?
Thou that didst beare the key of all my counsailes,
That knew'st the very bottome of my soule,
That (almost) might'st haue coyn'd me into Golde,
Would'st thou haue practis'd on me, for thy vse?
May it be possible, that forraigne hyer
Could out of thee extract one sparke of euill
That might annoy my finger? 'Tis so strange,
That though the truth of it stands off as grosse
As blacke and white, my eye will scarsely see it.
Treason, and murther, euer kept together,
As two yoake diuels sworne to eythers purpose,
Working so grossely in an naturall cause,
That admiration did not hoope at them.
But thou (gainst all proportion) didst bring in
Wonder to waite on treason, and on murther:
And whatsoeuer cunning fiend it was
That wrought vpon thee so preposterously,
Hath got the voyce in hell for excellence:

And

The Life of Henry the Fift.

And other diuels that suggest by treasons,
Do botch and bungle vp damnation,
With patches, colours, and with formes being fetcht
From glist'ring semblances of piety:
But he that temper'd thee, bad thee stand vp,
Gaue thee no instance why thou shouldst do treason,
Vnlesse to dub thee with the name of Traitor.
If that same Dæmon that hath gull'd thee thus,
Should with his Lyon-gate walke the whole world,
He might returne to vastie Tartar backe,
And tell the Legions, I can neuer win
A soule so easie as that Englishmans.
Oh, how hast thou with iealousie infected
The sweetnesse of affiance? Shew men dutifull,
Why so didst thou: seeme they graue and learned?
Why so didst thou. Come they of Noble Family?
Why so didst thou. Seeme they religious?
Why so didst thou. Or are they spare in diet,
Free from grosse passion, or of mirth, or anger,
Constant in spirit, not sweruing with the blood,
Garnish'd and deck'd in modest complement,
Not working with the eye, without the eare,
And but in purged iudgement trusting neither,
Such and so finely boulted didst thou seeme:
And thus thy fall hath left a kinde of blot,
To make thee full fraught man, and best indued
With some suspition, I will weepe for thee.
For this reuolt of thine, me thinkes is like
Another fall of Man. Their faults are open,
Arrest them to the answer of the Law,
And God acquit them of their practises.

Exe. I arrest thee of High Treason, by the name of *Richard* Earle of *Cambridge*.

I arrest thee of High Treason, by the name of *Thomas* Lord *Scroope* of *Marsham*.

I arrest thee of High Treason, by the name of *Thomas Grey*, Knight of *Northumberland*.

Scro. Our purposes, God iustly hath discouer'd,
And I repent my fault more then my death,
Which I beseech your Highnesse to forgiue,
Although my body pay the price of it.

Cam. For me, the Gold of France did not seduce,
Although I did admit it as a motiue,
The sooner to effect what I intended:
But God be thanked for preuention,
Which in sufferance heartily will reioyce,
Beseeching God, and you, to pardon mee.

Gray. Neuer did faithfull subiect more reioyce
At the discouery of most dangerous Treason,
Then I do at this houre ioy ore my selfe,
Preuented from a damned enterprize;
My fault, but not my body, pardon Soueraigne.

King. God quit you in his mercy: Hear your sentence
You haue conspir'd against Our Royall person,
Ioyn'd with an enemy proclaim'd, and from his Coffers,
Receyu'd the Golden Earnest of Our death:
Wherein you would haue sold your King to slaughter,
His Princes, and his Peeres to seruitude,
His Subiects to oppression, and contempt,
And his whole Kingdome into desolation:
Touching our person, seeke we no reuenge,
But we our Kingdomes safety must so tender,
Whose ruine you sought, that to her Lawes
We do deliuer you. Get you therefore hence,
(Poore miserable wretches) to your death:
The taste whereof, God of his mercy giue
You patience to indure, and true Repentance
Of all your deare offences. Beare them hence. *Exit.*

Now Lords for France: the enterprise whereof
Shall be to you as vs, like glorious.
We doubt not of a faire and luckie Warre,
Since God so graciously hath brought to light
This dangerous Treason, lurking in our way,
To hinder our beginnings. We doubt not now,
But euery Rubbe is smoothed on our way.
Then forth, deare Countreymen: Let vs deliuer
Our Puissance into the hand of God,
Putting it straight in expedition.
Chearely to Sea, the signes of Warre aduance,
No King of England, if not King of France. *Flourish.*

Enter Pistoll, Nim, Bardolph, Boy, and Hostesse.

Hostesse. 'Prythee honey sweet Husband, let me bring thee to Staines.

Pistoll. No: for my manly heart doth erne. *Bardolph*, be blythe: *Nim*, rowse thy vaunting Veines: Boy, brisle thy Courage vp: for *Falstaffe* hee is dead, and wee must erne therefore.

Bard. Would I were with him, wheresomere hee is, eyther in Heauen, or in Hell.

Hostesse. Nay sure, hee's not in Hell: hee's in *Arthurs* Bosome, if euer man went to *Arthurs* Bosome: a made a finer end, and went away and it had beene any Christome Child: a parted eu'n iust betweene Twelue and One, eu'n at the turning o'th' Tyde: for after I saw him fumble with the Sheets, and play with Flowers, and smile vpon his fingers end, I knew there was but one way: for his Nose was as sharpe as a Pen, and a Table of greene fields. How now Sir *Iohn* (quoth I?) what man? be a good cheare: so a cryed out, God, God, God, three or foure times: now I, to comfort him, bid him a should not thinke of God; I hop'd there was no neede to trouble himselfe with any such thoughts yet: so a bad me lay more Clothes on his feet: I put my hand into the Bed, and felt them, and they were as cold as any stone: then I felt to his knees, and so vp-peer'd, and vpward, and all was as cold as any stone.

Nim. They say he cryed out of Sack.

Hostesse. I, that a did.

Bard. And of Women.

Hostesse. Nay, that a did not.

Boy. Yes that a did, and said they were Deules incarnate.

Woman. A could neuer abide Carnation, 'twas a Colour he neuer lik'd.

Boy. A said once, the Deule would haue him about Women.

Hostesse. A did in some sort (indeed) handle Women: but then hee was rumatique, and talk'd of the Whore of Babylon.

Boy. Doe you not remember a saw a Flea sticke vpon *Bardolphs* Nose, and a said it was a blacke Soule burning in Hell.

Bard. Well, the fuell is gone that maintain'd that fire: that's all the Riches I got in his seruice.

Nim. Shall wee shogg? the King will be gone from Southampton.

Pist. Come, let's away. My Loue, giue me thy Lippes: Looke to my Chattels, and my Moueables: Let Sences rule: The world is, Pitch and pay: trust none: for Oathes are Strawes, mens Faiths are Wafer-Cakes, and hold-fast is the onely Dogge: My Ducke, therefore *Caueto* bee thy Counsailor. Goe, cleare thy Chrystalls. Yoke-fellowes in Armes, let vs to France, like Horse-leeches

leeches my Boyes, to sucke, to sucke, the very blood to sucke.

  Boy. And that's but vnwholesome food, they say.
  Pist. Touch her soft mouth, and march.
  Bard. Farwell Hostesse.
  Nim. I cannot kisse, that is the humor of it: but adieu.
  Pist. Let Huswiferie appeare: keepe close, I thee command.
  Hostesse. Farwell: adieu.   *Exeunt*

Flourish.
Enter the French King, the Dolphin, the Dukes of Berry and Britaine.

  King. Thus comes the English with full power vpon vs,
And more then carefully it vs concernes,
To answer Royally in our defences.
Therefore the Dukes of Berry and of Britaine,
Of Brabant and of Orleance, shall make forth,
And you Prince Dolphin, with all swift dispatch
To lyne and new repayre our Townes of Warre
With men of courage, and with meanes defendant:
For England his approaches makes as fierce,
As Waters to the sucking of a Gulfe.
It fits vs then to be as prouident,
As feare may teach vs, out of late examples
Left by the fatall and neglected English,
Vpon our fields.
  Dolphin. My most redoubted Father,
It is most meet we arme vs 'gainst the Foe:
For Peace it selfe should not so dull a Kingdome,
(Though War nor no knowne Quarrel were in question)
But that Defences, Musters, Preparations,
Should be maintain'd, assembled, and collected,
As were a Warre in expectation.
Therefore I say, 'tis meet we all goe forth,
To view the sick and feeble parts of France:
And let vs doe it with no shew of feare,
No, with no more, then if we heard that England
Were busied with a Whitson Morris-dance:
For, my good Liege, shee is so idly King'd,
Her Scepter so phantastically borne,
By a vaine giddie shallow humorous Youth,
That feare attends her not.
  Const. O peace, Prince Dolphin,
You are too much mistaken in this King:
Question your Grace the late Embassadors,
With what great State he heard their Embassie,
How well supply'd with Noble Councellors,
How modest in exception; and withall,
How terrible in constant resolution:
And you shall find, his Vanities fore-spent,
Were but the out-side of the Roman *Brutus*,
Couering Discretion with a Coat of Folly;
As Gardeners doe with Ordure hide those Roots
That shall first spring, and be most delicate.
  Dolphin. Well, 'tis not so, my Lord High Constable.
But though we thinke it so, it is no matter:
In cases of defence, 'tis best to weigh
The Enemie more mightie then he seemes,
So the proportions of defence are fill'd:
Which of a weake and niggardly proiection,
Doth like a Miser spoyle his Coat, with scanting
A little Cloth.
  King. Thinke we King *Harry* strong:
And Princes, looke you strongly arme to meet him.
The Kindred of him hath beene flesht vpon vs:
And he is bred out of that bloodie straine,
That haunted vs in our familiar Pathes:
Witnesse our too much memorable shame,
When Cressy Battell fatally was strucke,
And all our Princes captiu'd, by the hand
Of that black Name, *Edward*, black Prince of Wales:
Whiles that his Mountaine Sire, on Mountaine standing
Vp in the Ayre, crown'd with the Golden Sunne,
Saw his Heroicall Seed, and smil'd to see him
Mangle the Worke of Nature, and deface
The Patternes, that by God and by French Fathers
Had twentie yeeres been made. This is a Stem
Of that Victorious Stock: and let vs feare
The Natiue mightinesse and fate of him.

Enter a Messenger.

  Mess. Embassadors from *Harry* King of England,
Doe craue admittance to your Maiestie.
  King. Weele giue them present audience.
Goe, and bring them.
You see this Chase is hotly followed, friends.
  Dolphin. Turne head, and stop pursuit: for coward Dogs
Most spend their mouths, whē what they seem to threaten
Runs farre before them. Good my Soueraigne
Take vp the English short, and let them know
Of what a Monarchie you are the Head:
Selfe-loue, my Liege, is not so vile a sinne,
As selfe-neglecting.

Enter Exeter.

  King. From our Brother of England?
  Exe. From him, and thus he greets your Maiestie:
He wills you in the Name of God Almightie,
That you deuest your selfe, and lay apart
The borrowed Glories, that by gift of Heauen,
By Law of Nature, and of Nations, longs
To him and to his Heires, namely, the Crowne,
And all wide-stretched Honors, that pertaine
By Custome, and the Ordinance of Times,
Vnto the Crowne of France: that you may know
'Tis no sinister, nor no awk-ward Clayme,
Pickt from the worme-holes of long-vanisht dayes,
Nor from the dust of old Obliuion rakt,
He sends you this most memorable Lyne,
In euery Branch truly demonstratiue;
Willing you ouer-looke this Pedigree:
And when you find him euenly deriu'd
From his most fam'd, of famous Ancestors,
Edward the third; he bids you then resigne
Your Crowne and Kingdome, indirectly held
From him the Natiue and true Challenger.
  King. Or else what followes?
  Exe. Bloody constraint: for if you hide the Crowne
Euen in your hearts, there will he rake for it.
Therefore in fierce Tempest is he comming,
In Thunder and in Earth-quake, like a *Ioue*:
That if requiring faile, he will compell.
And bids you, in the Bowels of the Lord,
Deliuer vp the Crowne, and to take mercie
On the poore Soules, for whom this hungry Warre
Opens his vastie Iawes: and on your head
Turning the Widdowes Teares, the Orphans Cryes,
The dead-mens Blood, the priuy Maidens Groanes,
For Husbands, Fathers, and betrothed Louers,
That shall be swallowed in this Controuersie.
This is his Clayme, his Threatning, and my Message:
Vnlesse the Dolphin be in presence here;
To whom expressely I bring greeting to.

The Life of Henry the Fift.

King. For vs, we will consider of this further:
To morrow shall you beare our full intent
Back to our Brother of England.

Dolph. For the Dolphin,
I stand here for him: what to him from England?

Exe. Scorne and defiance, sleight regard, contempt,
And any thing that may not mis-become
The mightie Sender, doth he prize you at.
Thus sayes my King: and if your Fathers Highnesse
Doe not, in graunt of all demands at large,
Sweeten the bitter Mock you sent his Maiestie;
Hee'le call you to so hot an Answer of it,
That Caues and Wombie Vaultages of France
Shall chide your Trespas, and returne your Mock
In second Accent of his Ordinance.

Dolph. Say: if my Father render faire returne,
It is against my will: for I desire
Nothing but Oddes with England.
To that end, as matching to his Youth and Vanitie,
I did present him with the Paris-Balls.

Exe. Hee'le make your Paris Louer shake for it,
Were it the Mistresse Court of mightie Europe:
And be assur'd, you'le find a diff'rence,
As we his Subiects haue in wonder found,
Betweene the promise of his greener dayes,
And these he masters now: now he weighes Time
Euen to the vtmost Graine: that you shall reade
In your owne Losses, if he stay in France.

King. To morrow shall you know our mind at full.
Flourish.

Exe. Dispatch vs with all speed, least that our King
Come here himselfe to question our delay;
For he is footed in this Land already.

King. You shalbe soone dispatcht, with faire conditions.
A Night is but small breathe, and little pawse,
To answer matters of this consequence. *Exeunt.*

Actus Secundus.

Flourish. Enter Chorus.
Thus with imagin'd wing our swift Scene flyes,
In motion of no lesse celeritie then that of Thought.
Suppose, that you haue seene
The well-appointed King at Douer Peer,
Embarke his Royaltie: and his braue Fleet,
With silken Streamers, the young *Phebus* fayning;
Play with your Fancies: and in them behold,
Vpon the Hempen Tackle, Ship-boyes climbing;
Heare the shrill Whistle, which doth order giue
To sounds confus'd: behold the threaden Sayles,
Borne with th'inuisible and creeping Wind,
Draw the huge Bottomes through the furrowed Sea,
Bresting the loftie Surge. O, doe but thinke
You stand vpon the Riuage, and behold
A Citie on th'inconstant Billowes dauncing:
For so appeares this Fleet Maiesticall,
Holding due course to Harflew. Follow, follow:
Grapple your minds to sternage of this Nauie,
And leaue your England as dead Mid-night, still,
Guarded with Grandsires, Babyes, and old Women,
Eyther past, or not arriu'd to pyth and puissance:
For who is he, whose Chin is but enricht
With one appearing Hayre, that will not follow
These cull'd and choyse-drawne Caualiers to France?
Worke, worke your Thoughts, and therein see a Siege:
Behold the Ordenance on their Carriages,
With fatall mouthes gaping on girded Harflew.
Suppose th'Embassador from the French comes back:
Tells *Harry*, That the King doth offer him
Katherine his Daughter, and with her to Dowrie,
Some petty and vnprofitable Dukedomes.
The offer likes not: and the nimble Gunner
With Lynstock now the diuellish Cannon touches,
Alarum, and Chambers goe off.
And downe goes all before them. Still be kind,
And eech out our performance with your mind. *Exit.*

Enter the King, Exeter, Bedford, and Gloucester.
Alarum: Scaling Ladders at Harflew.

King. Once more vnto the Breach,
Deare friends, once more;
Or close the Wall vp with our English dead:
In Peace, there's nothing so becomes a man,
As modest stillnesse, and humilitie:
But when the blast of Warre blowes in our eares,
Then imitate the action of the Tyger:
Stiffen the sinewes, commune vp the blood,
Disguise faire Nature with hard-fauour'd Rage:
Then lend the Eye a terrible aspect:
Let it pry through the portage of the Head,
Like the Brasse Cannon: let the Brow o'rewhelme it,
As fearefully, as doth a galled Rocke
O're-hang and iutty his confounded Base,
Swill'd with the wild and wastfull Ocean.
Now set the Teeth, and stretch the Nosthrill wide,
Hold hard the Breath, and bend vp euery Spirit
To his full height. On, on, you Noblish English,
Whose blood is fet from Fathers of Warre-proofe:
Fathers, that like so many *Alexanders*,
Haue in these parts from Morne till Euen fought,
And sheath'd their Swords, for lack of argument.
Dishonour not your Mothers: now attest,
That those whom you call'd Fathers, did beget you.
Be Coppy now to me of grosser blood,
And teach them how to Warre. And you good Yeomen,
Whose Lyms were made in England; shew vs here
The mettell of your Pasture: let vs sweare,
That you are worth your breeding: which I doubt not:
For there is none of you so meane and base,
That hath not Noble luster in your eyes.
I see you stand like Grey-hounds in the slips,
Straying vpon the Start. The Game's afoot:
Follow your Spirit; and vpon this Charge,
Cry, God for *Harry*, England, and S. *George.*
Alarum, and Chambers goe off.

Enter Nim, Bardolph, Pistoll, and Boy.
Bard. On, on, on, on, on, to the breach, to the breach.
Nim. 'Pray thee Corporall stay, the Knocks are too hot: and for mine owne part, I haue not a Case of Liues: the humor of it is too hot, that is the very plaine-Song of it.
Pist. The plaine-Song is most iust: for humors doe abound: Knocks goe and come: Gods Vassals drop and dye: and Sword and Shield, in bloody Field, doth winne immortall fame.
Boy. Would I were in an Ale-house in London, I would giue all my fame for a Pot of Ale, and safetie.
Pist. And

Pist. And I: If wishes would preuayle with me, my purpose should not fayle with me; but thither would I high.

Boy. As duly, but not as truly, as Bird doth sing on bough.

Enter Fluellen.

Flu. Vp to the breach, you Dogges; auaunt you Cullions.

Pist. Be mercifull great Duke to men of Mould: abate thy Rage, abate thy manly Rage; abate thy Rage, great Duke. Good Bawcock bate thy Rage: vse lenitie sweet Chuck.

Nim. These be good humors: your Honor wins bad humors. *Exit.*

Boy. As young as I am, I haue obseru'd these three Swashers: I am Boy to them all three, but all they three, though they would serue me, could not be Man to me; for indeed three such Antiques doe not amount to a man: for *Bardolph*, hee is white-liuer'd, and red-fac'd; by the meanes whereof, a faces it out, but fights not: for *Pistoll*, hee hath a killing Tongue, and a quiet Sword; by the meanes whereof, a breakes Words, and keepes whole Weapons: for *Nim*, hee hath heard, that men of few Words are the best men, and therefore hee scornes to say his Prayers, lest a should be thought a Coward: but his few bad Words are matcht with as few good Deeds; for a neuer broke any mans Head but his owne, and that was against a Post, when he was drunke. They will steale any thing, and call it Purchase. *Bardolph* stole a Lute-case, bore it twelue Leagues, and sold it for three halfepence. *Nim* and *Bardolph* are sworne Brothers in filching: and in Callice they stole a fire-shouell. I knew by that peece of Seruice, the men would carry Coales. They would haue me as familiar with mens Pockets, as their Gloues or their Hand-kerchers: which makes much against my Manhood, if I should take from anothers Pocket, to put into mine; for it is plaine pocketting vp of Wrongs. I must leaue them, and seeke some better Seruice: their Villany goes against my weake stomacke, and therefore I must cast it vp. *Exit.*

Enter Gower.

Gower. Captaine *Fluellen*, you must come presently to the Mynes; the Duke of Gloucester would speake with you.

Flu. To the Mynes? Tell you the Duke, it is not so good to come to the Mynes: for looke you, the Mynes is not according to the disciplines of the Warre; the concauities of it is not sufficient: for looke you, th'athuersarie, you may discusse vnto the Duke, looke you, is digt himselfe foure yard vnder the Countermines: by *Cheshu*, I thinke a will plowe vp all, if there is not better directions.

Gower. The Duke of Gloucester, to whom the Order of the Siege is giuen, is altogether directed by an Irish man, a very valiant Gentleman yfaith.

Welch. It is Captaine *Makmorrice*, is it not?

Gower. I thinke it be.

Welch. By *Cheshu* he is an Asse, as in the World, I will verifie as much in his Beard: he ha's no more directions in the true disciplines of the Warres, looke you, of the Roman disciplines, then is a Puppy-dog.

Enter Makmorrice, and Captaine Iamy.

Gower. Here a comes, and the Scots Captaine, Captaine *Iamy*, with him.

Welch. Captaine *Iamy* is a maruellous falorous Gentleman, that is certain, and of great expedition and knowledge in th'aunchiant Warres, vpon my particular knowledge of his directions: by *Cheshu* he will maintaine his Argument as well as any Militarie man in the World, in the disciplines of the Pristine Warres of the Romans.

Scot. I say gudday, Captaine *Fluellen*.

Welch. Godden to your Worship, good Captaine *Iames*.

Gower. How now Captaine *Mackmorrice*, haue you quit the Mynes? haue the Pioners giuen o're?

Irish. By Chrish Law tish ill done: the Worke ish giue ouer, the Trompet sound the Retreat. By my Hand I sweare, and my fathers Soule, the Worke ish ill done: it ish giue ouer: I would haue blowed vp the Towne, so Chrish saue me law, in an houre. O tish ill done, tish ill done: by my Hand tish ill done.

Welch. Captaine *Mackmorrice*, I beseech you now, will you voutsafe me, looke you, a few disputations with you, as partly touching or concerning the disciplines of the Warre, the Roman Warres, in the way of Argument, looke you, and friendly communication: partly to satisfie my Opinion, and partly for the satisfaction, looke you, of my Mind: as touching the direction of the Militarie discipline, that is the Point.

Scot. It sall be vary gud, gud feith, gud Captens bath, and I sall quit you with gud leue, as I may pick occasion: that sall I mary.

Irish. It is no time to discourse, so Chrish saue me: the day is hot, and the Weather, and the Warres, and the King, and the Dukes: it is no time to discourse, the Town is beseech'd: and the Trumpet call vs to the breech, and we talke, and be Chrish do nothing, tis shame for vs all: so God sa'me tis shame to stand still, it is shame by my hand: and there is Throats to be cut, and Workes to be done, and there ish nothing done, so Christ ta'me law.

Scot. By the Mes, ere theise eyes of mine take themselues to slomber, ayle de gud seruice, or Ile ligge i'th' grund for it; ay, or goe to death: and Ile pay't as valorously as I may, that sal I suerly do, that is the breff and the long: mary, I wad full faine heard some question tween you tway.

Welch. Captaine *Mackmorrice*, I thinke, looke you, vnder your correction, there is not many of your Nation.

Irish. Of my Nation? What ish my Nation? Ish a Villaine, and a Basterd, and a Knaue, and a Rascall. What ish my Nation? Who talkes of my Nation?

Welch. Looke you, if you take the matter otherwise then is meant, Captaine *Mackmorrice*, peraduenture I shall thinke you doe not vse me with that affabilitie, as in discretion you ought to vse me, looke you, being as good a man as your selfe, both in the disciplines of Warre, and in the deriuation of my Birth, and in other particularities.

Irish. I doe not know you so good a man as my selfe: so Chrish saue me, I will cut off your Head.

Gower. Gentlemen both, you will mistake each other.

Scot. A, that's a foule fault. *A Parley.*

Gower. The Towne sounds a Parley.

Welch. Captaine *Mackmorrice*, when there is more better oportunitie to be required, looke you, I will be so bold as to tell you, I know the disciplines of Warre: and there is an end. *Exit.*

Enter the King and all his Traine before the Gates.

King. How yet resolues the Gouernour of the Towne? This is the latest Parle we will admit:

There-

Therefore to our best mercy giue your selues,
Or like to men prowd of destruction,
Defie vs to our worst: for as I am a Souldier,
A Name that in my thoughts becomes me best;
If I begin the batt'rie once againe,
I will not leaue the halfe-atchieued Harflew,
Till in her ashes she lye buryed.
The Gates of Mercy shall be all shut vp,
And the flesh'd Souldier, rough and hard of heart,
In libertie of bloody hand, shall raunge
With Conscience wide as Hell, mowing like Grasse
Your fresh faire Virgins, and your flowring Infants.
What is it then to me, if impious Warre,
Arrayed in flames like to the Prince of Fiends,
Doe with his smyrcht complexion all fell feats,
Enlynckt to wast and desolation?
What is't to me, when you your selues are cause,
If your pure Maydens fall into the hand
Of hot and forcing Violation?
What Reyne can hold licentious Wickednesse,
When downe the Hill he holds his fierce Carriere?
We may as bootlesse spend our vaine Command
Vpon th'enraged Souldiers in their spoyle,
As send Precepts to the *Leuiathan*, to come ashore.
Therefore, you men of Harflew,
Take pitty of your Towne and of your People,
Whiles yet my Souldiers are in my Command,
Whiles yet the coole and temperate Wind of Grace
O're-blowes the filthy and contagious Clouds
Of headly Murther, Spoyle, and Villany.
If not: why in a moment looke to see
The blind and bloody Souldier, with foule hand
Desire the Locks of your shrill-shriking Daughters:
Your Fathers taken by the siluer Beards,
And their most reuerend Heads dasht to the Walls:
Your naked Infants spitted vpon Pykes,
Whiles the mad Mothers, with their howles confus'd,
Doe breake the Clouds; as did the Wiues of Iewry,
At *Herods* bloody-hunting slaughter-men.
What say you? Will you yeeld, and this auoyd?
Or guiltie in defence, be thus destroy'd.

Enter Gouernour.

Gouer. Our expectation hath this day an end:
The Dolphin, whom of Succours we entreated,
Returnes vs, that his Powers are yet not ready,
To rayse so great a Siege: Therefore great King,
We yeeld our Towne and Liues to thy soft Mercy:
Enter our Gates, dispose of vs and ours,
For we no longer are defensible.

King. Open your Gates: Come Vnckle *Exeter*,
Goe you and enter Harflew; there remaine,
And fortifie it strongly 'gainst the French:
Vse mercy to them all for vs, deare Vnckle.
The Winter comming on, and Sicknesse growing
Vpon our Souldiers, we will retyre to Calis.
To night in Harflew will we be your Guest,
To morrow for the March are we addrest.

Flourish, and enter the Towne.

Enter Katherine and an old Gentlewoman.

Kathe. Alice, tu as esté en Angleterre, & tu bien parlas
le Language.

Alice. En peu Madame.

Kath. Ie te prie m'enseigniez, il faut que ie apprend a parler: Coment appelle vous le main en Anglois?

Alice. Le main il & appelle de Hand.

Kath. De Hand.

Alice. E le doyts.

Kat. Le doyts, ma foy Ie oublie, e doyt mays, ie me souemeray
le doyts ie pense qu'ils ont appelle de fingres, ou de fingres.

Alice. Le main de Hand, le doyts le Fingres, ie pense que ie
suis le bon escholier.

Kath. I'ay gaynie diux mots d'Anglois vistement, coment
appelle vous le ongles?

Alice. Le ongles, les appellons de Nayles.

Kath. De Nayles escoute: dites moy, si ie parle bien: de
Hand, de Fingres, e de Nayles.

Alice. C'est bien dict Madame, il & fort bon Anglois.

Kath. Dites moy l'Anglois pour le bras.

Alice. De Arme, Madame.

Kath. E de coudee.

Alice. D'Elbow.

Kath. D'Elbow: Ie men fay le repiticio de touts les mots
que vous m'aues, apprins des a present.

Alice. Il & trop difficile Madame, comme Ie pense.

Kath. Excuse moy *Alice* escoute, d'Hand, de Fingre, de
Nayles, d'Arma, de Bilbow.

Alice. D'Elbow, Madame.

Kath. O Seigneur Dieu, ie men oublie d'Elbow, coment appelle vous le col.

Alice. De Nick, Madame.

Kath. De Nick, e le menton.

Alice. De Chin.

Kath. De Sin: le col de Nick, le menton de Sin.

Alice. Ouy. Sauf vostre honneur en verite vous pronoun-
cies les mots aussi droict, que le Natifs d'Angleterre.

Kath. Ie ne doute point d'apprendre par de grace de Dieu,
& en peu de temps.

Alice. N'aue vos y desia oublie ce que ie vous a enseigne.

Kath. Nome ie recitera a vous promptement, d'Hand, de
Fingre, de Maylees.

Alice. De Nayles, Madame.

Kath. De Nayles, de Arme, de Ilbow.

Alice. Sans vostre honeur d'Elbow.

Kath. Ainsi de ie d'Elbow, de Nick, & de Sin: coment appelle vous les pied & de roba.

Alice. Le Foot Madame, & le Count.

Kath. Le Foot, & le Count: O Seigneur Dieu, il sout le
mots de son mauvais corruptible grosse & impudique, & non
pour le Dames de Honeur d'vser: Ie ne voudray pronoucer ce
mots deuant le Seigneurs de France, pour toute le monde, fo le
Foot & le Count, neant moys, Ie recitera vn autrefoys ma leçon
ensembe, d'Hand, de Fingre, de Nayles, d'Arme, d'Elbow, de
Nick, de Sin, de Foot, le Count.

Alice. Excellent, Madame.

Kath. C'est asses pour vne foyes, alons nous a diner.

Exit.

*Enter the King of France, the Dolphin, the
Constable of France, and others.*

King. 'Tis certaine he hath past the Riuer Some.

Const. And if he be not fought withall, my Lord,
Let vs not liue in France: let vs quit all,
And giue our Vineyards to a barbarous People.

Dolph. O Dieu viuant: Shall a few Sprayes of vs,
The emptying of our Fathers Luxurie,
Our Syens, put in wilde and sauage Stock,
Spirt vp so suddenly into the Clouds,
And ouer-looke their Grafters?

Brit. Normans, but bastard Normans, Norman bastards:
Mort du ma vie, if they march along
Vnfought withall, but I will sell my Dukedome,

To buy a slobbry and a durtie Farme
In that nooke-shotten Ile of Albion.

  Const. *Dieu de Battailes,* where haue they this mettell?
Is not their Clymate foggy, raw, and dull?
On whom, as in despight, the Sunne lookes pale,
Killing their Fruit with frownes. Can sodden Water,
A Drench for sur-reyn'd Iades, their Barly broth,
Decoct their cold blood to such valiant heat?
And shall our quick blood, spirited with Wine,
Seeme frostie? O, for honor of our Land,
Let vs not hang like roping Isyckles
Vpon our Houses Thatch, whiles a more frostie People
Sweat drops of gallant Youth in our rich fields:
Poore we call them, in their Natiue Lords.

  Dolphin. By Faith and Honor,
Our Madames mock at vs, and plainely say,
Our Mettell is bred out, and they will giue
Their bodyes to the Lust of English Youth,
To new-store France with Bastard Warriors.

  Brit. They bid vs to the English Dancing-Schooles,
And teach *Lauoltas* high, and swift *Carranto's,*
Saying, our Grace is onely in our Heeles,
And that we are most lostie Run-awayes.

  King. Where is *Montioy* the Herald? speed him hence,
Let him greet England with our sharpe defiance.
Vp Princes, and with spirit of Honor edged,
More sharper then your Swords, high to the field:
Charles Delabreth, High Constable of France,
You Dukes of *Orleance, Burbon,* and of *Berry,*
Alanson, Brabant, Bar, and *Burgonie,*
Iaques Chattillion, Rambures, Vandemont,
Beumont, Grand Free, Roussi, and *Faulconbridge,*
Loys, Lestrale, Bouciquall, and *Charaloyes,*
High Dukes, great Princes, Barons, Lords, and Kings;
For your great Seats, now quit you of great shames:
Barre *Harry* England, that sweepes through our Land
With Penons painted in the blood of Harflew:
Rush on his Hoast, as doth the melted Snow
Vpon the Valleyes, whose low Vassall Seat,
The Alpes doth spit, and void his rhewme vpon.
Goe downe vpon him, you haue Power enough,
And in a Captiue Chariot, into Roan
Bring him our Prisoner.

  Const. This becomes the Great.
Sorry am I his numbers are so few,
His Souldiers sick, and famisht in their March:
For I am sure, when he shall see our Army,
Hee'le drop his heart into the sincke of feare,
And for atchieuement, offer vs his Ransome.

  King. Therefore Lord Constable, hast on *Montioy,*
And let him say to England, that we send,
To know what willing Ransome he will giue.
Prince *Dolphin,* you shall stay with vs in Roan.

  Dolph. Not so, I doe beseech your Maiestie.

  King. Be patient, for you shall remaine with vs,
Now forth Lord Constable, and Princes all,
And quickly bring vs word of Englands fall. *Exeunt.*

Enter Captaines, English and Welch, Gower
and Fluellen.

  Gower. How now Captaine *Fluellen,* come you from the Bridge?

  Flu. I assure you, there is very excellent Seruices committed at the Bridge.

  Gower. Is the Duke of Exeter safe?

  Flu. The Duke of Exeter is as magnanimous as *Aga-memnon,* and a man that I loue and honour with my soule, and my heart, and my dutie, and my liue, and my liuing, and my vttermost power. He is not, God be praysed and blessed, any hurt in the World, but keepes the Bridge most valiantly, with excellent discipline. There is an aunchient Lieutenant there at the Pridge, I thinke in my very conscience hee is as valiant a man as *Marke Anthony,* and hee is a man of no estimation in the World, but I did see him doe as gallant seruice.

  Gower. What doe you call him?

  Flu. Hee is call'd aunchient *Pistoll.*

  Gower. I know him not.

Enter Pistoll.

  Flu. Here is the man.

  Pist. Captaine, I thee beseech to doe me fauours: the Duke of Exeter doth loue thee well.

  Flu. I, I prayse God, and I haue merited some loue at his hands.

  Pist. Bardolph, a Souldier firme and sound of heart, and of buxome valour, hath by cruell Fate, and giddie Fortunes furious fickle Wheele, that Goddesse blind, that stands vpon the rolling restlesse Stone.

  Flu. By your patience, aunchient *Pistoll:* Fortune is painted blinde, with a Muffler afore his eyes, to signifie to you, that Fortune is blinde; and shee is painted also with a Wheele, to signifie to you, which is the Morall of it, that shee is turning and inconstant, and mutabilitie, and variation: and her foot, looke you, is fixed vpon a Sphericall Stone, which rowles, and rowles, and rowles: in good truth, the Poet makes a most excellent description of it: Fortune is an excellent Morall.

  Pist. Fortune is *Bardolphs* foe, and frownes on him: for he hath stolne a Pax, and hanged must a be: a damned death: let Gallowes gape for Dogge, let Man goe free, and let not Hempe his Wind-pipe suffocate: but *Exeter* hath giuen the doome of death, for Pax of little price. Therefore goe speake, the Duke will heare thy voyce; and let not *Bardolphs* vitall thred bee cut with edge of Penny-Cord, and vile reproach. Speake Captaine for his Life, and I will thee requite.

  Flu. Aunchient *Pistoll,* I doe partly vnderstand your meaning.

  Pist. Why then reioyce therefore.

  Flu. Certainly Aunchient, it is not a thing to reioyce at: for if, looke you, he were my Brother, I would desire the Duke to vse his good pleasure, and put him to execution; for discipline ought to be vsed.

  Pist. Dye, and be dam'd, and *Figo* for thy friendship.

  Flu. It is well.

  Pist. The Figge of Spaine. *Exit.*

  Flu. Very good.

  Gower. Why, this is an arrant counterfeit Rascall, I remember him now: a Bawd, a Cut-purse.

  Flu. Ile assure you, a vtt'red as praue words at the Pridge, as you shall see in a Summers day: but it is very well: what he ha's spoke to me, that is well I warrant you, when time is serue.

  Gower. Why 'tis a Gull, a Foole, a Rogue, that now and then goes to the Warres, to grace himselfe at his returne into London, vnder the forme of a Souldier: and such fellowes are perfit in the Great Commanders Names, and they will learne you by rote where Seruices were done; at such and such a Sconce, at such a Breach, at such a Conuoy: who came off brauely, who was shot, who disgrac'd, what termes the Enemy stood on: and this they conne perfitly in the phrase of Warre; which they tricke
vp

vp with new-tuned Oathes: and what a Beard of the Generalls Cut, and a horride Sute of the Campe, will doe among foming Bottles, and Ale-washt Wits, is wonderfull to be thought on: but you must learne to know such slanders of the age, or else you may be maruellously mistooke.

Flu. I tell you what, Captaine *Gower*: I doe perceiue hee is not the man that hee would gladly make shew to the World hee is: if I finde a hole in his Coat, I will tell him my minde: hearke you, the King is comming, and I must speake with him from the Pridge.

Drum and Colours. Enter the King and his poore Souldiers.

Flu. God plesse your Maiestie.

King. How now *Fluellen*, cam'st thou from the Bridge?

Flu. I, so please your Maiestie: The Duke of Exeter ha's very gallantly maintain'd the Pridge; the French is gone off, looke you, and there is gallant and most praue passages: marry, th'athuersarie was haue possession of the Pridge, but he is enforced to retyre, and the Duke of Exeter is Master of the Pridge: I can tell your Maiestie, the Duke is a praue man.

King. What men haue you lost, *Fluellen*?

Flu. The perdition of th'athuersarie hath beene very great, reasonable great: marry for my part, I thinke the Duke hath lost neuer a man, but one that is like to be executed for robbing a Church, one *Bardolph*, if your Maiestie know the man: his face is all bubukles and whelkes, and knobs, and flames a fire, and his lippes blowes at his nose, and it is like a coale of fire, sometimes plew, and sometimes red, but his nose is executed, and his fire's out.

King. Wee would haue all such offendors so cut off: and we giue expresse charge, that in our Marches through the Countrey, there be nothing compell'd from the Villages; nothing taken, but pay'd for: none of the French vpbrayded or abused in disdainefull Language; for when Leuitie and Crueltie play for a Kingdome, the gentler Gamester is the soonest winner.

Tucket. Enter Mountioy.

Mountioy. You know me by my habit.

King. Well then, I know thee: what shall I know of thee?

Mountioy. My Masters mind.

King. Vnfold it.

Mountioy. Thus sayes my King: Say thou to *Harry* of England, Though we seem'd dead, we did but sleepe: Aduantage is a better Souldier then rashnesse. Tell him, wee could haue rebuk'd him at Harflewe, but that wee thought not good to bruise an iniurie, till it were full ripe. Now wee speake vpon our Q. and our voyce is imperiall: England shall repent his folly, see his weakenesse, and admire our sufferance. Bid him therefore consider of his ransome, which must proportion the losses we haue borne, the subiects we haue lost, the disgrace we haue digested; which in weight to re-answer, his pettinesse would bow vnder. For our losses, his Exchequer is too poore; for th'effusion of our bloud, the Muster of his Kingdome too faint a number; and for our disgrace, his owne person kneeling at our feet, but a weake and worthlesse satisfaction. To this adde defiance: and tell him for conclusion, he hath betrayed his followers, whose condemnation is pronounc't: So farre my King and Master; so much my Office.

King. What is thy name? I know thy qualitie.

Mount. Mountioy.

King. Thou doo'st thy Office fairely. Turne thee back, And tell thy King, I doe not seeke him now, But could be willing to march on to Callice, Without impeachment: for to say the sooth, Though 'tis no wisdome to confesse so much Vnto an enemie of Craft and Vantage, My people are with sicknesse much enfeebled, My numbers lessen'd: and those few I haue, Almost no better then so many French; Who when they were in health, I tell thee Herald, I thought, vpon one payre of English Legges Did march three Frenchmen. Yet forgiue me God, That I doe bragge thus; this your ayre of France Hath blowne that vice in me. I must repent: Goe therefore tell thy Master, heere I am; My Ransome, is this frayle and worthlesse Trunke; My Army, but a weake and sickly Guard: Yet God before, tell him we will come on, Though France himselfe, and such another Neighbor Stand in our way. There's for thy labour *Mountioy*. Goe bid thy Master well aduise himselfe, If we may passe, we will: if we be hindred, We shall your tawnie ground with your red blood Discolour: and so *Mountioy*, fare you well. The summe of all our Answer is but this: We would not seeke a Battaile as we are, Nor as we are, we say we will not shun it: So tell your Master.

Mount. I shall deliuer so: Thankes to your Highnesse.

Glouc. I hope they will not come vpon vs now.

King. We are in Gods hand, Brother, not in theirs: March to the Bridge, it now drawes toward night, Beyond the Riuer wee'le encampe our selues, And on to morrow bid them march away. *Exeunt.*

Enter the Constable of France, the Lord Rambures, Orleance, Dolphin, with others.

Const. Tut, I haue the best Armour of the World: would it were day.

Orleance. You haue an excellent Armour: but let my Horse haue his due.

Const. It is the best Horse of Europe.

Orleance. Will it neuer be Morning?

Dolph. My Lord of Orleance, and my Lord High Constable, you talke of Horse and Armour?

Orleance. You are as well prouided of both, as any Prince in the World.

Dolph. What a long Night is this? I will not change my Horse with any that treades but on foure postures: ch' ha: he bounds from the Earth, as if his entrayles were hayres: *le Chenal volante*, the Pegasus, *ches les narines de feu.* When I bestryde him, I soare, I am a Hawke: he trots the ayre: the Earth sings, when he touches it: the basest horne of his hoofe, is more Musicall then the Pipe of *Hermes*.

Orleance. Hee's of the colour of the Nutmeg.

Dolph. And of the heat of the Ginger. It is a Beast for *Perseus*: hee is pure Ayre and Fire; and the dull Elements of Earth and Water neuer appeare in him, but onely in patient stillnesse while his Rider mounts him: hee is indeede a Horse, and all other Iades you may call Beasts.

Const. In-

Const. Indeed my Lord, it is a most absolute and excellent Horse.

Dolph. It is the Prince of Palfrayes, his Neigh is like the bidding of a Monarch, and his countenance enforces Homage.

Orleance. No more Cousin.

Dolph. Nay, the man hath no wit, that cannot from the rising of the Larke to the lodging of the Lambe, varie deserued prayse on my Palfray: it is a Theame as fluent as the Sea: Turne the Sands into eloquent tongues, and my Horse is argument for them all: 'tis a subiect for a Soueraigne to reason on, and for a Soueraignes Soueraigne to ride on: And for the World, familiar to vs, and vnknowne, to lay apart their particular Functions, and wonder at him, I once writ a Sonnet in his prayse, and began thus, *Wonder of Nature.*

Orleance. I haue heard a Sonnet begin so to ones Mistresse.

Dolph. Then did they imitate that which I compos'd to my Courser, for my Horse is my Mistresse.

Orleance. Your Mistresse beares well.

Dolph. Me well, which is the prescript prayse and perfection of a good and particular Mistresse.

Const. Nay, for me thought yesterday your Mistresse shrewdly shooke your back.

Dolph. So perhaps did yours.

Const. Mine was not bridled.

Dolph. O then belike she was old and gentle, and you rode like a Kerne of Ireland, your French Hose off, and in your strait Strossers.

Const. You haue good iudgement in Horsemanship.

Dolph. Be warn'd by me then: they that ride so, and ride not warily, fall into foule Boggs: I had rather haue my Horse to my Mistresse.

Const. I had as liue haue my Mistresse a Iade.

Dolph. I tell thee Constable, my Mistresse weares his owne hayre.

Const. I could make as true a boast as that, if I had a Sow to my Mistresse.

Dolph. Le chien est retourne a son propre vemissement est la leuye lauee au bourbier: thou mak'st vse of any thing.

Const. Yet doe I not vse my Horse for my Mistresse, or any such Prouerbe, so little kin to the purpose.

Ramb. My Lord Constable, the Armour that I saw in your Tent to night, are those Starres or Sunnes vpon it?

Const. Starres my Lord.

Dolph. Some of them will fall to morrow, I hope.

Const. And yet my Sky shall not want.

Dolph. That may be, for you beare a many superfluously, and 'twere more honor some were away.

Const. Eu'n as your Horse beares your prayses, who would trot as well, were some of your bragges dismounted.

Dolph. Would I were able to loade him with his desert. Will it neuer be day? I will trot to morrow a mile, and my way shall be paued with English Faces.

Const. I will not say so, for feare I should be fac't out of my way: but I would it were morning, for I would faine be about the eares of the English.

Ramb. Who will goe to Hazard with me for twentie Prisoners?

Const. You must first goe your selfe to hazard, ere you haue them.

Dolph. 'Tis Mid-night, Ile goe arme my selfe. *Exit.*

Orleance. The Dolphin longs for morning.

Ramb. He longs to eate the English.

Const. I thinke he will eate all he kills.

Orleance. By the white Hand of my Lady, hee's a gallant Prince.

Const. Sweare by her Foot, that she may tread out the Oath.

Orleance. He is simply the most actiue Gentleman of France.

Const. Doing is actiuitie, and he will still be doing.

Orleance. He neuer did harme, that I heard of.

Const. Nor will doe none to morrow: hee will keepe that good name still.

Orleance. I know him to be valiant.

Const. I was told that, by one that knowes him better then you.

Orleance. What's hee?

Const. Marry hee told me so himselfe, and hee sayd hee car'd not who knew it.

Orleance. Hee needes not, it is no hidden vertue in him.

Const. By my faith Sir, but it is: neuer any body saw it, but his Lacquey: 'tis a hooded valour, and when it appeares, it will bate.

Orleance. Ill will neuer sayd well.

Const. I will cap that Prouerbe with, There is flatterie in friendship.

Orleance. And I will take vp that with, Giue the Deuill his due.

Const. Well plac't: there stands your friend for the Deuill: haue at the very eye of that Prouerbe with, A Pox of the Deuill.

Orleance. You are the better at Prouerbs, by how much a Fooles Bolt is soone shot.

Const. You haue shot ouer.

Orleance. 'Tis not the first time you were ouer-shot.

Enter a Messenger.

Mess. My Lord high Constable, the English lye within fifteene hundred paces of your Tents.

Const. Who hath measur'd the ground?

Mess. The Lord *Grandpree.*

Const. A valiant and most expert Gentleman. Would it were day? Alas poore *Harry* of England: hee longs not for the Dawning, as wee doe.

Orleance. What a wretched and peeuish fellow is this King of England, to mope with his fat-brain'd followers so farre out of his knowledge.

Const. If the English had any apprehension, they would runne away.

Orleance. That they lack: for if their heads had any intellectuall Armour, they could neuer weare such heauie Head-pieces.

Ramb. That Iland of England breedes very valiant Creatures; their Mastiffes are of vnmatchable courage.

Orleance. Foolish Curres, that runne winking into the mouth of a Russian Beare, and haue their heads crusht like rotten Apples: you may as well say, that's a valiant Flea, that dare eate his breakefast on the Lippe of a Lyon.

Const. Iust, iust: and the men doe sympathize with the Mastiffes, in robustious and rough comming on, leauing their Wits with their Wiues: and then giue them great Meales of Beefe, and Iron and Steele; they will eate like Wolues, and fight like Deuils.

Orleance. I,

Orleance. I, but these English are shrowdly out of Beefe.

Const. Then shall we finde to morrow, they haue only stomackes to eate, and none to fight. Now is it time to arme: come, shall we about it?

Orleance. It is now two a Clock: but let me see, by ten Wee shall haue each a hundred English men. *Exeunt.*

Actus Tertius.

Chorus.

Now entertaine coniecture of a time,
When creeping Murmure and the poring Darke
Fills the wide Vessell of the Vniuerse.
From Camp to Camp, through the foule Womb of Night
The Humme of eyther Army stilly sounds;
That the fixt Centinels almost receiue
The secret Whispers of each others Watch.
Fire answers fire, and through their paly flames
Each Battaile sees the others vmber'd face.
Steed threatens Steed, in high and boastfull Neighs
Piercing the Nights dull Eare: and from the Tents,
The Armourers accomplishing the Knights,
With busie Hammers closing Riuets vp,
Giue dreadfull note of preparation.
The Countrey Cocks doe crow, the Clocks doe towle:
And the third howre of drowsie Morning nam'd,
Prowd of their Numbers, and secure in Soule,
The confident and ouer-lustie French,
Doe the low-rated English play at Dice;
And chide the creeple-tardy-gated Night,
Who like a foule and ougly Witch doth limpe
So tediously away. The poore condemned English,
Like Sacrifices, by their watchfull Fires
Sit patiently, and inly ruminate
The Mornings danger: and their gesture sad,
Inuesting lanke-leane Cheekes, and Warre-worne Coats,
Presented them vnto the gazing Moone
So many horride Ghosts. O now, who will behold
The Royall Captaine of this ruin'd Band
Walking from Watch to Watch, from Tent to Tent;
Let him cry, Prayse and Glory on his head:
For forth he goes, and visits all his Hoast,
Bids them good morrow with a modest Smyle,
And calls them Brothers, Friends, and Countreymen.
Vpon his Royall Face there is no note,
How dread an Army hath enrounded him;
Nor doth he dedicate one iot of Colour
Vnto the wearie and all-watched Night:
But freshly lookes, and ouer-beares Attaint,
With chearefull semblance, and sweet Maiestie:
That euery Wretch, pining and pale before,
Beholding him, plucks comfort from his Lookes.
A Largesse vniuersall, like the Sunne,
His liberall Eye doth giue to euery one,
Thawing cold feare, that meane and gentle all
Behold, as may vnworthinesse define.
A little touch of *Harry* in the Night,
And so our Scene must to the Battaile flye:
Where, O for pitty, we shall much disgrace,
With foure or fiue most vile and ragged foyles,
(Right ill dispos'd, in brawle ridiculous)
The Name of Agincourt: Yet sit and see,
Minding true things, by what their Mock'ries bee.
Exit.

Enter the King, Bedford, and Gloucester.

King. Gloster, 'tis true that we are in great danger,
The greater therefore should our Courage be.
God morrow Brother *Bedford*: God Almightie,
There is some soule of goodnesse in things euill,
Would men obseruingly distill it out.
For our bad Neighbour makes vs early stirrers,
Which is both healthfull, and good husbandry.
Besides, they are our outward Consciences,
And Preachers to vs all; admonishing,
That we should dresse vs fairely for our end.
Thus may we gather Honey from the Weed,
And make a Morall of the Diuell himselfe.

Enter Erpingham.

Good morrow old Sir *Thomas Erpingham*:
A good soft Pillow for that good white Head,
Were better then a churlish turfe of France.

Erping. Not so my Liege, this Lodging likes me better,
Since I may say, now lye I like a King.

King. 'Tis good for men to loue their present paines,
Vpon example, so the Spirit is eased:
And when the Mind is quickned, out of doubt
The Organs, though defunct and dead before,
Breake vp their drowsie Graue, and newly moue
With casted slough, and fresh legeritie.
Lend me thy Cloake Sir *Thomas*: Brothers both,
Commend me to the Princes in our Campe;
Doe my good morrow to them, and anon
Desire them all to my Pauillion.

Gloster. We shall, my Liege.

Erping. Shall I attend your Grace?

King. No, my good Knight:
Goe with my Brothers to my Lords of England:
I and my Bosome must debate a while,
And then I would no other company.

Erping. The Lord in Heauen blesse thee, Noble *Harry*. *Exeunt.*

King. God a mercy old Heart, thou speak'st chearefully. *Enter Pistoll.*

Pist. Che vous la?

King. A friend.

Pist. Discusse vnto me, art thou Officer, or art thou base, common, and popular?

King. I am a Gentleman of a Company.

Pist. Trayl'st thou the puissant Pyke?

King. Euen so: what are you?

Pist. As good a Gentleman as the Emperor.

King. Then you are a better then the King.

Pist. The King's a Bawcock, and a Heart of Gold, a Lad of Life, an Impe of Fame, of Parents good, of Fist most valiant: I kisse his durtie shooe, and from heart-string I loue the louely Bully. What is thy Name?

King. Harry le Roy.

Pist. Le Roy? a Cornish Name: art thou of Cornish Crew?

King. No, I am a Welchman.

Pist. Know'st thou *Fluellen*?

King. Yes.

Pist. Tell him Ile knock his Leeke about his Pate vpon S. *Dauies* day.

King. Doe not you weare your Dagger in your Cappe that day, least he knock that about yours.

Pist. Art thou his friend?
King. And his Kinſman too.
Pist. The *Figo* for thee then.
King. I thanke you: God be with you.
Pist. My name is *Pistol* call'd.   *Exit.*
King. It sorts well with your fierceneſſe.

Manet King.

Enter Fluellen and Gower.

Gower. Captaine *Fluellen.*

Flu. 'So, in the Name of Ieſu Chriſt, ſpeake fewer: it is the greateſt admiration in the vniuerſall World, when the true and aunchient Prerogatifes and Lawes of the Warres is not kept: if you would take the paines but to examine the Warres of *Pompey* the Great, you ſhall finde, I warrant you, that there is no tiddle tadle nor pibble bable in *Pompeyes* Campe: I warrant you, you ſhall finde the Ceremonies of the Warres, and the Cares of it, and the Formes of it, and the Sobrietie of it, and the Modeſtie of it, to be otherwiſe.

Gower. Why the Enemie is lowd, you heare him all Night.

Flu. If the Enemie is an Aſſe and a Foole, and a prating Coxcombe; is it meet, thinke you, that wee ſhould alſo, looke you, be an Aſſe and a Foole, and a prating Coxcombe, in your owne conſcience now?

Gow. I will ſpeake lower.

Flu. I pray you, and beſeech you, that you will. *Exit.*

King. Though it appeare a little out of faſhion,
There is much care and valour in this Welchman.

Enter three Souldiers, Iohn Bates, Alexander Court, and Michael Williams.

Court. Brother *Iohn Bates*, is not that the Morning which breakes yonder?

Bates. I thinke it be: but wee haue no great cauſe to deſire the approach of day.

Williams. Wee ſee yonder the beginning of the day, but I thinke wee ſhall neuer ſee the end of it. Who goes there?

King. A Friend.

Williams. Vnder what Captaine ſerue you?

King. Vnder Sir *Iohn Erpingham.*

Williams. A good old Commander, and a moſt kinde Gentleman: I pray you, what thinkes he of our eſtate?

King. Euen as men wrackt vpon a Sand, that looke to be waſht off the next Tyde.

Bates. He hath not told his thought to the King?

King. No: nor it is not meet he ſhould: for though I ſpeake it to you, I thinke the King is but a man, as I am: the Violet ſmells to him, as it doth to me; the Element ſhewes to him, as it doth to me; all his Sences haue but humane Conditions: his Ceremonies layd by, in his Nakedneſſe he appeares but a man; and though his affections are higher mounted then ours, yet when they ſtoupe, they ſtoupe with the like wing: therefore, when he ſees reaſon of feares, as we doe; his feares, out of doubt, be of the ſame relliſh as ours are: yet in reaſon, no man ſhould poſſeſſe him with any appearance of feare; leaſt hee, by ſhewing it, ſhould dis-hearten his Army.

Bates. He may ſhew what outward courage he will: but I beleeue, as cold a Night as 'tis, hee could wiſh himſelfe in Thames vp to the Neck; and ſo I would he were, and I by him, at all aduentures, ſo we were quit here.

King. By my troth, I will ſpeake my conſcience of the King: I thinke hee would not wiſh himſelfe any where, but where hee is.

Bates. Then I would he were here alone; ſo ſhould he be ſure to be ranſomed, and a many poore mens liues ſaued.

King. I dare ſay, you loue him not ſo ill, to wiſh him here alone: howſoeuer you ſpeake this to feele other mens minds, me thinks I could not dye any where ſo contented, as in the Kings company; his Cauſe being iuſt, and his Quarrell honorable.

Williams. That's more then we know.

Bates. I, or more then wee ſhould ſeeke after; for wee know enough, if wee know wee are the Kings Subiects: if his Cauſe be wrong, our obedience to the King wipes the Cryme of it out of vs.

Williams. But if the Cauſe be not good, the King himſelfe hath a heauie Reckoning to make, when all thoſe Legges, and Armes, and Heads, chopt off in a Battaile, ſhall ioyne together at the latter day, and cry all, Wee dyed at ſuch a place, ſome ſwearing, ſome crying for a Surgean; ſome vpon their Wiues, left poore behind them; ſome vpon the Debts they owe, ſome vpon their Children rawly left: I am afear'd, there are few dye well, that dye in a Battaile: for how can they charitably diſpoſe of any thing, when Blood is their argument? Now, if theſe men doe not dye well, it will be a black matter for the King, that led them to it; who to diſobey, were againſt all proportion of ſubiection.

King. So, if a Sonne that is by his Father ſent about Merchandize, doe ſinfully miſcarry vpon the Sea; the imputation of his wickedneſſe, by your rule, ſhould be impoſed vpon his Father that ſent him: or if a Seruant, vnder his Maſters command, tranſporting a ſumme of Money, be aſſayled by Robbers, and dye in many irreconcil'd Iniquities; you may call the buſineſſe of the Maſter the author of the Seruants damnation: but this is not ſo: The King is not bound to anſwer the particular endings of his Souldiers, the Father of his Sonne, nor the Maſter of his Seruant; for they purpoſe not their death, when they purpoſe their ſeruices. Beſides, there is no King, be his Cauſe neuer ſo ſpotleſſe, if it come to the arbitrement of Swords, can trye it out with all vnſpotted Souldiers: ſome (peraduenture) haue on them the guilt of premeditated and contriued Murther; ſome, of beguiling Virgins with the broken Seales of Periurie; ſome, making the Warres their Bulwarke, that haue before gored the gentle Boſome of Peace with Pillage and Robberie. Now, if theſe men haue defeated the Law, and outrunne Natiue puniſhment; though they can out-ſtrip men, they haue no wings to flye from God. Warre is his Beadle, Warre is his Vengeance: ſo that here men are puniſht, for before breach of the Kings Lawes, in now the Kings Quarrell: where they feared the death, they haue borne life away; and where they would bee ſafe, they periſh. Then if they dye vnprouided, no more is the King guiltie of their damnation, then hee was before guiltie of thoſe Impieties, for the which they are now viſited. Euery Subiects Dutie is the Kings, but euery Subiects Soule is his owne. Therefore ſhould euery Souldier in the Warres doe as euery ſicke man in his Bed, waſh euery Moth out of his Conſcience: and dying ſo, Death is to him aduantage; or not dying, the time was bleſſedly loſt, wherein ſuch preparation was gayned: and in him that eſcapes, it were not ſinne to thinke, that making God ſo free an offer, he let him outliue that day, to ſee his Greatneſſe, and to teach others how they ſhould prepare.

Will. 'Tis

Will. 'Tis certaine, euery man that dyes ill, the ill vpon his owne head, the King is not to answer it.

Bates. I doe not desire hee should answer for me, and yet I determine to fight lustily for him.

King. I my selfe heard the King say he would not be ransom'd.

Will. I, hee said so, to make vs fight chearefully: but when our throats are cut, hee may be ransom'd, and wee ne're the wiser.

King. If I liue to see it, I will neuer trust his word after.

Will. You pay him then: that's a perillous shot out of an Elder Gunne, that a poore and a priuate displeasure can doe against a Monarch: you may as well goe about to turne the Sunne to yce, with fanning in his face with a Peacocks feather: You'le neuer trust his word after; come, 'tis a foolish saying.

King. Your reproofe is something too round, I should be angry with you, if the time were conuenient.

Will. Let it bee a Quarrell betweene vs, if you liue.

King. I embrace it.

Will. How shall I know thee againe?

King. Giue me any Gage of thine, and I will weare it in my Bonnet: Then if euer thou dar'st acknowledge it, I will make it my Quarrell.

Will. Heere's my Gloue: Giue mee another of thine.

King. There.

Will. This will I also weare in my Cap: if euer thou come to me, and say, after to morrow, This is my Gloue, by this Hand I will take thee a box on the eare.

King. If euer I liue to see it, I will challenge it.

Will. Thou dar'st as well be hang'd.

King. Well, I will doe it, though I take thee in the Kings companie.

Will. Keepe thy word: fare thee well.

Bates. Be friends you English fooles, be friends, wee haue French Quarrels enow, if you could tell how to reckon.
Exit Souldiers.

King. Indeede the French may lay twentie French Crownes to one, they will beat vs, for they beare them on their shoulders: but it is no English Treason to cut French Crownes, and to morrow the King himselfe will be a Clipper.

Vpon the King, let vs our Liues, our Soules,
Our Debts, our carefull Wiues,
Our Children, and our Sinnes, lay on the King:
We must beare all.
O hard Condition, Twin-borne with Greatnesse,
Subiect to the breath of euery foole, whose sence
No more can feele, but his owne wringing.
What infinite hearts-ease must Kings neglect,
That priuate men enioy?
And what haue Kings, that Priuates haue not too,
Saue Ceremonie, saue generall Ceremonie?
And what art thou, thou Idoll Ceremonie?
What kind of God art thou? that suffer'st more
Of mortall griefes, then doe thy worshippers.
What are thy Rents? what are thy Commings in?
O Ceremonie, shew me but thy worth.
What? is thy Soule of Odoration?
Art thou ought else but Place, Degree, and Forme,
Creating awe and feare in other men?
Wherein thou art lesse happy, being fear'd,
Then they in fearing.
What drink'st thou oft, in stead of Homage sweet,
But poyson'd flatterie? O, be sick, great Greatnesse,
And bid thy Ceremonie giue thee cure.
Thinks thou the fierie Feuer will goe out
With Titles blowne from Adulation?
Will it giue place to flexure and low bending?
Canst thou, when thou command'st the beggers knee,
Command the health of it? No, thou prowd Dreame,
That play'st so subtilly with a Kings Repose.
I am a King that find thee: and I know,
'Tis not the Balme, the Scepter, and the Ball,
The Sword, the Mase, the Crowne Imperiall,
The enter-tissued Robe of Gold and Pearle,
The farsed Title running 'fore the King,
The Throne he sits on: nor the Tyde of Pompe,
That beates vpon the high shore of this World:
No, not all these, thrice-gorgeous Ceremonie;
Not all these, lay'd in Bed Maiesticall,
Can sleepe so soundly, as the wretched Slaue:
Who with a body fill'd, and vacant mind,
Gets him to rest, cram'd with distressefull bread,
Neuer sees horride Night, the Child of Hell:
But like a Lacquey, from the Rise to Set,
Sweates in the eye of *Phebus*; and all Night
Sleepes in *Elizium*: next day after dawne,
Doth rise and helpe *Hiperio* to his Horse,
And followes so the euer-running yeere
With profitable labour to his Graue:
And but for Ceremonie, such a Wretch,
Winding vp Dayes with toyle, and Nights with sleepe,
Had the fore-hand and vantage of a King.
The Slaue, a Member of the Countreyes peace,
Enioyes it; but in grosse braine little wots,
What watch the King keepes, to maintaine the peace;
Whose howres, the Pesant best aduantages.

Enter Erpingham.

Erp. My Lord, your Nobles iealous of your absence,
Seeke through your Campe to find you.

King. Good old Knight, collect them all together
At my Tent: Ile be before thee.

Erp. I shall doo't, my Lord. *Exit.*

King. O God of Battailes, steele my Souldiers hearts,
Possesse them not with feare: Take from them now
The sence of reckning of th'opposed numbers:
Pluck their hearts from them. Not to day, O Lord,
O not to day, thinke not vpon the fault
My Father made, in compassing the Crowne.
I *Richards* body haue interred new,
And on it haue bestowed more contrite teares,
Then from it issued forced drops of blood.
Fiue hundred poore I haue in yeerely pay,
Who twice a day their wither'd hands hold vp
Toward Heauen, to pardon blood:
And I haue built two Chauntries,
Where the sad and solemne Priests sing still
For *Richards* Soule. More will I doe:
Though all that I can doe, is nothing worth;
Since that my Penitence comes after all,
Imploring pardon.

Enter Gloucester.

Glouc. My Liege.

King. My Brother *Gloucesters* voyce? I:
I know thy errand, I will goe with thee:
The day, my friend, and all things stay for me.
Exeunt.

Enter the Dolphin, Orleance, Rambures, and Beaumont.

Orleance. The Sunne doth gild our Armour vp, my Lords.

Dolph. Monte Cheual: My Horse, Verlot Lacquay: Ha.

Orleance. Oh braue Spirit.

Dolph. Via les ewes & terre.

Orleance. Rien puis le air & feu.

Dolph. Cein, Cousin Orleance.   *Enter Constable.*
Now my Lord Constable?

Const. Hearke how our Steedes, for present Seruice neigh.

Dolph. Mount them, and make incision in their Hides,
That their hot blood may spin in English eyes,
And doubt them with superfluous courage: ha.

Ram. What, wil you haue them weep our Horses blood?
How shall we then behold their naturall teares?

Enter Messenger.

Messeng. The English are embattail'd, you French Peeres.

Const. To Horse you gallant Princes, straight to Horse.
Doe but behold yond poore and starued Band,
And your faire shew shall suck away their Soules,
Leauing them but the shales and huskes of men.
There is not worke enough for all our hands,
Scarce blood enough in all their sickly Veines,
To giue each naked Curtleax a stayne,
That our French Gallants shall to day draw out,
And sheath for lack of sport. Let vs but blow on them,
The vapour of our Valour will o're-turne them.
'Tis positiue against all exceptions, Lords,
That our superfluous Lacquies, and our Pesants,
Who in vnnecessarie action swarme
About our Squares of Battaile, were enow
To purge this field of such a hilding Foe;
Though we vpon this Mountaines Basis by,
Tooke stand for idle speculation:
But that our Honours must not. What's to say?
A very little little let vs doe,
And all is done: then let the Trumpets sound
The Tucket Sonuance, and the Note to mount:
For our approach shall so much dare the field,
That England shall couch downe in feare, and yeeld.

Enter Graundpree.

Grandpree. Why do you stay so long, my Lords of France?
Yond Iland Carrions, desperate of their bones,
Ill-fauoredly become the Morning field:
Their ragged Curtaines poorely are let loose,
And our Ayre shakes them passing scornefully.
Bigge Mars seemes banqu'rout in their begger'd Hoast,
And faintly through a rustie Beuer peepes.
The Horsemen sit like fixed Candlesticks,
With Torch-staues in their hand: and their poore Iades
Lob downe their heads, dropping the hides and hips:
The gumme downe roping from their pale-dead eyes,
And in their pale dull mouthes the Iymold Bitt
Lyes foule with chaw'd-grasse, still and motionlesse.
And their executors, the knauish Crowes,
Flye o're them all, impatient for their howre.
Description cannot sute it selfe in words,
To demonstrate the Life of such a Battaile,
In life so liuelesse, as it shewes it selfe.

Const. They haue said their prayers,
And they stay for death.

Dolph. Shall we goe send them Dinners, and fresh Sutes,
And giue their fasting Horses Prouender,
And after fight with them?

Const. I stay but for my Guard: on
To the field, I will the Banner from a Trumpet take,
And vse it for my haste. Come, come away,
The Sunne is high, and we out-weare the day. *Exeunt.*

Enter Gloucester, Bedford, Exeter, Erpingham with all his Hoast: Salisbury, and Westmerland.

Glouc. Where is the King?

Bedf. The King himselfe is rode to view their Battaile.

West. Of fighting men they haue full threescore thousand.

Exe. There's fiue to one, besides they all are fresh.

Salisb. Gods Arme strike with vs, 'tis a fearefull oddes.
God buy' you Princes all; Ile to my Charge:
If we no more meet, till we meet in Heauen;
Then ioyfully, my Noble Lord of Bedford,
My deare Lord Gloucester, and my good Lord Exeter,
And my kind Kinsman, Warriors all, adieu.

Bedf. Farwell good *Salisbury*, & good luck go with thee:
And yet I doe thee wrong, to mind thee of it,
For thou art fram'd of the firme truth of valour.

Exe. Farwell kind Lord: fight valiantly to day.

Bedf. He is as full of Valour as of Kindnesse,
Princely in both.

Enter the King.

West. O that we now had here
But one ten thousand of those men in England,
That doe no worke to day.

King. What's he that wishes so?
My Cousin *Westmerland*. No, my faire Cousin:
If we are markt to dye, we are enow
To doe our Countrey losse: and if to liue,
The fewer men, the greater share of honour.
Gods will, I pray thee wish not one man more.
By *Ioue*, I am not couetous for Gold,
Nor care I who doth feed vpon my cost:
It yernes me not, if men my Garments weare;
Such outward things dwell not in my desires.
But if it be a sinne to couet Honor,
I am the most offending Soule aliue.
No 'faith, my Couze, wish not a man from England:
Gods peace, I would not loose so great an Honor,
As one man more me thinkes would share from me,
For the best hope I haue. O, doe not wish one more:
Rather proclaime it (*Westmerland*) through my Hoast,
That he which hath no stomack to this fight,
Let him depart, his Pasport shall be made,
And Crownes for Conuoy put into his Purse:
We would not dye in that mans companie,
That feares his fellowship, to dye with vs.
This day is call'd the Feast of *Crispian*:
He that out-liues this day, and comes safe home,
Will stand a tip-toe when this day is named,
And rowse him at the Name of *Crispian*.
He that shall see this day, and liue old age,
Will yeerely on the Vigil feast his neighbours,
And say, to morrow is Saint *Crispian*.
Then will he strip his sleeue, and shew his skarres:
Old men forget; yet all shall be forgot:
But hee'le remember, with aduantages,
What feats he did that day. Then shall our Names,
Familiar in his mouth as houshold words,

Harry

Harry the King, *Bedford* and *Exeter*,
Warwick and *Talbot*, *Salisbury* and *Gloucester*,
Be in their flowing Cups freshly remembred.
This story shall the good man teach his sonne:
And *Crispine Crispian* shall ne're goe by,
From this day to the ending of the World,
But we in it shall be remembred;
We few, we happy few, we band of brothers:
For he to day that sheds his blood with me,
Shall be my brother: be he ne're so vile,
This day shall gentle his Condition.
And Gentlemen in England, now a bed,
Shall thinke themselues accurst they were not here;
And hold their Manhoods cheape, whiles any speakes,
That fought with vs vpon Saint *Crispines* day.

Enter Salisbury.

Sal. My Soueraign Lord, bestow your selfe with speed:
The French are brauely in their battailes set,
And will with all expedience charge on vs.

  King. All things are ready, if our minds be so.
  West. Perish the man, whose mind is backward now.
  King. Thou do'st not wish more helpe from England, Couze?
  West. Gods will, my Liege, would you and I alone,
Without more helpe, could fight this Royall battaile.
  King. Why now thou hast vnwisht fiue thousand men:
Which likes me better, then to wish vs one.
You know your places: God be with you all:

Tucket. Enter Montioy.

  Mont. Once more I come to know of thee King *Harry*,
If for thy Ransome thou wilt now compound,
Before thy most assured Ouerthrow:
For certainly, thou art so neere the Gulfe,
Thou needs must be englutted. Besides, in mercy
The Constable desires thee, thou wilt mind
Thy followers of Repentance; that their Soules
May make a peacefull and a sweet retyre
From off these fields: where (wretches) their poore bodies
Must lye and fester.
  King. Who hath sent thee now?
  Mont. The Constable of France.
  King. I pray thee beare my former Answer back:
Bid them atchieue me, and then sell my bones.
Good God, why should they mock poore fellowes thus?
The man that once did sell the Lyons skin
While the beast liu'd, was kill'd with hunting him.
A many of our bodyes shall no doubt
Find Natiue Graues: vpon the which, I trust
Shall witnesse liue in Brasse of this dayes worke.
And those that leaue their valiant bones in France,
Dying like men, though buryed in your Dunghills,
They shall be fam'd: for there the Sun shall greet them,
And draw their honors reeking vp to Heauen,
Leauing their earthly parts to choake your Clyme,
The smell whereof shall breed a Plague in France.
Marke then abounding valour in our English:
That being dead, like to the bullets crasing,
Breake out into a second course of mischiefe,
Killing in relapse of Mortalitie.
Let me speake prowdly: Tell the Constable,
We are but Warriors for the working day:
Our Gaynesse and our Gilt are all besmyrcht
With raynie Marching in the painefull field.
There's not a piece of feather in our Hoast:
Good argument (I hope) we will not flye:
And time hath worne vs into slouenrie.
But by the Masse, our hearts are in the trim:
And my poore Souldiers tell me, yet ere Night,
They'le be in fresher Robes, or they will pluck
The gay new Coats o're the French Souldiers heads,
And turne them out of seruice. If they doe this,
As if God please, they shall; my Ransome then
Will soone be leuyed.
Herauld, saue thou thy labour:
Come thou no more for Ransome, gentle Herauld,
They shall haue none, I sweare, but these my ioynts:
Which if they haue, as I will leaue vm them,
Shall yeeld them little, tell the Constable.
  Mont. I shall, King *Harry*. And so fare thee well:
Thou neuer shalt heare Herauld any more. *Exit.*
  King. I feare thou wilt once more come againe for a Ransome.

Enter Yorke.

  Yorke. My Lord, most humbly on my knee I begge
The leading of the Vaward.
  King. Take it, braue *Yorke*.
Now Souldiers march away,
And how thou pleasest God, dispose the day. *Exeunt.*

Alarum. Excursions.
Enter Pistoll, French Souldier, Boy.

  Pist. Yeeld Curre.
  French. Ie pense que vous estes le Gentilhome de bon qua-litee.
  Pist. Qualtitie calmie custure me. Art thou a Gentle-man? What is thy Name? discusse.
  French. O Seigneur Dieu.
  Pist. O Signieur Dewe should be a Gentleman: per-pend my words O Signieur Dewe, and marke: O Signieur Dewe, thou dyest on point of Fox, except O Signieur thou doe giue to me egregious Ransome.
  French. O prennes misericordie aye pitez de moy.
  Pist. Moy shall not serue, I will haue fortie Moyes: for I will fetch thy rymme out at thy Throat, in droppes of Crimson blood.
  French. Est il impossible d'eschapper le force de ton bras.
  Pist. Brasse, Curre? thou damned and luxurious Moun-taine Goat, offer'st me Brasse?
  French. O perdonne moy.
  Pist. Say'st thou me so? is that a Tonne of Moyes? Come hither boy, aske me this slaue in French what is his Name.
  Boy. Escoute comment estes vous appelle?
  French. Mounsieur le Fer.
  Boy. He sayes his Name is M. *Fer.*
  Pist. M. *Fer:* Ile fer him, and firke him, and ferret him: discusse the same in French vnto him.
  Boy. I doe not know the French for fer, and ferret, and firke.
  Pist. Bid him prepare, for I will cut his throat.
  French. Que dit il Mounsieur?
  Boy. Il me commande a vous dire que vous faite vous prest, car ce soldat icy est disposee tout asture de couppes vostre gorge.
  Pist. Owy, cuppele gorge permafoy pesant, vnlesse thou giue me Crownes, braue Crownes; or mangled shalt thou be by this my Sword.
  French. O Ie vous supplie pour l'amour de Dieu: ma par-donner, Ie suis le Gentilhome de bon maison, gards ma vie, & Ie vous donneray deux cent escus.
  Pist. What are his words?
  Boy. He

Boy. He prayes you to saue his life, he is a Gentleman of a good house, and for his ransom he will giue you two hundred Crownes.

Pist. Tell him my fury shall abate, and I the Crownes will take.

Fren. Petit Monsieur que dit il?

Boy. Encore qu'il et contra son Iurement, de pardonner aucune prisonner: neant-mous pour les escues que vous layt a promets, il est content a vous donnes le liberte le franchisement.

Fre. Sur mes genoux se vous donnes milles remercious, et Ie me estime heurex que Ie intombe, entre les main. d'vn Cheualier Ie pense le plus braue valiant et tres distime signieur d'Angleterre.

Pist. Expound vnto me boy.

Boy. He giues you vpon his knees a thousand thanks, and he esteemes himselfe happy, that he hath falne into the hands of one (as he thinkes) the most braue, valorous and thrice-worthy signeur of England.

Pist. As I sucke blood, I will some mercy shew. Follow mee.

Boy. Saaue vous le grand Capitaine?

I did neuer know so full a voyce issue from so emptie a heart: but the saying is true, The empty vessel makes the greatest sound, *Bardolfe* and *Nym* had tenne times more valour, then this roaring diuell i'th olde play, that euerie one may payre his nayles with a woodden dagger, and they are both hang'd, and so would this be, if hee durst steale any thing aduenturously. I must stay with the Lackies with the luggage of our camp, the French might haue a good pray of vs, if he knew of it, for there is none to guard it but boyes. *Exit.*

Enter Constable, Orleance, Burbon, Dolphin, and Ramburs.

Con. O Diable.

Orl. O signeur le iour et perdia, toute et perdie.

Dol. Mor Dieu ma vie, all is confounded all,
Reproach, and euerlasting shame
Sits mocking in our Plumes.   *A short Alarum.*
O meschante Fortune, do not runne away.

Con. Why all our rankes are broke.

Dol. O perdurable shame, let's stab our selues:
Be these the wretches that we plaid at dice for?

Orl. Is this the King we sent too, for his ransome?

Bur. Shame, and eternall shame, nothing but shame,
Let vs dye in once more backe againe,
And he that will not follow *Burbon* now,
Let him go hence, and with his cap in hand
Like a base Pander hold the Chamber doore,
Whilst a base slaue, no gentler then my dogge,
His fairest daughter is contaminated.

Con. Disorder that hath spoyl'd vs, friend vs now,
Let vs on heapes go offer vp our liues.

Orl. We are enow yet liuing in the Field,
To smother vp the English in our throngs,
If any order might be thought vpon.

Bur. The diuell take Order now, Ile to the throng;
Let life be short, else shame will be too long. *Exit.*

Alarum. Enter the King and his trayne, with Prisoners.

King. Well haue we done, thrice-valiant Countrimen,
But all's not done, yet keepe the French the field.

Exe. The D. of Yorke commends him to your Maiesty

King. Liues he good Vnckle: thrice within this houre
I saw him downe; thrice vp againe, and fighting,
From Helmet to the spurre, all blood he was.

Exe. In which array (braue Soldier) doth he lye,
Larding the plaine: and by his bloody side,
(Yoake-fellow to his honour-owing-wounds)
The Noble Earle of Suffolke also lyes.
Suffolke first dyed, and Yorke all hagled ouer
Comes to him, where in gore he lay insteeped,
And takes him by the Beard, kisses the gashes
That bloodily did yawne vpon his face.
He cryes aloud; Tarry my Cosin Suffolke,
My soule shall thine keepe company to heauen:
Tarry (sweet soule) for mine, then flye a-brest:
As in this glorious and well-foughten field
We kept together in our Chiualrie.
Vpon these words I came, and cheer'd him vp,
He smil'd me in the face, raught me his hand,
And with a feeble gripe, sayes: Deere my Lord,
Commend my seruice to my Soueraigne,
So did he turne, and ouer Suffolkes necke
He threw his wounded arme, and kist his lippes,
And so espous'd to death, with blood he seal'd
A Testament of Noble-ending-loue:
The prettie and sweet manner of it forc'd
Those waters from me, which I would haue stop'd,
But I had not so much of man in mee,
And all my mother came into mine eyes,
And gaue me vp to teares.

King. I blame you not,
For hearing this, I must perforce compound
With mixtfull eyes, or they will issue to. *Alarum*
But hearke, what new alarum is this same?
The French haue re-enforc'd their scatter'd men:
Then euery souldiour kill his Prisoners,
Giue the word through. *Exit.*

Actus Quartus.

Enter Fluellen and Gower.

Flu. Kill the poyes and the luggage, 'Tis expressely against the Law of Armes, tis as arrant a peece of knauery marke you now, as can bee offert in your Conscience now, is it not?

Gow. 'Tis certaine, there's not a boy left aliue, and the Cowardly Rascalls that ranne from the battaile ha' done this slaughter: besides they haue burned and carried away all that was in the Kings Tent, wherefore the King most worthily hath caus'd euery souldiour to cut his prisoners throat. O'tis a gallant King.

Flu. I, hee was porne at *Monmouth* Captaine *Gower*: What call you the Townes name where *Alexander* the pig was borne?

Gow. Alexander the Great.

Flu. Why I pray you, is not pig, great? The pig, or the great, or the mighty, or the huge, or the magnanimous, are all one reckonings, saue the phrase is a little variations.

Gower. I thinke *Alexander* the Great was borne in *Macedon*, his Father was called *Phillip* of *Macedon*, as I take it.

Flu. I thinke it is in *Macedon* where *Alexander* is porne.

porne: I tell you Captaine, if you looke in the Maps of the Orld, I warrant you sall finde in the comparisons betweene *Macedon* & *Monmouth*, that the situations looke you, is both alike. There is a Riuer in *Macedon*, & there is also moreouer a Riuer at *Monmouth*, it is call'd Wye at *Monmouth*: but it is out of my praines, what is the name of the other Riuer: but 'tis all one, tis alike as my fingers is to my fingers, and there is Salmons in both. If you marke *Alexanders* life well, *Harry of Monmouthes* life is come after it indifferent well, for there is figures in all things. *Alexander* God knowes, and you know, in his rages, and his furies, and his wraths, and his cholliers, and his moodes, and his displeasures, and his indignations, and also being a little intoxicates in his praines, did in his Ales and his angers (looke you) kill his best friend *Clytus*.

Gow. Our King is not like him in that, he neuer kill'd any of his friends.

Flu. It is not well done (marke you now) to take the tales out of my mouth, ere it is made and finished. I speak but in the figures, and comparisons of it: as *Alexander* kild his friend *Clytus*, being in his Ales and his Cuppes; so also *Harry Monmouth* being in his right wittes, and his good iudgements, turn'd away the fat Knight with the great belly doublet: he was full of iests, and gypes, and knaueries, and mockes, I haue forgot his name.

Gow. Sir *Iohn Falstaffe*.

Flu. That is he: Ile tell you, there is good men porne at *Monmonth*.

Gow. Heere comes his Maiesty.

Alarum. Enter King Harry and Burbon with prisoners. Flourish.

King. I was not angry since I came to France,
Vntill this instant. Take a Trumpet Herald,
Ride thou vnto the Horsemen on yond hill:
If they will fight with vs, bid them come downe,
Or voyde the field: they do offend our sight.
If they'l do neither, we will come to them,
And make them sker away, as swift as stones
Enforced from the old Assyrian slings:
Besides, wee'l cut the throats of those we haue,
And not a man of them that we shall take,
Shall taste our mercy. Go and tell them so.

Enter Montioy.

Exe. Here comes the Herald of the French, my Liege
Glou. His eyes are humbler then they vs'd to be.
King. How now, what meanes this Herald? Knowst thou not,
That I haue fin'd these bones of mine for ransome?
Com'st thou againe for ransome?

Her. No great King:
I come to thee for charitable License,
That we may wander ore this bloody field,
To booke our dead, and then to bury them,
To sort our Nobles from our common men.
For many of our Princes (woe the while)
Lye drown'd and soak'd in mercenary blood:
So do our vulgar drench their peasant limbes
In blood of Princes, and with wounded steeds
Fret fet-locke deepe in gore, and with wilde rage
Yerke out their armed heeles at their dead masters,
Killing them twice. O giue vs leaue great King,
To view the field in safety, and dispose
Of their dead bodies.

Kin. I tell thee truly Herald,
I know not if the day be ours or no,
For yet a many of your horsemen peere,
And gallop ore the field.

Her. The day is yours.

Kin. Praised be God, and not our strength for it:
What is this Castle call'd that stands hard by.

Her. They call it *Agincourt*.

King. Then call we this the field of *Agincourt*,
Fought on the day of *Crispin Crispianus*.

Flu. Your Grandfather of famous memory (an't please your Maiesty) and your great Vncle *Edward* the Placke Prince of Wales, as I haue read in the Chronicles, fought a most praue pattle here in France.

Kin. They did *Fluellen*.

Flu. Your Maiesty sayes very true: If your Maiesties is remembred of it, the Welchmen did good seruice in a Garden where Leekes did grow, wearing Leekes in their *Monmouth* caps, which your Maiesty know to this houre is an honourable badge of the seruice: And I do beleeue your Maiesty takes no scorne to weare the Leeke vppon S. Tauies day.

King. I weare it for a memorable honor:
For I am Welch you know good Countriman.

Flu. All the water in Wye, cannot wash your Maiesties Welsh plood out of your pody, I can tell you that: God plesse it, and preserue it, as long as it pleases his Grace, and his Maiesty too.

Kin. Thankes good my Countrymen.

Flu. By *Ieshu*, I am your Maiesties Countreyman, I care not who know it: I will confesse it to all the Orld, I need not to be ashamed of your Maiesty, praised be God so long as your Maiesty is an honest man.

King. Good keepe me so.

Enter Williams.

Our Heralds go with him,
Bring me iust notice of the numbers dead
On both our parts. Call yonder fellow hither.

Exe. Souldier, you must come to the King.

Kin. Souldier, why wear'st thou that Gloue in thy Cappe?

Will. And't please your Maiesty, tis the gage of one that I should fight withall, if he be aliue.

Kin. An Englishman?

Wil. And't please your Maiesty, a Rascall that swagger'd with me last night: who if aliue, and euer dare to challenge this Gloue, I haue sworne to take him a boxe a'th ere: or if I can see my Gloue in his cappe, which he swore as he was a Souldier he would weare (if aliue) I wil strike it out soundly.

Kin. What thinke you Captaine *Fluellen*, is it fit this souldier keepe his oath.

Flu. Hee is a Crauen and a Villaine else, and't please your Maiesty in my conscience.

King. It may bee, his enemy is a Gentleman of great sort quite from the answer of his degree.

Flu. Though he be as good a Ientleman as the diuel is, as Lucifer and Belzebub himselfe, it is necessary (looke your Grace) that he keepe his vow and his oath: If hee bee periur'd (see you now) his reputation is as arrant a villaine and a Iacke sawce, as euer his blacke shoo trodd vpon Gods ground, and his earth, in my conscience law

King. Then keepe thy vow sirrah, when thou meet'st the fellow.

Wil. So, I wil my Liege, as I liue.

King. Who seru'st thou vnder?

Wil.

Will. Vnder Captaine *Gower*, my Liege.

Flu. *Gower* is a good Captaine, and is good knowledge and literatured in the Warres.

King. Call him hither to me, Souldier.

Will. I will my Liege.   *Exit.*

King. Here *Fluellen*, weare thou this fauour for me, and sticke it in thy Cappe: when *Alanson* and my selfe were downe together, I pluckt this Gloue from his Helme: If any man challenge this, hee is a friend to *Alanson*, and an enemy to our Person; if thou encounter any such, apprehend him, and thou do'st me loue.

Flu. Your Grace doo's me as great Honors as can be desir'd in the hearts of his Subiects: I would faine see the man, that ha's but two legges, that shall find himselfe agreef'd at this Gloue; that is all: but I would faine see it once, and please God of his grace that I might see.

King. Know'st thou *Gower*?

Flu. He is my deare friend, and please you.

King. Pray thee goe seeke him, and bring him to my Tent.

Flu. I will fetch him.   *Exit.*

King. My Lord of *Warwick*, and my Brother *Gloster*,
Follow *Fluellen* closely at the heeles.
The Gloue which I haue giuen him for a fauour,
May haply purchase him a box a'th'eare.
It is the Souldiers: I by bargaine should
Weare it my selfe. Follow good Cousin *Warwick*:
If that the Souldier strike him, as I iudge
By his blunt bearing, he will keepe his word;
Some sodaine mischiefe may arise of it:
For I doe know *Fluellen* valiant,
And toucht with Choler, hot as Gunpowder,
And quickly will returne an iniurie.
Follow, and see there be no harme betweene them.
Goe you with me, Vnckle of Exeter.   *Exeunt.*

Enter Gower and Williams.

Will. I warrant it is to Knight you, Captaine.

Enter Fluellen.

Flu. Gods will, and his pleasure, Captaine, I beseech you now, come apace to the King: there is more good toward you peraduenture, then is in your knowledge to dreame of.

Will. Sir, know you this Gloue?

Flu. Know the Gloue? I know the Gloue is a Gloue.

Will. I know this, and thus I challenge it.
                                Strikes him.

Flu. 'Sblud, an arrant Traytor as anyes in the Vniuersall World, or in France, or in England.

Gower. How now Sir? you Villaine.

Will. Doe you thinke Ile be forsworne?

Flu. Stand away Captaine *Gower*, I will giue Treason his payment into plowes, I warrant you.

Will. I am no Traytor.

Flu. That's a Lye in thy Throat. I charge you in his Maiesties Name apprehend him, he's a friend of the Duke *Alansons*.

Enter Warwick and Gloucester.

Warw. How now, how now, what's the matter?

Flu. My Lord of Warwick, heere is, praysed be God for it, a most contagious Treason come to light, looke you, as you shall desire in a Summers day. Heere is his Maiestie.   *Enter King and Exeter.*

King. How now, what's the matter?

Flu. My Liege, heere is a Villaine, and a Traytor, that looke your Grace, ha's strooke the Gloue which your Maiestie is take out of the Helmet of *Alanson*.

Will. My Liege, this was my Gloue, here is the fellow of it: and he that I gaue it to in change, promis'd to weare it in his Cappe: I promis'd to strike him, if he did: I met this man with my Gloue in his Cappe, and I haue beene as good as my word.

Flu. Your Maiestie heare now, sauing your Maiesties Manhood, what an arrant rascally, beggerly, lowsie Knaue it is: I hope your Maiestie is peare me testimonie and witnesse, and will auouchment, that this is the Gloue of *Alanson*, that your Maiestie is giue me, in your Conscience now.

King. Giue me thy Gloue Souldier;
Looke, heere is the fellow of it:
'Twas I indeed thou promised'st to strike,
And thou hast giuen me most bitter termes.

Flu. And please your Maiestie, let his Neck answere for it, if there is any Marshall Law in the World.

King. How canst thou make me satisfaction?

Will. All offences, my Lord, come from the heart: neuer came any from mine, that might offend your Maiestie.

King. It was our selfe thou didst abuse.

Will. Your Maiestie came not like your selfe: you appear'd to me but as a common man: witnesse the Night, your Garments, your Lowlinesse: and what your Highnesse suffer'd vnder that shape, I beseech you take it for your owne fault, and not mine: for had you beene as I tooke you for, I made no offence; therefore I beseech your Highnesse pardon me.

King. Here Vnckle *Exeter*, fill this Gloue with Crownes, And giue it to this fellow. Keepe it fellow,
And weare it for an Honor in thy Cappe,
Till I doe challenge it. Giue him the Crownes:
And Captaine, you must needs be friends with him.

Flu. By this Day and this Light, the fellow ha's mettell enough in his belly: Hold, there is twelue-pence for you, and I pray you to serue God, and keepe you out of prawles and prabbles, and quarrels and dissentions, and I warrant you it is the better for you.

Will. I will none of your Money.

Flu. It is with a good will: I can tell you it will serue you to mend your shooes: come, wherefore should you be so pashfull, your shooes is not so good: 'tis a good silling I warrant you, or I will change it.

Enter Herauld.

King. Now Herauld, are the dead numbred?

Herald. Heere is the number of the slaught'red French.

King. What Prisoners of good sort are taken, Vnckle?

Exe. Charles Duke of Orleance, Nephew to the King, *Iohn* Duke of Burbon, and Lord *Bouchiquald*:
Of other Lords and Barons, Knights and Squires,
Full fifteene hundred, besides common men.

King. This Note doth tell me of ten thousand French
That in the field lye slaine: of Princes in this number,
And Nobles bearing Banners, there lye dead
One hundred twentie six: added to these,
Of Knights, Esquires, and gallant Gentlemen,
Eight thousand and foure hundred: of the which,
Fiue hundred were but yesterday dubb'd Knights.
So that in these ten thousand they haue lost,
There are but sixteene hundred Mercenaries:
The rest are Princes, Barons, Lords, Knights, Squires,
                                        And

And Gentlemen of bloud and qualitie.
The Names of those their Nobles that lye dead:
Charles Delabreth, High Constable of France,
Iaques of Chatilion, Admirall of France,
The Master of the Crosse-bowes, Lord *Rambures*,
Great Master of France, the braue Sir *Guichard Dolphin*,
Iohn Duke of Alanson, *Anthonie* Duke of Brabant,
The Brother to the Duke of Burgundie,
And *Edward* Duke of Barr: of lustie Earles,
Grandpree and *Rousse*, *Fauconbridge* and *Foyes*,
Beaumont and *Marle*, *Vandemont* and *Lestrale*.
Here was a Royall fellowship of death.
Where is the number of our English dead?
Edward the Duke of Yorke, the Earle of Suffolke,
Sir *Richard Ketly*, *Dauy Gam* Esquire;
None else of name: and of all other men,
But fiue and twentie.
 O God, thy Arme was heere:
And not to vs, but to thy Arme alone,
Ascribe we all: when, without stratagem,
But in plaine shock, and euen play of Battaile,
Was euer knowne so great and little losse?
On one part and on th'other, take it God,
For it is none but thine.

 Exet. 'Tis wonderfull.
 King. Come, goe we in procession to the Village:
And be it death proclaymed through our Hoast,
To boast of this, or take that prayse from God,
Which is his onely.

 Flu. Is it not lawfull and please your Maiestie, to tell how many is kill'd?
 King. Yes Captaine: but with this acknowledgement, That God fought for vs.
 Flu. Yes, my conscience, he did vs great good.
 King. Doe we all holy Rights:
Let there be sung *Non nobis*, and *Te Deum*,
The dead with charitie enclos'd in Clay:
And then to Callice, and to England then,
Where ne're from France arriu'd more happy men.
 Exeunt.

Actus Quintus.

Enter Chorus.

Vouchsafe to those that haue not read the Story,
That I may prompt them: and of such as haue,
I humbly pray them to admit th'excuse
Of time, of numbers, and due course of things,
Which cannot in their huge and proper life,
Be here presented. Now we beare the King
Toward Callice: Graunt him there; there seene,
Heaue him away vpon your winged thoughts,
Athwart the Sea: Behold the English beach
Pales in the flood; with Men, Wiues, and Boyes,
Whose shouts & claps out-voyce the deep-mouth'd Sea,
Which like a mightie Whiffler 'fore the King,
Seemes to prepare his way: So let him land,
And solemnly see him set on to London.
So swift a pace hath Thought, that euen now
You may imagine him vpon Black-Heath:
Where, that his Lords desire him, to haue borne
His bruised Helmet, and his bended Sword
Before him, through the Citie: he forbids it,
Being free from vain-nesse, and selfe-glorious pride;
Giuing full Trophee, Signall, and Ostent,
Quite from himselfe, to God. But now behold,
In the quick Forge and working-house of Thought,
How London doth powre out her Citizens,
The Maior and all his Brethren in best sort,
Like to the Senatours of th'antique Rome,
With the Plebeians swarming at their heeles,
Goe forth and fetch their Conqu'ring *Cæsar* in:
As by a lower, but by louing likelyhood,
Were now the Generall of our gracious Empresse,
As in good time he may, from Ireland comming,
Bringing Rebellion broached on his Sword;
How many would the peacefull Citie quit,
To welcome him? much more, and much more cause,
Did they this *Harry*. Now in London place him.
As yet the lamentation of the French
Inuites the King of Englands stay at home:
The Emperour's comming in behalfe of France,
To order peace betweene them: and omit
All the occurrences, what euer chanc't,
Till *Harryes* backe returne againe to France:
There must we bring him; and my selfe haue play'd
The *interim*, by remembring you 'tis past.
Then brooke abridgement, and your eyes aduance,
After your thoughts, straight backe againe to France.
 Exit.

Enter Fluellen and Gower.

 Gower. Nay, that's right: but why weare you your Leeke to day? S. *Dauies* day is past.
 Flu. There is occasions and causes why and wherefore in all things: I will tell you asse my friend, Captaine *Gower*; the rascally, scauld, beggerly, lowsie, pragging Knaue *Pistoll*, which you and your selfe, and all the World, know to be no petter then a fellow, looke you now, of no merits: hee is come to me, and prings me pread and sault yesterday, looke you, and bid me eate my Leeke: it was in a place where I could not breed no contention with him; but I will be so bold as to weare it in my Cap till I see him once againe, and then I will tell him a little piece of my desires.

Enter Pistoll.

 Gower. Why heere hee comes, swelling like a Turky-cock.
 Flu. 'Tis no matter for his swellings, nor his Turky-cocks. God plesse you aunchient *Pistoll*: you scuruie lowsie Knaue, God plesse you.
 Pist. Ha, art thou bedlam? doest thou thirst, base Troian, to haue me fold vp *Parcas* fatall Web? Hence; I am qualmish at the smell of Leeke.
 Flu. I peseech you heartily, scuruie lowsie Knaue, at my desires, and my requests, and my petitions, to eate, looke you, this Leeke: because, looke you, you doe not loue it, nor your affections, and your appetites and your dilgestions doo's not agree with it, I would desire you to eate it.
 Pist. Not for *Cadwallader* and all his Goats.
 Flu. There is one Goat for you. *Strikes him.*
Will you be so good, scauld Knaue, as eate it?
 Pist. Base Troian, thou shalt dye.
 Flu. You say very true, scauld Knaue, when Gods will is: I will desire you to liue in the meane time, and eate your Victuals: come, there is sawce for it. You call'd me yesterday Mountaine-Squier, but I will make
you

you to day a squire of low degree. I pray you fall too, if you can mocke a Leeke, you can eate a Leeke.

Gour. Enough Captaine, you haue astonisht him.

Flu. I say, I will make him eate some part of my leeke, or I will peate his pate foure dayes: bite I pray you, it is good for your greene wound, and your ploodie Coxecombe.

Pist. Must I bite.

Flu. Yes certainly, and out of doubt and out of question too, and ambiguities.

Pist. By this Leeke, I will most horribly reuenge I eate and eate I sweare.

Flu. Eate I pray you, will you haue some more sauce to your Leeke: there is not enough Leeke to sweare by.

Pist. Quiet thy Cudgell, thou dost see I eate.

Flu. Much good do you scald knaue, heartily. Nay, pray you throw none away, the skinne is good for your broken Coxcombe; when you take occasions to see Leekes heereafter, I pray you mocke at 'em, that is all.

Pist. Good.

Flu. I, Leekes is good: hold you, there is a groat to heale your pate.

Pist. Me a groat?

Flu. Yes verily, and in truth you shall take it, or I haue another Leeke in my pocket, which you shall eate.

Pist. I take thy groat in earnest of reuenge.

Flu. If I owe you any thing, I will pay you in Cudgels, you shall be a Woodmonger, and buy nothing of me but cudgels: God bu'y you, and keepe you, & heale your pate. *Exit*

Pist. All hell shall stirre for this.

Gow. Go, go, you are a counterfeit cowardly Knaue, will you mocke at an ancient Tradition began vppon an honourable respect, and worne as a memorable Trophee of predeceased valor, and dare not auouch in your deeds any of your words. I haue seene you glecking & galling at this Gentleman twice or thrice. You thought, because he could not speake English in the natiue garb, he could not therefore handle an English Cudgell: you finde it otherwise, and henceforth let a Welsh correction, teach you a good English condition, fare ye well. *Exit*

Pist. Doeth fortune play the huswife with me now? Newes haue I that my *Doll* is dead i'th Spittle of a malady of France, and there my rendeuous is quite cut off: Old I do waxe, and from my wearie limbes honour is Cudgeld. Well, Baud Ile turne, and something leane to Cut-purse of quicke hand: To England will I steale, and there Ile steale:
And patches will I get vnto these cudgeld scarres,
And swore I got them in the Gallia warres. *Exit*.

Enter at one doore, King Henry, Exeter, Bedford, Warwicke, and other Lords. At another, Queene Isabel, the King, the Duke of Bourgongne, and other French.

King. Peace to this meeting, wherefore we are met;
Vnto our brother France, and to our Sister
Health and faire time of day: Ioy and good wishes
To our most faire and Princely Cosine *Katherine*:
And as a branch and member of this Royalty,
By whom this great assembly is contriu'd,
We do salute you Duke of *Burgogne*,
And Princes French and Peeres health to you all.

Fra. Right ioyous are we to behold your face,
Most worthy brother England, fairely met,
So are you Princes (English) euery one.

Quee. So happy be the Issue brother Ireland
Of this good day, and of this gracious meeting,
As we are now glad to behold your eyes,
Your eyes which hitherto haue borne
In them against the French that met them in their bent,
The fatall Balls of murthering Basiliskes:
The venome of such Lookes we fairely hope
Haue lost their qualitie, and that this day
Shall change all griefes and quarrels into loue.

Eng. To cry Amen to that, thus we appeare.

Quee. You English Princes all, I doe salute you.

Burg. My dutie to you both, on equall loue.
Great Kings of France and England: that I haue labour'd
With all my wits, my paines, and strong endeuors,
To bring your most Imperiall Maiesties
Vnto this Barre, and Royall enterview;
Your Mightinesse on both parts best can witnesse.
Since then my Office hath so farre preuayl'd,
That Face to Face, and Royall Eye to Eye,
You haue congreeted: let it not disgrace me,
If I demand before this Royall view,
What Rub, or what Impediment there is,
Why that the naked, poore, and mangled Peace,
Deare Nourse of Arts, Plentyes, and ioyfull Births,
Should not in this best Garden of the World,
Our fertile France, put vp her louely Visage?
Alas, shee hath from France too long been chas'd,
And all her Husbandry doth lye on heapes,
Corrupting in it owne fertilitie.
Her Vine, the merry cheerer of the heart,
Vnpruned, dyes: her Hedges euen pleach'd,
Like Prisoners wildly ouer-growne with hayre,
Put forth disorder'd Twigs: her fallow Leas,
The Darnell, Hemlock, and ranke Femetary,
Doth root vpon; while that the Culter rusts,
That should deracinate such Sauagery:
The euen Meade, that erst brought sweetly forth
The freckled Cowslip, Burnet, and greene Clouer,
Wanting the Sythe, withall vncorrected, ranke;
Conceiues by idlenesse, and nothing teemes,
But hatefull Docks, rough Thistles, Keksyes, Burres,
Loosing both beautie and vtilitie;
And all our Vineyards, Fallowes, Meades, and Hedges,
Defectiue in their natures, grow to wildnesse.
Euen so our Houses, and our selues, and Children,
Haue lost, or doe not learne, for want of time,
The Sciences that should become our Countrey;
But grow like Sauages, as Souldiers will,
That nothing doe, but meditate on Blood,
To Swearing, and sterne Lookes, defus'd Attyre,
And euery thing that seemes vnnaturall.
Which to reduce into our former fauour,
You are assembled: and my speech entreats,
That I may know the Let, why gentle Peace
Should not expell these inconueniences,
And blesse vs with her former qualities.

Eng. If Duke of Burgonie, you would the Peace,
Whose want giues growth to th'imperfections
Which you haue cited; you must buy that Peace
With full accord to all our iust demands,
Whose Tenures and particular effects
You haue enschedul'd briefely in your hands.

Burg. The King hath heard them: to the which, as yet
There is no Answer made.

Eng. Well then: the Peace which you before so vrg'd,
Lyes in his Answer.

France.

France. I haue but with a curselarie eye
O're-glanc't the Articles: Pleaseth your Grace
To appoint some of your Councell presently
To sit with vs once more, with better heed
To re-suruey them; we will suddenly
Passe our accept and peremptorie Answer.

England. Brother we shall. Goe Vnckle *Exeter,*
And Brother *Clarence,* and you Brother *Gloucester,*
Warwick, and *Huntington,* goe with the King,
And take with you free power, to ratifie,
Augment, or alter, as your Wisdomes best
Shall see aduantageable for our Dignitie,
Any thing in or out of our Demands,
And wee'le consigne thereto. Will you, faire Sister,
Goe with the Princes, or stay here with vs?

Quee. Our gracious Brother, I will goe with them:
Happily a Womans Voyce may doe some good,
When Articles too nicely vrg'd, be stood on.

England. Yet leaue our Cousin *Katherine* here with vs,
She is our capitall Demand, compris'd
Within the fore-ranke of our Articles.

Quee. She hath good leaue.   *Exeunt omnes.*

Manet King and Katherine.

King. Faire *Katherine,* and most faire,
Will you vouchsafe to teach a Souldier tearmes,
Such as will enter at a Ladyes eare,
And pleade his Loue-suit to her gentle heart.

Kath. Your Maiestie shall mock at me, I cannot speake your England.

King. O faire *Katherine,* if you will loue me soundly with your French heart, I will be glad to heare you confesse it brokenly with your English Tongue. Doe you like me, *Kate?*

Kath. Pardonne moy, I cannot tell wat is like me.

King. An Angell is like you *Kate,* and you are like an Angell.

Kath. Que dit il que Ie suis semblable a les Anges?

Lady. Ouy verayment (sauf vostre Grace) ainsi dit il.

King. I said so, deare *Katherine,* and I must not blush to affirme it.

Kath. O bon Dieu, les langues des hommes sont plein de tromperies.

King. What sayes she, faire one? that the tongues of men are full of deceits?

Lady. Ouy, dat de tongeus of de mans is be full of deceits: dat is de Princesse.

King. The Princesse is the better English-woman: yfaith *Kate,* my wooing is fit for thy vnderstanding, I am glad thou canst speake no better English, for if thou could'st, thou would'st finde me such a plaine King, that thou wouldst thinke, I had sold my Farme to buy my Crowne. I know no wayes to mince it in loue, but directly to say, I loue you; then if you vrge me farther, then to say, Doe you in faith? I weare out my suite: Giue me your answer, yfaith doe, and so clap hands, and a bargaine: how say you, Lady?

Kath. Sauf vostre honeur, me vnderstand well.

King. Marry, if you would put me to Verses, or to Dance for your sake, *Kate,* why you vndid me: for the one I haue neither words nor measure; and for the other, I haue no strength in measure, yet a reasonable measure in strength. If I could winne a Lady at Leape-frogge, or by vawting into my Saddle, with my Armour on my backe; vnder the correction of bragging be it spoken. I should quickly leape into a Wife: Or if I might buffet for my Loue, or bound my Horse for her fauours, I could lay on like a Butcher, and sit like a Iack an Apes, neuer off. But before God *Kate,* I cannot looke greenely, nor gaspe out my eloquence, nor I haue no cunning in protestation; onely downe-right Oathes, which I neuer vse till vrg'd, nor neuer breake for vrging. If thou canst loue a fellow of this temper, *Kate,* whose face is not worth Sunne-burning? that neuer lookes in his Glasse, for loue of any thing he sees there? let thine Eye be thy Cooke. I speake to thee plaine Souldier: If thou canst loue me for this, take me? if not? to say to thee that I shall dye, is true; but for thy loue, by the L. No: yet I loue thee too. And while thou liu'st, deare *Kate,* take a fellow of plaine and vncoyned Constancie, for he perforce must do thee right, because he hath not the gift to wooe in other places: for these fellowes of infinit tongue, that can ryme themselues into Ladyes fauours, they doe alwayes reason themselues out againe. What? a speaker is but a prater, a Ryme is but a Ballad; a good Legge will fall, a strait Backe will stoope, a blacke Beard will turne white, a curl'd Pate will grow bald, a faire Face will wither, a full Eye will wax hollow: but a good Heart, *Kate,* is the Sunne and the Moone, or rather the Sunne, and not the Moone; for it shines bright, and neuer changes, but keepes his course truly. If thou would haue such a one, take me? and take me; take a Souldier: take a Souldier; take a King. And what say'st thou then to my Loue? speake my faire, and fairely, I pray thee.

Kath. Is it possible dat I sould loue de ennemie of Fraunce?

King. No, it is not possible you should loue the Enemie of France, *Kate*; but in louing me, you should loue the Friend of France: for I loue France so well, that I will not part with a Village of it; I will haue it all mine: and *Kate,* when France is mine, and I am yours; then yours is France, and you are mine.

Kath. I cannot tell wat is dat.

King. No, *Kate?* I will tell thee in French which I am sure will hang vpon my tongue, like a new-married Wife about her Husbands Necke, hardly to be shooke off; *Ie quand sur le possession de Fraunce, & quand vous aues le possession de moy,* (Let mee see, what then? Saint *Dennis* bee my speede) *Donc vostre est Fraunce, & vous estes mienne.* It is as easie for me, *Kate,* to conquer the Kingdome, as to speake so much more French: I shall neuer moue thee in French, vnlesse it be to laugh at me.

Kath. Sauf vostre honeur, le Francois ques vous parleis, il & melieus que l Anglois le quel Ie parle.

King. No faith is't not, *Kate*: but thy speaking of my Tongue, and I thine, most truely falsely, must needes be graunted to be much at one. But *Kate,* doo'st thou vnderstand thus much English? Canst thou loue mee?

Kath. I cannot tell.

King. Can any of your Neighbours tell, *Kate?* Ile aske them. Come, I know thou louest me: and at night, when you come into your Closet, you'le question this Gentlewoman about me; and I know, *Kate,* you will to her dispraise those parts in me, that you loue with your heart: but good *Kate,* mocke me mercifully, the rather gentle Princesse, because I loue thee cruelly. If euer thou beest mine, *Kate,* as I haue a sauing Faith within me tells me thou shalt; I get thee with skambling, and thou must therefore needes proue a good Souldier-breeder: Shall not thou and I, betweene Saint *Dennis* and Saint *George,* compound a Boy, halfe French halfe English,

k   that

that shall goe to Constantinople, and take the Turke by the Beard. Shall wee not? what say'st thou, my faire Flower-de-Luce.

Kate. I doe not know dat.

King. No: 'tis hereafter to know, but now to promise: doe but now promise *Kate*, you will endeauour for your French part of such a Boy; and for my English moytie, take the Word of a King, and a Batcheler. How answer you, *La plus belle Katherine du monde mon trescher & deuin deesse.*

Kath. Your Maiestee aue fauſe Frenche enough to deceiue de moſt ſage Damoiſeil dat is en Fraunce.

King. Now fye vpon my falſe French: by mine Honor in true English, I loue thee *Kate*; by which Honor, I dare not ſweare thou loueſt me, yet my blood begins to flatter me, that thou doo'ſt; notwithstanding the poore and vntempering effect of my Viſage. Now beſhrew my Fathers Ambition, hee was thinking of Ciuill Warres when hee got me, therefore was I created with a ſtubborne out-ſide, with an aſpect of Iron, that when I come to wooe Ladyes, I fright them: but in faith *Kate*, the elder I wax, the better I ſhall appeare. My comfort is, that Old Age, that ill layer vp of Beautie, can doe no more ſpoyle vpon my Face. Thou haſt me, if thou haſt me, at the worſt; and thou ſhalt weare me, if thou weare me, better and better: and therefore tell me, most faire *Katherine*, will you haue me? Put off your Maiden Bluſhes, auouch the Thoughts of your Heart with the Lookes of an Empreſſe, take me by the Hand, and ſay, *Harry of England, I am thine:* which Word thou ſhalt no ſooner bleſſe mine Eare withall, but I will tell thee alowd, England is thine, Ireland is thine, France is thine, and *Henry Plantaginet* is thine; who, though I ſpeake it before his Face, if he be not Fellow with the beſt King, thou ſhalt finde the beſt King of Good-fellowes. Come your Anſwer in broken Muſick; for thy Voyce is Muſick, and thy English broken: Therefore Queene of all, *Katherine*, breake thy minde to me in broken English; wilt thou haue me?

Kath. Dat is as it ſhall pleaſe *de Roy mon pere.*

King. Nay, it will pleaſe him well, *Kate*; it ſhall pleaſe him, *Kate.*

Kath. Den it ſall alſo content me.

King. Vpon that I kiſſe your Hand, and I call you my Queene.

Kath. Laiſſe mon Seigneur, laiſſe, laiſſe, may foy: Ie ne veux point que vous abbaiſſe voſtre grandeur, en baiſant le main d'une noſtre Seigneur indignie ſeruiteur excuſe moy. Ie vous ſupplie mon treſ-puiſſant Seigneur.

King. Then I will kiſſe your Lippes, *Kate.*

Kath. Les Dames & Damoiſels pour eſtre baiſee deuant leur nopceſe il net pas le coſtume de Fraunce.

King. Madame, my Interpreter, what ſayes ſhee?

Lady. Dat it is not be de faſhion pour le Ladies of Fraunce; I cannot tell wat is buiſſe en Angliſh.

King. To kiſſe.

Lady. Your Maieſtee *entendre bettre que moy.*

King. It is not a faſhion for the Maids in Fraunce to kiſſe before they are marryed, would ſhe ſay?

Lady. Ouy verayment.

King. O *Kate*, nice Cuſtomes curſie to great Kings. Deare *Kate*, you and I cannot bee confin'd within the weake Lyſt of a Countreyes faſhion: wee are the makers of Manners, *Kate*; and the libertie that followes our Places, ſtoppes the mouth of all finde-faults, as I will doe yours, for vpholding the nice faſhion of your Countrey, in denying me a Kiſſe: therefore patiently, and yeelding. You haue Witch-craft in your Lippes, *Kate*: there is more eloquence in a Sugar touch of them, then in the Tongues of the French Councell; and they ſhould ſooner perſwade *Harry* of England, then a generall Petition of Monarchs. Heere comes your Father.

Enter the French Power, and the English Lords.

Burg. God ſaue your Maieſtie, my Royall Couſin, teach you our Princeſſe English?

King. I would haue her learne, my faire Couſin, how perfectly I loue her, and that is good English.

Burg. Is ſhee not apt?

King. Our Tongue is rough, Coze, and my Condition is not ſmooth: ſo that hauing neyther the Voyce nor the Heart of Flatterie about me, I cannot ſo coniure vp the Spirit of Loue in her, that hee will appeare in his true likeneſſe.

Burg. Pardon the frankneſſe of my mirth, if I anſwer you for that. If you would coniure in her, you muſt make a Circle: if coniure vp Loue in her in his true likeneſſe, hee muſt appeare naked, and blinde. Can you blame her then, being a Maid, yet roſ'd ouer with the Virgin Crimſon of Modeſtie, if ſhee deny the apparance of a naked blinde Boy in her naked ſeeing ſelfe? It were (my Lord) a hard Condition for a Maid to conſigne to.

King. Yet they doe winke and yeeld, as Loue is blind and enforces.

Burg. They are then excus'd, my Lord, when they ſee not what they doe.

King. Then good my Lord, teach your Couſin to conſent winking.

Burg. I will winke on her to conſent, my Lord, if you will teach her to know my meaning: for Maides well Summer'd, and warme kept, are like Flyes at Bartholomew-tyde, blinde, though they haue their eyes, and then they will endure handling, which before would not abide looking on.

King. This Morall tyes me ouer to Time, and a hot Summer; and ſo I ſhall catch the Flye, your Couſin, in the latter end, and ſhee muſt be blinde to.

Burg. As Loue is my Lord, before it loues.

King. It is ſo: and you may, ſome of you, thanke Loue for my blindneſſe, who cannot ſee many a faire French Citie for one faire French Maid that ſtands in my way.

French King. Yes my Lord, you ſee them perſpectiuely: the Cities turn'd into a Maid; for they are all gyrdled with Maiden Walls, that Warre hath entred.

England. Shall *Kate* be my Wife?

France. So pleaſe you.

England. I am content, ſo the Maiden Cities you talke of, may wait on her: ſo the Maid that ſtood in the way for my Wiſh, ſhall ſhew me the way to my Will.

France. Wee haue conſented to all tearmes of reaſon.

England. Is't ſo, my Lords of England?

Weſt. The King hath graunted euery Article; His Daughter firſt; and in ſequele, all, According to their firme propoſed natures.

Exet. Onely

The Life of Henry the Fift.

Exet. Onely he hath not yet subscribed this:
Where your Maiestie demands, That the King of France hauing any occasion to write for matter of Graunt, shall name your Highnesse in this forme, and with this addition, in French: *Nostre trescher filz, Henry Roy d'Angleterre Heretere de Fraunce*: and thus in Latine; *Præclarissimus Filius noster Henricus Rex Angliæ & Heres Franciæ*.

France. Nor this I haue not Brother so deny'd,
But your request shall make me let it passe.

England. I pray you then, in loue and deare allyance,
Let that one Article ranke with the rest,
And thereupon giue me your Daughter.

France. Take her faire Sonne, and from her blood rayse vp
Issue to me, that the contending Kingdomes
Of France and England, whose very shoares looke pale,
With enuy of each others happinesse,
May cease their hatred; and this deare Coniunction
Plant Neighbour-hood and Christian-like accord
In their sweet Bosomes: that neuer Warre aduance
His bleeding Sword 'twixt England and faire France.

Lords. Amen.

King. Now welcome *Kate*: and beare me witnesse all,
That here I kisse her as my Soueraigne Queene.
Flourish.

Quee. God, the best maker of all Marriages,
Combine your hearts in one, your Realmes in one:
As Man and Wife being two, are one in loue,
So be there 'twixt your Kingdomes such a Spousall,
That neuer may ill Office, or fell Iealousie,
Which troubles oft the Bed of blessed Marriage,
Thrust in betweene the Pation of these Kingdomes,
To make diuorce of their incorporate League:
That English may as French, French Englishmen,
Receiue each other. God speake this Amen.

All. Amen.

King. Prepare we for our Marriage: on which day,
My Lord of Burgundy wee'le take your Oath
And all the Peeres, for suretie of our Leagues.
Then shall I sweare to *Kate*, and you to me,
And may our Oathes well kept and prosp'rous be.
Senet. *Exeunt.*

Enter Chorus.

Thus farre with rough, and all-vnable Pen,
Our bending Author hath pursu'd the Story,
In little roome confining mightie men,
Mangling by starts the full course of their glory.
Small time: but in that small, most greatly liued
This Starre of England. Fortune made his Sword;
By which, the Worlds best Garden he atchieued:
And of it left his Sonne Imperiall Lord.
Henry the Sixt, in Infant Bands crown'd King
Of France and England, did this King succeed:
Whose State so many had the managing,
That they lost France, and made his England bleed:
Which oft our Stage hath showne; and for their sake,
In your faire minds let this acceptance take.

FINIS.

The first Part of Henry the Sixt.

Actus Primus. Scœna Prima.

Dead March.

Enter the Funerall of King Henry the Fift, attended on by the Duke of Bedford, Regent of France; the Duke of Gloster, Protector; the Duke of Exeter War-wicke, the Bishop of Winchester, and the Duke of Somerset.

Bedford.
Vng be § heauens with black, yield day to night;
Comets importing change of Times and States,
Brandish your crystall Tresses in the Skie,
And with them scourge the bad reuolting Stars,
That haue consented vnto *Henries* death:
King *Henry* the Fift, too famous to liue long,
England ne're lost a King of so much worth.
  Glost. England ne're had a King vntill his time:
Vertue he had, deseruing to command,
His brandisht Sword did blinde men with his beames,
His Armes spred wider then a Dragons Wings:
His sparkling Eyes, repleat with wrathfull fire,
More dazled and droue back his Enemies,
Then mid-day Sunne, fierce bent against their faces.
What should I say? his Deeds exceed all speech:
He ne're lift vp his Hand, but conquered.
  Exe. We mourne in black, why mourn we not in blood?
Henry is dead, and neuer shall reuiue:
Vpon a Woodden Coffin we attend;
And Deaths dishonourable Victorie,
We with our stately presence glorifie,
Like Captiues bound to a Triumphant Carre.
What? shall we curse the Planets of Mishap,
That plotted thus our Glories ouerthrow?
Or shall we thinke the subtile-witted French,
Coniurers and Sorcerers, that afraid of him,
By Magick Verses haue contriu'd his end.
  Winch. He was a King, blest of the King of Kings.
Vnto the French, the dreadfull Iudgement-Day
So dreadfull will not be, as was his sight.
The Battailes of the Lord of Hosts he fought:
The Churches Prayers made him so prosperous.
  Glost. The Church? where is it?
Had not Church-men pray'd,
His thred of Life had not so soone decay'd.
None doe you like, but an effeminate Prince,
Whom like a Schoole-boy you may ouer-awe.
  Winch. Gloster, what ere we like, thou art Protector,
And lookest to command the Prince and Realme.
Thy Wife is prowd, she holdeth thee in awe,
More then God or Religious Church-men may.

  Glost. Name not Religion, for thou lou'st the Flesh,
And ne're throughout the yeere to Church thou go'st,
Except it be to pray against thy foes.
  Bed. Cease, cease these Iarres, & rest your minds in peace:
Let's to the Altar: Heralds wayt on vs;
In stead of Gold, wee'le offer vp our Armes,
Since Armes auayle not, now that *Henry's* dead,
Posteritie await for wretched yeeres,
When at their Mothers moistned eyes, Babes shall suck,
Our Ile be made a Nourish of salt Teares,
And none but Women left to wayle the dead.
Henry the Fift, thy Ghost I inuocate:
Prosper this Realme, keepe it from Ciuill Broyles,
Combat with aduerse Planets in the Heauens;
A farre more glorious Starre thy Soule will make,
Then *Iulius Cæsar*, or bright——

Enter a Messenger.
  Mess. My honourable Lords, health to you all:
Sad tidings bring I to you out of France,
Of losse, of slaughter, and discomfiture:
Guyen, Champaigne, Rheimes, Orleance,
Paris Guysors, Poictiers, are all quite lost.
  Bedf. What say'st thou man, before dead *Henry's* Coarse?
Speake softly, or the losse of those great Townes
Will make him burst his Lead, and rise from death.
  Glost. Is Paris lost? is Roan yeelded vp?
If *Henry* were recall'd to life againe,
These news would cause him once more yeeld the Ghost.
  Exe. How were they lost? what trecherie was vs'd?
  Mess. No trecherie, but want of Men and Money.
Amongst the Souldiers this is muttered,
That here you maintaine seuerall Factions:
And whil'st a Field should be dispatcht and fought,
You are disputing of your Generals.
One would haue lingring Warres, with little cost;
Another would flye swift, but wanteth Wings:
A third thinkes, without expence at all,
By guilefull faire words, Peace may be obtayn'd.
Awake, awake, English Nobilitie,
Let not slouth dimme your Honors, new begot;
Cropt are the Flower-de-Luces in your Armes
Of Englands Coat, one halfe is cut away.
  Exe. Were our Teares wanting to this Funerall,
These Tidings would call forth her flowing Tides.
  Bedf. Me they concerne, Regent I am of France:
Giue me my steeled Coat, Ile fight for France.
Away with these disgracefull wayling Robes;
Wounds will I lend the French, in stead of Eyes,
To weepe their intermissiue Miseries.

Enter

Enter to them another Messenger.

Mess. Lords view these Letters, full of bad mischance.
France is revolted from the English quite,
Except some petty Townes, of no import.
The Dolphin *Charles* is crowned King in Rheimes:
The Bastard of Orleance with him is ioyn'd:
Reynold Duke of Aniou, doth take his part,
The Duke of Alanson flyeth to his side. *Exit.*

Exe. The Dolphin crown'd King? all flye to him?
O whither shall we flye from this reproach?

Glost. We will not flye, but to our enemies throats.
Bedford, if thou be slacke, Ile fight it out.

Bed. *Gloster*, why doubt'st thou of my forwardnesse?
An Army haue I muster'd in my thoughts,
Wherewith already France is ouer-run.

Enter another Messenger.

Mes. My gracious Lords, to adde to your laments,
Wherewith you now bedew King *Henries* hearse,
I must informe you of a dismall fight,
Betwixt the stout Lord *Talbot*, and the French.

Win. What? wherein *Talbot* ouercame, is't so?

3. Mes. O no: wherein Lord *Talbot* was o'rethrown:
The circumstance Ile tell you more at large.
The tenth of August last, this dreadfull Lord,
Retyring from the Siege of Orleance,
Hauing full scarce six thousand in his troupe,
By three and twentie thousand of the French
Was round incompassed, and set vpon:
No leysure had he to enranke his men.
He wanted Pikes to set before his Archers:
Instead whereof, sharpe Stakes pluckt out of Hedges
They pitched in the ground confusedly,
To keepe the Horsemen off, from breaking in.
More then three houres the fight continued:
Where valiant *Talbot*, aboue humane thought,
Enacted wonders with his Sword and Lance.
Hundreds he sent to Hell, and none durst stand him:
Here, there, and euery where enrag'd, he slew.
The French exclaym'd, the Deuill was in Armes,
All the whole Army stood agaz'd on him.
His Souldiers spying his vndaunted Spirit,
A *Talbot*, a *Talbot*, cry'd out amaine,
And rusht into the Bowels of the Battaile.
Here had the Conquest fully been seal'd vp,
If Sir *Iohn Falstaffe* had not play'd the Coward.
He being in the Vauward, plac't behinde,
With purpose to relieue and follow them,
Cowardly fled, not hauing struck one stroake.
Hence grew the generall wrack and massacre:
Enclosed were they with their Enemies.
A base Wallon, to win the Dolphins grace,
Thrust *Talbot* with a Speare into the Back,
Whom all France, with their chiefe assembled strength,
Durst not presume to looke once in the face.

Bedf. Is *Talbot* slaine then? I will slay my selfe,
For liuing idly here, in pompe and ease,
Whil'st such a worthy Leader, wanting ayd,
Vnto his dastard foe-men is betray'd.

3. Mess. O no, he liues, but is tooke Prisoner,
And Lord *Scales* with him, and Lord *Hungerford*:
Most of the rest slaughter'd, or tooke likewise.

Bedf. His Ransome there is none but I shall pay.
Ile hale the Dolphin headlong from his Throne,
His Crowne shall be the Ransome of my friend:
Foure of their Lords Ile change for one of ours.

Farewell my Masters, to my Taske will I,
Bonfires in France forthwith I am to make,
To keepe our great Saint *Georges* Feast withall.
Ten thousand Souldiers with me I will take,
Whose bloody deeds shall make all Europe quake.

3. Mess. So you had need, for Orleance is besieg'd,
The English Army is growne weake and faint:
The Earle of Salisbury craueth supply,
And hardly keepes his men from mutinie,
Since they so few, watch such a multitude.

Exe. Remember Lords your Oathes to *Henry* sworne:
Eyther to quell the Dolphin vtterly,
Or bring him in obedience to your yoake.

Bedf. I doe remember it, and here take my leaue,
To goe about my preparation. *Exit Bedford.*

Glost. Ile to the Tower with all the hast I can,
To view th'Artillerie and Munition,
And then I will proclayme young *Henry* King.
Exit Gloster.

Exe. To Eltam will I, where the young King is,
Being ordayn'd his speciall Gouernor,
And for his safetie there Ile best deuise. *Exit.*

Winch. Each hath his Place and Function to attend:
I am left out; for me nothing remaines:
But long I will not be Iack out of Office.
The King from Eltam I intend to send,
And sit at chiefest Sterne of publique Weale.
Exit.

Sound a Flourish.

Enter Charles, Alanson, and Reigneir, marching with Drum and Souldiers.

Charles. *Mars* his true mouing, euen as in the Heauens,
So in the Earth, to this day is not knowne.
Late did he shine vpon the English side:
Now we are Victors, vpon vs he smiles.
What Townes of any moment, but we haue?
At pleasure here we lye, neere Orleance:
Otherwhiles, the famisht English, like pale Ghosts,
Faintly besiege vs one houre in a moneth.

Alan. They want their Porredge, & their fat Bul Beeues:
Eyther they must be dyeted like Mules,
And haue their Prouender ty'd to their mouthes,
Or pitteous they will looke, like drowned Mice.

Reigneir. Let's rayse the Siege: why liue we idly here?
Talbot is taken, whom we wont to feare:
Remayneth none but mad-brayn'd *Salisbury*,
And he may well in fretting spend his gall,
Nor men nor Money hath he to make Warre.

Charles. Sound, sound Alarum, we will rush on them.
Now for the honour of the forlorne French:
Him I forgiue my death, that killeth me,
When he sees me goe back one foot, or flye. *Exeunt.*

Here Alarum, they are beaten back by the English, with great losse.

Enter Charles, Alanson, and Reigneir.

Charles. Who euer saw the like? what men haue I?
Dogges, Cowards, Dastards: I would ne're haue fled,
But that they left me 'midst my Enemies.

Reigneir. *Salisbury* is a desperate Homicide,
He fighteth as one weary of his life:
The other Lords, like Lyons wanting foode,
Doe rush vpon vs as their hungry prey.

Alanson. Froysard, a Countreyman of ours, records,
England all *Oliuers* and *Rowlands* breed,
During the time *Edward* the third did raigne:
More truly now may this be verified;
For none but *Samsons* and *Goliasses*
It sendeth forth to skirmish: one to tenne?
Leane raw-bon'd Rascals, who would e're suppose,
They had such courage and audacitie?

Charles. Let's leaue this Towne,
For they are hayre-brayn'd Slaues,
And hunger will enforce them to be more eager:
Of old I know them; rather with their Teeth
The Walls they'le teare downe, then forsake the Siege.

Reigneir. I thinke by some odde Gimmors or Deuice
Their Armes are set, like Clocks, still to strike on;
Else ne're could they hold out so as they doe:
By my consent, wee'le euen let them alone.

Alanson. Be it so.

Enter the Bastard of Orleance.

Bastard. Where's the Prince Dolphin? I haue newes for him.

Dolph. Bastard of Orleance, thrice welcome to vs.

Bast. Me thinks your looks are sad, your cheare appal'd.
Hath the late ouerthrow wrought this offence?
Be not dismay'd, for succour is at hand:
A holy Maid hither with me I bring,
Which by a Vision sent to her from Heauen,
Ordayned is to rayse this tedious Siege,
And driue the English forth the bounds of France:
The spirit of deepe Prophecie she hath,
Exceeding the nine *Sibyls* of old Rome:
What's past, and what's to come, she can descry.
Speake, shall I call her in? beleeue my words,
For they are certaine, and vnfallible.

Dolph. Goe call her in: but first, to try her skill,
Reignier stand thou as Dolphin in my place;
Question her prowdly, let thy Lookes be sterne,
By this meanes shall we sound what skill she hath.

Enter Ioane Puzel.

Reigneir. Faire Maid, is't thou wilt doe these wondrous feats?

Puzel. *Reignier*, is't thou that thinkest to beguile me?
Where is the Dolphin? Come, come from behinde,
I know thee well, though neuer seene before.
Be not amaz'd, there's nothing hid from me;
In priuate will I talke with thee apart:
Stand back you Lords, and giue vs leaue a while.

Reigneir. She takes vpon her brauely at first dash.

Puzel. Dolphin, I am by birth a Shepheards Daughter,
My wit vntrayn'd in any kind of Art:
Heauen and our Lady gracious hath it pleas'd
To shine on my contemptible estate.
Loe, whilest I wayted on my tender Lambes,
And to Sunnes parching heat display'd my cheekes,
Gods Mother deigned to appeare to me,
And in a Vision full of Maiestie,
Will'd me to leaue my base Vocation,
And free my Countrey from Calamitie:
Her ayde she promis'd, and assur'd successe.
In compleat Glory shee reueal'd her selfe:
And whereas I was black and swart before,
With those cleare Rayes, which shee infus'd on me,
That beautie am I blest with, which you may see.
Aske me what question thou canst possible,
And I will answer vnpremeditated:
My Courage trie by Combat, if thou dar'st,
And thou shalt finde that I exceed my Sex.
Resolue on this, thou shalt be fortunate,
If thou receiue me for thy Warlike Mate.

Dolph. Thou hast astonisht me with thy high termes:
Onely this proofe Ile of thy Valour make,
In single Combat thou shalt buckle with me;
And if thou vanquishest, thy words are true,
Otherwise I renounce all confidence.

Puzel. I am prepar'd: here is my keene-edg'd Sword,
Deckt with fine Flower-de-Luces on each side,
The which at Touraine, in S. *Katherines* Church-yard,
Out of a great deale of old Iron, I chose forth.

Dolph. Then come a Gods name, I feare no woman.

Puzel. And while I liue, Ile ne're flye from a man.

Here they fight, and Ioane de Puzel ouercomes.

Dolph. Stay, stay thy hands, thou art an Amazon,
And fightest with the Sword of *Debora.*

Puzel. Christs Mother helpes me, else I were too weake.

Dolph. Who e're helps thee, 'tis thou that must help me:
Impatiently I burne with thy desire,
My heart and hands thou hast at once subdu'd.
Excellent *Puzel*, if thy name be so,
Let me thy seruant, and not Soueraigne be,
'Tis the French Dolphin sueth to thee thus.

Puzel. I must not yeeld to any rights of Loue,
For my Profession's sacred from aboue:
When I haue chased all thy Foes from hence,
Then will I thinke vpon a recompence.

Dolph. Meane time looke gracious on thy prostrate Thrall.

Reigneir. My Lord me thinkes is very long in talke.

Alanf. Doubtlesse he shriues this woman to her smock,
Else ne're could he so long protract his speech.

Reigneir. Shall wee disturbe him, since hee keepes no meane?

Alan. He may meane more then we poor men do know,
These women are shrewd tempters with their tongues.

Reigneir. My Lord, where are you? what deuise you on?
Shall we giue o're Orleance, or no?

Puzel. Why no, I say: distrustfull Recreants,
Fight till the last gaspe: Ile be your guard.

Dolph. What shee sayes, Ile confirme: wee'le fight it out.

Puzel. Assign'd am I to be the English Scourge.
This night the Siege assuredly Ile rayse:
Expect Saint *Martins* Summer, *Halcyons* dayes,
Since I haue entred into these Warres.
Glory is like a Circle in the Water,
Which neuer ceaseth to enlarge it selfe,
Till by broad spreading, it disperse to naught.
With *Henries* death, the English Circle ends,
Dispersed are the glories it included:
Now am I like that prowd insulting Ship,
Which *Cæsar* and his fortune bare at once.

Dolph. Was *Mahomet* inspired with a Doue?
Thou with an Eagle art inspired then.
Helen, the Mother of Great *Constantine*,
Nor yet S. *Philips* daughters were like thee.
Bright Starre of *Venus*, falne downe on the Earth,
How may I reuerently worship thee enough?

Alanson. Leaue off delayes, and let vs rayse the Siege.

Reigneir. Wo-

Reigneir. Woman, do what thou canst to saue our honors, Driue them from Orleance, and be immortaliz'd.

Dolph. Presently wee'le try: come, let's away about it, No Prophet will I trust, if shee proue false. *Exeunt.*

Enter Gloster, with his Seruing-men.

Glost. I am come to suruey the Tower this day; Since *Henries* death, I feare there is Conueyance: Where be these Warders, that they wait not here? Open the Gates, 'tis *Gloster* that calls.

1. Warder. Who's there, that knocks so imperiously?

Glost. 1. Man. It is the Noble Duke of Gloster.

2. Warder. Who ere he be, you may not be let in.

1. Man. Villaines, answer you so the Lord Protector?

1. Warder. The Lord protect him, so we answer him, We doe no otherwise then wee are will'd.

Glost. Who willed you? or whose will stands but mine? There's none Protector of the Realme, but I: Breake vp the Gates, Ile be your warrantize; Shall I be flowted thus by dunghill Groomes?

Glosters men rush at the Tower Gates, and Woodnile the Lieutenant speakes within.

Wooduile. What noyse is this? what Traytors haue wee here?

Glost. Lieutenant, is it you whose voyce I heare? Open the Gates, here's *Gloster* that would enter.

Wooduile. Haue patience Noble Duke, I may not open, The Cardinall of Winchester forbids: From him I haue expresse commandement, That thou nor none of thine shall be let in.

Glost. Faint-hearted *Wooduile*, prizest him 'fore me? Arrogant *Winchester*, that haughtie Prelate, Whom *Henry* our late Soueraigne ne're could brooke? Thou art no friend to God, or to the King: Open the Gates, or Ile shut thee out shortly.

Seruingmen. Open the Gates vnto the Lord Protector, Or wee'le burst them open, if that you come not quickly.

Enter to the Protector at the Tower Gates Winchester and his men in Tawney Coates.

Winchest. How now ambitious *Vmpheir*, what meanes this?

Glost. Piel'd Priest, doo'st thou command me to be shut out?

Winch. I doe, thou most vsurping Proditor, And not Protector of the King or Realme.

Glost. Stand back thou manifest Conspirator, Thou that contriued'st to murther our dead Lord, Thou that giu'st Whores Indulgences to sinne, Ile canuas thee in thy broad Cardinalls Hat, If thou proceed in this thy insolence.

Winch. Nay, stand thou back, I will not budge a foot: This be Damascus, be thou curled *Cain*, To slay thy Brother *Abel*, if thou wilt.

Glost. I will not slay thee, but Ile driue thee back: Thy Scarlet Robes, as a Childs bearing Cloth, Ile vse, to carry thee out of this place.

Winch. Doe what thou dar'st, I beard thee to thy face.

Glost. What? am I dar'd, and bearded to my face? Draw men, for all this priuiledged place, Blew Coates to Tawny Coates. Priest, beware your Beard, I meane to tugge it, and to cuffe you soundly. Vnder my feet I stampe thy Cardinalls Hat:

In spight of Pope, or dignities of Church, Here by the Cheekes Ile drag thee vp and downe.

Winch. Gloster, thou wilt answere this before the Pope.

Glost. Winchester Goose, I cry, a Rope, a Rope. Now beat them hence, why doe you let them stay? Thee Ile chase hence, thou Wolfe in Sheepes array. Out Tawney-Coates, out Scarlet Hypocrite.

Here Glosters men beat out the Cardinalls men, and enter in the hurly-burly the Maior of London, and his Officers.

Maior. Fye Lords, that you being supreme Magistrates, Thus contumeliously should breake the Peace.

Glost. Peace Maior, thou know'st little of my wrongs: Here's *Beauford*, that regards nor God nor King, Hath here distrayn'd the Tower to his vse.

Winch. Here's *Gloster*, a Foe to Citizens, One that still motions Warre, and neuer Peace, O're-charging your free Purses with large Fines; That seekes to ouerthrow Religion, Because he is Protector of the Realme; And would haue Armour here out of the Tower, To Crowne himselfe King, and suppresse the Prince.

Glost. I will not answer thee with words, but blowes.
Here they skirmish againe.

Maior. Naught rests for me, in this tumultuous strife, But to make open Proclamation. Come Officer, as lowd as e're thou canst, cry:

All manner of men, assembled here in Armes this day, against Gods Peace and the Kings, wee charge and command you, in his Highnesse Name, to repayre to your seuerall dwelling places, and not to weare, handle, or vse any Sword, Weapon, or Dagger hence-forward, vpon paine of death.

Glost. Cardinall, Ile be no breaker of the Law: But we shall meet, and breake our minds at large.

Winch. Gloster, wee'le meet to thy cost, be sure: Thy heart-blood I will haue for this dayes worke.

Maior. Ile call for Clubs, if you will not away: This Cardinall's more haughtie then the Deuill.

Glost. Maior farewell: thou doo'st but what thou may'st.

Winch. Abhominable *Gloster*, guard thy Head, For I intend to haue it ere long. *Exeunt.*

Maior. See the Coast clear'd, and then we will depart. Good God, these Nobles should such stomacks beare, I my selfe fight not once in fortie yeere. *Exeunt.*

Enter the Master Gunner of Orleance, and his Boy.

M. Gunner. Sirrha, thou know'st how Orleance is besieg'd, And how the English haue the Suburbs wonne.

Boy. Father I know, and oft haue shot at them, How e're vnfortunate, I miss'd my ayme.

M. Gunner. But now thou shalt not. Be thou rul'd by me: Chiefe Master Gunner am I of this Towne, Something I must doe to procure me grace: The Princes espyals haue informed me, How the English, in the Suburbs close entrencht, Went through a secret Grate of Iron Barres, In yonder Tower, to ouer-peere the Citie, And thence discouer, how with most aduantage They may vex vs with Shot or with Assault. To intercept this inconuenience, A Peece of Ordnance 'gainst it I haue plac'd,

And

And euen these three dayes haue I watcht,
If I could see them. Now doe thou watch,
For I can stay no longer.
If thou spy'st any, runne and bring me word,
And thou shalt finde me at the Gouernors. *Exit.*

Boy. Father, I warrant you, take you no care,
Ile neuer trouble you, if I may spye them. *Exit.*

Enter Salisbury and Talbot on the Turrets, with others.

Salisb. Talbot, my life, my ioy, againe return'd?
How wert thou handled, being Prisoner?
Or by what meanes got'st thou to be releas'd?
Discourse I prethee on this Turrets top.

Talbot. The Earle of Bedford had a Prisoner,
Call'd the braue Lord *Ponton de Santrayle*,
For him was I exchang'd, and ransom'd.
But with a baser man of Armes by farre,
Once in contempt they would haue barter'd me:
Which I disdaining, scorn'd, and craued death,
Rather then I would be so pil'd esteem'd:
In fine, redeem'd I was as I desir'd.
But O, the trecherous *Falstaffe* wounds my heart,
Whom with my bare fists I would execute,
If I now had him brought into my power.

Salisb. Yet tell'st thou not, how thou wert entertain'd.

Tal. With scoffes and scornes, and contumelious taunts,
In open Market-place produc't they me,
To be a publique spectacle to all:
Here, sayd they, is the Terror of the French,
The Scar-Crow that affrights our Children so.
Then broke I from the Officers that led me,
And with my nayles digg'd stones out of the ground,
To hurle at the beholders of my shame.
My grisly countenance made others flye,
None durst come neere, for feare of suddaine death.
In Iron Walls they deem'd me not secure:
So great feare of my Name 'mongst them were spread,
That they suppos'd I could rend Barres of Steele,
And spurne in pieces Posts of Adamant.
Wherefore a guard of chosen Shot I had,
That walkt about me euery Minute while:
And if I did but stirre out of my Bed,
Ready they were to shoot me to the heart.

Enter the Boy with a Linstock.

Salisb. I grieue to heare what torments you endur'd,
But we will be reueng'd sufficiently.
Now it is Supper time in Orleance:
Here, through this Grate, I count each one,
And view the Frenchmen how they fortifie:
Let vs looke in, the sight will much delight thee:
Sir *Thomas Gargraue*, and Sir *William Glansdale*,
Let me haue your expresse opinions,
Where is best place to make our Batt'ry next?

Gargraue. I thinke at the North Gate, for there stands Lords.

Glansdale. And I heere, at the Bulwarke of the Bridge.

Talb. For ought I see, this Citie must be famisht,
Or with light Skirmishes enfeebled. *Here they shoot, and Salisbury falls downe.*

Salisb. O Lord haue mercy on vs, wretched sinners.

Gargraue. O Lord haue mercy on me, wofull man.

Talb. What chance is this, that suddenly hath crost vs?
Speake *Salisbury*; at least, if thou canst, speake:
How far'st thou, Mirror of all Martiall men?
One of thy Eyes, and thy Cheekes side struck off?
Accursed Tower, accursed fatall Hand,
That hath contriu'd this wofull Tragedie.
In thirteene Battailes, *Salisbury* o'recame:
Henry the Fift he first trayn'd to the Warres.
Whil'st any Trumpe did sound, or Drum struck vp,
His Sword did ne're leaue striking in the field.
Yet liu'st thou *Salisbury*? though thy speech doth fayle,
One Eye thou hast to looke to Heauen for grace.
The Sunne with one Eye vieweth all the World.
Heauen be thou gracious to none aliue,
If *Salisbury* wants mercy at thy hands.
Beare hence his Body, I will helpe to bury it.
Sir *Thomas Gargraue*, hast thou any life?
Speake vnto *Talbot*, nay, looke vp to him.
Salisbury cheare thy Spirit with this comfort,
Thou shalt not dye whiles——
He beckens with his hand, and smiles on me:
As who should say, When I am dead and gone,
Remember to auenge me on the French.
Plantaginet I will, and like thee,
Play on the Lute, beholding the Townes burne:
Wretched shall France be onely in my Name.

Here an Alarum, and it Thunders and Lightens.

What stirre is this? what tumult's in the Heauens?
Whence commeth this Alarum, and the noyse?

Enter a Messenger.

Mess. My Lord, my Lord, the French haue gather'd head.
The Dolphin, with one *Ioane de Puzel* ioyn'd,
A holy Prophetesse, new risen vp,
Is come with a great Power, to rayse the Siege.

Here Salisbury lifteth himselfe vp, and groanes.

Talb. Heare, heare, how dying *Salisbury* doth groane,
It irkes his heart he cannot be reueng'd.
Frenchmen, Ile be a *Salisbury* to you.
Puzel or *Pussel*, Dolphin or Dog-fish,
Your hearts Ile stampe out with my Horses heeles,
And make a Quagmire of your mingled braines.
Conuey me *Salisbury* into his Tent,
And then wee'le try what these dastard Frenchmen dare.
Alarum. Exeunt.

Here an Alarum againe, and Talbot pursueth the Dolphin, and driueth him: Then enter Ioane de Puzel, driuing Englishmen before her. Then enter Talbot.

Talb. Where is my strength, my valour, and my force?
Our English Troupes retyre, I cannot stay them,
A Woman clad in Armour chaseth them.

Enter Puzel.

Here, here shee comes. Ile haue a bowt with thee:
Deuill, or Deuils Dam, Ile coniure thee:
Blood will I draw on thee, thou art a Witch,
And straightway giue thy Soule to him thou seru'st.

Puzel. Come, come, 'tis onely I that must disgrace thee. *Here they fight.*

Talb. Heauens, can you suffer Hell so to preuayle?
My brest Ile burst with straining of my courage,
And from my shoulders crack my Armes asunder,
But I will chastise this high-minded Strumpet.

They fight againe.

Puzel. Talbot farwell, thy houre is not yet come,
I must goe Victuall Orleance forthwith:

A short Alarum: then enter the Towne with Souldiers.

O're-take me if thou canst, I scorne thy strength.
Goe, goe, cheare vp thy hungry-starued men,
Helpe *Salisbury* to make his Testament,
This Day is ours, as many more shall be. *Exit.*
  Talb. My thoughts are whirled like a Potters Wheele,
I know not where I am, nor what I doe:
A Witch by feare, not force, like *Hannibal*,
Driues back our troupes, and conquers as she lists:
So Bees with smoake, and Doues with noysome stench,
Are from their Hyues and Houses driuen away.
They call'd vs, for our fierceneße, English Dogges,
Now like to Whelpes, we crying runne away.

A short Alarum.

Hearke Countreymen, eyther renew the fight,
Or teare the Lyons out of Englands Coat;
Renounce your Soyle, giue Sheepe in Lyons stead:
Sheepe run not halfe so trecherous from the Wolfe,
Or Horse or Oxen from the Leopard,
As you flye from your oft-subdued slaues.

  Alarum. Here another Skirmish.
It will not be, retyre into your Trenches:
You all consented vnto *Salisburies* death,
For none would strike a stroake in his reuenge.
Puzel is entred into Orleance,
In spight of vs, or ought that we could doe.
O would I were to dye with *Salisbury*,
The shame hereof, will make me hide my head.
                              Exit Talbot.

Alarum, Retreat, Flourish.

*Enter on the Walls, Puzel, Dolphin, Reigneir,
Alanson, and Souldiers.*

  Puzel. Aduance our wauing Colours on the Walls,
Rescu'd is Orleance from the English.
Thus *Ioane de Puzel* hath perform'd her word.
  Dolph. Diuinest Creature, *Astrea's* Daughter,
How shall I honour thee for this succeße?
Thy promises are like *Adonis* Garden,
That one day bloom'd, and fruitfull were the next.
France, triumph in thy glorious Prophetesse,
Recouer'd is the Towne of Orleance,
More blessed hap did ne're befall our State.
  Reigneir. Why ring not out the Bells alowd,
Throughout the Towne?
Dolphin command the Citizens make Bonfires,
And feast and banquet in the open streets,
To celebrate the ioy that God hath giuen vs.
  Alanſ. All France will be repleat with mirth and ioy,
When they shall heare how we haue play'd the men.
  Dolph. 'Tis *Ioane*, not we, by whom the day is wonne:
For which, I will diuide my Crowne with her,
And all the Priests and Fryers in my Realme,
Shall in procession sing her endleße prayse.
A statelyer Pyramis to her Ile reare,
Then *Rhodophe's* or *Memphis* euer was.
In memorie of her, when she is dead,
Her Ashes, in an Vrne more precious
Then the rich-iewel'd Coffer of *Darius*,
Transported, shall be at high Festiuals
Before the Kings and Queenes of France.
No longer on Saint *Dennis* will we cry,
But *Ioane de Puzel* shall be France's Saint.
Come in, and let vs Banquet Royally,
After this Golden Day of Victorie.
                Flourish.   Exeunt.

Actus Secundus. Scena Prima.

Enter a Sergeant of a Band, with two Sentinels.

  Ser. Sirs, take your places, and be vigilant:
If any noyse or Souldier you perceiue
Neere to the walles, by some apparant signe
Let vs haue knowledge at the Court of Guard.
  Sent. Sergeant you shall. Thus are poore Seruitors
(When others sleepe vpon their quiet beds)
Constrain'd to watch in darkneße, raine, and cold.

*Enter Talbot, Bedford, and Burgundy, with scaling
Ladders: Their Drummes beating a
Dead March.*

  Tal. Lord Regent, and redoubted *Burgundy*,
By whose approach, the Regions of *Artoys*,
Wallon, and *Picardy*, are friends to vs:
This happy night, the Frenchmen are secure,
Hauing all day carows'd and banquetted,
Embrace we then this opportunitie,
As fitting best to quittance their deceite,
Contriu'd by Art, and balefull Sorcerie.
  Bed. Coward of France, how much he wrongs his fame,
Dispairing of his owne armes fortitude,
To ioyne with Witches, and the helpe of Hell.
  Bur. Traitors haue neuer other company.
But what's that *Puzell* whom they tearme so pure?
  Tal. A Maid, they say.
  Bed. A Maid? And be so martiall?
  Bur. Pray God she proue not masculine ere long:
If vnderneath the Standard of the French
She carry Armour, as she hath begun.
  Tal. Well, let them practise and conuerse with spirits.
God is our Fortresse, in whose conquering name
Let vs resolue to scale their flinty bulwarkes.
  Bed. Ascend braue *Talbot*, we will follow thee.
  Tal. Not altogether: Better farre I gueße,
That we do make our entrance seuerall wayes:
That if it chance the one of vs do faile,
The other yet may rise against their force.
  Bed. Agreed; Ile to yond corner.
  Bur. And I to this.
  Tal. And heere will *Talbot* mount, or make his graue.
Now *Salisbury*, for thee and for the right
Of English *Henry*, shall this night appeare
How much in duty, I am bound to both.
  Sent. Arme, arme, the enemy doth make assault.

Cry, St. George, A Talbot.

*The French leape ore the walles in their shirts. Enter
seuerall wayes, Bastard, Alanson, Reignier,
halfe ready, and halfe vnready.*

  Alan. How now my Lords? what all vnreadie so?
  Bast. Vnready? I and glad we scap'd so well.
  Reig. 'Twas time (I trow) to wake and leaue our beds,
Hearing Alarums at our Chamber doores.
  Alan. Of all exploits since first I follow'd Armes,
Nere heard I of a warlike enterprize

More

More venturous, or desperate then this.
Bast. I thinke this *Talbot* be a Fiend of Hell.
Reig. If not of Hell, the Heauens sure fauour him.
Alans. Here commeth *Charles,* I maruell how he sped?

Enter Charles and Ioane.

Bast. Tut, holy *Ioane* was his defensiue Guard.
Charl. Is this thy cunning, thou deceitfull Dame?
Didst thou at first, to flatter vs withall,
Make vs partakers of a little gayne,
That now our losse might be ten times so much?

Ioane. Wherefore is *Charles* impatient with his friend?
At all times will you haue my Power alike?
Sleeping or waking, must I still preuayle,
Or will you blame and lay the fault on me?
Improuident Souldiors, had your Watch been good,
This sudden Mischiefe neuer could haue falne.

Charl. Duke of Alanson, this was your default,
That being Captaine of the Watch to Night,
Did looke no better to that weightie Charge.

Alans. Had all your Quarters been as safely kept,
As that whereof I had the gouernment,
We had not beene thus shamefully surpriz'd.

Bast. Mine was secure.
Reig. And so was mine, my Lord.
Charl. And for my selfe, most part of all this Night
Within her Quarter, and mine owne Precinct,
I was imploy'd in passing to and fro,
About relieuing of the Centinels.
Then how, or which way, should they first breake in?

Ioane. Question (my Lords) no further of the case,
How or which way; 'tis sure they found some place,
But weakely guarded, where the breach was made:
And now there rests no other shift but this,
To gather our Souldiors, scatter'd and dispers't,
And lay new Plat-formes to endammage them. *Exeunt.*

Alarum. Enter a Souldier, crying, a Talbot, a Talbot: they flye, leauing their Clothes behind.

Sould. Ile be so bold to take what they haue left:
The Cry of *Talbot* serues me for a Sword,
For I haue loaden me with many Spoyles,
Vsing no other Weapon but his Name. *Exit.*

Enter Talbot, Bedford, Burgundie.

Bedf. The Day begins to breake, and Night is fled,
Whose pitchy Mantle ouer-vayl'd the Earth.
Here sound Retreat, and cease our hot pursuit. *Retreat.*

Talb. Bring forth the Body of old *Salisbury,*
And here aduance it in the Market-Place,
The middle Centure of this cursed Towne.
Now haue I pay'd my Vow vnto his Soule:
For euery drop of blood was drawne from him,
There hath at least fiue Frenchmen dyed to night.
And that hereafter Ages may behold
What ruine happened in reuenge of him,
Within their chiefest Temple Ile erect
A Tombe, wherein his Corps shall be interr'd:
Vpon the which, that euery one may reade,
Shall be engrau'd the sacke of Orleance,
The trecherous manner of his mournefull death,
And what a terror he had beene to France.
But Lords, in all our bloudy Massacre,
I muse we met not with the Dolphins Grace,
His new-come Champion, vertuous *Ioane* of Acre,
Nor any of his false Confederates.

Bedf. 'Tis thought Lord *Talbot,* when the fight began,
Rows'd on the sudden from their drowsie Beds,
They did amongst the troupes of armed men,
Leape o're the Walls for refuge in the field.

Burg. My selfe, as farre as I could well discerne,
For smoake, and duskie vapours of the night,
Am sure I scar'd the Dolphin and his Trull,
When Arme in Arme they both came swiftly running,
Like to a payre of louing Turtle-Doues,
That could not liue asunder day or night.
After that things are set in order here,
Wee'le follow them with all the power we haue.

Enter a Messenger.

Mess. All hayle, my Lords: which of this Princely trayne
Call ye the Warlike *Talbot,* for his Acts
So much applauded through the Realme of France?

Talb. Here is the *Talbot,* who would speak with him?
Mess. The vertuous Lady, Countesse of Ouergne,
With modestie admiring thy Renowne,
By me entreats (great Lord) thou would'st vouchsafe
To visit her poore Castle where she lyes,
That she may boast she hath beheld the man,
Whose glory fills the World with lowd report.

Burg. Is it euen so? Nay, then I see our Warres
Will turne vnto a peacefull Comick sport,
When Ladyes craue to be encountred with.
You may not (my Lord) despise her gentle suit.

Talb. Ne're trust me then: for when a World of men
Could not preuayle with all their Oratorie,
Yet hath a Womans kindnesse ouer-rul'd:
And therefore tell her, I returne great thankes,
And in submission will attend on her.
Will not your Honors beare me company?

Bedf. No, truly, 'tis more then manners will:
And I haue heard it sayd, Vnbidden Guests
Are often welcommest when they are gone.

Talb. Well then, alone (since there's no remedie)
I meane to proue this Ladyes courtesie.
Come hither Captaine, you perceiue my minde. *Whispers.*

Capt. I doe my Lord, and meane accordingly. *Exeunt.*

Enter Countesse.

Count. Porter, remember what I gaue in charge,
And when you haue done so, bring the Keyes to me.
Port. Madame, I will. *Exit.*
Count. The Plot is layd, if all things fall out right,
I shall as famous be by this exploit,
As Scythian *Tomyris* by *Cyrus* death.
Great is the rumour of this dreadfull Knight,
And his atchieuements of no lesse account:
Faine would mine eyes be witnesse with mine eares,
To giue their censure of these rare reports.

Enter Messenger and Talbot.

Mess. Madame, according as your Ladyship desir'd,
By Message crau'd, so is Lord *Talbot* come.
Count. And he is welcome: what? is this the man?
Mess. Madame, it is.
Count. Is this the Scourge of France?
Is this the *Talbot,* so much fear'd abroad?
That with his Name the Mothers still their Babes?
I see Report is fabulous and false.

I thought I should haue seene some *Hercules*,
A second *Hector*, for his grim aspect,
And large proportion of his strong knit Limbes,
Alas, this is a Child, a silly Dwarfe:
It cannot be, this weake and writhled shrimpe
Should strike such terror to his Enemies.

  Talb. Madame, I haue beene bold to trouble you:
But since your Ladyship is not at leysure,
Ile sort some other time to visit you.

  Count. What meanes he now?
Goe aske him, whither he goes?

  Mess. Stay my Lord *Talbot*, for my Lady craues,
To know the cause of your abrupt departure?

  Talb. Marry, for that shee's in a wrong beleefe,
I goe to certifie her *Talbot's* here.

Enter Porter with Keyes.

  Count. If thou be he, then art thou Prisoner.
  Talb. Prisoner? to whom?
  Count. To me, blood-thirstie Lord:
And for that cause I trayn'd thee to my House.
Long time thy shadow hath been thrall to me,
For in my Gallery thy Picture hangs:
But now the substance shall endure the like,
And I will chayne these Legges and Armes of thine,
That hast by Tyrannie these many yeeres
Wasted our Countrey, slaine our Citizens,
And sent our Sonnes and Husbands captiuate.

  Talb. Ha, ha, ha.
  Count. Laughest thou Wretch?
Thy mirth shall turne to moone.
  Talb. I laugh to see your Ladyship so fond,
To thinke, that you haue ought but *Talbots* shadow,
Whereon to practise your seueritie.
  Count. Why? art not thou the man?
  Talb. I am indeede.
  Count. Then haue I substance too.
  Talb. No, no, I am but shadow of my selfe:
You are deceiu'd, my substance is not here;
For what you see, is but the smallest part,
And least proportion of Humanitie:
I tell you Madame, were the whole Frame here,
It is of such a spacious loftie pitch,
Your Roofe were not sufficient to contayn't.

  Count. This is a Riddling Merchant for the nonce,
He will be here, and yet he is not here:
How can these contrarieties agree?
  Talb. That will I shew you presently.

Winds his Horne, Drummes strike vp, a Peale
of Ordenance: Enter Souldiors.

How say you Madame? are you now perswaded,
That *Talbot* is but shadow of himselfe?
These are his substance, sinewes, armes, and strength,
With which he yoaketh your rebellious Neckes,
Razeth your Cities, and subuerts your Townes,
And in a moment makes them desolate.

  Count. Victorious *Talbot*, pardon my abuse,
I finde thou art no lesse then Fame hath bruited,
And more then may be gathered by thy shape.
Let my presumption not prouoke thy wrath,
For I am sorry, that with reuerence
I did not entertaine thee as thou art.

  Talb. Be not dismay'd, faire Lady, nor misconster
The minde of *Talbot*, as you did mistake
The outward composition of his body.
What you haue done, hath not offended me:
Nor other satisfaction doe I craue,
But onely with your patience, that we may
Taste of your Wine, and see what Cates you haue,
For Souldiers stomacks alwayes serue them well.

  Count. With all my heart, and thinke me honored,
To feast so great a Warrior in my House. *Exeunt.*

Enter Richard Plantagenet, Warwick, Somerset,
Poole, and others.

  Yorke. Great Lords and Gentlemen,
What meanes this silence?
Dare no man answer in a Case of Truth?
  Suff. Within the Temple Hall we were too lowd,
The Garden here is more conuenient.
  York. Then say at once, if I maintain'd the Truth:
Or else was wrangling *Somerset* in th'error?
  Suff. Faith I haue beene a Truant in the Law,
And neuer yet could frame my will to it,
And therefore frame the Law vnto my will.
  Som. Iudge you, my Lord of *Warwicke*, then betweene vs.
  War. Between two Hawks, which flyes the higher pitch,
Between two Dogs, which hath the deeper mouth,
Between two Blades, which beares the better temper,
Between two Horses, which doth beare him best,
Between two Girles, which hath the merryest eye,
I haue perhaps some shallow spirit of Iudgement:
But in these nice sharpe Quillets of the Law,
Good faith I am no wiser then a Daw.
  York. Tut, tut, here is a mannerly forbearance:
The truth appeares so naked on my side,
That any purblind eye may find it out.
  Som. And on my side it is so well apparrell'd,
So cleare, so shining, and so euident,
That it will glimmer through a blind-mans eye.
  York. Since you are tongue-ty'd, and so loth to speake,
In dumbe significants proclayme your thoughts:
Let him that is a true-borne Gentleman,
And stands vpon the honor of his birth,
If he suppose that I haue pleaded truth,
From off this Bryer pluck a white Rose with me.
  Som. Let him that is no Coward, nor no Flatterer,
But dare maintaine the partie of the truth,
Pluck a red Rose from off this Thorne with me.
  War. I loue no Colours: and without all colour
Of base insinuating flatterie,
I pluck this white Rose with *Plantagenet*.
  Suff. I pluck this red Rose, with young *Somerset*,
And say withall, I thinke he held the right.
  Vernon. Stay Lords and Gentlemen, and pluck no more
Till you conclude, that he vpon whose side
The fewest Roses are cropt from the Tree,
Shall yeeld the other in the right opinion.
  Som. Good Master *Vernon*, it is well obiected:
If I haue fewest, I subscribe in silence.
  York. And I.
  Vernon. Then for the truth, and plainnesse of the Case,
I pluck this pale and Maiden Blossome here,
Giuing my Verdict on the white Rose side.
  Som. Prick not your finger as you pluck it off,
Least bleeding, you doe paint the white Rose red,
And fall on my side so against your will.
  Vernon. If I, my Lord, for my opinion bleed,
Opinion shall be Surgeon to my hurt,
And keepe me on the side where still I am.
  Som. Well, well, come on, who else?

Lawyer. Vnlesse my Studie and my Bookes be false,
The argument you held, was wrong in you;
In signe whereof, I pluck a white Rose too.

Yorke. Now *Somerset*, where is your argument?

Som. Here in my Scabbard, meditating, that
Shall dye your white Rose in a bloody red.

York. Meane time your cheeks do counterfeit our Roses:
For pale they looke with feare, as witnessing
The truth on our side.

Som. No *Plantagenet*:
'Tis not for feare, but anger, that thy cheekes
Blush for pure shame, to counterfeit our Roses,
And yet thy tongue will not confesse thy error.

Yorke. Hath not thy Rose a Canker, *Somerset*?

Som. Hath not thy Rose a Thorne, *Plantagenet*?

Yorke. I, sharpe and piercing to maintaine his truth,
Whiles thy consuming Canker eates his falsehood.

Som. Well, Ile find friends to weare my bleeding Roses,
That shall maintaine what I haue said is true,
Where false *Plantagenet* dare not be seene.

Yorke. Now by this Maiden Blossome in my hand,
I scorne thee and thy fashion, peeuish Boy.

Suff. Turne not thy scornes this way, *Plantagenet*.

Yorke. Proud *Poole*, I will, and scorne both him and thee.

Suff. Ile turne my part thereof into thy throat.

Som. Away, away, good *William de la Poole*,
We grace the Yeoman, by conuersing with him.

Warw. Now by Gods will thou wrong'st him, *Somerset*:
His Grandfather was *Lyonel* Duke of Clarence,
Third Sonne to the third *Edward* King of England:
Spring Crestlesse Yeomen from so deepe a Root?

Yorke. He beares him on the place's Priuiledge,
Or durst not for his crauen heart say thus.

Som. By him that made me, Ile maintaine my words
On any Plot of Ground in Christendome.
Was not thy Father, *Richard*, Earle of Cambridge,
For Treason executed in our late Kings dayes?
And by his Treason, stand'st not thou attainted,
Corrupted, and exempt from ancient Gentry?
His Trespas yet liues guiltie in thy blood,
And till thou be restor'd, thou art a Yeoman.

Yorke. My Father was attached, not attainted,
Condemn'd to dye for Treason, but no Traytor;
And that Ile proue on better men then *Somerset*,
Were growing time once ripened to my will.
For your partaker *Poole*, and you your selfe,
Ile note you in my Booke of Memorie,
To scourge you for this apprehension:
Looke to it well, and say you are well warn'd.

Som. Ah, thou shalt finde vs ready for thee still:
And know vs by these Colours for thy Foes,
For these, my friends in spight of thee shall weare.

Yorke. And by my Soule, this pale and angry Rose,
As Cognizance of my blood-drinking hate,
Will I for euer, and my Faction weare,
Vntill it wither with me to my Graue,
Or flourish to the height of my Degree.

Suff. Goe forward, and be choak'd with thy ambition:
And so farwell, vntill I meet thee next. *Exit.*

Som. Haue with thee *Poole*: Farwell ambitious *Richard*. *Exit.*

Yorke. How I am brau'd, and must perforce endure it?

Warw. This blot that they obiect against your House,
Shall be whipt out in the next Parliament,
Call'd for the Truce of *Winchester* and *Gloucester*:
And if thou be not then created *Yorke*,
I will not liue to be accounted *Warwicke*.
Meane time, in signall of my loue to thee,
Against prowd *Somerset*, and *William Poole*,
Will I vpon thy partie weare this Rose.
And here I prophecie: this brawle to day,
Growne to this faction in the Temple Garden,
Shall send betweene the Red-Rose and the White,
A thousand Soules to Death and deadly Night.

Yorke. Good Master *Vernon*, I am bound to you,
That you on my behalfe would pluck a Flower.

Ver. In your behalfe still will I weare the same.

Lawyer. And so will I.

Yorke. Thankes gentle.
Come, let vs foure to Dinner: I dare say,
This Quarrell will drinke Blood another day.

Exeunt.

Enter Mortimer, brought in a Chayre, and Iaylors.

Mort. Kind Keepers of my weake decaying Age,
Let dying *Mortimer* here rest himselfe.
Euen like a man new haled from the Wrack,
So fare my Limbes with long Imprisonment:
And these gray Locks, the Pursuiuants of death,
Nestor-like aged, in an Age of Care,
Argue the end of *Edmund Mortimer*.
These Eyes, like Lampes, whose wasting Oyle is spent,
Waxe dimme, as drawing to their Exigent.
Weake Shoulders, ouer-borne with burthening Griefe,
And pyth-lesse Armes, like to a withered Vine,
That droupes his sappe-lesse Branches to the ground.
Yet are these Feet, whose strength-lesse stay is numme,
(Vnable to support this Lumpe of Clay)
Swift-winged with desire to get a Graue,
As witting I no other comfort haue.
But tell me, Keeper, will my Nephew come?

Keeper. Richard *Plantagenet*, my Lord, will come:
We sent vnto the Temple, vnto his Chamber,
And answer was return'd, that he will come.

Mort. Enough: my Soule shall then be satisfied.
Poore Gentleman, his wrong doth equall mine.
Since *Henry Monmouth* first began to reigne,
Before whose Glory I was great in Armes,
This loathsome sequestration haue I had;
And euen since then, hath *Richard* beene obscur'd,
Depriu'd of Honor and Inheritance.
But now, the Arbitrator of Despaires,
Iust Death, kinde Vmpire of mens miseries,
With sweet enlargement doth dismisse me hence:
I would his troubles likewise were expir'd,
That so he might recouer what was lost.

Enter Richard.

Keeper. My Lord, your louing Nephew now is come.

Mor. Richard *Plantagenet*, my friend, is he come?

Rich. I, Noble Vnckle, thus ignobly vs'd,
Your Nephew, late despised *Richard*, comes.

Mort. Direct mine Armes, I may embrace his Neck,
And in his Bosome spend my latter gaspe.
Oh tell me when my Lippes doe touch his Cheekes,
That I may kindly giue one fainting Kisse.
And now declare sweet Stem from *Yorkes* great Stock,
Why didst thou say of late thou wert despis'd?

Rich. First

Rich. First, leane thine aged Back against mine Arme,
And in that ease, Ile tell thee my Disease.
This day in argument vpon a Case,
Some words there grew 'twixt *Somerset* and me:
Among which tearmes, he vs'd his lauish tongue,
And did vpbrayd me with my Fathers death;
Which obloquie set barres before my tongue,
Else with the like I had requited him.
Therefore good Vnckle, for my Fathers sake,
In honor of a true *Plantagenet*,
And for Alliance sake, declare the cause
My Father, Earle of Cambridge, lost his Head.

Mort. That cause (faire Nephew) that imprison'd me,
And hath detayn'd me all my flowring Youth,
Within a loathsome Dungeon, there to pyne,
Was cursed Instrument of his decease.

Rich. Discouer more at large what cause that was,
For I am ignorant, and cannot guesse.

Mort. I will, if that my fading breath permit,
And Death approach not, ere my Tale be done.
Henry the Fourth, Grandfather to this King,
Depos'd his Nephew *Richard*, *Edwards* Sonne,
The first begotten, and the lawfull Heire
Of *Edward* King, the Third of that Descent.
During whose Reigne, the *Percies* of the North,
Finding his Vsurpation most vniust,
Endeuour'd my aduancement to the Throne.
The reason mou'd these Warlike Lords to this,
Was, for that (young *Richard* thus remou'd,
Leauing no Heire begotten of his Body)
I was the next by Birth and Parentage:
For by my Mother, I deriued am
From *Lionel* Duke of Clarence, third Sonne
To King *Edward* the Third; whereas hee,
From *Iohn* of Gaunt doth bring his Pedigree,
Being but fourth of that Heroick Lyne.
But marke: as in this haughtie great attempt,
They laboured, to plant the rightfull Heire,
I lost my Libertie, and they their Liues.
Long after this, when *Henry* the Fift
(Succeeding his Father *Bullingbrooke*) did reigne;
Thy Father, Earle of Cambridge, then deriu'd
From famous *Edmund Langley*, Duke of Yorke,
Marrying my Sister, that thy Mother was;
Againe, in pitty of my hard distresse,
Leuied an Army, weening to redeeme,
And haue install'd me in the Diademe:
But as the rest, so fell that Noble Earle,
And was beheaded. Thus the *Mortimers*,
In whom the Title rested, were supprest.

Rich. Of which, my Lord, your Honor is the last.

Mort. True; and thou seest, that I no Issue haue,
And that my fainting words doe warrant death:
Thou art my Heire; the rest, I wish thee gather:
But yet be wary in thy studious care.

Rich. Thy graue admonishments preuayle with me:
But yet me thinkes, my Fathers execution
Was nothing lesse then bloody Tyranny.

Mort. With silence, Nephew, be thou pollitick,
Strong fixed is the House of *Lancaster*,
And like a Mountaine, not to be remou'd.
But now thy Vnckle is remouing hence,
As Princes doe their Courts, when they are cloy'd
With long continuance in a setled place.

Rich. O Vnckle, would some part of my young yeeres
Might but redeeme the passage of your Age.

Mort. Thou do'st then wrong me, as ye slaughterer doth,
Which giueth many Wounds, when one will kill.
Mourne not, except thou sorrow for my good,
Onely giue order for my Funerall.
And so farewell, and faire be all thy hopes,
And prosperous be thy Life in Peace and Warre. *Dyes.*

Rich. And Peace, no Warre, befall thy parting Soule.
In Prison hast thou spent a Pilgrimage,
And like a Hermite ouer-past thy dayes.
Well, I will locke his Councell in my Brest,
And what I doe imagine, let that rest.
Keepers conuey him hence, and I my selfe
Will see his Buryall better then his Life. *Exit.*
Here dyes the duskie Torch of *Mortimer*,
Choakt with Ambition of the meaner sort.
And for those Wrongs, those bitter Iniuries,
Which *Somerset* hath offer'd to my House,
I doubt not, but with Honor to redresse.
And therefore haste I to the Parliament,
Eyther to be restored to my Blood,
Or make my will th'aduantage of my good. *Exit.*

Actus Tertius. Scena Prima.

*Flourish. Enter King, Exeter, Gloster, Winchester, Warwick,
Somerset, Suffolk, Richard Plantagenet. Gloster offers
to put vp a Bill: Winchester snatches it, teares it.*

Winch. Com'st thou with deepe premeditated Lines?
With written Pamphlets, studiously deuis'd?
Humfrey of Gloster, if thou canst accuse,
Or ought intend'st to lay vnto my charge,
Doe it without inuention, suddenly,
As I with sudden, and extemporall speech,
Purpose to answer what thou canst obiect.

Glo. Presumptuous Priest, this place comends my patiēce,
Or thou should'st finde thou hast dis-honor'd me.
Thinke not, although in Writing I preferr'd
The manner of thy vile outragious Crymes,
That therefore I haue forg'd, or am not able
Verbatim to rehearse the Methode of my Penne.
No Prelate, such is thy audacious wickednesse,
Thy lewd, pestiferous, and dissentious prancks,
As very Infants prattle of thy pride.
Thou art a most pernitious Vsurer,
Froward by nature, Enemie to Peace,
Lasciuious, wanton, more then well beseemes
A man of thy Profession, and Degree.
And for thy Trecherie, what's more manifest?
In that thou layd'st a Trap to take my Life,
As well at London Bridge, as at the Tower.
Beside, I feare me, if thy thoughts were sifted,
The King, thy Soueraigne, is not quite exempt
From enuious mallice of thy swelling heart.

Winch. Gloster, I doe defie thee. Lords vouchsafe
To giue me hearing what I shall reply.
If I were couetous, ambitious, or peruerse,
As he will haue me: how am I so poore?
Or how haps it, I seeke not to aduance
Or rayse my selfe? but keepe my wonted Calling.
And for Dissention, who preferreth Peace
More then I doe? except I be prouok'd.
No, my good Lords, it is not that offends,
It is not that, that hath incens'd the Duke:
It is because no one should sway but hee,
No one, but hee, should be about the King;
And that engenders Thunder in his breast,

And

And makes him rore these Accusations forth.
But he shall know I am as good.

  Glost. As good?
Thou Bastard of my Grandfather.

  Winch. I, Lordly Sir: for what are you, I pray,
But one imperious in anothers Throne?

  Glost. Am I not Protector, sawcie Priest?

  Winch. And am not I a Prelate of the Church?

  Glost. Yes, as an Out-law in a Castle keepes,
And vseth it, to patronage his Theft.

  Winch. Vnreuerent *Glocester*.

  Glost. Thou art reuerent,
Touching thy Spirituall Function, not thy Life.

  Winch. Rome shall remedie this.

  Warw. Roame thither then,
My Lord, it were your dutie to forbeare.

  Som. I, see the Bishop be not ouer-borne:
Me thinkes my Lord should be Religious,
And know the Office that belongs to such.

  Warw. Me thinkes his Lordship should be humbler,
It fitteth not a Prelate so to plead.

  Som. Yes, when his holy State is toucht so neere.

  Warw. State holy, or vnhallow'd, what of that?
Is not his Grace Protector to the King?

  Rich. *Plantagenet* I see must hold his tongue,
Least it be said, Speake Sirrha when you should:
Must your bold Verdict enter talke with Lords?
Else would I haue a fling at *Winchester*.

  King. Vnckles of *Gloster*, and of *Winchester*,
The speciall Watch-men of our English Weale,
I would preuayle, if Prayers might preuayle,
To ioyne your hearts in loue and amitie.
Oh, what a Scandall is it to our Crowne,
That two such Noble Peeres as ye should iarre?
Beleeue me, Lords, my tender yeeres can tell,
Ciuill dissention is a viperous Worme,
That gnawes the Bowels of the Common-wealth.

  A noyse within, Downe with the
  Tawny-Coats.

  King. What tumult's this?

  Warw. An Vprore, I dare warrant,
Begun through malice of the Bishops men.

  A noyse againe, Stones, Stones.

  Enter Maior.

  Maior. Oh my good Lords, and vertuous *Henry*,
Pitty the Citie of London, pitty vs:
The Bishop, and the Duke of Glosters men,
Forbidden late to carry any Weapon,
Haue fill'd their Pockets full of peeble stones;
And banding themselues in contrary parts,
Doe pelt so fast at one anothers Pate,
That many haue their giddy braynes knockt out:
Our Windowes are broke downe in euery Street,
And we, for feare, compell'd to shut our Shops.

  Enter in skirmish with bloody Pates.

  King. We charge you, on allegeance to our selfe,
To hold your slaughtring hands, and keepe the Peace:
Pray' Vnckle *Gloster* mittigate this strife.

  1. Seruing. Nay, if we be forbidden Stones, wee'le fall
to it with our Teeth.

  2. Seruing. Doe what ye dare, we are as resolute.

  Skirmish againe.

  Glost. You of my houshold, leaue this peeuish broyle,
And set this vnaccustom'd fight aside.

  3. Seru. My Lord, we know your Grace to be a man
Iust, and vpright; and for your Royall Birth,
Inferior to none, but to his Maiestie:
And ere that we will suffer such a Prince,
So kinde a Father of the Common-weale,
To be disgraced by an Inke-horne Mate,
Wee and our Wiues and Children all will fight,
And haue our bodyes slaughtred by thy foes.

  1. Seru. I, and the very parings of our Nayles
Shall pitch a Field when we are dead.

  Begin againe.

  Glost. Stay, stay, I say:
And if you loue me, as you say you doe,
Let me perswade you to forbeare a while.

  King. Oh, how this discord doth afflict my Soule.
Can you, my Lord of Winchester, behold
My sighes and teares, and will not once relent?
Who should be pittifull, if you be not?
Or who should study to preferre a Peace,
If holy Church-men take delight in broyles?

  Warw. Yeeld my Lord Protector, yeeld *Winchester*,
Except you meane with obstinate repulse
To slay your Soueraigne, and destroy the Realme.
You see what Mischiefe, and what Murther too,
Hath beene enacted through your enmitie:
Then be at peace, except ye thirst for blood.

  Winch. He shall submit, or I will neuer yeeld.

  Glost. Compassion on the King commands me stoupe,
Or I would see his heart out, ere the Priest
Should euer get that priuiledge of me.

  Warw. Behold my Lord of Winchester, the Duke
Hath banisht moodie discontented fury,
As by his smoothed Browes it doth appeare:
Why looke you still so sterne, and tragicall?

  Glost. Here *Winchester*, I offer thee my Hand.

  King. Fie Vnckle *Beauford*, I haue heard you preach,
That Mallice was a great and grieuous sinne:
And will not you maintaine the thing you teach?
But proue a chiefe offendor in the same.

  Warw. Sweet King: the Bishop hath a kindly gyrd:
For shame my Lord of Winchester relent;
What, shall a Child instruct you what to doe?

  Winch. Well, Duke of Gloster, I will yeeld to thee
Loue for thy Loue, and Hand for Hand I giue.

  Glost. I, but I feare me with a hollow Heart.
See here my Friends and louing Countreymen,
This token serueth for a Flagge of Truce,
Betwixt our selues, and all our followers:
So helpe me God, as I dissemble not.

  Winch. So helpe me God, as I intend it not.

  King. Oh louing Vnckle, kinde Duke of Gloster,
How ioyfull am I made by this Contract.
Away my Masters, trouble vs no more,
But ioyne in friendship, as your Lords haue done.

  1. Seru. Content, Ile to the Surgeons.

  2. Seru. And so will I.

  3. Seru. And I will see what Physick the Tauerne affords. *Exeunt.*

  Warw. Accept this Scrowle, most gracious Soueraigne,
Which in the Right of *Richard Plantagenet*,
We doe exhibite to your Maiestie.

  Glo. Well vrg'd, my Lord of Warwick: for sweet Prince,
And if your Grace marke euery circumstance,
You haue great reason to doe *Richard* right,
Especially for those occasions
At Eltam Place I told your Maiestie.

  King. And

King. And those occasions, Vnckle, were of force:
Therefore my louing Lords, our pleasure is,
That *Richard* be restored to his Blood.

Warw. Let *Richard* be restored to his Blood,
So shall his Fathers wrongs be recompenc't.

Winch. As will the rest, so willeth *Winchester*.

King. If *Richard* will be true, not that all alone,
But all the whole Inheritance I giue,
That doth belong vnto the House of *Yorke*,
From whence you spring, by Lineall Descent.

Rich. Thy humble seruant vowes obedience,
And humble seruice, till the point of death.

King. Stoope then, and set your Knee against my Foot,
And in reguerdon of that dutie done,
I gyrt thee with the valiant Sword of *Yorke*:
Rise *Richard*, like a true *Plantagenet*,
And rise created Princely Duke of *Yorke*.

Rich. And so thriue *Richard*, as thy foes may fall,
And as my dutie springs, so perish they,
That grudge one thought against your Maiesty.

All. Welcome high Prince, the mighty Duke of *Yorke*.

Som. Perish base Prince, ignoble Duke of *Yorke*.

Glost. Now will it best auaile your Maiestie,
To crosse the Seas, and to be Crown'd in France:
The presence of a King engenders loue
Amongst his Subiects, and his loyall Friends,
As it dis-animates his Enemies.

King. When *Gloster* sayes the word, King *Henry* goes,
For friendly counsaile cuts off many Foes.

Glost. Your Ships alreadie are in readinesse.

Senet. Flourish. Exeunt.

Manet Exeter.

Exet. I, we may march in England, or in France,
Not seeing what is likely to ensue:
This late dissention growne betwixt the Peeres,
Burnes vnder fained ashes of forg'd loue,
And will at last breake out into a flame,
As festred members rot but by degree,
Till bones and flesh and sinewes fall away,
So will this base and enuious discord breed.
And now I feare that fatall Prophecie,
Which in the time of *Henry*, nam'd the Fift,
Was in the mouth of euery sucking Babe,
That *Henry* borne at Monmouth should winne all,
And *Henry* borne at Windsor, loose all:
Which is so plaine, that *Exeter* doth wish,
His dayes may finish, ere that haplesse time. *Exit.*

Scœna Secunda.

Enter Pucell disguis'd, with foure Souldiors with Sacks vpon their backs.

Pucell. These are the Citie Gates, the Gates of Roan,
Through which our Pollicy must make a breach.
Take heed, be wary how you place your words,
Talke like the vulgar sort of Market men,
That come to gather Money for their Corne.
If we haue entrance, as I hope we shall,
And that we finde the slouthfull Watch but weake,
Ile by a signe giue notice to our friends,
That *Charles* the Dolphin may encounter them.

Souldier. Our Sacks shall be a meane to sack the City,
And we be Lords and Rulers ouer Roan,
Therefore wee'le knock. *Knock.*

Watch. Che la.

Pucell. Peasauns la pouure gens de Fraunce,
Poore Market folkes that come to sell their Corne.

Watch. Enter, goe in, the Market Bell is rung.

Pucell. Now Roan, Ile shake thy Bulwarkes to the ground. *Exeunt.*

Enter Charles, Bastard, Alanson.

Charles. Saint *Dennis* blesse this happy Stratageme,
And once againe wee'le sleepe secure in Roan.

Bastard. Here entred *Pucell*, and her Practisants:
Now she is there, how will she specifie?
Here is the best and safest passage in.

Reig. By thrusting out a Torch from yonder Tower,
Which once discern'd, shewes that her meaning is,
No way to that (for weaknesse) which she entred.

Enter Pucell on the top, thrusting out a Torch burning.

Pucell. Behold, this is the happy Wedding Torch,
That ioyneth Roan vnto her Countreymen,
But burning fatall to the *Talbonites*.

Bastard. See Noble *Charles*, the Beacon of our friend,
The burning Torch in yonder Turret stands.

Charles. Now shine it like a Commet of Reuenge,
A Prophet to the fall of all our Foes.

Reig. Deferre no time, delayes haue dangerous ends,
Enter and cry, the Dolphin, presently,
And then doe execution on the Watch. *Alarum.*

An Alarum. Talbot in an Excursion.

Talb. France, thou shalt rue this Treason with thy teares,
If *Talbot* but suruiue thy Trecherie.
Pucell that Witch, that damned Sorceresse,
Hath wrought this Hellish Mischiefe vnawares,
That hardly we escap't the Pride of France. *Exit.*

An Alarum: Excursions. Bedford brought in sicke in a Chayre.

Enter Talbot and Burgonie without: within, Pucell, Charles, Bastard, and Reigneir on the Walls.

Pucell. God morrow Gallants, want ye Corn for Bread?
I thinke the Duke of Burgonie will fast,
Before hee'le buy againe at such a rate.
'Twas full of Darnell: doe you like the taste?

Burg. Scoffe on vile Fiend, and shamelesse Curtizan,
I trust ere long to choake thee with thine owne,
And make thee curse the Haruest of that Corne.

Charles. Your Grace may starue (perhaps) before that time.

Bedf. Oh let no words, but deedes, reuenge this Treason.

Pucell. What will you doe, good gray-beard?
Breake a Launce, and runne a-Tilt at Death,
Within a Chayre.

Talb. Foule Fiend of France, and Hag of all despight,
Incompass'd with thy lustfull Paramours,
Becomes it thee to taunt his valiant Age,
And twit with Cowardise a man halfe dead?
Damsell, Ile haue a bowt with you againe,
Or else let *Talbot* perish with this shame.

Pucell. Are ye so hot, Sir: yet *Pucell* hold thy peace,
If *Talbot* doe but Thunder, Raine will follow.

They whisper together in counsell.

God speed the Parliament: who shall be the Speaker?

Talb. Dare

Talb. Dare yee come forth, and meet vs in the field?

Pucell. Belike your Lordship takes vs then for fooles,
To try if that our owne be ours, or no.

Talb. I speake not to that rayling *Hecate*,
But vnto thee *Alanson*, and the rest.
Will ye, like Souldiors, come and fight it out?

Alanf. Seignior no.

Talb. Seignior hang: base Muleters of France,
Like Pesant foot-Boyes doe they keepe the Walls,
And dare not take vp Armes, like Gentlemen.

Pucell. Away Captaines, let's get vs from the Walls,
For *Talbot* meanes no goodnesse by his Lookes.
God b'uy my Lord, we came but to tell you
That wee are here. *Exeunt from the Walls.*

Talb. And there will we be too, ere it be long,
Or else reproach be *Talbots* greatest fame.
Vow *Burgonie*, by honor of thy House,
Prickt on by publike Wrongs sustain'd in France,
Either to get the Towne againe, or dye.
And I, as sure as English *Henry* liues,
And as his Father here was Conqueror;
As sure as in this late betrayed Towne,
Great *Cordelions* Heart was buryed;
So sure I sweare, to get the Towne, or dye.

Burg. My Vowes are equall partners with thy Vowes.

Talb. But ere we goe, regard this dying Prince,
The valiant Duke of Bedford: Come my Lord,
We will bestow you in some better place,
Fitter for sicknesse, and for crasie age.

Bedf. Lord *Talbot*, doe not so dishonour me:
Here will I sit, before the Walls of Roan,
And will be partner of your weale or woe.

Burg. Couragious *Bedford*, let vs now perswade you.

Bedf. Not to be gone from hence: for once I read,
That stout *Pendragon*, in his Litter sick,
Came to the field, and vanquished his foes.
Me thinkes I should reuiue the Souldiors hearts,
Because I euer found them as my selfe.

Talb. Vndaunted spirit in a dying breast,
Then be it so: Heauens keepe old *Bedford* safe.
And now no more adoe, braue *Burgonie*,
But gather we our Forces out of hand,
And set vpon our boasting Enemie. *Exit.*

*An Alarum: Excursions. Enter Sir Iohn
Falstaffe, and a Captaine.*

Capt. Whither away Sir *Iohn Falstaffe*, in such haste?

Falst. Whither away? to saue my selfe by flight,
We are like to haue the ouerthrow againe.

Capt. What? will you flye, and leaue Lord *Talbot*?

Falst. I, all the *Talbots* in the World, to saue my life. *Exit.*

Capt. Cowardly Knight, ill fortune follow thee. *Exit.*

*Retreat. Excursions. Pucell, Alanson, and
Charles flye.*

Bedf. Now quiet Soule, depart when Heauen please,
For I haue seene our Enemies ouerthrow.
What is the trust or strength of foolish man?
They that of late were daring with their scoffes,
Are glad and faine by flight to saue themselues.

Bedford dyes, and is carryed in by two in his Chaire.

*An Alarum. Enter Talbot, Burgonie, and
the rest.*

Talb. Lost, and recouered in a day againe,
This is a double Honor, *Burgonie*:
Yet Heauens haue glory for this Victorie.

Burg. Warlike and Martiall *Talbot*, *Burgonie*
Inshrines thee in his heart, and there erects
Thy noble Deeds, as Valors Monuments.

Talb. Thanks gentle Duke: but where is *Pucel* now?
I thinke her old Familiar is asleepe.
Now where's the Bastards braues, and *Charles* his glikes?
What all amort? Roan hangs her head for griefe,
That such a valiant Company are fled.
Now will we take some order in the Towne,
Placing therein some expert Officers,
And then depart to Paris, to the King,
For there young *Henry* with his Nobles lye.

Burg. What wills Lord *Talbot*, pleaseth *Burgonie*.

Talb. But yet before we goe, let's not forget
The Noble Duke of Bedford, late deceas'd,
But see his Exequies fulfill'd in Roan.
A brauer Souldier neuer couched Launce,
A gentler Heart did neuer sway in Court.
But Kings and mightiest Potentates must die,
For that's the end of humane miserie. *Exeunt.*

Scæna Tertia.

Enter Charles, Bastard, Alanson, Pucell.

Pucell. Dismay not (Princes) at this accident,
Nor grieue that Roan is so recouered:
Care is no cure, but rather corrosiue,
For things that are not to be remedy'd.
Let franticke *Talbot* triumph for a while,
And like a Peacock sweepe along his tayle,
Wee'le pull his Plumes, and take away his Trayne,
If Dolphin and the rest will be but rul'd.

Charles. We haue been guided by thee hitherto,
And of thy Cunning had no diffidence,
One sudden Foyle shall neuer breed distrust.

Bastard. Search out thy wit for secret pollicies,
And we will make thee famous through the World.

Alanf. Wee'le set thy Statue in some holy place,
And haue thee reuerenc't like a blessed Saint,
Employ thee then, sweet Virgin, for our good.

Pucell. Then thus it must be, this doth *Ioane* deuise:
By faire perswasions, mixt with sugred words,
We will entice the Duke of Burgonie
To leaue the *Talbot*, and to follow vs.

Charles. I marry Sweeting, if we could doe that,
France were no place for *Henryes* Warriors,
Nor should that Nation boast it so with vs,
But be extirped from our Prouinces.

Alanf. For euer should they be expuls'd from France,
And not haue Title of an Earledome here.

Pucell. Your Honors shall perceiue how I will worke,
To bring this matter to the wished end.
Drumme sounds a farre off.
Hearke, by the sound of Drumme you may perceiue
Their Powers are marching vnto Paris-ward.

Here sound an English March.
There goes the *Talbot*, with his Colours spred,
And all the Troupes of English after him. *French*

French March.
Now in the Rereward comes the Duke and his:
Fortune in fauor makes him lagge behinde.
Summon a Parley, we will talke with him.
Trumpets sound a Parley.

Charles. A Parley with the Duke of Burgonie.

Burg. Who craues a Parley with the Burgonie?

Pucell. The Princely *Charles* of France, thy Countrey-man.

Burg. What say'st thou *Charles*? for I am marching hence.

Charles. Speake *Pucell*, and enchaunt him with thy words.

Pucell. Braue *Burgonie*, vndoubted hope of France,
Stay, let thy humble Hand-maid speake to thee.

Burg. Speake on, but be not ouer-tedious.

Pucell. Looke on thy Country, look on fertile France,
And see the Cities and the Townes defac't,
By wasting Ruine of the cruell Foe,
As lookes the Mother on her lowly Babe,
When Death doth close his tender-dying Eyes.
See, see the pining Maladie of France:
Behold the Wounds, the most vnnaturall Wounds,
Which thou thy selfe hast giuen her wofull Brest.
Oh turne thy edged Sword another way,
Strike those that hurt, and hurt not those that helpe:
One drop of Blood drawne from thy Countries Bosome,
Should grieue thee more then streames of forraine gore.
Returne thee therefore with a floud of Teares,
And wash away thy Countries stayned Spots.

Burg. Either she hath bewitcht me with her words,
Or Nature makes me suddenly relent.

Pucell. Besides, all French and France exclaimes on thee,
Doubting thy Birth and lawfull Progenie.
Who ioyn'st thou with, but with a Lordly Nation,
That will not trust thee, but for profits sake?
When *Talbot* hath set footing once in France,
And fashion'd thee that Instrument of Ill,
Who then, but English *Henry*, will be Lord,
And thou be thrust out, like a Fugitiue?
Call we to minde, and marke but this for proofe:
Was not the Duke of Orleance thy Foe?
And was he not in England Prisoner?
But when they heard he was thine Enemie,
They set him free, without his Ransome pay'd,
In spight of *Burgonie* and all his friends.
See then, thou fight'st against thy Countreymen,
And ioyn'st with them will be thy slaughter-men.
Come, come, returne; returne thou wandering Lord,
Charles and the rest will take thee in their armes.

Burg. I am vanquished:
These haughtie wordes of hers
Haue batt'red me like roaring Cannon-shot,
And made me almost yeeld vpon my knees.
Forgiue me Countrey, and sweet Countreymen:
And Lords accept this heartie kind embrace.
My Forces and my Power of Men are yours.
So farwell *Talbot*, Ile no longer trust thee.

Pucell. Done like a Frenchman: turne and turne againe.

Charles. Welcome braue Duke, thy friendship makes vs fresh.

Bastard. And doth beget new Courage in our Breasts.

Alans. *Pucell* hath brauely play'd her part in this,
And doth deserue a Coronet of Gold.

Charles. Now let vs on, my Lords,
And ioyne our Powers,
And seeke how we may preiudice the Foe. *Exeunt.*

Scœna Quarta.

Enter the King, Gloucester, Winchester, Yorke, Suffolke, Somerset, Warwicke, Exeter: To them, with his Souldiors, Talbot.

Talb. My gracious Prince, and honorable Peeres,
Hearing of your arriuall in this Realme,
I haue a while giuen Truce vnto my Warres,
To doe my dutie to my Soueraigne.
In signe whereof, this Arme, that hath reclaym'd
To your obedience, fiftie Fortresses,
Twelue Cities, and seuen walled Townes of strength,
Beside fiue hundred Prisoners of esteeme;
Lets fall his Sword before your Highnesse feet:
And with submissiue loyaltie of heart
Ascribes the Glory of his Conquest got,
First to my God, and next vnto your Grace.

King. Is this the Lord *Talbot*, Vnckle *Gloucester*,
That hath so long beene resident in France?

Glost. Yes, if it please your Maiestie, my Liege.

King. Welcome braue Captaine, and victorious Lord.
When I was young (as yet I am not old)
I doe remember how my Father said,
A stouter Champion neuer handled Sword.
Long since we were resolued of your truth,
Your faithfull seruice, and your toyle in Warre:
Yet neuer haue you tasted our Reward,
Or beene reguerdon'd with so much as Thanks,
Because till now, we neuer saw your face.
Therefore stand vp, and for these good deserts,
We here create you Earle of Shrewsbury,
And in our Coronation take your place.

Senet. Flourish. Exeunt.

Manet Vernon and Basset.

Vern. Now Sir, to you that were so hot at Sea,
Disgracing of these Colours that I weare,
In honor of my Noble Lord of Yorke,
Dar'st thou maintaine the former words thou spak'st?

Bass. Yes Sir, as well as you dare patronage
The enuious barking of your sawcie Tongue,
Against my Lord the Duke of Somerset.

Vern. Sirrha, thy Lord I honour as he is.

Bass. Why, what is he? as good a man as *Yorke*.

Vern. Hearke ye: not so: in witnesse take ye that.
Strikes him.

Bass. Villaine, thou knowest
The Law of Armes is such,
That who so drawes a Sword, 'tis present death,
Or else this Blow should broach thy dearest Bloud.
But Ile vnto his Maiestie, and craue,
I may haue libertie to venge this Wrong,
When thou shalt see, Ile meet thee to thy cost.

Vern. Well miscreant, Ile be there as soone as you,
And after meete you, sooner then you would.
Exeunt.

Actus Quartus. Scena Prima.

Enter King, Glocester, Winchester, Yorke, Suffolke, Somerset, Warwicke, Talbot, and Gouernor Exeter.

Glo. Lord Bishop set the Crowne vpon his head.
Win. God saue King *Henry* of that name the sixt.
Glo. Now Gouernour of Paris take your oath,
That you elect no other King but him;
Esteeme none Friends, but such as are his Friends,
And none your Foes, but such as shall pretend
Malicious practises against his State:
This shall ye do, so helpe you righteous God.

Enter Falstaffe.

Fal. My gracious Soueraigne, as I rode from Calice,
To haste vnto your Coronation:
A Letter was deliuer'd to my hands,
Writ to your Grace, from th'Duke of Burgundy.

Tal. Shame to the Duke of Burgundy, and thee:
I vow'd (base Knight) when I did meete the next,
To teare the Garter from thy Crauens legge,
Which I haue done, because (vnworthily)
Thou was't installed in that High Degree.
Pardon me Princely *Henry*, and the rest:
This Dastard, at the battell of *Poictiers*,
When (but in all) I was sixe thousand strong,
And that the French were almost ten to one,
Before we met, or that a stroke was giuen,
Like to a trustie Squire, did run away.
In which assault, we lost twelue hundred men.
My selfe, and diuers Gentlemen beside,
Were there surpriz'd, and taken prisoners.
Then iudge (great Lords) if I haue done amisse:
Or whether that such Cowards ought to weare
This Ornament of Knighthood, yea or no?

Glo. To say the truth, this fact was infamous,
And ill beseeming any common man;
Much more a Knight, a Captaine, and a Leader.

Tal. When first this Order was ordain'd my Lords,
Knights of the Garter were of Noble birth;
Valiant, and Vertuous, full of haughtie Courage,
Such as were growne to credit by the warres:
Not fearing Death, nor shrinking for Distresse,
But alwayes resolute, in most extreames.
He then, that is not furnish'd in this sort,
Doth but vsurpe the Sacred name of Knight,
Prophaning this most Honourable Order,
And should (if I were worthy to be Iudge)
Be quite degraded, like a Hedge-borne Swaine,
That doth presume to boast of Gentle blood.

K. Staine to thy Countrymen, thou hear'st thy doom:
Be packing therefore, thou that was't a knight:
Henceforth we banish thee on paine of death.
And now Lord Protector, view the Letter
Sent from our Vnckle Duke of Burgundy.

Glo. What meanes his Grace, that he hath chaung'd his Stile?
No more but plaine and bluntly? *(To the King.)*
Hath he forgot he is his Soueraigne?
Or doth this churlish Superscription
Pretend some alteration in good will?
What's heere? *I haue vpon especiall cause,
Mou'd with compassion of my Countries wracke,
Together with the pittifull complaints
Of such as your oppression feedes vpon,
Forsaken your pernitious Faction,
And ioyn'd with Charles, the rightfull king of France.*
O monstrous Treachery: Can this be so?
That in alliance, amity, and oathes,
There should be found such false dissembling guile?

King. What? doth my Vnckle Burgundy reuolt?
Glo. He doth my Lord, and is become your foe.
King. Is that the worst this Letter doth containe?
Glo. It is the worst, and all (my Lord) he writes.
King. Why then Lord *Talbot* there shal talk with him,
And giue him chasticement for this abuse.
How say you (my Lord) are you not content?

Tal. Content, my Liege? Yes: But y̑ I am preuented,
I should haue begg'd I might haue bene employd.

King. Then gather strength, and march vnto him straight:
Let him perceiue how ill we brooke his Treason,
And what offence it is to flout his Friends.

Tal. I go my Lord, in heart desiring still
You may behold confusion of your foes.

Enter Vernon and Bassit.

Ver. Grant me the Combate, gracious Soueraigne.
Bas. And me (my Lord) grant me the Combate too.
Yorke. This is my Seruant, heare him Noble Prince.
Som. And this is mine (sweet *Henry*) fauour him.
King. Be patient Lords, and giue them leaue to speak.
Say Gentlemen, what makes you thus exclaime,
And wherefore craue you Combate? Or with whom?
Ver. With him (my Lord) for he hath done me wrong.
Bas. And I with him, for he hath done me wrong.
King. What is that wrong, wherof you both complain
First let me know, and then Ile answer you.

Bas. Crossing the Sea, from England into France,
This Fellow heere with enuious carping tongue,
Vpbraided me about the Rose I weare,
Saying, the sanguine colour of the Leaues
Did represent my Masters blushing cheekes:
When stubbornly he did repugne the truth,
About a certaine question in the Law,
Argu'd betwixt the Duke of Yorke, and him:
With other vile and ignominious tearmes.
In confutation of which rude reproach,
And in defence of my Lords worthinesse,
I craue the benefit of Law of Armes.

Ver. And that is my petition (Noble Lord:)
For though he seeme with forged queint conceite
To set a glosse vpon his bold intent,
Yet know (my Lord) I was prouok'd by him,
And he first tooke exceptions at this badge,
Pronouncing that the palenesse of this Flower,
Bewray'd the faintnesse of my Masters heart.

Yorke. Will not this malice Somerset be left?
Som. Your priuate grudge my Lord of York, wil out,
Though ne're so cunningly you smother it.

King. Good Lord, what madnesse rules in braine-sicke men,
When for so slight and friuolous a cause,
Such factious æmulations shall arise?
Good Cosins both of Yorke and Somerset,
Quiet your selues (I pray) and be at peace.

Yorke. Let this dissention first be tried by fight,
And then your Highnesse shall command a Peace.

Som. The quarrell toucheth none but vs alone,
Betwixt our selues let vs decide it then.

Yorke. There is my pledge, accept it Somerset.
Ver. Nay, let it rest where it began at first.

Bas.

Baß. Confirme it so, mine honourable Lord.
Glo. Confirme it so? Confounded be your strife,
And perish ye with your audacious prate,
Presumptuous vassals, are you not asham'd
With this immodest clamorous outrage,
To trouble and disturbe the King, and Vs?
And you my Lords, me thinkes you do not well
To beare with their peruerse Obiections:
Much lesse to take occasion from their mouthes,
To raise a mutiny betwixt your selues.
Let me perswade you take a better course.

Exet. It greeues his Highnesse,
Good my Lords, be Friends.

King. Come hither you that would be Combatants:
Henceforth I charge you, as you loue our fauour,
Quite to forget this Quarrell, and the cause.
And you my Lords: Remember where we are,
In France, amongst a fickle wauering Nation:
If they perceyue dissention in our lookes,
And that within our selues we disagree;
How will their grudging stomackes be prouok'd
To wilfull Disobedience, and Rebell?
Beside, What infamy will there arise,
When Forraigne Princes shall be certified,
That for a toy, a thing of no regard,
King *Henries* Peeres, and cheefe Nobility,
Destroy'd themselues, and lost the Realme of France?
Oh thinke vpon the Conquest of my Father,
My tender yeares, and let vs not forgoe
That for a trifle, that was bought with blood.
Let me be Vmper in this doubtfull strife:
I see no reason if I weare this Rose,
That any one should therefore be suspitious
I more incline to Somerset, than Yorke:
Both are my kinsmen, and I loue them both.
As well they may vpbray'd me with my Crowne,
Because (forsooth) the King of Scots is Crown'd.
But your discretions better can perswade,
Then I am able to instruct or teach:
And therefore, as we hither came in peace,
So let vs still continue peace, and loue.
Cosin of Yorke, we institute your Grace
To be our Regent in these parts of France:
And good my Lord of Somerset, vnite
Your Troopes of horsemen, with his Bands of foote,
And like true Subiects, sonnes of your Progenitors,
Go cheerefully together, and digest
Your angry Choller on your Enemies.
Our Selfe, my Lord Protector, and the rest,
After some respit, will returne to Calice;
From thence to England, where I hope ere long
To be presented by your Victories,
With *Charles, Alanson,* and that Traiterous rout.

Exeunt. Manet Yorke, Warwick, Exeter, Vernon.

War. My Lord of Yorke, I promise you the King
Prettily (me thought) did play the Orator.)

Yorke. And so he did, but yet I like it not,
In that he weares the badge of Somerset.

War. Tush, that was but his fancie, blame him not,
I dare presume (sweet Prince) he thought no harme.

York. And if I wish he did. But let it rest,
Other affayres must now be managed. *Exeunt.*

Flourish. Manet Exeter.

Exet. Well didst thou *Richard* to suppresse thy voice:
For had the passions of thy heart burst out,
I feare we should haue seene decipher'd there
More rancorous spight, more furious raging broyles,
Then yet can be imagin'd or suppos'd:
But howsoere, no simple man that sees
This iarring discord of Nobilitie,
This shouldering of each other in the Court,
This factious bandying of their Fauourites,
But that it doth presage some ill euent.
'Tis much, when Scepters are in Childrens hands:
But more, when Enuy breeds vnkinde deuision,
There comes the ruine, there begins confusion. *Exit.*

*Enter Talbot with Trumpe and Drumme,
before Burdeaux.*

Talb. Go to the Gates of Burdeaux Trumpeter,
Summon their Generall vnto the Wall. *Sounds.*

Enter Generall aloft.

English *Iohn Talbot* (Captaines) call you forth,
Seruant in Armes to *Harry* King of England,
And thus he would. Open your Citie Gates,
Be humble to vs, call my Soueraigne yours,
And do him homage as obedient Subiects,
And Ile withdraw me, and my bloody power.
But if you frowne vpon this proffer'd Peace,
You tempt the fury of my three attendants,
Leane Famine, quartering Steele, and climbing Fire,
Who in a moment, eeuen with the earth,
Shall lay your stately, and ayre-brauing Towers,
If you forsake the offer of their loue.

Cap. Thou ominous and fearefull Owle of death,
Our Nations terror, and their bloody scourge,
The period of thy Tyranny approacheth,
On vs thou canst not enter but by death:
For I protest we are well fortified,
And strong enough to issue out and fight.
If thou retire, the Dolphin well appointed,
Stands with the snares of Warre to tangle thee.
On either hand thee, there are squadrons pitcht,
To wall thee from the liberty of Flight;
And no way canst thou turne thee for redresse,
But death doth front thee with apparant spoyle,
And pale destruction meets thee in the face:
Ten thousand French haue tane the Sacrament,
To ryue their dangerous Artillerie
Vpon no Christian soule but English *Talbot*:
Loe, there thou standst a breathing valiant man
Of an inuincible vnconquer'd spirit:
This is the latest Glorie of thy praise,
That I thy enemy dew thee withall:
For ere the Glasse that now begins to runne,
Finish the processe of his sandy houre,
These eyes that see thee now well coloured,
Shall see thee withered, bloody, pale, and dead.

Drum a farre off.

Harke, harke, the Dolphins drumme, a warning bell,
Sings heauy Musicke to thy timorous soule,
And mine shall ring thy dire departure out. *Exit*

Tal. He Fables not, I heare the enemie:
Out some light Horsemen, and peruse their Wings.
O negligent and heedlesse Discipline,
How are we park'd and bounded in a pale?
A little Heard of Englands timorous Deere,
Maz'd with a yelping kennell of French Curres.
If we be English Deere, be then in blood,
Not Rascall-like to fall downe with a pinch,
But rather moodie mad: And desperate Stagges,

Turne

Turne on the bloody Hounds with heads of Steele,
And make the Cowards stand aloofe at bay:
Sell euery man his life as deere as mine,
And they shall finde deere Deere of vs my Friends.
God, and S. *George*, *Talbot* and Englands right,
Prosper our Colours in this dangerous fight.

Enter a Messenger that meets Yorke. Enter Yorke with Trumpet, and many Soldiers.

Yorke. Are not the speedy scouts return'd againe,
That dog'd the mighty Army of the Dolphin?
Mess. They are return'd my Lord, and giue it out,
That he is march'd to Burdeaux with his power
To fight with *Talbot* as he march'd along.
By your espyals were discouered
Two mightier Troopes then that the Dolphin led,
Which ioyn'd with him, and made their march for
(Burdeaux

Yorke. A plague vpon that Villaine Somerset,
That thus delayes my promised supply
Of horsemen, that were leuied for this siege.
Renowned *Talbot* doth expect my ayde,
And I am lowted by a Traitor Villaine,
And cannot helpe the noble Cheualier:
God comfort him in this necessity:
If he miscarry, farewell Warres in France.

Enter another Messenger.

2. *Mes.* Thou Princely Leader of our English strength,
Neuer so needfull on the earth of France,
Spurre to the rescue of the Noble *Talbot*,
Who now is girdled with a waste of Iron,
And hem'd about with grim destruction:
To Burdeaux warlike Duke, to Burdeaux Yorke,
Else farwell *Talbot*, France, and Englands honor.

Yorke. O God, that Somerset who in proud heart
Doth stop my Cornets, were in *Talbots* place,
So should wee saue a valiant Gentleman,
By forfeyting a Traitor, and a Coward:
Mad ire, and wrathfull fury makes me weepe,
That thus we dye, while remisse Traitors sleepe.

Mes. O send some succour to the distrest Lord.

Yorke. He dies, we loose: I breake my warlike word:
We mourne, France smiles: We loose, they dayly get,
All long of this vile Traitor Somerset.

Mes. Then God take mercy on braue *Talbots* soule,
And on his Sonne yong *Iohn*, who two houres since,
I met in trauaile toward his warlike Father;
This seuen yeeres did not *Talbot* see his sonne,
And now they meete where both their liues are done.

Yorke. Alas, what ioy shall noble *Talbot* haue,
To bid his yong sonne welcome to his Graue:
Away, vexation almost stoppes my breath,
That sundred friends greete in the houre of death.
Lucie farewell, no more my fortune can,
But curse the cause I cannot ayde the man.
Maine, Bloys, Poytiers, and *Toures,* are wonne away,
Long all of Somerset, and his delay. *Exit*

Mes. Thus while the Vulture of sedition,
Feedes in the bosome of such great Commanders,
Sleeping neglection doth betray to losse:
The Conquest of our scarse-cold Conqueror,
That euer-liuing man of Memorie,
Henrie the fift: Whiles they each other crosse,
Liues, Honours, Lands, and all, hurrie to losse.

Enter Somerset with his Armie.

Som. It is too late, I cannot send them now:
This expedition was by Yorke and Talbot,
Too rashly plotted. All our generall force,
Might with a sally of the very Towne
Be buckled with: the ouer-daring *Talbot*
Hath sullied all his glosse of former Honor
By this vnheedfull, desperate, wilde aduenture:
Yorke set him on to fight, and dye in shame,
That *Talbot* dead, great *Yorke* might beare the name.

Cap. Heere is Sir *William Lucie*, who with me
Set from our ore-matcht forces forth for ayde.

Som. How now Sir *William*, whether were you sent?

Lu. Whether my Lord, from bought & sold L. *Talbot*,
Who ring'd about with bold aduersitie,
Cries out for noble Yorke and Somerset,
To beate assayling death from his weake Regions,
And whiles the honourable Captaine there
Drops bloody swet from his warre-wearied limbes,
And in aduantage lingring lookes for rescue,
You his false hopes, the trust of Englands honor,
Keepe off aloofe with worthlesse emulation:
Let not your priuate discord keepe away
The leuied succours that should lend him ayde,
While he renowned Noble Gentleman
Yeeld vp his life vnto a world of oddes.
Orleance the Bastard, *Charles, Burgundie,
Alanson, Reignard,* compasse him about,
And *Talbot* perisheth by your default.

Som. Yorke set him on, Yorke should haue sent him
ayde.

Luc. And Yorke as fast vpon your Grace exclaimes,
Swearing that you with-hold his leuied hoast,
Collected for this expidition.

Som. York lyes: He might haue sent, & had the Horse:
I owe him little Dutie, and lesse Loue,
And take foule scorne to fawne on him by sending.

Lu. The fraud of England, not the force of France,
Hath now intrapt the Noble-minded *Talbot*:
Neuer to England shall he beare his life,
But dies betraid to fortune by your strife.

Som. Come go, I will dispatch the Horsemen strait:
Within sixe houres, they will be at his ayde.

Lu. Too late comes rescue, he is tane or slaine,
For flye he could not, if he would haue fled:
And flye would *Talbot* neuer though he might.

Som. If he be dead, braue *Talbot* then adieu.

Lu. His Fame liues in the world. His Shame in you.
Exeunt.

Enter Talbot and his Sonne.

Tal. O yong *Iohn Talbot*, I did send for thee
To tutor thee in stratagems of Warre,
That *Talbots* name might be in thee reuiu'd,
When saplesse Age, and weake vnable limbes
Should bring thy Father to his drooping Chaire.
But O malignant and ill-boading Starres,
Now thou art come vnto a Feast of death,
A terrible and vnauoyded danger:
Therefore deere Boy, mount on my swiftest horse,
And Ile direct thee how thou shalt escape
By sodaine flight. Come, dally not, be gone.

Iohn. Is my name *Talbot*? and am I your Sonne?
Shall

And shall I flye? O, if you loue my Mother,
Dishonor not her Honorable Name,
To make a Bastard, and a Slaue of me:
The World will say, he is not Talbots blood,
That basely fled, when Noble Talbot stood.

Talb. Flye, to reuenge my death, if I be slaine.
Iohn. He that flyes so, will ne're returne againe.
Talb. If we both stay, we both are sure to dye.
Iohn. Then let me stay, and Father doe you flye:
Your losse is great, so your regard should be;
My worth vnknowne, no losse is knowne in me.
Vpon my death, the French can little boast;
In yours they will, in you all hopes are lost.
Flight cannot stayne the Honor you haue wonne,
But mine it will, that no Exploit haue done.
You fled for Vantage, euery one will sweare:
But if I bow, they'le say it was for feare.
There is no hope that euer I will stay,
If the first howre I shrinke and run away:
Here on my knee I begge Mortalitie,
Rather then Life, preseru'd with Infamie.

Talb. Shall all thy Mothers hopes lye in one Tombe?
Iohn. I, rather then Ile shame my Mothers Wombe.
Talb. Vpon my Blessing I command thee goe.
Iohn. To fight I will, but not to flye the Foe.
Talb. Part of thy Father may be sau'd in thee.
Iohn. No part of him, but will be shame in mee.
Talb. Thou neuer hadst Renowne, nor canst not lose it.
Iohn. Yes, your renowned Name: shall flight abuse it?
Talb. Thy Fathers charge shal cleare thee from ỹ staine.
Iohn. You cannot witnesse for me, being slaine.
If Death be so apparant, then both flye.
Talb. And leaue my followers here to fight and dye?
My Age was neuer tainted with such shame.
Iohn. And shall my Youth be guiltie of such blame?
No more can I be seuered from your side,
Then can your selfe, your selfe in twaine diuide:
Stay, goe, doe what you will, the like doe I;
For liue I will not, if my Father dye.
Talb. Then here I take my leaue of thee, faire Sonne,
Borne to eclipse thy Life this afternoone:
Come, side by side, together liue and dye,
And Soule with Soule from France to Heauen flye. *Exit.*

*Alarum: Excursions, wherein Talbots Sonne
is hemm'd about, and Talbot
rescues him.*

Talb. Saint *George*, and Victory; fight Souldiers, fight:
The Regent hath with *Talbot* broke his word,
And left vs to the rage of France his Sword.
Where is *Iohn Talbot*? pawse, and take thy breath,
I gaue thee Life, and rescu'd thee from Death.
Iohn. O twice my Father, twice am I thy Sonne:
The Life thou gau'st me first, was lost and done,
Till with thy Warlike Sword, despight of Fate,
To my determin'd time thou gau'st new date.
Talb. When frō the *Dolphins* Crest thy Sword struck fire,
It warm'd thy Fathers heart with prowd desire
Of bold-fac't Victorie. Then Leaden Age,
Quicken'd with Youthfull Spleene, and Warlike Rage,
Beat downe *Alanson*, *Orleance*, *Burgundie*,
And from the Pride of *Gallia* rescued thee.
The irefull Bastard *Orleance*, that drew blood
From thee my Boy, and had the Maidenhood
Of thy first fight, I soone encountred,
And interchanging blowes, I quickly shed
Some of his Bastard blood, and in disgrace
Bespoke him thus: Contaminated, base,
And mis-begotten blood, I spill of thine,
Meane and right poore, for that pure blood of mine,
Which thou didst force from *Talbot*, my braue Boy.
Here purposing the Bastard to destroy,
Came in strong rescue. Speake thy Fathers care:
Art thou not wearie, *Iohn*? How do'st thou fare?
Wilt thou yet leaue the Battaile, Boy, and flie,
Now thou art seal'd the Sonne of Chiualrie?
Flye, to reuenge my death when I am dead,
The helpe of one stands me in little stead.
Oh, too much folly is it, well I wot,
To hazard all our liues in one small Boat.
If I to day dye not with Frenchmens Rage,
To morrow I shall dye with mickle Age.
By me they nothing gaine, and if I stay,
'Tis but the shortning of my Life one day.
In thee thy Mother dyes, our Households Name,
My Deaths Reuenge, thy Youth, and Englands Fame:
All these, and more, we hazard by thy stay;
All these are sau'd, if thou wilt flye away.

Iohn. The Sword of *Orleance* hath not made me smart,
These words of yours draw Life-blood from my Heart.
On that aduantage, bought with such a shame,
To saue a paltry Life, and slay bright Fame,
Before young *Talbot* from old *Talbot* flye,
The Coward Horse that beares me, fall and dye:
And like me to the pesant Boyes of France,
To be Shames scorne, and subiect of Mischance.
Surely, by all the Glorie you haue wonne,
And if I flye, I am not *Talbots* Sonne.
Then talke no more of flight, it is no boot,
If Sonne to *Talbot*, dye at *Talbots* foot.
Talb. Then follow thou thy desp'rate Syre of *Creet*,
Thou *Icarus*, thy Life to me is sweet:
If thou wilt fight, fight by thy Fathers side,
And commendable prou'd, let's dye in pride. *Exit.*

*Alarum. Excursions. Enter old
Talbot led.*

Talb. Where is my other Life? mine owne is gone.
O, where's young *Talbot*? where is valiant *Iohn*?
Triumphant Death, smear'd with Captiuitie,
Young *Talbots* Valour makes me smile at thee.
When he perceiu'd me shrinke, and on my Knee,
His bloodie Sword he brandisht ouer mee,
And like a hungry Lyon did commence
Rough deeds of Rage, and sterne Impatience:
But when my angry Guardant stood alone,
Tendring my ruine, and assayl'd of none,
Dizzie-ey'd Furie, and great rage of Heart,
Suddenly made him from my side to start
Into the clustring Battaile of the French:
And in that Sea of Blood, my Boy did drench
His ouer-mounting Spirit; and there di'de
My *Icarus*, my Blossome, in his pride.

Enter with Iohn Talbot, borne.

Seru. O my deare Lord, loe where your Sonne is borne.
Tal. Thou antique Death, which laugh'st vs here to scorn,
Anon from thy insulting Tyrannie,
Coupled in bonds of perpetuitie,
Two *Talbots* winged through the lither Skie,
In thy despight shall scape Mortalitie.

O thou whose wounds become hard fauoured death,
Speake to thy father, ere thou yeeld thy breath,
Braue death by speaking, whither he will or no:
Imagine him a Frenchman, and thy Foe.
Poore Boy, he smiles, me thinkes, as who should say,
Had Death bene French, then Death had dyed to day.
Come, come, and lay him in his Fathers armes,
My spirit can no longer beare these harmes.
Souldiers adieu: I haue what I would haue,
Now my old armes are yong *Iohn Talbots* graue. *Dyes*

*Enter Charles, Alanson, Burgundie, Bastard,
and Pucell.*

Char. Had Yorke and Somerset brought rescue in,
We should haue found a bloody day of this.
Bast. How the yong whelpe of *Talbots* raging wood,
Did flesh his punie-sword in Frenchmens blood.
Puc. Once I encountred him, and thus I said:
Thou Maiden youth, be vanquisht by a Maide.
But with a proud Maiesticall high scorne
He answer'd thus: Yong *Talbot* was not borne
To be the pillage of a Giglot Wench:
So rushing in the bowels of the French,
He left me proudly, as vnworthy fight.
Bur. Doubtlesse he would haue made a noble Knight:
See where he lyes inherced in the armes
Of the most bloody Nursser of his harmes.
Bast. Hew them to peeces, hack their bones assunder,
Whose life was Englands glory, Gallia's wonder.
Char. Oh no forbeare: For that which we haue fled
During the life, let vs not wrong it dead.

Enter Lucie.

Lu. Herald, conduct me to the Dolphins Tent,
To know who hath obtain'd the glory of the day.
Char. On what submissiue message art thou sent?
Lucy. Submission Dolphin? Tis a meere French word:
We English Warriours wot not what it meanes.
I come to know what Prisoners thou hast tane,
And to suruey the bodies of the dead.
Char. For prisoners askst thou? Hell our prison is.
But tell me whom thou seek'st?
Luc. But where's the great Alcides of the field,
Valiant Lord *Talbot* Earle of Shrewsbury?
Created for his rare successe in Armes,
Great Earle of *Washford, Waterford*, and *Valence*,
Lord *Talbot* of *Goodrig* and *Vrchinfield*,
Lord *Strange* of *Blackmere*, Lord *Verdon* of *Alton*,
Lord *Cromwell* of *Wingefield*, Lord *Furniuall* of *Sheffeild*,
The thrice victorious Lord of *Falconbridge*,
Knight of the Noble Order of *S. George*,
Worthy *S. Michael*, and the *Golden Fleece*,
Great Marshall to *Henry* the sixt,
Of all his Warres within the Realme of France.
Puc. Heere's a silly stately stile indeede:
The Turke that two and fiftie Kingdomes hath,
Writes not so tedious a Stile as this.
Him that thou magnifi'st with all these Titles,
Stinking and fly-blowne lyes heere at our feete.
Lucy. Is *Talbot* slaine, the Frenchmens only Scourge,
Your Kingdomes terror, and blacke *Nemesis*?
Oh were mine eye-balles into Bullets turn'd,
That I in rage might shoot them at your faces.
Oh, that I could but call these dead to life,
It were enough to fright the Realme of France.
Were but his Picture left amongst you here,

It would amaze the prowdest of you all.
Giue me their Bodyes, that I may beare them hence,
And giue them Buriall, as beseemes their worth.
Pucel. I thinke this vpstart is old *Talbots* Ghost,
He speakes with such a proud commanding spirit:
For Gods sake let him haue him, to keepe them here,
They would but stinke, and putrifie the ayre.
Char. Go take their bodies hence.
Lucy. Ile beare them hence: but from their ashes shal
    be reard
A Phœnix that shall make all France affear'd.
Char. So we be rid of them, do with him what y wilt.
And now to Paris in this conquering vaine,
All will be ours, now bloody *Talbots* slaine. *Exit.*

Scena secunda.

SENNET.

Enter King, Glocester, and Exeter.

King. Haue you perus'd the Letters from the Pope,
The Emperor, and the Earle of Arminack?
Glo. I haue my Lord, and their intent is this,
They humbly sue vnto your Excellence,
To haue a godly peace concluded of,
Betweene the Realmes of England, and of France.
King. How doth your Grace affect their motion?
Glo. Well (my good Lord) and as the only meanes
To stop effusion of our Christian blood,
And stablish quietnesse on euery side.
King. I marry Vnckle, for I alwayes thought
It was both impious and vnnaturall,
That such immanity and bloody strife
Should reigne among Professors of one Faith.
Glo. Beside my Lord, the sooner to effect,
And surer binde this knot of amitie,
The Earle of Arminacke neere knit to *Charles*,
A man of great Authoritie in France,
Proffers his onely daughter to your Grace,
In marriage, with a large and sumptuous Dowrie.
King. Marriage Vnckle? Alas my yeares are yong:
And fitter is my studie, and my Bookes,
Than wanton dalliance with a Paramour.
Yet call th'Embassadors, and as you please,
So let them haue their answeres euery one:
I shall be well content with any choyce
Tends to Gods glory, and my Countries weale.

Enter Winchester, and three Ambassadors.

Exet. What, is my Lord of *Winchester* install'd,
And call'd vnto a Cardinalls degree?
Then I perceiue, that will be verified
Henry the Fift did sometime prophesie.
If once he come to be a Cardinall,
Hee'l make his cap coequall with the Crowne.
King. My Lords Ambassadors, your seuerall suites
Haue bin consider'd and debated on,
Your purpose is both good and reasonable:
And therefore are we certainly resolu'd,
To draw conditions of a friendly peace,

Which

Which by my Lord of Winchester we meane
Shall be transported presently to France.

  Glo. And for the proffer of my Lord your Master,
I haue inform'd his Highnesse so at large,
As liking of the Ladies vertuous gifts,
Her Beauty, and the valew of her Dower,
He doth intend she shall be Englands Queene.

  King. In argument and proofe of which contract,
Beare her this Iewell, pledge of my affection.
And so my Lord Protector see them guarded,
And safely brought to *Douer*, wherein ship'd
Commit them to the fortune of the sea.   *Exeunt.*

  Win. Stay my Lord Legate, you shall first receiue
The summe of money which I promised
Should be deliuered to his Holinesse,
For cloathing me in these graue Ornaments.

  Legat. I will attend vpon your Lordships leysure.

  Win. Now Winchester will not submit, I trow,
Or be inferiour to the proudest Peere;
Humfrey of Gloster, thou shalt well perceiue,
That neither in birth, or for authoritie,
The Bishop will be ouer-borne by thee:
Ile either make thee stoope, and bend thy knee,
Or sacke this Country with a mutiny.   *Exeunt*

Scœna Tertia.

*Enter Charles, Burgundy, Alanson, Bastard,
Reignier, and Ione.*

  Char. These newes (my Lords) may cheere our droo-
      ping spirits:
'Tis said, the stout Parisians do reuolt,
And turne againe vnto the warlike French.

  Alan. Then march to Paris Royall *Charles* of France,
And keepe not backe your powers in dalliance.

  Pucel. Peace be amongst them if they turne to vs,
Else ruine combate with their Pallaces.

Enter Scout.

  Scout. Successe vnto our valiant Generall,
And happinesse to his accomplices.

  Char. What tidings send our Scouts? I prethee speak.

  Scout. The English Army that diuided was
Into two parties, is now conioyn'd in one,
And meanes to giue you battell presently.

  Char. Somewhat too sodaine Sirs, the warning is,
But we will presently prouide for them.

  Bur. I trust the Ghost of *Talbot* is not there:
Now he is gone my Lord, you neede not feare.

  Pucel. Of all base passions, Feare is most accurst.
Command the Conquest *Charles*, it shall be thine:
Let *Henry* fret, and all the world repine.

  Char. Then on my Lords, and France be fortunate.
    Exeunt.   Alarum.   Excursions.

Enter Ione de Pucell.

  Puc. The Regent conquers, and the Frenchmen flye.
Now helpe ye charming Spelles and Periapts,
And ye choise spirits that admonish me,
And giue mesignes of future accidents.   *Thunder.*
You speedy helpers, that are substitutes
Vnder the Lordly Monarch of the North,
Appeare, and ayde me in this enterprize.

Enter Fiends.

This speedy and quicke appearance argues proofe
Of your accustom'd diligence to me.
Now ye Familiar Spirits, that are cull'd
Out of the powerfull Regions vnder earth,
Helpe me this once, that France may get the field.
    They walke, and speake not.
Oh hold me not with silence ouer-long:
Where I was wont to feed you with my blood,
Ile lop a member off, and giue it you,
In earnest of a further benefit:
So you do condiscend to helpe me now.
    They hang their heads.
No hope to haue redresse? My body shall
Pay recompence, if you will graunt my suite.
    They shake their heads.
Cannot my body, nor blood-sacrifice,
Intreate you to your wonted furtherance?
Then take my soule; my body, soule, and all,
Before that England giue the French the foyle.
    They depart.
See, they forsake me. Now the time is come,
That France must vale her lofty plumed Crest,
And let her head fall into Englands lappe.
My ancient Incantations are too weake,
And hell too strong for me to buckle with:
Now France, thy glory droopeth to the dust.   *Exit.*

*Excursions. Burgundie and Yorke fight hand to
hand. French flye.*

  Yorke. Damsell of France, I thinke I haue you fast,
Vnchaine your spirits now with spelling Charmes,
And try if they can gaine your liberty.
A goodly prize, fit for the diuels grace.
See how the vgly Witch doth bend her browes,
As if with *Circe*, she would change my shape.

  Puc. Chang'd to a worser shape thou canst not be:

  Yor. Oh, *Charles* the Dolphin is a proper man,
No shape but his can please your dainty eye.

  Puc. A plaguing mischeefe light on *Charles*, and thee,
And may ye both be sodainly surpriz'd
By bloudy hands, in sleeping on your beds.

  Yorke. Fell banning Hagge, Inchantresse hold thy
      tongue.

  Puc. I prethee giue me leaue to curse awhile.

  Yorke. Curse Miscreant, when thou comst to the stake
    Exeunt.

*Alarum. Enter Suffolke with Margaret
in his hand.*

  Suff. Be what thou wilt, thou art my prisoner.
    Gazes on her.
Oh Fairest Beautie, do not feare, nor flye:
For I will touch thee but with reuerend hands,
I kisse these fingers for eternall peace,
And lay them gently on thy tender side.
Who art thou, say? that I may honor thee.

  Mar. *Margaret* my name, and daughter to a King,
The King of Naples, who so ere thou art.

  Suff. An Earle I am, and Suffolke am I call'd.
Be not offended Natures myracle,
Thou art alotted to be tane by me:
So doth the Swan her downie Signets saue,
    Oh stay:

Keeping them prisoner vnderneath his wings:
Yet if this seruile vsage once offend,
Go, and be free againe, as Suffolkes friend.   *She is going*
Oh stay: I haue no power to let her passe,
My hand would free her, but my heart sayes no.
As playes the Sunne vpon the glassie streames,
Twinkling another counterfetted beame,
So seemes this gorgeous beauty to mine eyes.
Faine would I woe her, yet I dare not speake:
Ile call for Pen and Inke, and write my minde:
Fye *De la Pole*, disable not thy selfe:
Hast not a Tongue? Is she not heere?
Wilt thou be daunted at a Womans sight?
I: Beauties Princely Maiesty is such,
'Confounds the tongue, and makes the senses rough.

  Mar. Say Earle of Suffolke, if thy name be so,
What ransome must I pay before I passe?
For I perceiue I am thy prisoner.

  Suf. How canst thou tell she will deny thy suite,
Before thou make a triall of her loue?

  M. Why speak'st thou not? What ransom must I pay?

  Suf. She's beautifull; and therefore to be Wooed:
She is a Woman; therefore to be Wonne.

  Mar. Wilt thou accept of ransome, yea or no?

  Suf. Fond man, remember that thou hast a wife,
Then how can *Margaret* be thy Paramour?

  Mar. I were best to leaue him, for he will not heare.

  Suf. There all is marr'd: there lies a cooling card.

  Mar. He talkes at randon: sure the man is mad.

  Suf. And yet a dispensation may bee had.

  Mar. And yet I would that you would answer me.

  Suf. Ile win this Lady *Margaret*. For whom?
Why for my King: Tush, that's a woodden thing.

  Mar. He talkes of wood: It is some Carpenter.

  Suf. Yet so my fancy may be satisfied,
And peace established betweene these Realmes.
But there remaines a scruple in that too:
For though her Father be the King of *Naples*,
Duke of *Anion* and *Mayne*, yet is he poore,
And our Nobility will scorne the match.

  Mar. Heare ye Captaine? Are you not at leysure?

  Suf. It shall be so, disdaine they ne're so much:
Henry is youthfull, and will quickly yeeld.
Madam, I haue a secret to reueale.

  Mar. What though I be inthral'd, he seems a knight
And will not any way dishonor me.

  Suf. Lady, vouchsafe to listen what I say.

  Mar. Perhaps I shall be rescu'd by the French,
And then I need not craue his curtesie.

  Suf. Sweet Madam, giue me hearing in a cause.

  Mar. Tush, women haue bene captiuate ere now.

  Suf. Lady, wherefore talke you so?

  Mar. I cry you mercy, 'tis but *Quid* for *Quo*.

  Suf. Say gentle Princesse, would you not suppose
Your bondage happy, to be made a Queene?

  Mar. To be a Queene in bondage, is more vile,
Than is a slaue, in base seruility:
For Princes should be free.

  Suf. And so shall you,
If happy Englands Royall King be free.

  Mar. Why what concernes his freedome vnto mee?

  Suf. Ile vndertake to make thee *Henries* Queene,
To put a Golden Scepter in thy hand,
And set a precious Crowne vpon thy head,
If thou wilt condiscend to be my——

  Mar. What?

  Suf. His loue.

  Mar. I am vnworthy to be *Henries* wife.

  Suf. No gentle Madam, I vnworthy am
To woe so faire a Dame to be his wife,
And haue no portion in the choice my selfe.
How say you Madam, are ye so content?

  Mar. And if my Father please, I am content.

  Suf. Then call our Captaines and our Colours forth,
And Madam, at your Fathers Castle walles,
Wee'l craue a parley, to conferre with him.

Sound. Enter Reignier on the Walles.

See *Reignier* see, thy daughter prisoner.

  Reig. To whom?

  Suf. To me.

  Reig. Suffolke, what remedy?
I am a Souldier, and vnapt to weepe,
Or to exclaime on Fortunes ficklenesse.

  Suf. Yes, there is remedy enough my Lord,
Consent, and for thy Honor giue consent,
Thy daughter shall be wedded to my King,
Whom I with paine haue wooed and wonne thereto:
And this her easie held imprisonment,
Hath gain'd thy daughter Princely libertie.

  Reig. Speakes Suffolke as he thinkes?

  Suf. Faire *Margaret* knowes,
That Suffolke doth not flatter, face, or faine.

  Reig. Vpon thy Princely warrant, I descend,
To giue thee answer of thy iust demand.

  Suf. And heere I will expect thy comming.

Trumpets sound. Enter Reignier.

  Reig. Welcome braue Earle into our Territories,
Command in *Anion* what your Honor pleases.

  Suf. Thankes *Reignier*, happy for so sweet a Childe,
Fit to be made companion with a King:
What answer makes your Grace vnto my suite?

  Reig. Since thou dost daigne to woe her little worth,
To be the Princely Bride of such a Lord:
Vpon condition I may quietly
Enioy mine owne, the Country *Maine* and *Anion*,
Free from oppression, or the stroke of Warre,
My daughter shall be *Henries*, if he please.

  Suf. That is her ransome, I deliuer her,
And those two Counties I will vndertake
Your Grace shall well and quietly enioy.

  Reig. And I againe in *Henries* Royall name,
As Deputy vnto that gracious King,
Giue thee her hand for signe of plighted faith.

  Suf. *Reignier* of France, I giue thee Kingly thankes,
Because this is in Trafficke of a King.
And yet me thinkes I could be well content
To be mine owne Atturney in this case.
Ile ouer then to England with this newes,
And make this marriage to be solemniz'd:
So farewell *Reignier*, set this Diamond safe
In Golden Pallaces as it becomes.

  Reig. I do embrace thee, as I would embrace
The Christian Prince King *Henrie* were he heere.

  Mar. Farewell my Lord, good wishes, praise, & praiers,
Shall Suffolke euer haue of *Margaret*.   *Shee is going.*

  Suf. Farwell sweet Madam: but hearke you *Margaret*,
No Princely commendations to my King?

  Mar. Such commendations as becomes a Maide,
A Virgin, and his Seruant, say to him.

  Suf. Words sweetly plac'd, and modestie directed,

But

The first Part of Henry the Sixt.

But Madame, I must trouble you againe,
No louing Token to his Maiestie?

Mar. Yes, my good Lord, a pure vnspotted heart,
Neuer yet taint with loue, I send the King.

Suf. And this withall. *Kisse her.*

Mar. That for thy selfe, I will not so presume,
To send such peeuish tokens to a King.

Suf. Oh wert thou for my selfe: but *Suffolke* stay,
Thou mayest not wander in that Labyrinth,
There Minotaurs and vgly Treasons lurke,
Solicite *Henry* with her wonderous praise.
Bethinke thee on her Vertues that surmount,
Mad naturall Graces that extinguish Art,
Repeate their semblance often on the Seas,
That when thou com'st to kneele at *Henries* feete,
Thou mayest bereaue him of his wits with wonder. *Exit*

Enter Yorke, Warwicke, Shepheard, Pucell.

Yor. Bring forth that Sorceresse condemn'd to burne.

Shep. Ah *Ione*, this kils thy Fathers heart out-right,
Haue I sought euery Country farre and neere,
And now it is my chance to finde thee out,
Must I behold thy timelesse cruell death:
Ah *Ione*, sweet daughter *Ione*, Ile die with thee.

Pucel. Decrepit Miser, base ignoble Wretch,
I am descended of a gentler blood.
Thou art no Father, nor no Friend of mine.

Shep. Out, out: My Lords, and please you, 'tis not so
I did beget her, all the Parish knowes:
Her Mother liueth yet, can testifie
She was the first fruite of my Bach'ler-ship.

War. Gracelesse, wilt thou deny thy Parentage?

Yorke. This argues what her kinde of life hath beene,
Wicked and vile, and so her death concludes.

Shep. Fye *Ione*, that thou wilt be so obstacle:
God knowes, thou art a collop of my flesh,
And for thy sake haue I shed many a teare:
Deny me not, I prythee, gentle *Ione*.

Pucell. Pezant auant. You haue suborn'd this man
Of purpose, to obscure my Noble birth.

Shep. 'Tis true, I gaue a Noble to the Priest,
The morne that I was wedded to her mother.
Kneele downe and take my blessing, good my Gyrle.
Wilt thou not stoope? Now cursed be the time
Of thy natiuitie: I would the Milke
Thy mother gaue thee when thou suck'st her brest,
Had bin a little Rats-bane for thy sake.
Or else, when thou didst keepe my Lambes a-field,
I wish some rauenous Wolfe had eaten thee.
Doest thou deny thy Father, cursed Drab?
O burne her, burne her, hanging is too good. *Exit.*

Yorke. Take her away, for she hath liu'd too long,
To fill the world with vicious qualities.

Puc. First let me tell you whom you haue condemn'd;
Not me, begotten of a Shepheard Swaine,
But issued from the Progeny of Kings,
Vertuous and Holy, chosen from aboue,
By inspiration of Celestiall Grace,
To worke exceeding myracles on earth.
I neuer had to do with wicked Spirits.
But you that are polluted with your lustes,
Stain'd with the guiltlesse blood of Innocents,
Corrupt and tainted with a thousand Vices:
Because you want the grace that others haue,
You iudge it straight a thing impossible
To compasse Wonders, but by helpe of diuels.

No misconceyued, *Ione* of *Aire* hath beene
A Virgin from her tender infancie,
Chaste, and immaculate in very thought,
Whose Maiden-blood thus rigorously effus'd,
Will cry for Vengeance, at the Gates of Heauen.

Yorke. I, I: away with her to execution.

War. And hearke ye sirs: because she is a Maide,
Spare for no Faggots, let there be enow:
Place barrelles of pitch vpon the fatall stake,
That so her torture may be shortned.

Puc. Will nothing turne your vnrelenting hearts?
Then *Ione* discouer thine infirmity,
That warranteth by Law, to be thy priuiledge.
I am with childe ye bloody Homicides:
Murther not then the Fruite within my Wombe,
Although ye hale me to a violent death.

Yor. Now heauen forfend, the holy Maid with child?

War. The greatest miracle that ere ye wrought.
Is all your strict precisenesse come to this?

Yorke. She and the Dolphin haue bin iugling,
I did imagine what would be her refuge.

War. Well go too, we'll haue no Bastards liue,
Especially since *Charles* must Father it.

Puc. You are deceyu'd, my childe is none of his,
It was *Alanson* that inioy'd my loue.

Yorke. Alanson that notorious Macheuile?
It dyes, and if it had a thousand liues.

Puc. Oh giue me leaue, I haue deluded you,
'Twas neyther *Charles*, nor yet the Duke I nam'd,
But *Reignier* King of *Naples* that preuayl'd.

War. A married man, that's most intollerable.

Yor. Why here's a Gyrle: I think she knowes not wel
(There were so many) whom she may accuse.

War. It's signe she hath beene liberall and free.

Yor. And yet forsooth she is a Virgin pure.
Strumpet, thy words condemne thy Brat, and thee.
Vse no intreaty, for it is in vaine.

Pu. Then lead me hence: with whom I leaue my curse.
May neuer glorious Sunne reflex his beames
Vpon the Countrey where you make abode:
But darknesse, and the gloomy shade of death
Inuiron you, till Mischeefe and Dispaire,
Driue you to break your necks, or hang your selues. *Exit*

Enter Cardinall.

Yorke. Breake thou in peeces, and consume to ashes,
Thou fowle accursed minister of Hell.

Car. Lord Regent, I do greete your Excellence
With Letters of Commission from the King.
For know my Lords, the States of Christendome,
Mou'd with remorse of these out-ragious broyles,
Haue earnestly implor'd a generall peace,
Betwixt our Nation, and the aspyring French;
And heere at hand, the Dolphin and his Traine
Approacheth, to conferre about some matter.

Yorke. Is all our trauell turn'd to this effect,
After the slaughter of so many Peeres,
So many Captaines, Gentlemen, and Soldiers,
That in this quarrell haue beene ouerthrowne,
And sold their bodyes for their Countryes benefit,
Shall we at last conclude effeminate peace?
Haue we not lost most part of all the Townes,
By Treason, Falshood, and by Treacherie,
Our great Progenitors had conquered:
Oh *Warwicke, Warwicke*, I foresee with greefe
The vtter losse of all the Realme of France.

War. Be patient Yorke, if we conclude a Peace

m It

It shall be with such strict and severe Couenants,
As little shall the Frenchmen gaine thereby.

Enter Charles, Alanson, Bastard, Reignier.

Char. Since Lords of England, it is thus agreed,
That peacefull truce shall be proclaim'd in France,
We come to be informed by your selues,
What the conditions of that league must be.

Yorke. Speake Winchester, for boyling choller chokes
The hollow passage of my poyson'd voyce,
By sight of these our balefull enemies.

Win. Charles, and the rest, it is enacted thus:
That in regard King *Henry* giues consent,
Of meere compassion, and of lenity,
To ease your Countrie of distressefull Warre,
And suffer you to breath in fruitfull peace,
You shall become true Liegemen to his Crowne.
And *Charles*, vpon condition thou wilt sweare
To pay him tribute, and submit thy selfe,
Thou shalt be plac'd as Viceroy vnder him,
And still enioy thy Regall dignity.

Alan. Must he be then as shadow of himselfe?
Adorne his Temples with a Coronet,
And yet in substance and authority,
Retaine but priuiledge of a priuate man?
This proffer is absurd, and reasonlesse.

Char. 'Tis knowne already that I am possest
With more then halfe the Gallian Territories,
And therein reuerenc'd for their lawfull King.
Shall I for lucre of the rest vn-vanquisht,
Detract so much from that prerogatiue,
As to be call'd but Viceroy of the whole?
No Lord Ambassador, Ile rather keepe
That which I haue, than coueting for more
Be cast from possibility of all.

Yorke. Insulting *Charles*, hast thou by secret meanes
Vs'd intercession to obtaine a league,
And now the matter growes to compremize,
Stand'st thou aloofe vpon Comparison.
Either accept the Title thou vsurp'st,
Of benefit proceeding from our King,
And not of any challenge of Desert,
Or we will plague thee with incessant Warres.

Reig. My Lord, you do not well in obstinacy,
To cauill in the course of this Contract:
If once it be neglected, ten to one
We shall not finde like opportunity.

Alan. To say the truth, it is your policie,
To saue your Subiects from such massacre
And ruthlesse slaughters as are dayly seene
By our proceeding in Hostility,
And therefore take this compact of a Truce,
Although you breake it, when your pleasure serues.

War. How sayst thou *Charles*?
Shall our Condition stand?

Char. It Shall:
Onely reseru'd, you claime no interest
In any of our Townes of Garrison.

Yor. Then sweare Allegeance to his Maiesty,
As thou art Knight, neuer to disobey,
Nor be Rebellious to the Crowne of England,
Thou nor thy Nobles, to the Crowne of England.
So, now dismisse your Army when ye please:
Hang vp your Ensignes, let your Drummes be still,
For heere we entertaine a solemne peace. *Exeunt*

Actus Quintus.

*Enter Suffolke in conference with the King,
Glocester, and Exeter.*

King. Your wondrous rare description (noble Earle)
Of beauteous *Margaret* hath astonish'd me:
Her vertues graced with externall gifts,
Do breed Loues setled passions in my heart,
And like as rigour of tempestuous gustes
Prouokes the mightiest Hulke against the tide,
So am I driuen by breath of her Renowne,
Either to suffer Shipwracke, or arriue
Where I may haue fruition of her Loue.

Suf. Tush my good Lord, this superficiall tale,
Is but a preface of her worthy praise:
The cheefe perfections of that louely Dame,
(Had I sufficient skill to vtter them)
Would make a volume of inticing lines,
Able to rauish any dull conceit.
And which is more, she is not so Diuine,
So full replete with choice of all delights,
But with as humble lowlinesse of minde,
She is content to be at your command:
Command I meane, of Vertuous chaste intents,
To Loue, and Honor *Henry* as her Lord.

King. And otherwise, will *Henry* ne're presume:
Therefore my Lord Protector, giue consent,
That *Marg'ret* may be Englands Royall Queene.

Glo. So should I giue consent to flatter sinne,
You know (my Lord) your Highnesse is betroath'd
Vnto another Lady of esteeme,
How shall we then dispense with that contract,
And not deface your Honor with reproach?

Suf. As doth a Ruler with vnlawfull Oathes,
Or one that at a Triumph, hauing vow'd
To try his strength, forsaketh yet the Listes
By reason of his Aduersaries oddes.
A poore Earles daughter is vnequall oddes,
And therefore may be broke without offence.

Gloucester. Why what (I pray) is *Margaret* more
then that?
Her Father is no better than an Earle,
Although in glorious Titles he excell.

Suf. Yes my Lord, her Father is a King,
The King of Naples, and Ierusalem,
And of such great Authoritie in France,
As his alliance will confirme our peace,
And keepe the Frenchmen in Allegeance.

Glo. And so the Earle of Arminacke may doe,
Because he is neere Kinsman vnto *Charles*.

Exet. Beside, his wealth doth warrant a liberal dower,
Where *Reignier* sooner will receyue, than giue.

Suf. A Dowre my Lords? Disgrace not so your King,
That he should be so abiect, base, and poore,
To choose for wealth, and not for perfect Loue.
Henry is able to enrich his Queene,
And not to seeke a Queene to make him rich,
So worthlesse Pezants bargaine for their Wiues,
As Market men for Oxen, Sheepe, or Horse.
Marriage is a matter of more worth,
Then to be dealt in by Atturney-ship:
Not whom we will, but whom his Grace affects,

Must

Must be companion of his Nuptiall bed.
And therefore Lords, since he affects her most,
Most of all these reasons bindeth vs,
In our opinions she should be preferr'd.
For what is wedlocke forced? but a Hell,
An Age of discord and continuall strife,
Whereas the contrarie bringeth blisse,
And is a patterne of Celestiall peace.
Whom should we match with *Henry* being a King,
But *Margaret*, that is daughter to a King:
Her peerelesse feature, ioyned with her birth,
Approues her fit for none, but for a King.
Her valiant courage, and vndaunted spirit,
(More then in women commonly is seene)
Will answer our hope in issue of a King.
For *Henry*, sonne vnto a Conqueror,
Is likely to beget more Conquerors,
If with a Lady of so high resolue,
(As is faire *Margaret*) he be link'd in loue.
Then yeeld my Lords, and heere conclude with mee,
That *Margaret* shall be Queene, and none but shee.

  King. Whether it be through force of your report,
My Noble Lord of Suffolke: Or for that
My tender youth was neuer yet attaint
With any passion of inflaming loue,
I cannot tell: but this I am assur'd,
I feele such sharpe dissention in my breast,
Such fierce alarums both of Hope and Feare,
As I am sicke with working of my thoughts.
Take therefore shipping, poste my Lord to France,
Agree to any couenants, and procure
That Lady *Margaret* do vouchsafe to come
To crosse the Seas to England, and be crown'd
King *Henries* faithfull and annointed Queene.
For your expences and sufficient charge,
Among the people gather vp a tenth.
Be gone I say, for till you do returne,
I rest perplexed with a thousand Cares.
And you (good Vnckle) banish all offence:
If you do censure me, by what you were,
Not what you are, I know it will excuse
This sodaine execution of my will.
And so conduct me, where from company,
I may reuolue and ruminate my greefe. *Exit.*
  Glo. I greefe I feare me, both at first and last.
Exit Glocester.
  Suf. Thus Suffolke hath preuail'd, and thus he goes
As did the youthfull *Paris* once to Greece,
With hope to finde the like euent in loue,
But prosper better than the Troian did:
Margaret shall now be Queene, and rule the King:
But I will rule both her, the King, and Realme. *Exit*

FINIS.

The second Part of Henry the Sixt,
with the death of the Good Duke HVMFREY.

Actus Primus. Scœna Prima.

Flourish of Trumpets: Then Hoboyes.

Enter King, Duke Humfrey, Salisbury, Warwicke, and Beauford on the one side.
The Queene, Suffolke, Yorke, Somerset, and Buckingham, on the other.

Suffolke.

AS by your high Imperiall Maiesty,
I had in charge at my depart for France,
As Procurator to your Excellence,
To marry Princes *Margaret* for your Grace;
So in the Famous Ancient City, *Toures*,
In presence of the Kings of *France*, and *Sicill*,
The Dukes of *Orleance, Calaber, Britaigne*, and *Alanson*,
Seuen Earles, twelue Barons, & twenty reuerend Bishops
I haue perform'd my Taske, and was espous'd,
And humbly now vpon my bended knee,
In sight of England, and her Lordly Peeres,
Deliuer vp my Title in the Queene
To your most gracious hands, that are the Substance
Of that great Shadow I did represent:
The happiest Gift, that euer Marquesse gaue,
The Fairest Queene, that euer King receiu'd.

King. Suffolke arise. Welcome Queene *Margaret*,
I can expresse no kinder signe of Loue
Then this kinde kisse: O Lord, that lends me life,
Lend me a heart repleate with thankfulnesse:
For thou hast giuen me in this beauteous Face
A world of earthly blessings to my soule,
If Simpathy of Loue vnite our thoughts.

Queen. Great King of England, & my gracious Lord,
The mutuall conference that my minde hath had,
By day, by night; waking, and in my dreames,
In Courtly company, or at my Beades,
With you mine *Alder liefest* Soueraigne,
Makes me the bolder to salute my King,
With ruder termes, such as my wit affoords,
And ouer ioy of heart doth minister.

King. Her sight did rauish, but her grace in Speech,
Her words yclad with wisedomes Maiesty,
Makes me from Wondring, fall to Weeping ioyes,
Such is the Fulnesse of my hearts content.
Lords, with one cheerefull voice, Welcome my Loue.

All kneel. Long liue Qu. *Margaret*, Englands happines.
Queene. We thanke you all. *Florish*

Suf. My Lord Protector, so it please your Grace,
Heere are the Articles of contracted peace,
Betweene our Soueraigne, and the French King *Charles*,
For eighteene moneths concluded by consent.

Glo. Reads. Inprimis, *It is agreed betweene the French K.*
Charles, and William de la Pole Marquesse of Suffolke, Am-
bassador for Henry King of England, That the said Henry shal
espouse the Lady Margaret, daughter vnto Reignier King of
Naples, Sicillia, and Ierusalem, and Crowne her Queene of
England, ere the thirtieth of May next ensuing.
Item, *That the Dutchy of Aniou, and the County of Main,*
shall be released and deliuered to the King her father.

King. Vnkle, how now?
Glo. Pardon me gracious Lord,
Some sodaine qualme hath strucke me at the heart,
And dim'd mine eyes, that I can reade no further.
King. Vnckle of Winchester, I pray read on.

Win. Item, *It is further agreed betweene them, That the*
Dutchesse of Aniou and Maine, shall be released and deliuered
ouer to the King her Father, and shee sent ouer of the King of
Englands owne proper Cost and Charges, without hauing any
Dowry.

King. They please vs well. Lord Marques kneel down,
We heere create thee the first Duke of Suffolke,
And girt thee with the Sword. Cosin of Yorke,
We heere discharge your Grace from being Regent
I'th parts of France, till terme of eighteene Moneths
Be full expyr'd. Thankes Vncle Winchester,
Gloster, Yorke, Buckingham, Somerset,
Salisburie, and Warwicke.
We thanke you all for this great fauour done,
In entertainment to my Princely Queene.
Come, let vs in, and with all speede prouide
To see her Coronation be perform'd.

Exit King, Queene, and Suffolke.

Manet the rest.

Glo. Braue Peeres of England, Pillars of the State,
To you Duke *Humfrey* must vnload his greefe:
Your greefe, the common greefe of all the Land.
What? did my brother *Henry* spend his youth,
His valour, coine, and people in the warres?
Did he so often lodge in open field:
In Winters cold, and Summers parching heate,
To conquer France, his true inheritance?
And did my brother *Bedford* toyle his wits,

To keepe by policy what *Henrie* got:
Haue you your selues, *Somerset, Buckingham,*
Braue *Yorke, Salisbury*, and victorious *Warwicke,*
Receiud deepe scarres in France and Normandie:
Or hath mine Vnckle *Beauford*, and my selfe,
With all the Learned Counsell of the Realme,
Studied so long, sat in the Councell house,
Early and late, debating too and fro
How France and Frenchmen might be kept in awe,
And hath his Highnesse in his infancie,
Crowned in Paris in despight of foes,
And shall these Labours, and these Honours dye?
Shall *Henries* Conquest, *Bedfords* vigilance,
Your Deeds of Warre, and all our Counsell dye?
O Peeres of England, shamefull is this League,
Fatall this Marriage, cancelling your Fame,
Blotting your names from Bookes of memory,
Racing the Charracters of your Renowne,
Defacing Monuments of Conquer'd France,
Vndoing all, as all had neuer bin.

Car. Nephew, what meanes this passionate discourse?
This preroration with such circumstance:
For France, 'tis ours; and we will keepe it still.

Glo. I Vnckle, we will keepe it, if we can:
But now it is impossible we should.
Suffolke, the new made Duke that rules the rost,
Hath giuen the Dutchy of *Aniou* and *Mayne,*
Vnto the poore King *Reignier*, whose large style
Agrees not with the leannesse of his purse.

Sal. Now by the death of him that dyed for all,
These Counties were the Keyes of *Normandie* :
But wherefore weepes *Warwicke*, my valiant sonne?

War. For greefe that they are past recouerie.
For were there hope to conquer them againe,
My sword should shed hot blood, mine eyes no teares.
Aniou and *Maine*? My selfe did win them both:
Those Prouinces, these Armes of mine did conquer,
And are the Citties that I got with wounds,
Deliuer'd vp againe with peacefull words?
Mort Dieu.

Yorke. For Suffolkes Duke, may he be suffocate,
That dims the Honor of this Warlike Isle:
France should haue torne and rent my very hart,
Before I would haue yeelded to this League.
I neuer read but Englands Kings haue had
Large summes of Gold, and Dowries with their wiues,
And our King *Henry* giues away his owne,
To match with her that brings no vantages.

Hum. A proper iest, and neuer heard before,
That Suffolke should demand a whole Fifteenth,
For Costs and Charges in transporting her:
She should haue staid in France, and steru'd in France
Before——

Car. My Lord of Gloster, now ye grow too hot,
It was the pleasure of my Lord the King.

Hum. My Lord of Winchester I know your minde.
'Tis not my speeches that you do mislike:
But 'tis my presence that doth trouble ye,
Rancour will out, proud Prelate, in thy face
I see thy furie: If I longer stay,
We shall begin our ancient bickerings:
Lordings farewell, and say when I am gone,
I prophesied, France will be lost ere long. *Exit Humfrey.*

Car. So, there goes our Protector in a rage:
'Tis knowne to you he is mine enemy:
Nay more, an enemy vnto you all,
And no great friend, I feare me to the King;
Consider Lords, he is the next of blood,
And heyre apparant to the English Crowne:
Had *Henrie* got an Empire by his marriage,
And all the wealthy Kingdomes of the West,
There's reason he should be displeas'd at it:
Looke to it Lords, let not his smoothing words
Bewitch your hearts, be wise and circumspect.
What though the common people fauour him,
Calling him, *Humfrey the good Duke of Gloster,*
Clapping their hands, and crying with loud voyce,
Iesu maintaine your Royall Excellence,
With God preserue the good Duke *Humfrey*:
I feare me Lords, for all this flattering glosse,
He will be found a dangerous Protector.

Buc. Why should he then protect our Soueraigne?
He being of age to gouerne of himselfe.
Cosin of Somerset, ioyne you with me,
And altogether with the Duke of Suffolke,
Wee'l quickly hoyse Duke *Humfrey* from his seat.

Car. This weighty businesse will not brooke delay,
Ile to the Duke of Suffolke presently. *Exit Cardinall.*

Som. Cosin of Buckingham, though *Humfries* pride
And greatnesse of his place be greefe to vs,
Yet let vs watch the haughtie Cardinall,
His insolence is more intollerable
Then all the Princes in the Land beside,
If Gloster be displac'd, hee'l be Protector.

Buc. Or thou, or I Somerset will be Protectors,
Despite Duke *Humfrey*, or the Cardinall.
Exit Buckingham, and Somerset.

Sal. Pride went before, Ambition followes him.
While these do labour for their owne preferment,
Behooues it vs to labor for the Realme.
I neuer saw but Humfrey Duke of Gloster,
Did beare him like a Noble Gentleman:
Oft haue I seene the haughty Cardinall,
More like a Souldier then a man o'th' Church,
As stout and proud as he were Lord of all,
Sweare like a Ruffian, and demeane himselfe
Vnlike the Ruler of a Common-weale.
Warwicke my sonne, the comfort of my age,
Thy deeds, thy plainnesse, and thy house-keeping,
Hath wonne the greatest fauour of the Commons,
Excepting none but good Duke Humfrey.
And Brother Yorke, thy Acts in Ireland,
In bringing them to ciuill Discipline:
Thy late exploits done in the heart of France,
When thou wert Regent for our Soueraigne,
Haue made thee fear'd and honor'd of the people,
Ioyne we together for the publike good,
In what we can, to bridle and suppresse
The pride of Suffolke, and the Cardinall,
With Somersets and Buckinghams Ambition,
And as we may, cherish Duke Humfries deeds,
While they do tend the profit of the Land.

War. So God helpe Warwicke, as he loues the Land,
And common profit of his Countrey.

Yor. And so sayes Yorke,
For he hath greatest cause.

Salisbury. Then lets make hast away,
And looke vnto the maine.

Warwicke. Vnto the maine?
Oh Father, *Maine* is lost,
That *Maine*, which by maine force Warwicke did winne,
And would haue kept, so long as breath did last:

Main-chance father you meant, but I meant *Maine*,
Which I will win from France, or else be slaine.

Exit Warwicke, and Salisbury. Manet Yorke.

Yorke. Anion and Maine are giuen to the French,
Paris is lost, the state of Normandie
Stands on a tickle point, now they are gone:
Suffolke concluded on the Articles,
The Peeres agreed, and *Henry* was well pleas'd,
To change two Dukedomes for a Dukes faire daughter.
I cannot blame them all, what is't to them?
'Tis thine they giue away, and not their owne.
Pirates may make cheape penyworths of their pillage,
And purchase Friends, and giue to Curtezans,
Still reuelling like Lords till all be gone,
While as the silly Owner of the goods
Weepes ouer them, and wrings his haplesse hands,
And shakes his head, and trembling stands aloofe,
While all is shar'd, and all is borne away,
Ready to sterue, and dare not touch his owne.
So Yorke must sit, and fret, and bite his tongue,
While his owne Lands are bargain'd for, and sold:
Me thinkes the Realmes of England, France, & Ireland,
Beare that proportion to my flesh and blood,
As did the fatall brand *Althæa* burnt,
Vnto the Princes heart of *Calidon*:
Aniou and Maine both giuen vnto the French?
Cold newes for me: for I had hope of France,
Euen as I haue of fertile Englands soile.
A day will come, when Yorke shall claime his owne,
And therefore I will take the *Neuils* parts,
And make a shew of loue to proud Duke *Humfrey*,
And when I spy aduantage, claime the Crowne,
For that's the Golden marke I seeke to hit:
Nor shall proud Lancaster vsurpe my right,
Nor hold the Scepter in his childish Fist,
Nor weare the Diadem vpon his head,
Whose Church-like humors fits not for a Crowne.
Then Yorke be still a-while, till time do serue:
Watch thou, and wake when others be asleepe,
To prie into the secrets of the State,
Till *Henrie* surfetting in ioyes of loue,
With his new Bride, & Englands deere bought Queen,
And *Humfrey* with the Peeres be falne at iarres:
Then will I raise aloft the Milke-white-Rose,
With whose sweet smell the Ayre shall be perfum'd,
And in my Standard beare the Armes of Yorke,
To grapple with the house of Lancaster,
And force perforce Ile make him yeeld the Crowne,
Whose bookish Rule, hath pull'd faire England downe.

Exit Yorke.

Enter Duke Humfrey and his wife Elianor.

Elia. Why droopes my Lord like ouer-ripen'd Corn,
Hanging the head at Ceres plenteous load?
Why doth the Great Duke *Humfrey* knit his browes,
As frowning at the Fauours of the world?
Why are thine eyes fixt to the sullen earth,
Gazing on that which seemes to dimme thy sight?
What seest thou there? King *Henries* Diadem,
Inchac'd with all the Honors of the world?
If so, Gaze on, and grouell on thy face,
Vntill thy head be circled with the same.
Put forth thy hand, reach at the glorious Gold.
What, is't too short? Ile lengthen it with mine,
And hauing both together heau'd it vp,
Wee'l both together lift our heads to heauen,
And neuer more abase our sight so low,
As to vouchsafe one glance vnto the ground.

Hum. O *Nell*, sweet *Nell*, if thou dost loue thy Lord,
Banish the Canker of ambitious thoughts:
And may that thought, when I imagine ill
Against my King and Nephew, vertuous *Henry*,
Be my last breathing in this mortall world.
My troublous dreames this night, doth make me sad.

Eli. What dream'd my Lord, tell me, and Ile requite it
With sweet rehearsall of my mornings dreame?

Hum. Me thought this staffe mine Office-badge in Court
Was broke in twaine: by whom, I haue forgot,
But as I thinke, it was by'th Cardinall,
And on the peeces of the broken Wand
Were plac'd the heads of *Edmond* Duke of Somerset,
And *William de la Pole* first Duke of Suffolke.
This was my dreame, what it doth bode God knowes.

Eli. Tut, this was nothing but an argument,
That he that breakes a sticke of Glosters groue,
Shall loose his head for his presumption.
But list to me my *Humfrey*, my sweete Duke:
Me thought I sate in Seate of Maiesty,
In the Cathedrall Church of Westminster,
And in that Chaire where Kings & Queens wer crownd,
Where *Henrie* and Dame *Margaret* kneel'd to me,
And on my head did set the Diadem.

Hum. Nay *Elinor*, then must I chide outright:
Presumptuous Dame, ill-nurter'd *Elianor*,
Art thou not second Woman in the Realme?
And the Protectors wife belou'd of him?
Hast thou not worldly pleasure at command,
Aboue the reach or compasse of thy thought?
And wilt thou still be hammering Treachery,
To tumble downe thy husband, and thy selfe,
From top of Honor, to Disgraces feete?
Away from me, and let me heare no more.

Elia. What, what, my Lord? Are you so chollericke
With *Elianor*, for telling but her dreame?
Next time Ile keepe my dreames vnto my selfe,
And not be check'd.

Hum. Nay be not angry, I am pleas'd againe.

Enter Messenger.

Mess. My Lord Protector, 'tis his Highnes pleasure,
You do prepare to ride vnto S. *Albons*,
Where as the King and Queene do meane to Hawke.

Hu. I go, Come *Nel* thou wilt ride with vs? *Ex. Hum*

Eli. Yes my good Lord, Ile follow presently.
Follow I must, I cannot go before,
While Gloster beares this base and humble minde.
Were I a Man, a Duke, and next of blood,
I would remoue these tedious stumbling blockes,
And smooth my way vpon their headlesse neckes.
And being a woman, I will not be slacke
To play my part in Fortunes Pageant.
Where are you there? Sir *Iohn*; nay feare not man,
We are alone, here's none but thee, & I. *Enter Hume.*

Hume. Iesus preserue your Royall Maiesty.

Elia. What saist thou? Maiesty: I am but Grace.

Hume. But by the grace of God, and *Humes* aduice,
Your Graces Title shall be multiplied.

Elia. What saist thou man? Hast thou as yet confer'd
With *Margerie Iordane* the cunning Witch,
With *Roger Bollingbrooke* the Coniurer?
And will they vndertake to do me good?

Hume. This they haue promised to shew your Highnes
A Spirit rais'd from depth of vnder ground,

That

That shall make answere to such Questions,
As by your Grace shall be propounded him.

Elianor. It is enough, Ile thinke vpon the Questions:
When from Saint *Albones* we doe make returne,
Wee'le see these things effected to the full.
Here *Hume*, take this reward, make merry man
With thy Confederates in this weightie cause.
Exit Elianor.

Hume. Hume must make merry with the Duchesse Gold:
Marry and shall: but how now, Sir *Iohn Hume*?
Seale vp your Lips, and giue no words but Mum,
The businesse asketh silent secrecie.
Dame *Elianor* giues Gold, to bring the Witch:
Gold cannot come amisse, were she a Deuill.
Yet haue I Gold flyes from another Coast:
I dare not say, from the rich Cardinall,
And from the great and new-made Duke of Suffolke;
Yet I doe finde it so: for to be plaine,
They (knowing Dame *Elianors* aspiring humor)
Haue hyred me to vnder-mine the Duchesse,
And buzze these Coniurations in her brayne.
They say, A craftie Knaue do's need no Broker,
Yet am I *Suffolke* and the Cardinalls Broker.
Hume, if you take not heed, you shall goe neare
To call them both a payre of craftie Knaues.
Well, so it stands: and thus I feare at last,
Humes Knauerie will be the Duchesse Wracke,
And her Attainture, will be *Humphreyes* fall:
Sort how it will, I shall haue Gold for all. *Exit*

Enter three or foure Petitioners, the Armorers Man being one.

1. *Pet.* My Masters, let's stand close, my Lord Protector will come this way by and by, and then wee may deliuer our Supplications in the Quill.

2. *Pet.* Marry the Lord protect him, for hee's a good man, Iesu blesse him.

Enter Suffolke, and Queene.

Peter. Here a comes me thinkes, and the Queene with him: Ile be the first sure.

2. *Pet.* Come backe foole, this is the Duke of Suffolk, and not my Lord Protector.

Suff. How now fellow: would'st any thing with me?

1. *Pet.* I pray my Lord pardon me, I tooke ye for my Lord Protector.

Queene. To my Lord Protector? Are your Supplications to his Lordship? Let me see them: what is thine?

1. *Pet.* Mine is, and't please your Grace, against *Iohn Goodman*, my Lord Cardinals Man, for keeping my House, and Lands, and Wife and all, from me.

Suff. Thy Wife too? that's some Wrong indeede. What's yours? What's heere? Against the Duke of Suffolke, for enclosing the Commons of Melforde. How now, Sir Knaue?

2. *Pet.* Alas Sir, I am but a poore Petitioner of our whole Towneship.

Peter. Against my Master *Thomas Horner*, for saying, That the Duke of Yorke was rightfull Heire to the Crowne.

Queene. What say'st thou? Did the Duke of Yorke say, hee was rightfull Heire to the Crowne?

Peter. That my Mistresse was? No forsooth: my Master said, That he was, and that the King was an Vsurper.

Suff. Who is there?
Enter Seruant.
Take this fellow in, and send for his Master with a Purseuant presently: wee'le heare more of your matter before the King. *Exit.*

Queene. And as for you that loue to be protected
Vnder the Wings of our Protectors Grace,
Begin your Suites anew, and sue to him.
Teare the Supplication.
Away, base Cullions: *Suffolke* let them goe.

All. Come, let's be gone. *Exit.*

Queene. My Lord of Suffolke, say, is this the guise?
Is this the Fashions in the Court of England?
Is this the Gouernment of Britaines Ile?
And this the Royaltie of *Albions* King?
What, shall King *Henry* be a Pupill still,
Vnder the surly *Glosters* Gouernance?
Am I a Queene in Title and in Stile,
And must be made a Subiect to a Duke?
I tell thee *Poole*, when in the Citie *Tours*
Thou ran'st a-tilt in honor of my Loue,
And stol'st away the Ladies hearts of France;
I thought King *Henry* had resembled thee,
In Courage, Courtship, and Proportion:
But all his minde is bent to Holinesse,
To number *Aue-Maries* on his Beades:
His Champions, are the Prophets and Apostles,
His Weapons, holy Sawes of sacred Writ,
His Studie is his Tilt-yard, and his Loues
Are brazen Images of Canonized Saints.
I would the Colledge of the Cardinalls
Would chuse him Pope, and carry him to Rome,
And set the Triple Crowne vpon his Head;
That were a State fit for his Holinesse.

Suff. Madame be patient: as I was cause
Your Highnesse came to England, so will I
In England worke your Graces full content.

Queene. Beside the haughtie Protector, haue we *Beauford*
The imperious Churchman; *Somerset*, *Buckingham*,
And grumbling *Yorke*: and not the least of these,
But can doe more in England then the King.

Suff. And he of these, that can doe most of all,
Cannot doe more in England then the *Neuils*:
Salisbury and *Warwick* are no simple Peeres.

Queene. Not all these Lords do vex me halfe so much,
As that prowd Dame, the Lord Protectors Wife:
She sweepes it through the Court with troups of Ladies,
More like an Empresse, then Duke *Humphreyes* Wife:
Strangers in Court, doe take her for the Queene:
She beares a Dukes Reuenewes on her backe,
And in her heart she scornes our Pouertie:
Shall I not liue to be aueng'd on her?
Contemptuous base-borne Callot as she is,
She vaunted 'mongst her Minions t'other day,
The very trayne of her worst wearing Gowne,
Was better worth then all my Fathers Lands,
Till *Suffolke* gaue two Dukedomes for his Daughter.

Suff. Madame, my selfe haue lym'd a Bush for her,
And plac't a Quier of such enticing Birds,
That she will light to listen to the Layes,
And neuer mount to trouble you againe.
So let her rest: and Madame list to me,
For I am bold to counsaile you in this;
Although we fancie not the Cardinall,
Yet must we ioyne with him and with the Lords,
Till we haue brought Duke *Humphrey* in disgrace.

As

As for the Duke of Yorke, this late Complaint
Will make but little for his benefit:
So one by one wee'le weed them all at last,
And you your selfe shall steere the happy Helme. *Exit.*

Sound a Sennet.

Enter the King, Duke Humfrey, Cardinall, Buckingham, Yorke, Salisbury, Warwicke, and the Duchesse.

King. For my part, Noble Lords, I care not which,
Or *Somerset*, or *Yorke*, all's one to me.

Yorke. If *Yorke* haue ill demean'd himselfe in France,
Then let him be denay'd the Regent-ship.

Som. If *Somerset* be vnworthy of the Place,
Let *Yorke* be Regent, I will yeeld to him.

Warw. Whether your Grace be worthy, yea or no,
Dispute not that, *Yorke* is the worthyer.

Card. Ambitious *Warwicke*, let thy betters speake.

Warw. The Cardinall's not my better in the field.

Buck. All in this presence are thy betters, *Warwicke*.

Warw. Warwicke may liue to be the best of all.

Salisb. Peace Sonne, and shew some reason *Buckingham*
Why *Somerset* should be preferr'd in this?

Queene. Because the King forsooth will haue it so.

Humf. Madame, the King is old enough himselfe
To giue his Censure: These are no Womens matters.

Queene. If he be old enough, what needs your Grace
To be Protector of his Excellence?

Humf. Madame, I am Protector of the Realme,
And at his pleasure will resigne my Place.

Suff. Resigne it then, and leaue thine insolence.
Since thou wert King; as who is King, but thou?
The Common-wealth hath dayly run to wrack,
The Dolphin hath preuayl'd beyond the Seas,
And all the Peeres and Nobles of the Realme
Haue beene as Bond-men to thy Soueraigntie.

Card. The Commons hast thou rackt, the Clergies Bags
Are lanke and leane with thy Extortions.

Som. Thy sumptuous Buildings, and thy Wiues Attyre
Haue cost a masse of publique Treasurie.

Buck. Thy Crueltie in execution
Vpon Offendors, hath exceeded Law,
And left thee to the mercy of the Law.

Queene. Thy sale of Offices and Townes in France,
If they were knowne, as the suspect is great,
Would make thee quickly hop without thy Head.
Exit Humfrey.
Giue me my Fanne: what, Mynion, can ye not?
She giues the Duchesse a box on the eare.
I cry you mercy, Madame: was it you?

Duch. Was't I? yea, I it was, prowd French-woman:
Could I come neere your Beautie with my Nayles,
I could set my ten Commandements in your face.

King. Sweet Aunt be quiet, 'twas against her will.

Duch. Against her will, good King? looke to't in time,
Shee'le hamper thee, and dandle thee like a Baby:
Though in this place most Master weare no Breeches,
She shall not strike Dame *Elianor* vnreueng'd.
Exit Elianor.

Buck. Lord Cardinall, I will follow *Elianor*,
And listen after *Humfrey*, how he proceeds:
Shee's tickled now, her Fume needs no spurres,
Shee'le gallop farre enough to her destruction.
Exit Buckingham.

Enter Humfrey.

Humf. Now Lords, my Choller being ouer-blowne,
With walking once about the Quadrangle,
I come to talke of Common-wealth Affayres.
As for your spightfull false Obiections,
Proue them, and I lye open to the Law:
But God in mercie so deale with my Soule,
As I in dutie loue my King and Countrey.
But to the matter that we haue in hand:
I say, my Soueraigne, *Yorke* is meetest man
To be your Regent in the Realme of France.

Suff. Before we make election, giue me leaue
To shew some reason, of no little force,
That *Yorke* is most vnmeet of any man.

Yorke. Ile tell thee, *Suffolke* why I am vnmeet.
First, for I cannot flatter thee in Pride:
Next, if I be appointed for the Place,
My Lord of Somerset will keepe me here,
Without Discharge, Money, or Furniture,
Till France be wonne into the Dolphins hands:
Last time I danc't attendance on his will,
Till Paris was besieg'd, famisht, and lost.

Warw. That can I witnesse, and a fouler fact
Did neuer Traytor in the Land commit.

Suff. Peace head-strong *Warwicke*.

Warw. Image of Pride, why should I hold my peace?

Enter Armorer and his Man.

Suff. Because here is a man accused of Treason,
Pray God the Duke of Yorke excuse himselfe.

Yorke. Doth any one accuse *Yorke* for a Traytor?

King. What mean'st thou, *Suffolke*? tell me, what are these?

Suff. Please it your Maiestie, this is the man
That doth accuse his Master of High Treason;
His words were these: That *Richard*, Duke of Yorke,
Was rightfull Heire vnto the English Crowne,
And that your Maiestie was an Vsurper.

King. Say man, were these thy words?

Armorer. And't shall please your Maiestie, I neuer sayd
nor thought any such matter: God is my witnesse, I am
falsely accus'd by the Villaine.

Peter. By these tenne bones, my Lords, hee did speake
them to me in the Garret one Night, as wee were scowring my Lord of Yorkes Armor.

Yorke. Base Dunghill Villaine, and Mechanicall,
Ile haue thy Head for this thy Traytors speech:
I doe beseech your Royall Maiestie,
Let him haue all the rigor of the Law.

Armorer. Alas, my Lord, hang me if euer I spake the
words: my accuser is my Prentice, and when I did correct him for his fault the other day, he did vow vpon his
knees he would be euen with me: I haue good witnesse
of this; therefore I beseech your Maiestie, doe not cast
away an honest man for a Villaines accusation.

King. Vnckle, what shall we say to this in law?

Humf. This doome, my Lord, if I may iudge:
Let *Somerset* be Regent o're the French,
Because in *Yorke* this breedes suspition;
And let these haue a day appointed them
For single Combat, in conuenient place,
For he hath witnesse of his seruants malice:
This is the Law, and this Duke *Humfreyes* doome.

Som. I

Som. I humbly thanke your Royall Maiestie.
Armorer. And I accept the Combat willingly.
Peter. Alas, my Lord, I cannot fight; for Gods sake pitty my case: the spight of man preuayleth against me. O Lord haue mercy vpon me, I shall neuer be able to fight a blow: O Lord my heart.
Humf. Sirrha, or you must fight, or else be hang'd.
King. Away with them to Prison: and the day of Combat, shall be the last of the next moneth. Come *Somerset*, wee'le see thee sent away.

Flourish. Exeunt.

Enter the Witch, the two Priests, and Bullingbrooke.

Hume. Come my Masters, the Duchesse I tell you expects performance of your promises.
Bulling. Master *Hume*, we are therefore prouided: will her Ladyship behold and heare our Exorcismes?
Hume. I, what else? feare you not her courage.
Bulling. I haue heard her reported to be a Woman of an inuincible spirit: but it shall be conuenient, Master *Hume*, that you be by her aloft, while wee be busie below; and so I pray you goe in Gods Name, and leaue vs. *Exit Hume.*
Mother *Iordan*, be you prostrate, and grouell on the Earth; *Iohn Southwell* reade you, and let vs to our worke.

Enter Elianor aloft.

Elianor. Well said my Masters, and welcome all: To this geere, the sooner the better.
Bullin. Patience, good Lady, Wizards know their times: Deepe Night, darke Night, the silent of the Night,
The time of Night when Troy was set on fire,
The time when Screech-owles cry, and Bandogs howle,
And Spirits walke, and Ghosts breake vp their Graues;
That time best fits the worke we haue in hand.
Madame, sit you, and feare not: whom wee rayse,
Wee will make fast within a hallow'd Verge.

Here doe the Ceremonies belonging, and make the Circle, Bullingbrooke or Southwell reades, Coniuro te, &c. It Thunders and Lightens terribly: then the Spirit riseth.

Spirit. Ad sum.
Witch. Asmath, by the eternall God,
Whose name and power thou tremblest at,
Answere that I shall aske: for till thou speake,
Thou shalt not passe from hence.
Spirit. Aske what thou wilt; that I had sayd, and done.
Bulling. First of the King: What shall of him become?
Spirit. The Duke yet liues, that *Henry* shall depose:
But him out-liue, and dye a violent death.
Bulling. What fates await the Duke of Suffolke?
Spirit. By Water shall he dye, and take his end.
Bulling. What shall befall the Duke of Somerset?
Spirit. Let him shun Castles,
Safer shall he be vpon the sandie Plaines,
Then where Castles mounted stand.
Haue done, for more I hardly can endure.
Bulling. Discend to Darknesse, and the burning Lake: False Fiend auoide.

Thunder and Lightning. Exit Spirit.

Enter the Duke of Yorke and the Duke of Buckingham with their Guard, and breake in.

Yorke. Lay hands vpon these Traytors, and their trash:
Beldam I thinke we watcht you at an ynch.
What Madame, are you there? the King & Commonweale
Are deepely indebted for this peece of paines;
My Lord Protector will, I doubt it not,
See you well guerdon'd for these good deserts.
Elianor. Not halfe so bad as thine to Englands King,
Iniurious Duke, that threatest where's no cause.
Buck. True Madame, none at all: what call you this?
Away with them, let them be clapt vp close,
And kept asunder: you Madame shall with vs.
Stafford take her to thee.
Wee'le see your Trinkets here all forth-comming.
All away. *Exit.*
Yorke. Lord *Buckingham*, me thinks you watcht her well:
A pretty Plot, well chosen to build vpon.
Now pray my Lord, let's see the Deuils Writ.
What haue we here? *Reades.*
*The Duke yet liues, that Henry shall depose:
But him out-line, and dye a violent death.*
Why this is iust, *Aio Æacida Romanos vincere posso.*
Well, to the rest:
*Tell me what fate awaits the Duke of Suffolke?
By Water shall he dye, and take his end.
What shall betide the Duke of Somerset?
Let him shunne Castles,
Safer shall he be vpon the sandie Plaines,
Then where Castles mounted stand.*
Come, come, my Lords,
These Oracles are hardly attain'd,
And hardly vnderstood.
The King is now in progresse towards Saint *Albones*,
With him, the Husband of this louely Lady:
Thither goes these Newes,
As fast as Horse can carry them:
A sorry Breakfast for my Lord Protector.
Buck. Your Grace shal giue me leaue, my Lord of York,
To be the Poste, in hope of his reward.
Yorke. At your pleasure, my good Lord.
Who's within there, hoe?

Enter a Seruingman.

Inuite my Lords of Salisbury and Warwick
To suppe with me to morrow Night. Away.
Exeunt.

Enter the King, Queene, Protector, Cardinall, and Suffolke, with Faulkners hallowing.

Queene. Beleeue me Lords, for flying at the Brooke,
I saw not better sport these seuen yeeres day:
Yet by your leaue, the Winde was very high,
And ten to one, old *Ioane* had not gone out.
King. But what a point, my Lord, your Faulcon made,
And what a pytch she flew aboue the rest:
To see how God in all his Creatures workes,
Yea Man and Birds are fayne of climbing high.
Suff. No maruell, and it like your Maiestie,
My Lord Protectors Hawkes doe towre so well,
They know their Master loues to be aloft,
And beares his thoughts aboue his Faulcons Pitch.
Glost. My Lord, 'tis but a base ignoble minde,
That mounts no higher then a Bird can sore:

Card. I

Card. I thought as much, hee would be aboue the Clouds.

Glost. I my Lord Cardinall, how thinke you by that? Were it not good your Grace could flye to Heauen?

King. The Treasurie of euerlasting Ioy.

Card. Thy Heauen is on Earth, thine Eyes & Thoughts Beat on a Crowne, the Treasure of thy Heart, Pernitious Protector, dangerous Peere, That smooth'st it so with King and Common-weale.

Glost. What, Cardinall? Is your Priest-hood growne peremptorie? *Tantæne animis Cœlestibus iræ*, Church-men so hot? Good Vnckle hide such mallice: With such Holynesse can you doe it?

Suff. No mallice Sir, no more then well becomes So good a Quarrell, and so bad a Peere.

Glost. As who, my Lord?

Suff. Why, as you, my Lord, An't like your Lordly Lords Protectorship.

Glost. Why *Suffolke*, England knowes thine insolence.

Queene. And thy Ambition, *Gloster*.

King. I prythee peace, good Queene, And whet not on these furious Peeres, For blessed are the Peace-makers on Earth.

Card. Let me be blessed for the Peace I make Against this prowd Protector with my Sword.

Glost. Faith holy Vnckle, would't were come to that.

Card. Marry, when thou dar'st.

Glost. Make vp no factious numbers for the matter, In thine owne person answere thy abuse.

Card. I, where thou dar'st not peepe: And if thou dar'st, this Euening, On the East side of the Groue.

King. How now, my Lords?

Card. Beleeue me, Cousin *Gloster*, Had not your man put vp the Fowle so suddenly, We had had more sport, Come with thy two-hand Sword.

Glost. True Vnckle, are ye aduis'd? The East side of the Groue: Cardinall, I am with you.

King. Why how now, Vnckle *Gloster*?

Glost. Talking of Hawking; nothing else, my Lord. Now by Gods Mother, Priest, Ile shaue your Crowne for this, Or all my Fence shall fayle.

Card. Medice teipsum, Protector see to't well, protect your selfe.

King. The Windes grow high, So doe your Stomacks, Lords: How irkesome is this Musick to my heart? When such Strings iarre, what hope of Harmony? I pray my Lords let me compound this strife.

Enter one crying a Miracle.

Glost. What meanes this noyse? Fellow, what Miracle do'st thou proclayme?

One. A Miracle, a Miracle.

Suffolke. Come to the King, and tell him what Miracle.

One. Forsooth, a blinde man at Saint *Albones* Shrine, Within this halfe houre hath receiu'd his sight, A man that ne're saw in his life before.

King. Now God be prays'd, that to beleeuing Soules Giues Light in Darknesse, Comfort in Despaire.

Enter the Maior of Saint Albones, and his Brethren, bearing the man betweene two in a Chayre.

Card. Here comes the Townes-men, on Procession, To present your Highnesse with the man.

King. Great is his comfort in this Earthly Vale, Although by his sight his sinne be multiplyed.

Glost. Stand by, my Masters, bring him neere the King, His Highnesse pleasure is to talke with him.

King. Good-fellow, tell vs here the circumstance, That we for thee may glorifie the Lord. What, hast thou beene long blinde, and now restor'd?

Simpc. Borne blinde, and't please your Grace.

Wife. I indeede was he.

Suff. What Woman is this?

Wife. His Wife, and't like your Worship.

Glost. Hadst thou been his Mother, thou could'st haue better told.

King. Where wert thou borne?

Simpc. At Barwick in the North, and't like your Grace.

King. Poore Soule, Gods goodnesse hath beene great to thee: Let neuer Day nor Night vnhallowed passe, But still remember what the Lord hath done.

Queene. Tell me, good-fellow, Cam'st thou here by Chance, or of Deuotion, To this holy Shrine?

Simpc. God knowes of pure Deuotion, Being call'd a hundred times, and oftner, In my sleepe, by good Saint *Albon*: Who said; *Symon*, come; come offer at my Shrine, And I will helpe thee.

Wife. Most true, forsooth: And many time and oft my selfe haue heard a Voyce, To call him so.

Card. What, art thou lame?

Simpc. I, God Almightie helpe me.

Suff. How cam'st thou so?

Simpc. A fall off of a Tree.

Wife. A Plum-tree, Master.

Glost. How long hast thou beene blinde?

Simpc. O borne so, Master.

Glost. What, and would'st climbe a Tree?

Simpc. But that in all my life, when I was a youth.

Wife. Too true, and bought his climbing very deare.

Glost. 'Masse, thou lou'dst Plummes well, that would'st venture so.

Simpc. Alas, good Master, my Wife desired some Damsons, and made me climbe, with danger of my Life.

Glost. A subtill Knaue, but yet it shall not serue: Let me see thine Eyes; winck now, now open them, In my opinion, yet thou seest not well.

Simpc. Yes Master, cleare as day, I thanke God and Saint *Albones*.

Glost. Say'st thou me so: what Colour is this Cloake of?

Simpc. Red Master, Red as Blood.

Glost. Why that's well said: What Colour is my Gowne of?

Simpc. Black forsooth, Coale-Black, as Iet.

King. Why then, thou know'st what Colour Iet is of?

Suff. And yet I thinke, Iet did he neuer see.

Glost. But

Glost. But Cloakes and Gownes, before this day, a many.

Wife. Neuer before this day, in all his life.

Glost. Tell me Sirrha, what's my Name?

Simpc. Alas Master, I know not.

Glost. What's his Name?

Simpc. I know not.

Glost. Nor his?

Simpc. No indeede, Master.

Glost. What's thine owne Name?

Simpc. Saunder Simpcoxe, and if it please you, Master.

Glost. Then *Saunder*, sit there,
The lying'st Knaue in Christendome.
If thou hadst beene borne blinde,
Thou might'st as well haue knowne all our Names,
As thus to name the seuerall Colours we doe weare.
Sight may distinguish of Colours:
But suddenly to nominate them all,
It is impossible.
My Lords, Saint *Albone* here hath done a Miracle:
And would ye not thinke it, Cunning to be great,
That could restore this Cripple to his Legges againe.

Simpc. O Master, that you could?

Glost. My Masters of Saint *Albones*,
Haue you not Beadles in your Towne,
And Things call'd Whippes?

Maior. Yes, my Lord, if it please your Grace.

Glost. Then send for one presently.

Maior. Sirrha, goe fetch the Beadle hither straight.
Exit.

Glost. Now fetch me a Stoole hither by and by.
Now Sirrha, if you meane to saue your selfe from Whipping, leape me ouer this Stoole, and runne away.

Simpc. Alas Master, I am not able to stand alone:
You goe about to torture me in vaine.

Enter a Beadle with Whippes.

Glost. Well Sir, we must haue you finde your Legges.
Sirrha Beadle, whippe him till he leape ouer that same Stoole.

Beadle. I will, my Lord.
Come on Sirrha, off with your Doublet, quickly.

Simpc. Alas Master, what shall I doe? I am not able to stand.

After the Beadle hath hit him once, he leapes ouer the Stoole, and runnes away: and they follow, and cry, A Miracle.

King. O God, seest thou this, and bearest so long?

Queene. It made me laugh, to see the Villaine runne.

Glost. Follow the Knaue, and take this Drab away.

Wife. Alas Sir, we did it for pure need.

Glost. Let them be whipt through euery Market Towne,
Till they come to Barwick, from whence they came.
Exit.

Card. Duke *Humfrey* ha's done a Miracle to day.

Suff. True: made the Lame to leape and flye away.

Glost. But you haue done more Miracles then I:
You made in a day, my Lord, whole Townes to flye.

Enter Buckingham.

King. What Tidings with our Cousin *Buckingham*?

Buck. Such as my heart doth tremble to vnfold:
A sort of naughtie persons, lewdly bent,
Vnder the Countenance and Confederacie
Of Lady *Elianor*, the Protectors Wife,
The Ring-leader and Head of all this Rout,
Haue practis'd dangerously against your State,
Dealing with Witches and with Coniurers,
Whom we haue apprehended in the Fact,
Raysing vp wicked Spirits from vnder ground,
Demanding of King *Henries* Life and Death,
And other of your Highnesse Priuie Councell,
As more at large your Grace shall vnderstand.

Card. And so my Lord Protector, by this meanes
Your Lady is forth-comming, yet at London.
This Newes I thinke hath turn'd your Weapons edge;
'Tis like, my Lord, you will not keepe your houre.

Glost. Ambitious Church-man, leaue to afflict my heart:
Sorrow and griefe haue vanquisht all my powers;
And vanquisht as I am, I yeeld to thee,
Or to the meanest Groome.

King. O God, what mischiefes work the wicked ones?
Heaping confusion on their owne heads thereby.

Queene. *Gloster*, see here the Tainctture of thy Nest,
And looke thy selfe be faultlesse, thou wert best.

Glost. Madame, for my selfe, to Heauen I doe appeale,
How I haue lou'd my King, and Common-weale:
And for my Wife, I know not how it stands,
Sorry I am to heare what I haue heard.
Noble shee is: but if shee haue forgot
Honor and Vertue, and convers't with such,
As like to Pytch, defile Nobilitie;
I banish her my Bed, and Companie,
And giue her as a Prey to Law and Shame,
That hath dis-honored *Glosters* honest Name.

King. Well, for this Night we will repose vs here:
To morrow toward London, back againe,
To looke into this Businesse thorowly,
And call these foule Offendors to their Answeres;
And poyse the Cause in Iustice equall Scales,
Whose Beame stands sure, whose rightful cause preuailes.
Flourish. *Exeunt.*

Enter Yorke, Salisbury, and Warwick.

Yorke. Now my good Lords of Salisbury & Warwick,
Our simple Supper ended, giue me leaue,
In this close Walke, to satisfie my selfe,
In crauing your opinion of my Title,
Which is infallible, to Englands Crowne.

Salisb. My Lord, I long to heare it at full.

Warw. Sweet *Yorke* begin: and if thy clayme be good,
The *Neuills* are thy Subiects to command.

Yorke. Then thus:
Edward the third, my Lords, had seuen Sonnes:
The first, *Edward* the Black-Prince, Prince of Wales;
The second, *William* of Hatfield; and the third,
Lionel, Duke of Clarence; next to whom,
Was *Iohn* of Gaunt, the Duke of Lancaster;
The sift, was *Edmond Langley*, Duke of Yorke;
The sixt, was *Thomas* of Woodstock, Duke of Gloster;
William of Windsor was the seuenth, and last.
Edward the Black-Prince dyed before his Father,
And left behinde him *Richard*, his onely Sonne,
Who after *Edward* the third's death, raign'd as King,
Till *Henry Bullingbrooke*, Duke of Lancaster,
The eldest Sonne and Heire of *Iohn* of Gaunt,
Crown'd by the Name of *Henry* the fourth,
Seiz'd on the Realme, depos'd the rightfull King,
Sent his poore Queene to France, from whence she came,
And

And him to Pumfret; where, as all you know,
Harmelesse *Richard* was murthered traiterously.

  Warw. Father, the Duke hath told the truth;
Thus got the House of *Lancaster* the Crowne.

  Yorke. Which now they hold by force, and not by right:
For *Richard*, the first Sonnes Heire, being dead,
The Issue of the next Sonne should haue reign'd.

  Salisb. But *William* of Hatfield dyed without an Heire.

  Yorke. The third Sonne, Duke of Clarence,
From whose Line I clayme the Crowne,
Had Issue *Phillip*, a Daughter,
Who married *Edmond Mortimer*, Earle of March:
Edmond had Issue, *Roger*, Earle of March;
Roger had Issue, *Edmond, Anne*, and *Elianor*.

  Salisb. This *Edmond*, in the Reigne of *Bullingbrooke*,
As I haue read, layd clayme vnto the Crowne,
And but for *Owen Glendour*, had beene King;
Who kept him in Captiuitie, till he dyed.
But, to the rest.

  Yorke. His eldest Sister, *Anne*,
My Mother, being Heire vnto the Crowne,
Marryed *Richard*, Earle of Cambridge,
Who was to *Edmond Langley*,
Edward the thirds fift Sonnes Sonne;
By her I clayme the Kingdome:
She was Heire to *Roger*, Earle of March,
Who was the Sonne of *Edmond Mortimer*,
Who marryed *Phillip*, sole Daughter
Vnto *Lionel*, Duke of Clarence.
So, if the Issue of the elder Sonne
Succeed before the younger, I am King.

  Warw. What plaine proceedings is more plain then this?
Henry doth clayme the Crowne from *Iohn* of Gaunt,
The fourth Sonne, *Yorke* claymes it from the third:
Till *Lionels* Issue fayles, his should not reigne.
It fayles not yet, but flourishes in thee,
And in thy Sonnes, faire slippes of such a Stock.
Then Father *Salisbury*, kneele we together,
And in this priuate Plot be we the first,
That shall salute our rightfull Soueraigne
With honor of his Birth-right to the Crowne.

  Both. Long liue our Soueraigne *Richard*, Englands King.

  Yorke. We thanke you Lords:
But I am not your King, till I be Crown'd,
And that my Sword be stayn'd
With heart-blood of the House of *Lancaster*:
And that's not suddenly to be perform'd,
But with aduice and silent secrecie.
Doe you as I doe in these dangerous dayes,
Winke at the Duke of Suffolkes insolence,
At *Beaufords* Pride, at *Somersets* Ambition,
At *Buckingham*, and all the Crew of them,
Till they haue snar'd the Shepheard of the Flock,
That vertuous Prince, the good Duke *Humfrey*:
'Tis that they seeke; and they, in seeking that,
Shall finde their deaths, if *Yorke* can prophecie.

  Salisb. My Lord, breake we off; we know your minde at full.

  Warw. My heart assures me, that the Earle of Warwick
Shall one day make the Duke of Yorke a King.

  Yorke. And *Neuill*, this I doe assure my selfe,
Richard shall liue to make the Earle of Warwick
The greatest man in England, but the King. *Exeunt.*

Sound Trumpets. Enter the King and State, with Guard, to banish the Duchesse.

  King. Stand forth Dame *Elianor Cobham*,
Glosters Wife:
In sight of God, and vs, your guilt is great,
Receiue the Sentence of the Law for sinne,
Such as by Gods Booke are adiudg'd to death.
You foure from hence to Prison, back againe;
From thence, vnto the place of Execution:
The Witch in Smithfield shall be burnt to ashes,
And you three shall be strangled on the Gallowes.
You Madame, for you are more Nobly borne,
Despoyled of your Honor in your Life,
Shall, after three dayes open Penance done,
Liue in your Countrey here, in Banishment,
With Sir *Iohn Stanly*, in the Ile of Man.

  Elianor. Welcome is Banishment, welcome were my Death.

  Glost. *Elianor*, the Law thou seest hath iudged thee,
I cannot iustifie whom the Law condemnes:
Mine eyes are full of teares, my heart of griefe.
Ah *Humfrey*, this dishonor in thine age,
Will bring thy head with sorrow to the ground.
I beseech your Maiestie giue me leaue to goe;
Sorrow would sollace, and mine Age would ease.

  King. Stay *Humfrey*, Duke of Gloster,
Ere thou goe, giue vp thy Staffe,
Henry will to himselfe Protector be,
And God shall be my hope, my stay, my guide,
And Lanthorne to my feete:
And goe in peace, *Humfrey*, no lesse belou'd,
Then when thou wert Protector to thy King.

  Queene. I see no reason, why a King of yeeres
Should be to be protected like a Child,
God and King *Henry* gouerne Englands Realme:
Giue vp your Staffe, Sir, and the King his Realme.

  Glost. My Staffe? Here, Noble *Henry*, is my Staffe:
As willingly doe I the same resigne,
As ere thy Father *Henry* made it mine;
And euen as willingly at thy feete I leaue it,
As others would ambitiously receiue it.
Farewell good King: when I am dead, and gone,
May honorable Peace attend thy Throne. *Exit Gloster.*

  Queene. Why now is *Henry* King, and *Margaret* Queen,
And *Humfrey*, Duke of Gloster, scarce himselfe,
That beares so shrewd a mayme: two Pulls at once;
His Lady banisht, and a Limbe lopt off.
This Staffe of Honor raught, there let it stand,
Where it best fits to be, in *Henries* hand.

  Suff. Thus droupes this loftie Pyne, & hangs his sprayes,
Thus *Elianors* Pride dyes in her youngest dayes.

  Yorke. Lords, let him goe. Please it your Maiestie,
This is the day appointed for the Combat,
And ready are the Appellant and Defendant,
The Armorer and his Man, to enter the Lists,
So please your Highnesse to behold the fight.

  Queene. I, good my Lord: for purposely therefore
Left I the Court, to see this Quarrell try'de.

  King. A Gods Name see the Lysts and all things fit,
Here let them end it, and God defend the right.

  Yorke. I neuer saw a fellow worse bestead,
Or more afraid to fight, then is the Appellant,
The seruant of this Armorer, my Lords.

Enter at one Doore the Armorer and his Neighbors, drinking to him so much, that hee is drunke; and he enters with a Drumme before him, and his Staffe, with a Sand-bagge fastened to it: and at the other Doore his Man, with a Drumme and Sand-bagge, and Prentices drinking to him.

1. Neighbor. Here Neighbour *Horner*, I drinke to you in a Cup of Sack; and feare not Neighbor, you shall doe well enough.

2. Neighbor. And here Neighbour, here's a Cuppe of Charneco.

3. Neighbor. And here's a Pot of good Double-Beere Neighbor: drinke, and feare not your Man.

Armorer. Let it come yfaith, and Ile pledge you all, and a figge for *Peter*.

1. Prent. Here *Peter*, I drinke to thee, and be not afraid.

2. Prent. Be merry *Peter*, and feare not thy Master, fight for credit of the Prentices.

Peter. I thanke you all: drinke, and pray for me, I pray you, for I thinke I haue taken my last Draught in this World. Here *Robin*, and if I dye, I giue thee my Aporne; and *Will*, thou shalt haue my Hammer: and here *Tom*, take all the Money that I haue. O Lord blesse me, I pray God, for I am neuer able to deale with my Master, hee hath learnt so much fence already.

Salisb. Come, leaue your drinking, and fall to blowes. Sirrha, what's thy Name?

Peter. Peter forsooth.

Salisb. Peter? what more?

Peter. Thumpe.

Salisb. Thumpe? Then see thou thumpe thy Master well.

Armorer. Masters, I am come hither as it were vpon my Mans instigation, to proue him a Knaue, and my selfe an honest man: and touching the Duke of Yorke, I will take my death, I neuer meant him any ill, nor the King, nor the Queene: and therefore *Peter* haue at thee with a downe-right blow.

Yorke. Dispatch, this Knaues tongue begins to double. Sound Trumpets, Alarum to the Combattants.

They fight, and Peter strikes him downe.

Armorer. Hold *Peter*, hold, I confesse, I confesse Treason.

Yorke. Take away his Weapon: Fellow thanke God, and the good Wine in thy Masters way.

Peter. O God, haue I ouercome mine Enemies in this presence? O *Peter*, thou hast preuayl'd in right.

King. Goe, take hence that Traytor from our sight, For by his death we doe perceiue his guilt, And God in Iustice hath reueal'd to vs The truth and innocence of this poore fellow, Which he had thought to haue murther'd wrongfully. Come fellow, follow vs for thy Reward.

Sound a flourish.   Exeunt.

Enter Duke Humfrey and his Men in Mourning Cloakes.

Glost. Thus sometimes hath the brightest day a Cloud:
And after Summer, euermore succeedes
Barren Winter, with his wrathfull nipping Cold;
So Cares and Ioyes abound, as Seasons fleet.
Sirs, what's a Clock?

Seru. Tenne, my Lord.

Glost. Tenne is the houre that was appointed me,
To watch the comming of my punisht Duchesse:
Vnneath may shee endure the Flintie Streets,
To treade them with her tender-feeling feet.
Sweet *Nell*, ill can thy Noble Minde abrooke
The abiect People, gazing on thy face,
With enuious Lookes laughing at thy shame,
That erst did follow thy prowd Chariot-Wheeles,
When thou didst ride in triumph through the streets.
But soft, I thinke she comes, and Ile prepare
My teare-stayn'd eyes, to see her Miseries.

Enter the Duchesse in a white Sheet, and a Taper burning in her hand, with the Sherife and Officers.

Seru. So please your Grace, wee'le take her from the Sherife.

Gloster. No, stirre not for your liues, let her passe by.

Elianor. Come you, my Lord, to see my open shame?
Now thou do'st Penance too. Looke how they gaze,
See how the giddy multitude doe point,
And nodde their heads, and throw their eyes on thee.
Ah *Gloster*, hide thee from their hatefull lookes,
And in thy Closet pent vp, rue my shame,
And banne thine Enemies, both mine and thine.

Glost. Be patient, gentle *Nell*, forget this griefe.

Elianor. Ah *Gloster*, teach me to forget my selfe:
For whilest I thinke I am thy married Wife,
And thou a Prince, Protector of this Land,
Me thinkes I should not thus be led along,
Mayl'd vp in shame, with Papers on my back,
And follow'd with a Rabble, that reioyce
To see my teares, and heare my deepe-fet groanes.
The ruthlesse Flint doth cut my tender feet,
And when I start, the enuious people laugh,
And bid me be aduised how I treade.
Ah *Humfrey*, can I beare this shamefull yoake?
Trowest thou, that ere Ile looke vpon the World,
Or count them happy, that enioyes the Sunne?
No: Darke shall be my Light, and Night my Day.
To thinke vpon my Pompe, shall be my Hell.
Sometime Ile say, I am Duke *Humfreyes* Wife,
And he a Prince, and Ruler of the Land:
Yet so he rul'd, and such a Prince he was,
As he stood by, whilest I, his forlorne Duchesse,
Was made a wonder, and a pointing stock
To euery idle Rascall follower.
But be thou milde, and blush not at my shame,
Nor stirre at nothing, till the Axe of Death
Hang ouer thee, as sure it shortly will.
For *Suffolke*, he that can doe all in all
With her, that hateth thee and hates vs all,
And *Yorke*, and impious *Beauford*, that false Priest,
Haue all lym'd Bushes to betray thy Wings,
And flye thou how thou canst, they'le tangle thee.
But feare not thou, vntill thy foot be snar'd,
Nor neuer seeke preuention of thy foes.

Glost. Ah *Nell*, forbeare: thou aymest all awry.
I must offend, before I be attainted:
And had I twentie times so many foes,
And each of them had twentie times their power,
All these could not procure me any scathe,
So long as I am loyall, true, and crimelesse.
Would'st haue me rescue thee from this reproach?

Why yet thy scandall were not wipt away,
But I in danger for the breach of Law.
Thy greatest helpe is quiet, gentle *Nell*:
I pray thee sort thy heart to patience,
These few dayes wonder will be quickly worne:

Enter a Herald.

Her. I summon your Grace to his Maiesties Parliament,
Holden at Bury, the first of this next Moneth.

Glost. And my consent ne're ask'd herein before?
This is close dealing. Well, I will be there.
My *Nell*, I take my leaue: and Master Sherife,
Let not her Penance exceede the Kings Commission.

Sh. And't please your Grace, here my Commission stayes:
And Sir *Iohn Stanly* is appointed now,
To take her with him to the Ile of Man.

Glost. Must you, Sir *Iohn*, protect my Lady here?

Stanly. So am I giuen in charge, may't please your Grace.

Glost. Entreat her not the worse, in that I pray
You vse her well: the World may laugh againe,
And I may liue to doe you kindnesse, if you doe it her.
And so Sir *Iohn*, farewell.

Elianor. What, gone my Lord, and bid me not farewell?

Glost. Witnesse my teares, I cannot stay to speake.
Exit Gloster.

Elianor. Art thou gone too? all comfort goe with thee,
For none abides with me: my Ioy, is Death;
Death, at whose Name I oft haue beene afear'd,
Because I wish'd this Worlds eternitie.
Stanley, I prethee goe, and take me hence,
I care not whither, for I begge no fauor;
Onely conuey me where thou art commanded.

Stanley. Why, Madame, that is to the Ile of Man,
There to be vs'd according to your State.

Elianor. That's bad enough, for I am but reproach:
And shall I then be vs'd reproachfully?

Stanley. Like to a Duchesse, and Duke *Humfreyes* Lady,
According to that State you shall be vs'd.

Elianor. Sherife farewell, and better then I fare,
Although thou hast beene Conduct of my shame.

Sherife. It is my Office, and Madame pardon me.

Elianor. I, I, farewell, thy Office is discharg'd:
Come *Stanley*, shall we goe?

Stanley. Madame, your Penance done,
Throw off this Sheet,
And goe we to attyre you for our Iourney.

Elianor. My shame will not be shifted with my Sheet:
No, it will hang vpon my richest Robes,
And shew it selfe, attyre me how I can.
Goe, leade the way, I long to see my Prison. *Exeunt*

Sound a Senet. Enter King, Queene, Cardinall, Suffolke,
Yorke, Buckingham, Salisbury, and Warwicke,
to the Parliament.

King. I muse my Lord of Gloster is not come:
'Tis not his wont to be the hindmost man,
What e're occasion keepes him from vs now.

Queene. Can you not see? or will ye not obserue
The strangenesse of his alter'd Countenance?
With what a Maiestie he beares himselfe,
How insolent of late he is become,
How prowd, how peremptorie, and vnlike himselfe.
We know the time since he was milde and affable,
And if we did but glance a farre-off Looke,
Immediately he was vpon his Knee,
That all the Court admir'd him for submission.
But meet him now, and be it in the Morne,
When euery one will giue the time of day,
He knits his Brow, and shewes an angry Eye,
And passeth by with stiffe vnbowed Knee,
Disdaining dutie that to vs belongs.
Small Curres are not regarded when they grynne,
But great men tremble when the Lyon rores,
And *Humfrey* is no little Man in England.
First note, that he is neere you in discent,
And should you fall, he is the next will mount:
Me seemeth then, it is no Pollicie,
Respecting what a rancorous minde he beares,
And his aduantage following your decease,
That he should come about your Royall Person,
Or be admitted to your Highnesse Councell.
By flatterie hath he wonne the Commons hearts:
And when he please to make Commotion,
'Tis to be fear'd they all will follow him.
Now 'tis the Spring, and Weeds are shallow-rooted,
Suffer them now, and they'le o're-grow the Garden,
And choake the Herbes for want of Husbandry.
The reuerent care I beare vnto my Lord,
Made me collect these dangers in the Duke.
If it be fond, call it a Womans feare:
Which feare, if better Reasons can supplant,
I will subscribe, and say I wrong'd the Duke.
My Lord of Suffolke, Buckingham, and Yorke,
Reproue my allegation, if you can,
Or else conclude my words effectuall.

Suff. Well hath your Highnesse seene into this Duke:
And had I first beene put to speake my minde,
I thinke I should haue told your Graces Tale.
The Duchesse, by his subornation,
Vpon my Life began her diuellish practises:
Or if he were not priuie to those Faults,
Yet by reputing of his high discent,
As next the King, he was successiue Heire,
And such high vaunts of his Nobilitie,
Did instigate the Bedlam braine-sick Duchesse,
By wicked meanes to frame our Soueraignes fall.
Smooth runnes the Water, where the Brooke is deepe,
And in his simple shew he harbours Treason.
The Fox barkes not, when he would steale the Lambe.
No, no, my Soueraigne, *Glouster* is a man
Vnsounded yet, and full of deepe deceit.

Card. Did he not, contrary to forme of Law,
Deuise strange deaths, for small offences done?

Yorke. And did he not, in his Protectorship,
Leuie great summes of Money through the Realme,
For Souldiers pay in France, and neuer sent it?
By meanes whereof, the Townes each day reuolted.

Buck. Tut, these are petty faults to faults vnknowne,
Which time will bring to light in smooth Duke *Humfrey*.

King. My Lords at once: the care you haue of vs,
To mowe downe Thornes that would annoy our Foot,
Is worthy prayse: but shall I speake my conscience,
Our Kinsman *Gloster* is as innocent,
From meaning Treason to our Royall Person,
As is the sucking Lambe, or harmelesse Doue:
The Duke is vertuous, milde, and too well giuen,
To dreame on euill, or to worke my downefall.

Qu. Ah what's more dangerous, then this fond affiance?
Seemes he a Doue? his feathers are but borrow'd,
For hee's disposed as the hatefull Rauen.
Is he a Lambe? his Skinne is surely lent him,

For

The second Part of Henry the Sixt.

For hee's enclin'd as is the rauenous Wolues.
Who cannot steale a shape, that meanes deceit?
Take heed, my Lord, the welfare of vs all,
Hangs on the cutting short that fraudfull man.

Enter Somerset.

Som. All health vnto my gracious Soueraigne.
King. Welcome Lord *Somerset*: What Newes from France?
Som. That all your Interest in those Territories,
Is vtterly bereft you: all is lost.
King. Cold Newes, Lord *Somerset*: but Gods will be done.
Yorke. Cold Newes for me: for I had hope of France,
As firmely as I hope for fertile England.
Thus are my Blossomes blasted in the Bud,
And Caterpillers eate my Leaues away;
But I will remedie this geare ere long,
Or sell my Title for a glorious Graue.

Enter Gloucester.

Glost. All happinesse vnto my Lord the King:
Pardon, my Liege, that I haue stay'd so long.
Suff. Nay *Gloster*, know that thou art come too soone,
Vnlesse thou wert more loyall then thou art:
I doe arrest thee of High Treason here.
Glost. Well *Suffolke*, thou shalt not see me blush,
Nor change my Countenance for this Arrest:
A Heart vnspotted, is not easily daunted.
The purest Spring is not so free from mudde,
As I am cleare from Treason to my Soueraigne.
Who can accuse me? wherein am I guiltie?
Yorke. 'Tis thought, my Lord,
That you tooke Bribes of France,
And being Protector, stay'd the Souldiers pay,
By meanes whereof, his Highnesse hath lost France.
Glost. Is it but thought so?
What are they that thinke it?
I neuer rob'd the Souldiers of their pay,
Nor euer had one penny Bribe from France.
So helpe me God, as I haue watcht the Night,
I, Night by Night, in studying good for England.
That Doyt that ere I wrested from the King,
Or any Groat I hoorded to my vse,
Be brought against me at my Tryall day.
No: many a Pound of mine owne proper store,
Because I would not taxe the needie Commons,
Haue I dis-pursed to the Garrisons,
And neuer ask'd for restitution.
Card. It serues you well, my Lord, to say so much.
Glost. I say no more then truth, so helpe me God.
Yorke. In your Protectorship, you did deuise
Strange Tortures for Offendors, neuer heard of,
That England was defam'd by Tyrannie.
Glost. Why 'tis well known, that whiles I was Protector,
Pittie was all the fault that was in me:
For I should melt at an Offendors teares,
And lowly words were Ransome for their fault:
Vnlesse it were a bloody Murtherer,
Or foule felonious Theefe, that fleec'd poore passengers,
I neuer gaue them condigne punishment.
Murther indeede, that bloodie sinne, I tortur'd
Aboue the Felon, or what Trespas else.
Suff. My Lord, these faults are easie, quickly answer'd:
But mightier Crimes are lay'd vnto your charge,
Whereof you cannot easily purge your selfe.
I doe arrest you in his Highnesse Name,
And here commit you to my Lord Cardinall
To keepe, vntill your further time of Tryall.
King. My Lord of Gloster, 'tis my speciall hope,
That you will cleare your selfe from all suspence,
My Conscience tells me you are innocent.
Glost. Ah gracious Lord, these dayes are dangerous:
Vertue is choakt with foule Ambition,
And Charitie chas'd hence by Rancours hand;
Foule Subornation is predominant,
And Equitie exil'd your Highnesse Land.
I know, their Complot is to haue my Life:
And if my death might make this Iland happy,
And proue the Period of their Tyrannie,
I would expend it with all willingnesse.
But mine is made the Prologue to their Play:
For thousands more, that yet suspect no perill,
Will not conclude their plotted Tragedie.
Beaufords red sparkling eyes blab his hearts mallice,
And *Suffolks* cloudie Brow his stormie hate;
Sharpe *Buckingham* vnburthens with his tongue,
The enuious Load that lyes vpon his heart:
And dogged *Yorke*, that reaches at the Moone,
Whose ouer-weening Arme I haue pluckt back,
By false accuse doth leuell at my Life.
And you, my Soueraigne Lady, with the rest,
Causelesse haue lay'd disgraces on my head,
And with your best endeuour haue stirr'd vp
My liefest Liege to be mine Enemie:
I, all of you haue lay'd your heads together,
My selfe had notice of your Conuenticles,
And all to make away my guiltlesse Life.
I shall not want false Witnesse, to condemne me,
Nor store of Treasons, to augment my guilt:
The ancient Prouerbe will be well effected,
A Staffe is quickly found to beat a Dogge.
Card. My Liege, his rayling is intollerable.
If those that care to keepe your Royall Person
From Treasons secret Knife, and Traytors Rage,
Be thus vpbrayded, chid, and rated at,
And the Offendor graunted scope of speech,
'Twill make them coole in zeale vnto your Grace.
Suff. Hath he not twit our Soueraigne Lady here
With ignominious words, though Clarkely coucht?
As if she had suborned some to sweare
False allegations, to o'rethrow his state.
Qu. But I can giue the loser leaue to chide.
Glost. Farre truer spoke then meant: I lose indeede,
Beshrew the winners, for they play'd me false,
And well such losers may haue leaue to speake.
Buck. Hee'le wrest the sence, and hold vs here all day.
Lord Cardinall, he is your Prisoner.
Card. Sirs, take away the Duke, and guard him sure.
Glost. Ah, thus King *Henry* throwes away his Crutch,
Before his Legges be firme to beare his Body.
Thus is the Shepheard beaten from thy side,
And Wolues are gnarling, who shall gnaw thee first.
Ah that my feare were false, ah that it were;
For good King *Henry*, thy decay I feare. *Exit Gloster.*
King. My Lords, what to your wisdomes seemeth best,
Doe, or vndoe, as if our selfe were here.
Queene. What, will your Highnesse leaue the Parliament?
King. I *Margaret*: my heart is drown'd with griefe,
Whose floud begins to flowe within mine eyes;
My Body round engyrt with miserie:

For what's more miserable then Discontent?
Ah Vnckle *Humfrey*, in thy face I see
The Map of Honor, Truth, and Loyaltie:
And yet, good *Humfrey*, is the houre to come,
That ere I prou'd thee false, or fear'd thy faith.
What lowring Starre now enuies thy estate?
That these great Lords, and *Margaret* our Queene,
Doe seeke subuersion of thy harmelesse Life.
Thou neuer didst them wrong, nor no man wrong:
And as the Butcher takes away the Calfe,
And binds the Wretch, and beats it when it strayes,
Bearing it to the bloody Slaughter-house;
Euen so remorselesse haue they borne him hence:
And as the Damme runnes lowing vp and downe,
Looking the way her harmelesse young one went,
And can doe naught but wayle her Darlings losse;
Euen so my selfe bewayles good *Glosters* case
With sad vnhelpefull teares, and with dimn'd eyes;
Looke after him, and cannot doe him good:
So mightie are his vowed Enemies.
His fortunes I will weepe, and 'twixt each groane,
Say, who's a Traytor? *Gloster* he is none. *Exit.*

Queene. Free Lords:
Cold Snow melts with the Sunnes hot Beames:
Henry, my Lord, is cold in great Affaires,
Too full of foolish pittie: and *Glosters* shew
Beguiles him, as the mournefull Crocodile
With sorrow snares relenting passengers;
Or as the Snake, roll'd in a flowring Banke,
With shining checker'd slough doth sting a Child,
That for the beautie thinkes it excellent.
Beleeue me Lords, were none more wise then I,
And yet herein I iudge mine owne Wit good;
This *Gloster* should be quickly rid the World,
To rid vs from the feare we haue of him.

Card. That he should dye, is worthie pollicie,
But yet we want a Colour for his death:
'Tis meet he be condemn'd by course of Law.

Suff. But in my minde, that were no pollicie:
The King will labour still to saue his Life,
The Commons haply rise, to saue his Life;
And yet we haue but triuiall argument,
More then mistrust, that shewes him worthy death.

Yorke. So that by this, you would not haue him dye.

Suff. Ah *Yorke*, no man aliue, so faine as I.

Yorke. 'Tis *Yorke* that hath more reason for his death.
But my Lord Cardinall, and you my Lord of Suffolke,
Say as you thinke, and speake it from your Soules:
Wer't not all one, an emptie Eagle were set,
To guard the Chicken from a hungry Kyte,
As place Duke *Humfrey* for the Kings Protector?

Queene. So the poore Chicken should be sure of death.

Suff. Madame 'tis true: and wer't not madnesse then,
To make the Fox suruey or of the Fold?
Who being accus'd a craftie Murtherer,
His guilt should be but idly posted ouer,
Because his purpose is not executed.
No: let him dye, in that he is a Fox,
By nature prou'd an Enemie to the Flock,
Before his Chaps be stayn'd with Crimson blood,
As *Humfrey* prou'd by Reasons to my Liege.
And doe not stand on Quillets how to slay him:
Be it by Gynnes, by Snares, by Subtletie,
Sleeping, or Waking, 'tis no matter how,
So he be dead; for that is good deceit,
Which mates him first, that first intends deceit.

Queene. Thrice Noble *Suffolke*, 'tis resolutely spoke.

Suff. Not resolute, except so much were done,
For things are often spoke, and seldome meant,
But that my heart accordeth with my tongue,
Seeing the deed is meritorious,
And to preserue my Soueraigne from his Foe,
Say but the word, and I will be his Priest.

Card. But I would haue him dead, my Lord of Suffolke,
Ere you can take due Orders for a Priest:
Say you consent, and censure well the deed,
And Ile prouide his Executioner,
I tender so the safetie of my Liege.

Suff. Here is my Hand, the deed is worthy doing.

Queene. And so say I.

Yorke. And I: and now we three haue spoke it,
It skills not greatly who impugnes our doome.

Enter a Poste.

Post. Great Lords, from Ireland am I come amaine,
To signifie, that Rebels there are vp,
And put the Englishmen vnto the Sword.
Send Succours (Lords) and stop the Rage betime,
Before the Wound doe grow vncurable;
For being greene, there is great hope of helpe.

Card. A Breach that craues a quick expedient stoppe.
What counsaile giue you in this weightie cause?

Yorke. That *Somerset* be sent as Regent thither:
'Tis meet that luckie Ruler be imploy'd,
Witnesse the fortune he hath had in France.

Som. If *Yorke*, with all his farre-fet pollicie,
Had beene the Regent there, in stead of me,
He neuer would haue stay'd in France so long.

Yorke. No, not to lose it all, as thou hast done.
I rather would haue lost my Life betimes,
Then bring a burthen of dis-honour home,
By staying there so long, till all were lost.
Shew me one skarre, character'd on thy Skinne,
Mens flesh preseru'd so whole, doe seldome winne.

Qu. Nay then, this sparke will proue a raging fire,
If Wind and Fuell be brought, to feed it with:
No more, good *Yorke*; sweet *Somerset* be still.
Thy fortune, *Yorke*, hadst thou beene Regent there,
Might happily haue prou'd farre worse then his.

Yorke. What, worse then naught? nay, then a shame take all.

Somerset. And in the number, thee, that wishest shame.

Card. My Lord of *Yorke*, trie what your fortune is:
Th' vnciuill Kernes of Ireland are in Armes,
And temper Clay with blood of Englishmen.
To Ireland will you leade a Band of men,
Collected choycely, from each Countie some,
And trie your hap against the Irishmen?

Yorke. I will, my Lord, so please his Maiestie.

Suff. Why, our Authoritie is his consent,
And what we doe establish, he confirmes:
Then, Noble *Yorke*, take thou this Taske in hand.

Yorke. I am content: Prouide me Souldiers, Lords,
Whiles I take order for mine owne affaires.

Suff. A charge, Lord *Yorke*, that I will see perform'd.
But now returne we to the false Duke *Humfrey*.

Card. No more of him: for I will deale with him,
That henceforth he shall trouble vs no more:
And so breake off, the day is almost spent,
Lord *Suffolke*, you and I must talke of that euent.

Yorke. My

Yorke. My Lord of Suffolke, within foureteene dayes
At Bristow I expect my Souldiers,
For there Ile shippe them all for Ireland.
Suff. Ile see it truly done, my Lord of Yorke. *Exeunt.*
Manet Yorke.

Yorke. Now *Yorke*, or neuer, steele thy fearfull thoughts,
And change misdoubt to resolution;
Be that thou hop'st to be, or what thou art;
Resigne to death, it is not worth th'enioying:
Let pale-fac't feare keepe with the meane-borne man,
And finde no harbor in a Royall heart.
Faster then Spring-time showres, comes thoght on thoght,
And not a thought, but thinkes on Dignitie.
My Brayne, more busie then the laboring Spider,
Weaues tedious Snares to trap mine Enemies.
Well Nobles, well: 'tis politikely done,
To send me packing with an Hoast of men:
I feare me, you but warme the starued Snake,
Who cherisht in your breasts, will sting your hearts.
'Twas men I lackt, and you will giue them me;
I take it kindly: yet be well assur'd,
You put sharpe Weapons in a mad-mans hands.
Whiles I in Ireland nourish a mightie Band,
I will stirre vp in England some black Storme,
Shall blowe ten thousand Soules to Heauen, or Hell:
And this fell Tempest shall not cease to rage,
Vntill the Golden Circuit on my Head,
Like to the glorious Sunnes transparant Beames,
Doe calme the furie of this mad-bred Flawe.
And for a minister of my intent,
I haue seduc'd a head-strong Kentishman,
Iohn Cade of Ashford,
To make Commotion, as full well he can,
Vnder the Title of *Iohn Mortimer*.
In Ireland haue I seene this stubborne *Cade*
Oppose himselfe against a Troupe of Kernes,
And fought so long, till that his thighes with Darts
Were almost like a sharpe-quill'd Porpentine:
And in the end being rescued, I haue seene
Him capre vpright, like a wilde Morisco,
Shaking the bloody Darts, as he his Bells.
Full often, like a shag-hayr'd craftie Kerne,
Hath he conuersed with the Enemie,
And vndiscouer'd, come to me againe,
And giuen me notice of their Villanies.
This Deuill here shall be my substitute;
For that *Iohn Mortimer*, which now is dead,
In face, in gate, in speech he doth resemble.
By this, I shall perceiue the Commons minde,
How they affect the House and Clayme of *Yorke*.
Say he be taken, rackt, and tortured;
I know, no paine they can inflict vpon him,
Will make him say, I mou'd him to those Armes.
Say that he thriue, as 'tis great like he will,
Why then from Ireland come I with my strength,
And reape the Haruest which that Rascall sow'd.
For *Humfrey*; being dead, as he shall be,
And *Henry* put apart: the next for me. *Exit.*

*Enter two or three running ouer the Stage, from the
Murther of Duke Humfrey.*

1. Runne to my Lord of Suffolke: let him know
We haue dispatcht the Duke, as he commanded.
2. Oh, that it were to doe: what haue we done?
Didst euer heare a man so penitent? *Enter Suffolke.*
1. Here comes my Lord.

Suff. Now Sirs, haue you dispatcht this thing?
1. I, my good Lord, hee's dead.
Suff. Why that's well said. Goe, get you to my House,
I will reward you for this venturous deed:
The King and all the Peeres are here at hand.
Haue you layd faire the Bed? Is all things well,
According as I gaue directions?
1. 'Tis, my good Lord.
Suff. Away, be gone. *Exeunt.*

*Sound Trumpets. Enter the King, the Queene,
Cardinall, Suffolke, Somerset, with
Attendants.*

King. Goe call our Vnckle to our presence straight:
Say, we intend to try his Grace to day,
If he be guiltie, as 'tis published.
Suff. Ile call him presently, my Noble Lord. *Exit.*
King. Lords take your places: and I pray you all
Proceed no straiter 'gainst our Vnckle *Gloster*,
Then from true euidence, of good esteeme,
He be approu'd in practise culpable.
Queene. God forbid any Malice should preuayle,
That faultlesse may condemne a Noble man:
Pray God he may acquit him of suspition.
King. I thanke thee *Nell*, these wordes content mee
much.

Enter Suffolke.

How now? why look'st thou paie? why tremblest thou?
Where is our Vnckle? what's the matter, *Suffolke*?
Suff. Dead in his Bed, my Lord: *Gloster* is dead.
Queene. Marry God forfend.
Card. Gods secret Iudgement: I did dreame to Night,
The Duke was dumbe, and could not speake a word.
King sounds.
Qu. How fares my Lord? Helpe Lords, the King is
dead.
Som. Rere vp his Body, wring him by the Nose.
Qu. Runne, goe, helpe, helpe: Oh *Henry* ope thine eyes.
Suff. He doth reuiue againe, Madame be patient.
King. Oh Heauenly God.
Qu. How fares my gracious Lord?
Suff. Comfort my Soueraigne, gracious *Henry* comfort.
King. What, doth my Lord of Suffolke comfort me?
Came he right now to sing a Rauens Note,
Whose dismall tune bereft my Vitall powres:
And thinkes he, that the chirping of a Wren,
By crying comfort from a hollow breast,
Can chase away the first-conceiued sound?
Hide not thy poyson with such sugred words,
Lay not thy hands on me: forbeare I say,
Their touch affrights me as a Serpents sting.
Thou balefull Messenger, out of my sight:
Vpon thy eye-balls, murderous Tyrannie
Sits in grim Maiestie, to fright the World.
Looke not vpon me, for thine eyes are wounding;
Yet doe not goe away: come Basiliske,
And kill the innocent gazer with thy sight:
For in the shade of death, I shall finde ioy;
In life, but double death, now *Gloster's* dead.
Queene. Why do you rate my Lord of Suffolke thus?
Although the Duke was enemie to him,
Yet he most Christian-like laments his death:
And for my selfe, Foe as he was to me,
Might liquid teares, or heart-offending groanes,
Or blood-consuming sighes recall his Life;

I would be blinde with weeping, sicke with grones,
Looke pale as Prim-rose with blood-drinking sighes,
And all to haue the Noble Duke aliue.
What know I how the world may deeme of me?
For it is knowne we were but hollow Friends:
It may be iudg'd I made the Duke away,
So shall my name with Slanders tongue be wounded,
And Princes Courts be fill'd with my reproach:
This get I by his death: Aye me vnhappie,
To be a Queene, and Crown'd with infamie.

   King. Ah woe is me for Gloster, wretched man.
   Queen. Be woe for me, more wretched then he is.
What, Dost thou turne away, and hide thy face?
I am no loathsome Leaper, looke on me.
What? Art thou like the Adder waxen deafe?
Be poysonous too, and kill thy forlorne Queene.
Is all thy comfort shut in Glosters Tombe?
Why then Dame *Elianor* was neere thy ioy.
Erect his Statue, and worship it,
And make my Image but an Ale-house signe.
Was I for this nye wrack'd vpon the Sea,
And twice by aukward winde from Englands banke
Droue backe againe vnto my Natiue Clime.
What boaded this? but well fore-warning winde
Did seeme to say, seeke not a Scorpions Nest,
Nor set no footing on this vnkinde Shore.
What did I then? But curst the gentle gusts,
And he that loos'd them forth their Brazen Caues,
And bid them blow towards Englands blessed shore,
Or turne our Sterne vpon a dreadfull Rocke:
Yet Æolus would not be a murtherer,
But left that hatefull office vnto thee.
The pretty vaulting Sea refus'd to drowne me,
Knowing that thou wouldst haue me drown'd on shore
With teares as salt as Sea, through thy vnkindnesse.
The splitting Rockes cowr'd in the sinking sands,
And would not dash me with their ragged sides,
Because thy flinty heart more hard then they,
Might in thy Pallace, perish *Elianor.*
As farre as I could ken thy Chalky Cliffes,
When from thy Shore, the Tempest beate vs backe,
I stood vpon the Hatches in the storme:
And when the duskie sky, began to rob
My earnest-gaping-sight of thy Lands view,
I tooke a costly Iewell from my necke,
A Hart it was bound in with Diamonds,
And threw it towards thy Land: The Sea receiu'd it,
And so I wish'd thy body might my Heart:
And euen with this, I lost faire Englands view,
And bid mine eyes be packing with my Heart,
And call'd them blinde and duskie Spectacles,
For loosing ken of *Albions* wished Coast.
How often haue I tempted Suffolkes tongue
(The agent of thy foule inconstancie)
To sit and watch me as *Ascanius* did,
When he to madding *Dido* would vnfold
His Fathers Acts, commenc'd in burning Troy.
Am I not witcht like her? Or thou not false like him?
Aye me, I can no more: Dye *Elinor,*
For *Henry* weepes, that thou dost liue so long.

   Noyse within. Enter Warwicke, and many Commons.

   War. It is reported, mighty Soueraigne,
That good Duke *Humfrey* Traiterously is murdred

By Suffolke, and the Cardinall *Beaufords* meanes:
The Commons like an angry Hiue of Bees
That want their Leader, scatter vp and downe,
And care not who they sting in his reuenge.
My selfe haue calm'd their spleenfull mutinie,
Vntill they heare the order of his death.

   King. That he is dead good Warwick, 'tis too true,
But how he dyed, God knowes, not *Henry:*
Enter his Chamber, view his breathlesse Corpes,
And comment then vpon his sodaine death.

   War. That shall I do my Liege; Stay Salsburie
With the rude multitude, till I returne.

   King. O thou that iudgest all things, stay my thoghts:
My thoughts, that labour to perswade my soule,
Some violent hands were laid on *Humfries* life:
If my suspect be false, forgiue me God,
For iudgement onely doth belong to thee:
Faine would I go to chafe his palie lips,
With twenty thousand kisses, and to draine
Vpon his face an Ocean of salt teares,
To tell my loue vnto his dumbe deafe trunke,
And with my fingers feele his hand, vnfeeling:
But all in vaine are these meane Obsequies,

   Bed put forth.
And to suruey his dead and earthy Image:
What were it but to make my sorrow greater?

   Warw. Come hither gracious Soueraigne, view this body.
   King. That is to see how deepe my graue is made;
For with his soule fled all my worldly solace:
For seeing him, I see my life in death.

   War. As surely as my soule intends to liue
With that dread King that tooke our state vpon him,
To free vs from his Fathers wrathfull curse,
I do beleeue that violent hands were laid
Vpon the life of this thrice-famed Duke.

   Suf. A dreadfull Oath, sworne with a solemn tongue:
What instance giues Lord Warwicke for his vow.

   War. See how the blood is setled in his face.
Oft haue I seene a timely-parted Ghost,
Of ashy semblance, meager, pale, and bloodlesse,
Being all descended to the labouring heart,
Who in the Conflict that it holds with death,
Attracts the same for aydance 'gainst the enemy,
Which with the heart there cooles, and ne're returneth,
To blush and beautifie the Cheeke againe.
But see, his face is blacke, and full of blood:
His eye-balles further out, than when he liued,
Staring full gastly, like a strangled man:
His hayre vprear'd, his nostrils stretcht with strugling:
His hands abroad display'd, as one that graspt
And tugg'd for Life, and was by strength subdude.
Looke on the sheets his haire (you see) is sticking,
His well proportion'd Beard, made ruffe and rugged,
Like to the Summers Corne by Tempest lodged:
It cannot be but he was murdred heere,
The least of all these signes were probable.

   Suf. Why Warwicke, who should do the D. to death?
My selfe and *Beauford* had him in protection,
And we I hope sir, are no murtherers.

   War. But both of you were vowed D. Humfries foes,
And you (forsooth) had the good Duke to keepe:
Tis like you would not feast him like a friend,
And 'tis well seene, he found an enemy.

   Queen. Than you belike suspect these Noblemen,
As guilty of Duke *Humfries* timelesse death.

War.

Warw. Who finds the Heyfer dead, and bleeding fresh,
And sees fast-by, a Butcher with an Axe,
But will suspect, 'twas he that made the slaughter?
Who finds the Partridge in the Puttocks Nest,
But may imagine how the Bird was dead,
Although the Kyte soare with vnbloudied Beake?
Euen so suspitious is this Tragedie.

Qu. Are you the Butcher, *Suffolke*? where's your Knife?
Is *Beauford* tearm'd a Kyte? where are his Tallons?

Suff. I weare no Knife, to slaughter sleeping men,
But here's a vengefull Sword, rusted with ease,
That shall be scowred in his rancorous heart,
That slanders me with Murthers Crimson Badge.
Say, if thou dar'st, prowd Lord of Warwickshire,
That I am faultie in Duke *Humfreyes* death.

Warw. What dares not *Warwick*, if false *Suffolke* dare him?

Qu. He dares not calme his contumelious Spirit,
Nor cease to be an arrogant Controller,
Though *Suffolke* dare him twentie thousand times.

Warw. Madame be still: with reuerence may I say,
For euery word you speake in his behalfe,
Is slander to your Royall Dignitie.

Suff. Blunt-witted Lord, ignoble in demeanor,
If euer Lady wrong'd her Lord so much,
Thy Mother tooke into her blamefull Bed
Some sterne vntutur'd Churle; and Noble Stock
Was graft with Crab-tree slippe, whose Fruit thou art,
And neuer of the *Neuils* Noble Race.

Warw. But that the guilt of Murther bucklers thee,
And I should rob the Deaths-man of his Fee,
Quitting thee thereby of ten thousand shames,
And that my Soueraignes presence makes me milde,
I would, false murd'rous Coward, on thy Knee
Make thee begge pardon for thy passed speech,
And say, it was thy Mother that thou meant'st,
That thou thy selfe wast borne in Bastardie;
And after all this fearefull Homage done,
Giue thee thy hyre, and send thy Soule to Hell,
Pernicious blood-sucker of sleeping men.

Suff. Thou shalt be waking, while I shed thy blood,
If from this presence thou dar'st goe with me.

Warw. Away euen now, or I will drag thee hence:
Vnworthy though thou art, Ile cope with thee,
And doe some seruice to Duke *Humfreyes* Ghost.

Exeunt.

King. What stronger Brest-plate then a heart vntainted?
Thrice is he arm'd, that hath his Quarrell iust;
And he but naked, though lockt vp in Steele,
Whose Conscience with Iniustice is corrupted.

A noyse within.

Queene. What noyse is this?

*Enter Suffolke and Warwicke, with their
Weapons drawne.*

King. Why how now Lords?
Your wrathfull Weapons drawne,
Here in our presence? Dare you be so bold?
Why what tumultuous clamor haue we here?

Suff. The trayt'rous *Warwick*, with the men of Bury,
Set all vpon me, mightie Soueraigne.

Enter Salisbury.

Salisb. Sirs stand apart, the King shall know your minde.

Dread Lord, the Commons send you word by me,
Vnlesse Lord *Suffolke* straight be done to death,
Or banished faire Englands Territories,
They will by violence teare him from your Pallace,
And torture him with grieuous lingring death.
They say, by him the good Duke *Humfrey* dy'de:
They say, in him they feare your Highnesse death;
And meere instinct of Loue and Loyaltie,
Free from a stubborne opposite intent,
As being thought to contradict your liking,
Makes them thus forward in his Banishment.
They say, in care of your most Royall Person,
That if your Highnesse should intend to sleepe,
And charge, that no man should disturbe your rest,
In paine of your dislike, or paine of death;
Yet notwithstanding such a strait Edict,
Were there a Serpent seene, with forked Tongue,
That slyly glyded towards your Maiestie,
It were but necessarie you were wak't:
Least being suffer'd in that harmefull slumber,
The mortall Worme might make the sleepe eternall.
And therefore doe they cry, though you forbid,
That they will guard you, where you will, or no,
From such fell Serpents as false *Suffolke* is;
With whose inuenomed and fatall sting,
Your louing Vnckle, twentie times his worth,
They say is shamefully bereft of life.

Commons within. An answer from the King, my Lord of Salisbury.

Suff. 'Tis like the Commons, rude vnpolisht Hindes,
Could send such Message to their Soueraigne:
But you, my Lord, were glad to be imploy'd,
To shew how queint an Orator you are.
But all the Honor *Salisbury* hath wonne,
Is, that he was the Lord Embassador,
Sent from a sort of Tinkers to the King.

Within. An answer from the King, or wee will all breake in.

King. Goe *Salisbury*, and tell them all from me,
I thanke them for their tender louing care;
And had I not beene cited so by them,
Yet did I purpose as they doe entreat:
For sure, my thoughts doe hourely prophecie,
Mischance vnto my State by *Suffolkes* meanes.
And therefore by his Maiestie I sweare,
Whose farre-vnworthie Deputie I am,
He shall not breathe infection in this ayre,
But three dayes longer, on the paine of death.

Qu. Oh *Henry*, let me pleade for gentle *Suffolke*.

King. Vngentle Queene, to call him gentle *Suffolke*.
No more I say: if thou do'st pleade for him,
Thou wilt but adde encrease vnto my Wrath.
Had I but sayd, I would haue kept my Word;
But when I sweare, it is irreuocable:
If after three dayes space thou here bee'st found,
On any ground that I am Ruler of,
The World shall not be Ransome for thy Life.
Come *Warwicke*, come good *Warwicke*, goe with mee,
I haue great matters to impart to thee. *Exit.*

Qu. Mischance and Sorrow goe along with you,
Hearts Discontent, and sowre Affliction,
Be play-fellowes to keepe you companie:
There's two of you, the Deuill make a third,
And three-fold Vengeance tend vpon your steps.

Suff. Cease, gentle Queene, these Execrations,
And let thy *Suffolke* take his heauie leaue.

Queene. Fye

Queen. Fye Coward woman, and soft harted wretch,
Hast thou not spirit to curse thine enemy.

Suf. A plague vpon them: wherefore should I curse them?
Would curses kill, as doth the Mandrakes grone,
I would inuent as bitter searching termes,
As curst, as harsh, and horrible to heare,
Deliuer'd strongly through my fixed teeth,
With full as many signes of deadly hate,
As leane-fac'd enuy in her loathsome caue.
My tongue should stumble in mine earnest words,
Mine eyes should sparkle like the beaten Flins,
Mine haire be fixt an end, as one distract:
I, euery ioynt should seeme to curse and ban,
And euen now my burthen'd heart would breake
Should I not curse them. Poyson be their drinke.
Gall, worse then Gall, the daintiest that they taste:
Their sweetest shade, a groue of Cypresse Trees:
Their cheefest Prospect, murd'ring Basiliskes:
Their softest Touch, as smart as Lyzards stings:
Their Musicke, frightfull as the Serpents hisse,
And boading Screech-Owles, make the Consort full.
All the foule terrors in darke seated hell——

Q. Enough sweet Suffolke, thou torment'st thy selfe,
And these dread curses like the Sunne 'gainst glasse,
Or like an ouer-charged Gun, recoile,
And turnes the force of them vpon thy selfe.

Suf. You bad me ban, and will you bid me leaue?
Now by the ground that I am banish'd from,
Well could I curse away a Winters night,
Though standing naked on a Mountaine top,
Where byting cold would neuer let grasse grow,
And thinke it but a minute spent in sport.

Qu. Oh, let me intreat thee cease, giue me thy hand,
That I may dew it with my mournfull teares:
Nor let the raine of heauen wet this place,
To wash away my wofull Monuments.
Oh, could this kisse be printed in thy hand,
That thou might'st thinke vpon these by the Seale,
Through whom a thousand sighes are breath'd for thee.
So get thee gone, that I may know my greefe,
'Tis but surmiz'd, whiles thou art standing by,
As one that surfets, thinking on a want:
I will repeale thee, or be well assur'd,
Aduenture to be banished my selfe:
And banished I am, if but from thee.
Go, speake not to me; euen now be gone.
Oh go not yet. Euen thus, two Friends condemn'd,
Embrace, and kisse, and take ten thousand leaues,
Loather a hundred times to part then dye;
Yet now farewell, and farewell Life with thee.

Suf. Thus is poore Suffolke ten times banished,
Once by the King, and three times thrice by thee.
'Tis not the Land I care for, wer't thou thence,
A Wildernesse is populous enough,
So Suffolke had thy heauenly company:
For where thou art, there is the World it selfe,
With euery seuerall pleasure in the World:
And where thou art not, Desolation.
I can no more: Liue thou to ioy thy life;
My selfe no ioy in nought, but that thou liu'st.

Enter Vaux.

Queene. Whether goes *Vaux* so fast? What newes I prethee?

Vaux. To signifie vnto his Maiesty,
That Cardinall *Beauford* is at point of death:
For sodainly a greeuous sicknesse tooke him,
That makes him gaspe, and stare, and catch the aire,
Blaspheming God, and cursing men on earth.
Sometime he talkes, as if Duke *Humfries* Ghost
Were by his side: Sometime, he calles the King,
And whispers to his pillow, as to him,
The secrets of his ouer-charged soule,
And I am sent to tell his Maiestie,
That euen now he cries alowd for him.

Qu. Go tell this heauy Message to the King. *Exit*
Aye me! What is this World? What newes are these?
But wherefore greeue I at an houres poore losse,
Omitting Suffolkes exile, my soules Treasure?
Why onely Suffolke mourne I not for thee?
And with the Southerne clouds, contend in teares?
Theirs for the earths encrease, mine for my sorrowes.
Now get thee hence, the King thou know'st is comming,
If thou be found by me, thou art but dead.

Suf. If I depart from thee, I cannot liue,
And in thy sight to dye, what were it else,
But like a pleasant slumber in thy lap?
Heere could I breath my soule into the ayre,
As milde and gentle as the Cradle-babe,
Dying with mothers dugge betweene it's lips.
Where from thy sight, I should be raging mad,
And cry out for thee to close vp mine eyes:
To haue thee with thy lippes to stop my mouth:
So should'st thou eyther turne my flying soule,
Or I should breathe it so into thy body,
And then it liu'd in sweete Elizium.
To dye by thee, were but to dye in iest,
From thee to dye, were torture more then death:
Oh let me stay, befall what may befall.

Queen. Away: Though parting be a fretfull corosiue,
It is applyed to a deathfull wound.
To France sweet Suffolke: Let me heare from thee:
For wheresoere thou art in this worlds Globe,
Ile haue an *Iris* that shall finde thee out.

Suf. I go.

Qu. And take my heart with thee.

Suf. A Iewell lockt into the wofulst Caske,
That euer did containe a thing of worth,
Euen as a splitted Barke, so sunder we:
This way fall I to death.

Qu. This way for me. *Exeunt*

Enter the King, Salisbury, and Warwicke, to the Cardinal in bed.

King. How fare's my Lord? Speake *Beauford* to thy Soueraigne.

Ca. If thou beest death, Ile giue thee Englands Treasure,
Enough to purchase such another Island,
So thou wilt let me liue, and feele no paine.

King. Ah, what a signe it is of euill life,
Where death's approach is seene so terrible.

War. *Beauford*, it is thy Soueraigne speakes to thee.

Beau. Bring me vnto my Triall when you will.
Dy'de he not in his bed? Where should he dye?
Can I make men liue where they will or no?
Oh torture me no more, I will confesse.
Aliue againe? Then shew me where he is,
Ile giue a thousand pound to looke vpon him.
He hath no eyes, the dust hath blinded them.

Combe downe his haire; looke, looke, it stands vpright,
Like Lime-twigs set to catch my winged soule:
Giue me some drinke, and bid the Apothecarie
Bring the strong poyson that I bought of him.

King. Oh thou eternall mouer of the heauens,
Looke with a gentle eye vpon this Wretch,
Oh beate away the busie medling Fiend,
That layes strong siege vnto this wretches soule,
And from his bosome purge this blacke dispaire.

War. See how the pangs of death do make him grin.

Sal. Disturbe him not, let him passe peaceably.

King. Peace to his soule, if Gods good pleasure be.
Lord Card'nall, if thou think'st on heauens blisse,
Hold vp thy hand, make signall of thy hope.
He dies and makes no signe: Oh God forgiue him.

War. So bad a death, argues a monstrous life.

King. Forbeare to iudge, for we are sinners all.
Close vp his eyes, and draw the Curtaine close,
And let vs all to Meditation. *Exeunt.*

Alarum. Fight at Sea. Ordnance goes off.

Enter Lieutenant, Suffolke, and others.

Lieu. The gaudy blabbing and remorsefull day,
Is crept into the bosome of the Sea:
And now loud houling Wolues arouse the Iades
That dragge the Tragicke melancholy night:
Who with their drowsie, slow, and flagging wings
Cleape dead-mens graues, and from their misty Iawes,
Breath foule contagious darknesse in the ayre:
Therefore bring forth the Souldiers of our prize,
For whilst our Pinnace Anchors in the Downes,
Heere shall they make their ransome on the sand,
Or with their blood staine this discoloured shore.
Maister, this Prisoner freely giue I thee,
And thou that art his Mate, make boote of this:
The other *Walter Whitmore* is thy share.

1. Gent. What is my ransome Master, let me know.

Ma. A thousand Crownes, or else lay down your head.

Mate. And so much shall you giue, or off goes yours.

Lieu. What thinke you much to pay 2000. Crownes,
And beare the name and port of Gentlemen?
Cut both the Villaines throats, for dy you shall:
The liues of those which we haue lost in fight,
Be counter-poys'd with such a pettie summe.

1. Gent. Ile giue it sir, and therefore spare my life.

2. Gent. And so will I, and write home for it straight.

Whitm. I lost mine eye in laying the prize aboord,
And therefore to reuenge it, shalt thou dye,
And so should these, if I might haue my will.

Lieu. Be not so rash, take ransome, let him liue.

Suf. Looke on my George, I am a Gentleman,
Rate me at what thou wilt, thou shalt be payed.

Whit. And so am I: my name is *Walter Whitmore.*
How now? why starts thou? What doth death affright?

Suf. Thy name affrights me, in whose sound is death:
A cunning man did calculate my birth,
And told me that by Water I should dye:
Yet let not this make thee be bloody-minded,
Thy name is *Gualtier*, being rightly sounded.

Whit. *Gualtier* or *Walter*, which it is I care not,
Neuer yet did base dishonour blurre our name,
But with our sword we wip'd away the blot.
Therefore, when Merchant-like I sell reuenge,
Broke be my sword, my Armes torne and defac'd,
And I proclaim'd a Coward through the world.

Suf. Stay *Whitmore*, for thy Prisoner is a Prince,
The Duke of Suffolke, *William de la Pole.*

Whit. The Duke of Suffolke, muffled vp in ragges?

Suf. I, but these ragges are no part of the Duke.

Lieu. But Ioue was neuer slaine as thou shalt be,
Obscure and lowsie Swaine, King *Henries* blood.

Suf. The honourable blood of Lancaster
Must not be shed by such a iaded Groome:
Hast thou not kist thy hand, and held my stirrop?
Bare-headed plodded by my foot-cloth Mule,
And thought thee happy when I shooke my head.
How often hast thou waited at my cup,
Fed from my Trencher, kneel'd downe at the boord,
When I haue feasted with Queene *Margaret*?
Remember it, and let it make thee Crest-falne,
I, and alay this thy abortiue Pride:
How in our voyding Lobby hast thou stood,
And duly wayted for my comming forth?
This hand of mine hath writ in thy behalfe,
And therefore shall it charme thy riotous tongue.

Whit. Speak Captaine, shall I stab the forlorn Swain.

Lieu. First let my words stab him, as he hath me.

Suf. Base slaue, thy words are blunt, and so art thou.

Lieu. Conuey him hence, and on our long boats side,
Strike off his head.   *Suf.* Thou dar'st not for thy owne.

Lieu. *Poole*, Sir *Poole*? Lord,
I kennell, puddle, sinke, whose filth and dirt
Troubles the siluer Spring, where England drinkes:
Now will I dam vp this thy yawning mouth,
For swallowing the Treasure of the Realme.
Thy lips that kist the Queene, shall sweepe the ground:
And thou that smil'dst at good Duke *Humfries* death,
Against the senselesse windes shall grin in vaine,
Who in contempt shall hisse at thee againe.
And wedded be thou to the Hagges of hell,
For daring to affye a mighty Lord
Vnto the daughter of a worthlesse King,
Hauing neyther Subiect, Wealth, nor Diadem:
By diuellish policy art thou growne great,
And like ambitious Sylla ouer-gorg'd,
With gobbets of thy Mother-bleeding heart.
By thee *Aniou* and *Maine* were sold to France.
The false reuolting Normans thorough thee,
Disdaine to call vs Lord, and *Piccardie*
Hath slaine their Gouernors, surpriz'd our Forts,
And sent the ragged Souldiers wounded home.
The Princely Warwicke, and the *Neuils* all,
Whose dreadfull swords were neuer drawne in vaine,
As hating thee, and rising vp in armes.
And now the House of Yorke thrust from the Crowne,
By shamefull murther of a guiltlesse King,
And lofty proud incroaching tyranny,
Burnes with reuenging fire, whose hopefull colours
Aduance our halfe-fac'd Sunne, striuing to shine;
Vnder the which is writ, *Innitis nubibus.*
The Commons heere in Kent are vp in armes,
And to conclude, Reproach and Beggerie,
Is crept into the Pallace of our King,
And all by thee: away, conuey him hence.

Suf. O that I were a God, to shoot forth Thunder
Vpon these paltry, seruile, abiect Drudges:
Small things make base men proud. This Villaine heere,
Being Captaine of a Pinnace, threatens more
Then *Bargulus* the strong Illyrian Pyrate.
Drones sucke not Eagles blood, but rob Bee-hiues:
It is impossible that I should dye

By

By such a lowly Vassall as thy selfe.
Thy words moue Rage, and not remorse in me:
I go of Message from the Queene to France:
I charge thee waft me safely crosse the Channell.

Lieu. Water: W. Come Suffolke, I must waft thee to thy death.

Suf. *Pine gelidus timor occupat artus*, it is thee I feare.

Wal. Thou shalt haue cause to feare before I leaue thee.
What, are ye daunted now? Now will ye stoope.

1.Gent. My gracious Lord intreat him, speak him fair.

Suf. Suffolkes Imperiall tongue is sterne and rough:
Vs'd to command, vntaught to pleade for fauour.
Farre be it, we should honor such as these
With humble suite: no, rather let my head
Stoope to the blocke, then these knees bow to any,
Saue to the God of heauen, and to my King:
And sooner dance vpon a bloody pole,
Then stand vncouer'd to the Vulgar Groome.
True Nobility, is exempt from feare:
More can I beare, then you dare execute.

Lieu. Hale him away, and let him talke no more:
Come Souldiers, shew what cruelty ye can.

Suf. That this my death may neuer be forgot.
Great men oft dye by vilde Bezonions.
A Romane Sworder, and Bandetto slaue
Murder'd sweet *Tully.* *Brutus* Bastard hand
Stab'd *Iulius Cæsar.* Sauage Islanders
Pompey the Great, and *Suffolke* dyes by Pyrats.
Exit Water with Suffolke.

Lieu. And as for these whose ransome we haue set,
It is our pleasure one of them depart:
Therefore come you with vs, and let him go.
Exit Lieutenant, and the rest.

Manet the first Gent. *Enter Walter with the body.*

Wal. There let his head, and liuelesse bodie lye,
Vntill the Queene his Mistris bury it. *Exit Walter.*

1.Gent. O barbarous and bloudy spectacle,
His body will I beare vnto the King:
If he reuenge it not, yet will his Friends,
So will the Queene, that liuing, held him deere.

Enter Beuis, and Iohn Holland.

Beuis. Come and get thee a sword, though made of a Lath, they haue bene vp these two dayes.

Hol. They haue the more neede to sleepe now then.

Beuis. I tell thee, *Iacke Cade* the Cloathier, meanes to dresse the Common-wealth and turne it, and set a new nap vpon it.

Hol. So he had need, for 'tis thred-bare. Well, I say, it was neuer merrie world in England, since Gentlemen came vp.

Beuis. O miserable Age: Vertue is not regarded in Handy-crafts men.

Hol. The Nobilitie thinke scorne to goe in Leather Aprons.

Beuis. Nay more, the Kings Councell are no good Workemen.

Hol. True: and yet it is said, Labour in thy Vocation: which is as much to say, as let the Magistrates be labouring men, and therefore should we be Magistrates.

Beuis. Thou hast hit it: for there's no better signe of a braue minde, then a hard hand.

Hol. I see them, I see them: There's *Bests* Sonne, the Tanner of Wingham.

Beuis. Hee shall haue the skinnes of our enemies, to make Dogges Leather of.

Hol. And Dicke the Butcher.

Beuis. Then is sin strucke downe like an Oxe, and iniquities throate cut like a Calfe.

Hol. And Smith the Weauer.

Beu. Argo, their thred of life is spun.

Hol. Come, come, let's fall in with them.

Drumme. *Enter Cade, Dicke Butcher, Smith the Weauer, and a Sawyer, with infinite numbers.*

Cade. Wee *Iohn Cade,* so tearm'd of our supposed Father.

But. Or rather of stealing a Cade of Herrings.

Cade. For our enemies shall faile before vs, inspired with the spirit of putting downe Kings and Princes, Command silence.

But. Silence.

Cade. My Father was a *Mortimer.*

But. He was an honest man, and a good Bricklayer.

Cade. My mother a *Plantagenet.*

Butch. I knew her well, she was a Midwife.

Cade. My wife descended of the *Lacies.*

But. She was indeed a Pedlers daughter, & sold many Laces.

Weauer. But now of late, not able to trauell with her furr'd Packe, she washes buckes here at home.

Cade. Therefore am I of an honorable house.

But. I by my faith, the field is honourable, and there was he borne, vnder a hedge: for his Father had neuer a house but the Cage.

Cade. Valiant I am.

Weauer. A must needs, for beggery is valiant.

Cade. I am able to endure much.

But. No question of that: for I haue seene him whipt three Market dayes together.

Cade. I feare neither sword, nor fire.

Wea. He neede not feare the sword, for his Coate is of proofe.

But. But me thinks he should stand in feare of fire, being burnt i'th hand for stealing of Sheepe.

Cade. Be braue then, for your Captaine is Braue, and Vowes Reformation. There shall be in England, seuen halfe peny Loaues sold for a peny: the three hoop'd pot, shall haue ten hoopes, and I wil make it Fellony to drink small Beere. All the Realme shall be in Common, and in Cheapside shall my Palfrey go to grasse: and when I am King, as King I will be.

All. God saue your Maiesty.

Cade. I thanke you good people. There shall bee no mony, all shall eate and drinke on my score, and I will apparrell them all in one Liuery, that they may agree like Brothers, and worship me their Lord.

But. The first thing we do, let's kill all the Lawyers.

Cade. Nay, that I meane to do. Is not this a lamentable thing, that of the skin of an innocent Lambe should be made Parchment; that Parchment being scribed ore, should vndoe a man. Some say the Bee stings, but I say, 'tis the Bees waxe: for I did but seale once to a thing, and I was neuer mine owne man since. How now? Who's there?

Enter a Clearke.

Weauer. The Clearke of Chartam: hee can write and reade, and cast accompt.

Cade. O monstrous.

Wea. We tooke him setting of boyes Copies.

Cade.

Cade. Here's a Villaine.
Wea. Ha's a Booke in his pocket with red Letters in't
Cade. Nay then he is a Coniurer.
But. Nay, he can make Obligations, and write Court hand.
Cade. I am sorry for't: The man is a proper man of mine Honour: vnlesse I finde him guilty, he shall not die. Come hither sirrah, I must examine thee: What is thy name?
Clearke. Emanuell.
But. They vse to writ it on the top of Letters: 'Twill go hard with you.
Cade. Let me alone: Dost thou vse to write thy name? Or hast thou a marke to thy selfe, like a honest plain dealing man?
Clearke. Sir I thanke God, I haue bin so well brought vp, that I can write my name.
All. He hath confest: away with him: he's a Villaine and a Traitor.
Cade. Away with him I say: Hang him with his Pen and Inke-horne about his necke.

Exit one with the Clearke
Enter Michael.

Mich. Where's our Generall?
Cade. Heere I am thou particular fellow.
Mich. Fly, fly, fly, Sir *Humfrey Stafford* and his brother are hard by, with the Kings Forces.
Cade. Stand villaine, stand, or Ile fell thee downe: he shall be encountred with a man as good as himselfe. He is but a Knight, is a?
Mich. No.
Cade. To equall him I will make my selfe a knight presently; Rise vp Sir *Iohn Mortimer*. Now haue at him.

Enter Sir Humfrey Stafford, and his Brother,
with Drum and Soldiers.

Staf. Rebellious Hinds, the filth and scum of Kent,
Mark'd for the Gallowes: Lay your Weapons downe,
Home to your Cottages: forsake this Groome.
The King is mercifull, if you reuolt.
Bro. But angry, wrathfull, and inclin'd to blood,
If you go forward: therefore yeeld, or dye.
Cade. As for these silken-coated slaues I passe not,
It is to you good people, that I speake,
Ouer whom (in time to come) I hope to raigne:
For I am rightfull heyre vnto the Crowne.
Staf. Villaine, thy Father was a Playsterer,
And thou thy selfe a Sheareman, art thou not?
Cade. And *Adam* was a Gardiner.
Bro. And what of that?
Cade. Marry, this *Edmund Mortimer* Earle of March, married the Duke of *Clarence* daughter, did he not?
Staf. I sir.
Cade. By her he had two children at one birth.
Bro. That's false.
Cade. I, there's the question; But I say, 'tis true:
The elder of them being put to nurse,
Was by a begger-woman stolne away,
And ignorant of his birth and parentage,
Became a Bricklayer, when he came to age.
His sonne am I, deny it if you can.
But. Nay, 'tis too true, therefore he shall be King.
Wea. Sir, he made a Chimney in my Fathers house, & the brickes are aliue at this day to testifie it: therefore deny it not.

Staf. And will you credit this base Drudges Wordes, that speakes he knowes not what.
All. I marry will we: therefore get ye gone.
Bro. *Iacke Cade*, the D. of York hath taught you this.
Cade. He lyes, for I inuented it my selfe. Go too Sirrah, tell the King from me, that for his Fathers sake *Henry* the fift, (in whose time, boyes went to Span-counter for French Crownes) I am content he shall raigne, but Ile be Protector ouer him.
Butcher. And furthermore, wee'l haue the Lord *Sayes* head, for selling the Dukedome of *Maine*.
Cade. And good reason: for thereby is England main'd And faine to go with a staffe, but that my puissance holds it vp. Fellow-Kings, I tell you, that that Lord Say hath gelded the Commonwealth, and made it an Eunuch: & more then that, he can speake French, and therefore hee is a Traitor.
Staf. O grosse and miserable ignorance.
Cade. Nay answer if you can: The Frenchmen are our enemies: go too then, I ask but this: Can he that speaks with the tongue of an enemy, be a good Councellour, or no?
All. No, no, and therefore wee'l haue his head.
Bro. Well, seeing gentle words will not preuayle,
Assaile them with the Army of the King.
Staf. Herald away, and throughout euery Towne,
Proclaime them Traitors that are vp with *Cade*,
That those which flye before the battell ends,
May euen in their Wiues and Childrens sight,
Be hang'd vp for example at their doores:
And you that be the Kings Friends follow me. *Exit.*
Cade. And you that loue the Commons, follow me:
Now shew your selues men, 'tis for Liberty.
We will not leaue one Lord, one Gentleman:
Spare none, but such as go in clouted shooen,
For they are thrifty honest men, and such
As would (but that they dare not) take our parts.
But. They are all in order, and march toward vs.
Cade. But then are we in order, when we are most out of order. Come, march forward.

Alarums to the fight, wherein both the Staffords are slaine.
Enter Cade and the rest.

Cade. Where's *Dicke*, the Butcher of Ashford?
But. Heere sir.
Cade. They fell before thee like Sheepe and Oxen, & thou behaued'st thy selfe, as if thou hadst beene in thine owne Slaughter-house: Therfore thus will I reward thee, the Lent shall bee as long againe as it is, and thou shalt haue a License to kill for a hundred lacking one.
But. I desire no more.
Cade. And to speake truth, thou deseru'st no lesse.
This Monument of the victory will I beare, and the bodies shall be dragg'd at my horse heeles, till I do come to London, where we will haue the Maiors sword born before vs.
But. If we meane to thriue, and do good, breake open the Gaoles, and let out the Prisoners.
Cade. Feare not that I warrant thee, Come, let's march towards London. *Exeunt.*

Enter the King with a Supplication, and the Queene with Suffolkes head, the Duke of Buckingham, and the Lord Say.

Queene. Oft haue I heard that greefe softens the mind,
And

And makes it fearefull and degenerate,
Thinke therefore on reuenge, and cease to weepe.
But who can cease to weepe, and looke on this.
Heere may his head lye on my throbbing brest:
But where's the body that I should imbrace?

  Buc. What answer makes your Grace to the Rebells Supplication?
  King. Ile send some holy Bishop to intreat:
For God forbid, so many simple soules
Should perish by the Sword. And I my selfe,
Rather then bloody Warre shall cut them short,
Will parley with *Iacke Cade* their Generall.
But stay, Ile read it ouer once againe.
  Qu. Ah barbarous villaines: Hath this louely face,
Rul'd like a wandering Plannet ouer me,
And could it not inforce them to relent,
That were vnworthy to behold the same.
  King. Lord *Say*, *Iacke Cade* hath sworne to haue thy head.
  Say. I, but I hope your Highnesse shall haue his.
  King. How now Madam?
Still lamenting and mourning for Suffolkes death?
I feare me (Loue) if that I had beene dead,
Thou would'st not haue mourn'd so much for me.
  Qu. No my Loue, I should not mourne, but dye for thee.

Enter a Messenger.

  King. How now? What newes? Why com'st thou in such haste?
  Mes. The Rebels are in Southwarke: Fly my Lord:
Iacke Cade proclaimes himselfe Lord *Mortimer*,
Descended from the Duke of *Clarence* house,
And calles your Grace Vsurper, openly,
And vowes to Crowne himselfe in Westminster.
His Army is a ragged multitude
Of Hindes and Pezants, rude and mercilesse:
Sir *Humfrey Stafford*, and his Brothers death,
Hath giuen them heart and courage to proceede:
All Schollers, Lawyers, Courtiers, Gentlemen,
They call false Catterpillers, and intend their death.
  Kin. Oh gracelesse men: they know not what they do.
  Buck. My gracious Lord, retire to Killingworth,
Vntill a power be rais'd to put them downe.
  Qu. Ah were the Duke of Suffolke now aliue,
These Kentish Rebels would be soone appeas'd.
  King. Lord *Say*, the Traitors hateth thee,
Therefore away with vs to Killingworth.
  Say. So might your Graces person be in danger:
The sight of me is odious in their eyes:
And therefore in this Citty will I stay,
And liue alone as secret as I may.

Enter another Messenger.

  Mess. *Iacke Cade* hath gotten London-bridge.
The Citizens flye and forsake their houses:
The Rascall people, thirsting after prey,
Ioyne with the Traitor, and they ioyntly sweare
To spoyle the City, and your Royall Court.
  Buc. Then linger not my Lord, away, take horse.
  King. Come *Margaret*, God our hope will succor vs.
  Qu. My hope is gone, now Suffolke is deceast.
  King. Farewell my Lord, trust not the Kentish Rebels
  Buc. Trust no body for feare you betraid.
  Say. The trust I haue, is in mine innocence,
And therefore am I bold and resolute. *Exeunt.*

Enter Lord Scales vpon the Tower walking. Then enters two or three Citizens below.

  Scales. How now? Is *Iacke Cade* slaine?
  1.*Cit.* No my Lord, nor likely to be slaine:
For they haue wonne the Bridge,
Killing all those that withstand them:
The L. Maior craues ayd of your Honor from the Tower
To defend the City from the Rebels.
  Scales. Such ayd as I can spare you shall command,
But I am troubled heere with them my selfe,
The Rebels haue assay'd to win the Tower.
But get you to Smithfield, and gather head,
And thither I will send you *Mathew Goffe*.
Fight for your King, your Countrey, and your Liues,
And so farwell, for I must hence againe. *Exeunt*

Enter Iacke Cade and the rest, and strikes his staffe on London stone.

  Cade. Now is *Mortimer* Lord of this City,
And heere sitting vpon London Stone,
I charge and command, that of the Cities cost
The pissing Conduit run nothing but Clarret Wine
This first yeare of our raigne.
And now henceforward it shall be Treason for any,
That calles me other then Lord *Mortimer*.

Enter a Soldier running.

  Soul. *Iacke Cade*, *Iacke Cade*.
  Cade. Knocke him downe there. *They kill him.*
  But. If this Fellow be wise, hee'l neuer call yee *Iacke Cade* more, I thinke he hath a very faire warning.
  Dicke. My Lord, there's an Army gathered together in Smithfield.
  Cade. Come, then let's go fight with them:
But first, go and set London Bridge on fire,
And if you can, burne downe the Tower too.
Come, let's away. *Exeunt omnes.*

Alarums. Mathew Goffe is slain, and all the rest. Then enter Iacke Cade, with his Company.

  Cade. So firs: now go some and pull down the Sauoy: Others to'th Innes of Court, downe with them all.
  But. I haue a suite vnto your Lordship.
  Cade. Bee it a Lordshippe, thou shalt haue it for that word.
  But. Onely that the Lawes of England may come out of your mouth.
  Iohn. Masse 'twill be sore Law then, for he was thrust in the mouth with a Speare, and 'tis not whole yet.
  Smith. Nay *Iohn*, it wil be stinking Law, for his breath stinkes with eating toasted cheese.
  Cade. I haue thought vpon it, it shall bee so. Away, burne all the Records of the Realme, my mouth shall be the Parliament of England.
  Iohn. Then we are like to haue biting Statutes Vnlesse his teeth be pull'd out.
  Cade. And hence-forward all things shall be in Common. *Enter a Messenger.*
  Mess. My Lord, a prize, a prize, heeres the Lord *Say*, which sold the Townes in France. He that made vs pay one and twenty Fifteenes, and one shilling to the pound, the last Subsidie. *Enter*

Enter George, with the Lord Say.

Cade. Well, hee shall be beheaded for it ten times: Ah thou Say, thou Surge, nay thou Buckram Lord, now art thou within point-blanke of our Iurisdiction Regall. What canst thou answer to my Maiesty, for giuing vp of Normandie vnto Mounsieur *Basimecu*, the Dolphine of France? Be it knowne vnto thee by these presence, euen the presence of Lord *Mortimer*, that I am the Beesome that must sweepe the Court cleane of such filth as thou art: Thou hast most traiterously corrupted the youth of the Realme, in erecting a Grammar Schoole: and whereas before, our Fore-fathers had no other Bookes but the Score and the Tally, thou hast caused printing to be vs'd, and contrary to the King, his Crowne, and Dignity, thou hast built a Paper-Mill. It will be prooued to thy Face, that thou hast men about thee, that vsually talke of a Nowne and a Verbe, and such abhominable wordes, as no Christian eare can endure to heare. Thou hast appointed Iustices of Peace, to call poore men before them, about matters they were not able to answer. Moreouer, thou hast put them in prison, and because they could not reade, thou hast hang'd them, when (indeede) onely for that cause they haue beene most worthy to liue. Thou dost ride in a foot-cloth, dost thou not?

Say. What of that?

Cade. Marry, thou ought'st not to let thy horse weare a Cloake, when honester men then thou go in their Hose and Doublets.

Dicke. And worke in their shirt to, as my selfe for example, that am a butcher.

Say. You men of Kent.

Dic. What say you of Kent.

Say. Nothing but this: 'Tis *bona terra, mala gens.*

Cade. Away with him, away with him, he speaks Latine.

Say. Heare me but speake, and beare mee wher'e you will:
Kent, in the Commentaries *Cæsar* writ,
Is term'd the ciuel'st place of all this Isle:
Sweet is the Covntry, because full of Riches,
The People Liberall, Valiant, Actiue, Wealthy,
Which makes me hope you are not void of pitty.
I sold not *Maine*, I lost not *Normandie*,
Yet to recouer them would loose my life:
Iustice with fauour haue I alwayes done,
Prayres and Teares haue mou'd me, Gifts could neuer.
When haue I ought exacted at your hands?
Kent to maintaine, the King, the Realme and you,
Large gifts haue I bestow'd on learned Clearkes,
Because my Booke preferr'd me to the King.
And seeing Ignorance is the curse of God,
Knowledge the Wing wherewith we flye to heauen.
Vnlesse you be possest with diuellish spirits,
You cannot but forbeare to murther me:
This Tongue hath parlied vnto Forraigne Kings
For your behoofe.

Cade. Tut, when struck'st thou one blow in the field?

Say. Great men haue reaching hands: oft haue I strucke Those that I neuer saw, and strucke them dead.

Geo. O monstrous Coward! What, to come behinde Folkes?

Say. These cheekes are pale for watching for your good

Cade. Giue him a box o'th'eare, and that wil make 'em red againe.

Say. Long sitting to determine poore mens causes,
Hath made me full of sicknesse and diseases.

Cade. Ye shall haue a hempen Candle then, & the help of hatchet.

Dicke. Why dost thou quiuer man?

Say. The Palsie, and not feare prouokes me.

Cade. Nay, he noddes at vs, as who should say, Ile be euen with you. Ile see if his head will stand steddier on a pole, or no: Take him away, and behead him.

Say. Tell me: wherein haue I offended most?
Haue I affected wealth, or honor? Speake.
Are my Chests fill'd vp with extorted Gold?
Is my Apparrell sumptuous to behold?
Whom haue I iniur'd, that ye seeke my death?
These hands are free from guiltlesse bloodshedding,
This breast from harbouring foule deceitfull thoughts.
O let me liue.

Cade. I feele remorse in my selfe with his words: but Ile bridle it: he shall dye, and it bee but for pleading so well for his life. Away with him, he ha's a Familiar vnder his Tongue, he speakes not a Gods name. Goe, take him away I say, and strike off his head presently, and then breake into his Sonne in Lawes house, Sir *Iames Cromer*, and strike off his head, and bring them both vppon two poles hither.

All. It shall be done.

Say. Ah Countrimen: If when you make your prair's, God should be so obdurate as your selues:
How would it fare with your departed soules,
And therefore yet relent, and saue my life.

Cade. Away with him, and do as I command ye: the proudest Peere in the Realme, shall not weare a head on his shoulders, vnlesse he pay me tribute: there shall not a maid be married, but she shall pay to me her Maydenhead ere they haue it: Men shall hold of mee in *Capite*. And we charge and command, that their wiues be as free as heart can wish, or tongue can tell.

Dicke. My Lord,
When shall we go to Cheapside, and take vp commodities vpon our billes?

Cade. Marry presently.

All. O braue.

Enter one with the heads.

Cade. But is not this brauer:
Let them kisse one another: For they lou'd well
When they were aliue. Now part them againe,
Least they consult about the giuing vp
Of some more Townes in France. Soldiers,
Deferre the spoile of the Citie vntill night:
For with these borne before vs, in steed of Maces,
Will we ride through the streets, & at euery Corner
Haue them kisse. Away. *Exit*

Alarum, and Retreat. Enter againe Cade, and all his rabblement.

Cade. Vp Fish-streete, downe Saint Magnes corner, kill and knocke downe, throw them into Thames:

Sound a parley.

What noise is this I heare?
Dare any be so bold to sound Retreat or Parley
When I command them kill?

Enter

Enter Buckingham, and old Clifford.

Buc. I heere they be, that dare and will disturb thee:
Know *Cade*, we come Ambassadors from the King
Vnto the Commons, whom thou hast misled,
And heere pronounce free pardon to them all,
That will forsake thee, and go home in peace.

Clif. What say ye Countrimen, will ye relent
And yeeld to mercy, whil'st 'tis offered you,
Or let a rabble leade you to your deaths.
Who loues the King, and will imbrace his pardon,
Fling vp his cap, and say, God saue his Maiesty.
Who hateth him, and honors not his Father,
Henry the fift, that made all France to quake,
Shake he his weapon at vs, and passe by.

All. God saue the King, God saue the King.

Cade. What Buckingham and Clifford are ye so braue?
And you base Pezants, do ye beleeue him, will you needs
be hang'd with your Pardons about your neckes? Hath
my sword therefore broke through London gates, that
you should leaue me at the White-heart in Southwarke.
I thought ye would neuer haue giuen out these Armes til
you had recouered your ancient Freedome. But you are
all Recreants and Dastards, and delight to liue in slauerie
to the Nobility. Let them breake your backes with burthens, take your houses ouer your heads, rauish your
Wiues and Daughters before your faces. For me, I will
make shift for one, and so Gods Cursse light vppon you
all.

All. Wee'l follow *Cade*,
Wee'l follow *Cade*.

Clif. Is *Cade* the sonne of *Henry* the fift,
That thus you do exclaime you'l go with him.
Will he conduct you through the heart of France,
And make the meanest of you Earles and Dukes?
Alas, he hath no home, no place to flye too:
Nor knowes he how to liue, but by the spoile,
Vnlesse by robbing of your Friends, and vs.
Wer't not a shame, that whilst you liue at iarre,
The fearfull French, whom you late vanquished
Should make a start ore-seas, and vanquish you?
Me thinkes alreadie in this ciuill broyle,
I see them Lording it in London streets,
Crying *Villiago* vnto all they meete.
Better ten thousand base-borne *Cades* miscarry,
Then you should stoope vnto a Frenchmans mercy.
To France, to France, and get what you haue lost:
Spare England, for it is your Natiue Coast:
Henry hath mony, you are strong and manly:
God on our side, doubt not of Victorie.

All. A Clifford, a Clifford,
Wee'l follow the King, and Clifford.

Cade. Was euer Feather so lightly blowne too & fro,
as this multitude? The name of Henry the fift, hales them
to an hundred mischiefes, and makes them leaue mee desolate. I see them lay their heades together to surprize
me. My sword make way for me, for heere is no staying:
in despight of the diuels and hell, haue through the verie
middest of you, and heauens and honor be witnesse, that
no want of resolution in mee, but onely my Followers
base and ignominious treasons, makes me betake mee to
my heeles. *Exit*

Buck. What, is he fled? Go some and follow him,
And he that brings his head vnto the King,
Shall haue a thousand Crownes for his reward.
Exeunt some of them.

Follow me souldiers, wee'l deuise a meane,
To reconcile you all vnto the King. *Exeunt omnes.*

Sound Trumpets. Enter King, Queene, and Somerset on the Tarras.

King. Was euer King that ioy'd an earthly Throne,
And could command no more content then I?
No sooner was I crept out of my Cradle,
But I was made a King, at nine months olde.
Was neuer Subiect long'd to be a King,
As I do long and wish to be a Subiect.

Enter Buckingham and Clifford.

Buc. Health and glad tydings to your Maiesty.
Kin. Why Buckingham, is the Traitor *Cade* surpris'd?
Or is he but retir'd to make him strong?

Enter Multitudes with Halters about their Neckes.

Clif. He is fled my Lord, and all his powers do yeeld,
And humbly thus with halters on their neckes,
Expect your Highnesse doome of life, or death.

King. Then heauen set ope thy euerlasting gates,
To entertaine my vowes of thankes and praise.
Souldiers, this day haue you redeem'd your liues,
And shew'd how well you loue your Prince & Countrey:
Continue still in this so good a minde,
And *Henry* though he be infortunate,
Assure your selues will neuer be vnkinde:
And so with thankes, and pardon to you all,
I do dismisse you to your seuerall Countries.

All. God saue the King, God saue the King.

Enter a Messenger.

Mes. Please it your Grace to be aduertised,
The Duke of Yorke is newly come from Ireland,
And with a puissant and a mighty power
Of Gallow-glasses and stout Kernes,
Is marching hitherward in proud array,
And still proclaimeth as he comes along,
His Armes are onely to remoue from thee
The Duke of Somerset, whom he tearmes a Traitor.

King. Thus stands my state, 'twixt Cade and Yorke distrest,
Like to a Ship, that hauing scap'd a Tempest,
Is straight way calme, and boorded with a Pyrate.
But now is Cade driuen backe, his men dispierc'd,
And now is Yorke in Armes, to second him.
I pray thee Buckingham go and meete him,
And aske him what's the reason of these Armes:
Tell him, Ile send Duke *Edmund* to the Tower,
And *Somerset* we will commit thee thither,
Vntill his Army be dismist from him.

Somerset. My Lord,
Ile yeelde my selfe to prison willingly,
Or vnto death, to do my Countrey good.

King. In any case, be not to rough in termes,
For he is fierce, and cannot brooke hard Language.

Buc. I will my Lord, and doubt not so to deale,
As all things shall redound vnto your good.

King. Come wife, let's in, and learne to gouern better,
For yet may England curse my wretched raigne.
Flourish. *Exeunt.*

Enter Cade.

Cade. Fye on Ambitions: fie on my selfe, that haue a sword, and yet am ready to famish. These fiue daies haue I hid me in these Woods, and durst not peepe out, for all the Country is laid for me: but now am I so hungry, that if I might haue a Lease of my life for a thousand yeares, I could stay no longer. Wherefore on a Bricke wall haue I climb'd into this Garden, to see if I can eate Grasse, or picke a Sallet another while, which is not amisse to coole a mans stomacke this hot weather: and I think this word Sallet was borne to do me good: for many a time but for a Sallet, my braine-pan had bene cleft with a brown Bill; and many a time when I haue beene dry, & brauely marching, it hath seru'd me insteede of a quart pot to drinke in: and now the word Sallet must serue me to feed on.

Enter Iden.

Iden. Lord, who would liue turmoyled in the Court,
And may enioy such quiet walkes as these?
This small inheritance my Father left me,
Contenteth me, and worth a Monarchy.
I seeke not to waxe great by others warning,
Or gather wealth I care not with what enuy:
Sufficeth, that I haue maintaines my state,
And sends the poore well pleased from my gate.

Cade. Heere's the Lord of the soile come to seize me for a stray, for entering his Fee-simple without leaue. A Villaine, thou wilt betray me, and get a 1000. Crownes of the King by carrying my head to him, but Ile make thee eate Iron like an Ostridge, and swallow my Sword like a great pin ere thou and I part.

Iden. Why rude Companion, whatsoere thou be,
I know thee not, why then should I betray thee?
Is't not enough to breake into my Garden,
And like a Theefe to come to rob my grounds:
Climbing my walles inspight of me the Owner,
But thou wilt braue me with these sawcie termes?

Cade. Braue thee? I by the best blood that euer was broach'd, and beard thee to. Looke on mee well, I haue eate no meate these fiue dayes, yet come thou and thy fiue men, and if I doe not leaue you all as dead as a doore naile, I pray God I may neuer eate grasse more.

Iden. Nay, it shall nere be said, while England stands,
That *Alexander Iden* an Esquire of Kent,
Tooke oddes to combate a poore famisht man.
Oppose thy stedfast gazing eyes to mine,
See if thou canst out-face me with thy lookes:
Set limbe to limbe, and thou art farre the lesser:
Thy hand is but a finger to my fist,
Thy legge a sticke compared with this Truncheon,
My foote shall fight with all the strength thou hast,
And if mine arme be heaued in the Ayre,
Thy graue is digg'd already in the earth:
As for words, whose greatnesse answer's words,
Let this my sword report what speech forbeares.

Cade. By my Valour: the most compleate Champion that euer I heard. Steele, if thou turne the edge, or cut not out the burly bon'd Clowne in chines of Beefe, ere thou sleepe in thy Sheath, I beseech Ioue on my knees thou mayst be turn'd to Hobnailes.

Heere they Fight.

O I am slaine, Famine and no other hath slaine me, let ten thousand diuelles come against me, and giue me but the ten meales I haue lost, and I'de defie them all. Wither Garden, and be henceforth a burying place to all that do dwell in this house, because the vnconquered soule of *Cade* is fled.

Iden. Is't *Cade* that I haue slain, that monstrous traitor?
Sword, I will hallow thee for this thy deede,
And hang thee o're my Tombe, when I am dead.
Ne're shall this blood be wiped from thy point,
But thou shalt weare it as a Heralds coate,
To emblaze the Honor that thy Master got.

Cade. *Iden* farewell, and be proud of thy victory: Tell Kent from me, she hath lost her best man, and exhort all the World to be Cowards: For I that neuer feared any, am vanquished by Famine, not by Valour. *Dyes.*

Id. How much thou wrong'st me, heauen be my iudge;
Die damned Wretch, the curse of her that bare thee:
And as I thrust thy body in with my sword,
So wish I, I might thrust thy soule to hell.
Hence will I dragge thee headlong by the heeles
Vnto a dunghill, which shall be thy graue,
And there cut off thy most vngracious head,
Which I will beare in triumph to the King,
Leauing thy trunke for Crowes to feed vpon. *Exit.*

Enter Yorke, and his Army of Irish, with Drum and Colours.

Yor. From Ireland thus comes York to claim his right,
And plucke the Crowne from feeble *Henries* head.
Ring Belles alowd, burne Bonfires cleare and bright
To entertaine great Englands lawfull King.
Ah *Sancta Maiestas*! who would not buy thee deere?
Let them obey, that knowes not how to Rule.
This hand was made to handle nought but Gold.
I cannot giue due action to my words,
Except a Sword or Scepter ballance it.
A Scepter shall it haue, haue I a soule,
On which Ile tosse the Fleure-de-Luce of France.

Enter Buckingham.

Whom haue we heere? Buckingham to disturbe me?
The king hath sent him sure: I must dissemble.

Buc. Yorke, if thou meanest wel, I greet thee well.

Yor. *Humfrey* of Buckingham, I accept thy greeting.
Art thou a Messenger, or come of pleasure.

Buc. A Messenger from *Henry*, our dread Liege,
To know the reason of these Armes in peace.
Or why, thou being a Subiect, as I am,
Against thy Oath, and true Allegeance sworne,
Should raise so great a power without his leaue?
Or dare to bring thy Force so neere the Court?

Yor. Scarse can I speake, my Choller is so great.
Oh I could hew vp Rockes, and fight with Flint,
I am so angry at these abiect tearmes.
And now like *Aiax Telamonius*,
On Sheepe or Oxen could I spend my furie.
I am farre better borne then is the king:
More like a King, more Kingly in my thoughts.
But I must make faire weather yet a while,
Till *Henry* be more weake, and I more strong.
Buckingham, I prethee pardon me,
That I haue giuen no answer all this while:
My minde was troubled with deepe Melancholly.
The cause why I haue brought this Armie hither,

Is to remoue proud Somerset from the King,
Seditious to his Grace, and to the State.

  Buc. That is too much presumption on thy part:
But if thy Armes be to no other end,
The King hath yeelded vnto thy demand:
The Duke of Somerset is in the Tower.

  Yorke. Vpon thine Honor is he Prisoner?
  Buck. Vpon mine Honor he is Prisoner.
  Yorke. Then Buckingham I do dismisse my Powres.
Souldiers, I thanke you all: disperse your selues:
Meet me to morrow in S. Georges Field,
You shall haue pay, and euery thing you wish.
And let my Soueraigne, vertuous *Henry*,
Command my eldest sonne, nay all my sonnes,
As pledges of my Fealtie and Loue,
Ile send them all as willing as I liue:
Lands, Goods, Horse, Armor, any thing I haue
Is his to vse, so Somerset may die.

  Buc. Yorke, I commend this kinde submission,
We twaine will go into his Highnesse Tent.

Enter King and Attendants.

  King. Buckingham, doth Yorke intend no harme to vs
That thus he marcheth with thee arme in arme?
  Yorke. In all submission and humility,
Yorke doth present himselfe vnto your Highnesse.
  K. Then what intends these Forces thou dost bring?
  Yor. To heaue the Traitor Somerset from hence,
And fight against that monstrous Rebell *Cade*,
Who since I heard to be discomfited.

Enter Iden with Cades head.

  Iden. If one so rude, and of so meane condition
May passe into the presence of a King:
Loe, I present your Grace a Traitors head,
The head of *Cade*, whom I in combat slew.
  King. The head of *Cade*? Great God, how iust art thou?
Oh let me view his Visage being dead,
That liuing wrought me such exceeding trouble.
Tell me my Friend, art thou the man that slew him?
  Iden. I was, an't like your Maiesty.
  King. How art thou call'd? And what is thy degree?
  Iden. Alexander Iden, that's my name,
A poore Esquire of Kent, that loues his King.
  Buc. So please it you my Lord, 'twere not amisse
He were created Knight for his good seruice.
  King. Iden, kneele downe, rise vp a Knight:
We giue thee for reward a thousand Markes,
And will, that thou henceforth attend on vs.
  Iden. May *Iden* liue to merit such a bountie,
And neuer liue but true vnto his Liege.

Enter Queene and Somerset.

  K. See Buckingham, Somerset comes with th'Queene,
Go bid her hide him quickly from the Duke.
  Qu. For thousand Yorkes he shall not hide his head,
But boldly stand, and front him to his face.
  Yor. How now? is Somerset at libertie?
Then Yorke vnloose thy long imprisoned thoughts,
And let thy tongue be equall with thy heart.
Shall I endure the sight of Somerset?
False King, why hast thou broken faith with me,
Knowing how hardly I can brooke abuse?
King did I call thee? No: thou art not King:
Not fit to gouerne and rule multitudes,
Which dar'st not, no nor canst not rule a Traitor.

That Head of thine doth not become a Crowne:
Thy Hand is made to graspe a Palmers staffe,
And not to grace an awefull Princely Scepter.
That Gold, must round engirt these browes of mine,
Whose Smile and Frowne, like to *Achilles* Speare
Is able with the change, to kill and cure.
Heere is a hand to hold a Scepter vp,
And with the same to acte controlling Lawes:
Giue place: by heauen thou shalt rule no more
O're him, whom heauen created for thy Ruler.

  Som. O monstrous Traitor! I arrest thee Yorke
Of Capitall Treason 'gainst the King and Crowne:
Obey audacious Traitor, kneele for Grace.

  York. Wold'st haue me kneele? First let me ask of thee,
If they can brooke I bow a knee to man:
Sirrah, call in my sonne to be my bale:
I know ere they will haue me go to Ward,
They'l pawne their swords of my infranchisement.

  Qu. Call hither *Clifford*, bid him come amaine,
To say, if that the Bastard boyes of Yorke
Shall be the Surety for their Traitor Father.

  Yorke. O blood-bespotted Neopolitan,
Out-cast of *Naples*, Englands bloody Scourge,
The sonnes of Yorke, thy betters in their birth,
Shall be their Fathers baile, and bane to those
That for my Surety will refuse the Boyes.

Enter Edward and Richard.

See where they come, Ile warrant they'l make it good.

Enter Clifford.

  Qu. And here comes *Clifford* to deny their baile.
  Clif. Health, and all happinesse to my Lord the King.
  Yor. I thanke thee *Clifford*: Say, what newes with thee?
Nay, do not fright vs with an angry looke:
We are thy Soueraigne *Clifford*, kneele againe;
For thy mistaking so, We pardon thee.
  Clif. This is my King Yorke, I do not mistake,
But thou mistakes me much to thinke I do,
To Bedlem with him, is the man growne mad.
  King. I Clifford, a Bedlem and ambitious humor
Makes him oppose himselfe against his King.
  Clif. He is a Traitor, let him to the Tower,
And chop away that factious pate of his.
  Qu. He is arrested, but will not obey:
His sonnes (he sayes) shall giue their words for him.
  Yor. Will you not Sonnes?
  Edw. I Noble Father, if our words will serue.
  Rich. And if words will not, then our Weapons shal.
  Clif. Why what a brood of Traitors haue we heere?
  Yorke. Looke in a Glasse, and call thy Image so.
I am thy King, and thou a false-heart Traitor:
Call hither to the stake my two braue Beares,
That with the very shaking of their Chaines,
They may astonish these fell-lurking Curres,
Bid Salsbury and Warwicke come to me.

*Enter the Earles of Warwicke, and
Salisbury.*

  Clif. Are these thy Beares? Wee'l bate thy Bears to death,
And manacle the Berard in their Chaines,
If thou dar'st bring them to the bayting place.
  Rich. Oft haue I seene a hot ore-weening Curre,
Run backe and bite, because he was with-held,
Who being suffer'd with the Beares fell paw,
Hath clapt his taile, betweene his legges and cride,
And such a peece of seruice will you do,

The second Part of Henry the Sixt.

If you oppose your selues to match Lord Warwicke.
  Clif. Hence heape of wrath, foule indigested lumpe,
As crooked in thy manners, as thy shape.
  Yor. Nay we shall heate you thorowly anon.
  Clif. Take heede least by your heate you burne your selues:
  King. Why Warwicke, hath thy knee forgot to bow?
Old Salsbury, shame to thy siluer haire,
Thou mad misleader of thy brain-sicke sonne,
What wilt thou on thy death-bed play the Ruffian?
And seeke for sorrow with thy Spectacles?
Oh where is Faith? Oh, where is Loyalty?
If it be banisht from the frostie head,
Where shall it finde a harbour in the earth?
Wilt thou go digge a graue to finde out Warre,
And shame thine honourable Age with blood?
Why art thou old, and want'st experience?
Or wherefore doest abuse it, if thou hast it?
For shame in dutie bend thy knee to me,
That bowes vnto the graue with mickle age.
  Sal. My Lord, I haue considered with my selfe
The Title of this most renowned Duke,
And in my conscience, do repute his grace
The rightfull heyre to Englands Royall seate.
  King. Hast thou not sworne Allegeance vnto me?
  Sal. I haue.
  Ki. Canst thou dispense with heauen for such an oath?
  Sal. It is great sinne, to sweare vnto a sinne:
But greater sinne to keepe a sinfull oath:
Who can be bound by any solemne Vow
To do a murd'rous deede, to rob a man,
To force a spotlesse Virgins Chastitie,
To reaue the Orphan of his Patrimonie,
To wring the Widdow from her custom'd right,
And haue no other reason for this wrong,
But that he was bound by a solemne Oath?
  Qu. A subtle Traitor needs no Sophister.
  King. Call Buckingham, and bid him arme himselfe.
  Yorke. Call Buckingham, and all the friends thou hast,
I am resolu'd for death and dignitie.
  Old Clif. The first I warrant thee, if dreames proue true
  War. You were best to go to bed, and dreame againe,
To keepe thee from the Tempest of the field.
  Old Clif. I am resolu'd to beare a greater storme,
Then any thou canst coniure vp to day:
And that Ile write vpon thy Burgonet,
Might I but know thee by thy housed Badge.
  War. Now by my Fathers badge, old *Neuils* Crest,
The rampant Beare chain'd to the ragged staffe,
This day Ile weare aloft my Burgonet,
As on a Mountaine top, the Cedar shewes,
That keepes his leaues in spight of any storme,
Euen so affright thee with the view thereof.
  Old Clif. And from thy Burgonet Ile rend thy Beare,
And tread it vnder foot with all contempt,
Despight the Bearard, that protects the Beare.
  Yo. Clif. And so to Armes victorious Father,
To quell the Rebels, and their Complices.
  Rich. Fie, Charitie for shame, speake not in spight,
For you shall sup with Iesu Christ to night.
  Yo. Clif. Foule stygmaticke that's more then thou canst tell.
  Ric. If not in heauen, you'l surely sup in hell. *Exeunt*

Enter Warwicke.

  War. Clifford of Cumberland, 'tis Warwicke calles:
And if thou dost not hide thee from the Beare,
Now when the angrie Trumpet sounds alarum,
And dead mens cries do fill the emptie ayre,
Clifford I say, come forth and fight with me,
Proud Northerne Lord, Clifford of Cumberland,
Warwicke is hoarse with calling thee to armes.

Enter Yorke.

  War. How now my Noble Lord? What all a-foot.
  Yor. The deadly handed Clifford slew my Steed:
But match to match I haue encountred him,
And made a prey for Carrion Kytes and Crowes
Euen of the bonnie beast he loued so well.

Enter Clifford.

  War. Of one or both of vs the time is come.
  Yor. Hold Warwick: seek thee out some other chace
For I my selfe must hunt this Deere to death.
  War. Then nobly Yorke, 'tis for a Crown thou fightst:
As I intend Clifford to thriue to day,
It greeues my soule to leaue theee vnassail'd. *Exit War.*
  Clif. What seest thou in me Yorke?
Why dost thou pause?
  Yorke. With thy braue bearing should I be in loue,
But that thou art so fast mine enemie.
  Clif. Nor should thy prowesse want praise & esteeme,
But that 'tis shewne ignobly, and in Treason.
  Yorke. So let it helpe me now against thy sword,
As I in iustice, and true right expresse it.
  Clif. My soule and bodie on the action both.
  Yor. A dreadfull lay, addresse thee instantly.
  Clif. La fin Corrone les eumenes.
  Yor. Thus Warre hath giuen thee peace, for y art still,
Peace with his soule, heauen if it be thy will.

Enter yong Clifford.

  Clif. Shame and Confusion all is on the rout,
Feare frames disorder, and disorder wounds
Where it should guard. O Warre, thou sonne of hell,
Whom angry heauens do make their minister,
Throw in the frozen bosomes of our part,
Hot Coales of Vengeance. Let no Souldier flye.
He that is truly dedicate to Warre,
Hath no selfe-loue: nor he that loues himselfe,
Hath not essentially, but by circumstance
The name of Valour. O let the vile world end,
And the premised Flames of the Last day,
Knit earth and heauen together.
Now let the generall Trumpet blow his blast,
Particularities, and pettie sounds
To cease. Was't thou ordain'd (deere Father)
To loose thy youth in peace, and to atcheeue
The Siluer Liuery of aduised Age,
And in thy Reuerence, and thy Chaire-dayes, thus
To die in Ruffian battell? Euen at this sight,
My heart is turn'd to stone: and while 'tis mine,
It shall be stony. Yorke, not our old men spares:
No more will I their Babes, Teares Virginall,
Shall be to me, euen as the Dew to Fire,
And Beautie, that the Tyrant oft reclaimes,
Shall to my flaming wrath, be Oyle and Flax:
Henceforth, I will not haue to do with pitty.
Meet I an infant of the house of Yorke,
Into as many gobbits will I cut it
As wilde *Medea* yong *Absirtis* did.
In cruelty, will I seeke out my Fame.
Come thou new ruine of olde Cliffords house:
As did *Aeneas* old *Anchyses* beare,
So beare I thee vpon my manly shoulders:
But then, *Aeneas* bare a liuing loade;

Nothing

Nothing so heauy as these woes of mine.

Enter Richard, and Somerset to fight.

Rich. So lye thou there:
For vnderneath an Ale-house palsry signe,
The Castle in S. *Albons*, Somerset
Hath made the Wizard famous in his death:
Sword, hold thy temper; Heart, be wrathfull still:
Priests pray for enemies, but Princes kill.
Fight. Excursions.

Enter King, Queene, and others.

Qu. Away my Lord, you are slow, for shame away.
King. Can we outrun the Heauens? Good *Margaret* stay.
Qu. What are you made of? You'l nor fight nor fly:
Now is it manhood, wisedome, and defence,
To giue the enemy way, and to secure vs
By what we can, which can no more but flye.
Alarum a farre off.
If you be tane, we then should see the bottome
Of all our Fortunes: but if we haply scape,
(As well we may, if not through your neglect)
We shall to London get, where you are lou'd,
And where this breach now in our Fortunes made
May readily be stopt.

Enter Clifford.

Clif. But that my hearts on future mischeefe set,
I would speake blasphemy ere bid you flye:
But flye you must: Vncureable discomfite.
Reignes in the hearts of all our present parts.
Away for your releefe, and we will liue
To see their day, and them our Fortune giue.
Away my Lord, away. *Exeunt.*

Alarum. Retreat. Enter Yorke, Richard, Warwicke, and Soldiers, with Drum & Colours.

Yorke. Of Salsbury, who can report of him,
That Winter Lyon, who in rage forgets
Aged contusions, and all brush of Time:
And like a Gallant, in the brow of youth,
Repaires him with Occasion. This happy day
Is not it selfe, nor haue we wonne one foot,
If Salsbury be lost.
Rich. My Noble Father:
Three times to day I holpe him to his horse,
Three times bestrid him: Thrice I led him off,
Perswaded him from any further act:
But still where danger was, still there I met him,
And like rich hangings in a homely house,
So was his Will, in his old feeble body,
But Noble as he is, looke where he comes.
Enter Salsbury.
Sal. Now by my Sword, well hast thou fought to day:
By th'Masse so did we all. I thanke you *Richard.*
God knowes how long it is I haue to liue:
And it hath pleas'd him that three times to day
You haue defended me from imminent death.
Well Lords, we haue not got that which we haue,
'Tis not enough our foes are this time fled,
Being opposites of such repayring Nature.
Yorke. I know our safety is to follow them,
For (as I heare) the King is fled to London,
To call a present Court of Parliament:
Let vs pursue him ere the Writs go forth.
What sayes Lord Warwicke, shall we after them?
War. After them: nay before them if we can:
Now by my hand (Lords) 'twas a glorious day.
Saint Albons battell wonne by famous Yorke,
Shall be eterniz'd in all Age to come.
Sound Drumme and Trumpets, and to London all,
And more such dayes as these, to vs befall. *Exeunt.*

FINIS.

The third Part of Henry the Sixt,
with the death of the Duke of YORKE.

Actus Primus. Scœna Prima.

Alarum.
Enter Plantagenet, Edward, Richard, Norfolke, Mountague, Warwicke, and Souldiers.

Warwicke.

I Wonder how the King escap'd our hands?
 Pl. While we pursu'd the Horsmen of ỹ North,
He slyly stole away, and left his men:
Whereat the great Lord of Northumberland,
Whose Warlike eares could neuer brooke retreat,
Chear'd vp the drouping Army, and himselfe.
Lord *Clifford* and Lord *Stafford* all a-brest
Charg'd our maine Battailes Front: and breaking in,
Were by the Swords of common Souldiers slaine.
 Edw. Lord *Staffords* Father, Duke of *Buckingham*,
Is either slaine or wounded dangerous.
I cleft his Beauer with a down-right blow:
That this is true (Father) behold his blood.
 Mount. And Brother, here's the Earle of Wiltshires blood,
Whom I encountred as the Battels ioyn'd.
 Rich. Speake thou for me, and tell them what I did.
 Plan. *Richard* hath best deseru'd of all my sonnes:
But is your Grace dead, my Lord of Somerset?
 Nor. Such hope haue all the line of *Iohn of Gaunt*.
 Rich. Thus do I hope to shake King *Henries* head.
 Warw. And so doe I, victorious Prince of *Yorke*.
Before I see thee seated in that Throne,
Which now the House of *Lancaster* vsurpes,
I vow by Heauen, these eyes shall neuer close.
This is the Pallace of the fearefull King,
And this the Regall Seat: possesse it *Yorke*,
For this is thine, and not King *Henries* Heires.
 Plant. Assist me then, sweet *Warwick*, and I will,
For hither we haue broken in by force.
 Norf. Wee'le all assist you: he that flyes, shall dye:
 Plant. Thankes gentle *Norfolke*, stay by me my Lords,
And Souldiers stay and lodge by me this Night.
            They goe vp.
 Warw. And when the King comes, offer him no violence,
Vnlesse he seeke to thrust you out perforce.
 Plant. The Queene this day here holds her Parliament,
But little thinkes we shall be of her counsaile,
By words or blowes here let vs winne our right.
 Rich. Arm'd as we are, let's stay within this House.
 Warw. The bloody Parliament shall this be call'd,
Vnlesse *Plantagenet*, Duke of Yorke, be King,
And bashfull *Henry* depos'd, whose Cowardize
Hath made vs by-words to our enemies.
 Plant. Then leaue me not, my Lords be resolute,
I meane to take possession of my Right.
 Warw. Neither the King, nor he that loues him best,
The prowdest hee that holds vp *Lancaster*,
Dares stirre a Wing, if *Warwick* shake his Bells.
Ile plant *Plantagenet*, root him vp who dares:
Resolue thee *Richard*, clayme the English Crowne.

Flourish. Enter King Henry, Clifford, Northumberland, Westmerland, Exeter, and the rest.

 Henry. My Lords, looke where the sturdie Rebell sits,
Euen in the Chayre of State: belike he meanes,
Backt by the power of *Warwicke*, that false Peere,
To aspire vnto the Crowne, and reigne as King.
Earle of Northumberland, he slew thy Father,
And thine, Lord *Clifford*, & you both haue vow'd reuenge
On him, his sonnes, his fauorites, and his friends.
 Northumb. If I be not, Heauens be reueng'd on me.
 Clifford. The hope thereof, makes *Clifford* mourne in Steele.
 Westm. What, shall we suffer this? lets pluck him down,
My heart for anger burnes, I cannot brooke it.
 Henry. Be patient, gentle Earle of Westmerland.
 Clifford. Patience is for Poultroones, such as he:
He durst not sit there, had your Father liu'd.
My gracious Lord, here in the Parliament
Let vs assayle the Family of *Yorke*.
 North. Well hast thou spoken, Cousin be it so.
 Henry. Ah, know you not the Citie fauours them,
And they haue troupes of Souldiers at their beck?
 Westm. But when the Duke is slaine, they'le quickly flye.
 Henry. Farre be the thought of this from *Henries* heart,
To make a Shambles of the Parliament House.
Cousin of Exeter, frownes, words, and threats,
Shall be the Warre that *Henry* meanes to vse.
Thou factious Duke of Yorke descend my Throne,
And kneele for grace and mercie at my feet,
I am thy Soueraigne.
 Yorke. I am thine.
 Exet. For shame come downe, he made thee Duke of Yorke.
 Yorke. It was my Inheritance, as the Earledome was.
            Exet. Thy

Exet. Thy Father was a Traytor to the Crowne.
Warw. Exeter thou art a Traytor to the Crowne,
In following this vsurping *Henry*.

Clifford. Whom should hee follow, but his naturall King?

Warw. True *Clifford*, that's *Richard* Duke of Yorke.

Henry. And shall I stand, and thou sit in my Throne?

Yorke. It must and shall be so, content thy selfe.

Warw. Be Duke of Lancaster, let him be King.

Westm. He is both King, and Duke of Lancaster,
And that the Lord of Westmerland shall maintaine.

Warw. And *Warwick* shall disproue it. You forget,
That we are those which chas'd you from the field,
And slew your Fathers, and with Colours spread
Marcht through the Citie to the Pallace Gates.

Northumb. Yes *Warwicke*, I remember it to my griefe,
And by his Soule, thou and thy House shall rue it.

Westm. Plantagenet, of thee and these thy Sonnes,
Thy Kinsmen, and thy Friends, Ile haue more liues
Then drops of bloud were in my Fathers Veines.

Cliff. Vrge it no more, lest that in stead of words,
I send thee, *Warwicke*, such a Messenger,
As shall reuenge his death, before I stirre.

Warw. Poore *Clifford*, how I scorne his worthlesse Threats.

Plant. Will you we shew our Title to the Crowne?
If not, our Swords shall pleade it in the field.

Henry. What Title hast thou Traytor to the Crowne?
My Father was as thou art, Duke of Yorke,
Thy Grandfather *Roger Mortimer*, Earle of March.
I am the Sonne of *Henry* the Fift,
Who made the Dolphin and the French to stoupe,
And seiz'd vpon their Townes and Prouinces.

Warw. Talke not of France, sith thou hast lost it all.

Henry. The Lord Protector lost it, and not I:
When I was crown'd, I was but nine moneths old.

Rich. You are old enough now,
And yet me thinkes you loose:
Father teare the Crowne from the Vsurpers Head.

Edward. Sweet Father doe so, set it on your Head.

Mount. Good Brother,
As thou lou'st and honorest Armes,
Let's fight it out, and not stand cauilling thus.

Richard. Sound Drummes and Trumpets, and the King will flye.

Plant. Sonnes peace.

Henry. Peace thou, and giue King *Henry* leaue to speake.

Warw. Plantagenet shal speake first: Heare him Lords,
And be you silent and attentiue too,
For he that interrupts him, shall not liue.

Hen. Think'st thou, that I will leaue my Kingly Throne,
Wherein my Grandsire and my Father sat?
No: first shall Warre vnpeople this my Realme;
I, and their Colours often borne in France,
And now in England, to our hearts great sorrow,
Shall be my Winding-sheet. Why faint you Lords?
My Title's good, and better farre then his.

Warw. Proue it *Henry*, and thou shalt be King.

Hen. Henry the Fourth by Conquest got the Crowne.

Plant. 'Twas by Rebellion against his King.

Henry. I know not what to say, my Titles weake:
Tell me, may not a King adopt an Heire?

Plant. What then?

Henry. And if he may, then am I lawfull King:
For *Richard*, in the view of many Lords,
Resign'd the Crowne to *Henry* the Fourth,
Whose Heire my Father was, and I am his.

Plant. He rose against him, being his Soueraigne,
And made him to resigne his Crowne perforce.

Warw. Suppose, my Lords, he did it vnconstrayn'd,
Thinke you 'twere preiudiciall to his Crowne?

Exet. No: for he could not so resigne his Crowne,
But that the next Heire should succeed and reigne.

Henry. Art thou against vs, Duke of Exeter?

Exet. His is the right, and therefore pardon me.

Plant. Why whisper you, my Lords, and answer not?

Exet. My Conscience tells me he is lawfull King.

Henry. All will reuolt from me, and turne to him.

Northumb. Plantagenet, for all the Clayme thou lay'st,
Thinke not, that *Henry* shall be so depos'd.

Warw. Depos'd he shall be, in despight of all.

Northumb. Thou art deceiu'd:
'Tis not thy Southerne power
Of Essex, Norfolke, Suffolke, nor of Kent,
Which makes thee thus presumptuous and prowd,
Can set the Duke vp in despight of me.

Clifford. King *Henry*, be thy Title right or wrong,
Lord *Clifford* vowes to fight in thy defence:
May that ground gape, and swallow me aliue,
Where I shall kneele to him that slew my Father.

Henry. Oh *Clifford*, how thy words reuiue my heart.

Plant. Henry of Lancaster, resigne thy Crowne:
What mutter you, or what conspire you Lords?

Warw. Doe right vnto this Princely Duke of Yorke,
Or I will fill the House with armed men,
And ouer the Chayre of State, where now he sits,
Write vp his Title with vsurping blood.

He stampes with his foot, and the Souldiers shew themselues.

Henry. My Lord of Warwick, heare but one word,
Let me for this my life time reigne as King.

Plant. Confirme the Crowne to me and to mine Heires,
And thou shalt reigne in quiet while thou liu'st.

Henry. I am content: *Richard Plantagenet*
Enioy the Kingdome after my decease.

Clifford. What wrong is this vnto the Prince, your Sonne?

Warw. What good is this to England, and himselfe?

Westm. Base, fearefull, and despayring *Henry*.

Clifford. How hast thou iniur'd both thy selfe and vs?

Westm. I cannot stay to heare these Articles.

Northumb. Nor I.

Clifford. Come Cousin, let vs tell the Queene these Newes.

Westm. Farwell faint-hearted and degenerate King,
In whose cold blood no sparke of Honor bides.

Northumb. Be thou a prey vnto the House of Yorke,
And dye in Bands, for this vnmanly deed.

Cliff. In dreadfull Warre may'st thou be ouercome,
Or liue in peace abandon'd and despis'd.

Warw. Turne this way *Henry*, and regard them not.

Exeter. They seeke reuenge, and therefore will not yeeld.

Henry. Ah Exeter.

Warw. Why should you sigh, my Lord?

Henry. Not for my selfe Lord *Warwick*, but my Sonne,
Whom I vnnaturally shall dis-inherite.
But be it as it may: I here entayle
The Crowne to thee and to thine Heires for euer,
Conditionally, that heere thou take an Oath,
To cease this Ciuill Warre; and whil'st I liue,

The third Part of Henry the Sixt.

To honor me as thy King, and Soueraigne:
And neyther by Treason nor Hostilitie,
To seeke to put me downe, and reigne thy selfe.

Plant. This Oath I willingly take, and will performe.

Warw. Long liue King *Henry*: *Plantagenet* embrace him.

Henry. And long liue thou, and these thy forward Sonnes.

Plant. Now *Yorke* and *Lancaster* are reconcil'd.

Exet. Accurst be he that seekes to make them foes.

Senet. Here they come downe.

Plant. Farewell my gracious Lord, Ile to my Castle.

Warw. And Ile keepe London with my Souldiers.

Norf. And I to Norfolke with my followers.

Mount. And I vnto the Sea, from whence I came.

Henry. And I with griefe and sorrow to the Court.

Enter the Queene.

Exeter. Heere comes the Queene,
Whose Lookes bewray her anger:
Ile steale away.

Henry. Exeter so will I.

Queene. Nay, goe not from me, I will follow thee.

Henry. Be patient gentle Queene, and I will stay.

Queene. Who can be patient in such extreames?
Ah wretched man, would I had dy'de a Maid?
And neuer seene thee, neuer borne thee Sonne,
Seeing thou hast prou'd so vnnaturall a Father.
Hath he deseru'd to loose his Birth-right thus?
Hadst thou but lou'd him halfe so well as I,
Or felt that paine which I did for him once,
Or nourisht him, as I did with my blood;
Thou would'st haue left thy dearest heart-blood there,
Rather then haue made that sauage Duke thine Heire,
And dis-inherited thine onely Sonne.

Prince. Father, you cannot dis-inherite me:
If you be King, why should not I succeede?

Henry. Pardon me *Margaret*, pardon me sweet Sonne,
The Earle of Warwick and the Duke enforc't me.

Quee. Enforc't thee? Art thou King, and wilt be forc't?
I shame to heare thee speake: ah timorous Wretch,
Thou hast vndone thy selfe, thy Sonne, and me,
And giu'n vnto the House of *Yorke* such head,
As thou shalt reigne but by their sufferance.
To entayle him and his Heires vnto the Crowne,
What is it, but to make thy Sepulcher,
And creepe into it farre before thy time?
Warwick is Chancelor, and the Lord of Callice,
Sterne *Falconbridge* commands the Narrow Seas,
The Duke is made Protector of the Realme,
And yet shalt thou be safe? Such safetie findes
The trembling Lambe, inuironned with Wolues.
Had I beene there, which am a silly Woman,
The Souldiers should haue toss'd me on their Pikes,
Before I would haue granted to that Act.
But thou preferr'st thy Life, before thine Honor.
And seeing thou do'st, I here diuorce my selfe,
Both from thy Table *Henry*, and thy Bed,
Vntill that Act of Parliament be repeal'd,
Whereby my Sonne is dis-inherited.
The Northerne Lords, that haue forsworne thy Colours,
Will follow mine, if once they see them spread:
And spread they shall be, to thy foule disgrace,
And vtter ruine of the House of *Yorke*:
Thus doe I leaue thee: Come Sonne, let's away,
Our Army is ready; come, wee'le after them.

Henry. Stay gentle *Margaret*, and heare me speake.

Queene. Thou hast spoke too much already: get thee gone.

Henry. Gentle Sonne *Edward*, thou wilt stay me?

Queene. I, to be murther'd by his Enemies.

Prince. When I returne with victorie to the field,
Ile see your Grace: till then, Ile follow her.

Queene. Come Sonne away, we may not linger thus.

Henry. Poore Queene,
How loue to me, and to her Sonne,
Hath made her breake out into termes of Rage.
Reueng'd may she be on that hatefull Duke,
Whose haughtie spirit, winged with desire,
Will cost my Crowne, and like an emptie Eagle,
Tyre on the flesh of me, and of my Sonne.
The losse of those three Lords torments my heart:
Ile write vnto them, and entreat them faire;
Come Cousin, you shall be the Messenger.

Exet. And I, I hope, shall reconcile them all. *Exit.*

Flourish. Enter Richard, Edward, and Mountague.

Richard. Brother, though I bee youngest, giue mee leaue.

Edward. No, I can better play the Orator.

Mount. But I haue reasons strong and forceable.

Enter the Duke of Yorke.

Yorke. Why how now Sonnes, and Brother, at a strife?
What is your Quarrell? how began it first?

Edward. No Quarrell, but a slight Contention.

Yorke. About what?

Rich. About that which concernes your Grace and vs,
The Crowne of England, Father, which is yours.

Yorke. Mine Boy? not till King *Henry* be dead.

Richard. Your Right depends not on his life, or death.

Edward. Now you are Heire, therefore enioy it now:
By giuing the House of *Lancaster* leaue to breathe,
It will out-runne you, Father, in the end.

Yorke. I tooke an Oath, that hee should quietly reigne.

Edward. But for a Kingdome any Oath may be broken:
I would breake a thousand Oathes, to reigne one yeere.

Richard. No: God forbid your Grace should be for-sworne.

Yorke. I shall be, if I clayme by open Warre.

Richard. Ile proue the contrary, if you'le heare mee speake.

Yorke. Thou canst not, Sonne: it is impossible.

Richard. An Oath is of no moment, being not tooke
Before a true and lawfull Magistrate,
That hath authoritie ouer him that sweares.
Henry had none, but did vsurpe the place.
Then seeing 'twas he that made you to depose,
Your Oath, my Lord, is vaine and friuolous.
Therefore to Armes: and Father doe but thinke,
How sweet a thing it is to weare a Crowne,
Within whose Circuit is *Elizium*,
And all that Poets faine of Blisse and Ioy.
Why doe we linger thus? I cannot rest,
Vntill the White Rose that I weare, be dy'de
Euen in the luke-warme blood of *Henries* heart.

Yorke. *Richard* ynough: I will be King, or dye.
Brother, thou shalt to London presently,
And whet on *Warwick* to this Enterprise.

Thou

Thou *Richard* shalt to the Duke of Norfolke,
And tell him priuily of our intent.
You *Edward* shall vnto my Lord *Cobham*,
With whom the Kentishmen will willingly rise.
In them I trust: for they are Souldiors,
Wittie, courteous, liberall, full of spirit.
While you are thus imploy'd, what resteth more?
But that I seeke occasion how to rise,
And yet the King not priuie to my Drift,
Nor any of the House of *Lancaster*.

Enter Gabriel.

But stay, what Newes? Why comm'st thou in such poste?
  Gabriel. The Queene,
With all the Northerne Earles and Lords,
Intend here to besiege you in your Castle.
She is hard by, with twentie thousand men:
And therefore fortifie your Hold, my Lord.
  Yorke. I, with my Sword.
What? think'st thou, that we feare them?
Edward and *Richard*, you shall stay with me,
My Brother *Mountague* shall poste to London.
Let Noble *Warwicke*, *Cobham*, and the rest,
Whom we haue left Protectors of the King,
With powrefull Pollicie strengthen themselues,
And trust not simple *Henry*, nor his Oathes.
  Mount. Brother, I goe: Ile winne them, feare it not.
And thus most humbly I doe take my leaue.
                                Exit Mountague.

Enter Mortimer, and his Brother.

  York. Sir *Iohn*, and Sir *Hugh Mortimer*, mine Vnckles,
You are come to Sandall in a happie houre.
The Armie of the Queene meane to besiege vs.
  Iohn. Shee shall not neede, wee'le meete her in the field.
  Yorke. What, with fiue thousand men?
  Richard. I, with fiue hundred, Father, for a neede.
A Woman's generall: what should we feare?
                            A March afarre off.
  Edward. I heare their Drummes:
Let's set our men in order,
And issue forth, and bid them Battaile straight.
  Yorke. Fiue men to twentie: though the oddes be great,
I doubt not, Vnckle, of our Victorie.
Many a Battaile haue I wonne in France,
When as the Enemie hath beene tenne to one:
Why should I not now haue the like successe?
                    Alarum.   *Exit.*

Enter Rutland, and his Tutor.

  Rutland. Ah, whither shall I flye, to scape their hands?
Ah Tutor, looke where bloody *Clifford* comes.

Enter Clifford.

  Clifford. Chaplaine away, thy Priesthood saues thy life.
As for the Brat of this accursed Duke,
Whose Father slew my Father, he shall dye.
  Tutor. And I, my Lord, will beare him company.
  Clifford. Souldiers, away with him.
  Tutor. Ah *Clifford*, murther not this innocent Child,
Least thou be hated both of God and Man. *Exit.*

  Clifford. How now? is he dead alreadie?
Or is it feare, that makes him close his eyes?
Ile open them.
  Rutland. So lookes the pent-vp Lyon o're the Wretch,
That trembles vnder his deuouring Pawes:
And so he walkes, insulting o're his Prey,
And so he comes, to rend his Limbes asunder.
Ah gentle *Clifford*, kill me with thy Sword,
And not with such a cruell threatning Looke.
Sweet *Clifford* heare me speake, before I dye:
I am too meane a subiect for thy Wrath,
Be thou reueng'd on men, and let me liue.
  Clifford. In vaine thou speak'st, poore Boy:
My Fathers blood hath stopt the passage
Where thy words should enter.
  Rutland. Then let my Fathers blood open it againe,
He is a man, and *Clifford* cope with him.
  Clifford. Had I thy Brethren here, their liues and thine
Were not reuenge sufficient for me:
No, if I digg'd vp thy fore-fathers Graues,
And hung their rotten Coffins vp in Chaynes,
It could not slake mine ire, nor ease my heart.
The sight of any of the House of *Yorke*,
Is as a furie to torment my Soule:
And till I root out their accursed Line,
And leaue not one aliue, I liue in Hell.
Therefore---
  Rutland. Oh let me pray, before I take my death:
To thee I pray; sweet *Clifford* pitty me.
  Clifford. Such pitty as my Rapiers point affords.
  Rutland. I neuer did thee harme: why wilt thou slay me?
  Clifford. Thy Father hath.
  Rutland. But 'twas ere I was borne.
Thou hast one Sonne, for his sake pitty me,
Least in reuenge thereof, sith God is iust,
He be as miserably slaine as I.
Ah, let me liue in Prison all my dayes,
And when I giue occasion of offence,
Then let me dye, for now thou hast no cause.
  Clifford. No cause? thy Father slew my Father: therefore dye.
  Rutland. Dij faciant laudis summa sit ista tuæ.
  Clifford. Plantagenet, I come *Plantagenet*:
And this thy Sonnes blood cleauing to my Blade,
Shall rust vpon my Weapon, till thy blood
Congeal'd with this, doe make me wipe off both. *Exit.*

Alarum. Enter Richard, Duke of Yorke.

  Yorke. The Army of the Queene hath got the field:
My Vnckles both are slaine, in rescuing me;
And all my followers, to the eager foe
Turne back, and flye, like Ships before the Winde,
Or Lambes pursu'd by hunger-starued Wolues.
My Sonnes, God knowes what hath bechanced them:
But this I know, they haue demean'd themselues
Like men borne to Renowne, by Life or Death.
Three times did *Richard* make a Lane to me,
And thrice cry'de, Courage Father, fight it out:
And full as oft came *Edward* to my side,
With Purple Faulchion, painted to the Hilt,
In blood of those that had encountred him:
And when the hardyest Warriors did retyre,
Richard cry'de, Charge, and giue no foot of ground,
And cry'de, A Crowne, or else a glorious Tombe,

A Scepter, or an Earthly Sepulchre.
With this we charg'd againe: but out alas,
We bodg'd againe, as I haue seene a Swan
With bootlesse labour swimme against the Tyde,
And spend her strength with ouer-matching Waues.
A short Alarum within.
Ah hearke, the fatall followers doe pursue,
And I am faint, and cannot flye their furie:
And were I strong, I would not shunne their furie.
The Sands are numbred, that makes vp my Life,
Here must I stay, and here my Life must end.

*Enter the Queene, Clifford, Northumberland,
the young Prince, and Souldiers.*

Come bloody *Clifford*, rough *Northumberland*,
I dare your quenchlesse furie to more rage:
I am your Butt, and I abide your Shot.
 Northumb. Yeeld to our mercy, proud *Plantagenet*.
 Clifford. I, to such mercy, as his ruthlesse Arme
With downe-right payment, shew'd vnto my Father.
Now *Phaeton* hath tumbled from his Carre,
And made an Euening at the Noone-tide Prick.
 Yorke. My ashes, as the Phœnix, may bring forth
A Bird, that will reuenge vpon you all:
And in that hope, I throw mine eyes to Heauen,
Scorning what ere you can afflict me with.
Why come you not? what, multitudes, and feare?
 Cliff. So Cowards fight, when they can flye no further,
So Doues doe peck the Faulcons piercing Tallons,
So desperate Theeues, all hopelesse of their Liues,
Breathe out Inuectiues 'gainst the Officers.
 Yorke. Oh *Clifford*, but bethinke thee once againe,
And in thy thought ore-run my former time:
And if thou canst, for blushing, view this face,
And bite thy tongue, that slanders him with Cowardice,
Whose frowne hath made thee faint and flye ere this.
 Clifford. I will not bandie with thee word for word,
But buckler with thee blowes twice two for one.
 Queene. Hold valiant *Clifford*, for a thousand causes
I would prolong a while the Traytors Life:
Wrath makes him deafe; speake thou *Northumberland*.
 Northumb. Hold *Clifford*, doe not honor him so much,
To prick thy finger, though to wound his heart.
What valour were it, when a Curre doth grinne,
For one to thrust his Hand betweene his Teeth,
When he might spurne him with his Foot away?
It is Warres prize, to take all Vantages,
And tenne to one, is no impeach of Valour.
 Clifford. I, I, so striues the Woodcocke with the Gynne.
 Northumb. So doth the Connie struggle in the Net.
 York. So triumph Theeues vpon their conquer'd Booty,
So True men yeeld with Robbers, so o're-matcht.
 Northumb. What would your Grace haue done vnto him now?
 Queene. Braue Warriors, *Clifford* and *Northumberland*,
Come make him stand vpon this Mole-hill here,
That raught at Mountaines with out-stretched Armes,
Yet parted but the shadow with his Hand.
What, was it you that would be Englands King?
Was't you that reuell'd in our Parliament,
And made a Preachment of your high Descent?
Where are your Messe of Sonnes, to back you now,
The wanton *Edward*, and the lustie *George*?

And where's that valiant Crook-back Prodigie,
Dickie, your Boy, that with his grumbling voyce
Was wont to cheare his Dad in Mutinies?
Or with the rest, where is your Darling, *Rutland*?
Looke *Yorke*, I stayn'd this Napkin with the blood
That valiant *Clifford*, with his Rapiers point,
Made issue from the Bosome of the Boy:
And if thine eyes can water for his death,
I giue thee this to drie thy Cheekes withall.
Alas poore *Yorke*, but that I hate thee deadly,
I should lament thy miserable state.
I prythee grieue, to make me merry, *Yorke*.
What, hath thy fierie heart so parcht thine entrayles,
That not a Teare can fall, for *Rutlands* death?
Why art thou patient, man? thou should'st be mad:
And I, to make thee mad, doe mock thee thus.
Stampe, raue, and fret, that I may sing and dance.
Thou would'st be fee'd, I see, to make me sport:
Yorke cannot speake, vnlesse he weare a Crowne.
A Crowne for *Yorke*; and Lords, bow lowe to him:
Hold you his hands, whilest I doe set it on.
I marry Sir, now lookes he like a King:
I, this is he that tooke King *Henries* Chaire,
And this is he was his adopted Heire.
But how is it, that great *Plantagenet*
Is crown'd so soone, and broke his solemne Oath?
As I bethinke me, you should not be King,
Till our King *Henry* had shooke hands with Death.
And will you pale your head in *Henries* Glory,
And rob his Temples of the Diademe,
Now in his Life, against your holy Oath?
Oh 'tis a fault too too vnpardonable.
Off with the Crowne; and with the Crowne, his Head,
And whilest we breathe, take time to doe him dead.
 Clifford. That is my Office, for my Fathers sake.
 Queene. Nay stay, let's heare the Orizons hee makes.
 Yorke. Shee-Wolfe of France,
But worse then Wolues of France,
Whose Tongue more poysons then the Adders Tooth:
How ill-beseeming is it in thy Sex,
To triumph like an Amazonian Trull,
Vpon their Woes, whom Fortune captiuates?
But that thy Face is Vizard-like, vnchanging,
Made impudent with vse of euill deedes.
I would assay, prowd Queene, to make thee blush.
To tell thee whence thou cam'st, of whom deriu'd,
Were shame enough, to shame thee,
Wert thou not shamelesse.
Thy Father beares the type of King of Naples,
Of both the Sicils, and Ierusalem,
Yet not so wealthie as an English Yeoman.
Hath that poore Monarch taught thee to insult?
It needes not, nor it bootes thee not, prowd Queene,
Vnlesse the Adage must be verify'd,
That Beggers mounted, runne their Horse to death.
'Tis Beautie that doth oft make Women prowd,
But God he knowes, thy share thereof is small.
'Tis Vertue, that doth make them most admir'd,
The contrary, doth make thee wondred at.
'Tis Gouernment that makes them seeme Diuine,
The want thereof, makes thee abhominable.
Thou art as opposite to euery good,
As the *Antipodes* are vnto vs,
Or as the South to the *Septentrion*.
Oh Tygres Heart, wrapt in a Womans Hide,

How

How could'st thou drayne the Life-blood of the Child,
To bid the Father wipe his eyes withall,
And yet be seene to beare a Womans face?
Women are soft, milde, pittifull, and flexible;
Thou, sterne, obdurate, flintie, rough, remorselesse.
Bid'st thou me rage? why now thou hast thy wish.
Would'st haue me weepe? why now thou hast thy will.
For raging Wind blowes vp incessant showers,
And when the Rage allayes, the Raine begins.
These Teares are my sweet *Rutlands* Obsequies,
And euery drop cryes vengeance for his death,
'Gainst thee fell *Clifford*, and thee false French-woman.

Northumb. Beshrew me, but his passions moues me so,
That hardly can I check my eyes from Teares.

Yorke. That Face of his,
The hungry Caniballs would not haue toucht,
Would not haue stayn'd with blood:
But you are more inhumane, more inexorable,
Oh, tenne times more then Tygers of Hyrcania.
See, ruthlesse Queene, a haplesse Fathers Teares:
This Cloth thou dipd'st in blood of my sweet Boy,
And I with Teares doe wash the blood away.
Keepe thou the Napkin, and goe boast of this,
And if thou tell'st the heauie storie right,
Vpon my Soule, the hearers will shed Teares:
Yea, euen my Foes will shed fast-falling Teares,
And say, Alas, it was a pittious deed.
There, take the Crowne, and with the Crowne, my Curse,
And in thy need, such comfort come to thee,
As now I reape at thy too cruell hand.
Hard-hearted *Clifford*, take me from the World,
My Soule to Heauen, my Blood vpon your Heads.

Northumb. Had he been slaughter-man to all my Kinne,
I should not for my Life but weepe with him,
To see how inly Sorrow gripes his Soule.

Queen. What, weeping ripe, my Lord *Northumberland*?
Thinke but vpon the wrong he did vs all,
And that will quickly drie thy melting Teares.

Clifford. Heere's for my Oath, heere's for my Fathers Death.

Queene. And heere's to right our gentle-hearted King.

Yorke. Open thy Gate of Mercy, gracious God,
My Soule flyes through these wounds, to seeke out thee.

Queene. Off with his Head, and set it on Yorke Gates,
So *Yorke* may ouer-looke the Towne of Yorke.

Flourish.   Exit.

*A March. Enter Edward, Richard,
and their power.*

Edward. I wonder how our Princely Father scap't:
Or whether he be scap't away, or no,
From *Cliffords* and *Northumberlands* pursuit?
Had he been ta'ne, we should haue heard the newes;
Had he beene slaine, we should haue heard the newes:
Or had he scap't, me thinkes we should haue heard
The happy tidings of his good escape.
How fares my Brother? why is he so sad?

Richard. I cannot ioy, vntill I be resolu'd
Where our right valiant Father is become.
I saw him in the Battaile range about,
And watcht him how he singled *Clifford* forth.
Me thought he bore him in the thickest troupe,
As doth a Lyon in a Heard of Neat,
Or as a Beare encompass'd round with Dogges:
Who hauing pincht a few, and made them cry,
The rest stand all aloofe, and barke at him.
So far'd our Father with his Enemies,
So fled his Enemies my Warlike Father:
Me thinkes 'tis prize enough to be his Sonne.
See how the Morning opes her golden Gates,
And takes her farwell of the glorious Sunne.
How well resembles it the prime of Youth,
Trimm'd like a Yonker, prauncing to his Loue?

Ed. Dazle mine eyes, or doe I see three Sunnes?

Rich. Three glorious Sunnes, each one a perfect Sunne,
Not seperated with the racking Clouds,
But seuer'd in a pale cleare-shining Skye.
See, see, they ioyne, embrace, and seeme to kisse,
As if they vow'd some League inuiolable.
Now are they but one Lampe, one Light, one Sunne:
In this, the Heauen figures some euent.

Edward. 'Tis wondrous strange,
The like yet neuer heard of.
I thinke it cites vs (Brother) to the field,
That wee, the Sonnes of braue *Plantagenet*,
Each one alreadie blazing by our meedes,
Should notwithstanding ioyne our Lights together,
And ouer-shine the Earth, as this the World.
What ere it bodes, hence-forward will I beare
Vpon my Targuet three faire shining Sunnes.

Richard. Nay, beare three Daughters:
By your leaue, I speake it,
You loue the Breeder better then the Male.

Enter one blowing.

But what art thou, whose heauie Lookes fore-tell
Some dreadfull story hanging on thy Tongue?

Mess. Ah, one that was a wofull looker on,
When as the Noble Duke of Yorke was slaine,
Your Princely Father, and my louing Lord.

Edward. Oh speake no more, for I haue heard too much.

Richard. Say how he dy'de, for I will heare it all.

Mess. Enuironed he was with many foes,
And stood against them, as the hope of Troy
Against the Greekes, that would haue entred Troy.
But *Hercules* himselfe must yeeld to oddes:
And many stroakes, though with a little Axe,
Hewes downe and fells the hardest-tymber'd Oake.
By many hands your Father was subdu'd,
But onely slaught'red by the irefull Arme
Of vn-relenting *Clifford*, and the Queene:
Who crown'd the gracious Duke in high despight,
Laugh'd in his face: and when with griefe he wept,
The ruthlesse Queene gaue him, to dry his Cheekes,
A Napkin, steeped in the harmelesse blood
Of sweet young *Rutland*, by rough *Clifford* slaine:
And after many scornes, many foule taunts,
They tooke his Head, and on the Gates of Yorke
They set the same, and there it doth remaine,
The saddest spectacle that ere I view'd.

Edward. Sweet Duke of Yorke, our Prop to leane vpon,
Now thou art gone, wee haue no Staffe, no Stay.
Oh *Clifford*, boyst'rous *Clifford*, thou hast slaine
The flowre of Europe, for his Cheualrie,
And trecherously hast thou vanquisht him,
For hand to hand he would haue vanquisht thee.
Now my Soules Pallace is become a Prison:
Ah, would she breake from hence, that this my body
                                                    Might

Might in the ground be closed vp in rest:
For neuer henceforth shall I ioy againe:
Neuer, oh neuer shall I see more ioy.

 Rich. I cannot weepe: for all my bodies moysture
Scarse serues to quench my Furnace-burning hart:
Nor can my tongue vnloade my hearts great burthen,
For selfe-same winde that I should speake withall,
Is kindling coales that fires all my brest,
And burnes me vp with flames, that tears would quench.
To weepe, is to make lesse the depth of greefe:
Teares then for Babes; Blowes, and Reuenge for mee.
Richard, I beare thy name, Ile venge thy death,
Or dye renowned by attempting it.

 Ed. His name that valiant Duke hath left with thee:
His Dukedome, and his Chaire with me is left.

 Rich. Nay, if thou be that Princely Eagles Bird,
Shew thy descent by gazing 'gainst the Sunne:
For Chaire and Dukedome, Throne and Kingdome say,
Either that is thine, or else thou wer't not his.

*March. Enter Warwicke, Marquesse Mountacute,
and their Army.*

 Warwick. How now faire Lords? What faire? What
newes abroad?

 Rich. Great Lord of Warwicke, if we should recompt
Our balefull newes, and at each words deliuerance
Stab Poniards in our flesh, till all were told,
The words would adde more anguish then the wounds.
O valiant Lord, the Duke of Yorke is slaine.

 Edw. O Warwicke, Warwicke, that *Plantagenet*
Which held thee deerely, as his Soules Redemption,
Is by the sterne Lord *Clifford* done to death.

 War. Ten dayes ago, I drown'd these newes in teares.
And now to adde more measure to your woes,
I come to tell you things sith then befalne.
After the bloody Fray at Wakefield fought,
Where your braue Father breath'd his latest gaspe,
Tydings, as swiftly as the Postes could runne,
Were brought me of your Losse, and his Depart.
I then in London, keeper of the King,
Muster'd my Soldiers, gathered flockes of Friends,
Marcht toward S. Albans, to intercept the Queene,
Bearing the King in my behalfe along:
For by my Scouts, I was aduertised
That she was comming with a full intent
To dash our late Decree in Parliament,
Touching King *Henries* Oath, and your Succession:
Short Tale to make, we at S. Albans met,
Our Battailes ioyn'd, and both sides fiercely fought:
But whether 'twas the coldnesse of the King,
Who look'd full gently on his warlike Queene,
That robb'd my Soldiers of their heated Spleene.
Or whether 'twas report of her successe,
Or more then common feare of *Cliffords* Rigour,
Who thunders to his Captiues, Blood and Death,
I cannot iudge: but to conclude with truth,
Their Weapons like to Lightning, came and went:
Our Souldiers like the Night-Owles lazie flight,
Or like a lazie Thresher with a Flaile,
Fell gently downe, as if they strucke their Friends.
I cheer'd them vp with iustice of our Cause,
With promise of high pay, and great Rewards:
But all in vaine, they had no heart to fight,
And we (in them) no hope to win the day,
So that we fled: the King vnto the Queene,
Lord *George,* your Brother, Norfolke, and my Selfe,
In haste, post haste, are come to ioyne with you:
For in the Marches heere we heard you were,
Making another Head, to fight againe.

 Ed. Where is the Duke of Norfolke, gentle Warwick?
And when came *George* from Burgundy to England?

 War. Some six miles off the Duke is with the Soldiers,
And for your Brother he was lately sent
From your kinde Aunt Dutchesse of Burgundie,
With ayde of Souldiers to this needfull Warre.

 Rich. 'Twas oddes belike, when valiant Warwick fled;
Oft haue I heard his praises in Pursuite,
But ne're till now, his Scandall of Retire.

 War. Nor now my Scandall *Richard,* dost thou heare:
For thou shalt know this strong right hand of mine,
Can plucke the Diadem from faint *Henries* head,
And wring the awefull Scepter from his Fist,
Were he as famous, and as bold in Warre,
As he is fam'd for Mildnesse, Peace, and Prayer.

 Rich. I know it well Lord Warwick, blame me not,
'Tis loue I beare thy glories make me speake:
But in this troublous time, what's to be done?
Shall we go throw away our Coates of Steele,
And wrap our bodies in blacke mourning Gownes,
Numb'ring our Aue-Maries with our Beads?
Or shall we on the Helmets of our Foes
Tell our Deuotion with reuengefull Armes?
If for the last, say I, and to it Lords.

 War. Why therefore Warwick came to seek you out,
And therefore comes my Brother *Mountague*:
Attend me Lords, the proud insulting Queene,
With *Clifford,* and the haught Northumberland,
And of their Feather, many moe proud Birds,
Haue wrought the easie-melting King, like Wax.
He swore consent to your Succession,
His Oath enrolled in the Parliament.
And now to London all the crew are gone,
To frustrate both his Oath, and what beside
May make against the house of Lancaster.
Their power (I thinke) is thirty thousand strong:
Now, if the helpe of Norfolke, and my selfe,
With all the Friends that thou braue Earle of March,
Among'st the louing Welshmen can'st procure,
Will but amount to fiue and twenty thousand,
Why Via, to London will we march,
And once againe, bestride our foaming Steeds,
And once againe cry Charge vpon our Foes,
But neuer once againe turne backe and flye.

 Rich. I, now me thinks I heare great Warwick speak;
Ne're may he liue to see a Sun-shine day,
That cries Retire, if Warwicke bid him stay.

 Ed. Lord Warwicke, on thy shoulder will I leane,
And when thou failst (as God forbid the houre)
Must *Edward* fall, which perill heauen forefend.

 War. No longer Earle of March, but Duke of Yorke:
The next degree, is Englands Royall Throne:
For King of England shalt thou be proclaim'd
In euery Burrough as we passe along,
And he that throwes not vp his cap for ioy,
Shall for the Fault make forfeit of his head.
King *Edward,* valiant *Richard Mountague*:
Stay we no longer, dreaming of Renowne,
But sound the Trumpets, and about our Taske.

 Rich. Then *Clifford,* were thy heart as hard as Steele,
As thou hast shewne it flintie by thy deeds,
I come to pierce it, or to giue thee mine.

 Ed. Then strike vp Drums, God and S. George for vs.

P *War.*

Enter a Messenger.

War. How now? what newes?

Mes. The Duke of Norfolke sends you word by me,
The Queene is comming with a puissant Hoast,
And craues your company, for speedy counsell.

War. Why then it sorts, braue Warriors, let's away.
Exeunt Omnes.

*Flourish. Enter the King, the Queene, Clifford, Northum-
and Yong Prince, with Drumme and
Trumpettes.*

Qu. Welcome my Lord, to this braue town of Yorke,
Yonders the head of that Arch-enemy,
That sought to be incompast with your Crowne.
Doth not the obiect cheere your heart, my Lord.

K. I, as the rockes cheare them that feare their wrack,
To see this sight, it irkes my very soule:
With-hold reuenge (deere God) 'tis not my fault,
Nor wittingly haue I infring'd my Vow.

Clif. My gracious Liege, this too much lenity
And harmfull pitty must be layd aside:
To whom do Lyons cast their gentle Lookes?
Not to the Beast, that would vsurpe their Den.
Whose hand is that the Forrest Beare doth licke?
Not his that spoyles her yong before her face.
Who scapes the lurking Serpents mortall sting?
Not he that sets his foot vpon her backe.
The smallest Worme will turne, being troden on,
And Doues will pecke in safegard of their Brood.
Ambitious Yorke, did leuell at thy Crowne,
Thou smiling, while he knit his angry browes.
He but a Duke, would haue his Sonne a King,
And raise his issue like a louing Sire.
Thou being a King, blest with a goodly sonne,
Did'st yeeld consent to disinherit him:
Which argued thee a most vnlouing Father.
Vnreasonable Creatures feed their young,
And though mans face be fearefull to their eyes,
Yet in protection of their tender ones,
Who hath not seene them euen with those wings,
Which sometime they haue vs'd with fearfull flight,
Make warre with him that climb'd vnto their nest,
Offering their owne liues in their yongs defence?
For shame, my Liege, make them your President:
Were it not pitty that this goodly Boy
Should loose his Birth-right by his Fathers fault,
And long heereafter say vnto his childe,
What my great Grandfather, and Grandsire got,
My carelesse Father fondly gaue away.
Ah, what a shame were this? Looke on the Boy,
And let his manly face, which promiseth
Successefull Fortune steele thy melting heart,
To hold thine owne, and leaue thine owne with him.

King. Full well hath *Clifford* plaid the Orator,
Inferring arguments of mighty force:
But *Clifford* tell me, did'st thou neuer heare,
That things ill got, had euer bad successe.
And happy alwayes was it for that Sonne,
Whose Father for his hoording went to hell:
Ile leaue my Sonne my Vertuous deeds behinde,
And would my Father had left me no more:
For all the rest is held at such a Rate,
As brings a thousand fold more care to keepe,
Then in possession any iot of pleasure.
Ah Cosin Yorke, would thy best Friends did know,
How it doth grieue me that thy head is heere.

Qu. My Lord cheere vp your spirits, our foes are nye,
And this soft courage makes your Followers faint:
You promist Knighthood to our forward sonne,
Vnsheath your sword, and dub him presently.
Edward, kneele downe.

King. Edward Plantagenet, arise a Knight,
And learne this Lesson; Draw thy Sword in right.

Prin. My gracious Father, by your Kingly leaue,
Ile draw it as Apparant to the Crowne,
And in that quarrell, vse it to the death.

Clif. Why that is spoken like a toward Prince.

Enter a Messenger.

Mess. Royall Commanders, be in readinesse,
For with a Band of thirty thousand men,
Comes Warwicke backing of the Duke of Yorke,
And in the Townes as they do march along,
Proclaimes him King, and many flye to him,
Darraigne your battell, for they are at hand.

Clif. I would your Highnesse would depart the field,
The Queene hath best successe when you are absent.

Qu. I good my Lord, and leaue vs to our Fortune.

King. Why, that's my fortune too, therefore Ile stay.

North. Be it with resolution then to fight.

Prin. My Royall Father, cheere these Noble Lords,
And hearten those that fight in your defence:
Vnsheath your Sword, good Father: Cry S. George.

*March. Enter Edward, Warwicke, Richard, Clarence,
Norfolke, Mountague, and Soldiers.*

Edw. Now periur'd *Henry*, wilt thou kneel for grace?
And set thy Diadem vpon my head?
Or bide the mortall Fortune of the field.

Qu. Go rate thy Minions, proud insulting Boy,
Becomes it thee to be thus bold in termes,
Before thy Soueraigne, and thy lawfull King?

Ed. I am his King, and he should bow his knee:
I was adopted Heire by his consent.

Cla. Since when, his Oath is broke: for as I heare,
You that are King, though he do weare the Crowne,
Haue caus'd him by new Act of Parliament,
To blot out me, and put his owne Sonne in.

Clif. And reason too,
Who should succeede the Father, but the Sonne.

Rich. Are you there Butcher? O, I cannot speake.

Clif. I Crooke-back, here I stand to answer thee,
Or any he, the proudest of thy sort.

Rich. 'Twas you that kill'd yong Rutland, was it not?

Clif. I, and old Yorke, and yet not satisfied.

Rich. For Gods sake Lords giue signall to the fight.

War. What say'st thou *Henry*,
Wilt thou yeeld the Crowne? (you speak?)

Qu. Why how now long-tongu'd Warwicke, dare
When you and I, met at S. *Albons* last,
Your legges did better seruice then your hands.

War. Then 'twas my turne to fly, and now 'tis thine:

Clif. You said so much before, and yet you fled.

War. 'Twas not your valor *Clifford* droue me thence.

Nor. No, nor your manhood that durst make you stay.

Rich. Northumberland, I hold thee reuerently,
Breake off the parley, for scarse I can refraine
The execution of my big-swolne heart
Vpon that *Clifford*, that cruell Child-killer.

Clif. I slew thy Father, cal'st thou him a Child?

Rich.

Rich. I like a Dastard, and a treacherous Coward,
As thou didd'st kill our tender Brother Rutland,
But ere Sunset, Ile make thee curse the deed.

King. Haue done with words (my Lords) and heare me speake.

Qu. Defie them then, or els hold close thy lips.

King. I prythee giue no limits to my Tongue,
I am a King, and priuiledg'd to speake.

Clif. My Liege, the wound that bred this meeting here,
Cannot be cur'd by Words, therefore be still.

Rich. Then Executioner vnsheath thy sword:
By him that made vs all, I am resolu'd,
That *Cliffords* Manhood, lyes vpon his tongue.

Ed. Say *Henry*, shall I haue my right, or no:
A thousand men haue broke their Fasts to day,
That ne're shall dine, vnlesse thou yeeld the Crowne.

War. If thou deny, their Blood vpon thy head,
For *Yorke* in iustice put's his Armour on.

Pr. Ed. If that be right, which *Warwick* saies is right,
There is no wrong, but euery thing is right.

War. Who euer got thee, there thy Mother stands,
For well I wot, thou hast thy Mothers tongue.

Qu. But thou art neyther like thy Sire nor Damme,
But like a foule mishapen Stygmaticke,
Mark'd by the Destinies to be auoided,
As venome Toades, or Lizards dreadfull stings.

Rich. Iron of Naples, hid with English gilt,
Whose Father beares the Title of a King,
(As if a Channell should be call'd the Sea)
Sham'st thou not, knowing whence thou art extraught,
To let thy tongue detect thy base-borne heart.

Ed. A wispe of straw were worth a thousand Crowns,
To make this shamelesse Callet know her selfe:
Helen of Greece was fayrer farre then thou,
Although thy Husband may be *Menelaus*;
And ne're was *Agamemnons* Brother wrong'd
By that false Woman, as this King by thee.
His Father reuel'd in the heart of France,
And tam'd the King, and made the Dolphin stoope:
And had he match'd according to his State,
He might haue kept that glory to this day.
But when he tooke a begger to his bed,
And grac'd thy poore Sire with his Bridall day,
Euen then that Sun-shine brew'd a showre for him,
That washt his Fathers fortunes forth of France,
And heap'd sedition on his Crowne at home:
For what hath broach'd this tumult but thy Pride?
Had'st thou bene meeke, our Title still had slept,
And we in pitty of the Gentle King,
Had slipt our Claime, vntill another Age.

Cla. But when we saw, our Sunshine made thy Spring,
And that thy Summer bred vs no increase,
We set the Axe to thy vsurping Roote:
And though the edge hath something hit our selues,
Yet know thou, since we haue begun to strike,
Wee'l neuer leaue, till we haue hewne thee downe,
Or bath'd thy growing, with our heated bloods.

Edw. And in this resolution, I defie thee,
Not willing any longer Conference,
Since thou denied'st the gentle King to speake.
Sound Trumpets, let our bloody Colours waue,
And either Victorie, or else a Graue.

Qu. Stay *Edward*.

Ed. No wrangling Woman, wee'l no longer stay,
These words will cost ten thousand liues this day.

Exeunt omnes.

Alarum. Excursions. Enter Warwicke.

War. Fore-spent with Toile, as Runners with a Race,
I lay me downe a little while to breath:
For strokes receiu'd, and many blowes repaid,
Haue robb'd my strong knit sinewes of their strength,
And spight of spight, needs must I rest a-while.

Enter Edward running.

Ed. Smile gentle heauen, or strike vngentle death,
For this world frownes, and *Edwards* Sunne is clowded.

War. How now my Lord, what happe? what hope of good?

Enter Clarence.

Cla. Our hap is losse, our hope but sad dispaire,
Our rankes are broke, and ruine followes vs.
What counsaile giue you? whether shall we flye?

Ed. Bootlesse is flight, they follow vs with Wings,
And weake we are, and cannot shun pursuite.

Enter Richard.

Rich. Ah *Warwicke*, why hast ŷ withdrawn thy selfe?
Thy Brothers blood the thirsty earth hath drunk,
Broach'd with the Steely point of *Cliffords* Launce:
And in the very pangs of death, he cryde,
Like to a dismall Clangor heard from farre,
Warwicke, reuenge; Brother, reuenge my death.
So vnderneath the belly of their Steeds,
That stain'd their Fetlockes in his smoaking blood,
The Noble Gentleman gaue vp the ghost.

War. Then let the earth be drunken with our blood:
Ile kill my Horse, because I will not flye:
Why stand we like soft-hearted women heere,
Wayling our losses, whiles the Foe doth Rage,
And looke vpon, as if the Tragedie
Were plaid in iest, by counterfetting Actors.
Heere on my knee, I vow to God aboue,
Ile neuer pawse againe, neuer stand still,
Till either death hath clos'd these eyes of mine,
Or Fortune giuen me measure of Reuenge.

Ed. Oh *Warwicke*, I do bend my knee with thine,
And in this vow do chaine my soule to thine:
And ere my knee rise from the Earths cold face,
I throw my hands, mine eyes, my heart to thee,
Thou setter vp, and plucker downe of Kings:
Beseeching thee (if with thy will it stands)
That to my Foes this body must be prey,
Yet that thy brazen gates of heauen may ope,
And giue sweet passage to my sinfull soule.
Now Lords, take leaue vntill we meete againe,
Where ere it be, in heauen, or in earth.

Rich. Brother,
Giue me thy hand, and gentle *Warwicke*,
Let me imbrace thee in my weary armes:
I that did neuer weepe, now melt with wo,
That Winter should cut off our Spring-time so.

War. Away, away:
Once more sweet Lords farwell.

Cla. Yet let vs altogether to our Troopes,
And giue them leaue to flye, that will not stay:
And call them Pillars that will stand to vs:
And if we thriue, promise them such rewards
As Victors weare at the Olympian Games.
This may plant courage in their quailing breasts,
For yet is hope of Life and Victory:

Foreslow no longer, make we hence amaine. *Exeunt*

Excursions. Enter Richard and Clifford.

Rich. Now *Clifford*, I haue singled thee alone,
Suppose this arme is for the Duke of Yorke,
And this for Rutland, both bound to reuenge,
Wer't thou inuiron'd with a Brazen wall.

Clif. Now *Richard*, I am with thee heere alone,
This is the hand that stabb'd thy Father *Yorke*,
And this the hand, that slew thy Brother *Rutland*,
And here's the heart, that triumphs in their death,
And cheeres these hands, that slew thy Sire and Brother,
To execute the like vpon thy selfe,
And so haue at thee.

They Fight, Warwicke comes, Clifford flies.

Rich. Nay *Warwicke*, single out some other Chace,
For I my selfe will hunt this Wolfe to death. *Exeunt.*

Alarum. Enter King Henry alone.

Hen. This battell fares like to the mornings Warre,
When dying clouds contend, with growing light,
What time the Shepheard blowing of his nailes,
Can neither call it perfect day, nor night.
Now swayes it this way, like a Mighty Sea,
Forc'd by the Tide, to combat with the Winde:
Now swayes it that way, like the selfe-same Sea,
Forc'd to retyre by furie of the Winde.
Sometime, the Flood preuailes; and than the Winde:
Now, one the better: then, another best;
Both tugging to be Victors, brest to brest:
Yet neither Conqueror, nor Conquered.
So is the equall poise of this fell Warre.
Heere on this Mole-hill will I sit me downe,
To whom God will, there be the Victorie:
For *Margaret* my Queene, and *Clifford* too
Haue chid me from the Battell: Swearing both,
They prosper best of all when I am thence.
Would I were dead, if Gods good will were so;
For what is in this world, but Greefe and Woe.
Oh God! me thinkes it were a happy life,
To be no better then a homely Swaine,
To sit vpon a hill, as I do now,
To carue out Dialls queintly, point by point,
Thereby to see the Minutes how they runne:
How many makes the Houre full compleate,
How many Houres brings about the Day,
How many Dayes will finish vp the Yeare,
How many Yeares, a Mortall man may liue.
When this is knowne, then to diuide the Times:
So many Houres, must I tend my Flocke;
So many Houres, must I take my Rest:
So many Houres, must I Contemplate:
So many Houres, must I Sport my selfe:
So many Dayes, my Ewes haue bene with yong:
So many weekes, ere the poore Fooles will Eane:
So many yeares, ere I shall sheere the Fleece:
So Minutes, Houres, Dayes, Monthes, and Yeares,
Past ouer to the end they were created,
Would bring white haires, vnto a Quiet graue.
Ah! what a life were this? How sweet? how louely?
Giues not the Hawthorne bush a sweeter shade
To Shepheards. looking on their silly Sheepe,
Then doth a rich Imbroider'd Canopie
To Kings, that feare their Subiects treacherie?
Oh yes, it doth; a thousand fold it doth.
And to conclude, the Shepherds homely Curds,
His cold thinne drinke out of his Leather Bottle,
His wonted sleepe, vnder a fresh trees shade,
All which secure, and sweetly he enioyes,
Is farre beyond a Princes Delicates:
His Viands sparkling in a Golden Cup,
His bodie couched in a curious bed,
When Care, Mistrust, and Treason waits on him.

Alarum. Enter a Sonne that hath kill'd his Father, at one doore: and a Father that hath kill'd his Sonne at another doore.

Son. Ill blowes the winde that profits no body,
This man whom hand to hand I slew in fight,
May be possessed with some store of Crownes,
And I that (haply) take them from him now,
May yet (ere night) yeeld both my Life and them
To some man else, as this dead man doth me.
Who's this? Oh God! It is my Fathers face,
Whom in this Conflict, I (vnwares) haue kill'd:
Oh heauy times! begetting such Euents.
From London, by the King was I prest forth,
My Father being the Earle of Warwickes man,
Came on the part of Yorke, prest by his Master:
And I, who at his hands receiu'd my life,
Haue by my hands, of Life bereaued him.
Pardon me God, I knew not what I did:
And pardon Father, for I knew not thee.
My Teares shall wipe away these bloody markes:
And no more words, till they haue flow'd their fill.

King. O pitteous spectacle! O bloody Times!
Whiles Lyons Warre, and battaile for their Dennes,
Poore harmlesse Lambes abide their enmity.
Weepe wretched man: Ile ayde thee Teare for Teare,
And let our hearts and eyes, like Ciuill Warre,
Be blinde with teares, and break ore-charg'd with griefe

Enter Father, bearing of his Sonne.

Fa. Thou that so stoutly hath resisted me,
Giue me thy Gold, if thou hast any Gold:
For I haue bought it with an hundred blowes.
But let me see: Is this our Foe-mans face?
Ah, no, no, no, it is mine onely Sonne.
Ah Boy, if any life be left in thee,
Throw vp thine eye: see, see, what showres arise,
Blowne with the windie Tempest of my heart,
Vpon thy wounds, that killes mine Eye, and Heart.
O pitty God, this miserable Age!
What Stragems? how fell? how Butcherly?
Erroneous, mutinous, and vnnaturall,
This deadly quarrell daily doth beget?
O Boy! thy Father gaue thee life too soone,
And hath bereft thee of thy life too late.

King. Wo aboue wo: greefe, more thẽ common greefe
O that my death would stay these ruthfull deeds:
O pitty, pitty, gentle heauen pitty:
The Red Rose and the White are on his face,
The fatall Colours of our striuing Houses:
The one, his purple Blood right well resembles,
The other his pale Cheekes (me thinkes) presenteth:
Wither one Rose, and let the other flourish:
If you contend, a thousand liues must wither.

Son. How will my Mother, for a Fathers death
Take on with me, and ne're be satisfi'd?

Fa. How will my Wife, for slaughter of my Sonne,
Shed seas of Teares, and ne're be satisfi'd?

King. How will the Country, for these wofull chances,
Mis-thinke

The third Part of King Henry the Sixt.

Mis-thinke the King, and not be satisfied?

Son. Was euer sonne, so rew'd a Fathers death?

Fath. Was euer Father so bemoan'd his Sonne?

Hen. Was euer King so greeu'd for Subiects woe?
Much is your sorrow; Mine, ten times so much.

Son. Ile beare thee hence, where I may weepe my fill.

Fath. These armes of mine shall be thy winding sheet:
My heart (sweet Boy) shall be thy Sepulcher,
For from my heart, thine Image ne're shall go.
My sighing brest, shall be thy Funerall bell;
And so obsequious will thy Father be,
Men for the losse of thee, hauing no more,
As *Priam* was for all his Valiant Sonnes,
Ile beare thee hence, and let them fight that will,
For I haue murthered where I should not kill. *Exit*

Hen. Sad-hearted-men, much ouergone with Care;
Heere sits a King, more wofull then you are.

Alarums. Excursions. Enter the Queen, the Prince, and Exeter.

Prin. Fly Father, flye: for all your Friends are fled,
And *Warwicke* rages like a chafed Bull:
Away, for death doth hold vs in pursuite.

Qu. Mount you my Lord, towards Barwicke post a-maine:
Edward and *Richard* like a brace of Grey-hounds,
Hauing the fearfull flying Hare in sight,
With fiery eyes, sparkling for very wrath,
And bloody steele graspt in their yrefull hands
Are at our backes, and therefore hence amaine.

Exet. Away: for vengeance comes along with them.
Nay, stay not to expostulate, make speed,
Or else come after, Ile away before.

Hen. Nay take me with thee, good sweet Exeter:
Not that I feare to stay, but loue to go
Whether the Queene intends. Forward, away. *Exeunt*

A lowd alarum. Enter Clifford Wounded.

Clif. Heere burnes my Candle out; I, heere it dies,
Which whiles it lasted, gaue King *Henry* light.
O Lancaster! I feare thy ouerthrow,
More then my Bodies parting with my Soule:
My Loue and Feare, glew'd many Friends to thee,
And now I fall. Thy tough Commixtures melts,
Impairing *Henry*, strength'ning misproud *Yorke*;
And whether flye the Gnats, but to the Sunne?
And who shines now, but *Henries* Enemies?
O *Phœbus*! had'st thou neuer giuen consent,
That *Phaeton* should checke thy fiery Steeds,
Thy burning Carre neuer had scorch'd the earth.
And *Henry*, had'st thou sway'd as Kings should do,
Or as thy Father, and his Father did,
Giuing no ground vnto the house of *Yorke*,
They neuer then had sprung like Sommer Flyes:
I, and ten thousand in this lucklesse Realme,
Had left no mourning Widdowes for our death,
And thou this day, had'st kept thy Chaire in peace.
For what doth cherrish Weeds, but gentle ayre?
And what makes Robbers bold, but too much lenity?
Bootlesse are Plaints, and Curelesse are my Wounds:
No way to flye, nor strength to hold out flight:
The Foe is mercilesse, and will not pitty:
For at their hands I haue deseru'd no pitty.
The ayre hath got into my deadly Wounds,
And much effuse of blood, doth make me faint:
Come *Yorke*, and *Richard*, *Warwicke*, and the rest,
I stab'd your Fathers bosomes; Split my brest.

Alarum & Retreat. Enter Edward, Warwicke, Richard, and Soldiers, Montague, & Clarence.

Ed. Now breath we Lords, good fortune bids vs pause,
And smooth the frownes of War, with peacefull lookes:
Some Troopes pursue the bloody-minded Queene,
That led calme *Henry*, though he were a King,
As doth a Saile, fill'd with a fretting Gust
Command an Argosie to stemme the Waues.
But thinke you (Lords) that *Clifford* fled with them?

War. No, 'tis impossible he should escape:
(For though before his face I speake the words)
Your Brother *Richard* markt him for the Graue.
And wheresoere he is, hee's surely dead. *Clifford grones*

Rich. Whose soule is that which takes hir heauy leaue?
A deadly grone, like life and deaths departing.
See who it is.

Ed. And now the Battailes ended,
If Friend or Foe, let him be gently vsed.

Rich. Reuoke that doome of mercy, for 'tis *Clifford*,
Who not contented that he lopp'd the Branch
In hewing *Rutland*, when his leaues put forth,
But set his murth'ring knife vnto the Roote,
From whence that tender spray did sweetly spring,
I meane our Princely Father, Duke of *Yorke*.

War. From off the gates of *Yorke*, fetch down y̆ head,
Your Fathers head, which *Clifford* placed there:
In stead whereof, let this supply the roome,
Measure for measure, must be answered.

Ed. Bring forth that fatall Schreechowle to our house,
That nothing sung but death, to vs and ours:
Now death shall stop his dismall threatning sound,
And his ill-boading tongue, no more shall speake.

War. I thinke is vnderstanding is bereft:
Speake *Clifford*, dost thou know who speakes to thee?
Darke cloudy death ore-shades his beames of life,
And he nor sees, nor heares vs, what we say.

Rich. O would he did, and so (perhaps) he doth,
'Tis but his policy to counterfet,
Because he would auoid such bitter taunts
Which in the time of death he gaue our Father.

Cla. If so thou think'st,
Vex him with eager Words.

Rich. Clifford, aske mercy, and obtaine no grace.

Ed. Clifford, repent in bootlesse penitence.

War. Clifford, deuise excuses for thy faults.

Cla. While we deuise fell Tortures for thy faults.

Rich. Thou didd'st loue Yorke, and I am son to Yorke.

Edw. Thou pittied'st Rutland, I will pitty thee:

Cla. Where's Captaine *Margaret*, to fence you now?

War. They mocke thee *Clifford*,
Sweare as thou was't wont.

Ric. What, not an Oath? Nay then the world go's hard
When *Clifford* cannot spare his Friends an oath:
I know by that he's dead, and by my Soule,
If this right hand would buy two houres life,
That I (in all despight) might rayle at him,
This hand should chop it off: & with the issuing Blood
Stifle the Villaine, whose vnstanched thirst
Yorke, and yong Rutland could not satisfie

War. I, but he's dead. Of with the Traitors head,
And reare it in the place your Fathers stands.
And now to London with Triumphant march,

There

There to be crowned Englands Royall King:
From whence, shall Warwicke cut the Sea to France,
And aske the Ladie *Bona* for thy Queene:
So shalt thou sinow both these Lands together,
And hauing France thy Friend, thou shalt not dread
The scattred Foe, that hopes to rise againe:
For though they cannot greatly sting to hurt,
Yet looke to haue them buz to offend thine eares:
First, will I see the Coronation,
And then to Britanny Ile crosse the Sea,
To effect this marriage, so it please my Lord.

  Ed. Euen as thou wilt sweet *Warwicke*, let it bee:
For in thy shoulder do I builde my Seate;
And neuer will I vndertake the thing
Wherein thy counsaile and consent is wanting:
Richard, I will create thee Duke of Gloucester,
And *George* of Clarence; *Warwicke* as our Selfe,
Shall do, and vndo as him pleaseth best.

  Rich. Let me be Duke of Clarence, *George* of Gloster,
For Glosters Dukedome is too ominous.

  War. Tut, that's a foolish obseruation:
Richard, be Duke of Gloster: Now to London,
To see these Honors in possession. *Exeunt*

*Enter Sinklo, and Humfrey with Crosse-bowes
in their hands.*

  Sink. Vnder this thicke growne brake, wee'l shrowd
our selues:
For through this Laund anon the Deere will come,
And in this couert will we make our Stand,
Culling the principall of all the Deere.

  Hum. Ile stay aboue the hill, so both may shoot.

  Sink. That cannot be, the noise of thy Crosse-bow
Will scarre the Heard, and so my shoot is lost:
Heere stand we both, and ayme we at the best:
And for the time shall not seeme tedious,
Ile tell thee what befell me on a day,
In this selfe-place, where now we meane to stand.

  Sink. Heere comes a man, let's stay till he be past.

Enter the King with a Prayer booke.

  Hen. From Scotland am I stolne euen of pure loue,
To greet mine owne Land with my wishfull sight:
No *Harry*, *Harry*, 'tis no Land of thine,
Thy place is fill'd, thy Scepter wrung from thee,
Thy Balme washt off, wherewith thou was Annointed:
No bending knee will call thee *Cæsar* now,
No humble suters preasse to speake for right:
No, not a man comes for redresse of thee:
For how can I helpe them, and not my selfe?

  Sink. I, heere's a Deere, whose skin's a Keepers Fee:
This is the quondam King; Let's seize vpon him.

  Hen. Let me embrace the sower Aduersaries,
For Wise men say, it is the wisest course.

  Hum. Why linger we? Let vs lay hands vpon him.

  Sink. Forbeare a-while, wee'l heare a little more.

  Hen. My Queene and Son are gone to France for aid:
And (as I heare) the great Commanding Warwicke
Is thither gone, to craue the French Kings Sister
To wife for *Edward*. If this newes be true,
Poore Queene, and Sonne, your labour is but lost:
For *Warwicke* is a subtle Orator:
And *Lewis* a Prince soone wonne with mouing words:
By this account then, *Margaret* may winne him,
For she's a woman to be pittied much:
Her sighes will make a batt'ry in his brest,
Her teares will pierce into a Marble heart:

The Tyger will be milde, whiles she doth mourne;
And *Nero* will be tainted with remorse,
To heare and see her plaints, her Brinish Teares.
I, but shee's come to begge, *Warwicke* to giue:
Shee on his left side, crauing ayde for *Henrie*;
He on his right, asking a wife for *Edward*.
Shee Weepes, and sayes, her *Henry* is depos'd:
He Smiles, and sayes, his *Edward* is instaul'd;
That she (poore Wretch) for greefe can speake no more:
Whiles *Warwicke* tels his Title, smooths the Wrong,
Inferreth arguments of mighty strength,
And in conclusion winnes the King from her,
With promise of his Sister, and what else,
To strengthen and support King *Edwards* place.
O *Margaret*, thus 'twill be, and thou (poore soule)
Art then forsaken, as thou went'st forlorne.

  Hum. Say, what art thou talk'st of Kings & Queens?

  King. More then I seeme, and lesse then I was borne to:
A man at least, for lesse I should not be:
And men may talke of Kings, and why not I?

  Hum. I, but thou talk'st, as if thou wer't a King.

  King. Why so I am (in Minde) and that's enough.

  Hum. But if thou be a King, where is thy Crowne?

  King. My Crowne is in my heart, not on my head:
Not deck'd with Diamonds, and Indian stones:
Nor to be seene: my Crowne, is call'd Content,
A Crowne it is, that sildome Kings enioy.

  Hum. Well, if you be a King crown'd with Content,
Your Crowne Content, and you, must be contented
To go along with vs. For (as we thinke)
You are the king King *Edward* hath depos'd:
And we his subiects, sworne in all Allegeance,
Will apprehend you, as his Enemie.

  King. But did you neuer sweare, and breake an Oath.

  Hum. No, neuer such an Oath, nor will not now.

  King. Where did you dwell when I was K. of England?

  Hum. Heere in this Country, where we now remaine.

  King. I was annointed King at nine monthes old,
My Father, and my Grandfather were Kings:
And you were sworne true Subiects vnto me:
And tell me then, haue you not broke your Oathes?

  Sin. No, for we were Subiects, but while you wer king

  King. Why? Am I dead? Do I not breath a Man?
Ah simple men, you know not what you sweare:
Looke, as I blow this Feather from my Face,
And as the Ayre blowes it to me againe,
Obeying with my winde when I do blow,
And yeelding to another, when it blowes,
Commanded alwayes by the greater gust:
Such is the lightnesse of you, common men.
But do not breake your Oathes, for of that sinne,
My milde intreatie shall not make you guiltie.
Go where you will, the king shall be commanded,
And be you kings, command, and Ile obey.

  Sinklo. We are true Subiects to the king,
King *Edward*.

  King. So would you be againe to *Henrie*,
If he were seated as king *Edward* is.

  Sinklo. We charge you in Gods name & the Kings,
To go with vs vnto the Officers.

  King. In Gods name lead, your Kings name be obeyd,
And what God will, that let your King performe,
And what he will, I humbly yeeld vnto. *Exeunt*

Enter K. Edward, Gloster, Clarence, Lady Gray.

  King. Brother of Gloster, at S. Albons field

This Ladyes Husband, Sir *Richard Grey*, was slaine,
His Land then seiz'd on by the Conqueror,
Her suit is now, to repossesse those Lands,
Which wee in Iustice cannot well deny,
Because in Quarrell of the House of *Yorke*,
The worthy Gentleman did lose his Life.

Rich. Your Highnesse shall doe well to graunt her suit:
It were dishonor to deny it her.

King. It were no lesse, but yet Ile make a pawse.

Rich. Yea, is it so:
I see the Lady hath a thing to graunt,
Before the King will graunt her humble suit.

Clarence. Hee knowes the Game, how true hee keepes the winde?

Rich. Silence.

King. Widow, we will consider of your suit,
And come some other time to know our minde.

Wid. Right gracious Lord, I cannot brooke delay:
May it please your Highnesse to resolue me now,
And what your pleasure is, shall satisfie me.

Rich. I Widow? then Ile warrant you all your Lands,
And if what pleases him, shall pleasure you:
Fight closer, or good faith you'le catch a Blow.

Clarence. I feare her not, vnlesse shee chance to fall.

Rich. God forbid that, for hee'le take vantages.

King. How many Children hast thou, Widow? tell me.

Clarence. I thinke he meanes to begge a Child of her.

Rich. Nay then whip me: hee'le rather giue her two.

Wid. Three, my most gracious Lord.

Rich. You shall haue foure, if you'le be rul'd by him.

King. 'Twere pittie they should lose their Fathers Lands.

Wid. Be pittifull, dread Lord, and graunt it then.

King. Lords giue vs leaue, Ile trye this Widowes wit.

Rich. I, good leaue haue you, for you will haue leaue,
Till Youth take leaue, and leaue you to the Crutch.

King. Now tell me, Madame, doe you loue your Children?

Wid. I, full as dearely as I loue my selfe.

King. And would you not doe much to doe them good?

Wid. To doe them good, I would sustayne some harme.

King. Then get your Husbands Lands, to doe them good.

Wid. Therefore I came vnto your Maiestie.

King. Ile tell you how these Lands are to be got.

Wid. So shall you bind me to your Highnesse seruice.

King. What seruice wilt thou doe me, if I giue them?

Wid. What you command, that rests in me to doe.

King. But you will take exceptions to my Boone.

Wid. No, gracious Lord, except I cannot doe it.

King. I, but thou canst doe what I meane to aske.

Wid. Why then I will doe what your Grace commands.

Rich. Hee plyes her hard, and much Raine weares the Marble.

Clar. As red as fire? nay then, her Wax must melt.

Wid. Why stoppes my Lord? shall I not heare my Taske?

King. An easie Taske, 'tis but to loue a King.

Wid. That's soone perform'd, because I am a Subiect.

King. Why then, thy Husbands Lands I freely giue thee.

Wid. I take my leaue with many thousand thankes.

Rich. The Match is made, shee seales it with a Curse.

King. But stay thee, 'tis the fruits of Loue I meane.

Wid. The fruits of Loue, I meane, my louing Liege.

King. I, but I feare me in another sence.
What Loue, think'st thou, I sue so much to get?

Wid. My loue till death, my humble thanks, my prayers,
That loue which Vertue begges, and Vertue graunts.

King. No, by my troth, I did not meane such loue.

Wid. Why then you meane not, as I thought you did.

King. But now you partly may perceiue my minde.

Wid. My minde will neuer graunt what I perceiue
Your Highnesse aymes at, if I ayme aright.

King. To tell thee plaine, I ayme to lye with thee.

Wid. To tell you plaine, I had rather lye in Prison.

King. Why then thou shalt not haue thy Husbands Lands.

Wid. Why then mine Honestie shall be my Dower,
For by that losse, I will not purchase them.

King. Therein thou wrong'st thy Children mightily.

Wid. Herein your Highnesse wrongs both them & me:
But mightie Lord, this merry inclination
Accords not with the sadnesse of my suit:
Please you dismisse me, eyther with I, or no.

King. I, if thou wilt say I to my request:
No, if thou do'st say No to my demand.

Wid. Then No, my Lord: my suit is at an end.

Rich. The Widow likes him not, shee knits her Browes.

Clarence. Hee is the bluntest Wooer in Christendome.

King. Her Looks doth argue her replete with Modesty,
Her Words doth shew her Wit incomparable,
All her perfections challenge Soueraigntie,
One way, or other, shee is for a King,
And shee shall be my Loue, or else my Queene.
Say, that King *Edward* take thee for his Queene?

Wid. 'Tis better said then done, my gracious Lord:
I am a subiect fit to ieast withall,
But farre vnfit to be a Soueraigne.

King. Sweet Widow, by my State I sweare to thee,
I speake no more then what my Soule intends,
And that is, to enioy thee for my Loue.

Wid. And that is more then I will yeeld vnto:
I know, I am too meane to be your Queene,
And yet too good to be your Concubine.

King. You cauill, Widow, I did meane my Queene.

Wid. 'Twill grieue your Grace, my Sonnes should call you Father.

King. No more, then when my Daughters Call thee Mother.
Thou art a Widow, and thou hast some Children,
And by Gods Mother, I being but a Batchelor,
Haue other-some. Why, 'tis a happy thing,
To be the Father vnto many Sonnes:
Answer no more, for thou shalt be my Queene.

Rich. The Ghostly Father now hath done his Shrift.

Clarence. When hee was made a Shriuer, 'twas for shift.

King. Brothers, you muse what Chat wee two haue had.

Rich. The Widow likes it not, for shee lookes very sad.

King. You'ld thinke it strange, if I should marrie her.

Clarence. To who, my Lord?

King. Why *Clarence*, to my selfe.

Rich. That

Rich. That would be tenne dayes wonder at the least.
Clarence. That's a day longer then a Wonder lasts.
Rich. By so much is the Wonder in extremes.
King. Well, ieast on Brothers: I can tell you both,
Her suit is graunted for her Husbands Lands.

Enter a Noble man.

Nob. My gracious Lord, *Henry* your Foe is taken,
And brought your Prisoner to your Pallace Gate.
King. See that he be conuey'd vnto the Tower:
And goe wee Brothers to the man that tooke him,
To question of his apprehension.
Widow goe you along: Lords vse her honourable.
Exeunt.

Manet Richard.

Rich. I, *Edward* will vse Women honourably:
Would he were wasted, Marrow, Bones, and all,
That from his Loynes no hopefull Branch may spring,
To crosse me from the Golden time I looke for:
And yet, betweene my Soules desire, and me,
The lustfull *Edwards* Title buryed,
Is *Clarence, Henry*, and his Sonne young *Edward*,
And all the vnlook'd-for Issue of their Bodies,
To take their Roomes, ere I can place my selfe:
A cold premeditation for my purpose.
Why then I doe but dreame on Soueraigntie,
Like one that stands vpon a Promontorie,
And spyes a farre-off shore, where hee would tread,
Wishing his foot were equall with his eye,
And chides the Sea, that sunders him from thence,
Saying, hee'le lade it dry, to haue his way:
So doe I wish the Crowne, being so farre off,
And so I chide the meanes that keepes me from it,
And so (I say) Ile cut the Causes off,
Flattering me with impossibilities:
My Eyes too quicke, my Heart o're-weenes too much,
Vnlesse my Hand and Strength could equall them.
Well, say there is no Kingdome then for *Richard*:
What other Pleasure can the World affoord?
Ile make my Heauen in a Ladies Lappe,
And decke my Body in gay Ornaments,
And 'witch sweet Ladies with my Words and Lookes.
Oh miserable Thought! and more vnlikely,
Then to accomplish twentie Golden Crownes.
Why Loue forswore me in my Mothers Wombe:
And for I should not deale in her soft Lawes,
Shee did corrupt frayle Nature with some Bribe,
To shrinke mine Arme vp like a wither'd Shrub,
To make an enuious Mountaine on my Back,
Where sits Deformitie to mocke my Body;
To shape my Legges of an vnequall size,
To dis-proportion me in euery part:
Like to a Chaos, or an vn-lick'd Beare-whelpe,
That carryes no impression like the Damme.
And am I then a man to be belou'd?
Oh monstrous fault, to harbour such a thought.
Then since this Earth affoords no Ioy to me,
But to command, to check, to o're-beare such,
As are of better Person then my selfe:
Ile make my Heauen, to dreame vpon the Crowne,
And whiles I liue, t'account this World but Hell,
Vntill my mis-shap'd Trunke, that beares this Head,
Be round impaled with a glorious Crowne.
And yet I know not how to get the Crowne,
For many Liues stand betweene me and home:

And I, like one lost in a Thornie Wood,
That rents the Thornes, and is rent with the Thornes,
Seeking a way, and straying from the way,
Not knowing how to finde the open Ayre,
But toyling desperately to finde it out,
Torment my selfe, to catch the English Crowne:
And from that torment I will free my selfe,
Or hew my way out with a bloody Axe.
Why I can smile, and murther whiles I smile,
And cry, Content, to that which grieues my Heart,
And wet my Cheekes with artificiall Teares,
And frame my Face to all occasions.
Ile drowne more Saylers then the Mermaid shall,
Ile slay more gazers then the Basiliske,
Ile play the Orator as well as *Nestor*,
Deceiue more slyly then *Vlisses* could,
And like a *Synon*, take another Troy.
I can adde Colours to the Camelion,
Change shapes with *Proteus*, for aduantages,
And set the murtherous *Macheuill* to Schoole.
Can I doe this, and cannot get a Crowne?
Tut, were it farther off, Ile plucke it downe. *Exit.*

Flourish.
Enter Lewis the French King, his Sister Bona, his
Admirall, call'd Bourbon: Prince Edward,
Queene Margaret, and the Earle of Oxford.
Lewis sits, and riseth vp againe.

Lewis. Faire Queene of England, worthy *Margaret*,
Sit downe with vs: it ill befits thy State,
And Birth, that thou should'st stand, while *Lewis* doth sit.
Marg. No, mightie King of France: now *Margaret*
Must strike her sayle, and learne a while to serue,
Where Kings command. I was (I must confesse)
Great Albions Queene, in former Golden dayes:
But now mischance hath trod my Title downe,
And with dis-honor layd me on the ground,
Where I must take like Seat vnto my fortune,
And to my humble Seat conforme my selfe.
Lewis. Why say, faire Queene, whence springs this
deepe despaire?
Marg. From such a cause, as fills mine eyes with teares,
And stops my tongue, while heart is drown'd in cares.
Lewis. What ere it be, be thou still like thy selfe,
And sit thee by our side. *Seats her by him.*
Yeeld not thy necke to Fortunes yoake,
But let thy dauntlesse minde still ride in triumph,
Ouer all mischance.
Be plaine, Queene *Margaret*, and tell thy griefe,
It shall be eas'd, if France can yeeld reliefe.
Marg. Those gracious words
Reuiue my drooping thoughts,
And giue my tongue-ty'd sorrowes leaue to speake.
Now therefore be it knowne to Noble *Lewis*,
That *Henry*, sole possessor of my Loue,
Is, of a King, become a banisht man,
And forc'd to liue in Scotland a Forlorne;
While prowd ambitious *Edward*, Duke of Yorke,
Vsurpes the Regall Title, and the Seat
Of Englands true anoynted lawfull King.
This is the cause that I, poore *Margaret*,
With this my Sonne, Prince *Edward, Henries* Heire,
Am come to craue thy iust and lawfull ayde:
And if thou faile vs, all our hope is done.
Scotland hath will to helpe, but cannot helpe:

Our

Our People, and our Peeres, are both mis-led,
Our Treasure seiz'd, our Souldiors put to flight,
And (as thou seest) our selues in heauie plight.

  Lewis. Renowned Queene,
With patience calme the Storme,
While we bethinke a meanes to breake it off.

  Marg. The more wee stay, the stronger growes our Foe.

  Lewis. The more I stay, the more Ile succour thee.

  Marg. O, but impatience waiteth on true sorrow.
And see where comes the breeder of my sorrow.

Enter Warwicke.

  Lewis. What's hee approacheth boldly to our presence?

  Marg. Our Earle of Warwicke, Edwards greatest Friend.

  Lewis. Welcome braue *Warwicke*, what brings thee to France?   *Hee descends. Shee ariseth.*

  Marg. I now begins a second Storme to rise,
For this is hee that moues both Winde and Tyde.

  Warw. From worthy *Edward*, King of Albion,
My Lord and Soueraigne, and thy vowed Friend,
I come (in Kindnesse, and vnfayned Loue)
First, to doe greetings to thy Royall Person,
And then to craue a League of Amitie:
And lastly, to confirme that Amitie
With Nuptiall Knot, if thou vouchsafe to graunt
That vertuous Lady *Bona*, thy faire Sister,
To Englands King, in lawfull Marriage.

  Marg. If that goe forward, *Henries* hope is done.

  Warw. And gracious Madame,   *Speaking to Bona.*
In our Kings behalfe,
I am commanded, with your leaue and fauor,
Humbly to kisse your Hand, and with my Tongue
To tell the passion of my Soueraignes Heart;
Where Fame, late entring at his heedfull Eares,
Hath plac'd thy Beauties Image, and thy Vertue.

  Marg. King *Lewis*, and Lady *Bona*, heare me speake,
Before you answer *Warwicke*. His demand
Springs not from *Edwards* well-meant honest Loue,
But from Deceit, bred by Necessitie:
For how can Tyrants safely gouerne home,
Vnlesse abroad they purchase great allyance?
To proue him Tyrant, this reason may suffice,
That *Henry* liueth still: but were hee dead,
Yet here Prince *Edward* stands, King *Henries* Sonne.
Looke therefore *Lewis*, that by this League and Mariage
Thou draw not on thy Danger, and Dis-honor:
For though Vsurpers sway the rule a while,
Yet Heau'ns are iust, and Time suppresseth Wrongs.

  Warw. Iniurious *Margaret*.

  Edw. And why not Queene?

  Warw. Because thy Father *Henry* did vsurpe,
And thou no more art Prince, then shee is Queene.

  Oxf. Then *Warwicke* disanulls great *Iohn* of Gaunt,
Which did subdue the greatest part of Spaine;
And after *Iohn* of Gaunt, *Henry* the Fourth,
Whose Wisdome was a Mirror to the wisest:
And after that wise Prince, *Henry* the Fift,
Who by his Prowesse conquered all France:
From these, our *Henry* lineally descends.

  Warw. Oxford, how haps it in this smooth discourse,
You told not, how *Henry* the Sixt hath lost
All that, which *Henry* the Fift had gotten:

Me thinkes these Peeres of France should smile at that.
But for the rest: you tell a Pedigree
Of threescore and two yeeres, a silly time
To make prescription for a Kingdomes worth.

  Oxf. Why *Warwicke*, canst thou speak against thy Liege,
Whom thou obeyd'st thirtie and six yeeres,
And not bewray thy Treason with a Blush?

  Warw. Can *Oxford*, that did euer fence the right,
Now buckler Falsehood with a Pedigree?
For shame leaue *Henry*, and call *Edward* King.

  Oxf. Call him my King, by whose iniurious doome
My elder Brother, the Lord *Aubrey Vere*
Was done to death? and more then so, my Father,
Euen in the downe-fall of his mellow'd yeeres,
When Nature brought him to the doore of Death?
No *Warwicke*, no: while Life vpholds this Arme,
This Arme vpholds the House of *Lancaster*.

  Warw. And I the House of *Yorke*.

  Lewis. Queene *Margaret*, Prince *Edward*, and *Oxford*,
Vouchsafe at our request, to stand aside,
While I vse further conference with *Warwicke*.
                      They stand aloofe.

  Marg. Heauens graunt, that *Warwickes* wordes bewitch him not.

  Lew. Now *Warwicke*, tell me euen vpon thy conscience
Is *Edward* your true King? for I were loth
To linke with him, that were not lawfull chosen.

  Warw. Thereon I pawne my Credit, and mine Honor.

  Lewis. But is hee gracious in the Peoples eye?

  Warw. The more, that *Henry* was vnfortunate.

  Lewis. Then further: all dissembling set aside,
Tell me for truth, the measure of his Loue
Vnto our Sister *Bona*.

  War. Such it seemes,
As may beseeme a Monarch like himselfe.
My selfe haue often heard him say, and sweare,
That this his Loue was an externall Plant,
Whereof the Root was fixt in Vertues ground,
The Leaues and Fruit maintain'd with Beauties Sunne,
Exempt from Enuy, but not from Disdaine,
Vnlesse the Lady *Bona* quit his paine.

  Lewis. Now Sister, let vs heare your firme resolue.

  Bona. Your graunt, or your denyall, shall be mine.
Yet I confesse, that often ere this day,   *Speaks to War.*
When I haue heard your Kings desert recounted,
Mine eare hath tempted iudgement to desire.

  Lewis. Then *Warwicke*, thus:
Our Sister shall be *Edwards*.
And now forthwith shall Articles be drawne,
Touching the Ioynture that your King must make,
Which with her Dowrie shall be counter-poys'd:
Draw neere, Queene *Margaret*, and be a witnesse,
That *Bona* shall be Wife to the English King.

  Pr. Edw. To *Edward*, but not to the English King.

  Marg. Deceitfull *Warwicke*, it was thy deuice,
By this alliance to make void my suit:
Before thy comming, *Lewis* was *Henries* friend.

  Lewis. And still is friend to him, and *Margaret*,
But if your Title to the Crowne be weake,
As may appeare by *Edwards* good successe;
Then 'tis but reason, that I be releas'd
From giuing ayde, which late I promised.
Yet shall you haue all kindnesse at my hand,
That your Estate requires, and mine can yeeld.

  Warw. Henry now liues in Scotland, at his ease;

Where

Where hauing nothing, nothing can he lose.
And as for you your selfe (our quondam Queene)
You haue a Father able to maintaine you,
And better 'twere, you troubled him, then France.

Mar. Peace impudent, and shamelesse Warwicke,
Proud setter vp, and puller downe of Kings,
I will not hence, till with my Talke and Teares
(Both full of Truth) I make King Lewis behold
Thy slye conueyance, and thy Lords false loue,
Post blowing a horne Within.
For both of you are Birds of selfe-same Feather.

Lewes. Warwicke, this is some poste to vs, or thee.
Enter the Poste.

Post. My Lord Ambassador,
These Letters are for you. *Speakes to Warwick.*
Sent from your Brother Marquesse *Montague*.
These from our King, vnto your Maiesty. *To Lewis.*
And Madam, these for you: *To Margaret*
From whom, I know not.
They all reade their Letters.

Oxf. I like it well, that our faire Queene and Mistris
Smiles at her newes, while *Warwicke* frownes at his.

Prince Ed. Nay marke how Lewis stampes as he were
netled. I hope, all's for the best.

Lew. Warwicke, what are thy Newes?
And yours, faire Queene.

Mar. Mine such, as fill my heart with vnhop'd ioyes.

War. Mine full of sorrow, and hearts discontent.

Lew. What? has your King married the Lady *Grey*?
And now to sooth your Forgery, and his,
Sends me a Paper to perswade me Patience?
Is this th'Alliance that he seekes with France?
Dare he presume to scorne vs in this manner?

Mar. I told your Maiesty as much before:
This proueth *Edwards* Loue, and *Warwickes* honesty.

War. King *Lewis*, I heere protest in sight of heauen,
And by the hope I haue of heauenly blisse,
That I am cleere from this misdeed of *Edwards*;
No more my King, for he dishonors me,
But most himselfe, if he could see his shame.
Did I forget, that by the House of Yorke
My Father came vntimely to his death?
Did I let passe th'abuse done to my Neece?
Did I impale him with the Regall Crowne?
Did I put *Henry* from his Natiue Right?
And am I guerdon'd at the last, with Shame?
Shame on himselfe, for my Desert is Honor.
And to repaire my Honor lost for him,
I heere renounce him, and returne to *Henry*.
My Noble Queene, let former grudges passe,
And henceforth, I am thy true Seruitour:
I will reuenge his wrong to Lady *Bona*,
And replant *Henry* in his former state.

Mar. Warwicke,
These words haue turn'd my Hate, to Loue,
And I forgiue, and quite forget old faults,
And ioy that thou becom'st King *Henries* Friend.

War. So much his Friend, I, his vnfained Friend,
That if King *Lewis* vouchsafe to furnish vs
With some few Bands of chosen Soldiours,
Ile vndertake to Land them on our Coast,
And force the Tyrant from his seat by Warre.
'Tis not his new-made Bride shall succour him.
And as for *Clarence*, as my Letters tell me,
Hee's very likely now to fall from him,
For matching more for wanton Lust, then Honor,

Or then for strength and safety of our Country.

Bona. Deere Brother, how shall *Bona* be reueng'd,
But by thy helpe to this distressed Queene?

Mar. Renowned Prince, how shall Poore *Henry* liue,
Vnlesse thou rescue him from foule dispaire?

Bona. My quarrel, and this English Queens, are one.

War. And mine faire Lady *Bona*, ioynes with yours.

Lew. And mine, with hers, and thine, and *Margarets*.
Therefore, at last, I firmely am resolu'd
You shall haue ayde.

Mar. Let me giue humble thankes for all, at once.

Lew. Then Englands Messenger, returne in Poste,
And tell false *Edward*, thy supposed King,
That *Lewis* of France, is sending ouer Maskers
To reuell it with him, and his new Bride.
Thou seest what's past, go feare thy King withall.

Bona. Tell him, in hope hee'l proue a widower shortly,
I weare the Willow Garland for his sake.

Mar. Tell him, my mourning weeds are layde aside,
And I am ready to put Armor on.

War. Tell him from me, that he hath done me wrong,
And therefore Ile vn-Crowne him, er't be long.
There's thy reward, be gone. *Exit Post.*

Lew. But Warwicke,
Thou and Oxford, with fiue thousand men
Shall crosse the Seas, and bid false *Edward* battaile:
And as occasion serues, this Noble Queen
And Prince, shall follow with a fresh Supply.
Yet ere thou go, but answer me one doubt:
What Pledge haue we of thy firme Loyalty?

War. This shall assure my constant Loyalty,
That if our Queene, and this young Prince agree,
Ile ioyne mine eldest daughter, and my Ioy,
To him forthwith, in holy Wedlocke bands.

Mar. Yes, I agree, and thanke you for your Motion,
Sonne *Edward*, she is Faire and Vertuous,
Therefore delay not, giue thy hand to Warwicke,
And with thy hand, thy faith irreuocable,
That onely Warwickes daughter shall be thine.

Prin. Ed. Yes, I accept her, for she well deserues it,
And heere to pledge my Vow, I giue my hand.
He giues his hand to War.

Lew. Why stay we now? These soldiers shalbe leuied,
And thou Lord Bourbon, our High Admirall
Shall waft them ouer with our Royall Fleete.
I long till *Edward* fall by Warres mischance,
For mocking Marriage with a Dame of France.
Exeunt. Manet Warwicke.

War. I came from *Edward* as Ambassador,
But I returne his sworne and mortall Foe:
Matter of Marriage was the charge he gaue me,
But dreadfull Warre shall answer his demand.
Had he none else to make a stale but me?
Then none but I, shall turne his Iest to Sorrow.
I was the Cheefe that rais'd him to the Crowne,
And Ile be Cheefe to bring him downe againe:
Not that I pitty *Henries* misery,
But seeke Reuenge on *Edwards* mockery. *Exit.*

Enter Richard, Clarence, Somerset, and
Mountague.

Rich. Now tell me Brother *Clarence*, what thinke you
Of this new Marriage with the Lady *Gray*?
Hath not our Brother made a worthy choice?

Cla. Alas, you know, 'tis farre from hence to France,
How

How could he stay till *Warwicke* made returne?
Som. My Lords, forbeare this talke: heere comes the King.

Flourish.

Enter King Edward, Lady Grey, Penbrooke, Stafford, Hastings: foure stand on one side, and foure on the other.

Rich. And his well-chosen Bride.
Clarence. I minde to tell him plainly what I thinke.
King. Now Brother of *Clarence*,
How like you our Choyce,
That you stand pensiue, as halfe malecontent?
Clarence. As well as *Lewis* of France,
Or the Earle of *Warwicke*,
Which are so weake of courage, and in iudgement,
That they'le take no offence at our abuse.
King. Suppose they take offence without a cause:
They are but *Lewis* and *Warwicke*, I am *Edward*,
Your King and *Warwickes*, and must haue my will.
Rich. And shall haue your will, because our King:
Yet hastie Marriage seldome proueth well.
King. Yea, Brother *Richard*, are you offended too?
Rich. Not I: no:
God forbid, that I should wish them seuer'd,
Whom God hath ioyn'd together:
I, and 'twere pittie, to sunder them,
That yoake so well together.
King. Setting your skornes, and your mislike aside,
Tell me some reason, why the Lady *Grey*
Should not become my Wife, and Englands Queene?
And you too, *Somerset*, and *Mountague*,
Speake freely what you thinke.
Clarence. Then this is mine opinion:
That King *Lewis* becomes your Enemie,
For mocking him about the Marriage
Of the Lady *Bona*.
Rich. And *Warwicke*, doing what you gaue in charge,
Is now dis-honored by this new Marriage.
King. What, if both *Lewis* and *Warwick* be appeas'd,
By such inuention as I can deuise?
Mount. Yet, to haue ioyn'd with France in such alliance,
Would more haue strength'ned this our Commonwealth
'Gainst forraine stormes, then any home-bred Marriage.
Hast. Why, knowes not *Mountague*, that of it selfe,
England is safe, if true within it selfe?
Mount. But the safer, when 'tis back'd with France.
Hast. 'Tis better vsing France, then trusting France:
Let vs be back'd with God, and with the Seas,
Which he hath giu'n for fence impregnable,
And with their helpes, onely defend our selues:
In them, and in our selues, our safetie lyes.
Clar. For this one speech, Lord *Hastings* well deserues
To haue the Heire of the Lord *Hungerford*.
King. I, what of that? it was my will, and graunt,
And for this once, my Will shall stand for Law.
Rich. And yet me thinks, your Grace hath not done well,
To giue the Heire and Daughter of Lord *Scales*
Vnto the Brother of your louing Bride;
Shee better would haue fitted me, or *Clarence*:
But in your Bride you burie Brotherhood.
Clar. Or else you would not haue bestow'd the Heire
Of the Lord *Bonuil* on your new Wiues Sonne,
And leaue your Brothers to goe speede elsewhere.
King. Alas, poore *Clarence*: is it for a Wife
That thou art malecontent? I will prouide thee.

Clarence. In chusing for your selfe,
You shew'd your iudgement:
Which being shallow, you shall giue me leaue
To play the Broker in mine owne behalfe;
And to that end, I shortly minde to leaue you.
King. Leaue me, or tarry, *Edward* will be King,
And not be ty'd vnto his Brothers will.
Lady Grey. My Lords, before it pleas'd his Maiestie
To rayse my State to Title of a Queene,
Doe me but right, and you must all confesse,
That I was not ignoble of Descent,
And meaner then my selfe haue had like fortune.
But as this Title honors me and mine,
So your dislikes, to whom I would be pleasing,
Doth cloud my ioyes with danger, and with sorrow.
King. My Loue, forbeare to fawne vpon their frownes:
What danger, or what sorrow can befall thee,
So long as *Edward* is thy constant friend,
And their true Soueraigne, whom they must obey?
Nay, whom they shall obey, and loue thee too,
Vnlesse they seeke for hatred at my hands:
Which if they doe, yet will I keepe thee safe,
And they shall feele the vengeance of my wrath.
Rich. I heare, yet say not much, but thinke the more.

Enter a Poste.

King. Now Messenger, what Letters, or what Newes from France?
Post. My Soueraigne Liege, no Letters, & few words,
But such, as I (without your speciall pardon)
Dare not relate.
King. Goe too, wee pardon thee:
Therefore, in briefe, tell me their words,
As neere as thou canst guesse them.
What answer makes King *Lewis* vnto our Letters?
Post. At my depart, these were his very words:
Goe tell false *Edward*, the supposed King,
That *Lewis* of France is sending ouer Maskers,
To reuell it with him, and his new Bride.
King. Is *Lewis* so braue? belike he thinkes me *Henry*.
But what said Lady *Bona* to my Marriage?
Post. These were her words, vtt'red with mild disdaine:
Tell him, in hope hee'le proue a Widower shortly,
Ile weare the Willow Garland for his sake.
King. I blame not her; she could say little lesse:
She had the wrong. But what said *Henries* Queene?
For I haue heard, that she was there in place.
Post. Tell him (quoth she)
My mourning Weedes are done,
And I am readie to put Armour on.
King. Belike she minds to play the Amazon.
But what said *Warwicke* to these iniuries?
Post. He, more incens'd against your Maiestie,
Then all the rest, discharg'd me with these words:
Tell him from me, that he hath done me wrong,
And therefore Ile vncrowne him, er't be long.
King. Ha? durst the Traytor breath out so prowd words?
Well, I will arme me, being thus fore-warn'd:
They shall haue Warres, and pay for their presumption.
But say, is *Warwicke* friends with *Margaret*?
Post. I, gracious Soueraigne,
They are so link'd in friendship,
That yong Prince *Edward* marryes *Warwicks* Daughter.
Clarence. Belike, the elder;
Clarence will haue the younger.

Now

Now Brother King farewell, and sit you fast,
For I will hence to *Warwickes* other Daughter,
That though I want a Kingdome, yet in Marriage
I may not proue inferior to your selfe.
You that loue me, and *Warwicke*, follow me.

Exit Clarence, and Somerset followes.

Rich. Not I:
My thoughts ayme at a further matter:
I stay not for the loue of *Edward*, but the Crowne.

King. *Clarence* and *Somerset* both gone to *Warwicke*?
Yet am I arm'd against the worst can happen:
And haste is needfull in this desp'rate case.
Pembrooke and *Stafford*, you in our behalfe
Goe leuie men, and make prepare for Warre;
They are alreadie, or quickly will be landed:
My selfe in person will straight follow you.

Exeunt Pembrooke and Stafford.

But ere I goe, *Hastings* and *Mountague*
Resolue my doubt: you twaine, of all the rest,
Are neere to *Warwicke*, by bloud, and by allyance:
Tell me, if you loue *Warwicke* more then me;
If it be so, then both depart to him:
I rather wish you foes, then hollow friends.
But if you minde to hold your true obedience,
Giue me assurance with some friendly Vow,
That I may neuer haue you in suspect.

Mount. So God helpe *Mountague*, as hee proues
true.

Hast. And *Hastings*, as hee fauours *Edwards* cause.

King. Now, Brother *Richard*, will you stand by vs?

Rich. I, in despight of all that shall withstand you.

King. Why so: then am I sure of Victorie.
Now therefore let vs hence, and lose no howre,
Till wee meet *Warwicke*, with his forreine powre.

Exeunt.

Enter Warwicke and Oxford in England,
with French Souldiors.

Warw. Trust me, my Lord, all hitherto goes well,
The common people by numbers swarme to vs.

Enter Clarence and Somerset.

But see where *Somerset* and *Clarence* comes:
Speake suddenly, my Lords, are wee all friends?

Clar. Feare not that, my Lord.

Warw. Then gentle *Clarence*, welcome vnto *Warwicke*,
And welcome *Somerset*: I hold it cowardize,
To rest mistrustfull, where a Noble Heart
Hath pawn'd an open Hand, in signe of Loue;
Else might I thinke, that *Clarence*, *Edwards* Brother,
Were but a fained friend to our proceedings:
But welcome sweet *Clarence*, my Daughter shall be thine.
And now, what rests? but in Nights Couerture,
Thy Brother being carelessely encamp'd,
His Souldiors lurking in the Towne about,
Wee may surprize and take him at our pleasure,
Our Scouts haue found the aduenture very easie:
That as *Vlysses*, and stout *Diomede*,
With sleight and manhood stole to *Rhesus* Tents,
And brought from thence the Thracian fatall Steeds;
So wee, well couer'd with the Nights black Mantle,
At vnawares may beat downe *Edwards* Guard,
And seize himselfe: I say not, slaughter him,
For I intend but onely to surprize him.
You that will follow me to this attempt,
Applaud the Name of *Henry*, with your Leader.

They all cry, Henry.

Why then, let's on our way in silent sort,
For *Warwicke* and his friends, God and Saint *George*.

Exeunt.

Enter three Watchmen to guard the Kings Tent.

1. Watch. Come on my Masters, each man take his stand,
The King by this, is set him downe to sleepe.

2. Watch. What, will he not to Bed?

1. Watch. Why, no: for he hath made a solemne Vow,
Neuer to lye and take his naturall Rest,
Till *Warwicke*, or himselfe, be quite supprest.

2. Watch. To morrow then belike shall be the day,
If *Warwicke* be so neere as men report.

3. Watch. But say, I pray, what Noble man is that,
That with the King here resteth in his Tent?

1. Watch. 'Tis the Lord *Hastings*, the Kings chiefest
friend.

3. Watch. O, is it so? but why commands the King,
That his chiefe followers lodge in Townes about him,
While he himselfe keepes in the cold field?

2. Watch. 'Tis the more honour, because more dangerous.

3. Watch. I, but giue me worship, and quietnesse,
I like it better then a dangerous honor.
If *Warwicke* knew in what estate he stands,
'Tis to be doubted he would waken him.

1. Watch. Vnlesse our Halberds did shut vp his passage.

2. Watch. I: wherefore else guard we his Royall Tent,
But to defend his Person from Night-foes?

Enter Warwicke, Clarence, Oxford, Somerset,
and French Souldiors, silent all.

Warw. This is his Tent, and see where stand his Guard:
Courage my Masters: Honor now, or neuer:
But follow me, and *Edward* shall be ours.

1. Watch. Who goes there?

2. Watch. Stay, or thou dyest.

Warwicke and the rest cry all, Warwicke, Warwicke,
and set vpon the Guard, who flye, crying, Arme, Arme,
Warwicke and the rest following them.

The Drumme playing, and Trumpet sounding.
Enter Warwicke, Somerset, and the rest, bringing the King
out in his Gowne, sitting in a Chaire: Richard
and Hastings flyes ouer the Stage.

Som. What are they that flye there?

Warw. *Richard* and *Hastings*: let them goe, heere is
the Duke.

K. Edw. The Duke?
Why *Warwicke*, when wee parted,
Thou call'dst me King.

Warw. I, but the case is alter'd,
When you disgrac'd me in my Embassade,
Then I degraded you from being King,
And come now to create you Duke of *Yorke*:
Alas, how should you gouerne any Kingdome,
That know not how to vse Embassadors,
Nor how to be contented with one Wife,
Nor how to vse your Brothers Brotherly,
Nor how to studie for the Peoples Welfare,
Nor how to shrowd your selfe from Enemies?

K. Edw. Yes,

The third Part of King Henry the Sixt. 167

K. Edw. Yea, Brother of Clarence,
Art thou here too?
Nay then I see, that *Edward* needs must downe.
Yet *Warwicke*, in despight of all mischance,
Of thee thy selfe, and all thy Complices,
Edward will alwayes beare himselfe as King:
Though Fortunes mallice ouerthrow my State,
My minde exceedes the compasse of her Wheele.

Warw. Then for his minde, be *Edward* Englands King;

Takes off his Crowne.

But *Henry* now shall weare the English Crowne,
And be true King indeede: thou but the shadow.
My Lord of Somerset, at my request,
See that forthwith Duke *Edward* be conuey'd
Vnto my Brother Arch-Bishop of Yorke:
When I haue fought with *Pembrooke*, and his fellowes,
Ile follow you, and tell what answer
Lewis and the Lady *Bona* send to him.
Now for a-while farewell good Duke of Yorke.

They leade him out forcibly.

K.Ed. What Fates impose, that men must needs abide;
It boots not to resist both winde and tide. *Exeunt.*

Oxf. What now remaines my Lords for vs to do,
But march to London with our Soldiers?

War. I, that's the first thing that we haue to do,
To free King *Henry* from imprisonment,
And see him seated in the Regall Throne. *exit.*

Enter Riuers, and Lady Gray.

Riu. Madam, what makes you in this sodain change?
Gray. Why Brother *Riuers*, are you yet to learne
What late misfortune is befalne King *Edward*?
Riu. What losse of some pitcht battell
Against *Warwicke*?
Gray. No, but the losse of his owne Royall person.
Riu. Then is my Soueraigne slaine?
Gray. I almost slaine, for he is taken prisoner,
Either betrayd by falshood of his Guard,
Or by his Foe surpriz'd at vnawares:
And as I further haue to vnderstand,
Is new committed to the Bishop of Yorke,
Fell *Warwickes* Brother, and by that our Foe.
Riu. These Newes I must confesse are full of greefe,
Yet gracious Madam, beare it as you may,
Warwicke may loose, that now hath wonne the day.
Gray. Till then, faire hope must hinder liues decay:
And I the rather waine me from dispaire
For loue of *Edwards* Off-spring in my wombe:
This is it that makes me bridle passion,
And beare with Mildnesse my misfortunes crosse:
I, I, for this I draw in many a teare,
And stop the rising of blood-sucking sighes,
Least with my sighes or teares, I blast or drowne
King *Edwards* Fruite, true heyre to th'English Crowne.
Riu. But Madam,
Where is *Warwicke* then become?
Gray. I am inform'd that he comes towards London,
To set the Crowne once more on *Henries* head,
Guesse thou the rest, King *Edwards* Friends must downe.
But to preuent the Tyrants violence,
(For trust not him that hath once broken Faith)
Ile hence forthwith vnto the Sanctuary,
To saue (at least) the heire of *Edwards* right:
There shall I rest secure from force and fraud:
Come therefore let vs flye, while we may flye,
If *Warwicke* take vs, we are sure to dye. *exeunt.*

Enter Richard, Lord Hastings, and Sir William Stanley.

Rich. Now my Lord *Hastings*, and Sir *William Stanley*
Leaue off to wonder why I drew you hither,
Into this cheefest Thicket of the Parke.
Thus stand the case: you know our King, my Brother,
Is prisoner to the Bishop here, at whose hands
He hath good vsage, and great liberty,
And often but attended with weake guard,
Come hunting this way to disport himselfe.
I haue aduertis'd him by secret meanes,
That if about this houre he make this way,
Vnder the colour of his vsuall game,
He shall heere finde his Friends with Horse and Men,
To set him free from his Captiuitie.

Enter King Edward, and a Huntsman with him.

Huntsman. This way my Lord,
For this way lies the Game.
King Edw. Nay this way man,
See where the Huntsmen stand.
Now Brother of Gloster, Lord Hastings, and the rest,
Stand you thus close to steale the Bishops Deere?
Rich. Brother, the time and case, requireth hast,
Your horse stands ready at the Parke-corner.
King Ed. But whether shall we then?
Hast. To Lyn my Lord,
And shipt from thence to Flanders.
Rich. Wel guest beleeue me, for that was my meaning
K.Ed. *Stanley*, I will require thy forwardnesse.
Rich. But wherefore stay we? 'tis no time to talke.
K.Ed. Huntsman, what say'st thou?
Wilt thou go along?
Hunts. Better do so, then tarry and be hang'd.
Rich. Come then away, lets ha no more adoo.
K.Ed. Bishop farwell,
Sheeld thee from *Warwickes* frowne,
And pray that I may re-possesse the Crowne. *exeunt*

Flourish. Enter King Henry the sixt, Clarence, Warwicke, Somerset, young Henry, Oxford, Mountague, and Lieutenant.

K.Hen. M.Lieutenant, now that God and Friends
Haue shaken *Edward* from the Regall seate,
And turn'd my captiue state to libertie,
My feare to hope, my sorrowes vnto ioyes,
At our enlargement what are thy due Fees?
Lieu. Subiects may challenge nothing of their Sou'rains
But, if an humble prayer may preuaile,
I then craue pardon of your Maiestie.
K.Hen. For what, Lieutenant? For well vsing me?
Nay, be thou sure, Ile well requite thy kindnesse.
For that it made my imprisonment, a pleasure:
I, such a pleasure, as incaged Birds
Conceiue; when after many moody Thoughts,
At last, by Notes of Houshold harmonie,
They quite forget their losse of Libertie.

q But

But *Warwicke*, after God, thou set'st me free,
And chiefely therefore, I thanke God, and thee,
He was the Author, thou the Instrument.
Therefore that I may conquer Fortunes spight,
By liuing low, where Fortune cannot hurt me,
And that the people of this blessed Land
May not be punisht with my thwarting starres,
Warwicke, although my Head still weare the Crowne,
I here resigne my Gouernment to thee,
For thou art fortunate in all thy deeds.

Warw. Your Grace hath still beene fam'd for vertuous,
And now may seeme as wise as vertuous,
By spying and auoiding Fortunes malice,
For few men rightly temper with the Starres:
Yet in this one thing let me blame your Grace,
For chusing me, when *Clarence* is in place.

Clar. No *Warwicke*, thou art worthy of the sway,
To whom the Heau'ns in thy Natiuitie,
Adiudg'd an Oliue Branch, and Lawrell Crowne,
As likely to be blest in Peace and Warre:
And therefore I yeeld thee my free consent.

Warw. And I chuse *Clarence* onely for Protector.

King. *Warwick* and *Clarence*, giue me both your Hands:
Now ioyne your Hands, & with your Hands your Hearts,
That no dissention hinder Gouernment:
I make you both Protectors of this Land,
While I my selfe will lead a priuate Life,
And in deuotion spend my latter dayes,
To sinnes rebuke, and my Creators prayse.

Warw. What answeres *Clarence* to his Soueraignes will?

Clar. That he consents, if *Warwicke* yeeld consent,
For on thy fortune I repose my selfe.

Warw. Why then, though loth, yet must I be content:
Wee'le yoake together, like a double shadow
To *Henries* Body, and supply his place;
I meane, in bearing weight of Gouernment,
While he enioyes the Honor, and his ease.
And *Clarence*, now then it is more then needfull,
Forthwith that *Edward* be pronounc'd a Traytor,
And all his Lands and Goods confiscate.

Clar. What else? and that Succession be determined.

Warw. I, therein *Clarence* shall not want his part.

King. But with the first, of all your chiefe affaires,
Let me entreat (for I command no more)
That *Margaret* your Queene, and my Sonne *Edward*,
Be sent for, to returne from France with speed:
For till I see them here, by doubtfull feare,
My ioy of libertie is halfe eclips'd.

Clar. It shall bee done, my Soueraigne, with all speede.

King. My Lord of Somerset, what Youth is that,
Of whom you seeme to haue so tender care?

Somers. My Liege, it is young *Henry*, Earle of Richmond.

King. Come hither, Englands Hope:
         Layes his Hand on his Head.
If secret Powers suggest but truth
To my diuining thoughts,
This prettie Lad will proue our Countries blisse.
His Lookes are full of peacefull Maiestie,
His Head by nature fram'd to weare a Crowne,
His Hand to wield a Scepter, and himselfe
Likely in time to blesse a Regall Throne:
Make much of him, my Lords; for this is hee
Must helpe you more, then you are hurt by mee.

Enter a Poste.

Warw. What newes, my friend?

Poste. That *Edward* is escaped from your Brother,
And fled (as hee heares since) to Burgundie.

Warw. Vnsauorie newes: but how made he escape?

Poste. He was conuey'd by *Richard*, Duke of Gloster,
And the Lord *Hastings*, who attended him
In secret ambush, on the Forrest side,
And from the Bishops Huntsmen rescu'd him:
For Hunting was his dayly Exercise.

Warw. My Brother was too carelesse of his charge,
But let vs hence, my Soueraigne, to prouide
A salue for any sore, that may betide.   *Exeunt.*

Manet Somerset, Richmond, and Oxford.

Som. My Lord, I like not of this flight of *Edwards*:
For doubtlesse, *Burgundie* will yeeld him helpe,
And we shall haue more Warres befor't be long.
As *Henries* late presaging Prophecie
Did glad my heart, with hope of this young *Richmond*:
So doth my heart mis-giue me, in these Conflicts,
What may befall him, to his harme and ours.
Therefore, Lord *Oxford*, to preuent the worst,
Forthwith wee'le send him hence to Brittanie,
Till stormes be past of Ciuill Enmitie.

Oxf. I: for if *Edward* re-possesse the Crowne,
'Tis like that *Richmond*, with the rest, shall downe.

Som. It shall be so: he shall to Brittanie.
Come therefore, let's about it speedily.   *Exeunt.*

*Flourish. Enter Edward, Richard, Hastings,
and Souldiers.*

Edw. Now Brother *Richard*, Lord *Hastings*, and the rest,
Yet thus farre Fortune maketh vs amends,
And sayes, that once more I shall enterchange
My wained state, for *Henries* Regall Crowne.
Well haue we pass'd, and now re-pass'd the Seas,
And brought desired helpe from Burgundie.
What then remaines, we being thus arriu'd
From Rauenspurre Hauen, before the Gates of Yorke,
But that we enter, as into our Dukedome?

Rich. The Gates made fast?
Brother, I like not this.
For many men that stumble at the Threshold,
Are well fore-told, that danger lurkes within.

Edw. Tush man, aboadments must not now affright vs:
By faire or foule meanes we must enter in,
For hither will our friends repaire to vs.

Hast. My Liege, Ile knocke once more, to summon them.

*Enter on the Walls, the Maior of Yorke,
and his Brethren.*

Maior. My Lords,
We were fore-warned of your comming,
And shut the Gates, for safetie of our selues;
For now we owe allegeance vnto *Henry*.

Edw. But, Master Maior, if *Henry* be your King,
Yet *Edward*, at the least, is Duke of Yorke.

Maior. True, my good Lord, I know you for no lesse.

Edw. Why, and I challenge nothing but my Dukedome,
As being well content with that alone.   *Rich.* But

Rich. But when the Fox hath once got in his Nose,
Hee'le soone finde meanes to make the Body follow.
Pet. Why, Master Maior, why stand you in a doubt?
Open the Gates, we are King *Henries* friends.
Maior. I, say you so? the Gates shall then be opened.
He descends.

Rich. A wise stout Captaine, and soone perswaded.
Hast. The good old man would faine that all were wel,
So 'twere not long of him: but being entred,
I doubt not I, but we shall soone perswade
Both him, and all his Brothers, vnto reason.

Enter the Maior, and two Aldermen.

Edw. So, Master Maior: these Gates must not be shut,
But in the Night, or in the time of Warre.
What, feare not man, but yeeld me vp the Keyes,
Takes his Keyes.
For *Edward* will defend the Towne, and thee,
And all those friends, that deine to follow mee.

March. Enter Mountgomerie, with Drumme and Souldiers.

Rich. Brother, this is Sir *Iohn Mountgomerie*,
Our trustie friend, vnlesse I be deceiu'd.
Edw. Welcome Sir *Iohn*: but why come you in Armes?
Mount. To helpe King *Edward* in his time of storme,
As euery loyall Subiect ought to doe.
Edw. Thankes good *Mountgomerie*:
But we now forget our Title to the Crowne,
And onely clayme our Dukedome,
Till God please to send the rest.
Mount. Then fare you well, for I will hence againe,
I came to serue a King, and not a Duke:
Drummer strike vp, and let vs march away.
The Drumme begins to march.
Edw. Nay stay, Sir *Iohn*, a while, and wee'le debate
By what safe meanes the Crowne may be recouer'd.
Mount. What talke you of debating? in few words,
If you'le not here proclaime your selfe our King,
Ile leaue you to your fortune, and be gone,
To keepe them back, that come to succour you.
Why shall we fight, if you pretend no Title?
Rich. Why Brother, wherefore stand you on nice points?
Edw. When wee grow stronger,
Then wee'le make our Clayme:
Till then, 'tis wisdome to conceale our meaning.
Hast. Away with scrupulous Wit, now Armes must rule.
Rich. And feareless minds clyme soonest vnto Crowns.
Brother, we will proclaime you out of hand,
The bruit thereof will bring you many friends.
Edw. Then be it as you will: for 'tis my right,
And *Henry* but vsurpes the Diademe.
Mount. I, now my Soueraigne speaketh like himselfe,
And now will I be *Edwards* Champion.
Hast. Sound Trumpet, *Edward* shal be here proclaim'd:
Come, fellow Souldior, make thou proclamation.
Flourish. Sound.
Soul. Edward the Fourth, by the Grace of God, King of England and Fraunce, and Lord of Ireland, &c.
Mount. And whosoe're gainsayes King *Edwards* right,
By this I challenge him to single fight.
Throwes downe his Gauntlet.
All. Long liue *Edward* the Fourth.

Edw. Thankes braue *Mountgomery*,
And thankes vnto you all:
If fortune serue me, Ile requite this kindnesse.
Now for this Night, let's harbor here in Yorke:
And when the Morning Sunne shall rayse his Carre
Aboue the Border of this Horizon,
Wee'le forward towards *Warwicke*, and his Mates;
For well I wot, that *Henry* is no Souldier.
Ah froward *Clarence*, how euill it beseemes thee,
To flatter *Henry*, and forsake thy Brother?
Yet as wee may, wee'le meet both thee and *Warwicke*.
Come on braue Souldiors: doubt not of the Day,
And that once gotten, doubt not of large Pay. *Exeunt.*

Flourish. Enter the King, Warwicke, Mountague, Clarence, Oxford, and Somerset.

War. What counsaile, Lords? *Edward* from Belgia,
With hastie Germanes, and blunt Hollanders,
Hath pass'd in safetie through the Narrow Seas,
And with his troupes doth march amaine to London,
And many giddie people flock to him.
King. Let's leuie men, and beat him backe againe.
Clar. A little fire is quickly trodden out,
Which being suffer'd, Riuers cannot quench.
War. In Warwickshire I haue true-hearted friends,
Not mutinous in peace, yet bold in Warre,
Those will I muster vp: and thou Sonne *Clarence*
Shalt stirre vp in Suffolke, Norfolke, and in Kent,
The Knights and Gentlemen, to come with thee:
Thou Brother *Mountague*, in Buckingham,
Northampton, and in Leicestershire, shalt find
Men well enclin'd to heare what thou command'st.
And thou, braue *Oxford*, wondrous well belou'd,
In Oxfordshire shalt muster vp thy friends.
My Soueraigne, with the louing Citizens,
Like to his Iland, gyrt in with the Ocean,
Or modest *Dyan*, circled with her Nymphs,
Shall rest in London, till we come to him:
Faire Lords take leaue, and stand not to reply.
Farewell my Soueraigne.
King. Farewell my *Hector*, and my Troyes true hope.
Clar. In signe of truth, I kisse your Highnesse Hand.
King. Well-minded *Clarence*, be thou fortunate.
Mount. Comfort, my Lord, and so I take my leaue.
Oxf. And thus I seale my truth, aud bid adieu.
King. Sweet *Oxford*, and my louing *Mountague*,
And all at once, once more a happy farewell.
War. Farewell, sweet Lords, let's meet at Couentry.
Exeunt.

King. Here at the Pallace will I rest a while.
Cousin of *Exeter*, what thinkes your Lordship?
Me thinkes, the Power that *Edward* hath in field,
Should not be able to encounter mine.
Exet. The doubt is, that he will seduce the rest.
King. That's not my feare, my meed hath got me fame:
I haue not stopt mine eares to their demands,
Nor posted off their suites with slow delayes,
My pittie hath beene balme to heale their wounds,
My mildnesse hath allay'd their swelling griefes,
My mercie dry'd their water-flowing teares.
I haue not been desirous of their wealth,
Nor much opprest them with great Subsidies,
Nor forward of reuenge, though they much err'd,
Then why should they loue *Edward* more then me?
No *Exeter*, these Graces challenge Grace:

And

And when the Lyon fawnes vpon the Lambe,
The Lambe will neuer cease to follow him.
Shout within, A Lancaster, A Lancaster.

Exet. Hearke, hearke, my Lord, what Shouts are these?

Enter Edward and his Souldiers.

Edw. Seize on the shamefac'd *Henry*, beare him hence,
And once againe proclaime vs King of England.
You are the Fount, that makes small Brookes to flow,
Now stops thy Spring, my Sea shall suck them dry,
And swell so much the higher, by their ebbe.
Hence with him to the Tower, let him not speake.
Exit with King Henry.
And Lords, towards Couentry bend we our course,
Where peremptorie *Warwicke* now remaines:
The Sunne shines hot, and if we vse delay,
Cold biting Winter marres our hop'd-for Hay.

Rich. Away betimes, before his forces ioyne,
And take the great-growne Traytor vnawares:
Braue Warriors, march amaine towards Couentry.
Exeunt.

Enter Warwicke, the Maior of Couentry, two Messengers, and others vpon the Walls.

War. Where is the Post that came from valiant *Oxford*?
How farre hence is thy Lord, mine honest fellow?

Mess.1. By this at Dunsmore, marching hitherward.

War. How farre off is our Brother *Mountague*?
Where is the Post that came from *Mountague*?

Mess.2. By this at Daintry, with a puissant troope.

Enter Someruile.

War. Say *Someruile*, what sayes my louing Sonne?
And by thy guesse, how nigh is *Clarence* now?

Somer. At Southam I did leaue him with his forces,
And doe expect him here some two howres hence.

War. Then *Clarence* is at hand, I heare his Drumme.

Someru. It is not his, my Lord, here Southam lyes:
The Drum your Honor heares, marcheth from *Warwicke*.

War. Who should that be? belike vnlook'd for friends.

Someru. They are at hand, and you shall quickly know.

March. Flourish. Enter Edward, Richard, and Souldiers.

Edw. Goe, Trumpet, to the Walls, and sound a Parle.

Rich. See how the surly *Warwicke* mans the Wall.

War. Oh vnbid spight, is sportfull *Edward* come?
Where slept our Scouts, or how are they seduc'd,
That we could heare no newes of his repayre.

Edw. Now *Warwicke*, wilt thou ope the Citie Gates,
Speake gentle words, and humbly bend thy Knee,
Call *Edward* King, and at his hands begge Mercy,
And he shall pardon thee these Outrages?

War. Nay rather, wilt thou draw thy forces hence,
Confesse who set thee vp, and pluckt thee downe,
Call *Warwicke* Patron, and be penitent,
And thou shalt still remaine the Duke of Yorke.

Rich. I thought at least he would haue said the King,
Or did he make the Ieast against his will?

War. Is not a Dukedome, Sir, a goodly gift?

Rich. I, by my faith, for a poore Earle to giue,
Ile doe thee seruice for so good a gift.

War. 'Twas I that gaue the Kingdome to thy Brother.

Edw. Why then 'tis mine, if but by *Warwickes* gift.

War. Thou art no *Atlas* for so great a weight:
And Weakeling, *Warwicke* takes his gift againe,
And *Henry* is my King, *Warwicke* his Subiect.

Edw. But *Warwickes* King is *Edwards* Prisoner:
And gallant *Warwicke*, doe but answer this,
What is the Body, when the Head is off?

Rich. Alas, that *Warwicke* had no more fore-cast,
But whiles he thought to steale the single Ten,
The King was slyly finger'd from the Deck:
You left poore *Henry* at the Bishops Pallace,
And tenne to one you'le meet him in the Tower.

Edw. 'Tis euen so, yet you are *Warwicke* still.

Rich. Come *Warwicke*,
Take the time, kneele downe, kneele downe:
Nay when? strike now, or else the Iron cooles.

War. I had rather chop this Hand off at a blow,
And with the other, fling it at thy face,
Then beare so low a sayle, to strike to thee.

Edw. Sayle how thou canst,
Haue Winde and Tyde thy friend,
This Hand, fast wound about thy coale-black hayre,
Shall, whiles thy Head is warme, and new cut off,
Write in the dust this Sentence with thy blood,
Wind-changing *Warwicke* now can change no more.

Enter Oxford, with Drumme and Colours.

War. Oh chearefull Colours, see where *Oxford* comes.

Oxf. *Oxford, Oxford*, for *Lancaster*.

Rich. The Gates are open, let vs enter too.

Edw. So other foes may set vpon our backs.
Stand we in good array: for they no doubt
Will issue out againe, and bid vs battaile;
If not, the Citie being but of small defence,
Wee'le quickly rowze the Traitors in the same.

War. Oh welcome *Oxford*, for we want thy helpe.

Enter Mountague, with Drumme and Colours.

Mount. *Mountague, Mountague*, for *Lancaster*.

Rich. Thou and thy Brother both shall buy this Treason
Euen with the dearest blood your bodies beare.

Edw. The harder matcht, the greater Victorie,
My minde presageth happy gaine, and Conquest.

Enter Somerset, with Drumme and Colours.

Som. *Somerset, Somerset*, for *Lancaster*.

Rich. Two of thy Name, both Dukes of Somerset,
Haue sold their Liues vnto the House of *Yorke*,
And thou shalt be the third, if this Sword hold.

Enter Clarence, with Drumme and Colours.

War. And loe, where *George* of Clarence sweepes along,
Of force enough to bid his Brother Battaile:
With whom, in vpright zeale to right, preuailes
More then the nature of a Brothers Loue.
Come *Clarence*, come: thou wilt, if *Warwicke* call.

Clar. Father of Warwick, know you what this meanes?
Looke here, I throw my infamie at thee:
I will not ruinate my Fathers House,
Who gaue his blood to lyme the stones together,
And set vp *Lancaster*. Why, trowest thou, *Warwicke*,
That *Clarence* is so harsh, so blunt, vnnaturall,
To bend the fatall Instruments of Warre

Against

Against his Brother, and his lawfull King.
Perhaps thou wilt obiect my holy Oath:
To keepe that Oath, were more impietie,
Than Iephah, when he sacrific'd his Daughter.
I am so sorry for my Trespas made,
That to deserue well at my Brothers hands,
I there proclayme my selfe thy mortall foe:
With resolution, wheresoe're I meet thee,
(As I will meet thee, if thou stirre abroad)
To plague thee, for thy soule mis-leading me.
And so, prowd-hearted *Warwicke*, I defie thee,
And to my Brother turne my blushing Cheekes.
Pardon me *Edward*, I will make amends:
And *Richard*, doe not frowne vpon my faults,
For I will henceforth be no more vnconstant.

  Edw. Now welcome more, and ten times more belou'd,
Then if thou neuer hadst deseru'd our hate.

  Rich. Welcome good *Clarence*, this is Brother-like.

  Warw. Oh passing Traytor, periur'd and vniust.

  Edw. What *Warwicke*,
Wilt thou leaue the Towne, and fight?
Or shall we beat the Stones about thine Eares?

  Warw. Alas, I am not coop'd here for defence:
I will away towards Barnet presently,
And bid thee Battaile, *Edward*, if thou dar'st.

  Edw. Yes *Warwicke*, *Edward* dares, and leads the way:
Lords to the field: Saint *George*, and Victorie. *Exeunt.*

March. Warwicke and his companie followes.

*Alarum, and Excursions. Enter Edward bringing
forth Warwicke wounded.*

  Edw. So, lye thou there: dye thou, and dye our feare,
For *Warwicke* was a Bugge that fear'd vs all.
Now *Mountague* sit fast, I seeke for thee,
That *Warwickes* Bones may keepe thine companie. *Exit.*

  Warw. Ah, who is nigh? come to me, friend, or foe,
And tell me who is Victor, *Yorke*, or *Warwicke*?
Why aske I that? my mangled body shewes,
My blood, my want of strength, my sicke heart shewes,
That I must yeeld my body to the Earth,
And by my fall, the conquest to my foe.
Thus yeelds the Cedar to the Axes edge,
Whose Armes gaue shelter to the Princely Eagle,
Vnder whose shade the ramping Lyon slept,
Whose top-branch ouer-peer'd *Ioues* spreading Tree,
And kept low Shrubs from Winters pow'rfull Winde.
These Eyes, that now are dim'd with Deaths black Veyle,
Haue beene as piercing as the Mid-day Sunne,
To search the secret Treasons of the World:
The Wrinckles in my Browes, now fill'd with blood,
Were lik'ned oft to Kingly Sepulchers:
For who liu'd King, but I could digge his Graue?
And who durst smile, when *Warwicke* bent his Brow?
Loe, now my Glory smear'd in dust and blood.
My Parkes, my Walkes, my Mannors that I had,
Euen now forsake me; and of all my Lands,
Is nothing left me, but my bodies length.
Why, what is Pompe, Rule, Reigne, but Earth and Dust?
And liue we how we can, yet dye we must.

Enter Oxford and Somerset.

  Som. Ah *Warwicke*, *Warwicke*, wert thou as we are,
We might recouer all our Losse againe:
The Queene from France hath brought a puissant power.
Euen now we heard the newes: ah, could'st thou flye.

  Warw. Why then I would not flye. Ah *Mountague*,
If thou be there, sweet Brother, take my Hand,
And with thy Lippes keepe in my Soule a while.
Thou lou'st me not: for, Brother, if thou didst,
Thy teares would wash this cold congealed blood,
That glewes my Lippes, and will not let me speake.
Come quickly *Mountague*, or I am dead.

  Som. Ah *Warwicke*, *Mountague* hath breath'd his last,
And to the latest gaspe, cry'd out for *Warwicke*:
And said, Commend me to my valiant Brother.
And more he would haue said, and more he spoke,
Which sounded like a Cannon in a Vault,
That mought not be distinguisht: but at last,
I well might heare, deliuered with a groane,
Oh farewell *Warwicke*.

  Warw. Sweet rest his Soule:
Flye Lords, and saue your selues,
For *Warwicke* bids you all farewell, to meet in Heauen.

  Oxf. Away, away, to meet the Queenes great power.

Here they beare away his Body. *Exeunt.*

*Flourish. Enter King Edward in triumph, with
Richard, Clarence, and the rest.*

  King. Thus farre our fortune keepes an vpward course,
And we are grac'd with wreaths of Victorie:
But in the midst of this bright-shining Day,
I spy a black suspicious threatning Cloud,
That will encounter with our glorious Sunne,
Ere he attaine his easefull Westerne Bed:
I meane, my Lords, those powers that the Queene
Hath rays'd in Gallia, haue arriued our Coast,
And, as we heare, march on to fight with vs.

  Clar. A little gale will soone disperse that Cloud,
And blow it to the Source from whence it came,
Thy very Beames will dry those Vapours vp,
For euery Cloud engenders not a Storme.

  Rich. The Queene is valued thirtie thousand strong,
And *Somerset*, with *Oxford*, fled to her:
If she haue time to breathe, be well assur'd
Her faction will be full as strong as ours.

  King. We are aduertis'd by our louing friends,
That they doe hold their course toward Tewksbury.
We hauing now the best at Barnet field,
Will thither straight, for willingnesse rids way,
And as we march, our strength will be augmented:
In euery Countie as we goe along,
Strike vp the Drumme, cry courage, and away. *Exeunt.*

*Flourish. March. Enter the Queene, young
Edward, Somerset, Oxford, and
Souldiers.*

  Qu. Great Lords, wise men ne'r sit and waile their losse,
But chearely seeke how to redresse their harmes.
What though the Mast be now blowne ouer-boord,
The Cable broke, the holding-Anchor lost,
And halfe our Saylors swallow'd in the flood?
Yet liues our Pilot still. Is't meet, that hee
Should leaue the Helme, and like a fearefull Lad,
With tearefull Eyes adde Water to the Sea,
And giue more strength to that which hath too much,
Whiles in his moane, the Ship splits on the Rock,
Which Industrie and Courage might haue sau'd?
Ah what a shame, ah what a fault were this.
Say *Warwicke* was our Anchor: what of that?

And *Mountague* our Top-Mast: what of him?
Our slaught'red friends, the Tackles: what of these?
Why is not *Oxford* here, another Anchor?
And *Somerset*, another goodly Mast?
The friends of France our Shrowds and Tacklings?
And though vnskilfull, why not *Ned* and I,
For once allow'd the skilfull Pilots Charge?
We will not from the Helme, to sit and weepe,
But keepe our Course (though the rough Winde say no)
From Shelues and Rocks, that threaten vs with Wrack,
As good to chide the Waues, as speake them faire.
And what is *Edward*, but a ruthlesse Sea?
What *Clarence*, but a Quick-sand of Deceit?
And *Richard*, but a raged fatall Rocke?
All these, the Enemies to our poore Barke.
Say you can swim, alas 'tis but a while:
Tread on the Sand, why there you quickly sinke,
Bestride the Rock, the Tyde will wash you off,
Or else you famish, that's a three-fold Death.
This speake I (Lords) to let you vnderstand,
If case some one of you would flye from vs,
That there's no hop'd-for Mercy with the Brothers,
More then with ruthlesse Waues, with Sands and Rocks.
Why courage then, what cannot be auoided,
'Twere childish weakenesse to lament, or feare.

Prince. Me thinkes a Woman of this valiant Spirit,
Should, if a Coward heard her speake these words,
Infuse his Breast with Magnanimitie,
And make him, naked, foyle a man at Armes.
I speake not this, as doubting any here:
For did I but suspect a fearefull man,
He should haue leaue to goe away betimes,
Least in our need he might infect another,
And make him of like spirit to himselfe.
If any such be here, as God forbid,
Let him depart, before we neede his helpe.

Oxf. Women and Children of so high a courage,
And Warriors faint, why 'twere perpetuall shame.
Oh braue young Prince: thy famous Grandfather
Doth liue againe in thee; long may'st thou liue,
To beare his Image, and renew his Glories.

Som. And he that will not fight for such a hope,
Goe home to Bed, and like the Owle by day,
If he arise, be mock'd and wondred at.

Qu. Thankes gentle *Somerset*, sweet *Oxford* thankes.

Prince. And take his thankes, that yet hath nothing else.

Enter a Messenger.

Mess. Prepare you Lords, for *Edward* is at hand,
Readie to fight: therefore be resolute.

Oxf. I thought no lesse: it is his Policie,
To haste thus fast, to finde vs vnprouided.

Som. But hee's deceiu'd, we are in readinesse.

Qu. This cheares my heart, to see your forwardnesse.

Oxf. Here pitch our Battaile, hence we will not budge.

Flourish, and march. Enter Edward, Richard, Clarence, and Souldiers.

Edw. Braue followers, yonder stands the thornie Wood,
Which by the Heauens assistance, and your strength,
Must by the Roots be hew'ne vp yet ere Night.
I need not adde more fuell to your fire,
For well I wot, ye blaze, to burne them out:
Giue signall to the fight, and to it Lords.

Qu. Lords, Knights, and Gentlemen, what I should say,
My teares gaine-say: for euery word I speake,
Ye see I drinke the water of my eye.
Therefore no more but this: *Henry* your Soueraigne
Is Prisoner to the Foe, his State vsurp'd,
His Realme a slaughter-house, his Subiects slaine,
His Statutes cancell'd, and his Treasure spent:
And yonder is the Wolfe, that makes this spoyle.
You fight in Iustice: then in Gods Name, Lords,
Be valiant, and giue signall to the fight.

Alarum, Retreat, Excursions. *Exeunt.*

Flourish. Enter Edward, Richard, Queene, Clarence, Oxford, Somerset.

Edw. Now here a period of tumultuous Broyles,
Away with *Oxford* to Hames Castle straight:
For *Somerset*, off with his guiltie Head.
Goe beare them hence, I will not heare them speake.

Oxf. For my part, Ile not trouble thee with words.

Som. Nor I, but stoupe with patience to my fortune.

Exeunt.

Qu. So part we sadly in this troublous World,
To meet with Ioy in sweet Ierusalem.

Edw. Is Proclamation made, That who finds *Edward*,
Shall haue a high Reward, and he his Life?

Rich. It is, and loe where youthfull *Edward* comes.

Enter the Prince.

Edw. Bring forth the Gallant, let vs heare him speake.
What? can so young a Thorne begin to prick?
Edward, what satisfaction canst thou make,
For bearing Armes, for stirring vp my Subiects,
And all the trouble thou hast turn'd me to?

Prince. Speake like a Subiect, prowd ambitious *Yorke*.
Suppose that I am now my Fathers Mouth,
Resigne thy Chayre, and where I stand, kneele thou,
Whil'st I propose the selfe-same words to thee,
Which (Traytor) thou would'st haue me answer to.

Qu. Ah, that thy Father had beene so resolu'd.

Rich. That you might still haue worne the Petticoat,
And ne're haue stolne the Breech from *Lancaster*.

Prince. Let *Æsop* fable in a Winters Night,
His Currish Riddles sorts not with this place.

Rich. By Heauen, Brat, Ile plague ye for that word.

Qu. I, thou wast borne to be a plague to men.

Rich. For Gods sake, take away this Captiue Scold.

Prince. Nay, take away this scolding Crooke-backe, rather.

Edw. Peace wilfull Boy, or I will charme your tongue.

Clar. Vntutor'd Lad, thou art too malapert.

Prince. I know my dutie, you are all vndutifull:
Lasciuious *Edward*, and thou periur'd *George*,
And thou mis-shapen *Dicke*, I tell ye all,
I am your better, Traytors as ye are,
And thou vsurp'st my Fathers right and mine.

Edw. Take that, the likenesse of this Rayler here.
Stabs him.

Rich. Sprawl'st thou? take that, to end thy agonie.
Rich. stabs him.

Clar. And ther's for twitting me with periurie.
Clar. stabs him.

Qu. Oh, kill me too.

Rich. Marry, and shall. *Offers to kill her.*

Edw. Hold, *Richard*, hold, for we haue done too much.

Rich. Why

Rich. Why should shee liue, to fill the World with words.

Edw. What? doth shee swowne? vse meanes for her recouerie.

Rich. *Clarence* excuse me to the King my Brother:
Ile hence to London on a serious matter,
Ere ye come there, be sure to heare some newes.

Cla. What? what?

Rich. Tower, the Tower.   *Exit.*

Qu. Oh *Ned*, sweet *Ned*, speake to thy Mother Boy.
Can'st thou not speake? O Traitors, Murtherers!
They that stabb'd *Cæsar*, shed no blood at all:
Did not offend, nor were not worthy Blame,
If this foule deed were by, to equall it.
He was a Man; this (in respect) a Childe,
And Men, ne're spend their fury on a Childe.
What's worse then Murtherer, that I may name it?
No, no, my heart will burst, and if I speake,
And I will speake, that so my heart may burst.
Butchers and Villaines, bloudy Caniballes,
How sweet a Plant haue you vntimely cropt:
You haue no children (Butchers) if you had,
The thought of them would haue stirr'd vp remorse,
But if you euer chance to haue a Childe,
Looke in his youth to haue him so cut off,
As deathsmen you haue rid this sweet yong Prince.

King. Away with her, go beare her hence perforce.

Qu. Nay, neuer beare me hence, dispatch me heere:
Here sheath thy Sword, Ile pardon thee my death:
What? wilt thou not? Then *Clarence* do it thou.

Cla. By heauen, I will not do thee so much ease.

Qu. Good *Clarence* do: sweet *Clarence* do thou do it.

Cla. Did'st thou not heare me sweare I would not do it?

Qu. I, but thou vsest to forsweare thy selfe.
'Twas Sin before, but now 'tis Charity.
What wilt y not? Where is that diuels butcher *Richard*?
Hard fauor'd *Richard*? *Richard*, where art thou?
Thou art not heere; Murther is thy Almes-deed:
Petitioners for Blood, thou ne're put'st backe.

Ed. Away I say, I charge ye beare her hence,

Qu. So come to you, and yours, as to this Prince.
 Exit Queene.

Ed. Where's *Richard* gone.

Cla. To London all in post, and as I guesse,
To make a bloody Supper in the Tower.

Ed. He's sodaine if a thing comes in his head.
Now march we hence, discharge the common sort
With Pay and Thankes, and let's away to London,
And see our gentle Queene how well she fares,
By this (I hope) she hath a Sonne for me.   *Exit.*

Enter Henry the sixt, and Richard, with the Lieutenant on the Walles.

Rich. Good day, my Lord, what at your Booke so hard?

Hen. I my good Lord: my Lord I should say rather,
Tis sinne to flatter, Good was little better:
Good *Gloster*, and good *Deuill*, were alike,
And both preposterous: therefore, not Good Lord.

Rich. Sirra, leaue vs to our selues, we must conferre.

Hen. So flies the wreakelesse shepherd from y Wolfe:
So first the harmlesse Sheepe doth yeeld his Fleece,
And next his Throate, vnto the Butchers Knife.
What Scene of death hath *Rossius* now to Acte?

Rich. Suspition alwayes haunts the guilty minde,
The Theefe doth feare each bush an Officer,

Hen. The Bird that hath bin limed in a bush,
With trembling wings misdoubteth euery bush;
And I the haplesse Male to one sweet Bird,
Haue now the fatall Obiect in my eye,
Where my poore yong was lim'd, was caught, and kill'd.

Rich. Why what a peuish Foole was that of Creet,
That taught his Sonne the office of a Fowle,
And yet for all his wings, the Foole was drown'd.

Hen. I *Dedalus*, my poore Boy *Icarus*,
Thy Father *Minos*, that deni'de our course,
The Sunne that sear'd the wings of my sweet Boy.
Thy Brother *Edward*, and thy Selfe, the Sea
Whose enuious Gulfe did swallow vp his life:
Ah, kill me with thy Weapon, not with words,
My brest can better brooke thy Daggers point,
Then can my eares that Tragicke History.
But wherefore dost thou come? Is't for my Life?

Rich. Think'st thou I am an Executioner?

Hen. A Persecutor I am sure thou art,
If murthering Innocents be Executing,
Why then thou art an Executioner.

Rich. Thy Son I kill'd for his presumption.

Hen. Hadst thou bin kill'd, when first y didst presume,
Thou had'st not liu'd to kill a Sonne of mine:
And thus I prophesie, that many a thousand,
Which now mistrust no parcell of my feare,
And many an old mans sighe, and many a Widdowes,
And many an Orphans water-standing-eye,
Men for their Sonnes, Wiues for their Husbands,
Orphans, for their Parents timeles death,
Shall rue the houre that euer thou was't borne.
The Owle shriek'd at thy birth, an euill signe,
The Night-Crow cry'de, aboding luckless time,
Dogs howl'd, and hiddeous Tempest shook down Trees:
The Rauen rook'd her on the Chimnies top,
And chatt'ring Pies in dismall Discords sung:
Thy Mother felt more then a Mothers paine,
And yet brought forth lesse then a Mothers hope,
To wit, an indigested and deformed lumpe,
Not like the fruit of such a goodly Tree.
Teeth had'st thou in thy head, when thou was't borne,
To signifie, thou cam'st to bite the world:
And if the rest be true, which I haue heard,
Thou cam'st——

Rich. Ile heare no more:
Dye Prophet in thy speech,   *Stabbes him.*
For this (among'st the rest) was I ordain'd.

Hen. I, and for much more slaughter after this,
O God forgiue my sinnes, and pardon thee.   *Dyes.*

Rich. What? will the aspiring blood of Lancaster
Sinke in the ground? I thought it would haue mounted.
See how my sword weepes for the poore Kings death.
O may such purple teares be alway shed
From those that wish the downfall of our house.
If any sparke of Life be yet remaining,
Downe, downe to hell, and say I sent thee thither.
 Stabs him againe.
I that haue neyther pitty, loue, nor feare,
Indeed 'tis true that *Henrie* told me of:
For I haue often heard my Mother say,
I came into the world with my Legges forward.
Had I not reason (thinke ye) to make hast,
And seeke their Ruine, that vsurp'd our Right?
The Midwife wonder'd, and the Women cri'de
O Iesus blesse vs, he is borne with teeth,

And

And so I was, which plainly signified,
That I should snarle, and bite, and play the dogge:
Then since the Heauens haue shap'd my Body so,
Let Hell make crook'd my Minde to answer it.
I haue no Brother, I am like no Brother:
And this word [Loue] which Gray-beards call Diuine,
Be resident in men like one another,
And not in me: I am my selfe alone.
Clarence beware, thou keept'st me from the Light,
But I will sort a pitchy day for thee:
For I will buzze abroad such Prophesies,
That Edward shall be fearefull of his life,
And then to purge his feare, Ile be thy death.
King Henry, and the Prince his Son are gone,
Clarence thy turne is next, and then the rest,
Counting my selfe but bad, till I be best.
Ile throw thy body in another roome,
And Triumph Henry, in thy day of Doome. *Exit.*

Flourish. Enter King, Queene, Clarence, Richard, Hastings, Nurse, and Attendants.

  King. Once more we sit in Englands Royall Throne,
Re-purchac'd with the Blood of Enemies:
What valiant Foe-men, like to Autumnes Corne,
Haue we mow'd downe in tops of all their pride?
Three Dukes of Somerset, threefold Renowne,
For hardy and vndoubted Champions:
Two Cliffords, as the Father and the Sonne,
And two Northumberlands: two brauer men,
Ne're spurr'd their Coursers at the Trumpets sound.
With them, the two braue Beares, Warwick & Montague,
That in their Chaines fetter'd the Kingly Lyon,
And made the Forrest tremble when they roar'd.
Thus haue we swept Suspition from our Seate,
And made our Footstoole of Security.
Come hither Besse, and let me kisse my Boy:
Yong Ned, for thee, thine Vnckles, and my selfe,
Haue in our Armors watcht the Winters night,
Went all afoote in Summers scalding heate,
That thou might'st repossesse the Crowne in peace,
And of our Labours thou shalt reape the gaine.
  Rich. Ile blast his Haruest, if your head were laid,
For yet I am not look'd on in the world.
This shoulder was ordain'd so thicke, to heaue,
And heaue it shall some waight, or breake my backe,
Worke thou the way, and that shalt execute.
  King. Clarence and Gloster, loue my louely Queene,
And kis your Princely Nephew Brothers both.
  Cla. The duty that I owe vnto your Maiesty,
I Seale vpon the lips of this sweet Babe.
  Cla. Thanke Noble Clarence, worthy brother thanks.
  Rich. And that I loue the tree frō whence ÿ sprang'st:
Witnesse the louing kisse I giue the Fruite,
To say the truth, so Iudas kist his master,
And cried all haile, when as he meant all harme.
  King. Now am I seated as my soule delights,
Hauing my Countries peace, and Brothers loues.
  Cla. What will your Grace haue done with Margaret,
Reynard her Father, to the King of France
Hath pawn'd the Sicils and Ierusalem,
And hither haue they sent it for her ransome.
  King. Away with her, and waft her hence to France,
And now what rests, but that we spend the time
With stately Triumphes, mirthfull Comicke shewes,
Such as befits the pleasure of the Court.
Sound Drums and Trumpets, farwell sowre annoy,
For heere I hope begins our lasting ioy. *Exeunt omnes*

FINIS.

The Tragedy of Richard the Third:
with the Landing of Earle Richmond, and the Battell at Bosworth Field.

Actus Primus. Scœna Prima.

Enter Richard Duke of Gloster, solus.

Now is the Winter of our Discontent,
Made glorious Summer by this Son of Yorke:
And all the clouds that lowr'd vpon our house
In the deepe bosome of the Ocean buried.
Now are our browes bound with Victorious Wreathes,
Our bruised armes hung vp for Monuments;
Our sterne Alarums chang'd to merry Meetings;
Our dreadfull Marches, to delightfull Measures.
Grim-visag'd Warre, hath smooth'd his wrinkled Front:
And now, in stead of mounting Barbed Steeds,
To fright the Soules of fearfull Aduersaries,
He capers nimbly in a Ladies Chamber,
To the lasciuious pleasing of a Lute.
But I, that am not shap'd for sportiue trickes,
Nor made to court an amorous Looking-glasse:
I, that am Rudely stampt, and want loues Maiesty,
To strut before a wonton ambling Nymph:
I, that am curtail'd of this faire Proportion,
Cheated of Feature by dissembling Nature,
Deform'd, vn-finish'd, sent before my time
Into this breathing World, scarse halfe made vp,
And that so lamely and vnfashionable,
That dogges barke at me, as I halt by them.
Why I (in this weake piping time of Peace)
Haue no delight to passe away the time,
Vnlesse to see my Shadow in the Sunne,
And descant on mine owne Deformity.
And therefore, since I cannot proue a Louer,
To entertaine these faire well spoken dayes,
I am determined to proue a Villaine,
And hate the idle pleasures of these dayes.
Plots haue I laide, Inductions dangerous,
By drunken Prophesies, Libels, and Dreames,
To set my Brother Clarence and the King
In deadly hate, the one against the other:
And if King *Edward* be as true and iust,
As I am Subtle, False, and Treacherous,
This day should *Clarence* closely be mew'd vp:
About a Prophesie, which sayes that G,
Of *Edwards* heyres the murtherer shall be.
Diue thoughts downe to my soule, here *Clarence* comes.

Enter Clarence, and Brakenbury, guarded.

Brother, good day: What meanes this armed guard
That waites vpon your Grace?

Cla. His Maiesty tendring my persons safety,
Hath appointed this Conduct, to conuey me to th' Tower

Rich. Vpon what cause?

Cla. Because my name is *George*.

Rich. Alacke my Lord, that fault is none of yours:
He should for that commit your Godfathers.
O belike, his Maiesty hath some intent,
That you should be new Christned in the Tower.
But what's the matter *Clarence*, may I know?

Cla. Yea *Richard*, when I know: but I protest
As yet I do not: But as I can learne,
He hearkens after Prophesies and Dreames,
And from the Crosse-row pluckes the letter G:
And sayes, a Wizard told him, that by G,
His issue disinherited should be.
And for my name of *George* begins with G,
It followes in his thought, that I am he.
These (as I learne) and such like toyes as these,
Hath moou'd his Highnesse to commit me now.

Rich. Why this it is, when men are rul'd by Women:
'Tis not the King that sends you to the Tower,
My Lady *Grey* his Wife, *Clarence* 'tis shee,
That tempts him to this harsh Extremity.
Was it not shee, and that good man of Worship,
Anthony Woodeuille her Brother there,
That made him send Lord *Hastings* to the Tower?
From whence this present day he is deliuered?
We are not safe *Clarence*, we are not safe.

Cla. By heauen, I thinke there is no man secure
But the Queenes Kindred, and night-walking Heralds,
That trudge betwixt the King, and Mistris *Shore*.
Heard you not what an humble Suppliant
Lord *Hastings* was, for her deliuery?

Rich. Humbly complaining to her Deitie,
Got my Lord Chamberlaine his libertie.
Ile tell you what, I thinke it is our way,
If we will keepe in fauour with the King,
To be her men, and weare her Liuery.
The iealous ore-worne Widdow, and her selfe,
Since that our Brother dub'd them Gentlewomen,
Are mighty Gossips in our Monarchy.

Bra. I beseech your Graces both to pardon me,
His Maiesty hath straightly giuen in charge,
That no man shall haue priuate Conference
(Of what degree soeuer) with your Brother.

Rich.

Rich. Euen so, and please your Worship *Brakenbury*,
You may partake of any thing we say:
We speake no Treason man; We say the King
Is wise and vertuous, and his Noble Queene
Well strooke in yeares, faire, and not iealious.
We say, that *Shores* Wife hath a pretty Foot,
A cherry Lip, a bonny Eye, a passing pleasing tongue:
And that the Queenes Kindred are made gentle Folkes.
How say you sir? can you deny all this?

Bra. With this (my Lord) my selfe haue nought to doo.

Rich. Naught to do with Mistris *Shore*?
I tell thee Fellow, he that doth naught with her
(Excepting one) were best to do it secretly alone.

Bra. What one, my Lord?

Rich. Her Husband Knaue, would'st thou betray me?

Bra. I do beseech your Grace
To pardon me, and withall forbeare
Your Conference with the Noble Duke.

Cla. We know thy charge *Brakenbury*, and wil obey.

Rich. We are the Queenes abiects, and must obey.
Brother farewell, I will vnto the King,
And whatsoe're you will imploy me in,
Were it to call King *Edwards* Widdow, Sister,
I will performe it to infranchise you.
Meane time, this deepe disgrace in Brotherhood,
Touches me deeper then you can imagine.

Cla. I know it pleaseth neither of vs well.

Rich. Well, your imprisonment shall not be long,
I will deliuer you, or else lye for you:
Meane time, haue patience.

Cla. I must perforce: Farewell. *Exit Clar.*

Rich. Go treade the path that thou shalt ne're returne:
Simple plaine *Clarence*, I do loue thee so,
That I will shortly send thy Soule to Heauen,
If Heauen will take the present at our hands.
But who comes heere? the new deliuered *Hastings*?

Enter Lord Hastings.

Hast. Good time of day vnto my gracious Lord.

Rich. As much vnto my good Lord Chamberlaine:
Well are you welcome to this open Ayre,
How hath your Lordship brook'd imprisonment?

Hast. With patience (Noble Lord) as prisoners must:
But I shall liue (my Lord) to giue them thankes
That were the cause of my imprisonment.

Rich. No doubt, no doubt, and so shall *Clarence* too,
For they that were your Enemies, are his,
And haue preuail'd as much on him, as you.

Hast. More pitty, that the Eagles should be mew'd,
Whiles Kites and Buzards play at liberty.

Rich. What newes abroad?

Hast. No newes so bad abroad, as this at home:
The King is sickly, weake, and melancholly,
And his Physitians feare him mightily.

Rich. Now by S. *Iohn*, that Newes is bad indeed.
O he hath kept an euill Diet long,
And ouer-much consum'd his Royall Person:
'Tis very greeuous to be thought vpon.
Where is he, in his bed?

Hast. He is.

Rich. Go you before, and I will follow you.
Exit Hastings.
He cannot liue I hope, and must not dye,
Till *George* be pack'd with post-horse vp to Heauen.
Ile in to vrge his hatred more to *Clarence*,
With Lyes well steel'd with weighty Arguments,
And if I faile not in my deepe intent,
Clarence hath not another day to liue:
Which done, God take King *Edward* to his mercy,
And leaue the world for me to bussle in.
For then, Ile marry *Warwickes* yongest daughter.
What though I kill'd her Husband, and her Father,
The readiest way to make the Wench amends,
Is to become her Husband, and her Father:
The which will I, not all so much for loue,
As for another secret close intent,
By marrying her, which I must reach vnto:
But yet I run before my horse to Market:
Clarence still breathes, *Edward* still liues and raignes,
When they are gone, then must I count my gaines. *Exit*

Scena Secunda.

Enter the Coarse of Henrie the sixt with Halberds to guard it, Lady Anne being the Mourner.

Anne. Set downe, set downe your honourable load,
If Honor may be shrowded in a Herse;
Whil'st I a-while obsequiously lament
Th'vntimely fall of Vertuous Lancaster.
Poore key-cold Figure of a holy King,
Pale Ashes of the House of Lancaster;
Thou bloodlesse Remnant of that Royall Blood,
Be it lawfull that I inuocate thy Ghost,
To heare the Lamentations of poore *Anne*,
Wife to thy *Edward*, to thy slaughtred Sonne,
Stab'd by the selfesame hand that made these wounds.
Loe, in these windowes that let forth thy life,
I powre the helplesse Balme of my poore eyes.
O cursed be the hand that made these holes:
Cursed the Heart, that had the heart to do it:
Cursed the Blood, that let this blood from hence:
More direfull hap betide that hated Wretch
That makes vs wretched by the death of thee,
Then I can wish to Wolues, to Spiders, Toades,
Or any creeping venom'd thing that liues.
If euer he haue Childe, Abortiue be it,
Prodigeous, and vntimely brought to light,
Whose vgly and vnnaturall Aspect
May fright the hopefull Mother at the view,
And that be Heyre to his vnhappinesse.
If euer he haue Wife, let her be made
More miserable by the death of him,
Then I am made by my young Lord, and thee.
Come now towards Chertsey with your holy Lode,
Taken from Paules, to be interred there.
And still as you are weary of this waight,
Rest you, whiles I lament King *Henries* Coarse.

Enter Richard Duke of Gloster.

Rich. Stay you that beare the Coarse, & set it down.

An. What blacke Magitian coniures vp this Fiend,
To stop deuoted charitable deeds?

Rich. Villaines set downe the Coarse, or by S. *Paul*,
Ile make a Coarse of him that disobeyes.

Gen. My Lord stand backe, and let the Coffin passe.
Rich. Vnmanner'd Dogge,
Stand'st thou when I commaund:
Aduance thy Halbert higher then my brest,
Or by S. Paul Ile strike thee to my Foote,
And spurne vpon thee Begger for thy boldnesse.

Anne. What do you tremble? are you all affraid?
Alas, I blame you not, for you are Mortall,
And Mortall eyes cannot endure the Diuell.
Auant thou dreadfull minister of Hell;
Thou had'st but power ouer his Mortall body,
His Soule thou canst not haue: Therefore be gone.

Rich. Sweet Saint, for Charity, be not so curst.

An. Foule Diuell,
For Gods sake hence, and trouble vs not,
For thou hast made the happy earth thy Hell:
Fill'd it with cursing cries, and deepe exclaimes:
If thou delight to view thy heynous deeds,
Behold this patterne of thy Butcheries.
Oh Gentlemen, see, see dead *Henries* wounds,
Open their congeal'd mouthes, and bleed afresh.
Blush, blush, thou lumpe of fowle Deformitie:
For 'tis thy presence that exhales this blood
From cold and empty Veines where no blood dwels.
Thy Deeds inhumane and vnnaturall,
Prouokes this Deluge most vnnaturall.
O God! which this Blood mad'st, reuenge his death:
O Earth! which this Blood drink'st, reuenge his death.
Either Heau'n with Lightning strike the murth'rer dead:
Or Earth gape open wide, and eate him quicke,
As thou dost swallow vp this good Kings blood,
Which his Hell-gouern'd arme hath butchered.

Rich. Lady, you know no Rules of Charity,
Which renders good for bad, Blessings for Curses.

An. Villaine, thou know'st nor law of God nor Man,
No Beast so fierce, but knowes some touch of pitty.

Rich. But I know none, and therefore am no Beast.

An. O wonderfull, when diuels tell the truth!

Rich. More wonderfull, when Angels are so angry:
Vouchsafe (diuine perfection of a Woman)
Of these supposed Crimes, to giue me leaue
By circumstance, but to acquit my selfe.

An. Vouchsafe (defus'd infection of man)
Of these knowne euils, but to giue me leaue
By circumstance, to curse thy cursed Selfe.

Rich. Fairer then tongue can name thee, let me haue
Some patient leysure to excuse my selfe.

An. Fouler then heart can thinke thee,
Thou can'st make no excuse currant,
But to hang thy selfe.

Rich. By such dispaire, I should accuse my selfe.

An. And by dispairing shalt thou stand excused,
For doing worthy Vengeance on thy selfe,
That did'st vnworthy slaughter vpon others.

Rich. Say that I slew them not.

An. Then say they were not slaine:
But dead they are, and diuellish slaue by thee.

Rich. I did not kill your Husband.

An. Why then he is aliue.

Rich. Nay, he is dead, and slaine by Edwards hands.

An. In thy foule throat thou Ly'st,
Queene *Margaret* saw
Thy murd'rous Faulchion smoaking in his blood;
The which, thou once didd'st bend against her brest,
But that thy Brothers beate aside the point.

Rich. I was prouoked by her sland'rous tongue,
That laid their guilt, vpon my guiltlesse Shoulders.

An. Thou was't prouoked by thy bloody minde,
That neuer dream'st on ought but Butcheries:
Did'st thou not kill this King?

Rich. I graunt ye.

An. Do'st grant me Hedge-hogge,
Then God graunt me too
Thou may'st be damned for that wicked deede,
O he was gentle, milde, and vertuous.

Rich. The better for the King of heauen that hath him.

An. He is in heauen, where thou shalt neuer come.

Rich. Let him thanke me, that holpe to send him thither:
For he was fitter for that place then earth.

An. And thou vnfit for any place, but hell.

Rich. Yes one place else, if you will heare me name it.

An. Some dungeon.

Rich. Your Bed-chamber.

An. Ill rest betide the chamber where thou lyest.

Rich. So will it Madam, till I lye with you.

An. I hope so.

Rich. I know so. But gentle Lady *Anne*,
To leaue this keene encounter of our wittes,
And fall something into a slower method.
Is not the causer of the timelesse deaths
Of these *Plantagenets*, *Henrie* and *Edward*,
As blamefull as the Executioner.

An. Thou was't the cause, and most accurst effect.

Rich. Your beauty was the cause of that effect:
Your beauty, that did haunt me in my sleepe,
To vndertake the death of all the world,
So I might liue one houre in your sweet bosome.

An. If I thought that, I tell thee Homicide,
These Nailes should rent that beauty from my Cheekes.

Rich. These eyes could not endure y beauties wrack,
You should not blemish it, if I stood by;
As all the world is cheared by the Sunne,
So I by that: It is my day, my life.

An. Blacke night ore-shade thy day, & death thy life.

Rich. Curse not thy selfe faire Creature,
Thou art both.

An. I would I were, to be reueng'd on thee.

Rich. It is a quarrell most vnnaturall,
To be reueng'd on him that loueth thee.

An. It is a quarrell iust and reasonable,
To be reueng'd on him that kill'd my Husband.

Rich. He that bereft the Lady of thy Husband,
Did it to helpe thee to a better Husband.

An. His better doth not breath vpon the earth.

Rich. He liues, that loues thee better then he could.

An. Name him.

Rich. Plantagenet.

An. Why that was he.

Rich. The selfesame name, but one of better Nature.

An. Where is he?

Rich. Heere: *Spits at him.*
Why dost thou spit at me.

An. Would it were mortall poyson, for thy sake.

Rich. Neuer came poyson from so sweet a place.

An. Neuer hung poyson on a fowler Toade.
Out of my sight, thou dost infect mine eyes.

Rich. Thine eyes (sweet Lady) haue infected mine.

An. Would they were Basiliskes, to strike thee dead.

Rich. I would they were, that I might dye at once:
For now they kill me with a liuing death.
Those eyes of thine, from mine haue drawne salt Teares;

Sham'd their Aspects with store of childish drops:
These eyes, which neuer shed remorsefull teare,
No, when my Father Yorke, and *Edward* wept,
To heare the pittious moane that Rutland made
When black-fac'd *Clifford* shooke his sword at him.
Nor when thy warlike Father like a Childe,
Told the sad storie of my Fathers death,
And twenty times, made pause to sob and weepe:
That all the standers by had wet their cheekes
Like Trees bedash'd with raine. In that sad time,
My manly eyes did scorne an humble teare:
And what these sorrowes could not thence exhale,
Thy Beauty hath, and made them blinde with weeping.
I neuer sued to Friend, nor Enemy:
My Tongue could neuer learne sweet smoothing word.
But now thy Beauty is propos'd my Fee,
My proud heart sues, and prompts my tongue to speake.

She lookes scornfully at him.

Teach not thy lip such Scorne; for it was made
For kissing Lady, not for such contempt.
If thy reuengefull heart cannot forgiue,
Loe heere I lend thee this sharpe-pointed Sword,
Which if thou please to hide in this true brest,
And let the Soule forth that adoreth thee,
I lay it naked to the deadly stroke,
And humbly begge the death vpon my knee.

He layes his brest open, she offers at with his sword.

Nay do not pause: For I did kill King *Henrie*,
But 'twas thy Beauty that prouoked me.
Nay now dispatch: 'Twas I that stabb'd yong *Edward*,
But 'twas thy Heauenly face that set me on.

She fals the Sword.

Take vp the Sword againe, or take vp me.

 An. Arise Dissembler, though I wish thy death,
I will not be thy Executioner.

 Rich. Then bid me kill my selfe, and I will do it.

 An. I haue already.

 Rich. That was in thy rage:
Speake it againe, and euen with the word,
This hand, which for thy loue, did kill thy Loue,
Shall for thy loue, kill a farre truer Loue,
To both their deaths shalt thou be accessary.

 An. I would I knew thy heart.

 Rich. 'Tis figur'd in my tongue.

 An. I feare me, both are false.

 Rich. Then neuer Man was true.

 An. Well, well, put vp your Sword.

 Rich. Say then my Peace is made.

 An. That shalt thou know heereafter.

 Rich. But shall I liue in hope.

 An. All men I hope liue so.
Vouchsafe to weare this Ring.

 Rich. Looke how my Ring incompasseth thy Finger,
Euen so thy Brest incloseth my poore heart:
Weare both of them, for both of them are thine.
And if thy poore deuoted Seruant may
But beg one fauour at thy gracious hand,
Thou dost confirme his happinesse for euer.

 An. What is it?

 Rich. That it may please you leaue these sad designes,
To him that hath most cause to be a Mourner,
And presently repayre to Crosbie House:
Where (after I haue solemnly interr'd
At Chertsey Monast'ry this Noble King,
And wet his Graue with my Repentant Teares)
I will with all expedient duty see you,
For diuers vnknowne Reasons, I beseech you,
Grant me this Boon.

 An. With all my heart, and much it ioyes me too,
To see you are become so penitent.
Tressel and *Barkley*, go along with me.

 Rich. Bid me farwell.

 An. 'Tis more then you deserue:
But since you teach me how to flatter you,
Imagine I haue saide farewell already.

Exit two with Anne.

 Gent. Towards Chertsey, Noble Lord?

 Rich. No, to White Friars, there attend my comming

Exit Corse.

Was euer woman in this humour woo'd?
Was euer woman in this humour wonne?
Ile haue her, but I will not keepe her long.
What? I that kill'd her Husband, and his Father,
To take her in her hearts extreamest hate,
With curses in her mouth, Teares in her eyes,
The bleeding witnesse of my hatred by,
Hauing God, her Conscience, and these bars against me,
And I, no Friends to backe my suite withall,
But the plaine Diuell, and dissembling lookes?
And yet to winne her? All the world to nothing.
Hah!
Hath she forgot alreadie that braue Prince,
Edward, her Lord, whom I (some three monthes since)
Stab'd in my angry mood, at Tewkesbury?
A sweeter, and a louelier Gentleman,
Fram'd in the prodigallity of Nature:
Yong, Valiant, Wise, and (no doubt) right Royal,
The spacious World cannot againe affoord:
And will she yet abase her eyes on me,
That cropt the Golden prime of this sweet Prince,
And made her Widdow to a wofull Bed?
On me, whose All not equals *Edwards* Moytie?
On me, that halts, and am mishapen thus?
My Dukedome, to a Beggerly denier!
I do mistake my person all this while:
Vpon my life she findes (although I cannot)
My selfe to be a maru'llous proper man.
Ile be at Charges for a Looking-glasse,
And entertaine a score or two of Taylors,
To study fashions to adorne my body:
Since I am crept in fauour with my selfe,
I will maintaine it with some little cost.
But first Ile turne yon Fellow in his Graue,
And then returne lamenting to my Loue.
Shine out faire Sunne, till I haue bought a glasse,
That I may see my Shadow as I passe. *exit.*

Scena Tertia.

*Enter the Queene Mother, Lord Riuers,
and Lord Gray.*

 Riu. Haue patience Madam, ther's no doubt his Maiesty
Will soone recouer his accustom'd health.

 Gray. In that you brooke it ill, it makes him worse,
Therefore for Gods sake entertaine good comfort,
And cheere his Grace with quicke and merry eyes

 Qu. If he were dead, what would betide on me?

 Gray.

If he were dead, what would betide on me?
 Gray. No other harme, but losse of such a Lord.
 Qu. The losse of such a Lord, includes all harmes.
 Gray. The Heauens haue blest you with a goodly Son,
To be your Comforter, when he is gone.
 Qu. Ah! he is yong; and his minority
Is put vnto the trust of *Richard Glouster*,
A man that loues not me, nor none of you.
 Riu. Is it concluded he shall be Protector?
 Qu. It is determin'd, not concluded yet:
But so it must be, if the King miscarry.

Enter Buckingham and Derby.

 Gray. Here comes the Lord of Buckingham & Derby.
 Buc. Good time of day vnto your Royall Grace.
 Der. God make your Maiesty ioyful, as you haue bin.
 Qu. The Countesse *Richmond*, good my L. of *Derby*.
To your good prayer, will scarsely say, Amen.
Yet *Derby*, notwithstanding shee's your wife,
And loues not me, be you good Lord assur'd,
I hate not you for her proud arrogance.
 Der. I do beseech you, either not beleeue
The enuious slanders of her false Accusers:
Or if shee be accus'd on true report,
Beare with her weaknesse, which I thinke proceeds
From wayward sicknesse, and no grounded malice.
 Qu. Saw you the King to day my Lord of *Derby*.
 Der. But now the Duke of Buckingham and I,
Are come from visiting his Maiesty.
 Que. What likelyhood of his amendment Lords.
 Buc. Madam good hope, his Grace speaks chearfully.
 Qu. God grant him health, did you confer with him?
 Buc. I Madam, he desires to make attonement
Betweene the Duke of Glouster, and your Brothers,
And betweene them, and my Lord Chamberlaine,
And sent to warne them to his Royall presence.
 Qu. Would all were well, but that will neuer be,
I feare our happinesse is at the height.

Enter Richard.

 Rich. They do me wrong, and I will not indure it,
Who is it that complaines vnto the King,
That I (forsooth) am sterne, and loue them not?
By holy *Paul*, they loue his Grace but lightly,
That fill his eares with such dissentious Rumors.
Because I cannot flatter, and looke faire,
Smile in mens faces, smooth, deceiue, and cogge,
Ducke with French nods, and Apish curtesie,
I must be held a rancorous Enemy.
Cannot a plaine man liue, and thinke no harme,
But thus his simple truth must be abus'd,
With silken, slye, insinuating Iackes?
 Grey. To who in all this presence speaks your Grace?
 Rich. To thee, that hast nor Honesty, nor Grace:
When haue I iniur'd thee? When done thee wrong?
Or thee? or thee? or any of your Faction?
A plague vpon you all. His Royall Grace
(Whom God preserue better then you would wish)
Cannot be quiet scarse a breathing while,
But you must trouble him with lewd complaints.
 Qu. Brother of Glouster, you mistake the matter:
The King on his owne Royall disposition,
(And not prouok'd by any Sutor else)
Ayming (belike) at your interiour hatred,
That in your outward action shewes it selfe
Against my Children, Brothers, and my Selfe,
Makes him to send, that he may learne the ground.
 Rich. I cannot tell, the world is growne so bad,
That Wrens make prey, where Eagles dare not pearch.
Since euerie Iacke became a Gentleman,
There's many a gentle person made a Iacke.
 Qu. Come, come, we know your meaning Brother
You enuy my aduancement, and my friends: (Gloster
God grant we neuer may haue neede of you.
 Rich. Meane time, God grants that I haue need of you.
Our Brother is imprison'd by your meanes,
My selfe disgrac'd, and the Nobilitie
Held in contempt, while great Promotions
Are daily giuen to ennoble those
That scarse some two dayes since were worth a Noble.
 Qu. By him that rais'd me to this carefull height,
From that contented hap which I inioy'd,
I neuer did incense his Maiestie
Against the Duke of *Clarence*, but haue bin
An earnest aduocate to plead for him.
My Lord you do me shamefull iniurie,
Falsely to draw me in these vile suspects.
 Rich. You may deny that you were not the meane
Of my Lord *Hastings* late imprisonment.
 Riu. She may my Lord, for——
 Rich. She may Lord *Riuers*, why who knowes not so?
She may do more sir then denying that:
She may helpe you to many faire preferments,
And then deny her ayding hand therein,
And lay those Honors on your high desert.
What may she not, she may, I marry may she.
 Riu. What marry may she?
 Ric. What marrie may she? Marrie with a King,
A Batcheller, and a handsome stripling too,
I wis your Grandam had a worser match.
 Qu. My Lord of Glouster, I haue too long borne
Your blunt vpbraidings, and your bitter scoffes:
By heauen, I will acquaint his Maiestie
Of those grosse taunts that oft I haue endur'd.
I had rather be a Countrie seruant maide
Then a great Queene, with this condition,
To be so baited, scorn'd, and stormed at,
Small ioy haue I in being Englands Queene.

Enter old Queene Margaret.

 Mar. And lesned be that small, God I beseech him,
Thy honor, state, and seate, is due to me.
 Rich. What? threat you me with telling of the King?
I will auouch't in presence of the King:
I dare aduenture to be sent to th'Towre.
'Tis time to speake,
My paines are quite forgot.
 Margaret. Out Diuell,
I do remember them too well:
Thou kill'dst my Husband *Henrie* in the Tower,
And *Edward* my poore Son, at Tewkesburie.
 Rich. Ere you were Queene,
I, or your Husband King:
I was a packe-horse in his great affaires:
A weeder out of his proud Aduersaries,
A liberall rewarder of his Friends,
To royalize his blood, I spent mine owne.
 Margaret. I and much better blood
Then his, or thine.

Rich. In all which time, you and your Husband *Grey*
Were factious, for the House of *Lancaster*;
And *Riuers*, so were you: Was not your Husband,
In *Margarets* Battaile, at Saint *Albons* slaine?
Let me put in your mindes, if you forget
What you haue beene ere this, and what you are:
Withall, what I haue beene, and what I am.

Q.M. A murth'rous Villaine, and so still thou art.

Rich. Poore *Clarence* did forsake his Father *Warwicke*,
I, and forswore himselfe (which Iesu pardon.)

Q.M. Which God reuenge.

Rich. To fight on *Edwards* partie, for the Crowne,
And for his meede, poore Lord, he is mewed vp:
I would to God my heart were Flint, like *Edwards*,
Or *Edwards* soft and pittifull, like mine;
I am too childish foolish for this World.

Q.M. High thee to Hell for shame, & leaue this World
Thou Cacodemon, there thy Kingdome is.

Riu. My Lord of Gloster: in those busie dayes,
Which here you vrge, to proue vs Enemies,
We follow'd then our Lord, our Soueraigne King,
So should we you, if you should be our King.

Rich. If I should be? I had rather be a Pedler:
Farre be it from my heart, the thought thereof.

Qu. As little ioy (my Lord) as you suppose
You should enioy, were you this Countries King,
As little ioy you may suppose in me,
That I enioy, being the Queene thereof.

Q.M. A little ioy enioyes the Queene thereof,
For I am shee, and altogether ioylesse:
I can no longer hold me patient.
Heare me, you wrangling Pyrates, that fall out,
In sharing that which you haue pill'd from me:
Which off you trembles not, that lookes on me?
If not, that I am Queene, you bow like Subiects;
Yet that by you depos'd, you quake like Rebells.
Ah gentle Villaine, doe not turne away. (sight?

Rich. Foule wrinckled Witch, what mak'st thou in my

Q.M. But repetition of what thou hast marr'd,
That will I make, before I let thee goe.

Rich. Wert thou not banished, on paine of death?

Q.M. I was: but I doe find more paine in banishment,
Then death can yeeld me here, by my abode.
A Husband and a Sonne thou ow'st to me,
And thou a Kingdome; all of you, allegeance:
This Sorrow that I haue, by right is yours,
And all the Pleasures you vsurpe, are mine.

Rich. The Curse my Noble Father layd on thee,
When thou didst Crown his Warlike Brows with Paper,
And with thy scornes drew'st Riuers from his eyes,
And then to dry them, gau'st the Duke a Clowt,
Steep'd in the faultlesse blood of prettie *Rutland*:
His Curses then, from bitternesse of Soule,
Denounc'd against thee, are all falne vpon thee:
And God, not we, hath plagu'd thy bloody deed.

Qu. So iust is God, to right the innocent.

Hast. O, 'twas the foulest deed to slay that Babe,
And the most mercilesse, that ere was heard of.

Riu. Tyrants themselues wept when it was reported.

Dors. No man but prophecied reuenge for it.

Buck. *Northumberland*, then present, wept to see it.

Q.M. What? were you snarling all before I came,
Ready to catch each other by the throat,
And turne you all your hatred now on me?
Did *Yorkes* dread Curse preuaile so much with Heauen,
That *Henries* death, my louely *Edwards* death,
Their Kingdomes losse, my wofull Banishment,
Should all but answer for that peeuish Brat?
Can Curses pierce the Clouds, and enter Heauen?
Why then giue way dull Clouds to my quick Curses.
Though not by Warre, by Surfet dye your King,
As ours by Murther, to make him a King.
Edward thy Sonne, that now is Prince of Wales,
For *Edward* our Sonne, that was Prince of Wales,
Dye in his youth, by like vntimely violence.
Thy selfe a Queene, for me that was a Queene,
Out-liue thy glory, like my wretched selfe:
Long may'st thou liue, to wayle thy Childrens death,
And see another, as I see thee now,
Deck'd in thy Rights, as thou art stall'd in mine.
Long dye thy happie dayes, before thy death,
And after many length'ned howres of griefe,
Dye neyther Mother, Wife, nor Englands Queene.
Riuers and *Dorset*, you were standers by,
And so wast thou, Lord *Hastings*, when my Sonne
Was stab'd with bloody Daggers: God, I pray him,
That none of you may liue his naturall age,
But by some vnlook'd accident cut off.

Rich. Haue done thy Charme, y̆ hateful wither'd Hagge.

Q.M. And leaue out thee? stay Dog, for y̆ shalt heare me.
If Heauen haue any grieuous plague in store,
Exceeding those that I can wish vpon thee,
O let them keepe it, till thy sinnes be ripe,
And then hurle downe their indignation
On thee, the troubler of the poore Worlds peace,
The Worme of Conscience still begnaw thy Soule,
Thy Friends suspect for Traytors while thou liu'st,
And take deepe Traytors for thy dearest Friends:
No sleepe close vp that deadly Eye of thine,
Vnlesse it be while some tormenting Dreame
Affrights thee with a Hell of ougly Deuills.
Thou eluish mark'd, abortiue rooting Hogge,
Thou that wast seal'd in thy Natiuitie
The slaue of Nature, and the Sonne of Hell:
Thou slander of thy heauie Mothers Wombe,
Thou loathed Issue of thy Fathers Loynes,
Thou Ragge of Honor, thou detested—

Rich. *Margaret*.

Q.M. *Richard*.   *Rich.* Ha.

Q.M. I call thee not.

Rich. I cry thee mercie then: for I did thinke,
That thou hadst call'd me all these bitter names.

Q.M. Why so I did, but look'd for no reply.
Oh let me make the Period to my Curse.

Rich. 'Tis done by me, and ends in *Margaret*.

Qu. Thus haue you breath'd your Curse against your self.

Q.M. Poore painted Queen, vain flourish of my fortune,
Why strew'st thou Sugar on that Bottel'd Spider,
Whose deadly Web ensnareth thee about?
Foole, foole, thou whet'st a Knife to kill thy selfe:
The day will come, that thou shalt wish for me,
To helpe thee curse this poysonous Bunch-backt Toade.

Hast. False boding Woman, end thy frantick Curse,
Least to thy harme, thou moue our patience.

Q.M. Foule shame vpon you, you haue all mou'd mine.

Ri. Were you wel seru'd, you would be taught your duty.

Q.M. To serue me well, you all should do me duty,
Teach me to be your Queene, and you my Subiects:
O serue me well, and teach your selues that duty.

Dors. Dispute not with her, shee is lunaticke.

Q.M. Peace Master Marquesse, you are malapert,
Your fire-new stampe of Honor is scarce currant.

O that your yong Nobility could iudge
What 'twere to lose it, and be miserable.
They that stand high, haue many blasts to shake them,
And if they fall, they dash themselues to peeces.

  Rich. Good counsaile marry, learne it, learne it Marquesse.
  Dor. It touches you my Lord, as much as me.
  Rich. I, and much more: but I was borne so high:
Our ayerie buildeth in the Cedars top,
And dallies with the winde, and scornes the Sunne.
  Mar. And turnes the Sun to shade: alas, alas,
Witnesse my Sonne, now in the shade of death,
Whose bright out-shining beames, thy cloudy wrath
Hath in eternall darknesse folded vp.
Your ayery buildeth in our ayeries Nest:
O God that seest it, do not suffer it,
As it is wonne with blood, lost be it so.
  Buc. Peace, peace for shame: If not, for Charity.
  Mar. Vrge neither charity, nor shame to me:
Vncharitably with me haue you dealt,
And shamefully my hopes (by you) are butcher'd.
My Charity is outrage, Life my shame,
And in that shame, still liue my sorrowes rage.
  Buc. Haue done, haue done.
  Mar. O Princely Buckingham, Ile kisse thy hand,
In signe of League and amity with thee:
Now faire befall thee, and thy Noble house:
Thy Garments are not spotted with our blood:
Nor thou within the compasse of my curse.
  Buc. Nor no one heere: for Curses neuer passe
The lips of those that breath them in the ayre.
  Mar. I will not thinke but they ascend the sky,
And there awake Gods gentle sleeping peace.
O Buckingham, take heede of yonder dogge:
Looke when he fawnes, he bites; and when he bites,
His venom tooth will rankle to the death.
Haue not to do with him, beware of him,
Sinne, death, and hell haue set their markes on him,
And all their Ministers attend on him.
  Rich. What doth she say, my Lord of Buckingham.
  Buc. Nothing that I respect my gracious Lord.
  Mar. What dost thou scorne me
For my gentle counsell?
And sooth the diuell that I warne thee from.
O but remember this another day:
When he shall split thy very heart with sorrow:
And say (poore *Margaret*) was a Prophetesse:
Liue each of you the subiects to his hate,
And he to yours, and all of you to Gods. *Exit.*
  Buc. My haire doth stand an end to heare her curses.
  Riu. And so doth mine, I muse why she's at libertie.
  Rich. I cannot blame her, by Gods holy mother,
She hath had too much wrong, and I repent
My part thereof, that I haue done to her.
  Mar. I neuer did her any to my knowledge.
  Rich. Yet you haue all the vantage of her wrong:
I was too hot, to do somebody good,
That is too cold in thinking of it now:
Marry as for *Clarence*, he is well repayed:
He is frank'd vp to fatting for his paines,
God pardon them, that are the cause thereof.
  Riu. A vertuous, and a Christian-like conclusion
To pray for them that haue done scath to vs.
  Rich. So do I euer, being well aduis'd.
                      Speakes to himselfe.
For had I curst now, I had curst my selfe.

  Enter Catesby.

  Cates. Madam, his Maiesty doth call for you,
And for your Grace, and yours my gracious Lord.
  Qu. Catesby I come, Lords will you go with mee.
  Riu. We wait vpon your Grace.
                      Exeunt all but Gloster.
  Rich. I do the wrong, and first begin to brawle.
The secret Mischeefes that I set abroach,
I lay vnto the greeuous charge of others.
Clarence, who I indeede haue cast in darknesse,
I do beweepe to many simple Gulles,
Namely to *Derby*, *Hastings*, *Buckingham*,
And tell them 'tis the Queene, and her Allies,
That stirre the King against the Duke my Brother.
Now they beleeue it, and withall whet me
To be reueng'd on *Riuers*, *Dorset*, *Grey*.
But then I sigh, and with a peece of Scripture,
Tell them that God bids vs do good for euill:
And thus I cloath my naked Villanie
With odde old ends, stolne forth of holy Writ,
And seeme a Saint, when most I play the deuill.

  Enter two murtherers.

But soft, heere come my Executioners,
How now my hardy stout resolued Mates,
Are you now going to dispatch this thing?
  Vil. We are my Lord, and come to haue the Warrant,
That we may be admitted where he is.
  Ric. Well thought vpon, I haue it heare about me:
When you haue done, repayre to *Crosby* place;
But sirs be sodaine in the execution,
Withall obdurate, do not heare him pleade;
For *Clarence* is well spoken, and perhappes
May moue your hearts to pitty, if you marke him.
  Vil. Tut, tut, my Lord, we will not stand to prate,
Talkers are no good dooers, be assur'd:
We go to vse our hands, and not our tongues.
  Rich. Your eyes drop Mill-stones, when Fooles eyes fall Teares:
I like you Lads, about your businesse straight.
Go, go, dispatch.
  Vil. We will my Noble Lord.

Scena Quarta.

  Enter Clarence and Keeper.
  Keep. Why lookes your Grace so heauily to day.
  Cla. O, I haue past a miserable night,
So full of fearefull Dreames, of vgly sights,
That as I am a Christian faithfull man,
I would not spend another such a night
Though 'twere to buy a world of happy daies:
So full of dismall terror was the time.
  Keep. What was your dream my Lord, I pray you tel me
  Cla. Me thoughts that I had broken from the Tower,
And was embark'd to crosse to Burgundy,
And in my company my Brother Glouster,
Who from my Cabin tempted me to walke,
Vpon the Hatches: There we look'd toward England,
And cited vp a thousand heauy times,

During the warres of Yorke and Lancaster
That had befalne vs. As we pac'd along
Vpon the giddy footing of the Hatches,
Me thought that Glouster stumbled, and in falling
Strooke me (that thought to stay him) ouer-boord,
Into the tumbling billowes of the maine.
O Lord, me thought what paine it was to drowne,
What dreadfull noise of water in mine eares,
What sights of vgly death within mine eyes.
Me thoughts, I saw a thousand fearfull wrackes:
A thousand men that Fishes gnaw'd vpon:
Wedges of Gold, great Anchors, heapes of Pearle,
Inestimable Stones, vnvalewed Iewels,
All scattred in the bottome of the Sea,
Some lay in dead-mens Sculles, and in the holes
Where eyes did once inhabit, there were crept
(As 'twere in scorne of eyes) reflecting Gemmes,
That woo'd the slimy bottome of the deepe,
And mock'd the dead bones that lay scattred by.

Keep. Had you such leysure in the time of death
To gaze vpon these secrets of the deepe?

Cla. Me thought I had, and often did I striue
To yeeld the Ghost: but still the enuious Flood
Stop'd in my soule, and would not let it forth
To find the empty, vast, and wand'ring ayre:
But smother'd it within my panting bulke,
Who almost burst, to belch it in the Sea.

Keep. Awak'd you not in this sore Agony?

Clar. No, no, my Dreame was lengthen'd after life.
O then, began the Tempest to my Soule.
I past (me thought) the Melancholly Flood,
With that sowre Ferry-man which Poets write of,
Vnto the Kingdome of perpetuall Night.
The first that there did greet my Stranger-soule,
Was my great Father-in-Law, renowned Warwicke,
Who spake alowd: What scourge for Periurie,
Can this darke Monarchy affoord false *Clarence*?
And so he vanish'd. Then came wand'ring by,
A Shadow like an Angell, with bright hayre
Dabbel'd in blood, and he shriek'd out alowd
Clarence is come, false, fleeting, periur'd *Clarence*,
That stabb'd me in the field by Tewkesbury:
Seize on him Furies, take him vnto Torment.
With that (me thought) a Legion of foule Fiends
Inuiron'd me, and howled in mine eares
Such hiddeous cries, that with the very Noise,
I (trembling) wak'd, and for a season after,
Could not beleeue, but that I was in Hell,
Such terrible Impression made my Dreame.

Keep. No maruell Lord, though it affrighted you,
I am affraid (me thinkes) to heare you tell it.

Cla. Ah Keeper, Keeper, I haue done these things
(That now giue euidence against my Soule)
For *Edwards* sake, and see how he requits mee.
O God! if my deepe prayres cannot appease thee,
But thou wilt be aueng'd on my misdeeds,
Yet execute thy wrath in me alone:
O spare my guiltlesse Wife, and my poore children.
Keeper, I prythee sit by me a-while,
My Soule is heauy, and I faine would sleepe.

Keep. I will my Lord, God giue your Grace good rest.

Enter Brakenbury the Lieutenant.

Bra. Sorrow breakes Seasons, and reposing houres,
Makes the Night Morning, and the Noon-tide night:
Princes haue but their Titles for their Glories,
An outward Honor, for an inward Toyle,
And for vnfelt Imaginations
They often feele a world of restlesse Cares:
So that betweene their Titles, and low Name,
There's nothing differs, but the outward fame.

Enter two Murtherers.

1. *Mur.* Ho, who's heere?

Bra. What would'st thou Fellow? And how camm'st thou hither.

2. *Mur.* I would speak with *Clarence*, and I came hither on my Legges.

Bra. What so breefe?

1. 'Tis better (Sir) then to be tedious:
Let him see our Commission, and talke no more. *Reads*

Bra. I am in this, commanded to deliuer
The Noble Duke of *Clarence* to your hands.
I will not reason what is meant heereby,
Because I will be guiltlesse from the meaning.
There lies the Duke asleepe, and there the Keyes.
Ile to the King, and signifie to him,
That thus I haue resign'd to you my charge. *Exit.*

1 You may sir, 'tis a point of wisedome:
Far you well.

2 What, shall we stab him as he sleepes.

1 No: hee'l say 'twas done cowardly, when he wakes

2 Why he shall neuer wake, vntill the great Iudgement day.

1 Why then hee'l say, we stab'd him sleeping.

2 The vrging of that word Iudgement, hath bred a kinde of remorse in me.

1 What? art thou affraid?

2 Not to kill him, hauing a Warrant,
But to be damn'd for killing him, from the which
No Warrant can defend me.

1 I thought thou had'st bin resolute.

2 So I am, to let him liue.

1 Ile backe to the Duke of Glouster, and tell him so.

2 Nay, I prythee stay a little:
I hope this passionate humor of mine, will change,
It was wont to hold me but while one tels twenty.

1 How do'st thou feele thy selfe now?

2 Some certaine dregges of conscience are yet within mee.

1 Remember our Reward, when the deed's done.

2 Come, he dies: I had forgot the Reward.

1 Where's thy conscience now.

2 O, in the Duke of Gloufters purse.

1 When hee opens his purse to giue vs our Reward, thy Conscience flyes out.

2 'Tis no matter, let it goe: There's few or none will entertaine it.

1 What if it come to thee againe?

2 Ile not meddle with it, it makes a man a Coward:
A man cannot steale, but it accuseth him: A man cannot
Sweare, but it Checkes him: A man cannot lye with his
Neighbours Wife, but it detects him. 'Tis a blushing
shamefac'd spirit, that mutinies in a mans bosome: It
filles a man full of Obstacles. It made me once restore a
Purse of Gold that (by chance) I found: It beggars any
man that keepes it: It is turn'd out of Townes and Cities for a dangerous thing, and euery man that means to
liue well, endeuours to trust to himselfe, and liue without it.

1 'Tis

1 'Tis euen now at my elbow, perswading me not to kill the Duke.
2 Take the diuell in thy minde, and beleeue him not: He would insinuate with thee but to make thee sigh.
1 I am strong fram'd, he cannot preuaile with me.
2 Spoke like a tall man, that respects thy reputation. Come, shall we fall to worke?
1 Take him on the Costard, with the hiltes of thy Sword, and then throw him into the Malmesey-Butte in the next roome.
2 O excellent deuice; and make a sop of him.
1 Soft, he wakes.
2 Strike.
1 No, wee'l reason with him.
Cla. Where art thou Keeper? Giue me a cup of wine.
2 You shall haue Wine enough my Lord anon.
Cla. In Gods name, what art thou?
1 A man, as you are.
Cla. But not as I am Royall.
1 Nor you as we are, Loyall.
Cla. Thy voice is Thunder, but thy looks are humble.
1 My voice is now the Kings, my lookes mine owne.
Cla. How darkly, and how deadly dost thou speake? Your eyes do menace me: why looke you pale? Who sent you hither? Wherefore do you come?
2 To, to, to—
Cla. To murther me?
Both. I, I.
Cla. You scarsely haue the hearts to tell me so, And therefore cannot haue the hearts to do it. Wherein my Friends haue I offended you?
1 Offended vs you haue not, but the King.
Cla. I shall be reconcil'd to him againe.
2 Neuer my Lord, therefore prepare to dye.
Cla. Are you drawne forth among a world of men To slay the innocent? What is my offence? Where is the Euidence that doth accuse me? What lawfull Quest haue giuen their Verdict vp Vnto the frowning Iudge? Or who pronounc'd The bitter sentence of poore Clarence death, Before I be conuict by course of Law? To threaten me with death, is most vnlawfull. I charge you, as you hope for any goodnesse, That you depart, and lay no hands on me: The deed you vndertake is damnable.
1 What we will do, we do vpon command.
2 And he that hath commanded, is our King.
Cla. Erroneous Vassals, the great King of Kings Hath in the Table of his Law commanded That thou shalt do no murther. Will you then Spurne at his Edict, and fulfill a Mans? Take heed: for he holds Vengeance in his hand, To hurle vpon their heads that breake his Law.
2 And that same Vengeance doth he hurle on thee, For false Forswearing, and for murther too: Thou did'st receiue the Sacrament, to fight In quarrell of the House of Lancaster.
1 And like a Traitor to the name of God, Did'st breake that Vow, and with thy treacherous blade, Vnrip'st the Bowels of thy Sou'raignes Sonne.
2 Whom thou was't sworne to cherish and defend.
1 How canst thou vrge Gods dreadfull Law to vs, When thou hast broke it in such deere degree?
Cla. Alas! for whose sake did I that ill deede? For Edward, for my Brother, for his sake. He sends you not to murther me for this:

For in that sinne, he is as deepe as I. If God will be auenged for the deed, O know you yet, he doth it publiquely, Take not the quarrell from his powrefull arme: He needs no indirect, or lawlesse course, To cut off those that haue offended him.
1 Who made thee then a bloudy minister, When gallant springing braue Plantagenet, That Princely Nouice was strucke dead by thee?
Cla. My Brothers loue, the Diuell, and my Rage.
1 Thy Brothers Loue, our Duty, and thy Faults, Prouoke vs hither now, to slaughter thee.
Cla. If you do loue my Brother, hate not me: I am his Brother, and I loue him well. If you are hyr'd for meed, go backe againe, And I will send you to my Brother Glouster: Who shall reward you better for my life, Then Edward will for tydings of my death.
2 You are deceiu'd, Your Brother Glouster hates you.
Cla. Oh no, he loues me, and he holds me deere: Go you to him from me.
1 I so we will.
Cla. Tell him, when that our Princely Father Yorke, Blest his three Sonnes with his victorious Arme, He little thought of this diuided Friendship: Bid Glouster thinke on this, and he will weepe.
1 I Milstones, as he lessoned vs to weepe.
Cla. O do not slander him, for he is kinde.
1 Right, as Snow in Haruest: Come, you deceiue your selfe, 'Tis he that sends vs to destroy you heere.
Cla. It cannot be, for he bewept my Fortune, And hugg'd me in his armes, and swore with sobs, That he would labour my deliuery.
1 Why so he doth, when he deliuers you From this earths thraldome, to the ioyes of heauen.
2 Make peace with God, for you must die my Lord.
Cla. Haue you that holy feeling in your soules, To counsaile me to make my peace with God, And are you yet to your owne soules so blinde, That you will warre with God, by murd'ring me. O sirs consider, they that set you on To do this deede, will hate you for the deede.
2 What shall we do?
Clar. Relent, and saue your soules: Which of you, if you were a Princes Sonne, Being pent from Liberty, as I am now, If two such murtherers as your selues came to you, Would not intreat for life, as you would begge Were you in my distresse.
1 Relent? no: 'Tis cowardly and womanish.
Cla. Not to relent, is beastly, sauage, diuellish: My Friend, I spy some pitty in thy lookes: O, if thine eye be not a Flatterer, Come thou on my side, and intreate for mee, A begging Prince, what begger pitties not.
2 Looke behinde you, my Lord.
1 Take that, and that, if all this will not do, Stabs him. Ile drowne you in the Malmesey-But within. Exit.
2 A bloody deed, and desperately dispatcht: How faine (like Pilate) would I wash my hands Of this most greeuous murther. Enter 1. Murtherer
1 How now? what mean'st thou that thou help'st me not? By Heauen the Duke shall know how slacke you haue beene.

2. *Mur.* I would he knew that I had sau'd his brother,
Take thou the Fee, and tell him what I say,
For I repent me that the Duke is slaine. *Exit.*

1. *Mur.* So do not I: go Coward as thou art.
Well, Ile go hide the body in some hole,
Till that the Duke giue order for his buriall:
And when I haue my meede, I will away,
For this will out, and then I must not stay. *Exit*

Actus Secundus. Scœna Prima.

*Flourish.
Enter the King sicke, the Queene, Lord Marquesse
Dorset, Riuers, Hastings, Catesby,
Buckingham, Wooduill.*

King. Why so: now haue I done a good daies work.
You Peeres, continue this vnited League:
I, euery day expect an Embassage
From my Redeemer, to redeeme me hence.
And more to peace my soule shall part to heauen,
Since I haue made my Friends at peace on earth.
Dorset and Riuers, take each others hand,
Dissemble not your hatred, Sweare your loue.

Riu. By heauen, my soule is purg'd from grudging hate
And with my hand I seale my true hearts Loue.

Hast. So thriue I, as I truly sweare the like.

King. Take heed you dally not before your King,
Lest he that is the supreme King of Kings
Confound your hidden falshood, and award
Either of you to be the others end.

Hast. So prosper I, as I sweare perfect loue.

Ri. And I, as I loue *Hastings* with my heart.

King. Madam, your selfe is not exempt from this:
Nor you Sonne *Dorset*, *Buckingham* nor you;
You haue bene factious one against the other.
Wife, loue Lord *Hastings*, let him kisse your hand,
And what you do, do it vnfeignedly.

Qu. There *Hastings*, I will neuer more remember
Our former hatred, so thriue I, and mine.

King. Dorset, imbrace him:
Hastings, loue Lord Marquesse.

Dor. This interchange of loue, I heere protest
Vpon my part, shall be inuiolable.

Hast. And so sweare I.

King. Now Princely *Buckingham*, seale ỹ this league
With thy embracements to my wiues Allies,
And make me happy in your vnity.

Buc. When euer *Buckingham* doth turne his hate
Vpon your Grace, but with all dutious loue,
Doth cherish you, and yours, God punish me
With hate in those where I expect most loue,
When I haue most need to imploy a Friend,
And most assured that he is a Friend,
Deepe, hollow, treacherous, and full of guile,
Be he vnto me: This do I begge of heauen,
When I am cold in loue, to you, or yours. *Embrace*

King. A pleasing Cordiall, Princely *Buckingham*,
Is this thy Vow, vnto my sickely heart:
There wanteth now our Brother Gloster heere,
To make the blessed period of this peace.

Buc. And in good time,
Heere comes Sir *Richard Ratcliffe*, and the Duke.

Enter Ratcliffe, and Gloster.

Rich. Good morrow to my Soueraigne King & Queen
And Princely Peeres, a happy time of day.

King. Happy indeed, as we haue spent the day:
Gloster, we haue done deeds of Charity,
Made peace of enmity, faire loue of hate,
Betweene these swelling wrong incensed Peeres.

Rich. A blessed labour my most Soueraigne Lord:
Among this Princely heape, if any heere
By false intelligence, or wrong surmize
Hold me a Foe: If I vnwillingly, or in my rage,
Haue ought committed that is hardly borne,
To any in this presence, I desire
To reconcile me to his Friendly peace:
'Tis death to me to be at enmitie:
I hate it, and desire all good mens loue,
First Madam, I intreate true peace of you,
Which I will purchase with my dutious seruice,
Of you my Noble Cosin Buckingham,
If euer any grudge were lodg'd betweene vs,
Of you and you, Lord *Riuers* and of *Dorset*,
That all without desert haue frown'd on me:
Of you Lord *Wooduill*, and Lord *Scales* of you,
Dukes, Earles, Lords, Gentlemen, indeed of all.
I do not know that Englishman aliue,
With whom my soule is any iot at oddes,
More then the Infant that is borne to night:
I thanke my God for my Humility.

Qu. A holy day shall this be kept heereafter:
I would to God all strifes were well compounded.
My Soueraigne Lord, I do beseech your Highnesse
To take our Brother *Clarence* to your Grace.

Rich. Why Madam, haue I offred loue for this,
To be so flowted in this Royall presence?
Who knowes not that the gentle Duke is dead? *They*
You do him iniurie to scorne his Coarse. *all start.*

King. Who knowes not he is dead?
Who knowes he is?

Qu. All-seeing heauen, what a world is this?

Buc. Looke I so pale Lord *Dorset*, as the rest?

Dor. I my good Lord, and no man in the presence,
But his red colour hath forsooke his cheekes.

King. Is *Clarence* dead? The Order was reuerst.

Rich. But he (poore man) by your first order dyed,
And that a winged Mercurie did beare:
Some tardie Cripple bare the Countermand,
That came too lagge to see him buried.
God grant, that some lesse Noble, and lesse Loyall,
Neerer in bloody thoughts, and not in blood,
Deserue not worse then wretched *Clarence* did,
And yet go currant from Suspition.

Enter Earle of Derby.

Der. A boone my Soueraigne for my seruice done.

King. I prethee peace, my soule is full of sorrow.

Der. I will not rise, vnlesse your Highnes heare me.

King. Then say at once, what is it thou requests.

Der. The forfeit (Soueraigne) of my seruants life,
Who slew to day a Riotous Gentleman,
Lately attendant on the Duke of Norfolke.

King. Haue I a tongue to doome my Brothers death,
And shall that tongue giue pardon to a slaue?
My Brother kill'd no man, his fault was Thought,
And yet his punishment was bitter death.

Who sued to me for him? Who (in my wrath)
Kneel'd and my feet, and bid me be aduis'd?
Who spoke of Brother-hood? who spoke of loue?
Who told me how the poore soule did forsake
The mighty Warwicke, and did fight for me?
Who told me in the field at Tewkesbury,
When Oxford had me downe, he rescued me:
And said deare Brother liue, and be a King?
Who told me, when we both lay in the Field,
Frozen (almost) to death, how he did lap me
Euen in his Garments, and did giue himselfe
(All thin and naked) to the numbe cold night?
All this from my Remembrance, brutish wrath
Sinfully pluckt, and not a man of you
Had so much grace to put it in my minde.
But when your Carters, or your wayting Vassalls
Haue done a drunken Slaughter, and defac'd
The precious Image of our deere Redeemer,
You straight are on your knees for Pardon, pardon,
And I (vniustly too) must grant it you.
But for my Brother, not a man would speake,
Nor I (vngracious) speake vnto my selfe
For him poore Soule. The proudest of you all,
Haue bin beholding to him in his life:
Yet none of you, would once begge for his life.
O God! I feare thy iustice will take hold
On me, and you; and mine, and yours for this.
Come *Hastings* helpe me to my Closset.
Ah poore *Clarence*. *Exeunt some with K. & Queen.*

  Rich. This is the fruits of rashnes: Markt you not,
How that the guilty Kindred of the Queene
Look'd pale, when they did heare of *Clarence* death.
O! they did vrge it still vnto the King,
God will reuenge it. Come Lords will you go,
To comfort *Edward* with our company.
  Buc. We wait vpon your Grace. *exeunt.*

Scena Secunda.

Enter the old Dutchesse of Yorke, with the two
children of Clarence.

  Edw. Good Grandam tell vs, is our Father dead?
  Dutch. No Boy.
  Daugh. Why do weepe so oft? And beate your Brest?
And cry, O *Clarence*, my vnhappy Sonne.
  Boy. Why do you looke on vs, and shake your head,
And call vs Orphans, Wretches, Castawayes,
If that our Noble Father were aliue?
  Dut. My pretty Cosins, you mistake me both,
I do lament the sicknesse of the King,
As loath to lose him, not your Fathers death:
It were lost sorrow to waile one that's lost.
  Boy. Then you conclude, (my Grandam) he is dead:
The King mine Vnckle is too blame for it.
God will reuenge it, whom I will importune
With earnest prayers, all to that effect.
  Daugh. And so will I.
  Dut. Peace children peace, the King doth loue you wel.
Incapeable, and shallow Innocents,
You cannot guesse who caus'd your Fathers death.
  Boy. Grandam we can: for my good Vnkle Gloster

Told me, the King prouok'd to it by the Queene,
Deuis'd impeachments to imprison him;
And when my Vnckle told me so, he wept,
And pittied me, and kindly kist my cheeke:
Bad me rely on him, as on my Father,
And he would loue me deerely as a childe.
  Dut. Ah! that Deceit should steale such gentle shape,
And with a vertuous Vizor hide deepe vice.
He is my sonne, I, and therein my shame,
Yet from my dugges, he drew not this deceit.
  Boy. Thinke you my Vnkle did dissemble Grandam?
  Dut. I Boy.
  Boy. I cannot thinke it. Hearke, what noise is this?

Enter the Queene with her haire about her ears,
Riuers & Dorset after her.

  Qu. Ah! who shall hinder me to waile and weepe?
To chide my Fortune, and torment my Selfe.
Ile ioyne with blacke dispaire against my Soule,
And to my selfe, become an enemie.
  Dut. What meanes this Scene of rude impatience?
  Qu. To make an act of Tragicke violence.
Edward my Lord, thy Sonne, our King is dead.
Why grow the Branches, when the Roote is gone?
Why wither not the leaues that want their sap?
If you will liue, Lament: if dye, be breefe,
That our swift-winged Soules may catch the Kings,
Or like obedient Subiects follow him,
To his new Kingdome of nere-changing night.
  Dut. Ah so much interest haue in thy sorrow,
As I had Title in thy Noble Husband:
I haue bewept a worthy Husbands death,
And liu'd with looking on his Images:
But now two Mirrors of his Princely semblance,
Are crack'd in pieces, by malignant death,
And I for comfort, haue but one false Glasse,
That greeues me, when I see my shame in him.
Thou art a Widdow: yet thou art a Mother,
And hast the comfort of thy Children left,
But death hath snatch'd my Husband from mine Armes,
And pluckt two Crutches from my feeble hands,
Clarence, and *Edward*. O, what cause haue I,
(Thine being but a moity of my moane)
To ouer-go thy woes, and drowne thy cries.
  Boy. Ah Aunt! you wept not for our Fathers death:
How can we ayde you with our Kindred teares?
  Daugh. Our fatherlesse distresse was left vnmoan'd,
Your widdow-dolour, likewise be vnwept.
  Qu. Giue me no helpe in Lamentation,
I am not barren to bring forth complaints:
All Springs reduce their currents to mine eyes,
That I being gouern'd by the waterie Moone,
May send forth plenteous teares to drowne the World.
Ah, for my Husband, for my deere Lord *Edward*.
  Chil. Ah for our Father, for our deere Lord *Clarence*.
  Dut. Alas for both, both mine *Edward* and *Clarence*.
  Qu. What stay had I but *Edward*, and hee's gone?
  Chil. What stay had we but *Clarence*? and he's gone.
  Dut. What stayes had I, but they? and they are gone.
  Qu. Was neuer widdow had so deere a losse.
  Chil. Were neuer Orphans had so deere a losse.
  Dut. Was neuer Mother had so deere a losse.
Alas! I am the Mother of these Greefes,
Their woes are parcell'd, mine is generall.
She for an *Edward* weepes, and so do I:

I for a *Clarence* weepes, so doth not shee:
These Babes for *Clarence* weepe, so do not they.
Alas! you three, on me threefold distrest:
Power all your teares, I am your sorrowes Nurse,
And I will pamper it with Lamentation.

  Dor. Comfort deere Mother, God is much displeas'd,
That you take with vnthankfulnesse his doing.
In common worldly things, 'tis call'd vngratefull,
With dull vnwillingnesse to repay a debt,
Which with a bounteous hand was kindly lent:
Much more to be thus opposite with heauen,
For it requires the Royall debt it lent you.

  Riuers. Madam, bethinke you like a carefull Mother
Of the young Prince your sonne: send straight for him,
Let him be Crown'd, in him your comfort liues.
Drowne desperate sorrow in dead *Edwards* graue,
And plant your ioyes in liuing *Edwards* Throne.

Enter Richard, Buckingham, Derbie, Hastings, and Ratcliffe.

  Rich. Sister haue comfort, all of vs haue cause
To waile the dimming of our shining Starre:
But none can helpe our harmes by wayling them.
Madam, my Mother, I do cry you mercie,
I did not see your Grace. Humbly on my knee,
I craue your Blessing.

  Dut. God blesse thee, and put meeknes in thy breast,
Loue Charity, Obedience, and true Dutie.

  Rich. Amen, and make me die a good old man,
That is the butt-end of a Mothers blessing;
I maruell that her Grace did leaue it out.

  Buc. You cloudy-Princes, & hart-sorowing-Peeres,
That beare this heauie mutuall loade of Moane,
Now cheere each other, in each others Loue:
Though we haue spent our Haruest of this King,
We are to reape the Haruest of his Sonne.
The broken rancour of your high-swolne hates,
But lately splinter'd, knit, and ioyn'd together,
Must gently be preseru'd, cherisht, and kept:
Me seemeth good, that with some little Traine,
Forthwith from Ludlow, the young Prince be set
Hither to London, to be crown'd our King.

  Riuers. Why with some little Traine,
My Lord of Buckingham?

  Buc. Marrie my Lord, least by a multitude,
The new-heal'd wound of Malice should breake out,
Which would be so much the more dangerous,
By how much the estate is greene, and yet vngouern'd.
Where euery Horse beares his commanding Reine,
And may direct his course as please himselfe,
As well the feare of harme, as harme apparant,
In my opinion, ought to be preuented.

  Rich. I hope the King made peace with all of vs,
And the compact is firme, and true in me.

  Riu. And so in me, and so (I thinke) in all.
Yet since it is but greene, it should be put
To no apparant likely-hood of breach,
Which haply by much company might be vrg'd:
Therefore I say with Noble Buckingham,
That it is meete so few should fetch the Prince.

  Hast. And so say I.

  Rich. Then be it so, and go we to determine
Who they shall be that strait shall poste to London.
Madam, and you my Sister, will you go
To giue your censures in this businesse. *Exeunt.*

Manet Buckingham, and Richard.

  Buc. My Lord, who euer iournies to the Prince,
For God sake let not vs two stay at home:
For by the way, Ile sort occasion,
As Index to the story we late talk'd of,
To part the Queenes proud Kindred from the Prince.

  Rich. My other selfe, my Counsailes Consistory,
My Oracle, My Prophet, my deere Cosin,
I, as a childe, will go by thy direction,
Toward London then, for wee'l not stay behinde. *Exeunt.*

Scena Tertia.

Enter one Citizen at one doore, and another at the other.

  1. *Cit.* Good morrow Neighbour, whether away so fast?

  2. *Cit.* I promise you, I scarsely know my selfe:
Heare you the newes abroad?

  1. Yes, that the King is dead.

  2. Ill newes byrlady, seldome comes the better:
I feare, I feare, 'twill proue a giddy world.

Enter another Citizen.

  3. Neighbours, God speed.

  1. Giue you good morrow sir.

  3. Doth the newes hold of good king *Edwards* death?

  2. I sir, it is too true, God helpe the while.

  3. Then Masters looke to see a troublous world.

  1. No, no, by Gods good grace, his Son shall reigne.

  3. Woe to that Land that's gouern'd by a Childe,

  2. In him there is a hope of Gouernment,
Which in his nonage, counsell vnder him,
And in his full and ripened yeares, himselfe
No doubt shall then, and till then gouerne well.

  1. So stood the State, when *Henry* the sixt
Was crown'd in Paris, but at nine months old.

  3. Stood the State so? No, no, good friends, God wot
For then this Land was famously enrich'd
With politike graue Counsell; then the King
Had vertuous Vnkles to protect his Grace.

  1. Why so hath this, both by his Father and Mother.

  3. Better it were they all came by his Father:
Or by his Father there were none at all:
For emulation, who shall now be neerest,
Will touch vs all too neere, if God preuent not.
O full of danger is the Duke of Glouster,
And the Queenes Sons, and Brothers, haught and proud:
And were they to be rul'd, and not to rule,
This sickly Land, might solace as before.

  1. Come, come, we feare the worst: all will be well.

  3. When Clouds are seen, wisemen put on their cloaks;
When great leaues fall, then Winter is at hand;
When the Sun sets, who doth not looke for night?
Vntimely stormes, makes men expect a Dearth:
All may be well; but if God sort it so,
'Tis more then we deserue, or I expect.

  2. Truly, the hearts of men are full of feare:
You cannot reason (almost) with a man,
That lookes not heauily, and full of dread.

  3. Before the dayes of Change, still is it so,
By a diuine instinct, mens mindes mistrust

Ensuing

Pursuing danger: as by proofe we see
The Water swell before a boyst'rous storme:
But leaue it all to God. Whither away?
2 Marry we were sent for to the Iustices.
3 And so was I: Ile beare you company. *Exeunt.*

Scena Quarta.

Enter Arch-bishop, yong Yorke, the Queene, and the Dutchesse.

Arch. Last night I heard they lay at Stony Stratford,
And at Northampton they do rest to night:
Tomorrow, or next day, they will be heere.

Dut. I long with all my heart to see the Prince:
I hope he is much growne since last I saw him.

Qu. But I heare no, they say my sonne of Yorke
Ha's almost ouertane him in his growth.

Yorke. I Mother, but I would not haue it so.

Dut. Why my good Cosin, it is good to grow.

Yor. Grandam, one night as we did sit at Supper,
My Vnkle *Riuers* talk'd how I did grow
More then my Brother. I, quoth my Vnkle *Glouster*,
Small Herbes haue grace, great Weeds do grow apace.
And since, me thinkes I would not grow so fast,
Because sweet Flowres are slow, and Weeds make hast.

Dut. Good faith, good faith, the saying did not hold
In him that did obiect the same to thee.
He was the wretched'st thing when he was yong,
So long a growing, and so leysurely,
That if his rule were true, he should be gracious.

Yor. And so no doubt he is, my gracious Madam.

Dut. I hope he is, but yet let Mothers doubt.

Yor. Now by my troth, if I had beene remembred,
I could haue giuen my Vnkles Grace, a flout,
To touch his growth, neerer then he toucht mine.

Dut. How my yong Yorke,
I prythee let me heare it.

Yor. Marry (they say) my Vnkle grew so fast,
That he could gnaw a crust at two houres old,
'Twas full two yeares ere I could get a tooth.
Grandam, this would haue beene a byting Iest.

Dut. I prythee pretty Yorke, who told thee this?

Yor. Grandam, his Nurse.

Dut. His Nurse? why she was dead, ere ỹ wast borne.

Yor. If 'twere not she, I cannot tell who told me.

Qu. A parlous Boy: go too, you are too shrew'd.

Dut. Good Madam, be not angry with the Childe.

Qu. Pitchers haue eares.

Enter a Messenger.

Arch. Heere comes a Messenger: What Newes?

Mes. Such newes my Lord, as greeues me to report.

Qu. How doth the Prince?

Mes. Well Madam, and in health.

Dut. What is thy Newes?

Mess. Lord *Riuers*, and Lord *Grey*,
Are sent to Pomfret, and with them,
Sir *Thomas Vaughan*, Prisoners.

Dut. Who hath committed them?

Mes. The mighty Dukes, *Glouster* and *Buckingham*.

Arch. For what offence?

Mes. The summe of all I can, I haue disclos'd:
Why, or for what, the Nobles were committed,
Is all vnknowne to me, my gracious Lord.

Qu. Aye me! I see the ruine of my House:
The Tyger now hath seiz'd the gentle Hinde,
Insulting Tiranny beginnes to Iutt
Vpon the innocent and awelesse Throne:
Welcome Destruction, Blood, and Massacre,
I see (as in a Map) the end of all.

Dut. Accursed, and vnquiet wrangling dayes,
How many of you haue mine eyes beheld?
My Husband lost his life, to get the Crowne,
And often vp and downe my sonnes were tost
For me to ioy, and weepe, their gaine and losse.
And being seated, and Domesticke broyles
Cleane ouer-blowne, themselues the Conquerors,
Make warre vpon themselues, Brother to Brother;
Blood to blood, selfe against selfe: O preposterous
And franticke outrage, end thy damned spleene,
Or let me dye, to looke on earth no more.

Qu. Come, come my Boy, we will to Sanctuary.
Madam, farwell.

Dut. Stay, I will go with you.

Qu. You haue no cause.

Arch. My gracious Lady go,
And thether beare your Treasure and your Goodes,
For my part, Ile resigne vnto your Grace
The Seale I keepe, and so betide to me,
As well I tender you, and all of yours.
Go, Ile conduct you to the Sanctuary. *Exeunt*

Actus Tertius. Scœna Prima.

The Trumpets sound.
Enter yong Prince, the Dukes of Glocester, and Buckingham,
Lord Cardinall, with others.

Buc. Welcome sweete Prince to London,
To your Chamber.

Rich. Welcome deere Cosin, my thoughts Soueraign
The wearie way hath made you Melancholly.

Prin. No Vnkle, but our crosses on the way,
Haue made it tedious, wearisome, and heauie.
I want more Vnkles heere to welcome me.

Rich. Sweet Prince, the vntainted vertue of your yeers
Hath not yet diu'd into the Worlds deceit:
No more can you distinguish of a man,
Then of his outward shew, which God he knowes,
Seldome or neuer iumpeth with the heart.
Those Vnkles which you want, were dangerous:
Your Grace attended to their Sugred words,
But look'd not on the poyson of their hearts:
God keepe you from them, and from such false Friends.

Prin. God keepe me from false Friends,
But they were none.

Rich. My Lord, the Maior of London comes to greet you.

Enter Lord Maior.

Lo. Maior. God blesse your Grace, with health and happie dayes.

Prin. I thanke you, good my Lord, and thank you all:

I thought my Mother,and my Brother *Yorke*,
Would long,ere this,haue met vs on the way.
Fie, what a Slug is *Hastings*, that he comes not
To tell vs, whether they will come, or no.

Enter Lord Hastings.

Buck. And in good time, heere comes the sweating Lord.

Prince. Welcome, my Lord : what, will our Mother come?

Hast. On what occasion God he knowes,not I;
The Queene your Mother,and your Brother *Yorke*,
Haue taken Sanctuarie : The tender Prince
Would faine haue come with me, to meet your Grace,
But by his Mother was perforce with-held.

Buck. Fie,what an indirect and peeuish course
Is this of hers ? Lord Cardinall, will your Grace
Perswade the Queene, to send the Duke of Yorke
Vnto his Princely Brother presently ?
If she denie, Lord *Hastings* goe with him,
And from her iealous Armes pluck him perforce.

Card. My Lord of Buckingham, if my weake Oratorie
Can from his Mother winne the Duke of Yorke,
Anon expect him here : but if she be obdurate
To milde entreaties, God forbid
We should infringe the holy Priuiledge
Of blessed Sanctuarie : not for all this Land,
Would I be guiltie of so great a sinne.

Buck. You are too sencelesse obstinate, my Lord,
Too ceremonious, and traditionall.
Weigh it but with the grossenesse of this Age,
You breake not Sanctuarie, in seizing him :
The benefit thereof is alwayes granted
To those, whose dealings haue deseru'd the place,
And those who haue the wit to clayme the place :
This Prince hath neyther claym'd it, nor deseru'd it,
And therefore, in mine opinion, cannot haue it.
Then taking him from thence, that is not there,
You breake no Priuiledge, nor Charter there :
Oft haue I heard of Sanctuarie men,
But Sanctuarie children, ne're till now.

Card. My Lord, you shall o're-rule my mind for once.
Come on, Lord *Hastings*, will you goe with me ?

Hast. I goe, my Lord. *Exit Cardinall and Hastings.*

Prince. Good Lords, make all the speedie hast you may.
Say, Vnckle *Glocester*, if our Brother come,
Where shall we soiourne, till our Coronation ?

Glo. Where it think'st best vnto your Royall selfe.
If I may counsaile you, some day or two
Your Highnesse shall repose you at the Tower :
Then where you please, and shall be thought most fit
For your best health, and recreation.

Prince. I doe not like the Tower, of any place :
Did *Iulius Cæsar* build that place, my Lord ?

Buck. He did, my gracious Lord, begin that place,
Which since, succeeding Ages haue re-edify'd.

Prince. Is it vpon record ? or else reported
Successiuely from age to age, he built it ?

Buck. Vpon record, my gracious Lord.

Prince. But say, my Lord, it were not registred,
Me thinkes the truth should liue from age to age,
As 'twere retayl'd to all posteritie,
Euen to the generall ending day.

Glo. So wise, so young, they say doe neuer liue long.

Prince. What say you, Vnckle ?

Glo. I say, without Characters, Fame liues long.
Thus, like the formall Vice, Iniquitie,
I moralize two meanings in one word.

Prince. That *Iulius Cæsar* was a famous man,
With what his Valour did enrich his Wit,
His Wit set downe, to make his Valour liue :
Death makes no Conquest of his Conqueror,
For now he liues in Fame, though not in Life.
Ile tell you what, my Cousin *Buckingham*.

Buck. What, my gracious Lord ?

Prince. And if I liue vntill I be a man,
Ile win our ancient Right in France againe,
Or dye a Souldier, as I liu'd a King.

Glo. Short Summers lightly haue a forward Spring.

Enter young Yorke, Hastings, and Cardinall.

Buck. Now in good time, heere comes the Duke of Yorke.

Prince. Richard of Yorke, how fares our Noble Brother ?

Yorke. Well, my deare Lord, so must I call you now.

Prince. I, Brother, to our griefe, as it is yours :
Too late he dy'd, that might haue kept that Title,
Which by his death hath lost much Maiestie.

Glo. How fares our Cousin, Noble Lord of Yorke?

Yorke. I thanke you, gentle Vnckle. O my Lord,
You said, that idle Weeds are fast in growth :
The Prince, my Brother, hath out-growne me farre.

Glo. He hath, my Lord.

Yorke. And therefore is he idle ?

Glo. Oh my faire Cousin, I must not say so.

Yorke. Then he is more beholding to you, then I.

Glo. He may command me as my Soueraigne,
But you haue power in me, as in a Kinsman.

Yorke. I pray you, Vnckle, giue me this Dagger.

Glo. My Dagger, little Cousin? with all my heart.

Prince. A Begger, Brother ?

Yorke. Of my kind Vnckle, that I know will giue,
And being but a Toy, which is no griefe to giue.

Glo. A greater gift then that, Ile giue my Cousin.

Yorke. A greater gift ? O, that's the Sword to it.

Glo. I, gentle Cousin, were it light enough.

Yorke. O then I see, you will part but with light gifts,
In weightier things you'le say a Begger nay.

Glo. It is too weightie for your Grace to weare.

Yorke. I weigh it lightly, were it heauier.

Glo. What, would you haue my Weapon, little Lord?

Yorke. I would that I might thanke you, as, as, you call me.

Glo. How ?

Yorke. Little.

Prince. My Lord of Yorke will still be crosse in talke:
Vnckle, your Grace knowes how to beare with him.

Yorke. You meane to beare me, not to beare with me:
Vnckle, my Brother mockes both you and me,
Because that I am little, like an Ape,
He thinkes that you should beare me on your shoulders.

Buck. With what a sharpe prouided wit he reasons:
To mittigate the scorne he giues his Vnckle,
He prettily and aptly taunts himselfe :
So cunning, and so young, is wonderfull.

Glo. My Lord, wilt please you passe along ?
My selfe, and my good Cousin *Buckingham*,
Will to your Mother, to entreat of her
To meet you at the Tower, and welcome you.

Yorke. What,

Yorke. What, will you goe vnto the Tower, my Lord?
Prince. My Lord Protector will haue it so.
Yorke. I shall not sleepe in quiet at the Tower.
Glo. Why, what should you feare?
Yorke. Marry, my Vnckle *Clarence* angry Ghost:
My Grandam told me he was murther'd there.
Prince. I feare no Vnckles dead.
Glo. Nor none that liue, I hope.
Prince. And if they liue, I hope I need not feare.
But come my Lord: and with a heauie heart,
Thinking on them, goe I vnto the Tower.

A Senet. Exeunt Prince, Yorke, Hastings, and Dorset.

Manet Richard, Buckingham, and Catesby.

Buck. Thinke you, my Lord, this little prating *Yorke*
Was not incensed by his subtile Mother,
To taunt and scorne you thus opprobriously?
Glo. No doubt, no doubt: Oh 'tis a perillous Boy,
Bold, quicke, ingenious, forward, capable:
Hee is all the Mothers, from the top to toe.
Buck. Well, let them rest: Come hither *Catesby*,
Thou art sworne as deepely to effect what we intend,
As closely to conceale what we impart:
Thou know'st our reasons vrg'd vpon the way.
What think'st thou? is it not an easie matter,
To make *William* Lord *Hastings* of our minde,
For the installment of this Noble Duke
In the Seat Royall of this famous Ile?
Cates. He for his fathers sake so loues the Prince,
That he will not be wonne to ought against him.
Buck. What think'st thou then of *Stanley*? Will not hee?
Cates. Hee will doe all in all as *Hastings* doth.
Buck. Well then, no more but this:
Goe gentle *Catesby*, and as it were farre off,
Sound thou Lord *Hastings*,
How he doth stand affected to our purpose,
And summon him to morrow to the Tower,
To sit about the Coronation.
If thou do'st finde him tractable to vs,
Encourage him, and tell him all our reasons:
If he be leaden, ycie, cold, vnwilling,
Be thou so too, and so breake off the talke,
And giue vs notice of his inclination:
For we to morrow hold diuided Councels,
Wherein thy selfe shalt highly be employ'd.
Rich. Commend me to Lord *William*: tell him *Catesby*,
His ancient Knot of dangerous Aduersaries
Tomorrow are let blood at Pomfret Castle,
And bid my Lord, for ioy of this good newes,
Giue Mistresse *Shore* one gentle Kisse the more.
Buck. Good *Catesby*, goe effect this businesse soundly.
Cates. My good Lords both, with all the heed I can.
Rich. Shall we heare from you, *Catesby*, ere we sleepe?
Cates. You shall, my Lord.
Rich. At *Crosby* House, there shall you find vs both.

Exit Catesby.

Buck. Now, my Lord,
What shall wee doe, if wee perceiue
Lord *Hastings* will not yeeld to our Complots?
Rich. Chop off his Head:
Something wee will determine:
And looke when I am King, clayme thou of me
The Earledome of Hereford, and all the moueables
Whereof the King, my Brother, was possest.

Buck. Ile clayme that promise at your Graces hand.
Rich. And looke to haue it yeelded with all kindnesse.
Come, let vs suppe betimes, that afterwards
Wee may digest our complots in some forme.

Exeunt.

Scena Secunda.

Enter a Messenger to the Doore of Hastings.

Mess. My Lord, my Lord.
Hast. Who knockes?
Mess. One from the Lord *Stanley*.
Hast. What is't a Clocke?
Mess. Vpon the stroke of foure.

Enter Lord Hastings.

Hast. Cannot my Lord *Stanley* sleepe these tedious Nights?
Mess. So it appeares, by that I haue to say:
First, he commends him to your Noble selfe.
Hast. What then?
Mess. Then certifies your Lordship, that this Night
He dreamt, the Bore had rased off his Helme:
Besides, he sayes there are two Councels kept;
And that may be determin'd at the one,
Which may make you and him to rue at th'other.
Therefore he sends to know your Lordships pleasure,
If you will presently take Horse with him,
And with all speed post with him toward the North,
To shun the danger that his Soule diuines.
Hast. Goe fellow, goe, returne vnto thy Lord,
Bid him not feare the seperated Councell:
His Honor and my selfe are at the one,
And at the other, is my good friend *Catesby*;
Where nothing can proceede, that toucheth vs,
Whereof I shall not haue intelligence:
Tell him his Feares are shallow, without instance.
And for his Dreames, I wonder hee's so simple,
To trust the mock'ry of vnquiet slumbers.
To flye the Bore, before the Bore pursues,
Were to incense the Bore to follow vs,
And make pursuit, where he did meane no chase.
Goe, bid thy Master rise, and come to me,
And we will both together to the Tower,
Where he shall see the Bore will vse vs kindly.
Mess. Ile goe, my Lord, and tell him what you say.

Exit.

Enter Catesby.

Cates. Many good morrowes to my Noble Lord.
Hast. Good morrow *Catesby*, you are early stirring:
What newes, what newes, in this our tott'ring State?
Cates. It is a reeling World indeed, my Lord:
And I beleeue will neuer stand vpright,
Till *Richard* weare the Garland of the Realme.
Hast. How weare the Garland?
Doest thou meane the Crowne?
Cates. I, my good Lord.
Hast. Ile haue this Crown of mine cut fro my shoulders,
Before Ile see the Crowne so foule mis-plac'd:
But canst thou guesse, that he doth ayme at it?

Cates. I,

Cates. I, on my life, and hopes to find you forward,
Vpon his partie, for the gaine thereof:
And thereupon he sends you this good newes,
That this same very day your enemies,
The Kindred of the Queene, must dye at Pomfret.

Hast. Indeed I am no mourner for that newes,
Because they haue beene still my aduersaries:
But, that Ile giue my voice on *Richards* side,
To barre my Masters Heires in true Descent,
God knowes I will not doe it, to the death.

Cates. God keepe your Lordship in that gracious
minde.

Hast. But I shall laugh at this a twelue-month hence,
That they which brought me in my Masters hate,
I liue to looke vpon their Tragedie.
Well *Catesby*, ere a fort-night make me older,
Ile send some packing, that yet thinke not on't.

Cates. 'Tis a vile thing to dye, my gracious Lord,
When men are vnprepar'd, and looke not for it.

Hast. O monstrous, monstrous! and so falls it out
With *Riuers, Vaughan, Grey:* and so 'twill doe
With some men else, that thinke themselues as safe
As thou and I, who (as thou know'st) are deare
To Princely *Richard*, and to *Buckingham*.

Cates. The Princes both make high account of you,
For they account his Head vpon the Bridge.

Hast. I know they doe, and I haue well deseru'd it.

Enter Lord Stanley.

Come on, come on, where is your Bore-speare man?
Feare you the Bore, and goe so vnprouided?

Stan. My Lord good morrow, good morrow *Catesby:*
You may ieast on, but by the holy Rood,
I doe not like these seuerall Councels, I.

Hast. My Lord, I hold my Life as deare as yours,
And neuer in my dayes, I doe protest,
Was it so precious to me, as 'tis now:
Thinke you, but that I know our state secure,
I would be so triumphant as I am?

Sta. The Lords at Pomfret, whē they rode from London,
Were iocund, and suppos'd their states were sure,
And they indeed had no cause to mistrust:
But yet you see, how soone the Day o're-cast.
This sudden stab of Rancour I misdoubt:
Pray God (I say) I proue a needlesse Coward.
What, shall we toward the Tower? the day is spent.

Hast. Come, come, haue with you:
Wot you what, my Lord,
To day the Lords you talke of, are beheaded.

Sta. They, for their truth, might better wear their Heads,
Then some that haue accus'd them, weare their Hats.
But come, my Lord, let's away.

Enter a Pursuiuant.

Hast. Goe on before, Ile talke with this good fellow.
     Exit Lord Stanley, and Catesby.
How now, Sirrha? how goes the World with thee?

Purs. The better, that your Lordship please to aske.

Hast. I tell thee man, 'tis better with me now,
Then when thou met'st me last, where now we meet:
Then was I going Prisoner to the Tower,
By the suggestion of the Queenes Allyes.
But now I tell thee (keepe it to thy selfe)
This day those Enemies are put to death,
And I in better state then ere I was.

Purs. God hold it, to your Honors good content.

Hast. Gramercie fellow: there, drinke that for me.
     Throwes him his Purse.

Purs. I thanke your Honor.   *Exit Pursuiuant.*

Enter a Priest.

Priest. Well met, my Lord, I am glad to see your Honor.

Hast. I thanke thee, good Sir *Iohn*, with all my heart.
I am in your debt, for your last Exercise:
Come the next Sabboth, and I will content you.

Priest. Ile wait vpon your Lordship.

Enter Buckingham.

Buc. What, talking with a Priest, Lord Chamberlaine?
Your friends at Pomfret, they doe need the Priest,
Your Honor hath no shriuing worke in hand.

Hast. Good faith, and when I met this holy man,
The men you talke of, came into my minde.
What, goe you toward the Tower?

Buc. I doe, my Lord, but long I cannot stay there:
I shall returne before your Lordship, thence.

Hast. Nay like enough, for I stay Dinner there.

Buc. And Supper too, although thou know'st it not.
Come, will you goe?

Hast. Ile wait vpon your Lordship.   *Exeunt.*

Scena Tertia.

Enter Sir Richard Ratcliffe, with Halberds, carrying
the Nobles to death at Pomfret.

Riuers. Sir *Richard Ratcliffe*, let me tell thee this,
To day shalt thou behold a Subiect die,
For Truth, for Dutie, and for Loyaltie.

Grey. God blesse the Prince from all the Pack of you,
A Knot you are, of damned Blood-suckers.

Vaugh. You liue, that shall cry woe for this heereafter.

Rat. Dispatch, the limit of your Liues is out.

Riuers. O Pomfret, Pomfret! O thou bloody Prison!
Fatall and ominous to Noble Peeres:
Within the guiltie Closure of thy Walls,
Richard the Second here was hackt to death:
And for more slander to thy dismall Seat,
Wee giue to thee our guiltlesse blood to drinke.

Grey. Now *Margarets* Curse is falne vpon our Heads,
When shee exclaim'd on *Hastings*, you, and I,
For standing by, when *Richard* stab'd her Sonne.

Riuers. Then curs'd shee *Richard*,
Then curs'd shee *Buckingham*,
Then curs'd shee *Hastings*. Oh remember God,
To heare her prayer for them, as now for vs:
And for my Sister, and her Princely Sonnes,
Be satisfy'd, deare God, with our true blood,
Which, as thou know'st, vniustly must be spilt.

Rat. Make haste, the houre of death is expiate.

Riuers. Come *Grey*, come *Vaughan*, let vs here embrace.
Farewell, vntill we meet againe in Heauen.
     Exeunt.

Scæna Quarta.

Enter Buckingham, Darby, Hastings, Bishop of Ely, Norfolke, Ratcliffe, Louell, with others, at a Table.

Hast. Now Noble Peeres, the cause why we are met,
Is to determine of the Coronation:
In Gods Name speake, when is the Royall day?
  Buck. Is all things ready for the Royall time?
  Darb. It is, and wants but nomination.
  Ely. To morrow then I iudge a happie day.
  Buck. Who knowes the Lord Protectors mind herein?
Who is most inward with the Noble Duke?
  Ely. Your Grace, we thinke, should soonest know his minde.
  Buck. We know each others Faces: for our Hearts,
He knowes no more of mine, then I of yours,
Or I of his, my Lord, then you of mine:
Lord *Hastings*, you and he are neere in loue.
  Hast. I thanke his Grace, I know he loues me well:
But for his purpose in the Coronation,
I haue not sounded him, nor he deliuer'd
His gracious pleasure any way therein:
But you, my Honorable Lords, may name the time,
And in the Dukes behalfe Ile giue my Voice,
Which I presume hee'le take in gentle part.

Enter Gloucester.

  Ely. In happie time, here comes the Duke himselfe.
  Rich. My Noble Lords, and Cousins all, good morrow:
I haue beene long a sleeper: but I trust,
My absence doth neglect no great designe,
Which by my presence might haue beene concluded.
  Buck. Had you not come vpon your Q, my Lord,
William, Lord *Hastings*, had pronounc'd your part;
I meane your Voice, for Crowning of the King.
  Rich. Then my Lord *Hastings*, no man might be bolder,
His Lordship knowes me well, and loues me well.
My Lord of Ely, when I was last in Holborne,
I saw good Strawberries in your Garden there,
I doe beseech you, send for some of them.
  Ely. Mary and will, my Lord, with all my heart.
Exit Bishop.
  Rich. Cousin of Buckingham, a word with you.
Catesby hath sounded *Hastings* in our businesse,
And findes the testie Gentleman so hot,
That he will lose his Head, ere giue consent
His Masters Child, as worshipfully he tearmes it,
Shall lose the Royaltie of Englands Throne.
  Buck. Withdraw your selfe a while, Ile goe with you.
Exeunt.
  Darb. We haue not yet set downe this day of Triumph:
To morrow, in my iudgement, is too sudden,
For I my selfe am not so well prouided,
As else I would be, were the day prolong'd.

Enter the Bishop of Ely.

  Ely. Where is my Lord, the Duke of Gloster?
I haue sent for these Strawberries.
  Ha. His Grace looks chearfully & smooth this morning,
There's some conceit or other likes him well,
When that he bids good morrow with such spirit.
I thinke there's neuer a man in Christendome
Can lesser hide his loue, or hate, then hee,
For by his Face straight shall you know his Heart.
  Darb. What of his Heart perceiue you in his Face,
By any liuelyhood he shew'd to day?
  Hast. Mary, that with no man here he is offended:
For were he, he had shewne it in his Lookes.

Enter Richard, and Buckingham.

  Rich. I pray you all, tell me what they deserue,
That doe conspire my death with diuellish Plots
Of damned Witchcraft, and that haue preuail'd
Vpon my Body with their Hellish Charmes.
  Hast. The tender loue I beare your Grace, my Lord,
Makes me most forward, in this Princely presence,
To doome th'Offendors, whosoe're they be:
I say, my Lord, they haue deserued death.
  Rich. Then be your eyes the witnesse of their euill.
Looke how I am bewitch'd: behold, mine Arme
Is like a blasted Sapling, wither'd vp:
And this is *Edwards* Wife, that monstrous Witch,
Consorted with that Harlot, Strumpet *Shore*,
That by their Witchcraft thus haue marked me.
  Hast. If they haue done this deed, my Noble Lord.
  Rich. If? thou Protector of this damned Strumpet,
Talk'st thou to me of Ifs: thou art a Traytor,
Off with his Head; now by Saint *Paul* I sweare,
I will not dine, vntill I see the same.
Louell and *Ratcliffe*, looke that it be done: *Exeunt.*
The rest that loue me, rise, and follow me.

Manet Louell and Ratcliffe, with the Lord Hastings.

  Hast. Woe, woe for England, not a whit for me,
For I, too fond, might haue preuented this:
Stanley did dreame, the Bore did rowse our Helmes,
And I did scorne it, and disdaine to flye:
Three times to day my Foot-Cloth-Horse did stumble,
And started, when he look'd vpon the Tower,
As loth to beare me to the slaughter-house.
O now I need the Priest, that spake to me:
I now repent I told the Pursuiuant,
As too triumphing, how mine Enemies
To day at Pomfret bloodily were butcher'd,
And I my selfe secure, in grace and fauour.
Oh *Margaret*, *Margaret*, now thy heauie Curse
Is lighted on poore *Hastings* wretched Head.
  Ra. Come, come, dispatch, the Duke would be at dinner:
Make a short Shrift, he longs to see your Head.
  Hast. O momentarie grace of mortall men,
Which we more hunt for, then the grace of God!
Who builds his hope in ayre of your good Lookes,
Liues like a drunken Sayler on a Mast,
Readie with euery Nod to tumble downe,
Into the fatall Bowels of the Deepe.
  Lou. Come, come, dispatch, 'tis bootlesse to exclaime.
  Hast. O bloody *Richard*: miserable England,
I prophecie the fearefull'st time to thee,
That euer wretched Age hath look'd vpon.
Come, lead me to the Block, beare him my Head,
They smile at me, who shortly shall be dead.
Exeunt.

Enter Richard, and Buckingham, in rotten Armour, maruellous ill-fauoured.

Richard. Come Cousin,
Canst thou quake, and change thy colour,
Murther thy breath in middle of a word,
And then againe begin, and stop againe,
As if thou were distraught, and mad with terror?

Buck. Tut, I can counterfeit the deepe Tragedian,
Speake, and looke backe, and prie on euery side,
Tremble and start at wagging of a Straw:
Intending deepe suspition, gastly Lookes
Are at my seruice, like enforced Smiles;
And both are readie in their Offices,
At any time to grace my Stratagemes.
But what, is *Catesby* gone?

Rich. He is, and see he brings the Maior along.

Enter the Maior, and Catesby.

Buck. Lord Maior.
Rich. Looke to the Draw-Bridge there.
Buck. Hearke, a Drumme.
Rich. Catesby, o're-looke the Walls.
Buck. Lord Maior, the reason we haue sent.
Rich. Looke back, defend thee, here are Enemies.
Buck. God and our Innocencie defend, and guard vs.

Enter Louell and Ratcliffe, with Hastings Head.

Rich. Be patient, they are friends: *Ratcliffe*, and *Louell.*
Louell. Here is the Head of that ignoble Traytor,
The dangerous and vnsuspected *Hastings.*

Rich. So deare I lou'd the man, that I must weepe:
I tooke him for the plainest harmelesse Creature,
That breath'd vpon the Earth, a Christian.
Made him my Booke, wherein my Soule recorded
The Historie of all her secret thoughts.
So smooth he dawb'd his Vice with shew of Vertue,
That his apparant open Guilt omitted,
I meane, his Conuersation with *Shores* Wife,
He liu'd from all attainder of suspects.

Buck. Well, well, he was the couertst sheltred Traytor
That euer liu'd.
Would you imagine, or almost beleeue,
Wert not, that by great preseruation
We liue to tell it, that the subtill Traytor
This day had plotted, in the Councell-House,
To murther me, and my good Lord of Gloster.

Maior. Had he done so?

Rich. What? thinke you we are Turkes, or Infidels?
Or that we would, against the forme of Law,
Proceed thus rashly in the Villaines death,
But that the extreme perill of the case,
The Peace of England, and our Persons safetie,
Enforc'd vs to this Execution.

Maior. Now faire befall you, he deseru'd his death,
And your good Graces both haue well proceeded,
To warne false Traytors from the like Attempts.

Buck. I neuer look'd for better at his hands,
After he once fell in with Mistresse *Shore*:
Yet had we not determin'd he should dye,
Vntill your Lordship came to see his end,
Which now the louing haste of these our friends,
Something against our meanings, haue preuented;
Because, my Lord, I would haue had you heard
The Traytor speake, and timorously confesse
The manner and the purpose of his Treasons:
That you might well haue signify'd the same
Vnto the Citizens, who haply may
Misconster vs in him, and wayle his death.

Ma. But, my good Lord, your Graces words shal serue,
As well as I had seene, and heard him speake:
And doe not doubt, right Noble Princes both,
But Ile acquaint our dutious Citizens
With all your iust proceedings in this case.

Rich. And to that end we wish'd your Lordship here,
T'auoid the Censures of the carping World.

Buck. Which since you come too late of our intent,
Yet witnesse what you heare we did intend:
And so, my good Lord Maior, we bid farwell.

Exit Maior.

Rich. Goe after, after, Cousin *Buckingham.*
The Maior towards Guild-Hall hyes him in all poste:
There, at your meetest vantage of the time,
Inferre the Bastardie of *Edwards* Children:
Tell them, how *Edward* put to death a Citizen,
Onely for saying, he would make his Sonne
Heire to the Crowne, meaning indeed his House,
Which, by the Signe thereof, was tearmed so.
Moreouer, vrge his hatefull Luxurie,
And beastiall appetite in change of Lust,
Which stretcht vnto their Seruants, Daughters, Wiues,
Euen where his raging eye, or sauage heart,
Without controll, lusted to make a prey.
Nay, for a need, thus farre come neere my Person:
Tell them, when that my Mother went with Child
Of that insatiate *Edward*; Noble *Yorke*,
My Princely Father, then had Warres in France,
And by true computation of the time,
Found, that the Issue was not his begot:
Which well appeared in his Lineaments,
Being nothing like the Noble Duke, my Father:
Yet touch this sparingly, as 'twere farre off,
Because, my Lord, you know my Mother liues.

Buck. Doubt not, my Lord, Ile play the Orator,
As if the Golden Fee, for which I plead,
Were for my selfe: and so, my Lord, adue.

Rich. If you thriue wel, bring them to Baynards Castle,
Where you shall finde me well accompanied
With reuerend Fathers, and well-learned Bishops.

Buck. I goe, and towards three or foure a Clocke
Looke for the Newes that the Guild-Hall affoords.

Exit Buckingham.

Rich. Goe *Louell* with all speed to Doctor *Shaw*,
Goe thou to Fryer *Penker*, bid them both
Meet me within this houre at Baynards Castle. *Exit.*
Now will I goe to take some priuie order,
To draw the Brats of *Clarence* out of sight,
And to giue order, that no manner person
Haue any time recourse vnto the Princes. *Exeunt.*

Enter a Scriuener.

Scr. Here is the Indictment of the good Lord *Hastings*,
Which in a set Hand fairely is engross'd,
That it may be to day read o're in *Paules.*
And marke how well the sequell hangs together:
Eleuen houres I haue spent to write it ouer,
For yester-night by *Catesby* was it sent me,
The Precedent was full as long a doing,
And yet within these fiue houres *Hastings* liu'd,
Vntainted, vnexamin'd, free, at libertie.
Here's a good World the while.
Who is so grosse, that cannot see this palpable deuice?
Yet

Yet who so bold, but sayes he sees it not?
Bad is the World, and all will come to nought,
When such ill dealing must be seene in thought. *Exit.*

Enter Richard and Buckingham at seuerall Doores.

Rich. How now, how now, what say the Citizens?
Buck. Now by the holy Mother of our Lord,
The Citizens are mum, say not a word.
Rich. Toucht you the Bastardie of *Edwards* Children?
Buck. I did, with his Contract with Lady *Lucy*,
And his Contract by Deputie in France,
Th'vnsatiate greedinesse of his desire,
And his enforcement of the Citie Wiues,
His Tyrannie for Trifles, his owne Bastardie,
As being got, your Father then in France,
And his resemblance, being not like the Duke.
Withall, I did inferre your Lineaments,
Being the right *Idea* of your Father,
Both in your forme, and Noblenesse of Minde:
Layd open all your Victories in Scotland,
Your Discipline in Warre, Wisdome in Peace,
Your Bountie, Vertue, faire Humilitie:
Indeed, left nothing fitting for your purpose,
Vntoucht, or sleightly handled in discourse.
And when my Oratorie drew toward end,
I bid them that did loue their Countries good,
Cry, God saue *Richard*, Englands Royall King.
 Rich. And did they so?
 Buck. No, so God helpe me, they spake not a word,
But like dumbe Statues, or breathing Stones,
Star'd each on other, and look'd deadly pale:
Which when I saw, I reprehended them,
And ask'd the Maior, what meant this wilfull silence?
His answer was, the people were not vsed
To be spoke to, but by the Recorder.
Then he was vrg'd to tell my Tale againe:
Thus sayth the Duke, thus hath the Duke inferr'd,
But nothing spoke, in warrant from himselfe.
When he had done, some followers of mine owne,
At lower end of the Hall, hurld vp their Caps,
And some tenne voyces cry'd, God saue King *Richard*:
And thus I tooke the vantage of those few.
Thankes gentle Citizens, and friends, quoth I,
This generall applause, and chearefull showt,
Argues your wisdome, and your loue to *Richard*:
And euen here brake off, and came away.
 Rich. What tongue-lesse Blockes were they,
Would they not speake?
Will not the Maior then, and his Brethren, come?
 Buck. The Maior is here at hand: intend some feare,
Be not you spoke with, but by mightie suit:
And looke you get a Prayer-Booke in your hand,
And stand betweene two Church-men, good my Lord,
For on that ground Ile make a holy Descant:
And be not easily wonne to our requests,
Play the Maids part, still answer nay, and take it.
 Rich. I goe: and if you plead as well for them,
As I can say nay to thee for my selfe,
No doubt we bring it to a happie issue.
 Buck. Go, go vp to the Leads, the Lord Maior knocks.

Enter the Maior, and Citizens.

Welcome, my Lord, I dance attendance here,
I thinke the Duke will not be spoke withall.

Enter Catesby.

 Buck. Now *Catesby*, what sayes your Lord to my request?
 Catesby. He doth entreat your Grace, my Noble Lord,
To visit him to morrow, or next day:
He is within, with two right reuerend Fathers,
Diuinely bent to Meditation,
And in no Worldly suites would he be mou'd,
To draw him from his holy Exercise.
 Buck. Returne, good *Catesby*, to the gracious Duke,
Tell him, my selfe, the Maior and Aldermen,
In deepe designes, in matter of great moment,
No lesse importing then our generall good,
Are come to haue some conference with his Grace.
 Catesby. Ile signifie so much vnto him straight. *Exit.*
 Buck. Ah ha, my Lord, this Prince is not an *Edward*,
He is not lulling on a lewd Loue-Bed,
But on his Knees, at Meditation:
Not dallying with a Brace of Curtizans,
But meditating with two deepe Diuines:
Not sleeping, to engrosse his idle Body,
But praying, to enrich his watchfull Soule.
Happie were England, would this vertuous Prince
Take on his Grace the Soueraigntie thereof.
But sure I feare we shall not winne him to it.
 Maior. Marry God defend his Grace should say vs nay.
 Buck. I feare he will: here *Catesby* comes againe.

Enter Catesby.

Now *Catesby*, what sayes his Grace?
 Catesby. He wonders to what end you haue assembled
Such troopes of Citizens, to come to him,
His Grace not being warn'd thereof before:
He feares, my Lord, you meane no good to him.
 Buck. Sorry I am, my Noble Cousin should
Suspect me, that I meane no good to him:
By Heauen, we come to him in perfit loue,
And so once more returne, and tell his Grace. *Exit.*
When holy and deuout Religious men
Are at their Beades, 'tis much to draw them thence,
So sweet is zealous Contemplation.

Enter Richard aloft, betweene two Bishops.

 Maior. See where his Grace stands, tweene two Clergie men.
 Buck. Two Props of Vertue, for a Christian Prince,
To stay him from the fall of Vanitie:
And see a Booke of Prayer in his hand,
True Ornaments to know a holy man.
Famous *Plantagenet*, most gracious Prince,
Lend fauourable eare to our requests,
And pardon vs the interruption
Of thy Deuotion, and right Christian Zeale.
 Rich. My Lord, there needes no such Apologie:
I doe beseech your Grace to pardon me,
Who earnest in the seruice of my God,
Deferr'd the visitation of my friends.
But leauing this, what is your Graces pleasure?
 Buck. Euen that (I hope) which pleaseth God aboue,
And all good men, of this vngouern'd Ile.
 Rich. I doe suspect I haue done some offence,
That seemes disgracious in the Cities eye,
And that you come to reprehend my ignorance.

Buck. You haue, my Lord:
Would it might please your Grace,
On our entreaties, to amend your fault.

　Rich. Else wherefore breathe I in a Christian Land.

　Buck. Know then, it is your fault, that you resigne
The Supreme Seat, the Throne Maiesticall,
The Sceptred Office of your Ancestors,
Your State of Fortune, and your Deaw of Birth,
The Lineall Glory of your Royall House,
To the corruption of a blemisht Stock;
Whiles in the mildnesse of your sleepie thoughts,
Which here we waken to our Countries good,
The Noble Ile doth want his proper Limmes:
His Face defac'd with skarres of Infamie,
His Royall Stock grafft with ignoble Plants,
And almost shouldred in the swallowing Gulfe
Of darke Forgetfulnesse, and deepe Obliuion.
Which to recure, we heartily solicite
Your gracious selfe to take on you the charge
And Kingly Gouernment of this your Land:
Not as Protector, Steward, Substitute,
Or lowly Factor, for anothers gaine;
But as successiuely, from Blood to Blood,
Your Right of Birth, your Empyrie, your owne.
For this, consorted with the Citizens,
Your very Worshipfull and louing friends,
And by their vehement instigation,
In this iust Cause come I to moue your Grace.

　Rich. I cannot tell, if to depart in silence,
Or bitterly to speake in your reproofe,
Best fitteth my Degree, or your Condition.
If not to answer, you might haply thinke,
Tongue-ty'd Ambition, not replying, yeelded
To beare the Golden Yoake of Soueraigntie,
Which fondly you would here impose on me.
If to reproue you for this suit of yours,
So season'd with your faithfull loue to me,
Then on the other side I check'd my friends.
Therefore to speake, and to auoid the first,
And then in speaking, not to incurre the last,
Definitiuely thus I answer you.
Your loue deserues my thankes, but my desert
Vnmeritable, shunnes your high request.
First, if all Obstacles were cut away,
And that my Path were euen to the Crowne,
As the ripe Reuenue, and due of Birth:
Yet so much is my pouertie of spirit,
So mightie, and so manie my defects,
That I would rather hide me from my Greatnesse,
Being a Barke to brooke no mightie Sea;
Then in my Greatnesse couet to be hid,
And in the vapour of my Glory smother'd.
But God be thank'd, there is no need of me,
And much I need to helpe you, were there need:
The Royall Tree hath left vs Royall Fruit,
Which mellow'd by the stealing howres of time,
Will well become the Seat of Maiestie,
And make (no doubt) vs happy by his Reigne.
On him I lay that, you would lay on me,
The Right and Fortune of his happie Starres,
Which God defend that I should wring from him.

　Buck. My Lord, this argues Conscience in your Grace,
But the respects thereof are nice, and triuiall,
All circumstances well considered.
You say, that *Edward* is your Brothers Sonne,
So say we too, but not by *Edwards* Wife:
For first was he contract to Lady *Lucie*,
Your Mother liues a Witnesse to his Vow;
And afterward by substitute betroth'd
To *Bona*, Sister to the King of France.
These both put off, a poore Petitioner,
A Care-cras'd Mother to a many Sonnes,
A Beautie-waining, and distressed Widow,
Euen in the after-noone of her best dayes,
Made prize and purchase of his wanton Eye,
Seduc'd the pitch, and height of his degree,
To base declension, and loath'd Bigamie.
By her, in his vnlawfull Bed, he got
This *Edward*, whom our Manners call the Prince.
More bitterly could I expostulate,
Saue that for reuerence to some aliue,
I giue a sparing limit to my Tongue.
Then good, my Lord, take to your Royall selfe
This proffer'd benefit of Dignitie:
If not to blesse vs and the Land withall,
Yet to draw forth your Noble Ancestrie
From the corruption of abusing times,
Vnto a Lineall true deriued course.

　Maior. Do good my Lord, your Citizens entreat you.

　Buck. Refuse not, mightie Lord, this proffer'd loue.

　Catesb. O make them ioyfull, grant their lawfull suit.

　Rich. Alas, why would you heape this Care on me?
I am vnfit for State, and Maiestie:
I doe beseech you take it not amisse,
I cannot, nor I will not yeeld to you.

　Buck. If you refuse it, as in loue and zeale,
Loth to depose the Child, your Brothers Sonne,
As well we know your tendernesse of heart,
And gentle, kinde, effeminate remorse,
Which we haue noted in you to your Kindred,
And egally indeede to all Estates:
Yet know, where you accept our suit, or no,
Your Brothers Sonne shall neuer reigne our King,
But we will plant some other in the Throne,
To the disgrace and downe-fall of your House:
And in this resolution here we leaue you.
Come Citizens, we will entreat no more.   *Exeunt.*

　Catesb. Call him againe, sweet Prince, accept their suit:
If you denie them, all the Land will rue it.

　Rich. Will you enforce me to a world of Cares.
Call them againe, I am not made of Stones,
But penetrable to your kinde entreaties,
Albeit against my Conscience and my Soule.

　　Enter Buckingham, and the rest.

Cousin of Buckingham, and sage graue men,
Since you will buckle fortune on my back,
To beare her burthen, where I will or no.
I must haue patience to endure the Load:
But if black Scandall, or foule-fac'd Reproach,
Attend the sequell of your Imposition,
Your meere enforcement shall acquittance me
From all the impure blots and staynes thereof;
For God doth know, and you may partly see,
How farre I am from the desire of this.

　Maior. God blesse your Grace, wee see it, and will
say it.

　Rich. In saying so, you shall but say the truth.

　Buck. Then I salute you with this Royall Title,
Long liue King *Richard*, Englands worthie King.

　All. Amen.

　Buck. To morrow may it please you to be Crown'd.

　Rich. Euen when you please, for you will haue it so.

　　　　　　　　　　　　　　　　　　　　Buck. To

Buck. To morrow then we will attend your Grace,
And so most ioyfully we take our leaue.
Rich. Come, let vs to our holy Worke againe.
Farewell my Cousins, farewell gentle friends. *Exeunt.*

Actus Quartus. Scena Prima.

*Enter the Queene, Anne Duchesse of Gloucester, the
Duchesse of Yorke, and Marquesse Dorset.*

Duch. Yorke. Who meetes vs heere?
My Neece *Plantagenet*,
Led in the hand of her kind Aunt of Gloster?
Now, for my Life, shee's wandring to the Tower,
On pure hearts loue, to greet the tender Prince.
Daughter, well met.
 Anne. God giue your Graces both, a happie
And a ioyfull time of day.
 Qu. As much to you, good Sister: whither away?
 Anne. No farther then the Tower, and as I guesse,
Vpon the like deuotion as your selues,
To gratulate the gentle Princes there.
 Qu. Kind Sister thankes, wee'le enter all together:

Enter the Lieutenant.

And in good time, here the Lieutenant comes.
Master Lieutenant, pray you, by your leaue,
How doth the Prince, and my young Sonne of *Yorke*?
 Lieu. Right well, deare Madame: by your patience,
I may not suffer you to visit them,
The King hath strictly charg'd the contrary.
 Qu. The King? who's that?
 Lieu. I meane, the Lord Protector.
 Qu. The Lord protect him from that Kingly Title.
Hath he set bounds betweene their loue, and me?
I am their Mother, who shall barre me from them?
 Duch. Yorke. I am their Fathers Mother, I will see
them.
 Anne. Their Aunt I am in law, in loue their Mother:
Then bring me to their sights, Ile beare thy blame,
And take thy Office from thee, on my perill.
 Lieu. No, Madame, no; I may not leaue it so:
I am bound by Oath, and therefore pardon me.
 Exit Lieutenant.

Enter Stanley.

Stanley. Let me but meet you Ladies one howre hence,
And Ile salute your Grace of Yorke as Mother,
And reuerend looker on of two faire Queenes.
Come Madame, you must straight to Westminster,
There to be crowned *Richards* Royall Queene.
 Qu. Ah, cut my Lace asunder,
That my pent heart may haue some scope to beat,
Or else I swoone with this dead-killing newes.
 Anne. Despightfull tidings, O vnpleasing newes.
 Dorf. Be of good cheare: Mother, how fares your
Grace?
 Qu. O *Dorset*, speake not to me, get thee gone,
Death and Destruction dogges thee at thy heeles,
Thy Mothers Name is ominous to Children.

If thou wilt out-strip Death, goe crosse the Seas,
And liue with *Richmond*, from the reach of Hell.
Goe hye thee, hye thee from this slaughter-house,
Lest thou encrease the number of the dead,
And make me dye the thrall of *Margarets* Curse,
Nor Mother, Wife, nor Englands counted Queene.
 Stanley. Full of wise care, is this your counsaile, Madame:
Take all the swift aduantage of the howres:
You shall haue Letters from me to my Sonne,
In your behalfe, to meet you on the way:
Be not ta'ne tardie by vnwise delay.
 Duch. Yorke. O ill dispersing Winde of Miserie,
O my accursed Wombe, the Bed of Death:
A Cockatrice hast thou hatcht to the World,
Whose vnauoided Eye is murtherous.
 Stanley. Come, Madame, come, I in all haste was sent.
 Anne. And I with all vnwillingnesse will goe.
O would to God, that the inclusiue Verge
Of Golden Mettall, that must round my Brow,
Were red hot Steele, to seare me to the Braines,
Anoynted let me be with deadly Venome,
And dye ere men can say, God saue the Queene.
 Qu. Goe, goe, poore soule, I enuie not thy glory,
To feed my humor, wish thy selfe no harme.
 Anne. No: why? When he that is my Husband now,
Came to me, as I follow'd *Henries* Corse,
When scarce the blood was well washt from his hands,
Which issued from my other Angell Husband,
And that deare Saint, which then I weeping follow'd:
O, when I say I look'd on *Richards* Face,
This was my Wish: Be thou (quoth I) accurst,
For making me, so young, so old a Widow:
And when thou wed'ft, let sorrow haunt thy Bed;
And be thy Wife, if any be so mad,
More miserable, by the Life of thee,
Then thou hast made me, by my deare Lords death.
Loe, ere I can repeat this Curse againe,
Within so small a time, my Womans heart
Grossely grew captiue to his honey words,
And prou'd the subiect of mine owne Soules Curse,
Which hitherto hath held mine eyes from rest:
For neuer yet one howre in his Bed
Did I enioy the golden deaw of sleepe,
But with his timorous Dreames was still awak'd.
Besides, he hates me for my Father *Warwicke*,
And will (no doubt) shortly be rid of me.
 Qu. Poore heart adieu, I pittie thy complaining.
 Anne. No more, then with my soule I mourne for
yours.
 Dorf. Farewell, thou wofull welcommer of glory.
 Anne. Adieu, poore soule, that tak'st thy leaue
of it.
 Du. Y. Go thou to *Richmond*, & good fortune guide thee,
Go thou to *Richard*, and good Angels tend thee,
Go thou to Sanctuarie, and good thoughts possesse thee,
I to my Graue, where peace and rest lye with mee.
Eightie odde yeeres of sorrow haue I seene,
And each howres ioy wrackt with a weeke of teene.
 Qu. Stay, yet looke backe with me vnto the Tower.
Pitty, you ancient Stones, those tender Babes,
Whom Enuie hath immur'd within your Walls,
Rough Cradle for such little prettie ones,
Rude ragged Nurse, old sullen Play-fellow,
For tender Princes: vse my Babies well;
So foolish Sorrowes bids your Stones farewell.
 Exeunt.

Scena Secunda.

Sound a Sennet. Enter Richard in pompe, Buckingham, Catesby, Ratcliffe, Louel.

Rich. Stand all apart. Cousin of Buckingham.
Buck. My gracious Soueraigne.
Rich. Giue me thy hand. *Sound.*
Thus high, by thy aduice, and thy assistance,
Is King *Richard* seated:
But shall we weare these Glories for a day?
Or shall they last, and we reioyce in them?
 Buck. Still liue they, and for euer let them last.
 Rich. Ah *Buckingham*, now doe I play the Touch,
To trie if thou be currant Gold indeed:
Young *Edward* liues, thinke now what I would speake.
 Buck. Say on my louing Lord.
 Rich. Why *Buckingham*, I say I would be King.
 Buck. Why so you are, my thrice-renowned Lord.
 Rich. Ha? am I King? 'tis so: but *Edward* liues.
 Buck. True, Noble Prince.
 Rich. O bitter consequence!
That *Edward* still should liue true Noble Prince.
Cousin, thou wast not wont to be so dull.
Shall I be plaine? I wish the Bastards dead,
And I would haue it suddenly perform'd.
What say'st thou now? speake suddenly, be briefe.
 Buck. Your Grace may doe your pleasure.
 Rich. Tut, tut, thou art all Ice, thy kindnesse freezes:
Say, haue I thy consent, that they shall dye?
 Buc. Giue me some litle breath, some pawse, deare Lord,
Before I positiuely speake in this:
I will resolue you herein presently. *Exit Buck.*
 Catesby. The King is angry, see he gnawes his Lippe.
 Rich. I will conuerse with Iron-witted Fooles,
And vnrespectiue Boyes: none are for me,
That looke into me with considerate eyes,
High-reaching *Buckingham* growes circumspect.
Boy.
 Page. My Lord.
 Rich. Know'st thou not any, whom corrupting Gold
Will tempt vnto a close exploit of Death?
 Page. I know a discontented Gentleman,
Whose humble meanes match not his haughtie spirit:
Gold were as good as twentie Orators,
And will (no doubt) tempt him to any thing.
 Rich. What is his Name?
 Page. His Name, my Lord, is *Tirrell*.
 Rich. I partly know the man: goe call him hither,
Boy. *Exit.*
The deepe reuoluing wittie *Buckingham*,
No more shall be the neighbor to my counsailes.
Hath he so long held out with me, vntyr'd,
And stops he now for breath? Well, be it so.

Enter Stanley.

How now, Lord *Stanley*, what's the newes?
 Stanley. Know my louing Lord, the Marquesse *Dorset*
As I heare, is fled to *Richmond*,
In the parts where he abides.
 Rich. Come hither *Catesby*, rumor it abroad,
That *Anne* my Wife is very grieuous sicke,
I will take order for her keeping close.
Inquire me out some meane poore Gentleman,
Whom I will marry straight to *Clarence* Daughter:
The Boy is foolish, and I feare not him.
Looke how thou dream'st: I say againe, giue out,
That *Anne*, my Queene, is sicke, and like to dye.
About it, for it stands me much vpon
To stop all hopes, whose growth may dammage me.
I must be marryed to my Brothers Daughter,
Or else my Kingdome stands on brittle Glasse:
Murther her Brothers, and then marry her,
Vncertaine way of gaine. But I am in
So farre in blood, that sinne will pluck on sinne,
Teare-falling Pittie dwells not in this Eye.

Enter Tyrrel.

Is thy Name *Tyrrel*?
 Tyr. *Iames Tyrrel*, and your most obedient subiect.
 Rich. Art thou indeed?
 Tyr. Proue me, my gracious Lord.
 Rich. Dar'st thou resolue to kill a friend of mine?
 Tyr. Please you:
But I had rather kill two enemies.
 Rich. Why then thou hast it: two deepe enemies,
Foes to my Rest, and my sweet sleepes disturbers,
Are they that I would haue thee deale vpon:
Tyrrel, I meane those Bastards in the Tower.
 Tyr. Let me haue open meanes to come to them,
And soone Ile rid you from the feare of them.
 Rich. Thou sing'st sweet Musique:
Hearke, come hither *Tyrrel*,
Goe by this token: rise, and lend thine Eare, *Whispers.*
There is no more but so: say it is done,
And I will loue thee, and preferre thee for it.
 Tyr. I will dispatch it straight. *Exit.*

Enter Buckingham.

 Buck. My Lord, I haue consider'd in my minde,
The late request that you did sound me in.
 Rich. Well, let that rest: *Dorset* is fled to *Richmond.*
 Buck. I heare the newes, my Lord.
 Rich. *Stanley*, hee is your Wiues Sonne: well, looke
vnto it.
 Buck. My Lord, I clayme the gift, my due by promise,
For which your Honor and your Faith is pawn'd,
Th'Earledome of Hertford, and the moueables,
Which you haue promised I shall possesse.
 Rich. *Stanley* looke to your Wife: if she conuey
Letters to *Richmond*, you shall answer it.
 Buck. What sayes your Highnesse to my iust request?
 Rich. I doe remember me, *Henry* the Sixt
Did prophecie, that *Richmond* should be King,
When *Richmond* was a little peeuish Boy.
A King perhaps.
 Buck. May it please you to resolue me in my suit.
 Rich. Thou troublest me, I am not in the vaine. *Exit.*
 Buck. And is it thus? repayes he my deepe seruice
With such contempt? made I him King for this?
O let me thinke on *Hastings*, and be gone
To Brecnock, while my fearefull Head is on. *Exit.*

Enter Tyrrel.

 Tyr. The tyrannous and bloodie Act is done,
The most arch deed of pittious massacre

That euer yet this Land was guilty of:
Dighton and Forrest, who I did suborne
To do this peece of ruthfull Butchery,
Albeit they were flesht Villaines, bloody Dogges,
Melted with tendernesse, and milde compassion,
Wept like to Children, in their deaths sad Story.
O thus (quoth Dighton) lay the gentle Babes:
Thus, thus (quoth Forrest) girdling one another
Within their Alablaster innocent Armes:
Their lips were foure red Roses on a stalke,
And in their Summer Beauty kist each other.
A Booke of Prayers on their pillow lay,
Which one (quoth Forrest) almost chang'd my minde:
But oh the Diuell, there the Villaine stopt:
When Dighton thus told on, we smothered
The most replenished sweet worke of Nature,
That from the prime Creation ere she framed.
Hence both are gone with Conscience and Remorse,
They could not speake, and so I left them both,
To beare this tydings to the bloody King.

Enter Richard.

And heere he comes. All health my Soueraigne Lord.
 Ric. Kinde *Tirrell*, am I happy in thy Newes.
 Tir. If to haue done the thing you gaue in charge,
Beget your happinesse, be happy then,
For it is done.
 Rich. But did'st thou see them dead.
 Tir. I did my Lord.
 Rich. And buried gentle *Tirrell*.
 Tir. The Chaplaine of the Tower hath buried them,
But where (to say the truth) I do not know.
 Rich. Come to me *Tirrel* soone, and after Supper,
When thou shalt tell the processe of their death.
Meane time, but thinke how I may do the good,
And be inheritor of thy desire.
Farewell till then.
 Tir. I humbly take my leaue.
 Rich. The Sonne of *Clarence* haue I pent vp close,
His daughter meanly haue I matcht in marriage,
The Sonnes of *Edward* sleepe in *Abrahams* bosome,
And *Anne* my wife hath bid this world good night.
Now for I know the Britaine *Richmond* aymes
At yong *Elizabeth* my brothers daughter,
And by that knot lookes proudly on the Crowne,
To her go I, a iolly thriuing wooer.

Enter Ratcliffe.

 Rat. My Lord.
 Rich. Good or bad newes, that thou com'st in so bluntly?
 Rat. Bad news my Lord, *Mourton* is fled to Richmond,
And Buckingham backt with the hardy Welshmen
Is in the field, and still his power encreaseth.
 Rich. Ely with Richmond troubles me more neere,
Then Buckingham and his rash leuied Strength.
Come, I haue learn'd, that fearfull commenting
Is leaden seruitor to dull delay.
Delay leds impotent and Snaile-pac'd Beggery:
Then fierie expedition be my wing,
Ioues Mercury, and Herald for a King:
Go muster men: My counsaile is my Sheeld,
We must be breefe, when Traitors braue the Field.
Exeunt.

Scena Tertia.

Enter old Queene Margaret.

 Mar. So now prosperity begins to mellow,
And drop into the rotten mouth of death:
Heere in these Confines slily haue I lurkt,
To watch the waining of mine enemies.
A dire induction, am I witnesse to,
And will to France, hoping the consequence
Will proue as bitter, blacke, and Tragicall.
Withdraw thee wretched *Margaret*, who comes heere?

Enter Dutchesse and Queene.

 Qu. Ah my poore Princes! ah my tender Babes:
My vnblowed Flowres, new appearing sweets:
If yet your gentle soules flye in the Ayre,
And be not fixt in doome perpetuall,
Houer about me with your ayery wings,
And heare your mothers Lamentation.
 Mar. Houer about her, say that right for right
Hath dim'd your Infant morne, to Aged night.
 Dut. So many miseries haue craz'd my voyce,
That my woe-wearied tongue is still and mute.
Edward Plantagenet, why art thou dead?
 Mar. *Plantagenet* doth quit *Plantagenet*,
Edward for *Edward*, payes a dying debt.
 Qu. Wilt thou, O God, flye from such gentle Lambs,
And throw them in the intrailes of the Wolfe?
When didst thou sleepe, when such a deed was done?
 Mar. When holy *Harry* dyed, and my sweet Sonne.
 Dut. Dead life, blind sight, poore mortall liuing ghost,
Woes Scene, Worlds shame, Graues due, by life vsurpt,
Breefe abstract and record of tedious dayes,
Rest thy vnrest on Englands lawfull earth,
Vnlawfully made drunke with innocent blood.
 Qu. Ah that thou would'st assoone affoord a Graue,
As thou canst yeeld a melancholly seate:
Then would I hide my bones, not rest them heere,
Ah who hath any cause to mourne but wee?
 Mar. If ancient sorrow be most reuerent,
Giue mine the benefit of signeurie,
And let my greefes frowne on the vpper hand
If sorrow can admit Society.
I had an *Edward*, till a *Richard* kill'd him:
I had a Husband, till a *Richard* kill'd him:
Thou had'st an *Edward*, till a *Richard* kill'd him:
Thou had'st a *Richard*, till a *Richard* kill'd him.
 Dut. I had a *Richard* too, and thou did'st kill him;
I had a *Rutland* too, thou hop'st to kill him.
 Mar. Thou had'st a *Clarence* too,
And *Richard* kill'd him.
From forth the kennell of thy wombe hath crept
A Hell-hound that doth hunt vs all to death:
That Dogge, that had his teeth before his eyes,
To worry Lambes, and lap their gentle blood:
That foule defacer of Gods handy worke:
That reignes in gauled eyes of weeping soules:
That excellent grand Tyrant of the earth,
Thy wombe let loose to chase vs to our graues.
O vpright, iust, and true-disposing God,
How do I thanke thee, that this carnall Curre
Prayes

Prayes on the issue of his Mothers body,
And makes her Pue-fellow with others mone.

Dut. Oh *Harries* wife, triumph not in my woes:
God witnesse with me, I haue wept for thine.

Mar. Beare with me: I am hungry for reuenge,
And now I cloy me with beholding it.
Thy *Edward* he is dead, that kill'd my *Edward*,
The other *Edward* dead, to quit my *Edward*:
Yong *Yorke*, he is but boote, because both they
Matcht not the high perfection of my losse.
Thy *Clarence* he is dead, that stab'd my *Edward*,
And the beholders of this franticke play,
Th'adulterate *Hastings, Riuers, Vaughan, Gray,*
Vntimely smother'd in their dusky Graues.
Richard yet liues, Hels blacke Intelligencer,
Onely reseru'd their Factor, to buy soules,
And send them thither: But at hand, at hand
Insues his pittious and vnpittied end.
Earth gapes, Hell burnes, Fiends roare, Saints pray,
To haue him sodainly conuey'd from hence:
Cancell his bond of life, deere God I pray,
That I may liue and say, The Dogge is dead.

Qu. O thou did'st prophesie, the time would come,
That I should wish for thee to helpe me curse
That bottel'd Spider, that foule bunch-back'd Toad.

Mar. I call'd thee then, vaine flourish of my fortune:
I call'd thee then, poore Shadow, painted Queen,
The presentation of but what I was;
The flattering Index of a direfull Pageant;
One heau'd a high, to be hurl'd downe below:
A Mother onely mockt with two faire Babes;
A dreame of what thou wast, a garish Flagge
To be the ayme of euery dangerous Shot;
A signe of Dignity, a Breath, a Bubble;
A Queene in ieast, onely to fill the Scene.
Where is thy Husband now? Where be thy Brothers?
Where be thy two Sonnes? Wherein dost thou Ioy?
Who sues, and kneeles, and sayes, God saue the Queene?
Where be the bending Peeres that flattered thee?
Where be the thronging Troopes that followed thee?
Decline all this, and see what now thou art.
For happy Wife, a most distressed Widdow:
For ioyfull Mother, one that wailes the name:
For one being sued too, one that humbly sues:
For Queene, a very Caytiffe, crown'd with care:
For she that scorn'd at me, now scorn'd of me:
For she being feared of all, now fearing one:
For she commanding all, obey'd of none.
Thus hath the course of Iustice whirl'd about,
And left thee but a very prey to time,
Hauing no more but Thought of what thou wast.
To torture thee the more, being what thou art,
Thou didst vsurpe my place, and dost thou not
Vsurpe the iust proportion of my Sorrow?
Now thy proud Necke, beares halfe my burthen'd yoke,
From which, euen heere I slip my wearied head,
And leaue the burthen of it all, on thee.
Farwell Yorkes wife, and Queene of sad mischance,
These English woes, shall make me smile in France.

Qu. O thou well skill'd in Curses, stay a-while,
And teach me how to curse mine enemies.

Mar. Forbeare to sleepe the night, and fast the day:
Compare dead happinesse, with liuing woe:
Thinke that thy Babes were sweeter then they were,
And he that slew them fowler then he is:
Bett'ring thy losse, makes the bad causer worse,
Reuoluing this, will teach thee how to Curse.

Qu. My words are dull, O quicken them with thine.

Mar. Thy woes will make them sharpe,
And pierce like mine. *Exit Margaret.*

Dut. Why should calamity be full of words?

Qu. Windy Atturnies to their Clients Woes,
Ayery succeeders of intestine ioyes,
Poore breathing Orators of miseries,
Let them haue scope, though what they will impart,
Helpe nothing els, yet do they ease the hart.

Dut. If so then, be not Tongue-ty'd: go with me,
And in the breath of bitter words, let's smother
My damned Son, that thy two sweet Sonnes smother'd,
The Trumpet sounds, be copious in exclaimes.

Enter King Richard, and his Traine.

Rich. Who intercepts me in my Expedition?

Dut. O she, that might haue intercepted thee
By strangling thee in her accursed wombe,
From all the slaughters (Wretch) that thou hast done.

Qu. Hid'st thou that Forhead with a Golden Crowne
Where't should be branded, if that right were right?
The slaughter of the Prince that ow'd that Crowne,
And the dyre death of my poore Sonnes, and Brothers.
Tell me thou Villaine-slaue, where are my Children?

Dut. Thou Toad, thou Toade,
Where is thy Brother *Clarence*?
And little *Ned Plantagenet* his Sonne?

Qu. Where is the gentle *Riuers, Vaughan, Gray*?

Dut. Where is kinde *Hastings*?

Rich. A flourish Trumpets, strike Alarum Drummes:
Let not the Heauens heare these Tell-tale women
Raile on the Lords Annointed. Strike I say.
Flourish. Alarums.
Either be patient, and intreat me fayre,
Or with the clamorous report of Warre,
Thus will I drowne your exclamations.

Dut. Art thou my Sonne?

Rich. I, I thanke God, my Father, and your selfe.

Dut. Then patiently heare my impatience.

Rich. Madam, I haue a touch of your condition,
That cannot brooke the accent of reproofe.

Dut. O let me speake.

Rich. Do then, but Ile not heare.

Dut. I will be milde, and gentle in my words.

Rich. And breefe (good Mother) for I am in hast.

Dut. Art thou so hasty? I haue staid for thee
(God knowes) in torment and in agony.

Rich. And came I not at last to comfort you?

Dut. No by the holy Rood, thou know'st it well,
Thou cam'st on earth, to make the earth my Hell.
A greeuous burthen was thy Birth to me,
Tetchy and wayward was thy Infancie.
Thy School-daies frightfull, desp'rate, wilde, and furious,
Thy prime of Manhood, daring, bold, and venturous:
Thy Age confirm'd, proud, subtle, slye, and bloody,
More milde, but yet more harmfull; Kinde in hatred:
What comfortable houre canst thou name,
That euer grac'd me with thy company?

Rich. Faith none, but *Humfrey Hower*,
That call'd your Grace
To Breakefast once, forth of my company.
If I be so disgracious in your eye,
Let me march on, and not offend you Madam.
Strike vp the Drumme.

Dut. I prythee heare me speake. *Rich.*

Rich. You speake too bitterly.
Dut. Heare me a word:
For I shall neuer speake to thee againe.
Rich. So.
Dut. Either thou wilt dye, by Gods iust ordinance
Ere from this warre thou turne a Conqueror:
Or I with greefe and extreame Age shall perish,
And neuer more behold thy face againe.
Therefore take with thee my most greeuous Curse,
Which in the day of Battell tyre thee more
Then all the compleat Armour that thou wear'st.
My Prayers on the aduerse party fight,
And there the little soules of *Edwards* Children,
Whisper the Spirits of thine Enemies,
And promise them Successe and Victory:
Bloody thou art, bloody will be thy end:
Shame serues thy life, and doth thy death attend. *Exit.*

Qu. Though far more cause, yet much lesse spirit to curse
Abides in me, I say Amen to her.

Rich. Stay Madam, I must talke a word with you.
Qu. I haue no more sonnes of the Royall Blood
For thee to slaughter. For my Daughters (*Richard*)
They shall be praying Nunnes, not weeping Queenes:
And therefore leuell not to hit their liues.

Rich. You haue a daughter call'd *Elizabeth*,
Vertuous and Faire, Royall and Gracious?
Qu. And must she dye for this? O let her liue,
And Ile corrupt her Manners, staine her Beauty,
Slander my Selfe, as false to *Edwards* bed:
Throw ouer her the vaile of Infamy,
So she may liue vnscarr'd of bleeding slaughter,
I will confesse she was not *Edwards* daughter.

Rich. Wrong not her Byrth, she is a Royall Princesse.
Qu. To saue her life, Ile say she is not so.
Rich. Her life is safest onely in her byrth.
Qu. And onely in that safety, dyed her Brothers.
Rich. Loe at their Birth, good starres were opposite.
Qu. No, to their liues, ill friends were contrary.
Rich. All vnauoyded is the doome of Destiny.
Qu. True: when auoyded grace makes Destiny.
My Babes were destin'd to a fairer death,
If grace had blest thee with a fairer life.

Rich. You speake as if that I had slaine my Cosins?
Qu. Cosins indeed, and by their Vnckle couzend,
Of Comfort, Kingdome, Kindred, Freedome, Life,
Whose hand soeuer lanch'd their tender hearts,
Thy head (all indirectly) gaue direction.
No doubt the murd'rous Knife was dull and blunt,
Till it was whetted on thy stone-hard heart,
To reuell in the Intrailes of my Lambes.
But that still vse of greefe, makes wilde greefe tame,
My tongue should to thy eares not name my Boyes,
Till that my Nayles were anchor'd in thine eyes:
And I in such a desp'rate Bay of death,
Like a poore Barke, of sailes and tackling reft,
Rush all to peeces on thy Rocky bosome.

Rich. Madam, so thriue I in my enterprize
And dangerous successe of bloody warres,
As I intend more good to you and yours,
Then euer you and yours by me were harm'd.

Qu. What good is couer'd with the face of heauen,
To be discouered, that can do me good.

Rich. Th'aduancement of your children, gentle Lady
Qu. Vp to some Scaffold, there to lose their heads.
Rich. Vnto the dignity and height of Fortune,
The high Imperiall Type of this earths glory.

Qu. Flatter my sorrow with report of it:
Tell me, what State, what Dignity, what Honor,
Canst thou demise to any childe of mine.
Rich. Euen all I haue; I, and my selfe and all,
Will I withall indow a childe of thine:
So in the Lethe of thy angry soule,
Thou drowne the sad remembrance of those wrongs,
Which thou supposest I haue done to thee.
Qu. Be breefe, least that the processe of thy kindnesse
Last longer telling then thy kindnesse date.
Rich. Then know,
That from my Soule, I loue thy Daughter.
Qu. My daughters Mother thinkes it with her soule.
Rich. What do you thinke?
Qu. That thou dost loue my daughter from thy soule
So from thy Soules loue didst thou loue her Brothers,
And from my hearts loue, I do thanke thee for it.
Rich. Be not so hasty to confound my meaning:
I meane that with my Soule I loue thy daughter,
And do intend to make her Queene of England.
Qu. Well then, who dost ỹ meane shallbe her King.
Rich. Euen he that makes her Queene:
Who else should bee?
Qu. What, thou?
Rich. Euen so: How thinke you of it?
Qu. How canst thou woo her?
Rich. That I would learne of you,
As one being best acquainted with her humour.
Qu. And wilt thou learne of me?
Rich. Madam, with all my heart.
Qu. Send to her by the man that slew her Brothers,
A paire of bleeding hearts: thereon ingraue
Edward and *Yorke*, then haply will she weepe:
Therefore present to her, as sometime *Margaret*
Did to thy Father, steept in Rutlands blood,
A hand-kercheefe, which say to her did dreyne
The purple sappe from her sweet Brothers body,
And bid her wipe her weeping eyes withall.
If this inducement moue her not to loue,
Send her a Letter of thy Noble deeds:
Tell her, thou mad'st away her Vnckle *Clarence*,
Her Vnckle *Riuers*, I (and for her sake)
Mad'st quicke conueyance with her good Aunt *Anne*.
Rich. You mocke me Madam, this not the way
To win your daughter.
Qu. There is no other way,
Vnlesse thou could'st put on some other shape,
And not be *Richard*, that hath done all this.
Ric. Say that I did all this for loue of her.
Qu. Nay then indeed she cannot choose but hate thee
Hauing bought loue, with such a bloody spoyle.
Rich. Looke what is done, cannot be now amended:
Men shall deale vnaduisedly sometimes,
Which after-houres giues leysure to repent.
If I did take the Kingdome from your Sonnes,
To make amends, Ile giue it to your daughter:
If I haue kill'd the issue of your wombe,
To quicken your encrease, I will beget
Mine yssue of your blood, vpon your Daughter:
A Grandams name is little lesse in loue,
Then is the doting Title of a Mother;
They are as Children but one steppe below,
Euen of your mettall, of your very blood:
Of all one paine, saue for a night of groanes
Endur'd of her, for whom you bid like sorrow.
Your Children were vexation to your youth,

But

But mine shall be a comfort to your Age,
The losse you haue, is but a Sonne being King,
And by that losse, your Daughter is made Queene.
I cannot make you what amends I would,
Therefore accept such kindnesse as I can.
Dorset your Sonne, that with a fearfull soule
Leads discontented steppes in Forraine soyle,
This faire Alliance, quickly shall call home
To high Promotions, and great Dignity.
The King that calles your beauteous Daughter Wife,
Familiarly shall call thy *Dorset*, Brother:
Againe shall you be Mother to a King:
And all the Ruines of distressefull Times,
Repayr'd with double Riches of Content.
What? we haue many goodly dayes to see:
The liquid drops of Teares that you haue shed,
Shall come againe, transform'd to Orient Pearle,
Aduantaging their Loue, with interest
Often-times double gaine of happinesse.
Go then (my Mother) to thy Daughter go,
Make bold her bashfull yeares, with your experience,
Prepare her eares to heare a Woers Tale.
Put in her tender heart, th'aspiring Flame
Of Golden Soueraignty: Acquaint the Princesse
With the sweet silent houres of Marriage ioyes:
And when this Arme of mine hath chastised
The petty Rebell, dull-brain'd *Buckingham*,
Bound with Triumphant Garlands will I come,
And leade thy daughter to a Conquerors bed:
To whom I will retaile my Conquest wonne,
And she shalbe sole Victoresse, *Cæsars Cæsar*.

Qu. What were I best to say, her Fathers Brother
Would be her Lord? Or shall I say her Vnkle?
Or he that slew her Brothers, and her Vnkles?
Vnder what Title shall I woo for thee,
That God, the Law, my Honor, and her Loue,
Can make seeme pleasing to her tender yeares?

 Rich. Inferre faire Englands peace by this Alliance.
 Qu. Which she shall purchase with stil lasting warre.
 Rich. Tell her, the King that may command, intreats.
 Qu. That at her hands, which the kings King forbids.
 Rich. Say she shall be a High and Mighty Queene.
 Qu. To vaile the Title, as her Mother doth.
 Rich. Say I will loue her euerlastingly.
 Qu. But how long shall that title euer last?
 Rich. Sweetly in force, vnto her faire liues end.
 Qu. But how long fairely shall her sweet life last?
 Rich. As long as Heauen and Nature lengthens it.
 Qu. As long as Hell and *Richard* likes of it.
 Rich. Say, I her Soueraigne, am her Subiect low.
 Qu. But she your Subiect, lothes such Soueraignty.
 Rich. Be eloquent in my behalfe to her.
 Qu. An honest tale speeds best, being plainly told.
 Rich. Then plainly to her, tell my louing tale.
 Qu. Plaine and not honest, is too harsh a style.
 Rich. Your Reasons are too shallow, and to quicke.
 Qu. O no, my Reasons are too deepe and dead,
Too deepe and dead (poore Infants) in their graues,
Harpe on it still shall I, till heart-strings breake.
 Rich. Harpe not on that string Madam, that is past.
Now by my George, my Garter, and my Crowne.
 Qu. Prophan'd, dishonor'd, and the third vsurpt.
 Rich. I sweare.
 Qu. By nothing, for this is no Oath:
Thy George prophan'd, hath lost his Lordly Honor;
Thy Garter blemish'd, pawn'd his Knightly Vertue;
Thy Crowne vsurp'd, disgrac'd his Kingly Glory:
If something thou would'st sweare to be beleeu'd,
Sweare then by something, that thou hast not wrong'd.
 Rich. Then by my Selfe.
 Qu. Thy Selfe, is selfe-misvs'd.
 Rich. Now by the World.
 Qu. 'Tis full of thy foule wrongs.
 Rich. My Fathers death.
 Qu. Thy life hath it dishonor'd.
 Rich. Why then, by Heauen.
 Qu. Heauens wrong is most of all:
If thou didd'st feare to breake an Oath with him,
The vnity the King my husband made,
Thou had'st not broken, nor my Brothers died.
If thou had'st fear'd to breake an oath by him,
Th'Imperiall mettall, circling now thy head,
Had grac'd the tender temples of my Child,
And both the Princes had bene breathing heere,
Which now two tender Bed-fellowes for dust,
Thy broken Faith hath made the prey for Wormes.
What can'st thou sweare by now.
 Rich. The time to come.
 Qu. That thou hast wronged in the time ore-past:
For I my selfe haue many teares to wash
Heereafter time, for time past, wrong'd by thee.
The Children liue, whose Fathers thou hast slaughter'd,
Vngouern'd youth, to waile it with their age:
The Parents liue, whose Children thou hast butcher'd,
Old barren Plants, to waile it with their Age.
Sweare not by time to come, for that thou hast
Misvs'd ere vs'd, by times ill-vs'd repast.
 Rich. As I entend to prosper, and repent:
So thriue I in my dangerous Affayres
Of hostile Armes: My selfe, my selfe confound:
Heauen, and Fortune barre me happy houres:
Day, yeeld me not thy light; nor Night, thy rest.
Be opposite all Planets of good lucke
To my proceeding, if with deere hearts loue,
Immaculate deuotion, holy thoughts,
I tender not thy beautious Princely daughter.
In her, consists my Happinesse, and thine:
Without her, followes to my selfe, and thee;
Her selfe, the Land, and many a Christian soule,
Death, Desolation, Ruine, and Decay:
It cannot be auoyded, but by this:
It will not be auoyded, but by this.
Therefore deare Mother (I must call you so)
Be the Atturney of my loue to her:
Pleade what I will be, not what I haue beene;
Not my deserts, but what I will deserue:
Vrge the Necessity and state of times,
And be not peeuish found, in great Designes.
 Qu. Shall I be tempted of the Diuel thus?
 Rich. I, if the Diuell tempt you to do good.
 Qu. Shall I forget my selfe, to be my selfe.
 Rich. I, if your selfes remembrance wrong your selfe.
 Qu. Yet thou didst kil my Children.
 Rich. But in your daughters wombe I bury them.
Where in that Nest of Spicery they will breed
Selues of themselues, to your recomforture.
 Qu. Shall I go win my daughter to thy will?
 Rich. And be a happy Mother by the deed.
 Qu. I go, write to me very shortly,
And you shal vnderstand from me her mind. *Exit Q.*
 Rich. Beare her my true loues kisse, and so farewell.
Relenting Foole, and shallow-changing Woman.

The Life and Death of Richard the Third.

How now, what newes?

Enter Ratcliffe.

Rat. Most mightie Soueraigne, on the Westerne Coast
Rideth a puissant Nauie: to our Shores
Throng many doubtfull hollow-hearted friends,
Vnarm'd, and vnresolu'd to beat them backe.
'Tis thought, that *Richmond* is their Admirall:
And there they hull, expecting but the aide
Of *Buckingham*, to welcome them ashore.

Rich. Some light-foot friend post to ye Duke of Norfolk:
Ratcliffe thy selfe, or *Catesby*, where is hee?

Cat. Here, my good Lord.

Rich. Catesby, flye to the Duke.

Cat. I will, my Lord, with all conuenient haste.

Rich. Catesby come hither, poste to Salisbury:
When thou com'st thither: Dull vnmindfull Villaine,
Why stay'st thou here, and go'st not to the Duke?

Cat. First, mighty Liege, tell me your Highnesse pleasure,
What from your Grace I shall deliuer to him.

Rich. O true, good *Catesby*, bid him leuie straight
The greatest strength and power that he can make,
And meet me suddenly at Salisbury.

Cat. I goe. *Exit.*

Rat. What, may it please you, shall I doe at Salisbury?

Rich. Why, what would'st thou doe there, before I goe?

Rat. Your Highnesse told me I should poste before.

Rich. My minde is chang'd:

Enter Lord Stanley.

Stanley, what newes with you?

Sta. None, good my Liege, to please you with ye hearing,
Nor none so bad, but well may be reported.

Rich. Hoyday, a Riddle, neither good nor bad:
What need'st thou runne so many miles about,
When thou mayest tell thy Tale the neerest way?
Once more, what newes?

Stan. Richmond is on the Seas.

Rich. There let him sinke, and be the Seas on him,
White-liuer'd Runnagate, what doth he there?

Stan. I know not, mightie Soueraigne, but by guesse.

Rich. Well, as you guesse.

Stan. Stirr'd vp by *Dorset, Buckingham*, and *Morton*,
He makes for England, here to clayme the Crowne.

Rich. Is the Chayre emptie? is the Sword vnsway'd?
Is the King dead? the Empire vnpossest?
What Heire of *Yorke* is there aliue, but wee?
And who is Englands King, but great *Yorkes* Heire?
Then tell me, what makes he vpon the Seas?

Stan. Vnlesse for that, my Liege, I cannot guesse.

Rich. Vnlesse for that he comes to be your Liege,
You cannot guesse wherefore the Welchman comes.
Thou wilt reuolt, and flye to him, I feare.

Stan. No, my good Lord, therefore mistrust me not.

Rich. Where is thy Power then, to beat him back?
Where be thy Tenants, and thy followers?
Are they not now vpon the Westerne Shore,
Safe-conducting the Rebels from their Shippes?

Stan. No, my good Lord, my friends are in the North.

Rich. Cold friends to me: what do they in the North,
When they should serue their Soueraigne in the West?

Stan. They haue not been commanded, mighty King:
Pleaseth your Maiestie to giue me leaue,
Ile muster vp my friends, and meet your Grace,
Where, and what time your Maiestie shall please.

Rich. I, thou would'st be gone, to ioyne with *Richmond*:
But Ile not trust thee.

Stan. Most mightie Soueraigne,
You haue no cause to hold my friendship doubtfull,
I neuer was, nor neuer will be false.

Rich. Goe then, and muster men: but leaue behind
Your Sonne *George Stanley*: looke your heart be firme,
Or else his Heads assurance is but fraile.

Stan. So deale with him, as I proue true to you.
Exit Stanley.

Enter a Messenger.

Mess. My gracious Soueraigne, now in Deuonshire,
As I by friends am well aduertised,
Sir *Edward Courtney*, and the haughtie Prelate,
Bishop of Exeter, his elder Brother,
With many moe Confederates, are in Armes.

Enter another Messenger.

Mess. In Kent, my Liege, the *Guilfords* are in Armes,
And euery houre more Competitors
Flocke to the Rebels, and their power growes strong.

Enter another Messenger.

Mess. My Lord, the Armie of great *Buckingham*.

Rich. Out on ye, Owles, nothing but Songs of Death,
He striketh him.
There, take thou that, till thou bring better newes.

Mess. The newes I haue to tell your Maiestie,
Is, that by sudden Floods, and fall of Waters,
Buckinghams Armie is dispers'd and scatter'd,
And he himselfe wandred away alone,
No man knowes whither.

Rich. I cry thee mercie:
There is my Purse, to cure that Blow of thine.
Hath any well-aduised friend proclaym'd
Reward to him that brings the Traytor in?

Mess. Such Proclamation hath been made, my Lord.

Enter another Messenger.

Mess. Sir *Thomas Louell*, and Lord Marquesse *Dorset*,
'Tis said, my Liege, in Yorkeshire are in Armes:
But this good comfort bring I to your Highnesse,
The Brittaine Nauie is dispers'd by Tempest.
Richmond in Dorsetshire sent out a Boat
Vnto the shore, to aske those on the Banks,
If they were his Assistants, yea, or no?
Who answer'd him, they came from *Buckingham*,
Vpon his partie: he mistrusting them,
Hoys'd sayle, and made his course againe for Brittaine.

Rich. March on, march on, since we are vp in Armes,
If not to fight with forraine Enemies,
Yet to beat downe these Rebels here at home.

Enter Catesby.

Cat. My Liege, the Duke of Buckingham is taken,
That is the best newes: that the Earle of Richmond

Is

Is with a mighty power Landed at Milford,
Is colder Newes, but yet they must be told.

  Rich. Away towards Salsbury, while we reason here,
A Royall battell might be wonne and lost:
Some one take order Buckingham be brought
To Salsbury, the rest march on with me. *Florish. Exeunt*

Scena Quarta.

Enter Derby, and Sir Christopher.

  Der. Sir *Christopher*, tell *Richmond* this from me,
That in the stye of the most deadly Bore,
My Sonne *George Stanley* is frankt vp in hold:
If I reuolt, off goes yong *Georges* head,
The feare of that, holds off my present ayde.
So get thee gone: commend me to thy Lord.
Withall say, that the Queene hath heartily consented
He should espouse *Elizabeth* hit daughter.
But tell me, where is Princely Richmond now?
  Chri. At Penbroke, or at Hertford West in *Wales*.
  Der. What men of Name resort to him.
  Chri. Sir *Walter Herbert*, a renowned Souldier,
Sir *Gilbert Talbot*, Sir *William Stanley*,
Oxford, redoubted *Pembroke*, Sir *Iames Blunt*,
And *Rice ap Thomas*, with a valiant Crew,
And many other of great name and worth:
And towards London do they bend their power,
If by the way they be not fought withall.
  Der. Well hye thee to thy Lord: I kisse his hand,
My Letter will resolue him of my minde.
Farewell. *Exeunt*

Actus Quintus. Scena Prima.

*Enter Buckingham with Halberds, led
to Execution.*

  Buc. Will not King *Richard* let me speake with him?
  Sher. No my good Lord, therefore be patient.
  Buc. Hastings, and *Edwards* children, *Gray* & *Riuers*,
Holy King *Henry*, and thy faire Sonne *Edward*,
Vaughan, and all that haue miscarried
By vnder-hand corrupted foule iniustice,
If that your moody discontented soules,
Do through the clowds behold this present houre,
Euen for reuenge mocke my destruction.
This is All-soules day (Fellow) is it not?
  Sher. It is.
  Buc. Why then Al-soules day, is my bodies doomsday
This is the day, which in King *Edwards* time
I wish'd might fall on me, when I was found
False to his Children, and his Wiues Allies.
This is the day, wherein I wisht to fall
By the false Faith of him whom most I trusted.
This, this All-soules day to my fearfull Soule,
Is the determin'd respit of my wrongs:
That high All-seer, which I dallied with,
Hath turn'd my fained Prayer on my head,
And giuen in earnest, what I begg'd in iest.
Thus doth he force the swords of wicked men
To turne their owne points in their Masters bosomes.
Thus *Margarets* curse falles heauy on my necke:
When he (quoth she) shall split thy heart with sorrow,
Remember *Margaret* was a Prophetesse:
Come leade me Officers to the blocke of shame,
Wrong hath but wrong, and blame the due of blame.
  Exeunt Buckingham with Officers.

Scena Secunda.

*Enter Richmond, Oxford, Blunt, Herbert, and
others, with drum and colours.*

  Richm. Fellowes in Armes, and my most louing Frends
Bruis'd vnderneath the yoake of Tyranny,
Thus farre into the bowels of the Land,
Haue we marcht on without impediment;
And heere receiue we from our Father *Stanley*
Lines of faire comfort and encouragement:
The wretched, bloody, and vsurping Boare,
(That spoyl'd your Summer Fields, and fruitfull Vines)
Swilles your warm blood like wash, & makes his trough
In your embowel'd bosomes: This foule Swine
Is now euen in the Centry of this Isle,
Ne're to the Towne of Leicester, as we learne:
From Tamworth thither, is but one dayes march.
In Gods name cheerely on, couragious Friends,
To reape the Haruest of perpetuall peace,
By this one bloody tryall of sharpe Warre.
  Oxf. Euery mans Conscience is a thousand men,
To fight against this guilty Homicide.
  Her. I doubt not but his Friends will turne to vs.
  Blunt. He hath no friends, but what are friends for fear,
Which in his deerest neede will flye from him.
  Richm. All for our vantage, then in Gods name march,
True Hope is swift, and flyes with Swallowes wings,
Kings it makes Gods, and meaner creatures Kings.
  Exeunt Omnes.

*Enter King Richard in Armes, with Norfolke, Ratcliffe,
and the Earle of Surrey.*

  Rich. Here pitch our Tent, euen here in Bosworth field,
My Lord of Surrey, why looke you so sad?
  Sur. My heart is ten times lighter then my lookes.
  Rich. My Lord of Norfolke.
  Nor. Heere most gracious Liege.
  Rich. Norfolke, we must haue knockes:
Ha, must we not?
  Nor. We must both giue and take my louing Lord.
  Rich. Vp with my Tent, heere wil I lye to night,
But where to morrow? Well, all's one for that.
Who hath descried the number of the Traitors?
  Nor. Six or seuen thousand is their vtmost power.
  Rich. Why our Battalia trebbles that account:
Besides, the Kings name is a Tower of strength,
Which they vpon the aduerse Faction want.
Vp with the Tent: Come Noble Gentlemen,
Let vs suruey the vantage of the ground.
Call for some men of sound direction:

Let's lacke no Discipline, make no delay,
For Lords, to morrow is a busie day.   *Exeunt*

Enter Richmond, Sir William Brandon, Oxford, and Dorset.

Richm. The weary Sunne, hath made a Golden set,
And by the bright Tract of his fiery Carre,
Giues token of a goodly day to morrow,
Sir *William Brandon*, you shall beare my Standard:
Giue me some Inke and Paper in my Tent:
Ile draw the Forme and Modell of our Battaile,
Limit each Leader to his seuerall Charge,
And part in iust proportion our small Power.
My Lord of Oxford, you Sir *William Brandon*,
And your Sir *Walter Herbert* stay with me:
The Earle of Pembroke keepes his Regiment;
Good Captaine *Blunt*, beare my goodnight to him,
And by the second houre in the Morning,
Desire the Earle to see me in my Tent:
Yet one thing more (good Captaine) do for me:
Where is Lord *Stanley* quarter'd, do you know?

Blunt. Vnlesse I haue mistane his Colours much,
(Which well I am assur'd I haue not done)
His Regiment lies halfe a Mile at least
South, from the mighty Power of the King.

Richm. If without perill it be possible,
Sweet *Blunt*, make some good meanes to speak with him
And giue him from me, this most needfull Note.

Blunt. Vpon my life, my Lord, Ile vndertake it,
And so God giue you quiet rest to night.

Richm. Good night good Captaine *Blunt*:
Come Gentlemen,
Let vs consult vpon to morrowes Businesse;
Into my Tent, the Dew is rawe and cold.
    They withdraw into the Tent.

Enter Richard, Ratcliffe, Norfolke, & Catesby.

Rich. What is't a Clocke?
Cat. It's Supper time my Lord, it's nine a clocke.
King. I will not sup to night,
Giue me some Inke and Paper:
What, is my Beauer easier then it was?
And all my Armour laid into my Tent?
Cat. It is my Liege: and all things are in readinesse.
Rich. Good Norfolke, hye thee to thy charge,
Vse carefull Watch, choose trusty Centinels.
Nor. I go my Lord.
Rich. Stir with the Larke to morrow, gentle Norfolk.
Nor. I warrant you my Lord.   *Exit*
Rich. Ratcliffe.
Rat. My Lord.
Rich. Send out a Pursuiuant at Armes
To *Stanleys* Regiment: bid him bring his power
Before Sun-rising, least his Sonne *George* fall
Into the blinde Caue of eternall night.
Fill me a Bowle of Wine: Giue me a Watch,
Saddle white Surrey for the Field to morrow:
Look that my Staues be sound, & not too heauy. *Ratcliff.*
Rat. My Lord.
Rich. Saw'st the melancholly Lord Northumberland?
Rat. Thomas the Earle of Surrey, and himselfe,
Much about Cockshut time, from Troope to Troope
Went through the Army, chearing vp the Souldiers.
King. So, I am satisfied: Giue me a Bowle of Wine,
I haue not that Alacrity of Spirit,
Nor cheere of Minde that I was wont to haue.
Set it downe. Is Inke and Paper ready?
Rat. It is my Lord.
Rich. Bid my Guard watch. Leaue me.
Ratcliffe, about the mid of night come to my Tent
And helpe to arme me. Leaue me I say.   *Exit Ratclif.*

Enter Derby to Richmond in his Tent.

Der. Fortune, and Victory sit on thy Helme.
Rich. All comfort that the darke night can affoord,
Be to thy Person, Noble Father in Law.
Tell me, how fares our Noble Mother?
Der. I by Attourney, blesse thee from thy Mother,
Who prayes continually for Richmonds good:
So much for that. The silent houres steale on,
And flakie darkenesse breakes within the East.
In breefe, for so the season bids vs be,
Prepare thy Battell early in the Morning,
And put thy Fortune to th'Arbitrement
Of bloody stroakes, and mortall staring Warre:
I, as I may, that which I would, I cannot,
With best aduantage will deceiue the time,
And ayde thee in this doubtfull shocke of Armes.
But on thy side I may not be too forward,
Least being seene, thy Brother, tender *George*
Be executed in his Fathers sight.
Farewell: the leysure, and the fearfull time
Cuts off the ceremonious Vowes of Loue,
And ample enterchange of sweet Discourse,
Which so long sundred Friends should dwell vpon:
God giue vs leysure for these rites of Loue.
Once more Adieu, be valiant, and speed well.

Richm. Good Lords conduct him to his Regiment:
Ile striue with troubled noise, to take a Nap,
Lest leaden slumber peize me downe to morrow,
When I should mount with wings of Victory:
Once more, good night kinde Lords and Gentlemen.
    Exeunt. Manet Richmond.
O thou, whose Captaine I account my selfe,
Looke on my Forces with a gracious eye:
Put in their hands thy bruising Irons of wrath,
That they may crush downe with a heauy fall,
Th'vsurping Helmets of our Aduersaries:
Make vs thy ministers of Chasticement,
That we may praise thee in thy victory:
To thee I do commend my watchfull soule,
Ere I let fall the windowes of mine eyes:
Sleeping, and waking, oh defend me still.   *Sleeps.*

Enter the Ghost of Prince Edward, Sonne to Henry the sixt.

Gh. to Ri. Let me sit heauy on thy soule to morrow:
Thinke how thou stab'st me in my prime of youth
At Teukesbury: Dispaire therefore, and dye.

Ghost to Richm. Be chearefull Richmond,
For the wronged Soules
Of butcher'd Princes, fight in thy behalfe:
King *Henries* issue Richmond comforts thee.

Enter the Ghost of Henry the sixt.

Ghost. When I was mortall, my Annointed body
By thee was punched full of holes;
Thinke on the Tower, and me: Dispaire, and dye.
Harry the sixt, bids thee dispaire, and dye.

To Richm. Vertuous and holy be thou Conqueror:
Harry that prophesied thou should'st be King,
Doth comfort thee in sleepe: Liue, and flourish.

Enter

Enter the Ghost of Clarence.

Ghost. Let me sit heauy in thy soule to morrow.
I that was wash'd to death with Fulsome Wine:
Poore *Clarence* by thy guile betray'd to death:
To morrow in the battell thinke on me,
And fall thy edgelesse Sword, dispaire and dye.

To Richm. Thou off-spring of the house of Lancaster
The wronged heyres of Yorke do pray for thee,
Good Angels guard thy battell, Liue and Flourish.

Enter the Ghosts of Riuers, Gray, and Vaughan.

Riu. Let me sit heauy in thy soule to morrow,
Riuers, that dy'de at Pomfret: dispaire, and dye.

Grey. Thinke vpon *Grey*, and let thy soule dispaire.

Vaugh. Thinke vpon *Vaughan*, and with guilty feare
Let fall thy Lance, dispaire and dye.

All to Richm. Awake,
And thinke our wrongs in *Richards* Bosome,
Will conquer him. Awake, and win the day.

Enter the Ghost of Lord Hastings.

Gho. Bloody and guilty: guiltily awake,
And in a bloody Battell end thy dayes.
Thinke on Lord Hastings: dispaire, and dye.

Hast. to Rich. Quiet vntroubled soule,
Awake, awake:
Arme, fight, and conquer, for faire Englands sake.

Enter the Ghosts of the two yong Princes.

Ghosts. Dreame on thy Cousins
Smothered in the Tower:
Let vs be laid within thy bosome *Richard*,
And weigh thee downe to ruine, shame, and death,
Thy Nephewes soule bids thee dispaire and dye.

Ghosts to Richm. Sleepe Richmond,
Sleepe in Peace, and wake in Ioy,
Good Angels guard thee from the Boares annoy,
Liue, and beget a happy race of Kings,
Edwards vnhappy Sonnes, do bid thee flourish.

Enter the Ghost of Anne, his Wife.

Ghost to Rich. Richard, thy Wife,
That wretched *Anne* thy Wife,
That neuer slept a quiet houre with thee,
Now filles thy sleepe with perturbations,
To morrow in the Battaile, thinke on me,
And fall thy edgelesse Sword, dispaire and dye:

Ghost to Richm. Thou quiet soule,
Sleepe thou a quiet sleepe:
Dreame of Successe, and Happy Victory,
Thy Aduersaries Wife doth pray for thee.

Enter the Ghost of Buckingham.

Ghost to Rich. The first was I
That help'd thee to the Crowne:
The last was I that felt thy Tyranny.
O, in the Battaile think on Buckingham,
And dye in terror of thy guiltinesse.
Dreame on, dreame on, of bloody deeds and death,
Fainting dispaire; dispairing yeeld thy breath.

Ghost to Richm. I dyed for hope
Ere I could lend thee Ayde;
But cheere thy heart, and be thou not dismayde:
God, and good Angels fight on Richmonds side,
And *Richard* fall in height of all his pride.

Richard starts out of his dreame.

Rich. Giue me another Horse, bind vp my Wounds:
Haue mercy Iesu. Soft, I did but dreame.
O coward Conscience! how dost thou afflict me?
The Lights burne blew. It is not dead midnight.
Cold fearefull drops stand on my trembling flesh.
What? do I feare my Selfe? There's none else by,
Richard loues *Richard*, that is, I am I.
Is there a Murtherer heere? No; Yes, I am:
Then flye; What from my Selfe? Great reason: why?
Lest I Reuenge. What? my Selfe vpon my Selfe?
Alacke, I loue my Selfe. Wherefore? For any good
That I my Selfe, haue done vnto my Selfe?
O no. Alas, I rather hate my Selfe,
For hatefull Deeds committed by my Selfe.
I am a Villaine: yet I Lye, I am not.
Foole, of thy Selfe speake well: Foole, do not flatter.
My Conscience hath a thousand seuerall Tongues,
And euery Tongue brings in a seuerall Tale,
And euerie Tale condemnes me for a Villaine;
Periurie, in the high'st Degree,
Murther, sterne murther, in the dyr'st degree,
All seuerall sinnes, all vs'd in each degree,
Throng all to'th'Barre, crying all, Guilty, Guilty.
I shall dispaire, there is no Creature loues me;
And if I die, no soule shall pittie me.
Nay, wherefore should they? Since that I my Selfe,
Finde in my Selfe, no pittie to my Selfe.
Me thought, the Soules of all that I had murther'd
Came to my Tent, and euery one did threat
To morrowes vengeance on the head of *Richard*.

Enter Ratcliffe.

Rat. My Lord.

King. Who's there?

Rat. *Ratcliffe* my Lord, 'tis I: the early Village Cock
Hath twice done salutation to the Morne,
Your Friends are vp, and buckle on their Armour.

King. O *Ratcliffe*, I feare, I feare.

Rat. Nay good my Lord, be not affraid of Shadows.

King. By the Apostle *Paul*, shadowes to night
Haue stroke more terror to the soule of *Richard*,
Then can the substance of ten thousand Souldiers
Armed in proofe, and led by shallow *Richmond*.
'Tis not yet neere day. Come go with me,
Vnder our Tents Ile play the Ease-dropper,
To heare if any meane to shrinke from me.

Exeunt Richard & Ratliffe.

Enter the Lords to Richmond sitting in his Tent.

Richm. Good morrow Richmond.

Rich. Cry mercy Lords, and watchfull Gentlemen,
That you haue tane a tardie sluggard heere?

Lords. How haue you slept my Lord?

Rich. The sweetest sleepe,
And fairest boading Dreames,
That euer entred in a drowsie head,
Haue I since your departure had my Lords.
Me thought their Soules, whose bodies *Rich.* murther'd,
Came to my Tent, and cried on Victory:
I promise you my Heart is very iocond,
In the remembrance of so faire a dreame,
How farre into the Morning is it Lords?

Lov. Vpon the stroke of foure.

Rich. Why then 'tis time to Arme, and giue direction.

His Oration to his Souldiers.

More then I haue said, louing Countrymen,
The leysure and inforcement of the time
Forbids to dwell vpon: yet remember this,

God

God, and our good cause, fight vpon our side,
The Prayers of holy Saints and wronged soules,
Like high rear'd Bulwarkes, stand before our Faces,
(Richard except) those whom we fight against,
Had rather haue vs win, then him they follow.
For, what is he they follow? Truly Gentlemen,
A bloudy Tyrant, and a Homicide:
One rais'd in blood, and one in blood establish'd;
One that made meanes to come by what he hath,
And slaughter'd those that were the meanes to help him:
A base foule Stone, made precious by the foyle
Of Englands Chaire, where he is falsely set:
One that hath euer beene Gods Enemy.
Then if you fight against Gods Enemy,
God will in iustice ward you as his Soldiers.
If you do sweare to put a Tyrant downe,
You sleepe in peace, the Tyrant being slaine:
If you do fight against your Countries Foes,
Your Countries Fat shall pay your paines the hyre.
If you do fight in safegard of your wiues,
Your wiues shall welcome home the Conquerors.
If you do free your Children from the Sword,
Your Childrens Children quits it in your Age.
Then in the name of God and all these rights,
Aduance your Standards, draw your willing Swords.
For me, the ransome of my bold attempt,
Shall be this cold Corpes on the earth's cold face.
But if I thriue, the gaine of my attempt,
The least of you shall share his part thereof.
Sound Drummes and Trumpets boldly, and cheerefully,
God, and Saint *George*, Richmond, and Victory.

Enter King Richard, Ratcliffe, and Catesby.

K. What said Northumberland as touching Richmond?
Rat. That he was neuer trained vp in Armes.
King. He said the truth: and what said Surrey then?
Rat. He smil'd and said, the better for our purpose.
King. He was in the right, and so indeed it is.
Tell the clocke there. *Clocke strikes.*
Giue me a Kalender: Who saw the Sunne to day?
Rat. Not I my Lord.
King. Then he disdaines to shine: for by the Booke
He should haue brau'd the East an houre ago,
A blacke day will it be to somebody. *Ratcliffe.*
Rat. My Lord.
King. The Sun will not be seene to day,
The sky doth frowne, and lowre vpon our Army.
I would these dewy teares were from the ground.
Not shine to day? Why, what is that to me
More then to Richmond? For the selfe-same Heauen
That frownes on me, lookes sadly vpon him.

Enter Norfolke.

Nor. Arme, arme, my Lord: the foe vaunts in the field.
King. Come, bustle, bustle. Caparison my horse.
Call vp Lord *Stanley*, bid him bring his power,
I will leade forth my Soldiers to the plaine,
And thus my Battell shal be ordred.
My Foreward shall be drawne in length,
Consisting equally of Horse and Foot:
Our Archers shall be placed in the mid'st;
Iohn Duke of Norfolke, *Thomas* Earle of Surrey,
Shall haue the leading of the Foot and Horse.
They thus directed, we will follow

In the maine Battell, whose puissance on either side
Shall be well-winged with our cheefest Horse:
This, and Saint George to boote.
What think'st thou Norfolke.
Nor. A good direction warlike Soueraigne,
This found I on my Tent this Morning.

Iockey of Norfolke, be not so bold,
For Dickon thy maister is bought and sold.

King. A thing deuised by the Enemy.
Go Gentlemen, euery man to his Charge,
Let not our babling Dreames affright our soules:
For Conscience is a word that Cowards vse,
Deuis'd at first to keepe the strong in awe,
Our strong armes be our Conscience, Swords our Law.
March on, ioyne brauely, let vs too't pell mell,
If not to heauen, then hand in hand to Hell.
What shall I say more then I haue inferr'd?
Remember whom you are to cope withall,
A sort of Vagabonds, Rascals, and Run-awayes,
A scum of Brittaines, and base Lackey Pezants,
Whom their o're-cloyed Country vomits forth
To desperate Aduentures, and assur'd Destruction.
You sleeping safe, they bring you to vnrest:
You hauing Lands, and blest with beauteous wiues,
They would restraine the one, distaine the other,
And who doth leade them, but a paltry Fellow?
Long kept in Britaine at our Mothers cost,
A Milke-sop, one that neuer in his life
Felt so much cold, as ouer shooes in Snow:
Let's whip these straglers o're the Seas againe,
Lash hence these ouer-weening Ragges of France,
These famish'd Beggers, weary of their liues,
Who (but for dreaming on this fond exploit)
For want of meanes (poore Rats) had hang'd themselues.
If we be conquered, let men conquer vs,
And not these bastard Britaines, whom our Fathers
Haue in their owne Land beaten, bobb'd, and thump'd,
And on Record, left them the heires of shame.
Shall these enioy our Lands? lye with our Wiues?
Rauish our daughters? *Drum afarre off*
Hearke, I heare their Drumme,
Right Gentlemen of England, fight boldly yeomen,
Draw Archers draw your Arrowes to the head,
Spurre your proud Horses hard, and ride in blood,
Amaze the welkin with your broken staues.

Enter a Messenger.

What sayes Lord *Stanley*, will he bring his power?
Mes. My Lord, he doth deny to come.
King. Off with his sonne *Georges* head.
Nor. My Lord, the Enemy is past the Marsh:
After the battaile, let *George Stanley* dye.
King. A thousand hearts are great within my bosom.
Aduance our Standards, set vpon our Foes,
Our Ancient word of Courage, faire S. *George*
Inspire vs with the spleene of fiery Dragons:
Vpon them, Victorie sits on our helpes.

Alarum, excursions. Enter Catesby.

Cat. Rescue my Lord of Norfolke,
Rescue, Rescue:
The King enacts more wonders then a man,
Daring an opposite to euery danger:
His horse is slaine, and all on foot he fights,
Seeking for Richmond in the throat of death:
Rescue faire Lord, or else the day is lost.

Alarums. *Enter*

Enter Richard.

Rich. A Horse, a Horse, my Kingdome for a Horse.
Cates. Withdraw my Lord, Ile helpe you to a Horse
Rich. Slaue, I haue set my life vpon a cast,
And I will stand the hazard of the Dye:
I thinke there be sixe Richmonds in the field,
Fiue haue I slaine to day, in stead of him.
A Horse, a Horse, my Kingdome for a Horse.

Alarum, Enter Richard and Richmond, they fight, Richard is slaine.

Retreat, and Flourish. Enter Richmond, Derby bearing the Crowne, with diuers other Lords.

Richm. God, and your Armes
Be prais'd Victorious Friends;
The day is ours, the bloudy Dogge is dead.
Der. Couragious Richmond,
Well hast thou acquit thee: Loe,
Heere these long vsurped Royalties,
From the dead Temples of this bloudy Wretch,
Haue I pluck'd off, to grace thy Browes withall.
Weare it, and make much of it.
Richm. Great God of Heauen, say Amen to all.
But tell me, is yong *George Stanley* liuing?
Der. He is my Lord, and safe in Leicester Towne,
Whither (if you please) we may withdraw vs.
Richm. What men of name are slaine on either side?
Der. *Iohn* Duke of Norfolke, *Walter* Lord Ferris,
Sir *Robert Brokenbury*, and Sir *William Brandon*.
Richm. Interre their Bodies, as become their Births,
Proclaime a pardon to the Soldiers fled,
That in submission will returne to vs,
And then as we haue tane the Sacrament,
We will vnite the White Rose, and the Red.
Smile Heauen vpon this faire Coniunction,
That long haue frown'd vpon their Enmity:
What Traitor heares me, and sayes not Amen?
England hath long beene mad, and scarr'd her selfe;
The Brother blindely shed the Brothers blood;
The Father, rashly slaughtered his owne Sonne;
The Sonne compell'd, beene Butcher to the Sire;
All this diuided Yorke and Lancaster,
Diuided, in their dire Diuision.
O now, let *Richmond* and *Elizabeth*,
The true Succeeders of each Royall House,
By Gods faire ordinance, conioyne together:
And let thy Heires (God if thy will be so)
Enrich the time to come, with Smooth-fac'd Peace,
With smiling Plenty, and faire Prosperous dayes.
Abate the edge of Traitors, Gracious Lord,
That would reduce these bloudy dayes againe,
And make poore England weepe in Streames of Blood;
Let them not liue to taste this Lands increase,
That would with Treason, wound this faire Lands peace.
Now Ciuill wounds are stopp'd, Peace liues agen;
That she may long liue heere, God say, Amen. *Exeunt*

FINIS.

The Famous History of the Life of
King HENRY the Eight.

THE PROLOGUE.

I Come no more to make you laugh, Things now,
That beare a Weighty, and a Serious Brow,
Sad, high, and working, full of State and Woe:
Such Noble Scænes, as draw the Eye to flow
We now present. Those that can Pitty, heere
May (if they thinke it well) let fall a Teare,
The Subiect will deserue it. Such as giue
Their Money out of hope they may beleeue,
May heere finde Truth too. Those that come to see
Onely a show or two, and so agree,
The Play may passe: If they be still, and willing,
Ile vndertake may see away their shilling
Richly in two short houres. Onely they
That come to heare a Merry, Bawdy Play,
A noyse of Targets: Or to see a Fellow
In a long Motley Coate, garded with Yellow,
Will be deceyu'd. For gentle Hearers, know
To ranke our chosen Truth with such a show
As Foole, and Fight is, beside forfeyting
Our owne Braines, and the Opinion that we bring
To make that onely true, we now intend,
Will leaue vs neuer an vnderstanding Friend.
Therefore, for Goodnesse sake, and as you are knowne
The First and Happiest Hearers of the Towne,
Be sad, as we would make ye. Thinke ye see
The very Persons of our Noble Story,
As they were Liuing: Thinke you see them Great,
And follow'd with the generall throng, and sweat
Of thousand Friends: Then, in a moment, see
How soone this Mightinesse, meets Misery:
And if you can be merry then, Ile say,
A Man may weepe vpon his Wedding day.

Actus Primus. Scœna Prima.

Enter the Duke of Norfolke at one doore. At the other, the Duke of Buckingham, and the Lord Aburgauenny.

Buckingham.
Good morrow, and well met. How haue ye done
Since last we saw in France?

Norf. I thanke your Grace:
Healthfull, and euer since a fresh Admirer
Of what I saw there.

Buck. An vntimely Ague
Staid me a Prisoner in my Chamber, when
Those Sunnes of Glory, those two Lights of Men
Met in the vale of Andren.

Nor. 'Twixt Guynes and Arde,
I was then present, saw them salute on Horsebacke,
Beheld them when they lighted, how they clung
In their Embracement, as they grew together,
Which had they,
What foure Thron'd ones could haue weigh'd
Such a compounded one?

Buck. All the whole time
I was my Chambers Prisoner.

Nor. Then you lost
The view of earthly glory: Men might say
Till this time Pompe was single, but now married
To one aboue it selfe. Each following day
Became the next dayes master, till the last
Made former Wonders, it's. To day the French,
All Clinquant all in Gold, like Heathen Gods
Shone downe the English; and to morrow, they
Made Britaine, India: Euery man that stood,
Shew'd like a Mine. Their Dwarfish Pages were
As Cherubins, all gilt: the Madams too,
Not vs'd to toyle, did almost sweat to beare
The Pride vpon them, that their very labour
Was to them, as a Painting. Now this Maske
Was cry'de incompareable; and th'ensuing night
Made it a Foole, and Begger. The two Kings
Equall in lustre, were now best, now worst
As presence did present them: Him in eye,
Still him in praise, and being present both,
'Twas said they saw but one, and no Discerner
Durst wagge his Tongue in censure, when these Sunnes
(For so they phrase 'em) by their Heralds challeng'd
The Noble Spirits to Armes, they did performe

Beyond

Beyond thoughts Compasse, that former fabulous Storie
Being now seene, possible enough, got credit
That *Beuis* was beleeu'd.

Buc. Oh you go farre.

Nor. As I belong to worship, and affect
In Honor, Honesty, the tract of eu'ry thing,
Would by a good Discourser loose some life,
Which Actions selfe, was tongue too.

Buc. All was Royall,
To the disposing of it nought rebell'd,
Order gaue each thing view. The Office did
Distinctly his full Function: who did guide,
I meane who set the Body, and the Limbes
Of this great Sport together?

Nor. As you guesse:
One certes, that promises no Element
In such a businesse.

Buc. I pray you who, my Lord?

Nor. All this was ordred by the good Discretion
Of the right Reuerend Cardinall of Yorke.

Buc. The diuell speed him: No mans Pye is freed
From his Ambitious finger. What had he
To do in these fierce Vanities? I wonder,
That such a Keech can with his very bulke
Take vp the Rayes o'th'beneficiall Sun,
And keepe it from the Earth.

Nor. Surely Sir,
There's in him stuffe, that put's him to these ends:
For being not propt by Auncestry, whose grace
Chalkes Successors their way; nor call'd vpon
For high feats done to'th'Crowne; neither Allied
To eminent Assistants; but Spider-like
Out of his Selfe-drawing Web. O giues vs note,
The force of his owne merit makes his way
A guift that heauen giues for him, which buyes
A place next to the King.

Abur. I cannot tell
What Heauen hath giuen him: let some Grauer eye
Pierce into that, but I can see his Pride
Peepe through each part of him: whence ha's he that,
If not from Hell? The Diuell is a Niggard,
Or ha's giuen all before, and he begins
A new Hell in himselfe.

Buc. Why the Diuell,
Vpon this French going out, tooke he vpon him
(Without the priuity o'th'King) t'appoint
Who should attend on him? He makes vp the File
Of all the Gentry; for the most part such
To whom as great a Charge, as little Honor
He meant to lay vpon: and his owne Letter
The Honourable Board of Councell, out
Must fetch him in, he Papers.

Abur. I do know
Kinsmen of mine, three at the least, that haue
By this, so sicken'd their Estates, that neuer
They shall abound as formerly.

Buc. O many
Haue broke their backes with laying Mannors on 'em
For this great Iourney. What did this vanity
But minister communication of
A most poore issue.

Nor. Greeuingly I thinke,
The Peace betweene the French and vs, not valewes
The Cost that did conclude it.

Buc. Euery man,
After the hideous storme that follow'd, was
A thing Inspir'd, and not consulting, broke
Into a generall Prophesie; That this Tempest
Dashing the Garment of this Peace, aboaded
The sodaine breach on't.

Nor. Which is budded out,
For France hath flaw'd the League, and hath attach'd
Our Merchants goods at Burdeux.

Abur. Is it therefore
Th'Ambassador is silenc'd?

Nor. Marry is't.

Abur. A proper Title of a Peace, and purchas'd
At a superfluous rate.

Buc. Why all this Businesse
Our Reuerend Cardinall carried.

Nor. Like it your Grace,
The State takes notice of the priuate difference
Betwixt you, and the Cardinall. I aduise you
(And take it from a heart, that wishes towards you
Honor, and plenteous safety) that you reade
The Cardinals Malice, and his Potency
Together; To consider further, that
What his high Hatred would effect, wants not
A Minister in his Power. You know his Nature,
That he's Reuengefull; and I know, his Sword
Hath a sharpe edge: It's long, and't may be saide
It reaches farre, and where 'twill not extend,
Thither he darts it. Bosome vp my counsell,
You'l finde it wholesome. Loe, where comes that Rock
That I aduice your shunning.

*Enter Cardinall Wolsey, the Purse borne before him, certaine
of the Guard, and two Secretaries with Papers: The
Cardinall in his passage, fixeth his eye on Buck-
ham, and Buckingham on him,
both full of disdaine.*

Car. The Duke of *Buckinghams* Surueyor? Ha?
Where's his Examination?

Secr. Heere so please you.

Car. Is he in person, ready?

Secr. I, please your Grace.

Car. Well, we shall then know more, & *Buckingham*
Shall lessen this bigge looke.

Exeunt Cardinall, and his Traine.

Buc. This Butchers Curre is venom'd-mouth'd, and I
Haue not the power to muzzle him, therefore best
Not wake him in his slumber. A Beggers booke,
Out-worths a Nobles blood.

Nor. What are you chaff'd?
Aske God for Temp'rance, that's th'appliance onely
Which your disease requires.

Buc. I read in's looks
Matter against me, and his eye reuil'd
Me as his abiect obiect, at this instant
He bores me with some tricke; He's gone to'th'King:
Ile follow, and out-stare him.

Nor. Stay my Lord,
And let your Reason with your Choller question
What 'tis you go about: to climbe steepe hilles
Requires slow pace at first. Anger is like
A full hot Horse, who being allow'd his way
Selfe-mettle tyres him: Not a man in England
Can aduise me like you: Be to your selfe,
As you would to your Friend.

Buc. Ile to the King,
And from a mouth of Honor, quite cry downe

This

This *Ipswich* fellowes insolence; or proclaime,
There's difference in no persons.

  Norf. Be aduis'd;
Heat not a Furnace for your foe so hot
That it do singe your selfe. We may out-runne
By violent swiftnesse that which we run at;
And lose by ouer-running: know you not,
The fire that mounts the liquor til't run ore,
In seeming to augment it, wasts it: be aduis'd;
I say againe there is no English Soule
More stronger to direct you then your selfe;
If with the sap of reason you would quench,
Or but allay the fire of passion.

  Buck. Sir,
I am thankfull to you, and Ile goe along
By your prescription: but this top-proud fellow,
Whom from the flow of gall I name not, but
From sincere motions, by Intelligence,
And proofes as cleere as Founts in *Iuly*, when
Wee see each graine of grauell; I doe know
To be corrupt and treasonous.

  Norf. Say not treasonous.

  Buck. To th'King Ile say't, & make my vouch as strong
As shore of Rocke: attend. This holy Foxe,
Or Wolfe, or both (for he is equall rau'nous
As he is subtile, and as prone to mischiefe,
As able to perform't) his minde, and place
Infecting one another, yea reciprocally,
Only to shew his pompe, as well in France,
As here at home, suggests the King our Master
To this last costly Treaty: Th'enteruiew,
That swallowed so much treasure, and like a glasse
Did breake ith'wrenching.

  Norf. Faith, and so it did.

  Buck. Pray giue me fauour Sir: This cunning Cardinall
The Articles o'th' Combination drew
As himselfe pleas'd; and they were ratified
As he cride thus let be, to as much end,
As giue a Crutch to th'dead. But our Count-Cardinall
Has done this, and tis well: for worthy *Wolsey*
(Who cannot erre) he did it. Now this followes,
(Which as I take it, is a kinde of Puppie
To th'old dam Treason) *Charles* the Emperour,
Vnder pretence to see the Queene his Aunt,
(For twas indeed his colour, but he came
To whisper *Wolsey*) here makes visitation,
His feares were that the Interview betwixt
England and France, might through their amity
Breed him some preiudice; for from this League,
Peep'd harmes that menac'd him. Priuily
Deales with our Cardinall, and as I troa
Which I doe well; for I am sure the Emperour
Paid ere he promis'd, whereby his Suit was granted
Ere it was ask'd. But when the way was made
And pau'd with gold: the Emperor thus desir'd,
That he would please to alter the Kings course,
And breake the foresaid peace. Let the King know
(As soone he shall by me) that thus the Cardinall
Does buy and sell his Honour as he pleases,
And for his owne aduantage.

  Norf. I am sorry
To heare this of him; and could wish he were
Somthing mistaken in't.

  Buck. No, not a sillable:
I doe pronounce him in that very shape
He shall appeare in proofe.

Enter Brandon, a Sergeant at Armes before him, and two or three of the Guard.

  Brandon. Your Office Sergeant: execute it.

  Sergeant. Sir,
My Lord the Duke of *Buckingham*, and Earle
Of *Hertford, Stafford* and *Northampton*, I
Arrest thee of High Treason, in the name
Of our most Soueraigne King.

  Buck. Lo you my Lord,
The net has falne vpon me, I shall perish
Vnder deuice, and practise:

  Bran. I am sorry,
To see you tane from liberty, to looke on
The busines present. Tis his Highnes pleasure
You shall to th' Tower.

  Buck. It will helpe me nothing
To plead mine Innocence; for that dye is on me
Which makes my whit'st part, black. The will of Heau'n
Be done in this and all things: I obey.
O my Lord *Aburgany*: Fare you well.

  Bran. Nay, he must beare you company. The King
Is pleas'd you shall to th'Tower, till you know
How he determines further.

  Abur. As the Duke said,
The will of Heauen be done, and the Kings pleasure
By me obey'd.

  Bran. Here is a warrant from
The King, t'attach Lord *Mountacute*, and the Bodies
Of the Dukes Confessor, *Iohn de la Car*,
One *Gilbert Pecke*, his Councellour.

  Buck. So, so;
These are the limbs o'th' Plot: no more I hope.

  Bra. A Monke o'th' *Chartreux*.

  Buck. O *Michaell Hopkins*?

  Bra. He.

  Buck. My Surueyor is falce: The ore-great *Cardinall*
Hath shew'd him gold; my life is spand already:
I am the shadow of poore *Buckingham*,
Whose Figure euen this instant Clowd puts on,
By Darkning my cleere Sunne. My Lords farewell. *Exe.*

Scena Secunda.

Cornets. Enter King Henry, leaning on the Cardinals shoulder, the Nobles, and Sir Thomas Louell: the Cardinall places himselfe vnder the Kings feete on his right side.

  King. My life it selfe, and the best heart of it,
Thankes you for this great care: I stood i'th' leuell
Of a full-charg'd confederacie, and giue thankes
To you that choak'd it. Let be cald before vs
That Gentleman of *Buckinghams*, in person,
Ile heare him his confessions iustifie,
And point by point the Treasons of his Maister,
He shall againe relate.

A noyse within crying roome for the Queene, vsher'd by the Duke of Norfolke. Enter the Queene, Norfolke and Suffolke: she kneels. King riseth from his State, takes her vp, kisses and placeth her by him.

  Queen. Nay, we must longer kneele; I am a Suitor.

  King. Arise, and take place by vs; halfe your Suit
Neuer name to, vs; you haue halfe our power:

The

The other moity ere you aske is giuen,
Repeat your will, and take it.
  Queen. Thanke your Maiesty
That you would loue your selfe, and in that loue
Not vnconsidered leaue your Honour, nor
The dignity of your Office; is the poynt
Of my Petition.
  Kin. Lady mine proceed.
  Queen. I am solicited not by a few,
And those of true condition; That your Subiects
Are in great grieuance: There haue beene Commissions
Sent downe among 'em, which hath flaw'd the heart
Of all their Loyalties; wherein, although
My good Lord Cardinall, they vent reproches
Most bitterly on you, as putter on
Of these exactions: yet the King, our Maister (not
Whose Honor Heauen shield from soile; euen he escapes
Language vnmannerly; yea, such which breakes
The sides of loyalty, and almost appeares
In lowd Rebellion.
  Norf. Not almost appeares,
It doth appeare; for, vpon these Taxations,
The Clothiers all not able to maintaine
The many to them longing, haue put off
The Spinsters, Carders, Fullers, Weauers, who
Vnfit for other life, compeld by hunger
And lack of other meanes, in desperate manner
Daring th'euent too th'teeth, are all in vprore,
And danger serues among them.
  Kin. Taxation?
Wherein? and what Taxation? My Lord Cardinall,
You that are blam'd for it alike with vs,
Know you of this Taxation?
  Card. Please you Sir,
I know but of a single part in ought
Pertaines to th'State; and front but in that File
Where others tell steps with me.
  Queen. No, my Lord?
You know no more then others? But you frame
Things that are knowne alike, which are not wholsome
To those which would not know them, and yet must
Perforce be their acquaintance. These exactions
(Whereof my Soueraigne would haue note) they are
Most pestilent to th'hearing, and to beare 'em,
The Backe is Sacrifice to th'load; They say
They are deuis'd by you, or else you suffer
Too hard an exclamation.
  Kin. Still Exaction:
The nature of it, in what kinde let's know,
Is this Exaction?
  Queen. I am much too venturous
In tempting of your patience; but am boldned
Vnder your promis'd pardon. The Subiects griefe
Comes through Commissions, which compels from each
The sixt part of his Substance, to be leuied
Without delay; and the pretence for this
Is nam'd, your warres in France: this makes bold mouths,
Tongues spit their duties out, and cold hearts freeze
Allegeance in them; their curses now
Liue where their prayers did: and it's come to passe,
This tractable obedience is a Slaue
To each incensed Will: I would your Highnesse
Would giue it quicke consideration; for
There is no primer basenesse.
  Kin. By my life,
This is against our pleasure.

  Card. And for me,
I haue no further gone in this, then by
A single voice, and that not past me, but
By learned approbation of the Iudges: If I am
Traduc'd by ignorant Tongues, which neither know
My faculties nor person, yet will be
The Chronicles of my doing: Let me say,
'Tis but the fate of Place, and the rough Brake
That Vertue must goe through: we must not stint
Our necessary actions, in the feare
To cope malicious Censurers, which euer,
As rau'nous Fishes doe a Vessell follow
That is new trim'd; but benefit no further
Then vainly longing. What we oft doe best,
By sicke Interpreters (once weake ones) is
Not ours, or not allow'd; what worst, as oft
Hitting a grosser quality, is cride vp
For our best Act: if we shall stand still,
In feare our motion will be mock'd, or carp'd at,
We should take roote here, where we sit;
Or sit State-Statues onely.
  Kin. Things done well,
And with a care, exempt themselues from feare:
Things done without example, in their issue
Are to be fear'd. Haue you a President
Of this Commission? I beleeue, not any.
We must not rend our Subiects from our Lawes,
And sticke them in our Will. Sixt part of each?
A trembling Contribution; why we take
From euery Tree, lop, barke, and part o'th' Timber:
And though we leaue it with a roote thus hackt,
The Ayre will drinke the Sap. To euery County
Where this is question'd, send our Letters, with
Free pardon to each man that has deny'de
The force of this Commission: pray looke too't;
I put it to your care.
  Card. A word with you.
Let there be Letters writ to euery Shire,
Of the Kings grace and pardon: the greeued Commons
Hardly conceiue of me. Let it be nois'd,
That through our Intercession, this Reuokement
And pardon comes: I shall anon aduise you
Further in the proceeding.   *Exit Secret.*

Enter Surueyor.

  Queen. I am sorry, that the Duke of *Buckingham*
Is run in your displeasure.
  Kin. It grieues many:
The Gentleman is Learn'd, and a most rare Speaker,
To Nature none more bound; his trayning such,
That he may furnish and instruct great Teachers,
And neuer seeke for ayd out of himselfe: yet see,
When these so Noble benefits shall proue
Not well dispos'd, the minde growing once corrupt,
They turne to vicious formes, ten times more vgly
Then euer they were faire. This man so compleat,
Who was enrold 'mongst wonders; and when we
Almost with rauish'd listning, could not finde
His houre of speech, a minute: He, (my Lady)
Hath into monstrous habits put the Graces
That once were his, and is become as blacke,
As if besmear'd in hell. Sit by Vs, you shall heare
(This was his Gentleman in trust) of him
Things to strike Honour sad. Bid him recount
The fore-recited practises, whereof
We cannot feele too little, heare too much.

Card.

Card. Stand forth, & with bold spirit relate what you
Most like a carefull Subiect haue collected
Out of the Duke of *Buckingham.*

Kin. Speake freely.

Sur. First, it was vsuall with him; euery day
It would infect his Speech: That if the King
Should without issue dye; hee'l carry it so
To make the Scepter his. These very words
I'ue heard him vtter to his Sonne in Law,
Lord *Aburgany*, to whom by oth he menac'd
Reuenge vpon the *Cardinall.*

Card. Please your Highnesse note
This dangerous conception in this point,
Not frended by his wish to your High person;
His will is most malignant, and it stretches
Beyond you to your friends.

Queen. My learn'd Lord *Cardinall*,
Deliuer all with Charity.

Kin. Speake on;
How grounded hee his Title to the Crowne
Vpon our faile; to this poynt hast thou heard him,
At any time speake ought?

Sur. He was brought to this,
By a vaine Prophesie of *Nicholas Henton.*

Kin. What was that *Henton*?

Sur. Sir, a *Chartreux* Fryer,
His Confessor, who fed him euery minute
With words of Soueraignty.

Kin. How know'st thou this?

Sur. Not long before your Highnesse sped to France,
The Duke being at the Rose, within the Parish
Saint *Laurence Poultney*, did of me demand
What was the speech among the Londoners,
Concerning the French Iourney. I replide,
Men feare the French would proue perfidious
To the Kings danger: presently, the Duke
Said, 'twas the feare indeed, and that he doubted
'Twould proue the verity of certaine words
Spoke by a holy Monke, that oft, sayes he,
Hath sent to me, wishing me to permit
Iohn de la Car, my Chaplaine, a choyce howre
To heare from him a matter of some moment:
Whom after vnder the Commissions Seale,
He sollemnly had sworne, that what he spoke
My Chaplaine to no Creature liuing, but
To me, should vtter, with demure Confidence,
This pausingly ensu'de; neither the King, nor's Heyres
(Tell you the Duke) shall prosper, bid him striue
To the loue o'th' Commonalty, the Duke
Shall gouerne England.

Queen. If I know you well,
You were the Dukes Suruey or, and lost your Office
On the complaint o'th' Tenants; take good heed
You charge not in your spleene a Noble person,
And spoyle your nobler Soule; I say, take heed;
Yes, heartily beseech you.

Kin. Let him on: Goe forward.

Sur. On my Soule, Ile speake but truth.
I told my Lord the Duke, by th' Diuels illusions
The Monke might be deceiu'd, and that 'twas dangerous
For this to ruminate on this so farre, vntill
It forg'd him some designe, which being beleeu'd
It was much like to doe: He answer'd, Tush,
It can doe me no damage; adding further,
That had the King in his last Sicknesse faild,
The Cardinals and Sir *Thomas Louels* heads
Should haue gone off.

Kin. Ha? What, so rancke? Ah, ha,
There's mischiefe in this man; canst thou say further?

Sur. I can my Liedge.

Kin. Proceed.

Sur. Being at *Greenwich*,
After your Highnesse had reprou'd the Duke
About Sir *William Blumer.*

Kin. I remember of such a time, being my sworn ser-
The Duke retein'd him his. But on: what hence? (uant,

Sur. If (quoth he) I for this had beene committed,
As to the Tower, I thought; I would haue plaid
The Part my Father meant to act vpon
Th' Vsurper *Richard*, who being at *Salsbury*,
Made suit to come in's presence; which if granted,
(As he made semblance of his duty) would
Haue put his knife into him.

Kin. A Gyant Traytor.

Card. Now Madam, may his Highnes liue in freedome,
And this man out of Prison.

Queen. God mend all.

Kin. Ther's somthing more would out of thee; what (say'st?

Sur. After the Duke his Father, with the knife
He stretch'd him, and with one hand on his dagger,
Another spread on's breast, mounting his eyes,
He did discharge a horrible Oath, whose tenor
Was, were he euill vs'd, he would outgoe
His Father, by as much as a performance
Do's an irresolute purpose.

Kin. There's his period,
To sheath his knife in vs: he is attach'd,
Call him to present tryall: if he may
Finde mercy in the Law, 'tis his; if none,
Let him not seek't of vs: By day and night
Hee's Traytor to th' height. *Exeunt.*

Scæna Tertia.

Enter L. Chamberlaine and L. Sandys.

L. Ch. Is't possible the spels of France should iuggle
Men into such strange mysteries?

L. San. New customes,
Though they be neuer so ridiculous,
(Nay let 'em be vnmanly) yet are follow'd.

L. Ch. As farre as I see, all the good our English
Haue got by the late Voyage, is but meerely
A fit or two o'th' face, (but they are shrewd ones)
For when they hold 'em, you would sweare directly
Their very noses had been Councellours
To *Pepin* or *Clotharius*, they keepe State so.

L. San. They haue all new legs,
And lame ones; one would take it,
That neuer see 'em pace before, the Spauen
A Spring-halt rain'd among 'em.

L. Ch. Death my Lord,
Their cloathes are after such a Pagan cut too't,
That sure th' haue worne out Christendome: how now?
What newes, Sir *Thomas Louell?*

Enter Sir Thomas Louell.

Louell. Faith my Lord,
I heare of none but the new Proclamation,
That's clapt vpon the Court Gate.

L. Cham. What is't for?
Lou. The reformation of our trauel'd Gallants,
That fill the Court with quarrels, talke, and Taylors.
  L. Cham. I'm glad 'tis there;
Now I would pray our Monsieurs
To thinke an English Courtier may be wise,
And neuer see the *Louure*.
  Lou. They must either
(For so run the Conditions) leaue those remnants
Of Foole and Feather, that they got in France,
With all their honourable points of ignorance
Pertaining thereunto; as Fights and Fire-workes,
Abusing better men then they can be
Out of a forreigne wisedome, renouncing cleane
The faith they haue in Tennis and tall Stockings,
Short blistred Breeches, and those types of Trauell;
And vnderstand againe like honest men,
Or pack to their old Playfellowes; there, I take it,
They may *Cum Priuilegio*, wee away
The lag end of their lewdnesse, and be laugh'd at.
  L. San. Tis time to giue 'em Physicke, their diseases
Are growne so catching.
  L. Cham. What a losse our Ladies
Will haue of these trim vanities?
  Louell. I marry,
There will be woe indeed Lords, the slye whorsons
Haue got a speeding tricke to lay downe Ladies.
A French Song, and a Fiddle, ha's no Fellow.
  L. San. The Diuell fiddle 'em,
I am glad they are going,
For sure there's no conuerting of 'em: now
An honest Country Lord as I am, besten
A long time out of play, may bring his plaine song,
And haue an houre of hearing, and by'r Lady
Held currant Musicke too.
  L. Cham. Well said Lord *Sands*,
Your Colts tooth is not cast yet?
  L. San. No my Lord,
Nor shall not while I haue a stumpe.
  L. Cham. Sir *Thomas*,
Whither were you a going?
  Lou. To the Cardinals;
Your Lordship is a guest too.
  L. Cham. O, 'tis true;
This night he makes a Supper, and a great one,
To many Lords and Ladies; there will be
The Beauty of this Kingdome Ile assure you.
  Lou. That Churchman
Beares a bounteous minde indeed,
A hand as fruitfull as the Land that feeds vs,
His dewes fall euery where.
  L. Cham. No doubt hee's Noble;
He had a blacke mouth that said other of him.
  L. San. He may my Lord,
Ha's wherewithall in him;
Sparing would shew a worse sinne, then ill Doctrine,
Men of his way, should be most liberall,
They are set heere for examples.
  L. Cham. True, they are so;
But few now giue so great ones:
My Barge stayes;
Your Lordship shall along: Come, good Sir *Thomas*,
We shall be late else, which I would not be,
For I was spoke to, with Sir *Henry Guilford*
This night to be Comptrollers.
  L. San. I am your Lordships.   *Exeunt.*

Scena Quarta.

Hoboies. A small Table vnder a State for the Cardinall, a longer Table for the Guests. Then Enter Anne Bullen, and diuers other Ladies, & Gentlemen, as Guests at one Doore; at an other Doore enter Sir Henry Guilford.

  S. Hen. Guilf. Ladyes,
A generall welcome from his Grace
Salutes ye all; This Night he dedicates
To faire content, and you: None heere he hopes
In all this Noble Beuy, has brought with her
One care abroad: hee would haue all as merry:
As first, good Company, good wine, good welcome,
Can make good people.

  Enter L. Chamberlaine L. Sands and Louell.
O my Lord, y'are tardy;
The very thought of this faire Company,
Clapt wings to me.
  Cham. You are young Sir *Harry Guilford*.
  San. Sir *Thomas Louell*, had the Cardinall
But halfe my Lay-thoughts in him, some of these
Should finde a running Banket, ere they rested,
I thinke would better please 'em: by my life,
They are a sweet society of faire ones.
  Lou. O that your Lordship were but now Confessor,
To one or two of these.
  San. I would I were,
They should finde easie pennance.
  Lou. Faith how easie?
  San. As easie as a downe bed would affoord it.
  Cham. Sweet Ladies will it please you sit; Sir *Harry*
Place you that side, Ile take the charge of this:
His Grace is entring. Nay, you must not freeze,
Two women plac'd together, makes cold weather:
My Lord *Sands*, you are one will keepe 'em waking:
Pray sit betweene these Ladies.
  San. By my faith,
And thanke your Lordship: by your leaue sweet Ladies,
If I chance to talke a little wilde, forgiue me:
I had it from my Father.
  An. Bul. Was he mad Sir?
  San. O very mad, exceeding mad, in loue too;
But he would bite none, iust as I doe now,
He would Kisse you Twenty with a breath.
  Cham. Well said my Lord:
So now y'are fairely seated: Gntlemen,
The pennance lyes on you; if these faire Ladies
Passe away frowning.
  San. For my little Cure,
Let me alone.

  Hoboyes. Enter Cardinall Wolsey, and takes his State.
  Card. Y'are welcome my faire Guests; that noble Lady
Or Gentleman that is not freely merry
Is not my Friend. This to confirme my welcome,
And to you all good health.
  San. Your Grace is Noble,
Let me haue such a Bowle may hold my thankes,
And saue me so much talking.
  Card. My Lord *Sands*,

I am beholding to you : cheere your neighbours :
Ladies you are not merry ; Gentlemen,
Whose fault is this?

San. The red wine first must rise
In their faire cheekes my Lord, then wee shall haue 'em,
Talke vs to silence.

An.B. You are a merry Gamster
My Lord *Sands*.

San. Yes, if I make my play:
Heer's to your Ladiship, and pledge it Madam:
For 'tis to such a thing.

An.B. You cannot shew me.

Drum and Trumpet, Chambers discharg'd.

San. I told your Grace, they would talke anon.

Card. What's that?

Cham. Looke out there, some of ye.

Card. What warlike voyce,
And to what end is this? Nay, Ladies, feare not;
By all the lawes of Warre y'are priuiledg'd.

Enter a Seruant.

Cham. How now, what is't?

Seru. A noble troupe of Strangers,
For so they seeme; th'haue left their Barge and landed,
And hither make, as great Embassadors
From forraigne Princes.

Card. Good Lord Chamberlaine,
Go, giue 'em welcome; you can speake the French tongue
And pray receiue 'em Nobly, and conduct 'em
Into our presence, where this heauen of beauty
Shall shine at full vpon them. Some attend him.

All rise, and Tables remou'd.

You haue now a broken Banket, but wee'l mend it.
A good digestion to you all; and once more
I showre a welcome on yee : welcome all.

Hoboyes. Enter King and others as Maskers, habited like Shepheards, vsher'd by the Lord Chamberlaine. They passe directly before the Cardinall, and gracefully salute him.

A noble Company : what are their pleasures?

Cham. Because they speak no English, thus they prai'd
To tell your Grace : That hauing heard by fame
Of this so Noble and so faire assembly,
This night to meet heere they could doe no lesse,
(Out of the great respect they beare to beauty)
But leaue their Flockes, and vnder your faire Conduct
Craue leaue to view these Ladies, and entreat
An houre of Reuels with 'em.

Card. Say, Lord *Chamberlaine*,
They haue done my poore house grace :
For which I pay 'em a thousand thankes,
And pray 'em take their pleasures.

Choose Ladies, King and An Bullen.

King. The fairest hand I euer touch'd: O Beauty,
Till now I neuer knew thee.

Musicke, Dance.

Card. My Lord.

Cham. Your Grace.

Card. Pray tell 'em thus much from me :
There should be one amongst 'em by his person
More worthy this place then my selfe, to whom
(If I but knew him) with my loue and duty
I would surrender it. *Whisper.*

Cham. I will my Lord.

Card. What say they?

Cham. Such a one, they all confesse
There is indeed, which they would haue your Grace
Find out, and he will take it.

Card. Let me see then,
By all your good leaues Gentlemen; heere Ile make
My royall choyce.

Kin. Ye haue found him Cardinall,
You hold a faire Assembly ; you doe well Lord :
You are a Churchman, or Ile tell you Cardinall,
I should iudge now vnhappily.

Card. I am glad
Your Grace is growne so pleasant.

Kin. My Lord Chamberlaine,
Prethee come hither, what faire Ladie's that?

Cham. An't please your Grace,
Sir *Thomas Bullens* Daughter, the Viscount *Rochford*,
One of her Highnesse women.

Kin. By Heauen she is a dainty one, Sweet heart,
I were vnmannerly to take you out,
And not to kisse you. A health Gentlemen,
Let it goe round.

Card. Sir *Thomas Louell*, is the Banket ready
I'th' Priuy Chamber?

Lou. Yes, my Lord.

Card. Your Grace
I feare, with dancing is a little heated.

Kin. I feare too much.

Card. There's fresher ayre my Lord,
In the next Chamber.

Kin. Lead in your Ladies eu'ry one : Sweet Partner,
I must not yet forsake you : Let's be merry,
Good my Lord Cardinall : I haue halfe a dozen healths,
To drinke to these faire Ladies, and a measure
To lead 'em once againe, and then let's dreame
Who's best in fauour. Let the Musicke knock it.

Exeunt with Trumpets.

Actus Secundus. Scena Prima.

Enter two Gentlemen at seuerall Doores.

1. Whether away so fast?

2. O, God saue ye:
Eu'n to the Hall, to heare what shall become
Of the great Duke of Buckingham.

1. Ile saue you
That labour Sir. All's now done but the Ceremony
Of bringing backe the Prisoner.

2. Were you there?

1. Yes indeed was I.

2. Pray speake what ha's happen'd.

1. You may guesse quickly what.

2. Is he found guilty?

1. Yes truely is he,
And condemn'd vpon't.

2. I am sorry for't.

1. So are a number more.

2. But pray how past it?

1. Ile tell you in a little. The great Duke
Came to the Bar; where, to his accusations
He pleaded still not guilty, and alleadged
Many sharpe reasons to defeat the Law.
The Kings Atturney on the contrary,
Vrg'd on the Examinations, proofes, confessions

Of diuers witnesses, which the Duke desir'd
To him brought *viua voce* to his face;
At which appear'd against him, his Surueyor
Sir *Gilbert Pecke* his Chancellour, and *Iohn Car*,
Confessor to him, with that Diuell Monke,
Hopkins, that made this mischiefe.

  2. That was hee
That fed him with his Prophecies.

  1. The same,
All these accus'd him strongly, which he faine
Would haue flung from him; but indeed he could not;
And so his Peeres vpon this euidence,
Haue found him guilty of high Treason. Much
He spoke, and learnedly for life: But all
Was either pittied in him, or forgotten.

  2. After all this, how did he beare himselfe?

  1. When he was brought agen to th' Bar, to heare
His Knell rung out, his Iudgement, he was stir'd
With such an Agony, he sweat extreamly,
And somthing spoke in choller, ill, and hasty:
But he fell to himselfe againe, and sweetly,
In all the rest shew'd a most Noble patience.

  2. I doe not thinke he feares death.

  1. Sure he does not,
He neuer was so womanish, the cause
He may a little grieue at.

  2. Certainly,
The Cardinall is the end of this.

  1. Tis likely,
By all coniectures: First *Kildares* Attendure;
Then Deputy of Ireland, who remou'd
Earle *Surrey*, was sent thither, and in hast too,
Least he should helpe his Father.

  2. That tricke of State
Was a deepe enuious one,

  1. At his returne,
No doubt he will requite it; this is noted
(And generally) who euer the King fauours,
The Cardnall instantly will finde imployment,
And farre enough from Court too.

  2. All the Commons
Hate him perniciously, and o' my Conscience
Wish him ten faddom deepe: This Duke as much
They loue and doate on: call him bounteous *Buckingham*,
The Mirror of all courtesie.

Enter Buckingham from his Arraignment, Tipstaues before him, the Axe with the edge towards him, Halberds on each side, accompanied with Sir Thomas Louell, Sir Nicholas Vaux, Sir Walter Sands, and common people, &c.

  1. Stay there Sir,
And see the noble ruin'd man you speake of.

  2. Let's stand close and behold him.

  Buck. All good people,
You that thus farre haue come to pitty me;
Heare what I say, and then goe home and lose me.
I haue this day receiu'd a Traitors iudgement,
And by that name must dye; yet Heauen beare witnes,
And if I haue a Conscience, let it sincke me,
Euen as the Axe falls, if I be not faithfull.
The Law I beare no mallice for my death,
T'has done vpon the premisses, but Iustice:
But those that sought it, I could wish more Christians:
(Be what they will) I heartily forgiue 'em;
Yet let 'em looke they glory not in mischiefe;
Nor build their euils on the graues of great men;
For then, my guiltlesse blood must cry against 'em.
For further life in this world I ne're hope,
Nor will I sue, although the King haue mercies
More then I dare make faults.
You few that lou'd me,
And dare be bold to weepe for *Buckingham*,
His Noble Friends and Fellowes; whom to leaue
Is only bitter to him, only dying:
Goe with me like good Angels to my end,
And as the long diuorce of Steele fals on me,
Make of your Prayers one sweet Sacrifice,
And lift my Soule to Heauen.
Lead on a Gods name.

  Louell. I doe beseech your Grace, for charity
If euer any malice in your heart
Were hid against me, now to forgiue me frankly.

  Buck. Sir *Thomas Louell*, I as free forgiue you
As I would be forgiuen: I forgiue all.
There cannot be those numberlesse offences
Gainst me, that I cannot take peace with:
No blacke Enuy shall make my Graue,
Commend mee to his Grace:
And if he speake of *Buckingham*; pray tell him,
You met him halfe in Heauen: my vowes and prayers
Yet are the Kings; and till my Soule forsake,
Shall cry for blessings on him. May he liue
Longer then I haue time to tell his yeares;
Euer belou'd and louing, may his Rule be;
And when old Time shall lead him to his end,
Goodnesse and he, fill vp one Monument.

  Lou. To th' water side I must conduct your Grace;
Then giue my Charge vp to Sir *Nicholas Vaux*,
Who vndertakes you to your end.

  Vaux. Prepare there,
The Duke is comming: See the Barge be ready;
And fit it with such furniture as suites
The Greatnesse of his Person.

  Buck. Nay, Sir *Nicholas*,
Let it alone; my State now will but mocke me.
When I came hither, I was Lord High Constable,
And Duke of *Buckingham*: now, poore *Edward Bohun*;
Yet I am richer then my base Accusers,
That neuer knew what Truth meant: I now seale it;
And with that blood will make 'em one day groane for't.
My noble Father *Henry* of *Buckingham*,
Who first rais'd head against Vsurping *Richard*,
Flying for succour to his Seruant *Banister*,
Being distrest; was by that wretch betraid,
And without Tryall, fell; Gods peace be with him.
Henry the Seauenth succeeding, truly pittying
My Fathers losse; like a most Royall Prince
Restor'd me to my Honours: and out of ruines
Made my Name once more Noble. Now his Sonne,
Henry the Eight, Life, Honour, Name and all
That made me happy; at one stroake ha's taken
For euer from the World. I had my Tryall,
And must needs say a Noble one; which makes me
A little happier then my wretched Father:
Yet thus farre we are one in Fortunes; both
Fell by our Seruants, by those Men we lou'd most:
A most vnnaturall and faithlesse Seruice.
Heauen ha's an end in all: yet, you that heare me,
This from a dying man receiue as certaine:
Where you are liberall of your loues and Councels,
Be sure you be not loose; for those you make friends,

And giue your hearts to; when they once perceiue
The least rub in your fortunes, fall away
Like water from ye, neuer found againe
But where they meane to sinke ye: all good people
Pray for me, I must now forsake ye; the last houre
Of my long weary life is come vpon me:
Farewell; and when you would say somthing that is sad,
Speake how I fell.
I haue done; and God forgiue me.
Exeunt Duke and Traine.

1. O, this is full of pitty; Sir, it cals
I feare, too many curses on their heads
That were the Authors.

2. If the Duke be guiltlesse,
'Tis full of woe: yet I can giue you inckling
Of an ensuing euill, if it fall,
Greater then this.

1. Good Angels keepe it from vs:
What may it be? you doe not doubt my faith Sir?

2. This Secret is so weighty, 'twill require
A strong faith to conceale it.

1. Let me haue it:
I doe not talke much.

2. I am confident;
You shall Sir: Did you not of late dayes heare
A buzzing of a Separation
Betweene the King and *Katherine*?

1. Yes, but it held not;
For when the King once heard it, out of anger
He sent command to the Lord Mayor straight
To stop the rumor; and allay those tongues
That durst disperse it.

2. But that slander Sir,
Is found a truth now: for it growes agen
Fresher then e're it was; and held for certaine
The King will venture at it. Either the Cardinall,
Or some about him neere, haue out of malice
To the good Queene, possest him with a scruple
That will vndoe her: To confirme this too,
Cardinall *Campeius* is arriu'd, and lately,
As all thinke for this busines.

1. Tis the Cardinall;
And meerely to reuenge him on the Emperour,
For not bestowing on him at his asking,
The Archbishopricke of *Toledo*, this is purpos'd.

2. I thinke
You haue hit the marke; but is't not cruell,
That she should feele the smart of this: the Cardinall
Will haue his will, and she must fall.

1. 'Tis wofull.
Wee are too open heere to argue this:
Let's thinke in priuate more. *Exeunt.*

Scena Secunda.

Enter Lord Chamberlaine, reading this Letter.

MY Lord, the Horses your Lordship sent for, with all the care I had, I saw well chosen, ridden, and furnish'd. They were young and handsome, and of the best breed in the North. When they were ready to set out for London, a man of my Lord Cardinalls, by Commission, and maine power tooke em from me, with this reason: his maister would bee seru'd before a Subiect, if not before the King, which stop'd our mouthes Sir.

I feare he will indeede; well, let him haue them; hee will haue all I thinke.

Enter to the Lord Chamberlaine, the Dukes of Norfolke and Suffolke.

Norf. Well met my Lord Chamberlaine.
Cham. Good day to both your Graces.
Suff. How is the King imployd?
Cham. I left him priuate,
Full of sad thoughts and troubles.
Norf. What's the cause?
Cham. It seemes the Marriage with his Brothers Wife
Ha's crept too neere his Conscience.
Suff. No, his Conscience
Ha's crept too neere another Ladie.
Norf. Tis so;
This is the Cardinals doing: The King-Cardinall,
That blinde Priest, like the eldest Sonne of Fortune,
Turnes what he list. The King will know him one day.
Suff. Pray God he doe,
Hee'l neuer know himselfe else.
Norf. How holily he workes in all his businesse,
And with what zeale? For now he has crackt the League
Between vs & the Emperor (the Queens great Nephew)
He diues into the Kings Soule, and there scatters
Dangers, doubts, wringing of the Conscience,
Feares, and despaires, and all these for his Marriage.
And out of all these, to restore the King,
He counsels a Diuorce, a losse of her
That like a Iewell, ha's hung twenty yeares
About his necke, yet neuer lost her lustre;
Of her that loues him with that excellence,
That Angels loue good men with: Euen of her,
That when the greatest stroake of Fortune falls
Will blesse the King: and is not this course pious?
Cham. Heauen keep me from such councel: tis most true
These newes are euery where, euery tongue speaks 'em,
And euery true heart weepes for't. All that dare
Looke into these affaires, see this maine end,
The French Kings Sister. Heauen will one day open
The Kings eyes, that so long haue slept vpon
This bold bad man.
Suff. And free vs from his slauery.
Norf. We had need pray,
And heartily, for our deliuerance;
Or this imperious man will worke vs all
From Princes into Pages: all mens honours
Lie like one lumpe before him, to be fashion'd
Into what pitch he please.
Suff. For me, my Lords,
I loue him not, nor feare him, there's my Creede:
As I am made without him, so Ile stand.
If the King please: his Curses and his blessings
Touch me alike: th'are breath I not beleeue in.
I knew him, and I know him: so I leaue him
To him that made him proud; the Pope.
Norf. Let's in;
And with some other busines, put the King
From these sad thoughts, that work too much vpon him:
My Lord, youle beare vs company?
Cham. Excuse me,
The King ha's sent me otherwhere: Besides
You'l finde a most vnfit time to disturbe him:
Health to your Lordships.

Nor.

Norfolke. Thankes my good Lord *Chamberlaine.*
Exit Lord Chamberlaine, and the King drawes the Curtaine
and sits reading pensiuely.

Suff. How sad he lookes; sure he is much afflicted.
Kin. Who's there? Ha?
Norff. Pray God he be not angry.
Kin. Who's there I say? How dare you thrust your selues
Into my priuate Meditations?
Who am I? Ha?

Norff. A gracious King, that pardons all offences
Malice ne're meant: Our breach of Duty this way,
Is businesse of Estate; in which, we come
To know your Royall pleasure.

Kin. Ye are too bold:
Go too; Ile make ye know your times of businesse:
Is this an howre for temporall affaires? Ha?

Enter Wolsey and Campeius with a Commission.

Who's there? my good Lord Cardinall? O my *Wolsey,*
The quiet of my wounded Conscience;
Thou art a cure fit for a King; you'r welcome
Most learned Reuerend Sir, into our Kingdome,
Vse vs, and it: My good Lord, haue great care,
I be not found a Talker.

Wol. Sir, you cannot;
I would your Grace would giue vs but an houre
Of priuate conference.

Kin. We are busie; goe.
Norff. This Priest ha's no pride in him?
Suff. Not to speake of:
I would not be so sicke though for his place:
But this cannot continue.
Norff. If it doe, Ile venture one; haue at him.
Suff. I another.

Exeunt Norfolke and Suffolke.

Wol. Your Grace ha's giuen a President of wisedome
Aboue all Princes, in committing freely
Your scruple to the voyce of Christendome:
Who can be angry now? What Enuy reach you?
The Spaniard tide by blood and fauour to her,
Must now confesse, if they haue any goodnesse,
The Tryall, iust and Noble. All the Clerkes,
(I meane the learned ones in Christian Kingdomes)
Haue their free voyces. Rome (the Nurse of Iudgement)
Inuited by your Noble selfe, hath sent
One generall Tongue vnto vs. This good man,
This iust and learned Priest, Cardnall *Campeius,*
Whom once more, I present vnto your Highnesse.

Kin. And once more in mine armes I bid him welcome,
And thanke the holy Conclaue for their loues,
They haue sent me such a Man, I would haue wish'd for.
Cam. Your Grace must needs deserue all strangers loues,
You are so Noble: To your Highnesse hand
I tender my Commission; by whose vertue,
The Court of Rome commanding. You my Lord
Cardinall of *Yorke,* are ioyn'd with me their Seruant,
In the vnpartiall iudging of this Businesse.

Kin. Two equall men: The Queene shall be acquainted
Forthwith for what you come. Where's *Gardiner?*
Wol. I know your Maiesty, ha's alwayes lou'd her
So deare in heart, not to deny her that
A Woman of lesse Place might aske by Law;
Schollers allow'd freely to argue for her.

Kin. I, and the best she shall haue; and my fauour
To him that does best, God forbid els: Cardinall,
Prethee call *Gardiner* to me, my new Secretary.
I find him a fit fellow.

Enter Gardiner.

Wol. Giue me your hand: much ioy & fauour to you;
You are the Kings now.
Gard. But to be commanded
For euer by your Grace, whose hand ha's rais'd me.
Kin. Come hither *Gardiner.*

Walkes and whispers.

Camp. My Lord of *Yorke,* was not one Doctor *Pace*
In this mans place before him?
Wol. Yes, he was.
Camp. Was he not held a learned man?
Wol. Yes surely.
Camp. Beleeue me, there's an ill opinion spread then,
Euen of your selfe Lord Cardinall.
Wol. How? of me?
Camp. They will not sticke to say, you enuide him;
And fearing he would rise (he was so vertuous)
Kept him a forraigne man still, which so greeu'd him,
That he ran mad, and dide.
Wol. Heau'ns peace be with him:
That's Christian care enough: for liuing Murmurers,
There's places of rebuke. He was a Foole;
For he would needs be vertuous. That good Fellow,
If I command him followes my appointment,
I will haue none so neere els. Learne this Brother,
We liue not to be grip'd by meaner persons.
Kin. Deliuer this with modesty to th' Queene.

Exit Gardiner.

The most conuenient place, that I can thinke of
For such receipt of Learning, is Black-Fryers:
There ye shall meete about this waighty busines.
My *Wolsey,* see it furnish'd, O my Lord,
Would it not grieue an able man to leaue
So sweet a Bedfellow? But Conscience, Conscience;
O 'tis a tender place, and I must leaue her. *Exeunt.*

Scena Tertia.

Enter Anne Bullen, and an old Lady.

An. Not for that neither; here's the pang that pinches.
His Highnesse, hauing liu'd so long with her, and she
So good a Lady, that no Tongue could euer
Pronounce dishonour of her; by my life,
She neuer knew harme-doing: Oh, now after
So many courses of the Sun enthroaned,
Still growing in a Maiesty and pompe, the which
To leaue, a thousand fold more bitter, then
'Tis sweet at first t'acquire. After this Processe,
To giue her the auaunt, it is a pitty
Would moue a Monster.

Old La. Hearts of most hard temper
Melt and lament for her.
An. Oh Gods will, much better
She ne're had knowne pompe; though't be temporall,
Yet if that quarrell. Fortune, do diuorce
It from the bearer, 'tis a sufferance, panging
As soule and bodies seuering.
Old L. Alas poore Lady,
Shee's a stranger now againe.
An. So much the more
Must pitty drop vpon her; verily
I sweare, tis better to be lowly borne,

And range with humble liuers in Content,
Then to be perk'd vp in a glistring griefe,
And weare a golden sorrow.

Old L. Our content
Is our best hauing.

Anne. By my troth, and Maidenhead,
I would not be a Queene.

Old. L. Beshrew me, I would,
And venture Maidenhead for't, and so would you
For all this spice of your Hipocrisie:
You that haue so faire parts of Woman on you,
Haue (too) a Womans heart, which euer yet
Affected Eminence, Wealth, Soueraignty;
Which, to say sooth, are Blessings; and which guifts
(Sauing your mincing) the capacity
Of your soft Chiuerell Conscience, would receiue,
If you might please to stretch it.

Anne. Nay, good troth.

Old L. Yes troth, & troth; you would not be a Queen?

Anne. No, not for all the riches vnder Heauen.

Old. L. Tis strange; a threepence bow'd would hire me
Old as I am, to Queene it: but I pray you,
What thinke you of a Dutchesse? Haue you limbs
To beare that load of Title?

An. No in truth.

Old. L. Then you are weakly made; plucke off a little,
I would not be a young Count in your way,
For more then blushing comes to: If your backe
Cannot vouchsafe this burthen, tis too weake
Euer to get a Boy.

An. How you doe talke;
I sweare againe, I would not be a Queene,
For all the world:

Old. L. In faith, for little England
You'ld venture an emballing: I my selfe
Would for *Carnaruanshire*, although there long'd
No more to th' Crowne but that: Lo, who comes here?

Enter Lord Chamberlaine.

L. Cham. Good morrow Ladies; what wer't worth to
The secret of your conference? (know

An. My good Lord,
Not your demand; it values not your asking:
Our Mistris Sorrowes we were pittying.

Cham. It was a gentle businesse, and becomming
The action of good women, there is hope
All will be well.

An. Now I pray God, *Amen*.

Cham. You beare a gentle minde, & heau'nly blessings
Follow such Creatures. That you may, faire Lady
Perceiue I speake sincerely, and high notes
Tane of your many vertues; the Kings Maiesty
Commends his good opinion of you, to you; and
Doe's purpose honour to you no lesse flowing,
Then Marchionesse of *Pembrooke*; to which Title,
A Thousand pound a yeare, Annuall support,
Out of his Grace, he addes.

An. I doe not know
What kinde of my obedience, I should tender;
More then my All, is Nothing: Nor my Prayers
Are not words duely hallowed; nor my Wishes
More worth, then empty vanities: yet Prayers & Wishes
Are all I can returne. 'Beseech your Lordship,
Vouchsafe to speake my thankes, and my obedience,
As from a blushing Handmaid, to his Highnesse;
Whose health and Royalty I pray for.

Cham. Lady;
I shall not faile t'approue the faire conceit
The King hath of you. I haue perus'd her well,
Beauty and Honour in her are so mingled,
That they haue caught the King: and who knowes yet
But from this Lady, may proceed a Iemme,
To lighten all this Ile. I'le to the King,
And say I spoke with you.

Exit Lord Chamberlaine.

An. My honour'd Lord.

Old. L. Why this it is: See, see,
I haue beene begging sixteene yeares in Court
(Am yet a Courtier beggerly) nor could
Come pat betwixt too early, and too late
For any suit of pounds: and you, (oh fate)
A very fresh Fish heere; fye, fye, fye vpon
This compel'd fortune: haue your mouth fild vp,
Before you open it.

An. This is strange to me.

Old L. How tasts it? Is it bitter? Forty pence, no:
There was a Lady once (tis an old Story)
That would not be a Queene, that would she not
For all the mud in Egypt; haue you heard it?

An. Come you are pleasant.

Old. L. With your Theame, I could
O're-mount the Larke: The Marchionesse of *Pembrooke*?
A thousand pounds a yeare, for pure respect?
No other obligation? by my Life,
That promises mo thousands: Honours traine
Is longer then his fore-skirt; by this time
I know your backe will beare a Dutchesse. Say,
Are you not stronger then you were?

An. Good Lady,
Make your selfe mirth with your particular fancy,
And leaue me out on't. Would I had no being
If this salute my blood a iot; it faints me
To thinke what followes.
The Queene is comfortlesse, and wee forgetfull
In our long absence: pray doe not deliuer,
What heere y'haue heard to her.

Old L. What doe you thinke me ——— *Exeunt.*

Scena Quarta.

Trumpets, Sennet, and Cornets.
*Enter two Vergers, with short siluer wands; next them two
Scribes in the habite of Doctors; after them, the Bishop of
Canterbury alone; after him, the Bishops of Lincolne, Ely,
Rochester, and S. Asaph: Next them, with some small
distance, followes a Gentleman bearing the Purse, with the
great Seale, and a Cardinals Hat: Then two Priests, bearing each a Siluer Crosse: Then a Gentleman Vsher bare-
headed, accompanyed with a Sergeant at Armes, bearing a
Siluer Mace: Then two Gentlemen bearing two great
Siluer Pillers: After them, side by side, the two Cardinals,
two Noblemen, with the Sword and Mace. The King takes
place vnder the Cloth of State. The two Cardinalls sit
vnder him as Iudges. The Queene takes place some distance from the King. The Bishops place themselues on
each side the Court in manner of a Consistory: Below them
the Scribes. The Lords sit next the Bishops. The rest of the
Attendants stand in conuenient order about the Stage.*

Car. Whil'st our Commission from Rome is read,
Let silence be commanded.

King. What's the need?
It hath already publiquely bene read,
And on all sides th'Authority allow'd,
You may then spare that time.

Car. Bee't so, proceed.

Scri. Say, *Henry* K. of England, come into the Court.

Crier. *Henry* King of England, &c.

King. Heere.

Scribe. Say, *Katherine* Queene of England,
Come into the Court.

Crier. *Katherine* Queene of England, &c.

The Queene makes no answer, rises out of her Chaire, goes about the Court, comes to the King, and kneeles at his Feete. Then speakes.

Sir, I desire you do me Right and Iustice,
And to bestow your pitty on me; for
I am a most poore Woman, and a Stranger,
Borne out of your Dominions: hauing heere
No Iudge indifferent, nor no more assurance
Of equall Friendship and Proceeding. Alas Sir:
In what haue I offended you? What cause
Hath my behauiour giuen to your displeasure,
That thus you should proceede to put me off,
And take your good Grace from me? Heauen witnesse,
I haue bene to you, a true and humble Wife,
At all times to your will conformable:
Euer in feare to kindle your Dislike,
Yea, subiect to your Countenance: Glad, or sorry,
As I saw it inclin'd? When was the houre
I euer contradicted your Desire?
Or made it not mine too? Or which of your Friends
Haue I not stroue to loue, although I knew
He were mine Enemy? What Friend of mine,
That had to him deriu'd your Anger, did I
Continue in my Liking? Nay, gaue notice
He was from thence discharg'd? Sir, call to minde,
That I haue beene your Wife, in this Obedience,
Vpward of twenty yeares, and haue bene blest
With many Children by you. If in the course
And processe of this time, you can report,
And proue it too, against mine Honor, aught;
My bond to Wedlocke, or my Loue and Dutie
Against your Sacred Person; in Gods name
Turne me away: and let the fowl'st Contempt
Shut doore vpon me, and so giue me vp
To the sharp'st kinde of Iustice. Please you, Sir,
The King your Father, was reputed for
A Prince most Prudent; of an excellent
And vnmatch'd Wit, and Iudgement. *Ferdinand*
My Father, King of Spaine, was reckon'd one
The wisest Prince, that there had reign'd, by many
A yeare before. It is not to be question'd,
That they had gather'd a wise Councell to them
Of euery Realme, that did debate this Businesse,
Who deem'd our Marriage lawful. Wherefore I humbly
Beseech you Sir, to spare me, till I may
Be by my Friends in Spaine, aduis'd; whose Counsaile
I will implore. If not, i'th'name of God
Your pleasure be fulfill'd.

Wol. You haue heere Lady,
(And of your choice) these Reuerend Fathers, men
Of singular Integrity, and Learning;
Yea, the elect o'th'Land, who are assembled
To pleade your Cause. It shall be therefore bootlesse,
That longer you desire the Court, as well
For your owne quiet, as to rectifie
What is vnsetled in the King.

Camp. His Grace
Hath spoken well, and iustly: Therefore Madam,
It's fit this Royall Session do proceed,
And that (without delay) their Arguments
Be now produc'd, and heard.

Qu. Lord Cardinall, to you I speake.

Wol. Your pleasure, Madam.

Qu. Sir, I am about to weepe; but thinking that
We are a Queene (or long haue dream'd so) certaine
The daughter of a King, my drops of teares,
Ile turne to sparkes of fire.

Wol. Be patient yet.

Qu. I will, when you are humble; Nay before,
Or God will punish me. I do beleeue
(Induc'd by potent Circumstances) that
You are mine Enemy, and make my Challenge,
You shall not be my Iudge. For it is you
Haue blowne this Coale, betwixt my Lord, and me;
(Which Gods dew quench) therefore, I say againe,
I vtterly abhorre; yea, from my Soule
Refuse you for my Iudge, whom yet once more
I hold my most malicious Foe, and thinke not
At all a Friend to truth.

Wol. I do professe
You speake not like your selfe: who euer yet
Haue stood to Charity, and displayd th'effects
Of disposition gentle, and of wisedome,
Ore-topping womans powre. Madam, you do me wrong
I haue no Spleene against you, nor iniustice
For you, or any: how farre I haue proceeded,
Or how farre further (Shall) is warranted
By a Commission from the Consistorie,
Yea, the whole Consistorie of Rome. You charge me,
That I haue blowne this Coale: I do deny it,
The King is present: If it be knowne to him,
That I gainsay my Deed, how may he wound,
And worthily my Falsehood, yea, as much
As you haue done my Truth. If he know
That I am free of your Report, he knowes
I am not of your wrong. Therefore in him
It lies to cure me, and the Cure is to
Remoue these Thoughts from you. The which before
His Highnesse shall speake in, I do beseech
You (gracious Madam) to vnthinke your speaking,
And to say so no more.

Queen. My Lord, my Lord,
I am a simple woman, much too weake
T'oppose your cunning. Y'are meek, & humble-mouth'd
You signe your Place, and Calling, in full seeming,
With Meekenesse and Humilitie: but your Heart
Is cramm'd with Arrogancie, Spleene, and Pride.
You haue by Fortune, and his Highnesse fauors,
Gone slightly o're lowe steppes, and now are mounted
Where Powres are your Retainers, and your words
(Domestickes to you) serue your will, as't please
Your selfe pronounce their Office. I must tell you,
You tender more your persons Honor, then
Your high profession Spirituall. That agen
I do refuse you for my Iudge, and heere
Before you all, Appeale vnto the Pope,
To bring my whole Cause 'fore his Holinesse,
And to be iudg'd by him.

She Curtsies to the King, and offers to depart.

Camp.

Camp. The Queene is obstinate,
Stubborne to Iustice, apt to accuse it, and
Disdainfull to be tride by't; tis not well.
Shee's going away.

Kin. Call her againe.

Crier. Katherine Q. of England, come into the Court.

Gent. Ush. Madam, you are cald backe.

Que. What need you note it? pray you keepe your way,
When you are cald returne. Now the Lord helpe,
They vexe me past my patience, pray you passe on;
I will not tarry: no, nor euer more
Vpon this businesse my appearance make,
In any of their Courts.

Exit Queene, and her Attendants.

Kin. Goe thy wayes *Kate*,
That man i'th' world, who shall report he ha's
A better Wife, let him in naught be trusted,
For speaking false in that; thou art alone
(If thy rare qualities, sweet gentlenesse,
Thy meeknesse Saint-like, Wife-like Gouernment,
Obeying in commanding, and thy parts
Soueraigne and Pious els, could speake thee out)
The Queene of earthly Queenes: Shee's Noble borne;
And like her true Nobility, she ha's
Carried her selfe towards me.

Wol. Most gracious Sir,
In humblest manner I require your Highnes,
That it shall please you to declare in hearing
Of all these eares (for where I am rob'd and bound,
There must I be vnloos'd, although not there
At once, and fully satisfide) whether euer I
Did broach this busines to your Highnes, or
Laid any scruple in your way, which might
Induce you to the question on't, or euer
Haue to you, but with thankes to God for such
A Royall Lady, spake one, the least word that might
Be to the preiudice of her present State,
Or touch of her good Person?

Kin. My Lord Cardinall,
I doe excuse you; yea, vpon mine Honour,
I free you from't: You are not to be taught
That you haue many enemies, that know not
Why they are so; but like to Village Curres,
Barke when their fellowes doe. By some of these
The Queene is put in anger; y'are excus'd:
But will you be more iustifi'de? You euer
Haue wish'd the sleeping of this busines, neuer desir'd
It to be stir'd; but oft haue hindred, oft
The passages made toward it; on my Honour,
I speake my good Lord Cardnall, to this point;
And thus farre cleare him.
Now, what mou'd me too't,
I will be bold with time and your attention: (too't:
Then marke th'inducement. Thus it came; giue heede
My Conscience first receiu'd a tendernes,
Scruple, and pricke, on certaine Speeches vtter'd
By th' Bishop of *Bayon*, then French Embassador,
Who had beene hither sent on the debating
And Marriage 'twixt the Duke of *Orleance*, and
Our Daughter *Mary*: I'th' Progresse of this busines,
Ere a determinate resolution, hee
(I meane the Bishop) did require a respite,
Wherein he might the King his Lord aduertise,
Whether our Daughter were legitimate,
Respecting this our Marriage with the Dowager,
Sometimes our Brothers Wife. This respite shooke
The bosome of my Conscience, enter'd me;
Yea, with a spitting power, and made to tremble
The region of my Breast, which forc'd such way,
That many maz'd considerings, did throng
And prest in with this Caution. First, me thought
I stood not in the smile of Heauen, who had
Commanded Nature, that my Ladies wombe
If it conceiu'd a male-child by me, should
Doe no more Offices of life too't; then
The Graue does to th' dead: For her Male Issue,
Or di'de where they were made, or shortly after
This world had ayr'd them. Hence I tooke a thought,
This was a Iudgement on me, that my Kingdome
(Well worthy the best Heyre o'th' World) should not
Be gladded in't by me. Then followes, that
I weigh'd the danger which my Realmes stood in
By this my Issues faile, and that gaue to me
Many a groaning throw: thus hulling in
The wild Sea of my Conscience, I did steere
Toward this remedy, whereupon we are
Now present heere together: that's to say,
I meant to rectifie my Conscience, which
I then did feele full sicke, and yet not well,
By all the Reuerend Fathers of the Land,
And Doctors learn'd. First I began in priuate,
With you my Lord of *Lincolne*; you remember
How vnder my oppression I did reeke
When I first mou'd you.

B. Lin. Very well my Liedge.

Kin. I haue spoke long, be pleas'd your selfe to say
How farre you satisfide me.

Lin. So please your Highnes,
The question did at first so stagger me,
Bearing a State of mighty moment in't,
And consequence of dread, that I committed
The daringst Counsaile which I had to doubt,
And did entreate your Highnes to this course,
Which you are running heere.

Kin. I then mou'd you,
My Lord of *Canterbury*, and got your leaue
To make this present Summons vnsolicited.
I left no Reuerend Person in this Court;
But by particular consent proceeded
Vnder your hands and Seales; therefore goe on,
For no dislike i'th' world against the person
Of the good Queene; but the sharpe thorny points
Of my alleadged reasons, driues this forward:
Proue but our Marriage lawfull, by my Life
And Kingly Dignity, we are contented
To weare our mortall State to come, with her,
(*Katherine* our Queene) before the primest Creature
That's Parragon'd o'th' World.

Camp. So please your Highnes,
The Queene being absent, 'tis a needfull fitnesse,
That we adiourne this Court till further day;
Meane while, must be an earnest motion
Made to the Queene to call backe her Appeale
She intends vnto his Holinesse.

Kin. I may perceiue
These Cardinals trifle with me: I abhorre
This dilatory sloth, and trickes of Rome.
My learn'd and welbeloued Seruant *Cranmer*,
Prethee returne, with thy approch: I know,
My comfort comes along: breake vp the Court;
I say, set on.

Exeunt, in manner as they enter'd.

Actus Tertius. Scena Prima.

Enter Queene and her Women as at worke.

Queen. Take thy Lute wench,
My Soule growes sad with troubles,
Sing, and disperse 'em if thou canst: leaue working:

SONG.

Orpheus with his Lute made Trees,
And the Mountaine tops that freeze,
  Bow themselues when he did sing.
To his Musicke, Plants and Flowers
Euer sprung; as Sunne and Showers,
  There had made a lasting Spring.
Euery thing that heard him play,
Euen the Billowes of the Sea,
  Hung their heads, & then lay by.
In sweet Musicke is such Art,
Killing care, & griefe of heart,
  Fall asleepe, or hearing dye.

Enter a Gentleman.

Queen. How now?
Gent. And't please your Grace, the two great Cardinals
Wait in the presence.
Queen. Would they speake with me?
Gent. They wil'd me say so Madam.
Queen. Pray their Graces
To come neere: what can be their busines
With me, a poore weake woman, falne from fauour?
I doe not like their comming; now I thinke on't,
They should bee good men, their affaires as righteous:
But all Hoods, make not Monkes.

Enter the two Cardinalls, Wolsey & Campian.

Wols. Peace to your Highnesse.
Queen. Your Graces find me heere part of a Houswife,
(I would be all) against the worst may happen:
What are your pleasures with me, reuerent Lords?
Wol. May it please you Noble Madam, to withdraw
Into your priuate Chamber; we shall giue you
The full cause of our comming.
Queen. Speake it heere.
There's nothing I haue done yet o' my Conscience
Deserues a Corner: would all other Women
Could speake this with as free a Soule as I doe.
My Lords, I care not (so much I am happy
Aboue a number) if my actions
Were tri'de by eu'ry tongue, eu'ry eye saw 'em,
Enuy and base opinion set against 'em,
I know my life so euen. If your busines
Seeke me out, and that way I am Wife in;
Out with it boldly: Truth loues open dealing.
Card. Tanta est erga te mentis integritas Regina serenissima.
Queen. O good my Lord, no Latin;
I am not such a Truant since my comming,
As not to know the Language I haue liu'd in:
A strange Tongue makes my cause more strange, suspiti-
Pray speake in English; heere are some will thanke you, (ous:
If you speake truth, for their poore Mistris sake;
Beleeue me she ha's had much wrong. Lord Cardinall,
The willing'st sinne I euer yet committed,
May be absolu'd in English.
Card. Noble Lady,
I am sorry my integrity shoul breed,
(And seruice to his Maiesty and you)
So deepe suspition, where all faith was meant;
We come not by the way of Accusation,
To taint that honour euery good Tongue blesses;
Nor to betray you any way to sorrow;
You haue too much good Lady: But to know
How you stand minded in the waighty difference
Betweene the King and you, and to deliuer
(Like free and honest men) our iust opinions,
And comforts to our cause.
Camp. Most honour'd Madam,
My Lord of Yorke, out of his Noble nature,
Zeale and obedience he still bore your Grace,
Forgetting (like a good man) your late Censure
Both of his truth and him (which was too farre)
Offers, as I doe, in a signe of peace,
His Seruice, and his Counsell.
Queen. To betray me.
My Lords, I thanke you both for your good wills,
Ye speake like honest men, (pray God ye proue so)
But how to make ye sodainly an Answere
In such a poynt of weight, so neere mine Honour,
(More neere my Life I feare) with my weake wit;
And to such men of grauity and learning;
In truth I know not. I was set at worke,
Among my Maids, full little (God knowes) looking
Either for such men, or such businesse;
For her sake that I haue beene, for I feele
The last fit of my Greatnesse; good your Graces
Let me haue time and Councell for my Cause:
Alas, I am a Woman frendlesse, hopelesse.
Wol. Madam,
You wrong the Kings loue with these feares,
Your hopes and friends are infinite.
Queen. In England,
But little for my profit can you thinke Lords,
That any English man dare giue me Councell?
Or be a knowne friend 'gainst his Highnes pleasure,
(Though he be growne so desperate to be honest)
And liue a Subiect? Nay forsooth, my Friends,
They that must weigh out my afflictions,
They that my trust must grow to, liue not heere,
They are (as all my other comforts) far hence
In mine owne Countrey Lords.
Camp. I would your Grace
Would leaue your greefes, and take my Counsell.
Queen. How Sir?
Camp. Put your maine cause into the Kings protection,
Hee's louing and most gracious. 'Twill be much,
Both for your Honour better, and your Cause:
For if the tryall of the Law o'retake ye,
You'l part away disgrac'd.
Wol. He tels you rightly.
Queen. Ye tell me what ye wish for both, my ruine:
Is this your Christian Councell? Out vpon ye.
Heauen is aboue all yet; there sits a Iudge,
That no King can corrupt.
Camp. Your rage mistakes vs.
Queen. The more shame for ye; holy men I thought ye,
Vpon my Soule two reuerend Cardinall Vertues:
But Cardinall Sins, and hollow hearts I feare ye:
Mend 'em for shame my Lords: Is this your comfort?
The Cordiall that ye bring a wretched Lady?
A woman lost among ye, laugh't at, scornd?
I will not wish ye halfe my miseries,

I haue more Charity. But say I warn'd ye;
Take heed, for heauens sake take heed, least at once
The burthen of my sorrowes, fall vpon ye.
  Car. Madam, this is a meere distraction,
You turne the good we offer, into enuy.
  Quee. Ye turne me into nothing. Woe vpon ye,
And all such false Professors. Would you haue me
(If you haue any Iustice, any Pitty,
If ye be any thing but Churchmens habits)
Put my sicke cause into his hands, that hates me?
Alas, ha's banish'd me his Bed already,
His Loue, too long ago. I am old my Lords,
And all the Fellowship I hold now with him
Is onely my Obedience. What can happen
To me, aboue this wretchednesse? All your Studies
Make me a Curse, like this.
  Camp. Your feares are worse.
  Qu. Haue I liu'd thus long (let me speake my selfe,
Since Vertue findes no friends) a Wife, a true one?
A Woman (I dare say without Vainglory)
Neuer yet branded with Suspition?
Haue I, with all my full Affections
Still met the King? Lou'd him next Heau'n? Obey'd him?
Bin (out of fondnesse) superstitious to him?
Almost forgot my Prayres to content him?
And am I thus rewarded? 'Tis not well Lords.
Bring me a constant woman to her Husband,
One that ne're dream'd a Ioy, beyond his pleasure;
And to that Woman (when she has done most)
Yet will I adde an Honor; a great Patience.
  Car. Madam, you wander from the good
We ayme at.
  Qu. My Lord,
I dare not make my selfe so guiltie,
To giue vp willingly that Noble Title
Your Master wed me to: nothing but death
Shall e're diuorce my Dignities.
  Car. Pray heare me.
  Qu. Would I had neuer trod this English Earth,
Or felt the Flatteries that grow vpon it:
Ye haue Angels Faces; but Heauen knowes your hearts.
What will become of me now, wretched Lady?
I am the most vnhappy Woman liuing.
Alas (poore Wenches) where are now your Fortunes?
Shipwrack'd vpon a Kingdome, where no Pitty,
No Friends, no Hope, no Kindred weepe for me?
Almost no Graue allow'd me? Like the Lilly
That once was Mistris of the Field, and flourish'd,
Ile hang my head, and perish.
  Car. If your Grace
Could but be brought to know, our Ends are honest,
You'ld feele more comfort. Why shold we (good Lady)
Vpon what cause wrong you? Alas, our Places,
The way of our Profession is against it;
We are to Cure such sorrowes, not to sowe 'em.
For Goodnesse sake, consider what you do,
How you may hurt your selfe: I, vtterly
Grow from the Kings Acquaintance, by this Carriage.
The hearts of Princes kisse Obedience,
So much they loue it. But to stubborne Spirits,
They swell and grow, as terrible as stormes.
I know you haue a Gentle, Noble temper,
A Soule as euen as a Calme; Pray thinke vs,
Those we professe, Peace-makers, Friends, and Seruants.
  Camp. Madam, you'l finde it so:
You wrong your Vertues
With these weake Womens feares. A Noble Spirit
As yours was, put into you, euer casts
Such doubts as false Coine from it. The King loues you,
Beware you loose it not: For vs (if you please
To trust vs in your businesse) we are ready
To vse our vtmost Studies, in your seruice.
  Qu. Do what ye will, my Lords:
And pray forgiue me;
If I haue vs'd my selfe vnmannerly,
You know I am a Woman, lacking wit
To make a seemely answer to such persons.
Pray do my seruice to his Maiestie,
He ha's my heart yet, and shall haue my Prayers
While I shall haue my life. Come reuerend Fathers,
Bestow your Councels on me. She now begges
That little thought when she set footing heere,
She should haue bought her Dignities so deere. *Exeunt*

Scena Secunda.

Enter the Duke of Norfolke, Duke of Suffolke, Lord Surrey, and Lord Chamberlaine.

  Norf. If you will now vnite in your Complaints,
And force them with a Constancy, the Cardinall
Cannot stand vnder them. If you omit
The offer of this time, I cannot promise,
But that you shall sustaine moe new disgraces,
With these you beare alreadie.
  Sur. I am ioyfull
To meete the least occasion, that may giue me
Remembrance of my Father-in-Law, the Duke,
To be reueng'd on him.
  Suf. Which of the Peeres
Haue vncontemn'd gone by him, or at least
Strangely neglected? When did he regard
The stampe of Noblenesse in any person
Out of himselfe?
  Cham. My Lords, you speake your pleasures:
What he deserues of you and me, I know:
What we can do to him (though now the time
Giues way to vs) I much feare. If you cannot
Barre his accesse to'th'King, neuer attempt
Any thing on him: for he hath a Witchcraft
Ouer the King in's Tongue.
  Nor. O feare him not,
His spell in that is out: the King hath found
Matter against him, that for euer marres
The Hony of his Language. No, he's setled
(Not to come off) in his displeasure.
  Sur. Sir,
I should be glad to heare such Newes as this
Once euery houre.
  Nor. Beleeue it, this is true.
In the Diuorce, his contrarie proceedings
Are all vnfolded: wherein he appeares,
As I would wish mine Enemy.
  Sur. How came
His practises to light?
  Suf. Most strangely.
  Sur. O how? how?
  Suf. The Cardinals Letters to the Pope miscarried,

And came to th'eye o'th'King, wherein was read
How that the Cardinall did intreat his Holinesse
To stay the Iudgement o'th'Diuorce; for if
It did take place, I do (quoth he) perceiue
My King is tangled in affection, to
A Creature of the Queenes, Lady *Anne Bullen*.

Sur. Ha's the King this?

Suf. Beleeue it.

Sur. Will this worke?

Cham. The King in this perceiues him, how he coasts
And hedges his owne way. But in this point,
All his trickes founder, and he brings his Physicke
After his Patients death; the King already
Hath married the faire Lady.

Sur. Would he had.

Suf. May you be happy in your wish my Lord,
For I professe you haue it.

Sur. Now all my ioy
Trace the Coniunction.

Suf. My Amen too't.

Nor. All mens.

Suf. There's order giuen for her Coronation:
Marry this is yet but yong, and may be left
To some eares vnrecounted. But my Lords
She is a gallant Creature, and compleate
In minde and feature. I perswade me, from her
Will fall some blessing to this Land, which shall
In it be memoriz'd.

Sur. But will the King
Digest this Letter of the Cardinals?
The Lord forbid.

Nor. Marry Amen.

Suf. No, no:
There be moe Waspes that buz about his Nose,
Will make this sting the sooner. Cardinall *Campeius*,
Is stolne away to Rome, hath 'tane no leaue,
Ha's left the cause o'th'King vnhandled, and
Is posted as the Agent of our Cardinall,
To second all his plot. I do assure you,
The King cry'de Ha, at this.

Cham. Now God incense him,
And let him cry Ha, lowder.

Norf. But my Lord
When returnes *Cranmer*?

Suf. He is return'd in his Opinions, which
Haue satisfied the King for his Diuorce,
Together with all famous Colledges
Almost in Christendome: shortly (I beleeue)
His second Marriage shall be publish'd, and
Her Coronation. *Katherine* no more
Shall be call'd Queene, but Princesse Dowager,
And Widdow to Prince *Arthur*.

Nor. This same *Cranmer's*
A worthy Fellow, and hath tane much paine
In the Kings businesse.

Suf. He ha's, and we shall see him
For it, an Arch-byshop.

Nor. So I heare.

Suf. Tis so.

Enter Wolsey and Cromwell.

The Cardinall.

Nor. Obserue, obserue, hee's moody.

Car. The Packet Cromwell,
Gau't you the King?

Crom. To his owne hand, in's Bed-chamber.

Card. Look'd he o'th'inside of the Paper?

Crom. Presently
He did vnseale them, and the first he view'd,
He did it with a Serious minde: a heede
Was in his countenance. You he bad
Attend him heere this Morning.

Card. Is he ready to come abroad?

Crom. I thinke by this he is.

Card. Leaue me a while. *Exit Cromwell.*
It shall be to the Dutches of Alanson,
The French Kings Sister; He shall marry her.
Anne Bullen? No: Ile no *Anne Bullens* for him,
There's more in't then faire Visage. *Bullen*?
No, wee'l no *Bullens*: Speedily I wish
To heare from Rome. The Marchionesse of Penbroke?

Nor. He's discontented.

Suf. May be he heares the King
Does whet his Anger to him.

Sur. Sharpe enough,
Lord for thy Iustice.

Car. The late Queenes Gentlewoman?
A Knights Daughter
To be her Mistris Mistris? The Queenes, Queene?
This Candle burnes not cleere, 'tis I must snuffe it,
Then out it goes. What though I know her vertuous
And well deseruing? yet I know her for
A spleeny Lutheran, and not wholsome to
Our cause, that she should lye i'th'bosome of
Our hard rul'd King. Againe, there is sprung vp
An Heretique, an Arch-one; *Cranmer*, one
Hath crawl'd into the fauour of the King,
And is his Oracle.

Nor. He is vex'd at something.

Enter King, reading of a Scedule.

Sur. I would 'twer somthing y would fret the string,
The Master-cord on's heart.

Suf. The King, the King.

King. What piles of wealth hath he accumulated
To his owne portion? And what expence by th'houre
Seemes to flow from him? How, i'th'name of Thrift
Does he rake this together? Now my Lords,
Saw you the Cardinall?

Nor. My Lord, we haue
Stood heere obseruing him. Some strange Commotion
Is in his braine: He bites his lip, and starts,
Stops on a sodaine, lookes vpon the ground,
Then layes his finger on his Temple: straight
Springs out into fast gate, then stops againe,
Strikes his brest hard, and anon, he casts
His eye against the Moone: in most strange Postures
We haue seene him set himselfe.

King. It may well be,
There is a mutiny in's minde. This morning,
Papers of State he sent me, to peruse
As I requir'd: and wot you what I found
There (on my Conscience put vnwittingly)
Forsooth an Inuentory, thus importing
The seuerall parcels of his Plate, his Treasure,
Rich Stuffes and Ornaments of Houshold, which
I finde at such proud Rate, that it out-speakes
Possession of a Subiect.

Nor. It's Heauens will,
Some Spirit put this paper in the Packet,
To blesse your eye withall.

King. If we did thinke

His Contemplation were aboue the earth,
And fixt on Spirituall obiect, he should still
Dwell in his Musings, but I am affraid
His Thinkings are below the Moone, not worth
His serious considering.

King takes his Seat, whispers Louell, who goes to the Cardinall.

Car. Heauen forgiue me,
Euer God blesse your Highnesse.

King. Good my Lord,
You are full of Heauenly stuffe, and beare the Inuentory
Of your best Graces, in your minde; the which
You were now running o're: you haue scarse time
To steale from Spirituall leysure, a briefe span
To keepe your earthly Audit, sure in that
I deeme you an ill Husband, and am glad
To haue you therein my Companion.

Car. Sir,
For Holy Offices I haue a time; a time
To thinke vpon the part of businesse, which
I beare i'th'State: and Nature does require
Her times of preseruation, which perforce
I her fraile sonne, among'st my Brethren mortall,
Must giue my tendance to.

King. You haue said well.

Car. And euer may your Highnesse yoake together,
(As I will lend you cause) my doing well,
With my well saying.

King. 'Tis well said agen,
And 'tis a kinde of good deede to say well,
And yet words are no deeds. My Father lou'd you,
He said he did, and with his deed did Crowne
His word vpon you. Since I had my Office,
I haue kept you next my Heart, haue not alone
Imploy'd you where high Profits might come home,
But par'd my present Hauings, to bestow
My Bounties vpon you.

Car. What should this meane?

Sur. The Lord increase this businesse.

King. Haue I not made you
The prime man of the State? I pray you tell me,
If what I now pronounce, you haue found true:
And if you may confesse it, say withall
If you are bound to vs, or no. What say you?

Car. My Soueraigne, I confesse your Royall graces
Showr'd on me daily, haue bene more then could
My studied purposes requite, which went
Beyond all mans endeauors. My endeauors,
Haue euer come too short of my Desires,
Yet fill'd with my Abilities: Mine owne ends
Haue beene mine so, that euermore they pointed
To th'good of your most Sacred Person, and
The profit of the State. For your great Graces
Heap'd vpon me (poore Vndeseruer) I
Can nothing render but Allegiant thankes,
My Prayres to heauen for you; my Loyaltie
Which euer ha's, and euer shall be growing,
Till death (that Winter) kill it.

King. Fairely answer'd:
A Loyall, and obedient Subiect is
Therein illustrated, the Honor of it
Does pay the Act of it, as i'th'contrary
The fowlenesse is the punishment. I presume,
That as my hand ha's open'd Bounty to you,
My heart drop'd Loue, my powre rain'd Honor, more
On you, then any: So your Hand, and Heart,
Your Braine, and euery Function of your power,
Should, notwithstanding that your bond of duty,
As 'twer in Loues particular, be more
To me your Friend, then any.

Car. I do professe,
That for your Highnesse good, I euer labour'd
More then mine owne: that am, haue, and will be
(Though all the world should cracke their duty to you,
And throw it from their Soule, though perils did
Abound, as thicke as thought could make 'em, and
Appeare in formes more horrid) yet my Duty,
As doth a Rocke against the chiding Flood,
Should the approach of this wilde Riuer breake,
And stand vnshaken yours.

King. 'Tis Nobly spoken:
Take notice Lords, he ha's a Loyall brest,
For you haue seene him open't. Read o're this,
And after this, and then to Breakfast with
What appetite you haue.

Exit King, frowning vpon the Cardinall, the Nobles throng after him smiling, and whispering.

Car. What should this meane?
What sodaine Anger's this? How haue I reap'd it?
He parted Frowning from me, as if Ruine
Leap'd from his Eyes. So lookes the chafed Lyon
Vpon the daring Huntsman that has gall'd him:
Then makes him nothing. I must reade this paper:
I feare the Story of his Anger. 'Tis so:
This paper ha's vndone me: 'Tis th'Accompt
Of all that world of Wealth I haue drawne together
For mine owne ends, (Indeed to gaine the Popedome,
And fee my Friends in Rome.) O Negligence!
Fit for a Foole to fall by: What crosse Diuell
Made me put this maine Secret in the Packet
I sent the King? Is there no way to cure this?
No new deuice to beate this from his Braines?
I know 'twill stirre him strongly; yet I know
A way, if it take right, in spight of Fortune
Will bring me off againe. What's this? *To th'Pope?*
The Letter (as I liue) with all the Businesse
I writ too's Holinesse. Nay then, farewell:
I haue touch'd the highest point of all my Greatnesse,
And from that full Meridian of my Glory,
I haste now to my Setting. I shall fall
Like a bright exhalation in the Euening,
And no man see me more.

Enter to Woolsey, the Dukes of Norfolke and Suffolke, the Earle of Surrey, and the Lord Chamberlaine.

Nor. Heare the Kings pleasure Cardinall,
Who commands you
To render vp the Great Seale presently
Into our hands, and to Confine your selfe
To Asher-house, my Lord of Winchesters,
Till you heare further from his Highnesse.

Car. Stay:
Where's your Commission? Lords, words cannot carrie
Authority so weighty.

Suf. Who dare crosse 'em,
Bearing the Kings will from his mouth expressely?

Car. Till I finde more then will, or words to do it,
(I meane your malice) know, Officious Lords,
I dare, and must deny it. Now I feele
Of what course Mettle ye are molded, Enuy,
How eagerly ye follow my Disgraces

As if it fed ye, and how sleeke and wanton
Ye appeare in euery thing may bring my ruine?
Follow your enuious courses, men of Malice;
You haue Christian warrant for 'em, and no doubt
In time will finde their fit Rewards. That Seale
You aske with such a Violence, the King
(Mine, and your Master) with his owne hand, gaue me:
Bad me enioy it, with the Place, and Honors
During my life; and to confirme his Goodnesse,
Ti'de it by Letters Patents. Now, who'll take it?

Sur. The King that gaue it.

Car. It must be himselfe then.

Sur. Thou art a proud Traitor, Priest.

Car. Proud Lord, thou lyest:
Within these fortie houres, Surrey durst better
Haue burnt that Tongue, then saide so.

Sur. Thy Ambition
(Thou Scarlet sinne) robb'd this bewailing Land
Of Noble Buckingham, my Father-in-Law,
The heads of all thy Brother-Cardinals,
(With thee, and all thy best parts bound together)
Weigh'd not a haire of his. Plague of your policie,
You sent me Deputie for Ireland,
Farre from his succour; from the King, from all
That might haue mercie on the fault, thou gau'st him:
Whil'st your great Goodnesse, out of holy pitty,
Absolu'd him with an Axe.

Wol. This, and all else
This talking Lord can lay vpon my credit,
I answer, is most false. The Duke by Law
Found his deserts. How innocent I was
From any priuate malice in his end,
His Noble Iurie, and foule Cause can witnesse.
If I lou'd many words, Lord, I should tell you,
You haue as little Honestie, as Honor,
That in the way of Loyaltie, and Truth,
Toward the King, my euer Roiall Master,
Dare mate a sounder man then Surrie can be,
And all that loue his follies.

Sur. By my Soule,
Your long Coat (Priest) protects you,
Thou should'st feele
My Sword i'th'life blood of thee else. My Lords,
Can ye endure to heare this Arrogance?
And from this Fellow? If we liue thus tamely,
To be thus Iaded by a peece of Scarlet,
Farewell Nobilitie: let his Grace go forward,
And dare vs with his Cap, like Larkes.

Card. All Goodnesse
Is poyson to thy Stomacke.

Sur. Yes, that goodnesse
Of gleaning all the Lands wealth into one,
Into your owne hands (Card'nall) by Extortion:
The goodnesse of your intercepted Packets
You writ to'th Pope, against the King: your goodnesse
Since you prouoke me, shall be most notorious.
My Lord of Norfolke, as you are truly Noble,
As you respect the common good, the State
Of our despis'd Nobilitie, our Issues,
(Whom if he liue, will scarse be Gentlemen)
Produce the grand summe of his sinnes, the Articles
Collected from his life. Ile startle you
Worse then the Sacring Bell, when the browne Wench
Lay kissing in your Armes, Lord Cardinall.

Car. How much me thinkes, I could despise this man,
But that I am bound in Charitie against it.

Nor. Those Articles, my Lord, are in the Kings hand:
But thus much, they are foule ones.

Wol. So much fairer
And spotlesse, shall mine Innocence arise,
When the King knowes my Truth.

Sur. This cannot saue you:
I thanke my Memorie, I yet remember
Some of these Articles, and out they shall.
Now, if you can blush, and crie guiltie Cardinall,
You'l shew a little Honestie.

Wol. Speake on Sir,
I dare your worst Obiections: If I blush,
It is to see a Nobleman want manners.

Sur. I had rather want those, then my head;
Haue at you.
First, that without the Kings assent or knowledge,
You wrought to be a Legate, by which power
You maim'd the Iurisdiction of all Bishops.

Nor. Then, That in all you writ to Rome, or else
To Forraigne Princes, *Ego & Rex meus*
Was still inscrib'd: in which you brought the King
To be your Seruant.

Suf. Then, that without the knowledge
Either of King or Councell, when you went
Ambassador to the Emperor, you made bold
To carry into Flanders, the Great Seale.

Sur. Item, You sent a large Commission
To *Gregory de Cassado*, to conclude
Without the Kings will, or the States allowance,
A League betweene his Highnesse, and *Ferrara*.

Suf. That out of meere Ambition, you haue caus'd
Your holy-Hat to be stampt on the Kings Coine.

Sur. Then, That you haue sent inumerable substance,
(By what meanes got, I leaue to your owne conscience)
To furnish Rome, and to prepare the wayes
You haue for Dignities, to the meere vndooing
Of all the Kingdome. Many more there are,
Which since they are of you, and odious,
I will not taint my mouth with.

Cham. O my Lord,
Presse not a falling man too farre: 'tis Vertue:
His faults lye open to the Lawes, let them
(Not you) correct him. My heart weepes to see him
So little, of his great Selfe.

Sur. I forgiue him.

Suf. Lord Cardinall, the Kings further pleasure is,
Because all those things you haue done of late
By your power Legatiue within this Kingdome,
Fall into'th'compasse of a Premunire;
That therfore such a Writ be sued against you,
To forfeit all your Goods, Lands, Tenements,
Castles, and whatsoeuer, and to be
Out of the Kings protection. This is my Charge.

Nor. And so wee'l leaue you to your Meditations
How to liue better. For your stubborne answer
About the giuing backe the Great Seale to vs,
The King shall know it, and (no doubt) shal thanke you.
So fare you well, my little good Lord Cardinall.

Exeunt all but Wolsey.

Wol. So farewell, to the little good you beare me.
Farewell? A long farewell to all my Greatnesse.
This is the state of Man; to day he puts forth
The tender Leaues of hopes, to morrow Blossomes,
And beares his blushing Honors thicke vpon him:
The third day, comes a Frost; a killing Frost,
And when he thinkes, good easie man, full surely

The Life of King Henry the Eight.

His Greatnesse is a ripening, nippes his roote,
And then he fals as I do. I haue ventur'd
Like little wanton Boyes that swim on bladders:
This many Summers in a Sea of Glory,
But farre beyond my depth: my high-blowne Pride
At length broke vnder me, and now ha's left me
Weary, and old with Seruice, to the mercy
Of a rude streame, that must for euer hide me.
Vaine pompe, and glory of this World, I hate ye,
I feele my heart new open'd. Oh how wretched
Is that poore man, that hangs on Princes fauours?
There is betwixt that smile we would aspire too,
That sweet Aspect of Princes, and their ruine,
More pangs, and feares then warres, or women haue;
And when he falles, he falles like Lucifer,
Neuer to hope againe.

Enter Cromwell, standing amazed.

Why how now *Cromwell*?

Crom. I haue no power to speake Sir.

Car. What, amaz'd
At my misfortunes? Can thy Spirit wonder
A great man should decline. Nay, and you weep
I am falne indeed.

Crom. How does your Grace.

Card. Why well:
Neuer so truly happy, my good *Cromwell*,
I know my selfe now, and I feele within me,
A peace aboue all earthly Dignities,
A still, and quiet Conscience. The King ha's cur'd me,
I humbly thanke his Grace: and from these shoulders
These ruin'd Pillers, out of pitty, taken
A loade, would sinke a Nauy, (too much Honor.)
O 'tis a burden *Cromwel*, 'tis a burden
Too heauy for a man, that hopes for Heauen.

Crom. I am glad your Grace,
Ha's made that right vse of it.

Card. I hope I haue:
I am able now (me thinkes)
(Out of a Fortitude of Soule, I feele)
To endure more Miseries, and greater farre
Then my Weake-hearted Enemies, dare offer.
What Newes abroad?

Crom. The heauiest, and the worst,
Is your displeasure with the King.

Card. God blesse him.

Crom. The next is, that Sir *Thomas Moore* is chosen
Lord Chancellor, in your place.

Card. That's somewhat sodain.
But he's a Learned man. May he continue
Long in his Highnesse fauour, and do Iustice
For Truths-sake, and his Conscience; that his bones,
When he ha's run his course, and sleepes in Blessings,
May haue a Tombe of Orphants teares wept on him.
What more?

Crom. That *Cranmer* is return'd with welcome;
Install'd Lord Arch-byshop of Canterbury.

Card. That's Newes indeed.

Crom. Last, that the Lady *Anne*,
Whom the King hath in secrecie long married,
This day was view'd in open, as his Queene,
Going to Chappell: and the voyce is now
Onely about her Corronation.

Card. There was the waight that pull'd me downe.
O *Cromwell*,
The King ha's gone beyond me: All my Glories
In that one woman, I haue lost for euer.
No Sun, shall euer vsher forth mine Honors,
Or gilde againe the Noble Troopes that waighted
Vpon my smiles. Go get thee from me *Cromwel*,
I am a poore falne man, vnworthy now
To be thy Lord, and Master. Seeke the King
(That Sun, I pray may neuer set) I haue told him,
What, and how true thou art; he will aduance thee:
Some little memory of me, will stirre him
(I know his Noble Nature) not to let
Thy hopefull seruice perish too. Good *Cromwell*
Neglect him not; make vse now, and prouide
For thine owne future safety.

Crom. O my Lord,
Must I then leaue you? Must I needes forgo
So good, so Noble, and so true a Master?
Beare witnesse, all that haue not hearts of Iron,
With what a sorrow *Cromwel* leaues his Lord.
The King shall haue my seruice; but my prayres
For euer, and for euer shall be yours.

Card. *Cromwel*, I did not thinke to shed a teare
In all my Miseries: But thou hast forc'd me
(Out of thy honest truth) to play the Woman.
Let's dry our eyes: And thus farre heare me *Cromwel*,
And when I am forgotten, as I shall be,
And sleepe in dull cold Marble, where no mention
Of me, more must be heard of: Say I taught thee;
Say *Wolsey*, that once trod the wayes of Glory,
And sounded all the Depths, and Shoales of Honor,
Found thee a way (out of his wracke) to rise in:
A sure, and safe one, though thy Master mist it.
Marke but my Fall, and that that Ruin'd me:
Cromwel, I charge thee, fling away Ambition,
By that sinne fell the Angels: how can man then
(The Image of his Maker) hope to win by it?
Loue thy selfe last, cherish those hearts that hate thee;
Corruption wins not more then Honesty.
Still in thy right hand, carry gentle Peace
To silence enuious Tongues. Be iust, and feare not;
Let all the ends thou aym'st at, be thy Countries,
Thy Gods, and Truths. Then if thou fall'st (O *Cromwell*)
Thou fall'st a blessed Martyr.
Serue the King: And prythee leade me in:
There take an Inuentory of all I haue,
To the last peny, 'tis the Kings. My Robe,
And my Integrity to Heauen, is all,
I dare now call mine owne. O *Cromwel*, *Cromwel*,
Had I but seru'd my God, with halfe the Zeale
I seru'd my King: he would not in mine Age
Haue left me naked to mine Enemies.

Crom. Good Sir, haue patience.

Card. So I haue. Farewell
The Hopes of Court, my Hopes in Heauen do dwell.

Exeunt.

Actus Quartus. Scena Prima.

Enter two Gentlemen, meeting one another.

1 Y'are well met once againe.

2 So are you.

1 You come to take your stand heere, and behold
The Lady *Anne*, passe from her Corronation.

2. 'Tis all my businesse. At our last encounter,
The Duke of Buckingham came from his Triall.

1. 'Tis very true. But that time offer'd sorrow,
This generall ioy.

2. 'Tis well: The Citizens
I am sure haue shewne at full their Royall minds,
As let 'em haue their rights, they are euer forward
In Celebration of this day with Shewes,
Pageants, and Sights of Honor.

1. Neuer greater,
Nor Ile assure you better taken Sir.

2. May I be bold to aske what that containes,
That Paper in your hand.

1. Yes, 'tis the List
Of those that claime their Offices this day,
By custome of the Coronation.
The Duke of Suffolke is the first, and claimes
To be high Steward; Next the Duke of Norfolke,
He to be Earle Marshall: you may reade the rest.

1. I thanke you Sir: Had I not known those customs,
I should haue beene beholding to your Paper:
But I beseech you, what's become of *Katherine*
The Princesse Dowager? How goes her businesse?

1. That I can tell you too. The Archbishop
Of Canterbury, accompanied with other
Learned, and Reuerend Fathers of his Order,
Held a late Court at Dunstable; sixe miles off
From Ampthill, where the Princesse lay, to which
She was often cyted by them, but appear'd not:
And to be short, for not Appearance, and
The Kings late Scruple, by the maine assent
Of all these Learned men, she was diuorc'd,
And the late Marriage made of none effect:
Since which, she was remou'd to Kymmalton,
Where she remaines now sicke.

2. Alas good Lady.
The Trumpets sound; Stand close,
The Queene is comming. *Ho-boyes.*

The Order of the Coronation.

1. *A liuely Flourish of Trumpets.*
2. *Then, two Iudges.*
3. *Lord Chancellor, with Purse and Mace before him.*
4. *Quiristers singing. Musicke.*
5. *Maior of London, bearing the Mace. Then Garter, in his Coate of Armes, and on his head he wore a Gilt Copper Crowne.*
6. *Marquesse Dorset, bearing a Scepter of Gold, on his head, a Demy Coronall of Gold. With him, the Earle of Surrey, bearing the Rod of Siluer with the Doue, Crowned with an Earles Coronet. Collars of Esses.*
7. *Duke of Suffolke, in his Robe of Estate, his Coronet on his head, bearing a long white Wand, as High Steward. With him, the Duke of Norfolke, with the Rod of Marshalship, a Coronet on his head. Collars of Esses.*
8. *A Canopy, borne by foure of the Cinque-Ports, vnder it the Queene in her Robe, in her haire, richly adorned with Pearle, Crowned. On each side her, the Bishops of London, and Winchester.*
9. *The Olde Dutchesse of Norfolke, in a Coronall of Gold, wrought with Flowers, bearing the Queenes Traine.*
10. *Certaine Ladies or Countesses, with plaine Circlets of Gold, without Flowers.*

Exeunt, first passing ouer the Stage in Order and State, and then, A great Flourish of Trumpets.

2. A Royall Traine beleeue me: These I know:
Who's that that beares the Scepter?

1. Marquesse Dorset,
And that the Earle of Surrey, with the Rod.

2. A bold braue Gentleman. That should bee
The Duke of Suffolke.

1. 'Tis the same: high Steward.

2. And that my Lord of Norfolke?

1. Yes.

2. Heauen blesse thee,
Thou hast the sweetest face I euer look'd on.
Sir, as I haue a Soule, she is an Angell;
Our King ha's all the Indies in his Armes,
And more, and richer, when he straines that Lady,
I cannot blame his Conscience.

1. They that beare
The Cloath of Honour ouer her, are foure Barons
Of the Cinque Ports.

2. Those men are happy,
And so are all, are neere her.
I take it, she that carries vp the Traine,
Is that old Noble Lady, Dutchesse of Norfolke.

1. It is, and all the rest are Countesses.

2. Their Coronets say so. These are Starres indeed,
And sometimes falling ones.

2. No more of that.

Enter a third Gentleman.

1. God saue you Sir. Where haue you bin broiling?

3. Among the crow'd i'th' Abbey, where a finger
Could not be wedg'd in more: I am stifled
With the meere ranknesse of their ioy.

2. You saw the Ceremony?

3. That I did.

1. How was it?

3. Well worth the seeing.

2. Good Sir, speake it to vs?

3. As well as I am able. The rich streame
Of Lords, and Ladies, hauing brought the Queene
To a prepar'd place in the Quire, fell off
A distance from her; while her Grace sate downe
To rest a while, some halfe an houre, or so,
In a rich Chaire of State, opposing freely
The Beauty of her Person to the People.
Beleeue me Sir, she is the goodliest Woman
That euer lay by man: which when the people
Had the full view of, such a noyse arose,
As the shrowdes make at Sea, in a stiffe Tempest,
As lowd, and to as many Tunes. Hats, Cloakes,
(Doublets, I thinke) flew vp, and had their Faces
Bin loose, this day they had beene lost. Such ioy
I neuer saw before. Great belly'd women,
That had not halfe a weeke to go, like Rammes
In the old time of Warre, would shake the prease
And make 'em reele before 'em. No man liuing
Could say this is my wife there, all were wouen
So strangely in one peece.

2. But what follow'd?

3. At length, her Grace rose, and with modest paces
Came to the Altar, where she kneel'd, and Saint-like
Cast her faire eyes to Heauen, and pray'd deuoutly.
Then rose againe, and bow'd her to the people:
When by the Arch-byshop of Canterbury,
She had all the Royall makings of a Queene;
As holy Oyle, *Edward* Confessors Crowne,
The Rod, and Bird of Peace, and all such Emblemes
Laid Nobly on her: which perform'd, the Quire

With all the choysest Musicke of the Kingdome,
Together sung *Te Deum*. So she parted,
And with the same full State pac'd backe againe
To Yorke-Place, where the Feast is held.

  1 Sir,
You must no more call it Yorke-place, that's past:
For since the Cardinall fell, that Titles lost,
'Tis now the Kings, and call'd White-Hall.

  3 I know it:
But 'tis so lately alter'd, that the old name
Is fresh about me.

  2 What two Reuerend Byshops
Were those that went on each side of the Queene?

  3 *Stokeley* and *Gardiner*, the one of Winchester,
Newly preferr'd from the Kings Secretary:
The other London.

  2 He of Winchester
Is held no great good louer of the Archbishops,
The vertuous *Cranmer*.

  3 All the Land knowes that:
How euer, yet there is no great breach, when it comes
Cranmer will finde a Friend will not shrinke from him.

  2 Who may that be, I pray you.

  3 *Thomas Cromwell*,
A man in much esteeme with th'King, and truly
A worthy Friend. The King ha's made him
Master o'th'Iewell House,
And one already of the Priuy Councell.

  2 He will deserue more.

  3 Yes without all doubt.
Come Gentlemen ye shall go my way,
Which is to'th Court, and there ye shall be my Guests:
Something I can command. As I walke thither,
Ile tell ye more.

  Both. You may command vs Sir.   *Exeunt*.

Scena Secunda.

*Enter Katherine Dowager, sicke, lead betweene Griffith,
her Gentleman Vsher, and Patience
her Woman.*

  Grif. How do's your Grace?
  Kath. O *Griffith*, sicke to death:
My Legges like loaden Branches bow to'th'Earth,
Willing to leaue their burthen: Reach a Chaire,
So now (me thinkes) I feele a little ease.
Did'st thou not tell me *Griffith*, as thou lead'st mee,
That the great Childe of Honor, Cardinall *Wolsey*
Was dead?
  Grif. Yes Madam: but I thanke your Grace
Out of the paine you suffer'd, gaue no eare too't.
  Kath. Pre'thee good *Griffith*, tell me how he dy'de.
If well, he stept before me happily
For my example.
  Grif. Well, the voyce goes Madam,
For after the stout Earle Northumberland
Arrested him at Yorke, and brought him forward
As a man sorely tainted, to his Answer,
He fell sicke sodainly, and grew so ill
He could not sit his Mule.
  Kath. Alas poore man.
  Grif. At last, with easie Rodes, he came to Leicester,
Lodg'd in the Abbey; where the reuerend Abbot
With all his Couent, honourably receiu'd him;
To whom he gaue these words. O Father Abbot,
An old man, broken with the stormes of State,
Is come to lay his weary bones among ye:
Giue him a little earth for Charity.
So went to bed; where eagerly his sicknesse
Pursu'd him still, and three nights after this,
About the houre of eight, which he himselfe
Foretold should be his last, full of Repentance,
Continuall Meditations, Teares, and Sorrowes,
He gaue his Honors to the world agen,
His blessed part to Heauen, and slept in peace.

  Kath. So may he rest,
His Faults lye gently on him:
Yet thus farre *Griffith*, giue me leaue to speake him,
And yet with Charity. He was a man
Of an vnbounded stomacke, euer ranking
Himselfe with Princes. One that by suggestion
Ty'de all the Kingdome. Symonie, was faire play,
His owne Opinion was his Law. I'th'presence
He would say vntruths, and be euer double
Both in his words, and meaning. He was neuer
(But where he meant to Ruine) pittifull.
His Promises, were as he then was, Mighty:
But his performance, as he is now, Nothing:
Of his owne body he was ill, and gaue
The Clergy ill example.

  Grif. Noble Madam:
Mens euill manners, liue in Brasse, their Vertues
We write in Water. May it please your Highnesse
To heare me speake his good now?

  Kath. Yes good *Griffith*,
I were malicious else.

  Grif. This Cardinall,
Though from an humble Stocke, vndoubtedly
Was fashion'd to much Honor. From his Cradle
He was a Scholler, and a ripe, and good one:
Exceeding wise, faire spoken, and perswading:
Lofty, and sowre to them that lou'd him not:
But, to those men that sought him, sweet as Summer.
And though he were vnsatisfied in getting,
(Which was a sinne) yet in bestowing, Madam,
He was most Princely: Euer witnesse for him
Those twinnes of Learning, that he rais'd in you,
Ipswich and Oxford: one of which, fell with him,
Vnwilling to out-liue the good that did it.
The other (though vnfinish'd) yet so Famous,
So excellent in Art, and still so rising,
That Christendome shall euer speake his Vertue.
His Ouerthrow, heap'd Happinesse vpon him:
For then, and not till then, he felt himselfe,
And found the Blessednesse of being little.
And to adde greater Honors to his Age
Then man could giue him; he dy'de, fearing God.

  Kath. After my death, I wish no other Herald,
No other speaker of my liuing Actions,
To keepe mine Honor, from Corruption,
But such an honest Chronicler as *Griffith*.
Whom I most hated Liuing, thou hast made mee
With thy Religious Truth, and Modestie,
(Now in his Ashes) Honor: Peace be with him.
Patience, be neere me still, and set me lower.
I haue not long to trouble thee. Good *Griffith*,
Cause the Musitians play me that sad note
I nam'd my Knell; whil'st I sit meditating

x   On

On that Cœlestiall Harmony I go too.
Sad and solemne Musicke.

Grif. She is asleep: Good wench, let's sit down quiet,
For feare we wake her. Softly, gentle *Patience.*

The Vision.
Enter solemnely tripping one after another, sixe Personages, clad in white Robes, wearing on their heades Garlands of Bayes, and golden Vizards on their faces, Branches of Bayes or Palme in their hands. They first Conge vnto her, then Dance: and at certaine Changes, the first two hold a spare Garland ouer her Head, at which the other foure make reuerend Curtsies. Then the two that held the Garland, deliuer the same to the other next two, who obserue the same order in their Changes, and holding the Garland ouer her head. Which done, they deliuer the same Garland to the last two: who likewise obserue the same Order. At which (as it were by inspiration) she makes (in her sleepe) signes of reioycing, and holdeth vp her hands to heauen. And so, in their Dancing vanish, carrying the Garland with them. The Musicke continues.

Kath. Spirits of peace, where are ye? Are ye all gone?
And leaue me heere in wretchednesse, behinde ye?

Grif. Madam, we are heere.

Kath. It is not you I call for,
Saw ye none enter since I slept?

Grif. None Madam.

Kath. No? Saw you not euen now a blessed Troope
Inuite me to a Banquet, whose bright faces
Cast thousand beames vpon me, like the Sun?
They promis'd me eternall Happinesse,
And brought me Garlands (*Griffith*) which I feele
I am not worthy yet to weare: I shall assuredly.

Grif. I am most ioyfull Madam, such good dreames
Possesse your Fancy.

Kath. Bid the Musicke leaue,
They are harsh and heauy to me.   *Musicke ceases.*

Pati. Do you note
How much her Grace is alter'd on the sodaine?
How long her face is drawne? How pale she lookes,
And of an earthy cold? Marke her eyes?

Grif. She is going Wench. Pray, pray.

Pati. Heauen comfort her.

Enter a Messenger.

Mes. And't like your Grace——

Kath. You are a sawcy Fellow,
Deserue we no more Reuerence?

Grif. You are too blame,
Knowing she will not loose her wonted Greatnesse
To vse so rude behauiour. Go too, kneele.

Mes. I humbly do entreat your Highnesse pardon,
My hast made me vnmannerly. There is staying
A Gentleman sent from the King, to see you.

Kath. Admit him entrance *Griffith.* But this Fellow
Let me ne're see againe.   *Exit Messeng.*

Enter Lord Capuchius.

If my sight faile not,
You should be Lord Ambassador from the Emperor,
My Royall Nephew, and your name *Capuchius.*

Cap. Madam the same. Your Seruant.

Kath. O my Lord,
The Times and Tides now are alter'd strangely
With me, since first you knew me.
But I pray you,
What is your pleasure with me?

Cap. Noble Lady,
First mine owne seruice to your Grace, the next
The Kings request, that I would visit you,
Who greeues much for your weaknesse, and by me
Sends you his Princely Commendations,
And heartily entreats you take good comfort.

Kath. O my good Lord, that comfort comes too late,
'Tis like a Pardon after Execution;
That gentle Physicke giuen in time, had cur'd me:
But now I am past all Comforts heere, but Prayers.
How does his Highnesse?

Cap. Madam, in good health.

Kath. So may he euer do, and euer flourish,
When I shall dwell with Wormes, and my poore name
Banish'd the Kingdome. *Patience,* is that Letter
I caus'd you write, yet sent away?

Pat. No Madam.

Kath. Sir, I most humbly pray you to deliuer
This to my Lord the King.

Cap. Most willing Madam.

Kath. In which I haue commended to his goodnesse
The Modell of our chaste loues: his yong daughter,
The dewes of Heauen fall thicke in Blessings on her,
Beseeching him to giue her vertuous breeding.
She is yong, and of a Noble modest Nature,
I hope she will deserue well; and a little
To loue her for her Mothers sake, that lou'd him,
Heauen knowes how deerely.
My next poore Petition,
Is, that his Noble Grace would haue some pittie
Vpon my wretched women, that so long
Haue follow'd both my Fortunes, faithfully,
Of which there is not one, I dare auow
(And now I should not lye) but will deserue
For Vertue, and true Beautie of the Soule,
For honestie, and decent Carriage
A right good Husband (let him be a Noble)
And sure those men are happy that shall haue 'em.
The last is for my men, they are the poorest,
(But pouerty could neuer draw 'em from me)
That they may haue their wages, duly paid 'em,
And something ouer to remember me by.
If Heauen had pleas'd to haue giuen me longer life
And able meanes, we had not parted thus.
These are the whole Contents, and good my Lord,
By that you loue the deerest in this world,
As you wish Christian peace to soules departed,
Stand these poore peoples Friend, and vrge the King
To do me this last right.

Cap. By Heauen I will,
Or let me loose the fashion of a man.

Kath. I thanke you honest Lord. Remember me
In all humilitie vnto his Highnesse:
Say his long trouble now is passing
Out of this world. Tell him in death I blest him
(For so I will) mine eyes grow dimme. Farewell
My Lord. *Griffith* farewell. Nay *Patience,*
You must not leaue me yet. I must to bed,
Call in more women. When I am dead, good Wench,
Let me be vs'd with Honor; strew me ouer
With Maiden Flowers, that all the world may know
I was a chaste Wife, to my Graue: Embalme me,
Then lay me forth (although vnqueen'd) yet like
A Queene, and Daughter to a King enterre me.
I can no more.

Exeunt leading Katherine.

Actus Quintus. Scena Prima.

Enter Gardiner Bishop of Winchester, a Page with a Torch before him, met by Sir Thomas Lovell.

Gard. It's one a clocke Boy, is't not?
Boy. It hath strooke.
Gard. These should be houres for necessities,
Not for delights: Times to repayre our Nature
With comforting repose, and not for vs
To waste these times. Good houre of night Sir *Thomas*:
Whether so late?
Lou. Came you from the King, my Lord?
Gar. I did Sir *Thomas*, and left him at Primero
With the Duke of Suffolke.
Lou. I must to him too
Before he go to bed. Ile take my leaue.
Gard. Not yet Sir *Thomas Lovell*: what's the matter?
It seemes you are in hast: and if there be
No great offence belongs too't, giue your Friend
Some touch of your late businesse: Affaires that walke
(As they say Spirits do) at midnight, haue
In them a wilder Nature, then the businesse
That seekes dispatch by day.
Lou. My Lord, I loue you;
And durst commend a secret to your eare
Much waightier then this worke. The Queens in Labor
They say in great Extremity, and fear'd
Shee'l with the Labour, end.
Gard. The fruite she goes with
I pray for heartily, that it may finde
Good time, and liue: but for the Stocke Sir *Thomas*,
I wish it grubb'd vp now.
Lou. Me thinkes I could
Cry the Amen, and yet my Conscience sayes
Shee's a good Creature, and sweet-Ladie do's
Deserue our better wishes.
Gard. But Sir, Sir,
Heare me Sir *Thomas*, y'are a Gentleman
Of mine owne way. I know you Wise, Religious,
And let me tell you, it will ne're be well,
'Twill not Sir *Thomas Lovell*, tak't of me,
Till *Cranmer*, *Cromwel*, her two hands, and shee
Sleepe in their Graues.
Lovell. Now Sir, you speake of two
The most remark'd i'th'Kingdome: as for *Cromwell*,
Beside that of the Iewell-House, is made Master
O'th'Rolles, and the Kings Secretary. Further Sir,
Stands in the gap and Trade of moe Preferments,
With which the Time will loade him. Th'Archbyshop
Is the Kings hand, and tongue, and who dare speake
One syllable against him?
Gard. Yes, yes, Sir *Thomas*,
There are that Dare, and I my selfe haue ventur'd
To speake my minde of him: and indeed this day,
Sir (I may tell it you) I thinke I haue
Incenst the Lords o'th'Councell, that he is
(For so I know he is, they know he is)
A most Arch-Heretique, a Pestilence
That does infect the Land: with which, they moued
Haue broken with the King, who hath so farre
Giuen eare to our Complaint, of his great Grace,
And Princely Care, fore-seeing those fell Mischieses,
Our Reasons layd before him, hath commanded
To morrow Morning to the Councell Boord
He be conuented. He's a ranke weed Sir *Thomas*,
And we must root him out. From your Affaires
I hinder you too long: Good night, Sir *Thomas*.
Exit Gardiner and Page.
Lou. Many good nights, my Lord, I rest your seruant.

Enter King and Suffolke.

King. Charles, I will play no more to night,
My mindes not on't, you are too hard for me.
Suff. Sir, I did neuer win of you before.
King. But little *Charles*,
Nor shall not when my Fancies on my play.
Now *Lovel*, from the Queene what is the Newes.
Lou. I could not personally deliuer to her
What you commanded me, but by her woman,
I sent your Message, who return'd her thankes
In the great'st humblenesse, and desir'd your Highnesse
Most heartily to pray for her.
King. What say'st thou? Ha?
To pray for her? What, is she crying out?
Lou. So said her woman, and that her suffrance made
Almost each pang, a death.
King. Alas good Lady.
Suf. God safely quit her of her Burthen, and
With gentle Trauaile, to the gladding of
Your Highnesse with an Heire.
King. 'Tis midnight *Charles*,
Prythee to bed, and in thy Prayres remember
Th'estate of my poore Queene. Leaue me alone,
For I must thinke of that, which company
Would not be friendly too.
Suf. I wish your Highnesse
A quiet night, and my good Mistris will
Remember in my Prayers.
King. *Charles* good night. *Exit Suffolke.*
Well Sir, what followes?

Enter Sir Anthony Denny.

Den. Sir, I haue brought my Lord the Arch-byshop,
As you commanded me.
King. Ha? Canterbury?
Den. I my good Lord.
King. 'Tis true: where is he *Denny*?
Den. He attends your Highnesse pleasure.
King. Bring him to Vs.
Lou. This is about that, which the Byshop spake,
I am happily come hither.

Enter Cranmer and Denny.

King. Auoyd the Gallery. *Lovel seemes to stay.*
Ha? I haue said. Be gone.
What? *Exeunt Lovell and Denny.*
Cran. I am fearefull: Wherefore frownes he thus?
'Tis his Aspect of Terror. All's not well.
King. How now my Lord?
You do desire to know wherefore
I sent for you.
Cran. It is my dutie
T'attend your Highnesse pleasure.
King. Pray you arise
My good and gracious Lord of Canterburie:
Come, you and I must walke a turne together:
I haue Newes to tell you.
Come, come, giue me your hand.
Ah my good Lord, I greeue at what I speake,
And am right sorrie to repeat what followes.
I haue, and most vnwillingly of late

Heard

Heard many greeuous. I do say my Lord
Greeuous complaints of you; which being consider'd,
Haue mou'd Vs, and our Councell, that you shall
This Morning come before vs, where I know
You cannot with such freedome purge your selfe,
But that till further Triall, in those Charges
Which will require your Answer, you must take
Your patience to you, and be well contented
To make your house our Towre: you, a Brother of vs
It fits we thus proceed, or else no witnesse
Would come against you.

   Cran. I humbly thanke your Highnesse,
And am right glad to catch this good occasion
Most throughly to be winnowed, where my Chaffe
And Corne shall flye asunder. For I know
There's none stands vnder more calumnious tongues,
Then I my selfe, poore man.

   King. Stand vp, good Canterbury,
Thy Truth, and thy Integrity is rooted
In vs thy Friend. Giue me thy hand, stand vp,
Prythee let's walke. Now by my Holydame,
What manner of man are you? My Lord, I look'd
You would haue giuen me your Petition, that
I should haue tane some paines, to bring together
Your selfe, and your Accusers, and to haue heard you
Without indurance further.

   Cran. Most dread Liege,
The good I stand on, is my Truth and Honestie:
If they shall faile, I with mine Enemies
Will triumph o're my person, which I waigh not,
Being of those Vertues vacant. I feare nothing
What can be said against me.

   King. Know you not
How your state stands i'th'world, with the whole world?
Your Enemies are many, and not small; their practises
Must beare the same proportion, and not euer
The Iustice and the Truth o'th'question carries
The dew o'th'Verdict with it; at what ease
Might corrupt mindes procure, Knaues as corrupt
To sweare against you: Such things haue bene done.
You are Potently oppos'd, and with a Malice
Of as great Size. Weene you of better lucke,
I meane in periur'd Witnesse, then your Master,
Whose Minister you are, whiles heere he liu'd
Vpon this naughty Earth? Go too, go too,
You take a Precepit for no leape of danger,
And woe your owne destruction.

   Cran. God, and your Maiesty
Protect mine innocence, or I fall into
The trap is laid for me.

   King. Be of good cheere,
They shall no more preuaile, then we giue way too:
Keepe comfort to you, and this Morning see
You do appeare before them. If they shall chance
In charging you with matters, to commit you:
The best perswasions to the contrary
Faile not to vse, and with what vehemencie
Th'occasion shall instruct you. If intreaties
Will render you no remedy, this Ring
Deliuer them, and your Appeale to vs
There make before them. Looke, the goodman weeps:
He's honest on mine Honor. Gods blest Mother,
I sweare he is true-hearted, and a soule
None better in my Kingdome. Get you gone,
And do as I haue bid you.   *Exit Cranmer.*
He ha's strangled his Language in his teares.

   Enter Olde Lady.

   Gent. within. Come backe: what meane you?
   Lady. Ile not come backe, the tydings that I bring
Will make my boldnesse, manners. Now good Angels
Fly o're thy Royall head, and shade thy person
Vnder their blessed wings.

   King. Now by thy lookes
I gesse thy Message. Is the Queene deliuer'd?
Say I, and of a boy.

   Lady. I, I my Liege,
And of a louely Boy: the God of heauen
Both now, and euer blesse her: 'Tis a Gyrle
Promises Boyes heereafter. Sir, your Queen
Desires your Visitation, and to be
Acquainted with this stranger; 'tis as like you,
As Cherry, is to Cherry.

   King. Louell.
   Lou. Sir.
   King. Giue her an hundred Markes.
Ile to the Queene.   *Exit King.*
   Lady. An hundred Markes? By this light, Ile ha more.
An ordinary Groome is for such payment.
I will haue more, or scold it out of him.
Said I for this, the Gyrle was like to him? Ile
Haue more, or else vnsay't: and now, while 'tis hot,
Ile put it to the issue.   *Exit Lady.*

Scena Secunda.

Enter Cranmer, Archbyshop of Canterbury.

   Cran. I hope I am not too late, and yet the Gentleman
That was sent to me from the Councell, pray'd me
To make great hast. All fast? What meanes this? Hoa?
Who waites there? Sure you know me?

   Enter Keeper.

   Keep. Yes, my Lord:
But yet I cannot helpe you.
   Cran. Why?
   Keep. Your Grace must waight till you be call'd for.

   Enter Doctor Buts.

   Cran. So.
   Buts. This is a Peere of Malice: I am glad
I came this way so happily. The King
Shall vnderstand it presently.   *Exit Buts*
   Cran. 'Tis Buts,
The Kings Physitian, as he past along
How earnestly he cast his eyes vpon me:
Pray heauen he sound not my disgrace: for certaine
This is of purpose laid by some that hate me,
(God turne their hearts, I neuer sought their malice)
To quench mine Honor; they would shame to make me
Wait else at doore: a fellow Councellor
'Mong Boyes, Groomes, and Lackeyes.
But their pleasures
Must be fulfill'd, and I attend with patience.

   Enter the King, and Buts, at a Windowe aboue.

   Buts. Ile shew your Grace the strangest sight.
   King. What's that Buts?

Butts. I thinke your Highnesse saw this many a day.
Kin. Body a me : where is it?
Butts. There my Lord :
The high promotion of his Grace of *Canterbury*,
Who holds his State at dore 'mongst Pursuants,
Pages, and Foot-boyes.

Kin. Ha? 'Tis he indeed.
Is this the Honour they doe one another?
'Tis well there's one aboue 'em yet; I had thought
They had parted so much honesty among 'em,
At least good manners; as not thus to suffer
A man of his Place, and so neere our fauour
To dance attendance on their Lordships pleasures.
And at the dore too, like a Post with Packets :
By holy *Mary* (*Butts*) there's knauery;
Let 'em alone, and draw the Curtaine close :
We shall heare more anon.

A Councell Table brought in with Chayres and Stooles, and placed vnder the State. Enter Lord Chancellour, plases himselfe at the vpper end of the Table, on the left hand : A Seate being left void aboue him, as for Canterburies Seate. Duke of Suffolke, Duke of Norfolke, Surrey, Lord Chamberlaine, Gardiner, seat themselues in Order on each side. Cromwell at lower end, as Secretary.

Chan. Speake to the businesse, M. Secretary;
Why are we met in Councell?
Crom. Please your Honours,
The chiefe cause concernes his Grace of *Canterbury*.
Gard. Ha's he had knowledge of it?
Crom. Yes.
Norf. Who waits there?
Keep. Without my Noble Lords?
Gard. Yes.
Keep. My Lord Archbishop :
And ha's done halfe an houre to know your pleasures.
Cham. Let him come in.
Keep. Your Grace may enter now.

Cranmer approches the Councell Table.

Cham. My good Lord Archbishop, I'm very sorry
To sit heere at this present, and behold
That Chayre stand empty : But we all are men
In our owne natures fraile, and capable
Of our flesh, few are Angels; out of which frailty
And want of wisedome, you that best should teach vs,
Haue misdemean'd your selfe, and not a little :
Toward the King first, then his Lawes, in filling
The whole Realme, by your teaching & your Chaplaines
(For so we are inform'd) with new opinions,
Diuers and dangerous; which are Heresies;
And not reform'd, may proue pernicious.

Gard. Which Reformation must be sodaine too
My Noble Lords; for those that tame wild Horses,
Pace 'em not in their hands to make 'em gentle;
But stop their mouthes with stubborn Bits & spurre 'em,
Till they obey the mannage. If we suffer
Out of our easinesse and childish pitty
To one mans Honour, this contagious sicknesse;
Farewell all Physicke : and what followes then?
Commotions, vprores, with a generall Taint
Of the whole State; as of late dayes our neighbours,
The vpper *Germany* can deerely witnesse :
Yet freshly pittied in our memories.

Cran. My good Lords; Hitherto, in all the Progresse
Both of my Life and Office, I haue labour'd,
And with no little study, that my teaching
And the strong course of my Authority,
Might goe one way, and safely; and the end
Was euer to doe well : nor is there liuing,
(I speake it with a single heart, my Lords)
A man that more detests, more stirres against,
Both in his priuate Conscience, and his place,
Defacers of a publique peace then I doe :
Pray Heauen the King may neuer find a heart
With lesse Allegeance in it. Men that make
Enuy, and crooked malice, nourishment;
Dare bite the best. I doe beseech your, Lordships,
That in this case of Iustice, my Accusers,
Be what they will, may stand forth face to face,
And freely vrge against me.

Suff. Nay, my Lord,
That cannot be; you are a Counsellor,
And by that vertue no man dare accuse you.
Gard. My Lord, because we haue busines of more moment,
We will be short with you. 'Tis his Highnesse pleasure
And our consent, for better tryall of you,
From hence you be committed to the Tower,
Where being but a priuate man againe,
You shall know many dare accuse you boldly,
More then (I feare) you are prouided for.

Cran. Ah my good Lord of *Winchester* : I thanke you,
You are alwayes my good Friend, if your will passe,
I shall both finde your Lordship, Iudge and Iuror,
You are so mercifull. I see your end,
'Tis my vndoing. Loue and meekenesse, Lord
Become a Churchman, better then Ambition :
Win straying Soules with modesty againe,
Cast none away : That I shall cleere my selfe,
Lay all the weight ye can vpon my patience,
I make as little doubt as you doe conscience,
In doing dayly wrongs. I could say more,
But reuerence to your calling, makes me modest.

Gard. My Lord, my Lord, you are a Sectary,
That's the plaine truth; your painted glosse discouers
To men that vnderstand you, words and weaknesse.

Crom. My Lord of *Winchester*, y'are a little,
By your good fauour, too sharpe; Men so Noble,
How euer faultly, yet should finde respect
For what they haue beene : 'tis a cruelty,
To load a falling man.

Gard. Good M. Secretary,
I cry your Honour mercie; you may worst
Of all this Table say so.
Crom. Why my Lord?
Gard. Doe not I know you for a Fauourer
Of this new Sect? ye are not sound.
Crom. Not sound?
Gard. Not sound I say.
Crom. Would you were halfe so honest :
Mens prayers then would seeke you, not their feares.
Gard. I shall remember this bold Language.
Crom. Doe.
Remember your bold life too.
Cham. This is too much;
Forbeare for shame my Lords.
Card. I haue done.
Crom. And I.
Cham. Then thus for you my Lord, it stands agreed
I take it, by all voyces : That forthwith,
You be conuaid to th' Tower a Prisoner;
There to remaine till the Kings further pleasure
Be knowne vnto vs : are you all agreed Lords.

All

All. We are.

Cran. Is there no other way of mercy,
But I must needs to th' Tower my Lords?

Gard. What other,
Would you expect? You are strangely troublesome:
Let some o' th' Guard be ready there.

Enter the Guard.

Cran. For me?
Must I goe like a Traytor thither?

Gard. Receiue him,
And see him safe i' th' Tower.

Cran. Stay good my Lords,
I haue a little yet to say. Looke there my Lords,
By vertue of that Ring, I take my cause
Out of the gripes of cruell men, and giue it
To a most Noble Iudge, the King my Maister.

Cham. This is the Kings Ring.

Sur. 'Tis no counterfeit.

Suff. 'Ts the right Ring, by Heau'n: I told ye all,
When we first put this dangerous stone a rowling,
'Twold fall vpon our selues.

Norf. Doe you thinke my Lords
The King will suffer but the little finger
Of this man to be vex'd?

Cham. 'Tis now too certaine;
How much more is his Life in value with him?
Would I were fairely out on't.

Crom. My mind gaue me,
In seeking tales and Informations
Against this man, whose honesty the Diuell
And his Disciples onely enuy at,
Ye blew the fire that burnes ye: now haue at ye.

Enter King frowning on them, takes his Seate.

Gard. Dread Soueraigne,
How much are we bound to Heauen,
In dayly thankes; that gaue vs such a Prince;
Not onely good and wise, but most religious:
One that in all obedience, makes the Church
The cheefe ayme of his Honour, and to strengthen
That holy duty out of deare respect,
His Royall selfe in Iudgement comes to heare
The cause betwixt her, and this great offender.

Kin. You were euer good at sodaine Commendations,
Bishop of *Winchester.* But know I come not
To heare such flattery now, and in my presence
They are too thin, and base to hide offences,
To me you cannot reach. You play the Spaniell,
And thinke with wagging of your tongue to win me:
But whatsoere thou tak'st me for; I'm sure
Thou hast a cruell Nature and a bloody.
Good man sit downe: Now let me see the proudest
Hee, that dares most, but wag his finger at thee.
By all that's holy, he had better starue,
Then but once thinke his place becomes thee not.

Sur. May it please your Grace;——

Kin. No Sir, it doe's not please me,
I had thought, I had had men of some vnderstanding,
And wisedome of my Councell; but I finde none:
Was it discretion Lords, to let this man,
This good man (few of you deserue that Title)
This honest man, wait like a lowsie Foot-boy
At Chamber dore? and one, as great as you are?
Why, what a shame was this? Did my Commission
Bid ye so farre forget your selues? I gaue ye
Power, as he was a Counsellour to try him,
Not as a Groome: There's some of ye, I see,
More out of Malice then Integrity,
Would trye him to the vtmost, had ye meane,
Which ye shall neuer haue while I liue.

Chan. Thus farre
My most dread Soueraigne, may it like your Grace,
To let my tongue excuse all. What was purpos'd
Concerning his Imprisonment, was rather
(If there be faith in men) meant for his Tryall,
And faire purgation to the world then malice,
I'm sure in me.

Kin. Well, well my Lords respect him,
Take him, and vse him well; hee's worthy of it.
I will say thus much for him, if a Prince
May be beholding to a Subiect; I
Am for his loue and seruice, so to him.
Make me no more adoe, but all embrace him;
Be friends for shame my Lords: My Lord of *Canterbury*
I haue a Suite which you must not deny mee.
That is, a faire young Maid that yet wants Baptisme,
You must be Godfather, and answere for her.

Cran. The greatest Monarch now aliue may glory
In such an honour: how may I deserue it,
That am a poore and humble Subiect to you?

Kin. Come, come my Lord, you'd spare your spoones;
You shall haue two noble Partners with you: the old
Duchesse of *Norfolke*, and Lady Marquesse *Dorset*? will
these please you?
Once more my Lord of *Winchester*, I charge you
Embrace, and loue this man.

Gard. With a true heart,
And Brother; loue I doe it.

Cran. And let Heauen
Witnesse how deare, I hold this Confirmation. (heares,

Kin. Good Man, those ioyfull teares shew thy true
The common voyce I see is verified
Of thee, which sayes thus: Doe my Lord of *Canterbury*
A shrewd turne, and hee's your friend for euer:
Come Lords, we trifle time away: I long
To haue this young one made a Christian.
As I haue made ye one Lords, one remaine:
So I grow stronger, you more Honour gaine. *Exeunt.*

Scena Tertia.

Noyse and Tumult within: Enter Porter and his man.

Port. You'l leaue your noyse anon ye Rascals: doe
you take the Court for Parish Garden: ye rude Slaues,
leaue your gaping:

Within. Good M. Porter I belong to th' Larder.

Port. Belong to th' Gallowes, and be hang'd ye Rogue:
Is this a place to roare in? Fetch me a dozen Crab-tree
staues, and strong ones; these are but switches to 'em:
Ile scratch your heads; you must be seeing Christenings?
Do you looke for Ale, and Cakes heere, you rude
Raskalls?

Man. Pray Sir be patient; 'tis as much impossible,
Vnlesse wee sweepe 'em from the dore with Cannons,
To scatter 'em, as 'tis to make 'em sleepe
On May-day Morning, which will neuer be:
We may as well push against Powles as stirre 'em.

Por. How got they in, and be hang'd?

The Life of King Henry the Eight.

Man. Alas I know not, how gets the Tide in?
As much as one sound Cudgell of foure foote,
(You see the poore remainder) could distribute,
I made no spare Sir.

Port. You did nothing Sir.

Man. I am not *Sampson*, nor Sir *Guy*, nor *Colebrand*,
To mow 'em downe before me: but if I spar'd any
That had a head to hit, either young or old,
He or shee, Cuckold or Cuckold-maker:
Let me ne're hope to see a Chine againe,
And that I would not for a Cow, God saue her.

Within. Do you heare M. Porter?

Port. I shall be with you presently, good M. *Puppy*,
Keepe the dore close Sirha.

Man. What would you haue me doe?

Por. What should you doe,
But knock 'em downe by th' dozens? Is this More fields
to muster in? Or haue wee some strange Indian with the
great *Toole*, come to Court, the women so besiege vs?
Blesse me, what a fry of Fornication is at dore? On my
Christian Conscience this one Christening will beget a
thousand, here will bee Father, God-father, and all together.

Man. The Spoones will be the bigger Sir: There is
a fellow somewhat neere the doore, he should be a Brasi-
er by his face, for o' my conscience twenty of the Dog-
dayes now reigne in's Nose; all that stand about him are
vnder the Line, they need no other pennance: that Fire-
Drake did I hit three times on the head, and three times
was his Nose discharged against mee; hee stands there
like a Morter-piece to blow vs. There was a Habberda-
shers Wife of small wit, neere him, that rail'd vpon me,
till her pinck'd porrenger fell off her head, for kindling
such a combustion in the State. I mist the Meteor once,
and hit that Woman, who cryed out Clubbes, when I
might see from farre, some forty Truncheoners draw to
her succour, which were the hope o' th' Strond where she
was quartered; they fell on, I made good my place; at
length they came to th' broome staffe to me, I defide 'em
still, when sodainly a File of Boyes behind 'em, loose shot,
deliuer'd such a showre of Pibbles, that I was faine to
draw mine Honour in, and let 'em win the Worke, the
Diuell was amongst 'em I thinke surely.

Por. These are the youths that thunder at a Playhouse,
and fight for bitten Apples, that no Audience but the
tribulation of Tower Hill, or the Limbes of Limehouse,
their deare Brothers are able to endure. I haue some of
'em in *Limbo Patrum*, and there they are like to dance
these three dayes; besides the running Banquet of two
Beadles, that is to come.

Enter Lord Chamberlaine.

Cham. Mercy o' me: what a Multitude are heere?
They grow still too; from all Parts they are comming,
As if we kept a Faire heere? Where are these Porters?
These lazy knaues? Y' haue made a fine hand fellowes?
Theres a trim rabble let in: are all these
Your faithfull friends o' th' Suburbs? We shall haue
Great store of roome no doubt, left for the Ladies,
When they passe backe from the Christening?

Por. And't please your Honour,
We are but men; and what so many may doe,
Not being torne a pieces, we haue done:
An Army cannot rule 'em.

Cham. As I liue,
If the King blame me for't; Ile lay ye all
By th' heeles, and sodainly: and on your heads
Clap round Fines for neglect: y' are lazy knaues,
And heere ye lye baiting of Bombards, when
Ye should doe Seruice. Harke the Trumpets sound,
Th' are come already from the Christening,
Go breake among the preasse, and finde away out
To let the Troope passe fairely; or Ile finde
A Marshallsey, shall hold ye play these two Monthes.

Por. Make way there, for the Princesse.

Man. You great fellow,
Stand close vp, or Ile make your head ake.

Por. You i' th' Chamblet, get vp o' th' raile,
Ile pecke you o're the pales else. *Exeunt.*

Scena Quarta.

*Enter Trumpets sounding: Then two Aldermen, L. Maior,
Garter, Cranmer, Duke of Norfolke with his Marshals
Staffe, Duke of Suffolke, two Noblemen, bearing great
standing Bowles for the Christening Guifts: Then foure
Noblemen bearing a Canopy, vnder which the Dutchesse of
Norfolke, Godmother, bearing the Childe richly habited in
a Mantle, &c. Traine borne by a Lady: Then followes
the Marchionesse Dorset, the other Godmother, and Ladies. The Troope passe once about the Stage, and Garter speakes.*

Gart. Heauen
From thy endlesse goodnesse, send prosperous life,
Long, and euer happie, to the high and Mighty
Princesse of England *Elizabeth*.

Flourish. Enter King and Guard.

Cran. And to your Royall Grace, & the good Queen,
My Noble Partners, and my selfe thus pray
All comfort, ioy in this most gracious Lady,
Heauen euer laid vp to make Parents happy,
May hourely fall vpon ye.

Kin. Thanke you good Lord Archbishop:
What is her Name?

Cran. *Elizabeth.*

Kin. Stand vp Lord,
With this Kisse, take my Blessing: God protect thee,
Into whose hand, I giue thy Life.

Cran. *Amen.*

Kin. My Noble Gossips, y' haue beene too Prodigall;
I thanke ye heartily: So shall this Lady,
When she ha's so much English.

Cran. Let me speake Sir,
For Heauen now bids me; and the words I vtter,
Let none thinke Flattery; for they' l finde 'em Truth.
This Royall Infant, Heauen still moue about her;
Though in her Cradle; yet now promises
Vpon this Land a thousand thousand Blessings,
Which Time shall bring to ripenesse: She shall be,
(But few now liuing can behold that goodnesse)
A Patterne to all Princes liuing with her,
And all that shall succeed: *Saba* was neuer
More couetous of Wisedome, and faire Vertue
Then this pure Soule shall be. All Princely Graces
That mould vp such a mighty Piece as this is,
With all the Vertues that attend the good,
Shall still be doubled on her. Truth shall Nurse her,

Holy and Heauenly thoughts still Counsell her:
She shall be lou'd and fear'd. Her owne shall blesse her;
Her Foes shake like a Field of beaten Corne,
And hang their heads with sorrow:
Good growes with her.
In her dayes, Euery Man shall eate in safety,
Vnder his owne Vine what he plants; and sing
The merry Songs of Peace to all his Neighbours.
God shall be truely knowne, and those about her,
From her shall read the perfect way of Honour,
And by those claime their greatnesse; not by Blood.
Nor shall this peace sleepe with her: But as when
The Bird of Wonder dyes, the Mayden Phoenix,
Her Ashes new create another Heyre,
As great in admiration as her selfe.
So shall she leaue her Blessednesse to One,
(When Heauen shal call her from this clowd of darknes)
Who, from the sacred Ashes of her Honour
Shall Star-like rise, as great in fame as she was,
And so stand fix'd. Peace, Plenty, Loue, Truth, Terror,
That were the Seruants to this chosen Infant,
Shall then be his, and like a Vine grow to him;
Where euer the bright Sunne of Heauen shall shine,
His Honour, and the greatnesse of his Name,
Shall be, and make new Nations. He shall flourish,
And like a Mountaine Cedar, reach his branches,
To all the Plaines about him: Our Childrens Children
Shall see this, and blesse Heauen.

Kin. Thou speakest wonders.

Cran. She shall be to the happinesse of England,
An aged Princesse; many dayes shall see her,
And yet no day without a deed to Crowne it.
Would I had knowne no more: But she must dye,
She must, the Saints must haue her; yet a Virgin,
A most vnspotted Lilly shall she passe
To th' ground, and all the World shall mourne her.

Kin. O Lord Archbishop
Thou hast made me now a man, neuer before
This happy Child, did I get any thing.
This Oracle of comfort, ha's so pleas'd me,
That when I am in Heauen, I shall desire
To see what this Child does, and praise my Maker.
I thanke ye all. To you my good Lord Maior,
And you good Brethren, I am much beholding:
I haue receiu'd much Honour by your presence,
And ye shall find me thankfull. Lead the way Lords,
Ye must all see the Queene, and she must thanke ye,
She will be sicke els. This day, no man thinke
'Has businesse at his house; for all shall stay:
This Little-One shall make it Holy-day. *Exeunt.*

THE EPILOGVE.

'Tis ten to one, this Play can neuer please
All that are heere: Some come to take their ease,
And sleepe an Act or two; but those we feare
W'haue frighted with our Trumpets: so 'tis cleare,
They'l say 'tis naught. Others to heare the City
Abus'd extreamly, and to cry that's witty,
Which wee haue not done neither; that I feare
All the expected good w'are like to heare.
For this Play at this time, is onely in
The mercifull construction of good women,
For such a one we shew'd 'em: If they smile,
And say twill doe; I know within a while,
 All the best men are ours; for 'tis ill hap,
 If they hold, when their Ladies bid 'em clap.

FINIS.

The Prologue.

IN Troy there lyes the Scene: From Iles of Greece
The Princes Orgillous, their high blood chaf'd
Haue to the Port of Athens sent their shippes
Fraught with the ministers and instruments
Of cruell Warre: Sixty and nine that wore
Their Crownets Regall, from th' Athenian bay
Put forth toward Phrygia, and their vow is made
To ransacke Troy, within whose strong emures
The rauish'd Helen, Menelaus Queene,
With wanton Paris sleepes, and that's the Quarrell.
To Tenedos they come,
And the deepe-drawing Barke do there disgorge
Their warlike frautage: now on Dardan Plaines
The fresh and yet vnbruised Greekes do pitch
Their braue Pauillions. Priams six-gated City,
Dardan and Timbria, Helias, Chetas, Troien,
And Antenonidus with massie Staples
And corresponsiue and fulfilling Bolts
Stirre vp the Sonnes of Troy.
Now Expectation tickling skittish spirits,
On one and other side, Troian and Greeke,
Sets all on hazard. And hither am I come,
A Prologue arm'd, but not in confidence
Of Authors pen, or Actors voyce; but suited
In like conditions, as our Argument;
To tell you (faire Beholders) that our Play
Leapes ore the vaunt and firstlings of those broyles,
Beginning in the middle: starting thence away,
To what may be digested in a Play:
Like, or finde fault, do as your pleasures are,
Now good, or bad, 'tis but the chance of Warre.

THE TRAGEDIE OF
Troylus and Cressida.

Actus Primus. Scœna Prima.

Enter Pandarus and Troylus.

Troylus.
Call here my Varlet, Ile vnarme againe.
Why should I warre without the wals of Troy
That finde such cruell battell here within?
Each Troian that is master of his heart,
Let him to field, *Troylus* alas hath none.

Pan. Will this geere nere be mended?

Troy. The Greeks are strong, & skilful to their strength,
Fierce to their skill, and to their fiercenesse Valiant:
But I am weaker then a womans teare;
Tamer then sleepe, fonder then ignorance;
Lesse valiant then the Virgin in the night,
And skillesse as vnpractis'd Infancie.

Pan. Well, I haue told you enough of this: For my part, Ile not meddle nor make no farther. Hee that will haue a Cake out of the Wheate, must needes tarry the grinding.

Troy. Haue I not tarried?

Pan. I the grinding; but you must tarry the bolting.

Troy. Haue I not tarried?

Pan. I the boulting; but you must tarry the leau'ing.

Troy. Still haue I tarried.

Pan. I, to the leauening: but heeres yet in the word hereafter, the Kneading, the making of the Cake, the heating of the Ouen, and the Baking; nay, you must stay the cooling too, or you may chance to burne your lips.

Troy. Patience her selfe, what Goddesse ere she be,
Doth lesser blench at sufferance, then I doe:
At *Priams* Royall Table doe I sit;
And when faire *Cressid* comes into my thoughts,
So (Traitor) then she comes, when she is thence.

Pan. Well:
She look'd yesternight fairer, then euer I saw her looke,
Or any woman else.

Troy. I was about to tell thee, when my heart,
As wedged with a sigh, would riue in twaine,
Least *Hector*, or my Father should perceiue me:
I haue (as when the Sunne doth light a-scorne)
Buried this sigh, in wrinkle of a smile:
But sorrow, that is couch'd in seeming gladnesse,
Is like that mirth, Fate turnes to sudden sadnesse.

Pan. And her haire were not somewhat darker then *Helens*, well go too, there were no more comparison betweene the Women. But for my part she is my Kinswoman, I would not (as they tearme it) praise it, but I wold some-body had heard her talke yesterday as I did: I will not disprayse your sister *Cassandra's* wit, but——

Troy. Oh *Pandarus*! I tell thee *Pandarus*;
When I doe tell thee, there my hopes lye drown'd:
Reply not in how many Fadomes deepe
They lye indrench'd. I tell thee, I am mad
In *Cressids* loue. Thou answer'st she is Faire,
Powr'st in the open Vlcer of my heart,
Her Eyes, her Haire, her Cheeke, her Gate, her Voice,
Handlest in thy discourse. O that her Hand
(In whose comparison, all whites are Inke)
Writing their owne reproach; to whose soft seizure,
The Cignets Downe is harsh, and spirit of Sense
Hard as the palme of Plough-man. This thou tel'st me;
As true thou tel'st me, when I say I loue her:
But saying thus, instead of Oyle and Balme,
Thou lai'st in euery gash that loue hath giuen me,
The Knife that made it.

Pan. I speake no more then truth.

Troy. Thou do'st not speake so much.

Pan. Faith, Ile not meddle in't: Let her be as shee is, if she be faire, 'tis the better for her: and she be not, she ha's the mends in her owne hands.

Troy. Good *Pandarus*: How now *Pandarus*?

Pan. I haue had my Labour for my trauell, ill thought on of her, and ill thought on of you: Gone betweene and betweene, but small thankes for my labour.

Troy. What art thou angry *Pandarus*? what with me?

Pan. Because she's Kinne to me, therefore shee's not so faire as *Helen*, and she were not kin to me, she would be as faire on Friday, as *Helen* is on Sunday. But what care I? I care not and she were a Black-a-Moore, 'tis all one to me.

Troy. Say I she is not faire?

Troy. I doe not care whether you doe or no. Shee's a Foole to stay behinde her Father: Let her to the Greeks, and so Ile tell her the next time I see her: for my part, Ile meddle nor make no more i'th'matter.

Troy. Pandarus?   *Pan.* Not I.

Troy. Sweete *Pandarus.*

Pan. Pray you speake no more to me, I will leaue all as I found it, and there an end. *Exit Pand.*

Sound Alarum.

Tro. Peace you vngracious Clamors, peace rude sounds,
Fooles on both sides, *Helen* must needs be faire,
When with your bloud you daily paint her thus.
I cannot fight vpon this Argument:

It is too staru'd a subiect for my Sword,
But *Pandarus*: O Gods! How do you plague me?
I cannot come to *Cressid* but by *Pandar*,
And he's as teachy to be woo'd to woe,
As she is stubborne, chaft, against all suite.
Tell me *Apollo* for thy *Daphnes* Loue
What *Cressid* is, what *Pandar*, and what we:
Her bed is *India*, there she lies, a Pearle,
Between our *Illium*, and where shee recides
Let it be cald the wild and wandring flood,
Our selfe the Merchant, and this sayling *Pandar*,
Our doubtfull hope, our conuoy and our Barke.

Alarum. Enter Æneas.

Æne. How now Prince *Troylus*?
Wherefore not a field?

Troy. Because not there; this womans answer forts.
For womanish it is to be from thence:
What newes *Æneas* from the field to day?

Æne. That *Paris* is returned home, and hurt.

Troy. By whom *Æneas*?

Æne. *Troylus* by *Menelaus*.

Troy. Let *Paris* bleed, 'tis but a scar to scorne.
Paris is gor'd with *Menelaus* horne. *Alarum.*

Æne. Harke what good sport is out of Towne to day.

Troy. Better at home, if would I might were may:
But to the sport abroad, are you bound thither?

Æne. In all swift haft.

Troy. Come goe wee then togither. *Exeunt.*

Enter Cressid and her man.

Cre. Who were those went by?

Man. Queene *Hecuba*, and *Hellen*.

Cre. And whether go they?

Man. Vp to the Easterne Tower,
Whose height commands as subiect all the vaile,
To see the battell: *Hector* whose pacience,
Is as a Vertue fixt, to day was mou'd:
He chides *Andromache* and strooke his Armorer,
And like as there were husbandry in Warre
Before the Sunne rose, hee was harneft lyte,
And to the field goe's he; where euery flower
Did as a Prophet weepe what it forsaw,
In *Hectors* wrath.

Cre. What was his cause of anger?

Man. The noise goe's this;
There is among the Greekes,
A Lord of Troian blood, Nephew to *Hector*,
They call him *Aiax*.

Cre. Good; and what of him?

Man. They say he is a very man *per se* and stands alone.

Cre. So do all men, vnlesse they are drunke, sicke, or haue no legges.

Man. This man Lady, hath rob'd many beasts of their particular additions, he is as valiant as the Lyon, churlish as the Beare, slow as the Elephant: a man into whom nature hath so crowded humors, that his valour is crusht into folly, his folly sauced with discretion: there is no man hath a vertue, that he hath not a glimpse of, nor any man an attaint, but he carries some staine of it. He is melancholy without cause, and merry against the haire, hee hath the ioynts of euery thing, but euery thing so out of ioynt, that hee is a gowtie *Briareus*, many hands and no vse; or purblinded *Argus*, all eyes and no sight.

Cre. But how should this man that makes me smile, make *Hector* angry?

Man. They say he yesterday cop'd *Hector* in the battell and stroke him downe, the disdaind & shame whereof, hath euer since kept *Hector* fasting and waking.

Enter Pandarus.

Cre. Who comes here?

Man. Madam your Vncle *Pandarus*.

Cre. *Hectors* a gallant man.

Man. As may be in the world Lady.

Pan. What's that? what's that?

Cre. Good morrow Vncle *Pandarus*.

Pan. Good morrow Cozen *Cressid*: what do you talke of? good morrow *Alexander*: how do you Cozen? when were you at Illium?

Cre. This morning Vncle.

Pan. What were you talking of when I came? Was *Hector* arm'd and gon ere yea came to Illium? *Hellen* was not vp? was she?

Cre. *Hector* was gone but *Hellen* was not vp?

Pan. E'ene so; *Hector* was stirring early.

Cre. That were we talking of, and of his anger.

Pan. Was he angry?

Cre. So he saies here.

Pan. True he was so; I know the cause too, heele lay about him to day I can tell them that, and there's *Troylus* will not come farre behind him, let them take heede of *Troylus*; I can tell them that too.

Cre. What is he angry too?

Pan. Who *Troylus*?
Troylus is the better man of the two.

Cre. Oh *Iupiter*; there's no comparison.

Pan. What not betweene *Troylus* and *Hector*? do you know a man if you see him?

Cre. I, if I euer saw him before and knew him.

Pan. Well I say *Troylus* is *Troylus*.

Cre. Then you say as I say,
For I am sure he is not *Hector*.

Pan. No not *Hector* is not *Troylus* in some degrees.

Cre. 'Tis iust, to each of them he is himselfe.

Pan. Himselfe? alas poore *Troylus* I would he were.

Cre. So he is.

Pan. Condition I had gone bare-foote to India.

Cre. He is not *Hector*.

Pan. Himselfe? no, or hee's not himselfe, would a were himselfe: well, the Gods are aboue, time must friend or end: well *Troylus* well, I would my heart were in her body; no, *Hector* is not a better man then *Troylus*.

Cre. Excuse me.

Pan. He is elder.

Cre. Pardon me, pardon me.

Pan. Th'others not come too't, you shall tell me another tale when th'others come too't: *Hector* shall not haue his will this yeare.

Cre. He shall not neede it if he haue his owne.

Pan. Nor his qualities.

Cre. No matter.

Pan. Nor his beautie.

Cre. 'Twould not become him, his own's better.

Pan. You haue no iudgement Neece; *Hellen* her selfe swore th'other day, that *Troylus* for a browne fauour (for so 'tis I must confesse) not browne neither.

Cre. No, but browne.

Pan. Faith to say truth, browne and not browne.

Cre. To say the truth, true and not true.

Pan. She prais'd his complexion aboue *Paris*.

Cre. Why *Paris* hath colour inough.

Pan. So he has.

Cre. Then *Troylus* should haue too much, if she prais'd him aboue, his complexion is higher then his, he hauing
colour

colour enough, and the other higher, is too flaming a praise for a good complexion, I had as liue Hellens golden tongue had commended Troylus for a copper nose.

Pan. I sweare to you,
I thinke Hellen loues him better then Paris.

Cre. Then shee's a merry Greeke indeed.

Pan. Nay I am sure she does, she came to him th'other day into the compast window, and you know he has not past three or foure haires on his chinne.

Cres. Indeed a Tapsters Arithmetique may soone bring his particulars therein, to a totall.

Pand. Why he is very yong, and yet will he within three pound lift as much as his brother Hector.

Cres. Is he is so younga man, and so old a lifter?

Pan. But to prooue to you that Hellen loues him, she came and puts me her white hand to his clouen chin.

Cres. Iuno haue mercy, how came it clouen?

Pan. Why, you know 'tis dimpled,
I thinke his smyling becomes him better then any man in all Phrigia.

Cre. Oh he smiles valiantly.

Pan. Dooes hee not?

Cre. Oh yes, and 'twere a clow'd in Autumne.

Pan. Why go to then, but to prooue to you that Hellen loues Troylus.

Cre. Troylus wil stand to thee
Proofe, if youle prooue it so.

Pan. Troylus? why he esteemes her no more then I esteeme an addle egge.

Cre. If you loue an addle egge as well as you loue an idle head, you would eate chickens i'th'shell.

Pan. I cannot chuse but laugh to thinke how she tickled his chin, indeed shee has a maruel's white hand I must needs confesse.

Cre. Without the racke.

Pan. And shee takes vpon her to spie a white haire on his chinne.

Cre. Alas poore chin? many a wart is richer.

Pand. But there was such laughing, Queene Hecuba laught that her eyes ran ore.

Cre. With Milstones.

Pan. And Cassandra laught.

Cre. But there was more temperate fire vnder the pot of her eyes: did her eyes run ore too?

Pan. And Hector laught.

Cre. At what was all this laughing?

Pand. Marry at the white haire that Hellen spied on Troylus chin.

Cres. And 't had beene a greene haire, I should haue laught too.

Pand. They laught not so much at the haire, as at his pretty answere.

Cre. What was his answere?

Pan. Quoth shee, heere's but two and fifty haires on your chinne; and one of them is white.

Cre. This is her question.

Pand. That's true, make no question of that, two and fiftie haires quoth hee, and one white, that white haire is my Father, and all the rest are his Sonnes. Iupiter quoth she, which of these haires is Paris my husband? The forked one quoth he, pluckt out and giue it him: but there was such laughing, and Hellen so blusht, and Paris so chaft, and all the rest so laught, that it past.

Cre. So let it now,
For is has beene a great while going by.

Pan. Well Cozen,
I told you a thing yesterday, think on't.

Cre. So I does.

Pand. Ile be sworne 'tis true, he will weepe you an'twere a man borne in Aprill. *Sound a retreate.*

Cres. And Ile spring vp in his teares, an'twere a nettle against May.

Pan. Harke they are comming from the field, shal we stand vp here and see them, as they passe toward illium, good Neece do, sweet Neece Cressida.

Cre. At your pleasure.

Pan. Heere, heere, here's an excellent place, heere we may see most brauely, Ile tel you them all by their names, as they passe by, but marke Troylus aboue the rest.

Enter Æneas.

Cre. Speake not so low'd.

Pan. That's Æneas, is not that a braue man, hee's one of the flowers of Troy I can you, but marke Troylus, you shal see anon.

Cre. Who's that?

Enter Antenor.

Pan. That's Antenor, he has a shrow'd wit I can tell you, and hee's a man good inough, hee's one o'th soundest iudgement in Troy whosoeuer, and a proper man of person: when comes Troylus? Ile shew you Troylus anon, if hee see me, you shall see him him nod at me.

Cre. Will he giue you the nod?

Pan. You shall see.

Cre. If he do, the rich shall haue, more.

Enter Hector.

Pan. That's Hector, that, that, looke you, that there's a fellow. Goe thy way Hector, there's a braue man Neece, O braue Hector! Looke how hee lookes? there's a countenance; ist not a braue man?

Cre. O braue man!

Pan. Is a not? It dooes a mans heart good, looke you what hacks are on his Helmet, looke you yonder, do you see? Looke you there? There's no iesting, laying on, tak't off, who ill as they say, there be hacks.

Cre. Be those with Swords?

Enter Paris.

Pan. Swords, any thing he cares not, and the diuell come to him, it's all one, by Gods lid it dooes ones heart good. Yonder comes Paris, yonder comes Paris: looke yee yonder Neece, ist not a gallant man to, ist not? Why this is braue now: who said he came hurt home to day? Hee's not hurt, why this will do Hellens heart good now, ha? Would I could see Troylus now, you shall Troylus anon.

Cre. Whose that?

Enter Hellenus

Pan. That's Hellenus, I maruell where Troylus is, that's Helenus, I thinke he went not forth to day: that's Helenus.

Cre. Can Hellenus fight Vncle?

Pan. Hellenus no: yes heele fight indifferent, well, I maruell where Troylus is; harke, do you not haere the people crie Troylus? Hellenus is a Priest.

Cre. What sneaking fellow comes yonder?

Enter Trylus.

Pan. Where? Yonder? That's Dæphobus. 'Tis Troylus! Ther's a man Neece, hem? Braue Troylus the Prince of Chiualrie.

Cre. Peace, for shame peace.

Pand. Marke him, not him: O braue Troylus: looke well vpon him Neece, looke you how his Sword is blou died, and his Helme more hackt then Hectors, and how he lookes,

lookes, and how he goes. O admirable youth! he ne're saw three and twenty. Go thy way *Troylus*, go thy way, had I a sister were a *Grace*, or a daughter a Goddesse, hee should take his choice. O admirable man! *Paris*? *Paris* is durt to him, and I warrant, *Helen* to change, would giue money to boot.

Enter common Souldiers.

Cres. Heere come more.
Pan. Asses, fooles, dolts, chaffe and bran, chaffe and bran; porredge after meat. I could liue and dye i'th'eyes of *Troylus*. Ne're looke, ne're looke; the Eagles are gon, Crowes and Dawes, Crowes and Dawes: I had rather be such a man as *Troylus* then *Agamemnon*, and all Greece.
Cres. There is among the Greekes *Achilles*, a better man then *Troylus*.
Pan. *Achilles*? a Dray-man, a Porter, a very Camell.
Cres. Well, well.
Pan. Well, well? Why haue you any discretion? haue you any eyes? Do you know what a man is? Is not birth, beauty, good shape, discourse, manhood, learning, gentlenesse, vertue, youth, liberality, and so forth: the Spice, and salt that seasons a man?
Cres. I, a minc'd man, and then to be bak'd with no Date in the pye, for then the mans dates out.
Pan. You are such another woman, one knowes not at what ward you lye.
Cres. Vpon my backe, to defend my belly; vpon my wit, to defend my wiles; vppon my secrecy, to defend mine honesty; my Maske, to defend my beauty, and you to defend all these: and at all these wardes I lye at, at a thousand watches.
Pan. Say one of your watches.
Cres. Nay Ile watch you for that, and that's one of the cheefest of them too: If I cannot ward what I would not haue hit, I can watch you for telling how I tooke the blow, vnlesse it swell past hiding, and then it's past watching.

Enter Boy.

Pan. You are such another.
Boy. Sir, my Lord would instantly speake with you.
Pan. Where?
Boy. At your owne house.
Pan. Good Boy tell him I come, I doubt he bee hurt. Fare ye well good Neece.
Cres. Adieu Vnkle.
Pan. Ile be with you Neece by and by.
Cres. To bring Vnkle.
Pan. I, a token from *Troylus*.
Cres. By the same token, you are a Bawd. *Exit Pand.*
Words, vowes, gifts, teares, & loues full sacrifice,
He offers in anothers enterprise:
But more in *Troylus* thousand fold I see,
Then in the glasse of *Pandar's* praise may be;
Yet hold I off. Women are Angels wooing,
Things won are done, ioyes soule lyes in the dooing:
That she belou'd, knowes nought, that knowes not this;
Men prize the thing vngain'd, more then it is.
That she was neuer yet, that euer knew
Loue got so sweet, as when desire did sue:
Therefore this maxime out of loue I teach;
"Atchieuement, is command; vngain'd, beseech.
That though my hearts Contents firme loue doth beare,
Nothing of that shall from mine eyes appeare. *Exit.*

Senet. Enter Agamemnon, Nestor, Vlysses, Diomedes, Menelaus, with others.

Agam. Princes:
What greefe hath set the Iaundies on your cheekes?
The ample proposition that hope makes
In all designes, begun on earth below
Fayles in the promist largenesse: cheekes and disasters
Grow in the veines of actions highest rear'd.
As knots by the conflux of meeting sap,
Infect the sound Pine, and diuerts his Graine
Tortiue and erant from his course of growth.
Nor Princes, is it matter new to vs,
That we come short of our suppose so farre,
That after seuen yeares siege, yet Troy walles stand;
Sith euery action that hath gone before,
Whereof we haue Record, Triall did draw
Bias and thwart, not answering the ayme:
And that vnbodied figure of the thought
That gaue't surmised shape. Why then (you Princes)
Do you with cheekes abash'd, behold our workes,
And thinke them shame, which are (indeed) nought else
But the protractiue trials of great Ioue,
To finde persistiue constancie in men?
The finenesse of which Mettall is not found
In Fortunes loue: for then, the Bold and Coward,
The Wise and Foole, the Artist and vn-read,
The hard and soft, seeme all affin'd, and kin.
But in the Winde and Tempest of her frowne,
Distinction with a lowd and powrefull fan,
Puffing at all, winnowes the light away;
And what hath masse, or matter by it selfe,
Lies rich in Vertue, and vnmingled.

Nestor. With due Obseruance of thy godly seat,
Great *Agamemnon*, *Nestor* shall apply
Thy latest words.
In the reproofe of Chance,
Lies the true proofe of men: The Sea being smooth,
How many shallow bauble Boates dare saile
Vpon her patient brest, making their way
With those of Nobler bulke?
But let the Ruffian *Boreas* once enrage
The gentle *Thetis*, and anon behold
The strong ribb'd Barke through liquid Mountaines cut,
Bounding betweene the two moyst Elements
Like *Persesus* Horse. Where's then the sawcy Boate,
Whose weake vntimber'd sides but euen now
Co-riual'd Greatnesse? Either to harbour fled,
Or made a Toste for Neptune. Euen so,
Doth valours shew, and valours worth diuide
In stormes of Fortune.
For, in her ray and brightnesse,
The Heard hath more annoyance by the Brieze
Then by the Tyger: But, when the splitting winde
Makes flexible the knees of knotted Oakes,
And Flies fled vnder shade, why then
The thing of Courage,
As rowz'd with rage, with rage doth sympathize,
And with an accent tun'd in selfe-same key,
Retyres to chiding Fortune.

Vlys. Agamemnon:
Thou great Commander, Nerue, and Bone of Greece,
Heart of our Numbers, soule, and onely spirit,
In whom the tempers, and the mindes of all
Should be shut vp: Heare what *Vlysses* speakes,
Besides the applause and approbation
The which most mighty for thy place and sway,

Troylus and Cressida.

And thou most reuerend for thy stretcht-out life,
I giue to both your speeches: which were such,
As *Agamemnon* and the hand of Greece
Should hold vp high in Brasse: and such againe
As venerable *Nestor* (hatch'd in Siluer)
Should with a bond of ayre, strong as the Axletree
In which the Heauens ride, knit all Greekes eares
To his experienc'd tongue: yet let it please both
(Thou Great, and Wise) to heare *Vlysses* speake.

Aga. Speak Prince of *Ithaca*, and be't of lesse expect:
That matter needlesse of importlesse burthen
Diuide thy lips; then we are confident
When ranke *Thersites* opes his Masticke iawes,
We shall heare Musicke, Wit, and Oracle.

Vlyss. Troy yet vpon his basis had bene downe,
And the great *Hectors* sword had lack'd a Master
But for these instances.
The specialty of Rule hath beene neglected;
And looke how many Grecian Tents do stand
Hollow vpon this Plaine, so many hollow Factions.
When that the Generall is not like the Hiue,
To whom the Forragers shall all repaire,
What Hony is expected? Degree being vizarded,
Th'vnworthiest shewes as fairely in the Maske.
The Heauens themselues, the Planets, and this Center,
Obserue degree, priority, and place,
Insisture, course, proportion, season, forme,
Office, and custome, in all line of Order:
And therefore is the glorious Planet Sol
In noble eminence, enthron'd and sphear'd
Amid'st the other, whose med'cinable eye
Corrects the ill Aspects of Planets euill,
And postes like the Command'ment of a King,
Sans checke, to good and bad. But when the Planets
In euill mixture to disorder wander,
What Plagues, and what portents, what mutiny?
What raging of the Sea? shaking of Earth?
Commotion in the Windes? Frights, changes, horrors,
Diuert, and cracke, rend and deracinate
The vnity, and married calme of States
Quite from their fixure? O, when Degree is shak'd,
(Which is the Ladder to all high designes)
The enterprize is sicke. How could Communities,
Degrees in Schooles, and Brother-hoods in Cities,
Peacefull Commerce from diuidable shores,
The primogenitiue, and due of Byrth,
Prerogatiue of Age, Crownes, Scepters, Lawrels,
(But by Degree) stand in Authentique place?
Take but Degree away, vn-tune that string,
And hearke what Discord followes: each thing meetes
In meere oppugnancie. The bounded Waters,
Should lift their bosomes higher then the Shores,
And make a soppe of all this solid Globe:
Strength should be Lord of imbecility,
And the rude Sonne should strike his Father dead:
Force should be right, or rather, right and wrong,
(Betweene whose endlesse iarre, Iustice recides)
Should loose her names, and so should Iustice too.
Then euery thing includes it selfe in Power,
Power into Will, Will into Appetite,
And Appetite (an vniuersall Wolfe,
So doubly seconded with Will, and Power)
Must make perforce an vniuersall prey,
And last, eate vp himselfe.
Great *Agamemnon*:
This Chaos, when Degree is suffocate,
Followes the choaking:
And this neglection of Degree, is it
That by a pace goes backward in a purpose
It hath to climbe. The Generall's disdain'd
By him one step below; he, by the next,
That next, by him beneath: so euery step
Exampled by the first pace that is sicke
Of his Superiour, growes to an enuious Feauer
Of pale, and bloodlesse Emulation.
And 'tis this Feauer that keepes Troy on foote,
Not her owne sinewes. To end a tale of length,
Troy in our weaknesse liues, not in her strength.

Nest. Most wisely hath *Vlysses* heere discouer'd
The Feauer, whereof all our power is sicke.

Aga. The Nature of the sicknesse found (*Vlysses*)
What is the remedie?

Vlyss. The great *Achilles*, whom Opinion crownes,
The sinew, and the fore-hand of our Hoste,
Hauing his eare full of his ayery Fame,
Growes dainty of his worth, and in his Tent
Lyes mocking our designes. With him, *Patroclus*,
Vpon a lazie Bed, the liue-long day
Breakes scurrill Iests,
And with ridiculous and aukward action,
(Which Slanderer, he imitation call's)
He Pageants vs. Sometime great *Agamemnon*,
Thy toplesse deputation he puts on;
And like a strutting Player, whose conceit
Lies in his Ham-string, and doth thinke it rich
To heare the woodden Dialogue and sound
'Twixt his stretcht footing, and the Scaffolage,
Such to be pittied, and ore-rested seeming
He acts thy Greatnesse in: and when he speakes,
'Tis like a Chime a mending. With tearmes vnsquar'd,
Which from the tongue of roaring *Typhon* dropt,
Would seemes Hyperboles. At this fusty stuffe,
The large *Achilles* (on his prest-bed lolling)
From his deepe Chest, laughes out a lowd applause,
Cries excellent, 'tis *Agamemnon* iust.
Now play me *Nestor*; hum, and stroke thy Beard
As he, being drest to some Oration:
That's done, as neere as the extreamest ends
Of paralels; as like, as *Vulcan* and his wife,
Yet god *Achilles* still cries excellent,
'Tis *Nestor* right. Now play him (me) *Patroclus*,
Arming to answer in a night-Alarme,
And then (forsooth) the faint defects of Age
Must be the Scene of myrth, to cough, and spit,
And with a palsie fumbling on his Gorget,
Shake in and out the Riuet: and at this sport
Sir Valour dies; cries, O enough *Patroclus*,
Or, giue me ribs of Steele, I shall split all
In pleasure of my Spleene. And in this fashion,
All our abilities, gifts, natures, shapes,
Seuerals and generals of grace exact,
Atchieuments, plots, orders, preuentions,
Excitements to the field, or speech for truce,
Successe or losse, what is, or is not, serues
As stuffe for these two, to make paradoxes.

Nest. And in the imitation of these twaine,
Who (as *Vlysses* sayes) Opinion crownes
With an Imperiall voyce, many are infect:
Aiax is growne selfe-will'd, and beares his head
In such a reyne, in full as proud a place
As broad *Achilles*, and keepes his Tent like him;
Makes factious Feasts, railes on our state of Warre

Bold

Troylus and Cressida.

Bold as an Oracle, and fets *Therfites*
A flaue, whose Gall coines flanders like a Mint,
To match vs in comparisons with durt,
To weaken and discredit our expofure,
How ranke foeuer rounded in with danger.

Vlyf. They taxe our policy, and call it Cowardice,
Count Wifedome as no member of the Warre,
Fore-ftall prefcience, and esteeme no acte
But that of hand: The still and mentall parts,
That do contriue how many hands shall strike
When fitneffe call them on, and know by meafure
Of their obferuant toyle, the Enemies waight,
Why this hath not a fingers dignity:
They call this Bed-worke, Mappry, Closset-Warre:
So that the Ramme that batters downe the wall,
For the great fwing and rudeneffe of his poize,
They place before his hand that made the Engine,
Or those that with the fineneffe of their foules,
By Reafon guide his execution.

Nest. Let this be granted, and *Achilles* horfe
Makes many *Thetis* fonnes. *Tucket*

Aga. What Trumpet? Looke *Menelaus.*
Men. From Troy. *Enter Aeneas.*
Aga. What would you 'fore our Tent?
Aene. Is this great *Agamemnons* Tent, I pray you?
Aga. Euen this.
Aene. May one that is a Herald, and a Prince,
Do a faire meffage to his Kingly eares?
Aga. With furety ftronger then *Achilles* arme,
'Fore all the Greekish heads, which with one voyce
Call *Agamemnon* Head and Generall.
Aene. Faire leaue, and large fecurity. How may
A ftranger to those most Imperial lookes,
Know them from eyes of other Mortals?
Aga. How?
Aene. I: I aske, that I might waken reuerence,
And on the cheeke be ready with a blush
Modeft as morning, when she coldly eyes
The youthfull Phoebus:
Which is that God in office guiding men?
Which is the high and mighty *Agamemnon*?
Aga. This Troyan fcornes vs, or the men of Troy
Are ceremonious Courtiers.
Aene. Courtiers as free, as debonnaire; vnarm'd,
As bending Angels: that's their Fame, in peace:
But when they would feeme Souldiers, they haue galles,
Good armes, ftrong ioynts, true fwords, & *Ioues* accord,
Nothing fo full of heart. But peace *Aeneas*,
Peace Troyan, lay thy finger on thy lips,
The worthineffe of praife diftaines his worth:
If that he prais'd himselfe, bring the praife forth.
But what the repining enemy commends,
That breath Fame blowes, that praife fole pure tranfcēds.

Aga. Sir, you of Troy, call you your felfe *Aeneas*?
Aene. I Greeke, that is my name.
Aga. What's your affayre I pray you?
Aene. Sir pardon, 'tis for *Agamemnons* eares.
Aga. He heares nought priuatly
That comes from Troy.
Aene. Nor I from Troy come not to whisper him,
I bring a Trumpet to awake his eare,
To fet his fence on the attentiue bent,
And then to fpeake.
Aga. Speake frankely as the winde,
It is not *Agamemnons* fleeping houre;
That thou fhalt know Troyan he is awake,
He tels thee fo himfelfe.

Aene. Trumpet blow loud,
Send thy Braffe voyce through all these lazie Tents,
And euery Greeke of mettle, let him know,
What Troy meanes fairely, fhall be fpoke alowd.
The Trumpets found.
We haue great *Agamemnon* heere in Troy,
A Prince call'd *Hector*, *Priam* is his Father:
Who in this dull and long-continew'd Truce
Is rufty growne. He bad me take a Trumpet,
And to this purpose fpeake: Kings, Princes, Lords,
If there be one among'ft the fayr'ft of Greece,
That holds his Honor higher then his eafe,
That feekes his praife, more then he feares his perill,
That knowes his Valour, and knowes not his feare,
That loues his Miftris more then in confession,
(With truant vowes to her owne lips he loues)
And dare avow her Beauty, and her Worth,
In other armes then hers: to him this Challenge.
Hector, in view of Troyans, and of Greekes,
Shall make it good, or do his beft to do it.
He hath a Lady, wifer, fairer, truer,
Then euer Greeke did compaffe in his armes,
And will to morrow with his Trumpet call,
Midway betweene your Tents, and walles of Troy,
To rowze a Grecian that is true in loue.
If any come, *Hector* fhal honour him:
If none, hee'l fay in Troy when he retyres,
The Grecian Dames are fun-burnt, and not worth
The fplinter of a Lance: Euen fo much.

Aga. This shall be told our Louers Lord *Aeneas*,
If none of them haue foule in fuch a kinde,
We left them all at home: But we are Souldiers,
And may that Souldier a meere recreant proue,
That meanes not, hath not, or is not in loue:
If then one is, or hath, or meanes to be,
That one meets *Hector*; if none elfe, Ile be he.

Nest. Tell him of *Nestor*, one that was a man
When *Hectors* Grandfire fuckt: he is old now,
But if there be not in our Grecian mould,
One Noble man, that hath one fparke of fire
To anfwer for his Loue; tell him from me,
Ile hide my Siluer beard in a Gold Beauer,
And in my Vantbrace put this wither'd brawne,
And meeting him, wil tell him, that my Lady
Was fayrer then his Grandame, and as chafte
As may be in the world: his youth in flood,
Ile pawne this truth with my three drops of blood.

Aene. Now heauens forbid fuch fcarfitie of youth.
Vlyf. Amen.

Aga. Faire Lord *Aeneas*,
Let me touch your hand:
To our Pauillion fhal I leade you firft:
Achilles shall haue word of this intent,
So fhall each Lord of Greece from Tent to Tent:
Your felfe fhall Feast with vs before you goe,
And finde the welcome of a Noble Foe. *Exeunt.*

Manet Vlysses, and Nestor.

Vlyf. *Nestor.*
Nest. What fayes *Vlysses*?
Vlyf. I haue a young conception in my braine,
Be you my time to bring it to fome fhape.
Nest. What is't?
Vlysses. This 'tis:
Blunt wedges riue hard knots: the feeded Pride
That hath to this maturity blowne vp

In ranke *Achilles*, must or now be cropt,
Or shedding breed a Nursery of like euil
To ouer-bulke vs all.

Nest. Wel, and how?

Ulyss. This challenge that the gallant *Hector* sends,
How euer it is spred in general name,
Relates in purpose onely to *Achilles*.

Nest. The purpose is perspicuous euen as substance,
Whose grossenesse little charracters summe vp,
And in the publication make no straine,
But that *Achilles*, were his braine as barren
As bankes of Lybia, though (*Apollo* knowes)
'Tis dry enough, wil with great speede of iudgement,
I, with celerity, finde *Hectors* purpose
Pointing on him.

Ulyss. And wake him to the answer, thinke you?

Nest. Yes, 'tis most meet; who may you else oppose
That can from *Hector* bring his Honor off,
If not *Achilles*; though't be a sportfull Combate,
Yet in this triall, much opinion dwels.
For heere the Troyans taste our deer'st repute
With their fin'st Pallate: and trust to me *Vlysses*,
Our imputation shall be oddely poiz'd
In this wilde action. For the successe
(Although particular) shall giue a scantling
Of good or bad, vnto the Generall:
And in such Indexes, although small prickes
To their subsequent Volumes, there is seene
The baby figure of the Gyant-masse
Of things to come at large. It is suppos'd,
He that meets *Hector*, issues from our choyse;
And choise being mutuall acte of all our soules,
Makes Merit her election, and doth boyle
As 'twere, from forth vs all: a man distill'd
Out of our Vertues; who miscarrying,
What heart from hence receyues the conqu'ring part
To steele a strong opinion to themselues,
Which entertain'd, Limbes are in his instruments,
In no lesse working, then are Swords and Bowes
Directiue by the Limbes.

Vlyss. Giue pardon to my speech:
Therefore 'tis meet, *Achilles* meet not *Hector*:
Let vs (like Merchants) shew our fowlest Wares,
And thinke perchance they'l sell: If not,
The lustre of the better yet to shew,
Shall shew the better. Do not consent,
That euer *Hector* and *Achilles* meete:
For both our Honour, and our Shame in this,
Are dogg'd with two strange Followers.

Nest. I see them not with my old eies: what are they?

Vlyss. What glory our *Achilles* shares from *Hector*,
(Were he not proud) we all should weare with him:
But he already is too insolent,
And we were better parch in Affricke Sunne,
Then in the pride and salt scorne of his eyes
Should he scape *Hector* faire. If he were foyld,
Why then we did our maine opinion crush
In taint of our best man. No, make a Lott'ry,
And by deuice let blockish *Aiax* draw
The sort to fight with *Hector*: Among our selues,
Giue him allowance as the worthier man,
For that will physicke the great Myrmidon
Who broyles in lowd applause, and make him fall
His Crest, that prouder then blew Iris bends.
If the dull brainlesse *Aiax* come safe off,
Wee'l dresse him vp in voyces: if he faile,
Yet go we vnder our opinion still,
That we haue better men. But hit or misse,
Our proiects life this shape of sence assumes,
Aiax imploy'd, pluckes downe *Achilles* Plumes.

Nest. Now *Vlysses*, I begin to rellish thy aduice,
And I wil giue a taste of it forthwith
To *Agamemnon*, go we to him straight:
Two Curres shal tame each other, Pride alone
Must tarre the Mastiffes on, as 'twere their bone. *Exeunt.*

Enter Aiax, and Thersites.

Aia. Thersites?

Ther. *Agamemnon*, how if he had Biles (ful) all ouer generally.

Aia. Thersites?

Ther. And those Byles did runne, say so; did not the General run, were not that a botchy core?

Aia. Dogge.

Ther. Then there would come some matter from him: I see none now.

Aia. Thou Bitch-Wolfes-Sonne, canst ÿ not heare? Feele then. *Strikes him.*

Ther. The plague of Greece vpon thee thou Mungrell beefe-witted Lord.

Aia. Speake then you whinid'st leauen speake, I will beate thee into handsomnesse.

Ther. I shal sooner rayle thee into wit and holinesse: but I thinke thy Horse wil sooner con an Oration, then ÿ learn a prayer without booke: Thou canst strike, canst thou? A red Murren o'th thy iades trickes.

Aia. Toads stoole, learne me the Proclamation.

Ther. Doest thou thinke I haue no sence thou strik'st

Aia. The Proclamation. (me thus?

Ther. Thou art proclaim'd a foole, I thinke.

Aia. Do not Porpentine, do not; my fingers itch.

Ther. I would thou didst itch from head to foot, and I had the scratching of thee, I would make thee the lothsom'st scab in Greece.

Aia. I say the Proclamation.

Ther. Thou grumblest & railest euery houre on *Achilles*, and thou art as ful of enuy at his greatnes, as *Cerberus* is at *Proserpina's* beauty. I, that thou barkst at him.

Aia. Mistresse *Thersites*.

Ther. Thou should'st strike him.

Aia. Coblofe.

Ther. He would pun thee into shiuers with his fist, as a Sailor breakes a bisket.

Aia. You horson Curre. *Ther.* Do, do.

Aia. Thou stoole for a Witch.

Ther. I, do, do, thou sodden-witted Lord: thou hast no more braine then I haue in mine elbows: An Asinico may tutor thee. Thou scuruy valiant Asse, thou art heere but to thresh Troyans, and thou art bought and solde among those of any wit, like a Barbarian slaue. If thou vse to beat me, I wil begin at thy heele and tel what thou art by inches, thou thing of no bowels thou.

Aia. You dogge.

Ther. You scuruy Lord.

Aia. You Curre.

Ther. *Mars* his Ideot: do rudenes, do Camell, do, do.

Enter Achilles, and Patroclus.

Achil. Why how now *Aiax*? wherefore do you this? How now *Thersites*? what's the matter man?

Ther. You see him there, do you?

Achil. I, what's the matter.

Ther. Nay looke vpon him.

Achil. So I do: what's the matter?

Ther.

Troylus and Cressida.

Ther. Nay but regard him well.
Achil. Well, why I do so.
Ther. But yet you looke not well vpon him: for who some euer you take him to be, he is *Aiax*.
Achil. I know that foole.
Ther. I, but that foole knowes not himselfe.
Aiax. Therefore I beate thee.
Ther. Lo, lo, lo, lo, what *modicums* of wit he vtters: his euasions haue eares thus long. I haue bobb'd his Braine more then he has beate my bones: I will buy nine Sparrowes for a peny, and his *Piamater* is not worth the ninth part of a Sparrow. This Lord (*Achilles*) *Aiax* who wears his wit in his belly, and his guttes in his head, Ile tell you what I say of him.
Achil. What?
Ther. I say this *Aiax*——
Achil. Nay good *Aiax*.
Ther. Has not so much wit.
Achil. Nay, I must hold you.
Ther. As will stop the eye of *Helens* Needle, for whom he comes to fight.
Achil. Peace foole.
Ther. I would haue peace and quietnes, but the foole will not: he there, that he, looke you there.
Aiax. O thou damn'd Curre, I shall——
Achil. Will you set your wit to a Fooles.
Ther. No I warrant you, for a fooles will shame it.
Pat. Good words *Thersites*.
Achil. What's the quarrell?
Aiax. I bad thee vile Owle, goe learne me the tenure of the Proclamation, and he rayles vpon me.
Ther. I serue thee not.
Aiax. Well, go too, go too.
Ther. I serue heere voluntary.
Achil. Your last seruice was sufferance, 'twas not voluntary, no man is beaten voluntary: *Aiax* was heere the voluntary, and you as vnder an Impresse.
Ther. E'neto, a great deale of your wit too lies in your sinnewes, or else there be Liars. *Hector* shall haue a great catch, if he knocke out either of your braines, he were as good cracke a fustie nut with no kernell.
Achil. What with me to *Thersites*?
Ther. There's *Vlysses*, and old *Nestor*, whose Wit was mouldy ere their Grandsires had nails on their toes, yoke you like draft-Oxen, and make you plough vp the warre.
Achil. What? what?
Ther. Yes good sooth, to *Achilles*, to *Aiax*, to——
Aiax. I shall cut out your tongue.
Ther. 'Tis no matter, I shall speake as much as thou afterwards.
Pat. No more words *Thersites*.
Ther. I will hold my peace when *Achilles* Brooch bids me, shall I?
Achil. There's for you *Patroclus*.
Ther. I wil see you hang'd like Clotpoles ere I come any more to your Tents; I will keepe where there is wit stirring, and leaue the faction of fooles. *Exit*.
Pat. A good riddance.
Achil. Marry this Sir is proclaim'd through al our host, That *Hector* by the fift houre of the Sunne, Will with a Trumpet, 'twixt our Tents and Troy To morrow morning call some Knight to Armes, That hath a stomacke, and such a one that dare Maintaine I know not what: 'tis trash. Farewell.
Aiax. Farewell? who shall answer him?
Achil. I know not, 'tis put to Lottry: otherwise

He knew his man.
Aiax. O meaning you, I will go learne more of it. *Exit*.

Enter Priam, Hector, Troylus, Paris and Helenus.

Pri. After so many houres, liues, speeches spent,
Thus once againe sayes *Nestor* from the Greekes,
Deliuer *Helen*, and all damage else
(As honour, losse of time, trauaile, expence,
Wounds, friends, and what els deere that is consum'd
In hot digestion of this cormorant Warre)
Shall be stroke off. *Hector*, what say you too't.

Hect. Though no man lesser feares the Greeks then I,
As farre as touches my particular: yet dread *Priam*,
There is no Lady of more softer bowels,
More spungie, to sucke in the sense of feare,
More ready to cry out, who knowes what followes
Then *Hector* is: the wound of peace is surety,
Surety secure: but modest Doubt is cal'd
The Beacon of the wise: the tent that searches
To'th'bottome of the worst. Let *Helen* go,
Since the first sword was drawne about this question,
Euery tythe soule 'mongst many thousand dismes,
Hath bin as deere as *Helen*: I meane of ours:
If we haue lost so many tenths of ours
To guard a thing not ours, nor worth to vs
(Had it our name) the valew of one ten;
What merit's in that reason which denies
The yeelding of her vp.

Troy. Fie, fie, my Brother;
Weigh you the worth and honour of a King
(So great as our dread Father) in a Scale
Of common Ounces? Wil you with Counters summe
The past proportion of his infinite,
And buckle in a waste most fathomlesse,
With spannes and inches so diminutiue,
As feares and reasons? Fie for godly shame?

Hel. No maruel though you bite so sharp at reasons,
You are so empty of them, should not our Father
Beare the great sway of his affayres with reasons,
Because your speech hath none that tels him so.

Troy. You are for dreames & slumbers brother Priest
You furre your gloues with reason: here are your reasons
You know an enemy intends you harme,
You know, a sword imploy'd is perillous,
And reason flyes the obiect of all harme.
Who maruels then when *Helenus* beholds
A Grecian and his sword, if he do set
The very wings of reason to his heeles:
Or like a Starre disorb'd. Nay, if we talke of Reason,
And flye like chidden Mercurie from *Ioue*,
Let's shut our gates and sleepe: Manhood and Honor
Should haue hard hearts, wold they but fat their thoghts
With this cramm'd reason: reason and respect,
Makes Liuers pale, and lustyhood deiect.

Hect. Brother, she is not worth
What she doth cost the holding.

Troy. What's aught, but as 'tis valew'd?

Hect. But value dwels not in particular will,
It holds his estimate and dignitie
As well, wherein 'tis precious of it selfe,
As in the prizer: 'Tis made Idolatrie,
To make the seruice greater then the God,
And the will dotes that is inclineable
To what infectiously it selfe affects,
Without some image of th'affected merit.

Troy. I take to day a Wife, and my election
Is led on in the conduct of my Will;

My

My Will enkindled by mine eyes and eares,
Two traded Pylots 'twixt the dangerous shores
Of Will, and Iudgement. How may I auoyde
(Although my will distaste what it elected)
The Wife I chose, there can be no euasion
To blench from this, and to stand firme by honour.
We turne not backe the Silkes vpon the Merchant
When we haue spoyl'd them; nor the remainder Viands
We do not throw in vnrespectiue same,
Because we now are full. It was thought meete
Paris should do some vengeance on the Greekes;
Your breath of full consent bellied his Sailes,
The Seas and Windes (old Wranglers) tooke a Truce,
And did him seruice; he touch'd the Ports desir'd,
And for an old Aunt whom the Greekes held Captiue,
He brought a Grecian Queen, whose youth & freshnesse
Wrinkles *Apolloes*, and makes stale the morning.
Why keepe we her? the Grecians keepe our Aunt:
Is she worth keeping? Why she is a Pearle,
Whose price hath launch'd aboue a thousand Ships,
And turn'd Crown'd Kings to Merchants.
If you'l auouch, 'twas wisedome *Paris* went,
(As you must needs, for you all cride, Go, go:)
If you'l confesse, he brought home Noble prize,
(As you must needs) for you all clapt your hands,
And cride inestimable; why do you now
The issue of your proper Wisedomes rate,
And do a deed that Fortune neuer did?
Begger the estimation which you priz'd,
Richer then Sea and Land? O Theft most base!
That we haue stolne what we do feare to keepe.
But Theeues vnworthy of a thing so stolne,
That in their Country did them that disgrace,
We feare to warrant in our Natiue place.

Enter Cassandra with her haire about her eares.

Cas. Cry Troyans, cry.
Priam. What noyse? what shreeke is this?
Troy. 'Tis our mad sister, I do know her voyce.
Cas. Cry Troyans.
Hect. It is *Cassandra*.
Cas. Cry Troyans cry; lend me ten thousand eyes,
And I will fill them with Propheticke teares.
Hect. Peace sister, peace.
Cas. Virgins, and Boyes; mid-age & wrinkled old,
Soft infancie, that nothing can but cry,
Adde to my clamour: let vs pay betimes
A moity of that masse of moane to come.
Cry Troyans cry, practise your eyes with teares,
Troy must not be, nor goodly Illion stand,
Our fire-brand Brother *Paris* burnes vs all.
Cry Troyans cry, a *Helen* and a woe;
Cry, cry, Troy burnes, or else let *Helen* goe. *Exit.*

Hect. Now youthfull *Troylus*, do not these hie straines
Of diuination in our Sister, worke
Some touches of remorse? Or is your bloud
So madly hot, that no discourse of reason,
Nor feare of bad successe in a bad cause,
Can qualifie the same?
Troy. Why Brother *Hector*,
We may not thinke the iustnesse of each acte
Such, and no other then euent doth forme it,
Nor once deiect the courage of our mindes;
Because *Cassandra's* mad, her brainsicke raptures
Cannot distaste the goodnesse of a quarrell,
Which hath our seuerall Honours all engag'd
To make it gracious. For my priuate part,
I am no more touch'd, then all *Priams* sonnes,
And Ioue forbid there should be done among'st vs
Such things as might offend the weakest spleene,
To fight for, and maintaine.

Par. Else might the world conuince of leuitie,
As well my vnder-takings as your counsels:
But I attest the gods, your full consent
Gaue wings to my propension, and cut off
All feares attending on so dire a proiect.
For what (alas) can these my single armes?
What propugnation is in one mans valour
To stand the push and enmity of those
This quarrell would excite? Yet I protest,
Were I alone to passe the difficulties,
And had as ample power, as I haue will,
Paris should ne're retract what he hath done,
Nor faint in the pursuite.

Pri. Paris, you speake
Like one be-sotted on your sweet delights;
You haue the Hony still, but these the Gall,
So to be valiant, is no praise at all.

Par. Sir, I propose not meerely to my selfe,
The pleasures such a beauty brings with it:
But I would haue the soyle of her faire Rape
Wip'd off in honourable keeping her.
What Treason were it to the ransack'd Queene,
Disgrace to your great worths, and shame to me,
Now to deliuer her possession vp
On termes of base compulsion? Can it be,
That so degenerate a straine as this,
Should once set footing in your generous bosomes?
There's not the meanest spirit on our partie,
Without a heart to dare, or sword to draw,
When *Helen* is defended: nor none so Noble,
Whose life were ill bestow'd, or death vnfam'd,
Where *Helen* is the subiect. Then (I say)
Well may we fight for her, whom we know well,
The worlds large spaces cannot paraiell.

Hect. Paris and *Troylus*, you haue both said well:
And on the cause and question now in hand,
Haue gloz'd, but superficially; not much
Vnlike young men, whom *Aristotle* thought
Vnfit to heare Morall Philosophie.
The Reasons you alledge, do more conduce
To the hot passion of distemp'red blood,
Then to make vp a free determination
'Twixt right and wrong: For pleasure, and reuenge,
Haue eares more deafe then Adders, to the voyce
Of any true decision. Nature craues
All dues be rendred to their Owners: now
What neerer debt in all humanity,
Then Wife is to the Husband? If this law
Of Nature be corrupted through affection,
And that great mindes of partiall indulgence,
To their benummed wills resist the same,
There is a Law in each well-ordred Nation,
To curbe those raging appetites that are
Most disobedient and refractorie.
If *Helen* then be wife to Sparta's King
(As it is knowne she is) these Morall Lawes
Of Nature, and of Nation, speake alowd
To haue her backe return'd. Thus to persist
In doing wrong, extenuates not wrong,
But makes it much more heauie. *Hectors* opinion

Is this in way of truth: yet nere the lesse,
My spritely brethren, I propend to you
In resolution to keepe *Helen* still;
For 'tis a cause that hath no meane dependance,
Vpon our ioynt and seuerall dignities.

  Tro. Why? there you toucht the life of our designe:
Were it not glory that we more affected,
Then the performance of our heauing spleenes,
I would not wish a drop of *Troian* blood,
Spent more in her defence. But worthy *Hector*,
She is a theame of honour and renowne,
A spurre to valiant and magnanimous deeds,
Whose present courage may beate downe our foes,
And fame in time to come canonize vs.
For I presume braue *Hector* would not loose
So rich aduantage of a promis'd glory,
As smiles vpon the fore-head of this action,
For the wide worlds reuenew.

  Hect. I am yours,
You valiant off-spring of great *Priamus*,
I haue a roisting challenge sent among'st
The dull and factious nobles of the Greekes,
Will strike amazement to their drowsie spirits,
I was aduertiz'd, their Great generall slept,
Whil'st emulation in the armie crept:
This I presume will wake him.   *Exeunt.*

         Enter Thersites *solus.*

  How now *Thersites?* what lost in the Labyrinth of thy
furie? shall the Elephant *Aiax* carry it thus? he beates
me, and I raile at him: O worthy satisfaction, would it
were otherwise: that I could beate him, whil'st he rail'd
at me: Sfoote, Ile learne to coniure and raise Diuels, but
Ile see some issue of my spitefull execrations. Then ther's
Achilles, a rare Enginer. If *Troy* be not taken till these two
vndermine it, the wals will stand till they fall of themselues. O thou great thunder-darter of Olympus, forget
that thou art *Ioue* the King of gods: and *Mercury*, loose
all the Serpentine craft of thy Caduceus, if thou take not
that little little lesse then little wit from them that they
haue, which short-arm'd ignorance it selfe knowes, is so
abundant scarse, it will not in circumuention deliuer a
Flye from a Spider, without drawing the massie Irons and
cutting the web: after this, the vengeance on the whole
Camp, or rather the bone-ach, for that me thinkes is the
curse dependant on those that warre for a placket. I haue
said my prayers and diuell, enuie, say Amen: What ho?
my Lord *Achilles*?

         Enter Patroclus.

  Patr. Who's there? *Thersites*, Good *Thersites* come
in and raile.

  Ther. If I could haue remembred a guilt counterfeit,
thou would'st not haue slipt out of my contemplation,
but it is no matter, thy selfe vpon thy selfe. The common
curse of mankinde, follie and ignorance be thine in great
reuenew; heauen blesse thee from a Tutor, and Discipline
come not neere thee. Let thy bloud be thy direction till
thy death, then if she that laies thee out sayes thou art a
faire coarse, Ile be sworne and sworne vpon't she neuer
shrowded any but Lazars, Amen. Wher's *Achilles*?

  Patr. What art thou deuout? wast thou in a prayer?
  Ther. I, the heauens heare me.
         Enter Achilles.
  Achil. Who's there?
  Patr. Thersites, my Lord.

  Achil. Where, where, art thou come? why my cheese,
my digestion, why hast thou not seru'd thy selfe into my
Table, so many meales? Come, what's *Agamemnon*?
  Ther. Thy Commander *Achilles*, then tell me *Patro-
clus*, what's *Achilles*?
  Patr. Thy Lord *Thersites*: then tell me I pray thee,
what's thy selfe?
  Ther. Thy knower *Patroclus*: then tell me *Patroclus*,
what art thou?
  Patr. Thou maist tell that know'st.
  Achil. O tell, tell.
  Ther. Ile declin the whole question: *Agamemnon* com-
mands *Achilles*, *Achilles* is my Lord, I am *Patroclus* know-
er, and *Patroclus* is a foole.
  Patro. You rascall.
  Ter. Peace foole, I haue not done.
  Achil. He is a priuiledg'd man, proceede *Thersites*.
  Ther. Agamemnon is a foole, *Achilles* is a foole, *Ther-
sites* is a foole, and as aforesaid, *Patroclus* is a foole.
  Achil. Deriue this? come?
  Ther. Agamemnon is a foole to offer to command *A-
chilles*, *Achilles* is a foole to be commanded of *Agamemnon*,
Thersites is a foole to serue such a foole: and *Patroclus* is a
foole positiue.
  Patr. Why am I a foole?

*Enter Agamemnon, Vlisses, Nestor, Diomedes,
         Aiax, and Chalcas.*

  Ther. Make that demand to the Creator, it suffises me
thou art. Looke you, who comes here?
  Achil. Patroclus, Ile speake with no body: come in
with me *Thersites*.   *Exit.*
  Ther. Here is such patcherie, such iugling, and such
knauerie: all the argument is a Cuckold and a Whore, a
good quarrel to draw emulations, factions, and bleede to
death vpon: Now the dry Suppeago on the Subiect, and
Warre and Lecherie confound all.
  Agam. Where is *Achilles*?
  Patr. Within his Tent, but ill dispos'd my Lord.
  Agam. Let it be knowne to him that we are here:
He sent our Messengers, and we lay by
Our appertainments, visiting of him:
Let him be told of, so perchance he thinke
We dare not moue the question of our place,
Or know not what we are.
  Pat. I shall so say to him.
  Vlis. We saw him at the opening of his Tent,
He is not sicke.
  Aia. Yes, Lyon sicke, sicke of proud heart; you may
call it Melancholly if will fauour the man, but by my
head, it is pride; but why, why, let him show vs the cause?
A word my Lord.
  Nes. What moues *Aiax* thus to bay at him?
  Vlis. Achillis hath inueigled his Foole from him.
  Nes. Who, *Thersites*?
  Vlis. He.
  Nes. Then will *Aiax* lacke matter, if he haue lost his
Argument.
  Vlis. No, you see he is his argument that has his argu-
ment *Achilles*.
  Nes. All the better, their fraction is more our wish
then their faction; but it was a strong counsell that a
Foole could disunite.
  Vlis. The amitie that wisedome knits, not folly may
easily vntie.   *Enter Patroclus.*

Here

Here comes *Patroclus*.

Nest. No *Achilles* with him?

Vliss. The Elephant hath ioynts, but none for curtesie:
His legge are legs for necessitie, not for flight.

Patro. *Achilles* bids me say he is much sorry:
If any thing more then your sport and pleasure,
Did moue your greatnesse, and this noble State,
To call vpon him; he hopes it is no other,
But for your health, and your digestion sake;
An after Dinners breath.

Aga. Heare you *Patroclus*:
We are too well acquainted with these answers:
But his euasion winged thus swift with scorne,
Cannot outflye our apprehensions.
Much attribute he hath, and much the reason,
Why we ascribe it to him, yet all his vertues,
Not vertuously of his owne part beheld,
Doe in our eyes, begin to loose their glosse;
Yea, and like faire Fruit in an vnholdsome dish,
Are like to rot vntasted: goe and tell him,
We came to speake with him; and you shall not sinne,
If you doe say, we thinke him ouer proud,
And vnder honest; in selfe-assumption greater
Then in the note of iudgement: & worthier then himselfe
Here tends the sauage strangenesse he puts on,
Disguise the holy strength of their command:
And vnder write in an obseruing kinde
His humorous predominance, yea watch
His pettish lines, his ebs, his flowes, as if
The passage and whole carriage of this action
Rode on his tyde. Goe tell him this, and adde,
That if he ouerhold his price so much,
Weele none of him; but let him, like an Engin
Not portable, lye vnder this report.
Bring action hither, this cannot goe to warre:
A stirring Dwarfe, we doe allowance giue,
Before a sleeping Gyant: tell him so.

Pat. I shall, and bring his answere presently.

Aga. In second voyce weele not be satisfied,
We come to speake with him, *Ulisses* enter you,
Exit Ulisses.

Aiax. What is he more then another?

Aga. No more then what he thinkes he is.

Aia. Is he so much, doe you not thinke, he thinkes himselfe a better man then I am?

Ag. No question.

Aiax. Will you subscribe his thought, and say he is?

Ag. No, Noble *Aiax*, you are as strong, as valiant, as wise, no lesse noble, much more gentle, and altogether more tractable

Aiax. Why should a man be proud? How doth pride grow? I know not what it is.

Aga. Your minde is the cleerer *Aiax*, and your vertues the fairer; he that is proud, eates vp himselfe; Pride is his owne Glasse, his owne trumpet, his owne Chronicle, and what euer praises it selfe but in the deede, deuoures the deede in the praise.

Enter Ulisses.

Aiax. I do hate a proud man, as I hate the ingendring of Toades.

Nest. Yet he loues himselfe: is't not strange?

Vliss. *Achilles* will not to the field to morrow.

Ag. What's his excuse?

Vliss. He doth relye on none,
But carries on the streame of his dispose,
Without obseruance or respect of any,
In will peculiar, and in selfe admission.

Aga. Why, will he not vpon our faire request,
Vntent his person, and share the ayre with vs?

Vliss. Things small as nothing, for requests sake onely
He makes important; possest he is with greatnesse,
And speakes not to himselfe, but with a pride
That quarrels at selfe-breath. Imagin'd wroth
Holds in his bloud such swolne and hot discourse,
That twixt his mentall and his actiue parts,
Kingdom'd *Achilles* in commotion rages,
And batters gainst it selfe; what should I say?
He is so plaguy proud, that the death tokens of it,
Cry no recouery.

Ag. Let *Aiax* goe to him.
Deare Lord, goe you and greete him in his Tent;
'Tis said he holds you well, and will be led
At your request a little from himselfe.

Vliss. O *Agamemnon*, let it not be so.
Weele consecrate the steps that *Aiax* makes,
When they goe from *Achilles*; shall the proud Lord,
That bastes his arrogance with his owne seame,
And neuer suffers matter of the world,
Enter his thoughts: saue such as doe reuolue
And ruminate himselfe. Shall he be worshipt,
Of that we hold an Idoll, more then hee?
No, this thrice worthy and right valiant Lord,
Must not so staule his Palme, nobly acquir'd,
Nor by my will assubiugate his merit,
As amply titled as *Achilles* is: by going to *Achilles*,
That were to enlard his fat already, pride,
And adde more Coles to Cancer, when he burnes
With entertaining great *Hiperion*.
This L. goe to him? *Iupiter* forbid,
And say in thunder, *Achilles* goe to him.

Nest. O this is well, he rubs the veine of him.

Dio. And how his silence drinkes vp this applause.

Aia. If I goe to him, with my armed fist, Ile pash him ore the face.

Ag. O no, you shall not goe.

Aia. And a be proud with me, ile pheeze his pride: let me goe to him.

Vliss. Not for the worth that hangs vpon our quarrel.

Aia. A paultry insolent fellow.

Nest. How he describes himselfe.

Aia. Can he not be sociable?

Vliss. The Rauen chides blacknesse.

Aia. Ile let his humours bloud.

Ag. He will be the Physitian that should be the patient.

Aia. And all men were a my minde.

Vliss. Wit would be out of fashion.

Aia. A should not beare it so, a should eate Swords first: shall pride carry it?

Nest. And 'twould, you'ld carry halfe.

Vliss. A would haue ten shares.

Aia. I will knede him, Ile make him supple, hee's not yet through warme.

Nest. Force him with praises, poure in, poure in: his ambition is dry.

Vliss. My L. you feede too much on this dislike.

Nest. Our noble Generall, doe not doe so.

Diom. You must prepare to fight without *Achilles*.

Vliss. Why, 'tis this naming of him doth him harme.
Here is a man, but 'tis before his face,
I will be silent.

Nest. Wherefore should you so?

He is not emulous, as *Achilles* is.

Vliss. 'Know the whole world, he is as valiant.

Aia. A horson dog, that shal palter thus with vs, would he were a *Troian*.

Nest. What a vice were it in *Aiax* now──

Vliss. If he were proud,

Dio. Or couetous of praise,

Vliss. I, or surley borne,

Dio. Or strange, or selfe affected.

Vl. Thank the heauens L. thou art of sweet composure;
Praise him that got thee, she that gaue thee sucke:
Fame be thy Tutor, and thy parts of nature
Thrice fam'd beyond, beyond all erudition;
But he that disciplin'd thy armes to fight,
Let *Mars* deuide Eternity in twaine,
And giue him halfe, and for thy vigour,
Bull-bearing *Milo*: his addition yeelde
To sinnowie *Aiax*: I will not praise thy wisdome,
Which like a bourne, a pale, a shore confines
Thy spacious and dilated parts; here's *Nestor*
Instructed by the Antiquary times:
He must, he is, he cannot but be wise.
But pardon Father *Nestor*, were your dayes
As greene as *Aiax* and your braine so temper'd,
You should not haue the eminence of him,
But be as *Aiax*.

Aia. Shall I call you Father?

Vliss. I my good Sonne.

Dio. Be rul'd by him Lord *Aiax*.

Vliss. There is no tarrying here, the Hart *Achilles*
Keepes thicket: please it our Generall,
To call together all his state of warre,
Fresh Kings are come to *Troy*; to morrow
We must with all our maine of power stand fast:
And here's a Lord, come Knights from East to West,
And cull their flowre, *Aiax* shall cope the best.

Ag. Goe we to Counsaile, let *Achilles* sleepe;
Light Botes may saile swift, though greater bulkes draw deepe. *Exeunt. Musicke sounds within.*

Enter *Pandarus* and a Seruant.

Pan. Friend, you, pray you a word: Doe not you follow the yong Lord *Paris*?

Ser. I sir, when he goes before me.

Pan. You depend vpon him I meane?

Ser. Sir, I doe depend vpon the Lord.

Pan. You depend vpon a noble Gentleman: I must needes praise him.

Ser. The Lord be praised.

Pa. You know me, doe you not?

Ser. Faith sir, superficially,

Pa. Friend know me better, I am the Lord *Pandarus*.

Ser. I hope I shall know your honour better.

Pa. I doe desire it.

Ser. You are in the state of Grace?

Pa. Grace, not so friend, honor and Lordship are my title: What Musique is this?

Ser. I doe but partly know sir: it is Musicke in parts.

Pa. Know you the Musitians.

Ser. Wholly sir.

Pa. Who play they to?

Ser. To the hearers sir.

Pa. At whose pleasur friend?

Ser. At mine sir, and theirs that loue Musicke.

Pa. Command, I meane friend.

Ser. Who shall I command sir?

Pa. Friend, we vnderstand not one another: I am too courtly, and thou art too cunning. At whose request doe these men play?

Ser. That's too't indeede sir: marry sir, at the request of *Paris* my L. who's there in person; with him the mortall *Venus*, the heart bloud of beauty, loues inuisible soule.

Pa. Who? my Cosin *Cressida*.

Ser. No sir, *Helen*, could you not finde out that by her attributes?

Pa. It should seeme fellow, that thou hast not seen the Lady *Cressida*. I come to speake with *Paris* from the Prince *Troylus*: I will make a complementall assault vpon him, for my businesse seethes.

Ser. Sodden businesse, there's a stewed phrase indeede.

Enter *Paris* and *Helena*.

Pan. Faire be to you my Lord, and to all this faire company: faire desires in all faire measure fairely guide them, especially to you faire Queene, faire thoughts be your faire pillow.

Hel. Deere L. you are full of faire words.

Pan. You speake your faire pleasure sweete Queene: faire Prince, here is good broken Musicke.

Par. You haue broke it cozen: and by my life you shall make it whole againe, you shall peece it out with a peece of your performance. *Nel*, he is full of harmony.

Pan. Truely Lady no.

Hel. O sir.

Pan. Rude in sooth, in good sooth very rude.

Paris. Well said my Lord: well, you say so in fits.

Pan. I haue businesse to my Lord, deere Queene: my Lord will you vouchsafe me a word.

Hel. Nay, this shall not hedge vs out, weele heare you sing certainely.

Pan. Well sweete Queene you are pleasant with me, but, marry thus my Lord, my deere Lord, and most esteemed friend your brother *Troylus*.

Hel. My Lord *Pandarus*, hony sweete Lord.

Pan. Go too sweete Queene, goe to,
Commends himselfe most affectionately to you.

Hel. You shall not bob vs out of our melody: If you doe, our melancholly vpon your head.

Pan. Sweete Queene, sweete Queene, that's a sweete Queene Ifaith──

Hel. And to make a sweet Lady sad, is a sower offence.

Pan. Nay, that shall not serue your turne, that shall it not in truth la. Nay, I care not for such words, no, no. And my Lord he desires you, that if the King call for him at Supper, you will make his excuse.

Hel. My Lord *Pandarus*?

Pan. What saies my sweete Queene, my very, very sweete Queene?

Par. What exploit's in hand, where sups he to night?

Hel. Nay but my Lord?

Pan. What saies my sweete Queene? my cozen will fall out with you.

Hel. You must not know where he sups.

Par. With my disposer *Cressida*.

Pan. No, no; no such matter, you are wide, com'your disposer is sicke.

Par. Well, Ile make excuse.

Pan. I good my Lord: why should you say *Cressida*? no, your poore disposer's sicke.

Par. I spie.

Pan. You

Pan. You spie, what doe you spie: come, giue me an Instrument now sweete Queene.

Hel. Why this is kindely done?

Pan. My Neece is horrible in loue with a thing you haue sweete Queene.

Hel. She shall haue it my Lord, if it be not my Lord *Paris.*

Pand. Hee? no, sheele none of him, they two are twaine.

Hel. Falling in after falling out, may make them three.

Pan. Come, come, Ile heare no more of this, Ile sing you a song now.

Hel. I, I, prethee now: by my troth sweet Lord thou hast a fine fore-head.

Pan. I you may, you may.

Hel. Let thy song be loue: this loue will vndoe vs all. Oh *Cupid, Cupid, Cupid.*

Pan. Loue? I that it shall yfaith.

Par. I, good now loue, loue, no thing but loue.

Pan. In good troth it begins so.

> Loue, loue, nothing but loue, still more:
> For O loues Bow,
> Shootes Backe and Doe:
> The Shaft confounds not that it wounds,
> But tickles still the sore:
> These Louers cry, oh ho they dye;
> Yet that which seemes the wound to kill,
> Doth turne oh ho, to ha ha he:
> So dying loue liues still,
> O ho a while, but ha ha ha;
> O ho groanes out for ha ha ha-----hey ho.

Hel. In loue yfaith to the very tip of the nose.

Par. He eates nothing but doues loue, and that breeds hot bloud, and hot bloud begets hot thoughts, and hot thoughts beget hot deedes, and hot deedes is loue.

Pan. Is this the generation of loue? Hot bloud, hot thoughts, and hot deedes, why they are Vipers, is Loue a generation of Vipers? Sweete Lord whose a field to day?

Par. Hector, Deiphœbus, Helenus, Anthenor, and all the ga'lantry of *Troy.* I would faine haue arm'd to day, but my *Nell* would not haue it so. How chance my brother *Troylus* went not?

Hel. He hangs the lippe at something; you know all Lord *Pandarus?*

Pan. Not I hony sweete Queene: I long to heare how they sped to day: Youle remember your brothers excuse?

Par. To a hayre.

Pan. Farewell sweete Queene.

Hel. Commend me to your Neece.

Par. I will sweete Queene.   *Sound a retreat.*

Par. They're come from fielde: let vs to *Priams* Hall To greete the Warriers. Sweet *Hellen,* I must woe you, To helpe vnarme our *Hector*: his stubborne Buckles, With these your white enchanting fingers toucht, Shall more obey then to the edge of Steele, Or force of Greekish sinewes: you shall doe more Then all the Iland Kings, disarme great *Hector.*

Hel. 'Twill make vs proud to be his seruant *Paris:* Yea what he shall receiue of vs in duetie, Giues vs more palme in beautie then we haue: Yea ouershines our selfe. Sweete aboue thought I loue thee.   *Exeunt.*

Enter Pandarus and Troylus Man.

Pan. How now, where's thy Maister, at my Cozen *Cressidas?*

Man. No sir, he stayes for you to conduct him thither.

Enter Troylus.

Pan. O here he comes: How now, how now?

Troy. Sirra walke off.

Pan. Haue you seene my Cousin?

Troy. No *Pandarus*: I stalke about her doore Like a strange soule vpon the Stigian bankes Staying for waftage. O be thou my *Charon,* And giue me swift transportance to those fields, Where I may wallow in the Lilly beds Propos'd for the deseruer. O gentle *Pandarus,* From *Cupids* shoulder plucke his painted wings, And flye with me to *Cressid.*

Pan. Walke here ith'Orchard, Ile bring her straight.
      Exit Pandarus.

Troy. I am giddy; expectation whirles me round, Th'imaginary relish is so sweete, That it inchants my sence: what will it be When that the watry pallats taste indeede Loues thrice reputed Nectar? Death I feare me Sounding distruction, or some ioy too fine, Too subtile, potent, and too sharpe in sweetnesse, For the capacitie of my ruder powers; I feare it much, and I doe feare besides, That I shall loose distinction in my ioyes, As doth a battaile, when they charge on heapes The enemy flying.   *Enter Pandarus.*

Pan. Shee's making her ready, sheele come straight; you must be witty now, she does so blush, & fetches her winde so short, as if she were fraid with a sprite: Ile fetch her; it is the prettiest villaine, she fetches her breath so short as a new tane Sparrow.   *Exit Pand.*

Troy. Euen such a passion doth imbrace my bosome: My heart beates thicker then a feauorous pulse, And all my powers doe their bestowing loose, Like vassallage at vnawares encountring The eye of Maiestie.

Enter Pandarus and Cressida.

Pan. Come, come, what neede you blush? Shames a babie; here she is now; sweare the oathes now to her, that you haue sworne to me. What are you gone againe, you must be watcht ere you be made tame, must you? come your wayes, come your wayes, and you draw backward weele put you i'th fils: why doe you not speak to her? Come draw this curtaine, & let's see your picture. Alasse the day, how loath you are to offend day light: and 'twere darke you'ld close sooner: So, so, rub on, and kisse the mistresse; how now, a kisse in fee-farme? build there Carpenter, the ayre is sweete. Nay, you shall fight your hearts out ere I part you. The Faulcon, as the Tercell, for all the Ducks ith Riuer: go too, go too.

Troy. You haue bereft me of all words Lady.

Pan. Words pay no debts; giue her deedes: but sheele bereaue you 'oth' deeds too, if shee call your actiuity in question: what billing againe? here's in witnesse whereof the Parties interchangeably. Come in, come in, Ile go get a fire?

Cres. Will you walke in my Lord?

Troy. O *Cressida,* how often haue I wisht me thus?

Cres. Wisht my Lord? the gods grant? O my Lord.

Troy. What should they grant? what makes this pretty abruption: what too curious dreg espies my sweete Lady in the fountaine of our loue?

Cres. More

Troylus and Cressida.

Cref. More dregs then water, if my teares haue eyes.

Troy. Feares make diuels of Cherubins, they neuer see truely.

Cref. Blinde feare, that feeing reason leads, findes safe footing, then blinde reason, ftumbling without feare: to feare the worst, oft cures the worse.

Troy. Oh let my Lady apprehend no feare, In all *Cupids* Pageant there is prefented no monfter.

Cref. Not nothing monftrous neither?

Troy. Nothing but our vndertakings, when we vowe to weepe seas, liue in fire, eate rockes, tame Tygers; thinking it harder for our Miftreffe to deuife impofition inough, then for vs to vndergoe any difficultie impofed. This is the monftruofitie in loue Lady, that the will is infinite, and the execution confin'd; that the defire is boundleffe, and the act a flaue to limit.

Cref. They say all Louers fweare more performance then they are able, and yet referue an ability that they neuer performe: vowing more then the perfection of ten; and difcharging leffe then the tenth part of one. They that haue the voyce of Lyons, and the act of Hares: are they not Monfters?

Troy. Are there fuch? fuch are not we: Praife vs as we are tafted, allow vs as we proue: our head fhall goe bare till merit crowne it: no perfection in reuerfion fhall haue a praife in prefent: wee will not name defert before his birth, and being borne his addition fhall be humble: few words to faire faith. *Troylus* fhall be fuch to *Creffid*, as what enuie can fay worft, fhall be a mocke for his truth; and what truth can fpeake trueft, not truer then *Troylus*.

Cref. Will you walke in my Lord?

Enter Pandarus.

Pan. What blufhing ftill? haue you not done talking yet?

Cref. Well Vnckle, what folly I commit, I dedicate to you.

Pan. I thanke you for that: if my Lord get a Boy of you, youle giue him me: be true to my Lord, if he flinch, chide me for it.

Tro. You know now your hoftages: your Vnckles word and my firme faith.

Pan. Nay, Ile giue my word for her too: our kindred though they be long ere they are wooed, they are conftant being wonne: they are Burres I can tell you, they'le fticke where they are throwne.

Cref. Boldneffe comes to mee now, and brings mee heart: Prince *Troylus*, I haue lou'd you night and day, for many weary moneths.

Troy. Why was my *Creffid* then fo hard to win?

Cref. Hard to feeme won: but I was won my Lord With the firft glance; that euer pardon me, If I confeffe much you will play the tyrant: I loue you now, but not till now fo much But I might maifter it; infaith I lye: My thoughts were like vnbrideled children grow Too head-ftrong for their mother: fee we fooles, Why haue I blab'd: who fhall be true to vs When we are fo vnfecret to our felues? But though I lou'd you well, I woed you not, And yet good faith I wifht my felfe a man; Or that we women had mens priuiledge Of fpeaking firft. Sweet, bid me hold my tongue, For in this rapture I fhall furely fpeake The thing I fhall repent: fee, fee, your filence Comming in dumbneffe, from my weakeneffe drawes My foule of counfell from me. Stop my mouth.

Troy. And fhall, albeit fweete Muficke iffues thence.

Pan. Pretty yfaith.

Cref. My Lord, I doe befeech you pardon me, 'Twas not my purpofe thus to beg a kiffe: I am afham'd; O Heauens, what haue I done! For this time will I take my leaue my Lord.

Troy. Your leaue fweete *Creffid*?

Pan. Leaue: and you take leaue till to morrow morning.

Cref. Pray you content you.

Troy. What offends you Lady?

Cref. Sir, mine owne company.

Troy. You cannot fhun your felfe.

Cref. Let me goe and try: I haue a kinde of felfe recides with you: But an vnkinde felfe, that it felfe will leaue, To be anothers foole. Where is my wit? I would be gone: I fpeake I know not what.

Troy. Well know they what they fpeake, that fpeakes fo wifely.

Cre. Perchance my Lord, I fhew more craft then loue, And fell fo roundly to a large confeffion, To Angle for your thoughts: but you are wife, Or elfe you loue not: for to be wife and loue, Exceedes mans might, that dwels with gods aboue.

Troy. O that I thought it could be in a woman: As if it can, I will prefume in you, To feede for aye her lampe and flames of loue. To keepe her conftancie in plight and youth, Out-liuing beauties outward, with a minde That doth renew fwifter then blood decaies: Or that perfwafion could but thus conuince me, That my integritie and truth to you, Might be affronted with the match and waight Of fuch a winnowed puritirie in loue: How were I then vp-lifted! but alas, I am as true, as truths fimplicitie, And fimpler then the infancie of truth.

Crf. In that Ile warre with you.

Troy. O vertuous fight, When right with right wars who fhall be moft right: True fwaines in loue, fhall in the world to come Approue their truths by *Troylus*, when their rimes, Full of proteft, of oath and big compare; Wants fimiles, truth tir'd with iteration, As true as fteele, as plantage to the Moone: As Sunne to day: as Turtle to her mate: As Iron to Adamant: as Earth to th'Center: Yet after all comparifons of truth, (As truths authenticke author to be cited) As true as *Troylus*, fhall crowne vp the Verfe, And fanctifie the numbers.

Cref. Prophet may you be: If I be falfe, or fwerue a haire from truth, When time is old and hath forgot it felfe: When water drops haue worne the Stones of *Troy*: And blinde obliuion fwallow'd Cities vp; And mightie States characterleffe are grated To duftie nothing; yet let memory, From falfe to falfe, among falfe Maids in loue, Vpbraid my falfehood, when they'aue faid as falfe, As Aire, as Water as Winde, as fandie earth; As Foxe to Lambe; as Wolfe to Heifers Calfe; Pard to the Hinde, or Stepdame to her Sonne; Yea, let them fay, to fticke the heart of falfehood,

Troylus and Cressida.

As false as *Cressid*.

Pand. Go too, a bargaine made: seale it, seale it, Ile be the witnesse here I hold your hand: here my Cousins, if euer you proue false one to another, since I haue taken such paines to bring you together, let all pittifull goers betweene be cal'd to the worlds end after my name: call them all Panders; let all constant men be *Troylusses*, all false women *Cressids*, and all brokers betweene, Panders: say, Amen.

Troy. Amen.
Cres. Amen.
Pan. Amen.

Whereupon I will shew you a Chamber, which bed, because it shall not speake of your prettie encounters, presse it to death: away.

And *Cupid* grant all tong-tide Maidens heere,
Bed, Chamber, and Pander, to prouide this geere. *Exeunt.*

Enter Vlysses, Diomedes, Nestor, Agamemnon, Menelaus and Chalcas. Florish.

Cal. Now Princes for the seruice I haue done you,
Th'aduantage of the time prompts me aloud,
To call for recompence: appeare it to your minde,
That through the sight I beare in things to loue,
I haue abandon'd Troy, left my possession,
Incur'd a Traitors name, expos'd my selfe,
From certaine and possest conueniences,
To doubtfull fortunes, sequestring from me all
That time, acquaintance, custome and condition,
Made tame, and most familiar to my nature:
And here to doe you seruice am become,
As new into the world, strange, vnacquainted,
I doe beseech you, as in way of taste,
To giue me now a little benefit:
Out of those many registred in promise,
Which you say, liue to come in my behalfe.

Agam. What would'st thou of vs Troian? make demand?

Cal. You haue a Troian prisoner, cal'd *Anthenor*,
Yesterday tooke: Troy holds him very deere.
Oft haue you (often haue you, thankes therefore)
Desir'd my *Cressid* in right great exchange.
Whom Troy hath still deni'd: but this *Anthenor*,
I know is such a wrest in their affaires;
That their negotiations all must slacke,
Wanting his mannage: and they will almost,
Giue vs a Prince of blood, a Sonne of *Priam*,
In change of him. Let him be sent great Princes,
And he shall buy my Daughter: and her presence,
Shall quite strike off all seruice I haue done,
In most accepted paine.

Aga. Let *Diomedes* beare him,
And bring vs *Cressid* hither: *Calcas* shall haue
What he requests of vs: good *Diomed*
Furnish you fairely for this enterchange;
Withall bring word, if *Hector* will to morrow
Be answer'd in his challenge. *Aiax* is ready.

Dio. This shall I vndertake, and 'tis a burthen
Which I am proud to beare. *Exit.*

Enter Achilles and Patroclus in their Tent.

Vlis. *Achilles* stands i'th entrance of his Tent;
Please it our Generall to passe strangely by him,
As if he were forgot: and Princes all,
Lay negligent and loose regard vpon him;
I will come last, 'tis like heele question me,

Why such vnplausiue eyes are bent? why turn'd on him?
If so, I haue derision medicinable,
To vse betweene your strangenesse and his pride,
Which his owne will shall haue desire to drinke;
It may doe good, pride hath no other glasse
To show it selfe, but pride: for supple knees,
Feede arrogance, and are the proud mans fees.

Agam. Weele execute your purpose, and put on
A forme of strangenesse as we passe along,
So doe each Lord, and either greete him not,
Or else disdainfully, which shall shake him more,
Then if not lookt on. I will lead the way.

Achil. What comes the Generall to speake with me?
You know my minde, Ile fight no more 'gainst Troy.

Aga. What saies *Achilles*, would he ought with vs?
Nes. Would you my Lord ought with the Generall?
Achil. No.
Nes. Nothing my Lord.
Aga. The better.
Achil. Good day, good day.
Men. How doe you? how doe you?
Achi. What, do's the Cuckold scorne me?
Aiax. How now *Patroclus*?
Achil. Good morrow *Aiax*?
Aiax. Ha.
Achil. Good morrow.
Aiax. I, and good next day too. *Exeunt.*

Achil. What meane these fellowes? know they not *Achilles*?

Patr. They passe by strangely: they were vs'd to bend
To send their smiles before them to *Achilles*:
To come as humbly as they vs'd to creepe to holy Altars.

Achil. What am I poore of late?
'Tis certaine, greatnesse once falne out with fortune,
Must fall out with men too: what the declin'd is,
He shall as soone reade in the eyes of others,
As feele in his owne fall: for men like butter-flies,
Shew not their mealie wings, but to the Summer:
And not a man for being simply man,
Hath any honour; but honour'd for those honours
That are without him; as place, riches, and fauour,
Prizes of accident, as oft as merit:
Which when they fall, as being slippery standers;
The loue that leand on them as slippery too,
Doth one plucke downe another, and together
Dye in the fall. But 'tis not so with me;
Fortune and I are friends, I doe enioy
At ample point, all that I did possesse,
Saue these mens lookes: who do me thinkes finde out
Something not worth in me such rich beholding,
As they haue often giuen. Here is *Vlisses*,
Ile interrupt his reading: how now *Vlisses*?

Vlis. Now great *Thetis* Sonne.
Achil. What are you reading?
Vlis. A strange fellow here
Writes me, that man, how dearely euer parted,
How much in hauing, or without, or in,
Cannot make boast to haue that which he hath;
Nor feeles not what he owes, but by reflection:
As when his vertues shining vpon others,
Heate them, and they retort that heate againe
To the first giuer.

Achil. This is not strange *Vlisses*:
The beautie that is borne here in the face,
The bearer knowes not, but commends it selfe,
Not going from it selfe: but eye to eye oppos'd, *Salutes*

Salutes each other with each others forme.
For speculation turnes not to it selfe,
Till it hath trauail'd, and is married there
Where it may see it selfe : this is not strange at all.

Ulis. I doe not straine it at the position,
It is familiar; but at the Authors drift,
Who in his circumstance, expresly proues
That no may is the Lord of any thing,
(Though in and of him there is much consisting,)
Till he communicate his parts to others:
Nor doth he of himselfe know them for ought,
Till he behold them formed in th'applause,
Where they are extended: who like an arch reuerb'rate
The voyce againe; or like a gate of steele,
Fronting the Sunne, receiues and renders backe
His figure, and his heate. I was much rapt in this,
And apprehended here immediately:
The vnknowne *Aiax*;
Heauens what a man is there? a very Horse, (are-
That has he knowes not what. Nature, what things there
Most abiect in regard, and deare in vse.
What things againe most deere in the esteeme,
And poore in worth: now shall we see to morrow,
An act that very chance doth throw vpon him?
Aiax renown'd? O heauens, what some men doe,
While some men leaue to doe!
How some men creepe in skittish fortunes hall,
Whiles others play the Ideots in her eyes:
How one man eates into anothers pride,
While pride is feasting in his wantonnesse
To see these Grecian Lords; why, euen already,
They clap the lubber *Aiax* on the shoulder,
As if his foote were on braue *Hectors* brest,
And great *Troy* shrinking.

Achil. I doe beleeue it:
For they past by me, as mysers doe by beggars,
Neither gaue to me good word, nor looke:
What are my deedes forgot?

Ulis. Time hath (my Lord) a wallet at his backe,
Wherein he puts almes for obliuion:
A great siz'd monster of ingratitudes:
Those scraps are good deedes past,
Which are deuour'd as fast as they are made,
Forgot as soone as done: perseuerance, deere my Lord,
Keepes honor bright, to haue done, is to hang
Quite out of fashion, like a rustie male,
In monumentall mockrie: take the instant way,
For honour trauels in a straight so narrow,
Where one but goes a breast, keepe then the path:
For emulation hath a thousand Sonnes,
That one by one pursue; if you giue way,
Or hedge aside from the direct forth right;
Like to an entred Tyde, they all rush by,
And leaue you hindmost:
Or like a gallant Horse falne in first ranke,
Lye there for pauement to the abiect, neere
Ore-run and trampled on: then what they doe in present,
Though lesse then yours in past, must ore-top yours:
For time is like a fashionable Hoste,
That slightly shakes his parting Guest by th'hand;
And with his armes out-stretcht, as he would flye,
Graspes in the commer: the welcome euer smiles,
And farewels goes out sighing: O let not vertue seeke
Remuneration for the thing it was: for beautie, wit,
High birth, vigor of bone, desert in seruice,
Loue, friendship, charity, are subiects all
To enuious and calumniating time:
One touch of nature makes the whole world kin:
That all with one consent praise new borne gaudes,
Though they are made and moulded of things past,
And goe to dust, that is a little guilt,
More laud then guilt oredusted.
The present eye praises the present obiect:
Then maruell not thou great and compleat man,
That all the Greekes begin to worship *Aiax*;
Since things in motion begin to catch the eye,
Then what not stirs: the cry went out on thee,
And still it might, and yet it may againe,
If thou would'st not entombe thy selfe aliue,
And case thy reputation in thy Tent;
Whose glorious deedes, but in these fields of late,
Made emulous missions 'mongst the gods themselues,
And draue great *Mars* to faction.

Achil. Of this my priuacie,
I haue strong reasons.

Ulis. But 'gainst your priuacie
The reasons are more potent and heroycall:
'Tis knowne *Achilles*, that you are in loue
With one of *Priams* daughters.

Achil. Ha? knowne?

Ulis. Is that a wonder?
The prouidence that's in a watchfull State,
Knowes almost euery graine of *Plutoes* gold;
Findes bottome in th'vncomprehensiue deepes;
Keepes place with thought; and almost like the gods,
Doe thoughts vnuaile in their dumbe cradles:
There is a mysterie (with whom relation
Durst neuer meddle) in the soule of State;
Which hath an operation more diuine,
Then breath or pen can giue expressure to:
All the commerse that you haue had with *Troy*,
As perfectly is ours, as yours, my Lord.
And better would it fit *Achilles* much,
To throw downe *Hector* then *Polixena*.
But it must grieue yong *Pirhus* now at home;
When fame shall in her Hand sound her trumpe;
And all the Greekish Girles shall tripping sing,
Great *Hectors* sister did *Achilles* winne;
But our great *Aiax* brauely beate downe him.
Farewell my Lord : I as your louer speake;
The foole slides ore the Ice that you should breake.

Patr. To this effect *Achilles* haue I mou'd you;
A woman impudent and mannish growne,
Is not more loth'd, then an effeminate man.
In time of action: I stand condemn'd for this;
They thinke my little stomacke to the warre,
And your great loue to me, restraines you thus:
Sweete, rouse your selfe; and the weake wanton *Cupid*
Shall from your necke vnloose his amorous fould,
And like a dew drop from the Lyons mane,
Be shooke to ayrie ayre.

Achil. Shall *Aiax* fight with *Hector*?

Patr. I, and perhaps receiue much honor by him.

Achil. I see my reputation is at stake,
My fame is shrowdly gored.

Patr. O then beware :
Those wounds heale ill, that men doe giue themselues :
Omission to doe what is necessary,
Seales a commission to a blanke of danger,
And danger like an ague subtly taints
Euen then when we sit idely in the sunne.

Achil. Goe call *Thersites* hither sweet *Patroclus*,

Ile send the foole to *Aiax*, and desire him
T'inuite the Troian Lords after the Combat
To see vs here vnarm'd: I haue a womans longing,
An appetite that I am sicke withall,
To see great *Hector* in his weedes of peace; *Enter Thersi.*
To talke with him, and to behold his visage,
Euen to my full of view. A labour sau'd.

Ther. A wonder.

Achil. What?

Ther. Aiax goes vp and downe the field, asking for himselfe.

Achil. How so?

Ther. Hee must fight singly to morrow with *Hector*, and is so prophetically proud of an heroicall cudgelling, that he raues in saying nothing.

Achil. How can that be?

Ther. Why he stalkes vp and downe like a Peacock, a stride and a stand: ruminates like an hostesse, that hath no Arithmatique but her braine to set downe her reckoning: bites his lip with a politique regard, as who should say, there were wit in his head and twoo'd out; and so there is: but it lyes as coldly in him, as fire in a flint, which will not shew without knocking. The mans vndone for euer; for if *Hector* breake not his necke i'th' combat, heele break't himselfe in vaine-glory. He knowes not mee: I said, good morrow *Aiax*; And he replyes, thankes *Agamemnon*. What thinke you of this man, that takes me for the Generall? Hee's growne a very land-fish, languagelesse, a monster: a plague of opinion, a man may weare it on both sides like a leather Ierkin.

Achil. Thou must be my Ambassador to him *Thersites*.

Ther. Who, I: why, heele answer no body: he professes not answering; speaking is for beggers: he weares his tongue in's armes: I will put on his presence; let *Patroclus* make his demands to me, you shall see the Pageant of *Aiax*.

Achil. To him *Patroclus*; tell him, I humbly desire the valiant *Aiax*, to inuite the most valorous *Hector*, to come vnarm'd to my Tent, and to procure safe conduct for his person, of the magnanimious and most illustrious, sixe or seauen times honour'd Captaine, Generall of the Grecian Armie *Agamemnon*, &c. doe this.

Patro. Ioue blesse great *Aiax*.

Ther. Hum.

Patr. I come from the worthy *Achilles*.

Ther. Ha?

Patr. Who most humbly desires you to inuite *Hector* to his Tent.

Ther. Hum.

Patr. And to procure safe conduct from *Agamemnon*.

Ther. Agamemnon?

Patr. I my Lord.

Ther. Ha?

Patr. What say you too't.

Ther. God buy you with all my heart.

Patr. Your answer sir.

Ther. If to morrow be a faire day, by eleuen a clocke it will goe one way or other; howsoeuer, he shall pay for me ere he has me.

Patr. Your answer sir.

Ther. Fare you well withall my heart.

Achil. Why, but he is not in this tune, is he?

Ther. No, but he's out a tune thus: what musicke will be in him when *Hector* has knockt out his braines, I know not: but I am sure none, vnlesse the Fidler *Apollo* get his sinewes to make catlings on.

Achil. Come, thou shalt beare a Letter to him straight.

Ther. Let me carry another to his Horse; for that's the more capable creature.

Achil. My minde is troubled like a Fountaine stir'd, And I my selfe see not the bottome of it.

Ther. Would the Fountaine of your minde were cleere againe, that I might water an Asse at it: I had rather be a Ticke in a Sheepe, then such a valiant ignorance.

Enter at one doore Æneas with a Torch, at another Paris, Diephœbus, Anthenor, Diomed the Grecian, with Torches.

Par. See hoa, who is that there?

Dieph. It is the Lord *Æneas*.

Æne. Is the Prince there in person?
Had I so good occasion to lye long
As you Prince *Paris*, nothing but heauenly businesse,
Should rob my bed-mate of my company.

Diom. That's my minde too: good morrow Lord *Æneas*.

Par. A valiant Greeke *Æneas*, take his hand,
Witnesse the processe of your speech within;
You told how *Diomed*, in a whole weeke by dayes
Did haunt you in the Field.

Æne. Health to you valiant sir,
During all question of the gentle truce:
But when I meete you arm'd, as blacke defiance,
As heart can thinke, or courage execute.

Diom. The one and other *Diomed* embraces,
Our blouds are now in calme; and so long health:
But when contention, and occasion meetes,
By *Ioue*, Ile play the hunter for thy life,
With all my force, pursuite and pollicy.

Æne. And thou shalt hunt a Lyon that will flye
With his face backward, in humaine gentlenesse:
Welcome to Troy; now by *Anchises* life,
Welcome indeede: by *Venus* hand I sweare,
No man aliue can loue in such a sort,
The thing he meanes to kill, more excellently.

Diom. We simpathize. *Ioue* let *Æneas* liue
(If to my sword his fate be not the glory)
A thousand compleate courses of the Sunne,
But in mine emulous honor let him dye:
With euery ioynt a wound, and that to morrow.

Æne. We know each other well.

Dio. We doe, and long to know each other worse.

Par. This is the most, despightfull'st gentle greeting;
The noblest hatefull loue, that ere I heard of.
What businesse Lord so early?

Æne. I was sent for to the King; but why, I know not.

Par. His purpose meets you; it was to bring this Greeke
To *Calcha's* house; and there to render him,
For the enfreed *Anthenor*, the faire *Cressid*:
Lets haue your company; or if you please,
Haste there before vs. I constantly doe thinke
(Or rather call my thought a certaine knowledge)
My brother *Troylus* lodges there to night.
Rouse him, and giue him note of our approach,
With the whole quality whereof, I feare
We shall be much vnwelcome.

Æne. That I assure you:
Troylus had rather Troy were borne to Greece,
Then *Cressid* borne from Troy.

Par. There

Par. There is no helpe:
The bitter disposition of the time will haue it so.
Oh Lord, weele follow you.

Æne. Good morrow all. *Exit Æneas*

Par. And tell me noble *Diomed*; faith tell me true,
Euen in the soule of sound good fellowship,
Who in your thoughts merits faire *Helen* most?
My selfe, or *Menelaus*?

Diom. Both alike.
He merits well to haue her, that doth seeke her,
Not making any scruple of her soylure,
With such a hell of paine, and world of charge.
And you as well to keepe her, that defend her,
Not pallating the taste of her dishonour,
With such a costly losse of wealth and friends:
He like a puling Cuckold, would drinke vp
The lees and dregs of a flat tamed peece:
You like a letcher, out of whorish loynes,
Are pleas'd to breede out your inheritors:
Both merits poyz'd, each weighs no lesse nor more,
But he as he, which heauier for a whore.

Par. You are too bitter to your country-woman.

Dio. Shee's bitter to her countrey: heare me *Paris*,
For euery false drop in her baudy veines,
A Grecians life hath sunke: for euery scruple
Of her contaminated carrion weight,
A Troian hath beene slaine. Since she could speake,
She hath not giuen so many good words breath,
As for her, Greekes and Troians suffred death.

Par. Faire *Diomed*, you doe as chapmen doe,
Dispraise the thing that you desire to buy:
But we in silence hold this vertue well;
Weele not commend, what we intend to sell.
Here lyes our way. *Exeunt.*

Enter Troylus and Cressida.

Troy. Deere trouble not your selfe: the morne is cold.

Cres. Then sweet my Lord, Ile call mine Vnckle down;
He shall vnbolt the Gates.

Troy. Trouble him not:
To bed, to bed: sleepe kill those pritty eyes,
And giue as soft attachment to thy sences,
As Infants empty of all thought.

Cres. Good morrow then.

Troy. I prithee now to bed.

Cres. Are you a weary of me?

Troy. O *Cressida*! but that the busie day
Wak't by the Larke, hath rouz'd the ribauld Crowes,
And dreaming night will hide our eyes no longer,
I would not from thee.

Cres. Night hath beene too briefe. (stayes.

Troy. Beshrew the witch! with venemous wights she
As hidiously as hell; but flies the graspes of loue,
With wings more momentary, swift then thought:
You will catch cold, and curse me.

Cres. Prithee tarry, you men will neuer tarry;
O foolish *Cressid*, I might haue still held off,
And then you would haue tarried. Harke, ther's one vp?

Pand. within. What's all the doores open here?

Troy. It is your Vnckle. *Enter Pandarus.*

Cres. A pestilence on him: now will he be mocking:
I shall haue such a life.

Pan. How now, how now? how goe maiden-heads?
Heare you Maide: wher's my cozin *Cressid*?

Cres. Go hang your selfe, you naughty mocking Vnckle:
You bring me to doo------and then you floute me too.

Pan. To do what? to do what? let her say what:
What haue I brought you to doe?

Cres. Come, come, beshrew your heart: youle nere be
good, nor suffer others.

Pan. Ha, ha: alas poore wretch: a poore *Chipochia*, hast
not slept to night? would he not (a naughty man) let it
sleepe: a bug-beare take him. *One knocks.*

Cres. Did not I tell you? would he were knockt ith'
head. Who's that at doore? good Vnckle goe and see.
My Lord, come you againe into my Chamber:
You smile and mocke me, as if I meant naughtily.

Troy. Ha, ha.

Cre. Come you are deceiu'd, I thinke of no such thing.
How earnestly they knocke: pray you come in. *Knocke.*
I would not for halfe *Troy* haue you seene here. *Exeunt.*

Pan. Who's there? what's the matter? will you beate
downe the doore? How now, what's the matter?

Æne. Good morrow Lord, good morrow.

Pan. Who's there my Lord *Æneas*? by my troth I
knew you not: what newes with you so early?

Æne. Is not Prince *Troylus* here?

Pan. Here? what should he doe here?

Æne. Come he is here, my Lord, doe not deny him:
It doth import him much to speake with me.

Pan. Is he here say you? 'tis more then I know, Ile be
sworne: For my owne part I came in late: what should
he doe here?

Æne. Who, nay then: Come, come, youle doe him
wrong, ere y'are ware: youle be so true to him, to be
false to him: Doe not you know of him, but yet goe fetch
him hither, goe.

Enter Troylus.

Troy. How now, what's the matter?

Æne. My Lord, I scarce haue leisure to salute you,
My matter is so rash: there is at hand,
Paris your brother, and *Deiphœbus*,
The Grecian *Diomed*, and our *Anthenor*
Deliuer'd to vs, and for him forth-with,
Ere the first sacrifice, within this houre,
We must giue vp to *Diomeds* hand
The Lady *Cressida*.

Troy. Is it concluded so?

Æne. By *Priam*, and the generall state of *Troy*,
They are at hand, and ready to effect it.

Troy. How my atchieuements mocke me;
I will goe meete them: and my Lord *Æneas*,
We met by chance; you did not finde me here.

Æn. Good, good, my Lord, the secrets of nature
Haue not more gift in taciturnitie. *Exeunt.*

Enter Pandarus and Cressid.

Pan. Is't possible? no sooner got but lost: the diuell
take *Anthenor*; the yong Prince will goe mad: a plague
vpon *Anthenor*; I would they had brok's necke.

Cres. How now? what's the matter? who was here?

Pan. Ah, ha?

Cres. Why sigh you so profoundly? wher's my Lord?
gone? tell me sweet Vnckle, what's the matter?

Pan. Would I were as deepe vnder the earth as I am
aboue.

Cres. O the gods! what's the matter?

Pan. Prythee get thee in: would thou had'st nere been
borne; I knew thou would'st be his death. O poore Gentleman: a plague vpon *Anthenor*.

Cres. Good

Cref. Good Vnckle I beseech you, on my knees, I beseech you what's the matter?

Pan. Thou must be gone wench, thou must be gone; thou art chang'd for *Anthenor*: thou must to thy Father, and be gone from *Troylus*: 'twill be his death: 'twill be his bane, he cannot beare it.

Cref. O you immortall gods! I will not goe.

Pan. Thou must.

Cref. I will not Vnckle: I haue forgot my Father:
I know no touch of consanguinitie:
No kin, no loue, no bloud, no soule, so neere me,
As the sweet *Troylus*: O you gods diuine!
Make *Cressids* name the very crowne of falshood!
If euer she leaue *Troylus*: time, orce and death,
Do to this body what extremitie you can;
But the strong base and building of my loue,
Is as the very Center of the earth,
Drawing all things to it. I will goe in and weepe.

Pan. Doe, doe.

Cref. Teare my bright heire, and scratch my praised cheekes,
Cracke my cleere voyce with sobs, and breake my heart
With sounding *Troylus*. I will not goe from *Troy*. *Exeunt.*

Enter Paris, Troylus, Aeneas, Deiphebus, Anthenor and Diomedes.

Par. It is great morning, and the houre prefixt
Of her deliuerie to this valiant Greeke
Comes fast vpon: good my brother *Troylus*,
Tell you the Lady what she is to doe,
And hast her to the purpose.

Troy. Walke into her house:
Ile bring her to the Grecian presently;
And to his hand, when I deliuer her,
Thinke it an Altar, and thy brother *Troylus*
A Priest, there offring to it his heart.

Par. I know what 'tis to loue,
And would, as I shall pittie, I could helpe.
Please you walke in, my Lords. *Exeunt.*

Enter Pandarus and Cressid.

Pan. Be moderate, be moderate.

Cref. Why tell you me of moderation?
The griefe is fine, full perfect that I taste,
And no lesse in a sense as strong
As that which causeth it. How can I moderate it?
If I could temporise with my affection,
Or brew it to a weake and colder pallat,
The like alaiment could I giue my griefe:
My loue admits no qualifying crosse; *Enter Troylus.*
No more my griefe, in such a precious losse.

Pan. Here, here, here, he comes, a sweet ducke.

Cref. O *Troylus*, *Troylus*!

Pan. What a paire of spectacles is here? let me embrace too: oh hart, as the goodly saying is; O heart, heauie heart, why sighest thou without breaking? where he answers againe; because thou canst not ease thy smart by friendship, nor by speaking: there was neuer a truer rime; let vs cast away nothing, for we may liue to haue neede of such a Verse: we see it, we see it: how now Lambs?

Troy. *Cressid*: I loue thee in so strange a puritie;
That the blest gods, as angry with my fancie,
More bright in zeale, then the deuotion which
Cold lips blow to their Deities: take thee from me.

Cref. Haue the gods enuie?

Pan. I, I, I, I, 'tis too plaine a case.

Cref. And is it true, that I must goe from Troy?

Troy. A hatefull truth.

Cref. What, and from *Troylus* too?

Troy. From Troy, and *Troylus*.

Cref. Ist possible?

Troy. And sodainely, where iniurie of chance
Puts backe leaue-taking, iustles roughly by
All time of pause; rudely beguiles our lips
Of all reioyndure: forcibly preuents
Our lockt embrasures; strangles our deare vowes,
Euen in the birth of our owne laboring breath,
We two, that with so many thousand sighes
Did buy each other, must poorely sell our selues,
With the rude breuitie and discharge of our
Iniurious time; now with a robbers haste
Crams his rich theeuerie vp, he knowes not how.
As many farwels as be starrs in heauen,
With distinct breath, and consign'd kisses to them,
He fumbles vp into a loose adieu;
And scants vs with a single famisht kisse,
Distasting with the salt of broken teares. *Enter Aeneas.*

Aeneas within. My Lord, is the Lady ready?

Troy. Harke, you are call'd: some say the genius so
Cries, come to him that instantly must dye.
Bid them haue patience: she shall come anon.

Pan. Where are my teares? raine, to lay this winde,
or my heart will be blowne vp by the root.

Cref. I must then to the Grecians?

Troy. No remedy.

Cref. A wofull *Cressid* 'mong'st the merry Greekes.

Troy. When shall we see againe?

Troy. Here me my loue: be thou but true of heart.

Cref. I true? how now? what wicked deeme is this?

Troy. Nay, we must vse expostulation kindely,
For it is parting from vs:
I speake not, be thou true, as fearing thee:
For I will throw my Gloue to death himselfe,
That there's no maculation in thy heart:
But be thou true, say I, to fashion in
My sequent protestation: be thou true,
And I will see thee.

Cref. O you shall be expos'd, my Lord to dangers
As infinite, as imminent: but Ile be true.

Troy. And Ile grow friend with danger;
Weare this Sleeue.

Cref. And you this Gloue.
When shall I see you?

Troy. I will corrupt the Grecian Centinels,
To giue thee nightly visitation.
But yet be true.

Cref. O heauens: be true againe?

Troy. Heare why I speake it; Loue:
The Grecian youths are full of qualitie,
Their louing well compos'd, with guift of nature,
Flawing and swelling ore with Arts and exercise:
How nouelties may moue, and parts with person.
Alas, a kinde of godly iealousie;
Which I beseech you call a vertuous sinne:
Makes me affraid.

Cref. O heauens, you loue me not!

Troy. Dye I a villaine then:
In this I doe not call your faith in question
So mainely as my merit: I cannot sing,
Nor heele the high Lauolt; nor sweeten talke;
Nor play at subtill games; faire vertues all;

Troylus and Cressida.

To which the Grecians are most prompt and pregnant:
But I can tell that in each grace of these,
There lurkes a still and dumb-discoursiue diuell,
That tempts most cunningly: but be not tempted.

Cres. Doe you thinke I will:

Troy. No, but something may be done that we wil not:
And sometimes we are diuels to our selues,
When we will tempt the frailtie of our powers,
Presuming on their changefull potencie.

Æneas within. Nay, good my Lord?

Troy. Come kisse, and let vs part.

Paris within. Brother *Troylus*?

Troy. Good brother come you hither,
And bring *Æneas* and the Grecian with you.

Cres. My Lord, will you be true?   *Exit.*

Troy. Who I? alas it is my vice, my fault:
Whiles others fish with craft for great opinion,
I, with great truth, catch meere simplicitie;
Whil'st some with cunning guild their copper crownes,
With truth and plainnesse I doe weare mine bare:

Enter the Greekes.

Feare not my truth; the morrall of my wit
Is plaine and true, ther's all the reach of it.
Welcome sir *Diomed*, here is the Lady
Which for *Antenor*, we deliuer you.
At the port (Lord) Ile giue her to thy hand,
And by the way possesse thee what she is.
Entreate her faire; and by my soule, faire Greeke,
If ere thou stand at mercy of my Sword,
Name *Cressid*, and thy life shall be as safe
As *Priam* is in Illion?

Diom. Faire Lady *Cressid*,
So please you sauethe thankes this Prince expects:
The lustre in youreye, heauen in your cheeke,
Pleades your faire visage, and to *Diomed*
You shall be mistresse, and command him wholly.

Troy. Grecian, thou do'st not vse me curteously,
To shame the seale of my petition towards,
I praising her. I tell thee Lord of Greece:
Shee is as farre high soaring o're thy praises,
As thou vnworthy to be cal'd her seruant:
I charge thee vse her well, euen for my charge:
For by the dreadfull *Pluto*, if thou do'st not,
(Though the great bulke *Achilles* be thy guard)
Ile cut thy throate.

Diom. Oh be not mou'd Prince *Troylus*;
Let me be priuiledg'd by my place and message,
To be a speaker free? when I am hence,
Ile answer to my lust: and know my Lord;
Ile nothing doe on charge: to her owne worth
She shall be priz'd: but that you say, be't so;
Ilespeake it in my spirit and honor, no.

Troy. Come to the Port. Ile tell thee *Diomed*,
This braue, shall oft make thee to hide thy head:
Lady giue me your hand, and as we walke,
To our owne selues bend we our needefull talke.

Sound Trumpet.

Par. Harke, *Hectors* Trumpet.

Æne. How haue we spent this morning
The Prince must thinke me tardy and remisse,
That swore to ride before him in the field.

Par. 'Tis *Troylus* fault: come, come, to field with him.
                                                                 Exeunt.

Dio. Let vs make ready straight.

Æne. Yea, with a Bridegroomes fresh alacritie
Let vs addresse to tend on *Hectors* heeles:
The glory of our *Troy* doth this day lye
On his faire worth, and single Chiualrie.

*Enter Aiax armed, Achilles, Patroclus, Agamemnon,
Menelaus, Vlisses, Nestor, Calcas, &c.*

Aga. Here art thou in appointment fresh and faire,
Anticipating time. With starting courage,
Giue with thy Trumpet a loud note to Troy
Thou dreadfull *Aiax*, that the appauled aire
May pierce the head of the great Combatant,
And hale him hither.

Aia. Thou, Trumpet, ther's my purse;
Now cracke thy lungs, and split thy brasen pipe:
Blow villaine, till thy sphered Bias cheeke
Out-swell the collicke of puft *Aquilon*:
Come, stretch thy chest, and let thy eyes spout bloud:
Thou blowest for *Hector*.

Vlis. No Trumpet answers.

Achil. 'Tis but early dayes.

Aga. Is not yong *Diomed* with *Calcas* daughter?

Vlis. 'Tis he, I ken the manner of his gate,
He rises on the toe: that spirit of his
In aspiration lifts him from the earth.

Aga. Is this the Lady *Cressid*?

Dio. Euen she.

Aga. Most deerely welcome to the Greekes, sweete
Lady.

Nest. Our Generall doth salute you with a kisse.

Vlis. Yet is the kindenesse but particular; 'twere better she were kist in generall.

Nest. And very courtly counsell: Ile begin. So much
for *Nestor*.

Achil. Ile take that winter from your lips faire Lady
Achilles bids you welcome.

Mene. I had good argument for kissing once.

Patro. But that's no argument for kissing now;
For thus pop't *Paris* in his hardiment.

Vlis. Oh deadly gall, and theame of all our scornes,
For which we loose our heads, to gild his hornes.

Patro. The first was *Menelaus* kisse, this mine:
Patroclus kisses you.

Mene. Oh this is trim.

Patr. *Paris* and I kisse euermore for him.

Mene. Ile haue my kisse sir: Lady by your leaue.

Cres. In kissing doe you render, or receiue.

Patr. Both take and giue.

Cres. Ile make my match to liue,
The kisse you take is better then you giue: therefore no
kisse.

Mene. Ile giue you boote, Ile giue you three for one.

Cres. You are an odde man, giue euen, or giue none.

Mene. An odde man Lady, euery man is odde.

Cres. No, *Paris* is not; for you know 'tis true,
That you are odde, and he is euen with you.

Mene. You fillip me a'th' head.

Cres. No, Ile be sworne.

Vlis. It were no match, your naile against his horne:
May I sweete Lady beg a kisse of you?

Cres. You may.

Vlis. I doe desire it.

Cres. Why begge then?

Vlis. Why then for *Venus* sake, giue me a kisse;
When *Hellen* is a maide againe, and his——

Cres. I am your debter, claime it when 'tis due.

Troylus and Cressida.

Vliss. Neuer's my day, and then a kisse of you.
Diom. Lady a word, Ile bring you to your Father.
Nest. A woman of quicke sence.
Vliss. Fie, fie, vpon her:
Ther's a language in her eye, her cheeke, her lip;
Nay, her foote speakes, her wanton spirites looke out
At euery ioynt, and motiue of her body:
Oh these encounterers so glib of tongue,
That giue a coasting welcome ere it comes;
And wide vnclaspe the tables of their thoughts,
To euery tickling reader: set them downe,
For sluttish spoyles of opportunitie;
And daughters of the game. *Exeunt.*

Enter all of Troy, Hector, Paris, Æneas, Helenus and Attendants. Florish.

All. The Troians Trumpet.
Aga. Yonder comes the troope.
Æne. Haile all you state of Greece: what shalbe done
To him that victory commands? or doe you purpose,
A victor shall be knowne: will you the Knights
Shall to the edge of all extremitie
Pursue each other; or shall be diuided
By any voyce, or order of the field: *Hector* bad aske?
Aga. Which way would *Hector* haue it?
Æne. He cares not, heele obey conditions.
Aga. 'Tis done like *Hector*, but securely done,
A little proudly, and great deale disprising
The Knight oppos'd.
Æne. If not *Achilles* sir, what is your name?
Achil. If not *Achilles*, nothing.
Æne. Therefore *Achilles*: but what ere, know this,
In the extremity of great and little:
Valour and pride excell themselues in *Hector*;
The one almost as infinite as all;
The other blanke as nothing: weigh him well:
And that which lookes like pride, is curtesie:
This *Aiax* is halfe made of *Hectors* bloud;
In loue whereof, halfe *Hector* staies at home:
Halfe heart, halfe hand, halfe *Hector*, comes to seeke
This blended Knight, halfe Troian, and halfe Greeke.
Achil. A maiden battaile then? O I perceiue you.
Aga. Here is sir, *Diomed*: goe gentle Knight,
Stand by our *Aiax*: as you and Lord *Æneas*
Consent vpon the order of their fight,
So be it: either to the yttermost,
Or else a breach: the Combatants being kin,
Halfe stints their strife, before their strokes begin.
Vliss. They are oppos'd already.
Aga. What Troian is that same that lookes so heauy?
Vliss. The yongest Sonne of *Priam*;
A true Knight; they call him *Troylus*;
Not yet mature, yet matchlesse, firme of word,
Speaking in deedes, and deedelesse in his tongue;
Not soone prouok't, nor being prouok't, soone calm'd;
His heart and hand both open, and both free:
For what he has, he giues; what thinkes, he shewes;
Yet giues he not till iudgement guide his bounty,
Nor dignifies an impaire thought with breath:
Manly as *Hector*, but more dangerous;
For *Hector* in his blaze of wrath subscribes
To tender obiects; but he, in heate of action,
Is more vindecatiue then iealous loue.
They call him *Troylus*; and on him erect,
A second hope, as fairely built as *Hector*.
Thus saies *Æneas*, one that knowes the youth,
Euen to his inches: and with priuate soule,
Did in great Illion thus translate him to me.
Aga. They are in action. *Alarum.*
Nest. Now *Aiax* hold thine owne.
Troy. *Hector*, thou sleep'st, awake thee.
Aga. His blowes are wel dispos'd there *Aiax*. *trumpets*
Diom. You must no more. *ceasse.*
Æne. Princes enough, so please you.
Aia. I am not warme yet, let vs fight againe.
Diom. As *Hector* pleases.
Hect. Why then will I no more:
Thou art great Lord, my Fathers sisters Sonne;
A cousen german to great *Priams* seede:
The obligation of our bloud forbids
A gorie emulation 'twixt vs twaine:
Were thy commixion, Greeke and Troian so,
That thou could'st say, this hand is Grecian all,
And this is Troian: the sinewes of this Legge,
All Greeke, and this all Troy: my Mothers bloud
Runs on the dexter cheeke, and this sinister
Bounds in my fathers: by *Ioue* multipotent,
Thou should'st not beare from me a Greekish member
Wherein my sword had not impressure made
Of our ranke feud: but the iust gods gainsay,
That any drop thou borrwd'st from thy mother,
My sacred Aunt, should by my mortall Sword
Be drained. Let me embrace thee *Aiax*:
By him that thunders, thou hast lustie Armes;
Hector would haue them fall vpon him thus.
Cozen, all honor to thee.
Aia. I thanke thee *Hector*:
Thou art too gentle, and too free a man:
I came to kill thee Cozen, and beare hence
A great addition, earned in thy death.
Hect. Not *Neoptolymus* so mirable,
On whose bright crest, fame with her lowd'st (O yes)
Cries, This is he; could'st promise to himselfe,
A thought of added honor, torne from *Hector*.
Æne. There is expectance here from both the sides,
What further you will doe?
Hect. Weele answere it:
The issue is embracement: *Aiax*, farewell.
Aia. If I might in entreaties finde successe,
As seld I haue the chance; I would desire
My famous Cousin to our Grecian Tents.
Diom. 'Tis *Agamemnons* wish, and great *Achilles*
Doth long to see vnarm'd the valiant *Hector*.
Hect. *Æneas*, call my brother *Troylus* to me:
And signifie this louing enteruiew
To the expecters of our Troian part:
Desire them home. Giue me thy hand, my Cousin:
I will goe eate with thee, and see your Knights.

Enter Agamemnon and the rest.

Aia. Great *Agamemnon* comes to meete vs here.
Hect. The worthiest of them, tell me name by name:
But for *Achilles*, mine owne serching eyes
Shall finde him by his large and portly size.
Aga. Worthy of Armes: as welcome as to one
That would be rid of such an enemie.
But that's no welcome: vnderstand more cleere
What's past, and what's to come, is strew'd with huskes,
And formelesse ruine of obliuion:
But in this extant moment, faith and troth,
Strain'd purely from all hollow bias drawing:
Bids thee with most diuine integritie,
From heart of very heart, great *Hector* welcome.
Hect. I thanke thee most imperious *Agamemnon*.
Aga. M

Aga. My well-fam'd Lord of Troy, no lesse to you.
Men. Let me confirme my Princely brothers greeting,
You brace of warlike Brothers, welcome hither.
Hect. Who must we answer?
Æne. The Noble *Menelaus.*
Hect. O, you my Lord, by *Mars* his gauntlet thanks,
Mocke not, that I affect th'vntraded Oath,
Your *quondam* wife sweares still by *Venus* Gloue
Shee's well, but bad me not commend her to you.
Men. Name her not now sir, she's a deadly Theame.
Hect. O pardon, I offend.
Nest. I haue (thou gallant Troyan) seene thee oft
Labouring for destiny, make cruell way
Through rankes of Greekish youth: and I haue seen thee
As hot as *Perseus*, spurre thy Phrygian Steed,
And seene thee scorning forfeits and subduments,
When thou hast hung thy aduanced sword i'th'ayre,
Not letting it decline, on the declined :
That I haue said vnto my standers by,
Loe Iupiter is yonder, dealing life.
And I haue seene thee pause, and take thy breath,
When that a ring of Greekes haue hem'd thee in,
Like an Olympian wrestling. This haue I seene,
But this thy countenance (still lockt in steele)
I neuer saw till now. I knew thy Grandsire,
And once fought with him ; he was a Souldier good,
But by great Mars, the Captaine of vs all,
Neuer like thee. Let an oldman embrace thee,
And (worthy Warriour) welcome to our Tents.
Æne. 'Tis the old *Nestor.*
Hect. Let me embrace thee good old Chronicle,
That hast so long walk'd hand in hand with time:
Most reuerend *Nestor*, I am glad to claspe thee.
Ne. I would my armes could match thee in contention
As they contend with thee in courtesie.
Hect. I would they could.
Nest. Ha? by this white beard I'ld fight with thee to
morrow. Well, welcom, welcome : I haue seen the time.
Vlys. I wonder now, how yonder City stands,
When we haue heere her Base and pillar by vs.
Hect. I know your fauour Lord *Vlysses* well.
Ah sir, there's many a Greeke and Troyan dead,
Since first I saw your selfe, and *Diomed*
In Illion, on your Greekish Embassie.
Vlys. Sir, I foretold you then what would ensue,
My prophesie is but halfe his iourney yet ;
For yonder wals that pertly front your Towne,
Yond Towers, whose wanton tops do busse the clouds,
Must kisse their owne feet.
Hect. I must not beleeue you :
There they stand yet : and modestly I thinke,
The fall of euery Phrygian stone will cost
A drop of Grecian blood : the end crownes all,
And that old common Arbitrator, Time,
Will one day end it.
Vlys. So to him we leaue it.
Most gentle, and most valiant *Hector*, welcome ;
After the Generall, I beseech you next
To Feast with me, and see me at my Tent.
Achil. I shall forestall thee Lord *Vlysses*, thou:
Now *Hector* I haue fed mine eyes on thee,
I haue with exact view perus'd thee *Hector*,
And quoted ioynt by ioynt.
Hect. Is this *Achilles* ?
Achil. I am *Achilles.*
Hect. Stand faire I prythee, let me looke on thee.

Achil. Behold thy fill.
Hect. Nay, I haue done already.
Achil. Thou art to breefe, I will the second time,
As I would buy thee, view thee, limbe by limbe.
Hect. O like a Booke of sport thou'lt reade me ore :
But there's more in me then thou vnderstand'st.
Why doest thou so oppresse me with thine eye?
Achil. Tell me you Heauens, in which part of his body
Shall I destroy him? Whether there, or there, or there,
That I may giue the locall wound a name,
And make distinct the very breach, where-our
Hectors great spirit flew. Answer me heauens.
Hect. It would discredit the blest Gods, proud man,
To answer such a question : Stand againe ;
Think'st thou to catch my life so pleasantly,
As to prenominate in nice coniecture
Where thou wilt hit me dead?
Achil. I tell thee yea.
Hect. Wert thou the Oracle to tell me so,
I'ld not beleeue thee : henceforth guard thee well,
For Ile not kill thee there, nor there, nor there,
But by the forge that stythied Mars his helme,
Ile kill thee euery where, yea, ore and ore.
You wisest Grecians, pardon me this bragge,
His insolence drawes folly from my lips,
But Ile endeuour deeds to match these words,
Or may I neuer——
Aiax. Do not chafe thee Cosin ;
And you *Achilles*, let these threats alone
Till accident, or purpose bring you too't.
You may euery day enough of *Hector*
If you haue stomacke. The generall state I feare,
Can scarse intreat you to be odde with him.
Hect. I pray you let vs see you in the field,
We haue had pelting Warres since you refus'd
The Grecians cause.
Achil. Dost thou intreat me *Hector*?
To morrow do I meete thee fell as death,
To night, all Friends.
Hect. Thy hand vpon that match.
Aga. First, all you Peeres of Greece go to my Tent,
There in the full conuiue you : Afterwards,
As *Hectors* leysure, and your bounties shall
Concurre together, seuerally intreat him.
Beate lowd the Taborins, let the Trumpets blow,
That this great Souldier may his welcome know. *Exeunt*
Troy. My Lord *Vlysses*, tell me I beseech you,
In what place of the Field doth *Calchas* keepe?
Vlys. At *Menelaus* Tent, most Princely *Troylus*,
There *Diomed* doth feast with him to night,
Who neither lookes on heauen, nor on earth,
But giues all gaze and bent of amorous view
On the faire *Cressid.*
Troy. Shall I (sweet Lord) be bound to thee so much,
After we part from *Agamemnons* Tent,
To bring me thither?
Vlys. You shall command me sir :
As gentle tell me, of what Honour was
This *Cressida* in Troy, had she no Louer there
That wailes her absence?
Troy. O sir, to such as boasting shew their scarres,
A mocke is due : will you walke on my Lord?
She was belou'd, she lou'd ; she is, and dooth ;
But still sweet Loue is food for Fortunes tooth. *Exeunt*

Enter Achilles, and Patroclus.

Achil. Ile heat his blood with Greekish wine to night,
Which

Which with my Cemitar Ile coole to morrow:
Patroclus, let vs Feast him to the hight.

  Pat. Heere comes *Thersites*.   *Enter Thersites.*

  Achil. How now, thou core of Enuy?
Thou crusty batch of Nature, what's the newes?

  Ther. Why thou picture of what thou seem'st, & Idoll
of Ideot-worshippers, here's a Letter for thee.

  Achil. From whence, Fragment?

  Ther. Why thou full dish of Foole, from Troy.

  Pat. Who keepes the Tent now?

  Ther. The Surgeons box, or the Patients wound.

  Patr. Well said aduersity, and what need these tricks?

  Ther. Prythee be silent boy, I profit not by thy talke,
thou art thought to be *Achilles* male Varlot.

  Patro. Male Varlot you Rogue? What's that?

  Ther. Why his masculine Whore. Now the rotten
diseases of the South, guts-griping Ruptures, Catarres,
Loades a grauell i'th'backe, Lethargies, cold Palsies, and
the like, take and take againe, such preposterous discoueries.

  Pat. Why thou damnable box of enuy thou, what
mean'st thou to curse thus?

  Ther. Do I curse thee?

  Patr. Why no, you ruinous But, you whorson indi-
stinguishable Curre.

  Ther. No? why art thou then exasperate, thou idle,
immateriall skiene of Sleyd silke; thou greene Sarcenet
flap for a sore eye, thou tassell of a Prodigals purse thou:
Ah how the poore world is pestred with such water-flies,
diminutiues of Nature.

  Pat. Out gall.

  Ther. Finch Egge.

  Ach. My sweet *Patroclus*, I am thwarted quite
From my great purpose in to morrowes battell:
Heere is a Letter from Queene *Hecuba*,
A token from her daughter, my faire Loue,
Both taxing me, and gaging me to keepe
An Oath that I haue sworne. I will not breake it,
Fall Greekes, faile Fame, Honor or go, or stay,
My maior vow lyes heere; this Ile obay:
Come, come *Thersites*, helpe to trim my Tent,
This night in banquetting must all be spent.
Away *Patroclus*.   *Exit.*

  Ther. With too much bloud, and too little Brain, these
two may run mad: but if with too much braine, and too
little blood, they do, Ile be a curer of madmen. Heere's
Agamemnon, an honest fellow enough, and one that loues
Quailes, but he has not so much Braine as eare-wax; and
the goodly transformation of Iupiter there his Brother,
the Bull, the primatiue Statue, and oblique memoriall of
Cuckolds, a thrifty shooing-horne in a chaine, hanging
at his Brothers legge, to what forme but that he is, shold
wit larded with malice, and malice forced with wit, turne
him too: to an Asse were nothing; hee is both Asse and
Oxe; to an Oxe were nothing, hee is both Oxe and Asse:
to be a Dogge, a Mule, a Cat, a Fitchew, a Toade, a Li-
zard, an Owle, a Puttocke, or a Herring without a Roe,
I would not care: but to be *Menelaus*, I would conspire
against Destiny. Aske me not what I would be, if I were
not *Thersites*: for I care not to bee the lowse of a Lazar,
so I were not *Menelaus*. Hoy-day, spirits and fires.

*Enter Hector, Aiax, Agamemnon, Vlysses, Ne-
stor, Diomed, with Lights.*

  Aga. We go wrong, we go wrong.

  Aiax. No yonder 'tis, there where we see the light.

  Hect. I trouble you.

  Aiax. No, not a whit.

Enter Achilles.

  Vlys. Heere comes himselfe to guide you?

  Achil. Welcome braue *Hector*, welcome Princes all.

  Agam. So now faire Prince of Troy, I bid goodnight,
Aiax commands the guard to tend on you.

  Hect. Thanks, and goodnight to the Greeks generall.

  Men. Goodnight my Lord.

  Hect. Goodnight sweet Lord *Menelaus*.

  Ther. Sweet draught: sweet quoth-a? sweet sinke,
sweet sure.

  Achil. Goodnight and welcom, both at once, to those
that go, or tarry.

  Aga. Goodnight.

  Achil. Old *Nestor* tarries, and you too *Diomed*,
Keepe *Hector* company an houre, or two.

  Dio. I cannot Lord, I haue important businesse,
The tide whereof is now, goodnight great *Hector*.

  Hect. Giue me your hand.

  Vlys. Follow his Torch, he goes to *Chalcas* Tent,
Ile keepe you company.

  Troy. Sweet sir, you honour me.

  Hect. And so good night.

  Achil. Come, come, enter my Tent.   *Exeunt.*

  Ther. That same *Diomed's* a false-hearted Rogue, a
most vniust Knaue; I will no more trust him when hee
leeres, then I will a Serpent when he hisses: he will spend
his mouth & promise, like Brabler the Hound; but when
he performes, Astronomers foretell it, that it is prodigious, there will come some change: the Sunne borrowes
of the Moone when *Diomed* keepes his word. I will rather leaue to see *Hector*, then not to dogge him: they say,
he keepes a Troyan Drab, and vses the Traitour *Chalcas*
his Tent. Ile after——— Nothing but Letcherie? All
incontinent Varlets.   *Exeunt.*

Enter Diomed.

  Dio. What are you vp here ho? speake?

  Chal. Who cals?

  Dio. Diomed, Chalcas (I thinke) wher's you Daughter?

  Chal. She comes to you.

Enter Troylus and Vlisses.

  Vlis. Stand where the Torch may not discouer vs.

Enter Cressid.

  Troy. Cressid comes forth to him.

  Dio. How now my charge?

  Cres. Now my sweet gardian: harke a word with you.

  Troy. Yea, so familiar?

  Vlis. She will sing any man at first sight.

  Ther. And any man may finde her, if he can take her
life: she's noted.

  Dio. Will you remember?

  Cal. Remember? yes.

  Dio. Nay, but doe then; and let your minde be coupled with your words.

  Troy. What should she remember?

  Vlis. List?

  Cres. Sweete hony Greek, tempt me no more to folly.

  Ther. Roguery.

  Dio. Nay then.

  Cres. Ile tell you what.

  Dio. Fo, fo, come tell a pin, you are a forsworne.

  Cres. In faith I cannot: what would you haue me do?

  Ther. A iugling tricke, to be secretly open.

  Dio. What did you sweare you would bestow on me?

  Cres. I prethee do not hold me to mine oath,
Bid me doe not any thing but that sweete Greeke.

                                              Dio. Goo

Troylus and Cressida.

Dio. Good night.
Troy. Hold, patience.
Ulis. How now Troian?
Cres. Diomed.
Dio. No, no, good night: Ile be your foole no more.
Trsy. Thy better must.
Cres. Harke one word in your eare.
Troy. O plague and madnesse!
Ulis. You are moued Prince, let vs depart I pray you,
Lest your displeasure should enlarge it selfe
To wrathfull tearmes: this place is dangerous;
The time right deadly: I beseech you goe.
Troy. Behold, I pray you.
Ulis. Nay, good my Lord goe off:
You flow to great distraction: come my Lord?
Troy. I pray thee stay?
Ulis. You haue not patience, come.
Troy. I pray you stay? by hell and hell torments,
I will not speake a word.
Dio. And so good night.
Cres. Nay, but you part in anger.
Troy. Doth that grieue thee? O withered truth!
Ulis. Why, how now Lord?
Troy. By Ioue I will be patient.
Cres. Gardian? why Greeke?
Dio. Fo, fo, adew, you palter.
Cres. In faith I doe not: come hither once againe.
Ulis. You shake my Lord at something; will you goe?
you will breake out.
Troy. She stroakes his cheeke.
Ulis. Come, come.
Troy. Nay stay, by Ioue I will not speake a word.
There is betweene my will, and all offences,
A guard of patience; stay a little while.
Ther. How the diuell Luxury with his fat rumpe and
potato finger, tickles these together: frye lechery, frye.
Dio. But will you then?
Cres. In faith I will lo; neuer trust me else.
Dio. Giue me some token for the surety of it.
Cres. Ile fetch you one. *Exit.*
Ulis. You haue sworne patience.
Troy. Feare me not sweete Lord.
I will not be my selfe, nor haue cognition
Of what I feele: I am all patience. *Enter Cressid.*
Ther. Now the pledge, now, now, now.
Cres. Here Diomed, keepe this Sleeue.
Troy. O beautie! where is thy Faith?
Ulis. My Lord.
Troy. I will be patient, outwardly I will.
Cres. You looke vpon that Sleeue? behold it well:
He lou'd me: O false wench: giue't me againe.
Dio. Whose was't?
Cres. It is no matter now I haue't againe.
I will not meete with you to morrow night:
I prythee Diomed visite me no more.
Ther. Now she sharpens: well said Whetstone.
Dio. I shall haue it.
Cres. What, this?
Dio. I that.
Cres. O all you gods! O prettie, prettie pledge;
Thy Maister now lies thinking in his bed
Of thee and me, and sighes, and takes my Gloue,
And giues memoriall daintie kisses to it;
As I kisse thee.
Dio. Nay, doe not snatch it from me.
Cres. He that takes that, takes my heart withall.

Dio. I had your heart before, this followes it.
Troy. I did sweare patience.
Cres. You shall not haue it Diomed; faith you shall not:
Ile giue you something else.
Dio. I will haue this: whose was it?
Cres. It is no matter.
Dio. Come tell me whose it was?
Cres. 'Twas one that lou'd me better then you will.
But now you haue it, take it.
Dio. Whose was it?
Cres. By all Dianas waiting women yond;
And by her selfe, I will not tell you whose.
Dio. To morrow will I weare it on my Helme,
And grieue his spirit that dares not challenge it.
Troy. Wert thou the diuell, and wor'st it on thy horne,
It should be challeng'd.
Cres. Well, well, 'tis done, 'tis past; and yet it is not:
I will not keepe my word.
Dio. Why then farewell,
Thou neuer shalt mocke Diomed againe.
Cres. You shall not goe: one cannot speake a word,
But it strait starts you.
Dio. I doe not like this fooling.
Ther. Nor I by Pluto: but that that likes not me, pleases me best.
Dio. What shall I come? the houre.
Cres. I, come: O Ioue! doe, come: I shall be plagu'd.
Dio. Farewell till then. *Exit.*
Cres. Goodnight: I prythee come:
Troylus farewell; one eye yet lookes on thee;
But with my heart, the other eye, doth see.
Ah poore our sexe; this fault in vs I finde:
The errour of our eye, directs our minde.
What errour leads, must erre; O then conclude,
Mindes swai'd by eyes, are full of turpitude. *Exit.*
Ther. A proofe of strength she could not publish more;
Vnlesse she say, my minde is now turn'd whore.
Ulis. Al's done my Lord.
Troy. It is.
Ulis. Why stay we then?
Troy. To make a recordation to my soule
Of euery syllable that here was spoke;
But if I tell how these two did coact;
Shall I not lye, in publishing a truth?
Sith yet there is a credence in my heart:
An esperance so obstinately strong,
That doth inuert that test of eyes and eares;
As if those organs had deceptious functions,
Created onely to calumniate.
Was Cressed here?
Ulis. I cannot coniure Troian.
Troy. She was not sure.
Ulis. Most sure she was.
Troy. Why my negation hath no taste of madnesse?
Ulis. Nor mine my Lord: Cressid was here but now.
Troy. Let it not be beleeu'd for womanhood:
Thinke we had mothers; doe not giue aduantage
To stubborne Criticks, apt without a theame
For deprauation, to square the generall sex
By Cressids rule. Rather thinke this not Cressid.
Ulis. What hath she done Prince, that can soyle our mothers?
Troy. Nothing at all, vnlesse that this were she.
Ther. Will he swagger himselfe out on's owne eyes?
Troy. This she? no, this is Diomids Cressida:
If beautie haue a soule, this is not she:

If soules guide vowes; if vowes are sanctimonie;
If sanctimonie be the gods delight:
If there be rule in vnitie it selfe,
This is not she: O madnesse of discourse!
That cause sets vp, with, and against thy selfe
By foule authoritie: where reason can revolt
Without perdition, and losse assume all reason,
Without revolt. This is, and is not Cressid:
Within my soule, there doth conduce a fight
Of this strange nature, that a thing inseperate,
Diuides more wider then the skie and earth:
And yet the spacious bredth of this diuision,
Admits no Orifex for a point as subtle,
As *Ariachnes* broken woofe to enter:
Instance, O instance! strong as *Plutoes* gates:
Cressid is mine, tied with the bonds of heauen;
Instance, O instance, strong as heauen it selfe:
The bonds of heauen are slipt, dissolu'd, and loos'd,
And with another knot fiue finger tied,
The fractions of her faith, orts of her loue:
The fragments, scraps, the bits, and greazie reliques,
Of her ore-eaten faith, are bound to *Diomed*.

Vlis. May worthy *Troylus* be halfe attached
With that which here his passion doth expresse?

Troy. I Greeke: and that shall be divulged well
In Characters, as red as *Mars* his heart
Inflam'd with *Venus*: neuer did yong man fancy
With so eternall, and so fixt a soule.
Harke Greek: as much I doe *Cressida* loue;
So much by weight, hate I her *Diomed*,
That Sleeue is mine, that heele beare in his Helme:
Were it a Caske compos'd by *Vulcans* skill,
My Sword should bite it: Not the dreadfull spout,
Which Shipmen doe the Hurricano call,
Constring'd in masse by the almighty Fenne,
Shall dizzie with more clamour Neptunes eare
In his difcent; then shall my prompted sword,
Falling on *Diomed*.

Ther. Heele tickle it for his concupie.

Troy. O *Cressid*! O false *Cressid*! false, false, false:
Let all vntruths stand by thy stained name,
And theyle seeme glorious.

Vlis. O containe your selfe:
Your passion drawes eares hither.

Enter Aeneas.

Aene. I haue beene seeking you this houre my Lord:
Hector by this is arming him in Troy.
Aiax your Guard, staies to conduct you home.

Troy. Haue with you Prince: my curteous Lord adew:
Farewell revolted faire: and *Diomed*,
Stand fast, and weare a Castle on thy head.

Vli. Ile bring you to the Gates.

Troy. Accept distracted thankes.

Exeunt Troylus, Aeneas, and Ulisses.

Ther. Would I could meete that rogue *Diomed*, I
would croke like a Rauen: I would bode, I would bode:
Patroclus will giue me any thing for the intelligence of
this whore: the Parrot will not doe more for an Almond,
then he for a commodious drab: Lechery, lechery, still
warres and lechery, nothing else holds fashion. A burning
diuell take them.

Enter Hector and Andromache.

And. When was my Lord so much vngently temper'd,
To stop his eares against admonishment?
Vnarme, vnarme, and doe not fight to day.

Hect. You traine me to offend you: get you gone.
By the everlasting gods, Ile goe.

And. My dreames will sure proue ominous to the day.

Hect. No more I say. *Enter Cassandra.*

Cassa. Where is my brother *Hector*?

And. Here sister, arm'd, and bloudy in intent:
Consort with me in loud and deere petition:
pursue we him on knees: for I haue dreampt
Of bloudy turbulence; and this whole night
Hath nothing beene but shapes, and formes of slaughter.

Cass. O, 'tis true.

Hect. Ho? bid my Trumpet sound.

Cass. No notes of sallie, for the heauens, sweet brother.

Hect. Begon I say: the gods haue heard me sweare.

Cass. The gods are deafe to hot and peeuish vowes;
They are polluted offrings, more abhord
Then spotted Liuers in the sacrifice.

And. O be perswaded, doe not count it holy,
To hurt by being iust; it is as lawfull:
For we would count giue much to as violent thefts,
And rob in the behalfe of charitie.

Cass. It is the purpose that makes strong the vowe;
But vowes to every purpose must not hold:
Vnarme sweete *Hector*.

Hect. Hold you still I say;
Mine honour keepes the weather of my fate:
Life euery man holds deere, but the deere man
Holds honor farre more precious, deere, then life.

Enter Troylus.

How now yong man? mean'st thou to fight to day?

And. *Cassandra*, call my father to perswade.

Exit Cassandra.

Hect. No faith yong *Troylus*; doffe thy harnesse youth;
I am to day ith'vaine of Chiualrie:
Let grow thy Sinewes till their knots be strong;
And tempt not yet the brushes of the warre.
Vnarme thee, goe; and doubt thou not braue boy,
Ile stand to day, for thee, and me, and Troy.

Troy. Brother, you haue a vice of mercy in you;
Which better fits a Lyon, then a man.

Hect. What vice is that? good *Troylus* chide me for it.

Troy. When many times the captiue Grecians fals,
Euen in the fanne and winde of your faire Sword:
You bid them rise, and liue.

Hect. O 'tis faire play.

Troy. Fooles play, by heauen *Hector*.

Hect. How now? how now?

Troy. For th'loue of all the gods
Let's leaue the Hermit Pitty with our Mothers;
And when we haue our Armors buckled on,
The venom'd vengeance ride vpon our swords,
Spur them to ruthfull worke, reine them from ruth.

Hect. Fie sauage, fie.

Troy. *Hector*, then 'tis warres.

Hect. *Troylus*, I would not haue you fight to day.

Troy. Who should with-hold me?
Not fate, obedience, nor the hand of *Mars*,
Beckning with fierie trunchion my retire;
Not *Priamus*, and *Hecuba* on knees;
Their eyes ore-galled with recourse of teares;
Nor you my brother, with your true sword drawne
Oppos'd to hinder me, should stop my way:
But by my ruine.

Enter Priam and Cassandra.

Cass. Lay hold vpon him *Priam*, hold him fast:
He is thy crutch; now if thou loose thy stay,
Thou on him leaning, and all Troy on thee,

Fall all together.
  Priam. Come Hector, come, goe backe:
Thy wife hath dreampt: thy mother hath had visions;
Cassandra doth foresee; and I my selfe,
Am like a Prophet suddenly enrapt,
to tell thee that this day is ominous:
Therefore come backe.
  Hect. Æneas is a field,
And I do stand engag'd to many Greekes,
Euen in the faith of valour, to appeare
This morning to them.
  Priam. I, but thou shalt not goe.
  Hect. I must not breake my faith:
You know me dutifull, therefore deare sir,
Let me not shame respect; but giue me leaue
To take that course by your content and voice,
Which you doe here forbid me, Royall Priam.
  Cass. O Priam, yeelde not to him.
  And. Doe not deere father.
  Hect. Andromache I am offended with you:
Vpon the loue you beare me, get you in.
                    Exit Andromache.
  Troy. This foolish, dreaming, superstitious girle,
Makes all these bodements.
  Cass. O farewell, deere Hector:
Looke how thou diest; looke how thy eye turnes pale:
Looke how thy wounds doth bleede at many vents:
Harke how Troy roares; how Hecuba cries out;
How poore Andromache shrils her dolour forth;
Behold distraction, frenzie, and amazement,
Like witlesse Antickes one another meete,
And all cry Hector, Hectors dead: O Hector!
  Troy. Away, away.
  Cass. Farewell: yes, soft: Hector I take my leaue;
Thou do'st thy selfe, and all our Troy deceiue.   Exit.
  Hect. You are amaz'd, my Liege, at her exclaime:
Goe in and cheere the Towne, weele forth and fight:
Doe deedes of praise, and tell you them at night.
  Priam. Farewell: the gods with safetie stand about
thee.   Alarum.
  Troy. They are at it, harke: proud Diomed, beleeue
I come to loose my arme, or winne my sleeue.

        Enter Pandar.

  Pand. Doe you heare my Lord? do you heare?
  Troy. What now?
  Pand. Here's a Letter come from yond poore girle.
  Troy. Let me reade.
  Pand. A whorson tisicke, a whorson rascally tisicke,
so troubles me; and the foolish fortune of this girle, and
what one thing, what another, that I shall leaue you one
o'th's dayes: and I haue a rheume in mine eyes too; and
such an ache in my bones; that vnlesse a man were curst,
I cannot tell what to thinke on't. What sayes shee
there?
  Troy. Words, words, meere words, no matter from
the heart;
Th'effect doth operate another way.
Goe winde to winde, there turne and change together:
My loue with words and errors still she feedes;
But edifies another with her deedes.
  Pand. Why, but heare you?
  Troy. Hence brother lackie; ignomie and shame
Pursue thy life, and liue aye with thy name.
      A Larum.   Exeunt.

        Enter Thersites in excursion.

  Ther. Now they are clapper-clawing one another, Ile
goe looke on: that dissembling abhominable varlet Diomede, has got that same scuruie, doting, foolish yong
knaues Sleeue of Troy, there in his Helme: I would faine
see them meet; that, that same yong Troian asse, that loues
the whore there, might send that Greekish whore-mai-
sterly villaine, with the Sleeue, backe to the dissembling
luxurious drabbe, of a sleeuelesse errant. O 'th' other side,
the pollicie of those craftie swearing rascals; that stole
old Mouse-eaten dry cheese, Nestor: and that same dog-
foxe Vlisses is not prou'd worth a Black-berry. They set
me vp in pollicy, that mungrill curre Aiax, against that
dogge of as bad a kinde, Achilles. And now is the curre
Aiax prouder then the curre Achilles, and will not arme
to day. Whereupon, the Grecians began to proclaime
barbarisme; and pollicie growes into an ill opinion.
        Enter Diomed and Troylus.
Soft, here come Sleeue, and th'other.
  Troy. Flye not: for should'st thou take the Riuer Stix,
I would swim after.
  Diom. Thou do'st miscall retire:
I doe not flye; but aduantagious care
Withdrew me from the oddes of multitude:
Haue at thee?
  Ther. Hold thy whore Grecian: now for thy whore
Troian: Now the Sleeue, now the Sleeue.
        Enter Hector.
  Hect. What art thou Greek? art thou for Hectors match?
Art thou of bloud, and honour?
  Ther. No, no: I am a rascall: a scuruie railing knaue:
a very filthy roague.
  Hect. I doe beleeue thee, liue.
  Ther. God a mercy, that thou wilt beleeue me; but a
plague breake thy necke——for frighting me: what's be-
come of the wenching rogues? I thinke they haue
swallowed one another. I would laugh at that mira-
cle——yet in a sort, lecherie eates it selfe: Ile seeke them.
                                            Exit.
        Enter Diomed and Seruants.
  Dio. Goe, goe, my seruant, take thou Troylus Horse;
Present the faire Steede to my Lady Cressid:
Fellow, commend my seruice to her beauty;
Tell her, I haue chastis'd the amorous Troyan.
And am her Knight by proofe.
  Ser. I goe my Lord.   Enter Agamemnon.
  Aga. Renew, renew, the fierce Polidamus
Hath beate downe Menon: bastard Margarelon
Hath Doreus prisoner.
And stands Calossus-wise wauing his beame,
Vpon the pashed courses of the Kings:
Epistropus and Cedius, Polixines is slaine;
Amphimacus, and Thoas deadly hurt;
Patroclus tane or slaine, and Palamedes
Sore hurt and bruised; the dreadfull Sagittary
Appauls our numbers, haste we Diomed
To re-enforcement, or we perish all.
        Enter Nestor.
  Nest. Goe beare Patroclus body to Achilles,
And bid the snaile-pac'd Aiax arme for shame:
There is a thousand Hectors in the field:
Now here he fights on Galathe his Horse,
And there lacks worke: anon he's there a foote,
And there they flye or dye, like scaled sculs,

                                            Before

Troylus and Cressida.

Before the belching Whale; then is he yonder,
And there the straying Greekes, ripe for his edge,
Fall downe before him, like the mowers swath;
Here, there, and euery where, he leaues and takes;
Dexteritie so obaying appetite,
That what he will, he does, and does so much,
That proofe is call'd impossibility.

Enter Vlisses.

Vlis. Oh, courage, courage Princes: great *Achilles*
Is arming, weeping, cursing, vowing vengeance;
Patroclus wounds haue rouz'd his drowzie bloud,
Together with his mangled *Myrmidons*,
That noselesse, handlesse, hackt and chipt, come to him;
Crying on *Hector*. *Aiax* hath lost a friend,
And foames at mouth, and he is arm'd, and at it:
Roaring for *Troylus*; who hath done to day,
Mad and fantasticke execution;
Engaging and redeeming of himselfe,
With such a carelesse force, and forcelesse care,
As if that luck in very spight of cunning, bad him win all.

Enter Aiax.

Aia. Troylus, thou coward Troylus. *Exit.*
Dio. I, there, there.
Nest. So, so, we draw together. *Exit.*

Enter Achilles.

Achil. Where is this *Hector*?
Come, come, thou boy-queller, shew thy face:
Know what it is to meete *Achilles* angry.
Hector, wher's *Hector*? I will none but *Hector*. *Exit.*

Enter Aiax.

Aia. Troylus, thou coward Troylus, shew thy head.

Enter Diomed.

Diom. Troylus, I say, wher's Troylus?
Aia. What would'st thou?
Diom. I would correct him.
Aia. Were I the Generall,
Thou should'st haue my office,
Ere that correction: Troylus I say, what Troylus?

Enter Troylus.

Troy. Oh traitour *Diomed*!
Turne thy false face thou traytor,
And pay thy life thou owest me for my horse.
Dio. Ha, art thou there?
Aia. Ile fight with him alone, stand *Diomed*.
Dio. He is my prize, I will not looke vpon.
Troy. Come both you coging Greekes, haue at you
both. *Exit Troylus.*

Enter Hector.

Hect. Yea Troylus? O well fought my yongest Brother.

Enter Achilles.

Achil. Now doe I see thee; haue at thee Hector.
Hect. Pause if thou wilt.
Achil. I doe disdaine thy curtesie, proud Troian;
Be happy that my armes are out of vse:
My rest and negligence befriends thee now,
But thou anon shalt heare of me againe:
Till when, goe seeke thy fortune. *Exit.*
Hect. Fare thee well:
I would haue beene much more a fresher man,
Had I expected thee: how now my Brother?

Enter Troylus.

Troy. Aiax hath tane *Æneas*; shall it be?
No, by the flame of yonder glorious heauen,
He shall not carry him: Ile be tane too,
Or bring him off: Fate heare me what I say;
I wreake not, though thou end my life to day. *Exit.*

Enter one in Armour.

Hect. Stand, stand, thou Greeke,
Thou art a goodly marke:
No? wilt thou not? I like thy armour well,
Ile frush it, and vnlocke the riuets all,
But Ile be maister of it: wilt thou not beast abide?
Why then flye on, Ile hunt thee for thy hide. *Exit.*

Enter Achilles with Myrmidons.

Achil. Come here about me you my *Myrmidons*:
Marke what I say; attend me where I wheele:
Strike not a stroake, but keepe your selues in breath;
And when I haue the bloudy *Hector* found,
Empale him with your weapons round about:
In fellest manner execute your arme.
Follow me sirs, and my proceedings eye;
It is decreed, *Hector* the great must dye. *Exit.*

Enter Thersites, Menelaus, and Paris.

Ther. The Cuckold and the Cuckold maker are at it:
now bull, now dogge, lowe; *Paris* lowe; now my double hen'd sparrow; lowe *Paris*, lowe; the bull has the
game: ware hornes ho?

Exit Paris and Menelaus.

Enter Bastard.

Bast. Turne slaue and fight.
Ther. What art thou?
Bast. A Bastard Sonne of *Priams*.
Ther. I am a Bastard too, I loue Bastards, I am a Bastard begot, Bastard instructed, Bastard in minde, Bastard
in valour, in euery thing illegitimate: one Beare will not
bite another; and wherefore should one Bastard? take
heede, the quarrel's most ominous to vs: if the Sonne of a
whore fight for a whore, he tempts iudgement: farewell
Bastard.
Bast. The diuell take thee coward. *Exeunt.*

Enter Hector.

Hect. Most putrified core so faire without:
Thy goodly armour thus hath cost thy life.
Now is my daies worke done; Ile take good breath:
Rest Sword, thou hast thy fill of bloud and death.

Enter Achilles and his Myrmidons.

Achil. Looke Hector how the Sunne begins to set;
How vgly night comes breathing at his heeles,
Euen with the vaile and darking of the Sunne.
To close the day vp, *Hectors* life is done.
Hect. I am vnarm'd, forgoe this vantage Greeke.
Achil. Strike fellowes, strike, this is the man I seeke.
So Illion fall thou: now Troy sinke downe;
Here lyes thy heart, thy sinewes, and thy bone.
On *Myrmidons*, cry you all a maine,
Achilles hath the mighty *Hector* slaine. *Retreat.*
Harke, a retreat vpon our Grecian part.
Gree. The Troian Trumpets sounds the like my Lord.
Achi. The dragon wing of night ore-spreds the earth
And stickler-like the Armies seperates
My halfe supt Sword, that frankly would haue fed,
Pleas'd with this dainty bed; thus goes to bed.
Come, tye his body to my horses tayle;
Along the field, I will the Troian traile. *Exeunt.*

Sound Retreat. Shout.

*Enter Agamemnon, Aiax, Menelaus, Nestor,
Diomed, and the rest marching.*

Aga. Harke, harke, what shout is that?
Nest. Peace Drums.

Sol. Achill.

Troylus and Cressida.

Sold. Achilles, Achilles, *Hector's* slaine, Achilles.
Dio. The bruite is, *Hector's* slaine, and by *Achilles*.
Aia. If it be so, yet braglesse let it be:
Great *Hector* was a man as good as he.
Agam. March patiently along; let one be sent
To pray *Achilles* see vs at our Tent.
If in his death the gods haue vs befrended,
Great Troy is ours, and our sharpe wars are ended.
Exeunt.

Enter Æneas, Paris, Anthenor and Deiphœbus.

Æne. Stand hoe, yet are we maisters of the field,
Neuer goe home; here starue we out the night.

Enter Troylus.

Troy. *Hector* is slaine.
All. *Hector*? the gods forbid.
Troy. Hee's dead: and at the murtherers Horses taile,
In beastly sort, drag'd through the shamefull Field.
Frowne on you heauens, effect your rage with speede:
Sit gods vpon your throanes, and smile at Troy.
I say at once, let your briefe plagues be mercy,
And linger not our sure destructions on.
Æne. My Lord, you doe discomfort all the Hoste.
Troy. You vnderstand me not, that tell me so:
I doe not speake of flight, of feare, of death,
But dare all imminence that gods and men,
Addresse their dangers in. *Hector* is gone:
Who shall tell *Priam* so? or *Hecuba*?
Let him that will a screechoule aye be call'd,
Goe in to Troy, and say there, *Hector's* dead:
There is a word will *Priam* turne to stone;
Make wels, and *Niobes* of the maides and wiues;
Coole statues of the youth: and in a word,
Scarre Troy out of it selfe. But march away,
Hector is dead: there is no more to say.

Stay yet: you vile abhominable Tents,
Thus proudly pight vpon our Phrygian plaines:
Let Titan rise as early as he dare,
Ile through, and through you; & thou great siz'd coward:
No space of Earth shall sunder our two hates,
Ile haunt thee, like a wicked conscience still,
That mouldeth goblins swift as frensies thoughts.
Strike a free march to Troy, with comfort goe:
Hope of reuenge, shall hide our inward woe.

Enter Pandarus.

Pand. But heare you? heare you?
Troy. Hence broker, lackie, ignomy, and shame
Pursue thy life, and liue aye with thy name.
Exeunt.

Pan. A goodly medcine for mine akingbones: oh world,
world, world! thus is the poore agent dispisde: Oh traitours and bawdes; how earnestly are you set aworke, and
how ill requited? why should our indeuour be so desir'd,
and the performance so loath'd? What Verse for it? what
instance for it? let me see.
Full merrily the humble Bee doth sing,
Till he hath lost his hony, and his sting.
And being once subdu'd in armed taile,
Sweete hony, and sweete notes together faile.
Good traders in the flesh, set this in your painted cloathes;
As many as be here of Panders hall,
Your eyes halfe out, weepe out at *Pandar's* fall:
Or if you cannot weepe, yet giue some grones;
Though not for me, yet for your akingbones:
Brethren and sisters of the hold-dore trade,
Some two months hence, my will shall here be made:
It should be now, but that my feare is this:
Some galled Goose of Winchester would hisse:
Till then, Ile sweate, and seeke about for eases;
And at that time bequeath you my diseases.
Exeunt.

¶¶¶

FINIS.

The Tragedy of Coriolanus.

Actus Primus: Scœna Prima.

Enter a Company of Mutinous Citizens, with Staues, Clubs, and other weapons.

1. Citizen.

Before we proceed any further, heare me speake.

All. Speake, speake.

1. Cit. You are all resolu'd rather to dy then to famish?

All. Resolu'd, resolu'd.

1. Cit. First you know, *Caius Martius* is chiefe enemy to the people.

All. We know't, we know't.

1. Cit. Let vs kill him, and wee'l haue Corne at our own price. Is't a Verdict?

All. No more talking on't; Let it be done, away, away

2. Cit. One word, good Citizens.

1. Cit. We are accounted poore Citizens, the Patricians good: what Authority surfets one, would releeue vs. If they would yeelde vs but the superfluitie while it were wholsome, wee might guesse they releeued vs humanely: But they thinke we are too deere, the leannesse that afflicts vs, the obiect of our misery, is as an inuentory to particularize their abundance, our sufferance is a gaine to them. Let vs reuenge this with our Pikes, ere we become Rakes. For the Gods know, I speake this in hunger for Bread, not in thirst for Reuenge.

2. Cit. Would you proceede especially against *Caius Martius*.

All. Against him first: He's a very dog to the Commonalty.

2. Cit. Consider you what Seruices he ha's done for his Country?

1. Cit. Very well, and could bee content to giue him good report for't, but that hee payes himselfe with beeing proud.

All. Nay, but speak not maliciously.

1. Cit. I say vnto you, what he hath done Famouslie, he did it to that end: though soft conscienc'd men can be content to say it was for his Countrey, he did it to please his Mother, and to be partly proud, which he is, euen to the altitude of his vertue.

2. Cit. What he cannot helpe in his Nature, you account a Vice in him: You must in no way say he is couetous.

1. Cit. If I must not, I neede not be barren of Accusations he hath faults (with surplus) to tyre in repetition. *Showts within.*
What showts are these? The other side a'th City is risen: why stay we prating heere? To th'Capitoll.

All. Come, come.

1 Cit. Soft, who comes heere?

Enter Menenius Agrippa.

2 Cit. Worthy *Menenius Agrippa*, one that hath alwaye lou'd the people.

1 Cit. He's one honest enough, wold al the rest wer so.

Mv. What work's my Countrimen in hand? Where go you with Bats and Clubs? The matter Speak I pray you.

2 Cit. Our busines is not vnknowne to th'Senat, they haue had inkling this fortnight what we intend to do, w̄ now wee'l shew em in deeds: they say poore Suters haue strong breaths, they shal know we haue strong arms too.

Menen. Why Masters, my good Friends, mine honest Neighbours, will you vndo your selues?

2 Cit. We cannot Sir, we are vndone already.

Men. I tell you Friends, most charitable care
Haue the Patricians of you for your wants.
Your suffering in this dearth, you may as well
Strike at the Heauen with your staues, as lift them
Against the Roman State, whose course will on
The way it takes: cracking ten thousand Curbes
Of more strong linke assunder, then can euer
Appeare in your impediment. For the Dearth,
The Gods, not the Patricians make it, and
Your knees to them (not armes) must helpe. Alacke,
You are transported by Calamity
Thether, where more attends you, and you slander
The Helmes o'th State; who care for you like Fathers,
When you curse them, as Enemies.

2 Cit. Care for vs? True indeed, they nere car'd for vs yet. Suffer vs to famish, and their Store-houses cramm'd with Graine: Make Edicts for Vsurie, to support Vsurers; repeale daily any wholsome Act established against the rich, and prouide more piercing Statutes daily, to chaine vp and restraine the poore. If the Warres eate vs not vppe, they will; and there's all the loue they beare vs.

Menen. Either you must
Confesse your selues wondrous Malicious,
Or be accus'd of Folly. I shall tell you
A pretty Tale, it may be you haue heard it,
But since it serues my purpose, I will venture
To scale't a little more.

2 Citizen. Well,
Ile heare it Sir: yet you must not thinke
To fobbe off our disgrace with a tale:
But and't please you deliuer.

Men. There was a time, when all the bodies members
Rebell'd against the Belly; thus accus'd it:
That onely like a Gulfe it did remaine

I'th midd'st a th'body, idle and vnactiue,
Still cubbording the Viand, neuer bearing
Like labour with the rest, where th'other Instments
Did see, and heare, deuise, instruct, walke, feele
And mutually participate, did minister
Vnto the appetite; and affection common
Of the whole body, the Belly answer'd.

  2. Cit. Well sir, what answer made the Belly
  Men. Sir, I shall tell you with a kinde of Smile,
Which ne're came from the Lungs, but euen thus:
For looke you I may make the belly Smile,
As well as speake, it tauntingly replyed
To'th'discontented Members, the mutinous part
That enuied his receite : euen so most fitly,
As you maligne our Senators, for that
They are not such as you.

  2. Cit. Your Bellies answer: What
The Kingly crown'd head, the vigilant eye,
The Counsailor Heart, the Arme our Souldier,
Our Steed the Legge, the Tongue our Trumpeter,
With other Muniments and petty helpes
In this our Fabricke, if that they——

  Men. What then? Fore me, this Fellow speakes.
What then? What then?

  2 Cit. Should by the Cormorant belly be restain'd,
Who is the sinke a th'body.

  Men. Well, what then?
  2. Cit. The former Agents, if they did complaine,
What could the Belly answer?

  Men. I will tell you,
If you'l bestow a small (of what you haue little)
Patience awhile; you'st heare the Bellies answer.

  2. Cit. Y'are long about it.
  Men. Note me this good Friend;
Your most graue Belly was deliberate,
Not rash like his Accusers, and thus answered.
True is it my Incorporate Friends (quoth he)
That I receiue the generall Food at first
Which you do liue vpon : and fit it is,
Because I am the Store-house, and the Shop
Of the whole Body. But, if you do remember,
I send it through the Riuers of your blood
Euen to the Court, the Heart, to th'seate o'th'Braine,
And through the Crankes and Offices of man,
The strongest Nerues, and small inferiour Veines
From me receiue that naturall competencie
Whereby they liue. And though that all at once
(You my good Friends, this sayes the Belly) marke me.

  2. Cit. I sir, well, well.
  Men. Though all at once, cannot
See what I do deliuer out to each,
Yet I can make my Awdit vp, that all
From me do backe receiue the Flowre of all,
And leaue me but the Bran. What say you too't?

  2. Cit. It was an answer, how apply you this?
  Men. The Senators of Rome, are this good Belly,
And you the mutinous Members : For examine
Their Counsailes, and their Cares; disgest things rightly,
Touching the Weale a'th Common, you shall finde
No publique benefit which you receiue,
But it proceeds, or comes from them to you,
And no way from your selues. What do you thinke?
You, the great Toe of this Assembly?

  2. Cit. I the great Toe? Why the great Toe?
  Men. For that being one o'th lowest, basest, poorest
Of this most wise Rebellion, thou goest formost :

Thou Rascall, that art worst in blood to run,
Lead'st first to win some vantage,
But make you ready your stiffe bats and clubs,
Rome, and her Rats, are at the point of battell,
The one side must haue baile.

  Enter Caius Martius.

Hayle, Noble *Martius.*
  Mar. Thanks. What's the matter you dissentious rogues
That rubbing the poore Itch of your Opinion,
Make your selues Scabs.

  2. Cit. We haue euer your good word.
  Mar. He that will giue good words to thee, wil flatter
Beneath abhorring. What would you haue, you Curres,
That like nor Peace, nor Warre? The one affrights you,
The other makes you proud. He that trusts to you,
Where he should finde you Lyons, findes you Hares:
Where Foxes, Geese you are : No surer, no,
Then is the coale of fire vpon the Ice,
Or Hailstone in the Sun. Your Vertue is,
To make him worthy, whose offence subdues him,
And curse that Iustice did it. Who deserues Greatnes,
Deserues your Hate : and your Affections are
A sickmans Appetite; who desires most that
Which would encrease his euill. He that depends
Vpon your fauours, swimmes with finnes of Leade,
And hewes downe Oakes, with rushes. Hang ye: trust ye?
With euery Minute you do change a Minde,
And call him Noble, that was now your Hate:
Him vilde, that was your Garland. What's the matter,
That in these seuerall places of the Citie,
You cry against the Noble Senate, who
(Vnder the Gods) keepe you in awe, which else
Would feede on one another? What's their seeking?

  Men. For Corne at their owne rates, whereof they say
The Citie is well stor'd.

  Mar. Hang 'em : They say?
They'l sit by th'fire, and presume to know
What's done i'th Capitoll : Who's like to rise,
Who thriues, & who declines: Side factions, & giue out
Coniecturall Marriages, making parties strong,
And feebling such as stand not in their liking,
Below their cobled Shooes. They say ther's graine enough?
Would the Nobility lay aside their ruth,
And let me vse my Sword, I'de make a Quarrie
With thousands of these quarter'd slaues, as high
As I could picke my Lance.

  Menen. Nay these are almost thoroughly perswaded:
For though abundantly they lacke discretion
Yet are they passing Cowardly. But I beseech you,
What sayes the other Troope?

  Mar. They are dissolu'd : Hang 'em;
They said they were an hungry, sigh'd forth Prouerbes
That Hunger-broke stone wals: that dogges must eate
That meate was made for mouths. That the gods sent not
Corne for the Richmen onely : With these shreds
They vented their Complainings, which being answer'd
And a petition granted them, a strange one,
To breake the heart of generosity,
And make bold power looke pale, they threw their caps
As they would hang them on the hornes a'th Moone,
Shooting their Emulation.

  Menen. What is graunted them?
  Mar. Fiue Tribunes to defend their vulgar wisdoms
Of their owne choice. One's *Iunius Brutus,*
Sicinius Velutus, and I know not. Sdeath,

The Tragedie of Coriolanus.

The rabble should haue first vnroo'st the City
Ere so preuayl'd with me; it will in time
Win vpon power, and throw forth greater Theames
For Insurrections arguing.

Menen. This is strange.

Mar. Go get you home you Fragments.

Enter a Messenger hastily.

Mess. Where's *Caius Martius?*

Mar. Heere: what's the matter?

Mes. The newes is sir, the Volcies are in Armes.

Mar. I am glad on't, then we shall ha meanes to vent
Our mustie superfluity. See our best Elders.

Enter Sicinius Velutus, Annius Brutus Cominius, Titus Lartius, with other Senatours.

1.Sen. *Martius* 'tis true, that you haue lately told vs,
The Volces are in Armes.

Mar. They haue a Leader,
Tullus Auffidius that will put you too't:
I sinne in enuying his Nobility:
And were I any thing but what I am,
I would wish me onely he.

Com. You haue fought together?

Mar. Were halfe to halfe the world by th'eares, & he
vpon my partie, I'de reuolt to make
Onely my warres with him. He is a Lion
That I am proud to hunt.

1.Sen. Then worthy *Martius*,
Attend vpon *Cominius* to these Warres.

Com. It is your former promise.

Mar. Sir it is,
And I am constant: *Titus Lucius*, thou
Shalt see me once more strike at *Tullus* face.
What art thou stiffe? Stand'st out?

Tit. No *Caius Martius*,
Ile leane vpon one Crutch, and fight with tother,
Ere stay behinde this Businesse.

Men. Oh true-bred.

Sen. Your Company to'th'Capitoll, where I know
Our greatest Friends attend vs.

Tit. Lead you on: Follow *Cominius*, we must followe
you, right worthy you Priority.

Com. Noble *Martius*.

Sen. Hence to your homes, be gone.

Mar. Nay let them follow,
The Volces haue much Corne: take these Rats thither,
To gnaw their Garners. Worshipfull Mutiners,
Your valour puts well forth: Pray follow. *Exeunt.*

Citizens steale away. Manet Sicin.& Brutus.

Sicin. Was euer man so proud as is this *Martius?*

Bru. He has no equall.

Sicin. When we were chosen Tribunes for the people.

Bru. Mark'd you his lip and eyes.

Sicin. Nay, but his taunts.

Bru. Being mou'd, he will not spare to gird the Gods.

Sicin. Bemocke the modest Moone.

Bru. The present Warres deuoure him, he is growne
Too proud to be so valiant.

Sicin. Such a Nature, tickled with good successe, disdaines the shadow which he treads on at noone, but I do
wonder, his insolence can brooke to be commanded vnder *Cominius?*

Bru. Fame, at the which he aymes,
In whom already he's well grac'd, cannot
Better be held, nor more attain'd then by

A place below the first: for what miscarries
Shall be the Generals fault, though he performe
To th'vtmost of a man, and giddy censure
Will then cry out of *Martius*: Oh, if he
Had borne the businesse.

Sicin. Besides, if things go well,
Opinion that so stickes on *Martius*, shall
Of his demerits rob *Cominius*.

Bru. Come: halfe all *Cominius* Honors are to *Martius*
Though *Martius* earn'd them not: and all his faults
To *Martius* shall be Honors, though indeed
In ought he merit not.

Sicin. Let's hence, and heare
How the dispatch is made, and in what fashion
More then his singularity, he goes
Vpon this present Action.

Bru. Let's along. *Exeunt.*

Enter Tullus Auffidius with Senators of Coriolus.

1.Sen. So, your opinion is *Auffidius*,
That they of Rome are entred in our Counsailes,
And know how we proceede,

Auf. Is it not yours?
What euer haue bin thought one in this State
That could be brought to bodily act, ere Rome
Had circumuention: 'tis not foure dayes gone
Since I heard thence, these are the words, I thinke
I haue the Letter heere: yes, heere it is;
They haue prest a Power, but it is not knowne
Whether for East or West: the Dearth is great,
The people Mutinous: And it is rumour'd,
Cominius, Martius your old Enemy
(Who is of Rome worse hated then of you)
And *Titus Lartius*, a most valiant Roman,
These three leade on this Preparation
Whether 'tis bent: most likely, 'tis for you:
Consider of it.

1.Sen. Our Armie's in the Field:
We neuer yet made doubt but Rome was ready
To answer vs.

Auf. Nor did you thinke it folly,
To keepe your great pretences vayl'd, till when
They needs must shew themselues, which in the hatching
It seem'd appear'd to Rome. By the discouery,
We shalbe shortned in our ayme, which was
To take in many Townes, ere (almost) Rome
Should know we were a-foot.

2.Sen. Noble *Auffidius*,
Take your Commission, hye you to your Bands,
Let vs alone to guard *Corioles*
If they set downe before's: for the remoue
Bring vp your Army: but (I thinke) you'l finde
Th'haue not prepar'd for vs.

Auf. O doubt not that,
I speake from Certainties. Nay more,
Some parcels of their Power are forth already,
And onely hitherward. I leaue your Honors.
If we, and *Caius Martius* chance to meete,
'Tis sworne betweene vs, we shall euer strike
Till one can do no more.

All. The Gods assist you.

Auf. And keepe your Honors safe.

1.Sen. Farewell.

2.Sen. Farewell.

All. Farewell. *Exeunt omnes.*

Enter Volumnia and Virgilia, mother and wife to Martius: They set them downe on two lowe stooles and sowe.

Volum. I pray you daughter sing, or expresse your selfe in a more comfortable sort : If my Sonne were my Husband, I should freelier reioyce in that absence wherein he wonne Honor, then in the embracements of his Bed, where he would shew most loue. When yet hee was but tender-bodied, and the onely Sonne of my womb; when youth with comelinesse pluck'd all gaze his way; when for a day of Kings entreaties, a Mother should not sel him an houre from her beholding; I considering how Honour would become such a person, that it was no better then Picture-like to hang by th'wall, if renowne made it not stirre, was pleas'd to let him seeke danger, where he was like to finde fame : To a cruell Warre I sent him, from whence he return'd, his browes bound with Oake. I tell thee Daughter, I sprang not more in ioy at first hearing he was a Man-child, then now in first seeing he had proued himselfe a man.

Virg. But had he died in the Businesse Madame, how then?

Volum. Then his good report should haue beene my Sonne, I therein would haue found issue. Heare me professe sincerely, had I a dozen sons each in my loue alike, and none lesse deere then thine, and my good *Martius*, I had rather had eleuen dye Nobly for their Countrey, then one voluptuously surfet out of Action.

Enter a Gentlewoman.

Gent. Madam, the Lady *Valeria* is come to visit you.

Virg. Beseech you giue me leaue to retire my selfe.

Volum. Indeed you shall not:
Me thinkes, I heare hither your Husbands Drumme:
See him plucke *Auffidius* downe by th'haire :
(As children from a Beare) the *Volces* shunning him :
Me thinkes I see him stampe thus, and call thus,
Come on you Cowards, you were got in feare
Though you were borne in Rome ; his bloody brow
With his mail'd hand, then wiping, forth he goes
Like to a Haruest man, that task'd to mowe
Or all, or loose his hyre.

Virg. His bloody Brow? Oh Iupiter, no blood.

Volum. Away you Foole ; it more becomes a man
Then gilt his Trophe. The brests of *Hecuba*
When she did suckle *Hector*, look'd not louelier
Then *Hectors* forhead, when it spit forth blood
At Grecian sword. *Contenning*, tell *Valeria*
We are fit to bid her welcome. *Exit Gent.*

Vir. Heauens blesse my Lord from fell *Auffidius*.

Vol. He'l beat *Auffidius* head below his knee,
And treade vpon his necke.

Enter Valeria with an Vsher, and a Gentlewoman.

Val. My Ladies both good day to you.

Vol. Sweet Madam.

Vir. I am glad to see your Ladyship.

Val. How do you both? You are manifest house-keepers. What are you sowing heere? A fine spotte in good faith. How does your little Sonne?

Vir. I thanke your Lady-ship: Well good Madam.

Vol. He had rather see the swords, and heare a Drum, then looke vpon his Schoolmaster.

Val. A my word the Fathers Sonne: Ile sweare 'tis a very pretty boy. A my troth, I look'd vpon him a Wensday halfe an houre together: ha's such a confirm'd countenance. I saw him run after a gilded Butterfly, & when he caught it, he let it go againe, and after it againe, and ouer and ouer he comes, and vp againe: catcht it again: or whether his fall enrag'd him, or how 'twas, hee did so set his teeth, and teare it. Oh, I warrant how he mammockt it.

Vol. One on's Fathers moods.

Val. Indeed la, tis a Noble childe.

Virg. A Cracke Madam.

Val. Come, lay aside your stitchery, I must haue you play the idle Huswife with me this afternoone.

Virg. No (good Madam)
I will not out of doores.

Val. Not out of doores?

Volum. She shall, she shall.

Virg. Indeed no, by your patience; Ile not ouer the threshold, till my Lord returne from the Warres.

Val. Fye, you confine your selfe most vnreasonably: Come, you must go visit the good Lady that lies in.

Virg. I will wish her speedy strength, and visite her with my prayers: but I cannot go thither.

Volum. Why I pray you.

Virg. 'Tis not to saue labour, nor that I want loue.

Val. You would be another *Penelope*: yet they say, all the yearne she spun in *Vlisses* absence, did but fill Athica full of Mothes. Come, I would your Cambrick were sensible as your finger, that you might leaue pricking it for pitie. Come you shall go with vs.

Vir. No good Madam, pardon me, indeed I will not foorth.

Val. In truth la go with me, and Ile tell you excellent newes of your Husband.

Virg. Oh good Madam, there can be none yet.

Val. Verily I do not iest with you: there came newes from him last night.

Vir. Indeed Madam.

Val. In earnest it's true; I heard a Senatour speake it. Thus it is: the Volcies haue an Army forth, against who *Cominius* the Generall is gone, with one part of our Romane power. Your Lord, and *Titus Lartius*, are set down before their Citie *Carioles*, they nothing doubt preuailing, and to make it breefe Warres. This is true on mine Honor, and so I pray go with vs.

Virg. Giue me excuse good Madame, I will obey you in euery thing heereafter.

Vol. Let her alone Ladie, as she is now: She will but disease our better mirth.

Valeria. In troth I thinke she would:
Fare you well then. Come good sweet Ladie.
Prythee *Virgilia* turne thy solemnesse out a doore,
And go along with vs.

Virgil. No
At a word Madam; Indeed I must not,
I wish you much mirth.

Val. Well, then farewell. *Exeunt Ladies*

Enter Martius, Titus Lartius, with Drumme and Colours, with Captaines and Souldiers, as before the City Corialus: to them a Messenger.

Martius. Yonder comes Newes:
A Wager they haue met.

Lar. My horse to yours, no.

Mar. Tis done.

Lart. Agreed.

The Tragedie of Coriolanus.

Mar. Say, ha's our Generall met the Enemy?
Mess. They lye in view, but haue not spoke as yet.
Lart. So, the good Horse is mine.
Mart. Ile buy him of you.
Lart. No, Ile nor sel, nor giue him: Lend you him I will
For halfe a hundred yeares: Summon the Towne.
Mar. How farre off lie these Armies?
Mess. Within this mile and halfe.
Mar. Then shall we heare their Larum, & they Ours.
Now Mars, I prythee make vs quicke in worke,
That we with smoaking swords may march from hence
To helpe our fielded Friends. Come, blow thy blast.

They Sound a Parley: Enter two Senators with others on the Walles of Corialus.

Tullus Auffidious, is he within your Walles?
1. Senat. No, nor a man that feares you lesse then he,
That's lesser then a little: *Drum a farre off.*
Hearke, our Drummes
Are bringing forth our youth: Wee'l breake our Walles
Rather then they shall pound vs vp our Gates,
Which yet seeme shut, we haue but pin'd with Rushes,
They'le open of themselues. Harke you, farre off
                Alarum farre off.
There is *Auffidious*. List what worke he makes
Among'st your clouen Army.
Mart. Oh they are at it.
Lart. Their noise be our instruction. Ladders hoa.

Enter the Army of the Volces.

Mar. They feare vs not, but issue forth their Citie.
Now put your Shields before your hearts, and fight
With hearts more proofe then Shields.
Aduance braue *Titus*,
They do disdaine vs much beyond our Thoughts,
which makes me sweat with wrath. Come on my fellows
He that retires, Ile take him for a *Volce*,
And he shall feele mine edge.

Alarum, the Romans are beat back to their Trenches Enter Martius Cursing.

Mar. All the contagion of the South, light on you,
You Shames of Rome: you Heard of Byles and Plagues
Plaister you o're, that you may be abhorr'd
Farther then seene, and one infect another
Against the Winde a mile: you soules of Geese,
That beare the shapes of men, how haue you run
From Slaues, that Apes would beate; *Pluto* and Hell,
All hurt behinde, backes red, and faces pale
With flight and agued feare, mend and charge home,
Or by the fires of heauen, Ile leaue the Foe,
And make my Warres on you: Looke too't: Come on,
If you'l stand fast, wee'l beate them to their Wiues,
As they vs to our Trenches followes.

Another Alarum, and Martius followes them to gates, and is shut in.

So, now the gates are ope: now proue good Seconds,
'Tis for the followers Fortune, widens them,
Not for the flyers: Marke me, and do the like.

Enter the Gati.

1.Sol. Foole-hardinesse, not I.
2.Sol. Nor I.
1.Sol. See they haue shut him in.   *Alarum continues*
All. To th'pot I warrant him.   *Enter Titus Lartius*
Tit. What is become of *Martius*?
All. Slaine (Sir) doubtlesse.
2.Sol. Following the Flyers at the very heeles,

With them he enters: who vpon the sodaine
Clapt to their Gates, he is himselfe alone,
To answer all the City.
Lar. Oh Noble Fellow!
Who sensibly out-dares his sencelesse Sword,
And when it bowes, stand'st vp: Thou art left *Martius*,
A Carbuncle intire: as big as thou art
Weare not so rich a Iewell. Thou was't a Souldier
Euen to *Calues* wish, not fierce and terrible
Onely in strokes, but with thy grim lookes, and
The Thunder-like percussion of thy sounds
Thou mad'st thine enemies shake, as if the World
Were Feauorous, and did tremble.

Enter Martius bleeding, assaulted by the Enemy.

1.Sol. Looke Sir.
Lar. O 'tis *Martius*.
Let's fetch him off, or make remaine alike.
            They fight, and all enter the City.
Enter certaine Romanes with spoiles.

1.Rom. This will I carry to *Rome*.
2.Rom. And I this.
3.Rom. A Murrain on't, I tooke this for Siluer.   *exeunt.*
            Alarum continues still a-farre off.
Enter Martius, and Titus with a Trumpet.

Mar. See heere these mouers, that do prize their hours
At a crack'd Drachme: Cushions, Leaden Spoones,
Irons of a Doit, Dublets that Hangmen would
Bury with those that wore them. These base slaues,
Ere yet the fight be done, packe vp, downe with them.
And harke, what noyse the Generall makes: To him
There is the man of my soules hate, *Auffidious*,
Piercing our Romanes: Then Valiant *Titus* take
Conuenient Numbers to make good the City,
Whil'st I with those that haue the spirit, wil haste
To helpe *Cominius*.
Lar. Worthy Sir, thou bleed'st,
Thy exercise hath bin too violent,
For a second course of Fight.
Mar. Sir, praise me not:
My worke hath yet not warm'd me. Fare you well:
The blood I drop, is rather Physicall
Then dangerous to me: To *Auffidious* thus, I will appear
Lar. Now the faire Goddesse Fortune,   (and fight.
Fall deepe in loue with thee, and her great charmes
Misguide thy Opposers swords, Bold Gentleman:
Prosperity be thy Page.
Mar. Thy Friend no lesse,
Then those she placeth highest: So farewell.
Lar. Thou worthiest *Martius*,
Go sound thy Trumpet in the Market place,
Call thither all the Officers a'th'Towne,
Where they shall know our minde. Away.   *Exeunt*
Enter Cominius as it were in retire, with soldiers.
Com. Breath you my friends, wel fought, we are come
Like Romans, neither foolish in our stands,   (off,
Nor Cowardly in retyre: Beleeue me Sirs,
We shall be charg'd againe. Whiles we haue strooke
By Interims and conueying gusts, we haue heard
The Charges of our Friends. The Roman Gods,
Leade their successes, as we wish our owne,
That both our powers, with smiling Fronts encountring,
May giue you thankfull Sacrifice. Thy Newes?
            Enter a Messenger.
Mess. The Cittizens of *Corioles* haue yssued,
And giuen to *Lartius* and to *Martius* Battaile:

I saw

I saw our party to their Trenches driuen,
And then I came away.

  Com. Though thou speakest truth,
Me thinkes thou speak'st not well. How long is't since?
  Mes. Aboue an houre, my Lord.
  Com. 'Tis not a mile: briefely we heard their drummes.
How could'st thou in a mile confound an houre,
And bring thy Newes so late?
  Mes. Spies of the *Volces*
Held me in chace, that I was forc'd to wheele
Three or foure miles about, else had I sir
Halfe an houre since brought my report.

Enter Martius.

  Com. Whose yonder,
That doe's appeare as he were Flead? O Gods,
He has the stampe of *Martius*, and I haue
Before time seene him thus.
  Mar. Come I too late?
  Com. The Shepherd knowes not Thunder frō a Taber,
More then I know the sound of *Martius* Tongue
From euery meaner man.
  Martius. Come I too late?
  Com. I, if you come not in the blood of others,
But mantled in your owne.
  Mart. Oh! let me clip ye
In Armes as sound, as when I woo'd in heart;
As merry, as when our Nuptiall day was done,
And Tapers burnt to Bedward.
  Com. Flower of Warriors, how is't with *Titus Lartius*?
  Mar. As with a man busied about Decrees:
Condemning some to death, and some to exile,
Ransoming him, or pittying, threatning th'other;
Holding *Corioles* in the name of Rome,
Euen like a fawning Grey-hound in the Leash,
To let him slip at will.
  Com. Where is that Slaue
Which told me they had beate you to your Trenches?
Where is he? Call him hither.
  Mar. Let him alone,
He did informe the truth: but for our Gentlemen,
The common file, (a plague-Tribunes for them)
The Mouse ne're shunn'd the Cat, as they did budge
From Rascals worse then they.
  Com. But how preuail'd you?
  Mar. Will the time serue to tell, I do not thinke:
Where is the enemy? Are you Lords a'th Field?
If not, why cease you till you are so?
  Com. *Martius*, we haue at disaduantage fought,
And did retyre to win our purpose.
  Mar. How lies their Battell? Know you on w side
They haue plac'd their men of trust?
  Com. As I guesse *Martius*,
Their Bands i'th Vaward are the Antients
Of their best trust: O're them *Auffidious*,
Their very heart of Hope.
  Mar. I do beseech you,
By all the Battailes wherein we haue fought,
By th'Blood we haue shed together,
By th'Vowes we haue made
To endure Friends, that you directly set me
Against *Affidious*, and his *Antiats*,
And that you not delay the present (but
Filling the aire with Swords aduanc'd) and Darts,
We proue this very houre.
  Com. Though I could wish,

You were conducted to a gentle Bath,
And Balmes applyed to you, yet dare I neuer
Deny your asking, take your choice of those
That best can ayde your action.
  Mar. Those are they
That most are willing; if any such be heere,
(As it were sinne to doubt) that loue this painting
Wherein you see me smear'd, if any feare
Lessen his person, then an ill report:
If any thinke, braue death out-weighes bad life,
And that his Countries deerer then himselfe,
Let him alone: Or so many so minded,
Waue thus to expresse his disposition,
And follow *Martius*.

They all shout and waue their swords, take him vp in their Armes, and cast vp their Caps.

Oh me alone, make you a sword of me:
If these shewes be not outward, which of you
But is foure *Volces*? None of you, but is
Able to beare against the great *Auffidious*
A Shield, as hard as his. A certaine number
(Though thankes to all) must I select from all:
The rest shall beare the businesse in some other fight
(As cause will be obey'd:) please you to March,
And foure shall quickly draw out my Command,
Which men are best inclin'd.
  Com. March on my Fellowes:
Make good this ostentation, and you shall
Diuide in all, with vs. *Exeunt*

Titus Lartius, hauing set a guard vpon Carioles, going with Drum and Trumpet toward Cominius, and Caius Martius, Enters with a Lieutenant, other Souldiours, and a Scout.

  Lar. So, let the Ports be guarded; keepe your Duties
As I haue set them downe. If I do send, dispatch
Those Centuries to our ayd, the rest will serue
For a short holding, if we loose the Field,
We cannot keepe the Towne.
  Lieu. Feare not our care Sir.
  Lart. Hence; and shut your gates vpon's:
Our Guider come, to th'Roman Campe conduct vs. *Exit*
Alarum, as in Battaile.

Enter Martius and Auffidius at seueral doores.
  Mar. Ile fight with none but thee, for I do hate thee
Worse then a Promise-breaker.
  Auffid. We hate alike:
Not Affricke ownes a Serpent I abhorre
More then thy Fame and Enuy: Fix thy foot.
  Mar. Let the first Budger dye the others Slaue,
And the Gods doome him after.
  Auf. If I flye *Martius*, hollow me like a Hare.
  Mar. Within these three houres *Tullus*
Alone I fought in your *Corioles* walles,
And made what worke I pleas'd: 'Tis not my blood,
Wherein thou seest me maskt, for thy Reuenge
Wrench vp thy power to th'highest.
  Auf. Wer't thou the *Hector*,
That was the whip of your bragg'd Progeny,
Thou should'st not scape me heere.

Heere they fight, and certaine Volces come in the ayde of Auffi. Martius fights til they be driuen in breathles.

Officious and not valiant, you haue sham'd me
In your condemned Seconds. *Flourish.*

Flourish. Alarum. A Retreat is sounded. Enter at one Doore Cominius, with the Romanes: At another Doore Martius, with his Arme in a Scarfe.

Com. If I should tell thee o're this thy dayes Worke,
Thou't not beleeue thy deeds: but Ile report it,
Where Senators shall mingle teares with smiles,
Where great Patricians shall attend, and shrug,
I'th'end admire: where Ladies shall be frighted,
And gladly quak'd, heare more: where the dull Tribunes,
That with the fustie Plebeans, hate thine Honors,
Shall say against their hearts, We thanke the Gods
Our Rome hath such a Souldier.
Yet cam'st thou to a Morsell of this Feast,
Hauing fully din'd before.

Enter Titus with his Power, from the Pursuit.

Titus Lartius. Oh Generall:
Here is the Steed, wee the Caparison:
Hadst thou beheld——

Martius. Pray now, no more:
My Mother, who ha's a Charter to extoll her Bloud,
When she do's prayse me, grieues me:
I haue done as you haue done, that's what I can,
Induc'd as you haue beene, that's for my Countrey:
He that ha's but effected his good will,
Hath ouerta'ne mine Act.

Com. You shall not be the Graue of your deseruing,
Rome must know the value of her owne:
'Twere a Concealement worse then a Theft,
No lesse then a Traducement,
To hide your doings, and to silence that,
Which to the spire, and top of prayses vouch'd,
Would seeme but modest: therefore I beseech you,
In signe of what you are, not to reward
What you haue done, before our Armie heare me.

Martius. I haue some Wounds vpon me, and they smart
To heare themselues remembred.

Com. Should they not:
Well might they fester 'gainst Ingratitude,
And tent themselues with death: of all the Horses,
Whereof we haue ta'ne good, and good store of all,
The Treasure in this field atchieued, and Citie,
We render you the Tenth, to be ta'ne forth,
Before the common distribution,
At your onely choyse.

Martius. I thanke you Generall:
But cannot make my heart consent to take
A Bribe, to pay my Sword: I doe refuse it,
And stand vpon my common part with those,
That haue beheld the doing.

A long flourish. They all cry, Martius, Martius, cast vp their Caps and Launces: Cominius and Lartius stand bare.

Mar. May these same Instruments, which you prophane,
Neuer sound more: when Drums and Trumpets shall
I'th'field proue flatterers, let Courts and Cities be
Made all of false-fac'd soothing:
When Steele growes soft, as the Parasites Silke,
Let him be made an Ouerture for th' Warres:
No more I say, for that I haue not wash'd
My Nose that bled, or foyl'd some debile Wretch,
Which without note, here's many else haue done,
You shoot me forth in acclamations hyperbolicall,
As if I lou'd my little should be dieted
In prayses, sawc'st with Lyes.

Com. Too modest are you:
More cruell to your good report, then gratefull
To vs, that giue you truly: by your patience,
If 'gainst your selfe you be incens'd, wee'le put you
(Like one that meanes his proper harme) in Manacles,
Then reason safely with you: Therefore be it knowne,
As to vs, to all the World, That *Caius Martius*
Weares this Warres Garland: in token of the which,
My Noble Steed, knowne to the Campe, I giue him,
With all his trim belonging; and from this time,
For what he did before *Corioles*, call him,
With all th'applause and Clamor of the Hoast,
Marcus Caius Coriolanus. Beare th'addition Nobly euer?

Flourish. Trumpets sound, and Drums.

Omnes. Marcus Caius Coriolanus.

Martius. I will goe wash:
And when my Face is faire, you shall perceiue
Whether I blush, or no: howbeit, I thanke you,
I meane to stride your Steed, and at all times
To vnder-crest your good Addition,
To th'fairenesse of my power.

Com. So, to our Tent:
Where ere we doe repose vs, we will write
To Rome of our successe: you *Titus Lartius*
Must to *Corioles* backe, send vs to Rome
The best, with whom we may articulate,
For their owne good, and ours.

Lartius. I shall, my Lord.

Martius. The Gods begin to mocke me:
I that now refus'd most Princely gifts,
Am bound to begge of my Lord Generall.

Com. Tak't, 'tis yours: what is't?

Martius. I sometime lay here in *Corioles*,
At a poore mans house: he vs'd me kindly,
He cry'd to me: I saw him Prisoner:
But then *Auffidius* was within my view,
And Wrath o're-whelm'd my pittie: I request you
To giue my poore Host freedome.

Com. Oh well begg'd:
Were he the Butcher of my Sonne, he should
Be free, as is the Winde: deliuer him, *Titus.*

Lartius. Martius, his Name.

Martius. By *Iupiter* forgot:
I am wearie, yea, my memorie is tyr'd:
Haue we no Wine here?

Com. Goe we to our Tent:
The bloud vpon your Visage dryes, 'tis time
It should be lookt too: come. *Exeunt.*

A flourish. Cornets. Enter Tullus Auffidius bloudie, with two or three Souldiors.

Auffi. The Towne is ta'ne.

Sould. 'Twill be deliuer'd backe on good Condition.

Auffid. Condition?
I would I were a Roman, for I cannot,
Being a *Volce,* be that I am. Condition?
What good Condition can a Treatie finde
I'th'part that is at mercy? fiue times, *Martius,*
I haue fought with thee; so often hast thou beat me;
And would'st doe so, I thinke, should we encounter

As often as we eate. By th'Elements,
If ere againe I meet him beard to beard,
He's mine, or I am his: Mine Emulation
Hath not that Honor in't it had: For where
I thought to crush him in an equall Force,
True Sword to Sword: Ile potche at him some way,
Or Wrath, or Craft may get him.

Sol. He's the diuell.

Auf. Bolder, though not so subtle: my valors poison'd,
With onely suff'ring staine by him: for him
Shall flye out of it selfe, nor sleepe, nor sanctuary,
Being naked, sicke; nor Phane, nor Capitoll,
The Prayers of Priests, nor times of Sacrifice:
Embarquements all of Fury, shall lift vp
Their rotten Priuiledge, and Custome 'gainst
My hate to *Martius*. Where I finde him, were it
At home, vpon my Brothers Guard, euen there
Against the hospitable Canon, would I
Wash my fierce hand in's heart. Go you to th'Citie,
Learne how 'tis held, and what they are that must
Be Hostages for Rome.

Soul. Will not you go?

Auf. I am attended at the Cyprus groue. I pray you
('Tis South the City Mils) bring me word thither
How the world goes: that to the pace of it
I may spurre on my iourney.

Soul. I shall sir.

Actus Secundus.

*Enter Menenius with the two Tribunes of the
people, Sicinius & Brutus.*

Men. The Augurer tels me, wee shall haue Newes to night.

Bru. Good or bad?

Men. Not according to the prayer of the people, for they loue not *Martius*.

Sicin. Nature teaches Beasts to know their Friends.

Men. Pray you, who does the Wolfe loue?

Sicin. The Lambe.

Men. I, to deuour him, as the hungry Plebeians would the Noble *Martius*.

Bru. He's a Lambe indeed, that baes like a Beare.

Men. Hee's a Beare indeede, that liues like a Lambe. You two are old men, tell me one thing that I shall aske you.

Both. Well sir.

Men. In what enormity is *Martius* poore in, that you two haue not in abundance?

Bru. He's poore in no one fault, but stor'd withall.

Sicin. Especially in Pride.

Bru. And topping all others in boasting.

Men. This is strange now: Do you two know, how you are censured heere in the City, I mean of vs a'th'right hand File, do you?

Both. Why? ho ware we censur'd?

Men. Because you talke of Pride now, will you not be angry.

Both. Well, well sir, well.

Men. Why 'tis no great matter: for a very little theefe of Occasion, will rob you of a great deale of Patience: Giue your dispositions the reines, and bee angry at your pleasures (at the least) if you take it as a pleasure to you, in being so: you blame *Martius* for being proud.

Brut. We do it not alone, sir.

Men. I know you can doe very little alone, for your helpes are many, or else your actions would growe wondrous single: your abilities are to Infant-like, for dooing much alone. You talke of Pride: Oh, that you could turn your eyes toward the Napes of your neckes, and make but an Interiour suruey of your good selues. Oh that you could.

Both. What then sir?

Men. Why then you should discouer a brace of vnmeriting, proud, violent, testie Magistrates (alias Fooles) as any in Rome.

Sicin. Menenius, you are knowne well enough too.

Men. I am knowne to be a humorous *Patritian*, and one that loues a cup of hot Wine, with not a drop of alaying Tiber in't: Said, to be something imperfect in fauouring the first complaint, hasty and Tinder-like vppon, to triuiall motion: One, that conuerses more with the Buttocke of the night, then with the forhead of the morning. What I think, I vtter, and spend my malice in my breath. Meeting two such Weales men as you are (I cannot call you *Licurgusses*,) if the drinke you giue me, touch my Palat aduersly, I make a crooked face at it, I can say, your Worshippes haue deliuer'd the matter well, when I finde the Asse in compound, with the Maior part of your syllables. And though I must be content to beare with those, that say you are reuerend graue men, yet they lye deadly, that tell you haue good faces, if you see this in the Map of my Microcosme, followes it that I am knowne well enough too? What harme can your beesome Conspectuities gleane out of this Cherracter, if I be knowne well enough too.

Bru. Come sir come, we know you well enough.

Menen. You know neither mee, your selues, nor any thing: you are ambitious, for poore knaues cappes and legges: you weare out a good wholesome Forenoone, in hearing a cause betweene an Orendge wife, and a Forsetseller, and then reiourne the Controuersie of three-pence to a second day of Audience. When you are hearing a matter betweene party and party, if you chaunce to bee pinch'd with the Collicke, you make faces like Mummers, set vp the bloodie Flagge against all Patience, and in roaring for a Chamber-pot, dismisse the Controuersie bleeding, the more intangled by your hearing: All the peace you make in their Cause, is calling both the parties Knaues. You are a payre of strange ones.

Bru. Come, come, you are well vnderstood to bee a perfecter gyber for the Table, then a necessary Bencher in the Capitoll.

Men. Our very Priests must become Mockers, if they shall encounter such ridiculous Subiects as you are, when you speake best vnto the purpose. It is not woorth the wagging of your Beards, and your Beards deserue not so honourable a graue, as to stuffe a Botchers Cushion, or to be intomb'd in an Asses Packe-saddle; yet you must bee saying, *Martius* is proud: who in a cheape estimation, is worth all your predecessors, since *Deucalion*, though peraduenture some of the best of 'em were hereditarie hangmen. Godden to your Worships, more of your conuersation would infect my Braine, being the Heardsmen of the Beastly Plebeans. I will be bold to take my leaue of you.

Bru. and Scic.   *Aside.*
                                                    Enter

The Tragedie of Coriolanus.

Enter Volumina, Virgilia, and Valeria.

How now (my as faire as Noble) Ladyes, and the Moone were shee Earthly, no Nobler; whither doe you follow your Eyes so fast?

Volum. Honorable *Menenius*, my Boy *Martius* approches: for the loue of *Iuno* let's goe.

Menen. Ha? *Martius* comming home?

Volum. I, worthy *Menenius*, and with most prosperous approbation.

Menen. Take my Cappe *Iupiter*, and I thanke thee: hoo, *Martius* comming home?

2.Ladies. Nay, 'tis true.

Volum. Looke, here's a Letter from him, the State hath another, his Wife another, and (I thinke) there's one at home for you.

Menen. I will make my very house reele to night: A Letter for me?

Virgil. Yes certaine, there's a Letter for you, I saw't.

Menen. A Letter for me? it giues me an Estate of seuen yeeres health; in which time, I will make a Lippe at the Physician: The most soueraigne Prescription in *Galen*, is but Emperickqutique; and to this Preseruatiue, of no better report then a Horse-drench. Is he not wounded? he was wont to come home wounded?

Virgil. Oh no, no, no.

Volum. Oh, he is wounded, I thanke the Gods for't.

Menen. So doe I too, if it be not too much: brings a Victorie in his Pocket? the wounds become him.

Volum. On's Browes: *Menenius*, hee comes the third time home with the Oaken Garland.

Menen. Ha's he disciplin'd *Auffidius* soundly?

Volum. *Titus Lartius* writes, they fought together, but *Auffidius* got off.

Menen. And 'twas time for him too, Ile warrant him that: and he had stay'd by him, I would not haue been so fiddious'd, for all the Chests in Carioles, and the Gold that's in them. Is the Senate possest of this?

Volum. Good Ladies let's goe. Yes, yes, yes: The Senate ha's Letters from the Generall, wherein hee giues my Sonne the whole Name of the Warre: he hath in this action out-done his former deeds doubly.

Valer. In troth, there's wondrous things spoke of him.

Menen. Wondrous: I, I warrant you, and not without his true purchasing.

Virgil. The Gods graunt them true.

Volum. True? pow waw.

Mene. True? Ile be sworne they are true: where is hee wounded, God saue your good Worships? *Martius* is comming home: hee ha's more cause to be prowd: where is he wounded?

Volum. Ith' Shoulder, and ith' left Arme: there will be large Cicatrices to shew the People, when hee shall stand for his place: he receiued in the repulse of *Tarquin* seuen hurts ith' Body.

Mene. One ith' Neck, and two ith' Thigh, there's nine that I know.

Volum. Hee had, before this last Expedition, twentie fiue Wounds vpon him.

Mene. Now it's twentie seuen; euery gash was an Enemies Graue. Hearke, the Trumpets.

A showt, and flourish.

Volum. These are the Vshers of *Martius*:
Before him, hee carryes Noyse;
And behinde him, hee leaues Teares:
Death, that darke Spirit, in's neruie Arme doth lye,
Which being aduanc'd, declines, and then men dye.

A Sennet. Trumpets sound.
Enter Cominius the Generall, and Titus Latius: be-
tweene them Coriolanus, crown'd with an Oaken
Garland, with Captaines and Soul-
diers, and a Herauld.

Herauld. Know Rome, that all alone *Martius* did fight
Within Corioles Gates: where he hath wonne,
With Fame, a Name to *Martius Caius*:
These in honor followes *Martius Caius Coriolanus*.
Welcome to Rome, renowned *Coriolanus*.

Sound. Flourish.

All. Welcome to Rome, renowned *Coriolanus*.

Coriol. No more of this, it does offend my heart: pray now no more.

Com. Looke, Sir, your Mother.

Coriol. Oh! you haue, I know, petition'd all the Gods for my prosperitie. *Kneeles.*

Volum. Nay, my good Souldier, vp;
My gentle *Martius*, worthy *Caius*,
And by deed-atchieuing Honor newly nam'd,
What is it (*Coriolanus*) must I call thee?
But oh, thy Wife.

Corio. My gracious silence, hayle:
Would'st thou haue laugh'd, had I come Coffin'd home,
That weep'st to see me triumph? Ah my deare,
Such eyes the Widowes in Carioles were,
And Mothers that lacke Sonnes.

Mene. Now the Gods Crowne thee.

Com. And liue you yet? Oh my sweet Lady, pardon.

Volum. I know not where to turne.
Oh welcome home: and welcome Generall,
And y'are welcome all.

Mene. A hundred thousand Welcomes:
I could weepe, and I could laugh,
I am light, and heauie; welcome:
A Curse begin at very root on's heart,
That is not glad to see thee.
You are three, that Rome should dote on:
Yet by the faith of men, we haue
Some old Crab-trees here at home,
That will not be grafted to your Rallish.
Yet welcome Warriors:
Wee call a Nettle, but a Nettle;
And the faults of fooles, but folly.

Com. Euer right.

Cor. *Menenius*, euer, euer.

Herauld. Giue way there, and goe on.

Cor. Your Hand, and yours?
Ere in our owne house I doe shade my Head,
The good Patricians must be visited,
From whom I haue receiu'd not onely greetings,
But with them, change of Honors.

Volum. I haue liued,
To see inherited my very Wishes,
And the Buildings of my Fancie:
Onely there's one thing wanting,
Which (I doubt not) but our Rome
Will cast vpon thee.

Cor. Know, good Mother,
I had rather be their seruant in my way,
Then sway with them in theirs.

Com. On, to the Capitall. *Flourish. Cornets.*

Exeunt in State, as before.

Enter

Enter Brutus and Scicinius.

Bru. All tongues speake of him, and the bleared sights
Are spectacled to see him. Your pratling Nurse
Into a rapture lets her Baby crie,
While she chats him: the Kitchin *Malkin* pinnes
Her richest Lockram 'bout her reechie necke,
Clambring the Walls to eye him:
Stalls, Bulkes, Windowes, are smother'd vp,
Leades fill'd, and Ridges hors'd
With variable Complexions; all agreeing
In earnestnesse to see him: seld-showne Flamins
Doe presse among the popular Throngs, and puffe
To winne a vulgar station: our veyl'd Dames
Commit the Warre of White and Damaske
In their nicely gawded Cheekes, toth' wanton spoyle
Of *Phœbus* burning Kisses: such a poother,
As if that whatsoeuer God, who leades him,
Were slyly crept into his humane powers,
And gaue him gracefull posture.

Scicin. On the suddaine, I warrant him Consull.

Brutus. Then our Office may, during his power, goe sleepe.

Scicin. He cannot temp'rately transport his Honors,
From where he should begin, and end, but will
Lose those he hath wonne.

Brutus. In that there's comfort.

Scici. Doubt not,
The Commoners, for whom we stand, but they
Vpon their ancient mallice, will forget
With the least cause, these his new Honors,
Which that he will giue them, make I as little question,
As he is prowd to doo't.

Brutus. I heard him sweare,
Were he to stand for Consull, neuer would he
Appeare i'th' Market place, nor on him put
The Naples Vesture of Humilitie,
Nor shewing (as the manner is) his Wounds
Toth' People, begge their stinking Breaths.

Scicin. 'Tis right.

Brutus. It was his word:
Oh he would misse it, rather then carry it,
But by the suite of the Gentry to him,
And the desire of the Nobles.

Scicin. I wish no better, then haue him hold that purpose, and to put it in execution.

Brutus. 'Tis most like he will.

Scicin. It shall be to him then, as our good wills; a sure destruction.

Brutus. So it must fall out
To him, or our Authorities, for an end.
We must suggest the People, in what hatred
He still hath held them: that to's power he would
Haue made them Mules, silenc'd their Pleaders,
And dispropertied their Freedomes; holding them,
In humane Action, and Capacitie,
Of no more Soule, nor fitnesse for the World,
Then Cammels in their Warre, who haue their Prouand
Onely for bearing Burthens, and sore blowes
For sinking vnder them.

Scicin. This (as you say) suggested,
At some time, when his soaring Insolence
Shall teach the People, which time shall not want,
If he be put vpon't, and that's as easie,
As to set Dogges on Sheepe, will be his fire
To kindle their dry Stubble: and their Blaze
Shall darken him for euer.

Enter a Messenger.

Brutus. What's the matter?

Mess. You are sent for to the Capitoll:
'Tis thought, that *Martius* shall be Consull:
I haue seene the dumbe men throng to see him,
And the blind to heare him speak: Matrons flong Gloues,
Ladies and Maids their Scarffes, and Handkerchers,
Vpon him as he pass'd: the Nobles bended
As to *Ioues* Statue, and the Commons made
A Shower, and Thunder, with their Caps, and Showts:
I neuer saw the like.

Brutus. Let's to the Capitoll,
And carry with vs Eares and Eyes for th' time,
But Hearts for the euent.

Scicin. Haue with you.   *Exeunt.*

*Enter two Officers, to lay Cushions, as it were,
in the Capitoll.*

1. *Off.* Come, come, they are almost here: how many stand for Consulships?

2. *Off.* Three, they say: but 'tis thought of euery one, *Coriolanus* will carry it.

1. *Off.* That's a braue fellow: but hee's vengeance prowd, and loues not the common people.

2. *Off.* 'Faith, there hath beene many great men that haue flatter'd the people, who ne're loued them; and there be many that they haue loued, they know not wherefore: so that if they loue they know not why, they hate vpon no better a ground. Therefore, for *Coriolanus* neyther to care whether they loue, or hate him, manifests the true knowledge he ha's in their disposition, and out of his Noble carelesnesse lets them plainely see't.

1. *Off.* If he did not care whether he had their loue, or no, hee waued indifferently, 'twixt doing them neyther good, nor harme: but hee seekes their hate with greater deuotion, then they can render it him; and leaues nothing vndone, that may fully discouer him their opposite. Now to seeme to affect the mallice and displeasure of the People, is as bad, as that which he dislikes, to flatter them for their loue.

2. *Off.* Hee hath deserued worthily of his Countrey, and his assent is not by such easie degrees as those, who hauing beene supple and courteous to the People, Bonnetted, without any further deed, to haue them at all into their estimation, and report: but hee hath so planted his Honors in their Eyes, and his actions in their Hearts, that for their Tongues to be silent, and not confesse so much, were a kinde of ingratefull Iniurie: to report otherwise, were a Mallice, that giuing it selfe the Lye, would plucke reproofe and rebuke from euery Eare that heard it.

1. *Off.* No more of him, hee's a worthy man: make way, they are comming.

*A Sennet. Enter the Patricians, and the Tribunes of
the People, Lictors before them: Coriolanus, Menenius, Cominius the Consul. Scicinius and Brutus
take their places by themselues: Coriolanus stands.*

Menen. Hauing determin'd of the Volces,
And to send for *Titus Lartius*: it remaines,
As the maine Point of this our after-meeting,

To gratifie his Noble seruice, that hath
Thus stood for his Countrey. Therefore please you,
Most reuerend and graue Elders, to desire
The present Consull, and last Generall,
In our well-found Successes, to report
A little of that worthy Worke, perform'd
By *Martius Caius Coriolanus*: whom
We met here, both to thanke, and to remember,
With Honors like himselfe.

1. Sen. Speake, good *Cominius*:
Leaue nothing out for length, and make vs thinke
Rather our states defectiue for requitall,
Then we to stretch it out. Masters a'th' People,
We doe request your kindest eares: and after
Your louing motion toward the common Body,
To yeeld what passes here.

Scicin. We are conuented vpon a pleasing Treatie, and
haue hearts inclinable to honor and aduance the Theame
of our Assembly.

Brutus. Which the rather wee shall be blest to doe, if
he remember a kinder value of the People, then he hath
hereto priz'd them at.

Menen. That's off, that's off: I would you rather had
been silent: Please you to heare *Cominius* speake?

Brutus. Most willingly: but yet my Caution was
more pertinent then the rebuke you giue it.

Menen. He loues your People, but tye him not to be
their Bed-fellow: Worthie *Cominius* speake.

Coriolanus rises, and offers to goe away.
Nay, keepe your place.

Senat. Sit *Coriolanus*: neuer shame to heare
What you haue Nobly done.

Coriol. Your Honors pardon:
I had rather haue my Wounds to heale againe,
Then heare say how I got them.

Brutus. Sir, I hope my words dis-bench'd you not?

Coriol. No Sir: yet oft,
When blowes haue made me stay, I fled from words.
You sooth'd not, therefore hurt not: but your People,
I loue them as they weigh—

Menen. Pray now sit downe.

Corio. I had rather haue one scratch my Head i'th' Sun,
When the Alarum were strucke, then idly sit
To heare my Nothings monster'd. *Exit Coriolanus*

Menen. Masters of the People,
Your multiplying Spawne, how can he flatter?
That's thousand to one good one, when you now see
He had rather venture all his Limbes for Honor,
Then on ones Eares to heare it. Proceed *Cominius*.

Com. I shall lacke voyce: the deeds of *Coriolanus*
Should not be vtter'd feebly: it is held,
That Valour is the chiefest Vertue,
And most dignifies the hauer: if it be,
The man I speake of, cannot in the World
Be singly counter-poys'd. At sixteene yeeres,
When *Tarquin* made a Head for Rome, he fought
Beyond the marke of others: our then Dictator,
Whom with all prayse I point at, saw him fight,
When with his Amazonian Shinne he droue
The brizled Lippes before him: he bestrid
An o're-prest Roman, and i'th' Consuls view
Slew three Opposers: *Tarquins* selfe he met,
And strucke him on his Knee: in that dayes feates,
When he might act the Woman in the Scene,
He prou'd best man i'th' field, and for his meed
Was Brow-bound with the Oake. His Pupill age

Man-entred thus, he waxed like a Sea,
And in the brunt of seuenteene Battailes since,
He lurcht all Swords of the Garland: for this last,
Before, and in Corioles, let me say
I cannot speake him home: he stopt the flyers,
And by his rare example made the Coward
Turne terror into sport: as Weeds before
A Vessell vnder sayle, so men obey'd,
And fell below his Stem: his Sword, Deaths stampe,
Where it did marke, it tooke from face to foot:
He was a thing of Blood, whose euery motion
Was tim'd with dying Cryes: alone he entred
The mortall Gate of th' Citie, which he painted
With shunlesse destinie: aydelesse came off,
And with a sudden re-inforcement strucke
Carioles like a Planet: now all's his,
When by and by the dinne of Warre gan pierce
His readie sence: then straight his doubled Spirit
Requickned what in flesh was fatigate,
And to the Battaile came he, where he did
Runne reeking o're the liues of men, as if 'twere
A perpetuall spoyle: and till we call'd
Both Field and Citie ours, he neuer stood
To ease his Brest with panting.

Menen. Worthy man.

Senat. He cannot but with measure fit the Honors
which we deuise him.

Com. Our spoyles he kickt at,
And look'd vpon things precious, as they were
The common Muck of the World: he couets lesse
Then Miserie it selfe would giue, rewards his deeds
With doing them, and is content
To spend the time, to end it.

Menen. Hee's right Noble, let him be call'd for.

Senat. Call *Coriolanus*.

Off. He doth appeare.

Enter Coriolanus.

Menen. The Senate, *Coriolanus*, are well pleas'd to make
thee Consull.

Corio. I doe owe them still my Life, and Seruices.

Menen. It then remaines, that you doe speake to the
People.

Corio. I doe beseech you,
Let me o're-leape that custome: for I cannot
Put on the Gowne, stand naked, and entreat them
For my Wounds sake, to giue their suffrage:
Please you that I may passe this doing.

Scicin. Sir, the People must haue their Voyces,
Neyther will they bate one iot of Ceremonie.

Menen. Put them not too't:
Pray you goe fit you to the Custome,
And take to you, as your Predecessors haue,
Your Honor with your forme.

Corio. It is a part that I shall blush in acting,
And might well be taken from the People.

Brutus. Marke you that.

Corio. To brag vnto them, thus I did, and thus
Shew them th' vnaking Skarres, which I should hide,
As if I had receiu'd them for the hyre
Of their breath onely.

Menen. Doe not stand vpon't:
We recommend to you Tribunes of the People
Our purpose to them, and to our Noble Consull
Wish we all Ioy, and Honor.

Senat. To

Senat. To *Coriolanus* come all ioy and Honor.
Flourish Cornets.
Then Exeunt. Manet Sicinius and Brutus.

Bru. You see how he intends to vse the people.

Scicin. May they perceiue's intent: he wil require them
As if he did contemne what he requested,
Should be in them to giue.

Bru. Come, wee'l informe them
Of our proceedings heere on th'Market place,
I know they do attend vs.

Enter seuen or eight Citizens.

1. Cit. Once if he do require our voyces, wee ought not to deny him.

2. Cit. We may Sir if we will.

3. Cit. We haue power in our selues to do it, but it is a power that we haue no power to do: For, if hee shew vs his wounds, and tell vs his deeds, we are to put our tongues into those wounds, and speake for them: So if he tel vs his Noble deeds, we must also tell him our Noble acceptance of them. Ingratitude is monstrous, and for the multitude to be ingratefull, were to make a Monster of the multitude; of the which, we being members, should bring our selues to be monstrous members.

1. Cit. And to make vs no better thought of a little helpe will serue: for once we stood vp about the Corne, he himselfe stucke not to call vs the many-headed Multitude.

3. Cit. We haue beene call'd so of many, not that our heads are some browne, some blacke, some Abram, some bald; but that our wits are so diuersly Coulord; and truely I thinke, if all our wittes were to issue out of one Scull, they would flye East, West, North, South, and their consent of one direct way, should be at once to all the points a'th Compasse.

2. Cit. Thinke you so? Which way do you iudge my wit would flye.

3. Cit. Nay your wit will not so soone out as another mans will, 'tis strongly wadg'd vp in a blocke-head: but if it were at liberty, 'twould sure Southward.

2. Cit. Why that way?

3. Cit. To loose it selfe in a Fogge, where being three parts melted away with rotten Dewes, the fourth would returne for Conscience sake, to helpe to get thee a Wife.

2. Cit. You are neuer without your trickes, you may, you may.

3. Cit. Are you all resolu'd to giue your voyces? But that's no matter, the greater part carries it, I say. If hee would incline to the people, there was neuer a worthier man.

Enter Coriolanus in a gowne of Humility, with Menenius.

Heere he comes, and in the Gowne of humility, marke his behauiour: we are not to stay altogether, but to come by him where he stands, by ones, by twoes, & by threes. He's to make his requests by particulars, wherein euerie one of vs ha's a single Honor, in giuing him our own voices with our owne tongues, therefore follow me, and Ile direct you how you shall go by him.

All. Content, content.

Men. Oh Sir, you are not right: haue you not knowne The worthiest men haue don't?

Corio. What must I say, I pray Sir?
Plague vpon't, I cannot bring
My tongue to such a pace. Looke Sir, my wounds,
I got them in my Countries Seruice, when
Some certaine of your Brethren roar'd, and ranne
From th'noise of our owne Drummes.

Menen. Oh me the Gods, you must not speak of that, You must desire them to thinke vpon you.

Coriol. Thinke vpon me? Hang 'em,
I would they would forget me, like the Vertues
Which our Diuines lose by em.

Men. You'l marre all,
Ile leaue you: Pray you speake to em, I pray you
In wholsome manner. *Exit*

Enter three of the Citizens.

Corio. Bid them wash their Faces,
And keepe their teeth cleane: So, heere comes a brace,
You know the cause (Sir) of my standing heere.

3 Cit. We do Sir, tell vs what hath brought you too't.

Corio. Mine owne desert.

2 Cit. Your owne desert.

Corio. I, but mine owne desire.

3 Cit. How not your owne desire?

Corio. No Sir, 'twas neuer my desire yet to trouble the poore with begging.

3 Cit. You must thinke if we giue you any thing, we hope to gaine by you.

Corio. Well then I pray, your price a'th Consulship.

1 Cit. The price is, to aske it kindly.

Corio. Kindly sir, I pray let me ha't: I haue wounds to shew you, which shall bee yours in priuate: your good voice Sir, what say you?

2 Cit. You shall ha't worthy Sir.

Corio. A match Sir, there's in all two worthie voyces begg'd: I haue your Almes, Adieu.

3 Cit. But this is something odde.

2 Cit. And 'twere to giue againe: but 'tis no matter.
Exeunt. *Enter two other Citizens.*

Coriol. Pray you now, if it may stand with the tune of your voices, that I may bee Consull, I haue heere the Customarie Gowne.

1. You haue deserued Nobly of your Country, and you haue not deserued Nobly.

Coriol. Your Ænigma.

1. You haue bin a scourge to her enemies, you haue bin a Rod to her Friends, you haue not indeede loued the Common people.

Coriol. You should account mee the more Vertuous, that I haue not bin common in my Loue, I will sir flatter my sworne Brother the people to earne a deerer estimation of them, 'tis a condition they account gentle: & since the wisedome of their choice, is rather to haue my Hat, then my Heart, I will practice the insinuating nod, and be off to them most counterfetly, that is sir, I will counterfet the bewitchment of some popular man, and giue it bountifull to the desirers: Therefore beseech you, I may be Consull.

2. Wee hope to finde you our friend: and therefore giue you our voices heartily.

1. You haue receyued, many wounds for your Countrey.

Coriol. I wil not Seale your knowledge with shewing them. I will make much of your voyces, and so trouble you no farther.

Both. The Gods giue you ioy Sir heartily.

Coriol. Most sweet Voyces:
Better it is to dye, better to sterue,
Then craue the higher, which first we do deserue.
Why in this Wooluish tongue should I stand heere,
To begge of Hob and Dicke, that does appeere

Their

Their needlesse Vouches: Custome calls me too't.
What Custome wills in all things, should we doo't?
The Dust on antique Time would lye vnswept,
And mountainous Error be too highly heapt,
For Truth to o're-peere. Rather then foole it so,
Let the high Office and the Honor go
To one that would doe thus. I am halfe through,
The one part suffered, the other will I doe.

Enter three Citizens more.

Here come moe Voyces.
Your Voyces? for your Voyces I haue fought,
Watcht for your Voyces: for your Voyces, beare
Of Wounds, two dozen odde: Battailes thrice six
I haue seene, and heard of: for your Voyces,
Haue done many things, some lesse, some more:
Your Voyces? Indeed I would be Consull.

1.Cit. Hee ha's done Nobly, and cannot goe without any honest mans Voyce.

2.Cit. Therefore let him be Consull: the Gods giue him ioy, and make him good friend to the People.

All. Amen, Amen. God saue thee, Noble Consull.

Corio. Worthy Voyces.

Enter Menenius, with Brutus and Sicinius.

Mene. You haue stood your Limitation:
And the Tribunes endue you with the Peoples Voyce,
Remaines, that in th'Officiall Markes inuested,
You anon doe meet the Senate.

Corio. Is this done?

Scicin. The Custome of Request you haue discharg'd:
The People doe admit you, and are summon'd
To meet anon, vpon your approbation.

Corio. Where? at the Senate-house?

Scicin. There, *Coriolanus*.

Corio. May I change these Garments?

Scicin. You may, Sir.

Cori. That Ile straight do: and knowing my selfe againe,
Repayre toth' Senate-house.

Mene. Ile keepe you company. Will you along?

Brut. We stay here for the People.

Scicin. Fare you well.   *Exeunt Coriol. and Mene.*
He ha's it now: and by his Lookes, me thinkes,
'Tis warme at's heart.

Brut. With a prowd heart he wore his humble Weeds:
Will you dismisse the People?

Enter the Plebeians.

Scici. How now, my Masters, haue you chose this man?

1.Cit. He ha's our Voyces, Sir.

Brut. We pray the Gods, he may deserue your loues.

2.Cit. Amen, Sir: to my poore vnworthy notice,
He mock'd vs, when he begg'd our Voyces.

3.Cit. Certainely, he flowted vs downe-right.

1.Cit. No, 'tis his kind of speech, he did not mock vs.

2.Cit. Not one amongst vs, saue your selfe, but sayes
He vs'd vs scornefully: he should haue shew'd vs
His Marks of Merit, Wounds receiu'd for's Countrey.

Scicin. Why so he did, I am sure.

All. No, no: no man saw 'em.

3.Cit. Hee said hee had Wounds,
Which he could shew in priuate:
And with his Hat, thus wauing it in scorne,
I would be Consull, sayes he: aged Custome,
But by your Voyces, will not so permit me.
Your Voyces therefore: when we graunted that,
Here was, I thanke you for your Voyces, thanke you

Your most sweet Voyces: now you haue left your Voyces,
I haue no further with you. Was not this mockerie?

Scicin. Why eyther were you ignorant to see't?
Or seeing it, of such Childish friendlinesse,
To yeeld your Voyces?

Brut. Could you not haue told him,
As you were lesson'd: When he had no Power,
But was a pettie seruant to the State,
He was your Enemie, euer spake against
Your Liberties, and the Charters that you beare
I'th' Body of the Weale: and now arriuing
A place of Potencie, and sway o'th' State,
If he should still malignantly remaine
Fast Foe toth' *Plebeij,* your Voyces might
Be Curses to your selues. You should haue said,
That as his worthy deeds did clayme no lesse
Then what he stood for: so his gracious nature
Would thinke vpon you, for your Voyces,
And translate his Mallice towards you, into Loue,
Standing your friendly Lord.

Scicin. Thus to haue said,
As you were fore-aduis'd, had toucht his Spirit,
And try'd his Inclination: from him pluckt
Eyther his gracious Promise, which you might
As cause had call'd you vp, haue held him to;
Or else it would haue gall'd his surly nature,
Which easily endures not Article,
Tying him to ought, so putting him to Rage,
You should haue ta'ne th'aduantage of his Choller,
And pass'd him vnelected.

Brut. Did you perceiue,
He did sollicite you in free Contempt,
When he did need your Loues: and doe you thinke,
That his Contempt shall not be brusing to you,
When he hath power to crush? Why, had your Bodyes
No Heart among you? Or had you Tongues, to cry
Against the Rectorship of Iudgement?

Scicin. Haue you, ere now, deny'd the asker:
And now againe, of him that did not aske, but mock,
Bestow your su'd-for Tongues?

3.Cit. Hee's not confirm'd, we may deny him yet.

2.Cit. And will deny him:
Ile haue fiue hundred Voyces of that sound.

1.Cit. I twice fiue hundred, & their friends, to piece 'em.

Brut. Get you hence instantly, and tell those friends,
They haue chose a Consull, that will from them take
Their Liberties, make them of no more Voyce
Then Dogges, that are as often beat for barking,
As therefore kept to doe so.

Scici. Let them assemble: and on a safer Iudgement,
All reuoke your ignorant election: Enforce his Pride,
And his old Hate vnto you: besides, forget not
With what Contempt he wore the humble Weed,
How in his Suit he scorn'd you: but your Loues,
Thinking vpon his Seruices, tooke from you
Th'apprehension of his present portance,
Which most gibingly, vngrauely, he did fashion
After the inueterate Hate he beares you.

Brut. Lay a fault on vs, your Tribunes,
That we labour'd (no impediment betweene)
But that you must cast your Election on him.

Scici. Say you chose him, more after our commandment,
Then as guided by your owne true affections, and that
Your Minds pre-occupy'd with what you rather must do,
Then what you should, made you against the graine
To Voyce him Consull. Lay the fault on vs.

Brut. I, spare vs not: Say, we read Lectures to you,
How youngly he began to serue his Countrey,
How long continued, and what stock he springs of,
The Noble House o'th' *Martians*: from whence came
That *Ancus Martius*, *Numaes* Daughters Sonne:
Who after great *Hostilius* here was King,
Of the same House *Publius* and *Quintus* were,
That our best Water, brought by Conduits hither,
And Nobly nam'd, so twice being Censor,
Was his great Ancestor.

Scicin. One thus descended,
That hath beside well in his person wrought,
To be set high in place, we did commend
To your remembrances: but you haue found,
Skaling his present bearing with his past,
That hee's your fixed enemie; and reuoke
Your suddaine approbation.

Brut. Say you ne're had don't,
(Harpe on that still) but by our putting on:
And presently, when you haue drawne your number,
Repaire toth' Capitoll.

All. We will so: almost all repent in their election.
Exeunt Plebeians.

Brut. Let them goe on:
This Mutinie were better put in hazard,
Then stay past doubt, for greater:
If, as his nature is, he fall in rage
With their refusall, both obserue and answer
The vantage of his anger.

Scicin. Toth' Capitoll, come:
We will be there before the streame o'th' People:
And this shall seeme, as partly 'tis, their owne,
Which we haue goaded on-ward. *Exeunt.*

Actus Tertius.

Cornets. Enter Coriolanus, Menenius, all the Gentry,
Cominius, Titus Latius, and other Senators.

Corio. *Tullus Auffidius* then had made new head.
Latius. He had my Lord, and that it was which caus'd
Our swifter Composition.

Corio. So then the Volces stand but as at first,
Readie when time shall prompt them, to make roade
Vpon's againe.

Com. They are worne (Lord Consull) so,
That we shall hardly in our ages see
Their Banners waue againe.

Corio. Saw you *Auffidius*?
Latius. On safegard he came to me, and did curse
Against the Volces, for they had so vildly
Yeelded the Towne: he is retyred to Antium.

Corio. Spoke he of me?
Latius. He did, my Lord.
Corio. How? what?
Latius. How often he had met you Sword to Sword:
That of all things vpon the Earth, he hated
Your person most: That he would pawne his fortunes
To hopelesse restitution, so he might
Be call'd your Vanquisher.

Corio. At Antium liues he?
Latius. At Antium.
Corio. I wish I had a cause to seeke him there,
To oppose his hatred fully. Welcome home.
Enter Scicinius and Brutus.
Behold, these are the Tribunes of the People,
The Tongues o'th' Common Mouth, I do despise them:
For they doe pranke them in Authoritie,
Against all Noble sufferance.

Scicin. Passe no further.
Cor. Hah? what is that?
Brut. It will be dangerous to goe on--No further.
Corio. What makes this change?
Mene. The matter?
Com. Hath he not pass'd the Noble, and the Common?
Brut. Cominius, no.
Corio. Haue I had Childrens Voyces?
Senat. Tribunes giue way, he shall toth' Market place.
Brut. The People are incens'd against him.
Scicin. Stop, or all will fall in broyle.
Corio. Are these your Heard?
Must these haue Voyces, that can yeeld them now,
And straight disclaim their toungs? what are your Offices?
You being their Mouthes, why rule you not their Teeth?
Haue you not set them on?

Mene. Be calme, be calme.
Corio. It is a purpos'd thing, and growes by Plot,
To curbe the will of the Nobilitie:
Suffer't, and liue with such as cannot rule,
Nor euer will be ruled.

Brut. Call't not a Plot:
The People cry you mockt them: and of late,
When Corne was giuen them *gratis*, you repin'd,
Scandal'd the Suppliants: for the People, call'd them
Time-pleasers, flatterers, foes to Noblenesse.

Corio. Why this was knowne before.
Brut. Not to them all.
Corio. Haue you inform'd them sithence?
Brut. How? I informe them?
Com. You are like to doe such businesse.
Brut. Not vnlike each way to better yours.
Corio. Why then should I be Consull? by yond Clouds
Let me deserue so ill as you, and make me
Your fellow Tribune.

Scicin. You shew too much of that,
For which the People stirre: if you will passe
To where you are bound, you must enquire your way,
Which you are out of, with a gentler spirit,
Or neuer be so Noble as a Consull,
Nor yoake with him for Tribune.

Mene. Let's be calme.
Com. The People are abus'd: set on, this paltring
Becomes not Rome: nor ha's *Coriolanus*
Deseru'd this so dishonor'd Rub, layd falsely
I'th' plaine Way of his Merit.

Corio. Tell me of Corne: this was my speech,
And I will speak't againe.

Mene. Not now, not now.
Senat. Not in this heat, Sir, now.
Corio. Now as I liue, I will.
My Nobler friends, I craue their pardons:
For the mutable ranke-sented Meynie,
Let them regard me, as I doe not flatter,
And therein behold themselues: I say againe,
In soothing them, we nourish 'gainst our Senate
The Cockle of Rebellion, Insolence, Sedition,
Which we our selues haue plowed for, sow'd, & scatter'd,
By mingling them with vs, the honor'd Number,
Who lack not Vertue, no, nor Power, but that
Which they haue giuen to Beggers.

Mene. Well, no more.
Senat. No more words, we beseech you.
Corio. How? no more?

The Tragedie of Coriolanus.

As for my Country, I haue shed my blood,
Not fearing outward force: So shall my Lungs
Coine words till their decay, against those Meazels
Which we disdaine should Tetter vs, yet sought
The very way to catch them.

  Bru. You speake a'th'people, as if you were a God,
To punish; Not a man, of their Infirmity.

  Sicin. 'Twere well we let the people know't.

  Mene. What, what? His Choller?

  Cor. Choller? Were I as patient as the midnight sleep,
By Ioue, 'twould be my minde.

  Sicin. It is a minde that shall remain a poison
Where it is: not poyson any further.

  Corio. Shall remaine?
Heare you this Triton of the *Minnoues*? Marke you
His absolute Shall?

  Com. 'Twas from the Cannon.

  Cor. Shall? O God! but most vnwise Patricians: why
You graue, but wreakleffe Senators, haue you thus
Giuen Hidra heere to choose an Officer,
That with his peremptory Shall, being but
The horne, and noise o'th' Monsters, wants not spirit
To say, hee'l turne your Current in a ditch,
And make your Channell his? If he haue power,
Then vale your Ignorance: If none, awake
Your dangerous Lenity: If you are Learn'd,
Be not as common Fooles; if you are not,
Let them haue Cushions by you. You are Plebeians,
If they be Senators: and they are no leffe,
When both your voices blended, the great'st taste
Most pallates theirs. They choose their Magistrate,
And such a one as he, who puts his Shall,
His popular Shall, against a grauer Bench
Then euer frown'd in Greece. By Ioue himselfe,
It makes the Consuls base; and my Soule akes
To know, when two Authorities are vp,
Neither Supreame; How soone Confusion
May enter 'twixt the gap of Both, and take
The one by th'other.

  Com. Well, on to'th'Market place.

  Corio. Who euer gaue that Counsell, to giue forth
The Corne a'th'Store-house gratis, as 'twas vs'd
Sometime in Greece.

  Mene. Well, well, no more of that.

  Cor. Thogh there the people had more absolute powre
I say they norisht disobedience: fed, the ruin of the State.

  Bru. Why shall the people giue
One that speakes thus, their voyce?

  Corio. Ile giue my Reasons,
More worthier then their Voyces. They know the Corne
Was not our recompence, resting well assur'd
They ne're did seruice for't; being prest to'th'Warre,
Euen when the Nauell of the State was touch'd,
They would not thred the Gates: This kinde of Seruice
Did not deserue Corne gratis. Being i'th'Warre,
There Mutinies and Reuolts, wherein they shew'd
Most Valour, spoke not for them. Th'Accusation
Which they haue often made against the Senate,
All cause vnborne, could neuer be the Natiue
Of our so franke Donation. Well, what then?
How shall this Bosome-multiplied, digest
The Senates Courtesie? Let deeds expresse
What's like to be their words, We did request it,
We are the greater pole, and in true feare
They gaue vs our demands. Thus we debase
The Nature of our Seats, and make the Rabble

Call our Cares, Feares; which will in time
Breake ope the Lockes a'th'Senate, and bring in
The Crowes to pecke the Eagles.

  Mene. Come enough.

  Bru. Enough, with ouer measure.

  Corio. No, take more.
What may be sworne by, both Diuine and Humane,
Seale what I end withall. This double worship,
Whereon part do's disdaine with cause, the other
Insult without all reason: where Gentry, Title, wisedom
Cannot conclude, but by the yea and no
Of generall Ignorance, it must omit
Reall Necessities, and giue way the while
To vnstable Slightnesse. Purpose so barr'd, it followes,
Nothing is done to purpose. Therefore beseech you,
You that will be lesse fearefull, then discreet,
That loue the fundamentall part of State
More then you doubt the change on't: That preferre
A Noble life, before a Long, and Wish,
To iumpe a Body with a dangerous Physicke,
That's sure of death without it: at once plucke out
The Multitudinous Tongue, let them not licke
The sweet which is their poyson. Your dishonor
Mangles true iudgement, and bereaues the State
Of that Integrity which should becom't:
Not hauing the power to do the good it would
For th'ill which doth controul't.

  Bru. Has said enough.

  Sicin. Ha's spoken like a Traitor, and shall answer
As Traitors do.

  Corio. Thou wretch, despight ore-whelme thee:
What should the people do with these bald Tribunes?
On whom depending, their obedience failes
To'th'greater Bench, in a Rebellion:
When what's not meet, but what must be, was Law,
Then were they chosen: in a better houre,
Let what is meet, be saide it must be meet,
And throw their power i'th'dust.

  Bru. Manifest Treason.

  Sicin. This a Consull? No.

Enter an Ædile.

  Bru. The Ediles hoe: Let him be apprehended:

  Sicin. Go call the people, in whose name my Selfe
Attach thee as a Traitorous Innouator:
A Foe to'th'publike Weale. Obey I charge thee,
And follow to thine answer.

  Corio. Hence old Goat.

  All. Wee'l Surety him.

  Com. Ag'd sir, hands off.

  Corio. Hence rotten thing, or I shall shake thy bones
Out of thy Garments.

  Sicin. Helpe ye Citizens.

Enter a rabble of Plebeians with the Ædiles.

  Mene. On both sides more respect.

  Sicin. Heere's hee, that would take from you all your
power.

  Bru. Seize him Ædiles.

  All. Downe with him, downe with him.

  2 Sen. Weapons, weapons, weapons:

They all bustle about Coriolanus.

Tribunes, Patricians, Citizens: what ho:
Sicinius, Brutus, Coriolanus, Citizens.

  All. Peace, peace, peace, stay, hold, peace.

  Mene. What is about to be? I am out of Breath,
Confusions neere, I cannot speake. You, Tribunes
To'th'people: *Coriolanus* patience: Speak good *Sicinius*.

Scici. Heare me, People peace.

All. Let's here our Tribune: peace, speake, speake, speake.

Scici. You are at point to lose your Liberties: *Martius* would haue all from you; *Martius*, Whom late you haue nam'd for Consull.

Mene. Fie, fie, fie, this is the way to kindle, not to quench.

Sena. To vnbuild the Citie, and to lay all flat.

Scici. What is the Citie, but the People?

All. True, the People are the Citie.

Brut. By the consent of all, we were establish'd the Peoples Magistrates.

All. You so remaine.

Mene. And so are like to doe.

Com. That is the way to lay the Citie flat, To bring the Roofe to the Foundation, And burie all, which yet distinctly raunges In heapes, and piles of Ruine.

Scici. This deserues Death.

Brut. Or let vs stand to our Authoritie, Or let vs lose it: we doe here pronounce, Vpon the part o'th' People, in whose power We were elected theirs, *Martius* is worthy Of present Death.

Scici. Therefore lay hold of him: Beare him to th' Rock Tarpeian, and from thence Into destruction cast him.

Brut. Ædiles seize him.

All Ple. Yeeld *Martius*, yeeld.

Mene. Heare me one word, beseech you Tribunes, heare me but a word.

Ædiles. Peace, peace.

Mene. Be that you seeme, truly your Countries friend, And temp'rately proceed to what you would Thus violently redresse.

Brut. Sir, those cold wayes, That seeme like prudent helpes, are very poysonous, Where the Disease is violent. Lay hands vpon him, And beare him to the Rock.   *Corio. drawes his Sword.*

Corio. No, Ile die here: There's some among you haue beheld me fighting, Come trie vpon your selues, what you haue seene me.

Mene. Downe with that Sword, Tribunes withdraw a while.

Brut. Lay hands vpon him.

Mene. Helpe *Martius*, helpe: you that be noble, helpe him young and old.

All. Downe with him, downe with him.   *Exeunt.*

In this Mutinie, the Tribunes, the Ædiles, and the People are beat in.

Mene. Goe, get you to our House: be gone, away, All will be naught else.

2. Sena. Get you gone.

Com. Stand fast, we haue as many friends as enemies.

Mene. Shall it be put to that?

Sena. The Gods forbid: I prythee noble friend, home to thy House; Leaue vs to cure this Cause.

Mene. For 'tis a Sore vpon vs, You cannot Tent your selfe: be gone, beseech you.

Corio. Come Sir, along with vs.

Mene. I would they were Barbarians, as they are, Though in Rome litter'd: not Romans, as they are not, Though calued i'th' Porch o'th' Capitoll: Be gone, put not your worthy Rage into your Tongue, One time will owe another.

Corio. On faire ground, I could beat fortie of them.

Mene. I could my selfe take vp a Brace o'th' best of them, yea, the two Tribunes.

Com. But now 'tis oddes beyond Arithmetick, And Manhood is call'd Foolerie, when it stands Against a falling Fabrick. Will you hence, Before the Tagge returne? whose Rage doth rend Like interrupted Waters, and o're-beare What they are vs'd to beare.

Mene. Pray you be gone: Ile trie whether my old Wit be in request With those that haue but little: this must be patcht With Cloth of any Colour.

Com. Nay, come away.   *Exeunt Coriolanus and Cominius.*

Patri. This man ha's marr'd his fortune.

Mene. His nature is too noble for the World: He would not flatter *Neptune* for his Trident, Or *Ioue*, for's power to Thunder: his Heart's his Mouth: What his Brest forges, that his Tongue must vent, And being angry, does forget that euer He heard the Name of Death.   *A Noyse within.*
Here's goodly worke.

Patri. I would they were a bed.

Mene. I would they were in Tyber.
What the vengeance, could he not speake 'em faire?

Enter Brutus and Sicinius with the rabble againe.

Sicin. Where is this Viper, That would depopulate the city, & be euery man himself.

Mene. You worthy Tribunes.

Sicin. He shall be throwne downe the Tarpeian rock With rigorous hands: he hath resisted Law, And therefore Law shall scorne him further Triall Then the seuerity of the publike Power, Which he so sets at naught.

1 Cit. He shall well know the Noble Tribunes are The peoples mouths, and we their hands.

All. He shall sure on't.

Mene. Sir, sir.   *Sicin.* Peace.

Me. Do not cry hauocke, where you shold but hunt With modest warrant.

Sicin. Sir, how com'st that you haue holpe To make this rescue?

Mene. Heare me speake? As I do know The Consuls worthinesse, so can I name his Faults.

Sicin. Consull? what Consull?

Mene. The Consull *Coriolanus*.

Bru. He Consull.

All. No, no, no, no, no.

Mene. If by the Tribunes leaue, And yours good people, I may be heard, I would craue a word or two, The which shall turne you to no further harme, Then so much losse of time.

Sic. Speake breefely then, For we are peremptory to dispatch This Viporous Traitor: to eiect him hence Were but one danger, and to keepe him heere Our certaine death: therefore it is decreed, He dyes to night.

Menen. Now the good Gods forbid, That our renowned Rome, whose gratitude Towards her deserued Children, is enroll'd In Ioues owne Booke, like an vnnaturall Dam Should now eate vp her owne.

Sicin.

The Tragedie of Coriolanus.

Sicin. He's a Disease that must be cut away.

Mene. Oh he's a Limbe, that ha's but a Disease
Mortall, to cut it off: to cure it, easie.
What ha's he done to Rome, that's worthy death?
Killing our Enemies, the blood he hath lost
(Which I dare vouch, is more then that he hath
By many an Ounce) he dropp'd it for his Country:
And what is left, to loose it by his Countrey,
Were to vs all that doo't, and suffer it
A brand to th'end a'th World.

Sicin. This is cleane kamme.

Brut. Meerely awry:
When he did loue his Country, it honour'd him.

Menen. The seruice of the foote
Being once gangren'd, is not then respected
For what before it was.

Bru. Wee'l heare no more:
Pursue him to his house, and plucke him thence,
Least his infection being of catching nature,
Spred further.

Menen. One word more, one word:
This Tiger-footed-rage, when it shall find
The harme of vnskan'd swiftnesse, will (too late)
Tye Leaden pounds too's heeles. Proceed by Processe,
Least parties (as he is belou'd) breake out,
And sacke great Rome with Romanes.

Brut. If it were so?

Sicin. What do ye talke?
Haue we not had a taste of his Obedience?
Our Ediles smot: our selues resisted: come.

Mene. Consider this: He ha's bin bred i'th'Warres
Since a could draw a Sword, and is ill-school'd
In boulted Language: Meale and Bran together
He throwes without distinction. Giue me leaue,
Ile go to him, and vndertake to bring him in peace,
Where he shall answer by a lawfull Forme
(In peace) to his vtmost perill.

1.Sen. Noble Tribunes,
It is the humane way: the other course
Will proue to bloody: and the end of it,
Vnknowne to the Beginning.

Sic. Noble *Menenius*, be you then as the peoples officer:
Masters, lay downe your Weapons.

Bru. Go not home.

Sic. Meet on the Market place: wee'l attend you there:
Where if you bring not *Martius*, wee'l proceede
In our first way.

Menen. Ile bring him to you.
Let me desire your company: he must come,
Or what is worst will follow.

Sena. Pray you let's to him. *Exeunt Omnes.*

Enter Coriolanus with Nobles.

Corio. Let them pull all about mine eares, present me
Death on the Wheele, or at wilde Horses heeles,
Or pile ten hilles on the Tarpeian Rocke,
That the precipitation might downe stretch
Below the beame of sight; yet will I still
Be thus to them.

Enter Volumnia.

Noble. You do the Nobler.

Corio. I muse my Mother
Do's not approue me further, who was wont
To call them Wollen Vassailes, things created
To buy and sell with Groats, to shew bare heads
In Congregations, to yawne, be still, and wonder,
When one but of my ordinance stood vp
To speake of Peace, or Warre. I talke of you,
Why did you wish me milder? Would you haue me
False to my Nature? Rather say, I play
The man I am.

Volum. Oh sir, sir, sir,
I would haue had you put your power well on
Before you had worne it out.

Corio. Let go.

Vol. You might haue beene enough the man you are,
With striuing lesse to be so: Lesser had bin
The things of your dispositions, if
You had not shew'd them how ye were dispos'd
Ere they lack'd power to crosse you.

Corio. Let them hang.

Volum. I, and burne too.

Enter Menenius with the Senators.

Men. Come, come, you haue bin too rough, somthing
too rough: you must returne, and mend it.

Sen. There's no remedy,
Vnlesse by not so doing, our good Citie
Cleaue in the midd'st, and perish.

Volum. Pray be counsail'd;
I haue a heart as little apt as yours,
But yet a braine, that leades my vse of Anger
To better vantage.

Mene. Well said, Noble woman:
Before he should thus stoope to'th'heart, but that
The violent fit a'th'time craues it as Physicke
For the whole State; I would put mine Armour on,
Which I can scarsely beare.

Corio. What must I do?

Mene. Returne to th'Tribunes.

Corio. Well, what then? what then?

Mene. Repent, what you haue spoke.

Corio. For them, I cannot do it to the Gods,
Must I then doo't to them?

Volum. You are too absolute,
Though therein you can neuer be too Noble,
But when extremities speake. I haue heard you say,
Honor and Policy, like vnseuer'd Friends,
I'th'Warre do grow together: Grant that, and tell me
In Peace, what each of them by th'other loose,
That they combine not there?

Corio. Tush, tush.

Mene. A good demand.

Volum. If it be Honor in your Warres, to seeme
The same you are not, which for your best ends
You adopt your policy: How is it lesse or worse
That it shall hold Companionship in Peace
With Honour, as in Warre; since that to both
It stands in like request.

Corio. Why force you this?

Volum. Because, that
Now it lyes you on to speake to th'people:
Not by your owne instruction, nor by'th'matter
Which your heart prompts you, but with such words
That are but roated in your Tongue;
Though but Bastards, and Syllables
Of no allowance, to your bosomes truth.
Now, this no more dishonors you at all,
Then to take in a Towne with gentle words,
Which else would put you to your fortune, and
The hazard of much blood.
I would dissemble with my Nature, where
My Fortunes and my Friends at stake, requir'd
I should do so in Honor. I am in this

Your Wife, your Sonne: These Senators, the Nobles,
And you, will rather shew our generall Lowts,
How you can frowne, then spend a fawne vpon 'em,
For the inheritance of their loues, and safegard
Of what that want might ruine.

Menen. Noble Lady,
Come goe with vs, speake faire: you may salue so,
Not what is dangerous present, but the losse
Of what is past.

Volum. I pry thee now, my Sonne,
Goe to them, with this Bonnet in thy hand,
And thus farre hauing stretcht it (here be with them)
Thy Knee bussing the stones: for in such businesse
Action is eloquence, and the eyes of th'ignorant
More learned then the eares, wauing thy head,
Which often thus correcting thy stout heart,
Now humble as the ripest Mulberry,
That will not hold the handling: or say to them,
Thou art their Souldier, and being bred in broyles,
Hast not the soft way, which thou do'st confesse
Were fit for thee to vse, as they to clayme,
In asking their good loues, but thou wilt frame
Thy selfe (forsooth) hereafter theirs so farre,
As thou hast power and person.

Menen. This but done,
Euen as she speakes, why their hearts were yours:
For they haue Pardons, being ask'd, as free,
As words to little purpose.

Volum. Prythee now,
Goe, and be rul'd: although I know thou hadst rather
Follow thine Enemie in a fierie Gulfe,
Then flatter him in a Bower. *Enter Cominius.*
Here is Cominius.

Com. I haue beene i'th' Market place: and Sir 'tis fit
You make strong partie, or defend your selfe
By calmenesse, or by absence: all's in anger.

Menen. Onely faire speech.

Com. I thinke 'twill serue, if he can thereto frame his
spirit.

Volum. He must, and will:
Prythee now say you will, and goe about it.

Corio. Must I goe shew them my vnbarb'd Sconce?
Must I with my base Tongue giue to my Noble Heart
A Lye, that it must beare well? I will doo't:
Yet were there but this single Plot, to loose
This Mould of *Martius,* they to dust should grinde it,
And throw't against the Winde. Toth' Market place:
You haue put me now to such a part, which neuer
I shall discharge toth' Life.

Com. Come, come, wee'le prompt you.

Volum. I prythee now sweet Son, as thou hast said
My praises made thee first a Souldier; so
To haue my praise for this, performe a part
Thou hast not done before.

Corio. Well, I must doo't:
Away my disposition, and possesse me
Some Harlots spirit: My throat of Warre be turn'd,
Which quier'd with my Drumme into a Pipe,
Small as an Eunuch, or the Virgin voyce
That Babies lull a-sleepe: The smiles of Knaues
Tent in my cheekes, and Schoole-boyes Teares take vp
The Glasses of my sight: A Beggars Tongue
Make motion through my Lips, and my Arm'd knees
Who bow'd but in my Stirrop, bend like his
That hath receiu'd an Almes. I will not doo't,
Least I surcease to honor mine owne truth,
And by my Bodies action, teach my Minde
A most inherent Basenesse.

Volum. At thy choice then:
To begge of thee, it is my more dis-honor,
Then thou of them. Come all to ruine, let
Thy Mother rather feele thy Pride, then feare
Thy dangerous Stoutnesse: for I mocke at death
With as bigge heart as thou. Do as thou list,
Thy Valiantnesse was mine, thou suck'st it from me:
But owe thy Pride thy selfe.

Corio. Pray be content:
Mother, I am going to the Market place:
Chide me no more. Ile Mountebanke their Loues,
Cogge their Hearts from them, and come home belou'd
Of all the Trades in Rome. Looke, I am going:
Commend me to my Wife, Ile returne Consull,
Or neuer trust to what my Tongue can do
I'th way of Flattery further.

Volum. Do your will. *Exit Volumnia*

Com. Away, the Tribunes do attend you: arm your self
To answer mildely: for they are prepar'd
With Accusations, as I heare more strong
Then are vpon you yet.

Corio. The word is, Mildely. Pray you let vs go,
Let them accuse me by inuention: I
Will answer in mine Honor.

Menen. I, but mildely.

Corio. Well mildely be it then, Mildely. *Exeunt*

Enter Sicinius and Brutus.

Bru. In this point charge him home, that he affects
Tyrannicall power: If he euade vs there,
Inforce him with his enuy to the people,
And that the Spoile got on the *Antiats*
Was ne're distributed. What, will he come?

Enter an Edile.

Edile. Hee's comming.

Bru. How accompanied?

Edile. With old *Menenius,* and those Senators
That alwayes fauour'd him.

Sicin. Haue you a Catalogue
Of all the Voices that we haue procur'd, set downe by'th
Edile. I haue: 'tis ready. (Pole?

Sicin. Haue you collected them by Tribes?

Edile. I haue.

Sicin. Assemble presently the people hither:
And when they heare me say, it shall be so,
I'th'right and strength a'th' Commons: be it either
For death, for fine, or Banishment, then let them
If I say Fine, cry Fine; if Death, cry Death,
Insisting on the olde prerogatiue
And power i'th Truth a'th Cause.

Edile. I shall informe them.

Bru. And when such time they haue begun to cry,
Let them not cease, but with a dinne confus'd
Inforce the present Execution
Of what we chance to Sentence.

Edi. Very well.

Sicin. Make them be strong, and ready for this hint
When we shall hap to giu't them.

Bru. Go about it,
Put him to Choller straite, he hath bene vs'd
Euer to conquer, and to haue his worth
Of contradiction. Being once chaft, he cannot
Be rein'd againe to Temperance, then he speakes
What's

The Tragedie of Coriolanus.

What's in his heart, and that is there which lookes
With vs to breake his necke.

Enter Coriolanus, Menenius, and Cominius, with others.

Sicin. Well, heere he comes.
Mene. Calmely, I do beseech you.
Corio. I, as an Hostler, that fourth poorest peece
Will beare the Knaue by th'Volume:
Th'honor'd Goddes
Keepe Rome in safety, and the Chaires of Iustice
Supplied with worthy men, plant loue amongs
Through our large Temples with y shewes of peace
And not our streets with Warre.
1 Sen. Amen, Amen.
Mene. A Noble wish.

Enter the Edile with the Plebeians.

Sicin. Draw neere ye people.
Edile. List to your Tribunes. Audience:
Peace I say.
Corio. First heare me speake.
Both Tri. Well, say: Peace hoe.
Corio. Shall I be charg'd no further then this present?
Must all determine heere?
Sicin. I do demand,
If you submit you to the peoples voices,
Allow their Officers, and are content
To suffer lawfull Censure for such faults
As shall be prou'd vpon you.
Corio. I am Content.
Mene. Lo Citizens, he sayes he is Content.
The warlike Seruice he ha's done, consider: Thinke
Vpon the wounds his body beares, which shew
Like Graues i'th holy Church-yard.
Corio. Scratches with Briars, scarres to moue
Laughter onely.
Mene. Consider further:
That when he speakes not like a Citizen,
You finde him like a Soldier: do not take
His rougher Actions for malicious sounds:
But as I say, such as become a Soldier,
Rather then enuy you.
Com. Well, well, no more.
Corio. What is the matter,
That being past for Consull with full voyce:
I am so dishonour'd, that the very houre
You take it off againe.
Sicin. Answer to vs.
Corio. Say then: 'tis true, I ought so
Sicin. We charge you, that you haue contriu'd to take
From Rome all season'd Office, and to winde
Your selfe into a power tyrannicall,
For which you are a Traitor to the people.
Corio. How? Traytor?
Mene. Nay temperately: your promise.
Corio. The fires i'th'lowest hell. Fould in the people:
Call me their Traitor, thou iniurious Tribune.
Within thine eyes sate twenty thousand deaths
In thy hands clutcht: as many Millions in
Thy lying tongue, both numbers. I would say
Thou lyest vnto thee, with a voice as free,
As I do pray the Gods.
Sicin. Marke you this people?
All. To th'Rocke, to th'Rocke with him.
Sicin. Peace:
We neede not put new matter to his charge:
What you haue seene him do, and heard him speake:

Beating your Officers, cursing your selues,
Opposing Lawes with stroakes, and heere defying
Those whose great power must try him.
Euen this so criminall, and in such capitall kinde
Deserues th'extreamest death.
Bru. But since he hath seru'd well for Rome.
Corio. What do you prate of Seruice.
Brut. I talke of that, that know it.
Corio. You?
Mene. Is this the promise that you made your mother.
Com. Know, I pray you.
Corio. Ile know no further:
Let them pronounce the steepe Tarpeian death,
Vagabond exile, Fleaing, pent to linger
But with a graine a day, I would not buy
Their mercie, at the price of one faire word,
Nor checke my Courage for what they can giue,
To haue't with saying, Good morrow.
Sicin. For that he ha's
(As much as in him lies) from time to time
Enui'd against the people; seeking meanes
To plucke away their power: as now at last,
Giuen Hostile strokes, and that not in the presence
Of dreaded Iustice, but on the Ministers
That doth distribute it. In the name a'th'people,
And in the power of vs the Tribunes, wee
(Eu'n from this instant) banish him our Citie
In perill of precipitation
From off the Rocke Tarpeian, neuer more
To enter our Rome gates. I'th'Peoples name,
I say it shall bee so.
All. It shall be so, it shall be so: let him away:
Hee's banish'd, and it shall be so.
Com. Heare me my Masters, and my common friends.
Sicin. He's sentenc'd: No more hearing.
Com. Let me speake:
I haue bene Consull, and can shew from Rome
Her Enemies markes vpon me. I do loue
My Countries good, with a respect more tender,
More holy, and profound, then mine owne life,
My deere Wiues estimate, her wombes encrease,
And treasure of my Loynes: then if I would
Speake that.
Sicin. We know your drift. Speake what?
Bru. There's no more to be said, but he is banish'd
As Enemy to the people, and his Countrey.
It shall bee so.
All. It shall be so, it shall be so.
Corio. You common cry of Curs, whose breath I hate,
As recke a'th'rotten Fennes: whose Loues I prize,
As the dead Carkasses of vnburied men,
That do corrupt my Ayre: I banish you,
And heere remaine with your vncertaintie.
Let euery feeble Rumor shake your hearts:
Your Enemies, with nodding of their Plumes
Fan you into dispaire: Haue the power still
To banish your Defenders, till at length
Your ignorance (which findes not till it feeles,
Making but reseruation of your selues,
Still your owne Foes) deliuer you
As most abated Captiues, to some Nation
That wonne you without blowes, despising
For you the City. Thus I turne my backe;
There is a world elsewhere.

Exeunt Coriolanus, Cominius, with Cumalys.
They all shout, and throw vp their Caps.

Edile

Edile. The peoples Enemy is gone, is gone.
All. Our enemy is banish'd, he is gone: Hoo, oo.
Sicin. Go see him out at Gates, and follow him
As he hath follow'd you, with all despight,
Giue him deseru'd vexation. Let a guard
Attend vs through the City.
All. Come, come, lets see him out at gates, come:
The Gods preserue our Noble Tribunes, come. *Exeunt.*

Actus Quartus.

Enter Coriolanus, Volumnia, Virgilia, Menenius, Cominius, with the yong Nobility of Rome.

Corio. Come leaue your teares: a briefe farwel: the beast
With many heads butts me away. Nay Mother,
Where is your ancient Courage? You were vs'd
To say, Extreamities was the trier of spirits,
That common chances. Common men could beare,
That when the Sea was calme, all Boats alike
Shew'd Mastership in floating. Fortunes blowes,
When most strooke home, being gentle wounded, craues
A Noble cunning. You were vs'd to load me
With Precepts that would make inuincible
The heart that conn'd them.

Virg. Oh heauens! O heauens!

Corio. Nay, I prythee woman.

Vol. Now the Red Pestilence strike al Trades in Rome,
And Occupations perish.

Corio. What, what, what:
I shall be lou'd when I am lack'd. Nay Mother,
Resume that Spirit, when you were wont to say,
If you had beene the Wife of *Hercules,*
Six of his Labours you'd haue done, and sau'd
Your Husband so much sweat. *Cominius,*
Droope not, Adieu: Farewell my Wife, my Mother,
Ile do well yet. Thou old and true *Menenius,*
Thy teares are salter then a yonger mans,
And venomous to thine eyes. My (sometime) Generall,
I haue seene the Sterne, and thou hast oft beheld
Heart-hardning spectacles. Tell these sad women,
'Tis fond to waile ineuitable strokes,
As 'tis to laugh at 'em. My Mother, you wot well
My hazards still haue beene your solace, and
Beleeu't not lightly, though I go alone
Like to a lonely Dragon, that his Fenne
Makes fear'd, and talk'd of more then seene: your Sonne
Will or exceed the Common, or be caught
With cautelous baits and practice.

Volum. My first sonne,
Whether will thou go? Take good *Cominius*
With thee awhile: Determine on some course
More then a wilde exposture, to each chance
That start's i'th'way before thee.

Corio. O the Gods!

Com. Ile follow thee a Moneth, deuise with thee
Where thou shalt rest, that thou may'st heare of vs,
And we of thee. So if the time thrust forth
A cause for thy Repeale, we shall not send
O're the vast world, to seeke a single man,
And loose aduantage, which doth euer coole
Ith'absence of the needer.

Corio. Fare ye well:
Thou hast yeares vpon thee, and thou art too full
Of the warres surfets, to go roue with one
That's yet vnbruis'd: bring me but out at gate.
Come my sweet wife, my deerest Mother, and
My Friends of Noble touch: when I am forth,
Bid me farewell, and smile. I pray you come:
While I remaine aboue the ground, you shall
Heare from me still, and neuer of me ought
But what is like me formerly.

Menen. That's worthily
As any eare can heare. Come, let's not weepe,
If I could shake off but one seuen yeeres
From these old armes and legges, by the good Gods
I'd with thee, euery foot.

Corio. Giue me thy hand, come. *Exeunt.*

Enter the two Tribunes, Sicinius, and Brutus, with the Edile.

Sicin. Bid them all home, he's gone: & wee'l no further,
The Nobility are vexed, whom we see haue sided
In his behalfe.

Brut. Now we haue shewne our power,
Let vs seeme humbler after it is done,
Then when it was a dooing.

Sicin. Bid them home: say their great enemy is gone,
And they, stand in their ancient strength.

Brut. Dismisse them home. Here comes his Mother.

Enter Volumnia, Virgilia, and Menenius.

Sicin. Let's not meet her.

Brut. Why?

Sicin. They say she's mad.

Brut. They haue tane note of vs: keepe on your way.

Volum. Oh y'are well met:
Th'hoorded plague a'th'Gods requit your loue.

Menen. Peace, peace, be not so loud.

Volum. If that I could for weeping, you should heare,
Nay, and you shall heare some. Will you be gone?

Virg. You shall stay too: I would I had the power
To say so to my Husband.

Sicin. Are you mankinde?

Volum. I foole, is that a shame. Note but this Foole,
Was not a man my Father? Had'st thou Foxship
To banish him that strooke more blowes for Rome
Then thou hast spoken words.

Sicin. Oh blessed Heauens!

Volum. Moe Noble blowes, then euer ỹ wise words.
And for Romes good, Ile tell thee what: yet goe:
Nay but thou shalt stay too: I would my Sonne
Were in Arabia, and thy Tribe before him,
His good Sword in his hand.

Sicin. What then?

Virg. What then? Hee'ld make an end of thy posterity

Volum. Bastards, and all.
Good man, the Wounds that he does beare for Rome!

Menen. Come, come, peace.

Sicin. I would he had continued to his Country
As he began, and not vnknit himselfe
The Noble knot he made.

Bru. I would he had.

Volum. I would he had? 'Twas you incenst the rable.
Cats, that can iudge as fitly of his worth,
As I can of those Mysteries which heauen
Will not haue earth to know.

Brut. Pray let's go.

Volum. Now pray sir get you gone.
You haue done a braue deede: Ere you go, heare this:
As farre as doth the Capitoll exceede
The meanest house in Rome; so farre my Sonne

This Ladies Husband heere; this (do you see)
Whom you haue banish'd, does exceed you all.
  Bru. Well, well, wee'l leaue you.
  Sicin. Why stay we to be baited
With one that wants her Wits.   *Exit Tribunes.*
  Volum. Take my Prayers with you.
I would the Gods had nothing else to do,
But to confirme my Cursses. Could I meete 'em
But once a day, it would vnclogge my heart
Of what lyes heauy too't.
  Mene. You haue told them home,
And by my troth you haue cause: you'l Sup with me.
  Volum. Angers my Meate: I suppe vpon my selfe,
And so shall sterue with Feeding: Come, let's go,
Leaue this faint-puling, and lament as I do,
In Anger, *Iuno*-like: Come, come, come.   *Exeunt.*
  Mene. Fie, fie, fie.   *Exit.*

        Enter a Roman, and a Volce.

  Rom. I know you well sir, and you know mee: your
name I thinke is *Adrian*.
  Volce. It is so sir, truly I haue forgot you.
  Rom. I am a Roman, and my Seruices are as you are,
against 'em. Know you me yet.
  Volce. Nicanor: no.
  Rom. The same sir.
  Volce. You had more Beard when I last saw you, but
your fauour is well appear'd by your Tongue. What's
the Newes in Rome: I haue a Note from the Volcean
state to finde you out there. You haue well sauc'd mee a
dayes iourney.
  Rom. There hath beene in Rome straunge Insurrections: The people, against the Senatours, Patricians, and
Nobles.
  Vol. Hath bin; is it ended then? Our State thinks not
so, they are in a most warlike preparation, & hope to com
vpon them, in the heate of their diuision
  Rom. The maine blaze of it is past, but a small thing
would make it flame againe. For the Nobles receyue so
to heart, the Banishment of that worthy *Coriolanus*, that
they are in a ripe aptnesse, to take al power from the people, and to plucke from them their Tribunes for euer.
This lyes glowing I can tell you, and is almost mature for
the violent breaking out.
  Vol. Coriolanus Banisht?
  Rom. Banish'd sir.
  Vol. You will be welcome with this intelligence *Nicanor*.
  Rom. The day serues well for them now. I haue heard
it saide, the fittest time to corrupt a mans Wife, is when
shee's falne out with her Husband. Your Noble *Tullus
Auffidius* well appeare well in these Warres, his great
Opposer *Coriolanus* being now in no request of his countrey.
  Volce. He cannot choose: I am most fortunate, thus
accidentally to encounter you. You haue ended my Businesse, and I will merrily accompany you home.
  Rom. I shall betweene this and Supper, tell you most
strange things from Rome: all tending to the good of
their Aduersaries. Haue you an Army ready say you?
  Vol. A most Royall one: The Centurions, and their
charges distinctly billetted already in th'entertainment,
and to be on foot at an houres warning.
  Rom. I am ioyfull to heare of their readinesse, and am
the man I thinke, that shall set them in present Action. So
sir, heartily well met, and most glad of your Company.
  Volce. You take my part from me sir, I haue the most

cause to be glad of yours.
  Rom. Well, let vs go together.   *Exeunt.*

    *Enter Coriolanus in meane Apparrell, Dis-
           guisd, and muffled.*

  Corio. A goodly City is this *Antium*. Citty,
'Tis I that made thy Widdowes: Many an heyre
Of these faire Edifices fore my Warres
Haue I heard groane, and drop: Then know me not,
Least that thy Wiues with Spits, and Boyes with stones
In puny Battell slay me. Saue you sir.
        Enter a Citizen.
  Cit. And you.
  Corio. Direct me, if it be your will, where great *Auf-
fidius* lies: Is he in *Antium*?
  Cit. He is, and Feasts the Nobles of the State, at his
house this night.
  Corio. Which is his house, beseech you?
  Cit. This heere before you.
  Corio. Thanke you sir, farewell.   *Exit Citizen*
Oh World, thy slippery turnes! Friends now fast sworn,
Whose double bosomes seemes to weare one heart,
Whose Houres, whose Bed, whose Meale and Exercise
Are still together: who Twin (as 'twere) in Loue,
Vnseparable, shall within this houre,
On a dissention of a Doit, breake out
To bitterest Enmity: So fellest Foes,
Whose Passions, and whose Plots haue broke their sleep
To take the one the other, by some chance,
Some tricke not worth an Egge, shall grow deere friends
And inter-ioyne their yssues. So with me,
My Birth-place haue I, and my loues vpon
This Enemie Towne: Ile enter, if he slay me
He does faire Iustice: if he giue me way,
Ile do his Country Seruice.   *Exit.*

       Musicke playes. Enter a Seruingman.

  1 Ser. Wine, Wine, Wine: What seruice is heere? I
thinke our Fellowes are asleepe.
          Enter another Seruingman.
  2 Ser. Where's *Cotus*? my M.cals for him: *Cotus. Exit.*
          Enter Coriolanus.
  Corio. A goodly House:
The Feast smels well: but I appeare not like a Guest.
        Enter the first Seruingman.
  1 Ser. What would you haue Friend? whence are you?
Here's no place for you: Pray go to the doore?   *Exit*
  Corio. I haue deseru'd no better entertainment, in being *Coriolanus*.   *Enter second Seruant.*
  2 Ser. Whence are you sir? Ha's the Porter his eyes in
his head, that he giues entrance to such Companions?
Pray get you out.
  Corio. Away.
  2 Ser. Away? Get you away.
  Corio. Now th'art troublesome.
  2 Ser. Are you so braue: Ile haue you talkt with anon
      Enter 3 Seruingman, the 1 meets him.
  3 What Fellowes this?
  1 A strange one as euer I look'd on: I cannot get him
out o'th'house: Prythee call my Master to him.
  3 What haue you to do here fellow? Pray you auoid
the house.
  Corio. Let me but stand, I will not hurt your Harth.
  3 What are you?
  Corio. A Gentleman.
  3 A maruellous poore one.
  Corio. True, so I am.
  3 Pray you poore Gentleman, take vp some other sta-
                                              tion.

tion: Heere's no place for you, pray you auoid: Come.

Corio. Follow your Function, go, and batten on colde bits. *Pushes him away from him.*

3 What you will not? Prythee tell my Maister what a strange Guest he ha's heere.

2 And I shall. *Exit second Seruingman.*

3 Where dwel'st thou?

Corio. Vnder the Canopy.

3 Vnder the Canopy?

Corio. I.

3 Where's that?

Corio. I'th City of Kites and Crowes.

3 I'th City of Kites and Crowes? What an Asse it is, then thou dwel'st with Dawes too?

Corio. No, I serue not thy Master.

3 How sir? Do you meddle with my Master?

Corio. I, 'tis an honester seruice, then to meddle with thy Mistris: Thou prat'st, and prat'st, serue with thy trencher: Hence. *Beats him away.*

Enter Auffidius with the Seruingman.

Auf. Where is this Fellow?

2 Here sir, I'de haue beaten him like a dogge, but for disturbing the Lords within.

Auf. Whence com'st thou? What wold'st y? Thy name? Why speak'st not? Speake man: What's thy name?

Corio. If *Tullus* not yet thou know'st me, and seeing me, dost not thinke me for the man I am, necessitie commands me name my selfe.

Auf. What is thy name?

Corio. A name vnmusicall to the Volcians eares, And harsh in sound to thine.

Auf. Say, what's thy name?
Thou hast a Grim apparance, and thy Face
Beares a Command in't: Though thy Tackles torne,
Thou shew'st a Noble Vessell: What's thy name?

Corio. Prepare thy brow to frowne: knowst y me yet?

Auf. I know thee not? Thy Name?

Corio. My name is *Caius Martius*, who hath done
To thee particularly, and to all the Volces
Great hurt and Mischiefe: thereto witnesse may
My Surname *Coriolanus.* The painfull Seruice,
The extreme Dangers, and the droppes of Blood
Shed for my thanklesse Country, are requitted:
But with that Surname, a good memorie
And witnesse of the Malice and Displeasure
Which thou should'st beare me, only that name remains.
The Cruelty and Enuy of the people,
Permitted by our dastard Nobles, who
Haue all forsooke me, hath deuour'd the rest:
And suffer'd me by th'voyce of Slaues to be
Hoop'd out of Rome. Now this extremity,
Hath brought me to thy Harth, not out of Hope
(Mistake me not) to saue my life: for if
I had fear'd death, of all the Men i'th' World
I would haue voided thee. But in meere spight
To be full quit of those my Banishers,
Stand I before thee heere: Then if thou hast
A heart of wreake in thee, that wilt reuenge
Thine owne particular wrongs, and stop those maimes
Of shame seene through thy Country, speed thee straight
And make my misery serue thy turne: So vse it,
That my reuengefull Seruices may proue
As Benefits to thee. For I will fight
Against my Cankred Countrey, with the Spleene
Of all the vnder Fiends. But if so be,
Thou dar'st not this, and that to proue more Fortunes

Th'art tyr'd, then in a word, I also am
Longer to liue most wearie: and present
My throat to thee, and to thy Ancient Malice:
Which not to cut, would shew thee but a Foole,
Since I haue euer followed thee with hate,
Drawne Tunnes of Blood out of thy Countries brest,
And cannot liue but to thy shame, vnlesse
It be to do thee seruice.

Auf. Oh *Martius, Martius*;
Each word thou hast spoke, hath weeded from my heart
A roote of Ancient Enuy. If *Iupiter*
Should from yond clowd speake diuine things,
And say 'tis true; I'de not beleeue them more
Then thee all-Noble *Martius.* Let me twine
Mine armes about that body, where against
My grained Ash an hundred times hath broke,
And scarr'd the Moone with splinters: heere I cleep
The Anuile of my Sword, and do contest
As hotly, and as Nobly with thy Loue,
As euer in Ambitious strength, I did
Contend against thy Valour. Know thou first,
I lou'd the Maid I married; neuer man
Sigh'd truer breath. But that I see thee heere
Thou Noble thing, more dances my rapt heart,
Then when I first my wedded Mistris saw
Bestride my Threshold. Why, thou Mars I tell thee,
We haue a Power on foote: and I had purpose
Once more to hew thy Target from thy Brawne,
Or loose mine Arme for't: Thou hast beate mee out
Twelue seuerall times, and I haue nightly since
Dreamt of encounters 'twixt thy selfe and me:
We haue beene downe together in my sleepe,
Vnbuckling Helmes, fisting each others Throat,
And wak'd halfe dead with nothing. Worthy *Martius*,
Had we no other quarrell else to Rome, but that
Thou art thence Banish'd, we would muster all
From twelue, to seuentie: and powring Warre
Into the bowels of vngratefull Rome,
Like a bold Flood o're-beate. Oh come, go in,
And take our Friendly Senators by'th'hands
Who now are heere, taking their leaues of mee,
Who am prepar'd against your Territories,
Though not for Rome it selfe.

Corio. You blesse me Gods.

Auf. Therefore most absolute Sir, if thou wilt haue
The leading of thine owne Reuenges, take
Th'one halfe of my Commission, and set downe
As best thou art experienc'd, since thou know'st
Thy Countries strength and weaknesse, thine own waies
Whether to knocke against the Gates of Rome,
Or rudely visit them in parts remote,
To fright them, ere destroy. But come in,
Let me commend thee first, to those that shall
Say yea to thy desires. A thousand welcomes,
And more a Friend, then ere an Enemie,
Yet *Martius* that was much. Your hand: most welcome. *Exeunt*

Enter two of the Seruingmen.

1 Heere's a strange alteration?

2 By my hand, I had thought to haue stroken him with a Cudgell, and yet my minde gaue me, his cloathes made a false report of him.

1 What an Arme he has, he turn'd me about with his finger and his thumbe, as one would set vp a Top.

2 Nay, I knew by his face that there was some-thing in him. He had sir, a kinde of face me thought, I cannot tell

tell how to tearme it.

1 He had so, looking as it were, would I were hang'd but I thought there was more in him, then I could think.

2 So did I, Ile be sworne: He is simply the rarest man i'th'world.

1 I thinke he is: but a greater soldier then he, You wot one.

2 Who my Master?

1 Nay, it's no matter for that.

2 Worth six on him.

1 Nay not so neither: but I take him to be the greater Souldiour.

2 Faith looke you, one cannot tell how to say that: for the Defence of a Towne, our Generall is excellent.

1 I, and for an assault too.

Enter the third Seruingman.

3 Oh Slaues, I can tell you Newes, Newes you Rascals

Both. What, what, what? Let's partake.

3 I would not be a Roman of all Nations; I had as liue be a condemn'd man.

Both. Wherefore? Wherefore?

3 Why here's he that was wont to thwacke our Generall, *Caius Martius.*

1 Why do you say, thwacke our Generall?

3 I do not say thwacke our Generall, but he was alwayes good enough for him

2 Come we are fellowes and friends: he was euer too hard for him, I haue heard him say so himselfe.

1 He was too hard for him directly, to say the Troth on't before *Corioles*, he scotcht him, and notcht him like a Carbinado.

2 And hee had bin Cannibally giuen, hee might haue boyld and eaten him too.

1 But more of thy Newes.

3 Why he is so made on heere within, as if hee were Son and Heire to Mars, set at vpper end o'th'Table: No question askt him by any of the Senators, but they stand bald before him. Our Generall himselfe makes a Mistris of him, Sanctifies himselfe with's hand, and turnes vp the white o'th'eye to his Discourse. But the bottome of the Newes is, our Generall is cut i'th'middle, & but one halfe of what he was yesterday. For the other ha's halfe, by the intreaty and graunt of the whole Table. Hee'l go he sayes, and sole the Porter of Rome Gates by th'eares. He will mowe all downe before him, and leaue his passage poul'd.

2 And he's as like to do't, as any man I can Imagine.

3 Doo't? he will doo't: for look you sir, he has as many Friends as Enemies: which Friends sir as it were, durst not (looke you sir) shew themselues (as we terme it) his Friends, whilest he's in Directitude.

1 Directitude? What's that?

3 But when they shall see sir, his Crest vp againe, and the man in blood, they will out of their Burroughes (like Conies after Raine) and reuell all with him.

1 But when goes this forward?

3 To morrow, to day, presently, you shall haue the Drum strooke vp this afternoone: 'Tis as it were a parcel of their Feast, and to be executed ere they wipe their lips.

2 Why then wee shall haue a stirring World againe: This peace is nothing, but to rust Iron, encrease Taylors, and breed Ballad-makers.

1 Let me haue Warre say I, it exceeds peace as farre as day do's night: It's sprightly walking, audible, and full of Vent. Peace, is a very Apoplexy, Lethargie, mull'd, deafe, sleepe, insensible, a getter of more bastard Children, then warres a destroyer of men.

2 'Tis so, and as warres in some sort may be saide to be a Rauisher, so it cannot be denied, but peace is a great maker of Cuckolds.

1 I, and it makes men hate one another.

3 Reason, because they then lesse neede one another: The Warres for my money. I hope to see Romanes as cheape as Volcians. They are rising, they are rising.

Both. In, in, in, in. *Exeunt*

Enter the two Tribunes, Sicinius, and Brutus.

Sicin. We heare not of him, neither need we fear him, His remedies are tame, the present peace, And quietnesse of the people, which before Were in wilde hurry. Heere do we make his Friends Blush, that the world goes well: who rather had, Though they themselues did suffer by't, behold Dissentious numbers pestring streets, then see Our Tradesmen singing in their shops, and going About their Functions friendly.

Enter Menenius.

Bru. We stood too't in good time. Is this *Menenius*?

Sicin. 'Tis he, 'tis he: O he is grown most kind of late: Haile Sir. *Mene.* Haile to you both.

Sicin. Your *Coriolanus* is not much mist, but with his Friends: the Commonwealth doth stand, and so would do, were he more angry at it.

Mene. All's well, and might haue bene much better, if he could haue temporiz'd.

Sicin. Where is he, heare you?

Mene. Nay I heare nothing: His Mother and his wife, heare nothing from him.

Enter three or foure Citizens.

All. The Gods preserue you both.

Sicin. Gooden our Neighbours.

Bru. Gooden to you all, gooden to you all.

1 Our selues, our wiues, and children, on our knees, Are bound to pray for you both.

Sicin. Liue, and thriue.

Bru. Farewell kinde Neighbours: We wisht *Coriolanus* had lou'd you as we did.

All. Now the Gods keepe you.

Both Tri. Farewell, farewell. *Exeunt Citizens*

Sicin. This is a happier and more comely time, Then when these Fellowes ran about the streets, Crying Confusion.

Bru. Caius Martius was A worthy Officer i'th'Warre, but Insolent, O'recome with Pride, Ambitious, past all thinking Selfe-louing.

Sicin. And affecting one sole Throne, without assistace

Mene. I thinke not so.

Sicin. We should by this, to all our Lamention, If he had gone forth Consull, found it so.

Bru. The Gods haue well preuented it, and Rome Sits safe and still, without him.

Enter an Ædile.

Ædile. Worthy Tribunes, There is a Slaue whom we haue put in prison, Reports the Volces with two seuerall Powers Are entred in the Roman Territories, And with the deepest malice of the Warre, Destroy, what lies before 'em.

Mene. 'Tis *Auffidius*, Who hearing of our *Martius* Banishment, Thrusts forth his hornes againe into the world Which were In-shell'd, when *Martius* stood for Rome,

And

And durst not once peepe out.
  Sicin. Come, what talke you of *Martius*.
  Bru. Go see this Rumorer whipt, it cannot be,
The Volces dare breake with vs.
  Mene. Cannot be?
We haue Record, that very well it can,
And three examples of the like, hath beene
Within my Age. But reason with the fellow
Before you punish him, where he heard this,
Leaft you shall chance to whip your Information,
And beate the Messenger, who bids beware
Of what is to be dreaded.
  Sicin. Tell not me: I know this cannot be.
  Bru. Not possible.

Enter a Messenger.

  Mes. The Nobles in great earneftnesse are going
All to the Senate-house: some newes is comming
That turnes their Countenances.
  Sicin. 'Tis this Slaue:
Go whip him fore the peoples eyes: His raising,
Nothing but his report.
  Mes. Yes worthy Sir,
The Slaues report is seconded, and more
More fearfull is deliuer'd.
  Sicin. What more fearefull?
  Mes. It is spoke freely out of many mouths,
How probable I do not know, that *Martius*
Ioyn'd with *Auffidius*, leads a power 'gainst Rome,
And vowes Reuenge as spacious, as betweene
The yong'ft and oldeft thing.
  Sicin. This is most likely.
  Bru. Rais'd onely, that the weaker sort may wish
Good *Martius* home againe.
  Sicin. The very tricke on't.
  Mene. This is vnlikely,
He, and *Auffidius* can no more attone
Then violent'ft Contrariety.

Enter Messenger.

  Mes. You are sent for to the Senate:
A fearefull Army, led by *Caius Martius*,
Associated with *Auffidius*, Rages
Vpon our Territories, and haue already
O're-borne their way, consum'd with fire, and tooke
What lay before them.

Enter Cominius.

  Com. Oh you haue made good worke.
  Mene. What newes? What newes?
  Com. You haue holp to rauish your owne daughters, &
To melt the Citty Leades vpon your pates,
To see your Wiues dishonour'd to your Noses.
  Mene. What's the newes? What's the newes?
  Com. Your Temples burned in their Ciment, and
Your Franchises, whereon you stood, confin'd
Into an Augors boare.
  Mene. Pray now, your Newes:
You haue made faire worke I feare me: pray your newes,
If *Martius* should be ioyn'd with Volceans.
  Com. If? He is their God, he leads them like a thing
Made by some other Deity then Nature,
That shapes man Better: and they follow him
Against vs Brats, with no lesse Confidence,
Then Boyes pursuing Summer Butter-flies,
Or Butchers killing Flyes.
  Mene. You haue made good worke,
You and your Apron men: you, that stood so much
Vpon the voyce of occupation, and
The breath of Garlicke-eaters.
  Com. Hee'l shake your Rome about your eares.
  Mene. As *Hercules* did shake downe Mellow Fruite:
You haue made faire worke.
  Brut. But is this true sir?
  Com. I, and you'l looke pale
Before you finde it other. All the Regions
Do smilingly Reuolt, and who resifts
Are mock'd for valiant Ignorance,
And perish constant Fooles: who is't can blame him?
Your Enemies and his, finde something in him,
  Mene. We are all vndone, vnlesse
The Noble man haue mercy.
  Com. Who shall aske it?
The Tribunes cannot doo't for shame; the people
Deserue such pitty of him, as the Wolfe
Doe's of the Shepheards: For his best Friends, if they
Should say be good to Rome, they charg'd him, euen
As those should do that had deseru'd his hate,
And therein shew'd like Enemies.
  Me. 'Tis true, if he were putting to my house, the brand
That should consume it, I haue not the face
To say, beseech you cease. You haue made faire hands,
You and your Crafts, you haue crafted faire.
  Com. You haue brought
A Trembling vpon Rome, such as was neuer
S'incapeable of helpe.
  Tri. Say not, we brought it.
  Mene. How? Was't we? We lou'd him,
But like Beasts, and Cowardly Nobles,
Gaue way vnto your Clusters, who did hoote
Him out o'th'Citty.
  Com. But I feare
They'l roare him in againe. *Tullus Auffidius*,
The second name of men, obeyes his points
As if he were his Officer: Desperation,
Is all the Policy, Strength, and Defence
That Rome can make against them.

Enter a Troope of Citizens.

  Mene. Heere come the Clusters.
And is *Auffidius* with him? You are they
That made the Ayre vnwholsome, when you cast
Your stinking, greasie Caps, in hooting
At *Coriolanus* Exile. Now he's comming,
And not a haire vpon a Souldiers head
Which will not proue a whip: As many Coxcombes
As you threw Caps vp, will he tumble downe,
And pay you for your voyces. 'Tis no matter,
If he could burne vs all into one coale,
We haue deseru'd it.
  Omnes. Faith, we heare fearfull Newes.
  1 Cit. For mine owne part,
When I said banish him, I said 'twas pitty.
  2 And so did I.
  3 And so did I: and to say the truth, so did very many of vs, that we did we did for the best, and though wee willingly consented to his Banishment, yet it was against our will.
  Com. Y'are goodly things, you Voyces.
  Mene. You haue made good worke
You and your cry. Shal's to the Capitoll?
  Com. Oh I, what else? *Exeunt both.*
  Sicin. Go Masters get you home, be not dismaid,
These are a Side, that would be glad to haue
This true, which they so seeme to feare. Go home,
And shew no signe of Feare. *1. Cit.*

The Tragedie of Coriolanus.

1 Cit. The Gods bee good to vs: Come Masters let's home, I euer said we were i'th wrong, when we banish'd him.

2 Cit. So did we all. But come, let's home. *Exit Cit.*

Bru. I do not like this Newes.

Sicin. Nor I.

Bru. Let's to the Capitoll: would halfe my wealth Would buy this for a lye.

Sicin. Pray let's go. *Exeunt Tribunes.*

Enter Auffidius with his Lieutenant.

Auf. Do they still flye to'th'Roman?

Lieu. I do not know what Witchcraft's in him: but Your Soldiers vse him as the Grace 'fore meate, Their talke at Table, and their Thankes at end, And you are darkned in this action Sir, Euen by your owne.

Auf. I cannot helpe it now, Vnlesse by vsing meanes I lame the foote Of our designe. He beares himselfe more proudlier, Euen to my person, then I thought he would When first I did embrace him. Yet his Nature In that's no Changeling, and I must excuse What cannot be amended.

Lieu. Yet I wish Sir, (I meane for your particular) you had not Ioyn'd in Commission with him: but either haue borne The action of your selfe, or else to him, had left it soly.

Auf. I vnderstand thee well, and be thou sure When he shall come to his account, he knowes not What I can vrge against him, although it seemes And so he thinkes, and is no lesse apparant To th'vulgar eye, that he beares all things fairely: And shewes good Husbandry for the Volcian State, Fights Dragon-like, and does atcheeue as soone As draw his Sword: yet he hath left vndone That which shall breake his necke, or hazard mine, When ere we come to our account.

Lieu. Sir, I beseech you, think you he'l carry Rome?

Auf. All places yeelds to him ere he sits downe, And the Nobility of Rome are his: The Senators and Patricians loue him too: The Tribunes are no Soldiers: and their people Will be as rash in the repeale, as hasty To expell him thence. I thinke hee'l be to Rome As is the Aspray to the Fish, who takes it By Soueraignty of Nature. First, he was A Noble seruant to them, but he could not Carry his Honors euen: whether 'was Pride Which out of dayly Fortune euer taints The happy man; whether defect of iudgement, To faile in the disposing of those chances Which he was Lord of: or whether Nature, Not to be other then one thing, not moouing From th'Caske to th'Cushion: but commanding peace Euen with the same austerity and garbe, As he controll'd the warre. But one of these (As he hath spices of them all) not all, For I dare so farre free him, made him fear'd, So hated, and so banish'd: but he ha's a Merit To choake it in the vtt'rance: So our Vertue, Lie in th'interpretation of the time, And power vnto it selfe most commendable, Hath not a Tombe so euident as a Chaire T'extoll what it hath done.
One fire driues out one fire; one Naile, one Naile; Rights by rights fouler, strengths by strengths do faile.
Come let's away: when *Caius* Rome is thine, Thou art poor'st of all; then shortly art thou mine. *exeunt*

Actus Quintus.

Enter Menenius, Cominius, Sicinius, Brutus, the two Tribunes, with others.

Menen. No, Ile not go: you heare what he hath said Which was sometime his Generall: who loued him In a most deere particular. He call'd me Father: But what o'that? Go you that banish'd him A Mile before his Tent, fall downe, and knee The way into his mercy: Nay, if he coy'd To heare *Cominius* speake, Ile keepe at home.

Com. He would not seeme to know me.

Menen. Do you heare?

Com. Yet one time he did call me by my name: I vrg'd our old acquaintance, and the drops That we haue bled together. *Coriolanus* He would not answer too: Forbad all Names, He was a kinde of Nothing, Titlelesse, Till he had forg'd himselfe a name a'th'fire Of burning Rome.

Menen. Why so: you haue made good worke: A paire of Tribunes, that haue wrack'd for Rome, To make Coales cheape: A Noble memory.

Com. I minded him, how Royall 'twas to pardon When it was lesse expected. He replyed It was a bare petition of a State To one whom they had punish'd.

Menen. Very well, could he say lesse.

Com. I offered to awaken his regard For's priuate Friends. His answer to me was He could not stay to picke them, in a pile Of noysome musty Chaffe. He said, 'twas folly For one poore graine or two, to leaue vnburnt And still to nose th'offence.

Menen. For one poore graine or two? I am one of those: his Mother, Wife, his Childe, And this braue Fellow too: we are the Graines, You are the musty Chaffe, and you are smelt Aboue the Moone. We must be burnt for you.

Sicin. Nay, pray be patient: If you refuse your ayde In this so neuer-needed helpe, yet do not Vpbraid's with our distresse. But sure if you Would be your Countries Pleader, your good tongue More then the instant Armie we can make Might stop our Countryman.

Mene. No: Ile not meddle.

Sicin. Pray you go to him.

Mene. What should I do?

Bru. Onely make triall what your Loue can do, For Rome, towards *Martius*.

Mene. Well, and say that *Martius* returne mee, As *Cominius* is return'd, vnheard: what then? But as a discontented Friend, greefe-shot With his vnkindnesse. Say't be so?

Sicin. Yet your good will Must haue that thankes from Rome, after the measure As you intended well.

Mene. Ile vndertak't: I thinke hee'l heare me. Yet to bite his lip, And humme at good *Cominius*, much vnhearts mee.

He was not taken well, he had not din'd,
The Veines vnfill'd, our blood is cold, and then
We powt vpon the Morning, are vnapt
To giue or to forgiue: but when we haue stufft
These Pipes, and these Conueyances of our blood
With Wine and Feeding, we haue suppler Soules
Then in our Priest-like Fasts: therefore Ile watch him
Till he be dieted to my request,
And then Ile set vpon him.

  Bru. You know the very rode into his kindnesse,
And cannot lose your way.

  Mene. Good faith Ile proue him,
Speed how it will. I shall ere long, haue knowledge
Of my successe.   *Exit.*

  Com. Hee'l neuer heare him.
  Sicin. No.
  Com. I tell you, he doe's sit in Gold, his eye
Red as 'twould burne Rome: and his Iniury
The Gaoler to his pitty. I kneel'd before him,
'Twas very faintly he said Rise: dismist me
Thus with his speechlesse hand. What he would do
He sent in writing after me: what he would not,
Bound with an Oath to yeeld to his conditions:
So that all hope is vaine, vnlesse his Noble Mother,
And his Wife, who (as I heare) meane to solicite him
For mercy to his Countrey: therefore let's hence,
And with our faire intreaties hast them on.   *Exeunt*

  Enter Menenius to the Watch or Guard.

  1. *Wat.* Stay: whence are you.
  2. *War.* Stand, and go backe.
  Me. You guard like men, 'tis well. But by your leaue,
I am an Officer of State, & come to speak with *Coriolanus*
  1 From whence?   *Mene.* From Rome.
  1 You may not passe, you must returne: our Generall
will no more heare from thence.
  2 You'l see your Rome embrac'd with fire, before
You'l speake with *Coriolanus.*
  Mene. Good my Friends,
If you haue heard your Generall talke of Rome,
And of his Friends there, it is Lots to Blankes,
My name hath touch't your eares: it is *Menenius.*
  1 Be it so, go back: the vertue of your name,
Is not heere passable.
  Mene. I tell thee Fellow,
Thy Generall is my Louer: I haue beene
The booke of his good Acts, whence men haue read
His Fame vnparalell'd, happely amplified:
For I haue euer verified my Friends,
(Of whom hee's cheefe) with all the size that verity
Would without lapsing suffer: Nay, sometimes,
Like to a Bowle vpon a subtle ground
I haue tumbled past the throw: and in his praise
Haue (almost) stampt the Leasing. Therefore Fellow,
I must haue leaue to passe.
  1 Faith Sir, if you had told as many lies in his behalfe,
as you haue vttered words in your owne, you should not
passe heere: no, though it were as vertuous to lye, as to
liue chastly. Therefore go backe.
  Men. Prythee fellow, remember my name is *Menenius*,
alwayes factionary on the party of your Generall.
  2 Howsoeuer you haue bin his Lier, as you say you
haue, I am one that telling true vnder him, must say you
cannot passe. Therefore go backe.
  Mene. Ha's he din'd can'st thou tell? For I would not
speake with him, till after dinner.
  1 You are a Roman, are you?

  Mene. I am as thy Generall is.
  1 Then you should hate Rome, as he do's. Can you,
when you haue pusht out your gates, the very Defender
of them, and in a violent popular ignorance, giuen your
enemy your shield, thinke to front his reuenges with the
easie groanes of old women, the Virginall Palms of your
daughters, or with the palsied intercession of such a decay'd
Dotant as you seeme to be? Can you think to blow
out the intended fire, your City is ready to flame in, with
such weake breath as this? No, you are deceiu'd, therfore
backe to Rome, and prepare for your execution: you are
condemn'd, our Generall has sworne you out of repreeue
and pardon.
  Mene. Sirra, if thy Captaine knew I were heere,
He would vse me with estimation.
  1 Come, my Captaine knowes you not.
  Mene. I meane thy Generall.
  1 My Generall cares not for you. Back I say, go: least
I let forth your halfe pinte of blood. Backe, that's the vtmost
of your hauing, backe.
  Mene. Nay but Fellow, Fellow.

  Enter Coriolanus with Auffidius.

  Corio. What's the matter?
  Mene. Now you Companion: Ile say an arrant for you:
you shall know now that I am in estimation: you shall
perceiue, that a Iacke gardant cannot office me from my
Son *Coriolanus*, guesse but my entertainment with him: if
thou stand'st not i'th state of hanging, or of some death
more long in Spectatorship, and crueller in suffering, behold
now presently, and swoond for what's to come vpon
thee. The glorious Gods sit in hourely Synod about thy
particular prosperity, and loue thee no worse then thy old
Father *Menenius* do's. O my Son, my Son! thou art preparing
fire for vs: looke thee, heere's water to quench it.
I was hardly moued to come to thee: but beeing assured
none but my selfe could moue thee, I haue bene blowne
out of your Gates with sighes: and coniure thee to pardon
Rome, and thy petitionary Countrimen. The good
Gods asswage thy wrath, and turne the dregs of it, vpon
this Varlet heere: This, who like a blocke hath denyed
my accesse to thee.
  Corio. Away.
  Mene. How? Away?
  Corio. Wife, Mother, Child, I know not. My affaires
Are Seruanted to others: Though I owe
My Reuenge properly, my remission lies
In Volcean brests. That we haue beene familiar,
Ingrate forgetfulnesse shall poison rather
Then pitty: Note how much, therefore be gone.
Mine eares against your suites, are stronger then
Your gates against my force. Yet for I loued thee,
Take this along, I writ it for thy sake,
And would haue sent it. Another word *Menenius*,
I will not heare thee speake. This man *Auffidius*
Was my belou'd in Rome: yet thou behold'st.
  Auffid. You keepe a constant temper.   *Exeunt*

  Manet the Guard and Menenius.

  1 Now sir, is your name *Menenius*?
  2 'Tis a spell you see of much power:
You know the way home againe.
  1 Do you heare how wee are shent for keeping your
greatnesse backe?
  2 What cause do you thinke I haue to swoond?
  Mene. I neither care for th'world, nor your Generall:
for such things as you. I can scarse thinke ther's any, y'are
so slight. He that hath a will to die by himselfe, feares it
not

The Tragedie of Coriolanus.

not from another: Let your Generall do his worst. For
you, bee that you are, long; and your misery encrease
with your age. I say to you, as I was said to, Away. *Exit*

1 A Noble Fellow I warrant him.

2 The worthy Fellow is our General. He's the Rock,
The Oake not to be winde-shaken. *Exit Watch.*

Enter Coriolanus and Auffidius.

Corio. We will before the walls of Rome to morrow
Set downe our Hoast. My partner in this Action,
You must report to th'Volcian Lords, how plainly
I haue borne this Businesse.

Auf. Onely their ends you haue respected,
Stopt your eares against the generall suite of Rome:
Neuer admitted a priuat whisper, no not with such frends
That thought them sure of you.

Corio. This last old man,
Whom with a crack'd heart I haue sent to Rome,
Lou'd me, aboue the measure of a Father,
Nay godded me indeed. Their latest refuge
Was to send him: for whose old Loue I haue
(Though I shew'd sowrely to him) once more offer'd
The first Conditions which they did refuse,
And cannot now accept, to grace him onely,
That thought he could do more: A very little
I haue yeelded too. Fresh Embasses, and Suites,
Nor from the State, nor priuate friends heereafter
Will I lend eare to. Ha? what shout is this? *Shout within*
Shall I be tempted to infringe my vow
In the same time 'tis made? I will not.

Enter Virgilia, Volumnia, Valeria, yong Martius,
with Attendants.

My wife comes formost, then the honour'd mould
Wherein this Trunke was fram'd, and in her hand
The Grandchilde to her blood. But out affection,
All bond and priuiledge of Nature breake;
Let it be Vertuous to be Obstinate.
What is that Curt'sie worth? Or those Doues eyes,
Which can make Gods forsworne? I melt, and am not
Of stronger earth then others: my Mother bowes,
As if Olympus to a Mole-hill should
In supplication Nod: and my yong Boy
Hath an Aspect of intercession, which
Great Nature cries, Deny not. Let the Volces
Plough Rome, and harrow Italy, Ile neuer
Be such a Gosling to obey instinct; but stand
As if a man were Author of himself, & knew no other kin

Virgil. My Lord and Husband.

Corio. These eyes are not the same I wore in Rome.

Virg. The sorrow that deliuers vs thus chang'd,
Makes you thinke so.

Corio. Like a dull Actor now, I haue forgot my part,
And I am out, euen to a full Disgrace. Best of my Flesh,
Forgiue my Tyranny: but do not say,
For that forgiue our Romanes. O a kisse
Long as my Exile, sweet as my Reuenge!
Now by the iealous Queene of Heauen, that kisse
I carried from thee deare; and my true Lippe
Hath Virgin'd it ere since. You Gods, I pray,
And the most noble Mother of the world
Leaue vnsaluted: Sinke my knee i'th'earth, *Kneeles*
Of thy deepe duty, more impression shew
Then that of common Sonnes.

Volum. Oh stand vp blest!
Whil'st with no softer Cushion then the Flint
I kneele before thee, and vnproperly
Shew duty as mistaken, all this while,

Betweene the Childe, and Parent.

Corio. What's this? your knees to me?
To your Corrected Sonne?
Then let the Pibbles on the hungry beach
Fillop the Starres: Then, let the mutinous windes
Strike the proud Cedars 'gainst the fiery Sun:
Murd'ring Impossibility, to make
What cannot be, slight worke.

Volum. Thou art my Warriour, I hope to frame thee
Do you know this Lady?

Corio. The Noble Sister of *Publicola*;
The Moone of Rome: Chaste as the Isicle
That's curdied by the Frost, from purest Snow,
And hangs on *Dians* Temple: Deere *Valeria.*

Volum. This is a poore Epitome of yours,
Which by th'interpretation of full time,
May shew like all your selfe.

Corio. The God of Souldiers:
With the consent of supreame Ioue, informe
Thy thoughts with Noblenesse, that thou mayst proue
To shame vnvulnerable, and sticke i'th Warres
Like a great Sea-marke standing euery flaw,
And sauing those that eye thee.

Volum. Your knee, Sirrah.

Corio. That's my braue Boy.

Volum. Euen he, your wife, this Ladie, and my selfe,
Are Sutors to you.

Corio. I beseech you peace:
Or if you'ld aske, remember this before;
The thing I haue forsworne to graunt, may neuer
Be held by you denials. Do not bid me
Dismisse my Soldiers, or capitulate
Againe, with Romes Mechanickes. Tell me not
Wherein I seeme vnnaturall: Desire not t'allay
My Rages and Reuenges, with your colder reasons.

Volum. Oh no more, no more:
You haue said you will not grant vs any thing:
For we haue nothing else to aske, but that
Which you deny already: yet we will aske,
That if you faile in our request, the blame
May hang vpon your hardnesse, therefore heare vs.

Corio. Auffidius, and you Volces marke, for wee'l
Heare nought from Rome in priuate. Your request?

Volum. Should we be silent & not speak, our Raiment
And state of Bodies would bewray what life
We haue led since thy Exile. Thinke with thy selfe,
How more vnfortunate then all liuing women
Are we come hither; since that thy sight, which should
Make our eies flow with ioy, harts dance with comforts,
Constraines them weepe, and shake with feare & sorow,
Making the Mother, wife, and Childe to see,
The Sonne, the Husband, and the Father tearing
His Countries Bowels out; and to poore we
Thine enmities most capitall: Thou barr'st vs
Our prayers to the Gods, which is a comfort
That all but we enioy. For how can we?
Alas! how can we, for our Country pray?
Whereto we are bound, together with thy victory:
Whereto we are bound: Alacke, or we must loose
The Countrie our deere Nurse, or else thy person
Our comfort in the Country. We must finde
An euident Calamity, though we had
Our wish, which side should win. For either thou
Must as a Forraine Recreant be led
With Manacles through our streets, or else
Triumphantly treade on thy Countries ruine,

And beare the Palme, for hauing brauely shed
Thy Wife and Childrens blood: For my selfe, Sonne,
I purpose not to waite on Fortune, till
These warres determine: If I cannot perswade thee,
Rather to shew a Noble grace to both parts,
Then seeke the end of one; thou shalt no sooner
March to assault thy Country, then to treade
(Trust too't, thou shalt not) on thy Mothers wombe
That brought thee to this world.

Virg. I, and mine, that brought you forth this boy,
To keepe your name liuing to time.

Boy. A shall not tread on me: Ile run away
Till I am bigger, but then Ile fight.

Corio. Not of a womans tendernesse to be,
Requires nor Childe, nor womans face to see:
I haue sate too long.

Volum. Nay, go not from vs thus:
If it were so, that our request did tend
To saue the Romanes, thereby to destroy
The Volces whom you serue, you might condemne vs
As poysonous of your Honour. No, our suite
Is that you reconcile them: While the Volces
May say, this mercy we haue shew'd: the Romanes,
This we receiu'd, and each in either side
Giue the All-haile to thee, and cry be Blest
For making vp this peace. Thou know'st (great Sonne)
The end of Warres vncertaine: but this certaine,
That if thou conquer Rome, the benefit
Which thou shalt thereby reape, is such a name
Whose repetition will be dogg'd with Curses:
Whose Chronicle thus writ, The man was Noble,
But with his last Attempt, he wip'd it out:
Destroy'd his Country, and his name remaines
To th'insuing Age, abhorr'd. Speake to me Son:
Thou hast affected the fiue straines of Honor,
To imitate the graces of the Gods.
To teare with Thunder the wide Cheekes a'th'Ayre,
And yet to change thy Sulphure with a Boult
That should but riue an Oake. Why do'st not speake?
Think'st thou it Honourable for a Nobleman
Still to remember wrongs? Daughter, speake you:
He cares not for your weeping. Speake thou Boy,
Perhaps thy childishnesse will moue him more
Then can our Reasons. There's no man in the world
More bound to's Mother, yet heere he let's me prate
Like one i'th' Stockes. Thou hast neuer in thy life,
Shew'd thy deere Mother any curtesie,
When she (poore Hen) fond of no second brood,
Ha's clock'd thee to the Warres: and safelie home
Loden with Honor. Say my Request's vniust,
And spurne me backe: But, if it be not so
Thou art not honest, and the Gods will plague thee
That thou restrain'st from me the Duty, which
To a Mothers part belongs. He turnes away:
Down Ladies: let vs shame him with him without knees
To his sur-name *Coriolanus* longs more pride
Then pitty to our Prayers. Downe: an end,
This is the last. So, we will home to Rome,
And dye among our Neighbours: Nay, behold's,
This Boy that cannot tell what he would haue,
But kneeles, and holds vp hands for fellowship,
Doe's reason our Petition with more strength
Then thou hast to deny't. Come, let vs go:
This Fellow had a Volcean to his Mother:
His Wife is in *Corioles*, and his Childe
Like him by chance: yet giue vs our dispatch:
I am husht vntill our City be afire, & then Ile speak a little
Holds her by the hand silent.

Corio. O Mother, Mother!
What haue you done? Behold, the Heauens do ope,
The Gods looke downe, and this vnnaturall Scene
They laugh at. Oh my Mother, Mother: Oh!
You haue wonne a happy Victory to Rome.
But for your Sonne, beleeue it: Oh beleeue it,
Most dangerously you haue with him preuail'd,
If not most mortall to him. But let it come:
Auffidius, though I cannot make true Warres,
Ile frame conuenient peace. Now good *Auffidius*,
Were you in my steed, would you haue heard
A Mother lesse? or granted lesse *Auffidius*?

Auf. I was mou'd withall.

Corio. I dare be sworne you were:
And sir, it is no little thing to make
Mine eyes to sweat compassion. But (good sir:)
What peace you'l make, aduise me: For my part,
Ile not to Rome, Ile backe with you, and pray you
Stand to me in this cause. Oh Mother! Wife!

Auf. I am glad thou hast set thy mercy, & thy Honor
At difference in thee: Out of that Ile worke
My selfe a former Fortune.

Corio. I by and by; But we will drinke together:
And you shall beare
A better witnesse backe then words, which we
On like conditions, will haue Counter-seal'd,
Come enter with vs: Ladies you deserue
To haue a Temple built you: All the Swords
In Italy, and her Confederate Armes,
Could not haue made this peace. *Exeunt.*

Enter Menenius and Sicinius.

Mene. See you yon'd Coin a'th Capitol, yon' corner?
Sicin. Why what of that?
Mene. If it be possible for you to displace it with your little finger, there is some hope the Ladies of Rome, especially his Mother, may preuaile with him. But I say, there is no hope in't, our throats are sentenc'd, and stay vppon execution.

Sicin. Is't possible, that so short a time can alter the condition of a man.

Mene. There is differency between a Grub & a Butterfly, yet your Butterfly was a Grub: this *Martius* is growne from Man to Dragon: He has wings, hee's more then a creeping thing.

Sicin. He lou'd his Mother deerely.

Mene. So did he mee: and he no more remembers his Mother now, then an eight yeare old horse. The tartnesse of his face, sowres ripe Grapes. When he walks, he moues like an Engine, and the ground shrinkes before his Treading. He is able to pierce a Corslet with his eye: Talkes like a knell, and his hum is a Battery. He sits in his State, as a thing made for *Alexander*. What he bids bee done, is finisht with his bidding. He wants nothing of a God but Eternity, and a Heauen to Throne in.

Sicin. Yes, mercy, if you report him truly.

Mene. I paint him in the Character. Mark what mercy his Mother shall bring from him: There is no more mercy in him, then there is milke in a male-Tyger, that shall our poore City finde: and all this is long of you.

Sicin. The Gods be good vnto vs.

Mene. No, in such a case the Gods will not bee good vnto vs. When we banish'd him, we respected not them: and he returning to breake our necks, they respect not vs.

Enter a Messenger.

Mess.

The Tragedie of Coriolanus.

Mef. Sir, if you'ld saue your life, flye to your House,
The Plebeians haue got your Fellow Tribune,
And hale him vp and downe; all swearing, if
The Romane Ladies bring not comfort home,
They'l giue him death by Inches.

Enter another Messenger.

Sicin. What's the Newes?
Mess. Good Newes, good newes, the Ladies haue preuayl'd,
The Volcians are dislodg'd, and *Martius* gone:
A merrier day did neuer yet greet Rome,
No, not th'expulsion of the *Tarquins*.

Sicin. Friend, art thou certaine this is true?
Is't most certaine.

Mes. As certaine as I know the Sun is fire:
Where haue you lurk'd that you make doubt of it:
Ne're through an Arch so hurried the blowne Tide,
As the recomforted through th'gates. Why harke you:

Trumpets, Hoboyes, Drums beate, altogether.

The Trumpets, Sack-buts, Psalteries, and Fifes,
Tabors, and Symboles, and the showting Romans,
Make the Sunne dance. Hearke you. *A shout within*

Mene. This is good Newes:
I will go meete the Ladies. This *Volumnia*,
Is worth of Consuls, Senators, Patricians,
A City full: Of Tribunes such as you,
A Sea and Land full: you haue pray'd well to day:
This Morning, for ten thousand of your throates,
I'de not haue giuen a doit. Harke, how they ioy.

Sound still with the Shouts.

Sicin. First, the Gods blesse you for your tydings:
Next, accept my thankefulnesse.

Mess. Sir, we haue all great cause to giue great thanks.
Sicin. They are neere the City.
Mes. Almost at point to enter.
Sicin. Wee'l meet them, and helpe the ioy. *Exeunt.*

Enter two Senators, with Ladies, passing ouer the Stage, with other Lords.

Sena. Behold our Patronnesse, the life of Rome:
Call all your Tribes together, praise the Gods,
And make triumphant fires, strew Flowers before them:
Vnshoot the noise that Banish'd *Martius*;
Repeale him, with the welcome of his Mother:
Cry welcome Ladies, welcome.

All. Welcome Ladies, welcome.

A Flourish with Drummes & Trumpets.

Enter Tullus Auffidius, with Attendants.

Auf. Go tell the Lords a'th'City, I am heere:
Deliuer them this Paper: hauing read it,
Bid them repayre to th'Market place, where I
Euen in theirs, and in the Commons eares
Will vouch the truth of it. Him I accuse:
The City Ports by this hath enter'd, and
Intends t'appeare before the People, hoping
To purge himselfe with words. Dispatch.

Enter 3 or 4 Conspirators of Auffidius Faction.

Most Welcome.
1. *Con.* How is it with our Generall?
Auf. Euen so, as with a man by his owne Almes im-poyson'd, and with his Charity slaine.
2. *Con.* Most Noble Sir, If you do hold the same intent
Wherein you wisht vs parties: Wee'l deliuer you
Of your great danger.
Auf. Sir, I cannot tell,
We must proceed as we do finde the People.

3. *Con.* The People will remaine vncertaine, whil'st
'Twixt you there's difference: but the fall of either
Makes the Suruiuor heyre of all.

Auf. I know it:
And my pretext to strike at him, admits
A good construction. I rais'd him, and I pawn'd
Mine Honor for his truth: who being so heighten'd,
He watered his new Plants with dewes of Flattery,
Seducing so my Friends: and to this end,
He bow'd his Nature, neuer knowne before,
But to be rough, vnswayable, and free.

3. *Consp.* Sir, his stoutnesse
When he did stand for Consull, which he lost
By lacke of stooping.

Auf. That I would haue spoke of:
Being banish'd for't, he came vnto my Harth,
Presented to my knife his Throat: I tooke him,
Made him ioynt-seruant with me: Gaue him way
In all his owne desires: Nay, let him choose
Out of my Files, his proiects, to accomplish
My best and freshest men, seru'd his designements
In mine owne person: holpe to reape the Fame
Which he did end all his; and tooke some pride
To do my selfe this wrong: Till at the last
I seem'd his Follower, not Partner; and
He wadg'd me with his Countenance, as if
I had bin Mercenary.

1. *Con.* So he did my Lord:
The Army marueyl'd at it, and in the last,
When he had carried Rome, and that we look'd
For no lesse Spoile, then Glory.

Auf. There was it:
For which my sinewes shall be stretcht vpon him,
At a few drops of Womens rheume, which are
As cheape as Lies; he sold the Blood and Labour
Of our great Action; therefore shall he dye,
And Ile renew me in his fall. But hearke.

Drummes and Trumpets sounds, with great showts of the people.

1. *Con.* Your Natiue Towne you enter'd like a Poste,
And had no welcomes home, but he returnes
Splitting the Ayre with noyse.

2. *Con.* And patient Fooles,
Whose children he hath slaine, their base throats teare
With giuing him glory.

3. *Con.* Therefore at your vantage,
Ere he expresse himselfe, or moue the people
With what he would say, let him feele your Sword:
Which we will second, when he lies along
After your way. His Tale pronounc'd, shall bury
His Reasons, with his Body.

Auf. Say no more. Heere come the Lords,

Enter the Lords of the City.

All Lords. You are most welcome home.
Auff. I haue not deseru'd it.
But worthy Lords, haue you with heede perused
What I haue written to you?

All. We haue.
1. *Lord.* And greeue to heare't:
What faults he made before the last, I thinke
Might haue found easie Fines: But there to end
Where he was to begin, and giue away
The benefit of our Leuies, answering vs
With our owne charge: making a Treatie, where
There was a yeelding; this admits no excuse.

Auf. He approaches, you shall heare him.

Enter Coriolanus marching with Drumme, and Colours. The Commoners being with him.

Corio. Haile Lords, I am return'd your Souldier:
No more infected with my Countries loue
Then when I parted hence: but still subsisting
Vnder your great Command. You are to know,
That prosperously I haue attempted, and
With bloody passage led your Warres, euen to
The gates of Rome: Our spoiles we haue brought home
Doth more then counterpoize a full third part
The charges of the Action. We haue made peace
With no lesse Honor to the *Antiates*
Then shame to th'Romaines. And we heere deliuer
Subscrib'd by'th'Consuls, and Patricians,
Together with the Seale a'th Senat, what
We haue compounded on.

Auf. Read it not Noble Lords,
But tell the Traitor in the highest degree
He hath abus'd your Powers.

Corio. Traitor? How now?

Auf. I Traitor, *Martius*.

Corio. *Martius*?

Auf. I *Martius*, *Caius Martius*: Do'st thou thinke
Ile grace thee with that Robbery, thy stolne name
Coriolanus in *Corioles*?
You Lords and Heads a'th'State, perfidiously
He ha's betray'd your businesse, and giuen vp
For certaine drops of Salt, your City Rome:
I say your City to his Wife and Mother,
Breaking his Oath and Resolution, like
A twist of rotten Silke, neuer admitting
Counsaile a'th'warre: But at his Nurses teares
He whin'd and roar'd away your Victory,
That Pages blush'd at him, and men of heart
Look'd wond'ring each at others.

Corio. Hear'st thou Mars?

Auf. Name not the God, thou boy of Teares.

Corio. Ha?

Aufid. No more.

Corio. Measurelesse Lyar, thou hast made my heart
Too great for what containes it. Boy? Oh Slaue,
Pardon me Lords, 'tis the first time that euer
I was forc'd to scoul'd. Your iudgments my graue Lords
Must giue this Curre the Lye: and his owne Notion,
Who weares my stripes imprest vpon him, that
Must beare my beating to his Graue, shall ioyne
To thrust the Lye vnto him.

1 Lord. Peace both, and heare me speake.

Corio. Cut me to peeces Volces men and Lads,
Staine all your edges on me. Boy, false Hound:
If you haue writ your Annales true, 'tis there,
That like an Eagle in a Doue-coat, I
Flatter'd your Volcians in *Corioles*.
Alone I did it, Boy.

Auf. Why Noble Lords,
Will you be put in minde of his blinde Fortune,
Which was your shame, by this vnholy Braggart?
'Fore your owne eyes, and eares?

All Consp. Let him dye for't.

All People. Teare him to peeces, do it presently:
He kill'd my Sonne, my daughter, he kill'd my Cosine
Marcus, he kill'd my Father.

2. Lord. Peace hoe: no outrage, peace:
The man is Noble, and his Fame folds in
This Orbe o'th'earth: His last offences to vs
Shall haue Iudicious hearing. Stand *Auffidius*,
And trouble not the peace.

Corio. O that I had him, with six *Auffidius's*, or more
His Tribe, to vse my lawfull Sword.

Auf. Insolent Villaine.

All Consp. Kill, kill, kill, kill, kill him.

Draw both the Conspirators, and kils Martius, who falles, Auffidius stands on him.

Lords. Hold, hold, hold, hold.

Auf. My Noble Masters, heare me speake.

1. Lord. O *Tullus*.

2. Lord. Thou hast done a deed, whereat
Valour will weepe.

3. Lord. Tread not vpon him Masters, all be quiet,
Put vp your Swords.

Auf. My Lords,
When you shall know (as in this Rage
Prouok'd by him, you cannot) the great danger
Which this mans life did owe you, you'l reioyce
That he is thus cut off. Please it your Honours
To call me to your Senate, Ile deliuer
My selfe your loyall Seruant, or endure
Your heauiest Censure.

1. Lord. Beare from hence his body,
And mourne you for him. Let him be regarded
As the most Noble Coarse, that euer Herald
Did follow to his Vrne.

2. Lord. His owne impatience,
Takes from *Auffidius* a great part of blame:
Let's make the Best of it.

Auf. My Rage is gone,
And I am strucke with sorrow. Take him vp:
Helpe three a'th'cheefest Souldiers, Ile be one.
Beate thou the Drumme that it speake mournfully:
Traile your steele Pikes. Though in this City hee
Hath widdowed and vnchilded many a one,
Which to this houre bewaile the Iniury,
Yet he shall haue a Noble Memory. Assist.

Exeunt bearing the Body of Martius. A dead March Sounded.

FINIS.

The Lamentable Tragedy of Titus Andronicus.

Actus Primus. Scœna Prima.

Flourish. Enter the Tribunes and Senators aloft. And then enter Saturninus and his Followers at one doore, and Bassianus and his Followers at the other, with Drum & Colours.

Saturninus.
Noble Patricians, Patrons of my right,
Defend the iustice of my Cause with Armes.
And Countrey-men, my louing Followers,
Pleade my Successiue Title with your Swords.
I was the first borne Sonne, that was the last
That wore the Imperiall Diadem of Rome:
Then let my Fathers Honours liue in me,
Nor wrong mine Age with this indignitie.

Bassianus. Romaines, Friends, Followers,
Fauourers of my Right:
If euer *Bassianus*, *Cæsars* Sonne,
Were gracious in the eyes of Royall Rome,
Keepe then this passage to the Capitoll:
And suffer not Dishonour to approach
Th'Imperiall Seate to Vertue: consecrate
To Iustice, Continence, and Nobility:
But let Desert in pure Election shine;
And Romanes, fight for Freedome in your Choice.

Enter Marcus Andronicus aloft with the Crowne.

Princes, that striue by Factions, and by Friends,
Ambitiously for Rule and Empery:
Know, that the people of Rome for whom we stand
A speciall Party, haue by Common voyce
In Election for the Romane Emperie,
Chosen *Andronicus*, Sur-named *Pious*,
For many good and great deserts to Rome.
A Nobler man, a brauer Warriour,
Liues not this day within the City Walles.
He by the Senate is accited home
From weary Warres against the barbarous Gothes,
That with his Sonnes (a terror to our Foes)
Hath yoak'd a Nation strong, train'd vp in Armes.
Ten yeares are spent, since first he vndertooke
This Cause of Rome, and chasticed with Armes
Our Enemies pride. Fiue times he hath return'd
Bleeding to Rome, bearing his Valiant Sonnes
In Coffins from the Field.
And now at last, laden with Honours Spoyles,
Returnes the good *Andronicus* to Rome,
Renowned *Titus*, flourishing in Armes.
Let vs intreat, by Honour of his Name,
Whom (worthily) you would haue now succeede,
And in the Capitoll and Senates right,
Whom you pretend to Honour and Adore,
That you withdraw you, and abate your Strength,
Dismisse your Followers, and as Suters should,
Pleade your Deserts in Peace and Humblenesse.

Saturnine. How fayre the Tribune speakes,
To calme my thoughts.

Bassia. *Marcus Andronicus*, so I do affie
In thy vprightnesse and Integrity:
And so I Loue and Honor thee, and thine,
Thy Noble Brother *Titus*, and his Sonnes,
And Her (to whom my thoughts are humbled all)
Gracious *Lauinia*, Romes rich Ornament,
That I will heere dismisse my louing Friends:
And to my Fortunes, and the Peoples Fauour,
Commit my Cause in ballance to be weigh'd.
Exit Souldiours.

Saturnine. Friends, that haue beene
Thus forward in my Right,
I thanke you all, and heere Dismisse you all,
And to the Loue and Fauour of my Countrey,
Commit my Selfe, my Person, and the Cause:
Rome, be as iust and gracious vnto me,
As I am confident and kinde to thee.
Open the Gates, and let me in.

Bassia. Tribunes, and me, a poore Competitor.
Flourish. *They go vp into the Senat house.*

Enter a Captaine.
Cap. Romanes make way: the good *Andronicus*,
Patron of Vertue, Romes best Champion,
Successefull in the Battailes that he fights,
With Honour and with Fortune is return'd,
From whence he circumscribed with his Sword,
And brought to yoke the Enemies of Rome.

Sound Drummes and Trumpets. And then enter two of Titus Sonnes; After them, two men bearing a Coffin couered with blacke, then two other Sonnes. After them, Titus Andronicus, and then Tamora the Queene of Gothes, & her two Sonnes Chiron and Demetrius, with Aaron the Moore, and others, as many as can bee: They set downe the Coffin, and Titus speakes.

Andronicus. Haile Rome:
Victorious in thy Mourning Weedes:

Loe as the Barke that hath discharg'd his fraught,
Returnes with precious lading to the Bay,
From whence at first she weigh'd her Anchorage:
Commeth Andronicus bound with Lawrell bowes,
To resalute his Country with his teares,
Teares of true ioy for his returne to Rome,
Thou great defender of this Capitoll,
Stand gracious to the Rites that we intend.
Romaines, of fiue and twenty Valiant Sonnes,
Halfe of the number that King Priam had,
Behold the poore remaines aliue and dead!
These that Suruiue, let Rome reward with Loue:
These that I bring vnto their latest home,
With buriall amongst their Auncestors.
Heere Gothes haue giuen me leaue to sheath my Sword:
Titus vnkinde, and carelesse of thine owne,
Why suffer'st thou thy Sonnes vnburied yet,
To houer on the dreadfull shore of Stix?
Make way to lay them by their Bretheren.

They open the Tombe.

There greete in silence as the dead are wont,
And sleepe in peace, slaine in your Countries warres:
O sacred receptacle of my ioyes,
Sweet Cell of vertue and Noblitie,
How many Sonnes of mine hast thou in store,
That thou wilt neuer render to me more?

Luc. Giue vs the proudest prisoner of the Gothes,
That we may hew his limbes, and on a pile
Ad manus fratrum, sacrifice his flesh:
Before this earthly prison of their bones,
That so the shadowes be not vnappeas'd,
Nor we disturb'd with prodigies on earth.

Tit. I giue him you, the Noblest that Suruiues,
The eldest Son of this distressed Queene.

Tam. Stay Romaine Bretheren, gracious Conqueror,
Victorious Titus, rue the teares I shed,
A Mothers teares in passion for her sonne:
And if thy Sonnes were euer deere to thee,
Oh thinke my sonnes to be as deere to mee.
Sufficeth not, that we are brought to Rome
To beautifie thy Triumphs, and returne
Captiue to thee, and to thy Romaine yoake,
But must my Sonnes be slaughtred in the streetes,
For Valiant doings in their Countries cause?
O! If to fight for King and Common-weale,
Were pietie in thine, it is in these:
Andronicus, staine not thy Tombe with blood.
Wilt thou draw neere the nature of the Gods?
Draw neere them then in being mercifull.
Sweet mercy is Nobilities true badge,
Thrice Noble Titus, spare my first borne sonne.

Tit. Patient your selfe Madam, and pardon me.
These are the Brethren, whom you Gothes beheld
Aliue and dead, and for their Bretheren slaine,
Religiously they aske a sacrifice:
To this your sonne is markt, and die he must,
T'appease their groaning shadowes that are gone.

Luc. Away with him, and make a fire straight,
And with our Swords vpon a pile of wood,
Let's hew his limbes till they be cleane consum'd.

Exit Sonnes with Alarbus.

Tamo. O cruell irreligious piety.
Chi. Was euer Scythia halfe so barbarous?
Dem. Oppose me Scythia to ambitious Rome,

Alarbus goes to rest, and we suruiue,
To tremble vnder Titus threatning lookes,
Then Madam stand resolu'd, but hope withall,
The selfe same Gods that arm'd the Queene of Troy
With opportunitie of sharpe reuenge
Vpon the Thracian Tyrant in his Tent,
May fauour Tamora the Queene of Gothes,
(When Gothes were Gothes, and Tamora was Queene)
To quit the bloody wrongs vpon her foes.

Enter the Sonnes of Andronicus againe.

Luci. See Lord and Father, how we haue perform'd
Our Romaine rightes, Alarbus limbs are lopt,
And intrals feede the sacrifising fire,
Whose smoke like incense doth perfume the skie.
Remaineth nought but to interre our Brethren,
And with low'd Larums welcome them to Rome.

Tit. Let it be so, and let Andronicus
Make this his latest farewell to their soules.

Flourish.

Then Sound Trumpets, and lay the Coffins in the Tombe.
In peace and Honour rest you heere my Sonnes,
Romes readiest Champions, repose you heere in rest,
Secure from worldly chaunces and mishaps:
Heere lurks no Treason, heere no enuie swels,
Heere grow no damned grudges, heere are no stormes,
No noyse, but silence and Eternall sleepe,
In peace and Honour rest you heere my Sonnes.

Enter Lauinia.

Laui. In peace and Honour, liue Lord Titus long,
My Noble Lord and Father, liue in Fame:
Loe at this Tombe my tributarie teares,
I render for my Bretherens Obsequies:
And at thy feete I kneele, with teares of ioy
Shed on the earth for thy returne to Rome.
O blesse me heere with thy victorious hand,
Whose Fortune Romes best Citizens applau'd.

Ti. Kind Rome,
That hast thus louingly reseru'd
The Cordiall of mine age to glad my hart,
Lauinia liue, out-liue thy Fathers dayes:
And Fames eternall date for vertues praise.

Marc. Long liue Lord Titus, my beloued brother,
Gracious Triumpher in the eyes of Rome.

Tit. Thankes Gentle Tribune,
Noble brother Marcus.

Mar. And welcome Nephews from successfull wars,
You that suruiue and you that sleepe in Fame:
Faire Lords your Fortunes are all alike in all,
That in your Countries seruice drew your Swords.
But safer Triumph is this Funerall Pompe,
That hath aspir'd to Solons Happines,
And Triumphs ouer chaunce in honours bed.
Titus Andronicus, the people of Rome,
Whose friend in iustice thou hast euer bene,
Send thee by me their Tribune and their trust,
This Palliament of white and spotlesse Hue,
And name thee in Election for the Empire,
With these our late deceased Emperours Sonnes:
Be Candidatus then, and put it on,
And helpe to set a head on headlesse Rome.

Tit. A better head her Glorious body fits,
Then his that shakes for age and feeblenesse:

What

The Tragedie of Titus Andronicus.

What should I d'on this Robe and trouble you,
Be chosen with proclamations to day,
To morrow yeeld vp rule, resigne my life,
And set abroad new businesse for you all.
Rome I haue bene thy Souldier forty yeares,
And led my Countries strength successfully,
And buried one and twenty Valiant Sonnes,
Knighted in Field, slaine manfully in Armes,
In right and Seruice of their Noble Countrie:
Giue me a staffe of Honour for mine age,
But not a Scepter to controule the world,
Vpright he held it Lords, that held it last.

Mar. *Titus* thou shalt obtaine and aske the Emperie.

Sat. Proud and ambitious Tribune can'st thou tell?

Titus. Patience Prince *Saturninus*.

Sat. Romaines do me right.
Patricians draw your Swords, and sheath them not
Till *Saturninus* be Romes Emperour:
Andronicus would thou wert shipt to hell,
Rather then rob me of the peoples harts.

Luc. Proud *Saturnine*, interrupter of the good
That Noble minded *Titus* meanes to thee.

Tit. Content thee Prince, I will restore to thee
The peoples harts, and weane them from themselues.

Bass. *Andronicus*, I do not flatter thee
But Honour thee, and will doe till I die:
My Faction if thou strengthen with thy Friend?
I will most thankefull be, and thankes to men
Of Noble mindes, is Honourable Meede.

Tit. People of Rome, and Noble Tribunes heere,
I aske your voyces and your Suffrages,
Will you bestow them friendly on *Andronicus*?

Tribunes. To gratifie the good *Andronicus*,
And Gratulate his safe returne to Rome,
The people will accept whom he admits.

Tit. Tribunes I thanke you, and this sure I make,
That you Create your Emperours eldest sonne,
Lord *Saturnine*, whose Vertues will I hope,
Reflect on Rome as Tytans Rayes on earth,
And ripen Iustice in this Common-weale:
Then if you will elect by my aduise,
Crowne him, and say: Long liue our Emperour.

Mar. An. With Voyces and applause of euery sort,
Patricians and Plebeans we Create
Lord *Saturninus* Romes Great Emperour.
And say, *Long liue our Emperour Saturnine.*

A long Flourish till they come downe.

Satu. *Titus Andronicus*, for thy Fauours done,
To vs in our Election this day,
I giue thee thankes in part of thy Deserts,
And will with Deeds requite thy gentlenesse:
And for an Onset *Titus* to aduance
Thy Name, and Honorable Familie,
Lauinia will I make my Empresse,
Romes Royall Mistris, Mistris of my hart
And in the Sacred *Pathan* her espouse:
Tell me *Andronicus* doth this motion please thee?

Tit. It doth my worthy Lord, and in this match,
I hold me Highly Honoured of your Grace,
And heere in sight of Rome, to *Saturnine*,
King and Commander of our Common-weale,
The Wide-worlds Emperour, do I Consecrate,
My Sword, my Chariot, and my Prisoners,
Presents well Worthy Romes Imperiall Lord:
Receiue them then, the Tribute that I owe,
Mine Honours Ensignes humbled at my feete.

Satu. Thankes Noble *Titus* Father of my life,
How proud I am of thee, and of thy gifts
Rome shall record, and when I do forget
The least of these vnspeakable Deserts,
Romans forget your Fealtie to me.

Tit. Now Madam are your prisoner to an Emperour,
To him that for you Honour and your State,
Will vse you Nobly and your followers.

Satu. A goodly Lady, trust me of the Hue
That I would choose, were I to choose a new:
Cleere vp Faire Queene that cloudy countenance,
Though chance of warre
Hath wrought this change of cheere,
Thou com'st not to be made a scorne in Rome:
Princely shall be thy vsage euery way.
Rest on my word, and let not discontent
Daunt all your hopes: Madam he comforts you,
Can make your Greater then the Queene of Gothes?
Lauinia you are not displeas'd with this?

Lau. Not I my Lord, sith true Nobilitie,
Warrants these words in Princely curtesie.

Sat. Thankes sweete *Lauinia*, Romans let vs goe:
Ransomlesse heere we set our Prisoners free,
Proclaime our Honors Lords with Trumpe and Drum.

Bass. Lord *Titus* by your leaue, this Maid is mine.

Tit. How sir? Are you in earnest then my Lord?

Bass. I Noble *Titus*, and resolu'd withall,
To doe my selfe this reason, and this right.

Marc. *Suum cuiquam*, is our Romane Iustice,
This Prince in Iustice ceazeth but his owne.

Luc. And that he will and shall, if *Lucius* liue.

Tit. Traytors auant, where is the Emperours Guarde?
Treason my Lord, *Lauinia* is surpris'd.

Sat. Surpris'd, by whom?

Bass. By him that iustly may
Beare his Betroth'd, from all the world away.

Muti. Brothers helpe to conuey her hence away,
And with my Sword Ile keepe this doore safe.

Tit. Follow my Lord, and Ile soone bring her backe.

Mut. My Lord you passe not heere.

Tit. What villaine Boy, bar'st me my way in Rome?

Mut. Helpe *Lucius* helpe.   *He kils him.*

Luc. My Lord you are vniust, and more then so,
In wrongfull quarrell, you haue slaine your son.

Tit. Nor thou, nor he are any sonnes of mine,
My sonnes would neuer so dishonour me.
Traytor restore *Lauinia* to the Emperour.

Luc. Dead if you will, but not to be his wife,
That is anothers lawfull promist Loue.

Enter aloft the Emperour with Tamora and her two
sonnes, and Aaron the Moore.

Empe. No *Titus*, no, the Emperour needs her not,
Nor her, nor thee, nor any of thy stocke:
Ile trust by Leisure him that mocks me once,
Thee neuer: nor thy Trayterous haughty sonnes,
Confederates all, thus to dishonour me.
Was none in Rome to make a stale
But *Saturnine*? Full well *Andronicus*
Agree these Deeds, with that proud bragge of thine,
That said'st, I beg'd the Empire at thy hands?

Tit. O monstrous, what reproachfull words are these?

Sat. But goe thy wayes, goe giue that changing peece,
To him that flourisht for her with his Sword:
A Valliant sonne in-law thou shalt enioy:
One, fit to bandy with thy lawlesse Sonnes,

To

To ruffle in the Common-wealth of Rome.

  Tit. These words are Razors to my wounded hart.

  Sat. And therefore louely *Tamora* Queene of Gothes,
That like the stately *Thebe* mong'st her Nimphs
Dost ouer-shine the Gallant'st Dames of Rome,
If thou be pleas'd with this my sodaine choyse,
Behold I choose thee *Tamora* for my Bride,
And will Create thee Empresse of Rome.
Speake Queene of Goths dost thou applau'd my choyse?
And heere I sweare by all the Romaine Gods,
Sith Priest and Holy-water are so neere,
And Tapers burne so bright, and euery thing
In readines for *Hymeneus* stand,
I will not resalute the streets of Rome,
Or clime my Pallace, till from forth this place,
I leade espous'd my Bride along with me,

  Tamo. And heere in sight of heauen to Rome I sweare,
If *Saturnine* aduance the Queen of Gothes,
Shee will a Hand-maid be to his desires,
A louing Nurse, a Mother to his youth.

  Satur. Ascend Faire Qeene,
Panthean Lords, accompany
Your Noble Emperour and his louely Bride,
Sent by the heauens for Prince *Saturnine*,
Whose wisedome hath her Fortune Conquered,
There shall we Consummate our Spousall rites.
    Exeunt omnes.

  Tit. I am not bid to waite vpon this Bride:
Titus when wer't thou wont to walke alone,
Dishonoured thus and Challenged of wrongs?

Enter Marcus and Titus Sonnes.

  Mar. O *Titus* see! O see what thou hast done!
In a bad quarrell, slaine a Vertuous sonne.

  Tit. No foolish Tribune, no: No sonne of mine,
Nor thou, nor these Confederates in the deed,
That hath dishonoured all our Family,
Vnworthy brother, and vnworthy Sonnes.

  Luci. But let vs giue him buriall as becomes:
Giue *Mutius* buriall with our Bretheren.

  Tit. Traytors away, he rest's not in this Tombe:
This Monument fiue hundreth yeares hath stood,
Which I haue Sumptuously re-edified:
Heere none but Souldiers, and Romes Seruitors,
Repose in Fame: None basely slaine in braules,
Bury him where you can, he comes not heere.

  Mar. My Lord this is impiety in you,
My Nephew *Mutius* deeds do plead for him,
He must be buried with his bretheren.

Titus two Sonnes speakes.

And shall, or him we will accompany.

  Ti. And shall! What villaine was it spake that word?

Titus sonne speakes.

He that would vouch'd it in any place but heere.

  Tit. What would you bury him in my despight?

  Mar. No Noble *Titus*, but intreat of thee,
To pardon *Mutius*, and to bury him.

  Tit. Marcus, Euen thou hast stroke vpon my Crest,
And with these Boyes mine Honour thou hast wounded,
My foes I doe repute you euery one.
So trouble me no more, but get you gone.

  1. Sonne. He is not himselfe, let vs withdraw.

  2. Sonne. Not I tell *Mutius* bones be buried.

The Brother and the sonnes kneele.

  Mar. Brother, for in that name doth nature plea'd.

  2. Sonne. Father, and in that name doth nature speake,

  Tit. Speake thou no more if all the rest will speede.

  Mar. Renowned *Titus* more then halfe my soule.

  Luc. Deare Father, soule and substance of vs all.

  Mar. Suffer thy brother *Marcus* to interre
His Noble Nephew heere in vertues nest,
That died in Honour and *Lauinia's* cause,
Thou art a Romaine, be not barbarous:
The Greekes vpon aduise did bury *Aiax*
That slew himselfe: And *Laertes* sonne,
Did graciously plead for his Funerals:
Let not young *Mutius* then that was thy ioy,
Be bar'd his entrance heere.

  Tit. Rise *Marcus*, rise,
The dismall'st day is this that ere I saw,
To be dishonored by my Sonnes in Rome:
Well, bury him, and bury me the next.

They put him in the Tombe.

  Luc. There lie thy bones sweet *Mutius* with thy friends
Till we with Trophees do adorne thy Tombe.

They all kneele and say.

No man shed teares for Noble *Mutius*,
He liues in Fame, that di'd in vertues cause.   *Exit.*

  Mar. My Lord to step out of these sudden dumps,
How comes it that the subtile Queene of Gothes,
Is of a sodaine thus aduanc'd in Rome?

  Tit. I know not *Marcus*: but I know it is,
(Whether by deuise or no) the heauens can tell,
Is she not then beholding to the man,
That brought her for this high good turne so farre?
Yes, and will Nobly him remunerate.

Flourish.
Enter the Emperor, Tamora, and her two sons, with the Moore at one doore. Enter at the other doore Bassianus and Lauinia with others.

  Sat. So *Bassianus*, you haue plaid your prize,
God giue you ioy sir of your Gallant Bride.

  Bass. And you of yours my Lord: I say no more,
Nor wish no lesse, and so I take my leaue.

  Sat. Traytor, if Rome haue law, or we haue power,
Thou and thy Faction shall repent this Rape.

  Bass. Rape call you it my Lord, to cease my owne,
My true betrothed Loue, and now my wife?
But let the lawes of Rome determine all,
Meane while I am possest of that is mine.

  Sat. 'Tis good sir: you are very short with vs,
But if we liue, weele be as sharpe with you.

  Bass. My Lord, what I haue done as best I may,
Answere I must, and shall do with my life,
Onely thus much I giue your Grace to know,
By all the duties that I owe to Rome,
This Noble Gentleman Lord *Titus* heere,
Is in opinion and in honour wrong'd,
That in the rescue of *Lauinia*,
With his owne hand did slay his youngest Son,
In zeale to you, and highly mou'd to wrath,
To be controul'd in that he frankly gaue:
Receiue him then to fauour *Saturnine*,
That hath expre'st himselfe in all his deeds,
A Father and a friend to thee, and Rome.

  Tit. Prince *Bassianus* leaue to plead my Deeds,
'Tis thou, and those, that haue dishonoured me,
Rome and the righteous heauens be my iudge,
How I haue lou'd and Honour'd *Saturnine*.

  Tam. My worthy Lord if euer *Tamora*,

Were

The Tragedie of Titus Andronicus.

Were gracious in those Princely eyes of thine,
Then heare me speake indifferently for all:
And at my sute (sweet) pardon what is past.

Satu. What Madam, be dishonoured openly,
And basely put it vp without reuenge?

Tam. Not so my Lord,
The Gods of Rome for-fend,
I should be Authour to dishonour you,
But on mine honour dare, I vndertake
For good Lord *Titus* innocence in all:
Whose fury not dissembled speakes his griefes:
Then at my sute looke graciously on him,
Loose not so noble a friend on vaine suppose,
Nor with sowre lookes afflict his gentle heart,
My Lord, be rul'd by me, be wonne at last,
Dissemble all your griefes and discontents,
You are but newly planted in your Throne,
Least then the people, and Patricians too,
Vpon a iust suruey take *Titus* part,
And so supplant vs for ingratitude,
Which Rome reputes to be a hainous sinne.
Yeeld at intreats, and then let me alone:
Ile finde a day to massacre them all,
And race their faction, and their familie,
The cruell Father, and his trayt'rous sonnes,
To whom I sued for my deare sonnes life.
And make them know what 'tis to let a Queene.
Kneele in the streetes, and beg for grace in vaine.
Come, come, sweet Emperour, (come *Andronicus*)
Take vp this good old man, and cheere the heart,
That dies in tempest of thy angry frowne.

King. Rise *Titus*, rise,
My Empresse hath preuail'd.

Titus. I thanke your Maiestie,
And her my Lord.
These words, these lookes,
Infuse new life in me.

Tamo. *Titus*, I am incorparate in Rome,
A Roman now adopted happily.
And must aduise the Emperour for his good,
This day all quarrels die *Andronicus*.
And let it be mine honour good my Lord,
That I haue reconcil'd your friends and you.
For you Prince *Bassianus*, I haue past
My word and promise to the Emperour,
That you will be more milde and tractable.
And feare not Lords:
And you *Lauinia*,
By my aduise all humbled on your knees,
You shall aske pardon of his Maiestie.

Son. We doe,
And vow to heauen, and to his Highnes,
That what we did, was mildly, as we might,
Tendring our sisters honour and our owne.

Mar. That on mine honour heere I do protest.

King. Away and talke not, trouble vs no more.

Tamora. Nay, nay,
Sweet Emperour, we must all be friends,
The Tribune and his Nephews kneele for grace,
I will not be denied, sweet hart looke back.

King. Marcus,
For thy sake and thy brothers heere,
And at my louely *Tamora's* intreats,
I doe remit these young mens haynous faults.
Stand vp: *Lauinia*, though you left me like a churle,
I found a friend, and sure as death I sware,

I would not part a Batchellour from the Priest.
Come, if the Emperours Court can feast two Brides,
You are my guest *Lauinia*, and your friends:
This day shall be a Loue-day *Tamora*.

Tit. To morrow and it please your Maiestie,
To hunt the Panther and the Hart with me,
With horne and Hound,
Weele giue your Grace *Bon iour*.

Satur. Be it so *Titus*, and Gramercy to. *Exeunt*.

Actus Secunda.

Flourish. *Enter Aaron alone.*

Aron. Now climbeth *Tamora* Olympus toppe,
Safe out of Fortunes shot, and sits aloft,
Secure of Thunders cracke or lightning flash,
Aduanc'd about pale enuies threatning reach:
As when the golden Sunne salutes the morne,
And hauing gilt the Ocean with his beames,
Gallops the Zodiacke in his glistering Coach,
And ouer-lookes the highest piering hills:
So *Tamora*:
Vpon her wit doth earthly honour waite,
And vertue stoopes and trembles at her frowne.
Then *Aaron* arme thy hart, and fit thy thoughts,
To mount aloft with thy Emperiall Mistris,
And mount her pitch, whom thou in triumph long
Hast prisoner held, fettred in amorous chaines,
And faster bound to *Aarons* charming eyes,
Then is *Prometheus* ti'de to *Caucasus*.
Away with slauish weedes, and idle thoughts,
I will be bright and shine in Pearle and Gold,
To waite vpon this new made Empresse.
To waite said I? To wanton with this Queene,
This Goddesse, this *Semiramis*, this Queene,
This Syren, that will charme Romes *Saturnine*,
And see his shipwracke, and his Common weales.
Hollo, what storme is this?

Enter Chiron and Demetrius brauing.

Dem. *Chiron* thy yeres wants wit, thy wit wants edge
And manners to intru'd where I am grac'd,
And may for ought thou know'st affected be.

Chi. *Demetrius*, thou doo'st ouer-weene in all,
And so in this, to beare me downe with braues,
'Tis not the difference of a yeere or two
Makes me lesse gracious, or thee more fortunate:
I am as able, and as fit, as thou,
To serue, and to deserue my Mistris grace,
And that my sword vpon thee shall approue,
And plead my passions for *Lauinia's* loue.

Aron. Clubs, clubs, these louers will not keep the peace.

Dem. Why Boy, although our mother (vnaduised)
Gaue you a daunting Rapier by your side,
Are you so desperate growne to threat your friends?
Goe too: haue your Lath glued within your sheath,
Till you know better how to handle it.

Chi. Meane while sir, with the little skill I haue,
Full well shalt thou perceiue how much I dare.

Deme. I Boy, grow ye so braue? *They drawe.*

Aron. Why how now Lords?
So nere the Emperours Pallace dare you draw,

And

And maintaine such a quarrell openly?
Full well I wote, the ground of all this grudge.
I would not for a million of Gold,
The cause were knowne to them it most concernes,
Nor would your noble mother for much more
Be so dishonored in the Court of Rome:
For shame put vp.

Deme. Not I, till I haue sheath'd
My rapier in his bosome, and withall
Thrust these reprochfull speeches downe his throat,
That he hath breath'd in my dishonour heere.

Chi. For that I am prepar'd, and full resolu'd,
Foule spoken Coward,
That thundrest with thy tongue,
And with thy weapon nothing dar'st performe.

Aron. Away I say.
Now by the Gods that warlike Gothes adore,
This pretty brabble will vndoo vs all:
Why Lords, and thinke you not how dangerous
It is to set vpon a Princes right?
What is Lauinia then become so loose,
Or Bassianus so degenerate,
That for her loue such quarrels may be broacht,
Without controulement, Iustice, or reuenge?
Young Lords beware, and should the Empresse know,
This discord ground, the musicke would not please.

Chi. I care not I, knew she and all the world,
I loue Lauinia more then all the world.

Demet. Youngling,
Learne thou to make some meaner choise,
Lauinia is thine elder brothers hope.

Aron. Why are ye mad? Or know ye not in Rome,
How furious and impatient they be,
And cannot brooke Competitors in loue?
I tell you Lords, you doe but plot your deaths,
By this deuise.

Chi. Aaron, a thousand deaths would I propose,
To atchieue her whom I do loue.

Aron. To atchieue her, how?

Deme. Why, mak'st thou it so strange?
Shee is a woman, therefore may be woo'd,
Shee is a woman, therfore may be wonne,
Shee is Lauinia therefore must be lou'd.
What man, more water glideth by the Mill
Then wots the Miller of, and easie it is
Of a cut loafe to steale a shiue we know:
Though Bassianus be the Emperours brother,
Better then he haue worne Vulcans badge.

Aron. I, and as good as Saturnius may.

Deme. Then why should he dispaire that knowes to
With words, faire lookes, and liberality: (court it
What hast not thou full often strucke a Doe,
And borne her cleanly by the Keepers nose?

Aron. Why then it seemes some certaine snatch or so
Would serue your turnes.

Chi. I so the turne were serued.

Deme. Aaron thou hast hit it.

Aron. Would you had hit it too,
Then should not we be tir'd with this adoo:
Why harke yee, harke yee, and are you such fooles,
To square for this? Would it offend you then?

Chi. Faith not me.

Deme. Nor me, so I were one.

Aron. For shame be friends, & ioyne for that you iar:
'Tis pollicie, and stratageme must doe
That you affect, and so must you resolue,
That what you cannot as you would atcheiue,
You must perforce accomplish as you may:
Take this of me, Lucrece was not more chast
Then this Lauinia, Bassianus loue,
A speedier course this lingring languishment
Must we pursue, and I haue found the path:
My Lords, a solemne hunting is in hand,
There will the louely Roman Ladies troope:
The Forrest walkes are wide and spacious,
And many vnfrequented plots there are,
Fitted by kinde for rape and villanie:
Single you thither then this dainty Doe,
And strike her home by force, if not by words:
This way or not at all, stand you in hope.
Come, come, our Empresse with her sacred wit
To villainie and vengance consecrate,
Will we acquaint with all that we intend,
And she shall file our engines with aduise,
That will not suffer you to square your selues,
But to your wishes height aduance you both.
The Emperours Court is like the house of Fame,
The pallace full of tongues, of eyes, of eares:
The Woods are ruthlesse, dreadfull, deafe, and dull:
There speake, and strike braue Boyes, & take your turnes,
There serue your lusts, shadow'd from heauens eye,
And reuell in Lauinia's Treasurie.

Chi. Thy counsell Lad smells of no cowardise.

Deme. Sit fas aut nefas, till I finde the streames,
To coole this heat, a Charme to calme their fits,
Per Stigia per manes Vehor. *Exeunt.*

*Enter Titus Andronicus and his three sonnes, making a noyse
with hounds and hornes, and Marcus.*

Tit. The hunt is vp, the morne is bright and gray,
The fields are fragrant, and the Woods are greene,
Vncouple heere, and let vs make a bay,
And wake the Emperour, and his louely Bride,
And rouze the Prince, and ring a hunters peale,
That all the Court may eccho with the noyse.
Sonnes let it be your charge, as it is ours,
To attend the Emperours person carefully:
I haue bene troubled in my sleepe this night,
But dawning day new comfort hath inspir'd.

Winde Hornes.
*Heere a cry of houndes, and winde hornes in a peale, then
Enter Saturninus, Tamora, Bassianus, Lauinia, Chiron, De-
metrius, and their Attendants.*

Ti. Many good morrowes to your Maiestie,
Madam to you as many and as good.
I promised your Grace, a Hunters peale.

Satur. And you haue rung it lustily my Lords,
Somewhat to earely for new married Ladies.

Bass. Lauinia, how say you?

Laui. I say no:
I haue bene awake two houres and more.

Satur. Come on then, horse and Chariots letts haue,
And to our sport: Madam, now shall ye see,
Our Romaine hunting.

Mar. I haue dogges my Lord,
Will rouze the proudest Panther in the Chase,
And clime the highest Pormontary top.

Tit. And I haue horse will follow where the game
Makes way, and runnes likes Swallowes ore the plaine
Deme. Chiron

The Tragedie of Titus Andronicus.

Deme. Chiron we hunt not we, with Horse nor Hound
But hope to plucke a dainty Doe to ground. *Exeunt*

Enter Aaron alone.

Aron. He that had wit, would thinke that I had none,
To bury so much Gold vnder a Tree,
And neuer after to inherit it.
Let him that thinks of me so abiectly,
Know that this Gold must coine a stratageme,
Which cunningly effected, will beget
A very excellent peece of villany:
And so repose sweet Gold for their vnrest,
That haue their Almes out of the Empresse Chest.

Enter Tamora to the Moore.

Tamo. My louely *Aaron*,
Wherefore look'st thou sad,
When euery thing doth make a Gleefull boast?
The Birds chaunt melody on euery bush,
The Snake lies rolled in the chearefull Sunne,
The greene leaues quiuer, with the cooling winde,
And make a cheker'd shadow on the ground:
Vnder their sweete shade, *Aaron* let vs sit,
And whil'st the babling Eccho mock's the Hounds,
Replying shrilly to the well tun'd-Hornes,
As if a double hunt were heard at once,
Let vs sit downe, and marke their yelping noyse:
And after conflict, such as was suppos'd.
The wandring Prince and *Dido* once enioy'd,
When with a happy storme they were surpris'd,
And Curtain'd with a Counsaile-keeping Caue,
We may each wreathed in the others armes,
(Our pastimes done) possesse a Golden slumber,
Whiles Hounds and Hornes, and sweet Melodious Birds
Be vnto vs, as is a Nurses Song
Of Lullabie, to bring her Babe asleepe.

Aron. Madame,
Though *Venus* gouerne your desires,
Saturne is Dominator ouer mine:
What signifies my deadly standing eye,
My silence, and my Cloudy Melancholie,
My fleece of Woolly haire, that now vncurles,
Euen as an Adder when she doth vnrowle
To do some fatall execution?
No Madam, these are no Veneriall signes,
Vengeance is in my heart, death in my hand,
Blood, and reuenge, are Hammering in my head.
Harke *Tamora*, the Empresse of my Soule,
Which neuer hopes more heauen, then rests in thee,
This is the day of Doome for *Bassianus*:
His *Philomel* must loose her tongue to day,
Thy Sonnes make Pillage of her Chastity,
And wash their hands in *Bassianus* blood.
Seest thou this Letter, take it vp I pray thee,
And giue the King this fatall plotted Scrowle,
Now question me no more, we are espied,
Heere comes a parcell of our hopefull Booty,
Which dreads not yet their liues destruction.

Enter Bassianus and Lauinia.

Tamo. Ah my sweet *Moore*:
Sweeter to me then life.

Aron. No more great Empresse, *Bassianus* comes,
Be crosse with him, and Ile goe fetch thy Sonnes
To backe thy quarrell what so ere they be.

Bassi. Whom haue we heere?
Romes Royall Empresse,
Vnfurnisht of our well beseeming troope?
Or is it *Dian* habited like her,
Who hath abandoned her holy Groues,
To see the generall Hunting in this Forrest?

Tamo. Sawcie controuler of our priuate steps:
Had I the power, that some say *Dian* had,
Thy Temples should be planted presently,
With Hornes, as was *Acteons*, and the Hounds
Should driue vpon his new transformed limbes,
Vnmannerly Intruder as thou art.

Laui. Vnder your patience gentle Empresse,
'Tis thought you haue a goodly gift in Horning,
And to be doubted, that your *Moore* and you
Are singled forth to try experiments:
Ioue sheild your husband from his Hounds to day,
'Tis pitty they should take him for a Stag.

Bassi. Beleeue me Queene, your swarth Cymerion,
Doth make your Honour of his bodies Hue,
Spotted, detested, and abhominable.
Why are you sequestred from all your traine?
Dismounted from your Snow-white goodly Steed,
And wandred hither to an obscure plot,
Accompanied with a barbarous *Moore*,
If foule desire had not conducted you?

Laui. And being intercepted in your sport,
Great reason that my Noble Lord, be rated
For Saucinesse, I pray you let vs hence,
And let her ioy her Rauen coloured loue,
This valley fits the purpose passing well.

Bassi. The King my Brother shall haue notice of this
Laui. I, for these slips haue made him noted long,
Good King, to be so mightily abused.

Tamora. Why I haue patience to endure all this?

Enter Chiron and Demetrius.

Dem. How now deere Soueraigne
And our gracious Mother,
Why doth your Highnes looke so pale and wan?

Tamo. Haue I not reason thinke you to looke pale.
These two haue tic'd me hither to this place,
A barren, detested vale you see it is.
The Trees though Sommer, yet forlorne and leane,
Ore-come with Mosse, and balefull Misselto.
Heere neuer shines the Sunne, heere nothing breeds,
Vnlesse the nightly Owle, or fatall Rauen:
And when they shew'd me this abhorred pit,
They told me heere at dead time of the night,
A thousand Fiends, a thousand hissing Snakes,
Ten thousand swelling Toades, as many Vrchins,
Would make such fearefull and confused cries,
As any mortall body hearing it,
Should straite fall mad, or else die suddenly.
No sooner had they told this hellish tale,
But strait they told me they would binde me heere,
Vnto the body of a dismall yew,
And leaue me to this miserable death.
And then they call'd me foule Adulteresse,
Lasciuious Goth, and all the bitterest tearmes
That euer eare did heare to such effect.
And had you not by wondrous fortune come,
This vengeance on me had they executed:
Reuenge it, as you loue your Mothers life,
Or be ye not henceforth cal'd my Children.

Dem. This is a witnesse that I am thy Sonne. *Stab him.*
Chi. And this for me,
Strook home to shew my strength.

Laui. I come *Semeramis*, nay Barbarous *Tamora*.

d d For

For no name fits thy nature but thy owne.

　Tam. Giue me thy poyniard, you shal know my boyes
Your Mothers hand shall right your Mothers wrong.

　Deme. Stay Madam heere is more belongs to her,
First thrash the Corne, then after burne the straw:
This Minion stood vpon her chastity,
Vpon her Nuptiall vow, her loyaltie.
And with that painted hope, braues your Mightinesse,
And shall she carry this vnto her graue?

　Chi. And if she doe,
I would I were an Eunuch,
Drag hence her husband to some secret hole,
And make his dead Trunke-Pillow to our lust.

　Tamo. But when ye haue the hony we desire,
Let not this Waspe out-liue vs both to sting.

　Chir. I warrant you Madam we will make that sure:
Come Mistris, now perforce we will enioy,
That nice-preserued honesty of yours.

　Lani. Oh *Tamora*, thou bear'st a woman face.

　Tamo. I will not heare her speake, away with her.

　Laui. Sweet Lords intreat her heare me but a word.

　Demet. Listen faire Madam, let it be your glory
To see her teares, but be your hart to them,
As vnrelenting flint to drops of raine.

　Laui. When did the Tigers young-ones teach the dam?
O doe not learne her wrath, she taught it thee,
The milke thou suck'st from her did turne to Marble,
Euen at thy Teat thou had'st thy Tyranny,
Yet euery Mother breeds not Sonnes alike,
Do thou intreat her shew a woman pitty.

　Chiro. What,
Would'st thou haue me proue my selfe a bastard?

　Laui. 'Tis true,
The Rauen doth not hatch a Larke,
Yet haue I heard, Oh could I finde it now,
The Lion mou'd with pitty, did indure
To haue his Princely pawes par'd all away.
Some say, that Rauens foster forlorne children,
The whil'st their owne birds famish in their nests:
Oh be to me though thy hard hart say no,
Nothing so kind but something pittifull.

　Tamo. I know not what it meanes, away with her.

　Lauin. Oh let me teach thee for my Fathers sake,
That gaue thee life when well he might haue slaine thee:
Be not obdurate, open thy deafe eares.

　Tamo. Had'st thou in person nere offended me,
Euen for his sake am I pittilesse:
Remember Boyes I powr'd forth teares in vaine,
To saue your brother from the sacrifice,
But fierce *Andronicus* would not relent,
Therefore away with her, and vse her as you will,
The worse to her, the better lou'd of me.

　Laui. Oh *Tamora*,
Be call'd a gentle Queene,
And with thine owne hands kill me in this place,
For 'tis not life that I haue beg'd so long,
Poore I was slaine, when *Bassianus* dy'd.

　Tam. What beg'st thou then? fond woman let me go?

　Laui. 'Tis present death I beg, and one thing more,
That womanhood denies my tongue to tell:
Oh keepe me from their worse then killing lust,
And tumble me into some loathsome pit,
Where neuer mans eye may behold my body,
Doe this, and be a charitable murderer.

　Tam. So should I rob my sweet Sonnes of their fee,
No let them satisfie their lust on thee.

　Deme. Away,
For thou hast staid vs heere too long.

　Lauinia. No Grace,
No womanhood? Ah beastly creature,
The blot and enemy to our generall name,
Confusion fall——

　Chi. Nay then Ile stop your mouth
Bring thou her husband,
This is the Hole where *Aaron* bid vs hide him.

　Tam. Farewell my Sonnes, see that you make her sure,
Nere let my heart know merry cheere indeed,
Till all the *Andronici* be made away:
Now will I hence to seeke my louely *Moore*,
And let my spleenefull Sonnes this Trull defloure. *Exit.*

Enter Aaron with two of Titus Sonnes.

　Aron. Come on my Lords, the better foote before,
Straight will I bring you to the lothsome pit,
Where I espied the Panther fast asleepe.

　Quin. My sight is very dull what ere it bodes.

　Marti. And mine I promise you, were it not for shame,
Well could I leaue our sport to sleepe a while.

　Quin. What art thou fallen?
What subtile Hole is this,
Whose mouth is couered with Rude growing Briers,
Vpon whose leaues are drops of new-shed-blood,
As fresh as mornings dew distil'd on flowers,
A very fatall place it seemes to me:
Speake Brother hast thou hurt thee with the fall?

　Martius. Oh Brother,
With the dismal'st obiect
That euer eye with sight made heart lament.

　Aron. Now will I fetch the King to finde them heere,
That he thereby may haue a likely gesse,
How these were they that made away his Brother.
Exit Aron.

　Marti. Why dost not comfort me and helpe me out,
From this vnhallow'd and blood-stained Hole?

　Quintus. I am surprised with an vncouth feare,
A chilling sweat ore-runs my trembling ioynts,
My heart suspects more then mine eie can see.

　Marti. To proue thou hast a true diuining heart,
Aaron and thou looke downe into this den,
And see a fearefull sight of blood and death.

　Quintus. *Aaron* is gone,
And my compassionate heart
Will not permit mine eyes once to behold
The thing whereat it trembles by surmise:
Oh tell me how it is, for nere till now
Was I a child, to feare I know not what.

　Marti. Lord *Bassianus* lies embrewed heere,
All on a heape like to the slaughtred Lambe,
In this detested, darke, blood-drinking pit.

　Quin. If it be darke, how doost thou know 'tis he?

　Mart. Vpon his bloody finger he doth weare
A precious Ring, that lightens all the Hole:
Which like a Taper in some Monument,
Doth shine vpon the dead mans earthly cheekes,
And shewes the ragged intrailes of the pit:
So pale did shine the Moone on *Piramus*,
When he by night lay bath'd in Maiden blood:
O Brother helpe me with thy fainting hand,
If feare hath made thee faint, as mee it hath,
Out of this fell deuouring receptacle,
As hatefull as *Ocitus* mistie mouth.

　Quint. Reach me thy hand, that I may helpe thee out,

Or wanting strength to doe thee so much good,
I may be pluckt into the swallowing wombe,
Of this deepe pit, poore *Bassianus* graue.
I haue no strength to plucke thee to the brinke.

  Martius. Not I no strength to clime without thy help.
  Quin. Thy hand once more, I will not loose againe,
Till thou art heere aloft, or I below,
Thou can'st not come to me, I come to thee. *Both fall in.*

Enter the Emperour, Aaron the Moore.

  Satur. Along with me, Ile see what hole is heere,
And what he is that now is leapt into it.
Say, who art thou that lately did'st descend,
Into this gaping hollow of the earth?
  Marti. The vnhappie sonne of old *Andronicus*,
Brought hither in a most vnluckie houre,
To finde thy brother *Bassianus* dead.
  Satur. My brother dead? I know thou dost but iest,
He and his Lady both are at the Lodge,
Vpon the North-side of this pleasant Chase,
'Tis not an houre since I left him there.
  Marti. We know not where you left him all aliue,
But out alas, heere haue we found him dead.

Enter Tamora, Andronicus, and Lucius.

  Tamo. Where is my Lord the King?
  King. Heere *Tamora*, though grieu'd with killing griefe.
  Tam. Where is thy brother *Bassianus*?
  King. Now to the bottome dost thou search my wound,
Poore *Bassianus* heere lies murthered.
  Tam. Then all too late I bring this fatall writ,
The complot of this timelesse Tragedie,
And wonder greatly that mans face can fold,
In pleasing smiles such murderous Tyrannie.

She giueth Saturnine a Letter.

Saturninus reads the Letter.
And if we misse to meete him hansomely,
Sweet huntsman, Bassianus 'tis we meane,
Doe thou so much as dig the graue for him,
Thou know'st our meaning, looke for thy reward
Among the Nettles at the Elder tree:
Which ouer-shades the mouth of that same pit:
Where we decreed to bury Bassianus,
Doe this and purchase vs thy lasting friends.

  King. Oh *Tamora*, was euer heard the like?
This is the pit, and this the Elder tree,
Looke sirs, if you can finde the huntsman out,
That should haue murthered *Bassianus* heere.
  Aron. My gracious Lord heere is the bag of Gold.
  King. Two of thy whelpes, fell Curs of bloody kind
Haue heere bereft my brother of his life:
Sirs drag them from the pit vnto the prison,
There let them bide vntill we haue deuis'd
Some neuer heard-of tortering paine for them.
  Tamo. What are they in this pit,
Oh wondrous thing!
How easily murder is discouered?
  Tit. High Emperour, vpon my feeble knee,
I beg this boone, with teares, not lightly shed,
That this fell fault of my accursed Sonnes,
Accursed, if the faults be prou'd in them.
  King. If it be prou'd? you see it is apparant,

Who found this Letter, *Tamora* was it you?
  Tamora. *Andronicus* himselfe did take it vp.
  Tit. I did my Lord,
Yet let me be their baile,
For by my Fathers reuerent Tombe I vow
They shall be ready at your Highnes will,
To answere their suspition with their liues.
  King. Thou shalt not baile them, see thou follow me:
Some bring the murthered body, some the murtherers,
Let them not speake a word, the guilt is plaine,
For by my soule, were there worse end then death,
That end vpon them should be executed.
  Tamo. *Andronicus* I will entreat the King,
Feare not thy Sonnes, they shall do well enough.
  Tit. Come *Lucius* come,
Stay not to talke with them. *Exeunt.*

Enter the Empresse Sonnes, with Lauinia, her hands cut off and her tongue cut out, and rauisht.

  Deme. So now goe tell and if thy tongue can speake,
Who t'was that cut thy tongue and rauisht thee.
  Chi. Write downe thy mind, bewray thy meaning so,
And if thy stumpes will let thee play the Scribe.
  Dem. See how with signes and tokens she can scowle.
  Chi. Goe home,
Call for sweet water, wash thy hands.
  Dem. She hath no tongue to call, nor hands to wash.
And so let's leaue her to her silent walkes.
  Chi. And t'were my cause, I should goe hang my selfe.
  Dem. If thou had'st hands to helpe thee knit the cord.
Exeunt.

Winde Hornes.
Enter Marcus from hunting, to Lauinia.
Who is this, my Neece that flies away so fast?
Cosen a word, where is your husband?
If I do dreame, would all my wealth would wake me,
If I doe wake, some Planet strike me downe,
That I may slumber in eternall sleepe.
Speake gentle Neece, what sterne vngentle hands
Hath lopt, and hew'd, and made thy body bare
Of her two branches, those sweet Ornaments
Whose circkling shadowes, Kings haue sought to sleep in
And might not gaine so great a happines
As halfe thy Loue: Why doest not speake to me?
Alas, a Crimson riuer of warme blood,
Like to a bubling fountaine stir'd with winde,
Doth rise and fall betweene thy Rosed lips,
Comming and going with thy hony breath.
But sure some *Tereus* hath defloured thee,
And least thou should'st detect them, cut thy tongue.
Ah, now thou turn'st away thy face for shame:
And notwithstanding all this losse of blood,
As from a Conduit with their issuing Spouts,
Yet doe thy cheekes looke red as *Titans* face,
Blushing to be encountred with a Cloud,
Shall I speake for thee? shall I say 'tis so?
Oh that I knew thy hart, and knew the beast
That I might raile at him to ease my mind.
Sorrow concealed, like an Ouen stopt,
Doth burne the hart to Cinders where it is.
Faire *Philomela* she but lost her tongue,
And in a tedious Sampler sowed her minde.
But louely Neece, that meane is cut from thee,
A craftier *Tereus* hast thou met withall,
And he hath cut those pretty fingers off,

That could haue better sowed then *Philomel*.
Oh had the monster seene those Lilly hands,
Tremble like Aspen leaues vpon a Lute,
And make the silken strings delight to kisse them,
He would not then haue toucht them for his life.
Or had he heard the heauenly Harmony,
Which that sweet tongue hath made,
He would haue dropt his knife and fell asleepe,
As *Cerberus* at the Thracian Poets feete.
Come, let vs goe, and make thy father blinde,
For such a sight will blinde a fathers eye.
One houres storme will drowne the fragrant meades,
What, will whole months of teares thy Fathers eyes?
Doe not draw backe, for we will mourne with thee:
Oh could our mourning ease thy misery. *Exeunt*

Actus Tertius.

Enter the Iudges and Senatours with Titus two sonnes bound, passing on the Stage to the place of execution, and Titus going before pleading.

Ti. Heare me graue fathers, noble Tribunes stay,
For pitty of mine age, whose youth was spent
In dangerous warres, whilst you securely slept:
For all my blood in Romes great quarrell shed,
For all the frosty nights that I haue watcht,
And for these bitter teares, which now you see,
Filling the aged wrinkles in my cheekes,
Be pittifull to my condemned Sonnes,
Whose soules is not corrupted as 'tis thought:
For two and twenty sonnes I neuer wept,
Because they died in honours lofty bed.

Andronicus lyeth downe, and the Iudges passe by him.

For these, Tribunes, in the dust I write
My harts deepe languor, and my soules sad teares:
Let my teares stanch the earths drie appetite.
My sonnes sweet blood, will make it shame and blush:
O earth! I will be friend thee more with raine *Exeunt*
That shall distill from these two ancient ruines,
Then youthfull Aprill shall with all his showres
In summers drought: Ile drop vpon thee still,
In Winter with warme teares Ile melt the snow,
And keepe erernall spring time on thy face,
So thou refuse to drinke my deare sonnes blood.

Enter Lucius, with his weapon drawne.

Oh reuerent Tribunes, oh gentle aged men,
Vnbinde my sonnes, reuerse the doome of death,
And let me say (that neuer wept before)
My teares are now preuailing Oratours.
    Lu. Oh noble father, you lament in vaine,
The Tribunes heare not, no man is by,
And you recount your sorrowes to a stone.
    Ti. Ah *Lucius* for thy brothers let me plead,
Graue Tribunes, once more I intreat of you.
    Lu. My gracious Lord, no Tribune heares you speake.
    Ti. Why 'tis no matter man, if they did heare
They would not marke me: oh if they did heare
They would not pitty me.
Therefore I tell my sorrowes bootles to the stones.

Who though they cannot answere my distresse,
Yet in some sort they are better then the Tribunes,
For that they will not intercept my tale;
When I doe weepe, they humbly at my feete
Receiue my teares, and seeme to weepe with me,
And were they but attired in graue weedes,
Rome could afford no Tribune like to these,
A stone is as soft waxe,
Tribunes more hard then stones:
A stone is silent, and offendeth not,
And Tribunes with their tongues doome men to death.
But wherefore stand'st thou with thy weapon drawne?
    Lu. To rescue my two brothers from their death,
For which attempt the Iudges haue pronounc'st
My euerlasting doome of banishment.
    Ti. O happy man, they haue befriended thee:
Why foolish *Lucius*, dost thou not perceiue
That Rome is but a wildernes of Tigers?
Tigers must pray, and Rome affords no prey
But me and and mine: how happy art thou then,
From these deuourers to be banished?
But who comes with our brother *Marcus* heere?

Enter Marcus and Lauinia.

Mar. Titus, prepare thy noble eyes to weepe,
Or if not so, thy noble heart to breake:
I bring consuming sorrow to thine age.
    Ti. Will it consume me? Let me see it then.
    Mar. This was thy daughter.
    Ti. Why *Marcus* so she is.
    Luc. Aye me this obiect kils me.
    Ti. Faint-harted boy, arise and looke vpon her,
Speake *Lauinia*, what accursed hand
Hath made thee handlesse in thy Fathers sight?
What foole hath added water to the Sea?
Or brought a faggot to bright burning Troy?
My griefe was at the height before thou cam'st,
And now like *Nylus* it disdaineth bounds:
Giue me a sword, Ile chop off my hands too,
For they haue fought for Rome, and all in vaine:
And they haue nur'st this woe,
In feeding life:
In bootelesse prayer haue they bene held vp,
And they haue seru'd me to effectlesse vse.
Now all the seruice I require of them,
Is that the one will helpe to cut the other:
'Tis well *Lauinia*, that thou hast no hands,
For hands to do Rome seruice, is but vaine.
    Luci. Speake gentle sister, who hath martyr'd thee?
    Mar. O that delightfull engine of her thoughts,
That blab'd them with such pleasing eloquence,
Is torne from forth that pretty hollow cage,
Where like a sweet meliodius bird it sung,
Sweet varied notes inchanting euery eare.
    Luci. Oh say thou for her,
Who hath done this deed?
    Marc. Oh thus I found her straying in the Parke,
Seeking to hide herselfe as doth the Deare
That hath receiude some vnrecuring wound.
    Tit. It was my Deare,
And he that wounded her,
Hath hurt me more, then had he kild me dead:
For now I stand as one vpon a Rocke,
Inuiron'd with a wildernesse of Sea.
Who markes the waxing tide,
Grow waue by waue,

Expecting

Expecting euer when some enuious surge,
Will in his brinish bowels swallow him.
This way to death my wretched sonnes are gone:
Heere stands my other sonne, a banisht man,
And heere my brother weeping at my woes.
But that which giues my soule the greatest spurne,
Is deere Lauinia, deerer then my soule.
Had I but seene thy picture in this plight,
It would haue madded me. What shall I doe?
Now I behold thy liuely body so?
Thou hast no hands to wipe away thy teares,
Nor tongue to tell me who hath martyr'd thee:
Thy husband he is dead, and for his death
Thy brothers are condemn'd, and dead by this.
Looke Marcus, ah sonne Lucius looke on her:
When I did name her brothers, then fresh teares
Stood on her cheekes, as doth the hony dew,
Vpon a gathred Lillie almost withered.

Mar. Perchance she weepes because they kil'd her husband,
Perchance because she knowes him innocent.

Ti. If they did kill thy husband then be ioyfull,
Because the law hath tane reuenge on them.
No, no, they would not doe so foule a deede,
Witnes the sorrow that their sister makes.
Gentle Lauinia let me kisse thy lips,
Or make some signes how I may do thee ease:
Shall thy good Vncle, and thy brother Lucius,
And thou and I sit round about some Fountaine,
Looking all downewards to behold our cheekes
How they are stain'd in meadowes, yet not dry
With miery slime left on them by a flood:
And in the Fountaine shall we gaze so long,
Till the fresh taste be taken from that cleerenes,
And made a brine pit with our bitter teares?
Or shall we cut away our hands like thine?
Or shall we bite our tongues, and in dumbe shewes
Passe the remainder of our hatefull dayes?
What shall we doe? Let vs that haue our tongues
Plot some deuise of further miseries
To make vs wondred at in time to come.

Lu. Sweet Father cease your teares, for at your griefe
See how my wretched sister sobs and weeps.

Mar. Patience deere Neece, good Titus drie thine eyes.

Ti. Ah Marcus, Marcus, Brother well I wot,
Thy napkin cannot drinke a teare of mine,
For thou poore man hast drown'd it with thine owne.

Lu. Ah my Lauinia I will wipe thy cheekes.

Ti. Marke Marcus marke, I vnderstand her signes,
Had she a tongue to speake, now would she say
That to her brother which I said to thee,
His Napkin with her true teares all bewet,
Can do no seruice on her sorrowfull cheekes.
Oh what a simpathy of woe is this!
As farre from helpe as Limbo is from blisse.

Enter Aron the Moore alone.

Moore. Titus Andronicus, my Lord the Emperour,
Sends thee this word, that if thou loue thy sonnes,
Let Marcus, Lucius, or thy selfe old Titus,
Or any one of you, chop off your hand,
And send it to the King: he for the same,
Will send thee hither both thy sonnes aliue,
And that shall be the ransome for their fault.

Ti. Oh gracious Emperour, oh gentle Aaron,
Did euer Rauen sing so like a Larke,
That giues sweet tydings of the Sunnes vprise?
With all my heart, Ile send the Emperour my hand,
Good Aron wilt thou help to chop it off?

Lu. Stay Father, for that noble hand of thine,
That hath throwne downe so many enemies,
Shall not be sent: my hand will serue the turne,
My youth can better spare my blood then you,
And therfore mine shall saue my brothers liues.

Mar. Which of your hands hath not defended Rome,
And rear'd aloft the bloody Battleaxe,
Writing destruction on the enemies Castle?
Oh none of both but are of high desert:
My hand hath bin but idle, let it serue
To ransome my two nephewes from their death,
Then haue I kept it to a worthy end.

Moore. Nay come agree, whose hand shall goe along
For feare they die before their pardon come.

Mar. My hand shall goe.

Lu. By heauen it shall not goe.

Ti. Sirs striue no more, such withered hearbs as these
Are meete for plucking vp, and therefore mine.

Lu. Sweet Father, if I shall be thought thy sonne,
Let me redeeme my brothers both from death.

Mar. And for our fathers sake, and mothers care,
Now let me shew a brothers loue to thee.

Ti. Agree betweene you, I will spare my hand.

Lu. Then Ile goe fetch an Axe.

Mar. But I will vse the Axe. *Exeunt*

Ti. Come hither Aaron, Ile deceiue them both,
Lend me thy hand, and I will giue thee mine.

Moore. If that be cal'd deceit, I will be honest,
And neuer whil'st I liue deceiue men so:
But Ile deceiue you in another sort,
And that you'l say ere halfe an houre passe.

He cuts off Titus hand.

Enter Lucius and Marcus againe.

Ti. Now stay you strife, what shall be, is dispatche,
Good Aron giue his Maiestie me hand,
Tell him, it was a hand that warded him
From thousand dangers: bid him bury it,
More hath it merited: That let it haue.
As for my sonnes, say I account of them,
As iewels purchast at an easie price,
And yet deere too, because I bought mine owne.

Aron. I goe Andronicus, and for thy hand,
Looke by and by to haue thy sonnes with thee:
Their heads I meane: Oh how this villany
Doth fat me with the very thoughts of it.
Let fooles doe good, and faire men call for grace,
Aron will haue his soule blacke like his face. *Exit.*

Ti. O heere I lift this one hand vp to heauen,
And bow this feeble ruine to the earth,
If any power pitties wretched teares,
To that I call: what wilt thou kneele with me?
Doe then deare heart, for heauen shall heare our prayers,
Or with our sighs weele breath the welkin dimme,
And staine the Sun with fogge as somtime cloudes,
When they do hug him in their melting bosomes.

Mar. Oh brother speake with possibilities,
And do not breake into these deepe extreames.

Ti. Is not my sorrow deepe, hauing no bottome?

Then be my passions bottomlesse with them.

Mar. But yet let reason gouerne thy lament.

Titus. If there were reason for these miseries,
Then into limits could I binde my woes :
When heauen doth weepe, doth not the earth oreflow?
If the windes rage, doth not the Sea wax mad,
Threatning the welkin with his big-swolne face?
And wilt thou haue a reason for this coile?
I am the Sea. Harke how her sighes doe flow:
Shee is the weeping welkin, I the earth :
Then must my Sea be moued with her sighes,
Then must my earth with her continuall teares,
Become a deluge : ouerflow'd and drown'd :
For why, my bowels cannot hide her woes,
But like a drunkard must I vomit them;
Then giue me leaue, for loosers will haue leaue,
To ease their stomackes with their bitter tongues.

Enter a messenger with two heads and a hand.

Mess. Worthy *Andronicus*, ill art thou repaid,
For that good hand thou sentst the Emperour :
Heere are the heads of thy two noble sonnes.
And heeres thy hand in scorne to thee sent backe :
Thy griefes, their sports : Thy resolution mockt,
That woe is me to thinke vpon thy woes,
More then remembrance of my fathers death. *Exit.*

Marc. Now let hot Ætna coole in Cicilie,
And be my heart an euer-burning hell :
These miseries are more then may be borne.
To weepe with them that weepe, doth ease some deale,
But sorrow flouted at, is double death.

Luci. Ah that this sight should make so deep a wound,
And yet detested life not shrinke thereat :
That euer death should let life beare his name,
Where life hath no more interest but to breath.

Mar. Alas poore hart that kisse is comfortlesse,
As frozen water to a starued snake.

Titus. When will this fearefull slumber haue an end?

Mar. Now farwell flatterie, die *Andronicus*,
Thou dost not slumber, see thy two sons heads,
Thy warlike hands, thy mangled daughter here :
Thy other banisht sonnes with this deere sight
Strucke pale and bloodlesse, and thy brother I,
Euen like a stony Image, cold and numme.
Ah now no more will I controule my griefes,
Rent off thy siluer haire, thy other hand
Gnawing with thy teeth, and be this dismall sight
The closing vp of our most wretched eyes :
Now is a time to storme, why art thou still?

Titus. Ha,ha,ha.

Mar. Why dost thou laugh? it fits not with this houre.

Ti. Why I haue not another teare to shed :
Besides, this sorrow is an enemy,
And would vsurpe vpon my watry eyes,
And make them blinde with tributarie teares.
Then which way shall I finde Reuenges Caue?
For these two heads doe seeme to speake to me,
And threat me, I shall neuer come to blisse,
Till all these mischiefes be returned againe,
Euen in their throats that haue committed them.
Come let me see what taske I haue to doe,
You heauie people, circle me about,
That I may turne me to each one of you,
And sweare vnto my soule to right your wrongs.
The vow is made, come Brother take a head,
And in this hand the other will I beare.
And *Lauinia* thou shalt be employd in these things:
Beare thou my hand sweet wench betweene thy teeth:
As for thee boy, goe get thee from my sight,
Thou art an Exile, and thou must not stay,
Hie to the *Gothes*, and raise an army there,
And if you loue me, as I thinke you doe,
Let's kisse and part, for we haue much to doe. *Exeunt.*

Manet Lucius.

Luci. Farewell *Andronicus* my noble Father:
The woful'st man that euer liu'd in Rome:
Farewell proud Rome, til *Lucius* come againe,
He loues his pledges dearer then his life:
Farewell *Lauinia* my noble sister,
O would thou wert as thou tofore hast beene,
But now, nor *Lucius* nor *Lauinia* liues
But in obliuion and hateful griefes:
If *Lucius* liue, he will requit your wrongs,
And make proud *Saturnine* and his Empresse
Beg at the gates likes *Tarquin* and his Queene.
Now will I to the *Gothes* and raise a power,
To be reueng'd on Rome and *Saturnine*. *Exit Lucius.*

A Banket.
Enter Andronicus, Marcus, Lauinia, and the Boy.

An. So,so, now sit, and looke you eate no more
Then will preserue iust so much strength in vs
As will reuenge these bitter woes of ours.
Marcus vnknit that sorrow-wreathen knot:
Thy Neece and I (poore Creatures) want our hands
And cannot passionate our tenfold griefe,
With foulded Armes. This poore right hand of mine,
Is left to tirranize vppon my breast.
Who when my hart all mad with misery,
Beats in this hollow prison of my flesh,
Then thus I thumpe it downe.
Thou Map of woe, that thus dost talk in signes,
When thy poore hart beates without ragious beating,
Thou canst not strike it thus to make it still?
Wound it with sighing girle, kil it with grones:
Or get some little knife betweene thy teeth,
And iust against thy hart make thou a hole,
That all the teares that thy poore eyes let fall
May run into that sinke, and soaking in,
Drowne the lamenting foole, in Sea salt teares.

Mar. Fy brother fy, teach her not thus to lay
Such violent hands vppon her tender life.

An. How now! Has sorrow made thee doate already?
Why *Marcus*, no man should be mad but I:
What violent hands can she lay on her life :
Ah, wherefore dost thou vrge the name of hands,
To bid *Æneas* tell the tale twice ore
How Troy was burnt, and he made miserable?
O handle not the rheame, to talke of hands,
Least we remember still that we haue none,
Fie, fie, how Frantiquely I square my talke
As if we should forget we had no hands :
If *Marcus* did not name the word of hands.
Come, lets fall too, and gentle girle eate this,
Heere is no drinke? Harke *Marcus* what she saies,
I can interpret all her martir'd signes,
She saies, she drinkes no other drinke but teares
Breu'd with her sorrow : mesh'd vppon her cheekes,
Speech.

Speechlesse complaynet, I will learne thy thought:
In thy dumb action, will I be as perfect
As begging Hermits in their holy prayers.
Thou shalt not sighe nor hold thy stumps to heauen,
Nor winke, nor nod, nor kneele, nor make a signe,
But I (of these) will wrest an Alphabet,
And by still practice, learne to know thy meaning.

 Boy. Good grandsire leaue these bitter deepe laments,
Make my Aunt merry, with some pleasing tale.

 Mar. Alas, the tender boy in passion mou'd,
Doth weepe to see his grandsires heauinesse.

 An. Peace tender Sapling, thou art made of teares,
And teares will quickly melt thy life away.

 Marcus strikes the dish with a knife.
What doest thou strike at *Marcus* with knife.

 Mar. At that that I haue kil'd my Lord, a Flye.

 An. Out on the murderour: thou kil'st my hart,
Mine eyes cloi'd with view of Tirranie:
A deed of death done on the Innocent
Becoms not *Titus* brother: get thee gone,
I see thou art not for my company.

 Mar. Alas (my Lord) I haue but kild a flie.

 An. But? How: if that Flie had a father and mother?
How would he hang his slender gilded wings
And buz lamenting doings in the ayer,
Poore harmelesse Fly,
That with his pretty buzing melody,
Came heere to make vs merry,
And thou hast kil'd him.

 Mar. Pardon me sir,
It was a blacke illfauour'd Fly,
Like to the Empresse Moore, therefore I kild him.

 An. O, o, o,
Then pardon me for reprehending thee,
For thou hast done a Charitable deed:
Giue me thy knife, I will insult on him,
Flattering my selfes, as if it were the Moore,
Come hither purposely to poyson me.
There's for thy selfe, and thats for *Tamira*: Ah sirra,
Yet I thinke we are not brought so low,
But that betweene vs, we can kill a Fly,
That comes in likenesse of a Cole-blacke Moore.

 Mar. Alas poore man, griefe ha's so wrought on him,
He takes false shadowes, for true substances.

 An. Come, take away: *Lauinia*, goe with me,
Ile to thy closset, and goe read with thee
Sad stories, chanced in the times of old.
Come boy, and goe with me, thy sight is young,
And thou shalt read, when mine begin to dazell. *Exeunt*

Actus Quartus.

Enter young Lucius and Lauinia running after him, and the Boy flies from her with his bookes vnder his arme.
Enter Titus and Marcus.

 Boy. Helpe Grandsier helpe, my Aunt *Lauinia*,
Followes me euery where I know not why.
Good Vncle *Marcus* see how swift she comes,
Alas sweet Aunt, I know not what you meane.

 Mar. Stand by me *Lucius*, doe not feare thy Aunt.

 Titus. She loues thee boy too well to doe thee harme

 Boy. I when my father was in Rome she did.

 Mar. What meanes my Neece *Lauinia* by these signes?

 Ti. Feare not *Lucius*, somewhat doth she meane:
See *Lucius* see, how much she makes of thee:
Some whether would she haue thee goe with her.
Ah boy, *Cornelia* neuer with more care
Read to her sonnes, then she hath read to thee,
Sweet Poetry, and *Tullies* Oratour:
Canst thou not gesse wherefore she plies thee thus?

 Boy. My Lord I know not I, nor can I gesse,
Vnlesse some fit or frenzie do possesse her:
For I haue heard my Grandsier say full oft,
Extremitie of griefes would make men mad.
And I haue read that *Hecuba* of Troy,
Ran mad through sorrow, that made me to feare,
Although my Lord, I know my noble Aunt,
Loues me as deare as ere my mother did,
And would not but in fury fright my youth,
Which made me downe to throw my bookes, and flie
Causles perhaps, but pardon me sweet Aunt,
And Madam, if my Vncle *Marcus* goe,
I will most willingly attend your Ladyship.

 Mar. *Lucius* I will.

 Ti. How now *Lauinia*, *Marcus* what meanes this?
Some booke there is that she desires to see,
Which is it girle of these? Open them boy,
But thou art deeper read and better skild,
Come and take choyse of all my Library,
And so beguile thy sorrow, till the heauens
Reueale the damn'd contriuer of this deed.
What booke?
Why lifts she vp her armes in sequence thus?

 Mar. I thinke she meanes that ther was more then one
Confederate in the fact, I more there was:
Or else to heauen she heaues them to reuenge.

 Ti. *Lucius* what booke is that she tosseth so?

 Boy. Grandsier 'tis *Ouids* Metamorphosis,
My mother gaue it me.

 Mar. For loue of her that's gone,
Perhahs she culd it from among the rest.

 Ti. Soft, so busily she turnes the leaues,
Helpe her, what would she finde? *Lauinia* shall I read?
This is the tragicke tale of *Philomel*?
And treates of *Tereus* treason and his rape,
And rape I feare was roote of thine annoy.

 Mar. See brother see, note how she quotes the leaues

 Ti. *Lauinia*, wert thou thus surpriz'd sweet girle,
Rauisht and wrong'd as *Philomela* was?
Forc'd in the ruthlesse, vast, and gloomy woods?
See, see, I such a place there is where we did hunt,
(O had we neuer, neuer hunted there)
Patern'd by that the Poet heere describes,
By nature made for murthers and for rapes.

 Mar. O why should nature build so foule a den,
Vnlesse the Gods delight in tragedies?

 Ti. Giue signes sweet girle, for heere are none but friends
What Romaine Lord it was durst do the deed?
Or slunke not *Saturnine*, as *Tarquin* erstt,
That left the Campe to sinne in *Lucrece* bed.

 Mar. Sit downe sweet Neece, brother sit downe by me,
Appollo, *Pallas*, *Ioue*, or *Mercury*,
Inspire me that I may this treason finde.
My Lord looke heere, looke heere *Lauinia*.

He writes his Name with his staffe, and guides it
with feete and mouth.
This sandie plot is plaine, guide if thou canst

This

This after me, I haue writ my name,
Without the helpe of any hand at all.
Curst be that hart that forc'st vs to that shift:
Write thou good Neece, and heere display at last,
What God will haue discouered for reuenge,
Heauen guide thy pen to print thy sorrowes plaine,
That we may know the Traytors and the truth.

She takes the staffe in her mouth, and guides it with her stumps and writes.

Ti. Oh doe ye read my Lord what she hath writes?
Stuprum, Chiron, Demetrius.

Mar. What, what, the lustfull sonnes of *Tamora*,
Performers of this hainous bloody deed?

Ti. Magni Dominator poli,
Tam lentus audis scelera, tam lentus vides?

Mar. Oh calme thee gentle Lord: Although I know
There is enough written vpon this earth,
To stirre a mutinie in the mildest thoughts,
And arme the mindes of infants to exclaimes.
My Lord kneele downe with me: *Lauinia* kneele,
And kneele sweet boy, the Romaine *Hectors* hope,
And sweare with me, as with the wofull Feere
And father of that chast dishonoured Dame,
Lord *Iunius Brutus* sweare for *Lucrece* rape,
That we will prosecute (by good aduise)
Mortall reuenge vpon these traytorous Gothes,
And see their blood, or die with this reproach.

Ti. Tis sure enough, and you knew how.
But if you hunt these Beare-whelpes, then beware
The Dam will wake, and if she winde you once,
Shee's with the Lyon deepely still in league.
And lulls him whilst she palyeth on her backe,
And when he sleepes will she do what she list.
You are a young huntsman *Marcus*, let it alone:
And come, I will goe get a leafe of brasse,
And with a Gad of steele will write these words,
And lay it by: the angry Northerne winde
Will blow these sands like *Sibels* leaues abroad,
And wheres your lesson then. Boy what say you?

Boy. I say my Lord, that if I were a man,
Their mothers bed-chamber should not be safe,
For these bad bond-men to the yoake of Rome.

Mar. I that's my boy, thy father hath full oft,
For his vngratefull country done the like.

Boy. And Vncle so will I, and if I liue.

Ti. Come goe with me into mine Armorie,
Lucius Ile fit thee, and withall, my boy
Shall carry from me to the Empresse sonnes,
Presents that I intend to send them both,
Come, come, thou'lt do thy message, wilt thou not?

Boy. I with my dagger in their bosomes Grandsire:

Ti. No boy not so, Ile teach thee another course,
Lauinia come, *Marcus* looke to my house,
Lucius and Ile goe braue it at the Court,
I marry will we sir, and weele be waited on. *Exeunt.*

Mar. O heauens! Can you heare a good man grone
And not relent, or not compassion him?
Marcus attend him in his extasie,
That hath more scars of sorrow in his heart,
Then foe-mens markes vpon his batter'd shield,
But yet so iust, that he will not reuenge,
Reuenge the heauens for old *Andronicus*. *Exit*

Enter Aron, Chiron and Demetrius at one dore: and at another dore young Lucius and another, with a bundle of weapons, and verses writ vpon them.

Chi. Demetrius heeres the sonne of *Lucius*,
He hath some message to deliuer vs.

Aron. I some mad message from his mad Grandfather.

Boy. My Lords, with all the humblenesse I may,
I greete your honours from *Andronicus*,
And pray the Romane Gods confound you both.

Deme. Gramercie louely *Lucius*, what's the newes?
For villanie's markt with rape. May it please you,
My Grandsire well aduis'd hath sent by me,
The goodliest weapons of his Armorie,
To gratifie your honourable youth,
The hope of Rome, for so he bad me say:
And so I do and with his gifts present
Your Lordships, when euer you haue need,
You may be armed and appointed well,
And so I leaue you both: like bloody villaines. *Exit*

Deme. What's heere? a scrole, & written round about?
Let's see.
Integer vitæ scelerisque purus, non egit maury iaculis nec arcus.

Chi. O'tis a verse in *Horace*, I know it well.
I read it in the Grammer long agoe.

Moore. I iust, a verse in *Horace*: right, you haue it,
Now what a thing it is to be an Asse?
Heer's no sound iest, the old man hath found their guilt,
And sends the weapons wrapt about with lines,
That wound (beyond their feeling) to the quick:
But were our witty Empresse well a foot,
She would applaud *Andronicus* conceit:
But let her rest, in her vnrest a while.
And now young Lords, wa's tnot a happy starre
Led vs to Rome strangers, and more then so,
Captiues, to be aduanced to this height?
It did me good before the Pallace gate,
To braue the Tribune in his brothers hearing.

Deme. But me more good, to see so great a Lord
Balely insinuate, and send vs gifts.

Moore. Had he not reason Lord *Demetrius*?
Did you not vse his daughter very friendly?

Deme. I would we had a thousand Romane Dames
At such a bay, by turne to serue out lust.

Chi. A charitable wish, and full of loue.

Moore. Heere lack's but you mother for to say, Amen.

Chi. And that would she for twenty thousand more.

Deme. Come, let vs go, and pray to all the Gods
For our beloued mother in her paines.

Moore. Pray to the deuils, the gods haue giuen vs ouer.

Flourish.

Dem. Why do the Emperors trumpets flourish thus?

Chi. Belike for ioy the Emperour hath a sonne.

Deme. Soft, who comes heere?

Enter Nurse with a blacke a Moore childe.

Nur. Good morrow Lords:
O tell me, did you see *Aaron* the Moore?

Aron. Well, more or lesse, or nere a whit at all,
Heere *Aaron* is, and what with *Aaron* now?

Nurse. Oh gentle *Aaron*, we are all vndone,
Now helpe, or woe betide thee euermore.

Aron. Why, what a catterwalling dost thou keepe?
What dost thou wrap and fumble in thine armes?

Nurse. O that which I would hide from heauens eye,
Our Empresse shame, and stately Romes disgrace,
She is deliuered Lords, she is deliuered.

Aron. To whom?

Nurse. I meane she is brought a bed?

Aron. Wel God giue her good rest,

What

The Tragedie of Titus Andronicus.

What hath he sent her?
  Nurse. A deuill.
  Aron. Why then she is the Deuils Dam: a ioyfull issue.
  Nurse. A ioylesse, dismall, blacke &, sorrowfull issue,
Heere is the babe as loathsome as a toad,
Amongst the fairest breeders of our clime,
The Empresse sends it thee, thy stampe, thy seale,
And bids thee christen it with thy daggers point.
  Aron. Out you whore, is black so base a hue?
Sweet blowse, you are a beautious blossome sure.
  Deme. Villaine what hast thou done?
  Aron. That which thou canst not vndoe.
  Chi. Thou hast vndone our mother.
  Deme. And therein hellish dog, thou hast vndone,
Woe to her chance, and damn'd her loathed choyce,
Accur'st the off-spring of so soule a fiend.
  Chi. It shall not liue.
  Aron. It shall not die.
  Nurse. Aaron it must, the mother wils it so.
  Aron. What, must it *Nurse*? Then let no man but I
Doe execution on my flesh and blood.
  Deme. Ile broach the Tadpole on my Rapiers point:
Nurse giue it me, my sword shall soone dispatch it.
  Aron. Sooner this sword shall plough thy bowels vp.
Stay murtherous villaines, will you kill your brother?
Now by the burning Tapers of the skie,
That sh'one so brightly when this Boy was got,
He dies vpon my Semitars sharpe point,
That touches this my first borne sonne and heire.
I tell you young-lings, not *Enceladus*
With all his threatning band of *Typhons* broode,
Nor great *Alcides*, nor the God of warre,
Shall ceaze this prey out of his fathers hands:
What, what, ye sanguine shallow harted Boyes,
Ye white-limb'd walls, ye Ale-house painted signes,
Cole-blacke is better then another hue,
In that it scornes to beare another hue:
For all the water in the Ocean,
Can neuer turne the Swans blacke legs to white,
Although she laue them hourely in the flood:
Tell the Empresse from me, I am of age
To keepe mine owne, excuse it how she can.
  Deme. Wilt thou betray thy noble mistris thus?
  Aron. My mistris is my mistris: this my selfe,
The vigour, and the picture of my youth:
This, before all the world do I preferre,
This mauger all the world will I keepe safe,
Or some of you shall smoake for it in Rome.
  Deme. By this our mother is for euer sham'd.
  Chi. Rome will despise her for this foule escape.
  Nur. The Emperour in his rage will doome her death.
  Chi. I blush to thinke vpon this ignominie.
  Aron. Why ther's the priniledge your beauty beares:
Fie trecherous hue, that will betray with blushing
The close enacts and counsels of the hart:
Heer's a young Lad fram'd of another leere,
Looke how the blacke slaue smiles vpon the father;
As who should say, old Lad I am thine owne.
He is your brother Lords, sensibly fed
Of that selfe blood that first gaue life to you,
And from that wombe where you imprisoned were
He is infranchised and come to light:
Nay he is your brother by the surer side,
Although my seale be stamped in his face.
  Nurse. Aaron what shall I say vnto the Empresse?
  Dem. Aduise thee *Aaron*, what is to be done,
And we will all subscribe to thy aduise:
Saue thou the child, so we may all be safe.
  Aron. Then sit we downe and let vs all consult.
My sonne and I will haue the winde of you:
Keepe there, now talke at pleasure of your safety.
  Deme. How many women saw this childe of his?
  Aron. Why so braue Lords, when we ioyne in league
I am a Lambe: but if you braue the *Moore*,
The chafed Bore, the mountaine Lyonesse,
The Ocean swells not so at *Aaron* stormes:
But say againe, how many saw the childe?
  Nurse. *Cornelia*, the midwife, and my selfe,
And none else but the deliuered Empresse.
  Aron. The Empresse, the Midwife, and your selfe,
Two may keepe counsell, when the third's away:
Goe to the Empresse, tell her this I said,   *He kils her*
Weeke, weeke, so cries a Pigge prepared to th'spit.
  Deme. What mean'st thou *Aaron*?
Wherefore did'st thou this?
  Aron. O Lord sir, 'tis a deed of pollicie?
Shall she liue to betray this guilt of our's:
A long tongu'd babling Gossip? No Lords no:
And now be it knowne to you my full intent.
Not farre, one *Muliteus* my Country-man
His wife but yesternight was brought to bed,
His childe is like to her, faire as you are:
Goe packe with him, and giue the mother gold,
And tell them both the circumstance of all,
And how by this their Childe shall be aduaunc'd,
And be receiued for the Emperours heyre,
And substituted in the place of mine,
To calme this tempest whirling in the Court,
And let the Emperour dandle him for his owne.
Harke ye Lords, ye see I haue giuen her physicke,
And you must needs bestow her funerall,
The fields are neere, and you are gallant Groomes:
This done, see that you take no longer daies
But send the Midwife presently to me.
The Midwife and the Nurse well made away,
Then let the Ladies tattle what they please.
  Chi. Aaron I see thou wilt not trust the ayre with se
  Deme. For this care of *Tamora*,   (crets.
Her selfe, and hers are highly bound to thee. *Exeunt.*
  Aron. Now to the Gothes, as swift as Swallow flies,
There to dispose this treasure in mine armes,
And secretly to greete the Empresse friends:
Come on you thick-lipt-slaue, Ile beare you hence,
For it is you that puts vs to our shifts:
Ile make you feed on berries, and on rootes,
And feed on curds and whay, and sucke the Goate,
And cabbin in a Caue, and bring you vp
To be a warriour, and command a Campe.   *Exit*

*Enter Titus, old Marcus, young Lucius, and other gentlemen
with bowes, and Titus beares the arrowes with
Letters on the end of them.*

  Tit. Come *Marcus*, come, kinsmen this is the way.
Sir Boy let me see your Archerie,
Looke yee draw home enough, and 'tis there straight:
Terras Astrea reliquit, be you remembred *Marcus*.
She's gone, she's fled, sirs take you to your tooles,
You Cosens shall goe sound the Ocean:
And cast your nets, haply you may find her in the Sea,
Yet ther's as little iustice as at Land:
No *Publius* and *Sempronius*, you must doe it,

Tis

'Tis you must dig with Mattocke, and with Spade,
And pierce the inmost Center of the earth:
Then when you come to *Plutoes* Region,
I pray you deliuer him this petition,
Tell him it is for iustice, and for aide,
And that it comes from old *Andronicus*,
Shaken with sorrowes in vngratefull Rome.
Ah Rome! Well, well, I made thee miserable,
What time I threw the peoples suffrages
On him that thus doth tyrannize ore me.
Goe get you gone, and pray be carefull all,
And leaue you not a man of warre vnsearcht,
This wicked Emperour may haue shipt her hence,
And kinsmen then we may goe pipe for iustice.

  Marc. O *Publius* is not this a heauie case
To see thy Noble Vnckle thus distract?

  Publ. Therefore my Lords it highly vs concernes,
By day and night t'attend him carefully:
And feede his humour kindely as we may,
Till time beget some carefull remedie.

  Marc. Kinsmen, his sorrowes are past remedie.
Ioyne with the Gothes, and with reuengefull warre,
Take wreake on Rome for this ingraticude,
And vengeance on the Traytor *Saturnine*.

  Tit. *Publius* how now? how now my Maisters?
What haue you met with her?

  Publ. No my good Lord, but *Pluto* sends you word,
If you will haue reuenge from hell you shall,
Marrie for iustice she is so imploy'd,
He thinkes with *Ioue* in heauen, or some where else:
So that perforce you must needs stay a time.

  Tit. He doth me wrong to feed me with delayes,
Ile diue into the burning Lake below,
And pull her out of *Acaron* by the heeles.
Marcus we are but shrubs, no Cedars we,
No big-bon'd-men, fram'd of the Cyclops size,
But mettall *Marcus*, steele to the very backe,
Yet wrung with wrongs more then our backe can beare:
And sith there's no iustice in earth nor hell,
We will sollicite heauen, and moue the Gods
To send downe Iustice for to wreake'our wongs:
Come to this geare, you are a good Archer *Marcus*.

  He giues them the Arrowes.

Ad Iouem, that's for you: here *ad Appollonem*,
Ad Martem, that's for my selfe,
Heere Boy to *Pallas*, heere to *Mercury*,
To *Saturnine*, to *Caius*, not to *Saturnine*,
You were as good to shoote against the winde.
Too it Boy, *Marcus* loose when I bid:
Of my word, I haue written to effect,
Ther's not a God left vnsollicited.

  Marc. Kinsmen, shoot all your shafts into the Court,
We will afflict the Emperour in his pride.

  Tit. Now Maisters draw, Oh well said *Lucius*:
Good Boy in *Virgoes* lap, giue it *Pallas*.

  Marc. My Lord, I aime a Mile beyond the Moone,
Your letter is with *Iupiter* by this.

  Tit. Ha, ha, *Publius*, *Publius*, what hast thou done?
See, see, thou hast shot off one of *Taurus* hornes.

  Mar. This was the sport my Lord, when *Publius* shot,
The Bull being gal'd, gaue *Aries* such a knocke,
That downe fell both the Rams hornes in the Court,
And who should finde them but the Empresse villaine:
She laught, and told the Moore he should not choose
But giue them to his Maister for a present.

  Tit. Why there it goes, God giue your Lordship ioy.

Enter the Clowne with a basket and two Pigeons in it.

  Titus. Newes, newes, from heauen,
Marcus the poast is come.
Sirrah, what tydings? haue you any letters?
Shall I haue Iustice, what sayes *Iupiter*?

  Clowne. Ho the Iibbetmaker, he sayes that he hath taken them downe againe, for the man must not be hang'd till the next weeke.

  Tit. But what sayes *Iupiter* I aske thee?

  Clowne. Alas sir I know not *Iupiter*:
I neuer dranke with him in all my life.

  Tit. Why villaine art not thou the Carrier?

  Clowne. I of my Pigions sir, nothing else.

  Tit. Why, did'st thou not come from heauen?

  Clowne. From heauen? Alas sir, I neuer came there, God forbid I should be so bold, to presse to heauen in my young dayes. Why I am going with my pigeons to the Tribunall Plebs, to take vp a matter of brawle, betwixt my Vncle, and one of the Emperialls men.

  Mar. Why sir, that is as fit as can be to serue for your Oration, and let him deliuer the Pigions to the Emperour from you.

  Tit. Tell mee, can you deliuer an Oration to the Emperour with a Grace?

  Clowne. Nay truely sir, I could neuer say grace in all my life.

  Tit. Sirrah come hither, make no more adoe,
But giue your Pigeons to the Emperour,
By me thou shalt haue Iustice at his hands.
Hold, hold, meane while her's money for thy charges.
Giue me pen and inke.
Sirrah, can you with a Grace deliuer a Supplication?

  Clowne. I sir.

  Titus. Then here is a Supplication for you, and when you come to him, at the first approach you must kneele, then kisse his foote, then deliuer vp your Pigeons, and then looke for your reward. Ile be at hand sir, see you do it brauely.

  Clowne. I warrant you sir, let me alone.

  Tit. Sirrha hast thou a knife? Come let me see it.
Heere *Marcus*, fold it in the Oration,
For thou hast made it like an humble Suppliant:
And when thou hast giuen it the Emperour,
Knocke at my dore, and tell me what he sayes.

  Clowne. God be with you sir, I will. *Exit.*

  Tit. Come *Marcus* let vs goe, *Publius* follow me.
Exeunt.

*Enter Emperour and Empresse, and her two sonnes, the
Emperour brings the Arrowes in his hand
that Titus shot at him.*

  Satur. Why Lords,
What wrongs are these? was euer seene
An Emperour in Rome thus ouerborne,
Troubled, Confronted thus, and for the extent
Of egall iustice, vs'd in such contempt?
My Lords, you know the mightfull Gods,
(How euer these disturbers of our peace
Buz in the peoples eares) there nought hath past,
But euen with law against the willfull Sonnes
Of old *Andronicus*. And what and if
His sorrowes haue so ouerwhelm'd his wits,
Shall we be thus afflicted in his wreakes,
His fits, his frenzie, and his bitternesse?
And now he writes to heauen for his redresse.
See, heeres to *Ioue*, and this to *Mercury*,

This

This to *Apollo*, this to the God of warre:
Sweet scrowles to flie about the streets of Rome:
What's this but Libelling against the Senate,
And blazoning our Iniustice euery where?
A goodly humour, is it not my Lords?
As who would say, in Rome no Iustice were.
But if I liue, his fained extasies
Shall be no shelter to these outrages:
But he and his shall know, that Iustice liues
In *Saturninus* health; whom if he sleepe,
Hee'l so awake, as he in fury shall
Cut off the proud'st Conspirator that liues.

  Tamo. My gracious Lord, my louely *Saturnine*,
Lord of my life, Commander of my thoughts,
Calme thee, and beare the faults of *Titus* age,
Th'effects of sorrow for his valiant Sonnes,
Whose losse hath pier'st him deepe, and scar'd his heart;
And rather comfort his distressed plight,
Then prosecute the meanest or the best
For these contempts. Why thus it shall become
High witted *Tamora* to glose with all: *Aside.*
But *Titus*, I haue touch'd thee to the quicke,
Thy life blood out: If *Aaron* now be wise,
Then is all safe, the Anchor's in the Port.

  Enter Clowne.

How now good fellow, would'st thou speake with vs?
  Clow. Yea forsooth, and your Mistership be Emperiall.
  Tam. Empresse I am, but yonder sits the Emperour.
  Clo. 'Tis he; God & Saint Stephen giue you good den;
I haue brought you a Letter, & a couple of Pigions heere.
                              He reads the Letter.
  Satu. Goe take him away, and hang him presently.
  Clowne. How much money must I haue?
  Tam. Come sirrah you must be hang'd.
  Clow. Hang'd? berLady, then I haue brought vp a neck
to a faire end.   *Exit.*

  Satu. Despightfull and intollerable wrongs,
Shall I endure this monstrous villany?
I know from whence this same deuise proceedes:
May this be borne? As if his traytrous Sonnes,
That dy'd by law for murther of our Brother,
Haue by my meanes beene butcher'd wrongfully?
Goe dragge the villaine hither by the haire,
Nor Age, nor Honour, shall shape priuiledge:
For this proud mocke, Ile be thy slaughter man:
Sly franticke wretch, that holp'st to make me great,
In hope thy selfe should gouerne Rome and me.

  Enter Nuntius Emillius.

  Satur. What newes with thee *Emillius*?
  Emil. Arme my Lords, Rome neuer had more cause,
The Gothes haue gather'd head, and with a power
Of high resolued men, bent to the spoyle
They hither march amaine, vnder conduct
Of *Lucius*, Sonne to old *Andronicus*:
Who threats in course of this reuenge to do
As much as euer *Coriolanus* did.
  King. Is warlike *Lucius* Generall of the Gothes?
These tydings nip me, and I hang the head
As flowers with frost, or grasse beat downe with stormes:
I, now begins our sorrowes to approach,
'Tis he the common people loue so much,
My selfe hath often-heard them say,
(When I haue walked like a priuate man)
That *Lucius* banishment was wrongfully,
And they haue wisht that *Lucius* were their Emperour.
  Tam. Why should you feare? Is not our City strong?

  King. I, but the Cittizens fauour *Lucius*,
And will reuolt from me, to succour him.
  Tam. King, be thy thoughts Imperious like thy name.
Is the Sunne dim'd, that Gnats do flie in it?
The Eagle suffers little Birds to sing,
And is not carefull what they meane thereby,
Knowing that with the shadow of his wings,
He can at pleasure stint their melodie.
Euen so mayest thou, the giddy men of Rome,
Then cheere thy spirit, for know thou Emperour,
I will enchaunt the old *Andronicus*,
With words more sweet, and yet more dangerous
Then baites to fish, or hony stalkes to sheepe,
When as the one is wounded with the baite,
The other rotted with delicious foode.
  King. But he will not entreat his Sonne for vs.
  Tam. If *Tamora* entreat him, then he will,
For I can smooth and fill his aged eare,
With golden promises, that were his heart
Almost Impregnable, his old eares deafe,
Yet should both eare and heart obey my tongue.
Goe thou before to our Embassadour,
Say, that the Emperour requests a parly
Of warlike *Lucius*, and appoint the meeting.
  King. Emillius do this message Honourably,
And if he stand in Hostage for his safety,
Bid him demaund what pledge will please him best.
  Emill. Your bidding shall I do effectually.   *Exit.*
  Tam. Now will I to that old *Andronicus*,
And temper him with all the Art I haue,
To plucke proud *Lucius* from the warlike Gothes.
And now sweet Emperour be blithe againe,
And bury all thy feare in my deuises.
  Satu. Then goe successantly and plead for him. *Exit.*

Actus Quintus.

Flourish. Enter Lucius with an Army of Gothes,
with Drum and Souldiers.

  Luci. Approued warriours, and my faithfull Friends,
I haue receiued Letters from great Rome,
Which signifies what hate they beare their Emperour,
And how desirous of our sight they are.
Therefore great Lords, be as your Titles witnesse,
Imperious and impatient of your wrongs,
And wherein Rome hath done you any scathe,
Let him make treble satisfaction.
  Goth. Braue slip, sprung from the Great *Andronicus*,
Whose name was once our terrour, now our comfort,
Whose high exploits, and honourable Deeds,
Ingratefull Rome requites with foule contempt:
Behold in vs, weele follow where thou lead'st,
Like stinging Bees in hottest Sommers day,
Led by their Maister to the flowred fields,
And be aueng'd on cursed *Tamora*:
And as he saith, so say we all with him.
  Luci. I humbly thanke him, and I thanke you all.
But who comes heere, led by a lusty *Goth*?

  Enter a Goth leading of Aaron with his child
  in his armes.

  Goth. Renowned *Lucius*, from our troups I straid,
To gaze vpon a ruinous Monasterie,

And as I earnestly did fixe mine eye
Vpon the wasted building, suddainely
I heard a childe cry vnderneath a wall:
I made vnto the noyse, when soone I heard,
The crying babe control'd with this discourse:
Peace Tawny slaue, halfe me, and halfe thy Dam,
Did not thy Hue bewray whose brat thou art?
Had nature lent thee, but thy Mothers looke,
Villaine thou might'st haue bene an Emperour.
But where the Bull and Cow are both milk-white,
They neuer do beget a cole-blacke-Calfe:
Peace, villaine peace, euen thus he rates the babe,
For I must beare thee to a trusty Goth,
Who when he knowes thou art the Empresse babe,
Will hold thee dearely for thy Mothers sake.
With this, my weapon drawne I rusht vpon him,
Surpriz'd him suddainely, and brought him hither
To vse, as you thinke needefull of the man.

  Luci. Oh worthy Goth, this is the incarnate deuill,
That rob'd *Andronicus* of his good hand:
This is the Pearle that pleas'd your Empresse eye,
And heere's the Base Fruit of his burning lust.
Say wall-ey'd slaue, whether would'st thou conuay
This growing Image of thy fiend-like face?
Why dost not speake? what deafe? Not a word?
A halter Souldiers, hang him on this Tree,
And by his side his Fruite of Bastardie.

  Aron. Touch not the Boy, he is of Royall blood.
  Luci. Too like the Syre for euer being good.
First hang the Child that he may see it spraull,
A sight to vexe the Fathers soule withall.

  Aron. Get me a Ladder *Lucius*, saue the Childe,
And beare it from me to the Empresse:
If thou do this, Ile shew thee wondrous things,
That highly may aduantage thee to heare;
If thou wilt not, befall what may befall,
Ile speake no more: but vengeance rot you all.

  Luci. Say on, and if it please me which thou speak'st,
Thy child shall liue, and I will see it Nourisht.

  Aron. And if it please thee? why assure thee *Lucius*,
'Twill vexe thy soule to heare what I shall speake:
For I must talke of Murthers, Rapes, and Massacres,
Acts of Blacke-night, abhominable Deeds,
Complots of Mischiefe, Treason, Villanies
Ruthfull to heare, yet pittiously performd,
And this shall all be buried by my death,
Vnlesse thou sweare to me my Childe shall liue.

  Luci. Tell on thy minde,
I say thy Childe shall liue.

  Aron. Sweare that he shall, and then I will begin.
  Luci. Who should I sweare by,
Thou beleeuest no God,
That graunted, how can'st thou beleeue an oath?

  Aron. What if I do not, as indeed I do not,
Yet for I know thou art Religious,
And hast a thing within thee, called Conscience,
With twenty Popish trickes and Ceremonies,
Which I haue seene thee carefull to obserue:
Therefore I vrge thy oath, for that I know
An Ideot holds his Bauble for a God,
And keepes the oath which by that God he sweares,
To that Ile vrge him: therefore thou shalt vow
By that same God, what God so ere it be
That thou adorest, and hast in reuerence,
To saue my Boy, to nourish and bring him vp,
Ore else I will discouer nought to thee.

  Luci. Euen by my God I sweare to to thee I will.
  Aron. First know thou,
I be got him on the Empresse.
  Luci. Oh most Insatiate luxurious woman!
  Aron. Tut *Lucius*, this was but a deed of Charitie,
To that which thou shalt heare of me anon,
'Twas her two Sonnes that murdered *Bassianus*,
They cut thy Sisters tongue, and rauisht her,
And cut her hands off, and trim'd her as thou saw'st.
  Lucius. Oh detestable villaine!
Call'st thou that Trimming?
  Aron. Why she was washt, and cut, and trim'd,
And 'twas trim sport for them that had the doing of it.
  Luci. Oh barbarous beastly villaines like thy selfe!
  Aron. Indeede, I was their Tutor to instruct them,
That Codding spirit had they from their Mother,
As sure a Card as euer wonne the Set:
That bloody minde I thinke they learn'd of me,
As true a Dog as euer fought at head.
Well, let my Deeds be witnesse of my worth:
I trayn'd thy Bretheren to that guilefull Hole,
Where the dead Corps of *Bassianus* lay:
I wrote the Letter, that thy Father found,
And hid the Gold within the Letter mention'd,
Confederate with the Queene, and her two Sonnes,
And what not done, that thou hast cause to rue,
Wherein I had no stroke of Mischeife in it.
I play'd the Cheater for thy Fathers hand,
And when I had it, drew my selfe apart,
And almost broke my heart with extreame laughter.
I pried me through the Creuice of a Wall,
When for his hand, he had his two Sonnes heads,
Beheld his teares, and laught so hartily,
That both mine eyes were rainie like to his:
And when I told the Empresse of this sport,
She sounded almost at my pleasing tale,
And for my tydings, gaue me twenty kisses.
  Goth. What canst thou say all this, and neuer blush?
  Aron. I, like a blacke Dogge, as the saying is.
  Luci. Art thou not sorry for these hainous deedes?
  Aron. I, that I had not done a thousand more:
Euen now I curse the day, and yet I thinke
Few come within few compasse of my curse,
Wherein I did not some Notorious ill,
As kill a man, or else deuise his death,
Rauish a Maid, or plot the way to do it,
Accuse some Innocent, and forsweare my selfe,
Set deadly Enmity betweene two Friends,
Make poore mens Cattell breake their neckes,
Set fire on Barnes and Haystackes in the night,
And bid the Owners quench them with the teares:
Oft haue I dig'd vp dead men from their graues,
And set them vpright at their deere Friends doore,
Euen when their sorrowes almost was forgot,
And on their skinnes, as on the Barke of Trees,
Haue with my knife carued in Romaine Letters,
Let not your sorrow die, though I am dead.
Tut, I haue done a thousand dreadfull things
As willingly, as one would kill a Fly.
And nothing greeues me hartily indeede,
But that I cannot doe ten thousand more.
  Luci. Bring downe the diuell, for he must not die
So sweet a death as hanging presently.
  Aron. If there be diuels, would I were a deuill,
To liue and burne in euerlasting fire,
So I might haue your company in hell,

But to torment you with my bitter tongue.

Luci. Sirs stop his mouth, & let him speake no more.

Enter Emillius.

Goth. My Lord, there is a Messenger from Rome
Desires to be admitted to your presence.

Luc. Let him come neere.
Welcome *Emillius*, what the newes from Rome?

Emi. Lord *Lucius*, and you Princes of the Gothes,
The Romaine Emperour greetes you all by me,
And for he vnderstands you are in Armes,
He craues a parly at your Fathers house
Willing you to demand your Hostages,
And they shall be immediately deliuered.

Goth. What saies our Generall?

Luc. Emillius, let the Emperour giue his pledges
Vnto my Father, and my Vncle *Marcus*, *Flourish*.
And we will come: march away. *Exeunt.*

Enter Tamora, and her two Sonnes disguised.

Tam. Thus in this strange and sad Habilliament,
I will encounter with *Andronicus*,
And say, I am Reuenge sent from below,
To ioyne with him and right his hainous wrongs:
Knocke at his study where they say he keepes,
To ruminate strange plots of dire Reuenge,
Tell him Reuenge is come to ioyne with him,
And worke confusion on his Enemies.

They knocke and Titus opens his study dore.

Tit. Who doth mollest my Contemplation?
Is it your tricke to make me ope the dore,
That so my sad decrees may flie away,
And all my studie be to no effect?
You are deceiu'd, for what I meane to do,
See heere in bloody lines I haue set downe:
And what is written shall be executed.

Tam. Titus, I am come to talke with thee,

Tit. No not a word: how can I grace my talke,
Wanting a hand to giue it action,
Thou hast the ods of me, therefore no more.

Tam. If thou did'st know me,
Thou would'st talke with me.

Tit. I am not mad, I know thee well enough,
Witnesse this wretched stump,
Witnesse these crimson lines,
Witnesse these Trenches made by griefe and care,
Witnesse the tyring day, and heauie night,
Witnesse all sorrow, that I know thee well
For our proud Empresse, Mighty *Tamora*:
Is not thy comming for my other hand?

Tamo. Know thou sad man, I am not *Tamora*,
She is thy Enemie, and I thy Friend,
I am Reuenge sent from th'infernall Kingdome,
To ease the gnawing Vulture of the mind,
By working wreakefull vengeance on my Foes:
Come downe and welcome me to this worlds light,
Conferre with me of Murder and of Death,
Ther's not a hollow Caue or lurking place,
No Vast obscurity, or Misty vale,
Where bloody Murther or detested Rape,
Can couch for feare, but I will finde them out,
And in their eares tell them my dreadfull name,
Reuenge, which makes the foule offenders quake.

Tit. Art thou Reuenge? and art thou sent to me,
To be a torment to mine Enemies?

Tam. I am, therefore come downe and welcome me.

Tit. Doe me some seruice ere I come to thee:
Loe by thy side where Rape and Murder stands,
Now giue some surance that thou art Reuenge,
Stab them, or teare them on thy Chariot wheeles,
And then Ile come and be thy Waggoner,
And whirle along with thee about the Globes.
Prouide thee two proper Palfries, as blacke as Iet,
To hale thy vengefull Waggon swift away,
And finde out Murder in their guilty cares.
And when thy Car is loaden with their heads,
I will dismount, and by the Waggon wheele,
Trot like a Seruile footeman all day long,
Euen from *Eptons* rising in the East,
Vntill his very downefall in the Sea.
And day by day Ile do this heauy taske,
So thou destroy Rapine and Murder there.

Tam. These are my Ministers, and come with me.

Tit. Are them thy Ministers, what are they call'd?

Tam. Rape and Murder, therefore called so,
Cause they take vengeance of such kind of men.

Tit. Good Lord how like the Empresse Sons they are,
And you the Empresse: But we worldly men,
Haue miserable mad mistaking eyes:
Oh sweet Reuenge, now do I come to thee,
And if one armes imbracement will content thee,
I will imbrace thee in it by and by.

Tam. This closing with him, fits his Lunacie,
What ere I forge to feede his braine-sicke fits,
Do you vphold, and maintaine in your speeches,
For now he firmely takes me for Reuenge,
And being Credulous in this mad thought,
Ile make him send for *Lucius* his Sonne,
And whil'st I at a Banquet hold him sure,
Ile find some cunning practise out of hand
To scatter and disperse the giddie Gothes,
Or at the least make them his Enemies:
See heere he comes, and I must play my theame.

Tit. Long haue I bene forlorne, and all for thee,
Welcome dread Fury to my woefull house,
Rapine and Murther, you are welcome too,
How like the Empresse and her Sonnes you are.
Well are you fitted, had you but a Moore,
Could not all hell afford you such a deuill?
For well I wote the Empresse neuer wags;
But in her company there is a Moore,
And would you represent our Queene aright
It were conuenient you had such a deuill:
But welcome as you are, what shall we doe?

Tam. What would'st thou haue vs doe *Andronicus*?

Dem. Shew me a Murtherer, Ile deale with him.

Chi. Shew me a Villaine that hath done a Rape,
And I am sent to be reueng'd on him.

Tam. Shew me a thousand that haue done thee wrong,
And Ile be reuenged on them all.

Tit. Looke round about the wicked streets of Rome,
And when thou find'st a man that's like thy selfe,
Good Murder stab him, hee's a Murtherer.
Goe thou with him, and when it is thy hap
To finde another that is like to thee,
Good Rapine stab him, he is a Rauisher.
Go thou with them, and in the Emperours Court,
There is a Queene attended by a Moore,
Well maist thou know her by thy owne proportion,
For vp and downe she doth resemble thee,
I pray thee doe on them some violent death,
They haue bene violent to me and mine.

ee *Tamora*.

Tam. Well hast thou lesson'd vs, this shall we do.
But would it please thee good *Andronicus*,
To send for *Lucius* thy thrice Valiant Sonne,
Who leades towards Rome a Band of Warlike Gothes,
And bid him come and Banquet at thy house.
When he is heere, euen at thy Solemne Feast,
I will bring in the Empresse and her Sonnes,
The Emperour himselfe, and all thy Foes,
And at thy mercy shall they stoop, and kneele,
And on them shalt thou ease, thy angry heart:
What saies *Andronicus* to this deuise?

Enter Marcus.

Tit. *Marcus* my Brother, 'tis sad *Titus* calls,
Go gentle *Marcus* to thy Nephew *Lucius*,
Thou shalt enquire him out among the Gothes,
Bid him repaire to me, and bring with him
Some of the chiefest Princes of the Gothes,
Bid him encampe his Souldiers where they are,
Tell him the Emperour, and the Empresse too,
Feasts at my house, and he shall Feast with them,
This do thou for my loue, and so let him,
As he regards his aged Fathers life.

Mar. This will I do, and soone returne againe.
Tam. Now will I hence about thy businesse,
And take my Ministers along with me.
Tit. Nay, nay let Rape and Murder stay with me,
Or els Ile call my Brother backe againe,
And cleaue to no reuenge but *Lucius*.
Tam. What say you Boyes, will you bide with him,
Whiles I goe tell my Lord the Emperour,
How I haue gouern'd our determined iest?
Yeeld to his Humour, smooth and speake him faire,
And tarry with him till I turne againe.
Tit. I know them all, though they suppose me mad,
And will ore-reach them in their owne deuises,
A payre of cursed hell-hounds and their Dam.
Dem. Madam depart at pleasure, leaue vs heere.
Tam. Farewell *Andronicus*, reuenge now goes
To lay a complot to betray thy Foes.
Tit. I know thou doo'st, and sweet reuenge farewell.
Chi. Tell vs old man, how shall we be imploy'd?
Tit. Tut, I haue worke enough for you to doe,
Publius come hither, *Caius*, and *Valentine*.
Pub. What is your will?
Tit. Know you these two?
Pub. The Empresse Sonnes
I take them, *Chiron, Demetrius*.
Titus. Fie *Publius*, fie, thou art too much deceau'd,
The one is Murder, Rape is the others name,
And therefore bind them gentle *Publius*,
Caius, and *Valentine* lay hands on them,
Oft haue you heard me wish for such an houre,
And now I find it, therefore binde them sure,
Chi. Villaines forbeare, we are the Empresse Sonnes.
Pub. And therefore do we, what we are commanded.
Stop close their mouthes, let them not speake a word,
Is he sure bound, looke that you binde them fast. *Exeunt.*

Enter Titus Andronicus with a knife, and Lauinia with a Bason.

Tit. Come, come *Lauinia*, looke, thy Foes are bound,
Sirs stop their mouthes, let them not speake to me,
But let them heare what fearefull words I vtter.
Oh Villaines, *Chiron*, and *Demetrius*,
Here stands the spring whom you haue stain'd with mud,
This goodly Sommer with your Winter mixt,
You kil'd her husband, and for that vil'd fault,
Two of her Brothers were condemn'd to death,
My hand cut off, and made a merry iest,
Both her sweet Hands, her Tongue, and that more deere
Then Hands or tongue, her spotlesse Chastity,
Inhumaine Traytors, you constrain'd and for'st.
What would you say, if I should let you speake?
Villaines for shame you could not beg for grace.
Harke Wretches, how I meane to martyr you,
This one Hand yet is left, to cut your throats,
Whil'st that *Lauinia* tweene her stumps doth hold:
The Bason that receiues your guilty blood.
You know your Mother meanes to feast with me,
And calls herselfe Reuenge, and thinkes me mad.
Harke Villaines, I will grin'd your bones to dust,
And with your blood and it, Ile make a Paste,
And of the Paste a Coffen I will reare,
And make two Pasties of your shamefull Heads,
And bid that strumpet your vnhallowed Dam,
Like to the earth swallow her increase.
This is the Feast, that I haue bid her to,
And this the Banquet she shall surfet on,
For worse then *Philomel* you vs'd my Daughter,
And worse then *Progne*, I will be reueng'd,
And now prepare your throats: *Lauinia* come,
Receiue the blood, and when that they are dead,
Let me goe grin'd their Bones to powder small,
And with this hatefull Liquor temper it,
And in that Paste let their vil'd Heads be bakte,
Come, come, be euery one officious,
To make this Banket, which I wish might proue,
More sterne and bloody then the Centaures Feast.

He cuts their throats.

So now bring them in, for Ile play the Cooke,
And see them ready, gainst their Mother comes. *Exeunt.*

Enter Lucius, Marcus, and the Gothes.

Luc. Vnckle *Marcus*, since 'tis my Fathers minde
That I repair to Rome, I am content.
Goth. And ours with thine befall, what Fortune will.
Luc. Good Vnckle take you in this barbarous Moor,
This Rauenous Tiger, this accursed deuill,
Let him receiue no sustenance, fetter him,
Till he be brought vnto the Emperous face,
For testimony of her foule proceedings.
And see the Ambush of our Friends be strong,
If ere the Emperour meanes no good to vs.
Aron. Some deuill whisper curses in my eare,
And prompt me that my tongue may vtter forth,
The Venemous Mallice of my swelling heart.
Luc. Away Inhumaine Dogge, Vnhallowed Slaue,
Sirs, helpe our Vnckle, to conuey him in, *Flourish.*
The Trumpets shew the Emperour is at hand.

Sound Trumpets. Enter Emperour and Empresse, with Tribunes and others.

Sat. What, hath the Firemament more Suns then one?
Luc. What bootes it thee to call thy selfe a Sunne?
Mar. Romes Emperour & Nephewe breake the parle
These quarrels must be quietly debated,
The Feast is ready which the carefull *Titus,*

Hath

Hath ordained to an Honourable end,
For Peace, for Loue, for League, and good to Rome:
please you therfore draw nie and take your places.
  Satur. *Marcus* we will.   *Hoboyes.*
      A Table brought in.
  *Enter Titus like a Cooke, placing the meat on
  the Table, and Lauinia with a vale ouer her face.*

  Titus. Welcome my gracious Lord,
Welcome Dread Queene,
Welcome ye Warlike Gothes, welcome *Lucius*,
And welcome all: although the cheere be poore,
'Twill fill your stomacks, please you eat of it.
  Sat. Why art thou thus attir'd *Andronicus*?
  Tit. Because I would be sure to haue all well,
To entertaine your Highnesse, and your Empresse.
  Tam. We are beholding to you good *Andronicus*?
  Tit. And if your Highnesse knew my heart, you were:
My Lord the Emperour resolue me this,
Was it well done of rash *Virginius*,
To slay his daughter with his owne right hand,
Because she was enfor'st, stain'd, and deflowr'd?
  Satur. It was *Andronicus*.
  Tit. Your reason, Mighty Lord?
  Sat. Because the Girle, should not suruine her shame,
And by her presence still renew his sorrowes.
  Tit. A reason mighty, strong, and effectuall,
A patterne, president, and liuely warrant,
For me (most wretched) to performe the like:
Die, die, *Lauinia*, and thy shame with thee,
And with thy shame, thy Fathers sorrow die.
                                        He kils her.
  Sat. What hast done, vnnaturall and vnkinde?
  Tit. Kil'd her for whom my teares haue made me blind.
I am as wofull as *Virginius* was,
And haue a thousand times more cause then he.
  Sat. What was she rauisht? tell who did the deed,
  Tit. Wilt please you eat,
Wilt please your Hignesse feed?
  Tam. Why hast thou slaine thine onely Daughter?
  Titus. Not I, 'twas *Chiron* and *Demetrius*,
They rauisht her, and cut away her tongue,
And they, 'twas they, that did her all this wrong.
  Satu. Go fetch them hither to vs presently.
  Tit. Why there they are both, baked in that Pie,
Whereof their Mother dantily hath fed,
Eating the flesh that she herselfe hath bred.
'Tis true, 'tis true, witnesse my kniues sharpe point.
                              He stabs the Empresse.
  Satu. Die franticke wretch, for this accursed deed.
  Luc. Can the Sonnes eye, behold his Father bleed?
There's meede for meede, death for a deadly deed.
  Mar. You sad fac'd men, people and Sonnes of Rome,
By vprores seuer'd like a flight of Fowle,
Scattred by windes and high tempestuous gusts:
Oh let me teach you how, to knit againe
This scattred Corne, into one mutuall sheafe,
These broken limbs againe into one body.
  Goth. Let Rome herselfe be bane vnto herselfe,
And shee whom mightie kingdomes curtsie too,
Like a forlorne and desperate castaway,
Doe shamefull execution on her selfe.
But if my frostie signes and chaps of age,
Graue witnesses of true experience,
Cannot induce you to attend my words,
Speake Romes deere friend, as 'erst our Auncestor,

When with his solemne tongue he did discourse
To loue-sicke *Didoes* sad attending eare,
The story of that balefull burning night,
When subtil Greekes surpriz'd King *Priams* Troy:
Tell vs what *Sinon* hath bewicht our eares,
Or who hath brought the fatall engine in,
That giues our Troy, our Rome the ciuill wound.
My heart is not compact of flint nor steele,
Nor can I vtter all our bitter griefe,
But floods of teares will drowne my Oratorie,
And breake my very vtterance, euen in the time
When it should moue you to attend me most,
Lending your kind hand Commiseration.
Heere is a Captaine, let him tell the tale,
Your hearts will throb and weepe to heare him speake.
  Luc. This Noble Auditory, be it knowne to you,
That cursed *Chiron* and *Demetrius*
Were they that murdred our Emperours Brother,
And they it were that rauished our Sister,
For their fell faults our Brothers were beheaded,
Our Fathers teares despis'd, and basely cousen'd,
Of that true hand that fought Romes quarrell out,
And sent her enemies vnto the graue.
Lastly, my selfe vnkindly banished,
The gates shut on me, and turn'd weeping out,
To beg reliefe among Romes Enemies,
Who drown'd their enmity in my true teares,
And op'd their armes to imbrace me as a Friend:
And I am turned forth, be it knowne to you,
That haue preseru'd her welfare in my blood,
And from her bosome tooke the Enemies point,
Sheathing the steele in my aduentrous body,
Alas you know, I am no Vaunter I,
My scars can witnesse, dumbe although they are,
That my report is iust and full of truth:
But soft, me thinkes I do digresse too much,
Cyting my worthlesse praise: Oh pardon me,
For when no Friends are by, men praise themselues.
  Marc. Now is my turne to speake: Behold this Child,
Of this was *Tamora* deliuered,
The issue of an Irreligious *Moore*,
Chiefe Architect and plotter of these woes,
The Villaine is aliue in *Titus* house,
And as he is, to witnesse this is true.
Now iudge what course had *Titus* to reuenge
These wrongs, vnspeakeable past patience,
Or more then any liuing man could beare.
Now you haue heard the truth, what say you Romaines?
Haue we done ought amisse? shew vs wherein,
And from the place where you behold vs now,
The poore remainder of *Andronici*,
Will hand in hand all headlong cast vs downe,
And on the ragged stones beat forth our braines,
And make a mutuall closure of our house:
Speake Romaines speake, and if you say we shall,
Loe hand in hand, *Lucius* and I will fall.
  Emilli. Come come, thou reuerent man of Rome,
And bring our Emperour gently in thy hand,
Lucius our Emperour: for well I know,
The common voyce do cry it shall be so.
  Mar. *Lucius*, all haile Romes Royall Emperour,
Goe, goe into old *Titus* sorrowfull house,
And hither hale that misbeliening *Moore*,
To be adiudg'd some direfull slaughtering death,
As punishment for his most wicked life.
Lucius all haile to Romes gracious Gouernour.

The Tragedie of Titus Andronicus.

Luc. Thankes gentle Romanes, may I gouerne so,
To heale Romes harmes, and wipe away her woe.
But gentle people, giue me ayme a-while,
For Nature puts me to a heauy taske:
Stand all aloofe, but Vnckle draw you neere,
To shed obsequious teares vpon this Trunke:
Oh take this warme kisse on thy pale cold lips,
These sorrowfull drops vpon thy bloud-slaine face,
The last true Duties of thy Noble Sonne.

Mar. Teare for teare, and louing kisse for kisse,
Thy Brother *Marcus* tenders on thy Lips:
O were the summe of these that I should pay
Countlesse, and infinit, yet would I pay them.

Luc. Come hither Boy, come, come, and learne of vs
To melt in showres: thy Grandsire lou'd thee well:
Many a time he danc'd thee on his knee:
Sung thee asleepe, his Louing Brest, thy Pillow:
Many a matter hath he told to thee,
Meete, and agreeing with thine Infancie:
In that respect then, like a louing Childe,
Shed yet some small drops from thy tender Spring,
Because kinde Nature doth require it so:
Friends, should associate Friends, in Greefe and Wo.
Bid him farwell, commit him to the Graue,
Do him that kindnesse, and take leaue of him.

Boy. O Grandsire, Grandsire: euen with all my heart
Would I were Dead, so you did Liue againe.
O Lord, I cannot speake to him for weeping,
My teares will choake me, if I ope my mouth.

Romans. You sad *Andronici*, haue done with woes,
Giue sentence on this execrable Wretch,
That hath beene breeder of these dire euents.

Luc. Set him brest deepe in earth, and famish him:
There let him stand, and raue, and cry for foode:
If any one releeues, or pitties him,
For the offence, he dyes. This is our doome:
Some stay, to see him fast'ned in the earth.

Aron. O why should wrath be mute, & Fury dumbe?
I am no Baby I, that with base Prayers
I should repent the Euils I haue done.
Ten thousand worse, then euer yet I did,
Would I performe if I might haue my will:
If one good Deed in all my life I did,
I do repent it from my very Soule.

Lucius. Some louing Friends conuey the Emp. hence,
And giue him buriall in his Fathers graue.
My Father, and *Lauinia*, shall forthwith
Be closed in our Housholds Monument:
As for that heynous Tyger *Tamora*,
No Funerall Rite, nor man in mournfull Weeds,
No mournfull Bell shall ring her Buriall:
But throw her foorth to Beasts and Birds of prey:
Her life was Beast-like, and deuoid of pitty,
And being so, shall haue like want of pitty.
See Iustice done on *Aaron* that damn'd Moore,
From whom, our heauy happes had their beginning:
Then afterwards, to Order well the State,
That like Euents, may ne're it Ruinate. *Exeunt omnes.*

FINIS.

THE TRAGEDIE OF ROMEO and IVLIET.

Actus Primus. Scœna Prima.

Enter Sampson and Gregory, with Swords and Bucklers, of the House of Capulet.

Sampson.

Gregory: A my word wee'l not carry coales.

Greg. No, for then we should be Colliars.

Samp. I meane, if we be in choller, wee'l draw.

Greg. I, While you liue, draw your necke out o'th Collar.

Samp. I strike quickly, being mou'd.

Greg. But thou art not quickly mou'd to strike.

Samp. A dog of the house of *Mountague*, moues me.

Greg. To moue, is to stir: and to be valiant, is to stand: Therefore, if thou art mou'd, thou runst away.

Samp. A dogge of that house shall moue me to stand. I will take the wall of any Man or Maid of *Mountagues*.

Greg. That shewes thee a weake slaue, for the weakest goes to the wall.

Samp. True, and therefore women being the weaker Vessels, are euer thrust to the wall: therefore I will push *Mountagues* men from the wall, and thrust his Maides to the wall.

Greg. The Quarrell is betweene our Masters, and vs (their men.

Samp. 'Tis all one, I will shew my selfe a tyrant: when I haue fought with the men, I will bee ciuill with the Maids, and cut off their heads.

Greg. The heads of the Maids?

Sam. I, the heads of the Maids, or their Maiden-heads, Take it in what sence thou wilt.

Greg. They must take it sence, that feele it.

Samp. Me they shall feele while I am able to stand: And 'tis knowne I am a pretty peece of flesh.

Greg. 'Tis well thou art not Fish: If thou had'st, thou had'st beene poore *Iohn*. Draw thy Toole, here comes of the House of the *Mountagues*.

Enter two other Seruingmen.

Sam. My naked weapon is out: quarrel, I wil back thee

Gre. How? Turne thy backe, and run.

Sam. Feare me not.

Gre. No marry: I feare thee.

Sam. Let vs take the Law of our sides: let them begin.

Gr. I wil frown as I passe by, & let thē take it as they list

Sam. Nay, as they dare. I wil bite my Thumb at them, which is a disgrace to them, if they beare it.

Abra. Do you bite your Thumbe at vs sir?

Samp. I do bite my Thumbe, sir.

Abra. Do you bite your Thumb at vs, sir?

Sam. Is the Law of our side, if I say I? *Gre.* No.

Sam. No sir, I do not bite my Thumbe at you sir: but I bite my Thumbe sir.

Greg. Do you quarrell sir?

Abra. Quarrell sir? no sir. (as you

Sam. If you do sir, I am for you, I serue as good a man

Abra. No better? *Samp.* Well sir.

Enter Benuolio.

Gr. Say better: here comes one of my masters kinsmen.

Samp. Yes, better.

Abra. You Lye.

Samp. Draw if you be men. *Gregory*, remember thy washing blow. *They Fight.*

Ben. Part Fooles, put vp your Swords, you know not what you do.

Enter Tibalt.

Tyb. What art thou drawne, among these heartlesse Hindes? Turne thee *Benuolio*, looke vpon thy death.

Ben. I do but keepe the peace, put vp thy Sword, Or manage it to part these men with me.

Tyb. What draw, and talke of peace? I hate the word As I hate hell, all *Mountagues*, and thee: Haue at thee Coward. *Fight.*

Enter three or foure Citizens with Clubs.

Offi. Clubs, Bils, and Partisons, strike, beat them down Downe with the *Capulets*, downe with the *Mountagues*.

Enter old Capulet in his Gowne, and his wife.

Cap. What noise is this? Giue me my long Sword ho.

Wife. A crutch, a crutch: why call you for a Sword?

Cap. My Sword I say: Old *Mountague* is come, And flourishes his Blade in spight of me.

Enter old Mountague, & his wife.

Moun. Thou villaine *Capulet*. Hold me not, let me go

2.Wife. Thou shalt not stir a foote to seeke a Foe.

Enter Prince Eskales, with his Traine.

Prince. Rebellious Subiects, Enemies to peace, Prophaners of this Neighbor-stained Steele, Will they not heare? What hoe, you Men, you Beasts, That quench the fire of your pernitious Rage, With purple Fountaines issuing from your Veines: On paine of Torture, from those bloody hands Throw your mistemper'd Weapons to the ground, And heare the Sentence of your mooued Prince. Three ciuill Broyles, bred of an Ayery word, By thee old *Capulet* and *Mountague*, Haue thrice disturb'd the quiet of our streets, And made *Verona*'s ancient Citizens Cast by their Graue beseeming Ornaments, To wield old Partizans, in hands as old,

ee 3 Cankred

Cankred with peace, to part your Cankred hate,
If euer you disturbe our streets againe,
Your liues shall pay the forfeit of the peace.
For this time all the rest depart away:
You *Capulet* shall goe along with me,
And *Mountague* come you this afternoone,
To know our Fathers pleasure in this case:
To old Free-towne, our common iudgement place:
Once more on paine of death, all men depart. *Exeunt.*

Moun. Who set this auncient quarrell new abroach?
Speake Nephew, were you by, when it began:

Ben. Heere were the seruants of your aduersarie,
And yours close fighting ere I did approach,
I drew to part them, in the instant came
The fiery *Tibalt*, with his sword prepar'd,
Which as he breath'd defiance to my eares,
He swong about his head, and cut the windes,
Who nothing hurt withall, hist him in scorne.
While we were enterchanging thrusts and blowes,
Came more and more, and fought on part and part,
Till the Prince came, who parted either part.

Wife. O where is *Romeo*, saw you him to day?
Right glad am I he was not at this fray.

Ben. Madam, an houre before the worshipt Sun
Peer'd forth the golden window of the East,
A troubled mind draue me to walke abroad,
Where vnderneath the groue of Sycamour,
That West-ward rooteth from this City side:
So earely walking did I see your Sonne:
Towards him I made, but he was ware of me,
And stole into the couert of the wood,
I measuring his affections by my owne,
Which then most sought, wher most might not be found:
Being one too many by my weary selfe,
Pursued my Honour, not pursuing his
And gladly shunn'd, who gladly fled from me.

Mount. Many a morning hath he there beene seene,
With teares augmenting the fresh mornings deaw,
Adding to cloudes, more cloudes with his deepe sighes,
But all so soone as the all-cheering Sunne,
Should in the farthest East begin to draw
The shadie Curtaines from *Auroras* bed,
Away from light steales home my heauy Sonne,
And priuate in his Chamber pennes himselfe,
Shuts vp his windowes, lockes faire day-light out,
And makes himselfe an artificiall night:
Blacke and portendous must this humour proue,
Vnlesse good counsell may the cause remoue.

Ben. My Noble Vncle doe you know the cause?
Moun. I neither know it, nor can learne of him.
Ben. Haue you importun'd him by any meanes?
Moun. Both by my selfe and many others Friends,
But he his owne affections counseller,
Is to himselfe (I will not say how true)
But to himselfe so secret and so close,
So farre from sounding and discouery,
As is the bud bit with an enuious worme,
Ere he can spread his sweete leaues to the ayre,
Or dedicate his beauty to the same.
Could we but learne from whence his sorrowes grow,
We would as willingly giue cure, as know.

Enter Romeo.

Ben. See where he comes, so please you step aside,
Ile know his greeuance, or be much denide.

Moun. I would thou wert so happy by thy stay,
To heare true shrift. Come Madam let's away. *Exeunt.*

Ben. Good morrow Cousin.
Rom. Is the day so young?
Ben. But new strooke nine.
Rom. Aye me, sad houres seeme long:
Was that my Father that went hence so fast?
Ben. It was: what sadnes lengthens *Romeo's* houres?
Ro. Not hauing that, which hauing, makes them short
Ben. In loue.
Romeo. Out.
Ben. Of loue.
Rom. Out of her fauour where I am in loue.
Ben. Alas that loue so gentle in his view,
Should be so tyrannous and rough in proofe.
Rom. Alas that loue, whose view is muffled still,
Should without eyes see path-wayes to his will:
Where shall we dine? O me: what fray was heere?
Yet tell me not, for I haue heard it all:
Heere's much to do with hate, but more with loue:
Why then, O brawling loue, O louing hate,
O any thing, of nothing first created:
O heauie lightnesse, serious vanity,
Mishapen Chaos of welseeing formes,
Feather of lead, bright smoake, cold fire, sicke health,
Still waking sleepe, that is not what it is:
This loue feele I, that feele no loue in this.
Doest thou not laugh?

Ben. No Coze, I rather weepe.
Rom. Good heart, at what?
Ben. At thy good hearts oppression.
Rom. Why such is loues transgression.
Griefes of mine owne lie heauie in my breast,
Which thou wilt propagate to haue it preast
With more of thine, this loue that thou hast showne,
Doth adde more griefe, to too much of mine owne.
Loue, is a smoake made with the fume of sighes,
Being purg'd, a fire sparkling in Louers eyes,
Being vext, a Sea nourisht with louing teares,
What is it else? a madnesse, most discreet,
A choking gall, and a preseruing sweet:
Farewell my Coze.

Ben. Soft I will goe along.
And if you leaue me so, you do me wrong.
Rom. Tut I haue lost my selfe, I am not here,
This is not *Romeo*, hee's some other where.
Ben. Tell me in sadnesse, who is that you loue?
Rom. What shall I grone and tell thee?
Ben. Grone, why no: but sadly tell me who.
Rom. A sicke man in sadnesse makes his will:
A word ill vrg'd to one that is so ill:
In sadnesse Cozin, I do loue a woman.
Ben. I aym'd so neare, when I suppos'd you lou'd.
Rom. A right good marke man, and shee's faire I loue
Ben. A right faire marke, faire Coze, is soonest hit.
Rom. Well in that hit you misse, sheel not be hit
With Cupids arrow, she hath *Dians* wit:
And in strong proofe of chastity well arm'd:
From loues weake childish Bow, she liues vncharm'd.
Shee will not stay the siege of louing tearmes,
Nor bid th'incounter of assailing eyes,
Nor open her lap to Sainct-seducing Gold:
O she is rich in beautie, onely poore,
That when she dies, with beautie dies her store.
Ben. Then she hath sworne, that she will still liue chast?
Rom. She hath, and in that sparing make huge wast?
For beauty steru'd with her seuerity,
Cuts beauty off from all posteritie.

The Tragedie of Romeo and Iuliet.

She is too faire, too wise, wisely too faire,
To merit blisse by making me dispaire:
She hath forsworne to loue, and in that vow
Do I liue dead, that liue to tell it now.

Ben. Be rul'd by me, forget to thinke of her.

Rom. O teach me how I should forget to thinke.

Ben. By giuing liberty vnto thine eyes,
Examine other beauties,

Ro. 'Tis the way to cal hers (exquisit) in question more,
These happy maskes that kisse faire Ladies browes,
Being blacke, puts vs in mind they hide the faire:
He that is strooken blind, cannot forget
The precious treasure of his eye-sight lost:
Shew me a Mistresse that is passing faire,
What doth her beauty serue but as a note,
Where I may read who past that passing faire.
Farewell thou can'st not teach me to forget.

Ben. I.e pay that doctrine, or else die in debt. *Exeunt.*

Enter Capulet, Countie Paris, and the Clowne.

Capu. Mountague is bound as well as I,
In penalty alike, and 'tis not hard I thinke,
For men so old as wee, to keepe the peace.

Par. Of Honourable reckoning are you both,
And pittie 'tis you liu'd at ods so long:
But now my Lord, what say you to my sute?

Capu. But saying ore what I haue said before,
My Child is yet a stranger in the world,
Shee hath not seene the change of fourteene yeares,
Let two more Summers wither in their pride,
Ere we may thinke her ripe to be a Bride.

Pari. Younger then she, are happy mothers made.

Capu. And too soone mar'd are those so early made:
Earth hath swallowed all my hopes but she,
Shee's the hopefull Lady of my earth:
But wooe her gentle *Paris*, get her heart,
My will to her consent, is but a part,
And shee agree, within her scope of choise,
Lyes my consent, and faire according voice:
This night I hold an old accustom'd Feast,
Whereto I haue inuited many a Guest,
Such as I loue, and you among the store,
One more, most welcome makes my number more:
At my poore house, looke to behold this night,
Earth-treading starres, that make darke heauen light,
Such comfort as do lusty young men feele,
When well apparel'd Aprill on the heele
Of limping Winter treads, euen such delight
Among fresh Fennell buds shall you this night
Inherit at my house: heare all, all see:
And like her most, whose merit most shall be:
Which one more veiw, of many, mine being one,
May stand in number, though in reckning none.
Come, goe with me: goe sirrah trudge about,
Through faire *Verona*, find those persons out,
Whose names are written there, and to them say,
My house and welcome, on their pleasure stay. *Exit.*

Ser. Find them out whose names are written. Heere it is written, that the Shoo-maker should meddle with his Yard, and the Tayler with his Last, the Fisher with his Pensill, and the Painter with his Nets. But I am sent to find those persons whose names are writ, & can neuer find what names the writing person hath here writ: (I must to the learned) in good time.

Enter Benuolio and Romeo.

Ben. Tut man, one fire burnes out anothers burning,
One paine is lesned by anothers anguish:
Turne giddie, and be holpe by backward turning:
One desparate greefe, cures with anothers languish:
Take thou some new infection to the eye,
And the rank poyson of the old wil die.

Rom. Your Plantan leafe is excellent for that.

Ben. For what I pray thee?

Rom. For your broken shin.

Ben. Why *Romeo* art thou mad?

Rom. Not mad, but bound more then a mad man is:
Shut vp in prison, kept without my foode,
Whipt and tormented: and Godden good fellow,

Ser. Godgigoden, I pray sir can you read?

Rom. I mine owne fortune in my miserie.

Ser. Perhaps you haue learn'd it without booke:
But I pray can you read any thing you see?

Rom. I, if I know the Letters and the Language.

Ser. Ye say honestly, rest you merry.

Rom. Stay fellow, I can read.

He reades the Letter.

SEigneur *Martino*, and his wife and daughter: County An-selme and his beautious sisters: the Lady widdow of Vtru-uio, Seigneur *Placentio*, and his louely Neeces: *Mercutio* and his brother *Valentine*: mine vncle *Capulet* his wife and daughters: my faire Neece *Rosaline*, *Liuia*, Seigneur *Valentio*, & his Cosen *Tybalt*: *Lucio* and the liuely *Helena*.

A faire assembly, whither should they come?

Ser. Vp.

Rom. Whither? to supper?

Ser. To our house.

Rom. Whose house?

Ser. My Maisters.

Rom. Indeed I should haue askt you that before.

Ser. Now Ile tell you without asking. My maister is the great rich *Capulet*, and if you be not of the house of *Mountagues* I pray come and crush a cup of wine. Rest you merry. *Exit.*

Ben. At this same auncient Feast of *Capulets*
Sups the faire *Rosaline*, whom thou so loues:
With all the admired Beauties of *Verona*,
Go thither and with vnattainted eye,
Compare her face with some that I shall show,
And I will make thee thinke thy Swan a Crow.

Rom. When the deuout religion of mine eye
Maintaines such falshood, then turne teares to fire:
And these who often drown'd could neuer die,
Transparent Heretiques be burnt for liers.
One fairer then my loue: the all-seeing Sun
Nere saw her match, since first the world begun.

Ben. Tut, you saw her faire, none else being by,
Herselfe poyz'd with herselfe in either eye:
But in that Christall scales, let there be waid,
Your Ladies loue against some other Maid
That I will show you, shining at this Feast,
And she shew scant shell, well, that now shewes best.

Rom. Ile goe along, no such sight to be showne,
But to reioyce in splendor of mine owne.

Enter Capulets Wife and Nurse.

Wife Nurse wher's my daughter? call her forth to me.

Nurse. Now by my Maidenhead, at twelue yeare old
I bad her come, what Lamb: what Ladi-bird, God forbid,
Where's this Girle? what *Iuliet*?

Enter Iuliet.

Iuliet. How now, who calls?

Nur. Your Mother.

Iuliet. Madam I am heere, what is your will?

Wife. This is the matter: Nurse giue leaue awhile, we must

must talke in secret. Nurse come backe againe, I haue remembred me, thou'se heare our counsell. Thou knowest my daughter's of a prety age.

  Nurse. Faith I can tell her age vnto an houre.
  Wife. Shee's not fourteene.
  Nurse. Ile lay fourteene of my teeth,
And yet to my teene be it spoken,
I haue but foure, shee's not fourteene.
How long is it now to *Lammas* tide?
  Wife. A fortnight and odde dayes.
  Nurse. Euen or odde, of all daies in the yeare come Lammas Eue at night shall she be fourteene. *Susan* & she, God rest all Christian soules, were of an age. Well *Susan* is with God, she was too good for me. But as I said, on Lammas Eue at night shall she be fourteene, that shall she marie, I remember it well. 'Tis since the Earth-quake now eleuen yeares, and she was wean'd I neuer shall forget it, of all the daies of the yeare, vpon that day: for I had then laid Worme-wood to my Dug sitting in the Sunne vnder the Douehouse wall, my Lord and you were then at *Mantua*, nay I doe beare a braine. But as I said, when it did tast the Worme-wood on the nipple of my Dugge, and felt it bitter, pretty foole, to see it teachie, and fall out with the Dugge, Shake quoth the Doue-house, 'twas no neede I trow to bid mee trudge: and since that time it is a eleuen yeares, for then she could stand alone, nay bi'th' roode she could haue runne, & wadled all about: for euen the day before she broke her brow, & then my Husband God be with his soule, a was a merrie man, tooke vp the Child, yea quoth hee, doest thou fall vpon thy face? thou wilt fall backeward when thou hast more wit, wilt thou not *Iule*? And by my holy-dam, the pretty wretch lefte crying, & said I: to see now how a Iest shall come about. I warrant, & I shall liue a thousand yeares, I neuer should forget it: wilt thou not *Iulet* quoth he? and pretty foole it stinted, and said I.
  Old La. Inough of this, I pray thee hold thy peace.
  Nurse. Yes Madam, yet I cannot chuse but laugh, to thinke it should leaue crying, & say I: and yet I warrant it had vpon it brow, a bumpe as big as a young Cockrels stone? A perilous knock, and it cryed bitterly. Yea quoth my husband, fall'st vpon thy face, thou wilt fall backward when thou commest to age: wilt thou not *Iule*? It stinted: and said I.
  Iule. And stint thou too, I pray thee *Nurse*, say I.
  Nur. Peace I haue done: God marke thee too his grace thou wast the prettiest Babe that ere I nurst, and I might liue to see thee married once, I haue my wish.
  Old La. Marry that marry is the very theame
I came to talke of, tell me daughter *Iuliet*,
How stands your disposition to be Married?
  Iuli. It is an houre that I dreame not of.
  Nur. An houre, were not I thine onely Nurse, I would say thou had'st suckt wisedome from thy teat.
  Old La. Well thinke of marriage now, yonger then you
Heere in *Verona*, Ladies of esteeme,
Are made already Mothers. By my count
I was your Mother, much vpon these yeares
That you are now a Maide, thus then in briefe:
The valiant *Paris* seekes you for his loue.
  Nurse. A man young Lady, Lady, such a man as all the world. Why hee's a man of waxe.
  Old La. *Veronas* Summer hath not such a flower.
  Nurse. Nay hee's a flower, infaith a very flower.
  Old La. What say you, can you loue the Gentleman?
This night you shall behold him at our Feast,
Read ore the volume of young *Paris* face,
And find delight, writ there with Beauties pen:
Examine euery seuerall liniament,
And see how one another lends content:
And what obscur'd in this faire volume lies,
Find written in the Margent of his eyes.
This precious Booke of Loue, this vnbound Louer,
To Beautifie him, onely lacks a Couer.
The fish liues in the Sea, and 'tis much pride
For faire without, the faire within to hide:
That Booke in manies eyes doth share the glorie,
That in Gold claspes, Lockes in the Golden storie:
So shall you share all that he doth possesse,
By hauing him, making your selfe no lesse.
  Nurse. No lesse, nay bigger: women grow by men.
  Old La. Speake briefly, can you like of *Paris* loue?
  Iuli. Ile looke to like, if looking liking moue.
But no more deepe will I endart mine eye,
Then your consent giues strength to make flye.

  Enter a Seruing man.

  Ser. Madam, the guests are come, supper seru'd vp, you cal'd, my young Lady askt for, the Nurse cur'st in the Pantery, and euery thing in extremitie: I must hence to wait, I beseech you follow straight. *Exit.*
  Mo. We follow thee, *Iuliet*, the Countie staies.
  Nurse. Goe Gyrle, seeke happie nights to happy daies.
Exeunt.

  Enter Romeo, Mercutio, Benuolio, with fiue or sixe other Maskers, Torch-bearers.

  Rom. What shall this speech be spoke for our excuse?
Or shall we on without Apologie?
  Ben. The date is out of such prolixitie,
Weele haue no *Cupid* hood winkt with a skarfe,
Bearing a Tartars painted Bow of lath,
Skaring the Ladies like a Crow-keeper.
But let them measure vs by what they will,
Weele measure them a Measure, and be gone.
  Rom. Giue me a Torch, I am not for this ambling.
Being but heauy I will beare the light.
  Mer. Nay gentle *Romeo*, we must haue you dance.
  Rom. Not I beleeue me, you haue dancing shooes
With nimble soles, I haue a soale of Lead
So stakes me to the ground, I cannot moue.
  Mer. You are a Louer, borrow *Cupids* wings,
And soare with them aboue a common bound.
  Rom. I am too sore enpearced with his shaft,
To soare with his light feathers, and to bound:
I cannot bound a pitch aboue dull woe,
Vnder loues heauy burthen doe I sinke.
  Hora. And to sinke in it should you burthen loue,
Too great oppression for a tender thing.
  Rom. Is loue a tender thing? it is too rough,
Too rude, too boysterous, and it prickes like thorne.
  Mer. If loue be rough with you, be rough with loue,
Pricke loue for pricking, and you beat loue downe,
Giue me a Case to put my visage in,
A Visor for a Visor, what care I
What curious eye doth quote deformities:
Here are the Beetle-browes shall blush for me.
  Ben. Come knocke and enter, and no sooner in,
But euery man betake him to his legs.
  Rom. A Torch for me, let wantons light of heart
Tickle the sencelesse rushes with their heeles:
For I am prouerb'd with a Grandsier Phrase,
Ile be a Candle-holder and looke on,
The game was nere so faire, and I am done.
  Mer. Tut,

Mer. Tut, duns the Mouse, the Constables owne word,
If thou art dun, weele draw thee from the mire.
Or saue your reuerence loue, wherein thou stickest
Vp to the eares, come we burne day-light ho.

Rom. Nay that's not so.

Mer. I meane sir I delay,
We wast our lights in vaine, lights, lights, by day;
Take our good meaning, for our Iudgement sits
Fiue times in that, ere once in our fine wits.

Rom. And we meane well in going to this Maske,
But 'tis no wit to go.

Mer. Why may one aske?

Rom. I dreampt a dreame to night.

Mer. And so did I.

Rom. Well what was yours?

Mer. That dreamers often lye.

Ro. In bed a sleepe while they do dreame things true.

Mer. O then I see Queene Mab hath beene with you:
She is the Fairies Midwife, & she comes in shape no bigger then Agat-stone, on the fore-finger of an Alderman, drawne with a teeme of little Atomies, ouer mens noses as they lie asleepe: her Waggon Spokes made of long Spinners legs: the Couer of the wings of Grashoppers, her Traces of the smallest Spiders web, her coullers of the Moonshines watry Beames, her Whip of Crickets bone, the Lash of Philome, her Waggoner, a small gray-coated Gnat, not halfe so bigge as a round little Worme, prickt from the Lazie-finger of a man. Her Chariot is an emptie Haselnut, made by the Ioyner Squirrel or old Grub, time out a mind, the Faries Coach-makers: & in this state she gallops night by night, through Louers braines: and then they dreame of Loue. On Courtiers knees, that dreame on Cursies strait: ore Lawyers fingers, who strait dreamt on Fees, ore Ladies lips, who strait on kisses dreame, which oft athe angry Mab with blisters plagues, because their breath with Sweet meats tainted are. Sometime she gallops ore a Courtiers nose, & then dreames he of smelling out a sute: & somtime comes she with Tith pigs tale, tickling a Parsons nose as a lies asleepe, then he dreames of another Benefice. Sometime she driueth ore a Souldiers necke, & then dreames he of cutting Forraine throats, of Breaches, Ambuscados, Spanish Blades: Of Healths fiue Fadome deepe, and then anon drums in his eares, at which he startes and wakes; and being thus frighted, sweares a prayer or two & sleepes againe: this is that very Mab that plats the manes of Horses in the night: & bakes the Elklocks in foule sluttish haires, which once vntangled, much misfortune bodes,
This is the hag, when Maides lie on their backs,
That presses them, and learnes them first to beare,
Making them women of good carriage:
This is she.

Rom. Peace, peace, *Mercutio* peace,
Thou talk'st of nothing.

Mer. True, I talke of dreames:
Which are the children of an idle braine,
Begot of nothing, but vaine phantasie,
Which is as thin of substance as the ayre,
And more inconstant then the wind, who wooes
Euen now the frozen bosome of the North:
And being anger'd, puffes away from thence,
Turning his side to the dew dropping South.

Ben. This wind you talke of blowes vs from our selues,
Supper is done, and we shall come too late.

Rom. I feare too early, for my mind misgiues,
Some consequence yet hanging in the starres,
Shall bitterly begin his fearefull date
With this nights reuels, and expire the tearme
Of a despised life clos'd in my brest:
By some vile forfeit of vntimely death,
But he that hath the stirrage of my course,
Direct my sute: on lustie Gentlemen.

Ben. Strike Drum.

They march about the Stage, and Seruingmen come forth with their napkins.

Enter Seruant.

Ser. Where's *Potpan*, that he helpes not to take away?
He shift a Trencher? he scrape a Trencher?

1. When good manners, shall lie in one or two mens hands, and they vnwasht too, 'tis a foule thing.

Ser. Away with the Ioynstooles, remoue the Courtcubbord, looke to the Plate: good thou, saue mee a piece of Marchpane, and as thou louest me, let the Porter let in *Susan Grindstone*, and *Nell*, *Anthonie* and *Potpan*.

2. I Boy readie.

Ser. You are lookt for, and cal'd for, askt for, & sought for, in the great Chamber.

1 We cannot be here and there too, chearly Boyes,
Be brisk awhile, and the longer liuer take all.

Exeunt.

Enter all the Guests and Gentlewomen to the Maskers.

1. Caps. Welcome Gentlemen,
Ladies that haue their toes
Vnplagu'd with Cornes, will walke about with you:
Ah my Mistresses, which of you all
Will now deny to dance? She that makes dainty,
She Ile sweare hath Cornes: am I come neare ye now?
Welcome Gentlemen, I haue seene the day
That I haue worne a Visor, and could tell
A whispering tale in a faire Ladies eare:
Such as would please: 'tis gone, 'tis gone, 'tis gone,
You are welcome Gentlemen, come Musitians play:

Musicke plaies: and the dance.

A Hall, Hall, giue roome, and foote it Girles,
More light you knaues, and turne the Tables vp:
And quench the fire, the Roome is growne too hot,
Ah sirrah, this vnlookt for sport comes well:
Nay sit, nay sit, good Cozin *Capulet*,
For you and I are past our dauncing daies:
How long 'ist now since last your selfe and I
Were in a Maske?

2. Capu. Berlady thirty yeares.

1. Capu. What man: 'tis not so much, 'tis not so much,
'Tis since the Nuptiall of *Lucentio*,
Come Pentycost as quickely as it will,
Some fiue and twenty yeares, and then we Maske.

2. Cap. 'Tis more, 'tis more, his Sonne is elder sir:
His Sonne is thirty.

3. Cap. Will you tell me that?
His Sonne was but a Ward two yeares agoe.

Rom. What Ladie is that which doth ni rich the hand
Of yonder Knight?

Ser. I know not sir.

Rom. O she doth teach the Torches to burne bright:
It seemes she hangs vpon the cheeke of night,
As a rich Iewel in an Æthiops eare:
Beauty too rich for vse, for earth too deare:
So shewes a Snowy Doue trooping with Crowes,
As yonder Lady ore her fellowes showes;
The measure done, Ile watch her place of stand,
And touching hers, make blessed my rude hand.

Did

Did my heart loue till now, forsweare it sight,
For I neuer saw true Beauty till this night.

Tib. This by his voice, should be a *Mountague*.
Fetch me my Rapier Boy, what dares the slaue
Come hither couer'd with an antique face,
To fleere and scorne at our Solemnitie?
Now by the stocke and Honour of my kin,
To strike him dead I hold it not a sin.

Cap. Why how now kinsman,
Wherefore storme you so?

Tib. Vncle this is a *Mountague*, our foe:
A Villaine that is hither come in spight,
To scorne at our Solemnitie this night.

Cap. Young *Romeo* is it?

Tib. 'Tis he, that Villaine *Romeo*.

Cap. Content thee gentle Coz, let him alone,
A beares him like a portly Gentleman:
And to say truth, *Verona* brags of him,
To be a vertuous and well gouern'd youth:
I would not for the wealth of all the towne,
Here in my house do him disparagement:
Therfore be patient, take no note of him,
It is my will, the which if thou respect,
Shew a faire presence, and put off these frownes,
An ill beseeming semblance for a Feast.

Tib. It fits when such a Villaine is a guest,
Ile not endure him.

Cap. He shall be endu'rd.
What goodman boy, I say he shall, go too,
Am I the Maister here or you? go too,
Youle not endure him, God shall mend my soule,
Youle make a Mutinie among the Guests:
You will set cocke a hoope, youle be the man.

Tib. Why Vncle, 'tis a shame.

Cap. Go too, go too,
You are a sawcy Boy, ist so indeed?
This tricke may chance to scath you, I know what,
You must contrary me, marry 'tis time.
Well said my hearts, you are a Princox, goe,
Be quiet, or more light, more light for shame,
Ile make you quiet. What, chearely my hearts.

Tib. Patience perforce, with wilfull choler meeting,
Makes my flesh tremble in their different greeting:
I will withdraw, but this intrusion shall
Now seeming sweet, conuert to bitter gall. *Exit.*

Rom. If I prophane with my vnworthiest hand,
This holy shrine, the gentle sin is this,
My lips to blushing Pilgrims did ready stand,
To smooth that rough touch, with a tender kisse.

Iul. Good Pilgrime,
You do wrong your hand too much.
Which mannerly deuotion shewes in this,
For Saints haue hands, that Pilgrims hands do tuch,
And palme to palme, is holy Palmers kisse.

Rom. Haue not Saints lips, and holy Palmers too?

Iul. I Pilgrim, lips that they must vse in prayer.

Rom. O then deare Saint, let lips do what hands do,
They pray (grant thou) least faith turne to dispaire.

Iul. Saints do not moue,
Though grant for prayers sake.

Rom. Then moue not while my prayers effect I take:
Thus from my lips, by thine my sin is purg'd.

Iul. Then haue my lips the sin that they haue tooke.

Rom. Sin from my lips? O trespasse sweetly vrg'd:
Giue me my sin againe.

Iul. You kisse by th'booke.

Nur. Madam your Mother craues a word with you.

Rom. What is her Mother?

Nurs. Marrie Batcheler,
Her Mother is the Lady of the house,
And a good Lady, and a wise, and Vertuous,
I Nur'st her Daughter that you talkt withall:
I tell you, he that can lay hold of her,
Shall haue the chinckes.

Rom. Is she a *Capulet*?
O deare account! My life is my foes debt.

Ben. Away, be gone, the sport is at the best.

Rom. I so I feare, the more is my vnrest.

Cap. Nay Gentlemen prepare not to be gone,
We haue a trifling foolish Banquet towards:
Is it e'ne so? why then I thanke you all.
I thanke you honest Gentlemen, good night:
More Torches here: come on, then let's to bed.
Ah sirrah, by my faie it waxes late,
Ile to my rest.

Iuli. Come hither Nurse,
What is yond Gentleman:

Nur. The Sonne and Heire of old *Tyberio*.

Iuli. What's he that now is going out of doore?

Nur. Marrie that I thinke be young *Petruchio*.

Iul. What's he that follows here that would not dance?

Nur. I know not.

Iul. Go aske his name: if he be married,
My graue is like to be my wedded bed.

Nur. His name is *Romeo*, and a *Mountague*,
The onely Sonne of your great Enemie.

Iul. My onely Loue sprung from my onely hate,
Too early seene, vnknowne, and knowne too late,
Prodigious birth of Loue it is to me,
That I must loue a loathed Enemie.

Nur. What's this? whats this?

Iul. A rime, I learne euen now
Of one I dan'st withall.
One cals within, Iuliet.

Nur. Anon, anon:
Come let's away, the strangers all are gone. *Exeunt.*

Chorus.

Now old desire doth in his death bed lie,
And yong affection gapes to be his Heire,
That faire, for which Loue gron'd for and would die,
With tender *Iuliet* matcht, is now not faire.
Now *Romeo* is beloued, and Loues againe,
A like bewitched by the charme of lookes:
But to his foe suppos'd he must complaine,
And she steale Loues sweet bait from fearefull hookes:
Being held a foe, he may not haue accesse
To breath such vowes as Louers vse to sweare,
And she as much in Loue, her meanes much lesse,
To meete her new Beloued any where:
But passion lends them Power, time, meanes to meete,
Temp'ring extremities with extreame sweete.

Enter Romeo alone.

Rom. Can I goe forward when my heart is here?
Turne backe dull earth, and find thy Center out.

Enter Benuolio, with Mercutio.

Ben. *Romeo*, my Cozen *Romeo*, *Romeo*.

Mer. He is wise,
And on my life hath stolne him home to bed.

Ben. He ran this way and leapt this Orchard wall.
Call good *Mercutio*:
Nay, Ile coniure too.

Mer.

Mer. *Romeo*, Humours, Madman, Passion, Louer,
Appeare thou in the likenesse of a sigh,
Speake but one rime, and I am satisfied:
Cry me but ay me, Prouant, but Loue and day,
Speake to my goship *Venus* one faire word,
One Nickname for her purblind Sonne and her,
Young *Abraham Cupid* he that shot so true,
When King *Cophetua* lou'd the begger Maid,
He heareth not, he stirreth not, he mouethn ot,
The Ape is dead, I must coniure him,
I coniure thee by *Rosalines* bright eyes,
By her High forehead, and her Scarlet lip,
By her Fine foote, Straight leg, and Quiuering thigh,
And the Demeanes, that there Adiacent lie,
That in thy likenesse thou appeare to vs.

Ben. And if he heare thee thou wilt anger him.

Mer. This cannot anger him, t'would anger him
To raise a spirit in his Mistresse circle,
Of some strange nature, letting it stand
Till she had laid it, and coniured it downe,
That were some spight.
My inuocation is faire and honest, & in his Mistris name,
I coniure onely but to raise vp him.

Ben. Come, he hath hid himselfe among these Trees
To be consorted with the Humerous night:
Blind is his Loue, and best befits the darke.

Mer. If Loue be blind, Loue cannot hit the marke,
Now will he sit vnder a Medler tree,
And wish his Mistresse were that kind of Fruite,
As Maides call Medlers when they laugh alone,
O *Romeo* that she were, O that she were
An open, or thou a Poprin Peare,
Romeo goodnight, Ile to my Truckle bed,
This Field-bed is to cold for me to sleepe,
Come shall we go?

Ben. Go then, for 'tis in vaine to seeke him here
That meanes not to be found. *Exeunt.*

Rom. He ieasts at Scarres that neuer felt a wound,
But soft, what light through yonder window breaks?
It is the East, and *Iuliet* is the Sunne,
Arise faire Sun and kill the enuious Moone,
Who is already sicke and pale with griefe,
That thou her Maid art far more faire then she:
Be not her Maid since she is enuious,
Her Vestal liuery is but sicke and greene,
And none but fooles do weare it, cast it off:
It is my Lady, O it is my Loue, O that she knew she were,
She speakes, yet she sayes nothing, what of that?
Her eye discourses, I will answere it:
I am too bold 'tis not to me she speakes:
Two of the fairest starres in all the Heauen,
Hauing some businesse do entreat her eyes,
To twinckle in their Spheres till they returne.
What if her eyes were there, they in her head,
The brightnesse of her cheeke would shame those starres,
As day-light doth a Lampe, her eye in heauen,
Would through the ayrie Region streame so bright,
That Birds would sing, and thinke it were not night:
See how she leanes her cheeke vpon her hand.
O that I were a Gloue vpon that hand,
That I might touch that cheeke.

Iul. Ay me.

Rom. She speakes.
Oh speake againe bright Angell, for thou art
As glorious to this night being ore my head,
As is a winged messenger of heauen

Vnto the white vpturned wondring eyes
Of mortalls that fall backe to gaze on him,
When he bestrides the lazie puffing Cloudes,
And sailes vpon the bosome of the ayre.

Iul. O *Romeo, Romeo*, wherefore art thou *Romeo*?
Denie thy Father and refuse thy name:
Or if thou wilt not, be but sworne my Loue,
And Ile no longer be a *Capulet.*

Rom. Shall I heare more, or shall I speake at this?

Iu. 'Tis but thy name that is my Enemy:
Thou art thy selfe, though not a *Mountague*,
What's *Mountague*? it is nor hand nor foote,
Nor arme, nor face, O be some other name
Belonging to a man.
What? in a names that which we call a Rose,
By any other word would smell as sweete,
So *Romeo* would, were he not *Romeo* cal'd,
Retaine that deare perfection which he owes,
Without that title *Romeo*, doffe thy name,
And for thy name which is no part of thee,
Take all my selfe.

Rom. I take thee at thy word:
Call me but Loue, and Ile be new baptiz'd,
Hence foorth I neuer will be *Romeo.*

Iuli. What man art thou, that thus bescreen'd in night
So stumblest on my counsell?

Rom. By a name,
I know not how to tell thee who I am:
My name deare Saint, is hatefull to my selfe,
Because it is an Enemy to thee,
Had I it written, I would teare the word.

Iuli. My eares haue yet not drunke a hundred words
Of thy tongues vttering, yet I know the sound.
Art thou not *Romeo*, and a *Montague*?

Rom. Neither faire Maid, if either thee dislike.

Iul. How cam'st thou hither.
Tell me, and wherefore?
The Orchard walls are high, and hard to climbe,
And the place death, considering who thou art,
If any of my kinsmen find thee here,

Rom. With Loues light wings
Did I ore-perch these Walls,
For stony limits cannot hold Loue out,
And what Loue can do, that dares Loue attempt:
Therefore thy kinsmen are no stop to me.

Iul. If they do see thee, they will murther thee.

Rom. Alacke there lies more perill in thine eye,
Then twenty of their Swords, looke thou but sweete,
And I am proofe against their enmity.

Iul. I would not for the world they saw thee here.

Rom. I haue nights cloake to hide me from their eyes
And but thou loue me, let them finde me here,
My life were better ended by their hate,
Then death proroged wanting of thy Loue.

Iul. By whose direction found'st thou out this place?

Rom. By Loue that first did promp me to enquire,
He lent me counsell, and I lent him eyes,
I am no Pylot, yet wert thou as far
As that vast-shore-washet with the fartheft Sea,
I should aduenture for such Marchandise.

Iul. Thou knowest the maske of night is on my face,
Else would a Maiden blush bepaint my cheeke,
For that which thou hast heard me speake to night,
Faine would I dwell on forme, faine, faine, denie
What I haue spoke, but farewell Complement,
Doest thou Loue? I know thou wilt say I,

And

And I will take thy word, yet if thou swear'st,
Thou maiest proue false: at Louers periuries
They say *Ioue* laught, oh gentle *Romeo*,
If thou dost Loue, pronounce it faithfully:
Or if thou thinkest I am too quickly wonne,
Ile frowne and be peruerse, and say thee nay,
So thou wilt wooe: But else not for the world.
In truth faire *Mountague* I am too fond:
And therefore thou maiest thinke my behauiour light,
But trust me Gentleman, Ile proue more true,
Then those that haue coying to be strange,
I should haue beene more strange, I must confesse,
But that thou ouer heard'st ere I was ware
My true Loues passion, therefore pardon me,
And not impute this yeelding to light Loue,
Which the darke night hath so discouered.

Rom. Lady, by yonder Moone I vow,
That tips with siluer all these Fruite tree tops.

Iul. O sweare not by the Moone, th'inconstant Moone,
That monethly changes in her circled Orbe,
Least that thy Loue proue likewise variable.

Rom. What shall I sweare by?

Iul. Do not sweare at all:
O rif thou wilt sweare by thy gratious selfe,
Which is the God of my Idolatry,
And Ile beleeue thee.

Rom. If my hearts deare loue.

Iuli. Well do not sweare, although I ioy in thee:
I haue no ioy of this contract to night,
It is too rash, too vnaduis'd, too sudden,
Too like the lightning which doth cease to be
Ere, one can say, it lightens, Sweete good night:
This bud of Loue by Summers ripening breath,
May proue a beautious Flower when next we meete:
Goodnight, goodnight, as sweete repose and rest,
Come to thy heart, as that within my brest.

Rom. O wilt thou leaue me so vnsatisfied?

Iuli. What satisfaction can'st thou haue to night?

Ro. Th'exchange of thy Loues faithfull vow for mine.

Iul. I gaue thee mine before thou did'st request it:
And yet I would it were to giue againe.

Rom. Would'st thou withdraw it,
For what purpose Loue?

Iul. But to be franke and giue it thee againe,
And yet I wish but for the thing I haue,
My bounty is as boundlesse as the Sea,
My Loue as deepe, the more I giue to thee
The more I haue, for both are Infinite:
I heare some noyse within deare Loue adue:
Cals within.

Anon good Nurse, sweet *Mountague* be true:
Stay but alittle, I will come againe.

Rom. O blessed blessed night, I am afear'd
Being in night, all this is but a dreame,
Too flattering sweet to be substantiall.

Iul. Three words deare *Romeo*,
And goodnight indeed,
If that thy bent of Loue be Honourable,
Thy purpose marriage, send me word to morrow,
By one that Ile procure to come to thee,
Where and what time thou wilt performe the right,
And all my Fortunes at thy foote Ile lay,
And follow thee my Lord throughout the world.
Within: Madam.
I come, anon: but if thou meanest not well,
I do beseech thee *Within: Madam.*
(By and by I come)
To cease thy strife, and leaue me to my griefe,
To morrow will I send.

Rom. So thriue my soule.

Iu. A thousand times goodnight. *Exit.*

Rome. A thousand times the worse to want thy light,
Loue goes toward Loue as school-boyes frō thier books
But Loue frō Loue, towards schoole with heauie lookes.

Enter Iuliet againe.

Iul. Hist *Romeo* hist: O for a Falkners voice,
To lure this Tassell gentle backe againe,
Bondage is hoarse, and may not speake aloud,
Else would I teare the Caue where Eccho lies,
And make her ayrie tongue more hoarse, then
With repetition of my *Romeo*.

Rom. It is my soule that calls vpon my name,
How siluer sweet, sound Louers tongues by night,
Like softest Musicke to attending eares.

Iul. *Romeo*.

Rom. My Neece.

Iul. What a clock to morrow
Shall I send to thee?

Rom. By the houre of nine.

Iul. I will not faile, 'tis twenty yeares till then,
I haue forgot why I did call thee backe.

Rom. Let me stand here till thou remember it.

Iul. I shall forget, to haue thee still stand there,
Remembring how I Loue thy company.

Rom. And Ile still stay, to haue thee still forget,
Forgetting any other home but this.

Iul. 'Tis almost morning, I would haue thee gone,
And yet no further then a wantons Bird,
That let's it hop a little from his hand,
Like a poore prisoner in his twisted Gyues,
And with a silken thred plucks it backe againe,
So louing Iealous of his liberty.

Rom. I would I were thy Bird.

Iul. Sweet so would I,
Yet I should kill thee with much cherishing:
Good night, good night.

Rom. Parting is such sweete sorrow,
That I shall say goodnight, till it be morrow.

Iul. Sleepe dwell vpon thine eyes, peace in thy brest.

Rom. Would I were sleepe and peace so sweet to rest,
The gray ey'd morne smiles on the frowning night,
Checkring the Easterne Clouds with streakes of light,
And darknesse fleckel'd like a drunkard reeles,
From forth dayes pathway, made by *Titans* wheeles.
Hence will I to my ghostly Fries close Cell,
His helpe to craue, and my deare hap to tell. *Exit.*

Enter Frier alone with a basket.

Fri. The gray ey'd morne smiles on the frowning night,
Checkring the Easterne Cloudes with streaks of light:
And fleckled darknesse like a drunkard reeles,
From forth daies path, and *Titans* burning wheeles:
Now ere the Sun aduance his burning eye,
The day to cheere, and nights danke dew to dry,
I must vpfill this Osier Cage of ours,
With balefull weedes, and precious Iuiced flowers,
The earth that's Natures mother, is her Tombe,
What is her burying graue that is her wombe:
And from her wombe children of diuers kind

We sucking on her naturall bosome find:
Many for many vertues excellent:
None but for some, and yet all different.
O mickle is the powerfull grace that lies
In Plants, Hearbs, stones, and their true qualities:
For nought so vile, that on the earth doth liue,
But to the earth some speciall good doth giue.
Nor ought so good, but strain'd from that faire vse,
Reuolts from true birth, stumbling on abuse.
Vertue it selfe turnes vice being misapplied,
And vice sometime by action dignified.

Enter Romeo.

Within the infant rin'd of this weake flower,
Poyson hath residence, and medicine power:
For this being smelt, with that part cheares each part,
Being tasted slayes all sences with the heart.
Two such opposed Kings encampe them still,
In man as well as Hearbes, grace and rude will:
And where the worser is predominant,
Full soone the Canker death eates vp that Plant.

Rom. Good morrow Father.

Fri. Benedecite.
What early tongue so sweet saluteth me?
Young Sonne, it argues a distempered head,
So soone to bid goodmorrow to thy bed:
Care keepes his watch in euery old mans eye,
And where Care lodges, sleepe will neuer lye:
But where vnbrused youth with vnstuft braine
Doth couch his lims, there, golden sleepe doth raigne:
Therefore thy earlinesse doth me assure,
Thou art vprous'd with some distemprature;
Or if not so, then here I hit it right,
Our *Romeo* hath not beene in bed to night.

Rom. That last is true, the sweeter rest was mine.

Fri. God pardon sin: wast thou with *Rosaline*?

Rom. With *Rosaline*, my ghostly Father? No,
I haue forgot that name, and that names woe.

Fri. That's my good Son, but wher hast thou bin then?

Rom. Ile tell thee ere thou aske it me agen:
I haue beene feasting with mine enemie,
Where on a sudden one hath wounded me,
That's by me wounded: both our remedies
Within thy helpe and holy phisicke lies:
I beare no hatred, blessed man: for loe
My intercession likewise steads my foe.

Fri. Be plaine good Son, rest homely in thy drift,
Ridling confession, findes but ridling shrift.

Rom. Then plainly know my hearts deare Loue is set,
On the faire daughter of rich *Capulet*:
As mine on hers, so hers is set on mine;
And all combin'd, saue what thou must combine
By holy marriage: when and where, and how,
We met, we wooed, and made exchange of vow:
Ile tell thee as we passe, but this I pray,
That thou consent to marrie vs to day.

Fri. Holy S. *Francis*, what a change is heere?
Is *Rosaline* that thou didst Loue so deare
So soone forsaken? young mens Loue then lies
Not truely in their hearts, but in their eyes.
Iesu *Maria*, what a deale of brine
Hath washt thy sallow cheekes for *Rosaline*?
How much salt water throwne away in waste,
To season Loue that of it doth not tast.
The Sun not yet thy sighes, from heauen cleares,
Thy old grones yet ringing in my auncient eares:
Lo here vpon thy cheeke the staine doth sit,
Of an old teare that is not washt off yet.
If ere thou wast thy selfe, and these woes thine,
Thou and these woes, were all for *Rosaline*.
And art thou chang'd? pronounce this sentence then,
Women may fall, when there's no strength in men.

Rom. Thou chid'st me oft for louing *Rosaline*.

Fri. For doting, not for louing pupill mine.

Rom. And bad'st me bury Loue.

Fri. Not in a graue,
To lay one in, another out to haue.

Rom. I pray thee chide me not, her I Loue now
Doth grace for grace, and Loue for Loue allow:
The other did not so.

Fri. O she knew well,
Thy Loue did read by rote, that could not spell:
But come young wauerer, come goe with me,
In one respect, Ile thy assistant be:
For this alliance may so happy proue,
To turne your houshould rancor to pure Loue.

Rom. O let vs hence, I stand on sudden hast.

Fri. Wisely and slow, they stumble that run fast.

Exeunt

Enter Benuolio and Mercutio.

Mer. Where the deu'le should this *Romeo* be? came he not home to night?

Ben. Not to his Fathers, I spoke with his man.

Mer. Why that same pale hard-harted wench, that *Rosaline* torments him so, that he will sure run mad.

Ben. *Tibalt*, the kinsman to old *Capulet*, hath sent a Letter to his Fathers house.

Mer. A challenge on my life.

Ben. *Romeo* will answere it.

Mer. Any man that can write, may answere a Letter.

Ben. Nay, he will answere the Letters Maister how he dares, being dared.

Mer. Alas poore *Romeo*, he is already dead stab'd with a white wenches blacke eye, runne through the eare with a Loue song, the very pinne of his heart, cleft with the blind Bowe-boyes but-shaft, and is he a man to encounter *Tybalt*?

Ben. Why what is *Tibalt*?

Mer. More then Prince of Cats. Oh hee's the Couragious Captaine of Complements: he fights as you sing pricksong, keeps time, distance, and proportion, he rests his minum, one, two, and the third in your bosom: the very butcher of a silk button, a Dualist, a Dualist: a Gentleman of the very first house of the first and second cause: ah the immortall Passado, the Punto reuerso, the Hay.

Ben. The what?

Mer. The Pox of such antique lisping affecting phantacies, these new tuners of accent: Iesu a very good blade, a very tall man, a very good whore. Why is not this a lamentable thing Grandsire, that we should be thus afflicted with these strange flies: these fashion Mongers, these pardon-mee's, who stand so much on the new form, that they cannot sit at ease on the old bench. O their bones, their bones.

Enter Romeo.

Ben. Here comes *Romeo*, here comes *Romeo*.

Mer. Without his Roe, like a dryed Hering. O flesh, flesh, how art thou fishified? Now is he for the numbers that *Petrarch* flowed in: *Laura* to his Lady, was a kitchen wench, marrie she had a better Loue to berime her: *Dido* a dowdie, *Cleopatra* a Gipsie, *Hellen* and *Hero*, hildings and Harlots: *Thisbie* a gray eie or so, but not to the purpose. Signior *Romeo*, *Bon iour*, there's a French salutation to your

French slop: you gaue vs the the counterfait fairely last night.

Romeo. Good morrow to you both, what counterfeit did I giue you?

Mer. The slip sir, the slip, can you not conceiue?

Rom. Pardon *Mercutio*, my businesse was great, and in such a case as mine, a man may straine curtesie.

Mer. That's as much as to say, such a case as yours constrains a man to bow in the hams.

Rom. Meaning to cursie.

Mer. Thou hast most kindly hit it.

Rom. A most curteous exposition.

Mer. Nay, I am the very pinck of curtesie.

Rom. Pinke for flower.

Mer. Right.

Rom. Why then is my Pump well flowr'd.

Mer. Sure wit, follow me this ieast, now till thou hast worne out thy Pump, that when the single sole of it is worne, the ieast may remaine after the wearing, sole-singular.

Rom. O single sol'd ieast,
Soly singular for the singlenesse.

Mer. Come betweene vs good *Benuolio*, my wits faints.

Rom. Swits and spurs,
Swits and spurs, or Ile crie a match.

Mer. Nay, if our wits run the Wild-Goose chase, I am done: For thou hast more of the Wild-Goose in one of thy wits, then I am sure I haue in my whole fiue. Was I with you there for the Goose?

Rom. Thou wast neuer with mee for any thing, when thou wast not there for the Goose.

Mer. I will bite thee by the eare for that iest.

Rom. Nay, good Goose bite not.

Mer. Thy wit is a very Bitter-sweeting,
It is a most sharpe sawce.

Rom. And is it not well seru'd into a Sweet-Goose?

Mer. Oh here's a wit of Cheuerell, that stretches from an ynch narrow, to an ell broad.

Rom. I stretch it out for that word, broad, which added to the Goose, proues thee farre and wide, abroad Goose.

Mer. Why is not this better now, then groning for Loue, now art thou sociable, now art thou *Romeo*: now art thou what thou art, by Art as well as by Nature, for this driueling Loue is like a great Naturall, that runs lolling vp and downe to hid his bable in a hole.

Ben. Stop there, stop there.

Mer. Thou desir'st me to stop in my tale against the haire.

Ben. Thou would'st else haue made thy tale large.

Mer. O thou art deceiu'd, I would haue made it short, or I was come to the whole depth of my tale, and meant indeed to occupie the argument no longer.

Enter Nurse and her man.

Rom. Here's goodly geare.
A sayle, a sayle.

Mer. Two, two: a Shirt and a Smocke.

Nur. Peter?

Peter. Anon.

Nur. My Fan *Peter*?

Mer. Good *Peter* to hide her face?
For her Fans the fairer face?

Nur. God ye good morrow Gentlemen.

Mer. God ye gooden faire Gentlewoman.

Nur. Is it gooden?

Mer. 'Tis no lesse I tell you: for the bawdy hand of the Dyall is now vpon the pricke of Noone.

Nur. Out vpon you: what a man are you?

Rom. One Gentlewoman,
That God hath made, himselfe to mar.

Nur. By my troth it is said, for himselfe to, mar quo-tha: Gentlemen, can any of you tel me where I may find the young *Romeo*?

Romeo. I can tell you: but young *Romeo* will be older when you haue found him, then he was when you sought him: I am the youngest of that name, for fault of a worse.

Nur. You say well.

Mer. Yea is the worst well,
Very well tooke: Ifaith, wisely, wisely.

Nur. If you be he sir,
I desire some confidence with you?

Ben. She will endite him to some Supper.

Mer. A baud, a baud, a baud. So ho.

Rom. What hast thou found?

Mer. No Hare sir, vnlesse a Hare sir in a Lenten pie, that is something stale and hoare ere it be spent.
An old Hare hoare, and an old Hare hoare is very good meat in Lent.
But a Hare that is hoare is too much for a score, when it hoares ere it be spent,
Romeo will you come to your Fathers? Weele to dinner thither.

Rom. I will follow you.

Mer. Farewell auncient Lady:
Farewell Lady, Lady, Lady.

Exit. Mercutio, Benuolio.

Nur. I pray you sir, what sawcie Merchant was this that was so full of his roperie?

Rom. A Gentleman Nurse, that loues to heare himselfe talke, and will speake more in a minute, then he will stand to in a Moneth.

Nur. And a speake any thing against me, Ile take him downe, & a were lustier then he is, and twentie such Iacks: and if I cannot, Ile finde those that shall: scuruie knaue, I am none of his flurt-gils, I am none of his skaines mates, and thou must stand by too and suffer euery knaue to vse me at his pleasure.

Pet. I saw no man vse you at his pleasure: if I had, my weapon should quickly haue beene out, I warrant you, I dare draw assoone as another man, if I see occasion in a good quarrell, and the law on my side.

Nur. Now afore God, I am so vext, that euery part about me quiuers, skuruy knaue: pray you sir a word: and as I told you, my young Lady bid me enquire you out, what she bid me say, I will keepe to my selfe: but first let me tell ye, if ye should leade her in a fooles paradise, as they say, it were a very grosse kind of behauiour, as they say: for the Gentlewoman is yong: & therefore, if you should deale double with her, truely it were an ill thing to be offered to any Gentlewoman, and very weake dealing.

Nur. Nurse commend me to thy Lady and Mistresse, I protest vnto thee.

Nur. Good heart, and yfaith I will tell her as much: Lord, Lord she will be a ioyfull woman.

Rom. What wilt thou tell her Nurse? thou doest not marke me?

Nur. I will tell her sir, that you do protest, which as I take it, is a Gentleman-like offer.

Rom. Bid her deuise some meanes to come to shrift this afternoone,
And there she shall at Frier *Lawrence* Cell
Beshriu'd and married: here is for thy paines.

Nur. No truly sir not a penny.

Rom. Go too, I say you shall.

Nur. This afternoone sir? well she shall be there.

Ro. And stay thou good Nurse behind the Abbey wall,
Within this houre my man shall be with thee,
And bring thee Cords made like a tackled staire,
Which to the high top gallant of my ioy,
Must be my conuoy in the secret night.
Farewell, be trustie and Ile quite thy paines:
Farewell, commend me to thy Mistresse.

Nur. Now God in heauen blesse thee: harke you sir,

Rom. What saist thou my deare Nurse?

Nurse. Is your man secret, did you nere heare say two may keepe counsell putting one away.

Ro. Warrant thee my man as true as steele.

Nur. We'l sir, my Mistresse is the sweetest Lady, Lord, Lord, when 'twas a little prating thing. O there is a Nobleman in Towne one *Paris*, that would faine lay knife aboard: but she good soule had as leeue a see Toade, a very Toade as see him: I anger her sometimes, and tell her that *Paris* is the properer man, but Ile warrant you, when I say so, shee lookes as pale as any clout in the versall world. Doth not Rosemarie and *Romeo* begin both with a letter?

Rom. I Nurse, what of that? Both with an R

Nur. A mocker that's the dogs name. R. is for the no, I know it begins with some other letter, and she hath the prettiest sententious of it, of you and Rosemary, that it would do you good to heare it.

Rom. Commend me to thy Lady.

Nur. I a thousand times. *Peter*?

Pet. Anon.

Nur. Before and apace.   *Exit Nurse and Peter.*

Enter Iuliet.

Iul. The clocke strook nine, when I did send the Nurse,
In halfe an houre she promised to returne,
Perchance she cannot meete him: that's not so:
Oh she is lame, Loues Herauld should be thoughts,
Which ten times faster glides then the Sunnes beames,
Driuing backe shadowes ouer lowring hils.
Therefore do nimble Pinion'd Doues draw Loue,
And therefore hath the wind-swift *Cupid* wings:
Now is the Sun vpon the highmost hill
Of this daies iourney, and from nine till twelue,
I three long houres, yet she is not come.
Had she affections and warme youthfull blood,
She would be as swift in motion as a ball,
My words would bandy her to my sweete Loue,
And his to me, but old folkes,
Many faine as they were dead,
Vnwieldie, slow, heauy, and pale as lead.

Enter Nurse.

O God she comes, O hony Nurse what newes?
Hast thou met with him? send thy man away.

Nur. Peter stay at the gate.

Iul. Now good sweet Nurse:
O Lord, why lookest thou sad?
Though newes be sad, yet tell them merrily.
If good thou sham'st the musicke of sweet newes,
By playing it to me, with so sower a face.

Nur. I am a weary, giue me leaue awhile,
Fie how my bones ake, what a iaunt haue I had?

Iul. I would thou had'st my bones, and I thy newes:
Nay come I pray thee speake, good good Nurse speake.

Nur. Iesu what hast? can you not stay a while?
Do you not see that I am out of breath?

Iul. How art thou out of breath, when thou hast breth
To say to me, that thou art out of breath?
The excuse that thou dost make in this delay,
Is longer then the tale thou dost excuse.
Is thy newes good or bad? answere to that,
Say either, and Ile stay the circustance:
Let me be satisfied, ist good or bad?

Nur. Well, you haue made a simple choice, you know not how to chuse a man: *Romeo*, no not he though his face be better then any mans, yet his legs excels all mens, and for a hand, and a foote, and a body, though they be not to be talkt on, yet they are past compare: he is not the flower of curtesie, but Ile warrant him as gentle a Lambe: go thy waies wench, serue God. What haue you din'd at home?

Iul. No no: but all this this did I know before
What saies he of our marriage? what of that?

Nur. Lord how my head akes, what a head haue I?
It beates as it would fall in twenty peeces.
My backe a tother side: o my backe, my backe:
Beshrew your heart for sending me about
To catch my death with iaunting vp and downe.

Iul. Ifaith: I am sorrie that that thou art so well.
Sweet sweet, sweet Nurse, tell me what saies my Loue?

Nur. Your Loue saies like an honest Gentleman,
And a courteous, and a kind, and a handsome,
And I warrant a vertuous: where is your Mother?

Iul. Where is my Mother?
Why she is within, where should she be?
How odly thou repli'st:
Your Loue saies like an honest Gentleman:
Where is your Mother?

Nur. O Gods Lady deare,
Are you so hot? marrie come vp I trow,
Is this the Poultis for my aking bones?
Henceforward do your messages your selfe.

Iul. Heere's such a coile, come what saies *Romeo*?

Nur. Haue you got leaue to go to shrift to day?

Iul. I haue.

Nur. Then high you hence to Frier *Lawrence* Cell,
There staies a Husband to make you a wife:
Now comes the wanton bloud vp in your cheekes,
Thei'le be in Scarlet straight at any newes:
Hie you to Church, I must an other way,
To fetch a Ladder by the which your Loue
Must climbe a birds nest Soone when it is darke:
I am the drudge, and toile in your delight:
But you shall beare the burthen soone at night.
Go Ile to dinner, hie you to the Cell.

Iul. Hie to high Fortune, honest Nurse, farewell. *Exeunt.*

Enter Frier and Romeo.

Fri. So smile the heauens vpon this holy act,
That after houres, with sorrow chide vs not.

Rom. Amen, amen, but come what sorrow can,
It cannot counteruaile the exchange of ioy
That one short minute giues me in her sight:
Do thou but close our hands with holy words,
Then Loue-deuouring death do what he dare,
It is inough. I may but call her mine.

Fri. These violent delights haue violent endes,
And in their triumph: die like fire and powder,
Which as they kisse consume. The sweetest honey
Is loathsome in his owne deliciousnesse,
And in the taste confoundes the appetite.
Therefore Loue moderately, long Loue doth so,
Too swift arriues as tardie as too slow.

Enter Iuliet.

Here comes the Lady. Oh so light a foot
Will nere weare out the euerlasting flint,

A Louer may bestride the Gossamours,
That ydles in the wanton Summer ayre,
And yet not fall, so light is vanitie.

Iul. Good euen to my ghostly Confessor.

Fri. Romeo shall thanke thee Daughter for vs both.

Iul. As much to him, else in his thanks too much.

Fri. Ah *Iuliet*, if the measure of thy ioy
Be heapt like mine, and that thy skill be more
To blason it, then sweeten with thy breath
This neighbour ayre, and let rich musickes tongue,
Vnfold the imagin'd happinesse that both
Recciue in either, by this deere encounter.

Iul. Conceit more rich in matter then in words,
Brags of his substance, not of Ornament:
They are but beggers that can count their worth,
But my true Loue is growne to such such excesse,
I cannot sum vp some of halfe my wealth.

Fri. Come, come with me, & we will make short worke,
For by your leaues, you shall not stay alone,
Till holy Church incorporate two in one.

Enter Mercutio, Benuolio, and men.

Ben. I pray thee good *Mercutio* lets retire,
The day is hot, the *Capulets* abroad:
And if we meet, we shal not scape a brawle, for now these
hot dayes, is the mad blood stirring.

Mer. Thou art like one of these fellowes, that when he
enters the confines of a Tauerne, claps me his Sword vpon
the Table, and sayes, God send me no need of thee: and by
the operation of the second cup, drawes him on the Drawer, when indeed there is no need.

Ben. Am I like such a Fellow?

Mer. Come, come, thou art as hot a Iacke in thy mood,
as any in *Italie*: and assoone moued to be moodie, and assoone moodie to be mou'd.

Ben. And what too?

Mer. Nay, and there were two such, we should haue
none shortly, for one would kill the other: thou, why thou
wilt quarrell with a man that hath a haire more, or a haire
lesse in his beard, then thou hast: thou wilt quarrell with a
man for cracking Nuts, hauing no other reason, but because thou hast hasell eyes: what eye, but such an eye,
would spie out such a quarrell? thy head is as full of quarrels, as an egge is full of meat, and yet thy head hath bin
beaten as addle as an egge for quarreling: thou hast quarrel'd with a man for coffing in the street, because he hath
wakened thy Dog that hath laine asleepe in the Sun. Did'st
thou not fall out with a Tailor for wearing his new Doublet before Easter? with another, for tying his new shooes
with old Riband, and yet thou wilt Tutor me from quarrelling?

Ben. And I were so apt to quarell as thou art, any man
should buy the Fee-simple of my life, for an houre and a
quarter.

Mer. The Fee-simple? O simple.

Enter Tybalt, Petruchio, and others.

Ben. By my head here comes the *Capulets*.

Mer. By my heele I care not.

Tyb. Follow me close, for I will speake to them.
Gentlemen, Good den, a word with one of you.

Mer. And but one word with one of vs? couple it with
something, make it a word and a blow.

Tib. You shall find me apt inough to that sir, and you
will giue me occasion.

Mercu. Could you not take some occasion without
giuing?

Tib. *Mercutio* thou consort'st with *Romeo*.

Mer. Consort? what dost thou make vs Minstrels? &
thou make Minstrels of vs, looke to heare nothing but discords: heere's my fiddlesticke, heere's that shall make you
daunce. Come consort.

Ben. We talke here in the publike haunt of men:
Either withdraw vnto some priuate place,
Or reason coldly of your greeuances:
Or else depart, here all eies gaze on vs.

Mer. Mens eyes were made to looke, and let them gaze,
I will not budge for no mans pleasure I.

Enter Romeo.

Tib. Well peace be with you sir, here comes my man.

Mer. But Ile be hang'd sir if he weare your Liuery:
Marry go before to field, heele be your follower,
Your worship in that sense, may call him man.

Tib. *Romeo*, the loue I beare thee, can affoord
No better terme then this: Thou art a Villaine.

Rom. *Tibalt*, the reason that I haue to loue thee,
Doth much excuse the appertaining rage
To such a greeting: Villaine am I none;
Therefore farewell, I see thou know'st me not.

Tib. Boy, this shall not excuse the iniuries
That thou hast done me, therefore turne and draw.

Rom. I do protest I neuer iniur'd thee,
But lou'd thee better then thou can'st deuise:
Till thou shalt know the reason of my loue,
And so good *Capulet*, which name I tender
As dearely as my owne, be satisfied.

Mer. O calme, dishonourable, vile submission:
Alla stucatho carries it away.
Tybalt, you Rat-catcher, will you walke?

Tib. What woulds thou haue with me?

Mer. Good King of Cats, nothing but one of your nine
liues, that I meane to make bold withall, and as you shall
vse me hereafter dry beate the rest of the eight. Will you
pluck your Sword out of his Pilcher by the eares? Make
hast, least mine be about your eares ere it be out.

Tib. I am for you.

Rom. Gentle *Mercutio*, put thy Rapier vp.

Mer. Come sir, your Passado.

Rom. Draw *Benuolio*, beat downe their weapons:
Gentlemen, for shame forbeare this outrage,
Tibalt, *Mercutio*, the Prince expresly hath
Forbidden bandying in *Verona* streetes.
Hold *Tybalt*, good *Mercutio*.

Exit Tybalt.

Mer. I am hurt.
A plague a both the Houses, I am sped:
Is he gone and hath nothing?

Ben. What art thou hurt?

Mer. I, I, a scratch, a scratch, marry 'tis inough,
Where is my Page? go Villaine fetch a Surgeon.

Rom. Courage man, the hurt cannot be much.

Mer. No: 'tis not so deepe as a well, nor so wide as a
Church doore, but 'tis inough, 'twill serue: aske for me to
morrow, and you shall find me a graue man. I am pepper'd
I warrant, for this world: a plague a both your houses.
What, a Dog, a Rat, a Mouse, a Cat to scratch a man to
death: a Braggart, a Rogue, a Villaine, that fights by the
booke of Arithmeticke, why the deu'le came you betweene vs? I was hurt vnder your arme.

Rom. I thought all for the best.

Mer. Helpe me into some house *Benuolio*,
Or I shall faint: a plague a both your houses.
They haue made wormes meat of me,

The Tragedie of Romeo and Iuliet

I haue it, and soundly to your Houses. *Exit.*

Rom. This Gentleman the Princes neere Alie,
My very Friend hath got his mortall hurt
In my behalfe, my reputation stain'd
With *Tybalts* slaunder, *Tybalt* that an houre
Hath beene my Cozin: O Sweet *Iuliet*,
Thy Beauty hath made me Effeminate,
And in my temper softned Valours steele.

Enter Benuolio.

Ben. O *Romeo, Romeo*, braue *Mercutio's* is dead,
That Gallant spirit hath aspir'd the Cloudes,
Which too vntimely here did scorne the earth.

Rom. This daies blacke Fate, on mo daies doth depend,
This but begins, the wo others must end.

Enter Tybalt.

Ben. Here comes the Furious *Tybalt* backe againe.

Rom. He gon in triumph, and *Mercutio* slaine?
Away to heauen respectiue Lenitie,
And fire and Fury, be my conduct now.
Now *Tybalt* take the Villaine backe againe
That late thou gau'st me, for *Mercutios* soule
Is but a little way aboue our heads,
Staying for thine to keepe him companie:
Either thou or I, or both, must goe with him.

Tib. Thou wretched Boy that didst consort him here,
Shalt with him hence.

Rom. This shall determine that.

They fight. Tybalt falles.

Ben. Romeo, away be gone:
The Citizens are vp, and *Tybalt* slaine,
Stand not amaz'd, the Prince will Doome thee death
If thou art taken: hence, be gone, away.

Rom. O! I am Fortunes foole.

Ben. Why dost thou stay?

Exit Romeo.

Enter Citizens.

Citi. Which way ran he that kild *Mercutio*?
Tibalt that Murtherer, which way ran he?

Ben. There lies that *Tybalt*.

Citi. Vp sir go with me:
I charge thee in the Princes names obey.

Enter Prince, old Montague, Capulet, their Wiues and all.

Prin. Where are the vile beginners of this Fray?

Ben. O Noble Prince, I can discouer all
The vnluckie Mannage of this fatall brall:
There lies the man slaine by young *Romeo*,
That slew thy kinsman braue *Mercutio*.

Cap. Wi. Tybalt, my Cozin? O my Brothers Child,
O Prince, O Cozin, Husband, O the blood is spild
Of my deare kinsman, Prince as thou art true,
For bloud of ours, shed bloud of *Mountague*.
O Cozin, Cozin.

Prin. Benuolio, who began this Fray?

Ben. Tybalt here slaine, whom *Romeo's* hand did slay,
Romeo that spoke him faire, bid him bethinke
How nice the Quarrell was, and vrg'd withall
Your high displeasure: all this vttered,
With gentle breath, calme looke, knees humbly bow'd
Could not take truce with the vnruly spleene
Of *Tybalts* deafe to peace, but that he Tilts
With Peircing steele at bold *Mercutio's* breast,
Who all as hot, turnes deadly point to point,
And with a Martiall scorne, with one hand beates
Cold death aside, and with the other sends
It back to *Tybalt*, whose dexterity
Retorts it: *Romeo* he cries aloud,
Hold Friends, Friends part, and swifter then his tongue,
His aged arme, beats downe their fatall points,
And twixt them rushes, vnderneath whose arme,
An enuious thrust from *Tybalt*, hit the life
Of stout *Mercutio*, and then *Tybalt* fled.
But by and by comes backe to *Romeo*,
Who had but newly entertained Reuenge,
And too't they goe like lightning, for ere I
Could draw to part them, was stout *Tybalt* slaine:
And as he fell, did *Romeo* turne and flie:
This is the truth, or let *Benuolio* die.

Cap. Wi. He is a kinsman to the *Mountague*,
Affection makes him false, he speakes not true:
Some twenty of them fought in this blacke strife,
And all those twenty could but kill one life.
I beg for Iustice, which thou Prince must giue:
Romeo slew *Tybalt*, *Romeo* must not liue.

Prin. Romeo slew him, he slew *Mercutio*,
Who now the price of his deare blood doth owe.

Cap. Not *Romeo* Prince, he was *Mercutios* Friend,
His fault concludes, but what the law should end,
The life of *Tybalt*.

Prin. And for that offence,
Immediately we doe exile him hence:
I haue an interest in your hearts proceeding:
My bloud for your rude brawles doth lie a bleeding.
But Ile Amerce you with so strong a fine,
That you shall all repent the losse of mine.
It will be deafe to pleading and excuses,
Nor teares, nor prayers shall purchase our abuses.
Therefore vse none, let *Romeo* hence in hast,
Else when he is found, that houre is his last.
Beare hence this body, and attend our will:
Mercy not Murders, pardoning those that kill.

Exeunt.

Enter Iuliet alone.

Iul. Gallop apece, you fiery footed steedes,
Towards *Phœbus* lodging, such a Wagoner
As *Phaeton* would whip you to the west,
And bring in Cloudie night immediately.
Spred thy close Curtaine Loue-performing night,
That run-awayes eyes may wincke, and *Romeo*
Leape to these armes, vntalkt of and vnseene,
Louers can see to doe their Amorous rights,
And by their owne Beauties: or if Loue be blind,
It best agrees with night: come ciuill night,
Thou sober suted Matron all in blacke,
And learne me how to loose a winning match,
Plaid for a paire of stainlesse Maidenhoods,
Hood my vnman'd blood bayting in my Cheekes,
With thy Blacke mantle, till strange Loue grow bold,
Thinke true Loue acted simple modestie:
Come night, come *Romeo*, come thou day in night,
For thou wilt lie vpon the wings of night
Whiter then new Snow vpon a Rauens backe:
Come gentle night, come louing blackebrow'd night,
Giue me my *Romeo*, and when I shall die,
Take him and cut him out in little starres,
And he will make the Face of heauen so fine,
That all the world will be in Loue with night,
And pay no worship to the Garish Sun,
O I haue bought the Mansion of a Loue,
But not possest it, and though I am sold,
Not yet enioy'd, so tedious is this day,
As is the night before some Festiuall,

To

To an impatient child that hath new robes
And may not weare them, O here comes my Nurse:
Enter Nurse with cords.
And she brings newes and euery tongue that speaks
But *Romeos*, name, speakes heauenly eloquence:
Now Nurse, what newes? what hast thou there?
The Cords that *Romeo* bid thee fetch?

Nur. I, I, the Cords.

Iuli. Ay me, what newes?
Why dost thou wring thy hands.

Nur. A welady, hee's dead, hee's dead,
We are vndone Lady, we are vndone.
Alacke the day, hee's gone, hee's kil'd, he's dead.

Iul. Can heauen be so enuious?

Nur. Romeo can,
Though heauen cannot. O *Romeo, Romeo*,
Who euer would haue thought it *Romeo*.

Iuli. What diuell art thou,
That dost torment me thus?
This torture should be roar'd in dismall hell,
Hath *Romeo* slaine himselfe? say thou but I,
And that bare vowell I shall poyson more
Then the death-darting eye of Cockatrice,
I am not I, if there be such an I.
Or those eyes shot, that makes thee answere I:
If he be slaine say I, or if not, no.
Briefe, sounds, determine of my weale or wo.

Nur. I saw the wound, I saw it with mine eyes,
God saue the marke, here on his manly brest,
A pitteous Coarse, a bloody piteous Coarse:
Pale, pale as ashes, all bedawb'd in blood,
All in gore blood, I sounded at the sight.

Iul. O breake my heart,
Poore Banckrout breake at once,
To prison eyes, nere looke on libertie.
Vile earth to earth resigne, end motion here,
And thou and *Romeo* presse on heauie beere.

Nur. O *Tybalt, Tybalt*, the best Friend I had:
O curteous *Tybalt* honest Gentleman,
That euer I should liue to see thee dead.

Iul. What storme is this that blowes so contrarie?
Is *Romeo* slaughtred? and is *Tybalt* dead?
My dearest Cozen, and my dearer Lord:
Then dreadfull Trumpet sound the generall doome,
For who is liuing, if those two are gone?

Nur. Tybalt is gone, and *Romeo* banished,
Romeo that kil'd him, he is banished.

Iul. O God!
Did *Rom'os* hand shed *Tybalts* blood
It did, it did, alas the day, it did.

Nur. O Serpent heart, hid with a flowring face.

Iul. Did euer Dragon keepe so faire a Caue?
Beautifull Tyrant, fiend Angelicall:
Rauenous Doue-feather'd Rauen,
Woluish-rauening Lambe,
Dispised substance of Diuinest show:
Iust opposite to what thou iustly seem'st,
A dimne Saint, an Honourable Villaine:
O Nature! what had'st thou to dee in hell,
When thou did'st bower the spirit of a fiend
In mortall paradise of such sweet flesh?
Was euer booke containing such vile matter
So fairely bound? O that deceit should dwell
In such a gorgeous Pallace.

Nur. There's no trust, no faith, no honestie in men,
All periur'd, all forsworne, all naught, all dissemblers,
Ah where's my man? giue me some Aqua-vitæ?
These griefes, these woes, these sorrowes make me old:
Shame come to *Romeo*.

Iul. Blister'd be thy tongue
For such a wish, he was not borne to shame:
Vpon his brow shame is asham'd to sit;
For 'tis a throane where Honour may be Crown'd
Sole Monarch of the vniuersall earth:
O what a beast was I to chide him?

Nur. Will you speake well of him,
That kil'd your Cozen?

Iul. Shall I speake ill of him that is my husband?
Ah poore my Lord, what tongue shall smooth thy name,
When I thy three houres wife haue mangled it.
But wherefore Villaine did'st thou kill my Cozin?
That Villaine Cozin would haue kil'd my husband:
Backe foolish teares, backe to your natiue spring,
Your tributarie drops belong to woe,
Which you mistaking offer vp to ioy:
My husband liues that *Tibalt* would haue slaine,
And *Tibalt* dead that would haue slaine my husband:
All this is comfort, wherefore weepe I then?
Some words there was worser then *Tybalts* death
That murdered me, I would forget it feine,
But oh, it presses to my memory,
Like damned guilty deedes to sinners minds,
Tybalt is dead and *Romeo* banished:
That banished, that one word banished,
Hath slaine ten thousand *Tibalts*: *Tibalts* death
Was woe inough if it had ended there:
Or if sower woe delights in fellowship,
And needly will be rankt with other griefes,
Why followed not when she said *Tibalts* dead,
Thy Father or thy Mother, nay or both,
Which moderne lamentation might haue mou'd.
But which a rere-ward following *Tybalts* death
Romeo is banished to speake that word,
Is Father, Mother, *Tybalt, Romeo, Iuliet*,
All slaine, all dead: *Romeo* is banished,
There is no end, no limit, measure, bound,
In that words death, no words can that woe sound.
Where is my Father and my Mother Nurse?

Nur. Weeping and wailing ouer *Tybalts* Coarse,
Will you go to them? I will bring you thither.

Iu. Wash they his wounds with teares: mine shal be spent
When theirs are drie for *Romeo's* banishment.
Take vp those Cordes, poore ropes you are beguil'd,
Both you and I for *Romeo* is exild:
He made you for a high-way to my bed,
But I a Maid, die Maiden widowed.
Come Cord, come Nurse, Ile to my wedding bed,
And death not *Romeo*, take my Maiden head.

Nur. Hie to your Chamber, Ile find *Romeo*
To comfort you, I wot well where he is:
Harke ye your *Romeo* will be heere at night,
Ile to him, he is hid at *Lawrence* Cell.

Iul. O find him, giue this Ring to my true Knight,
And bid him come, to take his last farewell. *Exit.*

Enter Frier and Romeo.

Fri. Romeo come forth,
Come forth thou fearfull man,
Affliction is enamor'd of thy parts:
And thou art wedded to calamitie.

Rom. Father what newes?

What is the Princes Doome?
What sorrow craues acquaintance at my hand,
That I yet know not?
  Fri. Too familiar
Is my deare Sonne with such sowre Company:
I bring thee tydings of the Princes Doome.
  Rom. What lesse then Doomesday,
Is the Princes Doome?
  Fri. A gentler iudgement vanisht from his lips,
Not bodies death, but bodies banishment.
  Rom. Ha, banishment? be mercifull, say death:
For exile hath more terror in his looke,
Much more then death: do not say banishment.
  Fri. Here from *Verona* art thou banished:
Be patient, for the world is broad and wide.
  Rom. There is no world without *Verona* walles,
But Purgatorie, Torture, hell it selfe:
Hence banished, is banisht from the world,
And worlds exile is death. Then banished,
Is death, mistearm'd, calling death banished,
Thou cut'st my head off with a golden Axe,
And smilest vpon the stroke that murders me.
  Fri. O deadly sin, O rude vnthankefulnesse!
Thy falt our Law calles death, but the kind Prince
Taking thy part, hath rusht aside the Law,
And turn'd that blacke word death, to banishment.
This is deare mercy, and thou seest it not.
  Rom. 'Tis Torture and not mercy, heauen is here
Where *Iuliet* liues, and euery Cat and Dog,
And little Mouse, euery vnworthy thing
Liue here in Heauen and may looke on her,
But *Romeo* may not. More Validitie,
More Honourable state, more Courtship liues
In carrion Flies, then *Romeo*: they may seaze
On the white wonder of deare *Iuliets* hand,
And steale immortall blessing from her lips,
Who euen in pure and vestall modestie
Still blush, as thinking their owne kisses sin.
This may Flies doe, when I from this must flie,
And saist thou yet, that exile is not death?
But *Romeo* may not, hee is banished.
Had'st thou no poyson mixt, no sharpe ground knife,
No sudden meane of death, though nere so meane,
But banished to kill me? Banished?
O Frier, the damned vse that word in hell:
Howlings attends it, how hast thou the hart
Being a Diuine, a Ghostly Confessor,
A Sin-Absoluer, and my Friend profest:
To mangle me with that word, banished?
  Fri. Then fond Mad man, heare me speake.
  Rom. O thou wilt speake againe of banishment.
  Fri. Ile giue thee Armour to keepe off that word,
Aduersities sweete milke, Philosophie,
To comfort thee, though thou art banished.
  Rom. Yet banished? hang vp Philosophie:
Vnlesse Philosohpie can make a *Iuliet*,
Displant a Towne, reuerse a Princes Doome,
It helpes not, it preuailes not, talke no more.
  Fri. O then I see, that Mad men haue no eares.
  Rom. How should they,
When wisemen haue no eyes?
  Fri. Let me dispaire with thee of thy estate,
  Rom. Thou can'st not speake of that y dost not feele,
Wert thou as young as *Iuliet* my Loue,
An houre but married, *Tybalt* murdered,
Doting like me, and like me banished,
Then mightest thou speake,
Then mightest thou teare thy hayre,
And fall vpon the ground as I doe now,
Taking the measure of an vnmade graue.
    Enter Nurse, and knockes.
  Frier. Arise one knockes,
Good *Romeo* hide thy selfe.
  Rom. Not I,
Vnlesse the breath of Hartsicke groanes
Mist-like infold me from the search of eyes. *Knocke*
  Fri. Harke how they knocke:
(Who's there) *Romeo* arise,
Thou wilt be taken, stay a while, stand vp: *Knocke.*

Run to my study: by and by, Gods will
What simplenesse is this: I come, I come. *Knocke.*

Who knocks so hard?
Whence come you? what's your will?
    Enter Nurse.
  Nur. Let me come in,
And you shall know my errand:
I come from Lady *Iuliet*.
  Fri. Welcome then.
  Nur. O holy Frier, O tell me holy Frier,
Where's my Ladies Lord? where's *Romeo*?
  Fri. There on the ground,
With his owne teares made drunke.
  Nur. O he is euen in my Mistresse case,
Iust in her case. O wofull simpathy:
Pittious predicament, euen so lies she,
Blubbring and weeping, weeping and blubbring,
Stand vp, stand vp, stand and you be a man,
For *Iuliets* sake, for her sake rise and stand:
Why should you fall into so deepe an O.
  Rom. Nurse.
  Nur. Ah sir, ah sir, deaths the end of all.
  Rom. Speak'st thou of *Iuliet*? how is it with her?
Doth not she thinke me an old Murtherer,
Now I haue stain'd the Childhood of our ioy,
With blood remoued, but little from her owne?
Where is she? and how doth she? and what sayes
My conceal'd Lady to our conceal'd Loue?
  Nur. Oh she sayes nothing sir, but weeps and weeps,
And now fals on her bed, and then starts vp,
And *Tybalt* calls, and then on *Romeo* cries,
And then downe falls againe.
  Ro. As if that name shot from the dead leuell of a Gun,
Did murder her, as that names cursed hand
Murdred her kinsman. Oh tell me Frier, tell me,
In what vile part of this Anatomie
Doth my name lodge? Tell me, that I may sacke
The hatefull Mansion.
  Fri. Hold thy desperate hand:
Art thou a man? thy forme cries out thou art:
Thy teares are womanish, thy wild acts denote
The vnreasonable Furie of a beast.
Vnseemely woman, in a seeming man,
And ill beseeming beast in seeming both,
Thou hast amaz'd me. By my holy order,
I thought thy disposition better temper'd.
Hast thou slaine *Tybalt*? wilt thou slay thy selfe?
And slay thy Lady, that in thy life lies,
By doing damned hate vpon thy selfe?
Why rayl'st thou on thy birth? the heauen and earth?

Since birth, and heauen and earth, all three do meete
In thee at once, which thou at once would'st loose.
Fie, fie, thou sham'st thy shape, thy loue, thy wit,
Which like a Vsurer abound'st in all :
And vsest none in that true vse indeed,
Which should bedecke thy shape, thy loue, thy wit:
Thy Noble shape, is but a forme of waxe,
Digressing from the Valour of a man,
Thy deare Loue sworne but hollow periurie,
Killing that Loue which thou hast vow'd to cherish.
Thy wit, that Ornament, to shape and Loue,
Mishapen in the conduct of them both :
Like powder in a skillesse Souldiers flaske,
Is set a fire by thine owne ignorance,
And thou dismembred with thine owne defence.
What, rowse thee man, thy *Iuliet* is aliue,
For whose deare sake thou wast but lately dead.
There art thou happy. *Tybalt* would kill thee,
But thou slew'st *Tybalt*, there art thou happie.
The law that threatned death became thy Friend,
And turn'd it to exile, there art thou happy.
A packe or blessing light vpon thy backe,
Happinesse Courts thee in her best array,
But like a mishaped and sullen wench,
Thou puttest vp thy Fortune and thy Loue:
Take heed, take heed, for such die miserable.
Goe get thee to thy Loue as was decreed,
Ascend her Chamber, hence and comfort her :
But looke thou stay not till the watch be set,
For then thou canst not passe to *Mantua*,
Where thou shalt liue till we can finde a time
To blaze your marriage, reconcile your Friends,
Beg pardon of thy Prince, and call thee backe,
With twenty hundred thousand times more ioy
Then thou went'st forth in lamentation.
Goe before Nurse, commend me to thy Lady,
And bid her hasten all the house to bed,
Which heauy sorrow makes them apt vnto.
Romeo is comming.

 Nur. O Lord, I could haue staid here all night,
To heare good counsell: oh what learning is !
My Lord Ile tell my Lady you will come.

 Rom. Do so, and bid my Sweete prepare to chide.

 Nur. Heere sir, a Ring she bid me giue you sir:
Hie you, make hast, for it growes very late.

 Rom. How well my comfort is reuiu'd by this.

 Fri. Go hence,
Goodnight, and here stands all your state :
Either be gone before the watch be set,
Or by the breake of day disguis'd from hence,
Soiourne in *Mantua*, Ile find out your man,
And he shall signifie from time to time,
Euery good hap to you, that chaunces heere:
Giue me thy hand, 'tis late, farewell, goodnight.

 Rom. But that a ioy past ioy, calls out on me,
It were a griefe, so briefe to part with thee :
Farewell.   *Exeunt.*

Enter old Capulet, his Wife and Paris.

 Cap. Things haue falne out sir so vnluckily,
That we haue had no time to moue our Daughter :
Looke you, she Lou'd her kinsman *Tybalt* dearely,
And so did I. Well, we were borne to die.
'Tis very late, she'l not come downe to night :
I promise you, but for your company,
I would haue bin a bed an houre ago.

 Par. These times of wo, affoord no times to wooe:
Madam goodnight, commend me to your Daughter.

 Lady. I will, and know her mind early to morrow,
To night, she is mewed vp to her heauinesse.

 Cap. Sir *Paris*, I will make a desperate tender
Of my Childes loue : I thinke she will be rul'd
In all respects by me : nay more, I doubt it not.
Wife, go you to her ere you go to bed,
Acquaint her here, of my Sonne *Paris* Loue,
And bid her, marke you me, on Wendsday next,
But soft, what day is this?

 Par. Monday my Lord.

 Cap. Monday, ha ha: well Wendsday is too soone,
A Thursday let it be: a Thursday tell her,
She shall be married to this Noble Earle :
Will you be ready ? do you like this hast?
Weele keepe no great adoe, a Friend or two,
For harke you, *Tybalt* being slaine so late,
It may be thought we held him carelesly,
Being our kinsman, if we reuell much :
Therefore weele haue some halfe a dozen Friends,
And there an end. But what say you to Thursday?

 Paris. My Lord,
I would that Thursday were to morrow.

 Cap. Well, get you gone, a Thursday, be it then:
Go you to *Iuliet* ere you go to bed,
Prepare her wife, against this wedding day.
Farewell my Lord, light to my Chamber hoa,
Afore me, it is so late, that we may call it early by and by,
Goodnight.   *Exeunt.*

Enter Romeo and Iuliet aloft.

 Iul. Wilt thou be gone ? It is not yet neere day :
It was the Nightingale, and not the Larke,
That pierc'st the fearefull hollow of thine eare,
Nightly she sings on yond Pomgranet tree,
Beleeue me Loue, it was the Nightingale.

 Rom. It was the Larke the Herauld of the Morne:
No Nightingale: looke Loue what enuious streakes
Do lace the seuering Cloudes in yonder East :
Nights Candles are burnt out, and Iocond day
Stands tipto on the mistie Mountaines tops,
I must be gone and liue, or stay and die.

 Iul. Yond light is not daylight, I know it I :
It is some Meteor that the Sun exhales,
To be to thee this night a Torch-bearer,
And light thee on thy way to *Mantua*.
Therefore stay yet, thou need'st not to be gone.

 Rom. Let me be tane, let me be put to death,
I am content, so thou wilt haue it so.
Ile say yon gray is not the mornings eye,
'Tis but the pale reflexe of *Cinthias* brow.
Nor that is not Larke whose noates do beate
The vaulty heauen so high aboue our heads,
I haue more care to stay, then will to go :
Come death and welcome, *Iuliet* wills it so.
How ist my soule, lets talke, it is not day.

 Iuli. It is, it is, hie hence be gone away :
It is the Larke that sings so out of tune,
Straining harsh Discords, and vnpleasing Sharpes.
Some say the Larke makes sweete Diuision;
This doth not so: for she diuideth vs.
Some say, the Larke and loathed Toad change eyes,
O now I would they had chang'd voyces too:

Since

The Tragedie of Romeo and Iuliet. 69

Since arme from arme that voyce doth vs affray,
Hunting thee hence, with Hunt s-vp to the day,
O now be gone, more light and it light growes.
  Rom. More light & light, more darke & darke our woes.

Enter Madam and Nurse.

  Nur. Madam.
  Iul. Nurse.
  Nur. Your Lady Mother is comming to your chamber,
The day is broke, be wary, looke about.
  Iul. Then window let day in, and let life out.
  Rom. Farewell, farewell, one kisse and Ile descend.
  Iul. Art thou gone so? Loue, Lord, ay Husband, Friend,
I must heare from thee euery day in the houre,
For in a minute there are many dayes,
O by this count I shall be much in yeares,
Ere I againe behold my *Romeo*.
  Rom. Farewell:
I will omit no oportunitie,
That may conuey my greetings Loue, to thee.
  Iul. O thinkest thou we shall euer meet againe?
  Rom. I doubt it not, and all these woes shall serue
For sweet discourses in our time to come.
  Iulet. O God! I haue an ill Diuining soule,
Me thinkes I see thee now, thou art so lowe,
As one dead in the bottome of a Tombe,
Either my eye-sight failes, or thou look'st pale.
  Rom. And trust me Loue, in my eye so do you:
Drie sorrow drinkes our blood. Adue, adue.   *Exit.*
  Iul. O Fortune, Fortune, all men call thee fickle,
If thou art fickle, what dost thou with him
That is renown'd for faith? be fickle Fortune:
For then I hope thou wilt not keepe him long,
But send him backe.

Enter Mother.

  Lad. Ho Daughter, are you vp?
  Iul. Who ist that calls? Is it my Lady Mother.
Is she not downe so late, or vp so early?
What vnaccustom'd cause procures her hither?
  Lad. Why how now *Iuliet*?
  Iul. Madam I am not well.
  Lad. Euermore weeping for your Cozins death?
What wilt thou wash him from his graue with teares?
And if thou could'st, thou could'st not make him liue:
Therefore haue done, some griefe shewes much of Loue,
But much of griefe, shewes still some want of wit.
  Iul. Yet let me weepe, for such a feeling losse.
  Lad. So shall you feele the losse, but not the Friend
Which you weepe for.
  Iul. Feeling so the losse,
I cannot chuse but euer weepe the Friend.
  La. Well Girle, thou weep'st not so much for his death,
As that the Villaine liues which slaughter'd him.
  Iul. What Villaine, Madam?
  Lad. That same Villaine *Romeo*.
  Iul. Villaine and he, be many Miles assunder:
God pardon, I doe with all my heart:
And yet no man like he, doth grieue my heart.
  Lad. That is because the Traitor liues.
  Iul. I Madam from the reach of these my hands:
Would none but I might venge my Cozins death.
  Lad. We will haue vengeance for it, feare thou not.
Then weepe no more, Ile send to one in *Mantua*,
Where that same banisht Run-agate doth liue,
Shall giue him such an vnaccustom'd dram,
That he shall soone keepe *Tybalt* company:
And then I hope thou wilt be satisfied.

  Iul. Indeed I neuer shall be satisfied
With *Romeo*, till I behold him. Dead
Is my poore heart so for a kinsman vext:
Madam if you could find out but a man
To beare a poyson, I would temper it;
That *Romeo* should vpon receit thereof,
Soone sleepe in quiet. O how my heart abhors
To heare him nam'd, and cannot come to him,
To wreake the Loue I bore my Cozin,
Vpon his body that hath slaughter'd him.
  Mo. Find thou the meanes, and Ile find such a man.
But now Ile tell thee ioyfull tidings Gyrle.
  Iul. And ioy comes well, in such a needy time,
What are they, beseech your Ladyship?
  Mo. Well, well, thou hast a carefull Father Child?
One who to put thee from thy heauinesse,
Hath sorted out a sudden day of ioy,
That thou expects not, nor I lookt not for.
  Iul. Madam in happy time, what day is this?
  Mo. Marry my Child, early next Thursday morne,
The gallant, young, and Noble Gentleman,
The Countie *Paris* at Saint *Peters* Church,
Shall happily make thee a ioyfull Bride.
  Iul. Now by Saint *Peters* Church, and *Peter* too,
He shall not make me there a ioyfull Bride.
I wonder at this hast, that I must wed
Ere he that should be Husband comes to woe:
I pray you tell my Lord and Father Madam,
I will not marrie yet, and when I doe, I sweare
It shallbe *Romeo*, whom you know I hate
Rather then *Paris*. These are newes indeed.
  Mo. Here comes your Father, tell him so your selfe,
And see how he will take it at your hands.

Enter Capulet and Nurse.

  Cap. When the Sun sets, the earth doth drizzle daew
But for the Sunset of my Brothers Sonne,
It raines downright.
How now? A Conduit Gyrle, what still in teares?
Euermore showring in one little body?
Thou counterfaits a Barke, a Sea, a Wind:
For still thy eyes, which I may call the Sea,
Do ebbe and flow with teares, the Barke thy body is
Sayling in this salt floud, the windes thy sighes,
Who raging with the teares and they with them,
Without a sudden calme will ouer set
Thy tempest tossed body. How now wife?
Haue you deliuered to her our decree?
  Lady. I sir;
But she will none, she giues you thankes,
I would the foole were married to her graue.
  Cap. Soft, take me with you, take me with you wife,
How, will she none? doth she not giue vs thanks?
Is she not proud? doth she not count her blest,
Vnworthy as she is, that we haue wrought
So worthy a Gentleman, to be her Bridegroome
  Iul. Not proud you haue,
But thankfull that you haue:
Proud can I neuer be of what I haue,
But thankfull euen for hate, that is meant Loue.
  Cap. How now?
How now? Chopt Logicke? what is this?
Proud, and I thanke you: and I thanke you not,
Thanke me no thankings, nor proud me no prouds,
But settle your fine ioints 'gainst Thursday next,

To

To go with *Paris* to Saint *Peters* Church:
Or I will drag thee,on a Hurdle thither.
Out you greene sicknesse carrion,out you baggage,
You tallow face.

Lady. Fie,fie,what are you mad?

Iul. Good Father,I beseech you on my knees,
Heare me with patience,but to speake a word.

Fa. Hang thee young baggage,disobedient wretch,
I tell thee what,get thee to Church a Thursday,
Or neuer after looke me in the face.
Speake not,reply not,do not answere me.
My fingers itch,wife: we scarce thought vs blest,
That God had lent vs but this onely Child,
But now I see this one is one too much,
And that we haue a curse in hauing her:
Out on her Hilding.

Nur. God in heauen blesse her,
You are too blame my Lord to rate her so.

Fa. And why my Lady wisedome? hold your tongue,
Good Prudence,smatter with your gossip,go.

Nur. I speake no treason,
Father,O Godigoden,
May not one speake?

Fa. Peace you mumbling foole,
Vtter your grauitie ore a Gossips bowles
For here we need it not.

La. You are too hot.

Fa. Gods bread, it makes me mad:
Day,night,houre,tide,time,worke,play,
Alone in companie,still my care hath bin
To haue her matcht,and hauing now prouided
A Gentleman of Noble Parentage,
Of faire Demeanes, Youthfull,and Nobly Allied,
Stuft as they say with Honourable parts,
Proportion'd as ones thought would wish a man,
And then to haue a wretched puling foole,
A whining mammet,in her Fortunes tender,
To answer,Ile not wed,I cannot Loue:
I am too young,I pray you pardon me.
But, and you will not wed,Ile pardon you.
Graze where you will,you shall not house with me:
Looke too't,thinke on't,I do not vse to iest.
Thursday is neere,lay hand on heart,aduise,
And you be mine,Ile giue you to my Friend:
And you be not,hang,beg,starue,die in the streets,
For by my soule,Ile nere acknowledge thee,
Nor what is mine shall neuer do thee good:
Trust too't,bethinke you,Ile not be forsworne   *Exit.*

Iuli. Is there no pittie sitting in the Cloudes,
That sees into the bottome of my griefe?
O sweet my Mother cast me not away,
Delay this marriage,for a month,a weeke,
Or if you do not,make the Bridall bed
In that dim Monument where *Tybalt* lies.

Mo. Talke not to me,for Ile not speake a word,
Do as thou wilt,for I haue done with thee.   *Exit.*

Iul. O God!
O Nurse,how shall this be preuented?
My Husband is on earth,my faith in heauen,
How shall that faith returne againe to earth,
Vnlesse that Husband send it me from heauen,
By leauing earth? Comfort me,counsaile me:
Alacke,alacke,that heauen should practise stratagems
Vpon so soft a subiect as my selfe.
What saist thou? hast thou not a word of ioy?
Some comfort Nurse.

Nur. Faith here it is,
Romeo is banished,and all the world to nothing,
That he dares nere come backe to challenge you:
Or if he do,it needs must be by stealth.
Then since the case so stands as now it doth,
I thinke it best you married with the Countie,
O hee's a Louely Gentleman:
Romeos a dish-clout to him: an Eagle Madam
Hath not so greene,so quicke,so faire an eye
As *Paris* hath,beshrow my very heart,
I thinke you are happy in this second match,
For it excels your first:or if it did not,
Your first is dead,or 'twere as good he were,
As liuing here and you no vse of him.

Iul. Speakest thou from thy heart?

Nur. And from my soule too,
Or else beshrew them both.

Iul. Amen.

Nur. What?

Iul. Well,thou hast comforted me marue'lous much,
Go in,and tell my Lady I am gone,
Hauing displeas'd my Father,to *Lawrence* Cell,
To make confession,and to be absolu'd.

Nur. Marrie I will,and this is wisely done.

Iul. Auncient damnation,O most wicked fiend!
It is more sin to wish me thus forsworne,
Or to dispraise my Lord with that same tongue
Which she hath prais'd him with aboue compare,
So many thousand times? Go Counsellor,
Thou and my bosom chencbforth shall be twaine:
Ile to the Frier to know his remedie,
If all else faile,my selfe haue power to die.   *Exeunt.*

Enter Frier and Countie Paris.

Fri. On Thursday sir?the time is very short.

Par. My Father *Capulet* will haue it so,
And I am nothing slow to slack his hast.

Fri. You say you do not know the Ladies mind?
Vneuen is the course, I like it not.

Pa. Immoderately she weepes for *Tybalts* death,
And therfore haue I little talke of Loue,
For *Venus* smiles not in a house of teares.
Now sir,her Father counts it dangerous
That she doth giue her sorrow so much sway:
And in his wisedome,hasts our marriage,
To stop the inundation of her teares,
Which it too much minded by her selfe alone,
May be put from her by societie.
Now doe you know the reason of this hast?

Fri. I would I knew not why it should be slow'd.
Looke sir,here comes the Lady towards my Cell.

Enter Iuliet.

Par. Happily met,my Lady and my wife.

Iul. That may be sir,when I may be a wife.

Par. That may be,must be Loue,on Thursday next.

Iul. What must be shall be.

Fri. That's a certaine text.

Par. Come you to make confession to this Father?

Iul. To answere that, I should confesse to you.

Par. Do not denie to him,that you Loue me.

Iul. I will confesse to you that I Loue him.

Par. So will ye,I am sure that you Loue me.

Iul. If I do so,it will be of more price,
Being spoke behind your backe,then to your face.

Par. Poore soule,thy face is much abus'd with teares.

Iuli. The

The Tragedie of Romeo and Iuliet.

Iul. The teares haue got small victorie by that:
For it was bad inough before their spight.

Pa. Thou wrong'st it more then teares with that report.

Iul. That is no slaunder sir, which is a truth,
And what I spake, I spake it to thy face.

Par. Thy face is mine, and thou hast slaundred it.

Iul. It may be so, for it is not mine owne.
Are you at leisure, Holy Father now,
Or shall I come to you at euening Masse?

Fri. My leisure serues me pensiue daughter now.
My Lord you must intreat the time alone.

Par. Godsheild: I should disturbe Deuotion,
Iuliet, on Thursday early will I rowse yee,
Till then adue, and keepe this holy kisse. *Exit Paris.*

Iul. O shut the doore, and when thou hast done so,
Come weepe with me, past hope, past care, past helpe.

Fri. O *Iuliet*, I alreadie know thy griefe,
It streames me past the compasse of my wits:
I heare thou must, and nothing may prorogue it,
On Thursday next be married to this Countie.

Iul. Tell me not Frier that thou hearest of this,
Vnlesse thou tell me how I may preuent it:
If in thy wisedome, thou canst giue no helpe,
Do thou but call my resolution wise,
And with his knife, Ile helpe it presently.
God ioyn'd my heart, and *Romeos*, thou our hands,
And ere this hand by thee to *Romeo* seal'd,
Shall be the Labell to another Deede,
Or my true heart with trecherous reuolt,
Turne to another, this shall slay them both:
Therefore out of thy long expetien'tl time,
Giue me some present counsell, or behold
Twixt my extreames and me, this bloody knife
Shall play the vmpeere, arbitrating that,
Which the commission of thy yeares and art,
Could to no issue of true honour bring:
Be not so long to speak, I long to die,
If what thou speak'st, speake not of remedy.

Fri. Hold Daughter, I doe spie a kind of hope,
Which craues as desperate an execution.
As that is desperate which we would preuent.
If rather then to marrie Countie *Paris*
Thou hast the strength of will to slay thy selfe,
Then is it likely thou wilt vndertake
A thing like death to chide away this shame,
That coap'st with death himselfe, to scape fro it:
And if thou dar'st, Ile giue thee remedie.

Iul. Oh bid me leape, rather then marrie *Paris*,
From of the Battlements of any Tower,
Or walke in theeuish waies, or bid me lurke
Where Serpents are: chaine me with roaring Beares
Or hide me nightly in a Charnell house,
Orecouered quite with dead mens ratling bones,
With reekie shankes and yellow chappels sculls:
Or bid me go into a new made graue,
And hide me with a dead man in his graue,
Things that to heare them told, haue made me tremble,
And I will doe it without feare or doubt,
To liue an vnstained wife to my sweet Loue.

Fri. Hold then: goe home, be merrie, giue consent,
To marrie *Paris*: wensday is to morrow,
To morrow night looke that thou lie alone,
Let not thy Nurse lie with thee in thy Chamber:
Take thou this Violl being then in bed,
And this distilling liquor drinke thou off,
When presently through all thy veines shall run,
A cold and drowsie humour: for no pulse
Shall keepe his natiue progresse, but surcease:
No warmth, no breath shall testifie thou liuest,
The Roses in thy lips and cheekes shall fade
To many ashes, the eyes windowes fall
Like death when he shut vp the day of life:
Each part depriu'd of supple gouernment,
Shall stiffe and starke, and cold appeare like death,
And in this borrowed likenesse of shrunke death
Thou shalt continue two and forty houres,
And then awake, as from a pleasant sleepe.
Now when the Bridegroome in the morning comes,
To rowse thee from thy bed, there art thou dead:
Then as the manner of our country is,
In thy best Robes vncouer'd on the Beere,
Be borne to buriall in thy kindreds graue:
Thou shalt be borne to that same ancient vault,
Where all the kindred of the *Capulets* lie,
In the meane time against thou shalt awake,
Shall *Romeo* by my Letters know our drift,
And hither shall he come, and that very night
Shall *Romeo* beare thee hence to *Mantua*.
And this shall free thee from this present shame,
If no inconstant toy nor womanish feare,
Abate thy valour in the acting it.

Iul. Giue me, giue me, O tell not me of care.

Fri. Hold get you gone, be strong and prosperous:
In this resolue, Ile send a Frier with speed
To *Mantua* with my Letters to thy Lord.

Iu. Loue giue me strength,
And strength shall helpe afford:
Farewell deare father. *Exit*

*Enter Father Capulet, Mother, Nurse, and
Seruing men, two or three.*

Cap. So many guests inuite as here are writ,
Sirrah, go hire me twenty cunning Cookes.

Ser. You shall haue none ill sir, for Ile trie if they can licke their fingers.

Cap. How canst thou trie them so?

Ser. Marrie sir, 'tis an ill Cooke that cannot licke his owne fingers: therefore he that cannot licke his fingers goes not with me.

Cap. Go be gone, we shall be much vnfurnisht for this time: what is my Daughter gone to Frier *Lawrence*?

Nur. I forsooth.

Cap. Well he may chance to do some good on her,
A peeuish selfe-wild harlotry it is.
Enter Iuliet.

Nur. See where she comes from shrift
With merrie looke.

Cap. How now my headstrong,
Where haue you bin gadding?

Iul. Where I haue learnt me to repent the sin
Of disobedient opposition:
To you and your behests, and am enioyn'd
By holy *Lawrence*, to fall prostrate here,
To beg your pardon: pardon I beseech you,
Henceforward I am euer rul'd by you.

Cap. Send for the Countie, goe tell him of this,
Ile haue this knot knit vp to morrow morning.

Iul. I met the youthfull Lord at *Lawrence* Cell,
And gaue him what becomed Loue I might,
Not stepping ore the bounds of modestie.

Cap. Why I am glad on't, this is well, stand vp,

This

This is as't should be, let me see the County:
I marrie go I say, and fetch him hither.
Now afore God, this reuerend holy Frier,
All our whole Cittie is much bound to him.

Iul. Nurse will you goe with me into my Closet,
To helpe me sort such needfull ornaments,
As you thinke fit to furnish me to morrow?

Mo. No not till Thursday, there's time inough.

Fa. Go Nurse, go with her,
Weele to Church to morrow.

Exeunt Iuliet and Nurse.

Mo. We shall be short in our prouision,
'Tis now neere night.

Fa. Tush, I will stirre about,
And all things shall be well, I warrant thee wife:
Go thou to *Iuliet*, helpe to deckeup her,
Ile not to bed to night, let me alone:
Ile play the huswife for this once. What ho?
They are all forth, well I will walke my selfe
To Countie *Paris*, to prepare him vp
Against to morrow, my heart is wondrous light,
Since this same way-ward Gyrle is so reclaim'd.

Exeunt Father and Mother.

Enter Iuliet and Nurse.

Iul. I those attires are best, but gentle Nurse
I pray thee leaue me to my selfe to night:
For I haue need of many Orysons,
To moue the heauens to smile vpon my state,
Which well thou know'st, is crosse and full of sin.

Enter Mother.

Mo. What are you busie ho? need you my help?

Iul. No Madam, we haue cul'd such necessaries
As are behoouefull for our state to morrow:
So please you, let me now be left alone;
And let the Nurse this night sit vp with you,
For I am sure, you haue your hands full all,
In this so sudden businesse.

Mo. Goodnight.
Get thee to bed and rest, for thou hast need. *Exeunt.*

Iul. Farewell:
God knowes when we shall meete againe.
I haue a faint cold feare thrills through my veines,
That almost freezes vp the heate of fire:
Ile call them backe againe to comfort me.
Nurse, what should she do here?
My dismall Sceane, I needs must act alone:
Come Viall, what if this mixture do not worke at all?
Shall I be married then to morrow morning?
No, no, this shall forbid it. Lie thou there,
What if it be a poyson which the Frier
Subtilly hath ministred to haue me dead,
Least in this marriage he should be dishonour'd,
Because he married me before to *Romeo*?
I feare it is, and yet me thinkes it should not,
For he hath still beene tried a holy man.
How, if when I am laid into the Tombe,
I wake before the time that *Romeo*
Come to redeeme me? There's a fearefull point:
Shall I not then be stifled in the Vault?
To whose foule mouth no healthsome ayre breaths in,
And there die strangled ere my *Romeo* comes.
Or if I liue, is it not very like,
The horrible conceit of death and night,
Together with the terror of the place,
As in a Vaulte, an ancient receptacle,

Where for these many hundred yeeres the bones
Of all my buried Auncestors are packt,
Where bloody *Tybalt*, yet but greene in earth,
Lies festring in his shrow'd, where as they say,
At some houres in the night, Spirits resort:
Alacke, alacke, is it not like that I
So early waking, what with loathsome smels,
And shrikes like Mandrakes torne out of the earth,
That liuing mortalls hearing them, run mad.
O if I walke, shall I not be distraught,
Inuironed with all these hidious feares,
And madly play with my forefathers ioynts?
And plucke the mangled *Tybalt* from his shrow'd?
And in this rage, with some great kinsmans bone,
As (with a club) dash out my desperate braines.
O looke, me thinks I see my Cozins Ghost,
Seeking out *Romeo* that did spit his body
Vpon my Rapiers point: stay *Tybalt*, stay;
Romeo, Romeo, Romeo, here's drinke: I drinke to thee.

Enter Lady of the house, and Nurse.

Lady. Hold,
Take these keies, and fetch more spices Nurse.

Nur. They call for Dates and Quinces in the Pastrie.

Enter old Capulet.

Cap. Come, stir, stir, stir,
The second Cocke hath Crow'd,
The Curphew Bell hath rung, 'tis three a clocke:
Looke to the bakte meates, good *Angelica*,
Spare not for cost.

Nur. Go you Cot-queane, go,
Get you to bed, faith youle be sicke to morrow
For this nights watching.

Cap. No not a whit: what? I haue watcht ere now
All night for lesse cause, and nere beene sicke.

La. I you haue bin a Mouse-hunt in your time,
But I will watch you from such watching now.

Exit Lady and Nurse.

Cap. A iealous hood, a iealous hood,
Now fellow, what there?

Enter three or foure with spits, and logs, and baskets.

Fel. Things for the Cooke sir, but I know not what.

Cap. Make hast, make hast, sirrah, fetch drier Logs.
Call *Peter*, he will shew thee where they are.

Fel. I haue a head sir, that will find out logs,
And neuer trouble *Peter* for the matter.

Cap. Masse and well said, a merrie horson, ha,
Thou shalt be loggerhead; good Father, 'tis day.

Play Musicke.

The Countie will be here with Musicke straight,
For so he said he would, I heare him neere,
Nurse, wife, what ho? what Nurse I say?

Enter Nurse.

Go waken *Iuliet*, go and trim her vp,
Ile go and chat with *Paris*: hie, make hast,
Make hast, the Bridegroome, he is come already:
Make hast I say.

Nur. Mistris, what Mistris? *Iuliet*? Fast I warrant her she.
Why Lambe, why Lady, fie you sluggabed,
Why Loue I say? Madam, sweet heart: why Bride?
What not a word? You take your peniworths now.
Sleepe for a weeke, for the next night I warrant
The Countie *Paris* hath set vp his rest,
That you shall rest but little, God forgiue me:
Marrie and Amen: how sound is she asleepe?

I must needs wake her: Madam, Madam, Madam,
I, let the Countie take you in your bed,
Heele fright you vp yfaith. Will it not be?
What drest, and in your clothes, and downe againe?
I must needs wake you: Lady, Lady, Lady?
Alas, alas, helpe, helpe, my Ladyes dead,
Oh weladay, that euer I was borne,
Some Aqua-vitæ ho, my Lord, my Lady?

  Mo. What noise is heere?   *Enter Mother.*
  Nur. O lamentable day.
  Mo. What is the matter?
  Nur. Looke, looke, oh heauie day.
  Mo. O me, O me, my Child, my onely life:
Reuiue, looke vp, or I will die with thee:
Helpe, helpe, call helpe.

    Enter Father.
  Fa. For shame bring *Iuliet* forth, her Lord is come.
  Nur. Shee's dead: deceast, shee's dead: alacke the day.
  M. Alacke the day, shee's dead, shee's dead, shee's dead.
  Fa. Ha? Let me see her: out alas shee's cold,
Her blood is setled and her ioynts are stiffe:
Life and these lips haue long bene seperated:
Death lies on her like an vntimely frost
Vpon the sweetest flower of all the field.
  Nur. O Lamentable day!
  Mo. O wofull time.
  Fa. Death that hath tane her hence to make me waile,
Ties vp my tongue, and will not let me speake.

    Enter Frier and the Countie.
  Fri. Come, is the Bride ready to go to Church?
  Fa. Ready to go, but neuer to returne.
O Sonne, the night before thy wedding day,
Hath death laine with thy wife: there she lies,
Flower as she was, deflowred by him.
Death is my Sonne in law, death is my Heire,
My Daughter he hath wedded. I will die,
And leaue him all life liuing, all is deaths.
  Pa. Haue I thought long to see this mornings face,
And doth it giue me such a sight as this?
  Mo. Accur'st, vnhappie, wretched hatefull day,
Most miserable houre, that ere time saw
In lasting labour of his Pilgrimage.
But one, poore one, one poore and louing Child,
But one thing to reioyce and solace in,
And cruell death hath catcht it from my sight.
  Nur. O wo, O wofull, wofull, wofull day,
Most lamentable day, most wofull day,
That euer, euer, I did yet behold.
O day, O day, O day, O hatefull day,
Neuer was seene so blacke a day as this:
O wofull day, O wofull day.
  Pa. Beguild, diuorced, wronged, spighted, slaine,
Most detestable death, by thee beguil'd,
By cruell, cruell thee, quite ouerthrowne:
O loue, O life; not life, but loue in death.
  Fat. Despis'd, distressed, hated, martir'd, kil'd,
Vncomfortable time, why cam'st thou now
To murther, murther our solemnitie?
O Child, O Child; my soule, and not my Child,
Dead art thou, alacke my Child is dead,
And with my Child, my ioyes are buried.
  Fri. Peace ho for shame, confusions: Care liues not
In these confusions, heauen and your selfe
Had part in this faire Maid, now heauen hath all,
And all the better is it for the Maid:
Your part in her, you could not keepe from death,
But heauen keepes his part in eternall life:
The most you sought was her promotion,
For 'twas your heauen, she shouldst be aduan'st,
And weepe ye now, seeing she is aduan'st
Aboue the Cloudes, as high as Heauen it selfe?
O in this loue, you loue your Child so ill,
That you run mad, seeing that she is well:
Shee's not well married, that liues married long,
But shee's best married, that dies married yong.
Drie vp your teares, and sticke your Rosemarie
On this faire Coarse, and as the custome is,
And in her best array beare her to Church:
For though some Nature bids all vs lament,
Yet Natures teares are Reasons merriment.

  Fa. All things that we ordained Festiuall,
Turne from their office to blacke Funerall:
Our instruments to melancholy Bells,
Our wedding cheare, to a sad buriall Feast:
Our solemne Hymnes, to sullen Dyrges change:
Our Bridall flowers serue for a buried Coarse:
And all things change them to the contrarie.
  Fri. Sir go you in; and Madam, go with him,
And go sir *Paris*, euery one prepare
To follow this faire Coarse vnto her graue:
The heauens do lowre vpon you, for some ill:
Moue them no more, by crossing their high will. *Exeunt*
  Mu. Faith we may put vp our Pipes and be gone.
  Nur. Honest goodfellowes: Ah put vp, put vp,
For well you know, this is a pitifull case.
  Mu. I by my troth, the case may be amended.

    Enter Peter.
  Pet. Musitions, oh Musitions,
Hearts ease, hearts ease,
O, and you will haue me liue, play hearts ease.
  Mu. Why hearts ease;
  Pet. O Musitions,
Because my heart it selfe plaies, my heart is full.
  Mu. Not a dump we, 'tis no time to play now.
  Pet. You will not then?
  Mu. No.
  Pet. I will then giue it you soundly.
  Mu. What will you giue vs?
  Pet. No money on my faith, but the gleeke.
I will giue you the Minstrell.
  Mu. Then will I giue you the Seruing creature.
  Peter. Then will I lay the seruing Creatures Dagger
on your pate. I will carie no Crochets, Ile Re you, Ile Fa
you, do you note me?
  Mu. And you Re vs, and Fa vs, you Note vs.
  2.M. Pray you put vp your Dagger,
And put out your wit.
Then haue at you with my wit.
  Peter. I will drie-beate you with an yron wit,
And put vp my yron Dagger.
Answere me like men:
When griping griefes the heart doth wound, then Mu-
sicke with her siluer sound.
Why siluer sound? why Musicke with her siluer sound?
what say you *Simon Catling*?
  Mu. Mary sir, because siluer hath a sweet sound.
  Pet. Pratest, what say you *Hugh Rebicke*?
  2.M. I say siluer sound, because Musitions sound for sil-
  Pet. Pratest to, what say you *Iames Sound-Post*? (uer
  3.Mu. Faith I know not what to say.
  Pet. O I cry you mercy, you are the Singer.
I will say for you; it is Musicke with her siluer sound,

Because Musitions haue no gold for sounding:
Then Musicke with her siluer sound, with speedy helpe
doth lend redresse. *Exit.*

Mu. What a pestilent knaue is this same?

M. 2. Hang him Iacke, come weele in here, tarrie for
the Mourners, and stay dinner. *Exit.*

Enter Romeo.

Rom. If I may trust the flattering truth of sleepe,
My dreames presage some ioyfull newes at hand:
My bosomes L. sits lightly in his throne:
And all thisan day an vccustom'd spirit,
Lifts me aboue the ground with cheerefull thoughts.
I dreamt my Lady came and found me dead,
(Strange dreame that giues a dead man leaue to thinke,)
And breath'd such life with kisses in my lips,
That I reuiu'd and was an Emperour.
Ah me, how sweet is loue it selfe possest,
When but loues shadowes are so rich in ioy.

Enter Romeo's man.

Newes from *Verona*, how now *Balthazer*?
Dost thou not bring me Letters from the Frier?
How doth my Lady? Is my Father well?
How doth my Lady *Iuliet*? that I aske againe,
For nothing can be ill, if she be well.

Man. Then she is well, and nothing can be ill.
Her body sleepes in *Capels* Monument,
And her immortall part with Angels liue,
I saw her laid low in her kindreds Vault,
And presently tooke Poste to tell it you:
O pardon me for bringing these ill newes,
Since you did leaue it for my office Sir.

Rom. Is it euen so?
Then I denie you Starres.
Thou knowest my lodging, get me inke and paper,
And hire Post-Horses, I will hence to night.

Man. I do beseech you sir, haue patience:
Your lookes are pale and wild, and do import
Some misaduenture.

Rom. Tush, thou art deceiu'd,
Leaue me, and do the thing I bid thee do.
Hast thou no Letters to me from the Frier?

Man. No my good Lord. *Exit Man.*

Rom. No matter: Get thee gone,
And hyre those Horses, Ile be with thee straight.
Well *Iuliet*, I will lie with thee to night:
Lets see for meanes: O mischiefe thou art swift,
To enter in the thoughts of desperate men:
I do remember an Appothecarie,
And here abouts dwells, which late I noted
In tattred weeds, with ouerwhelming browes,
Culling of Simples, meager were his lookes,
Sharpe miserie had worne him to the bones:
And in his needie shop a Tortoyrs hung,
An Allegater stuft, and other skins
Of ill shap'd fishes, and about his shelues,
A beggerly account of emptie boxes,
Greene earthen pots, Bladders, and mustie seedes,
Remnants of packthred, and old cakes of Roses
Were thinly scattered, to make vp a shew.
Noting this penury, to my selfe I said,
An if a man did need a poyson now,
Whose sale is persent death in *Mantua*,
Here liues a Caitiffe wretch would sell it him.
O this same thought did but fore-run my need,
And this same needie man must sell it me.
As I remember, this should be the house,
Being holy day, the beggers shop is shut,
What ho? Appothecarie?

Enter Appothecarie.

App. Who call's so low'd?

Rom. Come hither man, I see that thou art poore,
Hold, there is fortie Duckets, let me haue
A dram of poyson, such soone speeding geare,
As will disperse it selfe through all the veines,
That the life-wearie-taker may fall dead,
And that the Trunke may be discharg'd of breath,
As violently, as hastie powder fier'd
Doth hurry from the fatall Canons wombe.

App. Such mortall drugs I haue, but *Mantuas* law
Is death to any he, that vtters them.

Rom. Art thou so bare and full of wretchednesse,
And fear'st to die? Famine is in thy cheekes,
Need and opression starueth in thy eyes,
Contempt and beggery hangs vpon thy backe:
The world is not thy friend, nor the worlds law:
The world affords no law to make thee rich.
Then be not poore, but breake it, and take this.

App. My pouerty, but not my will consents.

Rom. I pray thy pouerty, and not thy will.

App. Put this in any liquid thing you will
And drinke it off, and if you had the strength
Of twenty men, it would dispatch you straight.

Rom. There's thy Gold,
Worse poyson to mens soules,
Doing more murther in this loathsome world,
Then these poore compounds that thou maiest not sell,
I sell thee poyson, thou hast sold me none,
Farewell, buy food, and get thy selfe in flesh,
Come Cordiall, and not poyson, go with me
To *Iuliets* graue, for there must I vse thee. *Exeunt.*

Enter Frier Iohn to Frier Lawrence.

Iohn. Holy *Franciscan* Frier, Brother, ho?

Enter Frier Lawrence.

Law. This same should be the voice of Frier *Iohn*.
Welcome from *Mantua*, what sayes *Romeo*?
Or if his mind be writ, giue me his Letter.

Iohn. Going to find a bare-foote Brother out,
One of our order to associate me,
Here in this Citie visiting the sick,
And finding him, the Searchers of the Towne
Suspecting that we both were in a house
Where the infectious pestilence did raigne,
Seal'd vp the doores, and would not let vs forth,
So that my speed to *Mantua* there was staid.

Law. Who bare my Letter then to *Romeo*?

Iohn. I could not send it, here it is againe,
Nor get a messenger to bring it thee,
So fearefull were they of infection.

Law. Vnhappie Fortune: by my Brotherhood
The Letter was not nice, but full of charge,
Of deare import, and the neglecting it
May do much danger: Frier *Iohn* go hence,
Get me an Iron Crow, and bring it straight
Vnto my Cell. *Exit.*

Iohn. Brother Ile go and bring it thee.

Law. Now must I to the Monument alone,
Within this three houres will faire *Iuliet* wake,
Shee will beshrew me much that *Romeo*
Hath had no notice of these accidents:
But I will write againe to *Mantua*,

And

The Tragedie of Romeo and Iuliet.

And keepe her at my Cell till *Romeo* come,
Poore liuing Coarse, clos'd in a dead mans Tombe, *Exit.*

Enter Paris and his Page.

Par. Giue me thy Torch Boy, hence and stand aloft,
Yet put it out, for I would not be seene:
Vnder yond young Trees lay thee all along,
Holding thy eare close to the hollow ground,
So shall no foot vpon the Churchyard tread,
Being loose, vnfirme with digging vp of Graues,
But thou shalt heare it: whistle then to me,
As signall that thou hear'st some thing approach,
Giue me those flowers. Do as I bid thee, go.

Page. I am almost afraid to stand alone
Here in the Churchyard, yet I will aduenture.

Pa. Sweet Flower with flowers thy Bridall bed I strew:
O woe, thy Canopie is dust and stones,
Which with sweet water nightly I will dewe,
Or wanting that, with teares destil'd by mones;
The obsequies that I for thee will keepe,
Nightly shall be, to strew thy graue, and weepe.
Whistle Boy.
The Boy giues warning, something doth approach,
What cursed foot wanders this wayes to night,
To crosse my obsequies, and true loues right?
What with a Torch? Muffle me night a while.

Enter Romeo, and Peter.

Rom. Giue me that Mattocke, & the wrenching Iron,
Hold take this Letter, early in the morning
See thou deliuer it to my Lord and Father,
Giue me the light; vpon thy life I charge thee,
What ere thou hear'st or seest, stand all aloofe,
And do not interrupt me in my course.
Why I descend into this bed of death,
Is partly to behold my Ladies face:
But chiefly to take thence from her dead finger,
A precious Ring: a Ring that I must vse,
In deare employment, therefore hence be gone:
But if thou iealous dost returne to prie
In what I further shall intend to do,
By heauen I will teare thee ioynt by ioynt,
And strew this hungry Churchyard with thy limbs:
The time, and my intents are sauage wilde:
More fierce and more inexorable farre,
Then emptie Tygers, or the roaring Sea.

Pet. I will be gone sir, and not trouble you

Ro. So shalt thou shew me friendship: take thou that,
Liue and be prosperous, and farewell good fellow.

Pet. For all this same, Ile hide me here about,
His lookes I feare, and his intents I doubt.

Rom. Thou detestable mawe, thou wombe of death,
Gorg'd with the dearest morsell of the earth:
Thus I enforce thy rotten Iawes to open,
And in despight, Ile cram thee with more food.

Par. This is that banisht haughtie *Mountague*,
That murdred my Loues Cozin; with which griefe,
It is supposed the faire Creature died,
And here is come to do some villanous shame
To the dead bodies: I will apprehend him.
Stop thy vnhallowed toyle, vile *Mountague*:
Can vengeance be pursued further then death?
Condemned vallaine, I do apprehend thee.
Obey and go with me, for thou must die,

Rom. I must indeed, and therfore came I hither:
Good gentle youth, tempt not a desperate man,
Flie hence and leaue me, thinke vpon those gone,
Let them affright thee. I beseech thee Youth,
Put not an other sin vpon my head,
By vrging me to furie. O be gone,
By heauen I loue thee better then my selfe,
For I come hither arm'd against my selfe:
Stay not, be gone, liue, and hereafter say,
A mad mans mercy bid thee run away.

Par. I do defie thy commiseration,
And apprehend thee for a Fellon here.

Ro. Wilt thou prouoke me? Then haue at thee Boy.

Pet. O Lord they fight, I will go call the Watch.

Pa. O I am slaine, if thou be mercifull,
Open the Tombe, lay me with *Iuliet*.

Rom. In faith I will, let me peruse this face:
Mercutius kinsman, Noble Countie *Paris*,
What said my man, when my betossed soule
Did not attend him as we rode? I thinke
He told me *Paris* should haue married *Iuliet*.
Said he not so? Or did I dreame it so?
Or am I mad, hearing him talke of *Iuliet*,
To thinke it was so? O giue me thy hand,
One, writ with me in sowre misfortunes booke.
Ile burie thee in a triumphant graue.
A Graue; O no, a Lanthorne; slaughtred Youth:
For here lies *Iuliet*, and her beautie makes
This Vault a feasting presence full of light.
Death lie thou there, by a dead man inter'd.
How oft when men are at the point of death,
Haue they beene merrie? Which their Keepers call
A lightning before death? Oh how may I
Call this a lightning? O my Loue, my Wife,
Death that hath suckt the honey of thy breath,
Hath had no power yet vpon thy Beautie:
Thou art not conquer'd: Beauties ensigne yet
Is Crymson in thy lips, and in thy cheekes,
And Deaths pale flag is not aduanced there.
Tybalt, ly'st thou there in thy bloudy sheet?
O what more fauour can I do to thee,
Then with that hand that cut thy youth in twaine,
To sunder his that was thy enemie?
Forgiue me Cozen. Ah deare *Iuliet*:
Why art thou yet so faire? I will beleeue,
Shall I beleeue, that vnsubstantiall death is amorous?
And that the leane abhorred Monster keepes
Thee here in darke to be his Paramour?
For feare of that, I still will stay with thee,
And neuer from this Pallace of dym night
Depart againe: come lie thou in my armes,
Heere's to thy health, where ere thou tumblest in.
O true Appothecarie!
Thy drugs are quicke. Thus with a kisse I die.
Depart againe; here, here will I remaine,
With Wormes that are thy Chambermaides: O here
Will I set vp my euerlasting rest:
And shake the yoke of inauspicious starres
From this world-wearied flesh: Eyes looke your last:
Armes take your last embrace: And lips, O you
The doores of breath, seale with a righteous kisse
A datelesse bargaine to ingrossing death:
Come bitter conduct, come vnsauoury guide,
Thou desperate Pilot, now at once run on
The dashing Rocks, thy Sea-sicke wearie Barke:
Heere's to my Loue. O true Appothecary:

Thy drugs are quicke. Thus with a kisse I die.
Enter Frier with Lanthorne, Crow, and Spade.

Fri. St. Francis be my speed, how oft to night
Haue my old feet stumbled at graues? Who's there?

Man. Here's one, a Friend, & one that knowes you well.

Fri. Blisse be vpon you. Tell me good my Friend
What Torch is yond that vainely lends his light
To grubs, and eyelesse Sculles? As I discerne,
It burneth in the *Capels* Monument.

Man. It doth so holy sir,
And there's my Master, one that you loue.

Fri. Who is it?

Man. *Romeo.*

Fri. How long hath he bin there?

Man. Full halfe an houre.

Fri. Go with me to the Vault.

Man. I dare not Sir.
My Master knowes not but I am gone hence,
And fearefully did menace me with death,
If I did stay to looke on his entents.

Fri. Stay, then Ile go alone, feares comes vpon me,
O much I feare some ill vnluckie thing.

Man. As I did sleepe vnder this young tree here,
I dreamt my maister and another fought,
And that my Maister slew him.

Fri. Romeo.
Alacke, alacke, what blood is this which staines
The stony entrance of this Sepulcher?
What meane these Masterlesse, and goarie Swords
To lie discolour'd by this place of peace?
Romeo, oh pale: who else? what *Paris* too?
And steept in blood? Ah what an vnknd houre
Is guiltie of this lamentable chance?
The Lady stirs.

Iul. O comfortable Frier, where's my Lord?
I do remember well where I should be:
And there I am, where is my *Romeo*?

Fri. I heare some noyse Lady, come from that nest
Of death, contagion, and vnnaturall sleepe,
A greater power then we can contradict
Hath thwarted our entents, come, come away,
Thy husband in thy bosome there lies dead:
And *Paris* too: come Ile dispose of thee,
Among a Sisterhood of holy Nunnes:
Stay not to question, for the watch is comming.
Come, go good *Iuliet*, I dare no longer stay. *Exit.*

Iul. Go get thee hence, for I will not away,
What's here? A cup clos'd in my true loues hand?
Poyson I see hath bin his timelesse end
O churle, drinke all? and left no friendly drop,
To helpe me after, I will kisse thy lips,
Happlie some poyson yet doth hang on them,
To make me die wth a restoratiue.
Thy lips are warme.

Enter Boy and Watch.

Watch. Lead Boy, which way?

Iul. Yea noise?
Then ile be briefe. O happy Dagger.
'Tis in thy sheath, there rust and let me die *Kils herselfe.*

Boy. This is the place,
There where the Torch doth burne

Watch. The ground is bloody,
Search about the Churchyard.
Go some of you, who ere you find attach.
Pittifull sight, here lies the Countie slaine,
And *Iuliet* bleeding, warme and newly dead

Who here hath laine these two dayes buried.
Go tell the Prince, runne to the *Capulets*,
Raise vp the *Mountagues*, some others search,
We see the ground whereon these woes do lye,
But the true ground of all these piteous woes,
We cannot without circumstance descry.

Enter Romeo's man.

Watch. Here's *Romeo*'r man,
We found him in the Churchyard.

Con. Hold him in safety, till the Prince come hither.

Enter Frier, and another Watchman.

3. Wat. Here is a Frier that trembles, sighes, and weepes:
We tooke this Mattocke and this Spade from him,
As he was comming from this Church-yard side.

Con. A great suspition, stay the Frier too.

Enter the Prince.

Prin. What misaduenture is so earely vp,
That calls our person from our mornings rest?

Enter Capulet and his Wife.

Cap. What should it be that they so shrike abroad?

Wife. O the people in the streete crie *Romeo*,
Some *Iuliet*, and some *Paris*, and all runne
With open outcry toward our Monument.

Pri. What feare is this which startles in your eares?

Wat. Soueraigne, here lies the Countie *Paris* slaine,
And *Romeo* dead, and *Iuliet* dead before,
Warme and new kil'd.

Prin. Search,
Seeke, and know how, this foule murder comes.

Wat. Here is a Frier, and Slaughter'd *Romeos* man,
With Instruments vpon them fit to open
These dead mens Tombes.

Cap. O heauen!
O wife looke how our Daughter bleedes!
This Dagger hath mistaine, for loe his house
Is empty on the backe of *Mountague*,
And is misheathed in my Daughters bosome.

Wife. O me, this sight of death, is as a Bell
That warnes my old age to a Sepulcher.

Enter Mountague.

Pri. Come *Mountague*, for thou art early vp
To see thy Sonne and Heire, now early downe.

Moun. Alas my liege, my wife is dead to night,
Griefe of my Sonnes exile hath stopt her breath:
What further woe conspires against my age?

Prin. Looke, and thou shalt see.

Moun. O thou vntaught, what manners in is this,
To presse before thy Father to a graue?

Prin. Seale vp the mouth of outrage for a while,
Till we can cleare these ambiguities,
And know their spring, their head, their true descent,
And then will I be generall of your woes,
And lead you euen to death? meane time forbeare,
And let mischance be slaue to patience,
Bring forth the parties of suspition.

Fri. I am the greatest, able to doe least,
Yet most suspected as the time and place
Doth make against me of this direfull murther:
And heere I stand both to impeach and purge
My selfe condemned, and my selfe excus'd.

Prin. Then say at once, what thou dost know in this?

Fri. I will be briefe, for my short date of breath
Is not so long as is a tedious tale.
Romeo there dead, was husband to that *Iuliet*,
And she there dead, that's *Romeos* faithfull wife:

The Tragedie of Romeo and Iuliet.   79

I married them; and their stolne marriage day
Was *Tybalts* Doomesday: whose vntimely death
Banish'd the new-made Bridegroome from this Citie:
For whom (and not for *Tybalt*) *Iuliet* pinde.
You, to remoue that siege of Greefe from her,
Betroth'd, and would haue married her perforce
To Countie *Paris*. Then comes she to me,
And (with wilde lookes) bid me deuise some meanes
To rid her from this second Marriage,
Or in my Cell there would she kill her selfe.
Then gaue I her (so Tutor'd by my Art)
A sleeping Potion, which so tooke effect
As I intended, for it wrought on her
The forme of death. Meane time, I writ to *Romeo*,
That he should hither come, as this dyre night,
To helpe to take her from her borrowed graue,
Being the time the Potions force should cease.
But he which bore my Letter, Frier *Iohn*,
Was stay'd by accident; and yesternight
Return'd my Letter backe. Then all alone,
At the prefixed houre of her waking,
Came I to take her from her Kindreds vault,
Meaning to keepe her closely at my Cell,
Till I conueniently could send to *Romeo*.
But when I came (some Minute ere the time
Of her awaking) heere vntimely lay
The Noble *Paris*, and true *Romeo* dead.
Shee wakes, and I intreated her come foorth,
And beare this worke of Heauen, with patience:
But then, a noyse did scarre me from the Tombe,
And she (too desperate) would not go with me,
But (as it seemes) did violence on her selfe.
All this I know, and to the Marriage her Nurse is priuy:
And if ought in this miscarried by my fault,
Let my old life be sacrific'd, some houre before the time,
Vnto the rigour of seuerest Law.

 Prin. We still haue knowne thee for a Holy man.
Where's *Romeo's* man? What can he say to this?

 Boy. I brought my Master newes of *Iuliets* death,
And then in poste he came from *Mantua*
To this same place, to this same Monument.
This Letter he early bid me giue his Father,
And threatned me with death, going in the Vault,
If I departed not, and left him there.

 Prin. Giue me the Letter, I will look on it.
Where is the Counties Page that rais'd the Watch?
Sirra, what made your Master in this place?

 Page. He came with flowres to strew his Ladies graue,
And bid me stand aloofe, and so I did:
Anon comes one with light to ope the Tombe,
And by and by my Maister drew on him,
And then I ran away to call the Watch.

 Prin. This Letter doth make good the Friers words,
Their course of Loue, the tydings of her death:
And heere he writes, that he did buy a poyson
Of a poore Pothecarie, and therewithall
Came to this Vault to dye, and lye with *Iuliet*.
Where be these Enemies? *Capulet, Mountague,*
See what a scourge is laide vpon your hate,
That Heauen finds meanes to kill your ioyes with Loue;
And I, for winking at your discords too,
Haue lost a brace of Kinsmen: All are punish'd.

 Cap. O Brother *Mountague*, giue me thy hand,
This is my Daughters ioynture, for no more
Can I demand.

 Moun. But I can giue thee more:
For I will raise her Statue in pure Gold,
That whiles *Verona* by that name is knowne,
There shall no figure at that Rate be set,
As that of True and Faithfull *Iuliet*.

 Cap. As rich shall *Romeo* by his Lady ly,
Poore sacrifices of our enmity.

 Prin. A glooming peace this morning with it brings,
The Sunne for sorrow will not shew his head;
Go hence, to haue more talke of these sad things,
Some shall be pardon'd, and some punished.
For neuer was a Storie of more Wo,
Then this of *Iuliet*, and her *Romeo*. *Exeunt omnes*

Gg

FINIS.

THE LIFE OF TYMON OF ATHENS.

Actus Primus. Scœna Prima.

Enter Poet, Painter, Ieweller, Merchant, and Mercer, at seuerall doores.

Poet. Good day Sir.
  Pain. I am glad y'are well.
  Poet. I haue not seene you long, how goes the World?
  Pain. It weares sir, as it growes.
  Poet. I that's well knowne:
But what particular Rarity? What strange,
Which manifold record not matches: see
Magicke of Bounty, all these spirits thy power
Hath conjur'd to attend. I know the Merchant.
  Pain. I know them both: th'other's a Ieweller.
  Mer. O 'tis a worthy Lord.
  Iew. Nay that's most fixt.
  Mer. A most incomparable man, breath'd as it were,
To an vntyreable and continuate goodnesse:
He passes.
  Iew. I haue a Iewell heere.
  Mer. O pray let's see't. For the Lord *Timon*, sir?
  Iewel. If he will touch the estimate. But for that——
  Poet. When we for recompence haue prais'd the vild,
It staines the glory in that happy Verse,
Which aptly sings the good.
  Mer. 'Tis a good forme.
  Iewel. And rich: heere is a Water looke ye.
  Pain. You are rapt sir, in some worke, some Dedication to the great Lord.
  Poet. A thing slipt idlely from me.
Our Poesie is as a Gowne, which vses
From whence 'tis nourisht: the fire i'th'Flint
Shewes not, till it be strooke: our gentle flame
Prouokes it selfe, and like the currant flyes
Each bound it chafes. What haue you there?
  Pain. A Picture sir: when comes your Booke forth?
  Poet. Vpon the heeles of my presentment sir.
Let's see your peece.
  Pain. 'Tis a good Peece.
  Poet. So 'tis, this comes off well, and excellent.
  Pain. Indifferent.
  Poet. Admirable: How this grace
Speakes his owne standing: what a mentall power
This eye shootes forth? How bigge imagination
Moues in this Lip, to th'dumbnesse of the gesture,
One might interpret.
  Pain. It is a pretty mocking of the life:
Heere is a touch: Is't good?
  Poet. I will say of it,
It Tutors Nature, Artificiall strife
Liues in these touches, liuelier then life.

Enter certaine Senators.

  Pain. How this Lord is followed.
  Poet. The Senators of Athens, happy men.
  Pain. Looke moe.
  Po. You see this confluence, this great flood of visitors,
I haue in this rough worke, shap'd out a man
Whom this beneath world doth embrace and hugge
With amplest entertainment: My free drift
Halts not particularly, but moues it selfe
In a wide Sea of wax, no leuell'd malice
Infects one comma in the course I hold,
But flies an Eagle flight, bold, and forth on,
Leauing no Tract behinde.
  Pain. How shall I vnderstand you?
  Poet. I will vnboult to you.
You see how all Conditions, how all Mindes,
As well of glib and slipp'ry Creatures, as
Of Graue and austere qualitie, tender downe
Their seruices to Lord *Timon*: his large Fortune,
Vpon his good and gracious Nature hanging,
Subdues and properties to his loue and tendance
All sorts of hearts; yea, from the glasse-fac'd Flatterer
To *Apemantus*, that few things loues better
Then to abhorre himselfe: euen hee drops downe
The knee before him, and returnes in peace
Most rich in *Timons* nod.
  Pain. I saw them speake together.
  Poet. Sir, I haue vpon a high and pleasant hill
Feign'd Fortune to be thron'd.
The Base o'th'Mount
Is rank'd with all deserts, all kinde of Natures
That labour on the bosome of this Sphere,
To propagate their states; among'st them all,
Whose eyes are on this Soueraigne Lady fixt,
One do I personate of Lord *Timons* frame,
Whom Fortune with her Iuory hand wafts to her,
Whose present grace, to present slaues and seruants
Translates his Riuals.
  Pain. 'Tis conceyu'd, to scope
This Throne, this Fortune, and this Hill me thinkes

With one man becken'd from the rest below,
Bowing his head against the steepy Mount
To climbe his happinesse, would be well exprest
In our Condition.

Poet. Nay Sir, but heare me on:
All those which were his Fellowes but of late,
Some better then his valew; on the moment
Follow his strides, his Lobbies fill with tendance,
Raine Sacrificiall whisperings in his eare,
Make Sacred euen his styrrop, and through him
Drinke the free Ayre.

Pain. I marry, what of these?

Poet. When Fortune in her shift and change of mood
Spurnes downe her late beloued; all his Dependants
Which labour'd after him to the Mountaines top,
Euen on their knees and hand, let him sit downe,
Not one accompanying his declining foot.

Pain. Tis common:
A thousand morall Paintings I can shew,
That shall demonstrate these quicke blowes of Fortunes,
More pregnantly then words. Yet you do well,
To shew Lord *Timon*, that meane eyes haue seene
The foot aboue the head.

Trumpets sound.
Enter Lord Timon, addressing himselfe curteously to euery Suter.

Tim. Imprison'd is he, say you?
Mes. I my good Lord, fiue Talents is his debt,
His meanes most short, his Creditors most straite:
Your Honourable Letter he desires
To those haue shut him vp, which failing,
Periods his comfort.

Tim. Noble *Ventidius* well:
I am not of that Feather, to shake off
My Friend when he must neede me. I do know him
A Gentleman, that well deserues a helpe,
Which he shall haue. Ile pay the debt, and free him.

Mes. Your Lordship euer bindes him.

Tim. Commend me to him, I will send his ransome,
And being enfranchized bid him come to me;
'Tis not enough to helpe the Feeble vp,
But to support him after. Fare you well.

Mes. All happinesse to your Honor. *Exit.*

Enter an old Athenian.

Oldm. Lord *Timon*, heare me speake.
Tim. Freely good Father.
Oldm. Thou hast a Seruant nam'd *Lucilius*.
Tim. I haue so: What of him?
Oldm. Most Noble *Timon*, call the man before thee.
Tim. Attends he heere, or no? *Lucillius*.
Luc. Heere at your Lordships seruice.
Oldm. This Fellow heere, L. *Timon*, this thy Creature,
By night frequents my house. I am a man
That from my first haue beene inclin'd to thrift,
And my estate deserues an Heyre more rais'd,
Then one which holds a Trencher.

Tim. Well: what further?

Old. One onely Daughter haue I, no Kin else,
On whom I may conferre what I haue got:
The Maid is faire, a'th'youngest for a Bride,
And I haue bred her at my deerest cost
In Qualities of the best. This man of thine
Attempts her loue: I prythee (Noble Lord)
Ioyne with me to forbid him her resort,
My selfe haue spoke in vaine.

Tim. The man is honest.
Oldm. Therefore he will be *Timon*,
His honesty rewards him in it selfe,
It must not beare my Daughter.

Tim. Does she loue him?
Oldm. She is yong and apt:
Our owne precedent passions do instruct vs
What leuities in youth.

Tim. Loue you the Maid?
Luc. I my good Lord, and she accepts of it.
Oldm. If in her Marriage my consent be missing,
I call the Gods to witnesse, I will choose.
Mine heyre from forth the Beggers of the world,
And dispossesse her all.

Tim. How shall she be endowed,
If she be mated with an equall Husband?
Oldm. Three Talents on the present; in future, all.
Tim. This Gentleman of mine
Hath seru'd me long:
To build his Fortune, I will straine a little,
For 'tis a Bond in men. Giue him thy Daughter,
What you bestow, in him Ile counterpoize,
And make him weigh with her.

Oldm. Most Noble Lord,
Pawne me to this your Honour, she is his.
Tim. My hand to thee,
Mine Honour on my promise.
Luc. Humbly I thanke your Lordship, neuer may
That state or Fortune fall into my keeping,
Which is not owed to you. *Exit*

Poet. Vouchsafe my Labour,
And long liue your Lordship.
Tim. I thanke you, you shall heare from me anon:
Go not away. What haue you there, my Friend?
Pain. A peece of Painting, which I do beseech
Your Lordship to accept.
Tim. Painting is welcome.
The Painting is almost the Naturall man:
For since Dishonor Traffickes with mans Nature,
He is but out-side: These Pensil'd Figures are
Euen such as they giue out. I like your worke,
And you shall finde I like it; Waite attendance
Till you heare further from me.

Pain. The Gods preserue ye.
Tim. Well fare you Gentleman: giue me your hand.
We must needs dine together: sir your Iewell
Hath suffered vnder praise.

Iewel. What my Lord, dispraise?
Tim. A meere saciety of Commendations,
If I should pay you for't as 'tis extold,
It would vnclew me quite.

Iewel. My Lord, 'tis rated
As those which sell would giue: but you well know,
Things of like valew differing in the Owners,
Are prized by their Masters. Beleeu't deere Lord,
You mend the Iewell by the wearing it.

Tim. Well mock'd. *Enter Apermantus.*
Mer. No my good Lord, he speakes y common toong
Which all men speake with him.

Tim. Looke who comes heere, will you be chid?
Iewel. Wee'l beare with your Lordship.
Mer. Hee'l spare none.
Tim. Good morrow to thee,
Gentle *Apermantus*.

Aper.

Ape. Till I be gentle, stay thou for thy good morrow. When thou art *Timons* dogge, and these Knaues honest.

Tim. Why dost thou call them Knaues, thou know'st them not?

Ape. Are they not Athenians?

Tim. Yes.

Ape. Then I repent not.

Iew. You know me, *Apemantus*?

Ape. Thou know'st I do, I call'd thee by thy name.

Tim. Thou art proud *Apemantus*?

Ape. Of nothing so much, as that I am not like *Timon*

Tim. Whether art going?

Ape. To knocke out an honest Athenians braines.

Tim. That's a deed thou't dye for.

Ape. Right, if doing nothing be death by th'Law.

Tim. How lik'st thou this picture *Apemantus*?

Ape. The best, for the innocence.

Tim. Wrought he not well that painted it.

Ape. He wrought better that made the Painter, and yet he's but a filthy peece of worke.

Pain. Y'are a Dogge.

Ape. Thy Mothers of my generation : what's she, if I be a Dogge?

Tim. Wilt dine with me *Apemantus*?

Ape. No : I eate not Lords.

Tim. And thou should'st, thoud'st anger Ladies.

Ape. O they eate Lords ; So they come by great bellies.

Tim. That's a lasciuious apprehension.

Ape. So, thou apprehend'st it, Take it for thy labour.

Tim. How dost thou like this Iewell, *Apemantus*?

Ape. Not so well as plain-dealing, which will not cast a man a Doit.

Tim. What dost thou thinke 'tis worth?

Ape. Not worth my thinking. How now Poet?

poet. How now Philosopher?

pe. Thou lyest.

Poet. Art not one?

Ape. Yes.

Poet. Then I lye not.

Ape. Art not a Poet?

Poet. Yes.

Ape. Then thou lyest : Looke in thy last worke, where thou hast fegin'd him a worthy Fellow.

Poet. That's not feign'd, he is so.

Ape. Yes he is worthy of thee, and to pay thee for thy labour. He that loues to be flattered, is worthy o'th flatterer. Heauens, that I were a Lord.

Tim. What wouldst do then *Apemantus*?

Ape. E'ne as *Apemantus* does now, hate a Lord with my heart.

Tim. What thy selfe?

Ape. I.

Tim. Wherefore?

Ape. That I had no angry wit to be a Lord. Art not thou a Merchant?

Mer. I *Apemantus*.

Ape. Traffick confound thee, if the Gods will not.

Mer. If Trafficke do it, the Gods do it.

Ape. Traffickes thy God, & thy God confound thee.

Trumpet sounds. Enter a Messenger.

Tim. What Trumpets that?

Mes. 'Tis *Alcibiades*, and some twenty Horse All of Companionship.

Tim. Pray entertaine them, giue them guide to vs. You must needs dine with me : go not you hence Till I haue thankt you : when dinners done Shew me this peece. I am ioyfull of your sights.

Enter Alcibiades with the rest.

Most welcome Sir.

Ape. So, so ; their Aches contract, and sterue your supple ioynts : that there should bee small loue amongst these sweet Knaues, and all this Curtesie. The straine of mans bred out into Baboon and Monkey.

Alc. Sir, you haue sau'd my longing, and I feed Most hungerly on your sight.

Tim. Right welcome Sir : Ere we depart, wee'l share a bounteous time In different pleasures. Pray you let vs in.

Exeunt.

Enter two Lords.

1. *Lord* What time a day is't *Apemantus*?

Ape. Time to be honest.

1 That time serues still.

Ape. The most accursed thou that still omitst it.

2 Thou art going to Lord *Timons* Feast.

Ape. I, to see meate fill Knaues, and Wine heat fooles.

2 Farthee well, farthee well.

Ape. Thou art a Foole to bid me farewell twice.

2 Why *Apemantus*?

Ape. Should'st haue kept one to thy selfe, for I meane to giue thee none.

1 Hang thy selfe.

Ape. No I will do nothing at thy bidding : Make thy requests to thy Friend.

2 Away vnpeaceable Dogge, Or Ile spurne thee hence.

Ape. I will flye like a dogge, the heeles a'th'Asse.

1 Hee's opposite to humanity. Comes shall we in, And taste Lord *Timons* bountie : he out-goes The verie heart of kindnesse.

2 He powres it out : *Plutus* the God of Gold Is but his Steward : no meede but he repayes Seuen-fold aboue it selfe : No guift to him, But breeds the giuer a returne : exceeding All vse of quittance.

1 The Noblest minde he carries, That euer gouern'd man.

2 Long may he liue in Fortunes. Shall we in? Ile keepe you Company.

Exeunt.

Hoboyes Playing lowd Musicke.

A great Banquet seru'd in : and then, Enter Lord Timon, the States, the Athenian Lords, Ventigius which Timon redeem'd from prison. Then comes dropping after all Apemantus discontentedly like himselfe.

Ventig. Most honoured *Timon*, It hath pleas'd the Gods to remember my Fathers age, And call him to long peace : He is gone happy, and has left me rich : Then, as in gratefull Vertue I am bound To your free heart, I do returne those Talents Doubled with thankes and seruice, from whose helpe I deriu'd libertie.

Tim. O by no meanes, Honest *Ventigius* : You mistake my loue,

I gaue

Timon of Athens.

I gaue it freely euer, and ther's none
Can truely say he giues, if he recciues:
If our betters play at that game, we must not dare
To imitate them: faults that are rich are faire.

Vint. A Noble spirit.

Tim. Nay my Lords, Ceremony was but deuis'd at first
To set a glosse on faint deeds, hollow welcomes,
Recanting goodnesse, sorry ere 'tis showne:
But where there is true friendship, there needs none.
Pray sit, more welcome are ye to my Fortunes,
Then my Fortunes to me.

1. Lord. My Lord, we alwaies haue confest it.

Aper. Ho ho, confest it? Handg'd it? Haue you not?

Tim. O *Apermantus*, you are welcome.

Aper. No: You shall not make me welcome:
I come to haue thee thrust me out of doores.

Tim. Fie, th'art a churle, ye'haue got a humour there
Does not become a man, 'tis much too blame:
They say my Lords, *Ira furor breuis est*,
But yond man is verie angrie.
Go, let him haue a Table by himselfe:
For he does neither affect companie,
Nor is he fit for't indeed.

Aper. Let me stay at thine apperill *Timon*,
I come to obserue, I giue thee warning on't.

Tim. I take no heede of thee: Th'art an *Athenian*,
therefore welcome: I my selfe would haue no power,
prythee let my meate make thee silent.

Aper. I scorne thy meate, 'twould choake me: for I
should nere flatter thee. Oh you Gods! What a number
of men eats *Timon*, and he sees 'em not? It greeues me
to see so many dip there meate in one mans blood, and
all the madnesse is, he cheeres them vp too.
I wonder men dare trust themselues with men,
Me thinks they should enuite them without kniues,
Good for there meate, and safer for their liues.
There's much example for't, the fellow that sits next him,
now parts bread with him, pledges the breath of him in
a diuided draught: is the readiest man to kill him. 'Tas
beene proued, if I were a huge man I should feare to
drinke at meales, least they should spie my wind-pipes
dangerous noates, great men should drinke with harnesse
on their throates.

Tim. My Lord in heart: and let the health go round.

2. Lord. Let it flow this way my good Lord.

Aper. Flow this way? A braue fellow. He keepes his
tides well, those healths will make thee and thy state
looke ill, *Timon*.
Heere's that which is too weake to be a sinner,
Honest water, which nere left man i'th'mire:
This and my food are equals, there's no ods,
Feasts are to proud to giue thanks to the Gods.

Apermantus Grace.

Immortall Gods, I craue no pelfe,
I pray for no man but my selfe,
Grannt I may neuer proue so fond,
To trust man on his Oath or Bond.
Or a Harlot for her weeping,
Or a Dogge that seemes asleeping,
Or a keeper with my freedome,
Or my friends if I should need 'em.
Amen. So fall too't:
Richmen sin, and I eat roots.
Much good dich thy good heart, *Apermantus*

Tim. Captaine,
Alcibiades, your hearts in the field now.

Alci. My heart is euer at your seruice, my Lord.

Tim. You had rather be at a breakefast of Enemies,
then a dinner of Friends.

Alc. So they were bleeding new my Lord, there's no
meat like 'em, I could wish my best friend at such a Feast.

Aper. Would all those Flatterers were thine Enemies
then, that then thou might'st kill 'em: & bid me to 'em.

1. Lord. Might we but haue that happinesse my Lord,
that you would once vse our hearts, whereby we might
expresse some part of our zeales, we should thinke our
selues for euer perfect.

Timon. Oh no doubt my good Friends, but the Gods
themselues haue prouided that I shall haue much helpe
from you: how had you beene my Friends else. Why
haue you that charitable title from thousands? Did not
you chiefely belong to my heart? I haue told more of
you to my selfe, then you can with modestie speake in
your owne behalfe. And thus farre I confirme you. O h
you Gods(thinke I,)what need we haue any Friends, if
we should nere haue need of 'em? They were the most
needlesse Creatures liuing; should we nere haue vse for
'em? And would most resemble sweete Instruments
hung vp in Cases, that keepes there sounds to themselues. Why I haue often wisht my selfe poorer, that
I might come neerer to you: we are borne to do benefits. And what better or properer can we call our owne,
then the riches of our Friends? Oh what a pretious comfort 'tis, to haue so many like Brothers commanding
one anothers Fortunes. Oh ioyes, e'ne made away er't
can be borne: mine eies cannot hold out water me thinks:
to forget their Faults. I drinke to you.

Aper. Thou weep'st to make them drinke, *Timon*.

2. Lord. Ioy had the like conception in our eies,
And at that instant, like a babe sprung vp.

Aper. Ho, ho: I laugh to thinke that babe a bastard.

3. Lord. I promise you my Lord you mou'd me much.

Aper. Much.

*Sound Tucket. Enter the Maskers of Amazons, with
Lutes in their hands, dauncing and playing.*

Tim. What meanes that Trumpe? How now?

Enter Seruant.

Ser. Please you my Lord, there are certaine Ladies
Most desirous of admittance.

Tim. Ladies? what are their wils?

Ser. There comes with them a fore-runner my Lord,
which beares that office, to signifie their pleasures.

Tim. I pray let them be admitted.

Enter Cupid with the Maske of Ladies.

Cup. Haile to thee worthy *Timon* and to all that of
his Bounties taste: the fiue best Sences acknowledge thee
their Patron, and come freely to gratulate thy plentious
bosome.
There taft, touch all, pleas'd from thy Table rise;
They onely now come but to Feast thine eies.

Timo. They'r wecome all, let 'em haue kind admittance. Musicke make their welcome.

Luc. You see my Lord, how ample y'are belou'd.

Aper. Hoyday,
What a sweepe of vanitie comes this way.
They daunce? They are madwomen,

Like Madnesse is the glory of this life,
As this pompe shewes to a little oyle and roote.
We make our selues Fooles, to disport our selues,
And spend our Flatteries, to drinke those men,
Vpon whose Age we voyde it vp agen
With poysonous Spight and Enuy.
Who liues, that's not depraued, or depraues;
Who dyes, that beares not one spurne to their graues
Of their Friends guift:
I should feare, those that dance before me now,
Would one day stampe vpon me: 'Tas bene done,
Men shut their doores against a setting Sunne.

The Lords rise from Table, with much adoring of Timon, and to shew their loues, each single out an Amazon, and all Dance, men with women, a loftie straine or two to the Hoboyes, and cease.

Tim. You haue done our pleasures
Much grace (faire Ladies)
Set a faire fashion on our entertainment,
Which was not halfe so beautifull, and kinde:
You haue added worth vntoo't, and luster,
And entertain'd me with mine owne deuice.
I am to thanke you for't.

1 Lord. My Lord you take vs euen at the best.

Aper. Faith for the worst is filthy, and would not hold taking, I doubt me.

Tim. Ladies, there is an idle banquet attends you,
Please you to dispose your selues.

All La. Most thankfully, my Lord. *Exeunt.*

Tim. Flauius.

Fla. My Lord.

Tim. The little Casket bring me hither.

Fla. Yes, my Lord. More Iewels yet?
There is no crossing him in's humor,
Else I should tell him well, yfaith I should;
When all's spent, hee'ld be crost then, and he could:
'Tis pitty Bounty had not eyes behinde,
That man might ne're be wretched for his minde. *Exit.*

1 Lord. Where be our men?

Ser. Heere my Lord, in readinesse.

2 Lord. Our Horses.

Tim. O my Friends:
I haue one word to say to you: Looke you, my good L.
I must intreat you honour me so much,
As to aduance this Iewell, accept it, and weare it,
Kinde my Lord.

1 Lord. I am so farre already in your guifts.

All. So are we all.

Enter a Seruant.

Ser. My Lord, there are certaine Nobles of the Senate newly alighted, and come to visit you.

Tim. They are fairely welcome.

Enter Flauius.

Fla. I beseech your Honor, vouchsafe me a word, it does concerne you neere.

Tim. Neere? why then another time Ile heare thee.
I prythee let's be prouided to shew them entertainment.

Fla. I scarse know how.

Enter another Seruant.

Ser. May it please your Honor, Lord *Lucius*
(Out of his free loue) hath presented to you
Foure Milke-white Horses, trapt in Siluer.

Tim. I shall accept them fairely: let the Presents
Be worthily entertain'd.

Enter a third Seruant.

How now? What newes?

3. Ser. Please you my Lord, that honourable Gentleman Lord *Lucullus*, entreats your companie to morrow, to hunt with him, and ha's sent your Honour two brace of Grey-hounds.

Tim. Ile hunt with him,
And let them be receiu'd, not without faire Reward.

Fla. What will this come to?
He commands vs to prouide, and giue great guifts,
   and all out of an empty Coffer:
Nor will he know his Purse, or yeeld me this,
To shew him what a Begger his heart is,
Being of no power to make his wishes good.
His promises flye so beyond his state,
That what he speaks is all in debt, he ows for eu'ry word:
He is so kinde, that he now payes interest for't;
His Land's put to their Bookes. Well, would I were
Gently put out of Office, before I were forc'd out:
Happier is he that has no friend to feede,
Then such that do e'ne Enemies exceede.
I bleed inwardly for my Lord. *Exit*

Tim. You do your selues much wrong,
You bate too much of your owne merits.
Heere my Lord, a trifle of our Loue.

2 Lord. With more then common thankes
I will receyue it.

3 Lord. O he's the very soule of Bounty.

Tim. And now I remember my Lord, you gaue good words the other day of a Bay Courser I rod on. Tis yours because you lik'd it.

1. L. Oh, I beseech you pardon mee, my Lord, in that.

Tim. You may take my word my Lord: I know no man can iustly praise, but what he does affect. I weighe my Friends affection with mine owne: Ile tell you true, Ile call to you.

All Lor. O none so welcome.

Tim. I take all, and your seuerall visitations
So kinde to heart, 'tis not enough to giue:
Me thinkes, I could deale Kingdomes to my Friends,
And nere be wearie. *Alcibiades*,
Thou art a Soldiour, therefore sildome rich,
It comes in Charitie to thee: for all thy liuing
Is mong'st the dead: and all the Lands thou hast
Lye in a pitcht field.

Alc. I, defil'd Land, my Lord.

1. Lord. We are so vertuously bound.

Tim. And so am I to you.

2. Lord. So infinitely endeer'd.

Tim. All to you. Lights, more Lights.

1. Lord. The best of Happines, Honor, and Fortunes Keepe with you Lord *Timon*.

Tim. Ready for his Friends. *Exeunt Lords*

Aper. What a coiles heere, seruing of beckes, and iutting out of bummes. I doubt whether their Legges be worth the summes that are giuen for 'em.
Friendships full of dregges,
Me thinkes false hearts, should neuer haue sound legges.
Thus honest Fooles lay out their wealth on Curtsies.

Tim. Now *Apermantus* (if thou wert not sullen)
I would be good to thee.

Aper. No, Ile nothing; for if I should be brib'd too, there would be none left to raile vpon thee, and then thou wouldst sinne the faster. Thou giu'st so long *Timon* (I feare me) thou wilt giue away thy selfe in paper shortly. What needs these Feasts, pompes, and Vaine-glories?

Tim.

Timon of Athens.

Tim. Nay, and you begin to raile on Societie once, I am sworne not to giue regard to you. Farewell, & come with better Musicke. *Exit*

Aper. So: Thou wilt not heare mee now, thou shalt not then. Ile locke thy heauen from thee:
Oh that mens eares should be
To Counsell deafe, but not to Flatterie. *Exit*

Enter a Senator.

Sen. And late fiue thousand: to *Varro* and to *Isidore*
He owes nine thousand, besides my former summe,
Which makes it fiue and twenty. Still in motion
Of raging waste? It cannot hold; it will not.
If I want Gold, steale but a beggers Dogge,
And giue it *Timon*, why the Dogge coines Gold.
If I would sell my Horse, and buy twenty moe
Better then he; why giue my Horse to *Timon*,
Aske nothing, giue it him, it Foles me straight
And able Horses: No Porter at his gate,
But rather one that smiles, and still inuites
All that passe by. It cannot hold, no reason
Can found his state in safety. *Caphis* hoa,
Caphis I say.

Enter Caphis.

Ca. Heere sir, what is your pleasure.
Sen. Get on your cloake, & haste you to Lord *Timon*,
Importune him for my Moneyes, be not ceast
With slight deniall; nor then silenc'd, when
Commend me to your Master, and the Cap
Playes in the right hand, thus: but tell him,
My Vses cry to me; I must serue my turne
Out of mine owne, his dayes and times are past,
And my reliances on his fracted dates
Haue smit my credit. I loue, and honour him,
But must not breake my backe, to heale his finger.
Immediate are my needs, and my releefe
Must not be tost and turn'd to me in words,
But finde supply immediate. Get you gone,
Put on a most importunate aspect,
A visage of demand: for I do feare
When euery Feather stickes in his owne wing,
Lord *Timon* will be left a naked gull,
Which flashes now a Phœnix, get you gone.
Ca. I go sir.
Sen. I go sir?
Take the Bonds along with you,
And haue the dates in. Come.
Ca. I will Sir.
Sen. Go. *Exeunt*

Enter Steward, with many billes in his hand.

Stew. No care, no stop, so senselesse of expence,
That he will neither know how to maintaine it,
Nor cease his flow of Riot. Takes no accompt
How things go from him, nor resume no care
Of what is to continue: neuer minde,
Was to be so vnwise, to be so kinde.
What shall be done, he will not heare, till feele:
I must be round with him, now he comes from hunting.
Fye, fie, fie, fie.

Enter Caphis, Isidore, and Varro.

Cap. Good euen *Varro*: what, you come for money?
Var. Is't not your businesse too?
Cap. It is, and yours too, *Isidore*?
Isid. It is so.

Cap. Would we were all discharg'd.
Var. I feare it,
Cap. Heere comes the Lord.

Enter Timon, and his Traine.

Tim. So soone as dinners done, wee'l forth againe
My *Alcibiades*. With me, what is your will?
Cap. My Lord, heere is a note of certaine dues.
Tim. Dues? whence are you?
Cap. Of Athens heere, my Lord.
Tim. Go to my Steward.
Cap. Please it your Lordship, he hath put me off
To the succession of new dayes this moneth:
My Master is awak'd by great Occasion,
To call vpon his owne, and humbly prayes you,
That with your other Noble parts, you'l suite,
In giuing him his right.
Tim. Mine honest Friend,
I prythee but repaire to me next morning.
Cap. Nay, good my Lord.
Tim. Containe thy selfe, good Friend.
Var. One *Varroes* seruant, my good Lord.
Isid. From *Isidore*, he humbly prayes your speedy payment.
Cap. If you did know my Lord, my Masters wants.
Var. 'Twas due on forfeyture my Lord, sixe weekes, and past.
Isi. Your Steward puts me off my Lord, and I
Am sent expressely to your Lordship.
Tim. Giue me breath:
I do beseech you good my Lords keepe on,
Ile waite vpon you instantly. Come hither: pray you
How goes the world, that I am thus encountred
With clamorous demands of debt, broken Bonds,
And the detention of long since due debts
Against my Honor?
Stew. Please you Gentlemen,
The time is vnagreeable to this businesse:
Your importunacie cease, till after dinner,
That I may make his Lordship vnderstand,
Wherefore you are not paid.
Tim. Do so my Friends, see them well entertain'd.
Stew. Pray draw neere. *Exit*

Enter Apemantus and Foole.

Caph. Stay, stay, here comes the Foole with *Apemantus*, let's ha some sport with 'em.
Var. Hang him, hee'l abuse vs.
Isid. A plague vpon him dogge.
Var. How dost Foole?
Ape. Dost Dialogue with thy shadow?
Var. I speake not to thee.
Ape. No 'tis to thy selfe. Come away.
Isi. There's the Foole hangs on your backe already.
Ape. No thou stand'st single, th'art not on him yet.
Cap. Where's the Foole now?
Ape. He last ask'd the question. Poore Rogues, and Vsurers men, Bauds betweene Gold and want.
Al. What are we *Apemantus*?
Ape. Asses.
All. Why?
Ape. That you ask me what you are, & do not know your selues. Speake to 'em Foole.
Foole. How do you Gentlemen?
All. Gramercies good Foole:
How does your Mistris?

Foole.

Foole. She's e'ne setting on water to scal'd such Chickens as you are. Would we could see you at Corinth.

Ape. Good, Gramercy.

Enter Page.

Foole. Looke you, heere comes my Masters Page.

Page. Why how now Captaine? what do you in this wise Company. How dost thou *Apermantus*?

Ape. Would I had a Rod in my mouth, that I might answer thee profitably.

Boy. Prythee *Apemantus* reade me the superscription of these Letters, I know not which is which.

Ape. Canst not read?

Page. No.

Ape. There will little Learning dye then that day thou art hang'd. This is to Lord *Timon*, this to *Alcibiades*. Go thou was't borne a Bastard, and thou't dye a Bawd.

Page. Thou was't whelpt a Dogge, and thou shalt famish a Dogges death. Answer not, I am gone. *Exit*

Ape. E'ne so thou out-runst Grace, Foole I will go with you to Lord *Timons*.

Foole. Will you leaue me there?

Ape. If *Timon* stay at home. You three serue three Vsurers?

All. I would they seru'd vs.

Ape. So would I: As good a tricke as euer Hangman seru'd Theefe.

Foole. Are you three Vsurers men?

All. I Foole.

Foole. I thinke no Vsurer, but ha's a Foole to his Seruant. My Mistris is one, and I am her Foole: when men come to borrow of your Masters, they approach sadly, and go away merry: but they enter my Masters house merrily, and go away sadly. The reason of this?

Var. I could render one.

Ap. Do it then, that we may account thee a Whoremaster, and a Knaue, which notwithstanding thou shalt be no lesse esteemed.

Varro. What is a Whoremaster Foole?

Foole. A Foole in good cloathes, and something like thee. 'Tis a spirit, sometime t'appeares like a Lord, somtime like a Lawyer, sometime like a Philosopher, with two stones moe then's artificiall one. Hee is verie often like a Knight; and generally, in all shapes that man goes vp and downe in, from fourescore to thirteen, this spirit walkes in.

Var. Thou art not altogether a Foole.

Foole. Nor thou altogether a Wise man, As much foolerie as I haue, so much wit thou lack'st.

Ape. That answer might haue become *Apemantus*.

All. Aside, aside, heere comes Lord *Timon*.

Enter Timon and Steward.

Ape. Come with me (Foole) come.

Foole. I do not alwayes follow Louer, elder Brother, and Woman, sometime the Philosopher.

Stew. Pray you walke neere, Ile speake with you anon. *Exeunt.*

Tim. You make me meruell wherefore ere this time Had you not fully laide my state before me, That I might so haue rated my expence As I had leaue of meanes.

Stew. You would not heare me;

At many leysures I propose.

Tim. Go too: Perchance some single vantages you tooke, When my indisposition put you backe, And that vnaptnesse made your minister Thus to excuse your selfe.

Stew. O my good Lord, At many times I brought in my accompts, Laid them before you, you would throw them off, And say you found them in mine honestie, When for some trifling present you haue bid me Returne so much, I haue shooke my head, and wept: Yes 'gainst th'Authoritie of manners, pray'd you To hold your hand more close: I did indure Not sildome, nor no slight checkes, when I haue Prompted you in the ebbe of your estate, And your great flow of debts; my lou'd Lord, Though you heare now (too late) yet now's a time, The greatest of your hauing, lackes a halfe, To pay your present debts.

Tim. Let all my Land be sold.

Stew. 'Tis all engag'd, some forfeyted and gone, And what remaines will hardly stop the mouth Of present dues; the future comes apace: What shall defend the interim, and at length How goes our reck'ning?

Tim. To Lacedemon did my Land extend.

Stew. O my good Lord, the world is but a word, Were it all yours, to giue it in a breath, How quickely were it gone.

Tim. You tell me true.

Stew. If you suspect my Husbandry or Falshood, Call me before th'exactest Auditors, And set me on the proofe. So the Gods blesse me, When all our Offices haue beene opprest With riotous Feeders, when our Vaults haue wept With drunken spilth of Wine; when euery roome Hath blaz'd with Lights, and braid with Minstrelsie, I haue retyr'd me to a wastefull cocke, And set mine eyes at flow.

Tim. Prythee no more,

Stew. Heauens, haue I said, the bounty of this Lord: How many prodigall bits haue Slaues and Pezants This night englutted: who is not *Timons*, What heart, head, sword, force, meanes, but is L. *Timons*: Great *Timon*, Noble, Worthy, Royall *Timon*: Ah, when the meanes are gone, that buy this praise, The breath is gone, whereof this praise is made: Feast won, fast lost; one cloud of Winter showres, These flyes are couch't.

Tim. Come sermon me no further. No villanous bounty yet hath past my heart; Vnwisely, not ignobly haue I giuen. Why dost thou weepe, can'st thou the conscience lacke, To thinke I shall lacke friends: secure thy heart, If I would broach the vessels of my loue, And try the argument of hearts, by borrowing, Men, and mens fortunes could I frankely vse As I can bid thee speake.

Ste. Assurance blesse your thoughts.

Tim. And in some sort these wants of mine are crown'd, That I account them blessings. For by these Shall I trie Friends. You shall perceiue How you mistake my Fortunes: I am wealthie in my Friends. Within there, *Flauius, Seruilius*?

Timon of Athens.   85

Enter three Seruants.

Ser. My Lord, my Lord.

Tim. I will dispatch you seuerally.
You to Lord *Lucius*, to Lord *Lucullus* you, I hunted
with his Honor to day; you to *Sempronius*; commend me
to their loues; and I am proud say, that my occasions
haue found time to vse 'em toward a supply of mony: let
the request be fifty Talents.

Flam. As you haue said, my Lord.

Stew. Lord *Lucius* and *Lucullus*? Humh.

Tim. Go you sir to the Senators;
Of whom, euen to the States best health; I haue
Deseru'd this Hearing: bid 'em send o'th'instant
A thousand Talents to me.

Ste. I haue beene bold
(For that I knew it the most generall way)
To them, to vse your Signet, and your Name,
But they do shake their heads, and I am heere
No richer in returne.

Tim. Is't true? Can't be?

Stew. They answer in a ioynt and corporate voice,
That now they are at fall, want Treasure cannot
Do what they would, are sorrie: you are Honourable,
But yet they could haue wisht, they know not,
Something hath beene amisse; a Noble Nature
May catch a wrench; would all were well; 'tis pitty,
And so intending other serious matters,
After distastefull lookes; and these hard Fractions
With certaine halfe-caps, and cold mouing nods,
They froze me into Silence.

Tim. You Gods reward them:
Prythee man looke cheerely. These old Fellowes
Hiue their ingratitude in them Hereditary:
Their blood is cak'd, 'tis cold, it sildome flowes,
'Tis lacke of kindely warmth, they are not kinde;
And Nature, as it growes againe toward earth,
Is fashion'd for the iourney, dull and heauy.
Go to *Ventiddius* (prythee be not sad,
Thou art true, and honest; Ingeniously I speake,
No blame belongs to thee:) *Ventiddius* lately
Buried his Father, by whose death hee's stepp'd
Into a great estate: When he was poore,
Imprison'd, and in scarsitie of Friends,
I cleer'd him with fiue Talents: Greet him from me,
Bid him suppose, some good necessity
Touches his Friend, which craues to be remembred
With those fiue Talents; that had, giue't these Fellowes
To whom 'tis instant due. Neu'r speake, or thinke,
That *Timons* fortunes 'mong his Friends can sinke.

Stew. I would I could not thinke it:
That thought is Bounties Foe;
Being free it selfe, it thinkes all others so.   *Exeunt*

*Flaminius waiting to speake with a Lord from his Master,
enters a seruant to him.*

Ser. I haue told my Lord of you, he is comming down
to you.

Flam. I thanke you Sir.

Enter Lucullus.

Ser. Heere's my Lord.

Luc. One of Lord *Timons* men? A Guift I warrant.
Why this hits right: I dreampt of a Siluer Bason & Ewre
to night. *Flaminius*, honest *Flaminius*, you are verie re-
spectiuely welcome sir. Fill me some Wine. And how
does that Honourable, Compleate, Free-hearted Gentleman of Athens, thy very bountifull good Lord and Mayster?

Flam. His health is well sir.

Luc. I am right glad that his health is well sir: and
what hast thou there vnder thy Cloake, pretty *Flaminius*?

Flam. Faith, nothing but an empty box Sir, which in
my Lords behalfe, I come to intreat your Honor to supply: who hauing great and instant occasion to vse fiftie
Talents, hath sent to your Lordship to furnish him: nothing doubting your present assistance therein.

Luc. La, la, la, la: Nothing doubting sayes hee? Alas
good Lord, a Noble Gentleman 'tis, if he would not keep
so good a house. Many a time and often I ha din'd with
him, and told him on't, and come againe to supper to him
of purpose, to haue him spend lesse, and yet he wold embrace no counsell, take no warning by my comming, euery man has his fault, and honesty is his, I ha told him on't,
but I could nere get him from't.

Enter Seruant with Wine.

Ser. Please your Lordship, heere is the Wine.

Luc. Flaminius, I haue noted thee alwayes wise.
Heere's to thee.

Flam. Your Lordship speakes your pleasure.

Luc. I haue obserued thee alwayes for a towardlie
prompt spirit, giue thee thy due, and one that knowes
what belongs to reason; and canst vse the time wel, if the
time vse thee well. Good parts in thee; get you gone sirrah. Draw neerer honest *Flaminius*. Thy Lords a bountifull Gentleman, but thou art wise, and thou know'st
well enough (although thou com'st to me) that this is no
time to lend money, especially vpon bare friendshippe
without securitie. Here's three *Solidares* for thee, good
Boy winke at me, and say thou saw'st mee not. Fare thee
well.

Flam. Is't possible the world should so much differ,
And we aliue that liued? Fly damned basenesse
To him that worships thee.

Luc. Ha? Now I see thou art a Foole, and fit for thy
Master.   *Exit L.*

Flam May these adde to the number ỹ may scald thee:
Let moulten Coine be thy damnation,
Thou disease of a friend, and not himselfe:
Has friendship such a faint and milkie heart,
It turnes in lesse then two nights? O you Gods!
I feele my Masters passion. This Slaue vnto his Honor,
Has my Lords meate in him:
Why should it thriue, and turne to Nutriment,
When he is turn'd to poyson?
O may Diseases onely worke vpon't:
And when he's sicke to death, let not that part of Nature
Which my Lord payd for, be of any power
To expell sicknesse, but prolong his hower.   *Exit.*

Enter Lucius, with three strangers.

Luc. Who the Lord *Timon*? He is my very good friend
and an Honourable Gentleman.

1 We know him for no lesse, thogh we are but strangers to him. But I can tell you one thing my Lord, and
which I heare from common rumours, now Lord *Timons*
happie howres are done and past, and his estate shrinkes
from him.

Lucius. Fye no, doe not beleeue it: hee cannot want
for money.

2 But beleeue you this my Lord, that not long agoe,
one of his men was with the Lord *Lucullus*, to borrow so
many Talents, nay vrg'd extreamly for't, and shewed
                                                                                  what

what necessity belong'd too't, and yet was deny'de.
  Luci. How?
  2 I tell you, deny'de my Lord.
  Luci. What a strange case was that? Now before the Gods I am asham'd on't. Denied that honourable man? There was verie little Honour shew'd in't. For my owne part, I must needes confesse, I haue receyued some small kindnesses from him, as Money, Plate, Iewels, and such like Trifles; nothing comparing to his: yet had hee mistooke him, and sent to me, I should ne're haue denied his Occasion so many Talents.

  Enter Seruilius.
  Seruil. See, by good hap yonders my Lord, I haue swet to see his Honor. My Honor'd Lord.
  Lucil. Seruilius? You are kindely met sir. Farthewell, commend me to thy Honourable vertuous Lord, my very exquisite Friend.
  Seruil. May it please your Honour, my Lord hath sent——
  Luci. Ha? what ha's he sent? I am so much endeered to that Lord; hee's euer sending: how shall I thank him think'st thou? And what has he sent now?
  Seruil. Has onely sent his present Occasion now my Lord: requesting your Lordship to supply his instant vse with so many Talents.
  Lucil. I know his Lordship is but merry with me, He cannot want fifty fiue hundred Talents.
  Seruil. But in the mean time he wants lesse my Lord. If his occasion were not vertuous, I should not vrge it halfe so faithfully.
  Luc. Dost thou speake seriously Seruilius?
  Seruil. Vpon my soule 'tis true Sir.
  Luci. What a wicked Beast was I to disfurnish my selfe against such a good time, when I might ha shewn my selfe Honourable? How vnluckily it hapned, that I shold Purchase the day before for a little part, and vndo a great deale of Honour? Seruilius, now before the Gods I am not able to do (the more beast I say) I was sending to vse Lord Timon my selfe, these Gentlemen can witnesse; but I would not for the wealth of Athens I had done't now. Commend me bountifully to his good Lordship, and I hope his Honor will conceiue the fairest of mee, because I haue no power to be kinde. And tell him this from me, I count it one of my greatest afflictions say, that I cannot pleasure such an Honourable Gentleman. Good Seruilius, will you befriend mee so farre, as to vse mine owne words to him?
  Ser. Yes sir, I shall. Exit Seruil.
  Lucil. Ile looke you out a good turne Seruilius.
True as you said, Timon is shrunke indeede,
And he that's once deny'de, will hardly speede. Exit.
  1 Do you obserue this Hostilius?
  2 I, too well.
  1 Why this is the worlds soule,
And iust of the same peece
Is euery Flatterers sport: who can call him his Friend
That dips in the same dish? For in my knowing
Timon has bin this Lords Father,
And kept his credit with his purse:
Supported his estate, nay Timons money
Has paid his men their wages. He ne're drinkes,
But Timons Siluer treads vpon his Lip,
And yet, oh see the monstrousnesse of man,
When he lookes out in an vngratefull shape;
He does deny him (in respect of his)

What charitable men affoord to Beggers.
  3 Religion grones at it.
  1 For mine owne part, I neuer tasted Timon in my life
Nor came any of his bounties ouer me,
To marke me for his Friend. Yet I protest,
For his right Noble minde, illustrious Vertue,
And Honourable Carriage,
Had his necessity made vse of me,
I would haue put my wealth into Donation,
And the best halfe should haue return'd to him,
So much I loue his heart: But I perceiue,
Men must learne now with pitty to dispence,
For Policy sits aboue Conscience. Exeunt.

  Enter a third seruant with Sempronius, another
  of Timons Friends.

  Semp. Must he needs trouble me in't? Hum.
'Boue all others?
He might haue tried Lord Lucius, or Lucullus,
And now Ventidgius is wealthy too,
Whom he redeem'd from prison. All these
Owes their estates vnto him.
  Ser. My Lord,
They haue all bin touch'd, and found Base-Mettle,
For they haue all denied him.
  Semp. How? Haue they deny'de him?
Has Ventidgius and Lucullus deny'de him,
And does he send to me? Three? Humh?
It shewes but little loue, or iudgement in him.
Must I be his last Refuge? His Friends (like Physitians)
Thriue, giue him ouer: Must I take th'Cure vpon me?
Has much disgrac'd me in't, I'me angry at him,
That might haue knowne my place. I see no sense for't,
But his Occasions might haue wooed me first:
For in my conscience, I was the first man
That ere receiued guift from him.
And does he thinke so backwardly of me now,
That Ile requite it last? No:
So it may proue an Argument of Laughter
To th'rest, and 'mong'st Lords be thought a Foole:
I'de rather then the worth of thrice the summe,
Had sent to me first, but for my mindes sake:
I'de such a courage to do him good. But now returne,
And with their faint reply, this answer ioyne;
Who bates mine Honor, shall not know my Coyne. Exit.
  Ser. Excellent: Your Lordships a goodly Villain: the diuell knew not what he did, when hee made man Politicke; he crossed himselfe by't: and I cannot thinke, but in the end, the Villanies of man will set him cleere. How fairely this Lord striues to appeare foule? Takes Vertuous Copies to be wicked: like those, that vnder hotte ardent zeale, would set whole Realmes on fire, of such a nature is his politike loue.
This was my Lords best hope, now all are fled
Saue onely the Gods. Now his Friends are dead,
Doores that were ne're acquainted with their Wards
Many a bounteous yeere, must be imploy'd
Now to guard sure their Master:
And this is all a liberall course allowes,
Who cannot keepe his wealth, must keep his house. Exit.

  Enter Varro's man, meeting others. All Timons Creditors to
  wait for his comming out. Then enter Lucius
  and Hortensius.

  Var. man. Well met, goodmorrow Titus & Hortensius.
  Titus

Timon of Athens.

Tit. The like to you kinde *Varro*.
Hort. Lucius, what do we meet together?
Luci. I, and I thinke one businesse do's command vs all,
For mine is money.
Tit. So is theirs, and ours.

Enter Philotus.

Luci. And sir *Philotus* too.
Phil. Good day at once.
Luci. Welcome good Brother.
What do you thinke the houre?
Phil. Labouring for Nine.
Luci. So much?
Phil. Is not my Lord seene yet?
Luci. Not yet.
Phil. I wonder on't, he was wont to shine at seauen.
Luci. I, but the dayes are waxt shorter with him:
You must consider, that a Prodigall course
Is like the Sunnes, but not like his recouerable, I feare:
'Tis deepest Winter in Lord *Timons* purse, that is: One
may reach deepe enough, and yet finde little.
Phil. I am of your feare, for that.
Tit. Ile shew you how t'obserue a strange euent:
Your Lord sends now for Money?
Hort. Most true, he doe's.
Tit. And he weares Iewels now of *Timons* guift,
For which I waite for money.
Hort. It is against my heart.
Luci. Marke how strange it showes,
Timon in this, should pay more then he owes:
And e'ne as if your Lord should weare rich Iewels,
And send for money for 'em.
Hort. I'me weary of this Charge,
The Gods can witnesse:
I know my Lord hath spent of *Timons* wealth,
And now Ingratitude, makes it worse then stealth.
Varro. Yes, mine's three thousand Crownes:
What's yours?
Luci. Fiue thousand mine.
Varro. 'Tis much deepe, and it should seem by th'sum
Your Masters confidence was aboue mine,
Else surely his had equall'd.

Enter Flaminius.

Tit. One of Lord *Timons* men.
Luc. *Flaminius*? Sir, a word: Pray is my Lord readie
to come forth?
Flam. No, indeed he is not.
Tit. We attend his Lordship: pray signifie so much.
Flam. I need not tell him that, he knowes you are too
diligent.

Enter Steward in a Cloake, muffled.

Luci. Ha: is not that his Steward muffled so?
He goes away in a Clowd: Call him, call him.
Tit. Do you heare, sir?
2. Varro. By your leaue, sir.
Stew. What do ye aske of me, my Friend.
Tit. We waite for certaine Money heere, sir.
Stew. I, if Money were as certaine as your waiting,
'Twere sure enough.
Why then preferr'd you not your summes and Billes
When your false Masters eate of my Lords meat?
Then they could smile, and fawne vpon his debts,
And take downe th'Interest into their glutt'nous Mawes.
You do your selues but wrong, to stirre me vp,
Let me passe quietly:
Beleeue't, my Lord and I haue made an end,
I haue no more to reckon, he to spend.
Luci. I, but this answer will not serue.
Stew. If't 'twill not serue, 'tis not so base as you,
For you serue Knaues.
1. Varro. How? What does his casheer'd Worship
mutter?
2. Varro. No matter what, 'hee's poore, and that's re-
uenge enough. Who can speake broader, then hee that
has no house to put his head in? Such may rayle against
great buildings.

Enter Seruilius.

Tit. Oh heere's *Seruilius*: now wee shall know some
answere.
Seru. If I might beseech you Gentlemen, to repayre
some other houre, I should deriue much from't. For tak't
of my soule, my Lord leanes wondrously to discontent:
His comfortable temper has forsooke him, he's much out
of health, and keepes his Chamber.
Luci. Many do keepe their Chambers, are not sicke:
And if it be so farre beyond his health,
Me thinkes he should the sooner pay his debts,
And make a cleere way to the Gods.
Seruil. Good Gods.
Titus. We cannot take this for answer, sir.
Flaminius within. *Seruilius* helpe, my Lord, my Lord.

Enter Timon in a rage.

Tim. What, are my dores oppos'd against my passage?
Haue I bin euer free, and must my house
Be my retentiue Enemy? My Gaole?
The place which I haue Feasted, does it now
(Like all Mankinde) shew me an Iron heart?
Luci. Put in now *Titus*.
Tit. My Lord, heere is my Bill.
Luci. Here's mine.
1. Var. And mine, my Lord.
2. Var. And ours, my Lord.
Philo. All our Billes.
Tim. Knocke me downe with 'em, cleaue mee to the
Girdle.
Luc. Alas, my Lord.
Tim. Cut my heart in summes.
Tit. Mine, fifty Talents.
Tim. Tell out my blood.
Luc. Fiue thousand Crownes, my Lord.
Tim. Fiue thousand drops payes that.
What yours? and yours?
1. Var. My Lord.
2. Var. My Lord.
Tim. Teare me, take me, and the Gods fall vpon you.
Exit Timon.
Hort. Faith I perceiue our Masters may throwe their
caps at their money, these debts may well be call'd despe-
rate ones, for a madman owes 'em. *Exeunt.*

Enter Timon.

Timon. They haue e'ene put my breath from mee the
slaues. Creditors? Diuels.
Stew. My deere Lord.
Tim. What if it should be so?
Stew. My Lord.
Tim. Ile haue it so. My Steward?
Stew. Heere my Lord.
Tim. So fitly? Go, bid all my Friends againe,
Lucius, Lucullus, and *Sempronius Vllorxa*: All,
Ile once more feast the Rascals.
Stew. O my Lord, you onely speake from your distra-
cted soule; there's not so much left to, furnish out a mo-
derate Table.

Timon

Tim. Be it not in thy care:
Go I charge thee, inuite them all, let in the tide
Of Knaues once more: my Cooke and Ile prouide. *Exeunt.*

*Enter three Senators at one doore, Alcibiades meeting them,
with Attendants.*

1. *Sen.* My Lord, you haue my voyce, too't,
The faults Bloody:
'Tis necessary he should dye:
Nothing imboldens sinne so much, as Mercy.

2. Most true; the Law shall bruise 'em.

Alc. Honor, health, and compassion to the Senate.

1. Now Captaine.

Alc. I am an humble Sutor to your Vertues;
For pitty is the vertue of the Law,
And none but Tyrants vse it cruelly.
It pleases time and Fortune to lye heauie
Vpon a Friend of mine, who in hot blood
Hath stept into the Law: which is past depth
To those that (without heede) do plundge intoo't.
He is a Man (setting his Fate aside) of comely Vertues,
Nor did he soyle the fact with Cowardice,
(And Honour in him, which buyes out his fault)
But with a Noble Fury, and faire spirit,
Seeing his Reputation touch'd to death,
He did oppose his Foe:
And with such sober and vnnoted passion
He did behooue his anger ere 'twas spent,
As if he had but prou'd an Argument.

1. *Sen.* You vndergo too strict a Paradox,
Striuing to make an vgly deed looke faire:
Your words haue tooke such paines, as if they labour'd
To bring Man-slaughter into forme, and set Quarrelling
Vpon the head of Valour; which indeede
Is Valour mis-begot, and came into the world,
When Sects, and Factions were newly borne.
Hee's truly Valiant, that can wisely suffer
The worst that man can breath,
And make his Wrongs, his Out-sides,
To weare them like his Rayment, carelessely,
And ne're preferre his iniuries to his heart,
To bring it into danger.
If Wrongs be euilles, and inforce vs kill,
What Folly 'tis, to hazard life for Ill.

Alci. My Lord.

1. *Sen.* You cannot make grosse sinnes looke cleare,
To reuenge is no Valour, but to beare.

Alci. My Lords, then vnder fauour, pardon me,
If I speake like a Captaine.
Why do fond men expose themselues to Battell,
And not endure all threats? Sleepe vpon't,
And let the Foes quietly cut their Throats
Without repugnancy? If there be
Such Valour in the bearing, what make wee
Abroad? Why then, Women are more valiant
That stay at home, if Bearing carry it:
And the Asse, more Captaine then the Lyon?
The fellow loaden with Irons, wiser then the Iudge?
If Wisedome be in suffering, Oh my Lords,
As you are great, be pittifully Good,
Who cannot condemne rashnesse in cold blood?
To kill, I grant, is sinnes extreamest Gust,
But in defence, by Mercy, 'tis most iust.
To be in Anger, is impietie:
But who is Man, that is not Angrie.
Weigh but the Crime with this.

2. *Sen.* You breath in vaine.

Alci. In vaine?
His seruice done at Lacedemon, and Bizantium,
Were a sufficient briber for his life.

1. What's that?

Alc. Why say my Lords ha's done faire seruice,
And slaine in fight many of your enemies:
How full of valour did he beare himselfe
In the last Conflict, and made plenteous wounds?

2. He has made too much plenty with him:
He's a sworne Rioter, he has a sinne
That often drownes him, and takes his valour prisoner.
If there were no Foes, that were enough
To ouercome him. In that Beastly furie,
He has bin knowne to commit outrages,
And cherrish Factions. 'Tis inferr'd to vs,
His dayes are foule, and his drinke dangerous.

1. He dyes.

Alci. Hard fate: he might haue dyed in warre.
My Lords, if not for any parts in him,
Though his right arme might purchase his owne time,
And be in debt to none: yet more to moue you,
Take my deserts to his, and ioyne 'em both.
And for I know, your reuerend Ages loue Security,
Ile pawne my Victories, all my Honour to you
Vpon his good returnes.
If by this Crime, he owes the Law his life,
Why let the Warre receiue't in valiant gore,
For Law is strict, and Warre is nothing more.

1. We are for Law, he dyes, vrge it no more
On height of our displeasure: Friend, or Brother,
He forfeits his owne blood, that spilles another.

Alc. Must it be so? It must not bee:
My Lords, I do beseech you know mee.

2. How?

Alc. Call me to your remembrances.

3. What.

Alc. I cannot thinke but your Age has forgot me,
It could not else be, I should proue so base,
To sue and be deny'de such common Grace.
My wounds ake at you.

1. Do you dare our anger?
'Tis in few words, but spacious in effect:
We banish thee for euer.

Alc. Banish me?
Banish your dotage, banish vsurie,
That makes the Senate vgly.

1. If after two dayes shine, Athens containe thee,
Attend our waightier Iudgement.
And not to swell our Spirit,
He shall be executed presently. *Exeunt.*

Alc. Now the Gods keepe you old enough,
That you may liue
Onely in bone, that none may looke on you.
I'm worse then mad: I haue kept backe their Foes
While they haue told their Money, and let out
Their Coine vpon large interest. I my selfe,
Rich onely in large hurts. All those, for this?
Is this the Balsome, that the vsuring Senat
Powres into Captaines wounds? Banishment.
It comes not ill: I hate not to be banisht,
It is a cause worthy my Spleene and Furie,
That I may strike at Athens. Ile cheere vp
My discontented Troopes, and lay for hearts;
'Tis Honour with most Lands to be at ods,
Souldiers should brooke as little wrongs as Gods. *Exit.*

Enter

Timon of Athens.

Enter divers Friends at severall doores.

1. The good time of day to you, sir.
2. I also wish it to you: I thinke this Honorable Lord did but try vs this other day.
1. Vpon that were my thoughts tyring when wee encountred. I hope it is not so low with him as he made it seeme in the triall of his severall Friends.
2. It should not be, by the perswasion of his new Feasting.
1. I should thinke so. He hath sent mee an earnest inuiting, which many my neere occasions did vrge mee to put off: but he hath coniur'd mee beyond them, and I must needs appeare.
2. In like manner was I in debt to my importunat businesse, but he would not heare my excuse. I am sorrie, when he sent to borrow of mee, that my Prouision was out.
1. I am sicke of that greefe too, as I vnderstand how all things go.
2. Euery man heares so: what would hee haue borrowed of you?
1. A thousand Peeces.
2. A thousand Peeces?
1. What of you?
2. He sent to me sir——Heere he comes.

Enter Timon and Attendants.

Tim. With all my heart Gentlemen both; and how fare you?
1. Euer at the best, hearing well of your Lordship.
2. The Swallow followes not Summer more willing, then we your Lordship.
Tim. Nor more willingly leaues Winter, such Summer Birds are men. Gentlemen, our dinner will not recompence this long stay: Feast your eares with the Musicke awhile: If they will fare so harshly o'th' Trumpets sound: we shall too't presently.
1. I hope it remaines not vnkindely with your Lordship, that I return'd you an empty Messenger.
Tim. O sir, let it not trouble you.
2. My Noble Lord,
Tim. Ah my good Friend, what cheere?

The Banket brought in.

2. My most Honorable Lord, I am e'ne sick of shame, that when your Lordship this other day sent to me, I was so vnfortunate a Beggar.
Tim. Thinke not on't, sir.
2. If you had sent but two houres before.
Tim. Let it not cumber your better remembrance. Come bring in all together.
2. All couer'd Dishes.
1. Royall Cheare, I warrant you.
3. Doubt not that, if money and the season can yeild it
1. How do you? What's the newes?
3. *Alcibiades* is banish'd: heare you of it?
Both. Alcibiades banish'd?
3. 'Tis so, be sure of it.
1. How? How?
2. I pray you vpon what?
Tim. My worthy Friends, will you draw neere?
3. Ile tell you more anon. Here's a Noble feast toward
2. This is the old man still.
3. Wilt hold? Wilt hold?
2. It do's: but time will, and so.

3. I do conceyue.
Tim. Each man to his stoole, with that spurre as hee would to the lip of his Mistris: your dyet shall bee in all places alike. Make not a Citie Feast of it, to let the meat coole, ere we can agree vpon the first place. Sit, sit.
The Gods require our Thankes.

You great Benefactors, sprinkle our Society with Thankefulnesse. For your owne guifts, make your selues prais'd: But reserue still to giue, least your Deities be despised. Lend to each man enough, that one neede not lend to another. For were your Godheads to borrow of men, men would forsake the Gods. Make the Meate be beloued, more then the Man that giues it. Let no Assembly of Twenty, be without a score of Villaines. If there sit twelue Women at the Table, let a dozen of them bee as they are. The rest of your Fees, O Gods, the Senators of Athens, together with the common legge of People, what is amisse in them, you Gods, make suteable for destruction. For these my present Friends, as they are to mee nothing, so in nothing blesse them, and to nothing are they welcome.

Vncouer Dogges, and lap.
Some speake. What do's his Lordship meane?
Some other. I know not.
Timon. May you a better Feast neuer behold
You knot of Mouth-Friends: Smoke, & lukewarm water
Is your perfection. This is *Timons* last,
Who stucke and spangled you with Flatteries,
Washes it off, and sprinkles in your faces
Your reeking villany. Liue loath'd, and long
Most smiling, smooth, detested Parasites,
Curteous Destroyers, affable Wolues, meeke Beares:
You Fooles of Fortune, Trencher-friends, Times Flyes,
Cap and knee-Slaues, vapours, and Minute Iackes.
Of Man and Beast, the infinite Maladie
Crust you quite o're. What do'st thou go?
Soft, take thy Physicke first; thou too, and thou:
Stay I will lend thee money, borrow none.
What? All in Motion? Henceforth be no Feast,
Whereat a Villaine's not a welcome Guest.
Burne house, sinke Athens, henceforth hated be
Of *Timon* Man, and all Humanity. *Exit*

Enter the Senators, with other Lords.

1. How now, my Lords?
2. Know you the quality of Lord *Timons* fury?
3. Push, did you see my Cap?
4. I haue lost my Gowne.
1. He's but a mad Lord, & nought but humors swaies him. He gaue me a Iewell th'other day, and now hee has beate it out of my hat. Did you see my Iewell?
2. Did you see my Cap.
3. Heere 'tis.
4. Heere lyes my Gowne.
1. Let's make no stay.
2. Lord *Timons* mad.
3. I feel't vpon my bones.
4. One day he giues vs Diamonds, next day stones.

Exeunt the Senators.

Enter Timon.

Tim. Let me looke backe vpon thee. O thou Wall
That girdles in those Wolues, diue in the earth,
And fence not Athens. Matrons, turne incontinent,
Obedience fayle in Children: Slaues and Fooles

Plucke the graue wrinkled Senate from the Bench,
And minister in their steeds, to generall Filthes.
Conuert o'th'Instant greene Virginity,
Doo't in your Parents eyes. Bankrupts, hold fast
Rather then render backe; out with your Kniues,
And cut your Trusters throates. Bound Seruants, steale,
Large-handed Robbers your graue Masters are,
And pill by Law. Maide, to thy Masters bed,
Thy Mistris is o'th'Brothell. Some of sixteen,
Plucke the lyn'd Crutch from thy old limping Sire,
With it, beate out his Braines. Piety, and Feare,
Religion to the Gods, Peace, Iustice, Truth,
Domesticke awe, Night-rest, and Neighbour-hood,
Instruction, Manners, Mysteries, and Trades,
Degrees, Obseruances, Customes, and Lawes,
Decline to your confounding contraries.
And yet Confusion liue: Plagues incident to men,
Your potent and infectious Feauors, heape
On Athens ripe for stroke. Thou cold Sciatica,
Cripple our Senators, that their limbes may halt
As lamely as their Manners. Lust, and Libertie
Creepe in the Mindes and Marrowes of our youth,
That 'gainst the streame of Vertue they may strine,
And drowne themselues in Riot. Itches, Blaines,
Sowe all th'Athenian bosomes, and their crop
Be generall Leprosie: Breath, infect breath,
That their Society (as their Friendship) may
Be meerely poyson. Nothing Ile beare from thee
But nakednesse, thou detestable Towne,
Take thou that too, with multiplying Bannes:
Timon will to the Woods, where he shall finde
Th'vnkindest Beast, more kinder then Mankinde.
The Gods confound (heare me you good Gods all)
Th'Athenians both within and out that Wall:
And graunt as *Timon* growes, his hate may grow
To the whole race of Mankinde, high and low.
Amen.   *Exit.*

Enter Steward with two or three Seruants.

1 Heare you M. Steward, where's our Master?
Are we vndone, cast off, nothing remaining?
  Stew. Alack my Fellowes, what should I say to you?
Let me be recorded by the righteous Gods,
I am as poore as you.
  1 Such a House broke?
So Noble a Master falne, all gone, and not
One Friend to take his Fortune by the arme,
And go along with him.
  2 As we do turne our backes
From our Companion, throwne into his graue,
So his Familiars to his buried Fortunes
Slinke all away, leaue their false vowes with him
Like empty purses pickt; and his poore selfe
A dedicated Beggar to the Ayre,
With his disease, of all shunn'd pouerty,
Walkes like contempt alone. More of our Fellowes.

Enter other Seruants.

  Stew. All broken Implements of a ruin'd house.
  3 Yet do our hearts weare *Timons* Liuery,
That see I by our Faces: we are Fellowes still,
Seruing alike in sorrow: Leak'd is our Barke,
And we poore Mates, stand on the dying Decke,
Hearing the Surges threat: we must all part
Into this Sea of Ayre.
  Stew. Good Fellowes all,

The latest of my wealth Ile share among'st you.
Where euer we shall meete, for *Timons* sake,
Let's yet be Fellowes. Let's shake our heads, and say
As 'twere a Knell vnto our Masters Fortunes,
We haue seene better dayes. Let each take some:
Nay put out all your hands: Not one word more,
Thus part we rich in sorrow, parting poore.

Embrace and part seuerall wayes.

Oh the fierce wretchednesse that Glory brings vs!
Who would not wish to be from wealth exempt,
Since Riches point to Misery and Contempt?
Who would be so mock'd with Glory, or to liue
But in a Dreame of Friendship,
To haue his pompe, and all what state compounds,
But onely painted like his varnisht Friends:
Poore honest Lord, brought lowe by his owne heart,
Vndone by Goodnesse: Strange vnvsuall blood,
When mans worst sinne is, He do's too much Good.
Who then dares to be halfe so kinde agen?
For Bounty that makes Gods, do still marre Men.
My deerest Lord, blest to be most accurst,
Rich onely to be wretched; thy great Fortunes
Are made thy cheefe Afflictions. Alas (kinde Lord)
Hee's flung in Rage from this ingratefull Seate
Of monstrous Friends:
Nor ha's he with him to supply his life,
Or that which can command it:
Ile follow and enquire him out.
Ile euer serue his minde, with my best will,
Whilst I haue Gold, Ile be his Steward still.   *Exit.*

Enter Timon in the woods.

  Tim. O blessed breeding Sun, draw from the earth
Rotten humidity: below thy Sisters Orbe
Infect the ayre. Twin'd Brothers of one wombe,
Whose procreation, residence, and birth,
Scarse is diuidant; touch them with seuerall fortunes,
The greater scornes the lesser. Not Nature
(To whom all sores lay siege) can beare great Fortune
But by contempt of Nature.
Raise me this Begger, and deny't that Lord,
The Senators shall beare contempt Hereditary,
The Begger Natiue Honor.
It is the Pastour Lards, the Brothers sides,
The want that makes him leaue: who dares? who dares
In puritie of Manhood stand vpright
And say, this mans a Flatterer. If one be,
So are they all: for euerie grize of Fortune
Is smooth'd by that below. The Learned pate
Duckes to the Golden Foole. All's obliquie:
There 'snothing leuell in our cursed Natures
But direct villanie. Therefore be abhorr'd,
All Feasts, Societies, and Throngs of men.
His semblable, yea himselfe *Timon* disdaines,
Destruction phang mankinde; Earth yeeld me Rootes,
Who seekes for better of thee, sawce his pallate
With thy most operant Poyson. What is heere?
Gold? Yellow, glittering, precious Gold?
No Gods, I am no idle Votarist,
Roots you cleere Heauens. Thus much of this will make
Blacke, white; fowle, faire; wrong, right;
Base, Noble; Old, young; Coward, valiant.
Ha you Gods! why this? what this you Gods? why this
Will lugge your Priests and Seruants from your sides:
Plucke stout mens pillowes from below their heads.

This yellow Slaue,
Will knit and breake Religions, blesse th'accurst,
Make the hoare Leprosie ador'd, place Theeues,
And giue them Title, knee, and approbation
With Senators on the Bench: This is it
That makes the wappen'd Widdow wed againe;
Shee, whom the Spittle-house, and vlcerous sores,
Would cast the gorge at. This Embalmes and Spices
To'th'Aprill day againe. Come damn'd Earth,
Thou common whore of Mankinde, that puttes oddes
Among the rout of Nations, I will make thee
Do thy right Nature.   *March afarre off.*
Ha? A Drumme? Th'art quicke,
But yet Ile bury thee: Thou't go (strong Theefe)
When Gowty keepers of thee cannot stand:
Nay stay thou out for earnest.

Enter Alcibiades with Drumme and Fife in warlike manner, and Phrynia and Timandra.

  Alc. What art thou there? speake.
  Tim. A Beast as thou art. The Canker gnaw thy hart
For shewing me againe the eyes of Man.
  Alc. What is thy name? Is man so hatefull to thee,
That art thy selfe a Man?
  Tim. I am *Misantropos*, and hate Mankinde.
For thy part, I do wish thou wert a dogge,
That I might loue thee something.
  Alc. I know thee well:
But in thy Fortunes am vnlearn'd, and strange.
  Tim. I know thee too, and more then that I know thee
I not desire to know. Follow thy Drumme,
With mans blood paint the ground Gules, Gules:
Religious Cannons, ciuill Lawes are cruell,
Then what should warre be? This fell whore of thine,
Hath in her more destruction then thy Sword,
For all her Cherubin looke.
  Phrin. Thy lips rot off.
  Tim. I will not kisse thee, then the rot returnes
To thine owne lippes againe.
  Alc. How came the Noble *Timon* to this change?
  Tim. As the Moone do's, by wanting light to giue:
But then renew I could not like the Moone,
There were no Sunnes to borrow of.
  Alc. Noble *Timon*, what friendship may I do thee?
  Tim. None, but to maintaine my opinion.
  Alc. What is it *Timon*?
  Tim. Promise me Friendship, but performe none.
If thou wilt not promise, the Gods plague thee, for thou
art a man: if thou do'st performe, confound thee, for
thou art a man.
  Alc. I haue heard in some sort of thy Miseries.
  Tim. Thou saw'st them when I had prosperitie.
  Alc. I see them now, then was a blessed time.
  Tim. As thine is now, held with a brace of Harlots.
  Timan. Is this th'Athenian Minion, whom the world
Voic'd so regardfully?
  Tim. Art thou *Timandra*?   *Timan.* Yes.
  Tim. Be a whore still, they loue thee not that vse thee,
giue them diseases, leauing with thee their Lust. Make
vse of thy salt houres, season the slaues for Tubbes and
Bathes, bring downe Rose-cheekt youth to the Fubfast,
and the Diet.
  Timan. Hang thee Monster.
  Alc. Pardon him sweet *Timandra* for his wits
Are drown'd and lost in his Calamities.

I haue but little Gold of late, braue *Timon*,
The want whereof, doth dayly make reuolt
In my penurious Band. I haue heard and greeu'd
How cursed Athens, mindelesse of thy worth,
Forgetting thy great deeds, when Neighbour states
But for thy Sword and Fortune trod vpon them.
  Tim. I prythee beate thy Drum, and get thee gone.
  Alc. I am thy Friend, and pitty thee deere *Timon*.
  Tim. How doest thou pitty him whom ỹ dost troble,
I had rather be alone.
  Alc. Why fare thee well:
Heere is some Gold for thee.
  Tim. Keepe it, I cannot eate it.
  Alc. When I haue laid proud Athens on a heape.
  Tim. Warr'st thou 'gainst Athens.
  Alc. I *Timon*, and haue cause.
  Tim. The Gods confound them all in thy Conquest,
And thee after, when thou hast Conquer'd.
  Alc. Why me, *Timon*?
  Tim. That by killing of Villaines
Thou was't borne to conquer my Country.
Put vp thy Gold. Go on, heeres Gold, go on;
Be as a Plannetary plague, when *Ioue*
Will o're some high-Vic'd City, hang his poyson
In the sicke ayre: let not thy sword skip one:
Pitty not honour'd Age for his white Beard,
He is an Vsurer. Strike me the counterfet Matron,
It is her habite onely, that is honest.
Her selfe's a Bawd. Let not the Virgins cheeke
Make soft thy trenchant Sword: for those Milke pappes
That through the window Barne bore at mens eyes,
Are not within the Leafe of pitty writ,
But set them down horrible Traitors. Spare not the Babe
Whose dimpled smiles from Fooles exhaust their mercy;
Thinke it a Bastard, whom the Oracle
Hath doubtfully pronounced, the throat shall cut,
And mince it sans remorse. Sweare against Obiects,
Put Armour on thine eares, and on thine eyes,
Whose proofe, nor yels of Mothers, Maides, nor Babes,
Nor sight of Priests in holy Vestments bleeding,
Shall pierce a iot. There's Gold to pay thy Souldiers,
Make large confusion: and thy fury spent,
Confounded be thy selfe. Speake not, be gone.
  Alc. Hast thou Gold yet, Ile take the Gold thou giuest me, not all thy Counsell.
  Tim. Dost thou or dost thou not, Heauens curse vpon
thee.
  Both. Giue vs some Gold good *Timon*, hast ỹ more?
  Tim. Enough to make a Whore forsweare her Trade,
And to make Whores, a Bawd. Hold vp you Sluts
Your Aprons mountant; you are not Othable,
Although I know you'l sweare, terribly sweare
Into strong shudders, and to heauenly Agues
Th'immortall Gods that heare you. Spare your Oathes:
Ile trust to your Conditions, be whores still.
And he whose pious breath seekes to conuert you,
Be strong in Whore, allure him, burne him vp,
Let your close fire predominate his smoke,
And be no turne-coats: yet may your paines six months
Be quite contrary, And Thatch
Your poore thin Rooses with burthens of the dead,
(Some that were hang'd) no matter:
Weare them, betray with them; Whore still,
Paint till a horse may myre vpon your face:
A pox of wrinkles.
  Both. Well, more Gold, what then?

hh 2   *Beleeue't*

Beleeue't that wee'l do any thing for Gold.

  Tim. Consumptions sowe
In hollow bones of man, strike their sharpe shinnes,
And marre mens spurring. Cracke the Lawyers voyce,
That he may neuer more false Title pleade,
Nor sound his Quillets shrilly: Hoare the Flamen,
That scold'st against the quality of flesh,
And not beleeues himselfe. Downe with the Nose,
Downe with it flat, take the Bridge quite away
Of him, that his particular to foresee (bald
Smels from the generall weale. Make curld'pate Ruffians
And let the vnscar'd Braggerts of the Warre
Deriue some paine from you. Plague all,
That your Actiuity may defeate and quell
The source of all Erection. There's more Gold.
Do you damne others, and let this damne you,
And ditches graue you all.

  Both. More counsell with more Money, bounteous *Timon.*

  Tim. More whore, more Mischeefe first, I haue giuen you earnest.

  Alc. Strike vp the Drum towardes Athens, farewell *Timon*: if I thriue well, Ile visit thee againe.

  Tim. If I hope well, Ile neuer see thee more.

  Alc. I neuer did thee harme.

  Tim. Yes, thou spok'st well of me.

  Alc. Call'st thou that harme?

  Tim. Men dayly finde it. Get thee away,
And take thy Beagles with thee.

  Alc. We but offend him, strike. *Exeunt.*

  Tim. That Nature being sicke of mans vnkindnesse
Should yet be hungry: Common Mother, thou
Whose wombe vnmeasureable, and infinite brest
Teemes and feeds all: whose selfesame Mettle
Whereof thy proud Childe (arrogant man) is puft,
Engenders the blacke Toad, and Adder blew,
The gilded Newt, and eyelesse venom'd Worme,
With all th'abhorred Births below Crispe Heauen,
Whereon *Hyperions* quickning fire doth shine:
Yeeld him, who all the humane Sonnes do hate,
From foorth thy plenteous bosome, one poore roote:
Enseare thy Fertile and Conceptious wombe,
Let it no more bring out ingratefull man.
Goe great with Tygers, Dragons, Wolues, and Beares,
Teeme with new Monsters, whom thy vpward face
Hath to the Marbled Mansion all aboue
Neuer presented. O, a Root, deare thankes:
Dry vp thy Marrowes, Vines, and Plough-torne Leas,
Whereof ingratefull man with Licourish draughts
And Morsels Vnctious, greases his pure minde,
That from it all Consideration slippes——

  Enter Apemantus.

More man? Plague, plague.

  Ape. I was directed hither. Men report,
Thou dost affect my Manners, and dost vse them.

  Tim. 'Tis then, because thou dost not keepe a dogge
Whom I would imitate. Consumption catch thee.

  Ape. This is in thee a Nature but infected,
A poore vnmanly Melancholly sprung
From change of future. Why this Spade? this place?
This Slaue-like Habit, and these lookes of Care?
Thy Flatterers yet weare Silke, drinke Wine, lye soft,
Hugge their diseas'd Perfumes, and haue forgot
That euer *Timon* was. Shame not these Woods,
By putting on the cunning of a Carper.
Be thou a Flatterer now, and seeke to thriue

By that which ha's vndone thee; hindge thy knee,
And let his very breath whom thou'lt obserue
Blow off thy Cap: praise his most vicious straine,
And call it excellent: thou wast told thus:
Thou gau'st thine eares (like Tapsters, that bad welcom)
To Knaues, and all approachers: 'Tis most iust
That thou turne Rascall, had'st thou wealth againe,
Rascals should haue't. Do not assume my likenesse.

  Tim. Were I like thee, I'de throw away my selfe.

  Ape. Thou hast cast away thy selfe, being like thy self
A Madman so long, now a Foole: what think'st
That the bleake ayre, thy boysterous Chamberlaine
Will put thy shirt on warme? Will these moyst Trees,
That haue out-liu'd the Eagle, page thy heeles
And skip when thou point'st out? Will the cold brooke
Candied with Ice, Cawdle thy Morning taste
To cure thy o're-nights surfet? Call the Creatures,
Whose naked Natures liue in all the spight
Of wrekefull Heauen, whose bare vnhoused Trunkes,
To the conflicting Elements expos'd
Answer meere Nature: bid them flatter thee,
O thou shalt finde.

  Tim. A Foole of thee: depart.

  Ape. I loue thee better now, then ere I did.

  Tim. I hate thee worse.

  Ape. Why?

  Tim. Thou flatter'st misery.

  Ape. I flatter not, but say thou art a Caytiffe.

  Tim. Why do'st thou seeke me out?

  Ape. To vex thee.

  Tim. Alwayes a Villaines Office, or a Fooles.
Dost please thy selfe in't?

  Ape. I.

  Tim. What, a Knaue too?

  Ape. If thou did'st put this sowre cold habit on
To castigate thy pride, 'twere well: but thou
Dost it enforcedly: Thou'dst Courtier be againe
Wert thou not Beggar: willing misery
Out-liues: incertaine pompe, is crown'd before:
The one is filling still, neuer compleat:
The other, at high wish: best state Contentlesse,
Hath a distracted and most wretched being,
Worse then the worst, Content.
Thou should'st desire to dye, being miserable.

  Tim. Not by his breath, that is more miserable.
Thou art a Slaue, whom Fortunes tender arme
With fauour neuer claspt: but bred a Dogge.
Had'st thou like vs from our first swath proceeded,
The sweet degrees that this breefe world affords,
To such as may the passiue drugges of it
Freely command'st: thou would'st haue plung'd thy self
In generall Riot, melted downe thy youth
In different beds of Lust, and neuer learn'd
The Icie precepts of respect, but followed
The Sugred game before thee. But my selfe,
Who had the world as my Confectionarie,
The mouthes, the tongues, the eyes, and hearts of men,
At duty more then I could frame employment;
That numberlesse vpon me stucke, as leaues
Do on the Oake, haue with one Winters brush
Fell from their boughes, and left me open, bare,
For euery storme that blowes. I to beare this,
That neuer knew but better, is some burthen:
Thy Nature, did commence in sufferance, Time
Hath made thee hard in't. Why should'st $\bar{y}$ hate Men?
They neuer flatter'd thee. What hast thou giuen?

If thou wilt curse; thy Father (that poore ragge)
Must be thy subiect; who in spight put stuffe
To some shee-Begger, and compounded thee
Poore Rogue, hereditary. Hence, be gone,
If thou hadst not bene borne the worst of men,
Thou hadst bene a Knaue and Flatterer.

Ape. Art thou proud yet?

Tim. I, that I am not thee.

Ape. I, that I was no Prodigall.

Tim. I, that I am one now.
Were all the wealth I haue shut vp in thee,
I'ld giue thee leaue to hang it. Get thee gone:
That the whole life of Athens were in this,
Thus would I eate it.

Ape. Heere, I will mend thy Feast.

Tim. First mend thy company, take away thy selfe.

Ape. So I shall mend mine owne, by th'lacke of thine

Tim. 'Tis not well mended so, it is but botcht;
If not, I would it were.

Ape. What would'st thou haue to Athens?

Tim. Thee thither in a whirlewind: if thou wilt,
Tell them there I haue Gold, looke, so I haue.

Ape. Heere is no vse for Gold.

Tim. The best, and truest:
For heere it sleepes, and do's no hyred harme.

Ape. Where lyest a nights *Timon*?

Tim. Vnder that's aboue me.
Where feed'st thou a-dayes *Apemantus*?

Ape. Where my stomacke findes meate, or rather
where I eate it.

Tim. Would poyson were obedient, & knew my mind

Ape. Where would'st thou send it?

Tim. To sawce thy dishes.

Ape. The middle of Humanity thou neuer knewest,
but the extremitie of both ends. When thou wast in thy
Gilt, and thy Perfume, they mockt thee for too much
Curiositie: in thy Ragges thou know'st none, but art despis'd for the contrary. There's a medler for thee, eate it.

Tim. On what I hate, I feed not.

Ape. Do'st hate a Medler?

Tim. I, though it looke like thee.

Ape. And th'hadst hated Medlers sooner, ỹ should'st
haue loued thy selfe better now. What man didd'st thou
euer know vnthrift, that was beloued after his meanes?

Tim. Who without those meanes thou talk'st of, didst
thou euer know belou'd?

Ape. My selfe.

Tim. I vnderstand thee: thou hed'st some meanes to
keepe a Dogge.

Apem. What things in the world canst thou neerest
compare to thy Flatterers?

Tim. Women neerest, but men: men are the things
themselues. What would'st thou do with the world *Apemantus*, if it lay in thy power?

Ape. Giue it the Beasts, to be rid of the men.

Tim. Would'st thou haue thy selfe fall in the confusion of men, and remaine a Beast with the Beasts.

Ape. I *Timon*.

Tim. A beastly Ambition, which the Goddes graunt
thee t'attaine to. If thou wert the Lyon, the Fox would
beguile thee: if thou wert the Lambe, the Foxe would
eate thee: if thou wert the Fox, the Lion would suspect
thee, when peraduenture thou wert accus'd by the Asse:
If thou wert the Asse, thy dulnesse would torment thee;
and still thou lin'dst but as a Breakefast to the Wolfe. If
thou wert the Wolfe, thy greedinesse would afflict thee,
& oft thou should'st hazard thy life for thy dinner. Wert
thou the Vnicorne, pride and wrath would confound
thee, and make thine owne selfe the conquest of thy fury.
Wert thou a Beare, thou would'st be kill'd by the Horse:
wert thou a Horse, thou would'st be seaz'd by the Leopard: wert thou a Leopard, thou wert Germane to the
Lion, and the spottes of thy Kindred, were Iurors on thy
life. All thy safety were remotion, and thy defence absence. What Beast could'st thou bee, that were not subiect to a Beast: and what a Beast art thou already, that
seest not thy losse in transformation.

Ape. If thou could'st please me
With speaking to me, thou might'st
Haue hit vpon it heere.
The Commonwealth of Athens, is become
A Forrest of Beasts.

Tim. How ha's the Asse broke the wall, that thou art
out of the Citie.

Ape. Yonder comes a Poet and a Painter:
The plague of Company light vpon thee:
I will feare to catch it, and giue way.
When I know not what else to do,
Ile see thee againe.

Tim. When there is nothing liuing but thee,
Thou shalt be welcome.
I had rather be a Beggers Dogge,
Then *Apemantus*.

Ape. Thou art the Cap
Of all the Fooles aliue.

Tim. Would thou wert cleane enough
To spit vpon.

Ape. A plague on thee,
Thou art too bad to curse.

Tim. All Villaines
That do stand by thee, are pure.

Ape. There is no Leprosie,
But what thou speak'st.

Tim. If I name thee, Ile beate thee;
But I should infect my hands.

Ape. I would my tongue
Could rot them off.

Tim. Away thou issue of a mangie dogge,
Choller does kill me,
That thou art aliue, I swoond to see thee.

Ape. Would thou would'st burst.

Tim. Away thou tedious Rogue, I am sorry I shall
lose a stone by thee.

Ape. Beast.

Tim. Slaue.

Ape. Toad.

Tim. Rogue, Rogue, Rogue.
I am sicke of this false world, and will loue nought
But euen the meere necessities vpon't:
Then *Timon* presently prepare thy graue:
Lye where the light Fome of the Sea may beate
Thy graue stone dayly, make thine Epitaph,
That death in me, at others liues may laugh.
O thou sweete King-killer, and deare diuorce
Twixt naturall Sunne and fire: thou bright defiler
Of *Hmens* purest bed, thou valiant Mars,
Thou euer, yong, fresh, loued, and delicate wooer,
Whose blush doth thawe the consecrated Snow
That lyes on Dians lap.
Thou visible God,
That souldrest close Impossibilities,
And mak'st them kisse; that speak'st with euerie Tongue

To euerie purpose: O thou touch of hearts,
Thinke thy slaue-man rebels, and by thy vertue
Set them into confounding oddes, that Beasts
May haue the world in Empire.

Ape. Would 'twere so,
But not till I am dead. Ile say th' hast Gold:
Thou wilt be throng'd too shortly.

Tim. Throng'd too?

Ape. I.

Tim. Thy backe I prythee.

Ape. Liue, and loue thy misery.

Tim. Long liue so, and so dye. I am quit.

Ape. Mo things like men,
Eate *Timon*, and abhorre then.   *Exit Apeman.*

Enter the Bandetti.

1 Where should he haue this Gold? It is some poore Fragment, some slender Ort of his remainder: the meere want of Gold, and the falling from of his Friendes, droue him into this Melancholly.

2 It is nois'd
He hath a masse of Treasure.

3 Let vs make the assay vpon him, if he care not for't, he will supply vs easily: if he couetously reserue it, how shall's get it?

2 True: for he beares it not about him:
'Tis hid.

1 Is not this hee?

All. Where?

2 'Tis his description.

3 He? I know him.

All. Saue thee *Timon.*

Tim. Now Theeues.

All. Soldiers, not Theeues.

Tim. Both too, and womens Sonnes.

All. We are not Theeues, but men
That much do want.

Tim. Your greatest want is, you want much of meat:
Why should you want? Behold, the Earth hath Rootes:
Within this Mile breake forth a hundred Springs:
The Oakes beare Mast, the Briars Scarlet Heps,
The bounteous Huswife Nature, on each bush,
Layes her full Messe before you. Want? why Want?

1 We cannot liue on Grasse, on Berries, Water,
As Beasts, and Birds, and Fishes.

Ti. Nor on the Beasts themselues, the Birds & Fishes,
You must eate men. Yet thankes I must you con,
That you are Theeues profest: that you worke not
In holier shapes: For there is boundlesse Theft
In limited Professions. Rascall Theeues
Heere's Gold. Go, sucke the subtle blood o'th' Grape,
Till the high Feauor seeth your blood to froth,
And so scape hanging. Trust not the Physitian,
His Antidotes are poyson, and he slayes
Moe then you Rob: Take wealth, and liues together,
Do Villaine do, since you protest to doo't.
Like Workemen, Ile example you with Theeuery:
The Sunnes a Theefe, and with his great attraction
Robbes the vaste Sea. The Moones an arrant Theefe,
And her pale fire, she snatches from the Sunne.
The Seas a Theefe, whose liquid Surge, resolues
The Moone into Salt teares. The Earth's a Theefe,
That feeds and breeds by a composture stolne
From gen'rall excrement: each thing's a Theefe.
The Lawes, your curbe and whip, in their rough power

Ha's vncheck'd Theft. Loue not your selues, away,
Rob one another, there's more Gold, cut throates,
All that you meete are Theeues: to Athens go,
Breake open shoppes, nothing can you steale
But Theeues do loose it: steale lesse, for this I giue you,
And Gold confound you howsoere: Amen.

3 Has almost charm'd me from my Profession, by perswading me to it.

1 'Tis in the malice of mankinde, that he thus aduises vs not to haue vs thriue in our mystery.

2 Ile beleeue him as an Enemy,
And giue ouer my Trade.

1 Let vs first see peace in Athens, there is no time so miserable, but a man may be true.   *Exit Theeues.*

Enter the Steward to Timon.

Stew. Oh you Gods!
Is yon'd despis'd and ruinous man my Lord?
Full of decay and fayling? Oh Monument
And wonder of good deeds, euilly bestow'd!
What an alteration of Honor has desp'rate want made?
What vilder thing vpon the earth, then Friends,
Who can bring Noblest mindes, to basest ends.
How rarely does it meete with this times guise,
When man was wisht to loue his Enemies:
Grant I may euer loue, and rather woo
Those that would mischeefe me, then those that doo.
Has caught me in his eye, I will present my honest griefe
vnto him; and as my Lord, still serue him with my life.
My deerest Master.

Tim. Away: what art thou?

Stew. Haue you forgot me, Sir?

Tim. Why dost aske that? I haue forgot all men.
Then, if thou grunt'st, th'art a man,
I haue forgot thee.

Stew. An honest poore seruant of yours.

Tim. Then I know thee not:
I neuer had honest man about me, I all
I kept were Knaues, to serue in meate to Villaines.

Stew. The Gods are witnesse,
Neu'r did poore Steward weare a truer greefe
For his vndone Lord, then mine eyes for you.

Tim. What, dost thou weepe?
Come neerer, then I loue thee
Because thou art a woman, and disclaim'st
Flinty mankinde: whose eyes do neuer giue,
But thorow Lust and Laughter: pittie's sleeping:
Strange times y weepe with laughing, not with weeping.

Stew. I begge of you to know me, good my Lord,
T'accept my greefe, and whil'st this poore wealth lasts,
To entertaine me as your Steward still.

Tim. Had I a Steward
So true, so iust, and now so comfortable?
It almost turnes my dangerous Nature wilde.
Let me behold thy face: Surely, this man
Was borne of woman.
Forgiue my generall, and exceptlesse rashnesse
You perpetuall sober Gods. I do proclaime
One honest man: Mistake me not, but one:
No more I pray, and hee's a Steward.
How faine would I haue hated all mankinde,
And thou redeem'st thy selfe. But all saue thee,
I fell with Curses.
Me thinkes thou art more honest now, then wise:
For, by oppressing and betraying mee,

Thou

Thou might'st haue sooner got another Seruice:
For many so arriue at second Masters,
Vpon their first Lords necke. But tell me true,
(For I must euer doubt, though ne're so sure)
Is not thy kindnesse subtle, couetous,
If not a Vsuring kindnesse, and as rich men deale Guifts,
Expecting in returne twenty for one?

Stew. No my most worthy Master, in whose brest
Doubt, and suspect (alas) are plac'd too late:
You should haue fear'd false times, when you did Feast.
Suspect still comes, where an estate is least.
That which I shew, Heauen knowes, is meerely Loue,
Dutie, and Zeale, to your vnmatched minde;
Care of your Food and Liuing, and beleeue it,
My most Honour'd Lord,
For any benefit that points to mee,
Either in hope, or present, I'de exchange
For this one wish, that you had power and wealth
To requite me, by making rich your selfe.

Tim. Looke thee, 'tis so: thou singly honest man,
Heere take: the Gods out of my miserie
Ha's sent thee Treasure. Go, liue rich and happy,
But thus condition'd: Thou shalt build from men:
Hate all, curse all, shew Charity to none,
But let the famisht flesh slide from the Bone,
Ere thou releeue the Begger. Giue to dogges
What thou denyest to men. Let Prisons swallow 'em,
Debts wither 'em to nothing, be men like blasted woods
And may Diseases licke vp their false bloods,
And so fare well, and thriue.

Stew. O let me stay, and comfort you, my Master.

Tim. If thou hat'st Curses
Stay not: flye, whil'st thou art blest and free:
Ne're see thou man, and let me ne're see thee. *Exit*

Enter Poet, and Painter.

Pain. As I tooke note of the place, it cannot be farre
where he abides.

Poet. What's to be thought of him?
Does the Rumor hold for true,
That hee's so full of Gold?

Painter. Certaine.
Alcibiades reports it: *Phrinica* and *Timandylo*
Had Gold of him. He likewise enrich'd
Poore stragling Souldiers, with great quantity.
'Tis saide, he gaue vnto his Steward
A mighty summe.

Poet. Then this breaking of his,
Ha's beene but a Try for his Friends?

Painter. Nothing else:
You shall see him a Palme in Athens againe,
And flourish with the highest:
Therefore, 'tis not amisse, we tender our loues
To him, in this suppos'd distresse of his:
It will shew honestly in vs,
And is very likely, to loade our purposes
With what they trauaile for,
If it be a iust and true report, that goes
Of his hauing.

Poet. What haue you now
To present vnto him?

Painter. Nothing at this time
But my Visitation: onely I will promise him
An excellent Peece.

Poet. I must serue him so too;
Tell him of an intent that's comming toward him.

Painter. Good as the best.
Promising, is the verie Ayre o'th' Time;
It opens the eyes of Expectation.
Performance, is euer the duller for his acte,
And but in the plainer and simpler kinde of people,
The deede of Saying is quite out of vse.
To Promise, is most Courtly and fashionable;
Performance, is a kinde of Will or Testament
Which argues a great sicknesse in his iudgement
That makes it.

Enter Timon from his Caue.

Timon. Excellent Workeman,
Thou canst not paint a man so badde
As is thy selfe.

Po.t. I am thinking
What I shall say I haue prouided for him:
It must be a personating of himselfe:
A Satyre against the softnesse of Prosperity,
With a Discouerie of the infinite Flatteries
That follow youth and opulencie.

Timon. Must thou needes
Stand for a Villaine in thine owne Worke?
Wilt thou whip thine owne faults in other men?
Do so, I haue Gold for thee.

Poet. Nay let's seeke him.
Then do we sinne against our owne estate,
When we may profit meete, and come too late.

Painter. True:
When the day serues before blacke-corner'd night;
Finde what thou want'st, by free and offer'd light.
Come.

Tim. Ile meete you at the turne:
What a Gods Gold, that he is worshipt
In a baser Temple, then where Swine feede?
'Tis thou that rigg'st the Barke, and plow'st the Fome,
Setlest admired reuerence in a Slaue,
To thee be worshipt, and thy Saints for aye:
Be crown'd with Plagues, that thee alone obay.
Fit I meet them.

Poet. Haile worthy *Timon.*

Pain. Our late Noble Master.

Timon. Haue I once liu'd
To see two honest men?

Poet. Sir:
Hauing often of your open Bounty tasted,
Hearing you were retyr'd, your Friends falne off,
Whose thankelesse Natures (O abhorred Spirits)
Not all the Whippes of Heauen, are large enough;
What, to you,
Whose Starre-like Noblenesse gaue life and influence
To their whole being? I am rapt, and cannot couer
The monstrous bulke of this Ingratitude
With any size of words.

Timon. Let it go,
Naked men may see't the better:
You that are honest, by being what you are,
Make them best seene, and knowne.

Pain. He, and my selfe
Haue trauail'd in the great showre of your guifts,
And sweetly felt it.

Timon. I, you are honest man.

Painter. We are hither come
To offer you our seruice.

Timon. Most honest men:

Why how shall I requite you?
Can you eate Roots, and drinke cold water, no?
  Both. What we can do,
Wee'l do to do you seruice.
  Tim. Y'are honest men,
Y'haue heard that I haue Gold,
I am sure you haue, speake truth, y'are honest men.
  Pain. So it is said my Noble Lord, but therefore
Came not my Friend, nor I.
  Timon. Good honest men: Thou draw'st a counterfet
Best in all Athens, th'art indeed the best,
Thou counterfet'st most liuely.
  Pain. So, so, my Lord.
  Tim. E'ne so sir as I say. And for thy fiction,
Why thy Verse swels with stuffe so fine and smooth,
That thou art euen Naturall in thine Art.
But for all this (my honest Natur'd friends)
I must needs say you haue a little fault,
Marry 'tis not monstrous in you, neither wish I
You take much paines to mend.
  Both. Beseech your Honour
To make it knowne to vs.
  Tim. You'l take it ill.
  Both. Most thankefully, my Lord.
  Timon. Will you indeed?
  Both. Doubt it not worthy Lord.
  Tim. There's neuer a one of you but trusts a Knaue,
That mightily deceiues you.
  Both. Do we, my Lord?
  Tim. I, and you heare him cogge,
See him dissemble,
Know his grosse patchery, loue him, feede him,
Keepe in your bosome, yet remaine assur'd
That he's a made-vp-Villaine.
  Pain. I know none such, my Lord.
  Poet. Nor I.
  Timon. Looke you,
I loue you well, Ile giue you Gold
Rid me these Villaines from your companies;
Hang them, or stab them, drowne them in a draught,
Confound them by some course, and come to me,
Ile giue you Gold enough.
  4. Both. Name them my Lord, let's know them.
  Tim. You that way, and you this:
But two in Company:
Each man apart, all single, and alone,
Yet an arch Villaine keepes him company:
If where thou art, two Villaines shall not be,
Come not neere him. If thou would'st not recide
But where one Villaine is, then him abandon.
Hence, packe, there's Gold, you came for Gold ye slaues:
You haue worke for me; there's payment, hence,
You are an Alcumist, make Gold of that:
Out Rascall dogges.   *Exeunt*

Enter Steward, and two Senators.

  Stew. It is vaine that you would speake with Timon:
For he is set so onely to himselfe,
That nothing but himselfe, which lookes like man,
Is friendly with him.
  1. Sen. Bring vs to his Caue.
It is our part and promise to th'Athenians
To speake with Timon.
  2. Sen. At all times alike
Men are not still the same: 'twas Time and Greefes
That fram'd him thus. Time with his fairer hand,
Offering the Fortunes of his former dayes,
The former man may make him: bring vs to him
And chanc'd it as it may.
  Stew. Heere is his Caue:
Peace and content be heere. Lord Timon, Timon,
Looke out, and speake to Friends: Th'Athenians
By two of their most reuerend Senate greet thee:
Speake to them Noble Timon.

Enter Timon out of his Caue.

  Tim. Thou Sunne that comforts burne,
Speake and be hang'd:
For each true word, a blister, and each false
Be as a Cantherizing to the root o'th'Tongue,
Consuming it with speaking.
  1 Worthy Timon.
  Tim. Of none but such as you,
And you of Timon.
  1 The Senators of Athens, greet thee Timon.
  Tim. I thanke them,
And would send them backe the plague,
Could I but catch it for them.
  1 O forget
What we are sorry for our selues in thee:
The Senators, with one consent of loue,
Intreate thee backe to Athens, who haue thought
On speciall Dignities, which vacant lye
For thy best vse and wearing.
  2 They confesse
Toward thee, forgetfulnesse too generall grosse;
Which now the publike Body, which doth sildome
Play the re-canter, feeling in it selfe
A lacke of Timons ayde, hath since withall
Of it owne fall, restraining ayde to Timon,
And send forth vs, to make their sorrowed render,
Together, with a recompence more fruitfull
Then their offence can weigh downe by the Dramme,
I euen such heapes and summes of Loue and Wealth,
As shall to thee blot out, what wrongs were theirs,
And write in thee the figures of their loue,
Euer to read them chine.
  Tim. You witch me in it;
Surprize me to the very brinke of teares;
Lend me a Fooles heart, and a womans eyes,
And Ile beweepe these comforts, worthy Senators.
  1 Therefore so please thee to returne with vs,
And of our Athens, thine and ours to take
The Captainship, thou shalt be met with thankes,
Allowed with absolute power, and thy good name
Liue with Authoritie: so soone we shall driue backe
Of Alcibiades th'approaches wild,
Who like a Bore too sauage, doth root vp
His Countries peace.
  2 And shakes his threatning Sword
Against the walles of Athens.
  1 Therefore Timon.
  Tim. Well sir, I will: therefore I will sir thus:
If Alcibiades kill my Countrymen,
Let Alcibiades know this of Timon,
That Timon cares not. But if he sacke faire Athens,
And take our goodly aged men by'th'Beards,
Giuing our holy Virgins to the staine
Of contumelious, beastly, mad-brain'd warre:
Then let him know, and tell him Timon speakes it,

In pitty of our aged, and our youth,
I cannot choose but tell him that I care not,
And let him tak't at worst: For their Kniues care not,
While you haue throats to answer. For my selfe,
There's not a whittle, in th'vnruly Campe,
But I do prize it at my loue, before
The reuerends Throat in Athens. So I leaue you
To the protection of the prosperous Gods,
As Theeues to Keepers.

Stew. Stay not, all's in vaine.

Tim. Why I was writing of my Epitaph,
It will be seene to morrow. My long sicknesse
Of Health, and Liuing, now begins to mend,
And nothing brings me all things. Go, liue still,
Be *Alcibiades* your plague; you his,
And last so long enough.

1. We speake in vaine.

Tim. But yet I loue my Country, and am not
One that reioyces in the common wracke,
As common bruite doth put it.

1. That's well spoke.

Tim. Commend me to my louing Countreymen.

1. These words become your lippes as they passe thorow them.

2. And enter in our eares, like great Triumphers
In their applauding gates.

Tim. Commend me to them,
And tell them, that to ease them of their greefes,
Their feares of Hostile strokes, their Aches losses,
Their pangs of Loue, with other incident throwes
That Natures fragile Vessell doth sustaine
In lifes vncertaine voyage, I will some kindnes do them,
Ile teach them to preuent wilde *Alcibiades* wrath.

1. I like this well, he will returne againe.

Tim. I haue a Tree which growes heere in my Close,
That mine owne vse inuites me to cut downe,
And shortly must I fell it. Tell my Friends,
Tell Athens, in the sequence of degree,
From high to low throughout, that who so please
To stop Affliction, let him take his haste;
Come hither ere my Tree hath felt the Axe,
And hang himselfe. I pray you do my greeting.

Stew. Trouble him no further, thus you still shall finde him.

Tim. Come not to me againe, but say to Athens,
Timon hath made his euerlasting Mansion
Vpon the Beached Verge of the salt Flood,
Who once a day with his embossed Froth
The turbulent Surge shall couer; thither come,
And let my graue-stone be your Oracle:
Lippes, let foure words go by, and Language end:
What is amisse, Plague and Infection mend.
Graues onely be mens workes, and Death their gaine;
Sunne, hide thy Beames, *Timon* hath done his Raigne.
Exit Timon.

1. His discontents are vnremoueably coupled to Nature.

2. Our hope in him is dead: let vs returne,
And straine what other meanes is left vnto vs
In our deere perill.

1. It requires swift foot. *Exeunt.*

Enter two other Senators, with a Messenger.

1. Thou hast painfully discouer'd: are his Files
As full as thy report?

Mes. I haue spoke the least.
Besides his expedition promises present approach.

2. We stand much hazard, if they bring not *Timon*.

Mes. I met a Currier, one mine ancient Friend,
Whom though in generall part we were oppos'd,
Yet our old loue made a particular force,
And made vs speake like Friends. This man was riding
From *Alcibiades* to *Timons* Caue,
With Letters of intreaty, which imported
His Fellowship i'th'cause against your City,
In part for his sake mou'd.

Enter the other Senators.

1. Heere come our Brothers.

3. No talke of *Timon*, nothing of him expect,
The Enemies Drumme is heard, and fearefull scouring
Doth choake the ayre with dust: In, and prepare,
Ours is the fall I feare, our Foes the Snare. *Exeunt.*

Enter a Souldier in the Woods, seeking Timon.

Sol. By all description this should be the place.
Whose heere? Speake hoa. No answer? What is this?
Tymon is dead, who hath out-stretcht his span,
Some Beast reade this; There do's not liue a Man.
Dead sure, and this his Graue, what's on this Tomb,
I cannot read: the Charracter Ile take with wax,
Our Captaine hath in euery Figure skill;
An ag'd Interpreter, though yong in dayes:
Before proud Athens hee's set downe by this,
Whose fall the marke of his Ambition is. *Exit.*

Trumpets sound. Enter Alcibiades with his Powers before Athens.

Alc. Sound to this Coward, and lasciuious Towne,
Our terrible approach. *Sounds a Parly.*

The Senators appeare vpon the wals.

Till now you haue gone on, and fill'd the time
With all Licentious measure, making your willes
The scope of Iustice. Till now, my selfe and such
As slept within the shadow of your power
Haue wander'd with our trauerst Armes, and breath'd
Our sufferance vainly: Now the time is flush,
When crouching Marrow in the bearer strong
Cries (of it selfe) no more: Now breathlesse wrong,
Shall sit and pant in your great Chaires of ease,
And purse Insolence shall breake his winde
With feare and horrid flight.

1. Sen. Noble, and young;
When thy first greefes were but a meere conceit,
Ere thou had'st power, or we had cause of feare,
We sent to thee, to giue thy rages Balme,
To wipe out our Ingratitude, with Loues
Aboue their quantitie.

2. So did we wooe
Transformed *Timon*, to our Citties loue
By humble Message, and by promist meanes:
We were not all vnkinde, nor all deserue
The common stroke of warre.

1. These walles of ours,
Were not erected by their hands, from whom
You haue receyu'd your greefe: Nor are they such,
That these great Towres, Trophees, & Schools shold fall
For priuate faults in them.

2. Nor are they liuing
Who

Who were the motiues that you first went out,
(Shame that they wanted, cunning in excesse)
Hath broke their hearts. March, Noble Lord,
Into our City with thy Banners spred,
By decimation and a tythed death;
If thy Reuenges hunger for that Food
Which Nature loathes, take thou the destin'd tenth,
And by the hazard of the spotted dye,
Let dye the spotted.

  1 All haue not offended:
For those that were, it is not square to take
On those that are, Reuenge: Crimes, like Lands
Are not inherited, then deere Countryman,
Bring in thy rankes, but leaue without thy rage,
Spare thy Athenian Cradle, and those Kin
Which in the bluster of thy wrath must fall
With those that haue offended, like a Shepheard,
Approach the Fold, and cull th'infected forth,
But kill not altogether.

  2 What thou wilt,
Thou rather shalt inforce it with thy smile,
Then hew too't, with thy Sword.

  1 Set but thy foot
Against our rampyr'd gates, and they shall ope:
So thou wilt send thy gentle heart before,
To say thou't enter Friendly.

  2 Throw thy Gloue,
Or any Token of thine Honour else,
That thou wilt vse the warres as thy redresse,
And not as our Confusion: All thy Powers
Shall make their harbour in our Towne, till wee
Haue seal'd thy full desire.

  Alc. Then there's my Gloue,
Defend and open your vncharged Ports,
Those Enemies of *Timons*, and mine owne
Whom you your selues shall set out for reproofe,
Fall and no more; and to attone your feares
With my more Noble meaning, not a man
Shall passe his quarter, or offend the streame
Of Regular Iustice in your Cities bounds,
But shall be remedied to your publique Lawes
At heauiest answer.

  Both. 'Tis most Nobly spoken.
  Alc. Descend, and keepe your words.

Enter a Messenger.

  Mes. My Noble Generall, *Timon* is dead,
Entomb'd vpon the very hemme o'th'Sea,
And on his Grauestone, this Insculpture which
With wax I brought away: whose soft Impression
Interprets for my poore ignorance.

Alcibiades reades the Epitaph.
Heere lies a wretched Coarse, of wretched Soule bereft,
Seek not my name: A Plague consume you, wicked Caitifs left:
Heere lye I Timon, who aliue, all liuing men did hate,
Passe by, and curse thy fill, but passe and stay not here thy gate.
These well expresse in thee thy latter spirits:
Though thou abhorrd'st in vs our humane griefes,
Scorn'd'st our Braines flow, and those our droplets, which
From niggard Nature fall; yet Rich Conceit
Taught thee to make vast Neptune weepe for aye
On thy low Graue, on faults forgiuen. Dead
Is Noble *Timon*, of whose Memorie
Heereafter more. Bring me into your Citie,
And I will vse the Oliue, with my Sword:
Make war breed peace; make peace stint war, make each
Prescribe to other, as each others Leach.
Let our Drummes strike.   *Exeunt.*

FINIS.

THE ACTORS NAMES.

TYMON of Athens.
Lucius, And
Lucullus, two Flattering Lords.
Appemantus, a Churlish Philosopher.
Sempronius another flattering Lord.
Alcibiades, an Athenian Captaine.
Poet.
Painter.
Jeweller.
Merchant.
Certaine Senatours.
Certaine Maskers.
Certaine Theeues.

Flaminius, one of Tymons Seruants.
Seruilius, another.
Caphis.
Varro.
Philo.   } Seuerall Seruants to Vsurers.
Titus.
Lucius.
Hortensis
Ventigius. one of Tymons false Friends.
Cupid.
Sempronius.
With diuers other Seruants,
And Attendants.

THE TRAGEDIE OF IVLIVS CÆSAR.

Actus Primus. Scœna Prima.

Enter Flauius, Murellus, and certaine Commoners ouer the Stage.

Flauius.

HEnce: home you idle Creatures, get you home:
Is this a Holiday? What, know you not
(Being Mechanicall) you ought not walke
Vpon a labouring day, without the signe
Of your Profession? Speake, what Trade art thou?

Car. Why Sir, a Carpenter.

Mur. Where is thy Leather Apron, and thy Rule?
What dost thou with thy best Apparrell on?
You sir, what Trade are you?

Cobl. Truely Sir, in respect of a fine Workman, I am but as you would say, a Cobler.

Mur. But what Trade art thou? Answer me directly.

Cob. A Trade Sir, that I hope I may vse, with a safe Conscience, which is indeed Sir, a Mender of bad soules.

Fla. What Trade thou knaue? Thou naughty knaue, what Trade?

Cobl. Nay I beseech you Sir, be not out with me: yet if you be out Sir, I can mend you.

Mur. What mean'st thou by that? Mend mee, thou sawcy Fellow?

Cob. Why sir, Cobble you.

Fla. Thou art a Cobler, art thou?

Cob. Truly sir, all that I liue by, is with the Aule: I meddle with no Tradesmans matters, nor womens matters; but withal I am indeed Sir, a Surgeon to old shooes: when they are in great danger, I recouer them. As proper men as euer trod vpon Neats Leather, haue gone vpon my handy-worke.

Fla. But wherefore art not in thy Shop to day?
Why do'st thou leade these men about the streets?

Cob. Truly sir, to weare out their shooes, to get my selfe into more worke. But indeede sir, we make Holyday to see *Cæsar*, and to reioyce in his Triumph.

Mur. Wherefore reioyce?
What Conquest brings he home?
What Tributaries follow him to Rome,
To grace in Captiue bonds his Chariot Wheeles?
You Blockes, you stones, you worse then senselesse things:
O you hard hearts, you cruell men of Rome,
Knew you not *Pompey* many a time and oft?
Haue you climb'd vp to Walles and Battlements,
To Towres and Windowes? Yea, to Chimney tops,
Your Infants in your Armes, and there haue sate
The liue-long day, with patient expectation,
To see great *Pompey* passe the streets of Rome:
And when you saw his Chariot but appeare,
Haue you not made an Vniuersall shout,
That Tyber trembled vnderneath her bankes
To heare the replication of your sounds,
Made in her Concaue Shores?
And do you now put on your best attyre?
And do you now cull out a Holyday?
And do you now strew Flowers in his way,
That comes in Triumph ouer *Pompeyes* blood?
Be gone,
Runne to your houses, fall vpon your knees,
Pray to the Gods to intermit the plague
That needs must light on this Ingratitude.

Fla. Go, go, good Countrymen, and for this fault
Assemble all the poore men of your sort;
Draw them to Tyber bankes, and weepe your teares
Into the Channell, till the lowest streame
Do kisse the most exalted Shores of all.

Exeunt all the Commoners.

See where their basest mettle be not mou'd,
They vanish tongue-tyed in their guiltinesse:
Go you downe that way towards the Capitoll,
This way will I: Disrobe the Images,
If you do finde them deckt with Ceremonies.

Mur. May we do so?
You know it is the Feast of Lupercall.

Fla. It is no matter, let no Images
Be hung with *Cæsars* Trophees: Ile about,
And driue away the Vulgar from the streets;
So do you too, where you perceiue them thicke.
These growing Feathers, pluckt from *Cæsars* wing,
Will make him flye an ordinary pitch,
Who else would soare aboue the view of men,
And keepe vs all in seruile fearefulnesse. *Exeunt*

Enter Cæsar, Antony for the Course, Calphurnia, Portia, Decius, Cicero, Brutus, Cassius, Caska, a Soothsayer: after them Murellus and Flauius.

Cæs. *Calphurnia*.

Cask. Peace ho, *Cæsar* speakes.

Cæs. *Calphurnia*.

Calp. Heere my Lord.

Cæs. Stand you directly in *Antonio's* way,
When he doth run his course. *Antonio*.

Ant. *Cæsar*, my Lord.

Cæs. Forget not in your speed *Antonio*,
To touch *Calphurnia*: for our Elders say,

The Barren touched in this holy chace,
Shake off their sterrile curse.

Ant. I shall remember,
When *Cæsar* sayes, Do this; it is perform'd.

Cæs. Set on, and leaue no Ceremony out.

Sooth. Cæsar.

Cæs. Ha? Who calles?

Cask. Bid euery noyse be still: peace yet againe.

Cæs. Who is it in the presse, that calles on me?
I heare a Tongue shriller then all the Musicke
Cry, *Cæsar*: Speake, *Cæsar* is turn'd to heare.

Sooth. Beware the Ides of March.

Cæs. What man is that?

Br. A Sooth-sayer bids you beware the Ides of March

Cæs. Set him before me, let me see his face.

Cassi. Fellow, come from the throng, look vpon *Cæsar*.

Cæs. What sayst thou to me now? Speak once againe.

Sooth. Beware the Ides of March.

Cæs. He is a Dreamer, let vs leaue him: Passe.

Sennet.   *Exeunt. Manet Brut. & Cass.*

Cassi. Will you go see the order of the course?

Brut. Not I.

Cassi. I pray you do.

Brut. I am not Gamesom: I do lacke some part
Of that quicke Spirit that is in *Antony*:
Let me not hinder *Cassius* your desires;
Ile leaue you.

Cassi. *Brutus*, I do obserue you now of late:
I haue not from your eyes, that gentlenesse
And shew of Loue, as I was wont to haue:
You beare too stubborne, and too strange a hand
Ouer your Friend, that loues you.

Bru. Cassius,
Be not deceiu'd: If I haue veyl'd my looke,
I turne the trouble of my Countenance
Meerely vpon my selfe. Vexed I am
Of late, with passions of some difference,
Conceptions onely proper to my selfe,
Which giue some soyle (perhaps) to my Behauiours:
But let not therefore my good Friends be greeu'd
(Among which number *Cassius* be you one)
Nor construe any further my neglect,
Then that poore *Brutus* with himselfe at warre,
Forgets the shewes of Loue to other men.

Cassi. Then *Brutus*, I haue much mistook your passion,
By meanes whereof, this Brest of mine hath buried
Thoughts of great value, worthy Cogitations.
Tell me good *Brutus*, Can you see your face?

Brutus. No *Cassius*:
For the eye sees not it selfe but by reflection,
By some other things.

Cassius. 'Tis iust,
And it is very much lamented *Brutus*,
That you haue no such Mirrors, as will turne
Your hidden worthinesse into your eye,
That you might see your shadow:
I haue heard,
Where many of the best respect in Rome,
(Except immortall *Cæsar*) speaking of *Brutus*,
And groaning vnderneath this Ages yoake,
Haue wish'd, that Noble *Brutus* had his eyes.

Bru. Into what dangers, would you
Leade me *Cassius*?
That you would haue me seeke into my selfe,
For that which is not in me?

Cas. Therefore good *Brutus*, be prepar'd to heare:
And since you know, you cannot see your selfe
So well as by Reflection; I your Glasse,
Will modestly discouer to your selfe
That of your selfe, which you yet know not of.
And be not iealous on me, gentle *Brutus*:
Were I a common Laughter, or did vse
To stale with ordinary Oathes my loue
To euery new Protester: if you know,
That I do fawne on men, and hugge them hard,
And after scandall them: Or if you know,
That I professe my selfe in Banquetting
To all the Rout, then hold me dangerous.

Flourish, and Shout.

Bru. What meanes this Showting?
I do feare, the People choose *Cæsar*
For their King.

Cassi. I, do you feare it?
Then must I thinke you would not haue it so.

Bru. I would not *Cassius*, yet I loue him well:
But wherefore do you hold me heere so long?
What is it, that you would impart to me?
If it be ought toward the generall good,
Set Honor in one eye, and Death i'th other,
And I will looke on both indifferently:
For let the Gods so speed mee, as I loue
The name of Honor, more then I feare death.

Cassi. I know that vertue to be in you *Brutus*,
As well as I do know your outward fauour.
Well, Honor is the subiect of my Story:
I cannot tell, what you and other men
Thinke of this life: But for my single selfe,
I had as liefe not be, as liue to be
In awe of such a Thing, as I my selfe.
I was borne free as *Cæsar*, so were you,
We both haue fed as well, and we can both
Endure the Winters cold, as well as hee.
For once, vpon a Rawe and Gustie day,
The troubled Tyber, chafing with her Shores,
Cæsar saide to me, Dar'st thou *Cassius* now
Leape in with me into this angry Flood,
And swim to yonder Point? Vpon the word,
Accoutred as I was, I plunged in,
And bad him follow: so indeed he did.
The Torrent roar'd, and we did buffet it
With lusty Sinewes, throwing it aside,
And stemming it with hearts of Controuersie,
But ere we could arriue the Point propos'd,
Cæsar cride, Helpe me *Cassius*, or I sinke.
I (as *Æneas*, our great Ancestor,
Did from the Flames of Troy, vpon his shoulder
The old *Anchyses* beare) so, from the waues of Tyber
Did I the tyred *Cæsar*: And this Man,
Is now become a God, and *Cassius* is
A wretched Creature, and must bend his body,
If *Cæsar* carelesly but nod on him.
He had a Feauer when he was in Spaine,
And when the Fit was on him, I did marke
How he did shake: Tis true, this God did shake,
His Coward lippes did from their colour flye,
And that same Eye, whose bend doth awe the World,
Did loose his Lustre: I did heare him grone:
I, and that Tongue of his, that bad the Romans
Marke him, and write his Speeches in their Bookes,
Alas, it cried, Giue me some drinke *Titinius*,

As a sicke Girle : Ye Gods, it doth amaze me,
A man of such a feeble temper should
So get the start of the Maiesticke world,
And beare the Palme alone.
               Shout.   Flourish.
  Bru. Another generall shout?
I do beleeue, that these applauses are
For some new Honors, that are heap'd on Cæsar.
  Cassi. Why man, he doth bestride the narrow world
Like a Colossus, and we petty men
Walke vnder his huge legges, and peepe about
To finde our selues dishonourable Graues.
Men at sometime, are Masters of their Fates.
The fault (deere Brutus) is not in our Starres,
But in our Selues, that we are vnderlings.
Brutus and Cæsar: What should be in that Cæsar?
Why should that name be sounded more then yours?
Write them together: Yours, is as faire a Name:
Sound them, it doth become the mouth as well:
Weigh them, it is as heauy: Coniure with 'em,
Brutus will start a Spirit as soone as Cæsar.
Now in the names of all the Gods at once,
Vpon what meate doth this our Cæsar feede,
That he is growne so great? Age, thou art sham'd.
Rome, thou hast lost the breed of Noble Bloods.
When went there by an Age, since the great Flood,
But it was fam'd with more then with one man?
When could they say (till now) that talk'd of Rome,
That her wide Walkes incompast but one man?
Now is't Rome indeed, and Roome enough
When there is in it but one onely man.
O! you and I, haue heard our Fathers say,
There was a Brutus once, that would haue brook'd
Th'eternall Diuell to keepe his State in Rome,
As easily as a King.
  Bru. That you do loue me, I am nothing iealous:
What you would worke me too, I haue some ayme:
How I haue thought of this, and of these times
I shall recount heereafter. For this present,
I would not so (with loue I might intreat you)
Be any further moou'd: What you haue said,
I will consider: what you haue to say
I will with patience heare, and finde a time
Both meete to heare, and answer such high things.
Till then, my Noble Friend, chew vpon this:
Brutus had rather be a Villager,
Then to repute himselfe a Sonne of Rome
Vnder these hard Conditions, as this time
Is like to lay vpon vs.
  Cassi. I am glad that my weake words
Haue strucke but thus much shew of fire from Brutus.

            Enter Cæsar and his Traine.

  Bru. The Games are done,
And Cæsar is returning.
  Cassi. As they passe by,
Plucke Caska by the Sleeue,
And he will (after his sowre fashion) tell you
What hath proceeded worthy note to day.
  Bru. I will do so: but looke you Cassius,
The angry spot doth glow on Cæsars brow,
And all the rest, looke like a chidden Traine;
Calphurnia's Cheeke is pale, and Cicero
Lookes with such Ferret, and such fiery eyes
As we haue seene him in the Capitoll

Being crost in Conference, by some Senators.
  Cassi. Caska will tell vs what the matter is.
  Cæs. Antonio.
  Ant. Cæsar.
  Cæs. Let me haue men about me, that are fat,
Sleeke-headed men, and such as sleepe a-nights:
Yond Cassius has a leane and hungry looke,
He thinkes too much: such men are dangerous.
  Ant. Feare him not Cæsar, he's not dangerous,
He is a Noble Roman, and well giuen.
  Cæs. Would he were fatter; But I feare him not:
Yet if my name were lyable to feare,
I do not know the man I should auoyd
So soone as that spare Cassius. He reades much,
He is a great Obseruer, and he lookes
Quite through the Deeds of men. He loues no Playes,
As thou dost Antony: he heares no Musicke;
Seldome he smiles, and smiles in such a sort
As if he mock'd himselfe, and scorn'd his spirit
That could be mou'd to smile at any thing.
Such men as he, be neuer at hearts ease,
Whiles they behold a greater then themselues,
And therefore are they very dangerous.
I rather tell thee what is to be fear'd,
Then what I feare: for alwayes I am Cæsar.
Come on my right hand, for this eare is deafe,
And tell me truely, what thou think'st of him. Sennit.
            Exeunt Cæsar and his Traine.

  Cask. You pul'd me by the cloake, would you speake
with me?
  Bru. I Caska, tell vs what hath chanc'd to day
That Cæsar lookes so sad.
  Cask. Why you were with him, were you not?
  Bru. I should not then aske Caska what had chanc'd.
  Cask. Why there was a Crowne offer'd him; & being
offer'd him, he put it by with the backe of his hand thus,
and then the people fell a shouting.
  Bru. What was the second noyse for?
  Cask. Why for that too.
  Cassi. They shouted thrice: what was the last cry for?
  Cask. Why for that too.
  Bru. Was the Crowne offer'd him thrice?
  Cask. I marry was't, and hee put it by thrice, euerie
time gentler then other; and at euery putting by, mine
honest Neighbors showted.
  Cassi. Who offer'd him the Crowne?
  Cask. Why Antony.
  Bru. Tell vs the manner of it, gentle Caska.
  Caska. I can as well bee hang'd as tell the manner of
it: It was meere Foolerie, I did not marke it. I sawe
Marke Antony offer him a Crowne, yet 'twas not a
Crowne neyther, 'twas one of these Coronets: and as I
told you, hee put it by once: but for all that, to my thinking, he would faine haue had it. Then hee offered it to
him againe: then hee put it by againe: but to my thinking, he was very loath to lay his fingers off it. And then
he offered it the third time; hee put it the third time by,
and still as hee refus'd it, the rabblement howted, and
clapp'd their chopt hands, and threw vppe their sweatie
Night-cappes, and vttered such a deale of stinking
breath, because Cæsar refus'd the Crowne, that it had
(almost) choaked Cæsar: for hee swoonded, and fell
downe at it: And for mine owne part, I durst not laugh,
for feare of opening my Lippes, and receyuing the bad
Ayre.

                        kk 2   Cassi.

Cassi. But soft I pray you: what, did *Cæsar* swound?

Cask. He fell downe in the Market-place, and foam'd at mouth, and was speechlesse.

Brut. 'Tis very like he hath the Falling sicknesse.

Cassi. No, *Cæsar* hath it not: but you, and I, And honest *Caska*, we haue the Falling sicknesse.

Cask. I know not what you meane by that, but I am sure *Cæsar* fell downe. If the tag-ragge people did not clap him, and hisse him, according as he pleas'd, and displeas'd them, as they vse to doe the Players in the Theatre, I am no true man.

Brut. What said he, when he came vnto himselfe?

Cask. Marry, before he fell downe, when he perceiu'd the common Heard was glad he refus'd the Crowne, he pluckt me ope his Doublet, and offer'd them his Throat to cut: and I had beene a man of any Occupation, if I would not haue taken him at a word, I would I might goe to Hell among the Rogues, and so hee fell. When he came to himselfe againe, hee said, If hee had done, or said any thing amisse, he desir'd their Worships to thinke it was his infirmitie. Three or foure Wenches where I stood, cryed, Alasse good Soule, and forgaue him with all their hearts: But there's no heed to be taken of them; if *Cæsar* had stab'd their Mothers, they would haue done no lesse.

Brut. And after that, he came thus sad away.

Cask. I.

Cassi. Did *Cicero* say any thing?

Cask. I, he spoke Greeke.

Cassi. To what effect?

Cask. Nay, and I tell you that, Ile ne're looke you i'th' face againe. But those that vnderstood him, smil'd at one another, and shooke their heads: but for mine owne part, it was Greeke to me. I could tell you more newes too: *Murrellus* and *Flauius*, for pulling Scarffes off *Cæsars* Images, are put to silence. Fare you well. There was more Foolerie yet, if I could remember it.

Cassi. Will you suppe with me to Night, *Caska*?

Cask. No, I am promis'd forth.

Cassi. Will you Dine with me to morrow?

Cask. I, if I be aliue, and your minde hold, and your Dinner worth the eating.

Cassi. Good, I will expect you.

Cask. Doe so: farewell both. *Exit.*

Brut. What a blunt fellow is this growne to be? He was quick Mettle, when he went to Schoole.

Cassi. So is he now, in execution
Of any bold, or Noble Enterprize,
How-euer he puts on this tardie forme:
This Rudenesse is a Sawce to his good Wit,
Which giues men stomacke to disgest his words
With better Appetite.

Brut. And so it is:
For this time I will leaue you:
To morrow, if you please to speake with me,
I will come home to you: or if you will,
Come home to me, and I will wait for you.

Cassi. I will doe so: till then, thinke of the World.
Exit Brutus.
Well *Brutus*, thou art Noble: yet I see,
Thy Honorable Mettle may be wrought
From that it is dispos'd: therefore it is meet,
That Noble mindes keepe euer with their likes:
For who so firme, that cannot be seduc'd?
Cæsar doth beare me hard, but he loues *Brutus*.
If I were *Brutus* now, and he were *Cassius*,
He should not humor me. I will this Night,
In seuerall Hands, in at his Windowes throw,
As if they came from seuerall Citizens,
Writings, all tending to the great opinion
That Rome holds of his Name: wherein obscurely
Cæsars Ambition shall be glanced at.
And after this, let *Cæsar* seat him sure,
For wee will shake him, or worse dayes endure.
Exit.

Thunder, and Lightning. Enter Caska, and Cicero.

Cic. Good euen, *Caska*: brought you *Cæsar* home?
Why are you breathlesse, and why stare you so?

Cask. Are not you mou'd, when all the sway of Earth
Shakes, like a thing vnfirme? O *Cicero*,
I haue seene Tempests, when the scolding Winds
Haue riu'd the knottie Oakes, and I haue seene
Th'ambitious Ocean swell, and rage, and foame,
To be exalted with the threatning Clouds:
But neuer till to Night, neuer till now,
Did I goe through a Tempest-dropping-fire.
Eyther there is a Ciuill strife in Heauen,
Or else the World, too sawcie with the Gods,
Incenses them to send destruction.

Cic. Why, saw you any thing more wonderfull?

Cask. A common slaue, you know him well by sight,
Held vp his left Hand, which did flame and burne
Like twentie Torches ioyn'd; and yet his Hand,
Not sensible of fire, remain'd vnscorch'd.
Besides, I ha' not since put vp my Sword,
Against the Capitoll I met a Lyon,
Who glaz'd vpon me, and went surly by,
Without annoying me. And there were drawne
Vpon a heape, a hundred gastly Women,
Transformed with their feare, who swore, they saw
Men, all in fire, walke vp and downe the streetes.
And yesterday, the Bird of Night did sit,
Euen at Noone-day, vpon the Market place,
Howting, and shreeking. When these Prodigies
Doe so conioyntly meet, let not men say,
These are their Reasons, they are Naturall:
For I beleeue, they are portentous things
Vnto the Clymate, that they point vpon.

Cic. Indeed, it is a strange disposed time:
But men may construe things after their fashion,
Cleane from the purpose of the things themselues.
Comes *Cæsar* to the Capitoll to morrow?

Cask. He doth: for he did bid *Antonio*
Send word to you, he would be there to morrow.

Cic. Good-night then, *Caska*:
This disturbed Skie is not to walke in.

Cask. Farewell *Cicero*. *Exit Cicero.*

Enter Cassius.

Cassi. Who's there?

Cask. A Romane.

Cassi. Caska, by your Voyce.

Cask. Your Eare is good.
Cassius, what Night is this?

Cassi. A very pleasing Night to honest men.

Cask. Who euer knew the Heauens menace so?

Cassi. Those that haue knowne the Earth so full of faults.

For

For my part, I haue walk'd about the streets,
Submitting me vnto the perillous Night;
And thus vnbraced, Caska, as you see,
Haue bar'd my Bosome to the Thunder-stone:
And when the crosse blew Lightning seem'd to open
The Brest of Heauen, I did present my selfe
Euen in the ayme, and very flash of it.

 Cask. But wherefore did you so much tempt the Hea-
It is the part of men, to feare and tremble, (uens?
When the most mightie Gods, by tokens send
Such dreadfull Heraulds, to astonish vs.

 Cassi. You are dull, Caska:
And those sparkes of Life, that should be in a Roman,
You doe want, or else you vse not.
You looke pale, and gaze, and put on feare,
And cast your selfe in wonder,
To see the strange impatience of the Heauens:
But if you would consider the true cause,
Why all these Fires, why all these gliding Ghosts,
Why Birds and Beasts, from qualitie and kinde,
Why Old men, Fooles, and Children calculate,
Why all these things change from their Ordinance,
Their Natures, and pre-formed Faculties,
To monstrous qualitie; why you shall finde,
That Heauen hath infus'd them with these Spirits,
To make them Instruments of feare, and warning,
Vnto some monstrous State.
Now could I (Caska) name to thee a man,
Most like this dreadfull Night,
That Thunders, Lightens, opens Graues, and roares,
As doth the Lyon in the Capitoll:
A man no mightier then thy selfe, or me,
In personall action; yet prodigious growne,
And fearefull, as these strange eruptions are.

 Cask. 'Tis Cæsar that you meane:
Is it not, Cassius?

 Cassi. Let it be who it is: for Romans now
Haue Thewes, and Limbes, like to their Ancestors;
But woe the while, our Fathers mindes are dead,
And we are gouern'd with our Mothers spirits,
Our yoake, and sufferance, shew vs Womanish.

 Cask. Indeed, they say, the Senators to morrow
Meane to establish Cæsar as a King:
And he shall weare his Crowne by Sea, and Land,
In euery place, saue here in Italy.

 Cassi. I know where I will weare this Dagger then;
Cassius from Bondage will deliuer Cassius:
Therein, yee Gods, you make the weake most strong;
Therein, yee Gods, you Tyrants doe defeat.
Nor Stonie Tower, nor Walls of beaten Brasse,
Nor ayre-lesse Dungeon, nor strong Linkes of Iron,
Can be retentiue to the strength of spirit:
But Life being wearie of these worldly Barres,
Neuer lacks power to dismisse it selfe.
If I know this, know all the World besides,
That part of Tyrannie that I doe beare,
I can shake off at pleasure.   Thunder still.

 Cask. So can I:
So euery Bond-man in his owne hand beares
The power to cancell his Captiuitie.

 Cassi. And why should Cæsar be a Tyrant then?
Poore man, I know he would not be a Wolfe,
But that he sees the Romans are but Sheepe:
He were no Lyon, were not Romans Hindes.
Those that with haste will make a mightie fire,
Begin it with weake Strawes. What trash is Rome?
What Rubbish, and what Offall? when it serues
For the base matter, to illuminate
So vile a thing as Cæsar. But oh Griefe,
Where hast thou led me? I (perhaps) speake this
Before a willing Bond-man: then I know
My answere must be made. But I am arm'd,
And dangers are to me indifferent.

 Cask. You speake to Caska, and to such a man,
That is no fleering Tell-tale. Hold, my Hand:
Be factious for redresse of all these Griefes,
And I will set this foot of mine as farre,
As who goes farthest.

 Cassi. There's a Bargaine made.
Now know you, Caska, I haue mou'd already
Some certaine of the Noblest minded Romans
To vnder-goe, with me, an Enterprize,
Of Honorable dangerous consequence;
And I doe know by this, they stay for me
In Pompeyes Porch: for now this fearefull Night,
There is no stirre, or walking in the streetes;
And the Complexion of the Element
Is Fauors, like the Worke we haue in hand,
Most bloodie, fierie, and most terrible.

Enter Cinna.

 Caska. Stand close a while, for heere comes one in haste.

 Cassi. 'Tis Cinna, I doe know him by his Gate,
He is a friend. Cinna, where haste you so?

 Cinna. To finde out you: Who's that, Metellus Cymber?

 Cassi. No, it is Caska, one incorporate
To our Attempts. Am I not stay'd for, Cinna?

 Cinna. I am glad on't.
What a fearefull Night is this?
There's two or three of vs haue seene strange sights.

 Cassi. Am I not stay'd for? tell me.

 Cinna. Yes, you are. O Cassius,
If you could but winne the Noble Brutus
To our party——

 Cassi. Be you content. Good Cinna, take this Paper,
And looke you lay it in the Pretors Chayre,
Where Brutus may but finde it: and throw this
In at his Window; set this vp with Waxe
Vpon old Brutus Statue: all this done,
Repaire to Pompeyes Porch, where you shall finde vs.
Is Decius Brutus and Trebonius there?

 Cinna. All, but Metellus Cymber, and hee's gone
To seeke you at your house. Well, I will hie,
And so bestow these Papers as you bad me.

 Cassi. That done, repayre to Pompeyes Theater.
                                                Exit Cinna.
Come Caska, you and I will yet, ere day,
See Brutus at his house: three parts of him
Is ours alreadie, and the man entire
Vpon the next encounter, yeelds him ours.

 Cask. O, he sits high in all the Peoples hearts:
And that which would appeare Offence in vs,
His Countenance, like richest Alchymie,
Will change to Vertue, and to Worthinesse.

 Cassi. Him, and his worth, and our great need of him,
You haue right well conceited: let vs goe,
For it is after Mid-night, and ere day,
We will awake him, and be sure of him.
                                                Exeunt.

Actus Secundus.

Enter Brutus in his Orchard.

Brut. What *Lucius*, hoe?
I cannot, by the progresse of the Starres,
Giue guesse how neere to day. *Lucius*, I say?
I would it were my fault to sleepe so soundly.
When *Lucius*, when? awake, I say: what *Lucius*?
 Enter Lucius.

Luc. Call'd you, my Lord?
 Brut. Get me a Tapor in my Study, *Lucius*:
When it is lighted, come and call me here.
 Luc. I will, my Lord. *Exit.*
 Brut. It must be by his death: and for my part,
I know no personall cause, to spurne at him,
But for the generall. He would be crown'd:
How that might change his nature, there's the question?
It is the bright day, that brings forth the Adder,
And that craues warie walking: Crowne him that,
And then I graunt we put a Sting in him,
That at his will he may doe danger with.
Th'abuse of Greatnesse, is, when it dis-ioynes
Remorse from Power: And to speake truth of *Cæsar*,
I haue not knowne, when his Affections sway'd
More then his Reason. But 'tis a common proofe,
That Lowlynesse is young Ambitions Ladder,
Whereto the Climber vpward turnes his Face:
But when he once attaines the vpmost Round,
He then vnto the Ladder turnes his Backe,
Lookes in the Clouds, scorning the base degrees
By which he did ascend: so *Cæsar* may;
Then least he may, preuent. And since the Quarrell
Will beare no colour, for the thing he is,
Fashion it thus; that what he is, augmented,
Would runne to these, and these extremities:
And therefore thinke him as a Serpents egge,
Which hatch'd, would as his kinde grow mischieuous;
And kill him in the shell.
 Enter Lucius.

Luc. The Taper burneth in your Closet, Sir:
Searching the Window for a Flint, I found
This Paper, thus seal'd vp, and I am sure
It did not lye there when I went to Bed.
 Giues him the Letter.

Brut. Get you to Bed againe, it is not day:
Is not to morrow (Boy) the first of March?
 Luc. I know not, Sir.
 Brut. Looke in the Calender, and bring me word.
 Luc. I will, Sir. *Exit.*
 Brut. The exhalations, whizzing in the ayre,
Giue so much light, that I may reade by them.
 Opens the Letter, and reades.
Brutus thou sleep'st; awake, and see thy selfe:
Shall Rome, &c. speake, strike, redresse.
Brutus, thou sleep'st: awake.
Such instigations haue beene often dropt,
Where I haue tooke them vp:
Shall Rome, &c. Thus must I piece it out:
Shall Rome stand vnder one mans awe? What Rome?
My Ancestors did from the streetes of Rome
The *Tarquin* driue, when he was call'd a King.
Speake, strike, redresse. Am I entreated
To speake, and strike? O Rome, I make thee promise,
If the redresse will follow, thou receiuest
Thy full Petition at the hand of *Brutus*.
 Enter Lucius.

Luc. Sir, March is wasted fifteene dayes.
 Knocke within.
Brut. 'Tis good. Go to the Gate, some body knocks:
Since *Cassius* first did whet me against *Cæsar*,
I haue not slept.
Betweene the acting of a dreadfull thing,
And the first motion, all the *Interim* is
Like a *Phantasma*, or a hideous Dreame:
The *Genius*, and the mortall Instruments
Are then in councell; and the state of a man,
Like to a little Kingdome, suffers then
The nature of an Insurrection.
 Enter Lucius.

Luc. Sir, 'tis your Brother *Cassius* at the Doore,
Who doth desire to see you.
 Brut. Is he alone?
 Luc. No, Sir, there are moe with him.
 Brut. Doe you know them?
 Luc. No, Sir, their Hats are pluckt about their Eares,
And halfe their Faces buried in their Cloakes,
That by no meanes I may discouer them,
By any marke of fauour.
 Brut. Let 'em enter:
They are the Faction. O Conspiracie,
Sham'st thou to shew thy dang'rous Brow by Night,
When euills are most free? O then, by day
Where wilt thou finde a Cauerne darke enough,
To maske thy monstrous Visage? Seek none Conspiracie,
Hide it in Smiles, and Affabilitie:
For if thou path thy natiue semblance on,
Not *Erebus* it selfe were dimme enough,
To hide thee from preuention.

Enter the Conspirators, Cassius, Caska, Decius,
Cinna, Metellus, and Trebonius.

Cass. I thinke we are too bold vpon your Rest:
Good morrow *Brutus*, doe we trouble you?
 Brut. I haue beene vp this howre, awake all Night:
Know I these men, that come along with you?
 Cass. Yes, euery man of them; and no man here
But honors you: and euery one doth wish,
You had but that opinion of your selfe,
Which euery Noble Roman beares of you.
This is *Trebonius*.
 Brut. He is welcome hither.
 Cass. This, *Decius Brutus*.
 Brut. He is welcome too.
 Cass. This, *Caska*; this, *Cinna*; and this, *Metellus Cymber*.
 Brut. They are all welcome.
What watchfull Cares doe interpose themselues
Betwixt your Eyes, and Night?
 Cass. Shall I entreat a word? *They whisper.*
 Decius. Here lyes the East: doth not the Day breake heere?
 Cask. No.
 Cin. O pardon, Sir, it doth; and yon grey Lines,
That fret the Clouds, are Messengers of Day.
 Cask. You shall confesse, that you are both deceiu'd:
Heere, as I point my Sword, the Sunne arises,
Which is a great way growing on the South,

Weigh-

Weighing the youthfull Season of the yeare.
Some two moneths hence, vp higher toward the North
He first presents his fire, and the high East
Stands as the Capitoll, directly heere.

Bru. Giue me your hands all ouer, one by one.

Caſ. And let vs sweare our Resolution.

Brut. No, not an Oath: if not the Face of men,
The sufferance of our Soules, the times Abuse;
If these be Motiues weake, breake off betimes,
And euery man hence, to his idle bed:
So let high-sighted-Tyranny range on,
Till each man drop by Lottery. But if these
(As I am sure they do) beare fire enough
To kindle Cowards, and to steele with valour
The melting Spirits of women. Then Countrymen,
What neede we any spurre, but our owne cause,
To pricke vs to redresse? What other Bond,
Then secret Romans, that haue spoke the word,
And will not palter? And what other Oath,
Then Honesty to Honesty ingag'd,
That this shall be, or we will fall for it.
Sweare Priests and Cowards, and men Cautelous
Old feeble Carrions, and such suffering Soules
That welcome wrongs: Vnto bad causes, sweare
Such Creatures as men doubt; but do not staine
The euen vertue of our Enterprize,
Nor th'insuppressiue Mettle of our Spirits,
To thinke, that or our Cause, or our Performance
Did neede an Oath. When euery drop of blood
That euery Roman beares, and Nobly beares
Is guilty of a seuerall Bastardie,
If he do breake the smallest Particle
Of any promise that hath past from him.

Caſ. But what of *Cicero*? Shall we sound him?
I thinke he will stand very strong with vs.

Cask. Let vs not leaue him out.

Cyn. No, by no meanes.

Metel. O let vs haue him, for his Siluer haires
Will purchase vs a good opinion:
And buy mens voyces, to commend our deeds:
It shall be sayd, his iudgement rul'd our hands,
Our youths, and wildenesse, shall no whit appeare,
But all be buried in his Grauity.

Bru. O name him not; let vs not breake with him,
For he will neuer follow any thing
That other men begin.

Caſ. Then leaue him out.

Cask. Indeed, he is not fit.

Decius. Shall no man else be toucht, but onely *Cæsar*?

Caſ. Decius well vrg'd: I thinke it is not meet,
Marke Antony, so well belou'd of *Cæsar*,
Should out-liue *Cæsar*, we shall finde of him
A shrew'd Contriuer. And you know, his meanes
If he improue them, may well stretch so farre
As to annoy vs all: which to preuent,
Let *Antony* and *Cæsar* fall together.

Bru. Our course will seeme too bloody, *Caius Cassius*,
To cut the Head off, and then hacke the Limbes:
Like Wrath in death, and Enuy afterwards:
For *Antony*, is but a Limbe of *Cæsar*.
Let's be Sacrificers, but not Butchers *Caius*:
We all stand vp against the spirit of *Cæsar*,
And in the Spirit of men, there is no blood:
O that we then could come by *Cæsars* Spirit,
And not dismember *Cæsar*! But (alas)
Cæsar must bleed for it. And gentle Friends,
Let's kill him Boldly, but not Wrathfully:
Let's carue him, as a Dish fit for the Gods,
Not hew him as a Carkasse fit for Hounds:
And let our Hearts, as subtle Masters do,
Stirre vp their Seruants to an acte of Rage,
And after seeme to chide 'em. This shall make
Our purpose Necessary, and not Enuious.
Which so appearing to the common eyes,
We shall be call'd Purgers, not Murderers.
And for *Marke Antony*, thinke not of him:
For he can do no more then *Cæsars* Arme,
When *Cæsars* head is off.

Caſ. Yet I feare him,
For in the ingrafted loue he beares to *Cæsar*.

Bru. Alas, good *Cassius*, do not thinke of him:
If he loue *Cæsar*, all that he can do
Is to himselfe; take thought, and dye for *Cæsar*,
And that were much he should: for he is giuen
To sports, to wildenesse, and much company.

Treb. There is no feare in him; let him not dye,
For he will liue, and laugh at this heereafter.

Clocke strikes.

Bru. Peace, count the Clocke.

Caſ. The Clocke hath stricken three.

Treb. 'Tis time to part.

Caſſ. But it is doubtfull yet,
Whether *Cæsar* will come forth to day, or no:
For he is Superstitious growne of late,
Quite from the maine Opinion he held once,
Of Fantasie, of Dreames, and Ceremonies:
It may be, these apparant Prodigies,
The vnaccustom'd Terror of this night,
And the perswasion of his Augurers,
May hold him from the Capitoll to day.

Decius. Neuer feare that: If he be so resolu'd,
I can ore-sway him: For he loues to heare,
That Vnicornes may be betray'd with Trees,
And Beares with Glasses, Elephants with Holes,
Lyons with Toyles, and men with Flatterers.
But, when I tell him, he hates Flatterers,
He sayes, he does; being then most flattered.
Let me worke:
For I can giue his humour the true bent;
And I will bring him to the Capitoll.

Caſ. Nay, we will all of vs, be there to fetch him.

Bru. By the eight houre, is that the vttermost?

Cin. Be that the vttermost, and faile not then.

Met. Caius Ligarius doth beare *Cæsar* hard,
Who rated him for speaking well of *Pompey*;
I wonder none of you haue thought of him.

Bru. Now good *Metellus* go along by him:
He loues me well, and I haue giuen him Reasons,
Send him but hither, and Ile fashion him.

Caſ. The morning comes vpon's:
Wee'l leaue you *Brutus*,
And friends disperse your selues; but all remember
What you haue said, and shew your selues true Romans.

Bru. Good Gentlemen, looke fresh and merrily,
Let not our lookes put on our purposes,
But beare it as our Roman Actors do,
With vntyr'd Spirits, and formall Constancie,
And so good morrow to you euery one. *Exeunt.*

Manet Brutus.

Boy: *Lucius:* Fast asleepe? It is no matter,
Enioy the hony-heauy-Dew of Slumber:
Thou hast no Figures, nor no Fantasies,

Which busie care drawes, in the braines of men;
Therefore thou sleep'st so sound.

Enter Portia.

Por. Brutus, my Lord.

Bru. Portia: What meane you? wherfore rise you now?
It is not for your health, thus to commit
Your weake condition, to the raw cold morning.

Por. Nor for yours neither. Y'haue vngently Brutus
Stole from my bed: and yesternight at Supper
You sodainly arose, and walk'd about,
Musing, and sighing, with your armes a-crosse:
And when I ask'd you what the matter was,
You star'd vpon me, with vngentle lookes.
I vrg'd you further, then you scratch'd your head,
And too impatiently stampt with your foote:
Yet I insisted, yet you answer'd not,
But with an angry wafter of your hand
Gaue signe for me to leaue you: So I did,
Fearing to strengthen that impatience
Which seem'd too much inkindled; and withall,
Hoping it was but an effect of Humor,
Which sometime hath his houre with euery man.
It will not let you eate, nor talke, nor sleepe;
And could it worke so much vpon your shape,
As it hath much preuayl'd on your Condition,
I should not know you Brutus. Deare my Lord,
Make me acquainted with your cause of greefe.

Bru. I am not well in health, and that is all.

Por. Brutus is wise, and were he not in health,
He would embrace the meanes to come by it.

Bru. Why so I do: good Portia go to bed.

Por. Is Brutus sicke? And is it Physicall
To walke vnbraced, and sucke vp the humours
Of the danke Morning? What, is Brutus sicke?
And will he steale out of his wholsome bed
To dare the vile contagion of the Night?
And tempt the Rhewmy, and vnpurged Ayre,
To adde vnto his sicknesse? No my Brutus,
You haue some sicke Offence within your minde,
Which by the Right and Vertue of my place
I ought to know of: And vpon my knees,
I charme you, by my once commended Beauty,
By all your vowes of Loue, and that great Vow
Which did incorporate and make vs one,
That you vnfold to me, your selfe; your halfe
Why you are heauy: and what men to night
Haue had resort to you: for heere haue beene
Some sixe or seuen, who did hide their faces
Euen from darknesse.

Bru. Kneele not gentle Portia.

Por. I should not neede, if you were gentle Brutus.
Within the Bond of Marriage, tell me Brutus,
Is it excepted, I should know no Secrets
That appertaine to you? Am I your Selfe,
But as it were in sort, or limitation?
To keepe with you at Meales, comfort your Bed,
And talke to you sometimes? Dwell I but in the Suburbs
Of your good pleasure? If it be no more,
Portia is Brutus Harlot, not his Wife.

Bru. You are my true and honourable Wife,
As deere to me, as are the ruddy droppes
That visit my sad heart.

Por. If this were true, then should I know this secret.
I graunt I am a Woman; but withall,
A Woman that Lord Brutus tooke to Wife:
I graunt I am a Woman; but withall,
A Woman well reputed: Cato's Daughter.
Thinke you, I am no stronger then my Sex
Being so Father'd, and so Husbanded?
Tell me your Counsels, I will not disclose 'em:
I haue made strong proofe of my Constancie,
Giuing my selfe a voluntary wound
Heere, in the Thigh: Can I beare that with patience,
And not my Husbands Secrets?

Bru. O ye Gods!
Render me worthy of this Noble Wife. *Knocke.*
Harke, harke, one knockes: Portia go in a while,
And by and by thy bosome shall partake
The secrets of my Heart.
All my engagements, I will construe to thee,
All the Charractery of my sad browes:
Leaue me with hast. *Exit Portia.*

Enter Lucius and Ligarius.

Lucius, who's that knockes.

Luc. Heere is a sicke man that would speak with you.

Bru. Caius Ligarius, that Metellus spake of.
Boy, stand aside. Caius Ligarius, how?

Cai. Vouchsafe good morrow from a feeble tongue.

Bru. O what a time haue you chose out braue Caius
To weare a Kerchiefe? Would you were not sicke.

Cai. I am not sicke, if Brutus haue in hand
Any exploit worthy the name of Honor.

Bru. Such an exploit haue I in hand Ligarius,
Had you a healthfull eare to heare of it.

Cai. By all the Gods that Romans bow before,
I heere discard my sicknesse. Soule of Rome,
Braue Sonne, deriu'd from Honourable Loines,
Thou like an Exorcist, hast coniur'd vp
My mortified Spirit. Now bid me runne,
And I will striue with things impossible,
Yea get the better of them. What's to do?

Bru. A peece of worke,
That will make sicke men whole.

Cai. But are not some whole, that we must make sicke?

Bru. That must we also. What it is my Caius,
I shall vnfold to thee, as we are going,
To whom it must be done.

Cai. Set on your foote,
And with a heart new-fir'd, I follow you,
To do I know not what: but it sufficeth
That Brutus leads me on. *Thunder.*

Bru. Follow me then. *Exeunt*

Thunder & Lightning.
Enter Iulius Cæsar in his Night-gowne.

Cæsar. Nor Heauen, nor Earth,
Haue beene at peace to night:
Thrice hath Calphurnia, in her sleepe cryed out,
Helpe, ho: They murther Cæsar. Who's within?

Enter a Seruant.

Ser. My Lord.

Cæs. Go bid the Priests do present Sacrifice,
And bring me their opinions of Successe. *Exit*

Ser. I will my Lord.

Enter Calphurnia.

Cal. What mean you Cæsar? Think you to walk forth?
You shall not stirre out of your house to day.

Cæs. Cæsar shall forth; the things that threaten'd me,
Ne're look'd but on my backe: When they shall see
The face of Cæsar, they are vanished. *Calp.*

The Tragedie of Julius Cæsar.

Calp. Cæsar, I neuer stood on Ceremonies,
Yet now they fright me: There is one within,
Besides the things that we haue heard and seene,
Recounts most horrid sights seene by the Watch.
A Lionnesse hath whelped in the streets,
And Graues haue yawn'd, and yeelded vp their dead;
Fierce fiery Warriours fight vpon the Clouds
In Rankes and Squadrons, and right forme of Warre
Which drizel'd blood vpon the Capitoll:
The noise of Battell hurtled in the Ayre:
Horsses do neigh, and dying men did grone,
And Ghosts did shrieke and squeale about the streets.
O Cæsar, these things are beyond all vse,
And I do feare them.

Cæs. What can be auoyded
Whose end is purpos'd by the mighty Gods?
Yet Cæsar shall go forth: for these Predictions
Are to the world in generall, as to Cæsar.

Calp. When Beggers dye, there are no Comets seen,
The Heauens themselues blaze forth the death of Princes

Cæs. Cowards dye many times before their deaths,
The valiant neuer taste of death but once:
Of all the Wonders that I yet haue heard,
It seemes to me most strange that men should feare,
Seeing that death, a necessary end
Will come, when it will come.

Enter a Seruant.

What say the Augurers?

Ser. They would not haue you to stirre forth to day.
Plucking the intrailes of an Offering forth,
They could not finde a heart within the beast.

Cæs. The Gods do this in shame of Cowardice:
Cæsar should be a Beast without a heart
If he should stay at home to day for feare:
No Cæsar shall not; Danger knowes full well
That Cæsar is more dangerous then he.
We heare two Lyons litter'd in one day,
And I the elder and more terrible,
And Cæsar shall go foorth.

Calp. Alas my Lord,
Your wisedome is consum'd in confidence:
Do not go forth to day: Call it my feare,
That keepes you in the house, and not your owne.
Wee'l send Mark Antony to the Senate house,
And he shall say, you are not well to day:
Let me vpon my knee, preuaile in this.

Cæs. Mark Antony shall say I am not well,
And for thy humor, I will stay at home.

Enter Decius.

Heere's Decius Brutus, he shall tell them so.

Deci. Cæsar, all haile: Good morrow worthy Cæsar,
I come to fetch you to the Senate house.

Cæs. And you are come in very happy time,
To beare my greeting to the Senators,
And tell them that I will not come to day:
Cannot, is false: and that I dare not, falser:
I will not come to day, tell them so Decius.

Calp. Say he is sicke.

Cæs. Shall Cæsar send a Lye?
Haue I in Conquest stretcht mine Arme so farre,
To be afear'd to tell Gray-beards the truth:
Decius, go tell them, Cæsar will not come.

Deci. Most mighty Cæsar, let me know some cause,
Lest I be laught at when I tell them so.

Cæs. The cause is in my Will, I will not come,
That is enough to satisfie the Senate.
But for your priuate satisfaction,
Because I loue you, I will let you know.
Calphurnia heere my wife, stayes me at home:
She dreampt to night, she saw my Statue,
Which like a Fountaine, with an hundred spouts
Did run pure blood: and many lusty Romans
Came smiling, & did bathe their hands in it:
And these does she apply, for warnings and portents,
And euils imminent; and on her knee
Hath begg'd, that I will stay at home to day.

Deci. This Dreame is all amisse interpreted,
It was a vision, faire and fortunate:
Your Statue spouting blood in many pipes,
In which so many smiling Romans bath'd,
Signifies, that from you great Rome shall sucke
Reuiuing blood, and that great men shall presse
For Tinctures, Staines, Reliques, and Cognisance.
This by Calphurnia's Dreame is signified.

Cæs. And this way haue you well expounded it.

Deci. I haue, when you haue heard what I can say:
And know it now, the Senate haue concluded
To giue this day, a Crowne to mighty Cæsar.
If you shall send them word you will not come,
Their mindes may change. Besides, it were a mocke
Apt to be render'd, for some one to say,
Breake vp the Senate, till another time:
When Cæsars wife shall meete with better Dreames.
If Cæsar hide himselfe, shall they not whisper
Loe Cæsar is affraid?
Pardon me Cæsar, for my deere deere loue
To your proceeding, bids me tell you this:
And reason to my loue is liable.

Cæs. How foolish do your fears seeme now Calphurnia?
I am ashamed I did yeeld to them.
Giue me my Robe, for I will go.

Enter Brutus, Ligarius, Metellus, Caska, Trebonius, Cynna, and Publius.

And looke where Publius is come to fetch me.

Pub. Good morrow Cæsar.

Cæs. Welcome Publius.
What Brutus, are you stirr'd so earely too?
Good morrow Caska: Caius Ligarius,
Cæsar was ne're so much your enemy,
As that same Ague which hath made you leane.
What is't a Clocke?

Bru. Cæsar, 'tis strucken eight.

Cæs. I thanke you for your paines and curtesie.

Enter Antony.

See, Antony that Reuels long a-nights
Is notwithstanding vp. Good morrow Antony.

Ant. So to most Noble Cæsar.

Cæs. Bid them prepare within:
I am too blame to be thus waited for.
Now Cynna, now Metellus: what Trebonius,
I haue an houres talke in store for you:
Remember that you call on me to day:
Be neere me, that I may remember you.

Treb. Cæsar I will: and so neere will I be,
That your best Friends shall wish I had beene further.

Cæs. Good Friends go in, and taste some wine with me
And we (like Friends) will straight way go together.

Bru. That euery like is not the same, O Cæsar,
The heart of Brutus earnes to thinke vpon. *Exeunt*

Enter Artemidorus.

Cæsar, beware of Brutus, take heede of Cassius; come not
neere

neere Caska, haue an eye to Cynna, trust not Trebonius, marke well Metellus Cymber, Decius Brutus loues thee not: Thou hast wrong'd Caius Ligarius. There is but one minde in all these men, and it is bent against Cæsar: If thou beest not Immortall, looke about you: Security giues way to Conspiracie. The mighty Gods defend thee.

Thy Louer, Artemidorus.

Heere will I stand, till Cæsar passe along,
And as a Sutor will I giue him this:
My heart laments, that Vertue cannot liue
Out of the teeth of Emulation.
If thou reade this, O Cæsar, thou mayest liue;
If not, the Fates with Traitors do contriue. Exit.

Enter Portia and Lucius.

Por. I prythee Boy, run to the Senate-house,
Stay not to answer me, but get thee gone.
Why doest thou stay?

Luc. To know my errand Madam.

Por. I would haue had thee there and heere agen
Ere I can tell thee what thou should'st do there:
O Constancie, be strong vpon my side,
Set a huge Mountaine tweene my Heart and Tongue:
I haue a mans minde, but a womans might:
How hard it is for women to keepe counsell.
Art thou heere yet?

Luc. Madam, what should I do?
Run to the Capitoll, and nothing else?
And so returne to you, and nothing else?

Por. Yes, bring me word Boy, if thy Lord look well,
For he went sickly forth: and take good note
What Cæsar doth, what Sutors presse to him.
Hearke Boy, what noyse is that?

Luc. I heare none Madam.

Por. Prythee listen well:
I heard a bustling Rumor like a Fray,
And the winde brings it from the Capitoll.

Luc. Sooth Madam, I heare nothing.

Enter the Soothsayer.

Por. Come hither Fellow, which way hast thou bin?
Sooth. At mine owne house, good Lady.
Por. What is't a clocke?
Sooth. About the ninth houre Lady.
Por. Is Cæsar yet gone to the Capitoll?
Sooth. Madam not yet, I go to take my stand,
To see him passe on to the Capitoll.
Por. Thou hast some suite to Cæsar, hast thou not?
Sooth. That I haue Lady, if it will please Cæsar
To be so good to Cæsar, as to heare me:
I shall beseech him to befriend himselfe.
Por. Why know'st thou any harme's intended towards him?
Sooth. None that I know will be,
Much that I feare may chance:
Good morrow to you: heere the street is narrow:
The throng that followes Cæsar at the heeles,
Of Senators, of Prætors, common Sutors,
Will crowd a feeble man (almost) to death:
Ile get me to a place more voyd, and there
Speake to great Cæsar as he comes along. Exit

Por. I must go in:
Aye me! How weake a thing
The heart of woman is? O Brutus,
The Heauens speede thee in thine enterprize.
Sure the Boy heard me: Brutus hath a suite
That Cæsar will not grant. O, I grow faint:
Run Lucius, and commend me to my Lord,
Say I am merry; Come to me againe,
And bring me word what he doth say to thee. Exeunt.

Actus Tertius.

Flourish.
Enter Cæsar, Brutus, Cassius, Caska, Decius, Metellus, Trebonius, Cynna, Antony, Lepidus, Artimedorus, Publius, and the Soothsayer.

Cæs. The Ides of March are come.
Sooth. I Cæsar, but not gone.
Art. Haile Cæsar: Read this Scedule.
Deci. Trebonius doth desire you to ore-read
(At your best leysure) this his humble suite.
Art. O Cæsar, reade mine first: for mine's a suite
That touches Cæsar neerer. Read it great Cæsar.
Cæs. What touches vs our selfe, shall be last seru'd.
Art. Delay not Cæsar, read it instantly.
Cæs. What, is the fellow mad?
Pub. Sirra, giue place.
Cassi. What, vrge you your Petitions in the street?
Come to the Capitoll.
Popil. I wish your enterprize to day may thriue.
Cassi. What enterprize Popillius?
Popil. Fare you well.
Bru. What said Popillius Lena?
Cassi. He wisht to day our enterprize might thriue:
I feare our purpose is discouered.
Bru. Looke how he makes to Cæsar: marke him.
Cassi. Caska be sodaine, for we feare preuention.
Brutus what shall be done? If this be knowne,
Cassius or Cæsar neuer shall turne backe,
For I will slay my selfe.
Bru. Cassius be constant:
Popillius Lena speakes not of our purposes,
For looke he smiles, and Cæsar doth not change.
Cassi. Trebonius knowes his time: for look you Brutus
He drawes Mark Antony out of the way.
Deci. Where is Metellus Cimber, let him go,
And presently preferre his suite to Cæsar.
Bru. He is addrest: presse neere, and second him.
Cin. Caska, you are the first that reares your hand.
Cæs. Are we all ready? What is now amisse,
That Cæsar and his Senate must redresse?
Metel. Most high, most mighty, and most puisant Cæsar
Metellus Cymber throwes before thy Seate
An humble heart.
Cæs. I must preuent thee Cymber:
These couchings, and these lowly courtesies
Might fire the blood of ordinary men,
And turne pre-Ordinance, and first Decree
Into the lane of Children. Be not fond,
To thinke that Cæsar beares such Rebell blood
That will be thaw'd from the true quality
With that which melteth Fooles, I meane sweet words,
Low-crooked-curtsies, and base Spaniell fawning:
Thy Brother by decree is banished:
If thou doest bend, and pray, and fawne for him,
I spurne thee like a Curre out of my way:
Know, Cæsar doth not wrong, nor without cause
Will he be satisfied.
Metel. Is there no voyce more worthy then my owne,

The Tragedie of Julius Cæsar. 119

To sound more sweetly in great *Cæsars* eare,
For the repealing of my banish'd Brother?

 Bru. I kisse thy hand, but not in flattery *Cæsar*:
Desiring thee, that *Publius Cymber* may
Haue an immediate freedome of repeale.

 Cæs. What *Brutus*?

 Cassi. Pardon *Cæsar*: *Cæsar* pardon:
As lowe as to thy foote doth *Cassius* fall,
To begge infranchisement for *Publius Cymber*.

 Cæs. I could be well mou'd, if I were as you,
If I could pray to mooue, Prayers would mooue me:
But I am constant as the Northerne Starre,
Of whose true fixt, and resting quality,
There is no fellow in the Firmament.
The Skies are painted with vnnumbred sparkes,
They are all Fire, and euery one doth shine:
But, there's but one in all doth hold his place.
So, in the World; 'Tis furnish'd well with Men,
And Men are Flesh and Blood, and apprehensiue;
Yet in the number, I do know but One
That vnassayleable holds on his Ranke,
Vnshak'd of Motion: and that I am he,
Let me a little shew it, euen in this:
That I was constant *Cymber* should be banish'd,
And constant do remaine to keepe him so.

 Cinna. O *Cæsar*.

 Cæs. Hence: Wilt thou lift vp Olympus?

 Decius. Great *Cæsar*.

 Cæs. Doth not *Brutus* bootlesse kneele?

 Cask. Speake hands for me.

They stab Cæsar.

 Cæs. Et Tu Brutè?——Then fall *Cæsar*. *Dyes*

 Cin. Liberty, Freedome; Tyranny is dead,
Run hence, proclaime, cry it about the Streets.

 Cassi. Some to the common Pulpits, and cry out
Liberty, Freedome, and Enfranchisement.

 Bru. People and Senators, be not affrighted:
Fly not, stand still: Ambitions debt is paid.

 Cask. Go to the Pulpit *Brutus*.

 Dec. And *Cassius* too.

 Bru. Where's *Publius*?

 Cin. Heere, quite confounded with this mutiny.

 Met. Stand fast together, least some Friend of *Cæsars*
Should chance——

 Bru. Talke not of standing. *Publius* good cheere,
There is no harme intended to your person,
Nor to no Roman else: so tell them *Publius*.

 Cassi. And leaue vs *Publius*, least that the people
Rushing on vs, should do your Age some mischiefe.

 Bru. Do so, and let no man abide this deede,
But we the Doers.

Enter Trebonius.

 Cassi. Where is *Antony*?

 Treb. Fled to his House amaz'd:
Men, Wiues, and Children, stare, cry out, and run,
As it were Doomesday.

 Bru. Fates, we will know your pleasures:
That we shall dye we know, 'tis but the time
And drawing dayes out, that men stand vpon.

 Cask. Why he that cuts off twenty yeares of life,
Cuts off so many yeares of fearing death.

 Bru. Grant that, and then is Death a Benefit:
So are we *Cæsars* Friends, that haue abridg'd
His time of fearing death. Stoope Romans, stoope,
And let vs bathe our hands in *Cæsars* blood
Vp to the Elbowes, and besmeare our Swords:
Then walke we forth, euen to the Market place,
And wauing our red Weapons o're our heads,
Let's all cry Peace, Freedome, and Liberty.

 Cassi. Stoop then, and wash. How many Ages hence
Shall this our lofty Scene be acted ouer,
In State vnborne, and Accents yet vnknowne?

 Bru. How many times shall *Cæsar* bleed in sport,
That now on *Pompeyes* Basis lye along,
No worthier then the dust?

 Cassi. So oft as that shall be,
So often shall the knot of vs be call'd,
The Men that gaue their Country liberty.

 Dec. What, shall we forth?

 Cassi. I, euery man away.
Brutus shall leade, and we will grace his heeles
With the most boldest, and best hearts of Rome.

Enter a Seruant.

 Bru. Soft, who comes heere? A friend of *Antonies*.

 Ser. Thus *Brutus* did my Master bid me kneele;
Thus did *Mark Antony* bid me fall downe,
And being prostrate, thus he bad me say:
Brutus is Noble, Wise, Valiant, and Honest;
Cæsar was Mighty, Bold, Royall, and Louing:
Say, I loue *Brutus*, and I honour him;
Say, I fear'd *Cæsar*, honour'd him, and lou'd him.
If *Brutus* will vouchsafe, that *Antony*
May safely come to him, and be resolu'd
How *Cæsar* hath deseru'd to lye in death,
Mark Antony, shall not loue *Cæsar* dead
So well as *Brutus* liuing; but will follow
The Fortunes and Affayres of Noble *Brutus*,
Thorough the hazards of this vntrod State,
With all true Faith. So sayes my Master *Antony*.

 Bru. Thy Master is a Wise and Valiant Romane,
I neuer thought him worse:
Tell him, so please him come vnto this place
He shall be satisfied: and by my Honor
Depart vntouch'd.

 Ser. Ile fetch him presently. *Exit Seruant.*

 Bru. I know that we shall haue him well to Friend.

 Cassi. I wish we may: But yet haue I a minde
That feares him much: and my misgiuing still
Falles shrewdly to the purpose.

Enter Antony.

 Bru. But heere comes *Antony*:
Welcome *Mark Antony*.

 Ant. O mighty *Cæsar*! Dost thou lye so lowe?
Are all thy Conquests, Glories, Triumphes, Spoiles,
Shrunke to this little Measure? Fare thee well.
I know not Gentlemen what you intend,
Who else must be let blood, who else is ranke:
If I my selfe, there is no houre so fit
As *Cæsars* deaths houre; nor no Instrument
Of halfe that worth, as those your Swords; made rich
With the most Noble blood of all this World.
I do beseech yee, if you beare me hard,
Now, whil'st your purpled hands do reeke and smoake,
Fulfill your pleasure. Liue a thousand yeeres,
I shall not finde my selfe so apt to dye.
No place will please me so, no meane of death,
As heere by *Cæsar*, and by you cut off,
The Choice and Master Spirits of this Age.

 Bru. O *Antony*! Begge not your death of vs:
Though now we must appeare bloody and cruell,
As by our hands, and this our present Acte
You see we do: Yet see you but our hands,

And

And this, the bleeding businesse they haue done:
Our hearts you see not, they are pittifull:
And pitty to the generall wrong of Rome,
As fire driues out fire, so pitty, pitty
Hath done this deed on *Cæsar*. For your part,
To you, our Swords haue leaden points *Marke Antony*:
Our Armes in strength of malice, and our Hearts
Of Brothers temper, do receiue you in,
With all kinde loue, good thoughts, and reuerence.

  Cassi. Your voyce shall be as strong as any mans,
In the disposing of new Dignities.

  Bru. Onely be patient, till we haue appeas'd
The Multitude, beside themselues with feare,
And then, we will deliuer you the cause,
Why I, that did loue *Cæsar* when I strooke him,
Haue thus proceeded.

  Ant. I doubt not of your Wisedome:
Let each man render me his bloody hand.
First *Marcus Brutus* will I shake with you;
Next *Caius Cassius* do I take your hand;
Now *Decius Brutus* yours; now yours *Metellus*;
Yours *Cinna*; and my valiant *Caska*, yours;
Though last, not least in loue, yours good *Trebonius*.
Gentlemen all: Alas, what shall I say,
My credit now stands on such slippery ground,
That one of two bad wayes you must conceit me,
Either a Coward, or a Flatterer.
That I did loue thee *Cæsar*, O 'tis true:
If then thy Spirit looke vpon vs now,
Shall it not greeue thee deerer then thy death,
To see thy *Antony* making his peace,
Shaking the bloody fingers of thy Foes?
Most Noble, in the presence of thy Coarse,
Had I as many eyes, as thou hast wounds,
Weeping as fast as they streame forth thy blood,
It would become me better, then to close
In tearmes of Friendship with thine enemies.
Pardon me *Iulius*, heere was't thou bay'd braue Hart,
Heere did'st thou fall, and heere thy Hunters stand
Sign'd in thy Spoyle, and Crimson'd in thy Lethee.
O World! thou wast the Forrest to this Hart,
And this indeed, O World, the Hart of thee.
How like a Deere, strooken by many Princes,
Dost thou heere lye?

  Cassi. Mark *Antony*.

  Ant. Pardon me *Caius Cassius*:
The Enemies of *Cæsar*, shall say this:
Then, in a Friend, it is cold Modestie.

  Cassi. I blame you not for praising *Cæsar* so,
But what compact meane you to haue with vs?
Will you be prick'd in number of our Friends,
Or shall we on, and not depend on you?

  Ant. Therefore I tooke your hands, but was indeed
Sway'd from the point, by looking downe on *Cæsar*.
Friends am I with you all, and loue you all,
Vpon this hope, that you shall giue me Reasons,
Why, and wherein, *Cæsar* was dangerous.

  Bru. Or else were this a sauage Spectacle:
Our Reasons are so full of good regard,
That were you *Antony*, the Sonne of *Cæsar*,
You should be satisfied.

  Ant. That's all I seeke,
And am moreouer sutor, that I may
Produce his body to the Market-place,
And in the Pulpit as becomes a Friend,
Speake in the Order of his Funerall.

  Bru. You shall *Marke Antony*.

  Cassi. Brutus, a word with you:
You know not what you do; Do not consent
That *Antony* speake in his Funerall:
Know you how much the people may be mou'd
By that which he will vtter.

  Bru. By your pardon:
I will my selfe into the Pulpit first,
And shew the reason of our *Cæsars* death.
What *Antony* shall speake, I will protest
He speakes by leaue, and by permission:
And that we are contented *Cæsar* shall
Haue all true Rites, and lawfull Ceremonies,
It shall aduantage more, then do vs wrong.

  Cassi. I know not what may fall, I like it not.

  Bru. Mark Antony, heere take you *Cæsars* body:
You shall not in your Funerall speech blame vs,
But speake all good you can deuise of *Cæsar*,
And say you doo't by our permission:
Else shall you not haue any hand at all
About his Funerall. And you shall speake
In the same Pulpit whereto I am going,
After my speech is ended.

  Ant. Be it so:
I do desire no more.

  Bru. Prepare the body then, and follow vs. *Exeunt.*
    Manet Antony.
O pardon me, thou bleeding peece of Earth:
That I am meeke and gentle with these Butchers.
Thou art the Ruines of the Noblest man
That euer liued in the Tide of Times.
Woe to the hand that shed this costly Blood.
Ouer thy wounds, now do I Prophesie,
(Which like dumbe mouthes do ope their Ruby lips,
To begge the voyce and vtterance of my Tongue)
A Curse shall light vpon the limbes of men;
Domesticke Fury, and fierce Ciuill strife,
Shall cumber all the parts of Italy:
Blood and destruction shall be so in vse,
And dreadfull Obiects so familiar,
That Mothers shall but smile, when they behold
Their Infants quartered with the hands of Warre:
All pitty choak'd with custome of fell deeds,
And *Cæsars* Spirit ranging for Reuenge,
With *Ate* by his side, come hot from Hell,
Shall in these Confines, with a Monarkes voyce,
Cry hauocke, and let slip the Dogges of Warre,
That this foule deede, shall smell aboue the earth
With Carrion men, groaning for Buriall.
    Enter Octauio's Seruant.
You serue *Octauius Cæsar*, do you not?

  Ser. I do *Marke Antony*.

  Ant. Cæsar did write for him to come to Rome.

  Ser. He did receiue his Letters, and is comming,
And bid me say to you by word of mouth———
O *Cæsar*!

  Ant. Thy heart is bigge: get thee a-part and weepe:
Passion I see is catching from mine eyes,
Seeing those Beads of sorrow stand in thine,
Began to water. Is thy Master comming?

  Ser. He lies to night within seuen Leagues of Rome.

  Ant. Post backe with speede,
And tell him what hath chanc'd:
Heere is a mourning Rome, a dangerous Rome,
No Rome of safety for *Octauius* yet,
Hie hence, and tell him so. Yet stay a-while,

Thou

Thou shalt not backe, till I haue borne this course
Into the Market place: There shall I try
In my Oration, how the People take
The cruell issue of these bloody men,
According to the which, thou shalt discourse
To yong *Octauius*, of the state of things.
Lend me your hand. *Exeunt*

Enter Brutus and goes into the Pulpit, and Cassius, with the Plebeians.

Ple. We will be satisfied: let vs be satisfied.

Bru. Then follow me, and giue me Audience friends.
Cassius go you into the other streete,
And part the Numbers:
Those that will heare me speake, let 'em stay heere;
Those that will follow *Cassius*, go with him,
And publike Reasons shall be rendred
Of *Cæsars* death.

1. *Ple.* I will heare *Brutus* speake.

2. I will heare *Cassius*, and compare their Reasons,
When seuerally we heare them rendred.

3. The Noble *Brutus* is ascended: Silence.

Bru. Be patient till the last.
Romans, Countrey-men, and Louers, heare mee for my
cause, and be silent, that you may heare. Beleeue me for
mine Honor, and haue respect to mine Honor, that you
may beleeue. Censure me in your Wisedom, and awake
your Senses, that you may the better Iudge. If there bee
any in this Assembly, any deere Friend of *Cæsars*, to him
I say, that *Brutus* loue to *Cæsar* was no lesse then his. If
then, that Friend demand, why *Brutus* rose against *Cæsar*, this is my answer: Not that I lou'd *Cæsar* lesse, but
that I lou'd Rome more. Had you rather *Cæsar* were liuing, and dye all Slaues; then that *Cæsar* were dead, to
liue all Free-men? As *Cæsar* lou'd mee, I weepe for him;
as he was Fortunate, I reioyce at it; as he was Valiant, I
honour him: But, as he was Ambitious, I slew him. There
is Teares, for his Loue: Ioy, for his Fortune: Honor, for
his Valour: and Death, for his Ambition. Who is heere
so base, that would be a Bondman? If any, speak, for him
haue I offended. Who is heere so rude, that would not
be a Roman? If any, speake, for him haue I offended. Who
is heere so vile, that will not loue his Countrey? If any,
speake, for him haue I offended. I pause for a Reply.

All. None *Brutus*, none.

Brutus. Then none haue I offended. I haue done no
more to *Cæsar*, then you shall do to *Brutus*. The Question of his death, is inroll'd in the Capitoll: his Glory not
extenuated, wherein he was worthy; nor his offences enforc'd, for which he suffered death.

Enter Mark Antony, with Cæsars body.

Heere comes his Body, mourn'd by *Marke Antony*, who
though he had no hand in his death, shall receiue the benefit of his dying, a place in the Cōmonwealth, as which
of you shall not. With this I depart, that as I slewe my
best Louer for the good of Rome, I haue the same Dagger for my selfe, when it shall please my Country to need
my death.

All. Liue *Brutus*, liue, liue.

1. Bring him with Triumph home vnto his house.
2. Giue him a Statue with his Ancestors.
3. Let him be *Cæsar*.
4. *Cæsars* better parts,

Shall be Crown'd in *Brutus*.

1. Wee'l bring him to his House,
With Showts and Clamors.

Bru. My Country-men.

2. Peace, silence, *Brutus* speakes.

1. Peace ho.

Bru. Good Countrymen, let me depart alone,
And (for my sake) stay heere with *Antony*:
Do grace to *Cæsars* Corpes, and grace his Speech
Tending to *Cæsars* Glories, which *Marke Antony*
(By our permission) is allow'd to make.
I do intreat you, not a man depart,
Saue I alone, till *Antony* haue spoke. *Exit*

1. Stay ho, and let vs heare *Mark Antony*.

3. Let him go vp into the publike Chaire,
Wee'l heare him: Noble *Antony* go vp.

Ant. For *Brutus* sake, I am beholding to you.

4. What does he say of *Brutus*?

3. He sayes, for *Brutus* sake
He findes himselfe beholding to vs all.

4. 'Twere best he speake no harme of *Brutus* heere?

1. This *Cæsar* was a Tyrant.

3. Nay that's certaine:
We are blest that Rome is rid of him.

2. Peace, let vs heare what *Antony* can say.

Ant. You gentle Romans.

All. Peace hoe, let vs heare him.

An. Friends, Romans, Countrymen, lend me your ears:
I come to bury *Cæsar*, not to praise him:
The euill that men do, liues after them,
The good is oft enterred with their bones,
So let it be with *Cæsar*. The Noble *Brutus*,
Hath told you *Cæsar* was Ambitious:
If it were so, it was a greeuous Fault,
And greeuously hath *Cæsar* answer'd it.
Heere, vnder leaue of *Brutus*, and the rest
(For *Brutus* is an Honourable man,
So are they all; all Honourable men)
Come I to speake in *Cæsars* Funerall.
He was my Friend, faithfull, and iust to me;
But *Brutus* sayes, he was Ambitious,
And *Brutus* is an Honourable man.
He hath brought many Captiues home to Rome,
Whose Ransomes, did the generall Coffers fill:
Did this in *Cæsar* seeme Ambitious?
When that the poore haue cry'de, *Cæsar* hath wept:
Ambition should be made of sterner stuffe,
Yet *Brutus* sayes, he was Ambitious:
And *Brutus* is an Honourable man.
You all did see, that on the *Lupercall*,
I thrice presented him a Kingly Crowne,
Which he did thrice refuse. Was this Ambition?
Yet *Brutus* sayes, he was Ambitious:
And sure he is an Honourable man.
I speake not to disprooue what *Brutus* spoke,
But heere I am, to speake what I do know;
You all did loue him once, not without cause,
What cause with-holds you then, to mourne for him?
O Iudgement! thou are fled to brutish Beasts,
And Men haue lost their Reason. Beare with me,
My heart is in the Coffin there with *Cæsar*,
And I must pawse, till it come backe to me.

1 Me thinkes there is much reason in his sayings.

2 If thou consider rightly of the matter,
Cæsar ha's had great wrong. (his place.

3 Ha's hee Masters? I feare there will a worse come in

4. Mark'd ye his words? he would not take ẏ Crown,
Therefore 'tis certaine, he was not Ambitious.

1. If it be found so, some will deere abide it.

2. Poore soule, his eyes are red as fire with weeping.

3. There's not a Nobler man in Rome then *Antony*.

4. Now marke him, he begins againe to speake.

Ant. But yesterday, the word of *Cæsar* might
Haue stood against the World: Now lies he there,
And none so poore to do him reuerence.
O Maisters! If I were dispos'd to stirre
Your hearts and mindes to Mutiny and Rage,
I should do *Brutus* wrong, and *Cassius* wrong:
Who (you all know) are Honourable men.
I will not do them wrong: I rather choose
To wrong the dead, to wrong my selfe and you,
Then I will wrong such Honourable men.
But heere's a Parchment, with the Seale of *Cæsar*,
I found it in his Closset, 'tis his Will:
Let but the Commons heare this Testament:
(Which pardon me) I do not meane to reade,
And they would go and kisse dead *Cæsars* wounds,
And dip their Napkins in his Sacred Blood;
Yea, begge a haire of him for Memory,
And dying, mention it within their Willes,
Bequeathing it as a rich Legacie
Vnto their issue.

4. Wee'l heare the Will, reade it *Marke Antony*.

All. The Will, the Will; we will heare *Cæsars* Will.

Ant. Haue patience gentle Friends, I must not read it.
It is not meete you know how *Cæsar* lou'd you:
You are not Wood, you are not Stones, but men:
And being men, hearing the Will of *Cæsar*,
It will inflame you, it will make you mad:
'Tis good you know not that you are his Heires,
For if you should, O what would come of it?

4. Read the Will, wee'l heare it *Antony*:
You shall reade vs the Will, *Cæsars* Will.

Ant. Will you be Patient? Will you stay a-while?
I haue o're-shot my selfe to tell you of it,
I feare I wrong the Honourable men,
Whose Daggers haue stabb'd *Cæsar*: I do feare it.

4. They were Traitors: Honourable men?

All. The Will, the Testament.

2. They were Villaines, Murderers: the Will, read the Will.

Ant. You will compell me then to read the Will:
Then make a Ring about the Corpes of *Cæsar*,
And let me shew you him that made the Will:
Shall I descend? And will you giue me leaue?

All. Come downe.

2 Descend.

3 You shall haue leaue.

4 A Ring, stand round.

1 Stand from the Hearse, stand from the Body.

2 Roome for *Antony*, most Noble *Antony*.

Ant. Nay presse not so vpon me, stand farre off.

All. Stand backe: roome, beare backe.

Ant. If you haue teares, prepare to shed them now.
You all do know this Mantle, I remember
The first time euer *Cæsar* put it on,
'Twas on a Summers Euening in his Tent,
That day he ouercame the *Neruij*.
Looke, in this place ran *Cassius* Dagger through:
See what a rent the enuious *Caska* made:
Through this, the wel-beloued *Brutus* stabb'd,
And as he pluck'd his cursed Steele away:
Marke how the blood of *Cæsar* followed it,
As rushing out of doores, to be resolu'd
If *Brutus* so vnkindely knock'd, or no:
For *Brutus*, as you know, was *Cæsars* Angel.
Iudge, O you Gods, how deerely *Cæsar* lou'd him:
This was the most vnkindest cut of all.
For when the Noble *Cæsar* saw him stab,
Ingratitude, more strong then Traitors armes,
Quite vanquish'd him: then burst his Mighty heart,
And in his Mantle, muffling vp his face,
Euen at the Base of *Pompeyes* Statue
(Which all the while ran blood) great *Cæsar* fell.
O what a fall was there, my Countrymen?
Then I, and you, and all of vs fell downe,
Whil'st bloody Treason flourish'd ouer vs.
O now you weepe, and I perceiue you feele
The dint of pitty: These are gracious droppes.
Kinde Soules, what weepe you, when you but behold
Our *Cæsars* Vesture wounded? Looke you heere,
Heere is Himselfe, marr'd as you see with Traitors.

1. O pitteous spectacle!

2. O Noble *Cæsar*!

3. O wofull day!

4. O Traitors, Villaines!

1. O most bloody sight!

2. We will be reueng'd: Reuenge
About, seeke, burne, fire, kill, slay,
Let not a Traitor liue.

Ant. Stay Country-men.

1. Peace there, heare the Noble *Antony*.

2. Wee'l heare him, wee'l follow him, wee'l dy with him.

Ant. Good Friends, sweet Friends, let me not stirre
To such a sodaine Flood of Mutiny:
They that haue done this Deede, are honourable.
What priuate greefes they haue, alas I know not,
That made them do it: They are Wise, and Honourable,
And will no doubt with Reasons answer you.
I come not (Friends) to steale away your hearts,
I am no Orator, as *Brutus* is;
But (as you know me all) a plaine blunt man
That loue my Friend, and that they know full well,
That gaue me publike leaue to speake of him:
For I haue neyther writ nor words, nor worth,
Action, nor Vtterance, nor the power of Speech,
To stirre mens Blood. I onely speake right on:
I tell you that, which you your selues do know,
Shew you sweet *Cæsars* wounds, poor poor dum mouths
And bid them speake for me: But were I *Brutus*,
And *Brutus Antony*, there were an *Antony*
Would ruffle vp your Spirits, and put a Tongue
In euery Wound of *Cæsar*, that should moue
The stones of Rome, to rise and Mutiny.

All. Wee'l Mutiny.

1 Wee'l burne the house of *Brutus*.

3 Away then, come, seeke the Conspirators.

Ant. Yet heare me Countrymen, yet heare me speake

All. Peace hoe, heare *Antony*, most Noble *Antony*.

Ant. Why Friends, you go to do you know not what:
Wherein hath *Cæsar* thus deseru'd your loues?
Alas you know not, I must tell you then:
You haue forgot the Will I told you of.

All. Most true, the Will, let's stay and heare the Will.

Ant. Heere is the Will, and vnder *Cæsars* Seale:
To euery Roman Citizen he giues,
To euery seuerall man, seuenty fiue Drachmaes.

The Tragedie of Julius Cæsar.

2. Ple. Most Noble *Cæsar*, wee'l reuenge his death.
3. Ple. O Royall *Cæsar*.
Ant. Heare me with patience.
All. Peace hoe.
Ant. Moreouer, he hath left you all his Walkes,
His priuate Arbors, and new-planted Orchards,
On this side Tyber, he hath left them you,
And to your heyres for euer: common pleasures
To walke abroad, and recreate your selues.
Heere was a *Cæsar*: when comes such another?
1. Ple. Neuer, neuer: come, away, away:
Wee'l burne his body in the holy place,
And with the Brands fire the Traitors houses.
Take vp the body.
2. Ple. Go fetch fire.
3. Ple. Plucke downe Benches.
4. Ple. Plucke downe Formes, Windowes, any thing.
Exit Plebeians.

Ant. Now let it worke: Mischeefe thou art a-foot,
Take thou what course thou wilt.
How now Fellow?

Enter Seruant.

Ser. Sir, *Octauius* is already come to Rome.
Ant. Where is hee?
Ser. He and *Lepidus* are at *Cæsars* house.
Ant. And thither will I straight, to visit him:
He comes vpon a wish. Fortune is merry,
And in this mood will giue vs any thing.
Ser. I heard him say, *Brutus* and *Cassius*
Are rid like Madmen through the Gates of Rome.
Ant. Belike they had some notice of the people
How I had moued them. Bring me to *Octauius*. *Exeunt*

Enter Cinna the Poet, and after him the Plebeians.

Cinna. I dreamt to night, that I did feast with *Cæsar*,
And things vnluckily charge my Fantasie:
I haue no will to wander foorth of doores,
Yet something leads me foorth.
1. What is your name?
2. Whether are you going?
3. Where do you dwell?
4. Are you a married man, or a Batchellor?
2. Answer euery man directly.
1. I, and breefely.
4. I, and wisely.
3. I, and truly, you were best.
Cin. What is my name? Whether am I going? Where
do I dwell? Am I a married man, or a Batchellour? Then
to answer euery man, directly and breefely, wisely and
truly: wisely I say, I am a Batchellor.
2 That's as much as to say, they are fooles that marrie: you'l beare me a bang for that I feare: proceede directly.
Cinna. Directly I am going to *Cæsars* Funerall.
1. As a Friend, or an Enemy?
Cinna. As a friend.
2. That matter is answered directly.
4. For your dwelling: breefely.
Cinna. Breefely, I dwell by the Capitoll.
3. Your name sir, truly.
Cinna. Truly, my name is *Cinna*.
1. Teare him to peeces, hee's a Conspirator.
Cinna. I am *Cinna* the Poet, I am *Cinna* the Poet.
4. Teare him for his bad verses, teare him for his bad Verses.

Cin. I am not *Cinna* the Conspirator.
4. It is no matter, his name's *Cinna*, plucke but his
name out of his heart, and turne him going.
3. Teare him, tear him; Come Brands hoe, Firebrands:
to *Brutus*, to *Cassius*, burne all. Some to *Decius* House,
and some to *Caska's*; some to *Ligarius*: Away, go.
Exeunt all the Plebeians.

Actus Quartus.

Enter Antony, Octauius, and Lepidus.

Ant. These many then shall die, their names are prickt
Octa. Your Brother too must dye: consent you *Lepidus*?
Lep. I do consent.
Octa. Pricke him downe *Antony*.
Lep. Vpon condition *Publius* shall not liue,
Who is your Sisters sonne, *Marke Antony*.
Ant. He shall not liue; looke, with a spot I dam him.
But *Lepidus*, go you to *Cæsars* house:
Fetch the Will hither, and we shall determine
How to cut off some charge in Legacies.
Lep. What? shall I finde you heere?
Octa. Or heere, or at the Capitoll. *Exit Lepidus*
Ant. This is a slight vnmeritable man,
Meet to be sent on Errands: is it fit
The three-fold World diuided, he should stand
One of the three to share it?
Octa. So you thought him,
And tooke his voyce who should be prickt to dye
In our blacke Sentence and Proscription.
Ant. Octauius, I haue seene more dayes then you,
And though we lay these Honours on this man,
To ease our selues of diuers sland'rous loads,
He shall but beare them, as the Asse beares Gold,
To groane and swet vnder the Businesse,
Either led or driuen, as we point the way:
And hauing brought our Treasure, where we will,
Then take we downe his Load, and turne him off
(Like to the empty Asse) to shake his eares,
And graze in Commons.
Octa. You may do your will:
But hee's a tried, and valiant Souldier.
Ant. So is my Horse *Octauius*, and for that
I do appoint him store of Prouender.
It is a Creature that I teach to fight,
To winde, to stop, to run directly on:
His corporall Motion, gouern'd by my Spirit,
And in some taste, is *Lepidus* but so:
He must be taught, and train'd, and bid go forth:
A barren spirited Fellow; one that feeds
On Obiects, Arts, and Imitations.
Which out of vse, and stal'de by other men
Begin his fashion. Do not talke of him,
But as a property: and now *Octauius*,
Listen great things. *Brutus* and *Cassius*
Are leuying Powers; We must straight make head:
Therefore let our Alliance be combin'd,
Our best Friends made, our meanes stretcht,
And let vs presently go sit in Councell,
How couert matters may be best disclos'd,
And open Perils surest answered.
Octa. Let vs do so: for we are at the stake,

And

And bayed about with many Enemies,
And some that smile haue in their hearts I feare
Millions of Mischeefes.   *Exeunt*

Drum. Enter Brutus, Lucillius, and the Army. Titinius and Pindarus meete them.

Bru. Stand ho.
Lucil. Giue the word ho, and Stand.
Bru. What now *Lucillius*, is *Cassius* neere?
Lucil. He is at hand, and *Pindarus* is come
To do you salutation from his Master.
Bru. He greets me well. Your Master *Pindarus*
In his owne change, or by ill Officers,
Hath giuen me some worthy cause to wish
Things done, vndone: But if he be at hand
I shall be satisfied.
Pin. I do not doubt
But that my Noble Master will appeare
Such as he is, full of regard, and Honour.
Bru. He is not doubted. A word *Lucillius*
How he receiu'd you: let me be resolu'd.
Lucil. With courtesie, and with respect enough,
But not with such familiar instances,
Nor with such free and friendly Conference
As he hath vs'd of old.
Bru. Thou hast describ'd
A hot Friend, cooling: Euer note *Lucillius*,
When Loue begins to sicken and decay
It vseth an enforced Ceremony.
There are no trickes, in plaine and simple Faith:
But hollow men, like Horses hot at hand,
Make gallant shew, and promise of their Mettle:
                                    Low March within.
But when they should endure the bloody Spurre,
They fall their Crests, and like deceitfull Iades
Sinke in the Triall. Comes his Army on?
Lucil. They meane this night in Sardis to be quarter'd:
The greater part, the Horse in generall
Are come with *Cassius*.

Enter Cassius and his Powers.

Bru. Hearke, he is arriu'd:
March gently on to meete him.
Cassi. Stand ho.
Bru. Stand ho, speake the word along.
Stand.
Stand.
Stand.
Cassi. Most Noble Brother, you haue done me wrong.
Bru. Iudge me you Gods; wrong I mine Enemies?
And if not so, how should I wrong a Brother.
Cassi. *Brutus*, this sober forme of yours, hides wrongs,
And when you do them——
Bru. *Cassius*, be content,
Speake your greefes softly, I do know you well.
Before the eyes of both our Armies heere
(Which should perceiue nothing but Loue from vs)
Let vs not wrangle. Bid them moue away:
Then in my Tent *Cassius* enlarge your Greefes,
And I will giue you Audience.
Cassi. *Pindarus*,
Bid our Commanders leade their Charges off
A little from this ground.
Bru. *Lucillius*, do you the like, and let no man
Come to our Tent, till we haue done our Conference.
Let *Lucius* and *Titinius* guard our doore.   *Exeunt*
Manet Brutus and Cassius.

Cassi. That you haue wrong'd me, doth appear in this
You haue condemn'd, and noted *Lucius Pella*
For taking Bribes heere of the Sardians;
Wherein my Letters, praying on his side,
Because I knew the man was slighted off.
Bru. You wrong'd your selfe to write in such a case.
Cassi. In such a time as this, it is not meet
That euery nice offence should beare his Comment.
Bru. Let me tell you *Cassius*, you your selfe
Are much condemn'd to haue an itching Palme,
To sell, and Mart your Offices for Gold
To Vndeseruers.
Cassi. I, an itching Palme?
You know that you are *Brutus* that speakes this,
Or by the Gods, this speech were else your last.
Bru. The name of *Cassius* Honors this corruption,
And Chasticement doth therefore hide his head.
Cassi. Chasticement?
Bru. Remember March, the Ides of March remēber:
Did not great *Iulius* bleede for Iustice sake?
What Villaine touch'd his body, that did stab,
And not for Iustice? What? Shall one of Vs,
That strucke the Formost man of all this World,
But for supporting Robbers: shall we now,
Contaminate our fingers, with base Bribes?
And sell the mighty space of our large Honors
For so much trash, as may be grasped thus?
I had rather be a Dogge, and bay the Moone,
Then such a Roman.
Cassi. *Brutus*, baite not me,
Ile not indure it: you forget your selfe
To hedge me in. I am a Souldier, I,
Older in practice, Abler then your selfe
To make Conditions.
Bru. Go too: you are not *Cassius*.
Cassi. I am.
Bru. I say, you are not.
Cassi. Vrge me no more, I shall forget my selfe:
Haue minde vpon your health: Tempt me no farther.
Bru. Away slight man.
Cassi. Is't possible?
Bru. Heare me, for I will speake.
Must I giue way, and roome to your rash Choller?
Shall I be frighted, when a Madman stares?
Cassi. O ye Gods, ye Gods, Must I endure all this?
Bru. All this? I more: Fret till your proud hart break.
Go shew your Slaues how Chollericke you are,
And make your Bondmen tremble. Must I bouge?
Must I obserue you? Must I stand and crouch
Vnder your Testie Humour? By the Gods,
You shall digest the Venom of your Spleene
Though it do Split you. For, from this day forth,
Ile vse you for my Mirth, yea for my Laughter
When you are Waspish.
Cassi. Is it come to this?
Bru. You say, you are a better Souldier:
Let it appeare so; make your vaunting true,
And it shall please me well. For mine owne part,
I shall be glad to learne of Noble men.
Cass. You wrong me euery way:
You wrong me *Brutus*:
I saide, an Elder Souldier, not a Better.
Did I say Better?
Bru. If you did, I care not.
Cassi. When *Cæsar* liu'd, he durst not thus haue mou'd me
Bru. Peace, peace, you durst not so haue tempted him.

Cassi. I durst not.
Bru. No.
Cassi. What? durst not tempt him?
Bru. For your life you durst not.
Cassi. Do not presume too much vpon my Loue,
I may do that I shall be sorry for.
Bru. You haue done that you should be sorry for.
There is no terror *Cassius* in your threats:
For I am Arm'd so strong in Honesty,
That they passe by me, as the idle winde,
Which I respect not. I did send to you
For certaine summes of Gold, which you deny'd me,
For I can raise no money by vile meanes:
By Heauen, I had rather Coine my Heart,
And drop my blood for Drachmaes, then to wring
From the hard hands of Peazants, their vile trash
By any indirection. I did send
To you for Gold to pay my Legions,
Which you deny'd me: was that done like *Cassius*?
Should I haue answer'd *Caius Cassius* so?
When *Marcus Brutus* growes so Couetous,
To locke such Rascall Counters from his Friends,
Be ready Gods with all your Thunder-bolts,
Dash him to peeces.
  Cassi. I deny'd you not.
  Bru. You did.
  Cassi. I did not. He was but a Foole
That brought my answer back. *Brutus* hath riu'd my hart:
A Friend should beare his Friends infirmities;
But *Brutus* makes mine greater then they are.
  Bru. I do not, till you practice them on me.
  Cassi. You loue me not.
  Bru. I do not like your faults.
  Cassi. A friendly eye could neuer see such faults.
  Bru. A Flatterers would not, though they do appeare
As huge as high Olympus.
  Cassi. Come *Antony*, and yong *Octauius* come,
Reuenge your selues alone on *Cassius*,
For *Cassius* is a-weary of the World:
Hated by one he loues, brau'd by his Brother,
Check'd like a bondman, all his faults obseru'd,
Set in a Note-booke, learn'd, and con'd by roate
To cast into my Teeth. O I could weepe
My Spirit from mine eyes. There is my Dagger,
And heere my naked Breast: Within, a Heart
Deerer then *Pluto's* Mine, Richer then Gold:
If that thou bee'st a Roman, take it foorth.
I that deny'd thee Gold, will giue my Heart:
Strike as thou did'st at *Cæsar*: For I know,
When thou did'st hate him worst, § loued'st him better
Then euer thou loued'st *Cassius*.
  Bru. Sheath your Dagger:
Be angry when you will, it shall haue scope:
Do what you will, Dishonor, shall be Humour.
O *Cassius*, you are yoaked with a Lambe
That carries Anger, as the Flint beares fire,
Who much inforced, shewes a hastie Sparke,
And straite is cold agen.
  Cassi. Hath *Cassius* liu'd
To be but Mirth and Laughter to his *Brutus*,
When greefe and blood ill temper'd, vexeth him?
  Bru. When I spoke that, I was ill temper'd too.
  Cassi. Do you confesse so much? Giue me your hand.
  Bru. And my heart too.
  Cassi. O *Brutus*!
  Bru. What's the matter?

  Cassi. Haue not you loue enough to beare with me,
When that rash humour which my Mother gaue me
Makes me forgetfull.
  Bru. Yes *Cassius*, and from henceforth
When you are ouer-earnest with your *Brutus*,
Hee'l thinke your Mother chides, and leaue you so.

Enter a Poet.

  Poet. Let me go in to see the Generals,
There is some grudge betweene 'em, 'tis not meete
They be alone.
  Lucil. You shall not come to them.
  Poet. Nothing but death shall stay me.
  Cas. How now? What's the matter?
  Poet. For shame you Generals; what do you meane?
Loue, and be Friends, as two such men should bee,
For I haue seene more yeeres I'me sure then yee.
  Cas. Ha, ha, how vildely doth this Cynicke rime?
  Bru. Get you hence sirra: Sawcy Fellow, hence.
  Cas. Beare with him *Brutus*, 'tis his fashion.
  Brut. Ile know his humor, when he knowes his time:
What should the Warres do with these Iigging Fooles?
Companion, hence.
  Cas. Away, away be gone. *Exit Poet*
  Bru. *Lucillius* and *Titinius* bid the Commanders
Prepare to lodge their Companies to night.
  Cas. And come your selues, & bring *Messala* with you
Immediately to vs.
  Bru. *Lucius*, a bowle of Wine.
  Cas. I did not thinke you could haue bin so angry.
  Bru. O *Cassius*, I am sicke of many greefes.
  Cas. Of your Philosophy you make no vse,
If you giue place to accidentall euils.
  Bru. No man beares sorrow better. *Portia* is dead.
  Cas. Ha? *Portia*?
  Bru. She is dead.
  Cas. How scap'd I killing, when I crost you so?
O insupportable, and touching losse!
Vpon what sicknesse?
  Bru. Impatient of my absence,
And greefe, that yong *Octauius* with *Mark Antony*
Haue made themselues so strong: For with her death
That tydings came. With this she fell distract,
And (her Attendants absent) swallow'd fire.
  Cas. And dy'd so?
  Bru. Euen so.
  Cas. O ye immortall Gods!

Enter Boy with Wine, and Tapers.

  Bru. Speak no more of her: Giue me a bowl of wine,
In this I bury all vnkindnesse *Cassius*. *Drinkes*
  Cas. My heart is thirsty for that Noble pledge.
Fill *Lucius*, till the Wine ore-swell the Cup:
I cannot drinke too much of *Brutus* loue.

Enter Titinius and Messala.

  Brutus. Come in *Titinius*:
Welcome good *Messala*:
Now sit we close about this Taper heere,
And call in question our necessities.
  Cass. *Portia*, art thou gone?
  Bru. No more I pray you.
Messala, I haue heere receiued Letters,
That yong *Octauius*, and *Marke Antony*
Come downe vpon vs with a mighty power,
Bending their Expedition toward *Philippi*.

Mess. My selfe haue Letters of the selfe-same Tenure.
Bru. With what Addition.
Mess. That by proscription, and billes of Outlarie,
Octauius, Antony, and *Lepidus,*
Haue put to death, an hundred Senators.
Bru. Therein our Letters do not well agree:
Mine speake of seuenty Senators, that dy'de
By their proscriptions, *Cicero* being one.
Cassi. *Cicero* one?
Messa. Cicero is dead, and by that order of proscription
Had you your Letters from your wife, my Lord?
Bru. No *Messala.*
Messa. Nor nothing in your Letters writ of her?
Bru. Nothing *Messala.*
Messa. That me thinkes is strange.
Bru. Why aske you?
Heare you ought of her, in yours?
Messa. No my Lord.
Bru. Now as you are a Roman tell me true.
Messa. Then like a Roman, beare the truth I tell,
For certaine she is dead, and by strange manner.
Bru. Why farewell *Portia*: We must die *Messala*:
With meditating that she must dye once,
I haue the patience to endure it now.
Messa. Euen so great men, great losses shold indure.
Cassi. I haue as much of this in Art as you,
But yet my Nature could not beare it so.
Bru. Well, to our worke aliue. What do you thinke
Of marching to *Philippi* presently.
Cassi. I do not thinke it good.
Bru. Your reason?
Cassi. This it is:
'Tis better that the Enemie seeke vs,
So shall he waste his meanes, weary his Souldiers,
Doing himselfe offence, whil'st we lying still,
Are full of rest, defence, and nimblenesse.
Bru. Good reasons must of force giue place to better:
The people 'twixt *Philippi*, and this ground
Do stand but in a forc'd affection:
For they haue grug'd vs Contribution:
The Enemy, marching along by them,
By them shall make a fuller number vp,
Come on refresht, new added, and encourag'd:
From which aduantage shall we cut him off.
If at *Philippi* we do face him there,
These people at our backe.
Cassi. Heare me good Brother.
Bru. Vnder your pardon. You must note beside,
That we haue tride the vtmost of our Friends:
Our Legions are brim full, our cause is ripe,
The Enemy encreaseth euery day,
We at the height, are readie to decline.
There is a Tide in the affayres of men,
Which taken at the Flood, leades on to Fortune:
Omitted, all the voyage of their life,
Is bound in Shallowes, and in Miseries.
On such a full Sea are we now a-float,
And we must take the current when it serues,
Or loose our Ventures.
Cassi. Then with your will go on: wee'l along
Our selues, and meet them at *Philippi.*
Bru. The deepe of night is crept vpon our talke,
And Nature must obey Necessitie,
Which we will niggard with a little rest:
There is no more to say.
Cassi. No more, goodnight,

Early to morrow will we rise, and hence.
Enter Lucius.
Bru. Lucius my Gowne: farewell good *Messala,*
Good night *Titinius*: Noble, Noble *Cassius,*
Good night, and good repose.
Cassi. O my deere Brother:
This was an ill beginning of the night:
Neuer come such diuision 'tweene our soules:
Let it not *Brutus.*
Enter Lucius with the Gowne.
Bru. Euery thing is well.
Cassi. Good night my Lord.
Bru. Good night good Brother.
Tit. Messa. Good night Lord *Brutus.*
Bru. Farewell euery one.   *Exeunt.*
Giue me the Gowne. Where is thy Instrument?
Luc. Heere in the Tent.
Bru. What, thou speak'st drowsily?
Poore knaue I blame thee not, thou art ore-watch'd.
Call *Claudio,* and some other of my men,
Ile haue them sleepe on Cushions in my Tent.
Luc. Varrus, and *Claudio.*
Enter Varrus and Claudio.
Var. Cals my Lord?
Bru. I pray you sirs, lye in my Tent and sleepe,
It may be I shall raise you by and by
On businesse to my Brother *Cassius.*
Var. So please you, we will stand,
And watch your pleasure.
Bru. I will it not haue it so: Lye downe good sirs,
It may be I shall otherwise bethinke me.
Looke *Lucius,* heere's the booke I sought for so:
I put it in the pocket of my Gowne.
Luc. I was sure your Lordship did not giue it me.
Bru. Beare with me good Boy, I am much forgetfull.
Canst thou hold vp thy heauie eyes a-while,
And touch thy Instrument a straine or two.
Luc. I my Lord, an't please you.
Bru. It does my Boy:
I trouble thee too much, but thou art willing.
Luc. It is my duty Sir.
Brut. I should not vrge thy duty past thy might,
I know yong bloods looke for a time of rest.
Luc. I haue slept my Lord already.
Bru. It was well done, and thou shalt sleepe againe:
I will not hold thee long. If I do liue,
I will be good to thee.
Musicke, and a Song.
This is a sleepy Tune: O Murd'rous slumber!
Layest thou thy Leaden Mace vpon my Boy,
That playes thee Musicke? Gentle knaue good night:
I will not do thee so much wrong to wake thee:
If thou do'st nod, thou break'st thy Instrument,
Ile take it from thee, and (good Boy) good night.
Let me see, let me see; is not the Leafe turn'd downe
Where I left reading? Heere it is I thinke.
Enter the Ghost of Cæsar.
How ill this Taper burnes. Ha! Who comes heere?
I thinke it is the weakenesse of mine eyes
That shapes this monstrous Apparition.
It comes vpon me: Art thou any thing?
Art thou some God, some Angell, or some Diuell,
That mak'st my blood cold, and my haire to stare?
Speake to me, what thou art.
Ghost. Thy euill Spirit *Brutus?*
Bru. Why com'st thou?
                                                                Ghost.

Ghost. To tell thee thou shalt see me at *Philippi.*
Brut. Well: then I shall see thee againe?
Ghost. I, at *Philippi.*
Brut. Why I will see thee at *Philippi* then:
Now I haue taken heart, thou vanishest.
Ill Spirit, I would hold more talke with thee.
Boy, *Lucius, Varrus, Claudio,* Sirs: Awake:
Claudio.

Luc. The strings my Lord, are false.
Bru. He thinkes he still is at his Instrument.
Lucius, awake.
Luc. My Lord.
Bru. Did'st thou dreame *Lucius*, that thou so cryedst out?
Luc. My Lord, I do not know that I did cry.
Bru. Yes that thou did'st: Did'st thou see any thing?
Luc. Nothing my Lord.
Bru. Sleepe againe *Lucius*: Sirra *Claudio,* Fellow,
Thou: Awake.
Var. My Lord.
Clau. My Lord.
Bru. Why did you so cry out sirs, in your sleepe?
Both. Did we my Lord?
Bru. I: saw you any thing?
Var. No my Lord, I saw nothing.
Clau. Nor I my Lord.
Bru. Go, and commend me to my Brother *Cassius*:
Bid him set on his Powres betimes before,
And we will follow.
Both. It shall be done my Lord. *Exeunt*

Actus Quintus.

Enter Octauius, Antony, and their Army.
Octa. Now *Antony,* our hopes are answered,
You said the Enemy would not come downe,
But keepe the Hilles and vpper Regions:
It proues not so: their battailes are at hand,
They meane to warne vs at *Philippi* heere:
Answering before we do demand of them.
Ant. Tut I am in their bosomes, and I know
Wherefore they do it: They could be content
To visit other places, and come downe
With fearefull brauery: thinking by this face
To fasten in our thoughts that they haue Courage;
But 'tis not so.

Enter a Messenger.
Mes. Prepare you Generals,
The Enemy comes on in gallant shew:
Their bloody signe of Battell is hung out,
And something to be done immediately.
Ant. *Octauius*, leade your Battaile softly on
Vpon the left hand of the euen Field.
Octa. Vpon the right hand I, keepe thou the left.
Ant. Why do you crosse me in this exigent.
Octa. I do not crosse you: but I will do so. *March.*

Drum. Enter Brutus, Cassius, & their Army.
Bru. They stand, and would haue parley.
Cassi. Stand fast *Titinius*, we must out and talke.
Octa. Mark Antony, shall we giue signe of Battaile?
Ant. No *Cæsar*, we will answer on their Charge.

Make forth, the Generals would haue some words.
Oct. Stirre not vntill the Signall.
Bru. Words before blowes: is it so Countrymen?
Octa. Not that we loue words better, as you do.
Bru. Good words are better then bad strokes *Octauius.*
An. In your bad strokes *Brutus*, you giue good words
Witnesse the hole you made in *Cæsars* heart,
Crying long liue, Haile *Cæsar.*
Cassi. Antony,
The posture of your blowes are yet vnknowne;
But for your words, they rob the *Hibla* Bees,
And leaue them Hony-lesse.
Ant. Not stinglesse too.
Bru. O yes, and soundlesse too:
For you haue stolne their buzzing *Antony,*
And very wisely threat before you sting.
Ant. Villains: you did not so, when your vile daggers
Hackt one another in the sides of *Cæsar*:
You shew'd your teethes like Apes,
And fawn'd like Hounds,
And bow'd like Bondmen, kissing *Cæsars* feete;
Whil'st damned *Caska*, like a Curre, behinde
Strooke *Cæsar* on the necke. O you Flatterers.
Cassi. Flatterers? Now *Brutus* thanke your selfe,
This tongue had not offended so to day,
If *Cassius* might haue rul'd.
Octa. Come, come, the cause. If arguing make vs swet,
The proofe of it will turne to redder drops:
Looke, I draw a Sword against Conspirators,
When thinke you that the Sword goes vp againe?
Neuer till *Cæsars* three and thirtie wounds
Be well aueng'd; or till another *Cæsar*
Haue added slaughter to the Sword of Traitors.
Brut. Cæsar, thou canst not dye by Traitors hands,
Vnlesse thou bring'st them with thee.
Octa. So I hope:
I was not borne to dye on *Brutus* Sword.
Bru. O if thou wer't the Noblest of thy Straine,
Yong-man, thou could'st not dye more honourable.
Cassi. A peeuish School-boy, worthles of such Honor
Ioyn'd with a Masker, and a Reueller.
Ant. Old *Cassius* still.
Octa. Come *Antony*: away:
Defiance Traitors, hurle we in your teeth.
If you dare fight to day, come to the Field;
If not, when you haue stomackes.
Exit Octauius. Antony, and Army
Cassi. Why now blow winde, swell Billow,
And swimme Barke:
The Storme is vp, and all is on the hazard.
Bru. Ho *Lucillius*, hearke, a word with you.
Lucillius and Messala stand forth.
Luc. My Lord.
Cassi. Messala.
Messa. What sayes my Generall?
Cassi. Messala, this is my Birth-day: as this very day
Was *Cassius* borne. Giue me thy hand *Messala*:
Be thou my witnesse, that against my will
(As *Pompey* was) am I compell'd to set
Vpon one Battell all our Liberties.
You know, that I held *Epicurus* strong,
And his Opinion: Now I change my minde,
And partly credit things that do presage.
Comming from *Sardis*, on our former Ensigne
Two mighty Eagles fell, and there they pearch'd,
Gorging and feeding from our Soldiers hands,

Who

Who to *Philippi* heere consorted vs:
This Morning are they fled away, and gone,
And in their steeds, do Rauens, Crowes, and Kites
Fly ore our heads, and downward looke on vs
As we were sickely prey; their shadowes seeme
A Canopy most fatall, vnder which
Our Army lies, ready to giue vp the Ghost.

  Messa. Beleeue not so.
  Cassi. I but beleeue it partly,
For I am fresh of spirit, and resolu'd
To meete all perils, very constantly.
  Bru. Euen so *Lucillius*.
  Cassi. Now most Noble *Brutus*,
The Gods to day stand friendly, that we may
Louers in peace, leade on our dayes to age.
But since the affayres of men rests still incertaine,
Let's reason with the worst that may befall.
If we do lose this Battaile, then is this
The very last time we shall speake together:
What are you then determined to do?
  Bru. Euen by the rule of that Philosophy,
By which I did blame *Cato*, for the death
Which he did giue himselfe, I know not how:
But I do finde it Cowardly, and vile,
For feare of what might fall, so to preuent
The time of life, arming my selfe with patience,
To stay the prouidence of some high Powers,
That gouerne vs below.
  Cassi. Then, if we loose this Battaile,
You are contented to be led in Triumph
Thorow the streets of Rome.
  Bru. No *Cassius*, no:
Thinke not thou Noble Romane,
That euer *Brutus* will go bound to Rome,
He beares too great a minde. But this same day
Must end that worke, the Ides of March begun.
And whether we shall meete againe, I know not:
Therefore our euerlasting farewell take:
For euer, and for euer, farewell *Cassius*,
If we do meete againe, why we shall smile;
If not, why then this parting was well made.
  Cassi. For euer, and for euer, farewell *Brutus*:
If we do meete againe, wee'l smile indeede;
If not, 'tis true, this parting was well made.
  Bru. Why then leade on. O that a man might know
The end of this dayes businesse, ere it come:
But it sufficeth, that the day will end,
And then the end is knowne. Come ho, away. *Exeunt.*

Alarum. Enter Brutus and Messala.

  Bru. Ride, ride *Messala*, ride and giue these Billes
Vnto the Legions, on the other side.   *Lowd Alarum.*
Let them set on at once: for I perceiue
But cold demeanor in *Octauio's* wing:
And sodaine push giues them the ouerthrow:
Ride, ride *Messala*, let them all come downe. *Exeunt.*

Alarums. Enter Cassius and Titinius.

  Cassi. O looke *Titinius*, looke, the Villaines flye:
My selfe haue to mine owne turn'd Enemy:
This Ensigne heere of mine was turning backe,
I slew the Coward, and did take it from him.
  Titin. O *Cassius*, *Brutus* gaue the word too early,
Who hauing some aduantage on *Octauius*,
Tooke it too eagerly: his Soldiers fell to spoyle,
Whil'st we by *Antony* are all inclos'd.

Enter Pindarus.

  Pind. Fly further off my Lord: flye further off,
Mark Antony is in your Tents my Lord:
Flye therefore Noble *Cassius*, flye farre off.
  Cassi. This Hill is farre enough. Looke, look *Titinius*
Are those my Tents where I perceiue the fire?
  Tit. They are, my Lord.
  Cassi. *Titinius*, if thou louest me,
Mount thou my horse, and hide thy spurres in him,
Till he haue brought thee vp to yonder Troopes
And heere againe, that I may rest assur'd
Whether yond Troopes, are Friend or Enemy.
  Tit. I will be heere againe, euen with a thought. *Exit.*
  Cassi. Go *Pindarus*, get higher on that hill,
My sight was euer thicke: regard *Titinius*,
And tell me what thou not'st about the Field.
This day I breathed first, Time is come round,
And where I did begin, there shall I end,
My life is run his compasse. Sirra, what newes?
  Pind. Aboue. O my Lord.
  Cassi. What newes?
  Pind. *Titinius* is enclosed round about
With Horsemen, that make to him on the Spurre,
Yet he spurres on. Now they are almost on him:
Now *Titinius*. Now some light: O he lights too.
Hee's tane.   *Showt.*
And hearke, they shout for ioy.
  Cassi. Come downe, behold no more:
O Coward that I am, to liue so long,
To see my best Friend tane before my face.

Enter Pindarus.

Come hither sirrah: In Parthia did I take thee Prisoner,
And then I swore thee, sauing of thy life,
That whatsoeuer I did bid thee do,
Thou should'st attempt it. Come now, keepe thine oath,
Now be a Free-man, and with this good Sword
That ran through *Cæsars* bowels, search this bosome.
Stand not to answer: Heere, take thou the Hilts,
And when my face is couer'd, as 'tis now,
Guide thou the Sword ——— *Cæsar*, thou art reueng'd,
Euen with the Sword that kill'd thee.
  Pin. So, I am free,
Yet would not so haue beene
Durst I haue done my will. O *Cassius*,
Farre from this Country *Pindarus* shall run,
Where neuer Roman shall take note of him.

Enter Titinius and Messala.

  Messa. It is but change, *Titinius*: for *Octauius*
Is ouerthrowne by Noble *Brutus* power,
As *Cassius* Legions are by *Antony*.
  Titin. These tydings will well comfort *Cassius*.
  Messa. Where did you leaue him.
  Titin. All disconsolate,
With *Pindarus* his Bondman, on this Hill.
  Messa. Is not that he that lyes vpon the ground?
  Titin. He lies not like the Liuing. O my heart!
  Messa. Is not that hee?
  Titin. No, this was he *Messala*,
But *Cassius* is no more. O setting Sunne:
As in thy red Rayes thou doest sinke to night;

The Tragedie of Julius Cæsar.

So in his red blood *Cassius* day is set.
The Sunne of Rome is set. Our day is gone,
Clowds, Dewes, and Dangers come; our deeds are done:
Mistrust of my successe hath done this deed.

Messa. Mistrust of good successe hath done this deed.
O hatefull Error, Melancholies Childe:
Why do'st thou shew to the apt thoughts of men
The things that are not? O Error soone conceyu'd,
Thou neuer com'st vnto a happy byrth,
But kil'st the Mother that engendred thee.

Tit. What *Pindarus*? Where art thou *Pindarus*?

Messa. Seeke him *Titinius*, whilst I go to meet
The Noble *Brutus*, thrusting this report
Into his eares; I may say thrusting it:
For piercing Steele, and Darts inuenomed,
Shall be as welcome to the eares of *Brutus*,
As tydings of this sight.

Tit. Hye you *Messala*,
And I will seeke for *Pindarus* the while:
Why did'st thou send me forth braue *Cassius*?
Did I not meet thy Friends, and did not they
Put on my Browes this wreath of Victorie,
And bid me giue it thee? Did'st thou not heare their
Alas, thou hast misconstrued euery thing. (*showts?*
But hold thee, take this Garland on thy Brow,
Thy *Brutus* bid me giue it thee, and I
Will do his bidding. *Brutus*, come apace,
And see how I regarded *Caius Cassius*:
By your leaue Gods: This is a Romans part,
Come *Cassius* Sword, and finde *Titinius* hart. *Dies*

*Alarum. Enter Brutus, Messala, yong Cato,
Strato, Volumnius, and Lucillius.*

Bru. Where, where *Messala*, doth his body lye?
Messa. Loe yonder, and *Titinius* mourning it.
Bru. *Titinius* face is vpward.
Cato. He is slaine.
Bru. O *Iulius Cæsar*, thou art mighty yet,
Thy Spirit walkes abroad, and turnes our Swords
In our owne proper Entrailes. *Low Alarums.*
Cato. Braue *Titinius*,
Looke where he haue not crown'd dead *Cassius*.
Bru. Are yet two Romans liuing such as these?
The last of all the Romans, far thee well:
It is impossible, that euer Rome
Should breed thy fellow. Friends I owe mo teares
To this dead man, then you shall see me pay.
I shall finde time, *Cassius*: I shall finde time.
Come therefore, and to *Tharsus* send his body,
His Funerals shall not be in our Campe,
Least it discomfort vs. *Lucillius* come,
And come yong *Cato*, let vs to the Field,
Labio and *Flauio* set our Battailes on:
'Tis three a clocke, and Romans yet ere night,
We shall try Fortune in a second fight. *Exeunt.*

*Alarum. Enter Brutus, Messala, Cato, Lucillius,
and Flauius.*

Bru. Yet Country-men: O yet, hold vp your heads.
Cato. What Bastard doth not? Who will go with me?
I will proclaime my name about the Field.
I am the Sonne of *Marcus Cato*, hoe.
A Foe to Tyrants, and my Countries Friend.
I am the Sonne of *Marcus Cato*, hoe.

Enter Souldiers, and fight.

And I am *Brutus*, *Marcus Brutus*, I,
Brutus my Countries Friend: Know me for *Brutus*.

Luc. O yong and Noble *Cato*, art thou downe?
Why now thou dyest, as brauely as *Titinius*,
And may'st be honour'd, being *Cato*'s Sonne.

Sold. Yeeld, or thou dyest.
Luc. Onely I yeeld to dye:
There is so much, that thou wilt kill me straight:
Kill *Brutus*, and be honour'd in his death.
Sold. We must not: a Noble Prisoner.

Enter Antony.

2. *Sold.* Roome hoe: tell *Antony*, *Brutus* is tane.
1. *Sold.* Ile tell thee newes. Heere comes the Generall,
Brutus is tane, *Brutus* is tane my Lord.
Ant. Where is hee?
Luc. Safe *Antony*, *Brutus* is safe enough:
I dare assure thee, that no Enemy
Shall euer take aliue the Noble *Brutus*:
The Gods defend him from so great a shame,
When you do finde him, or aliue, or dead,
He will be found like *Brutus*, like himselfe.

Ant. This is not *Brutus* friend, but I assure you,
A prize no lesse in worth; keepe this man safe,
Giue him all kindnesse. I had rather haue
Such men my Friends, then Enemies. Go on,
And see where *Brutus* be aliue or dead,
And bring vs word, vnto *Octauius* Tent:
How euery thing is chanc'd. *Exeunt.*

*Enter Brutus, Dardanius, Clitus, Strato,
and Volumnius.*

Brut. Come poore remaines of friends, rest on this
Rocke.
Clit. *Statilius* shew'd the Torch-light, but my Lord
He came not backe: he is or tane, or slaine.
Brut. Sit thee downe, *Clitus*: slaying is the word,
It is a deed in fashion. Hearke thee, *Clitus*.
Clit. What I, my Lord? No, not for all the World.
Brut. Peace then, no words.
Clit. Ile rather kill my selfe.
Brut. Hearke thee, *Dardanius*.
Dard. Shall I doe such a deed?
Clit. O *Dardanius*.
Dard. O *Clitus*.
Clit. What ill request did *Brutus* make to thee?
Dard. To kill him, *Clitus*: looke he meditates.
Clit. Now is that Noble Vessell full of griefe,
That it runnes ouer euen at his eyes.
Brut. Come hither, good *Volumnius*, list a word.
Volum. What sayes my Lord?
Brut. Why this, *Volumnius*:
The Ghost of *Cæsar* hath appear'd to me
Two seuerall times by Night: at Sardis, once;
And this last Night, here in Philippi fields:
I know my houre is come.
Volum. Not so, my Lord.
Brut. Nay, I am sure it is, *Volumnius*.
Thou seest the World, *Volumnius*, how it goes,
Our Enemies haue beat vs to the Pit: *Low Alarums.*
It is more worthy, to leape in our selues,
Then tarry till they push vs. Good *Volumnius*,
Thou know'st, that we two went to Schoole together:
Euen for that our loue of old, I prethee
Hold thou my Sword Hilts, whilest I runne on it.
Vol. That's not an Office for a friend, my Lord.
Alarum still.

Clit. Fly,

Cly. Fly, flye my Lord, there is no tarrying heere.
Bru. Farewell to you, and you, and you *Volumnius*.
Strato, thou hast bin all this while asleepe:
Farewell to thee, to *Strato*, Countrymen:
My heart doth ioy, that yet in all my life,
I found no man, but he was true to me.
I shall haue glory by this loosing day
More then *Octauius*, and *Marke Antony*,
By this vile Conquest shall attaine vnto.
So fare you well at once, for *Brutus* tongue
Hath almost ended his liues History:
Night hangs vpon mine eyes, my Bones would rest,
That haue but labour'd, to attaine this houre.

Alarum. Cry within, Flye, flye, flye.

Cly. Fly my Lord, flye.
Bru. Hence: I will follow:
I prythee *Strato*, stay thou by thy Lord,
Thou art a Fellow of a good respect:
Thy life hath had some smatch of Honor in it,
Hold then my Sword, and turne away thy face,
While I do run vpon it. Wilt thou *Strato*?
Stra. Giue me your hand first. Fare you wel my Lord.
Bru. Farewell good *Strato*. —— *Cæsar*, now be still,
I kill'd not thee with halfe so good a will.   *Dyes.*

Alarum. Retreat. Enter Antony, Octauius, Messala,
Lucillius, and the Army.

Octa. What man is that?
Messa. My Masters man. *Strato*, where is thy Master?
Stra. Free from the Bondage you are in *Messala*,
The Conquerors can but make a fire of him:
For *Brutus* onely ouercame himselfe,
And no man else hath Honor by his death.
Lucil. So *Brutus* should be found. I thank thee *Brutus*
That thou hast prou'd *Lucillius* saying true.
Octa. All that seru'd *Brutus*, I will entertaine them,
Fellow, wilt thou bestow thy time with me?
Stra. I, if *Messala* will preferre me to you.
Octa. Do so, good *Messala*.
Messa. How dyed my Master *Strato*?
Stra. I held the Sword, and he did run on it.
Messa. *Octauius*, then take him to follow thee,
That did the latest seruice to my Master.
Ant. This was the Noblest Roman of them all:
All the Conspirators saue onely hee,
Did that they did, in enuy of great *Cæsar*:
He, onely in a generall honest thought,
And common good to all, made one of them.
His life was gentle, and the Elements
So mixt in him, that Nature might stand vp,
And say to all the world; This was a man.
Octa. According to his Vertue, let vs vse him
Withall Respect, and Rites of Buriall.
Within my Tent his bones to night shall ly,
Most like a Souldier ordered Honourably:
So call the Field to rest, and let's away,
To part the glories of this happy day.   *Exeunt omnes.*

FINIS.

THE TRAGEDIE OF MACBETH.

Actus Primus. Scœna Prima.

Thunder and Lightning. Enter three Witches.

1. Hen shall we three meet againe?
In Thunder, Lightning, or in Raine?
2. When the Hurley-burley's done,
When the Battaile's lost, and wonne.
3. That will be ere the set of Sunne.
1. Where the place?
2. Vpon the Heath.
3. There to meet with *Macbeth*.
1. I come, *Gray-Malkin*.
All. Padock calls anon: faire is foule, and foule is faire,
Houer through the fogge and filthie ayre. *Exeunt.*

Scena Secunda.

Alarum within. Enter King Malcome, Donalbaine, Lenox, with attendants, meeting a bleeding Captaine.

King. What bloody man is that? he can report,
As seemeth by his plight, of the Reuolt
The newest state.

Mal. This is the Serieant,
Who like a good and hardie Souldier fought
'Gainst my Captiuitie: Haile braue friend;
Say to the King, the knowledge of the Broyle,
As thou didst leaue it.

Cap. Doubtfull it stood,
As two spent Swimmers, that doe cling together,
And choake their Art: The mercilesse *Macdonwald*
(Worthie to be a Rebell, for to that
The multiplying Villanies of Nature
Doe swarme vpon him) from the Westerne Isles
Of Kernes and Gallowgrosses is supply'd,
And Fortune on his damned Quarry smiling,
Shew'd like a Rebells Whore: but all's too weake:
For braue *Macbeth* (well hee deserues that Name)
Disdayning Fortune, with his brandisht Steele,
Which smoak'd with bloody execution
(Like Valours Minion) caru'd out his passage,
Till hee fac'd the Slaue:
Which neu'r shooke hands, nor bad farwell to him,
Till he vnseam'd him from the Naue toth' Chops,
And fix'd his Head vpon our Battlements.

King. O valiant Cousin, worthy Gentleman.
Cap. As whence the Sunne 'gins his reflection,
Shipwracking Stormes, and direfull Thunders:
So from that Spring, whence comfort seem'd to come,
Discomfort swells: Marke King of Scotland, marke,
No sooner Iustice had, with Valour arm'd,
Compell'd these skipping Kernes to trust their heeles,
But the Norweyan Lord, surueying vantage,
With furbusht Armes, and new supplyes of men,
Began a fresh assault.

King. Dismay'd not this our Captaines, *Macbeth* and
Banquoh?

Cap. Yes, as Sparrowes, Eagles;
Or the Hare, the Lyon:
If I say sooth, I must report they were
As Cannons ouer-charg'd with double Cracks,
So they doubly redoubled stroakes vpon the Foe:
Except they meant to bathe in reeking Wounds,
Or memorize another *Golgotha*,
I cannot tell: but I am faint,
My Gashes cry for helpe.

King. So well thy words become thee, as thy wounds,
They smack of Honor both: Goe get him Surgeons.

Enter Rosse and Angus.

Who comes here?
Mal. The worthy *Thane* of Rosse.
Lenox. What a haste lookes through his eyes?
So should he looke, that seemes to speake things strange.
Rosse. God saue the King.
King. Whence cam'st thou, worthy *Thane*?
Rosse. From Fiffe, great King,
Where the Norweyan Banners flowt the Skie,
And fanne our people cold.
Norway himselfe, with terrible numbers,
Assisted by that most disloyall Traytor,
The *Thane* of Cawdor, began a dismall Conflict,
Till that *Bellona's* Bridegroome, lapt in proofe,
Confronted him with selfe-comparisons,
Point against Point, rebellious Arme 'gainst Arme,
Curbing his lauish spirit: and to conclude,
The Victorie fell on vs.

King. Great happinesse.
Rosse. That now *Sweno*, the Norwayes King,
Craues composition:
Nor would we deigne him buriall of his men,
Till he disbursed, at Saint *Colmes* ynch,
Ten thousand Dollars, to our generall vse.

King. No

King. No more that Thane of Cawdor shall deceiue
Our Bosome interest: Goe pronounce his present death,
And with his former Title greet *Macbeth*.

Rosse. Ile see it done.

King. What he hath lost, Noble *Macbeth* hath wonne.

Exeunt.

Scena Tertia.

Thunder. Enter the three Witches.

1. Where hast thou beene, Sister?
2. Killing Swine.
3. Sister, where thou?
1. A Saylors Wife had Chestnuts in her Lappe,
And mouncht, & mouncht, and mouncht:
Giue me, quoth I.
Aroynt thee, Witch, the rumpe-fed Ronyon cryes.
Her Husband's to Aleppo gone, Master o'th' *Tiger*:
But in a Syue Ile thither sayle,
And like a Rat without a tayle,
Ile doe, Ile doe, and Ile doe.
2. Ile giue thee a Winde.
1. Th'art kinde.
3. And I another.
1. I my selfe haue all the other,
And the very Ports they blow,
All the Quarters that they know,
I'th' Ship-mans Card.
Ile dreyne him drie as Hay:
Sleepe shall neyther Night nor Day
Hang vpon his Pent-house Lid:
He shall liue a man forbid:
Wearie Seu'nights, nine times nine,
Shall he dwindle, peake, and pine:
Though his Barke cannot be lost,
Yet it shall be Tempest-tost.
Looke what I haue.
2. Shew me, shew me.
1. Here I haue a Pilots Thumbe,
Wrackt, as homeward he did come. *Drum within.*
3. A Drumme, a Drumme:
Macbeth doth come.
All. The weyward Sisters, hand in hand,
Posters of the Sea and Land,
Thus doe goe, about, about,
Thrice to thine, and thrice to mine,
And thrice againe, to make vp nine.
Peace, the Charme's wound vp.

Enter Macbeth and Banquo.

Macb. So foule and faire a day I haue not seene.

Banquo. How farre is't call'd to Soris? What are these,
So wither'd, and so wilde in their attyre,
That looke not like th'Inhabitants o'th' Earth,
And yet are on't? Liue you, or are you aught
That man may question? you seeme to vnderstand me,
By each at once her choppie finger laying
Vpon her skinnie Lips: you should be Women,
And yet your Beards forbid me to interprete
That you are so.

Mac. Speake if you can: what are you?

1. All haile *Macbeth*, haile to thee Thane of Glamis.
2. All haile *Macbeth*, haile to thee Thane of Cawdor.
3. All haile *Macbeth*, that shalt be King hereafter.

Banq. Good Sir, why doe you start, and seeme to feare
Things that doe sound so faire? i'th' name of truth
Are ye fantasticall, or that indeed
Which outwardly ye shew? My Noble Partner
You greet with present Grace, and great prediction
Of Noble hauing, and of Royall hope,
That he seemes wrapt withall: to me you speake not,
If you can looke into the Seedes of Time,
And say, which Graine will grow, and which will not,
Speake then to me, who neyther begge, nor feare
Your fauors, nor your hate.

1. Hayle.
2. Hayle.
3. Hayle.
1. Lesser then *Macbeth*, and greater.
2. Not so happy, yet much happyer.
3. Thou shalt get Kings, though thou be none:
So all haile *Macbeth*, and *Banquo*.
1. *Banquo*, and *Macbeth*, all haile.

Macb. Stay you imperfect Speakers, tell me more:
By *Sinells* death, I know I am Thane of Glamis,
But how, of Cawdor? the Thane of Cawdor liues
A prosperous Gentleman: And to be King,
Stands not within the prospect of beleefe,
No more then to be Cawdor. Say from whence
You owe this strange Intelligence, or why
Vpon this blasted Heath you stop our way
With such Prophetique greeting?
Speake, I charge you. *Witches vanish.*

Banq. The Earth hath bubbles, as the Water ha's,
And these are of them: whither are they vanish'd?

Macb. Into the Ayre: and what seem'd corporall,
Melted, as breath into the Winde.
Would they had stay'd.

Banq. Were such things here, as we doe speake about?
Or haue we eaten on the insane Root,
That takes the Reason Prisoner?

Macb. Your Children shall be Kings.

Banq. You shall be King.

Macb. And Thane of Cawdor too: went it not so?

Banq. Toth' selfe-same tune, and words: who's here?

Enter Rosse and Angus.

Rosse. The King hath happily receiu'd, *Macbeth*,
The newes of thy successe: and when he reades
Thy personall Venture in the Rebels fight,
His Wonders and his Prayses doe contend,
Which should be thine, or his: silenc'd with that,
In viewing o're the rest o'th' selfe-same day,
He findes thee in the stout Norweyan Rankes,
Nothing afeard of what thy selfe didst make
Strange Images of death, as thick as Tale
Can post with post, and euery one did beare
Thy prayses in his Kingdomes great defence,
And powr'd them downe before him.

Ang. Wee are sent,
To giue thee from our Royall Master thanks,
Onely to harrold thee into his sight,
Not pay thee.

Rosse. And for an earnest of a greater Honor,
He bad me, from him, call thee Thane of Cawdor:

In

The Tragedie of Macbeth.

In which addition, haile most worthy *Thane*,
For it is thine.

Banq. What, can the Deuill speake true?

Macb. The *Thane* of Cawdor liues:
Why doe you dresse me in borrowed Robes?

Ang. Who was the *Thane*, liues yet,
But vnder heauie Iudgement beares that Life,
Which he deserues to loose.
Whether he was combin'd with those of Norway,
Or did lyne the Rebell with hidden helpe,
And vantage; or that with both he labour'd
In his Countreyes wracke, I know not:
But Treasons Capitall, confess'd, and prou'd,
Haue ouerthrowne him.

Macb. Glamys, and *Thane* of Cawdor:
The greatest is behinde. Thankes for your paines.
Doe you not hope your Children shall be Kings,
When those that gaue the *Thane* of Cawdor to me,
Promis'd no lesse to them.

Banq. That trusted home,
Might yet enkindle you vnto the Crowne,
Besides the *Thane* of Cawdor. But 'tis strange:
And oftentimes, to winne vs to our harme,
The Instruments of Darknesse tell vs Truths,
Winne vs with honest Trifles, to betray's
In deepest consequence.
Cousins, a word, I pray you.

Macb. Two Truths are told,
As happy Prologues to the swelling Act
Of the Imperiall Theame. I thanke you Gentlemen:
This supernaturall solliciting
Cannot be ill; cannot be good.
If ill? why hath it giuen me earnest of successe,
Commencing in a Truth? I am *Thane* of Cawdor.
If good? why doe I yeeld to that suggestion,
Whose horrid Image doth vnfixe my Heire,
And make my seated Heart knock at my Ribbes,
Against the vse of Nature? Present Feares
Are lesse then horrible Imaginings:
My Thought, whose Murther yet is but fantasticall,
Shakes so my single state of Man,
That Function is smother'd in surmise,
And nothing is, but what is not.

Banq. Looke how our Partner's rapt.

Macb. If Chance will haue me King,
Why Chance may Crowne me,
Without my stirre.

Banq. New Honors come vpon him
Like our strange Garments, cleaue not to their mould,
But with the aid of vse.

Macb. Come what come may,
Time, and the Houre, runs through the roughest Day.

Banq. Worthy *Macbeth*, wee stay vpon your leysure.

Macb. Giue me your fauour:
My dull Braine was wrought with things forgotten.
Kinde Gentlemen, your paines are registred,
Where euery day I turne the Leafe,
To reade them.
Let vs toward the King: thinke vpon
What hath chanc'd: and at more time,
The *Interim* hauing weigh'd it, let vs speake
Our free Hearts each to other.

Banq. Very gladly.

Macb. Till then enough:
Come friends. *Exeunt.*

Scena Quarta.

Flourish. Enter King, Lenox, Malcolme, Donalbaine, and Attendants.

King. Is execution done on *Cawdor*?
Or not those in Commission yet return'd?

Mal. My Liege, they are not yet come back.
But I haue spoke with one that saw him die:
Who did report, that very frankly hee
Confess'd his Treasons, implor'd your Highnesse Pardon,
And set forth a deepe Repentance:
Nothing in his Life became him,
Like the leauing it. Hee dy'de,
As one that had beene studied in his death,
To throw away the dearest thing he ow'd,
As 'twere a carelesse Trifle.

King. There's no Art,
To finde the Mindes construction in the Face:
He was a Gentleman, on whom I built
An absolute Trust.

Enter Macbeth, Banquo, Rosse, and Angus.

O worthyest Cousin,
The sinne of my Ingratitude euen now
Was heauie on me. Thou art so farre before,
That swiftest Wing of Recompence is slow,
To ouertake thee. Would thou hadst lesse deseru'd,
That the proportion both of thanks, and payment,
Might haue beene mine: onely I haue left to say,
More is thy due, then more then all can pay.

Macb. The seruice, and the loyaltie I owe,
In doing it, payes it selfe.
Your Highnesse part, is to receiue our Duties:
And our Duties are to your Throne, and State,
Children, and Seruants; which doe but what they should,
By doing euery thing safe toward your Loue
And Honor.

King. Welcome hither:
I haue begun to plant thee, and will labour
To make thee full of growing. Noble *Banquo*,
That hast no lesse deseru'd, nor must be knowne
No lesse to haue done so: Let me enfold thee,
And hold thee to my Heart.

Banq. There if I grow,
The Haruest is your owne.

King. My plenteous Ioyes,
Wanton in fulnesse, seeke to hide themselues
In drops of sorrow. Sonnes, Kinsmen, *Thanes*,
And you whose places are the nearest, know,
We will establish our Estate vpon
Our eldest, *Malcolme*, whom we name hereafter,
The Prince of Cumberland: which Honor must
Not vnaccompanied, inuest him onely,
But signes of Noblenesse, like Starres, shall shine
On all deseruers. From hence to Enuernes,
And binde vs further to you.

Macb. The Rest is Labor, which is not vs'd for you:
Ile be my selfe the Herbenger, and make ioyfull
The hearing of my Wife, with your approach:
So humbly take my leaue.

King. My worthy *Cawdor*.

Macb. The Prince of Cumberland: that is a step,
On which I must fall downe, or else o're-leape,

The Tragedie of Macbeth.

For in my way it lyes. Starres hide your fires,
Let not Light see my black and deepe desires:
The Eye winke at the Hand; yet let that bee,
Which the Eye feares, when it is done to see. *Exit.*

King. True, worthy *Banquo*: he is full so valiant,
And in his commendations, I am fed:
It is a Banquet to me. Let's after him,
Whose care is gone before, to bid vs welcome:
It is a peerelesse Kinsman. *Flourish. Exeunt.*

Scena Quinta.

Enter Macbeths Wife alone with a Letter.

Lady. They met me in the day of successe: and I haue learn'd by the perfect'st report, they haue more in them, then mortall knowledge. When I burnt in desire to question them further, they made themselues Ayre, into which they vanish'd. Whiles I stood rapt in the wonder of it, came Missiues from the King, who all-hail'd me Thane of Cawdor, by which Title before, these weyward Sisters saluted me, and referr'd me to the comming on of time, with haile King that shalt be. This haue I thought good to deliuer thee (my dearest Partner of Greatnesse) that thou might'st not loose the dues of reioycing by being ignorant of what Greatnesse is promis'd thee. Lay it to thy heart, and farewell.

Glamys thou art, and Cawdor, and shalt be
What thou art promis'd: yet doe I feare thy Nature,
It is too full o'th' Milke of humane kindnesse,
To catch the neerest way. Thou would'st be great,
Art not without Ambition, but without
The illnesse should attend it. What thou would'st highly,
That would'st thou holily: would'st not play false,
And yet would'st wrongly winne.
Thould'st haue, great Glamys, that which cryes,
Thus thou must doe, if thou haue it;
And that which rather thou do'st feare to doe,
Then wishest should be vndone. High thee hither,
That I may powre my Spirits in thine Eare,
And chastise with the valour of my Tongue
All that impeides thee from the Golden Round,
Which Fate and Metaphysicall ayde doth seeme
To haue thee crown'd withall. *Enter Messenger.*
What is your tidings?

Mess. The King comes here to Night.

Lady. Thou'rt mad to say it.
Is not thy Master with him? who, wer't so,
Would haue inform'd for preparation.

Mess. So please you, it is true: our Thane is comming:
One of my fellowes had the speed of him;
Who almost dead for breath, had scarcely more
Then would make vp his Message.

Lady. Giue him tending,
He brings great newes. *Exit Messenger.*
The Rauen himselfe is hoarse,
That croakes the fatall entrance of *Duncan*
Vnder my Battlements. Come you Spirits,
That tend on mortall thoughts, vnsex me here,
And fill me from the Crowne to the Toe, top-full
Of direst Crueltie: make thick my blood,
Stop vp th'accesse, and passage to Remorse,
That no compunctious visitings of Nature

Shake my fell purpose, nor keepe peace betweene
Th'effect, and hit. Come to my Womans Brests,
And take my Milke for Gall, you murth'ring Ministers,
Where-euer, in your sightlesse substances,
You wait on Natures Mischiefe. Come thick Night,
And pall thee in the dunnest smoake of Hell,
That my keene Knife see not the Wound it makes,
Nor Heauen peepe through the Blanket of the darke,
To cry, hold, hold. *Enter Macbeth.*

Great Glamys, worthy Cawdor,
Greater then both, by the all-haile hereafter,
Thy Letters haue transported me beyond
This ignorant present, and I feele now
The future in the instant.

Macb. My dearest Loue,
Duncan comes here to Night.

Lady. And when goes hence?

Macb. To morrow, as he purposes.

Lady. O neuer,
Shall Sunne that Morrow see.
Your Face, my Thane, is as a Booke, where men
May reade strange matters, to beguile the time.
Looke like the time, beare welcome in your Eye,
Your Hand, your Tongue: looke like th'innocent flower,
But be the Serpent vnder't. He that's comming,
Must be prouided for: and you shall put
This Nights great Businesse into my dispatch,
Which shall to all our Nights, and Dayes to come,
Giue solely soueraigne sway, and Masterdome.

Macb. We will speake further.

Lady. Onely looke vp cleare:
To alter fauor, euer is to feare:
Leaue all the rest to me. *Exeunt.*

Scena Sexta.

Hoboyes, and Torches. Enter King, Malcolme, Donalbaine, Banquo, Lenox, Macduff, Rosse, Angus, and Attendants.

King. This Castle hath a pleasant seat,
The ayre nimbly and sweetly recommends it selfe
Vnto our gentle sences.

Banq. This Guest of Summer,
The Temple-haunting Barlet does approue,
By his loued Mansonry, that the Heauens breath
Smells wooingly here: no Iutty frieze,
Buttrice, nor Coigne of Vantage, but this Bird
Hath made his pendant Bed, and procreant Cradle,
Where they must breed, and haunt: I haue obseru'd
The ayre is delicate. *Enter Lady.*

King. See, see, our honor'd Hostesse:
The Loue that followes vs, sometime is our trouble,
Which still we thanke as Loue. Herein I teach you,
How you shall bid God-eyld vs for your paines,
And thanke vs for your trouble.

Lady. All our seruice,
In euery point twice done, and then done double,
Were poore, and single Businesse, to contend
Against those Honors deepe, and broad,
Wherewith your Maiestie loades our House:
For those of old, and the late Dignities,
Heap'd vp to them, we rest your Ermites.

King. Where's

The Tragedie of Macbeth.

King. Where's the Thane of Cawdor?
We courst him at the heeles, and had a purpose
To be his Purueyor: But he rides well,
And his great Loue (sharpe as his Spurre) hath holp him
To his home before vs: Faire and Noble Hostesse
We are your guest to night.
  La. Your Seruants euer,
Haue theirs, themselues, and what is theirs in compt,
To make their Audit at your Highnesse pleasure,
Still to returne your owne.
  King. Giue me your hand:
Conduct me to mine Host we loue him highly,
And shall continue, our Graces towards him.
By your leaue Hostesse. *Exeunt.*

Scena Septima.

Ho-boyes. Torches.
Enter a Sewer, and diuers Seruants with Dishes and Seruice ouer the Stage. Then enter Macbeth.

  Macb. If it were done, when 'tis done, then 'twer well,
It were done quickly: If th'Assassination
Could trammell vp the Consequence, and catch
With his surcease, Successe: that but this blow
Might be the be all, and the end all. Heere,
But heere, vpon this Banke and Schoole of time,
Wee'ld iumpe the life to come. But in these Cases,
We still haue iudgement heere, that we but teach
Bloody Instructions, which being taught, returne
To plague th'Inuenter, This euen-handed Iustice
Commends th'Ingredience of our poyson'd Challice
To our owne lips. Hee's heere in double trust;
First, as I am his Kinsman, and his Subiect,
Strong both against the Deed: Then, as his Host,
Who should against his Murtherer shut the doore,
Not beare the knife my selfe. Besides, this Duncane
Hath borne his Faculties so meeke; hath bin
So cleere in his great Office, that his Vertues
Will pleade like Angels, Trumpet-tongu'd against
The deepe damnation of his taking off:
And Pitty, like a naked New-borne-Babe,
Striding the blast, or Heauens Cherubin, hors'd
Vpon the sightlesse Curriors of the Ayre,
Shall blow the horrid deed in euery eye,
That teares shall drowne the winde. I haue no Spurre
To pricke the sides of my intent, but onely
Vaulting Ambition, which ore-leapes it selfe,
And falles on th'other. *Enter Lady.*
How now? What Newes?
  La. He has almost supt: why haue you left the chamber?
  Mac. Hath he ask'd for me?
  La. Know you not, he ha's?
  Mac. We will proceed no further in this Businesse:
He hath Honour'd me of late, and I haue bought
Golden Opinions from all sorts of people,
Which would be worne now in their newest glosse,
Not cast aside so soone.
  La. Was the hope drunke,
Wherein you drest your selfe? Hath it slept since?
And wakes it now to looke so greene, and pale,
At what it did so freely? From this time,
Such I account thy loue. Art thou affear'd
To be the same in thine owne Act, and Valour,
As thou art in desire? Would'st thou haue that
Which thou esteem'st the Ornament of Life,
And liue a Coward in thine owne Esteeme?
Letting I dare not, wait vpon I would,
Like the poore Cat i'th'Addage.
  Macb. Prythee peace:
I dare do all that may become a man,
Who dares no more, is none.
  La. What Beast was't then
That made you breake this enterprize to me?
When you durst do it, then you were a man:
And to be more then what you were, you would
Be so much more the man. Nor time, nor place
Did then adhere, and yet you would make both:
They haue made themselues, and that their fitnesse now
Do's vnmake you. I haue giuen Sucke, and know
How tender 'tis to loue the Babe that milkes me,
I would, while it was smyling in my Face,
Haue pluckt my Nipple from his Bonelesse Gummes,
And dasht the Braines out, had I so sworne
As you haue done to this.
  Macb. If we should faile?
  Lady. We faile?
But screw your courage to the sticking place,
And wee'le not fayle: when Duncan is asleepe,
(Whereto the rather shall his dayes hard Iourney
Soundly inuite him) his two Chamberlaines
Will I with Wine, and Wassell, so conuince,
That Memorie, the Warder of the Braine,
Shall be a Fume, and the Receit of Reason
A Lymbeck onely: when in Swinish sleepe,
Their drenched Natures lyes as in a Death,
What cannot you and I performe vpon
Th'vnguarded Duncan? What not put vpon
His spungie Officers? who shall beare the guilt
Of our great quell.
  Macb. Bring forth Men-Children onely:
For thy vndaunted Mettle should compose
Nothing but Males. Will it not be receiu'd,
When we haue mark'd with blood those sleepie two
Of his owne Chamber, and vs'd their very Daggers,
That they haue don't?
  Lady. Who dares receiue it other,
As we shall make our Griefes and Clamor rore,
Vpon his Death?
  Macb. I am settled, and bend vp
Each corporall Agent to this terrible Feat.
Away, and mock the time with fairest show,
False Face must hide what the false Heart doth know.
Exeunt.

Actus Secundus. Scena Prima.

Enter Banquo, and Fleance, with a Torch before him.

  Banq. How goes the Night, Boy?
  Fleance. The Moone is downe: I haue not heard the Clock.
  Banq. And she goes downe at Twelue.
  Fleance. I take't, 'tis later, Sir.
  Banq. Hold, take my Sword:
There's Husbandry in Heauen,
Their Candles are all out: take thee that too.

A heauie Summons lyes like Lead vpon me,
And yet I would not sleepe:
Mercifull Powers, restraine in me the cursed thoughts
That Nature giues way to in repose.

Enter Macbeth, and a Seruant with a Torch.

Giue me my Sword: who's there?
  Macb. A Friend.
  Banq. What Sir, not yet at rest? the King's a bed.
He hath beene in vnusuall Pleasure,
And sent forth great Largesse to your Offices.
This Diamond he greetes your Wife withall,
By the name of most kind Hostesse,
And shut vp in measurelesse content.
  Mac. Being vnprepar'd,
Our will became the seruant to defect,
Which else should free haue wrought.
  Banq. All's well.
I dreamt last Night of the three weyward Sisters:
To you they haue shew'd some truth.
  Macb. I thinke not of them:
Yet when we can entreat an houre to serue,
We would spend it in some words vpon that Businesse,
If you would graunt the time.
  Banq. At your kind'st leysure.
  Macb. If you shall cleaue to my consent,
When 'tis, it shall make Honor for you.
  Banq. So I lose none,
In seeking to augment it, but still keepe
My Bosome franchis'd, and Allegeance cleare,
I shall be counsail'd.
  Macb. Good repose the while.
  Banq. Thankes Sir: the like to you. *Exit Banquo.*
  Macb. Goe bid thy Mistresse, when my drinke is ready,
She strike vpon the Bell. Get thee to bed. *Exit.*
Is this a Dagger, which I see before me,
The Handle toward my Hand? Come, let me clutch thee:
I haue thee not, and yet I see thee still.
Art thou not fatall Vision, sensible
To feeling, as to sight? or art thou but
A Dagger of the Minde, a false Creation,
Proceeding from the heat-oppressed Braine?
I see thee yet, in forme as palpable,
As this which now I draw.
Thou marshall'st me the way that I was going,
And such an Instrument I was to vse.
Mine Eyes are made the fooles o'th'other Sences,
Or else worth all the rest: I see thee still;
And on thy Blade, and Dudgeon, Gouts of Blood,
Which was not so before. There's no such thing:
It is the bloody Businesse, which informes
Thus to mine Eyes. Now o're the one halfe World
Nature seemes dead, and wicked Dreames abuse
The Curtain'd sleepe: Witchcraft celebrates
Pale *Heccats* Offrings: and wither'd Murther,
Alarum'd by his Centinell, the Wolfe,
Whose howle's his Watch, thus with his stealthy pace,
With *Tarquins* rauishing sides, towards his designe
Moues like a Ghost. Thou sowre and firme-set Earth
Heare not my steps, which they may walke, for feare
Thy very stones prate of my where-about,
And take the present horror from the time,
Which now sutes with it. Whiles I threat, he liues:
Words to the heat of deedes too cold breath giues.
                                A Bell rings.

I goe, and it is done: the Bell inuites me.
Heare it not, *Duncan*, for it is a Knell,
That summons thee to Heauen, or to Hell. *Exit.*

Scena Secunda.

Enter Lady.

  La. That which hath made thē drunk, hath made me bold:
What hath quench'd them, hath giuen me fire.
Hearke, peace: it was the Owle that shriek'd,
The fatall Bell-man, which giues the stern'st good-night.
He is about it, the Doores are open:
And the surfeted Groomes doe mock their charge
With Snores. I haue drugg'd their Possets,
That Death and Nature doe contend about them,
Whether they liue, or dye.

Enter Macbeth.

  Macb. Who's there? what hoa?
  Lady. Alack, I am afraid they haue awak'd,
And 'tis not done: th'attempt, and not the deed,
Confounds vs: hearke: I lay'd their Daggers ready,
He could not misse 'em. Had he not resembled
My Father as he slept, I had don't.
My Husband?
  Macb. I haue done the deed:
Didst thou not heare a noyse?
  Lady. I heard the Owle schreame, and the Crickets cry.
Did not you speake?
  Macb. When?
  Lady. Now.
  Macb. As I descended?
  Lady. I.
  Macb. Hearke, who lyes i'th'second Chamber?
  Lady. *Donalbaine.*
  Mac. This is a sorry sight.
  Lady. A foolish thought, to say a sorry sight.
  Macb. There's one did laugh in's sleepe,
And one cry'd Murther, that they did wake each other:
I stood, and heard them: But they did say their Prayers,
And addrest them againe to sleepe.
  Lady. There are two lodg'd together.
  Macb. One cry'd God blesse vs, and Amen the other,
As they had seene me with these Hangmans hands:
Listning their feare, I could not say Amen,
When they did say God blesse vs.
  Lady. Consider it not so deepely.
  Mac. But wherefore could not I pronounce Amen?
I had most need of Blessing, and Amen stuck in my throat.
  Lady. These deeds must not be thought
After these wayes: so, it will make vs mad.
  Macb. Me thought I heard a voyce cry, Sleep no more:
Macbeth does murther Sleepe, the innocent Sleepe,
Sleepe that knits vp the rauel'd Sleeue of Care,
The death of each dayes Life, sore Labors Bath,
Balme of hurt Mindes, great Natures second Course,
Chiefe nourisher in Life's Feast.
  Lady. What doe you meane?
  Macb. Still it cry'd, Sleepe no more to all the House:
Glamis hath murther'd Sleepe, and therefore *Cawdor*
Shall sleepe no more: *Macbeth* shall sleepe no more.
  Lady. Who was it, that thus cry'd? why worthy *Thane*,
You doe vnbend your Noble strength, to thinke
So braine-sickly of things: Goe get some Water,
                                                And

The Tragedie of Macbeth.

nd wash this filthie Witnesse from your Hand.
Why did you bring these Daggers from the place?
They must lye there: goe carry them, and smeare
The sleepie Groomes with blood.

  Macb. Ile goe no more:
I am afraid, to thinke what I haue done:
Looke on't againe, I dare not.

  Lady. Infirme of purpose:
Giue me the Daggers: the sleeping, and the dead,
Are but as Pictures: 'tis the Eye of Child-hood,
That feares a painted Deuill. If he doe bleed,
Ile guild the Faces of the Groomes withall,
For it must seeme their Guilt.   *Exit.*
                        Knocke within.

  Macb. Whence is that knocking?
How is't with me, when euery noyse appalls me?
What Hands are here? hah: they pluck out mine Eyes.
Will all great *Neptunes* Ocean wash this blood
Cleane from my Hand? no: this my Hand will rather
The multitudinous Seas incarnardine,
Making the Greene one, Red.

                Enter Lady.

  Lady. My Hands are of your colour: but I shame
To weare a Heart so white.   *Knocke.*
I heare a knocking at the South entry:
Retyre we to our Chamber:
A little Water cleares vs of this deed.
How easie is it then? your Constancie
Hath left you vnattended.   *Knocke.*
Hearke, more knocking.
Get on your Night-Gowne, least occasion call vs,
And shew vs to be Watchers: be not lost
So poorely in your thoughts.

  Macb. To know my deed,   *Knocke.*
'Twere best not know my selfe.
Wake *Duncan* with thy knocking:
I would thou could'st.   *Exeunt.*

Scena Tertia.

                Enter a Porter.
                        Knocking within.

  Porter. Here's a knocking indeede: if a man were
Porter of Hell Gate, hee should haue old turning the
Key. *Knock.* Knock, Knock, Knock. Who's there
i'th' name of *Belzebub*? Here's a Farmer, that hang'd
himselfe on th'expectation of Plentie: Come in time, haue
Napkins enow about you, here you'le sweat for't. *Knock.*
Knock, knock. Who's there in th'other Deuils Name?
Faith here's an Equiuocator, that could sweare in both
the Scales against eyther Scale, who committed Treason
enough for Gods sake, yet could not equiuocate to Hea-
uen: oh come in, Equiuocator. *Knock.* Knock,
Knock, Knock. Who's there? 'Faith here's an English
Taylor come hither, for stealing out of a French Hose:
Come in Taylor, here you may rost your Goose. *Knock.*
Knock, Knock. Neuer at quiet: What are you? but this
place is too cold for Hell. Ile Deuill-Porter it no further:
I had thought to haue let in some of all Professions, that
goe the Primrose way to th'euerlasting Bonfire. *Knock.*
Anon, anon, I pray you remember the Porter.

            Enter Macduff, and Lenox.

  Macd. Was it so late, friend, ere you went to Bed,
That you doe lye so late?
  Port. Faith Sir, we were carowsing till the second Cock:
And Drinke, Sir, is a great prouoker of three things.
  Macd. What three things does Drinke especially
prouoke?
  Port. Marry, Sir, Nose-painting, Sleepe, and Vrine.
Lecherie, Sir, it prouokes, and vnprouokes: it prouokes
the desire, but it takes away the performance. Therefore
much Drinke may be said to be an Equiuocator with Lecherie: it makes him, and it marres him; it sets him on,
and it takes him off; it perswades him, and dis-heartens
him; makes him stand too, and not stand too: in conclusion, equiuocates him in a sleepe, and giuing him the Lye,
leaues him.
  Macd. I beleeue, Drinke gaue thee the Lye last Night.
  Port. That it did, Sir, i'the very Throat on me: but I
requited him for his Lye, and (I thinke) being too strong
for him, though he tooke vp my Legges sometime, yet I
made a Shift to cast him.

                Enter Macbeth.

  Macd. Is thy Master stirring?
Our knocking ha's awak'd him: here he comes.
  Lenox. Good morrow, Noble Sir.
  Macb. Good morrow both.
  Macd. Is the King stirring, worthy *Thane*?
  Macb. Not yet.
  Macd. He did command me to call timely on him,
I haue almost slipt the houre.
  Mab. Ile bring you to him.
  Macd. I know this is a ioyfull trouble to you:
But yet 'tis one.
  Macb. The labour we delight in, Physicks paine:
This is the Doore.
  Macd. Ile make so bold to call, for 'tis my limitted
seruice.   *Exit Macduffe.*
  Lenox. Goes the King hence to day?
  Macb. He does: he did appoint so.
  Lenox. The Night ha's been vnruly:
Where we lay, our Chimneys were blowne downe,
And (as they say) lamentings heard i'th'Ayre;
Strange Schreemes of Death,
And Prophecying, with Accents terrible,
Of dyre Combustion, and confus'd Euents,
New hatch'd toth' wofull time.
The obscure Bird clamor'd the liue-long Night.
Some say, the Earth was feuorous,
And did shake.
  Macb. 'Twas a rough Night.
  Lenox. My young remembrance cannot paralell
A fellow to it.

                Enter Macduff.

  Macd. O horror, horror, horror,
Tongue nor Heart cannot conceiue, nor name thee.
  Macb. and Lenox. What's the matter?
  Macd. Confusion now hath made his Master-peece:
Most sacrilegious Murther hath broke ope
The Lords anoynted Temple, and stole thence
The Life o'th' Building.
  Macb. What is't you say, the Life?
  Lenox. Meane you his Maiestie?
  Macd. Approch the Chamber, and destroy your sight
With a new *Gorgon.* Doe not bid me speake:
                                            See,

The Tragedie of Macbeth.

See, and then speake your selues: awake, awake,

Exeunt Macbeth and Lenox.

Ring the Alarum Bell: Murther, and Treason,
Banquo, and Donalbaine: Malcolme awake,
Shake off this Downey sleepe, Deaths counterfeit,
And looke on Death it selfe: vp, vp, and see
The great Doomes Image: Malcolme, Banquo,
As from your Graues rise vp, and walke like Sprights,
To countenance this horror. Ring the Bell.

Bell rings. Enter Lady.

Lady. What's the Businesse?
That such a hideous Trumpet calls to parley
The sleepers of the House? speake, speake.

Macd. O gentle Lady,
'Tis not for you to heare what I can speake:
The repetition in a Womans eare,
Would murther as it fell.

Enter Banquo.

O Banquo, Banquo, Our Royall Master's murther'd.

Lady. Woe, alas:
What, in our House?

Ban. Too cruell, any where.
Deare Duff, I prythee contradict thy selfe,
And say, it is not so.

Enter Macbeth, Lenox, and Rosse.

Macb. Had I but dy'd an houre before this chance,
I had liu'd a blessed time: for from this instant,
There's nothing serious in Mortalitie:
All is but Toyes: Renowne and Grace is dead,
The Wine of Life is drawne, and the meere Lees
Is left this Vault, to brag of.

Enter Malcolme and Donalbaine.

Donal. What is amisse?

Macb. You are, and doe not know't:
The Spring, the Head, the Fountaine of your Blood
Is stopt, the very Source of it is stopt.

Macd. Your Royall Father's murther'd.

Mal. Oh, by whom?

Lenox. Those of his Chamber, as it seem'd, had don't:
Their Hands and Faces were all badg'd with blood,
So were their Daggers, which vnwip'd, we found
Vpon their Pillowes: they star'd, and were distracted,
No mans Life was to be trusted with them.

Macb. O, yet I doe repent me of my furie,
That I did kill them.

Macd. Wherefore did you so?

Macb. Who can be wise, amaz'd, temp'rate, & furious,
Loyall, and Neutrall, in a moment? No man:
Th'expedition of my violent Loue
Out-run the pawser, Reason. Here lay Duncan,
His Siluer skinne, lac'd with his Golden Blood,
And his gash'd Stabs, look'd like a Breach in Nature,
For Ruines wastfull entrance: there the Murtherers,
Steep'd in the Colours of their Trade; their Daggers
Vnmannerly breech'd with gore: who could refraine,
That had a heart to loue; and in that heart,
Courage, to make's loue knowne?

Lady. Helpe me hence, hoa.

Macd. Looke to the Lady.

Mal. Why doe we hold our tongues,
That most may clayme this argument for ours?

Donal. What should be spoken here,
Where our Fate hid in an augure hole,
May rush, and seize vs? Let's away,
Our Teares are not yet brew'd.

Mal. Nor our strong Sorrow
Vpon the foot of Motion.

Banq. Looke to the Lady:
And when we haue our naked Frailties hid,
That suffer in exposure; let vs meet,
And question this most bloody piece of worke,
To know it further. Feares and scruples shake vs:
In the great Hand of God I stand, and thence,
Against the vndivulg'd pretence, I fight
Of Treasonous Mallice.

Macd. And so doe I.

All. So all.

Macb. Let's briefely put on manly readinesse,
And meet i'th' Hall together.

All. Well contented. *Exeunt.*

Malc. What will you doe?
Let's not consort with them:
To shew an vnfelt Sorrow, is an Office
Which the false man do's easie.
Ile to England.

Don. To Ireland, I:
Our seperated fortune shall keepe vs both the safer:
Where we are, there's Daggers in mens Smiles;
The neere in blood, the neerer bloody.

Malc. This murtherous Shaft that's shot,
Hath not yet lighted: and our safest way,
Is to auoid the ayme. Therefore to Horse,
And let vs not be daintie of leaue-taking,
But shift away: there's warrant in that Theft,
Which steales it selfe, when there's no mercie left.

Exeunt.

Scena Quarta.

Enter Rosse, with an Old man.

Old man. Threescore and ten I can remember well,
Within the Volume of which Time, I haue seene
Houres dreadfull, and things strange: but this sore Night
Hath trifled former knowings.

Rosse. Ha, good Father,
Thou seest the Heauens, as troubled with mans Act,
Threatens his bloody Stage: byth' Clock 'tis Day,
And yet darke Night strangles the trauailing Lampe:
Is't Nights predominance, or the Dayes shame,
That Darknesse does the face of Earth intombe,
When liuing Light should kisse it?

Old man. 'Tis vnnaturall,
Euen like the deed that's done: On Tuesday last,
A Faulcon towring in her pride of place,
Was by a Mowsing Owle hawkt at, and kill'd.

Rosse. And Duncans Horses,
(A thing most strange, and certaine)
Beauteous, and swift, the Minions of their Race,
Turn'd wilde in nature, broke their stalls, flong out,
Contending 'gainst Obedience, as they would
Make Warre with Mankinde.

Old man. 'Tis said, they eate each other.

Rosse. They did so:

To th'amazement of mine eyes that look'd vpon't.
Enter Macduffe.
Heere comes the good *Macduffe.*
How goes the world Sir, now?
  Macd. Why see you not?
  Rosse. Is't known who did this more then bloody deed?
  Macd. Those that *Macbeth* hath slaine.
  Rosse. Alas the day,
What good could they pretend?
  Macd. They were subborned,
Malcolme, and *Donalbaine* the Kings two Sonnes
Are stolne away and fled, which puts vpon them
Suspition of the deed.
  Rosse. 'Gainst Nature still,
Thriftlesse Ambition, that will rauen vp
Thine owne liues meanes: Then 'tis most like,
The Soueraignty will fall vpon *Macbeth.*
  Macd. He is already nam'd, and gone to Scone
To be inuested.
  Rosse. Where is *Duncans* body?
  Macd. Carried to Colmekill,
The Sacred Store-house of his Predecessors,
And Guardian of their Bones.
  Rosse. Will you to Scone?
  Macd. No Cosin, Ile to Fife.
  Rosse. Well, I will thither.
  Macd. Well may you see things wel done there: Adieu
Least our old Robes sit easier then our new.
  Rosse. Farewell, Father.
  Old M. Gods benyson go with you, and with those
That would make good of bad, and Friends of Foes.
Exeunt omnes

Actus Tertius. Scena Prima.

Enter Banquo.

  Banq. Thou hast it now, King, Cawdor, Glamis, all,
As the weyard Women promis'd, and I feare
Thou play'd'st most fowly for't: yet it was saide
It should not stand in thy Posterity,
But that my selfe should be the Roote, and Father
Of many Kings. If there come truth from them,
As vpon thee *Macbeth,* their Speeches shine,
Why by the verities on thee made good,
May they not be my Oracles as well,
And set me vp in hope. But hush, no more.

Senit sounded. Enter Macbeth as King, Lady Lenox,
Rosse, Lords, and Attendants.

  Macb. Heere's our chiefe Guest.
  La. If he had beene forgotten,
It had bene as a gap in our great Feast,
And all-thing vnbecomming.
  Macb. To night we hold a solemne Supper sir,
And Ile request your presence.
  Banq. Let your Highnesse
Command vpon me, to the which my duties
Are with a most indissoluble tye
For euer knit.
  Macb. Ride you this afternoone?
  Ban. I, my good Lord.
  Macb. We should haue else desir'd your good aduice

(Which still hath been both graue, and prosperous)
In this dayes Councell: but wee'le take to morrow.
Is't farre you ride?
  Ban. As farre, my Lord, as will fill vp the time
'Twixt this, and Supper. Goe not my Horse the better,
I must become a borrower of the Night,
For a darke houre, or twaine.
  Macb. Faile not our Feast.
  Ban. My Lord, I will not.
  Macb. We heare our bloody Cozens are bestow'd
In England, and in Ireland, not confessing
Their cruell Parricide, filling their hearers
With strange inuention. But of that to morrow,
When therewithall, we shall haue cause of State,
Crauing vs ioyntly. Hye you to Horse:
Adieu, till you returne at Night.
Goes *Fleance* with you?
  Ban. I, my good Lord: our time does call vpon's.
  Macb. I wish your Horses swift, and sure of foot:
And so I doe commend you to their backs.
Farewell. *Exit Banquo.*
Let euery man be master of his time,
Till seuen at Night, to make societie
The sweeter welcome:
We will keepe our selfe till Supper time alone:
While then, God be with you. *Exeunt Lords.*
Sirrha, a word with you: Attend those men
Our pleasure?
  Seruant. They are, my Lord, without the Pallace Gate.
  Macb. Bring them before vs. *Exit Seruant.*
To be thus, is nothing, but to be safely thus:
Our feares in *Banquo* sticke deepe,
And in his Royaltie of Nature reignes that
Which would be fear'd. 'Tis much he dares,
And to that dauntlesse temper of his Minde,
He hath a Wisdome, that doth guide his Valour,
To act in safetie. There is none but he,
Whose being I doe feare: and vnder him,
My *Genius* is rebuk'd, as it is said
Mark Anthonies was by *Cæsar.* He chid the Sisters,
When first they put the Name of King vpon me,
And bad them speake to him. Then Prophet-like,
They hayl'd him Father to a Line of Kings.
Vpon my Head they plac'd a fruitlesse Crowne,
And put a barren Scepter in my Gripe,
Thence to be wrencht with an vnlineall Hand,
No Sonne of mine succeeding: if't be so,
For *Banquo's* Issue haue I fil'd my Minde,
For them, the gracious *Duncan* haue I murther'd,
Put Rancours in the Vessell of my Peace
Onely for them, and mine eternall Iewell
Giuen to the common Enemie of Man,
To make them Kings, the Seedes of *Banquo* Kings.
Rather then so, come Fate into the Lyst,
And champion me to th' vtterance.
Who's there?

Enter Seruant, and two Murtherers.

Now goe to the Doore, and stay there till we call.
Exit Seruant.
Was it not yesterday we spoke together?
  Murth. It was, so please your Highnesse.
  Macb. Well then,
Now haue you consider'd of my speeches:

The Tragedie of Macbeth.

Know, that it was he, in the times past,
Which held you so vnder fortune,
Which you thought had been our innocent selfe.
This I made good to you, in our last conference,
Past in probation with you:
How you were borne in hand, how crost:
The Instruments: who wrought with them:
And all things else, that might
To halfe a Soule, and to a Notion craz'd,
Say, Thus did *Banquo*.

   1. *Murth.* You made it knowne to vs.
   Macb. I did so:
And went further, which is now
Our point of second meeting.
Doe you finde your patience so predominant,
In your nature, that you can let this goe?
Are you so Gospell'd, to pray for this good man,
And for his Issue, whose heauie hand
Hath bow'd you to the Graue, and begger'd
Yours for euer?

   1. *Murth.* We are men, my Liege.
   Macb. I, in the Catalogue ye goe for men,
As Hounds, and Greyhounds, Mungrels, Spaniels, Curres,
Showghes, Water-Rugs, and Demy-Wolues are clipt
All by the Name of Dogges: the valued file
Distinguishes the swift, the slow, the subtle,
The House-keeper, the Hunter, euery one
According to the gift, which bounteous Nature
Hath in him clos'd: whereby he does receiue
Particular addition, from the Bill,
That writes them all alike: and so of men.
Now, if you haue a station in the file,
Not i'th' worst ranke of Manhood, say't,
And I will put that Businesse in your Bosomes,
Whose execution takes your Enemie off,
Grapples you to the heart; and loue of vs,
Who weare our Health but sickly in his Life,
Which in his Death were perfect.

   2. *Murth.* I am one, my Liege,
Whom the vile Blowes and Buffets of the World
Hath so incens'd, that I am recklesse what I doe,
To spight the World.

   1. *Murth.* And I another,
So wearie with Disasters, tugg'd with Fortune,
That I would set my Life on any Chance,
To mend it, or be rid on't.

   Macb. Both of you know *Banquo* was your Enemie.
   Murth. True, my Lord.
   Macb. So is he mine: and in such bloody distance,
That euery minute of his being, thrusts
Against my neer'st of Life: and though I could
With bare-fac'd power sweepe him from my sight,
And bid my will auouch it; yet I must not,
For certaine friends that are both his, and mine,
Whose loues I may not drop, but wayle his fall,
Who I my selfe struck downe: and thence it is,
That I to your assistance doe make loue,
Masking the Businesse from the common Eye,
For sundry weightie Reasons.

   2. *Murth.* We shall, my Lord,
Performe what you command vs.

   1. *Murth.* Though our Liues--
   Macb. Your Spirits shine through you.
Within this houre, at most,
I will aduise you where to plant your selues,
Acquaint you with the perfect Spy o'th' time,
The moment on't, for't must be done to Night,
And something from the Pallace: alwayes thought,
That I require a clearenesse; and with him,
To leaue no Rubs nor Botches in the Worke:
Fleans, his Sonne, that keepes him companie,
Whose absence is no lesse materiall to me,
Then is his Fathers, must embrace the fate
Of that darke houre: resolue your selues apart,
Ile come to you anon.

   Murth. We are resolu'd, my Lord.
   Macb. Ile call vpon you straight: abide within,
It is concluded: *Banquo* thy Soules flight,
If it finde Heauen, must finde it out to Night. *Exeunt.*

Scena Secunda.

Enter Macbeths Lady, and a Seruant.

   Lady. Is *Banquo* gone from Court?
   Seruant. I, Madame, but returnes againe to Night.
   Lady. Say to the King, I would attend his leysure,
For a few words.
   Seruant. Madame, I will.   *Exit.*
   Lady. Nought's had, all's spent,
Where our desire is got without content:
'Tis safer, to be that which we destroy,
Then by destruction dwell in doubtfull ioy.

Enter Macbeth.

How now, my Lord, why doe you keepe alone?
Of sorryest Fancies your Companions making,
Vsing those Thoughts, which should indeed haue dy'd
With them they thinke on: things without all remedie
Should be without regard: what's done, is done.

   Macb. We haue scorch'd the Snake, not kill'd it:
Shee'le close, and be her selfe, whilest our poore Mallice
Remaines in danger of her former Tooth.
But let the frame of things dis-ioynt,
Both the Worlds suffer,
Ere we will eate our Meale in feare, and sleepe
In the affliction of these terrible Dreames,
That shake vs Nightly: Better be with the dead,
Whom we, to gayne our peace, haue sent to peace,
Then on the torture of the Minde to lye
In restlesse extasie.
Duncane is in his Graue:
After Lifes fitfull Feuer, he sleepes well,
Treason ha's done his worst: nor Steele, nor Poyson,
Mallice domestique, forraine Leuie, nothing,
Can touch him further.

   Lady. Come on:
Gentle my Lord, sleeke o're your rugged Lookes,
Be bright and Iouiall among your Guests to Night.

   Macb. So shall I Loue, and so I pray be you:
Let your remembrance apply to *Banquo*,
Present him Eminence, both with Eye and Tongue:
Vnsafe the while, that wee must laue
Our Honors in these flattering streames,
And make our Faces Vizards to our Hearts,
Disguising what they are.

   Lady. You must leaue this.
   Macb. O, full of Scorpions is my Minde, deare Wife:
Thou know'st, that *Banquo* and his *Fleans* liues.
                                                    Lady. But

Lady. But in them, Natures Coppie's not eterne.
Macb. There's comfort yet, they are assaileable,
Then be thou iocund: ere the Bat hath flowne
His Cloyster'd flight, ere to black *Heccats* summons
The shard-borne Beetle, with his drowsie hums,
Hath rung Nights yawning Peale,
There shall be done a deed of dreadfull note.
Lady. What's to be done?
Macb. Be innocent of the knowledge, dearest Chuck,
Till thou applaud the deed: Come, seeling Night,
Skarfe vp the tender Eye of pittifull Day,
And with thy bloodie and inuisible Hand
Cancell and teare to pieces that great Bond,
Which keepes me pale. Light thickens,
And the Crow makes Wing toth' Rookie Wood:
Good things of Day begin to droope, and drowse,
Whiles Nights black Agents to their Prey's doe rowse.
Thou maruell'st at my words: but hold thee still,
Things bad begun, make strong themselues by ill:
So prythee goe with me. *Exeunt.*

Scena Tertia.

Enter three Murtherers.

1. But who did bid thee ioyne with vs?
3. *Macbeth.*
2. He needes not our mistrust, since he deliuers
Our Offices, and what we haue to doe,
To the direction iust.
1. Then stand with vs:
The West yet glimmers with some streakes of Day.
Now spurres the lated Traueller apace,
To gayne the timely Inne, end neere approches
The subiect of our Watch.
3. Hearke, I heare Horses.
Banquo within. Giue vs a Light there, hoa.
2. Then 'tis hee:
The rest, that are within the note of expectation,
Alreadie are i'th' Court.
1. His Horses goe about.
3. Almost a mile: but he does vsually,
So all men doe, from hence toth' Pallace Gate
Make it their Walke.

Enter Banquo and Fleans, with a Torch.

2. A Light, a Light.
3. 'Tis hee.
1. Stand too't.
Ban. It will be Rayne to Night.
1. Let it come downe.
Ban. O, Trecherie!
Flye good *Fleans*, flye, flye, flye,
Thou may'st reuenge. O Slaue!
3. Who did strike out the Light?
1. Was't not the way?
3. There's but one downe: the Sonne is fled.
2. We haue lost
Best halfe of our Affaire.
1. Well, let's away, and say how much is done.
Exeunt.

Scæna Quarta.

Banquet prepar'd. Enter Macbeth, Lady, Rosse, Lenox, Lords, and Attendants.

Macb. You know your owne degrees, sit downe:
At first and last, the hearty welcome.
Lords. Thankes to your Maiesty.
Macb. Our selfe will mingle with Society,
And play the humble Host:
Our Hostesse keepes her State, but in best time
We will require her welcome.
La. Pronounce it for me Sir, to all our Friends,
For my heart speakes, they are welcome.

Enter first Murtherer.

Macb. See they encounter thee with their harts thanks
Both sides are euen: heere Ile sit i'th' mid'st,
Be large in mirth, anon wee'l drinke a Measure
The Table round. There's blood vpon thy face.
Mur. 'Tis *Banquo's* then.
Macb. 'Tis better thee without, then he within.
Is he dispatch'd?
Mur. My Lord his throat is cut, that I did for him.
Mac. Thou art the best o'th' Cut-throats,
Yet hee's good that did the like for *Fleans*:
If thou did'st it, thou art the Non-pareill.
Mur. Most Royall Sir
Fleans is scap'd.
Macb. Then comes my Fit againe:
I had else beene perfect;
Whole as the Marble, founded as the Rocke,
As broad, and generall, as the casing Ayre:
But now I am cabin'd, crib'd, confin'd, bound in
To sawcy doubts, and feares. But *Banquo's* safe?
Mur. I, my good Lord: safe in a ditch he bides,
With twenty trenched gashes on his head;
The least a Death to Nature.
Macb. Thankes for that:
There the growne Serpent lyes, the worme that's fled
Hath Nature that in time will Venom breed,
No teeth for th' present. Get thee gone, to morrow
Wee'l heare our selues againe. *Exit Murderer.*
Lady. My Royall Lord,
You do not giue the Cheere, the Feast is sold
That is not often vouch'd, while 'tis a making:
'Tis giuen, with welcome: to feede were best at home:
From thence, the sawce to meate is Ceremony,
Meeting were bare without it.

Enter the Ghost of Banquo, and sits in Macbeths place.

Macb. Sweet Remembrancer:
Now good digestion waite on Appetite,
And health on both.
Lenox. May't please your Highnesse sit.
Macb. Here had we now our Countries Honor, roof'd,
Were the grac'd person of our *Banquo* present:
Who, may I rather challenge for vnkindnesse,
Then pitty for Mischance.
Rosse. His absence (Sir)
Layes blame vpon his promise. Pleas't your Highnesse
To grace vs with your Royall Company?

Macb. The Table's full.
Lenox. Heere is a place reseru'd Sir.
Macb. Where?
Lenox. Heere my good Lord.
What is't that moues your Highnesse?
Macb. Which of you haue done this?
Lords. What, my good Lord?
Macb. Thou canst not say I did it: neuer shake
Thy goary lockes at me.
Rosse. Gentlemen rise, his Highnesse is not well.
Lady. Sit worthy Friends: my Lord is often thus,
And hath beene from his youth. Pray you keepe Seat,
The fit is momentary, vpon a thought
He will againe be well. If much you note him
You shall offend him, and extend his Passion,
Feed, and regard him not. Are you a man?
Macb. I, and a bold one, that dare looke on that
Which might appall the Diuell.
La. O proper stuffe:
This is the very painting of your feare:
This is the Ayre-drawne-Dagger which you said
Led you to *Duncan.* O, these flawes and starts
(Impostors to true feare) would well become
A womans story, at a Winters fire
Authoriz'd by her Grandam: shame it selfe,
Why do you make such faces? When all's done
You looke but on a stoole.
Macb. Prythee see there:
Behold, looke, loe, how say you:
Why what care I, if thou canst nod, speake too.
If Charnell houses, and our Graues must send
Those that we bury, backe; our Monuments
Shall be the Mawes of Kytes.
La. What? quite vnmann'd in folly.
Macb. If I stand heere, I saw him.
La. Fie for shame.
Macb. Blood hath bene shed ere now, i'th'olden time
Ere humane Statute purg'd the gentle Weale:
I, and since too, Murthers haue bene perform'd
Too terrible for the eare. The times has bene,
That when the Braines were out, the man would dye,
And there an end: But now they rise againe
With twenty mortall murthers on their crownes,
And push vs from our stooles. This is more strange
Then such a murther is.
La. My worthy Lord
Your Noble Friends do lacke you.
Macb. I do forget:
Do not muse at me my most worthy Friends,
I haue a strange infirmity, which is nothing
To those that know me. Come, loue and health to all,
Then Ile sit downe: Giue me some Wine, fill full:

Enter Ghost.

I drinke to th'generall ioy o'th'whole Table,
And to our deere Friend *Banquo*, whom we misse:
Would he were heere: to all, and him we thirst,
And all to all.
Lords. Our duties, and the pledge.
Mac. Auant, & quit my sight, let the earth hide thee:
Thy bones are marrowlesse, thy blood is cold:
Thou hast no speculation in those eyes
Which thou dost glare with.
La. Thinke of this good Peeres
But as a thing of Custome: 'Tis no other,
Onely it spoyles the pleasure of the time.
Macb. What man dare, I dare:
Approach thou like the rugged Russian Beare,
The arm'd Rhinoceros, or th'Hircan Tiger,
Take any shape but that, and my firme Nerues
Shall neuer tremble. Or be aliue againe,
And dare me to the Desart with thy Sword:
If trembling I inhabit then, protest mee
The Baby of a Girle. Hence horrible shadow,
Vnreall mock'ry hence. Why so, being gone
I am a man againe: pray you sit still.
La. You haue displac'd the mirth,
Broke the good meeting, with most admir'd disorder.
Macb. Can such things be,
And ouercome vs like a Summers Clowd,
Without our speciall wonder? You make me strange
Euen to the disposition that I owe,
When now I thinke you can behold such sights,
And keepe the naturall Rubie of your Cheekes,
When mine is blanch'd with feare.
Rosse. What sights, my Lord?
La. I pray you speake not: he growes worse & worse
Question enrages him: at once, goodnight.
Stand not vpon the order of your going,
But go at once.
Len. Good night, and better health
Attend his Maiesty.
La. A kinde goodnight to all. *Exit Lords.*
Macb. It will haue blood they say:
Blood will haue Blood:
Stones haue beene knowne to moue, & Trees to speake:
Augures, and vnderstood Relations, haue
By Maggot Pyes, & Choughes, & Rookes brought forth
The secret'st man of Blood. What is the night?
La. Almost at oddes with morning, which is which.
Macb. How say'st thou that *Macduff* denies his person
At our great bidding.
La. Did you send to him Sir?
Macb. I heare it by the way: But I will send:
There's not a one of them but in his house
I keepe a Seruant Feed. I will to morrow
(And betimes I will) to the weyard Sisters.
More shall they speake: for now I am bent to know
By the worst meanes, the worst, for mine owne good,
All causes shall giue way. I am in blood
Stept in so farre, that should I wade no more,
Returning were as tedious as go ore:
Strange things I haue in head, that will to hand,
Which must be acted, ere they may be scand.
La. You lacke the season of all Natures, sleepe.
Macb. Come, wee'l to sleepe: My strange & self-abuse
Is the initiate feare, that wants hard vse:
We are yet but yong indeed. *Exeunt.*

Scena Quinta.

Thunder. Enter the three Witches, meeting Hecat.

1. Why how now *Hecat*, you looke angerly?
Hec. Haue I not reason (Beldams) as you are?
Sawcy, and ouer-bold, how did you dare
To Trade, and Trafficke with *Macbeth*,
In Riddles, and Affaires of death;

And

The Tragedie of Macbeth.

And I the Mistris of your Charmes,
The close contriuer of all harmes,
Was neuer call'd to beare my part,
Or shew the glory of our Art?
And which is worse, all you haue done
Hath bene but for a wayward Sonne,
Spightfull, and wrathfull, who (as others do)
Loues for his owne ends, not for you.
But make amends now: Get you gon,
And at the pit of Acheron
Meete me i'th'Morning: thither he
Will come, to know his Destinie.
Your Vessels, and your Spels prouide,
Your Charmes, and euery thing beside;
I am for th'Ayre: This night Ile spend
Vnto a dismall, and a Fatall end.
Great businesse must be wrought ere Noone.
Vpon the Corner of the Moone
There hangs a vap'rous drop, profound,
Ile catch it ere it come to ground;
And that distill'd by Magicke slights,
Shall raise such Artificiall Sprights,
As by the strength of their illusion,
Shall draw him on to his Confusion.
He shall spurne Fate, scorne Death, and beare
His hopes 'boue Wisedome, Grace, and Feare:
And you all know, Security
Is Mortals cheefest Enemie.

Musicke, and a Song.

Hearke, I am call'd: my little Spirit see
Sits in a Foggy cloud, and stayes for me.

Sing within. Come away, come away, &c.

1 Come, let's make hast, shee'l soone be
Backe againe.   *Exeunt.*

Scæna Sexta.

Enter Lenox, and another Lord.

Lenox. My former Speeches,
Haue but hit your Thoughts
Which can interpret farther: Onely I say
Things haue bin strangely borne. The gracious *Duncan*
Was pittied of *Macbeth*: marry he was dead:
And the right valiant *Banquo* walk'd too late,
Whom you may say (if't please you) *Fleans* kill'd,
For *Fleans* fled: Men must not walke too late.
Who cannot want the thought, how monstrous
It was for *Malcolme*, and for *Donalbane*
To kill their gracious Father? Damned Fact,
How it did greeue *Macbeth*? Did he not straight
In pious rage, the two delinquents teare,
That were the Slaues of drinke, and thralles of sleepe?
Was not that Nobly done? I, and wisely too:
For 'twould haue anger'd any heart aliue
To heare the men deny't. So that I say,
He ha's borne all things well, and I do thinke,
That had he *Duncans* Sonnes vnder his Key,
(As, and't please Heauen he shall not) they should finde
What 'twere to kill a Father: So should *Fleans*.
But peace; for from broad words, and cause he fayl'd
His presence at the Tyrants Feast, I heare
Macduffe liues in disgrace. Sir, can you tell
Where he bestowes himselfe?

Lord. The Sonnes of *Duncane*
(From whom this Tyrant holds the due of Birth)
Liues in the English Court, and is receyu'd
Of the most Pious *Edward*, with such grace,
That the maleuolence of Fortune, nothing
Takes from his high respect. Thither *Macduffe*
Is gone, to pray the Holy King, vpon his ayd
To wake Northumberland, and warlike *Seyward*,
That by the helpe of these (with him aboue)
To ratifie the Worke) we may againe
Giue to our Tables meate, sleepe to our Nights:
Free from our Feasts, and Banquets bloody kniues;
Do faithfull Homage, and receiue free Honors,
All which we pine for now. And this report
Hath so exasperate their King, that hee
Prepares for some attempt of Warre.

Len. Sent he to *Macduffe*?

Lord. He did: and with an absolute Sir, not I
The clowdy Messenger turnes me his backe,
And hums; as who should say, you'l rue the time
That clogges me with this Answer.

Lenox. And that well might
Aduise him to a Caution, t'hold what distance
His wisedome can prouide. Some holy Angell
Flye to the Court of England, and vnfold
His Message ere he come, that a swift blessing
May soone returne to this our suffering Country,
Vnder a hand accurs'd.

Lord. Ile send my Prayers with him.   *Exeunt*

Actus Quartus. Scena Prima.

Thunder. Enter the three Witches.

1 Thrice the brinded Cat hath mew'd.
2 Thrice, and once the Hedge-Pigge whin'd.
3 Harpier cries, 'tis time, 'tis time.
1 Round about the Caldron go:
In the poysond Entrailes throw
Toad, that vnder cold stone,
Dayes and Nights, ha's thirty one:
Sweltred Venom sleeping got,
Boyle thou first i'th'charmed pot.

All. Double, double, toile and trouble;
Fire burne, and Cauldron bubble.

2 Fillet of a Fenny Snake,
In the Cauldron boyle and bake:
Eye of Newt, and Toe of Frogge,
Wooll of Bat, and Tongue of Dogge:
Adders Forke, and Blinde-wormes Sting,
Lizards legge, and Howlets wing:
For a Charme of powrefull trouble,
Like a Hell-broth, boyle and bubble.

All. Double, double, toyle and trouble,
Fire burne, and Cauldron bubble.

3 Scale of Dragon, Tooth of Wolfe,
Witches Mummey, Maw, and Gulfe
Of the rauin'd salt Sea sharke:
Roote of Hemlocke, digg'd i'th'darke:
Liuer of Blaspheming Iew,
Gall of Goate, and Slippes of Yew,
Sliuer'd in the Moones Ecclipse:

Nose of Turke, and Tartars lips:
Finger of Birth-strangled Babe,
Ditch-deliuer'd by a Drab,
Make the Grewell thicke, and slab.
Adde thereto a Tigers Chawdron,
For th'Ingredience of our Cawdron.

All. Double, double, toyle and trouble,
Fire burne, and Cauldron bubble.

2 Coole it with a Baboones blood,
Then the Charme is firme and good.

Enter Hecat, and the other three Witches.

Hec. O well done: I commend your paines,
And euery one shall share i'th'gaines:
And now about the Cauldron sing
Like Elues and Fairies in a Ring,
Inchanting all that you put in.

Musicke and a Song. Blacke Spirits, &c.

2 By the pricking of my Thumbes,
Something wicked this way comes:
Open Lockes, who euer knockes.

Enter Macbeth.

Macb. How now you secret, black, & midnight Hags?
What is't you do?

All. A deed without a name.

Macb. I coniure you, by that which you Professe,
(How ere you come to know it) answer me:
Though you vntye the Windes, and let them fight
Against the Churches: Though the yesty Waues
Confound and swallow Nauigation vp:
Though bladed Corne be lodg'd, & Trees blown downe,
Though Castles topple on their Warders heads:
Though Pallaces, and Pyramids do slope
Their heads to their Foundations: Though the treasure
Of Natures Germaine, tumble altogether,
Euen till destruction sicken: Answer me
To what I aske you.

1 Speake.
2 Demand.
3 Wee'l answer.
1 Say, if th'hadst rather heare it from our mouthes,
Or from our Masters.

Macb. Call 'em: let me see 'em.

1 Powre in Sowes blood, that hath eaten
Her nine Farrow: Greaze that's sweaten
From the Murderers Gibbet, throw
Into the Flame.

All. Come high or low:
Thy Selfe and Office deaftly show. *Thunder.*

1. Apparation, an Armed Head.

Macb. Tell me, thou vnknowne power.

1 Appar. He knowes thy thought:
Heare his speech, but say thou nought.

1 Appar. Macbeth, Macbeth, Macbeth:
Beware Macduffe,
Beware the Thane of Fife: dismisse me. Enough.
He Descends.

Macb. What ere thou art, for thy good caution, thanks
Thou hast harp'd my feare aright. But one word more.

1 He will not be commanded: heere's another
More potent then the first. *Thunder.*

2 Apparition, a Bloody Childe.

2 Appar. Macbeth, Macbeth, Macbeth.

Macb. Had I three eares, I'd heare thee.

2 Appar. Be bloudy, bold, & resolute:
Laugh to scorne
The powre of man: For none of woman borne
Shall harme *Macbeth*. *Descends.*

Mac. Then liue *Macduffe*: what need I feare of thee?
But yet Ile make assurance: double sure,
And take a Bond of Fate: thou shalt not liue,
That I may tell pale-hearted Feare, it lies;
And sleepe in spight of Thunder. *Thunder.*

3 Apparition, a Childe Crowned, with a Tree in his hand.
What is this, that rises like the issue of a King,
And weares vpon his Baby-brow, the round
And top of Soueraignty?

All. Listen, but speake not too't.

3 Appar. Be Lyon metled, proud, and take no care:
Who chafes, who frets, or where Conspirers are:
Macbeth shall neuer vanquish'd be, vntill
Great Byrnam Wood, to high Dunsmane Hill
Shall come against him. *Descend.*

Macb. That will neuer bee:
Who can impresse the Forrest, bid the Tree
Vnfixe his earth-bound Root? Sweet boadments, good:
Rebellious dead, rise neuer till the Wood
Of Byrnan rise, and our high plac'd *Macbeth*
Shall liue the Lease of Nature, pay his breath
To time, and mortall Custome. Yet my Hart
Throbs to know one thing: Tell me, if your Art
Can tell so much: Shall *Banquo's* issue euer
Reigne in this Kingdome?

All. Seeke to know no more.

Macb. I will be satisfied. Deny me this,
And an eternall Curse fall on you: Let me know.
Why sinkes that Caldron? & what noise is this? *Hoboyes*

1 Shew.
2 Shew.
3 Shew.

All. Shew his Eyes, and greeue his Hart,
Come like shadowes, so depart.

A shew of eight Kings, and Banquo last, with a glasse in his hand.

Macb. Thou art too like the Spirit of *Banquo*: Down:
Thy Crowne do's seare mine Eye-bals. And thy haire
Thou other Gold-bound-brow, is like the first:
A third, is like the former. Filthy Hagges,
Why do you shew me this?——A fourth? Start eyes!
What will the Line stretch out to'th'cracke of Doome?
Another yet? A seauenth? Ile see no more:
And yet the eight appeares, who beares a glasse,
Which shewes me many more: and some I see,
That two-fold Balles, and trebble Scepters carry.
Horrible sight: Now I see 'tis true,
For the Blood-bolter'd *Banquo* smiles vpon me,
And points at them for his. What? is this so?

1 I Sir, all this is so. But why
Stands *Macbeth* thus amazedly?
Come Sisters, cheere we vp his sprights,
And shew the best of our delights.
Ile Charme the Ayre to giue a sound,
While you performe your Antique round:
That this great King may kindly say,
Our duties, did his welcome pay. *Musicke.*

The Witches Dance, and vanish.

Macb. Where are they? Gone?
Let this pernitious houre,
Stand aye accursed in the Kalender.
Come in, without there. *Enter Lenox.*

Lenox. What's your Graces will.

Macb.

Macb. Saw you the Weyard Sisters?
Lenox. No my Lord.
Macb. Came they not by you?
Lenox. No indeed my Lord.
Macb. Infected be the Ayre whereon they ride,
And damn'd all those that trust them. I did heare
The gallopping of Horse. Who was't came by?
Len. 'Tis two or three my Lord, that bring you word:
Macduff is fled to England.
Macb. Fled to England?
Len. I, my good Lord.
Macb. Time, thou anticipat'st my dread exploits:
The flighty purpose neuer is o're-tooke
Vnlesse the deed go with it. From this moment,
The very firstlings of my heart shall be
The firstlings of my hand. And euen now
To Crown my thoughts with Acts: be it thoght & done:
The Castle of *Macduff*, I will surprize,
Seize vpon Fife; giue to th'edge o'th'Sword
His Wife, his Babes, and all vnfortunate Soules
That trace him in his Line. No boasting like a Foole,
This deed Ile do, before this purpose coole,
But no more sights. Where are these Gentlemen?
Come bring me where they are. *Exeunt*

Scena Secunda.

Enter Macduffes Wife, her Son, and Rosse.

Wife. What had he done, to make him fly the Land?
Rosse. You must haue patience Madam.
Wife. He had none:
His flight was madnesse: when our Actions do not,
Our feares do make vs Traitors.
Rosse. You know not
Whether it was his wisedome, or his feare.
Wife. Wisedom? to leaue his wife, to leaue his Babes,
His Mansion, and his Titles, in a place
From whence himselfe do's flye? He loues vs not,
He wants the naturall touch. For the poore Wren
(The most diminitiue of Birds) will fight,
Her yong ones in her Nest, against the Owle:
All is the Feare, and nothing is the Loue;
As little is the Wisedome, where the flight
So runnes against all reason.
Rosse. My deerest Cooz,
I pray you schoole your selfe. But for your Husband,
He is Noble, Wise, Iudicious, and best knowes
The fits o'th'Season. I dare not speake much further,
But cruell are the times, when we are Traitors
And do not know our selues: when we hold Rumor
From what we feare, yet know not what we feare,
But floate vpon a wilde and violent Sea
Each way, and moue. I take my leaue of you:
Shall not be long but Ile be heere againe:
Things at the worst will cease, or else climbe vpward,
To what they were before. My pretty Cosine,
Blessing vpon you.
Wife. Father'd he is,
And yet hee's Father-lesse.
Rosse. I am so much a Foole, should I stay longer
It would be my disgrace, and your discomfort.
I take my leaue at once. *Exit Rosse.*

Wife. Sirra, your Fathers dead,
And what will you do now? How will you liue?
Son. As Birds do Mother.
Wife. What with Wormes, and Flyes?
Son. With what I get I meane, and so do they.
Wife. Poore Bird,
Thou'dst neuer Feare the Net, nor Lime,
The Pitfall, nor the Gin.
Son. Why should I Mother?
Poore Birds they are not set for:
My Father is not dead for all your saying.
Wife. Yes, he is dead:
How wilt thou do for a Father?
Son. Nay how will you do for a Husband?
Wife. Why I can buy me twenty at any Market.
Son. Then you'l by 'em to sell againe.
Wife. Thou speak'st withall thy wit,
And yet I'faith with wit enough for thee.
Son. Was my Father a Traitor, Mother?
Wife. I, that he was.
Son. What is a Traitor?
Wife. Why one that sweares, and lyes.
Son. And be all Traitors, that do so?
Wife. Euery one that do's so, is a Traitor,
And must be hang'd.
Son. And must they all be hang'd, that swear and lye?
Wife. Euery one.
Son. Who must hang them?
Wife. Why, the honest men.
Son. Then the Liars and Swearers are Fools: for there
are Lyars and Swearers enow, to beate the honest men,
and hang vp them.
Wife. Now God helpe thee, poore Monkie:
But how wilt thou do for a Father?
Son. If he were dead, you'ld weepe for him: if you
would not, it were a good signe, that I should quickly
haue a new Father.
Wife. Poore pratler, how thou talk'st?
Enter a Messenger.
Mes. Blesse you faire Dame: I am not to you known,
Though in your state of Honor I am perfect;
I doubt some danger do's approach you neerely.
If you will take a homely mans aduice,
Be not found heere: Hence with your little ones
To fright you thus. Me thinkes I am too sauage:
To do worse to you, were fell Cruelty,
Which is too nie your person. Heauen preserue you,
I dare abide no longer. *Exit Messenger*
Wife. Whether should I flye?
I haue done no harme. But I remember now
I am in this earthly world: where to do harme
Is often laudable, to do good sometime
Accounted dangerous folly. Why then (alas)
Do I put vp that womanly defence,
To say I haue done no harme?
What are these faces?
Enter Murtherers.
Mur. Where is your Husband?
Wife. I hope in no place so vnsanctified,
Where such as thou may'st finde him.
Mur. He's a Traitor.
Son. Thou ly'st thou shagge-ear'd Villaine.
Mur. What you Egge?
Yong fry of Treachery?
Son. He ha's kill'd me Mother,
Run away I pray you. *Exit crying Murther.*

Scæna Tertia.

Enter Malcolme and Macduffe.

Mal. Let vs seeke out some desolate shade, & there
Weepe our sad bosomes empty.

Macd. Let vs rather
Hold fast the mortall Sword: and like good men,
Bestride our downfall Birthdome: each new Morne,
New Widdowes howle, new Orphans cry, new sorowes
Strike heauen on the face, that it resounds
As if it felt with Scotland, and yell'd out
Like Syllable of Dolour.

Mal. What I beleeue, Ile waile;
What know, beleeue; and what I can redresse,
As I shall finde the time to friend: I wil.
What you haue spoke, it may be so perchance.
This Tyrant, whose sole name blisters our tongues,
Was once thought honest: you haue lou'd him well,
He hath not touch'd you yet. I am yong, but something
You may discerne of him through me, and wisedome
To offer vp a weake, poore innocent Lambe
T'appease an angry God.

Macd. I am not treacherous.

Male. But *Macbeth* is.
A good and vertuous Nature may recoyle
In an Imperiall charge. But I shall craue your pardon:
That which you are, my thoughts cannot transpose;
Angels are bright still, though the brightest fell.
Though all things foule, would wear the brows of grace
Yet Grace must still looke so.

Macd. I haue lost my Hopes.

Male. Perchance euen there
Where I did finde my doubts.
Why in that rawnesse left you Wife, and Childe?
Those precious Motiues, those strong knots of Loue,
Without leaue-taking. I pray you,
Let not my Iealousies, be your Dishonors,
But mine owne Safeties: you may be rightly iust,
What euer I shall thinke.

Macd. Bleed, bleed poore Country,
Great Tyrrany, lay thou thy basis sure,
For goodnesse dare not check thee: wear ÿ thy wrongs,
The Title, is affear'd. Far thee well Lord,
I would not be the Villaine that thou think'st,
For the whole Space that's in the Tyrants Graspe,
And the rich East to boot.

Mal. Be not offended:
I speake not as in absolute feare of you:
I thinke our Country sinkes beneath the yoake,
It weepes, it bleeds, and each new day a gash
Is added to her wounds. I thinke withall,
There would be hands vplifted in my right:
And heere from gracious England haue I offer
Of goodly thousands. But for all this,
When I shall treade vpon the Tyrants head,
Or weare it on my Sword; yet my poore Country
Shall haue more vices then it had before,
More suffer, and more sundry wayes then euer,
By him that shall succeede.

Macd. What should he be?

Mal. It is my selfe I meane: in whom I know
All the particulars of Vice so grafted,
That when they shall be open'd, blacke *Macbeth*
Will seeme as pure as Snow, and the poore State
Esteeme him as a Lambe, being compar'd
With my confinelesse harmes.

Macd. Not in the Legions
Of horrid Hell, can come a Diuell more damn'd
In euils, to top *Macbeth*.

Mal. I grant him Bloody,
Luxurious, Auaricious, False, Deceitfull,
Sodaine, Malicious, smacking of euery sinne
That ha's a name. But there's no bottome, none
In my Voluptuousnesse: Your Wiues, your Daughters,
Your Matrons, and your Maides, could not fill vp
The Cesterne of my Lust, and my Desire
All continent Impediments would ore-beare
That did oppose my will. Better *Macbeth*,
Then such an one to reigne.

Macd. Boundlesse intemperance
In Nature is a Tyranny: It hath beene
Th'vntimely emptying of the happy Throne,
And fall of many Kings. But feare not yet
To take vpon you what is yours: you may
Conuey your pleasures in a spacious plenty,
And yet seeme cold. The time you may so hoodwinke:
We haue willing Dames enough: there cannot be
That Vulture in you, to deuoure so many
As will to Greatnesse dedicate themselues,
Finding it so inclinde.

Mal. With this, there growes
In my most ill-compos'd Affection, such
A stanchlesse Auarice, that were I King,
I should cut off the Nobles for their Lands,
Desire his Iewels, and this others House,
And my more-hauing, would be as a Sawce
To make me hunger more, that I should forge
Quarrels vniust against the Good and Loyall,
Destroying them for wealth.

Macd. This Auarice
stickes deeper: growes with more pernicious roote
Then Summer-seeming Lust: and it hath bin
The Sword of our slaine Kings: yet do not feare,
Scotland hath Foysons, to fill vp your will
Of your meere Owne. All these are portable,
With other Graces weigh'd.

Mal. But I haue none. The King-becoming Graces,
As Iustice, Verity, Temp'rance, Stablenesse,
Bounty, Perseuerance, Mercy, Lowlinesse,
Deuotion, Patience, Courage, Fortitude,
I haue no rellish of them, but abound
In the diuision of each seuerall Crime,
Acting it many wayes. Nay, had I powre, I should
Poure the sweet Milke of Concord, into Hell,
Vprore the vniuersall peace, confound
All vnity on earth.

Macd. O Scotland, Scotland.

Mal. If such a one be fit to gouerne, speake:
I am as I haue spoken.

Mac. Fit to gouern? No not to liue. O Natiõ miserable!
With an vntitled Tyrant, bloody Sceptred,
When shalt thou see thy wholsome dayes againe?
Since that the truest Issue of thy Throne
By his owne Interdiction stands accust,
And do's blaspheme his breed? Thy Royall Father
Was a most Sainted-King: the Queene that bore thee,
Oftner vpon her knees, then on her feet,
Dy'de euery day she liu'd. Fare thee well,

These

These Euils thou repeat'st vpon thy selfe,
Hath banish'd me from Scotland. O my Brest,
Thy hope ends heere.

 Mal. Macduff, this Noble passion
Childe of integrity, hath from my soule
Wip'd the blacke Scruples, reconcil'd my thoughts
To thy good Truth, and Honor. Diuellish *Macbeth*,
By many of these traines, hath sought to win me
Into his power: and modest Wisedome plucks me
From ouer-credulous hast: but God aboue
Deale betweene thee and me; For euen now
I put my selfe to thy Direction, and
Vnspeake mine owne detraction. Heere abiure
The taints, and blames I laide vpon my selfe,
For strangers to my Nature. I am yet
Vnknowne to Woman, neuer was forsworne,
Scarsely haue coueted what was mine owne:
At no time broke my Faith, would not betray
The Deuill to his Fellow, and delight
No lesse in truth then life. My first false speaking
Was this vpon my selfe. What I am truly
Is thine, and my poore Countries to command:
Whither indeed, before they heere approach
Old *Seyward* with ten thousand warlike men
Already at a point, was setting foorth:
Now wee'l together, and the chance of goodnesse
Be like our warranted Quarrell. Why are you silent?

 Macd. Such welcome, and vnwelcom things at once
'Tis hard to reconcile.

Enter a Doctor.

 Mal. Well, more anon. Comes the King forth
I pray you?

 Doct. I Sir: there are a crew of wretched Soules
That stay his Cure: their malady conuinces
The great assay of Art. But at his touch,
Such sanctity hath Heauen giuen his hand,
They presently amend. *Exit.*

 Mal. I thanke you Doctor.

 Macd. What's the Disease he meanes?

 Mal. Tis call'd the Euill.
A most myraculous worke in this good King,
Which often since my heere remaine in England,
I haue seene him do: How he solicites heauen
Himselfe best knowes: but strangely visited people
All swolne and Vlcerous, pittifull to the eye,
The meere dispaire of Surgery, he cures,
Hanging a golden stampe about their neckes,
Put on with holy Prayers, and 'tis spoken
To the succeeding Royalty he leaues
The healing Benediction. With this strange vertue,
He hath a heauenly guift of Prophesie,
And sundry Blessings hang about his Throne,
That speake him full of Grace.

Enter Rosse.

 Macd. See who comes heere.

 Malc. My Countryman: but yet I know him not.

 Macd. My euer gentle Cozen, welcome hither.

 Malc. I know him now. Good God betimes remoue
The meanes that makes vs Strangers.

 Rosse. Sir, Amen.

 Macd. Stands Scotland where it did?

 Rosse. Alas poore Countrey,
Almost affraid to know it selfe. It cannot
Be call'd our Mother, but our Graue; where nothing
But who knowes nothing, is once seene to smile:
Where sighes, and groanes, and shrieks that rent the ayre
Are made, not mark'd: Where violent sorrow seemes
A Moderne extasie: The Deadmans knell,
Is there scarse ask'd for who, and good mens liues
Expire before the Flowers in their Caps,
Dying, or ere they sicken.

 Macd. Oh Relation; too nice, and yet too true.

 Malc. What's the newest griefe?

 Rosse. That of an houres age, doth hisse the speaker,
Each minute teemes a new one.

 Macd. How do's my Wife?

 Rosse. Why well.

 Macd. And all my Children?

 Rosse. Well too.

 Macd. The Tyrant ha's not batter'd at their peace?

 Rosse. No, they were wel at peace, when I did leaue 'em

 Macd. Be not a niggard of your speech: How gos't?

 Rosse. When I came hither to transport the Tydings
Which I haue heauily borne, there ran a Rumour
Of many worthy Fellowes, that were out,
Which was to my beleefe witnest the rather,
For that I saw the Tyrants Power a-foot.
Now is the time of helpe: your eye in Scotland
Would create Soldiours, make our women fight,
To dosse their dire distresses.

 Malc. Bee't their comfort
We are comming thither: Gracious England hath
Lent vs good *Seyward*, and ten thousand men,
An older, and a better Souldier, none
That Christendome giues out.

 Rosse. Would I could answer
This comfort with the like. But I haue words
That would be howl'd out in the desert ayre,
Where hearing should not latch them.

 Macd. What concerne they,
The generall cause, or is it a Fee-griefe
Due to some single brest?

 Rosse. No minde that's honest
But in it shares some woe, though the maine part
Pertaines to you alone.

 Macd. If it be mine
Keepe it not from me, quickly let me haue it.

 Rosse. Let not your eares dispise my tongue for euer,
Which shall possesse them with the heauiest sound
That euer yet they heard.

 Macd. Humh: I guesse at it.

 Rosse. Your Castle is surpriz'd: your Wife, and Babes
Sauagely slaughter'd: To relate the manner
Were on the Quarry of these murther'd Deere
To adde the death of you.

 Malc. Mercifull Heauen:
What man, ne're pull your hat vpon your browes;
Giue sorrow words; the griefe that do's not speake,
Whispers the o're-fraught heart, and bids it breake.

 Macd. My Children too?

 Ro. Wife, Children, Seruants, all that could be found.

 Macd. And I must be from thence? My wife kil'd too?

 Rosse. I haue said.

 Malc. Be comforted.
Let's make vs Med'cines of our great Reuenge,
To cure this deadly greefe.

 Macd. He ha's no Children. All my pretty ones?
Did you say All? Oh Hell-Kite! All?
What, All my pretty Chickens, and their Damme
At one fell swoope?

 Malc. Dispute it like a man.

 Macd. I shall do so:

But I must also feele it as a man;
I cannot but remember such things were
That were most precious to me: Did heauen looke on,
And would not take their part? Sinfull *Macduff*,
They were all strooke for thee: Naught that I am,
Not for their owne demerits, but for mine
Fell slaughter on their soules: Heauen rest them now.

  Mal. Be this the Whetstone of your sword, let griefe
Conuert to anger: blunt not the heart, enrage it.

  Macd. O I could play the woman with mine eyes,
And Braggart with my tongue. But gentle Heauens,
Cut short all intermission: Front to Front,
Bring thou this Fiend of Scotland, and my selfe
Within my Swords length set him, if he scape
Heauen forgiue him too.

  Mal. This time goes manly:
Come go we to the King, our Power is ready,
Our lacke is nothing but our leaue. *Macbeth*
Is ripe for shaking, and the Powres aboue
Put on their Instruments: Receiue what cheere you may,
The Night is long, that neuer findes the Day. *Exeunt*

Actus Quintus. Scena Prima.

Enter a Doctor of Physicke, and a Wayting Gentlewoman.

  Doct. I haue too Nights watch'd with you, but can perceiue no truth in your report. When was it shee last walk'd?

  Gent. Since his Maiesty went into the Field, I haue seene her rise from her bed, throw her Night-Gown vp-pon her, vnlocke her Closset, take foorth paper, folde it, write vpon't, read it, afterwards Seale it, and againe re-turne to bed; yet all this while in a most fast sleepe.

  Doct. A great perturbation in Nature, to receyue at once the benefit of sleep, and do the effects of watching. In this slumbry agitation, besides her walking, and other actuall performances, what (at any time) haue you heard her say?

  Gent. That Sir, which I will not report after her.

  Doct. You may to me, and 'tis most meet you should.

  Gent. Neither to you, nor any one, hauing no witnesse
to confirme my speech.   *Enter Lady, with a Taper.*
Lo you, heere she comes: This is her very guise, and vp-on my life fast asleepe: obserue her, stand close.

  Doct. How came she by that light?

  Gent. Why it stood by her: she ha's light by her con-tinually, 'tis her command.

  Doct. You see her eyes are open.

  Gent. I but their sense are shut.

  Doct. What is it she do's now?
Looke how she rubbes her hands.

  Gent. It is an accustom'd action with her, to seeme thus washing her hands: I haue knowne her continue in this a quarter of an houre.

  Lad. Yet heere's a spot.

  Doct. Heark, she speaks, I will set downe what comes from her, to satisfie my remembrance the more strongly.

  La. Out damned spot: out I say. One: Two: Why then 'tis time to doo't: Hell is murky. Fye, my Lord, fie, a Souldier, and affear'd? what need we feare? who knowes it, when none can call our powre to accompt: yet who would haue thought the olde man to haue had so much blood in him.

  Doct. Do you marke that?

  Lad. The Thane of Fife, had a wife: where is she now? What will these hands ne're be cleane? No more o'that my Lord, no more o'that: you marre all with this star-ting.

  Doct. Go too, go too:
You haue knowne what you should not.

  Gent. She ha's spoke what shee should not, I am sure of that: Heauen knowes what she ha's knowne.

  La. Heere's the smell of the blood still: all the per-fumes of Arabia will not sweeten this little hand. Oh, oh, oh.

  Doct. What a sigh is there? The hart is sorely charg'd.

  Gent. I would not haue such a heart in my bosome, for the dignity of the whole body.

  Doct. Well, well, well.

  Gent. Pray God it be sir.

  Doct. This disease is beyond my practise: yet I haue knowne those which haue walkt in their sleep, who haue dyed holily in their beds.

  Lad. Wash your hands, put on your Night-Gowne, looke not so pale: I tell you yet againe *Banquo's* buried; he cannot come out on's graue.

  Doct. Euen so?

  Lady. To bed, to bed: there's knocking at the gate: Come, come, come, come, giue me your hand: What's done, cannot be vndone. To bed, to bed, to bed. *Exit Lady.*

  Doct. Will she go now to bed?

  Gent. Directly.

  Doct. Foule whisp'rings are abroad: vnnaturall deeds
Do breed vnnaturall troubles: infected mindes
To their deafe pillowes will discharge their Secrets:
More needs she the Diuine, then the Physitian:
God, God forgiue vs all. Looke after her,
Remoue from her the meanes of all annoyance,
And still keepe eyes vpon her: So goodnight,
My minde she ha's mated, and amaz'd my sight.
I thinke, but dare not speake.

  Gent. Good night good Doctor.   *Exeunt.*

Scena Secunda.

Drums and Colours. Enter Menteth, Cathnes, Angus, Lenox, Soldiers.

  Ment. The English powre is neere, led on by *Malcolm*, His Vnkle *Seyward*, and the good *Macduff*.
Reuenges burne in them: for their deere causes
Would to the bleeding, and the grim Alarme
Excite the mortified man.

  Ang. Neere Byrnan wood
Shall we well meet them, that way are they comming.

  Cath. Who knowes if *Donalbane* be with his brother?

  Len. For certaine Sir, he is not: I haue a File
Of all the Gentry; there is *Seywards* Sonne,
And many vnruffe youths, that euen now
Protest their first of Manhood.

  Ment. What do's the Tyrant.

  Cath. Great Dunsinane he strongly Fortifies:
Some say hee's mad: Others, that lesser hate him,
Do call it valiant Fury, but for certaine

The Tragedie of Macbeth.

He cannot buckle his distemper'd cause
Within the belt of Rule.

Ang. Now do's he feele
His secret Murthers sticking on his hands,
Now minutely Reuolts vpbraid his Faith-breach:
Those he commands, moue onely in command,
Nothing in loue: Now do's he feele his Title
Hang loose about him, like a Giants Robe
Vpon a dwarfish Theefe.

Ment. Who then shall blame
His pester'd Senses to recoyle, and start,
When all that is within him, do's condemne
It selfe, for being there.

Cath. Well, march we on,
To giue Obedience, where 'tis truly ow'd:
Meet we the Med'cine of the sickly Weale,
And with him poure we in our Countries purge,
Each drop of vs.

Lenox. Or so much as it needes,
To dew the Soueraigne Flower, and drowne the Weeds:
Make we our March towards Birnan. *Exeunt marching.*

Scæna Tertia.

Enter Macbeth, Doctor, and Attendants.

Macb. Bring me no more Reports, let them flye all:
Till Byrnane wood remoue to Dunsinane,
I cannot taint with Feare. What's the Boy *Malcolme*?
Was he not borne of woman? The Spirits that know
All mortall Consequences, haue pronounc'd me thus:
Feare not *Macbeth*, no man that's borne of woman
Shall ere haue power vpon thee. Then fly false Thanes,
And mingle with the English Epicures,
The minde I sway by, and the heart I beare,
Shall neuer sagge with doubt, nor shake with feare.

Enter Seruant.

The diuell damne thee blacke, thou cream-fac'd Loone:
Where got'st thou that Goose-looke.

Ser. There is ten thousand.

Macb. Geese Villaine?

Ser. Souldiers Sir.

Macb. Go pricke thy face, and ouer-red thy feare
Thou Lilly-liuer'd Boy. What Soldiers, Patch?
Death of thy Soule, those Linnen cheekes of thine
Are Counsailers to feare. What Soldiers Whay-face?

Ser. The English Force, so please you.

Macb. Take thy face hence. *Seyton*, I am sick at hart,
When I behold: *Seyton*, I say, this push
Will cheere me euer, or dis-eate me now.
I haue liu'd long enough: my way of life
Is falne into the Seare, the yellow Leafe,
And that which should accompany Old-Age,
As Honor, Loue, Obedience, Troopes of Friends,
I must not looke to haue: but in their steed,
Curses, not lowd but deepe, Mouth-honor, breath
Which the poore heart would faine deny, and dare not.
Seyton?

Enter Seyton.

Sey. What's your gracious pleasure?

Macb. What Newes more?

Sey. All is confirm'd my Lord, which was reported.

Macb. Ile fight, till from my bones, my flesh be hackt.
Giue me my Armor.

Seyt. 'Tis not needed yet.

Macb. Ile put it on:
Send out moe Horses, skirre the Country round,
Hang those that talke of Feare. Giue me mine Armor:
How do's your Patient, Doctor?

Doct. Not so sicke my Lord,
As she is troubled with thicke-comming Fancies
That keepe her from her rest.

Macb. Cure her of that:
Can'st thou not Minister to a minde diseas'd,
Plucke from the Memory a rooted Sorrow,
Raze out the written troubles of the Braine,
And with some sweet Obliuious Antidote
Cleanse the stufft bosome, of that perillous stuffe
Which weighes vpon the heart?

Doct. Therein the Patient
Must minister to himselfe.

Macb. Throw Physicke to the Dogs, Ile none of it.
Come, put mine Armour on: giue me my Staffe:
Seyton, send out: Doctor, the Thanes flye from me:
Come sir, dispatch. If thou could'st Doctor, cast
The Water of my Land, finde her Disease,
And purge it to a sound and pristine Health,
I would applaud thee to the very Eccho,
That should applaud againe. Pull't off I say,
What Rubarb, Cyme, or what Purgatiue drugge
Would scowre these English hence: hear'st ÿ of them?

Doct. I my good Lord: your Royall Preparation
Makes vs heare something.

Macb. Bring it after me:
I will not be affraid of Death and Bane,
Till Birnane Forrest come to Dunsinane.

Doct. Were I from Dunsinane away, and cleere,
Profit againe should hardly draw me heere. *Exeunt*

Scena Quarta.

Drum and Colours. Enter Malcolme, Seyward, Macduffe, Seywards Sonne, Menteth, Cathnes, Angus, and Soldiers Marching.

Malc. Cosins, I hope the dayes are neere at hand
That Chambers will be safe.

Ment. We doubt it nothing.

Syew. What wood is this before vs?

Ment. The wood of Birnane.

Malc. Let euery Souldier hew him downe a Bough,
And bear't before him, thereby shall we shadow
The numbers of our Hoast, and make discouery
Erre in report of vs.

Sold. It shall be done.

Syw. We learne no other, but the confident Tyrant
Keepes still in Dunsinane, and will indure
Our setting downe befor't.

Malc. 'Tis his maine hope:
For where there is aduantage to be giuen,
Both more and lesse haue giuen him the Reuolt,
And none serue with him, but constrained things,
Whose hearts are absent too.

Macd. Let our iust Censures
Attend the true euent, and put we on

Industrious

The Tragedie of Macbeth.

Industrious Souldiership.

Sey. The time approaches,
That will with due decision make vs know
What we shall say we haue, and what we owe:
Thoughts speculatiue, their vnsure hopes relate,
But certaine issue, stroakes must arbitrate,
Towards which, aduance the warre. *Exeunt marching*

Scena Quinta.

Enter Macbeth, Seyton, & Souldiers, with Drum and Colours.

Macb. Hang out our Banners on the outward walls,
The Cry is still, they come: our Castles strength
Will laugh a Siedge to scorne: Heere let them lye,
Till Famine and the Ague eate them vp:
Were they not forc'd with those that should be ours,
We might haue met them darefull, beard to beard,
And beate them backward home. What is that noyse?
A Cry within of Women.

Sey. It is the cry of women, my good Lord.

Macb. I haue almost forgot the taste of Feares:
The time ha's beene, my sences would haue cool'd
To heare a Night-shrieke, and my Fell of haire
Would at a dismall Treatise rowze, and stirre
As life were in't. I haue supt full with horrors,
Direnesse familiar to my slaughterous thoughts
Cannot once start me. Wherefore was that cry?

Sey. The Queene (my Lord) is dead.

Macb. She should haue dy'de heereafter;
There would haue beene a time for such a word:
To morrow, and to morrow, and to morrow,
Creepes in this petty pace from day to day,
To the last Syllable of Recorded time:
And all our yesterdayes, haue lighted Fooles
The way to dusty death. Out, out, breefe Candle,
Life's but a walking Shadow, a poore Player,
That struts and frets his houre vpon the Stage,
And then is heard no more. It is a Tale
Told by an Ideot, full of sound and fury
Signifying nothing. *Enter a Messenger.*
Thou com'st to vse thy Tongue: thy Story quickly.

Mes. Gracious my Lord,
I should report that which I say I saw,
But know not how to doo't.

Macb. Well, say sir.

Mes. As I did stand my watch vpon the Hill
I look'd toward Byrnane, and anon me thought
The Wood began to moue.

Macb. Lyar, and Slaue.

Mes. Let me endure your wrath, if't be not so:
Within this three Mile may you see it comming.
I say, a mouing Groue.

Macb. If thou speak'st false,
Vpon the next Tree shall thou hang aliue
Till Famine cling thee: If thy speech be sooth,
I care not if thou dost for me as much.
I pull in Resolution, and begin
To doubt th'Equiuocation of the Fiend,
That lies like truth. Feare not, till Byrnane Wood
Do come to Dunsinane, and now a Wood

Comes toward Dunsinane. Arme, Arme, and out,
If this which he auouches, do's appeare,
There is nor flying hence, nor tarrying here,
I 'ginne to be a-weary of the Sun,
And wish th'estate o'th'world were now vndon.
Ring the Alarum Bell, blow Winde, come wracke,
At least wee'l dye with Harnesse on our backe. *Exeunt*

Scena Sexta.

Drumme and Colours.
Enter Malcolme, Seyward, Macduffe, and their Army, with Boughes.

Mal. Now neere enough:
Your leauy Skreenes throw downe,
And shew like those you are: You (worthy Vnkle)
Shall with my Cosin your right Noble Sonne
Leade our first Battell. Worthy *Macduffe*, and wee
Shall take vpon's what else remaines to do,
According to our order.

Sey. Fare you well:
Do we but finde the Tyrants power to night,
Let vs be beaten, if we cannot fight.

Macd. Make all our Trumpets speak, giue th̄ all breath
Those clamorous Harbingers of Blood, & Death. *Exeunt*
Alarums continued.

Scena Septima.

Enter Macbeth.

Macb. They haue tied me to a stake, I cannot flye,
But Beare-like I must fight the course. What's he
That was not borne of Woman? Such a one
Am I to feare, or none.
Enter young Seyward.

Y. Sey. What is thy name?

Macb. Thou'lt be affraid to heare it.

Y. Sey. No: though thou call'st thy selfe a hoter name
Then any is in hell.

Macb. My name's *Macbeth*.

Y. Sey. The diuell himselfe could not pronounce a Title
More hatefull to mine eare.

Macb. No: nor more fearefull.

Y. Sey. Thou lyest abhorred Tyrant, with my Sword
Ile proue the lye thou speak'st.
Fight, and young Seyward slaine.

Macb. Thou was't borne of woman;
But Swords I smile at, Weapons laugh to scorne,
Brandish'd by man that's of a Woman borne. *Exit.*
Alarums. Enter Macduffe.

Macd. That way the noise is: Tyrant shew thy face,
If thou beest slaine, and with no stroake of mine,
My Wife and Childrens Ghosts will haunt me still:
I cannot strike at wretched Kernes, whose armes
Are hyr'd to beare their Staues; either thou *Macbeth*,
Or else my Sword with an vnbattered edge
I sheath againe vndeeded. There thou should'st be,
By this great clatter, one of greatest note

Seemes

The Tragedie of Macbeth.

Seemes bruited. Let me finde him Fortune,
And more I begge not.　　*Exit.*　　*Alarums.*

Enter Malcolme and Seyward.

Sey. This way my Lord, the Castles gently rendred:
The Tyrants people, on both sides do fight,
The Noble Thanes do brauely in the Warre,
The day almost it selfe professes yours,
And little is to do.

Malc. We haue met with Foes
That strike beside vs.

Sey. Enter Sir, the Castle.　　*Exeunt.*　　*Alarum*

Enter Macbeth.

Macb. Why should I play the Roman Foole, and dye
On mine owne sword? whiles I see liues, the gashes
Do better vpon them.

Enter Macduffe.

Macd. Turne Hell-hound, turne.

Macb. Of all men else I haue auoyded thee:
But get thee backe, my soule is too much charg'd
With blood of thine already.

Macd. I haue no words,
My voice is in my Sword, thou bloodier Villaine
Then tearmes can giue thee out.　　*Fight: Alarum*

Macb. Thou loosest labour,
As easie may'st thou the intrenchant Ayre
With thy keene Sword impresse, as make me bleed:
Let fall thy blade on vulnerable Crests,
I beare a charmed Life, which must not yeeld
To one of woman borne.

Macd. Dispaire thy Charme,
And let the Angell whom thou still hast seru'd
Tell thee, *Macduffe* was from his Mothers womb
Vntimely ript.

Macb. Accursed be that tongue that tels mee so;
For it hath Cow'd my better part of man:
And be these Iugling Fiends no more beleeu'd,
That palter with vs in a double sence,
That keepe the word of promise to our eare,
And breake it to our hope. Ile not fight with thee.

Macd. Then yeeld thee Coward,
And liue to be the shew, and gaze o'th'time.
Wee'l haue thee, as our rarer Monsters are
Painted vpon a pole, and vnder-writ,
Heere may you see the Tyrant.

Macb. I will not yeeld
To kisse the ground before young *Malcolmes* feet,
And to be baited with the Rabbles curse.
Though Byrnane wood be come to Dunsinane,
And thou oppos'd, being of no woman borne,
Yet I will try the last. Before my body,
I throw my warlike Shield: Lay on *Macduffe*,
And damn'd be him, that first cries hold, enough.
　　Exeunt fighting.　　*Alarums.*

Enter Fighting, and Macbeth slaine.

Retreat, and Flourish. Enter with Drumme and Colours,
Malcolm, Seyward, Rosse, Thanes, & Soldiers.

Mal. I would the Friends we misse, were safe arriu'd.

Sey. Some must go off: and yet by these I see,
So great a day as this is cheapely bought.

Mal. *Macduffe* is missing, and your Noble Sonne.

Rosse. Your son my Lord, ha's paid a souldiers debt,
He onely liu'd but till he was a man,
The which no sooner had his Prowesse confirm'd
In the vnshrinking station where he fought,
But like a man he dy'de.

Sey. Then he is dead?

Rosse. I, and brought off the field: your cause of sorrow
Must not be measur'd by his worth, for then
It hath no end.

Sey. Had he his hurts before?

Rosse. I, on the Front.

Sey. Why then, Gods Soldier be he:
Had I as many Sonnes, as I haue haires,
I would not wish them to a fairer death:
And so his Knell is knoll'd.

Mal. Hee's worth more sorrow,
And that Ile spend for him.

Sey. He's worth no more,
They say he parted well, and paid his score,
And so God be with him. Here comes newer comfort.

Enter Macduffe; with Macbeths head.

Macd. Haile King, for so thou art.
Behold where stands
Th'Vsurpers cursed head: the time is free:
I see thee compast with thy Kingdomes Pearle,
That speake my salutation in their minds:
Whose voyces I desire alowd with mine.
Haile King of Scotland.

All. Haile King of Scotland.　　*Flourish.*

Mal. We shall not spend a large expence of time,
Before we reckon with your seuerall loues,
And make vs euen with you. My Thanes and Kinsmen
Henceforth be Earles, the first that euer Scotland
In such an Honor nam'd: What's more to do,
Which would be planted newly with the time,
As calling home our exil'd Friends abroad,
That fled the Snares of watchfull Tyranny,
Producing forth the cruell Ministers
Of this dead Butcher, and his Fiend-like Queene;
Who (as 'tis thought) by selfe and violent hands,
Tooke off her life. This, and what needfull else
That call's vpon vs, by the Grace of Grace,
We will performe in measure, time, and place:
So thankes to all at once, and to each one,
Whom we inuite, to see vs Crown'd at Scone.
　　Flourish.　　*Exeunt Omnes.*

FINIS.

THE TRAGEDIE OF
HAMLET, Prince of Denmarke.

Actus Primus. Scœna Prima.

Enter Barnardo and Francisco two Centinels.

Barnardo.
Ho's there?
Fran. Nay answer me: Stand & vnfold your selfe.
Bar. Long liue the King.
Fran. Barnardo?
Bar. He.
Fran. You come most carefully vpon your houre.
Bar. 'Tis now strook twelue, get thee to bed *Francisco.*
Fran. For this releefe much thankes: 'Tis bitter cold,
And I am sicke at heart.
Barn. Haue you had quiet Guard?
Fran. Not a Mouse stirring.
Bar. Well, goodnight. If you do meet *Horatio* and *Marcellus*, the Riuals of my Watch, bid them make hast.

Enter Horatio and Marcellus.

Fran. I thinke I heare them. Stand: who's there?
Hor. Friends to this ground.
Mar. And Leige-men to the Dane.
Fran. Giue you good night.
Mar. O farwel honest Soldier, who hath relieu'd you?
Fra. Barnardo ha's my place: giue you goodnight.
Exit Fran.

Mar. Holla Barnardo.
Bar. Say, what is *Horatio* there?
Hor. A peece of him.
Bar. Welcome *Horatio*, welcome good *Marcellus.*
Mar. What, ha's this thing appear'd againe to night.
Bar. I haue seene nothing.
Mar. *Horatio* saies, 'tis but our Fantasie,
And will not let beleefe take hold of him
Touching this dreaded sight, twice seene of vs,
Therefore I haue intreated him along
With vs, to watch the minutes of this Night,
That if againe this Apparition come,
He may approue our eyes, and speake to it.
Hor. Tush, tush, 'twill not appeare.
Bar. Sit downe a-while,
And let vs once againe assaile your eares,
That are so fortified against our Story,
What we two Nights haue seene.
Hor. Well, sit we downe,
And let vs heare *Barnardo* speake of this.
Barn. Last night of all,
When yond same Starre that's Westward from the Pole
Had made his course t'illume that part of Heauen
Where now it burnes, *Marcellus* and my selfe,
The Bell then beating one.
Mar. Peace, breake thee of: *Enter the Ghost.*
Looke where it comes againe.
Barn. In the same figure, like the King that's dead.
Mar. Thou art a Scholler; speake to it *Horatio.*
Barn. Lookes it not like the King? Marke it *Horatio.*
Hora. Most like: It harrowes me with fear & wonder
Barn. It would be spoke too.
Mar. Question it *Horatio.*
Hor. What art thou that vsurp'st this time of night,
Together with that Faire and Warlike forme
In which the Maiesty of buried Denmarke
Did sometimes march: By Heauen I charge thee speake.
Mar. It is offended.
Barn. See, it stalkes away.
Hor. Stay: speake; speake: I Charge thee, speake.
Exit the Ghost.
Mar. 'Tis gone, and will not answer.
Barn. How now *Horatio*? You tremble & look pale:
Is not this something more then Fantasie?
What thinke you on't?
Hor. Before my God, I might not this beleeue
Without the sensible and true auouch
Of mine owne eyes.
Mar. Is it not like the King?
Hor. As thou art to thy selfe,
Such was the very Armour he had on,
When th'Ambitious Norwey combatted:
So frown'd he once, when in an angry parle
He smot the sledded Pollax on the Ice.
'Tis strange.
Mar. Thus twice before, and iust at this dead houre,
With Martiall stalke, hath he gone by our Watch.
Hor. In what particular thought to work, I know not:
But in the grosse and scope of my Opinion,
This boades some strange erruption to our State.
Mar. Good now sit downe, & tell me he that knowes
Why this same strict and most obseruant Watch,
So nightly toyles the subiect of the Land,
And why such dayly Cast of Brazon Cannon
And Forraigne Mart for Implements of warre:
Why such impresse of Ship-wrights, whose sore Taske
Do's not diuide the Sunday from the weeke,
What might be toward, that this sweaty hast
Doth make the Night ioynt-Labourer with the day:
Who is't that can informe me?
Hor. That can I,

At least the whisper goes so : Our last King,
Whose Image euen but now appear'd to vs,
Was (as you know) by *Fortinbras* of Norway,
(Thereto prick'd on by a most emulate Pride)
Dar'd to the Combate. In which, our Valiant *Hamlet*,
(For so this side of our knowne world esteem'd him)
Did slay this *Fortinbras*: who by a Seal'd Compact,
Well ratified by Law, and Heraldrie,
Did forfeite (with his life) all those his Lands
Which he stood seiz'd on, to the Conqueror :
Against the which, a Moity competent
Was gaged by our King : which had return'd
To the Inheritance of *Fortinbras*,
Had he bin Vanquisher, as by the same Cou'nant
And carriage of the Article designe,
His fell to *Hamlet*. Now sir, young *Fortinbras*,
Of vnimproued Mettle, hot and full,
Hath in the skirts of Norway, heere and there,
Shark'd vp a List of Landlesse Resolutes,
For Foode and Diet, to some Enterprize
That hath a stomacke in't : which is no other
(And it doth well appeare vnto our State)
But to recouer of vs by strong hand
And termes Compulsatiue, those foresaid Lands
So by his Father lost : and this (I take it)
Is the maine Motiue of our Preparations,
The Sourse of this our Watch, and the cheefe head
Of this post-hast, and Romage in the Land.
  Enter Ghost againe.
But soft, behold : Loe, where it comes againe :
Ile crosse it, though it blast me. Stay Illusion :
If thou hast any sound, or vse of Voyce,
Speake to me. If there be any good thing to be done,
That may to thee do ease, and grace to me ; speak to me.
If thou art priuy to thy Countries Fate
(Which happily foreknowing may auoyd) Oh speake.
Or, if thou hast vp-hoorded in thy life
Extorted Treasure in the wombe of Earth,
(For which, they say, you Spirits oft walke in death)
Speake of it. Stay, and speake. Stop it *Marcellus*.
  Mar. Shall I strike at it with my Partizan ?
  Hor. Do, if it will not stand.
  Barn. 'Tis heere.
  Hor. 'Tis heere.
  Mar. 'Tis gone.   *Exit Ghost.*
We do it wrong, being so Maiesticall
To offer it the shew of Violence,
For it is as the Ayre, invulnerable,
And our vaine blowes, malicious Mockery.
  Barn. It was about to speake, when the Cocke crew.
  Hor. And then it started, like a guilty thing
Vpon a fearfull Summons. I haue heard,
The Cocke that is the Trumpet to the day,
Doth with his lofty and shrill-sounding Throate
Awake the God of Day : and at his warning,
Whether in Sea, or Fire, in Earth, or Ayre,
Th'extrauagant, and erring Spirit, hyes
To his Confine. And of the truth heerein,
This present Obiect made probation.
  Mar. It faded on the crowing of the Cocke.
Some sayes, that euer 'gainst that Season comes
Wherein our Sauiours Birth is celebrated,
The Bird of Dawning singeth all night long :
And then (they say) no Spirit can walke abroad,
The nights are wholsome, then no Planets strike,
No Faiery talkes, nor Witch hath power to Charme :
So hallow'd, and so gracious is the time.
  Har. So haue I heard, and do in part beleeue it.
But looke, the Morne in Russet mantle clad,
Walkes o're the dew of yon high Easterne Hill,
Breake we our Watch vp, and by my aduice
Let vs impart what we haue seene to night
Vnto yong *Hamlet*. For vpon my life,
This Spirit dumbe to vs, will speake to him :
Do you consent we shall acquaint him with it,
As needfull in our Loues, fitting our Duty ?
  Mar. Let do't I pray, and I this morning know
Where we shall finde him most conueniently.   *Exeunt*

Scena Secunda.

*Enter Claudius King of Denmarke, Gertrude the Queene,
Hamlet, Polonius, Laertes, and his Sister O-
phelia, Lords Attendants.*

  King. Though yet of *Hamlet* our deere Brothers death
The memory be greene : and that it vs befitted
To beare our hearts in greefe, and our whole Kingdome
To be contracted in one brow of woe :
Yet so farre hath Discretion fought with Nature,
That we with wisest sorrow thinke on him,
Together with remembrance of our selues.
Therefore our sometimes Sister, now our Queen,
Th'Imperiall Ioyntresse of this warlike State,
Haue we, as 'twere, with a defeated ioy,
With one Auspicious, and one Dropping eye,
With mirth in Funerall, and with Dirge in Marriage,
In equall Scale weighing Delight and Dole
Taken to Wife ; nor haue we heerein barr'd
Your better Wisedomes, which haue freely gone
With this affaire along, for all our Thankes.
Now followes, that you know young *Fortinbras*,
Holding a weake supposall of our worth ;
Or thinking by our late deere Brothers death,
Our State to be disioynt, and out of Frame,
Colleagued with the dreame of his Aduantage ;
He hath not fayl'd to pester vs with Message,
Importing the surrender of those Lands
Lost by his Father : with all Bonds of Law
To our most valiant Brother. So much for him.
  Enter Voltemand and Cornelius.
Now for our selfe, and for this time of meeting
Thus much the businesse is. We haue heere writ
To Norway, Vncle of young *Fortinbras*,
Who Impotent and Bedrid, scarsely heares
Of this his Nephewes purpose, to suppresse
His further gate heerein. In that the Leuies,
The Lists, and full proportions are all made
Out of his subiect : and we heere dispatch
You good *Cornelius*, and you *Voltemand*,
For bearing of this greeting to old Norway,
Giuing to you no further personall power
To businesse with the King, more then the scope
Of these dilated Articles allow :
Farewell, and let your hast commend your duty.
  Volt. In that, and all things, will we shew our duty.
  King. We doubt it nothing, heartily farewell.
       Exit Voltemand and Cornelius.
And now *Laertes*, what's the newes with you ?

You

You told vs of some suite. What is't *Laertes*?
You cannot speake of Reason to the Dane,
And loose your voyce. What would'st thou beg *Laertes*,
That shall not be my Offer, not thy Asking?
The Head is not more Natiue to the Heart,
The Hand more Instrumentall to the Mouth,
Then is the Throne of Denmarke to thy Father.
What would'st thou haue *Laertes*?

 Laer. Dread my Lord,
Your leaue and fauour to returne to France,
From whence, though willingly I came to Denmarke
To shew my duty in your Coronation,
Yet now I must confesse, that duty done,
My thoughts and wishes bend againe towards France,
And bow them to your gracious leaue and pardon.

 King. Haue you your Fathers leaue?
What sayes *Pollonius*?

 Pol. He hath my Lord:
I do beseech you giue him leaue to go.

 King. Take thy faire houre *Laertes*, time be thine,
And thy best graces spend it at thy will:
But now my Cosin *Hamlet*, and my Sonne?

 Ham. A little more then kin, and lesse then kinde.

 King. How is it that the Clouds still hang on you?

 Ham. Not so my Lord, I am too much i'th'Sun.

 Queen. Good *Hamlet* cast thy nightly colour off,
And let thine eye looke like a Friend on Denmarke.
Do not for euer with thy veyled lids
Seeke for thy Noble Father in the dust;
Thou know'st 'tis common, all that liues must dye,
Passing through Nature, to Eternity.

 Ham. I Madam, it is common.

 Queen. If it be;
Why seemes it so particular with thee.

 Ham. Seemes Madam? Nay, it is: I know not Seemes:
'Tis not alone my Inky Cloake (good Mother)
Nor Customary suites of solemne Blacke,
Nor windy suspiration of forc'd breath,
No, nor the fruitfull Riuer in the Eye,
Nor the deiected hauiour of the Visage,
Together with all Formes, Moods, shewes of Griefe,
That can denote me truly. These indeed Seeme,
For they are actions that a man might play:
But I haue that Within, which passeth show;
These, but the Trappings, and the Suites of woe.

 King. 'Tis sweet and commendable
In your Nature *Hamlet*,
To giue these mourning duties to your Father:
But you must know, your Father lost a Father,
That Father lost, lost his; and the Suruiuer bound
In filiall Obligation, for some terme
To do obsequious Sorrow. But to perseuer
In obstinate Condolement, is a course
Of impious stubbornnesse. 'Tis vnmanly greefe,
It shewes a will most incorrect to Heauen,
A Heart vnfortified, a Minde impatient,
An Vnderstanding simple, and vnschool'd:
For, what we know must be, and is as common
As any the most vulgar thing to sence,
Why should we in our peeuish Opposition
Take it to heart? Fye, 'tis a fault to Heauen,
A fault against the Dead, a fault to Nature,
To Reason most absurd, whose common Theame
Is death of Fathers, and who still hath cried,
From the first Coarse, till he that dyed to day,
This must be so. We pray you throw to earth
This vnpreuayling woe, and thinke of vs
As of a Father; For let the world take note,
You are the most immediate to our Throne,
And with no lesse Nobility of Loue,
Then that which deerest Father beares his Sonne,
Do I impart towards you. For your intent
In going backe to Schoole in Wittenberg,
It is most retrograde to our desire:
And we beseech you, bend you to remaine
Heere in the cheere and comfort of our eye,
Our cheefest Courtier Cosin, and our Sonne.

 Qu. Let not thy Mother lose her Prayers *Hamlet*:
I prythee stay with vs, go not to Wittenberg.

 Ham. I shall in all my best
Obey you Madam.

 King. Why 'tis a louing, and a faire Reply,
Be as our selfe in Denmarke. Madam come,
This gentle and vnforc'd accord of *Hamlet*
Sits smiling to my heart; in grace whereof,
No iocond health that Denmarke drinkes to day,
But the great Cannon to the Clowds shall tell,
And the Kings Rouce, the Heauens shall bruite againe,
Respeaking earthly Thunder. Come away. *Exeunt*

Manet Hamlet.

 Ham. Oh that this too too solid Flesh, would melt,
Thaw, and resolue it selfe into a Dew:
Or that the Euerlasting had not fixt
His Cannon 'gainst Selfe-slaughter. O God, O God!
How weary, stale, flat, and vnprofitable
Seemes to me all the vses of this world?
Fie on't? Oh fie, fie, 'tis an vnweeded Garden
That growes to Seed: Things rank, and grosse in Nature
Possesse it meerely. That it should come to this:
But two months dead: Nay, not so much; not two,
So excellent a King, that was to this
Hiperion to a Satyre: so louing to my Mother,
That he might not beteene the windes of heauen
Visit her face too roughly. Heauen and Earth
Must I remember: why she would hang on him,
As if encrease of Appetite had growne
By what it fed on; and yet within a month?
Let me not thinke on't: Frailty, thy name is woman.
A little Month, or ere those shooes were old,
With which she followed my poore Fathers body
Like *Niobe*, all teares. Why she, euen she.
(O Heauen! A beast that wants discourse of Reason
Would haue mourn'd longer) married with mine Vnkle,
My Fathers Brother: but no more like my Father,
Then I to *Hercules*. Within a Moneth?
Ere yet the salt of most vnrighteous Teares
Had left the flushing of her gauled eyes,
She married. O most wicked speed, to post
With such dexterity to Incestuous sheets:
It is not, nor it cannot come to good.
But breake my heart, for I must hold my tongue.

Enter Horatio, Barnard, and Marcellus.

 Hor. Haile to your Lordship.

 Ham. I am glad to see you well:
Horatio, or I do forget my selfe.

 Hor. The same my Lord,
And your poore Seruant euer.

 Ham. Sir my good friend,
Ile change that name with you:
And what make you from Wittenberg *Horatio*?

The Tragedie of Hamlet.

Marcellus.

Mar. My good Lord.

Ham. I am very glad to see you: good euen Sir.
But what in faith make you from *Wittemberge*?

Hor. A truant disposition, good my Lord.

Ham. I would not haue your Enemy say so;
Nor shall you doe mine eare that violence,
To make it truster of your owne report
Against your selfe. I know you are no Truant:
But what is your affaire in *Elsenour*?
Wee'l teach you to drinke deepe, ere you depart.

Hor. My Lord, I came to see your Fathers Funerall.

Ham. I pray thee doe not mock me (fellow Student)
I thinke it was to see my Mothers Wedding.

Hor. Indeed my Lord, it followed hard vpon.

Ham. Thrift, thrift *Horatio*: the Funerall Bakt-meats
Did coldly furnish forth the Marriage Tables;
Would I had met my dearest foe in heauen,
Ere I had euer seene that day *Horatio*.
My father, me thinkes I see my father.

Hor. Oh where my Lord?

Ham. In my minds eye (*Horatio*)

Hor. I saw him once; he was a goodly King.

Ham. He was a man, take him for all in all:
I shall not look vpon his like againe.

Hor. My Lord, I thinke I saw him yesternight.

Ham. Saw? Who?

Hor. My Lord, the King your Father.

Ham. The King my Father?

Hor. Season your admiration for a while
With an attent eare; till I may deliuer
Vpon the witnesse of these Gentlemen,
This maruell to you.

Ham. For Heauens loue let me heare.

Hor. Two nights together, had these Gentlemen
(*Marcellus* and *Barnardo*) on their Watch
In the dead wast and middle of the night
Beene thus encountred. A figure like your Father,
Arm'd at all points exactly, *Cap a Pe*,
Appeares before them, and with sollemne march
Goes slow and stately: By them thrice he walkt,
By their opprest and feare-surprized eyes,
Within his Truncheons length; whilst they bestil'd
Almost to Ielly with the Act of feare,
Stand dumbe and speake not to him. This to me
In dreadfull secrecie impart they did,
And I with them the third Night kept the Watch,
Whereas they had deliuer'd both in time,
Forme of the thing; each word made true and good,
The Apparition comes. I knew your Father:
These hands are not more like.

Ham. But where was this?

Mar. My Lord, vpon the platforme where we watcht.

Ham. Did you not speake to it?

Hor. My Lord, I did;
But answere made it none: yet once me thought
It lifted vp it head, and did addresse
It selfe to motion, like as it would speake:
But euen then, the Morning Cocke crew lowd;
And at the sound it shrunke in hast away,
And vanisht from our sight.

Ham. Tis very strange.

Hor. As I doe liue my honour'd Lord 'tis true;
And we did thinke it writ downe in our duty
To let you know of it.

Ham. Indeed, indeed Sirs; but this troubles me.
Hold you the watch to Night?

Both. We doe my Lord.

Ham. Arm'd, say you?

Both. Arm'd, my Lord.

Ham. From top to toe?

Both. My Lord, from head to foote.

Ham. Then saw you not his face?

Hor. O yes, my Lord, he wore his Beauer vp.

Ham. What, lookt he frowningly?

Hor. A countenance more in sorrow then in anger.

Ham. Pale, or red?

Hor. Nay very pale.

Ham. And fixt his eyes vpon you?

Hor. Most constantly.

Ham. I would I had beene there.

Hor. It would haue much amaz'd you.

Ham. Very like, very like: staid it long?

Hor. While one with moderate hast might tell a hundred.

All. Longer, longer.

Hor. Not when I saw't.

Ham. His Beard was grisly? no.

Hor. It was, as I haue seene it in his life,
A Sable Siluer'd.

Ham. Ile watch to Night; perchance 'twill wake a-
gaine.

Hor. I warrant you it will.

Ham. If it assume my noble Fathers person,
Ile speake to it, though Hell it selfe should gape
And bid me hold my peace. I pray you all,
If you haue hitherto conceal'd this sight;
Let it bee treble in your silence still:
And whatsoeuer els shall hap to night,
Giue it an vnderstanding but no tongue;
I will requite your loues; so, fare ye well:
Vpon the Platforme twixt eleuen and twelue,
Ile visit you.

All. Our duty to your Honour. *Exeunt.*

Ham. Your loue, as mine to you: farewell.
My Fathers Spirit in Armes? All is not well:
I doubt some foule play: would the Night were come;
Till then sit still my soule; foule deeds will rise,
Though all the earth orewhelm them to mens eies. *Exit.*

Scena Tertia.

Enter Laertes and Ophelia.

Laer. My necessaries are imbark't; Farewell:
And Sister, as the Winds giue Benefit,
And Conuoy is assistant; doe not sleepe,
But let me heare from you.

Ophel. Doe you doubt that?

Laer. For *Hamlet*, and the trifling of his fauours,
Hold it a fashion and a toy in Bloud;
A Violet in the youth of Primy Nature;
Froward, not permanent; sweet not lasting
The suppliance of a minute? No more.

Ophel. No more but so.

Laer. Thinke it no more:
For nature cressant does not grow alone,
In thewes and Bulke: but as his Temple waxes,
The inward seruice of the Minde and Soule
Growes wide withall. Perhaps he loues you now,
And now no soyle nor cautell doth besmerch
The vertue of his feare: but you must feare

His greatnesse weigh'd, his will is not his owne;
For hee himselfe is subiect to his Birth:
Hee may not, as vnuallued persons doe,
Carue for himselfe; for, on his choyce depends
The sanctity and health of the weole State.
And therefore must his choyce be circumscrib'd
Vnto the voyce and yeelding of that Body,
Whereof he is the Head. Then if he sayes he loues you,
It fits your wisedome so farre to beleeue it;
As he in his peculiar Sect and force
May giue his saying deed: which is no further,
Then the maine voyce of *Denmarke* goes withall.
Then weigh what losse your Honour may sustaine,
If with too credent eare you list his Songs;
Or lose your Heart; or your chast Treasure open
To his vnmastred importunity.
Feare it *Ophelia*, feare it my deare Sister,
And keepe within the reare of your Affection;
Out of the shot and danger of Desire.
The chariest Maid is Prodigall enough,
If she vnmaske her beauty to the Moone:
Vertue it selfe scapes not calumnious stroakes,
The Canker Galls, the Infants of the Spring
Too oft before the buttons be disclos'd,
And in the Morne and liquid dew of Youth,
Contagious blastments are most imminent.
Be wary then, best safety lies in feare;
Youth to it selfe rebels, though none else neere.

Ophe. I shall th'effect of this good Lesson keepe,
As watchmen to my heart: but good my Brother
Doe not as some vngracious Pastors doe,
Shew me the steepe and thorny way to Heauen;
Whilst like a puft and reckelesse Libertine
Himselfe, the Primrose path of dalliance treads,
And reaks not his owne reade.

Laer. Oh, feare me not.

Enter Polonius.

I stay too long; but here my Father comes:
A double blessing is a double grace;
Occasion smiles vpon a second leaue.

Polon. Yet heere *Laertes*? Aboord, aboord for shame,
The winde sits in the shoulder of your saile,
And you are staid for there: my blessing with you;
And these few Precepts in thy memory,
See thou Character. Giue thy thoughts no tongue,
Nor any vnproportion'd thought his Act:
Be thou familiar; but by no meanes vulgar:
The friends thou hast, and their adoption tride,
Grapple them to thy Soule, with hoopes of Steele:
But doe not dull thy palme, with entertainment
Of each vnhatch't, vnfledg'd Comrade. Beware
Of entrance to a quarrell: but being in
Bear't that th'opposed may beware of thee.
Giue euery man thine eare; but few thy voyce:
Take each mans censure; but reserue thy iudgement:
Costly thy habit as thy purse can buy;
But not exprest in fancie; rich, not gawdie:
For the Apparell oft proclaimes the man.
And they in France of the best ranck and station,
Are of a most select and generous cheff in that.
Neither a borrower, nor a lender be;
For lone oft loses both it selfe and friend:
And borrowing duls the edge of Husbandry.
This aboue all; to thine owne selfe be true:
And it must follow, as the Night the Day,
Thou canst not then be false to any man.
Farewell: my Blessing season this in thee.

Laer. Most humbly doe I take my leaue, my Lord.

Polon. The time inuites you, goe, your seruants tend.

Laer. Farewell *Ophelia*, and remember well
What I haue said to you.

Ophe. 'Tis in my memory lockt,
And you your selfe shall keepe the key of it.

Laer. Farewell. *Exit Laer.*

Polon. What ist *Ophelia* he hath said to you?

Ophe. So please you, somthing touching the L. *Hamlet.*

Polon. Marry, well bethought:
Tis told me he hath very oft of late
Giuen priuate time to you; and you your selfe
Haue of your audience beene most free and bounteous.
If it be so, as so tis put on me;
And that in way of caution: I must tell you,
You doe not vnderstand your selfe so cleerely,
As it behoues my Daughter, and your Honour.
What is betweene you, giue me vp the truth?

Ophe. He hath my Lord of late, made many tenders
Of his affection to me.

Polon. Affection, puh. You speake like a greene Girle,
Vnsifted in such perillous Circumstance.
Doe you beleeue his tenders, as you call them?

Ophe. I do not know, my Lord, what I should thinke.

Polon. Marry Ile teach you; thinke your selfe a Baby,
That you haue tane his tenders for true pay,
Which are not starling. Tender your selfe more dearly;
Or not to crack the winde of the poore Phrase,
Roaming it thus, you'l tender me a foole.

Ophe. My Lord, he hath importun'd me with loue,
In honourable fashion.

Polon. I, fashion you may call it, go too, go too.

Ophe. And hath giuen countenance to his speech,
My Lord, with all the vowes of Heauen.

Polon. I, Springes to catch Woodcocks. I doe know
When the Bloud burnes, how Prodigall the Soule
Giues the tongue vowes: these blazes, Daughter,
Giuing more light then heate; extinct in both,
Euen in their promise, as it is a making;
You must not take for fire. For this time Daughter,
Be somewhat scanter of your Maiden presence;
Set your entreatments at a higher rate,
Then a command to parley. For Lord *Hamlet*,
Beleeue so much in him, that he is young,
And with a larger tether may he walke,
Then may be giuen you. In few, *Ophelia*,
Doe not beleeue his vowes; for they are Broakers,
Not of the eye, which their Inuestments show:
But meere implorators of vnholy Sutes,
Breathing like sanctified and pious bonds,
The better to beguile. This is for all:
I would not, in plaine tearmes, from this time forth,
Haue you so slander any moment leisure,
As to giue words or talke with the Lord *Hamlet*:
Looke too't, I charge you; come your wayes.

Ophe. I shall obey my Lord. *Exeunt.*

Enter Hamlet, Horatio, Marcellus.

Ham. The Ayre bites shrewdly: is it very cold?

Hor. It is a nipping and an eager ayre.

Ham. What hower now?

Hor. I thinke it lacks of twelue.

Mar. No, it is strooke.

Hor. Indeed I heard it not: then it drawes neere the season,
Wherein the Spirit held his wont to walke.

What

The Tragedie of Hamlet.

What does this meane my Lord? (rouse,
  Ham. The King doth wake to night, and takes his
Keepes wassels and the swaggering vpspring reeles,
And as he dreines his draughts of Renish downe,
The kettle Drum and Trumpet thus bray out
The triumph of his Pledge.
  Horat. Is it a custome?
  Ham. I marry is't;
And to my mind, though I am natiue heere,
And to the manner borne: It is a Custome
More honour'd in the breach, then the obseruance.

Enter Ghost.

  Hor. Looke my Lord, it comes.
  Ham. Angels and Ministers of Grace defend vs:
Be thou a Spirit of health, or Goblin damn'd,
Bring with thee ayres from Heauen, or blasts from Hell,
Be thy euents wicked or charitable,
Thou com'st in such a questionable shape
That I will speake to thee. Ile call thee *Hamlet*,
King, Father, Royall Dane: Oh, oh, answer me,
Let me not burst in Ignorance; but tell
Why thy Canoniz'd bones Hearsed in death,
Haue burst their cerments, why the Sepulcher
Wherein we saw thee quietly enurn'd,
Hath op'd his ponderous and Marble iawes,
To cast thee vp againe? What may this meane?
That thou dead Coarse againe in compleat steele,
Reuisits thus the glimpses of the Moone,
Making Night hidious? And we fooles of Nature,
So horridly to shake our disposition,
With thoughts beyond thee; reaches of our Soules,
Say, why is this? wherefore? what should we doe?

Ghost beckens Hamlet.

  Hor. It beckons you to goe away with it,
As if it some impartment did desire
To you alone.
  Mar. Looke with what courteous action
It wafts you to a more remoued ground:
But doe not goe with it.
  Hor. No, by no meanes.
  Ham. It will not speake: then will I follow it.
  Hor. Doe not my Lord.
  Ham. Why, what should be the feare?
I doe not set my life at a pins fee;
And for my Soule, what can it doe to that?
Being a thing immortall as it selfe:
It waues me forth againe; Ile follow it.
  Hor. What if it tempt you toward the Floud my Lord?
Or to the dreadfull Sonnet of the Cliffe,
That beetles o're his base into the Sea,
And there assumes some other horrible forme,
Which might depriue your Soueraignty of Reason,
And draw you into madnesse thinke of it?
  Ham. It wafts me still: goe on, Ile follow thee.
  Mar. You shall not goe my Lord.
  Ham. Hold off your hand.
  Hor. Be rul'd, you shall not goe.
  Ham. My fate cries out,
And makes each petty Artire in this body,
As hardy as the Nemian Lions nerue:
Still am I cal'd? Vnhand me Gentlemen:
By Heau'n, Ile make a Ghost of him that lets me:
I say away, goe on, Ile follow thee.

Exeunt Ghost & Hamlet.

  Hor. He waxes desperate with imagination.
  Mar. Let's follow; 'tis not fit thus to obey him.

  Hor. Haue after, to what issue will this come?
  Mar. Something is rotten in the State of Denmarke.
  Hor. Heauen will direct it.
  Mar. Nay, let's follow him. *Exeunt.*

Enter Ghost and Hamlet.

  Ham. Where wilt thou lead me? speak; Ile go no fur-
  Gho. Marke me. (ther.
  Ham. I will.
  Gho. My hower is almost come,
When I to sulphurous and tormenting Flames
Must render vp my selfe.
  Ham. Alas poore Ghost.
  Gho. Pitty me not, but lend thy serious hearing
To what I shall vnfold.
  Ham. Speake, I am bound to heare.
  Gho. So art thou to reuenge, when thou shalt heare.
  Ham. What?
  Gho. I am thy Fathers Spirit,
Doom'd for a certaine terme to walke the night;
And for the day confin'd to fast in Fiers,
Till the foule crimes done in my dayes of Nature
Are burnt and purg'd away? But that I am forbid
To tell the secrets of my Prison-House;
I could a Tale vnfold, whose lightest word
Would harrow vp thy soule, freeze thy young blood,
Make thy two eyes like Starres, start from their Spheres,
Thy knotty and combined locks to part,
And each particular haire to stand an end,
Like Quilles vpon the fretfull Porpentine:
But this eternall blason must not be
To eares of flesh and blood; list *Hamlet*, oh list,
If thou didst euer thy deare Father loue.
  Ham. Oh Heauen!
  Gho. Reuenge his foule and most vnnaturall Murther.
  Ham. Murther?
  Ghost. Murther most foule, as in the best it is;
But this most foule, strange, and vnnaturall.
  Ham. Hast, hast me to know it,
That with wings as swift
As meditation, or the thoughts of Loue,
May sweepe to my Reuenge.
  Ghost. I finde thee apt,
And duller should'st thou be then the fat weede
That rots it selfe in ease, on Lethe Wharfe,
Would'st thou not stirre in this. Now *Hamlet* heare:
It's giuen out, that sleeping in mine Orchard,
A Serpent stung me: so the whole eare of Denmarke,
Is by a forged processe of my death
Rankly abus'd: But know thou Noble youth,
The Serpent that did sting thy Fathers life,
Now weares his Crowne.
  Ham. O my Propheticke soule: mine Vncle?
  Ghost. I that incestuous, that adulterate Beast
With witchcraft of his wits, hath Traitorous guifts.
Oh wicked Wit, and Gifts, that haue the power
So to seduce? Won to to this shamefull Lust
The will of my most seeming vertuous Queene:
Oh *Hamlet*, what a falling off was there,
From me, whose loue was of that dignity,
That it went hand in hand, euen with the Vow
I made to her in Marriage; and to decline
Vpon a wretch, whose Naturall gifts were poore
To those of mine. But Vertue, as it neuer wil be moued,
Though Lewdnesse court it in a shape of Heauen:
So Lust, though to a radiant Angell link'd,
Will sate it selfe in a Celestiall bed, & prey on Garbage.

Oo But

But soft, me thinkes I sent the Mornings Ayre;
Briefe let me be: Sleeping within mine Orchard,
My custome alwayes in the afternoone;
Vpon my secure hower thy Vncle stole
With iuyce of cursed Hebenon in a Violl,
And in the Porches of mine eares did poure
The leaperous Distilment; whose effect
Holds such an enmity with bloud of Man,
That swift as Quick-siluer, it courses through
The naturall Gates and Allies of the Body;
And with a sodaine vigour it doth posset
And curd, like Aygre droppings into Milke,
The thin and wholsome blood: so did it mine;
And a most instant Tetter bak'd about,
Most Lazar-like, with vile and loathsome crust,
All my smooth Body.
Thus was I, sleeping, by a Brothers hand,
Of Life, of Crowne, and Queene at once dispatcht;
Cut off euen in the Blossomes of my Sinne,
Vnhouzzled, disappointed, vnnaneld,
No reckoning made, but sent to my account
With all my imperfections on my head;
Oh horrible, Oh horrible, most horrible:
If thou hast nature in thee beare it not;
Let not the Royall Bed of Denmarke be
A Couch for Luxury and damned Incest.
But howsoeuer thou pursuest this Act,
Taint not thy mind; nor let thy Soule contriue
Against thy Mother ought; leaue her to heauen,
And to those Thornes that in her bosome lodge,
To pricke and sting her. Fare thee well at once;
The Glow-worme showes the Matine to be neere,
And gins to pale his vneffectuall Fire:
Adue, adue, *Hamlet*: remember me.   *Exit*.

   Ham. Oh all you host of Heauen! Oh Earth; what els?
And shall I couple Hell? Oh fie: hold my heart;
And you my sinnewes, grow not instant Old;
But beare me stiffely vp: Remember thee?
I, thou poore Ghost, while memory holds a seate
In this distracted Globe: Remember thee?
Yea, from the Table of my Memory,
Ile wipe away all triuiall fond Records,
All sawes of Bookes, all formes, all presures past,
That youth and obseruation coppied there;
And thy Commandment all alone shall liue
Within the Booke and Volume of my Braine,
Vnmixt with baser matter; yes, yes, by Heauen:
Oh most pernicious woman!
Oh Villaine, Villaine, smiling damned Villaine!
My Tables, my Tables; meet it is I set it downe,
That one may smile, and smile and be a Villaine;
At least I'm sure it may be so in Denmarke;
So Vnckle there you are: now to my word;
It is; Adue, Adue, Remember me: I haue sworn't.
  Hor. & Mar. within. My Lord, my Lord.
    Enter Horatio and Marcellus.
  Mar. Lord *Hamlet*.
  Hor. Heauen secure him.
  Mar. So be it.
  Hor. Illo, ho, ho, my Lord.
  Ham. Hillo, ho, ho, boy; come bird, come.
  Mar. How ist my Noble Lord?
  Hor. What newes, my Lord?
  Ham. Oh wonderfull!
  Hor. Good my Lord tell it.
  Ham. No you'l reueale it.
  Hor. Not I, my Lord, by Heauen.
  Mar. Nor I, my Lord.
  Ham. How say you then, would heart of man once think it?
But you'l be secret?
  Both. I, by Heau'n, my Lord.
  Ham. There's nere a villaine dwelling in all Denmarke
But hee's an arrant knaue.
  Hor. There needs no Ghost my Lord, come from the
Graue, to tell vs this.
  Ham. Why right, you are i'th' right;
And so, without more circumstance at all,
I hold it fit that we shake hands, and part:
You, as your busines and desires shall point you:
For euery man ha's businesse and desire,
Such as it is: and for mine owne poore part,
Looke you, Ile goe pray.
  Hor. These are but wild and hurling words, my Lord.
  Ham. I'm sorry they offend you heartily:
Yes faith, heartily.
  Hor. There's no offence my Lord.
  Ham. Yes, by Saint *Patricke*, but there is my Lord,
And much offence too, touching this Vision heere:
It is an honest Ghost, that let me tell you:
For your desire to know what is betweene vs,
O're-master't as you may. And now good friends,
As you are Friends, Schollers and Soldiers,
Giue me one poore request.
  Hor. What is't my Lord? we will.
  Ham. Neuer make knowne what you haue seen to night.
  Both. My Lord, we will not.
  Ham. Nay, but swear't.
  Hor. Infaith my Lord, not I.
  Mar. Nor I my Lord: in faith.
  Ham. Vpon my sword.
  Marcell. We haue sworne my Lord already.
  Ham. Indeed, vpon my sword, Indeed.
  Gho. Sweare.   *Ghost cries vnder the Stage.*
  Ham. Ah ha boy, sayest thou so. Art thou there true-
penny? Come one you here this fellow in the selleredge
Consent to sweare.
  Hor. Propose the Oath my Lord.
  Ham. Neuer to speake of this that you haue seene,
Sweare by my sword.
  Gho. Sweare.
  Ham. Hic & vbique? Then wee'l shift for grownd,
Come hither Gentlemen,
And lay your hands againe vpon my sword,
Neuer to speake of this that you haue heard:
Sweare by my Sword.
  Gho. Sweare.
  Ham. Well said old Mole, can'st worke i'th' ground so fast?
A worthy Pioner, once more remoue good friends.
  Hor. Oh day and night: but this is wondrous strange.
  Ham. And therefore as a stranger giue it welcome.
There are more things in Heauen and Earth, *Horatio*,
Then are dream't of in our Philosophy. But come,
Here as before, neuer so helpe you mercy,
How strange or odde so ere I beare my selfe;
(As I perchance heereafter shall thinke meet
To put an Anticke disposition on:)
That you at such time seeing me, neuer shall
With Armes encombred thus, or thus, head shake;
Or by pronouncing of some doubtfull Phrase;
As well, we know, or we could and if we would,
Or if we list to speake; or there be and if there might,
Or such ambiguous giuing out to note,

The Tragedie of Hamlet.

That you know ought of me; this not to doe:
So grace and mercy at your most neede helpe you:
Sweare.

Ghost. Sweare.

Ham. Rest, rest perturbed Spirit: so Gentlemen,
With all my loue I doe commend me to you;
And what so poore a man as *Hamlet* is,
May doe t'expresse his loue and friending to you,
God willing shall not lacke: let vs goe in together,
And still your fingers on your lippes I pray,
The time is out of ioynt: Oh cursed spight,
That euer I was borne to set it right.
Nay, come let's goe together. *Exeunt.*

Actus Secundus.

Enter Polonius, and Reynoldo.

Polon. Giue him his money, and these notes *Reynoldo*.

Reynol. I will my Lord.

Polon. You shall doe maruels wisely: good *Reynoldo*,
Before you visite him you make inquiry
Of his behauiour.

Reynol. My Lord, I did intend it.

Polon. Marry, well said;
Very well said. Looke you Sir,
Enquire me first what Danskers are in Paris;
And how, and who; what meanes; and where they keepe:
What company, at what expence: and finding
By this encompasement and drift of question,
That they doe know my sonne: Come you more neerer
Then your particular demands will touch it,
Take you as 'twere some distant knowledge of him,
And thus I know his father and his friends,
And in part him. Doe you marke this *Reynoldo*?

Reynol. I, very well my Lord.

Polon. And in part him, but you may say not well;
But if't be hee I meane, hees very wilde;
Addicted so and so; and there put on him
What forgeries you please: marry, none so ranke,
As may dishonour him; take heed of that:
But Sir, such wanton, wild, and vsuall slips,
As are Companions noted and most knowne
To youth and liberty.

Reynol. As gaming my Lord.

Polon. I, or drinking, fencing, swearing,
Quarelling, drabbing. You may goe so farre.

Reynol. My Lord that would dishonour him.

Polon. Faith no, as you may season it in the charge;
You must not put another scandall on him,
That hee is open to Incontinencie;
That's not my meaning: but breath his faults so quaintly,
That they may seeme the taints of liberty;
The flash and out-breake of a fiery minde,
A sauagenes in vnreclaim'd bloud of generall assault.

Reynol. But my good Lord.

Polon. Wherefore should you doe this?

Reynol. I my Lord, I would know that.

Polon. Marry Sir, heere's my drift,
And I belieue it is a fetch of warrant:
You laying these slight sulleyes on my Sonne,
As 'twere a thing a little soil'd i'th' working: (sound,
Marke you your party in conuerse; him you would
Hauing euer seene. In the prenominate crimes,

The youth you breath of guilty, be assur'd
He closes with you in this consequence:
Good sir, or so, or friend, or Gentleman.
According to the Phrase and the Addition,
Of man and Country.

Reynol. Very good my Lord.

Polon. And then Sir does he this?
He does: what was I about to say?
I was about to say somthing: where did I leaue?

Reynol. At closes in the consequence:
At friend, or so, and Gentleman.

Polon. At closes in the consequence, I marry,
He closes with you thus. I know the Gentleman,
I saw him yesterday, or tother day;
Or then or then, with such and such; and as you say,
There was he gaming, there o're-tooke in's Rouse,
There falling out at Tennis; or perchance,
I saw him enter such a house of saile;
Videlicet, a Brothell, or so forth. See you now;
Your bait of falshood, takes this Cape of truth;
And thus doe we of wisedome and of reach
With windlesses, and with assaies of Bias,
By indirections finde directions out:
So by my former Lecture and aduice
Shall you my Sonne; you haue me, haue you not?

Reynol. My Lord I haue.

Polon. God buy you; fare you well.

Reynol. Good my Lord.

Polon. Obserue his inclination in your selfe.

Reynol. I shall my Lord.

Polon. And let him plye his Musicke.

Reynol. Well, my Lord. *Exit.*

Enter Ophelia.

Polon. Farewell.
How now *Ophelia,* what's the matter?

Ophe. Alas my Lord, I haue beene so affrighted.

Polon. With what, in the name of Heauen?

Ophe. My Lord, as I was sowing in my Chamber,
Lord *Hamlet* with his doublet all vnbrac'd,
No hat vpon his head, his stockings foul'd,
Vngartred, and downe giued to his Anckle,
Pale as his shirt, his knees knocking each other,
And with a looke so pitious in purport,
As if he had been loosed out of hell,
To speake of horrors: he comes before me.

Polon. Mad for thy Loue?

Ophe. My Lord, I doe not know: but truly I do feare it.

Polon. What said he?

Ophe. He tooke me by the wrist, and held me hard;
Then goes he to the length of all his arme;
And with his other hand thus o're his brow,
He fals to such perusall of my face,
As he would draw it. Long staid he so,
At last, a little shaking of mine Arme:
And thrice his head thus wauing vp and downe,
He rais'd a sigh, so pittious and profound,
That it did seeme to shatter all his bulke,
And end his being. That done, he lets me goe,
And with his head ouer his shoulders turn'd,
He seem'd to finde his way without his eyes,
For out adores he went without their helpe;
And to the last, bended their light on me.

Polon. Goe with me, I will goe seeke the King,
This is the very extasie of Loue,
Whose violent property foredoes it selfe,

And

And leads the will to desperate Vndertakings,
As oft as any passion vnder Heauen,
That does afflict our Natures. I am sorrie,
What haue you giuen him any hard words of late?

Ophe. No my good Lord: but as you did command,
I did repell his Letters, and deny'de
His accesse to me.

Pol. That hath made him mad.
I am sorrie that with better speed and iudgement
I had not quoted him. I feare he did but trifle,
And meant to wracke thee: but beshrew my iealousie:
It seemes it is as proper to our Age,
To cast beyond our selues in our Opinions,
As it is common for the yonger sort
To lacke discretion. Come, go we to the King,
This must be knowne, w being kept close might moue
More greefe to hide, then hate to vtter loue. *Exeunt.*

Scena Secunda.

Enter King, Queene, Rosincrane, and Guildensterne Cumalijs.

King. Welcome deere *Rosincrance* and *Guildensterne.*
Moreouer, that we much did long to see you,
The neede we haue to vse you, did prouoke
Our hastie sending. Something haue you heard
Of *Hamlets* transformation: so I call it,
Since not th'exterior, nor the inward man
Resembles that it was. What it should bee
More then his Fathers death, that thus hath put him
So much from th'vnderstanding of himselfe,
I cannot deeme of. I intreat you both,
That being of so young dayes brought vp with him:
And since so Neighbour'd to his youth, and humour,
That you vouchsafe your rest heere in our Court
Some little time: so by your Companies
To draw him on to pleasures, and to gather
So much as from Occasions you may gleane,
That open'd lies within our remedie.

Qu. Good Gentlemen, he hath much talk'd of you,
And sure I am, two men there are not liuing,
To whom he more adheres. If it will please you
To shew vs so much Gentrie, and good will,
As to expend your time with vs a-while,
For the supply and profit of our Hope,
Your Visitation shall receiue such thankes
As fits a Kings remembrance.

Rosin. Both your Maiesties
Might by the Soueraigne power you haue of vs,
Put your dread pleasures, more into Command
Then to Entreatie.

Guil. We both obey,
And here giue vp our selues, in the full bent,
To lay our Seruices freely at your feete,
To be commanded.

King. Thankes *Rosincrance*, and gentle *Guildensterne.*
Qu. Thankes *Guildensterne* and gentle *Rosincrance.*
And I beseech you instantly to visit
My too much changed Sonne.
Go some of ye,
And bring the Gentlemen where *Hamlet is.*

Guil. Heauens make our presence and our practises
Pleasant and helpfull to him. *Exit.*

Queene. Amen.

Enter Polonius.

Pol. Th'Ambassadors from Norwey, my good Lord,
Are ioyfully return'd.

King. Thou still hast bin the Father of good Newes.

Pol. Haue I, my Lord? Assure you, my good Liege,
I hold my dutie, as I hold my Soule,
Both to my God, one to my gracious King:
And I do thinke, or else this braine of mine
Hunts not the traile of Policie, so sure
As I haue vs'd to do: that I haue found
The very cause of *Hamlets* Lunacie.

King. Oh speake of that, that I do long to heare.

Pol. Giue first admittance to th'Ambassadors,
My Newes shall be the Newes to that great Feast.

King. Thy selfe do grace to them, and bring them in.
He tels me my sweet Queene, that he hath found
The head and sourse of all your Sonnes distemper.

Qu. I doubt it is no other, but the maine,
His Fathers death, and our o're-hasty Marriage.

Enter Polonius, Voltumand, and Cornelius.

King. Well, we shall sift him. Welcome good Frends:
Say *Voltumand*, what from our Brother Norwey?

Volt. Most faire returne of Greetings, and Desires.
Vpon our first, he sent out to suppresse
His Nephewes Leuies, which to him appear'd
To be a preparation 'gainst the Poleak:
But better look'd into, he truly found
It was against your Highnesse, whereat greeued,
That so his Sicknesse, Age, and impotence
Was falsely borne in hand, sends out Arrests
On *Fortinbras*, which he (in breefe) obeyes,
Receiues rebuke from Norwey: and in fine,
Makes Vow before his Vnkle, neuer more
To giue th'assay of Armes against your Maiestie.
Whereon old *Norwey*, ouercome with ioy,
Giues him three thousand Crownes in Annuall Fee,
And his Commission to imploy those Soldiers
So leuied as before, against the Poleak:
With an intreaty heerein further shewne,
That it might please you to giue quiet passe
Through your Dominions, for his Enterprize,
On such regards of safety and allowance,
As therein are set downe.

King. It likes vs well:
And at our more consider'd time wee'l read,
Answer, and thinke vpon this Businesse.
Meane time we thanke you, for your well-tooke Labour.
Go to your rest, at night wee'l Feast together.
Most welcome home. *Exit Ambass.*

Pol. This businesse is very well ended.
My Liege, and Madam, to expostulate
What Maiestie should be, what Dutie is,
Why day is day; night, night; and time is time,
Were nothing but to waste Night, Day, and Time.
Therefore, since Breuitie is the Soule of Wit,
And tediousnesse, the limbes and outward flourishes,
I will be breefe. Your Noble Sonne is mad:
Mad call I it; for to define true Madnesse,
What is't, but to be nothing else but mad.
But let that go.

Qu. More matter, with lesse Art.

Pol. Madam, I sweare I vse no Art at all:
That he is mad, 'tis true: 'Tis true 'tis pittie,
And pittie it is true: A foolish figure,
But farewell it: for I will vse no Art.

Mad

The Tragedie of Hamlet.

Mad let vs grant him then: and now remaines
That we finde out the cause of this effect,
Or rather say, the cause of this defect;
For this effect defectiue, comes by cause,
Thus it remaines, and the remainder thus. Perpend,
I haue a daughter: haue, whil'st she is mine,
Who in her Dutie and Obedience, marke,
Hath giuen me this: now gather, and surmise.

The Letter.

To the Celestiall, and my Soules Idoll, the most beautified Ophelia.

That's an ill Phrase, a vilde Phrase, beautified is a vilde Phrase: but you shall heare these in her excellent white bosome, these.

  Qu. Came this from *Hamlet* to her.
  Pol. Good Madam stay awhile, I will be faithfull.

Doubt thou, the Starres are fire,
Doubt, that the Sunne doth moue:
Doubt Truth to be a Lier,
But neuer Doubt, I loue.

O deere Ophelia, I am ill at these Numbers: I haue not Art to reckon my groanes; but that I loue thee best, oh most Best beleeue it. Adieu.

Thine euermore most deere Lady, whilst this Machine is to him, Hamlet.

This in Obedience hath my daughter shew'd me:
And more aboue hath his soliciting,
As they fell out by Time, by Meanes, and Place,
All giuen to mine eare.
  King. But how hath she receiu'd his Loue?
  Pol. What do you thinke of me?
  King. As of a man, faithfull and Honourable.
  Pol. I wold faine proue so. But what might you think?
When I had seene this hot loue on the wing,
As I perceiued it, I must tell you that
Before my Daughter told me, what might you
Or my deere Maiestie your Queene heere, think,
If I had playd the Deske or Table-booke,
Or giuen my heart a winking, mute and dumbe,
Or look'd vpon this Loue, with idle sight,
What might you thinke? No, I went round to worke,
And (my yong Mistris) thus I did bespeake
Lord *Hamlet* is a Prince out of thy Starre,
This must not be: and then, I Precepts gaue her,
That she should locke her selfe from his Resort,
Admit no Messengers, receiue no Tokens:
Which done, she tooke the Fruites of my Aduice,
And he repulsed. A short Tale to make,
Fell into a Sadnesse, then into a Fast,
Thence to a Watch, thence into a Weaknesse,
Thence to a Lightnesse, and by this declension
Into the Madnesse whereon now he raues,
And all we waile for.
  King. Do you thinke 'tis this?
  Qu. It may be very likely.
  Pol. Hath there bene such a time, I'de fain know that,
That I haue possitiuely said, 'tis so,
When it prou'd otherwise?
  King. Not that I know.
  Pol. Take this from this; if this be otherwise,
If Circumstances leade me, I will finde
Where truth is hid, though it were hid indeede
Within the Center.
  King. How may we try it further?
  Pol. You know sometimes
He walkes foure houres together, heere
In the Lobby.
  Qu. So he ha's indeed.
  Pol. At such a time I'le loose my Daughter to him,
Be you and I behinde an Arras then,
Marke the encounter: If he loue her not,
And be not from his reason falne thereon;
Let me be no Assistant for a State,
And keepe a Farme and Carters.
  King. We will try it.

Enter Hamlet reading on a Booke.

  Qu. But looke where sadly the poore wretch
Comes reading.
  Pol. Away I do beseech you, both away,
Ile boord him presently.   *Exit King & Queen.*
Oh giue me leaue. How does my good Lord *Hamlet*?
  Ham. Well, God-a-mercy.
  Pol. Do you know me, my Lord?
  Ham. Excellent, excellent well: y'are a Fishmonger.
  Pol. Not I my Lord.
  Ham. Then I would you were so honest a man.
  Pol. Honest, my Lord?
  Ham. I sir, to be honest as this world goes, is to bee one man pick'd out of two thousand.
  Pol. That's very true, my Lord.
  Ham. For if the Sun breed Magots in a dead dogge, being a good kissing Carrion——
Haue you a daughter?
  Pol. I haue my Lord.
  Ham. Let her not walke i'th'Sunne: Conception is a blessing, but not as your daughter may conceiue. Friend looke too't.
  Pol. How say you by that? Still harping on my daughter: yet he knew me not at first; he said I was a Fishmonger: he is farre gone, farre gone: and truly in my youth, I suffred much extreamity for loue: very neere this. Ile speake to him againe. What do you read my Lord?
  Ham. Words, words, words.
  Pol. What is the matter, my Lord?
  Ham. Betweene who?
  Pol. I meane the matter you meane, my Lord.
  Ham. Slanders Sir: for the Satyricall slaue saies here, that old men haue gray Beards; that their faces are wrinkled; their eyes purging thicke Amber, or Plum-Tree Gumme: and that they haue a plentifull locke of Wit, together with weake Hammes. All which Sir, though I most powerfully, and potently beleeue; yet I holde it not Honestie to haue it thus set downe: For you your selfe Sir, should be old as I am, if like a Crab you could go backward.
  Pol. Though this be madnesse,
Yet there is Method in't: will you walke
Out of the ayre my Lord?
  Ham. Into my Graue?
  Pol. Indeed that is out o'th'Ayre:
How pregnant (sometimes) his Replies are?
A happinesse,
That often Madnesse hits on,
Which Reason and Sanitie could not
So prosperously be deliuer'd of.
I will leaue him,
And sodainely contriue the meanes of meeting
Betweene him, and my daughter.
My Honourable Lord, I will most humbly
Take my leaue of you.

Ham. You cannot Sir take from me any thing, that I will more willingly part withall, except my life, my life.

Polon. Fare you well my Lord.

Ham. These tedious old fooles.

Polon. You goe to seeke my Lord *Hamlet*; there hee is.

Enter Rosincran and Guildensterne.

Rosin. God saue you Sir.

Guild. Mine honour'd Lord?

Rosin. My most deare Lord?

Ham. My excellent good friends? How do'st thou *Guildensterne*? Oh, *Rosincrane*; good Lads: How doe ye both?

Rosin. As the indifferent Children of the earth.

Guild. Happy, in that we are not ouer-happy: on Fortunes Cap, we are not the very Button.

Ham. Nor the Soales of her Shoo?

Rosin. Neither my Lord.

Ham. Then you liue about her waste, or in the middle of her fauour?

Guil. Faith, her priuates, we.

Ham. In the secret parts of Fortune? Oh, most true: she is a Strumpet. What's the newes?

Rosin. None my Lord; but that the World's growne honest.

Ham. Then is Doomesday neere: But your newes is not true. Let me question more in particular: what haue you my good friends, deserued at the hands of Fortune, that she sends you to Prison hither?

Guil. Prison, my Lord?

Ham. Denmark's a Prison.

Rosin. Then is the World one.

Ham. A goodly one, in which there are many Confines, Wards, and Dungeons; *Denmarke* being one o'th' worst.

Rosin. We thinke not so my Lord.

Ham. Why then 'tis none to you; for there is nothing either good or bad, but thinking makes it so: to me it is a prison.

Rosin. Why then your Ambition makes it one: 'tis too narrow for your minde.

Ham. O God, I could be bounded in a nutshell, and count my selfe a King of infinite space; were it not that I haue bad dreames.

Guil. Which dreames indeed are Ambition: for the very substance of the Ambitious, is meerely the shadow of a Dreame.

Ham. A dreame it selfe is but a shadow.

Rosin. Truely, and I hold Ambition of so ayry and light a quality, that it is but a shadowes shadow.

Ham. Then are our Beggers bodies; and our Monarchs and out-stretcht Heroes the Beggers Shadowes: shall wee to th' Court: for, by my fey I cannot reason?

Both. Wee'l wait vpon you.

Ham. No such matter. I will not sort you with the rest of my seruants: for to speake to you like an honest man: I am most dreadfully attended; but in the beaten way of friendship, What make you at *Elsonower*?

Rosin. To visit you my Lord, no other occasion.

Ham. Begger that I am, I am euen poore in thankes; but I thanke you: and sure deare friends my thanks are too deare a halfepeny; were you not sent for? Is it your owne inclining? Is it a free visitation? Come, deale iustly with me: come, come; nay speake.

Guil. What should we say my Lord?

Ham. Why any thing. But to the purpose; you were sent for; and there is a kinde confession in your lookes; which your modesties haue not craft enough to color, I know the good King & Queene haue sent for you.

Rosin. To what end my Lord?

Ham. That you must teach me: but let mee coniure you by the rights of our fellowship, by the consonancy of our youth, by the Obligation of our euer-preserued loue, and by what more deare, a better proposer could charge you withall; be euen and direct with me, whether you were sent for or no.

Rosin. What say you?

Ham. Nay then I haue an eye of you: if you loue me hold not off.

Guil. My Lord, we were sent for.

Ham. I will tell you why; so shall my anticipation preuent your discouery of your secricie to the King and Queene: moult no feather, I haue of late, but wherefore I know not, lost all my mirth, forgone all custome of exercise; and indeed, it goes so heauenly with my disposition; that this goodly frame the Earth, seemes to me a sterrill Promontory; this most excellent Canopy the Ayre, look you, this braue ore-hanging, this Maiesticall Roofe, fretted with golden fire: why, it appeares no other thing to mee, then a foule and pestilent congregation of vapours. What a piece of worke is a man! how Noble in Reason? how infinite in faculty? in forme and mouing how expresse and admirable? in Action, how like an Angel? in apprehension, how like a God? the beauty of the world, the Parragon of Animals; and yet to me, what is this Quintessence of Dust? Man delights not me; no, nor Woman neither; though by your smiling you seeme to say so.

Rosin. My Lord, there was no such stuffe in my thoughts.

Ham. Why did you laugh, when I said, Man delights not me?

Rosin. To thinke, my Lord, if you delight not in Man, what Lenton entertainment the Players shall receiue from you: wee coated them on the way, and hither are they comming to offer you Seruice.

Ham. He that playes the King shall be welcome; his Maiesty shall haue Tribute of mee: the aduenturous Knight shal vse his Foyle and Target: the Louer shall not sigh *gratis*, the humorous man shall end his part in peace: the Clowne shall make those laugh whose lungs are tickled a'th' sere: and the Lady shall say her minde freely; or the blanke Verse shall halt for't: what Players are they?

Rosin. Euen those you were wont to take delight in the Tragedians of the City.

Ham. How chances it they trauaile? their residence both in reputation and profit was better both wayes.

Rosin. I thinke their Inhibition comes by the meanes of the late Innouation?

Ham. Doe they hold the same estimation they did when I was in the City? Are they so follow'd?

Rosin. No indeed, they are not.

Ham. How comes it? doe they grow rusty?

Rosin. Nay, their indeauour keepes in the wonted pace; But there is Sir an ayrie of Children, little Yases, that crye out on the top of question; and are most tyrannically clap't for't: these are now the
fashi-

fashion, and so be-ratled the common Stages (so they call them) that many wearing Rapiers, are affraide of Goose-quils, and dare scarse come thither.

Ham. What are they Children? Who maintains 'em? How are they escoted? Will they pursue the Quality no longer then they can sing? Will they not say afterwards if they should grow themselues to common Players (as it is like most if their meanes are no better) their Writers do them wrong, to make them exclaim against their owne Succession.

Rosin. Faith there ha's bene much to do on both sides: and the Nation holds it no sinne, to tarre them to Controuersie. There was for a while, no mony bid for argument, vnlesse the Poet and the Player went to Cuffes in the Question.

Ham. Is't possible?

Guild. Oh there ha's beene much throwing about of Braines.

Ham. Do the Boyes carry it away?

Rosin. I that they do my Lord, *Hercules* & his load too.

Ham. It is not strange: for mine Vnckle is King of Denmarke, and those that would make mowes at him while my Father liued; giue twenty, forty, an hundred Ducates a peece, for his picture in Little. There is something in this more then Naturall, if Philosophie could finde it out.

Flourish for the Players.

Guil. There are the Players.

Ham. Gentlemen, you are welcom to *Elsonower*: your hands, come: The appurtenance of Welcome, is Fashion and Ceremony. Let me comply with you in the Garbe, lest my extent to the Players (which I tell you must shew fairely outward) should more appeare like entertainment then yours. You are welcome: but my Vnckle Father, and Aunt Mother are deceiu'd.

Guil. In what my deere Lord?

Ham. I am but mad North, North-West: when the Winde is Southerly, I know a Hawke from a Handsaw.

Enter Polonius.

Pol. Well be with you Gentlemen.

Ham. Hearke you *Guildensterne*, and you too: at each eare a hearer: that great Baby you see there, is not yet out of his swathing clouts.

Rosin. Happily he's the second time come to them: for they say, an old man is twice a childe.

Ham. I will Prophesie. Hee comes to tell me of the Players. Mark it, you say right Sir: for a Monday morning 'twas so indeed.

Pol. My Lord, I haue Newes to tell you.

Ham. My Lord, I haue Newes to tell you. When *Rossius* an Actor in Rome——

Pol. The Actors are come hither my Lord.

Ham. Buzze, buzze.

Pol. Vpon mine Honor.

Ham. Then can each Actor on his Asse——

Polon. The best Actors in the world, either for Tragedie, Comedie, Historie, Pastorall: Pastoricall-Comicall-Historicall-Pastorall: Tragicall-Historicall: Tragicall-Comicall-Historicall-Pastorall: Scene indiuible, or Poem vnlimited. *Seneca* cannot be too heauy, nor *Plautus* too light, for the law of Writ, and the Liberty. These are the onely men.

Ham. O *Iephta* Iudge of Israel, what a Treasure had'st thou?

Pol. What a Treasure had he, my Lord?

Ham. Why one faire Daughter, and no more, The which he loued passing well.

Pol. Still on my Daughter.

Ham. Am I not i'th'right old *Iephta*?

Polon. If you call me *Iephta* my Lord, I haue a daughter that I loue passing well.

Ham. Nay that followes not.

Polon. What followes then, my Lord?

Ha. Why, As by lot, God wot: and then you know, It came to passe, as most like it was: The first rowe of the *Pons Chanson* will shew you more. For looke where my Abridgements come.

Enter foure or fiue Players.

Y'are welcome Masters, welcome all. I am glad to see thee well: Welcome good Friends. O my olde Friend? Thy face is valiant since I saw thee last: Com'st thou to beard me in Denmarke? What, my yong Lady and Mistris? Byrlady your Ladiship is neerer Heauen then when I saw you last, by the altitude of a Choppine. Pray God your voice like a peece of vncurrant Gold be not crack'd within the ring. Masters, you are all welcome: wee'l e'ne to't like French Faulconers, flie at any thing we see: wee'l haue a Speech straight. Come giue vs a tast of your quality: come, a passionate speech.

1. Play. What speech, my Lord?

Ham. I heard thee speak me a speech once, but it was neuer Acted: or if it was, not aboue once, for the Play I remember pleas'd not the Million, 'twas *Cauiarie* to the Generall: but it was (as I receiu'd it, and others, whose iudgement in such matters, cried in the top of mine) an excellent Play; well digested in the Scœnes, set downe with as much modestie, as cunning. I remember one said, there was no Sallets in the lines, to make the matter sauoury; nor no matter in the phrase, that might indite the Author of affectation, but cal'd it an honest method. One cheefe Speech in it, I cheefely lou'd, 'twas *Aeneas* Tale to *Dido*, and thereabout of it especially, where he speaks of *Priams* slaughter. If it liue in your memory, begin at this Line, let me see, let me see: The rugged *Pyrrhus* like th' *Hyrcanian* Beast. It is not so: it begins with *Pyrrhus*
The rugged *Pyrrhus*, he whose Sable Armes
Blacke as his purpose, did the night resemble
When he lay couched in the Ominous Horse,
Hath now this dread and blacke Complexion smear'd
With Heraldry more dismall. Head to foote
Now is he to take Geulles, horridly Trick'd
With blood of Fathers, Mothers, Daughters, Sonnes,
Bak'd and impasted with the parching streets,
That lend a tyrannous, and damned light
To their vilde Murthers, roasted in wrath and fire,
And thus o're-sized with coagulate gore,
VVith eyes like Carbuncles, the hellish *Pyrrhus*
Old Grandsire *Priam* seekes.

Pol. Fore God, my Lord, well spoken, with good accent, and good discretion.

1. Player. Anon he findes him,
Striking too short at Greekes. His anticke Sword,
Rebellious to his Arme, lyes where it falles
Repugnant to command: vnequall match,
Pyrrhus at *Priam* driues, in Rage strikes wide:
But with the whiffe and winde of his fell Sword,
Th'vnnerued Father fals. Then senseleffe Illium,
Seeming to feele his blow, with flaming top
Stoopes to his Base, and with a hideous crash
Takes Prisoner *Pyrrhus* eare. For loe, his Sword
Which was declining on the Milkie head
Of Reuerend *Priam*, seem'd i'th'Ayre to sticke:

So as a painted Tyrant *Pyrrhus* stood,
And like a Newtrall to his will and matter, did nothing.
But as we often see against some storme,
A silence in the Heauens, the Racke stand still,
The bold windes speechlesse, and the Orbe below
As hush as death: Anon the dreadfull Thunder
Doth rend the Region. So after *Pyrrhus* pause,
A rowsed Vengeance sets him new a-worke,
And neuer did the Cyclops hammers fall
On Mars his Armours, forg'd for proofe Eterne,
With lesse remorse then *Pyrrhus* bleeding sword
Now falles on *Priam*.
Out, out, thou Strumpet-Fortune, all you Gods,
In generall Synod take away her power:
Breake all the Spokes and Fallies from her wheele,
And boule the round Naue downe the hill of Heauen,
As low as to the Fiends.

Pol. This is too long.

Ham. It shall to'th Barbars, with your beard. Prythee say on: He's for a Iigge, or a tale of Baudry, or hee sleepes. Say on; come to *Hecuba*.

1. *Play.* But who, O who, had seene the inobled Queen.

Ham. The inobled Queene?

Pol. That's good: Inobled Queene is good.

1. *Play.* Run bare-foot vp and downe,
Threatning the flame
With Bisson Rheume: A clout about that head,
Where late the Diadem stood, and for a Robe
About her lanke and all ore-teamed Loines,
A blanket in th'Alarum of feare caught vp.
Who this had seene, with tongue in Venome steep'd,
'Gainst Fortunes State, would Treason haue pronounc'd?
But if the Gods themselues did see her then,
When she saw *Pyrrhus* make malicious sport
In mincing with his Sword her Husbands limbes,
The instant Burst of Clamour that she made
(Vnlesse things mortall moue them not at all)
Would haue made milche the Burning eyes of Heauen,
And passion in the Gods.

Pol. Looke where he ha's not turn'd his colour, and ha's teares in's eyes. Pray you no more.

Ham. 'Tis well, Ile haue thee speake out the rest, soone. Good my Lord, will you see the Players wel bestow'd. Do ye heare, let them be well vs'd: for they are the Abstracts and breefe Chronicles of the time. After your death, you were better haue a bad Epitaph, then their ill report while you liued.

Pol. My Lord, I will vse them according to their desart.

Ham. Gods bodykins man, better. Vse euerie man after his desart, and who should scape whipping: vse them after your own Honor and Dignity. The lesse they deserue, the more merit is in your bountie. Take them in.

Pol. Come sirs. *Exit Polon.*

Ham. Follow him Friends: wee'l heare a play to morrow. Dost thou heare me old Friend, can you play the murther of *Gonzago*?

Play. I my Lord.

Ham. Wee'l ha't to morrow night. You could for a need study a speech of some dosen or sixteene lines, which I would set downe, and insert in't? Could ye not?

Play. I my Lord.

Ham. Very well. Follow that Lord, and looke you mock him not. My good Friends, Ile leaue you til night you are welcome to *Elsonower*?

Rosin. Good my Lord. *Exeunt.*

Manet Hamlet.

Ham. I so, God buy'ye: Now I am alone.
Oh what a Rogue and Pesant slaue am I?
Is it not monstrous that this Player heere,
But in a Fixion, in a dreame of Passion,
Could force his soule so to his whole conceit,
That from her working, all his visage warm'd;
Teares in his eyes, distraction in's Aspect,
A broken voyce, and his whole Function suiting
With Formes, to his Conceit? And all for nothing?
For *Hecuba*?
What's *Hecuba* to him, or he to *Hecuba*,
That he should weepe for her? What would he doe,
Had he the Motiue and the Cue for passion
That I haue? He would drowne the Stage with teares,
And cleaue the generall eare with horrid speech:
Make mad the guilty, and apale the free,
Confound the ignorant, and amaze indeed,
The very faculty of Eyes and Eares. Yet I,
A dull and muddy-mettled Rascall, peake
Like Iohn a-dreames, vnpregnant of my cause,
And can say nothing: No, not for a King,
Vpon whose property, and most deere life,
A damn'd defeate was made. Am I a Coward?
Who calles me Villaine? breakes my pate a-crosse?
Pluckes off my Beard, and blowes it in my face?
Tweakes me by'th'Nose? giues me the Lye i'th'Throate,
As deepe as to the Lungs? Who does me this?
Ha? Why I should take it: for it cannot be,
But I am Pigeon-Liuer'd, and lacke Gall
To make Oppression bitter, or ere this,
I should haue fatted all the Region Kites
With this Slaues Offall, bloudy: a Bawdy villaine,
Remorselesse, Treacherous, Letcherous, kindles villaine!
Oh Vengeance!
Who? What an Asse am I? I sure, this is most braue,
That I, the Sonne of the Deere murthered,
Prompted to my Reuenge by Heauen, and Hell,
Must (like a Whore) vnpacke my heart with words,
And fall a Cursing like a very Drab,
A Scullion? Fye vpon't: Foh. About my Braine.
I haue heard, that guilty Creatures sitting at a Play,
Haue by the very cunning of the Sceene,
Bene strooke so to the soule, that presently
They haue proclaim'd their Malefactions.
For Murther, though it haue no tongue, will speake
With most myraculous Organ. Ile haue these Players,
Play something like the murder of my Father,
Before mine Vnkle. Ile obserue his lookes,
Ile tent him to the quicke: If he but blench
I know my course. The Spirit that I haue seene
May be the Diuell, and the Diuel hath power
T'assume a pleasing shape, yea and perhaps
Out of my Weaknesse, and my Melancholly,
As he is very potent with such Spirits,
Abuses me to damne me. Ile haue grounds
More Relatiue then this: The Play's the thing,
Wherein Ile catch the Conscience of the King. *Exit*

Enter King, Queene, Polonius, Ophelia, Rosincrance, Guildenstern, and Lords.

King. And can you by no drift of circumstance
Get from him why he puts on this Confusion:
Grating so harshly all his dayes of quiet

With

With turbulent and dangerous Lunacy.

Rosin. He does confesse he feeles himselfe distracted,
But from what cause he will by no meanes speake.

Guil. Nor do we finde him forward to be sounded,
But with a crafty Madnesse keepes aloofe:
When we would bring him on to some Confession
Of his true state.

Qu. Did he receiue you well?

Rosin. Most like a Gentleman.

Guild. But with much forcing of his disposition.

Rosin. Niggard of question, but of our demands
Most free in his reply.

Qu. Did you assay him to any pastime?

Rosin. Madam, it so fell out, that certaine Players
We ore-wrought on the way: of these we told him,
And there did seeme in him a kinde of ioy
To heare of it: They are about the Court,
And (as I thinke) they haue already order
This night to play before him.

Pol. 'Tis most true:
And he beseech'd me to intreate your Maiesties
To heare, and see the matter.

King. With all my heart, and it doth much content me
To heare him so inclin'd. Good Gentlemen,
Giue him a further edge, and driue his purpose on
To these delights.

Rosin. We shall my Lord.   *Exeunt.*

King. Sweet *Gertrude* leaue vs too,
For we haue closely sent for *Hamlet* hither,
That he, as 'twere by accident, may there
Affront *Ophelia.* Her Father, and my selfe (lawful espials)
Will so bestow our selues, that seeing vnseene
We may of their encounter frankely iudge,
And gather by him, as he is behaued,
If't be th'affliction of his loue, or no.
That thus he suffers for.

Qu. I shall obey you,
And for your part *Ophelia,* I do wish
That your good Beauties be the happy cause
Of *Hamlets* wildenesse: so shall I hope your Vertues
Will bring him to his wonted way againe,
To both your Honors.

Ophe. Madam, I wish it may.

Pol. Ophelia, walke you heere. Gracious so please ye
We will bestow our selues: Reade on this booke,
That shew of such an exercise may colour
Your lonelinesse. We are oft too blame in this,
'Tis too much prou'd, that with Deuotions visage,
And pious Action, we do surge o're
The diuell himselfe.

King. Oh 'tis true:
How smart a lash that speech doth giue my Conscience?
The Harlots Cheeke beautied with plaist'ring Art
Is not more vgly to the thing that helpes it,
Then is my deede, to my most painted word.
Oh heauie burthen!

Pol. I heare him comming, let's withdraw my Lord.
            Exeunt.

Enter Hamlet.

Ham. To be, or not to be, that is the Question:
Whether 'tis Nobler in the minde to suffer
The Slings and Arrowes of outragious Fortune,
Or to take Armes against a Sea of troubles,
And by opposing end them: to dye, to sleepe
No more; and by a sleepe, to say we end
The Heart-ake, and the thousand Naturall shockes
That Flesh is heyre too? 'Tis a consummation
Deuoutly to be wish'd. To dye to sleepe,
To sleepe, perchance to Dreame; I, there's the rub,
For in that sleepe of death, what dreames may come,
When we haue shuffel'd off this mortall coile,
Must giue vs pawse. There's the respect
That makes Calamity of so long life:
For who would beare the Whips and Scornes of time,
The Oppressors wrong, the poore mans Contumely,
The pangs of dispriz'd Loue, the Lawes delay,
The insolence of Office, and the Spurnes
That patient merit of the vnworthy takes,
When he himselfe might his *Quietus* make
With a bare Bodkin? Who would these Fardles beare
To grunt and sweat vnder a weary life,
But that the dread of something after death,
The vndiscouered Countrey, from whose Borne
No Traueller returnes, Puzels the will,
And makes vs rather beare those illes we haue,
Then flye to others that we know not of.
Thus Conscience does make Cowards of vs all,
And thus the Natiue hew of Resolution
Is sicklied o're, with the pale cast of Thought,
And enterprizes of great pith and moment,
With this regard their Currants turne away,
And loose the name of Action. Soft you now,
The faire *Ophelia?* Nimph, in thy Orizons
Be all my sinnes remembred.

Ophe. Good my Lord,
How does your Honor for this many a day?

Ham. I humbly thanke you: well, well, well.

Ophe. My Lord, I haue Remembrances of yours,
That I haue longed long to re-deliuer.
I pray you now, receiue them.

Ham. No, no, I neuer gaue you ought.

Ophe. My honor'd Lord, I know right well you did,
And with them words of so sweet breath compos'd,
As made the things more rich, then perfume left:
Take these againe, for to the Noble minde
Rich gifts wax poore, when giuers proue vnkinde.
There my Lord.

Ham. Ha, ha: Are you honest?

Ophe. My Lord.

Ham. Are you faire?

Ophe. What meanes your Lordship?

Ham. That if you be honest and faire, your Honesty
should admit no discourse to your Beautie.

Ophe. Could Beautie my Lord, haue better Comerce
then your Honestie?

Ham. I trulie: for the power of Beautie, will sooner
transforme Honestie from what it is, to a Bawd, then the
force of Honestie can translate Beautie into his likenesse.
This was sometime a Paradox, but now the time giues it
proofe. I did loue you once.

Ophe. Indeed my Lord, you made me beleeue so.

Ham. You should not haue beleeued me. For vertue
cannot so innocculate our old stocke, but we shall rellish
of it. I loued you not.

Ophe. I was the more deceiued.

Ham. Get thee to a Nunnerie. Why would'st thou
be a breeder of Sinners? I am my selfe indifferent honest,
but yet I could accuse me of such things, that it were better my Mother had not borne me. I am very prowd, reuengefull, Ambitious, with more offences at my becke,
then I haue thoughts to put them in imagination, to giue
them shape, or time to acte them in. What should such

Fel-

Fellowes as I do, crawling betweene Heauen and Earth. We are arrant Knaues all, beleeue none of vs. Goe thy wayes to a Nunnery. Where's your Father?

Ophe. At home, my Lord.

Ham. Let the doores be shut vpon him, that he may play the Foole no way, but in's owne house. Farewell.

Ophe. O helpe him, you sweet Heauens.

Ham. If thou doest Marry, Ile giue thee this Plague for thy Dowrie. Be thou as chast as Ice, as pure as Snow, thou shalt not escape Calumny. Get thee to a Nunnery. Go, Farewell. Or if thou wilt needs Marry, marry a fool: for Wise men know well enough, what monsters you make of them. To a Nunnery go, and quickly too. Farewell.

Ophe. O heauenly Powers, restore him.

Ham. I haue heard of your pratlings too wel enough. God has giuen you one pace, and you make your selfe another: you gidge, you amble, and you lispe, and nickname Gods creatures, and make your Wantonnesse, your Ignorance. Go too, Ile no more on't, it hath made me mad. I say, we will haue no more Marriages. Those that are married already, all but one shall liue, the rest shall keep as they are. To a Nunnery, go. *Exit Hamlet*

Ophe. O what a Noble minde is heere o're-throwne?
The Courtiers, Soldiers, Schollers: Eye, tongue, sword,
Th'expectansie and Rose of the faire State,
The glasse of Fashion, and the mould of Forme,
Th'obseru'd of all Obseruers, quite, quite downe.
Haue I of Ladies most deiect and wretched,
That suck'd the Honie of his Musicke Vowes:
Now see that Noble, and most Soueraigne Reason,
Like sweet Bels iangled out of tune, and harsh,
That vnmatch'd Forme and Feature of blowne youth,
Blasted with extasie. Oh woe is me,
T'haue seene what I haue seene: see what I see.

Enter King, and Polonius.

King. Loue? His affections do not that way tend,
Nor what he spake, though it lack'd Forme a little,
Was not like Madnesse. There's something in his soule?
O're which his Melancholly sits on brood,
And I do doubt the hatch, and the disclose
Will be some danger, which to preuent
I haue in quicke determination
Thus set it downe. He shall with speed to England
For the demand of our neglected Tribute:
Haply the Seas and Countries different
With variable Obiects, shall expell
This something setled matter in his heart:
Whereon his Braines still beating, puts him thus
From fashion of himselfe. What thinke you on't?

Pol. It shall do well. But yet do I beleeue
The Origin and Commencement of this greefe
Sprung from neglected loue. How now *Ophelia*?
You neede not tell vs, what Lord *Hamlet* saide,
We heard it all. My Lord, do as you please,
But if you hold it fit after the Play,
Let his Queene Mother all alone intreat him
To shew his Greefes: let her be round with him,
And Ile be plac'd so, please you in the eare
Of all their Conference. If she finde him not,
To England send him: Or confine him where
Your wisedome best shall thinke.

King. It shall be so:
Madnesse in great Ones, must not vnwatch'd go.
Exeunt.

Enter Hamlet, and two or three of the Players.

Ham. Speake the Speech I pray you, as I pronounc'd it to you trippingly on the Tongue: But if you mouth it, as many of your Players do, I had as liue the Town-Cryer had spoke my Lines: Nor do not saw the Ayre too much your hand thus, but vse all gently; for in the verie Torrent, Tempest, and (as I may say) the Whirle-winde of Passion, you must acquire and beget a Temperance that may giue it Smoothnesse. O it offends mee to the Soule, to see a robustious Pery-wig-pated Fellow, teare a Passion to tatters, to verie ragges, to split the eares of the Groundlings: who (for the most part) are capeable of nothing, but inexplicable dumbe shewes, & noise: I could haue such a Fellow whipt for o're-doing Termagant: it out-*Herod's* Herod. Pray you auoid it.

Player. I warrant your Honor.

Ham. Be not too tame neyther: but let your owne Discretion be your Tutor. Sute the Action to the Word, the Word to the Action, with this speciall obseruance: That you ore-stop not the modestie of Nature; for any thing so ouer-done, is fro the purpose of Playing, whose end both at the first and now, was and is, to hold as 'twer the Mirrour vp to Nature; to shew Vertue her owne Feature, Scorne her owne Image, and the verie Age and Bodie of the Time, his forme and pressure. Now, this ouer-done, or come tardie off, though it make the vnskilfull laugh, cannot but make the Iudicious greeue; The censure of the which One, must in your allowance o're-way a whole Theater of Others. Oh, there bee Players that I haue seene Play, and heard others praise, and that highly (not to speake it prophanely) that neyther hauing the accent of Christians, nor the gate of Christian, Pagan, or Norman, haue so strutted and bellowed, that I haue thought some of Natures Iouerney-men had made men, and not made them well, they imitated Humanity so abhominably.

Play. I hope we haue reform'd that indifferently with vs, Sir.

Ham. O reforme it altogether. And let those that play your Clownes, speake no more then is set downe for them. For there be of them, that will themselues laugh, to set on some quantitie of barren Spectators to laugh too, though in the meane time, some necessary Question of the Play be then to be considered: that's Villanous, & shewes a most pittifull Ambition in the Foole that vses it. Go make you readie. *Exit Players.*

Enter Polonius, Rosincrance, and Guildensterne.

How now my Lord,
Will the King heare this peece of Worke?

Pol. And the Queene too, and that presently.

Ham. Bid the Players make hast. *Exit Polonius.*
Will you two helpe to hasten them?

Both. We will my Lord. *Exeunt.*

Enter Horatio.

Ham. What hoa, *Horatio*?

Hora. Heere sweet Lord, at your Seruice.

Ham. Horatio, thou art eene as iust a man
As ere my Conuersation coap'd withall.

Hora. O my deere Lord.

Ham. Nay, do not thinke I flatter:
For what aduancement may I hope from thee,
That no Reuennew hast, but thy good spirits

To feed & cloath thee. Why shold the poor be flatter'd?
No, let the Candied tongue, like absurd pompe,
And crooke the pregnant Hindges of the knee,
Where thrift may follow faining? Dost thou heare,
Since my deere Soule was Mistris of my choyse,
And could of men distinguish, her election
Hath seal'd thee for her selfe. For thou hast bene
As one in suffering all, that suffers nothing.
A man that Fortunes buffets, and Rewards
Hath 'tane with equall Thankes. And blest are those,
Whose Blood and Iudgement are so well co-mingled,
That they are not a Pipe for Fortunes finger,
To sound what stop she please. Giue me that man,
That is not Passions Slaue, and I will weare him
In my hearts Core: I, in my Heart of heart,
As I do thee. Something too much of this.
There is a Play to night before the King,
One Scoene of it comes neere the Circumstance
Which I haue told thee, of my Fathers death.
I prythee, when thou see'st that Acte a-foot,
Euen with the verie Comment of my Soule
Obserue mine Vnkle: If his occulted guilt,
Do not it selfe vnkennell in one speech,
It is a damned Ghost that we haue seene:
And my Imaginations are as foule
As Vulcans Stythe. Giue him needfull note,
For I mine eyes will riuet to his Face:
And after we will both our iudgements ioyne,
To censure of his seeming.

Hora. Well my Lord.
If he steale ought the whil'st this Play is Playing,
And scape detecting, I will pay the Theft.

Enter King, Queene, Polonius, Ophelia, Rosincrance,
Guildensterne, and other Lords attendant with
his Guard carrying Torches. Danish
March. Sound a Flourish.

Ham. They are comming to the Play: I must be idle.
Get you a place.

King. How fares our Cosin *Hamlet*?

Ham. Excellent Ifaith, of the Camelions dish: I eate
the Ayre promise-cramm'd, you cannot feed Capons so.

King. I haue nothing with this answer *Hamlet*, these
words are not mine.

Ham. No, nor mine. Now my Lord, you plaid once
i'th'Vniuersity, you say?

Polon. That I did my Lord, and was accounted a good
Actor.

Ham. And what did you enact?

Pol. I did enact *Iulius Cæsar*, I was kill'd i'th'Capitol:
Brutus kill'd me.

Ham. It was a bruite part of him, to kill so Capitall a
Calfe there. Be the Players ready?

Rosin. I my Lord, they stay vpon your patience.

Qu. Come hither my good *Hamlet*, sit by me.

Ha. No good Mother, here's Mettle more attractiue.

Pol. Oh ho, do you marke that?

Ham. Ladie, shall I lye in your Lap?

Ophe. No my Lord.

Ham. I meane, my Head vpon your Lap?

Ophe. I my Lord.

Ham. Do you thinke I meant Country matters?

Ophe. I thinke nothing, my Lord.

Ham. That's a faire thought to ly between Maids legs

Ophe. What is my Lord?

Ham. Nothing.

Ophe. You are merrie, my Lord?

Ham. Who I?

Ophe. I my Lord.

Ham. Oh God, your onely Iigge-maker: what should
a man do, but be merrie. For looke you how cheerefully my Mother lookes, and my Father dyed within's two
Houres.

Ophe. Nay, 'tis twice two moneths, my Lord.

Ham. So long? Nay then let the Diuel weare blacke,
for Ile haue a suite of Sables. Oh Heauens! dye two moneths ago, and not forgotten yet? Then there's hope, a
great mans Memorie, may out-liue his life halfe a yeare:
But byrlady he must builde Churches then: or else shall
he suffer not thinking on, with the Hoby-horsse, whose
Epitaph is, For o, For o, the Hoby-horse is forgot.

Hoboyes play. The dumbe shew enters.

Enter a King and Queene, very louingly; the Queene embra-
cing him. She kneeles, and makes shew of Protestation vnto
him. He takes her vp, and declines his head vpon her neck.
Layes him downe vpon a Banke of Flowers. She seeing him
a-sleepe, leaues him. Anon comes in a Fellow, takes off his
Crowne, kisses it, and powres poyson in the Kings eares, and
Exits. The Queene returnes, findes the King dead, and
makes passionate Action. The Poysoner, with some two or
three Mutes comes in againe, seeming to lament with her.
The dead body is carried away: The Poysoner Wooes the
Queene with Gifts, she seemes loath and vnwilling awhile,
but in the end, accepts his loue. Exeunt

Ophe. What meanes this, my Lord?

Ham. Marry this is Miching *Malicho*, that meanes
Mischeefe.

Ophe. Belike this shew imports the Argument of the
Play?

Ham. We shall know by these Fellowes: the Players
cannot keepe counsell, they'l tell all.

Ophe. Will they tell vs what this shew meant?

Ham. I, or any shew that you'l shew him. Bee not
you asham'd to shew, hee'l not shame to tell you what it
meanes.

Ophe. You are naught, you are naught, Ile marke the
Play.

Enter Prologue.
For vs, and for our Tragedie,
Heere stooping to your Clemencie:
We begge your hearing Patientlie.

Ham. Is this a Prologue, or the Poesie of a Ring?

Ophe. 'Tis briefe my Lord.

Ham. As Womans loue.

Enter King and his Queene.
King. Full thirtie times hath Phœbus Cart gon round,
Neptunes salt Wash, and *Tellus* Orbed ground:
And thirtie dozen Moones with borrowed sheene,
About the World haue times twelue thirties beene,
Since loue our hearts, and *Hymen* did our hands
Vnite comutuall, in most sacred Bands.

Bap. So many iournies may the Sunne and Moone
Make vs againe count o're, ere loue be done.
But woe is me, you are so sicke of late,
So farre from cheere, and from your forme state,
That I distrust you: yet though I distrust,
Discomfort you (my Lord) it nothing must:
For womens Feare and Loue, holds quantitie,

In neither ought, or in extremity:
Now what my loue is, proofe hath made you know,
And as my Loue is siz'd, my Feare is so.

  King. Faith I must leaue thee Loue, and shortly too:
My operant Powers my Functions leaue to do:
And thou shalt liue in this faire world behinde,
Honour'd, belou'd, and haply, one as kinde.
For Husband shalt thou——

  Bap. Oh confound the rest:
Such Loue, must needs be Treason in my brest:
In second Husband, let me be accurst,
None wed the second, but who kill'd the first.

  Ham. Wormwood, Wormwood.

  Bapt. The instances that second Marriage moue,
Are base respects of Thrift, but none of Loue.
A second time, I kill my Husband dead,
When second Husband kisses me in Bed.

  King. I do beleeue you. Think what now you speak:
But what we do determine, oft we breake:
Purpose is but the slaue to Memorie,
Of violent Birth, but poore validitie:
Which now like Fruite vnripe stickes on the Tree,
But fall vnshaken, when they mellow bee.
Most necessary 'tis, that we forget
To pay our selues, what to our selues is debt:
What to our selues in passion we propose,
The passion ending, doth the purpose lose.
The violence of other Greefe or Ioy,
Their owne ennactors with themselues destroy:
Where Ioy most Reuels, Greefe doth most lament;
Greefe ioyes, Ioy greeues on slender accident.
This world is not for aye, nor 'tis not strange
That euen our Loues should with our Fortunes change.
For 'tis a question left vs yet to proue,
Whether Loue lead Fortune, or else Fortune Loue.
The great man downe, you marke his fauourites flies,
The poore aduanc'd, makes Friends of Enemies:
And hitherto doth Loue on Fortune tend,
For who not needs, shall neuer lacke a Frend:
And who in want a hollow Friend doth try,
Directly seasons him his Enemie.
But orderly to end, where I begun,
Our Willes and Fates do so contrary run,
That our Deuices still are ouerthrowne,
Our thoughts are ours, their ends none of our owne.
So thinke thou wilt no second Husband wed.
But die thy thoughts, when thy first Lord is dead.

  Bap. Nor Earth to giue me food, nor Heauen light,
Sport and repose locke from me day and night:
Each opposite that blankes the face of ioy,
Meet what I would haue well, and it destroy:
Both heere, and hence, pursue me lasting strife,
If once a Widdow, euer I be Wife.

  Ham. If she should breake it now.

  King. 'Tis deepely sworne:
Sweet, leaue me heere a while,
My spirits grow dull, and faine I would beguile
The tedious day with sleepe.

  Qu. Sleepe rocke thy Braine, *Sleepes*
And neuer come mischance betweene vs twaine. *Exit*

  Ham. Madam, how like you this Play?

  Qu. The Lady protests to much me thinkes.

  Ham. Oh but shee'l keepe her word.

  King. Haue you heard the Argument, is there no Offence in't?

  Ham. No, no, they do but iest, poyson in iest, no Offence i'th'world.

  King. What do you call the Play?

  Ham. The Mouse-trap: Marry how? Tropically:
This Play is the Image of a murder done in *Vienna: Gonzago* is the Dukes name, his wife *Baptista*: you shall see anon: 'tis a knauish peece of worke: But what o'that? Your Maiestie, and wee that haue free soules, it touches vs not: let the gall'd iade winch: our withers are vnrung.

Enter Lucianus.

This is one *Lucianus* nephew to the King.

  Ophe. You are a good Chorus, my Lord.

  Ham. I could interpret betweene you and your loue:
if I could see the Puppets dallying.

  Ophe. You are keene my Lord, you are keene.

  Ham. It would cost you a groaning, to take off my edge.

  Ophe. Still better and worse.

  Ham. So you mistake Husbands.
Begin Murderer. Pox, leaue thy damnable Faces, and begin. Come, the croaking Rauen doth bellow for Reuenge.

  Lucian. Thoughts blacke, hands apt,
Drugges fit, and Time agreeing:
Confederate season, else no Creature seeing:
Thou mixture ranke, of Midnight Weeds collected,
With Hecats Ban, thrice blasted, thrice infected,
Thy naturall Magicke, and dire propertie,
On wholsome life, vsurpe immediately.

Powres the poyson in his eares.

  Ham. He poysons him i'th'Garden for's estate: His name's *Gonzago*: the Story is extant and writ in choyce Italian. You shall see anon how the Murtherer gets the loue of *Gonzago's* wife.

  Ophe. The King rises.

  Ham. What, frighted with false fire.

  Qu. How fares my Lord?

  Pol. Giue o're the Play.

  King. Giue me some Light. Away.

  All. Lights, Lights, Lights. *Exeunt*

Manet Hamlet & Horatio.

  Ham. Why let the strucken Deere go weepe,
The Hart vngalled play:
For some must watch, while some must sleepe;
So runnes the world away.
Would not this Sir, and a Forrest of Feathers, if the rest of my Fortunes turne Turke with me; with two Prouinciall Roses on my rac'd Shooes, get me a Fellowship in a crie of Players sir.

  Hor. Halfe a share.

  Ham. A whole one I,
For thou dost know: Oh *Damon* deere,
This Realme dismantled was of Ioue himselfe,
And now reignes heere.
A verie verie Paiocke.

  Hora. You might haue Rim'd.

  Ham. Oh good *Horatio*, Ile take the Ghosts word for a thousand pound. Did'st perceiue?

  Hora. Verie well my Lord.

  Ham. Vpon the talke of the poysoning?

  Hora. I did verie well note him.

Enter Rosincrance and Guildensterne.

  Ham. Oh, ha? Come some Musick. Come § Recorders:
For if the King like not the Comedie,
Why then belike he likes it not perdie.
Come some Musicke.

  Guild. Good my Lord, vouchsafe me a word with you.
  Ham.

The Tragedie of Hamlet.

Ham. Sir, a whole History.
Guild. The King, sir.
Ham. I sir, what of him?
Guild. Is in his retyrement, maruellous distemper'd.
Ham. With drinke Sir?
Guild. No my Lord, rather with choller.
Ham. Your wisedome should shew it selfe more richer, to signifie this to his Doctor: for for me to put him to his Purgation, would perhaps plundge him into farre more Choller.
Guild. Good my Lord put your discourse into some frame, and start not so wildely from my affayre.
Ham. I am tame Sir, pronounce.
Guild. The Queene your Mother, in most great affliction of spirit, hath sent me to you.
Ham. You are welcome.
Guild. Nay, good my Lord, this courtesie is not of the right breed. If it shall please you to make me a wholsome answer, I will doe your Mothers command'ment: if not, your pardon, and my returne shall bee the end of my Businesse.
Ham. Sir, I cannot.
Guild. What, my Lord?
Ham. Make you a wholsome answere: my wits diseas'd. But sir, such answers as I can make, you shal command: or rather you say, my Mother: therfore no more but to the matter. My Mother you say.
Rosin. Then thus she sayes: your behauior hath stroke her into amazement, and admiration.
Ham. Oh wonderfull Sonne, that can so astonish a Mother. But is there no sequell at the heeles of this Mothers admiration?
Rosin. She desires to speake with you in her Closset, ere you go to bed.
Ham. We shall obey, were she ten times our Mother. Haue you any further Trade with vs?
Rosin. My Lord, you once did loue me.
Ham. So I do still, by these pickers and stealers.
Rosin. Good my Lord, what is your cause of distemper? You do freely barre the doore of your owne Libertie, if you deny your greefes to your Friend.
Ham. Sir I lacke Aduancement.
Rosin. How can that be, when you haue the voyce of the King himselfe, for your Succession in Denmarke?
Ham. I, but while the grasse growes, the Prouerbe is something musty.

Enter one with a Recorder.

O the Recorder. Let me see, to withdraw with you, why do you go about to recouer the winde of mee, as if you would driue me into a toyle?
Guild. O my Lord, if my Dutie be too bold, my loue is too vnmannerly.
Ham. I do not well vnderstand that. Will you play vpon this Pipe?
Guild. My Lord, I cannot.
Ham. I pray you.
Guild. Beleeue me, I cannot.
Ham. I do beseech you.
Guild. I know no touch of it, my Lord.
Ham. 'Tis as easie as lying: gouerne these Ventiges with your finger and thumbe, giue it breath with your mouth, and it will discourse most excellent Musicke. Looke you, these are the stoppes.
Guild. But these cannot I command to any vtterance of harmony, I haue not the skill.
Ham. Why looke you now, how vnworthy a thing you make of me: you would play vpon mee; you would seeme to know my stops: you would pluck out the heart of my Mysterie; you would sound mee from my lowest Note, to the top of my Compasse: and there is much Musicke, excellent Voice, in this little Organe, yet cannot you make it. Why do you thinke, that I am easier to bee plaid on, then a Pipe? Call me what Instrument you will, though you can fret me, you cannot play vpon me. God blesse you Sir.

Enter Polonius.

Polon. My Lord; the Queene would speak with you, and presently.
Ham. Do you see that Clowd? that's almost in shape like a Camell.
Polon. By'th'Misse, and it's like a Camell indeed.
Ham. Me thinkes it is like a Weazell.
Polon. It is back'd like a Weazell.
Ham. Or like a Whale?
Polon. Verie like a Whale.
Ham. Then will I come to my Mother, by and by:
They foole me to the top of my bent.
I will come by and by.
Polon. I will say so. *Exit.*
Ham. By and by, is easily said. Leaue me Friends:
'Tis now the verie witching time of night,
When Churchyards yawne, and Hell it selfe breaths out
Contagion to this world. Now could I drink hot blood,
And do such bitter businesse as the day
Would quake to looke on. Soft now, to my Mother:
Oh Heart, loose not thy Nature; let not euer
The Soule of *Nero*, enter this firme bosome:
Let me be cruell, not vnnaturall,
I will speake Daggers to her, but vse none:
My Tongue and Soule in this be Hypocrites.
How in my words someuer she be shent,
To giue them Seales, neuer my Soule consent.

Enter King, Rosincrance, and Guildensterne.

King. I like him not, nor stands it safe with vs,
To let his madnesse range. Therefore prepare you,
I your Commission will forthwith dispatch,
And he to England shall along with you:
The termes of our estate, may not endure
Hazard so dangerous as doth hourely grow
Out of his Lunacies.
Guild. We will our selues prouide:
Most holie and Religious feare it is
To keepe those many many bodies safe
That liue and feede vpon your Maiestie.
Rosin. The single
And peculiar life is bound
With all the strength and Armour of the minde,
To keepe it selfe from noyance: but much more,
That Spirit, vpon whose spirit depends and rests
The liues of many, the cease of Maiestie
Dies not alone; but like a Gulfe doth draw
What's neere it, with it. It is a massie wheele
Fixt on the Sommet of the highest Mount,
To whose huge Spoakes, ten thousand lesser things
Are mortiz'd and adioyn'd: which when it falles,
Each small annexment, pettie consequence
Attends the boystrous Ruine. Neuer alone
Did the King sighe, but with a generall grone.
King. Arme you, I pray you to this speedie Voyage;
For we will Fetters put vpon this feare,

PP   Which

Which now goes too free-footed.

Both. We will haste vs. *Exeunt Gent.*

Enter Polonius.

Pol. My Lord, he's going to his Mothers Closset:
Behinde the Arras Ile conuey my selfe
To heare the Processe. Ile warrant shee'l tax him home,
And as you said, and wisely was it said,
'Tis meete that some more audience then a Mother,
Since Nature makes them partiall, should o're-heare
The speech of vantage. Fare you well my Liege,
Ile call vpon you ere you go to bed,
And tell you what I know.

King. Thankes deere my Lord.
Oh my offence is ranke, it smels to heauen,
It hath the primall eldest curse vpon't,
A Brothers murther. Pray can I not,
Though inclination be as sharpe as will:
My stronger guilt, defeats my strong intent,
And like a man to double businesse bound,
I stand in pause where I shall first begin,
And both neglect; what if this cursed hand
Were thicker then it selfe with Brothers blood,
Is there not Raine enough in the sweet Heauens
To wash it white as Snow? Whereto serues mercy,
But to confront the visage of Offence?
And what's in Prayer, but this two-fold force,
To be fore-stalled ere we come to fall,
Or pardon'd being downe? Then Ile looke vp,
My fault is past. But oh, what forme of Prayer
Can serue my turne? Forgiue me my foule Murther:
That cannot be, since I am still possest
Of those effects for which I did the Murther.
My Crowne, mine owne Ambition, and my Queene:
May one be pardon'd, and retaine th'offence?
In the corrupted currants of this world,
Offences gilded hand may shoue by Iustice,
And oft 'tis seene, the wicked prize it selfe
Buyes out the Law; but 'tis not so aboue,
There is no shuffling, there the Action lyes
In his true Nature, and we our selues compell'd
Euen to the teeth and forehead of our faults,
To giue in euidence. What then? What rests?
Try what Repentance can. What can it not?
Yet what can it, when one cannot repent?
Oh wretched state! Oh bosome, blacke as death!
Oh limed soule, that strugling to be free,
Art more ingag'd: Helpe Angels, make assay:
Bow stubborne knees, and heart with strings of Steele,
Be soft as sinewes of the new-borne Babe,
All may be well.

Enter Hamlet.

Ham. Now might I do it pat, now he is praying,
And now Ile doo't, and so he goes to Heauen,
And so am I reueng'd: that would be scann'd,
A Villaine killes my Father, and for that
I his foule Sonne, do this same Villaine send
To heauen. Oh this is hyre and Sallery, not Reuenge.
He tooke my Father grossely, full of bread,
With all his Crimes broad blowne, as fresh as May,
And how his Audit stands, who knowes, saue Heauen:
But in our circumstance and course of thought
'Tis heauie with him: and am I then reueng'd,
To take him in the purging of his Soule,
When he is fit and season'd for his passage? No.
Vp Sword, and know thou a more horrid hent

When he is drunke asleepe: or in his Rage,
Or in th'incestuous pleasure of his bed,
At gaming, swearing, or about some acte
That ha's no rellish of Saluation in't,
Then trip him, that his heeles may kicke at Heauen,
And that his Soule may be as damn'd and blacke
As Hell, whereto it goes. My Mother stayes,
This Physicke but prolongs thy sickly dayes. *Exit.*

King. My words flye vp, my thoughts remain below,
Words without thoughts, neuer to Heauen go. *Exit.*

Enter Queene and Polonius.

Pol. He will come straight:
Looke you lay home to him,
Tell him his prankes haue been too broad to beare with,
And that your Grace hath scree'nd, and stoode betweene
Much heate, and him. Ile silence me e'ene heere:
Pray you be round with him.

Ham. within. Mother, mother, mother.

Qu. Ile warrant you, feare me not.
Withdraw, I heare him comming.

Enter Hamlet.

Ham. Now Mother, what's the matter?

Qu. Hamlet, thou hast thy Father much offended.

Ham. Mother, you haue my Father much offended.

Qu. Come, come, you answer with an idle tongue.

Ham. Go, go, you question with an idle tongue.

Qu. Why how now Hamlet?

Ham. Whats the matter now?

Qu. Haue you forgot me?

Ham. No by the Rood, not so:
You are the Queene, your Husbands Brothers wife,
But would you were not so. You are my Mother.

Qu. Nay, then Ile set those to you that can speake.

Ham. Come, come, and sit you downe, you shall not boudge:
You go not till I set you vp a glasse,
Where you may see the inmost part of you?

Qu. What wilt thou do? thou wilt not murther me?
Helpe, helpe, hoa.

Pol. What hoa, helpe, helpe, helpe.

Ham. How now, a Rat? dead for a Ducate, dead.

Pol. Oh I am slaine. *Killes Polonius.*

Qu. Oh me, what hast thou done?

Ham. Nay I know not, is it the King?

Qu. Oh what a rash, and bloody deed is this?

Ham. A bloody deed, almost as bad good Mother,
As kill a King, and marrie with his Brother.

Qu. As kill a King?

Ham. I Lady, 'twas my word.
Thou wretched, rash, intruding foole farewell,
I tooke thee for thy Betters, take thy Fortune,
Thou find'st to be too busie, is some danger.
Leaue wringing of your hands, peace, sit you downe,
And let me wring your heart, for so I shall
If it be made of penetrable stuffe;
If damned Custome haue not braz'd it so,
That it is proofe and bulwarke against Sense.

Qu. What haue I done, that thou dar'st wag thy tong,
In noise so rude against me?

Ham. Such an Act
That blurres the grace and blush of Modestie,
Cals Vertue Hypocrite, takes off the Rose
From the faire forehead of an innocent loue,
And makes a blister there. Makes marriage vowes
As false as Dicers Oathes. Oh such a deed,

As from the body of Contraction pluckes
The very soule, and sweete Religion makes
A rapsidie of words. Heauens face doth glow,
Yea this solidity and compound masse,
With tristfull visage as against the doome,
Is thought-sicke at the act.

Qu. Aye me; what act, that roares so lowd, & thunders in the Index.

Ham. Looke heere vpon this Picture, and on this,
The counterfet presentment of two Brothers:
See what a grace was seated on his Brow.
Hyperions curles, the front of Ioue himselfe,
An eye like Mars, to threaten or command
A Station, like the Herald Mercurie
New lighted on a heauen-kissing hill:
A Combination, and a forme indeed,
Where euery God did seeme to set his Seale,
To giue the world assurance of a man.
This was your Husband. Looke you now what followes.
Heere is your Husband, like a Mildew'd eare
Blasting his wholsom breath. Haue you eyes?
Could you on this faire Mountaine leaue to feed,
And batten on this Moore? Ha? Haue you eyes?
You cannot call it Loue: For at your age,
The hey-day in the blood is tame, it's humble,
And waites vpon the Iudgement: and what Iudgement
Would step from this, to this? What diuell was't,
That thus hath cousend you at hoodman-blinde?
O Shame! where is thy Blush? Rebellious Hell,
If thou canst mutine in a Matrons bones,
To flaming youth, let Vertue be as waxe,
And melt in her owne fire. Proclaime no shame,
When the compulsiue Ardure giues the charge,
Since Frost it selfe, as actiuely doth burne,
As Reason panders Will.

Qu. O *Hamlet*, speake no more.
Thou turn'st mine eyes into my very soule,
And there I see such blacke and grained spots,
As will not leaue their Tinct.

Ham. Nay, but to liue
In the ranke sweat of an enseamed bed,
Stew'd in Corruption; honying and making loue
Ouer the nasty Stye.

Qu. Oh speake to me, no more,
These words like Daggers enter in mine eares.
No more sweet *Hamlet*.

Ham. A Murderer, and a Villaine:
A Slaue, that is not twentieth part the tythe
Of your precedent Lord. A vice of Kings,
A Cutpurse of the Empire and the Rule.
That from a shelfe, the precious Diadem stole,
And put it in his Pocket.

Qu. No more.

Enter Ghost.

Ham. A King of shreds and patches.
Saue me; and houer o're me with your wings
You heauenly Guards. What would you gracious figure?

Qu. Alas he's mad.

Ham. Do you not come your tardy Sonne to chide,
That laps't in Time and Passion, lets go by
Th'important acting of your dread command? Oh say.

Ghost. Do not forget: this Visitation
Is but to whet thy almost blunted purpose.
But looke, Amazement on thy Mother sits;
O step betweene her, and her fighting Soule,
Conceit in weakest bodies, strongest workes.
Speake to her *Hamlet*.

Ham. How is it with you Lady?

Qu. Alas, how is't with you?
That you bend your eye on vacancie,
And with their corporall ayre do hold discourse.
Forth at your eyes, your spirits wildely peepe,
And as the sleeping Soldiours in th'Alarme,
Your bedded haire, like life in excrements,
Start vp, and stand an end. Oh gentle Sonne,
Vpon the heate and flame of thy distemper
Sprinkle coole patience. Whereon do you looke?

Ham. On him, on him: look you how pale he glares,
His forme and cause conioyn'd, preaching to stones,
Would make them capeable. Do not looke vpon me,
Least with this pitteous action you conuert
My sterne effects: then what I haue to do,
Will want true colour; teares perchance for blood.

Qu. To who do you speake this?

Ham. Do you see nothing there?

Qu. Nothing at all, yet all that is I see.

Ham. Nor did you nothing heare?

Qu. No, nothing but our selues.

Ham. Why look you there: looke how it steals away:
My Father in his habite, as he liued,
Looke where he goes euen now out at the Portall. *Exit.*

Qu. This is the very coynage of your Braine,
This bodilesse Creation extasie is very cunning in.

Ham. Extasie?
My Pulse as yours doth temperately keepe time,
And makes as healthfull Musicke. It is not madnesse
That I haue vttered; bring me to the Test
And I the matter will re-word: which madnesse
Would gamboll from. Mother, for loue of Grace,
Lay not a flattering Vnction to your soule,
That not your trespasse, but my madnesse speakes:
It will but skin and filme the Vlcerous place,
Whil'st ranke Corruption mining all within,
Infects vnseene. Confesse your selfe to Heauen,
Repent what's past, auoyd what is to come,
And do not spred the Compost on the Weedes,
To make them ranke. Forgiue me this my Vertue,
For in the fatnesse of this pursie times,
Vertue it selfe, of Vice must pardon begge,
Yea courb, and woe, for leaue to do him good.

Qu. Oh *Hamlet*,
Thou hast cleft my heart in twaine.

Ham. O throw away the worser part of it,
And liue the purer with the other halfe.
Good night, but go not to mine Vnkles bed,
Assume a Vertue, if you haue it not, refraine to night,
And that shall lend a kinde of easinesse
To the next abstinence. Once more goodnight,
And when you are desirous to be blest,
Ile blessing begge of you. For this same Lord,
I do repent: but heauen hath pleas'd it so,
To punish me with this, and this with me,
That I must be their Scourge and Minister.
I will bestow him, and will answer well
The death I gaue him: so againe, good night.
I must be cruell, onely to be kinde;
Thus bad begins, and worse remaines behinde.

Qu. What shall I do?

Ham. Not this by no meanes that I bid you do:
Let the blunt King tempt you againe to bed,
Pinch Wanton on your cheeke, call you his Mouse,
And let him for a paire of reechie kisses,

Or padling in your necke with his damn'd Fingers,
Make you to rauell all this matter out,
That I essentially am not in madnesse,
But made in craft. 'Twere good you let him know,
For who that's but a Queene, faire, sober, wise,
Would from a Paddocke, from a Bat, a Gibbe,
Such deere concernings hide, Who would do so,
No in despight of Sense and Secrecie,
Vnpegge the Basket on the houses top:
Let the Birds flye, and like the famous Ape
To try Conclusions in the Basket, creepe
And breake your owne necke downe.

 Qu. Be thou assur'd, if words be made of breath,
And breath of life: I haue no life to breath
What thou hast saide to me.

 Ham. I must to England, you know that?
 Qu. Alacke I had forgot: 'Tis so concluded on.
 Ham. This man shall set me packing:
Ile lugge the Guts into the Neighbor roome,
Mother goodnight. Indeede this Counsellor
Is now most still, most secret, and most graue,
Who was in life, a foolish prating Knaue.
Come sir, to draw toward an end with you.
Good night Mother.

Exit Hamlet tugging in Polonius.
Enter King.

 King. There's matters in these sighes.
These profound heaues
You must translate; Tis fit we vnderstand them.
Where is your Sonne?

 Qu. Ah my good Lord, what haue I seene to night?
 King. What *Gertrude*? How do's *Hamlet*?
 Qu. Mad as the Seas, and winde, when both contend
Which is the Mightier, in his lawlesse fit
Behinde the Arras, hearing something stirre,
He whips his Rapier out, and cries a Rat, a Rat,
And in his brainish apprehension killes
The vnseene good old man.

 King. Oh heauy deed:
It had bin so with vs had we beene there:
His Liberty is full of threats to all,
To you your selfe, to vs, to euery one.
Alas, how shall this bloody deede be answered?
It will be laide to vs, whose prouidence
Should haue kept short, restrain'd, and out of haunt,
This mad yong man. But so much was our loue,
We would not vnderstand what was most fit,
But like the Owner of a foule disease,
To keepe it from divulging, let's it feede
Euen on the pith of life. Where is he gone?

 Qu. To draw apart the body he hath kild,
O're whom his very madnesse like some Oare
Among a Minerall of Mettels base
Shewes it selfe pure. He weepes for what is done.

 King. Oh *Gertrude*, come away?
The Sun no sooner shall the Mountaines touch,
But we will ship him hence, and this vilde deed,
We must with all our Maiesty and Skill
Both countenance, and excuse. *Enter Ros & Guild.*
Ho *Guildenstern*:
Friends both go ioyne you with some further ayde:
Hamlet in madnesse hath *Polonius* slaine,
And from his Mother Closset's hath he drag'd him.
Go seeke him out, speake faire, and bring the body
Into the Chappell. I pray you hast in this. *Exit Gent.*
Come *Gertrude*, wee'l call vp our wisest friends,

To let them know both what we meane to do,
And what's vntimely done. Oh come away,
My soule is full of discord and dismay. *Exeunt.*

Enter Hamlet.

 Ham. Safely stowed.
 Gentlemen within. *Hamlet*, Lord *Hamlet*.
 Ham. What noise? Who cals on *Hamlet*?
Oh heere they come. *Enter Ros. and Guildensterne.*

 Ro. What haue you done my Lord with the dead body?
 Ham. Compounded it with dust, whereto 'tis Kinne.
 Rosin. Tell vs where 'tis, that we may take it thence,
And beare it to the Chappell.

 Ham. Do not beleeue it.
 Rosin. Beleeue what?
 Ham. That I can keepe your counsell, and not mine
owne. Besides, to be demanded of a Spundge, what replication should be made by the Sonne of a King.

 Rosin. Take you me for a Spundge, my Lord?
 Ham. I sir, that sokes vp the Kings Countenance, his
Rewards, his Authorities (but such Officers do the King
best seruice in the end. He keepes them like an Ape in
the corner of his iaw, first mouth'd to be last swallowed,
when he needes what you haue glean'd, it is but squee-
zing you, and Spundge you shall be dry againe.

 Rosin. I vnderstand you not my Lord.
 Ham. I am glad of it: a knauish speech sleepes in a
foolish eare.

 Rosin. My Lord, you must tell vs where the body is,
and go with vs to the King.

 Ham. The body is with the King, but the King is not
with the body. The King, is a thing ———

 Guild. A thing my Lord?
 Ham. Of nothing: bring me to him, hide Fox, and all
after. *Exeunt*

Enter King.

 King. I haue sent to seeke him, and to find the bodie:
How dangerous is it that this man goes loose:
Yet must not we put the strong Law on him:
Hee's loued of the distracted multitude,
Who like not in their iudgement, but their eyes:
And where 'tis so, th'Offenders scourge is weigh'd
But neerer the offence: to beare all smooth, and euen,
This sodaine sending him away, must seeme
Deliberate pause, diseases desperate growne,
By desperate appliance are releeued,
Or not at all. *Enter Rosincrane.*
How now? What hath befalne?

 Rosin. Where the dead body is bestow'd my Lord,
We cannot get from him.

 King. But where is he?
 Rosin. Without my Lord, guarded to know your
pleasure.

 King. Bring him before vs.
 Rosin. Hoa, *Guildensterne*? Bring in my Lord.

Enter Hamlet and Guildensterne.

 King. Now *Hamlet*, where's *Polonius*?
 Ham. At Supper.
 King. At Supper? Where?
 Ham. Not where he eats, but where he is eaten, a certaine connocation of wormes are e'ne at him. Your worm
is your onely Emperor for diet. We fat all creatures else
to fat vs, and we fat our selfe for Magots. Your fat King,
and your leane Begger is but variable seruice to dishes,
but to one Table that's the end.

 King. What dost thou meane by this?
  Ham.

Ham. Nothing but to shew you how a King may go a Progresse through the guts of a Begger.

King. Where is *Polonius*.

Ham. In heauen, send thither to see. If your Messenger finde him not there, seeke him i'th other place your selfe: but indeed, if you finde him not this moneth, you shall nose him as you go vp the staires into the Lobby.

King. Go seeke him there.

Ham. He will stay till ye come.

K. *Hamlet*, this deed of thine, for thine especial safety Which we do tender, as we deerely greeue For that which thou hast done, must send thee hence With fierie Quicknesse. Therefore prepare thy selfe, The Barke is readie, and the winde at helpe, Th'Associates tend, and euery thing at bent For England.

Ham. For England?

King. I *Hamlet*.

Ham. Good.

King. So is it, if thou knew'st our purposes.

Ham. I see a Cherube that see's him: but come, for England. Farewell deere Mother.

King. Thy louing Father *Hamlet*.

Hamlet. My Mother: Father and Mother is man and wife: man & wife is one flesh, and so my mother. Come, for England. *Exit*

King. Follow him at foote, Tempt him with speed aboord: Delay it not, Ile haue him hence to night. Away, for euery thing is Seal'd and done That else leanes on th'Affaire, pray you make hast. And England, if my loue thou holdst at ought, As my great power thereof may giue thee sense, Since yet thy Cicatrice lookes raw and red After the Danish Sword, and thy free awe Payes homage to vs; thou maist not coldly set Our Soueraigne Processe, which imports at full By Letters coniuring to that effect The present death of *Hamlet*. Do it England, For like the Hecticke in my blood he rages, And thou must cure me: Till I know 'tis done, How ere my happes, my ioyes were ne're begun. *Exit*

Enter Fortinbras with an Armie.

For. Go Captaine, from me greet the Danish King, Tell him that by his licence, *Fortinbras* Claimes the conueyance of a promis'd March Ouer his Kingdome. You know the Rendeuous: If that his Maiesty would ought with vs, We shall expresse our dutie in his eye, And let him know so.

Cap. I will doo't, my Lord.

For. Go safely on. *Exit.*

Enter Queene and Horatio.

Qu. I will not speake with her.

Hor. She is importunate, indeed distract, her moode will needs be pittied.

Qu. What would she haue?

Hor. She speakes much of her Father; saies she heares There trickes i'th'world, and hems, and beats her heart, Spurns enuiously at Strawes, speakes things in doubt, That carry but halfe sense: Her speech is nothing, Yet the vnshaped vse of it doth moue The hearers to Collection; they ayme at it, And botch the words vp fit to their owne thoughts, Which as her winkes, and nods, and gestures yeeld them,

Indeed would make one thinke there would be thought, Though nothing sure, yet much vnhappily.

Qu. 'Twere good she were spoken with, For she may strew dangerous coniectures In ill breeding minds. Let her come in. To my sicke soule (as sinnes true Nature is) Each toy seemes Prologue, to some great amisse, So full of Artlesse iealousie is guilt, It spill's it selfe, in fearing to be spilt.

Enter Ophelia distracted.

Ophe. Where is the beauteous Maiesty of Denmark.

Qu. How now *Ophelia*?

Ophe. How should I your true loue know from another one? By his Cockle hat and staffe, and his Sandal shoone.

Qu. Alas sweet Lady: what imports this Song?

Ophe. Say you? Nay pray you marke.
He is dead and gone Lady, he is dead and gone,
At his head a grasse-greene Turfe, at his heeles a stone.

Enter King.

Qu. Nay but *Ophelia*.

Ophe. Pray you marke.
White his Shrow'd as the Mountaine Snow.

Qu. Alas, looke heere my Lord.

Ophe. Larded with sweet flowers:
Which bewept to the graue did not go,
With true-loue showres.

King. How do ye, pretty Lady?

Ophe. Well, God dil'd you. They say the Owle was a Bakers daughter. Lord, wee know what we are, but know not what we may be. God be at your Table.

King. Conceit vpon her Father.

Ophe. Pray you let's haue no words of this: but when they aske you what it meanes, say you this:
To morrow is S. Valentines day, all in the morning betime,
And I a Maid at your Window, to be your Valentine.
Then vp he rose, & don'd his clothes, & dupt the chamber dore,
Let in the Maid, that out a Maid, neuer departed more.

King. Pretty *Ophelia*.

Ophe. Indeed la? without an oath Ile make an end on't.
By gis, and by S. Charity,
Alacke, and fie for shame:
Yong men wil doo't, if they come too't,
By Cocke they are too blame.
Quoth she before you tumbled me,
You promis'd me to Wed:
So would I ha done by yonder Sunne,
And thou hadst not come to my bed.

King. How long hath she bin this?

Ophe. I hope all will be well. We must bee patient, but I cannot choose but weepe, to thinke they should lay him i'th'cold ground: My brother shall knowe of it, and so I thanke you for your good counsell. Come, my Coach: Goodnight Ladies: Goodnight sweet Ladies: Goodnight, goodnight. *Exit.*

King. Follow her close, Giue her good watch I pray you: Oh this is the poyson of deepe greefe, it springs All from her Fathers death. Oh *Gertrude, Gertrude*, When sorrowes comes, they come not single spies, But in Battaliaes. First, her Father slaine, Next your Sonne gone, and he most violent Author Of his owne iust remoue: the people muddied, Thicke and vnwholsome in their thoughts, and whispers For good *Polonius* death; and we haue done but greenly In hugger mugger to interre him. Poore *Ophelia* Diuided from her selfe, and her faire Iudgement,

Without

Without the which we are Pictures, or meere Beasts.
Last, and as much containing as all these,
Her Brother is in secret come from France,
Keepes on his wonder, keepes himselfe in clouds,
And wants not Buzzers to infect his eare
With pestilent Speeches of his Fathers death,
Where in necessitie of matter Beggard,
Will nothing sticke our persons to Arraigne
In eare and eare. O my deere *Gertrude*, this,
Like to a murdering Peece in many places,
Giues me superfluous death. *A Noise within.*

Enter a Messenger.

Qu. Alacke, what noyse is this?
King. Where are my *Switzers*?
Let them guard the doore. What is the matter?
Mes. Saue your selfe, my Lord.
The Ocean (ouer-peering of his List)
Eates not the Flats with more impittious haste
Then young *Laertes*, in a Riotous head,
Ore-beares your Officers, the rabble call him Lord,
And as the world were now but to begin,
Antiquity forgot, Custome not knowne,
The Ratifiers and props of euery word,
They cry choose we? *Laertes* shall be King.
Caps, hands, and tongues, applaud it to the clouds,
Laertes shall be King, *Laertes* King.

Qu. How cheerefully on the false Traile they cry,
Oh this is Counter you false *Danish Dogges.*

Noise within. *Enter Laertes.*

King. The doores are broke.
Laer. Where is the King, sirs? Stand you all without.
All. No, let's come in.
Laer. I pray you giue me leaue.
Al. We will, we will.
Laer. I thanke you: Keepe the doore.
Oh thou vilde King, giue me my Father.
Qu. Calmely good *Laertes.*
Laer. That drop of blood, that calmes
Proclaimes me Bastard:
Cries Cuckold to my Father, brands the Harlot
Euen heere betweene the chaste vnsmirched brow
Of my true Mother.
King. What is the cause *Laertes*,
That thy Rebellion lookes so Gyant-like?
Let him go *Gertrude*: Do not feare our person:
There's such Diuinity doth hedge a King,
That Treason can but peepe to what it would,
Acts little of his will. Tell me *Laertes*,
Why thou art thus Incenst? Let him go *Gertrude.*
Speake man.
Laer. Where's my Father?
King. Dead.
Qu. But not by him.
King. Let him demand his fill.
Laer. How came he dead? Ile not be Iuggel'd with.
To hell Allegeance: Vowes, to the blackest diuell.
Conscience and Grace, to the profoundest Pit.
I dare Damnation: to this point I stand,
That both the worlds I giue to negligence,
Let come what comes: onely Ile be reueng'd
Most throughly for my Father.
King. Who shall stay you?
Laer. My Will, not all the world,
And for my meanes, Ile husband them so well,
They shall go farre with little.

King. Good *Laertes*:
If you desire to know the certaintie
Of your deere Fathers death, if writ in your reuenge,
That Soop-stake you will draw both Friend and Foe,
Winner and Looser.
Laer. None but his Enemies.
King. Will you know them then.
La. To his good Friends, thus wide Ile ope my Armes:
And like the kinde Life-rend'ring Politician,
Repast them with my blood.
King. Why now you speake
Like a good Childe, and a true Gentleman,
That I am guiltlesse of your Fathers death,
And am most sensible in greefe for it,
It shall as leuell to your Iudgement pierce
As day do's to your eye.
A noise within. Let her come in.
Enter Ophelia.

Laer. How now? what noise is that?
Oh heate drie vp my Braines, teares seuen times salt,
Burne out the Sence and Vertue of mine eye.
By Heauen, thy madnesse shall be payed by waight,
Till our Scale turnes the beame. Oh Rose of May,
Deere Maid, kinde Sister, sweet *Ophelia*:
Oh Heauens, is't possible, a yong Maids wits,
Should be as mortall as an old mans life?
Nature is fine in Loue, and where 'tis fine,
It sends some precious instance of it selfe
After the thing it loues.
Ophe. *They bore him bare fac'd on the Beer,*
Hey non nony, nony, hey nony:
And on his graue raines many a teare,
Fare you well my Doue.

Laer. Had'st thou thy wits, and did'st pursuade Reuenge, it could not moue thus.
Ophe. You must sing downe a-downe, and you call him a-downe-a. Oh, how the wheele becomes it? It is the false Steward that stole his masters daughter.
Laer. This nothings more then matter.
Ophe. There's Rosemary, that's for Remembraunce. Pray loue remember: and there is Paconcies, that's for Thoughts.
Laer. A document in madnesse, thoughts & remembrance fitted.
Ophe. There's Fennell for you, and Columbnes: ther's Rew for you, and heere's some for me. Wee may call it Herbe-Grace a Sundaies: Oh you must weare your Rew with a difference. There's a Daysie, I would giue you some Violets, but they wither'd all when my father dyed: They say, he made a good end;

For bonny sweet Robin is all my ioy.

Laer. Thought, and Affliction, Passion, Hell it selfe:
She turnes to Fauour, and to prettinesse.
Ophe. *And will he not come againe,*
And will he not come againe:
No, no, he is dead, go to thy Death-bed,
He neuer wil come againe.
His Beard as white as Snow,
All Flaxen was his Pole:
He is gone, he is gone, and we cast away mone,
Gramercy on his Soule.
And of all Christian Soules, I pray God.
God buy ye. *Exeunt Ophelia*
Laer. Do you see this, you Gods?
King. Laertes, I must common with your greefe,
Or you deny me right: go but apart,

Make

Make choice of whom your wisest Friends you will,
And they shall heare and iudge 'twixt you and me;
If by direct or by Colaterall hand
They finde vs touch'd, we will our Kingdome giue,
Our Crowne, our Life, and all that we call Ours
To you in satisfaction. But if not,
Be you content to lend your patience to vs,
And we shall ioyntly labour with your soule
To giue it due content.

   Laer. Let this be so:
His meanes of death, his obscure buriall;
No Trophee, Sword, nor Hatchment o're his bones,
No Noble rite, nor formall ostentation,
Cry to be heard, as 'twere from Heauen to Earth,
That I must call in question.

   King. So you shall:
And where th'offence is, let the great Axe fall.
I pray you go with me.   *Exeunt*

Enter Horatio, with an Attendant.

   Hora. What are they that would speake with me?
   Ser. Saylors sir, they say they haue Letters for you.
   Hor. Let them come in,
I do not know from what part of the world
I should be greeted, if not from Lord *Hamlet.*

Enter Saylor.

   Say. God blesse you Sir.
   Hor. Let him blesse thee too.
   Say. Hee shall Sir, and't please him. There's a Letter for you Sir: It comes from th'Ambassadours that was bound for England, if your name be *Horatio*, as I am let to know it is.

Reads the Letter.

Horatio, *When thou shalt haue overlook'd this, giue these Fellowes some meanes to the King: They haue Letters for him. Ere we were two dayes old at Sea, a Pyrate of very Warlicke appointment gaue vs Chace. Finding our selues too slow of Saile, we put on a compelled Valour. In the Grapple, I boorded them: On the instant they got cleare of our Shippe, so I alone became their Prisoner. They haue dealt with mee, like Theeues of Mercy, but they knew what they did. I am to doe a good turne for them. Let the King haue the Letters I haue sent, and repaire thou to me with as much hast as thou wouldest flye death. I haue words to speake in your eare, will make thee dumbe, yet are they much too light for the bore of the Matter. These good Fellowes will bring thee where I am.* Rosincrance *and* Guildensterne, *hold their course for England. Of them I haue much to tell thee, Farewell.*

                  He that thou knowest thine,
                  Hamlet.

Come, I will giue you way for these your Letters,
And do't the speedier, that you may direct me
To him from whom you brought them.   *Exit.*

Enter King and Laertes.

   King. Now must your conscience my acquittance seal,
And you must put me in your heart for Friend,
Sith you haue heard, and with a knowing eare,
That he which hath your Noble Father slaine,
Pursued my life.

   Laer. It well appeares. But tell me,
Why you proceeded not against these feates,
So crimefull, and so Capitall in Nature,
As by your Safety, Wisedome, all things else,
You mainly were stirr'd vp?

   King. O for two speciall Reasons,
Which may to you (perhaps) seeme much vnsinnowed,
And yet to me they are strong. The Queen his Mother,
Liues almost by his lookes: and for my selfe,
My Vertue or my Plague, be it either which,
She's so coniunctiue to my life and soule;
That as the Starre moues not but in his Sphere,
I could not but by her. The other Motiue,
Why to a publike count I might not go,
Is the great loue the generall gender beare him,
Who dipping all his Faults in their affection,
Would like the Spring that turneth Wood to Stone,
Conuert his Gyues to Graces. So that my Arrowes
Too slightly timbred for so loud a Winde,
Would haue reuerted to my Bow againe,
And not where I had arm'd them.

   Laer. And so haue I a Noble Father lost,
A Sister driuen into desperate tearmes,
Who was (if praises may go backe againe)
Stood Challenger on mount of all the Age
For her perfections. But my reuenge will come.

   King. Breake not your sleepes for that,
You must not thinke
That we are made of stuffe, so flat, and dull,
That we can let our Beard be shooke with danger,
And thinke it pastime. You shortly shall heare more,
I lou'd your Father, and we loue our Selfe,
And that I hope will teach you to imagine——

Enter a Messenger.

How now? What Newes?
   Mes. Letters my Lord from *Hamlet.* This to your Maiesty: this to the Queene.
   King. From *Hamlet?* Who brought them?
   Mes. Saylors my Lord they say, I saw them not: They were giuen me by *Claudio*, he receiu'd them.
   King. Laertes you shall heare them:
Leaue vs.   *Exit Messenger*

High and Mighty, *you shall know I am set naked on your Kingdome. To morrow shall I begge leaue to see your Kingly Eyes. When I shall (first asking your Pardon thereunto) recount th'Occasions of my sodaine, and more strange returne.*
                  Hamlet.

What should this meane? Are all the rest come backe?
Or is it some abuse? Or no such thing?
   Laer. Know you the hand?
   Kin. 'Tis *Hamlets* Character, naked and in a Postscript here he sayes alone: Can you aduise me?
   Laer. I'm lost in it my Lord; but let him come,
It warmes the very sicknesse in my heart,
That I shall liue and tell him to his teeth;
Thus diddest thou.
   Kin. If it be so *Laertes*, as how should it be so:
How otherwise will you be rul'd by me?
   Laer. If so you'l not o'rerule me to a peace.
   Kin. To thine owne peace: if he be now return'd,
As checking at his Voyage, and that he meanes
No more to vndertake it; I will worke him
To an exployt now ripe in my Deuice,
Vnder the which he shall not choose but fall;
And for his death no winde of blame shall breath,
But euen his Mother shall vncharge the practice,
And call it accident: Some two Monthes hence
Here was a Gentleman of *Normandy*,
I'ue seene my selfe, and seru'd against the French,
And they ran well on Horsebacke; but this Gallant

Had witchcraft in't; he grew into his Seat,
And to such wondrous doing brought his Horse,
As had he beene encorps't and demy-Natur'd
With the braue Beast, so farre he past my thought,
That I in forgery of shapes and trickes,
Come short of what he did.

  Laer. A Norman was't?
  Kin. A Norman.
  Laer. Vpon my life *Lamound.*
  Kin. The very same.
  Laer. I know him well, he is the Brooch indeed,
And Iemme of all our Nation.
  Kin. Hee mad confession of you,
And gaue you such a Masterly report,
For Art and exercise in your defence;
And for your Rapier most especially,
That he cryed out, t'would be a sight indeed,
If one could match you Sir. This report of his
Did *Hamlet* so envenom with his Enuy,
That he could nothing doe but wish and begge,
Your sodaine comming ore to play with him;
Now out of this.
  Laer. Why out of this, my Lord?
  Kin. Laertes was your Father deare to you?
Or are you like the painting of a sorrow,
A face without a heart?
  Laer. Why aske you this?
  Kin. Not that I thinke you did not loue your Father,
But that I know Loue is begun by Time:
And that I see in passages of proofe,
Time qualifies the sparke and fire of it:
Hamlet comes backe: what would you vndertake,
To show your selfe your Fathers sonne indeed,
More then in words?
  Laer. To cut his throat i'th' Church.
  Kin. No place indeed should murder Sancturize;
Reuenge should haue no bounds: but good *Laertes*
Will you doe this, keepe close within your Chamber,
Hamlet return'd, shall know you are come home:
Wee'l put on those shall praise your excellence,
And set a double varnish on the fame
The Frenchman gaue you, bring you in fine together,
And wager on your heads, he being remisse,
Most generous, and free from all contriuing,
Will not peruse the Foiles? So that with ease,
Or with a little shuffling, you may choose
A Sword vnbaited, and in a passe of practice,
Requit him for your Father.
  Laer. I will doo't,
And for that purpose Ile annoint my Sword:
I bought an Vnction of a Mountebanke
So mortall, I but dipt a knife in it,
Where it drawes blood, no Cataplasme so rare,
Collected from all Simples that haue Vertue
Vnder the Moone, can saue the thing from death,
That is but scratcht withall: Ile touch my point,
With this contagion, that if I gall him slightly,
It may be death.
  Kin. Let's further thinke of this,
Weigh what conuenience both of time and meanes
May fit vs to our shape, if this should faile;
And that our drift looke through our bad performance,
'Twere better not assaid; therefore this Proiect
Should haue a backe or second, that might hold,
If this should blast in proofe: Soft, let me see
Wee'l make a solemne wager on your commings,
I ha't: when in your motion you are hot and dry,
As make your bowts more violent to the end,
And that he cals for drinke; Ile haue prepar'd him
A Challice for the nonce; whereon but sipping,
If he by chance escape your venom'd stuck,
Our purpose may hold there; how sweet Queene.

Enter Queene.

  Queen. One woe doth tread vpon anothers heele,
So fast they'l follow: your Sister's drown'd *Laertes.*
  Laer. Drown'd! O where?
  Queen. There is a Willow growes aslant a Brooke,
That shewes his hore leaues in the glassie streame:
There with fantasticke Garlands did she come,
Of Crow-flowers, Nettles, Daysies, and long Purples,
That liberall Shepheards giue a grosser name;
But our cold Maids doe Dead Mens Fingers call them:
There on the pendant boughes, her Coronet weeds
Clambring to hang; an enuious sliuer broke,
When downe the weedy Trophies, and her selfe,
Fell in the weeping Brooke, her cloathes spred wide,
And Mermaid-like, a while they bore her vp,
Which time she chaunted snatches of old tunes,
As one incapable of her owne distresse,
Or like a creature Natiue, and indued
Vnto that Element: but long it could not be,
Till that her garments, heauy with her drinke,
Pul'd the poore wretch from her melodious buy,
To muddy death.
  Laer. Alas then, is she drown'd?
  Queen. Drown'd, drown'd.
  Laer. Too much of water hast thou poore *Ophelia,*
And therefore I forbid my teares: but yet
It is our tricke, Nature her custome holds,
Let shame say what it will; when these are gone
The woman will be out: Adue my Lord,
I haue a speech of fire, that faine would blaze,
But that this folly doubts it.   *Exit.*
  Kin. Let's follow, *Gertrude:*
How much I had to doe to calme his rage?
Now feare I this will giue it start againe;
Therefore let's follow.   *Exeunt.*

Enter two Clownes.

  Clown. Is she to bee buried in Christian buriall, that wilfully seekes her owne saluation?
  Other. I tell thee she is, and therefore make her Graue straight, the Crowner hath sate on her, and finds it Christian buriall.
  Clo. How can that be, vnlesse she drowned her selfe in her owne defence?
  Other. Why 'tis found so.
  Clo. It must be *Se offendendo*, it cannot bee else: for heere lies the point; If I drowne my selfe wittingly, it argues an Act: and an Act hath three branches. It is an Act to doe and to performe; argall she drown'd her selfe wittingly.
  Other. Nay but heare you Goodman Deluer.
  Clown. Giue me leaue; heere lies the water; good: heere stands the man; good: If the man goe to this water and drowne himsele; it is will he, nill he, he goes; marke you that? But if the water come to him & drowne him; hee drownes not himselfe. Argall, hee that is not guilty of his owne death, shortens not his owne life.
  Other. But is this law?
  Clo. I marry is't, Crowners Quest Law.

Other. Will you ha the truth on't: if this had not beene a Gentlewoman, shee should haue beene buried out of Christian Buriall.

Clo. Why there thou say'st. And the more pitty that great folke should haue countenance in this world to drowne or hang themselues, more then their euen Christian. Come, my Spade; there is no ancient Gentlemen, but Gardiners, Ditchers and Graue-makers; they hold vp *Adams* Profession.

Other. Was he a Gentleman?

Clo. He was the first that euer bore Armes.

Other. Why he had none.

Clo. What, ar't a Heathen? how dost thou vnderstand the Scripture? the Scripture sayes *Adam* dig'd; could hee digge without Armes? Ile put another question to thee: if thou answerest me not to the purpose, confesse thy selfe——

Other. Go too.

Clo. What is he that builds stronger then either the Mason, the Shipwright, or the Carpenter?

Other. The Gallowes maker; for that Frame outliues a thousand Tenants.

Clo. I like thy wit well in good faith, the Gallowes does well; but how does it well? it does well to those that doe ill: now, thou dost ill to say the Gallowes is built stronger then the Church: Argall, the Gallowes may doe well to thee. Too't againe, Come.

Other. Who builds stronger then a Mason, a Shipwright, or a Carpenter?

Clo. I, tell me that, and vnyoake.

Other. Marry, now I can tell.

Clo. Too't.

Other. Masse, I cannot tell.

Enter Hamlet and Horatio a farre off.

Clo. Cudgell thy braines no more about it; for your dull Asse will not mend his pace with beating; and when you are ask't this question next, say a Graue-maker: the Houses that he makes, lasts till Doomesday: go, get thee to *Yaughan*, fetch me a stoupe of Liquor.

Sings.
In youth when I did loue, did loue,
me thought it was very sweete :
To contract O the time for a my behoue,
O me thought there was nothing meete.

Ham. Ha's this fellow no feeling of his businesse, that he sings at Graue-making?

Hor. Custome hath made it in him a property of easinesse.

Ham. 'Tis ee'n so; the hand of little Imployment hath the daintier sense.

Clowne sings.
But Age with his stealing steps
hath caught me in his clutch :
And hath shipped me intill the Land,
as if I had neuer beene such.

Ham. That Scull had a tongue in it, and could sing once: how the knaue iowles it to th' grownd, as if it were *Caines* Iaw-bone, that did the first murther: It might be the Pate of a Politician which this Asse o're Offices: one that could circumuent God, might it not?

Hor. It might, my Lord.

Ham. Or of a Courtier, which could say, Good Morrow sweet Lord: how dost thou, good Lord? this might be my Lord such a one, that prais'd my Lord such a ones Horse, when he meant to begge it; might it not?

Hor. I, my Lord.

Ham. Why ee'n so: and now my Lady Wormes, Chaplesse, and knockt about the Mazard with a Sextons Spade; heere's fine Reuolution, if wee had the tricke to see't. Did these bones cost no more the breeding, but to play at Loggets with 'em? mine ake to thinke on't.

Clowne sings.
A Pickhaxe and a Spade, a Spade,
for and a shrowding-Sheete :
O a Pit of Clay for to be made,
for such a Guest is meete.

Ham. There's another: why might not that bee the Scull of of a Lawyer? where be his Quiddits now? his Quillets? his Cases? his Tenures, and his Tricks? why doe's he suffer this rude knaue now to knocke him about the Sconce with a dirty Shouell, and will not tell him of his Action of Battery? hum. This fellow might be in's time a great buyer of Land, with his Statutes, his Recognizances, his Fines, his double Vouchers, his Recoueries: Is this the fine of his Fines, and the recouery of his Recoueries, to haue his fine Pate full of fine Dirt? will his Vouchers vouch him no more of his Purchases, and double ones too, then the length and breadth of a paire of Indentures? the very Conueyances of his Lands will hardly lye in this Boxe; and must the Inheritor himselfe haue no more? ha?

Hor. Not a iot more, my Lord.

Ham. Is not Parchment made of Sheep-skinnes?

Hor. I my Lord, and of Calue-skinnes too.

Ham. They are Sheepe and Calues that seek out assurance in that. I will speake to this fellow: whose Graue's this Sir?

Clo. Mine Sir:
O a Pit of Clay for to be made,
for such a Guest is meete.

Ham. I thinke it be thine indeed: for thou liest in't.

Clo. You lye out on't Sir, and therefore it is not yours: for my part, I doe not lye in't; and yet it is mine.

Ham. Thou dost lye in't, to be in't and say 'tis thine: 'tis for the dead, not for the quicke, therefore thou lyest.

Clo. 'Tis a quicke lye Sir, 'twill away againe from me to you.

Ham. What man dost thou digge it for?

Clo. For no man Sir.

Ham. What woman then?

Clo. For none neither.

Ham. Who is to be buried in't?

Clo. One that was a woman Sir; but rest her Soule, shee's dead.

Ham. How absolute the knaue is? wee must speake by the Carde, or equiuocation will vndoe vs: by the Lord *Horatio*, these three yeares I haue taken note of it, the Age is growne so picked, that the toe of the Pesant comes so neere the heeles of our Courtier, hee galls his Kibe. How long hast thou been a Graue-maker?

Clo. Of all the dayes i'th' yeare, I came too't that day that our last King *Hamlet* o'recame *Fortinbras.*

Ham. How long is that since?

Clo. Cannot you tell that? euery foole can tell that: It was the very day, that young *Hamlet* was borne, hee that was mad, and sent into England.

Ham. I marry, why was he sent into England?

Clo. Why, because he was mad; hee shall recouer his wits there; or if he do not, it's no great matter there.

Ham.

Ham. Why?

Clo. 'Twill not be seene in him, there the men are as mad as he.

Ham. How came he mad?

Clo. Very strangely they say.

Ham. How strangely?

Clo. Faith e'ene with loosing his wits.

Ham. Vpon what ground?

Clo. Why heere in Denmarke: I haue bin sixeteene heere, man and Boy thirty yeares.

Ham. How long will a man lie 'ith' earth ere he rot?

Clo. Ifaith, if he be not rotten before he die (as we haue many pocky Coarses now adaies, that will scarce hold the laying in) he will last you some eight yeare, or nine yeare. A Tanner will last you nine yeare.

Ham. Why he, more then another?

Clo. Why sir, his hide is so tan'd with his Trade, that he will keepe out water a great while. And your water, is a sore Decayer of your horson dead body. Heres a Scull now: this Scul, has laine in the earth three & twenty years.

Ham. Whose was it?

Clo. A whoreson mad Fellowes it was; Whose doe you thinke it was?

Ham. Nay, I know not.

Clo. A pestilence on him for a mad Rogue, a pou'rd a Flaggon of Renish on my head once: This same Scull Sir, this same Scull sir, was *Yoricks* Scull, the Kings lester.

Ham. This?

Clo. E'ene that.

Ham. Let me see. Alas poore *Yorick*, I knew him *Horatio*, a fellow of infinite Iest; of most excellent fancy, he hath borne me on his backe a thousand times: And how abhorred my Imagination is, my gorge rises at it. Heere hung those lipps, that I haue kist I know not how oft. VVhere be your Iibes now? Your Gambals? Your Songs? Your flashes of Merriment that were wont to set the Table on a Rore? No one now to mock your own Ieering? Quite chopfalne? Now get you to my Ladies Chamber, and tell her, let her paint an inch thicke, to this fauour she must come. Make her laugh at that: prythee *Horatio* tell me one thing.

Hor. What's that my Lord?

Ham. Dost thou thinke *Alexander* lookt o'this fashion i'th' earth?

Hor. E'ene so.

Ham. And smelt so? Puh.

Hor. E'ene so, my Lord.

Ham. To what base vses we may returne *Horatio*. Why may not Imagination trace the Noble dust of *Alexander*, till he find it stopping a bunghole.

Hor. 'Twere to consider: to curiously to consider so.

Ham. No faith, not a iot. But to follow him thether with modestie enough, & likelichood to lead it; as thus. *Alexander* died: *Alexander* was buried: *Alexander* returneth into dust; the dust is earth; of earth we make Lome, and why of that Lome (whereto he was conuerted) might they not stopp a Beere-barrell? Imperiall *Cæsar*, dead and turn'd to clay, Might stop a hole to keepe the winde away. Oh, that that earth, which kept the world in awe, Should patch a Wall, t'expell the winters flaw. But soft, but soft, aside; heere comes the King.

Enter King, Queene, Laertes, and a Coffin, with Lords attendant.

The Queene, the Courtiers. Who is that they follow, And with such maimed rites? This doth betoken, The Coarse they follow, did with disperate hand, Fore do it owne life; 'twas some Estate. Couch we a while, and mark.

Laer. What Cerimony else?

Ham. That is *Laertes*, a very Noble youth: Marke.

Laer. What Cerimony else?

Priest. Her Obsequies haue bin as farre inlarg'd, As we haue warrantis, her death was doubtfull, And but that great Command, o're-swaies the order, She should in ground vnsanctified haue lodg'd, Till the last Trumpet. For charitable praier, Shardes, Flints, and Peebles, should be throwne on her: Yet heere she is allowed her Virgin Rites, Her Maiden strewments, and the bringing home Of Bell and Buriall.

Laer. Must there no more be done?

Priest. No more be done: We should prophane the seruice of the dead, To sing sage *Requiem*, and such rest to her As to peace-parted Soules.

Laer. Lay her i'th' earth, And from her faire and vnpolluted flesh, May Violets spring. I tell thee (churlish Priest) A Ministring Angell shall my Sister be, When thou liest howling?

Ham. What, the faire *Ophelia*?

Queene. Sweets, to the sweet farewell. I hop'd thou should'st haue bin my *Hamlets* wife: I thought thy Bride-bed to haue deckt (sweet Maid) And not t'haue strew'd thy Graue.

Laer. Oh terrible woer, Fall ten times trebble, on that cursed head Whose wicked deed, thy most Ingenious sence Depriu'd thee of. Hold off the earth a while, Till I haue caught her once more in mine armes:

Leaps in the graue.

Now pile your dust, vpon the quicke, and dead, Till of this flat a Mountaine you haue made, To o're top old *Pelion*, or the skyish head Of blew *Olympus*.

Ham. What is he, whose griefes Beares such an Emphasis? whose phrase of Sorrow Coniure the wandring Starres, and makes them stand Like wonder-wounded hearers? This is I, *Hamlet* the Dane.

Laer. The deuill take thy soule.

Ham. Thou prai'st not well, I prythee take thy fingers from my throat; Sir though I am not Spleenatiue, and rash, Yet haue I something in me dangerous, Which let thy wisenesse feare. Away thy hand.

King. Pluck them asunder.

Qu. *Hamlet*, *Hamlet*.

Gen. Good my Lord be quiet.

Ham. Why I will fight with him vppon this Theme, Vntill my eielids will no longer wag.

Qu. Oh my Sonne, what Theame?

Ham. I lou'd *Ophelia*; fortie thousand Brothers Could not (with all there quantitie of Loue) Make vp my summe. What wilt thou do for her?

King. Oh he is mad *Laertes*,

Qu. For loue of God forbeare him.

Ham. Come show me what thou'lt doe. Woo't weepe? Woo't fight? Woo't teare thy selfe? Woo't drinke vp *Esile*, eate a Crocodile?

The Tragedie of Hamlet.

Ile doo't. Dost thou come heere to whine;
To outface me with leaping in her Graue?
Be buried quicke with her, and so will I.
And if thou prate of Mountaines; let them throw
Millions of Akers on vs; till our ground
Sindging his pate against the burning Zone,
Make *Ossa* like a wart. Nay, and thou't mouth,
Ile rant as well as thou.

Kin. This is meere Madnesse:
And thus awhile the fit will worke on him:
Anon as patient as the female Doue,
When that her golden Cuplet are disclos'd;
His silence will sit drooping.

Ham. Heare you Sir:
What is the reason that you vse me thus?
I lou'd vp you euer; but it is no matter:
Let *Hercules* himselfe doe what he may,
The Cat will Mew, and Dogge will haue his day. *Exit.*

Kin. I pray you good *Horatio* wait vpon him,
Strengthen your patience in our last nights speech,
Wee'l put the matter to the present push:
Good *Gertrude* set some watch ouer your Sonne,
This Graue shall haue a liuing Monument:
An houre of quiet shortly shall we see;
Till then, in patience our proceeding be. *Exeunt.*

Enter Hamlet and Horatio.

Ham. So much for this Sir; now let me see the other,
You doe remember all the Circumstance.

Hor. Remember it my Lord?

Ham. Sir, in my heart there was a kinde of fighting,
That would not let me sleepe; me thought I lay
Worse then the mutines in the Bilboes, rashly,
(And praise be rashnesse for it) let vs know,
Our indiscretion sometimes serues vs well,
When our deare plots do paule, and that should teach vs,
There's a Diuinity that shapes our ends,
Rough-hew them how we will.

Hor. That is most certaine.

Ham. Vp from my Cabin
My sea-gowne scarft about me in the darke,
Grop'd I to finde out them; had my desire,
Finger'd their Packet, and in fine, withdrew
To mine owne roome againe, making so bold,
(My feares forgetting manners) to vnseale
Their grand Commission, where I found *Horatio*,
Oh royall knauery: An exact command,
Larded with many seuerall sorts of reason;
Importing Denmarks health, and Englands too,
With hoo, such Bugges and Goblins in my life;
That on the superuize no leasure bated,
No not to stay the grinding of the Axe,
My head shoud be struck off.

Hor. Ist possible?

Ham. Here's the Commission, read it at more leysure:
But wilt thou heare me how I did proceed?

Hor. I beseech you.

Ham. Being thus benetted round with Villaines,
Ere I could make a Prologue to my braines,
They had begun the Play. I sate me downe,
Deuis'd a new Commission, wrote it faire,
I once did hold it as our Statists doe,
A basenesse to write faire; and laboured much
How to forget that learning: but Sir now,
It did me Yeomans seruice: wilt thou know
The effects of what I wrote?

Hor. I, good my Lord.

Ham. An earnest Coniuration from the King,
As England was his faithfull Tributary,
As loue betweene them, as the Palme should flourish,
As Peace should still her wheaten Garland weare,
And stand a Comma 'tweene their amities,
And many such like Assis of great charge,
That on the view and know of these Contents,
Without debatement further, more or lesse,
He should the bearers put to sodaine death,
Not shriuing time allowed.

Hor. How was this seal'd?

Ham. Why, euen in that was Heauen ordinate;
I had my fathers Signet in my Purse,
Which was the Modell of that Danish Seale:
Folded the Writ vp in forme of the other,
Subscrib'd it, gau't th' impression, plac't it safely,
The changeling neuer knowne: Now, the next day
Was our Sea Fight, and what to this was sement,
Thou know'st already.

Hor. So *Guildensterne* and *Rosincrance*, go too't.

Ham. Why man, they did make loue to this imployment
They are not neere my Conscience; their debate
Doth by their owne insinuation grow:
'Tis dangerous, when the baser nature comes
Betweene the passe, and fell incensed points
Of mighty opposites.

Hor. Why, what a King is this?

Ham. Does it not, thinkst thee, stand me now vpon
He that hath kil'd my King, and whor'd my Mother,
Popt in betweene th' election and my hopes,
Throwne out his Angle for my proper life,
And with such coozenage; is't not perfect conscience,
To quit him with this arme? And is't not to be damn'd
To let this Canker of our nature come
In further euill.

Hor. It must be shortly knowne to him from England
What is the issue of the businesse there.

Ham. It will be short,
The *interim's* mine, and a mans life's no more
Then to say one: but I am very sorry good *Horatio*,
That to *Laertes* I forgot my selfe;
For by the image of my Cause, I see
The Portraiture of his; Ile count his fauours:
But sure the brauery of his griefe did put me
Into a Towring passion.

Hor. Peace, who comes heere?

Enter young Osricke.

Osr. Your Lordship is right welcome back to Den-

Ham. I humbly thank you Sir, dost know this waterflie?

Hor. No my good Lord.

Ham. Thy state is the more gracious; for 'tis a vice to know him: he hath much Land, and fertile; let a Beast be Lord of Beasts, and his Crib shall stand at the Kings Messe; 'tis a Chowgh; but as I saw spacious in the possession of dirt.

Osr. Sweet Lord, if your friendship were at leysure, I should impart a thing to you from his Maiesty.

Ham. I will receiue it with all diligence of spirit; put your Bonet to his right vse, 'tis for the head.

Osr. I thanke your Lordship, 'tis very hot.

Ham. No, beleeue mee 'tis very cold, the winde is Northerly.

Osr. It is indifferent cold my Lord indeed.

Ham. Mee thinkes it is very soultry, and hot for my Complexion.

Osr. Exceedingly, my Lord, it is very soultry, as 'twere I cannot tell how: but my Lord, his Maiesty bad me signifie to you, that he ha's laid a great wager on your head: Sir, this is the matter.

Ham. I beseech you remember.

Osr. Nay, in good faith, for mine ease in good faith: Sir, you are not ignorant of what excellence *Laertes* is at his weapon.

Ham. What's his weapon?

Osr. Rapier and dagger.

Ham. That's two of his weapons; but well.

Osr. The sir King ha's wag'd with him six Barbary Horses, against the which he impon'd as I take it, sixe French Rapiers and Poniards, with their assignes, as Girdle, Hangers or so: three of the Carriages infaith are very deare to fancy, very responsiue to the hilts, most delicate carriages, and of very liberall conceit.

Ham. What call you the Carriages?

Osr. The Carriages Sir, are the hangers.

Ham. The phrase would bee more Germaine to the matter: If we could carry Cannon by our sides; I would it might be Hangers till then; but on sixe Barbary Horses against sixe French Swords: their Assignes, and three liberall conceited Carriages, that's the French but against the Danish; why is this impon'd as you call it?

Osr. The King Sir, hath laid that in a dozen passes betweene you and him, hee shall not exceed you three hits; He hath one twelue for mine, and that would come to imediate tryall, if your Lordship would vouchsafe the Answere.

Ham. How if I answere no?

Osr. I meane my Lord, the opposition of your person in tryall.

Ham. Sir, I will walke heere in the Hall; if it please his Maiestie, 'tis the breathing time of day with me; let the Foyles bee brought, the Gentleman willing, and the King hold his purpose; I will win for him if I can: if not, Ile gaine nothing but my shame, and the odde hits.

Osr. Shall I redeliuer you ee'n so?

Ham. To this effect Sir, after what flourish your nature will.

Osr. I commend my duty to your Lordship.

Ham. Yours, yours; hee does well to commend it himselfe, there are no tongues else for's tongue.

Hor. This Lapwing runs away with the shell on his head.

Ham. He did Complie with his Dugge before hee suck't it: thus had he and mine more of the same Beauy that I know the drossie age dotes on; only got the tune of the time, and outward habite of encounter, a kinde of yesty collection, which carries them through & through the most fond and winnowed opinions; and doe but blow them to their tryalls; the Bubbles are out.

Hor. You will lose this wager, my Lord.

Ham. I doe not thinke so, since he went into France, I haue beene in continuall practice; I shall winne at the oddes: but thou wouldest not thinke how all heere about my heart: but it is no matter.

Hor. Nay, good my Lord.

Ham. It is but foolery; but it is such a kinde of gain-giuing, as would perhaps trouble a woman.

Hor. If your minde dislike any thing, obey. I will forestall their repaire hither, and say you are not fit.

Ham. Not a whit, we defie Augury; there's a speciall Prouidence in the fall of a sparrow. If it be now, 'tis not to come: if it bee not to come, it will bee now: if it be not now; yet it will come; the readinesse is all, since no man ha's ought of what he leaues. What is't to leaue betimes?

Enter King, Queene, Laertes and Lords, with other Attendants with Foyles, and Gauntlets, a Table and Flagons of Wine on it.

Kin. Come *Hamlet*, come, and take this hand from me.

Ham. Giue me your pardon Sir, I'ue done you wrong, But pardon't as you are a Gentleman.
This presence knowes,
And you must needs haue heard how I am punisht
With sore distraction? What I haue done
That might your nature honour, and exception
Roughly awake, I heere proclaime was madnesse:
Was't *Hamlet* wrong'd *Laertes*? Neuer *Hamlet*.
If *Hamlet* from himselfe be tane away:
And when he's not himselfe, do's wrong *Laertes*,
Then *Hamlet* does it not, *Hamlet* denies it:
Who does it then? His Madnesse? If't be so,
Hamlet is of the Faction that is wrong'd,
His madnesse is poore *Hamlets* Enemy.
Sir, in this Audience,
Let my disclaiming from a purpos'd euill,
Free me so farre in your most generous thoughts,
That I haue shot mine Arrow o're the house,
And hurt my Mother.

Laer. I am satisfied in Nature,
Whose motiue in this case should stirre me most
To my Reuenge. But in my termes of Honor
I stand aloofe, and will no reconcilement,
Till by some elder Masters of knowne Honor,
I haue a voyce, and president of peace
To keepe my name vngorg'd. But till that time,
I do receiue your offer'd loue like loue,
And wil not wrong it.

Ham. I do embrace it freely,
And will this Brothers wager frankely play.
Giue vs the Foyles: Come on.

Laer. Come one for me.

Ham. He be your foile *Laertes*, in mine ignorance,
Your Skill shall like a Starre i'th'darkest night,
Sticke fiery off indeede.

Laer. You mocke me Sir.

Ham. No by this hand.

King. Giue them the Foyles yong *Osricke*,
Cousen *Hamlet*, you know the wager.

Ham. Verie well my Lord,
Your Grace hath laide the oddes a'th'weaker side.

King. I do not feare it,
I haue seene you both:
But since he is better'd, we haue therefore oddes.

Laer. This is too heauy,
Let me see another.

Ham. This likes me well,
These Foyles haue all a length.   *Prepare to play.*

Osricke. I my good Lord.

King. Set me the Stopes of wine vpon that Table:
If *Hamlet* giue the first, or second hit,
Or quit in answer of the third exchange,
Let all the Battlements their Ordinance fire,
The King shal drinke to *Hamlets* better breath,
And in the Cup an vnion shal he throw
Richer then that, which foure successiue Kings
In Denmarkes Crowne haue worne.

Giue

The Tragedie of Hamlet.

Giue me the Cups,
And let the Kettle to the Trumpets speake,
The Trumpet to the Cannoneer without,
The Cannons to the Heauens, the Heauen to Earth,
Now the King drinkes to *Hamlet*. Come, begin,
And you the Iudges beare a wary eye.

Ham. Come on sir.
Laer. Come on sir. *They play.*
Ham. One.
Laer. No.
Ham. Iudgement.
Osr. A hit, a very palpable hit.
Laer. Well: againe.
King. Stay, giue me drinke.
Hamlet, this Pearle is thine,
Here's to thy health. Giue him the cup,
Trumpets sound, and shot goes off.
Ham. Ile play this bout first, set by a-while.
Come: Another hit; what say you?
Laer. A touch, a touch, I do confesse.
King. Our Sonne shall win.
Qu. He's fat, and scant of breath.
Heere's a Napkin, rub thy browes,
The Queene Carowses to thy fortune, *Hamlet*.
Ham. Good Madam.
King. Gertrude, do not drinke.
Qu. I will my Lord;
I pray you pardon me.
King. It is the poyson'd Cup, it is too late.
Ham. I dare not drinke yet Madam,
By and by.
Qu. Come, let me wipe thy face.
Laer. My Lord, Ile hit him now.
King. I do not thinke't.
Laer. And yet 'tis almost 'gainst my conscience.
Ham. Come for the third.
Laertes, you but dally,
I pray you passe with your best violence,
I am affear'd you make a wanton of me.
Laer. Say you so? Come on. *Play.*
Osr. Nothing neither way.
Laer. Haue at you now.
In scuffling they change Rapiers.
King. Part them, they are incens'd.
Ham. Nay come, againe.
Osr. Looke to the Queene there hoa.
Hor. They bleed on both sides. How is't my Lord?
Osr. How is't *Laertes*?
Laer. Why as a Woodcocke
To mine Sprindge, *Osricke*,
I am iustly kill'd with mine owne Treacherie.
Ham. How does the Queene?
King. She sounds to see them bleede.
Qu. No, no, the drinke, the drinke.
Oh my deere *Hamlet*, the drinke, the drinke,
I am poyson'd.
Ham. Oh Villany! How? Let the doore be lock'd.
Treacherie, seeke it out.
Laer. It is heere *Hamlet*.
Hamlet, thou art slaine,
No Medicine in the world can do thee good.
In thee, there is not halfe an houre of life;
The Treacherous Instrument is in thy hand,
Vnbated and envenom'd: the foule practise
Hath turn'd it selfe on me. Loe, heere I lye,
Neuer to rise againe: Thy Mothers poyson'd:

I can no more, the King, the King's too blame.
Ham. The point envenom'd too,
Then venome to thy worke. *Hurts the King.*
All. Treason, Treason.
King. O yet defend me Friends, I am but hurt.
Ham. Heere thou incestuous, murdrous,
Damned Dane,
Drinke off this Potion: Is thy Vnion heere?
Follow my Mother. *King Dyes.*
Laer. He is iustly seru'd.
It is a poyson temp'red by himselfe:
Exchange forgiuenesse with me, Noble *Hamlet*;
Mine and my Fathers death come not vpon thee,
Nor thine on me. *Dyes.*
Ham. Heauen make thee free of it, I follow thee.
I am dead *Horatio*, wretched Queene adiew,
You that looke pale, and tremble at this chance,
That are but Mutes or audience to this acte:
Had I but time (as this fell Sergeant death
Is strick'd in his Arrest) oh I could tell you.
But let it be: *Horatio*, I am dead,
Thou liu'st, report me and my causes right
To the vnsatisfied.
Hor. Neuer beleeue it.
I am more an Antike Roman then a Dane:
Heere's yet some Liquor left.
Ham. As th'art a man, giue me the Cup.
Let go, by Heauen Ile haue't.
Oh good *Horatio*, what a wounded name,
(Things standing thus vnknowne) shall liue behind me.
If thou did'st euer hold me in thy heart,
Absent thee from felicitie awhile,
And in this harsh world draw thy breath in paine,
To tell my Storie.
March afarre off, and shout within.
What warlike noyse is this?

Enter Osricke.

Osr. Yong *Fortinbras*, with conquest come frō Poland
To th'Ambassadors of England giues this warlike volly.
Ham. O I dye *Horatio*:
The potent poyson quite ore-crowes my spirit,
I cannot liue to heare the Newes from England,
But I do prophesie th'election lights
On *Fortinbras*, he ha's my dying voyce,
So tell him with the occurrents more and lesse,
Which haue solicited. The rest is silence. O, o, o, o. *Dyes*
Hora. Now cracke a Noble heart:
Goodnight sweet Prince,
And flights of Angels sing thee to thy rest,
Why do's the Drumme come hither?

Enter Fortinbras and English Ambassador, with Drumme, Colours, and Attendants.

Fortin. Where is this sight?
Hor. What is it ye would see;
If ought of woe, or wonder, cease your search.
For. His quarry cries on hauocke. Oh proud death,
What feast is toward in thine eternall Cell,
That thou so many Princes, at a shoote,
So bloodily hast strooke.
Amb. The sight is dismall,
And our affaires from England come too late,
The eares are senselesse that should giue vs hearing,
To tell him his comma'ndment is fulfill'd,

qq That

That *Rosincrance* and *Guildensterne* are dead:
Where should we haue our thankes?

  Hor. Not from his mouth,
Had it th'abilitie of life to thanke you:
He neuer gaue command'ment for their death.
But since so iumpe vpon this bloodie question,
You from the Polake warres, and you from England
Are heere arriued. Giue order that these bodies
High on a stage be placed to the view,
And let me speake to th'yet vnknowing world,
How these things came about. So shall you heare
Of carnall, bloudie, and vnnaturall acts,
Of accidentall iudgements, casuall slaughters
Of death's put on by cunning, and forc'd cause,
And in this vpshot, purposes mistooke,
Falne on the Inuentors heads. All this can I
Truly deliuer.

  For. Let vs hast to heare it,
And call the Noblest to the Audience.
For me, with sorrow, I embrace my Fortune,
I haue some Rites of memory in this Kingdome,
Which are to claime, my vantage doth
Inuite me,

  Hor. Of that I shall haue alwayes cause to speake,
And from his mouth
Whose voyce will draw on more:
But let this same be presently perform'd,
Euen whiles mens mindes are wilde,
Lest more mischance
On plots, and errors happen.

  For. Let foure Captaines
Beare *Hamlet* like a Soldier to the Stage,
For he was likely, had he beene put on
To haue prou'd most royally:
And for his passage,
The Souldiours Musicke, and the rites of Warre
Speake lowdly for him.
Take vp the body; Such a sight as this
Becomes the Field, but heere shewes much amis.
Go, bid the Souldiers shoote.

Exeunt Marching: after the which, a Peale of Ordenance are shot off.

FINIS.

THE TRAGEDIE OF KING LEAR.

Actus Primus. Scœna Prima.

Enter Kent, Gloucester, and Edmond.

Kent.

I Thought the King had more affected the Duke of *Albany*, then *Cornwall*.

Glou. It did alwayes seeme so to vs: But now in the diuision of the Kingdome, it appeares not which of the Dukes hee valewes most, for qualities are so weigh'd, that curiosity in neither, can make choise of eithers moity.

Kent. Is not this your Son, my Lord?

Glou. His breeding Sir, hath bin at my charge. I haue so often blush'd to acknowledge him, that now I am braz'd too't.

Kent. I cannot conceiue you.

Glou. Sir, this yong Fellowes mother could; whereupon she grew round womb'd, and had indeede (Sir) a Sonne for her Cradle, ere she had a husband for her bed. Do you smell a fault?

Kent. I cannot wish the fault vndone, the issue of it, being so proper.

Glou. But I haue a Sonne, Sir, by order of Law, some yeere elder then this; who, yet is no deerer in my account, though this Knaue came somthing sawcily to the world before he was sent for: yet was his Mother fayre, there was good sport at his making, and the horson must be acknowledged. Doe you know this Noble Gentleman, *Edmond*?

Edm. No, my Lord.

Glou. My Lord of Kent: Remember him heereafter, as my Honourable Friend.

Edm. My seruices to your Lordship.

Kent. I must loue you, and sue to know you better.

Edm. Sir, I shall study deseruing.

Glou. He hath bin out nine yeares, and away he shall againe. The King is comming.

Sennet. Enter King Lear, Cornwall, Albany, Gonerill, Regan, Cordelia, and attendants.

Lear. Attend the Lords of France & Burgundy, Gloster.

Glou. I shall, my Lord. *Exit.*

Lear. Meane time we shal expresse our darker purpose. Giue me the Map there. Know, that we haue diuided In three our Kingdome: and 'tis our fast intent, To shake all Cares and Businesse from our Age, Conferring them on yonger strengths, while we Vnburthen'd crawle toward death. Our son of *Cornwal*, And you our no lesse louing Sonne of *Albany*, We haue this houre a constant will to publish Our daughters seuerall Dowers, that future strife May be preuented now. The Princes, *France* & *Burgundy*, Great Riuals in our yongest daughters loue, Long in our Court, haue made their amorous soiourne, And heere are to be answer'd. Tell me my daughters (Since now we will diuest vs both of Rule, Interest of Territory, Cares of State) Which of you shall we say doth loue vs most, That we, our largest bountie may extend Where Nature doth with merit challenge. *Generill*, Our eldest borne, speake first.

Gon. Sir, I loue you more then word can weild $\tilde{y}$ matter, Deerer then eye-sight, space, and libertie, Beyond what can be valewed, rich or rare, No lesse then life, with grace, health, beauty, honor: As much as Childe ere lou'd, or Father found. A loue that makes breath poore, and speech vnable, Beyond all manner of so much I loue you.

Cor. What shall *Cordelia* speake? Loue, and be silent.

Lear. Of all these bounds euen from this Line, to this, With shadowie Forrests, and with Champains rich'd With plenteous Riuers, and wide-skirted Meades We make thee Lady. To thine and *Albanies* issues Be this perpetuall. What sayes our second Daughter? Our deerest *Regan*, wife of *Cornwall*?

Reg. I am made of that selfe-mettle as my Sister, And prize me at her worth. In my true heart, I finde she names my very deede of loue: Onely she comes too short, that I professe My selfe an enemy to all other ioyes, Which the most precious square of sense professes, And finde I am alone felicitate In your deere Highnesse loue.

Cor. Then poore *Cordelia*, And yet not so, since I am sure my loue's More ponderous then my tongue.

Lear. To thee, and thine hereditarie euer, Remaine this ample third of our faire Kingdome, No lesse in space, validitie, and pleasure Then that conferr'd on *Generill*. Now our Ioy, Although our last and least: to whose yong loue, The Vines of France, and Milke of Burgundie, Striue to be interest. What can you say, to draw A third, more opilent then your Sisters? speake.

Cor. Nothing my Lord.

Lear. Nothing?

Cor. Nothing.

Lear. Nothing will come of nothing, speake againe.

Cor. Vnhappie that I am, I cannot heaue
My heart into my mouth: I loue your Maiesty
According to my bond, no more nor lesse.

Lear. How, how *Cordelia*? Mend your speech a little,
Least you may marre your Fortunes.

Cor. Good my Lord,
You haue begot me, bred me, lou'd me.
I returne those duties backe as are right fit,
Obey you, Loue you, and most Honour you.
Why haue my Sisters Husbands, if they say
They loue you all? Happily when I shall wed,
That Lord, whose hand must take my plight, shall carry
Halfe my loue with him, halfe my Care, and Dutie,
Sure I shall neuer marry like my Sisters.

Lear. But goes thy heart with this?

Cor. I my good Lord.

Lear. So young, and so vntender?

Cor. So young my Lord, and true.

Lear. Let it be so, thy truth then be thy dowre:
For by the sacred radience of the Sunne,
The misteries of *Heccat* and the night:
By all the operation of the Orbes,
From whom we do exist, and cease to be,
Heere I disclaime all my Paternall care,
Propinquity and property of blood,
And as a stranger to my heart and me,
Hold thee from this for euer. The barbarous *Scythian*,
Or he that makes his generation messes
To gorge his appetite, shall to my bosome
Be as well neighbour'd, pittied, and releeu'd,
As thou my sometime Daughter.

Kent. Good my Liege.

Lear. Peace *Kent*,
Come not betweene the Dragon and his wrath,
I lou'd her most, and thought to set my rest
On her kind nursery. Hence and avoid my sight:
So be my graue my peace, as here I giue
Her Fathers heart from her; call *France*, who stirres?
Call *Burgundy, Cornwall*, and *Albanie*,
With my two Daughters Dowres, digest the third,
Let pride, which she cals plainnesse, marry her:
I doe inuest you ioyntly with my power,
Preheminence, and all the large effects
That troope with Maiesty. Our selfe by Monthly course,
With reseruation of an hundred Knights,
By you to be sustain'd, shall our abode
Make with you by due turne, onely we shall retaine
The name, and all th'addition to a King: the Sway,
Reuennew, Execution of the rest,
Beloued Sonnes be yours, which to confirme,
This Coronet part betweene you.

Kent. Royall *Lear*,
Whom I haue euer honor'd as my King,
Lou'd as my Father, as my Master follow'd,
As my great Patron thought on in my praiers.

Le. The bow is bent & drawne, make from the shaft.

Kent. Let it fall rather, though the forke inuade
The region of my heart, be *Kent* vnmannerly,
When *Lear* is mad, what wouldest thou do old man?
Think'st thou that dutie shall haue dread to speake,
When power to flattery bowes?
To plainnesse honour's bound,
When Maiesty falls to folly, reserue thy state,
And in thy best consideration checke

This hideous rashnesse, answere my life, my iudgement:
Thy yongest Daughter do's not loue thee least,
Nor are those empty hearted, whose low sounds
Reuerbe no hollownesse.

Lear. *Kent*, on thy life no more.

Kent. My life I neuer held but as pawne
To wage against thine enemies, nere feare to loose it,
Thy safety being motiue.

Lear. Out of my sight.

Kent. See better *Lear*, and let me still remaine
The true blanke of thine eie.

Lear. Now by *Apollo*,

Kent. Now by *Apollo*, King
Thou swear'st thy Gods in vaine.

Lear. O Vassall! Miscreant.

Alb. Cor. Deare Sir forbeare.

Kent. Kill thy Physition, and thy fee bestow
Vpon the foule disease, reuoke thy guift,
Or whil'st I can vent clamour from my throate,
Ile tell thee thou dost euill.

Lea. Heare me recreant, on thine allegeance heare me;
That thou hast sought to make vs breake our vowes,
Which we durst neuer yet; and with strain'd pride,
To come betwixt our sentences, and our power,
Which, nor our nature, nor our place can beare;
Our potencie made good, take thy reward.
Fiue dayes we do allot thee for prouision,
To shield thee from disasters of the world,
And on the sixt to turne thy hated backe
Vpon our kingdome; if on the tenth day following,
Thy banisht trunke be found in our Dominions,
The moment is thy death, away. By *Iupiter*,
This shall not be reuok'd.

Kent. Fare thee well King, sith thus thou wilt appeare,
Freedome liues hence, and banishment is here;
The Gods to their deere shelter take thee Maid,
That iustly think'st, and hast most rightly said:
And your large speeches, may your deeds approue,
That good effects may spring from words of loue:
Thus *Kent*, O Princes, bids you all adew,
Hee'l shape his old course, in a Country new. *Exit.*

Flourish. Enter *Gloster* with *France*, and *Burgundy, Attendants.*

Cor. Heere's *France* and *Burgundy*, my Noble Lord.

Lear. My Lord of *Burgundie*,
We first addresse toward you, who with this King
Hath riuald for our Daughter; what in the least
Will you require in present Dower with her,
Or cease your quest of Loue?

Bur. Most Royall Maiesty,
I craue no more then hath your Highnesse offer'd,
Nor will you tender lesse?

Lear. Right Noble *Burgundy*,
When she was deare to vs, we did hold her so,
But now her price is fallen: Sir, there she stands,
If ought within that little seeming substance,
Or all of it with our displeasure piec'd,
And nothing more may fitly like your Grace,
Shee's there, and she is yours.

Bur. I know no answer.

Lear. Will you with those infirmities she owes,
Vnfriended, new adopted to our hate,
Dow'rd with our curse, and stranger'd with our oath,
Take her or, leaue her.

Bur. Par-

The Tragedie of King Lear.

Bur. Pardon me Royall Sir,
Election makes not vp in such conditions.

Le. Then leaue her sir, for by the powre that made me,
I tell you all her wealth. For you great King,
I would not from your loue make such a stray,
To match you where I hate, therefore beseech you
T'auert your liking a more worthier way,
Then on a wretch whom Nature is asham'd
Almost t'acknowledge hers.

Fra. This is most strange,
That she whom euen but now, was your obiect,
The argument of your praise, balme of your age,
The best, the deerest, should in this trice of time
Commit a thing so monstrous, to dismantle
So many folds of fauour: sure her offence
Must be of such vnnaturall degree,
That monsters it : Or your fore-voucht affection
Fall into taint, which to beleeue of her
Must be a faith that reason without miracle
Should neuer plant in me.

Cor. I yet beseech your Maiesty.
If for I want that glib and oylie Art,
To speake and purpose not, since what I will intend,
Ile do't before I speake, that you make knowne
It is no vicious blot, murther, or foulenesse,
No vnchaste action or dishonoured step
That hath depriu'd me of your Grace and fauour,
But euen for want of that, for which I am richer,
A still soliciting eye, and such a tongue,
That I am glad I haue not, though not to haue it,
Hath lost me in your liking.

Lear. Better thou had'st
Not beene borne, then not t'haue pleas'd me better.

Fra. Is it but this ? A tardinesse in nature,
Which often leaues the history vnspoke
That it intends to do : my Lord of *Burgundy*,
What say you to the Lady ? Loue's not loue
When it is mingled with regards, that stands
Aloofe from th'intire point, will you haue her ?
She is herselfe a Dowrie.

Bur. Royall King,
Giue but that portion which your selfe propos'd,
And here I take *Cordelia* by the hand,
Dutchesse of *Burgundie*.

Lear. Nothing, I haue sworne, I am firme.

Bur. I am sorry then you haue so lost a Father,
That you must loose a husband.

Cor. Peace be with *Burgundie*,
Since that respect and Fortunes are his loue,
I shall not be his wife.

Fra. Fairest *Cordelia*, that art most rich being poore,
Most choise forsaken, and most lou'd despis'd,
Thee and thy vertues here I seize vpon,
Be it lawfull I take vp what's cast away.
Gods, Gods ! 'Tis strange, that from their cold'st neglect
My Loue should kindle to enflam'd respect.
Thy dowrelesse Daughter King, throwne to my chance,
Is Queene of vs, of ours, and our faire *France* :
Not all the Dukes of watrish *Burgundy*,
Can buy this vnpriz'd precious Maid of me.
Bid them farewell *Cordelia*, though vnkinde,
Thou loosest here a better where to finde.

Lear. Thou hast her *France*, let her be thine, for we
Haue no such Daughter, nor shall euer see
That face of hers againe, therfore be gone,
Without our Grace, our Loue, our Benizon :
Come Noble *Burgundie*.   *Flourish. Exeunt.*

Fra. Bid farwell to your Sisters.

Cor. The Iewels of our Father, with wash'd eies
Cordelia leaues you, I know you what you are,
And like a Sister am most loth to call
Your faults as they are named. Loue well our Father:
To your professed bosomes I commit him,
But yet alas, stood I within his Grace,
I would prefer him to a better place,
So farewell to you both.

Regn. Prescribe not vs our dutie.

Gon. Let your study
Be to content your Lord, who hath receiu'd you
At Fortunes almes, you haue obedience scanted,
And well are worth the want that you haue wanted.

Cor. Time shall vnfold what plighted cunning hides,
Who couers faults, at last with shame derides:
Well may you prosper.

Fra. Come my faire *Cordelia*. *Exit France and Cor.*

Gon. Sister, it is not little I haue to say,
Of what most neerely appertaines to vs both,
I thinke our Father will hence to night.

Reg. That's most certaine, and with you: next moneth
with vs.

Gon. You see how full of changes his age is, the obseruation we haue made of it hath beene little; he alwaies
lou'd our Sister most, and with what poore iudgement he
hath now cast her off, appeares too grossely.

Reg. 'Tis the infirmity of his age, yet he hath euer but
slenderly knowne himselfe.

Gon. The best and soundest of his time hath bin but
rash, then must we looke from his age, to receiue not a-
lone the imperfections of long ingraffed condition, but
therewithall the vnruly way-wardnesse, that infirme and
cholericke yeares bring with them.

Reg. Such vnconstant starts are we like to haue from
him, as this of *Kents* banishment.

Gon. There is further complement of leaue-taking betweene *France* and him, pray you let vs sit together, if our
Father carry authority with such disposition as he beares,
this last surrender of his will but offend vs.

Reg. We shall further thinke of it.

Gon. We must do something, and i'th' heate. *Exeunt.*

Scena Secunda.

Enter Bastard.

Bast. Thou Nature art my Goddesse, to thy Law
My seruices are bound, wherefore should I
Stand in the plague of custome, and permit
The curiosity of Nations, to depriue me?
For that I am some twelue, or fourteene Moonshines
Lag of a Brother ? Why Bastard ? Wherefore base ?
When my Dimensions are as well compact,
My minde as generous, and my shape as true
As honest Madams issue ? Why brand they vs
With Base ? With basenes Bastardie ? Base, Base ?
Who in the lustie stealth of Nature, take
More composition, and fierce qualitie,
Then doth within a dull stale tyred bed
Goe to th'creating a whole tribe of Fops
Got 'tweene a sleepe, and wake ? Well then,
Legitimate *Edgar*, I must haue your land,
Our Fathers loue, is to the Bastard *Edmond*,
As to th'legitimate : fine word : Legitimate.

Well, my Legittimate, if this Letter speed,
And my inuention thriue, *Edmond* the base
Shall to'th'Legitimate: I grow, I prosper:
Now Gods, stand vp for Bastards.

Enter Gloucester.

Glo. Kent banish'd thus? and France in choller parted?
And the King gone to night? Prescrib'd his powre,
Confin'd to exhibition? All this done
Vpon the gad? *Edmond*, how now? What newes?

Bast. So please your Lordship, none.

Glou. Why so earnestly seeke you to put vp ye Letter?

Bast. I know no newes, my Lord.

Glou. What Paper were you reading?

Bast. Nothing my Lord.

Glou. No? what needed then that terrible dispatch of it into your Pocket? The quality of nothing, hath not such neede to hide it selfe. Let's see: come, if it bee nothing, I shall not neede Spectacles.

Bast. I beseech you Sir, pardon mee; it is a Letter from my Brother, that I haue not all ore-read; and for so much as I haue perus'd, I finde it not fit for your ore-looking.

Glou. Giue me the Letter, Sir.

Bast. I shall offend, either to detaine, or giue it: The Contents, as in part I vnderstand them, Are too blame.

Glou. Let's see, let's see.

Bast. I hope for my Brothers iustification, hee wrote this but as an essay, or taste of my Vertue.

Glou. reads. This policie, and reuerence of Age, makes the world bitter to the best of our times: keepes our Fortunes from vs, till our oldnesse cannot rellish them. I begin to finde an idle and fond bondage, in the oppression of aged tyranny, who swayes not as it hath power, but as it is suffer'd. Come to me, that of this I may speake more. If our Father would sleepe till I wak'd him, you should enioy halfe his Reuennew for euer, and liue the beloued of your Brother. *Edgar.*

Hum? Conspiracy? Sleepe till I wake him, you should enioy halfe his Reuennew: my Sonne *Edgar*, had hee a hand to write this? A heart and braine to breede it in? When came you to this? Who brought it?

Bast. It was not brought mee, my Lord; there's the cunning of it. I found it throwne in at the Casement of my Closset.

Glou. You know the character to be your Brothers?

Bast. If the matter were good my Lord, I durst swear it were his: but in respect of that, I would faine thinke it were not.

Glou. It is his.

Bast. It is his hand, my Lord: but I hope his heart is not in the Contents.

Glo. Has he neuer before sounded you in this busines?

Bast. Neuer my Lord. But I haue heard him oft maintaine it to be fit, that Sonnes at perfect age, and Fathers declin'd, the Father should bee as Ward to the Son, and the Sonne manage his Reuennew.

Glou. O Villain, villain: his very opinion in the Letter. Abhorred Villaine, vnnaturall, detested, brutish Villaine; worse then brutish: Go sirrah, seeke him: Ile apprehend him. Abhominable Villaine, where is he?

Bast. I do not well know my L. If it shall please you to suspend your indignation against my Brother, til you can deriue from him better testimony of his intent, you should run a certaine course: where, if you violently proceed against him, mistaking his purpose, it would make a great gap in your owne Honor, and shake in peeces, the heart of his obedience. I dare pawne downe my life for him, that he hath writ this to feele my affection to your Honor, & to no other pretence of danger.

Glou. Thinke you so?

Bast. If your Honor iudge it meete, I will place you where you shall heare vs conferre of this, and by an Auricular assurance haue your satisfaction, and that without any further delay, then this very Euening.

Glou. He cannot bee such a Monster. *Edmond* seeke him out: winde me into him, I pray you: frame the Businesse after your owne wisedome. I would vnstate my selfe, to be in a due resolution.

Bast. I will seeke him Sir, presently: conuey the businesse as I shall find meanes, and acquaint you withall.

Glou. These late Eclipses in the Sun and Moone portend no good to vs: though the wisedome of Nature can reason it thus, and thus, yet Nature finds it selfe scourg'd by the sequent effects. Loue cooles, friendship falls off, Brothers diuide. In Cities, mutinies; in Countries, discord; in Pallaces, Treason; and the Bond crack'd, 'twixt Sonne and Father. This villaine of mine comes vnder the prediction; there's Son against Father, the King fals from byas of Nature, there's Father against Childe. We haue seene the best of our time. Machinations, hollownesse, treacherie, and all ruinous disorders follow vs disquietly to our Graues. Find out this Villain *Edmond*, it shall lose thee nothing, do it carefully: and the Noble & true-harted Kent banish'd; his offence, honesty. 'Tis strange. *Exit.*

Bast. This is the excellent foppery of the world, that when we are sicke in fortune, often the surfets of our own behauiour, we make guilty of our disasters, the Sun, the Moone, and Starres, as if we were villaines on necessitie, Fooles by heauenly compulsion, Knaues, Theeues, and Treachers by Sphericall predominance. Drunkards, Lyars, and Adulterers by an inforc'd obedience of Planatary influence; and all that we are euill in, by a diuine thrusting on. An admirable euasion of Whore-master-man, to lay his Goatish disposition on the charge of a Starre, My father compounded with my mother vnder the Dragons taile, and my Natiuity was vnder *Vrsa Maior*, so that it followes, I am rough and Leacherous. I should haue bin that I am, had the maidenlest Starre in the Firmament twinkled on my bastardizing.

Enter Edgar.

Pat: he comes like the Catastrophe of the old Comedie: my Cue is villanous Melancholly, with a sighe like *Tom* o'Bedlam. ———— O these Eclipses do portend these diuisions. Fa, Sol, La, Me.

Edg. How now Brother *Edmond*, what serious contemplation are you in?

Bast. I am thinking Brother of a prediction I read this other day, what should follow these Eclipses.

Edg. Do you busie your selfe with that?

Bast. I promise you, the effects he writes of, succeede vnhappily. When saw you my Father last?

Edg. The night gone by.

Bast. Spake you with him?

Edg. I, two houres together.

Bast. Parted you in good termes? Found you no displeasure in him, by word, nor countenance?

Edg. None at all,

Bast. Bethink your selfe wherein you may haue offended him: and at my entreaty forbeare his presence, vntill some little time hath qualified the heat of his displeasure, which at this instant so rageth in him, that with the mischiefe

chiefe of your person, it would scarsely alay.

Edg. Some Villaine hath done me wrong.

Edm. That's my feare, I pray you haue a continent forbearance till the speed of his rage goes slower: and as I say, retire with me to my lodging, from whence I will fitly bring you to heare my Lord speake: pray ye goe, there's my key: if you do stirre abroad, goe arm'd.

Edg. Arm'd, Brother?

Edm. Brother, I aduise you to the best, I am no honest man, if ther be any good meaning toward you: I haue told you what I haue seene, and heard: But faintly. Nothing like the image, and horror of it, pray you away.

Edg. Shall I heare from you anon? *Exit.*

Edm. I do serue you in this businesse:
A Credulous Father, and a Brother Noble,
Whose nature is so farre from doing harmes,
That he suspects none: on whose foolish honestie
My practises ride easie: I see the businesse.
Let me, if not by birth, haue lands by wit,
All with me's meete, that I can fashion fit. *Exit.*

Scena Tertia.

Enter Gonerill, and Steward.

Gon. Did my Father strike my Gentleman for chiding of his Foole?

Ste. I Madam.

Gon. By day and night, he wrongs me, euery howre
He flashes into one grosse crime, or other,
That sets vs all at ods: Ile not endure it;
His Knights grow riotous, and himselfe vpbraides vs
On euery trifle. When he returnes from hunting,
I will not speake with him, say I am sicke,
If you come slacke of former seruices,
You shall do well, the fault of it Ile answer.

Ste. He's comming Madam, I heare him.

Gon. Put on what weary negligence you please,
You and your Fellowes: I'de haue it come to question;
If he distaste it, let him to my Sister,
Whose mind and mine I know in that are one,
Remember what I haue said.

Ste. Well Madam.

Gon. And let his Knights haue colder lookes among you: what growes of it no matter, aduise your fellowes so, Ile write straight to my Sister to hold my course: prepare for dinner. *Exeunt.*

Scena Quarta.

Enter Kent.

Kent. If but as will I other accents borrow,
That can my speech defuse, my good intent
May carry through it selfe to that full issue
For which I raiz'd my likenesse. Now banisht *Kent*,
If thou canst serue where thou dost stand condemn'd,
So may it come, thy Master whom thou lou'st,
Shall find thee full of labours.

Horses within. Enter Lear and Attendants.

Lear. Let me not stay a iot for dinner, go get it ready, how now, what art thou?

Kent. A man Sir.

Lear. What dost thou professe? What would'st thou with vs?

Kent. I do professe to be no lesse then I seeme; to serue him truely that will put me in trust, to loue him that is honest, to conuerse with him that is wise and saies little, to feare iudgement, to fight when I cannot choose, and to eate no fish.

Lear. What art thou?

Kent. A very honest hearted Fellow, and as poore as the King.

Lear. If thou be'st as poore for a subiect, as hee's for a King, thou art poore enough. What wouldst thou?

Kent. Seruice.

Lear. Who wouldst thou serue?

Kent. You.

Lear. Do'st thou know me fellow?

Kent. No Sir, but you haue that in your countenance, which I would faine call Master.

Lear. What's that?

Kent. Authority.

Lear. What seruices canst thou do?

Kent. I can keepe honest counsaile, ride, run, marre a curious tale in telling it, and deliuer a plaine message bluntly: that which ordinary men are fit for, I am qualified in, and the best of me, is Dilligence.

Lear. How old art thou?

Kent. Not so young Sir to loue a woman for singing, nor so old to dote on her for any thing. I haue yeares on my backe forty eight.

Lear. Follow me, thou shalt serue me, if I like thee no worse after dinner, I will not part from thee yet. Dinner ho, dinner, where's my knaue? my Foole? Go you and call my Foole hither. You you Sirrah, where's my Daughter?

Enter Steward.

Ste. So please you —— *Exit.*

Lear. What saies the Fellow there? Call the Clotpole backe: wher's my Foole? Ho, I thinke the world's asleepe, how now? Where's that Mungrell?

Knigh. He saies my Lord, your Daughters is not well.

Lear. Why came not the slaue backe to me when I call'd him?

Knigh. Sir, he answered me in the roundest manner, he would not.

Lear. He would not?

Knight. My Lord, I know not what the matter is, but to my iudgement your Highnesse is not entertain'd with that Ceremonious affection as you were wont, theres a great abatement of kindnesse appeares as well in the generall dependants, as in the Duke himselfe also, and your Daughter.

Lear. Ha? Saist thou so?

Knigh. I beseech you pardon me my Lord, if I bee mistaken, for my duty cannot be silent, when I thinke your Highnesse wrong'd.

Lear. Thou but remembrest me of mine owne Conception, I haue perceiued a most faint neglect of late, which I haue rather blamed as mine owne iealous curiositie, then as a very pretence and purpose of vnkindnesse; I will looke further into't: but where's my Foole? I haue not seene him this two daies.

Knight. Since my young Ladies going into *France*

Sir,

Sir, the Foole hath much pined away.

Lear. No more of that, I haue noted it well, goe you and tell my Daughter, I would speake with her. Goe you call hither my Foole; Oh you Sir, you, come you hither Sir, who am I Sir?

Enter Steward.

Ste. My Ladies Father.

Lear. My Ladies Father? my Lords knaue, you whorson dog, you slaue, you curre.

Ste. I am none of these my Lord, I beseech your pardon.

Lear. Do you bandy lookes with me, you Rascall?

Ste. Ile not be strucken my Lord.

Kent. Nor tript neither, you base Foot-ball plaier.

Lear. I thanke thee fellow. Thou seru'st me, and Ile loue thee.

Kent. Come sir, arise, away, Ile teach you differences: away, away, if you will measure your lubbers length againe, tarry, but away, goe too, haue you wisedome, so.

Lear. Now my friendly knaue I thanke thee, there's earnest of thy seruice.

Enter Foole.

Foole. Let me hire him too, here's my Coxcombe.

Lear. How now my pretty knaue, how dost thou?

Foole. Sirrah, you were best take my Coxcombe.

Lear. Why my Boy?

Foole. Why? for taking ones part that's out of fauour, nay, & thou canst not smile as the wind sits, thou'lt catch colde shortly, there take my Coxcombe; why this fellow ha's banish'd two on's Daughters, and did the third a blessing against his will, if thou follow him, thou must needs weare my Coxcombe. How now Nunckle? would I had two Coxcombes and two Daughters.

Lear. Why my Boy?

Fool. If I gaue them all my liuing, I'ld keepe my Coxcombes my selfe, there's mine, beg another of thy Daughters.

Lear. Take heed Sirrah, the whip.

Foole. Truth's a dog must to kennell, hee must bee whipt out, when the Lady Brach may stand by th'fire and stinke.

Lear. A pestilent gall to me.

Foole. Sirha, Ile teach thee a speech.

Lear. Do.

Foole. Marke it Nuncle;
Haue more then thou showest,
Speake lesse then thou knowest,
Lend lesse then thou owest,
Ride more then thou goest,
Learne more then thou trowest,
Set lesse then thou throwest;
Leaue thy drinke and thy whore,
And keepe in a dore,
And thou shalt haue more,
Then two tens to a score.

Kent. This is nothing Foole.

Foole. Then 'tis like the breath of an vnfeed Lawyer, you gaue me nothing for't, can you make no vse of nothing Nuncle?

Lear. Why no Boy, Nothing can be made out of nothing.

Foole. Prythee tell him, so much the rent of his land comes to, he will not beleeue a Foole.

Lear. A bitter Foole.

Foole. Do'st thou know the difference my Boy, betweene a bitter Foole, and a sweet one.

Lear. No Lad, teach me.

Foole. Nunckle, giue me an egge, and Ile giue thee two Crownes.

Lear. What two Crownes shall they be?

Foole. Why after I haue cut the egge i'th'middle and eate vp the meate, the two Crownes of the egge: when thou clouest thy Crownes i'th'middle, and gau'st away both parts, thou boar'st thine Asse on thy backe o're the durt, thou had'st little wit in thy bald crowne, when thou gau'st thy golden one away; if I speake like my selfe in this, let him be whipt that first findes it so.
Fooles had nere lesse grace in a yeere,
For wise men are growne foppish,
And know not how their wits to weare,
Their manners are so apish.

Le. When were you wont to be so full of Songs sirrah?

Foole. I haue vsed it Nunckle, ere since thou mad'st thy Daughters thy Mothers, for when thou gau'st them the rod, and put'st downe thine owne breeches, then they
For sodaine ioy did weepe,
And I for sorrow sung,
That such a King should play bo-peepe,
And goe the Foole among.
Pry'thy Nunckle keepe a Schoolemaster that can teach thy Foole to lie, I would faine learne to lie.

Lear. And you lie sirrah, wee'l haue you whipt.

Foole. I maruell what kin thou and thy daughters are, they'l haue me whipt for speaking true: thou'lt haue me whipt for lying, and sometimes I am whipt for holding my peace. I had rather be any kind o'thing then a foole, and yet I would not be thee Nunckle, thou hast pared thy wit o'both sides, and left nothing i'th'middle; heere comes one o'the parings.

Enter Gonerill.

Lear. How now Daughter? what makes that Frontlet on? You are too much of late i'th'frowne.

Foole. Thou wast a pretty fellow when thou hadst no need to care for her frowning, now thou art an O without a figure, I am better then thou art now, I am a Foole, thou art nothing. Yes forsooth I will hold my tongue, so your face bids me, though you say nothing.
Mum, mum, he that keepes nor crust, nor crum,
Weary of all, shall want some. That's a sheal'd Pescod.

Gon. Not only Sir this, your all-lycenc'd Foole,
But other of your insolent retinue
Do hourely Carpe and Quarrell, breaking forth
In ranke, and (not to be endur'd) riots Sir.
I had thought by making this well knowne vnto you,
To haue found a safe redresse, but now grow fearefull
By what your selfe too late haue spoke and done,
That you protect this course, and put it on
By your allowance, which if you should, the fault
Would not scape censure, nor the redresses sleepe,
Which in the tender of a wholesome weale,
Might in their working do you that offence,
Which else were shame, that then necessitie
Will call discreet proceeding.

Fool. For you know Nunckle, the Hedge-Sparrow fed the Cuckoo so long, that it's had it head bit off by it young, so out went the Candle, and we were left darkling.

Lear. Are you our Daughter? (dome

Gon. I would you would make vse of your good wise(Whereof I know you are fraught), and put away
These dispositions, which of late transport you
From what you rightly are.

Foole. May

Foole. May not an Asse know, when the Cart drawes the Horse?
Whoop Iugge I loue thee.
  Lear. Do's any heere know me?
This is not *Lear*:
Do's *Lear* walke thus? Speake thus? Where are his eies?
Either his Notion weakens, his Discernings
Are Lethargied. Ha! Waking? 'Tis not so?
Who is it that can tell me who I am?
  Foole. Lears shadow.
  Lear. Your name, faire Gentlewoman?
  Gon. This admiration Sir, is much o'th'sauour
Of other your new prankes. I do beseech you
To vnderstand my purposes aright:
As you are Old, and Reuerend, should be Wise.
Heere do you keepe a hundred Knights and Squires,
Men so disorder'd, so debosh'd, and bold,
That this our Court infected with their manners,
Shewes like a riotous Inne; Epicurisme and Lust
Makes it more like a Tauerne, or a Brothell,
Then a grac'd Pallace. The shame it selfe doth speake
For instant remedy. Be then desir'd
By her, that else will take the thing she begges,
A little to disquantity your Traine,
And the remainders that shall still depend,
To be such men as may besort your Age,
Which know themselues, and you.
  Lear. Darknesse, and Diuels.
Saddle my horses: call my Traine together.
Degenerate Bastard, Ile not trouble thee;
Yet haue I left a daughter.
  Gon. You strike my people, and your disorder'd rable,
make Seruants of their Betters.

Enter Albany.

  Lear. Woe, that too late repents:
Is it your will, speake Sir? Prepare my Horses.
Ingratitude! thou Marble-hearted Fiend,
More hideous when thou shew'st thee in a Child,
Then the Sea-monster.
  Alb. Pray Sir be patient.
  Lear. Detested Kite, thou lyest.
My Traine are men of choice, and rarest parts,
That all particulars of dutie know,
And in the most exact regard, support
The worships of their name. O most small fault,
How vgly did'st thou in *Cordelia* shew?
Which like an Engine, wrencht my frame of Nature
From the fixt place: drew from my heart all loue,
And added to the gall. O *Lear, Lear, Lear!*
Beate at this gate that let thy Folly in,
And thy deere Iudgement out. Go, go, my people.
  Alb. My Lord, I am guiltlesse, as I am ignorant
Of what hath moued you.
  Lear. It may be so, my Lord.
Heare Nature, heare deere Goddesse, heare:
Suspend thy purpose, if thou did'st intend
To make this Creature fruitfull:
Into her Wombe conuey stirrility,
Drie vp in her the Organs of increase,
And from her derogate body, neuer spring
A Babe to honor her. If she must teeme,
Create her childe of Spleene, that it may liue
And be a thwart disnatur'd torment to her.
Let it stampe wrinkles in her brow of youth,
With cadent Teares fret Channels in her cheekes,
Turne all her Mothers paines, and benefits
To laughter, and contempt: That she may feele,
How sharper then a Serpents tooth it is,
To haue a thanklesse Childe. Away, away. *Exit.*
  Alb. Now Gods that we adore,
Whereof comes this?
  Gon. Neuer afflict your selfe to know more of it:
But let his disposition haue that scope
As dotage giues it.

Enter Lear.

  Lear. What fiftie of my Followers at a clap?
Within a fortnight?
  Alb. What's the matter, Sir?
  Lear. Ile tell thee:
Life and death, I am asham'd
That thou hast power to shake my manhood thus,
That these hot teares, which breake from me perforce
Should make thee worth them.
Blastes and Fogges vpon thee:
Th'vntented woundings of a Fathers curse
Pierce euerie sense about thee. Old fond eyes,
Beweepe this cause againe, Ile plucke ye out,
And cast you with the waters that you loose
To temper Clay. Ha? Let it be so.
I haue another daughter,
Who I am sure is kinde and comfortable:
When she shall heare this of thee, with her nailes
Shee'l flea thy Wolusih visage. Thou shalt finde,
That Ile resume the shape which thou dost thinke
I haue cast off for euer. *Exit*
  Gon. Do you marke that?
  Alb. I cannot be so partiall *Gonerill*,
To the great loue I beare you.
  Gon. Pray you content. What *Oswald*, hoa?
You Sir, more Knaue then Foole, after your Master.
  Foole. Nunkle *Lear*, Nunkle *Lear*,
Tarry, take the Foole with thee:
A Fox, when one has caught her,
And such a Daughter,
Should sure to the Slaughter,
If my Cap would buy a Halter,
So the Foole followes after. *Exit*
  Gon. This man hath had good Counseli,
A hundred Knights?
'Tis politike, and safe to let him keepe
At point a hundred Knights: yes, that on euerie dreame,
Each buz, each fancie, each complaint, dislike,
He may enguard his dotage with their powres,
And ho'd our liues in mercy. *Oswald*, I say.
  Alb. Well, you may feare too farre.
  Gon. Safer then trust too farre;
Let me still take away the harmes I feare,
Not feare still to be taken. I know his heart,
What he hath vtter'd I haue writ my Sister:
If she sustaine him, and his hundred Knights
When I haue shew'd th'vnfitnesse.

Enter Steward.

How now *Oswald*?
What haue you writ that Letter to my Sister?
  Stew. I Madam.
  Gon. Take you some company, and away to horse,
Informe her full of my particular feare,
And thereto adde such reasons of your owne,
As may compact it more. Get you gone,

And

And hasten your returne; no, no, my Lord,
This milky gentlenesse, and course of yours
Though I condemne not, yet vnder pardon
Your are much more at task for want of wisedome,
Then prai'sd for harmefull mildnesse.

Alb. How farre your eies may pierce I cannot tell;
Striuing to better, oft we marre what's well.

Gon. Nay then ——

Alb. Well, well, the'uent. *Exeunt*

Scena Quinta.

Enter Lear, Kent, Gentleman, and Foole.

Lear. Go you before to *Gloster* with these Letters; acquaint my Daughter no further with any thing you know, then comes from her demand out of the Letter, if your Dilligence be not speedy, I shall be there afore you.

Kent. I will not sleepe my Lord, till I haue deliuered your Letter. *Exit.*

Foole. If a mans braines were in's heeles, wert not in danger of kybes?

Lear. I Boy.

Foole. Then I prythee be merry, thy wit shall not go slip-shod.

Lear. Ha, ha, ha.

Fool. Shalt see thy other Daughter will vse thee kindly, for though she's as like this, as a Crabbe's like an Apple, yet I can tell what I can tell.

Lear. What can'st tell Boy?

Foole. She will taste as like this as, a Crabbe do's to a Crab: thou canst tell why ones nose stands i'th'middle on's face?

Lear. No.

Foole. Why to keepe ones eyes of either side's nose, that what a man cannot smell out, he may spy into.

Lear. I did her wrong.

Foole. Can'st tell how an Oyster makes his shell?

Lear. No.

Foole. Nor I neither; but I can tell why a Snaile ha's a house.

Lear. Why?

Foole. Why to put's head in, not to giue it away to his daughters, and leaue his hornes without a case.

Lear. I will forget my Nature, so kind a Father? Be my Horsses ready?

Foole. Thy Asses are gone about 'em; the reason why the seuen Starres are no mo then seuen, is a pretty reason.

Lear. Because they are not eight.

Foole. Yes indeed, thou would'st make a good Foole.

Lear. To tak't againe perforce; Monster Ingratitude!

Foole. If thou wert my Foole Nunckle, I'd haue thee beaten for being old before thy time.

Lear. How's that?

Foole. Thou shouldst not haue bin old, till thou hadst bin wise.

Lear. O let me not be mad, not mad sweet Heauen: keepe me in temper, I would not be mad. How now are the Horses ready?

Gent. Ready my Lord.

Lear. Come Boy.

Fool. She that's a Maid now, & laughs at my departure, Shall not be a Maid long, vnlesse things be cut shorter.
Exeunt.

Actus Secundus. Scena Prima.

Enter Bastard, and Curan, seuerally.

Bast. Saue thee *Curan.*

Cur. And your Sir, I haue bin With your Father, and giuen him notice That the Duke of *Cornwall*, and *Regan* his Duchesse Will be here with him this night.

Bast. How comes that?

Cur. Nay I know not, you haue heard of the newes abroad, I meane the whisper'd ones, for they are yet but ear-kissing arguments.

Bast. Not I: pray you what are they?

Cur. Haue you heard of no likely Warres toward, 'Twixt the Dukes of *Cornwall*, and *Albany*?

Bast. Not a word.

Cur. You may do then in time,
Fare you well Sir. *Exit.*

Bast. The Duke be here to night? The better best,
This weaues it selfe perforce into my businesse,
My Father hath set guard to take my Brother,
And I haue one thing of a queazie question
Which I must act, Briefenesse, and Fortune worke,

Enter Edgar.
Brother, a word, discend; Brother I say,
My Father watches: O Sir, fly this place,
Intelligence is giuen where you are hid;
You haue now the good aduantage of the night,
Haue you not spoken 'gainst the Duke of *Cornewall?*
Hee's comming hither, now i'th' night, i'th' haste,
And *Regan* with him, haue you nothing said
Vpon his partie 'gainst the Duke of *Albany?*
Aduise your selfe.

Edg. I am sure on't, not a word.

Bast. I heare my Father comming, pardon me:
In cunning, I must draw my Sword vpon you:
Draw, seeme to defend your selfe,
Now quit you well.
Yeeld, come before my Father, light hoa, here,
Fly Brother, Torches, Torches, so farewell. *Exit Edgar.*

Some blood drawne on me, would beget opinion
Of my more fierce endeauour. I haue seene drunkards
Do more then this in sport; Father, Father,
Stop, stop, no helpe?

Enter Gloster, and Seruants with Torches.

Glo. Now *Edmund*, where's the villaine?

Bast. Here stood he in the dark, his sharpe Sword out, Mumbling of wicked charmes, coniuring the Moone To stand auspicious Mistris.

Glo. But where is he?

Bast. Looke Sir, I bleed.

Glo. Where is the villaine, *Edmund*?

Bast. Fled this way Sir, when by no meanes he could.

Glo. Pursue him, ho, go after. By no meanes, what?

Bast. Perswade me to the murther of your Lordship,
But

But that I told him the reuenging Gods,
'Gainst Paricides did all the thunder bend,
Spoke with how manifold, and strong a Bond
The Child was bound to'th' Father; Sir in fine,
Seeing how lothly opposite I stood
To his vnnaturall purpose, in fell motion
With his prepared Sword, he charges home
My vnprouided body, latch'd mine armes;
And when he saw my best alarum'd spirits
Bold in the quarrels right, rouz'd to th'encounter,
Or whether gasted by the noyse I made,
Full sodainely he fled.

  Glost. Let him fly farre:
Nor in this Land shall he remaine vncaught
And found; dispatch, the Noble Duke my Master,
My worthy Arch and Patron comes to night,
By his authoritie I will proclaime it,
That he which finds him shall deserue our thankes,
Bringing the murderous Coward to the stake:
He that conceales him death.

  Bast. When I dissuaded him from his intent,
And found him pight to doe it, with curst speech
I threaten'd to discouer him; he replied,
Thou vnpossessing Bastard, dost thou thinke,
If I would stand against thee, would the reposall
Of any trust, vertue, or worth in thee
Make thy words faith'd? No, what should I denie,
(As this I would, though thou didst produce
My very Character) I'ld turne it all
To thy suggestion, plot, and damned practise:
And thou must make a dullard of the world,
If they not thought the profits of my death
Were very pregnant and potentiall spirits
To make thee seeke it.   *Tucket within.*

  Glo. O strange and fastned Villaine,
Would he deny his Letter, said he?
Harke, the Dukes Trumpets, I know not wher he comes;
All Ports Ile barre, the villaine shall not scape,
The Duke must grant me that: besides, his picture
I will send farre and neere, that all the kingdome
May haue due note of him, and of my land,
(Loyall and naturall Boy) Ile worke the meanes
To make thee capable.

Enter Cornewall, Regan, and Attendants.

  Corn. How now my Noble friend, since I came hither
(Which I can call but now,) I haue heard strangenesse.
  Reg. If it be true, all vengeance comes too short
Which can pursue th'offender; how dost my Lord?
  Glo. O Madam, my old heart is crack'd, it's crack'd.
  Reg. What, did my Fathers Godsonne seeke your life?
He whom my Father nam'd, your *Edgar*?
  Glo. O Lady, Lady, shame would haue it hid.
  Reg. Was he not companion with the riotous Knights
That tended vpon my Father?
  Glo. I know not Madam, 'tis too bad, too bad.
  Bast. Yes Madam, he was of that consort.
  Reg. No maruaile then, though he were ill affected,
'Tis they haue put him on the old mans death,
To haue th'expence and wast of his Reuenues:
I haue this present euening from my Sister
Beene well inform'd of them, and with such cautions,
That if they come to soiourne at my house,
Ile not be there.
  Cor. Nor I, assure thee *Regan*;

Edmund, I heare that you haue shewne your Father
A Child-like Office.
  Bast. It was my duty Sir.
  Glo. He did bewray his practise, and receiu'd
This hurt you see, striuing to apprehend him.
  Cor. Is he pursued?
  Glo. I my good Lord.
  Cor. If he be taken, he shall neuer more
Be feat'd of doing harme, make your owne purpose,
How in my strength you please: for you *Edmund*,
Whose vertue and obedience doth this instant
So much commend it selfe, you shall be ours,
Nature's of such deepe trust, we shall much need:
You we first seize on.
  Bast. I shall serue you Sir truely, how euer else.
  Glo. For him I thanke your Grace.
  Cor. You know not why we came to visit you?
  Reg. Thus out of season, thredding darke ey'd night,
Occasions Noble *Gloster* of some prize,
Wherein we must haue vse of your aduise.
Our Father he hath writ, so hath our Sister,
Of differences, which I best though it fit
To answere from our home: the seuerall Messengers
From hence attend dispatch, our good old Friend,
Lay comforts to your bosome, and bestow
Your needfull counsaile to our businesses,
Which craues the instant vse.
  Glo. I serue you Madam,
Your Graces are right welcome.   *Exeunt. Flourish.*

Scena Secunda.

Enter Kent, and Steward seuerally.

  Stew. Good dawning to thee Friend, art of this house?
  Kent. I.
  Stew. Where may we set our horses?
  Kent. I'th'myre.
  Stew. Prythee, if thou lou'st me, tell me.
  Kent. I loue thee not.
  Ste. Why then I care not for thee.
  Kent. If I had thee in *Lipsbury* Pinfold, I would make
thee care for me.
  Ste. Why do'st thou vse me thus? I know thee not.
  Kent. Fellow I know thee.
  Ste. What do'st thou know me for?
  Kent. A Knaue, a Rascall, an eater of broken meates, a
base, proud, shallow, beggerly, three-suited-hundred
pound, filthy woosted-stocking knaue, a Lilly-liuered,
action-taking, whoreson glasse-gazing super-seruiceable
finicall Rogue, one Trunke-inheriting slaue, one that
would'st be a Baud in way of good seruice, and art nothing but the composition of a Knaue, Begger, Coward,
Pandar, and the Sonne and Heire of a Mungrill Bitch,
one whom I will beate into clamours whining, if thou
deny'st the least sil'able of thy addition.
  Stew. Why, what a monstrous Fellow art thou, thus
to raile on one, that is neither knowne of thee, nor
knowes thee?
  Kent. What a brazen-fac'd Varlet art thou, to deny
thou knowest me? Is it two dayes since I tript vp thy
heeles, and beate thee before the King? Draw you rogue,

for though it be night, yet the Moone shines, Ile make a sop oth' Moonshine of you, you whoreson Cullyenly Barber-monger, draw.

Stew. Away, I haue nothing to do with thee.

Kent. Draw you Rascall, you come with Letters against the King, and take Vanitie the puppets part, against the Royaltie of her Father: draw you Rogue, or Ile so carbonado your shanks, draw you Rascall, come your waies.

Ste. Helpe, ho, murther, helpe.

Kent. Strike you slaue: stand rogue, stand you neat slaue, strike.

Stew. Helpe hoa, murther, murther.

Enter Bastard, Cornewall, Regan, Gloster, Seruants.

Bast. How now, what's the matter? Part.

Kent. With you goodman Boy, if you please, come, Ile flesh ye, come on yong Master.

Glo. Weapons? Armes? what's the matter here?

Cor. Keepe peace vpon your liues, he dies that strikes againe, what is the matter?

Reg. The Messengers from our Sister, and the King?

Cor. What is your difference, speake?

Stew. I am scarce in breath my Lord.

Kent. No Maruell, you haue so bestir'd your valour, you cowardly Rascall, nature disclaimes in thee: a Taylor made thee.

Cor. Thou art a strange fellow, a Taylor make a man?

Kent. A Taylor Sir, a Stone-cutter, or a Painter, could not haue made him so ill, though they had bin but two yeares oth' trade.

Cor. Speake yet, how grew your quarrell?

Ste. This ancient Ruffian Sir, whose life I haue spar'd at sute of his gray-beard.

Kent. Thou whoreson Zed, thou vnnecessary letter: my Lord, if you will giue me leaue, I will tread this vnboulted villaine into morter, and daube the wall of a Iakes with him. Spare my gray-beard, you wagtaile?

Cor. Peace sirrah,
You beastly knaue, know you no reuerence?

Kent. Yes Sir, but anger hath a priuiledge.

Cor. Why art thou angrie?

Kent. That such a slaue as this should weare a Sword,
Who weares no honesty: such smiling rogues as these,
Like Rats oft bite the holy cords a twaine,
Which are t'intrince, t'vnloose: smooth euery passion
That in the natures of their Lords rebell,
Being oile to fire, snow to the colder moodes,
Reuenge, affirme, and turne their Halcion beakes
With euery gall, and vary of their Masters,
Knowing naught (like dogges) but following:
A plague vpon your Epilepticke visage,
Smoile you my speeches, as I were a Foole?
Goose, if I had you vpon *Sarum* Plaine,
I'ld driue ye cackling home to *Camelot.*

Corn. What art thou mad old Fellow?

Glost. How fell you out, say that?

Kent. No contraries hold more antipathy,
Then I, and such a knaue.

Corn. Why do'st thou call him Knaue?
What is his fault?

Kent. His countenance likes me not.

Cor. No more perchance do's mine, nor his, nor hers.

Kent. Sir, 'tis my occupation to be plaine,
I haue seene better faces in my time,
Then stands on any shoulder that I see
Before me, at this instant.

Corn. This is some Fellow,
Who hauing beene prais'd for bluntnesse, doth affect
A saucy roughnes, and constraines the garb
Quite from his Nature. He cannot flatter he,
An honest mind and plaine, he must speake truth,
And they will take it so, if not, hee's plaine.
These kind of Knaues I know, which in this plainnesse
Harbour more craft, and more corrupter ends,
Then twenty silly-ducking obseruants,
That stretch their duties nicely.

Kent. Sir, in good faith, in sincere verity,
Vnder th'allowance of your great aspect,
Whose influence like the wreath of radient fire
On flicking *Phœbus* front.

Corn. What mean'st by this?

Kent. To go out of my dialect, which you discommend so much; I know Sir, I am no flatterer, he that beguild you in a plaine accent, was a plaine Knaue, which for my part I will not be, though I should win your displeasure to entreat me too't.

Corn. What was th'offence you gaue him?

Ste. I neuer gaue him any:
It pleas'd the King his Master very late
To strike at me vpon his misconstruction,
When he compact, and flattering his displeasure
Tript me behind: being downe, insulted, rail'd,
And put vpon him such a deale of Man,
That worthied him, got praises of the King,
For him attempting, who was selfe-subdued,
And in the fleshment of this dead exploit,
Drew on me here againe.

Kent. None of these Rogues, and Cowards
But *Aiax* is there Foole.

Corn. Fetch forth the Stocks?
You stubborne ancient Knaue, you reuerent Bragart,
Wee'l teach you.

Kent. Sir, I am too old to learne:
Call not your Stocks for me, I serue the King.
On whose imployment I was sent to you,
You shall doe small respects, show too bold malice
Against the Grace, and Person of my Master,
Stocking his Messenger.

Corn. Fetch forth the Stocks;
As I haue life and Honour, there shall he sit till Noone.

Reg. Till noone? till night my Lord, and all night too.

Kent. Why Madam, if I were your Fathers dog,
You should not vse me so.

Reg. Sir, being his Knaue, I will.   *Stocks brought out.*

Cor. This is a Fellow of the selfe same colour,
Our Sister speakes of. Come, bring away the Stocks.

Glo. Let me beseech your Grace, not to do so,
The King his Master, needs must take it ill
That he so slightly valued in his Messenger,
Should haue him thus restrained.

Cor. Ile answere that.

Reg. My Sister may recieue it much more worsse,
To haue her Gentleman abus'd, assaulted.

Corn. Come my Lord, away.   *Exit.*

Glo. I am sorry for thee friend, 'tis the Duke pleasure,
Whose disposition all the world well knowes
Will not be rub'd nor stopt, Ile entreat for thee.

Kent. Pray do not Sir, I haue watch'd and trauail'd hard,
Some time I shall sleepe out, the rest Ile whistle:
A good mans fortune may grow out at heeles:

Giue

The Tragedie of King Lear.

Giue you good morrow.

Glo. The Duke's too blame in this,
'Twill be ill taken. *Exit.*

Kent. Good King, that must approue the common saw,
Thou out of Heauens benediction com'st
To the warme Sun.
Approach thou Beacon to this vnder Globe,
That by thy comfortable Beames I may
Peruse this Letter. Nothing almost sees miracles
But miserie. I know 'tis from *Cordelia*,
Who hath most fortunately beene inform'd
Of my obscured course. And shall finde time
From this enormous State, seeking to giue
Losses their remedies. All weary and o're-watch'd,
Take vantage heauie eyes, not to behold
This shamefull lodging. Fortune goodnight,
Smile once more, turne thy wheele.

Enter Edgar.

Edg. I heard my selfe proclaim'd,
And by the happy hollow of a Tree,
Escap'd the hunt. No Port is free, no place
That guard, and most vnusall vigilance
Do's not attend my taking. Whiles I may scape
I will preserue myselfe: and am bethought
To take the basest, and most poorest shape
That euer penury in contempt of man,
Brought neere to beast; my face Ile grime with filth,
Blanket my loines, elfe all my haires in knots,
And with presented nakednesse out-face
The Windes, and persecutions of the skie;
The Country giues me proofe, and president
Of Bedlam beggers, who with roaring voices,
Strike in their num'd and mortified Armes,
Pins, Wodden-prickes, Nayles, Sprigs of Rosemarie:
And with this horrible obiect, from low Farmes,
Poore pelting Villages, Sheeps-Coates, and Milles,
Sometimes with Lunaticke bans, sometime with Praiers
Inforce their charitie: poore *Turlygod*, poore *Tom*,
That's something yet: *Edgar* I nothing am. *Exit.*

Enter Lear, Foole, and Gentleman.

Lea. 'Tis strange that they should so depart from home,
And not send backe my Messengers.

Gent. As I learn'd,
The night before, there was no purpose in them
Of this remoue.

Kent. Haile to thee Noble Master.

Lear. Ha? Mak'st thou this shame ahy pastime?

Kent. No my Lord.

Foole. Hah, ha, he weares Cruell Garters Horses are
tide by the heads, Dogges and Beares by'th'necke,
Monkies by'th'loynes, and Men by'th'legs: when a man
ouerlustie at legs, then he weares wodden nether-stocks.

Lear. What's he,
That hath so much thy place mistooke
To set thee heere?

Kent. It is both he and she,
Your Son, and Daughter.

Lear. No.

Kent. Yes.

Lear. No I say.

Kent. I say yea.

Lear. By *Iupiter* I sweare no.

Kent. By *Iuno*, I sweare I.

Lear. They durst not do't:
They could not, would not do't: 'tis worse then murther,
To do vpon respect such violent outrage:
Resolue me with all modest haste, which way
Thou might'st deserue, or they impose this vsage,
Comming from vs.

Kent. My Lord, when at their home
I did commend your Highnesse Letters to them,
Ere I was risen from the place, that shewed
My dutie kneeling, came there a reeking Poste,
Stew'd in his haste, halfe breathlesse, painting forth
From *Gonerill* his Mistris, salutations;
Deliuer'd Letters spight of intermission,
Which presently they read; on those contents
They summon'd vp their meiney, straight tooke Horse,
Commanded me to follow, and attend
The leisure of their answer, gaue me cold lookes,
And meeting heere the other Messenger,
Whose welcome I perceiu'd had poison'd mine,
Being the very fellow which of late
Displaid so sawcily against your Highnesse,
Hauing more man then wit about me, drew;
He rais'd the house, with loud and coward cries,
Your Sonne and Daughter found this trespasse worth
The shame which heere it suffers. (way,

Foole. Winters not gon yet, if the wil'd Geese fly that
Fathers that weare rags, do make their Children blind,
But Fathers that beare bags, shall see their children kind.
Fortune that arrant whore, nere turns the key toth' poore.
But for all this thou shalt haue as many Dolors for thy
Daughters, as thou canst tell in a yeare.

Lear. Oh how this Mother swels vp toward my heart!
Historica passio, downe thou clining sorrow,
Thy Elements below where is this Daughter?

Kent. With the Earle Sir, here within.

Lear. Follow me not, stay here. *Exit.*

Gen. Made you no more offence,
But what you speake of?

Kent. None:
How chance the the King comes with so small a number?

Foole. And thou hadst beene set i'th' Stockes for that
question, thou'dst well deseru'd it.

Kent. Why Foole?

Foole. Wee'l set thee to schoole to an Ant, to teach
thee ther's no labouring i'th' winter. All that follow their
noses, are led by their eyes, but blinde men, and there's
not a nose among twenty, but can smell him that's stinking; let go thy hold, when a greatwheele runs downe a
hill, least it breake thy necke with following. But the
great one that goes vpward, let him drawthee after:
when a wiseman giues thee better counsell giue me mine
againe, I would haue none but knaues follow it, since a
Foole giues it.

That Sir, which serues and seekes for gaine,
And followes but for forme;
Will packe, when it begins to raine,
And leaue thee in the storme,
But I will tarry, the Foole will stay,
And let the wiseman flie:
The knaue turnes Foole that runnes away,
The Foole no knaue perdie.

Enter Lear, and Glofter.

Kent. Where learn'd you this Foole?

Foole. Not i'th' Stocks Foole.

Lear.

Lear. Deny to speake with me?
They are sicke, they are weary,
They haue trauail'd all the night? meere fetches,
The images of reuolt and flying off.
Fetch me a better answer.

Glo. My deere Lord,
You know the fiery quality of the Duke,
How vnremoueable and fixt he is
In his owne course.

Lear. Vengeance, Plague, Death, Confusion:
Fiery? What quality? Why *Gloster, Gloster,*
I'ld speake with the Duke of *Cornewall,* and his wife.

Glo. Well my good Lord, I haue inform'd them so.

Lear. Inform'd them? Do'st thou vnderstand me man.

Glo. I my good Lord.

Lear. The King would speake with *Cornwall,*
The deere Father
Would with his Daughter speake, commands, tends, ser-
Are they inform'd of this? My breath and blood: (uice,
Fiery? The fiery Duke, tell the hot Duke that——
No, but not yet, may be he is not well,
Infirmity doth still neglect all office,
Whereto our health is bound, we are not our selues,
When Nature being opprest, commands the mind
To suffer with the body; Ile forbeare,
And am fallen out with my more headier will,
To take the indispos'd and sickly fit,
For the sound man. Death on my state: wherefore
Should he sit heere? This act perswades me,
That this remotion of the Duke and her
Is practise only. Giue me my Seruant forth;
Goe tell the Duke, and's wife, I'ld speake with them:
Now, presently: bid them come forth and heare me,
Or at their Chamber doore Ile beate the Drum,
Till it crie sleepe to death.

Glo. I would haue all well betwixt you. *Exit.*

Lear. Oh me my heart! My rising heart! But downe.

Foole. Cry to it Nunckle, as the Cockney did to the
Eeles, when she put 'em i'th' Paste aliue, she knapt 'em
o'th' coxcombs with a sticke, and cryed downe wantons,
downe; 'twas her Brother, that in pure kindnesse to his
Horse buttered his Hay.

Enter Cornewall, Regan, Gloster, Seruants.

Lear. Good morrow to you both.

Corn. Haile to your Grace. *Kent here set at liberty.*

Reg. I am glad to see your Highnesse.

Lear. *Regan,* I thinke your are. I know what reason
I haue to thinke so, if thou should'st not be glad,
I would diuorce me from thy Mother Tombe,
Sepulchring an Adultresse. O are you free?
Some other time for that. Beloued *Regan,*
Thy Sisters naught: oh *Regan,* she hath tied
Sharpe tooth'd vnkindnesse, like a vulture heere,
I can scarce speake to thee, thou'lt not beleeue
With how deprau'd a quality. Oh *Regan.*

Reg. I pray you Sir, take patience, I haue hope
You lesse know how to value her desert,
Then she to scant her dutie.

Lear. Say? How is that?

Reg. I cannot thinke my Sister in the least
Would faile her Obligation. If Sir perchance
She haue restrained the Riots of your Followres,
'Tis on such ground, and to such wholesome end,
As cleeres her from all blame.

Lear. My curses on her.

Reg. O Sir, you are old,
Nature in you stands on the very Verge
Of his confine: you should be rul'd, and led
By some discretion, that discernes your state
Better then you your selfe: therefore I pray you,
That to our Sister, you do make returne,
Say you haue wrong'd her.

Lear. Aske her forgiuenesse?
Do you but marke how this becomes the house?
Deere daughter, I confesse that I am old;
Age is vnnecessary: on my knees I begge,
That you'l vouchsafe me Rayment, Bed, and Food.

Reg. Good Sir, no more: these are vnsightly trickes:
Returne you to my Sister.

Lear. Neuer *Regan:*
She hath abated me of halfe my Traine;
Look'd blacke vpon me, strooke me with her Tongue
Most Serpent-like, vpon the very Heart.
All, the stor'd Vengeances of Heauen, fall
On her ingratefull top: strike her yong bones
You taking Ayres, with Lamenesse.

Corn. Fye sir, fie.

Le. You nimble Lightnings, dart your blinding flames
Into her scornfull eyes: Infect her Beauty,
You Fen-suck'd Fogges, drawne by the powrfull Sunne,
To fall, and blister.

Reg. O the blest Gods!
So will you wish on me, when the rash moode is on.

Lear. No *Regan,* thou shalt neuer haue my curse:
Thy tender-hefted Nature shall not giue
Thee o're to harshnesse: Her eyes are fierce, but thine
Do comfort, and not burne. 'Tis not in thee
To grudge my pleasures, to cut off my Traine,
To bandy hasty words, to scant my sizes,
And in conclusion, to oppose the bolt
Against my comming in. Thou better know'st
The Offices of Nature, bond of Childhood,
Effects of Curtesie, dues of Gratitude;
Thy halfe o'th' Kingdome hast thou not forgot,
Wherein I thee endow'd.

Reg. Good Sir, to th' purpose. *Tucket within.*

Lear. Who put my man i'th' Stockes?

Enter Steward.

Corn. What Trumpet's that?

Reg. I know't, my Sisters: this approues her Letter,
That she would soone be heere. Is your Lady come?

Lear. This is a Slaue, whose easie borrowed pride
Dwels in the sickly grace of her he followes.
Out Varlet, from my sight.

Corn. What meanes your Grace?

Enter Gonerill.

Lear. Who stockt my Seruant? *Regan,* I haue good hope
Thou did'st not know on't.
Who comes here? O Heauens!
If you do loue old men; if your sweet sway
Allow Obedience; if you your selues are old,
Make it your cause: Send downe, and take my part.
Art not asham'd to looke vpon this Beard?
O *Regan,* will you take her by the hand?

Gon. Why not by'th' hand Sir? How haue I offended?
All's not offence that indiscretion findes,
And dotage termes so.

Lear. O sides, you are too tough!
Will you yet hold?
How came my man i'th' Stockes?

Corn. I set him there, Sir: but his owne Disorders
Deseru'd

Deseru'd much lesse aduancement.

 Lear. You? Did you?

 Reg. I pray you Father being weake, seeme so;
If till the expiration of your Moneth
You will returne and soiourne with my Sister,
Dismissing halfe your traine, come then to me,
I am now from home, and out of that prouision
Which shall be needfull for your entertainement.

 Lear. Returne to her? and fifty men dismiss'd?
No, rather I abiure all roofes, and chuse
To wage against the enmity oth'ayre,
To be a Comrade with the Wolfe, and Owle,
Necessities sharpe pinch. Returne with her?
Why the hot-bloodied *France*, that dowerlesse tooke
Our yongest borne, I could as well be brought
To knee his Throne, and Squire-like pension beg,
To keepe base life afoote; returne with her?
Perswade me rather to be slaue and sumpter
To this detested groome.

 Gon. At your choice Sir.

 Lear. I prythee Daughter do not make me mad,
I will not trouble thee my Child; farewell:
Wee'l no more meete, no more see one another.
But yet thou art my flesh, my blood, my Daughter,
Or rather a disease that's in my flesh,
Which I must needs call mine. Thou art a Byle,
A plague sore, or imbossed Carbuncle
In my corrupted blood. But Ile not chide thee,
Let shame come when it will, I do not call it,
I do not bid the Thunder-bearer shoote,
Nor tell tales of thee to high-iudging *Ioue*,
Mend when thou can'st, be better at thy leisure,
I can be patient, I can stay with *Regan*,
I and my hundred Knights.

 Reg. Not altogether so,
I look'd not for you yet, nor am prouided
For your fit welcome, giue eare Sir to my Sister,
For those that mingle reason with your passion,
Must be content to thinke you old, and so,
But she knowes what she do's.

 Lear. Is this well spoken?

 Reg. I dare auouch it Sir, what fifty Followers?
Is it not well? What should you need of more?
Yea, or so many? Sith that both charge and danger,
Speake 'gainst so great a number? How in one house
Should many people, vnder two commands
Hold amity? 'Tis hard, almost impossible.

 Gon. Why might not you my Lord, receiue attendance
From those that she cals Seruants, or from mine?

 Reg. Why not my Lord?
If then they chanc'd to slacke ye,
We could comptroll them; if you will come to me,
(For now I spie a danger) I entreate you
To bring but fiue and twentie, to no more
Will I giue place or notice.

 Lear. I gaue you all.

 Reg. And in good time you gaue it.

 Lear. Made you my Guardians, my Depositaries,
But kept a reseruation to be followed
With such a number? What, must I come to you
With fiue and twenty? *Regan*, said you so?

 Reg. And speak't againe my Lord, no more with me.

 Lea. Those wicked Creatures yet do look wel fauor'd
When others are more wicked, not being the worst
Stands in some ranke of praise, Ile go with thee,
Thy fifty yet doth double fiue and twenty,
And thou art twice her Loue.

 Gon. Heare me my Lord;
What need you fiue and twenty? Ten? Or fiue?
To follow in a house, where twice so many
Haue a command to tend you?

 Reg. What need one?

 Lear. O reason not the need: our basest Beggers
Are in the poorest thing superfluous,
Allow not Nature, more then Nature needs:
Mans life is cheape as Beastes. Thou art a Lady;
If onely to go warme were gorgeous,
Why Nature needs not what thou gorgeous wear'st,
Which scarcely keepes thee warme, but for true need:
You Heauens, giue me that patience, patience I need,
You see me heere (you Gods) a poore old man,
As full of griefe as age, wretched in both,
If it be you that stirres these Daughters hearts
Against their Father, foole me not so much,
To beare it tamely: touch me with Noble anger,
And let not womens weapons, water drops,
Staine my mans cheekes. No you vnnaturall Hags,
I will haue such reuenges on you both,
That all the world shall——I will do such things,
What they are yet, I know not, but they shalbe
The terrors of the earth? you thinke Ile weepe,
No, Ile not weepe, I haue full cause of weeping.

Storme and Tempest.

But this heart shal break into a hundred thousand flawes
Or ere Ile weepe: O Foole, I shall go mad. *Exeunt.*

 Corn. Let vs withdraw, 'twill be a Storme.

 Reg. This house is little, the old man an'ds people,
Cannot be well bestow'd.

 Gon. 'Tis his owne blame hath put himselfe from rest,
And must needs taste his folly.

 Reg. For his particular, ile receiue him gladly,
But not one follower.

 Gon. So am I purpos'd.
Where is my Lord of *Gloster*?

Enter Gloster.

 Corn. Followed the old man forth, he is return'd.

 Glo. The King is in high rage.

 Corn. Whether is he going?

 Glo. He cals to Horse, but will I know not whether.

 Corn. 'Tis best to giue him way, he leads himselfe.

 Gon. My Lord, entreate him by no meanes to stay.

 Glo. Alacke the night comes on, and the high windes
Do sorely ruffle, for many Miles about
There's scarce a Bush.

 Reg. O Sir, to wilfull men,
The iniuries that they themselues procure,
Must be their Schoole-Masters: shut vp your doores,
He is attended with a desperate traine,
And what they may incense him too, being apt,
To haue his eare abus'd, wisedome bids feare.

 Cor. Shut vp your doores my Lord, 'tis a wil'd night,
My *Regan* counsels well: come out oth' storme. *Exeunt.*

Actus Tertius. Scena Prima.

Storme still. Enter Kent, and a Gentleman, seuerally.

 Kent. Who's there besides foule weather?

 Gen. One minded like the weather, most vnquietly.

Kent. I know you: Where's the King?

Gent. Contending with the fretfull Elements;
Bids the winde blow the Earth into the Sea,
Or swell the curled Waters 'boue the Maine,
That things might change, or cease.

Kent. But who is with him?

Gent. None but the Foole, who labours to out-iest
His heart-strooke iniuries.

Kent. Sir, I do know you,
And dare vpon the warrant of my note
Commend a deere thing to you. There is diuision
(Although as yet the face of it is couer'd
With mutuall cunning) 'twixt Albany, and Cornwall:
Who haue, as who haue not, that their great Starres
Thron'd and set high; Seruants, who seeme no lesse,
Which are to France the Spies and Speculations
Intelligent of our State. What hath bin seene,
Either in snuffes, and packings of the Dukes,
Or the hard Reine which both of them hath borne
Against the old kinde King; or something deeper,
Whereof (perchance) these are but furnishings.

Gent. I will talke further with you.

Kent. No, do not;
For confirmation that I am much more
Then my out-wall; open this Purse, and take
What it containes. If you shall see *Cordelia*,
(As feare not but you shall) shew her this Ring,
And she will tell you who that Fellow is
That yet you do not know. Fye on this Storme,
I will go seeke the King.

Gent. Giue me your hand,
Haue you no more to say?

Kent. Few words, but to effect more then all yet;
That when we haue found the King, in which your pain
That way, Ile this: He that first lights on him,
Holla the other. *Exeunt.*

Scena Secunda.

Storme still. Enter Lear, and Foole.

Lear. Blow windes, & crack your cheekes; Rage, blow
You Cataracts, and Hyrricano's spout,
Till you haue drench'd our Steeples, 'drown the Cockes.
You Sulph'rous and Thought-executing Fires,
Vaunt-curriors of Oake-cleauing Thunder-bolts,
Sindge my white head. And thou all-shaking Thunder,
Strike flat the thicke Rotundity o'th'world,
Cracke Natures moulds, all germaines spill at once
That makes ingratefull Man.

Foole. O Nunkle, Court holy-water in a dry house, is
better then this Rain-water out o'doore. Good Nunkle,
in, aske thy Daughters blessing, heere's a night pitties
neither Wisemen, nor Fooles.

Lear. Rumble thy belly full: spit Fire, spowt Raine:
Nor Raine, Winde, Thunder, Fire are my Daughters;
I taxe not you, you Elements with vnkindnesse.
I neuer gaue you Kingdome, call'd you Children;
You owe me no subscription. Then let fall
Your horrible pleasure. Heere I stand your Slaue,
A poore, infirme, weake, and dispis'd old man:
But yet I call you Seruile Ministers,
That will with two pernicious Daughters ioyne
Your high-engender'd Battailes, 'gainst a head
So old, and white as this. O, ho! 'tis foule.

Foole. He that has a house to put's head in, has a good
Head-peece:
The Codpiece that will house, before the head has any;
The Head, and he shall Lowse: so Beggers marry many.
The man ỹ makes his Toe, what he his Hart should make,
Shall of a Corne cry woe, and turne his sleepe to wake.
For there was neuer yet faire woman, but shee made
mouthes in a glasse.

Enter Kent.

Lear. No, I will be the patterne of all patience,
I will say nothing.

Kent. Who's there?

Foole. Marry here's Grace, and a Codpiece, that's a
Wiseman, and a Foole.

Kent. Alas Sir are you here? Things that loue night,
Loue not such nights as these: The wrathfull Skies
Gallow the very wanderers of the darke
And make them keepe their Caues: Since I was man,
Such sheets of Fire, such bursts of horrid Thunder,
Such groanes of roaring Winde, and Raine, I neuer
Remember to haue heard. Mans Nature cannot carry
Th'affliction, nor the feare.

Lear. Let the great Goddes
That keepe this dreadfull pudder o're our heads,
Finde out their enemies now. Tremble thou Wretch,
That hast within thee vndivulged Crimes
Vnwhipt of Iustice. Hide thee, thou Bloudy hand;
Thou Periur'd, and thou Simular of Vertue
That art Incestuous. Caytiffe, to peeces shake
That vnder couert, and conuenient seeming
Ha's practis'd on mans life. Close pent-vp guilts,
Riue your concealing Continents, and cry
These dreadfull Summoners grace. I am a man,
More sinn'd against, then sinning.

Kent. Alacke, bare-headed?
Gracious my Lord, hard by heere is a Houell,
Some friendship will it lend you 'gainst the Tempest:
Repose you there, while I to this hard house,
(More harder then the stones whereof 'tis rais'd,
Which euen but now, demanding after you,
Deny'd me to come in) returne, and force
Their scanted curtesie.

Lear. My wits begin to turne.
Come on my boy. How dost my boy? Art cold?
I am cold my selfe. Where is this straw, my Fellow?
The Art of our Necessities is strange,
And can make vilde things precious. Come, your Houel;
Poore Foole, and Knaue, I haue one part in my heart
That's sorry yet for thee.

Foole. He that has and a little-tyne wit,
With heigh-ho, the Winde and the Raine,
Must make content with his Fortunes fit,
Though the Raine it raineth euery day.

Le. True Boy: Come bring vs to this Houell. *Exit.*

Foole. This is a braue night to coole a Curtizan:
Ile speake a Prophesie ere I go:
When Priests are more in word, then matter;
When Brewers marre their Malt with water;
When Nobles are their Taylors Tutors,
No Heretiques burn'd, but wenches Sutors;
When euery Case in Law, is right:
No Squire in debt, nor no poore Knight;
When Slanders do not liue in Tongues;
Nor Cut-purses come not to throngs;
When Vsurers tell their Gold i'th'Field,

The Tragedie of King Lear.

And Baudes, and whores, do Churches build,
Then shal the Realme of *Albion*, come to great confusion:
Then comes the time, who liues to see't,
That going shalbe vs'd with feet. (time.
This prophecie *Merlin* shall make, for I liue before his
                                                    Exit.

Scæna Tertia.

Enter Gloster, and Edmund.

Glo. Alacke, alacke *Edmund*, I like not this vnnaturall dealing; when I desired their leaue that I might pity him, they tooke from me the vse of mine owne house, charg'd me on paine of perpetuall displeasure, neither to speake of him, entreat for him, or any way sustaine him.

Bast. Most sauage and vnnaturall.

Glo. Go too; say you nothing. There is diuision betweene the Dukes, and a worsse matter then that: I haue receiued a Letter this night, 'tis dangerous to be spoken, I haue lock'd the Letter in my Closset, these iniuries the King now beares, will be reuenged home; ther is part of a Power already footed, we must incline to the King, I will looke him, and priuily relieue him; goe you and maintaine talke with the Duke, that my charity be not of him perceiued; If he aske for me, I am ill, and gone to bed, if I die for it, (as no lesse is threatned me) the King my old Master must be relieued. There is strange things toward *Edmund*, pray you be carefull.   *Exit.*

Bast. This Curtesie forbid thee, shall the Duke
Instantly know, and of that Letter too;
This seemes a faire deseruing, and must draw me
That which my Father looses: no lesse then all,
The yonger rises, when the old doth fall.   *Exit.*

Scena Quarta.

Enter Lear, Kent, and Foole.

Kent. Here is the place my Lord, good my Lord enter,
The tirrany of the open night's too rough
For Nature to endure.   *Storme still.*
  Lear. Let me alone.
  Kent. Good my Lord enter heere.
  Lear. Wilt breake my heart?
  Kent. I had rather breake mine owne,
Good my Lord enter.
  Lear. Thou think'st 'tis much that this contentious
Inuades vs to the skin so: 'tis to thee,   (storme
But where the greater malady is fixt,
The lesser is scarce felt. Thou'dst shun a Beare,
But if thy flight lay toward the roaring Sea,
Thou'dst meete the Beare i'th' mouth, when the mind's
The bodies delicate: the tempest in my mind,   free,
Doth from my sences take all feeling else,
Saue what beates there, Filliall ingratitude,
Is it not as this mouth should teare this hand
For lifting food too't? But I will punish home;
No, I will weepe no more; in such a night,
To shut me out? Poure on, I will endure:
In such a night as this? O *Regan, Gonerill,*
Your old kind Father, whose franke heart gaue all,
O that way madnesse lies, let me shun that:
No more of that.
  Kent. Good my Lord enter here.
  Lear. Prythee go in thy selfe, seeke thine owne ease,
This tempest will not giue me leaue to ponder
On things would hurt me more, but Ile goe in,
In Boy, go first. You houselesse pouertie,   *Exit.*
Nay get thee in; Ile pray, and then Ile sleepe.
Poore naked wretches, where so ere you are
That bide the pelting of this pittilesse storme,
How shall your House-lesse heads, and vnfed sides,
Your lop'd, and window'd raggednesse defend you
From seasons such as these? O I haue tane
Too little care of this: Take Physicke, Pompe,
Expose thy selfe to feele what wretches feele,
That thou maist shake the superflux to them,
And shew the Heauens more iust.

Enter Edgar, and Foole.

Edg. Fathom, and halfe, Fathom and halfe; poore *Tom.*
Foole. Come not in heere Nuncle, here's a spirit, helpe me, helpe me.
Kent. Giue me thy hand, who's there?
Foole. A spirite, a spirite, he sayes his name's poore *Tom.*
Kent. What art thou that dost grumble there i'th' straw? Come forth.
Edg. Away, the foule Fiend followes me, through the sharpe Hauthorne blow the windes. Humh, goe to thy bed and warme thee.
Lear. Did'st thou giue all to thy Daughters? And art thou come to this?
Edgar. Who giues any thing to poore *Tom?* Whom the foule fiend hath led though Fire, and through Flame, through Sword, and Whirle-Poole, o're Bog, and Quagmire, that hath laid Kniues vnder his Pillow, and Halters in his Pue, set Rats-bane by his Porredge, made him Proud of heart, to ride on a Bay trotting Horse, ouer foure incht Bridges, to course his owne shadow for a Traitor. Blisse thy fiue Wits, *Toms* a cold. O do, de, do, de, do de, blisse thee from Whirle-Windes, Starre-blasting, and taking, do poore *Tom* some charitie, whom the foule Fiend vexes. There could I haue him now, and there, and there ag ai ne, and there.   *Storme still.*
Lear. Ha's his Daughters brought him to this passe?
Could'st thou saue nothing? Would'st thou giue 'em all?
Foole. Nay, he reseru'd a Blanket, else we had bin all sham'd.
Lea. Now all the plagues that in the pendulous ayre
Hang fated o're mens faults, light on thy Daughters.
Kent. He hath no Daughters Sir.
Lear. Death Traitor, nothing could haue subdu'd
To such a lownesse, but his vnkind Daughters. (Nature
Is it the fashion, that discarded Fathers,
Should haue thus little mercy on their flesh:
Iudicious punishment, 'twas this flesh begot
Those Pelicane Daughters.
Edg. Pillicock sat on Pillicock hill, alow: alow, loo, loo.
Foole. This cold night will turne vs all to Fooles, and Madmen.
Edgar. Take heed o'th' foule Fiend, obey thy Parents, keepe thy words Iustice, sweare not, commit not,

with mans sworne Spouse; set not thy Sweet-heart on proud array. *Tom's a cold*.

Lear. What hast thou bin?

Edg. A Seruingman? Proud in heart, and minde; that curl'd my haire, wore Gloues in my cap; seru'd the Lust of my Mistris heart, and did the acte of darkenesse with her. Swore as many Oathes, as I spake words, & broke them in the sweet face of Heauen. One, that slept in the contriuing of Lust, and wak'd to doe it. Wine lou'd I deerely, Dice deerely; and in Woman, out-Paramour'd the Turke. False of heart, light of eare, bloody of hand; Hog in sloth, Foxe in stealth, Wolfe in greedinesse, Dog in madnes, Lyon in prey. Let not the creaking of shooes, Nor the rustling of Silkes, betray thy poore heart to woman. Keepe thy foote out of Brothels, thy hand out of Plackets, thy pen from Lenders Bookes, and defye the foule Fiend. Still through the Hauthorne blowes the cold winde: Sayes suum, mun, nonny, Dolphin my Boy, Boy *Sesey*: let him trot by. *Storme still*.

Lear. Thou wert better in a Graue, then to answere with thy vncouer'd body, this extremitie of the Skies. Is man no more then this? Consider him well. Thou ow'st the Worme no Silke; the Beast, no Hide; the Sheepe, no Wooll; the Cat, no perfume. Ha? Here's three on's are sophisticated. Thou art the thing it selfe; vnaccommodated man, is no more but such a poore, bare, forked Animall as thou art. Off, off you Lendings: Come, vnbutton heere.

Enter Gloucester, with a Torch.

Foole. Prythee Nunckle be contented, 'tis a naughtie night to swimme in. Now a little fire in a wilde Field, were like an old Letchers heart, a small spark, all the rest on's body, cold: Looke, heere comes a walking fire.

Edg. This is the foule Flibbertigibbet; hee begins at Curfew, and walkes at first Cocke: Hee giues the Web and the Pin, squints the eye, and makes the Hare-lippe; Mildewes the white Wheate, and hurts the poore Creature of earth.

Swithold footed thrice the old,
He met the Night-Mare, and her nine-fold;
Bid her a-light, and her troth-plight,
And aroynt thee Witch, aroynt thee.

Kent. How fares your Grace?

Lear. What's he?

Kent. Who's there? What is't you seeke?

Glou. What are you there? Your Names?

Edg. Poore Tom, that eates the swimming Frog, the Toad, the Tod-pole, the wall-Neut, and the water: that in the furie of his heart, when the foule Fiend rages, eats Cow-dung for Sallets; swalloowes the old Rat, and the ditch-Dogge; drinkes the green Mantle of the standing Poole; who is whipt from Tything to Tything, and stockt, punish'd, and imprison'd: who hath three Suites to his backe, sixe shirts to his body:

Horse to ride, and weapon to weare:
But Mice, and Rats, and such small Deare,
Haue bin Toms food, for seuen long yeare:

Beware my Follower. Peace Smulkin, peace thou Fiend.

Glou. What, hath your Grace no better company?

Edg. The Prince of Darkenesse is a Gentleman. *Modo* he's call'd, and *Mahu*.

Glou. Our flesh and blood, my Lord, is growne so vilde, that it doth hate what gets it.

Edg. Poore Tom's a cold.

Glou. Go in with me; my duty cannot suffer T'obey in all your daughters hard commands: Though their Iniunction be to barre my doores, And let this Tyrannous night take hold vpon you, Yet haue I ventured to come seeke you out, And bring you where both fire, and food is ready.

Lear. First let me talke with this Philosopher, What is the cause of Thunder?

Kent. Good my Lord take his offer, Go into th'house.

Lear. Ile talke a word with this same lerned Theban: What is your study?

Edg. How to preuent the Fiend, and to kill Vermine.

Lear. Let me aske you one word in priuate.

Kent. Importune him once more to go my Lord, His wits begin t'vnsettle.

Glou. Canst thou blame him? *Storm still* His Daughters seeke his death: Ah, that good Kent, He said it would be thus: poore banish'd man: Thou sayest the King growes mad, Ile tell thee Friend I am almost mad my selfe. I had a Sonne, Now out-law'd from my blood: he sought my life But lately: very late: I lou'd him (Friend) No Father his Sonne deerer: true to tell thee, The greefe hath craz'd my wits. What a night's this? I do beseech your grace.

Lear. O cry you mercy, Sir: Noble Philosopher, your company.

Edg. Tom's a cold.

Glou. In fellow there, into th'Houel; keep thee warm.

Lear. Come, let's in all.

Kent. This way, my Lord.

Lear. With him; I will keepe still with my Philosopher.

Kent. Good my Lord, sooth him: Let him take the Fellow.

Glou. Take him you on.

Kent. Sirra, come on: go along with vs.

Lear. Come, good Athenian.

Glou. No words, no words, hush.

Edg. Childe *Rowland* to the darke Tower came, His word was still, fie, foh, and fumme, I smell the blood of a Brittish man. *Exeunt*

Scena Quinta.

Enter Cornwall, and Edmund.

Corn. I will haue my reuenge, ere I depart his house.

Bast. How my Lord, I may be censured, that Nature thus giues way to Loyaltie, something feares mee to thinke of.

Cornw. I now perceiue, it was not altogether your Brothers euill disposition made him seeke his death: but a prouoking merit set a-worke by a reprouable badnesse in himselfe.

Bast. How malicious is my fortune, that I must repent to be iust? This is the Letter which hee spoake of; which approues him an intelligent partie to the aduantages of France. O Heauens! that this Treason were not; or not I the detector.

Corn. Go with me to the Dutchesse.

Bast. If the matter of this Paper be certain, you haue mighty businesse in hand.

Corn.

The Tragedie of King Lear.   299

Corn. True or false, it hath made thee Earle of Gloucester: seeke out where thy Father is, that hee may bee ready for our apprehension.

Bast. If I finde him comforting the King, it will stuffe his suspition more fully. I will perseuer in my course of Loyalty, though the conflict be sore betweene that, and my blood.

Corn. I will lay trust vpon thee: and thou shalt finde a deere Father in my loue. *Exeunt.*

Scena Sexta.

Enter Kent, and Gloucester.

Glou. Heere is better then the open ayre, take it thankfully: I will peece out the comfort with what addition I can: I will not be long from you. *Exit*

Kent. All the powre of his wits, haue giuen way to his impatience: the Gods reward your kindnesse.

Enter Lear, Edgar, and Foole.

Edg. Fraterretto cals me, and tells me *Nero* is an Angler in the Lake of Darknesse: pray Innocent, and beware the foule Fiend.

Foole. Prythee Nunkle tell me, whether a madman be a Gentleman, or a Yeoman.

Lear. A King, a King.

Foole. No, he's a Yeoman, that ha's a Gentleman to his Sonne: for hee's a mad Yeoman that sees his Sonne a Gentleman before him.

Lear. To haue a thousand with red burning spits Come hizzing in vpon 'em.

Edg. Blesse thy fiue wits.

Kent. O pitty: Sir, where is the patience now That you so oft haue boasted to retaine?

Edg. My teares begin to take his part so much, They marre my counterfetting.

Lear. The little dogges, and all;
Trey, Blanch, and Sweet-heart: see, they barke at me.

Edg. Tom, will throw his head at them: Auaunt you Curres, be thy mouth or blacke or white:
Tooth that poysons if it bite:
Mastiffe, Grey-hound, Mongrill, Grim,
Hound or Spaniell, Brache, or Hym:
Or Bobtaile tight, or Troudle taile,
Tom will make him weepe and waile,
For with throwing thus my head;
Dogs leapt the hatch, and all are fled.
Do, de, de, de: sese: Come, march to Wakes and Fayres, And Market Townes: poore Tom thy horne is dry.

Lear. Then let them Anatomize *Regan*: See what breeds about her heart. Is there any cause in Nature that make these hard-hearts. You sir, I entertaine for one of my hundred; only, I do not like the fashion of your garments. You will say they are Persian; but let them bee chang'd.

Enter Gloster.

Kent. Now good my Lord, lye heere, and rest awhile.

Lear. Make no noise, make no noise, draw the Curtaines: so, so, wee'l go to Supper i'th'morning.

Foole. And Ile go to bed at noone.

Glou. Come hither Friend:
Where is the King my Master?

Kent. Here Sir, but trouble him not, his wits are gon.

Glou. Good friend, I prythee take him in thy armes;
I haue ore-heard a plot of death vpon him:
There is a Litter ready, lay him in't,
And driue toward Douer friend, where thou shalt meete Both welcome, and protection. Take vp thy Master, If thou should'st dally halfe an houre, his life
With thine, and all that offer to defend him,
Stand in assured losse. Take vp, take vp,
And follow me, that will to some prouision
Giue thee quicke conduct. Come, come, away. *Exeunt*

Scena Septima.

Enter Cornwall, Regan, Gonerill, Bastard, and Seruants.

Corn. Poste speedily to my Lord your husband, shew him this Letter, the Army of France is landed: seeke out the Traitor Glouster.

Reg. Hang him instantly.

Gon. Plucke out his eyes.

Corn. Leaue him to my displeasure. *Edmond*, keepe you our Sister company: the reuenges wee are bound to take vppon your Traitorous Father, are not fit for your beholding. Aduice the Duke where you are going, to a most festiuate preparation: we are bound to the like. Our Postes shall be swift, and intelligent betwixt vs. Farewell deere Sister, farewell my Lord of Glouster.

Enter Steward.

How now? Where's the King?

Stew. My Lord of Glouster hath conuey'd him hence Some fiue or six and thirty of his Knights
Hot Questrists after him, met him at gate,
Who, with some other of the Lords, dependants,
Are gone with him toward Douer; where they boast To haue well armed Friends.

Corn. Get horses for your Mistris.

Gon. Farewell sweet Lord, and Sister. *Exit*

Corn. Edmund farewell: go seek the Traitor Gloster, Pinnion him like a Theefe, bring him before vs:
Though well we may not passe vpon his life
Without the forme of Iustice: yet our power
Shall do a curt'sie to our wrath, which men
May blame, but not comptroll.

Enter Gloucester, and Seruants.

Who's there? the Traitor?

Reg. Ingratefull Fox, 'tis he.

Corn. Binde fast his corky armes.

Glou. What meanes your Graces?
Good my Friends consider you are my Ghests:
Do me no foule play, Friends.

Corn. Binde him I say.

Reg. Hard, hard: O filthy Traitor.

Glou. Vnmercifull Lady, as you are, I'me none.

Corn. To this Chaire binde him,
Villaine, thou shalt finde.

Glou. By the kinde Gods, 'tis most ignobly done To plucke me by the Beard.

Reg. So white, and such a Traitor?

Glou. Naughty Ladie,
These haires which thou dost rauish from my chin Will quicken and accuse thee. I am your Host,
With Robbers hands, my hospitable fauours

You

You should not ruffle thus. What will you do?
  Corn. Come Sir,
What Letters had you late from France?
  Reg. Be simple answer'd, for we know the truth.
  Corn. And what confederacie haue you with the Traitors, late footed in the Kingdome?
  Reg. To whose hands
You haue sent the Lunaticke King: Speake.
  Glou. I haue a Letter guessingly set downe
Which came from one that's of a newtrall heart,
And not from one oppos'd.
  Corn. Cunning.
  Reg. And false.
  Corn. Where hast thou sent the King?
  Glou. To Douer.
  Reg. Wherefore to Douer?
Was't thou not charg'd at perill.
  Corn. Wherefore to Douer? Let him answer that.
  Glou. I am tyed to th'Stake,
And I must stand the Course.
  Reg. Wherefore to Douer?
  Glou. Because I would not see thy cruell Nailes
Plucke out his poore old eyes: nor thy fierce Sister,
In his Annointed flesh, sticke boarish phangs.
The Sea, with such a storme as his bare head,
In Hell-blacke-night indur'd, would haue buoy'd vp
And quench'd the Stelled fires:
Yet poore old heart, he holpe the Heauens to raine.
If Wolues had at thy Gate howl'd that sterne time,
Thou should'st haue said, good Porter turne the Key:
All Cruels else subscribe: but I shall see
The winged Vengeance ouertake such Children.
  Corn. See't shalt thou neuer. Fellowes hold ỹ Chaire,
Vpon these eyes of thine, Ile set my foote.
  Glou. He that will thinke to liue, till he be old,
Giue me some helpe.——O cruell! O you Gods.
  Reg. One side will mocke another: Th'other too.
  Corn. If you see vengeance.
  Seru. Hold your hand, my Lord:
I haue seru'd you euer since I was a Childe:
But better seruice haue I neuer done you,
Then now to bid you hold.
  Reg. How now, you dogge?
  Ser. If you did weare a beard vpon your chin,
I'ld shake it on this quarrell. What do you meane?
  Corn. My Villaine?
  Seru. Nay then come on, and take the chance of anger.
  Reg. Giue me thy Sword. A pezant stand vp thus?
                                    Killes him.
  Ser. Oh I am slaine: my Lord, you haue one eye left
To see some mischefe on him. Oh.
  Corn. Least it see more, preuent it; Out vilde gelly:
Where is thy luster now?
  Glou. All darke and comfortlesse?
Where's my Sonne Edmund?
Edmund, enkindle all the sparkes of Nature
To quit this horrid acte.
  Reg. Out treacherous Villaine,
Thou call'st on him, that hates thee. It was he
That made the ouerture of thy Treasons to vs:
Who is too good to pitty thee.
  Glou. O my Follies! then Edgar was abus'd,
Kinde Gods, forgiue me that, and prosper him.
  Reg. Go thrust him out at gates, and let him smell
His way to Douer.   Exit with Glouster.
How is't my Lord? How looke you?
  Corn. I haue receiu'd a hurt: Follow me Lady;
Turne out that eyelesse Villaine: throw this Slaue
Vpon the Dunghill: Regan, I bleed apace,
Vntimely comes this hurt. Giue me your arme. Exeunt.

Actus Quartus. Scena Prima.

Enter Edgar.

  Edg. Yet better thus, and knowne to be contemn'd,
Then still contemn'd and flatter'd, to be worst:
The lowest, and most deiected thing of Fortune,
Stands still in esperance, liues not in feare:
The lamentable change is from the best,
The worst returnes to laughter. Welcome then,
Thou vnsubstantiall ayre that I embrace:
The Wretch that thou hast blowne vnto the worst,
Owes nothing to thy blasts.
    Enter Glouster, and an Oldman.
But who comes heere? My Father poorely led?
World, World, O world!
But that thy strange mutations make vs hate thee,
Life would not yeelde to age.
  Oldm. O my good Lord, I haue bene your Tenant,
And your Fathers Tenant, these fourescore yeares.
  Glou. Away, get thee away: good Friend be gone,
Thy comforts can do me no good at all,
Thee, they may hurt.
  Oldm. You cannot see your way.
  Glou. I haue no way, and therefore want no eyes:
I stumbled when I saw. Full oft 'tis seene,
Our meanes secure vs, and our meere defects
Proue our Commodities. Oh deere Sonne Edgar,
The food of thy abused Fathers wrath:
Might I but liue to see thee in my touch,
I'ld say I had eyes againe.
  Oldm. How now? who's there?
  Edg. O Gods! Who is't can say I am at the worst?
I am worse then ere I was.
  Old. 'Tis poore mad Tom.
  Edg. And worse I may be yet: the worst is not,
So long as we can say this is the worst.
  Oldm. Fellow, where goest?
  Glou. Is it a Beggar-man?
  Oldm. Madman, and beggar too.
  Glou. He has some reason, else he could not beg.
I'th'last nights storme, I such a fellow saw;
Which made me thinke a Man, a Worme. My Sonne
Came then into my minde, and yet my minde
Was then scarse Friends with him.
I haue heard more since:
As Flies to wanton Boyes, are we to th'Gods,
They kill vs for their sport.
  Edg. How should this be?
Bad is the Trade that must play Foole to sorrow,
Ang'ring it selfe, and others. Blesse thee Master.
  Glou. Is that the naked Fellow?
  Oldm. I, my Lord.
  Glou. Get thee away: If for my sake
Thou wilt ore-take vs hence a mile or twaine
I'th'way toward Douer, do it for ancient loue,
And bring some couering for this naked Soule,
Which Ile intreate to leade me.
  Old. Alacke sir, he is mad.

The Tragedie of King Lear.

Glou. 'Tis the times plague,
When Madmen leade the blinde:
Do as I bid thee, or rather do thy pleasure:
Aboue the rest, be gone.

Oldm. Ile bring him the best Parrell that I haue
Come on't, what will. *Exit*

Glou. Sirrah, naked fellow.

Edg. Poore Tom's a cold. I cannot daub it further.

Glou. Come hither fellow.

Edg. And yet I must:
Blesse thy sweete eyes, they bleede.

Glou. Know'st thou the way to Douer?

Edg. Both stile, and gate; Horseway, and foot-path:
poore Tom hath bin scarr'd out of his good wits. Blesse
thee good mans sonne, from the foule Fiend.

Glou. Here take this purse, ỹ whom the heau'ns plagues
Haue humbled to all strokes: that I am wretched
Makes thee the happier: Heauens deale so still:
Let the superfluous, and Lust-dieted man,
That slaues your ordinance, that will not see
Because he do's not feele, feele your powre quickly:
So distribution should vndoo excesse,
And each man haue enough. Dost thou know Douer?

Edg. I Master.

Glou. There is a Cliffe, whose high and bending head
Lookes fearfully in the confined Deepe:
Bring me but to the very brimme of it,
And Ile repayre the misery thou do'st beare
With something rich about me: from that place,
I shall no leading neede.

Edg. Giue me thy arme;
Poore Tom shall leade thee. *Exeunt.*

Scena Secunda.

Enter Gonerill, Bastard, and Steward.

Gon. Welcome my Lord. I meruell our mild husband
Not met vs on the way. Now, where's your Master?

Stew. Madam within, but neuer man so chang'd:
I told him of the Army that was Landed:
He smil'd at it. I told him you were comming,
His answer was, the worse. Of Glosters Treachery,
And of the loyall Seruice of his Sonne
When I inform'd him, then he call'd me Sot,
And told me I had turn'd the wrong side out:
What most he should dislike, seemes pleasant to him;
What like, offensiue.

Gon. Then shall you go no further.
It is the Cowish terror of his spirit
That dares not vndertake: Hee'l not feele wrongs
Which tye him to an answer: our wishes on the way
May proue effects. Backe *Edmond* to my Brother,
Hasten his Musters, and conduct his powres.
I must change names at home, and giue the Distaffe
Into my Husbands hands. This trustie Seruant
Shall passe betweene vs: ere long you are like to heare
(If you dare venture in your owne behalfe)
A Mistresses command. Weare this; spare speech,
Decline your head. This kisse, if it durst speake
Would stretch thy Spirits vp into the ayre:
Conceiue, and fare thee well.

Bast. Yours in the rankes of death. *Exit.*

Gon. My most deere Gloster.

Oh, the difference of man, and man,
To thee a Womans seruices are due,
My Foole vsurpes my body.

Stew. Madam, here come's my Lord.

Enter Albany.

Gon. I haue beene worth the whistle.

Alb. Oh *Gonerill*,
You are not worth the dust which the rude winde
Blowes in your face.

Gon. Milke-Liuer'd man,
That bear'st a cheeke for blowes, a head for wrongs,
Who hast not in thy browes an eye-discerning
Thine Honor, from thy suffering.

Alb. See thy selfe diuell:
Proper deformitie seemes not in the Fiend
So horrid as in woman.

Gon. Oh vaine Foole.

Enter a Messenger.

Mes. Oh my good Lord, the Duke of *Cornwals* dead,
Slaine by his Seruant, going to put out
The other eye of Glouster.

Alb. Gloufters eyes.

Mes. A Seruant that he bred, thrill'd with remorse,
Oppos'd against the act: bending his Sword
To his great Master, who, threat-enrag'd
Flew on him, and among'st them fell'd him dead,
But not without that harmefull stroke, which since
Hath pluckt him after.

Alb. This shewes you are aboue
You Iustices, that these our neather crimes
So speedily can venge. But (O poore Glouster)
Lost he his other eye?

Mes. Both, both, my Lord.
This Leter Madam, craues a speedy answer:
'Tis from your Sister.

Gon. One way I like this well.
But being widdow, and my Glouster with her,]
May all the building in my fancie plucke
Vpon my hatefull life. Another way
The Newes is not so tart. Ile read, and answer.

Alb. Where was his Sonne,
When they did take his eyes?

Mes. Come with my Lady hither.

Alb. He is not heere.

Mes. No my good Lord, I met him backe againe.

Alb. Knowes he the wickednesse?

Mes. I my good Lord: 'twas he inform'd against him
And quit the house on purpose, that their punishment
Might haue the freer course.

Alb. Glouster, I liue
To thanke thee for the loue thou shew'dst the King,
And to reuenge thine eyes. Come hither Friend,
Tell me what more thou know'st. *Exeunt.*

Scena Tertia.

Enter with Drum and Colours, Cordelia, Gentlemen,
and Souldiours.

Cor. Alacke, 'tis he: why he was met euen now
As mad as the vext Sea, singing alowd,
Crown'd with ranke Fenitar, and furrow weeds,
With Hardokes, Hemlocke, Nettles, Cuckoo flowres,
Darnell

Darnell, and all the idle weedes that grow
In our sustaining Corne. A Centery send forth;
Search euery Acre in the high-growne field,
And bring him to our eye. What can mans wisedome
In the restoring his bereaued Sense; he that helpes him,
Take all my outward worth.

Gent. There is meanes Madam:
Our foster Nurse of Nature, is repose,
The which he lackes: that to prouoke in him
Are many Simples operatiue, whose power
Will close the eye of Anguish.

Cord. All blest Secrets,
All you vnpublish'd Vertues of the earth
Spring with my teares; be aydant, and remediate
In the Goodmans desires: seeke, seeke for him,
Least his vngouern'd rage, dissolue the life
That wants the meanes to leade it.

Enter Messenger.

Mes. Newes Madam,
The Brittish Powres are marching hitherward.

Cor. 'Tis knowne before. Our preparation stands
In expectation of them. O deere Father,
It is thy businesse that I go about: Therfore great France
My mourning, and importun'd teares hath pittied:
No blowne Ambition doth our Armes incite,
But loue, deere loue, and our ag'd Fathers Rite:
Soone may I heare, and see him. *Exeunt.*

Scena Quarta.

Enter Regan, and Steward.

Reg. But are my Brothers Powres set forth?
Stew. I Madam.
Reg. Himselfe in person there?
Stew. Madam with much ado:
Your Sister is the better Souldier.
Reg. Lord *Edmund* spake not with your Lord at home?
Stew. No Madam.
Reg. What might import my Sisters Letter to him?
Stew. I know not, Lady.
Reg. Faith he is posted hence on serious matter:
It was great ignorance, Gloustes eyes being out
To let him liue. Where he arriues, he moues
All hearts against vs: *Edmund*, I thinke is gone
In pitty of his misery, to dispatch
His nighted life: Moreouer to descry
The strength o'th'Enemy.
Stew. I must needs after him, Madam, with my Letter.
Reg. Our troopes set forth to morrow, stay with vs:
The wayes are dangerous.
Stew. I may not Madam:
My Lady charg'd my dutie in this busines.
Reg. Why should she write to *Edmund*?
Might not you transport her purposes by word? Belike,
Some things, I know not what. Ile loue thee much
Let me vnseale the Letter.
Stew. Madam, I had rather——
Reg. I know your Lady do's not loue her Husband,
I am sure of that: and at her late being heere,
She gaue strange Eliads, and most speaking lookes
To Noble *Edmund*. I know you are of her bosome.
Stew. I, Madam?
Reg. I speake in vnderstanding: Y'are; I know't,
Therefore I do aduise you take this note:
My Lord is dead: *Edmond*, and I haue talk'd,
And more conuenient is he for my hand
Then for your Ladies: You may gather more:
If you do finde him, pray you giue him this;
And when your Mistris heares thus much from you,
I pray desire her call her wisedome to her.
So fare you well:
If you do chance to heare of that blinde Traitor,
Preferment fals on him, that cuts him off.
Stew. Would I could meet Madam, I should shew
What party I do follow.
Reg. Fare thee well. *Exeunt.*

Scena Quinta.

Enter Gloucester, and Edgar.

Glou. When shall I come to th'top of that same hill?
Edg. You do climbe vp it now. Look how we labor.
Glou. Me thinkes the ground is euen.
Edg. Horrible steepe.
Hearke, do you heare the Sea?
Glou. No truly.
Edg. Why then your other Senses grow imperfect
By your eyes anguish.
Glou. So may it be indeed.
Me thinkes thy voyce is alter'd, and thou speak'st
In better phrase, and matter then thou did'st.
Edg. Y'are much deceiu'd: In nothing am I chang'd
But in my Garments.
Glou. Me thinkes y'are better spoken.
Edg. Come on Sir,
Heere's the place: stand still: how fearefull
And dizie 'tis, to cast ones eyes so low,
The Crowes and Choughes, that wing the midway ayre
Shew scarse so grosse as Beetles. Halfe way downe
Hangs one that gathers Sampire: dreadfull Trade:
Me thinkes he seemes no bigger then his head.
The Fishermen, that walk'd vpon the beach
Appeare like Mice: and yond tall Anchoring Barke,
Diminish'd to her Cocke: her Cocke, a Buoy
Almost too small for sight. The murmuring Surge,
That on th'vnnumbred idle Pebble chafes
Cannot be heard so high. Ile looke no more,
Least my braine turne, and the deficient sight
Topple downe headlong.
Glou. Set me where you stand.
Edg. Giue me your hand:
You are now within a foote of th'extreme Verge:
For all beneath the Moone would I not leape vpright.
Glou. Let go my hand:
Heere Friend's another purse: in it, a Iewell
Well worth a poore mans taking. Fayries, and Gods
Prosper it with thee. Go thou further off,
Bid me farewell, and let me heare thee going.
Edg. Now fare ye well, good Sir.
Glou. With all my heart.
Edg. Why I do trifle thus with his dispaire,
Is done to cure it.
Glou. O you mighty Gods!
This world I do renounce, and in your sights

Shake patiently my great affliction off:
If I could beare it longer, and not fall
To quarrell with your great opposelesse willes,
My snuffe, and loathed part of Nature should
Burne it selfe out. If *Edgar* liue, O blesse him:
Now Fellow, fare thee well.

Edg. Gone Sir, farewell:
And yet I know not how conceit may rob
The Treasury of life, when life it selfe
Yeelds to the Theft. Had he bin where he thought,
By this had thought bin past. Aliue, or dead?
Hoa, you Sir: Friend, heare you Sir, speake:
Thus might he passe indeed: yet he reuiues.
What are you Sir?

Glou. Away, and let me dye.

Edg. Had'st thou beene ought
But Gozemore, Feathers, Ayre,
(So many fathome downe precipitating)
Thou'dst shiuer'd like an Egge: but thou do'st breath:
Hast heauy substance, bleed'st not, speak'st, art sound,
Ten Masts at each, make not the altitude
Which thou hast perpendicularly fell,
Thy life's a Myracle. Speake yet againe.

Glou. But haue I falne, or no?

Edg. From the dread Somnet of this Chalkie Bourne
Looke vp a height, the shrill-gorg'd Larke so farre
Cannot be seene, or heard: Do but looke vp.

Glou. Alacke, I haue no eyes:
Is wretchednesse depriu'd that benefit
To end it selfe by death? 'Twas yet some comfort,
When misery could beguile the Tyrants rage,
And frustrate his proud will.

Edg. Giue me your arme.
Vp, so: How is't? Feele you your Legges? You stand.

Glou. Too well, too well.

Edg. This is aboue all strangenesse,
Vpon the crowne o'th'Cliffe. What thing was that
Which parted from you?

Glou. A poore vnfortunate Beggar.

Edg. As I stood heere below, me thought his eyes
Were two full Moones: he had a thousand Noses,
Hornes wealk'd, and waued like the enraged Sea:
It was some Fiend: Therefore thou happy Father,
Thinke that the cleerest Gods, who make them Honors
Of mens Impossibilities, haue preserued thee.

Glou. I do remember now: henceforth Ile beare
Affliction, till it do cry out it selfe
Enough, enough, and dye. That thing you speake of,
I tooke it for a man: often 'twould say
The Fiend, the Fiend, he led me to that place.

Edgar. Beare free and patient thoughts.

Enter Lear.

But who comes heere?
The safer sense will ne're accommodate
His Master thus.

Lear. No, they cannot touch me for crying. I am the King himselfe.

Edg. O thou side-piercing sight!

Lear. Nature's aboue Art, in that respect. Ther's your Presse-money. That fellow handles his bow, like a Crow-keeper: draw mee a Cloathiers yard. Looke, looke, a Mouse: peace, peace, this peece of toasted Cheese will doo't. There's my Gauntlet, Ile proue it on a Gyant. Bring vp the browne Billes. O well flowne Bird: i'th' clout, i'th'clout: Hewgh. Giue the word.

Edg. Sweet Mariorum.

Lear. Passe.

Glou. I know that voice.

Lear. Ha! *Gonerill* with a white beard? They flatter'd me like a Dogge, and told mee I had the white hayres in my Beard, ere the blacke ones were there. To say I, and no, to euery thing that I said: I, and no too, was no good Diuinity. When the raine came to wet me once, and the winde to make me chatter: when the Thunder would not peace at my bidding, there I found 'em, there I smelt 'em out. Go too, they are not men o'their words; they told me, I was euery thing: 'Tis a Lye, I am not Agu-proofe.

Glou. The tricke of that voyce, I do well remember: Is't not the King?

Lear. I, euery inch a King.
When I do stare, see how the Subiect quakes.
I pardon that mans life. What was thy cause?
Adultery? thou shalt not dye: dye for Adultery?
No, the Wren goes too't, and the small gilded Fly
Do's letcher in my sight. Let Copulation thriue:
For Gloucesters bastard Son was kinder to his Father,
Then my Daughters got 'tweene the lawfull sheets.
Too't Luxury pell-mell, for I lacke Souldiers.
Behold yond simpring Dame, whose face betweene her
Forkes presages Snow; that minces Vertue, & do's shake
the head to heare of pleasures name. The Fitchew, nor
the soyled Horse goes too't with a more riotous appetite. Downe from the waste they are Centaures, though
Women all aboue: but to the Girdle do the Gods inherit, beneath is all the Fiends. There's hell, there's darkenes, there is the sulphurous pit; burning, scalding, stench,
consumption: Fye, fie, fie; pah, pah: Giue me an Ounce
of Ciuet; good Apothecary sweeten my immagination:
There's money for thee.

Glou. O let me kisse that hand.

Lear. Let me wipe it first,
It smelles of Mortality.

Glou. O ruin'd peece of Nature, this great world
Shall so weare out to naught.
Do'st thou know me?

Lear. I remember thine eyes well enough: dost thou squiny at me? No, doe thy worst blinde Cupid, Ile not loue. Reade thou this challenge, marke but the penning of it.

Glou. Were all thy Letters Sunnes, I could not see.

Edg. I would not take this from report,
It is, and my heart breakes at it.

Lear. Read.

Glou. What with the Case of eyes?

Lear. Oh ho, are you there with me? No eies in your head, nor no mony in your purse? Your eyes are in a heauy case, your purse in a light, yet you see how this world goes.

Glou. I see it feelingly.

Lear. What, art mad? A man may see how this world goes, with no eyes. Looke with thine eares: See how yond Iustice railes vpon yond simple theefe. Hearke in thine eare: Change places, and handy-dandy, which is the Iustice, which is the theefe: Thou hast seene a Farmers dogge barke at a Beggar?

Glou. I Sir.

Lear. And the Creature run from the Cur: there thou might'st behold the great image of Authoritie, a Dogg's obey'd in Office. Thou, Rascall Beadle, hold thy bloody hand: why dost thou lash that Whore? Strip thy owne backe, thou hotly lusts to vse her in that kind, for which thou whip'st her. The Vsurer hangs the Cozener. Thorough

rough tatter'd cloathes great Vices do appeare: Robes, and Furr'd gownes hide all. Place sinnes with Gold, and the strong Lance of Iustice, hurtlesse breakes: Arme it in ragges, a Pigmies straw do's pierce it. None do's offend, none, I say none, Ile able 'em; take that of me my Friend, who haue the power to seale th'accusers lips. Get thee glasse-eyes, and like a scuruy Politician, seeme to see the things thou dost not. Now, now, now, now. Pull off my Bootes: harder, harder, so.

Edg. O matter, and impertinency mixt,
Reason in Madnesse.

Lear. If thou wilt weepe my Fortunes, take my eyes,
I know thee well enough, thy name is Glouster:
Thou must be patient; we came crying hither:
Thou know'st, the first time that we smell the Ayre
We wawle, and cry. I will preach to thee: Marke.

Glou. Alacke, alacke the day.

Lear. When we are borne, we cry that we are come
To this great stage of Fooles. This a good blocke:
It were a delicate stratagem, to shoo
A Troope of Horse with Felt: Ile put't in proofe,
And when I haue stolne vpon these Son in Lawes,
Then kill, kill, kill, kill, kill, kill.

Enter a Gentleman.

Gent. Oh heere he is: lay hand vpon him, Sir.
Your most deere Daughter——

Lear. No rescue? What, a Prisoner? I am euen
The Naturall Foole of Fortune. Vse me well,
You shall haue ransome. Let me haue Surgeons,
I am cut to'th'Braines.

Gent. You shall haue any thing.

Lear. No Seconds? All my selfe?
Why, this would make a man, a man of Salt
To vse his eyes for Garden water-pots. I wil die brauely,
Like a smugge Bridegroome. What? I will be Iouiall:
Come, come, I am a King, Masters, know you that?

Gent. You are a Royall one, and we obey you.

Lear. Then there's life in't. Come, and you get it,
You shall get it by running: Sa, sa, sa, sa. *Exit.*

Gent. A sight most pittifull in the meanest wretch,
Past speaking of in a King. Thou hast a Daughter
Who redeemes Nature from the generall curse
Which twaine haue brought her to.

Edg. Haile gentle Sir.

Gent. Sir, speed you: what's your will?

Edg. Do you heare ought (Sir) of a Battell toward.

Gent. Most sure, and vulgar:
Euery one heares that, which can distinguish sound.

Edg. But by your fauour:
How neere's the other Army?

Gent. Neere, and on speedy foot: the maine descry
Stands on the hourely thought.

Edg. I thanke you Sir, that's all.

Gent. Though that the Queen on special cause is here
Her Army is mou'd on. *Exit.*

Edg. I thanke you Sir.

Glou. You euer gentle Gods, take my breath from me,
Let not my worser Spirit tempt me againe
To dye before you please.

Edg. Well pray you Father.

Glou. Now good sir, what are you?

Edg. A most poore man, made tame to Fortunes blows
Who, by the Art of knowne, and feeling sorrowes,
Am pregnant to good pitty. Giue me your hand,
Ile leade you to some biding.

Glou. Heartie thankes:
The bountie, and the benizon of Heauen
To boot, and boot.

Enter Steward.

Stew. A proclaim'd prize: most happie
That eyelesse head of thine, was first fram'd flesh
To raise my fortunes. Thou old, vnhappy Traitor,
Breefely thy selfe remember: the Sword is out
That must destroy thee.

Glou. Now let thy friendly hand
Put strength enough too't.

Stew. Wherefore, bold Pezant,
Dar'st thou support a publish'd Traitor? Hence,
Least that th'infection of his fortune take
Like hold on thee. Let go his arme.

Edg. Chill not let go Zir,
Without vurther 'casion.

Stew. Let go Slaue, or thou dy'st.

Edg. Good Gentleman goe your gate, and let poore volke passe: and 'chud ha' bin zwaggerd out of my life, 'twould not ha' bin zo long as 'tis, by a vortnight. Nay, come not neere th'old man: keepe out che vor'ye, or ice try whither your Costard, or my Ballow be the harder; chill be plaine with you.

Stew. Out Dunghill.

Edg. Chill picke your teeth Zir: come, no matter vor your foynes.

Stew. Slaue thou hast slaine me: Villain, take my purse; If euer thou wilt thriue, bury my bodie,
And giue the Letters which thou find'st about me,
To *Edmund* Earle of Glouster: seeke him out
Vpon the English party. Oh vntimely death, death.

Edg. I know thee well. A seruiceable Villaine,
As duteous to the vices of thy Mistris,
As badnesse would desire.

Glou. What, is he dead?

Edg. Sit you downe Father: rest you.
Let's see these Pockets; the Letters that he speakes of
May be my Friends: hee's dead; I am onely sorry
He had no other Deathsman. Let vs see:
Leaue gentle waxe, and manners: blame vs not
To know our enemies mindes, we rip their hearts,
Their Papers is more lawfull.

Reads the Letter.

*L*Et our reciprocall vowes be remembred. *You haue manie opportunities to cut him off: if your will want not, time and place will be fruitfully offer'd. There is nothing done. If hee returne the Conqueror, then am I the Prisoner, and his bed, my Gaole, from the loathed warmth whereof, deliuer me, and supply the place for your Labour.*

Your (Wife, so I would say) affectionate Seruant. Gonerill.

Oh indinguish'd space of Womans will,
A plot vpon her vertuous Husbands life,
And the exchange my Brother: heere, in rhe sands
Thee Ile rake vp, the poste vnsanctified
Of murtherous Letchers: and in the mature time,
With this vngracious paper strike the sight
Of the death-practis'd Duke: for him 'tis well,
That of thy death, and businesse, I can tell.

Glou. The King is mad:
How stiffe is my vilde sense
That I stand vp, and haue ingenious feeling
Of my huge Sorrowes? Better I were distract,
So should my thoughts be seuer'd from my greefes,

Drum afarre off.

And woes, by wrong imaginations loose

The knowledge of themselues.
  Edg. Giue me your hand :
Farre off methinkes I heare the beaten Drumme.
Come Father, Ile bestow you with a Friend. *Exeunt.*

Scæna Septima.

Enter Cordelia, Kent, and Gentleman.

  Cor. O thou good *Kent,*
How shall I liue and worke
To match thy goodnesse?
My life will be too short,
And euery measure faile me.
  Kent. To be acknowledg'd Madam is ore-pai'd,
All my reports go with the modest truth,
Nor more, nor clipt, but so.
  Cor. Be better suited,
These weedes are memories of those worser houres :
I prythee put them off.
  Kent. Pardon deere Madam,
Yet to be knowne shortens my made intent,
My boone I make it, that you know me not,
Till time, and I, thinke meet.
  Cor. Then be't so my good Lord :
How do's the King?
  Gent. Madam sleepes still.
  Cor. O you kind Gods!
Cure this great breach in his abused Nature,
Th'vntun'd and iarring senses, O winde vp,
Of this childe-changed Father.
  Gent. So please your Maiesty,
That we may wake the King, he hath slept long?
  Cor. Be gouern'd by your knowledge, and proceede
I'th'sway of your owne will : is he array'd?

Enter Lear in a chaire carried by Seruants

  Gent. I Madam: in the heauinesse of sleepe,
We put fresh garments on him.
Be by good Madam when we do awake him,
I doubt of his Temperance.
  Cor. O my deere Father, restauratian hang
Thy medicine on my lippes, and let this kisse
Repaire those violent harmes, that my two Sisters
Haue in thy Reuerence made.
  Kent. Kind and deere Princesse.
  Cor. Had you not bin their Father, these white flakes
Did challenge pitty of them. Was this a face
To be oppos'd against the iarring windes?
Mine Enemies dogge, though he had bit me,
Should haue stood that night against my fire,
And was't thou faine (poore Father)
To houell thee with Swine and Rogues forlorne,
In short, and musty straw? Alacke, alacke,
'Tis wonder that thy life and wits, at once
Had not concluded all. He wakes, speake to him.
  Gen. Madam do you, 'tis fittest.
  Cor. How does my Royall Lord?
How fares your Maiesty?
  Lear. You do me wrong to take me out o'th'graue,
Thou art a Soule in blisse, but I am bound
Vpon a wheele of fire, that mine owne teares
Do scal'd, like molten Lead.
  Cor. Sir, do you know me?
  Lear. You are a spirit I know, where did you dye?
  Cor. Still, still, farre wide.
  Gen. He's scarse awake,
Let him alone a while.
  Lear. Where haue I bin?
Where am '? Faire day light?
I am mightily abus'd; I should eu'n dye with pitty
To see another thus. I know not what to say :
I will not sweare these are my hands : let's see,
I feele this pin pricke, would I were assur'd
Of my condition.
  Cor. O looke vpon me Sir,
And hold your hand in benediction o're me,
You must not kneele.
  Lear. Pray do not mocke me :
I am a very foolish fond old man,
Fourescore and vpward,
Not an houre more, nor lesse :
And to deale plainely,
I feare I am not in my perfect mind.
Me thinkes I should know you, and know this man,
Yet I am doubtfull : For I am mainely ignorant
What place this is : and all the skill I haue
Remembers not these garments : nor I know not
Where I did lodge last night. Do not laugh at me,
For (as I am a man) I thinke this Lady
To be my childe *Cordelia.*
  Cor. And so I am : I am.
  Lear. Be your teares wet?
Yes faith : I pray weepe not,
If you haue poyson for me, I will drinke it :
I know you do not loue me, for your Sisters
Haue (as I do remember) done me wrong.
You haue some cause, they haue not.
  Cor. No cause, no cause.
  Lear. Am I in France?
  Kent. In your owne kingdome Sir.
  Lear. Do not abuse me.
  Gent. Be comforted good Madam, the great rage
You see is kill'd in him : desire him to go in,
Trouble him no more till further setling.
  Cor. Wilt please your Highnesse walke?
  Lear. You must beare with me :
Pray you now forget, and forgiue,
I am old and foolish. *Exeunt*

Actus Quintus. Scena Prima.

Enter with Drumme and Colours, Edmund, Regan.
Gentlemen, and Souldiers.

  Bast. Know of the Duke if his last purpose hold,
Or whether since he is aduis'd by ought
To change the course, he's full of alteration,
And selfereprouing, bring his constant pleasure.
  Reg. Our Sisters man is certainely miscarried.
  Bast. 'Tis to be doubted Madam.
  Reg. Now sweet Lord,
You

You know the goodnesse I intend vpon you:
Tell me but truly, but then speake the truth,
Do you not loue my Sister?
  Bast. In honour'd Loue.
  Reg. But haue you neuer found my Brothers way,
To the fore-fended place?
  Bast. No by mine honour, Madam.
  Reg. I neuer shall endure her, deere my Lord
Be not familiar with her.
  Bast. Feare not, she and the Duke her husband.

Enter with Drum and Colours, Albany, Gonerill, Soldiers.

  Alb. Our very louing Sister, well be-met:
Sir, this I heard, the King is come to his Daughter
With others, whom the rigour of our State
Forc'd to cry out.
  Regan. Why is this reason'd?
  Gone. Combine together 'gainst the Enemie:
For these domesticke and particurlar broiles,
Are not the question heere.
  Alb. Let's then determine with th'ancient of warre
On our proceeding.
  Reg. Sister you'le go with vs?
  Gon. No.
  Reg. 'Tis most conuenient, pray go with vs.
  Gon. Oh ho, I know the Riddle, I will goe.
          Exeunt both the Armies.

Enter Edgar.

  Edg. If ere your Grace had speech with man so poore,
Heare me one word.
  Alb. Ile ouertake you, speake.
  Edg. Before you fight the Battaile, ope this Letter:
If you haue victory, let the Trumpet sound
For him that brought it: wretched though I seeme,
I can produce a Champion, that will proue
What is auouched there. If you miscarry,
Your businesse of the world hath so an end,
And machination ceases. Fortune loues you.
  Alb. Stay till I haue read the Letter.
  Edg. I was forbid it:
When time shall serue, let but the Herald cry,
And Ile appeare againe.   Exit.
  Alb. Why farethee well, I will o're-looke thy paper.

Enter Edmund.

  Bast. The Enemy's in view, draw vp your powers,
Heere is the guesse of their true strength and Forces,
By dilligent discouerie, but your hast
Is now vrg'd on you.
  Alb. We will greet the time.   Exit.
  Bast. To both these Sisters haue I sworne my loue:
Each iealous of the other, as the stung
Are of the Adder. Which of them shall I take?
Both? One? Or neither? Neither can be enioy'd
If both remaine aliue: To take the Widdow,
Exasperates, makes mad her Sister Gonerill,
And hardly shall I carry out my side,
Her husband being aliue. Now then, wee'l vse
His countenance for the Battaile, which being done,
Let her who would be rid of him, deuise
His speedy taking off. As for the mercie
Which he intends to Lear and to Cordelia,
The Battaile done, and they within our power,
Shall neuer see his pardon: for my state,
Stands on me to defend, not to debate.   Exit.

Scena Secunda.

Alarum within. Enter with Drumme and Colours, Lear,
Cordelia, and Souldiers, ouer the Stage, and Exeunt.

Enter Edgar, and Gloster.

  Edg. Heere Father, take the shadow of this Tree
For your good hoast: pray that the right may thriue:
If euer I returne to you againe,
Ile bring you comfort.
  Glo. Grace go with you Sir.   Exit.
          Alarum and Retreat within.
Enter Edgar.
  Egdar. Away old man, giue me thy hand, away:
King Lear hath lost, he and his Daughter tane,
Giue me thy hand: Come on.
  Glo. No further Sir, a man may rot euen heere.
  Edg. What in ill thoughts againe?
Men must endure
Their going hence, euen as their comming hither,
Ripenesse is all come on.
  Glo. And that's true too.   Exeunt.

Scena Tertia.

Enter in conquest with Drum and Colours, Edmund, Lear,
and Cordelia, as prisoners, Souldiers, Captaine.

  Bast. Some Officers take them away: good guard,
Vntill their greater pleasures first be knowne
That are to censure them.
  Cor. We are not the first,
Who with best meaning haue incurr'd the worst:
For thee oppressed King I am cast downe,
My selfe could else out-frowne false Fortunes frowne.
Shall we not see these Daughters, and these Sisters?
  Lear. No, no, no, no: come let's away to prison,
We two alone will sing like Birds i'th'Cage:
When thou dost aske me blessing, Ile kneele downe
And aske of thee forgiuenesse: So wee'l liue,
And pray, and sing, and tell old tales, and laugh
At gilded Butterflies: and heere (poore Rogues)
Talke of Court newes, and wee'l talke with them too,
Who loofes, and who wins; who's in, who's out;
And take vpon's the mystery of things,
As if we were Gods spies: And wee'l weare out
In a wall'd prison, packs and sects of great ones,
That ebbe and flow by th'Moone.
  Bast. Take them away.
  Lear. Vpon such sacrifices my Cordelia,
The Gods themselues throw Incense.
Haue I caught thee?
He that parts vs, shall bring a Brand from Heauen,
And fire vs hence, like Foxes: wipe thine eyes,
The good yeares shall deuoure them, flesh and fell,
                                                      Ere

Ere they shall make vs weepe?
Weele see e'm staru'd first: come. *Exit.*

Bast. Come hither Captaine, hearke.
Take thou this note, go follow them to prison,
One step I haue aduanc'd thee, if thou do'st
As this instructs thee, thou dost make thy way
To Noble Fortunes: know thou this, that men
Are as the time is; to be tender minded
Do's not become a Sword, thy great imployment
Will not beare question: either say thou'lt do't,
Or thriue by other meanes.

Capt. Ile do't my Lord.

Bast. About it, and write happy, when th'hast done,
Marke I say instantly, and carry it so
As I haue set it downe. *Exit Captaine.*

Flourish. Enter Albany, Gonerill, Regan, Soldiers.

Alb. Sir, you haue shew'd to day your valiant straine
And Fortune led you well: you haue the Captiues
Who were the opposites of this dayes strife:
I do require them of you so to vse them,
As we shall find their merites, and our safety
May equally determine.

Bast. Sir, I thought it fit,
To send the old and miserable King to some retention,
Whose age had Charmes in it, whose Title more,
To plucke the common bosome on his side,
And turne our imprest Launces in our eies
Which do command them. With him I sent the Queen:
My reason all the same, and they are ready
To morrow, or at further space, t'appeare
Where you shall hold your Session.

Alb. Sir, by your patience,
I hold you but a subiect of this Warre,
Not as a Brother.

Reg. That's as we list to grace him.
Methinkes our pleasure might haue bin demanded
Ere you had spoke so farre. He led our Powers,
Bore the Commission of my place and person,
The which immediacie may well stand vp,
And call it selfe your Brother.

Gon. Not so hot:
In his owne grace he doth exalt himselfe,
More then in your addition.

Reg. In my rights,
By me inuested, he compeeres the best.

Alb. That were the most, if he should husband you.

Reg. Iesters do oft proue Prophets.

Gon. Hola, hola,
That eye that told you so, look'd but a squint.

Rega. Lady I am not well, else I should answere
From a full flowing stomack. Generall,
Take thou my Souldiers, prisoners, patrimony,
Dispose of them, of me, the walls is thine:
Witnesse the world, that I create thee heere
My Lord, and Master.

Gon. Meane you to enioy him?

Alb. The let alone lies not in your good will.

Bast. Nor in thine Lord.

Alb. Halfe-blooded fellow, yes.

Reg. Let the Drum strike, and proue my title thine.

Alb. Stay yet, heare reason: *Edmund,* I arrest thee
On capitall Treason; and in thy arrest,
This guilded Serpent: for your claime faire Sisters,
I bare it in the interest of my wife,
'Tis she is sub-contracted to this Lord,
And I her husband contradict your Banes.
If you will marry, make your loues to me,
My Lady is bespoke.

Gon. An enterlude.

Alb. Thou art armed *Gloster,*
Let the Trmpet sound:
If none appeare to proue vpon thy person,
Thy heynous, manifest, and many Treasons,
There is my pledge: Ile make it on thy heart
Ere I taste bread, thou art in nothing lesse
Then I haue heere proclaim'd thee.

Reg. Sicke, O sicke.

Gon. If not, Ile nere trust medicine.

Bast. There's my exchange, what in the world he's
That names me Traitor, villain-like he lies,
Call by the Trumpet: he that dares approach;
On him, on you, who not, I will maintaine
My truth and honor firmely.

Enter a Herald.

Alb. A Herald, ho.
Trust to thy single vertue, for thy Souldiers
All leuied in my name, haue in my name
Tooke their discharge.

Regan. My sicknesse growes vpon me.

Alb. She is not well, conuey her to my Tent.
Come hither Herald, let the Trumpet sound,
And read out this. *A Trumpet sounds.*

Herald reads.

IF any man of qualitie or degree, within the lists of the Army, will maintaine vpon Edmund, supposed Earle of Gloster, that he is a manifold Traitor, let him appeare by the third sound of the Trumpet: he is bold in his defence. 1 Trumpet.

Her. Againe. 2 Trumpet.
Her. Againe. 3 Trumpet.

Trumpet answers within.

Enter Edgar armed.

Alb. Aske him his purposes, why he appeares
Vpon this Call o'th'Trumpet.

Her. What are you?
Your name, your quality, and why you answer
This present Summons?

Edg. Know my name is lost
By Treasons tooth: bare-gnawne, and Canker-bit,
Yet am I Noble as the Aduersary
I come to cope.

Alb. Which is that Aduersary?

Edg. What's he that speakes for *Edmund* Earle of Glo-

Bast. Himselfe, what saist thou to him? (ster?

Edg. Draw thy Sword,
That if my speech offend a Noble heart,
Thy arme may do thee Iustice, heere is mine:
Behold it is my priuiledge,
The priuiledge of mine Honours,
My oath, and my profession. I protest,
Maugre thy strength, place, youth, and eminence,
Despise thy victor-Sword, and fire new Fortune,
Thy valor, and thy heart, thou art a Traitor:
False to thy Gods, thy Brother, and thy Father,
Conspirant 'gainst this high illustirous Prince,
And from th'extremest vpward of thy head,
To the discent and dust below thy foote,

A most Toad-spotted Traitor. Say thou no,
This Sword, this arme, and my best spirits are bent
To proue vpon thy heart, whereto I speake,
Thou lyest.

Bast. In wisedome I should aske thy name,
But since thy out-side lookes so faire and Warlike,
And that thy tongue (some say) of breeding breathes,
What safe, and nicely I might well delay,
By rule of Knight-hood, I disdaine and spurne:
Backe do I tosse these Treasons to thy head,
With the hell-hated Lye, ore-whelme thy heart,
Which for they yet glance by, and scarely bruise,
This Sword of mine shall giue them instant way,
Where they shall rest for euer. Trumpets speake.

Alb. Saue him, saue him. *Alarums. Fights.*
Gon. This is practise *Gloster*,
By th'law of Warre, thou wast not bound to answer
An vnknowne opposite: thou art not vanquish'd,
But cozend, and beguild.

Alb. Shut your mouth Dame,
Or with this paper shall I stop it: hold Sir,
Thou worse then any name, reade thine owne euill:
No tearing Lady, I perceiue you know it.

Gon. Say if I do, the Lawes are mine not thine,
Who can araigne me for't? *Exit.*

Alb. Most monstrous! O, know'st thou this paper?
Bast. Aske me not what I know.
Alb. Go after her, she's desperate, gouerne her.
Bast. What you haue charg'd me with,
That haue I done,
And more, much more, the time will bring it out.
'Tis past, and so am I: But what art thou
That hast this Fortune on me? If thou'rt Noble,
I do forgiue thee.

Edg. Let's exchange charity:
I am no lesse in blood then thou art *Edmond*,
If more, the more th'hast wrong'd me.
My name is *Edgar* and thy Fathers Sonne,
The Gods are iust, and of our pleasant vices
Make instruments to plague vs:
The darke and vitious place where thee he got,
Cost him his eyes.

Bast. Th'hast spoken right, 'tis true,
The Wheele is come full circle, I am heere.

Alb. Me thought thy very gate did prophesie
A Royall Noblenesse: I must embrace thee,
Let sorrow split my heart, if euer I
Did hate thee, or thy Father.

Edg. Worthy Prince I know't.
Alb. Where haue you hid your selfe?
How haue you knowne the miseries of your Father?

Edg. By nursing them my Lord. List a breefe tale,
And when 'tis told, O that my heart would burst.
The bloody proclamation to escape
That follow'd me so neere, (O our liues sweetnesse,
That we the paine of death would hourely dye,
Rather then die at once) taught me to shift
Into a mad-mans rags, t'assume a semblance
That very Dogges disdain'd: and in this habit
Met I my Father with his bleeding Rings,
Their precious Stones new lost: became his guide,
Led him, begg'd for him, sau'd him from dispaire.
Neuer (O fault) reueal'd my selfe vnto him,
Vntill some halfe houre past when I was arm'd,
Not sure, though hoping of this good successe,
I ask'd his blessing, and from first to last
Told him our pilgrimage. But his flaw'd heart
(Alacke too weake the conflict to support)
Twixt two extremes of passion, ioy and greefe,
Burst smilingly.

Bast. This speech of yours hath mou'd me,
And shall perchance do good, but speake you on,
You looke as you had something more to say.

Alb. If there be more, more wofull, hold it in,
For I am almost ready to dissolue,
Hearing of this.

Enter a Gentleman.

Gen. Helpe, helpe: O helpe.
Edg. What kinde of helpe?
Alb. Speake man.
Edg. What meanes this bloody Knife?
Gen. 'Tis hot, it smoakes, it came euen from the heart
of------O she's dead.
Alb. Who dead? Speake man.
Gen. Your Lady Sir, your Lady; and her Sister
By her is poyson'd: she confesses it.
Bast. I was contracted to them both, all three
Now marry in an instant.
Edg. Here comes *Kent*.

Enter Kent.

Alb. Produce the bodies, be they aliue or dead;
Gonerill and Regans bodies brought out.
This iudgement of the Heauens that makes vs tremble,
Touches vs not with pitty: O, is this he?
The time will not allow the complement
Which very manners vrges.

Kent. I am come
To bid my King and Master aye good night.
Is he not here?

Alb. Great thing of vs forgot,
Speake *Edmund*, where's the King? and where's *Cordelia?*
Seest thou this obiect *Kent?*

Kent. Alacke, why thus?
Bast. Yet *Edmund* was belou'd:
The one the other poison'd for my sake,
And after slew herselfe.

Alb. Euen so: couer their faces.
Bast. I pant for life: some good I meane to do
Despight of mine owne Nature. Quickly send,
(Be briefe in it) to th'Castle, for my Writ
Is on the life of *Lear*, and on *Cordelia*:
Nay, send in time.

Alb. Run, run, O run.
Edg. To who my Lord? Who ha's the Office?
Send thy token of repreeue.

Bast. Well thought on, take my Sword,
Giue it the Captaine.

Edg. Hast thee for thy life.
Bast. He hath Commission from thy Wife and me,
To hang *Cordelia* in the prison, and
To lay the blame vpon her owne dispaire,
That she for-did her selfe.

Alb. The Gods defend her, beare him hence awhile.

Enter Lear with Cordelia in his armes.

Lear. Howle, howle, howle: O your are men of stones,
Had I your tongues and eyes, Il'd vse them so,
That Heauens vault should crack: she's gone for euer.
I know when one is dead, and when one liues,
She's dead as earth: Lend me a Looking-glasse,

If that her breath will mist or staine the stone,
Why then she liues.
  Kent. Is this the promis'd end?
  Edg. Or image of that horror.
  Alb. Fall and cease.
  Lear. This feather stirs, she liues: if it be so,
It is a chance which do's redeeme all sorrowes
That euer I haue felt.
  Kent. O my good Master.
  Lear. Prythee away.
  Edg. 'Tis Noble *Kent* your Friend.
  Lear. A plague vpon you Murderors, Traitors all,
I might haue sau'd her, now she's gone for euer:
Cordelia, Cordelia, stay a little. Ha:
What is't thou saist? Her voice was euer soft,
Gentle, and low, an excellent thing in woman.
I kill'd the Slaue that was a hanging thee.
  Gent. 'Tis true (my Lords) he did.
  Lear. Did I not fellow?
I haue seene the day, with my good biting Faulchion
I would haue made him skip: I am old now,
And these same crosses spoile me. Who are you?
Mine eyes are not o'th'best, Ile tell you straight.
  Kent. If Fortune brag of two, she lou'd and hated,
One of them we behold.
  Lear. This is a dull sight, are you not *Kent*?
  Kent. The same: your Seruant *Kent*,
Where is your Seruant *Caius*?
  Lear. He's a good fellow, I can tell you that,
He'le strike and quickly too, he's dead and rotten.
  Kent. No my good Lord, I am the very man.
  Lear. Ile see that straight.
  Kent. That from your first of difference and decay,
Haue follow'd your sad steps.
  Lear. Your are welcome hither.
  Kent. Nor no man else:
All's cheerlesse, darke, and deadly,
Your eldest Daughters haue fore-done themselues,
And desperately are dead
  Lear. I so I thinke.
  Alb. He knowes not what he saies, and vaine is it
That we present vs to him,

  Enter a Messenger.

  Edg. Very bootlesse.
  Mess. Edmund is dead my Lord.
  Alb. That's but a trifle heere:
You Lords and Noble Friends, know our intent,
What comfort to this great decay may come,
Shall be appli'd. For vs we will resigne,
During the life of this old Maiesty.
To him our absolute power, you to your rights,
With boote, and such addition as your Honours
Haue more then merited. All Friends shall
Taste the wages of their vertue, and all Foes
The cup of their deseruings: O see, see.
  Lear. And my poore Foole is hang'd: no, no, no life?
Why should a Dog, a Horse, a Rat haue life,
And thou no breath at all? Thou'lt come no more,
Neuer, neuer, neuer, neuer, neuer.
Pray you vndo this Button. Thanke you Sir,
Do you see this? Looke on her? Looke her lips,
Looke there, looke there. *He dies.*
  Edg. He faints, my Lord, my Lord.
  Kent. Breake heart, I prythee breake.
  Edg. Looke vp my Lord.
  Kent. Vex not his ghost, O let him passe, he hates him,
That would vpon the wracke of this tough world
Stretch him out longer.
  Edg. He is gon indeed.
  Kent. The wonder is, he hath endur'd so long,
He but vsurpt his life.
  Alb. Beare them from hence, our present businesse
Is generall woe: Friends of my soule, you twaine,
Rule in this Realme, and the gor'd state sustaine.
  Kent. I haue a iourney Sir, shortly to go,
My Master calls me, I must not say no.
  Edg. The waight of this sad time we must obey,
Speake what we feele, not what we ought to say:
The oldest hath borne most, we that are yong,
Shall neuer see so much, nor liue so long.

  Exeunt with a dead March.

FINIS.

THE TRAGEDIE OF
Othello, the Moore of Venice.

Actus Primus. Scœna Prima.

Enter Rodorigo, and Iago.

Rodorigo.

Euer tell me, I take it much vnkindly
That thou (*Iago*) who hast had my purse,
As if ỹ strings were thine, should'st know of this.

  Ia. But you'l not heare me: If euer I did dream
Of such a matter, abhorre me.

  Rodo. Thou told'st me,
Thou did'st hold him in thy hate.

  Iago. Despise me
If I do not. Three Great-ones of the Cittie,
(In personall suite to make me his Lieutenant)
Off-capt to him: and by the faith of man
I know my price, I am worth no worsse a place.
But he (as louing his owne pride, and purposes)
Euades them, with a bumbast Circumstance,
Horribly stufft with Epithites of warre,
Non-suites my Mediators. For certes, saies he,
I haue already chose my Officer. And what was he?
For-sooth, a great Arithmatician,
One *Michaell Cassio*, a Florentine,
(A Fellow almost damn'd in a faire Wife)
That neuer set a Squadron in the Field,
Nor the deuision of a Battaile knowes
More then a Spinster. Vnlesse the Bookish Theoricke:
Wherein the Tongued Consuls can propose
As Masterly as he. Meere pratle (without practise)
Is all his Souldiership. But he (Sir) had th'election;
And I (of whom his eies had seene the proofe
At Rhodes, at Ciprus, and on others grounds
Christen'd, and Heathen) must be be-leed, and calm'd
By Debitor, and Creditor. This Counter-caster,
He (in good time) must his Lieutenant be,
And I (blesse the marke) his Mooreships Auntient.

  Rod. By heauen, I rather would haue bin his hangman.

  Iago. Why, there's no remedie.
'Tis the curfse of Seruice;
Preferment goes by Letter, and affection,
And not by old gradation, where each second
Stood Heire to'th'first. Now Sir, be iudge your selfe,
Whether I in any iust terme am Affin'd
To loue the *Moore*?

  Rod. I would not follow him then.

  Iago. O Sir content you.
I follow him, to serue my turne vpon him.
We cannot all be Masters, nor all Masters
Cannot be truely follow'd. You shall marke
Many a dutious and knee-crooking knaue;
That (doting on his owne obsequious bondage)
Weares out his time, much like his Masters Asse,
For naught but Prouender, & when he's old Casheer'd.
Whip me such honest knaues. Others there are
Who trym'd in Formes, and visages of Dutie,
Keepe yet their hearts attending on themselues,
And throwing but showes of Seruice on their Lords
Doe well thriue by them.
And when they haue lin'd their Coates
Doe themselues Homage.
These Fellowes haue some soule,
And such a one do I professe my selfe. For (Sir)
It is as sure as you are *Rodorigo*,
Were I the Moore, I would not be *Iago*:
In following him, I follow but my selfe.
Heauen is my Iudge, not I for loue and dutie,
But seeming so, for my peculiar end:
For when my outward Action doth demonstrate
The natiue act, and figure of my heart
In Complement externe, 'tis not long after
But I will weare my heart vpon my sleeue
For Dawes to pecke at; I am not what I am.

  Rod. What a full Fortune do's the Thicks-lips owe
If he can carry't thus?

  Iago. Call vp her Father:
Rowse him, make after him, poyson his delight,
Proclaime him in the Streets. Incense her kinsmen,
And though he in a fertile Clymate dwell,
Plague him with Flies: though that his Ioy be Ioy,
Yet throw such chances of vexation on't,
As it may loose some colour.

  Rodo. Heere is her Fathers house, Ile call aloud.

  Iago. Doe, with like timerous accent, and dire yell,
As when (by Night and Negligence) the Fire
Is spied in populus Citties.

  Rodo. What hoa: *Brabantio*, Signior *Brabantio*, hoa.

  Iago. Awake: what hoa, *Brabantio*: Theeues, Theeues.
Looke to your house, your daughter, and your Bags,
Theeues, Theeues.

  Bra. Aboue. What is the reason of this terrible
Summons? What is the matter there?

  Rodo. Signior is all your Familie within?

  Iago. Are your Doores lock'd?

  Bra. Why? Wherefore ask you this?

  Iago. Sir, y'are rob'd, for shame put on your Gowne,
Your

Your heart is burst, you haue lost halfe your soule
Euen now, now, very now, an old blacke Ram
Is tupping your white Ewe. Arise, arise,
Awake the snorting Cittizens with the Bell,
Or else the deuill will make a Grand-sire of you.
Arise I say.

  Bra. What, haue you lost your wits?
  Rod. Most reuerend Signior, do you know my voice?
  Bra. Not I: what are you?
  Rod. My name is *Rodorigo.*
  Bra. The worsser welcome:
I haue charg'd thee not to haunt about my doores:
In honest plainenesse thou hast heard me say,
My Daughter is not for thee, And now in madnesse
(Being full of Supper, and distempring draughtes)
Vpon malitious knauerie, dost thou come
To start my quiet.
  Rod. Sir, Sir, Sir.
  Bra. But thou must needs be sure,
My spirits and my place haue in their power
To make this bitter to thee.
  Rodo. Patience good Sir.
  Bra. What tell'st thou me of Robbing?
This is Venice: my house is not a Grange.
  Rodo. Most graue *Brabantio,*
In simple and pure soule, I come to you.
  Ia. Sir: you are one of those that will not serue God,
if the deuill bid you. Because we come to do you seruice,
and you thinke we are Ruffians, you'le haue your Daughter
couer'd with a Barbary horse, you'le haue your Nephewes
neigh to you, you'le haue Coursers for Cozens:
and Gennets for Germaines.
  Bra. What prophane wretch art thou?
  Ia. I am one Sir, that comes to tell you, your Daughter
and the Moore, are making the Beast with two backs.
  Bra. Thou art a Villaine.
  Iago. You are a Senator.
  Bra. This thou shalt answere. I know thee *Rodorigo.*
  Rod. Sir, I will answere any thing. But I beseech you
If't be your pleasure, and most wise consent,
(As partly I find it is) that your faire Daughter,
At this odde Euen and dull watch o'th'night
Transported with no worse nor better guard,
But with a knaue of common hire, a Gundelier,
To the grosse claspes of a Lasciuious Moore:
If this be knowne to you, and your Allowance,
We then haue done you bold, and saucie wrongs.
But if you know not this, my Manners tell me,
We haue your wrong rebuke. Do not beleeue
That from the sence of all Ciuilitie,
I thus would play and trifle with your Reuerence.
Your Daughter (if you haue not giuen her leaue)
I say againe, hath made a grosse reuolt,
Tying her Dutie, Beautie, Wit, and Fortunes
In an extrauagant, and wheeling Stranger,
Of here, and euery where: straight satisfie your selfe.
If she be in her Chamber, or your house,
Let loose on me the Iustice of the State
For thus deluding you.
  Bra. Strike on the Tinder, hoa:
Giue me a Taper: call vp all my people,
This Accident is not vnlike my dreame,
Beleefe of it oppresses me alreadie.
Light, I say, light.   *Exit.*
  Iag. Farewell: for I must leaue you.
It seemes not meete, nor wholesome to my place
To be producted, (as if I stay, I shall,)
Against the Moore. For I do know the State,
(How euer this may gall him with some checke)
Cannot with safetie cast him. For he's embark'd
With such loud reason to the Cyprus Warres,
(Which euen now stands in Act) that for their soules
Another of his Fadome, they haue none,
To lead their Businesse. In which regard,
Though I do hate him as I do hell paines,
Yet, for necessitie of present life,
I must show out a Flag, and signe of Loue,
(Which is indeed but signe) that you shal surely find him
Lead to the Sagitary the raised Search:
And there will I be with him. So farewell.   *Exit.*

Enter Brabantio, with Seruants and Torches.

  Bra. It is too true an euill. Gone she is,
And what's to come of my despised time,
Is naught but bitternesse. Now *Rodorigo,*
Where didst thou see her? (Oh vnhappie Girle)
With the Moore saist thou? (Who would be a Father?)
How didst thou know 'twas she? (Oh she deceaues me
Past thought:) what said she to you? Get moe Tapers:
Raise all my Kindred. Are they married thinke you?
  Rodo. Truely I thinke they are.
  Bra. Oh Heauen: how got she out?
Oh treason of the blood.
Fathers, from hence trust not your Daughters minds
By what you see them act. Is there not Charmes,
By which the propertie of Youth, and Maidhood
May be abus'd? Haue you not read *Rodorigo,*
Of some such thing?
  Rod. Yes Sir: I haue indeed.
  Bra. Call vp my Brother: oh would you had had her,
Some one way, some another. Doe you know
Where we may apprehend her, and the Moore?
  Rod. I thinke I can discouer him, if you please
To get good Guard, and go along with me.
  Bra. Pray you lead on. At euery house Ile call,
(I may command at most) get Weapons (hoa)
And raise some speciall Officers of might:
On good *Rodorigo,* I will deserue your paines.   *Exeunt.*

Scena Secunda.

Enter Othello, Iago, Attendants, with Torches.

  Ia. Though in the trade of Warre I haue slaine men,
Yet do I hold it very stuffe o'th'conscience
To do no contriu'd Murder: I lacke Iniquitie
Sometime to do me seruice. Nine, or ten times
I had thought t'haue yerk'd him here vnder the Ribbes.
  Othello. 'Tis better as it is.
  Iago. Nay but he prated,
And spoke such scuruy, and prouoking termes
Against your Honor, that with the little godlinesse I haue
I did full hard forbeare him. But I pray you Sir,
Are you fast married? Be assur'd of this,
That the Magnifico is much belou'd,
And hath in his effect a voice potentiall
As double as the Dukes. He will diuorce you.
Or put vpon you, what restraint or greeuance,

The Law (with all his might, to enforce it on)
Will giue him Cable.
  Othel. Let him do his spight;
My Seruices, which I haue done the Signorie
Shall out-tongue his Complaints. 'Tis yet to know,
Which when I know, that boasting is an Honour,
I shall promulgate. I fetch my life and being,
From Men of Royall Seige. And my demerites
May speake (vnbonnetted) to as proud a Fortune
As this that I haue reach'd. For know *Iago,*
But that I loue the gentle *Desdemona,*
I would not my vnhoused free condition
Put into Circumscription, and Confine,
For the Seas worth. But looke, what Lights come yond?

  Enter Cassio, with Torches.

  Iago. Those are the raised Father, and his Friends:
You were best go in.
  Othel. Not I: I must be found.
My Parts, my Title, and my perfect Soule
Shall manifest me rightly. Is it they?
  Iago. By *Ianus,* I thinke no.
  Othel. The Seruants of the Dukes?
And my Lieutenant?
The goodnesse of the Night vpon you (Friends)
What is the Newes?
  Cassio. The Duke do's greet you (Generall)
And he requires your haste, Post-haste appearance,
Euen on the instant.
  Othello. What is the matter, thinke you?
  Cassio. Something from Cyprus, as I may diuine:
It is a businesse of some heate. The Gallies
Haue sent a dozen sequent Messengers
This very night, at one anothers heeles:
And many of the Consuls, rais'd and met,
Are at the Dukes already. You haue bin hotly call'd for,
When being not at your Lodging to be found,
The Senate hath sent about three seuerall Quests,
To search you out.
  Othel. 'Tis well I am found by you:
I will but spend a word here in the house,
And goe with you.
  Cassio. Aunciant, what makes he heere?
  Iago. Faith, he to night hath boarded a Land Carract,
If it proue lawfull prize, he'- made for euer.
  Cassio. I do not vnderstand.
  Iago. He's married.
  Cassio. To who?
  Iago. Marry to —— Come Captaine, will you go?
  Othel. Haue with you.
  Cassio. Here comes another Troope to seeke for you.

  Enter Brabantio, Rodorigo, with Officers, and Torches.

  Iago. It is *Brabantio:* Generall be aduis'd,
He comes to bad intent.
  Othello. Holla, stand there.
  Rodo. Signior, it is the Moore.
  Bra. Downe with him, Theefe.
  Iago. You, *Rodorigo?* Cme Sir, I am for you.
  Othe. Keepe vp your bright Swords, for the dew will
rust them. Good Signior, you shall more command with
yeares, then with your Weapons.
  Bra. Oh thou foule Theefe,
Where hast thou stow'd my Daughter?
Damn'd as thou art, thou hast enchaunted her
For Ile referre me to all things of sense,
(If she in Chaines of Magick were not bound)
Whether a Maid, so tender, Faire, and Happie,
So opposite to Marriage, that she shun'd
The wealthy curled Deareling of our Nation,
Would euer haue (t'encurre a generall mocke)
Run from her Guardage to the sootie bosome,
Of such a thing as thou: to feare, not to delight?
Iudge me the world, if 'tis not grosse in sense,
That thou hast practis'd on her with foule Charmes,
Abus'd her delicate Youth, with Drugs or Minerals,
That weakens Motion. Ile haue't disputed on,
'Tis probable, and palpable to thinking;
I therefore apprehend and do attach thee,
For an abuser of the World, a practiser
Of Arts inhibited, and out of warrant;
Lay hold vpon him, if he do resist
Subdue him, at his perill.
  Othe. Hold your hands
Both you of my inclining, and the rest.
Were it my Cue to fight, I should haue knowne it
Without a Prompter. Whether will you that I goe
To answere this your charge?
  Bra. To Prison, till fit time
Of Law, and course of direct Session
Call thee to answer.
  Othe. What if I do obey?
How may the Duke be therewith satisfi'd,
Whose Messengers are heere about my side,
Vpon some present businesse of the State,
To bring me to him.
  Officer. 'Tis true most worthy Signior,
The Dukes in Counsell, and your Noble selfe,
I am sure is sent for.
  Bra. How? The Duke in Counsell?
In this time of the night? Bring him away;
Mine's not an idle Cause. The Duke himselfe,
Or any of my Brothers of the State,
Cannot but feele this wrong, as 'twere their owne:
For if such Actions may haue passage free,
Bond-slaues, and Pagans shall our Statesmen be. *Exeunt*

Scæna Tertia.

  Enter Duke, Senators, and Officers.

  Duke. There's no composition in this Newes,
That giues them Credite.
  1. Sen. Indeed, they are disproportioned;
My Letters say, a Hundred and seuen Gallies.
  Duke. And mine a Hundred fortie.
  2. Sena. And mine two Hundred:
But though they iumpe not on a iust accompt,
(As in these Cases where the ayme reports,
'Tis oft with difference) yet do they all confirme
A Turkish Fleete, and bearing vp to Cyprus.
  Duke. Nay, it is possible enough to iudgement:
I do not so secure me in the Error,
But the maine Article I do approue
In fearefull sense.
  Saylor within. What hoa, what hoa, what hoa.
  Enter Saylor.
  Officer.

Officer. A Messenger from the Gallies.
Duke. Now? What's the businesse?
Sailor. The Turkish Preparation makes for Rhodes,
So was I bid report here to the State,
By Signior *Angelo*.
  Duke. How say you by this change?
  1. Sen. This cannot be
By no assay of reason. 'Tis a Pageant
To keepe vs in false gaze, when we consider
Th'importancie of Cyprus to the Turke;
And let our selues againe but vnderstand,
That as it more concernes the Turke then Rhodes,
So may he with more facile question beare it,
For that it stands not in such Warrelike brace,
But altogether lackes th'abilities
That Rhodes is dress'd in. If we make thought of this,
We must not thinke the Turke is so vnskilfull,
To leaue that latest, which concernes him first,
Neglecting an attempt of ease, and gaine
To wake, and wage a danger profitlesse.
  Duke. Nay, in all confidence he's not for Rhodes.
  Officer. Here is more Newes.

Enter a Messenger.

  Messen. The Ottamites, Reueren'd, and Gracious,
Steering with due course toward the Ile of Rhodes,
Haue there inioynted them with an after Fleete.
  1. Sen. I, so I thought: how many, as you guesse?
  Mess. Of thirtie Saile: and now they do re-stem
Their backward course, bearing with frank appearance
Their purposes toward Cyprus. Signior *Montano*,
Your trustie and most Valiant Seruitour,
With his free dutie, recommends you thus,
And prayes you to beleeue him.
  Duke. 'Tis certaine then for Cyprus:
Marcus Luccicos is not he in Towne?
  1. Sen. He's now in Florence.
  Duke. Write from vs,
To him, Post, Post-haste, dispatch.
  2. Sen. Here comes *Brabantio*, and the Valiant Moore.

Enter Brabantio, Othello, Cassio, Iago, Rodorigo,
and Officers.

  Duke. Valiant *Othello*, we must straight employ you,
Against the generall Enemy Ottoman.
I did not see you: welcome gentle Signior,
We lack't your Counsaile, and your helpe to night.
  Bra. So did I yours: Good your Grace pardon me.
Neither my place, nor ought I heard of businesse
Hath rais'd me from my bed; nor doth the generall care
Take hold on me. For my perticular griefe
Is of so flood-gate, and ore-bearing Nature,
That it engluts, and swallowes other sorrowes,
And it is still it selfe.
  Duke. Why? What's the matter?
  Bra. My Daughter: oh my Daughter!
  Sen. Dead?
  Bra. I, to me.
She is abus'd, stolne from me, and corrupted
By Spels, and Medicines, bought of Mountebanks;
For Nature, so prepostrously to erre,
(Being not deficient, blind, or lame of sense,)
Sans witch-craft could not.
  Duke. Who ere he be, that in this foule proceeding
Hath thus beguil'd your Daughter of her selfe,
And you of her; the bloodie Booke of Law,
You shall your selfe read, in the bitter letter,
After your owne sense: yea, though our proper Son
Stood in your Action.
  Bra. Humbly I thanke your Grace,
Here is the man; this Moore, whom now it seemes
Your speciall Mandate, for the State affaires
Hath hither brought.
  All. We are verie sorry for't.
  Duke. What in your owne part, can you say to this?
  Bra. Nothing, but this is so.
  Othe. Most Potent, Graue, and Reueren'd Signiors,
My very Noble, and approu'd good Masters;
That I haue tane away this old mans Daughter,
It is most true: true I haue married her;
The verie head, and front of my offending,
Hath this extent; no more. Rude am I, in my speech,
And little bless'd with the soft phrase of Peace;
For since these Armes of mine, had seuen yeares pith,
Till now, some nine Moones wasted, they haue vs'd
Their deerest action, in the Tented Field:
And little of this great world can I speake,
More then pertaines to Feats of Broiles, and Battaile,
And therefore little shall I grace my cause,
In speaking for my selfe. Yet, (by your gratious patience)
I will a round vn-varnish'd uTale deliuer,
Of my whole course of Loue.
What Drugges, what Charmes,
What Coniuration, and what mighty Magicke,
(For such proceeding I am charg'd withall)
I won his Daughter.
  Bra. A Maiden, neuer bold:
Of Spirit so still, and quiet, that her Motion
Blush'd at her selfe, and she, in spight of Nature,
Of Yeares, of Country, Credite, euery thing
To fall in Loue, with what she fear'd to looke on;
It is a iudgement main'd, and most imperfect.
That will confesse Perfection so could erre
Against all rules of Nature, and must be driuen
To find out practises of cunning hell
Why this should be. I therefore vouch againe,
That with some Mixtures, powrefull o're the blood,
Or with some Dram, (coniur'd to this effect)
He wrought vp on her.
To vouch this, is no proofe,
Without more wider, and more ouer Test
Then these thin habits, and poore likely-hoods
Of moderne seeming, do prefer against him.
  Sen. But *Othello*, speake,
Did you, by indirect, and forced courses
Subdue, and poyson this yong Maides affections?
Or came it by request, and such faire question
As soule, to soule affordeth?
  Othel. I do beseech you,
Send for the Lady to the Sagitary,
And let her speake of me before her Father;
If you do finde me foule, in her report,
The Trust, the Office, I do hold of you,
Not onely take away, but let your Sentence
Euen fall vpon my life.
  Duke. Fetch *Desdemona* hither.
  Othe. Aunciant, conduct them:
You best know the place.
And tell she come, as truely as to heauen,
I do confesse the vices of my blood,
So iustly to your Graue eares, Ile present

How

How I did thriue in this faire Ladies loue,
And she in mine.
  Duke. Say it *Othello.*
  Othe. Her Father lou'd me, oft inuited me:
Still question'd me the Storie of my life,
From yeare to yeare: the Battaile, Sieges, Fortune,
That I haue past.
I ran it through, euen from my boyish daies,
Toth'very moment that he bad me tell it.
Wherein I spoke of most disastrous chances:
Of mouing Accidents by Flood and Field,
Of haire-breadth scapes i'th'imminent deadly breach;
Of being taken by the Insolent Foe,
And sold to slauery. Of my redemption thence,
And portance in my Trauellours historie.
Wherein of Antars vast, and Desarts idle,
Rough Quarries, Rocks, Hills, whose head touch heauen,
It was my hint to speake. Such was my Processe,
And of the Canibals that each others eate,
The *Antropophague,* and men whose heads
Grew beneath their shoulders. These things to heare,
Would *Desdemona* seriously incline:
But still the house Affaires would draw her hence:
Which euer as she could with haste dispatch,
She'l'd come againe, and with a greedie eare
Deuoure vp my discourse. Which I obseruing,
Tooke once a pliant houre, and found good meanes
To draw from her a prayer of earnest heart,
That I would all my Pilgrimage dilate,
Whereof by parcels she had something heard,
But not instinctiuely: I did consent,
And often did beguile her of her teares,
When I did speake of some distressefull stroke
That my youth suffer'd: My Storie being done,
She gaue me for my paines a world of kisses:
She swore in faith 'twas strange: 'twas passing strange,
'Twas pittifull: 'twas wondrous pittifull.
She wish'd she had not heard it, yet she wish'd
That Heauen had made her such a man. She thank'd me,
And bad me, if I had a Friend that lou'd her,
I should but teach him how to tell my Story,
And that would wooe her. Vpon this hint I spake,
She lou'd me for the dangers I had past,
And I lou'd her, that she did pitty them.
This onely is the witch-craft I haue vs'd.
Here comes the Ladie: Let her witnesse it.

Enter Desdemona, Iago, Attendants.

  Duke. I thinke this tale would win my Daughter too,
Good *Brabantio,* take vp this mangled matter at the best:
Men do their broken Weapons rather vse,
Then their bare hands.
  Bra. I pray you heare her speake?
If she confesse that she was halfe the wooer,
Destruction on my head, if my bad blame
Light on the man. Come hither gentle Mistris,
Do you perceiue in all this Noble Companie,
Where most you owe obedience?
  Des. My Noble Father,
I do perceiue heere a diuided dutie.
To you I am bound for life, and education:
My life and education both do learne me,
How to respect you. You are the Lord of duty,
I am hitherto your Daughter. But heere's my Husband;
And so much dutie, as my Mother shew'd
To you, preferring you before her Father:
So much I challenge, that I may professe
Due to the Moore my Lord.
  Bra. God be with you: I haue done.
Please it your Grace, on to the State Affaires;
I had rather to adopt a Child, then get it.
Come hither Moore;
I here do giue thee that with all my heart,
Which but thou hast already, with all my heart
I would keepe from thee. For your sake (Iewell)
I am glad at soule, I haue no other Child,
For thy escape would teach me Tirranie
To hang clogges on them. I haue done my Lord.
  Duke. Let me speake like your selfe:
And lay a Sentence,
Which as a grise, or step may helpe these Louers.
When remedies are past, the griefes are ended
By seeing the worst, which late on hopes depended.
To mourne a Mischeefe that is past and gon,
Is the next way to draw new mischiefe on.
What cannot be preseru'd, when Fortune takes:
Patience, her Iniury a mock'ry makes.
The rob'd that smiles, steales something from the Thiefe,
He robs himselfe, that spends a bootelesse griefe.
  Bra. So let the Turke of Cyprus vs beguile,
We loose it not so long as we can smile:
He beares the Sentence well, that nothing beares,
But the free comfort which from thence he heares.
But he beares both the Sentence, and the sorrow,
That to pay griefe, must of poore Patience borrow.
These Sentences, to Sugar, or to Gall,
Being strong on both sides, are Equiuocall.
But words are words, I neuer yet did heare:
That the bruized heart was pierc'd through the eares.
I humbly beseech you proceed to th'Affaires of State.
  Duke. The Turke with a most mighty Preparation
makes for Cyprus: *Othello,* the Fortitude of the place is
best knowne to you. And though we haue there a Substitute of most allowed sufficiencie; yet opinion, a more
soueraigne Mistris of Effects, throwes a more safer
voice on you: you must therefore be content to slubber
the glosse of your new Fortunes, with this more stubborne, and boysirous expedition.
  Othe. The Tirant Custome, most Graue Senators,
Hath made the flinty and Steele Coach of Warre
My thrice-driuen bed of Downe. I do agnize
A Naturall and prompt Alacartie,
I finde in hardnesse: and do vndertake
This present Warres against the *Ottamites.*
Most humbly therefore bending to your State,
I craue fit disposition for my Wife,
Due reference of Place, and Exhibition,
With such Accomodation and besort
As leuels with her breeding.
  Duke. Why at her Fathers?
  Bra. I will not haue it so.
  Othe. Nor I.
  Des. Nor would I there recide,
To put my Father in impatient thoughts
By being in his eye. Most Grcaious Duke,
To my vnfolding, lend your prosperous eare,
And let me finde a Charter in your voice
T'assist my simplenesse.
  Duke. What would you *Desdemona?*
  Des. That I loue the Moore, to liue with him,
My downe-right violence, and storme of Fortunes,

May trumpet to the world. My heart's subdu'd
Euen to the very quality of my Lord;
I saw Othello's visage in his mind,
And to his Honours and his valiant parts,
Did I my soule and Fortunes consecrate.
So that (deere Lords) if I be left behind
A Moth of Peace, and he go to the Warre,
The Rites for why I loue him, are bereft me:
And I a heauie interim shall support
By his deere absence. Let me go with him.

Othe. Let her haue your voice.

Vouch with me Heauen, I therefore beg it not
To please the pallate of my Appetite:
Nor to comply with heat the yong affects
In my defunct, and proper satisfaction.
But to be free, and bounteous to her minde:
And Heauen defend your good soules, that you thinke
I will your serious and great businesse scant
When she is with me. No, when light wing'd Toyes
Of feather'd *Cupid*, seele with wanton dulnesse
My speculatiue, and offic'd Instrument:
That my Disports corrupt, and taint my businesse:
Let House-wiues make a Skillet of my Helme,
And all indigne, and base aduersities,
Make head against my Estimation.

Duke. Be it as you shall priuately determine,
Either for her stay, or going: th'Affaire cries hast:
And speed must answer it.

Sen. You must away to night.

Othe. With all my heart.

Duke. At nine i'th'morning, here wee'l meete againe.
Othello, leaue some Officer behind
And he shall our Commission bring to you:
And such things else of qualitie and respect
As doth import you.

Othe. So please your Grace, my Ancient,
A man he is of honesty and trust:
To his conueyance I assigne my wife,
With what else needfull, your good Grace shall think
To be sent after me.

Duke. Let it be so:
Good night to euery one. And Noble Signior,
If Vertue no delighted Beautie lacke,
Your Son-in-law is farre more Faire then Blacke.

Sen. Adieu braue Moore, vse *Desdemona* well.

Bra. Looke to her (Moore) if thou hast eies to see:
She ha's deceiu'd her Father, and may thee. *Exit.*

Othe. My life vpon her faith. Honest *Iago*,
My *Desdemona* must I leaue to thee:
I prythee let thy wife attend on her,
And bring them after in the best aduantage.
Come *Desdemona*, I haue but an houre
Of Loue, of wordly matter, and direction
To spend with thee. We must obey the the time. *Exit.*

Rod. Iago.

Iago. What saist thou Noble heart?

Rod. What will I do, think'st thou?

Iago. Why go to bed and sleepe.

Rod. I will incontinently drowne my selfe.

Iago. If thou do'st, I shall neuer loue thee after. Why thou silly Gentleman?

Rod. It is sillynesse to liue, when to liue is torment: and then haue we a prescription to dye, when death is our Physition.

Iago. Oh villanous: I haue look'd vpon the world for foure times seuen yeares, and since I could distinguish betwixt a Benefit, and an Iniurie: I neuer found man that knew how to loue himselfe. Ere I would say, I would drowne my selfe for the loue of a Gynney Hen, I would change my Humanity with a Baboone.

Rod. What should I do? I confesse it is my shame to be so fond, but it is not in my vertue to amend it.

Iago. Vertue? A figge, 'tis in our selues that we are thus, or thus. Our Bodies are our Gardens, to the which, our Wills are Gardiners. So that if we will plant Nettels, or sowe Lettice: Set Hisope, and weede vp Time: Supplie it with one gender of Hearbes, or distract it with many: either to haue it sterrill with idlenesse, or manured with Industry, why the power, and Corrigeable authoritie of this lies in our Wills. If the braine of our liues had not one Scale of Reason, to poize another of Sensualitie, the blood, and basenesse of our Natures would conduct vs to most preposterous Conclusions. But we haue Reason to coole our raging Motions, our carnall Stings, or vnbitted Lusts: whereof I take this, that you call Loue, to be a Sect, or Seyen.

Rod. It cannot be.

Iago. It is meerly a Lust of the blood, and a permission of the will. Come, be a man: drowne thy selfe? Drown Cats, and blind Puppies. I haue profest me thy Friend, and I confesse me knit to thy deseruing, with Cables of perdurable toughnesse. I could neuer better steed thee then now. Put Money in thy purse: follow thou the Warres, defeate thy fauour, with an vsurp'd Beard. I say put Money in thy purse. It cannot be long that *Desdemona* should continue her loue to the Moore. Put Money in thy purse: nor he his to her. It was a violent Commencement in her, and thou shalt see an answerable Sequestration, put but Money in thy purse. These Moores are changeable in their wils: fill thy purse with Money. The Food that to him now is as lushious as Locusts, shalbe to him shortly, as bitter as Coloquintida. She must change for youth: when she is sated with his body she will find the errors of her choice. Therefore, put Money in thy purse. If thou wilt needs damne thy selfe, do it a more delicate way then drowning. Make all the Money thou canst: If Sanctimonie, and a fraile vow, betwixt an erring Barbarian, and super-subtle Venetian be not too hard for my wits, and all the Tribe of hell, thou shalt enioy her: therefore make Money: a pox of drowning thy selfe, it is cleane out of the way. Seeke thou rather to be hang'd in Compassing thy ioy, then to be drown'd, and go without her.

Rodo. Wilt thou be fast to my hopes, if I depend on the issue?

Iago. Thou art sure of me: Go make Money: I haue told thee often, and I re-tell thee againe, and againe, I hate the Moore. My cause is hearted; thine hath no lesse reason. Let vs be coniunctiue in our reuenge, against him. If thou canst Cuckold him, thou dost thy selfe a pleasure, me a sport. There are many Euents in the Wombe of Time, which wilbe deliuered. Trauerse, go, provide thy Money. We will haue more of this to morrow. Adieu.

Rod. Where shall we meete i'th'morning?

Iago. At my Lodging.

Rod. Ile be with thee betimes.

Iago. Go too, farewell. Do you heare *Rodorigo*?

Rod. Ile sell all my Land. *Exit.*

Iago. Thus do I euer make my Foole, my purse:
For I mine owne gain'd knowledge should prophane
If I would time expend with such Snpe,

But

But for my Sport, and Profit: I hate the Moore,
And it is thought abroad, that 'twixt my sheets
She ha's done my Office. I know not if't be true,
But I, for meere suspition in that kinde,
Will do, as if for Surety. He holds me well,
The better shall my purpose worke on him:
Cassio's a proper man: Let me see now,
To get his Place, and to plume vp my will
In double Knauery. How? How? Let's see.
After some time, to abuse *Othello's* eares,
That he is too familiar with his wife:
He hath a person, and a smooth dispose
To be suspected: fram'd to make women false.
The Moore is of a free, and open Nature,
That thinkes men honest, that but seeme to be so,
And will as tenderly be lead by'th'Nose
As Asses are:
I haue't: it is engendred: Hell, and Night,
Must bring this monstrous Birth, to the worlds light.

Actus Secundus. Scena Prima.

Enter Montano, and two Gentlemen.

Mon. What from the Cape, can you discerne at Sea?
1. Gent. Nothing at all, it is a high wrought Flood:
I cannot 'twixt the Heauen, and the Maine,
Descry a Saile.
Mon. Me thinks, the wind hath spoke aloud at Land,
A fuller blast ne're shooke our Battlements:
If it hath ruffiand so vpon the Sea,
What ribbes of Oake, when Mountaines melt on them,
Can hold the Mortise. What shall we heare of this?
2. A Segregation of the Turkish Fleet:
For do but stand vpon the Foaming Shore,
The chidden Billow seemes to pelt the Clowds,
The winde-shak'd-Surge, with high & monstrous Maine
Seemes to cast water on the burning Beare,
And quench the Guards of th'euer-fixed Pole:
I neuer did like mollestation view
On the enchafed Flood.
Mon. If that the Turkish Fleete
Be not enshelter'd, and embay'd, they are drown'd,
It is impossible to beare it out.

Enter a Gentleman.

3. Newes Laddes: our warres are done:
The desperate Tempest hath so bang'd the Turkes,
That their designement halts. A Noble ship of Venice,
Hath seene a greeuous wracke and sufferance
On most part of their Fleet.
Mon. How? Is this true?
3. The Ship is heere put in: A *Verennessa*, *Michael Cassio*
Lieutenant to the warlike Moore, *Othello*,
Is come on Shore, the Moore himselfe at Sea,
And is in full Commission heere for Cyprus.
Mon. I am glad on't:
'Tis a worthy Gouernour.
3. But this same *Cassio*, though he speake of comfort,
Touching the Turkish losse, yet he lookes sadly,
And prayes the Moore be safe; for they were parted
With fowle and violent Tempest.
Mon. Pray Heauens he be:

For I haue seru'd him, and the man commands
Like a full Soldier. Let's to the Sea-side (hoa)
As well to see the Vessell that's come in,
As to throw-out our eyes for braue *Othello*,
Euen till we make the Maine, and th'Eriall blew,
An indistinct regard.
Gent. Come, let's do so;
For euery Minute is expectancie
Of more Arriuancie.

Enter Cassio.

Cassi. Thankes you, the valiant of the warlike Isle,
That so approoue the Moore: Oh let the Heauens
Giue him defence against the Elements,
For I haue lost him on a dangerous Sea.
Mon. Is he well ship'd?
Cassio. His Barke is stoutly Timber'd, and his Pylot
Of verie expert, and approu'd Allowance;
Therefore my hope's (not surfetted to death)
Stand in bold Cure.
Within. A Saile, a Saile, a Saile.
Cassio. What noise?
Gent. The Towne is empty; on the brow o'th'Sea
Stand rankes of People, and they cry, a Saile.
Cassio. My hopes do shape him for the Gouernor.
Gent. They do discharge their Shot of Courtesie,
Our Friends, at least.
Cassio. I pray you Sir, go forth,
And giue vs truth who 'tis that is arriu'd.
Gent. I shall.   *Exit.*
Mon. But good Lieutenant, is your Generall wiu'd?
Cassio. Most fortunately: he hath atchieu'd a Maid
That paragons description, and wilde Fame:
One that excels the quirkes of Blazoning pens,
And in th'essentiall Vesture of Creation,
Do's tyre the Ingeniuer.

Enter Gentleman.

How now? Who ha's put in?
Gent. 'Tis one *Iago*, Auncient to the Generall.
Cassio. Ha's had most fauourable, and happie speed:
Tempests themselues, high Seas, and howling windes,
The gutter'd-Rockes, and Congregated Sands,
Traitors ensteep'd, to enclogge the guiltlesse Keele,
As hauing sence of Beautie, do omit
Their mortall Natures, letting go safely by
The Diuine *Desdemona.*
Mon. What is she?
Cassio. She that I spake of:
Our great Captains Captaine,
Left in the conduct of the bold *Iago*,
Whose footing heere anticipates our thoughts,
A Senights speed. Great Ioue, *Othello* guard,
And swell his Saile with thine owne powrefull breath,
That he may blesse this Bay with his tall Ship,
Make Ioues quicke pants in *Desdemonaes* Armes,
Giue renew'd fire to our extincted Spirits.

Enter Desdemona, Iago, Rodorigo, and Æmilia.

Oh behold,
The Riches of the Ship is come on shore:
You men of Cyprus, let her haue your knees.
Haile to thee Ladie: and the grace of Heauen,
Before, behinde thee, and on euery hand
Enwheele thee round.
Des. I thanke you, Valiant *Cassio*,
What tydings can you tell of my Lord?

Cas. He is not yet arriu'd, nor know I ought
But that he's well, and will be shortly heere.

Des. Oh, but I feare:
How lost you company?

Cassio. The great Contention of Sea, and Skies
Parted our fellowship. But hearke, a Saile.

Within. A Saile, a Saile.

Gent. They giue this greeting to the Cittadell:
This likewise is a Friend.

Cassio. See for the Newes:
Good Ancient, you are welcome. Welcome Mistris:
Let it not gaule your patience (good *Iago*)
That I extend my Manners. 'Tis my breeding,
That giues me this bold shew of Curtesie.

Iago. Sir, would she giue you so much of her lippes,
As of her tongue she oft bestowes on me,
You would haue enough.

Des. Alas: she ha's no speech.

Iago. Infaith too much:
I finde it still, when I haue leaue to sleepe.
Marry before your Ladyship, I grant,
She puts her tongue a little in her heart,
And chides with thinking.

Æmil. You haue little cause to say so.

Iago. Come on, come on: you are Pictures out of
doore: Bells in your Parlours: Wilde-Cats in your Kitchens: Saints in your Iniuries: Diuels being offended:
Players in your Huswiferie, and Huswiues in your
Beds.

Des. Oh, fie vpon thee, Slanderer.

Iago. Nay, it is true: or else I am a Turke,
You rise to play, and go to bed to worke.

Æmil. You shall not write my praise.

Iago. No, let me not.

Desde. What would'st write of me, if thou should'st
praise me?

Iago. Oh, gentle Lady, do not put me too't,
For I am nothing, if not Criticall.

Des. Come on, assay.
There's one gone to the Harbour?

Iago. I Madam.

Des. I am not merry: but I do beguile
The thing I am, by seeming otherwise.
Come, how would'st thou praise me?

Iago. I am about it, but indeed my inuention comes
from my pate, as Birdlyme do's from Freeze, it pluckes
out Braines and all. But my Muse labours, and thus she
is deliuer'd.

If she be faire, and wise: fairenesse, and wit,
The ones for vse, the other vseth it.

Des. Well prais'd:
How if she be Blacke and Witty?

Iago. *If she be blacke, and thereto haue a wit,*
She'le find a white, that shall her blacknesse fit.

Des. Worse, and worse.

Æmil. How if Faire, and Foolish?

Iago. *She neuer yet was foolish that was faire,*
For euen her folly helpt her to an heire.

Desde. These are old fond Paradoxes, to make Fooles
laugh i'th' Alehouse. What miserable praise hast thou
for her that's Foule, and Foolish.

Iago. *There's none so foule and foolish thereunto,*
But do's foule pranks, which faire, and wise-ones do.

Desde. Oh heauy ignorance: thou prais'est the worst
best. But what praise could'st thou bestow on a deseruing woman indeed? One, that in the authoritly of her
merit, did iustly put on the vouch of very malice it
selfe.

Iago. *She that was euer faire, and neuer proud,*
Had Tongue at will, and yet was neuer loud:
Neuer lackt Gold, and yet went neuer gay,
Fled from her wish, and yet said now I may.
She that being angred, her reuenge being nie,
Bad her wrong stay, and her displeasure flie:
She that in wisedome neuer was so fraile,
To change the Cods-head for the Salmons taile:
She that could thinke, and neu'r disclose her mind,
See Suitors following, and not looke behind:
She was a wight, (if euer such wightes were)

Des. To do what?

Iago. *To suckle Fooles, and chronicle small Beere.*

Desde. Oh most lame and impotent conclusion. Do
not learne of him *Æmillia*, though he be thy husband.
How say you (*Cassio*) is he not a most prophane, and liberall Counsailor?

Cassio. He speakes home (Madam) you may rellish
him more in the Souldier, then in the Scholler.

Iago. He takes her by the palme: I, well said, whisper. With as little a web as this, will I ensnare as great
a Fly as *Cassio*. I smile vpon her, do: I will giue thee
in thine owne Courtship. You say true, 'tis so indeed.
If such tricks as these strip you out of your Lieutenantrie, it had beene better you had not kiss'd your three fingers so oft, which now againe you are most apt to play
the Sir, in. Very good: well kiss'd, and excellent Curtsie: 'tis so indeed. Yet againe, your fingers to your
lippes? Would they were Cluster-pipes for your
sake.
The Moore I know his Trumpet.

Cassio. 'Tis truely so.

Des. Let's meere him, and recieue him.

Cassio. Loe, where he comes.

Enter Othello, and Attendants.

Oth. O, my faire Warriour.

Des. My deere *Othello*.

Othe. It giues me wonder great, as my content
To see you heere before me.
Oh my Soules Ioy:
If after euery Tempest, come such Calmes,
May the windes blow, till they haue waken'd death:
And let the labouring Barke climbe hills of Seas
Olympus high: and duck againe as low,
As hell's from Heauen. If it were now to dye,
'Twere now to be most happy. For I feare,
My Soule hath her content so absolute,
That not another comfort like to this,
Succeedes in vnknowne Fate.

Des. The Heauens forbid
But that our Loues
And Comforts should encrease
Euen as our dayes do grow.

Othe. Amen to that (sweet Powers)
I cannot speake enough of this content,
It stoppes me heere: it is too much of ioy.
And this, and this the greatest discords be
That ere our hearts shall make.

Iago. Oh you are well tun'd now: But Ile set downe
the peggs that make this Musicke, as honest as I am.

Othe.

Othe. Come: let vs to the Castle.
Newes (Friends) our Warres are done:
The Turkes are drown'd.
How do's my old Acquaintance of this Isle?
(Hony) you shall be well desir'd in Cyprus,
I haue found great loue among'st them. Oh my Sweet,
I prattle out of fashion, and I doate
In mine owne comforts. I prythee, good *Iago*,
Go to the Bay, and disimbarke my Coffers:
Bring thou the Master to the Cittadell,
He is a good one, and his worthynesse
Do's challenge much respect. Come *Desdemona*,
Once more well met at Cyprus.

Exit Othello and Desdemona.

Iago. Do thou meet me presently at the Harbour. Come thither, if thou be'st Valiant, (as they say base men being in Loue, haue then a Nobilitie in their Natures, more then is natiue to them) list-me; the Lieutenant to night watches on the Court of Guard. First, I must tell thee this: *Desdemona*, is directly in loue with him.

Rod. With him? Why, 'tis not possible.

Iago. Lay thy finger thus: and let thy soule be instructed. Marke me with what violence she first lou'd the Moore, but for bragging, and telling her fantasticall lies. To loue him still for prating, let not thy discreet heart thinke it. Her eye must be fed. And what delight shall she haue to looke on the diuell? When the Blood is made dull with the Act of Sport, there should be a game to enflame it, and to giue Satiety a fresh appetite. Louelinesse in fauour, simpathy in yeares, Manners, and Beauties: all which the Moore is defectiue in. Now for want of these requir'd Conueniences, her delicate tendernesse wil finde it selfe abus'd, begin to heaue the gorge, disrellish and abhorre the Moore, very Nature wil instruct her in it, and compell her to some second choice. Now Sir, this granted (as it is a most pregnant and vnforc'd position) who stands so eminent in the degree of this Forune, as *Cassio* do's: a knaue very voluble: no further conscionable, then in putting on the meere forme of Ciuill, and Humaine seeming, for the better compasse of his salt, and most hidden loose Affection? Why none, why none: A slipper, and subtle knaue, a finder of occasion: that he's an eye can stampe, and counterfeit Aduantages, though true Aduantage neuer present it selfe. A diuelish knaue: besides, the knaue is handsome, young: and hath all those requisites in him, that folly and greene mindes looke after. A pestilent compleat knaue, and the woman hath found him already.

Rodo. I cannot beleeue that in her, she's full of most bless'd condition.

Iago. Bless'd figges-end. The Wine she drinkes is made of grapes. If shee had beene bless'd, shee would neuer haue lou'd the Moore: Bless'd pudding. Didst thou not see her paddle with the palme of his hand? Didst not marke that?

Rod. Yes, that I did: but that was but curtesie.

Iago. Leacherie by this hand: an Index, and obscure prologue to the History of Lust and foule Thoughts. They met so neere with their lippes, that their breathes embrac'd together. Villanous thoughts *Rodorigo*, when these mutabilities so marthall the way, hard at hand comes the Master, and maine exercise, th'incorporate conclusion: Pish. But Sir, be you rul'd by me. I haue brought you from Venice. Watch you to night: for the Command, Ile lay't vpon you. *Cassio* knowes you not: Ile not be farre from you. Do you finde some occasion to anger *Cassio*, either by speaking too loud, or tainting his discipline, or from what other course you please, which the time shall more fauorably minister.

Rod. Well.

Iago. Sir, he's rash, and very sodaine in Choller: and happely may strike at you, prouoke him that he may: for euen out of that will I cause these of Cyprus to Mutiny. Whose qualification shall come into no true taste againe, but by the displanting of *Cassio*. So shall you haue a shorter iourney to your desires, by the meanes I shall then haue to preferre them. And the impediment most profitably remoued, without the which there were no expectation of our prosperitie.

Rodo. I will do this, if you can bring it to any opportunity.

Iago. I warrant thee. Meete me by and by at the Cittadell. I must fetch his Necessaries a Shore. Farewell.

Rodo. Adieu. *Exit.*

Iago. That *Cassio* loues her, I do well beleeu't:
That she loues him, 'tis apt, and of great Credite.
The Moore (how beit that I endure him not)
Is of a constant, louing, Noble Nature,
And I dare thinke, he'le proue to *Desdemona*
A most deere husband. Now I do loue her too,
Not out of absolute Lust, (though peraduenture
I stand accomptant for as great a sin)
But partely led to dyet my Reuenge,
For that I do suspect the lustie Moore
Hath leap'd into my Seate. The thought whereof,
Doth (like a poysonous Minerall) gnaw my Inwardes:
And nothing can, or shall content my Soule
Till I am euen'd with him, wife, for wife.
Or fayling so, yet that I put the Moore,
At least into a Ielouzie so strong
That iudgement cannot cure. Which thing to do,
If this poore Trash of Venice, whom I trace
For his quicke hunting, stand the putting on,
Ile haue our *Michael Cassio* on the hip,
Abuse him to the Moore, in the right garbe
(For I feare *Cassio* with my Night-Cape too)
Make the Moore thanke me, loue me, and reward me,
For making him egregiously an Asse,
And practising vpon his peace, and quiet,
Euen to madnesse. 'Tis heere: but yet confus'd,
Knaueries plaine face, is neuer seene, till vs'd. *Exit.*

Scena Secunda.

Enter Othello's, Herald with a Proclamation.

Herald. It is *Othello's* pleasure, our Noble and Valiant Generall. That vpon certaine tydings now arriu'd, importing the meere perdition of the Turkish Fleete: euery man put himselfe into Triumph. Some to daunce, some to make Bonfires, each man, to what Sport and Reuels his addition leads him. For besides these beneficiall Newes, it is the Celebration of his Nuptiall. So much was his pleasure should be proclaimed. All offices are open, & there is full libertie of Feasting from this pre-

present houre of fiue, till the Bell haue told eleuen. Blesse the Isle of Cyprus, and our Noble Generall Othello.   *Exit.*

Enter Othello, Desdemona, Cassio, and Attendants.

Othe. Good *Michael*, looke you to the guard to night.
Let's teach our selues that Honourable stop,
Not to out-sport discretion.

Cas. *Iago*, hath direction what to do.
But notwithstanding with my personall eye
Will I looke to't.

Othe. *Iago*, is most honest:
Michael, goodnight. To morrow with your earliest,
Let me haue speech with you. Come my deere Loue,
The purchase made, the fruites are to ensue,
That profit's yet to come 'tweene me, and you.
Goodnight.   *Exit.*

Enter Iago.

Cas. Welcome *Iago*: we must to the Watch.

Iago. Not this houre Lieutenant: 'tis not yet ten o'th'clocke. Our Generall cast vs thus earely for the loue of his *Desdemona*: Who, let vs not therefore blame; he hath not yet made wanton the night with her: and she is sport for *Ioue*.

Cas. She's a most exquisite Lady.

Iago. And Ile warrant her, full of Game.

Cas. Indeed shes a most fresh and delicate creature.

Iago. What an eye she ha's?
Methinkes it sounds a parley to prouocation.

Cas. An inuiting eye:
And yet me thinkes right modest.

Iago. And when she speakes,
Is it not an Alarum to Loue?

Cas. She is indeed perfection.

Iago. Well: happinesse to their Sheetes. Come Lieutenant, I haue a stope of Wine, and heere without are a brace of Cyprus Gallants, that would faine haue a measure to the health of blacke *Othello*.

Cas. Not to night, good *Iago*, I haue very poore, and vnhappie Braines for drinking. I could well wish Curtesie would inuent some other Custome of entertainment.

Iago. Oh, they are our Friends: but one Cup, Ile drinke for you.

Cassio. I haue drunke but one Cup to night, and that was craftily qualified too: and behold what inouation it makes heere. I am infortunate in the infirmity, and dare not taske my weakenesse with any more.

Iago. What man? 'Tis a night of Reuels, the Gallants desire it.

Cas. Where are they?

Iago. Heere, at the doore: I pray you call them in.

Cas. Ile do't, but it dislikes me.   *Exit.*

Iago. If I can fasten but one Cup vpon him
With that which he hath drunke to night alreadie,
He'l be as full of Quarrell, and offence
As my yong Mistris dogge.
Now my sicke Foole *Rodorigo*,
Whom Loue hath turn'd almost the wrong side out,
To *Desdemona* hath to night Carrows'd.
Potations, pottle-deepe; and he's to watch.
Three else of Cyprus, Noble swelling Spirites,
(That hold their Honours in a wary distance,
The very Elements of this Warrelike Isle)
Haue I to night fluster'd with flowing Cups,
And they Watch too.
Now 'mongst this Flocke of drunkards
Am I put to our *Cassio* in some Action
That may offend the Isle. But here they come.

Enter Cassio, Montano, and Gentlemen.
If Consequence do but approue my dreame,
My Boate sailes freely, both with winde and Streame.

Cas. 'Fore heauen, they haue giuen me a rowse already.

Mon. Good-faith a litle one: not past a pint, as I am a Souldier.

Iago. Some Wine hoa.
And let me the Cannakin clinke, clinke:
And let me the Cannakin clinke.
A Souldiers a man: Oh, mans life's but a span,
Why then let a Souldier drinke.
Some Wine Boyes.

Cas. 'Fore Heauen: an excellent Song.

Iago. I learn'd it in England: where indeed they are most potent in Potting. Your Dane, your Germaine, and your swag-belly'd Hollander, (drinke hoa) are nothing to your English.

Cassio. Is your Englishmen so exquisite in his drinking?

Iago. Why, he drinkes you with facillitie, your Dane dead drunke. He sweates not to ouerthrow your Almaine. He giues your Hollander a vomit, ere the next Pottle can be fill'd.

Cas. To the health of our Generall.

Mon. I am for it Lieutenant: and Ile do you Iustice.

Iago. Oh sweet England.
King Stephen was and-a worthy Peere,
His Breeches cost him but a Crowne,
He held them Six pence all to deere,
With that he cal'd the Tailor Lowne:
He was a wight of high Renowne,
And thou art but of low degree:
'Tis Pride that pulls the Country downe,
And take thy awl'd Cloake about thee.
Some Wine hoa.

Cassio. Why this is a more exquisite Song then the other.

Iago. Will you heare't againe?

Cas. No: for I hold him to be vnworthy of his Place, that do's those things. Well: heau'ns aboue all: and there be soules must be saued, and there be soules must not be saued.

Iago. It's true, good Lieutenant.

Cas. For mine owne part, no offence to the Generall, nor any man of qualitie: I hope to be saued.

Iago. And so do I too Lieutenant.

Cassio. I: (but by your leaue) not before me. The Lieutenant is to be saued before the Ancient. Let's haue no more of this: let's to our Affaires. Forgiue vs our sinnes: Gentlemen let's looke to our businesse. Do not thinke Gentlemen, I am drunke: this is my Ancient, this is my right hand, and this is my left. I am not drunke now: I can stand well enough, and I speake well enough.

Gent. Excellent well.

Cas. Why very well then: you must not thinke then, that I am drunke.   *Exit.*

Monta. To th'Platforme (Masters) come, let's set the Watch.

Iago. You see this Fellow, that is gone before,
He's a Souldier, fit to stand by *Cæsar*,
And giue direction. And do but see his vice,
'Tis to his vertue, a iust Equinox,

The one as long as th'other. 'Tis pittie of him:
I feare the trust Othello puts him in,
On some odde time of his infirmitie
Will shake this Island.

  Mont. But is he often thus?
  Iago. 'Tis euermore his prologue to his sleepe,
He'le watch the Horologe a double Set,
If Drinke rocke not his Cradle.
  Mont. It were well
The Generall were put in mind of it:
Perhaps he sees it not, or his good nature
Prizes the vertue that appeares in *Cassio*,
And lookes not on his euills: is not this true?

  Enter Rodorigo.

  Iago. How now *Rodorigo*?
I pray you after the Lieutenant, go.
  Mon. And 'tis great pitty, that the Noble Moore
Should hazard such a Place, as his owne Second
With one of an ingraft Infirmitie,
It were an honest Action, to say so
To the Moore.
  Iago. Not I, for this faire Island,
I do loue *Cassio* well: and would do much
To cure him of this euill, But hearke, what noise?

  Enter Cassio pursuing Rodorigo.

  Cas. You Rogue: you Rascall.
  Mon. What's the matter Lieutenant?
  Cas. A Knaue teach me my dutie? Ile beate the
Knaue into a Twiggen-Bottle.
  Rod. Beate me?
  Cas. Dost thou prate, Rogue?
  Mon. Nay, good Lieutenant:
I pray you Sir, hold your hand.
  Cassio. Let me go (Sir)
Or Ile knocke you o're the Mazard.
  Mon. Come, come: you're drunke.
  Cassio. Drunke?
  Iago. Away I say: go out and cry a Mutinie.
Nay good Lieutenant. Alas Gentlemen:
Helpe hoa. Lieutenant. Sir *Montano*:
Helpe Masters. Heere's a goodly Watch indeed.
Who's that which rings the Bell: Diablo, hoa:
The Towne will rise. Fie, fie Lieutenant,
You'le be asham'd for euer.

  Enter Othello, and Attendants.

  Othe. What is the matter heere?
  Mon. I bleed still, I am hurt to th'death. He dies.
  Othe. Hold for your liues.
  Iag. Hold hoa: Lieutenant, Sir *Montano*, Gentlemen:
Haue you forgot all place of sense and dutie?
Hold. The Generall speaks to you: hold for shame.
  Oth. Why how now hoa? From whence ariseth this?
Are we turn'd Turkes? and to our selues do that
Which Heauen hath forbid the *Ottamittes*.
For Christian shame, put by this barbarous Brawle:
He that stirs next, to carue for his owne rage,
Holds his soule light: He dies vpon his Motion.
Silence that dreadfull Bell, it frights the Isle,
From her propriety. What is the matter, Masters?
Honest *Iago*, that lookes dead with greeuing,
Speake: who began this? On thy loue I charge thee?
  Iago. I do not know: Friends all, but now, euen now.
In Quarter, and in termes like Bride, and Groome
Deuesting them for Bed: and then, but now:
(As if some Planet had vnwitted men)
Swords out, and tilting one at others breastes,
In opposition bloody. I cannot speake
Any begining to this peeuish oddes.
And would, in Action glorious, I had lost
Those legges, that brought me to a part of it.
  Othe. How comes it (*Michaell*) you are thus forgot?
  Cas. I pray you pardon me, I cannot speake.
  Othe. Worthy *Montano*, you were wont to be ciuill:
The grauitie, and stillnesse of your youth
The world hath noted. And your name is great
In mouthes of wisest Censure. What's the matter
That you vnlace your reputation thus,
And spend your rich opinion, for the name
Of a night-brawler? Giue me answer to it.
  Mon. Worthy *Othello*, I am hurt to danger,
Your Officer *Iago* can informe you,
While I spare speech which something now offends me,
Of all that I do know, nor know I ought
By me, that's said, or done amisse this night,
Vnlesse selfe-charitie be sometimes a vice,
And to defend our selues, it be a sinne
When violence assailes vs.
  Othe. Now by Heauen,
My blood begins my safer Guides to rule,
And passion (hauing my best iudgement collied)
Assaies to leade the way. If I once stir,
Or do but lift this Arme, the best of you
Shall sinke in my rebuke. Giue me to know
How this foule Rout began: Who set it on,
And he that is approu'd in this offence,
Though he had twinn'd with me, both at a birth,
Shall loose me. What in a Towne of warre,
Yet wilde, the peoples hearts brim-full of feare,
To Manage priuate, and domesticke Quarrell?
In night, and on the Court and Guard of safetie?
'Tis monstrous: *Iago*, who began't?
  Mon. If partially Affin'd, or league in office,
Thou dost deliuer more, or lesse then Truth,
Thou art no Souldier.
  Iago. Touch me not so neere,
I had rather haue this tongue cut from my mouth,
Then it should do offence to *Michaell Cassio*.
Yet I perswade my selfe, to speake the truth
Shall nothing wrong him. This it is Generall:
Montano and my selfe being in speech,
There comes a Fellow crying out for helpe,
And *Cassio* following him with determin'd Sword
To execute vpon him. Sir, this Gentleman,
Steppes in to *Cassio*, and entreats his pause:
My selfe, the crying Fellow did pursue,
Least by his clamour (as it so fell out)
The Towne might fall in fright. He, (swift of foote)
Out-ran my purpose: and I return'd then rather
For that I heard the clinke, and fall of Swords,
And *Cassio* high in oath: Which till to night
I nere might say before. When I came backe
(For this was briefe) I found them close together
At blow, and thrust, euen as againe they were
When you your selfe did part them.
More of this matter cannot I report.
But Men are Men: The best sometimes forget,
Though *Cassio* did some little wrong to him,
As men in rage strike those that wish them best,
Yet surely *Cassio* I beleeue receiu'd
From him that fled some strange Indignitie,
Which patience could not passe.

Othe.

Othe. I know *Iago*
Thy honestie, and loue doth mince this matter,
Making it light to *Cassio*: *Cassio*, I loue thee,
But neuer more be Officer of mine.

Enter Desdemona attended.

Looke if my gentle Loue be not rais'd vp:
Ile make thee an example.

Des. What is the matter (Deere?)
Othe. All's well, Sweeting:
Come away to bed. Sir for your hurts,
My selfe will be your Surgeon. Lead him off:
Iago, looke with care about the Towne,
And silence those whom this vil'd brawle distracted.
Come *Desdemona*, 'tis the Soldiers life,
To haue their Balmy slumbers wak'd with strife. *Exit.*

Iago. What are you hurt Lieutenant?
Cas. I, past all Surgery.
Iago. Marry Heauen forbid.
Cas. Reputation, Reputation, Reputation: Oh I haue lost my Reputation. I haue lost the immortall part of myselfe, and what remaines is bestiall. My Reputation, *Iago*, my Reputation.
Iago. As I am an honest man I had thought you had receiued some bodily wound; there is more sence in that then in Reputation. Reputation is an idle, and most false imposition; oft got without merit, and lost without deseruing. You haue lost no Reputation at all, vnlesse you repute your selfe such a looser. What man, there are more wayes to recouer the Generall againe. You are but now cast in his moode, (a punishment more in policie, then in malice) euen so as one would beate his offencelesse dogge, to affright an Imperious Lyon. Sue to him againe, and he's yours.
Cas. I will rather sue to be despis'd, then to deceiue so good a Commander, with so slight, so drunken, and so indiscreet an Officer. Drunke? And speake Parrat? And squabble? Swagger? Sweare? And discourse Fustian with (ones owne shadow? Oh thou inuisible spirit of Wine, if thou hast no name to be knowne by, let vs call thee Diuell.
Iago. What was he that you follow'd with your Sword? What had he done to you?
Cas. I know not.
Iago. Is't possible?
Cas. I remember a masse of things, but nothing distinctly: a Quarrell, but nothing wherefore. Oh, that men should put an Enemie in their mouthes, to steale away their Braines? that we should with ioy, pleasance, reuell and applause, transforme our selues into Beasts.
Iago. Why? But you are now well enough: how came you thus recouered?
Cas. It hath pleas'd the diuell drunkennesse, to giue place to the diuell wrath, one vnperfectnesse, shewes me another to make me frankly despise my selfe.
Iago. Come, you are too seuere a Moraller. As the Time, the Place, & the Condition of this Country stands I could hartily wish this had not befalne: but since it is, as it is, mend it for your owne good.
Cas. I will aske him for my Place againe, he shall tell me, I am a drunkard: had I as many mouthes as *Hydra*, such an answer would stop them all. To be now a sensible man, by and by a Foole, and presently a Beast. Oh strange! Euery inordinate cup is vnbless'd, and the Ingredient is a diuell.

Iago. Come, come: good wine, is a good famillar Creature, if it be well vs'd: exclaime no more against it. And good Lieutenant, I thinke, you thinke I loue you.
Cassio. I haue well approued it, Sir. I drunke?
Iago. You, or any man liuing, may be drunke at a time man. I tell you what you shall do: Our Generall's Wife, is now the Generall. I may say so, in this respect, for that he hath deuoted, and giuen vp himselfe to the Contemplation, marke: and deuotement of her parts and Graces. Confesse your selfe freely to her: Importune her helpe to put you in your place againe. She is of so free, so kinde, so apt, so blessed a disposition, she holds it a vice in her goodnesse, not to do more then she is requested. This broken ioynt betweene you, and her husband, entreat her to splinter. And my Fortunes against any lay worth naming, this cracke of your Loue, shall grow stonger, then it was before.
Cassio. You aduise me well.
Iago. I protest in the sinceritie of Loue, and honest kindnesse.
Cassio. I thinke it freely: and betimes in the morning, I will beseech the vertuous *Desdemona* to vndertake for me: I am desperate of my Fortunes if they check me.
Iago. You are in the right: good night Lieutenant, I must to the Watch.
Cassio. Good night, honest *Iago*.

Exit Cassio.

Iago. And what's he then,
That saies I play the Villaine?
When this aduise is free I giue, and honest,
Proball to thinking, and indeed the course
To win the Moore againe,
For 'tis most easie
Th'inclyning *Desdemona* to subdue
In any honest Suite. She's fram'd as fruitefull
As the free Elements. And then for her
To win the Moore, were to renownce his Baptisme,
All Seales, and Simbols of redeemed sin:
His Soule is so enfetter'd to her Loue,
That she may make, vnmake, do what she list,
Euen as her Appetite shall play the God,
With his weake Function. How am I then a Villaine;
To Counsell *Cassio* to this paralell course,
Directly to his good? Diuinitie of hell,
When diuels will the blackest sinnes put on,
They do suggest at first with heauenly shewes,
As I do now. For whiles this honest Foole
Plies *Desdemona*, to repaire his Fortune,
And she for him, pleades strongly to the Moore,
Ile powre this pestilence into his eare:
That she repeales him, for her bodies Lust.
And by how much she striues to do him good,
She shall vndo her Credite with the Moore.
So will I turne her vertue into pitch,
And out of her owne goodnesse make the Net,
That shall en-mash them all.
How now *Rodorigo*?

Enter Rodorigo.

Rodorigo. I do follow heere in the Chace, not like a Hound that hunts, but one that filles vp the Crie. My Money is almost spent; I haue bin to night exceedingly well Cudgell'd: And I thinke the issue

will bee, I shall haue so much experience for my paines;
And so, with no money at all, and a little more Wit, returne againe to Venice.

  Iago. How poore are they that haue not Patience?
What wound did euer heale but by degrees?
Thou know'st we worke by Wit, and not by Witchcraft
And Wit depends on dilatory time:
Dos't not go well? *Cassio* hath beaten thee,
And thou by that small hurt hath casheer'd *Cassio*:
Though other things grow faire against the Sun,
Yet Fruites that blossome first, will first be ripe:
Content thy selfe, a-while. Introth'tis Morning;
Pleasure, and Action, make the houres seeme short.
Retire thee, go where thou art Billited:
Away, I say, thou shalt know more heereafter:
Nay get thee gone.   *Exit Roderigo.*
Two things are to be done:
My Wife must moue for *Cassio* to her Mistris:
Ile set her on my selfe, a while, to draw the Moor apart,
And bring him iumpe, when he may *Cassio* finde
Soliciting his wife: I, that's the way:
Dull not Deuice, by coldnesse, and delay.   *Exit.*

Actus Tertius. Scena Prima.

Enter Cassio, Musitians, and Clowne.

  Cassio. Masters, play heere, I wil content your paines,
Something that's briefe: and bid, goodmorrow General.
  Clo. Why Masters, haue your Instruments bin in Na-
ples, that they speake i'th'Nose thus?
  Mus. How Sir? how?
  Clo. Are these I pray you, winde Instruments?
  Mus. I marry are they sir.
  Clo. Oh, thereby hangs a tale.
  Mus. Whereby hangs a tale, sir?
  Clow. Marry sir, by many a winde Instrument that I
know. But Masters, heere's money for you: and the Ge-
nerall so likes your Musicke, that he desires you for loues
sake to make no more noise with it.
  Mus. Well Sir, we will not.
  Clo. If you haue any Musicke that may not be heard,
too't againe. But (as they say) to heare Musicke, the Ge-
nerall do's not greatly care.
  Mus. We haue none such, sir.
  Clow. Then put vp your Pipes in your bagge, for Ile
away. Go, vanish into ayre, away.   *Exit Mu.*
  Cassio Dost thou heare me, mine honest Friend?
  Clo. No, I heare not your honest Friend:
I heare you.
  Cassio. Prythee keepe vp thy Quillets, ther's a poore
peece of Gold for thee: if the Gentlewoman that attends
the Generall be stirring, tell her, there's one *Cassio* en-
treats her a little fauour of Speech. Wilt thou do this?
  Clo. She is stirring sir: if she will stirre hither, I shall
seeme to notifie vnto her.   *Exit Clo.*

Enter Iago.

In happy time, *Iago.*
  Iago. You haue not bin a-bed then?
  Cassio. Why no: the day had broke before we parted.
I haue made bold (*Iago*) to send in to your wife:
My suite to her is, that she will to vertuous *Desdemona*
Procure me some accesse.
  Iago. Ile send her to you presently:
And Ile deuise a meane to draw the Moore
Out of the way, that your conuerse and businesse
May be more free.   *Exit.*
  Cassio. I humbly thanke you for't. I neuer knew
A Florentine more kinde, and honest.

Enter Æmilia.

  Æmil. Goodmorrow (good Lieutenant) I am sorrie
For your displeasure: but all will sure be well.
The Generall and his wife are talking of it,
And she speakes for you stoutly. The Moore replies,
That he you hurt is of great Fame in Cyprus,
And great Affinitie: and that in wholsome Wisedome
He might not but refuse you. But he protests he loues you
And needs no other Suitor, but his likings
To bring you in againe.
  Cassio. Yet I beseech you,
If you thinke fit, or that it may be done,
Giue me aduantage of some breefe Discourse
With *Desdemon* alone.
  Æmil. Pray you come in:
I will bestow you where you shall haue time
To speake your bosome freely.
  Cassio. I am much bound to you.

Scœna Secunda.

Enter Othello, Iago, and Gentlemen.

  Othe. These Letters giue (*Iago*) to the Pylot,
And by him do my duties to the Senate:
That done, I will be walking on the Workes,
Repaire there to mee.
  Iago. Well, my good Lord, Ile doo't.
  Oth. This Fortification (Gentlemen) shall we see't?
  Gent. We'll waite vpon your Lordship.   *Exeunt*

Scœna Tertia.

Enter Desdemona, Cassio, and Æmilia.

  Des. Be thou assur'd (good *Cassio*) I will do
All my abilities in thy behalfe.
  Æmil. Good Madam do:
I warrant it greeues my Husband,
As if the cause were his.
  Des. Oh that's an honest Fellow, Do not doubt *Cassio*
But I will haue my Lord, and you againe
As friendly as you were.
  Cassio. Bounteous Madam,
What euer shall become of *Michael Cassio*,
He's neuer any thing but your true Seruant.
  Des. I know't: I thanke you: you do loue my Lord:
You haue knowne him long, and be you well assur'd
He shall in strangenesse stand no farther off,
Then in a politique distance.
  Cassio. I, but Lady,
That policie may either last so long,
Or feede vpon such nice and waterish diet,
Or breede it selfe so out of Circumstances,
That I being absent, and my place supply'd,
My Generall will forget my Loue, and Seruice.
  Des. Do not doubt that: before *Æmilia* here,

I giue thee warrant of thy place. Assure thee,
If I do vow a friendship, Ile performe it
To the last Article. My Lord shall neuer rest,
Ile watch him tame, and talke him out of patience;
His Bed shall seeme a Schoole, his Boord a Shrift,
Ile intermingle euery thing he do's
With *Cassio's* suite: Therefore be merry *Cassio*,
For thy Solicitor shall rather dye,
Then giue thy cause away.

Enter Othello, and Iago.

Æmil. Madam, heere comes my Lord.
Cassio. Madam, Ile take my leaue.
Des. Why stay, and heare me speake.
Cassio. Madam, not now: I am very ill at ease,
Vnfit for mine owne purposes.
Des. Well, do your discretion. *Exit Cassio.*
Iago. Hah? I like not that.
Othel. What dost thou say?
Iago. Nothing my Lord; or if—I know not what.
Othel. Was not that *Cassio* parted from my wife?
Iago. Cassio my Lord? No sure, I cannot thinke it
That he would steale away so guilty-like,
Seeing your comming.
Oth. I do beleeue 'twas he.
Des. How now my Lord?
I haue bin talking with a Suitor heere,
A man that languishes in your displeasure.
Oth. Who is't you meane?
Des. Why your Lieutenant *Cassio*: Good my Lord,
If I haue any grace, or power to moue you,
His present reconciliation take.
For if he be not one, that truly loues you,
That erres in Ignorance, and not in Cunning,
I haue no iudgement in an honest face.
I prythee call him backe.
Oth. Went he hence now?
Des. I sooth; so humbled,
That he hath left part of his greefe with mee
To suffer with him. Good Loue, call him backe.
Othel. Not now (sweet *Desdemon*) some other time.
Des. But shall't be shortly?
Oth. The sooner (Sweet) for you.
Des. Shall't be to night, at Supper?
Oth. No, not to night.
Des. To morrow Dinner then?
Oth. I shall not dine at home:
I meete the Captaines at the Cittadell.
Des. Why then to morrow night, on Tuesday morne,
On Tuesday noone, or night; on Wensday Morne.
I prythee name the time, but let it not
Exceed three dayes. Infaith hee's penitent:
And yet his Trespasse, in our common reason
(Saue that they say the warres must make example)
Out of her best, is not almost a fault
T'encurre a priuate checke. When shall he come?
Tell me *Othello.* I wonder in my Soule
What you would aske me, that I should deny,
Or stand so mam'ring on? What? *Michael Cassio,*
That came a woing with you? and so many a time
(When I haue spoke of you dispraisingly)
Hath tane your part, to haue so much to do
To bring him in? Trust me, I could do much.
Oth. Prythee no more: Let him come when he will:
I will deny thee nothing.
Des. Why, this is not a Boone:

'Tis as I should entreate you weare your Gloues,
Or feede on nourishing dishes, or keepe you warme,
Or sue to you, to do a peculiar profit
To your owne person. Nay, when I haue a suite
Wherein I meane to touch your Loue indeed,
It shall be full of poize, and difficult waight,
And fearefull to be granted.
Oth. I will deny thee nothing.
Whereon, I do beseech thee, grant me this,
To leaue me but a little to my selfe.
Des. Shall I deny you? No: farewell my Lord.
Oth. Farewell my *Desdemona,* Ile come to thee strait.
Des. Æmilia come; be as your Fancies teach you;
What ere you be, I am obedient. *Exit.*
Oth. Excellent wretch: Perdition catch my Soule
But I do loue thee: and when I loue thee not,
Chaos is come againe.
Iago. My Noble Lord.
Oth. What dost thou say, *Iago?*
Iago. Did *Michael Cassio*
When he woo'd my Lady, know of your loue?
Oth. He did, from first to last:
Why dost thou aske?
Iago. But for a satisfaction of my Thought,
No further harme.
Oth. Why of thy thought, *Iago?*
Iago. I did not thinke he had bin acquainted with hir.
Oth. O yes, and went betweene vs very oft.
Iago. Indeed?
Oth. Indeed? I indeed. Discern'st thou ought in that?
Is he not honest?
Iago. Honest, my Lord?
Oth. Honest? I, Honest.
Iago. My Lord, for ought I know.
Oth. What do'st thou thinke?
Iago. Thinke, my Lord?
Oth. Thinke, my Lord? Alas, thou ecchost me;
As if there were some Monster in thy thought
Too hideous to be shewne. Thou dost meane somthing:
I heard thee say euen now, thou lik'st not that,
When *Cassio* left my wife. What didd'st not like?
And when I told thee, he was of my Counsaile,
Of my whole course of wooing; thou cried'st, Indeede?
And didd'st contract, and purse thy brow together,
As if thou then hadd'st shut vp in thy Braine
Some horrible Conceite. If thou do'st loue me,
Shew me thy thought.
Iago. My Lord, you know I loue you.
Oth. I thinke thou do'st:
And for I know thou'rt full of Loue, and Honestie,
And weigh'st thy words before thou giu'st them breath,
Therefore these stops of thine, fright me the more:
For such things in a false disloyall Knaue
Are trickes of Custome: but in a man that's iust,
They're close dilations, working from the heart,
That Passion cannot rule.
Iago. For *Michael Cassio,*
I dare be sworne, I thinke that he is honest.
Oth. I thinke so too.
Iago. Men should be what they seeme,
Or those that be not, would they might seeme none.
Oth. Certaine, men should be what they seeme.
Iago. Why then I thinke *Cassio's* an honest man.
Oth. Nay, yet there's more in this?
I prythee speake to me, as to thy thinkings,
As thou dost ruminate, and giue thy worst of thoughts

The

The worst of words.

Iago. Good my Lord pardon me,
Though I am bound to euery Acte of dutie,
I am not bound to that: All Slaues are free:
Vtter my Thoughts? Why say, they are vild, and false?
As where's that Palace, whereinto foule things
Sometimes intrude not? Who ha's that breast so pure,
Wherein vncleanly Apprehensions
Keepe Leetes, and Law-dayes, and in Sessions sit
With meditations lawfull?

Oth. Thou do'st conspire against thy Friend (*Iago*)
If thou but think'st him wrong'd, and mak'st his eare
A stranger to thy Thoughts.

Iago. I do beseech you,
Though I perchance am vicious in my guesse
(As I confesse it is my Natures plague
To spy into Abuses, and of my iealousie
Shapes faults that are not) that your wisedome
From one, that so imperfectly conceits,
Would take no notice, nor build your selfe a trouble
Out of his scattering, and vnsure obseruance:
It were not for your quiet, nor your good,
Nor for my Manhood, Honesty, and Wisedome,
To let you know my thoughts.

Oth. What dost thou meane?

Iago. Good name in Man, & woman (deere my Lord)
Is the immediate Iewell of their Soules;
Who steales my purse, steales trash:
'Tis something, nothing;
'Twas mine, 'tis his, and has bin slaue to thousands:
But he that filches from me my good Name,
Robs me of that, which not enriches him,
And makes me poore indeed.

Oth. Ile know thy Thoughts.

Iago. You cannot, if my heart were in your hand,
Nor shall not, whil'st 'tis in my custodie.

Oth. Ha?

Iago. Oh, beware my Lord, of iealousie,
It is the greene-ey'd Monster, which doth mocke
The meate it feeds on. That Cuckold liues in blisse,
Who certaine of his Fate, loues not his wronger:
But oh, what damned minutes tels he ore,
Who dotes, yet doubts: Suspects, yet soundly loues?

Oth. O miserie.

Iago. Poore, and Content, is rich, and rich enough,
But Riches finelesse, is as poore as Winter,
To him that euer feares he shall be poore:
Good Heauen, the Soules of all my Tribe defend
From Iealousie.

Oth. Why? why is this?
Think'st thou, I'ld make a Life of Iealousie;
To follow still the changes of the Moone
With fresh suspitions? No: to be once in doubt,
Is to be resolu'd: Exchange me for a Goat,
When I shall turne the businesse of my Soule
To such exufflicate, and blow'd Surmises,
Matching thy inference. 'Tis not to make me Iealious,
To say my wife is faire, feeds well, loues company,
Is free of Speech, Sings, Playes, and Dances:
Where Vertue is, these are more vertuous.
Nor from mine owne weake merites, will I draw
The smallest feare, or doubt of her reuolt,
For she had eyes, and chose me. No *Iago*,
Ile see before I doubt; when I doubt, proue;
And on the proofe, there is no more but this,
Away at once with Loue, or Iealousie.

Ia. I am glad of this: For now I shall haue reason
To shew the Loue and Duty that I beare you
With franker spirit. Therefore (as I am bound)
Receiue it from me. I speake not yet of proofe:
Looke to your wife, obserue her well with *Cassio*,
Weare your eyes, thus: not Iealious, nor Secure:
I would not haue your free, and Noble Nature,
Out of selfe-Bounty, be abus'd: Looke too't:
I know our Country disposition well:
In Venice, they do let Heauen see the prankes
They dare not shew their Husbands.
Their best Conscience,
Is not to leaue't vndone, but kept vnknowne.

Oth. Dost thou say so?

Iago. She did deceiue her Father, marrying you,
And when she seem'd to shake, and feare your lookes,
She lou'd them most.

Oth. And so she did.

Iago. Why go too then:
Shee that so young could giue out such a Seeming
To seele her Fathers eyes vp, close as Oake,
He thought 'twas Witchcraft.
But I am much too blame:
I humbly do beseech you of your pardon
For too much louing you.

Oth. I am bound to thee for euer.

Iago. I see this hath a little dash'd your Spirits:

Oth. Not a iot, not a iot.

Iago. Trust me, I feare it has:
I hope you will consider what is spoke
Comes from your Loue.
But I do see y'are moou'd:
I am to pray you, not to straine my speech
To grosser issues, nor to larger reach,
Then to Suspition.

Oth. I will not.

Iago. Should you do so (my Lord)
My speech should fall into such vilde successe,
Which my Thoughts aym'd not.
Cassio's my worthy Friend:
My Lord, I see y'are mou'd.

Oth. No, not much mou'd:
I do not thinke but *Desdemona's* honest.

Iago. Long liue she so;
And long liue you to thinke so.

Oth. And yet how Nature erring from it selfe.

Iago. I, there's the point:
As (to be bold with you)
Not to affect many proposed Matches
Of her owne Clime, Complexion, and Degree,
Whereto we see in all things, Nature tends:
Foh, one may smel in such, a will most ranke,
Foule disproportions. Thoughts vnnaturall.
But (pardon me) I do not in position
Distinctly speake of her, though I may feare
Her will, recoyling to her better iudgement,
May fal to match you with her Country formes,
And happily repent.

Oth. Farewell, farewell:
If more thou dost perceiue, let me know more:
Set on thy wife to obserue.
Leaue me *Iago*.

Iago. My Lord, I take my leaue.

Othel. Why did I marry?
This honest Creature (doubtlesse)
Sees, and knowes more, much more then he vnfolds.

Iago

Iago. My Lord, I would I might intreat your Honor
To scan this thing no farther: Leaue it to time,
Although 'tis fit that *Cassio* haue his Place;
For sure he filles it vp with great Ability;
Yet if you please, to him off a-while:
You shall by that perceiue him, and his meanes:
Note if your Lady straine his Entertainment
With any strong, or vehement importunitie,
Much will be seene in that: In the meane time,
Let me be thought too busie in my feares,
(As worthy cause I haue to feare I am)
And hold her free, I do beseech your Honor.

  Oth. Feare not my gouernment.
  Iago. I once more take my leaue.   *Exit.*
  Oth. This Fellow's of exceeding honesty,
And knowes all Quantities with a learn'd Spirit
Of humane dealings. If I do proue her Haggard,
Though that her Iesses were my deere heart-strings,
I'ld whistle her off, and let her downe the winde
To prey at Fortune. Haply, for I am blacke,
And haue not those soft parts of Conuersation
That Chamberers haue: Or for I am declin'd
Into the vale of yeares (yet that's not much)
Shee's gone. I am abus'd, and my releefe
Must be to loath her. Oh Curse of Marriage!
That we can call these delicate Creatures ours,
And not their Appetites? I had rather be a Toad,
And liue vpon the vapour of a Dungeon,
Then keepe a corner in the thing I loue
For others vses. Yet 'tis the plague to Great-ones,
Prerogatiu'd are they lesse then the Base,
'Tis destiny vnshunnable, like death:
Euen then, this forked plague is Fated to vs,
When we do quicken. Looke where she comes:

Enter Desdemona and Æmilia.

If she be false, Heauen mock'd it selfe:
Ile not beleeue't.
  Des. How now, my deere *Othello*?
Your dinner, and the generous Islanders
By you inuited, do attend your presence.
  Oth. I am too blame.
  Des. Why do you speake so faintly?
Are you not well?
  Oth. I haue a paine vpon my Forehead, heere.
  Des. Why that's with watching, 'twill away againe.
Let me but binde it hard, within this houre
It will be well.
  Oth. Your Napkin is too little:
Let it alone: Come, Ile go in with you.   *Exit.*
  Des. I am very sorry that you are not well.
  Æmil. I am glad I haue found this Napkin:
This was her first remembrance from the Moore,
My wayward Husband hath a hundred times
Woo'd me to steale it. But she so loues the Token,
(For he coniur'd her, she should euer keepe it)
That she reserues it euermore about her,
To kisse, and talke too. Ile haue the worke tane out,
And giu't *Iago*: what he will do with it
Heauen knowes, not I:
I nothing, but to please his Fantasie.

Enter Iago.

  Iago. How now? What do you heere alone?
  Æmil. Do not you chide: I haue a thing for you.

  Iago. You haue a thing for me?
It is a common thing——
  Æmil. Hah?
  Iago. To haue a foolish wife.
  Æmil. Oh, is that all? What will you giue me now
For that same Handkerchiefe.
  Iago. What Handkerchiefe?
  Æmil. What Handkerchiefe?
Why that the Moore first gaue to *Desdemona*,
That which so often you did bid me steale.
  Iago. Hast stolne it from her?
  Æmil. No; but she let it drop by negligence,
And to th'aduantage, I being heere, took't vp:
Looke, heere 'tis.
  Iago. A good wench, giue it me.
  Æmil. What will you do with't, that you haue bene
so earnest to haue me filch it?
  Iago. Why, what is that to you?
  Æmil. If it be not for some purpose of import,
Giu't me againe. Poore Lady, shee'l run mad
When she shall lacke it.
  Iago. Be not acknowne on't:
I haue vse for it. Go, leaue me.   *Exit Æmil.*
I will in *Cassio's* Lodging loose this Napkin,
And let him finde it. Trifles light as ayre,
Are to the iealious, confirmations strong,
As proofes of holy Writ. This may do something.
The Moore already changes with my poyson:
Dangerous conceites, are in their Natures poysons,
Which at the first are scarse found to distaste:
But with a little acte vpon the blood,
Burne like the Mines of Sulphure. I did say so.

Enter Othello.

Looke where he comes: Not Poppy, nor Mandragora,
Nor all the drowsie Syrrups of the world
Shall euer medicine thee to that sweete sleepe
Which thou owd'st yesterday.
  Oth. Ha, ha, false to mee?
  Iago. Why how now Generall? No more of that.
  Oth. Auant, be gone: Thou hast set me on the Racke:
I sweare 'tis better to be much abus'd,
Then but to know't a little.
  Iago. How now, my Lord?
  Oth. What sense had I, in her stolne houres of Lust?
I saw't not, thought it not: it harm'd not me:
I slept the next night well, fed well, was free, and merrie.
I found not *Cassio's* kisses on her Lippes:
He that is robb'd, not wanting what is stolne,
Let him not know't, and he's not robb'd at all.
  Iago. I am sorry to heare this?
  Oth. I had beene happy, if the generall Campe,
Pyoners and all, had tasted her sweet Body,
So I had nothing knowne. Oh now, for euer
Farewell the Tranquill minde; farewell Content;
Farewell the plumed Troopes, and the bigge Warres,
That makes Ambition, Vertue! Oh farewell,
Farewell the neighing Steed, and the shrill Trumpe,
The Spirit-stirring Drum, th'Eare-piercing Fife,
The Royall Banner, and all Qualitie,
Pride, Pompe, and Circumstance of glorious Warre:
And O you mortall Engines, whose rude throates
Th'immortall Ioues dread Clamours, counterfet,
Farewell: *Othello's* Occupation's gone.
  Iago. Is't possible, my Lord?
  Oth. Villaine, be sure thou proue my Loue a Whore;
Be sure of it: Giue me the Occular proofe,

Or by the worth of mine eternall Soule,
Thou had'st bin better haue bin borne a Dog
Then answer my wak'd wrath.

 Iago. Is't come to this?

 Oth. Make me to see't: or (at the least) so proue it,
That the probation beare no Hindge, nor Loope,
To hang a doubt on: Or woe vpon thy life.

 Iago. My Noble Lord.

 Oth. If thou dost slander her, and torture me,
Neuer pray more: Abandon all remorse
On Horrors head, Horrors accumulate:
Do deeds to make Heauen weepe, all Earth amaz'd;
For nothing canst thou to damnation adde,
Greater then that.

 Iago. O Grace! O Heauen forgiue me!
Are you a Man? Haue you a Soule? or Sense?
God buy you: take mine Office. Oh wretched Foole,
That lou'st to make thine Honesty, a Vice!
Oh monstrous world! Take note, take note (O World)
To be direct and honest, is not safe.
I thanke you for this profit, and from hence
Ile loue no Friend, sith Loue breeds such offence.

 Oth. Nay stay: thou should'st be honest.

 Iago. I should be wise; for Honestie's a Foole,
And looses that it workes for.

 Oth. By the World,
I thinke my Wife be honest, and thinke she is not:
I thinke that thou art iust, and thinke thou art not:
Ile haue some proofe. My name that was as fresh
As *Dians* Visage, is now begrim'd and blacke
As mine owne face. If there be Cords, or Kniues,
Poyson, or Fire, or suffocating streames,
Ile not indure it. Would I were satisfied.

 Iago. I see you are eaten vp with Passion:
I do repent me, that I put it to you.
You would be satisfied?

 Oth. Would? Nay, and I will.

 Iago. And may: but how? How satisfied, my Lord?
Would you the super-vision grossely gape on?
Behold her top'd?

 Oth. Death, and damnation. Oh!

 Iago. It were a tedious difficulty, I thinke,
To bring them to that Prospect: Damne them then,
If euer mortall eyes do see them boulster
More then their owne. What then? How then?
What shall I say? Where's Satisfaction?
It is impossible you should see this,
Were they as prime as Goates, as hot as Monkeyes,
As salt as Wolues in pride, and Fooles as grosse
As Ignorance, made drunke. But yet, I say,
If imputation, and strong circumstances,
Which leade directly to the doore of Truth,
Will giue you satisfaction, you might haue't.

 Oth. Giue me a liuing reason she's disloyall.

 Iago. I do not like the Office.
But sith I am entred in this cause so farre
(Prick'd too't by foolish Honesty, and Loue)
I will go on. I lay with *Cassio* lately,
And being troubled with a raging tooth,
I could not sleepe. There are a kinde of men,
So loose of Soule, that in their sleepes will mutter
Their Affayres: one of this kinde is *Cassio:*
In sleepe I heard him say, sweet *Desdemona,*
Let vs be wary, let vs hide our Loues,
And then (Sir) would he gripe, and wring my hand:
Cry, oh sweet Creature: then kisse me hard,
As if he pluckt vp kisses by the rootes,
That grew vpon my lippes, laid his Leg ore my Thigh,
And sigh, and kisse, and then cry cursed Fate,
That gaue thee to the Moore.

 Oth. O monstrous! monstrous!

 Iago. Nay, this was but his Dreame.

 Oth. But this denoted a fore-gone conclusion,
'Tis a shrew'd doubt, though it be but a Dreame.

 Iago. And this may helpe to thicken other proofes,
That do demonstrate thinly.

 Oth. Ile teare her all to peeces.

 Iago. Nay yet be wise; yet we see nothing done,
She may be honest yet: Tell me but this,
Haue you not sometimes seene a Handkerchiefe
Spotted with Strawberries, in your wiues hand?

 Oth. I gaue her such a one: 'twas my first gift.

 Iago. I know not that: but such a Handkerchiefe
(I am sure it was your wiues) did I to day
See *Cassio* wipe his Beard with.

 Oth. If it be that.

 Iago. If it be that, or any, it was hers.
It speakes against her with the other proofes.

 Othel. O that the Slaue had forty thousand liues:
One is too poore, too weake for my reuenge.
Now do I see 'tis true. Looke heere *Iago,*
All my fond loue thus do I blow to Heauen. 'Tis gone.
Arise blacke vengeance, from the hollow hell,
Yeeld vp (O Loue) thy Crowne, and hearted Throne
To tyrannous Hate. Swell bosome with thy fraught,
For 'tis of Aspickes tongues.

 Iago. Yet be content.

 Oth. Oh blood, blood, blood.

 Iago. Patience I say: your minde may change.

 Oth. Neuer *Iago.* Like to the Ponticke Sea,
Whose Icie Current, and compulsiue course,
Neu'r keepes retyring ebbe, but keepes due on
To the Proponticke, and the Hellespont:
Euen so my bloody thoughts, with violent pace
Shall neu'r looke backe, neu'r ebbe to humble Loue,
Till that a capeable, and wide Reuenge
Swallow them vp. Now by yond Marble Heauen,
In the due reuerence of a Sacred vow,
I heere engage my words.

 Iago. Do not rise yet:
Witnesse you euer-burning Lights aboue,
You Elements, that clip vs round about,
Witnesse that heere *Iago* doth giue vp
The execution of his wit, hands, heart,
To wrong'd *Othello's* Seruice. Let him command,
And to obey shall be in me remorse,
What bloody businesse euer.

 Oth. I greet thy loue,
Not with vaine thanks, but with acceptance bounteous,
And will vpon the instant put thee too't.
Within these three dayes let me heare thee say,
That *Cassio's* not aliue.

 Iago. My Friend is dead:
'Tis done at your Request.
But let her liue.

 Oth. Damne her lewde Minx:
O damne her, damne her.
Come go with me a-part, I will withdraw
To furnish me with some swift meanes of death
For the faire Diuell.
Now art thou my Lieutenant.

 Iago. I am your owne for euer. *Exeunt.*

Scena

Scæna Quarta.

Enter Desdemona, Æmilia, and Clown.

Des. Do you know Sirrah, where Lieutenant *Cassio* lyes?

Clow. I dare not say he lies any where.

Des. Why man?

Clo. He's a Soldier, and for me to say a Souldier lyes, 'tis stabbing.

Des. Go too: where lodges he?

Clo. To tell you where he lodges, is to tel you where I lye.

Des. Can any thing be made of this?

Clo. I know not where he lodges, and for mee to deuise a lodging, and say he lies heere, or he lies there, were to lye in mine owne throat.

Des. Can you enquire him out? and be edified by report?

Clo. I will Catechize the world for him, that is, make Questions, and by them answer.

Des. Seeke him, bidde him come hither: tell him, I haue moou'd my Lord on his behalfe, and hope all will be well.

Clo. To do this, is within the compasse of mans Wit, and therefore I will attempt the doing it. *Exit Clo.*

Des. Where should I loose the Handkerchiefe, Æmilia?

Æmil. I know not Madam.

Des. Beleeue me, I had rather haue lost my purse Full of Cruzadoes. And but my Noble Moore Is true of minde, and made of no such basenesse, As iealious Creatures are, it were enough To put him to ill-thinking.

Æmil. Is he not iealious?

Des. Who, he? I thinke the Sun where he was borne, Drew all such humors from him.

Æmil. Looke where he comes.

Enter Othello.

Des. I will not leaue him now, till *Cassio* be Call'd to him. How is't with you, my Lord?

Oth. Well my good Lady. Oh hardnes to dissemble! How do you, *Desdemona*?

Des. Well, my good Lord.

Oth. Giue me your hand. This hand is moist my Lady.

Des. It hath felt no age, nor knowne no sorrow.

Oth. This argues fruitfulnesse, and liberall heart: Hot, hot, and moyst. This hand of yours requires A sequester from Liberty: Fasting, and Prayer, Much Castigation, Exercise deuout, For heere's a yong, and sweating Diuell heere That commonly rebels: 'Tis a good hand, A franke one.

Des. You may (indeed) say so: For 'twas that hand that gaue away my heart.

Oth. A liberall hand. The hearts of old, gaue hands: But our new Heraldry is hands, not hearts.

Des. I cannot speake of this: Come, now your promise.

Oth. What promise, Chucke?

Des. I haue sent to bid *Cassio* come speake with you.

Oth. I haue a salt and sorry Rhewme offends me: Lend me thy Handkerchiefe.

Des. Heere my Lord.

Oth. That which I gaue you.

Des. I haue it not about me.

Oth. Not?

Des. No indeed, my Lord.

Oth. That's a fault: That Handkerchiefe Did an Ægyptian to my Mother giue: She was a Charmer, and could almost read The thoughts of people. She told her, while she kept it, 'T would make her Amiable, and subdue my Father Intirely to her loue: But if she lost it, Or made a Guift of it, my Fathers eye Should hold her loathed, and his Spirits should hunt After new Fancies. She dying, gaue it me, And bid me (when my Fate would haue me Wiu'd) To giue it her. I did so; and take heede on't, Make it a Darling, like your precious eye: To loose't, or giue't away, were such perdition, As nothing else could match.

Des. Is't possible?

Oth. 'Tis true: There's Magicke in the web of it: A *Sybill* that had numbred in the world The Sun to course, two hundred compasses, In her Prophetticke furie sow'd the Worke: The Wormes were hallowed, that did breede the Silke, And it was dyde in Mummey, which the Skilfull Conseru'd of Maidens hearts.

Des. Indeed? Is't true?

Oth. Most veritable, therefore looke too't well.

Des. Then would to Heauen, that I had neuer seene't?

Oth. Ha? wherefore?

Des. Why do you speake so startingly, and rash?

Oth. Is't lost? Is't gon? Speak, is't out o'th'way?

Des. Blesse vs.

Oth. Say you?

Des. It is not lost: but what and if it were?

Oth. How?

Des. I say it is not lost.

Oth. Fetcht, let me see't.

Des. Why so I can: but I will not now: This is a tricke to put me from my suite, Pray you let *Cassio* be receiu'd againe.

Oth. Fetch me the Handkerchiefe, My minde mis-giues.

Des. Come, come: you'l neuer meete a more sufficient man.

Oth. The Handkerchiefe.

Des. A man that all his time Hath founded his good Fortunes on your loue; Shar'd dangers with you.

Oth. The Handkerchiefe.

Des. Insooth, you are too blame.

Oth. Away. *Exit Othello.*

Æmil. Is not this man iealious?

Des. I neu'r saw this before. Sure, there's some wonder in this Handkerchikfe: I am most vnhappy in the losse of it.

Æmil. 'Tis not a yeare or two shewes vs a man: They are all but Stomackes, and we all but Food, They eate vs hongerly, and when they are full They belch vs.

Enter Iago, and Cassio.

Looke you, *Cassio* and my Husband.

Iago. There is no other way: 'tis she must doo't: And loe the happinesse: go, and importune her.

Des.

Des. How now (good *Cassio*) what's the newes with you?

Cassio. Madam, my former suite. I do beseech you,
That by your vertuous meanes, I may againe
Exist, and be a member of his loue,
Whom I, with all the Office of my heart
Intirely honour, I would not be delayd.
If my offence, be of such mortall kinde,
That nor my Seruice past, nor present Sorrowes,
Nor purpos'd merit in futurity,
Can ransome me into his loue againe,
But to know so, must be my benefit:
So shall I cloath me in a forc'd content,
And shut my selfe vp in some other course
To Fortunes Almes.

Des. Alas (thrice-gentle *Cassio*)
My Aduocation is not now in Tune;
My Lord, is not my Lord; nor should I know him,
Were he in Fauour, as in Humour alter'd.
So helpe me euery spirit sanctified,
As I haue spoken for you all my best,
And stood within the blanke of his displeasure
For my free speech. You must awhile be patient:
What I can do, I will: and more I will
Then for my selfe, I dare. Let that suffice you.

Iago. Is my Lord angry?

Æmil. He went hence but now:
And certainly in strange vnquietnesse.

Iago. Can he be angry? I haue scene the Cannon
When it hath blowne his Rankes into the Ayre,
And like the Diuell from his very Arme
Puff't his owne Brother: And is he angry?
Something of moment then: I will go meet him,
There's matter in't indeed, if he be angry.   *Exit*

Des. I prythee do so. Something sure of State,
Either from Venice, or some vnhatch'd practise
Made demonstrable heere in Cyprus, to him,
Hath pudled his cleare Spirit: and in such cases,
Mens Natures wrangle with inferiour things,
Though great ones are their obiect. 'Tis euen so.
For let our finger ake, and it endues
Our other healthfull members, euen to a sense
Of paine. Nay, we must thinke men are not Gods,
Nor of them looke for such obseruancie
As fits the Bridall. Beshrew me much, *Æmilia*,
I was (vnhandsome Warrior, as I am)
Arraigning his vnkindnesse with my soule:
But now I finde, I had suborn'd the Witnesse,
And he's Indited falsely.

Æmil. Pray heauen it bee
State matters, as you thinke, and no Conception,
Nor no Iealious Toy, concerning you.

Des. Alas the day, I neuer gaue him cause.

Æmil. But Iealious soules will not be answer'd so;
They are not euer iealious for the cause,
But iealious, for they're iealious. It is a Monster
Begot vpon it selfe, borne on it selfe.

Des. Heauen keepe the Monster from *Othello's* mind.

Æmil. Lady, Amen.

Des. I will go seeke him. *Cassio*, walke heere about:
If I doe finde him fit, Ile moue your suite,
And seeke to effect it to my vttermost.   *Exit*

Cas. I humbly thanke your Ladyship.

Enter Bianca.

Bian. 'Saue you (Friend *Cassio*.)

Cassio. What make you from home?
How is't with you, my most faire *Bianca*?
Indeed (sweet Loue) I was comming to your house.

Bian. And I was going to your Lodging, *Cassio*.
What? keepe a weeke away? Seuen dayes, and Nights?
Eight score eight houres? And Louers absent howres
More tedious then the Diall, eight score times?
Oh weary reck'ning.

Cassio. Pardon me, *Bianca*:
I haue this while with leaden thoughts beene prest,
But I shall in a more continuate time
Strike off this score of absence. Sweet *Bianca*
Take me this worke out.

Bianca. Oh *Cassio* whence came this?
This is some Token from a newer Friend,
To the felt-Absence: now I feele a Cause:
Is't come to this? Well, well.

Cassio. Go too, woman:
Throw your vilde gesses in the Diuels teeth,
From whence you haue them. You are iealious now,
That this is from some Mistris, some remembrance:
No, in good troth *Bianca*.

Bian. Why, who's is it?

Cassio. I know not neither:
I found it in my Chamber,
I like the worke well; Ere it be demanded
(As like enough it will) I would haue it coppied:
Take it, and doo't, and leaue me for this time.

Bian. Leaue you? Wherefore?

Cassio. I do attend heere on the Generall,
And thinke it no addition, nor my wish
To haue him see me woman'd.

Bian. Why, I pray you?

Cassio. Not that I loue you not.

Bian. But that you do not loue me.
I pray you bring me on the way a little,
And say, if I shall see you soone at night?

Cassio. 'Tis but a little way that I can bring you,
For I attend heere: But Ile see you soone.

Bian. 'Tis very good: I must be circumstanc'd.
                                    Exeunt omnes.

Actus Quartus. Scena Prima.

Enter Othello, and Iago.

Iago. Will you thinke so?

Oth. Thinke so, *Iago*?

Iago. What, to kisse in priuate?

Oth. An vnauthoriz'd kisse?

Iago. Or to be naked with her Friend in bed,
An houre, or more, not meaning any harme?

Oth. Naked in bed (*Iago*) and not meane harme?
It is hypocrisie against the Diuell:
They that meane vertuously, and yet do so,
The Diuell their vertue tempts, and they tempt Heauen.

Iago. If they do nothing, 'tis a Veniall slip:
But if I giue my wife a Handkerchiefe.

Oth. What then?

Iago. Why then 'tis hers (my Lord) and being hers,
She may (I thinke) bestow't on any man.

Oth. She is Protectresse of her honor too:
May she giue that?

Iago.

the Moore of Venice. 329

Iago. Her honor is an Essence that's not seene,
They haue it very oft, that haue it not.
But for the Handkerchiefe.

Othe. By heauen, I would most gladly haue forgot it:
Thou saidst (oh, it comes ore my memorie,
As doth the Rauen o're the infectious house:
Boading to all) he had my Handkerchiefe.

Iago. I: what of that?

Othe. That's not so good now.

Iag. What if I had said, I had seene him do you wrong?
Or heard him say (as Knaues be such abroad,
Who hauing by their owne importunate suit,
Or voluntary dotage of some Mistris,
Conuinced or supply'd them, cannot chuse
But they must blab.)

Oth. Hath he said any thing?

Iago. He hath (my Lord) but be you well assur'd,
No more then he'le vn-sweare.

Oth. What hath he said?

Iago. Why, that he did: I know not what he did.

Othe. What? What?

Iago. Lye.

Oth. With her?

Iago. With her? On her: what you will.

Othe. Lye with her? lye on her? We say lye on her,
when they be-lye-her. Lye with her: that's fullsome:
Handkerchiefe: Confessions: Handkerchiefe. To confesse, and be hang'd for his labour. First, to be hang'd,
and then to confesse: I tremble at it. Nature would not
inuest her selfe in such shadowing passion, without some
Instruction. It is not words that shakes me thus, (pish)
Noses, Eares, and Lippes: is't possible. Confesse? Handkerchiefe? O diuell. *Falls in a Traunce.*

Iago. Worke on,
My Medicine workes. Thus credulous Fooles are caught,
And many worthy, and chast Dames euen thus,
(All guiltlesse) meete reproach: what hoa? My Lord?
My Lord, I say: Othello.

Enter Cassio.

How now *Cassio*?

Cas. What's the matter?

Iago. My Lord is falne into an Epilepsie,
This is his second Fit: he had one yesterday.

Cas. Rub him about the Temples.

Iago. The Lethargie must haue his quyet course:
If not, he foames at mouth: and by and by
Breakes out to sauage madnesse. Looke, he stirres:
Do you withdraw your selfe a little while,
He will recouer straight: when he is gone,
I would on great occasion, speake with you.
How is it Generall? Haue you not hurt your head?

Othe. Dost thou mocke me?

Iago. I mocke you not, by Heauen:
Would you would beare your Fortune like a Man.

Othe. A Horned man's a Monster, and a Beast.

Iago. Ther's many a Beast then in a populous Citty,
And many a ciuill Monster.

Othe. Did he confesse it?

Iago. Good Sir, be a man:
Thinke euery bearded fellow that's but yoak'd
May draw with you. There's Millions now aliue,
That nightly lye in those vnproper beds,
Which they dare sweare peculiar. Your case is better.
Oh, 'tis the spight of hell, the Fiends Arch-mock,
To lip a wanton in a secure Cowch;

And to suppose her chast. No, let me know,
And knowing what I am, I know what she shallbe.

Oth. Oh, thou art wise: 'tis certaine.

Iago. Stand you a while apart,
Confine your selfe but in a patient List,
Whil'st you were heere, o're-whelmed with your griefe
(A passion most resulting such a man)
Cassio came hither. I shifted him away,
And layd good scuses vpon your Extasie,
Bad him anon returne: and heere speake with me,
The which he promis'd. Do but encaue your selfe,
And marke the Fleeres, the Gybes, and notable Scornes
That dwell in euery Region of his face.
For I will make him tell the Tale anew;
Where, how, how oft, how long ago, and when
He hath, and is againe to cope your wife.
I say, but marke his gesture: marry Patience,
Or I shall say y'are all in all in Spleene,
And nothing of a man.

Othe. Do'st thou heare, *Iago*,
I will be found most cunning in my Patience:
But (do'st thou heare) most bloody.

Iago. That's not amisse,
But yet keepe time in all: will you withdraw?
Now will I question *Cassio* of *Bianca*,
A Huswife, that by selling her desires
Buyes her selfe Bread, and Cloath. It is a Creature
That dotes on *Cassio*, (as 'tis the Strumpets plague
To be-guile many, and be be-guil'd by one)
He, when he heares of her, cannot restraine
From the excesse of Laughter. Heere he comes.

Enter Cassio.

As he shall smile, *Othello* shall go mad:
And his vnbookish Ielousie must conserue
Poore *Cassio's* smiles, gestures, and light behauiours
Quite in the wrong. How do you Lieutenant?

Cas. The worser, that you giue me the addition,
Whose want euen killes me.

Iago. Ply *Desdemona* well, and you are sure on't:
Now, if this Suit lay in *Bianca's* dowre,
How quickely should you speed?

Cas. Alas poore Caitiffe.

Oth. Looke how he laughes already.

Iago. I neuer knew woman loue man so.

Cas. Alas poore Rogue, I thinke indeed she loues me.

Oth. Now he denies it faintly: and laughes it out.

Iago. Do you heare *Cassio*?

Oth. Now he importunes him
To tell it o're: go too, well said, well said.

Iago. She giues it out, that you shall marry her.
Do you intend it?

Cas. Ha, ha, ha.

Oth. Do ye triumph, Romaine? do you triumph?

Cas. I marry. What? A customer; prythee beare
Some Charitie to my wit, do not thinke it
So vnwholesome. Ha, ha, ha.

Oth. So, so, so, so: they laugh, that winnes.

Iago. Why the cry goes, that you marry her.

Cas. Prythee say true.

Iago. I am a very Villaine else.

Oth. Haue you scoar'd me? Well.

Cas. This is the Monkeys owne giuing out:
She is perswaded I will marry her
Out of her owne loue & flattery, not out of my promise.

Oth. *Iago* becomes me: now he begins the story.

Cassio. She was heere euen now: she haunts me in euery place. I was the other day talking on the Sea-banke with certaine Venetians, and thither comes the Bauble, and falls me thus about my neck.

Oth. Crying oh deere *Cassio*, as it were: his iesture imports it.

Cassio. So hangs, and lolls, and weepes vpon me: So shakes, and pulls me. Ha, ha, ha.

Oth. Now he tells how she pluckt him to my Chamber: oh, I see that nose of yours, but not that dogge, I shall throw it to.

Cassio. Well, I must leaue her companie.

Iago. Before me: looke where she comes.

Enter Bianca.

Caf. 'Tis such another Fitchew: marry a perfum'd one? What do you meane by this haunting of me?

Bian. Let the diuell, and his dam haunt you: what did you meane by that same Hanskerchiefe, you gaue me euen now? I was a fine Foole to take it: I must take out the worke? A likely piece of worke, that you should finde it in your Chamber, and know not who left it there. This is some Minxes token, & I must take out the worke? There, giue it your Hobbey-horse, wheresoeuer you had it, Ile take out no worke on't.

Cassio. How now, my sweete *Bianca*? How now? How now?

Othe. By Heauen, that should be my Handkerchiefe.

Bian. If you'le come to supper to night you may, if you will not, come when you are next prepar'd for. *Exit*

Iago. After her: after her.

Caf. I must, shee'l rayle in the streets else.

Iago. Will you sup there?

Cassio. Yes, I intend so.

Iago. Well, I may chance to see you: for I would very faine speake with you.

Caf. Prythee come: will you?

Iago. Go too: say no more.

Oth. How shall I murther him, *Iago*.

Iago. Did you perceiue how he laugh'd at his vice?

Oth. Oh, *Iago*.

Iago. And did you see the Handkerchiefe?

Oth. Was that mine?

Iago. Yours by this hand: and to see how he prizes the foolish woman your wife: she gaue it him, and he hath giu'n it his whore.

Oth. I would haue him nine yeeres a killing: A fine woman, a faire woman, a sweete woman?

Iago. Nay, you must forget that.

Othello. I, let her rot and perish, and be damn'd to night, for she shall not liue. No, my heart is turn'd to stone: I strike it, and it hurts my hand. Oh, the world hath not a sweeter Creature: she might lye by an Emperours side, and command him Taskes.

Iago. Nay, that's not your way.

Othe. Hang her, I do but say what she is: so delicate with her Needle: an admirable Musitian. Oh she will sing the Sauagenesse out of a Beare: of so high and plenteous wit, and inuention?

Iago. She's the worse for all this.

Othe. Oh, a thousand, a thousand times: And then of so gentle a condition?

Iago. I too gentle.

Othe, Nay that's certaine: But yet the pitty of it, *Iago*: oh *Iago*, the pitty of it

Iago.

Iago. If you are so fond ouer her iniquitie: giue her pattent to offend, for if it touch not you, it comes neere no body.

Oth. I will chop her into Messes: Cuckold me?

Iago. Oh, 'tis foule in her.

Oth. With mine Officer?

Iago. That's fouler.

Othe. Get me some poyson, *Iago*, this night. Ile not expostulate with her: least her body and beautie vnprouide my mind againe: this night *Iago*.

Iago. Do it not with poyson, strangle her in her bed, Euen the bed she hath contaminated.

Oth. Good, good: The Iustice of it pleases: very good.

Iago. And for *Cassio*, let me be his vndertaker: You shall heare more by midnight.

Enter Lodouico, Desdemona, and Attendants.

Othe. Excellent good: What Trumpet is that same?

Iago. I warrant something from Venice, 'Tis *Lodouico* this, comes from the Duke. See, your wife's with him.

Lodo. Saue you worthy Generall.

Othe. With all my heart Sir.

Lod. The Duke, and the Senators of Venice greet you.

Othe. I kisse the Instrument of their pleasures.

Des. And what's the newes, good cozen *Lodouico*?

Iago. I am very glad to see you Signior: Welcome to Cyprus.

Lod. I thanke you: how do's Lieutenant *Cassio*?

Iago. Liues Sir,

Des. Cozen, there's falne betweene him, & my Lord, An vnkind breach: but you shall make all well.

Othe. Are you sure of that?

Des. My Lord?

Othe. This faile you not to do, as you will——

Lod. He did not call: he's busie in the paper. Is there deuision 'twixt my Lord, and *Cassio*?

Des. A most vnhappy one: I would do much T'attone them, for the loue I beare to *Cassio*.

Oth. Fire, and brimestone.

Des. My Lord.

Oth. Are you wise?

Des. What is he angrie?

Lod. May be th'Letter mou'd him. For as I thinke, they do command him home, Deputing *Cassio* in his Gouernment.

Des. Trust me, I am glad on't.

Othe. Indeed?

Des. My Lord?

Othe. I am glad to see you mad.

Des. Why, sweete *Othello*?

Othe. Diuell.

Des. I haue not deseru'd this.

Lod. My Lord, this would not be beleeu'd in Venice, Though I should sweare I saw't. 'Tis very much, Make her amends: she weepes.

Othe. Oh diuell, diuell: If that the Earth could teeme with womans teares, Each drop she falls, would proue a Crocodile: Out of my sight.

Des. I will not stay to offend you.

Lod. Truely obedient Lady: I do beseech your Lordship call her backe.

Oth.

Othe. Mistris.
Des. My Lord.
Othe. What would you with her, Sir?
Lod. Who I, my Lord?
Othe. I, you did wish, that I would make her turne:
Sir, she can turne, and turne: and yet go on
And turne againe. And she can weepe, Sir, weepe.
And she's obedient: as you say obedient.
Very obedient: proceed you in your teares.
Concerning this Sir, (oh well-painted passion)
I am commanded home: get you away:
Ile send for you anon. Sir I obey the Mandate,
And will returne to Venice. Hence, auaunt:
Cassio shall haue my Place. And Sir, to night
I do entreat, that we may sup together.
You are welcome Sir to Cyprus.
Goates, and Monkeys. *Exit.*

Lod. Is this the Noble Moore, whom our full Senate
Call all in all sufficient? Is this the Nature
Whom Passion could not shake? Whose solid vertue
The shot of Accident, nor dart of Chance
Could neither graze, nor pierce?

Iago. He is much chang'd.

Lod. Are his wits safe? Is he not light of Braine?

Iago. He's that he is: I may not breath my censure.
What he might be: if what he might, he is not,
I would to heauen he were.

Lod. What? Strike his wife?

Iago. 'Faith that was not so well: yet would I knew
That stroke would proue the worst.

Lod. Is it his vse?
Or did the Letters, worke vpon his blood,
And new create his fault?

Iago. Alas, alas:
It is not honestie in me to speake
What I haue seene, and knowne. You shall obserue him,
And his owne courses will denote him so,
That I may saue my speech: do but go after
And marke how he continues.

Lod. I am sorry that I am deceiu'd in him. *Exeunt.*

Scena Secunda.

Enter Othello, and Æmilia.

Othe. You haue seene nothing then?
Æmil. Nor euer heard: nor euer did suspect.
Othe. Yes, you haue seene *Cassio*, and she together.
Æmi. But then I saw no harme: and then I heard,
Each syllable that breath made vp betweene them.
Othe. What? Did they neuer whisper?
Æmil. Neuer my Lord.
Othe. Nor send you out o'th'way?
Æmil. Neuer.
Othe. To fetch her Fan, her Gloues, her Mask, nor nothing?
Æmil. Neuer my Lord.
Othe. That's strange.
Æmil. I durst (my Lord) to wager, she is honest:
Lay downe my Soule at stake: If you thinke other,
Remoue your thought. It doth abuse your bosome.
If any wretch haue put this in your head,
Let Heauen requit it with the Serpents curse,
For if she be not honest, chaste, and true,
There's no man happy. The purest of their Wiues
Is foule as Slander.

Othe. Bid her come hither: go. *Exit Æmilia.*
She saies enough: yet she's a simple Baud
That cannot say as much. This is a subtile Whore:
A Closset Locke and Key of Villanous Secrets,
And yet she'le kneele, and pray: I haue seene her do't.

Enter Desdemona, and Æmilia.

Des. My Lord, what is your will?
Othe. Pray you Chucke come hither.
Des. What is your pleasure?
Oth. Let me see your eyes: looke in my face.
Des. What horrible Fancie's this?
Othe. Some of your Function Mistris:
Leaue Procreants alone, and shut the doore:
Cough, or cry hem; if any body come:
Your Mystery, your Mystery: May dispatch. *Exit Æmi.*

Des. Vpon my knee, what doth your speech import?
I vnderstand a Fury in your words.

Othe. Why? What art thou?
Des. Your wife my Lord: your true and loyall wife.
Othello. Come sweare it: damne thy selfe, least
being like one of Heauen, the diuells themselues should
feare to ceaze thee. Therefore be double damn'd: sweare
thou art honest.

Des. Heauen doth truely know it.
Othe. Heauen truely knowes, that thou art false as hell.
Des. To whom my Lord?
With whom? How am I false?

Othe. Ah *Desdemon*, away, away, away.
Des. Alas the heauy day: why do you weepe?
Am I the motiue of these teares my Lord?
If happely you my Father do suspect,
An Instrument of this your calling backe,
Lay not your blame on me: if you haue lost him,
I haue lost him too.

Othe. Had it pleas'd Heauen,
To try me with Affliction, had they rain'd
All kind of Sores, and Shames on my bare-head:
Steep'd me in pouertie to the very lippes.
Giuen to Captiuitie, me, and my vtmost hopes,
I should haue found in some place of my Soule
A drop of patience. But alas, to make me
The fixed Figure for the time of Scorne,
To point his slow, and mouing finger at.
Yet could I beare that too, well, very well:
But there where I haue garnerd vp my heart,
Where either I must liue, or beare no life,
The Fountaine from the which my currant runnes,
Or else dries vp: to be discarded thence,
Or keepe it as a Cesterne, for foule Toades
To knot and gender in. Turne thy complexion there:
Patience, thou young and Rose-lip'd Cherubin,
I heere looke grim as hell.

Des. I hope my Noble Lord esteemes me honest.
Othe. Oh I, as Sommer Flyes are in the Shambles,
That quicken euen with blowing. Oh thou weed:
Who art so louely faire, and smell'st so sweete,
That the Sense akes at thee,
Would thou had'st neuer bin borne.

Des. Alas, what ignorant sin haue I committed?
Othe. Was this faire Paper? This most goodly Booke
Made to write Whore vpon? What commited,

Com.

Committed? Oh, thou publicke Commoner,
I should make very Forges of my cheekes,
That would to Cynders burne vp Modestie,
Did I but speake thy deedes. What commited?
Heauen stoppes the Nose at it, and the Moone winks:
The baudy winde that kisses all it meetes,
Is hush'd within the hollow Myne of Earth
And will not hear't. What commited?

Des. By Heauen you do me wrong.

Othe. Are not you a Strumpet?

Des. No, as I am a Cristian.
If to preserue this vessell for my Lord,
From any other foule vnlawfull touch
Be not to be a Strumpet, I am none.

Othe. What, not a Whore?

Des. No, as I shall be sau'd.

Othe. Is't possible?

Des. Oh Heauen forgiue vs.

Othe. I cry you mercy then.
I tooke you for that cunning Whore of Venice,
That married with *Othello*. You Mistris,

Enter Æmilia.

That haue the office opposite to Saint *Peter*,
And keepes the gate of hell. You, you: I you,
We haue done our course: there's money for your paines:
I pray you turne the key, and keepe our counsaile. *Exit.*

Æmil. Alas, what do's this Gentleman conceiue?
How do you Madam? how do you my good Lady?

Des. Faith, halfe a sleepe.

Æmi. Good Madam,
What's the matter with my Lord?

Des. With who?

Æmil. Why, with my Lord, Madam?

Des. Who is thy Lord?

Æmil. He that is yours, sweet Lady.

Des. I haue none: do not talke to me, *Æmilia*,
I cannot weepe: nor answeres haue I none,
But what should go by water. Prythee to night,
Lay on my bed my wedding sheetes, remember,
And call thy husband hither.

Æmil. Heere's a change indeed. *Exit.*

Des. 'Tis meete I should be vs'd so: very meete.
How haue I bin behau'd, that he might sticke
The small'st opinion on my least misuse?

Enter Iago, and Æmilia.

Iago. What is your pleasure Madam?
How is't with you?

Des. I cannot tell: those that do teach yong Babes
Do it with gentle meanes, and easie taskes.
He might haue chid me so: for in good faith
I am a Child to chiding.

Iago. What is the matter Lady?

Æmil. Alas (*Iago*) my Lord hath so bewhor'd her,
Throwne such dispight, and heauy termes vpon her
That true hearts cannot beare it.

Des. Am I that name, *Iago*?

Iago. What name, (faire Lady?)

Des. Such as she said my Lord did say I was.

Æmil. He call'd her whore: a Begger in his drinke:
Could not haue laid such termes vpon his Callet.

Iago. Why did he so?

Des. I do not know: I am sure I am none such.

Iago. Do not weepe, do not weepe: alas the day.

Æmil. Hath she forsooke so many Noble Matches?
Her Father? And her Country? And her Friends?
To be call'd Whore? Would it not make one weepe?

Des. It is my wretched Fortune.

Iago. Beshrew him for't:
How comes this Tricke vpon him?

Des. Nay, Heauen doth know.

Æmi. I will be hang'd, if some eternall Villaine,
Some busie and insinuating Rogue,
Some cogging, cozening Slaue, to get some Office,
Haue not deuis'd this Slander: I will be hang'd else.

Iago. Fie, there is no such man: it is impossible.

Des. If any such there be, Heauen pardon him.

Æmil. A halter pardon him:
And hell gnaw his bones.
Why should he call her Whore?
Who keepes her companie?
What Place? What Time?
What Forme? What liklyhood?
The Moore's abus'd by some most villanous Knaue,
Some base notorious Knaue, some scuruy Fellow.
Oh Heauens, that such companions thou'd'st vnfold,
And put in euery honest hand a whip
To lash the Rascalls naked through the world,
Euen from the East to th' West.

Iago. Speake within doore.

Æmil. Oh fie vpon them: some such Squire he was
That turn'd your wit, the seamy-side without,
And made you to suspect me with the Moore.

Iago. You are a Foole: go too.

Des. Alas *Iago*,
What shall I do to win my Lord againe?
Good Friend, go to him: for by this light of Heauen,
I know not how I lost him. Heere I kneele:
If ere my will did trespasse 'gainst his Loue,
Either in discourse of thought, or actuall deed,
Or that mine Eyes, mine Eares, or any Sence
Delighted them: or any other Forme.
Or that I do not yet, and euer did,
And euer will, (though he do shake me off
To beggerly diuorcement) Loue him deerely,
Comfort forsweare me. Vnkindnesse may do much,
And his vnkindnesse may defeat my life,
But neuer taynt my Loue. I cannot say Whore,
It do's abhorre me now I speake the word,
To do the Act, that might the addition earne,
Not the worlds Masse of vanitie could make me.

Iago. I pray you be content: 'tis but his humour:
The businesse of the State do's him offence.

Des. If 'twere no other.

Iago. It is but so, I warrant,
Hearke how these Instruments summon to supper:
The Messengers of Venice staies the meate,
Go in, and weepe not: all things shall be well.

Exeunt Desdemona and Æmilia.

Enter Rodorigo.

How now *Rodorigo*?

Rod. I do not finde
That thou deal'st iustly with me.

Iago. What in the contrarie?

Rodori. Euery day thou dafts me with some deuise
Iago, and rather, as it seemes to me now, keep'st from
me all conueniencie, then suppliest me with the least aduantage of hope: I will indeed no longer endure it. Nor
am I yet perswaded to put vp in peace, what already I
haue foolishly suffred.

Iago. Will you heare me *Rodorigo*?

Rodori.

Rodori. I haue heard too much: and your words and Performances are no kin together.

Iago. You charge me most vniustly.

Rodo. With naught but truth: I haue wasted my selfe out of my meanes. The Iewels you haue had from me to deliuer *Desdemona*, would halfe haue corrupted a Votarist. You haue told me she hath receiu'd them, and return'd me expectations and comforts of sodaine respect, and acquaintance, but I finde none.

Iago. Well, go too: very well.

Rod. Very well, go too: I cannot go too, (man) nor tis not very well. Nay I think it is scuruy: and begin to finde my selfe fopt in it.

Iago. Very well.

Rodor. I tell you, 'tis not very well: I will make my selfe knowne to *Desdemona*. If she will returne me my Iewels, I will giue ouer my Suit, and repent my vnlawfull solicitation. If not, assure your selfe, I will seeke satisfaction of you.

Iago. You haue said now.

Rodo. I: and said nothing but what I protest intendment of doing.

Iago. Why, now I see there's mettle in thee: and euen from this instant do build on thee a better opinion then euer before: giue me thy hand *Rodorigo*. Thou hast taken against me a most iust exception: but yet I protest I haue dealt most directly in thy Affaire.

Rod. It hath not appeer'd.

Iago. I grant indeed it hath not appeer'd: and your suspition is not without wit and iudgement. But *Rodorigo*, if thou hast that in thee indeed, which I haue greater reason to beleeue now then euer (I meane purpose, Courage, and Valour) this night shew it. If thou the next night following enioy not *Desdemona*, take me from this world with Treacherie, and deuise Engines for my life.

Rod. Well: what is it? Is it within reason and compasse?

Iago. Sir, there is especiall Commission come from Venice to depute *Cassio* in *Othello's* place.

Rod. Is that true? Why then *Othello* and *Desdemona* returne againe to Venice.

Iago. Oh no: he goes into Mauritania and taketh away with him the faire *Desdemona*, vnlesse his abode be lingred heere by some accident. Wherein none can be so determinate, as the remouing of *Cassio*.

Rod. How do you meane remouing him?

Iago. Why, by making him vncapable of *Othello's* place: knocking out his braines.

Rod. And that you would haue me to do.

Iago. I: if you dare do your selfe a profit, and a right. He sups to night with a Harlotry: and thither will I go to him. He knowes not yet of his Honourable Fortune, if you will watch his going thence (which I will fashion to fall out betweene twelue and one) you may take him at your pleasure. I will be neere to second your Attempt, and he shall fall betweene vs. Come, stand not amaz'd at it, but go along with me: I will shew you such a necessitie in his death, that you shall thinke your selfe bound to put it on him. It is now high supper time: and the night growes to wast. About it.

Rod. I will heare further reason for this.

Iago. And you shalbe satisfi'd. *Exeunt.*

Scena Tertia.

Enter Othello, Lodouico, Desdemona, Æmilia, and Atendants.

Lod. I do beseech you Sir, trouble your selfe no surther.

Oth. Oh pardon me: 'twill do me good to walke.

Lodoui. Madam, goodnight: I humbly thanke your Ladyship.

Des. Your Honour is most welcome.

Oth. Will you walke Sir? Oh *Desdemona*.

Des. My Lord.

Othello. Get you to bed on th'instant, I will be return'd forthwith: dismisse your Attendant there: look't be done. *Exit.*

Des. I will my Lord.

Æm. How goes it now? He lookes gentler then he did.

Des. He saies he will returne incontinent, And hath commanded me to go to bed, And bid me to dismisse you.

Æmi. Dismisse me?

Des. It was his bidding: therefore good *Æmilia*, Giue me my nightly wearing, and adieu, We must not now displease him.

Æmil. I, would you had neuer seene him.

Des. So would not I: my loue doth so approue him, That euen his stubbornesse, his checks, his frownes, (Prythee vn-pin me) haue grace and fauour.

Æmi. I haue laid those Sheetes you bad me on the bed.

Des. All's one: good Father, how foolish are our minds? If I do die before, prythee shrow'd me In one of these same Sheetes.

Æmil. Come, come: you talke.

Des. My Mother had a Maid call'd *Barbarie*, She was in loue: and he she lou'd prou'd mad, And did forsake her. She had a Song of Willough, An old thing 'twas: but it express'd her Fortune, And she dy'd singing it. That Song to night, Will not go from my mind: I haue much to do, But to go hang my head all at one side And sing it like poore *Brabarie*: prythee dispatch.

Æmi. Shall I go fetch your Night-gowne?

Des. No, vn-pin me here, This *Lodouico* is a proper man.

Æmi. A very handsome man.

Des. He speakes well.

Æmil. I know a Lady in Venice would haue walk'd barefoot to Palestine for a touch of his nether lip.

Des. The poore Soule sat singing, by a Sicamour tree.
Sing all a greene Willough:
Her hand on her bosome, her head on her knee,
Sing Willough, Willough, Willough.
The fresh Streames ran by her, and murmur'd her moanes
Sing Willough, &c.
Her salt teares fell from her, and softned the stones,
Sing Willough, &c. (Lay by these)
Willough, Willough. (Prythee high thee: he'le come anon)
Sing all a greene Willough must be my Garland.
Let no body blame him, his scorne I approue,
(Nay that's not next. Harke, who is't that knocks?

Æmil. It's the wind.

Des. I call'd my Loue false Loue: but what said he then?
Sing Willough, &c.
If I court mo women, you'le couch with mo men.

So get thee gone, good night: mine eyes do itch:
Doth that boade weeping?

Æmil. 'Tis neyther heere, nor there.

Def. I haue heard it said so. O these Men, these men!
Do'st thou in conscience thinke (tell me *Æmilia*)
That there be women do abuse their husbands
In such grosse kinde?

Æmil. There be some such, no question.

Def. Would'st thou do such a deed for all the world?

Æmil. Why, would not you?

Def. No, by this Heauenly light.

Æmil. Nor I neither, by this Heauenly light:
I might doo't as well i'th'darke.

Def. Would'st thou do such a deed for al the world?

Æmil. The world's a huge thing:
It is a great price, for a small vice.

Def. Introth, I thinke thou would'st not.

Æmil. Introth I thinke I should, and vndoo't when I had done. Marry, I would not doe such a thing for a ioynt Ring, nor for measures of Lawne, nor for Gownes, Petticoats, nor Caps, nor any petty exhibition. But for all the whole world: why, who would not make her husband a Cuckold, to make him a Monarch? I should venture Purgatory for't.

Def. Beshrew me, if I would do such a wrong
For the whole world.

Æmil. Why, the wrong is but a wrong i'th'world;
and hauing the world for your labour, 'tis a wrong in
your owne world, and you might quickly make it right.

Def. I do not thinke there is any such woman.

Æmil. Yes, a dozen: and as many to'th'vantage, as
would store the world they plaid for.
But I do thinke it is their Husbands faults
If Wiues do fall: (Say, that they slacke their duties,
And powre our Treasures into forraigne laps;
Or else breake out in peeuish Iealousies,
Throwing restraint vpon vs: Or say they strike vs,
Or scant our former hauing in despight)
Why we haue galles: and though we haue some Grace,
Yet haue we some Reuenge. Let Husbands know,
Their wiues haue sense like them: They see, and smell,
And haue their Palats both for sweet, and sowre,
As Husbands haue. What is it that they do,
When they change vs for others? Is it Sport?
I thinke it is: and doth Affection breed it?
I thinke it doth. Is't Frailty that thus erres?
It is so too. And haue not we Affections?
Desires for Sport? and Frailty, as men haue?
Then let them vse vs well: else let them know,
The illes we do, their illes instruct vs so.

Def. Goodnight, goodnight:
Heauen me such vses send,
Not to picke bad, from bad; but by bad, mend. *Exeunt*

Actus Quintus. Scena Prima.

Enter Iago, and Rodorigo.

Iago. Heere, stand behinde this Barke,
Straight will he come:
Weare thy good Rapier bare, and put it home:
Quicke, quicke, feare nothing; Ile be at thy Elbow,
It makes vs, or it marres vs, thinke on that,
And fixe most firme thy Resolution.

Rod. Be neere at hand, I may miscarry in't.

Iago. Heere, at thy hand: Be bold, & take thy stand.

Rod. I haue no great deuotion to the deed,
And yet he hath giuen me satisfying Reasons:
'Tis but a man gone. Forth my Sword: he dies.

Iago. I haue rub'd this yong Quat almost to the sense,
And he growes angry. Now, whether he kill *Cassio*,
Or *Cassio* him, or each do kill the other,
Euery way makes my gaine. Liue *Rodorigo*,
He calles me to a restitution large
Of Gold, and Iewels, that I bob'd from him,
As Guifts to *Desdemona*.
It must not be: If *Cassio* do remaine,
He hath a dayly beauty in his life,
That makes me vgly: and besides, the Moore
May vnfold me to him: there stand I in much perill:
No, he must dye. But so, I heard him comming.

Enter Cassio.

Rod. I know his gate, 'tis he: Villaine thou dyest.

Cas. That thrust had beene mine enemy indeed,
But that my Coate is better then thou know'st:
I will make proofe of thine.

Rod. Oh, I am slaine.

Cassio. I am maym'd for euer:
Helpe hoa: Murther, murther.

Enter Othello.

Oth. The voyce of *Cassio*, *Iago* keepes his word.

Rod. O Villaine that I am.

Oth. It is euen so.

Cas. Oh helpe hoa: Light, a Surgeon.

Oth. 'Tis he: O braue *Iago*, honest, and iust,
That hast such Noble sense of thy Friends wrong,
Thou teachest me. Minion, your deere lyes dead,
And your vnblest Fate highes: Strumpet I come:
For of my heart, those Charmes thine Eyes, are blotted.
Thy Bed lust-stain'd, shall with Lusts blood bee spotted.

Exit Othello.

Enter Lodouico and Gratiano.

Cas. What hoa? no Watch? No passage?
Murther, Murther.

Gra. 'Tis some mischance, the voyce is very direfull.

Cas. Oh helpe.

Lodo. Hearke.

Rod. Oh wretched Villaine.

Lod. Two or three groane. 'Tis heauy night;
These may be counterfeits: Let's think't vnsafe
To come into the cry, without more helpe.

Rod. Nobody come: then shall I bleed to death.

Enter Iago.

Lod. Hearke.

Gra. Here's one comes in his shirt, with Light, and Weapons.

Iago. Who's there?
Who's noyse is this that cries on murther?

Lodo. We do not know.

Iago. Do not you heare a cry?

Cas. Heere, heere: for heauen sake helpe me.

Iago. What's the matter?

Gra. This is *Othello*'s Ancient, as I take it.

Lodo. The same indeede, a very valiant Fellow.

Iago. What are you heere, that cry so greeuously?

Cas. *Iago?* Oh I am spoyl'd, vndone by Villaines:
Giue me some helpe.

Iago. O mee, Lieutenant!
What Villaines haue done this?

Cas. I thinke that one of them is heereabout,

And cannot make away.
  Iago. Oh treacherous Villaines:
What are you there? Come in, and giue some helpe.
  Rod. O helpe me there.
  Cassio. That's one of them.
  Iago. Oh murd'rous Slaue! O Villaine!
  Rod. O damn'd *Iago*! O inhumane Dogge!
  Iago. Kill men i'th'darke?
Where be these bloody Theeues?
How silent is this Towne? Hoa, murther, murther.
What may you be? Are you of good, or euill?
  Lod. As you shall proue vs, praise vs.
  Iago. Signior *Lodouico*?
  Lod. He Sir.
  Iago. I cry you mercy: here's *Cassio* hurt by Villaines.
  Gra. Cassio?
  Iago. How is't Brother?
  Cas. My Legge is cut in two.
  Iago. Marry heauen forbid:
Light Gentlemen, Ile binde it with my shirt.
        Enter Bianca.
  Bian. What is the matter hoa? Who is't that cry'd?
  Iago. Who is't that cry'd?
  Bian. Oh my deere *Cassio*,
My sweet *Cassio*: Oh *Cassio, Cassio, Cassio*.
  Iago. O notable Strumpet. *Cassio*, may you suspect
Who they should be, that haue thus mangled you?
  Cas. No.
  Gra. I am sorry to finde you thus;
I haue beene to seeke you.
  Iago. Lend me a Garter. So:——Oh for a Chaire
To beare him easily hence.
  Bian. Alas he faints. Oh *Cassio, Cassio, Cassio*.
  Iago. Gentlemen all, I do suspect this Trash
To be a party in this Iniurie.
Patience awhile, good *Cassio*. Come, come;
Lend me a Light: know we this face, or no?
Alas my Friend, and my deere Countryman
Rodorigo? No: Yes sure: Yes, 'tis *Rodorigo*.
  Gra. What, of Venice?
  Iago. Euen he Sir: Did you know him?
  Gra. Know him? I.
  Iago. Signior *Gratiano*? I cry your gentle pardon:
These bloody accidents must excuse my Manners,
That so neglected you.
  Gra. I am glad to see you.
  Iago. How do you *Cassio*? Oh, a Chaire, a Chaire.
  Gra. Rodorigo?
  Iago. He, he, 'tis he:
Oh that's well said, the Chaire.
Some good man beare him carefully from hence,
Ile fetch the Generall's Surgeon. For you Mistris,
Saue you your labour. He that lies slaine heere (*Cassio*)
Was my deere friend. What malice was between you?
  Cas. None in the world: nor do I know the man?
  Iago. What? looke you pale? Oh beare him o'th'Ayre.
Stay you good Gentlemen. Looke you pale, Mistris?
Do you perceiue the gastnesse of her eye?
Nay, if you stare, we shall heare more anon.
Behold her well: I pray you looke vpon her:
Do you see Gentlemen? Nay, guiltinesse will speake
Though tongues were out of vse.
  Æmil. Alas, what is the matter?
What is the matter, Husband?
  Iago. Cassio hath heere bin set on in the darke
By *Rodorigo*, and Fellowes that are scap'd:

He's almost slaine, and *Rodorigo* quite dead.
  Æmil. Alas good Gentleman: alas good *Cassio*.
  Iago. This is the fruits of whoring. Prythe *Æmilia*,
Go know of *Cassio* where he supt to night.
What, do you shake at that?
  Bian. He supt at my house, but I therefore shake not.
  Iago. O did he so? I charge you go with me.
  Æmil. Oh fie vpon thee Strumpet.
  Bian. I am no Strumpet, but of life as honest,
As you that thus abuse me.
  Æmil. As I? Fie vpon thee.
  Iago. Kinde Gentlemen:
Let's go see poore *Cassio* drest.
Come Mistris, you must tel's another Tale.
Æmilia, run you to the Cittadell,
And tell my Lord and Lady, what hath happ'd:
Will you go on afore? This is the night
That either makes me, or foredoes me quight. *Exeunt*

Scœna Secunda.

Enter Othello, and Desdemona in her bed.

  Oth. It is the Cause, it is the Cause (my Soule)
Let me not name it to you, you chaste Starres,
It is the Cause. Yet Ile not shed her blood,
Nor scarre that whiter skin of hers, then Snow,
And smooth as Monumentall Alablaster:
Yet she must dye, else shee'l betray more men:
Put out the Light, and then put out the Light:
If I quench thee, thou flaming Minister,
I can againe thy former light restore,
Should I repent me. But once put out thy Light,
Thou cunning'st Patterne of excelling Nature,
I know not where is that *Promethean* heate
That can thy Light re-Lume.
When I haue pluck'd thy Rose,
I cannot giue it vitall growth againe,
It needs must wither. Ile smell thee on the Tree.
Oh Balmy breath, that dost almost perswade
Iustice to breake her Sword. One more, one more:
Be thus when thou art dead, and I will kill thee,
And loue thee after. One more, and that's the last.
So sweet, was ne're so fatall. I must weepe,
But they are cruell Teares: This sorrow's heauenly,
It strikes, where it doth loue. She wakes.
  Des. Who's there? *Othello*?
  Othel. I *Desdemona*.
  Des. Will you come to bed, my Lord?
  Oth. Haue you pray'd to night, *Desdemon*?
  Des. I my Lord.
  Oth. If you bethinke your selfe of any Crime
Vnreconcil'd as yet to Heauen, and Grace,
Solicite for it straight.
  Des. Alacke, my Lord,
What may you meane by that?
  Oth. Well, do it, and be breefe, I will walke by:
I would not kill thy vnprepared Spirit,
No, Heauens fore-fend) I would not kill thy Soule.
  Des. Talke you of killing?
  Oth. I, I do.
  Des. Then Heauen haue mercy on mee.

Oth.

Oth. Amen, with all my heart.
Des. If you say, I hope you will not kill me.
Oth. Humh.
Des. And yet I feare you: for you're fatall then
When your eyes rowle so.
Why I should feare, I know not,
Since guiltinesse I know not: But yet I feele I feare.
Oth. Thinke on thy sinnes.
Des. They are Loues I beare to you.
Oth. I, and for that thou dy'st.
Des. That death's vnnaturall, that kils for louing.
Alas, why gnaw you so your nether-lip?
Some bloody passion shakes your very Frame:
These are portents: but yet I hope, I hope,
They do not point on me.
Oth. Peace, and be still.
Des. I will so: What's the matter?
Oth. That Handkerchiefe
Which I so lou'd, and gaue thee, thou gau'st to *Cassio*.
Des. No by my Life, and Soule: send for the man,
And aske him.
Oth. Sweet Soule, take heed, take heed of Periury,
Thou art on thy death-bed.
Des. I, but not yet to dye.
Oth. Presently.
Therefore confesse thee freely of thy sinne:
For to deny each Article with Oath,
Cannot remoue, nor choake the strong Conception
That I do grone withall. Thou art to dye.
Des. O Heauen haue mercy on me.
Oth. I say, Amen.
Des. And haue you mercy too. I neuer did
Offend you in my life: neuer lou'd *Cassio*,
But with such generall warrantie of Heauen,
As I might loue. I neuer gaue him Token.
Oth. By Heauen I saw my Handkerchiefe in's hand.
O periur'd woman, thou do'st stone my heart,
And makes me call, what I intend to do,
A Murther, which I thought a Sacrifice.
I saw the Handkerchiefe.
Des. He found it then:
I neuer gaue it him: Send for him hither:
Let him confesse a truth.
Oth. He hath confest.
Des. What, my Lord?
Oth. That he hath vs'd thee.
Des. How? vnlawfully?
Oth. I.
Des. He will not say so.
Oth. No: his mouth is stopp'd:
Honest *Iago* hath 'tane order for't.
Des. Oh, my feare interprets. What is he dead?
Oth. Had all his haires bin liues, my great Reuenge
Had stomacke for them all.
Des. Alas, he is betray'd, and I vndone.
Oth. Out Strumpet: weep'st thou for him to my face?
Des. O banish me, my Lord, but kill me not.
Oth. Downe Strumpet.
Des. Kill me to morrow, let me liue to night.
Oth. Nay, if you striue.
Des. But halfe an houre.
Oth. Being done, there is no pawse.
Des. But while I say one prayer.
Oth. It is too late.   *Smothers her.*

Æmilia at the doore.

Æmil. My Lord, my Lord? What hoa?
My Lord, my Lord.
Oth. What noise is this? Not dead? not yet quite dead?
I that am cruell, am yet mercifull,
I would not haue thee linger in thy paine?
So, so.
Æmil. within. What hoa? my Lord, my Lord?
Oth. Who's there?
Æmil. Oh good my Lord, I would speake a word with you.
Oth. Yes: 'Tis *Æmilia*: by and by. Shee's dead.
'Tis like she comes to speake of *Cassio*'s death:
The noise was high. Hah, no more moouing?
Still as the Graue. Shall she come in? Wer't good?
I thinke she stirres againe. No, what's best to do?
If she come in, shee'l sure speake to my wife:
My wife, my wife: what wife? I haue no wife.
Oh insupportable! Oh heauy houre!
Me thinkes, it should be now a huge Eclipse
Of Sunne, and Moone; and that th'affrighted Globe
Did yawne at Alteration.
Æmil. I do beseech you
That I may speake with you. Oh good my Lord.
Oth. I had forgot thee: oh come in *Æmilia*.
Soft, by and by, let me the Curtaines draw.
Where art thou? What's the matter with thee now?

Enter Æmilia.

Æmil. Oh my good Lord, yonders foule Murthers done.
Oth. What? now?
Æmil. But now, my Lord.
Oth. It is the very error of the Moone,
She comes more neerer Earth then she was wont,
And makes men mad.
Æmil. *Cassio*, my Lord, hath kill'd
A young Venetian, call'd *Rodorigo*.
Oth. *Rodorigo* kill'd? and *Cassio* kill'd?
Æmil. No. *Cassio* is not kill'd.
Oth. Not *Cassio* kill'd? Then Murther's out of tune,
And sweet Reuenge growes harsh.
Des. O falsely, falsely murder'd.
Æmil. Alas! what cry is that?
Oth. That? What?
Æmil. Out, and alas, that was my Ladies voice.
Helpe, helpe hoa, helpe. Oh Ladie speake againe,
Sweet *Desdemona*, oh sweet Mistris, speake.
Des. A guiltlesse death, I dye.
Æmil. Oh who hath done this deed?
Des. No body: I my selfe, farewell:
Commend me to my kinde Lord: oh farewell.
Oth. Why, how should she be murdred?
Æmil. Alas: who knowes?
Oth. You heare her say her selfe, it was not I.
Æmil. She said so: I must needs report the truth.
Oth. She's like a Liar gone to burning hell,
'Twas I that kill'd her.
Æmil. Oh the more Angell she, and you the blacker Diuell.
Oth. She turn'd to folly: and she was a whore.
Æmil. Thou do'st bely her, and thou art a diuell.
Oth. She was false as water.
Æmil. Thou art rash as fire, to say
That she was false. Oh she was heauenly true.
Oth. *Cassio* did top her: Ask thy husband else.
O, I were damn'd beneath all depth in hell:
But that I did proceed vpon iust grounds
To this extremity. Thy Husband knew it all.
                                                                    Æmil.

Æmil. My Husband?
Oth. Thy Husband.
Æmil. That she was falſe to Wedlocke?
Oth. I, with *Caſſio*: had ſhe bin true,
If Heauen would make me ſuch another world,
Of one entyre and perfect Chryſolite,
I'ld not haue ſold her for it.
 Æmil. My Husband?
Oth. I, 'twas he that told me on her firſt,
An honeſt man he is, and hates the ſlime
That ſtickes on filthy deeds.
 Æmil. My Husband?
Oth. What needs this itterance, Woman?
I ſay, thy Husband.
 Æmil. Oh Miſtris,
Villany hath made mockes with loue:
My Husband ſay ſhe was falſe?
 Oth. He, Woman;
I ſay thy Husband: Do'ſt vnderſtand the word?
My Friend, thy Husband; honeſt, honeſt *Iago*.
 Æmil. If he ſay ſo, may his pernicious Soule
Rot halfe a graine a day: he lyes to'th'heart,
She was too fond of her moſt filthy Bargaine.
 Oth. Hah?
 Æmil. Do thy worſt:
This deede of thine is no more worthy Heauen,
Then thou was't worthy her.
 Oth. Peace, you were beſt.
 Æmil. Thou haſt not halfe that powre to do me harm,
As I haue to be hurt. Oh Gull, oh dolt,
As ignorant as durt: thou haſt done a deed
(I care not for thy Sword) Ile make thee known,
Though I loſt twenty liues. Helpe, helpe, hoa, helpe:
The Moore hath kill'd my Miſtris. Murther, murther.

Enter Montano, Gratiano, and Iago.

Mon. What is the matter? How now Generall?
 Æmil. Oh, are you come, *Iago*: you haue done well,
That men muſt lay their Murthers on your necke.
 Gra. What is the matter?
 Æmil. Diſproue this Villaine, if thou bee'ſt a man:
He ſayes, thou told'ſt him that his wife was falſe:
I know thou did'ſt not: thou'rt not ſuch a Villain.
Speake, for my heart is full.
 Iago. I told him what I thought,
And told no more
Then what he found himſelfe was apt, and true.
 Æmil. But did you euer tell him,
She was falſe?
 Iago. I did.
 Æmil. You told a Lye an odious damned Lye:
Vpon my Soule, a Lye; a wicked Lye.
Shee falſe with *Caſſio*?
Did you ſay with *Caſſio*?
 Iago. With *Caſſio*, Miſtris?
Go too, charme your tongue.
 Emil. I will not charme my Tongue;
I am bound to ſpeake,
My Miſtris heere lyes murthered in her bed.
 All. Oh Heauens, foreſend.
 Emil. And your reports haue ſet the Murder on.
 Othello. Nay ſtare not Maſters,
It is true indeede.
 Gra. 'Tis a ſtrange Truth.
 Mont. O monſtrous Acte.

Emil. Villany, villany, villany:
I thinke vpon't, I thinke: I ſmel't: O Villany:
I thought ſo then: Ile kill my ſelfe for greefe.
O villany! villany!
 Iago. What, are you mad?
I charge you get you home.
 Emil. Good Gentlemen, let me haue leaue to ſpeake:
'Tis proper I obey him; but not now:
Perchance *Iago*, I will ne're go home.
 Oth. Oh, oh, oh.
 Emil. Nay, lay thee downe, and roare;
For thou haſt kill'd the ſweeteſt innocent,
That ere did lift vp eye.
 Oth. Oh ſhe was fowle!
I ſcarſe did know you Vnkle, there lies your Neece,
Whoſe breath (indeed) theſe hands haue newly ſtopp'd:
I know this acte ſhewes horrible and grim.
 Gra. Poore *Deſdemon*:
I am glad thy Father's dead,
Thy Match was mortall to him: and pure greefe
Shore his old thred in twaine. Did he liue now,
This ſight would make him do a deſperate turne:
Yea, curſe his better Angell from his ſide,
And fall to Reprobance.
 Oth. 'Tis pittifull: but yet *Iago* knowes
That ſhe with *Caſſio*, hath the Act of ſhame
A thouſand times committed. *Caſſio* confeſt it,
And ſhe did gratifie his amorous workes
With that Recognizance and pledge of Loue
Which I firſt gaue her: I ſaw it in his hand:
It was a Handkerchiefe, an Antique Token
My Father gaue my Mother.
 Emil. Oh Heauen! oh heauenly Powres!
 Iago. Come, hold your peace.
 Emil. 'Twill out, 'twill out. I peace?
No, I will ſpeake as liberall as the North;
Let Heauen, and Men, and Diuels, let them all,
All, all, crie ſhame againſt me, yet Ile ſpeake.
 Iago. Be wiſe, and get you home.
 Emil. I will not.
 Gra. Fye, your Sword vpon a Woman.
 Emil. Oh thou dull Moore,
That Handkerchiefe thou ſpeak'ſt of
I found by Fortune, and did giue my Husband:
For often, with a ſolemne earneſtneſſe,
(More then indeed belong'd to ſuch a Trifle)
He begg'd of me, to ſteale't.
 Iago. Villanous Whore.
 Emil. She giue it *Caſſio*? No, alas I found it,
And I did giu't my Husband.
 Iago. Filth, thou lyeſt.
 Emil. By Heauen I do not, I do not Gentlemen:
Oh murd'rous Coxcombe, what ſhould ſuch a Foole
Do with ſo good a wife?
 Oth. Are there no ſtones in Heauen,
But what ſerues for the Thunder?
Precious Villaine.
 Gra. The woman falles:
Sure he hath kill'd his Wife.
 Emil. I, I: oh lay me by my Miſtris ſide.
 Gra. Hee's gone, but his wife's kill'd.
 Mon. 'Tis a notorious Villain; take you this weapon
Which I haue recouer'd from the Moore:
Come guard the doore without, let him not paſſe,
But kill him rather. Ile after that ſame villaine,
For 'tis a damned Slaue. *Exit.*
Oth.

Oth. I am not valiant neither:
But euery Punie whipster gets my Sword.
But why should Honor out-liue Honesty?
Let it go all.

 Æmil. What did thy Song boad Lady?
Hearke, canst thou heare me? I will play the Swan,
And dye in Musicke: *Willough, Willough, Willough.*
Moore, she was chaste: She lou'd thee, cruell Moore,
So come my Soule to blisse, as I speake true:
So speaking as I thinke, alas, I dye.

 Oth. I haue another weapon in this Chamber,
It was a Sword of Spaine, the Ice brookes temper:
Oh heere it is: Vnkle I must come forth.

 Gra. If thou attempt it, it will cost thee deere;
Thou hast no weapon, and perforce must suffer.

 Oth. Looke in vpon me then, and speake with me,
Or naked as I am I will assault thee.

 Gra. What is the matter?

 Othel. Behold, I haue a weapon:
A better neuer did it selfe sustaine
Vpon a Soldiers Thigh. I haue seene the day,
That with this little Arme, and this good Sword,
I haue made my way through more impediments
Then twenty times your stop. But (oh vaine boast)
Who can controll his Fate? 'Tis not so now.
Be not affraid, though you do see me weapon'd:
Heere is my iournies end, heere is my butt
And verie Sea-marke of my vtmost Saile.
Do you go backe dismaid? 'Tis a lost feare:
Man but a Rush against *Othello's* brest,
And he retires. Where should *Othello* go?
Now: how dost thou looke now? Oh ill-Starr'd wench,
Pale as thy Smocke: when we shall meete at compt,
This looke of thine will hurle my Soule from Heauen,
And Fiends will snatch at it. Cold, cold, my Girle?
Euen like thy Chastity. O cursed, cursed Slaue!
Whip me ye Diuels,
From the possession of this Heauenly sight:
Blow me about in windes, roast me in Sulphure,
Wash me in steepe-downe gulfes of Liquid fire.
Oh *Desdemon*! dead *Desdemon*: dead. Oh, oh!

*Enter Lodouico, Cassio, Montano, and Iago,
with Officers.*

 Lod. Where is this rash, and most vnfortunate man?

 Oth. That's he that was *Othello*: heere I am.

 Lod. Where is that Viper?
Bring the Villaine forth.

 Oth. I look down towards his feet; but that's a Fable,
If that thou bee'st a Diuell, I cannot kill thee.

 Lod. Wrench his Sword from him.

 Iago. I bleed Sir, but not kill'd.

 Othel. I am not sorry neither, I'd haue thee liue:
For in my sense, 'tis happinesse to die.

 Lod. Oh thou *Othello*, that was once so good,
Falne in the practise of a cursed Slaue,
What shall be saide to thee.

 Oth. Why any thing:
An honourable Murderer, if you will:
For nought I did in hate, but all in Honour.

 Lod. This wretch hath part confest his Villany:
Did you and he consent in *Cassio's* death.

 Oth. I.

 Cas. Deere Generall, I neuer gaue you cause.

 Oth. I do beleeue it, and I aske your pardon:
Will you, I pray, demand that demy-Diuell,
Why he hath thus ensnar'd my Soule and Body.

 Iag. Demand me nothing: what you know, you know:
From this time forth, I neuer will speake word.

 Lod. What? not to pray?

 Gra. Torments will ope your lips.

 Oth. Well, thou dost best.

 Lod. Sir,
You shall vnderstand what hath befalne,
(Which, as I thinke, you know not) heere is a Letter
Found in the pocket of the slaine *Rodorigo*,
And heere another, the one of them imports
The death of *Cassio*, to be vndertooke
By *Rodorigo*.

 Oth. O Villaine!

 Cassio. Most Heathenish, and most grosse.

 Lod. Now, heere's another discontented paper
Found in his pocket too: and this it seemes
Rodorigo meant t'haue sent this damned villaine:
But that (belike) *Iago* in the interim
Came in, and satisfi'd him.

 Oth. Oh thou pernitious Caitiffe;
How came you (*Cassio*) by that Handkerchiefe
That was my wiues?

 Cassio. I found it in my Chamber:
And he himselfe confest it but euen now,
That there he dropt it for a speciall purpose,
Which wrought to his desire.

 Othel. O Foole, foole, foole!

 Cassio. There is besides, in *Rodorigo's* Letter,
How he vpbraides *Iago*, that he made him
Braue me vpon the Watch: whereon it came
That I was cast: and euen but now he spake
(After long seeming dead) *Iago* hurt him,
Iago set him on.

 Lod. You must forsake this roome, and go with vs:
Your Power, and your Command is taken off,
And *Cassio* rules in Cyprus. For this Slaue,
If there be any cunning Crueltie,
That can torment him much, and hold him long,
It shall be his. You shall close Prisoner rest,
Till that the Nature of your fault be knowne
To the Venetian State. Come, bring away.

 Oth. Soft you; a word or two before you goe:
I haue done the State some seruice, and they know't:
No more of that. I pray you in your Letters,
When you shall these vnluckie deeds relate,
Speake of me, as I am. Nothing extenuate,
Nor set downe ought in malice.
Then must you speake,
Of one that lou'd not wisely, but too well:
Of one, not easily Iealious, but being wrought,
Perplexed in the extreame: Of one, whose hand
(Like the base Iudean) threw a Pearle away
Richer then all his Tribe: Of one, whose subdu'd Eyes,
Albeit vn-vsed to the melting moode,
Drops teares as fast as the Arabian Trees
Their Medicinable gumme. Set you downe this:
And say besides, that in *Aleppo* once,
Where a malignant, and a Turbond-Turke
Beate a Venetian, and traduc'd the State,
I tooke by th'throat the circumcised Dogge,
And smoate him, thus.

 Lod. Oh bloody period.

 Gra. All that is spoke, is marr'd.

 Oth. I kist thee, ere I kill'd thee: No way but this,
Killing my selfe, to dye vpon a kisse.   *Dyes*
                                                                 Cassio.

Caf. This did I feare, but thought he had no weapon: For he was great of heart.	Let it be hid. *Gratiano*, keepe the houfe, And feize vpon the Fortunes of the Moore, For they fucceede on you. To you, Lord Gouernor,
Lod. Oh Sparton Dogge: More fell then Anguifh, Hunger, or the Sea: Looke on the Tragicke Loading of this bed: This is thy worke: The Obiect poyfons Sight.	Remaines the Cenfure of this hellifh villaine: The Time, the Place, the Torture, oh inforce it: My felfe will ftraight aboord, and to the State, This heauie Act, with heauie heart relate. *Exeunt.*

FINIS.

The Names of the Actors.
(:**:)

Othello, *the Moore.*
Brabantio, *Father to Defdemona.*
Caffio, *an Honourable Lieutenant.*
Iago, *a Villaine.*
Rodorigo, *a gull'd Gentleman.*
Duke *of Venice.*

Senators.
Montano, *Gouernour of Cyprus.*
Gentlemen of Cyprus.
Lodouico, *and* Gratiano, *two Noble Venetians.*
Saylors.
Clowne.

Defdemona, *wife to Othello.*
Æmilia, *wife to Iago.*
Bianca, *a Curtezan.*

THE TRAGEDIE OF
Anthonie, and Cleopatra.

Actus Primus. Scœna Prima.

Enter Demetrius and Philo.

Philo.
Ay, but this dotage of our Generals
Ore-flowes the measure: those his goodly eyes
That o're the Files and Musters of the Warre,
Haue glow'd like plated Mars:
Now bend, now turne
The Office and Deuotion of their view
Vpon a Tawny Front. His Captaines heart,
Which in the scuffles of great Fights hath burst
The Buckles on his brest, reneages all temper,
And is become the Bellowes and the Fan
To coole a Gypsies Lust.

Flourish. Enter Anthony, Cleopatra, her Ladies, the Traine, with Eunuchs fanning her.
Looke where they come:
Take but good note, and you shall see in him
(The triple Pillar of the world) transform'd
Into a Strumpets Foole. Behold and see.

Cleo. If it be Loue indeed, tell me how much.
Ant. There's beggery in the loue that can be reckon'd
Cleo. Ile set a bourne how farre to be belou'd.
Ant. Then must thou needes finde out new Heauen, new Earth.

Enter a Messenger.
Mes. Newes (my good Lord) from Rome.
Ant. Grates me, the summe.
Cleo. Nay heare them Anthony.
Fuluia perchance is angry: Or who knowes,
If the scarse-bearded Cæsar haue not sent
His powrefull Mandate to you, Do this, or this;
Take in that Kingdome, and Infranchise that:
Perform't, or else we damne thee.
Ant. How, my Loue?
Cleo. Perchance? Nay, and most like:
You must not stay heere longer, your dismission
Is come from Cæsar, therefore heare it Anthony.
Where's Fuluias Processe? (Cæsars I would say) both?
Call in the Messengers: As I am Egypts Queene,
Thou blushest Anthony, and that blood of thine
Is Cæsars homager: else so thy cheeke payes shame,
When shrill-tongu'd Fuluia scolds. The Messengers.
Ant. Let Rome in Tyber melt, and the wide Arch
Of the raing'd Empire fall: Heere is my space,
Kingdomes are clay: Our dungie earth alike

Feeds Beast as Man; the Noblenesse of life
Is to do thus: when such a mutuall paire,
And such a twaine can doo't, in which I binde
One paine of punishment, the world to weete
We stand vp Peerelesse.
Cleo. Excellent falshood:
Why did he marry Fuluia, and not loue her?
Ile seeme the Foole I am not. Anthony will be himselfe.
Ant. But stirr'd by Cleopatra.
Now for the loue of Loue, and her soft houres,
Let's not confound the time with Conference harsh;
There's not a minute of our liues should stretch
Without some pleasure now. What sport to night?
Cleo. Heare the Ambassadors.
Ant. Fye wrangling Queene:
Whom euery thing becomes, to chide, to laugh,
To weepe: who euery passion fully striues
To make it selfe (in Thee) faire, and admir'd.
No Messenger but thine, and all alone, to night
Wee'l wander through the streets, and note
The qualities of people. Come my Queene,
Last night you did desire it. Speake not to vs.
Exeunt with the Traine.

Dem. Is Cæsar with Anthonius priz'd so slight?
Philo. Sir sometimes when he is not Anthony,
He comes too short of that great Property
Which still should go with Anthony.
Dem. I am full sorry, that hee approues the common
Lyar, who thus speakes of him at Rome; but I will hope
of better deeds to morrow. Rest you happy. *Exeunt*

Enter Enobarbus, Lamprius, a Soothsayer, Rannius, Lucillius, Charmian, Iras, Mardian the Eunuch, and Alexas.

Char. L. Alexas, sweet Alexas, most any thing Alexas, almost most absolute Alexas, where's the Soothsayer that you prais'd so to th' Queene? Oh that I knewe this Husband, which you say, must change his Hornes with Garlands.
Alex. Soothsayer.
Sooth. Your will?
Char. Is this the Man? Is't you sir that know things?
Sooth. In Natures infinite booke of Secrecie, a little I can read.
Alex. Shew him your hand.
Enob. Bring in the Banket quickly: Wine enough,

Cleopa

Cleopatra's health to drinke.

Char. Good sir, giue me good Fortune.

Sooth. I make not, but foresee.

Char. Pray then, foresee me one.

Sooth. You shall be yet farre fairer then you are.

Char. He meanes in flesh.

Iras. No, you shall paint when you are old.

Char. Wrinkles forbid.

Alex. Vex not his prescience, be attentiue.

Char. Hush.

Sooth. You shall be more belouing, then beloued.

Char. I had rather heate my Liuer with drinking.

Alex. Nay, heare him.

Char. Good now some excellent Fortune: Let mee be married to three Kings in a forenoone, and Widdow them all: Let me haue a Childe at fifty, to whom *Herode* of Iewry may do Homage. Finde me to marrie me with *Octauius Cæsar*, and companion me with my Mistris.

Sooth. You shall out-liue the Lady whom you serue.

Char. Oh excellent, I loue long life better then Figs.

Sooth. You haue seene and proued a fairer former fortune, then that which is to approach.

Char. Then belike my Children shall haue no names: Prythee how many Boyes and Wenches must I haue.

Sooth. If euery of your wishes had a wombe, & foretell euery wish, a Million.

Char. Out Foole, I forgiue thee for a Witch.

Alex. You thinke none but your sheets are priuie to your wishes.

Char. Nay come, tell *Iras* hers.

Alex. Wee'l know all our Fortunes.

Enob. Mine, and most of our Fortunes to night, shall be drunke to bed.

Iras. There's a Palme presages Chastity, if nothing els.

Char. E'ne as the o're-flowing Nylus presageth Famine.

Iras. Go you wilde Bedfellow, you cannot Soothsay.

Char. Nay, if an oyly Palme bee not a fruitfull Prognostication, I cannot scratch mine eare. Prythee tel her but a worky day Fortune.

Sooth. Your Fortunes are alike.

Iras. But how, but how, giue me particulars.

Sooth. I haue said.

Iras. Am I not an inch of Fortune better then she?

Char. Well, if you were but an inch of fortune better then I: where would you choose it.

Iras. Not in my Husbands nose.

Char. Our worser thoughts Heauens mend.

Alexas. Come, his Fortune, his Fortune. Oh let him mary a woman that cannot go, sweet *Isis*, I beseech thee, and let her dye too, and giue him a worse, and let worse follow worse, till the worst of all follow him laughing to his graue, fifty-fold a Cuckold. Good *Isis* heare me this Prayer, though thou denie me a matter of more waight: good *Isis* I beseech thee.

Iras. Amen, deere Goddesse, heare that prayer of the people. For, as it is a heart-breaking to see a handsome man loose-Wiu'd, so it is a deadly sorrow, to beholde a foule Knaue vncuckolded: Therefore deere *Isis* keep decorum, and Fortune him accordingly.

Char. Amen.

Alex. Lo now, if it lay in their hands to make mee a Cuckold, they would make themselues Whores, but they'ld doo't.

Enter Cleopatra.

Enob. Hush, heere comes *Anthony*.

Char. Not he, the Queene.

Cleo. Saue you, my Lord.

Enob. No Lady.

Cleo. Was he not heere?

Char. No Madam.

Cleo. He was dispos'd to mirth, but on the sodaine A Romane thought hath strooke him. Enobarbus?

Enob. Madam.

Cleo. Seeke him, and bring him hither: wher's *Alexias*?

Alex. Heere at your seruice. My Lord approaches.

Enter Anthony, with a Messenger.

Cleo. We will not looke vpon him:
Go with vs. *Exeunt.*

Messen. *Fuluia* thy Wife,
First came into the Field.

Ant. Against my Brother *Lucius*?

Messen. I: but soone that Warre had end,
And the times state
Made friends of them, ioynting their force 'gainst *Cæsar*,
Whose better issue in the warre from Italy,
Vpon the first encounter draue them.

Ant. Well, what worst.

Mess. The Nature of bad newes infects the Teller.

Ant. When it concernes the Foole or Coward: On.
Things that are past, are done, with me. 'Tis thus,
Who tels me true, though in his Tale lye death,
I heare him as he flatter'd.

Mess. *Labienus* (this is stiffe-newes)
Hath with his Parthian Force
Extended Asia: from Euphrates his conquering
Banner shooke, from Syria to Lydia,
And to Ionia, whil'st——

Ant. *Anthony* thou would'st say.

Mes. Oh my Lord.

Ant. Speake to me home,
Mince not the generall tongue, name
Cleopatra as she is call'd in Rome:
Raile thou in *Fuluia's* phrase, and taunt my faults
With such full License, as both Truth and Malice
Haue power to vtter. Oh then we bring forth weeds,
When our quicke windes lye still, and our illes told vs
Is as our earing: fare thee well awhile.

Mes. At your Noble pleasure. *Exit Messenger.*

Enter another Messenger.

Ant. From *Scicion* how the newes? Speake there.

1. *Mes.* The man from *Scicion*,
Is there such an one?

2. *Mes.* He stayes vpon your will.

Ant. Let him appeare:
These strong Egyptian Fetters I must breake,
Or loose my selfe in dotage.

Enter another Messenger with a Letter.

What are you?

3. *Mes.* *Fuluia* thy wife is dead.

Ant. Where dyed she.

Mes. In *Scicion*, her length of sicknesse,
With what else more serious,
Importeth thee to know, this beares.

Antho. Forbeare me
There's a great Spirit gone, thus did I desire it:
What our contempts doth often hurle from vs,

We wish it ours againe. The present pleasure,
By reuolution lowring, does become
The opposite of it selfe: she's good being gon,
The hand could plucke her backe, that shou'd her on.
I must from this enchanting Queene breake off,
Ten thousand harmes, more then the illes I know
My idlenesse doth hatch.

Enter Enobarbus.

How now *Enobarbus*.

Eno. What's your pleasure, Sir?

Anth. I must with haste from hence.

Eno. Why then we kill all our Women. We see how mortall an vnkindnesse is to them, if they suffer our departure, death's the word.

Ant. I must be gone.

Eno. Vnder a compelling an occasion, let women die. It were pitty to cast them away for nothing, though betweene them and a great cause, they should be esteemed nothing. *Cleopatra* catching but the least noyse of this, dies instantly: I haue seene her dye twenty times vppon farre poorer moment: I do think there is mettle in death, which commits some louing acte vpon her, she hath such a celerity in dying.

Ant. She is cunning past mans thought.

Eno. Alacke Sir no, her passions are made of nothing but the finest part of pure Loue. We cannot cal her winds and waters, sighes and teares: They are greater stormes and Tempests then Almanackes can report. This cannot be cunning in her; if it be, she makes a showre of Raine as well as Ioue.

Ant. Would I had neuer seene her.

Eno. Oh sir, you had then left vnseene a wonderfull peece of worke, which not to haue beene blest withall, would haue discredited your Trauaile.

Ant. Fuluia is dead.

Eno. Sir.

Ant. Fuluia is dead.

Eno. Fuluia?

Ant. Dead.

Eno. Why sir, giue the Gods a thankefull Sacrifice: when it pleaseth their Deities to take the wife of a man from him, it shewes to man the Tailors of the earth: comforting therein, that when olde Robes are worne out, there are members to make new. If there were no more Women but *Fuluia*, then had you indeede a cut, and the case to be lamented: This greefe is crown'd with Consolation, your old Smocke brings foorth a new Petticoate, and indeed the teares liue in an Onion, that should water this sorrow.

Ant. The businesse she hath broached in the State, Cannot endure my obsence.

Eno. And the businesse you haue broach'd heere cannot be without you, especially that of *Cleopatra's*, which wholly depends on your abode.

Ant. No more light Answeres:
Let our Officers
Haue notice what we purpose. I shall breake
The cause of our Expedience to the Queene,
And get her loue to part. For not alone
The death of *Fuluia*, with more vrgent touches
Do strongly speake to vs: but the Letters too
Of many our contriuing Friends in Rome,
Petition vs at home. *Sextus Pompeius*
Haue giuen the dare to *Cesar*, and commands
The Empire of the Sea. Our slippery people,
Whose Loue is neuer link'd to the deseruer,
Till his deserts are past, begin to throw
Pompey the great, and all his Dignities
Vpon his Sonne, who high in Name and Power,
Higher then both in Blood and Life, stands vp
For the maine Souldier. Whose quality going on,
The sides o'th'world may danger. Much is breeding,
Which Like the Coursers heire, hath yet but life,
And not a Serpents poyson. Say our pleasure,
To such whose places vnder vs, require
Our quicke remoue from hence.

Enob. I shall doo't.

Enter Cleopatra, Charmian, Alexas, and Iras.

Cleo. Where is he?

Char. I did not see him since.

Cleo. See where he is,
Whose with him, what he does:
I did not send you. If you finde him sad,
Say I am dauncing: if in Myrth, report
That I am sodaine sicke. Quicke, and returne.

Char. Madam, me thinkes if you did loue him deerly,
You do not hold the method, to enforce
The like from him.

Cleo. What should I do, I do not?

Ch. In each thing giue him way, crosse him in nothing.

Cleo. Thou teachest like a foole: the way to lose him.

Char. Tempt him not so too farre. I wish forbeare,
In time we hate that which we often feare.

Enter Anthony.

But heere comes *Anthony*.

Cleo. I am sicke, and sullen.

An. I am sorry to giue breathing to my purpose.

Cleo. Helpe me away deere *Charmian*, I shall fall,
It cannot be thus long, the sides of Nature
Will not sustaine it.

Ant. Now my deerest Queene.

Cleo. Pray you stand farther from mee.

Ant. What's the matter?

Cleo. I know by that same eye ther's some good news.
What sayes the married woman you may goe?
Would she had neuer giuen you leaue to come.
Let her not say 'tis I that keepe you heere,
I haue no power vpon you: Hers you are.

Ant. The Gods best know.

Cleo. Oh neuer was there Queene
So mightily betrayed: yet at the first
I saw the Treasons planted.

Ant. Cleopatra.

Cleo. Why should I thinke you can be mine, & true,
(Though you in swearing shake the Throaned Gods)
Who haue beene false to *Fuluia*?
Riotous madnesse,
To be entangled with those mouth-made vowes,
Which breake themselues in swearing.

Ant. Most sweet Queene.

Cleo. Nay pray you seeke no colour for your going,
But bid farewell, and goe:
When you sued staying,
Then was the time for words: No going then,
Eternity was in our Lippes, and Eyes,
Blisse in our browes bent: none our parts so poore,
But was a race of Heauen. They are so still,
Or thou the greatest Souldier of the world,
Art turn'd the greatest Lyar.

Ant. How now Lady?

Cleo.

Cleo. I would I had thy inches, thou should'ſt know
There were a heart in Egypt.

Ant. Heare me Queene:
The ſtrong neceſſity of Time, commands
Our Seruicles a-while: but my full heart
Remaines in vſe with you. Our Italy,
Shines o're with ciuill Swords; *Sextus Pompeius*
Makes his approaches to the Port of Rome,
Equality of two Domeſticke powers,
Breed ſcrupulous faction: The hated growne to ſtrength
Are newly growne to Loue: The condemn'd *Pompey*,
Rich in his Fathers Honor, creepes apace
Into the hearts of ſuch, as haue not thriued
Vpon the preſent ſtate, whoſe Numbers threſten,
And quietneſſe growne ſicke of reſt, would purge
By any deſperate change: My more particular,
And that which moſt with you ſhould ſafe my going,
Is *Fuluias* death.

Cleo. Though age from folly could not giue me freedom
It does from childiſhneſſe. Can *Fuluia* dye?

Ant. She's dead my Queene.
Looke heere, and at thy Soueraigne leyſure read
The Garboyles ſhe awak'd: at the laſt, beſt,
See when, and where ſhee died.

Cleo. O moſt falſe Loue!
Where be the Sacred Violles thou ſhould'ſt fill
With ſorrowfull water? Now I ſee, I ſee,
In *Fuluias* death, how mine receiu'd ſhall be.

Ant. Quarrell no more, but bee prepar'd to know
The purpoſes I beare: which are, or ceaſe,
As you ſhall giue th'aduice. By the fire
That quickens Nylus ſlime, I go from hence
Thy Souldier, Seruant, making Peace or Warre,
As thou affects.

Cleo. Cut my Lace, *Charmian* come,
But let it be, I am quickly ill, and well,
So *Anthony* loues.

Ant. My precious Queene forbeare,
And giue true euidence to his Loue, which ſtands
An honourable Triall.

Cleo. So *Fuluia* told me.
I prythee turne aſide, and weepe for her,
Then bid adiew to me, and ſay the teares
Belong to Egypt. Good now, play one Scene
Of excellent diſſembling, and let it looke
Like perfect Honor.

Ant. You'l heat my blood no more?

Cleo. You can do better yet: but this is meetly.

Ant. Now by Sword.

Cleo. And Target. Still he mends.
But this is not the beſt. Looke prythee *Charmian*,
How this Herculean Roman do's become
The carriage of his chafe.

Ant. Ile leaue you Lady.

Cleo. Courteous Lord, one word:
Sir, you and I muſt part, but that's not it:
Sir, you and I haue lou'd, but there's not it:
That you know well, ſomething it is I would:
Oh, my Obliuion is a very *Anthony*,
And I am all forgotten.

Ant. But that your Royalty
Holds Idleneſſe your ſubiect, I ſhould take you
For Idleneſſe it ſelfe.

Cleo. 'Tis ſweating Labour,
To beare ſuch Idleneſſe ſo neere the heart
As *Cleopatra* this. But Sir, forgiue me,
Since my becommings kill me, when they do not
Eye well to you. Your Honor calles you hence,
Therefore be deafe to my vnpittied Folly.
And all the Gods go with you. Vpon your Sword
Sit Lawrell victory, and ſmooth ſucceſſe
Be ſtrew'd before your feete.

Ant. Let vs go. Come: Our ſeparation ſo abides and flies,
That thou reciding heere, goes yet with mee;
And I hence fleeting, heere remaine with thee.
Away. *Exeunt.*

Enter Octauius reading a Letter, Lepidus, and their Traine.

Cæſ. You may ſee *Lepidus*, and henceforth know,
It is not *Cæſars* Naturall vice, to hate
One great Competitor. From Alexandria
This is the newes: He fiſhes, drinkes, and waſtes
The Lampes of night in reuell: Is not more manlike
Then *Cleopatra*: nor the Queene of *Ptolomy*
More Womanly then he. Hardly gaue audience
Or vouchſafe to thinke he had Partners. You
Shall finde there a man, who is th'abſtracts of all faults,
That all men follow.

Lep. I muſt not thinke
There are, euils enow to darken all his goodneſſe:
His faults in him, ſeeme as the Spots of Heauen,
More fierie by nights Blackneſſe; Hereditarie,
Rather then purchaſte: what he cannot change,
Then what he chooſes.

Cæſ. You are too indulgent. Let's graunt it is not
Amiſſe to tumble on the bed of *Ptolomy*,
To giue a Kingdome for a Mirth, to ſit
And keepe the turne of Tipling with a Slaue,
To reele the ſtreets at noone, and ſtand the Buffet
With knaues that ſmels of ſweate: Say this becoms him
(As his compoſure muſt be rare indeed,
Whom theſe things cannot blemiſh) yet muſt *Anthony*
No way excuſe his foyles, when we do beare
So great waight in his lightneſſe. If he fill'd
His vacancie with his Voluptuouſneſſe,
Full ſurfets, and the drineſſe of his bones,
Call on him for't. But to confound ſuch time,
That drummes him from his ſport, and ſpeakes as lowd
As his owne State, and ours, 'tis to be chid:
As we rate Boyes, who being mature in knowledge,
Pawne their experience to their preſent pleaſure,
And ſo rebell to iudgement.

Enter a Meſſenger.

Lep. Heere's more newes.

Meſ. Thy biddings haue beene done, & euerie houre
Moſt Noble *Cæſar*, ſhalt thou haue report
How 'tis abroad. *Pompey* is ſtrong at Sea,
And it appeares, he is belou'd of thoſe
That only haue feard *Cæſar*: to the Ports
The diſcontents repaire, and mens reports
Giue him much wrong'd.

Cæſ. I ſhould haue knowne no leſſe,
It hath bin taught vs from the primall ſtate
That he which is was wiſht, vntill he were:
And the ebb'd man,
Ne're lou'd, till ne're worth loue,
Comes fear'd, by being lack'd. This common bodie,
Like to a Vagabond Flagge vpon the Streame,
Goes too, and backe, lacking the varrying tyde

To rot it selfe with motion.

   Mes. Cæsar I bring thee word,
Menacrates and *Menas* famous Pyrates
Makes the Sea serue them, which they eare and wound
With keeles of euery kinde. Many hot inrodes
They make in Italy, the Borders Maritime
Lacke blood to thinke on't, and flush youth reuolt,
No Vessell can peepe forth : but 'tis as soone
Taken as seene : for *Pompeyes* name strikes more
Then could his Warre resisted.

   Cæsar. Anthony,
Leaue thy lasciuious Vassailes. When thou once
Was beaten from *Medena*, where thou slew'st
Hirsius, and *Pausa* Consuls, at thy heele
Did Famine follow, whom thou fought'st against,
(Though daintily brought vp) with patience more
Then Sauages could suffer. Thou did'st drinke
The stale of Horses, and the gilded Puddle
Which Beasts would cough at. Thy pallat thē did daine
The roughest Berry, on the rudest Hedge.
Yea, like the Stagge, when Snow the Pasture sheets,
The barkes of Trees thou brows'd. On the Alpes,
It is reported thou did'st eate strange flesh,
Which some did dye to looke on : And all this
(It wounds thine Honor that I speake it now)
Was borne so like a Soldiour, that thy cheeke
So much as lank'd not.

   Lep. Tis pitty of him.

   Cæs. Let his shames quickely
Driue him to Rome, 'tis time we twaine
Did shew our selues i'th'Field, and to that end
Assemble me immediate counsell, *Pompey*
Thriues in our Idlenesse.

   Lep. To morrow *Cæsar*,
I shall be furnisht to informe you rightly
Both what by Sea and Land I can be able
To front this present time.

   Cæs. Til which encounter, it is my busines too. Farwell.

   Lep. Farwell my Lord, what you shal know mean time
Of stirres abroad, I shall beseech you Sir
To let me be partaker.

   Cæsar. Doubt not sir, I knew it for my Bond. *Exeunt*

   Enter Cleopatra, Charmian, Iras, & Mardian.

   Cleo. Charmian.

   Char. Madam.

   Cleo. Ha, ha, giue me to drinke *Mandragora*.

   Char. Why Madam?

   Cleo. That I might sleepe out this great gap of time:
My *Anthony* is away.

   Char. You thinke of him too much.

   Cleo. O 'tis Treason.

   Char. Madam, I trust not so.

   Cleo. Thou, Eunuch *Mardian*?

   Mar. What's your Highnesse pleasure?

   Cleo. Not now to heare thee sing. I take no pleasure
In ought an Eunuch ha's : Tis well for thee,
That being vnseminar'd, thy freer thoughts
May not flye forth of Egypt. Hast thou Affections?

   Mar. Yes gracious Madam.

   Cleo. Indeed?

   Mar. Not in deed Madam, for I can do nothing
But what in deede is honest to be done:
Yet haue I fierce Affections, and thinke
What Venus did with Mars.

   Cleo. Oh *Charmion*:
Where think'st thou he is now? Stands he, or sits he?
Or does he walke? Or is he on his Horse?
Oh happy horse to beare the weight of *Anthony*!
Do brauely Horse, for wot'st thou whom thou moou'st,
The demy *Atlas* of this Earth, the Arme
And Burganet of men. Hee's speaking now,
Or murmuring, where's my Serpent of old Nyle,
(For so he cals me:) Now I feede my selfe
With most delicious poyson. Thinke on me
That am with Phœbus amorous pinches blacke,
And wrinkled deepe in time. Broad-fronted *Cæsar*,
When thou was't heere aboue the ground, I was
A morsell for a Monarke : and great *Pompey*
Would stand and make his eyes grow in my brow,
There would he anchor his Aspect, and dye
With looking on his life.

   Enter Alexas from Cæsar.

   Alex. Soueraigne of Egypt, haile.

   Cleo. How much vnlike art thou *Marke Anthony*?
Yet comming from him, that great Med'cine hath
With his Tinct gilded thee.
How goes it with my braue *Marke Anthonie*?

   Alex. Last thing he did (deere Queene)
He kist the last of many doubled kisses
This Orient Pearle. His speech stickes in my heart.

   Cleo. Mine eare must plucke it thence.

   Alex. Good Friend, quoth he:
Say the firme Roman to great Egypt sends
This treasure of an Oyster : at whose foote
To mend the petty present, I will peece
Her opulent Throne, with Kingdomes. All the East,
(Say thou) shall call her Mistris. So he nodded,
And soberly did mount an Arme-gaunt Steede,
Who neigh'd so hye, that what I would haue spoke,
Was beastly dumbe by him.

   Cleo. What was he sad, or merry?

   Alex. Like to the time o'th'yeare, betweene ȳ extremes
Of hot and cold, he was nor sad, nor merrie.

   Cleo. Oh well diuided disposition: Note him,
Note him good *Charmian*, 'tis the man; but note him.
He was not sad, for he would shine on those
That make their lookes by his. He was not merrie,
Which seem'd to tell them, his remembrance lay
In Egypt with his ioy, but betweene both.
Oh heauenly mingle! Bee'st thou sad, or merrie,
The violence of either thee becomes,
So do's it no mans else. Met'st thou my Posts?

   Alex. I Madam, twenty seuerall Messengers.
Why do you send so thicke?

   Cleo. Who's borne that day, when I forget to send
to *Anthonie*, shall dye a Begger. Inke and paper *Charmian*. Welcome my good *Alexas*. Did I *Charmian*, e-
uer loue *Cæsar* so?

   Char. Oh that braue *Cæsar*!

   Cleo. Be choak'd with such another Emphasis,
Say the braue *Anthony*.

   Char. The valiant *Cæsar*.

   Cleo. By *Isis*, I will giue thee bloody teeth,
If thou with *Cæsar* Parago nagaine:
My man of men.

   Char. By your most gracious pardon,
I sing but after you.

   Cleo. My Sallad dayes,
When I was greene in iudgement, cold in blood,
To say, as I saide then. But come, away,
Get me Inke and Paper,

he shall haue euery day a seuerall greeting, or Ile vnpeople Egypt. *Exeunt*

Enter Pompey, Menecrates, and Menas, in warlike manner.

Pom. If the great Gods be iust, they shall assist
The deeds of iustest men.

Mene. Know worthy *Pompey,* that what they do delay, they not deny.

Pom. Whiles we are sutors to their Throne, decayes the thing we sue for.

Mene. We ignorant of our selues,
Begge often our owne harmes, which the wise Powres
Deny vs for our good: so finde we profit
By loosing of our Prayers.

Pom. I shall do well.
The people loue me, and the Sea is mine;
My powers are Crescent, and my Auguring hope
Sayes it will come to'th'full. Marke *Anthony*
In Egypt sits at dinner, and will make
No warres without doores. *Cæsar* gets money where
He looses hearts: *Lepidus* flatters both,
Of both is flatter'd: but he neither loues,
Nor either cares for him.

Mene. *Cæsar* and *Lepidus* are in the field,
A mighty strength they carry.

Pom. Where haue you this? 'Tis false.

Mene. From *Siluius,* Sir.

Pom. He dreames: I know they are in Rome together
Looking for *Anthony*: but all the charmes of Loue,
Salt *Cleopatra* soften thy wand lip,
Let Witchcraft ioyne with Beauty, Lust with both,
Tye vp the Libertine in a field of Feasts,
Keepe his Braine fuming. Epicurean Cookes,
Sharpen with cloylesse sawce his Appetite,
That sleepe and feeding may prorogue his Honour,
Euen till a Lethied dulnesse——

Enter Varrius.

How now *Varrius?*

Var. This is most certaine, that I shall deliuer:
Marke Anthony is euery houre in Rome
Expected. Since he went from Egypt, 'tis
A space for farther Trauaile.

Pom. I could haue giuen lesse matter
A better eare. *Menas,* I did not thinke
This amorous Surfetter would haue donn'd his Helme
For such a petty Warre: His Souldiership
Is twice the other twaine: But let vs reare
The higher our Opinion, that our stirring
Can from the lap of Egypts Widdow, plucke
The neere Lust-wearied *Anthony.*

Mene. I cannot hope,
Cæsar and *Anthony* shall well greet together;
His Wife that's dead, did trespasses to *Cæsar,*
His Brother wan'd vpon him, although I thinke
Not mou'd by *Anthony.*

Pom. I know not *Menas,*
How lesser Enmities may giue way to greater,
Were't not that we stand vp against them all:
'Twer pregnant they should square between themselues,
For they haue entertained cause enough
To draw their swords: but how the feare of vs
May Ciment their diuisions, and binde vp
The petty difference, we yet not know:
Bee't as our Gods will haue't; it onely stands
Our liues vpon, to vse our strongest hands
Come *Menas.* *Exeunt.*

Enter Enobarbus and Lepidus.

Lep. Good *Enobarbus,* 'tis a worthy deed,
And shall become you well, to intreat your Captaine
To soft and gentle speech.

Enob. I shall intreat him
To answer like himselfe: if *Cæsar* moue him,
Let *Anthony* looke ouer *Cæsars* head,
And speake as lowd as Mars. By Iupiter,
Were I the wearer of *Anthonio's* Beard,
I would not shaue't to day.

Lep. 'Tis not a time for priuate stomacking.

Eno. Euery time serues for the matter that is then borne in't.

Lep. But small to greater matters must giue way.

Eno. Not if the small come first.

Lep. Your speech is passion: but pray you stirre
No Embers vp. Heere comes the Noble *Anthony.*

Enter Anthony and Ventidius.

Eno. And yonder *Cæsar.*

Enter Cæsar, Mecenas, and Agrippa.

Ant. If we compose well heere, to Parthia:
Hearke *Ventidius.*

Cæsar. I do not know *Mecenas,* aske *Agrippa.*

Lep. Noble Friends:
That which combin'd vs was most great, and let not
A leaner action rend vs. What's amisse,
May it be gently heard. When we debate
Our triuiall difference loud, we do commit
Murther in healing wounds. Then Noble Partners,
The rather for I earnestly beseech,
Touch you the sowrest points with sweetest tearmes,
Nor curstnesse grow to'th'matter.

Ant. 'Tis spoken well:
Were we before our Armies, and to fight,
I should do thus. *Flourish.*

Cæs. Welcome to Rome.

Ant. Thanke you.

Cæs. Sir,

Ant. Sit sir.

Cæs. Nay then.

Ant. I learne, you take things ill, which are not so:
Or being, concerne you not.

Cæs. I must be laught at, if or for nothing, or a little, I
Should say my selfe offended, and with you
Chiefely i'th'world. More laught at, that I should
Once name you derogately: when to sound your name
It not concern'd me.

Ant. My being in Egypt *Cæsar,* what was't to you?

Cæs. No more then my reciding heere at Rome
Might be to you in Egypt: yet if you there
Did practise on my State, your being in Egypt
Might be my question.

Ant. How intend you, practis'd?

Cæs. You may be pleas'd to catch at mine intent,
By what did heere befall me. Your Wife and Brother
Made warres vpon me, and their contestation
Was Theame for you, you were the word of warre.

Ant. You do mistake your busines, my Brother neuer
Did vrge me in his Act: I did inquire it,
And haue my Learning from some true reports
That drew their swords with you, did he not rather
Discredit my authority with yours,
And make the warres alike against my stomacke,
Hauing alike your cause. Of this, my Letters
Before did satisfie you. If you'l patch a quarrell,
As matter whole you haue to make it with,

It must not be with this.

Caes. You praise your selfe, by laying defects of iudgement to me: but you patcht vp your excuses.

Anth. Not so, not so:
I know you could not lacke, I am certaine on't,
Very necessity of this thought, that I
Your Partner in the cause 'gainst which he fought,
Could not with gracefull eyes attend those Warres
Which fronted mine owne peace. As for my wife,
I would you had her spirit, in such another,
The third o'th'world is yours, which with a Snaffle,
You may pace easie, but not such a wife.

Enobar. Would we had all such wiues, that the men might go to Warres with the women.

Anth. So much vncurbable, her Garboiles (*Caesar*)
Made out of her impatience: which not wanted
Shrodenesse of policie to: I greeuing grant,
Did you too much disquiet, for that you must,
But say I could not helpe it.

Caesar. I wrote to you, when rioting in Alexandria you
Did pocket vp my Letters: and with taunts
Did gibe my Missiue out of audience.

Ant. Sir, he fell vpon me, ere admitted, then:
Three Kings I had newly feasted, and did want
Of what I was i'th'morning: but next day
I told him of my selfe, which was as much
As to haue askt him pardon. Let this Fellow
Be nothing of our strife: if we contend
Out of our question wipe him.

Caesar. You haue broken the Article of your oath, which you shall neuer haue tongue to charge me with.

Lep. Soft *Caesar*.

Ant. No *Lepidus*, let him speake,
The Honour is Sacred which he talks on now,
Supposing that I lackt it: but on *Caesar*,
The Article of my oath.

Caesar. To lend me Armes, and aide when I requir'd them, the which you both denied.

Anth. Neglected rather:
And then when poysoned houres had bound me vp
From mine owne knowledge, as neerely as I may,
Ile play the penitent to you. But mine honesty,
Shall not make poore my greatnesse, nor my power
Worke without it. Truth is, that *Fuluia*,
To haue me out of Egypt, made Warres heere,
For which my selfe, the ignorant motiue, do
So farre aske pardon, as befits mine Honour
To stoope in such a case.

Lep. 'Tis Noble spoken.

Mece. If it might please you, to enforce no further
The griefes betweene ye: to forget them quite,
Were to remember: that the present neede,
Speakes to attone you.

Lep. Worthily spoken *Mecenas*.

Enobar. Or if you borrow one anothers Loue for the instant, you may when you heare no more words of *Pompey* returne it againe: you shall haue time to wrangle in, when you haue nothing else to do.

Anth. Thou art a Souldier, onely speake no more.

Enob. That truth should be silent, I had almost forgot.

Anth. You wrong this presence, therefore speake no more.

Enob. Go too then: your Considerate stone.

Caesar. I do not much dislike the matter, but
The manner of his speech: for't cannot be,
We shall remaine in friendship, our conditions
So differing in their acts. Yet if I knew,
What Hoope should hold vs staunch from edge to edge
A th'world: I would persue it.

Agri. Giue me leaue *Caesar*.

Caesar. Speake *Agrippa*.

Agri. Thou hast a Sister by the Mothers side, admit'd *Octauia*: Great *Mark Anthony* is now a widdower.

Caesar. Say not, say *Agrippa*; if *Cleopater* heard you, your proofe were well deserued of rashnesse.

Anth. I am not marryed *Caesar*: let me heere *Agrippa* further speake.

Agri. To hold you in perpetuall amitie,
To make you Brothers, and to knit your hearts
With an vn-slipping knot, take *Anthony*,
Octauia to his wife: whose beauty claimes
No worse a husband then the best of men: whose
Vertue, and whose generall graces, speake
That which none else can vtter. By this marriage,
All little Ielousies which now seeme great,
And all great feares, which now import their dangers,
Would then be nothing. Truth's would be tales,
Where now halfe tales be truth's: her loue to both,
Would each to other, and all loues to both
Draw after her. Pardon what I haue spoke,
For 'tis a studied not a present thought,
By duty ruminated.

Anth. Will *Caesar* speake?

Caesar. Not till he heares how *Anthony* is toucht,
With what is spoke already.

Anth. What power is in *Agrippa*,
If I would say *Agrippa*, be it so,
To make this good?

Caesar. The power of *Caesar*,
And his power, vnto *Octauia*.

Anth. May I neuer
(To this good purpose, that so fairely shewes)
Dreame of impediment: let me haue thy hand
Further this act of Grace: and from this houre,
The heart of Brothers gouerne in our Loues,
And sway our great Designes.

Caesar. There's my hand:
A Sister I bequeath you, whom no Brother
Did euer loue so deerely. Let her liue
To ioyne our kingdomes, and our hearts, and neuer
Flie off our Loues againe.

Lepi. Happily, Amen.

Ant. I did not think to draw my Sword 'gainst *Pompey*,
For he hath laid strange courtesies, and great
Of late vpon me. I must thanke him onely,
Least my remembrance, suffer ill report:
At heele of that, defie him.

Lepi. Time cals vpon's,
Of vs must *Pompey* presently be sought,
Or else he seekes out vs.

Anth. Where lies he?

Caesar. About the Mount-Mesena.

Anth. What is his strength by land?

Caesar. Great, and encreasing:
But by Sea he is an absolute Master.

Anth. So is the Fame,
Would we had spoke together. Hast we for it,
Yet ere we put our selues in Armes, dispatch we
The businesse we haue talkt of.

Caesar. With most gladnesse,
And do inuite you to my Sisters view,

Whether straight Ile lead you.

Anth. Let vs *Lepidus* not lacke your companie.

Lep. Noble *Anthony*, not sickenesse should detaine me.

Flourish. Exit omnes.
Manet Enobarbus, Agrippa, Mecenas.

Mec. Welcome from Ægypt Sir.

Eno. Halfe the heart of *Cæsar*, worthy *Mecenas*. My honourable Friend *Agrippa*.

Agri. Good *Enobarbus*.

Mece. We haue cause to be glad, that matters are so well disgested: you staid well by't in Egypt.

Enob. I Sir, we did sleepe day out of countenaunce: and made the night light with drinking.

Mece. Eight Wilde-Boares rosted whole at a breakfast: and but twelue persons there. Is this true?

Eno. This was but as a Flye by an Eagle: we had much more monstrous matter of Feast, which worthily deserued noting.

Mecenas. She's a most triumphant Lady, if report be square to her.

Enob. When she first met *Marke Anthony*, she purst vp his heart vpon the Riuer of *Sidnis*.

Agri. There she appear'd indeed: or my reporter deuis'd well for her.

Eno. I will tell you,
The Barge she sat in, like a burnisht Throne
Burnt on the water: the Poope was beaten Gold,
Purple the Sailes: and so perfumed that
The Windes were Loue-sicke.
With them the Owers were Siluer,
Which to the tune of Flutes kept stroke, and made
The water which they beate, to follow faster;
As amorous of their strokes. For her owne person,
It beggerd all discription, she did lye
In her Pauillion, cloth of Gold, of Tissue,
O're-picturing that Venus, where we see
The fancie out-worke Nature. On each side her,
Stood pretty Dimpled Boyes, like smiling Cupids,
With diuers colour'd Fannes whose winde did seeme,
To gloue the delicate cheekes which they did coole,
And what they vndid did.

Agrip. Oh rare for *Anthony*.

Eno. Her Gentlewoman, like the *Nereides*,
So many Mer-maides tended her i'th'eyes,
And made their bends adornings. At the Helme,
A seeming Mer-maide steeres: The Silken Tackle,
Swell with the touches of those Flower-soft hands,
That yarely frame the office. From the Barge
A strange inuisible perfume hits the sense
Of the adiacent Wharfes. The Citty cast
Her people out vpon her: and *Anthony*
Enthron'd i'th' Market-place, did sit alone,
Whisling to th'ayre: which but for vacancie,
Had gone to gaze on *Cleopater* too,
And made a gap in Nature.

Agri. Rare Egiptian.

Eno. Vpon her landing, *Anthony* sent to her,
Inuited her to Supper: she replyed,
It should be better, he became her guest:
Which she entreated, our Courteous *Anthony*,
Whom nere the word of no woman hard speake,
Being barber'd ten times o're, goes to the Feast;
And for his ordinary, paies his heart,
For what his eyes eate onely.

Agri. Royall Wench:
She made great *Cæsar* lay his Sword to bed,
He ploughed her, and she cropt.

Eno. I saw her once
Hop forty Paces through the publicke streete,
And hauing lost her breath, she spoke, and panted,
That she did make defect, perfection,
And breathlesse powre breath forth.

Mece. Now *Anthony*, must leaue her vtterly.

Eno. Neuer he will not:
Age cannot wither her, nor custome stale
Her infinite variety: other women cloy
The appetites they feede, but she makes hungry,
Where most she satisfies. For vildest things
Become themselues in her, that the holy Priests
Blesse her, when she is Riggish.

Mece. If Beauty, Wisedome, Modesty, can settle
The heart of *Anthony*: *Octauia* is
A blessed Lottery to him.

Agrip. Let vs go. Good *Enobarbus*, make your selfe my guest, whilst you abide heere.

Eno. Humbly Sir I thanke you. *Exeunt*

Enter Anthony, Cæsar, Octauia betweene them.

Anth. The world, and my great office, will
Sometimes deuide me from your bosome.

Octa. All which time, before the Gods my knee shall
bowe my prayers to them for you.

Anth. Goodnight Sir. My *Octauia*
Read not my blemishes in the worlds report:
I haue not kept my square, but that to come
Shall all be done by th' Rule: good night deere Lady:
Good night Sir.

Cæsar. Goodnight. *Exit.*

Enter Soothsaier.

Anth. Now sirrah: you do wish your selfe in Egypt?

Sooth. Would I had neuer come from thence, nor you thither.

Ant. If you can, your reason?

Sooth. I see it in my motion: haue it not in my tongue,
But yet hie you to Egypt againe.

Antho. Say to me, whose Fortunes shall rise higher
Cæsars or mine?

Soot. *Cæsars.* Therefore (oh *Anthony*) stay not by his side
Thy Dæmon that thy spirit which keepes thee, is
Noble, Couragious, high vnmatchable,
Where *Cæsars* is not. But neere him, thy Angell
Becomes a feare: as being o're-powr'd, therefore
Make space enough betweene you.

Anth. Speake this no more.

Sooth. To none but thee no more but: when to thee,
If thou dost play with him at any game,
Thou art sure to loose: And of that Naturall lucke,
He beats thee 'gainst the oddes. Thy Luster thickens,
When he shines by: I say againe, thy spirit
Is all affraid to gouerne thee neere him:
But he alway 'tis Noble.

Anth. Get thee gone:
Say to *Ventigius* I would speake with him. *Exit.*
He shall to Parthia, be it Art or hap,
He hath spoken true. The very Dice obey him,
And in our sports my better cunning faints,
Vnder his chance, if we draw lots he speeds,
His Cocks do winne the Battaile, still of mine,
When it is all to naught: and his Quailes euer
Beate mine (in hoopt) at odd's. I will to Egypte:

And though I make this marriage for my peace,
I'th'East my pleasure lies. Oh come *Ventigius*.

Enter Ventigius.

You must to Parthia, your Commissions ready:
Follow me, and recieu't. *Exeunt.*

Enter Lepidus, Mecenas and Agrippa.

Lepidus. Trouble your selues no further: pray you
hasten your Generals after.

Agr. Sir, *Marke Anthony*, will e'ne but kisse *Octauia*,
and weele follow.

Lepi. Till I shall see you in your Souldiers dresse,
Which will become you both: Farewell.

Mece. We shall: as I conceiue the iourney, be at
Mount before you *Lepidus*.

Lepi. Your way is shorter, my purposes do draw me
much about, you'le win two dayes vpon me.

Both. Sir good successe.

Lepi. Farewell. *Exeunt.*

Enter Cleopater, Charmian, Iras, and Alexas.

Cleo. Giue me some Musicke: Musicke, moody foode
of vs that trade in Loue.

Omnes. The Musicke, hoa.

Enter Mardian the Eunuch.

Cleo. Let it alone, let's to Billards: come *Charmian*.

Char. My arme is sore, best play with *Mardian*.

Cleopa. As well a woman with an Eunuch plaide, as
with a woman. Come you'le play with me Sir?

Mardi. As well as I can Madam.

Cleo. And when good will is shewed,
Though't come to short
The Actor may pleade pardon. I'le none now,
Giue me mine Angle, weele to'th'Riuer there
My Musicke playing farre off. I will betray
Tawny fine fishes, my bended hooke shall pierce
Their slimy iawes: and as I draw them vp,
Ile thinke them euery one an *Anthony*,
And say, ah ha; y'are caught.

Char. 'Twas merry when you wager'd on your Angling, when your diuer did hang a salt fish on his hooke
which he with feruencie drew vp.

Cleo. That time? Oh times:
I laught him out of patience: and that night
I laught him into patience, and next morne,
Ere the ninth houre, I drunke him to his bed:
Then put my Tires and Mantles on him, whilst
I wore his Sword Phillippan. Oh from Italie,

Enter a Messenger.

Ramme thou thy fruitefull tidings in mine eares,
That long time haue bin barren.

Mes. Madam, Madam.

Cleo. Anthonyo's dead.
If thou say so Villaine, thou kil'st thy Mistris:
But well and free, if thou so yeild him.
There is Gold, and heere
My blewest vaines to kisse: a hand that Kings
Haue lipt, and trembled kissing.

Mes. First Madam, he is well.

Cleo. Why there's more Gold.
But sirrah marke, we vse
To say, the dead are well: bring it to that,
The Gold I giue thee, will I melt and powr
Downe thy ill vttering throate.

Mes. Good Madam heare me.

Cleo. Well, go too I will:
But there's no goodnesse in thy face if *Anthony*
Be free and healthfull; so tart a fauour
To trumpet such good tidings. If not well,
Thou shouldst come like a Furie crown'd with Snakes,
Not like a formall man.

Mes. Wilt please you heare me?

Cleo. I haue a mind to strike thee ere thou speak'st:
Yet if thou say *Anthony* liues, 'tis well,
Or friends with *Cæsar*, or not Captiue to him,
Ile set thee in a shower of Gold, and haile
Rich Pearles vpon thee.

Mes. Madam, he's well.

Cleo. Well said.

Mes. And Friends with *Cæsar*.

Cleo. Th'art an honest man.

Mes. Cæsar, and he, are greater Friends then euer.

Cleo. Make thee a Fortune from me.

Mes. But yet Madam.

Cleo. I do not like but yet, it does alay
The good precedence, fie vpon but yet,
But yet is as a Iaylor to bring foorth
Some monstrous Malefactor. Prythee Friend,
Powre out the packe of matter to mine eare,
The good and bad together: he's friends with *Cæsar*,
In state of health thou saist, and thou saist, free.

Mes. Free Madam, no: I made no such report,
He's bound vnto *Octauia*.

Cleo. For what good turne?

Mes. For the best turne i'th'bed.

Cleo. I am pale *Charmian*.

Mes. Madam, he's married to *Octauia*.

Cleo. The most infectious Pestilence vpon thee.
Strikes him downe.

Mes. Good Madam patience.

Cleo. What say you? *Strikes him.*
Hence horrible Villaine, or Ile spurne thine eyes
Like balls before me: Ile vnhaire thy head,
She hales him vp and downe.
Thou shalt be whipt with Wyer, and stew'd in brine,
Smarting in lingring pickle.

Mes. Gratious Madam,
I that do bring the newes, made not the match.

Cleo. Say 'tis not so, a Prouince I will giue thee,
And make thy Fortunes proud: the blow thou had'st
Shall make thy peace, for mouing me to rage,
And I will boot thee with what guift beside
Thy modestie can begge.

Mes. He's married Madam.

Cleo. Rogue, thou hast liu'd too long. *Draw a knife.*

Mes. Nay then ile runne:
What meane you Madam, I haue made no fault. *Exit.*

Char. Good Madam keepe your selfe within your selfe,
The man is innocent.

Cleo. Some Innocents scape not the thunderbolt:
Melt Egypt into Nyle: and kindly creatures
Turne all to Serpents. Call the slaue againe,
Though I am mad, I will not byte him: Call?

Char. He is afeard to come.

Cleo. I will not hurt him,
These hands do lacke Nobility, that they strike
A meaner then my selfe: since I my selfe
Haue giuen my selfe the cause. Come hither Sir.

Enter the Messenger againe.

Though it be honest, it is neuer good
To bring bad newes: giue to a gratious Message

An hoſt of tongues, but let ill tydings tell
Themſelues, when they be felt.

  Meſ. I haue done my duty.
  Cleo. Is he married?
I cannot hate thee worſer then I do,
If thou againe ſay yes.
  Meſ. He's married Madam.
  Cleo. The Gods confound thee,
Doſt thou hold there ſtill?
  Meſ. Should I lye Madame?
  Cleo. Oh, I would thou didſt:
So halfe my Egypt were ſubmerg'd and made
A Ceſterne for ſcal'd Snakes. Go get thee hence,
Had'ſt thou *Narciſſus* in thy face to me,
Thou would'ſt appeere moſt vgly: He is married?
  Meſ. I craue your Highneſſe pardon.
  Cleo. He is married?
  Meſ. Take no offence, that I would not offend you,
To punniſh me for what you make me do
Seemes much vnequall, he's married to *Octauia*.
  Cleo. Oh that his fault ſhould make a knaue of thee,
That art not what th'art ſure of. Get thee hence,
The Marchandize which thou haſt brought from Rome
Are all too deere for me:
Lye they vpon thy hand, and be vndone by em.
  Char. Good your Highneſſe patience.
  Cleo. In prayſing *Anthony*, I haue diſprais'd *Cæſar*.
  Char. Many times Madam.
  Cleo. I am paid for't now: lead me from hence,
I faint, oh *Iras, Charmian*: 'tis no matter.
Go to the Fellow, good *Alexas* bid him
Report the feature of *Octauia*: her yeares,
Her inclination, let him not leaue out
The colour of her haire. Bring me word quickly,
Let him for euer go, let him not *Charmian*,
Though he be painted one way like a Gorgon,
The other wayes a Mars. Bid you *Alexas*
Bring me word, how tall ſhe is: pitty me *Charmian*,
But do not ſpeake to me. Lead me to my Chamber.
                                                Exeunt.

Flouriſh. Enter Pompey, at one doore with Drum and Trumpet: at another Cæſar, Lepidus, Anthony, Enobarbus, Mæcenas, Agrippa, Menas with Souldiers Marching.

  Pom. Your Hoſtages I haue, ſo haue you mine:
And we ſhall talke before we fight.
  Cæſar. Moſt meete that firſt we come to words,
And therefore haue we
Our written purpoſes before vs ſent,
Which if thou haſt conſidered, let vs know,
If't will tye vp thy diſcontented Sword,
And carry backe to Cicelie much tall youth,
That elſe muſt periſh heere.
  Pom. To you all three,
The Senators alone of this great world,
Chiefe Factors for the Gods. I do not know,
Wherefore my Father ſhould reuengers want,
Hauing a Sonne and Friends, ſince *Iulius Cæſar*,
Who at Phillippi the good *Brutus* ghoſted,
There ſaw you labouring for him. What was't
That mou'd pale *Caſſius* to conſpire? And what
Made all-honor'd, honeſt, Romaine *Brutus*,
With the arm'd reſt, Courtiers of beautious freedome,
To drench the Capitoll, but that they would
Haue one man but a man, and that his it
Hath made me rigge my Nauie. At whoſe burthen,
The anger'd Ocean fomes, with which I meant
To ſcourge th'ingratitude, that deſpightfull Rome
Caſt on my Noble Father.
  Cæſar. Take your time.
  Ant. Thou can'ſt not feare vs *Pompey* with thy ſailes.
Weele ſpeake with thee at Sea. At land thou know'ſt
How much we do o're-count thee.
  Pom. At Land indeed
Thou doſt orecount me of my Fatherrs houſe:
But ſince the Cuckoo buildes not for himſelfe,
Remaine in't as thou maiſt.
  Lepi. Be pleas'd to tell vs,
(For this is from the preſent how you take)
The offers we haue ſent you.
  Cæſar. There's the point.
  Ant. Which do not be entreated too,
But waigh what it is worth imbrac'd
  Cæſar. And what may follow to try a larger Fortune.
  Pom. You haue made me offer
Of Cicelie, Sardinia: and I muſt
Rid all the Sea of Pirats. Then, to ſend
Meaſures of Wheate to Rome: this greed vpon,
To part with vnhackt edges, and beare backe
Our Targes vndinted.
  Omnes. That's our offer.
  Pom. Know then I came before you heere,
A man prepar'd
To take this offer. But *Marke Anthony*,
Put me to ſome impatience: though I looſe
The praiſe of it by telling. You muſt know
When *Cæſar* and your Brother were at blowes,
Your Mother came to Cicelie, and did finde
Her welcome Friendly.
  Ant. I haue heard it *Pompey*,
And am well ſtudied for a liberall thanks,
Which I do owe you.
  Pom. Let me haue your hand:
I did not thinke Sir, to haue met you heere.
  Ant. The beds i'th'Eaſt are ſoft, and thanks to you,
That cal'd me timelier then my purpoſe hither:
For I haue gained by't.
  Cæſar. Since I ſaw you laſt, ther's a change vpon you.
  Pom. Well, I know not,
What counts harſh Fortune caſt's vpon my face,
But in my boſome ſhall ſhe neuer come,
To make my heart her vaſſaile.
  Lep. Well met heere.
  Pom. I hope ſo *Lepidus*, thus we are agreed:
I craue our compoſion may be written
And ſeal'd betweene vs.
  Cæſar. That's the next to do.
  Pom. Weele feaſt each other, ere we part, and let's
Draw lots who ſhall begin.
  Ant. That will I *Pompey*.
  Pompey. No *Anthony* take the lot: but firſt or laſt,
your fine Egyptian cookerie ſhall haue the fame, I haue
heard that *Iulius Cæſar*, grew fat with feaſting there.
  Anth. You haue heard much.
  Pom. I haue faire meaning Sir.
  Ant. And faire words to them.
  Pom. Then ſo much haue I heard,
And I haue heard *Appolodorus* carried——
  Eno. No more that: he did ſo.
  Pom. What I pray you?
  Eno. A certaine Queene to *Cæſar* in a Matris.
  Pom. I know thee now, how far'ſt thou Souldier?
  Eno. Well, and well am like to do, for I perceiue

The Tragedie of

Foure Feasts are toward.

Pom. Let me shake thy hand,
I neuer hated thee: I haue seene thee fight,
When I haue enuied thy behauiour.

Enob. Sir, I neuer lou'd you much, but I ha'prais'd ye,
When you haue well deseru'd ten times as much,
As I haue said you did.

Pom. Inioy thy plainnesse,
It nothing ill becomes thee:
Aboord my Gally, I inuite you all.
Will you leade Lords?

All. Shew's the way, sir.

Pom. Come. *Exeunt. Manet Enob. & Menas*

Men. Thy Father *Pompey* would ne're haue made this Treaty. You, and I haue knowne sir.

Enob. At Sea, I thinke.

Men. We haue Sir.

Enob. You haue done well by water.

Men. And you by Land.

Enob. I will praise any man that will praise me, thogh it cannot be denied what I haue done by Land.

Men. Nor what I haue done by water.

Enob. Yes some-thing you can deny for your owne safety: you haue bin a great Theefe by Sea.

Men. And you by Land.

Enob. There I deny my Land seruice: but giue mee your hand *Menas*, if our eyes had authority, heere they might take two Theeues kissing.

Men. All mens faces are true, whatsomere their hands are.

Enob. But there is neuer a fayre Woman, ha's a true Face.

Men. No slander, they steale hearts.

Enob. We came hither to fight with you.

Men. For my part, I am sorry it is turn'd to a Drinking. *Pompey* doth this day laugh away his Fortune.

Enob. If he do, sure he cannot weep't backe againe.

Men. Y'haue said Sir, we look'd not for *Marke Anthony* heere, pray you, is he married to *Cleopatra*?

Enob. Cæsars Sister is call'd *Octauia*.

Men. True Sir, she was the wife of *Caius Marcellus*.

Enob. But she is now the wife of *Marcus Anthonius*.

Men. Pray'ye sir.

Enob. 'Tis true.

Men. Then is *Cæsar* and he, for euer knit together.

Enob. If I were bound to Diuine of this vnity, I wold not Prophesie so.

Men. I thinke the policy of that purpose, made more in the Marriage, then the loue of the parties.

Enob. I thinke so too. But you shall finde the band that seemes to tye their friendship together, will bee the very strangler of their Amity: *Octauia* is of a holy, cold, and still conuersation.

Men. Who would not haue his wife so?

Eno. Not he that himselfe is not so: which is *Marke Anthony*: he will to his Egyptian dish againe: then shall the sighes of *Octauia* blow the fire vp in *Cæsar*, and (as I said before) that which is the strength of their Amity, shall proue the immediate Author of their variance. *Anthony* will vse his affection where it is. Hee married but his occasion heere.

Men. And thus it may be. Come Sir, will you aboord? I haue a health for you.

Enob. I shall take it sir: we haue vs'd our Throats in Egypt.

Men. Come, let's away. *Exeunt.*

Musicke playes.
Enter two or three Seruants with a Banket.

1. Heere they'l be man: some o'th'their Plants are ill rooted already, the least winde i'th'world wil blow them downe.

2. *Lepidus* is high Conlord.

1. They haue made him drinke Almes drinke.

2. As they pinch one another by the disposition, hee cries out, no more; reconciles them to his entreatie, and himselfe to'th'drinke.

1. But it raises the greater warre betweene him & his discretion.

2. Why this it is to haue a name in great mens Fellowship: I had as liue haue a Reede that will doe me no seruice, as a Partizan I could not heaue.

1. To be call'd into a huge Sphere, and not to be seene to moue in't, are the holes where eyes should bee, which pittifully disaster the cheekes.

A Sennet sounded.
Enter Cæsar, Anthony, Pompey, Lepidus, Agrippa, Mecenas, Enobarbus, Menes, with other Captaines.

Ant. Thus do they Sir: they take the flow o'th'Nyle By certaine scales i'th'Pyramid: they know
By'th'height, the lownesse, or the meane: If dearth
Or Foizon follow. The higher Nilus swels,
The more it promises: as it ebbes, the Seedsman
Vpon the slime and Ooze scatters his graine,
And shortly comes to Haruest.

Lep. Y'haue strange Serpents there?

Anth. I *Lepidus*.

Lep. Your Serpent of Egypt, is bred now of your mud by the operation of your Sun: so is your Crocodile.

Ant. They are so.

Pom. Sit, and some Wine: A health to *Lepidus*.

Lep. I am not so well as I should be:
But Ile ne're out.

Enob. Not till you haue slept: I feare me you'l bee in till then.

Lep. Nay certainly, I haue heard the *Ptolomies* Pyramisis are very goodly things: without contradiction I haue heard that.

Menas. Pompey, a word.

Pomp. Say in mine eare, what is't.

Men. Forsake thy seate I do beseech thee Captaine, And heare me speake a word.

Pom. Forbeare me till anon. *Whispers in's Eare.*
This Wine for *Lepidus*.

Lep. What manner o'thing is your Crocodile?

Ant. It is shap'd sir like it selfe, and it is as broad as it hath bredth; It is iust so high as it is, and mooues with it owne organs. It liues by that which nourisheth it, and the Elements once out of it, it Transmigrates.

Lep. What colour is it of?

Ant. Of it owne colour too.

Lep. 'Tis a strange Serpent.

Ant. 'Tis so, and the teares of it are wet.

Cæs. Will this description satisfie him?

Ant. With the Health that *Pompey* giues him, else he is a very Epicure.

Pomp. Go hang sir, hang: tell me of that? Away: Do as I bid you. Where's this Cup I call'd for?

Men. If for the sake of Merit thou wilt heare mee,
Rise

Anthony and Cleopatra.

Rise from thy stoole.

Pom. I thinke th'art mad: the matter?

Men. I haue euer held my cap off to thy Fortunes.

Pom. Thou hast seru'd me with much faith: what's else to say? Be iolly Lords.

Anth. These Quicke-sands *Lepidus*,
Keepe off, them for you sinke.

Men. Wilt thou be Lord of all the world?

Pom. What saist thou?

Men. Wilt thou be Lord of the whole world?
That's twice.

Pom. How should that be?

Men. But entertaine it, and though thou thinke me poore, I am the man will giue thee all the world.

Pom. Hast thou drunke well.

Men. No *Pompey*, I haue kept me from the cup,
Thou art if thou dar'st be, the earthly Ioue:
What ere the Ocean pales, or skie inclippes,
Is thine, if thou wilt ha't.

Pom. Shew me which way?

Men. These three World-sharers, these Competitors
Are in thy vessell. Let me cut the Cable,
And when we are put off, fall to their throates:
All there is thine.

Pom. Ah, this thou shouldst haue done,
And not haue spoke on't. In me 'tis villanie,
In thee,'t had bin good seruice: thou must know,
'Tis not my profit that does lead mine Honour:
Mine Honour it, Repent that ere thy tongue,
Hath so betraide thine acte. Being done vnknowne,
I should haue found it afterwards well done,
But must condemne it now: desist, and drinke.

Men. For this, Ile neuer follow.
Thy paul'd Fortunes more,
Who seekes and will not take, when once 'tis offer'd,
Shall neuer finde it more.

Pom. This health to *Lepidus*.

Ant. Beare him ashore,
Ile pledge it for him *Pompey*.

Eno. Heere's to thee *Menas*.

Men. *Enobarbus*, welcome.

Pom. Fill till the cup be hid.

Eno. There's a strong Fellow *Menas*.

Men. Why?

Eno. A beares the third part of the world man: seest not?

Men. The third part, then he is drunk: would it were all, that it might go on wheeles.

Eno. Drinke thou: encrease the Reeles.

Men Come.

Pom. This is not yet an Alexandrian Feast.

Ant. It ripen's towards it: strike the Vessells hoa.
Heere's to *Cæsar*.

Cæsar. I could well forbear't, it's monstrous labour when I wash my braine, and it grow fouler.

Ant. Be a Child o'th'time.

Cæsar. Possesse it, Ile make answer: but I had rather fast from all, foure dayes, then drinke so much in one.

Enob. Ha my braue Emperour, shall we daunce now the Egyptian Backenals, and celebrate our drinke?

Pom. Let's ha't good Souldier.

Ant. Come, let's all take hands,
Till that the conquering Wine hath steep't our sense,
In soft and delicate Lethe.

Eno. All take hands:
Make battery to our eares with the loud Musicke,
The while, Ile place you, then the Boy shall sing.
The holding euery man shall beate as loud,
As his strong sides can volly.

Musicke Playes. *Enobarbus places them hand in hand.*

The Song.

Come thou Monarch of the Vine,
Plumpie Bacchus, with pinke eyne:
In thy Fattes our Cares be drown'd,
With thy Grapes our haires be Crown'd.
    Cup vs till the world go round,
    Cup vs till the world go round.

Cæsar. What would you more?
Pompey goodnight. Good Brother
Let me request you of our grauer businesse
Frownes at this leuitie. Gentle Lords let's part,
You see we haue burnt out our cheekes. Strong *Enobarbe*
Is weaker then the Wine, and mine owne tongue
Spleet's what it speakes: the wilde disguise hath almost
Antickt vs all. What needs more words? goodnight.
Good *Anthony* your hand.

Pom. Ile try you on the shore.

Anth. And shall Sir, giues your hand.

Pom. Oh *Anthony*, you haue my Father house.
But what, we are Friends?
Come downe into the Boate.

Eno. Take heed you fall not *Menas*: Ile not on shore,
No to my Cabin: these Drummes,
These Trumpets, Flutes: what
Let Neptune heare, we bid aloud farewell
To these great Fellowes. Sound and be hang'd, sound out.

Sound a Flourish with Drummes.

Enor. Hoo saies a there's my Cap.

Men. Hoa, Noble Captaine, come. *Exeunt.*

Enter Ventidius as it were in triumph, the dead body of Pacorus borne before him.

Ven. Now darting Parthya art thou stroke, and now
Pleas'd Fortune does of *Marcus Crassus* death
Make me reuenger. Beare the Kings Sonnes body,
Before our Army, thy *Pacorus* Orades,
Paies this for *Marcus Crassus*.

Romaine. Noble *Ventidius*,
Whil'st yet with Parthian blood thy Sword is warme,
The Fugitiue Parthians follow. Spurre through Media,
Mesapotamia, and the shelters, whether
The routed flie. So thy grand Captaine *Anthony*
Shall set thee on triumphant Chariots, and
Put Garlands on thy head.

Ven. Oh *Sillius, Sillius*,
I haue done enough. A lower place note well
May make too great an act. For learne this *Sillius*,
Better to leaue vndone, then by our deed
Acquire too high a Fame, when him we serues away.
Cæsar and *Anthony*, haue euer wonne
More in their officer, then person. *Sossius*
One of my place in Syria, his Lieutenant,
For quicke accumulation of renowne,
Which he atchiu'd by'th'minute, lost his fauour.
Who does i'th'Warres more then his Captaine can,
Becomes his Captaines Captaine: and Ambition
(The Souldiers vertue) rather makes choise of losse
Then gaine, which darkens him.
I could do more to do *Anthonius* good,
But 'twould offend him. And in his offence,

Should

Should my performance perish.

Rom. Thou hast *Ventidius* that, without the which a Souldier and his Sword graunts scarce distinction : thou wilt write to *Anthony*.

Ven. Ile humbly signifie what in his name,
That magicall word of Warre we haue effected,
How with his Banners, and his well paid ranks,
The nere-yet beaten Horse of Parthia,
We haue iaded out o'th' Field.

Rom. Where is he now?

Ven. He purposeth to Athens, whither with what hast
The waight we must conuay with's, will permit :
We shall appeare before him. On there, passe along.
Exeunt.

Enter Agrippa at one doore, Enobarbus at another.

Agri. What are the Brothers parted?

Eno. They haue dispatcht with *Pompey*, he is gone,
The other three are Sealing. *Octauia* weepes
To part from Rome : *Cæsar* is sad, and *Lepidus*
Since *Pompey's* feast, as *Menas* saies, is troubled
With the Greene-Sicknesse.

Agri. 'Tis a Noble *Lepidus*.

Eno. A very fine one : oh, how he loues *Cæsar*.

Agri. Nay but how deerely he adores *Mark Anthony*.

Eno. *Cæsar*? why he's the Iupiter of men.

Ant. What's *Anthony*, the God of Iupiter?

Eno. Spake you of *Cæsar*? How, the nou-pareill?

Agri. Oh *Anthony*, oh thou Arabian Bird!

Eno. Would you praise *Cæsar*, say *Cæsar* go no further.

Agr. Indeed he plied them both with excellent praises.

Eno. But he loues *Cæsar* best, yet he loues *Anthony* :
Hoo, Hearts, Tongues, Figure,
Scribes, Bards, Poets, cannot
Thinke speake, cast, write, sing, number : hoo,
His loue to *Anthony*. But as for *Cæsar*,
Kneele downe, kneele downe, and wonder.

Agri. Both he loues.

Eno. They are his Shards, and he their Beetle, so:
This is to horse : Adieu, Noble *Agrippa*.

Agri. Good Fortune worthy Souldier, and farewell.

Enter Cæsar, Anthony, Lepidus, and Octauia.

Antho. No further Sir.

Cæsar. You take from me a great part of my selfe:
Vse me well in't. Sister, proue such a wife
As my thoughts make thee, and as my fartheft Band
Shall passe on thy approofe : most Noble *Anthony*,
Let not the peece of Vertue which is set
Betwixt vs, as the Cyment of our loue
To keepe it builded, be the Ramme to batter
The Fortresse of it : for better might we
Haue lou'd without this meane, if onboth parts
This be not cherisht.

Ant. Make me not offended, in your distrust.

Cæsar. I haue said.

Ant. You shall not finde,
Though you be therein curious, the left cause
For what you seeme to feare, so the Gods keepe you,
And make the hearts of Romaines serue your ends :
We will heere part.

Cæsar. Farewell my deerest Sister, fare thee well,
The Elements be kind to thee, and make
Thy spirits all of comfort : fare thee well.

Octa. My Noble Brother.

Anth. The Aprill's in her eyes, it is Loues spring,
And these the showers to bring it on : be cheerfull.

Octa. Sir, looke well to my Husbands house : and

Cæsar. What *Octauia*?

Octa. Ile tell you in your eare.

Ant. Her tongue will not obey her heart, nor can
Her heart informe her tougne.
The Swannes downe feather
That stands vpon the Swell at the full of Tide :
And neither way inclines.

Eno. Will *Cæsar* weepe?

Agr. He ha's a cloud in's face.

Eno. He were the worse for that were he a Horse, so is he being a man.

Agri. Why *Enobarbus*:
When *Anthony* found *Iulius Cæsar* dead,
He cried almost to roaring : And he wept,
When at Phillippi he found *Brutus* slaine.

Eno. That yearindeed, he was trobled with a rheume,
What willingly he did confound, he wail'd,
Beleeu't till I weepe too.

Cæsar. No sweet *Octauia*,
You shall heare from me still : the time shall not
Out-go my thinking on you.

Ant. Come Sir, come,
Ile wrastle with you in my strength of loue,
Looke heere I haue you, thus I let you go,
And giue you to the Gods.

Cæsar. Adieu, be happy.

Lep. Let all the number of the Starres giue light
To thy faire way.

Cæsar. Farewell, farewell. *Kisses Octauia.*

Ant. Farewell. *Trumpets sound. Exeunt.*

Enter Cleopatra, Charmian, Iras, and Alexas.

Cleo. Where is the Fellow?

Alex. Halfe afeard to come.

Cleo. Go too, go too : Come hither Sir.

Enter the Messenger as before.

Alex. Good Maiestie: *Herod* of Iury dare not looke vpon you, but when you are well-pleas'd.

Cleo. That *Herods* head, Ile haue : but how? When *Anthony* is gone, through whom I might commaund it:
Come thou neere.

Mes. Most gratious Maiestie.

Cleo. Did'st thou behold *Octauia*?

Mes. I dread Queene.

Cleo. Where?

Mes. Madam in Rome, I lookt her in the face : and saw her led betweene her Brother, and *Marke Anthony*.

Cleo. Is she as tall as me?

Mes. She is not Madam.

Cleo. Didst heare her speake?
Is she shrill tongu'd or low?

Mes. Madam, I heard her speake, she is low voic'd.

Cleo. That's not so good : he cannot like her long.

Char. Like her? Oh *Isis* : 'tis impossible.

Cleo. I thinke so *Charmian*: dull of tongue, & dwarfish
What Maiestie is in her gate, remember
If ere thou look'st on Maiestie.

Mes. She creepes: her motion, & her station are as one:
She shewes a body, rather then a life,
A Statue, then a Breather.

Cleo. Is this certaine?

Mes. Or I haue no obseruance.

Cha. Three in Egypt cannot make better note.

Cleo. He's very knowing, I do perceiu't,
There's nothing in her yet.

The Fellow ha's good iudgement.

Char. Excellent.

Cleo. Guesse at her yeares, I prythee.

Mess. Madam, she was a widdow.

Cleo. Widdow? *Charmian*, hearke.

Mes. And I do thinke she's thirtie.

Cle. Bear'st thou her face in mind? is't long or round?

Mess. Round, euen to faultinesse.

Cleo. For the most part too, they are foolish that are so. Her haire what colour?

Mess. Browne Madam: and her forehead
As low as she would wish it.

Cleo. There's Gold for thee,
Thou must not take my former sharpenesse ill,
I will employ thee backe againe: I finde thee
Most fit for businesse. Go, make thee ready,
Our Letters are prepar'd.

Char. A proper man.

Cleo. Indeed he is so: I repent me much
That so I harried him. Why me think's by him,
This Creature's no such thing.

Char. Nothing Madam.

Cleo. The man hath seene some Maiesty, and should know.

Char. Hath he seene Maiestie? *Isis* else defend: and seruing you so long.

Cleopa. I haue one thing more to aske him yet good *Charmian*: but 'tis no matter, thou shalt bring him to me where I will write, all may be well enough.

Char. I warrant you Madam. *Exeunt.*

Enter Anthony and Octauia.

Ant. Nay, nay *Octauia*, not onely that,
That were excusable, that and thousands more
Of semblable import, but he hath wag'd
New Warres 'gainst *Pompey*. Made his will, and read it,
To publicke care, spoke scantly of me,
When perforce he could not
But pay me tearmes of Honour: cold and sickly
He vented then most narrow measure, lent me,
When the best hint was giuen him: he not look't,
Or did it from his teeth.

Octaui. Oh my good Lord,
Beleeue not all, or if you must beleeue,
Stomacke not all. A more vnhappie Lady,
If this deuision chance, ne're stood betweene
Praying for both parts:
The good Gods wil mocke me presently,
When I shall pray: Oh blesse my Lord and Husband,
Vndo that prayer, by crying out as loud,
Oh blesse my Brother. Husband winne, winne Brother,
Prayes, and distroyes the prayer, no midway
'Twixt these extreames at all.

Ant. Gentle *Octauia*,
Let your best loue draw to that point which seeks
Best to preserue it: if I loose mine Honour,
I loose my selfe: better I were not yours
Then your so branchlesse. But as you requested,
Your selfe shall go between's, the meane time Lady,
Ile raise the preparation of a Warre
Shall staine your Brother, make your soonest hast,
So your desires are yours.

Oct. Thankes to my Lord,
The loue of power make me most weake, most weake,
You reconciler: Warres 'twixt you twaine would be,
As if the world should cleaue, and that slaine men
Should soader vp the Rift.

Anth. When it appeeres to you where this begins,
Turne your displeasure that way, for our faults
Can neuer be so equall, that your loue
Can equally moue with them. Prouide your going,
Choose your owne company, and command what cost
Your heart he's mind too. *Exeunt.*

Enter Enobarbus, and Eros.

Eno. How now Friend *Eros*?

Eros. Ther's strange Newes come Sir.

Eno. What man?

Eros. Cæsar & *Lepidus* haue made warres vpon *Pompey*.

Eno. This is old, what is the successe?

Eros. Cæsar hauing made vse of him in the warres 'gainst *Pompey*: presently denied him riuality, would not let him partake in the glory of the action, and not resting here, accuses him of Letters he had formerly wrote to *Pompey*. Vpon his owne appeale seizes him, so the poore third is vp, till death enlarge his Confine.

Eno. Then would thou hadst a paire of chapsn o more, and throw betweene them all the food thou hast, they'le grinde the other. Where's *Anthony*?

Eros. He's walking in the garden thus, and spurnes
The rush that lies before him. Cries Foole *Lepidus*,
And threats the throate of that his Officer,
That murdred *Pompey*.

Eno. Our great Nauies rig'd.

Eros. For Italy and *Cæsar*, more *Domitius*,
My Lord desires you presently: my Newes
I might haue told heareafter.

Eno. 'Twillbe naught, but let it be: bring me to *Anthony*.

Eros. Come Sir. *Exeunt.*

Enter Agrippa, Mecenas, and Cæsar.

Cæs. Contemning Rome he ha's done all this, & more
In Alexandria: heere's the manner of't:
I'th' Market-place on a Tribunall siluer'd,
Cleopatra and himselfe in Chaires of Gold
Were publikely enthron'd: at the feet, sat
Cæsarion whom they call my Fathers Sonne,
And all the vnlawfull issue, that their Lust
Since then hath made betweene them. Vnto her,
He gaue the stablishment of Egypt, made her
Of lower Syria, Cyprus, Lydia, absolute Queene.

Mece. This in the publike eye?

Cæsar. I'th' common shew place, where they exercise,
His Sonnes hither proclaimed the King of Kings,
Great Media, Parthia, and Armenia
He gaue to *Alexander*. To *Ptolomy* he assign'd,
Syria, Silicia, and Phœnetia: she
In th'abiliments of the Goddesse *Isis*
That day appeer'd, and oft before gaue audience,
As 'tis reported so.

Mece. Let Rome be thus inform'd.

Agri. Who queazie with his insolence already,
Will their good thoughts call from him.

Cæsar. The people knowes it,
And haue now receiu'd his accusations.

Agri. Who does he accuse?

Cæsar. Cæsar, and that hauing in Cicilie
Sextus Pompeius spoil'd, we had not rated him
His part o'th' Isle. Then does he say, he lent me
Some shipping vnrestor'd. Lastly, he frets
That *Lepidus* of the Triumpherate, should be depos'd,
And being that, we detaine all his Reuenue.

Agri. Sir, this should be answer'd.

Cæsar. 'Tis done already, and the Messenger gone:
I haue told him *Lepidus* was growne too cruell,

That he his high Authority abus'd,
And did deserue his change: for what I haue conquer'd,
I grant him part: but then in his Armenia,
And other of his conquer'd Kingdoms, I demand the like

Mec. Hee'l neuer yeeld to that.

Cæs. Nor must not then be yeelded to in this.

Enter Octauia with her Traine.

Octa. Haile *Cæsar*, and my L. haile most deere *Cæsar*.

Cæsar. That euer I should call thee Cast-away:

Octa. You haue not call'd me so, nor haue you cause.

Cæs. Why haue you stoln vpon vs thus? you come not
Like *Cæsars* Sister, The wife of *Anthony*
Should haue an Army for an Vsher, and
The neighes of Horse to tell of her approach,
Long ere she did appeare. The trees by th'way
Should haue borne men, and expectation fainted,
Longing for what it had not. Nay, the dust
Should haue ascended to the Roofe of Heauen,
Rais'd by your populous Troopes: But you are come
A Market-maid to Rome, and haue preuented
The ostentation of our loue; which left vnshewne,
Is often left vnlou'd: we should haue met you
By Sea, and Land, supplying euery Stage
With an augmented greeting.

Octa. Good my Lord,
To come thus was I not constrain'd, but did it
On my free-will. My Lord *Marke Anthony*,
Hearing that you prepar'd for Warre, acquainted
My grieued eare withall: whereon I begg'd
His pardon for returne.

Cæs. Which soone he granted,
Being an abstract 'tweene his Lust, and him.

Octa. Do not say so, my Lord.

Cæs. I haue eyes vpon him,
And his affaires come to me on the wind: wher is he now?

Octa. My Lord, in Athens.

Cæsar. No my most wronged Sister, *Cleopatra*
Hath nodded him to her. He hath giuen his Empire
Vp to a Whore, who now are leuying
The Kings o'th' earth for Warre. He hath assembled,
Bochus the King of Lybia, *Archilaus*
Of Cappadocia, *Philadelphos* King
Of Paphlagonia: the Thracian King *Adallas*,
King *Mauchus* of Arabia, King of Pont,
Herod of Iewry, *Mithridates* King
Of Comageat, *Polemen* and *Amintas*,
The Kings of Mede, and Licoania,
With a more larger List of Scepters.

Octa. Aye me most wretched,
That haue my heart parted betwixt two Friends,
That does afflict each other. (*breaking forth*

Cæs. Welcom hither: your Letters did with-holde our
Till we perceiu'd both how you were wrong led,
And we in negligent danger: cheere your heart,
Be you not troubled with the time, which driues
O're your content, these strong necessities,
But let determin'd things to destinie
Hold vnbewayl'd their way. Welcome to Rome,
Nothing more deere to me: You are abus'd
Beyond the marke of thought: and the high Gods
To do you Iustice, makes his Ministers
Of vs, and those that loue you. Best of comfort,
And euer welcom to vs.   *Agrip.* Welcome Lady.

Mec. Welcome deere Madam,
Each heart in Rome does loue and pitty you,
Onely th'adulterous *Anthony*, most large
In his abhominations, turnes you off,
And giues his potent Regiment to a Trull
That noyses it against vs.

Octa. Is it so sir?

Cæs. Most certaine: Sister welcome: pray you
Be euer knowne to patience. My deer'st Sister. *Exeunt*

Enter Cleopatra, and Enobarbus.

Cleo. I will be euen with thee, doubt it not.

Eno. But why, why, why?

Cleo. Thou hast forespoke my being in these warres,
And say'st it it not fit.

Eno. Well: is it, is it.

Cleo. If not, denounc'd against vs, why should not
we be there in person.

Enob. Well, I could reply: if wee should serue with
Horse and Mares together, the Horse were meerly lost:
the Mares would beare a Soldiour and his Horse.

Cleo. What is't you say?

Enob. Your presence needs must puzle *Anthony*,
Take from his heart, take from his Braine, from's time,
What should not then be spar'd. He is already
Traduc'd for Leuity, and 'tis said in Rome,
That *Photinus* an Eunuch, and your Maides
Mannage this warre.

Cleo. Sinke Rome, and their tongues rot
That speake against vs. A Charge we beare i'th' Warre,
And as the president of my Kingdome will
Appeare there for a man. Speake not against it,
I will not stay behinde.

Enter Anthony and Camidias.

Eno. Nay I haue done, here comes the Emperor.

Ant. Is it not strange *Camidius*,
That from Tarrentum, and Brandusium,
He could so quickly cut the Ionian Sea,
And take in Troine. You haue heard on't (Sweet?)

Cleo. Celerity is neuer more admir'd,
Then by the negligent.

Ant. A good rebuke,
Which might haue well becom'd the best of men
To taunt at slacknesse. *Camidius*, wee
Will fight with him by Sea.

Cleo. By Sea, what else?

Cam. Why will my Lord, do so?

Ant. For that he dares vs too't.

Enob. So hath my Lord, dar'd him to single fight.

Cam. I, and to wage this Battell at Pharsalia,
Where *Cæsar* fought with *Pompey*. But these offers
Which serue not for his vantage, he shakes off,
And so should you.

Enob. Your Shippes are not well mann'd,
Your Marriners are Militers, Reapers, people
Ingrost by swift Impresse. In *Cæsars* Fleete,
Are those, that often haue 'gainst *Pompey* fought,
Their shippes are yare, yours heauy: no disgrace
Shall fall you for refusing him at Sea,
Being prepar'd for Land.

Ant. By Sea, by Sea.

Eno. Most worthy Sir, you therein throw away
The absolute Soldiership you haue by Land,
Distract your Armie, which doth most consist
Of Warre-markt-footmen, leaue vnexecuted
Your owne renowned knowledge, quite forgoe
The way which promises assurance, and
Giue vp your selfe meerly to chance and hazard,
From firme Securitie.

Ant. Ile fight at Sea.

Cleo. I haue sixty Sailes. *Cæsar* none better.

Ant. Our ouer-plus of shipping will we burne,
And with the rest full mann'd, from th'head of Action
Beate th'approaching *Cæsar*. But if we faile,
We then can doo't at Land.   *Enter a Messenger.*
Thy Businesse?

Mes. The Newes is true, my Lord, he is descried,
Cæsar ha's taken Toryne.

Ant. Can he be there in person? 'Tis impossible
Strange, that his power should be. *Camidius*,
Our nineteene Legions thou shalt hold by Land,
And our twelue thousand Horse. Wee'l to our Ship,
Away my *Thetis*.

Enter a Souldier.

How now worthy Souldier?

Sould. Oh Noble Emperor, do not fight by Sea,
Trust not to rotten plankes: Do you misdoubt
This Sword, and these my Wounds; let th'Egyptians
And the Phœnicians go a ducking: wee
Haue vs'd to conquer standing on the earth,
And fighting foot to foot.

Ant. Well, well, away.   *exit Ant. Cleo. & Enob.*

Soul. By *Hercules* I thinke I am i'th'right.

Cam. Souldier thou art: but his whole action growes
Not in the power on't: so our Leaders leade,
And we are Womens men.

Soul. You keepe by Land the Legions and the Horse
whole, do you not?

Ven. *Marcus Octauius*, *Marsus Iusteus*,
Publicola, and *Celius*, are for Sea:
But we keepe whole by Land. This speede of *Cæsars*
Carries beyond beleefe.

Soul. While he was yet in Rome,
His power went out in such distractions,
As beguilde all Spies.

Cam. Who's his Lieutenant, heare you?

Soul. They say, one *Towrus*.

Cam. Well, I know the man.

Enter a Messenger.

Mes. The Emperor cals *Camidius*.

Cam. With Newes the times with Labour,
And throwes forth each minute, some.   *exeunt*

Enter Cæsar with his Army, marching.

Cæs. *Towrus*?

Tow. My Lord.

Cæs. Strike not by Land,
Keepe whole, prouoke not Battaile
Till we haue done at Sea. Do not exceede
The Prescript of this Scroule: Our fortune lyes
Vpon this iumpe.   *exit.*

Enter Anthony, and Enobarbus.

Ant. Set we our Squadrons on yond side o'th'Hill,
In eye of *Cæsars* battaile, from which place
We may the number of the Ships behold,
And so proceed accordingly.   *exit.*

Camidius Marcheth with his Land Army one way ouer the stage, and Towrus the Lieutenant of Cæsar the other way: After their going in, is heard the noise of a Sea-fight.

Alarum. Enter Enobarbus and Scarus.

Eno. Naught, naught, al naught, I can behold no longer:
Thantoniad, the Egyptian Admirall,
With all their sixty flye, and turne the Rudder:
To see't, mine eyes are blasted.

Enter Scarrus.

Scar. Gods, & Goddesses, all the whol synod of them!

Eno. What's thy passion.

Scar. The greater Cantle of the world, is lost
With very ignorance, we haue kist away
Kingdomes, and Prouinces.

Eno. How appeares the Fight?

Scar. On our side, like the Token'd Pestilence,
Where death is sure. Yon ribaudred Nagge of Egypt,
(Whom Leprosie o're-take) i'th'midst o'th'fight,
When vantage like a payre of Twinnes appear'd
Both as the same, or rather ours the elder;
(The Breeze vpon her) like a Cow in Iune,
Hoists Sailes, and flyes.

Eno. That I beheld:
Mine eyes did sicken at the sight, and could not
Indure a further view.

Scar. She once being loost,
The Noble ruine of her Magicke, *Anthony*,
Claps on his Sea-wing, and (like a doting Mallard)
Leauing the Fight in heighth, flyes after her:
I neuer saw an Action of such shame;
Experience, Man-hood, Honor, ne're before,
Did violate so it selfe.

Enob. Alacke, alacke.

Enter Camidius.

Cam. Our Fortune on the Sea is out of breath,
And sinkes most lamentably. Had our Generall
Bin what he knew himselfe, it had gone well:
Oh his ha's giuen example for our flight,
Most grossely by his owne.

Enob. I, are you thereabouts? Why then goodnight indeede.

Cam. Toward Peloponnesus are they fled.

Scar. 'Tis easie toot,
And there I will attend what further comes.

Camid. To *Cæsar* will I render
My Legions and my Horse, sixe Kings alreadie
Shew me the way of yeelding.

Eno. Ile yet follow
The wounded chance of *Anthony*, though my reason
Sits in the winde against me.

Enter Anthony with Attendants.

Ant. Hearke, the Land bids me tread no more vpon't,
It is asham'd to beare me. Friends, come hither,
I am so lated in the world, that I
Haue lost my way for euer. I haue a shippe,
Laden with Gold, take that, diuide it: flye,
And make your peace with *Cæsar*.

Omnes. Fly? Not wee.

Ant. I haue fled my selfe, and haue instructed cowards
To runne, and shew their shoulders. Friends be gone,
I haue my selfe resolu'd vpon a course,
Which has no neede of you. Be gone,
My Treasure's in the Harbour. Take it: Oh,
I follow'd that I blush to looke vpon,
My very haires do mutiny: for the white
Reproue the browne for rashnesse, and they them
For feare, and doting. Friends be gone, you shall
Haue Letters from me to some Friends, that will
Sweepe your way for you. Pray you looke not sad,
Nor make replyes of loathnesse, take the hint
Which my dispaire proclaimes. Let them be left
Which leaues it selfe, to the Sea-side straight way;
I will possesse you of that ship and Treasure.

Leaue me, I pray a little: pray you now,
Nay do so: for indeede I haue lost command,
Therefore I pray you, Ile see you by and by. *Sits downe*

Enter Cleopatra led by Charmian and Eros.

Eros. Nay gentle Madam, to him, comfort him.

Iras. Do most deere Queene.

Char. Do, why, what else?

Cleo. Let me sit downe: Oh *Iuno*.

Ant. No, no, no, no, no.

Eros. See you heere, Sir?

Ant. Oh fie, fie, fie.

Char. Madam.

Iras. Madam, oh good Empresse.

Eros. Sir, sir.

Ant. Yes my Lord, yes; he at Philippi kept
His sword e'ne like a dancer, while I strooke
The leane and wrinkled *Cassius*, and 'twas I
That the mad *Brutus* ended: he alone
Dealt on Lieutenantry, and no practise had
In the braue squares of Warre: yet now: no matter.

Cleo. Ah stand by.

Eros. The Queene my Lord, the Queene.

Iras. Go to him, Madam, speake to him,
Hee's vnqualited with very shame.

Cleo. Well then, sustaine me: Oh.

Eros. Most Noble Sir arise, the Queene approaches,
Her head's declin'd, and death will cease her, but
Your comfort makes the rescue.

Ant. I haue offended Reputation,
A most vnnoble sweruing.

Eros. Sir, the Queene.

Ant. Oh whether hast thou lead me Egypt, see
How I conuey my shame, out of thine eyes,
By looking backe what I haue left behinde
Stroy'd in dishonor.

Cleo. Oh my Lord, my Lord,
Forgiue my fearfull sayles, I little thought
You would haue followed.

Ant. Egypt, thou knew'st too well,
My heart was to thy Rudder tyed by'th'strings,
And thou should'st stowe me after. O're my spirit
The full supremacie thou knew'st, and that
Thy becke, might from the bidding of the Gods
Command mee.

Cleo. Oh my pardon.

Ant. Now I must
To the young man send humble Treaties, dodge
And palter in the shifts of lownes, who
With halfe the bulke o'th'world plaid as I pleas'd,
Making, and marring Fortunes. You did know
How much you were my Conqueror, and that
My Sword, made weake by my affection, would
Obey it on all cause.

Cleo. Pardon, pardon.

Ant. Fall not a teare I say, one of them rates
All that is wonne and lost: Giue me a kisse,
Euen this repayes me.
We sent our Schoolemaster, is a come backe?
Loue I am full of Lead: some Wine
Within there, and our Viands: Fortune knowes,
We scorne her most, when most she offers blowes. *Exeunt*

Enter Cæsar, Agrippa, and Dollabello, with others.

Cæs. Let him appeare that's come from *Anthony*.
Know you him.

Dolla. *Cæsar*, 'tis his Schoolemaster,
An argument that he is pluckt, when hither
He sends so poore a Pinnion of his Wing,
Which had superfluous Kings for Messengers,
Not many Moones gone by.

Enter Ambassador from Anthony.

Cæsar. Approach, and speake.

Amb. Such as I am, I come from *Anthony*:
I was of late as petty to his ends,
As is the Morn-dew on the Mertle leafe
To his grand Sea.

Cæs. Bee't so, declare thine office.

Amb. Lord of his Fortunes he salutes thee, and
Requires to liue in Egypt, which not granted
He Lessons his Requests, and to thee sues
To let him breath betweene the Heauens and Earth
A priuate man in Athens: this for him.
Next, *Cleopatra* does confesse thy Greatnesse,
Submits her to thy might, and of thee craues
The Circle of the *Ptolomies* for her heyres,
Now hazarded to thy Grace.

Cæs. For *Anthony*,
I haue no eares to his request. The Queene,
Of Audience, nor Desire shall faile, so shee
From Egypt driue her all-disgraced Friend,
Or take his life there. This if shee performe,
She shall not sue vnheard. So to them both.

Amb. Fortune pursue thee.

Cæs. Bring him through the Bands:
To try thy Eloquence, now 'tis time, dispatch,
From *Anthony* winne *Cleopatra*, promise
And in our Name, what she requires, adde more
From thine inuention, offers. Women are not
In their best Fortunes strong; but want will periure
The ne're touch'd Vestall. Try thy cunning *Thidias*,
Make thine owne Edict for thy paines, which we
Will answer as a Law.

Thid. *Cæsar*, I go.

Cæsar. Obserue how *Anthony* becomes his flaw,
And what thou think'st his very action speakes
In euery power that mooues.

Thid. *Cæsar*, I shall. *exeunt.*

Enter Cleopatra, Enobarbus, Charmian, & Iras.

Cleo. What shall we do, *Enobarbus*?

Eno. Thinke, and dye.

Cleo. Is *Anthony*, or we in fault for this?

Eno. *Anthony* onely, that would make his will
Lord of his Reason. What though you fled,
From that great face of Warre, whose seuerall ranges
Frighted each other? Why should he follow?
The itch of his Affection should not then
Haue nickt his Captain-ship, at such a point,
When halfe to halfe the world oppos'd, he being
The meered question? 'Twas a shame no lesse
Then was his losse, to course your flying Flagges,
And leaue his Nauy gazing.

Cleo. Prythee peace.

Enter the Ambassador, with Anthony.

Ant. Is that his answer? *Amb.* I my Lord.

Ant. The Queene shall then haue courtesie,
So she will yeeld vs vp.

Am. He sayes so.

Antho. Let her know't. To the Boy *Cæsar* send this
grizled head, and he will fill thy wishes to the brimme,
With Principalities.

Cleo. That head my Lord?

Ant.

Anthony and Cleopatra.

Ant. To him againe, tell him he weares the Rose
Of youth vpon him: from which, the world should note
Something particular: His Coine, Ships, Legions,
May be a Cowards, whose Ministers would preuaile
Vnder the seruice of a Childe, as soone
As i'th'Command of *Cæsar*. I dare him therefore
To lay his gay Comparisons a-part,
And answer me declin'd, Sword against Sword,
Our selues alone: Ile write it: Follow me.

Eno. Yes like enough: hye battel'd *Cæsar* will
Vnstate his happinesse, and be Stag'd to'th'shew
Against a Sworder. I see mens Iudgements are
A parcell of their Fortunes, and things outward
Do draw the inward quality after them
To suffer all alike, that he should dreame,
Knowing all measures, the full *Cæsar* will
Answer his emptinesse; *Cæsar* thou hast subdu'de
His iudgement too.

Enter a Seruant.

Ser. A Messenger from *Cæsar*.

Cleo. What no more Ceremony? See my Women,
Against the blowne Rose may they stop their nose,
That kneel'd vnto the Buds. Admit him sir.

Eno. Mine honesty, and I, beginne to square,
The Loyalty well held to Fooles, does make
Our Faith meere folly: yet he that can endure
To follow with Allegeance a falne Lord,
Does conquer him that did his Master conquer,
And earnes a place i'th'Story.

Enter Thidias.

Cleo. *Cæsars* will.

Thid. Heare it apart.

Cleo. None but Friends: say boldly.

Thid. So haply are they Friends to *Anthony*.

Enob. He needs as many (Sir) as *Cæsar* ha's,
Or needs not vs. If *Cæsar* please, our Master
Will leape to be his Friend: For vs you know,
Whose he is, we are, and that is *Cæsars*.

Thid. So. Thus then thou most renown'd, *Cæsar* intreats,
Not to consider in what case thou stand'st
Further then he is *Cæsars*.

Cleo. Go on, right Royall.

Thid. He knowes that you embrace not *Anthony*
As you did loue, but as you feared him.

Cleo. Oh.

Thid. The scarre's vpon your Honor, therefore he
Does pitty, as constrained blemishes,
Not as deserued.

Cleo. He is a God,
And knowes what is most right. Mine Honour
Was not yeelded, but conquer'd meerely.

Eno. To be sure of that, I will aske *Anthony*.
Sir, sir, thou art so leakie
That we must leaue thee to thy sinking, for
Thy deerest quit thee.   *Exit Enob.*

Thid. Shall I say to *Cæsar*,
What you require of him: for he partly begges
To be desir'd to giue. It much would please him,
That of his Fortunes you should make a staffe
To leane vpon. But it would warme his spirits
To heare from me you had left *Anthony*,
And put your selfe vnder his shrowd, the vniuersal Land-
Cleo. What's your name?   (lord.
Thid. My name is *Thidias*.

Cleo. Most kinde Messenger,
Say to great *Cæsar* this in disputation,

I kisse his conqu'ring hand: Tell him, I am prompt
To lay my Crowne at's feete, and there to kneele.
Tell him, from his all-obeying breath, I heare
The doome of Egypt.

Thid. 'Tis your Noblest course:
Wisedome and Fortune combarting together,
If that the former dare but what it can,
No chance may shake it. Giue me grace to lay
My dutie on your hand.

Cleo. Your *Cæsars* Father oft,
(When he hath mus'd of taking kingdomes in)
Bestow'd his lips on that vnworthy place,
As it rain'd kisses.

Enter Anthony and Enobarbus.

Ant. Fauours? By Ioue that thunders. What art thou
Thid. One that but performes   (Fellow?
The bidding of the fullest man, and worthiest
To haue command obey'd.

Eno. You will be whipt.

Ant. Approch there: ah you Kite. Now Gods & diuels
Authority melts from me of late. When I cried hoa,
Like Boyes vnto a musse, Kings would start forth,
And cry, your will. Haue you no eares?
I am *Anthony* yet. Take hence this Iack, and whip him.

Enter a Seruant.

Eno. 'Tis better playing with a Lions whelpe,
Then with an old one dying.

Ant. Moone and Starres,
Whip him: wer't twenty of the greatest Tributaries
That do acknowledge *Cæsar*, should I finde them
So sawcy with the hand of she heere, what's her name
Since she was *Cleopatra*? Whip him Fellowes,
Till like a Boy you see him cridge his face,
And whine aloud for mercy. Take him hence.

Thid. Marke *Anthony*.

Ant. Tugge him away: being whipt
Bring him againe, the Iacke of *Cæsars* shall
Beare vs an arrant to him.   *Exeunt with Thidius.*
You were halfe blasted ere I knew you: Ha?
Haue I my pillow left vnprest in Rome,
Forborne the getting of a lawfull Race,
And by a iem of women, to be abus'd
By one that lookes on Feeders?

Cleo. Good my Lord.

Ant. You haue beene a boggeler euer,
But when we in our viciousnesse grow hard
(Oh misery on't) the wise Gods seele our eyes
In our owne filth, drop our cleare iudgements, make vs
Adore our errors, laugh at's while we strut
To our confusion.

Cleo. Oh, is't come to this?

Ant. I found you as a Morsell, cold vpon
Dead *Cæsars* Trencher: Nay, you were a Fragment
Of *Gneius Pompeyes*, besides what hotter houres
Vnregistred in vulgar Fame, you haue
Luxuriously pickt out. For I am sure,
Though you can guesse what Temperance should be,
You know not what it is.

Cleo. Wherefore is this?

Ant. To let a Fellow that will take rewards,
And say, God quit you, be familiar with
My play-fellow, your hand; this Kingly Seale,
And plighter of high hearts. O that I were
Vpon the hill of Basan, to out-roare
The horned Heard, for I haue sauage cause,
And to proclaime it ciuilly, were like

A halter'd necke, which do's the Hangman thanke,
For being yare about him. Is he whipt?

Enter a Seruant with Thidias.

Ser. Soundly, my Lord.
Ant. Cried he? and begg'd a Pardon?
Ser. He did aske fauour.
Ant. If that thy Father liue, let him repent
Thou was't not made his daughter, and be thou sorrie
To follow Cæsar in his Triumph, since
Thou hast bin whipt. For following him, henceforth
The white hand of a Lady Feauer thee,
Shake thou to looke on't. Get thee backe to Cæsar,
Tell him thy entertainment: looke thou say
He makes me angry with him. For he seemes
Proud and disdainfull, harping on what I am,
Not what he knew I was. He makes me angry,
And at this time most easie 'tis to doo't:
When my good Starres, that were my former guides
Haue empty left their Orbes, and shot their Fires
Into th' Abisme of hell. If he mislike,
My speech, and what is done, tell him he has
Hiparchus, my enfranched Bondman, whom
He may at pleasure whip, or hang, or torture,
As he shall like to quit me. Vrge it thou:
Hence with thy stripes, be gone. *Exit Thid.*

Cleo. Haue you done yet?
Ant. Alacke our Terrene Moone is now Eclipst,
And it portends alone the fall of Anthony.
Cleo. I must stay his time?
Ant. To flatter Cæsar, would you mingle eyes
With one that tyes his points.
Cleo. Not know me yet?
Ant. Cold-hearted toward me?
Cleo. Ah (Deere) if I be so,
From my cold heart let Heauen ingender haile,
And poyson it in the sourse, and the first stone
Drop in my necke: as it determines so
Dissolue my life, the next Cæsarian smile,
Till by degrees the memory of my wombe,
Together with my braue Egyptians all,
By the discandering of this pelleted storme,
Lye grauelesse, till the Flies and Gnats of Nyle
Haue buried them for prey.
Ant. I am satisfied:
Cæsar sets downe in Alexandria, where
I will oppose his Fate. Our force by Land,
Hath Nobly held, our seuer'd Nauie too
Haue knit againe, and Fleete, threatning most Sea-like.
Where hast thou bin my heart? Dost thou heare Lady?
If from the Field I shall returne once more
To kisse these Lips, I will appeare in Blood,
I, and my Sword, will earne our Chronicle,
There's hope in't yet.
Cleo. That's my braue Lord.
Ant. I will be trebble-sinewed, hearted, breath'd,
And fight maliciously: for when mine houres
Were nice and lucky, men did ransome liues
Of me for iests: But now, Ile set my teeth,
And send to darkenesse all that stop me. Come,
Let's haue one other gawdy night: Call to me
All my sad Captaines, fill our Bowles once more:
Let's mocke the midnight Bell.
Cleo. It is my Birth-day,
I had thought t'haue held it poore. But since my Lord
Is Anthony againe, I will be Cleopatra.
Ant. We will yet do well.

Cleo. Call all his Noble Captaines to my Lord,
Ant. Do so, wee'l speake to them,
And to night Ile force
The Wine peepe through their scarres:
Come on (my Queene)
There's sap in't yet. The next time I do fight
Ile make death loue me: for I will contend
Euen with his pestilent Sythe. *Exeunt.*

Eno. Now hee'l out-stare the Lightning, to be furious
Is to be frighted out of feare, and in that moode
The Doue will pecke the Estridge; and I see still
A diminution in our Captaines braine,
Restores his heart; when valour prayes in reason,
It eates the Sword it fights with: I will seeke
Some way to leaue him. *Exeunt.*

*Enter Cæsar, Agrippa, & Mecenas with his Army,
Cæsar reading a Letter.*

Cæs. He calles me Boy, and chides as he had power
To beate me out of Egypt. My Messenger
He hath whipt with Rods, dares me to personal Combat.
Cæsar to Anthony: let the old Ruffian know,
I haue many other wayes to dye: meane time
Laugh at his Challenge.
Mece. Cæsar must thinke,
When one so great begins to rage, hee's hunted
Euen to falling. Giue him no breath, but now
Make boote of his distraction: Neuer anger
Made good guard for it selfe.
Cæs. Let our best heads know,
That to morrow, the last of many Battailes
We meane to fight. Within our Files there are,
Of those that seru'd Marke Anthony but late,
Enough to fetch him in. See it done,
And Feast the Army, we haue store to doo't,
And they haue earn'd the waste. Poore Anthony. *Exeunt*

*Enter Anthony, Cleopatra, Enobarbus, Charmian,
Iras, Alexas, with others.*

Ant. He will not fight with me, Domitian?
Eno. No?
Ant. Why should he not?
Eno. He thinks, being twenty times of better fortune,
He is twenty men to one.
Ant. To morrow Soldier,
By Sea and Land Ile fight: or I will liue,
Or bathe my dying Honor in the blood
Shall make it liue againe. Woo't thou fight well.
Eno. Ile strike, and cry, Take all.
Ant. Well said, come on:
Call forth my Houshold Seruants, lets to night

Enter 3 or 4 Seruitors.

Be bounteous at our Meale. Giue me thy hand,
Thou hast bin rightly honest, so hast thou,
Thou, and thou, and thou: you haue seru'd me well,
And Kings haue beene your fellowes.
Cleo. What meanes this?
Eno. 'Tis one of those odde tricks which sorow shoots
Out of the minde.
Ant. And thou art honest too:
I wish I could be made so many men,
And all of you clapt vp together, in
An Anthony: that I might do you seruice,
So good as you haue done.

Omnes.

Anthony and Cleopatra. 359

Omnes. The Gods forbid.

Ant. Well, my good Fellowes, wait on me to night:
Scant not my Cups, and make as much of me,
As when mine Empire was your Fellow too,
And suffer'd my command.

Cleo. What does he meane?

Eno. To make his Followers weepe.

Ant. Tend me to night;
May be, it is the period of your duty,
Haply you shall not see me more, or if,
A mangled shadow. Perchance to morrow,
You'l serue another Master. I looke on you,
As one that takes his leaue. Mine honest Friends,
I turne you not away, but like a Master
Married to your good seruice, stay till death:
Tend me to night two houres, I aske no more,
And the Gods yeeld you for't.

Eno. What meane you (Sir)
To giue them this discomfort? Looke they weepe,
And I an Asse, am Onyon-ey'd; for shame,
Transforme vs not to women.

Ant. Ho, ho, ho:
Now the Witch take me, if I meant it thus.
Grace grow where those drops fall (my hearty Friends)
You take me in too dolorous a sense,
For I spake to you for your comfort, did desire you
To burne this night with Torches: Know (my hearts)
I hope well of to morrow, and will leade you,
Where rather Ile expect victorious life,
Then death, and Honor. Let's to Supper, come,
And drowne consideration. *Exeunt.*

Enter a Company of Souldiours.

1. Sol. Brother, goodnight: to morrow is the day.

2. Sol. It will determine one way: Fare you well.
Heard you of nothing strange about the streets.

1 Nothing: what newes?

2 Belike 'tis but a Rumour, goodnight to you.

1 Well sir, goodnight.

They meete other Soldiers.

2 Souldiers, haue carefull Watch.

1 And you: Goodnight, goodnight.

They place themselues in euery corner of the Stage.

2 Heere we: and if to morrow
Our Nauie thriue, I haue an absolute hope
Our Landmen will stand vp.

1 'Tis a braue Army, and full of purpose.

Musicke of the Hoboyes is vnder the Stage.

2 Peace, what noise?

1 List, list.

2 Hearke.

1 Musicke i'th'Ayre.

3 Vnder the earth.

4 It signes well, do's it not?

3 No.

1 Peace I say: What should this meane?

2 'Tis the God *Hercules*, whom *Anthony* loued,
Now leaues him.

1 Walke, let's see if other Watchmen
Do heare what we do?

2 How now Maisters? *Speak together.*

Omnes. How now? how now do you heare this?

1 I, is't not strange?

3 Do you heare Masters? Do you heare?

1 Follow the noyse so farre as we haue quarter.
Let's see how it will giue off.

Omnes. Content: 'Tis strange. *Exeunt.*

Enter Anthony and Cleopatra, with others.

Ant. Eros, mine Armour *Eros.*

Cleo. Sleepe a little.

Ant. No my Chucke. *Eros,* come mine Armor *Eros.*

Enter Eros.

Come good Fellow, put thine Iron on,
If Fortune be not ours to day, it is
Because we braue her. Come.

Cleo. Nay, Ile helpe too, *Anthony.*
What's this for? Ah let be, let be, thou art
The Armourer of my heart: False, false: This, this,
Sooth-law Ile helpe: Thus it must bee.

Ant. Well, well, we shall thriue now.
Seest thou my good Fellow. Go, put on thy defences.

Eros. Briefely Sir.

Cleo. Is not this buckled well?

Ant. Rarely, rarely:
He that vnbuckles this, till we do please
To daft for our Repose, shall heare a storme.
Thou fumblest *Eros,* and my Queenes a Squire
More tight at this, then thou: Dispatch. O Loue,
That thou couldst see my Warres to day, and knew'st
The Royall Occupation, thou should'st see
A Workeman in't.

Enter an Armed Soldier.

Good morrow to thee, welcome,
Thou look'st like him that knowes a warlike Charge:
To businesse that we loue, we rise betime,
And go too't with delight.

Soul. A thousand Sir, early though't be, haue on their
Riueted trim, and at the Port expect you. *Showts.*

Trumpets Flourish.

Enter Captaines, and Souldiers.

Alex. The Morne is faire: Good morrow Generall.

All. Good morrow Generall.

Ant. 'Tis well blowne Lads.
This Morning, like the spirit of a youth
That meanes to be of note, begins betimes.
So, so: Come giue me that, this way, well-sed.
Fare thee well Dame, what ere becomes of me,
This is a Soldiers kisse: rebukeable,
And worthy shamefull checke it were, to stand
On more Mechanicke Complement, Ile leaue thee.
Now like a man of Steele, you that will fight,
Follow me close, Ile bring you too't: Adieu. *Exeunt.*

Char. Please you retyre to your Chamber?

Cleo. Lead me:
He goes forth gallantly: That he and *Cæsar* might
Determine this great Warre in single fight;
Then *Anthony*; but now. Well on. *Exeunt.*

Trumpets sound. Enter Anthony, and Eros.

Eros. The Gods make this a happy day to *Anthony.*

Ant. Would thou, & those thy scars had once preuaild
To make me fight at Land.

Eros. Had'st thou done so,
The Kings that haue reuolted, and the Soldier
That has this morning left thee, would haue still
Followed thy heeles.

Ant. Whose gone this morning?

Eros. Who? one euer neere thee, call for *Enobarbus,*

Hee

He shall not heare thee, or from *Cæsars* Campe,
Say I am none of thine.
  Ant. What sayest thou?
  Sold. Sir he is with *Cæsar*.
  Eros. Sir, his Chests and Treasure he has not with him.
  Ant. Is he gone?
  Sol. Most certaine.
  Ant. Go *Eros*, send his Treasure after, do it,
Detaine no iot I charge thee : write to him,
(I will subscribe) gentle adieu's, and greetings;
Say, that I wish he neuer finde more cause
To change a Master. Oh my Fortunes haue
Corrupted honest men. Dispatch *Enobarbus*. *Exit*

  Flourish. Enter *Agrippa, Cæsar, with Enobarbus,*
    and Dollabella.

  Cæs. Go forth *Agrippa*, and begin the fight:
Our will is *Anthony* be tooke aliue :
Make it so knowne.
  Agrip. *Cæsar*, I shall.
  Cæsar. The time of vniuersall peace is neere:
Proue this a prosp'rous day, the three nook'd world
Shall beare the Oliue freely.
    Enter a Messenger.
  Mes. *Anthony* is come into the Field.
  Cæs. Go charge *Agrippa*,
Plant those that haue reuolted in the Vant,
That *Anthony* may seeme to spend his Fury
Vpon himselfe. *Exeunt.*

  Enob. *Alexas* did reuolt, and went to *Iewry* on
Affaires of *Anthony*, there did disswade
Great *Herod* to incline himselfe to *Cæsar*,
And leaue his Master *Anthony*. For this paines,
Cæsar hath hang'd him : *Camindius* and the rest
That fell away, haue entertainment, but
No honourable trust: I haue done ill,
Of which I do accuse my selfe so sorely,
That I will ioy no more.
    Enter a Soldier of Cæsars.
  Sol. *Enobarbus*, *Anthony*
Hath after thee sent all thy Treasure, with
His Bounty ouer-plus. The Messenger
Came on my guard, and at thy Tent is now
Vnloading of his Mules.
  Eno. I giue it you.
  Sol. Mocke not *Enobarbus*,
I tell you true : Best you saf't the bringer
Out of the hoast, I must attend mine Office,
Or would haue done't my selfe. Your Emperor
Continues still a Ioue. *Exit*

  Enob. I am alone the Villaine of the earth,
And feele I am so most. Oh *Anthony*,
Thou Mine of Bounty, how would'st thou haue payed
My better seruice, when my turpitude
Thou dost so Crowne with Gold. This blowes my hart,
If swift thought breake it not : a swifter meane
Shall out-strike thought, but thought will doo't. I feele
I fight against thee : No I will go seeke
Some Ditch, wherein to dye : the foul'st best fits
My latter part of life. *Exit.*

    Alarum, Drummes and Trumpets.
    Enter Agrippa.
  Agrip. Retire, we haue engag'd our selues too farre :
Cæsar himselfe ha's worke, and our oppression
Exceeds what we expected. *Exit.*

    Alarums.
    Enter Anthony, and Scarrus wounded.

  Scar. O my braue Emperor, this is fought indeed,
Had we done so at first, we had drouen them home
With clowts about their heads. *Far off.*
  Ant. Thou bleed'st apace.
  Scar. I had a wound heere that was like a T,
But now 'tis made an H.
  Ant. They do retyre.
  Scar. Wee'l beat 'em into Bench-holes, I haue yet
Roome for six scotches more.
    Enter Eros.
  Eros. They are beaten Sir, and our aduantage serues
For a faire victory.
  Scar. Let vs score their backes,
And snatch 'em vp, as we take Hares behinde,
'Tis sport to maul a Runner.
  Ant. I will reward thee
Once for thy sprightly comfort, and ten-fold
For thy good valour. Come thee on.
  Scar. Ile halt after. *Exeunt*

    Alarum. Enter *Anthony againe in a March.*
    Scarrus, with others.

  Ant. We haue beate him to his Campe : Runne one
Before, & let the Queen know of our guests: to morrow
Before the Sun shall see's, wee'l spill the blood
That ha's to day escap'd. I thanke you all,
For doughty handed are you, and haue fought
Not as you seru'd the Cause, but as't had beene
Each mans like mine : you haue shewne all *Hectors*.
Enter the Citty, clip your Wiues, your Friends,
Tell them your feats, whil'st they with ioyfull teares
Wash the congealement from your wounds, and kisse
The Honour'd-gashes whole.
    Enter Cleopatra.
Giue me thy hand,
To this great Faiery, Ile commend thy acts,
Make her thankes blesse thee. Oh thou day o'th'world,
Chaine mine arm'd necke, leape thou, Attyre and all
Through proofe of Harnesse to my heart, and there
Ride on the pants triumphing.
  Cleo. Lord of Lords.
Oh infinite Vertue, comm'st thou smiling from?
The worlds great snare vncaught.
  Ant. Mine Nightingale,
We haue beate them to their Beds.
What Gyrle, though gray
Do something mingle with our yonger brown, yet ha we
A Braine that nourishes our Nerues, and can
Get gole for gole of youth. Behold this man,
Commend vnto his Lippes thy sauouring hand,
Kisse it my Warriour : He hath fought to day,
As if a God in hate of Mankinde, had
Destroyed in such a shape.
  Cleo. Ile giue thee Friend
An Armour all of Gold : it was a Kings.
  Ant. He has deseru'd it, were it Carbunkled
Like holy Phœbus Carre. Giue me thy hand,
Through Alexandria make a iolly March,
Beare our backt Targets, like the men that owe them.
Had our great Pallace the capacity
To Campe this hoast, we all would sup together,
And drinke Carowses to the next dayes Fate
Which

Which promises Royall perill, Trumpetters
With brazen dinne blast you the Citties eare,
Make mingle with our ratling Tabourines,
That heauen and earth may strike their sounds together,
Applauding our approach. *Exeunt.*

Enter a Centerie, and his Company, Enobarbus followes.

Cent. If we be not releeu'd within this houre,
We must returne to'th'Court of Guard: the night
Is shiny, and they say, we shall embattaile
By'th'second houre i'th'Morne.

1. Watch. This last day was a shrew'd one too's.

Enob. Oh beare me witnesse night.

2 What man is this?

1 Stand close, and list him.

Enob. Be witnesse to me (O thou blessed Moone)
When men reuolted shall vpon Record
Beare hatefull memory: poore *Enobarbus* did
Before thy face repent.

Cent. Enobarbus?

2 Peace: Hearke further.

Enob. Oh Soueraigne Mistris of true Melancholly,
The poysonous dampe of night dispunge vpon me,
That Life, a very Rebell to my will,
May hang no longer on me. Throw my heart
Against the flint and hardnesse of my fault,
Which being dried with greefe, will breake to powder,
And finish all foule thoughts. Oh *Anthony*,
Nobler then my reuolt is Infamous,
Forgiue me in thine owne particular,
But let the world ranke me in Register
A Master leauer, and a fugitiue:
Oh *Anthony*! Oh *Anthony*!

1 Let's speake to him.

Cent. Let's heare him, for the things he speakes
May concerne *Cæsar*.

2 Let's do so, but he sleepes.

Cent. Swoonds rather, for so bad a Prayer as his
Was neuer yet for sleepe.

1 Go we to him.

2 Awake sir, awake, speake to vs.

1 Heare you sir?

Cent. The hand of death hath raught him.

Drummes afarre off.

Hearke the Drummes demurely wake the sleepers:
Let vs beare him to'th'Court of Guard: he is of note:
Our houre is fully out.

2 Come on then, he may recouer yet. *exeunt*

Enter Anthony and Scarrus, with their Army.

Ant. Their preparation is to day by Sea,
We please them not by Land.

Scar. For both, my Lord.

Ant. I would they'ld fight i'th'Fire, or i'th'Ayre,
Wee'ld fight there too. But this it is, our Foote
Vpon the hilles adioyning to the Citty
Shall stay with vs. Order for Sea is giuen,
They haue put forth the Hauen:
Where their appointment we may best discouer,
And looke on their endeuour. *exeunt*

Enter Cæsar, and his Army.

Cæs. But being charg'd, we will be still by Land,
Which as I tak't we shall, for his best force
Is forth to Man his Gallies. To the Vales,
And hold our best aduantage. *exeunt.*

Alarum afarre off, as at a Sea-fight.
Enter Anthony, and Scarrus.

Ant. Yet they are not ioyn'd:
Where yon'd Pine does stand, I shall discouer all,
Ile bring thee word straight, how 'tis like to go. *exit.*

Scar. Swallowes haue built
In *Cleopatra's* Sailes their nests. The Auguries
Say, they know not, they cannot tell, looke grimly,
And dare not speake their knowledge. *Anthony*,
Is valiant, and deiected, and by starts
His fretted Fortunes giue him hope and feare
Of what he has, and has not.

Enter Anthony.

Ant. All is lost:
This fowle Egyptian hath betrayed me:
My Fleete hath yeelded to the Foe, and yonder
They cast their Caps vp, and Carowse together
Like Friends long lost. Triple-turn'd Whore, 'tis thou
Hast sold me to this Nouice, and my heart
Makes onely Warres on thee. Bid them all flye:
For when I am reueng'd vpon my Charme,
I haue done all. Bid them all flye, be gone.
Oh Sunne, thy vprise shall I see no more,
Fortune, and *Anthony* part heere, euen heere
Do we shake hands? All come to this? The hearts
That pannelled me at heeles, to whom I gaue
Their wishes, do dis-Candie, melt their sweets
On blossoming *Cæsar*: And this Pine is barkt,
That ouer-top'd them all. Betray'd I am.
Oh this false Soule of Egypt! this graue Charme,
Whose eye beck'd forth my Wars, & cal'd them home:
Whose Bosome was my Crownet, my chiefe end,
Like a right Gypsie, hath at fast and loose
Beguil'd me, to the very heart of losse.
What *Eros, Eros*?

Enter Cleopatra.

Ah, thou Spell! Auaunt.

Cleo. Why is my Lord enrag'd against his Loue?

Ant. Vanish, or I shall giue thee thy deseruing,
And blemish *Cæsars* Triumph. Let him take thee,
And hoist thee vp to the shouting Plebeians,
Follow his Chariot, like the greatest spot
Of all thy Sex. Most Monster-like be shewne
For poor'st Diminitiues, for Dolts, and let
Patient *Octauia*, plough thy visage vp
With her prepared nailes. *exit Cleopatra.*
'Tis well th'art gone,
If it be well to liue. But better 'twere
Thou fell'st into my furie, for one death
Might haue preuented many. *Eros*, hoa?
The shirt of *Nessus* is vpon me, teach me
Alcides, thou mine Ancestor, thy rage.
Let me lodge *Licas* on the hornes o'th'Moone,
And with those hands that graspt the heauiest Club,
Subdue my worthiest selfe: The Witch shall die,
To the young Roman Boy she hath sold me, and I fall
Vnder this plot: She dyes for't. *Eros* hoa? *exit.*

Enter Cleopatra, Charmian, Iras, Mardian.

Cleo. Helpe me my women: Oh hee's more mad
Then *Telamon* for his Shield, the Boare of Thessaly
Was neuer so imbost.

Char. To'th'Monument, there locke your selfe,
And send him word you are dead:

The

The Soule and Body riue not more in parting,
Then greatnesse going off.

　Cleo. To'th'Monument:
Mardian, go tell him I haue slaine my selfe:
Say, that the last I spoke was *Anthony*,
And word it (prythee) pitteously. Hence *Mardian*,
And bring me how he takes my death to'th'Monument.
　　　　　　　　　　　　　　　　　Exeunt.

　　　　　　Enter Anthony, and Eros.
　Ant. *Eros*, thou yet behold'st me?
　Eros. I Noble Lord.
　Ant. Sometime we see a clowd that's Dragonish,
A vapour sometime, like a Beare, or Lyon,
A toward Cittadell, a pendant Rocke,
A forked Mountaine, or blew Promontorie
With Trees vpon't, that nodde vnto the world,
And mocke our eyes with Ayre.
Thou hast seene these Signes,
They are blacke Vespers Pageants.
　Eros. I my Lord.
　Ant. That which is now a Horse, euen with a thoght
the Racke dislimes, and makes it indistinct
As water is in water.
　Eros. It does my Lord.
　Ant. My good Knaue *Eros*, now thy Captaine is
Euen such a body: Heere I am *Anthony*,
Yet cannot hold this visible shape (my Knaue)
I made these warres for Egypt, and the Queene,
Whose heart I thought I had, for she had mine:
Which whil'st it was mine, had annext vntoo't
A Million moe, (now lost:) shee *Eros* has
Packt Cards with *Cæsars*, and false plaid my Glory
Vnto an Enemies triumph.
Nay, weepe not gentle *Eros*, there is left vs
Our selues to end our selues.
　　　　　　Enter Mardian.
Oh thy vilde Lady, she has rob'd me of my Sword.
　Mar. No *Anthony*,
My Mistris lou'd thee, and her Fortunes mingled
With thine intirely.
　Ant. Hence sawcy Eunuch peace, she hath betraid me,
And shall dye the death.
　Mar. Death of one person, can be paide but once,
And that she ha's discharg'd. What thou would'st do
Is done vnto thy hand: the last she spake
Was *Anthony*, most Noble *Anthony*,
Then in the midd'st a tearing grone did breake
The name of *Anthony*: it was diuided
Betweene her heart, and lips: she rendred life
Thy name so buried in her.
　Ant. Dead then?
　Mar. Dead.
　Ant. Vnarme *Eros*, the long dayes taske is done,
And we must sleepe: That thou depart'st hence safe
Does pay thy labour richly: Go. *exit Mardian.*
Off, plucke off,
The seuen-fold shield of *Aiax* cannot keepe
The battery from my heart. Oh cleaue my sides.
Heart, once be stronger then thy Continent,
Cracke thy fraile Case. Apace *Eros*, apace;
No more a Soldier: bruised peeces go,
You haue bin Nobly borne. From me awhile. *exit Eros*
I will o're-take thee *Cleopatra*, and
Weepe for my pardon. So it must be, for now
All length is Torture: since the Torch is out,
Lye downe and stray no farther. Now all labour

Marres what it does: yea, very force entangles
It selfe with strength: Seale then, and all is done.
Eros? I come my Queene. *Eros*? Stay for me,
Where Soules do couch on Flowers, wee'l hand in hand,
And with our sprightly Port make the Ghostes gaze:
Dido, and her *Æneas* shall want Troopes,
And all the haunt be ours. Come *Eros, Eros.*
　　　　　　Enter Eros.
　Eros. What would my Lord?
　Ant. Since *Cleopatra* dyed,
I haue liu'd in such dishonour, that the Gods
Detest my basenesse. I, that with my Sword,
Quarter'd the World, and o're greene Neptunes backe
With Ships, made Cities; condemne my selfe, to lacke
The Courage of a Woman, lesse Noble minde
Then she which by her death, our *Cæsar* telles
I am Conqueror of my selfe. Thou art sworne *Eros*,
That when the exigent should come, which now
Is come indeed: When I should see behinde me
Th'ineuitable prosecution of disgrace and horror,
That on my command, thou then would'st kill me.
Doo't, the time is come: Thou strik'st not me,
'Tis *Cæsar* thou defeat'st. Put colour in thy Cheeke.
　Eros. The Gods with-hold me,
Shall I do that which all the Parthian Darts,
(Though Enemy) lost ayme, and could not.
　Ant. *Eros*,
Would'st thou be window'd in great Rome, and see
Thy Master thus with pleacht Armes, bending downe
His corrigible necke, his face subdu'de
To penetratiue shame; whil'st the wheel'd seate
Of Fortunate *Cæsar* drawne before him, branded
His Basenesse that ensued.
　Eros. I would not see't.
　Ant. Come then: for with a wound I must be cur'd.
Draw that thy honest Sword, which thou hast worne
Most vsefull for thy Country.
　Eros. Oh sir, pardon me.
　Ant. When I did make thee free, swor'st ỹ not then
To do this when I bad thee? Do it at once,
Or thy precedent Seruices are all
But accidents vnpurpos'd. Draw, and come.
　Eros. Turne from me then that Noble countenance,
Wherein the worship of the whole world lyes.
　Ant. Loe thee.
　Eros. My sword is drawne.
　Ant. Then let it do at once
The thing why thou hast drawne it.
　Eros. My deere Master,
My Captaine, and my Emperor. Let me say
Before I strike this bloody stroke, Farwell.
　Ant. 'Tis said man, and farewell.
　Eros. Farewell great Chiefe. Shall I strike now?
　Ant. Now *Eros*. *Killes himselfe.*
　Eros. Why there then:
Thus I do escape the sorrow of *Anthonies* death.
　Ant. Thrice-Nobler then my selfe,
Thou teachest me: Oh valiant *Eros*, what
I should, and thou could'st not, my Queene and *Eros*
Haue by their braue instruction got vpon me
A Noblenesse in Record. But I will bee
A Bride-groome in my death, and run into't
As to a Louers bed. Come then, and *Eros*,
Thy Master dies thy Scholler; to do thus
I learnt of thee. How, not dead? Not dead?
The Guard, how? Oh dispatch me.
　　　　　　　　　　　　　　　　　Enter

Anthony and Cleopatra.

Enter a Guard.

1. Guard. What's the noise?
Ant. I haue done my worke ill Friends:
Oh make an end of what I haue begun.
2 The Starre is falne.
1 And time is at his Period.
All. Alas, and woe.
Ant. Let him that loues me, strike me dead.
1 Not I.
2 Nor I.
3 Nor any one. *exeunt*
Dercetus. Thy death and fortunes bid thy folowers fly
This sword but shewne to Cæsar with this tydings,
Shall enter me with him.

Enter Diomedes.

Dio. Where's Anthony?
Decre. There Diomed there.
Diom. Liues he: wilt thou not answer man?
Ant. Art thou there Diomed?
Draw thy sword, and giue mee,
Suffising strokes for death.
Diom. Most absolute Lord:
My Mistris Cleopatra sent me to thee.
Ant. When did shee send thee?
Diom. Now my Lord.
Anth. Where is she? *(feare*
Diom. Lockt in her Monument: she had a Prophesying
Of what hath come to passe: for when she saw
(Which neuer shall be found) you did suspect
She had dispos'd with Cæsar, and that your rage
Would not be purg'd, she sent you word she was dead:
But fearing since how it might worke, hath sent
Me to proclaime the truth, and I am come
I dread, too late.
Ant. Too late good Diomed: call my Guard I prythee.
Dio. What hoa: the Emperors Guard,
The Guard, what hoa? Come, your Lord calles.

Enter 4. or 5. of the Guard of Anthony.

Ant. Beare me good Friends where Cleopatra bides,
'Tis the last seruice that I shall command you.
1 Woe, woe are we sir, you may not liue to weare
All your true Followers out.
All. Most heauy day.
Ant. Nay good my Fellowes, do not please sharp fate
To grace it with your sorrowes. Bid that welcome
Which comes to punish vs, and we punish it
Seeming to beare it lightly. Take me vp,
I haue led you oft, carry me now good Friends,
And haue my thankes for all. *Exit bearing Anthony*

Enter Cleopatra, and her Maides aloft, with Charmian & Iras.

Cleo. Oh Charmian, I will neuer go from hence.
Char. Be comforted deere Madam.
Cleo. No, I will not:
All strange and terrible euents are welcome,
But comforts we dispise; our size of sorrow
Proportion'd to our cause, must be as great
As that which makes it.

Enter Diomed.

How now? is he dead?
Diom. His death's vpon him, but not dead.
Looke out o'th other side your Monument,
His Guard haue brought him thither.

Enter Anthony, and the Guard.

Cleo. Oh Sunne,
Burne the great Sphere thou mou'st in, darkling stand
The varrying shore o'th'world. O Antony, Antony, Antony
Helpe Charmian, helpe Iras helpe: helpe Friends
Below, let's draw him hither.
Ant. Peace,
Not Cæsars Valour hath o'rethrowne Anthony,
But Anthonie's hath Triumpht on it selfe.
Cleo. So it should be,
That none but Anthony should conquer Anthony,
But woe 'tis so.
Ant. I am dying Egypt, dying; onely
I heere importune death a-while, vntill
Of many thousand kisses, the poore last
I lay vpon thy lippes.
Cleo. I dare not Deere,
Deere my Lord pardon: I dare not,
Least I be taken: not th'Imperious shew
Of the full-Fortun'd Cæsar, euer shall
Be brooch'd with me, if Knife, Drugges, Serpents haue
Edge, sting, or operation. I am safe:
Your Wife Octauia, with her modest eyes,
And still Conclusion, shall acquire no Honour
Demuring vpon me: but come, come Anthony,
Helpe me my women, we must draw thee vp:
Assist good Friends.
Ant. Oh quicke, or I am gone.
Cleo. Heere's sport indeede:
How heauy weighes my Lord?
Our strength is all gone into heauinesse,
That makes the waight. Had I great Iuno's power,
The strong wing'd Mercury should fetch thee vp,
And set thee by Ioues side. Yet come a little,
Wishers were euer Fooles. Oh come, come, come,
They heaue Anthony aloft to Cleopatra.
And welcome, welcome. Dye when thou hast liu'd,
Quicken with kissing: had my lippes that power,
Thus would I weare them out.
All. A heauy sight.
Ant. I am dying Egypt, dying.
Giue me some Wine, and let me speake a little.
Cleo. No, let me speake, and let me rayle so hye,
That the false Huswife Fortune, breake her Wheele,
Prouok'd by my offence.
Ant. One word (sweet Queene)
Of Cæsar seeke your Honour, with your safety. Oh.
Cleo. They do not go together.
Ant. Gentle heare me,
None about Cæsar trust, but Proculeius.
Cleo. My Resolution, and my hands, Ile trust,
None about Cæsar.
Ant. The miserable change now at my end,
Lament nor sorrow at: but please your thoughts
In feeding them with those my former Fortunes
Wherein I liued. The greatest Prince o'th'world,
The Noblest: and do now not basely dye,
Not Cowardly put off my Helmet to
My Countreyman. A Roman, by a Roman
Valiantly vanquish'd. Now my Spirit is going,
I can no more.
Cleo. Noblest of men, woo't dye?
Hast thou no care of me, shall I abide
In this dull world, which in thy absence is
No better then a Stye? Oh see my women:
The Crowne o'th'earth doth melt. My Lord?
Oh wither'd is the Garland of the Warre,

The

The Souldiers pole is falne : young Boyes and Gyrles
Are leuell now with men : The oddes is gone,
And there is nothing left remarkeable
Beneath the visiting Moone.

  Char. Oh quietnesse, Lady.

  Iras. She's dead too, our Soueraigne.

  Char. Lady.

  Iras. Madam.

  Char. Oh Madam, Madam, Madam.

  Iras. Royall Egypt : Empresse.

  Char. Peace, peace, *Iras*.

  Cleo. No more but in a Woman, and commanded
By such poore passion, as the Maid that Milkes,
And doe's the meanest chares. It were for me,
To throw my Scepter at the iniurious Gods,
To tell them that this World did equall theyrs,
Till they had stolne our Iewell. All's but naught :
Patience is sottish, and impatience does
Become a Dogge that's mad : Then is it sinne,
To rush into the secret house of death,
Ere death dare come to vs. How do you Women?
What, what good cheere? Why how now *Charmian* ?
My Noble Gyrles? Ah Women, women! Looke
Our Lampe is spent, it's out. Good sirs, take heart,
Wee'l bury him : And then, what's braue, what's Noble,
Let's doo't after the high Roman fashion,
And make death proud to take vs. Come, away,
This case of that huge Spirit now is cold.
Ah Women, Women! Come, we haue no Friend
But Resolution, and the breefest end.

         Exeunt, bearing of Anthonies body.

Enter Cæsar, Agrippa, Dollabella, Menas, with
his Counsell of Warre.

  Cæsar. Go to him *Dollabella*, bid him yeeld,
Being so frustrate, tell him,
He mockes the pawses that he makes.

  Dol. Cæsar, I shall.

      Enter Decretas with the sword of Anthony.

  Cæs. Wherefore is that? And what art thou that dar'st
Appeare thus to vs?

  Dec. I am call'd *Decretas*,
Marke *Anthony* I seru'd, who best was worthie
Best to be seru'd : whil'st he stood vp, and spoke
He was my Master, and I wore my life
To spend vpon his haters. If thou please
To take me to thee, as I was to him,
Ile be to *Cæsar* : if y pleasest not, I yeild thee vp my life.

  Cæsar. What is't thou say'st?

  Dec. I say (Oh *Cæsar*) *Anthony* is dead.

  Cæsar. The breaking of so great a thing, should make
A greater cracke. The round World
Should haue shooke Lyons into ciuill streets,
And Citizens to their dennes. The death of *Anthony*
Is not a single doome, in the name lay
A moity of the world.

  Dec. He is dead *Cæsar*,
Not by a publike minister of Iustice,
Nor by a hyred Knife, but that selfe-hand
Which writ his Honor in the Acts it did,
Hath with the Courage which the heart did lend it,
Splitted the heart. This is his Sword,
I robb'd his wound of it, behold it stain'd
With his most Noble blood.

  Cæs. Looke you sad Friends,
The Gods rebuke me, but it is Tydings
To wash the eyes of Kings.

  Dol. And strange it is,
That Nature must compell vs to lament
Our most persisted deeds.

  Mec. His taints and Honours, wag'd equal with him.

  Dola. A Rarer spirit neuer
Did steere humanity : but you Gods will giue vs
Some faults to make vs men. Cæsar is touch'd.

  Mec. When such a spacious Mirror's set before him
He needes must see himselfe.

  Cæsar. Oh *Anthony*,
I haue followed thee to this, but we do launch
Diseases in our Bodies. I must perforce
Haue shewne to thee such a declining day,
Or looke on thine : we could not stall together,
In the whole world. But yet let me lament
With teares as Soueraigne as the blood of hearts,
That thou my Brother, my Competitor,
In top of all designe; my Mate in Empire,
Friend and Companion in the front of Warre,
The Arme of mine owne Body, and the Heart
Where mine his thoughts did kindle; that our Starres
Vnreconciliable, should diuide our equalnesse to this.
Heare me good Friends,
But I will tell you at some meeter Season,
The businesse of this man lookes out of him,
Wee'l heare him what he sayes.

       Enter an Ægyptian.
Whence are you?

  Ægyp. A poore Egyptian yet, the Queen my mistris
Confin'd in all, she has her Monument
Of thy intents, desires, instruction,
That she preparedly may frame her selfe
To th' way shee's forc'd too.

  Cæsar. Bid her haue good heart,
She soone shall know of vs, by some of ours,
How honourable, and how kindely Wee
Determine for her. For *Cæsar* cannot leaue to be vngentle

  Ægypt. So the Gods preserue thee.   *Exit.*

  Cæs. Come hither *Proculeius*. Go and say
We purpose her no shame : giue her what comforts
The quality of her passion shall require ;
Least in her greatnesse, by some mortall stroke
She do defeate vs. For her life in Rome,
Would be eternall in our Triumph : Go,
And with your speediest bring vs what she sayes,
And how you finde of her.

  Pro. Cæsar I shall.   *Exit Proculeius.*

  Cæs. Gallus go you along : where's *Dolabella*, to second *Proculeius* ?

  All. Dolabella.

  Cæs. Let him alone : for I remember now
How hee's imployd : he shall in time be ready.
Go with me to my Tent, where you shall see
How hardly I was drawne into this Warre,
How calme and gentle I proceeded still
In all my Writings. Go with me, and see
What I can shew in this.   *Exeunt.*

Enter Cleopatra, Charmian, Iras, and Mardian.

  Cleo. My desolation does begin to make
A better life : Tis paltry to be *Cæsar* :
Not being Fortune, hee's but Fortunes knaue,
A minister of her will : and it is great

To do that thing that ends all other deeds,
Which shackles accedents, and bolts vp change;
Which sleepes, and neuer pallates more the dung,
The beggers Nurse, and Cæsars.

Enter Proculeius.

Pro. Cæsar sends greeting to the Queene of Egypt,
And bids thee study on what faire demands
Thou mean'st to haue him grant thee.

Cleo. What's thy name?

Pro. My name is *Proculeius*.

Cleo. Anthony
Did tell me of you, bad me trust you, but
I do not greatly care to be deceiu'd
That haue no vse for trusting. If your Master
Would haue a Queene his begger, you must tell him,
That Maiesty to keepe *decorum*, must
No lesse begge then a Kingdome: If he please
To giue me conquer'd Egypt for my Sonne,
He giues me so much of mine owne, as I
Will kneele to him with thankes.

Pro. Be of good cheere:
Y'are falne into a Princely hand, feare nothing,
Make your full reference freely to my Lord,
Who is so full of Grace, that it flowes ouer
On all that neede. Let me report to him
Your sweet dependacie, and you shall finde
A Conqueror that will pray in ayde for kindnesse,
Where he for grace is kneel'd too.

Cleo. Pray you tell him,
I am his Fortunes Vassall, and I send him
The Greatnesse he has got. I hourely learne
A Doctrine of Obedience, and would gladly
Looke him i'th'Face.

Pro. This Ile report (deere Lady)
Haue comfort, for I know your plight is pittied
Of him that caus'd it.

Pro. You see how easily she may be surpriz'd:
Guard her till Cæsar come.

Iras. Royall Queene.

Char. Oh Cleopatra, thou art taken Queene.

Cleo. Quicke, quicke, good hands.

Pro. Hold worthy Lady, hold:
Doe not your selfe such wrong, who are in this
Releeu'd, but not betraid.

Cleo. What of death too that rids our dogs of languish

Pro. Cleopatra, do not abuse my Masters bounty, by
Th'vndoing of your selfe: Let the World see
His Noblenesse well acted, which your death
Will neuer let come forth.

Cleo. Where art thou Death?
Come hither come; Come, come, and take a Queene
Worth many Babes and Beggers.

Pro. Oh temperance Lady.

Cleo. Sir, I will eate no meate, Ile not drinke sir,
If idle talke will once be necessary
Ile not sleepe neither. This mortall house Ile ruine,
Do Cæsar what he can. Know sir, that I
Will not waite pinnion'd at your Masters Court,
Nor once be chastic'd with the sober eye
Of dull Octauia. Shall they hoyst me vp,
And shew me to the showting Varlotarie
Of censuring Rome? Rather a ditch in Egypt.
Be gentle graue vnto me, rather on Nylus mudde
Lay me starke-nak'd, and let the water-Flies
Blow me into abhorring; rather make
My Countries high pyramides my Gibbet,
And hang me vp in Chaines.

Pro. You do extend
These thoughts of horror further then you shall
Finde cause in Cæsar.

Enter Dolabella.

Dol. Proculeius,
What thou hast done, thy Master Cæsar knowes,
And he hath sent for thee: for the Queene,
Ile take her to my Guard.

Pro. So Dolabella,
It shall content me best: Be gentle to her,
To Cæsar I will speake, what you shall please,
If you'l imploy me to him. *Exit Proculeius*

Cleo. Say, I would dye.

Dol. Most Noble Empresse, you haue heard of me.

Cleo. I cannot tell.

Dol. Assuredly you know me.

Cleo. No matter sir, what I haue heard or knowne:
You laugh when Boyes or Women tell their Dreames,
Is't not your tricke?

Dol. I vnderstand not, Madam.

Cleo. I dreampt there was an Emperor *Anthony*.
Oh such another sleepe, that I might see
But such another man.

Dol. If it might please ye.

Cleo. His face was as the Heau'ns, and therein stucke
A Sunne and Moone, which kept their course, & lighted
The little o'th'earth.

Dol. Most Soueraigne Creature.

Cleo. His legges bestrid the Ocean, his rear'd arme
Crested the world: His voyce was propertied
As all the tuned Spheres, and that to Friends:
But when he meant to quaile, and shake the Orbe,
He was as ratling Thunder. For his Bounty,
There was no winter in't. An *Anthony* it was,
That grew the more by reaping: His delights
Were Dolphin-like, they shew'd his backe aboue
The Element they liu'd in: In his Liuery
Walk'd Crownes and Crownets: Realms & Islands were
As plates dropt from his pocket.

Dol. Cleopatra.

Cleo. Thinke you there was, or might be such a man
As this I dreampt of?

Dol. Gentle Madam, no.

Cleo. You Lye vp to the hearing of the Gods:
But if there be, nor euer were one such
It's past the size of dreaming: Nature wants stuffe
To vie strange formes with fancie, yet t'imagine
An *Anthony* were Natures peece, 'gainst Fancie,
Condemning shadowes quite.

Dol. Heare me, good Madam:
Your losse is as your selfe, great; and you beare it
As answering to the weight, would I might neuer
Ore-take pursu'de successe: But I do feele
By the rebound of yours, a greefe that suites
My very heart at roote.

Cleo. I thanke you sir:
Know you what Cæsar meanes to do with me?

Dol. I am loath to tell you what, I would you knew.

Cleo. Nay pray you sir.

Dol. Though he be Honourable.

Cleo. Hee'l leade me then in Triumph.

Dol. Madam he will, I know't. *Flourish.*

*Enter Proculeius, Cæsar, Gallus, Mecenas,
and others of his Traine.*

All. Make way there Cæsar.

Cæs. Which is the Queene of Egypt.
Dol. It is the Emperor Madam. *Cleo. kneeles.*
Cæsar. Arise, you shall not kneele:
I pray you rise, rise Egypt.
  Cleo. Sir, the Gods will haue it thus,
My Master and my Lord I must obey.
  Cæsar. Take to you no hard thoughts,
The Record of what iniuries you did vs,
Though written in our flesh, we shall remember
As things but done by chance.
  Cleo. Sole Sir o'th' World,
I cannot proiect mine owne cause so well
To make it cleare, but do confesse I haue
Bene laden with like frailties, which before
Haue often sham'd our Sex.
  Cæsar. Cleopatra know,
We will extenuate rather then inforce:
If you apply your selfe to our intents,
Which towards you are most gentle, you shall finde
A benefit in this change: but if you seeke
To lay on me a Cruelty, by taking
Anthonies course, you shall bereaue your selfe
Of my good purposes, and put your children
To that destruction which Ile guard them from,
If thereon you relye. Ile take my leaue.
  Cleo. And may through all the world: tis yours, & we
your Scutcheons, and your signes of Conquest shall
Hang in what place you please. Here my good Lord.
  Cæsar. You shall aduise me in all for *Cleopatra*.
  Cleo. This is the breefe: of Money, Plate, & Iewels
I am possest of, 'tis exactly valewed,
Not petty things admitted. Where's *Seleucus*?
  Seleu. Heere Madam.
  Cleo. This is my Treasurer, let him speake (my Lord)
Vpon his perill, that I haue reseru'd
To my selfe nothing. Speake the truth *Seleucus*.
  Seleu. Madam, I had rather seele my lippes,
Then to my perill speake that which is not.
  Cleo. What haue I kept backe.
  Sel. Enough to purchase what you haue made known
  Cæsar. Nay blush not *Cleopatra*, I approue
Your Wisedome in the deede.
  Cleo. See *Cæsar*: Oh behold,
How pompe is followed: Mine will now be yours,
And should we shift estates, yours would be mine.
The ingratitude of this *Seleucus*, does
Euen make me wilde. Oh Slaue, of no more trust
Then loue that's hyr'd? What goest thou backe, ŷ shalt
Go backe I warrant thee: but Ile catch thine eyes
Though they had wings. Slaue, Soule-lesse, Villain, Dog.
O rarely base!
  Cæsar. Good Queene, let vs intreat you.
  Cleo. O *Cæsar*, what a wounding shame is this,
That thou vouchsafing heere to visit me,
Doing the Honour of thy Lordlinesse
To one so meeke, that mine owne Seruant should
Parcell the summe of my disgraces, by
Addition of his Enuy. Say (good *Cæsar*)
That I some Lady trifles haue reseru'd,
Immoment toyes, things of such Dignitie
As we greet moderne Friends withall, and say
Some Nobler token I haue kept apart
For *Liuia* and *Octauia*, to induce
Their mediation, must I be vnfolded
With one that I haue bred: The Gods! it smites me
Beneath the fall I haue. Prythee go hence,

Or I shall shew the Cynders of my spirits
Through th'Ashes of my chance: Wer't thou a man,
Thou would'st haue mercy on me.
  Cæsar. Forbeare *Seleucus*.
  Cleo. Be it known, that we the greatest are mis-thoght
For things that others do: and when we fall,
We answer others merits, in our name
Are therefore to be pittied.
  Cæsar. Cleopatra,
Not what you haue reseru'd, nor what acknowledg'd
Put we i'th'Roll of Conquest: still bee't yours,
Bestow it at your pleasure, and beleeue
Cæsars no Merchant, to make prize with you
Of things that Merchants sold. Therefore be cheer'd,
Make not your thoughts your prisons: No deere Queen,
For we intend so to dispose you, as
Your selfe shall giue vs counsell: Feede, and sleepe:
Our care and pitty is so much vpon you,
That we remaine your Friend, and so adieu.
  Cleo. My Master, and my Lord.
  Cæsar. Not so: Adieu. *Flourish.*
    Exeunt Cæsar, and his Traine.
  Cleo. He words me Gyrles, he words me,
That I should not be Noble to my selfe.
But hearke thee *Charmian*.
  Iras. Finish good Lady, the bright day is done,
And we are for the darke.
  Cleo. Hye thee againe,
I haue spoke already, and it is prouided,
Go put it to the haste.
  Char. Madam, I will.
    Enter Dolabella.
  Dol. Where's the Queene?
  Char. Behold sir.
  Cleo. Dolabella.
  Dol. Madam, as thereto I sworne, by your command
(Which my loue makes Religion to obey)
I tell you this: *Cæsar* through Syria
Intends his iourney, and within three dayes,
You with your Children will he send before,
Make your best vse of this. I haue perform'd
Your pleasure, and my promise.
  Cleo. Dolabella, I shall remaine your debter.
  Dol. I your Seruant:
Adieu good Queene, I must attend on *Cæsar*. *Exit*
  Cleo. Farewell, and thankes.
Now *Iras*, what think'st thou?
Thou, an Egyptian Puppet shall be shewne
In Rome aswell as I: Mechanicke Slaues
With greazie Aprons, Rules, and Hammers shall
Vplift vs to the view. In their thicke breathes,
Ranke of grosse dyet, shall we be enclowded,
And forc'd to drinke their vapour.
  Iras. The Gods forbid.
  Cleo. Nay, 'tis most certaine *Iras*: sawcie Lictors
Will catch at vs like Strumpets, and scald Rimers
Ballads vs out a Tune. The quicke Comedians
Extemporally will stage vs, and present
Our Alexandrian Reuels: *Anthony*
Shall be brought drunken forth, and I shall see
Some squeaking *Cleopatra* Boy my greatnesse
I'th'posture of a Whore.
  Iras. O the good Gods!
  Cleo. Nay that's certaine.
  Iras. Ile neuer see't? for I am sure mine Nailes
Are stronger then mine eyes.

Cleo. Why that's the way to foole their preparation,
And to conquer their most absurd intents.
Enter Charmian.

Now *Charmian*.
Shew me my Women like a Queene: Go fetch
My best Attyres. I am againe for *Cidrus*,
To meete *Marke Anthony*. Sirra *Iras*, go
(Now Noble *Charmian*, wee'l dispatch indeede,)
And when thou hast done this chare, Ile giue thee leaue
To play till Doomesday: bring our Crowne, and all.
A noise within.

Wherefore's this noise?
Enter a Guardsman.

Gardf. Heere is a rurall Fellow,
That will not be deny'de your Highnesse presence,
He brings you Figges.

Cleo. Let him come in. *Exit Guardsman.*
What poore an Instrument
May do a Noble deede: he brings me liberty.
My Resolution's plac'd, and I haue nothing
Of woman in me: Now from head to foote
I am Marble constant: now the fleeting Moone
No Planet is of mine.
Enter Guardsman, and Clowne.

Guardf. This is the man.

Cleo. Auoid, and leaue him. *Exit Guardsman.*
Hast thou the pretty worme of *Nylus* there,
That killes and paines not?

Clow. Truly I haue him: but I would not be the partie that should desire you to touch him, for his byting is
immortall: those that doe dye of it, doe seldome or neuer recouer.

Cleo. Remember'st thou any that haue dyed on't?

Clow. Very many, men and women too. I heard of
one of them no longer then yesterday, a very honest woman, but something giuen to lye, as a woman should not
do, but in the way of honesty, how she dyed of the byting of it, what paine she felt: Truely, she makes a verie
good report o'th'worme: but he that wil beleeue all that
they say, shall neuer be saued by halfe that they do: but
this is most falliable, the Worme's an odde Worme.

Cleo. Get thee hence, farewell.

Clow. I wish you all ioy of the Worme.

Cleo. Farewell.

Clow. You must thinke this (looke you,) that the
Worme will do his kinde.

Cleo. I, I, farewell.

Clow. Looke you, the Worme is not to bee trusted,
but in the keeping of wise people: for indeede, there is
no goodnesse in the Worme.

Cleo. Take thou no care, it shall be heeded.

Clow. Very good: giue it nothing I pray you, for it
is not worth the feeding.

Cleo. Will it eate me?

Clow. You must not think I am so simple, but I know
the diuell himselfe will not eate a woman: I know, that
a woman is a dish for the Gods, if the diuell dresse her
not. But truly, these same whorson diuels doe the Gods
great harme in their women: for in euery tenne that they
make, the diuels marre fiue.

Cleo. Well, get thee gone, farewell.

Clow. Yes forsooth: I wish you ioy o'th'worm. *Exit*

Cleo. Giue me my Robe, put on my Crowne, I haue
Immortall longings in me. Now no more
The iuyce of Egypts Grape shall moyst this lip.
Yare, yare, good *Iras*; quicke: Me thinkes I heare
Anthony call: I see him rowse himselfe
To praise my Noble Act. I heare him mock
The lucke of *Cæsar*, which the Gods giue men
To excuse their after wrath. Husband, I come:
Now to that name, my Courage proue my Title.
I am Fire, and Ayre; my other Elements
I giue to baser life. So, haue you done?
Come then, and take the last warmth of my Lippes.
Farewell kinde *Charmian*, *Iras*, long farewell.
Haue I the Aspicke in my lippes? Dost fall?
If thou, and Nature can so gently part,
The stroke of death is as a Louers pinch,
Which hurts, and is desir'd. Dost thou lye still?
If thus thou vanishest, thou tell'st the world,
It is not worth leaue-taking.

Char. Dissolue thicke clowd, & Raine, that I may say
The Gods themselues do weepe.

Cleo. This proues me base:
If she first meete the Curled *Anthony*,
Hee'l make demand of her, and spend that kisse
Which is my heauen to haue. Come thou mortal wretch,
With thy sharpe teeth this knot intrinsicate,
Of life at once vntye: Poore venomous Foole,
Be angry, and dispatch. Oh could'st thou speake,
That I might heare thee call great *Cæsar* Asse, vnpolicied.

Char. Oh Easterne Starre.

Cleo. Peace, peace:
Dost thou not see my Baby at my breast,
That suckes the Nurse asleepe.

Char. O breake! O breake!

Cleo. As sweet as Balme, as soft as Ayre, as gentle.
O *Anthony*! Nay I will take thee too.
What should I stay—— *Dyes.*

Char. In this wilde World? So fare thee well:
Now boast thee Death, in thy possession lyes
A Lasse vnparalell'd. Downie Windowes cloze,
And golden Phœbus, neuer be beheld
Of eyes againe so Royall: your Crownes away,
Ile mend it, and then play——
Enter the Guard rustling in, and Dolabella.

1 Guard. Where's the Queene?

Char. Speake softly, wake her not.

1 *Cæsar* hath sent

Char. Too slow a Messenger.
Oh come apace, dispatch, I partly feele thee.

1 Approach hoa,
All's not well: *Cæsar's* beguild.

2 There's *Dolabella* sent from *Cæsar*: call him.

1 What worke is heere *Charmian*?
Is this well done?

Char. It is well done, and fitting for a Princesse
Descended of so many Royall Kings.
Ah Souldier. *Charmian dyes.*

Enter Dolabella.

Dol. How goes it heere?

2 Guard. All dead.

Dol. *Cæsar*, thy thoughts
Touch their effects in this: Thy selfe art comming
To see perform'd the dreaded Act which thou
So sought'st to hinder.

Enter Cæsar and all his Traine, marching.

All. A way there, a way for *Cæsar*.

The Tragedie of Anthony and Cleopatra.

Dol. Oh sir, you are too sure an Augurer:
That you did feare, is done.

Cæsar. Braueft at the last,
She leuell'd at our purposes, and being Royall
Tooke her owne way: the manner of their deaths,
I do not see them bleede.

Dol. Who was last with them?

1. Guard. A simple Countryman, that broght hir Figs:
This was his Basket.

Cæsar. Poyson'd then.

1. Guard. Oh *Cæsar*:
This *Charmian* liu'd but now, she stood and spake:
I found her trimming vp the Diadem;
On her dead Miftris tremblingly she stood,
And on the sodaine dropt.

Cæsar. Oh Noble weakenesse:
If they had swallow'd poyson, 'twould appeare
By externall swelling: but she lookes like sleepe,
As she would catch another *Anthony*
In her strong toyle of Grace.

Dol. Heere on her breft,
There is a vent of Bloud, and something blowne,
The like is on her Arme.

1. Guard. This is an Aspickes traile,
And these Figge-leaues haue slime vpon them, such
As th' Aspicke leaues vpon the Caues of Nyle.

Cæsar. Most probable
That so she dyed: for her Physitian tels mee
She hath pursu'de Conclusions infinite
Of easie wayes to dye. Take vp her bed,
And beare her Women from the Monument,
She shall be buried by her *Anthony*.
No Graue vpon the earth shall clip in it
A payre so famous: high euents as these
Strike those that make them: and their Story is
No lesse in pitty, then his Glory which
Brought them to be lamented. Our Army shall
In solemne shew, attend this Funerall,
And then to Rome. Come *Dolabella*, see
High Order, in this great Solmemnity. *Exeunt omnes*

FINIS.

THE TRAGEDIE OF CYMBELINE.

Actus Primus. Scœna Prima.

Enter two Gentlemen.

1. Gent.

You do not meet a man but Frownes.
Our bloods no more obey the Heauens
Then our Courtiers:
Still seeme, as do's the Kings.

2. Gent. But what's the matter?

1. His daughter, and the heire of's kingdome (whom
He purpos'd to his wiues sole Sonne, a Widdow
That late he married) hath referr'd her selfe
Vnto a poore, but worthy Gentleman. She's wedded,
Her Husband banish'd; she imprison'd, all
Is outward sorrow, though I thinke the King
Be touch'd at very heart.

2 None but the King?

1 He that hath lost her too: so is the Queene,
That most desir'd the Match. But not a Courtier,
Although they weare their faces to the bent
Of the Kings lookes, hath a heart that is not
Glad at the thing they scowle at.

2 And why so?

1 He that hath miss'd the Princesse, is a thing
Too bad, for bad report: and he that hath her,
(I meane, that married her, alacke good man,
And therefore banish'd) is a Creature, such,
As to seeke through the Regions of the Earth
For one, his like; there would be something failing
In him, that should compare. I do not thinke,
So faire an Outward, and such stuffe Within
Endowes a man, but hee.

2 You speake him farre.

1 I do extend him (Sir) within himselfe,
Crush him together, rather then vnfold
His measure duly.

2 What's his name, and Birth?

1 I cannot delue him to the roote: His Father
Was call'd *Sicillius*, who did ioyne his Honor
Against the Romanes, with *Cassibulan*,
But had his Titles by *Tenantius*, whom
He seru'd with Glory, and admir'd Successe:
So gain'd the Sur-addition, *Leonatus*.
And had (besides this Gentleman in question)
Two other Sonnes, who in the Warres o'th'time
Dy'de with their Swords in hand. For which, their Father
Then old, and fond of yssue, tooke such sorrow
That he quit Being; and his gentle Lady
Bigge of this Gentleman (our Theame) deceast
As he was borne. The King he takes the Babe
To his protection, cals him *Posthumus Leonatus*,
Breedes him, and makes him of his Bed-chamber,
Puts to him all the Learnings that his time
Could make him the receiuer of, which he tooke
As we do ayre, fast as 'twas ministred,
And in's Spring, became a Haruest: Liu'd in Court
(Which rare it is to do) most prais'd, most lou'd,
A sample to the yongest: to th'more Mature,
A glasse that feated them: and to the grauer,
A Childe that guided Dotards. To his Mistris,
(For whom he now is banish'd) her owne price
Proclaimes how she esteem'd him; and his Vertue
By her electiõ may be truly read, what kind of man he is.

2 I honor him, euen out of your report.
But pray you tell me, is she sole childe to'th'King?

1 His onely childe:
He had two Sonnes (if this be worth your hearing,
Marke it) the eldest of them, at three yeares old
I'th'swathing cloathes, the other from their Nursery
Were stolne, and to this houre, no ghesse in knowledge
Which way they went.

2 How long is this ago?

1 Some twenty yeares.

2 That a Kings Children should be so conuey'd,
So slackely guarded, and the search so slow
That could not trace them.

1 Howsoere, 'tis strange,
Or that the negligence may well be laugh'd at:
Yet is it true Sir.

2 I do well beleeue you.

1 We must forbeare. Heere comes the Gentleman,
The Queene, and Princesse. *Exeunt*

Scena Secunda.

Enter the Queene, Posthumus, and Imogen.

Qu. No, be assur'd you shall not finde me (Daughter)
After the slander of most Step-Mothers,
Euill-ey'd vnto you. You're my Prisoner, but
Your Gaoler shall deliuer you the keyes

That

The Tragedie of Cymbeline.

That locke vp your restraint. For you *Posthumus*,
So soone as I can win th'offended King,
I will be knowne your Aduocate: marry yet
The fire of Rage is in him, and 'twere good
You lean'd vnto his Sentence, with what patience
Your wisedome may informe you.

Post. 'Please your Highnesse,
I will from hence to day.

Qu. You know the perill:
Ile fetch a turne about the Garden, pittying
The pangs of barr'd Affections, though the King
Hath charg'd you should not speake together. *Exit*

Imo. O dissembling Curtesie! How fine this Tyrant
Can tickle where she wounds? My deerest Husband,
I something feare my Fathers wrath, but nothing
(Alwayes reseru'd my holy duty) what
His rage can do on me. You must be gone,
And I shall heere abide the hourely shot
Of angry eyes: not comforted to liue,
But that there is this Iewell in the world,
That I may see againe.

Post. My Queene, my Mistris:
O Lady, weepe no more, least I giue cause
To be suspected of more tendernesse
Then doth become a man. I will remaine
The loyall'st husband, that did ere plight troth.
My residence in Rome, at one *Filorio's*,
Who, to my Father was a Friend, to me
Knowne but by Letter; thither write (my Queene)
And with mine eyes, Ile drinke the words you send,
Though Inke be made of Gall.

Enter Queene.

Qu. Be briefe, I pray you:
If the King come, I shall incurre, I know not
How much of his displeasure: yet Ile moue him
To walke this way: I neuer do him wrong,
But he do's buy my Iniuries, to be Friends:
Payes deere for my offences.

Post. Should we be taking leaue
As long a terme as yet we haue to liue,
The loathnesse to depart, would grow: Adieu.

Imo. Nay, stay a little:
Were you but riding forth to ayre your selfe,
Such parting were too petty. Looke heere (Loue)
This Diamond was my Mothers; take it (Heart)
But keepe it till you woo another Wife,
When *Imogen* is dead.

Post. How, how? Another?
You gentle Gods, giue me but this I haue,
And seare vp my embracements from a next,
With bonds of death. Remaine, remaine thou heere,
While sense can keepe it on: And sweetest, fairest,
As I (my poore selfe) did exchange for you
To your so infinite losse; so in our trifles
I still winne of you. For my sake weare this,
It is a Manacle of Loue, Ile place it
Vpon this fayrest Prisoner.

Imo. O the Gods!
When shall we see againe?

Enter Cymbeline, and Lords.

Post. Alacke, the King.

Cym. Thou basest thing, auoyd hence, from my sight:
If after this command thou fraught the Court
With thy vnworthinesse, thou dyest. Away,
Thou'rt poyson to my blood.

Post. The Gods protect you,
And blesse the good Remainders of the Court:
I am gone. *Exit.*

Imo. There cannot be a pinch in death
More sharpe then this is.

Cym. O disloyall thing,
That should'st repayre my youth, thou heap'st
A yeares age on mee.

Imo. I beseech you Sir,
Harme not your selfe with your vexation,
I am senselesse of your Wrath; a Touch more rare
Subdues all pangs, all feares.

Cym. Past Grace? Obedience?

Imo. Past hope, and in dispaire, that way past Grace.

Cym. That might'st haue had
The sole Sonne of my Queene.

Imo. O blessed, that I might not: I chose an Eagle,
And did auoyd a Puttocke.

Cym. Thou took'st a Begger, would'st haue made my
Throne, a Seate for basenesse.

Imo. No, I rather added a lustre to it.

Cym. O thou vilde one!

Imo. Sir,
It is your fault that I haue lou'd *Posthumus*:
You bred him as my Play-fellow, and he is
A man, worth any woman: Ouer-buyes mee
Almost the summe he payes.

Cym. What? art thou mad?

Imo. Almost Sir: Heauen restore me: would I were
A Neat-heards Daughter, and my *Leonatus*
Our Neighbour-Shepheards Sonne.

Enter Queene.

Cym. Thou foolish thing;
They were againe together: you haue done
Not after our command. Away with her,
And pen her vp.

Qu. Beseech your patience: Peace
Deere Lady daughter, peace. Sweet Soueraigne,
Leaue vs to our selues, and make your self some comfort
Out of your best aduice.

Cym. Nay, let her languish
A drop of blood a day, and being aged
Dye of this Folly. *Exit.*

Enter Pisanio.

Qu. Fye, you must giue way:
Heere is your Seruant. How now Sir? What newes?

Pisa. My Lord your Sonne, drew on my Master.

Qu. Hah?
No harme I trust is done?

Pisa. There might haue beene,
But that my Master rather plaid, then fought,
And had no helpe of Anger: they were parted
By Gentlemen, at hand.

Qu. I am very glad on't.

Imo. Your Son's my Fathers friend, he takes his part
To draw vpon an Exile. O braue Sir,
I would they were in Affricke both together,
My selfe by with a Needle, that I might pricke
The goer backe. Why came you from your Master?

Pisa. On his command: he would not suffer mee
To bring him to the Hauen: left these Notes
Of what commands I should be subiect too,
When't pleas'd you to employ me.

Qu. This hath beene
Your faithfull Seruant: I dare lay mine Honour
He will remaine so.

Pisa. I humbly thanke your Highnesse.

Qu. Pray walke a-while.
Imo. About some halfe houre hence,
Pray you speake with me;
You shall (at least) go see my Lord aboord.
For this time leaue me. *Exeunt.*

Scena Tertia.

Enter Clotten, and two Lords.

1. Sir, I would aduise you to shift a Shirt; the Violence of Action hath made you reek as a Sacrifice: where ayre comes out, ayre comes in: There's none abroad so wholesome as that you vent.

Clot. If my Shirt were bloody, then to shift it. Haue I hurt him?

2 No faith: not so much as his patience.

1 Hurt him? His bodie's a passable Carkasse if he bee not hurt. It is a through-fare for Steele if it be not hurt.

2. His Steele was in debt, it went o'th'Backe-side the Towne.

Clot. The Villaine would not stand me.

2 No, but he fled forward still, toward your face.

1 Stand you? you haue Land enough of your owne: But he added to your hauing, gaue you some ground.

2 As many Inches, as you haue Oceans (Puppies.)

Clot. I would they had not come betweene vs.

2 So would I, till you had measur'd how long a Foole you were vpon the ground.

Clot. And that shee should loue this Fellow, and refuse mee.

2 If it be a sin to make a true election, she is damn'd.

1 Sir, as I told you alwayes: her Beauty & her Braine go not together. Shee's a good signe, but I haue seene small reflection of her wit.

2 She shines not vpon Fooles, least the reflection Should hurt her.

Clot. Come, Ile to my Chamber: would there had beene some hurt done.

2 I wish not so, vnlesse it had bin the fall of an Asse, which is no great hurt.

Clot. You'l go with vs?

1 Ile attend your Lordship.

Clot. Nay come, let's go together.

2 Well my Lord. *Exeunt.*

Scena Quarta.

Enter Imogen, and Pisanio.

Imo. I would thou grew'st vnto the shores o'th'Hauen, And questioned'st euery Saile: if he should write, And I not haue it, 'twere a Paper lost As offer'd mercy is: What was the last That he spake to thee?

Pisa. It was his Queene, his Queene.

Imo. Then wau'd his Handkerchiefe?

Pisa. And kist it, Madam.

Imo. Senselesse Linnen, happier therein then I: And that was all?

Pisa. No Madam: for so long As he could make me with his eye, or eare, Distinguish him from others, he did keepe The Decke, with Gloue, or Hat, or Handkerchife, Still wauing, as the fits and stirres of's mind Could best expresse how slow his Soule sayl'd on, How swift his Ship.

Imo. Thou should'st haue made him, As little as a Crow, or lesse, ere left To after-eye him.

Pisa. Madam, so I did.

Imo. I would haue broke mine eye-strings; Crack'd them, but to looke vpon him, till the diminution Of space, had pointed him sharpe as my Needle: Nay, followed him, till he had melted from The smalnesse of a Gnat, to ayre: and then Haue turn'd mine eye, and wept. But good *Pisanio*, When shall we heare from him.

Pisa. Be assur'd Madam, With his next vantage.

Imo. I did not take my leaue of him, but had Most pretty things to say: Ere I could tell him How I would thinke on him at certaine houres, Such thoughts, and such: Or I could make him sweare, The Shees of Italy should not betray Mine Interest, and his Honour: or haue charg'd him At the sixt houre of Morne, at Noone, at Midnight, T'encounter me with Orisons, for then I am in Heauen for him: Or ere I could, Giue him that parting kisse, which I had set Betwixt two charming words, comes in my Father, And like the Tyrannous breathing of the North, Shakes all our buddes from growing.

Enter a Lady.

La. The Queene (Madam) Desires your Highnesse Company.

Imo. Those things I bid you do, get them dispatch'd, I will attend the Queene.

Pisa. Madam, I shall. *Exeunt.*

Scena Quinta.

Enter Philario, Iachimo: a Frenchman, a Dutchman, and a Spaniard.

Iach. Beleeue it Sir, I haue seene him in Britaine; hee was then of a Cressent note, expected to proue so woorthy, as since he hath beene allowed the name of. But I could then haue look'd on him, without the help of Admiration, though the Catalogue of his endowments had bin tabled by his side, and I to peruse him by Items.

Phil. You speake of him when he was lesse furnish'd, then now hee is, with that which makes him both without, and within.

French. I haue seene him in France: wee had very many there, could behold the Sunne, with as firme eyes as hee.

Iach. This matter of marrying his Kings Daughter, wherein he must be weighed rather by her valew, then his owne, words him (I doubt not) a great deale from the matter.

French. And then his banishment.

Iach. I, and the approbation of those that weepe this lamentable diuorce vnder her colours, are wonderfully to extend him, be it but to fortifie her iudgement, which else an easie battery might lay flat, for taking a Begger without lesse quality. But how comes it, he is to soiourne with you? How creepes acquaintance?

Phil. His Father and I were Souldiers together, to whom I haue bin often bound for no lesse then my life.

Enter Posthumus.

Heere comes the Britaine. Let him be so entertained amongst you, as suites with Gentlemen of your knowing, to a Stranger of his quality. I beseech you all be better knowne to this Gentleman, whom I commend to you, as a Noble Friend of mine. How Worthy he is, I will leaue to appeare hereafter, rather then story him in his owne hearing.

French. Sir, we haue knowne togither in Orleance.

Post. Since when, I haue bin debtor to you for courtesies, which I will be euer to pay, and yet pay still.

French. Sir, you o're-rate my poore kindnesse, I was glad I did attone my Countryman and you: it had beene pitty you should haue beene put together, with so mortall a purpose, as then each bore, vpon importance of, so slight and triuiall a nature.

Post. By your pardon Sir, I was then a young Traueller, rather shun'd to go euen with what I heard, then in my euery action to be guided by others experiences: but vpon my mended iudgement (if I offend to say it is mended) my Quarrell was not altogether slight.

French. Faith yes, to be put to the arbiterment of Swords, and by such two, that would by all likelyhood haue confounded one the other, or haue falne both.

Iach. Can we with manners, aske what was the difference?

French. Safely, I thinke, 'twas a contention in publicke, which may (without contradiction) suffer the report. It was much like an argument that fell out last night, where each of vs fell in praise of our Country-Mistresses. This Gentleman, at that time vouching, (and vpon warrant of bloody affirmation) his to be more Faire, Vertuous, Wise, Chaste, Constant, Qualified, and lesse attemptible then any, the rarest of our Ladies in Fraunce.

Iach. That Lady is not now liuing; or this Gentlemans opinion by this, worne out.

Post. She holds her Vertue still, and I my mind.

Iach. You must not so farre preferre her, 'fore ours of Italy.

Posth. Being so farre prouok'd as I was in France: I would abate her nothing, though I professe my selfe her Adorer, not her Friend.

Iach. As faire, and as good: a kind of hand in hand comparison, had beene something too faire, and too good for any Lady in Britanie; if she went before others. I haue seene as that Diamond of yours out-lusters many I haue beheld, I could not beleeue she excelled many: but I haue not seene the most pretious Diamond that is, nor you the Lady.

Post. I prais'd her, as I rated her: so do I my Stone.

Iach. What do you esteeme it at?

Post. More then the world enioyes.

Iach. Either your vnparagon'd Mistirs is dead, or she's out-priz'd by a trifle.

Post. You are mistaken: the one may be solde or giuen, or if there were wealth enough for the purchases, or merite for the guift. The other is not a thing for sale, and onely the guift of the Gods.

Iach. Which the Gods haue giuen you?

Post. Which by their Graces I will keepe.

Iach. You may weare her in title yours: but you know strange Fowle light vpon neighbouring Ponds. Your Ring may be stolne too, so your brace of vnprizeable Estimations, the one is but fraile, and the other Casuall; A cunning Thiefe, or a (that way) accomplish'd Courtier, would hazzard the winning both of first and last.

Post. Your Italy, containes none so accomplish'd a Courtier to conuince the Honour of my Mistris: if in the holding or losse of that, you terme her fraile, I do nothing doubt you haue store of Theeues, notwithstanding I feare not my Ring.

Phil. Let vs leaue heere, Gentlemen?

Post. Sir, with all my heart. This worthy Signior I thanke him, makes no stranger of me, we are familiar at first.

Iach. With fiue times so much conuersation, I should get ground of your faire Mistris; make her go backe, euen to the yeilding, had I admittance, and opportunitie to friend.

Post. No, no.

Iach. I dare thereupon pawne the moytie of my Estate, to your Ring, which in my opinion o're-values it something: but I make my wager rather against your Confidence, then her Reputation. And to barre your offence heerein to, I durst attempt it against any Lady in the world.

Post. You are a great deale abus'd in too bold a perswasion, and I doubt not you sustaine what y'are worthy of, by your Attempt.

Iach. What's that?

Posth. A Repulse though your Attempt (as you call it) deserue more; a punishment too.

Phi. Gentlemen enough of this, it came in too sodainely, let it dye as it was borne, and I pray you be better acquainted.

Iach. Would I had put my Estate, and my Neighbors on th'approbation of what I haue spoke.

Post. What Lady would you chuse to assaile?

Iach. Yours, whom in constancie you thinke stands so safe. I will lay you ten thousands Duckets to your Ring, that commend me to the Court where your Lady is, with no more aduantage then the opportunitie of a second conference, and I will bring from thence, that Honor of hers, which you imagine so reseru'd.

Posthmus. I will wage against your Gold, Gold to it: My Ring I holde deere as my finger, 'tis part of it.

Iach. You are a Friend, and there in the wiser: if you buy Ladies flesh at a Million a Dram, you cannot preseure it from tainting; but I see you haue some Religion in you, that you feare.

Posthu. This is but a custome in your tongue: you beare a grauer purpose I hope.

Iach. I am the Master of my speeches, and would vnder-go what's spoken, I sweare.

Posthu. Will you? I shall but lend my Diamond till your returne: let there be Couenants drawne between's. My Mistris exceedes in goodnesse, the hugenesse of your vnworthy thinking. I dare you to this match: heere's my Ring.

Phil. I will haue it no lay.

Iach. By the Gods it is one: if I bring you no sufficient testimony that I haue enioy'd the deerest bodily part of your Mistris: my ten thousand Duckets are yours;

The Tragedy of Cymbeline.

so is your Diamond too: if I come off, and leaue her in such honour as you haue trust in; Shee your Iewell, this your Iewell, and my Gold are yours: prouided, I haue your commendation, for my more free entertainment.

Post. I embrace these Conditions, let vs haue Articles betwixt vs: onely thus farre you shall answere; if you make your voyage vpon her, and giue me directly to vnderstand, you haue preuayl'd, I am no further your Enemy, shee is not worth our debate. If shee remaine vnseduc'd, you not making it appeare otherwise: for your ill opinion, and th'assault you haue made to her chastity, you shall answer me with your Sword.

Iach. Your hand, a Couenant: wee will haue these things set downe by lawfull Counsell, and straight away for Britaine, least the Bargaine should catch colde, and sterue: I will fetch my Gold, and haue our two Wagers recorded.

Post. Agreed.

French. Will this hold, thinke you.

Phil. Signior *Iachimo* will not from it. Pray let vs follow 'em. *Exeunt.*

Scena Sexta.

Enter Queene, Ladies, and Cornelius.

Qu. Whiles yet the dewe's on ground,
Gather those Flowers,
Make haste. Who ha's the note of them?

Lady. I Madam.

Queen. Dispatch. *Exit Ladies.*
Now Master Doctor, haue you brought those drugges?

Cor. Pleaseth your Highnes, I: here they are, Madam:
But I beseech your Grace, without offence
(My Conscience bids me aske) wherefore you haue
Commanded of me these most poysonous Compounds,
Which are the moouers of a languishing death:
But though slow, deadly.

Qu. I wonder, Doctor,
Thou ask'st me such a Question: Haue I not bene
Thy Pupill long? Hast thou not learn'd me how
To make Perfumes? Distill? Preserue? Yea so,
That our great King himselfe doth woo me oft
For my Confections? Hauing thus farre proceeded,
(Vnlesse thou think'st me diuellish) is't not meete
That I did amplifie my iudgement in
Other Conclusions? I will try the forces
Of these thy Compounds, on such Creatures as
We count not worth the hanging (but none humane)
To try the vigour of them, and apply
Allayments to their Act, and by them gather
Their seuerall vertues, and effects.

Cor. Your Highnesse
Shall from this practise, but make hard your heart:
Besides, the seeing these effects will be
Both noysome, and infectious.

Qu. O content thee.

Enter Pisanio.

Heere comes a flattering Rascall, vpon him
Will I first worke: Hee's for his Master,
And enemy to my Sonne. How now *Pisanio*?
Doctor, your seruice for this time is ended,
Take your owne way.

Cor. I do suspect you, Madam,
But you shall do no harme.

Qu. Hearke thee, a word.

Cor. I do not like her. She doth thinke she ha's
Strange ling'ring poysons: I do know her spirit,
And will not trust one of her malice, with
A drugge of such damn'd Nature. Those she ha's,
Will stupifie and dull the Sense a-while,
Which first (perchance) shee'l proue on Cats and Dogs,
Then afterward vp higher: but there is
No danger in what shew of death it makes,
More then the locking vp the Spirits a time,
To be more fresh, reuiuing. She is fool'd
With a most false effect: and I, the truer,
So to be false with her.

Qu. No further seruice, Doctor,
Vntill I send for thee.

Cor. I humbly take my leaue. *Exit.*

Qu. Weepes she still (saist thou?)
Dost thou thinke in time
She will not quench, and let instructions enter
Where Folly now possesses? Do thou worke:
When thou shalt bring me word she loues my Sonne,
Ile tell thee on the instant, thou art then
As great as is thy Master: Greater, for
His Fortunes all lye speechlesse, and his name
Is at last gaspe. Returne he cannot, nor
Continue where he is: To shift his being,
Is to exchange one misery with another,
And euery day that comes, comes to decay
A dayes worke in him. What shalt thou expect
To be depender on a thing that leanes?
Who cannot be new built, nor ha's no Friends
So much, as but to prop him? Thou tak'st vp
Thou know'st not what: But take it for thy labour,
It is a thing I made, which hath the King
Fiue times redeem'd from death. I do not know
What is more Cordiall. Nay, I prythee take it,
It is an earnest of a farther good
That I meane to thee. Tell thy Mistris how
The case stands with her: doo't, as from thy selfe;
Thinke what a chance thou changest on, but thinke
Thou hast thy Mistris still, to boote, my Sonne,
Who shall take notice of thee. Ile moue the King
To any shape of thy Preferment, such
As thou'lt desire: and then my selfe, I cheefely,
That set thee on to this desert, am bound
To loade thy merit richly. Call my women. *Exit Pisa.*
Thinke on my words. A slye, and constant knaue,
Not to be shak'd: the Agent for his Master,
And the Remembrancer of her, to hold
The hand-fast to her Lord. I haue giuen him that,
Which if she take, shall quite vnpeople her
Of Leidgers for her Sweete: and which, she after
Except she bend her humor, shall be assur'd
To taste of too.

Enter Pisanio, and Ladies.

So, so: Well done, well done:
The Violets, Cowslippes, and the Prime-Roses
Beare to my Closset: Fare thee well, *Pisanio.*
Thinke on my words. *Exit Qu. and Ladies*

Pisa. And shall do:
But when to my good Lord, I proue vntrue,
Ile choake my selfe: there's all Ile do for you. *Exit.*

Scena

Scena Septima.

Enter Imogen alone.

Imo. A Father cruell, and a Stepdame false,
A Foolish Suitor to a Wedded-Lady,
That hath her Husband banish'd : O, that Husband,
My supreame Crowne of griefe, and those repeated
Vexations of it. Had I bin Theefe-stolne,
As my two Brothers, happy : but most miserable
Is the desires that's glorious. Blessed be those
How meane so ere, that haue their honest wills,
Which seasons comfort. Who may this be? Fye.

Enter Pisanio, and Iachimo.

Pisa. Madam, a Noble Gentleman of Rome,
Comes from my Lord with Letters.

Iach. Change you, Madam :
The Worthy *Leonatus* is in safety,
And greetes your Highnesse deerely.

Imo. Thanks good Sir,
You're kindly welcome.

Iach. All of her, that is out of doore, most rich :
If she be furnish'd with a mind so rare
She is alone th'Arabian-Bird; and I
Haue lost the wager. Boldnesse be my Friend :
Arme me Audacitie from head to foote,
Or like the Parthian I shall flying fight,
Rather directly fly.

Imogen reads.

He is one of the Noblest note, to whose kindnesses I am most infinitely tied. Reflect vpon him accordingly, as you value your trust. Leonatus.

So farre I reade aloud.
But euen the very middle of my heart
Is warm'd by th'rest, and take it thankefully.
You are as welcome (worthy Sir) as I
Haue words to bid you, and shall finde it so
In all that I can do.

Iach. Thankes fairest Lady :
What are men mad? Hath Nature giuen them eyes
To see this vaulted Arch, and the rich Crop
Of Sea and Land, which can distinguish 'twixt
The firie Orbes aboue, and the twinn'd Stones
Vpon the number'd Beach, and can we not
Partition make with Spectales so pretious
Twixt faire, and foule?

Imo. What makes your admiration?

Iach. It cannot be i'th'eye : for Apes, and Monkeys
'Twixt two such She's, would chatter this way, and
Contemne with mowes the other. Nor i'th'iudgment :
For Idiots in this case of fauour, would
Be wisely definit : Nor i'th'Appetite.
Sluttery to such neate Excellence, oppos'd
Should make desire vomit emptinesse,
Not so allur'd to feed.

Imo. What is the matter trow?

Iach. The Cloyed will :
That satiate yet vnsatisfi'd desire, that Tub
Both fill'd and running : Rauening first the Lambe,
Longs after for the Garbage.

Imo. What, deere Sir,
Thus rap's you? Are you well?

Iach. Thanks Madam well : Beseech you Sir,
Desire my Man's abode, where I did leaue him :
He's strange and peeuish.

Pisa. I was going Sir,
To giue him welcome. *Exit.*

Imo. Continues well my Lord?
His health beseech you?

Iach. Well, Madam.

Imo. Is he dispos'd to mirth? I hope he is.

Iach. Exceeding pleasant : none a stranger there,
So merry, and so gamesome : he is call'd
The Britaine Reueller.

Imo. When he was heere
He did incline to sadnesse, and oft times
Not knowiug why.

Iach. I neuer saw him sad.
There is a Frenchman his Companion, one
An eminent Monsieur, that it seemes much loues
A Gallian-Girle at home. He furnaces
The thicke sighes from him; whiles the iolly Britaine,
(Your Lord I meane) laughes from's free lungs cries oh,
Can my sides hold, to think that man who knowes
By History, Report, or his owne proofe
What woman is, yea what she cannot choose
But must be will's free houres languish :
For assured bondage?

Imo. Will my Lord say so?

Iach. I Madam, with his eyes in flood, with laughter,
It is a Recreation to be by
And heare him mocke the Frenchman :
But Heauen's know some men are much too blame.

Imo. Not he I hope.

Iach. Not he :
But yet Heauen's bounty towards him, might
Be vs'd more thankfully. In himselfe 'tis much;
In you which I account his beyond all Talents.
Whil'st I am bound to wonder, I am bound
To pitty too.

Imo. What do you pitty Sir?

Iach. Two Creatures heartyly.

Imo. Am I one Sir?
You looke on me : what wrack discerne you in me
Deserues your pitty?

Iach. Lamentable : what
To hide me from the radiant Sun, and solace
I'th'Dungeon by a Snuffe.

Imo. I pray you Sir,
Deliuer with more opennesse your answeres
To my demands. Why do you pitty me?

Iach. That others do,
(I was about to say) enioy your——but
It is an office of the Gods to venge it,
Not mine to speake on't.

Imo. You do seeme to know
Something of me, or what concernes me : pray you
Since doubting things go ill, often hurts more
Then to be sure they do. For Certainties
Either are past remedies; or timely knowing,
The remedy then borne. Discouer to me
What both you spur and stop.

Iach. Had I this cheeke
To bathe my lips vpon : this hand, whose touch,
(Whose euery touch) would force the Feelers soule
To th'oath of loyalty. This obiect, which
Takes prisoner the wild motion of mine eye,
Fiering it onely heere, should I (damn'd then)

Slauer

Slauuer with lippes as common as the stayres
That mount the Capitoll: Ioyne gripes, with hands
Made hard with hourely falshood (falshood as
With labour:) then by peeping in an eye
Base and illustrious as the smoakie light
That's fed with stinking Tallow: it were fit
That all the plagues of Hell should at one time
Encounter such reuolt.

  Imo. My Lord, I feare
Has forgot Brittaine.

  Iach. And himselfe, not I
Inclin'd to this intelligence, pronounce
The Beggery of his change: but 'tis your Graces
That from my mutest Conscience, to my tongue,
Charmes this report out.

  Imo. Let me heare no more.

  Iach. O deerest Soule: your Cause doth strike my hart
With pitty, that doth make me sicke. A Lady
So faire, and fasten'd to an Emperie
Would make the great'st King double, to be partner'd
With Tomboyes hyr'd, with that selfe exhibition
Which your owne Coffers yeeld: with diseas'd ventures
That play with all Infirmities for Gold,
Which rottennesse can lend Nature. Such boyl'd stuffe
As well might poyson Poyson. Be reueng'd,
Or she that bore you, was no Queene, and you
Recoyle from your great Stocke.

  Imo. Reueng'd:
How should I be reueng'd? If this be true,
(As I haue such a Heart, that both mine eares
Must not in haste abuse) if it be true,
How should I be reueng'd?

  Iach. Should he make me
Liue like *Diana's* Priest, betwixt cold sheets,
Whiles he is vaulting variable Rampes
In your despight, vpon your purse: reuenge it.
I dedicate my selfe to your sweet pleasure,
More Noble then that runnagate to your bed,
And will continue fast to your Affection,
Still close, as sure.

  Imo. What hoa, *Pisanio*?

  Iach. Let me my seruice tender on your lippes.

  Imo. Away, I do condemne mine eares, that haue
So long attended thee: If thou wert Honourable
Thou would'st haue told this tale for Vertue, not
For such an end thou seek'st, as base, as strange:
Thou wrong'st a Gentleman, who is as farre
From thy report, as thou from Honor: and
Solicites heere a Lady, that disdaines
Thee, and the Diuell alike. What hoa, *Pisanio*?
The King my Father shall be made acquainted
Of thy Assault: if he shall thinke it fit,
A sawcy Stranger in his Court, to Mart
As in a Romish Stew, and to expound
His beastly minde to vs; he hath a Court
He little cares for, and a Daughter, who
He not respects at all. What hoa, *Pisanio*?

  Iach. O happy *Leonatus* I may say,
The credit that thy Lady hath of thee
Deserues thy trust, and thy most perfect goodnesse
Her assur'd credit. Blessed liue you long,
A Lady to the worthiest Sir, that euer
Country call'd his; and you his Mistris, onely
For the most worthiest fit. Giue me your pardon,
I haue spoke this to know if your Affiance
Were deeply rooted, and shall make your Lord,

That which he is, new o're: And he is one
The truest manner'd: such a holy Witch,
That he enchants Societies into him:
Halfe all men hearts are his.

  Imo. You make amends.

  Iach. He sits 'mongst men, like a defended God;
He hath a kinde of Honor sets him off,
More then a mortall seeming. Be not angrie
(Most mighty Princesse) that I haue aduentur'd
To try your taking of a false report, which hath
Honour'd with confirmation your great Iudgement,
In the election of a Sir, so rare,
Which you know, cannot erre. The loue I beare him,
Made me to fan you thus, but the Gods made you
(Vnlike all others) chaffelesse. Pray your pardon.

  Imo. All's well Sir:
Take my powre i'th'Court for yours.

  Iach. My humble thankes: I had almost forgot
T'intreat your Grace, but in a small request,
And yet of moment too, for it concernes:
Your Lord, my selfe, and other Noble Friends
Are partners in the businesse.

  Imo. Pray what is't?

  Iach. Some dozen Romanes of vs, and your Lord
(The best Feather of our wing) haue mingled summes
To buy a Present for the Emperor:
Which I (the Factor for the rest) haue done
In France: 'tis Plate of rare deuice, and Iewels
Of rich, and exquisite forme, their valewes great,
And I am something curious, being strange
To haue them in safe stowage: May it please you
To take them in protection.

  Imo. Willingly:
And pawne mine Honor for their safety, since
My Lord hath interest in them, I will keepe them
In my Bed-chamber.

  Iach. They are in a Trunke
Attended by my men: I will make bold
To send them to you, onely for this night:
I must aboord to morrow.

  Imo. O no, no.

  Iach. Yes I beseech: or I shall short my word
By length'ning my returne. From Gallia,
I crost the Seas on purpose, and on promise
To see your Grace.

  Imo. I thanke you for your paines:
But not away to morrow.

  Iach. O I must Madam.
Therefore I shall beseech you, if you please
To greet your Lord with writing, doo't to night,
I haue out-stood my time, which is materiall
To'th'tender of our Present.

  Imo. I will write:
Send your Trunke to me, it shall safe be kept,
And truely yeelded you: you're very welcome. *Exeunt.*

Actus Secundus. Scena Prima.

Enter Clotten, and the two Lords.

  Clot. Was there euer man had such lucke? when I kist
the Iacke vpon an vp-cast, to be hit away? I had a hundred pound on't: and then a whorson Iacke-an-Apes,
must

The Tragedy of Cymbeline.

must take me vp for swearing, as if I borrowed mine oathes of him, and might not spend them at my pleasure.

1. What got he by that? you haue broke his pate with your Bowle.

2. If his wit had bin like him that broke it: it would haue run all out.

Clot. When a Gentleman is dispos'd to sweare: it is not for any standers by to curtall his oathes. Ha?

2. No my Lord; nor crop the eares of them.

Clot. Whorson dog: I gaue him satisfaction? would he had bin one of my Ranke.

2. To haue smell'd like a Foole.

Clot. I am not vext more at any thing in th'earth: a pox on't. I had rather not be so Noble as I am: they dare not fight with me, because of the Queene my Mother: euery Iacke-Slaue hath his belly full of Fighting, and I must go vp and downe like a Cock, that no body can match.

2. You are Cocke and Capon too, and you crow Cock, with your combe on.

Clot. Sayest thou?

2. It is not fit you Lordship should vndertake euery Companion, that you giue offence too.

Clot. No, I know that: but it is fit I should commit offence to my inferiors.

2. I, it is fit for your Lordship onely.

Clot. Why so I say.

1. Did you heere of a Stranger that's come to Court night?

Clot. A Stranger, and I not know on't?

2. He's a strange Fellow himselfe, and knowes it not.

1. There's an Italian come, and 'tis thought one of *Leonatus* Friends.

Clot. Leonatus? A banisht Rascall; and he's another, whatsoeuer he be. Who told you of this Stranger?

1. One of your Lordships Pages.

Clot. Is it fit I went to looke vpon him? Is there no derogation in't?

2. You cannot derogate my Lord.

Clot. Not easily I thinke.

2. You are a Foole graunted, therefore your Issues being foolish do not derogate.

Clot. Come, Ile go see this Italian: what I haue lost to day at Bowles, Ile winne to night of him. Come: go.

2. Ile attend your Lordship. *Exit.*

That such a craftie Diuell as is his Mother
Should yeild the world this Asse: A woman, that
Beares all downe with her Braine, and this her Sonne,
Cannot take two from twenty for his heart,
And leaue eighteene. Alas poore Princesse,
Thou diuine *Imogen*, what thou endur'st,
Betwixt a Father by thy Step-dame gouern'd,
A Mother hourely coyning plots: A Wooer,
More hatefull then the foule expulsion is,
Of thy deere Husband. Then that horrid Act
Of the diuorce, heel'd make the Heauens hold firme
The walls of thy deere Honour. Keepe vnshak'd
That Temple thy faire mind, that thou maist stand
T'enioy thy banish'd Lord: and this great Land. *Exeunt.*

Scena Secunda.

Enter Imogen, in her Bed, and a Lady.

Imo. Who's there? My woman: *Helene?*
La. Please you Madam.
Imo. What houre is it?

Lady. Almost midnight, Madam.
Imo. I haue read three houres then:
Mine eyes are weake,
Fold downe the leafe where I haue left: to bed.
Take not away the Taper, leaue it burning:
And if thou canst awake by foure o'th'clock,
I prythee call me: Sleepe hath ceiz'd me wholly.
To your protection I commend me, Gods,
From Fayries, and the Tempters of the night,
Guard me beseech yee. *Sleepes.*

Iach: mo from the Trunke.

Iach. The Crickets sing, and mans ore-labor'd sense
Repaires it selfe by rest: Our *Tarquine* thus
Did softly presse the Rushes, ere he waken'd
The Chastitie he wounded. *Cytherea,*
How brauely thou becom'st thy Bed; fresh Lilly,
And whiter then the Sheetes: that I might touch,
But kisse, one kisse. Rubies vnparagon'd,
How deerely they doo't: 'Tis her breathing that
Perfumes the Chamber thus: the Flame o'th'Taper
Bowes toward her, and would vnder-peepe her lids.
To see th'inclosed Lights, now Canopied
Vnder these windowes, White and Azure lac'd
With Blew of Heauens owne tinct. But my designe.
To note the Chamber, I will write all downe,
Such, and such pictures: There the window, such
Th'adronement of her Bed; the Arras, Figures,
Why such, and such: and the Contents o'th'Story.
Ah, but some naturall notes about her Body,
Aboue ten thousand meaner Moueables
Would testifie, t'enrich mine Inuentorie.
O sleepe, thou Ape of death, lye dull vpon her,
And be her Sense but as a Monument,
Thus in a Chappell lying. Come off, come off;
As slippery as the Gordian-knot was hard.
'Tis mine, and this will witnesse outwardly,
As strongly as the Conscience do's within:
To'th'madding of her Lord. On her left brest
A mole Cinque-spotted: Like the Crimson drops
I'th'bottome of a Cowslippe. Heere's a Voucher,
Stronger then euer Law could make; this Secret
Will force him thinke I haue pick'd the lock, and t'ane
The treasure of her Honour. No more: to what end?
Why should I write this downe, that's riueted,
Screw'd to my memorie. She hath bin reading late,
The Tale of *Tereus*, heere the leaffe's turn'd downe
Where *Philomele* gaue vp. I haue enough,
To'th'Truncke againe, and shut the spring of it.
Swift, swift, you Dragons of the night, that dawning
May beare the Rauens eye: I lodge in feare,
Though this a heauenly Angell: hell is heere. *Clocke strikes*

One, two, three: time, time. *Exit.*

Scena Tertia.

Enter Clotten, and Lords.

1. Your Lordship is the most patient man in losse, the most coldest that euer turn'd vp Ace.

Clot. It would make any man cold to loose.

1. But not euery man patient after the noble temper of your Lordship: You are most hot, and furious when you winne.

Clot.

The Tragedie of Cymbeline.

Winning will put any man into courage: if I could get this foolish *Imogen*, I should haue Gold enough: it's almost morning, is't not?

  1. Day, my Lord.

  Clot. I would this Musicke would come: I am aduised to giue her Musicke a mornings, they say it will penetrate.   *Enter Musitians.*

Come on, tune: If you can penetrate her with your fingering, so: wee'l try with tongue too: if none will do, let her remaine: but Ile neuer giue o're. First, a very excellent good conceyted thing; after a wonderful sweet aire, with admirable rich words to it, and then let her consider.

SONG.

Hearke, hearke, the Larke at Heauens gate sings,
  and Phœbus gins arise,
His Steeds to water at those Springs
  on chalic'd Flowres that lyes:
And winking Mary-buds begin to ope their Golden eyes
With euery thing that pretty is, my Lady sweet arise:
  Arise, arise.

So, get you gone: if this pen trate, I will consider your Musicke the better: if it do not, it is a voyce in her eares which Horse-haires, and Calues-guts, nor the voyce of vnpaued Eunuch to boot, can neuer amed.   *Enter Cymbaline, and Queene.*

  2 Heere comes the King.

  Clot. I am glad I was vp so late, for that's the reason I was vp so early: he cannot choose but take this Seruice I haue done, fatherly. Good morrow to your Maiesty, and to my gracious Mother.

  Cym. Attend you here the doore of our stern daughter Will she not forth?

  Clot. I haue assayl'd her with Musickes, but she vouchsafes no notice.

  Cym. The Exile of her Minion is too new, She hath not yet forgot him, some more time Must weare the print of his remembrance on't, And then she's yours.

  Qu. You are most bound to'th'King, Who let's go by no vantages, that may Preferre you to his daughter: Frame your selfe To orderly solicity, and be friended With aptnesse of the season: make denials Encrease your Seruices: so seeme, as if You were inspir'd to do those duties which You tender to her: that you in all obey her, Saue when command to your dismission tends, And therein you are senselesse.

  Clot. Senselesse? Not so.

  Mes. So like you (Sir) Ambassadors from Rome; The one is *Caius Lucius.*

  Cym. A worthy Fellow, Albeit he comes on angry purpose now; But that's no fault of his: we must receyue him According to the Honor of his Sender, And towards himselfe, his goodnesse fore-spent on vs We must extend our notice: Our deere Sonne, When you haue giuen good morning to your Mistris, Attend the Queene, and vs, we shall haue neede T'employ you towards this Romane. Come our Queene.   *Exeunt.*

  Clot. If she be vp, Ile speake with her: if not Let her lye still, and dreame: by your leaue hoa, I know her women are about her: what

If I do line one of their hands, 'tis Gold Which buyes admittance (oft it doth) yea, and makes *Diana's* Rangers false themselues, yeeld vp Their Deere to'th'stand o'th'Stealer: and 'tis Gold Which makes the True-man kill'd, and saues the Theefe: Nay, sometime hangs both Theefe, and True-man: what Can it not do, and vndoo? I will make One of her women Lawyer to me, for I yet not vnderstand the case my selfe.
By your leaue.   *Knockes.*
   Enter a Lady.

  La. Who's there that knockes?

  Clot. A Gentleman.

  La. No more.

  Clot. Yes, and a Gentlewomans Sonne.

  La. That's more Then some whose Taylors are as deere as yours, Can iustly boast of: what's your Lordships pleasure?

  Clot. Your Ladies person, is she ready?

  La. I, to keepe her Chamber.

  Clot. There is Gold for you, Sell me your good report.

  La. How, my good name? or to report of you What I shall thinke is good. The Princesse.

   Enter Imogen.

  Clot. Good morrow fairest, Sister your sweet hand.

  Imo. Good morrow Sir, you lay out too much paines For purchasing but trouble: the thankes I giue, Is telling you that I am poore of thankes, And scarse can spare them.

  Clot. Still I sweare I loue you.

  Imo. If you but said so, 'twere as deepe with me: If you sweare still, your recompence is still That I regard it not.

  Clot. This is no answer.

  Imo. But that you shall not say, I yeeld being silent, I would not speake. I pray you spare me, 'faith I shall vnfold equall discourtesie To your best kindnesse: one of your great knowing Should learne (being taught) forbearance.

  Clot. To leaue you in your madnesse, 'twere my sin, I will not.

  Imo. Fooles are not mad Folkes.

  Clot. Do you call me Foole?

  Imo. As I am mad, I do: If you'l be patient, Ile no more be mad, That cures vs both. I am much sorry (Sir) You put me to forget a Ladies manners By being so verball: and learne now, for all, That I which know my heart, do heer pronounse By th'very truth of it, I care not for you, And am so neere the lacke of Charitie To accuse my selfe, I hate you: which I had rather You felt, then make't my boast.

  Clot. You sinne against Obedience, which you owe your Father, for The Contract you pretend with that base Wretch, One, bred of Almes, and foster'd with cold dishes, With scraps o'th'Court: It is no Contract, none; And though it be allowed in meaner parties (Yet who then he more meane) to knit their soules (On whom there is no more dependancie But Brats and Beggery) in selfe-figur'd knot, Yet you are curb'd from that enlargement, by

aaa   The

The consequence o'th'Crowne, and must not foyle
The precious note of it; with a base Slaue,
A Hilding for a Liuorie, a Squires Cloth,
A Pantler; not so eminent.
  Imo. Prophane Fellow:
Wert thou the Sonne of *Iupiter*, and no more,
But what thou art besides: thou wer't too base,
To be his Groome: thou wer't dignified enough
Euen to the point of Enuie. If 'twere made
Comparatiue for your Vertues, to be stil'd
The vnder Hangman of his Kingdome; and hated
For being prefer'd so well.
  Clot. The South-Fog rot him.
  Imo. He neuer can meete more mischance, then come
To be but nam'd of thee. His mean'st Garment
That euer hath but clipt his body; is dearer
In my respect, then all the Heires aboue thee,
Were they all made such men: How now *Pisanio*?
    Enter Pisanio.
  Clot. His Garments? Now the diuell.
  Imo. To *Dorothy* my woman hie thee presently.
  Clot. His Garment?
  Imo. I am sprighted with a Foole,
Frighted, and angred worse: Go bid my woman
Search for a Iewell, that too casually
Hath left mine Arme: it was thy Masters. Shrew me
If I would loose it for a Reuenew,
Of any Kings in Europe. I do think,
I saw't this morning: Confident I am.
Last night 'twas on mine Arme; I kiss'd it,
I hope it be not gone, to tell my Lord
That I kisse aught but he.
  Pis. 'Twill not be lost.
  Imo. I hope so: go and search.
  Clot. You haue abus'd me:
His meanest Garment?
  Imo. I, I said so Sir,
If you will make't an Action, call witnesse to't.
  Clot. I will enferme your Father.
  Imo. Your Mother too:
She's my good Lady; and will conceiue, I hope
But the worst of me. So I leaue your Sir,
To th' worst of discontent.   *Exit.*
  Clot. Ile bereueng'd:
His mean'st Garment? Well.   *Exit.*

Scena Quarta.

Enter Posthumus, and Philario.

  Post. Feare it not Sir: I would I were so sure
To winne the King, as I am bold, her Honour
Will remaine her's.
  Phil. What meanes do you make to him?
  Post. Not any: but abide the change of Time,
Quake in the present winters state, and wish
That warmer dayes would come: In these fear'd hope
I barely gratifie your loue; they fayling,
I must die much your debtor.
  Phil. Your very goodnesse, and your company,
Ore-payes all I can do. By this your King,
Hath heard of Great *Augustus*: *Caius Lucius*,
Will do's Commission throughly. And I think

Hee'le grant the Tribute: send th' Arrerages,
Or looke vpon our Romaines, whose remembrance
Is yet fresh in their griefe.
  Post. I do beleeue
(Statist though I am none, nor like to be)
That this will proue a Warre; and you shall heare
The Legion now in Gallia, sooner landed
In our not-fearing-Britaine, then haue tydings
Of any penny Tribute paid. Our Countrymen
Are men more order'd, then when *Iulius Cæsar*
Smil'd at their lacke of skill, but found their courage
Worthy his frowning at. Their discipline,
(Now wing-led with their courages) will make knowne
To their Approuers, they are People, such
That 'mend vpon the world.   *Enter Iachimo.*
  Phi. See *Iachimo.*
  Post. The swiftest Harts, haue posted you by land;
And Windes of all the Corners kiss'd your Sailes,
To make your vessell nimble.
  Phil. Welcome Sir.
  Post. I hope the briefenesse of your answere, made
The speedinesse of your returne.
  Iachi. Your Lady,
Is one of the fayrest that I haue look'd vpon
  Post. And therewithall the best, or let her beauty
Looke thorough a Casement to allure false hearts,
And be false with them.
  Iachi. Heere are Letters for you.
  Post. Their tenure good I trust.
  Iach. 'Tis very like.
  Post. Was *Caius Lucius* in the Britaine Court,
When you were there?
  Iach. He was expected then,
But not approach'd.
  Post. All is well yet,
Sparkles this Stone as it was wont, or is't not
Too dull for your good wearing?
  Iach. If I haue lost it,
I should haue lost the worth of it in Gold,
Ile make a iourney twice as farre, t'enioy
A second night of such sweet shortnesse, which
Was mine in Britaine, for the Ring is wonne.
  Post. The Stones too hard to come by.
  Iach. Not a whit,
Your Lady being so easy.
  Post. Make note Sir
Your losse, your Sport: I hope you know that we
Must not continue Friends.
  Iach. Good Sir, we must
If you keepe Couenant: had I not brought
The knowledge of your Mistris home, I grant
We were to question farther; but I now
Professe my selfe the winner of her Honor,
Together with your Ring; and not the wronger
Of her, or you hauing proceeded but
By both your willes.
  Post. If you can mak't apparant
That you haue tasted her in Bed; my hand,
And Ring is yours. If not, the foule opinion
You had of her pure Honour; gaines, or looses,
Your Sword, or mine, or Masterlesse leaue both
To who shall finde them.
  Iach. Sir, my Circumstances
Being so nere the Truth, as I will make them;
Must first induce you to beleeue; whose strength
I will confirme with oath, which I doubt not
                                              You'l

You'l giue me leaue to spare, when you shall finde
You neede it not.
  Post. Proceed.
  Iach. First, her Bed-chamber
(Where I confesse I slept not, but professe
Had that was well worth watching) it was hang'd
With Tapistry of Silke, and Siluer, the Story
Proud *Cleopatra*, when she met her Roman,
And *Sidnus* swell'd aboue the Bankes, or for
The presse of Boates, or Pride. A peece of Worke
So brauely done, so rich, that it did striue
In Workemanship, and Value, which I wonder'd
Could be so rarely, and exactly wrought
Since the true life on't was——
  Post. This is true:
And this you might haue heard of heere, by me,
Or by some other.
  Iach. More particulars
Must iustifie my knowledge.
  Post. So they must,
Or doe your Honour iniury.
  Iach. The Chimney
Is South the Chamber, and the Chimney-peece
Chaste *Dian*, bathing: neuer saw I figures
So likely to report themselues; the Cutter
Was as another Nature dumbe, out-went her,
Motion, and Breath left out.
  Post. This is a thing
Which you might from Relation likewise reape,
Being, as it is, much spoke of.
  Iach. The Roofe o'th'Chamber,
With golden Cherubins is fretted. Her Andirons
(I had forgot them) were two winking Cupids
Of Siluer, each on one foote standing, nicely
Depending on their Brands.
  Post. This is her Honor:
Let it be granted you haue seene all this (and praise
Be giuen to your remembrance) the description
Of what is in her Chamber, nothing saues
The wager you haue laid.
  Iach. Then if you can
Be pale, I begge but leaue to ayre this Iewell: See,
And now 'tis vp againe: it must be married
To that your Diamond, Ile keepe them.
  Post. Ioue——
Once more let me behold it: Is it that
Which I left with her?
  Iach. Sir (I thanke her) that
She stript it from her Arme: I see her yet:
Her pretty Action, did out-sell her guift,
And yet enrich'd it too: she gaue it me,
And said, she priz'd it once.
  Post. May be, she pluck'd it off
To send it me.
  Iach. She writes so to you? doth shee?
  Post. O no, no, no, 'tis true. Heere, take this too,
It is a Basiliske vnto mine eye,
Killes me to looke on't: Let there be no Honor,
Where there is Beauty: Truth, where semblance: Loue,
Where there's another man. The Vowes of Women,
Of no more bondage be, to where they are made,
Then they are to their Vertues, which is nothing:
O, aboue measure false.
  Phil. Haue patience Sir,
And take your Ring againe, 'tis not yet wonne:
It may be probable she lost it: or

Who knowes if one her women, being corrupted
Hath stolne it from her.
  Post. Very true,
And so I hope he came by't: backe my Ring,
Render to me some corporall signe about her
More euident then this: for this was stolne.
  Iach. By Iupiter, I had it from her Arme.
  Post. Hearke you, he sweares: by Iupiter he sweares.
'Tis true, nay keepe the Ring, 'tis true: I am sure
She would not loose it: her Attendants are
All sworne, and honourable: they induc'd to steale it?
And by a Stranger? No, he hath enioy'd her,
The Cognisance of her incontinencie
Is this: she hath bought the name of Whore, thus deerly
There, take thy hyre, and all the Fiends of Hell
Diuide themselues betweene you.
  Phil. Sir, be patient:
This is not strong enough to be beleeu'd
Of one perswaded well of.
  Post. Neuer talke on't:
She hath bin colted by him.
  Iach. If you seeke
For further satisfying, vnder her Breast
(Worthy her pressing) lyes a Mole, right proud
Of that most delicate Lodging. By my life
I kist it, and it gaue me present hunger
To feede againe, though full. You do remember
This staine vpon her?
  Post. I, and it doth confirme
Another staine, as bigge as Hell can hold,
Were there no more but it.
  Iach. Will you heare more?
  Post. Spare your Arethmaticke,
Neuer count the Turnes: Once, and a Million.
  Iach. Ile be sworne.
  Post. No swearing:
If you will sweare you haue not done't, you lye,
And I will kill thee, if thou do'st deny
Thou'st made me Cuckold.
  Iach. Ile deny nothing.
  Post. O that I had her heere, to teare her Limb-meale:
I will go there and doo't, i'th' Court, before
Her Father. Ile do something.   *Exit.*
  Phil. Quite besides
The gouernment of Patience. You haue wonne:
Let's follow him, and peruert the present wrath
He hath against himselfe.
  Iach. With all my heart.   *Exeunt.*

Enter Posthumus.

  Post. Is there no way for Men to be, but Women
Must be halfe-workers? We are all Bastards,
And that most venerable man, which I
Did call my Father, was, I know not where
When I was stampt. Some Coyner with his Tooles
Made me a counterfeit: yet my Mother seem'd
The *Dian* of that time: so doth my Wife
The Non-pareill of this. Oh Vengeance, Vengeance!
Me of my lawfull pleasure she restrain'd,
And pray'd me oft forbearance: did it with
A pudencie so Rosie, the sweet view on't
Might well haue warm'd olde Saturne;
That I thought her
As Chaste, as vn-Sunn'd Snow. Oh, all the Diuels!
This yellow *Iachimo* in an houre, was't not?

Or leſſe; at firſt? Perchance he ſpoke not, but
Like a full Acorn'd Boare, a Iarmen on,
Cry'de oh, and mounted; found no oppoſition,
But what he look'd for, ſhould oppoſe, and ſhe
Should from encounter guard. Could I finde out
The Womans part in me, for there's no motion
That tends to vice in man, but I affirme
It is the Womans part: be it Lying, note it,
The womans: Flattering, hers; Deceiuing, hers:
Luſt, and ranke thoughts, hers, hers: Reuenges hers:
Ambitions, Couetings, change of Prides, Diſdaine,
Nice-longing, Slanders, Mutability;
All Faults that name, nay, that Hell knowes,
Why hers, in part, or all: but rather all For euen to Vice
They are not conſtant, but are changing ſtill;
One Vice, but of a minute old, for one
Not halfe ſo old as that. Ile write againſt them,
Deteſt them, curſe them: yet 'tis greater Skill
In a true Hate, to pray they haue their will:
The very Diuels cannot plague them better. *Exit.*

Actus Tertius. Scena Prima.

Enter in State, Cymbeline, Queene, Clotten, and Lords at one doore, and at another, Caius, Lucius, and Attendants.

Cym. Now ſay, what would *Auguſtus Cæſar* with vs?
Luc. When *Iulius Cæſar* (whoſe remembrance yet
Liues in mens eyes, and will to Eares and Tongues
Be Theame, and hearing euer) was in this Britain,
And Conquer'd it, *Caſſibulan* thine Vnkle
(Famous in *Cæſars* prayſes, no whit leſſe
Then in his Feats deſeruing it) for him,
And his Succeſſion, granted Rome a Tribute,
Yeerely three thouſand pounds; which (by thee) lately
Is left vntender'd.

Qu. And to kill the meruaile,
Shall be ſo euer.

Clot. There be many *Cæſars*,
Ere ſuch another *Iulius*: Britaine's a world
By it ſelfe, and we will nothing pay
For wearing our owne Noſes.

Qu. That opportunity
Which then they had to take from's, to reſume
We haue againe. Remember Sir, my Liege,
The Kings your Anceſtors, together with
The naturall brauery of your Iſle, which ſtands
As Neptunes Parke, ribb'd, and pal'd in
With Oakes vnskaleable, and roaring Waters,
With Sands that will not beare your Enemies Boates,
But ſucke them vp to th' Top-maſt. A kinde of Conqueſt
Cæſar made heere, but made not heere his bragge
Of Came, and Saw, and Ouer-came: with ſhame
(The firſt that euer touch'd him) he was carried
From off our Coaſt, twice beaten: and his Shipping
(Poore ignorant Baubles) on our terrible Seas
Like Egge-ſhels mou'd vpon their Surges, crack'd
As eaſily 'gainſt our Rockes. For ioy whereof,
The fam'd *Caſſibulan*, who was once at point
(Oh giglet Fortune) to maſter *Cæſars* Sword,
Made *Luds-Towne* with reioycing-Fires bright,
And Britaines ſtrut with Courage.

Clot. Come, there's no more Tribute to be paid: our
Kingdome is ſtronger then it was at that time: and (as I
ſaid) there is no moe ſuch *Cæſars*, other of them may haue
crook'd Noſes, but to owe ſuch ſtraite Armes, none.

Cym. Son, let your Mother end.

Clot. We haue yet many among vs, can gripe as hard
as *Caſſibulan*, I doe not ſay I am one: but I haue a hand.
Why Tribute? Why ſhould we pay Tribute? If *Cæſar*
can hide the Sun from vs with a Blanket, or put the Moon
in his pocket, we will pay him Tribute for light: elſe Sir,
no more Tribute, pray you now.

Cym. You muſt know,
Till the iniurious Romans, did extort
This Tribute from vs, we were free. *Cæſars* Ambition,
Which ſwell'd ſo much, that it did almoſt ſtretch
The ſides o'th' World, againſt all colour heere,
Did put the yoake vpon's; which to ſhake off
Becomes a warlike people, whom we reckon
Our ſelues to be, we do. Say then to *Cæſar*,
Our Anceſtor was that *Mulmutius*, which
Ordain'd our Lawes, whoſe vſe the Sword of *Cæſar*
Hath too much mangled; whoſe repayre, and franchiſe,
Shall (by the power we hold) be our good deed,
Tho Rome be therfore angry. *Mulmutius* made our lawes
Who was the firſt of Britaine, which did put
His browes within a golden Crowne, and call'd
Himſelfe a King.

Luc. I am ſorry *Cymbeline*,
That I am to pronounce *Auguſtus Cæſar*
(*Cæſar*, that hath moe Kings his Seruants, then
Thy ſelfe Domeſticke Officers) thine Enemy:
Receyue it from me then. Warre, and Confuſion
In *Cæſars* name pronounce I 'gainſt thee: Looke
For fury, not to be reſiſted. Thus defide,
I thanke thee for my ſelfe.

Cym. Thou art welcome *Caius*,
Thy *Cæſar* Knighted me; my youth I ſpent
Much vnder him; of him, I gather'd Honour,
Which he, to ſeeke of me againe, perforce,
Behooues me keepe at vtterance. I am perfect,
That the Pannonians and Dalmatians, for
Their Liberties are now in Armes: a Preſident
Which not to reade, would ſhew the Britaines cold:
So *Cæſar* ſhall not finde them.

Luc. Let proofe ſpeake.

Clot. His Maieſty biddes you welcome. Make pa-
ſtime with vs, a day, or two, or longer: if you ſeek vs afterwards in other tearmes, you ſhall finde vs in our Salt-
water-Girdle: if you beate vs out of it, it is yours: if you
fall in the aduenture, our Crowes ſhall fare the better for
you: and there's an end.

Luc. So ſir.

Cym. I know your Maſters pleaſure, and he mine:
All the Remaine, is welcome. *Exeunt.*

Scena Secunda.

Enter Piſanio reading of a Letter.

Piſ. How? of Adultery? Wherefore write you not
What Monſters her accuſe? *Leonatus*:
Oh Maſter, what a ſtrange infection

The Tragedie of Cymbeline.

Is falne into thy eare? What false Italian,
(As poysonous tongu'd, as handed) hath preuail'd
On thy too ready hearing? Disloyall? No.
She's punish'd for her Truth; and vndergoes
More Goddesse-like, then Wife-like; such Assaults
As would take in some Vertue. Oh my Master,
Thy mind to her, is now as lowe, as were
Thy Fortunes. How? That I should murther her,
Vpon the Loue, and Truth, and Vowes; which I
Haue made to thy command? I her? Her blood?
If it be so, to do good seruice, neuer
Let me be counted seruiceable. How looke I,
That I should seeme to lacke humanity,
So much as this Fact comes to? Doo't: The Letter.
That I haue sent her, by her owne command,
Shall giue thee opportunitie. Oh damn'd paper,
Blacke as the Inke that's on thee: senseless bauble,
Art thou a Fœdarie for this Act; and look'st
So Virgin-like without? Loe here she comes.

Enter Imogen.

I am ignorant in what I am commanded.

Imo. How now *Pisanio*?

Pis. Madam, heere is a Letter from my Lord.

Imo. Who, thy Lord? That is my Lord *Leonatus*?
Oh, learn'd indeed were that Astronomer
That knew the Starres, as I his Characters,
Heel'd lay the Future open. You good Gods,
Let what is heere contain'd, rellish of Loue,
Of my Lords health, of his content: yet not
That we two are asunder, let that grieue him;
Some griefes are medcinable, that is one of them,
For it doth physicke Loue, of his content,
All but in that. Good Wax, thy leaue: blest be
You Bees that make these Lockes of counsaile. Louers,
And men in dangerous Bondes pray not alike,
Though Forfeytours you cast in prison, yet
You clafpe young *Cupids* Tables: good Newes Gods.

Iustice and your Fathers wrath (should he take me in his
Dominion) could not be so cruell to me, as you: (oh the dee-
rest of Creatures) would euen renew me with your eyes. Take
notice that I am in Cambria *at* Milford-Hauen: *what your*
owne Loue, will out of this aduise you, follow. So he wishes you
all happinesse, that remaines loyall to his Vow, and your encrea-
sing in Loue. Leonatus Posthumus.

Oh for a Horse with wings: Hear'st thou *Pisanio*?
He is at Milford-Hauen: Read, and tell me
How farre 'tis thither. If one of meane affaires
May plod it in a weeke, why may not I
Glide thither in a day? Then true *Pisanio*,
Who long'st like me, to see thy Lord; who long'st
(Oh let me bate) but not like me: yet long'st
But in a fainter kinde. Oh not like me:
For mine's beyond, beyond: say, and speake thicke
(Loues Counsailor should fill the bores of hearing,
To'th'smothering of the Sense) how farre it is
To this same blessed Milford. And by'th'way
Tell me how Wales was made so happy, as
T'inherite such a Hauen. But first of all,
How we may steale from hence: and for the gap
That we shall make in Time, from our hence-going,
And our returne, to excuse: but first, how get hence.
Why should excuse be borne or ere begot?
Weele talke of that heereafter. Prythee speake,
How many store of Miles may we well rid

Twixt houre, and houre?

Pis. One score 'twixt Sun, and Sun,
Madam's enough for you: and too much too.

Imo. Why, one that rode to's Excution Man,
Could neuer go so slow: I haue heard of Riding wagers,
Where Horses haue bin nimbler then the Sands
That run i'th'Clocks behalfe. But this is Foolrie,
Go, bid my Woman faigne a Sicknesse, say
She'le home to her Father; and prouide me presently
A Riding Suit: No costlier then would fit
A Franklins Huswife.

Pis. Madam, you're best consider.

Imo. I see before me (Man) nor heere, not heere;
Nor what ensues but haue a Fog in them
That I cannot looke through. Away, I prythee,
Do as I bid thee: There's no more to say;
Accessible is none but Milford way. *Exeunt.*

Scena Tertia.

Enter Belarius, Guiderius, and Aruiragus.

Bel. A goodly day, not to keepe house with such,
Whose Roofe's as lowe as ours: Sleepe Boyes, this gate
Instructs you how t'adore the Heauens; and bowes you
To a mornings holy office. The Gates of Monarches
Are Arch'd so high, that Giants may iet through
And keepe their impious Turbonds on, without
Good morrow to the Sun. Haile thou faire Heauen,
We house i'th'Rocke, yet vse thee not so hardly
As prouder liuers do.

Guid. Haile Heauen.

Aruir. Haile Heauen.

Bela. Now for our Mountaine sport, vp to yond hill
Your legges are yong: Ile tread these Flats. Consider,
When you aboue perceiue me like a Crow,
That it is Place, which lessen's and sets off,
And you may then reuolue what Tales, I haue told you,
Of Courts, of Princes; of the Tricks in Warre.
This Seruice, is not Seruice; so being done,
But being so allowed. To apprehend thus,
Drawes vs a profit from all things we see:
And often to our comfort, shall we finde
The sharded-Beetle, in a safer hold
Then is the full-wing'd Eagle. Oh this life,
Is Nobler, then attending for a checke:
Richer, then doing nothing for a Babe:
Prouder, then rustling in vnpayd-for Silke:
Such gaine the Cap of him, that makes him fine,
Yet keepes his Booke vncros'd: no life to ours.

Gui. Out of your proofe you speak: we poore vnfledg'd
Haue neuer wing'd from view o'th'nest; nor knowes not
What Ayre's from home. Hap'ly this life is best,
(If quiet life be best) sweeter to you
That haue a sharper knowne. Well corresponding
With your stiffe Age; but vnto vs, it is
A Cell of Ignorance: trauailing a bed,
A Prison, or a Debtor, that not dares
To stride a limit.

Arui. What should we speake of
When we are old as you? When we shall heare
The Raine and winde beate darke December? How
In this our pinching Caue, shall we discourse

The

The freezing houres away? We haue seene nothing:
We are beastly; subtle as the Fox for prey,
Like warlike as the Wolfe, for what we eate:
Our Valour is to chace what flyes: Our Cage
We make a Quire, as doth the prison'd Bird,
And sing our Bondage freely.

Bel. How you speake.
Did you but know the Cities Vsuries,
And felt them knowingly: the Art o'th'Court,
As hard to leaue, as keepe: whose top to climbe
Is certaine falling: or so slipp'ry, that
The feare's as bad as falling. The toyle o'th'Warre,
A paine that onely seemes to seeke out danger
I'th' name of Fame, and Honor, which dyes i'th'search,
And hath as oft a sland'rous Epitaph,
As Record of faire Act. Nay, many times
Doth ill deserue, by doing well: what's worse
Must curt'sie at the Censure. Oh Boyes, this Storie
The World may reade in me: My bodie's mark'd
With Roman Swords; and my report, was once
First, with the best of Note. *Cymbeline* lou'd me,
And when a Souldier was the Theame, my name
Was not farre off: then was I as a Tree
Whose boughes did bend with fruit. But in one night,
A Storme, or Robbery (call it what you will)
Shooke downe my mellow hangings: nay my Leaues,
And left me bare to weather.

Gui. Vncertaine fauour.

Bel. My fault being nothing (as I haue told you oft)
But that two Villaines, whose false Oathes preuayl'd
Before my perfect Honor, swore to *Cymbeline*,
I was Confederate with the Romanes: so
Followed my Banishment, and this twenty yeeres,
This Rocke, and these Demesnes, haue bene my World,
Where I haue liu'd at honest freedome, payed
More pious debts to Heauen, then in all
The fore-end of my time. But, vp to'th'Mountaines,
This is not Hunters Language; he that strikes
The Venison first, shall be the Lord o'th'Feast,
To him the other two shall minister,
And we will feare no poyson, which attends
In place of greater State.
Ile meete you in the Valleyes. *Exeunt.*
How hard it is to hide the sparkes of Nature?
These Boyes know little they are Sonnes to'th'King,
Nor *Cymbeline* dreames that they are aliue.
They thinke they are mine,
And though train'd vp thus meanely
I'th'Caue, whereon the Bowe their thoughts do hit,
The Roofes of Palaces, and Nature prompts them
In simple and lowe things, to Prince it, much
Beyond the tricke of others. This *Paladour*,
The heyre of *Cymbeline* and Britaine, who
The King his Father call'd *Guiderius*. Ioue,
When on my three-foot stoole I sit, and tell
The warlike feats I haue done, his spirits flye out
Into my Story: say thus mine Enemy fell,
And thus I set my foote on's necke, euen then
The Princely blood flowes in his Cheeke, he sweats,
Straines his yong Nerues, and puts himselfe in posture
That acts my words. The yonger Brother *Cadwall*,
Once *Aruiragus*, in as like a figure
Strikes life into my speech, and shewes much more
His owne conceyuing. Hearke, the Game is rows'd,
Oh *Cymbeline*, Heauen and my Conscience knowes
Thou didd'st vniustly banish me: whereon

At three, and two yeeres old, I stole these Babes,
Thinking to barre thee of Succession, as
Thou refts me of my Lands. *Euriphile*,
Thou was't their Nurse, they took thee for their mother,
And euery day do honor to her graue:
My selfe *Belarius*, that am *Morgan* call'd
They take for Naturall Father. The Game is vp. *Exit.*

Scena Quarta.

Enter Pisanio and Imogen.

Imo. Thou told'st me when we came frō horse, ŷ place
Was neere at hand: Ne're long'd my Mother so
To see me first, as I haue now. *Pisanio*, Man:
Where is *Posthumus*? What is in thy mind
That makes thee stare thus? Wherefore breaks that sigh
From th'inward of thee? One, but painted thus
Would be interpreted a thing perplex'd
Beyond selfe-explication. Put thy selfe
Into a hauiour of lesse feare, ere wildnesse
Vanquish my stayder Senses. What's the matter?
Why tender'st thou that Paper to me, with
A looke vntender? Is't be Summer Newes
Smile too't before: if Winterly, thou need'st
But keepe that count'nance stil. My Husbands hand?
That Drug-damn'd Italy, hath out-crafted him,
And hee's at some hard point. Speake man, thy Tongue
May take off some extreamitie, which to reade
Would be euen mortall to me.

Pis. Please you reade,
And you shall finde me (wretched man) a thing
The most disdain'd of Fortune.

Imogen reades.

Thy *Mistris* (*Pisanio*) hath plaide the Strumpet in my Bed: the Testimonies whereof, lyes bleeding in me. I speak not out of weake Surmises, but from proofe as strong as my greefe, and as certaine as I expect my Reuenge. That part, thou (*Pisanio*) must acte for me, if thy Faith be not tainted with the breach of hers; let thine owne hands take away her life: I shall giue thee opportunity at *Milford Hauen*. She hath my Letter for the purpose; where, if thou feare to strike, and to make mee certaine it is done, thou art the Pander to her dishonour, and equally to me disloyall.

Pis. What shall I need to draw my Sword, the Paper
Hath cut her throat alreadie? No, 'tis Slander,
Whose edge is sharper then the Sword, whose tongue
Out-venomes all the Wormes of Nyle, whose breath
Rides on the posting windes, and doth belye
All corners of the World. Kings, Queenes, and States,
Maides, Matrons, nay the Secrets of the Graue
This viperous slander enters. What cheere, Madam?

Imo. False to his Bed? What is it to be false?
To lye in watch there, and to thinke on him?
To weepe 'twixt clock and clock? If sleep charge Nature,
To breake it with a fearfull dreame of him,
And cry my selfe awake? That's false to's bed? Is it?

Pisa. Alas good Lady.

Imo. I false? Thy Conscience witnesse: *Iachimo*,
Thou didd'st accuse him of Incontinencie,
Thou then look'dst like a Villaine: now, me thinkes
Thy

Thy fauours good enough. Some Iay of Italy
(Whose mother was her painting) hath betraid him:
Poore I am stale, a Garment out of fashion,
And for I am richer then to hang by th'walles,
I must be ript: To peeces with me: Oh!
Mens Vowes are womens Traitors. All good seeming
By thy reuolt (oh Husband) shall be thought
Put on for Villainy; not borne where't growes,
But worne a Baite for Ladies.

　Pisa. Good Madam, heare me.
　Imo. True honest men being heard, like false *Æneas*,
Were in his time thought false: and *Synons* weeping
Did scandall many a holy teare: tooke pitty
From most true wretchednesse. So thou, *Posthumus*
Wilt lay the Leauen on all proper men;
Goodly, and gallant, shall be false and periur'd
From thy great faile: Come Fellow, be thou honest,
Do thou thy Masters bidding. When thou seest him,
A little witnesse my obedience. Looke
I draw the Sword my selfe, take it, and hit
The innocent Mansion of my Loue (my Heart:)
Feare not, 'tis empty of all things, but Greefe:
Thy Master is not there, who was indeede
The riches of it. Do his bidding, strike,
Thou mayst be valiant in a better cause;
But now thou seem'st a Coward.

　Pis. Hence vile Instrument,
Thou shalt not damne my hand.
　Imo. Why, I must dye:
And if I do not by thy hand, thou art
No Seruant of thy Masters. Against Selfe-slaughter,
There is a prohibition so Diuine,
That crauens my weake hand: Come, heere's my heart:
Something's a-foot: Soft, soft, wee'l no defence,
Obedient as the Scabbard. What is heere,
The Scriptures of the Loyall *Leonatus*,
All turn'd to Heresie? Away, away
Corrupters of my Faith, you shall no more
Be Stomachers to my heart: thus may poore Fooles
Beleeue false Teachers: Though those that are betraid
Do feele the Treason sharpely, yet the Traitor
Stands in worse case of woe. And thou *Posthumus*,
That didd'st set vp my disobedience 'gainst the King
My Father, and makes me put into contempt the suites
Of Princely Fellowes, shalt heereafter finde
It is no acte of common passage, but
A straine of Rarenesse: and I greeue my selfe,
To thinke, when thou shalt be disedg'd by her,
That now thou tyrest on, how thy memory
Will then be pang'd by me. Prythee dispatch,
The Lambe entreats the Butcher. Where's thy knife?
Thou art too slow to do thy Masters bidding
When I desire it too.

　Pis. Oh gracious Lady:
Since I receiu'd command to do this businesse,
I haue not slept one winke.
　Imo. Doo't, and to bed then.
　Pis. Ile wake mine eye-balles first.
　Imo. Wherefore then
Didd'st vndertake it? Why hast thou abus'd
So many Miles, with a pretence? This place?
Mine Action? and thine owne? Our Horses labour?
The Time inuiting thee? The perturb'd Court
For my being absent? whereunto I neuer
Purpose returne. Why hast thou gone so farre
To be vn-bent? when thou hast 'tane thy stand,
Th'elected Deere before thee?

　Pis. But to win time
To loose so bad employment, in the which
I haue consider'd of a course: good Ladie
Heare me with patience.

　Imo. Talke thy tongue weary, speake:
I haue heard I am a Strumpet, and mine eare
Therein false strooke, can take no greater wound,
Nor tent, to bottome that. But speake.
　Pis. Then Madam,
I thought you would not backe againe.
　Imo. Most like,
Bringing me heere to kill me.
　Pis. Not so neither:
But if I were as wise, as honest, then
My purpose would proue well: it cannot be,
But that my Master is abus'd. Some Villaine,
I, and singular in his Art, hath done you both
This cursed iniurie.

　Imo. Some Roman Curtezan?
　Pisa. No, on my life:
Ile giue but notice you are dead, and send him
Some bloody signe of it. For 'tis commanded
I should do so: you shall be mist at Court,
And that will well confirme it.

　Imo. Why good Fellow,
What shall I do the while? Where bide? How liue?
Or in my life, what comfort, when I am
Dead to my Husband?
　Pis. If you'l backe to th'Court.
　Imo. No Court, no Father, nor no more adoe
With that harsh, noble, simple nothing:
That *Clotten*, whose Loue-suite hath bene to me
As fearefull as a Siege.
　Pis. If not at Court,
Then not in Britaine must you bide.
　Imo. Where then?
Hath Britaine all the Sunne that shines? Day? Night?
Are they not but in Britaine? I'th'worlds Volume
Our Britaine seemes as of it, but not in't:
In a great Poole, a Swannes-nest, prythee thinke
There's liuers out of Britaine.

　Pis. I am most glad
You thinke of other place: Th'Ambassador,
Lucius the Romane comes to Milford-Hauen
To morrow. Now, if you could weare a minde
Darke, as your Fortune is, and but disguise
That which t'appeare it selfe, must not yet be,
But by selfe-danger, you should tread a course
Pretty, and full of view: yea, happily, neere
The residence of *Posthumus*; so nie (at least)
That though his Actions were not visible, yet
Report should render him hourely to your eare,
As truely as he mooues.

　Imo. Oh for such meanes,
Though perill to my modestie, not death on't
I would aduenture.

　Pis. Well then, heere's the point:
You must forget to be a Woman: change
Command, into obedience. Feare, and Nicenesse
(The Handmaides of all Women, or more truely
Woman it pretty selfe) into a waggish courage,
Ready in gybes, quicke-answer'd, sawcie, and
As quarrellous as the Weazell: Nay, you must
Forget that rarest Treasure of your Cheeke,
Exposing it (but oh the harder heart,

Alacke no remedy) to the greedy touch
Of common-kissing *Titan*: and forget
Your laboursome and dainty Trimmes, wherein
You made great *Iuno* angry.

Imo. Nay be breefe?
I see into thy end, and am almost
A man already.

Pis. First, make your selfe but like one,
Fore-thinking this. I haue already fit
('Tis in my Cloake-bagge) Doublet, Hat, Hose, all
That answer to them: Would you in their seruing,
(And with what imitation you can borrow
From youth of such a season) 'fore Noble *Lucius*
Present your selfe, desire his seruice: tell him
Wherein you're happy; which will make him know,
If that his head haue eare in Musicke, doubtlesse
With ioy he will imbrace you: for hee's Honourable,
And doubling that, most holy. Your meanes abroad:
You haue me rich, and I will neuer faile
Beginning, nor supplyment.

Imo. Thou art all the comfort
The Gods will diet me with. Prythee away,
There's more to be consider'd: but wee'l euen
All that good time will giue vs. This attempt,
I am Souldier too, and will abide it with
A Princes Courage. Away, I prythee.

Pis. Well Madam, we must take a short farewell,
Least being mist, I be suspected of
Your carriage from the Court. My Noble Mistris,
Heere is a boxe, I had it from the Queene,
What's in't is precious: If you are sicke at Sea,
Or Stomacke-qualm'd at Land, a Dramme of this
Will driue away distemper. To some shade,
And fit you to your Manhood: may the Gods
Direct you to the best.

Imo. Amen: I thanke thee. *Exeunt.*

Scena Quinta.

Enter Cymbeline, Queene, Cloten, Lucius, and Lords.

Cym. Thus farre, and so farewell.

Luc. Thankes, Royall Sir:
My Emperor hath wrote, I must from hence,
And am right sorry, that I must report ye
My Masters Enemy.

Cym. Our Subiects (Sir)
Will not endure his yoake; and for our selfe
To shew lesse Soueraignty then they, must needs
Appeare vn-Kinglike.

Luc. So Sir: I desire of you
A Conduct ouer Land, to Milford-Hauen.
Madam, all ioy befall your Grace, and you.

Cym. My Lords, you are appointed for that Office:
The due of Honor, in no point omit:
So farewell Noble *Lucius*.

Luc. Your hand, my Lord.

Clot. Receiue it friendly: but from this time forth
I weare it as your Enemy.

Luc. Sir, the Euent
Is yet to name the winner. Fare you well.

Cym. Leaue not the worthy *Lucius*, good my Lords
Till he haue crost the Seuern. Happines. *Exit Lucius, &c*

Qu. He goes hence frowning: but it honours vs
That we haue giuen him cause.

Clot. 'Tis all the better,
Your valiant Britaines haue their wishes in it.

Cym. *Lucius* hath wrote already to the Emperor
How it goes heere. It fits vs therefore ripely
Our Chariots, and our Horsemen be in readinesse:
The Powres that he already hath in Gallia
Will soone be drawne to head, from whence he moues
His warre for Britaine.

Qu. 'Tis not sleepy businesse,
But must be look'd too speedily, and strongly.

Cym. Our expectation that it would be thus
Hath made vs forward. But my gentle Queene,
Where is our Daughter? She hath not appear'd
Before the Roman, nor to vs hath tender'd
The duty of the day. She looke vs like
A thing more made of malice, then of duty,
We haue noted it. Call her before vs, for
We haue beene too slight in sufferance.

Qu. Royall Sir,
Since the exile of *Posthumus*, most retyr'd
Hath her life bin: the Cure whereof, my Lord,
'Tis time must do. Beseech your Maiesty,
Forbeare sharpe speeches to her. Shee's a Lady
So tender of rebukes, that words are strokes,
And strokes death to her.

Enter a Messenger.

Cym. Where is she Sir? How
Can her contempt be answer'd?

Mes. Please you Sir,
Her Chambers are all lock'd, and there's no answer
That will be giuen to'th'lowd of noise, we make.

Qu. My Lord, when last I went to visit her,
She pray'd me to excuse her keeping close,
Whereto constrain'd by her infirmitie,
She should that dutie leaue vnpaide to you
Which dayly she was bound to proffer: this
She wish'd me to make knowne: but our great Court
Made me too blame in memory.

Cym. Her doores lock'd?
Not seene of late? Grant Heauens, that which I
Feare, proue false. *Exit.*

Qu. Sonne, I say, follow the King.

Clot. That man of hers, *Pisanio*, her old Seruant
I haue not seene these two dayes. *Exit.*

Qu. Go, looke after:
Pisanio, thou that stand'st so for *Posthumus*,
He hath a Drugge of mine: I pray, his absence
Proceed by swallowing that. For he beleeues
It is a thing most precious. But for her,
Where is she gone? Haply dispaire hath seiz'd her:
Or wing'd with feruour of her loue, she's flowne
To her desir'd *Posthumus*: gone she is,
To death, or to dishonor, and my end
Can make good vse of either. Shee being downe,
I haue the placing of the Brittish Crowne.

Enter Cloten.

How now, my Sonne?

Clot. 'Tis certaine she is fled:
Go in and cheere the King, he rages, none
Dare come about him.

Qu. All the better: may
This night fore-stall him of the comming day. *Exit Qu.*

Clo. I loue, and hate her: for she's Faire and Royall,
And that she hath all courtly parts more exquisite

Then

The Tragedie of Cymbeline. 385

Then Lady, Ladies, Woman, from euery one
The best she hath, and she of all compounded
Out-selles them all. I loue her therefore, but
Disdaining me, and throwing Fauours on
The low *Posthumus*, slanders so her iudgement,
That what's else rare, is choak'd: and in that point
I will conclude to hate her, nay indeede,
To be reueng'd vpon her. For, when Fooles shall——

Enter Pisanio.

Who is heere? What, are you packing sirrah?
Come hither: Ah you precious Pandar, Villaine,
Where is thy Lady? In a word, or else
Thou art straightway with the Fiends.

Pis. Oh, good my Lord.

Clo. Where is thy Lady? Or, by Iupiter,
I will not aske againe. Close Villaine,
Ile haue this Secret from thy heart, or rip
Thy heart to finde it. Is she with *Posthumus*?
From whose so many waights of basenesse, cannot
A dram of worth be drawne.

Pis. Alas, my Lord,
How can she be with him? When was she miss'd?
He is in Rome.

Clot. Where is she Sir? Come neerer:
No farther halting: satisfie me home,
What is become of her?

Pis. Oh, my all-worthy Lord.

Clo. All-worthy Villaine,
Discouer where thy Mistris is, at once,
At the next word: no more of worthy Lord:
Speake, or thy silence on the instant, is
Thy condemnation, and thy death.

Pis. Then Sir:
This Paper is the historie of my knowledge
Touching her flight.

Clo. Let's see't: I will pursue her
Euen to *Augustus* Throne.

Pis. Or this, or perish.
She's farre enough, and what he learnes by this,
May proue his trauell, not her danger.

Clo. Humh.

Pis. Ile write to my Lord she's dead: Oh *Imogen*,
Safe mayst thou wander, safe returne agen.

Clot. Sirra, is this Letter true?

Pis. Sir, as I thinke.

Clot. It is *Posthumus* hand, I know't. Sirrah, if thou
would'st not be a Villain, but do me true seruice: vndergo those Imployments wherin I should haue cause to vse
thee with a serious industry, that is, what villainy soere I
bid thee do to performe it, directly and truely, I would
thinke thee an honest man: thou should'st neither want
my meanes for thy releefe, nor my voyce for thy preferment.

Pis. Well, my good Lord.

Clot. Wilt thou serue mee? For since patiently and
constantly thou hast stucke to the bare Fortune of that
Begger *Posthumus*, thou canst not in the course of gratitude, but be a diligent follower of mine. Wilt thou serue
mee?

Pis. Sir, I will.

Clo. Giue mee thy hand, heere's my purse. Hast any
of thy late Masters Garments in thy possession?

Pisan. I haue (my Lord) at my Lodging, the same
Suite he wore, when he tooke leaue of my Ladie & Mistresse.

Clo. The first seruice thou dost mee, fetch that Suite
hither, let it be thy first seruice, go.

Pis. I shall my Lord. *Exit.*

Clo. Meet thee at Milford-Hauen: (I forgot to aske
him one thing, Ile remember't anon:) euen there, thou
villaine *Posthumus* will I kill thee. I would these Garments were come. She saide vpon a time (the bitternesse
of it, I now belch from my heart) that shee held the very
Garment of *Posthumus*, in more respect, then my Noble
and naturall person; together with the adornement of
my Qualities. With that Suite vpon my backe wil I rauish her: first kill him, and in her eyes; there shall she see
my valour, which wil then be a torment to hir contempt.
He on the ground, my speech of insulment ended on his
dead bodie, and when my Lust hath dined (which, as I
say, to vex her, I will execute in the Cloathes that she so
prais'd:) to the Court Ile knock her backe, foot her home
againe. She hath despis'd mee reioycingly, and Ile bee
merry in my Reuenge.

Enter Pisanio.

Be those the Garments?

Pis. I, my Noble Lord.

Clo. How long is't since she went to Milford-Hauen?

Pis. She can scarse be there yet.

Clo. Bring this Apparrell to my Chamber, that is
the second thing that I haue commanded thee. The third
is, that thou wilt be a voluntarie Mute to my designe. Be
but dutious, and true preferment shall tender it selfe to
thee. My Reuenge is now at Milford, would I had wings
to follow it. Come, and be true. *Exit*

Pis. Thou bid'st me to my losse: for true to thee,
Were to proue false, which I will neuer bee
To him that is most true. To Milford go,
And finde not her, whom thou pursuest. Flow, flow
You Heauenly blessings on her: This Fooles speede
Be crost with slownesse; Labour be his meede. *Exit*

Scena Sexta.

Enter Imogen alone.

Imo. I see a mans life is a tedious one,
I haue tyr'd my selfe: and for two nights together
Haue made the ground my bed. I should be sicke,
But that my resolution helpes me: Milford,
When from the Mountaine top, *Pisanio* shew'd thee,
Thou was't within a kenne. Oh Ioue, I thinke
Foundations flye the wretched: such I meane,
Where they should be releeu'd. Two Beggers told me,
I could not misse my way. Will poore Folkes lye
That haue Afflictions on them, knowing 'tis
A punishment, or Triall? Yes; no wonder,
When Rich-ones scarse tell true. To lapse in Fulnesse
Is sorer, then to lye for Neede: and Falshood
Is worse in Kings, then Beggers. My deere Lord,
Thou art one o'th'false Ones: Now I thinke on thee,
My hunger's gone; but euen before, I was
At point to sinke, for Food. But what is this?
Heere is a path too't: 'tis some sauage hold:
I were best not call; I dare not call: yet Famine
Ere cleane it o're-throw Nature, makes it valiant.
Plentie, and Peace breeds Cowards: Hardnesse euer
Of Hardinesse is Mother. Hoa? who's heere?
If any thing that's ciuill, speake: if sauage,

Take

Take, or lend. Hoa? No answer? Then Ile enter.
Best draw my Sword; and if mine Enemy
But feare the Sword like me, hee'l scarsely looke on't.
Such a Foe, good Heauens. *Exit.*

Scena Septima.

Enter Belarius, Guiderius, and Aruiragus.

Bel. You *Polidore* haue prou'd best Woodman, and
Are Master of the Feast: *Cadwall,* and I
Will play the Cooke, and Seruant, 'tis our match:
The sweat of industry would dry, and dye
But for the end it workes too. Come, our stomackes
Will make what's homely, sauoury: Wearinesse
Can snore vpon the Flint, when restie Sloth
Findes the Downe-pillow hard. Now peace be heere,
Poore house, that keep'st thy selfe.

Gui. I am throughly weary.

Arui. I am weake with toyle, yet strong in appetite.

Gui. There is cold meat i'th'Caue, we'l brouz on that
Whil'st what we haue kill'd, be Cook'd.

Bel. Stay, come not in:
But that it eates our victualles, I should thinke
Heere were a Faiery.

Gui. What's the matter, Sir?

Bel. By Iupiter an Angell: or if not
An earthly Paragon. Behold Diuinenesse
No elder then a Boy.

Enter Imogen.

Imo. Good masters harme me not:
Before I enter'd heere, I call'd, and thought
To haue begg'd, or bought, what I haue took: good troth
I haue stolne nought, nor wou'd not, though I had found
Gold strew'd i'th'Floore. Heere's money for my Meate,
I would haue left it on the Boord, so soone
As I had made my Meale; and parted
With Pray'rs for the Prouider.

Gui. Money? Youth.

Aru. All Gold and Siluer rather turne to durt,
As 'tis no better reckon'd, but of those
Who worship durty Gods.

Imo. I see you're angry:
Know, if you kill me for my fault, I should
Haue dyed, had I not made it.

Bel. Whether bound?

Imo. To Milford-Hauen.

Bel. What's your name?

Imo. Fidele Sir: I haue a Kinsman, who
Is bound for Italy; he embark'd at Milford,
To whom being going, almost spent with hunger,
I am falne in this offence.

Bel. Prythee (faire youth)
Thinke vs no Churles: nor measure our good mindes
By this rude place we liue in. Well encounter'd,
'Tis almost night, you shall haue better cheere
Ere you depart; and thankes to stay, and eate it:
Boyes, bid him welcome.

Gui. Were you a woman, youth,
I should woo hard, but be your Groome in honesty:
I bid for you, as I do buy.

Arui. Ile make't my Comfort
He is a man, Ile loue him as my Brother:
And such a welcome as I'ld giue to him
(After long absence) such is yours. Most welcome;
Be sprightly, for you fall 'mongst Friends.

Imo. 'Mongst Friends?
If Brothers: would it had bin so, that they
Had bin my Fathers Sonnes, then had my prize
Bin lesse, and so more equall ballasting
To thee *Posthumus.*

Bel. He wrings at some distresse.

Gui. Would I could free't.

Arui. Or I, what ere it be,
What paine it cost, what danger: Gods!

Bel. Hearke Boyes.

Imo. Great men
That had a Court no bigger then this Caue,
That did attend themselues, and had the vertue
Which their owne Conscience seal'd them: laying by
That nothing-guift of differing Multitudes
Could not out-peere these twaine. Pardon me Gods,
I'd change my sexe to be Companion with them,
Since *Leonatus* false.

Bel. It shall be so:
Boyes wee'l go dresse our Hunt. Faire youth come in:
Discourse is heauy, fasting: when we haue supp'd
Wee'l mannerly demand thee of thy Story,
So farre as thou wilt speake it.

Gui. Pray draw neere.

Arui. The Night to th'Owle,
And Morne to th'Larke lesse welcome.

Imo. Thankes Sir.

Arui. I pray draw neere. *Exeunt.*

Scena Octaua.

Enter two Roman Senators, and Tribunes.

1. Sen. This is the tenor of the Emperors Writ;
That since the common men are now in Action
'Gainst the Pannonians, and Dalmatians,
And that the Legions now in Gallia, are
Full weake to vndertake our Warres against
The falne-off Britaines, that we do incite
The Gentry to this businesse. He creates
Lucius Pro-Consull: and to you the Tribunes
For this immediate Leuy, he commands
His absolute Commission. Long liue *Cæsar.*

Tri. Is *Lucius* Generall of the Forces?

2. Sen. I.

Tri. Remaining now in Gallia?

1. Sen. With those Legions
Which I haue spoke of, whereunto your leuie
Must be suppliant: the words of your Commission
Will tye you to the numbers, and the time
Of their dispatch.

Tri. We will discharge our duty. *Exeunt.*

Actus Quartus. Scena Prima.

Enter Clotten alone.

Clot. I am neere to th'place where they should meet,
if *Pisanio* haue mapp'd it truely. How fit his Garments
serue me? Why should his Mistris who was made by him
that

that made the Taylor, not be fit too? The rather (sauing reuerence of the Word) for 'tis saide a Womans fitnesse comes by fits: therein I must play the Workman, I dare speake it to my selfe, for it is not Vaineglorie for a man, and his Glasse, to confer in his owne Chamber; I meane, the Lines of my body are as well drawne as his; no lesse young, more strong, not beneath him in Fortunes, beyond him in the aduantage of the time, aboue him in Birth, alike conuersant in generall seruices, and more remarkeable in single oppositions; yet this imperseuerant Thing loues him in my despight. What Mortalitie is? *Posthumus,* thy head (which now is growing vppon thy shoulders) shall within this houre be off, thy Mistris inforced, thy Garments cut to peeces before thy face: and all this done, spurne her home to her Father, who may (happily) be a little angry for my so rough vsage: but my Mother hauing power of his testinesse, shall turne all into my commendations. My Horse is tyed vp safe, out Sword, and to a sore purpose: Fortune put them into my hand: This is the very description of their meeting place and the Fellow dares not deceiue me. *Exit.*

Scena Secunda.

Enter Belarius, Guiderius, Aruiragus, and Imogen from the Caue.

Bel. You are not well: Remaine heere in the Caue,
Wee'l come to you after Hunting.
 Arui. Brother, stay heere:
Are we not Brothers?
 Imo. So man and man should be,
But Clay and Clay, differs in dignitie,
Whose dust is both alike. I am very sicke,
 Gui. Go you to Hunting, Ile abide with him.
 Imo. So sicke I am not, yet I am not well:
But not so Citizen a wanton, as
To seeme to dye, ere sicke: So please you, leaue me,
Sticke to your Iournall course: the breach of Custome,
Is breach of all. I am ill, but your being by me
Cannot amend me. Society, is no comfort
To one not sociable: I am not very sicke,
Since I can reason of it: pray you trust me heere,
Ile rob none but my selfe, and let me dye
Stealing so poorely.
 Gui. I loue thee: I haue spoke it,
How much the quantity, the waight as much,
As I do loue my Father.
 Bel. What? How? how?
 Arui. If it be sinne to say so (Sir) I yoake mee
In my good Brothers fault: I know not why
I loue this youth, and I haue heard you say,
Loue's reason's, without reason. The Beere at doore,
And a demand who is't shall dye, I'ld say
My Father, not this youth.
 Bel. Oh noble straine!
O worthinesse of Nature, breed of Greatnesse!
"Cowards father Cowards, & Base things Syre Base;
"Nature hath Meale, and Bran; Contempt, and Grace.
I'me not their Father, yet who this should bee,
Doth myracle it selfe, lou'd before mee.
'Tis the ninth houre o'th' Morne.
 Arui. Brother, farewell.

 Imo. I wish ye sport.
 Arui. You health.——So please you Sir.
 Imo. These are kinde Creatures.
Gods, what lyes I haue heard:
Our Courtiers say, all's sauage, but at Court;
Experience, oh thou disproou'st Report.
Th'emperious Seas breeds Monsters; for the Dish,
Poore Tributary Riuers, as sweet Fish:
I am sicke still, heart-sicke: *Pisanio,*
He now taste of thy Drugge.
 Gui. I could not stirre him:
He said he was gentle, but vnfortunate;
Dishonestly afflicted, but yet honest.
 Arui. Thus did he answer me: yet said heereafter,
I might know more.
 Bel. To'th' Field, to'th' Field:
Wee'l leaue you for this time, go in, and rest.
 Arui. Wee'l not be long away.
 Bel. Pray be not sicke,
For you must be our Huswife.
 Imo. Well, or ill,
I am bound to you. *Exit.*
 Bel. And shal't be euer.
This youth, how ere distrest, appeares he hath had
Good Ancestors.
 Arui. How Angell-like he sings?
 Gui. But his neate Cookerie?
 Arui. He cut our Rootes in Charracters,
And sawc't our Brothes, as *Iuno* had bin sicke,
And he her Dieter.
 Arui. Nobly he yoakes
A smiling, with a sigh; as if the sighe
Was that it was, for not being such a Smile:
The Smile, mocking the Sigh, that it would flye
From so diuine a Temple, to commix
With windes, that Saylors raile at.
 Gui. I do note,
That greefe and patience rooted in them both,
Mingle their spurres together.
 Arui. Grow patient,
And let the stinking-Elder (Greefe) vntwine
His perishing roote, with the encreasing Vine.
 Bel. It is great morning. Come away: Who's there?
Enter Cloten.
 Clo. I cannot finde those Runnagates, that Villaine
Hath mock'd me. I am faint.
 Bel. Those Runnagates?
Meanes he not vs? I partly know him, 'tis
Cloten, the Sonne o'th' Queene. I feare some Ambush:
I saw him not these many yeares, and yet
I know 'tis he: We are held as Out-Lawes: Hence.
 Gui. He is but one: you, and my Brother search
What Companies are neere: pray you away,
Let me alone with him.
 Clot. Soft, what are you
That flye me thus? Some villaine-Mountainers?
I haue heard of such. What Slaue art thou?
 Gui. A thing
More slauish did I ne're, then answering
A Slaue without a knocke.
 Clot. Thou art a Robber,
A Law-breaker, a Villaine: yeeld thee Theefe.
 Gui. To who? to thee? What art thou? Haue not I
An arme as bigge as thine? A heart, as bigge:
Thy words I grant are bigger: for I weare not
My Dagger in my mouth. Say what thou art:

Why

The Tragedy of Cymbeline.

Why I should yeeld to thee?

Clot. Thou Villaine base,
Know'st me not by my Cloathes?

Gui. No, nor thy Taylor, Rascall:
Who is thy Grandfather? He made those cloathes,
Which (as it seemes) make thee.

Clo. Thou precious Varlet,
My Taylor made them not.

Gui. Hence then, and thanke
The man that gaue them thee. Thou art some Foole,
I am loath to beate thee.

Clot. Thou iniurious Theefe,
Heare but my name, and tremble.

Gui. What's thy name?

Clo. *Cloten*, thou Villaine.

Gui. Cloten, thou double Villaine be thy name,
I cannot tremble at it, were it Toad, or Adder, Spider,
'Twould moue me sooner.

Clot. To thy further feare,
Nay, to thy meere Confusion, thou shalt know
I am Sonne to'th'Queene.

Gui. I am sorry for't: not seeming
So worthy as thy Birth.

Clot. Art not afeard?

Gui. Those that I reuerence, those I feare: the Wise:
At Fooles I laugh: not feare them.

Clot. Dye the death:
When I haue slaine thee with my proper hand,
Ile follow those that euen now fled hence:
And on the Gates of *Luds-Towne* set your heads:
Yeeld Rusticke Mountaineer. *Fight and Exeunt.*

Enter Belarius and Aruiragus.

Bel. No Companie's abroad?

Arui. None in the world: you did mistake him sure.

Bel. I cannot tell: Long is it since I saw him,
But Time hath nothing blurr'd those lines of Fauour
Which then he wore: the snatches in his voice,
And burst of speaking were as his: I am absolute
'Twas very *Cloten*.

Arui. In this place we left them:
I wish my Brother make good time with him,
You say he is so fell.

Bel. Being scarse made vp,
I meane to man; he had not apprehension
Of roaring terrors: For defect of iudgement
Is oft the cause of Feare.

Enter Guiderius.

But see thy Brother.

Gui. This *Cloten* was a Foole, an empty purse,
There was no money in't: Not *Hercules*
Could haue knock'd out his Braines, for he had none:
Yet I not doing this, the Foole had borne
My head, as I do his.

Bel. What hast thou done?

Gui. I am perfect what: cut off one *Clotens* head,
Sonne to the Queene (after his owne report)
Who call'd me Traitor, Mountaineer, and swore
With his owne single hand heel'd take vs in,
Displace our heads, where (thanks the Gods) they grow
And set them on *Luds-Towne.*

Bel. We are all vndone.

Gui. Why, worthy Father, what haue we to loose,
But that he swore to take, our Liues? the Law
Protects not vs, then why should we be tender,
To let an airogant peece of flesh threat vs?
Play Iudge, and Executioner, all himselfe?

For we do feare the Law. What company
Discouer you abroad?

Bel. No single soule
Can we set eye on: but in all safe reason
He must haue some Attendants. Though his Honor
Was nothing but mutation, I, and that
From one bad thing to worse: Not Frenzie,
Not absolute madnesse could so farre haue rau'd
To bring him heere alone: although perhaps
It may be heard at Court, that such as wee
Caue heere, hunt heere, are Out-lawes, and in time
May make some stronger head, the which he hearing,
(As it is like him) might breake out, and sweare
Heel'd fetch vs in, yet is't not probable
To come alone, either he so vndertaking,
Or they so suffering: then on good ground we feare,
If we do feare this Body hath a taile
More perillous then the head.

Arui. Let Ord'nance
Come as the Gods fore-say it: howsoere,
My Brother hath done well.

Bel. I had no minde
To hunt this day: The Boy *Fideles* sickenesse
Did make my way long forth.

Gui. With his owne Sword,
Which he did waue against my throat, I haue tane
His head from him: Ile throw't into the Creeke
Behinde our Rocke, and let it to the Sea,
And tell the Fishes, hee's the Queenes Sonne, *Cloten*,
Tha.'s all I reake. *Exit.*

Bel. I feare 'twill be reueng'd:
Would (*Polidore*) thou had'st not done't: though valour
Becomes thee well enough,

Arui. Would I had done't:
So the Reuenge alone pursu'de me: *Polidore*
I loue thee brotherly, but enuy much
Thou hast robb'd me of this deed: I would Reuenges
That possible strength might meet, wold seek vs through
And put vs to our answer.

Bel. Well, 'tis done:
Wee'l hunt no more to day, nor seeke for danger
Where there's no profit. I prythee to our Rocke,
You and *Fidele* play the Cookes: Ile stay
Till hasty *Polidore* returne, and bring him
To dinner presently.

Arui. Poore sicke *Fidele*.
Ile willingly to him, to gaine his colour,
Il'd let a parish of such *Clotens* blood,
And praise my selfe for charity. *Exit.*

Bel. Oh thou Goddesse,
Thou diuine Nature; thou thy selfe thou blazon'st
In these two Princely Boyes: they are as gentle
As Zephires blowing below the Violet,
Not wagging his sweet head; and yet, as rough
(Their Royall blood enchaf'd) as the rud'st winde,
That by the top doth take the Mountaine Pine,
And make him stoope to th'Vale. 'Tis wonder
That an inuisible instinct should frame them
To Royalty vnlearn'd, Honor vntaught,
Ciuility not seene from other: valour
That wildely growes in them, but yeelds a crop
As if it had beene sow'd: yet still it's strange
What *Clotens* being heere to vs portends,
Or what his death will bring vs.

Enter Guiderius.

Gui. Where's my Brother?

The Tragedie of Cymbeline.

I haue sent *Cloten* Clot-pole downe the streame,
In Embassie to his Mother; his Bodie's hostage
For his returne.   *Solemne Musick.*

  Bel. My ingenuous Instrument,
(Hearke *Polidore*) it sounds: but what occasion
Hath *Cadwal* now to giue it motion? Hearke.

  Gui. Is he at home?

  Bel. He went hence euen now.

  Gui. What does he meane?
Since death of my deer'st Mother
It did not speake before. All solemne things
Should answer solemne Accidents. The matter?
Triumphes for nothing, and lamenting Toyes,
Is iollity for Apes, and greefe for Boyes.
Is *Cadwall* mad?

*Enter Aruiragus, with Imogen dead, bearing
her in his Armes.*

  Bel. Looke, heere he comes,
And brings the dire occasion in his Armes,
Of what we blame him for.

  Arui. The Bird is dead
That we haue made so much on. I had rather
Haue skipt from sixteene yeares of Age, to sixty:
To haue turn'd my leaping time into a Crutch,
Then haue seene this.

  Gui. Oh sweetest, fayrest Lilly:
My Brother weares thee not the one halfe so well,
As when thou grew'st thy selfe.

  Bel. Oh Melancholly,
Who euer yet could sound thy bottome? Finde
The Ooze, to shew what Coast thy sluggish care
Might'st easilest harbour in. Thou blessed thing,
Ioue knowes what man thou might'st haue made: but I,
Thou dyed'st a most rare Boy, of Melancholly.
How found you him?

  Arui. Starke, as you see:
Thus smiling, as some Fly had tickled slumber,
Not as deaths dart being laugh'd at: his right Cheeke
Reposing on a Cushion.

  Gui. Where?

  Arui. O'th'floore:
His armes thus leagu'd, I thought he slept, and put
My clowted Brogues from off my feete, whose rudenesse
Answer'd my steps too lowd.

  Gui. Why, he but sleepes:
If he be gone, hee'l make his Graue, a Bed:
With female Fayries will his Tombe be haunted,
And Wormes will not come to thee.

  Arui. With fayrest Flowers
Whil'st Sommer lasts, and I liue heere, *Fidele,*
Ile sweeten thy sad graue: thou shalt not lacke
The Flower that's like thy face. Pale-Primrose, nor
The azur'd Hare-bell, like thy Veines: no, nor
The leafe of Eglantine, whom not to slander,
Out-sweetned not thy breath: the Raddocke would
With Charitable bill (Oh bill sore shaming
Those rich-left-heyres, that let their Fathers lye
Without a Monument) bring thee all this,
Yea, and furr'd Mosse besides. When Flowres are none
To winter-ground thy Coarse.

  Gui. Prythee haue done,
And do not play in Wench-like words with that
Which is so serious. Let vs bury him,
And not protract with admiration, what
Is now due debt. To th'graue.

  Arui. Say, where shall's lay him?

  Gui. By good *Euriphile,* our Mother.

  Arui. Bee't so:
And let vs (*Polidore*) though now our voyces
Haue got the mannish cracke, sing him to th'ground
As once to our Mother: vse like note, and words,
Saue that *Euriphile,* must be *Fidele.*

  Gui. *Cadwall,*
I cannot sing: Ile weepe, and word it with thee;
For Notes of sorrow, out of tune, are worse
Then Priests, and Phanes that lye.

  Arui. Wee'l speake it then.

  Bel. Great greefes I see med'cine the lesse: For *Cloten*
Is quite forgot. He was a Queenes Sonne, Boyes,
And though he came our Enemy, remember
He was paid for that: though meane, and mighty rotting
Together haue one dust, yet Reuerence
(That Angell of the world) doth make distinction
Of place 'tweene high, and low. Our Foe was Princely,
And though you tooke his life, as being our Foe,
Yet bury him, as a Prince.

  Gui. Pray you fetch him hither,
Thersites body is as good as *Aiax,*
When neyther are aliue.

  Arui. If you'l go fetch him,
Wee'l say our Song the whil'st: Brother begin.

  Gui. Nay *Cadwall,* we must lay his head to th'East,
My Father hath a reason for't.

  Arui. 'Tis true.

  Gui. Come on then, and remoue him.

  Arui. So, begin.

SONG.

  Guid. *Feare no more the heate o'th'Sun,
Nor the furious Winters rages,
Thou thy worldly task hast don,
Home art gon, and tane thy wages.
Golden Lads, and Girles all must,
As Chimney-Sweepers come to dust.*

  Arui. *Feare no more the frowne o'th'Great,
Thou art past the Tirants stroake,
Care no more to cloath and eate,
To thee the Reede is as the Oake:
The Scepter, Learning, Physicke must,
All follow this and come to dust.*

  Guid. *Feare no more the Lightning flash.*

  Arui. *Nor th'all-dreaded Thunderstone.*

  Gui. *Feare not Slander, Censure rash.*

  Arui. *Thou hast finish'd Ioy and mone.*

  Both. *All Louers young, all Louers must,
Consigne to thee and come to dust.*

  Guid. *No Exorcisor harme thee.*

  Arui. *Nor no witch-craft charme thee.*

  Guid. *Ghost vnlaid forbeare thee.*

  Arui. *Nothing ill come neere thee.*

  Both. *Quiet consumation haue,
And renowned be thy graue.*

Enter Belarius with the body of Cloten.

  Gui. We haue done our obsequies:
Come lay him downe.

  Bel. Heere's a few Flowres, but 'bout midnight more:
The hearbes that haue on them cold dew o'th'night
Are strewings fit'st for Graues: vpon their Faces.
You were as Flowres, now wither'd: euen so
These Herbelets shall, which we vpon you strew.
Come on, away, apart vpon our knees:
The ground that gaue them first, ha's them againe:
Their pleasures here are past, so are their paine. *Exeunt.*

bbb   *Imogen*

Imogen awakes.

Yes Sir, to Milford-Hauen, which is the way?
I thanke you: by yond bush? pray how farre thether?
'Ods pittikins: can it be sixe mile yet?
I haue gone all night: 'Faith, Ile lye downe, and sleepe.
But soft; no Bedfellow? Oh Gods, and Goddesses!
These Flowres are like the pleasures of the World;
This bloody man the care on't. I hope I dreame:
For so I thought I was a Caue-keeper,
And Cooke to honest Creatures. But 'tis not so:
'Twas but a bolt of nothing, shot at nothing,
Which the Braine makes of Fumes. Our very eyes,
Are sometimes like our Iudgements, blinde. Good faith
I tremble still with feare: but if there be
Yet left in Heauen, as small a drop of pittie
As a Wrens eye; fear'd Gods, a part of it.
The Dreame's heere still: euen when I wake it is
Without me, as within me: not imagin'd, felt.
A headlesse man? The Garments of *Posthumus*?
I know the shape of's Legge: this is his Hand:
His Foote Mercuriall: his martiall Thigh
The brawnes of *Hercules*: but his Iouiall face——
Murther in heauen? How? 'tis gone. *Pisanio*,
All Curses madded *Hecuba* gaue the Greekes,
And mine to boot, be darted on thee: thou
Conspir'd with that Irregulous diuell *Cloten*,
Hath heere cut off my Lord. To write, and read,
Be henceforth treacherous. Damn'd *Pisanio*,
Hath with his forged Letters (damn'd *Pisanio*)
From this most brauest vessell of the world
Strooke the maine top! Oh *Posthumus*, alas,
Where is thy head? where's that? Aye me! where's that?
Pisanio might haue kill'd thee at the heart,
And left this head on. How should this be, *Pisanio*?
'Tis he, and *Cloten*: Malice, and Lucre in them
Haue laid this Woe heere. Oh 'tis pregnant, pregnant!
The Drugge he gaue me, which hee said was precious
And Cordiall to me, haue I not found it
Murd'rous to'th'Senses? That confirmes it home:
This is *Pisanio*'s deede, and *Cloten*: Oh!
Giue colour to my pale cheeke with thy blood,
That we the horrider may seeme to those
Which chance to finde vs. Oh, my Lord! my Lord!

Enter Lucius, Captaines, and a Soothsayer.

Cap. To them, the Legions garrison'd in Gallia
After your will, haue crost the Sea, attending
You heere at Milford-Hauen, with your Shippes:
They are heere in readinesse.

Luc. But what from Rome?

Cap. The Senate hath stirr'd vp the Confiners,
And Gentlemen of Italy, most willing Spirits,
That promise Noble Seruice: and they come
Vnder the Conduct of bold *Iachimo*,
Syenna's Brother.

Luc. When expect you them?

Cap. With the next benefit o'th'winde.

Luc. This forwardnesse
Makes our hopes faire. Command our present numbers
Be muster'd: bid the Captaines looke too't. Now Sir,
What haue you dream'd of late of this warres purpose.

Sooth. Last night, the very Gods shew'd me a vision
(I fast, and pray'd for their Intelligence) thus:
I saw Ioues Bird, the Roman Eagle wing'd
From the spungy South, to this part of the West,
There vanish'd in the Sun-beames, which portends
(Vnlesse my sinnes abuse my Diuination)
Successe to th'Roman hoast.

Luc. Dreame often so,
And neuer false. Soft hoa, what truncke is heere?
Without his top? The ruine speakes, that sometime
It was a worthy building. How? a Page?
Or dead, or sleeping on him? But dead rather:
For Nature doth abhorre to make his bed
With the defunct, or sleepe vpon the dead.
Let's see the Boyes face.

Cap. Hee's aliue my Lord.

Luc. Hee'l then instruct vs of this body: Young one,
Informe vs of thy Fortunes, for it seemes
They craue to be demanded: who is this
Thou mak'st thy bloody Pillow? Or who was he
That (otherwise then noble Nature did)
Hath alter'd that good Picture? What's thy interest
In this sad wracke? How came't? Who is't?
What art thou?

Imo. I am nothing; or if not,
Nothing to be were better: This was my Master,
A very valiant Britaine, and a good,
That heere by Mountaineers lyes slaine: Alas,
There is no more such Masters: I may wander
From East to Occident, cry out for Seruice,
Try many, all good: serue truly: neuer
Finde such another Master.

Luc. 'Lacke, good youth:
Thou mou'st no lesse with thy complaining, then
Thy Maister in bleeding: say his name, good Friend.

Imo. *Richard du Champ*: If I do lye, and do
No harme by it, though the Gods heare, I hope
They'l pardon it. Say you Sir?

Luc. Thy name?

Imo. *Fidele* Sir.

Luc. Thou doo'st approue thy selfe the very same:
Thy Name well fits thy Faith; thy Faith, thy Name:
Wilt take thy chance with me? I will not say
Thou shalt be so well master'd, but be sure
No lesse belou'd. The Romane Emperors Letters
Sent by a Consull to me, should not sooner
Then thine owne worth preferre thee: Go with me.

Imo. Ile follow Sir. But first, and't please the Gods,
Ile hide my Master from the Flies, as deepe
As these poore Pickaxes can digge: and when
With wild wood-leaues & weeds, I ha' strew'd his graue
And on it said a Century of prayers
(Such as I can) twice o're, Ile weepe, and sighe,
And leauing so his seruice, follow you,
So please you entertaine mee.

Luc. I good youth,
And rather Father thee, then Master thee: My Friends,
The Boy hath taught vs manly duties: Let vs
Finde out the prettiest Dazied-Plot we can,
And make him with our Pikes and Partizans
A Graue: Come, Arme him: Boy hee's preferr'd
By thee, to vs, and he shall be interr'd
As Souldiers can. Be cheerefull; wipe thine eyes,
Some Falles are meanes the happier to arise. *Exeunt*

Scena Tertia.

Enter Cymbeline, Lords, and Pisanio.

Cym. Againe: and bring me word how 'tis with her,
A Feauour with the absence of her Sonne;

A madnesse, of which her life's in danger: Heauens,
How deeply you at once do touch me. Imogen,
The great part of my comfort, gone: My Queene
Vpon a desperate bed, and in a time
When fearefull Warres point at me: Her Sonne gone,
So needfull for this present? It strikes me, past
The hope of comfort. But for thee, Fellow,
Who needs must know of her departure, and
Dost seeme so ignorant, wee'l enforce it from thee
By a sharpe Torture.

 Pis. Sir, my life is yours,
I humbly set it at your will: But for my Mistris,
I nothing know where she remaines: why gone,
Nor when she purposes returne. Beseech your Highnes,
Hold me your loyall Seruant.

 Lord. Good my Liege,
The day that she was missing, he was heere;
I dare be bound hee's true, and shall performe
All parts of his subiection loyally. For *Cloten*,
There wants no diligence in seeking him,
And will no doubt be found.

 Cym. The time is troublesome:
Wee'l slip you for a season, but our iealousie
Do's yet depend.

 Lord. So please your Maiesty,
The Romaine Legions, all from Gallia drawne,
Are landed on your Coast, with a supply
Of Romaine Gentlemen, by the Senate sent.

 Cym. Now for the Counsaile of my Son and Queen,
I am amaz'd with matter.

 Lord. Good my Liege,
Your preparation can affront no lesse   (ready:
Then what you heare of. Come more, for more you're
The want is, but to put those Powres in motion,
That long to moue.

 Cym. I thanke you: let's withdraw
And meete the Time, as it seekes vs. We feare not
What can from Italy annoy vs, but
We greeue at chances heere. Away.   *Exeunt.*

 Pisa. I heard no Letter from my Master, since
I wrote him *Imogen* was slaine. 'Tis strange:
Nor heare I from my Mistris, who did promise
To yeeld me often tydings. Neither know I
What is betide to *Cloten*, but remaine
Perplext in all. The Heauens still must worke:
Wherein I am false, I am honest: not true, to be true.
These present warres shall finde I loue my Country,
Euen to the note o'th'King, or Ile fall in them:
All other doubts, by time let them be cleer'd,
Fortune brings in some Boats, that are not steer'd. *Exit.*

Scena Quarta.

Enter Belarius, Guiderius, & Aruiragus.

 Gui. The noyse is round about vs.
 Bel. Let vs from it.
 Arui. What pleasure Sir, we finde in life, to locke it
From Action, and Aduenture.
 Gui. Nay, what hope
Haue we in hiding vs? This way the Romaines
Must, or for Britaines slay vs or receiue vs
For barbarous and vnnaturall Reuolts
During their vse, and slay vs after.

 Bel. Sonnes,
Wee'l higher to the Mountaines, there secure v..
To the Kings party there's no going: newnesse
Of *Clotens* death (we being not knowne, not muster'd
Among the Bands) may driue vs to a render
Where we haue liu'd; and so extort from's that
Which we haue done, whose answer would be death
Drawne on with Torture.

 Gui. This is (Sir) a doubt
In such a time, nothing becomming you,
Nor satisfying vs.

 Arui. It is not likely,
That when they heare their Roman horses neigh,
Behold their quarter'd Fires; haue both their eyes
Aud eares so cloyd importantly as now,
That they will waste their time vpon our note,
To know from whence we are.

 Bel. Oh, I am knowne
Of many in the Army: Many yeeres
(Though *Cloten* then but young) you see, not wore him
From my remembrance. And besides, the King
Hath not deseru'd my Seruice, nor your Loues,
Who finde in my Exile, the want of Breeding;
The certainty of this heard life, aye hopelesse
To haue the courtesie your Cradle promis'd,
But to be still hot Summers Tanlings, and
The shrinking Slaues of Winter.

 Gui. Then be so,
Better to cease to be. Pray Sir, to th' Army:
I, and my Brother are not knowne; your selfe
So out of thought, and thereto so ore-growne,
Cannot be question'd.

 Arui. By this Sunne that shines
Ile thither: What thing is't, that I neuer
Did see man dye, scarfe euer look'd on blood,
But that of Coward Hares, hot Goats, and Venison?
Neuer bestrid a Horse saue one, that had
A Rider like my selfe, who ne're wore Rowell,
Nor Iron on his heele? I am asham'd
To looke vpon the holy Sunne, to haue
The benefit of his blest Beames, remaining
So long a poore vnknowne.

 Gui. By heauens Ile go,
If you will blesse me Sir, and giue me leaue,
Ile take the better care: but if you will not,
The hazard therefore due fall on me, by
The hands of Romaines.

 Arui. So say I, Amen.

 Bel. No reason I (since of your liues you set
So slight a valewation) should reserue
My crack'd one to more care. Haue with you Boyes:
If in your Country warres you chance to dye,
That is my Bed too (Lads) and there Ile lye.
Lead, lead; the time seems long, their blood thinks scorn
Till it flye out, and shew them Princes borne.   *Exeunt.*

Actus Quintus. Scena Prima.

Enter Posthumus alone.

 Post. Yea bloody cloth, Ile keep thee: for I am wisht
Thou should'st be colour'd thus. You married ones,
If each of you should take this course, how many
Must murther Wiues much better then themselues

For wrying but a little? Oh *Pisanio*,
Euery good Seruant do's not all Commands:
No Bond, but to do iust ones. Gods, if you
Should haue 'tane vengeance on my faults, I neuer
Had liu'd to put on this: so had you saued
The noble *Imogen*, to repent, and strooke
Me (wretch) more worth your Vengeance. But alacke,
You snatch some hence for little faults; that's loue
To haue them fall no more: you some permit
To second illes with illes, each elder worse,
And make them dread it, to the dooers thrift.
But *Imogen* is your owne, do your best willes,
And make me blest to obey. I am brought hither
Among th'Italian Gentry, and to fight
Against my Ladies Kingdome: 'Tis enough
That (Britaine) I haue kill'd thy Mistris: Peace,
Ile giue no wound to thee: therefore good Heauens,
Heare patiently my purpose. Ile disrobe me
Of these Italian weedes, and suite my selfe
As do's a *Britaine* Pezant: so Ile fight
Against the part I come with: so Ile dye
For thee (O *Imogen*) euen for whom my life
Is euery breath, a death: and thus, vnknowne,
Pittied, nor hated, to the face of perill
My selfe Ile dedicate. Let me make men know
More valour in me, then my habits show.
Gods, put the strength o'th'*Leonati* in me:
To shame the guize o'th'world, I will begin,
The fashion lesse without, and more within. *Exit.*

Scena Secunda.

Enter Lucius, Iachimo, and the Romane Army at one doore: and the Britaine Army at another: Leonatus Posthumus following like a poore Souldier. They march ouer, and goe out. Then enter againe in Skirmish Iachimo and Posthumus: he vanquisheth and disarmeth Iachimo, and then leaues him.

Iac. The heauinesse and guilt within my bosome,
Takes off my manhood: I haue belyed a Lady,
The Princesse of this Country; and the ayre on't
Reuengingly enfeebles me, or could this Carle,
A very drudge of Natures, haue subdu'de me
In my profession? Knighthoods, and Honors borne
As I weare mine) are titles but of scorne.
If that thy Gentry (Britaine) go before
This Lowt, as he exceeds our Lords, the oddes
Is, that we scarse are men, and you are Goddes. *Exit.*

The Battaile continues, the Britaines fly, Cymbeline is taken: Then enter to his rescue, Bellarius, Guiderius, and Aruiragus.

Bel. Stand, stand, we haue th'aduantage of the ground,
The Lane is guarded: Nothing rowts vs, but
The villany of our feares.

Gui. Aru. Stand, stand, and fight.

Enter Posthumus, and seconds the Britaines. They Rescue Cymbeline, and Exeunt.

Then enter Lucius, Iachimo, and Imogen.

Luc. Away boy from the Troopes, and saue thy selfe:
For friends kil friends, and the disorder's such
As warre were hood-wink'd.

Iac. 'Tis their fresh supplies.

Luc. It is a day turn'd strangely: or betimes
Let's re-inforce, or fly. *Exeunt.*

Scena Tertia.

Enter Posthumus, and a Britaine Lord.

Lor. Cam'st thou from where they made the stand?

Post. I did,
Though you it seemes come from the Fliers?

Lo. I did.

Post. No blame be to you Sir, for all was lost,
But that the Heauens fought: the King himselfe
Of his wings destitute, the Army broken,
And but the backes of Britaines seene; all flying
Through a strait Lane, the Enemy full-hearted,
Lolling the Tongue with slaught'ring: hauing worke
More plentifull, then Tooles to doo't: strooke downe
Some mortally, some slightly touch'd, some falling
Meerely through feare, that the strait passe was damm'd
With deadmen, hurt behinde, and Cowards liuing
To dye with length'ned shame.

Lo. Where was this Lane?

Post. Close by the battell, ditch'd, & wall'd with turph,
Which gaue aduantage to an ancient Souldiour
(An honest one I warrant) who deseru'd
So long a breeding, as his white beard came to,
In doing this for's Country. Athwart the Lane,
He, with two striplings (Lads more like to run
The Country base, then to commit such slaughter,
With faces fit for Maskes, or rather fayrer
Then those for preseruation cas'd, or shame)
Made good the passage, cryed to those that fled.
Our *Britaines* hearts dye flying, not our men,
To darknesse fleete soules that flye backwards; stand,
Or we are Romanes, and will giue you that
Like beasts, which you shun beastly, and may saue
But to looke backe in frowne: Stand, stand. These three,
Three thousand confident, in acte as many:
For three performers are the File, when all
The rest do nothing. With this word stand, stand,
Accomodated by the Place; more Charming
With their owne Noblenesse, which could haue turn'd
A Distaffe, to a'Lance, guilded pale lookes;
Part shame, part spirit renew'd, that some turn'd coward
But by example (Oh a sinne in Warre,
Damn'd in the first beginners) gan to looke
The way that they did, and to grin like Lyons
Vpon the Pikes o'th'Hunters. Then beganne
A stop i'th'Chaser; a Retyre: Anon
A Rowt, confusion thicke: forthwith they flye
Chickens, the way which they stopt Eagles: Slaues
The strides the Victors made: and now our Cowards
Like Fragments in hard Voyages became
The life o'th'need: hauing found the backe doore open
Of the vnguarded hearts: heauens, how they wound,
Some slaine before some dying; some their Friends
Ore-borne i'th'former waue, ten chac'd by one,
Are now each one the slaughter-man of twenty:
Those that would dye, or ere resist, are growne
The mortall bugs o'th'Field.

Lor.

Lord. This was strange chance:
A narrow Lane, an old man, and two Boyes.

Post. Nay, do not wonder at it: you are made
Rather to wonder at the things you heare,
Then to worke any. Will you Rime vpon't,
And vent it for a Mock'rie? Heere is one:
"*Two Boyes, an Oldman (twice a Boy) a Lane,*
"*Preseru'd the Britaines, was the Romanes bane.*

Lord. Nay, be not angry Sir.

Post. Lacke, to what end?
Who dares not stand his Foe, Ile be his Friend:
For if hee'l do, as he is made to doo,
I know hee'l quickly flye my friendship too.
You haue put me into Rime.

Lord. Farewell, you're angry.   *Exit.*

Post. Still going? This is a Lord: Oh Noble misery
To be i'th'Field, and aske what newes of me:
To day, how many would haue giuen their Honours
To haue sau'd their Carkasses? Tooke heele to doo't,
And yet dyed too. I, in mine owne woe charm'd
Could not finde death, where I did heare him groane,
Nor feele him where he strooke. Being an vgly Monster,
'Tis strange he hides him in fresh Cups, soft Beds,
Sweet words; or hath moe ministers then we
That draw his kniues i'th'War. Well I will finde him:
For being now a Fauourer to the Britaine,
No more a Britaine, I haue resum'd againe
The part I came in. Fight I will no more,
But yeeld me to the veriest Hinde, that shall
Once touch my shoulder. Great the slaughter is
Heere made by'th'Romane; great the Answer be
Britaines must take. For me, my Ransome's death,
On eyther side I come to spend my breath;
Which neyther heere Ile keepe, nor beare agen,
But end it by some meanes for *Imogen.*

Enter two Captaines, and Soldiers.

1 Great Iupiter be prais'd, *Lucius* is taken,
'Tis thought the old man, and his sonnes, were Angels.

2 There was a fourth man, in a silly habit,
That gaue th'Affront with them.

1 So 'tis reported:
But none of 'em can be found. Stand, who's there?

Post. A Roman,
Who had not now beene drooping heere, if Seconds
Had answer'd him.

2 Lay hands on him: a Dogge,
A legge of Rome shall not returne to tell
What Crows haue peckt them here: he brags his seruice
As if he were of note: bring him to'th'King.

*Enter Cymbeline, Belarius, Guiderius, Aruiragus, Pisanio, and
Romane Captiues. The Captaines present Posthumus to
Cymbeline, who deliuers him ouer to a Gaoler.*

Scena Quarta.

Enter Posthumus, and Gaoler.

Gao. You shall not now be stolne,
You haue lockes vpon you:
So graze, as you finde Pasture.

2. *Gao.* I, or a stomacke.

Post. Most welcome bondage; for thou art a way
(I thinke) to liberty: yet am I better
Then one that's sicke o'th'Gowt, since he had rather
Groane so in perpetuity, then be cur'd
By'th'sure Physitian, Death; who is the key
T'vnbarre these Lockes. My Conscience, thou art fetter'd
More then my shanks, & wrists: you good Gods giue me
The penitent Instrument to picke that Bolt,
Then free for euer. Is't enough I am sorry?
So Children temporall Fathers do appease;
Gods are more full of mercy. Must I repent,
I cannot do it better then in Gyues,
Desir'd, more then constrain'd, to satisfie
If of my Freedome 'tis the maine part, take
No stricter render of me, then my All.
I know you are more clement then vilde men,
Who of their broken Debtors take a third,
A sixt, a tenth, letting them thriue againe
On their abatement; that's not my desire.
For *Imogens* deere life, take mine, and though
'Tis not so deere, yet 'tis a life; you coyn'd it,
'Tweene man, and man, they waigh not euery stampe:
Though light, take Peeces for the figures sake,
(You rather) mine being yours: and so great Powres,
If you will take this Audit, take this life,
And cancell these cold Bonds. Oh *Imogen,*
Ile speake to thee in silence.

*Solemne Musicke. Enter (as in an Apparation) Sicillius Leo-
natus, Father to Posthumus, an old man, attyred like a warriour, leading in his hand an ancient Matron (his wife, &
Mother to Posthumus) with Musicke before them. Then,
after other Musicke, followes the two young Leonati (Brothers to Posthumus) with wounds as they died in the warrs.
They circle Posthumus round as he lies sleeping.*

Sicil. No more thou Thunder-Master
  shew thy spight, on Mortall Flies:
With Mars fall out with *Iuno* chide, that thy Adulteries
  Rates, and Reuenges.
Hath my poore Boy done ought but well,
  whose face I neuer saw:
I dy'de whil'st in the Wombe he staide,
  attending Natures Law.
Whose Father then (as men report,
  thou Orphanes Father art)
Thou should'st haue bin, and sheelded him,
  from this earth-vexing smart.

Moth. *Lucina* lent not me her ayde,
  but tooke me in my Throwes,
That from me was *Posthumus* ript,
  came crying 'mong'st his Foes.
A thing of pitty.

Sicil. Great Nature like his Ancestrie,
  moulded the stuffe so faire:
That he d'seru'd the praise o'th'World,
  as great *Sicilius* heyre.

1. *Bro.* When once he was mature for man,
  in Britaine where was hee
That could stand vp his paralell?
  Or fruitfull obiect bee?
In eye of *Imogen,* that best could deeme
  his dignitie.

Mo. With Marriage wherefore was he mockt
  to be exil'd, and throwne
From *Leonati* Seate, and cast from her,
  his deerest one:
Sweete *Imogen?*

Sic. Why did you suffer *Iachimo,* slight thing of Italy,

To taint his Nobler hart & braine, with needlesse iealousy,
And to become the geeke and scorne o'th'others vilany?

  2 Bro. For this, from stiller Seats we came,
    our Parents, and vs twaine,
  That striking in our Countries cause,
    fell brauely, and were slaine,
  Our Fealty, & *Tenantius* right, with Honor to maintaine.

  1 Bro. Like hardiment *Posthumus* hath
    to *Cymbeline* perform'd.
  Then Iupiter, y King of Gods, why hast y thus adiourn'd
  The Graces for his Merits due, being all to dolors turn'd?

  Sicil. Thy Christall window ope; looke,
    looke out, no longer exercise
  Vpon a valiant Race, thy harsh, and potent iniuries:

  Moth. Since (Iupiter) our Son is good,
    take off his miseries.

  Sicil. Peepe through thy Marble Mansion, helpe,
    or we poore Ghosts will cry
  To'th'shining Synod of the rest, against thy Deity.

  Brothers. Helpe (Iupiter) or we appeale,
    and from thy iustice flye.

Iupiter descends in Thunder and Lightning, sitting vppon an Eagle: hee throwes a Thunder-bolt. The Ghostes fall on their knees.

  Iupiter. No more you petty Spirits of Region low
  Offend our hearing: hush. How dare you Ghostes
  Accuse the Thunderer, whose Bolt (you know)
  Sky-planted, batters all rebelling Coasts.
  Poore shadowes of Elizium, hence, and rest
  Vpon your neuer-withering bankes of Flowres.
  Be not with mortall accidents opprest,
  No care of yours it is, you know 'tis ours.
  Whom best I loue, I crosse; to make my guift
  The more delay'd, delighted. Be content,
  Your low-laide Sonne, our Godhead will vplift:
  His Comforts thriue, his Trials well are spent:
  Our Iouiall Starre reign'd at his Birth, and in
  Our Temple was he married: Rise, and fade,
  He shall be Lord of Lady *Imogen*,
  And happier much by his Affliction made.
  This Tablet lay vpon his Brest, wherein
  Our pleasure, his full Fortune, doth confine,
  And so away: no farther with your dinne
  Expresse Impatience, least you stirre vp mine:
  Mount Eagle, to my Palace Christalline.   *Ascends*

  Sicil. He came in Thunder, his Celestiall breath
  Was sulphurous to smell: the holy Eagle
  Stoop'd, as to foote vs: his Ascension is
  More sweet then our blest Fields: his Royall Bird
  Prunes the immortall wing, and cloyes his Beake,
  As when his God is pleas'd.

  All. Thankes Iupiter.

  Sic. The Marble Pauement clozes, he is enter'd
  His radiant Roofe: Away, and to Be blest
  Let vs with care performe his great behest.   *Vanish*

  Post. Sleepe, thou hast bin a Grandsire, and begot
  A Father to me: and thou hast created
  A Mother, and two Brothers. But (oh scorne)
  Gone, they went hence so soone as they were borne:
  And so I am awake. Poore Wretches, that depend
  On Greatnesse, Fauour; Dreame as I haue done,
  Wake, and finde nothing. But (alas) I swerue:
  Many Dreame not to finde, neither deserue,
  And yet are steep'd in Fauours; so am I
  That haue this Golden chance, and know not why:
  What Fayeries haunt this ground? A Book? Oh rare one,

Be not, as is our fangled world, a Garment
Nobler then that it couers. Let thy effects
So follow, to be most vnlike our Courtiers,
As good, as promise.

Reades.

WHen as a Lyons whelpe, shall to himselfe vnknown, without seeking finde, and bee embrac'd by a peece of tender Ayre: And when from a stately Cedar shall be lopt branches, which being dead many yeares, shall after reuiue, bee ioynted to the old Stocke, and freshly grow, then shall *Posthumus* end his miseries, Britaine be fortunate, and flourish in Peace and Plentie.

'Tis still a Dreame: or else such stuffe as Madmen
Tongue, and braine not: either both, or nothing,
Or senselesse speaking, or a speaking such
As sense cannot vntye. Be what it is,
The Action of my life is like it, which Ile keepe
If but for simpathy.

Enter Gaoler.

  Gao. Come Sir, are you ready for death?

  Post. Ouer-roasted rather: ready long ago.

  Gao. Hanging is the word, Sir, if you bee readie for that, you are well Cook'd.

  Post. So if I proue a good repast to the Spectators, the dish payes the shot.

  Gao. A heauy reckoning for you Sir: But the comfort is you shall be called to no more payments, fear no more Tauerne Bils, which are often the sadnesse of parting, as the procuring of mirth: you come in faint for want of meate, depart reeling with too much drinke: sorrie that you haue payed too much, and sorry that you are payed too much: Purse and Braine, both empty: the Brain the heauier, for being too light; the Purse too light, being drawne of heauinesse. Oh, of this contradiction you shall now be quit: Oh the charity of a penny Cord, it summes vp thousands in a trice: you haue no true Debitor, and Creditor but it: of what's past, is, and to come, the discharge: your necke (Sir) is Pen, Booke, and Counters; so the Acquittance followes.

  Post. I am merrier to dye, then thou art to liue.

  Gao. Indeed Sir, he that sleepes, feeles not the Tooth-Ache: but a man that were to sleepe your sleepe, and a Hangman to helpe him to bed, I think he would change places with his Officer: for, look you Sir, you know not which way you shall go.

  Post. Yes indeed do I, fellow.

  Gao. Your death has eyes in's head then: I haue not seene him so pictur'd: you must either bee directed by some that take vpon them to know, or to take vpon your selfe that which I am sure you do not know: tor iump the after-enquiry on your owne perill: and how you shall speed in your iournies end, I thinke you'l neuer returne to tell one.

  Post. I tell thee, Fellow, there are none want eyes, to direct them the way I am going, but such as winke, and will not vse them.

  Gao. What an infinite mocke is this, that a man shold haue the best vse of eyes, to see the way of blindnesse: I am sure hanging's the way of winking.

Enter a Messenger.

  Mes. Knocke off his Manacles, bring your Prisoner to the King.

  Post. Thou bring'st good newes, I am call'd to bee made free.

  Gao. Ile be hang'd then.

  Post. Thou shalt be then freer then a Gaoler; no bolts
for

for the dead.

Gao. Vnlesse a man would marry a Gallowes, & beget yong Gibbets, I neuer saw one so prone: yet on my Conscience, there are verier Knaues desire to liue, for all he be a Roman; and there be some of them too that dye against their willes; so should I, if I were one. I would we were all of one minde, and one minde good: O there were desolation of Gaolers and Galowses: I speake against my present profit, but my wish hath a preferment in't. *Exeunt.*

Scena Quinta.

Enter Cymbeline, Bellarius, Guiderius, Aruiragus, Pisanio, and Lords.

Cym. Stand by my side you, whom the Gods haue made
Preseruers of my Throne: woe is my heart,
That the poore Souldier that so richly fought,
Whose ragges, sham'd gilded Armes, whose naked brest
Stept before Targes of proofe, cannot be found:
He shall be happy that can finde him, if
Our Grace can make him so.

Bel. I neuer saw
Such Noble fury in so poore a Thing;
Such precious deeds, in one that promist nought
But beggery, and poore lookes.

Cym. No tydings of him?

Pisa. He hath bin search'd among the dead, & liuing;
But no trace of him.

Cym. To my greefe, I am
The heyre of his Reward, which I will adde
To you (the Liuer, Heart, and Braine of Britaine)
By whom (I grant) she liues. 'Tis now the time
To aske of whence you are. Report it.

Bel. Sir,
In Cambria are we borne, and Gentlemen:
Further to boast, were neyther true, nor modest,
Vnlesse I adde, we are honest.

Cym. Bow your knees:
Arise my Knights o'th'Battell, I create you
Companions to our person, and will fit you
With Dignities becomming your estates.
Enter Cornelius and Ladies.
There's businesse in these faces: why so sadly
Greet you our Victory? you looke like Romaines,
And not o'th' Court of Britaine.

Corn. Hayle great King,
To sowre your happinesse, I must report
The Queene is dead.

Cym. Who worse then a Physitian
Would this report become? But I consider,
By Med'cine life may be prolong'd, yet death
Will seize the Doctor too. How ended she?

Cor. With horror, madly dying, like her life,
Which (being cruell to the world) concluded
Most cruell to her selfe. What she confest,
I will report, so please you: These her Women
Can trip me, if I erre, who with wet cheekes
Were present when she finish'd.

Cym. Prythee say.

Cor. First, she confest she neuer lou'd you: onely
Affected Greatnesse got by you: not you:
Married your Royalty, was wife to your place:

Abhorr'd your person.

Cym. She alone knew this:
And but she spoke it dying, I would not
Beleeue her lips in opening it. Proceed.

Corn. Your daughter, whom she bore in hand to loue
With such integrity, she did confesse
Was as a Scorpion to her sight, whose life
(But that her flight preuented it) she had
Tane off by poyson.

Cym. O most delicate Fiend!
Who is't can reade a Woman? Is there more?

Corn. More Sir, and worse. She did confesse she had
For you a mortall Minerall, which being tooke,
Should by the minute feede on life; and ling'ring,
By inches waste you. In which time, she purpos'd
By watching, weeping, tendance, kissing, to
Orecome you with her shew: and in time
(When she had fitted you with her craft, to worke
Her Sonne into th'adoption of the Crowne:
But fayling of her end by his strange absence,
Grew shamelesse desperate, open'd (in despight
Of Heauen, and Men) her purposes: repented
The euils she hatch'd, were not effected: so
Dispayring, dyed.

Cym. Heard you all this, her Women?

La. We did, so please your Highnesse.

Cym. Mine eyes
Were not in fault, for she was beautifull:
Mine eares that heare her flattery, not my heart,
That thought her like her seeming. It had beene vicious
To haue mistrusted her: yet (Oh my Daughter)
That it was folly in me, thou mayst say,
And proue it in thy feeling. Heauen mend all.

*Enter Lucius, Iachimo, and other Roman prisoners,
Leonatus behind, and Imogen.*

Thou comm'st not *Caius* now for Tribute, that
The Britaines haue rac'd out, though with the losse
Of many a bold one: whose Kinsmen haue made suite
That their good soules may be appeas'd, with slaughter
Of you their Captiues, which our selfe haue granted,
So thinke of your estate.

Luc. Consider Sir, the chance of Warre, the day
Was yours by accident: had it gone with vs,
We should not when the blood was cool, haue threatend
Our Prisoners with the Sword. But since the Gods
Will haue it thus, that nothing but our liues
May be call'd ransome, let it come: Sufficeth,
A Roman, with a Romans heart can suffer:
Augustus liues to thinke on't: and so much
For my peculiar care. This one thing onely
I will entreate, my Boy (a Britaine borne)
Let him be ransom'd: Neuer Master had
A Page so kinde, so duteous, diligent,
So tender ouer his occasions, true,
So feate, so Nurse-like: let his vertue ioyne
With my request, which Ile make bold, your Highnesse
Cannot deny: he hath done no Britaine harme,
Though he haue seru'd a Roman. Saue him (Sir)
And spare no blood beside.

Cym. I haue surely seene him:
His fauour is familiar to me: Boy,
Thou hast look'd thy selfe into my grace,
And art mine owne. I know not why, wherefore,
To say, liue boy: ne're thanke thy Master, liue;
And aske of *Cymbeline* what Boone thou wilt,
Fitting my bounty, and thy state, Ile giue it:

Yea, though thou do demand a Prisoner
The Noblest tane.

   Imo. I humbly thanke your Highnesse.

   Luc. I do not bid thee begge my life, good Lad,
And yet I know thou wilt.

   Imo. No, no, alacke,
There's other worke in hand: I see a thing
Bitter to me, as death: your life, good Master,
Must shuffle for it selfe.

   Luc. The Boy disdaines me,
He leaues me, scornes me: briefely dye their ioyes,
That place them on the truth of Gyrles, and Boyes.
Why stands he so perplext?

   Cym. What would'st thou Boy?
I loue thee more, and more: thinke more and more
What's best to aske. Know'st him thou look'st on? speak
Wilt haue him liue? Is he thy Kin? thy Friend?

   Imo. He is a Romane, no more kin to me,
Then I to your Highnesse, who being born your vassaile
Am something neerer.

   Cym. Wherefore ey'st him so?

   Imo. Ile tell you (Sir) in priuate, if you please
To giue me hearing.

   Cym. I, with all my heart,
And lend my best attention. What's thy name?

   Imo. Fidele Sir.

   Cym. Thou'rt my good youth: my Page
Ile be thy Master: walke with me: speake freely.

   Bel. Is not this Boy reuiu'd from death?

   Arui. One Sand another
Not more resembles that sweet Rosie Lad:
Who dyed, and was *Fidele*: what thinke you?

   Gui. The same dead thing aliue.

   Bel. Peace, peace, see further: he eyes vs not, forbeare
Creatures may be alike: were't he, I am sure
He would haue spoke to vs.

   Gui. But we see him dead.

   Bel. Be silent: let's see further.

   Pisa. It is my Mistris:
Since she is liuing, let the time run on,
To good, or bad.

   Cym. Come, stand thou by our side,
Make thy demand alowd. Sir, step you forth,
Giue answer to this Boy, and do it freely,
Or by our Greatnesse, and the grace of it
(Which is our Honor) bitter torture shall
Winnow the truth from falshood. One speake to him.

   Imo. My boone is, that this Gentleman may render
Of whom he had this Ring.

   Post. What's that to him?

   Cym. That Diamond vpon your Finger, say
How came it yours?

   Iach. Thou'lt torture me to leaue vnspoken, that
Which to be spoke, wou'd torture thee.

   Cym. How? me?

   Iach. I am glad to be constrain'd to vtter that
Which torments me to conceale. By Villany
I got this Ring: 'twas *Leonatus* Iewell,
Whom thou did'st banish: and which more may greeue
As it doth me: a Nobler Sir, ne're liu'd
'Twixt sky and ground. Wilt thou heare more my Lord? (thee,

   Cym. All that belongs to this.

   Iach. That Paragon, thy daughter,
For whom my heart drops blood, and my false spirits
Quaile to remember. Giue me leaue, I faint.

   Cym. My Daughter? what of hir? Renew thy strength
I had rather thou should'st liue, while Nature will,
Then dye ere I heare more: striue man, and speake.

   Iach. Vpon a time, vnhappy was the clocke
That strooke the houre: it was in Rome, accurst
The Mansion where: 'twas at a Feast, oh would
Our Viands had bin poyson'd (or at least
Those which I heau'd to head:) the good *Posthumus*,
(What should I say? he was too good to be
Where ill men were, and was the best of all
Among'st the rar'st of good ones) sitting sadly,
Hearing vs praise our Loues of Italy
For Beauty, that made barren the swell'd boast
Of him that best could speake: for Feature, laming
The Shrine of *Venus*, or straight-pight *Minerua*,
Postures, beyond breefe Nature. For Condition,
A shop of all the qualities, that man
Loues woman for, besides that hooke of Wiuing,
Fairenesse, which strikes the eye.

   Cym. I stand on fire. Come to the matter.

   Iach. All too soone I shall,
Vnlesse thou would'st greeue quickly. This *Posthumus*,
Most like a Noble Lord, in loue, and one
That had a Royall Louer, tooke his hint,
And (not dispraising whom we prais'd, therein
He was as calme as vertue) he began
His Mistris picture, which by his tongue, being made,
And then a minde put in't, either our bragges
Were crak'd of Kitchin-Trulles, or his description
Prou'd vs vnspeaking sottes.

   Cym. Nay, nay, to'th' purpose.

   Iach. Your daughters Chastity, (there it beginnes)
He spake of her, as *Dian* had hot dreames,
And she alone, were cold: Whereat, I wretch
Made scruple of his praise, and wager'd with him
Peeces of Gold, 'gainst this, which then he wore
Vpon his honour'd finger) to attaine
In suite the place of 's bed, and winne this Ring
By hers, and mine Adultery: he (true Knight)
No lesser of her Honour confident
Then I did truly finde her, stakes this Ring,
And would so, had it beene a Carbuncle
Of Phœbus Wheele; and might so safely, had it
Bin all the worth of 's Carre. Away to Britaine
Poste I in this designe: Well may you (Sir)
Remember me at Court, where I was taught
Of your chaste Daughter, the wide difference
'Twixt Amorous, and Villanous. Being thus quench'd
Of hope, not longing; mine Italian braine,
Gan in your duller Britaine operare
Most vildely: for my vantage excellent.
And to be breefe, my practise so preuayl'd
That I return'd with simular proofe enough,
To make the Noble *Leonatus* mad,
By wounding his beleefe in her Renowne,
With Tokens thus, and thus: auerring notes
Of Chamber-hanging, Pictures, this her Bracelet
(Oh cunning how I got) nay some markes
Of secret on her person, that he could not
But thinke her bond of Chastity quite crack'd,
I hauing 'tane the forfeyt. Whereupon,
Me thinkes I see him now.

   Post. I so thou do'st,
Italian Fiend. Aye me, most credulous Foole,
Egregious murtherer, Theefe, any thing
That's due to all the Villaines past, in being
To come. Oh giue me Cord, or knife, or poyson,

Some

The Tragedie of Cymbeline.

Some vpright Iusticer. Thou King, send out
For Torturors ingenious: it is I
That all th'abhorred things o'th'earth amend
By being worse then they. I am *Posthumus*,
That kill'd thy Daughter: Villain-like, I lye,
That caus'd a lesser villaine then my selfe,
A sacrilegious Theefe to doo't. The Temple
Of Vertue was she; yea, and she her selfe.
Spit, and throw stones, cast myre vpon me, set
The dogges o'th'street to bay me: euery villaine
Be call'd *Posthumus Leonatus*, and
Be villany lesse then 'twas. Oh *Imogen*!
My Queene, my life, my wife: oh *Imogen*,
Imogen, Imogen.

  Imo. Peace my Lord, heare, heare.
  Post. Shall's haue a play of this?
Thou scornfull Page, there lye thy part.
  Pis. Oh Gentlemen, helpe,
Mine and your Mistris: Oh my Lord *Posthumus*,
You ne're kill'd *Imogen* till now: helpe, helpe,
Mine honour'd Lady.
  Cym. Does the world go round?
  Posth. How comes these staggers on mee?
  Pisa. Wake my Mistris.
  Cym. If this be so, the Gods do meane to strike me
To death, with mortall ioy.
  Pisa. How fares my Mistris?
  Imo. Oh get thee from my sight,
Thou gau'st me poyson: dangerous Fellow hence,
Breath not where Princes are.
  Cym. The tune of *Imogen*.
  Pisa. Lady, the Gods throw stones of sulpher on me, if
That box I gaue you, was not thought by mee
A precious thing, I had it from the Queene.
  Cym. New matter still.
  Imo. It poyson'd me.
  Corn. Oh Gods!
I left out one thing which the Queene confest,
Which must approue thee honest. If *Pisanio*
Haue (said she) giuen his Mistris that Confection
Which I gaue him for Cordiall, she is seru'd,
As I would serue a Rat.
  Cym. What's this, *Cornelius*?
  Corn. The Queene (Sir) very oft importun'd me
To temper poysons for her, still pretending
The satisfaction of her knowledge, onely
In killing Creatures vilde, as Cats and Dogges
Of no esteeme. I dreading, that her purpose
Was of more danger, did compound for her
A certaine stuffe, which being tane, would cease
The present powre of life, but in short time,
All Offices of Nature, should againe
Do their due Functions. Haue you tane of it?
  Imo. Most like I did, for I was dead.
  Bel. My Boyes, there was our error.
  Gui. This is sure *Fidele*.
  Imo. Why did you throw your wedded Lady fro you?
Thinke that you are vpon a Rocke, and now
Throw me againe.
  Post. Hang there like fruite, my soule,
Till the Tree dye.
  Cym. How now, my Flesh? my Childe?
What, mak'st thou me a dullard in this Act?
Wilt thou not speake to me?
  Imo. Your blessing, Sir.
  Bel. Though you did loue this youth, I blame ye not,

You had a motiue for't.
  Cym. My teares that fall
Proue holy-water on thee; *Imogen*,
Thy Mothers dead.
  Imo. I am sorry for't, my Lord.
  Cym. Oh, she was naught; and long of her it was
That we meet heere so strangely: but her Sonne
Is gone, we know not how, nor where.
  Pisa. My Lord,
Now feare is from me, Ile speake troth. Lord *Cloten*
Vpon my Ladies missing, came to me
With his Sword drawne, foam'd at the mouth, and swore
If I discouer'd not which way she was gone,
It was my instant death. By accident,
I had a feigned Letter of my Masters
Then in my pocket, which directed him
To seeke her on the Mountaines neere to Milford,
Where in a frenzie, in my Masters Garments
(Which he inforc'd from me) away he postes
With vnchaste purpose, and with oath to violate
My Ladies honor, what became of him,
I further know not.
  Gui. Let me end the Story: I slew him there.
  Cym. Marry, the Gods forefend.
I would not thy good deeds, should from my lips
Plucke a hard sentence: Prythee valiant youth
Deny't againe.
  Gui. I haue spoke it, and I did it.
  Cym. He was a Prince.
  Gui. A most inciuill one. The wrongs he did mee
Were nothing Prince-like; for he did prouoke me
With Language that would make me spurne the Sea,
If it could so roare to me. I cut off's head,
And am right glad he is not standing heere
To tell this tale of mine.
  Cym. I am sorrow for thee:
By thine owne tongue thou art condemn'd, and must
Endure our Law: Thou'rt dead.
  Imo. That headlesse man I thought had bin my Lord
  Cym. Binde the Offender,
And take him from our presence.
  Bel. Stay, Sir King.
This man is better then the man he slew,
As well descended as thy selfe, and hath
More of thee merited, then a Band of *Clotens*
Had euer scarre for. Let his Armes alone,
They were not borne for bondage.
  Cym. Why old Soldier:
Wilt thou vndoe the worth thou art vnpayd for
By tasting of our wrath? How of descent
As good as we?
  Arui. In that he spake too farre.
  Cym. And thou shalt dye for't.
  Bel. We will dye all three,
But I will proue that two one's are as good
As I haue giuen out him. My Sonnes, I must
For mine owne part, vnfold a dangerous speech,
Though haply well for you.
  Arui. Your danger's ours.
  Guid. And our good his.
  Bel. Haue at it then, by leaue
Thou hadd'st (great King) a Subiect, who
Was call'd *Belarius*.
  Cym. What of him? He is a banish'd Traitor.
  Bel. He it is, that hath
Assum'd this age: indeed a banish'd man,

I know not how, a Traitor.

Cym. Take him hence,
The whole world shall not saue him.

Bel. Not too hot;
First pay me for the Nursing of thy Sonnes,
And let it be confiscate all, so soone
As I haue receyu'd it.

Cym. Nursing of my Sonnes?

Bel. I am too blunt, and sawcy: heere's my knee:
Ere I arise, I will preferre my Sonnes,
Then spare not the old Father. Mighty Sir,
These two young Gentlemen that call me Father,
And thinke they are my Sonnes, are none of mine,
They are the yssue of your Loynes, my Liege,
And blood of your begetting.

Cym. How? my Issue.

Bel. So sure as you, your Fathers: I (old *Morgan*)
Am that *Belarius*, whom you sometime banish'd:
Your pleasure was my neere offence, my punishment
It selfe, and all my Treason that I suffer'd,
Was all the harme I did. These gentle Princes
(For such, and so they are) these twenty yeares
Haue I train'd vp; those Arts they haue, as I
Could put into them. My breeding was (Sir)
As your Highnesse knowes: Their Nurse *Euriphile*
(Whom for the Theft I wedded) stole these Children
Vpon my Banishment: I moou'd her too't,
Hauing receyu'd the punishment before
For that which I did then. Beaten for Loyaltie,
Excited me to Treason. Their deere losse,
The more of you 'twas felt, the more it shap'd
Vnto my end of stealing them. But gracious Sir,
Heere are your Sonnes againe, and I must loose
Two of the sweet'st Companions in the World.
The benediction of these couering Heauens
Fall on their heads like dew, for they are worthie
To in-lay Heauen with Starres.

Cym. Thou weep'st, and speak'st:
The Seruice that you three haue done, is more
Vnlike, then this thou tell'st. I lost my Children,
If these be they, I know not how to wish
A payre of worthier Sonnes.

Bel. Be pleas'd awhile;
This Gentleman, whom I call *Polidore*,
Most worthy Prince, as yours, is true *Guiderius*:
This Gentleman, my *Cadwall*, *Aruiragus*.
Your yonger Princely Son, he Sir, was lapt
In a most curious Mantle, wrought by th'hand
Of his Queene Mother, which for more probation
I can with ease produce.

Cym. *Guiderius* had
Vpon his necke a Mole, a sanguine Starre,
It was a marke of wonder.

Bel. This is he,
Who hath vpon him still that naturall stampe:
It was wise Natures end, in the donation
To be his euidence now.

Cym. Oh, what am I
A Mother to the byrth of three? Nere Mother
Reioyc'd deliuerance more: Blest, pray you be,
That after this strange starting from your Orbes,
You may reigne in them now: Oh *Imogen*,
Thou hast lost by this a Kingdome.

Imo. No, my Lord:
I haue got two Worlds by't. Oh my gentle Brothers,
Haue we thus met? Oh neuer say heereafter

But I am truest speaker. You call'd me Brother
When I was but your Sister: I you Brothers,
When we were so indeed.

Cym. Did you ere meete?

Arui. I my good Lord.

Gui. And at first meeting lou'd,
Continew'd so, vntill we thought he dyed.

Corn. By the Queenes Dramme she swallow'd.

Cym. O rare instinct!
When shall I heare all through? This fierce abridgment,
Hath to it Circumstantiall branches, which
Distinction should be rich in. Where? how liu'd you?
And when came you to serue our Romane Captiue?
How parted with your Brother? How first met them?
Why fled you from the Court? And whether these?
And your three motiues to the Battaile? with
I know not how much more should be demanded,
And all the other by-dependances
From chance to chance? But nor the Time, nor Place
Will serue our long Interrogatories. See,
Posthumus Anchors vpon *Imogen*;
And she (like harmlesse Lightning) throwes her eye
On him: her Brothers, Me: her Master hitting
Each obiect with a Ioy: the Counter-change
Is seuerally in all. Let's quit this ground,
And smoake the Temple with our Sacrifices.
Thou art my Brother, so wee'l hold thee euer.

Imo. You are my Father too, and did releeue me:
To see this gracious season.

Cym. All ore-ioy'd
Saue these in bonds, let them be ioyfull too,
For they shall taste our Comfort.

Imo. My good Master, I will yet do you seruice.

Luc. Happy be you.

Cym. The forlorne Souldier, that so Nobly fought
He would haue well becom'd this place, and grac'd
The thankings of a King.

Post. I am Sir
The Souldier that did company these three
In poore beseeming: 'twas a fitment for
The purpose I then follow'd. That I was he,
Speake *Iachimo*, I had you downe, and might
Haue made you finish.

Iach. I am downe againe:
But now my heauie Conscience sinkes my knee,
As then your force did. Take that life, beseech you
Which I so often owe: but your Ring first,
And heere the Bracelet of the truest Princesse
That euer swore her Faith.

Post. Kneele not to me:
The powre that I haue on you, is to spare you:
The malice towards you, to forgiue you. Liue
And deale with others better.

Cym. Nobly doom'd:
Wee'l learne our Freenesse of a Sonne-in-Law:
Pardon's the word to all.

Arui. You holpe vs Sir,
As you did meane indeed to be our Brother,
Ioy'd are we, that you are.

Post. Your Seruant Princes. Good my Lord of Rome
Call forth your Sooth-sayer: As I slept, me thought
Great Iupiter vpon his Eagle back'd
Appear'd to me, with other sprightly shewes
Of mine owne Kindred. When I wak'd, I found
This Labell on my bosome; whose containing
Is so from sense in hardnesse, that I can

Make

The Tragedy of Cymbeline.

Make no Collection of it. Let him shew
His skill in the construction.

Luc. Philarmonus.

Sooth. Heere, my good Lord.

Luc. Read, and declare the meaning.

Reades.

When as a Lyons whelpe, shall to himselfe vnknown, without seeking finde, and bee embrac'd by a peece of tender Ayre: And when from a stately Cedar shall be lopt branches, which being dead many yeares, shall after reuiue, bee ioynted to the old Stocke, and freshly grow, then shall Posthumus end his miseries, Britaine be fortunate, and flourish in Peace and Plentie.

Thou *Leonatus* art the Lyons Whelpe,
The fit and apt Construction of thy name
Being *Leonatus*, doth import so much:
The peece of tender Ayre, thy vertuous Daughter,
Which we call *Mollis Aer*, and *Mollis Aer*
We terme it *Mulier*; which *Mulier* I diuine
Is this most constant Wife, who euen now
Answering the Letter of the Oracle,
Vnknowne to you vnsought, were clipt about
With this most tender Aire.

Cym. This hath some seeming.

Sooth. The lofty Cedar, Royall *Cymbeline*
Personates thee: And thy lopt Branches, point
Thy two Sonnes forth: who by *Belarius* stolne
For many yeares thought dead, are now reuiu'd
To the Maiesticke Cedar ioyn'd; whose Issue
Promises Britaine, Peace and Plenty.

Cym. Well,
My Peace we will begin: And *Caius Lucius*,
Although the Victor, we submit to *Cæsar*,
And to the Romane Empire; promising
To pay our wonted Tribute, from the which
We were disswaded by our wicked Queene,
Whom heauens in Iustice both on her, and hers,
Haue laid most heauy hand.

Sooth. The fingers of the Powres aboue, do tune
The harmony of this Peace: the Vision
Which I made knowne to *Lucius* ere the stroke
Of yet this scarse-cold-Battaile, at this instant
Is full accomplish'd. For the Romaine Eagle
From South to West, on wing soaring aloft
Lessen'd her selfe, and in the Beames o'th'Sun
So vanish'd; which fore-shew'd our Princely Eagle
Th'Imperiall *Cæsar*, should againe vnite
His Fauour, with the Radiant *Cymbeline*,
Which shines heere in the West.

Cym. Laud we the Gods,
And let our crooked Smoakes climbe to their Nostrils
From our blest Altars. Publish we this Peace
To all our Subiects. Set we forward: Let
A Roman, and a Brittish Ensigne waue
Friendly together: so through *Luds-Towne* march,
And in the Temple of great Iupiter
Our Peace wee'l ratifie: Seale it with Feasts.
Set on there: Neuer was a Warre did cease
(Ere bloodie hands were wash'd) with such a Peace.

Exeunt.

FINIS.

Printed at the Charges of *W. Iaggard, Ed. Blount, I. Smithweeke,*
and *W. Aspley,* 1623.

Fo.1 - no. 68
Cs 0443

STC 22273
Fo.1
no. 68

Perfect
(Small original defects in F1-2, H5-6, N1-3
Small defects in Tt6, V1-2.
Leaf of verses & last leaf mounted but
quite sound.
Every leaf is genuine & untouched)

pro B. Quaritch Ltd
Talbot
28.7.24

RECORD OF EXHIBITION

Date	Opening

Ex. # 189